University Casebook Series

BUSINESS TORTS (1972)

Milton Handler, Professor of Law Emeritus, Columbia University.

CIVIL PROCEDURE, see Procedure

COMMERCIAL AND CONSUMER TRANSACTIONS (1972) with 1973 Supplement

William E. Hogan, Professor of Law, Cornell University.
William D. Warren, Professor of Law, Stanford University.

COMMERCIAL AND 'INVESTMENT PAPER, Third Edition (1964) with Statutory Materials

Roscoe T. Steffen, Professor of Law, University of California, Hastings College of the Law.

COMMERCIAL LAW, CASES & MATERIALS ON, Second Edition (1968) with Statutory Supplement

E. Allan Farnsworth, Professor of Law, Columbia University.
John Honnold, Professor of Law, University of Pennsylvania.

COMMERCIAL PAPER (1968), with Statutory Supplement

E. Allan Farnsworth, Professor of Law, Columbia University.

COMMERCIAL PAPER AND BANK DEPOSITS AND COLLECTIONS (1967) with Statutory Supplement

William D. Hawkland, Professor of Law, University of Illinois.

COMMERCIAL TRANSACTIONS—Text, Cases and Problems, Fourth Edition (1968)

Robert Braucher, Professor of Law, Harvard University, and
The late Arthur E. Sutherland, Jr., Professor of Law, Harvard University.

COMPARATIVE LAW, Third Edition (1970)

Rudolf B. Schlesinger, Professor of Law, Cornell University.

COMPETITIVE PROCESS, LEGAL REGULATION OF THE (1972) with Statutory Supplement and 1975 Supplement

Edmund W. Kitch, Professor of Law, University of Chicago.
Harvey S. Perlman, Professor of Law, University of Nebraska.

CONFLICT OF LAWS, Sixth Edition (1971), with 1975 Supplement

Willis L. M. Reese, Professor of Law, Columbia University, and
Maurice Rosenberg, Professor of Law, Columbia University.

CONSTITUTIONAL LAW, Fourth Edition (1973), with 1975 Supplement

Edward L. Barrett, Jr., Professor of Law, University of California, Davis.
Paul W. Bruton, Professor of Law, University of Pennsylvania.

CONSTITUTIONAL LAW, Ninth Edition (1975)

Gerald Gunther, Professor of Law, Stanford University.

CONSTITUTIONAL LAW, INDIVIDUAL RIGHTS IN (1970) with 1974 Supplement

Gerald Gunther, Professor of Law, Stanford University.
Noel T. Dowling, late Professor of Law, Columbia University.

CONTRACT LAW AND ITS APPLICATION (1971)

Addison Mueller, Professor of Law, University of California, Los Angeles.
Arthur I. Rosett, Professor of Law, University of California, Los Angeles.

CONTRACT LAW, STUDIES IN (1970)

Edward J. Murphy, Professor of Law, University of Notre Dame.
Richard E. Speidel, Professor of Law, University of Virginia.

CONTRACTS AND CONTRACT REMEDIES, Fourth Edition (1957)

The late Harold Shepherd, Professor of Law Emeritus, Stanford University, and
Harry H. Wellington, Professor of Law, Yale University.

CONTRACTS AND CONTRACT REMEDIES, Second Edition (1969)

John P. Dawson, Professor of Law, Harvard University, and
Wm. Burnett Harvey, Professor of Law, Indiana University.

CONTRACTS, Second Edition (1972) with Statutory Supplement

E. Allan Farnsworth, Professor of Law, Columbia University.
William F. Young, Jr., Professor of Law, Columbia University.
Harry W. Jones, Professor of Law, Columbia University.

CONTRACTS (1971) with Statutory and Administrative Law Supplement

Ian R. Macneil, Professor of Law, Cornell University.

COPYRIGHT, Unfair Competition, and Other Topics Bearing on the Protection of Literary, Musical, and Artistic Works, Second Edition (1974)

Benjamin Kaplan, Professor of Law Emeritus, Harvard University, and
Ralph S. Brown, Jr., Professor of Law, Yale University.

CORPORATE FINANCE (1972)

Victor Brudney, Professor of Law, Harvard University.
Marvin A. Chirelstein, Professor of Law, Yale University.

CORPORATION LAW, with Statutory Supplement (1973)

Detlev F. Vagts, Professor of Law, Harvard University.

CORPORATIONS, Fourth Edition—Unabridged (1969) with Case Supplement and Special Supplement

William L. Cary, Professor of Law, Columbia University.

CORPORATIONS, Fourth Edition—Abridged (1970) with Case Supplement and Special Supplement

William L. Cary, Professor of Law, Columbia University.

CORPORATIONS (1972)

Reprinted with Conard, Knauss & Siegels' Enterprise Organization.

CORPORATIONS, see also Enterprise Organization

CORRECTIONAL PROCESS (1971) (Pamphlet)

Reprinted from Miller, Dawson, Dix and Parnas's Criminal Justice Administration & Related Processes.

CREDITORS' RIGHTS, Fifth Edition (1957)

The late John Hanna, Professor of Law Emeritus, Columbia University, and
The late James Angell MacLachlan, Professor of Law Emeritus, Harvard University.

CREDITORS' RIGHTS AND CORPORATE REORGANIZATION, Fifth Edition (1957)

> The late John Hanna, Professor of Law Emeritus, Columbia University, and The late James Angell MacLachlan, Professor of Law Emeritus, Harvard University.

CREDITORS' RIGHTS, see also Debtor-Creditor Law

CRIMINAL LAW (1973)

> Fred E. Inbau, Professor of Law, Northwestern University.
> James R. Thompson, U. S. Attorney for the Northern District of Illinois.
> Andre A. Moenssens, Professor of Law, University of Richmond.

CRIMINAL PROCEDURE (1974) with 1975 Supplement

> Fred E. Inbau, Professor of Law, Northwestern University.
> James R. Thompson, U. S. Attorney for the Northern District of Illinois.
> James B. Haddad, First Assistant State's Attorney, Cook County, Illinois.
> James B. Zagel, Chief, Criminal Justice Division, Office of Attorney General of Illinois.
> Gary L. Starkman, Assistant U. S. Attorney, Northern District of Illinois.

CRIMINAL JUSTICE, THE ADMINISTRATION OF, CASES AND MATERIALS ON, Second Edition (1969)

> Francis C. Sullivan, Professor of Law, Louisiana State University.
> Paul Hardin III, Professor of Law, Duke University.
> John Huston, Professor of Law, University of Washington.
> Frank R. Lacy, Professor of Law, University of Oregon.
> Daniel E. Murray, Professor of Law, University of Miami.
> George W. Pugh, Professor of Law, Louisiana State University.

CRIMINAL JUSTICE ADMINISTRATION AND RELATED PROCESSES (1971) with 1974 Supplement

> Frank W. Miller, Professor of Law, Washington University.
> Robert O. Dawson, Professor of Law, University of Texas.
> George E. Dix, Professor of Law, University of Texas.
> Raymond I. Parnas, Professor of Law, University of California, Davis.

CRIMINAL LAW, Second Edition (1975)

> Lloyd L. Weinreb, Professor of Law, Harvard University.

CRIMINAL LAW AND ITS ADMINISTRATION (1940), with 1956 Supplement

> The late Jerome Michael, Professor of Law, Columbia University, and Herbert Wechsler, Professor of Law, Columbia University.

CRIMINAL LAW AND PROCEDURE, Fourth Edition (1972)

> Rollin M. Perkins, Professor of Law, University of California, Hastings College of the Law.

CRIMINAL PROCESS, Second Edition (1974)

> Lloyd L. Weinreb, Professor of Law, Harvard University.

DAMAGES, Second Edition (1952)

> The late Charles T. McCormick, Professor of Law, University of Texas, and The late William F. Fritz, Professor of Law, University of Texas.

DEBTOR–CREDITOR LAW (1974) with 1975 Case-Statutory Supplement

> William D. Warren, Professor of Law, Stanford University.
> William E. Hogan, Professor of Law, Cornell University.

DECEDENTS' ESTATES (1971)

Max Rheinstein, Professor of Law Emeritus, University of Chicago.
Mary Ann Glendon, Professor of Law, Boston College Law School.

DECEDENTS' ESTATES AND TRUSTS, Fourth Edition (1971)

John Ritchie III, Professor of Law, University of Virginia,
Neill H. Alford, Jr., Dean of the School of Law, University of Georgia.
Richard W. Effland, Professor of Law, Arizona State University.

DECEDENTS' ESTATES AND TRUSTS (1968)

Howard R. Williams, Professor of Law, Stanford University.

DOMESTIC RELATIONS, Second Edition (1974)

Monrad G. Paulsen, Dean of the Law School, University of Virginia.
Walter Wadlington, Professor of Law, University of Virginia.
Julius Goebel, Jr., Professor of Law Emeritus, Columbia University.

DOMESTIC RELATIONS: STATUTORY MATERIALS, 1974 Edition

Monrad G. Paulsen, Dean of the Law School, University of Virginia.
Walter Wadlington, Professor of Law, University of Virginia.

DOMESTIC RELATIONS—Civil and Canon Law (1963)

Philip A. Ryan, Professor of Law, Georgetown University, and
Dom David Granfield, Associate Professor, Catholic University of America.

DYNAMICS OF AMERICAN LAW, THE: Courts, the Legal Process and Freedom of Expression (1968)

Marc A. Franklin, Professor of Law, Stanford University.

ENTERPRISE ORGANIZATION (1972)

Alfred F. Conard, Professor of Law, University of Michigan.
Robert L. Knauss, Dean of the School of Law, Vanderbilt University.
Stanley Siegel, Professor of Law, University of Michigan.

ENVIRONMENTAL PROTECTION, SELECTED LEGAL AND ECONOMIC ASPECTS OF (1971)

Charles J. Meyers, Professor of Law, Stanford University.
A. Dan Tarlock, Professor of Law, Indiana University.

EQUITY AND EQUITABLE REMEDIES (1975)

Edward D. Re, Adjunct Professor of Law, St. John's University.

EQUITY, RESTITUTION AND DAMAGES, Second Edition (1974)

Robert Childres, Professor of Law, Northwestern University.
William F. Johnson, Jr., Adjunct Professor of Law, New York University.

ESTATE PLANNING PROBLEMS (1973)

David Westfall, Professor of Law, Harvard University.

ETHICS, see Legal Profession

EVIDENCE, Second Edition (1972)

David W. Louisell, Professor of Law, University of California, Berkeley.
John Kaplan, Professor of Law, Stanford University.
Jon R. Waltz, Professor of Law, Northwestern University.

EVIDENCE, Sixth Edition (1973) with 1975 Supplement

John M. Maguire, Professor of Law Emeritus, Harvard University.
Jack B. Weinstein, Professor of Law, Columbia University.
James H. Chadbourn, Professor of Law, Harvard University.
John H. Mansfield, Professor of Law, Harvard University.

EVIDENCE (1968)

> Francis C. Sullivan, Professor of Law, Louisiana State University.
> Paul Hardin, III, Professor of Law, Duke University.

FEDERAL COURTS, Fifth Edition (1970) with 1975 Supplement

> The late Charles T. McCormick, Professor of Law, University of Texas.
> James H. Chadbourn, Professor of Law, Harvard University, and
> Charles Alan Wright, Professor of Law, University of Texas.

FEDERAL COURTS AND THE FEDERAL SYSTEM, Second Edition (1973)

> The late Henry M. Hart, Jr., Professor of Law, Harvard University.
> Herbert Wechsler, Professor of Law, Columbia University.
> Paul M. Bator, Professor of Law, Harvard University.
> Paul J. Mishkin, Professor of Law, University of California, Berkeley.
> David L. Shapiro, Professor of Law, Harvard University.

FEDERAL RULES OF CIVIL PROCEDURE, 1973 Edition

FEDERAL TAXATION, see Taxation

FREE ENTERPRISE AND ECONOMIC ORGANIZATION, Fourth Edition (1972)

> Louis B. Schwartz, Professor of Law, University of Pennsylvania.

FUTURE INTERESTS AND ESTATE PLANNING (1961) with 1962 Supplement

> The late W. Barton Leach, Professor of Law, Harvard University, and
> James K. Logan, Dean of the Law School, University of Kansas.

FUTURE INTERESTS (1958)

> The late Philip Mechem, Professor of Law Emeritus, University of Pennsylvania.

FUTURE INTERESTS (1970)

> Howard R. Williams, Professor of Law, Stanford University.

GOVERNMENT CONTRACTS, FEDERAL (1975)

> John W. Whelan, Professor of Law, Hastings College of the Law.
> Robert S. Pasley, Professor of Law, Cornell University.

HOUSING (THE ILL-HOUSED) (1971)

> Peter W. Martin, Professor of Law, Cornell University.

INJUNCTIONS (1972)

> Owen M. Fiss, Professor of Law, Yale University.

INSURANCE (1971)

> William F. Young, Professor of Law, Columbia University.

INTERNATIONAL LAW, See also Transnational Legal Problems and United Nations Law

INTERNATIONAL LEGAL SYSTEM (1973) with Documentary Supplement

> Noyes E. Leech, Professor of Law, University of Pennsylvania.
> Covey T. Oliver, Professor of Law, University of Pennsylvania.
> Joseph Modeste Sweeney, Dean of the School of Law, Tulane University.

INTERNATIONAL TRADE AND INVESTMENT, REGULATION OF (1970)

> Carl H. Fulda, Professor of Law, University of Texas.
> Warren F. Schwartz, Professor of Law, University of Virginia.

INTERNATIONAL TRANSACTIONS AND RELATIONS (1960)

Milton Katz, Professor of Law, Harvard University, and
Kingman Brewster, Jr., President, Yale University.

INTRODUCTION TO THE STUDY OF LAW (1970)

E. Wayne Thode, Professor of Law, University of Utah.
J. Leon Lebowitz, Professor of Law, University of Texas.
Lester J. Mazor, Professor of Law, University of Utah.

INTRODUCTION TO LAW, see also Legal Method, also On Law in Courts, also Dynamics of American Law

JUDICIAL CODE: Rules of Procedure in the Federal Courts with Excerpts from the Criminal Code, 1973 Edition

The late Henry M. Hart, Jr., Professor of Law, Harvard University, and
Herbert Wechsler, Professor of Law, Columbia University.

JURISPRUDENCE (Temporary Edition Hard Bound) (1949)

Lon L. Fuller, Professor of Law, Harvard University.

JUVENILE COURTS (1967)

Hon. Orman W. Ketcham, Juvenile Court of the District of Columbia.
Monrad G. Paulsen, Dean of the Law School, University of Virginia.

JUVENILE JUSTICE PROCESS (1971) (Pamphlet)

Reprinted from Miller, Dawson, Dix & Parnas's Criminal Justice Administration & Related Processes.

LABOR LAW, Seventh Edition (1969) with Statutory Supplement and 1973 Case Supplement

Archibald Cox, Professor of Law, Harvard University, and
Derek C. Bok, President, Harvard University.

LABOR LAW (1968) with Statutory Supplement

Clyde W. Summers, Professor of Law, University of Pennsylvania.
Harry H. Wellington, Professor of Law, Yale University.

LABOR RELATIONS (1949)

The late Harry Shulman, Dean of the Law School, Yale University, and
Neil Chamberlain, Professor of Economics, Columbia University.

LAND FINANCING (1970)

Norman Penney, Professor of Law, Cornell University.
Richard F. Broude, Professor of Law, Georgetown University.

LAW, LANGUAGE AND ETHICS (1972)

William R. Bishin, Professor of Law, University of Southern California.
Christopher D. Stone, Professor of Law, University of Southern California.

LEGAL METHOD, Second Edition (1952)

Noel T. Dowling, late Professor of Law, Columbia University,
The late Edwin W. Patterson, Professor of Law, Columbia University, and
Richard R. B. Powell, Professor of Law, University of California, Hastings College of the Law.
Second Edition by Harry W. Jones, Professor of Law, Columbia University.

LEGAL METHODS (1969)

>Robert N. Covington, Professor of Law, Vanderbilt University.
>E. Blythe Stason, Professor of Law, Vanderbilt University.
>John W. Wade, Professor of Law, Vanderbilt University.
>The late Elliott E. Cheatham, Professor of Law, Vanderbilt University.
>Theodore A. Smedley, Professor of Law, Vanderbilt University.

LEGAL PROFESSION (1970)

>Samuel D. Thurman, Dean of the College of Law, University of Utah.
>Ellis L. Phillips, Jr., Professor of Law, Columbia University.
>The late Elliott E. Cheatham, Professor of Law, Vanderbilt University.

LEGISLATION, Third Edition (1973)

>Horace E. Read, Vice President, Dalhousie University.
>John W. MacDonald, Professor of Law, Cornell Law School.
>Jefferson B. Fordham, Professor of Law, University of Utah, and
>William J. Pierce, Professor of Law, University of Michigan.

LOCAL GOVERNMENT LAW, Revised Edition (1975)

>Jefferson B. Fordham, Professor of Law, University of Utah.

MENTAL HEALTH PROCESS (1971) (Pamphlet)

>Reprinted from Miller, Dawson, Dix & Parnas's Criminal Justice Administration & Related Processes.

MODERN REAL ESTATE TRANSACTIONS, Second Edition (1958)

>Allison Dunham, Professor of Law, University of Chicago.

MUNICIPAL CORPORATIONS, see Local Government Law

NEGOTIABLE INSTRUMENTS, see Commercial Paper

NEW YORK PRACTICE, Third Edition (1973)

>Herbert Peterfreund, Professor of Law, New York University.
>Joseph M. McLaughlin, Dean of the Law School, Fordham University.

OIL AND GAS, Third Edition (1974)

>Howard R. Williams, Professor of Law, Stanford University,
>Richard C. Maxwell, Professor of Law, University of California, Los Angeles, and
>Charles J. Meyers, Professor of Law, Stanford University.

ON LAW IN COURTS (1965)

>Paul J. Mishkin, Professor of Law, University of California, Berkeley.
>Clarence Morris, Professor of Law, University of Pennsylvania.

OWNERSHIP AND DEVELOPMENT OF LAND (1965)

>Jan Krasnowiecki, Professor of Law, University of Pennsylvania.

PARTNERSHIP PLANNING (1970) (Pamphlet)

>William L. Cary, Professor of Law, Columbia University.

PATENT, TRADEMARK AND COPYRIGHT LAW (1959)

>E. Ernest Goldstein, Professor of Law, University of Texas.

PLEADING & PROCEDURE: STATE AND FEDERAL, Third Edition (1973)

>David W. Louisell, Professor of Law, University of California, Berkeley, and
>Geoffrey C. Hazard, Jr., Professor of Law, Yale University.

POLICE FUNCTION (1971) (Pamphlet)

Reprinted from Miller, Dawson, Dix & Parnas's Criminal Justice Administration and Related Processes.

PROCEDURE—Biography of a Legal Dispute (1968)

Marc A. Franklin, Professor of Law, Stanford University.

PROCEDURE—CIVIL PROCEDURE, Second Edition (1974)

James H. Chadbourn, Professor of Law, Harvard University, and
A. Leo Levin, Professor of Law, University of Pennsylvania.
Philip Shuchman, Professor of Law, University of Connecticut.

PROCEDURE—CIVIL PROCEDURE, Third Edition (1973)

Richard H. Field, Professor of Law, Harvard University, and
Benjamin Kaplan, Professor of Law, Harvard University.

PROCEDURE—CIVIL PROCEDURE, Second Edition (1970) with 1975 Supplement

Maurice Rosenberg, Professor of Law, Columbia University.
Jack B. Weinstein, Professor, of Law, Columbia University.
Hans Smit, Professor of Law, Columbia University.

PROCEDURE—FEDERAL RULES OF CIVIL PROCEDURE, 1975 Edition

PROCEDURE PORTFOLIO (1962)

James H. Chadbourn, Professor of Law, Harvard University, and
A. Leo Levin, Professor of Law, University of Pennsylvania.

PRODUCTS AND THE CONSUMER: DECEPTIVE PRACTICES (1972)

W. Page Keeton, Dean of the School of Law, University of Texas.
Marshall S. Shapo, Professor of Law, University of Virginia.

PRODUCTS AND THE CONSUMER: DEFECTIVE AND DANGEROUS PRODUCTS (1970)

W. Page Keeton, Dean of the School of Law, University of Texas.
Marshall S. Shapo, Professor of Law, University of Virginia.

PROPERTY, Third Edition (1972)

John E. Cribbet, Dean of the Law School, University of Illinois,
The late William F. Fritz, Professor of Law, University of Texas, and
Corwin W. Johnson, Professor of Law, University of Texas.

PROPERTY—PERSONAL (1953)

The late S. Kenneth Skolfield, Professor of Law Emeritus, Boston University.

PROPERTY—PERSONAL, Third Edition (1954)

The late Everett Fraser, Dean of the Law School Emeritus, University of Minnesota—Third Edition by
Charles W. Taintor II, late Professor of Law, University of Pittsburgh.

PROPERTY—REAL—INTRODUCTION, Third Edition (1954)

The late Everett Fraser, Dean of the Law School Emeritus, University of Minnesota.

PROPERTY—REAL PROPERTY AND CONVEYANCING (1954)

Edward E. Bade, late Professor of Law, University of Minnesota.

PROPERTY, MODERN REAL, FUNDAMENTALS OF (1974)

Edward H. Rabin, Professor of Law, University of California, Davis.

PROPERTY, REAL, PROBLEMS IN (Pamphlet) (1969)

Edward H. Rabin, Professor of Law, University of California, Davis.

PUBLIC UTILITY LAW, see Free Enterprise, also Regulated Industries

REAL ESTATE PLANNING (1974) with Problems and Statutory Supplement

Norton L. Steuben, Professor of Law, University of Colorado.

RECEIVERSHIP AND CORPORATE REORGANIZATION, see Creditors' Rights

REGULATED INDUSTRIES (1967) with Statutory Supplement

William K. Jones, Professor of Law, Columbia University.

RESTITUTION, Second Edition (1966)

John W. Wade, Professor of Law, Vanderbilt University.

SALES AND SECURITY, Fourth Edition (1962), with Statutory Supplement

George G. Bogert, James Parker Hall Professor of Law Emeritus, University of Chicago.
The late William E. Britton, Professor of Law, University of California, Hastings College of the Law, and
William D. Hawkland, Professor of Law, University of Illinois.

SALES AND SALES FINANCING, Third Edition (1968) with Statutory Supplement

John Honnold, Professor of Law, University of Pennsylvania.

SECURITY, Third Edition (1959)

The late John Hanna, Professor of Law Emeritus, Columbia University.

SECURITIES REGULATION, Third Edition (1972) with 1975 Statutory Supplement and 1975 Case Supplement

Richard W. Jennings, Professor of Law, University of California, Berkeley.
Harold Marsh, Jr., Professor of Law, University of California, Los Angeles.

SOCIAL WELFARE AND THE INDIVIDUAL (1971)

Robert J. Levy, Professor of Law, University of Minnesota.
Thomas P. Lewis, Professor of Law, Boston University.
Peter W. Martin, Professor of Law, Cornell University.

TAXATION, FEDERAL, Sixth Edition (1966) with 1972 Supplement

Erwin N. Griswold, Solicitor General of the United States.

TAXATION, FEDERAL ESTATE AND GIFT, 1961 Edition with 1973 Supplement

William C. Warren, Professor of Law, Columbia University, and
Stanley S. Surrey, Professor of Law, Harvard University.

TAXATION, FEDERAL INCOME (1972) with 1974 Supplement

James J. Freeland, Professor of Law, University of Florida.
Richard B. Stephens, Professor of Law, University of Florida.

TAXATION, FEDERAL INCOME, Volume I, Personal Tax (1972) with 1975 Supplement; Volume II, Corporate and Partnership Taxation (1973)

Stanley S. Surrey, Professor of Law, Harvard University.
William C. Warren, Professor of Law, Columbia University.
Paul R. McDaniel, Professor of Law, Boston College Law School.
Hugh J. Ault, Professor of Law, Boston College Law School.

UNIVERSITY CASEBOOK SERIES—Continued

TAXES AND FINANCE—STATE AND LOCAL (1974)

Oliver Oldman, Professor of Law, Harvard University.
Ferdinand P. Schoettle, Professor of Law, University of Minnesota.

TORT LAW AND ALTERNATIVES: INJURIES AND REMEDIES (1971)

Marc A. Franklin, Professor of Law, Stanford University.

TORTS, Second Edition (1952)

The late Harry Shulman, Dean of the Law School, Yale University, and
Fleming James, Jr., Professor of Law, Yale University.

TORTS, Fifth Edition (1971)

The late William L. Prosser, Professor of Law, University of California,
Hastings College of the Law.
John W. Wade, Professor of Law, Vanderbilt University.

TRADE REGULATION (1975)

Milton Handler, Professor of Law Emeritus, Columbia University.
Harlan M. Blake, Professor of Law, Columbia University.
Robert Pitofsky, Professor of Law, Georgetown University.
Harvey J. Goldschmid, Professor of Law, Columbia University.

TRADE REGULATION, see Free Enterprise

TRANSNATIONAL LEGAL PROBLEMS (1968) with 1973 Documentary Supplement

Henry J. Steiner, Professor of Law, Harvard University.
Detlev F. Vagts, Professor of Law, Harvard University.

TRIAL ADVOCACY (1968)

A. Leo Levin, Professor of Law, University of Pennsylvania.
Harold Cramer, Esq., Member of the Philadelphia Bar, (Maurice Rosenberg, Professor of Law, Columbia University, as consultant).

TRUSTS, Fourth Edition (1967)

George G. Bogert, James Parker Hall Professor of Law Emeritus, University of Chicago.
Dallin H. Oaks, President, Brigham Young University.

TRUSTS AND SUCCESSION, Second Edition (1968)

George E. Palmer, Professor of Law, University of Michigan.

UNFAIR COMPETITION, see Competitive Process and Business Torts

UNITED NATIONS IN ACTION (1968)

Louis B. Sohn, Professor of Law, Harvard University.

UNITED NATIONS LAW, Second Edition (1967) with Documentary Supplement (1968)

Louis B. Sohn, Professor of Law, Harvard University.

WATER RESOURCE MANAGEMENT (1971) with 1973 Supplement

Charles J. Meyers, Professor of Law, Stanford University.
A. Dan Tarlock, Professor of Law, Indiana University.

WILLS AND ADMINISTRATION, 5th Edition (1961)

The late Philip Mechem, Professor of Law, University of Pennsylvania, and
The late Thomas E. Atkinson, Professor of Law, New York University.

WORLD LAW, see United Nations Law

University Casebook Series

EDITORIAL BOARD

CASES AND MATERIALS

ON

CONSTITUTIONAL LAW

By
GERALD GUNTHER
William Nelson Cromwell Professor of Law,
Stanford University

NINTH EDITION

Mineola, N. Y.
THE FOUNDATION PRESS, INC.
1975

For Bobby, Daniel, Andrew

*

PREFACE

I have enjoyed writing this casebook. I have not enjoyed such post-writing tasks as the reading of galleys. So, too, with this final step: for me, writing a preface is a chore, not a joy. I do not think that prefaces are *necessary* evils: no prefatory capsule can provide an adequate overview of contents; after months of writing (and after preparing a detailed Table of Contents), I would prefer to have readers gather what this book is all about by examining the pages that follow. Nevertheless, I have not resisted the tradition of beginning with a preface. My reasons go beyond the pressures of conformity. There is independent ground for some introductory words in the need to explain the fact that, though this is the first edition of the book to bear solely my name, it carries the designation of a Ninth Edition. Sketching the history of the book in turn prompts some comments on my approach—and affords opportunity, too, for acknowledgments of aid and stimulation received.

Evolution. This book is the successor to a series begun by Noel T. Dowling, late Harlan Fiske Stone Professor of Constitutional Law at Columbia University. Noel Dowling's first edition was published in 1937. The final one bearing only his name, the Sixth Edition, appeared in 1959. In the late fifties, Noel Dowling urged that Herbert Wechsler and I undertake the continuation of the casebook. We ultimately agreed to do so, with the understanding that we would be free to elaborate (or depart from) the Dowling model in order to reflect our own ideas. Noel Dowling, that true and fine gentleman, readily concurred.

Early in the 1960's, Herbert Wechsler and I outlined an approach for a new edition. Other commitments kept us from carrying through our plans immediately. In the fall of 1964, I agreed to prepare an updating of Noel Dowling's last edition. That task, I found, provided the opportunity for considerable rewriting as well. Thus, the 1965 edition—the Seventh Edition, Dowling and Gunther—was a partial implementation of the sketch Herbert Wechsler and I had drawn. That revision proved extensive enough to prompt Herbert Wechsler to urge me to go ahead on my own in future editions.

I completed that substantial revision with the Eighth Edition—the 1970 edition, Gunther and Dowling. When I turned to the preparation of this Ninth Edition, then, I anticipated that the task would largely be one of updating my earlier revisions. I underestimated the changes in the intervening years, in constitutional doctrine and in my own thinking—and underestimated my own compulsiveness as well. As I worked on this edition, the effort to restrict my focus to recent changes proved too confining. My teaching and writing since the last edition had led me to rethink a wide range of problems. I accordingly found it far more satisfying to rewrite.

This edition, then, is a complete revision of the predecessors. It is, above all, a reflection of my own tastes, in organization and in analysis, as of

1975. Yet in casebook writing generally—and especially in revising a book with the history of this one—no author is an island. Though Noel Dowling and I never collaborated, his influence persists: as with earlier editions, I have tried to preserve the strengths which gained the Dowling book such wide acceptance for nearly three decades. And though Herbert Wechsler's name has never appeared as co-author in this series, his imprint remains strong—not only because of the sketch for a revision he and I prepared in the early sixties, but also, and primarily, because of the pervasive influence that friend and former Columbia colleague has had on my own thinking. Their efforts provided the base for this outlet for my own views and tastes.

Approach. My approach is best reflected in the materials which follow: as I have said, the detailed Table of Contents and the text convey my views about structure and analysis far better than anything I can say here. The book is fairly traditional in structure—but, I hope, original and stimulating in content. My aim is to promote serious, critical study of constitutional interpretation and decisionmaking. There are at least three ways of structuring a constitutional law casebook: the traditional topical organization, emphasizing doctrinal themes, functional problems, and constitutional provisions; the historical, chronological one; and the methodological, process-oriented one, focusing on pervasive problems of modes of adjudication, allocations of decisionmaking authority, and sources of constitutional interpretation, from text and history to structural and contemporary values. I believe that all three perspectives are essential ones. My choice of the traditional, topical organization rests on the belief that it continues to be the best vehicle for the pursuit of all the major themes.

No casebook writer's juggling capacities are equal to the task of keeping all of those themes at the forefront at all times. My major device for pursuit of that goal has been to intersperse extensive notes throughout the topical organization. Repeatedly, I call attention to the historical context. Even more often, I examine the recurrent questions of process, methodology, and allocations of decisionmaking authority. That far more extensive textual commentary in this edition marks one of the major changes from previous ones. I have gone beyond brief, occasionally rhetorical questions to attempt clearer exposition of groundwork and fuller analysis of interrelationships. I have also sought to promote a sharper focus on the most challenging questions by providing introductory overviews to chapters of special richness and complexity—e. g., those on equal protection, freedom of expression, and congressional power to implement, and perhaps to modify, rights under the post-Civil War Amendments.

The difficulties of intertwining a range of organizing themes are matched by the problems of assuring attention to several layers of issues. Identifying doctrinal developments—where we are, where we have been, where we may be going—is a necessary but not sufficient ingredient of constitutional law materials for an informed lawyer and decisionmaker. What are legitimate sources and adequate justifications for constitutional interpretation? What is the authority and responsibility of nonjudicial organs for

constitutional interpretation? What is the meaning of, and justification for, the varying modes of judicial review, the varying intensities of judicial scrutiny? Themes such as these, noted repeatedly in earlier editions, are more fully and more systematically traced in this one.

I have made some changes in the organization of the book, and more changes in relative space allocations. But the basic structure of recent editions remains intact: I begin with an examination of judicial review authority in Part I; Part II deals with problems of governmental structure; Part III turns to issues of individual rights. The major change in Part I has been the deferral of detailed consideration of jurisdictional themes in the exercise of judicial review. Consideration of "case or controversy" and related limitations on judicial authority now appears as chapter 15, the last chapter. Developments of those "jurisdictional" principles—issues such as standing and ripeness and abstention—have increasingly been influenced by the underlying substantive rights involved, and I have accordingly found it easier to deal with those problems after an examination of substantive materials.

Part II, on structure, continues to deal not only with questions of federalism, but also with problems of separation of powers. When I reintroduced a chapter on separation of powers in the last edition, some readers questioned its utility, on the ground that most of those concerns were obsolete and that there were in any event too few judicial decisions to make the problems "teachable." The events culminating in the Nixon impeachment proceedings and the War Powers Resolution of 1973 have quieted the charges of obsolescence; and, though there are more court decisions now, I have never thought that constitutional law was a subject to be pursued solely in judicial opinions. I have retained considerable emphasis on problems of federalism, though in condensed form. They are materials vital to an understanding of court roles and capacities; they provide illuminating historical perspective; and they retain sufficient practical significance to warrant contemporary study. The major deletion in Part II has been the long chapter on state taxation of interstate commerce: a fuller study of problems of state regulation of commerce seems to me to provide a more interesting and useful context for an examination of governing principles and competing considerations.

Part III, on individual rights, receives greater emphasis than ever: it now occupies about two-thirds of the book. That is an inevitable reflection of the direction and rapid pace of modern constitutional developments. When Noel Dowling wrote his Preface to his first edition in 1937, he began by saying that his principal aim was "to build a course [on] the major theme of the regulatory power of government." Preoccupation with governmental power was understandably central in a book published in the wake of the New Deal's Court-packing crisis. Preoccupation with individual rights is similarly understandable in a book published in the wake of Warren era changes and in the midst of Burger era modifications. Equal protection was the theme of one of the shortest chapters in Dowling's first edition; it is the title of the longest chapter in this one. My two chapters on freedom of expression exceed even the equal protection analysis in length.

Substantive due process developments have been reorganized to contrast more sharply the discredited use of that doctrine in an earlier era with its modern revival in the contraception and abortion decisions. And the powers of Congress under the post-Civil War Amendments, powers moribund in 1937, warrant an expanded chapter with detailed analytical notes in this edition. (That chapter, chapter 11, has been moved from Part II to Part III of the book to permit consideration of the legislative role after judicial interpretations of due process and equal protection are examined.)

Over the years, some areas once staples of constitutional law courses have developed such an identity and complexity of their own as to warrant treatment as separate disciplines. What was once the fate of administrative law, for example, has now become appropriate for the constitutional requirements of criminal procedure. Some samples of those developments are retained, for the light they throw on the general evolution of due process standards and the incorporation controversy; but full treatment of the details is left to other courses. Despite deletions such as that, this book is somewhat longer than the Eighth Edition—though considerably shorter than that edition plus the nearly 500 pages of its most recent Supplement. I believe I have kept the book to manageable size. But, as in the past, I have refused to permit editing of cases to degenerate into the gathering of skeletal segments of opinions. I have resorted to textual treatment and summaries even more frequently than before; but some of the space saved through that technique has been absorbed by the fuller descriptive and analytical notes.* But the selection of materials here, and their organization, should not be viewed as an effort at dogmatic prescription of essentials. I myself do not teach all the materials each year. Moreover, I make changes in sequence each time I teach a constitutional law course. Users of the book will no doubt continue to use individual judgments as to coverage and sequence. My aim has been to provide as stimulating and full a treatment of the covered problems as space permits. (This volume covers developments through early June, 1975.)

Perhaps more important than these comments about approach and coverage is the reiteration of a theme I stated in earlier editions: "Inevitably, I relied heavily upon my own experience with students and, above all, my own tastes: I have sought to compile the kind of volume I would most enjoy using in class." I expect to enjoy using this one, though its organization is probably closer to what I did the last time I taught than what I will do when I teach next. I think constitutional law is an important, serious, endlessly intriguing and constantly enjoyable subject. Conveying that sense to my students has always been my highest goal. To convey some of that sense to the users of this book is its chief purpose.

Acknowledgments. Adequate acknowledgment would include everyone I have talked with about constitutional law, and all I have read about it. A more circumscribed focus would reemphasize the debts I owe to Noel

---

* As in the past, I have been highly selective with regard to bibliographical references. I frequently cite Selected Essays 1938–62 (1963); the reference is to Selected Essays on Constitutional Law 1938–1962 (1963), compiled by a Committee of the Association of American Law Schools.

Dowling and Herbert Wechsler. In more recent years, I have benefited above all from the stimulating collegiality of Paul Brest and William Cohen. Both were engaged in casebook writing while I was at work on this edition. I have learned much from Paul Brest's brilliant, original, lucid Processes of Constitutional Decisionmaking (1975). I have benefited as well from portions of the manuscript of a book on civil liberties for undergraduates which William Cohen is preparing in collaboration with another colleague, John Kaplan. I have also been helped by valuable comments from those who have used my book at other schools: the late and much missed Alexander M. Bickel and Harry Kalven, Jr.; my recent colleagues at Harvard, John Hart Ely, Andrew L. Kaufman, and Laurence H. Tribe; and Gerhard Casper, Norman Dorsen, R. Kent Greenawalt, Kenneth L. Karst, Hans Linde, Arnold Loewy, Paul J. Mishkin, the Hon. Jon O. Newman, Michael E. Smith, and Frank R. Strong, among many others.

I am grateful, too, to the Stanford students who helped me with the chores of cite checking and proof reading. And over the years, I have been especially fortunate in having had the assistance of extraordinary secretaries. I acknowledged the great contributions of Bess Hitchcock in my earlier editions. I feared catastrophe when she retired; that prospect was averted when B Fahr came to work with me. I would praise her remarkable combination of intelligence and effectiveness even more loudly were I not afraid that a colleague would steal her. Without her—and without the classical music stations in the San Francisco area—timely completion of this book, and retention of my sanity, would have been impossible.

GERALD GUNTHER

Stanford, California
June, 1975

SUMMARY OF CONTENTS

TABLE OF CONTENTS

TABLE OF CONTENTS

PART II

THE STRUCTURE OF GOVERNMENT: NATION AND STATES IN THE FEDERAL SYSTEM

Section 1. State Regulation and the Dormant Commerce Clause —Continued

B. State Regulation of Transportation—Continued

TABLE OF CONTENTS

Page

PART III

INDIVIDUAL RIGHTS

TABLE OF CONTENTS

xlix

TABLE OF CONTENTS

Section 2. Expression in Public Places and the Maintenance of Local Peace and Order: Regulating the "Time, Place and Manner" Rather Than the Content of Speech in the "Public Forum"?—Continued

B. Evolving Doctrines: Noisy, Abrasive Speakers; Sensitive, Hostile Audiences—Continued

lix

TABLE OF CONTENTS

TABLE OF CASES

The major cases are in italic type. Other cases discussed are in roman type. References are to pages.

THE CONSTITUTION

OF THE

UNITED STATES OF AMERICA

We the People of the United States, in Order to form a more perfect Union, establish Justice, insure domestic Tranquility, provide for the common defence, promote the general Welfare, and secure the Blessings of Liberty to ourselves and our Posterity, do ordain and establish this Constitution for the United States of America.

ARTICLE I.

SECTION 1. All legislative Powers herein granted shall be vested in a Congress of the United States, which shall consist of a Senate and House of Representatives.

SECTION 2. The House of Representatives shall be composed of Members chosen every second Year by the People of the several States, and the Electors in each State shall have the Qualifications requisite for Electors of the most numerous Branch of the State Legislature.

No Person shall be a Representative who shall not have attained to the Age of twenty five Years, and been seven Years a Citizen of the United States, and who shall not, when elected, be an Inhabitant of that State in which he shall be chosen.

Representatives and direct Taxes shall be apportioned among the several States which may be included within this Union, according to their respective Numbers, which shall be determined by adding to the whole Number of free Persons, including those bound to Service for a Term of Years, and excluding Indians not taxed, three fifths of all other Persons. The actual Enumeration shall be made within three Years after the first Meeting of the Congress of the United States, and within every subsequent Term of ten Years, in such Manner as they shall by Law direct. The Number of Representatives shall not exceed one for every thirty Thousand, but each State shall have at Least one Representative; and until such enumeration shall be made, the State of New Hampshire shall be entitled to chuse three, Massachusetts eight, Rhode Island and Providence Plantations one, Connecticut five, New-York six, New Jersey four, Pennsylvania eight, Delaware one, Maryland six, Virginia ten, North Carolina five, South Carolina five, and Georgia three.

When vacancies happen in the Representation from any State, the Executive Authority thereof shall issue Writs of Election to fill such Vacancies.

The House of Representatives shall chuse their Speaker and other Officers; and shall have the sole Power of Impeachment.

SECTION 3. The Senate of the United States shall be composed of two Senators from each State, chosen by the Legislature thereof, for six Years; and each Senator shall have one Vote.

Immediately after they shall be assembled in Consequence of the first Election, they shall be divided as equally as may be into three Classes. The

Seats of the Senators of the first Class shall be vacated at the Expiration of the second Year, of the second Class at the Expiration of the fourth Year, and of the third Class at the Expiration of the sixth Year, so that one third may be chosen every second Year; and if Vacancies happen by Resignation, or otherwise, during the Recess of the Legislature of any State, the Executive thereof may make temporary Appointments until the next Meeting of the Legislature, which shall then fill such Vacancies.

No Person shall be a Senator who shall not have attained to the Age of thirty Years, and been nine Years a Citizen of the United States, and who shall not, when elected, be an Inhabitant of that State for which he shall be chosen.

The Vice President of the United States shall be President of the Senate, but shall have no Vote, unless they be equally divided.

The Senate shall chuse their other Officers, and also a President pro tempore, in the Absence of the Vice President, or when he shall exercise the Office of President of the United States.

The Senate shall have the sole Power to try all Impeachments. When sitting for that Purpose, they shall be on Oath or Affirmation. When the President of the United States is tried the Chief Justice shall preside: And no Person shall be convicted without the Concurrence of two thirds of the Members present.

Judgment in Cases of Impeachment shall not extend further than to removal from Office, and disqualification to hold and enjoy any Office of honor, Trust or Profit under the United States: but the Party convicted shall nevertheless be liable and subject to Indictment, Trial, Judgment and Punishment, according to Law.

SECTION 4. The Times, Places and Manner of holding Elections for Senators and Representatives, shall be prescribed in each State by the Legislature thereof; but the Congress may at any time by Law make or alter such Regulations, except as to the Places of chusing Senators.

The Congress shall assemble at least once in every Year, and such Meeting shall be on the first Monday in December, unless they shall by Law appoint a different Day.

SECTION 5. Each House shall be the Judge of the Elections, Returns and Qualifications of its own Members, and a Majority of each shall constitute a Quorum to do Business; but a smaller Number may adjourn from day to day, and may be authorized to compel the Attendance of absent Members, in such Manner, and under such Penalties as each House may provide.

Each House may determine the Rules of its Proceedings, punish its Members for disorderly Behaviour, and, with the Concurrence of two thirds, expel a Member.

Each House shall keep a Journal of its Proceedings, and from time to time publish the same, excepting such Parts as may in their Judgment require Secrecy; and the Yeas and Nays of the Members of either House on any question shall, at the Desire of one fifth of those Present, be entered on the Journal.

Neither House, during the Session of Congress, shall, without the Consent of the other, adjourn for more than three days, nor to any other Place than that in which the two Houses shall be sitting.

SECTION 6. The Senators and Representatives shall receive a Compensation for their Services, to be ascertained by Law, and paid out of the Treasury of the United States. They shall in all Cases, except Treason, Felony and Breach of the Peace, be privileged from Arrest during their Attendance at the Session of their respective Houses, and in going to and returning from the same; and for any Speech or Debate in either House, they shall not be questioned in any other Place.

No Senator or Representative shall, during the Time for which he was elected, be appointed to any civil Office under the Authority of the United States, which shall have been created, or the Emoluments whereof shall have been encreased during such time; and no Person holding any Office under the United States, shall be a Member of either House during his Continuance in Office.

SECTION 7. All Bills for raising Revenue shall originate in the House of Representatives; but the Senate may propose or concur with amendments as on other Bills.

Every Bill which shall have passed the House of Representatives and the Senate, shall, before it become a Law, be presented to the President of the United States; If he approve he shall sign it, but if not he shall return it, with his Objections to that House in which it shall have originated, who shall enter the Objections at large on their Journal, and proceed to reconsider it. If after such Reconsideration two thirds of that House shall agree to pass the Bill, it shall be sent, together with the Objections, to the other House, by which it shall likewise be reconsidered, and if approved by two thirds of that House, it shall become a Law. But in all such Cases the Votes of both Houses shall be determined by Yeas and Nays, and the Names of the Persons voting for and against the Bill shall be entered on the Journal of each House respectively. If any Bill shall not be returned by the President within ten Days (Sunday excepted) after it shall have been presented to him, the Same shall be a Law, in like Manner as if he had signed it, unless the Congress by their Adjournment prevent its Return, in which Case it shall not be a Law.

Every Order, Resolution, or Vote to which the Concurrence of the Senate and House of Representatives may be necessary (except on a question of Adjournment) shall be presented to the President of the United States; and before the Same shall take Effect, shall be approved by him, or being disapproved by him, shall be repassed by two thirds of the Senate and House of Representatives, according to the Rules and Limitations prescribed in the Case of a Bill.

SECTION 8. The Congress shall have Power To lay and collect Taxes, Duties, Imposts and Excises, to pay the Debts and provide for the common Defence and general Welfare of the United States; but all Duties, Imposts and Excises shall be uniform throughout the United States;

To borrow Money on the credit of the United States;

To regulate Commerce with foreign Nations, and among the several States, and with the Indian Tribes;

To establish an uniform Rule of Naturalization, and uniform Laws on the subject of Bankruptcies throughout the United States;

To coin Money, regulate the Value thereof, and of foreign Coin, and fix the Standard of Weights and Measures;

To provide for the Punishment of counterfeiting the Securities and current Coin of the United States;

To establish Post Offices and post Roads;

To promote the Progress of Science and useful Arts, by securing for limited Times to Authors and Inventors the exclusive Right to their respective Writings and Discoveries;

To constitute Tribunals inferior to the supreme Court;

To define and punish Piracies and Felonies committed on the high Seas, and Offences against the Law of Nations;

To declare War, grant Letters of Marque and Reprisal, and make Rules concerning Captures on Land and Water;

To raise and support Armies, but no Appropriation of Money to that Use shall be for a longer Term than two Years;

To provide and maintain a Navy;

To make Rules for the Government and Regulation of the land and naval Forces;

To provide for calling forth the Militia to execute the Laws of the Union, suppress Insurrections and repel Invasions;

To provide for organizing, arming, and disciplining, the Militia, and for governing such Part of them as may be employed in the Service of the United States, reserving to the States respectively, the Appointment of the Officers, and the Authority of training the Militia according to the discipline prescribed by Congress;

To exercise exclusive Legislation in all Cases whatsoever, over such District (not exceeding ten Miles square) as may, by Cession of particular States, and the Acceptance of Congress, become the Seat of the Government of the United States, and to exercise like Authority over all Places purchased by the Consent of the Legislature of the State in which the Same shall be, for the Erection of Forts, Magazines, Arsenals, dock-Yards, and other needful Buildings;—And

To make all Laws which shall be necessary and proper for carrying into Execution the foregoing Powers, and all other Powers vested by this Constitution in the Government of the United States, or in any Department or Officer thereof.

SECTION 9. The Migration or Importation of such Persons as any of the States now existing shall think proper to admit, shall not be prohibited by the Congress prior to the Year one thousand eight hundred and eight, but a Tax or duty may be imposed on such Importation, not exceeding ten dollars for each Person.

The Privilege of the Writ of Habeas Corpus shall not be suspended, unless when in Cases of Rebellion or Invasion the public Safety may require it.

No Bill of Attainder or ex post facto Law shall be passed.

No Capitation, or other direct, Tax shall be laid, unless in Proportion to the Census or Enumeration herein before directed to be taken.

No Tax or Duty shall be laid on Articles exported from any State.

No Preference shall be given by any Regulation of Commerce or Revenue to the Ports of one State over those of another; nor shall Vessels bound to, or from, one State, be obliged to enter, clear or pay Duties in another.

No Money shall be drawn from the Treasury, but in Consequence of Appropriations made by Law; and a regular Statement and Account of the Receipts and Expenditures of all public Money shall be published from time to time.

No Title of Nobility shall be granted by the United States: And no Person holding any Office of Profit or Trust under them, shall, without the Consent of the Congress, accept of any present, Emolument, Office, or Title, of any kind whatever, from any King, Prince or foreign State.

SECTION 10. No State shall enter into any Treaty, Alliance, or Confederation; grant Letters of Marque and Reprisal; coin Money; emit Bills of Credit; make any Thing but gold and silver Coin a Tender in Payment of Debts; pass any Bill of Attainder, ex post facto Law, or Law impairing the Obligation of Contracts, or grant any Title of Nobility.

No State shall, without the Consent of the Congress, lay any Imposts or Duties on Imports or Exports, except what may be absolutely necessary for executing its inspection Laws: and the net Produce of all Duties and Imposts, laid by any State on Imports or Exports, shall be for the Use of the Treasury of the United States; and all such Laws shall be subject to the Revision and Controul of the Congress.

No State shall, without the Consent of Congress, lay any Duty of Tonnage, keep Troops, or Ships of War in time of Peace, enter into any Agreement or Compact with another State, or with a foreign Power, or engage in War, unless actually invaded, or in such imminent Danger as will not admit of delay.

ARTICLE II.

SECTION 1. The executive Power shall be vested in a President of the United States of America. He shall hold his Office during the Term of four Years, and, together with the Vice President, chosen for the same Term, be elected, as follows

Each State shall appoint, in such Manner as the Legislature thereof may direct, a Number of Electors, equal to the whole Number of Senators and Representatives to which the State may be entitled in the Congress: but no Senator or Representative, or Person holding an Office of Trust or Profit under the United States, shall be appointed an Elector.

The Electors shall meet in their respective States, and vote by Ballot for two Persons, of whom one at least shall not be an Inhabitant of the same State with themselves. And they shall make a List of all the Persons voted for, and of the Number of Votes for each; which List they shall sign and certify, and transmit sealed to the Seat of the Government of the United States, directed to the President of the Senate. The President of the Senate shall, in the Presence of the Senate and House of Representatives, open all the Certificates, and the Votes shall then be counted. The Person having the greatest Number of Votes shall be the President, if such Number be a Majority of the whole Number of Electors appointed; and if there be more than one who have such Majority, and have an equal Number of Votes, then the House of Representatives shall immediately chuse by Ballot one of them for President; and if no Person have a Majority, then from the five highest on the List the said House shall in like Manner chuse the President. But in chusing the President, the Votes shall be taken by States, the Representation from each State having one Vote; a quorum for this Purpose shall consist of a Member or Members from two thirds of the States, and a Majority of all the States shall be necessary to a Choice. In every Case, after the Choice of the President, the Person having the greatest Number of Votes of the Electors shall be the Vice President. But if there should remain two or more who have equal Votes, the Senate shall chuse from them by Ballot the Vice President.

The Congress may determine the Time of chusing the Electors, and the Day on which they shall give their Votes; which Day shall be the same throughout the United States.

No Person except a natural born Citizen, or a Citizen of the United States, at the time of the Adoption of this Constitution, shall be eligible to the Office of President; neither shall any Person be eligible to that Office who shall not have attained to the Age of thirty five Years, and been fourteen Years a Resident within the United States.

In Case of the Removal of the President from Office, or of his Death, Resignation, or Inability to discharge the Powers and Duties of the said Office, the Same shall devolve on the Vice President, and the Congress may by Law provide for the Case of Removal, Death, Resignation or Inability, both of the President and Vice President, declaring what Officer shall then act as President, and such Officer shall act accordingly, until the Disability be removed, or a President shall be elected.

The President shall, at stated Times, receive for his Services, a Compensation, which shall neither be encreased nor diminished during the Period for which he shall have been elected, and he shall not receive within that Period any other Emolument from the United States, or any of them.

Before he enter on the Execution of his Office, he shall take the following Oath or Affirmation:—"I do solemnly swear (or affirm) that I will faithfully execute the Office of President of the United States, and will to the best of my Ability, preserve, protect and defend the Constitution of the United States."

SECTION 2. The President shall be Commander in Chief of the Army and Navy of the United States, and of the Militia of the several States, when called into the actual Service of the United States; he may require the Opinion, in writing, of the principal Officer in each of the executive Departments, upon any Subject relating to the Duties of their respective Offices, and he shall have Power to grant Reprieves and Pardons for Offences against the United States, except in Cases of Impeachment.

He shall have Power, by and with the Advice and Consent of the Senate, to make Treaties, provided two thirds of the Senators present concur; and he shall nominate, and by and with the Advice and Consent of the Senate, shall appoint Ambassadors, other public Ministers and Consuls, Judges of the supreme Court, and all other Officers of the United States, whose Appointments are not herein otherwise provided for, and which shall be established by Law: but the Congress may by Law vest the Appointment of such inferior Officers, as they think proper, in the President alone, in the Courts of Law, or in the Heads of Departments.

The President shall have Power to fill up all Vacancies that may happen during the Recess of the Senate, by granting Commissions which shall expire at the End of their next Session.

SECTION 3. He shall from time to time give to the Congress Information of the State of the Union, and recommend to their Consideration such Measures as he shall judge necessary and expedient; he may, on extraordinary Occasions, convene both Houses, or either of them, and in Case of Disagreement between them, with Respect to the Time of Adjournment, he may adjourn them to such Time as he shall think proper; he shall receive Ambassadors and other public Ministers; he shall take Care that the Laws be faithfully executed, and shall Commission all the Officers of the United States.

SECTION 4. The President, Vice President and all Civil Officers of the United States, shall be removed from Office on Impeachment for, and Conviction of, Treason, Bribery, or other high Crimes and Misdemeanors.

ARTICLE III.

SECTION 1. The judicial Power of the United States, shall be vested in one supreme Court, and in such inferior Courts as the Congress may from time to time ordain and establish. The Judges, both of the supreme and inferior Courts, shall hold their Offices during good Behaviour, and shall, at stated Times, receive for their Services, a Compensation, which shall not be diminished during their Continuance in Office.

SECTION 2. The judicial Power shall extend to all Cases, in Law and Equity, arising under this Constitution, the Laws of the United States, and Treaties made, or which shall be made, under their Authority;—to all Cases affecting Ambassadors, other public Ministers and Consuls;—to all Cases of admiralty and maritime Jurisdiction;—to Controversies to which the United States shall be a Party;—to Controversies between two or more States;—between a State and Citizens of another State;—between Citizens of different States;—between Citizens of the same State claiming Lands under Grants of different States, and between a State, or the Citizens thereof, and foreign States, Citizens or Subjects.

In all Cases affecting Ambassadors, other public Ministers and Consuls, and those in which a State shall be Party, the supreme Court shall have

original Jurisdiction. In all the other Cases before mentioned, the supreme Court shall have appellate Jurisdiction, both as to Law and Fact, with such Exceptions, and under such Regulations as the Congress shall make.

The Trial of all Crimes, except in Cases of Impeachment, shall be by Jury; and such Trial shall be held in the State where the said Crimes shall have been committed; but when not committed within any State, the Trial shall be at such Place or Places as the Congress may by Law have directed.

SECTION 3. Treason against the United States, shall consist only in levying War against them, or in adhering to their Enemies, giving them Aid and Comfort. No Person shall be convicted of Treason unless on the Testimony of two Witnesses to the same overt Act, or on Confession in open Court.

The Congress shall have Power to declare the Punishment of Treason, but no Attainder of Treason shall work Corruption of Blood, or Forfeiture except during the Life of the Person attainted.

ARTICLE IV.

SECTION 1. Full Faith and Credit shall be given in each State to the public Acts, Records, and judicial Proceedings of every other State. And the Congress may by general Laws prescribe the Manner in which such Acts, Records and Proceedings shall be proved, and the Effect thereof.

SECTION 2. The Citizens of each State shall be entitled to all Privileges and Immunities of Citizens in the several States.

A Person charged in any State with Treason, Felony, or other Crime, who shall flee from Justice, and be found in another State, shall on Demand of the executive Authority of the State from which he fled, be delivered up, to be removed to the State having Jurisdiction of the Crime.

No Person held to Service or Labour in one State, under the Laws thereof, escaping into another, shall, in Consequence of any Law or Regulation therein, be discharged from such Service or Labour, but shall be delivered up on Claim of the Party to whom such Service or Labour may be due.

SECTION 3. New States may be admitted by the Congress into this Union; but no new State shall be formed or erected within the Jurisdiction of any other State; nor any State be formed by the Junction of two or more States, or Parts of States, without the Consent of the Legislatures of the States concerned as well as of the Congress.

The Congress shall have Power to dispose of and make all needful Rules and Regulations respecting the Territory or other Property belonging to the United States; and nothing in this Constitution shall be so construed as to Prejudice any Claims of the United States, or of any particular State.

SECTION 4. The United States shall guarantee to every State in this Union a Republican Form of Government, and shall protect each of them against Invasion; and on Application of the Legislature, or of the Executive (when the Legislature cannnot be convened) against domestic Violence.

ARTICLE V.

The Congress, whenever two thirds of both Houses shall deem it necessary, shall propose Amendments to this Constitution, or, on the Application of the Legislatures of two thirds of the several States, shall call a Convention for proposing Amendments, which, in either Case, shall be valid to all Intents and Purposes, as Part of this Constitution, when ratified by the Legislatures of three fourths of the several States, or by Conventions in three fourths thereof, as the one or the other Mode of Ratification may be

proposed by the Congress; Provided that no Amendment which may be made prior to the Year One thousand eight hundred and eight shall in any Manner affect the first and fourth Clauses in the Ninth Section of the first Article; and that no State, without its Consent, shall be deprived of its equal Suffrage in the Senate.

ARTICLE VI.

All Debts contracted and Engagements entered into, before the Adoption of this Constitution, shall be as valid against the United States under this Constitution, as under the Confederation.

This Constitution, and the Laws of the United States which shall be made in Pursuance thereof; and all Treaties made, or which shall be made, under the Authority of the United States, shall be the supreme Law of the Land; and the Judges in every State shall be bound thereby, any Thing in the Constitution or Laws of any State to the Contrary notwithstanding.

The Senators and Representatives before mentioned, and the Members of the several State Legislatures, and all executive and judicial Officers, both of the United States and of the several States, shall be bound by Oath or Affirmation, to support this Constitution; but no religious Test shall ever be required as a Qualification to any Office or public Trust under the United States.

ARTICLE VII.

The Ratification of the Conventions of nine States, shall be sufficient for the Establishment of this Constitution between the States so ratifying the Same.*

* * *

ARTICLES IN ADDITION TO, AND AMENDMENT OF, THE CONSTITUTION OF THE UNITED STATES OF AMERICA, PROPOSED BY CONGRESS, AND RATIFIED BY THE SEVERAL STATES, PURSUANT TO THE FIFTH ARTICLE OF THE ORIGINAL CONSTITUTION.

AMENDMENT I(1791].

Congress shall make no law respecting an establishment of religion, or prohibiting the free exercise thereof; or abridging the freedom of speech, or of the press; or the right of the people peaceably to assemble, and to petition the Government for a redress of grievances.

AMENDMENT II[1791].

A well regulated Militia, being necessary to the security of a free State, the right of the people to keep and bear Arms, shall not be infringed.

AMENDMENT III[1791].

No Soldier shall, in time of peace be quartered in any house, without the consent of the Owner, nor in time of war, but in a manner to be prescribed by law.

AMENDMENT IV[1791].

The right of the people to be secure in their persons, houses, papers, and effects, against unreasonable searches and seizures, shall not be violated, and no Warrants shall issue, but upon probable cause, supported by Oath or affirmation, and particularly describing the place to be searched, and the persons or things to be seized.

AMENDMENT V[1791].

No person shall be held to answer for a capital, or otherwise infamous crime, unless on a presentment or indictment of a Grand Jury, except in cases arising in the land or naval forces, or in the Militia, when in actual service in time of War or public danger; nor shall any person be subject for the same offence to be twice put in jeopardy of life or limb; nor shall be compelled in any criminal case to be a witness against himself, nor be deprived of life, liberty, or property, without due process of law; nor shall private property be taken for public use, without just compensation.

AMENDMENT VI[1791].

In all criminal prosecutions, the accused shall enjoy the right to a speedy and public trial, by an impartial jury of the State and district wherein the crime shall have been committed, which district shall have been previously ascertained by law, and to be informed of the nature and cause of the accusation; to be confronted with the witnesses against him; to have compulsory process for obtaining Witnesses in his favor, and to have the Assistance of Counsel for his defence.

AMENDMENT VII[1791].

In Suits at common law, where the value in controversy shall exceed twenty dollars, the right of trial by jury shall be preserved, and no fact tried by a jury, shall be otherwise re-examined in any Court of the United States, than according to the rules of the common law.

AMENDMENT VIII[1791].

Excessive bail shall not be required, nor excessive fines imposed, nor cruel and unusual punishments inflicted.

AMENDMENT IX[1791].

The enumeration in the Constitution, of certain rights, shall not be construed to deny or disparage others retained by the people.

AMENDMENT X[1791].

The powers not delegated to the United States by the Constitution, nor prohibited by it to the States, are reserved to the States respectively, or to the people.

AMENDMENT XI[1798].

The Judicial power of the United States shall not be construed to extend to any suit in law or equity, commenced or prosecuted against one of the United States by Citizens of another State, or by Citizens or Subjects of any Foreign State.

AMENDMENT XII[1804].

The Electors shall meet in their respective states and vote by ballot for President and Vice-President, one of whom, at least, shall not be an inhabitant of the same state with themselves; they shall name in their ballots the person voted for as President, and in distinct ballots the person voted for as Vice-President, and they shall make distinct lists of all persons voted for as President, and of all persons voted for as Vice-President, and of the number of votes for each, which lists they shall sign and certify, and transmit sealed to the seat of the government of the United States, directed to the President of the Senate;—The President of the Senate shall, in the presence of the Senate and House of Representatives, open all the certificates and the votes shall then be counted;—The person having the greatest number of votes for President, shall be the President, if such number be a majority of the whole number of Electors appointed; and if no person have such majority, then from the persons having the highest numbers not exceeding three on the list of those voted for as President, the House of Representatives shall choose immediately, by ballot, the President. But in choosing the President, the votes shall be taken by states, the representation from each state having one vote; a quorum for this purpose shall consist of a member or members from two-thirds of the states, and a majority of all the states shall be necessary to a choice. And if the House of Representatives shall not choose a President whenever the right of choice shall devolve upon them, before the fourth day of March next following, then the Vice-President shall act as President, as in the case of the death or other constitutional disability of the President—The person having the greatest number of votes as Vice-President, shall be the Vice-President, if such number be a majority of the whole number of Electors appointed, and if no person have a majority, then from the two highest numbers on the list, the Senate shall choose the Vice-President; a quorum for the purpose shall consist of two-thirds of the whole number of Senators, and a majority of the whole number shall be necessary to a choice. But no person constitutionally ineligible to the office of President shall be eligible to that of Vice-President of the United States.

AMENDMENT XIII[1865].

SECTION 1. Neither slavery nor involuntary servitude, except as a punishment for crime whereof the party shall have been duly convicted, shall exist within the United States, or any place subject to their jurisdiction.

SECTION 2. Congress shall have power to enforce this article by appropriate legislation.

AMENDMENT XIV[1868].

SECTION 1. All persons born or naturalized in the United States and subject to the jurisdiction thereof, are citizens of the United States and of the State wherein they reside. No State shall make or enforce any law which shall abridge the privileges or immunities of citizens of the United States; nor shall any State deprive any person of life, liberty, or property, without due process of law; nor deny to any person within its jurisdiction the equal protection of the laws.

SECTION 2. Representatives shall be apportioned among the several States according to their respective numbers, counting the whole number of persons in each State, excluding Indians not taxed. But when the right to vote at any election for the choice of electors for President and Vice President of the United States, Representatives in Congress, the Executive and Judicial officers of a State, or the members of the Legislature thereof, is denied to any of the male inhabitants of such State, being twenty-one years of age, and citizens of the United States, or in any way abridged, except for participation in rebellion, or other crime, the basis of representation therein shall be reduced in the proportion which the number of such male citizens shall bear to the whole number of male citizens twenty-one years of age in such State.

SECTION 3. No person shall be a Senator or Representative in Congress, or elector of President and Vice President, or hold any office, civil or military, under the United States, or under any State, who, having previously taken an oath, as a member of Congress, or as an officer of the United States, or as a member of any State legislature, or as an executive or judicial officer of any State, to support the Constitution of the United States, shall have engaged in insurrection or rebellion against the same, or given aid or comfort to the enemies thereof. But Congress may by a vote of two-thirds of each House, remove such disability.

SECTION 4. The validity of the public debt of the United States, authorized by law, including debts incurred for payment of pensions and bounties for services in suppressing insurrection or rebellion, shall not be questioned. But neither the United States nor any State shall assume or pay any debt or obligation incurred in aid of insurrection or rebellion against the United States, or any claim for the loss or emancipation of any slave; but all such debts, obligations and claims shall be held illegal and void.

SECTION 5. The Congress shall have power to enforce, by appropriate legislation, the provisions of this article.

AMENDMENT XV[1870].

SECTION 1. The right of citizens of the United States to vote shall not be denied or abridged by the United States or by any State on account of race, color, or previous condition of servitude.

SECTION 2. The Congress shall have power to enforce this article by appropriate legislation.

AMENDMENT XVI[1913].

The Congress shall have power to lay and collect taxes on incomes, from whatever source derived, without apportionment among the several States, and without regard to any census or enumeration.

AMENDMENT XVII[1913].

The Senate of the United States shall be composed of two Senators from each State, elected by the people thereof, for six years; and each Senator shall have one vote. The electors in each State shall have the qualifications requisite for electors of the most numerous branch of the State legislatures.

When vacancies happen in the representation of any State in the Senate, the executive authority of such State shall issue writs of election to fill such vacancies: *Provided*, That the legislature of any State may empower the executive thereof to make temporary appointments until the people fill the vacancies by election as the legislature may direct.

This amendment shall not be so construed as to affect the election or term of any Senator chosen before it becomes valid as part of the Constitution.

AMENDMENT XVIII[1919].

SECTION 1. After one year from the ratification of this article the manufacture, sale, or transportation of intoxicating liquors within, the importation thereof into, or the exportation thereof from the United States and all territory subject to the jurisdiction thereof for beverage purposes is hereby prohibited.

SECTION 2. The Congress and the several States shall have concurrent power to enforce this article by appropriate legislation.

SECTION 3. This article shall be inoperative unless it shall have been ratified as an amendment to the Constitution by the legislatures of the several States, as provided in the Constitution, within seven years from the date of the submission hereof to the States by the Congress.

AMENDMENT XIX[1920].

The right of citizens of the United States to vote shall not be denied or abridged by the United States or by any State on account of sex.

Congress shall have power to enforce this article by appropriate legislation.

AMENDMENT XX[1933].

SECTION 1. The terms of the President and Vice President shall end at noon on the 20th day of January, and the terms of Senators and Representatives at noon on the 3d day of January, of the years in which such terms would have ended if this article had not been ratified; and the terms of their successors shall then begin.

SECTION 2. The Congress shall assemble at least once in every year, and such meeting shall begin at noon on the 3d day of January, unless they shall by law appoint a different day.

SECTION 3. If, at the time fixed for the beginning of the term of the President, the President elect shall have died, the Vice President elect shall become President. If a President shall not have been chosen before the time fixed for the beginning of his term, or if the President elect shall have failed to qualify, then the Vice President elect shall act as President until a President shall have qualified; and the Congress may by law provide for the case wherein neither a President elect nor a Vice President elect shall have qualified, declaring who shall then act as President, or the manner in which one who is to act shall be selected, and such person shall act accordingly until a President or Vice President shall have qualified.

c

SECTION 4. The Congress may by law provide for the case of the death of any of the persons from whom the House of Representatives may choose a President whenever the right of choice shall have devolved upon them, and for the case of the death of any of the persons from whom the Senate may choose a Vice President whenever the right of choice shall have devolved upon them.

SECTION 5. Sections 1 and 2 shall take effect on the 15th day of October following the ratification of this article.

SECTION 6. This article shall be inoperative unless it shall have been ratified as an amendment to the Constitution by the legislatures of three-fourths of the several States within seven years from the date of its submission.

AMENDMENT XXI[1933].

SECTION 1. The eighteenth article of amendment to the Constitution of the United States is hereby repealed.

SECTION 2. The transportation or importation into any State, Territory or possession of the United States for delivery or use therein of intoxicating liquors, in violation of the laws thereof, is hereby prohibited.

SECTION 3. This article shall be inoperative unless it shall have been ratified as an amendment to the Constitution by conventions in the several States, as provided in the Constitution, within seven years from the date of the submission hereof to the States by the Congress.

AMENDMENT XXII[1951].

SECTION 1. No person shall be elected to the office of the President more than twice, and no person who has held the office of President, or acted as President, for more than two years of a term to which some other person was elected President shall be elected to the office of the President more than once. But this Article shall not apply to any person holding the office of President when this Article was proposed by the Congress, and shall not prevent any person who may be holding the office of President, or acting as President, during the term within which this Article becomes operative from holding the office of President or acting as President during the remainder of such term.

SECTION 2. This article shall be inoperative unless it shall have been ratified as an amendment to the Constitution by the legislatures of three-fourths of the several States within seven years from the date of its submission to the States by the Congress.

AMENDMENT XXIII[1961].

SECTION 1. The District constituting the seat of Government of the United States shall appoint in such manner as the Congress may direct:

A number of electors of President and Vice President equal to the whole number of Senators and Representatives in Congress to which the District would be entitled if it were a State, but in no event more than the least populous State; they shall be in addition to those appointed by the States, but they shall be considered, for the purposes of the election of President and Vice President, to be electors appointed by a State; and they shall meet in the District and perform such duties as provided by the twelfth article of amendment.

SECTION 2. The Congress shall have power to enforce this article by appropriate legislation.

AMENDMENT XXIV[1964].

SECTION 1. The right of citizens of the United States to vote in any primary or other election for President or Vice President, for electors for President or Vice President, or for Senator or Representative in Congress, shall not be denied or abridged by the United States or any State by reason of failure to pay any poll tax or other tax.

SECTION 2. The Congress shall have power to enforce this article by appropriate legislation.

AMENDMENT XXV[1967].

SECTION 1. In case of the removal of the President from office or of his death or resignation, the Vice President shall become President.

SECTION 2. Whenever there is a vacancy in the office of the Vice President, the President shall nominate a Vice President who shall take office upon confirmation by a majority vote of both Houses of Congress.

SECTION 3. Whenever the President transmits to the President pro tempore of the Senate and the Speaker of the House of Representatives his written declaration that he is unable to discharge the powers and duties of his office, and until he transmits to them a written declaration to the contrary, such powers and duties shall be discharged by the Vice President as Acting President.

SECTION 4. Whenever the Vice President and a majority of either the principal officers of the executive departments or of such other body as Congress may by law provide, transmit to the President pro tempore of the Senate and the Speaker of the House of Representatives their written declaration that the President is unable to discharge the powers and duties of his office, the Vice President shall immediately assume the powers and duties of the office as Acting President.

Thereafter, when the President transmits to the President pro tempore of the Senate and the Speaker of the House of Representatives his written declaration that no inability exists, he shall resume the powers and duties of his office unless the Vice President and a majority of either the principal officers of the executive department or of such other body as Congress may by law provide, transmit within four days to the President pro tempore of the Senate and the Speaker of the House of Representatives their written declaration that the President is unable to discharge the powers and duties of his office. Thereupon Congress shall decide the issue, assembling within forty-eight hours for that purpose if not in session. If the Congress, within twenty-one days after receipt of the latter written declaration, or, if Congress is not in session, within twenty-one days after Congress is required to assemble, determines by two-thirds vote of both Houses that the President is unable to discharge the powers and duties of his office, the Vice President shall continue to discharge the same as Acting President; otherwise, the President shall resume the powers and duties of his office.

AMENDMENT XXVI[1971].*

SECTION 1. The right of citizens of the United States, who are eighteen years of age or older, to vote shall not be denied or abridged by the United States or by any State on account of age.

* The 26th Amendment was submitted to the States on March 23, 1971—three months after the Supreme Court deci- sion holding unconstitutional the provisions of the Voting Rights Act Amendments of 1970 which had sought

SECTION 2.   The Congress shall have power to enforce this article by appropriate legislation.

AMENDMENT XXVII [Proposed].†

SECTION 1.   Equality of rights under the law shall not be denied or abridged by the United States or by any State on account of sex.

SECTION 2.   The Congress shall have the power to enforce, by appropriate legislation, the provisions of this article.

SECTION 3.   This amendment shall take effect two years after the date of ratification.

to authorize 18-year-olds to vote in state elections.   See Oregon v. Mitchell, 400 U.S. 112 (1970), chap. 11, sec. 4, below.   Three months later, on June 30, 1971, the ratification process was completed.

† The proposed 27th Amendment was submitted to the states on March 22, 1972.   Although about half of the necessary number of states approved the Amendment in the first three months after submission, the drive for adoption of the Equal Rights Amendment slowed thereafter.   By June 1975, support for the Amendment still fell at least four short of the required 38 ratifying state legislatures.   (See also the materials on gender-based discrimination in chap. 10, sec. 3B, below.)

†

CASES AND MATERIALS ON
CONSTITUTIONAL LAW

Part I

THE JUDICIAL FUNCTION
IN CONSTITUTIONAL CASES

Chapter 1

THE NATURE AND SOURCES OF THE SUPREME
COURT'S AUTHORITY

Introduction. Constitutional law courses and materials emphasize Supreme Court decisions. But the Supreme Court is not the only court authorized to examine constitutional claims, and courts are not the only forums for significant constitutional debates. In the cases that follow, only a very few passages of the constitutional text get extensive scrutiny: the few words about judicial power in Art. III; the allocations of legislative powers found especially in Art. I, § 8; the individual rights guarantees in the Bill of Rights and the post-Civil War Amendments. Yet many of the other provisions significantly affect the operations of constitutional government: those dealing with selection and structure of Presidency and Congress are obvious illustrations. And some provisions (that on impeachment, for instance) have given rise to major constitutional controversies that have not reached the courts.

Yet more than pedagogical tradition supports the emphasis on the Supreme Court. On those questions that do get to court, the Supreme Court's last word makes it obviously the most important judicial voice. And a remarkable range of constitutional questions *has* reached the Court: the more than 400 volumes of reports of a Court increasingly preoccupied with constitutional questions are no doubt the richest source of constitutional law.

It is traditional, too, to begin the examination of constitutional law problems with opinions from the Court presided over by Chief Justice John Marshall early in the nineteenth century. Thus, Part I of this book begins with Marbury v. Madison; Part II, with McCulloch v. Maryland and Gibbons v. Ogden. Attention to Marshall Court cases is more than a ritualistic bow to historical landmarks: the reason is not simply that those cases were important in the development of judicial authority and federal power allocations; it is also that those cases of the early 1800's—much more so than many of the decisions of intervening years—are important *now*.

1

So it is with Marbury v. Madison. Some attention to it would be justified if it represented no more than the historical fact of the Court's first elaborate statement of its judicial review powers. But the extensive concern with Marbury here would not be warranted if it were merely a closed, albeit important, book. Instead, Marbury is very much alive: it rests on reasoning significant for the exercise of judicial power today.

To what extent, for example, is the authority asserted in Marbury simply an incidental by-product of the ordinary judicial function in deciding lawsuits: to look to the governing law, to consider the Constitution as one relevant source of law—and, in cases of conflicting legal statements, to give priority to the Constitution and to refuse enforcement of any contravening legal statement? To what extent does the Marbury authority rest instead on a claim that the Constitution thrust a more extraordinary mission upon the Supreme Court? Was the Court endowed with a roving commission to police the other branches—a charge to be the overseeing guardian of constitutional norms, to be the special enforcer of constitutional restrictions? In the proper reading of Marbury, in the answers to these questions, may lie answers to many of the questions raised in this chapter (and further pursued in chap. 15): May Congress curtail the Court's constitutional business? May the Court intervene in all constitutional disputes? Should it? Must it? When is resort to the Court appropriate? When permissible? Who may obtain answers to constitutional questions from the Court? When? As to what questions?

Understanding the core reasoning of Marbury, then, is essential to thinking about Court power today. And appreciation of the Marbury reasoning in turn requires some attention to historical antecedents and context. The assertions of the power, and the justifications for it, did not spring full-blown in 1803: they reflected a variety of earlier developments, some directly relevant, some tangentially so. And it was only because a concrete dispute had been brought to the Court that John Marshall had an opportunity to speak about judicial power. To develop these themes of intellectual and political history, as well as to explore a number of issues opened up by Marbury, is the purpose of the materials that follow the case.

SECTION 1.   JUDICIAL REVIEW: THE BASES AND IMPLICATIONS OF MARBURY v. MADISON

MARBURY v. MADISON

1 Cranch * 137, 2 L.Ed. 60 (1803).

On Petition for Mandamus.

[William Marbury was one of those named a justice of the peace for the District of Columbia at the very close of the Federalist Administration of President John Adams, during that rash of last minute judicial appointments in March 1801 described in the historical note which follows this case. The incoming Jefferson Administration chose to disregard those appointments for which formal commissions had not been delivered before the end of Adams' term.   Marbury and some disappointed colleagues then decided to go directly to the Supreme Court of the United States, in the December term 1801, to compel Jefferson's Secretary of State Madison to deliver their commissions.   The Court was not able to decide on their 1801 request until February 1803.   Before printing the opinion, the reporter summarized the earlier proceedings briefly.   His paragraph is reprinted here both to clarify the technical posture of the case and to dramatize (by adding some proper names in brackets) the involvement of John Marshall in the underlying dispute.]

At the last term, viz., December term, 1801, William Marbury, Dennis Ramsay, Robert Townsend Hooe, and William Harper, by their counsel, Charles Lee, Esq., late attorney general of the United States, severally moved the court for a rule to James Madison, Secretary of State of the United States, to show cause why a mandamus should not issue commanding him to cause to be delivered to them respectively their several commissions as justices of the peace in the District of Columbia.   This motion was supported by affidavits [including one by John Marshall's brother James] of the following facts: that notice of this motion had been given to Mr. Madison; that Mr. Adams, the late President of the United States, nominated the applicants to

---

* 1 Cranch was the first volume devoted wholly to the reports of cases in the Supreme Court, and it was not published until 1804.   The 1790's cases were reported by A. J. Dallas in volumes which also covered Pennsylvania decisions.   In 1816 Congress made provision for an official reporter.   Henry Wheaton of New York was the first incumbent.   He was succeeded in 1827 by Richard Peters, Jr., with whom he became involved in litigation, Wheaton v. Peters, 8 Pet. 591 (1834), on whether a reporter "has or can have any copyright in the written opinions delivered by this Court."   Wheaton lost. In 1884 it was announced (108 U.S. vi)

that it "is the custom of the Court to cite decisions reported since Wallace only by the number in the official series, as '91 U.S.,' '92 U.S.,' &c." Up to 91 U.S., the reporters, and number of volumes for each, were as follows: Dallas, 4;   Cranch, 9;   Wheaton, 12; Peters, 16;   Howard, 24;   Black, 2; Wallace, 23.

Almost all of the principal cases in this volume, and most of those discussed in the notes, are decisions of the United States Supreme Court.   Accordingly, the tribunal is not named in the materials below unless it is a court other than the Supreme Court.

the senate for their advice and consent to be appointed justices of the peace of the District of Columbia; that the senate advised and consented to the appointments; that commissions in due form were signed by the said President appointing them justices, &c.; and that the seal of the United States was in due form affixed to the said commissions by the Secretary of State [John Marshall]; that the applicants have requested Mr. Madison to deliver them their said commissions, who has not complied with that request; and that said commissions are withheld from them . . .. Whereupon a rule was laid to show cause. . . .

Afterwards, on the 24th of February [1803], the following opinion of the Court was delivered by the Chief Justice [MARSHALL]:

Opinion of the Court.

At the last term on the affidavits then read and filed with the clerk, a rule was granted in this case, requiring the Secretary of State to show cause why a mandamus should not issue, directing him to deliver to William Marbury his commission as a justice of the peace for the county of Washington, in the district of Columbia.

No cause has been shown, and the present motion is for a mandamus. The peculiar delicacy of this case, the novelty of some of its circumstances, and the real difficulty attending the points which occur in it, require a complete exposition of the principles on which the opinion to be given by the court is founded.

These principles have been, on the side of the applicant, very ably argued at the bar. In rendering the opinion of the court, there will be some departure in form, though not in substance, from the points stated in that argument.

In the order in which the court has viewed this subject, the following questions have been considered and decided:

1st. Has the applicant a right to the commission he demands?

2d. If he has a right, and that right has been violated, do the laws of this country afford him a remedy?

3d. If they do afford him a remedy, is it a mandamus issuing from this court?

The first object of inquiry is—1st. Has the applicant a right to the commission he demands? . . .

It is . . . decidedly the opinion of the court, that when a commission has been signed by the president, the appointment is made; and that the commission is complete, when the seal of the United States has been affixed to it by the secretary of state. . . .

Mr. Marbury, then, since his commission was signed by the president, and sealed by the secretary of state, was appointed; and as the law creating the office, gave the officer a right to hold for five years, independent of the executive, the appointment was not revocable, but vested in the officer legal rights, which are protected by the laws of his country.

To withhold his commission, therefore, is an act deemed by the court not warranted by law, but violative of a vested legal right.

This brings us to the second enquiry; which is 2dly. If he has a right, and that right has been violated, do the laws of his country afford him a remedy?

The very essence of civil liberty certainly consists in the right of every individual to claim the protection of the laws, whenever he receives an injury. One of the first duties of government is to afford that protection. . . .

The government of the United States has been emphatically termed a government of laws, and not of men. It will certainly cease to deserve this high appellation, if the laws furnish no remedy for the violation of a vested legal right.

If this obloquy is to be cast on the jurisprudence of our country, it must arise from the peculiar character of the case.

It behooves us then to enquire whether there be in its composition any ingredient which shall exempt it from legal investigation, or exclude the injured party from legal redress. . . .

Is it in the nature of the transaction? Is the act of delivering or withholding a commission to be considered as a mere political act, belonging to the executive department alone, for the performance of which entire confidence is placed by our constitution in the supreme executive; and for any misconduct respecting which, the injured individual has no remedy.

That there may be such cases is not to be questioned; but that every act of duty, to be performed in any of the great departments of government, constitutes such a case, is not to be admitted. . . .

It follows, then, that the question, whether the legality of an act of the head of a department be examinable in a court of justice or not, must always depend on the nature of that act. . . .

By the constitution of the United States, the President is invested with certain important political powers, in the exercise of which he is to use his own discretion, and is accountable only to his country in his political character, and to his own conscience. To aid him in the performance of these duties, he is authorized to appoint certain officers, who act by his authority and in conformity with his orders.

In such cases, their acts are his acts; and whatever opinion may be entertained of the manner in which executive discretion may be used, still there exists, and can exist, no power to control that discretion. The subjects are political. They respect the nation, not individual rights, and being entrusted to the executive, the decision of the executive is conclusive. The application of this remark will be perceived by adverting to the act of congress for establishing the department of foreign affairs. This officer, as his duties were prescribed by that act, is to conform precisely to the will of the President. He is the mere organ by whom that will is communicated. The acts of such an officer, as an officer, can never be examinable by the courts.

But when the legislature proceeds to impose on that officer other duties; when he is directed peremptorily to perform certain acts; when the rights of individuals are dependent on the performance of those acts; he is so

far the officer of the law; is amenable to the laws for his conduct; and cannot at his discretion sport away the vested rights of others.

The conclusion from this reasoning is, that where the heads of departments are the political or confidential agents of the executive, merely to execute the will of the President, or rather to act in cases in which the executive professes a constitutional or legal discretion, nothing can be more perfectly clear than that their acts are only politically examinable. But where a specific duty is assigned by law, and individual rights depend upon the performance of that duty, it seems equally clear that the individual who considers himself injured, has a right to resort to the laws of his country for a remedy. . . .

It is, then, the opinion of the Court [that Marbury has a] right to the commission; a refusal to deliver which is a plain violation of that right, for which the laws of his country afford him a remedy.

It remains to be enquired whether,

3dly. He is entitled to the remedy for which he applies. This depends on—1st. The nature of the writ applied for, and,

2dly. The power of this court.

1st. The nature of the writ. . . .

This writ, if awarded, would be directed to an officer of government, and its mandate to him would be, to use the words of Blackstone, "to do a particular thing therein specified, which appertains to his office and duty and which the court has previously determined, or at least supposes, to be consonant to right and justice." Or, in the words of Lord Mansfield, the applicant, in this case, has a right to execute an office of public concern, and is kept out of possession of that right.

These circumstances certainly concur in this case.

Still, to render the mandamus a proper remedy, the officer to whom it is to be directed, must be one to whom, on legal principles, such writ may be directed; and the person applying for it must be without any other specific and legal remedy.

1st. With respect to the officer to whom it would be directed. The intimate political relation, subsisting between the president of the United States and the heads of departments, necessarily renders any legal investigation of the acts of one of those high officers peculiarly irksome, as well as delicate; and excites some hesitation with respect to the propriety of entering into such investigation. Impressions are often received without much reflection or examination, and it is not wonderful, that in such a case as this, the assertion, by an individual, of his legal claims in a court of justice, to which claims it is the duty of that court to attend, should at first view be considered by some, as an attempt to intrude into the cabinet, and to intermeddle with the prerogatives of the executive.

It is scarcely necessary for the court to disclaim all pretensions to such a jurisdiction. An extravagance, so absurd and excessive, could not have been entertained for a moment. The province of the court is, solely, to decide on the rights of individuals, not to enquire how the executive, or executive officers, perform duties in which they have a discretion. Questions, in

their nature political, or which are, by the constitution and laws, submitted to the executive, can never be made in this court.

But, if this be not such a question; if so far from being an intrusion into the secrets of the cabinet, it respects a paper, which, according to law, is upon record, and to a copy of which the law gives a right, on the payment of ten cents; if it be no intermeddling with a subject, over which the executive can be considered as having exercised any control; what is there in the exalted station of the officer, which shall bar a citizen from asserting, in a court of justice, his legal rights, or shall forbid a court to listen to the claim; or to issue a mandamus, directing the performance of a duty, not depending on executive discretion, but on particular acts of congress and the general principles of law?

If one of the heads of departments commits any illegal act, under color of his office, by which an individual sustains an injury, it cannot be pretended that his office alone exempts him from being sued in the ordinary mode of proceeding, and being compelled to obey the judgment of the law. How then can his office exempt him from this particular mode of deciding on the legality of his conduct, if the case be such a case as would, were any other individual the party complained of, authorize the process?

It is not by the office of the person to whom the writ is directed, but the nature of the thing to be done that the propriety or impropriety of issuing a mandamus, is to be determined. Where the head of a department acts in a case, in which executive discretion is to be exercised; in which he is the mere organ of executive will; it is again repeated, that any application to a court to control, in any respect, his conduct, would be rejected without hesitation.

But where he is directed by law to do a certain act affecting the absolute rights of individuals, in the performance of which he is not placed under the particular direction of the President, and the performance of which, the President cannot lawfully forbid, and therefore is never presumed to have forbidden; as for example, to record a commission, or a patent for land, which has received all the legal solemnities; or to give a copy of such record; in such cases, it is not perceived on what ground the courts of the country are further excused from the duty of giving judgment, that right be done to an injured individual, than if the same services were to be performed by a person not the head of a department. . . .

This, then, is a plain case for a mandamus, either to deliver the commission, or a copy of it from the record; and it only remains to be enquired,

Whether it can issue from this court.

The act to establish the judicial courts of the United States authorizes the Supreme Court "to issue writs of mandamus in cases warranted by the principles and usages of law, to any courts appointed, or persons holding office, under the authority of the United States." *

---

* The full text of Section 13 of the Judiciary Act of 1789, 1 Stat. 73: *"And be it further enacted,* That the Supreme Court shall have exclusive jurisdiction of all controversies of a civil nature, where a state is a party, except between a state and its citizens; and except also between a state and citizens of other states, or aliens, in which latter case it shall have original but not exclusive jurisdiction. And shall have exclusively all such jurisdiction of suits or proceedings against ambassadors, or other public

The Secretary of State, being a person holding an office under the authority of the United States, is precisely within the letter of the description; and if this court is not authorized to issue a writ of mandamus to such an officer, it must be because the law is unconstitutional, and therefore absolutely incapable of conferring the authority, and assigning the duties which its words purport to confer and assign.

The constitution vests the whole judicial power of the United States in one Supreme Court, and such inferior courts as congress shall, from time to time, ordain and establish. This power is expressly extended to all cases arising under the laws of the United States; and, consequently, in some form, may be exercised over the present case; because the right claimed is given by a law of the United States.

In the distribution of this power it is declared that "the Supreme Court shall have original jurisdiction in all cases affecting ambassadors, other public ministers and consuls, and those in which a state shall be a party. In all other cases, the Supreme Court shall have appellate jurisdiction."

It has been insisted, at the bar, that as the original grant of jurisdiction, to the supreme and inferior courts, is general, and the clause, assigning original jurisdiction to the Supreme Court, contains no negative or restrictive words, the power remains to the legislature, to assign original jurisdiction to that court in other cases than those specified in the article which has been recited; provided those cases belong to the judicial power of the United States.

If it had been intended to leave it in the discretion of the legislature to apportion the judicial power between the supreme and inferior courts according to the will of that body, it would certainly have been useless to have proceeded further than to have defined the judicial power, and the tribunals in which it should be vested. The subsequent part of the section is mere surplusage, is entirely without meaning, if such is to be the construction. If congress remains at liberty to give this court appellate jurisdiction, where the constitution has declared their jurisdiction shall be original; and original jurisdiction where the constitution has declared it shall be appellate; the distribution of jurisdiction, made in the constitution, is form without substance.

Affirmative words are often, in their operation, negative of other objects than those affirmed; and in this case, a negative or exclusive sense must ge given to them or they have no operation at all.

It cannot be presumed that any clause in the constitution is intended to be without effect; and, therefore, such a construction is inadmissible, unless the words require it.

ministers, or their domestics, or domestic servants, as a court of law can have or exercise consistently with the law of nations; and original, but not exclusive jurisdiction of all suits brought by ambassadors, or other public ministers, or in which a consul, or vice consul, shall be a party. And the trial of issues of fact in the Supreme Court, in all actions at law against citizens of the United States, shall be by jury. *The Supreme Court shall also have appellate jurisdiction from the circuit courts and courts of the several states, in the cases herein after specially provided for; and shall have power to issue writs of prohibition to the district courts, when proceeding as courts of admiralty and maritime jurisdiction, and writs of mandamus, in cases warranted by the principles and usages of law, to any courts appointed, or persons holding office, under the authority of the United States.*" [Emphasis added.]

If the solicitude of the convention, respecting our peace with foreign powers, induced a provision that the supreme court should take original jurisdiction in cases which might be supposed to affect them; yet the clause would have proceeded no further than to provide for such cases, if no further restriction on the powers of congress had been intended. That they should have appellate jurisdiction in all other cases, with such exceptions as congress might make, is no restriction; unless the words be deemed exclusive of original jurisdiction.

When an instrument organizing fundamentally a judicial system, divides it into one supreme, and so many inferior courts as the legislature may ordain and establish; then enumerates its powers, and proceeds so far to distribute them, as to define the jurisdiction of the supreme court by declaring the cases in which it shall take original jurisdiction, and that in others it shall take appellate jurisdiction; the plain import of the words seems to be, that in one class of cases its jurisdiction is original, and not appellate; in the other it is appellate, and not original. If any other construction would render the clause inoperative, that is an additional reason for rejecting such other construction, and for adhering to their obvious meaning.

To enable this court, then, to issue a mandamus, it must be shown to be an exercise of appellate jurisdiction, or to be necessary to enable them to exercise appellate jurisdiction.

It has been stated at the bar that the appellate jurisdiction may be exercised in a variety of forms, and that if it be the will of the legislature that a mandamus should be used for that purpose, that will must be obeyed. This is true, yet the jurisdiction must be appellate, not original.

It is the essential criterion of appellate jurisdiction, that it revises and corrects the proceedings in a cause already instituted, and does not create that cause. Although, therefore, a mandamus may be directed to courts, yet to issue such a writ to an officer for the delivery of a paper, is in effect the same as to sustain an original action for that paper, and, therefore, seems not to belong to appellate, but to original jurisdiction. Neither is it necessary in such a case as this, to enable the court to exercise its appellate jurisdiction.

The authority, therefore, given to the Supreme Court, by the act establishing the judicial courts of the United States, to issue writs of mandamus to public officers, appears not to be warranted by the constitution; and it becomes necessary to enquire whether a jurisdiction, so conferred, can be exercised.

The question, whether an act, repugnant to the constitution, can become the law of the land, is a question deeply interesting to the United States; but, happily, not of an intricacy proportioned to its interest. It seems only necessary to recognize certain principles, supposed to have been long and well established, to decide it.

That the people have an original right to establish, for their future government, such principles as, in their opinion, shall most conduce to their own happiness, is the basis on which the whole American fabric has been erected. The exercise of this original right is a very great exertion; nor can it, nor ought it, to be frequently repeated. The principles, therefore, so established, are deemed fundamental. And as the authority from which they proceed is supreme, and can seldom act, they are designed to be permanent.

This original and supreme will organizes the government, and assigns to different departments their respective powers. It may either stop here, or establish certain limits not to be transcended by those departments.

The government of the United States is of the latter description. The powers of the legislature are defined and limited; and that those limits may not be mistaken, or forgotten, the constitution is written. To what purpose are powers limited, and to what purpose is that limitation committed to writing, if these limits may, at any time, be passed by those intended to be restrained? The distinction between a government with limited and unlimited powers is abolished, if those limits do not confine the persons on whom they are imposed, and if acts prohibited and acts allowed, are of equal obligation. It is a proposition too plain to be contested, that the constitution controls any legislative act repugnant to it; or, that the legislature may alter the constitution by an ordinary act.

Between these alternatives there is no middle ground. The constitution is either a superior, paramount law, unchangeable by ordinary means, or it is on a level with ordinary legislative acts, and, like other acts, is alterable when the legislature shall please to alter it.

If the former part of the alternative be true, then a legislative act contrary to the constitution is not law: if the latter part be true, then written constitutions are absurd attempts, on the part of the people, to limit a power in its own nature illimitable.

Certainly all those who have framed written constitutions contemplate them as forming the fundamental and paramount law of the nation, and consequently, the theory of every such government must be, that an act of the legislature, repugnant to the constitution, is void.

This theory is essentially attached to a written constitution, and is, consequently, to be considered, by this court, as one of the fundamental principles of our society. It is not therefore to be lost sight of in the further consideration of this subject.

If an act of the legislature, repugnant to the constitution, is void, does it, notwithstanding its invalidity, bind the courts, and oblige them to give it effect? Or, in other words, though it be not law, does it constitute a rule as operative as if it was a law? This would be to overthrow in fact what was established in theory; and would seem, at first view, an absurdity too gross to be insisted on. It shall, however, receive a more attentive consideration.

It is emphatically the province and duty of the judicial department to say what the law is. Those who apply the rule to particular cases, must of necessity expound and interpret that rule. If two laws conflict with each other, the courts must decide on the operation of each.

So if a law be in opposition to the constitution; if both the law and the constitution apply to a particular case, so that the court must either decide that case conformably to the law, disregarding the constitution; or conformably to the constitution, disregarding the law; the court must determine which of these conflicting rules governs the case. This is of the very essence of judicial duty.

If, then, the courts are to regard the constitution, and the constitution is superior to any ordinary act of the legislature, the constitution, and not such ordinary act, must govern the case to which they both apply.

Those then who controvert the principle that the constitution is to be considered, in court, as a paramount law, are reduced to the necessity of maintaining that courts must close their eyes on the constitution, and see only the law.

This doctrine would subvert the very foundation of all written constitutions. It would declare that an act which, according to the principles and theory of our government, is entirely void, is yet, in practice, completely obligatory. It would declare that if the legislature shall do what is expressly forbidden, such act, notwithstanding the express prohibition, is in reality effectual. It would be giving to the legislature a practical and real omnipotence, with the same breath which professes to restrict their powers within narrow limits. It is prescribing limits, and declaring that those limits may be passed at pleasure.

That it thus reduces to nothing what we have deemed the greatest improvement on political institutions—a written constitution—would of itself be sufficient, in America, where written constitutions have been viewed with so much reverence, for rejecting the construction. But the peculiar expressions of the constitution of the United States furnish additional arguments in favour of its rejection.

The judicial power of the United States is extended to all cases arising under the constitution.

Could it be the intention of those who gave this power, to say that in using it the constitution should not be looked into? That a case arising under the constitution should be decided without examining the instrument under which it arises?

This is too extravagant to be maintained.

In some cases, then, the constitution must be looked into by the judges. And if they can open it at all, what part of it are they forbidden to read or to obey?

There are many other parts of the constitution which serve to illustrate this subject. It is declared that "no tax or duty shall be laid on articles exported from any state." Suppose a duty on the export of cotton, of tobacco, or of flour; and a suit instituted to recover it. Ought judgment to be rendered in such a case? Ought the judges to close their eyes on the constitution, and only see the law?

The constitution declares that "no bill of attainder or ex post facto law shall be passed."

If, however, such a bill should be passed, and a person should be prosecuted under it; must the court condemn to death those victims whom the constitution endeavors to preserve?

"No person," says the constitution, "shall be convicted of treason unless on the testimony of two witnesses to the same overt act, or on confession in open court."

Here the language of the constitution is addressed especially to the courts. It prescribes, directly for them, a rule of evidence not to be departed from. If the legislature should change that rule, and declare *one* witness, or a confession *out* of court, sufficient for conviction, must the constitutional principle yield to the legislative act?

From these, and many other selections which might be made, it is apparent, that the framers of the constitution contemplated that instrument as a rule for the government of *courts,* as well as of the legislature.

Why otherwise does it direct the judges to take an oath to support it? This oath certainly applies, in an especial manner, to their conduct in their official character. How immoral to impose it on them, if they were to be used as the instruments, and the knowing instruments, for violating what they swear to support!

The oath of office, too, imposed by the legislature, is completely demonstrative of the legislative opinion on this subject. It is in these words: "I do solemnly swear that I will administer justice without respect to persons, and do equal right to the poor and to the rich; and that I will faithfully and impartially discharge all the duties incumbent on me as ———, according to the best of my abilities and understanding, agreeably to *the constitution*, and laws of the United States."

Why does a judge swear to discharge his duties agreeably to the constitution of the United States, if that constitution forms no rule for his government? If it is closed upon him, and cannot be inspected by him?

If such be the real state of things, this is worse than solemn mockery. To prescribe, or to take this oath, becomes equally a crime.

It is also not entirely unworthy of observation, that in declaring what shall be the *supreme* law of the land, the *constitution* itself is first mentioned; and not the laws of the United States generally, but those only which shall be made in *pursuance* of the constitution, have that rank.

Thus, the particular phraseology of the constitution of the United States confirms and strengthens the principle, supposed to be essential to all written constitutions, that a law repugnant to the constitution is void; and that *courts,* as well as other departments, are bound by that instrument.

The rule must be discharged.

THE HISTORICAL SETTING OF THE MARBURY CASE

1. *The political environment.*   a. *Judicial "reform."* The Marbury case was an early manifestation of the clashes between the Jeffersonian Republicans and the Marshall Court. John Marshall, Secretary of State in the Cabinet of lame-duck President John Adams, was nominated as Chief Justice in January 1801 and took his oath of office on February 4, 1801. On February 17, the House of Representatives elected Thomas Jefferson as President. Marshall continued to act as Secretary of State through March 3, 1801, the end of Adams' term. Indeed, he may have stayed on somewhat longer: on March 4, 1801—the day Marshall as Chief Justice administered the oath of office to new President Jefferson—he agreed to comply with

Jefferson's request "to perform the duties of Secretary of State until a successor be appointed." Oster, The Political and Economic Doctrines of John Marshall (1914), 182.

Four days before Jefferson's election, the Federalist Congress reorganized the federal judiciary. The Circuit Court Act of February 13, 1801, relieved the Justices of the Supreme Court of circuit-riding duty. In the past, Circuit Courts had been manned by District Court judges and Supreme Court Justices; the 1801 law established sixteen Circuit Court judgeships. The Jeffersonians were indignant: to them, the Circuit Court Act was the defeated Federalists' device to maintain control of one branch of the government. As expected, the new judgeships went to Federalists, for Adams hastily nominated his "midnight judges" during the last two weeks of his term. The Jeffersonians' concern went beyond patronage: the partisan enforcement of the Alien and Sedition Laws had been a major target of their attacks in the political warfare that preceded the election of 1800.

Marbury and his co-petitioners were not among the "midnight judges" named pursuant to the Circuit Court Act. Their positions had been created even later: the Organic Act of the District of Columbia was passed on February 27, 1801, less than a week before the end of Adams' term. The Act authorized the President to name justices of the peace for the District. Adams named forty-two justices on March 2, 1801, and the Senate confirmations came on March 3, Adams' last day in office. The commissions of the petitioners in the Marbury case had been signed by Adams—as well as signed and sealed by Acting Secretary of State Marshall—but they had not been delivered by the end of the day; and the new President chose to treat them as a "nullity." As John Marshall wrote two weeks later, "I should . . . have sent out the commissions which had been signed & sealed but for the extreme hurry of the time."

Marshall was therefore intimately acquainted with the facts of the Marbury controversy. Yet the issue of the existence of the commissions was extensively considered in the Court hearing in the Marbury case. For example, an affidavit by James Marshall—John Marshall's brother—was introduced to prove the existence of some of the commissions. (James Marshall stated that he was to deliver a number of the commissions but that, "finding he could not conveniently carry the whole," he returned "several of them" to his brother's office. 1 Cranch, at 146.) In view of his involvement in the controversy, should Marshall have disqualified himself from participation in the decision? Compare Martin v. Hunter's Lessee, sec. 2 below, where Marshall did not sit because he and his brother James were interested property owners.

The Jeffersonians soon demonstrated that they would not complacently accept Federalist entrenchment in the judiciary: they made repeal of the Circuit Court Act of 1801 an early item of business in the new Congress. The 1801 Act was repealed on March 31, 1802, while the Marbury case was pending in the Supreme Court. The 1802 Act essentially reestablished the old Circuit Court system, with Supreme Court Justices and District Judges once again manning the Circuit Court benches. During these congressional debates, a few Jeffersonians for the first time questioned the Court's authority to consider the constitutionality of congressional acts. There was still an-

other sign of the mounting hostility to the Court: Congress abolished the June and December Terms of the Supreme Court created by the 1801 Act and provided that there would be only one Term, in February. Accordingly, there was no Court session in 1802; the Court that had received Marbury's petition in December 1801 did not reconvene until February 1803.

b. *Impeachment.* The Jeffersonians soon unsheathed a still more potent weapon. Early in 1802, the House voted to impeach Federalist District Judge John Pickering of New Hampshire, and many feared that impeachment of Supreme Court Justices would follow. The choice of Pickering as the first target was a "tragic blunder," however. Pickering, an insane drunkard, was plainly incompetent to serve as a judge, but it took some stretching to convert this into "Treason, Bribery, or other high Crimes and Misdemeanors," as required by Article II, Section 4, of the Constitution. Nevertheless, the Senate voted to remove Pickering from office in March 1804. See Turner, "The Impeachment of John Pickering," 54 Am.Hist.Rev. 485 (1949).

On the day after Pickering's removal, Congress moved on to bigger game: the House impeached Supreme Court Justice Samuel Chase. To the Jeffersonians, Chase was a glaring example of Federalist abuse of judicial office: he had made electioneering statements from the bench in 1800, and he had conducted several vindictive sedition and treason trials. A few months after the Marbury decision, he provided the immediate provocation for his impeachment: in May 1803, in a partisan charge to the federal grand jury in Baltimore, he criticized the repeal of the 1801 Circuit Court Act and the activities of modern "reformers." The Senate trial of Chase was held early in 1805. Were judges impeachable for conduct that did not constitute an indictable offense? The debate was lengthy and important: if the case against Chase succeeded, it was widely expected, John Marshall and other federal judges would be next. But the Senate vote in March 1805 did not produce the constitutional majority necessary to convict Chase. The impeachment weapon was deflated—it was a "farce," "not even a scare-crow," as Jefferson reluctantly concluded. The Jefferson-Marshall dispute continued, but the Court had survived the most critical stage.*

2. *Were there alternative grounds of decision?* Most contemporary commentary on the Marbury decision ignored the passages on the authority of the courts to consider the constitutionality of congressional acts. Attention focused instead on the assertion of the right to examine some executive acts. Was Marshall's opinion a reflection of a "masterful sense of strategy," as is often alleged? Was it a shrewd scheme in which the denial of mandamus avoided an immediate confrontation with the executive and provided a shield for the Court's criticism of Jefferson's behavior—and for its assertion and exercise of judicial review over statutes? See, e. g., McCloskey, The American Supreme Court (1960), 40: "The decision is a masterwork of indirection, a brilliant example of Marshall's capacity to sidestep danger while seeming to

---

* See generally 1 Warren, The Supreme Court in United States History (rev. ed. 1926); III Beveridge, The Life of John Marshall (1919); Baker, John Marshall—A Life in Law (1974); Ellis, The Jeffersonian Crisis: Courts and Politics in the Young Republic (1971); and Dewey, Marshall versus Jefferson: The Political Background of Marbury v. Madison (1970).

court it, to advance in one direction while his opponents are looking in another."

Some critics of Marbury insist that, given Marshall's conclusion, the Court had no business saying any more than that it lacked jurisdiction. Were the opening parts of the opinion, on remedies against executive illegality, unnecessary or inappropriate? Jefferson insisted until the end of his life that most of the opinion was "merely an *obiter* dissertation of the Chief Justice." Jefferson to Justice William Johnson, June 12, 1823, I S. Car.His. & Gen.Mag. 1, 9–10 (1900). Compare the materials on avoidance of constitutional questions, chap. 15 below.

Other critics have insisted that Marshall could and should have made those important final pages on judicial review unnecessary by resolving the preliminary issues differently. For example, more than the signing and sealing might have been held necessary to complete the appointment, or greater presidential authority regarding appointees might have been recognized. See the material on the presidential removal power, chap. 7 below. And a position that mandamus was not available against Cabinet officials was possible. Note the further developments in Kendall v. United States, 12 Pet. 524 (1838), chap. 7 below.

Moreover, the Court's interpretations of Section 13 and Article III have come under special attack. Though the specific Marbury holding has held up, Marshall's underlying conception of mutually exclusive categories of original and appellate jurisdiction has not prevailed. Congress may not add to the Court's original jurisdiction; but it may grant lower courts jurisdiction over cases within the constitutional description of Supreme Court original jurisdiction—and cases of that description may then come to the Supreme Court on appeal. For example, Section 13 itself recognized concurrent original jurisdiction in the lower courts, and several Supreme Court Justices on circuit had sustained lower court jurisdiction in a foreign consul case as early as 1793, United States v. Ravara, 2 Dall. 297. Years later, the Supreme Court agreed. Börs v. Preston, 111 U.S. 252 (1884); see also Ames v. Kansas, 111 U.S. 449 (1884) (state against citizen of another state). And Marshall himself, in a rare admission, called some of the statements about Article III in Marbury unduly broad when he rejected Virginia's arguments against the Supreme Court's exercise of appellate jurisdiction in a case involving a state, in Cohens v. Virginia, 6 Wheat. 264 (1821), sec. 2 below. See generally Powell, Vagaries and Varieties in Constitutional Interpretation (1956), 3–19, and Van Alstyne, "A Critical Guide to Marbury v. Madison," 1969 Duke L.J. 1.*

---

* A few years after Marbury, the Marshall Court also exercised the power to hold a state statute unconstitutional. In Fletcher v. Peck, 6 Cranch 87 (1810), a case from a lower federal court, a statute of Georgia was held to be in violation of the contract clause (see chap. 9, sec. 2, below). Authority to review state court decisions was sustained in Martin v. Hunter's Lessee, sec. 2 below. After Marbury, the Court did not hold another federal law unconstitutional until the controversial and ill-fated decision in Dred Scott v. Sandford, 19 How. 393 (1857).

THE LEGITIMACY OF JUDICIAL REVIEW

Introduction. Was the judicial review authority asserted in Marbury v. Madison a usurpation? That question has long sparked controversy. See, e. g., the extensive attack on judicial review in Boudin, Government by Judiciary (1932). And the debate lives. See the elaborate defense of legitimacy in Berger, Congress v. The Supreme Court (1969).

The attackers say that Marshall's own opinion is question-begging and weak; that the Constitution does not explicitly authorize judicial review; that the Framers of the Constitution did not clearly intend to grant that extraordinary power; and that the pre-Convention theories and practices were not sufficiently clear and widespread to provide legitimation. The materials that follow reflect that ongoing debate, with particular emphasis on those aspects that bear on the contemporary justifications as well as historical legitimacy of judicial review. After a brief review of the historical roots of the authority and the Convention debates, there are longer excerpts from two significant early statements bearing on Marshall's reasoning: the most important anticipation of that reasoning, Alexander Hamilton's No. 78 of The Federalist; and the most important judicial attack on Marbury, the Gibson dissent in a Pennsylvania case, Eakin v. Raub. Professor Wechsler's debate with Judge Learned Hand illustrates the continuing controversy regarding the constitutional justification for Marbury—a controversy that bears immediately on contemporary evaluations and exercises of the Supreme Court's power.

1. *Historical antecedents.* Though Marshall's opinion in Marbury talked about general principles and constitutional text, not historical data, efforts to justify judicial review have often provoked explorations of historical roots. Some of the searches have been on rather remote and tangential byways. For example, there has been frequent mention of Lord Coke's famous statement in Dr. Bonham's Case, at 8 Rep. 118a (C.P. 1610), that "the common law will controul acts of Parliament, [and] adjudge them to be utterly void" when the acts are "against common right and reason." But that was hardly descriptive of British practice in the seventeenth century; by the eighteenth, it was not even respectable dictum. More in point was the appellate jurisdiction of the Privy Council over colonial courts; but invalidation of legislation through that route was rare and unpopular. The practice of state courts in the years immediately following independence holds the greatest promise as a source of relevant information. But here, too, the examples are few and controversial; and there is doubt that many people at the Convention or in the early national period knew about the scattered actual or alleged examples of judicial invalidation of state legislation such as Holmes v. Walton, a New Jersey case of 1780. For an extensive selection of articles examining antecedents such as these, see Volume I of Selected Essays on Constitutional Law (1938).* See also Berger, Con-

---

* Compare also the discussion of the antecedents of judicial review in Goebel, Antecedents and Beginnings to 1801 (1 History of the Supreme Court of the United States) (1971), with Nelson, "Changing Conceptions of Judicial Review: The Evolution of Con- stitutional Theory in the States, 1790– 1860," 120 U.Pa.L.Rev. 1166 (1972). On Goebel's conclusion that the doctrine of judicial review was "preached [during the 1780's] apparently without protest," Nelson comments that "Goebel some- what overstates his case."

gress v. The Supreme Court (1969), which finds support for judicial review in these precedents even while recognizing their spottiness: he insists, at 46, that the argument does not "hinge upon whether there existed an established *practice* of judicial review, but rather on the Founders' *belief*" that precedents and statements like Coke's supported court enforcement of constitutional limits.

The general spread of ideas conducive to the acceptance of judicial review was in any event probably more important than the existence of specific precedents.† A pervasive theme, and one reflected in Marshall's reasoning, was the development of written constitutions, with the assurance of limited government as a major purpose. Constitutionalism was hardly an American invention, but Americans had an unusually extensive experience with basic documents of government, from royal charters to state constitutions and the Articles of Confederation. Yet the constitutional historians who justify judicial review as a natural outgrowth of constitutionalism make an argument that is incomplete. It is possible to have a constitution without having judicial review. There is accordingly a large question-begging element in deriving judicial enforceability simply from the existence of written constitutions: to say that a government cannot exceed its constitutional powers does not demonstrate who is to decide whether there is conflict with the constitution. Viewing a constitution as a species of "law," then, becomes a vital link between constitutionalism and judicial competence to adjudicate constitutional issues. That link, hardly a prominent feature in the political theory of the Revolutionary era, is central in the Marbury opinion.

The background of practices and ideas amply demonstrates that the judicial review authority asserted in Marbury by Marshall was no sudden innovation or single-handed achievement. But the pre-Convention heritage hardly made the 1803 result inevitable. Nor does that heritage clearly tell us what was most important to Marshall when he wrote Marbury: Was his emphasis on a Constitution-interpreting function of courts as *incidental* to their ordinary role? Or did he insist upon a *special* Constitution-enforcing responsibility of courts as enforcers of limits on government? Was the main concern of Marbury the establishment of judicial *competence* to interpret the Constitution—because courts were in the business of deciding legal questions, because the Constitution was law, because Articles III and VI confirmed that the Constitution was a variety of law that might come before the courts? Or was Marshall more concerned with the broader theme of constitutions as an assurance of limited government, and with carving out for courts a role as *special*—supreme, perhaps even exclusive—guardians of constitutional norms?

† See generally Bailyn, The Ideological Origins of the American Revolution (1967), and Wood, The Creation of the American Republic, 1776–1787 (1969). See also Vile, Constitutionalism and the Separation of Powers (1967), and Katz, "The Origins of American Constitutional Thought," in 3 Perspectives in American History 474 (Bailyn & Fleming, eds., 1969).

The influential book by Wood finds an especially hospitable climate for the development for judicial review in the evolving theories of the 1780's, particularly the replacement of traditional notions of legislative sovereignty by emphasis on popular sovereignty. Note Hamilton's argument in No. 78 of the Federalist, below, that courts "were designed to be an intermediate body between the people and the legislature" —and the echoes of that theme in the Marbury opinion.

2. *The Constitutional Convention.* The Constitution does not explicitly grant the judicial review power asserted in Marbury. That silence has made the legitimacy debate possible. Did the Framers intend to grant the power? Some efforts to demonstrate an original understanding supporting judicial review have relied heavily on Framers' statements not made in Philadelphia in 1787. See Beard, The Supreme Court and the Constitution (1912). But the most persuasive data regarding Framers' intent are of course the Convention debates. See Farrand, The Records of the Federal Convention of 1787 (1911).

The Convention context in which the most important statements regarding judicial power were made was the discussion of the Council of Revision proposal—a proposal that Justices join with the President in the veto process. That provision was rejected, partly on grounds supporting the legitimacy of judicial review. According to Madison's Notes, Luther Martin, for example, thought "the association of the Judges with the Executive" a "dangerous innovation": "A knowledge of mankind, and of Legislative Affairs cannot be presumed to belong in a higher degree to the Judges than to the Legislature. And as to the Constitutionality of laws, that point will come before the Judges in their proper official character. In this character they have a negative on the laws. Join them with the Executive in the Revision and they will have a double negative. It is necessary that the Supreme Judiciary should have the confidence of the people. This will soon be lost, if they are employed in the task of remonstrating agst. popular measures of the Legislature." See also Elbridge Gerry's argument that judges should not sit on the Council of Revision because "they will have a sufficient check agst. encroachments on their own department by their exposition of the laws, which involved a power of deciding on their Constitutionality. . . . It was quite foreign from the nature of ye. office to make them judges of the policy of public measures."

An incisive brief survey of the debates concludes: "The grant of judicial power was to include the power, where necessary in the decision of cases, to disregard state or federal statutes found to be unconstitutional. Despite the curiously persisting myth of usurpation, the Convention's understanding on this point emerges from its records with singular clarity." * For an argument that courts were only to invalidate congressional acts interfering with judicial operations—and an attack on the accuracy of Madison's Notes—see Crosskey, Politics and the Constitution in the History of the United States (1953); for a criticism of Crosskey's "self-defense" theory, see Berger, Congress v. The Supreme Court (1969), 154–65.

Compare the survey of the historical data on legitimacy in Leonard W. Levy's excellent introduction to a paperback volume of selected essays edited by him, Judicial Review and the Supreme Court (1967). Levy quotes Edward S. Corwin's testimony on the 1937 Court-Packing Plan: "[I]n blunt language he declared, 'The people who say the framers intended [judicial review] are talking nonsense'—to which he hastily added, 'and the people who say they did not intend it are talking nonsense.'" Levy adds: "A close

---

* Bator, Mishkin, Shapiro and Wechsler, Hart and Wechsler's The Federal Courts and the Federal System (2d ed. 1973), 9. [This volume is cited hereinafter as Hart and Wechsler, Federal Courts (2d ed. 1973).]

textual and contextual examination of the evidence will not result in an improvement on these propositions." Raoul Berger, however, found support for a more decisive stance: he thought it "reasonably plain" after an extensive review of the debates at the Convention, during ratification, and in the First Congress, that there was "an assumption by the leadership that judicial review would be available to keep Congress within Constitutional 'limits,' " and that "review was part of the Constitutional scheme"; he concluded that "criticism of conventional reliance on the Founders' statements" is "strained and insubstantial." Berger, Congress v. The Supreme Court (1969), 198, 335–36 and chaps. 3–5.

    3. *The Federalist Papers.* Support for judicial review far more explicit than anything found in the Convention debates appears in The Federalist. Hamilton, Jay and Madison wrote these newspaper essays in defense and explanation of the proposed Constitution as campaign documents in the ratification battle in New York. They have become the classic commentaries on the Constitution. The papers most directly concerned with the judiciary were five written by Alexander Hamilton, Nos. 78 through 82 of The Federalist. No. 82, for example, supports Supreme Court review of state court decisions. And the most famous, No. 78, contains some striking parallels to —as well as some provocative variations on—the Marbury v. Madison theme.

Hamilton, Federalist No. 78

    . . . Whoever attentively considers the different departments of power must perceive, that in a government in which they are separated from each other, the judiciary, from the nature of its functions, will always be the least dangerous to the political rights of the constitution; because it will be least in a capacity to annoy or injure them. The executive not only dispenses the honors, but holds the sword of the community. The legislature not only commands the purse, but prescribes the rules by which the duties and rights of every citizen are to be regulated. The judiciary on the contrary has no influence over either the sword or the purse, no direction either of the strength or of the wealth of the society, and can take no active resolution whatever. It may truly be said to have neither Force nor Will, but merely judgment; and must ultimately depend upon the aid of the executive arm even for the efficacy of its judgments.

    This simple view of the matter suggests several important consequences. It proves incontestibly that the judiciary is beyond comparison the weakest of the three departments of power; that it can never attack with success either of the other two; and that all possible care is requisite to enable it to defend itself against their attacks. . . .

    The complete independence of the courts of justice is peculiarly essential in a limited constitution. By a limited constitution I understand one which contains certain specified exceptions to the legislative authority; such for instance as that it shall pass no bills of attainder, no ex post facto laws, and the like. Limitations of this kind can be preserved in practice no other way than through the medium of the courts of justice; whose duty it must be to declare all acts contrary to the manifest tenor of the constitution void. Without. this, all the reservations of particular rights or privileges would amount to nothing.

Some perplexity respecting the right of the courts to pronounce legislative acts void, because contrary to the constitution, has arisen from an imagination that the doctrine would imply a superiority of the judiciary to the legislative power. It is urged that the authority which can declare the acts of another void, must necessarily be superior to the one whose acts may be declared void. As this doctrine is of great importance in all the American constitutions, a brief discussion of the grounds on which it rests cannot be unacceptable.

There is no position which depends on clearer principles, than that every act of a delegated authority, contrary to the tenor of the commission under which it is exercised, is void. No legislative act therefore contrary to the constitution can be valid. To deny this would be to affirm that the deputy is greater than his principal; that the servant is above his master; that the representatives of the people are superior to the people themselves; that men acting by virtue of powers may do not only what their powers do not authorise, but what they forbid.

If it be said that the legislative body are themselves the constitutional judges of their own powers, and that the construction they put upon them is conclusive upon the other departments, it may be answered, that this cannot be the natural presumption, where it is not to be collected from any particular provisions in the constitution. It is not otherwise to be supposed that the constitution could intend to enable the representatives of the people to substitute their *will* to that of their constituents. It is far more rational to suppose that the courts were designed to be an intermediate body between the people and the legislature, in order, among other things, to keep the latter within the limits assigned to their authority. The interpretation of the laws is the proper and peculiar province of the courts. A constitution is in fact, and must be, regarded by the judges as a fundamental law. It therefore belongs to them to ascertain its meaning as well as the meaning of any particular act proceeding from the legislative body. If there should happen to be an irreconcilable variance between the two, that which has the superior obligation and validity ought of course to be preferred; or in other words, the constitution ought to be preferred to the statute, the intention of the people to the intention of their agents.

Nor does this conclusion by any means suppose a superiority of the judicial to the legislative power. It only supposes that the power of the people is superior to both; and that where the will of the legislature declared in its statutes, stands in opposition to that of the people declared in the constitution, the judges ought to be governed by the latter, rather than the former. They ought to regulate their decisions by the fundamental laws, rather than by those which are not fundamental. . . .

[The] independence of the judges is equally requisite to guard the constitution and the rights of individuals from the effects of those ill humours which the arts of designing men, or the influence of particular conjunctures, sometimes disseminate among the people themselves, and which, though they speedily give place to better information and more deliberate reflection, have a tendency in the meantime to occasion dangerous innovations in the government, and serious oppressions of the minor party in the community. . . .

4. *Justice Gibson's dissent in Eakin v. Raub, 12 S. & R. 330 (Pa. 1825)*. The following excerpts are from an opinion denying that the Pennsylvania Supreme Court was authorized to consider the constitutionality of acts of the state legislature. Five years after writing this dissent, Justice Gibson was a strong contender for a seat on the United States Supreme Court, but President Andrew Jackson ultimately named Gibson's fellow-Pennsylvanian, Henry Baldwin. Twenty years after Eakin v. Raub, when Gibson had become Pennsylvania's Chief Justice, he announced that he had changed his mind, both because an intervening state constitutional convention had silently "sanctioned the pretensions of the courts" and because of his "experience of the necessity of the case." Norris v. Clymer, 2 Pa. 277 (1845).

Gibson in Eakin v. Raub

I am aware, that a right to declare all unconstitutional acts void, without distinction as to either [state or federal] constitution, is generally held as a professional dogma; but I apprehend, rather as a matter of faith than of reason. [I]t is not a little remarkable, that although the right in question has all along been claimed by the judiciary, no judge has ventured to discuss it, except Chief Justice Marshall . . . ; and if the argument of a jurist so distinguished for the strength of his ratiocinative powers be found inconclusive, it may fairly be set down to the weakness of the position which he attempts to defend . . . .

[T]he constitution is said to be a law of superior obligation; and consequently, that if it were to come into collision with an act of the legislature, the latter would have to give way; this is conceded. But it is a fallacy, to suppose, that they can come into collision *before the judiciary.* . . .

The constitution and the *right* of the legislature to pass the act, may be in collision; but is that a legitimate subject for judicial determination? If it be, the judiciary must be a peculiar organ, to revise the proceedings of the legislature, and to correct its mistakes; and in what part of the constitution are we to look for this proud preeminence? [I]t is by no means clear, that to declare a law void, which has been enacted according to the forms prescribed in the constitution, is not a usurpation of legislative power. It is an act of sovereignty; and sovereignty and legislative power are said by Sir William *Blackstone* to be convertible terms. It is the business of the judiciary, to interpret the laws, not scan the authority of the lawgiver; and without the latter, it cannot take cognizance of a collision between a law and the constitution. So that, to affirm that the judiciary has a right to judge of the existence of such collision, is to take for granted the very thing to be proved . . . . .

But it has been said to be emphatically the business of the judiciary, to ascertain and pronounce what the law is; and that this necessarily involves a consideration of the constitution. It does so: but how far? If the judiciary will inquire into anything beside the form of enactment, where shall it stop? There must be some point of limitation to such an inquiry; for no one will pretend, that a judge would be justifiable in calling for the election returns, or scrutinizing the qualifications of those who composed the legislature. . . .

[I]t will not be pretended, that the legislature has not, at least, an equal right with the judiciary to put a construction on the constitution; nor that either of them is infallible; nor that either ought to be required to surrender its judgment to the other. Suppose, then, they differ in opinion as to the constitutionality of a particular law; if the organ whose business it first is to decide on the subject, is not to have its judgment treated with respect, what shall prevent it from securing the preponderance of its opinion by the strong arm of power? [T]he soundness of any construction which would bring one organ of the government into collision with another, is to be more than suspected; for where collision occurs, it is evident, the machine is working in a way the framers of it did not intend. . . .

But the judges are sworn to support the constitution, and are they not bound by it as the law of the land? . . . The oath to support the constitution is not peculiar to the judges, but is taken indiscriminately by every officer of the government, and is designed rather as a test of the political principles of the man, than to bind the officer in the discharge of his duty: otherwise, it were difficult to determine, what operation it is to have in the case of a recorder of deeds, for instance, who, in the execution of his office, has nothing to do with the constitution. But granting it to relate to the official conduct of the judge, as well as every other officer, and not to his political principles, still, it must be understood in reference to supporting the constitution, *only as far as that may be involved in his official duty;* and consequently, if his official duty does not comprehend an inquiry into the authority of the legislature, neither does his oath. . . .

But do not the judges do a *positive* act in violation of the constitution, when they give effect to an unconstitutional law? Not if the law has been passed according to the forms established in the constitution. The fallacy of the question is, in supposing that the judiciary adopts the acts of the legislature as its own; whereas, the enactment of a law and the interpretation of it are not concurrent acts, and as the judiciary is not required to concur in the enactment, neither is it in the breach of the constitution which may be the consequence of the enactment; the fault is imputable to the legislature, and on it the responsibility exclusively rests. . . . *

5. *The Hand-Wechsler debate.* For an illuminating revival of the legitimacy debate, and sharp disagreement about the basis for judicial review in the constitutional text, see Hand, The Bill of Rights (1958), 1–30, and Wechsler, "Toward Neutral Principles of Constitutional Law," in Principles, Politics, and Fundamental Law (1961), 4–10 [also printed in 73 Harv.L.Rev. 1 (1959) and Selected Essays 1938–62 (1963), 463]. Judge

---

* Justice Gibson was careful to limit his attack on the Marbury v. Madison rationale to the issue of judicial review of the acts of a coordinate legislature. Near the end of his opinion, he emphasized that state courts have not only the power but also the duty to invalidate state laws when they conflict with "supreme" federal obligations. He stated: "But in regard to an act of assembly, which is found to be in collision with the constitution, laws or treaties of the *United States,* I take the duty of the judiciary to be exactly the reverse. By becoming parties to the federal constitution, the states have agreed to several limitations of their individual sovereignty, to enforce which, it was thought to be absolutely necessary, to prevent them from giving effect to laws in violation of those limitations, through the instrumentality of their own judges." See the materials on Supreme Court review of state court judgments, sec. 2 below.

Learned Hand emphasized that there was "nothing in the United States Constitution that gave courts any authority to review the decisions of Congress," insisted that "it was a plausible—indeed to my mind an unanswerable—argument" that such an authority was inconsistent with separation of powers, and asserted that "when the Constitution emerged from the Convention in September 1787, the structure of the proposed government, if one looked to the text, gave no ground for inferring that the decisions of the Supreme Court . . . were to be authoritative upon the Executive and the Legislature." Judge Hand found justification for the Supreme Court's assumption of judicial review authority solely in the practical need "to prevent the defeat of the venture at hand"—to keep the government from foundering. Professor Wechsler, relying on the Article VI Supremacy Clause and on Article III, replied: "I believe the power of the courts is grounded in the language of the Constitution and is not a mere interpolation."

The Hand-Wechsler debate of the mid-twentieth century illustrates how the legitimacy issue may influence views regarding the contemporary exercise of the power. Thus, Judge Hand concluded that "since this power is not a logical deduction from the structure of the Constitution but only a practical condition upon its successful operation, it need not be exercised whenever a court sees, or thinks that it sees, an invasion of the Constitution. It is always a preliminary question how importunately the occasion demands an answer." (Compare the materials on discretionary abstention, chap. 15, sec. 4, below.) Professor Wechsler objected to so broad a discretion to decline to adjudicate a constitutional objection in a case properly before a court: "For me, as for anyone who finds the judicial power anchored in the Constitution, there is no such escape from the judicial obligations; the duty cannot be attenuated in this way." (The "duty," he added, was "not that of policing or advising legislatures or executives," but rather simply the duty "to decide the litigated case and to decide it in accordance with the law.")

The Hand-Wechsler debate illustrates, too, that evaluations of the content as well as the timing of contemporary court decisions may evolve from discussions beginning with concern over legitimacy. Since Wechsler's defense of legitimacy is so closely tied to implications of the judicial function, he insisted that Constitution-interpreting courts must above all act like courts. Accordingly, he warned against "ad hoc evaluation" as "the deepest problem of our constitutionalism" and insisted that decisions must rest on "neutral principles": "the main constituent of the judicial process is precisely that it must be genuinely principled, resting with respect to every step that is involved in reaching judgment on analysis and reasons quite transcending the immediate result that is achieved." To Judge Hand, judicial review of legislative choices inevitably turned courts into "a third, legislative, chamber," adding: "For myself it would be most irksome to be ruled by a bevy of Platonic Guardians, even if I knew how to choose them, which I assuredly do not."

6. *Judicial review and democracy.* As the Hand-Wechsler debate illustrates, concern with the bases of judicial review in constitutional history and text is often closely connected with explorations of the consistency between judicial review and democratic government. Views on that issue, too, may

profoundly affect exercises and evaluations of the judicial power, as is amply revealed in many of the opinions in this volume. Anxiety about the undemocratic aspects of judicial review, for example, tends to support the judicial self-restraint stance long associated with Justice Frankfurter—the reluctance to intervene in the judgments of other branches of government.

Leonard W. Levy's paperback, Judicial Review and the Supreme Court (1967), is a useful selection of essays, and his Introduction includes a critical analysis of the major contending arguments regarding the propriety of judicial invalidation of legislative decisions. Classic statements viewing judicial review as undemocratic and as undercutting popular responsibility are Thayer, "The Origin and Scope of the American Doctrine of Constitutional Law," 7 Harv.L.Rev. 129 (1893), 1 Selected Essays 503 (1938), and Commager, Majority Rule and Minority Rights (1943). Important defenses of judicial intervention are Rostow, "The Democratic Character of Judicial Review," 66 Harv.L.Rev. 193 (1952), Selected Essays 1938–62 (1963), 1, and C. L. Black, Jr., The People and the Court: Judicial Review in a Democracy (1960). For an especially provocative and sophisticated effort to justify judicial intervention while recognizing that it is countermajoritarian, see Bickel, The Least Dangerous Branch (1962). As noted, the issues in this debate are recurrent themes in judicial opinions and permeate any constitutional law course. The problems are best explored in the specific contexts of the cases below. See, e. g., the issues of judicial intervention and democratic processes raised by Justice Stone's Carolene Products case footnote, and by the opinions in Griswold v. Connecticut, both in chap. 9, sec. 3, below.

Closely related to this debate about the propriety and scope of judicial intervention are several other themes that recur throughout this volume. For example, views about the legitimacy of judicial review may influence attitudes about the appropriate sources of constitutional interpretation. To what extent must the Court confine itself to the text and history of the relevant constitutional provision? To what extent may it rely on inferences from the structures and relationships established by the basic document? See C. L. Black, Jr., Structure and Relationship in Constitutional Law (1969). To what extent is the Court authorized to implement values derived from sources outside the written document—e. g., the society's political and moral values, or the Justices' personal ones? See generally, Brest, Processes of Constitutional Decisionmaking (1975), and note especially chap. 9 below. Moreover, views about the legitimacy of judicial review and its consistency with democracy may influence positions about the appropriate deference the Court owes to legislative judgments. When should a legislative judgment be accorded a strong "presumption of constitutionality" and be sustained so long as it is merely "reasonable"? When may the Court properly apply stricter scrutiny and demand that more than mere rationality be shown in support of a legislative judgment? These themes surface in a variety of contexts, in every chapter of Parts II and III of this book. Note, e. g., the intense controversies about appropriate standards of review in the varying interpretations of the frequently litigated due process and equal protection clauses of the Fourteenth Amendment. And see especially the recent disputes about the proper occasions for "minimal scrutiny" and "strict scrutiny"—or some intermediate standard—in applying the equal protection clause, chap. 10 below.

7. *Judicial review abroad.* Since World War II, while Americans have continued to agonize over the justifiability of judicial review, more and more other nations have looked to courts to enforce constitutionalism. Judicial review has become especially important in Germany and Italy. Most judicial review mechanisms in civil law countries differ from the American in form: for example, creation of special Constitutional Courts has been the norm. But the American experience has been an important "persuasive authority" as to basic theory; and in practice there are signs of "a converging trend" in the exercise of judicial review in the American and civil law systems, as a sophisticated commentator suggests. Cappelletti, "The Significance of Judicial Review of Legislation in the Contemporary World," in Ius Privatum Gentium (Festschrift for Max Rheinstein, 1969), 147. See also Cappelletti and Adams, "Judicial Review of Legislation: European Antecedents and Adaptations," 79 Harv.L.Rev. 1207 (1966), and Gunther, "The Constitution of Ghana—An American's Impressions and Comparisons," 8 U.Ghana L.J. 2 (1971).

THE AUTHORITATIVENESS OF THE COURT'S CONSTITUTIONAL INTERPRETATIONS

Introduction. To what extent are other departments of government obligated to follow judicial interpretations of the Constitution? Must, or may, the President and Congress give independent consideration to questions of constitutionality in the exercise of their official functions? Are the courts the ultimate, even the exclusive, interpreters of the Constitution, or do other organs of government share in that authority? Questions such as these raise the issue of the true scope of the power of judicial review. Is judicial review simply a by-product of a court's duty to decide cases within its jurisdiction in accordance with law, including the Constitution; or do courts have special competence to interpret law, including the Constitution, so that they are ultimate, supreme interpreters of the Constitution? Even Marshall's reasoning in Marbury v. Madison, though clearly leaning to the former, more modest view, is not free from ambiguity. And later developments—not only popular expectations but also Court assertions such as those in the 1958 decision in Cooper v. Aaron, note 6 below—suggest a broader binding effect for judicial interpretations.

To promote examination of these questions, notes 1 to 4 below present a series of presidential statements claiming varying degrees of autonomy vis-à-vis judicial interpretations, in a variety of contexts. Consider, with regard to each statement, whether anything in the President's position is inconsistent with Marshall's justification for judicial review in Marbury. Consider, too, whether the presidential positions are inconsistent with other possible justifications for judicial review. And consider especially whether any of the presidential statements is inconsistent with the Court's claims in Cooper v. Aaron—claims which include the assertion that a Supreme Court interpretation of the Constitution "is the supreme law of the land." (Note also the additional comments and questions about the presidential assertions in note 5 below.)

Recall that much of Marshall's argument in Marbury was directed against contentions that courts lacked *competence* or *authority* to consider issues of constitutionality. Can it be argued on the basis of Marshall's position that a judicial interpretation is the *ultimate, final* one? That it is *binding* on those not parties to the litigation? That the judiciary is the *exclusive* source of constitutional interpretations? Recall Marshall's quite modest, defensive statement that the Constitution is "a rule for the government of *courts* as well as the legislature" and his conclusion that "*courts,* as well as other departments, are bound by that instrument." Yet Marshall also stated: "It is emphatically the province and duty of the judicial department to say what the law is." Is there enough ambiguity in that statement to support the inference of a *special* judicial competence, a superior role, in constitutional interpretation? Contrast Hamilton's stronger statement in No. 78 of The Federalist, above: "The interpretation of the laws is the proper and peculiar province of the courts."

1. *Thomas Jefferson.* a. *Letter to Abigail Adams, Sept. 11, 1804* (VIII The Writings of Thomas Jefferson (Ford ed. 1897), 310):

"You seem to think it devolved on the judges to decide on the validity of the sedition law. But nothing in the Constitution has given them a right to decide for the Executive, more than to the Executive to decide for them. Both magistracies are equally independent in the sphere of action assigned to them. The judges, believing the law constitutional, had a right to pass a sentence of fine and imprisonment; because that power was placed in their hands by the Constitution. But the Executive, believing the law to be unconstitutional, was bound to remit the execution of it; because that power has been confided to him by the Constitution. That instrument meant that its co-ordinate branches should be checks on each other. But the opinion which gives to the judges the right to decide what laws are constitutional, and what not, not only for themselves in their own sphere of action, but for the Legislature & Executive also, in their spheres, would make the judiciary a despotic branch."

b. *Letter to William C. Jarvis, Sept. 28, 1820* (X The Writings of Thomas Jefferson (Ford ed. 1899), 160):

"You seem . . . to consider the judges as the ultimate arbiters of all constitutional questions; a very dangerous doctrine indeed, and one which would place us under the despotism of an oligarchy. . . . The constitution has erected no such single tribunal, knowing that to whatever hands confided, with the corruptions of time and party, its members would become despots. It has more wisely made all the departments co-equal and co-sovereign within themselves. If the legislature fails to pass laws for a census, for paying the judges and other officers of government, for establishing a militia, for naturalization as prescribed by the constitution, or if they fail to meet in congress, the judges cannot issue their mandamus to them; if the President fails to supply the place of a judge, to appoint other civil or military officers, to issue requisite commissions, the judges cannot force him. . . . The judges certainly have more frequent occasion to act on constitutional questions, because the laws of *meum* and *tuum* and of criminal action, forming the great mass of the system of law, constitute their particular department."

2. *Andrew Jackson—Veto Message (on bill to recharter the Bank of the United States), July 10, 1832* (II Messages and Papers of the Presidents (Richardson ed. 1896), 576, 581–583):

"It is maintained by the advocates of the bank that its constitutionality in all its features ought to be considered as settled by precedent and by the decision of the Supreme Court. [McCulloch v. Maryland, 4 Wheat. 316 (1819) (see chap. 2 below). To this conclusion I can not assent. Mere precedent is a dangerous source of authority, and should not be regarded as deciding questions of constitutional power except where the acquiescence of the people and the States can be considered as well settled. . . . If the opinion of the Supreme Court covered the whole ground of this act, it ought not to control the coordinate authorities of this Government. The Congress, the Executive, and the Court must each for itself be guided by its own opinion of the Constitution. Each public officer who takes an oath to support the Constitution swears that he will support it as he understands it, and not as it is understood by others. It is as much the duty of the House of Representatives, of the Senate, and of the President to decide upon the constitutionality of any bill or resolution which may be presented to them for passage or approval as it is of the supreme judges when it may be brought before them for judicial decision. The opinion of the judges has no more authority over Congress than the opinion of Congress has over the judges, and on that point the President is independent of both. The authority of the Supreme Court must not, therefore, be permitted to control the Congress or the Executive when acting in their legislative capacities, but to have only such influence as the force of their reasoning may deserve.

"But in the case relied upon the Supreme Court have not decided that all the features of this corporation are compatible with the Constitution. . . . Under the decision of the Supreme Court . . . it is the exclusive province of Congress and the President to decide whether the particular features of this act are *necessary* and *proper* in order to enable the bank to perform conveniently and efficiently the public duties assigned to it as a fiscal agent, and therefore constitutional, or *unnecessary* and *improper*, and therefore unconstitutional.

"Without commenting on the general principle affirmed by the Supreme Court, let us examine the details of this act in accordance with the rule of legislative action which they have laid down. It will be found that many of the powers and privileges conferred on it can not be supposed necessary for the purpose for which it is proposed to be created, and are not, therefore, means necessary to attain the end in view, and consequently not justified by the Constitution."

3. *Abraham Lincoln.* a. *Speeches during the Lincoln-Douglas Senatorial Campaign, July, October 1858.* (II The Collected Works of Abraham Lincoln (Basler ed. 1953), 494, 516; III id. 255):

[July 10, 1858:] "I have expressed heretofore, and I now repeat, my opposition to the Dred Scott Decision [Dred Scott v. Sandford, 19 How. 393 (1857)], but I should be allowed to state the nature of that opposition, and I ask your indulgence while I do so. What is fairly implied by the term Judge Douglas has used, 'resistance to the Decision?' I do not resist it. If I wanted to take Dred Scott from his master, I would be interfering with

property, and that terrible difficulty that Judge Douglas speaks of, of interfering with property, would arise. But I am doing no such thing as that, but all that I am doing is refusing to obey it as a political rule. If I were in Congress, and a vote should come up on a question whether slavery should be prohibited in a new territory, in spite of that Dred Scott decision, I would vote that it should."

[July 17, 1858:] "I am opposed to [the Dred Scott] decision in a certain sense, but not in the sense which [Douglas] puts on it. I say that in so far as it decided in favor of Dred Scott's master and against Dred Scott and his family, I do not propose to disturb or resist the decision.

"I never have proposed to do any such thing. I think, that in respect for judicial authority, my humble history would not suffer in a comparison with that of Judge Douglas. He would have the citizen conform his vote to that decision; the Member of Congress, his; the President, his use of the veto power. He would make it a rule of political action for the people and all the departments of the government. I would not. By resisting it as a political rule, I disturb no right of property, create no disorder, excite no mobs."

[Oct. 13, 1858:] "We oppose the Dred Scott decision in a certain way, upon which I ought perhaps to address you a few words. We do not propose that when Dred Scott has been decided to be a slave by the court, we, as a mob, will decide him to be free. We do not propose that, when any other one, or one thousand, shall be decided by that court to be slaves, we will in any violent way disturb the rights of property thus settled; but we nevertheless do oppose that decision as a political rule which shall be binding on the voter, to vote for nobody who thinks it wrong, which shall be binding on the members of Congress or the President to favor no measure that does not actually concur with the principles of that decision. We do not propose to be bound by it as a political rule in that way, because we think it lays the foundation not merely of enlarging and spreading out what we consider an evil, but it lays the foundation for spreading that evil into the States themselves. We propose so resisting it as to have it reversed if we can, and a new judicial rule established upon this subject."

b. *First Inaugural Address, March 4, 1861* (VI Messages and Papers of the Presidents (Richardson ed. 1897), 5, 9–10):

"I do not forget the position assumed by some that constitutional questions are to be decided by the Supreme Court, nor do I deny that such decisions must be binding in any case upon the parties to a suit as to the object of that suit, while they are also entitled to very high respect and consideration in all parallel cases by all other departments of the Government. And while it is obviously possible that such decision may be erroneous in any given case, still the evil effect following it, being limited to that particular case, with the chance that it may be overruled and never become a precedent for other cases, can better be borne than could the evils of a different practice. At the same time, the candid citizen must confess that if the policy of the Government upon vital questions affecting the whole people is to be irrevocably fixed by decisions of the Supreme Court, the instant they are made in ordinary litigation between parties in personal actions the people will have ceased to be their own rulers, having to that extent practically resigned their Government into the hands of that eminent tribunal. Nor is there in this

view any assault upon the court or the judges.   It is a duty from which they may not shrink to decide cases properly brought before them, and it is no fault of theirs if others seek to turn their decisions to political purposes."

4. *Franklin D. Roosevelt*. a. *Letter to Congressman Hill, July 6, 1935* (4 The Public Papers and Addresses of Franklin D. Roosevelt (1938), 297–98): [The letter was written after the Supreme Court's 1935 decision in the Schechter case (chap. 3 below), the "sick chicken" case construing national regulatory powers narrowly and invalidating an important segment of New Deal emergency legislation, the National Industrial Recovery Act. President Roosevelt nevertheless urged Congress to enact a law establishing an NIRA-like regulatory scheme for the bituminous coal industry. The President's letter explained the need for the law, noted that its constitutionality depended on "whether production conditions directly affect, promote or obstruct interstate commerce," and added the passage which follows.] "Manifestly, no one is in a position to give assurance that the proposed act will withstand constitutional tests .   .   .. But the situation is so urgent and the benefits of the legislation so evident that all doubts should be resolved in favor of the bill, leaving to the courts, in an orderly fashion, the ultimate question of constitutionality. A decision by the Supreme Court relative to this measure would be helpful as indicating, with increasing clarity, the constitutional limits within which this Government must operate. .   .   . I hope your committee will not permit doubts as to constitutionality, however reasonable, to block the suggested legislation." *

b. *Proposed speech on the Gold Clause Cases, Feb. 1935:* (I F.D.R.— His Personal Letters, 1928–1945 (Elliott Roosevelt ed. 1950), 459–460): [This was a draft speech President Roosevelt planned to deliver in the event the Court decided against the Government on the constitutionality of abrogating "gold clauses" in federal obligations. In fact, the Court decided for the Roosevelt Administration, and the speech was not delivered. See Perry v. United States, 294 U.S. 330 (1935).] "I do not seek to enter into any controversy with the distinguished members of the Supreme Court of the United States who have participated in this .   .   . decision. They have decided these cases in accordance with the letter of the law as they read it. But it is appropriate to quote a sentence from the First Inaugural Address of President Lincoln: [quoting the "At the same time" sentence in note 3b, above].
.   .   .

"It is the duty of the Congress and the President to protect the people of the United States to the best of their ability. It is necessary to protect them from the unintended construction of voluntary acts, as well as from intolerable burdens involuntarily imposed. To stand idly by and to permit the decision of the Supreme Court to be carried through to its logical, inescapable conclusion would so imperil the economic and political security of this nation that the legislative and executive officers of the Government must look beyond the narrow letter of contractual obligations, so that they may sustain the substance of the promise originally made in accord with the actual intention of the parties. .   .   .   I shall immediately take such steps as may

---

* Congress promptly enacted the legislation urged by the President; but the Court, less than a year later, invalidated the Bituminous Coal Conservation Act of 1935, in the Carter case (chap. 3 below). On the Court crisis provoked by invalidations of New Deal laws, see chap. 3 below.

be necessary, by proclamation and by message to the Congress of the United States."

5. *The autonomy of the coordinate branches.* a. *Some comments on the Presidential statements.* If constitutional interpretation were a special or exclusive judicial function, most of the quoted presidential statements would be indefensible. Yet are not most of them consistent with the major thrust of Marshall's rationale in Marbury—the rationale that rests judicial review not on any special judicial guardianship of constitutional norms, but simply on the courts' duty to decide cases before them in accordance with the relevant law? Recall Herbert Wechsler's description of judicial duty in his "Neutral Principles" lecture, noted above: the duty is "not that of policing or advising Legislatures or Executives," but rather simply the duty "to decide the litigated case and to decide it in accordance with the law." As Wechsler has said elsewhere ["The Courts and the Constitution," 65 Colum.L.Rev. 1001 (1965)]: "That is, at least, what Marbury v. Madison was all about."

The presidential statements suggest, too, that attention to context is essential if uncritical condemnation is to be avoided whenever other branches claim some autonomy in constitutional judgments. In the Jackson bank veto situation (note 2 above), the Supreme Court had indeed spoken. But Jackson emphasized the autonomy of "the Congress or the Executive when acting in their legislative capacities": though bank recharter legislation would be constitutional, Congress or the President could refuse to enact new legislation because of constitutional doubts. Would the broader view of judicial authority in Cooper v. Aaron, below, deny that a member of Congress may (indeed, must) vote against legislation he believes to be unconstitutional, even though the law would be constitutional under the standards of prior Court decisions? Is there any greater difficulty as a matter of constitutional principle with the variety of legislative autonomy President Roosevelt urged upon Congressman Hill (note 4b above)?

Jefferson (note 1a) and Lincoln (note 3) were faced with prior judicial decisions that spoke with special immediacy to the problems that confronted them. Yet Jefferson was defending the exercise of the pardoning power, a power specifically vested in the President with broad discretion; he insisted simply on autonomy in his "own sphere of action." And Lincoln was careful to distinguish between direct interference with the Court decision in Dred Scott's case and acceptance of the constitutional interpretation of that case "as a political rule." All of these positions fell short of direct conflict with a court order; all recognized judicial authority to adjudicate constitutionality with respect to the case before the court and simply insisted on autonomy within their own "spheres of action."

Only President Roosevelt's proposed speech on the "gold clause" issue (note 4b above) suggests direct defiance of a court order, direct contravention of the narrow, classical justification of Marbury. And serious presidential considerations of direct defiance have been very rare indeed. There is a legend that President Jackson, shortly before his veto of the bank recharter bill, said of a Supreme Court decision: "John Marshall has made his decision. Now let him enforce it." The decision was Worcester v. Georgia, 6 Peters 515 (1832), where the Marshall Court held that Georgia had no legislative authority over Cherokee Nation lands. In fact, Jackson's support

for enforcement of the decision was never put to a test: though he was no doubt unhappy about it, the litigation was abandoned before any call for presidential assistance arose. See Burke, "The Cherokee Cases: A Study in Law, Politics, and Morality," 21 Stan.L.Rev. 500 (1969). More recently, while Special Prosecutor Jaworski's effort to gain access to Watergate tapes was pending before the courts, President Nixon and his counsel hinted that the President might not comply with an order to turn over the tapes. Yet on the day that the Supreme Court decision against the President was handed down, in United States v. Nixon, 418 U.S. 683 (1974) (chap. 7 below), President Nixon announced that he had instructed his counsel "to take whatever measures are necessary to comply with that decision in all respects."

If the Marbury rationale leaves to legislators and the President considerable autonomy even in the face of Supreme Court interpretations quite closely in point, their authority and obligation to consider constitutionality would seem even greater when they are writing on a relatively blank slate. Yet even in those situations, legislators sometimes suggest that problems of constitutionality are solely the courts' business. Is such a stance defensible under Marbury? Under Cooper v. Aaron, below? Under the Constitution? See, e. g., some of the comments during the hearings on the Civil Rights Act of 1964, noted in chap. 3 below. And see generally, Morgan, Congress and the Constitution (1966), and Brest, "The Conscientious Legislator's Guide to Constitutional Interpretation," 27 Stan.L.Rev. 585 (1975).

b. *Legitimate disagreement and improper defiance.* Is never-ending, chaotic questioning of Court interpretations inevitable if one takes a narrow view of authoritativeness pursuant to Marbury? Consider the solution advanced in Wechsler, "The Courts and the Constitution," 65 Colum.L.Rev. 1001, 1008 (1965), which draws on aspects of President Lincoln's position quoted in note 3b above. Lincoln spoke of the "chance" that the ruling "may be overruled and never become a precedent for other cases." Wechsler comments: "When that chance has been exploited and has run its course, with reaffirmation rather than reversal of decision, has not the time arrived when its acceptance is demanded, without insisting on repeated litigation? The answer here, it seems to me, must be affirmative, both as the necessary implication of our constitutional tradition and to avoid the greater evils that will otherwise ensue."

Does this position permit too broad a range of challenges to Court rulings, in theory or in practice? And is such criticism acceptable only so long as it is calm and rational? Note Professor Jaffe's observation that intense criticism is especially appropriate as well as probable in the area of constitutional adjudication: "There will be and there should be popular response to the Supreme Court's decision; not just the 'informed' criticism of law professors but the deep-felt, emotion-laden, unsophisticated reaction of the laity. This is so because more than any court in the modern world the Supreme Court 'makes policy,' and is at the same time so little subject to formal democratic control. . . . Yet those who urge the Court on to political innovation are outraged when its decisions arouse, as they must, resentment and political attack." Jaffe, "Impromptu Remarks," 76 Harv.L.Rev. 1111 (1963).

6. *Is the Court "the ultimate interpreter of the Constitution"?—Some modern assertions.*   a. *Cooper v. Aaron: Are Court interpretations "the supreme law of the land"?* The opinion in COOPER v. AARON, 358 U.S. 1 (1958), provides the major judicial support for a view widely held by the public, that the Court is the ultimate or supreme interpreter of the Constitution. Cooper v. Aaron arose against a background of opposition by Governor Faubus and other Arkansas officials against public school desegregation in Little Rock. The state officials claimed that they were not "bound" by the Supreme Court's basic school desegregation ruling, the 1954 decision in Brown v. Board of Education, 347 U.S. 483 (chap. 10 below). Arkansas did not appear in that case; but a subsequent lower court order directed desegregation by the Little Rock school board, and the state officials tried to prevent the school board from complying with that desegregation decree.* In that context, the Supreme Court could have limited itself to its reminder that state officials lacked "power to nullify a federal court order." But the Court's response—signed by each of the nine Justices—went considerably beyond: instead of confining itself to implementing the desegregation order entered by the lower federal court in Arkansas, it spoke broadly about the impact of the 1954 ruling in Brown on the state officials.† In that dictum, at 358 U.S. 1, 17–19, the Justices asserted:

"[W]e should answer the premise of the actions of the Governor and Legislature that they are not bound by our holding in the Brown case. It is necessary only to recall some basic constitutional propositions which are settled doctrine. Article VI of the Constitution makes the Constitution the 'supreme Law of the Land.' In 1803, Chief Justice Marshall, speaking for a unanimous Court, referring to the Constitution as 'the fundamental and paramount law of the nation,' declared in the notable case of Marbury v. Madison, 1 Cranch 137, 177, that 'It is emphatically the province and duty of the judicial department to say what the law is.' This decision declared the basic principle that the federal judiciary is supreme in the exposition of the law of the

---

* To recall the context and holding in Cooper v. Aaron somewhat more precisely: The Little Rock school board, seeking to desegregate the public schools pursuant to a plan approved by the lower federal court, was blocked in its efforts by Governor Faubus' action in calling out the National Guard in September 1957. The Governor placed Little Rock's Central High School "off limits" to Black students. After a trial court injunction against the Governor, the troops were withdrawn. Thereafter, Black students were able to attend school under the protection of federally-commanded troops. In February 1958, the school board sought a long postponement of the desegregation program. The U. S. District Court granted that relief, after noting the "chaos, bedlam and turmoil" and finding the situation "intolerable." The Court of Appeals reversed; and that decision was affirmed by the Supreme Court. The Su-

preme Court found that the school officials had acted in "entire good faith" but concluded that "the actions of the other state agencies responsible for those conditions compel us to reject the Board's legal position. . . . The constitutional rights of respondents are not to be sacrificed or yielded to the violence and disorder which have followed upon the actions of the Governor and Legislature."

† Note the suggestion of a "crucial difference" between Governor Faubus' stated opposition to the Brown decision and his efforts to block school board implementation of a desegregation plan approved by the federal court in Arkansas, in Horowitz and Karst, Law, Lawyers and Social Change (1969), 253. Are the authors persuasive in their analogy—"it is the difference between arguing with the umpire and refusing to leave the base when you are called out"?

Constitution, and that principle has ever since been respected by this Court and the Country as a permanent and indispensable feature of our constitutional system. It follows that the interpretation of the Fourteenth Amendment enunciated by this Court in the Brown case is the supreme law of the land, and Art. VI of the Constitution makes it of binding effect on the States 'any Thing in the Constitution or Laws of any State to the Contrary notwithstanding.' Every state legislator and executive and judicial officer is solemnly committed by oath taken pursuant to Art. VI, ¶ 3, 'to support this Constitution.' "

Was that Court view of its own powers truly a statement of "settled doctrine"? Was it merely a restatement of Marbury v. Madison—or was it a substantial expansion of the authority asserted by Chief Justice Marshall? Assuming that most of the presidential views noted above are consistent with Marbury, can they also be reconciled with Cooper v. Aaron? Note Gunther, "The Subtle Vices of the 'Passive Virtues'—A Comment on Principle and Expediency in Judicial Review," 64 Colum.L.Rev. 1, 25 (1964): "Bickel [Bickel, The Least Dangerous Branch (1962)] draws from Marbury v. Madison . . . the notion that the Court's 'doctrines are not to be questioned,' by citizens or by other departments of government. . . . That confuses Marshall's assertion of judicial authority to interpret the Constitution with judicial exclusiveness; that confuses Marbury v. Madison with statements in the Little Rock case, Cooper v. Aaron."

b. *Additional Court "restatements" of Marbury.* Since Cooper v. Aaron, the Court has found several other occasions to assert broad views of its judicial review authority. For example, in holding legislative reapportionment disputes justiciable in Baker v. Carr, 369 U.S. 186 (1962) (chap. 15 below), Justice Brennan's majority opinion referred in passing to the "responsibility of this Court as ultimate interpreter of the Constitution." And Chief Justice Warren relied on that comment a few years later in his majority opinion defending the Court's power to review the exclusion of Congressman Adam Clayton Powell from the House of Representatives: the Chief Justice stated in Powell v. McCormack, 395 U.S. 486, 549 (1969) (chap. 7 below), that "it is the responsibility of this Court to act as the ultimate interpreter of the Constitution. Marbury v. Madison . . . ."

Still more recently, the Burger Court invoked Marbury v. Madison for broad and questionable inferences in another context, in the Watergate tapes litigation, United States v. Nixon, 418 U.S. 683 (1974) (chap. 7 below). Chief Justice Burger's opinion in the Nixon case repeatedly cited Marbury and stated at one point: "The President's counsel . . . reads the Constitution as providing an absolute privilege of confidentiality for all presidential communications. Many decisions of this Court, however, have unequivocally reaffirmed the holding of [Marbury v. Madison] that 'it is emphatically the province and duty of the judicial department to say what the law is.' " Does that "however" make sense? Does acceptance of Marbury mean that the Constitution cannot be read to vest final authority to decide certain issues in other branches? Note the materials on "political questions," chaps. 7 and 15 below. And note Gunther, "Judicial Hegemony and Legislative Autonomy: The Nixon Case and the Impeachment Process," 22

UCLA L.Rev. 30 (1974).* [Chief Justice Burger's questionably broad reliance on Marbury does at least fall short of claiming constitutional interpretation as an *exclusively* judicial role. In the sentence preceding the passage quoted above, he conceded: "In the performance of assigned constitutional duties each branch of the Government must initially interpret the Constitution, and the interpretation of its powers by any branch is due great respect from the others."]

7. *The legal consequences of judicial "invalidation."* Under the classic Marbury theory, a court confronted with an unconstitutional statute simply refuses enforcement to that law in the case before it. In civil law countries, by contrast, a court exercising judicial review issues a ruling of general invalidity binding on all, not just on the parties before it. But here, too, civil law and American law are closer in practice than in theory. Thus, it does not tell the whole story to say, as an American court has said, that a decision upon constitutionality "affects the parties only, and there is no judgment against the statute." Shephard v. Wheeling, 4 S.E. 635 (W.Va. 1887). For example, some practical reach of a court ruling beyond the immediate parties is assured by the ordinary judicial adherence to stare decisis.

Yet to say that an invalidity ruling affects more than the parties is not to say that it is the same as wiping a statute off the books. It is as inaccurate to claim too broad an impact for a ruling as it is to state it too narrowly. The best-known example of overstatement is an assertion in Norton v. Shelby County, 118 U.S. 425 (1886), a statement that has required some important qualifications: "An unconstitutional act is not a law; it confers no rights; it imposes no duties; it affords no protection; it creates no office;

* The Gunther article suggests one possible answer to the questions: "That 'however' suggests that the Marbury passage helps answer the executive privilege contention . . . . But there is nothing in Marbury v. Madison that precludes a constitutional interpretation which gives final authority to another branch. "I do not believe that the Court intended to announce that every constitutional issue requires final adjudication on the merits by the judiciary. As in the past, there are likely to be issues in the future which the Court will find to have been 'committed by the Constitution to another branch of government . . . .' [Baker v. Carr.] For example, I would think (and hope) that a conviction on impeachment would be found unreviewable in the courts. Nor do I mean to suggest that the Court's result was wrong on the merits: I think checks and balances arguments make a non-absolute view of executive privilege appropriate. I simply suggest that the argument for absolute executive privilege deserved a more focused, careful, separable answer than the Court's invocation of Marbury v. Madison provides.

"In short, I think the Court's overbroad reliance on Marbury was at the least a non sequitur and at worst dangerous nonsense. And the Judiciary Committee debate on article III [of the Articles of Impeachment against Richard M. Nixon, based on the refusal to comply with congressional subpoenas] illustrates some of the danger. [Many of the Congressmen] who opposed article III did so on the basis of statements echoing the misleading tenor of the objectionable parts of the Court's opinion in United States v. Nixon: somehow it was incongruous in the American scheme that Congress should decide that constitutional issue on its own; somehow it was inappropriate to have the legislature rather than the judiciary resolve this dispute between the legislative and executive branches." [The article gives several examples of legislators' invocation of Marbury (and its "restatements" in the Powell and Nixon cases) during the course of the House Judiciary Committee impeachment debates. See chap. 7 below.]

it is, in legal contemplation, as inoperative as though it had never been passed."

But a law held unconstitutional in an American court is by no means so wholly a nullity, as the Attorney General quite persuasively advised President Roosevelt in 1937. The Supreme Court had held the District of Columbia minimum wage law unconstitutional in 1923, in the Adkins case; but in 1937, in sustaining a similar Washington law in the West Coast Hotel Co. case, the Court formally overruled Adkins. (The cases are in chap. 9, secs. 1B and 1C, below.) The Attorney General advised that the 1923 ruling had simply "suspend[ed]" enforcement, and that the act was valid and enforceable after the 1937 decision, explaining: "The decisions are practically in accord in holding that the courts have no power to repeal or abolish a statute, and that notwithstanding a decision holding it unconstitutional a statute continues to remain on the statute books." 39 Ops.Atty.Gen. 22 (1937).

The Supreme Court itself has had occasion to warn that the problem is more subtle and complex than the Norton language suggested. In Chicot County Drainage Dist. v. Baxter State Bank, 308 U.S. 371 (1940), for example, the Court held that an unappealed decision applying a federal statute was res judicata despite a subsequent Supreme Court ruling in another case that the law was unconstitutional. Chief Justice Hughes stated:

"The courts below have proceeded on the theory that the Act of Congress, having been found to be unconstitutional, was not a law; that it was inoperative, conferring no rights and imposing no duties . . . . [Norton.] It is quite clear, however, that such broad statements as to the effect of a determination of unconstitutionality must be taken with qualifications. The actual existence of a statute, prior to such a determination, is an operative fact and may have consequences which cannot justly be ignored. The past cannot always be erased by a new judicial declaration. The effect of the subsequent ruling as to invalidity may have to be considered in various aspects,—with respect to particular relations, individual and corporate, and particular conduct, private and official. [I]t is manifest from numerous decisions that an all-inclusive statement of a principle of absolute retroactive invalidity cannot be justified." See generally Field, The Effect of an Unconstitutional Statute (1935).*

Chief Justice Hughes in the Chicot County case stressed that "a principle of absolute retroactive invalidity" was unsupportable, while recognizing

---

* For a more recent rejection of the Norton overstatement that unconstitutional laws are wholly inoperative, see Chief Justice Burger's opinion in the second Lemon v. Kurtzman decision, 411 U.S. 192 (1973). There, the Court denied retroactive effect to its earlier decision in the case (chap. 14 below) holding a state's spending program in violation of the Establishment Clause and permitted payments to nonpublic schools for services rendered prior to that 1971 decision of unconstitutionality. The Chief Justice commented: "However appealing the logic of Norton may have been in the abstract, its abandonment reflected our recognition that statutory or even judge-made rules of law are hard facts on which people must rely in making decisions and in shaping their conduct. This fact of legal life underpins our modern decisions recognizing a doctrine of nonretroactivity. Appellants offer no persuasive reasons for confining the modern approach to those constitutional cases involving criminal procedure or municipal bonds, and we ourselves perceive none."

retroactivity as the normal consequence of judicial invalidation. But, as Chief Justice Burger's comment in the footnote suggests, more recent attention has shifted from the typical rule of retroactivity to the permissible range of prospectivity. That problem has been raised by the Court's rapid expansion of federal constitutional rights in criminal proceedings. (See chap. 8 below.) Could the Court announce new guarantees without permitting all those already convicted to benefit from those new rights? Beginning with Linkletter v. Walker, 381 U.S. 618 (1965), the Court decided that it could indeed withhold retroactive effect for its rulings. The Court found that "the Constitution neither prohibits nor requires retrospective effect," so that it was the Court's task to "weigh the merits and demerits" of retroactivity for the rule in question "by looking to the prior history," to the "purpose and effect" of the new constitutional rule, and to "whether retrospective operation will further or retard its operation." Determining which new rules should be limited to prospective effect under this approach—and deciding what "prospectivity" should mean—has given rise to repeated controversy since Linkletter. (See the additional materials on this problem at the end of chap. 8 below, and see generally Mishkin, "Foreword: The High Court, the Great Writ, and the Due Process of Time and Law," 79 Harv.L.Rev. 56 (1965).)

SECTION 2. SUPREME COURT AUTHORITY TO REVIEW STATE COURT JUDGMENTS: THE MARTIN v. HUNTER'S LESSEE ISSUES

MARTIN v. HUNTER'S LESSEE, 1 Wheat. 304 (1816), ranks second only to Marbury v. Madison among the important decisions of the Marshall era articulating the contours of federal judicial authority. The Martin decision defended the legitimacy of Supreme Court review of state court judgments resting on interpretations of federal law; it rejected the highest Virginia court's challenge to the constitutionality of § 25 of the Judiciary Act of 1789. Section 25 provided essentially for Supreme Court review of final decisions of the highest state courts rejecting claims based on federal law—including federal constitutional law. (The full text of § 25 is printed—together with its expanded modern counterpart, 28 U.S.C. § 1257 —in sec. 4 below.)

In many respects, the textual and historical support for the Supreme Court authority asserted in Martin is stronger than can be mustered in defense of Marbury v. Madison. The Court had sporadically exercised § 25 authority for years prior to the Virginia challenge in Martin. As Justice Story's opinion in Martin elaborates, some support for the authority can be drawn from the language of Articles III and VI of the Constitution. Moreover, an expectation of Supreme Court review of state court judgments runs through the Constitutional Convention debates. At the Convention, the establishment of inferior federal courts was a major source of controversy. The relevant provisions of Article III reflect a compromise between opposing views: one insisting on the mandatory creation of lower federal courts; the other leaving initial application of federal law entirely to the

state courts. The compromise left the creation and jurisdiction of lower federal courts largely to the discretion of Congress. That compromise, as well as the Supremacy Clause of Art. VI, contemplated that federal questions would initially arise in state as well as federal courts and assumed that Supreme Court review would insure any necessary uniformity.

Despite that strong support for the Supreme Court decision in Martin, some attention to the Martin controversy is warranted, because of contemporary as well as historical concerns. The excerpts below delineate the core of the contending positions of the Virginia judges and of Justice Story in the Supreme Court. They throw light not only on the question of what the fighting in the early 19th century was all about: for example, did the Virginians advocate a hopelessly unworkable, anarchical scheme of allocation of authority among state and federal courts? Beyond that, the Martin materials also introduce continuingly important themes: the existence of state as well as federal courts as interpreters of federal law; the obligation as well as authority of state courts to heed the "supreme" law; the complex interrelations between state and federal judiciaries in a system in which the function of interpreting federal (including constitutional) law is divided among the judicial structures of separate, state and federal, governments.*

1. *The background of the Martin litigation.* The immediate provocation for the Supreme Court's decision sustaining the constitutionality of § 25 of the Judiciary Act of 1789 was the refusal by the Virginia Court of Appeals (announced in 1815) to obey the Supreme Court mandate in Fairfax's Devisee v. Hunter's Lessee, 7 Cranch 603 (1813). That Fairfax ruling in turn was the culmination of land litigation that had been instituted many years earlier, in 1791. The dispute concerned the vast land holdings of Lord Fairfax. Virginia claimed that it had properly seized the Fairfax properties prior to 1783, as lands belonging to British loyalists during the Revolution. Virginia parceled out some of the land to its own citizens; and Hunter claimed the land in issue as such a grantee from the State of Virginia. Martin claimed title under a devise from Fairfax: he insisted that the Fairfax lands were protected against seizure because of the Peace Treaty of 1783 and the Jay Treaty of 1794. In short, Hunter's claim rested on a series of Virginia statutes relating to the forfeiture to the State of lands owned by British subjects; Martin's position, by contrast, was that title to the land acquired under the Fairfax will in 1781 had not vested in Virginia prior to 1783, and that it was thereafter protected by the treaty provisions.

Though Hunter had instituted his action to establish his right to the land as early as 1791, the litigation was in abeyance for almost two decades. In the interim, there were complicated negotiations—negotiations which involved John Marshall, for the future Chief Justice and his brother James had contracted for the purchase of the main part of the Fairfax estate from

---

* Additional aspects of the problem of federal-state court relations are noted later in this chapter. Note especially the consideration of the "adequate state grounds" obstacle to Supreme Court review of state court decisions (including the return to the Martin litigation as illustrative of that ob-stacle). See also chap. 15, sec. 4B, below, on federal court intervention in state court proceedings. Full exploration of these problems is left to courses on federal jurisdiction. See, e. g., Hart and Wechsler, Federal Courts (2d ed. 1973); Wright, Federal Courts (2d ed. 1970).

the Fairfax heirs.† It was not until 1810 that the Virginia Court of Appeals first ruled on the case—and decided for Hunter and the effectiveness of Virginia's seizure of the Fairfax lands. It was that decision that the Supreme Court reversed, siding with Martin in 1813. Pursuant to that 1813 decision, the Supreme Court mandate, in strong language, "instructed" and "commanded" the Virginia judges to enter judgment for Martin.

The issue of compliance with that mandate stirred considerable controversy in Virginia. It was a somewhat surprising time for states' rights agitation to reemerge in Virginia. A divided nation was at war with England; James Madison, the President from Virginia, was trying to unite the nation against vociferous states' rights criticisms from anti-war forces centered in New England; and yet the Virginia judges, with their ruling on § 25, initiated new waves of states' rights attacks that were to engulf the Marshall Court for years. As the state court reporter noted, the question whether the Supreme Court's mandate should be obeyed "excited all that attention from the Bench and Bar which its great importance truly merited." The issue was argued at length before the Virginia Court of Appeals in 1814. However, no decision was announced until well after a year later, in 1815: apparently, the Virginia judges delayed publication in order to avoid encouraging the secessionist feelings mounting in New England near the close of the War of 1812.

2. *The core of the Virginia judges' position in Martin.* a. The Virginia judges produced several opinions but united in a strongly worded joint conclusion: "The Court is unanimously of opinion, that the appellate power of the Supreme Court of the United States does not extend to this court, under a sound construction of the constitution of the United States; that so much of the 25th section of the act of Congress to establish the judicial courts of the United States, as extends the appellate jurisdiction of the Supreme Court to this court, is not in pursuance of the constitution of the United States; that the writ of error in this case was improvidently allowed under the authority of that act; that the proceedings thereon in the Supreme Court were *coram non judice* in relation to this court; and that obedience to its mandate be declined by this court." *

---

† Because of that involvement, John Marshall did not participate in the Supreme Court decisions in 1813 and 1816. The task of writing the opinions of the Court fell to Justice Joseph Story. Story, a Jeffersonian Republican from Massachusetts, had been appointed to the Court by President Madison in 1811. His nationalist positions in Martin and many other cases disappointed some Jeffersonians—including Thomas Jefferson himself. But the Jeffersonian heritage included nationalist as well as localist strands; and in a state such as Massachusetts nationalism was understandably popular with Jeffersonians. New England Federalists had increasingly turned to states' rights beliefs in opposition to a national government controlled by Jeffersonians; support for strong national institutions was accordingly an attractive ideology for Jeffersonians such as Story. The ambivalence in Jeffersonian thinking about national and state powers is illustrated by the contrasting reactions of ex-Presidents Jefferson and Madison to the controversial § 25 sustained in the Martin decision: Jefferson sided with the critics of decisions such as Martin; Madison dissociated himself from them and, in strong letters over many years, defended the legitimacy and necessity of § 25 review.

* The most influential member of the Virginia Court of Appeals was no doubt Spencer Roane—a life-long critic of John Marshall, an active political leader as well as eminent judge, a frequent contributor to the organ of the

The bases for the Virginia judges' joint conclusion are indicated by the following excerpts from the opinion of Judge Cabell: The power of the national government operates on "individuals in their individual capacity. No one presumes to contend, that the state governments can operate compulsively on the general government or any of its departments, even in cases of unquestionable encroachment on state authority . . . . Such encroachment of jurisdiction could neither be prevented nor redressed by the state government, or any of its departments, *by any procedure acting on the Federal Courts.* I can perceive nothing in the constitution which gives to the Federal Courts any stronger claim to prevent or redress, *by any procedure acting on the state* Courts, an equally obvious encroachment on the Federal jurisdiction. The constitution of the United States contemplates the independence of both governments, and regards the *residuary* sovereignty of the states, as not less inviolable, than the *delegated* sovereignty of the United States. It must have been foreseen that controversies would sometimes arise as to the boundaries of the two jurisdictions. Yet the constitution has provided no umpire, has erected no tribunal by which they shall be settled. The omission proceeded, probably, from the belief, that such a tribunal would produce evils greater than those of the occasional collisions which it would be designed to remedy. . . .

"If this Court should now proceed to enter a judgment in this case, according [to] instructions of the Supreme Court, the Judges of this Court, in doing so, must act either as Federal or as State Judges. But we cannot be made Federal Judges without our consent, and without commissions. Both these requisites being wanting, the act could not, therefore, be done by us, constitutionally, as Federal Judges. We must, then, in obeying this mandate, be considered still as State Judges. We are required, as State Judges to enter up a judgment, not our own, but dictated and prescribed to us by another Court. . . . But, before one Court can dictate to another, the judgment it shall pronounce, it must bear, to that other, the relation of an appellate Court. The term appellate, however, necessarily includes the idea of *superiority.* But one Court cannot be correctly said to be *superior* to another, unless both of them belong to the same sovereignty. It would be a misapplication of terms to say that a Court of Virginia is *superior* to a Court of Maryland, or vice versa. The Courts of the United States, therefore, belonging to one sovereignty, cannot be appellate Courts in relation to the State

Richmond leadership of Virginia politics, the "Richmond Enquirer," and a vociferous and articulate critic of Marshall Court opinions beginning with the Martin case.

Only in the Martin case did Spencer Roane have the opportunity to cross swords with Marshall Court decisions in his official capacity. His objections to later decisions—McCulloch v. Maryland in 1819 (chap. 2 below) and Cohens v. Virginia in 1821 (below) —were even stronger. That opposition was expressed in pseudonymous essays in the "Richmond Enquirer"; and John Marshall was so stung by them that he resorted to pseudonymous

newspaper responses of his own after McCulloch. See Gunther (ed.), John Marshall's Defense of McCulloch v. Maryland (1969). On Roane generally, see Note, "Judge Spencer Roane of Virginia: Champion of States' Rights —Foe of John Marshall," 66 Harv.L. Rev. 1242 (1953). And for fuller accounts of the Martin litigation, see IV Beveridge, The Life of John Marshall (1919), 144–67; 1 Warren, The Supreme Court in United States History (rev. ed. 1926), 442–53; and 2 Crosskey, Politics and the Constitution in the History of the United States (1953), 785–814.

Courts, which belong to a different sovereignty—and of course, their commands or instructions impose no obligation.

".   .   .   But the act of Congress now under consideration, attempts, in fact, to make the State Courts *Inferior Federal Courts*, and to exercise through them, jurisdiction over the subjects of federal cognizance. [T]he appellate jurisdiction of the Supreme Court of the United States [under Article III of the Constitution], must have reference to the inferior Courts of the United States, and not to State Courts.   .   .   .   It has been contended that the constitution contemplated only the objects of appeal, and not the tribunals from which the appeal is to be taken; and intended to give to the Supreme Court of the United States appellate jurisdiction in all the cases of federal cognizance. But this argument proves too much, and what is utterly inadmissible. It would give appellate jurisdiction, as well over the courts of England or France, as over the State courts; for, although I do not think the State Courts are *foreign* Courts in relation to the Federal Courts, yet I consider them not less *independent* than foreign Courts."

b.   In considering the feasibility and justifiability of a judicial scheme such as that contemplated by the Virginia judges, note that they did not deny the supremacy of valid federal law under Art. VI of the Constitution, nor their obligation to give effect to superior federal law in state court adjudication. In the Martin litigation, for example, they acknowledged that alien property holdings that existed at the time of the treaties of 1783 and 1794 were protected by those superior federal guarantees. They insisted, however, that the Fairfax interests had been validly seized by the State prior to 1783. Nor did the Virginia judges deny all claims to a valid federal judicial enforcement machinery. Paradoxically, their response to nationalist needs was to point to the congressional authority under Art. III to expand the number and jurisdiction of the lower federal courts. For example, to the argument that without the appellate jurisdiction "there will be no other mode by which congress can extend the judicial power of the United States to the cases of federal cognizance; that there will, consequently, be no uniformity of decision," Judge Cabell replied: "All the purposes of the constitution of the United States will be answered by the erection of Federal Courts, into which any party, plaintiff or defendant, concerned in a case of federal cognizance, *may* carry it for adjudication." In short, the Virginia position, rather than being a total flouting of federal supremacy or an advocacy of direct resistance to federal court orders, was a more moderate assertion of limited state judicial autonomy: to the extent judiciary legislation left federal questions to arise and make their way through the state courts, final adjudication had to be by that judicial system; if that channeling of cases proved unsatisfactory, the federal government's recourse was to route federal issues into lower federal courts at an earlier point. In that view, the only impermissible federal intervention was to tell the highest state court judges that they had interpreted federal law incorrectly: it was only that direct review of final state court decisions that was an impermissible trampling upon state judicial autonomy and state sovereignty.

3.   *The core of Justice Story's opinion for the Supreme Court in Martin.* The Virginia court's challenge stirred Justice Story into an elaborate response. To attack federal judicial power was to strike at a subject particularly close

to Joseph Story's heart. Even before Martin v. Hunter's Lessee came to the Supreme Court, Joseph Story had devoted some of his extra-judicial energies to the drafting and advocating of federal legislation which would have expanded federal jurisdiction to the maximum extent possible under the Constitution—to a point not reached even under modern judiciary legislation. (On those lobbying efforts by Story, see sec. 3 below.) The seriousness with which Story viewed the Virginia challenge is reflected in a passage near the beginning of his opinion: "The questions involved in this judgment are of great importance and delicacy. Perhaps it is not too much to affirm, that, upon their right decision, rest some of the most solid principles which have hitherto been supposed to sustain and protect the Constitution itself." At the outset of his detailed examination of Article III, Story inserted several paragraphs suggesting that its provisions were "mandatory upon the legislature." But he soon abandoned that theme † and rested most of his analysis on the assumption that Art. III left considerable discretion to Congress with respect to the allocation of jurisdiction to federal courts. He argued:

"But, even admitting that the language of the constitution is not mandatory, and that congress may constitutionally omit to vest the judicial power in courts of the United States, it cannot be denied that when it is vested, it may be exercised to the utmost constitutional extent.

"This leads us to the consideration of the great question, as to the nature and extent of the appellate jurisdiction of the United States. We have already seen, that appellate jurisdiction is given by the constitution to the supreme court, in all cases where it has not original jurisdiction; subject, however, to such exceptions and regulations as congress may prescribe. It is, therefore, capable of embracing every case enumerated in the constitution, which is not exclusively to be decided by way of original jurisdiction. [W]hat is there to restrain its exercise over state tribunals, in the enumerated cases? The appellate power is not limited by the terms of the third article to any particular courts. . . . It is the *case*, then, and not the *court*, that gives the jurisdiction. If the judicial power extends to the case, it will be in vain to search in the letter of the constitution for any qualification as to the tribunal where it depends. It is incumbent, then, upon those who assert such a qualification, to show its existence, by necessary implication. If the text be clear and distinct, no restriction upon its plain and obvious import ought to be admitted, unless the inference be irresistible. . . .

"[It must] be conceded that the constitution not only contemplated, but meant to provide for cases within the scope of the judicial power of the United States, which might yet depend before state tribunals. It was foreseen that in the exercise of their ordinary jurisdiction, state courts would incidentally take cognisance of cases arising under the constitution, the laws and treaties of the United States. Yet, to all these cases, the judicial power, by the very terms of the constitution, is to extend. It cannot extend by original jurisdiction if that was already rightfully and exclusively attached in the state courts, which (as has been already shown) may occur; it must, therefore, extend by appellate jurisdiction, or not at all. It would seem to follow that the appellate power of the United States must, in such cases,

† Justice Story's preliminary suggestions about the "mandatory" nature of Article III are considered more fully below, in sec. 3.

extend to state tribunals; and if in such cases, there is no reason why it should not equally attach upon all others within the purview of the constitution.

"It has been argued that such an appellate jurisdiction over state courts is inconsistent with the genius of our governments, and the spirit of the constitution. That the latter was never designed to act upon state sovereignties, but only upon the people, and that if the power exists, it will materially impair the sovereignty of the states, and the independence of their courts. We cannot yield to the force of this reasoning; it assumes principles which we cannot admit, and draws conclusions to which we do not yield our assent.

"It is a mistake that the constitution was not designed to operate upon states, in their corporate capacities. It is crowded with provisions which restrain or annul the sovereignty of the states in some of the highest branches of their prerogatives. The tenth section of the first article contains a long list of disabilities and prohibitions imposed upon the states. Surely, when such essential portions of state sovereignty are taken away, or prohibited to be exercised, it cannot be correctly asserted that the constitution does not act upon the states. The language of the constitution is also imperative upon the states as to the performance of many duties. It is imperative upon the state legislatures to make laws prescribing the time, places and manner of holding elections for senators and representatives, and for electors of president and vice-president. And in these, as well as some other cases, congress have a right to revise, amend, or supercede the laws which may be passed by state legislatures. When, therefore, the states are stripped of some of the highest attributes of sovereignty, and the same are given to the United States; when the legislatures of the states are, in some respects, under the control of congress, and in every case are, under the constitution, bound by the paramount authority of the United States; it is certainly difficult to support the argument that the appellate power over the decisions of state courts is contrary to the genius of our institutions. The courts of the United States can, without question, revise the proceedings of the executive and legislative authorities of the states, and if they are found to be contrary to the constitution, may declare them to be of no legal validity. Surely, the exercise of the same right over judicial tribunals is not a higher or more dangerous act of sovereign power.

"Nor can such a right be deemed to impair the independence of state judges. It is assuming the very ground in controversy to assert that they possess an absolute independence of the United States. In respect to the powers granted to the United States, they are not independent; they are expressly bound to obedience, by the letter of the constitution; and if they should unintentionally transcend their authority, or misconstrue the constitution, there is no more reason for giving their judgments an absolute and irresistible force, than for giving it to the acts of the other co-ordinate departments of state sovereignty.

"The argument urged from the possibility of the abuse of the revising power, is equally unsatisfactory. It is always a doubtful course, to argue against the use or existence of a power, from the possibility of its abuse. It is still more difficult, by such an argument, to ingraft upon a general power a restriction which is not to be found in the terms in which it is given. From the very nature of things, the absolute right of decision, in the last

resort, must rest somewhere—wherever it may be vested, it is susceptible of abuse. In all questions of jurisdiction, the inferior, or appellate court, must pronounce the final judgment; and common sense, as well as legal reasoning, has conferred it upon the latter. . . .

"It is further argued, that no great public mischief can result from a construction which shall limit the appellate power of the United States to cases in their own courts: first, because state judges are bound by an oath to support the constitution of the United States, and must be presumed to be men of learning and integrity; and secondly, because congress must have an unquestionable right to remove all cases within the scope of the judicial power from the state courts to the courts of the United States, at any time before final judgment, though not after final judgment. As to the first reason— admitting that the judges of the state courts are, and always will be, of as much learning, integrity and wisdom, as those of the courts of the United States, (which we very cheerfully admit,) it does not aid the argument. It is manifest that the constitution has proceeded upon a theory of its own, and given or withheld powers according to the judgment of the American people, by whom it was adopted. We can only construe its powers, and cannot in- quire into the policy or principles which induced the grant of them. The constitution has presumed (whether rightly or wrongly we do not inquire) that state attachments, state prejudices, state jealousies, and state interests, might sometimes obstruct, or control, or be supposed to obstruct or control, the regular administration of justice. Hence, in controversies between states; between citizens of different states; between citizens claiming grants under different states; between a state and its citizens, or foreigners, and between citizens and foreigners, it enables the parties, under the authority of congress, to have the controversies heard, tried and determined before the national tribunals. No other reason than that which has been stated can be assigned, why some, at least, of those cases should not have been left to the cognizance of the state courts. In respect to the other enumerated cases—the cases arising under the constitution, laws and treaties of the United States, cases affecting ambassadors and other public ministers, and cases of admiralty and maritime jurisdiction—reasons of a higher and more extensive nature, touch- ing the safety, peace and sovereignty of the nation, might well justify a grant of exclusive jurisdiction.

"This is not all. A motive of another kind, perfectly compatible with the most sincere respect for state tribunals, might induce the grant of appel- late power over their decisions. That motive is the importance, and even necessity of *uniformity* of decisions throughout the whole United States, upon all subjects within the purview of the constitution. Judges of equal learning and integrity, in different states, might differently interpret a statute, or a treaty of the United States, or even the constitution itself: if there were no revising authority to control these jarring and discordant judgments, and harmonize them into uniformity, the laws, the treaties and the constitution of the United States would be different in different states, and might, per- haps, never have precisely the same construction, obligation, or efficacy, in any two states. The public mischiefs that would attend such a state of things would be truly deplorable; and it cannot be believed that they could have escaped the enlightened convention which formed the constitution. What, indeed, might then have been only prophecy, has now become fact; and the

appellate jurisdiction must continue to be the only adequate remedy for such evils.

"There is an additional consideration, which is entitled to great weight. The constitution of the United States was designed for the common and equal benefit of all the people of the United States. The judicial power was granted for the same benign and salutary purposes. It was not to be exercised exclusively for the benefit of parties who might be plaintiffs, and would elect the national forum, but also for the protection of defendants who might be entitled to try their rights, or assert their privileges, before the same forum. Yet, if the construction contended for be correct, it will follow, that as the plaintiff may always elect the state court, the defendant may be deprived of all the security which the constitution intended in aid of his rights. Such a state of things can, in no respect, be considered as giving equal rights. To obviate this difficulty, we are referred to the power which, it is admitted, congress possess to remove suits from state courts to the national courts; and this forms the second ground upon which the argument we are considering has been attempted to be sustained.

"This power of removal is not to be found in express terms in any part of the constitution; if it be given, it is only given by implication, as a power necessary and proper to carry into effect some express power. [I]f the right of removal from state courts exist before judgment because it is included in the appellate power, it must, for the same reason, exist after judgment. And if the appellate power by the constitution does not include cases pending in state courts, the right of removal, which is but a mode of exercising that power, cannot be applied to them. Precisely the same objections, therefore, exist as to the right of removal before judgment, as after, and both must stand or fall together. Nor, indeed, would the force of the arguments on either side materially vary, if the right of removal were an exercise of original jurisdiction. It would equally trench upon the jurisdiction and independence of state tribunals. . . .

"On the whole, the court are of opinion, that the appellate power of the United States does extend to cases pending in the state courts; and that the 25th section of the judiciary act, which authorizes the exercise of this jurisdiction in the specified cases, by a writ of error, is supported by the letter and spirit of the constitution. We find no clause in that instrument which limits this power; and we dare not interpose a limitation where the people have not been disposed to create one.

"Strong as this conclusion stands upon the general language of the constitution, it may still derive support from other sources. It is an historical fact, that this exposition of the constitution, extending its appellate power to state courts, was, previous to its adoption, uniformly and publicly avowed by its friends, and admitted by its enemies, as the basis of their respective reasonings, both in and out of the state conventions. It is an historical fact, that at the time when the judiciary act was submitted to the deliberations of the first congress, composed as it was, not only of men of great learning and ability, but of men who had acted a principal part in framing, supporting or opposing that constitution, the same exposition was explicitly declared and admitted by the friends and by the opponents of that system. It is an historical fact, that the supreme court of the United States have, from time to time, sustained this appellate jurisdiction in a great variety of cases, brought

from the tribunals of many of the most important states in the Union, and that no state tribunal has ever breathed a judicial doubt on the subject, or declined to obey the mandate of the supreme court, until the present occasion. This weight of contemporaneous exposition by all parties, this acquiescence of enlightened state courts, and these judicial decisions of the supreme court through so long a period, do, as we think, place the doctrine upon a foundation of authority which cannot be shaken, without delivering over the subject to perpetual and irremediable doubts. . . . ."

At the end of the opinion, Justice Story avoided the abrasive "instruct" and "command" language in the 1813 judgment in Fairfax's Devisee v. Hunter's Lessee that had provoked the confrontation with the Virginia Court of Appeals. Instead, he concluded: "We have not thought it incumbent on us to give any opinion upon the question, whether this court have authority to issue a writ of mandamus to the court of appeals to enforce the former judgments, as we do not think it necessarily involved in the decision of this cause. It is the opinion of the whole court, that the judgment of the court of appeals of Virginia, rendered on the mandate in this cause, be reversed . . . ."

In a separate opinion, Justice William Johnson—President Jefferson's first appointee to the Marshall Court—stated: "It will be observed in this case, that the court disavows all intention to decide on the right to issue compulsory process to the state courts; thus leaving us, in my opinion, where the constitution and laws place us—supreme over persons and cases, as far as our judicial powers extend, but not asserting any compusory control over the state tribunals. In this view, I acquiesce in their opinion, but not altogether in the reasoning or opinion of my brother who delivered it."

4. *Cohens v. Virginia: Supreme Court review of state criminal cases.* Justice Story's confident and forceful opinion in Martin v. Hunter's Lessee did not end the agitation over the justifiability of § 25 of the 1789 Judiciary Act. Instead, the Martin dispute signalled the beginning of waves of attacks on § 25. Those attacks were symptoms of more pervasive states' rights concerns in the immediate post-Martin years. They were concerns stimulated especially by a series of Marshall Court decisions striking down a variety of state actions. For example, the 1819 decision in McCulloch v. Maryland (chap. 2 below), sustaining the constitutionality of the Bank of the United States and barring state taxation of the Bank as the nation was entering an economic depression, set off a wave of protests—including an effort by Ohio to provoke relitigation of the McCulloch issues by seizing more than $100,000 from the vaults of the Bank branch in Chillicothe, Ohio. John Marshall's repudiation of that effort produced not only a reaffirmation of McCulloch but also important new, expansive assertions about federal judicial authority. Osborn v. Bank of the United States, 9 Wheat. 738 (1824). Note also, e. g., two other decisions in the same Term as McCulloch that contributed to the mounting states' rights fervor: Dartmouth College v. Woodward, 4 Wheat. 518 (1819), finding the New Hampshire legislature's effort to modify the college charter a violation of the contract clause; and Sturges v. Crowninshield, 4 Wheat. 122 (1819), once again relying on the contract clause, to invalidate retroactive state insolvency legislation. (See chap. 9, sec. 2B, below.)

Section 25 was a common—though by no means the only—target of those states' rights attacks. Most often, hostility to § 25 manifested itself in efforts to obtain congressional repeal of the provision. See note 5 below. But there was one important post-Martin occasion for the Supreme Court to address the issue once again: it came in COHENS v. VIRGINIA, 6 Wheat. 264 (1821). That case arose from the conviction of the Cohen brothers in a Norfolk court for selling District of Columbia lottery tickets in violation of Virginia laws. The Cohens claimed that, under the Supremacy Clause, they were immune from state laws in selling congressionally authorized lottery tickets. The Supreme Court ultimately decided against them on the merits, reading the congressional statute as conferring no such immunity. But the major issue was the jurisdictional one: did the Supreme Court have constitutional authority to review state criminal judgments? * Virginia's counsel not only reiterated the arguments advanced in the Martin case, but found new ones. They emphasized that here, unlike Martin, the State was a named party in the case, and they argued especially that the grant of original jurisdiction to the Supreme Court of cases "in which a state shall be a party" excluded the exercise of appellate jurisdiction in such cases. They claimed, too, that the Constitution did not confer federal judicial power in controversies between a State and its own citizens and that the Eleventh Amendment in any event barred review. Those arguments gave the Court the opportunity not only to reaffirm but also to extend the principles of Martin v. Hunter's Lessee.

Cohens v. Virginia at last gave John Marshall the chance to say his piece on the § 25 issue officially. In 1816, in Martin, he had not sat and therefore could not join in repudiating the challenges by Spencer Roane and his Virginia colleagues. In 1819, spurred by Spencer Roane's newspaper criticisms of McCulloch, Marshall had gotten a defence of § 25 into print, but only in the course of pseudonymous essays signed by "A Friend of the Constitution." See Gunther, ed., John Marshall's Defense of McCulloch v. Maryland (1969). Now, with Cohens, it was Marshall's turn to speak officially, and Roane's to be relegated to sideline criticism in the newspapers: in his most vitriolic attack, the "Algernon Sidney" essays in the "Richmond Enquirer," Roane explained why Cohens was a "most monstrous and unexampled decision."

Marshall's Cohens opinion rejecting the jurisdictional challenge restated the defense of the constitutionality of § 25 and answered Virginia's new contentions by concluding "that the judicial power, as originally given, extends to all cases arising under the constitution or a law of the United States,

---

* Could it have been argued that § 25 was limited to civil cases and did not reach criminal cases? See the text of the provision, quoted in sec. 4 below. Justice Story—in his role as advocate of legislative reform—at one time read the language narrowly: at the time of Martin, he had unsuccessfully urged that Congress amend the Judiciary Act to reach state criminal cases. As Story described the provision he drafted, it would have given Supreme Court review in criminal cases "in the same manner as the exist-ing law (Judicial Act 1789, s. 25) gives it in relation to *civil suits*." The statement was in a memorandum printed in part in I The Life and Letters of Joseph Story (W. W. Story ed. 1851), 293.

Counsel for Virginia in Cohens did not, however, argue that § 25 was limited to civil cases. Chief Justice Marshall's opinion stated that § 25 "comprehends expressly the case under consideration," but it is doubtful that he had in mind the civil-criminal distinction that had troubled Justice Story in 1816.

whoever may be the parties." The fact that a state was a party made no difference: review authority in the Cohens case rested not on the nature of the parties but on the nature of the questions in the case. Marshall's opinion pointed out that cases to which the jurisdiction of the federal courts may extend fall into two classes: "In the first, their jurisdiction depends on the character of the cause, whoever may be the parties. This class comprehends 'all cases in law and equity arising under this constitution, the laws of the United States, and treaties made, or which shall be made, under their authority.' This clause extends the jurisdiction of the Court to all the cases described, without making in its terms any exception whatever, and without any regard to the condition of the party. . . . In the second class, the jurisdiction depends entirely on the character of the parties. In this are comprehended 'controversies between two or more States, between a State and citizens of another State,' and 'between a State and foreign States, citizens or subjects.' If these be the parties, it is entirely unimportant what may be the subject of controversy. Be it what it may, these parties have a constitutional right to come into the Courts of the Union."

Marshall's defense of Supreme Court review took a harsher view of the reliability of state judges than Story had expressed in Martin. Marshall's statements no doubt reflected his mounting anxieties about states' rights attacks in the 1816–21 period. For example, he commented: "In many States, the judges are dependent for office and for salary on the will of the legislature. . . . When we observe the importance which [the Constitution] attaches to the independence of judges, we are the less inclined to suppose that it can have intended to leave these constitutional questions to tribunals where this independence may not exist, in all cases where a State shall prosecute an individual who claims the protection of an act of Congress. [A constitution] is framed for ages to come. [Its] course cannot always be tranquil. It is exposed to storms and tempests, and its framers must be unwise statesmen indeed, if they have not provided it, as far as its nature will permit, with the means of self-preservation from the perils it may be destined to encounter. No government ought to be so defective in its organization, as not to contain within itself the means of securing the execution of its own laws against other dangers than those which occur every day."

5. *State challenges to Supreme Court authority and authoritativeness—19th century variants and 20th century emulations.* A number of states other than Virginia challenged the right of the Supreme Court to review state court decisions in the period before the Civil War—often on grounds far broader than those advanced by Virginia in the Martin and Cohens cases. See generally Warren, "Legislative and Judicial Attacks on the Supreme Court of the United States—A History of the Twenty-Fifth Section of the Judiciary Act," 47 Am.L.Rev. 1, 161 (1913); Reference Note, "Interposition vs. Judicial Power—A Study of Ultimate Authority in Constitutional Questions," 1 Race Rel.L.Rep. 465 (1956). Warren's article describes challenges from the courts of seven states and mentions several attempts in Congress to repeal Section 25—the first major one in 1821, immediately after Cohens; the most serious one in 1831, see H.Rep.No.43, 21st Cong., 2d Sess. (1831). The critical significance of § 25 was appreciated, for example, by John C. Calhoun, long before he emerged as the chief public spokesman for nullification—for the power of a state to block (at least temporarily, until the Constitu-

tion could be amended) enforcement of "unconstitutional" federal laws within the state. Months before he privately drafted the South Carolina Exposition of 1828, years before he publicly advocated nullification, Calhoun suggested that, if § 25 could be eliminated, more drastic remedies (such as nullification, and years later, secession) would be unnecessary.†

The position of Virginia in Martin should be distinguished from the more extreme positions denying the general authoritativeness—and occasionally the specific enforceability—of federal court decisions, on the ground of the states' right to "interpose" their own interpretations of the Constitution against federal action. These "interposition" statements ranged from the general protest of the Virginia and Kentucky Resolutions of 1798 to South Carolina's nullification efforts in 1832 and the later secession movement. Though these more extreme contentions tended to share common premises (e. g., the compact theory of the Union) and common language (e. g., "null and void" declarations), they, too, varied widely in operative consequences. An excellent sampling of the state resolutions appears in Ames, State Documents on Federal Relations (1906).

In examining the pre-Civil War state contentions, it is important to read the broad assertions in light of the specific remedial, operative portions of the state resolutions. As with the presidential statements quoted in the notes following Marbury v. Madison, above, it is useful to distinguish between statements (a) denying that constitutional interpretations are *exclusively* the function of the federal courts or that federal interpretations bind the nation, and (b) asserting that specific federal court orders may be directly disobeyed. Compare, for example, Madison's 1800 Report on the Virginia Resolutions [denying that "the judicial authority is to be regarded as the sole expositor of the Constitution in the last resort," in the context of urging congressional repeal of the Alien and Sedition Laws], with direct state defiance of federal court authority [e. g., the South Carolina Nullification Ordinance of 1832, making punishable as contempt the taking of certain appeals to the United States Supreme Court, 1 South Carolina Statutes at Large 330 (1836); the act of December 1832, carrying the Ordinance into effect, providing in Section 6 that anyone arrested pursuant to a federal court order enforcing the tariff shall be entitled to habeas corpus and to damages for unlawful im-

† See, e. g., a letter by John C. Calhoun to Senator Littleton W. Tazewell of Virginia, August 25, 1827 (in the Calhoun Papers, The Library of Congress), speculating about possible remedies for "the protection of one portion of the people against another." With the increasingly evident minority status of the South, he suggested, there was only "one effectual remedy, a veto on the part of the local interest, or, under our system, on the Part of the States." Months before he became a fervent advocate of nullification as the form of that "veto," he wrote as well: "There is one fact, however, of the greatest importance, that this negative would in truth exist were it not for a provision in a single act of Congress, I mean the 25th Section of the Judiciary act of 1789; the existence or non-existence of which provision, would make an entire change in the operation of our system. If the appellate power from the State courts to the U. States court provided for by the 25th Secn. did not exist, the practical consequence would be, that each government would have a negative on the other, and thus possess the most effectual remedy, that can be conceived against encroachment. Under this view, this provision becomes one of the deepest importance, much more so, than any other in the statute books; and altho' among the oldest, it ought not to be considered too late to enquire, by what authority Congress adopted it; and how far it can be reconciled with the Sovereignty of the States, as to their reserved rights?"

prisonment, id. at 372; Georgia's defiance of the mandate in Worcester v. Georgia, 6 Pet. 515 (1832), see Burke, "The Cherokee Cases: A Study in Law, Politics, and Morality," 21 Stan.L.Rev. 500 (1969); and the bill passed by the Georgia House of Representatives in 1793, stating that "any Federal Marshal, or any other person" seeking to execute the mandate in Chisholm v. Georgia, 2 Dall. 419 (1793), shall be "guilty of felony, and shall suffer death, without the benefit of clergy, by being hanged," Ames, above, 10].

For more recent state "interposition" resolutions, reviving the pre-Civil War tradition, see, e. g., 1 Race Rel.L.Rep. 437–447 (1956) (1956 legislative resolutions of Alabama, Georgia, Mississippi, South Carolina, and Virginia, in the wake of Brown v. Board of Education, the School Segregation Case). For Supreme Court replies, see Cooper v. Aaron, 358 U.S. 1 (1958), sec. 1 above, and Bush v. Orleans Parish School Board, 364 U.S. 500 (1960). In Bush, the Court, per curiam, denied motions for a stay of a three-judge District Court order enjoining the enforcement of Louisiana interposition laws directed at school desegregation. The Court quoted from the District Court decision, 188 F.Supp. 916, 926: "The conclusion is clear that interposition is not a *constitutional* doctrine. If taken seriously, it is illegal defiance of constitutional authority." The Supreme Court added: "The main basis for challenging this ruling is that the State of Louisiana 'has interposed itself in the field of public education over which it has exclusive control.' This objection is without substance, as we held, upon full consideration, in Cooper v. Aaron."

On the importance of Supreme Court review of cases challenging state laws, see, in addition to Martin and Cohens, Justice Holmes' well-known statement: "I do not think the United States would come to an end if we lost our power to declare an Act of Congress void. I do think the Union would be imperiled if we could not make that declaration as to the laws of the several States." Holmes, Collected Legal Papers (1920), 295.

6. *Enforcement of Court mandates.* A Supreme Court reversal of a state court judgment may not be determinative of the outcome of the case. Ordinarily, the Supreme Court merely remands for "proceedings not inconsistent with the opinion of this Court." Under such a mandate, the state court is free to consider any undetermined questions or even to reexamine already decided matters of state law. If it is contended that the state court failed to follow the Supreme Court mandate, the appropriate remedy, when available, is to seek a new review of the judgment. In cases of state recalcitrance, the Supreme Court has at times entered judgment and awarded execution, or remanded with specific directions to enter judgment. On the availability of mandamus to compel obedience to a Supreme Court mandate where the state court decision on remand is nonfinal and accordingly not directly reviewable under the jurisdictional statutes, see Deen v. Hickman, 358 U.S. 57 (1958). See generally 28 U.S.C. §§ 2106 and 1651, and Stern and Gressman, Supreme Court Practice (4th ed. 1969), 87, 142.

A number of statutory provisions suggest specific remedies to overcome resistance to federal court orders: e. g., as to the powers and duties of United States marshals in executing judgments, see, e. g., 28 U.S.C. § 672; as to the use of the contempt power in the event of "[d]isobedience

or resistance," see 18 U.S.C. §§ 401, 402; as to the use of armed forces by the executive "to enforce the laws of the United States," see 10 U.S.C. §§ 332, 333, 15. See generally Reference Note, "Enforcement of Court Orders—Federal Contempt Proceedings and Prevention of Obstruction," 2 Race Rel.L.Rep. 1051 (1957), and Pollitt, "Presidential Use of Troops to Execute the Laws: A Brief History," 36 N.C.L.Rev. 117 (1958).

SECTION 3. CONGRESSIONAL POWER TO CURTAIL THE JURISDICTION OF FEDERAL COURTS

EX PARTE McCARDLE

7 Wall. 506, 19 L.Ed. 264 (1869).

Appeal from the Circuit Court for the Southern District of Mississippi.

[Under the post-Civil War Reconstruction Acts, Congress imposed military government on a large number of the former Confederate States. McCardle was a Mississippi newspaper editor in military custody on charges of publishing "incendiary and libelous articles." He brought this habeas corpus proceeding under an Act of Congress of February 5, 1867, which authorized federal courts to grant habeas corpus to anyone restrained "in violation of the Constitution" and which also authorized appeals to the Supreme Court. After the Circuit Court denied McCardle's habeas petition, he appealed to the Supreme Court. After the Supreme Court sustained jurisdiction of that appeal, 6 Wall. 318 (1868), and after argument was heard on the merits, Congress passed the Act of March 27, 1868. That law stated that so much of the 1867 Act "as authorized an appeal from the judgment of the Circuit Court to the Supreme Court of the United States, or the exercise of any such jurisdiction by said Supreme Court, on appeals which have been, or may hereafter be taken, be, and the same is hereby repealed." The historical context is developed further in note 1 following the opinion dismissing the appeal.]

The Chief Justice [CHASE] delivered the opinion of the Court.

The first question necessarily is that of jurisdiction; for, if the act of March, 1868, takes away the jurisdiction defined by the act of February, 1867, it is useless, if not improper, to enter into any discussion of other questions.

It is quite true, as was argued by the counsel for the petitioner, that the appellate jurisdiction of this Court is not derived from acts of Congress. It is, strictly speaking, conferred by the Constitution. But it is conferred "with such exceptions and under such regulations as Congress shall make."

It is unnecessary to consider whether, if Congress had made no exceptions and no regulations, this court might not have exercised general appellate jurisdiction under rules prescribed by itself. For among the earliest acts of the first Congress, at its first session, was the act of September 24th, 1789, to establish the judicial courts of the United States. That act provided for the organization of this court, and prescribed regulations for the exercise of its jurisdiction.

The source of that jurisdiction, and the limitations of it by the Constitution and by statute, have been on several occasions subjects of consideration here. In the case of Durousseau v. The United States [6 Cranch 307], particularly, the whole matter was carefully examined, and the court held, that while "the appellate powers of this court are not given by the judicial act, but are given by the Constitution," they are, nevertheless, "limited and regulated by that act, and by such other acts as have been passed on the subject." The court said, further, that the judicial act was an exercise of the power given by the Constitution to Congress "of making exceptions to the appellate jurisdiction of the Supreme Court." "They have described affirmatively," said the court, "its jurisdiction, and this affirmative description has been understood to imply a negation of the exercise of such appellate power as is not comprehended within it."

The principle that the affirmation of appellate jurisdiction implies the negation of all such jurisdiction not affirmed having been thus established, it was an almost necessary consequence that acts of Congress, providing for the exercise of jurisdiction, should come to be spoken of as acts granting jurisdiction, and not as acts making exceptions to the constitutional grant of it.

The exception to appellate jurisdiction in the case before us, however, is not an inference from the affirmation of other appellate jurisdiction. It is made in terms. The provision of the act of 1867, affirming the appellate jurisdiction of this court in cases of habeas corpus is expressly repealed. It is hardly possible to imagine a plainer instance of positive exception.

We are not at liberty to inquire into the motives of the legislature. We can only examine into its power under the Constitution; and the power to make exceptions to the appellate jurisdiction of this court is given by express words.

What, then, is the effect of the repealing act upon the case before us? We cannot doubt as to this. Without jurisdiction the court cannot proceed at all in any cause. Jurisdiction is power to declare the law, and when it ceases to exist, the only function remaining to the court is that of announcing the fact and dismissing the cause. And this is not less clear upon authority than upon principle.

Several cases were cited by the counsel for the petitioner in support of the position that jurisdiction of this case is not affected by the repealing act. But none of them, in our judgment, afford any support to it. They are all cases of the exercise of judicial power by the legislature, or of legislative interference with courts in the exercising of continuing jurisdiction.

On the other hand, the general rule, supported by the best elementary writers, is, that "when an act of the legislature is repealed, it must be considered, except as to transactions past and closed, as if it never existed." And the effect of repealing acts upon suits under acts repealed, has been determined by the adjudications of this court. The subject was fully considered in Norris v. Crocker [13 How. 429], and more recently in Insurance Company v. Ritchie [5 Wall. 541]. In both of these cases it was held that no judgment could be rendered in a suit after the repeal of the act under which it was brought and prosecuted.

It is quite clear, therefore, that this court cannot proceed to pronounce judgment in this case, for it has no longer jurisdiction of the appeal; and judicial duty is not less fitly performed by declining ungranted jurisdiction than in exercising firmly that which the Constitution and the laws confer.

Counsel seem to have supposed, if effect be given to the repealing act in question, that the whole appellate power of the court, in cases of habeas corpus, is denied. But this is an error. The act of 1868 does not except from that jurisdiction any cases but appeals from Circuit Courts under the act of 1867. It does not affect the jurisdiction which was previously exercised.

The appeal of the petitioner in this case must be dismissed for want of jurisdiction.

————

THE SCOPE OF THE CONGRESSIONAL POWER

Introduction. Consider, in examining the principal case and the following notes: How far-reaching is the congressional power sustained in McCardle? Does the historical context of that case substantially weaken its force as precedent? Is it possible to state viable limits on the power of Congress to enact "Exceptions" and "Regulations" of the Supreme Court's appellate jurisdiction? Does Art. III impose significant limits? Do other provisions of the Constitution—for example, the Fifth Amendment? Do basic constitutional assumptions about judicial review impose enforceable limits on the power of Congress? Is the Court really vulnerable to serious political reprisals from Congress unless limiting principles on McCardle can be stated? Or are there significant practical restraints on the jurisdiction-limiting weapon?

1. *McCardle in historical context.* Congressional policies after the Civil War produced sharp conflicts with the other branches. President Andrew Johnson opposed the Reconstruction Acts, for example; and there were repeated efforts to test their constitutionality in the courts. The McCardle case moved to a climax at the height of the tension between Congress and President and after two earlier efforts to elicit Supreme Court rulings had failed.

Soon after the basic provisions of reconstruction legislation had been passed over the President's veto, challenges in the courts were launched. Prospects for success seemed good if the Court reached the merits: the military government features looked vulnerable in view of a case decided by the Supreme Court just before the reconstruction laws were passed. Ex parte Milligan, 4 Wall. 2 (1867). The first attack on the reconstruction laws in the Supreme Court came when the State of Mississippi challenged their constitutionality through an action to enjoin presidential enforcement. But in Mississippi v. Johnson, 4 Wall. 475 (1867), the Supreme Court concluded that it lacked power to issue such an order against the President. (Cf. United States v. Nixon, chap. 7 below.) The State of Georgia immediately brought a similar action against the Secretary of War. Once again, the Court dismissed on jurisdictional grounds: it held in Georgia v. Stanton, 6 Wall. 50 (1868), that the suit raised nonjusticiable political questions.

But then, while Congress was considering a variety of measures to curb the judicial threat to reconstruction, the Court took jurisdiction of McCardle's appeal.

With that constitutional challenge formally before the Court and with argument on the merits already concluded (but, as the official report noted, "before conference in regard to the decision proper to be made") Congress passed the 1868 law withdrawing appellate jurisdiction. By then, impeachment proceedings against President Johnson had begun. Nevertheless, he vetoed the law. With the Court standing by and withholding action on the case before it pending the outcome of the political battle, Congress overrode the veto. Argument on the jurisdiction-curtailing law was then sought in the Court. And, as one more manifestation of the political crisis hovering over the case, that argument had to be postponed because of (as the official report put it) "the Chief Justice being detained from his place here, by his duties in the Court of Impeachment."

There was one more effort to elicit a ruling on reconstruction after the dismissal of the McCardle appeal. In Ex parte Yerger, 8 Wall. 85 (1869), the Court took jurisdiction of a proceeding by another petitioner in military detention in Mississippi. Yerger, like McCardle, had unsuccessfully sought habeas in a lower federal court. But Yerger came to the Supreme Court by a route different from McCardle's: he did not invoke the appeal provision of the 1867 Act; accordingly, the Court found, the 1868 repeal did not apply. Yet a decision on the constitutionality of the Reconstruction Acts was once again averted: before the Court could rule on the merits, Yerger was released from military custody.*

2. *The search for limits on congressional power.* Understandably, the congressional power to make exceptions to appellate jurisdiction proved tempting to some critics of Warren Court decisions—as it has to Court critics since the days of the Marshall Court. And their efforts to curtail Court jurisdiction in turn spurred the search for principles to blunt that weapon. A limit on Art. III power articulated by Professor Henry M. Hart, Jr., has been widely resorted to by Court defenders in Congress and out. Hart urged that "the exceptions must not be such as will detroy the essential role of the Supreme Court in the constitutional plan." See Hart, "The Power of Congress to Limit the Jurisdiction of Federal Courts: An Exercise in Dialectic," 66 Harv.L.Rev. 1362, 1365 (1953). What is that "essential role"?

See also Ratner, "Congressional Power Over the Appellate Jurisdiction of the Supreme Court," 109 U.Pa.L.Rev. 157 (1960). Ratner would interpret the Article III congressional power as if it read: "With such exceptions and under such regulations as Congress may make, not inconsistent with the essential functions of the Supreme Court under this Constitution." He sees two such functions: to maintain the supremacy of federal law; and to provide "ultimate resolution of inconsistent or conflicting interpretations of federal law by state and federal courts." Would § 25 of the 1789 Act have met that test? Would the present jurisdictional pro-

* For the most thorough exploration of the background of McCardle, see Fairman, Reconstruction and Reunion 1864–88, Part One (6 History of the Supreme Court of the United States) (1971). See also Van Alstyne, "A Critical Guide to Ex Parte McCardle," 15 Ariz.L.Rev. 229 (1973).

visions? See the old and new statutory provisions, sec. 4 below. Ratner would hold unconstitutional any effort to bar review "in every case involving a particular subject."

Compare Wechsler, "The Courts and the Constitution," 65 Colum.L. Rev. 1001 (1965), commenting on constitutional arguments that would prohibit any alterations of appellate jurisdiction "motivated by hostility to the decisions of the Court": "I see no basis for this view and think it antithetical to the plan of the Constitution for the courts—which was quite simply that the Congress would decide from time to time how far the federal judicial institution should be used within the limits of the federal judicial power." †

Determining congressional power on the basis of the "constitutional plan" and the "essential functions" of the Supreme Court invites return to basic issues of Marbury v. Madison and judicial review. Thus, the Wechsler argument includes a reminder that federal courts do not pass on constitutional questions because of any "special function vested in them to enforce the Constitution or police the other agencies of government." And a lengthy defense of a broadly conceived view of judicial review is central in the most elaborate challenge to broad congressional power over appellate jurisdiction, Raoul Berger's book, Congress v. The Supreme Court (1969).

Berger concludes that "the express 'exceptions' power cannot bar access to judicial protection of constitutional rights." But only a small portion of his book-length attack on congressional power deals with the "exceptions" provision directly; most of the volume is a defense of the legitimacy of judicial review. Given the breadth of intended judicial power, he argues, it would be incongruous to authorize as much congressional control as the McCardle ruling and the Wechsler comment suggest: the Framers, he urges at 286, "were deeply concerned with, and in no little part designed judicial review as a restraint on, *Congressional* excesses. If the Court was intended to curb Congressional excesses in appropriately presented 'cases or controversies' and if an attempt to exercise that power might in turn be blocked by Congress as a judicial 'excess,' then the Convention was aimlessly going in circles." His narrow reading of the "exceptions" power is illustrated by his review, at 289, of the ratification debates: they "revolved almost exclusively about the retrial of facts found by a jury"; they contain "not the faintest intimation" that the "exceptions" clause "was designed to enable Congress to withdraw jurisdiction to declare an Act of Congress void." He agrees with Hart, moreover, that congressional power to regulate jurisdiction is subject to constitutional limits such as the Fifth Amendment. See Battaglia v. General Motors Corp., 169 F.2d 254, 257 (2d Cir. 1948).

Berger even invokes Franklin D. Roosevelt's resort to the Court-packing technique (see the note on the 1937 crisis in chap. 3, below) to support his narrow reading of the "exceptions" power. The New Deal Administration would not have sought to increase the size of the Court if hostile decisions could have been blocked via the jurisdictional route: "All the hullabaloo about 'Court-packing' was so easily avoidable if this alternative is so legitimate

---

† Recall also Chief Justice Chase's comment in McCardle: "We are not at liberty to inquire into the motives of the legislature." Why not? The Court's inhibitions about inquiring into legislative motives are examined further in later sections of this book.

and available. But are there not other explanations for that choice? For example, may not FDR's method of attacking the Court illustrate the severe practical limitation on the appellate-jurisdiction-curtailing technique? If Congress simply withdraws Supreme Court jurisdiction, inconsistent interpretations in lower courts are likely. Moreover, prior Supreme Court rulings would persist as precedents: "The jurisdictional withdrawal thus might work to freeze the very doctrines that had prompted its enactment, placing an intolerable moral burden on the lower courts." Wechsler, above, at 1006. Would Berger's "constitutional plan" premise for a narrow reading of the "exceptions" power not also bar all other Court-curbing weapons of Congress (such as Court-packing), with the possible exception of impeachment?

Note that even if Art. III cannot be persuasively read to curtail congressional power, other limitations in the Constitution, as in the Bill of Rights, are presumably applicable. Could Congress, for example, bar Supreme Court review for certain classes of litigants on the basis of their race or political beliefs? Note too, that there may be practical limitations on congressional resort to the power to curb appellate jurisdiction. If access to the Supreme Court were barred, decision would be left to lower courts, with inconsistent results and a threat to the uniformity need articulated by Justice Story in Martin v. Hunter's Lessee. Moreover, the unpopular Supreme Court decisions which prompted the congressional response would remain on the books as precedents. See the Wechsler article noted above, 65 Colum. L.Rev. 1001 (1965), and generally, Hart and Wechsler, Federal Courts (2d ed. 1973), chap. 4, sec. 1.

Can it be argued that a congressional power over appellate jurisdiction ultimately is a source of strength rather than weakness for the Supreme Court? The Hart and Wechsler volume suggests, at 363, that it may be "politically healthy" that "the limits of congressional power have never been completely clarified": "Does the existence of a Congressional power of unspecified scope help the maintenance of a desirable tension between Court and Congress? In some circumstances, may not attempts to restrict jurisdiction be an appropriate and important way for the political branches to register disagreement with the Court . . . ? And is it not enormously significant in this regard that, ever since McCardle, such 'attempts' have, in the main, been just that, that Congress has not significantly cut back the Supreme Court's jurisdiction in a 'vindictive' manner despite the enormous unpopularity from time to time of some of its rulings?"

3. *The vitality of McCardle and the Klein case.* Congress has not given the Court cause to reexamine McCardle directly, but Justice Douglas found occasion to call it in question in a footnote to a dissent a few years ago. "There is a serious question whether the McCardle case could command a majority view today," he said in an opinion joined by Justice Black in Glidden Co. v. Zdanok, 370 U.S. 530, 605 (1962).

The Glidden case, with a majority opinion by Justice Harlan, dealt mainly with the distinction between Art. I "legislative courts" and Art. III courts. The context of Justice Douglas' remark about McCardle was as follows: "The opinion of my Brother Harlan stirs a host of problems that need not be opened. What is done will, I fear, plague us for years. First, that opinion cites with approval Ex parte McCardle, 7 Wall. 506, in which

Congress withdrew jurisdiction of this Court to review a habeas corpus case that was *sub judice* and then apparently draws a distinction between that case and United States v. Klein, 13 Wall. 128, where such withdrawal was not permitted in a property claim. There is a serious question whether the McCardle case could command a majority view today. Certainly the distinction between liberty and property (which emanates from this portion of my Brother Harlan's opinion) has no vitality even in terms of the Due Process Clause."

Is that all there is to the Klein-McCardle distinction? Consider the fuller statement of Klein which follows. Does the Klein-McCardle difference reflect simply a preference of property over liberty? Or does the Klein case rest on a principle more acceptable today—a principle of continuing utility as a limit on congressional power over jurisdiction? Justice Harlan's reference to Klein came in the following passage in Glidden: "The authority [of Congress to control the jurisdiction of Article III courts] is not, of course, unlimited. In 1870, Congress purported to withdraw jurisdiction from the Court of Claims and from this Court on appeal over cases seeking indemnification for property captured during the Civil War, so far as eligibility therefor might be predicated upon an amnesty awarded by the President, as both courts had previously held that it might. Despite Ex parte McCardle, supra, the Court refused to apply the statute to a case in which the claimant had already been adjudged entitled to recover by the Court of Claims, calling it an unconstitutional attempt to invade the judicial province by prescribing a rule of decision in a pending case. United States v. Klein, 13 Wall. 128 [1872]."

In the Klein controversy, earlier rulings had held that a presidential pardon satisfied the requirement that a property claimant was not a supporter of the "rebellion." The new statute enacted while Klein's appeal was pending provided that a pardon was to be taken as showing quite the contrary, that the claimant *had* aided the rebellion, and went on to provide that the courts were to dismiss such claims for want of jurisdiction. The Court opinion holding the law unconstitutional stated that the Court would have upheld it as an exercise of the "exceptions" power if "it simply denied the right of appeal in a particular class of cases." But here the jurisdictional language was only "a means to an end": "to deny to pardons granted by the President the effect which this court had adjudged them to have." The Court concluded that dismissing the appeal would allow Congress to "prescribe rules of decision to the Judicial Department of the government in cases pending before it." There was a violation of separation of powers principles not only because of this legislative interference with judicial power but also because "impairing the effect of a pardon" infringed "the constitutional power of the Executive."

Note also Hart and Wechsler, Federal Courts (2d ed. 1973), 316, viewing Klein as holding that it is "an unconstitutional invasion of the judicial function when Congress purports, not to withdraw jurisdiction completely, but to bind the Court to decide a case in accordance with a rule of law independently unconstitutional on other grounds." Is the distinction between Klein and McCardle a viable one? Consider the modern Court-curbing proposals in the next note: Which are legitimate

jurisdictional controls and which are efforts to dictate the outcome of a case on the merits? Which are withdrawals of whole categories of cases, and which are simply efforts to withdraw particular issues from judicial consideration in cases before the courts? If Klein is read to bar withdrawal of particular issues where that is tantamount to directing the outcome of a case, does that draw into question as well the legitimacy of congressional withdrawal of jurisdiction of an entire class of cases, when that withdrawal of jurisdiction is prompted by a desire to affect the outcome? See Brest, Processes of Constitutional Decisionmaking (1975), chap. 15.

4. *Congressional control: Modern concerns.* a. *The Roberts defense.* During the Warren years, most congressional interest in appellate jurisdiction was prompted by proposals for piecemeal withdrawals. Yet not long before, there was serious attention to suggestions to deprive Congress of that weapon. Former Justice Roberts, for example, proposed a constitutional amendment to assure the Court's appellate jurisdiction in all constitutional cases. "Now is the Time: Fortifying the Supreme Court's Independence," 35 A.B.A.J. 1 (1949). Senator John Marshall Butler of Maryland, with the support of several bar associations, introduced an amendment including such an assurance in 1953. S.J.Res. 44, 83d Cong., 1st Sess. (1953). The Senate approved, but the House tabled. See 79 A.B.A.Rep. 242 (1954).

b. *The Jenner-Butler attack.* Within a few years, Congress became more concerned with curtailing jurisdiction than with safeguarding it. See, e. g., Senator Jenner's bill—provoked by several Warren Court decisions—eliminating appellate jurisdiction in cases involving, for example, the federal employees' security program, state subversive legislation, and state bar admissions. S. 2646, 85th Cong., 1st Sess. (1957). The rapid shift in political winds was symbolized by Senator John Marshall Butler: a sponsor of the pro-Court amendment in 1953, he now joined with Senator Jenner to sponsor a revised version of the Jenner proposal. The Jenner-Butler bill [S. 3386, 85th Cong., 2d Sess. (1958)] would have included the following provision— prompted by the 1957 decisions in Konigsberg v. State Bar, 353 U.S. 252, and Schware v. Board of Bar Examiners, 353 U.S. 232 (chap. 13, sec. 5, below)—: "Notwithstanding the provisions of sections 1253, 1254, and 1257 of [28 U.S.C.], the Supreme Court shall have no jurisdiction to review, either by appeal, writ of certiorari, or otherwise, any case where there is drawn into question the validity of any law, rule, or regulation of any State, or of any board of bar examiners, or similar body, or of any action or proceeding taken pursuant to any such law, rule, or regulation pertaining to the admission of persons to the practice of law within such State."

Would the Jenner-Butler provision have been constitutional? The bill was narrowly defeated. For the political struggle, see Murphy, Congress and the Court (1962), and Senate Judiciary Committee, Hearings on S. 2646, 85th Cong., Limitation of the Appellate Jurisdiction of the Supreme Court (1957–58). See generally Elliott, "Court-Curbing Proposals in Congress," 33 Notre Dame Law. 597 (1958).

Another provision in the Jenner-Butler omnibus proposal—in reaction to such cases as Watkins v. United States, 354 U.S. 178 (1957) (chap. 13, sec. 6)—would have amended 2 U.S.C. § 192, the congressional contempt statute. That law states that anyone "who having being summoned as a

witness" by any congressional committee and who wilfully "refuses to answer any question pertinent to the question under inquiry" shall be guilty of a misdemeanor. The Jenner-Butler bill would have added: "Provided, That for the purposes of this section any question shall be deemed pertinent unless timely objection is made thereto on the ground that such question lacks pertinency, or when such objection is made, if such question is ruled pertinent by the body conducting the hearing." Would this provision have been subject to substantial constitutional objections? Under McCardle? Under Klein?

c. *The Tuck and Dirksen bills.* Compare the unsuccessful congressional attempts in 1964 to curtail federal jurisdiction in legislative apportionment cases. The efforts were reactions to Baker v. Carr, 369 U.S. 186 (1962), and Reynolds v. Sims, 377 U.S. 533 (1964) (both in chap 15, sec. 5, below). The House adopted the Tuck bill, H.R. 11926, 88th Cong., 2d Sess.: "The Supreme Court shall not have the right to review the action of a Federal court or a State court of last resort concerning any action taken upon a petition or complaint seeking to apportion or reapportion any legislature of any State of the Union or any branch thereof. . . . The district courts shall not have jurisdiction to entertain any petition or complaint seeking to apportion or reapportion the legislature of any State of the Union or any branch thereof, nor shall any order or decree of any district or circuit court now pending and not finally disposed of by actual reapportionment be hereafter enforced."

In the Senate, Senator Dirksen proposed a bill, S. 3069, 88th Cong., 2d Sess., ultimately introduced as an amendment to a foreign aid bill. The Dirksen rider provided: "Upon application made by or on behalf of any State or by one or more citizens thereof in any action or proceeding in any court of the United States, or before any justice or judge of the United States, in which there is placed in question the validity of the composition of either house of the legislature of that State or the apportionment of the membership thereof, such action or proceeding shall be stayed until the end of the second regular session of the legislature of that State which begins after the date of enactment of this section." Debate on the proposal produced a "baby filibuster," various amendments, and finally Senate adoption of a "sense of Congress" resolution stating that in any reapportionment suit the federal court order "could properly, in the absence of unusual circumstances," allow postponement for a limited time to enable the state legislature to reapportion itself. The differing House and Senate provisions on reapportionment were, in the end, eliminated by the conference committee. See McKay, "Court, Congress, and Reapportionment," 63 Mich.L.Rev. 255 (1964).

d. *The 1968 crime control bill and some questions.* The Senate Judiciary Committee's version of the 1968 crime control bill—provoked by decisions such as Miranda v. Arizona, 384 U.S. 436 (1966)—included a provision which stated that neither the Supreme Court nor any other Article III court "shall have jurisdiction to review or to reverse, vacate, modify, or disturb in any way, a ruling of any trial court of any State in any criminal prosecution admitting in evidence as voluntarily made an admission or confession of any accused." See Title II of the amended S. 917, 90th Cong., 2d Sess., in Sen.Rep.No.1097. That Report contains an elaborate defense of congressional power over jurisdiction, but all anti-Miranda provisions couched in

jurisdictional terms were eliminated on the floor of the Senate prior to passage of the Omnibus Crime Control and Safe Streets Act of 1968.

Do any of these proposals raise constitutional questions? Under McCardle? Under Klein? Under Marbury v. Madison? Note the passage from Justice Rutledge's dissent in Yakus v. United States, 321 U.S. 414, 468 (1944): "It is one thing for Congress to withhold jurisdiction. It is entirely another to confer it and direct that it be exercised in a manner inconsistent with constitutional requirements or, what in some instances may be the same thing, without regard to them. . . . [W]henever the judicial power is called into play it is responsible directly to the fundamental law and no other authority can intervene to force or authorize the judicial body to disregard it." *

e. *Anti-busing legislation.* Note the range of restraints on the courts in the anti-busing proposals that followed in the wake of the 1971 Swann decision on school desegregation remedies. The proposals and their fate are noted below, chap. 10, sec. 2B. Are they supportable as exercises of Art. III power? Or does their validity turn on the scope of the substantive power of Congress over desegregation methods, under § 5 of the 14th Amendment (see chap. 11, sec. 4, below)?

CONGRESS AND THE LOWER FEDERAL COURTS

1. *Justice Story's position.* Most of Justice Story's opinion in Martin v. Hunter's Lessee, sec. 2 above, rested on the assumption that Art. III was "not mandatory, and that congress may constitutionally omit to vest the judicial power in courts of the United States." But before he reached that central portion of his opinion, Justice Story wrote several paragraphs of quite a different tenor, suggesting that the Judiciary Article of the Constitution was indeed to be "mandatory upon the legislature." Some have viewed Story's "mandatory" passages as meaning that Congress *must* establish lower federal courts with the fullest possible jurisdiction—something Congress has never done. Others have read the passages to mean that Congress must at least vest the fullest possible appellate jurisdiction in the Supreme Court in the absence of comprehensive lower federal court jurisdiction—again, something Congress has never done. (Think, for example, of cases between citizens of different states arising in the state courts: they are cases within the federal judicial power, but they have never been reviewable in the Supreme Court.)

---

* Yakus v. United States involved the congressional effort in the Emergency Price Control Act of 1942 to restrict constitutional litigation to a single federal court. It provided that the validity of OPA regulations could be tested only in an administrative proceeding, subject to review by a specially constituted Emergency Court of Appeals and ultimately by the Supreme Court. The Yakus petitioners had not resorted to this exclusive statutory procedure and were not permitted to raise the defense of invalidity in a criminal prosecution for violation of an OPA regulation. The Supreme Court majority affirmed the convictions: "There is no constitutional requirement that that test [of the validity of a regulation] be made in one tribunal rather than in another, so long as there is an opportunity to be heard and for judicial review which satisfies the demands of due process, as is the case here."

In Martin v. Hunter's Lessee, Justice Story's "mandatory" passages stated: "The language of [Art. III] throughout is manifestly designed to be mandatory upon the legislature. Its obligatory force is so imperative, that congress could not, without a violation of its duty, have refused to carry it into operation. The judicial power of the United States *shall be vested* (not may be vested) in one supreme court, and in such inferior courts as congress may, from time to time, ordain and establish. . . .

"If, then, it is a duty of congress to vest the judicial power of the United States, it is a duty to vest the *whole judicial power*. The language, if imperative as to one part, is imperative as to all. If it were otherwise, this anomaly would exist, that congress might successively refuse to vest the jurisdiction in any one class of cases enumerated in the constitution, and thereby defeat the jurisdiction as to all; for the constitution has not singled out any class on which congress are bound to act in preference to others.

"The next consideration is as to the courts in which the judicial power shall be vested. It is manifest that a supreme court must be established: but whether it be equally obligatory to establish inferior courts, is a question of some difficulty. If congress may lawfully omit to establish inferior courts, it might follow, that in some of the enumerated cases the judicial power could nowhere exist. The supreme court can have original jurisdiction in two classes of cases only, viz. in cases affecting ambassadors, other public ministers and consuls, and in cases in which a state is a party. Congress cannot vest any portion of the judicial power of the United States, except in courts ordained and established by itself; and if in any of the cases enumerated in the constitution, the state courts did not then possess jurisdiction, the appellate jurisdiction of the supreme court (admitting that it could act on state courts) could not reach those cases, and, consequently, the injunction of the constitution, that the judicial power "*shall be vested*," would be disobeyed. It would seem, therefore, to follow, that congress are bound to create some inferior courts, in which to vest all that jurisdiction which, under the constitution, is *exclusively* vested in the United States, and of which the supreme court cannot take original cognizance. They might establish one or more inferior courts; they might parcel out the jurisdiction among such courts, from time to time, at their own pleasure. But the whole judicial power of the United States should be, at all times, vested either in an original or appellate form, in some courts created under its authority. . . .

"It being, then, established that the language of this clause is imperative, the next question is as to the cases to which it shall apply. The answer is found in the constitution itself. The judicial power shall extend to all the cases enumerated in the constitution. As the mode is not limited, it may extend to all such cases, in any form, in which judicial power may be exercised. It may, therefore, extend to them in the shape of original or appellate jurisdiction, or both; for there is nothing in the nature of the cases which binds to the exercise of the one in preference to the other. . . ."

Were those Story remarks intended to be legally binding on Congress? Or were they merely a moral appeal to Congress? The latter explanation seems more consistent with Story's contemporaneous actions. In other cases, for example, he dismissed cases not within the jurisdictional statutes, on the

ground that the lower court "has no jurisdiction which is not given by some statute." White v. Fenner, 29 Fed.Cas. 1015, No. 17,547 (Cir.Ct.R.I.1818). Perhaps even more significant are his activities as legislative lobbyist at the time of Martin.

Story, who had seen state challenges to federal authority at close range in his New England circuit duties during the War of 1812, was particularly anxious to make use of the relative harmony at the end of the War to solidify national institutions. Over a period of years, he wrote letters to associates influential in Congress urging legislation and frequently enclosing drafts. In December 1815, for example, he asked the aid of the new Reporter, Henry Wheaton, in "vindicating the necessity of establishing other great national institutions: the extension of the jurisdiction of the courts of the U. S. over *the whole* extent contemplated in the Constitution; the appointment of national notaries public & national justices of the peace; national port wardens & pilots for all the ports of the U. S.; a national bank; & a national bankrupt law." I The Life and Letters of Joseph Story (W. W. Story ed. 1851), 271.

One of his favorite projects was a comprehensive judicial code. In submitting one of his drafts, he made it clear that he did not think that Article III automatically created lower courts with full jurisdiction: "The object of this section is to give to the Circuit Court *original* jurisdiction of all cases intended by the Constitution to be confided to the judicial power of the United States, where that jurisdiction has not been already delegated by law. If it was proper in the Constitution to provide for such a jurisdiction, it is wholly irreconcilable with the sound policy or interests of the Government to suffer it to slumber. . . . It is truly surprising and mortifying to know how little effective power now exists in this department. . . . I will barely illustrate my positions by a reference to a single class of cases. No Court of the United States has any general delegation of authority 'in all cases in law and equity arising under the Constitution, the laws of the United States, and the treaties made, or to be made, under its authority.' The consequence is, that in thousands of instances arising under the laws of the United States, the parties are utterly without remedy, or with a very inadequate remedy." Id. 293–94.

The general "federal question" jurisdiction Story desired in 1816 was not in fact vested in the lower federal courts until 1875. Story's dicta in Martin were, apparently, an appeal to Congress—an appeal that failed. Moreover, the view that the creation and jurisdiction of lower federal courts was largely left to Congress is supported by the debates at the Constitutional Convention. And the Convention compromise was reflected in the Judiciary Act of 1789 as well, creating some lower federal courts with some, but not nearly all, of the potential federal jurisdiction described in Art. III.

2. *Sheldon v. Sill.* Among the most explicit Court decisions sustaining that view is SHELDON v. SILL, 8 How. 441 (1850), upholding the assignee clause of the 1789 Judiciary Act against a claim that the statute could not bar lower court jurisdiction of a case within the description of cases in Art. III. Justice Grier's opinion explained:

"It must be admitted, that if the Constitution had ordained and established the inferior courts, and distributed to them their respective powers,

they could not be restricted or divested by Congress. But as it has made no such distribution, one of two consequences must result,—either that each inferior court created by Congress must exercise all the judicial powers not given to the Supreme Court, or that Congress, having the power to establish the courts, must define their respective jurisdictions. The first of these inferences has never been asserted, and could not be defended with any show of reason, and if not, the latter would seem to follow as a necessary consequence. And it would seem to follow, also, that, having a right to prescribe, Congress may withhold from any court of its creation jurisdiction of any of the enumerated controversies. Courts created by statute can have no jurisdiction but such as the statute confers. No one of them can assert a just claim to jurisdiction exclusively conferred on another, or withheld from all.

"The Constitution has defined the limits of the judicial power of the United States, but has not prescribed how much of it shall be exercised by the Circuit Court; consequently, the statute which does prescribe the limits of their jurisdiction, cannot be in conflict with the Constitution, unless it confers powers not enumerated therein."

3. *Congressional control: Arguable modern limitations?* The Con-suggest a broad congressional authority over lower federal court jurisdiction suggest a broad Congressional authority over lower federal court jurisdiction and remedies. Are there nevertheless constitutional limits on what Congress may do? Presumably, as with the congressional authority over Supreme Court appellate jurisdiction, the Bill of Rights applies to exercises of legislative power under Art. III as it does to other exercises of congressional authority. But are there limitations derivable from Art. III itself? Is there an "essential role" for lower federal courts, for example, analogous to that argued for Supreme Court appellate review? Note Eisenberg, "Congressional Authority to Restrict Lower Federal Court Jurisdiction," 83 Yale L.J. 498 (1974), concluding: "It can now be asserted that [the existence of lower federal courts] in some form is constitutionally required." Eisenberg relies on the "need" for lower federal courts to enforce "innovative" Supreme Court decisions in areas such as reapportionment and desegregation, and on the impossibility, given the Supreme Court's modern workload, of Supreme Court review of all state court cases involving federal issues.

Even if that argument is not persuasive in principle (and the total abolition of lower federal courts unlikely in practice), can it nevertheless be argued that Congress cannot impose limited restrictions on lower federal courts in response to unpopular court decisions? Recall, e. g., the Tuck bill noted above, which included provisions directed at the District Courts as well as the Supreme Court. The Supreme Court had no difficulty in sustaining the Norris-LaGuardia Act of 1932, depriving federal courts of "jurisdiction" to issue injunctions in labor disputes. Lauf v. E. G. Shinner & Co., 303 U.S. 323 (1938). See also Taylor v. St. Vincent's Hospital, 369 F.Supp. 948 (D. Mont.1973), relying on congressional power under Art. III to dismiss a suit against a hospital for refusing to perform a sterilization and invoking § 401 (b) of the Health Programs Extension Act of 1973. The Section was enacted in response to an earlier injunction in the case; it provides that receipt of federal aid by a hospital "does not authorize any court or any public official" to require the hospital to perform sterilizations or abortions if the

hospital prohibits them "on the basis of religious beliefs or moral convictions." *   Should provisions such as these be required to pass muster under congressional power pursuant to § 5 of the 14th Amendment (see chap. 11 below), or is reliance on Art. III adequate? †

SECTION 4.   THE MODERN FRAMEWORK OF JUDICIAL REVIEW: SUPREME COURT JURISDICTION AND PRACTICE

Introduction. What are the contemporary jurisdictional and procedural groundrules that govern the exercise of Supreme Court authority? The purpose of this Section is to give an overview of the main features and problems of the modern framework. Art. III of the Constitution provides, as always, the foundation. But on the few words of that Article has been built a complex superstructure, of congressional statutes and Supreme Court Rules and practices.

Art. III, § 1, for example, provides for "one supreme Court." But it is for Congress to set the size of the Court. There have been nine Justices since 1869. But earlier in the 19th century, the number fluctuated quite frequently: at the time of Marbury v. Madison, for example, it was six; and at the time of Martin v. Hunter's Lessee, it was seven. Most of the increases in the early years came because the number of federal judicial circuits grew with the expansion of the country. Sitting on circuit was a major part of a Supreme Court Justice's duties until well into the 19th century. But that congressional power over size is also a potential source of political checks on the Court. President Franklin D. Roosevelt's proposed Court-curbing weap-

---

* See generally Note, "Congressional Power Over State and Federal Court Jurisdiction: The Hill-Burton and Trans-Alaska Pipeline Examples," 49 N.Y.U.L.Rev. 131 (1974), arguing that the Taylor court should not have read § 401(b) as a jurisdictional provision.

† Note that limits on federal courts ordinarily leave state courts as available forums, so that curtailments of federal jurisdiction do not typically require confrontation with the difficult and unsettled problem of access to *some* judicial forum. Is there, for example a general due process right of access to courts to review adverse administrative determinations? That is a question which "this Court studiously has avoided," as Justice Douglas commented in his dissent in Ortwein v. Schwab, 410 U.S. 656 (1973) (chap. 10 below). In another dissent in that case, Justice Marshall argued that "it is at very least doubtful that the Due Process Clause permits a State to shield an ad-ministrative agency from all judicial review when that agency acts to revoke a benefit previously granted." See also Justice Brandeis' statement on review of administrative action, in a concurrence in St. Joseph Stock Yards Co. v. United States, 298 U.S. 38 (1936): "The supremacy of law demands that there shall be an opportunity to have some court decide whether the proceeding in which facts were adjudicated was conducted regularly." Where Congress has sought to curtail review of administrative action, the Court has typically strained to read the statute so as to permit review. See, e. g., the statutory interpretation to avoid "serious questions" of constitutionality in Johnson v. Robison, 415 U.S. 361 (1974). The problems of curtailment of all judicial review and of arguable rights of access to courts are pursued more fully in courses in administrative law and federal jurisdiction.

on was to expand the size of the Court. (See the materials on the Court-Packing Plan, chap. 3 below.) Even such relatively trivial-seeming legislation as that setting the time at which the Court shall convene can be made to serve political ends: recall the Jeffersonian legislation which caused the decision in Marbury to be postponed until 1803, as noted in sec. 1 above. Under present law (28 U.S.C. § 2), the Court is directed to convene for "a term of court commencing on the first Monday in October of each year." Because of that provision, a typical session—e. g., October 1974 to June 1975—is referred to as the "October Term 1974."

The more complex Art. III ingredients of the judicial framework are the provisions of Art. III, § 2, stating that the Judicial Power shall extend to certain specified "Cases" and "Controversies." What constitutes a "case" or "controversy" suitable for federal judicial resolution is a complex and much-litigated question; some of its ramifications are explored in chap. 15. After listing those categories of "Cases" and "Controversies" within the federal judicial power, Art. III, § 2, proceeds to address the Supreme Court's jurisdiction specifically: "In all Cases affecting Ambassadors, other public Ministers and Consuls, and those in which a State shall be a Party, the supreme Court shall have original Jurisdiction. In all the other Cases before mentioned, the supreme Court shall have appellate Jurisdiction, both as to Law and Fact, with such Exceptions, and under such Regulations as the Congress shall make." Some of the problems inherent in those words have already surfaced, in cases such as Marbury, Martin, and McCardle. What concerns us now is the congressional fleshing out of those jurisdictional categories. The original jurisdiction need not detain us: it is rarely invoked; and it is even more rarely the source of significant constitutional interpretations.* The present contours of the appellate jurisdiction—the avenues to review in the Supreme Court from lower federal and state courts—are the major concerns of the materials that follow. After sketching the outlines of contemporary jurisdictional provisions—and some of their problems—the materials look at the Supreme Court's Rules and practices governing the exercise of obligatory (appeal) and discretionary (certiorari) review. The section concludes with an examination of the contemporary concern about the Supreme Court's growing workload and the major and controversial proposals engendered by that concern—proposals for substantial changes in the way the Supreme Court conducts its business.

---

* For a rare example, see South Carolina v. Katzenbach, chap. 11 below. See generally, 28 U.S.C. § 1251 and Hart and Wechsler, Federal Courts (2d. ed 1973), chap. 3.

APPELLATE JURISDICTION: THE STATUTES

1. *Review of state court judgments.* a. *The modern provisions.* Review of state court proceedings is governed by Section 1257 of Title 28 of the United States Code:

"Final judgments or decrees rendered by the highest court of a State in which a decision could be had, may be reviewed by the Supreme Court as follows:

"(1) By appeal, where is drawn in question the validity of a treaty or statute of the United States and the decision is against its validity.

"(2) By appeal, where is drawn in question the validity of a statute of any state on the ground of its being repugnant to the Constitution, treaties or laws of the United States, and the decision is in favor of its validity.

"(3) By writ of certiorari, where the validity of a treaty or statute of the United States is drawn in question or where the validity of a State statute is drawn in question on the ground of its being repugnant to the Constitution, treaties or laws of the United States, or where any title, right, privilege or immunity is specially set up or claimed under the Constitution, treaties or statutes of, or commission held or authority exercised under, the United States."

b. *Assuring supremacy and uniformity.* Note the similarities and differences between that modern jurisdictional statute, 28 U.S.C. § 1257, and its earliest antecedent, § 25 of the Judiciary Act of 1789, considered in Martin v. Hunter's Lessee, above.† Note that under § 25 (and indeed well into the 20th century), Supreme Court review was available only if the state court *denied* federal claims—e. g., by sustaining a state statute against federal objections or setting aside a federal law. Jurisdiction was broadened in 1914, when Supreme Court review was for the first time extended to cases in which the state court had *sustained* rather than rejected the federal claim. Assurance of greater uniformity in federal law interpretation, not simply assurance of federal supremacy, thus became a major goal of the review statute.

---

† The text of § 25: "That a final judgment or decree in any suit, in the highest court of law or equity of a State in which a decision in the suit could be had, where is drawn in question the validity of a treaty or statute of, or an authority exercised under the United States, and the decision is against their validity; or where is drawn in question the validity of a statute of, or an authority exercised under any State, on the ground of their being repugnant to the constitution, treaties or laws of the United States, and the decision is in favour of such their validity, or where is drawn in question the construction of any clause of the constitution, or of a treaty, or statute of, or commission held under the United States, and the decision is against the title, right, privilege or exemption specially set up or claimed by either party, under such clause of the said Constitution, treaty, statute or commission, may be re-examined and reversed or affirmed in the Supreme Court of the United States upon a writ of error . . . .. But no other error shall be assigned or regarded as a ground of reversal in any such case as aforesaid, than such as appears on the face of the record, and immediately respects the before mentioned questions of validity or construction of the said constitution, treaties, statutes, commissions, or authorities in dispute."

Is the uniformity need adequately met today? Not even the 1914 extension, now reflected in 28 U.S.C. § 1257(3), provides for the correction of *all* errors in state court interpretations of federal law. The decision which provoked the 1914 change illustrates the point. In Ives v. South Buffalo Ry. Co., 201 N.Y. 271 (1911), the state court had held New York's workmen's compensation law unconstitutional under the due process clauses of the state as well as the federal constitution. The New York court's interpretation of the federal due process clause was thought to be more restrictive than the Supreme Court's position, yet no review was possible under the old jurisdictional statute. But, ironically, not even the 1914 expansion would have permitted review in the Ives case—because of the "adequate state grounds" barrier to Supreme Court review, considered in note 2 below.

c. *Appeals and certiorari.*   Under § 25 and its 19th century revisions, Supreme Court review was obligatory: all state cases within the statute could be taken to the Supreme Court as a matter of right, by writ of error. The 1914 expansion introduced review in the discretion of the Supreme Court in certain cases; and that method was expanded by the Judges' Bill of 1925. Obligatory review—with the modern terminology of "appeal" rather than "writ of error"—is covered by 28 U.S.C. § 1257(1) and (2); discretionary review by the "certiorari" provision, 28 U.S.C. § 1257(3).* As a byproduct of the debates in the 1970's about relieving the workload of the Supreme Court, proposals have been advanced to eliminate the obligatory "appeal" jurisdiction of the Court and to make the discretionary "certiorari" route the only one to the Supreme Court. (See the note on the "noncontroversial" aspects of the Freund Committee proposal, at the end of this section.)

At present, determination of whether appeal or certiorari is the appropriate review route lies to a considerable extent within the discretion of counsel in framing his federal objection in the state court. That control by litigants rests largely on the interpretation of a predecessor to 28 U.S.C. § 1257 in Dahnke-Walker Milling Co. v. Bondurant, 257 U.S. 282 (1921). There, a Tennessee corporation brought a contract suit against a Kentucky resident in a Kentucky court. The defendant successfully contended in the state court that the contract was unenforceable because the corporation had not qualified to do business in Kentucky pursuant to a state statute. The plaintiff objected that the commerce clause of the United States Constitution prevented the application of the statute to an interstate commerce transaction. The state court conceded that the statute could not be applied to transactions in interstate commerce, but held that the transaction in question was "strictly intrastate." The Supreme Court decided that the case was properly before it on writ of error (now appeal), since the plaintiff "did not simply claim a right or immunity under the Constitution of the United States, but distinctly insisted that as to the transaction in question the Kentucky statute

---

* On the practice in appeal and certiorari cases, and the extent to which discretionary elements play a role in the disposition of appeals, see the next group of notes and sec. 4A of chap. 15. The taking of an appeal in a case where certiorari is the appropriate mode of review is not ground for dismissal. Rather, 28 U.S.C. § 2103 requires that in such a case (whether from a state court or from a lower federal court) "the papers whereon the appeal was taken shall be regarded and acted on as a petition for writ of certiorari."

was void." When the state court nevertheless enforced the statute, its action constituted "an affirmation of its validity when so applied." Justice Brandeis, dissenting, insisted that "the validity of the statute is not actually drawn in question. Only the propriety of the application or use of the statute is questioned." He predicted: "If jurisdiction upon writ of error can be obtained by the mere claim in words that a state statute is invalid, if so construed as to 'apply' to a given state of facts, the right to a review will depend, in large classes of cases, not upon the nature of the constitutional question involved, but upon the skill of counsel."

2. *The "adequate and independent state grounds" barrier to Supreme Court review of state court decisions.* The Supreme Court does not review state court decisions resting on "adequate and independent state grounds." Efforts to obtain review of such decisions are dismissed for lack of jurisdiction. Determining whether a state court's reliance on an issue of state law bars Supreme Court review is a frequently encountered and complex problem. State grounds of decision may be substantive or procedural: a state court ruling may rest on a mixture of state and federal substantive grounds; or a state court may fail to reach a federal issue because of an allegedly dispositive state procedural ground. In either situation, assessing the "adequacy" and "independence" of the state ground may be difficult. The intricacies of these problems are pursued in federal jurisdiction courses.* But the theoretical underpinnings and a few of the practical consequences of the "adequate and independent state grounds" barrier are worth noting here.

Justice Jackson, in Herb v. Pitcairn, 324 U.S. 117 (1945), summarized the rule and its basis: "This Court from the time of its foundation has adhered to the principle that it will not review judgments of state courts that rest on adequate and independent state grounds. . . . The reason is so obvious that it has rarely been thought to warrant statement. It is found in the partitioning of power between the state and federal judicial systems and in the limitations of our own jurisdiction. Our only power over state judgments is to correct them to the extent that they incorrectly adjudge federal rights. And our power is to correct wrong judgments, not to revise opinions. We are not permitted to render an advisory opinion, and if the same judgment would be rendered by the state court after we corrected its views of federal laws, our review could amount to nothing more than an advisory opinion." Justice Jackson found the rule a constitutional necessity, in view of the Art. III preclusion of advisory opinions (see chap. 15); others have suggested that, whether or not the rule is constitutionally based, it is required by the jurisdictional statutes.†

* See generally, Hart and Wechsler, Federal Courts (2d ed. 1973), chap. 5, and Wright, Federal Courts (2d ed. 1970), chap. 12; see also Gunther and Dowling, Cases and Materials on Constitutional Law (8th ed. 1970), chap. 2, sec. 3.

† See, e. g. Justice Brennan's comments in reaffirming the "independent and adequate state grounds" barrier in Fay v. Noia, 372 U.S. 391 (1963): "The deletion [in 1867] of the express restriction [in the last sentence of Sec. 25 of the 1789 Judiciary Act] did not enlarge this Court's power in that regard. Murdock v. City of Memphis, 20 Wall. 590 [1875]." In a footnote, he added that it was unnecessary to decide "whether the adequate state-ground rule is constitutionally compelled or merely a matter of the con-

a. *State substantive law.* In constitutional litigation, the most common example of an independent and adequate state substantive ground is a state court ruling that a state law violates both the state and the federal constitutions. Even though the state court opinion may include an elaborate discussion of the meaning of the federal guarantee—an interpretation that may be wrong—the Supreme Court will not review if the state judges rest as well on their own constitutional provisions: a correction of the state court's interpretation would not change the outcome of the case. For example, the California Supreme Court has in recent years several times invalidated state laws in opinions primarily discussing the Federal Constitution, yet immune from review because of additional, brief statements that a similar state constitutional provision has been violated as well. And the California Supreme Court's non-reviewable statements about federal law have repeatedly had considerable impact on other courts. See, e. g., Serrano v. Priest, 5 Cal.3d 584, 487 P.2d 1241 (1971), sustaining a challenge to interdistrict inequalities in school financing in an opinion discussing federal law at length but immune from Supreme Court review. The California Court's approach was followed by several other state and federal courts before the Supreme Court took a different view of the federal equal protection clause in the Rodriguez case, chap. 10 below. Should such unreviewable state court ventures into federal constitutional law be praised as creative, or criticized as irresponsible? For an admiring evaluation, see Karst, "Serrano v. Priest: A State Court's Responsibilities and Opportunities in the Development of Federal Constitutional Law," 60 Calif.L.Rev. 720 (1972).*

struction of the statutes defining this Court's appellate review," since "the present statute governing our review of state court decisions, 28 U.S.C. § 1257, limited as it is to *judgments or decrees* rendered by the highest court of a State in which a decision could be had' (italics supplied), provides ample statutory warrant" for the rule.

* For an early manifestation of the complexities of interrelated state and federal substantive grounds (in a non-constitutional setting), recall Martin v. Hunter's Lessee, sec. 2 above. In deciding the merits of that litigation, the Virginia judges had not denied that federal treaties protected lands held by aliens as of 1783; they insisted instead that as a matter of Virginia law the Fairfax lands had been seized by the State prior to 1783. Moreover, most of the Virginia judges stated that their judgment for Hunter was independently supportable on the basis of a legislatively approved Compromise adopted while the litigation was in abeyance in the 1790's. Justice Story, in examining those asserted state grounds of decision in 1816, found neither acceptable. He rejected the relevance of the Act of Compromise because it was not pleaded on the face of the record and therefore was not properly before

the Supreme Court under the terms of § 25 of the Judiciary Act of 1789. And the state court's view as to who owned the lands in 1783 was not found controlling by Justice Story because of his concern about potential evasion of federal guarantees. In a sweeping statement, he argued: "How, indeed, can it be possible to decide whether a [land] title be within the protection of a treaty, until it is ascertained what that title is, and whether it have a legal validity?" He added: "If the court below should decide, that the title was bad, and therefore not protected by the treaty, must not this court have a power to decide the title to be good, and, therefore, protected by the treaty?"

Under modern practice, the Martin litigation would not be reviewable in the Supreme Court. The Court would take note of the existence of the Act of Compromise. The state property ruling would give more difficulty: the modern Supreme Court would not disregard it as readily and totally as Story did; its concern about state evasion of federal guarantees by disingenuous statements of state law would prompt only limited reexamination of the state property ruling, not a wholesale displacement. Cf. note 2b below.

b. *State procedural law.* An allegedly adequate and independent state ground may be procedural rather than substantive, as noted. And it is the problem of state procedural grounds that has been of the greatest practical significance and the most prolific source of litigation in recent years. The problem has taken on special importance with the expansion of federal constitutional rights for state criminal defendants. The posture of a typical state procedural grounds case differs from the state substantive grounds situation. In the substantive grounds model, the state court discusses federal as well as state issues; the problem on Supreme Court review is to assess the significance and acceptability of the state ground in the state-federal mix. In the usual procedural grounds case, by contrast, the state court does not get to the federal claim at all; rather, the state decision relies solely on the state law ground and holds that noncompliance with the state procedural requirement precludes adjudication of the federal issue. Suppose, for example, a state criminal defendant objects to introduction of evidence on the ground that it was illegally seized, or to a confession on the ground that it was coerced. Suppose, moreover, the state court refuses to rule on the merits of those objections on the ground that they were not raised in accordance with state procedural groundrules—e. g., "with fair precision" or "in due time." May the Supreme Court on review nevertheless get to the federal objections? Or are the state procedural grounds "adequate" to support the conviction? Will and should the Supreme Court entertain the federal issue despite a state court ruling that it was not properly raised?

That problem arises from the fact that state courts have from the beginning been a significant initial forum for the adjudication of federal claims. And from the beginning, a state's control of its judicial machinery has carried considerable autonomy in prescribing the processes for the raising of all claims (federal as well as state) in the state courts. Ordinarily, then, compliance with state procedural requirements as to the time and manner of raising and preserving federal questions is necessary in order to invoke Supreme Court review. Yet deference to state procedures has never been total: precluding all Supreme Court review upon a state court's mere recital of a state procedural ground would endanger vindication of federal rights. What, then, are the governing considerations in determining whether the asserted state procedural ground is "adequate" to preclude review? The Supreme Court has often said that a state court's refusal to decide a federal question must rest on "fair" and "substantial" grounds.

This is not the place to explore in depth what is necessary to establish unfairness or insubstantiality. But a statement from Justice Clark's dissent in Williams v. Georgia, 349 U.S. 375, 399 (1955), usefully summarizes the typical avenues of Supreme Court inquiry: "A purported state ground is not independent and adequate in two instances. *First,* where the circumstances give rise to an inference that the state court is guilty of an evasion—an interpretation of state law with the specific intent to deprive a litigant of a federal right. [A footnote at this point added: "This charge upon the integrity of a State Supreme Court is so serious that this Court has restricted such findings to cases where the state court decision lacked 'fair support' in the state law."] *Second,* where the state law, honestly applied though it may be, and even dictated by the precedents, throws such obstacles in the way of enforcement of federal rights that it must be

struck down as unreasonably interfering with the vindication of such rights." For a somewhat greater Court willingness to reexamine procedural grounds, see Henry v. Mississippi, 379 U.S. 443 (1965), where the majority—in examining an asserted state ground of "waiver"—suggested that state procedural grounds are subject to broader Supreme Court reexamination than state substantive grounds. Justice Brennan's majority opinion stated "that a litigant's procedural defaults in state proceedings do not prevent vindication of his federal rights unless the State's insistence on compliance with its procedural rules serves a legitimate state interest. In every case we must inquire whether the enforcement of a procedural forfeiture serves such a state interest. If it does not, the state procedural rule ought not be permitted to bar vindication of important federal rights."†

3. *Review of judgments of federal courts.* The most commonly invoked basis for review of federal court decisions is 28 U.S.C. § 1254, which provides for Supreme Court review of cases in the Courts of Appeals. Its most important provisions authorize review as follows:

"(1) By writ of certiorari granted upon the petition of any party to any civil or criminal case, before or after rendition of judgment or decree;

"(2) By appeal by a party relying on a State statute held by a court of appeals to be invalid as repugnant to the Constitution, treaties or laws of the United States, but such appeal shall preclude review by writ of certiorari at the instance of such appellant, and the review on appeal shall be restricted to the Federal questions presented."*

Obligatory review of Courts of Appeals decisions is rare: there is little occasion for Courts of Appeals to hold state statutes unconstitutional [see 28 U.S.C. § 1254(2)] because actions to enjoin state laws must be brought before a three-judge District Court under 28 U.S.C. § 2281. See Currie, "The Three-Judge District Court in Constitutional Litigation," 32 U.Chi.L. Rev. 1 (1964). Most lower federal court cases within the Supreme Court's obligatory appeal jurisdiction come from the three-judge District Courts rather than the Courts of Appeals. For example, 28 U.S.C. § 1253 permits a

---

† See generally Hill, "The Inadequate State Ground," 65 Colum.L.Rev. 943 (1965), and Sandalow, "Henry v. Mississippi and the Adequate State Ground: Proposals for a Revised Doctrine," 1965 Sup.Ct.Rev. 187. For the effect of failure to comply with state procedural requirement on the availability of federal habeas corpus relief, see Fay v. Noia, 372 U.S. 391 (1963), 28 U.S.C. § 2254, and the more recent proposals to bar federal habeas corpus relief if the constitutional claim could have been raised in a state court [see Note, "Proposed Modification of Federal Habeas Corpus for State Prisoners—Reform or Revocation?" 61 Georgetown L.J. 1221 (1973)].

* 28 U.S.C. § 1254 also authorizes a third route, a rarely used one: under § 1254(3), Courts of Appeals may "certify" questions in cases before them for Supreme Court "instructions." Note, too, that under § 1254, unlike the state court review provisions in § 1257, the lower court case need not reach final judgment before qualifying for Supreme Court review: certiorari may be granted "before or after rendition of judgment or decree" in the Court of Appeals. The Supreme Court, however, limits pre-judgment review to extraordinary cases. For an example, see United States v. Nixon, 418 U.S. 683 (1974) (chap. 7 below), the Watergate tapes case in which certiorari was sought and granted immediately upon filing of the appeal from Judge Sirica's order in the Court of Appeals. For a criticism of the Supreme Court's haste in that case, see Gunther, "Judicial Hegemony and Legislative Autonomy: The Nixon Case and the Impeachment Process," 22 UCLA L.Rev. 30 (1974).

direct appeal of any order granting or denying an injunction in any civil action required to be heard by three-judge District Courts. And three-judge courts are required in a number of situations beyond those seeking injunctions against unconstitutional laws. See, e. g., 28 U.S.C. § 2325 (injunctions against ICC orders). The Freund Committee proposal prompted by concern about the Supreme Court's workload, noted below, recommends "elimination of the three-judge court, and of direct review in these classes of cases." Should the obligatory appeal jurisdiction be eliminated entirely? Or would it be adequate to eliminate direct appeals from federal District Courts—channeling those cases through the Courts of Appeals—but retaining obligatory review in some classes of cases from state courts?

APPELLATE JURISDICTION:
SUPREME COURT RULES, PRACTICES, PROBLEMS

1. *Appeal.* a. Though the cases within the certiorari jurisdiction far outnumber those that come up on appeal, the several hundred efforts a year to invoke the appeal jurisdiction comprise an important portion of the Court's workload.† The appeal route is theoretically obligatory, but the Court does not afford oral argument and disposition with full opinion in every case allegedly within the appeal jurisdiction. Instead, the Court uses a screening mechanism: an appeal is initiated by filing a "jurisdictional statement." Its contents are prescribed by Rule 15 of the Supreme Court.* The jurisdictional statement is required to demonstrate not only why the case falls within the appeal provisions of the jurisdictional statutes, but also "why the questions presented are so substantial as to require plenary consideration, with briefs on the merits and oral argument, for their resolution." See Rule 15(e) and (f). Most appeals are handled solely on the basis of that jurisdictional statement and the response to it. Thus, even in cases satisfying the technical requirements of the jurisdictional statute, the Court may decide to dispose of the case summarily, for want of "substantiality." In cases from state courts, the Supreme Court denotes such dispositions by "dismissing" the appeal; in cases from lower federal courts, the judgment below is summarily "affirmed." When the Court's examination of the jurisdictional statement persuades it that plenary consideration is warranted, the Court enters an order to "note probable jurisdiction." As a matter of Court practice, the votes of four Justices are sufficient to grant a full hearing to an appeal.

---

† Note, e.g., the statistics for the October 1972 Term of the Court: though nearly 90% of the cases disposed of came to the Court via the certiorari rather than the appeal route, the 346 appeals (out of a total of 3452 dispositions) yielded 49 of the total of 138 cases decided with signed opinions. About 14% of all appeals were handled with full opinions; that was true of less than 3% of the certiorari cases. See Note, "The Freund Report: A Statistical Analysis and Critique," 27 Rutgers L.Rev. 378, 902 (Table I) (1974).

* The Supreme Court Rules were most recently revised in 1970 and are printed at 398 U.S. 1015. See generally Stern and Gressman, Supreme Court Practice (4th ed. 1969); Boskey and Gressman, "The 1970 Changes in the Supreme Court's Rules," 49 F.R.D. 679 (1970).

b. Are summary dispositions on "insubstantiality" grounds votes on the merits? They certainly are as a matter of theory: as Justice Brennan commented in Ohio ex rel. Eaton v. Price, 360 U.S. 246 (1959): "Votes to affirm summarily, and to dismiss for want of a substantial federal question, it hardly needs comment, are votes on the merits of a case . . . ." Yet the Court has increasingly resorted to summary dispositions of appeals even when the questions presented hardly seem frivolous. Over the years, "insubstantiality" dispositions of appeals have come to be viewed as less weighty precedents than cases decided with opinion after argument. Nevertheless, even summary "insubstantiality" dispositions of appeals can properly be cited as rulings on the merit—unlike denials of certiorari petitions (see note 2 below).

c. Under the statutory framework distinguishing appeals as of right from certiorari review within the Court's discretion, the Court seemingly has no escape from saying something on the merits in a case meeting all of the technical requirements of the appeal jurisdiction. Nevertheless, there have been some cases of that variety in which the Court has refused to exercise jurisdiction and has declined to decide on the merits. Can that practice be defended? May discretionary ingredients appropriate on certiorari properly enter the judgment on whether to entertain an appeal? That problem—of duty and discretion regarding adjudication—recurs throughout chap. 15. Note especially the "discretionary" dismissals of appeals considered in chap. 15, sec. 4A.

2. *Certiorari.* a. The Court's discretionary jurisdiction—the route by which review is sought in most cases—is invoked by filing a petition for writ of certiorari. Supreme Court Rule 23 prescribes the contents of the petition. The petition must include a showing that the Court has jurisdiction: in cases from state courts, for example, it must "show that the federal question was timely and properly raised so as to give this court jurisdiction to review." But the major purpose of the petition is to demonstrate that the case is "certworthy"—that it is of sufficient general significance, and not simply of importance to the parties in the case, to warrant review. The votes of four Justices are needed for a grant of review on certiorari.

The Court's Rule 19 is an attempt to state in general terms the "Considerations Governing Review on Certiorari." Rule 19(1) provides: "A review on writ of certiorari is not a matter of right, but of sound judicial discretion, and will be granted only where there are special and important reasons therefor. The following, while neither controlling nor fully measuring the court's discretion, indicate the character of reasons which will be considered:

"(a) Where a state court has decided a federal question of substance not theretofore determined by this court, or has decided it in a way probably not in accord with applicable decisions of this court.

"(b) Where a court of appeals has rendered a decision in conflict with the decision of another court of appeals on the same matter; or has decided an important state or territorial question in a way in conflict with applicable state or territorial law; or has decided an important question of federal law which has not been, but should be, settled by this court; or has decided a federal question in a way in conflict with applicable decisions of this court;

or has so far departed from the accepted and usual course of judicial proceedings, or so far sanctioned such a departure by a lower court, as to call for an exercise of this court's power of supervision."

Over the years, as the number of certiorari petitions has increased and the consequent workload has grown, Justices have repeatedly urged lawyers to use greater self-restraint in filing petitions. An early, typical appeal came in a speech by Chief Justice Vinson to the ABA in 1949 (69 S.Ct. v). He reported that "too many" of the certiorari petitions "reveal a serious misconception on the part of counsel concerning the role of the Supreme Court in our federal system." He added: "Lawyers might be well-advised, in preparing petitions for certiorari, to spend a little less time discussing the merits [and] a little more time demonstrating why it is important that the Court should hear them." See also, e. g., Justice Harlan's "Manning the Dikes," 13 Record N.Y.C. Bar Ass'n 541 (1958); but compare Justice Douglas' "The Supreme Court and Its Case Load," 45 Cornell L.Rev. 401 (1960). Despite these pleas, the number of petitions has grown: it is now more than double what it was when Chief Justice Vinson spoke. Some observers have argued that admonitions from the bench cannot curb the flow so long as other actions by the Court encourage filings—actions such as unpredictable grants of certiorari as well as changes in substantive doctrine stimulating litigation in new areas. Others have suggested that the Court could help by providing guidelines more specific than those in Rule 19 or by giving reasons when it denies a certiorari petition. [For the arguments rejecting the latter route, see Justice Frankfurter's comments in the next paragraph.] Most recent examinations of the certiorari workload assume that, if any relief is needed, it will require structural changes rather than admonitions to the bar. See the note on the Freund Committee proposal and related recommendations, at the end of this section.

b.   Unlike the summary disposition of an appeal for "insubstantiality," a denial of a petition for certiorari is not a decision on the merits. Justice Frankfurter explained the significance which should be (and usually is) given a denial of certiorari in a separate opinion in Maryland v. Baltimore Radio Show, 338 U.S. 912 (1950): "[A] denial simply means that fewer than four members of the Court deemed it desirable to review a decision of the lower court as a matter 'of sound judicial discretion.' . . . A variety of considerations underlie denials of the writ, and as to the same petition different reasons may lead different Justices to the same result. This is especially true of petitions for review on writ of certiorari to a State court. Narrowly technical reasons may lead to denials. Review may be sought too late; the judgment of the lower court may not be final; it may not be the judgment of a State court of last resort; the decision may be supportable as a matter of State law, not subject to review by this Court, even though the State court also passed on issues of federal law. A decision may satisfy all these technical requirements and yet may commend itself for review to fewer than four members of the Court. Pertinent considerations of judicial policy here come into play. A case may raise an important question but the record may be cloudy. It may be desirable to have different aspects of an issue further illumined by the lower courts. Wise adjudication has its own time for ripening.

"Since there are these conflicting and, to the uninformed, even confusing reasons for denying petitions for certiorari, it has been suggested from time to time that the Court indicate its reasons for denial. Practical considerations preclude. . . . If the Court is to do its work it would not be feasible to give reasons, however brief, for refusing to take these cases. The time that would be required is prohibitive, apart from the fact as already indicated that different reasons not infrequently move different members of the Court in concluding that a particular case at a particular time makes review undesirable. . . . Inasmuch, therefore, as all that a denial of a petition for a writ of certiorari means is that fewer than four members of the Court thought it should be granted, this Court has rigorously insisted that such a denial carries with it no implication whatever regarding the Court's views on the merits of a case which it has declined to review. The Court has said this again and again; again and again the admonition has to be repeated." [Though, as Justice Frankfurter noted, the Court does not give reasons for denial of certiorari, there has been a growing tendency for Justices to note their dissents from denials and occasionally to give their reasons in separate opinions.]

c. In recent decades, there have been sporadic controversies—on and off the Court—regarding Supreme Court practice in handling certiorari cases. Among the areas of dispute: (a) grants of certiorari in employees' injury actions under federal statutes, on the issue of the adequacy of the evidence, see Note, "Supreme Court Certiorari Policy in Cases Arising Under the FELA," 69 Harv.L.Rev. 1441 (1956), Wilkerson v. McCarthy, 336 U.S. 53 (1949), Ferguson v. Moore-McCormack Lines, Inc., 352 U.S. 521 (1957); (b) the obligation of a Justice to vote on the merits after certiorari has been granted, see Rogers v. Missouri Pac. R. R. Co., 352 U.S. 500 (1957), and Leiman, "The Rule of Four," 57 Colum.L.Rev. 975 (1957); (c) the dismissal of certiorari as "improvidently granted" after argument on the merits, see Rice v. Sioux City Cemetery, 349 U.S. 70 (1955); (d) the summary disposition of cases on the merits, in brief per curiam memoranda, see Note, "Supreme Court Per Curiam Practice: A Critique," 69 Harv.L.Rev. 707 (1956).

d. The Court's growing workload—largely attributable to the increase in certiorari petitions—is indicated by the statistics summarizing the business of the October 1973 Term: 3876 cases finally disposed of, with 157 opinions for the Court; 3347 certiorari petitions and jurisdictional statements considered, with review set for 183. See "The Supreme Court, 1973 Term," 88 Harv.L.Rev. 13, 277 (1974), and generally Hart, "Foreword: The Time Chart of the Justices," 73 Harv.L.Rev. 84 (1959). In recent decades, there has been a striking increase in the annual number of cases: compare, with the 3876 cases disposed of in the 1973 Term, 3117 in the 1968 Term, 2401 in the 1963 Term, 1670 in the 1956 Term, and 1278 in the 1952 Term. There has also been a remarkable increase in the size of the Court's Miscellaneous Docket—the Docket consisting mainly of in forma pauperis petitions from prisoners, and understandably expanding with the Court's proliferation of criminal procedure decisions. In recent years, the Miscellaneous Docket has become larger than the Appellate one: in the 1973 Term, 2004 Miscellaneous cases were disposed of, as against 1868 on the Appellate Docket. The percentage of grants of review on the "regular," Appellate Docket has

typically been much larger than on the Miscellaneous Docket. In the 1973 Term, for example, review was granted in 10.6 percent of Appellate Docket cases and in only 0.9 percent of Miscellaneous Docket ones. The number of cases disposed of with full opinion has not varied significantly over the years; accordingly, the percentage of cases in which review is granted has declined as the number of requests for review has grown.

Statistics such as these—growth in the size of the Dockets, decline in the percentage of cases reviewed—have formed the foundation for recent recommendations on the workload such as those considered in the next note. But these sheer numbers, like most statistics, can be somewhat misleading. Though the burden is no doubt heavy, the figures should not be read to suggest that the Court discusses every petition at its weekly conferences. Copies of each petition do indeed go to the chambers of each Justice. But many Justices use the assistance of their law clerks to prepare brief summaries of petitions.* Moreover, the Court has an internal procedure to avoid discussion of the large percentage of certiorari petitions that are clearly not "certworthy": before the conference, the Chief Justice prepares a "dead list"; unless one of the other Justices requests that a case on that list be discussed, review is automatically denied. In short, nearly 4000 cases on a Docket does not mean 4000 fungible cases requiring equal periods of time. Many indeed do require considerable attention, from the Justices and their clerks; many more—depending on the views and experience of each Justice—can be evaluated very quickly indeed.† But with all of these qualifications, the workload for each Justice remains considerable. Evaluation of the magnitude of the problem has divided the Justices and observers; and those divisions have surfaced in the debates on the recent reform proposals summarized in the materials that follow.

PROPOSALS TO REDUCE THE SUPREME COURT'S WORKLOAD

1. *The Freund Committee Report.* Major—and to some extent controversial—changes in Supreme Court jurisdiction were proposed in the December, 1972, report of a committee headed by Prof. Paul A. Freund. (Federal Judicial Center, Report of the Study Group on the Caseload of the Supreme Court.) Considerable criticism greeted one of the proposals, the creation of a National Court of Appeals to reduce the certiorari workload of the Court. The criticisms directed at that suggestion deflected attention from a number of other important, although less controversial, proposals. Most of the suggested changes stem from the Committee's perception

---

* On the often exaggerated role of the law clerks, see Wilkinson, Serving Justice—A Supreme Court Clerk's View (1974).

† See, e. g., former Justice Goldberg's comment that "an astonishing number of filed cases raise questions that a third-year law student can immediately recognize as inappropriate for the Su-

preme Court." Goldberg, "One Supreme Court," The New Republic, Feb. 10, 1973, at 15. On the internal work practices of the Court, see generally the Wilkinson book cited above, Clark, "The Decisional Processes of the Supreme Court," 50 Cornell L.Rev. 385 (1965), and Brennan, "State Court Decisions and the Supreme Court," 34 Fla.Bar.J. 269 (1960).

that the statistics of the Court's workload—"both in absolute terms and in the mounting trend"—indicate "that the conditions essential for the performance of the Court's mission do not exist." The pressures of the Court's docket are allegedly "incompatible with the appropriate fulfillment of its historic and essential functions." (Those functions, the Committee insists, are "distinctive and essential": the Court is "not simply another court of errors and appeals"; its task is "to define and vindicate the rights guaranteed by the Constitution, to assure the uniformity of federal law, and to maintain the constitutional distribution of powers in our federal union.")

a. *The noncontroversial proposals.* The Committee urges that all cases be brought to the Court (or to the new National Court of Appeals, if it is established) by certiorari rather than by appeal. The appeal route of obligatory review, from state as well as federal courts, would be abolished. The Committee also recommends "elimination of the three-judge court, and of direct review, in these classes of cases"—most significantly, constitutional challenges to statutes and review of ICC orders. Moreover, there would no longer be direct appeals in any of the situations where single-judge orders may now be taken immediately to the Supreme Court—e. g., certain criminal appeals. In addition, the Report urges "increased staff support" for the·Supreme Court. (Note also the suggestion for the establishment of a nonjudicial body as the initial federal forum to investigate and report on complaints of prisoners.)

b. *The controversial proposal for a National Court of Appeals, 1972.* The most widely debated Freund Committee proposal urges the establishment of a new court whose primary function would be to take over the bulk of the Supreme Court's certiorari-screening function. The National Court of Appeals would be composed of seven judges drawn on a rotating basis from the federal courts of appeals and serving staggered three-year terms. All review requests that now go to the Supreme Court would go initially to that new Court. That Court would have the final authority to deny review of the "majority" of cases. It could hear and finally decide cases of "true conflict between circuits." It would be expected to certify 400 to 450 cases a year to the Supreme Court. The Supreme Court would then select a limited number of those for full hearing on the merits.

The Committee recognizes that this would involve some "loss of control" by the Supreme Court over its docket, but it believes that this scheme would involve "the least possible loss." Balancing the "minimal" costs of the proposal against its expected benefits, the Committee is "entirely persuaded that the proposal is worth adopting." In the course of reaching that conclusion, the Committee rejected a number of more drastic proposals, including the limitation of Supreme Court jurisdiction to constitutional issues and the creation of specialized courts of administrative appeals. A suggestion to create a new national intermediate court primarily to handle cases referred to it by the Supreme Court was rejected as not really relieving the Supreme Court of its heavy screening burden. (Compare note 2 below.) Moreover, the Committee considered premature the suggestions for the establishment of a National Court of Review of fifteen judges, to sit in panels, with the Supreme Court's review jurisdiction limited to cases decided by that Court of Review. Creating such a "new court of great dignity" would be a "drastic" change, though "the time may come" when it may be necessary. The Committee

commented: "Such a change as this should not be made until the need is undeniable and the change unavoidable. In our judgment, the time is not yet. The change can still be avoided, and may never prove necessary."

Is that comment applicable as well to the Committee's recommendation of a National Court of Appeals? If the Committee's suggestion is rejected, what solutions are preferable? Or is there no genuine problem in need of a solution? Questions such as these provoked considerable debate; * and that critical debate spurred by the Freund Committee Report helped evolve the proposal for an alternate solution considered in the next note.

2. *The controversial proposal for a national division of the U. S. Court of Appeals.* a. *The 1974 proposal.* Some of the criticisms of the Freund Committee proposal might be met by the creation of a different variety of national appellate court inferior to the Supreme Court. Such a proposal, for a national division of the Court of Appeals, is contained in recommendations that surfaced early in 1974. The concept, though not the specifics, of the new proposal was endorsed by the American Bar Association's House of Delegates in February 1974, for transmittal to the Commission on Revision of the Federal Court Appellate System. The ABA-endorsed idea stemmed, in substantially similar form, from two sources: an ABA Special Committee on Coordination of Judicial Improvements; and the Advisory Council for Appellate Justice. See Hufstedler, "Courtship and Other Legal Arts," 60 A.B. A.J. 545 (1974) (Judge Shirley M. Hufstedler is a member of both the Council and the Committee).

The thrust of the new national division proposal is to avoid the criticism of having the Supreme Court's *screening function* delegated to a new body by having the Supreme Court instead delegate the power to *decide* classes of cases to the new tribunal, with a limited Supreme Court opportunity to reexamine the decisions below. Note Judge Hufstedler's summary of the criteria which presumably formed the backdrop for the evolution of the new proposal: "Any proposal for a new national court must be tested against negative criteria for which there is a growing consensus: Do not interfere with the Supreme Court's power to control its own docket, do not cut off access to the Supreme Court, do not unnecessarily elongate the appellate process, do not build a specialized tribunal, do not invidiously discriminate or appear to discriminate against any class of litigation, do not unduly expand the federal judiciary, do not create a tribunal on which able judges will not be willing to sit, and do not permit a method of selecting judges for the court that would allow dominance by any administration or political party. While avoiding these negatives, a new court must meet the positive requirements of providing enough decisional capacity to carry its anticipated load, of maintaining enough jurisdictional flexibility to adapt to changing needs, and of attracting good judges."

---

* See, e. g., Bickel (a member of the Freund Committee), The Caseload of the Supreme Court, and What, If Anything, To Do About It" (Amer.Enterprise Inst.1973); C. Black, "The National Court of Appeals: An Unwise Proposal," 83 Yale L.J. 883 (1974); Symposium, "Should the Appellate Jurisdiction of the United States Supreme Court Be Changed? . . .," 27 Rutgers L.Rev. 878 (1974); Casper and Posner, "A Study of the Supreme Court's Caseload," 3 J. Legal Studies 339 (1974); and Griswold, "The Supreme Court's Case Load . . . .," 1973 U.Ill.L.F. 615.

To implement principles such as these, the ABA's Special Committee proposed a new national court of appeals with the following "key features": "(1) Congress creates a national court of appeals, (2) the judges of which are selected from active United States Circuit Judges with not less than a specified number of years service, (3) it grants power to the Supreme Court, by Supreme Court rules, to confer jurisdiction on the new court, (4) within boundaries set by Congress, (5) to hear and to decide classes of litigation, or individual cases referred to it by the Supreme Court, and to recommend to the Supreme Court hearing or denial of hearing in such cases, (6) subject to the continuing power of the Supreme Court to accept or to reject any case for hearing, and further subject to the requirement (7) that no decision of the national court shall become final until the elapse of a specified period of time [e. g., 60 or 90 days] after the records, decisions and recommendations of the national court have been received by the Supreme Court, and the Court has not taken active action thereon, (8) Congress creates new circuit judgeships to replace the circuit judges who will be assigned to the national court."

Of greatest interest, in light of the criticisms of the Freund Committee Report, is the Committee's elaboration of the third "key feature." After noting that judges might be assigned to the national division by the Chief Justice with the concurrence of at least five of the Associate Justices and the consent of the Senate, the Committee suggested that "Congress should grant power to the Supreme Court to confer, by court rules, jurisdiction upon the national division within boundaries set by Congress, to decide classes of litigation. For example, the Supreme Court might refer (1) all petitions for review from Circuit Courts in criminal collateral attack proceedings, (2) all tax cases from the Tax Court and the Federal District Courts, (3) all petitions for review of federal administrative decisions, (4) all cases from state courts of last resort, etc. In addition, the Supreme Court might refer individual cases to the national division if it deemed this appropriate." [The similar proposal by the Advisory Council singles out review of state court criminal convictions and resolution of conflicts between Circuits as primary tasks for the new court.]

b. *The criticisms.* Is the new proposal more desirable than that of the Freund Committee? What are its problems? The new proposal, too has encountered criticisms. See especially that by the late Chief Justice Warren, "Let's Not Weaken the Supreme Court," 60 A.B.A.J. 77 (1974). He characterized the new proposal as "a way of providing some vague sort of relief to the lower courts by means of crippling the Supreme Court's exercise of jurisdiction over certain classes of litigation." He saw it as a "cynical and formidable" assault on the functions of the Supreme Court, and he insists that the "desired reduction in the workload of the lower federal courts cannot be achieved by carving up and delegating some of the decision-making processes of the Supreme Court." After referring to the Freund Committee proposal as "an unnecessary and unwarranted disruption of the Supreme Court's exercise of its own vested jurisdiction," he argued that the more recent suggestions "are even more ill-advised and irrelevant with respect to the workload problems of the Supreme Court." He perceived constitutional problems: "there is a serious question whether Congress has the constitutional power, once it has vested certain appellate jurisdiction in the Supreme Court,

to delegate or authorize the delegation of any part of that jurisdiction to an inferior court." [Is there merit to the constitutional questions raised about the new proposal, or about the Freund Committee Report?] The late Chief Justice also argued that a Court power to delegate portions of its jurisdiction to the new tribunal would throw the Court "into the political arena," and he argued that "these matters should always be left to our supreme political institution," Congress. He objected too, to the "passive role" of the Supreme Court as to cases delegated to the new court for decision. He concluded that "The Supreme Court must remain free to exercise the entirety of the jurisdiction vested in it," and he urged: "We must reject the cynical approach of those who would destroy or invade the functions of the Supreme Court merely to solve passing problems in the case intake of the lower federal judiciary." †

3. *The 1975 variation: The Hruska Commission's proposed National Court of Appeals.* Early in 1975, the Commission on Revision of the Federal Court Appellate System—the Commission (chaired by Senator Hruska) to whom the recommendations in note 2a were submitted—endorsed the creation of a National Court of Appeals.* The Commission, unlike earlier study groups, did not focus primarily on the Supreme Court's workload. Instead, it emphasized the problems of the courts of appeals. Its proposal for a new National Court stemmed from its perception of a need to "increase the system's capacity for definitive adjudication of issues of national law." The Commission tentatively proposed a new National Court of Appeals of seven Art. III judges. The new Court would be expected to decide at least 150 cases on the merits each year—"thus doubling the national appellate capacity"—and would have as its primary tasks not only the resolution of conflicts among the circuits but also the provision of "authoritative determinations of recurring issues before a conflict had ever arisen."

Cases could be brought to the new National Court of Appeals via two routes: first, "a 'transfer jurisdiction,' under which the regional courts of appeals could transfer cases that would otherwise be heard by those courts"; second, "a 'reference jurisdiction,' under which the Supreme Court could refer to the National Court any case within its jurisdiction [—i. e., cases from state as well as lower federal courts]." The National Court would have discretion to decline cases in the "transfer jurisdiction," but would

---

† The late Chief Justice carried that depth of concern to his deathbed. See Justice Brennan's "Chief Justice Warren," 88 Harv.L.Rev. 1, 4 (1974): "I last saw him only two hours before his death. He wouldn't talk with me about his health. He wanted an update on the status of the proposal to create a National Court of Appeals. He strongly opposed the proposal. Its adoption, he was convinced, threatened to shut the door of the Supreme Court to the poor, the friendless, the little man."

* Under the Commission's statutory mandate, its report was to be submitted to the President, the Congress and the Chief Justice by late June, 1975. Commission agreement on the National Court proposal was reported in January. See The New York Times, Jan. 18, 1975. The Commission's tentative recommendations were published in April, 1975. See Commission on Revision of the Federal Court Appellate System, Structure and Internal Procedures: Recommendations for Change —A Preliminary Report (1975). The Commission scheduled public hearings on that Preliminary Report to aid in its preparation of its Final Report.

be obligated to hear cases within the "reference jurisdiction." (The Commission did not seek to define how the Supreme Court might use its reference powers. Moreover, its Preliminary Report made no recommendations "on the extent to which the Congress should be involved in delineating the reference procedure.")

In effect, then, the new National Court would handle cases by reference from the existing courts of appeals when a prompt national precedent seemed desirable. And it would decide referrals from the Supreme Court presumably in cases warranting a resolution with national effect but not significant enough for immediate decision on the merits by the Supreme Court. All decisions of the National Court would be reviewable by the Supreme Court on certiorari. The Commission anticipated, however, "that few decisions of the National Court in cases which came to it from the Supreme Court would in fact be reviewed thereafter by the Supreme Court." It added: "To avoid prolonging the appellate process any more than absolutely necessary, the Commission would recommend that in such cases the Supreme Court give expedited consideration to requests for review of the National Court decision, and that such requests take the form of brief statements of the reasons why the Supreme Court should now hear a case that it has already once decided not to review."

Would adoption of the Hruska Commission's tentative recommendations significantly alleviate the Supreme Court's workload problem? Are the recommendations subject to the same criticisms generated by the earlier proposals regarding the Supreme Court's workload? Would adoption of the recommendations be desirable?

Transitional Note. This chapter has sketched only the framework of constitutional adjudication; it does not explore the additional "jurisdictional" and "procedural" ramifications essential to an adequate comprehension of the process of constitutional adjudication. Those added materials seem at times to be esoteric technicalities; but the rules about when the Court will speak, and as to what issues, go to the heart of the Court's place in the constitutional scheme. Those ramifications can usefully be considered at this point; but they are postponed in this edition to the last chapter, chap. 15. They are placed at the end of the book for two related reasons: first, further exploration of the Supreme Court review process at this point would unduly postpone consideration of the substantive content of governmental powers and individual rights; second, the Court's delineation of "jurisdictional" and "procedural" groundrules is often affected by the substantive doctrines at stake, so that examination of such issues as standing and ripeness can better take place after an examination of the substantive developments. The following chapters, accordingly, turn to those substantive problems; at the end, in chap. 15, the book returns to the groundrules governing the exercise of Court authority,† the theme opened up by this chapter.

---

† See also the preliminary consideration   bility in the separation of powers chap-
   of "political questions" and justicia-   ter, chap. 7 below.

Part II

THE STRUCTURE OF GOVERNMENT:
NATION AND STATES IN THE FEDERAL SYSTEM

Introduction. Stronger government was necessary, but government must not become too powerful: these were dominant concerns to the Framers, and the Constitution reflects their effort to accommodate these needs and risks. That document granted greater powers to the central government to cure some of the weaknesses under the Articles of Confederation; yet the Constitution also assured restraints on governmental power. To the drafters of 1787, protection against excessive concentrations of power lay less in explicit limits such as the "shall nots" of the Bill of Rights than in diffusions of power among a variety of governmental units. Thus, the Constitution allocated powers among nation and states: a federal division of powers was achieved by specifying (most notably in Art. I, § 8) those powers Congress might exercise and by emphasizing (in the Tenth Amendment) that undelegated powers were "reserved to the States respectively, or to the people." Moreover, the less-than-total powers given to the national government were diffused among three separate branches, separately described in the first three Articles of the Constitution.

Part II of this casebook deals with these grants and dispersals of power. These chapters explore not only the governmental actions these grants justify but also the limits these grants imply. How can the scope of national authority be articulated with an adequate regard for the interest in local autonomy? That is the focus of chapters 2 through 4: they examine the extent and limits of authority when national power seeks to reach arguably local affairs. (See also chapter 11, exploring the scope of congressional power under the post-Civil War Amendments.) Chapters 5 and 6 focus on the states rather than on national authority—and especially on the limits on state power imposed by national governmental concerns, particularly as reflected in the grant to Congress of the power to regulate interstate commerce. And chapter 7, finally, turns from the nation-state dimension to examine the restraints imposed by the separation of powers within the national government—by the distribution of national powers among executive, legislative, and judicial branches.

Chapter 2

NATIONAL POWERS AND LOCAL ACTIVITIES:
ORIGINS AND RECURRENT THEMES

Introduction: Federalism—Antiquarian Relic? Contemporary Value?
Federalism is the major concern of Part II of this book. The first three chapters of Part II, on the scope of the powers granted to Congress by the Constitutional Convention, include the most controversial impacts of federalism on American history. Again and again in these pages, legislation enacted with great popular support is held unconstitutional by the Supreme Court. And in a larger number of instances, states' rights arguments—some principled, some disingenuous—have defeated or delayed congressional action. The materials that follow focus on federalism-related limits on national power: limits developed in the interest of curtailing national intrusion into local affairs, as distinguished from restraints stemming from individual rights guarantees (considered in Part III of this book).

The controversial impacts of federalism-related limits suggest questions relevant to much of what follows: What were the historical justifications for American federalism? How successfully has the Supreme Court applied those values to changing circumstances? These questions in turn raise even more basic ones: Does federalism retain sufficient value in the modern context, or is it an obsolete obstruction to be dismissed with minimal lip service? And should the Supreme Court be the predominant custodian of federalism? Are substantial Court-imposed limits on congressional power unnecessary because local interests are adequately safeguarded by the political processes? Even if Court restraint vis-á-vis Congress is appropriate, is the Court nevertheless compelled to act as the interventionist umpire of the federal system vis-á-vis the states, by blocking state impingements on national interests? Recall Justice Holmes' famous remark: "I do not think the United States would come to an end if we lost our power to declare an Act of Congress void. I do think the Union would be imperiled if we could not make that declaration as to the laws of the several States." Holmes, Collected Legal Papers (1920), 295. But so long as the power "to declare an Act of Congress void" exists, is the Court justified in relinquishing parts of it, or in adopting a greater "hands-off" attitude in some areas than in others?

The appropriate role of the Court in the evolution of federalism is an issue apparent on the face of many of the materials that follow. Related, equally pervasive questions typically lurk beneath the surface: What are the values, historical and contemporary, of federalism? Can it still be said that federalism increases liberty, encourages diversity, promotes creative experimentation and responsive self-government? Or is it a legalistic obstruction, a harmful brake on governmental responses to pressing social issues, a shield for selfish vested interests? Is federalism a theme that constitutional law must grapple with simply because it is *there*, in the Constitution? Is the prime challenge it poses that of minimizing the obstacles that the complexities of

federalism put in the way of meeting modern needs? Or does federalism embody more appealing values that deserve some of the imaginative enthusiasm with which modern constitutional law embraces the promotion of such values as equality and freedom of speech?

"[D]iversity, pluralism, experimentation, protection from arbitrary majoritarianism and over-centralization, and a greater degree of citizen participation"—so a modern effort to articulate the values inherent in American federalism put it. Advisory Commission on Intergovernmental Relations, Urban America and the Federal System (1969), 105. Yet, as that Report illustrates, those values will not be adequately realized unless the federal system can respond more effectively to such pressing modern problems as "[t]he malaise of our metropolitan areas." That Report urges "aggressive and imaginative" structural and fiscal assistance so that states—with boundaries reflecting history rather than current functional needs—may help cure the "illness" of "the problem of making metropolitan areas governable."

Federalism has been not only the American response for governing large geographical areas with diverse local needs. The federal model has also provided a mechanism for governments of other nations, as well as for international cooperation. See generally Wheare, Federal Government (3d ed. 1953); Macmahon (ed.), Federalism: Mature and Emergent (1955); Friedrich, Trends of Federalism in Theory and Practice (1968). The frictions and accommodations during nearly two centuries of American experience—the concerns of the materials that follow—deserve consideration not only for their own sake but also for the light they shed on federalism's capacity to adapt to future needs, here and elsewhere.

McCULLOCH v. MARYLAND

4 Wheat. 316, 4 L.Ed. 579 (1819)

Error to the Court of Appeals of the State of Maryland.

[Congress chartered the Second Bank of the United States in 1816. The Bank soon established branches in many states. Its branch in Baltimore quickly became the most active of all. In April, 1818, the Maryland legislature adopted "An Act to impose a Tax on all Banks or Branches thereof in the State of Maryland, not chartered by the Legislature." The law provided that any banks operating in Maryland "without authority from the State" could issue bank notes only on stamped paper furnished by the State upon payment of a fee varying with the denomination of each note; but any bank subject to that requirement could "relieve itself" from it "by paying annually, in advance, . . . the sum of fifteen thousand dollars." The statute also provided for penalties for violators: for example, the president, cashier and all other officers of the bank were to "forfeit" five hundred dollars "for each and every offense." The penalties were enforceable by indictment or by "action of debt, in the County Court," "one half to the informer, and the other half to the use of the State."

[This action for the statutory penalty was brought in the County Court of Baltimore County by one John James, suing for himself and the State,

against James McCulloch, the Cashier of the Baltimore branch of the Bank of the United States. It was admitted that the Bank was doing business without authority from the State and that McCulloch had issued bank notes without complying with the Maryland law. The case was decided against McCulloch on the basis of the agreed statement of facts, and the decision was affirmed by the Maryland Court of Appeals. From there, the case was taken by writ of error to the Supreme Court.* For the historical context of the dispute, see the materials following the Court's opinion.]

Mr. Chief Justice MARSHALL delivered the opinion of the Court.

In the case now to be determined, the defendant, a sovereign State, denies the obligation of a law enacted by the legislature of the Union, and the plaintiff, on his part, contests the validity of an act which has been passed by the legislature of that State. The constitution of our country, in its most interesting and vital parts, is to be considered; the conflicting powers of the government of the Union and of its members, as marked in that constitution, are to be discussed; and an opinion given, which may essentially influence the great operations of the government. No tribunal can approach such a question without a deep sense of its importance, and of the awful responsibility involved in its decision. But it must be decided peacefully, or remain a source of hostile legislation, perhaps of hostility of a still more serious nature; and if it is to be so decided, by this tribunal alone can the decision be made. On the Supreme Court of the United States has the constitution of our country devolved this important duty.

The first question made in the cause is, has Congress power to incorporate a bank?

It has been truly said that this can scarcely be considered as an open question, entirely unprejudiced by the former proceedings of the nation respecting it. The principle now contested was introduced at a very early period of our history, has been recognised by many successive legislatures, and has been acted upon by the judicial department, in cases of peculiar delicacy, as a law of undoubted obligation.

It will not be denied, that a bold and daring usurpation might be resisted, after an acquiescence still longer and more complete than this. But it is conceived that a doubtful question, one on which human reason may pause, and the human judgment be suspended, in the decision of which the great principles of liberty are not concerned, but the respective powers of those who are equally the representatives of the people are to be adjusted; if not put at rest by the practice of the government, ought to receive a considerable impression from that practice. An exposition of the constitution, deliberately established by legislative acts, on the faith of which an immense property has been advanced, ought not to be lightly disregarded.

* Court Reporter Henry Wheaton noted that "[t]his case involving a constitutional question of great importance; and the sovereign rights of the United States and the State of Maryland; and the Government of the United States having directed their Attorney General to appear for the plaintiff in error, the Court dispensed with its general rule, permitting only two counsel to argue for each party." Six counsel (United States Attorney General William Wirt, Daniel Webster and William Pinkney for the Bank; State Attorney General Luther Martin, Joseph Hopkinson and Walter Jones for Maryland) argued the case over a period of nine days. The opinion was delivered only three days after the arguments had been concluded.

The power now contested was exercised by the first Congress elected under the present constitution. The bill for incorporating the bank of the United States did not steal upon an unsuspecting legislature, and pass unobserved. Its principle was completely understood, and was opposed with equal zeal and ability. After being resisted, first in the fair and open field of debate, and afterwards in the executive cabinet, with as much persevering talent as any measure has ever experienced, and being supported by arguments which convinced minds as pure and as intelligent as this country can boast, it became a law. The original act was permitted to expire; but a short experience of the embarrassments to which the refusal to revive it exposed the government, convinced those who were most prejudiced against the measure of its necessity, and induced the passage of the present law. It would require no ordinary share of intrepidity to assert that a measure adopted under these circumstances was a bold and plain usurpation, to which the constitution gave no countenance.

These observations belong to the cause; but they are not made under the impression that, were the question entirely new, the law would be found irreconcilable with the constitution.

In discussing this question, the counsel for the State of Maryland have deemed it of some importance, in the construction of the constitution, to consider that instrument not as emanating from the people, but as the act of sovereign and independent States. The powers of the general government, it has been said, are delegated by the States, who alone are truly sovereign; and must be exercised in subordination to the States, who alone possess supreme dominion.

It would be difficult to sustain this proposition. The Convention which framed the constitution was indeed elected by the State legislatures. But the instrument, when it came from their hands, was a mere proposal, without obligation, or pretensions to it. It was reported to the then existing Congress of the United States, with a request that it might "be submitted to a convention of delegates, chosen in each State by the people thereof, under the recommendation of its legislature, for their assent and ratification." This mode of proceeding was adopted; and by the convention, by Congress, and by the State legislatures, the instrument was submitted to the people. They acted upon it in the only manner in which they can act safely, effectively, and wisely, on such a subject, by assembling in convention. It is true, they assembled in their several States—and where else should they have assembled? No political dreamer was ever wild enough to think of breaking down the lines which separate the States, and of compounding the American people into one common mass. Of consequence, when they act, they act in their States. But the measures they adopt do not, on that account, cease to be the measures of the people themselves, or become the measures of the State governments.

From these conventions the constitution derives its whole authority. The government proceeds directly from the people; is "ordained and established" in the name of the people; and is declared to be ordained, "in order to form a more perfect union, establish justice, ensure domestic tranquillity, and secure the blessings of liberty to themselves and to their posterity." The assent of the States, in their sovereign capacity, is implied in calling a convention, and thus submitting that instrument to the people. But the people were at perfect

liberty to accept or reject it; and their act was final. It required not the affirmance, and could not be negatived, by the State governments. The constitution, when thus adopted, was of complete obligation, and bound the State sovereignties. . . .

The government of the Union, then, (whatever may be the influence of this fact on the case,) is, emphatically, and truly, a government of the people. In form and in substance it emanates from them. Its powers are granted by them, and are to be exercised directly on them, and for their benefit.

This government is acknowledged by all to be one of enumerated powers. The principle, that it can exercise only the powers granted to it, [is] now universally admitted. But the question respecting the extent of the powers actually granted, is perpetually arising, and will probably continue to arise, as long as our system shall exist. . . .

The government of the United States, [though] limited in its powers, is supreme; and its laws, when made in pursuance of the constitution, form the supreme law of the land, "any thing in the constitution or laws of any State to the contrary notwithstanding."

Among the enumerated powers, we do not find that of establishing a bank or creating a corporation. But there is no phrase in the instrument which, like the articles of confederation, excludes incidental or implied powers; and which requires that everything granted shall be expressly and minutely described. [The Articles of Confederation had provided that each state "retains" every power not "expressly delegated."] Even the 10th amendment, which was framed for the purpose of quieting the excessive jealousies which had been excited, omits the word "expressly," and declares only that the powers "not delegated to the United States, nor prohibited to the States, are reserved to the States or to the people"; thus leaving the question, whether the particular power which may become the subject of contest has been delegated to the one government, or prohibited to the other, to depend on a fair construction of the whole instrument. The men who drew and adopted this amendment had experienced the embarrassments resulting from the insertion of this word in the articles of confederation, and probably omitted it to avoid those embarrassments. A constitution, to contain an accurate detail of all the subdivisions of which its great powers will admit, and of all the means by which they may be carried into execution, would partake of the prolixity of a legal code, and could scarcely be embraced by the human mind. It would probably never be understood by the public. Its nature, therefore, requires, that only its great outlines should be marked, its important objects designated, and the minor ingredients which compose those objects be deduced from the nature of the objects themselves. That this idea was entertained by the framers of the American constitution, is not only to be inferred from the nature of the instrument, but from the language. Why else were some of the limitations, found in the ninth section of the 1st article, introduced? It is also, in some degree, warranted by their having omitted to use any restrictive term which might prevent its receiving a fair and just interpretation. In considering this question, then, we must never forget that it is *a constitution* we are expounding.

Although, among the enumerated powers of government, we do not find the word "bank" or "incorporation," we find the great powers to lay and

collect taxes; to borrow money; to regulate commerce; to declare and conduct a war; and to raise and support armies and navies. The sword and the purse, all the external relations, and no inconsiderable portion of the industry of the nation, are entrusted to its government. It can never be pretended that these vast powers draw after them others of inferior importance, merely because they are inferior. Such an idea can never be advanced. But it may with great reason be contended, that a government, entrusted with such ample powers, on the due execution of which the happiness and prosperity of the nation so vitally depends, must also be entrusted with ample means for their execution. The power being given, it is the interest of the nation to facilitate its execution. It can never be their interest, and cannot be presumed to have been their intention, to clog and embarrass its execution by withholding the most appropriate means. Throughout this vast republic, from the St. Croix to the Gulph of Mexico, from the Atlantic to the Pacific, revenue is to be collected and expended, armies are to be marched and supported. The exigencies of the nation may require that the treasure raised in the north should be transported to the south, *that* raised in the east conveyed to the west, or that this order should be reversed. Is that construction of the constitution to be preferred which would render these operations difficult, hazardous, and expensive? Can we adopt that construction, (unless the words imperiously require it,) which would impute to the framers of that instrument, when granting these powers for the public good, the intention of impeding their exercise by withholding a choice of means? If, indeed, such be the mandate of the constitution, we have only to obey; but that instrument does not profess to enumerate the means by which the powers it confers may be executed; nor does it prohibit the creation of a corporation, if the existence of such a being be essential to the beneficial exercise of those powers. It is, then, the subject of fair inquiry, how far such means may be employed.

It is not denied, that the powers given to the government imply the ordinary means of execution. That, for example, of raising revenue, and applying it to national purposes, is admitted to imply the power of conveying money from place to place, as the exigencies of the nation may require, and of employing the usual means of conveyance. But it is denied that the government has its choice of means; or, that it may employ the most convenient means, if, to employ them, it be necessary to erect a corporation.

On what foundation does this argument rest? On this alone: The power of creating a corporation, is one appertaining to sovereignty, and is not expressly conferred on Congress. This is true. But all legislative powers appertain to sovereignty. The original power of giving the law on any subject whatever, is a sovereign power; and if the government of the Union is restrained from creating a corporation, as a means for performing its functions, on the single reason that the creation of a corporation is an act of sovereignty; if the sufficiency of this reason be acknowledged, there would be some difficulty in sustaining the authority of Congress to pass other laws for the accomplishment of the same objects.

The government which has a right to do an act, and has imposed on it the duty of performing that act, must, according to the dictates of reason, be allowed to select the means; and those who contend that it may not select any appropriate means, that one particular mode of effecting the object is excepted, take upon themselves the burden of establishing that exception.

. . . The power of creating a corporation, though appertaining to sovereignty, is not, like the power of making war, or levying taxes, or of regulating commerce, a great substantive and independent power, which cannot be implied as incidental to other powers, or used as a means of executing them. It is never the end for which other powers are exercised, but a means by which other objects are accomplished. . . . The power of creating a corporation is never used for its own sake, but for the purpose of effecting something else. No sufficient reason is, therefore, perceived, why it may not pass as incidental to those powers which are expressly given, if it be a direct mode of executing them.

But the constitution of the United States has not left the right of Congress to employ the necessary means, for the execution of the powers conferred on the government, to general reasoning. To its enumeration of powers is added that of making "all laws which shall be necessary and proper, for carrying into execution the foregoing powers, and all other powers vested by this constitution, in the government of the United States, or in any department thereof."

The counsel for the State of Maryland have urged various arguments, to prove that this clause, though in terms a grant of power, is not so in effect; but is really restrictive of the general right, which might otherwise be implied, of selecting means for executing the enumerated powers. . . .

[T]he argument on which most reliance is placed, is drawn from the peculiar language of this clause. Congress is not empowered by it to make all laws, which may have relation to the powers conferred on the government, but such only as may be *"necessary and proper"* for carrying them into execution. The word *"necessary"* is considered as controlling the whole sentence, and as limiting the right to pass laws for the execution of the granted powers, to such as are indispensable, and without which the power would be nugatory. That it excludes the choice of means, and leaves to Congress, in each case, that only which is most direct and simple.

Is it true, that this is the sense in which the word "necessary" is always used? Does it always import an absolute physical necessity, so strong, that one thing, to which another may be termed necessary, cannot exist without that other? We think it does not. If reference be had to its use, in the common affairs of the world, or in approved authors, we find that it frequently imports no more than that one thing is convenient, or useful, or essential to another. To employ the means necessary to an end, is generally understood as employing any means calculated to produce the end, and not as being confined to those single means, without which the end would be entirely unattainable. Such is the character of human language, that no word conveys to the mind, in all situations, one single definite idea; and nothing is more common than to use words in a figurative sense. Almost all compositions contain words, which, taken in their rigorous sense, would convey a meaning different from that which is obviously intended. It is essential to just construction, that many words which import something excessive should be understood in a more mitigated sense—in that sense which common usage justifies. The word "necessary" is of this description. It has not a fixed character peculiar to itself. It admits of all degrees of comparison; and is often connected with other words, which increase or diminish the impression

the mind receives of the urgency it imports.   A thing may be necessary, very necessary, absolutely or indispensably necessary.   To no mind would the same idea be conveyed by these several phrases.   This comment on the word is well illustrated by the passage cited at the bar, from the 10th section of the 1st article of the constitution.   It is, we think, impossible to compare the sentence which prohibits a State from laying "imposts, or duties on imports or exports, except what may be *absolutely* necessary for executing its inspection laws," with that which authorizes Congress "to make all laws which shall be necessary and proper for carrying into execution" the powers of the general government, without feeling a conviction that the convention understood itself to change materially the meaning of the word "necessary," by prefixing the word "absolutely."   This word, then, like others, is used in various senses; and, in its construction, the subject, the context, the intention of the person using them, are all to be taken into view.

Let this be done in the case under consideration.   The subject is the execution of those great powers on which the welfare of a nation essentially depends.   It must have been the intention of those who gave these powers, to insure, as far as human prudence could insure, their beneficial execution. This could not be done by confiding the choice of means to such narrow limits as not to leave it in the power of Congress to adopt any which might be appropriate, and which were conducive to the end.   This provision is made in a constitution intended to endure for ages to come, and, consequently, to be adapted to the various *crises* of human affairs.   To have prescribed the means by which government should, in all future time, execute its powers, would have been to change, entirely, the character of the instrument, and give it the properties of a legal code.   It would have been an unwise attempt to provide, by immutable rules, for exigencies which, if foreseen at all, must have been seen dimly, and which can be best provided for as they occur.   To have declared that the best means shall not be used, but those alone without which the power given would be nugatory, would have been to deprive the legislature of the capacity to avail itself of experience, to exercise its reason, and to accommodate its legislation to circumstances.   If we apply this principle of construction to any of the powers of the government, we shall find it so pernicious in its operation that we shall be compelled to discard it.   .   .   .

So, with respect to the whole penal code of the United States: whence arises the power to punish in cases not prescribed by the constitution?   All admit that the government may, legitimately, punish any violation of its laws;   and yet, this is not among the enumerated powers of Congress.   The right to enforce the observance of law, by punishing its infraction, might be denied with the more plausibility, because it is expressly given in some cases. Congress is empowered "to provide for the punishment of counterfeiting the securities and current coin of the United States," and "to define and punish piracies and felonies committed on the high seas, and offences against the law of nations."   The several powers of Congress may exist, in a very imperfect state to be sure, but they may exist and be carried into execution, although no punishment should be inflicted in cases where the right to punish is not expressly given.

Take, for example, the power "to establish post offices and post roads." This power is executed by the single act of making the establishment.   But,

from this has been inferred the power and duty of carrying the mail along the post road, from one post office to another. And, from this implied power, has again been inferred the right to punish those who steal letters from the post office, or rob the mail. It may be said, with some plausibility, that the right to carry the mail, and to punish those who rob it, is not indispensably necessary to the establishment of a post office and post road. This right is indeed essential to the beneficial exercise of the power, but not indispensably necessary to its existence. So, of the punishment of the crimes of stealing or falsifying a record or process of a Court of the United States, or of perjury in such Court. To punish these offences is certainly conducive to the due administration of justice. But courts may exist, and may decide the causes brought before them, though such crimes escape punishment.

The baneful influence of this narrow construction on all the operations of the government, and the absolute impracticability of maintaining it without rendering the government incompetent to its great objects, might be illustrated by numerous examples drawn from the constitution, and from our laws. The good sense of the public has pronounced, without hesitation, that the power of punishment appertains to sovereignty, and may be exercised whenever the sovereign has a right to act, as incidental to his constitutional powers. It is a means for carrying into execution all sovereign powers, and may be used, although not indispensably necessary. It is a right incidental to the power, and conducive to its beneficial exercise.

If this limited construction of the word "necessary" must be abandoned in order to punish, whence is derived the rule which would reinstate it, when the government would carry its powers into execution by means not vindictive in their nature? If the word "necessary" means "needful," "requisite," "essential," "conducive to," in order to let in the power of punishment for the infraction of law; why is it not equally comprehensive when required to authorize the use of means which facilitate the execution of the powers of government without the infliction of punishment?

In ascertaining the sense in which the word "necessary" is used in this clause of the constitution, we may derive some aid from that with which it is associated. Congress shall have power "to make all laws which shall be necessary and *proper* to carry into execution" the powers of the government. If the word "necessary" was used in that strict and rigorous sense for which the counsel for the State of Maryland contend, it would be an extraordinary departure from the usual course of the human mind, as exhibited in composition, to add a word, the only possible effect of which is to qualify that strict and rigorous meaning; to present to the mind the idea of some choice of means of legislation not straitened and compressed within the narrow limits for which gentlemen contend.

But the argument which most conclusively demonstrates the error of the construction contended for by the counsel for the State of Maryland, is founded on the intention of the Convention, as manifested in the whole clause. To waste time and argument in proving that, without it, Congress might carry its powers into execution, would be not much less idle than to hold a lighted taper to the sun. As little can it be required to prove, that in the absence of this clause, Congress would have some choice of means. That it might employ those which, in its judgment, would most advantageously effect the ob-

ject to be accomplished.   That any means adapted to the end, any means which tended directly to the execution of the constitutional powers of the government, were in themselves constitutional.   This clause, as construed by the State of Maryland, would abridge, and almost annihilate this useful and necessary right of the legislature to select its means.   That this could not be intended, is, we should think, had it not been already controverted, too apparent for controversy.   We think so for the following reasons:

1st.   The clause is placed among the powers of Congress, not among the limitations on those powers.

2nd.   Its terms purport to enlarge, not to diminish the powers vested in the government.   It purports to be an additional power, not a restriction on those already granted.   .   .   .   Had the intention been to make this clause restrictive, it would unquestionably have been so in form as well as in effect.

The result of the most careful and attentive consideration bestowed upon this clause is, that if it does not enlarge, it cannot be construed to restrain the powers of Congress, or to impair the right of the legislature to exercise its best judgment in the selection of measures to carry into execution the constitutional powers of the government.   If no other motive for its insertion can be suggested, a sufficient one is found in the desire to remove all doubts respecting the right to legislate on that vast mass of incidental powers which must be involved in the constitution, if that instrument be not a splendid bauble.

We admit, as all must admit, that the powers of the government are limited, and that its limits are not to be transcended.   But we think the sound construction of the constitution must allow to the national legislature that discretion, with respect to the means by which the powers it confers are to be carried into execution, which will enable that body to perform the high duties assigned to it, in the manner most beneficial to the people.   Let the end be legitimate, let it be within the scope of the constitution, and all means which are appropriate, which are plainly adapted to that end, which are not prohibited, but consist with the letter and spirit of the constitution, are constitutional.

That a corporation must be considered as a means not less usual, not of higher dignity, not more requiring a particular specification than other means, has been sufficiently proved.   [B]eing considered merely as a means, to be employed only for the purpose of carrying into execution the given powers, there could be no motive for particularly mentioning it.   .   .   .   If a corporation may be employed indiscriminately with other means to carry into execution the powers of the government, no particular reason can be assigned for excluding the use of a bank, if required for its fiscal operations.   To use one, must be within the discretion of Congress, if it be an appropriate mode of executing the powers of government.   That it is a convenient, a useful, and essential instrument in the prosecution of its fiscal operations, is not now a subject of controversy.   All those who have been concerned in the administration of our finances, have concurred in representing its importance and necessity; and so strongly have they been felt, that statesmen of the first class, whose previous opinions against it had been confirmed by every circumstance which can fix the human judgment, have yielded those

opinions to the exigencies of the nation. . . . The time has passed away when it can be necessary to enter into any discussion in order to prove the importance of this instrument, as a means to effect the legitimate objects of the government.

But, were its necessity less apparent, none can deny its being an appropriate measure; and if it is, the degree of its necessity, as has been very justly observed, is to be discussed in another place. Should Congress, in the execution of its powers, adopt measures which are prohibited by the constitution; or should Congress, under the pretext of executing its powers, pass laws for the accomplishment of objects not entrusted to the government; it would become the painful duty of this tribunal, should a case requiring such a decision come before it, to say that such an act was not the law of the land. But where the law is not prohibited, and is really calculated to effect any of the objects entrusted to the government, to undertake here to inquire into the degree of its necessity, would be to pass the line which circumscribes the judicial department, and to tread on legislative ground. This court disclaims all pretensions to such a power.

After this declaration, it can scarcely be necessary to say that the existence of State banks can have no possible influence on the question. No trace is to be found in the constitution of an intention to create a dependence of the government of the Union on those of the States, for the execution of the great powers assigned to it. Its means are adequate to its ends; and on those means alone was it expected to rely for the accomplishment of its ends. To impose on it the necessity of resorting to means which it cannot control, which another government may furnish or withhold, would render its course precarious, the result of its measures uncertain, and create a dependence on other governments, which might disappoint its most important designs, and is incompatible with the language of the constitution. But were it otherwise, the choice of means implies a right to choose a national bank in preference to State banks, and Congress alone can make the election.

After the most deliberate consideration, it is the unanimous and decided opinion of this Court, that the act to incorporate the Bank of the United States is a law made in pursuance of the constitution, and is a part of the supreme law of the land.

The branches, proceeding from the same stock, and being conducive to the complete accomplishment of the object, are equally constitutional. It would have been unwise to locate them in the charter, and it would be unnecessarily inconvenient to employ the legislative power in making those subordinate arrangements. The great duties of the bank are prescribed; those duties require branches; and the bank itself may, we think, be safely trusted with the selection of places where those branches shall be fixed; reserving always to the government the right to require that a branch shall be located where it may be deemed necessary.

It being the opinion of the Court, that the act incorporating the bank is constitutional; and that the power of establishing a branch in the State of Maryland might be properly exercised by the bank itself, we proceed to inquire—

2. Whether the State of Maryland may, without violating the constitution, tax that branch? *

That the power of taxation is one of vital importance; that it is retained by the States; that it is not abridged by the grant of a similar power to the government of the Union; that it is to be concurrently exercised by the two governments: are truths which have never been denied. But, such is the paramount character of the constitution, that its capacity to withdraw any subject from the action of even this power, is admitted. The States are expressly forbidden to lay any duties on imports or exports, except what may be absolutely necessary for executing their inspection laws. If the obligation of this prohibition must be conceded—if it may restrain a State from the exercise of its taxing power on imports and exports; the same paramount character would seem to restrain, as it certainly may restrain, a State from such other exercise of this power, as is in its nature incompatible with, and repugnant to, the constitutional laws of the Union. A law, absolutely repugnant to another, as entirely repeals that other as if express terms of repeal were used.

On this ground the counsel for the bank place its claim to be exempted from the power of a State to tax its operations. There is no express provision for the case, but the claim has been sustained on a principle which so entirely pervades the constitution, is so intermixed with the materials which compose it, so interwoven with its web, so blended with its texture, as to be incapable of being separated from it, without rending it into shreds.

This great principle is, that the constitution and the laws made in pursuance thereof are supreme; that they control the constitution and laws of the respective States, and cannot be controlled by them. From this, which may be almost termed an axiom, other propositions are deduced as corollaries, on the truth or error of which, and on their application to this case, the cause has been supposed to depend. These are, 1st. that a power to create implies a power to preserve. 2nd. That a power to destroy, if wielded by a different hand, is hostile to, and incompatible with these powers to create and to preserve. 3d. That where this repugnancy exists, that authority which is supreme must control, not yield to that over which it is supreme.
. . .

That the power of taxing [the bank] by the States may be exercised so as to destroy it, is too obvious to be denied. But taxation is said to be an absolute power, which acknowledges no other limits than those expressly prescribed in the constitution, and like sovereign power of every other description, is trusted to the discretion of those who use it. But the very terms of this argument admit that the sovereignty of the State, in the article of taxation itself, is subordinate to, and may be controlled by, the constitution of the United States. How far it has been controlled by that instrument must be a question of construction. In making this construction, no principle not declared, can be admissable, which would defeat the legitimate operations of a supreme government. It is of the very essence of supremacy to remove

---

* Consideration of the details of Marshall's answer to this second question can be postponed to the further exploration of the problem of federal immunities from state legislation in chap. 6 (Intergovernmental Immunities and Interstate Relationships), below.

all obstacles to its action within its own sphere, and so to modify every power vested in subordinate governments, as to exempt its own operations from their own influence. This effect need not be stated in terms. It is so involved in the declaration of supremacy, so necessarily implied in it, that the expression of it could not make it more certain. We must, therefore, keep it in view while construing the constitution.

The argument on the part of the State of Maryland is, not that the States may directly resist a law of Congress, but that they may exercise their acknowledged powers upon it, and that the constitution leaves them this right in the confidence that they will not abuse it.

Before we proceed to examine this argument, and to subject it to the test of the constitution, we must be permitted to bestow a few considerations on the nature and extent of this original right of taxation, which is acknowledged to remain with the States. It is admitted that the power of taxing the people and their property is essential to the very existence of government, and may be legitimately exercised on the objects to which it is applicable, to the utmost extent to which the government may choose to carry it. The only security against the abuse of this power, is found in the structure of the government itself. In imposing a tax the legislature acts upon its constituents. This is in general a sufficient security against erroneous and oppressive taxation.

The people of a State, therefore, give to their government a right of taxing themselves and their property, and as the exigencies of government cannot be limited, they prescribe no limits to the exercise of this right, resting confidently on the interest of the legislator, and on the influence of the constituents over their representative, to guard them against its abuse. But the means employed by the government of the Union have no such security, nor is the right of a State to tax them sustained by the same theory. Those means are not given by the people of a particular State, not given by the constituents of the legislature, which claim the right to tax them, but by the people of all the States. They are given by all, for the benefit of all—and upon theory, should be subjected to that government only which belongs to all.

It may be objected to this definition, that the power of taxation is not confined to the people and property of a State. It may be exercised upon every object brought within its jurisdiction.

This is true. But to what source do we trace this right? It is obvious, that it is an incident of sovereignty, and is co-extensive with that to which it is an incident. All subjects over which the sovereign power of a State extends, are objects of taxation; but those over which it does not extend, are, upon the soundest principles, exempt from taxation. This proposition may almost be pronounced self-evident.

The sovereignty of a State extends to everything which exists by its own authority, or is introduced by its permission; but does it extend to those means which are employed by Congress to carry into execution powers conferred on that body by the people of the United States? We think it demonstrable that it does not. Those powers are not given by the people of a single State. They are given by the people of the United States, to a

government whose laws, made in pursuance of the constitution, are declared to be supreme. Consequently, the people of a single State cannot confer a sovereignty which will extend over them.

If we measure the power of taxation residing in a State, by the extent of sovereignty which the people of a single State possess, and can confer on its government, we have an intelligible standard, applicable to every case to which the power may be applied. We have a principle which leaves the power of taxing the people and property of a State unimpaired; which leaves to a State the command of all its resources, and which places beyond its reach, all those powers which are conferred by the people of the United States on the government of the Union, and all those means which are given for the purpose of carrying those powers into execution. We have a principle which is safe for the States, and safe for the Union. We are relieved, as we ought to be, from clashing sovereignty; from interfering powers; from a repugnancy between a right in one government to pull down what there is an acknowledged right in another to build up; from the incompatibility of a right in one government to destroy what there is a right in another to preserve. We are not driven to the perplexing inquiry, so unfit for the judicial department, what degree of taxation is the legitimate use, and what degree may amount to the abuse of the power. The attempt to use it on the means employed by the government of the Union, in pursuance of the constitution, is itself an abuse, because it is the usurpation of a power which the people of a single State cannot give.

We find, then, on just theory, a total failure of this original right to tax the means employed by the government of the Union, for the execution of its powers. The right never existed, and the question whether it has been surrendered, cannot arise.

But, waiving this theory for the present, let us resume the inquiry, whether this power can be exercised by the respective States, consistently with a fair construction of the constitution?

That the power to tax involves the power to destroy; that the power to destroy may defeat and render useless the power to create; that there is a plain repugnance, in conferring on one government a power to control the constitutional measures of another, which other, with respect to those very measures, is declared to be supreme over that which exerts the control, are propositions not to be denied. But all inconsistencies are to be reconciled by the magic of the word CONFIDENCE. Taxation, it is said, does not necessarily and unavoidably destroy. To carry it to the excess of destruction would be an abuse, to presume which, would banish that confidence which is essential to all government.

But is this a case of confidence? Would the people of any one State trust those of another with a power to control the most insignificant operations of their State government? We know they would not. Why, then, should we suppose that the people of any one State should be willing to trust those of another with a power to control the operations of a government to which they have confided their most important and most valuable interests? In the legislature of the Union alone, are all represented. The legislature of the Union alone, therefore, can be trusted by the people with the power of controlling measures which concern all, in the confidence that it will not be

abused. This, then, is not a case of confidence, and we must consider it as it really is.

If we apply the principle for which the State of Maryland contends, to the constitution generally, we shall find it capable of changing totally the character of that instrument. We shall find it capable of arresting all the measures of the government, and of prostrating it at the foot of the States. The American people have declared their constitution, and the laws made in pursuance thereof, to be supreme; but this principle would transfer the supremacy, in fact, to the States.

If the States may tax one instrument, employed by the government in the execution of its powers, they may tax any and every other instrument. They may tax the mail; they may tax the mint; they may tax patent rights; they may tax the papers of the custom-house; they may tax judicial process; they may tax all the means employed by the government, to an excess which would defeat all the ends of government. This was not intended by the American people. They did not design to make their government dependent on the States. . . .

. . . This is not all. If the controling power of the States be established; if their supremacy as to taxation be acknowledged; what is to restrain their exercising this control in any shape they may please to give it? Their sovereignty is not confined to taxation. That is not the only mode in which it might be displayed. The question is, in truth, a question of supremacy; and if the right of the States to tax the means employed by the general government be conceded, the declaration that the constitution, and the laws made in pursuance thereof, shall be the supreme law of the land, is empty and unmeaning declamation. . . .

It has also been insisted, that, as the power of taxation in the general and State governments is acknowledged to be concurrent, every argument which would sustain the right of the general government to tax banks chartered by the States, will equally sustain the right of the States to tax banks chartered by the general government.

But the two cases are not on the same reason. The people of all the States have created the general government, and have conferred upon it the general power of taxation. The people of all the States, and the States themselves, are represented in Congress, and, by their representatives, exercise this power. When they tax the chartered institutions of the States, they tax their constituents; and these taxes must be uniform. But, when a State taxes the operations of the government of the United States, it acts upon institutions created, not by their own constituents, but by people over whom they claim no control. It acts upon the measures of a government created by others as well as themselves, for the benefit of others in common with themselves. The difference is that which always exists, and always must exist, between the action of the whole on a part, and the action of a part on the whole—between the laws of a government declared to be supreme, and those of a government which, when in opposition to those laws, is not supreme.

But if the full application of this argument could be admitted, it might bring into question the right of Congress to tax the State banks, and could not prove the right of the States to tax the Bank of the United States.

The Court has bestowed on this subject its most deliberate consideration. The result is a conviction that the States have no power, by taxation or otherwise, to retard, impede, burden, or in any manner control, the operations of the constitutional laws enacted by Congress to carry into execution the powers vested in the general government. This is, we think, the unavoidable consequence of that supremacy which the constitution has declared.

We are unanimously of opinion, that the law passed by the legislature of Maryland, imposing a tax on the Bank of the United States, is unconstitutional and void.

This opinion does not deprive the States of any resources which they originally possessed. It does not extend to a tax paid by the real property of the bank, in common with the other real property within the State, nor to a tax imposed on the interest which the citizens of Maryland may hold in this institution, in common with other property of the same description throughout the State. But this is a tax on the operations of the bank, and is, consequently, a tax on the operation of an instrument employed by the government of the Union to carry its powers into execution. Such a tax must be unconstitutional.

[Reversed.]

IMPLIED POWERS AND THE NECESSARY AND PROPER CLAUSE—THE HISTORICAL CONTEXT

Introduction. The nation was thirty years old when the Bank case came to the Supreme Court. The issues presented were not novel ones in 1819: both the specific question of the constitutionality of the Bank and the general one regarding the scope of national powers had been repeatedly debated since the beginning. These notes can only suggest some of the highlights of the contentions before 1819 and during the following decade. But the McCulloch decision, important as it is, was no more the end than the beginning of the debate. The scope of the national legislature's authority to reach local affairs is a characteristic, never-ending problem of our federal system. It continues to breed conflicts and to generate searches for new accommodations; and the next two chapters will trace some of these conflicts and accommodations from Marshall's day to ours.

1. *The allocation of powers in the Articles of Confederation and the Constitution.* a. *The Confederation.* The American federal structure allocates powers between nation and states by enumerating the powers delegated to the national government and acknowledging the retention by the states of the remainder. That allocation technique did not originate at the Constitutional Convention. The Articles of Confederation followed a similar scheme. What the Convention contributed was an expansion of enumerated national powers to remedy perceived weaknesses under the Articles. Thus, the most important enumeration of congressional powers in the Constitution, Art. I, § 8, had a counterpart quite similar in form if not in scope in one of the Articles of Confederation:

"Article IX. The United States in Congress assembled, shall have the sole and exclusive right and power of determining on peace and war,

. . . —of sending and receiving ambassadors—entering into treaties and alliances, provided that no treaty of commerce shall be made whereby the legislative power of the respective States shall be restrained from imposing such imposts and duties on foreigners, as their own people are subjected to, or from prohibiting the exportation or importation of any species of goods or commodities whatsoever—of establishing rules for deciding in all cases, what captures on land or water shall be legal, and in what manner prizes taken by land or naval forces in the service of the United States shall be divided or appropriated—of granting letters of marque and reprisal in times of peace— appointing courts for the trial of piracies and felonies committed on the high seas and establishing courts for receiving and determining finally appeals in all cases of captures . . . .

"The United States in Congress assembled shall also have the sole and exclusive right and power of regulating the alloy and value of coin struck by their own authority, or by that of the respective States—fixing the standard of weights and measures throughout the United States—regulating the trade and managing all affairs with the Indians, not members of any of the States, provided that the legislative right of any State within its own limits be not infringed or violated—establishing or regulating post-offices from one State to another, throughout all the United States, and exacting such postage on the papers passing thro' the same as may be requisite to defray the expenses of the said office—appointing all officers of the land forces, in the service of the United States, excepting regimental officers—appointing all the officers of the naval forces, and commissioning all officers whatever in the service of the United States—making rules for the government and regulation of the said land and naval forces, and directing their operations. . . . ."

Note also the acknowledgment of power retained by the states in Art. II of the Articles, asserting that each state retained "every Power, Jurisdiction and right, which is not by this confederation expressly delegated to the United States." That provision had its counterpart in the Tenth Amendment of the Constitution, which omits the adverb "expressly" in assuring that the "powers not delegated to the United States" nor prohibited to the States "are reserved to the States respectively, or to the people." [Recall Marshall's reference to that change in the McCulloch opinion.] The move from Articles to Constitution was not, then, one from a central government of no powers to one with all powers; rather, it was a shift from one with less powers to one with more powers (and with improved machinery to enforce those powers, through a separate national executive and judiciary). And the Tenth Amendment was designed to allay fears that were an understandable concomitant of greater powers, fears frequently expressed in the ratification debates: the fears of an excessively powerful, excessively centralized national government.

Note the differences between the congressional power grants in the two documents. The most important new specifications were the grants of the power to levy taxes and regulate interstate and foreign commerce. It was the lack of those powers (the Confederation's funds, for example, came from the states, who had the sole power to impose taxes) that had been most widely blamed for the failures of the Articles. It was failures like these that were

central in the survey of the "insufficiency of the present Confederation to the preservation of the Union" in the Federalist Papers, and that led Hamilton to ask in Federalist No. 15: "[W]hat indication is there of national disorder, poverty, and insignificance that could befall a community so peculiarly blessed with natural advantages as we are, which does not form a part of the dark catalogue of our public misfortunes?"

b. *The Constitutional Convention.* Consensus that the new Constitution should strengthen national powers did not inevitably mean that a more ample enumeration of powers would be the chosen technique. Rather than building on the enumeration format of the Articles, a simpler, more general, more inclusive statement of congressional powers was conceivable. That, indeed, was the approach the Convention adopted initially. Is it significant that the specification route was ultimately followed in Art. I? At the Convention, the Virginia plan proposed "[t]hat the National Legislature ought to be empowered to enjoy the Legislative Rights vested in Congress by the Confederation; and moreover to legislate in all cases, to which the separate States are incompetent, or in which the harmony of the united States may be interrupted by exercise of individual legislation." And the Convention delegates, indeed, twice voted for formulations in similarly general terms. See I Farrand, The Records of the Federal Convention of 1787 (1911), 47, 53; II id. 21. The ultimate scheme of Art. I, § 8,—specifying the granted powers and ending with the Necessary and Proper Clause in paragraph 18— originated in the Convention's Committee of Detail.

There was virtually no discussion of the Necessary and Proper Clause at the Convention. Many of the fears of a powerful central government during the ratification discussions focused on that Clause, however. Defenders of the Constitution—such as Hamilton and Madison—insisted that the Clause was "harmless" and that objections to it were a "pretext." As Madison explained in No. 44 of the Federalist Papers: "Had the Constitution been silent on this head, there can be no doubt that all the particular powers, requisite as means of executing the general powers would have resulted to the government, by unavoidable implication." Recall the McCulloch opinion.

2. *The Jefferson–Hamilton debate on the Bank in 1791.* With the establishment of the new government, agreement on the general formulations among the supporters of the new Constitution soon gave way to conflict on applications. The best known dispute in Washington's Administration warrants special attention: it was characteristic of the emerging conflicts between broad and narrow constructionists; and it focused on the very issue that ultimately came to the Court in McCulloch—and provided some of the ideological heritage that found its way into Marshall's opinion on the constitutionality of the Bank.

In December 1790, Alexander Hamilton, Washington's Secretary of the Treasury, sent to the House of Representatives a lengthy Report urging the incorporation of a national bank. He listed as among its principal advantages "[t]he augmentation of the active or productive capital," a greater "facility as to the government in obtaining pecuniary aids, especially in sudden emergencies," and the "facilitating of the payment of taxes." Less than two months later, Congress enacted a law creating the First Bank of the United States— a law much like the one passed in 1816 and sustained in McCulloch. While

the bill was on Washington's desk, the President requested opinions on constitutionality from Attorney General Edmund Randolph, Secretary of State Thomas Jefferson, and Alexander Hamilton. Randolph's first response stated that the measure was unconstitutional. Jefferson's answer agreed with Randolph's result, but Hamilton insisted that his project was constitutional. The President followed his Treasury Secretary's advice. Excerpts from the Jefferson and Hamilton opinions follow.

Jefferson:

I consider the foundation of the Constitution as laid on this ground: That "all powers not delegated to the United States, by the Constitution, nor prohibited by it to the States, are reserved to the States or to the people." . . . To take a single step beyond the boundaries thus specially drawn around the powers of Congress, is to take possession of a boundless field of power, no longer susceptible of any definition.

The incorporation of a bank, and the powers assumed by this bill, have not, in my opinion, been delegated to the United States, by the Constitution.

I. They are not among the powers specially enumerated . . . . .

II. Nor are they within either of the general phrases, which are the two following:—

1. To lay taxes to provide for the general welfare of the United States, that is to say, "to lay taxes for *the purpose* of providing for the general welfare." For the laying of taxes is the *power,* and the general welfare the *purpose* for which the power is to be exercised. They are not to lay taxes *ad libitum for any purpose they please*; but only *to pay the debts or provide for the welfare of the Union.* In like manner, they are not *to do anything they please* to provide for the general welfare, but only to *lay taxes* for that purpose. To consider the latter phrase, not as describing the purpose of the first, but as giving a distinct and independent power to do any act they please, which might be for the good of the Union, would render all the preceding and subsequent enumerations of power completely useless.

It would reduce the whole instrument to a single phrase, that of instituting a Congress with power to do whatever would be for the good of the United States; and, as they would be the sole judges of the good or evil, it would be also a power to do whatever evil they please. [See chap. 4, sec. 2, below.] . . .

. . . It is known that the very power now proposed *as a means* was rejected as *an end* by the Convention which formed the Constitution. A proposition was made to them to authorize Congress to open canals, and an amendatory one to empower them to incorporate. But the whole was rejected, and one of the reasons for rejection urged in debate was, that then they would have a power to erect a bank, which would render the great cities, where there were prejudices and jealousies on the subject, adverse to the reception of the Constitution.

2. The second general phrase is, "to make all laws *necessary* and proper for carrying into execution the enumerated powers." But they can all be

carried into execution without a bank.   A bank therefore is not *necessary*, and consequently not authorized by this phrase.

It has been urged that a bank will give great facility or convenience in the collection of taxes.   Suppose this were true: yet the Constitution allows only the means which are *"necessary,"* not those which are merely "convenient" for effecting the enumerated powers.   If such a latitude of construction be allowed to this phrase as to give any non-enumerated power, it will go to every one, for there is not one which ingenuity may not torture into a *convenience* in some instance *or other,* to *some one* of so long a list of enumerated powers.   It would swallow up all the delegated powers, and reduce the whole to one power, as before observed.   Therefore it was that the Constitution restrained them to the *necessary* means, that is to say, to those means without which the grant of power would be nugatory.   .   .   .

Can it be thought that the Constitution intended that for a shade or two of *convenience*, more or less, Congress should be authorised to break down the most ancient and fundamental laws of the several States; such as those against Mortmain, the laws of Alienage, the rules of descent, the acts of distribution, the laws of escheat and forfeiture, the laws of monopoly? Nothing but a necessity invincible by any other means, can justify such a prostitution of laws, which constitute the pillars of our whole system of jurisprudence.   .   .   .

Hamilton:

.   .   .   [I]t is unquestionably incident to *sovereign power* to erect corporations, and consequently to *that* of the United States, in *relation* to the *objects* intrusted to the management of the government.   The difference is this: where the authority of the government is general, it can create corporations in *all cases;* where it is confined to certain branches of legislation, it can create corporations *only* in those cases.   .   .   .

.   .   .   It is conceded that *implied powers* are to be considered as delegated equally with *express ones.*   Then it follows, that as a power of erecting a corporation may as well be *implied* as any other thing, it may as well be employed as an *instrument* or *means* of carrying into execution any of the specified powers, as any other *instrument* or *means* whatever.   The only question must be in this, as in every other case, whether the means to be employed, or, in this instance, the corporation to be erected, has a natural relation to any of the acknowledged objects or lawful ends of the government. Thus a corporation may not be erected by Congress for superintending the police of the city of Philadelphia, because they are not authorized to *regulate* the *police* of that city.   But one may be erected in relation to the collection of taxes, or to the trade with foreign countries, or to the trade between the States, or with the Indian tribes; because it is the province of the Federal Government to *regulate* those objects, and because it is incident to a general *sovereign* or *legislative* power to *regulate* a thing, to employ all the means which relate to its regulation to the best and greatest advantage.

.   .   .   [T]he Secretary of State maintains, that no means are to be considered *necessary* but those without which the grant of the power would be *nugatory.*   Nay, so far does he go in his restrictive interpretation of the

word, as even to make the case of *necessity* which shall warrant the constitutional exercise of the power to depend on *casual* and *temporary* circumstances; an idea which alone refutes the construction. The *expediency* of exercising a particular power, at a particular time, must, indeed, depend on circumstances; but the constitutional right of exercising it must be uniform and invariable, the same today as tomorrow.

All the arguments, therefore, against the constitutionality of the bill derived from the accidental existence of certain State banks—institutions which happen to exist today, and, for aught that concerns the government of the United States, may disappear tomorrow—must not only be rejected as fallacious, but must be viewed as demonstrative that there is a *radical* source of error in the reasoning.

It is essential to the being of the national government, that so erroneous a conception of the meaning of the word *necessary* should be exploded.

It is certain, that neither the grammatical nor popular sense of the term requires that construction. According to both, *necessary* often means no more than *needful, requisite, incidental, useful* or *conducive to.* It is a common mode of expression to say, that it is *necessary* for a government or a person to do this or that thing, when nothing more is intended or understood, than that the interests of the government or person require, or will be promoted by, the doing of this or that thing. The imagination can be at no loss for exemplifications of the use of the word in this sense. And it is the true one in which it is to be understood as used in the Constitution. The whole turn of the clause containing it indicates, that it was the intent of the Convention, by that clause, to give a liberal latitude to the exercise of the specified powers. The expressions have peculiar comprehensiveness. They are, "to make all *laws* necessary and proper for *carrying into execution* the *foregoing powers,* and *all other powers* vested by the Constitution in the *Government* of the United States, or in any *department* or *officer* thereof."

To understand the word as the Secretary of State does, would be to depart from its obvious and popular sense, and to give it a restrictive operation, an idea never before entertained. It would be to give it the same force as if the word *absolutely* or *indispensably* had been prefixed to it.

Such a construction would beget endless uncertainty and embarrassment. The cases must be palpable and extreme, in which it could be pronounced, with certainty, that a measure was absolutely necessary, or one, without which the exercise of a given power would be nugatory. There are few measures of any government which would stand so severe a test. To insist upon it, would be to make the criterion of the exercise of any implied power, a *case of extreme necessity;* which is rather a rule to justify the overleaping of the bounds of constitutional authority, than to govern the ordinary exercise of it. . . .

The *degree* in which a measure is necessary can never be a *test* of the legal right to adopt it; that must be a matter of opinion, and can only be a *test* of expediency. The *relation* between the *measure* and the *end;* between the *nature* of the *means* employed towards the execution of a power, and the object of that power, must be the criterion of constitutionality, not the more or less of *necessity* or *utility.* . . .

This restrictive interpretation of the word *necessary* is also contrary to this sound maxim of construction; namely, that the powers contained in a

constitution of government, especially those which concern the general administration of the affairs of a country, its finances, trade, defence, etc., ought to be construed liberally in advancement of the public good. . . . The means by which national exigencies are to be provided for, national inconveniences obviated, national prosperity promoted, are of such infinite variety, extent, and complexity, that there must of necessity be great latitude of discretion in the selection and application of those means. Hence, consequently, the necessity and propriety of exercising the authorities intrusted to a government on principles of liberal construction. . . .

But while on the one hand the construction of the Secretary of State is deemed inadmissible, it will not be contended, on the other, that the clause in question gives any *new* or *independent* power. But it gives an explicit sanction to the doctrine of *implied powers*, and is equivalent to an admission of the proposition that the government, as to its *specified powers* and *objects*, has plenary and sovereign authority, in some cases paramount to the States; in others, co-ordinate with it. . . .

[The] criterion is the *end*, to which the measure relates as a *means*. If the *end* be clearly comprehended within any of the specified powers, and if the measure have an obvious relation to that *end*, and is not forbidden by any particular provision of the Constitution, it may safely be deemed to come within the compass of the national authority. There is also this further criterion, which may materially assist the decision: Does the proposed measure abridge a pre-existing right of any State or of any individual? If it does not, there is a strong presumption in favor of its constitutionality, and slighter relations to any declared object of the Constitution may be permitted to turn the scale. . . .

Another argument made use of by the Secretary of State is, the rejection of a proposition by the Convention to empower Congress to make corporations, either generally, or for some special purpose. [W]hatever may have been the nature of the proposition, or the reasons for rejecting it, it includes nothing in respect to the real merits of the question. The Secretary of State will not deny that, whatever may have been the intention of the framers of a constitution or of a law, that intention is to be sought for in the instrument itself, according to the usual and established rules of construction. Nothing is more common than for laws to *express* and *effect* more or less than was intended. If, then, a power to erect a corporation in any case be deducible, by fair inference, from the whole or any part of the numerous provisions of the Constitution of the United States, arguments drawn from extrinsic circumstances, regarding the intention of the Convention, must be rejected. . . .

[I]t remains to show the relation of such an institution to one or more of the specified powers of the government. Accordingly it is affirmed that it has a relation, more or less direct, to the power of collecting taxes, to that of borrowing money, to that of regulating trade between the States, and to those of raising and maintaining fleets and armies. To the two former the relation may be said to be immediate; and in the last place it will be argued, that it is clearly within the provision which authorizes the making of all *needful rules and regulations* concerning the *property* of the United States, as the same has been practised upon by the government.

A bank relates to the collection of taxes in two ways—*indirectly*, by increasing the quantity of circulating medium and quickening circulation, which facilitates the means of paying;　directly, by creating a *convenient species* of medium in which they are to be paid. . . .

A bank has a direct relation to the power of borrowing money, because it is a usual, and in sudden emergencies an essential, instrument in the obtaining of loans to government. . . .

The institution of a bank has also a natural relation to the regulation of trade between the States, in so far as it is conducive to the creation of a convenient medium of *exchange* between them, and to the keeping up a full circulation, by preventing the frequent displacement of the metals in reciprocal remittances. . . .

A hope is entertained that it has, by this time, been made to appear, to the satisfaction of the President, that a bank has a natural relation to the power of collecting taxes—to that of regulating trade—to that of providing for the common defence—and that, as the bill under consideration contemplates the government in the light of a joint proprietor of the stock of the bank, it brings the case within the provision of the clause of the Constitution which immediately respects the property of the United States. . . .

3. *Broad and narrow construction: The Jeffersonian positions and the 1805 Marshall reply.* The fear of "consolidation" of powers in the national government did not end with the 1791 Bank controversy.　Indeed, strict construction of congressional authority became a central plank in the opposition platform of the Jeffersonian Republicans later in the decade.　When Jefferson drafted the Kentucky Resolutions, and Madison those of Virginia, in 1798, their protests against the Federalists' Alien and Sedition Laws were not simply defenses of First Amendment freedoms.　The Resolutions also reflected an insistence on states' rights: a protest against the tendency of "the Federal Government to enlarge its powers by forced constructions" (Virginia Resolutions);　a protest against the "construction applied by the general government" to such provisions as the Necessary and Proper Clause, an assertion that "'words meant by [the Constitution] to be subsidiary only to the execution of the limited powers ought not to be so construed as themselves to give unlimited powers" (Kentucky Resolutions).

After the Republicans assumed power in 1801, the responsibilities of their offices compelled Jefferson and Madison to depart from consistent adherence to the strict construction position.　At times, it was left to such orthodox Republicans as John Randolph and John Taylor of Caroline and Spencer Roane to defend the traditional Jeffersonian creed.　Yet, from a number of sources—and for a variety of motives, from philosophical conviction to temporary self-interest—the opposing positions on national powers were kept alive to and beyond the year McCulloch was decided.

The purity of Jefferson's constitutional principles was more apparent in the years before and after his presidential terms than while he was in office.　President Jefferson found it possible, for example, to overcome his constitutional scruples regarding the purchase of Louisiana: though at first he thought it "important, in the present case, to set an example against broad construction," he ultimately dropped his plan to seek a constitutional amendment to ratify his actions: "If . . . our friends shall think differently,

certainly I shall acquiesce with satisfaction; confiding, that the good sense of our country will correct the evil of construction when it shall produce ill effects." See VIII The Writings of Thomas Jefferson (Ford ed.), 248, 262; and, generally, Levy, Jefferson and Civil Liberties—The Darker Side (1963). Compare Jefferson's colorful articulation of strict constructionists' fears when he commented, just before he was elected President, on a bill to grant a federal charter to a mining company: "Congress are authorized to defend the nation. Ships are necessary for defence; copper is necessary for ships; mines, necessary for copper; a company necessary to work the mines; and who can doubt this reasoning who has ever played at 'This is the House that Jack Built'? Under such a process of filiation of necessities the sweeping clause makes clean work." (Quoted in 1 Warren, The Supreme Court in United States History (rev. ed. 1926), 501.) (Note the recurrent manifestations of "House that Jack Built" arguments in the cases below.)

While Jefferson was in the White House, supporters of national legislation continued to maintain that congressional powers should be broadly construed. And an early opinion by Chief Justice Marshall gave support to that position, in a case anticipating the more elaborate discussion in McCulloch. In sustaining a law giving priority, in insolvency cases, to debts owing to the United States, Marshall said: "In construing [the Necessary and Proper Clause] it would be incorrect and would produce endless difficulties, if the opinion should be maintained that no law was authorised which was not indispensably necessary to give effect to a specified power. Where various systems might be adopted for that purpose, it might be said with respect to each, that it was not necessary, because the end might be obtained by other means. Congress must possess the choice of means, and must be empowered to use any means which are in fact conducive to the exercise of a power granted by the constitution." United States v. Fisher, 2 Cranch 358, 396 (1805).

4. *National powers after the War of 1812.* The controversy over the scope of congressional powers intensified in the years immediately before the McCulloch decision. Before and during the War, more and more Federalists hostile to the Jefferson and Madison Administrations began to embrace strict construction theories. By the end of the War, that Party was in its death throes. But proposals for ambitious congressional programs now came from a new generation of Republicans, especially in the short period of nationalistic optimism that followed the end of the War of 1812. Compare the broad-scale national action advocated by Justice Story at the time of Martin v. Hunter's Lessee, as noted above, chap. 1, sec. 3.

The drive to charter the Second Bank of the United States was only a small part of that wave of nationalism. In 1816, for example, John C. Calhoun was still more than a decade away from his role as chief theoretician of the Nullifiers; in 1816, Calhoun was the legislative leader who successfully steered the Bank bill through the House, supported the tariff, and proposed a national system of roads and canals. See generally 1 The Papers of John C. Calhoun (Meriwether ed. 1959). So with Henry Clay: as Speaker of the House early in 1817, he praised Calhoun's roads and canals bill and defended his American System—particularly those "most worthy" subjects, "Internal Improvements and Domestic Manufactures." 2 The Papers of Henry Clay (Hopkins ed. 1961), 308.

Yet each of these nationalistic proposals faced opponents—in Congress, where Daniel Webster was among the critics for a while, in the White House, and in the country at large. Moreover, the opposition arguments were frequently couched in constitutional terms. President Madison, for example, vetoed Calhoun's bill establishing an internal improvements fund from the bonus paid to the United States under the Bank charter. He found "insuperable difficulty [in] reconciling the bill with the Constitution," for authority for the congressional action was not "among the enumerated powers" and did not fall "by any just interpretation" within the Necessary and Proper Clause. (Compare the Butler case, chap. 4, sec. 2, below.) Madison's conscience would not permit him to endorse such a "constructive extension of the powers of Congress," such an "inadmissible latitude of construction." I Messages and Papers of the Presidents (Richardson ed. 1896), 584.

McCulloch v. Maryland, then, was not an abstract or novel exercise in constitutional interpretation. The scope of congressional powers had been a continuous and controversial issue in American debates from the start. The McCulloch opinion added a weighty ingredient to the debate—but the debate continued. President Monroe, for example, vetoed the Cumberland Road Bill in 1822—though the Justices, unofficially (and despite the barrier to advisory opinions), did not agree with his position.* With President John Quincy Adams' election in 1825, a strong supporter of broad congressional powers at last came into office. Thus, Adams' proposals included not only internal improvements but national action in aid of education and science as well (see II id., 311). But by now Congress was reluctant, and the Adams Administration faced increasingly hostile constitutional and political criticism.

Much of the constitutional criticism in the 1820's came from the state legislatures. The resolutions adopted illustrate both the pervasiveness of the criticism and the challenges to McCulloch inherent in the attacks. See generally Ames, State Documents on Federal Relations (1906). Late in 1825, for example, the South Carolina legislature—still years away from Nullification but increasingly discontent with national actions—asked a special committee to report on "the decisions of the federal judiciary and the acts of Congress contravening the letter and spirit of the Constitution." There was little doubt about the prime judicial target: as a similar committee reported two years later "with great pain," the "reasoning of the Court in the case of McCulloch vs. the State of Maryland" was "founded on a misconstruction" of the Constitution. I Statutes at Large of South Carolina 231 (1836). That was the premise that underlay the action of the South Carolina legislature in December 1825, when it adopted the special committee's recommended Resolutions (id., 229):

"1. *Resolved*, That Congress does not possess the power, under the constitution, to adopt a general system of internal improvement as a national measure.

---

* See letter of Justice William Johnson (purporting to report on behalf of his "Brother Judges" as well) to President James Monroe in 1822, ending with the suggestion that "it would not be unproductive of good, if the Secretary of State were to have the opinion of this Court on the Bank question, printed and dispersed through the Union." See 1 Warren, The Supreme Court in United States History (rev. ed. 1926), 597.

"2. *Resolved*, That a right to impose and collect taxes, does not authorize Congress to lay a tax for any other purposes than such as are necessarily embraced in the specific grants of power, and those necessarily implied therein.

"3. *Resolved*, That Congress ought not to exercise a power granted for particular objects, to effect other objects, the right to effect which has never been conceded.

"4. *Resolved*, That it is an unconstitutional exercise of power, on the part of Congress, to tax the citizens of one State to make roads and canals for the citizens of another State.

"5. *Resolved*, That it is an unconstitutional exercise of power, on the part of Congress, to lay duties to protect domestic manufacturers."

The impact of McCulloch v. Maryland extended far beyond the immediate issues of the case, far beyond its own day—not only to South Carolina in the 1820's, but also to the recurrent disputes about the scope of congressional power since. But it is not enough to view McCulloch in its larger setting; a word about the immediate context accordingly follows.

5. *The Bank controversy: Politics and economics.* The expiration of the charter of the First Bank of the United States in 1811 coincided with—and to some extent contributed to—increasing national fiscal difficulties. Financial problems were aggravated during the War of 1812, and demands for a new national bank proliferated. By the end of the War, even President Madison—who, in his 1800 Report on the Virginia Resolutions, had echoed Jefferson's argument that the first Bank was unconstitutional—began to urge consideration of a successor institution: in his Annual Message of December 1815, he advised Congress that "the probable operation of a national bank will merit consideration." I Messages and Papers of the Presidents (Richardson ed. 1896), 566.

The Republicans in Congress did not need that reminder. They had approved a new bank charter almost a year earlier, but the President had vetoed it in January 1815. But the Veto Message demonstrated that the Administration's constitutional position had shifted: while disapproving the details of the bill, President Madison had "waive[d]" the question of congressional power to incorporate a bank, "as being precluded in my judgment by repeated recognitions under varied circumstances of the validity of such an institution in acts of the legislative, executive, and judicial branches of the Government." Id., at 555. In 1816, Congress established a Second Bank acceptable to Madison; and Marshall's 1819 opinion sustaining its constitutionality took pains to remind the nation of Madison's "waiver."

The Bank got off to a flourishing start. In 1817 and for most of 1818, few questions about constitutionality were raised: the country was in a postwar economic boom, trade was active, prices were rising. And the Bank of the United States, which could have exercised some of the regulatory functions of a modern central bank by controlling credit expansion, chose instead to be "liberal" and to encourage the speculative boom. The harsh morning-after was not far off, however: by the fall of 1818, a financial panic and depression shook the economy. The Bank, short of specie reserves, called in its excessive loans—and the debtors, state banks and private individuals,

reacted with understandable anger toward the central "monied power," the "monster" Bank. In October 1818, a congressional investigation of the Bank began, and there was considerable support for repeal of its charter. The January 1819 report of the investigating committee found that the Bank had indeed suffered from loose management under its first president, William Jones. But the charter-repeal move failed in February 1819; instead, Jones resigned and was succeeded by the far more competent Langdon Cheves.

When the McCulloch case came before the Court, then, the Bank was the center of the most heated issue of the congressional session. Moreover, by early 1819, the Baltimore branch of the Bank—one of eighteen branches in existence at the time—was the most controversial of the Bank's operations, for reasons going quite beyond Maryland's tax. As cashier, James McCulloch was no minor functionary: in the Bank's structure, the branch cashiers were the chief executive agents of the central management in Philadelphia. And during the congressional investigation, McCulloch was the Bank's main legislative lobbyist in Washington. He was even more busy at home: the Baltimore branch was the most active of all, and McCulloch and his cohorts—branch president Buchanan and director Williams—were systematically looting the Bank by instigating unsecured loans and by sanctioning unreported overdrafts. Reports of Baltimore misconduct were circulating in Washington by late 1818; by the time the case was argued in March 1819, there were rumors that McCulloch was heavily implicated. But there were also indignant denials of the rumors, and widespread disbelief that McCulloch and his associates had acted improperly. Official charges of misconduct by McCulloch did not come until a month after the Court decision; and in May, Langdon Cheves ordered his removal from office. Criminal proceedings against McCulloch and his associates were brought by Maryland and continued for several years, with Bank counsel aiding the prosecution. But Maryland had no embezzlement statute as yet, and the difficult effort to obtain a common law conspiracy conviction failed.

The banner of national power and supremacy was thus carried by a most unsavory figure, a scoundrel whose schemes cost the Bank more than a million dollars. But the Bank controversy litigated in the McCulloch case was not merely a Baltimore matter. The hard times, and the antipathy of state banks under pressure from the Bank of the United States, produced anti-Bank measures in a number of states—some antedating the Maryland tax law. Indiana and Illinois flatly prohibited banks not chartered by the state. Tennessee, Georgia, North Carolina, Kentucky and Ohio—like Maryland—imposed taxes on "foreign" bank operations—taxes that were typically even more burdensome than Maryland's. Similar efforts in several other state legislatures failed by narrow margins. The Court's decision did not silence all of the attacks: in the face of the McCulloch decision in March, Ohio chose to collect its $50,000 per branch tax by force, in September 1819. Ohio agents seized more than $100,000 from the vaults of the branch Bank in Chillicothe, in order to stimulate a relitigation of the McCulloch issues. The Ohio leaders insisted that the issues had not been adequately and fully aired in the Maryland litigation. It took another Court decision—Osborn v. Bank of the United States, 9 Wheat. 738 (1824)—to settle the Ohio dispute, reaffirm McCulloch, and validate the Bank's statutory authority to sue in the federal courts. By that time, the Bank's difficulties had eased: it was man-

aged more competently—by Cheves' successor, Nicholas Biddle—and the nation had recovered from the depression. Not until the Jackson Administration did the Bank face another severe attack. And the Jackson challenge was fatal: the McCulloch decision was not an adequate shield against President Jackson's veto of the 1832 Bank recharter, and the Bank went out of existence in 1836.*

    6. *The Bank controversy: The constitutional contentions and John Marshall's pseudonymous defense.* By contrast with the often bitter and sometimes bizarre political controversies that engulfed the Bank, the constitutional submissions in the McCulloch case were calm and largely predictable. The arguments for the Bank, by Attorney General Wirt and William Pinkney and Daniel Webster—who had voted against the Bank bill as a Federalist Congressman three years earlier—are, to be sure, reflected in the Marshall opinion. But counsels' arguments were primarily conduits for constitutional contentions that had become staples in debates during the preceding three decades. Though Daniel Webster's reputation was substantially enhanced by his Court arguments in 1819, it was William Pinkney who was the major orator in the McCulloch case. And neither Webster nor Pinkney considered the McCulloch argument the chief challenge of the 1819 Term: they were preoccupied with other cases, especially their possible encounter if the Dartmouth College Case were to be reargued. As Pinkney wrote Webster in December 1818, a preargument "interchange of Ideas" among co-counsel for the Bank seemed unnecessary, since the argument probably would involve "little else than the threadbare topics connected with the constitutionality of the establishment of the Bank."

    The constitutional arguments were not novel, and the pro-Bank holding was no surprise. But to the far-sighted, the case signified more than the immediate result. For John Marshall and his Virginia states' rights critics, especially, what was truly at stake was McCulloch's impact on national programs other than the Bank and, above all, on the general scope of national powers. General principles of constitutional interpretation really mattered the most in the long run. And general principles were central in a fierce ideological newspaper debate that ensued—with Spencer Roane of Virginia as the chief pseudonymous critic in the Richmond Enquirer, and John Marshall himself, for the only time in his career, as chief pseudonymous newspaper defender of the Court.

    Within weeks of the McCulloch decision, the Richmond Enquirer, the chief organ of Virginia states' rights leaders, began publishing elaborate attacks. Marshall saw in them a revival of the feared strict constructionist principles of 1798: if they prevailed, "the constitution would be converted into the old confederation." The Chief Justice, afraid that no one else would make an adequate defense, took to the newspapers himself. In April 1819, he wrote two essays for a Philadelphia paper. But then Judge Spencer Roane —the chief participant in the defiant state court decision that was reversed in Martin v. Hunter's Lessee and a leading Virginia politician as well as ideologue—sharply attacked McCulloch in a series of essays signed "Hampden."

---

* For additional background on the Bank controversy, see Catterall, The Second Bank of the United States (1902), and Hammond, Banks and Politics in America—From the Revolution to the Civil War (1957).

Marshall, his letters disclose, found himself "more stimulated on this subject than on any other because I believe the design to be to injure the Judges & impair the constitution." Anxious and intense, he hastily wrote nine elaborate essays that were published in the Alexandria Gazette over the pseudonym "A Friend of the Constitution." [For these recently discovered essays and their background, see Gunther (ed.), John Marshall's Defense of McCulloch v. Maryland (1969).]

The Bank aspects of the case are hardly mentioned in this newspaper battle, either by the attackers or by Marshall. As Marshall realized, it was doctrine, not result, that troubled the Virginians: they would have preferred "an obsequious, silent opinion without reasons"; it was "our heretical reasoning" that was "pronounced most damnable." And it was that reasoning that concerned Marshall most: he defended it against charges that it legitimated unlimited congressional powers; he denied that McCulloch endorsed consolidation; he insisted that the decision struck a moderate balance between excessively broad and unduly narrow conceptions of national powers. (His elaborations are considered further in the next group of notes.)

7. *The national bank—A "private" or "public" institution?* a. *In 1819.* Note that Marshall in McCulloch said very little about the organization and operations of the Bank. Should he have said more? Recall also that the Bank's success was considerably greater during its prosperous first year, than in the depression months immediately preceding the decision. Could the 1819 circumstances have been relied on to challenge the constitutionality of the Bank, if the 1816 context provided substantial basis for the congressional judgment to charter the Bank? (See also the further questions about Marshall's opinion in the next group of notes.)

The Bank was manifestly not a purely governmental operation—not like a mint or an army fort. As long ago as 1790, Hamilton had argued, in proposing a national bank: "To attach full confidence to an institution of this nature, it appears to be an essential ingredient in its structure, that it shall be under a *private* not a *public* direction—under the guidance of *individual interest*, not of *public policy*." Any suspicion that the nationally chartered bank was "too much influenced by *public necessity*," he asserted, would "be a canker that would continually corrode the vitals of the credit of the bank." He added: "The keen, steady, and, as it were, magnetic sense of their own interest as proprietors, in the directors of a bank, pointing invariably to its true pole—the prosperity of the institution,—is the only security that can always be relied upon for a careful and prudent administration" and for "permanent confidence" in the bank. (Hamilton's Report to the House on a National Bank, December 13, 1790.) Obviously, Hamilton and, later, the proponents of the Second Bank of the United States expected substantial governmental benefits from a congressionally chartered bank, as a source of loans, as a depository and fiscal agent, and as a stabilizer of currency. But these benefits were to be byproducts of the bank's operations as a largely private, profit-making, commercial institution.

The charter of the Second Bank, accordingly, provided that eighty percent of the stock ownership and of the directors were to be private; twenty percent of the stock was government-owned, and the President nominated only five of the twenty-five directors. Walter Jones and Joseph Hopkinson

mentioned the "private" nature of the Bank in the course of their argument in McCulloch, though mainly on the question of the Bank's immunity from state taxation rather than its constitutionality under Article I. Were the "private" features relevant, on either question? Should Marshall have discussed them? Compare Plous and Baker, "McCulloch v. Maryland: Right Principle, Wrong Case," 9 Stan.L.Rev. 710 (1957). Should Marshall, moreover, have emphasized that the Maryland tax was discriminatory? (The problem of governmental tax immunities is considered further in chap. 6, below.)

b. *In 1968.* Note the recent comments on these aspects of McCulloch in First Agricultural Nat. Bank v. State Tax Comm'n, 392 U.S. 339 (1968) (see also chap. 6, sec. 1, below). The majority reaffirmed the immunity of national banks from state taxation on statutory grounds and accordingly did not directly confront the state court's position that "the status of national banks has been so changed by the establishment of the Federal Reserve System that they should no longer be considered nontaxable by the States as instrumentalities of the United States." But Justice Thurgood Marshall's dissent, joined by Justices Harlan and Stewart, was prepared to reach the constitutional issue: in light of "the present functions and role of national banks," they should not be considered "constitutionally immune from nondiscriminatory state taxation." McCulloch and other "hoary cases" could "and perhaps should" be read as banning only discriminatory taxes. A modern national bank, he explained, is "a privately owned corporation existing for the private profit of its shareholders. It performs no significant federal governmental function that is not performed equally by state-chartered banks." The Bank of the United States of the McCulloch case was quite different, he insisted: it "would clearly be a federal instrumentality under the Court's most recent discussion of the doctrine."

CONGRESSIONAL POWER, THE JUDICIAL FUNCTION, AND POLITICAL RESTRAINTS

1. *Restraints on congressional power: Some general questions about judicially-imposed limitations.* Consider, in examining the McCulloch opinion and the cases in the next two chapters, what principled limits courts can and should impose to guard against excessive intrusion of national authority into local affairs. Are courts capable of articulating effective federalism-related limits (as distinguished from limits designed to protect individual rights, considered in Part III below)? Or is the imposition of restraints best left largely or wholly to the political process, in view of the representation of local interest in the national government? (See the Wechsler argument in note 3 below.) Did Marshall's McCulloch opinion legitimate an unlimited congressional discretion? In intent? In language? In effect?

a. *Necessary and proper means to achieve enumerated ends: Judicial scrutiny of means-ends relationships.* Do Marshall's formulations regarding means-ends relationships constitute restraints on congressional choices that are judicially enforceable? Marshall spoke of means "which tended directly to the execution" of delegated powers, "means which are appropri-

ate" and "plainly adapted" to achieving legitimate ends. What are the limits on the chains of inferences—on the "House that Jack Built" arguments that Jefferson feared (noted above)—that may be put forth to justify a statute as a "necessary and proper" means to effectuate a granted power? Must that justification be considered by Congress, or may it be supplied subsequent to enactment, by counsel's argument or by the Court's speculation about the justifications a reasonable legislature *might* have relied on? Does the required "reasonable relation"—or "plausible relation"—nexus between means and ends turn on standards of logic? Of empiric observation? Is the required nexus "uniform and invariable, the same today as tomorrow," or does it depend on "circumstances" "at a particular time"? (See Hamilton's argument, noted above.) What "time": Date of enactment? Date of adjudication? *

Marshall wrote his pseudonymous "Friend of the Constitution" essays to counter Spencer Roane's charges that McCulloch gave "a *general* letter of attorney to the future legislators of the union," that in fact "the court had granted to congress unlimited powers under the pretext of a discretion in selecting means." See Gunther (ed.), John Marshall's Defense of McCulloch v. Maryland (1969). Marshall insisted that the required means-ends relationship was a judicially enforceable one, and some of his essays try to restate and elaborate the requirement. For example, "neither a feigned convenience nor a strict necessity; but a reasonable convenience, and a qualified necessity," had to be shown to demonstrate that means were constitutional; means must have "a plain relation to the end," they must be "direct, natural and appropriate." McCulloch, he insisted, denied "the unlimited power of congress to adopt any means whatever." (But to what "ends" *was* the Bank an appropriate "means"? Compare Marshall's cursory treatment of that question in McCulloch with Hamilton's more elaborate statement in 1791. Should Marshall have explored the actual structure and operation of the Bank more fully? Or was he justified in deferring to Congress (and to history) on the issue of the appropriateness of the Bank?)

Despite Marshall's insistence that the means-ends inquiry represented a significant judicial restraint on Congress, was not Roane right after all about the effective scope of congressional discretion after McCulloch, given the exercises of national power sustained by the Court in the cases that follow? Was he not right about the effect of McCulloch, if not about Marshall's purpose? Was that because McCulloch did not seriously look for limits? Because the McCulloch limits were inadequate? Could better limits have been stated? Consider Gunther (ed.), above, at 20: "The degree of centralization that has taken place [since McCulloch] may well have come about in the face of Marshall's intent rather than in accord with his expectations. That centralization may be the inevitable consequence of economic and social changes. And this development may suggest the impossibility of

---

* The problem of judicial scrutiny of means-ends relationships arises not only in the context of federalism limits on congressional power; it recurs throughout this volume. See, e. g., the discussion of a "means-oriented" scrutiny under the due process clause in chap. 9 below, and under the equal protection clause in chap. 10 below and in Gunther, "The Supreme Court, 1971 Term: Foreword: . . . A Model for a Newer Equal Protection," 86 Harv.L.Rev. 1 (1972). See also Flemming v. Nestor, chap. 4, sec. 2, below.

articulating general constitutional standards capable of limiting those central-izing forces, particularly through judicial action. But to say this is very dif-ferent from saying that Marshall knew he was engaging in a hopeless task."

b. *"Pretext": Judicial inquiry into congressional purposes and abuses of power.* In articulating limits on congressional choices, Marshall spoke not only of the required means-ends relationships, but also of congressional pur-poses. Can courts effectively assure legislative good faith in exercising pow-ers? Can and should courts scrutinize the nature and purity of legislative motives? * Marshall asserted in McCulloch—and emphatically reiterated in his newspaper replies to Roane—that the Court would invalidate laws "for the accomplishment of objects, not entrusted to the government," laws enacted "under the pretext" of exercising granted powers. See, e. g., Gunther (ed.), above, at 187; see also Marshall's statement at 173: "It is not pretended that this right of selection [of means] may be fraudulently used to the destruc-tion of the fair land marks of the constitution. Congress certainly may not, under the pretext of collecting taxes, or of guaranteeing to each state a re-publican form of government, alter the law of descents; but if the means have a plain relation to the end—if they be direct, natural and appropriate," they are constitutional.

Is the "pretext" limitation a viable one, capable of judicial enforce-ment? Does it require a judicial determination of the "true" object of the law—of congressional purposes and motives? Are otherwise constitutional laws invalidated by impermissible "pretext" statements by Congress? Do the Art. I, § 8, powers of Congress specify the permissible *aims* of legis-lation, or simply the permissible, objectively determinable *areas* of national regulation? Does the commerce clause, for example, authorize legislative control for any purpose so long as the *field* regulated is that of interstate commerce"? May Congress seek "morality," "police" objectives—may it, e. g., legislate against prostitution or for racial justice or against rioters—so long as the sanction of the law takes hold on some commerce-connected ac-tivity? Or must the regulation be enacted with a primarily commercial pur-pose? Or must the evil being regulated at least have commercial dimensions? May Congress enact a conditional prohibition of interstate movement of goods and persons with a major collateral objective of regulating intrastate activi-ties not directly reachable? [For further pursuit of these problems in the context of the commerce power, see Hammer v. Dagenhart and related ma-terials in chap. 3, below.]

2. *Some additional questions on the Marshall opinion in McCulloch.* a. How useful is Marshall's emphasis on the theme that "it is *a constitu-tion* we are expounding"? † Is that more than a truism? Was anyone deny-

---

* What are the institutional and prac-tical difficulties inhibiting such in-quiries? That problem will recur in later materials in this volume. See, e. g., chaps. 4 and 10, below. See generally, Ely, "Legislative and Ad-ministrative Motivation in Constitu-tional Law," 79 Yale L.J. 1205 (1970), and Brest, "Palmer v. Thompson: An Approach to the Problem of Unconsti-tutional Legislative Motive," 1971 Sup. Ct.Rev. 95.

† Justice Frankfurter once called this "the single most important utterance in the literature of constitutional law—most important because most compre-hensive and comprehending." Frank-furter, "John Marshall and the Ju-dicial Function," 69 Harv.L.Rev. 217 (1955).

ing that? Does the emphasis on *constitutional* interpretation aid in the delineation of implied powers? Is a broad construction of national powers an inevitable consequence of interpreting *"a constitution"*? Could not Spencer Roane and other states' righters have argued that their views, too, had in mind *"a constitution"*—that the Constitution as they interpreted it was no less *"a constitution"* because it provided for tighter controls on national power and greater protection of state authority in a federal scheme of divided sovereignty?

b.   How significant was the Necessary and Proper Clause to Marshall's result? Is it fair to say that he had established his conclusion even before he came to the consideration of that Clause in Art. I, § 8, cl. 18? How persuasive is Marshall's textual and contextual reading of the Necessary and Proper Clause once he reaches it? More broadly, consider the sources of Marshall's interpretation: to some extent he relies on text; to some extent, on history. Is there also considerable emphasis on "inference from the structures and relationships created by the constitution?" See C. L. Black, Jr., Structure and Relationship in Constitutional Law (1969), and chap. 6, sec. 1, below. Note Marshall's reliances on consideration of structure and relationship not only in justifying his views of national powers but also—and even more clearly—in elaborating his position on federal immunities from state legislation. Charles Black's lectures advocate a greater emphasis on structural interpretation as against often "manipulative" textual exegesis. Inferences from structures and relationships are often defensible; but are they more immune from the risk of manipulation than resort to other sources of constitutional interpretation? Cf. Blasi, "Creativity and Legitimacy in Constitutional Law," 80 Yale L.J. 176 (1970).

c.   The question of the Bank's immunity from the state tax is considered further in chap. 6, below; but consider now what the source of that immunity is in Marshall's view: Text? History? Structures and relationships? Marshall's personal nationalist views? Should Marshall have considered more fully, on the question of state taxing power, the practical operations of the Bank, including its largely private ownership? Should he have considered a narrower rule more responsive to Maryland discriminatory tax—a tax not applicable to all banks but only to those not chartered by the State? How farreaching are Marshall's implications as to governmental immunity? How can his principles justify what he suggests in the last paragraph of his opinion: a valid tax on the Bank's real property, or on Maryland citizens' holdings of Bank stock?

3.   *Restraints on congressional power: The Political Safeguards of Federalism.* Consider, in examining the Court's efforts to formulate limiting principles in the cases that follow, whether the need for judicial efforts to safeguard federalism values is minimal in view of the representation of local interests in the political structure of the national government. Do these "political safeguards" operate with equal effectiveness with regard to all kinds of congressional action? As effectively in cases of morals regulation as in cases of economic regulation? As effectively when the spending power is invoked (see chap. 4, sec. 2, below) as with proposals for direct regulation? Consider the following excerpts from Wechsler, "The Political Safeguards of Federalism—The Role of the States in the Composition and Selection of

the National Government," in Principles, Politics, and Fundamental Law (1961), 49–82: *

"Our constitution makers established a central government authorized to act directly upon individuals through its own agencies—and thus they formed a nation capable of function and of growth. To serve the ends of federalism they employed three main devices: (1) They preserved the states as separate sources of authority and organs of administration—a point on which they hardly had a choice. (2) They gave the states a role of great importance in the composition and selection of the central government. (3) They undertook to formulate a distribution of authority between the nation and the states, in terms which gave some scope at least to legal processes for its enforcement.

"Scholarship—not only legal scholarship—has given most attention to the last of these enumerated mechanisms, perhaps because it has been fascinated by the Supreme Court and its interpretations of the power distribution clauses of the Constitution. The continuous existence of the states as governmental entities and their strategic role in the selection of the Congress and the President are so immutable a feature of the system that their importance tends to be ignored. Of the framers' mechanisms, however, they have had and have today the larger influence upon the working balance of our federalism. The actual extent of central intervention in the governance of our affairs is determined far less by the formal power distribution than by the sheer existence of the states and their political power to influence the action of the national authority. . . .

"National action has . . . always been regarded as exceptional in our polity, an intrusion to be justified by some necessity, the special rather than the ordinary case. This point of view cuts even deeper than the concept of the central government as one of granted, limited authority, articulated in the tenth amendment. National power may be quite unquestioned in a given situation; those who would advocate its exercise must none the less answer the preliminary question why the matter should not be left to the states. Even when Congress acts, its tendency has been to frame enactments on an *ad hoc* basis to accomplish limited objectives, supplanting state-created norms only so far as may be necessary for the purpose. Indeed, with all the centralizing growth throughout the years, federal law is still a largely interstitial product, rarely occupying any field completely, building normally upon legal relationships established by the states. As Henry Hart and I have put it elsewhere: 'Congress acts . . . against the background of the total *corpus juris* of the states in much the way that a state legislature acts against the background of the common law, assumed to govern unless changed by legislation.' As a state legislature views the common law as something to be left alone unless a need for change has been established, so Congress has traditionally viewed the governance of matters by the states.

"The tradition plainly serves the values of our federalism in so far as it maintains a burden of persuasion on those favoring national intervention. . . .

* The excerpts are reprinted here with the permission of the publisher, © copyright 1961 by the President and Fellows of Harvard College. The substance of the essay also appears in 54 Colum.L.Rev. 543 (1954) and in Selected Essays 1938–62 (1963), 185.

"If I have drawn too much significance from the mere fact of the existence of the states, the error surely will be rectified by pointing also to their crucial role in the selection and the composition of the national authority. More is involved here than that aspect of the compromise between the larger and the smaller states that yielded their equality of status in the Senate. Representatives no less than Senators are allotted by the Constitution to the states, although their number varies with state population as determined by the census. Though the House was meant to be the 'grand depository of the democratic principle of the government,' as distinguished from the Senate's function as the forum of the states, the people to be represented with due deference to their respective numbers were *the people of the states*. And with the President, as with Congress, the crucial instrument of the selection— whether through electors, or, in the event of failure of majority, by the House voting as state units—is again the states. The consequence, of course, is that the states are the strategic yardsticks for the measurement of interest and opinion, the special centers of political activity, the separate geographical determinants of national as well as local politics. [But see the modern reapportionment decisions, chap. 15, sec. 5, below.] .   .   .

"To the extent that federalist values have real significance they must give rise to local sensitivity to central intervention; to the extent that such a local sensitivity exists, it cannot fail to find reflection in the Congress. Indeed, the problem of the Congress is and always has been to attune itself to national opinion and produce majorities for action called for by the voice of the entire nation. It is remarkable that it should function thus as well as it does, given its intrinsic sensitivity to any insular opinion that is dominant in a substantial number of the states.   .   .   .

"The President must be, as I have said above, the main repository of 'national spirit' in the central government. But both the mode of his selection and the future of his party require that he also be responsive to local values that have large support within the states. And since his programs must, in any case, achieve support in Congress—in so far as they involve new action—he must surmount the greater local sensitivity of Congress before anything is done.

"If this analysis is correct, the national political process in the United States—and especially the role of the states in the composition and selection of the central government—is intrinsically well adapted to retarding or restraining new intrusions by the center on the domain of the states. Far from a national authority that is expansionist by nature, the inherent tendency in our system is precisely the reverse, necessitating the widest support before intrusive measures of importance can receive significant consideration, reacting readily to opposition grounded in resistance within the states. Nor is this tendency effectively denied by pointing to the size or scope of the existing national establishment. However useful it may be to explore possible contractions in specific areas, such evidence points mainly to the magnitude of unavoidable responsibility under the circumstances of our time.

"It is in light of this inherent tendency, reflected most importantly in Congress, that the governmental power distribution clauses of the Constitution gain their largest meaning as an instrument for the protection of the

states. Those clauses, as is well known, have served far more to qualify or stop intrusive legislative measures in the Congress than to invalidate enacted legislation in the Supreme Court.

"This does not differ from the expectation of the framers quite as markedly as might be thought. For the containment of the national authority Madison did not emphasize the function of the Court; he pointed to the composition of the Congress and to the political processes. . . .

"The prime function envisaged for judicial review—in relation to federalism—was the maintenance of national supremacy against nullification or usurpation by the individual states, the national government having no part in their composition or their councils. This is made clear by the fact that reliance on the courts was substituted, apparently on Jefferson's suggestion, for the earlier proposal to give Congress a veto of state enactments deemed to trespass on the national domain. And except for the brief interlude that ended with the crisis of the thirties, it is mainly in the realm of such policing of the states that the Supreme Court has in fact participated in determining the balances of federalism.[1] This is not to say that the Court can decline to measure national enactments by the Constitution when it is called upon to face the question in the course of ordinary litigation; the supremacy clause governs there as well. It is rather to say that the Court is on weakest ground when it opposes its interpretation of the Constitution to that of Congress in the interest of the states, whose representatives control the legislative process and, by hypothesis, have broadly acquiesced in sanctioning the challenged Act of Congress.

"Federal intervention as against the states is thus primarily a matter for congressional determination in our system as it stands. So too, moreover, is the question whether state enactments shall be stricken down as an infringement on the national authority. For while the Court has an important function in this area, as I have noted, the crucial point is that its judgments here are subject to reversal by Congress, which can consent to action by the states that otherwise would be invalidated. The familiar illustrations in commerce and in state taxation of federal instrumentalities do not by any means exhaust the field. The Court makes the decisive judgment only when—and to the extent that—Congress has not laid down the resolving rule.

"To perceive that it is Congress rather than the Court that on the whole is vested with the ultimate authority for managing our federalism is not, of course, to depreciate the role played by the Court, subordinate though it may be. It is no accident that Congress has been slow to exercise its managerial authority, remitting to the Court so much of what it could determine by a legislative rule. The difficulties of reaching agreement on such matters, not

1. "Of the great controversies with respect to national power before the Civil War, only the Bank and slavery within the territories were carried to the Court and its participation with respect to slavery was probably its greatest failure. The question of internal improvements, for example, which raised the most acute problem of constitutional construction, was fought out politically and in Congress. After the War only the Civil Rights Cases and income tax decisions were important in setting limits on national power—until the Child Labor Case and the New Deal decisions. The recasting of constitutional positions since the crisis acknowledges much broader power in the Congress—as against the states—than it is likely soon or ever to employ." [Footnote by Professor Wechsler.]

to speak of drafting problems of immense complexity, lend obvious attractiveness to the *ad hoc* judicial method of adjustment. Whether Congress could contribute more effectively to the solution of these problems is a challenging and open question. The legislative possibilities within this area of our polity have hardly been explored."

A MODERN POSTCRIPT: A LIMITED REPUDIATION OF THE McCULLOCH APPROACH BY THE WARREN COURT?

Introduction: A narrower range of "necessary and proper" means in the individual rights context? The modern Supreme Court has frequently invoked Marshall's McCulloch approach to sustain broad readings of implied powers and to validate a wide congressional discretion to choose among "necessary and proper" means. Tracing that development is a major purpose of the next two chapters. [See especially chap. 3 on national regulation under the commerce power, including, e. g., Wickard v. Filburn (federal farm production controls applied to wheat grown for home consumption), and Katzenbach v. McClung (national ban on racial discrimination in "local" restaurants).] In cases such as those, as in McCulloch, it was federalism considerations that gave rise to the alleged limitations on national power. But the Constitution imposes restraints for reasons other than those stemming from the federal system. Most notably, the Constitution includes a range of individual rights guarantees—the theme of Part III of this book. Should the McCulloch approach to congressional discretion be modified or abandoned when the argued limitation on national power is an individual rights rather than a federalism one? Should the interpretation of the Necessary and Proper Clause change when the objection to a law rests on a non-federalism ground? Those are the central questions raised by the Warren era military jurisdiction cases in this group of notes. The prevailing opinions in these cases do indeed suggest an approach to national powers unlike that in McCulloch. The basic problem raised in these notes is whether that difference is explainable and justifiable.

No doubt, additional considerations properly come into play when exercises of national power impinge on individual rights rather than on federalism restraints. But should that individual rights concern be expressed by recasting Art. I powers and curtailing the McCulloch approach to congressional discretion under Art. I? Or should the concern be articulated more directly, by explicitly elaborating the individual rights limitations? Must the scope of congressional discretion be redefined when opposing interests other than those of localism come into play? Should restrictions on the choice of means rest directly on the constitutional provision (e. g., in the Bill of Rights) that may prohibit one of the possible "appropriate" means, rather than holding the prohibited means "inappropriate" under Art. I? Does it make a difference whether the reason for a ruling of unconstitutionality is (a) that the law is not "appropriate" to the effectuation of a delegated power in Art. I, or (b) that the law, though "appropriate" under

the broad choice legitimated by McCulloch, is barred by another provision of the Constitution, such as the First Amendment or the Fifth Amendment?

To explore these problems of doctrine and judicial technique in a preliminary way warrants this detour in time (to the Warren era) and area (to some individual rights restraints on national powers). The focus of these notes is on a group of Warren Court decisions rejecting congressional efforts to authorize the exercise of military jurisdiction over civilians. The reason for examining these cases here stems far less from their specific holdings than from the Court's approach to national power issues: Are the majority's criteria for delineating the scope of Art. I powers in these cases consistent with the McCulloch approach? Should the Court's rulings of unconstitutionality in these cases have rested directly on the limiting prohibitions protecting individual rights, instead of being articulated as an application of a purportedly general principle regarding the implementation of Art. I powers? Which of the contending positions in these cases is doctrinally sounder? Which is more consistent with the McCulloch approach?

1. *The constitutional framework of the military jurisdiction cases.* Art. I, § 8, cl. 14, empowers Congress "To make Rules for the Government and Regulation of the land and naval Forces." It has long been held that when Congress is properly exercising that power, the normal method of trial in civilian courts provided by Art. III and the Bill of Rights—e. g., trial by jury—is not required. And the Fifth Amendment explicitly exempts "cases arising in the land or naval forces" from the grand jury indictment guarantee. In a series of cases, the Court has refused to sustain governmental efforts to exercise court martial jurisdiction over civilians with some relationship to the armed forces.* For example, in REID v. COVERT, 354 U.S. 1 (1957), the Court had before it a challenge to a provision of the Uniform Code of Military Justice (UCMJ) subjecting to military jurisdiction "all persons serving with, employed by, or accompanying the armed forces without the continental limits of the United States." The Court held that that section could not be constitutionally applied to dependents of servicemen overseas charged with *capital* crimes. Justice Black's plurality opinion in Reid argued that "if the language of Clause 14 is given its natural meaning, the power granted does not extend to civilians—even though they may be dependents living with servicemen on a military base. The term 'land and naval Forces' refers to persons who are members of the armed services and not to their civilian wives, children and other dependents." He noted: "The Government argues that the Necessary and Proper Clause [18] when taken in conjunction with Clause 14 allows Congress to authorize a trial of Mrs. Smith and Mrs. Covert by military tribunals and under military law. The Government claims that the two clauses together can constitute a broad grant of power 'without limitation' authorizing Congress

---

* In addition to the Reid and Kinsella cases discussed in the text, see also the barriers to court-martial jurisdiction in United States ex rel. Toth v. Quarles, 350 U.S. 11 (1955) (discharged service personnel charged with crimes committed while in the service), and McElroy v. United States ex rel. Guagliardo, 361 U.S. 281 (1960) (civilian employees of the armed forces working abroad). Note also the later cases limiting court-martial jurisdiction over members of the armed forces to "service-connected" offenses. O'Callahan v. Parker, 395 U.S. 258 (1969); Relford v. U. S. Disciplinary Commandant, 401 U.S. 355 (1971).

to subject all persons, civilians and soldiers alike, to military trial if 'necessary and proper' to govern and regulate the land and naval forces." Justice Black rejected that contention: "[T]he Necessary and Proper Clause cannot operate to extend military jurisdiction to any group of persons beyond that class described in Clause 14—'the land and naval Forces.'"

The conflict between the contending positions as to the Necessary and Proper Clause is best illustrated by another decision, three years after Reid v. Covert. In KINSELLA v. UNITED STATES EX REL. SINGLETON, 361 U.S. 234 (1960), Justice Clark's majority opinion refused to distinguish Reid and held unconstitutional the application of the UCMJ provision to civilian dependents charged with *noncapital* offenses. Justice Harlan's dissent in the Kinsella case insisted that Justice Clark's approach ignored the lessons of McCulloch. Excerpts from the opposing positions follow.

2. *Justice Clark's view of the Necessary and Proper Clause in Kinsella.* In extending the Reid v. Covert analysis to noncapital cases in the Kinsella case, Justice Clark summarized the Reid interpretation of the Necessary and Proper Clause as follows: "[T]he power to 'make Rules for the Government and Regulation of the land and naval Forces' bears no limitation as to offenses. . . . If the exercise of the power is valid it is because it is granted in Clause 14 not because of the Necessary and Proper Clause. The latter clause is not itself a grant of power, but a *caveat* that the Congress possesses all the means necessary to carry out the specifically granted 'foregoing' powers of § 8 'and all other Powers vested by this Constitution. . . .' As James Madison explained, the Necessary and Proper Clause is 'but merely a declaration, for the removal of all uncertainty, that the means of carrying into execution those [powers] otherwise granted are included in the grant.' VI Writings of James Madison, edited by Gaillard Hunt, 383. There can be no question but that Clause 14 grants the Congress power to adopt the Uniform Code of Military Justice. Our initial inquiry is whether Congress can include civilian dependents within the term 'land and naval Forces' as a proper incident to this power and necessary to its execution. If answered in the affirmative then civilian dependents are amenable to the Code. In [Reid v. Covert], it was held they were not so amenable as to capital offenses. Our final inquiry, therefore, is narrowed to whether Clause 14, which under [Reid v. Covert] has been held not to include civilian dependents charged with capital offenses, may now be expanded to include civilian dependents who are charged with noncapital offenses. We again refer to James Madison:

'When the Constitution was under the discussions which preceded its ratification, it is well known that great apprehensions were expressed by many, lest the omission of some positive exception, from the powers delegated, of certain rights, . . . might expose them to the danger of being drawn, by construction, within some of the powers vested in Congress, more especially of the power to make all laws necessary and proper for carrying their other powers into execution. In reply to this objection, it was invariably urged to be a fundamental and characteristic principle of the Constitution, that all powers not given by it were reserved; that no powers were given beyond those enumerated in the Constitution, and such as were fairly incident to them; . . . .' Writings, supra, at 390.

We are therefore constrained to say that since this Court has said that the Necessary and Proper Clause cannot expand Clause 14 so as to include prosecution of civilian dependents for capital crimes, it cannot expand Clause 14 to include prosecution of them for noncapital offenses." Justice Clark was "not convinced that a critical impact upon discipline will result, as claimed by the Government . . ., if noncapital offenses are given the same treatment as capital ones."

3. *Justice Harlan's dissent in Kinsella.* Justices Harlan and Frankfurter had joined the majority's holding of unconstitutionality in Reid v. Covert, the capital crimes case. But in the noncapital crime situation of Kinsella, they were willing to find the exercise of military jurisdiction constitutional. Justice Harlan's dissent, joined by Justice Frankfurter, took sharp issue with Justice Clark's approach to the Necessary and Proper Clause:†

"The Court's view of the effect of [Reid v. Covert] in these noncapital cases stems from the basic premise that only persons occupying a military 'status' are within the scope of the Art. I, § 8, cl. 14 power. . . .

"I think the 'status' premise on which the Court has proceeded is unsound. Article I, § 8, cl. 14, speaks not in narrow terms of soldiers and sailors, but broadly gives Congress power to prescribe 'Rules for the Government and Regulation of the land and naval Forces.' This power must be read in connection with Clause 18 of the same Article [the Necessary and Proper Clause] . . . . Thus read, the power respecting the land and naval forces encompasses, in my opinion, all that Congress may appropriately deem 'necessary' for their good order. It does not automatically exclude the regulation of nonmilitary personnel.

"I think it impermissible to conclude . . . that the Necessary and Proper Clause may not be resorted to in judging constitutionality in cases of this type. The clause, itself a part of Art. I, § 8, in which the power to regulate the armed forces is also found, applies no less to that power than it does to the other § 8 congressional powers, and indeed is to be read 'as an integral part of each' such power. . . .

"Of course, the Necessary and Proper Clause cannot be used to 'expand' powers which are otherwise constitutionally limited, but that is only to say that when an asserted power is not appropriate to the exercise of an express power, to which all 'necessary and proper' powers must relate, the asserted power is not a 'proper' one. But to say, as the Court does now, that the Necessary and Proper Clause 'is not itself a grant of power' is to disregard Clause 18 as one of the enumerated powers of § 8 of Art. I.

---

† Note also the variations on the approach to the Necessary and Proper Clause in a separate opinion by Justice Whittaker, joined by Justice Stewart (agreeing with Justice Clark's result). Justice Whittaker stated: "The source of the power, if it exists, is Art. I, § 8, cl. 14, of the Constitution." At this point he added as a footnote: "This does not overlook the 'Necessary and Proper' Clause, Art. I, § 8, cl. 18, of the Constitution, but, in my view, that Clause, though applicable, adds nothing to Clause 14, because the latter Clause, empowering Congress 'To make Rules for the Government and Regulation of the land and naval Forces,' plainly means *all necessary and proper rules* for those purposes. Mr. Justice Stewart is of the view that Clause 14 must be read in connection with the 'Necessary and Proper' Clause, and agrees with the views expressed in Mr. Justice Harlan's separate opinion as to the applicability and effect of that clause."

"Viewing Congress' power to provide for the governing of the armed forces in connection with the Necessary and Proper Clause, it becomes apparent, I believe, that a person's 'status' with reference to the military establishment is but one, and not alone the determinative, factor in judging the constitutionality of a particular exercise of that power. By the same token, the major premise on which the Court ascribes to Covert a controlling effect in these noncapital cases disappears. . . .

"It is one thing to hold that nonmilitary personnel situated at our foreign bases may be tried abroad by courts-martial in times of peace for noncapital offenses, but quite another to say that they may be so tried where life is at stake. In the latter situation I do not believe that the Necessary and Proper Clause, which alone in cases like this brings the exceptional Article I jurisdiction into play, can properly be taken as justifying the trial of nonmilitary personnel without the full protections of an Article III court. . . . Before the constitutional existence of such a power can be found, for me a much more persuasive showing would be required that Congress had good reason for concluding that such a course is necessary to the proper maintenance of our military establishment abroad than has been made in any of the cases of this kind which have thus far come before the Court. . . .

". . . I believe that the true issue on this aspect of all such cases concerns the closeness or remoteness of the relationship between the person affected and the military establishment. Is that relationship close enough so that Congress may, in light of all the factors involved, appropriately deem it 'necessary' that the military be given jurisdiction to deal with offenses committed by such persons? "

4. *Implied powers and the Kinsella majority: A narrow reading of national powers?* Obviously, the arguments against constitutionality in Kinsella rest on different considerations than those encountered in cases such as McCulloch v. Maryland. The limiting factors on congressional powers here arise from Art. III, the Bill of Rights, and the history of American civil-military relations, not from the federal system. Is that difference sufficient justification for interpreting the Necessary and Proper Clause differently here? Would the prevailing opinion in Kinsella have been more viable if it had stated that military trial of civilians accompanying the armed forces *was,* in Art. I terms, an appropriate means to effectuate the Clause 14 power— but a means precluded by other provisions of the Constitution? Regulation of intrastate commerce is not a delegated power, yet that regulation is permissible when it is "necessary and proper" for the regulation of interstate commerce. (See chap. 4.) How can it be said, then, that the subject-matter of Clause 14 ("the land and naval Forces") defines the outermost reach of that power—that regulation reaching something other than individuals formally in "the land and naval Forces" cannot be an appropriate means to effectuate the Clause 14 power? Does this amount to a general repudiation of the broad interpretations of national powers in McCulloch v. Maryland and in many modern cases? Or is this only a pro tanto repudiation: is the broad Marshall reading still valid when states' rights objections are the only ones raised? Compare United States v. Oregon, note 6 below. In what circumstances is it appropriate to invoke the Kinsella substitute for the Marshall approach to congressional powers?

5. *The Kinsella majority's selection of historical antecedents: A preference for the spirit of 1798, not 1819?* Do the foregoing questions rest on an exaggerated view of the Kinsella majority's interpretation of Necessary and Proper Clause? Can that reading of the Clause be reconciled with Marshall's position? A closer look at a major source relied on by Justice Clark in Kinsella suggests that, at this late date, the anti-Marshall position did indeed win a victory—at least in this context.

Justice Clark in Kinsella quotes twice from James Madison's Writings for his interpretation of the Necessary and Proper Clause. The James Madison relied on was not, however, the Madison of 1788, the nationalist writer of such essays as No. 44 of the Federalist Papers. It was not the Madison of 1816, the President who reluctantly chose not to veto the charter of the Second Bank of the United States. Rather, the Madison relied on was the Madison of 1800, the states' rights publicist. Both quotations used by Justice Clark are from the lengthy Report of a committee of the Virginia legislature [VI Writings of James Madison (Hunt ed. 1906), 341–406] drafted by Madison to explain and justify the Virginia Resolutions of 1798. These Resolutions, like those of Kentucky, had protested the Alien and Sedition Acts, but the protests had encountered a hostile reception in other state legislatures. On the issue of national powers and the Necessary and Proper Clause, it is plain, the Madison Report was in the mainstream of strict construction doctrine—the *losing* side in McCulloch v. Maryland.

The Report defended, for example, the 1798 Virginia statement (also drafted by Madison) that condemned the "spirit . . . manifested by the Federal Government to enlarge its powers by forced constructions of the constitutional charter" and the "design to expound certain general phrases . . . so as to destroy the meaning and effect of the particular enumeration which necessarily explains and limits the general phrases." In addition to much general discussion of a two-fold emphasis on the "necessary" as well as the "proper" ingredient of Clause 18, Madison's Report contained a few examples of the objectionable "forced constructions for enlarging the Federal powers." The first and major example—"omitting others which have less occupied public attention, or been less extensively regarded as *unconstitutional*"—: "the *Bank Law,* which, from the circumstances of its passage, as well as the latitude of construction on which it was founded, strikes the attention with singular force." Id., 352–353. (Emphasis added.)

In short, Madison's 1800 view of the Necessary and Proper Clause—relied on by Justice Clark in 1960—was a reiteration of the Jeffersonian position against the chartering of the First Bank of the United States in 1791. In 1791, it will be recalled, Hamilton's view on the constitutionality of the Bank prevailed over Jefferson's, as noted above; and Hamilton's view in turn was that of the Marshall Court, in the supposedly authoritative exposition of the Necessary and Proper Clause in McCulloch v. Maryland. The Kinsella interpretation in 1960, then, appears to be a belated, albeit limited, victory for the position repudiated by Marshall.

6. *The scope of the belated victory for Virginia states' rights ideology.* a. *United States v. Oregon.* How limited a victory is it? Surely the result of McCulloch is not impaired by Kinsella. But can the Necessary and Proper Clause interpretation of the court-martial cases be restricted to non-

federalism issues? Justices Black and Clark appeared to think so, for they were both in the majority in United States v. Oregon, below; but Justice Douglas' dissent suggests that not all Justices are prepared to restrict application of the broadly stated Kinsella version of the 1800 position to the immediate context of the revival.

Justice Black wrote the majority opinion in UNITED STATES v. ORE-GON, 366 U.S. 643 (1961). He stated the facts as follows: "Adam Warpouske, an Oregon resident, died in a United States Veterans' Administration Hospital in Oregon without a will or legal heirs, leaving a net estate composed of personal property worth about $13,000. Oregon law provides that such property shall escheat to the State. A United States statute, on the other hand, provides that when a veteran dies without a will or legal heirs in a veterans' hospital, his personal property 'shall immediately vest in and become the property of the United States as trustee for the sole and benefit of the General Post Fund . . . .' [38 U.S.C. § 17.] In reliance upon those provisions of their respective statutes, both the State of Oregon and the Government of the United States filed claims for Warpouske's estate in the Oregon probate court having jurisdiction of the matter." The Supreme Court decided that the United States was entitled to the estate under the statute. Justice Black's opinion concluded: "We see no merit in the challenge to the constitutionality. . . . Congress undoubtedly has the power—under its constitutional powers to raise armies and navies and to conduct wars—to pay pensions, and to build hospitals and homes for veterans. We think it plain that the same sources of power authorize Congress to require that the personal property left by its wards when they die in government facilities shall be devoted to the comfort and recreation of other ex-service people who must depend upon the Government for care. The fact that this law pertains to the devolution of property does not render it invalid. Although it is true that this is an area normally left to the States, it is not immune under the Tenth Amendment from laws passed by the Federal Government which are, as is the law here, necessary and proper to the exercise of a delegated power."

But Justice Douglas, joined by Justice Whittaker, dissented: "I do not see how this decedent's estate can constitutionally pass to the United States. The succession of real and personal property is traditionally a state matter under our federal system. . . . That tradition continues. . . .

"The power to build hospitals and homes for veterans and to pay them pensions is plainly necessary and proper to the powers to raise and support armies and navies and to conduct wars. The power to provide for the administration of the estates of veterans (which are not made up of federal funds owing the veterans) is to me a far cry from any such power. But the present Act is of that character. . . .

"*Only recently we warned against an expansive construction of the Necessary and Proper Clause. We stated that it is 'not itself a grant of power but a caveat that the Congress possesses all the means necessary to carry out' the powers specifically granted. Kinsella v. Singleton, 361 U.S. 234, 247. Powers not given 'were reserved,' as Madison said. . . .*

"Veterans or anyone else may make the United States a beneficiary of their estate, absent a state law that precludes it. . . . But if it is 'fairly

incident' to raising and supporting armies and navies and conducting wars for the United States to take over the administration of the personal property of veterans who die intestate, I see no reason why Congress cannot take over their real estate too. I see no reason why, if the United States can go as far as we allow it to go today, it cannot supersede any will a veteran makes and thus better provide for the comfort, care, and recreation of other ex-service men and women who are dependent on the United States for care. And the more money the Federal Government collects for veterans the better the care they will receive. No greater collision with state law would be present where Congress took realty or displaced an entire will than here. . . .

"The Tenth Amendment does not, of course, dilute any power delegated to the national government. . . . But when the Federal Government enters a field as historically local as the administration of decedents' estates, some clear relation of the asserted power to one of the delegated powers should be shown. At times the exercise of a delegated power reaches deep into local problems. Wickard v. Filburn . . . .. But there is no semblance of likeness here. The need of the Government to enter upon the administration of veterans' estates—made up of funds not owing from the United States—is no crucial phase of the ability of the United States to care for ex-service men and women or to manage federal fiscal affairs.

"Today's decision does not square with our conception of federalism. There is nothing more deeply imbedded in the Tenth Amendment, as I read history, than the disposition of the estates of deceased people. I do not see how a scheme for administration of decedents' estates of the kind we have here can possibly be necessary and proper to any power delegated to Congress. . . ." [Emphasis added.]

   b. *National power and "historically local" fields.* Is there an independent justification for Justice Douglas' reading of national powers in the Oregon case, beyond the reliance on the arguably erratic interpretation of the Necessary and Proper Clause in Kinsella? Is there a justifiable general principle that "when the Federal Government enters a field" that is "historically local," an especially "clear relation of the asserted power to one of the delegated powers should be shown"? Recall the hints of a somewhat similar approach in Marshall and Hamilton. Note Alexander Hamilton's statement in 1791, printed above: "There is also this further criterion, which may materially assist the decision: Does the proposed measure abridge a pre-existing right of any state . . .?" Recall also Marshall's newspaper statement in 1819: "Congress certainly may not, under the pretext of collecting taxes, or of guaranteeing to each state a republican form of government, alter the law of descents . . . .." If asking whether "a field" is "historically local" is not an adequate guide for extraordinary judicial scrutiny of congressional action, is it nevertheless arguable that the federalism concern warrants special weight when congressional regulations impinge on "the organizational form and structure" of state and local governments? See the recurrent concern with those considerations of state autonomy below—e. g., in chap. 3, and chap. 6.*

---

* As the post-1937 cases in the next two chapters will show, the modern Court has rarely been receptive to state autonomy and states rights challenges to federal legislation. But as this edition goes to press, there are indica-

7. *A polemical postscript.* The point of this Kinsella to Madison to Oregon detour is not to suggest that Marshall's approach in McCulloch has in fact been broadly repudiated, or that the Kinsella and Oregon decisions are necessarily unsound in result. It is to suggest the importance of the *content* of the Court's elaborations of principle; it is to suggest that it is not enough to recognize that the limiting principles on national authority in the court-martial cases differ from those in Oregon; it is to suggest that a Court must not only perceive but also adequately articulate the differences. By resting the explanation in part on a general Necessary and Proper Clause interpretation, the Reid and Kinsella opinions convey doctrines of probably unintended breadth and assume the risk of application of the doctrines in such settings as United States v. Oregon. Could adequate opinions have been written in the court-martial cases without giving a somewhat unusual meaning to the Necessary and Proper Clause? By emphasizing Art. III and the Bill of Rights—rather than Art. I—as the sole sources of the limitations?

tions of a growing sensitivity to federalistic limits by a number of Justices. Note, e. g., Fry v. United States, 421 U.S. —— (May 27, 1975): though the Court sustained the application of temporary federal wage controls to state employees, Justice Thurgood Marshall's majority opinion was a narrow one. He emphasized that the federal action was an emergency measure of limited scope and that it did not appreciably intrude upon state sovereignty. Note especially his comment on a passage often viewed as a symbol of the modern disappearance of federalistic limits. Justice Marshall stated: "While the Tenth Amendment has been characterized as a 'truism', stating merely that 'all is retained which has not been surrendered,' United States v. Darby, 312 U.S. 100, 124 (1941) [p. 182 below], it is not without significance. The Amendment expressly declares the constitutional policy that Congress may not exercise power in a fashion that impairs the States' integrity or their ability to function effectively in a federal system."

Perhaps an even more important straw in the wind is the Court's action in National League of Cities v. Dunlop, a state autonomy challenge to a broad extension of the Fair Labor Standards Act to state and local employees. Though the lower court had thought the challenge barred by Maryland v. Wirtz, a 1968 decision noted at p. 206 below, Chief Justice Burger stayed enforcement of the new regulations, the Court heard argument on the merits in April 1975—and indicated that it found the challenge a substantial one when, on May 27, 1975, it set the case for reargument in the October 1975 Term. (See also the note on Dunlop at p. 387 below; and note Justice Rehnquist's dissent on the same day in the Fry case, above, urging that Maryland v. Wirtz be overruled.)

Chapter 3

THE COMMERCE POWER

Introduction. The poor condition of American commerce and the pro-liferating trade rivalries between the states were the immediate provocations for the calling of the Constitutional Convention. One of the new Constitution's major innovations was a response to those concerns: Congress was granted the power "To Regulate Commerce with foreign Nations, and among the Several States." That grant was to suppress the "interfering and un-neighbourly regulations of some States"—regulations which, "if not re-strained by a national controul," would prove to be ever more "serious sources of animosity and discord." (Hamilton's No. 22 of The Federalist.) The national commerce power, it was hoped, would put an end to hostile state restrictions, retaliatory trade regulations, protective tariffs on imports from other states.

That congressional power, designed to promote a national market and curb Balkanization of the economy, has been a subject of extensive and con-tinuous consideration by the Court since Marshall's day. The commerce power has had a two-fold impact: as a restraint on state action (considered in chap. 5), and as a source of national authority (the concern of this chap-ter). In the hundreds of cases in which state regulations and taxes have been challenged under the commerce clause, free trade is the national interest that claims protection, and the tie to the historical roots of the clause is plain. In the cases in which the clause is invoked to justify congressional regulation, the nexus with historical purposes is often more tenuous. But the modern pressures for national action on a widening range of problems have prompted increasingly intense searches for constitutional justifications among the enumerated powers. And in these searches, the commerce clause has proved to be a frequently attractive and often hospitable base for the assertion of regulatory authority.

This chapter examines in some detail the Court's efforts to articulate the scope and limits of the commerce power. That examination is worth-while not only for its own sake—for the sake of tracing the contours of con-gressional authority—but also for its institutional aspects, for the light it sheds on the Court's general capacity to develop enforceable limits on governmental powers. Many of the doctrines in these cases have proved ineffective as re-straints; some of them have been explicitly abandoned by the Court. Did these limits fail because they were unjustifiable in content? Because they were applied inconsistently and with result-oriented biases? What prin-cipled limits were possible? What limits remain? Does the history of commerce clause litigation suggest that judicially-developed doctrines limiting government tend to be facades for the personal preferences of the judges? Are restraints designed to protect individual rights likely to be more prin-cipled than the federalism-related limits considered here?

These general problems underlie the recurrent questions of commerce clause doctrine which surface in many of the cases in this chapter. Congress

has frequently sought to deal with problems far removed from the evils that gave rise to the commerce clause. Does the purpose of Congress determine the legitimacy of resort to the commerce power? Can a standard of constitutionality distinguish between "commercial" and "economic" legislation on the one hand and "moral," "police" regulation on the other? Can limits be stated that do not require an inquiry into congressional motives? Does the commerce clause curtail excessive intrusion of national power into local affairs? Are there adequate constitutional standards to distinguish between local affairs remote from commerce and intrastate activities with a sufficiently close connection to interstate commerce? Even if adequate judicially enforceable limits are beyond the Court's capacity (or proper institutional role), do the text and structure of the Constitution nevertheless establish federalism-related restraints which a legislator must heed in considering proposals for national action? *

SECTION 1. THE MARSHALL COURT'S GROUNDWORK

GIBBONS v. OGDEN

9 Wheat. 1, 6 L.Ed. 23 (1824).

Appeal from the Court for the Trial of Impeachments and Correction of Errors of the State of New York.

[The New York legislature granted to Robert Livingston and Robert Fulton the exclusive right to operate steamboats in New York waters. By assignment from Livingston and Fulton, Aaron Ogden acquired monopoly rights to operate steamboats between New York and New Jersey. Thomas Gibbons, a former partner of Ogden, began operating two steamboats between New York and Elizabethtown, New Jersey, in violation of Ogden's monopoly. Gibbons' boats were enrolled and licensed as "vessels employed in the coasting trade" under a federal law of 1793 (1 Stat. 305). Ogden obtained an injunction from the New York Court of Chancery ordering Gibbons to stop operating his ferries in New York waters. 4 Johns.Ch. 150 (1819). The highest New York court affirmed. 17 Johns. 488 (1820). Only a part of

---

* This chapter singles out the commerce power to explore federalist limits on national regulation: it is congressional resort to that power that has been the most prolific source of litigation. But the general problem of localist restraints on national power is not confined to commerce clause issues. There is some doctrinal, and an even closer historical, connection between the commerce cases in this chapter and the taxing and spending power materials in the opening sections of the next chapter. On the doctrinal relationship, compare, e. g., the problem of abuses of power—using a national power as a "pretext" to achieve ulterior ends— in the Child Labor Case, Hammer v. Dagenhart (sec. 3 below in this chapter), with the Child Labor Tax Case (sec. 1 of the next chapter). On the historical relationship, compare the Court's efforts to curb exercises of the commerce power in the early decades of this century with similar efforts to restrain congressional uses of other Art. I, § 8, powers: e. g., the 1936 decision in the Carter case (sec. 4 of this chapter) parallels the 1936 decision in a spending power case, United States v. Butler (sec. 2 of the next chapter). These and other doctrinal and historical interrelations are developed in several notes below.

Chief Justice Marshall's opinion sustaining Gibbons' appeal is printed here—
that portion discussing the national commerce power. The rest of the Marshall
opinion—the part dealing with the validity of the New York monopoly under
the Constitution and the federal law—appears later, with other materials on
limitations of state power in chap. 5, sec. 1.]

Mr. Chief Justice MARSHALL delivered the opinion of the Court
. . . :

The appellant contends that this decree is erroneous, because the laws
which purport to give the exclusive privilege it sustains, are repugnant to the
constitution and laws of the United States.

They are said to be repugnant—

1st. To that clause in the constitution which authorizes congress to
regulate commerce. . . .

This [Constitution] contains an enumeration of powers expressly granted
by the people to their government. It has been said, that these powers ought
to be construed strictly. But why ought they to be so construed? Is there
one sentence in the constitution which gives countenance to this rule? . . .
What do gentlemen mean, by a strict construction? If they contend only
against that enlarged construction, which would extend words beyond their
natural and obvious import, we might question the application of the term,
but should not controvert the principle. If they contend for that narrow
construction which, in support of some theory not to be found in the constitution, would deny to the government those powers which the words of the
grant, as usually understood, import, and which are consistent with the general views and objects of the instrument; for that narrow construction, which
would cripple the government, and render it unequal to the objects for which
it is declared to be instituted, and to which the powers given, as fairly understood, render it competent; then we cannot perceive the propriety of this
strict construction, nor adopt it as the rule by which the constitution is to be
expounded. . . . If, from the imperfection of human language, there
should be serious doubts respecting the extent of any given power, it is a
well settled rule, that the objects for which it was given, especially when those
objects are expressed in the instrument itself, should have great influence in
the construction. . . .

The words are, "Congress shall have power to regulate commerce with
foreign nations, and among the several States, and with the Indian tribes."

The subject to be regulated is commerce; and our constitution being,
as was aptly said at the bar, one of enumeration, and not of definition, to ascertain the extent of the power, it becomes necessary to settle the meaning of
the word. The counsel for the appellee would limit it to traffic, to buying
and selling, or the interchange of commodities, and do not admit that it comprehends navigation. This would restrict a general term, applicable to many
objects, to one of its significations. Commerce, undoubtedly, is traffic, but
it is something more: it is intercourse. It describes the commercial intercourse between nations, and parts of nations, in all its branches, and is
regulated by prescribing rules for carrying on that intercourse. The mind
can scarcely conceive a system for regulating commerce between nations,
which shall exclude all laws concerning navigation, which shall be silent on the

admission of the vessels of the one nation into the ports of the other, and be confined to prescribing rules for the conduct of individuals, in the actual employment of buying and selling, or of barter.

If commerce does not include navigation, the government of the Union has no direct power over that subject, and can make no law prescribing what shall constitute American vessels, or requiring that they shall be navigated by American seamen. Yet this power has been exercised from the commencement of the government, has been exercised with the consent of all, and has been understood by all to be a commercial regulation. All America understands, and has uniformly understood, the word "commerce" to comprehend navigation. It was so understood, and must have been so understood, when the constitution was framed. The power over commerce, including navigation, was one of the primary objects for which the people of America adopted their government, and must have been contemplated in forming it. The convention must have used the word in that sense; because all have understood it in that sense, and the attempt to restrict it comes too late. .   .   .

The word used in the constitution, then, comprehends, and has been always understood to comprehend, navigation within its meaning; and a power to regulate navigation is as expressly granted as if that term had been added to the word "commerce."

To what commerce does this power extend? The constitution informs us, to commerce "with foreign nations, and among the several States, and with the Indian tribes."

It has, we believe, been universally admitted that these words comprehend every species of commercial intercourse between the United States and foreign nations. No sort of trade can be carried on between this country and any other, to which this power does not extend. It has been truly said, that commerce, as the word is used in the constitution, is a unit, every part of which is indicated by the term.

If this be the admitted meaning of the word, in its application to foreign nations, it must carry the same meaning throughout the sentence, and remain a unit, unless there be some plain intelligible cause which alters it.

The subject to which the power is next applied, is to commerce "among the several States." The word "among" means intermingled with. A thing which is among others, is intermingled with them. Commerce among the States, cannot stop at the external boundary line of each State, but may be introduced into the interior.

It is not intended to say that these words comprehend that commerce which is completely internal, which is carried on between man and man in a State, or between different parts of the same State, and which does not extend to or affect other States. Such a power would be inconvenient, and is certainly unnecessary.

Comprehensive as the word "among" is, it may very properly be restricted to that commerce which concerns more States than one. The phrase is not one which would probably have been selected to indicate the completely interior traffic of a State, because it is not an apt phrase for that purpose; and the enumeration of the particular classes of commerce to which the power was to be extended, would not have been made, had the intention been to

extend the power to every description. The enumeration presupposes some-thing not enumerated; and that something, if we regard the language or the subject of the sentence, must be the exclusively internal commerce of a State. The genius and character of the whole government seem to be, that its action is to be applied to all the external concerns of the nation, and to those internal concerns which affect the States generally; but not to those which are com-pletely within a particular State, which do not affect other States, and with which it is not necessary to interfere, for the purpose of executing some of the general powers of the government. The completely internal commerce of a State, then, may be considered as reserved for the State itself.

But, in regulating commerce with foreign nations, the power of Congress does not stop at the jurisdictional lines of the several States. It would be a very useless power, if it could not pass those lines. The commerce of the United States with foreign nations, is that of the whole United States. Every district has a right to participate in it. The deep streams which penetrate our country in every direction, pass through the interior of almost every State in the Union, and furnish the means of exercising this right. If Congress has the power to regulate it, that power must be exercised whenever the subject exists. If it exists within the States, if a foreign voyage may commence or terminate at a port within a State, then the power of Congress may be exercised within a State. . . .

We are now arrived at the inquiry—What is this power?

It is the power to regulate; that is, to prescribe the rule by which com-merce is to be governed. This power, like all others vested in Congress, is complete in itself, may be exercised to its utmost extent, and acknowledges no limitations, other than are prescribed in the constitution. These are ex-pressed in plain terms, and do not affect the questions which arise in this case, or which have been discussed at the bar. If, as has always been understood, the sovereignty of Congress, though limited to specified objects, is plenary as to those objects, the power over commerce with foreign nations, and among the several States, is vested in Congress as absolutely as it would be in a single government, having in its constitution the same restrictions on the exercise of the power as are found in the constitution of the United States. The wisdom and the discretion of Congress, their identity with the people, and the influence which their constituents possess at elections, are, in this, as in many other instances, as that, for example, of declaring war, the sole restraints on which they have relied, to secure them from its abuse. They are the restraints on which the people must often rely solely, in all representative governments.

This principle is, if possible, still more clear, when applied to commerce "among the several States." They either join each other, in which case they are separated by a mathematical line, or they are remote from each other, in which case other States lie between them. What is commerce "among" them; and how is it to be conducted? Can a trading expedition between two adjoin-ing States, commence and terminate outside of each? And if the trading intercourse be between two States remote from each other, must it not com-mence in one, terminate in the other, and probably pass through a third? Commerce among the States must, of necessity, be commerce with the States. In the regulation of trade with the Indian tribes, the action of the law, especially when the constitution was made, was chiefly within a State. The

power of Congress, then, whatever it may be, must be exercised within the territorial jurisdiction of the several States. . . .

The power of Congress, then, comprehends navigation, within the limits of every State in the Union; so far as that navigation may be, in any manner, connected with "commerce with foreign nations, or among the several States, or with the Indian tribes." It may, of consequence, pass the jurisdictional line of New York, and act upon the very waters to which the prohibition now under consideration applies. . . .

Powerful and ingenious minds, taking, as postulates, that the powers expressly granted to the government of the Union, are to be contracted by construction, into the narrowest possible compass, and that the original powers of the States are retained, if any possible construction will retain them, may, by a course of well digested, but refined and metaphysical reasoning, founded on these premises, explain away the constitution of our country, and leave it, a magnificent structure, indeed, to look at, but totally unfit for use. They may so entangle and perplex the understanding, as to obscure principles, which were before thought quite plain, and induce doubts where, if the mind were to pursue its own course, none would be perceived. In such a case, it is peculiarly necessary to recur to safe and fundamental principles to sustain those principles, and, when sustained, to make them the tests of the arguments to be examined. [Additional excerpts from Chief Justice Marshall's opinion invalidating the New York monopoly grant appear in chap. 5, sec. 1, below. Justice Johnson's concurring opinion is omitted.]

THE MARSHALL COURT'S LEGACY AND MODERN PROBLEMS

1. *Gibbons v. Ogden: A doctrine for all needs?* Gibbons v. Ogden, like McCulloch v. Maryland, is frequently and prominently cited in modern decisions sustaining very expansive exercises of congressional powers. Is that modern reliance on Marshall justifiable? Consider Wickard v. Filburn, 317 U.S. 111 (1942) (sec. 5 below), one of the most important discussions of the commerce power. Justice Jackson's opinion for the Court in Wickard stated: "At the beginning Chief Justice Marshall described the federal commerce power with a breadth never yet exceeded. Gibbons v. Ogden, 9 Wheat. 1, 194–195. He made emphatic the embracing and penetrating nature of this power by warning that effective restraints on its exercise must proceed from political rather than from judicial processes." Is that a fair statement? Does Gibbons in effect abandon judicial restraints? Does Wickard v. Filburn? After McCulloch, Marshall vehemently denied Spencer Roane's charge that his principles gave Congress unlimited authority. Did Gibbons give Congress the carte blanche denied by McCulloch? What judicial limits did Marshall assert?

2. *Early commerce power legislation.* During the first century under our Constitution, most of the Court's discussions of the scope of the commerce power arose—as in Gibbons v. Ogden—in cases dealing with state action affecting interstate commerce. And in most of those cases (unlike Gibbons), Congress had not exercised its power at all. Rather, the com-

merce clause came into play only because state laws were challenged as infringing on the freedom of interstate commerce allegedly guaranteed by Art.
I, § 8, even though Congress' authority under that clause was unexercised
and "dormant." (Those limits on state regulation of commerce are developed in chap. 5 below.) Nevertheless, the concepts of interstate commerce
developed in those state regulation cases proved a source of limits on national action when Congress turned to major uses of the commerce power in
later years. See, e. g., the Knight case, sec. 2 below.

Large-scale regulatory action by Congress did not begin until the Interstate Commerce Act of 1887 and the Sherman Anti-Trust Act of 1890.
Challenges to those statutes—examined in the next section—initiated the
major modern confrontations between the Court and congressional authority over commerce. But there were occasional exercises of the national commerce power even before 1887. For example, Congress enacted laws to improve water and land transportation.* And there was also some commerce
legislation of a "police" character, as in United States v. Marigold, 9 How.
560 (1850) (prohibiting the importation of counterfeit money). But the
most troublesome problems about the reach of the national power did not
emerge until Congress turned to weightier legislative efforts. The rapid
19th century developments in industrialization, transportation and communication produced national economic problems and demands for congressional
regulation. Control of railroad rates and of restraints on competition were
the early congressional responses to these demands and yielded the Knight
and Shreveport cases below.

3. *Emerging doctrinal difficulties: Regulation of national economic
problems vs. regulation of "police" problems.* a. *The central problem of
sec. 2: Regulating intrastate activities because of their relationship to interstate commerce.* It was in cases such as Shreveport and Knight that the Court
tried to state the extent to which Congress might regulate local activities because of their relationship with interstate commerce. The doctrinal problems
of those cases foreshadow the difficulties encountered in subsequent efforts
at national economic regulation—especially the New Deal attempts considered
in the Schechter, Carter, Jones & Laughlin, Darby and Wickard v. Filburn
decisions below. How far, and with what justification, may Congress
reach intrastate activities related to national economic concerns? Can intrastate activities be regulated when they can be considered a part of interstate
commerce, within "the stream of commerce"? Is the production of goods not
reachable by the commerce power, because production neither is commerce
nor has a "direct" effect on commerce? Or can production and consumption
of goods be regulated because they "affect" commerce? It is problems such
as these that are the focus of sec. 2 below.

---

* See, e. g., Roberts v. Northern Pacific
R. Co., 158 U.S. 1 (1894) (creation of
a corporation for the purpose of building railroads); Luxton v. North River
Bridge Co., 153 U.S. 525 (1894) (creation of a corporation with authority
to construct a bridge); California v.
Central Pacific R. Co., 127 U.S. 1 (1888)
(chartering of interstate carrier). See
also The Daniel Ball, 10 Wall. 557
(1871) (federal inspection law for steam
vessels, applied to river steamers built
to operate solely within the boundaries
of one state; Court noted that ship
carried goods in interstate commerce
and accordingly was "an instrumentality of that commerce").

b. *The central problem of sec. 3: "Police" regulations—morality and the commerce power.* Efforts to deal with the emerging problems of the national economy were not the only examples of expanded congressional resort to the commerce power starting with the closing years of the 19th century. In a substantially contemporaneous development, Congress also manifested an increased interest in problems of morality and criminality— gambling, prostitution, theft. Those congressional "police" regulations came to the Court at about the same time as the new national economic regulations. Did the Court handle those two types of laws differently? Should they have been handled differently? Is it useful, or possible, to distinguish national legislation dealing with police problems—directed ultimately at "bad" local activities—from national laws concerned with economic problems? Is it constitutionally significant that police legislation typically relied, as the regulatory technique, on prohibition of interstate transportation, rather than direct control of local activities? (See, e. g., the Lottery Case and Hammer v. Dagenhart, below.) Did these police regulations represent invocations of the commerce power as a "pretext"? Should the Court consider the ulterior purpose of legislation, if its immediate focus is on the movement of commerce across state lines? Are laws directed at police problems less justifiable invocations of the commerce power than regulations of economic problems? Problems such as these are the concern of sec. 3 below.

The distinctions suggested in the preceding two paragraphs, even if valid, may be more difficult to apply than to state. What if economic and "police" objectives both underlie legislation? Can a distinction between economic and "police" purposes be applied, for example, to the Wagner Act or the Fair Labor Standards Acts (see sec. 5 below)? Can and should the Court make such a distinction, in terms of the primary purposes of the legislators? Even if the Court, for institutional reasons, finds it impossible to curb questionable invocations of the power, is the issue of congressional goals nevertheless a significant one for a legislator pondering a vote on a bill? Should a legislator be troubled by attempts to use the commerce clause for social or moral—predominantly noneconomic—objectives? Questions such as these should be borne in mind in examining the ensuing sections tracing the development of the modern commerce power. Note especially the emphasis on such questions in the final section below—sec. 6—on the public accommodations provisions of the Civil Rights Act of 1964.

SECTION 2. THE BEGINNINGS OF MODERN ECONOMIC REGULATION: JUSTIFYING NATIONAL REGULATION OF LOCAL ACTIVITIES ON THE BASIS OF THEIR RELATIONSHIP TO INTERSTATE COMMERCE

Introduction—The requisite "local"-"interstate" connection: Knight and Shreveport as sources of contending approaches. The two earliest examples of major modern regulatory legislation—the Sherman Anti-Trust Act of 1890 and the Interstate Commerce Act of 1887—produced important Court efforts to formulate commerce clause doctrine. The Sherman Act

came before the Court in 1895, in the Sugar Trust case, United States v. E. C. Knight Co., 156 U.S. 1 (1895). The most important early Court encounter with the Interstate Commerce Act came two decades later, in the Shreveport Rate Case, Houston E. & W. Texas Ry. Co. v. United States, 234 U.S. 342 (1914). The doctrinal approaches of these cases cast significant, and to some extent contradictory, shadows over subsequent litigation. Thus, when New Deal laws came before the Court in the 1930's, the differing progeny of the Knight and Shreveport cases offered the Justices a choice of standards. Until 1936, the Court drew on the Knight heritage; beginning with 1937, the Shreveport approach became central.

The Knight and Shreveport cases presented similar problems: What were the standards to be applied when Congress sought to invoke the commerce power to reach arguably "local" economic activities? What constituted an adequate connection between the "local" and the "interstate"? Was the required relationship one of logical nexus or of practical impact? The Knight case symbolizes the former; the Shreveport case the latter. Knight suggested that the local activity was not reachable unless it had a "direct" rather than an "indirect" effect on interstate commerce: an attempt to monopolize sugar refining, though of significant interstate economic consequences, was not controllable through federal legislation because the relationship between "manufacturing" and "commerce" was "indirect." In the Shreveport case, by contrast, "local" railroad rates were reachable because of their practical, economic impact on interstate transportation.

That issue of requisite relationships echoes a problem raised as early as Marshall's opinion in the McCulloch case. His was a broad but not unlimited interpretation of congressional powers. Recall chap. 2 above. As he stated in his opinion—and in his extrajudicial commentaries—congressional means must be "plainly adapted" to a "legitimate" end, must be "really calculated" to effect objects entrusted to the national government. And the means, he noted, must be "consistent with the letter and spirit of the constitution." In a sense, the 20th century Court's struggles with the reach of the commerce power represent efforts to give content to the "plainly adapted" and "really calculated" requirements. How adequate are those efforts? How consistent are they with the "spirit of the constitution" requirement—arguably, the implied limitations arising from the federal nature of the governmental structure established by the Constitution?

The next group of notes deals with the Knight case and its immediate consequences for antitrust enforcement. That group is followed by notes focusing on the Shreveport case and its related problems. The logical nexus, "direct"-"indirect" emphasis of Knight, it turned out, did not prove a significant barrier to application of the antitrust laws. But it did leave a deposit of doctrine capable of being invoked in other contexts; and that deposit proved decisive in the early New Deal cases. When the Court struck down national economic regulations in the 1930's, the "direct"-"indirect" distinction of Knight proved fatal to congressional efforts, in cases such as Schechter and Carter (sec. 4 below). But then, quite suddenly, in the wake of Franklin Delano Roosevelt's Court-packing plan of 1937, the Court adopted a more benign attitude toward national economic regulation. And the Shreveport heritage was invoked to provide support for that new constitutional direction: it is the emphasis on the substantial economic effect of the local

activity on interstate commerce that plays a central role in such modern cases as Jones & Laughlin and Wickard v. Filburn (sec. 5 below).

THE KNIGHT CASE, THE LOGICAL NEXUS STANDARD, AND ANTITRUST ENFORCEMENT

1. *The Knight approach and its sources.* In the Sugar Trust Case, UNITED STATES v. E. C. KNIGHT CO., 156 U.S. 1 (1895), the Supreme Court affirmed the dismissal of a Government civil action to set aside, under the Sherman Anti-Trust Act, the acquisition by the American Sugar Refining Company of the stock of four other sugar refineries.* The Government had alleged that the four acquired companies had produced about 33% of all sugar refined in the United States, and that American's acquisition gave it control of all refineries except one, producing about 2% of the total sugar refined. The Court's decision rested on a construction of the Act; but its statutory interpretation was premised on confining constitutional doctrines, especially the view that Congress could not under the commerce clause reach a monopoly in "manufacture."

Chief Justice Fuller's majority opinion indicated that, even conceding "the existence of a monopoly in manufacture"—a monopoly of 98% of sugar refining—the monopoly could not be "directly suppressed here." He stated: "Doubtless the power to control the manufacture of a given thing involves in a certain sense the control of its disposition, but this is a secondary and not the primary sense; and although the exercise of that power may result in bringing the operation of commerce into play, it does not control it, and affects it only incidentally and indirectly. Commerce succeeds to manufacture, and is not a part of it." Monopolies might sometimes be regulated under the commerce power, he suggested, but only when "the transaction is itself a monopoly of commerce." He emphasized that it was "vital that the independence of the commercial power and of the police power, and the delimitation between them, however sometimes perplexing, should always be recognized and observed."

In elaborating the distinction between "manufacture" and "commerce," Chief Justice Fuller relied heavily on decisions which had not involved congressional exercises of commerce power at all but rather questions of state authority in the face of the "dormant" commerce clause. What weight should have been given to those opinions stemming from a state rather than a national regulatory context? He relied particularly on Kidd v. Pearson, 128 U.S. 1 (1888), sustaining an Iowa prohibition of the manufacture of intoxicating liquors intended for export to other states. Chief Justice Fuller quoted from the Court's opinion in Kidd: "No distinction is more popular to the common mind, or more clearly expressed in economic and political literature, than that between manufacture and commerce. Manufacture is transformation—the fashioning of raw materials into a change of form for use. The functions of commerce are different. The buying and selling and the

---

* Section 1 of the Sherman Act prohibited any contract, combination or conspiracy "in restraint of trade or commerce among the several states." Section 2 provided penalties for any person "who shall monopolize, or combine or conspire . . . to monopolize any part of the trade or commerce among the several states."

transportation incidental thereto constitute commerce . . .. If it be held that [regulation of commerce] includes the regulation of all such manufactures as are intended to be the subject of commercial transactions in the future, it is impossible to deny that it would also include all productive industries that contemplate the same thing. The result would be that Congress would be invested, to the exclusion of the States, with the power to regulate, not only manufactures, but also agriculture, horticulture, stock raising, domestic fisheries, mining—in short every branch of human industry. For is there one of them that does not contemplate, more or less clearly, an interstate or foreign market? . . . The power being vested in Congress and denied to the States, it would follow as an inevitable result that the duty would devolve on Congress to regulate all of these delicate, multiform and vital interests—interests which in their nature are and must be local in all the details of their successful management."

That approach of the Kidd case governed Chief Justice Fuller's Knight analysis and led him to insist that the nexus between the local and the interstate was a qualitative one of logical relationships rather than an empiric one of economic impacts. As he put it: "Contracts, combinations, or conspiracies to control domestic enterprise in manufacture, agriculture, mining, production in all its forms, or to raise or lower prices or wages, might unquestionably tend to restrain external as well as domestic trade, but the restraint would be an indirect result, however inevitable and whatever its extent, and such result would not necessarily determine the object of the contract, combination, or conspiracy." He added: "Slight reflection will show that if the national power extends to all contracts and combinations in manufacture, agriculture, mining, and other productive industries, whose ultimate result may affect external commerce, comparatively little of business operations and affairs would be left for state control." †

Those standards barred the suit against the Sugar Trust: the challenged actions "related exclusively to the acquisition of the Philadelphia refineries" and "bore no direct relation to commerce between the States." Chief Justice Fuller added: "The object was manifestly private gain in the manufacture of the commodity, but not through the control of interstate or foreign commerce." To be sure, the sugar business was a national one; "but this was no more than to say that trade and commerce served manufacture to fulfil its function." In short, a monopoly of "the manufacture" could not be treated by the Court as an attempt "to monopolize commerce, even though, in order to dispose of the product, the instrumentality of commerce was necessarily invoked." The first Justice Harlan submitted a strong dissent.

† Passages such as this reflect the much-criticized notion of "dual federalism" characteristic of Court opinions of the pre-1937 era—the notion that the powers reserved to the states operated as an independent limitation on the scope of national powers, that state and national legislative domains were mutually exclusive areas. When Justice Stone remarked in United States v. Darby, 312 U.S. 100 (1941) (sec. 5 below), that the Tenth Amendment is "but a truism that all is retained which has not been surrendered," the statement was widely hailed as a reminder of the death of "dual federalism" after 1937. See Corwin, "The Passing of Dual Federalism," 36 Va.L.Rev. 1 (1950). But should the abandonment of rigid, mutually exclusive categories of state and federal competence carry with it abandonment of all concern with federalistic, structural limitations on the exercise of national powers? See secs. 5 and 6 below and recall p. 125 above.

2. *The limited impact of Knight on antitrust enforcement.* Though the Knight approach was to prove a major obstacle to national economic regulation in later years—see especially the early New Deal cases in sec. 4 below—it did not paralyze antitrust enforcement. In a number of cases soon after Knight, the Court perceived a range of constitutional justifications for applying the Sherman and Clayton Acts. Some examples follow:

a. In Addyston Pipe & Steel Co. v. United States, 175 U.S. 211 (1899), the Court sustained an action against six companies manufacturing iron pipe who had made agreements in restraint of competition. The Court found that "it was the purpose of the combination, to directly and by means of such combination increase the prices." This was held to be a "direct restraint upon interstate commerce."

b. In Northern Securities Co. v. United States, 193 U.S. 197 (1904), the Court, in a 5 to 4 decision, sustained an action to set aside the control acquired by Northern over two companies operating parallel railroad lines. Justice Holmes urged in dissent that the statute be construed in such a way as "not to raise grave doubts" about its constitutionality. Recalling the "indirect effect" language of Knight, he added: "Commerce depends upon population, but Congress could not, on that ground, undertake to regulate marriage and divorce. If the act before us is to be carried out according to what seems to be the logic of the argument for the Government, which I do not believe that it will be, I can see no part of the conduct of life with which on similar principles Congress might not interfere."

Could marriage and divorce be regulated under the theory of Justice Holmes' dissent (a dissent that became the majority view a generation later) in Hammer v. Dagenhart, sec. 3 below?

c. A year later, in Swift & Co. v. United States, 196 U.S. 375 (1905), Justice Holmes wrote for the Court in sustaining the application of the Sherman Act to a conspiracy to monopolize the supply and distribution of fresh meat throughout the United States. The bill charged "a combination of a dominant proportion of the dealers in fresh meat throughout the United States not to bid against each other in the livestock markets of the different States, to bid up prices for a few days in order to induce the cattle men to send their stock to the stock yards, to fix prices at which they will sell, and to that end to restrict shipments of meat when necessary, to establish a uniform rule of credit to dealers and to keep a black list, to make uniform and improper charges for cartage, and finally, to get less than lawful rates from the railroads to the exclusion of competitors." In answer to the objection that the bill "does not set forth a case of commerce among the States," Justice Holmes said: "[C]ommerce among the States is not a technical legal conception, but a practical one, drawn from the course of business." [The Swift case spoke of regulating activities in the "stream of commerce"—a view that was to provide important support for the expansive application of the commerce clause in other areas. Swift is noted further below.]

d. Application of the Sherman Act to labor activities began with Loewe v. Lawlor, 208 U.S. 274 (1908). That case involved an attempt to organize workers on hats through a boycott of hat manufacturers' products shipped in commerce. Despite the attempt to prevent application of the antitrust laws to organizing activities by labor, in the Clayton Act of 1914,

certain boycotts and strikes continued to be held illegal, as in Duplex Printing Press Co. v. Deering, 254 U.S. 443 (1921). In response, the Norris-LaGuardia Act of 1931 restricted federal injunctions in labor disputes.

It has been suggested that the Court's principles in these labor antitrust cases "were strikingly deficient in neutrality," especially in contrast with some of the cases—see sec. 4 below—in which Congress sought to aid labor. Wechsler, Principles, Politics & Fundamental Law (1961), 32. Were these Court principles also non-neutral in comparison with those found in antitrust suits against business activities?

e. It has been said that "Congress wanted to go to the utmost extent of its Constitutional power in restraining trust and monopoly agreements." United States v. South-Eastern Underwriters Ass'n, 322 U.S. 533, 558 (1944) (holding the business of insurance to be covered by the antitrust laws despite older rulings stating that insurance was not commerce). Nevertheless, some recent decisions find businesses outside antitrust coverage though within the reach of the commerce power. E. g., United States v. Yellow Cab Co., 332 U.S. 218 (1947). Perhaps the best-known example is professional baseball. In Toolsen v. New York Yankees, 346 U.S. 356 (1953), the Court found reserve clauses in players' contracts outside the antitrust laws. The Court pointed to a decision in 1922 in which Justice Holmes had stated for the Court that "personal effort, not related to production, is not a subject of commerce." Federal Baseball Club v. National League, 259 U.S. 200. In Toolsen, the Court stated: "The business [has] been left for thirty years to develop, on the understanding that it was not subject to existing antitrust legislation. . . . Without reexamination of the underlying issues, the judgments below are affirmed on the authority of Federal Baseball Club . . ., so far as that decision determines that Congress had no intention of including the business of baseball within the scope of the federal antitrust laws." The Court has adhered to Federal Baseball and Toolson: in a 5 to 3 decision in Flood v. Kuhn, 407 U.S. 258 (1972), Justice Blackmun's majority opinion, while recognizing that the exemption of baseball from the antitrust laws was "an anomaly" and "an aberration," refused "to overturn those cases judicially when Congress, by its positive inaction, has allowed those decisions to stand for so long." Other professional sports, however, have been held subject to the antitrust laws. See United States v. International Boxing Club, 348 U.S. 236 (1955), and Radovich v. National Football League, 352 U.S. 445 (1957).

THE SHREVEPORT CASE AND THE ORIGINS OF THE "SUBSTANTIAL ECONOMIC EFFECTS" APPROACH

Introduction. Even while the Knight approach and its emphasis on the "direct"-"indirect" distinction remained on the books, the Court began to develop a quite different analysis of the nexus necessary to justify regulation of "local" matters under the commerce power. The railroad context was the most prolific source of this alternate approach—an approach emphasizing the practical, quantitative rather than the logical, qualitative relationship between the "local" and the "interstate." Most of the early congressional

attempts to regulate the railroad industry withstood constitutional attack: the Court repeatedly sustained the laws under the commerce power because of the physical or economic effects of the intrastate activities regulated on interstate commerce. The Shreveport case (note 1 below) is the best example of this approach; and the analyses of Shreveport and other railroad cases (note 2 below) were to provide useful constitutional underpinnings for the Court's increasingly benign attitude toward national economic regulation since 1937 (see sec. 5 below).

But the Shreveport view was not the only route toward expanded national regulatory power opened by the cases of the early 20th century. There was also an occasional willingness to reach arguably "local" matters by viewing them as being "in" interstate commerce: in those cases, considered in note 3 below, the rationale for reaching intrastate activities was not the practical effect of the "local" on the "interstate," but rather the argument that seemingly local matters could be viewed as part of a continuous "stream" or "current" of commerce. That "current of commerce" approach shared with the Shreveport analysis the characteristic of emphasizing practical, economic relationships rather than qualitative, logical ones.

1. *The Shreveport Rate case.* In HOUSTON E. & W. TEXAS RY. CO. v. UNITED STATES (THE SHREVEPORT RATE CASE), 234 U.S. 342 (1914), Justice Hughes' majority opinion sustained congressional authority to reach intrastate rail rates discriminating against interstate railroad traffic. The Interstate Commerce Commission, after setting rates for transportation of goods between Shreveport, Louisiana, and points within Texas, ordered several railroads to end their practice of setting rates for hauls between points within Texas which were proportionately less than the rates for transportation from Texas points to Shreveport, Louisiana. For example, the rate to carry wagons from Marshall in East Texas to Dallas, a distance of 147.7 miles, was 36.8 cents; the rate from Marshall to Shreveport, Louisiana, only 42 miles away, was 56 cents. (Shreveport competed with Texas cities such as Dallas for shipments from East Texas.) The ICC found that this rate structure "unjustly discriminated in favor of traffic within the state of Texas, and against similar traffic between Louisiana and Texas," and ordered the railroads to end the discrimination. In challenging that ICC order, the railroads argued that "Congress is impotent to control the intrastate charges of an interstate carrier even to the extent necessary to prevent injurious discrimination against interstate traffic."

Justice Hughes rejected that challenge. He insisted that congressional authority, "extending to these interstate carriers as instruments of interstate commerce, necessarily embraces the right to control their operations in all matters having such a close and substantial relation to interstate traffic that the control is essential or appropriate to the security of that traffic, to the efficiency of the interstate service, and to the maintenance of conditions under which interstate commerce may be conducted upon fair terms and without molestation or hindrance. As it is competent for Congress to legislate to these ends, unquestionably it may seek their attainment by requiring that the agencies of interstate commerce shall not be used in such manner as to cripple, retard, or destroy it. The fact that carriers are instruments of intrastate commerce, as well as of interstate commerce, does not derogate from the complete

and paramount authority of Congress over the latter, or preclude the Federal power from being exerted to prevent the intrastate operations of such carriers from being made a means of injury to that which has been confided to Federal care. Whenever the interstate and intrastate transactions of carriers are so related that the government of the one involves the control of the other, it is Congress, and not the State, that is entitled to prescribe the final and dominant rule, for otherwise Congress would be denied the exercise of its constitutional authority and the State, and not the Nation, would be supreme within the national field."

Justice Hughes found support in earlier decisions authorizing congressional control of some intrastate activities in the interest of the safety of interstate railroad operations. (See also note 2b below.) He summarized some of those decisions as follows: "In Baltimore & Ohio Railroad Co. v. Interstate Commerce Commission [221 U.S. 612], the argument against the validity of the Hours of Service Act [of 1907] involved the consideration that the interstate and intrastate transactions of the carriers were so interwoven that it was utterly impracticable for them to divide their employés so that those who were engaged in interstate commerce should be confined to that commerce exclusively. Employés dealing with the movement of trains were employed in both sorts of commerce; but the court held that this fact did not preclude the exercise of Federal power. As Congress could limit the hours of labor of those engaged in interstate transportation, it necessarily followed that its will could not be frustrated by prolonging the period of service through other requirements of the carriers, or by the commingling of duties relating to interstate and intrastate operations. . . . So, in the Second Employers' Liability Cases [223 U.S. 1], it was insisted that while Congress had the authority to regulate the liability of a carrier for injuries sustained by one employee through the negligence of another, where all were engaged in interstate commerce, that power did not embrace instances where the negligent employee was engaged in intrastate commerce. The court said that this was a mistaken theory, as the causal negligence when operating injuriously upon an employee engaged in interstate commerce, had the same effect with respect to that commerce as if the negligent employee were also engaged therein."

In relating these decisions dealing with the physical impacts of local activities to the Shreveport problem of economic impacts, Justice Hughes explained: "While these decisions sustaining the Federal power relate to measures adopted in the interest of the safety of persons and property, they illustrate the principle that Congress in the exercise of its paramount power may prevent the common instrumentalities of interstate and intrastate commercial intercourse from being used in their intrastate operations to the injury of interstate commerce. This is not to say that Congress possesses the authority to regulate the internal commerce of a State, as such, but that it does possess the power to foster and protect interstate commerce, and to take all measures necessary or appropriate to that end, although intrastate transactions of interstate carriers may thereby be controlled." Justice Hughes accordingly concluded: "It is for Congress to supply the needed correction where the relation between intrastate and interstate rates presents the evil to be corrected, and this it may do completely, by reason of

its control over the interstate carrier in all matters having such a close and substantial relation to interstate commerce that it is necessary or appropriate to exercise the control for the effective government of that commerce." Justices Lurton and Pitney noted their dissents.

2. *Other examples of local railroad matters with an adequate impact on interstate commerce.* a. *Economic impacts—rate regulations.* The Shreveport case was only one of a series justifying the regulation of local rates structures because of the economic burdens imposed by the intrastate situation on interstate activities. See, e. g., Railroad Commission of Wisconsin v. Chicago, B. & Q. R. R., 257 U.S. 563 (1922). There, the Court sustained an ICC order requiring a blanket increase in all intrastate rates, even though state law prescribed a lower maximum. The justification for the order differed from that in the Shreveport Case: it was based on the expansion of the ICC's authority in the Transportation Act of 1920. As the Court explained: "Theretofore the control which Congress through the Interstate Commerce Commission exercised was primarily for the purpose of preventing injustice by unreasonable or discriminatory rates against persons and localities, and the only provisions of the law that inured to the benefit of the carriers were the requirement that the rates should be reasonable in the sense of furnishing an adequate compensation for the particular service rendered and the abolition of rebates. The new measure imposed an affirmative duty on the Interstate Commerce Commission to fix rates and to take other important steps to maintain an adequate railway service for the people of the United States." See also Dayton-Goose Creek Ry. Co. v. United States, 263 U.S. 456 (1924), upholding the power to control railroad earnings—intrastate as well as interstate—above a fair return, under the "recapture clause" of the 1920 Act; and Colorado v. United States, 271 U.S. 153 (1926), sustaining the power to order abandonment of an intrastate branch of a railroad, because the deficit incurred in operating that branch burdened the railroad's interstate activities.

b. *Physical impacts—safety regulations.* As noted in the excerpt from the Shreveport Case, Justice Hughes there drew on earlier decisions sustaining national regulation of local matters where the local activity imposed a tangible burden on interstate transportation. Safety regulations understandably were the easiest for the Court to sustain under this rationale, for they presented the most readily observable manifestations of local activities burdening interstate commerce: the obstruction to interstate movement caused by local accidents was a visible, physical one. See, in addition to the safety law decisions noted in the Shreveport excerpts, the approach in SOUTHERN RAILWAY CO. v. UNITED STATES, 222 U.S. 20 (1911). That case involved the Federal Safety Appliance Act. The Court sustained a penalty judgment imposed for operating railroad cars equipped with defective couplers. Three of the cars were used in moving intrastate traffic. The Act covered all cars "used on any railroad engaged in interstate commerce"; the Court found that this provision was satisfied because the cars were used "on a railroad which is a highway of interstate commerce," and that the law did not require that the cars be used "in moving interstate traffic." And application of the statute to vehicles used in moving intrastate traffic was found constitutional, "not because Congress possesses any power to regulate intrastate commerce as such, but because its power to regulate interstate commerce . . . may be exerted to secure the safety of the persons and

property transported therein and of those who are employed in such transportation no matter what may be the source of the dangers which threaten it." [Note the reliance on a related rationale in sustaining national regulation of labor relations (to avert the obstruction of commerce caused by strikes) in the Jones & Laughlin case, sec. 5 below.] The Court emphasized "practical considerations" that "are of common knowledge," including the fact that "the absence of appropriate safety appliances from any part of any train is a menace not only to that train, but to others."

3. *The "current of commerce" theory.* a. *The Swift case.* While the Court's emphasis on "practical considerations" was providing one type of rationale for demonstrating the impact of the local on the interstate (in cases such as Southern Railway), several other decisions were sketching an alternate basis for arguing that an intrastate activity should be reachable under the commerce power. The "current of commerce" rationale suggested that some local activities were controllable not because of their effects on commerce, but because they could themselves be viewed as "in" commerce or as an integral part of the "current of commerce." Justice Holmes' opinion in Swift & Co. v. United States, 196 U.S. 375 (1905), provided the impetus. In sustaining a Sherman Act injunction against price fixing by meat dealers (as noted above), Justice Holmes used the following language: "When cattle are sent for sale from a place in one State, with the expectation that they will end their transit, after purchase, in another, and when in effect they do so, with only the interruption necessary to find a purchaser at the stockyard, and when this is a typical, constantly recurring course, the current thus existing is a current of commerce among the States, and the purchase of the cattle is a part and incident of such commerce."

b. *The congressional reliance.* Congress successfully drew on this "current of commerce" concept in drafting subsequent regulation of stockyard practices. The Packers and Stockyards Act of 1921 was aimed primarily at preventing "unfair, discriminatory, or deceptive practices" by meat packers in interstate commerce. One of the provisions of the Act stated that "for the purpose of this Chapter . . . a transaction in respect to any article shall be considered to be in commerce if such article is part of that current of commerce usual in the livestock and meat packing industries, whereby livestock [and its products] are sent from one State with the expectation that they will end their transit, after purchase, in another. . . . Articles normally in such current of commerce shall not be considered out of such current through resort being had to any means or device intended to remove transactions in respect thereto from the provisions of this Act."

c. *Stafford v. Wallace.* Commission men and dealers in stockyards, subject to Secretary of Agriculture regulation of their charges and practices under the Act, challenged its constitutionality. The Supreme Court rejected the attack in STAFFORD v. WALLACE, 258 U.S. 495 (1922). Chief Justice Taft's opinion for the Court—with only Justice McReynolds dissenting —contained the following passages:

"The stockyards are not a place of rest or final destination. . . . The stockyards are but a throat through which the current flows, and the transactions which occur therein are only incident to this current from the West to the East, and from one State to another. Such transactions can not

be separated from the movement to which they contribute and necessarily take on its character. The commission men are essential in making the sales without which the flow of the current would be obstructed, and this, whether they are made to packers or dealers. The dealers are essential to the sales to the stock farmers and feeders. The sales are not in this aspect merely local transactions. They create a local change of title, it is true, but they do not stop the flow; they merely change the private interests in the subject of the current, not interfering with, but, on the contrary, being indispensable to its continuity. The origin of the livestock is in the West, its ultimate destination known to, and intended by, all engaged in the business is in the Middle West and East either as meat products or stock for feeding and fattening. This is the definite and well-understood course of business. The stockyards and the sales are necessary factors in the middle of this current of commerce. . . .

"The reasonable fear by Congress that such acts, usually lawful and affecting only intrastate commerce when considered alone, will probably and more or less constantly be used in conspiracies against interstate commerce or constitute a direct and undue burden on it, expressed in this remedial legislation, serves the same purpose as the intent charged in the Swift indictment to bring acts of a similar character into the current of interstate commerce for federal restraint. Whatever amounts to more or less constant practice, and threatens to obstruct or unduly to burden the freedom of interstate commerce is within the regulatory power of Congress under the commerce clause, and it is primarily for Congress to consider and decide the fact of the danger and meet it. This court will certainly not substitute its judgment for that of Congress in such a matter unless the relation of the subject to interstate commerce and its effect upon it are clearly non-existent."

Does Chief Justice Taft's last paragraph rest on a different theory of justification than the "current of commerce" approach of his first paragraph? Is there a significant difference between the "effect on commerce" and the "current of commerce" rationale? Note the attempts to rely on these justifications in subsequent commerce clause litigation, especially that considered in secs. 4 and 5 below.

SECTION 3. NATIONAL "POLICE" REGULATION: PROHIBITION OF INTERSTATE COMMERCE AS A TOOL

Introduction. In the cases in the preceding section, the Court confronted congressional efforts to impose direct regulations on local activities—regulations allegedly justified by the nexus between the local activity and interstate commerce. When that technique of regulation was used, the Court pursued a wavering course, from the restrictive interpretation of Knight to the more generous one of Shreveport. Yet in the same era, the Court rendered a series of decisions—reviewed in the first part of this section—consistently receptive to congressional regulation. The cases which follow differ from those in sec. 2 in two respects. First, the apparent objective of the legislation was primarily moral, as with efforts to control gambling and prostitu-

tion; the aim was typically quite far removed from the economic concerns that had prompted the commerce clause. Second, the technique of regulation differed: the congressional sanction was typically imposed at the state line, though the "harm" sought to be alleviated was primarily local; the form of regulation was to prohibit certain kinds of interstate movements; and that technique gave the Court far less trouble than when Congress sought to impose sanctions directly upon intrastate activity. But when legislators sought to apply the commerce-prohibiting technique to a problem with significant economic as well as moral dimensions, that of child labor, the Court called a halt, at least for a generation. See the Child Labor Case, printed below. In examining the materials in this section, consider whether there was any justification for the differing Court responses to the problems and techniques in the materials that follow and those considered in sec. 2. Which variety of legislation was closer to the original purposes of the commerce clause? Which technique of regulation was more susceptible to judicial scrutiny?

CHAMPION v. AMES
[THE LOTTERY CASE]

188 U.S. 321, 23 S.Ct. 321, 47 L.Ed. 492 (1903).

Appeal from the Circuit Court of the United States for the Northern District of Illinois.

[Appellant was arrested in Chicago to assure his appearance in a federal court in Texas, where he had been indicted for conspiracy to violate the Federal Lottery Act of 1895. The law prohibited importing, mailing, or transporting "from one State to another in the United States" any "ticket, chance, share or interest in or dependent upon the event of a lottery . . . offering prizes dependent upon lot or chance." The indictment charged shipment by Wells Fargo Express, from Texas to California, of a box containing Paraguayan lottery tickets. Appellant challenged the constitutionality of the Act by seeking release on habeas corpus in Chicago. The Circuit Court dismissed the writ.]

Mr. Justice HARLAN delivered the opinion of the Court. . . .

We are of opinion that lottery tickets are subjects of traffic and therefore are subjects of commerce, and the regulation of the carriage of such tickets from State to State, at least by independent carriers, is a regulation of commerce among the several States.

But it is said that the statute in question does not regulate the carrying of lottery tickets from State to State, but by punishing those who cause them to be so carried Congress in effect prohibits such carrying; that in respect of the carrying from one State to another of articles or things that are, in fact, or according to usage in business, the subjects of commerce, the authority given Congress was not to *prohibit,* but only to *regulate.* . . .

. . . Are we prepared to say that a provision which is, in effect, a *prohibition* of the carriage of such articles from State to State is not a fit or appropriate mode for the *regulation* of that particular kind of commerce?

If lottery traffic, *carried on through interstate commerce,* is a matter of which Congress may take cognizance and over which its power may be exerted, can it be possible that it must tolerate the traffic, and simply regulate the manner in which it may be carried on? Or may not Congress, for the protection of the people of all the States, and under the power to regulate interstate commerce, devise such means within the scope of the Constitution, and not prohibited by it, as will drive that traffic out of commerce among the States?

In determining whether regulation may not under some circumstances properly take the form or have the effect of prohibition, the nature of the interstate traffic which it was sought by the act of May 2, 1895, to suppress cannot be overlooked. When enacting that statute Congress no doubt shared the views upon the subject of lotteries heretofore expressed by this court. In Phalen v. Virginia, 8 How. 163, 168, after observing that the suppression of nuisances injurious to public health or morality is among the most important duties of Government, this court said: "Experience has shown that the common forms of gambling are comparatively innocuous when placed in contrast with the widespread pestilence of lotteries. The former are confined to a few persons and places, but the latter infests the whole community; it enters every dwelling; it reaches every class; it preys upon the hard earnings of the poor; it plunders the ignorant and simple." . . .

If a State, when considering legislation for the suppression of lotteries within its own limits, may properly take into view the evils that inhere in the raising of money, in that mode, why may not Congress, invested with the power to regulate commerce among the several States, provide that such commerce shall not be polluted by the carrying of lottery tickets from one State to another? In this connection it must not be forgotten that the power of Congress to regulate commerce among the States is plenary, is complete in itself, and is subject to no limitations except such as may be found in the Constitution. [S]urely it will not be said to be a part of any one's liberty, as recognized by the supreme law of the land, that he shall be allowed to introduce into commerce among the States an element that will be confessedly injurious to the public morals. . . .

[Congress] does not assume to interfere with traffic or commerce in lottery tickets carried on exclusively within the limits of any State, but has in view only commerce of that kind among the several States. It has not assumed to interfere with the completely internal affairs of any State, and has only legislated in respect of a matter which concerns the people of the United States. As a State may, for the purpose of guarding the morals of its own people, forbid all sales of lottery tickets within its limits, so Congress, for the purpose of guarding the people of the United States against the "widespread pestilence of lotteries" and to protect the commerce which concerns all the States, may prohibit the carrying of lottery tickets from one State to another. In legislating upon the subject of the traffic in lottery tickets, as carried on through interstate commerce, Congress only supplemented the action of those States—perhaps all of them—which, for the protection of the public morals, prohibit the drawing of lotteries, as well as the sale or circulation of lottery tickets, within their respective limits. It said, in effect, that it would not permit the declared policy of the

States, which sought to protect their people against the mischiefs of the lottery business, to be overthrown or disregarded by the agency of interstate commerce. We should hesitate long before adjudging that an evil of such appalling character, carried on through interstate commerce, cannot be met and crushed by the only power competent to that end. . . .

It is said, however, that if, in order to suppress lotteries carried on through interstate commerce, Congress may exclude lottery tickets from such commerce, that principle leads necessarily to the conclusion that Congress may arbitrarily exclude from commerce among the States any article, commodity or thing, of whatever kind or nature, or however useful or valuable, which it may choose, no matter with what motive, to declare shall not be carried from one State to another. It will be time enough to consider the constitutionality of such legislation when we must do so. The present case does not require the court to declare the full extent of the power that Congress may exercise in the regulation of commerce among the States. . . . It would not be difficult to imagine legislation that [would be] hostile to the objects for the accomplishment of which Congress was invested with the general power to regulate commerce among the several States. But, as often said, the possible abuse of a power is not an argument against its existence. There is probably no governmental power that may not be exerted to the injury of the public. If what is done by Congress is manifestly in excess of the powers granted to it, then upon the courts will rest the duty of adjudging that its action is neither legal nor binding upon the people. But if what Congress does is within the limits of its power, and is simply unwise or injurious, the remedy is that suggested by Chief Justice Marshall in Gibbons v. Ogden, when he said: "The wisdom and the discretion of Congress, their identity with the people, and the influence which their constituents possess at elections, are, in this, as in many other instances, as that, for example, of declaring war, the sole restraints on which they have relied, to secure them from its abuse. They are the restraints on which the people must often rely solely, in all representative governments." . . .

Affirmed.

Mr. Chief Justice FULLER, with whom concur Mr. Justice BREWER, Mr. Justice SHIRAS and Mr. Justice PECKHAM, dissenting. . . .
. . . That the purpose of Congress in this enactment was the suppression of lotteries cannot reasonably be denied. That purpose is avowed in the title of the act, and is its natural and reasonable effect, and by that its validity must be tested. . . .

The power of the State to impose restraints and burdens on persons and property in conservation and promotion of the public health, good order and prosperity is a power originally and always belonging to the States, [and is] essentially exclusive, and the suppression of lotteries as a harmful business falls within this power, commonly called of police. . . .

It is urged, however, that because Congress is empowered to regulate commerce between the several States, it, therefore, may suppress lotteries by prohibiting the carriage of lottery matter. Congress may indeed make all laws necessary and proper for carrying the powers granted to it into execution, and doubtless an act prohibiting the carriage of lottery matter would be

necessary and proper to the execution of a power to suppress lotteries; but that power belongs to the States and not to Congress. To hold that Congress has general police power would be to hold that it may accomplish objects not entrusted to the General Government, and to defeat the operation of the Tenth Amendment .   .   ..

But apart from the question of *bona fides,* this act cannot be brought within the power to regulate commerce among the several States, unless lottery tickets are articles of commerce, and, therefore, when carried across state lines, of interstate commerce; or unless the power to regulate interstate commerce includes the absolute and exclusive power to prohibit the transportation of any thing or anybody from one State to another. .   .   . Is the carriage of lottery tickets from one State to another commercial intercourse? [The dissent concluded that it was not "commercial intercourse."]

It will not do to say—a suggestion which has heretofore been made in this case—that state laws have been found to be ineffective for the suppression of lotteries, and therefore Congress should interfere. The scope of the commerce clause of the Constitution cannot be enlarged because of present views of public interest. .   .   .

"Should Congress," said [Marshall] in McCulloch v. Maryland, 4 Wheat. 316, 423, "under the pretext of executing its powers, pass laws for the accomplishment of objects not entrusted to the Government; it would become the painful duty of this tribunal, should a case requiring such a decision come before it, to say that such an act was not the law of the land."

.   .   .

The power to prohibit the transportation of diseased animals and infected goods over railroads or on steamboats is an entirely different thing, for they would be in themselves injurious to the transaction of interstate commerce, and, moreover, are essentially commercial in their nature. And the exclusion of diseased persons rests on different ground, for nobody would pretend that persons could be kept off the trains because they were going from one State to another to engage in the lottery business. However enticing that business may be, we do not understand these pieces of paper themselves can communicate bad principles by contact. .   .   .

I regard this decision as inconsistent with the views of the framers of the Constitution, and of Marshall, its great expounder. Our form of government may remain notwithstanding legislation or decision, but, as long ago observed, it is with governments, as with religions, the form may survive the substance of the faith. .   .   .

———

SUCCESSFUL EARLY USES OF THE COMMERCE–PROHIBITING POWER

1. *The ghost of Marshall.* Note the competing uses of Marshall statements in the Harlan and Fuller opinions. Was the "wisdom and discretion of Congress" quotation from Gibbons v. Ogden, used by Harlan, apposite to the problem of the principal case? Did that make it unnecessary to consider the "pretext" statement in McCulloch v. Maryland, quoted by

Fuller? Would it have been possible to sustain the statute on the assumption that its true "objects" were the control of a local "harm"—intrastate lottery-promoting activities? On the theory that these activities "affected" or "burdened" commerce? On the basis of the "current of commerce" theory? Should the Court have insisted on an adequate justification for reaching intrastate activities? Was the failure to require such a justification (and the acceptance of the "prohibition" rationale) fatal to the development of commerce power doctrine of sufficient integrity and viability? Note the questions following the Child Labor Case at the end of this section, and compare the later uses of the commerce-prohibiting power, sec. 5 below.

2. *The impact on Congress.* Early-twentieth century reformers seeking a constitutional basis for broader federal "police" measures quickly seized on the encouragement provided by the majority position in the Lottery Case. In 1906, for example, Senator Albert J. Beveridge—later John Marshall's biographer—successfully proposed a Meat Inspection Amendment to an appropriations bill. The Amendment, backed by President Theodore Roosevelt and by popular support generated by such exposés as Upton Sinclair's "The Jungle," became law: it prohibited interstate shipment of meats that had not been federally inspected. In the same session, Congress enacted the Pure Food and Drugs Act. Later that year, Senator Beveridge suggested a law excluding from commerce goods produced by child labor. He was confident that the Lottery Case "absolutely settled" the constitutionality of his proposal. But passage of a child labor law was still a decade away—and the Court found the 1916 Child Labor Act unconstitutional after all, in Hammer v. Dagenhart, the next principal case.*

3. *Exclusion of "harmful" goods.* The Lottery Case precedent was, however, adequate to sustain a wide variety of early-twentieth century laws excluding objects deemed harmful from interstate commerce. See Cushman, "The National Police Power under the Commerce Clause of the Constitution," 3 Minn.L.Rev. 289, 381 (1919). Decisions sustaining the Pure Food and Drugs Act and the Mann (White Slave) Act were especially important in building the hopes that were crushed by Hammer v. Dagenhart:

a. *Impure foods.* In HIPOLITE EGG CO. v. UNITED STATES, 220 U.S. 45 (1911), a shipment of adulterated preserved eggs had been confiscated under the Pure Food and Drugs Act of 1906. The action was challenged on the ground that "the shipment had passed out of interstate commerce before the seizure of the eggs." A unanimous Court rejected the attack. Justice McKenna emphasized that the case involved "illicit articles—articles which the law seeks to keep out of commerce, because they are debased by adulteration." There could therefore be no insistence that "the articles must be apprehended . . . before they have become a part of the general mass of property of the State." That argument, he claimed, "attempts to apply to articles of illegitimate commerce the rule which marks the line between the exercise of Federal power and state power over articles of legitimate commerce. [See chap. 5, below.] The contention misses the question

---

* See Braeman, "Albert J. Beveridge and the First National Child Labor Bill," 60 Indiana Magazine of History 1 (1964), and Braeman, "The Square Deal in Action: A Case Study in the Growth of the 'National Police Power,'" in Braeman, Bremner and Walter, Change and Continuity in Twentieth Century America (1964), 35–80.

in the case. There is here no conflict of national and state jurisdictions over property legally articles of trade. The question here is whether articles which are outlaws of commerce may be seized wherever found, and it certainly will not be contended that they are outside of the jurisdiction of the National Government when they are within the borders of a State. The question in the case, therefore is, What power has Congress over such articles? Can they escape the consequences of their illegal transportation by being mingled at the place of destination with other property? To give them such immunity would defeat, in many cases, the provision for their confiscation, and their confiscation or destruction is the especial concern of the law. The power to do so is certainly appropriate to the right to bar them from interstate commerce, and completes its purpose, which is not to prevent merely the physical movement of adulterated articles, but the use of them, or rather to prevent trade in them between the States by denying to them the facilities of interstate commerce. And appropriate means to that end, which we have seen is legitimate, are the seizure and condemnation of the articles at their point of destination. . . . McCulloch v. Maryland, 4 Wheat. 316."

How far-reaching is that application of McCulloch v. Maryland? Does it justify a direct ban on producing adulterated goods as a "means appropriate to the right to bar them from interstate commerce"? Only if the goods are intended for interstate shipment? Does it justify national marriage and divorce standards as an "appropriate means" to implement a ban on interstate movement of persons married or divorced in violation of national standards? Only if the persons getting married or divorced intend to travel interstate? Does it offer a bootstrap technique for reaching local affairs via the prohibition route: in order to regulate a local matter, simply prohibit interstate movements connected with it and then reach the local matter as an incidental means to implement the interstate prohibition? Note the elaboration of this justification of local control as an incident of interstate commerce prohibition in United States v. Darby, sec. 5 below.

b. *The Mann Act.* The Mann Act, prohibiting the transportation of women in interstate commerce for immoral purposes, was upheld in HOKE v. UNITED STATES, 227 U.S. 308 (1913). Again, Justice McKenna wrote for a unanimous Court. He cited, in addition to the Lottery Case, United States v. Popper, 98 Fed. 423 (N.D.Cal.1899), involving an 1897 law prohibiting the "carrying of obscene literature and articles designed for indecent and immoral use from one State to another."

The opinion in Hoke contained one of the broadest early statements of the commerce-prohibiting power: "[I]t must be kept in mind that we are one people; and the powers reserved to the States and those conferred on the Nation are adapted to be exercised, whether independently or concurrently, to promote the general welfare, material and moral. This is the effect of the decisions, and surely if the facility of interstate transportation can be taken away from the demoralization of lotteries, the debasement of obscene literature, the contagion of diseased cattle or persons, the impurity of food and drugs, the like facility can be taken away from the systematic enticement to and the enslavement in prostitution and debauchery of women, and, more insistently, of girls. . . . The principle established by the cases is the simple one, when rid of confusing and distracting considerations, that Con-

gress has power over transportation 'among the several States'; that the power is complete in itself, and that Congress, as an incident to it, may adopt not only means necessary but convenient to its exercise, and the means may have the quality of police regulations."

Justice McKenna dissented, however, when the Court, in a 5 to 3 decision, found the Mann Act applicable to activities not constituting "commercialized vice." CAMINETTI v. UNITED STATES, 242 U.S. 470 (1917). Justice Day wrote for the majority. The dissent argued that "everybody knows that there is a difference between the occasional immoralities of men and women and that systematized and mercenary immorality epitomized in the statute's graphic phrase 'White-slave traffic.' And it was such immorality that was in the legislative mind and not the other. The other is occasional, not habitual—inconspicuous—does not offensively obtrude upon public notice. Interstate commerce is not its instrument as it is of the other, nor is prostitution its object or its end. It may, indeed, in instances, find a convenience in crossing state lines, but this is its accident, not its aid."

Could this objection to the interpretation of the Act be the basis of a valid constitutional objection? One year after Caminetti, the Court held the Child Labor Law unconstitutional, in the case that follows. Note that Justice Day once again wrote the majority opinion—and that Justice McKenna was once again with the dissenters.

HAMMER v. DAGENHART
[THE CHILD LABOR CASE]

247 U.S. 251, 38 S.Ct. 529, 62 L.Ed. 1101 (1918).

Appeal from the District Court of the United States for the Western District of North Carolina.

Mr. Justice DAY delivered the opinion of the Court.

A bill was filed in the [District Court] by a father in his own behalf and as next friend of his two minor sons, one under the age of fourteen years and the other between the ages of fourteen and sixteen years, employees in a cotton mill at Charlotte, North Carolina, to enjoin the enforcement of the act of Congress [of 1916] intended to prevent interstate commerce in the products of child labor. . . .

The District Court held the act unconstitutional and entered a decree enjoining its enforcement. This appeal brings the case here. The first section of the act is in the margin.[1]

1. That no producer, manufacturer, or dealer shall ship or deliver for shipment in interstate or foreign commerce any article or commodity the product of any mine or quarry, situated in the United States, in which within thirty days prior to the time of the removal of such product therefrom children under the age of sixteen years have been employed or permitted to work, or any article or commodity the product of any mill, cannery, workshop, factory, or manufacturing establishment, situated in the United States, in which within thirty days prior to the removal of such product therefrom children under the age of fourteen years have been employed or permitted to work, or children between the ages of fourteen years and sixteen years have been employed or permitted to work more than eight hours in any

The attack upon the act rests upon three propositions: First: It is not a regulation of interstate and foreign commerce; second: It contravenes the Tenth Amendment to the Constitution; third: It conflicts with the Fifth Amendment to the Constitution. . . .

[I]t is insisted that adjudged cases in this court establish the doctrine that the power to regulate given to Congress incidentally includes the authority to prohibit the movement of ordinary commodities and therefore that the subject is not open for discussion. The cases demonstrate the contrary. They rest upon the character of the particular subjects dealt with and the fact that the scope of governmental authority, state or national, possessed over them is such that the authority to prohibit is as to them but the exertion of the power to regulate. [After discussing the Lottery Case, Hipolite, Hoke and similar decisions—see the preceding notes—the Court continued:]

In each of these instances the use of interstate transportation was necessary to the accomplishment of harmful results. In other words, although the power over interstate transportation was to regulate, that could only be accomplished by prohibiting the use of the facilities of interstate commerce to effect the evil intended.

This element is wanting in the present case. The thing intended to be accomplished by this statute is the denial of the facilities of interstate commerce to those manufacturers in the States who employ children within the prohibited ages. The act in its effect does not regulate transportation among the states, but aims to standardize the ages at which children may be employed in mining and manufacturing within the states. The goods shipped are of themselves harmless. The act permits them to be freely shipped after thirty days from the time of their removal from the factory. When offered for shipment, and before transportation begins, the labor of their production is over, and the mere fact that they were intended for interstate commerce transportation does not make their production subject to federal control under the commerce power. . . .

Over interstate transportation, or its incidents, the regulatory power of Congress is ample, but the production of articles, intended for interstate commerce, is a matter of local regulation. . . . If it were otherwise, all manufacture intended for interstate shipment would be brought under federal control to the practical exclusion of the authority of the States, a result certainly not contemplated by the framers of the Constitution when they vested in Congress the authority to regulate commerce among the States. Kidd v. Pearson, 128 U.S. 1, 21.

It is further contended that the authority of Congress may be exerted to control interstate commerce in the shipment of child-made goods because of the effect of the circulation of such goods in other States where the evil of this class of labor has been recognized by local legislation, and the right to thus employ child labor has been more rigorously restrained than in the State of production. In other words, that the unfair competition, thus engendered, may be controlled by closing the channels of interstate commerce

day, or more than six days in any week, or after the hour of seven o'clock postmeridian, or before the hour of six o'clock antemeridian. [Footnote by the Court.]

to manufacturers in those States where the local laws do not meet what Congress deems to be the more just standard of other States.

There is no power vested in Congress to require the States to exercise their police power so as to prevent possible unfair competition. Many causes may coöperate to give one State, by reason of local laws or conditions, an economic advantage over others. The Commerce Clause was not intended to give to Congress a general authority to equalize such conditions. In some of the States laws have been passed fixing minimum wages for women, in others the local law regulates the hours of labor of women in various employments. Business done in such States may be at an economic disadvantage when compared with States which have no such regulations; surely, this fact does not give Congress the power to deny transportation in interstate commerce to those who carry on business where the hours of labor and the rate of compensation for women have not been fixed by a standard in use in other States and approved by Congress. . . .

The grant of power to Congress over the subject of interstate commerce was to enable it to regulate such commerce, and not to give it authority to control the States in their exercise of the police power over local trade and manufacture. . . .

That there should be limitations upon the right to employ children in mines and factories in the interest of their own and the public welfare, all will admit. That such employment is generally deemed to require regulation is shown by the fact that the brief of counsel states that every State in the Union has a law upon the subject, limiting the right to thus employ children. . . . It may be desirable that such laws be uniform, but our Federal Government is one of enumerated powers; "this principle," declared Chief Justice Marshall in McCulloch v. Maryland, 4 Wheat. 316, "is universally admitted." . . . The maintenance of the authority of the States over matters purely local is as essential to the preservation of our institutions as is the conservation of the supremacy of the federal power in all matters entrusted to the Nation by the Federal Constitution. . . .

We have neither authority nor disposition to question the motives of Congress in enacting this legislation. The purposes intended must be attained consistently with constitutional limitations and not by an invasion of the powers of the States. This court has no more important function than that which devolves upon it the obligation to preserve inviolate the constitutional limitations upon the exercise of authority, federal and state, to the end that each may continue to discharge, harmoniously with the other, the duties entrusted to it by the Constitution.

In our view the necessary effect of this act is, by means of a prohibition against the movement in interstate commerce of ordinary commercial commodities, to regulate the hours of labor of children in factories and mines within the States, a purely state authority. Thus the act in a two-fold sense is repugnant to the Constitution. It not only transcends the authority delegated to Congress over commerce but also exerts a power as to a purely local matter to which the federal authority does not extend. The far reaching result of upholding the act cannot be more plainly indicated than by pointing out that if Congress can thus regulate matters entrusted to local authority by prohibition of the movement of commodities in interstate commerce, all

freedom of commerce will be at an end, and the power of the States over local matters may be eliminated, and thus our system of government be practically destroyed.   .   .   .

Affirmed.

Mr. Justice HOLMES, dissenting.

The single question in this case is whether Congress has power to prohibit the shipment in interstate or foreign commerce [of the products specified in the statute].   The objection urged against the power is that the States have exclusive control over their methods of production and that Congress cannot meddle with them, and taking the proposition in the sense of direct intermeddling I agree to it and suppose that no one denies it.   But if an act is within the powers specifically conferred upon Congress, it seems to me that it is not made any less constitutional because of the indirect effects that it may have, however obvious it may be that it will have those effects, and that we are not at liberty upon such grounds to hold it void.

The first step in my argument is to make plain what no one is likely to dispute—that the statute in question is within the power expressly given to Congress if considered only as to its immediate effects and that if invalid it is so only upon some collateral ground.   The statute confines itself to prohibiting the carriage of certain goods in interstate or foreign commerce. Congress is given power to regulate such commerce in unqualified terms. It would not be argued today that the power to regulate does not include the power to prohibit.   Regulation means the prohibition of something, and when interstate commerce is the matter to be regulated I cannot doubt that the regulation may prohibit any part of such commerce that Congress sees fit to forbid.   At all events it is established by the Lottery Case and others that have followed it that a law is not beyond the regulative power of Congress merely because it prohibits certain transportation out and out.   .   .   .   . So I repeat that this statute in its immediate operation is clearly within the Congress's constitutional power.

The question then is narrowed to whether the exercise of its otherwise constitutional power by Congress can be pronounced unconstitutional because of its possible reaction upon the conduct of the States in a matter upon which I have admitted that they are free from direct control.   I should have thought that that matter had been disposed of so fully as to leave no room for doubt. I should have thought that the most conspicuous decisions of this Court had made it clear that the power to regulate commerce and other constitutional powers could not be cut down or qualified by the fact that it might interfere with the carrying out of the domestic policy of any State.

The manufacture of oleomargarine is as much a matter of state regulation as the manufacture of cotton cloth.   Congress levied a tax upon the compound when colored so as to resemble butter that was so great as obviously to prohibit the manufacture and sale.   In a very elaborate discussion the present Chief Justice excluded any inquiry into the purpose of an act which apart from that purpose was within the power of Congress.   McCray v. United States, 195 U.S. 27.   [See chap. 4, sec. 1, below.]   .   .   .   And to come to cases upon interstate commerce, notwithstanding [the Knight case], the Sherman Act has been made an instrument for the breaking up of com-

binations in restraint of trade and monopolies, using the power to regulate commerce as a foothold, but not proceeding because that commerce was the end actually in mind. The objection that the control of the States over production was interfered with was urged again and again but always in vain. . . .

The [Pure Food and Drug Act] applies not merely to articles that the changing opinions of the time condemn as intrinsically harmful but to others innocent in themselves, simply on the ground that the order for them was induced by a preliminary fraud. Weeks v. United States, 245 U.S. 618. It does not matter whether the supposed evil precedes or follows the transportation. It is enough that in the opinion of Congress the transportation encourages the evil. I may add that in the cases on the so-called White Slave Act it was established that the means adopted by Congress as convenient to the exercise of its power might have the character of police regulations. . . .

The notion that prohibition is any less prohibition when applied to things now thought evil I do not understand. But if there is any matter upon which civilized countries have agreed—far more unanimously than they have with regard to intoxicants and some other matters over which this country is now emotionally aroused—it is the evil of premature and excessive child labor. I should have thought that if we were to introduce our own moral conceptions where in my opinion they do not belong, this was preëminently a case for upholding the exercise of all its powers by the United States. But I had thought that the propriety of the exercise of a power admitted to exist in some cases was for the consideration of Congress alone and that this Court always had disavowed the right to intrude its judgment upon questions of policy or morals. It is not for this Court to pronounce when prohibition is necessary to regulation if it ever may be necessary—to say that it is permissible as against strong drink but not as against the product of ruined lives.

The act does not meddle with anything belonging to the States. They may regulate their internal affairs and their domestic commerce as they like. But when they seek to send their products across the state line they are no longer within their rights. If there were no Constitution and no Congress their power to cross the line would depend upon their neighbors. Under the Constitution such commerce belongs not to the States but to Congress to regulate. It may carry out its views of public policy whatever indirect effect they may have upon the activities of the States. Instead of being encountered by a prohibitive tariff at her boundaries the State encounters the public policy of the United States which it is for Congress to express. The public policy of the United States is shaped with a view to the benefit of the nation as a whole. If, as has been the case within the memory of men still living, a State should take a different view of the propriety of sustaining a lottery from that which generally prevails, I cannot believe that the fact would require a different decision from that reached in Champion v. Ames. Yet in that case it would be said with quite as much force as in this that Congress was attempting to intermeddle with the State's domestic affairs. The national welfare as understood by Congress may require a different attitude within its sphere from that of some self-seeking State. It seems to me entirely con-

stitutional for Congress to enforce its understanding by all the means at its command.

Mr. Justice McKENNA, Mr. Justice BRANDEIS and Mr. Justice CLARKE concur in this opinion.

————

PROBLEMS AND CONSEQUENCES OF THE CHILD LABOR CASE

1. *Viable limits on the commerce power and the Holmes dissent.* a. Is the majority's distinction of earlier cases involving the commerce-prohibiting power persuasive? Is the dissent needlessly broad? Should Justice Holmes have paid greater attention to the "unfair competition" effects of interstate shipment of the goods? Are the evils produced by child labor-made goods more closely related to "commercial" concerns than the evils involved in the Mann Act decisions and Lottery Case? Is it possible to argue that the Child Labor Act was more "economic," "commercial" in purpose than most of the "police" regulations sustained in the cases between the Lottery Case and Hammer?

Recall that, in his Northern Securities dissent (noted in sec. 2 above), Justice Holmes could see "no part of the conduct of life with which on similar principles Congress might not interfere," if the "logic of the argument for the Government" were accepted. Can not the same be said of the "logic of the argument" of the Holmes dissent in Hammer? Was Justice Holmes simply ceasing to argue restrictions on the commerce-prohibiting power because the majority had abandoned the opportunity to adhere to viable limitations in the cases beginning with the Lottery Case? Was it necessary to ignore the "collateral" effects, to limit judicial vision to the "immediate effects" of the statute, to justify the Child Labor Law? Would it not have been possible to concede that the law in effect regulated local production for interstate commerce, and yet sustain it because the activities regulated "affected" commerce? Note that Holmes' dissent suggests that the states "are free from direct control" regarding child labor. If that is so, is his dissenting position not an endorsement of the "pretext" usage of power condemned by Marshall in McCulloch v. Maryland? *

b. Holmes' "hands-off" policy ultimately prevailed in 1941, in United States v. Darby (sec. 5 below), when the Court explicitly overruled Hammer v. Dagenhart. If the Holmesian position is justifiable— e. g., because of institutional limitations on the Court, such as the difficulties of identifying congressional "purposes" and "pretext" abuses of power— does it follow that a legislator is wholly free to vote for commerce power regulations with primarily moral rather than commercial objectives? Even when judicial unwillingness to invalidate is predictable, is not a legislator nevertheless compelled—given the lawmaker's constitutional oath—to

---

* The majority's position in Hammer did not wholly bar the use of the commerce-prohibiting technique in other areas of regulation. See, e. g., Brooks v. United States, 267 U.S. 432 (1925) (sustaining the constitutionality of the National Motor Vehicle Theft Act of 1919). For use of the commerce-prohibiting device in later years, see the notes after the Darby case, sec. 5 below.

scrutinize his or her purposes in supporting legislation and to determine whether those purposes are consistent with the constitutional allocations of power? See generally Brest, "The Conscientious Legislator's Guide to Constitutional Interpretation," 27 Stan.L.Rev. 585 (1975). Justice Holmes himself did perceive such a difference between the judge's and the legislator's approach to constitutional issues. In a letter of April 3, 1919, Holmes wrote to then District Judge Learned Hand, on problems such as those presented by the Child Labor Case: "In my opinion Congress may have what ulterior motives they please if the act passed in the immediate aspect is within its powers—though personally, were I a legislator I might think it dishonest to use powers in that way." [The letter is printed in Gunther, "Learned Hand and the Origins of Modern First Amendment Doctrine: Some Fragments of History," 27 Stan.L.Rev. 719 (1975).]

2. *Other efforts to control child labor.* After the Hammer decision, Congress sought to regulate child labor through the taxing power. That law was invalidated in the Child Labor Tax Case in 1922 (printed in sec. 1 of the next chapter). Justice Holmes was with the majority there. After the unsuccessful legislative efforts, Congress submitted to the states a proposed constitutional amendment authorizing national child labor laws. The amendment was never ratified; but the need for ratification largely disappeared in view of the Court's decision in United States v. Darby, 312 U.S. 100 (1941) (sec. 5, below).

SECTION 4.　THE COURT THREATENS THE NEW DEAL

Introduction. President Franklin D. Roosevelt took office in the midst of a grave economic crisis and with a call for "action, and action now." Symptoms of the Great Depression were everywhere: sharp drops in employment, production, income; business failures and home mortgage foreclosures. The response was swift: an unprecedented flow of far-reaching measures came from Congress—torrentially during the dramatic "First Hundred Days," with more deliberate speed thereafter.

Many New Deal measures were based on the commerce power, for the "problems were economic, and the Commerce Clause was the enumerated power most directly concerned with business and economic, or commercial matters." And the regulatory technique typically invoked to reach those economic problems was the "effect on commerce" one considered in sec. 2 above. The commerce-prohibiting technique appeared to have been blocked by the Child Labor Case (see sec. 3); and prohibitions of interstate movements seemed in any event an awkward approach to the New Deal's problems. Practically as well as legally, then, efforts to regulate intrastate affairs on the ground of their relationship to interstate commerce seemed the far more attractive approach. Cases such as the Shreveport decision were encouraging; yet cases like Knight looked the other way. Would the New Deal measures survive judicial scrutiny? There could be no certainty, for "there was ample authority in the Supreme Court opinions looking both ways." Stern, "The Commerce Clause and the National Economy, 1933–

1946," 59 Harv.L.Rev. 645, 646 (1946), Selected Essays, 1938–62 (1963), 218, 219.

The first signs from the Supreme Court were encouraging. Early in 1934, 5 to 4 decisions sustained state laws in the face of attacks that were clearly substantial under prior interpretations of the contract and due process clauses. [Home Building & Loan Ass'n v. Blaisdell, 290 U.S. 398 (1934) (mortgage moratorium law); Nebbia v. New York, 291 U.S. 502 (1934) (milk price regulation)—both considered in chap. 9 below.] A few months later, however, in the first Court test of a major New Deal law, the National Industrial Recovery Act of 1933 was wounded, though the reach of the commerce power was not discussed: in the "hot oil" case, the petroleum code under the NIRA was invalidated on the ground of excessive delegation of legislative power to the executive. Panama Refining Co. v. Ryan, 293 U.S. 388 (1935). But an important early New Deal measure—a 1933 Joint Resolution declaring "gold clauses" in private contracts to be "against public policy"—was sustained, Norman v. Baltimore & Ohio R. R. Co., 294 U.S. 240 (1935), though the Government won only a narrow victory in its attempt to avoid payment under gold clauses in public obligations, Perry v. United States, 294 U.S. 330 (1935).

There was still no ruling on New Deal regulation under the commerce clause, however. That did not come until later in 1935. In the first test, the Court invalidated a measure not central to the New Deal program, the Railroad Retirement Act of 1934. RAILROAD RETIREMENT BOARD v. ALTON RAILROAD CO., 295 U.S. 330 (1935). That decision was an especially gloomy omen because, as noted in sec. 2, Congress had long regulated railroad matters and had seldom encountered constitutional obstacles. Nevertheless, the 5 to 4 decision in Alton invalidated a law establishing a compulsory retirement and pension plan for all carriers subject to the Interstate Commerce Act. Justice Roberts' majority opinion concluded that the law was "not in purpose or effect a regulation of interstate commerce within the meaning of the Constitution." He rejected the argument that pensions were "related to efficiency of transportation." If "the fostering of a contented mind on the part of an employee" were accepted as "in any just sense a regulation of interstate transportation," he insisted, "obviously there is no limit to the field of so-called regulation." Was it not "apparent," he asked, that such regulations "are really and essentially related solely to the social welfare of the worker, and therefore remote from any regulation of commerce as such?" He concluded that they "obviously lie outside the orbit of Congressional Power."

Justice Roberts recognized that the Court had long sustained legislation such as the Safety Appliance Act, the Employers' Liability Act, and hours-of-service laws: those, he insisted, were distinguishable because they had "a direct and intimate connection with the actual operation of the railroads." He conceded, too, that Congress probably could enact a compulsory workmen's compensation law for railroad workers. But that variety of legislation was supposedly distinguishable because the pension law sought "to attach to the relation of employer and employee a new incident, without reference to any existing obligation or legal liability, solely in the interest of the employee, with no regard to the conduct of the business, or its safety or effi-

ciency, but purely for social ends." Chief Justice Hughes' dissent, joined by Justices Brandeis, Stone and Cardozo, insisted that it was "clear that the morale of railroad employees has an important bearing on the efficiency of the transportation service, and that a reasonable pension plan by its assurance of security is an appropriate means to that end."

The Alton decision proved to be an accurate omen of doom. Attempts to justify more important New Deal laws under the commerce power failed soon after: three weeks after Alton, the Government lost the "sick chicken" case challenging the National Industrial Recovery Act, Schechter Poultry Corp. v. United States, 295 U.S. 495 (1935)—a decision that seemed a return to "the horse-and-buggy age" to President Roosevelt. In the following year, the commerce clause basis once again failed when the Bituminous Coal Conservation Act of 1935 was held unconstitutional, Carter v. Carter Coal Co., 298 U.S. 238 (1936). And the New Deal's failures were not limited to commerce power cases: in the same year, for example, an effort to resort to the spending power as justification for national regulation of agricultural production was rejected by the Court, in United States v. Butler, 297 U.S. 1 (1936) (chap. 4, sec. 2, below).

The Schechter and Carter cases follow. Consider, with respect to those cases as well as Alton, whether the majority positions were consistent with earlier commerce clause rulings. Can any of the decisions be justified as "principled"—as a decision that rests on "reasons that in their generality and their neutrality transcend any immediate result that is involved"? Wechsler, "Toward Neutral Principles of Constitutional Law," 73 Harv.L.Rev. 1, 19 (1959); Selected Essays 1938–62 (1963), 463, 475. Or were those decisions simply willful fiats by a Supreme Court majority hostile to reform, as many New Deal critics of the Court charged?

THE SCHECHTER CASE AND ITS AFTERMATH

1. *The decision.* The most dramatic and most controversial New Deal effort to combat the Depression and revive the economy was the enactment of the National Industrial Recovery Act of 1933. The NIRA authorized the President—ordinarily upon application by trade associations—to promulgate "codes of fair competition for the trade or industry." Several hundred codes were soon adopted. The typical code contained provisions regarding unfair trade practices, minimum wages and prices, maximum hours and collective bargaining. Violation of any code provision "in any transaction in or affecting interstate commerce" was made punishable as a misdemeanor.

The Act was held unconstitutional in SCHECHTER POULTRY CORP. v. UNITED STATES, 295 U.S. 495 (1935). By then, the regime of the NIRA was near an end in any event; the Roosevelt Administration's fears, and the President's "horse-and-buggy age" comment, reflected concerns about the fate of more permanent New Deal innovations. The NIRA scheme had worked well at the outset, with widespread public support. But by the time the Schechter case came to the Court, the regulatory structure was disintegrating in the face of waning enthusiasm, administrative difficulties, and

lower court injunctions. The Supreme Court test of the Act was not sought by the Government: the record in the Schechter case contained few data to show the nexus between the slaughterer and the interstate poultry market; and application of the law to a relatively small segment of the national economy—a wholesale poultry market in Brooklyn—was hardly an ideal context to seek validation of the law. But after the Second Circuit invalidated the application of the wage and hour requirements to Schechter—though sustaining Schechter's convictions on most charges of code violation—the Government decided not to oppose Supreme Court review. The Court granted certiorari on April 15, 1935, only two months before the Act was to expire. And the decision came on May 27, 1935, just before the Act would have died of its own force.*

The Schechter case stemmed from convictions for violating the minimum wage, maximum hour, and trade practice provisions of the "Code of Fair Competition for the Live Poultry Industry of the Metropolitan Area in and about the City of New York." Ninety-six percent of the poultry marketed in New York came from other states; but Schechter sold only to local poultry dealers. Poultry was ordinarily purchased from commission men in New York City, trucked to Schechter's Brooklyn slaughterhouses, and sold there to retailers. Schechter's challenge had two prongs: first, that the Act unconstitutionally delegated legislative power [see chap. 7 below]; second, that the application of the Act to intrastate activities exceeded the commerce power. The Supreme Court agreed with both grounds of the attack and held that the wages and hours of Schechter's employees were not subject to federal control.

The Government's defense of the Act tried to rely on two strains in prior doctrine (see sec. 2 above): the "stream of commerce" rationale of the Swift and Stafford v. Wallace cases; and the "affecting commerce" legacy of the Shreveport case. Chief Justice Hughes' opinion for the Court rejected both analogies. These were not "transactions 'in' interstate commerce," he insisted: the interstate transactions regarding poultry ended when the shipments reached the Brooklyn slaughterhouses; neither the slaughtering nor the sale by Schechter were "transactions in interstate commerce." Schechter's activities, in short, were not "in a 'current' or 'flow' of interstate commerce."

Moreover, the Chief Justice refused to find that Schechter's transactions "directly 'affect' interstate commerce." In applying the "affecting commerce" rationale, he insisted, "there is a necessary and well-established distinction between direct and indirect effects." He elaborated: "The precise line can be drawn only as individual cases arise, but the distinction is clear in principle. Direct effects are illustrated by the railroad cases we have cited, as, e. g., the effect of failure to use prescribed safety appliances on railroads which are the highways of both interstate and intrastate commerce, injury to an employee engaged in interstate transportation by the negligence of an employee engaged in an intrastate movement, the fixing of rates for intrastate transportation which unjustly discriminate against interstate com-

* On the Government's litigation strategy regarding the NIRA and the Schechter case, see Stern, "The Commerce Clause and the National Economy, 1933–1946," 59 Harv.L.Rev. 645 (1946), Selected Essays, 1938–62 (1963), 218.

merce. But where the effect of intrastate transactions upon interstate commerce is merely indirect, such transactions remain within the domain of state power. If the commerce clause were construed to reach all enterprises and transactions which could be said to have an indirect effect upon interstate commerce, the federal authority would embrace practically all the activities of the people and the authority of the State over its domestic concerns would exist only by sufferance of the federal government."

Applying those principles to the Schechter operations, Chief Justice Hughes insisted that the hours and wages of Schechter employees "have no direct relation to interstate commerce." He rejected the Government argument "that hours and wages affect prices; that slaughterhouse men sell at a small margin above operating costs; that labor represents 50 to 60 per cent. of these costs; that a slaughterhouse operator paying lower wages or reducing his costs by exacting long hours of work, translates his saving into lower prices; that this results in demands for a cheaper grade of goods; and that the cutting of prices brings about a demoralization of the price structure." That argument, the Chief Justice found, "proves too much": "If the federal government may determine the wages and hours of employees in the internal commerce of a State, because of their relation to cost and prices and their indirect effect upon interstate commerce, it would seem that a similar control might be exerted over other elements of cost, also affecting prices, such as the number of employees, rent, advertising, methods of doing business, etc. All the processes of production and distribution that enter into costs could likewise be controlled. If the cost of doing an intrastate business is in itself the permitted object of federal control, the extent of the regulation of cost would be a question of discretion and not of power."

Finally, Chief Justice Hughes rejected an even broader argument "based upon the serious economic situation which led to the passage of the Recovery Act,—the fall in prices, the decline in wages and employment, and the curtailment of the market for commodities." He found no constitutional justification in "the great importance of maintaining wage distributions which would provide the necessary stimulus in starting 'the cumulative forces making for expanding commercial activity.' " To that argument † he replied: "Without in any way disparaging this motive, it is enough to say that the

† Note a similar argument paraphrased in the Stern article, footnote * above, emphasizing "that depressed business conditions had catastrophically affected all commerce" and "that a possible remedy was to increase the purchasing power of all wage earners through wage and hour regulation, thereby increasing the demand for products to be shipped in commerce." Such an argument, Stern notes, would apply to all workers, "irrespective of whether they themselves were in activities related to interstate activities." Wage and hour regulation of employees such as Schechter's would thus be "a reasonable means of improving the nation's business and the commerce—interstate or intrastate—of which that business consisted. The argument treats the whole national economy as inseparable into interstate and intrastate segments, insofar as the fluctuations of the business cycle are concerned." Stern notes that Government counsel realized in 1935 that such an argument had "little chance of success in the judicial climate of the period."

Was that argument a more plausible one factually than the "demoralization of the price structure" theme pressed by the Government and rejected by Chief Justice Hughes? Would a better record or a more substantial economic argument have persuaded the Court? Or would the "direct"-"indirect" distinction have proved an immovable obstacle? Note the continued invocation of that distinction in Carter, the next principal case.

recuperative efforts of the federal government must be made in a manner consistent with the authority granted by the Constitution." In a similar vein, he had said at the outset of his opinion: "Extraordinary conditions do not create or enlarge constitutional power."

Justice Cardozo, joined by Justice Stone, submitted a brief concurring opinion—a particularly notable one because they were among the Justices who typically dissented from other decisions invalidating New Deal legislation. Justice Cardozo agreed with Chief Justice Hughes on both grounds: not only was there "unlawful delegation"—"This is delegation running riot"—; there was also the "far-reaching and incurable" commerce power objection. On the latter, he elaborated: "There is a view of causation that would obliterate the distinction between what is national and what is local in the activities of commerce. Motion at the outer rim is communicated perceptibly, though minutely, to recording instruments at the center. A society such as ours 'is an elastic medium which transmits all tremors throughout its territory; the only question is of their size.' Per Learned Hand, J., in the court below. The law is not indifferent to considerations of degree. Activities local in their immediacy do not become interstate and national because of distant repercussions. What is near and what is distant may at times be uncertain. . . . . There is no penumbra of uncertainty obscuring judgment here. To find immediacy or directness here is to find it almost everywhere. If centripetal forces are to be isolated to the exclusion of the forces that oppose and counteract them, there will be an end to our federal system."

2. *The aftermath.* In a press conference soon after Schechter, President Roosevelt articulated the Administration's concerns about the decision. According to him, the case raised "the big issue in the country": "Does this decision mean that the United States Government has no control over any national economic problem?" He added that the decision "—if you accept the obiter dicta and all the phraseology of it—seems to be squarely on the side of restoring to the States forty-eight different controls over national economic problems. . . . . In some ways it may be the best thing that has happened to the country for a long time that such a decision has come from the Supreme Court, because it clarifies the issue." 4 The Public Papers and Addresses of Franklin D. Roosevelt (1938), 212, 218–19.

But the Schechter language was not necessarily fatal to the New Deal cause. As to doctrine, the "very weakness of the Schechter case, from the Government's viewpoint, was its saving grace." The Court had not yet passed on congressional power "to control trade practices or labor relations [in] any major industry, such as petroleum, lumber, coal or steel." In future litigation, "the case—and perhaps its language—could clearly be distinguished, when and if such regulation was attempted." *

The attempt to move the New Deal forward despite the Schechter language was made immediately. For example, the right of collective bargaining, recognized in the NIRA, was guaranteed in a more permanent statute: the National Labor Relations Act (Wagner Act) became law on July 5, 1935. And President Roosevelt quickly urged Congress to enact a law establishing an NIRA-like regulatory scheme for the bituminous coal industry. While that bill—introduced by Senator Joseph Guffey—was pending in a House

* Stern, "The Commerce Clause and the National Economy, 1933–1946," 59   Harv.L.Rev. 645, 662 (1946), Selected Essays 1938–62 (1963), 227.

subcommittee, President Roosevelt wrote his controversial letter to the chairman, Congressman Hill—the letter ending with the statement: "I hope your committee will not permit doubts as to constitutionality, however reasonable, to block the suggested legislation." (Recall the excerpts in chap. 1, sec. 1, above.) The bill became law soon after; and a court challenge was filed the next day. That test suit produced the Carter decision, which follows.

CARTER v. CARTER COAL CO.

298 U.S. 238, 56 S.Ct. 855, 80 L.Ed. 1160 (1936).

Certiorari to the United States Court of Appeals for the District of Columbia.

[The Bituminous Coal Conservation Act of 1935 imposed a 15 percent tax on the disposal of coal at the mine. Producers could receive a 90 percent reduction of the tax by accepting a code to be formulated by a National Bituminous Coal Commission, with the aid of district boards. Under Part II, minimum prices were to be set for each area. Under Part III, the labor provisions, code members were to recognize the employees' "right to organize and bargain collectively," and wage and hour agreements negotiated by a specified percentage of producers and workers' representatives were to be binding on all code members.

[Carter brought a stockholder's suit against his company to enjoin it from paying the tax and complying with the code. The Commissioner of Internal Revenue was joined as a defendant. The trial court sustained the Act and dismissed the suit. "Because of the importance of the question and the advantage of a speedy final determination thereof," the Supreme Court granted certiorari before argument or decision in the Court of Appeals.]

Mr. Justice SUTHERLAND delivered the opinion of the Court. . . . . [The majority opinion found the stockholders' suit appropriate and not premature. On the merits, it dealt almost entirely with Part III, the labor provisions of the code. The price provisions, Part II, were found inseparable from the labor provisions; hence the entire Act fell without separate consideration of the constitutionality of the price regulations. Before explaining why the labor provisions were unjustifiable under the commerce power, Justice Sutherland noted the Government's concession that the law could not be sustained under the taxing power (see the Child Labor Tax Case, chap. 4, sec. 1). The majority also found the maximum hour provisions unconstitutional and an arbitrary delegation of power, citing the Schechter case. Excerpts from Justice Sutherland's discussion of congressional power follow:]

Certain recitals contained in the act plainly suggest that its makers were of the opinion that its constitutionality could be sustained under some general federal power, thought to exist, apart from the specific grants of the Constitution [The recitals] are to the effect that the distribution of bituminous coal is of national interest, affecting the health and comfort of the people and the general welfare of the nation . . . .. These affirmations— and the further ones that the production and distribution of such coal "directly affect interstate commerce," because of which and of the waste of the

national coal resources and other circumstances, the regulation is necessary for the protection of such commerce—do not constitute an exertion of the *will* of Congress which is legislation, but a recital of considerations which in the *opinion* of that body existed and justified the expression of its will in the present act. Nevertheless, this preamble may not be disregarded. On the contrary it is important, because it makes clear, except for the pure assumption that the conditions described "directly" affect interstate commerce, that the powers which Congress undertook to exercise are not specific but of the most general character . . . .

The proposition, often advanced and as often discredited, that the power of the federal government inherently extends to purposes affecting the nation as a whole with which the states severally cannot deal or cannot adequately deal, and the related notion that Congress, entirely apart from those powers delegated by the Constitution, may enact laws to promote the general welfare, have never been accepted but always definitely rejected by this court.

. . .

[T]he general purposes which the act recites . . . are beyond the power of Congress except so far, and only so far, as they may be realized by an exercise of some specific power granted by the Constitution. [W]e find no grant of power which authorizes Congress to legislate in respect of these general purposes unless it be found in the commerce clause— and this we now consider. . . .

[T]he word "commerce" is the equivalent of the phrase "intercourse for the purposes of trade." Plainly, the incidents leading up to and culminating in the mining of coal do not constitute such intercourse. The employment of men, the fixing of their wages, hours of labor and working conditions, the bargaining in respect of these things—whether carried on separately or collectively—each and all constitute intercourse for the purposes of production, not of trade. The latter is a thing apart from the relation of employer and employee, which in all producing occupations is purely local in character. Extraction of coal from the mine is the aim and the completed result of local activities. Commerce in the coal mined is not brought into being by force of these activities, but by negotiations, agreements, and circumstances entirely apart from production. Mining brings the subject matter of commerce into existence. Commerce disposes of it.

[T]he effect of the labor provisions of the act, including those in respect of minimum wages, wage agreements, collective bargaining, and the Labor Board and its powers, primarily falls upon production and not upon commerce. [P]roduction is a purely local activity. It follows that none of these essential antecedents of production constitutes a transaction in or forms any part of interstate commerce. [Schechter.] Everything which moves in interstate commerce has had a local origin. Without local production somewhere, interstate commerce, as now carried on, would practically disappear. Nevertheless, the local character of mining, of manufacturing and of crop growing is a fact, and remains a fact, whatever may be done with the products. . . .

That the production of every commodity intended for interstate sale and transportation has some effect upon interstate commerce may be, if it has

not already been, freely granted; and we are brought to the final and decisive inquiry, whether here that effect is direct, as the "preamble" recites, or indirect. The distinction is not formal, but substantial in the highest degree, as we pointed out in the Schechter case. . . .

Whether the effect of a given activity or condition is direct or indirect is not always easy to determine. The word "direct" implies that the activity or condition invoked or blamed shall operate proximately—not mediately, remotely, or collaterally—to produce the effect. It connotes the absence of an efficient intervening agency or condition. And the extent of the effect bears no logical relation to its character. The distinction between a direct and an indirect effect turns, not upon the magnitude of either the cause or the effect, but entirely upon the manner in which the effect has been brought about. If the production by one man of a single ton of coal intended for interstate sale and shipment, and actually so sold and shipped, affects interstate commerce indirectly, the effect does not become direct by multiplying the tonnage, or increasing the number of men employed, or adding to the expense or complexities of the business, or by all combined. It is quite true that rules of law are sometimes qualified by considerations of degree, as the government argues. But the matter of degree has no bearing upon the question here, since that question is not—What is the *extent* of the local activity or condition, or the *extent* of the effect produced upon interstate commerce? but—What is the *relation* between the activity or condition and the effect?

Much stress is put upon the evils which come from the struggle between employers and employees over the matter of wages, working conditions, the right of collective bargaining, etc., and the resulting strikes, curtailment and irregularity of production and effect on prices; and it is insisted that interstate commerce is *greatly* affected thereby. But, in addition to what has just been said, the conclusive answer is that the evils are all local evils over which the federal government has no legislative control. The relation of employer and employee is a local relation. . . . And the controversies and evils, which it is the object of the act to regulate and minimize, are local controversies and evils affecting local work undertaken to accomplish that local result. Such effect as they may have upon commerce, however extensive it may be, is secondary and indirect. An increase in the greatness of the effect adds to its importance. It does not alter its character. . . .

. . . . A reading of the entire opinion [in Schechter] makes clear, what we now declare, that the want of power on the part of the federal government is the same whether the wages, hours of service, and working conditions, and the bargaining about them, are related to production before interstate commerce has begun, or to sale and distribution after it has ended. . . . .

Separate opinion of Mr. Chief Justice HUGHES. . . .

The power to regulate interstate commerce embraces the power to protect that commerce from injury, whatever may be the source of the dangers which threaten it, and to adopt any appropriate means to that end. . . . Congress thus has adequate authority to maintain the orderly conduct of interstate commerce and to provide for the peaceful settlement of disputes which threaten it. . . . But Congress may not use this protective authority as

a pretext for the exertion of power to regulate activities and relations within the States which affect interstate commerce only indirectly. . . .

But [the] Act also provides for the regulation of the prices of bituminous coal sold in interstate commerce and prohibits unfair methods of competition in interstate commerce. Undoubtedly transactions in carrying on interstate commerce are subject to the federal power to regulate that commerce and the control of charges and the protection of fair competition in that commerce are familiar illustrations of the exercise of the power, as the Interstate Commerce Act, the Packers and Stockyards Act, and the Anti-Trust Acts abundantly show. . . . The marketing provisions in relation to interstate commerce can be carried out as provided in Part II without regard to the labor provisions contained in Part III. That fact, in the light of the congressional declaration of separability, should be considered of controlling importance.

In this view, the Act, and the Code for which it provides, may be sustained in relation to the provisions for marketing in interstate commerce, and the decisions of the courts below, so far as they accomplish that result, should be affirmed.

Mr. Justice CARDOZO [dissenting].

 . . . I am satisfied that the Act is within the power of the central government in so far as it provides for minimum and maximum prices upon sales of bituminous coal in the transactions of interstate commerce and in those of intrastate commerce where interstate commerce is directly or intimately affected. Whether it is valid also in other provisions that have been considered and condemned in the opinion of the court, I do not find it necessary to determine at this time. Silence must not be taken as importing acquiescence. . . .

Regulation of prices being an exercise of the commerce power in respect of interstate transactions, the question remains whether it comes within that power as applied to intrastate sales where interstate prices are directly or intimately affected. Mining and agriculture and manufacture are not interstate commerce considered by themselves, yet their relation to that commerce may be such that for the protection of the one there is need to regulate the other. [Schechter.] Sometimes it is said that the relation must be "direct" to bring that power into play. In many circumstances such a description will be sufficiently precise to meet the needs of the occasion. But a great principle of constitutional law is not susceptible of comprehensive statement in an adjective. The underlying thought is merely this, that "the law is not indifferent to considerations of degree." [Schechter, concurring opinion.] It cannot be indifferent to them without an expansion of the commerce clause that would absorb or imperil the reserved powers of the states. At times, as in the case cited, the waves of causation will have radiated so far that their undulatory motion, if discernible at all, will be too faint or obscure, too broken by cross-currents, to be heeded by the law. In such circumstances the holding is not directed at prices or wages considered in the abstract, but at prices or wages in particular conditions. The relation may be tenuous or the opposite according to the facts. Always the setting of the facts is to be viewed if one would know the closeness of the tie. Perhaps, if one group of adjectives is to be chosen in preference to another, "intimate" and "remote" will

be found to be as good as any. At all events, "direct" and "indirect," even if accepted as sufficient, must not be read too narrowly. . . . A survey of the cases shows that the words have been interpreted with suppleness of adaptation and flexibility of meaning. The power is as broad as the need that evokes it.

One of the most common and typical instances of a relation characterized as direct has been that between interstate and intrastate rates for carriers by rail where the local rates are so low as to divert business unreasonably from interstate competitors. In such circumstances Congress has the power to protect the business of its carriers against disintegrating encroachments. . . . To be sure, the relation even then may be characterized as indirect if one is nice or over-literal in the choice of words. Strictly speaking, the intrastate rates have a primary effect upon the intrastate traffic and not upon any other, though the repercussions of the competitive system may lead to secondary consequences affecting interstate traffic also. . . . What the cases really mean is that the causal relation in such circumstances is so close and intimate and obvious as to permit it to be called direct without subjecting the word to an unfair or excessive strain. There is a like immediacy here. Within rulings the most orthodox, the prices for intrastate sales of coal have so inescapable a relation to those for interstate sales that a system of regulation for transactions of the one class is necessary to give adequate protection to the system of regulation adopted for the other. The argument is strongly pressed by intervening counsel that this may not be true in all communities or in exceptional conditions. If so, the operators unlawfully affected may show that the Act to that extent is invalid as to them. . . .

I am authorized to state that Mr. Justice BRANDEIS and Mr. Justice STONE join in this opinion.

THE COURT–PACKING PLAN

1. *The background and fate of the plan.* The foregoing decisions persuaded the Roosevelt Administration that strong measures were needed to save the New Deal. Several major New Deal laws had already been held unconstitutional; others—the National Labor Relations Act and the Social Security Act among them—might well meet a similar fate. The Carter decision confirmed the worst anticipations generated by Schechter. And there were others: the Agricultural Adjustment Act, sought to be justified under the spending power, was held unconstitutional in United States v. Butler, 297 U.S. 1 (1936) (chap. 4 below). And in a decision a few weeks after Carter, the divided Court confirmed that the federalism concern was not the only constitutional obstacle economic regulations would encounter: in Morehead v. New York ex rel. Tipaldo, 298 U.S. 587 (1936), the Court invalidated a state law establishing minimum wages for women as a violation of the due process clause of the 14th Amendment. (See chap. 9 below.) As a result of that course of decisions, conviction hardened within the Administration that something had to be done about the Court.

But President Roosevelt did not make Court reform an issue in the 1936 election. Rather, he waited until February 1937 to propose changes, giving reasons that seemed disingenuous to many. A month later, in a radio

address, he challenged the Court more directly and defended his plan on a more forthright basis. But the content of the plan and its original method of presentation provoked widespread opposition—including that of a number of New Deal supporters. After extensive hearings, the Senate Judiciary Committee rejected the proposal in June 1937. While the controversy was raging, the Court handed down a number of decisions sustaining regulatory statutes, and Justice Van Devanter retired. The final Senate debate was almost anti-climactic: proposed amendments by the proponents failed to save the heart of the plan, and in late July it was in effect killed. The following excerpts are from documents in the body or the appendixes of Sen.Rep. No. 711, 75th Cong., 1st Sess. (1937) (Reorganization of the Federal Judiciary—Adverse Report of the Committee on the Judiciary).

a. *The Proposed Bill:*

When any judge of a court of the United States, appointed to hold his office during good behavior, has heretofore or hereafter attained the age of seventy years and has held a commission or commissions as judge of any such court or courts at least ten years, continuously or otherwise, and within six months thereafter has neither resigned nor retired, the President, for each such judge who has not so resigned or retired, shall nominate, and by and with the advice and consent of the Senate, shall appoint one additional judge to the court to which the former is commissioned. . . . No more than fifty judges shall be appointed thereunder, nor shall any judge be so appointed if such appointment would result in (1) more than fifteen members of the Supreme Court of the United States . . . . [Six Justices were over seventy in 1937: Butler (71), Hughes (75), Sutherland (75), McReynolds (75), Van Devanter (78), and Brandeis (81).]

b. *The President's Message to Congress, Feb. 5, 1937:*

It is . . . one of the definite duties of the Congress constantly to maintain the effective functioning of the Federal judiciary. . . . The judiciary has often found itself handicapped by insufficient personnel with which to meet a growing and more complex business. . . . Even at the present time the Supreme Court is laboring under a heavy burden. . . . It seems clear . . . that the necessity of relieving present congestion extends to the enlargement of the capacity of all the Federal courts. A part of the problem of obtaining a sufficient number of judges to dispose of cases is the capacity of the judges themselves. This brings forward the question of aged or infirm judges—a subject of delicacy and yet one which requires frank discussion. . . . Modern complexities call also for a constant infusion of new blood in the courts, just as it is needed in executive functions of the Government and in private business. . . . I, therefore, earnestly recommend that the necessity of an increase in the number of judges be supplied by legislation providing for the appointment of additional judges in all Federal courts, without exception, where there are incumbent judges of retirement age who do not choose to retire or to resign.

c. *Letter of Chief Justice Charles Evans Hughes to Senator Burton K. Wheeler, March 21, 1937:*

"MY DEAR SENATOR WHEELER: In response to your inquiries, I have the honor to present the following statement with respect to the work of the Supreme Court:

"1.   The Supreme Court is fully abreast of its work. . . .

"7.   An increase in the number of Justices of the Supreme Court, apart from any question of policy, which I do not discuss, would not promote the efficiency of the Court. It is believed that it would impair that efficiency so long as the Court acts as a unit. There would be more judges to hear, more judges to confer, more judges to discuss, more judges to be convinced and to decide. The present number of Justices is thought to be large enough so far as the prompt, adequate, and efficient conduct of the work of the Court is concerned. . . .

"On account of the shortness of time I have not been able to consult with the members of the Court generally with respect to the foregoing statement, but I am confident that it is in accord with the views of the Justices. I should say, however, that I have been able to consult with Mr. Justice Van Devanter and Mr. Justice Brandeis, and I am at liberty to say that the statement is approved by them. . . ."

     d.   *Radio Address by President Roosevelt, March 9, 1937:*

   . . .   The American people have learned from the depression. For in the last three national·elections an overwhelming majority of them voted a mandate that the Congress and the President begin the task of providing that protection—not after long years of debate, but now.

The courts, however, have cast doubts on the ability of the elected Congress to protect us against catastrophe by meeting squarely our modern social and economic conditions. . . .

I want to talk with you very simply about the need for present action in this crisis—the need to meet the unanswered challenge of one-third of a nation ill-nourished, ill-clad, ill-housed. . . .

When the Congress has sought to stabilize national agriculture, to improve the conditions of labor, to safeguard business against unfair competition, to protect our national resources, and in many other ways to serve our clearly national needs, the majority of the Court has been assuming the power to pass on the wisdom of these acts of the Congress—and to approve or disapprove the public policy written into these laws.

This is not only my accusation, it is the accusation of most distinguished Justices of the present Supreme Court. [See especially Justice Stone's vigorous dissent in the Butler case in 1936, chap. 4 below.] . . .

We have, therefore, reached the point as a Nation where we must take action to save the Constitution from the Court and the Court from itself. We must find a way to take an appeal from the Supreme Court to the Constitution itself. We want a Supreme Court which will do justice under the Constitution—not over it. . . .

[My] plan has two chief purposes: By bringing into the judicial system a steady and continuing stream of new and younger blood, I hope, first, to make the administration of all Federal justice speedier and therefore less cost-

ly; secondly, to bring to the decision of social and economic problems younger men who have had personal experience and contact with modern facts and
circumstances under which average men have to live and work. This plan
will save our National Constitution from hardening of the judicial arteries.
. . .

We cannot rely on an amendment as the immediate or only answer to
our present difficulties. . . . Even if an amendment were passed, and
even if in the years to come it were to be ratified, its meaning would depend
upon the kind of Justices who would be sitting on the Supreme Court bench.
An amendment like the rest of the Constitution is what the Justices say it is
rather than what its framers or you might hope it is. . . .

e. *Conclusion of Adverse Report of Senate Judiciary Committee, June
14, 1937:*

We recommend the rejection of this bill as a needless, futile, and utterly
dangerous abandonment of constitutional principle. . . .

It would subjugate the courts to the will of Congress and the President
and thereby destroy the independence of the judiciary, the only certain shield
of individual rights. . . . It stands now before the country, acknowledged by its proponents as a plan to force judicial interpretation of the Constitution, a proposal that violates every sacred tradition of American democracy.

Under the form of the Constitution it seeks to do that which is unconstitutional. [Recall chap. 1, sec. 3, above.] [I]ts practical operation would
be to make the Constitution what the executive or legislative branches of the
Government choose to say it is—an interpretation to be changed with each
change of administration. It is a measure which should be so emphatically
rejected that its parallel will never again be presented to the free representatives of the free people of America.

2. *The impact of the plan.* Two years after the Court-packing debate,
President Roosevelt claimed that he had lost the battle but won the war. Do
the decisions from 1937 on support that estimate? The Jones & Laughlin
case, which follows, was decided on April 12, 1937, while the debate was
still raging. Observe, in examining the commerce power cases in sec. 5, the
fate of the "direct"-"indirect" standard of the Knight-Schechter-Carter line
of cases. Could any of the cases since 1937 have been decided the same way
if that standard had prevailed? As interpreted by the majority in the pre-
1937 cases? As interpreted by Justice Cardozo in Schechter and Carter?
Note the reliance on the Shreveport legacy of practical effects in the post-
1937 cases. Note also that, in several major decisions, the majority proved
itself willing to go further than the Government's narrower, more hesitant
arguments. And note the fuller economic record submitted by the Government in the cases that follow: contrast, e. g., the economic data in Jones &
Laughlin with those in Schechter.

The commerce power decisions were not the only indications of a changing judicial response. Two weeks after Jones & Laughlin, for example, the
Court overruled prior decisions invalidating minimum wage laws as violative
of due process. West Coast Hotel Co. v. Parrish, 300 U.S. 379, chap. 9 below.
West Coast Hotel, in particular, provoked the charge that Justice Roberts had

changed his position in the face of the Roosevelt challenge—the "switch in time" that supposedly "saved the Nine." But, as a memorandum left by the Justice demonstrates, the Court voted in West Coast Hotel weeks before the judicial reorganization plan was announced. See Frankfurter, "Mr. Justice Roberts," 104 U.Pa.L.Rev. 311 (1955). Compare Justice Roberts' votes in Alton, Schechter and Carter, above, with those in the commerce clause decisions which follow; and his position in United States v. Butler with that in Steward Machine Co. v. Davis (both in chap. 4 below). Note the changes in Court personnel from 1937 through 1941: President Roosevelt made seven appointments—Justices Black, Reed, Frankfurter, Douglas, Murphy, Byrnes and Jackson.*

SECTION 5. THE COMMERCE POWER SINCE 1937—CONSTITUTIONAL REVOLUTION OR CONTINUITY?

NATIONAL LABOR RELATIONS BOARD v. JONES & LAUGHLIN STEEL CORP.
301 U.S. 1, 57 S.Ct. 615, 81 L.Ed. 893 (1937).

Certiorari to the Circuit Court of Appeals for the Fifth Circuit.

[This was the major case testing the constitutionality of the National Labor Relations Act of 1935. Unlike the Schechter circumstances, this test arose in a context desired by the Government: labor practices in a large integrated industry. In a proceeding initiated by a union, the NLRB found that the company had engaged in "unfair labor practices" by discriminatory discharges of employees for union activity. The Board ordered the company to cease and desist from discrimination and coercion. When the company failed to comply, the NLRB sought judicial enforcement of its order, but the Court of Appeals denied the Board's petition on the ground that "the order lay beyond the range of federal power."]

Mr. Chief Justice HUGHES delivered the opinion of the Court. . . .

The facts as to the nature and scope of the business of the Jones & Laughlin Steel Corporation have been found by the Labor Board and, so far as they are essential to the determination of this controversy, they are not in dispute. The Labor Board has found: The corporation [is] engaged in the business of manufacturing iron and steel in plants situated in Pittsburgh and nearby Aliquippa, Pennsylvania. It manufactures and distributes a widely diversified line of steel and pig iron, being the fourth largest producer of steel in the United States. With its subsidiaries—nineteen in number—it is a completely integrated enterprise, owning and operating ore, coal and limestone

* The background and consequences for the Court-packing plan are discussed in Jackson, The Struggle for Judicial Supremacy (1941). For the political aspects of the controversy, see the useful contemporary account in Alsop and Catledge, The 168 Days (1938); the colorful modern review in Baker, Back to Back—The Duel Between FDR and the Supreme Court (1967); and the astute retrospective analysis in Chapter 15, "Court Packing: The Miscalculated Risk," Burns, Roosevelt: The Lion and the Fox (1956). See also Leuchtenburg, "The Origins of Franklin D. Roosevelt's 'Court-Packing Plan,'" 1966 Sup.Ct.Rev. 347.

properties, lake and river transportation facilities and terminal railroads located at its manufacturing plants. It owns or controls mines in Michigan and Minnesota. It operates four ore steamships on the Great Lakes, used in the transportation of ore to its factories. It owns coal mines in Pennsylvania. It operates towboats and steam barges used in carrying coal to its factories. It owns limestone properties in various places in Pennsylvania and West Virginia. It owns the Monongahela connecting railroad which connects the plants of the Pittsburgh works and forms an interconnection with the Pennsylvania, New York Central and Baltimore and Ohio Railroad systems. It owns the Aliquippa and Southern Railroad Company which connects the Aliquippa works with the Pittsburgh and Lake Erie, part of the New York Central system. Much of its product is shipped to its warehouses in Chicago, Detroit, Cincinnati and Memphis,—to the last two places by means of its own barges and transportation equipment. In Long Island City, New York, and in New Orleans it operates structural steel fabricating shops in connection with the warehousing of semi-finished materials sent from its works. Through one of its wholly-owned subsidiaries it owns, leases and operates stores, warehouses and yards for the distribution of equipment and supplies for drilling and operating oil and gas wells and for pipe lines, refineries and pumping stations. It has sales offices in twenty cities in the United States and a wholly-owned subsidiary which is devoted exclusively to distributing its product in Canada. Approximately 75 per cent. of its product is shipped out of Pennsylvania.

Summarizing these operations, the Labor Board concluded that the works in Pittsburgh and Aliquippa "might be likened to the heart of a self-contained, highly integrated body. They draw in the raw materials from Michigan, Minnesota, West Virginia, Pennsylvania in part through arteries and by means controlled by the respondent; they transform the materials and then pump them out to all parts of the nation through the vast mechanism which the respondent has elaborated."

To carry on the activities of the entire steel industry, 33,000 men mine ore, 44,000 men mine coal, 4,000 men quarry limestone, 16,000 men manufacture coke, 343,000 men manufacture steel, and 83,000 men transport its product. Respondent has about 10,000 employees in its Aliquippa plant, which is located in a community of about 30,000 persons. . . .

First. The scope of the Act.—The Act is challenged in its entirety as an attempt to regulate all industry, thus invading the reserved powers of the States over their local concerns. It is asserted that the references in the Act to interstate and foreign commerce are colorable at best; that the Act is not a true regulation of such commerce or of matters which directly affect it but on the contrary has the fundamental object of placing under the compulsory supervision of the federal government all industrial labor relations within the nation. . . .

We think it clear that the National Labor Relations Act may be construed so as to operate within the sphere of constitutional authority. The jurisdiction conferred upon the Board, and invoked in this instance, is found in § 10(a), which provides:

"Sec. 10(a). The Board is empowered, as hereinafter provided, to prevent any person from engaging in any unfair labor practice (listed in section 8) affecting commerce."

The critical words of this provision, prescribing the limits of the Board's authority in dealing with the labor practices, are "affecting commerce." The Act specifically defines the "commerce" to which it refers (§ 2(6)):

"The term 'commerce' means trade, traffic, commerce, transportation, or communication among the several States . . . ."

There can be no question that the commerce thus contemplated by the Act . . . is interstate and foreign commerce in the constitutional sense. The Act also defines the term "affecting commerce" (§ 2(7)):

"The term 'affecting commerce' means in commerce, or burdening or obstructing commerce or the free flow of commerce, or having led or tending to lead to a labor dispute burdening or obstructing commerce or the free flow of commerce."

. . . The grant of authority to the Board does not purport to extend to the relationship between all industrial employees and employers . . . regardless of effects upon interstate or foreign commerce. It purports to reach only what may be deemed to burden or obstruct that commerce and, thus qualified, it must be construed as contemplating the exercise of control within constitutional bounds. It is a familiar principle that acts which directly burden or obstruct interstate or foreign commerce, or its free flow, are within the reach of the congressional power. Acts having that effect are not rendered immune because they grow out of labor disputes. . . . It is the effect upon commerce, not the source of the injury, which is the criterion. . . . Whether or not particular action does affect commerce in such a close and intimate fashion as to be subject to federal control, and hence to lie within the authority conferred upon the Board, is left by the statute to be determined as individual cases arise. We are thus to inquire whether in the instant case the constitutional boundary has been passed. . . .

Third. The application of the Act to employees engaged in production. —The principle involved.—Respondent says that whatever may be said of employees engaged in interstate commerce, the industrial relations and activities in the manufacturing department of respondent's enterprise are not subject to federal regulation. The argument rests upon the proposition that manufacturing in itself is not commerce. [Kidd v. Pearson; Schechter; Carter.]

The Government distinguishes these cases. The various parts of respondent's enterprise are described as interdependent and as thus involving "a great movement of iron ore, coal and limestone along well-defined paths to the steel mills, thence through them, and thence in the form of steel products into the consuming centers of the country—a definite and well-understood course of business." It is urged that these activities constitute a "stream" or "flow" of commerce, of which the Aliquippa manufacturing plant is the focal point, and that industrial strife at that point would cripple the entire movement. Reference is made to our decision sustaining the Packers and Stockyards Act. Stafford v. Wallace, 258 U.S. 495. . . .

Respondent contends that the instant case presents material distinctions. . . . The raw materials which are brought to the plant are delayed for long periods and, after being subjected to manufacturing processes, "are changed substantially as to character, utility and value." The finished products which emerge "are to a large extent manufactured without reference to pre-exising orders and contracts and are entirely different from the raw materials which enter at the other end. . . ."

We do not find it necessary to determine whether these features of defendant's business dispose of the asserted analogy to the "stream of commerce" cases. The instances in which that metaphor has been used are but particular, and not exclusive, illustrations of the protective power which the Government invokes in support of the present Act. The congressional authority to protect interstate commerce from burdens and obstructions is not limited to transactions which can be deemed to be an essential part of a "flow" of interstate or foreign commerce. Burdens and obstructions may be due to injurious action springing from other sources. The fundamental principle is that the power to regulate commerce is the power to enact "all appropriate legislation" for "its protection and advancement"; to adopt measures "to promote its growth and insure its safety"; "to foster, protect, control and restrain." . . . That power is plenary and may be exerted to protect interstate commerce "no matter what the source of the dangers which threaten it." . . . Although activities may be intrastate in character when separately considered, if they have such a close and substantial relation to interstate commerce that their control is essential or appropriate to protect that commerce from burdens and obstructions, Congress cannot be denied the power to exercise that control. [Schechter.] Undoubtedly the scope of this power must be considered in the light of our dual system of government and may not be extended so as to embrace effects upon interstate commerce so indirect and remote that to embrace them, in view of our complex society, would effectually obliterate the distinction between what is national and what is local and create a completely centralized government. Id. The question is necessarily one of degree. . . .

That intrastate activities, by reason of close and intimate relation to interstate commerce, may fall within federal control is demonstrated in the case of carriers who are engaged in both interstate and intrastate transportation. . . . [Among the illustrations are] the broad requirements of the Safety Appliance Act and the Hours of Service Act. Southern Railway Co. v. United States, 222 U.S. 20 . . . . It is said that this exercise of federal power has relation to the maintenance of adequate instrumentalities of interstate commerce. But the agency is not superior to the commerce which uses it. The protective power extends to the former because it exists as to the latter.

The close and intimate effect which brings the subject within the reach of federal power may be due to activities in relation to productive industry although the industry when separately viewed is local. This has been abundantly illustrated in the application of the federal Anti-Trust Act. . . .

It is thus apparent that the fact that the employees here concerned were engaged in production is not determinative. The question remains as to the effect upon interstate commerce of the labor practice involved. In the

Schechter case, supra, we found that the effect there was so remote as to be beyond the federal power. To find "immediacy or directness" there was to find it "almost everywhere," a result inconsistent with the maintenance of our federal system. In the Carter case, supra, the Court was of the opinion that the provisions of the statute relating to production were invalid upon several grounds,—that there was improper delegation of legislative power, and that the requirements not only went beyond any sustainable measure of protection of interstate commerce but were also inconsistent with due process. These cases are not controlling here.

Fourth.   Effects of the unfair labor practice in respondent's enterprise. —Giving full weight to respondent's contention with respect to a break in the complete continuity of the "stream of commerce" by reason of respondent's manufacturing operations, the fact remains that the stoppage of those operations by industrial strife would have a most serious effect upon interstate commerce. In view of respondent's far-flung activities, it is idle to say that the effect would be indirect or remote. It is obvious that it would be immediate and might be catastrophic. We are asked to shut our eyes to the plainest facts of our national life and to deal with the question of direct and indirect effects in an intellectual vacuum. Because there may be but indirect and remote effects upon interstate commerce in connection with a host of local enterprises throughout the country, it does not follow that other industrial activities do not have such a close and intimate relation to interstate commerce as to make the presence of industrial strife a matter of the most urgent national concern. When industries organize themselves on a national scale, making their relation to interstate commerce the dominant factor in their activities, how can it be maintained that their industrial labor relations constitute a forbidden field into which Congress may not enter when it is necessary to protect interstate commerce from the paralyzing consequences of industrial war? We have often said that interstate commerce itself is a practical conception. It is equally true that interferences with that commerce must be appraised by a judgment that does not ignore actual experience.

Experience has abundantly demonstrated that the recognition of the right of employees to self-organization and to have representatives of their own choosing for the purpose of collective bargaining is often an essential condition of industrial peace. Refusal to confer and negotiate has been one of the most prolific causes of strife. This is such an outstanding fact in the history of labor disturbances that it is a proper subject of judicial notice and requires no citation of instances. . . .

Fifth.   The means which the Act employs.—*Questions under the due process clause and other constitutional restrictions.* [These objections were also rejected.]

Our conclusion is that the order of the Board was within its competency and that the Act is valid as here applied. . . .

Reversed.

Mr. Justice McREYNOLDS delivered the following dissenting opinion in the cases preceding. [The dissent was applicable to Jones & Laughlin and to two companion cases: NLRB v. Fruehauf Trailer Co., 301 U.S. 49, involved the largest trailer manufacturer in the United States, with sales

offices in twelve states; NLRB v. Friedman-Harry Marks Clothing Co., 301 U.S. 58, involved a Virginia clothing manufacturer. The majority emphasized that over 99 percent of the raw materials came from other states and that over 80 percent of the products were sold to other states. The dissent pointed out that the company produced "less than one-half of one per cent of the men's clothing produced in the United States and employs 800 of the 150,000 workmen engaged therein."]

Mr. Justice VAN DEVANTER, Mr. Justice SUTHERLAND, Mr. Justice BUTLER and I are unable to agree with the decisions.   .   .   .

The three respondents happen to be manufacturing concerns—one large, two relatively small. The Act is now applied to each upon grounds common to all. Obviously what is determined as to these concerns may gravely affect a multitude of employers who engage in a great variety of private enterprises—mercantile, manufacturing, publishing, stock-raising, mining, etc. It puts into the hands of a Board power of control over purely local industry beyond anything heretofore deemed permissible.   .   .   .

Any effect on interstate commerce by the discharge of employees shown here, would be indirect and remote in the highest degree, as consideration of the facts will show. In [Jones & Laughlin] ten men out of ten thousand were discharged; in the other cases only a few. The immediate effect in the factory may be to create discontent among all those employed and a strike may follow, which, in turn, may result in reducing production, which ultimately may reduce the volume of goods moving in interstate commerce. By this chain of indirect and progressively remote events we finally reach the evil with which it is said the legislation under consideration undertakes to deal. A more remote and indirect interference with interstate commerce or a more definite invasion of the powers reserved to the states is difficult, if not impossible, to imagine.   .   .   .

It is gravely stated that experience teaches that if an employer discourages membership in "any organization of any kind" "in which employees participate, and which exists for the purpose in whole or in part of dealing with employers concerning grievances, labor disputes, wages, rates of pay, hours of employment or conditions of work," discontent may follow and this in turn may lead to a strike, and as the outcome of the strike there may be a block in the stream of interstate commerce. Therefore Congress may inhibit the discharge! Whatever effect any cause of discontent may ultimately have upon commerce is far too indirect to justify Congressional regulation. Almost anything—marriage, birth, death—may in some fashion affect commerce.   .   .   .

––––––––

Transitional Note. Jones & Laughlin gave new life to the "affecting commerce" rationale—the rationale justifying national regulation of intrastate activities because of their practical effect on interstate commerce. Five years later, in Wickard v. Filburn (1942), the Court elaborated and expanded that rationale. Wickard is printed immediately below, to permit tracing the development of that "affecting commerce" doctrinal strand at this point. But in between Jones & Laughlin and Wickard, the Court made

another major contribution to an expansive reading of the commerce power, in United States v. Darby in 1941. Consideration of Darby is postponed until after Wickard, because Darby deals with the "commerce-prohibiting" device as well as the "affecting commerce" technique of regulation. Darby is printed below, after Wickard, to permit separate focus there on the modern aspects of the commerce-prohibiting problems first encountered in the Lottery Case and in Hammer v. Dagenhart, sec. 3 above.

The decisions sustaining national power in Wickard v. Filburn and United States v. Darby, unlike that in Jones & Laughlin, were unanimous ones. There were rapid changes in the composition of the Court after Jones & Laughlin: by the time of the Darby decision, all of the four dissenters in Jones & Laughlin had left. Justice McReynolds was the last to go: he retired just a few days before the Darby decision was announced.

WICKARD v. FILBURN

317 U.S. 111, 63 S.Ct. 82, 87 L.Ed. 122 (1942).

On appeal from the District Court of the United States for the Southern District of Ohio.

[Filburn, a farmer in Ohio, sued Wickard, the Secretary of Agriculture, to enjoin enforcement of a marketing penalty imposed under the Agricultural Adjustment Act of 1938, as amended, "upon that part of his 1941 wheat crop which was available for market in excess of the market quota established for his farm." He attacked the marketing quota provisions of the Act as, inter alia, beyond the commerce power. The lower court enjoined enforcement on other grounds, and Secretary Wickard appealed.]

Mr. Justice JACKSON delivered the opinion of the Court. . . .

The appellee for many years past has owned and operated a small farm in Montgomery County, Ohio, maintaining a herd of dairy cattle, selling milk, raising poultry, and selling poultry and eggs. It has been his practice to raise a small acreage of winter wheat, sown in the Fall and harvested in the following July; to sell a portion of the crop; to feed part to poultry and livestock on the farm, some of which is sold; to use some in making flour for home consumption; and to keep the rest for the following seeding. The intended disposition of the crop here involved has not been expressly stated.

In July of 1940, pursuant to the Agricultural Adjustment Act of 1938, as then amended, there was established for the appellee's 1941 crop a wheat acreage allotment of 11.1 acres and a normal yield of 20.1 bushels of wheat an acre. He was given notice of such allotment in July of 1940 before the Fall planting of his 1941 crop of wheat, and again in July of 1941, before it was harvested. He sowed, however, 23 acres, and harvested from his 11.9 acres of excess acreage 239 bushels, which under the terms of the Act as amended on May 26, 1941, constituted farm marketing excess, subject to a penalty of 49 cents a bushel, or $117.11 in all. The appellee has not paid the penalty and he has not postponed or avoided it by storing the excess under regulations of the Secretary of Agriculture, or by delivering it up to the Secretary. The Committee, therefore, refused him a marketing card,

which was, under the terms of Regulations promulgated by the Secretary, necessary to protect a buyer from liability to the penalty and upon its protecting lien.

The general scheme of the Agricultural Adjustment Act of 1938 as related to wheat is to control the volume moving in interstate and foreign commerce in order to avoid surpluses and shortages and the consequent abnormally low or high wheat prices and obstructions to commerce. Within prescribed limits and by prescribed standards the Secretary of Agriculture is directed to ascertain and proclaim each year a national acreage allotment for the next crop of wheat, which is then apportioned to the states and their counties, and is eventually broken up into allotments for individual farms.

. . .

It is urged that under the Commerce Clause of the Constitution, Article I, § 8, clause 3, Congress does not possess the power it has in this instance sought to exercise. The question would merit little consideration since our decision in [United States v. Darby], except for the fact that this Act extends federal regulation to production not intended in any part for commerce but wholly for consumption on the farm. The Act includes a definition of "market" and its derivatives, so that as related to wheat, in addition to its conventional meaning, it also means to dispose of "by feeding (in any form) to poultry or livestock which, or the products of which, are sold, bartered, or exchanged, or to be so disposed of." Hence, marketing quotas not only embrace all that may be sold without penalty but also what may be consumed on the premises. Wheat produced on excess acreage is designated as "available for marketing" as so defined and the penalty is imposed thereon. Penalties do not depend upon whether any part of the wheat, either within or without the quota, is sold or intended to be sold. The sum of this is that the Federal Government fixes a quota including all that the farmer may harvest for sale or for his own farm needs, and declares that wheat produced on excess acreage may neither be disposed of nor used except upon payment of the penalty or except it is stored as required by the Act or delivered to the Secretary of Agriculture.

Appellee says that this is a regulation of production and consumption of wheat. Such activities are, he urges, beyond the reach of Congressional power under the Commerce Clause, since they are local in character, and their effects upon interstate commerce are at most "indirect." In answer the Government argues that the statute regulates neither production nor consumption, but only marketing; and, in the alternative, that if the Act does go beyond the regulation of marketing it is sustainable as a "necessary and proper" implementation of the power of Congress over interstate commerce.

The Government's concern lest the Act be held to be a regulation of production or consumption, rather than of marketing, is attributable to a few dicta and decisions of this Court which might be understood to lay it down that activities such as "production," "manufacturing," and "mining" are strictly "local" and, except in special circumstances which are not present here, cannot be regulated under the commerce power because their effects upon interstate commerce are, as matter of law, only "indirect." Even today, when this power has been held to have great latitude, there is no decision of this Court that such activities may be regulated where no part of the

product is intended for interstate commerce or intermingled with the subjects thereof. We believe that a review of the course of decision under the Commerce Clause will make plain, however, that questions of the power of Congress are not to be decided by reference to any formula which would give controlling force to nomenclature such as "production" and "indirect" and foreclose consideration of the actual effects of the activity in question upon interstate commerce.

At the beginning Chief Justice Marshall described the federal commerce power with a breadth never yet exceeded. [Gibbons v. Ogden.] He made emphatic the embracing and penetrating nature of this power by warning that effective restraints on its exercise must proceed from political rather than from judicial processes. [Recall the comment on this passage in sec. 1 above. Justice Jackson proceeded to review commerce power decisions since Gibbons. He noted that cases such as Knight had established a "line of restrictive authority," but that "other cases" had "called forth broader interpretations of the Commerce Clause destined to supersede the earlier ones, and to bring about a return to the principles first enunciated by Chief Justice Marshall in Gibbons v. Ogden." He commented: "In some cases sustaining the exercise of federal power over intrastate matters the term 'direct' was used for the purpose of stating, rather than of reaching, a result; in others it was treated as synonymous with 'substantial' or 'material'; and in others it was not used at all. Of late its use has been abandoned in cases dealing with questions of federal power under the Commerce Clause." After quoting from the Shreveport Case, Justice Jackson continued:]

The Court's recognition of the relevance of the economic effects in the application of the Commerce Clause, exemplified by this statement, has made the mechanical application of legal formulas no longer feasible. Once an economic measure of the reach of the power granted to Congress in the Commerce Clause is accepted, questions of federal power cannot be decided simply by finding the activity in questions to be "production" nor can consideration of its economic effects be foreclosed by calling them "indirect."
. . . .

Whether the subject of the regulation in question was "production," "consumption," or "marketing" is, therefore, not material for purposes of deciding the question of federal power before us. That an activity is of local character may help in a doubtful case to determine whether Congress intended to reach it. The same consideration might help in determining whether in the absence of Congressional action it would be permissible for the state to exert its power on the subject matter, even though in so doing it to some degree affected interstate commerce. But even if appellee's activity be local and though it may not be regarded as commerce, it may still, whatever its nature, be reached by Congress if it exerts a substantial economic effect on interstate commerce, and this irrespective of whether such effect is what might at some earlier time have been defined as "direct" or "indirect."

The parties have stipulated a summary of the economics of the wheat industry. Commerce among the states in wheat is large and important. Although wheat is raised in every state but one, production in most states is not equal to consumption. . . .

The wheat industry has been a problem industry for some years. Largely as a result of increased foreign production and import restrictions, annual exports of wheat and flour from the United States during the ten-year period ending in 1940 averaged less than 10 per cent of total production, while during the 1920's they averaged more than 25 per cent. The decline in the export trade has left a large surplus in production which, in connection with an abnormally large supply of wheat and other grains in recent years, caused congestion in a number of markets; tied up railroad cars; and caused elevators in some instances to turn away grains, and railroads to institute embargoes to prevent further congestion. . . .

In the absence of regulation the price of wheat in the United States would be much affected by world conditions. During 1941, producers who coöperated with the Agricultural Adjustment program received an average price on the farm of about $1.16 a bushel, as compared with the world market price of 40 cents a bushel. . . .

The effect of consumption of homegrown wheat on interstate commerce is due to the fact that it constitutes the most variable factor in the disappearance of the wheat crop. Consumption on the farm where grown appears to vary in an amount greater than 20 per cent of average production. The total amount of wheat consumed as food varies but relatively little, and use as seed is relatively constant.

The maintenance by government regulation of a price for wheat undoubtedly can be accomplished as effectively by sustaining or increasing the demand as by limiting the supply. The effect of the statute before us is to restrict the amount which may be produced for market and the extent as well to which one may forestall resort to the market by producing to meet his own needs. That appellee's own contribution to the demand for wheat may be trivial by itself is not enough to remove him from the scope of federal regulation where, as here, his contribution, taken together with that of many others similarly situated, is far from trivial. . . .

It is well established by decisions of this Court that the power to regulate commerce includes the power to regulate the prices at which commodities in that commerce are dealt in and practices affecting such prices. One of the primary purposes of the Act in question was to increase the market price of wheat, and to that end to limit the volume thereof that could affect the market. It can hardly be denied that a factor of such volume and variability as home-consumed wheat would have a substantial influence on price and market conditions. This may arise because being in marketable condition such [home-grown] wheat overhangs the market and, if induced by rising prices, tends to flow into the market and check price increases. But if we assume that it is never marketed, it supplies a need of the man who grew it which would otherwise be reflected by purchases in the open market. Home-grown wheat in this sense competes with wheat in commerce. The stimulation of commerce is a use of the regulatory function quite as definitely as prohibitions or restrictions thereon. This record leaves us in no doubt that Congress may properly have considered that wheat consumed on the farm where grown, if wholly outside the scheme of regulation, would have a substantial effect in defeating and obstructing its purpose to stimulate trade therein at increased prices. . . . .

[The statute was also challenged as "a deprivation of property without due process of law contrary to the Fifth Amendment, both because of its regulatory effect on the appellee and because of its alleged retroactive effect." The contentions were rejected.]

Reversed.

THE COMMERCE POWER, THE NATIONAL MARKET, AND THE SCOPE OF THE WICKARD v. FILBURN RATIONALE

1. *Invocations of the market concept.* The concept of a national market in goods—a concept rooted in the historical origins of the commerce clause, sec. 1 above—proved a useful source of constitutional justifications for congressional regulation of activities "in" or "affecting" commerce in a number of modern cases, both before Wickard and Filburn and since. As an example, consider Mulford v. Smith: After the Court invalidated the Agricultural Adjustment Act of 1933 in United States v. Butler, 297 U.S. 1 (1936) (chap. 4 below), as an unconstitutional regulation of "local" production, Congress enacted the Agricultural Adjustment Act of 1938. The marketing quota provisions of the Act were sustained as a regulation of a channel of commerce. MULFORD v. SMITH, 307 U.S. 38 (1939). Penalties imposed by the Act were payments to the government of one-half the market price of all tobacco sold above quota, the fine to be paid by warehousemen and deducted by them from the purchase price paid to the farmer. The Court —three years after Butler—emphasized that the Act did not purport to control production and added: "It sets no limit upon the acreage which may be planted or produced and imposes no penalty for the planting and producing of tobacco in excess of the marketing quota. It purports to be solely a regulation of interstate commerce, which it reaches and affects at the throat where tobacco enters the stream of commerce,—the marketing warehouse. . . . Any rule, such as that embodied in the Act, which is intended to foster, protect and conserve that commerce, or to prevent the flow of commerce from working harm to the people of the nation, is within the competence of Congress." *

2. *The scope of the Wickard rationale.* Was the "national market" theory essential to sustain the sanction imposed in Wickard v. Filburn? Could Congress have imposed a limit on farm production directly, without the superstructure of the market control scheme, by simply invoking the "affecting commerce" argument?

---

* Note also Currin v. Wallace, 306 U.S. 1 (1939), sustaining the Tobacco Inspection Act of 1935, which authorized the Secretary of Agriculture to establish standards of tobacco and designate markets where tobacco moves in interstate and foreign commerce. See also the upholding of congressional efforts to fix prices of goods and services in transactions in or affecting commerce in United States v. Rock Royal Co-operative, 307 U.S. 533 (1939) (milk); Sunshine Coal & Anthracite Co. v. Adkins, 310 U.S. 381 (1940) (coal); and FPC v. Natural Gas Pipeline Co., 315 U.S. 575 (1942) (natural gas). And note United States v. Wrightwood Dairy Co., 315 U.S. 110 (1942), justifying federal regulation of milk handling in the Chicago marketing area on the "affecting commerce" theory and explaining that "the marketing of a local product in competition of a like commodity moving interstate may so interfere with interstate commerce or its regulation as to afford a basis for Congressional regulation of intrastate activity."

Justice Jackson in Wickard still required a showing of "substantial economic effect on interstate commerce." But is any real substance left to the notion of substantiality if that requirement is satisfied whenever the activity regulated, "taken together with that of many others similarly situated, is far from trivial"? Does that aggregate burden approach leave any local activities so minimal as to be unreachable? Is the scope of Wickard v. Filburn limited by Justice Jackson's emphasis on the economic magnitude of the wheat production problem? Is aggregation allowable only when the resultant economic problem is of truly substantial dimensions? Is the scope of Wickard limited by the fact that Congress was dealing with a genuine economic problem? Or is the aggregation theory also usable for national "police" regulations? Note Justice Rutledge's broad statement in Mandeville Island Farms v. American Crystal Sugar Co., 334 U.S. 219, 236 (1948): "Congress' power to keep the interstate market free of goods produced under conditions inimical to the general welfare [Darby case, below], may be exercised in individual cases without showing any specific effect upon interstate commerce"; 'it is enough that the individual activity when multiplied into a general practice is subject to federal control [Wickard v. Filburn], or that it contains a threat to the interstate economy that requires preventive regulation." But, as later notes elaborate, there may be reason for caution to avoid reading too much into broad dicta. Compare, for example, Justice Harlan's 1968 comment, noted below [in Maryland v. Wirtz, 392 U.S. 183], suggesting that Wickard v. Filburn did *not* mean "that Congress may use a relatively trivial impact on commerce as an excuse for broad general regulation of state or private activities." [The problems of potential limits, if any, on the contemporary scope of the commerce power are pursued in later notes in this chapter. See especially note 3d after Darby, below.]

UNITED STATES v. DARBY

312 U.S. 100, 61 S.Ct. 451, 85 L.Ed. 609 (1941).

Appeal from the District Court of the United States for the Southern District of Georgia.

Mr. Justice STONE delivered the opinion of the Court.

The two principal questions raised by the record in this case are, *first,* whether Congress has constitutional power to prohibit the shipment in interstate commerce of lumber manufactured by employees whose wages are less than a prescribed minimum or whose weekly hours of labor at that wage are greater than a prescribed maximum, and, *second,* whether it has power to prohibit the employment of workmen in the production of goods "for interstate commerce" at other than prescribed wages and hours. A subsidiary question is whether in connection with such prohibitions Congress can require the employer subject to them to keep records showing the hours worked each day and week by each of his employees including those engaged "in the production and manufacture of goods, to-wit, lumber, for "interstate commerce.'"

Appellee demurred to an indictment found in the district court for southern Georgia charging him with violation of § 15(a) (1) (2) and (5) of the Fair Labor Standards Act of 1938 . . . . The district court sustained

the demurrer and quashed the indictment and the case comes here on direct appeal under § 238 of the Judicial Code, as amended, . . . which authorizes an appeal to this Court when the judgment sustaining the demurrer "is based on the invalidity or construction of the statute upon which the indictment is founded."

The Fair Labor Standards Act set up a comprehensive legislative scheme for preventing the shipment in interstate commerce of certain products and commodities produced in the United States under labor conditions as respects wages and hours which fail to conform to standards set up by the Act. Its purpose, as we judicially know from the declaration of policy in § 2(a) of the Act, and the reports of Congressional committees proposing the legislation, . . . is to exclude from interstate commerce goods produced for the commerce and to prevent their production for interstate commerce, under conditions detrimental to the maintenance of the minimum standards of living necessary for health and general well-being; and to prevent the use of interstate commerce as the means of competition in the distribution of goods so produced, and as the means of spreading and perpetuating such substandard labor conditions among the workers of the several states. . . .

. . . Section 15(a)(1) makes unlawful the shipment in interstate commerce of any goods "in the production of which any employee was employed in violation of section 6 or section 7," which provide, among other things, that during the first year of operation of the Act a minimum wage of 25 cents per hour shall be paid to employees "engaged in [interstate] commerce or the production of goods for [interstate] commerce," § 6, and that the maximum hours of employment for employees "engaged in commerce or the production of goods for commerce" without increased compensation for overtime, shall be forty-four hours a week. § 7. § 15(a)(2) makes it unlawful to violate the provisions of §§ 6 and 7 including the minimum wage and maximum hour requirements just mentioned for employees engaged in production of goods for commerce. . . .

The indictment charges that appellee is engaged, in the state of Georgia, in the business of acquiring raw materials, which he manufactures into finished lumber with the intent, when manufactured, to ship it in interstate commerce to customers outside the state, and that he does in fact so ship a large part of the lumber so produced. . . .

The prohibition of shipment of the proscribed goods in interstate commerce. § 15(a)(1) prohibits, and the indictment charges, the shipment in interstate commerce, of goods produced for interstate commerce by employees whose wages and hours of employment do not conform to the requirements of the Act. [T]he only question arising under the commerce clause with respect to such shipments is whether Congress has the constitutional power to prohibit them.

While manufacture is not of itself interstate commerce the shipment of manufactured goods interstate is such commerce and the prohibition of such shipment by Congress is indubitably a regulation of the commerce. The power to regulate commerce is the power "to prescribe the rule by which commerce is governed." Gibbons v. Ogden, 9 Wheat. 1, 196. It extends not only to those regulations which aid, foster and protect the commerce, but embraces those which prohibit it. . . . . It is conceded that the pow-

er of Congress to prohibit transportation in interstate commerce includes noxious articles, stolen articles, kidnapped persons, and articles such as intoxicating liquor or convict made goods, traffic in which is forbidden or restricted by the laws of the state of destination. . . .

But it is said that the present prohibition falls within the scope of none of these categories; that while the prohibition is nominally a regulation of the commerce its motive or purpose is regulation of wages and hours of persons engaged in manufacture, the control of which has been reserved to the states and upon which Georgia and some of the states of destination have placed no restriction; that the effect of the present statute is not to exclude the prescribed articles from interstate commerce in aid of state regulation as in Kentucky Whip & Collar Co. v. Illinois Central R. R. Co.,* but instead, under the guise of a regulation of interstate commerce, it undertakes to regulate wages and hours within the state contrary to the policy of the state which has elected to leave them unregulated.

The power of Congress over interstate commerce [can] neither be enlarged nor diminished by the exercise or non-exercise of state power. Kentucky Whip & Collar Co. v. Illinois Central R. R. Co., supra. Congress, following its own conception of public policy concerning the restrictions which may appropriately be imposed on interstate commerce, is free to exclude from the commerce articles whose use in the states for which they are destined it may conceive to be injurious to the public health, morals or welfare, even though the state has not sought to regulate their use. . . .

Such regulation is not a forbidden invasion of state power merely because either its motive or its consequence is to restrict the use of articles of commerce within the states of destination; and is not prohibited unless by other Constitutional provisions. It is no objection to the assertion of the power to regulate interstate commerce that its exercise is attended by the same incidents which attend the exercise of the police power of the states. . . .

The motive and purpose of the present regulation is plainly to make effective the Congressional conception of public policy that interstate commerce should not be made the instrument of competition in the distribution of goods produced under substandard labor conditions, which competition is injurious to the commerce and to the states from and to which the commerce flows. The motive and purpose of a regulation of interstate commerce are matters for the legislative judgment upon the exercise of which the Constitution places no restriction and over which the courts are given no control. McCray v. United States, 195 U.S. 27; Sonzinsky v. United States, 300 U.S. 506, 513, and cases cited. "The judicial cannot prescribe to the legislative

---

* In Kentucky Whip & Collar Co. v. Illinois Central R. R. Co., 299 U.S. 334 (1937), the Court sustained the Ashurst-Summers Act which made it unlawful to transport convict-made goods into any state where the receipt, sale or possession of such goods violated state law. The Court said: "The Congress has not sought to exercise a power not granted or to usurp the police powers of the States. It has not acted on any assumption of a power enlarged by virtue of state action. The Congress has exercised its plenary power, which is subject to no limitation other than that which is founded in the Constitution itself. The Congress has formulated its own policy and established its own rule. The fact that it has adopted its rule in order to aid the enforcement of valid state laws affords no ground for constitutional objection."

department of the government limitations upon the exercise of its ackowledged power." Veazie Bank v. Fenno, 8 Wall. 533. [These taxing power cases are considered in chap. 4, sec. 1, below.] Whatever their motive and purpose, regulations of commerce which do not infringe some constitutional prohibition are within the plenary power conferred on Congress by the Commerce Clause. Subject only to that limitation, presently to be considered, we conclude that the prohibition of the shipment interstate of goods produced under the forbidden substandard labor conditions is within the constitutional authority of Congress.

[T]hese principles of constitutional interpretation have been so long and repeatedly recognized by this Court as applicable to the Commerce Clause, that there would be little occasion for repeating them now were it not for the decision of this Court twenty-two years ago in Hammer v. Dagenhart, 247 U.S. 251. In that case it was held by a bare majority of the Court over the powerful and now classic dissent of Mr. Justice Holmes setting forth the fundamental issues involved, that Congress was without power to exclude the products of child labor from interstate commerce. The reasoning and conclusion of the Court's opinion there cannot be reconciled with the conclusion which we have reached, that the power of Congress under the Commerce Clause is plenary to exclude any article from interstate commerce subject only to the specific prohibitions of the Constitution.

Hammer v. Dagenhart has not been followed. The distinction on which the decision was rested that Congressional power to prohibit interstate commerce is limited to articles which in themselves have some harmful or deleterious property—a distinction which was novel when made and unsupported by any provision of the Constitution—has long since been abandoned. . . The thesis of the opinion that the motive of the prohibition or its effect to control in some measure the use or production within the states of the article thus excluded from the commerce can operate to deprive the regulation of its constitutional authority has long since ceased to have force. . . .

The conclusion is inescapable that Hammer v. Dagenhart was a departure from the principles which have prevailed in the interpretation of the Commerce Clause both before and since the decision and that such vitality, as a precedent, as it then had has long since been exhausted. It should be and now is overruled.

Validity of the wage and hour requirements. Section 15(a) (2) and §§ 6 and 7 require employers to conform to the wage and hour provisions with respect to all employees engaged in the production of goods for interstate commerce. As appellees' employees are not alleged to be "engaged in interstate commerce" the validity of the prohibition turns on the question whether the employment, under other than the prescribed labor standards, of employees engaged in the production of goods for interstate commerce is so related to the commerce and so affects it as to be within the reach of the power of Congress to regulate it. . . .

The recognized need of drafting a workable statute and the well known circumstances in which it was to be applied are persuasive of the conclusion, which the legislative history supports, [that] the "production for commerce" intended includes at least production of goods, which, at the

time of production, the employer, according to the normal course of his business, intends or expects to move in interstate commerce although, through the exigencies of the business, all of the goods may not thereafter actually enter interstate commerce.

There remains the question whether such restriction on the production of goods for commerce is a permissible exercise of the commerce power. The power of Congress over interstate commerce is not confined to the regulation of commerce among the states. It extends to those activities intrastate which so affect interstate commerce or the exercise of the power of Congress over it as to make regulation of them appropriate means to the attainment of a legitimate end, the exercise of the granted power of Congress to regulate interstate commerce. [See McCulloch v. Maryland.] . . . [L]ong before the adoption of the National Labor Relations Act this Court had many times held that the power of Congress to regulate interstate commerce extends to the regulation through legislative action of activities intrastate which have a substantial effect on the commerce or the exercise of the Congressional power over it. . . .

In such legislation Congress has sometimes left it to the courts to determine whether the intrastate activities have the prohibited effect on the commerce, as in the Sherman Act. It has sometimes left it to an administrative board or agency to determine whether the activities sought to be regulated or prohibited have such effect, as in the case of the Interstate Commerce Act, and the National Labor Relations Act, or whether they come within the statutory definition of the prohibited Act, as in the Federal Trade Commission Act. And sometimes Congress itself has said that a particular activity affects the commerce, as it did in the present Act, the Safety Appliance Act and the Railway Labor Act. In passing on the validity of legislation of the class last mentioned the only function of courts is to determine whether the particular activity regulated or prohibited is within the reach of the federal power.

. . .

Congress, having by the present Act adopted the policy of excluding from interstate commerce all goods produced for the commerce which do not conform to the specified labor standards, it may choose the means reasonably adapted to the attainment of the permitted end, even though they involve control of intrastate activities. Such legislation has often been sustained with respect to powers, other than the commerce power granted to the national government, when the means chosen, although not themselves within the granted power, were nevertheless deemed appropriate aids to the accomplishment of some purpose within an admitted power of the national government. . . . A familiar like exercise of power is the regulation of intrastate transactions which are so commingled with or related to interstate commerce that all must be regulated if the interstate commerce is to be effectively controlled. Shreveport Case, 234 U.S. 342; Currin v. Wallace, 306 U.S. 1; Mulford v. Smith, supra. Similarly Congress may require inspection and preventive treatment of all cattle in a disease infected area in order to prevent shipment in interstate commerce of some of the cattle without the treatment. Thornton v. United States, 271 U.S. 414. It may prohibit the removal, at destination, of labels required by the Pure Food & Drugs Act to be affixed to articles transported in interstate commerce. McDermott v. Wisconsin, 228 U.S. 115. . . .

had received it as the direct consignee of an interstate shipment. These variants are not sufficient we think to detract from the applicability of the McDermott holding to the present decision. In both cases alike the question relates to the constitutional power of Congress under the commerce clause to regulate the branding of articles that have completed an interstate shipment and are being held for future sales in purely local or intrastate commerce. The reasons given for the McDermott holding therefore are equally applicable and persuasive here. And many cases decided since the McDermott decision lend support to the validity of § 301(k). See, e. g., . . . Wickard v. Filburn, 317 U.S. 111 . . .; United States v. Darby, 312 U.S. 100 . . . ." [Justice Rutledge concurred; Justice Frankfurter, joined by Justices Reed and Jackson, dissented on the construction of the Act, without mentioning the constitutional issue.]

b. *The adequacy of the justification.* What is the constitutional basis for this application of the Act? Use of "means reasonably adapted" to "implementing" the commerce-prohibiting provisions? (Section 301(c) forbids the "introduction . . . into interstate commerce" of misbranded drugs.) Control of local activities "affecting" commerce? Control of activities "in" commerce? Does the Court's opinion provide an adequate explanation? Do the citations of Darby and Wickard v. Filburn? Does the citation of McDermott v. Wisconsin, 228 U.S. 115 (1913)? (In McDermott, a grocer possessing cans labeled "corn syrup," as required by federal law, was convicted under a Wisconsin law requiring that such cans carry only a "glucose" label. The Court, in reversing the conviction, stated that "Congress may determine for itself the character of the means necessary to make its purpose effectual in preventing the shipment in interstate commerce of articles of a harmful character, and to this end may provide the means of inspection, examination and seizure necessary. . . . The real opportunity for Government inspection may only arise when, as in the present case, the goods as packed have been removed from the outside box in which they were shipped and remain, as the act provides, 'unsold.' " Note that in McDermott, the retailer had received the goods from a wholesaler in another state; and that the holding of the case was to reverse his conviction under a state law found to conflict with a federal act—under the Supremacy Clause and preemption principles considered in chap. 5 below. Did Justice Black give undue weight to the McDermott language?)

3. *Limitless power to regulate economic problems?—The Public Utility Holding Company Act cases.* a. *Introduction.* Though the commerce-prohibiting technique validated in the Darby case has been a particularly favored one for reaching "moral" problems ever since the days of the Lottery Case, it is of course available to deal with matters of genuinely substantial economic significance as well. A series of constitutional challenges to the Public Utility Holding Company Act of 1935 illustrates that usage and raises additional problems as well. In this series of cases, the "affecting commerce" approach occasionally surfaces as an added support for the congressional prohibition of commerce, as indeed it was resorted to as an alternative explanation in Darby itself. Perhaps more surprisingly, the Court's justifications in this series of cases are unusually detailed—more detailed than one might expect if the commerce-prohibiting technique were a virtually self-

validating device. In examining these cases, then, consider: To what extent do the decisions rest on commerce-prohibiting techniques of the Lottery Case-Darby variety? To what extent are they independently justified, or justifiable, on "in" commerce or "affecting" commerce grounds? Do these decisions demonstrate that no doctrinal limits on the modern commerce power exist when it is invoked to meet national economic needs? Can it be inferred from the elaborate justifications offered in these cases that legislation addressed to problems with less significant economic dimensions would encounter greater difficulty in the Court? (Note also the questions in 3d below.)

a. *Electric Bond & Share.* In Electric Bond & Share Co. v. SEC, 303 U.S. 419 (1938), the Court, with only Justice McReynolds dissenting, sustained provisions compelling registration of holding companies and prohibiting the use of the instrumentalities of commerce (and of the mails) by unregistered companies: "When Congress lays down a valid rule to govern those engaged in transactions in interstate commerce, Congress may deny to those who violate the rule the right to engage in such transactions. Champion v. Ames, 188 U.S. 321."

b. *North American Co.* In NORTH AMERICAN CO. v. SEC, 327 U.S. 686 (1946), the Court unanimously sustained a provision authorizing the SEC to require each holding company engaged in commerce to limit its operations to a single integrated public utility system. Justice Murphy wrote: "This broad commerce clause does not operate so as to render the nation powerless to defend itself against economic forces that Congress decrees inimical or destructive to the national economy. Rather it is an affirmative power commensurate with the national needs. . . . It is sufficient to reiterate the well-settled principle that Congress may impose relevant conditions and requirements on those who use the channels of interstate commerce in order that those channels will not become the means of promoting or spreading evil, whether of a physical, moral or economic nature. Brooks v. United States, 267 U.S. 432, 436–437. *This power permits Congress to attack an evil directly at its source, provided that the evil bears a substantial relationship to interstate commerce.* . . . The fact that an evil may involve a corporation's financial practices, its business structure or its security portfolio does not detract from the power of Congress under the commerce clause to promulgate rules in order to destroy that evil. Once it is established that the evil concerns or affects commerce in more states than one, Congress may act. [Congress in the Act] was concerned with the economic evils resulting from uncoordinated and unintegrated public utility holding company systems. These evils were found to be polluting the channels of interstate commerce and to take the form of transactions occurring in and concerning more states than one. Congress also found that the national welfare was thereby harmed, as well as the interests of investors and consumers. These evils, moreover, were traceable in large part to the nature and extent of the securities owned by the holding companies. Congress therefore had power under the commerce clause to attempt to remove those evils by ordering the holding companies to divest themselves of the securities that made such evils possible." [Emphasis added.]

Is the justification offered surprisingly detailed, given the Darby rationale? Could the corporate structure be controlled simply as an imple-

mentation of the conditional ban on the use of commerce facilities? Note the italicized sentence. Does it suggest a greater limitation on congressional power than that indicated by the alternative justifications given in Darby for the regulation of wages and hours in production activities?

c. *American Power & Light.* Compare AMERICAN POWER & LIGHT CO. v. SEC, 329 U.S. 90 (1946), involving the "death sentence" provision of the Act and sustaining an SEC order compelling the dissolution of the petitioning company because its corporate structure was "unduly and unnecessarily complicated" and "unfairly and inequitably distributed voting power among the security holders." Justice Murphy's opinion for the Court stated:

"The Bond and Share system, including American and Electric, possesses an undeniable interstate character which makes it properly subject, from the statutory standpoint, to the provisions of § 11(b) (2). This vast system embraces utility properties in no fewer than 32 states, from New Jersey to Oregon and from Minnesota to Florida, as well as 12 foreign countries. Bond and Share dominates and controls this system from its headquarters in New York City. As was the situation in the North American case, the proper control and functioning of such an extensive multi-state network of corporations necessitates continuous and substantial use of the mails and the instrumentalities of interstate commerce. . . . Congress, of course, has undoubted power under the commerce clause to impose relevant conditions and requirements on those who use the channels of interstate commerce so that those channels will not be conduits for promoting or perpetuating economic evils. . . . Thus to the extent that corporate business is transacted through such channels, affecting commerce in more states than one, Congress may act directly with respect to that business to protect what it conceives to be the national welfare. . . . To deny that Congress has power to eliminate evils connected with pyramided holding company systems, evils which have been found to be promoted and transmitted by means of interstate commerce, is to deny that Congress can effectively deal with problems concerning the welfare of the national economy. We cannot deny that power. Rather we reaffirm once more the constitutional authority resident in Congress by virtue of the commerce clause to undertake to solve national problems directly and realistically, giving due recognition to the scope of state power. That follows from the fact that the federal commerce power is as broad as the economic needs of the nation."

d. *Substantial limits on broad dicta?* The opinions in these Public Utility Holding Act cases are favorite sources for broad judicial phrases to support commentators' assertions that the modern commerce power is virtually limitless. Yet the limits may be somewhat more substantial than the broad phrases suggest, if the passages are read with a grain of salt and in context. If the commerce power is truly limitless, what explains the extensive Court justifications for uses of the power? Cases disposing of constitutional qualms as curtly as Sullivan (note 2) are rare. Note that even the generous language in the North American case (note 3b) repeatedly speaks of *"economic* evils" and states that the evil regulated must have a substantial relationship to commerce (not simply that the person or activity reached must have some nexus with commerce, whether or not the evil regulated relates to that nexus).

Consider, as an example of this problem, the issue suggested by Katzenbach v. McClung, sec. 6 below: May racial discrimination at a restaurant be prohibited simply because the restaurant has *some* nexus with commerce (e. g., it serves mustard produced out-of-state)? Or does the commerce clause require that it is *racial discrimination* (the evil regulated), not simply *any* aspect of the restaurant's operations, that must have a relationship to interstate commerce? Contrast the statements of Attorney General Kennedy and Assistant Attorney General Marshall in the Senate hearings on the 1964 Civil Rights Act, sec. 6 below.

The problem of reading broad dicta as to the reach of the commerce power with an eye to their particular contexts is not confined to cases focusing on the commerce-prohibiting technique. The widely held view that the modern commerce power is virtually limitless so far as judicially imposed restraints are concerned draws support from "affecting commerce" as well as "commerce-prohibiting" cases. Again, some caution against inferring too much from broad judicial statements may be warranted. For example, Wickard v. Filburn, an "affecting commerce" case, is a favorite citation to support assertions of de facto unlimited commerce power. Yet the broad statements in that case, it should be recalled, appear in an opinion articulating at length the factual and theoretical underpinnings for the justification relied on there. And note Justice Harlan's comment in a majority opinion a generation after Wickard v. Filburn, in Maryland v. Wirtz, 392 U.S. 183 (1968) (noted below), stating: "Neither here nor in Wickard has the Court declared that Congress may use a relatively trivial impact on commerce as an excuse for broad general regulation of state or private activities." Consider also the Five Gambling Devices case, in the next group of notes. It is a statutory interpretation case, to be sure. Yet if all the earlier dicta were to be taken at face value and for all that they might be worth, should not the Justices have accepted the Government's view of the reach of the statute without difficulty? Do the Justices' doubts suggest lingering constitutional limits on the commerce power? Note the statement on the scope of constitutional powers in the opinion by Justice Jackson (author of some of the broadest statements in Wickard v. Filburn, 11 years earlier): "While general statements, out of these different contexts, might bear upon the subject one way or another, it is apparent that the precise question tendered to us now is not settled by any prior decision." And note his reliance on "the implications and limitations of our federal system" and his sensitivity to "affairs considered normally reserved to the states" when he turns to the statutory interpretation problem. (See also the material on statutory interpretation in the final note in this section.)

THE COMMERCE POWER AND CRIME:
SOME MODERN PROBLEMS

Introduction. Expansion of federal criminal jurisdiction raises some of the most sensitive problems of potential congressional impingement upon the values of federalism. Criminal laws are among the clearest examples of federal regulation of "traditionally local" concerns. Moreover, the substan-

tial economic dimensions of the "evils" regulated are typically far less evident in federal criminal legislation than, for example, in the statutes of the New Deal era. The risks of abuse of national power were notable as early as the measures directed at gambling and prostitution at the beginning of the century. And the risks persist in the mounting modern resort to the commerce power as the basis for new federal criminal laws, relying both on the "commerce-prohibiting" and "affecting commerce" techniques.

This group of notes examines some of the modern uses of the power. Do they raise serious constitutional problems? Do they risk violating the "spirit" of the Constitution Marshall spoke of in the McCulloch case? Are the modern uses likely to encounter difficulties in the Court? Even if they pass muster in the Court, should members of Congress be troubled by these reliances on the commerce power? If the broad dicta of Darby and Wickard v. Filburn are taken at face value, few if any uses of the commerce power should give any real difficulty in the Court. And there is some evidence that the modern Court's "hands-off" attitude carries over to commerce power-based criminal laws. Yet there are some counter-signals as well: in the context of statutory interpretation, at least, there are indications from the Justices of hesitations and misgivings about the expansion of federal criminal jurisdiction.

Note 1 below examines some examples of recent congressional legislation. Note 2, on the Perez case, shows the Court sustaining the constitutionality of a modern criminal law, though not without dissent. And the cases in note 3 illustrate some of the modern Court's uneasiness: in the statutory interpretation context, federalism considerations have been resorted to repeatedly to justify narrow interpretations. In short, as Perez illustrates, the Court seems willing to sustain considerable congressional control of intrastate criminal activities when Congress clearly insists on pressing the commerce power so far; but, as the statutory interpretation cases indicate, the Court will not find that Congress has gone to the outer reaches of power unless the legislative intent is amply clear.

1. *Some examples of modern legislation.* a. *Organized crime.* Interest in commerce power-based crime laws received new impetus with the widely publicized war on crime that commenced during the 1960's.* Consid-

---

* See, e. g., President Johnson's message, Law Enforcement and Administration of Justice, H.Doc.No.103, 89th Cong., 1st Sess. (1965); Pollner, "Attorney General Robert F. Kennedy's Legislative Program to Curb Organized Crime and Racketeering," 28 Brooklyn L.Rev. 37 (1961).

Though recent crime laws have occasionally relied on the "affecting commerce" rationale (see, e. g., the provisions on "civil disorders" in note 1b below), the "commerce-prohibiting" technique has been the favorite device, as in 18 U.S.C. § 1952 in the text. Use of that technique, though somewhat curtailed by the Child Labor Case, never came to a complete halt after its early validation in the Lottery Case. Though early uses of the technique were primarily concerned with harm in the state of destination, harms in the state of origin of the interstate movement have also been included within the sweep of the general technique of using the commerce-prohibiting method for police power objectives—of closing the channels of commerce to movements deemed harmful to morals and welfare, even though the harm feared occurs primarily at the local level. Recall, e. g., the ban on interstate transportation of stolen motor vehicles, sustained in Brooks v. United States, 267 U.S. 432 (1925), and the limited ban on shipping convict-made goods, sustained in the Kentucky Whip & Collar case in 1937, as noted above. See also,

er the following section of 18 U.S.C., one of several anti-crime provisions enacted in response to Kennedy Administration proposals in 1961. Does it raise substantial constitutional difficulties in any of its applications?

§ 1952. *"Interstate and foreign travel or transportation in aid of racketeering enterprises.*

"(a) Whoever travels in interstate or foreign commerce or uses any facility in interstate or foreign commerce, including the mail, with intent to—

"(1) distribute the proceeds of any unlawful activity; or

"(2) commit any crime of violence to further any unlawful activity; or

"(3) otherwise promote, manage, establish, carry on, or facilitate the promotion, management, establishment or carrying on, of any unlawful activity, and thereafter performs or attempts to perform any of the acts specified in subparagraphs (1), (2), and (3), shall be fined not more than $10,000 or imprisoned for not more than five years, or both.

"(b) As used in this section 'unlawful activity' means (1) any business enterprise involving gambling, liquor on which the Federal excise tax has not been paid, narcotics, or prostitution offenses in violation of the laws of the State in which they are committed or of the United States, or (2) extortion, bribery, or arson in violation of the laws of the State in which committed or of the United States. . . ."

Note the Court's narrowing interpretation of the statute in the Rewis case, note 3 below. Do the final phrases of § 1952(a)(3) create any constitutional difficulty, by including as an element of the crime the performance of specified acts after the interstate travel has ended? Does the general reference to acts unlawful under state law in § 1952(b) create any difficulty?

b. *Riots and disorders.* The format of the Kennedy Administration's anti-racketeering law apparently inspired the scheme of the anti-riot amendments in Title I of the Civil Rights Act of 1968. Note the close similarity to the pattern of 18 U.S.C. § 1952 above (the anti-racketeering law) in the 1968 anti-riot law, 18 U.S.C. § 2101:

§ 2101. *"Riots.*

"(a) (1) Whoever travels in interstate or foreign commerce or uses any facility of interstate or foreign commerce, including, but not limited to, the mail, telegraph, telephone, radio, or television, with intent—

"(A) to incite a riot; or

"(B) to organize, promote, encourage, participate in, or carry on a riot; or

"(C) to commit any act of violence in furtherance of a riot; or

"(D) to aid or abet any person in inciting or participating in or carrying on a riot or committing any act of violence in furtherance of a riot;

e. g., the Federal Kidnapping Act, Gooch v. United States, 297 U.S. 124 (1936); the Fugitive Felon and Witness Act, see Hemans v. United States, 163 F.2d 228 (6th Cir. 1947); and the statutory prohibitions involved in the cases in note 3 below.

and who either during the course of any such travel or use or thereafter performs or attempts to perform any other overt act for any purpose specified in subparagraph (A), (B), (C), or (D) of this paragraph—

"Shall be fined not more than $10,000, or imprisoned not more than five years, or both.

"(b) In any prosecution under this section, proof that a defendant engaged or attempted to engage in one or more of the overt acts described in subparagraph (A), (B), (C), or (D) of paragraph (1) of subsection (a) and (1) has traveled in interstate or foreign commerce, or (2) has use of or used any facility of interstate or foreign commerce, including but not limited to, mail, telegraph, telephone, radio, or television, to communicate with or broadcast to any person or group of persons prior to such overt acts, such travel or use shall be admissible proof to establish that such defendant traveled in or used such facility of interstate or foreign commerce. . . . ." †

Compare Title X of the 1968 Civil Rights Act—a Title headed the "Civil Obedience Act of 1965." Note its greater reliance on the "affecting commerce" rather than "commerce-prohibiting" technique in portions of the statute. It includes the following addition to Title 18 of the United States Code:

§ 231. *"Civil disorders*

"(a) (1) Whoever teaches or demonstrates to any other person the use, application, or making of any firearm or explosive or incendiary device, or technique capable of causing injury or death to persons, knowing or having reason to know or intending that the same will be unlawfully employed for use in, or in furtherance of, a civil disorder which may in any way or degree obstruct, delay, or adversely affect commerce or the movement of any article or commodity in commerce or the conduct or performance of any federally protected function; or

"(2) Whoever transports or manufactures for transportation in commerce any firearm, or explosive or incendiary device, knowing or having reason to know or intending that the same will be used unlawfully in furtherance of a civil disorder; or

"(3) Whoever commits or attempts to commit any act to obstruct, impede, or interfere with any fireman or law enforcement officer lawfully engaged in the lawful performance of his official duties incident to and during the commission of a civil disorder which in any way or degree obstructs, delays, or adversely affects commerce or the movement of any article or commodity in commerce or the conduct or performance of any federally protected function—

"Shall be fined not more than $10,000 or imprisoned not more than five years, or both. . . . ."

---

† Is there a protected interest in interstate movement of persons that limits commerce power-based restraints on interstate travel? See, e. g., the decision invalidating durational residence requirements in welfare laws in Shapiro v. Thompson, 394 U.S. 618 (1969) (chap. 10, sec. 4, below). Note also, among earlier cases examining asserted rights to travel interstate, Crandall v. Nevada, 6 Wall. 35 (1867), Edwards v. California, 314 U.S. 160 (1941), United States v. Guest, 383 U.S. 745 (1966) (all below), and see especially the note on personal mobility and the Edwards case, chap. 5, sec. 1, below.

2. *The Perez case.* a. *The decision.* In the Consumer Credit Protection Act, Congress made criminal "extortionate credit transactions"— transactions involving, e. g., the threat of violence to collect debts. In PEREZ v. UNITED STATES, 402 U.S. 146 (1971), the Act was applied to a transaction that had taken place entirely within one state: petitioner, a "loan shark," had used threats of violence to collect $3000 he had loaned to the owner of a local butcher shop. A divided Court rejected the constitutional challenge to that application of the law. Justice Douglas' majority opinion conceded that the constitutional question was a "substantial one," but found adequate constitutional authority: "Extortionate credit transactions, though purely intrastate, may in the judgment of Congress affect interstate commerce." Here, he insisted, there was "a tie-in between local loan sharks and interstate crime." He found the critical tie-in in legislative hearings and reports indicating that organized crime depended heavily on revenue from loan sharking. Justice Douglas noted: "The essence of all these reports and hearings was summarized and embodied in formal congressional findings.* They supplied Congress with the knowledge that the loan shark racket provides organized crime with its second most lucrative source of revenue, exacts millions from the pockets of people, coerces its victims into the commission of crimes against property, and causes the takeover by racketeers of legitimate businesses." The findings, Justice Douglas concluded, rebutted the argument that loan sharking was "a traditionally local activity," for they showed "that loan sharking in its national setting is one way organized interstate crime . . . syphons funds from numerous localities to finance its national operations."

Justice Douglas found an adequate "affecting commerce" rationale even though petitioner's particular activities had not been shown to have any impact on interstate commerce: "Petitioner is clearly *a member of a class* which engages in extortionate credit transactions as defined by Congress. . . . Where the *class of activities* is regulated and that *class* is within the reach of federal power, the courts have no power 'to excise as trivial, individual instances' of the class. [Maryland v. Wirtz, noted below]." He noted that in the Darby case, *"a class of activities"* had been held "properly regulated by Congress without proof that the particular intrastate activity against which a sanction was laid had an effect on commerce."

Justice Stewart dissented, concluding: "Because I am unable to discern any rational distinction between loan sharking and other local crime, I cannot escape the conclusion that this statute was beyond the power of Congress to enact. The definition and prosecution of local, intrastate crimes are reserved to the States under the Ninth and Tenth Amendments." He insisted that "the Framers of the Constitution never intended that the national Govern-

---

* The statute included the following findings by Congress:

"(1) Organized crime is interstate and international in character. Its activities involve many billions of dollars each year. It is directly responsible for murders, willful injuries to person and property, corruption of officials, and terrorization of countless citizens. A substantial part of the income of organized crime is generat-

ed by extortionate credit transactions.
. . .

"(3) Extortionate credit transactions are carried on to a substantial extent in interstate and foreign commerce and through the means and instrumentalities of such commerce. Even where extortionate credit transactions are purely intrastate in character, they nevertheless directly affect interstate and foreign commerce."

ment might define as a crime and prosecute such wholly local activity." And he argued: "In order to sustain this law we would, in my view, have to be able at the least to say that Congress could rationally have concluded that loan sharking is an activity with interstate attributes which distinguish it in some substantial respect from other local crime. But it is not enough to say that loan sharking is a national problem, for all crime is a national problem. It is not enough to say that some loan sharking has interstate characteristics, for any crime may have an interstate setting. And the circumstance that loan sharking has an adverse impact on interstate business is not a distinguishing attribute, for interstate business suffers from almost all criminal activity, be it shoplifting or violence in the streets."

b. *Some comments: Another limitless "bootstrap" principle?* Note the comment on Perez by Robert L. Stern, formerly of the Solicitor General's Office, a participant in many Government efforts to apply the commerce power to national economic problems since the 1930's, and an author whose writings on the commerce clause have been cited earlier: "Even a lawyer who fought for a realistic interpretation which would recognize that in commercial matters the United States was one nation finds himself surprised at where we are now—and at how readily the recent expansion is accepted. . . . The ease with which the public and the judiciary now swallow the federal regulation of what were once deemed exclusively local matters undoubtedly reflects the general integration of the nation, in disregard of state lines." Stern, "The Commerce Clause Revisited—The Federalization of Intrastate Crime," 15 Ariz.L.Rev. 271, 284 (1973).

Is the majority's statement of the commerce power justification in Perez adequate? Compare Stern's suggestion: "The key to the Perez decision may be found in the difficulty of proving in each individual case that the loan shark had an interstate connection even when it existed." Id. at 278. Compare Westfall v. United States, 274 U.S. 256, 259 (1927), quoted by Stern: "[W]hen it is necessary in order to prevent an evil to make the law embrace more than the precise thing to be prevented it may do so." Is that remark by Justice Holmes—in another context—adequate to overcome federalism objections and to authorize all-embracing national regulation of a problem whenever it is "difficult" to prove the interstate elements of the problem?

How far-reaching is the Perez rationale? † Stern asks: "Can Congress forbid the possession or transfer of all pills, or all white pills, because of the difficulty of distinguishing dangerous pills from others and because some might move interstate?" If that question is answered in the affirmative, does the answer rest on another limitless "bootstrap" principle, subject only to the practical restraint that "Congress is unlikely to interject the federal government into local transactions without good reason"? Recall the "super-bootstrap" technique which served as an alternative ground in Darby, as noted in the comments after Darby, above. Do the cases in the next note suggest that the Court may yet require more of Congress than the conclusory findings in the loan shark statute? Note the comment in 49 Tex.L.Rev.

† Stern draws from it the principle that "Congress may regulate local acts which in themselves have no interstate nexus or effect if as a practical matter it is difficult to tell the good from the bad and the interstate from the intrastate." Id. at 280.

568, 573 (1971): "[W]hile Congress 'finds and declares' that purely intrastate extortionate extensions of credit affect interstate commerce, it fails to specify *how* interstate commerce is affected by those transactions."

3. *The "implications of the federal system" as a restraint on statutory interpretation.* Though Congress has used the commerce power extensively for criminal legislation (see note 1), and though the Court has been willing to sustain congressional action reaching local activity where congressional purposes are evident (see note 2), the Court has repeatedly rejected federal prosecutors' efforts to read less clear statutes as reaching deeply into traditionally local domains. Should the concerns voiced by the Court in statutory interpretation contexts find their way into constitutional interpretation as well? Should those concerns inhibit legislators faced with new proposals for federal criminal legislation?

a. *The Five Gambling Devices case.* UNITED STATES v. FIVE GAMBLING DEVICES, 346 U.S. 441 (1953), involved the interpretation of the "incidental registration and reporting provisions" of a 1951 statute prohibiting shipment of gambling machines in interstate commerce. The information-eliciting provisions of the law were applicable to "every manufacturer and dealer in gambling devices"; they were not expressly limited to persons with some nexus to interstate commerce. The case involved three companion proceedings: two criminal indictments, and one libel to forfeit several gambling machines seized by the FBI in a country club in Tennessee. The Government argued that the statute should be applied according to its literal terms, without any requirement that the particular activities be shown to have any relationship to interstate commerce. As to constitutional justification, the Government argued that, "to make effective the prohibition of transportation in interstate commerce, Congress may constitutionally require reporting of all intrastate transactions." In a 5 to 4 decision, the Supreme Court affirmed the dismissals of all the proceedings on statutory grounds. The case is of special interest because all of the Justices who commented on the commerce power issue found the hovering constitutional problems substantial. And most intriguing is the opinion in support of the majority result by Justice Jackson, joined by Justices Frankfurter and Minton.* Under a broad reading of the "super-bootstrap" analysis in the Darby case, the Government's "control-the-local-as-a-means-of-implementing-the-interstate-prohibition" argument should have been persuasive. And Justice Jackson, as the writer of the Wickard v. Filburn opinion, had been identified with broad, virtually limitless, reaches of the commerce power. Against that background, the undercurrents of constitutional doubts in Five Gambling Devices are especially notable.

On the constitutional issue, Justice Jackson commented: "We do not intimate any ultimate answer to the appellees' constitutional questions other than to observe that they cannot be dismissed as frivolous, nor as unimportant to the nature of our federation. No precedent of this Court sustains the power of Congress to enact legislation penalizing failure to report information concerning acts not shown to be in, or mingled with, or found to affect commerce." What about the "super-bootstrap" alternative theory of

---

* Justice Black, joined by Justice Douglas, concurred in the result because of the vagueness of the reporting provisions, without reaching the commerce power issue.

Darby? Justice Jackson's caveat may be applicable to that theory as well as to other broad dicta: "While general statements, out of these different contexts, might bear upon the subject one way or another, it is apparent that the precise question tendered to us now is not settled by any prior decision."

Rather than resolving the constitutional question, Justice Jackson chose to construe the statute narrowly to avoid problems of constitutionality. And as to the content of the statutory interpretation, federalism concerns again played a role: "We do not question that literal language of this Act is capable of the broad, unlimited construction urged by the Government. Indeed, if it were enacted for a unitary system of government, no other construction would be appropriate. But we must assume that the implications and limitations of our federal system constitute a major premise of all congressional legislation, though not repeatedly recited therein. Against the background of our tradition and system of government, we cannot say that the lower courts, which have held as a matter of statutory construction that this Act does not reach purely intrastate matters, have not made a permissible interpretation. We find in the text no unmistakable intention of Congress to raise the constitutional questions implicit in the Government's effort to apply the Act in its most extreme impact upon affairs considered normally reserved to the states."

Justice Jackson noted, too, that supporters of the bill had emphasized in the legislative deliberations that the law was not intended to displace state law enforcement. Yet "here it was the [FBI] which entered a country club and seized slot machines not shown ever to have had any connection with interstate commerce in any manner whatever. If this is not substituting federal for state enforcement, it is difficult to know how it could be accomplished. A more local and detailed act of enforcement is hardly conceivable. These cases, if sustained, would substantially take unto the Federal Government the entire pursuit of the gambling device."

Justice Clark, joined by Chief Justice Warren and Justices Reed and Burton, dissented; but even Justice Clark recognized that the constitutional issue was not a trivial one. He thought the information-eliciting requirements justifiable as "reasonably necessary, appropriate and probably essential means for enforcing the ban on interstate transportation of gambling devices." But he conceded that his conclusion was "not inevitably dictated by prior decisions of the Court." He noted, too, that the information requirements as to local transactions were "certainly not a mere ruse designed to invade areas of control reserved to the states," but were "naturally and reasonably adapted to the effective exercise of" the commerce power. Moreover, he emphasized that Congress had not "sought to *regulate* local activity": in such a case, "its power would no doubt be less clear." He thought the distinction between obtaining information and "regulating" a "substantial" one. [Has the distinction become less "substantial" since 1951? Recall the sustaining of a "regulatory" criminal law in the Perez case, note 2 above.]

b. *Rewis and Bass.* Two 1971 decisions adhered to the Five Gambling Devices approach of rejecting broad Government interpretations of new criminal statutes because of federalism considerations. In REWIS v. UNITED STATES, 401 U.S. 808 (1971), Justice Marshall's opinion for a

unanimous Court reversed convictions under the Travel Act, 18 U.S.C. § 1952 (note 1 above). Petitioners ran a lottery (numbers operation) in a small town a few miles south of the Georgia-Florida state line. In the trial court, they, as well as two Georgia residents who had come to the Florida lottery to place bets, were convicted. The Court of Appeals reversed the convictions of the Georgia residents on the ground that customers of gambling operations were not covered by the Act, but upheld petitioners' convictions on the ground that operators of gambling establishments are responsible for the interstate travel of their customers. The Supreme Court agreed that "mere customers" were not covered and limited the Act even further by holding "that conducting a gambling operation frequented by out-of-state bettors, by itself," does not violate the Act.

Justice Marshall explained: "Legislative history of the Act is limited, but does reveal that § 1952 was aimed primarily at organized crime and, more specifically, at persons who reside in one State while operating or managing illegal activities located in another. In addition, we are struck by what Congress did not say. Given the ease with which citizens of our Nation are able to travel and the existence of many multi-state metropolitan areas, substantial amounts of criminal activity, traditionally subject to state regulation, are patronized by out-of-state customers. In such a context, Congress would certainly recognize that an expansive Travel Act would alter sensitive federal-state relationships, could overextend limited federal police resources, and might well produce situations in which the geographic origin of customers, a matter of happenstance, would transform relatively minor state offenses into federal felonies."

Later that year, in UNITED STATES v. BASS, 404 U.S. 336 (1971), Justice Marshall once again wrote the prevailing opinion, but this time there was a dissent—by Justice Blackmun, joined by Chief Justice Burger. Appellee had been convicted for possession of firearms in violation of § 1202 (a)(1) of the Omnibus Crime Control and Safe Streets Act of 1968, which applies to any person convicted of a felony "who receives, possesses, or transports in interstate commerce or affecting commerce . . . any firearm." There had been no showing that appellee's firearms were commerce-related. The prosecution had assumed that the commerce limitations applied only to "transports" and that possession and receipt were therefore punishable without showing a connection with commerce in individual cases. The Court disagreed: "Because its sanctions are criminal and because, under the Government's broader reading, the statute would mark a major inroad into a domain traditionally left to the States, we refuse to adopt the broad reading in the absence of a clearer direction from Congress."

Justice Marshall explained: "[U]nless Congress conveys its purpose clearly, it will not be deemed to have significantly changed the federal-state balance. Congress has traditionally been reluctant to define as a federal crime conduct readily denounced as criminal by the States. [W]e will not be quick to assume that Congress has meant to effect a significant change in the sensitive relation between federal and state criminal jurisdiction. In traditionally sensitive areas, such as legislation affecting the federal balance, the requirement of clear statement assures that the legislature has in fact faced, and intended to bring into issue, the critical matters involved in the judicial decision."

[Note the continued reliance on that passage from Bass as a guide to statutory construction, in United States v. Enmons, 410 U.S. 396 (1973).]

RECENT USES OF THE "AFFECTING COMMERCE" RATIONALE: A FURTHER LOOK AT PRACTICAL AND THEORETICAL LIMITS

Introduction. The preceding groups of notes focused primarily on contemporary problems regarding invocations of the "commerce-prohibiting" technique, in noneconomic contexts. This final group of notes returns to the "affecting commerce" approach of the line of cases culminating in Wickard v. Filburn, and to regulations with primarily economic rather than "police" objectives. When these techniques and areas of regulation are involved, what, if any, limits to the reach of the modern commerce power can be identified? The first note calls attention to restraints in congressional exercises of power. The second note provides some illustrative examples of recent congressional uses of the power and asks whether any approaches the constitutional boundaries. The concluding materials return once more to the problem of judicially imposable limitations: Can proffered "affecting commerce" rationales be rejected as resting on too insubstantial a nexus between the local and the interstate? Even if the "substantial economic effect" requirement of Wickard v. Filburn is met, can congressional action be restrained when it impinges directly on the structures and operations of state government itself? * (Recall the note at p. 125 above.)

1. *Statutory reach short of constitutional limits.* As the scope of the commerce power has expanded, the actual range of national control has increasingly come to turn on congressional choices rather than constitutional limits.† But the fact that Congress chooses not to go as far as the Constitution permits does not make constitutional doctrines irrelevant. Thus, as the Five Gambling Devices case illustrated, constitutional limits affect statutory interpretation. Moreover, just as Congress has not in fact entered all areas of potential control, it frequently does not go to the constitutional limit in the areas actually regulated. Accordingly, the statutory formula of coverage often presents the major operative issue in drafting and interpreting modern commerce clause regulations. Compare, for example, the "affecting commerce" formula in the National Labor Relations Act (in the Jones & Laughlin case) with the narrower scope of the Fair Labor Standards Act (in the Darby case) as to employees engaged "in the production of goods for commerce." See Kirschbaum Co. v. Walling, 316 U.S. 517 (1942). See also the reliance on the narrowing "in commerce" language in the Clayton and Robinson-Patman Acts, in Gulf Oil Corp. v. Copp Paving Co., 419 U.S. 186 (1974).

---

* Many of the questions raised throughout this chapter recur in a particularized context in the final section, sec. 6, on the public accommodations provisions of the Civil Rights Act of 1964.

† Compare chap. 6, sec. 2, Congressional Ordering of Federal-State Relationships; and recall Herbert Wechsler on the "Political Safeguards of Federalism," at the end of chap. 2 above. See also Bogen, "The Hunting of the Shark: An Inquiry Into the Limits of Congressional Power Under the Commerce Clause," 8 Wake Forest L.Rev. 187 (1972).

2. *Recent legislation using the "affecting commerce" technique: Constitutional problems?* Do the following provisions (all but the last are additions to 21 U.S.C.) press "affecting commerce" justifications too far, in view of the scope of the commerce power in cases such as Wickard v. Filburn?

a. *Drugs.* § 360 [Added in 1962]. *"Registration of drug producers.*

. . .

"(b) On or before December 31 of each year every person who owns or operates any establishment in any State engaged in the manufacture, preparation, propagation, compounding, or processing of a drug or drugs shall register with the Secretary his name, places of business and all such establishments." **

b. *Oleomargarine.* § 347 [added in 1950]. *"Intrastate sales of colored oleomargarine—Law governing.*

"(a) Colored oleomargarine or colored margarine which is sold in the same State or Territory in which it is produced shall be subject in the same manner and to the same extent to the provisions of this chapter as if it had been introduced in interstate commerce. . . .

"(b) No person shall sell, or offer for sale, colored oleomargarine or colored margarine unless—

"(1) such oleomargarine or margarine is packaged,

"(2) the net weight of the contents of any package sold in a retail establishment is one pound or less,

"(3) there appears on the label of the package (A) the word 'oleomargarine' or 'margarine' in type or lettering at least as large as any other type or lettering on such label, and (B) a full and accurate statement of all the ingredients contained in such oleomargarine or margarine, and

"(4) each part of the contents of the package is contained in a wrapper which bears the word 'oleomargarine' or 'margarine' in type or lettering not smaller than 20-point type. . . .

"(c) No person shall possess in a form ready for serving colored oleomargarine or colored margarine at a public eating place unless a notice that oleomargarine or margarine is served is displayed prominently and conspicuously in such place and in such manner as to render it likely to be read and understood by the ordinary individual being served in such eating place or is printed or is otherwise set forth on the menu in type or lettering not smaller than that normally used to designate the serving of other food items. No per-

** Public Law 87–781, which included 21 U.S.C. § 360, contained the following statement as Section 301: "The Congress hereby finds and declares that in order to make regulation of interstate commerce in drugs effective, it is necessary to provide for registration and inspection of all establishments in which drugs are manufactured, prepared, propagated, compounded, or processed; that the products of all such establishments are likely to enter the channels of interstate commerce and directly affect such commerce; and that the regulation of interstate commerce in drugs without provision for registration and inspection of establishments that may be engaged only in intrastate commerce in such drugs would discriminate against and depress interstate commerce in such drugs, and adversely burden, obstruct, and affect such interstate commerce."

son shall serve colored oleomargarine or colored margarine at a public eating place, whether or not any charge is made therefor, unless (1) each separate serving bears or is accompanied by labeling identifying it as oleomargarine or margarine, or (2) each separate serving thereof is triangular in shape. . .

"(e) For the purpose of this section colored oleomargarine or colored margarine is oleomargarine or margarine having a tint or shade containing more than one and six-tenths degrees of yellow, or of yellow and red collectively, but with an excess of yellow over red, measured in terms of Lovibond tintometer scale or its equivalent."

§ 347a. *"Congressional declaration of policy regarding oleomargarine sales.*

"The Congress finds and declares that the sale, or the serving in public eating places, of colored oleomargarine or colored margarine without clear identification as such or which is otherwise adulterated or misbranded within the meaning of this chapter depresses the market in interstate commerce for butter and for oleomargarine or margarine clearly identified and neither adulterated nor misbranded, and constitutes a burden on interstate commerce in such articles. Such burden exists, irrespective of whether such oleomargarine or margarine originates from an interstate source or from the State in which it is sold."

c. *The significance of legislative findings.* What is the significance of congressional findings, such as those in Public Law 87–781 and in 21 U.S.C. § 347a above? Are they significant in congressional consideration? In constitutional litigation? Are they useful? Necessary? Determinative? Note the discussion and disposition of these problems in the consideration of Title II of the Civil Rights Act of 1964 (sec. 6 below).

d. *Air pollution.* Does the commerce clause authorize comprehensive federal control of air pollution? See Edelman, "Federal Air and Water Control: The Application of the Commerce Power to Abate Interstate and Intrastate Pollution," 33 Geo.Wash.L.Rev. 1067 (1965). Do the abatement provisions of the Federal Clean Air Act, 42 U.S.C. § 1857 et seq., raise constitutional problems? The Act authorized the U. S. Attorney General to bring an abatement action on behalf of the United States if the pollution is "endangering the health or welfare of persons in a state other than that in which the discharge or discharges (causing or contributing to such pollution) originate." But in those situations in which the pollution endangers "persons only in the state in which the discharge or discharges originate," the Attorney General may sue only on request of a Governor. Is that difference in the scope of authority in the two situations required by the commerce clause?†

† Note the congressional findings in the Act, 42 U.S.C. § 1857(a), which include the following:

"(1) that the predominant part of the Nation's population is located in its rapidly expanding metropolitan and other urban areas, which generally cross the boundary lines of local jurisdictions and often extend into two or more States;

"(2) that the growth in the amount and complexity of air pollution brought about by urbanization, industrial development, and the increasing use of motor vehicles, has resulted in mounting dangers to the public health and welfare, including injury to agricultural crops and livestock, damage to and the deterioration of property, and hazards to air and ground transportation;

"(3) that the prevention and control of air pollution at its source is the pri-

3. *Maryland v. Wirtz and potential limits of power: "Trivial"
economic impacts? State autonomy?* Coverage of the Fair Labor Standards
Act [see the Darby case, above] was extended by two amendments in the
1960's; and constitutional challenges to those 1961 and 1966 amendments
came to the Court in MARYLAND v. WIRTZ, 392 U.S. 183 (1968).
The Court sustained both amendments; and the opinions in the case cast
light on the contemporary availability of both "trivial impacts" and "state
autonomy" defenses to applications of commerce clause regulations.*

a. *"Trivial impacts."* The 1961 amendment considered in Wirtz
dealt with a major traditional concern of the FLSA, employees in private
industry. Prior to the amendment, coverage was limited to employees
"engaged in commerce or in the production of goods for commerce." The
1966 extension included every employee who "is employed in an enterprise
engaged in commerce or in the production of goods for commerce." In
effect, that amendment extended protection "to the fellow employees of any
employee who would have been protected by the original Act," but it did
not enlarge the class of employers subject to the Act. Justice Harlan's
majority opinion found this "enterprise concept" constitutionally justified on
alternative grounds: either under the original "unfair competition" theory
of Darby or on the Jones & Laughlin "labor dispute" theory. With regard
to the competition analysis, Justice Harlan noted: "There was obviously a
'rational basis' for the logical inference that the pay and hours of production
employees affect a company's competitive position. The logical inference
does not stop with production employees. When a company does an interstate business, its competition with companies elsewhere is affected by all its
significant labor costs, not merely by the wages and hours of those employees who have physical contact with the goods in question." With
respect to the labor dispute analysis, he commented that "there is a basis
in logic and experience for the conclusion that substandard labor conditions
among any group of employees, whether or not they are personally engaged
in commerce or production, may lead to strife disrupting an entire enterprise."

With regard to potential limits on the scope of the commerce power, a
footnote to the majority opinion (replying to the dissent by Justice Douglas
mainly concerned with the state autonomy issue, see note 3b below) is of particular interest. Justice Harlan stated: "The dissent suggests
that by use of an 'enterprise concept' such as that we have upheld here, Congress could under today's decision declare a whole State an 'enterprise' affecting commerce and take over its budgeting activities. This reflects, we think,
a misreading of the Act, of Wickard v. Filburn, supra, and of our decision.
. . . . We uphold the enterprise concept on the explicit premise that
an 'enterprise' is a set of operations whose activities in commerce would all
be expected to be affected by the wages and hours of any group of employees,
which is what Congress obviously intended. So defined, the term is quite
cognizant of limitations on the commerce power. Neither here nor in

mary responsibility of States and local
governments . . . ."
* Recall also, as another potential limit,
the advocacy of special judicial scrutiny when Congress seeks to regulate

a "historically local" field, in Justice
Douglas' dissent in United States v.
Oregon, 366 U.S. 643 (1961) (consider-
ed at the end of chap. 2 above).

Wickard has the Court declared that Congress may use a relatively trivial impact on commerce as an excuse for broad general regulation of state or private activities. The Court has said only that where a general regulatory statute bears a substantial relation to commerce, the de minimis character of individual instances arising under that statute is of no consequence."

b. *State autonomy.* A different variety of limitation was suggested in response to the 1966 amendment to the FLSA, which applied the Act to employees of state-operated schools and hospitals. The majority upheld that application against charges of interference with the autonomy of the operations of state government. Justice Harlan's majority opinion found the argument that the Act interfered with "sovereign state functions" untenable. He insisted that national actions under the commerce power "may override countervailing state interests whether these are described as 'governmental' or 'proprietary' in character." Justice Douglas' dissent, joined by Justice Stewart, thought the majority's position "unexceptionable" as "an exercise in semantics" if "congressional federalism is the standard," but insisted that "what is done here is nonetheless such a serious invasion of state sovereignty protected by the Tenth Amendment that it is in my belief not consistent with our constitutional federalism."

In elaborating, Justice Douglas stated that these statutory provisions "disrupt the fiscal policy of the States and threaten their autonomy in the regulation of health and education." He added: "It is one thing to force a State to purchase safety equipment for its railroad [sustained in United States v. California, 297 U.S. 175 (1936), chap. 6 below] and another to force it to spend several million more dollars on hospitals and schools or substantially reduce services in these areas." If the majority's rationale were accepted, he asked, "could Congress compel the States to build superhighways crisscrossing their territory in order to accommodate interstate vehicles, to provide inns and eating places for interstate travelers, to quadruple their police forces in order to prevent commerce-crippling riots, etc.? Could the Congress virtually draw up each State's budget to avoid 'disruptive effect[s] on . . . commercial intercourse'?" He concluded: "In this case the State as a sovereign power is being seriously tampered with, potentially crippled." (See also p. 125 above and p. 387 below.)

The state autonomy concerns raised by the dissenters as a limit on national regulatory authority in the Wirtz case have arisen in other contexts as well. For further exploration of the problem of intergovernmental regulatory immunities, see chap. 6, sec. 1, below. For an unsuccessful effort to assert state autonomy barriers to conditions on federal spending programs, see Oklahoma v. U. S. Civil Service Commission, 330 U.S. 127 (1947) (chap. 4, sec. 2, below). For a general discussion of the problem, and an argument that state autonomy concerns cast doubt on aspects of proposed federal no-fault auto insurance legislation, see Dorsen, "The National No-Fault Motor Vehicle Insurance Act: A Problem in Federalism," 49 N.Y.U.L.Rev. 45 (1974).* (See also the 1975 developments, p. 125 above.)

---

* Dorsen's criticism is directed at features of the National No-Fault Insurance Act adopted by the Senate in May, 1974, S. 354, 93d Cong., 2d Sess. Under Title II of the bill, national standards for state-enacted no-fault plans are established. Title III then sets forth an alternative state no-fault insurance plan which automatically goes into effect in states which do not voluntarily pass a no-fault law conforming to Title II within four years

SECTION 6. THE COMMERCE POWER AND RACIAL DISCRIMINATION: THE PUBLIC ACCOMMODATIONS TITLE OF THE CIVIL RIGHTS ACT OF 1964

Introduction. This section pursues the questions raised in the preceding materials by examining the use of the commerce power in a particular context: the controversial invocation of the power in the especially important context of banning racial discrimination in public accommodations. The focus here is on congressional consideration and judicial scrutiny of Title II of the Civil Rights Act of 1964. Excerpts from the hearings and the text of the statute precede the Court decisions on its constitutionality and scope. The legislative deliberations illustrate some of the problems of selecting appropriate constitutional bases and drafting adequate statutory coverage formulas. In examining the hearings, consider especially the legislator's independent obligation to consider constitutionality as well as policy in his or her lawmaking role. These excerpts remind that constitutional discussions are not an exclusive judicial function in our system of government. And the Court decisions sustaining the legislation raise anew the problems of acceptable rationales and potential limits in the exercise of the power to regulate interstate commerce.

This section also serves as a preview of constitutional problems in congressional civil rights legislation—a subject pursued more fully in later chapters. Congressional action to protect civil rights has been sporadic. After a period of intensive activity during Reconstruction, from 1866 to 1875, Congress was virtually silent for over three-quarters of a century. A revival of legislative productivity began with the Civil Rights Act of 1957. Most federal civil rights laws have been based on the post-Civil War Amendments. (Congressional authority under those Amendments—especially § 5 of the 14th Amendment—is the focus of chap. 11 below.) But, as the Civil Rights Act of 1964 illustrates, Art. I, § 8, may also provide authority for legislation to protect civil rights. The title of the Act reflects not only the wide-ranging content of legislation but also the varied sources of power invoked: there is reference not only to the commerce but also to the spending power in Art. I, § 8; there is also reference to legislative power under the 14th and 15th Amendments.* But it is the portion of the legislation drawing on the commerce power for constitutional support that is the special concern of this section.†

after enactment of the Act. As described by Dorsen, the detailed alternative plan "commands state officials to perform their duties and to spend state funds according to a federal mandate, even if the state has not authorized its officials to act." Dorsen concedes that the commerce power is ample to justify a wholly national no-fault plan under an "affecting commerce" rationale. But he questions the means proposed in Title III. He insists that the "coercive use of state officials to organize and manage a com-prehensive regulatory program is not typical of congressional legislation." And he suggests that "an effect of S. 354 could be to impair the essence of federalism by intruding on state autonomy in a manner not contemplated by the Constitution."

* The 1964 legislation is entitled: "An Act to enforce the constitutional right to vote, to confer jurisdiction upon the district courts of the United States to

† See footnote on p. 209.

A. THE COVERAGE OF THE STATUTE

TITLE II—INJUNCTIVE RELIEF AGAINST DISCRIMINATION IN PLACES OF PUBLIC ACCOMMODATION **

Sec. 201. (a) All persons shall be entitled to the full and equal enjoyment of the goods, services, facilities, privileges, advantages, and accommodations of any place of public accommodation, as defined in this section, without discrimination or segregation on the ground of race, color, religion, or national origin.

(b) Each of the following establishments which serves the public is a place of public accommodation within the meaning of this title if its operations affect commerce, or if discrimination or segregation by it is supported by State action:

(1) any inn, hotel, motel, or other establishment which provides lodging to transient guests, other than an establishment located within a building which contains not more than five rooms for rent or hire and which is actually occupied by the proprietor of such establishment as his residence;

(2) any restaurant, cafeteria, lunchroom, lunch counter, soda fountain, or other facility principally engaged in selling food for consumption on the premises, including, but not limited to, any such facility located on the premises of any retail establishment; or any gasoline station;

(3) any motion picture house, theater, concert hall, sports arena, stadium or other place of exhibition or entertainment; and

(4) any establishment (A)(i) which is physically located within the premises of any establishment otherwise covered by this subsection, or (ii) within the premises of which is physically located any such covered establishment, and (B) which holds itself out as serving patrons of such covered establishment.

(c) The operations of an establishment affect commerce within the meaning of this title if (1) it is one of the establishments described in paragraph (1) of subsection (b); (2) in the case of an establishment described in paragraph (2) of subsection (b), it serves or offers to serve interstate travelers or a substantial por-

provide injunctive relief against discrimination in public accommodations, to authorize the Attorney General to institute suits to protect constitutional rights in public facilities and public education, to extend the Commission on Civil Rights, to prevent discrimination in federally assisted programs, to establish a Commission on Equal Employment Opportunity, and for other purposes." Pub.L. 88–352, 78 Stat. 241. It became law on July 2, 1964, more than a year after President Kennedy had urged comprehensive civil rights legislation in a message to Congress. Enactment followed the first successful cloture vote on a civil rights bill (71 to 29), on June 10, 1964, after weeks of Senate debate.

† The public accommodations provisions are not the only modern anti-discrimination laws resting on the commerce power for constitutional support. For example, long before the 1964 Act, the Court had found that the general anti-discrimination provisions of the Interstate Commerce Act prohibited racial segregation by interstate carriers. See, e. g., Henderson v. United States, 339 U.S. 816 (1950). Moreover, as early as 1944, the Court had found a ban on racial discrimination implicit in a union's status as exclusive bargaining agent under federal labor legislation. Steele v. Louisville & N. R. R., 323 U.S. 192 (1944). More recently, statutory bans on discrimination have been made more explicit. See, e. g., Title VII, "Equal Employment Opportunity," of the 1964 Civil Rights Act, prohibiting discrimination on the basis of race, color, religion, sex, or national origin. See, e. g., Griggs v. Duke Power Co., 401 U.S. 424 (1971) (see chap. 10 below); and note also the Equal Employment Opportunity Act of 1972. Moreover, the 1968 Civil Rights Act included fair housing provisions (Title VIII). However, two months before the enactment of that law, the Court read a comprehensive ban against racial discrimination in housing into an 1866 statute based on the 13th Amendment. Jones v. Alfred H. Mayer Co., 392 U.S. 409 (1968). Are there any limits on commerce power-based legislation directed at housing discrimination? The Jones case, and the relationship between the 1866 and 1968 housing laws, are considered below, chap. 11, sec. 3.

** The text printed here follows the numbering in Pub.L. 88–352, 78 Stat. 241. See also the renumbered version, 42 U.S.C.A. §§ 2000a–2000a–6.

tion of the food which it serves, or gasoline or other products which it sells, has moved in commerce; (3) in the case of an establishment described in paragraph (3) of subsection (b), it customarily presents films, performances, athletic teams, exhibitions, or other sources of entertainment which move in commerce; and (4) in the case of an establishment described in paragraph (4) of subsection (b), it is physically located within the premises of, or there is physically located within its premises, an establishment the operations of which affect commerce within the meaning of this subsection. For purposes of this section, "commerce" means travel, trade, traffic, commerce, transportation, or communication among the several States, or between the District of Columbia and any State, or between any foreign country or any territory or possession and any State or the District of Columbia, or between points in the same State but through any other State or the District of Columbia or a foreign country.

(d) Discrimination or segregation by an establishment is supported by State action within the meaning of this title if such discrimination or segregation (1) is carried on under color of any law, statute, ordinance, or regulation; or (2) is carried on under color of any custom or usage required or enforced by officials of the State or political subdivision thereof; or (3) is required by action of the State or political subdivision thereof. [See chap. 11, sec. 2, below.]

(e) The provisions of this title shall not apply to a private club or other establishment not in fact open to the public, except to the extent that the facilities of such establishment are made available to the customers or patrons of an establishment within the scope of subsection (b).

Sec. 202. All persons shall be entitled to be free, at any establishment or place, from discrimination or segregation of any kind on the ground of race, color, religion, or national origin, if such discrimination or segregation is or purports to be required by any law, statute, ordinance, regulation, rule, or order of a State or any agency or political subdivision thereof.

Sec. 203. No person shall (a) withhold, deny, or attempt to withhold or deny, or deprive or attempt to deprive, any person of any right or privilege secured by section 201 or 202, or (b) intimidate, threaten, or coerce, or attempt to intimidate, threaten, or coerce any person with the purpose of interfering with any right or privilege secured by section 201 or 202, or (c) punish or attempt to punish any person for exercising or attempting to exercise any right or privilege secured by section 201 or 202. [Sec. 204 provides for private civil relief; Sec. 205, for civil actions by the Attorney General in certain cases.] . . .

B. THE CONGRESSIONAL DELIBERATIONS

Introduction. Consideration of the proposals that became the 1964 Act produced extensive hearings before several committees, and lengthy debates on the floor of both houses of Congress. Constitutional issues were discussed exhaustively. The selections that follow are from hearings in the early stages of the process, before the Senate Commerce Committee in July and August 1963. Hearings Before the Senate Committee on Commerce on S. 1732, 88th Cong., 1st Sess., parts 1 and 2. The Committee had before it the Administration proposal on public accommodations. Before the Administration bill was submitted to Congress in late June, it was widely reported that it would rely solely on the commerce clause. As introduced, it included references to the Fourteenth Amendment as well, but the commerce power focus predominated: for example, the proposed title was "Interstate Public Accommodations Act"; the introductory series of findings dealt almost entirely with commerce; the commerce emphases, and the afterthought nature of the Fourteenth Amendment reliance, were highlighted by the final "finding" that the "burdens on and obstructions to commerce which are de-

scribed above can best be removed by invoking the powers of Congress under the Fourteenth amendment and the commerce clause of the Constitution"; and the coverage provisions were entirely in commerce terms. (Section 201 (d) of the Act, on discrimination "supported by State action," was added subsequently, during the congressional consideration of the bill.) Note the Gunther comments made at the time when the proposal rested solely on the commerce power, printed below, after the excerpts from the hearings.

Examine the coverage provisions of Title II in light of the concerns expressed during the hearings. Note the reluctance of some Senators to utilize the commerce clause rather than the Fourteenth Amendment. Was there basis for that reluctance in the Constitution or in the Court's decisions? Should a Senator be concerned even if the Court's decisions left the matter doubtful—or should that issue be left to the Court? Suppose a legislator has no doubts that a commerce clause-based law would be sustained by the courts. May he nevertheless claim that it is his right, or duty, to consider questions of constitutional "propriety" in casting his vote? See generally Morgan, Congress and the Constitution (1966), and Brest, "The Conscientious Legislator's Guide to Constitutional Interpretation," 27 Stan.L.Rev. 585 (1975). (For further examination of the constitutional difficulties in the Fourteenth Amendment approach, see chap. 11 below.)

Note that the bill as enacted omitted the recital of findings. Were Senator Monroney's statements about the importance of findings justified? Were there significant differences regarding the scope of the commerce power between the views of Attorney General Kennedy and of Assistant Attorney General Marshall? Was there merit in Senator Magnuson's position on the respective roles of Congress and Court in determining the reach of the commerce clause?

THE SENATE COMMITTEE HEARINGS, 1963

MR. [ROBERT F.] KENNEDY [ATTORNEY GENERAL]. . . . We base this on the commerce clause which I think makes it clearly constitutional. In my personal judgment, basing it on the 14th amendment would also be constitutional. . . .   I think that there is argument about the 14th amendment basis—going back to the 1883 Supreme Court decision [Civil Rights Cases, 109 U.S. 3, chap. 11 below], and the fact that this is not State action—that therefore Congress would not have the right under the 14th amendment to pass any legislation dealing with it. . . .

Senator, I think that there is an injustice that needs to be remedied. We have to find the tools with which to remedy that injustice. . . .

There cannot be any legitimate question about the commerce clause. That is clearly constitutional. We need to obtain a remedy. The commerce clause will obtain a remedy and there won't be a problem about the constitutionality. . . .

SENATOR MONRONEY [DEM., OKLA.] . . . . Mr. Attorney General, I think most of the members of this committee are sincerely in agreement with your strong plea for the elimination of discrimination. I think most of them would like to have legislation that could achieve this end

instantly and totally. But many of us are worried about the use the interstate commerce clause will have on matters which have been for more than 170 years thought to be within the realm of local control under our dual system of State and Federal Government . . . .

Is the test whether the line of business has a substantial effect on interstate commerce? Lodgings are covered, if they are public, and transients are served. Does that mean that all lodging houses under your theory of the effect on interstate commerce would be under Federal regulation, regardless of whether the transients that were using the lodgings were intrastate or interstate?

MR. KENNEDY. That is correct. If it is a lodging, a motel, that opens its doors to the general public, invites the general public, then it would be covered. . . .

SENATOR MONRONEY. . . . If we pass this bill, even though the end we seek is good, I wonder how far we are stretching the Constitution. . . .

MR. KENNEDY. The point I would make, Senator, is that we are not going beyond any principle of the use of the commerce clause that has not already been clearly established, which has been passed in this Congress, and which has been ruled on by the courts. We are not stretching the commerce clause. We are not adding anything to the commerce clause. This is just like laws that have been passed by the Senate of the United States and the House of Representatives, and passed on by the courts of the United States.
. . .

SENATOR MONRONEY. I grant you that I can see ample evidence under all the historic interpretations of the interstate commerce clause that the Hilton hotel chain is in interstate commerce, that your national food stores are in interstate commerce, that your variety stores which have lunch counters are in interstate commerce. Many motels which are national in their operations are in interstate commerce. I raise no question about that. I think it is true. I think Congress does have the right to regulate those businesses under the commerce clause, because they operate in many States.

But I find it rather difficult to stretch the clause to cover an eating place simply because some of its meat moves from one State into another; or because the vegetables they serve come from Florida; or the oranges come from California. . . .

MR. KENNEDY. What I am saying is that there is precedent for passing this kind of legislation. With these precedents and with the great need that exists, the legislation should be as inclusive as possible, as long as it doesn't affect a personal or social relationship. . . .

SENATOR MONRONEY. I strongly doubt that we can stretch the Interstate Commerce Clause that far. . . . Under your summary of the court's actions, there would hardly be any field of business in any State that is exempt from Federal regulation under the interstate commerce clause.

MR. KENNEDY. No, I didn't say that, Senator. That is not my point. Excuse me.

SENATOR MONRONEY. I am trying to get it straight. I am not trying to misinterpret you. If the court decisions and all the precedents that

you have mentioned are, or have been construed to mean that a business, no matter how intrastate in its nature, comes under the interstate commerce clause, then we can legislate for other businesses in other fields in addition to the discrimination legislation that is asked for here.

MR. KENNEDY. If the establishment is covered by the commerce clause, then you can regulate; that is correct * . . ..

THE CHAIRMAN [SENATOR MAGNUSON, DEM., WASH.]. I think we ought to get this in perspective. Congress doesn't determine what is under the interstate commerce clause. The Constitution and court decisions determine that. Since it is regulatory in nature in passing any one of these bills, Congress can determine how far it wants to use the interstate commerce clause, how far down it wants to go, what it wants to cover, what it doesn't want to cover. This has been the case in all of these bills that come under the umbrella of the interstate commerce clause.

We can't pass a bill saying what is under interstate commerce, because the Constitution provides that; that would require a constitutional amendment. We are talking about how far you want to go or what you want to do in a particular field with a bill, or a number of bills. Whether a business is in interstate commerce or not is a question of the interpretation of the Constitution and of the courts' rules in these matters. . . .

SENATOR THURMOND [DEM. (now REP.), S. C.] Mr. Attorney General, isn't it true that all of the acts of Congress based on the commerce clause which you have mentioned in your statement were primarily designed to regulate economic affairs of life and that the basic purpose of this bill is to regulate moral and social affairs?

MR. KENNEDY. Well, Senator, let me say this: I think that the discrimination that is taking place at the present time is having a very adverse effect on our economy. So I think that it is quite clear that under the commerce clause even if it was just on that aspect and even if you get away from the moral aspect—I think it is quite clear that this kind of discrimination has an adverse effect on the economy. I think all you have to do is look at some of the southern communities at the present time and the difficult time that they are having.

SENATOR THURMOND. And you would base this bill on the economic features rather than the social and moral aspect?

MR. KENNEDY. I think the other is an extremely important aspect of it that we should keep in mind. . . .

SENATOR THURMOND. Now how could the denial of services to an individual who is a resident and has no intention of leaving that State be a burden on interstate commerce?

* Compare the testimony by Assistant Attorney General Marshall, below, and the following paragraph in a memorandum on the constitutionality of Title II subsequently submitted by the Justice Department and printed in an appendix to the Hearings (part II, at p. 1296):

"Of course, there are limits on congressional power under the Commerce Clause. It may be conceded that Congress does not hold the power to regulate all of a man's conduct solely because he has relationship with interstate commerce. What is required is that there be a relationship between interstate commerce and the evil to be regulated. Over the course of the years, various tests have been established for determining whether this relationship exists. The proposed legislation clearly meets these tests."

MR. KENNEDY. Because we are talking about a cumulative situation here, Senator. It is not just an individual. If this was just an individual situation and there was one restaurant or one motel or one hotel, we wouldn't all be sitting here today.

What this is is a general practice, and a practice that has existed for many, many, many years. What we are trying to do is to get at that general practice.

The cumulative effect of a number of establishments which take in transients, and some of which would be interstate, some of which would be intrastate—the cumulative effect of all these has a major effect on interstate commerce. That is the theory, and it is a theory that has been borne out in a number of decisions. And I suppose the best known is Wickard v. Filburn, where the man just ran his own wheat farm. . . .

SENATOR THURMOND. What does "substantial" mean when you say "substantial"? That is what I am trying to get at. . . .

MR. KENNEDY. I don't think you can have any mathematical precision and a cutoff line. There has been a good deal of legislation that has been passed by Congress, passed on by this committee where you have expressions such as this. What is "interstate commerce"? Even if you didn't have "substantial," Senator, how would you be able to define it? You can't define, with mathematical precision, "interstate commerce." You can't define, specifically and particularly, "due process of law" or "equal protection of the laws." These are terms that we use frequently in our legislation and in court decisions. So you can't do that. But I think you could work it out in the individual case. . . .

SENATOR THURMOND. I am just trying to find out what, so a fellow would know, for instance, if he got three-fourths of his business from interstate travelers, would he be covered by this bill?

MR. KENNEDY. I would think he would. . . .

SENATOR THURMOND. And only 30 percent was interstate; would that be covered?

MR. KENNEDY. I think it probably would. But I think it would depend somewhat where the [business] was established and perhaps a number of other factors. . . .

SENATOR THURMOND. Twenty percent?

MR. KENNEDY. Again, I think it would depend on other factors.

SENATOR THURMOND. What other factors?

MR. KENNEDY. Was he near an airport, Senator? I don't know.

SENATOR THURMOND. What difference does it make whether he is near an airport or 10 miles from the airport if 20 percent of his business came from out of State? Would he have to serve them?

MR. KENNEDY. I think these other factors play a role in it, Senator —whether an establishment deals with those in interstate commerce. That would be a factor you would have to take into consideration. I would say that perhaps it very well might be covered. But I think that he could, he wouldn't have any problem if he wouldn't discriminate. It wouldn't be difficult for him. He would decide, "I am not going to discriminate." . . .

SENATOR MONRONEY. I would like to ask the Attorney General for the purpose of the record to give us the effect in law, if any, of section 2, on page 1 through page 4 [the "Findings"]. This is the ordinary preamble of the bill, is it not; and would not have any effect before the courts in determining the scope of the law?

MR. KENNEDY. This is the ordinary preamble giving the purposes of the law, Senator; that is correct.

SENATOR MONRONEY. There is no law actually involved in it?

MR. KENNEDY. No.

SENATOR MONRONEY. The Court, whatever it decided on the scope of the interstate commerce clause, . . . would base its decision on the other sections of the bill, and this is merely, I guess, what the Court would call obiter dicta.

MR. KENNEDY. That is correct. . . .

THE CHAIRMAN [MAGNUSON]. When you use the commerce clause for a social objective there is plenty of precedent for that, too. We did that in the Mann Act; we did that in the Pinball Act, and the gambling regulations for social reasons. We don't have to do this. It is a matter of public policy.

The commerce clause is there. We can't stretch it, restrict it, or do anything with it. It is there. The Constitution will not change unless we have a constitutional amendment. . . .

SENATOR COOPER [REP., KY.]. I do not suppose that anyone would seriously contend that the administration is proposing legislation, or the Congress is considering legislation, because it has suddenly determined, after all these years, that segregation is a burden on interstate commerce. We are considering legislation because we believe, as the great majority of the people in our country believe, that all citizens have an equal right to have access to goods, services, and facilities which are held out to be available for public use and patronage.

If there is a right to the equal use of accommodations held out to the public, it is a right of citizenship and a constitutional right under the 14th amendment. It has nothing to do with whether a business is in interstate commerce or whether discrimination against individuals places a burden on commerce. It does not depend upon the commerce clause and cannot be limited by that clause, in my opinion, as the administration bill would do. . . .

If we are going to deal with this question of the use of public accommodations, I think it imperative that Congress should enact legislation which would meet it fully and squarely as a right under the 14th amendment, and not indirectly and partially as the administration's approach would do.

Rights under the Constitution apply to all citizens, and the integrity and dignity of the individual should not be placed on lesser grounds such as the commerce clause. . . .

MR. [BURKE] MARSHALL [ASSISTANT ATTORNEY GENERAL, CIVIL RIGHTS DIVISION]. . . . Let me dispel at the out-

set a possible misconception concerning the scope of S. 1732. We do not propose to regulate the businesses covered merely because they are engaged in some phase of interstate commerce. Discrimination by the establishments covered in the bill should be prohibited because it is that discrimination itself which adversely affects interstate commerce.

Section 2 of the bill describes in detail the effect of racial discrimination on national commerce. Discrimination burdens Negro interstate travelers and thereby inhibits interstate travel. It artificially restricts the market available for interstate goods and services. It leads to the withholding of patronage by potential customers for such goods and services. It inhibits the holding of conventions and meetings in segregated cities. It interferes with businesses that wish to obtain the services of persons who do not choose to subject themselves to segregation and discrimination. And it restricts business enterprises in their choice of location for offices and plants, thus preventing the most effective allocation of national resources.

Clearly, all of these are burdens on interstate commerce and they may therefore be dealt with by the Congress. . . .

SENATOR PASTORE [DEM., R.I.] . . . I believe in this bill, because I believe in the dignity of man, not because it impedes our commerce. I don't think any man has the right to say to another man, You can't eat in my restaurant because you have a dark skin; no matter how clean you are, you can't eat at my restaurant.

That deprives a man of his full stature as an American citizen. That shocks me. That hurts me. And that is the reason why I want to vote for this law.

Now, it might well be that I can effect the same remedy through the commerce clause. But I like to feel that what we are talking about is a moral issue, an issue that involves the morality of this great country of ours. And that morality, it seems to me, comes under the 14th amendment, where we speak about immunities and where we speak about equal protection of the law. I would like to feel that the Supreme Court of the United States is given another chance to review it, not under the commerce clause, but under the 14th amendment. . . . Do you see anything wrong in that?

MR. MARSHALL. Senator, I think it would be a mistake to rely solely on the 14th amendment. This bill, S. 1732, relies on the 14th amendment, and also relies on the commerce clause. I think it is plainly constitutional. I think if it relied solely on the 14th amendment, it might not be held constitutional. I think it would be a disservice to pass a bill that was later thrown out by the Supreme Court.

SENATOR PASTORE. I am not being critical of you. I am merely stating my own position. I am saying we are being a little too careful, cagey, and cautious, in debating this question of the 14th amendment. I realize you should bring all of the tools at your disposal and that is what you are doing. You are saying you are not only relying on the 14th amendment, you are relying on the commerce clause as well and you have every right to do that as a good lawyer. All I am saying here is that we have a perfect right to proceed under the 14th amendment and try it again.

MR. MARSHALL. Yes, Senator. . . .

THE CHAIRMAN [MAGNUSON]. [W]hat is in interstate commerce? As a matter of public policy, we may all come to the conclusion you wouldn't want to put this under that authority. But there is no use of us here belaboring the point of what the interstate commerce clause includes, how far it may or may not extend, because it is written.

MR. JAMES J. KILPATRICK [JOURNALIST]. [S]ir, this is your primary obligation before it ever hits that court, to make that judgment, to bring to bear on it all the thought, power, energy, and intellect that you can to make the primary decision as to whether it is or is not constitutional. . . .

MR. [BRUCE] BROMLEY [N. Y. ATTORNEY; FORMER JUDGE, N. Y. COURT OF APPEALS]. . . . Of course, I concede that Congress does not hold the power to regulate all of a man's conduct solely because he has at some time in the past imported goods in interstate commerce. And I not only concede, I assert there must be some connection between interstate commerce and the evil to be regulated. . . .

SENATOR MONRONEY. . . . I am still troubled on the interstate commerce clause. There are no restrictions on what we can rule to be in interstate commerce. Therefore, under the powers of the Federal Government is there any cutoff place—not just on bias, but on regulation, on policing powers of industry, corporate and otherwise—that the Federal Government would have?

I always presumed maybe it was just a tradition of the Government not to invade the States rights, but I also presumed there were certain definite limits beyond which we couldn't go in controlling matters which were intrastate in nature.

MR. BROMLEY. My dear Senator, I think there are plainly limits. Let's just take a very simple one.

You can't apply this law to a little barber shop whose activities have no substantial effect on interstate commerce. And you can't apply it in any area or any law under the commerce clause unless you are dealing with some activity which is either in the stream of commerce or has a substantial effect upon that flow in commerce.

I don't see, sir, why that worries you in the slightest. . . .

SOME COMMENTS FROM THE SIDELINES

a. *Gunther.* Consider the following excerpts from a letter by a Professor Gerald Gunther to the Department of Justice, dated June 5, 1963— several weeks before the Senate hearings printed above, two weeks before the submission of the Administration bill to Congress, while the Administration proposals still rested solely on the commerce power. Was there substance to the concerns expressed? Were all bases for concern removed by the testimony before Congress, as reflected in the Supreme Court opinions in Heart of Atlanta and McClung, below?

"I was happy to note that the Administration has put off for a few days the submission of its new civil rights proposals to Congress. I hope

that the additional time will permit the Justice Department to reexamine its reported decision to rely exclusively on the commerce clause. . . .

"My basic difficulties with the proposal in light of our constitutional structure may be briefly stated. If a federal ban on discrimination in such businesses as stores and restaurants is to be enacted, it should rest on the obviously most relevant source of national power, the Fourteenth Amendment, rather than the tenuously related commerce clause. The proposed end run by way of the commerce clause seems to me ill-advised in every respect. . . .

"Let me elaborate somewhat: I know of course that the commerce power is a temptingly broad one. But surely responsible statutory drafting should have a firmer basis than, for example, some of the loose talk in recent newspaper articles about the widely accepted, unrestricted availability of the commerce clause to achieve social ends. Some qualifications seem in order. Thus, most of the obviously 'social' laws, as with lottery and prostitution legislation, have their immediate impact on the interstate movement and rest on the power to prohibit that movement. Most 'social' laws are not directly aimed at intrastate affairs, are not attempts to regulate internal activities as such. Where immediate regulations of intrastate conduct have been imposed, a demonstrable economic effect on interstate commerce, business, trade has normally been required. That kind of showing has been made, for example, with regard to the control of 'local' affairs in the labor relations and agricultural production fields. The commerce clause 'hook' has been put to some rather strained uses in the past, I know; but the substantive content of the commerce clause would have to be drained beyond any point yet reached to justify the simplistic argument that all intrastate activity may be subjected to any kind of national regulation merely because some formal crossing of an interstate boundary once took place, without regard to the relationship between the aim of the regulation and interstate trade. The aim of the proposed anti-discrimination legislation, I take it, is quite unrelated to any concern with national commerce in any substantive sense.

"It would, I think, pervert the meaning and purpose of the commerce clause to invoke it as the basis for this legislation. And the strained use now suggested for the commerce power cannot even be justified by the argument that a national problem exists in an area to which the Constitution does not address itself. The Fourteenth Amendment, after all, . . . specifically focuses on the problem of racial discrimination; and the fifth section of the Amendment as well as the Necessary and Proper Clause speak to congressional power to enforce it. . . .

" . . . I would much prefer to see the Government channel its resources of ingenuity and advocacy into the development of a viable interpretation of the Fourteenth Amendment, the provision with a natural linkage to the race problem. That would seem to me a considerably less demeaning task than the construction of an artificial commerce facade; and it would carry the incidental benefit of giving the Department the opportunity to aid the Supreme Court in the fashioning of a more adequate rationale for the modern scope of the Fourteenth Amendment than is now apparent in this much criticized area of constitutional law. . . ."

b. *Wechsler.* Compare a July 18, 1963, letter by Professor Herbert Wechsler to the Chairman of the Senate Commerce Committee, Hearings on S. 1732, 88th Cong., 1st Sess., part 2, 1193–94, which included the following paragraph:

"I should add that I see nothing fictive in the proposition that the practices to which the measure is directed may occur in or affect 'the commerce that concerns more States than one' or, even more plainly, may occur, as the Taft-Hartley Act requires, in an industry which affects such commerce. There are, in fact, effects upon such matters as the free movement of individuals and goods across State lines, the level of demand for products of the national market and the freedom of enterprises engaged in interstate commerce to abandon the restrictions that some of their local competitors may impose. To legislate within the area of such effects on commerce seems to me to fall within the great tradition of the Congress in the exercise of this explicit power." †

C. THE COURT DECISIONS
HEART OF ATLANTA MOTEL v. UNITED STATES
379 U.S. 241, 85 S.Ct. 348, 13 L.Ed.2d 258 (1964).

Appeal from the United States District Court for the Northern District of Georgia.

Mr. Justice CLARK delivered the opinion of the Court.

This is a declaratory judgment action . . . attacking the constitutionality of Title II of the Civil Rights Act of 1964. . . . Appellant owns and operates the Heart of Atlanta Motel which has 216 rooms available to transient guests. The motel is located on Courtland Street, two blocks from downtown Peachtree Street. It is readily accessible to interstate highways 75 and 85 and state highways 23 and 41. Appellant solicits patronage from outside the State of Georgia through various national advertising media, including magazines of national circulation; it maintains over 50 billboards and highway signs within the State, soliciting patronage for the motel; it accepts convention trade from outside Georgia and approximately 75% of its registered guests are from out of State. Prior to passage of the Act the

---

† During the subsequent debates, a number of additional statements by constitutional law experts were introduced in support of the bill. An example is a March 30, 1964, letter by Harrison Tweed and Bernard G. Segal, for themselves and a number of other distinguished attorneys, to Senators Humphrey and Kuchel. Excerpts follow:

"With respect to title II, the congressional authority for its enactment is expressly stated in the bill to rest on the commerce clause of the Constitution and on the 14th amendment. The reliance upon both of these powers to accomplish the stated purpose of title II is sound. Discriminatory practices, though free from any State compulsion, support, or encouragement, may so burden the channels of interstate commerce as to justify, legally, congressional regulation under the commerce clause. . . .

"The grounding of the public accommodations title on the commerce clause is in keeping with a long tradition of Federal legislation, validated in many judicial decisions, and is not today open to substantial legal dispute. In exercising its power to regulate commerce among the States, Congress has enacted laws, encompassing the widest range of commercial transactions, similar to the regulatory scheme of title II of H.R. 7152."

motel had followed a practice of refusing to rent rooms to Negroes, and it alleged that it intended to continue to do so. In an effort to perpetuate that policy this suit was filed. [The District Court sustained the Act.] . . .

It is admitted that the operation of the motel brings it within the provisions of § 201(a) of the Act and that appellant refused to provide lodging for transient Negroes because of their race or color and that it intends to continue that policy unless restrained.

The sole question posed is, therefore, the constitutionality of the Civil Rights Act of 1964 as applied to these facts. The legislative history of the Act indicates that Congress based the Act on § 5 and the Equal Protection Clause of the Fourteenth Amendment as well as its power to regulate interstate commerce under Art. I, § 8, cl. 3 of the Constitution.

The Senate Commerce Committee made it quite clear that the fundamental object of Title II was to vindicate "the deprivation of personal dignity that surely accompanies denials of equal access to public establishments." At the same time, however, it noted that such an objective has been and could be readily achieved "by congressional action based on the commerce power of the Constitution." S.Rep.No. 872, at 16–17. Our study of the legislative record, made in the light of prior cases, has brought us to the conclusion that Congress possessed ample power in this regard, and we have therefore not considered the other grounds relied upon. This is not to say that the remaining authority upon which it acted was not adequate, a question upon which we do not pass, but merely that since the commerce power is sufficient for our decision here we have considered it alone. Nor is § 201(d) or § 202, having to do with state action, involved here and we do not pass upon either of those sections. . . .

While the Act as adopted carried no congressional findings the record of its passage through each house is replete with evidence of the burdens that discrimination by race or color places upon interstate commerce. . . . This testimony included the fact that our people have become increasingly mobile with millions of all races traveling from State to State; that Negroes in particular have been the subject of discrimination in transient accommodations, having to travel great distances to secure the same; that often they have been unable to obtain accommodations and have had to call upon friends to put them up overnight . . . ; and that these conditions had become so acute as to require the listing of available lodging for Negroes in a special guidebook which was itself "dramatic testimony of the difficulties" Negroes encounter in travel . . . . These exclusionary practices were found to be nationwide, the Under Secretary of Commerce testifying that there is "no question that this discrimination in the North still exists to a large degree" and in the West and Midwest as well. . . . This testimony indicated a qualitative as well as quantitative effect on interstate travel by Negroes. The former was the obvious impairment of the Negro traveler's pleasure and convenience that resulted when he continually was uncertain of finding lodging. As for the latter, there was evidence that this uncertainty stemming from racial discrimination had the effect of discouraging travel on the part of a substantial portion of the Negro community. . . . We shall not burden this opinion with further details since the voluminous testimony

presents overwhelming evidence that discrimination by hotels and motels impedes interstate travel. . . .

The power of Congress to deal with these obstructions depends on the meaning of the Commerce Clause. [T]he determinative test of the exercise of power by the Congress under the Commerce Clause is simply whether the activity sought to be regulated is "commerce which concerns more States than one" and has a real and substantial relation to the national interest. . . .

The same interest in protecting interstate commerce which led Congress to deal with segregation in interstate carriers and the white slave traffic has prompted it to extend the exercise of its power to gambling; to criminal enterprises; to deceptive practices in the sale of products; to fraudulent security transactions; to misbranding of drugs; to wages and hours; to members of labor unions; to crop control; to discrimination against shippers; to the protection of small business from injurious price cutting; to resale price maintenance; to professional football; and to racial discrimination by owners and managers of terminal restaurants.

That Congress was legislating against moral wrongs in many of these areas rendered its enactments no less valid. In framing Title II of this Act Congress was also dealing with what it considered a moral problem. But that fact does not detract from the overwhelming evidence of the disruptive effect that racial discrimination has had on commercial intercourse. It was this burden which empowered Congress to enact appropriate legislation, and, given this basis for the exercise of its power, Congress was not restricted by the fact that the particular obstruction to interstate commerce with which it was dealing was also deemed a moral and social wrong.

It is said that the operation of the motel here is of a purely local character. But, assuming this to be true, "if it is interstate commerce that feels the pinch, it does not matter how local the operation that applies the squeeze." United States v. Women's Sportswear Mfrs. Ass'n., 336 U.S. 460, 464 (1949). [A quotation from United States v. Darby is omitted.] Thus the power of Congress to promote interstate commerce also includes the power to regulate the local incidents thereof, including local activities in both the States of origin and destination, which might have a substantial and harmful effect upon that commerce. One need only examine the evidence which we have discussed above to see that Congress may—as it has—prohibit racial discrimination by motels serving travelers, however "local" their operations may appear. . . .

We, therefore, conclude that the action of the Congress in the adoption of the Act as applied here to a motel which concededly serves interstate travelers is within the power granted it by the Commerce Clause of the Constitution, as interpreted by this Court for 140 years. . . .

Affirmed.

[Excerpts from the concurring opinions of Justices Black, Douglas and Goldberg—applicable to this case and to McClung, which follows—appear after McClung.]

KATZENBACH v. McCLUNG

379 U.S. 294, 85 S.Ct. 377, 13 L.Ed.2d 290 (1964).

Appeal from the United States District Court for the Northern District of Alabama.

Mr. Justice CLARK delivered the opinion of the Court.

This case was argued with [Heart of Atlanta Motel]. This complaint for injunctive relief against appellants attacks the constitutionality of the [Civil Rights Act of 1964] as applied to a restaurant. [A]n injunction was issued restraining appellants from enforcing the Act against the restaurant. [We reverse.]

Ollie's Barbecue is a family-owned restaurant in Birmingham, Alabama, specializing in barbecued meats and homemade pies, with a seating capacity of 220 customers. It is located on a state highway 11 blocks from an interstate one and a somewhat greater distance from railroad and bus stations. The restaurant caters to a family and white-collar trade with a take-out service for Negroes. It employs 36 persons, two-thirds of whom are Negroes.

In the 12 months preceding the passage of the Act, the restaurant purchased locally approximately $150,000 worth of food, $69,683 or 46% of which was meat that it bought from a local supplier who had procured it from outside the State. The District Court expressly found that a substantial portion of the food served in the restaurant had moved in interstate commerce. The restaurant has refused to serve Negroes in its dining accommodations since its original opening in 1927, and since July 2, 1964, it has been operating in violation of the Act. The court below concluded that if it were required to serve Negroes it would lose a substantial amount of business. . . .

[The District Court concluded that Congress] had legislated a conclusive presumption that a restaurant affects interstate commerce if it serves or offers to serve interstate travelers or if a substantial portion of the food which it serves has moved in commerce. This, the court held, it could not do because there was no demonstrable connection between food purchased in interstate commerce and sold in a restaurant and the conclusion of Congress that discrimination in the restaurant would affect that commerce. . . .

. . . Sections 201(b) (2) and (c) place any "restaurant . . . principally engaged in selling food for consumption on the premises" under the Act "if . . . it serves or offers to serve interstate travelers or a substantial portion of the food which it serves . . . has moved in commerce."

Ollie's Barbecue admits that it is covered by these provisions of the Act. . . . The sole question, therefore, narrows down to whether Title II, as applied to a restaurant receiving about $70,000 worth of food which has moved in commerce, is a valid exercise of the power of Congress. The Government has contended that Congress had ample basis upon which to find that racial discrimination at restaurants which receive from out of state a substantial portion of the food served does, in fact, impose commercial burdens of national magnitude upon interstate commerce. The appellees'

major argument is directed to this premise. They urge that no such basis existed. It is to that question that we now turn. . . .

As we noted in Heart of Atlanta Motel both Houses of Congress conducted prolonged hearings on the Act. [W]hile no formal findings were made, which of course is not necessary, it is well that we make mention of the testimony at these hearings the better to understand the problem before Congress and determine whether the Act is a reasonable and appropriate means toward its solution. The record is replete with testimony of the burdens placed on interstate commerce by racial discrimination in restaurants. A comparion of per capita spending by Negroes in restaurant, theaters, and like establishments indicated less spending, after discounting income differences, in areas where discrimination is widely practiced. This condition, which was especially aggravated in the South, was attributed in the testimony of the Under Secretary of Commerce to racial segregation. . . . This diminutive spending springing from a refusal to serve Negroes and their total loss as customers has, regardless of the absence of direct evidence, a close connection to interstate commerce. The fewer customers a restaurant enjoys the less food it sells and consequently the less it buys. . . . In addition, the Attorney General testified that this type of discrimination imposed "an artificial restriction on the market" and interfered with the flow of merchandise. . . . In addition, there were many references to discriminatory situations causing wide unrest and having a depressant effect on general business conditions in the respective communities. . . .

Moreover there was an impressive array of testimony that discrimination in restaurants had a direct and highly restrictive effect upon interstate travel by Negroes. This resulted, it was said, because discriminatory practices prevent Negroes from buying prepared food served on the premises while on a trip, except in isolated and unkempt restaurants and under most unsatisfactory and often unpleasant conditions. This obviously discourages travel and obstructs interstate commerce for one can hardly travel without eating. Likewise, it was said, that discrimination deterred professional, as well as skilled, people from moving into areas where such practices occurred and thereby caused industry to be reluctant to establish there. . . .

We believe that this testimony afforded ample basis for the conclusion that established restaurants in such areas sold less interstate goods because of the discrimination, that interstate travel was obstructed directly by it, that business in general suffered and that many new businesses refrained from establishing there as a result of it. Hence the District Court was in error in concluding that there was no connection between discrimination and the movement of interstate commerce. The court's conclusion that such a connection is outside "common experience" flies in the face of stubborn fact.

It goes without saying that, viewed in isolation, the volume of food purchased by Ollie's Barbecue from sources supplied from out of state was insignificant when compared with the total foodstuffs moving in commerce. . . . [W]hile the focus of the legislation was on the individual restaurant's relation to interstate commerce, Congress appropriately considered the importance of that connection with the knowledge that the discrimination was but "representative of many others throughout the country, the total incidence

of which if left unchecked may well become far-reaching in its harm to commerce." Polish Alliance v. Labor Board, 322 U.S. 643, 648 (1944). . . .

. . . Much is said about a restaurant business being local but "even if appellee's activity be local and though it may not be regarded as commerce, it may still, whatever its nature, be reached by Congress if it exerts a substantial economic effect on interstate commerce . . . ." [Wickard v. Filburn.] . . .

The appellees contend that Congress has arbitrarily created a conclusive presumption that all restaurants meeting the criteria set out in the Act "affect commerce." Stated another way, they object to the omission of a provision for a case-by-case determination—judicial or administrative—that racial discrimination in a particular restaurant effects commerce. But Congress' action in framing this Act was not unprecedented. [United States v. Darby.]

Here, as [in Darby], Congress has determined for itself that refusals of service to Negroes have imposed burdens both upon the interstate flow of food and upon the movement of products generally. Of course, the mere fact that Congress has said when particular activity shall be deemed to affect commerce does not preclude further examination by this Court. But where we find that the legislators, in light of the facts and testimony before them, have a rational basis for finding a chosen regulatory scheme necessary to the protection of commerce, our investigation is at an end. The only remaining question—one answered in the affirmative by the court below—is whether the particular restaurant either serves or offers to serve interstate travelers or serves food a substantial portion of which has moved in interstate commerce.

The appellees urge that Congress, in passing the Fair Labor Standards Act and the National Labor Relations Act, made specific findings which were embodied in those statutes. Here, of course, Congress has included no formal findings. But their absence is not fatal to the validity of the statute, . . . for the evidence presented at the hearings fully indicated the nature and effect of the burdens on commerce which Congress meant to alleviate.

Confronted as we are with the facts laid before Congress, we must conclude that it had a rational basis for finding that racial discrimination in restaurants had a direct and adverse effect on the free flow of interstate commerce. . . . [We think] that Congress acted well within its power to protect and foster commerce in extending the coverage of Title II only to those restaurants offering to serve interstate travelers or serving food, a substantial portion of which has moved in interstate commerce.

The absence of direct evidence connecting discriminatory restaurant service with the flow of interstate food, a factor on which the appellees place much reliance, is not, given the evidence as to the effect of such practices on other aspects of commerce, a crucial matter.

The power of Congress in this field is broad and sweeping; where it keeps within its sphere and violates no express constitutional limitation it has been the rule of this Court, going back almost to the founding days of the Republic, not to interfere. The Civil Rights Act of 1964, as here applied, we find to be plainly appropriate in the resolution of what the Congress found to be a national commercial problem of the first magnitude. We find

it in no violation of any express limitations of the Constitution and we therefore declare it valid.

Reversed.

Mr. Justice BLACK, concurring. . . .

I recognize that every remote, possible, speculative effect on commerce should not be accepted as an adequate constitutional ground to uproot and throw into the discard all our traditional distinctions between what is purely local, and therefore controlled by state laws, and what affects the national interest and is therefore subject to control by federal laws. I recognize too that some isolated and remote lunch room which sells only to local people and buys almost all its supplies in the locality may possibly be beyond the reach of the power of Congress to regulate commerce, just as such an establishment is not covered by the present Act. But in deciding the constitutional power of Congress in cases like the two before us we do not consider the effect on interstate commerce of only one isolated, individual, local event, without regard to the fact that this single local event when added to many others of a similar nature may impose a burden on interstate commerce by reducing its volume or distorting its flow. . . . Measuring, as this Court has so often held is required, by the aggregate effect of a great number of such acts of discrimination, I am of the opinion that Congress has constitutional power under the Commerce and Necessary and Proper Clauses to protect interstate commerce from the injuries bound to befall it from these discriminatory practices. . . .

. . . Because the Civil Rights Act of 1964 as applied here is wholly valid under the Commerce Clause and the Necessary and Proper Clause, there is no need to consider whether this Act is also constitutionally supportable under section 5 of the Fourteenth Amendment which grants Congress "power to enforce, by appropriate legislation, the provisions of this article."

Mr. Justice DOUGLAS, concurring. . . .

Though I join the Court's opinions, I am somewhat reluctant here, as I was in Edwards v. California, 314 U.S. 160, 177 [chap. 5 below], to rest solely on the Commerce Clause. My reluctance is not due to any conviction that Congress lacks power to regulate commerce in the interests of human rights. It is rather my belief that the right of people to be free of state action that discriminates against them because of race, like the "right to persons to move freely from State to State" [Edwards v. California], "occupies a more protected position in our constitutional system than does the movement of cattle, fruit, steel and coal across state lines." [The] result reached by the Court is for me much more obvious as a protective measure under the Fourteenth Amendment than under the Commerce Clause. For the former deals with the constitutional status of the individual not with the impact on commerce of local activities or vice versa. . . .

A decision based on the Fourteenth Amendment would have a more settling effect, making unnecessary litigation over whether a particular restaurant or inn is within the commerce definitions of the Act or whether a particular customer is an interstate traveler. . . .

[W]hile I agree with the Court that Congress in fashioning the present Act used the Commerce Clause to regulate racial segregation, it also used (and properly so) some of its power under § 5 of the Fourteenth Amendment. [Our] decision should be based on the Fourteenth Amendment, thereby putting an end to all obstructionist strategies and allowing every person—whatever his race, creed, or color—to patronize all places of public accommodation without discrimination whether he travels interstate or intrastate.

Mr. Justice GOLDBERG, concurring.

I join in the opinions and judgments of the Court . . . .

The primary purpose of the Civil Rights Act of 1964, however, as the Court recognizes, and as I would underscore, is the vindication of human dignity and not mere economics. . . . Congress clearly had authority under both § 5 of the Fourteenth Amendment and the Commerce Clause to enact the Civil Rights Act of 1964.

THE 1964 ACT AND THE SCOPE OF THE COMMERCE POWER

1. *Daniel v. Paul.* Compare the concern expressed by Justice Black in McClung with the application of the Act five years later, in DANIEL v. PAUL, 395 U.S. 298 (1969). There, the Court, over Justice Black's dissent, held the Lake Nixon Club near Little Rock, Arkansas, to be a "public accommodation" whose operations "affect commerce," and therefore subject to the Act. The Club was described as "a 232-acre amusement area with swimming, boating, sun bathing, picnicking, miniature golf, dancing facilities and a snack bar." Justice Brennan's majority opinion found Lake Nixon's snack bar to be a covered public accommodation under §§ 201 (a)(2) and 201(c)(2); that status automatically brought the entire establishment within the Act, under §§ 201(b)(4) and 201(c)(4). The snack bar, he found, was covered under either criterion of § 201(c)(2): it offered "to serve interstate travelers"; and "a substantial portion of the food" served there "has moved in commerce."

With respect to the former standard, he noted that the owners' "choice of advertising media leaves no doubt" that they "were seeking broad-based patronage from an audience which they knew to include interstate travelers" in the Little Rock area. Moreover, "it would be unrealistic to assume that none of the 100,000 patrons actually served by the Club each season was an interstate traveler." And since the snack bar "was established to serve all patrons of the entire facility, we must conclude that the snack bar offered to serve and served out-of-state persons." With respect to the second criterion, Justice Brennan thought there could be "no serious doubt" that a "substantial portion of the food" had "moved in interstate commerce." Although he conceded that the record was "not as complete on this point as might be desired," he pointed to the "limited fare—hot dogs and hamburgers on buns, soft drinks, and milk"—served by the snack bar, and the trial court's judicial notice that some of the ingredients of the bread and of the soft drinks probably came from out-of-state sources. "Thus, at the very least," Justice Bren-

nan stated, "three of the four food items sold at the snack bar contain ingredients originating outside of the State."

The Court also found the Club a covered public accommodation under § 201(b) (3) of the Act, as a "place of entertainment" whose operations "affect commerce" because, under § 201(c) (3), its customary "sources of entertainment . . . move in commerce." Justice Brennan rejected the argument that "place of entertainment" referred only to establishments where patrons were spectators rather than direct participants, even though most of the legislative discussion admittedly "focused on places of spectator entertainment rather than recreational areas." And he was easily satisfied that the "sources of entertainment [here] move in commerce." He was able to state the supporting data in three sentences: "The Club leases 15 paddle boats on a royalty basis from an Oklahoma company. Another boat was purchased from the same company. The Club's juke box was manufactured outside Arkansas and plays records manufactured outside the State."

Justice Black's dissent stated that he would have agreed with the result if the public accommodations law had been based on § 5 of the Fourteenth Amendment. But instead Congress had "tied the Act and limited its protection" to the commerce power. That required a finding that the Club's operations "affect commerce" within the meaning of § 201(c), and the lower courts' findings did not support coverage. He concluded: "While it is the duty of courts to enforce this important Act, we are not called on to hold, nor should we hold subject to that Act this country people's recreation center, lying in what may be, so far as we know, a little 'sleepy hollow' between Arkansas hills miles away from any interstate highway. This would be stretching the Commerce Clause so as to give the Federal Government complete control over every little remote country place of recreation in every nook and cranny of every precinct and county in every one of the 50 States. This goes too far for me."

2. *A final word about the reach of the commerce power, in light of the 1964 Act.* Do the applications of the public accommodations provision to Ollie's Barbecue and to the Lake Nixon Club rest on persuasive commerce power justifications? Do the statutory coverage formulas adequately mesh with the constitutional rationales? Does the McClung opinion persuasively link restaurant discrimination with the interstate flow of food? Is it more persuasive in linking restaurant discrimination with obstruction of interstate travel? Were more persuasive commerce power rationales available? Recall the comments on Perez v. United States, sec. 5 above: Could the McClung and Daniel cases be justified on the ground that regulation of intrastate discrimination is necessary because of the difficulty of distinguishing discrimination which affects interstate commerce from that which may not? Would that rationale be limitless? Would that violate Marshall's "spirit" of the Constitution in McCulloch? Would it be inconsistent with the implications of the Constitution establishing a federalistic structure? Does the aggregating rationale of Wickard v. Filburn offer significant help in justifying McClung and Daniel? Could Congress have relied on the "commerce-prohibiting" technique—e. g., by prohibiting the shipment of interstate goods to racially discriminatory restaurants, and banning local restaurant discrimination as a means to implement that interstate prohibition?

Is concern about the federalistic structure and "spirit" of the Constitution made unnecessary by Chief Justice Stone's well-known statement in Darby that the Tenth Amendment "states but a truism that all is retained which has not been surrendered"? But did not Marshall in McCulloch recognize that truism in effect—and yet insist that legislation must also be consistent with the "spirit" as well as "letter" of the Constitution? What implications from the "spirit" or structure of the Constitution does, or should, the Court recognize today? If the Court refuses to recognize any such limitations—or feels itself incompetent to enforce any—are not legislators nevertheless bound to heed them in the lawmaking process? Was adequate heed paid to federalism limitations in the congressional deliberations that produced such modern laws as the criminal provisions surveyed in sec. 5 above—or Title II of the 1964 Act?

Is a revived sensitivity to federalistic limits suggested by the May 1975 developments noted at p. 125, above? Recall especially the comment on the Darby "truism" statement in Justice Marshall's majority opinion in Fry v. United States, 421 U.S. —— (1975): "While the Tenth Amendment has been characterized as a 'truism,' stating merely that 'all is retained which has not been surrendered' [Darby], it is not without significance. The Amendment expressly declares the constitutional policy that Congress may not exercise power in a fashion that impairs the States' integrity or their ability to function effectively in a federal system."

Chapter 4

OTHER NATIONAL POWERS
IN THE 1787 CONSTITUTION

Scope Note. Because of the central role of the commerce power as a source of national authority to regulate local activities, that power was the focus of the preceding chapter. This chapter turns more briefly to several other national powers granted by the Constitutional Convention—powers which have also had significant impacts on the allocation of authority within the federal system. The taxing and spending powers (secs. 1 and 2 below) are of special interest because of their close functional and doctrinal ties to the commerce power. The Constitutional Convention delegated the taxing and spending powers in the opening clause of Art. I, § 8: "The Congress shall have power To lay and collect Taxes, Duties, Imposts, and Excises, to pay the Debts and provide for the common Defence and general Welfare of the United States." The manner in which taxes are imposed and the way in which revenues are spent have significant regulatory impacts. As with the commerce power, the taxing and spending powers have been invoked to deal with "police" as well as economic problems. Not surprisingly, regulations through taxing and spending have been resorted to in periods, as in the early decades of this century, when the need for legislation seemed great and direct regulation through the commerce power was under constitutional clouds.

To what extent are the functions and limits pertaining to the taxing and spending power similar to, and to what extent are they different from, those considered in connection with the commerce power? Those are the primary themes of secs. 1 and 2. Sec. 3 briefly considers two other sources of national authority that are significant to the federal scheme, though even less frequently litigated: it deals with national powers relating to war and foreign relations (especially through treaties).* One other important basis for congressional action must be noted for a comprehensive view of national powers with significant impact on the division of authority in the federal system. That additional source lies not in the 1787 document itself but in the post-Civil War changes. The 13th, 14th, and 15th Amendments all specify that Congress may "enforce this article by appropriate legislation." That authority long lay dormant because of congressional inaction and restrictive judicial interpretations. But new legislative efforts and new Court approaches have dramatized the vast impact of those Amendments on the federal system. The examination of the effect of the post-Civil War Amendments on congressional powers appears in chap. 11 below.†

---

* For a summary of additional national powers—not examined in detail in this volume—see note * at the beginning of sec. 3 below.

† The important problem of congressional power under the post-Civil War Amendments is postponed to chap. 11 because those issues are best examined

SECTION 1. THE TAXING POWER

Introduction. To what extent may the national taxing power be used as a means of regulation? ** The materials in this section examine the Court's handling of that problem, and they are offered primarily for critical comparison with the preceding commerce power cases. A number of relationships between the two lines of cases has already been noted. For example, tax cases were relied on in the Hammer v. Dagenhart dissent and in Darby; and Congress has repeatedly invoked one of the powers when the other proved to be an inadequate basis for national regulation, as in the child labor area.

Consider, in examining these cases, the similarities and the differences in the development of limits on the commerce and taxing powers. Do the differences in doctrine reflect differences in the nature of the problems? Has the Court been more successful in curbing "abuses" of the taxing power than of the commerce power? Is it easier to detect an invocation of the power to tax as a "pretext"? In short, compare the search for "motive" and "purpose" in tax cases with that in commerce cases. Is it important to distinguish taxes whose regulatory impact depends on the immediate deterring effect on the taxed activity from those whose regulatory effect rests on collateral reporting and enforcement provisions of the tax statute?

CHILD LABOR TAX CASE
[BAILEY v. DREXEL FURNITURE CO.]

259 U.S. 20, 42 S.Ct. 449, 66 L.Ed. 817 (1922).

Error to the District Court of the United States for the Western District of North Carolina.

[A few months after the Court had held regulation of child labor through the commerce power unconstitutional in Hammer v. Dagenhart (chap. 3, sec. 3, above), Congress enacted the Child Labor Tax Law of 1919. That law imposed a federal excise tax of 10% of annual net profits on every employer of child labor in the covered businesses. The coverage provisions were very similar to those in the act invalidated in Hammer v. Dagenhart,

after exploring the judicial interpretations of the self-executing impacts of those Amendments, in the absence of implementing legislation by Congress. That postponement should not, however, obscure the great and growing impact of congressional power under the Amendments on federal-state allocations of power, as illustrated by such modern cases as Katzenbach v. Morgan, 384 U.S. 641 (1966) (chap. 11, sec. 4, below).

** This section does not deal with national taxation that is clearly for revenue purposes, but the power of Congress to tax for those purposes should of course be borne in mind. The Court has said that the power "is given in the Constitution, with only one exception and only two qualifications. Congress cannot tax exports, and it must impose direct taxes by the rule of apportionment, and indirect taxes by the rule of uniformity. Thus limited, and thus only, it reaches every subject, and may be exercised at discretion." License Tax Cases, 5 Wall. 462, 471 (1867).

except for the interstate commerce nexus.* After paying a tax of over $6000 assessed for 1919, the Drexel Furniture Company successfully brought a refund suit in the lower court.]

Mr. Chief Justice TAFT delivered the opinion of the Court. . . .

The law is attacked on the ground that it is a regulation of the employment of child labor in the States—an exclusively state function under the Federal Constitution and within the reservations of the Tenth Amendment. It is defended on the ground that it is a mere excise tax levied by the Congress of the United States under its broad power of taxation conferred by § 8, Article I, of the Federal Constitution. We must construe the law and interpret the intent and meaning of Congress from the language of the act. The words are to be given their ordinary meaning unless the context shows that they are differently used. Does this law impose a tax with only that incidental restraint and regulation which a tax must inevitably involve? Or does it regulate by the use of the so-called tax as a penalty? If a tax, it is clearly an excise. If it were an excise on a commodity or other thing of value we might not be permitted under previous decisions of this court to infer solely from its heavy burden that the act intends a prohibition instead of a tax. But this act is more. It provides a heavy exaction for a departure from a detailed and specified course of conduct in business. [The tax] is not to be proportioned in any degree to the extent or frequency of the departures, but is to be paid by the employer in full measure whether he employs five hundred children for a year, or employs only one for a day. Moreover, if he does not know the child is within the named age limit, he is not to pay; that is to say, it is only where he knowingly departs from the prescribed course that payment is to be exacted. Scienter is associated with penalties, not with taxes. The employer's factory is to be subject to inspection at any time not only by the taxing officers of the Treasury, the Department normally charged with the collection of taxes, but also by the Secretary of Labor and his subordinates whose normal function is the advancement and protection of the welfare of the workers. In the light of these features of the act, a court must be blind not to see that the so-called tax is imposed to stop the employment of children within the age limits prescribed. Its prohibitory and regulatory

---

* The 1919 law imposing a "Tax on Employment of Child Labor" included the following provisions:

"Sec. 1200. That every person . . . operating (a) any mine or quarry situated in the United States in which children under the age of sixteen years have been employed or permitted to work during any portion of the taxable year; or (b) any mill, cannery, workshop, factory, or manufacturing establishment situated in the United States in which children under the age of fourteen years have been employed or permitted to work, or children between the ages of fourteen and sixteen have been employed or permitted to work more than eight hours in any day or more than six days in any week, or after the hour of seven o'clock post meridian, or before the hour of six o'clock ante meridian, during any portion of the taxable year, shall pay for each taxable year, in addition to all other taxes imposed by law, an excise tax equivalent to 10 per centum of the entire net profits received or accrued for such year from the sale or disposition of the product of such mine, quarry, mill, cannery, workshop, factory, or manufacturing establishment."

Section 1203 relieved from liability any employer of child labor who believed the child to be of proper age. Section 1206 authorized the Commissioner of Internal Revenue "to enter and inspect at any time any mine, quarry, mill, cannery, workshop, factory, or manufacturing establishment." The Secretary of Labor was given similar authority.

effect and purpose are palpable. All others can see and understand this. How can we properly shut our minds to it?

It is the high duty and function of this court in cases regularly brought to its bar to decline to recognize or enforce seeming laws of Congress, dealing with subjects not entrusted to Congress but left or committed by the supreme law of the land to the control of the States. We can not avoid the duty even though it require us to refuse to give effect to legislation designed to promote the highest good. . . .

Out of a proper respect for the acts of a coördinate branch of the Government, this court has gone far to sustain taxing acts as such, even though there has been ground for suspecting from the weight of the tax it was intended to destroy its subject. But, in the act before us, the presumption of validity cannot prevail, because the proof of the contrary is found on the very face of its provisions. Grant the validity of this law, and all that Congress would need to do, hereafter, in seeking to take over to its control any one of the great number of subjects of public interest, jurisdiction of which the States have never parted with, and which are reserved to them by the Tenth Amendment, would be to enact a detailed measure of complete regulation of the subject and enforce it by a so-called tax upon departures from it. To give such magic to the word "tax" would be to break down all constitutional limitation of the powers of Congress and completely wipe out the sovereignty of the States.

The difference between a tax and a penalty is sometimes difficult to define and yet the consequences of the distinction in the required method of their collection often are important. Where the sovereign enacting the law has power to impose both tax and penalty the difference between revenue production and mere regulation may be immaterial, but not so when one sovereign can impose a tax only, and the power of regulation rests in another. Taxes are occasionally imposed in the discretion of the legislature on proper subjects with the primary motive of obtaining revenue from them and with the incidental motive of discouraging them by making their continuance onerous. They do not lose their character as taxes because of the incidental motive. But there comes a time in the extension of the penalizing features of the so-called tax when it loses its character as such and becomes a mere penalty with the characteristics of regulation and punishment. Such is the case in the law before us. Although Congress does not invalidate the contract of employment or expressly declare that the employment within the mentioned ages is illegal, it does exhibit its intent practically to achieve the latter result by adopting the criteria of wrongdoing and imposing its principal consequence on those who transgress its standard.

The case before us can not be distinguished from that of Hammer v. Dagenhart. . . . This case requires as did the Dagenhart Case the application of the principle announced by Chief Justice Marshall in [McCulloch v. Maryland], in a much quoted passage [—quoting the "pretext" passage].

But it is pressed upon us that this court has gone so far in sustaining taxing measures the effect or tendency of which was to accomplish purposes not directly within congressional power that we are bound by authority to maintain this law.

The first of these is Veazie Bank v. Fenno, 8 Wall. 533 [1869]. In that case, the validity of a law which increased a tax on the circulating notes of persons and state banks from one per centum to ten per centum was in question. . . . The second objection was stated by the court:

"It is insisted, however, that the tax in the case before us is excessive, and so excessive as to indicate a purpose on the part of Congress to destroy the franchise of the bank, and is, therefore, beyond the constitutional power of Congress."

To this the court answered:

"The first answer to this is that the judicial cannot prescribe to the legislative departments of the government limitations upon the exercise of its acknowledged powers. The power to tax may be exercised oppressively upon persons, but the responsibility of the legislature is not to the courts, but to the people by whom its members are elected. . . ."

It will be observed that the sole objection to the tax there was its excessive character. Nothing else appeared on the face of the act. It was an increase of a tax admittedly legal to a higher rate and that was all. There were no elaborate specifications on the face of the act, as here, indicating the purpose to regulate matters of state concern and jurisdiction through an exaction so applied as to give it the qualities of a penalty for violation of law rather than a tax. . . .

But more than this, what was charged to be the object of the excessive tax was within the congressional authority, as appears from the second answer which the court gave to the objection. After having pointed out the legitimate means taken by Congress to secure a national medium or currency, the court said:

"Having thus, in the exercise of undisputed constitutional powers, undertaken to provide a currency for the whole country, it cannot be questioned that Congress may, constitutionally, secure the benefit of it to the people by appropriate legislation. To this end, . . . Congress may restrain, by suitable enactments, the circulation as money of any notes not issued under its own authority. . . ."

The next case is that of McCray v. United States, 195 U.S. 27 [1904]. That, like the Veazie Bank Case, was the increase of an excise tax upon a subject properly taxable in which the taxpayers claimed that the tax had become invalid because the increase was excessive. It was a tax on oleomargarine, a substitute for butter. The tax on the white oleomargarine was one-quarter of a cent a pound, and on the yellow oleomargarine was first two cents and was then by the act in question increased to ten cents per pound. This court held that the discretion of Congress in the exercise of its constitutional powers to levy excise taxes could not be controlled or limited by the courts because the latter might deem the incidence of the tax oppressive or even destructive. It was the same principle as that applied in the Veazie Bank Case. . . . In neither of these cases did the law objected to show on its face as does the law before us the detailed specifications of a regulation of a state concern and business with a heavy exaction to promote the efficacy of such regulation. . . .

[And, finally,] United States v. Doremus, 249 U.S. 86 [1919], involved the validity of the Narcotic Drug Act, 38 Stat. 785, which imposed a

special tax on the manufacture, importation and sale or gift of opium or coca leaves or their compounds or derivatives. It required every person subject to the special tax to register with the Collector of Internal Revenue his name and place of business and forbade him to sell except upon the written order of the person to whom the sale was made on a form prescribed by the Commissioner of Internal Revenue. The vendor was required to keep the order for two years, and the purchaser to keep a duplicate for the same time and both were to be subject to official inspection. Similar requirements were made as to sales upon prescriptions of a physician and as to the dispensing of such drugs directly to a patient by a physician. The validity of a special tax in the nature of an excise tax on the manufacture, importation and sale of such drugs was, of course, unquestioned. The provisions for subjecting the sale and distribution of the drugs to official supervision and inspection were held to have a reasonable relation to the enforcement of the tax and were therefore held valid.*

The court said that the act could not be declared invalid just because another motive than taxation, not shown on the face of the act, might have contributed to its passage. This case does not militate against the conclusion we have reached in respect of the law now before us. The court, there, made manifest its view that the provisions of the so-called taxing act must be naturally and reasonably adapted to the collection of the tax and not solely to the achievement of some other purpose plainly within state power.

For the reasons given, we must hold the Child Labor Tax Law invalid and the judgment of the District Court is

Affirmed.

Mr. Justice CLARKE dissents.

THE USE OF THE TAXING POWER FOR REGULATORY PURPOSES

1. *The prior decisions.* The important regulatory tax cases before the Child Labor Tax Case—Veazie Bank v. Fenno, McCray v. United States, and United States v. Doremus—are described in Chief Justice Taft's opinion, above. Are the prior decisions distinguishable, or did the principal case manifest a significant shift in approach? Is the relationship of the principal case to those earlier decisions like that of Hammer v. Dagenhart to the earlier commerce-prohibiting cases (e. g., the Lottery Case, or the cases sustaining the Mann Act and the Pure Food and Drug Act)? See chap. 3, sec. 3, above and note 2 below.

---

* The "special tax" at the time of the Doremus case was $1 per year. Compare the later decision in Nigro v. United States, 276 U.S. 332 (1928), where the Court noted that the Narcotic Drug Act had been amended to produce substantial revenue from the tax and added: "If there was doubt of the character of this act as an alleged subterfuge, it has been removed by the change whereby what was a nominal tax before was made a substantial one." Note also Linder v. United States, 268 U.S. 5 (1925), construing the Act narrowly to avoid constitutional difficulties by holding it inapplicable to a physician "who acts bona fide and according to fair medical standards." The Court commented: "Obviously, direct control of medical practice in the States is beyond the power of the Federal Government."

2.   *Early 20th century commerce and tax cases: Parallels and contrasts.*
a.   Note that Justice Holmes was in the majority in the Child Labor Tax
Case—just four years after his dissent in Hammer v. Dagenhart. In the
principal case, the Child Labor Tax Case, he joined in looking beyond the
congressional label to invalidate because of forbidden purpose and effect;
in his dissent in Hammer v. Dagenhart, he had insisted that the Court could
not look to purposes and obvious collateral effects and was bound to sustain
a law where Congress had invoked the commerce-prohibiting technique. Are
Holmes' positions in the two cases reconcilable?

In Hammer v. Dagenhart, moreover, Holmes had relied on McCray, the
oleomargarine tax case, to show that judicial inquiry into congressional purpose was improper. And the McCray tax decision of 1904, in turn, had relied on the commerce power Lottery Case of 1903 in rejecting the notion
"that the judiciary may restrain the exercise of lawful power on the assumption that a wrongful purpose or motive has caused the power to be exerted."
At the time of Hammer v. Dagenhart in 1918, in short, Holmes was opposing judicial invalidation because of improper purpose in tax (McCray) as
well as commerce (Lottery, Child Labor) cases. By 1922, in the principal
case, had Holmes abandoned that position? In commerce as well as in tax
cases? Because he was in the minority in Hammer? Only in tax cases?
Only in some tax cases—because bad purpose was clearer in the principal
case than in McCray? [Note that the opinion in the principal case describes
and distinguishes the McCray case.] Compare Justice Frankfurter's "purpose" position in Kahriger, the next principal case, and note the questions on
tax-commerce parallels and contrasts after the Kahriger case.

b.   Shortly after the decision in the Doremus case—the Narcotic Drug
Act decision (joined by Holmes) discussed at the end of Chief Justice Taft's
opinion in the Child Labor Tax Case—Justice Holmes wrote to Judge Learned
Hand: "As to the [Drug Act case], *(between ourselves)* I am tickled at every
case of that sort as they seem to me to confirm the ground of my dissent in
the Child Labor case last term. Hammer v. Dagenhart, 247 U.S. 251, 277.
Also, I think the drug act cases rightly decided. In my opinion Congress
may have what ulterior motives they please if the act passed in the immediate
aspect is within their powers—though personally, were I a legislator I might
think it dishonest to use powers in that way." Oliver Wendell Holmes to
Learned Hand, April 3, 1919, quoted in Gunther, "Learned Hand and the
Origins of Modern First Amendment Doctrine," 27 Stan.L.Rev. 719 (1975).

Are Justice Holmes' positions in Doremus and the Child Labor Tax
Case reconcilable? Are the cases distinguishable because the economic sanction in the child labor situation (10% of net profits for noncompliance)
was more substantial than that in the narcotics situation ($1 a year at the
time of the Doremus case)? Which way does that distinction cut? Which
scheme was more justifiable as a regulatory device incidental to a revenue raising measure? Note generally Cushman, "Social and Economic Control
Through Federal Taxation," 18 Minn.L.Rev. 759, concluding, in 1934,
"that we have at present two available techniques for dealing with the validity of national police regulations under the taxing power": the criterion of
"objective constitutionality," or "judicial obtuseness," which permits the

Court to sustain a regulatory tax; and the "penalty" theory, which invalidates the statute because it "imposes a penalty, rather than levies a tax."

c. Hill v. Wallace, 259 U.S. 44 (1922), decided on the same day as—and with reliance on—the Child Labor Tax Case, again illustrates alternate uses of the taxing and commerce powers. In Hill, the Court invalidated the Future Trading Act, under which a tax of 20 cents was imposed on every bushel of grain involved in a contract or sale for future delivery—except sales on boards of trade certified as meeting the detailed regulatory requirements of the federal law. The Hill decision was urged upon the Court to show the invalidity of a subsequent commerce power-based regulation of boards of trade, the 1922 Grain Future Trading Act. But that Act was sustained in Chicago Board of Trade v. Olsen, 262 U.S. 1 (1923). For similar successive invocations of the fiscal and commerce powers, compare United States v. Butler, sec. 2 below, with Mulford v. Smith, chap. 3 above (agricultural production and marketing).

3. *From the Child Labor Tax Case to Kahriger.* a. In United States v. Constantine, 296 U.S. 287 (1935), defendant was convicted in a federal district court of conducting the business of retail dealer in malt liquor contrary to the law of Alabama without having paid the special excise tax of $1000 imposed by an Act of Congress. He had paid the normal tax of $25 for conducting the business, and the question presented was "whether the exaction of $1000 in addition, by reason solely of his violation of state law, is a tax or penalty." Justice Roberts' opinion for the Court concluded "that the indicia which the section exhibits of an intent to prohibit and to punish violations of state law as such are too strong to be disregarded, remove all semblance of a revenue act and stamp the sum it exacts as a penalty. In this view the statute is a clear invasion of the police power, inherent in the states, reserved from the grant of powers to the federal government by the Constitution. . . . Reference was made in the argument to decisions of this Court holding that where the power to tax is conceded the motive for the execution may not be questioned. . . . They are not authority where, as in the present instance, under the guise of a taxing act the purpose is to usurp the police powers of the state." Justice Cardozo, joined by Justices Brandeis and Stone, dissented: "Thus the process of psychoanalysis has spread to unaccustomed fields."

b. Sonzinsky v. United States, 300 U.S. 506 (1937), sustained the National Firearms Act of 1934, which imposed a $200 annual license tax on dealers in firearms. Noting that the tax "is productive of some revenue," the Court said "we are not free to speculate as to the motives which moved Congress to impose it, or as to the extent to which it may operate to restrict the activities taxed. As it is not attended by an offensive regulation, and since it operates as a tax, it is within the national taxing power." United States v. Sanchez, 340 U.S. 42 (1950), upheld the Marihuana Tax Act of 1937 which placed a tax ($100 per ounce) on the transfer of marihuana to an unregistered person, liability for its payment resting on the transferor in the event the transferee failed to pay. The statute contained no regulations other than the registration provisions and had for its primary objective the restriction of the traffic to accepted industrial and medicinal channels, with only a secondary objective of raising revenue. The tax was sustained as "a legitimate exercise of the taxing power despite its collateral regulatory purpose and effect."

UNITED STATES v. KAHRIGER

345 U.S. 22, 73 S.Ct. 510, 97 L.Ed. 754 (1953).

Appeal from the United States District Court for the Eastern District of Pennsylvania.

Mr. Justice REED delivered the opinion of the Court.

The issue raised by this appeal is the constitutionality of the occupational tax provisions of the Revenue Act of 1951, which levy a tax on persons engaged in the business of accepting wagers, and require such persons to register with the Collector of Internal Revenue.* [An attack on the tax scheme as violating the self-incrimination privilege of the Fifth Amendment was rejected by the majority. That aspect of Kahriger was overruled fifteen years later, in the Marchetti case, note 2 below. The passages from the opinion printed here focus on the other ground of the constitutional challenge: the claim that Congress, "under the pretense of exercising its power to tax, has attempted to penalize illegal intrastate gambling through the regulatory features of the Act" and "has thus infringed the police power which is reserved to the states." The District Court sustained that claim on the authority of United States v. Constantine, 296 U.S. 287 (1935), note 3a preceding this case. Justice Reed noted that Sonzinsky v. United States (note 3b above) had explained Constantine as turning on the fact that the subject of the tax was "described or treated as criminal by the taxing statute." Here, by contrast, the wagering tax "applies to all persons engaged in the business of receiving wagers, regardless of whether such activity violates state law." Justice Reed continued:]

Appellee would have us say that, because there is legislative history [1] indicating a congressional motive to suppress wagering, this tax is not a proper exercise of such taxing power. [But an] intent to curtail and hinder, as

---

* In a footnote, Justice Reed quoted the provisions of the Act imposing on covered persons an annual excise tax of 10% on all wages, a special tax of fifty dollars per year, and a requirement that name, residence, place of business, and name and residence of each employee, be registered with the Collector of Internal Revenue.

Justice Reed did not quote a number of other provisions of the law, including one requiring the Collector to "place and keep conspicuously in his office, for public inspection, an alphabetical list of the names" of all taxpayers under these provisions, and to furnish certified copies of those lists "upon application of any prosecuting officer of any State, county, or municipality."

Should Justice Reed have quoted those provisions as well? Compare footnote 1 below and see note 2 following this case.

I. There are suggestions in the debates that Congress sought to hinder, if not

prevent, the type of gambling taxed. See 97 Cong.Rec. 6892:

"Mr. HOFFMAN of Michigan. Then I will renew my observation that it might if properly construed be considered an additional penalty on the illegal activities.

"Mr. COOPER. Certainly, and we might indulge the hope that the imposition of this type of tax would eliminate that kind of activity." 97 Cong.Rec. 12236: "If the local official does not want to enforce the law and no one catches him winking at the law, he may keep on winking at it, but when the Federal Government identifies a law violator, and the local newspaper gets hold of it, and the local church organizations get hold of it, and the people who do want the law enforced get hold of it, they say, 'Mr. Sheriff, what about it? We understand that there is a place down here licensed to sell liquor.' He says, 'Is that so? I will put him out of business.'" [Footnote by the Court.]

well as tax, was also manifest [in the series of cases beginning with Veazie Bank v. Fenno], and in each of them the tax was upheld . . ..

It is conceded that a federal excise tax does not cease to be valid merely because it discourages or deters the activities taxed. Nor is the tax invalid because the revenue obtained is negligible. Appellee, however, argues that the sole purpose of the statute is to penalize only illegal gambling in the states through the guise of a tax measure. As with the above excise taxes which we have held to be valid, the instant tax has a regulatory effect. But regardless of its regulatory effect, the wagering tax produces revenue. As such it surpasses both the narcotics and firearms taxes which we have found valid.[2]

It is axiomatic that the power of Congress to tax is extensive and sometimes falls with crushing effect on businesses deemed unessential or inimical to the public welfare, or where, as in dealing with narcotics, the collection of the tax also is difficult. As is well known, the constitutional restraints on taxing are few. . . . The difficulty of saying when the power to lay uniform taxes is curtailed, because its use brings a result beyond the direct legislative power of Congress, has given rise to diverse decisions. In that area of abstract ideas, a final definition of the line between state and federal power has baffled judges and legislators.

While the Court has never questioned the above-quoted statement of Mr. Chief Justice Marshall in the McCulloch case [the "pretext" statement], the application of the rule has brought varying holdings on constitutionality. Where federal legislation has rested on other congressional powers, such as the Necessary and Proper Clause or the Commerce Clause, this Court has generally sustained the statutes, despite their effect on matters ordinarily considered state concern. When federal power to regulate is found, its exercise is a matter for Congress. Where Congress has employed the taxing clause a greater variation in the decisions has resulted. The division in this Court has been more acute. Without any specific differentiation between the power to tax and other federal powers, the indirect results from the exercise of the power to tax have raised more doubts. . . . It is hard to understand why the power to tax should raise more doubts because of indirect effects than other federal powers.

Penalty provisions in tax statutes added for breach of a regulation concerning activities in themselves subject only to state regulation have caused this Court to declare the enactments invalid. Unless there are provisions extraneous to any tax need, courts are without authority to limit the exercise of the taxing power. All the provisions of this excise are adapted to the collection of a valid tax.

Nor do we find the registration requirements of the wagering tax offensive. All that is required is the filing of names, addresses, and places of

2. One of the indicia which appellee offers to support his contention that the wagering tax is not a proper revenue measure is that the tax amount collected under it was $4,371,869, as compared with an expected amount of $400,000,000 a year. The figure of $4,371,869, however, is relatively large when it is compared with the $3,501 collected under the tax on adulterated and process or renovated butter and filled cheese, the $914,910 collected under the tax on narcotics, including marihuana and special taxes, and the $28,911 collected under the tax on firearms, transfer and occupational taxes. (Summary of Internal Revenue Collections, released by Bureau of Internal Revenue, October 3, 1952.) [Footnote by the Court.]

business. This is quite general in tax returns. Such data are directly and intimately related to the collection of the tax and are "obviously supportable as in aid of a revenue purpose." Sonzinsky v. United States, 300 U.S. 506, at 513. The registration provisions make the tax simpler to collect. . . .

Reversed.

Mr. Justice JACKSON, concurring.

I concur in the judgment and opinion of the Court, but with such doubt that if the minority agreed upon an opinion which did not impair legitimate use of the taxing power I probably would join it. But we deal here with important and contrasting values in our scheme of government, and it is important that neither be allowed to destroy the other. . . .

Of course, all taxation has a tendency, proportioned to its burdensomeness, to discourage the activity taxed. One cannot formulate a revenue-raising plan that would not have economic and social consequences. . . .

But here is a purported tax law which requires no reports and lays no tax except on specified gamblers whose calling in most states is illegal. It requires this group to step forward and identify themselves, not because they, like others, have income, but because of its source. This is difficult to regard as a rational or good-faith revenue measure, despite the deference that is due Congress. On the contrary, it seems to be a plan to tax out of existence the professional gambler whom it has been found impossible to prosecute out of existence. . . .

The United States has a system of taxation by confession. That a people so numerous, scattered and individualistic annually assesses itself with a tax liability, often in highly burdensome amounts, is a reassuring sign of the stability and vitality of our system of self-government. What surprised me in once trying to help administer these laws was not to discover examples of recalcitrance, fraud or self-serving mistakes in reporting, but to discover that such derelictions were so few. It will be a sad day for the revenues if the good will of the people toward their taxing system is frittered away in efforts to accomplish by taxation moral reforms that cannot be accomplished by direct legislation. But the evil that can come from this statute will probably soon make itself manifest to Congress. The evil of a judicial decision impairing the legitimate taxing power by extreme constitutional interpretations might not be transient. Even though this statute approaches the fair limits of constitutionality, I join the decision of the Court.

Mr. Justice BLACK, with whom Mr. Justice DOUGLAS concurs, dissenting [solely on the basis of the self-incrimination provision of the Fifth Amendment]. . . .

Mr. Justice FRANKFURTER, dissenting. . . .

To review in detail the decisions of this Court, beginning with Veazie Bank v. Fenno, 8 Wall. 533, dealing with this ambivalent type of revenue enactment, would be to rehash the familiar. Two generalizations may, however, safely be drawn from this series of cases. Congress may make an oblique use of the taxing power in relation to activities with which Congress may deal directly, as for instance, commerce between the States. Thus, if the dissenting views of Mr. Justice Holmes in Hammer v. Dagenhart, 247 U.S. 251, 277, had been the decision of the Court, as they became in United

States v. Darby, 312 U.S. 100, the effort to deal with the problem of child labor through an assertion of the taxing power in the statute considered in Child Labor Tax Case, 259 U.S. 20, would by the latter case have been sustained. However, when oblique use is made of the taxing power as to matters which substantively are not within the powers delegated to Congress, the Court cannot shut its eyes to what is obviously, because designedly, an attempt to control conduct which the Constitution left to the responsibility of the States, merely because Congress wrapped the legislation in the verbal cellophane of a revenue measure.

Concededly the constitutional questions presented by such legislation are difficult. On the one hand, courts should scrupulously abstain from hobbling congressional choice of policies, particularly when the vast reach of the taxing power is concerned. On the other hand, to allow what otherwise is excluded from congressional authority to be brought within it by casting legislation in the form of a revenue measure could, as so significantly expounded in the Child Labor Tax Case, supra, offer an easy way for the legislative imagination to control "any one of the great number of subjects of public interest, jurisdiction of which the States have never parted with . . . ." Child Labor Tax Case, at 38. I say "significantly" because Mr. Justice Holmes and two of the Justices who had joined his dissent in Hammer v. Dagenhart, McKenna and Brandeis, JJ., agreed with the opinion in the Child Labor Tax Case. . . .

What is relevant to judgment here is that, even if the history of this legislation as it went through Congress did not give one the libretto to the song, the context of the circumstances which brought forth this enactment— sensationally exploited disclosures regarding gambling in big cities and small, the relation of this gambling to corrupt politics, the impatient public response to these disclosures, the feeling of ineptitude or paralysis on the part of local law-enforcing agencies—emphatically supports what was revealed on the floor of Congress, namely, that what was formally a means of raising revenue for the Federal Government was essentially an effort to check if not to stamp out professional gambling.

A nominal taxing measure must be found an inadmissible intrusion into a domain of legislation reserved for the States not merely when Congress requires that such a measure is to be enforced through a detailed scheme of administration beyond the obvious fiscal needs, as in the Child Labor Tax Case, supra. That is one ground for holding that Congress was constitutionally disrespectful of what is reserved to the States. Another basis for deeming such a formal revenue measure inadmissible is presented by this case. In addition to the fact that Congress was concerned with activity beyond the authority of the Federal Government, the enforcing provision of this enactment is designed for the systematic confession of crimes with a view to prosecution for such crimes under State law.

. . . The motive of congressional legislation is not for our scrutiny, provided only that the ulterior purpose is not expressed in ways which negative what the revenue words on their face express and which do not seek enforcement of the formal revenue purpose through means that offend those standards of decency in our civilization against which due process is a barrier. [Cf. chap. 8 below.] . . .

Mr. Justice DOUGLAS, while not joining in the entire opinion, agrees with the views expressed herein that this tax is an attempt by the Congress to control conduct which the Constitution has left to the responsibility of the States.

THE TAXING POWER AFTER KAHRIGER

1. *The taxing and commerce powers: Modern parallels and contrasts.* a. Does Kahriger suggest more substantial modern limits on regulatory taxes than on commerce power-based legislation? Does it authorize greater judicial scrutiny of congressional action than the Court was willing to undertake in Darby and Wickard v. Filburn? Recall the questions in note 2 after the Child Labor Tax Case. With respect to judicial inquiry into the purposes and collateral effects of the commerce-prohibiting technique, the majority view in Hammer v. Dagenhart was overruled in Darby. Has there been a parallel development regarding the taxing power? Is the majority approach in the Child Labor Tax Case (1922) more respectable today than the discredited Hammer v. Dagenhart (1918) position?

Note that Justice Stone's opinion in Darby relied on McCray and Veazie Bank (the early taxing power cases discussed in the Child Labor Tax Case) in support of his refusal to inquire into the motive and purpose of commerce regulation; and Stone's opinion was for a unanimous Court. In the commerce area, in short, the modern Court has apparently abandoned all "pretext" control. Yet as to taxing, in Kahriger, there are several dissents on that abuse of power issue from members of the modern Court. Is the difference explainable?

b. Justice Reed in Kahriger thought it "hard to understand why the power to tax should raise more doubts because of indirect effects than other federal powers." What *is* the explanation of the difference? Is it because "ordinary," revenue-raising taxes are less likely to have "indirect effects" than "ordinary" commerce regulations? But see Justice Jackson's concurrence: "One cannot formulate a revenue-raising plan that would not have economic and social consequences." Is it because the federal scheme conveys clearer implications about the primary purpose of tax than of commerce legislation? Because it implies more clearly that taxes must have a primary revenue-raising objective, and that Congress may only pursue other objectives so long as they are ancillary to revenue-raising? But is there no historical guidance about the proper primary purpose of commerce regulations? And if some Justices are willing to distinguish between primary and ancillary objectives with respect to the taxing power, why are they unwilling—or view themselves as incompetent—to do so with respect to the commerce power?

Was the wagering tax a variety of tax that "discourages or deters the activities taxed" because of the impact of the taxing sanction? Or did the regulatory impact stem from the collateral reporting features, as in United States v. Doremus, noted above? Should Justice Reed have focused on those features rather than the "regulatory effect" of the tax itself? Or are the "abuse of power" problems raised by those two varieties of regulatory impacts essentially similar? Are the kinds of data Justice Frankfurter relies

on to identify "ulterior purpose" in Kahriger the kinds the Court *should* rely on? In taxing cases? In commerce power cases as well?

2. *The cases since Kahriger.* Kahriger was overruled solely on Fifth Amendment self-incrimination grounds in MARCHETTI v. UNITED STATES, 390 U.S. 39 (1968). Justice Harlan's majority opinion repeatedly referred to the statutory provision printed in footnote * to the Kahriger case, but not mentioned by Justice Reed in Kahriger. For example, he noted: "The terms of the wagering tax system make quite plain that Congress intended information obtained as a consequence of registration and payment of the occupational tax to be provided to interested prosecuting authorities." But a year after the Marchetti case, the Court rejected a constitutional challenge based on it and directed at the statutory prohibitions on selling narcotic drugs and marijuana without the written order forms required by law. MINOR v. UNITED STATES (and Buie v. United States), 396 U.S. 87 (1969). Though the majority spoke only of the Fifth Amendment claim, Justice Douglas' dissent, joined by Justice Black, reached the federalism problem as well. In urging the reversal of Minor's conviction for selling heroin without an order form, Justice Douglas insisted that the Fifth Amendment issue was "not the end of the matter for me." He noted that there was no way in which order forms to purchase heroin could be obtained. And he added: "The Federal Government does not have plenary power to define and punish criminal acts." Yet here, the Government was "punishing an individual for failing to do something that the Government has made it impossible for him to do." After quoting from Chief Justice Taft's opinion in Nigro v. United States (noted above), he added: "I do not see how the Government can make a crime out of not receiving an order form and at the same time allow no order forms for this category of sales."

Moreover, Justice Douglas was not persuaded by a suggestion that "a statute imposing a flat ban on sales of heroin might be sustainable under the Commerce Clause": "We are concerned in this case with what the Congress did, not with what it might have done or might yet do in the future. It is clear that what Congress did [was] to enact a taxing measure." The majority limited its response to that federalism objection to a footnote: "A statute does not cease to be a valid tax measure because it deters the activity taxed, because the revenue obtained is negligible, or because the activity is otherwise illegal. . . . Even viewing [the provision] as little more than a flat ban on certain sales, it is sustainable under the powers granted Congress in Art. I, § 8," citing cases such as United States v. Sullivan and United States v. Darby (chap. 3 above). Should congressional authority be tested in terms of the powers it *purports* to exercise? Or should the Court use its own imaginativeness to search for sources of power that *might* justify a statute? Compare Justice Douglas' majority opinion in Woods v. Miller Co., 333 U.S. 138 (1948) (a war power case, in sec. 3 below): "The question of the constitutionality of action taken by Congress does not depend on recitals of the power which it undertakes to exercise."

SECTION 2. THE SPENDING POWER

Introduction. The national spending power is probably the most important of all Art. I, § 8, powers in its impact on the actual functioning of the federal system. Whether in the context of payments to individuals for particular purposes (as with old age support under Social Security) or of conditional grants to states (as with education or welfare) or of direct financing of federal entrepreneurial operations (as with the TVA), national decisions about how money is to be spent involve pervasive policy choices and have significant regulatory consequences. Yet litigation about the scope of the power has been rare, for restrictive doctrines regarding standing to sue have traditionally barred taxpayer challenges to federal spending programs. (See chap. 15.) But the constitutional questions are no less real for the sparsity of judicial decisions. From the beginning, spending proposals have provoked disputes: at the time of McCulloch v. Maryland, for example, the constitutionality of federal spending for roads and canals was a subject of lively debate. (Recall the notes in chap. 2.) And the scope of the spending power has been a recurrent source of controversy ever since, as the opinions in the next principal case illustrate.

What are the legitimate purposes of national spending? What is the proper role of courts in assessing legitimacy when justiciability restraints permit decisions on the merits? What conditions may Congress impose on spending programs? What is constitutionally required with respect to the relationship between the condition, the particular program, and the "general welfare"? These are the questions for major attention in examining these selections from the rare encounters of the Court with the spending power.

UNITED STATES v. BUTLER
297 U.S. 1, 56 S.Ct. 312, 80 L.Ed. 477 (1936).

Certiorari to the Circuit Court of Appeals for the First Circuit.

[This case invalidated one of the major New Deal measures, the Agricultural Adjustment Act of 1933. The Act sought to raise farm prices by curtailing agricultural production. To do so, it authorized the Secretary of Agriculture to make contracts with farmers to reduce their productive acreage in exchange for benefit payments. The payments were to be made out of funds payable by the processor: a processing tax was imposed "upon the first domestic processing" of the particular commodity. A processing tax on cotton was imposed upon the Hoosac Mills Corporation. Butler and his co-receivers for the company challenged the tax, claiming that it was an integral part of an unconstitutional program to control agricultural production.

[The Government challenged Butler's standing to sue, insisting that under cases such as Frothingham v. Mellon (see chap. 15), taxpayers could not question federal spending programs. But the Court found that barrier inapplicable. It found that this was not merely a taxpayers' suit "to restrain the expenditure of the public monies." Rather, the taxpayers here "resist the exaction as a step in an authorized plan." The taxing and spending aspects

of a statute imposing an earmarked tax could not be separated: "The tax plays an indispensable part in the plan of regulation. . . . The whole revenue from the levy is appropriated in aid of crop control; none of it is made available for general governmental use." * Justice Roberts' majority opinion accordingly concluded on this aspect of the case "that the act is one regulating agricultural production; that the tax is a mere incident of such regulation; and that the respondents have standing to challenge the legality of the exaction."]

Mr. Justice ROBERTS delivered the opinion of the Court. . . .

The Government asserts that even if the respondents may question the propriety of the appropriation embodied in the statute their attack must fail because Article I, § 8 of the Constitution authorizes the contemplated expenditure of the funds raised by the tax. This contention presents the great and the controlling question in the case. . . .

There should be no misunderstanding as to the function of this court in such a case. It is sometimes said that the court assumes a power to overrule or control the action of the people's representatives. This is a misconception. The Constitution is the supreme law of the land ordained and established by the people. All legislation must conform to the principles it lays down. When an act of Congress is appropriately challenged in the courts as not conforming to the constitutional mandate the judicial branch of the Government has only one duty,—to lay the article of the Constitution which is invoked beside the statute which is challenged and to decide whether the latter squares with the former. All the court does, or can do, is to announce its considered judgment upon the question. The only power it has, if such it may be called, is the power of judgment. This court neither approves nor condemns any legislative policy. Its delicate and difficult office is to ascertain and declare whether the legislation is in accordance with, or in contravention of, the provisions of the Constitution; and, having done that, its duty ends. [After noting that the Government had not sought to justify the Act on the basis of the commerce power, Justice Roberts continued:]

The clause thought to authorize the legislation . . . confers upon the Congress power "to lay and collect Taxes, Duties, Imposts and Excises, to pay the Debts and provide for the common Defence and general Welfare of the United States. . . ." It is not contended that this provision grants power to regulate agricultural production upon the theory that such legislation would promote the general welfare. The Government concedes that the phrase "to provide for the general welfare" qualifies the power "to lay and collect taxes." The view that the clause grants power to provide for the general welfare, independently of the taxing power, has never been authoritatively accepted. Mr. Justice Story points out that if it were adopted "it is obvious that under color of the generality of the words, to 'provide for the common defence and general welfare,' the government of the United States is in reality, a government of general and unlimited powers, notwith-

---

* Justice Roberts' majority opinion defined a tax as "an exaction for the support of Government." He insisted that the word "tax" had "never been thought to connote the expropriation of money from one group for the benefit of another."

standing the subsequent enumeration of specific powers." The true construction undoubtedly is that the only thing granted is the power to tax for the purpose of providing funds for payment of the nation's debts and making provision for the general welfare.

Nevertheless, the Government asserts that warrant is found in this clause for the adoption of the Agricultural Adjustment Act. The argument is that Congress may appropriate and authorize the spending of moneys for the "general welfare"; that the phrase should be liberally construed to cover anything conducive to national welfare; that decision as to what will promote such welfare rests with Congress alone, and the courts may not review its determination; and finally that the appropriation under attack was in fact for the general welfare of the United States. . . .

Since the foundation of the Nation, sharp differences of opinion have persisted as to the true interpretation of the phrase. Madison asserted it amounted to no more than a reference to the other powers enumerated in the subsequent clauses of the same section; that, as the United States is a government of limited and enumerated powers, the grant of power to tax and spend for the general national welfare must be confined to the enumerated legislative fields committed to the Congress. In this view the phrase is mere tautology, for taxation and appropriation are or may be necessary incidents of the exercise of any of the enumerated legislative powers. Hamilton, on the other hand, maintained the clause confers a power separate and distinct from those later enumerated, is not restricted in meaning by the grant of them, and Congress consequently has a substantive power to tax and to appropriate, limited only by the requirement that it shall be exercised to provide for the general welfare of the United States. Each contention has had the support of those whose views are entitled to weight. This court has noticed the question, but has never found it necessary to decide which is the true construction. Mr. Justice Story, in his Commentaries, espouses the Hamiltonian position. We shall not review the writings of public men and commentators or discuss the legislative practice. Study of all these leads us to conclude that the reading advocated by Mr. Justice Story is the correct one. While, therefore, the power to tax is not unlimited, its confines are set in the clause which confers it, and not in those of § 8 which bestow and define the legislative powers of the Congress. It results that the power of Congress to authorize expenditure of public moneys for public purposes is not limited by the direct grants of legislative power found in the Constitution. . . .

We are not now required to ascertain the scope of the phrase "general welfare of the United States" or to determine whether an appropriation in aid of agriculture falls within it. Wholly apart from that question, another principle embedded in our Constitution prohibits the enforcement of the Agricultural Adjustment Act. The Act invades the reserved rights of the states. It is a statutory plan to regulate and control agricultural production, a matter beyond the powers delegated to the federal government. The tax, the appropriation of the funds raised, and the direction for their disbursement, are but parts of the plan. They are but means to an unconstitutional end. . . .

It is an established principle that the attainment of a prohibited end may not be accomplished under the pretext of the exertion of powers which are granted [quoting Marshall's "pretext" statement in McCulloch]. . . .

If the taxing power may not be used as the instrument to enforce a regulation of matters of state concern with respect to which the Congress has no authority to interfere, may it, as in the present case, be employed to raise the money necessary to purchase a compliance which the Congress is powerless to command? The Government asserts that whatever might be said against the validity of the plan if compulsory, it is constitutionally sound because the end is accomplished by voluntary co-operation. There are two sufficient answers to the contention. The regulation is not in fact voluntary. The farmer, of course, may refuse to comply, but the price of such refusal is the loss of benefits. The amount offered is intended to be sufficient to exert pressure on him to agree to the proposed regulation. The power to confer or withhold unlimited benefits is the power to coerce or destroy. If the cotton grower elects not to accept the benefits, he will receive less for his crops; those who receive payments will be able to undersell him. The result may well be financial ruin. The coercive purpose and intent of the statute is not obscured by the fact that it has not been perfectly successful. . . .

But if the plan were one for purely voluntary co-operation it would stand no better so far as federal power is concerned. At best, it is a scheme for purchasing with federal funds submission to federal regulation of a subject reserved to the states.

It is said that Congress has the undoubted right to appropriate money to executive officers for expenditure under contracts between the government and individuals; that much of the total expenditures is so made. But appropriations and expenditures under contracts for proper governmental purposes cannot justify contracts which are not within federal power. And contracts for the reduction of acreage and the control of production are outside the range of that power. An appropriation to be expended by the United States under contracts calling for violation of a state law clearly would offend the Constitution. Is a statute less objectionable which authorizes expenditure of federal moneys to induce action in a field in which the United States has no power to intermeddle? The Congress cannot invade state jurisdiction to compel individual action; no more can it purchase such action. . . . .

We are not here concerned with a conditional appropriation of money, nor with a provision that if certain conditions are not complied with the appropriation shall no longer be available. By the Agricultural Adjustment Act the amount of the tax is appropriated to be expended only in payment under contracts whereby the parties bind themselves to regulation by the Federal Government. There is an obvious difference between a statute stating the conditions upon which moneys shall be expended and one effective only upon assumption of a contractual obligation to submit to a regulation which otherwise could not be enforced. Many examples pointing the distinction might be cited. We are referred to appropriations in aid of education, and it is said that no one has doubted the power of Congress to stipulate the sort of education for which money shall be expended. But an ap-

propriation to an educational institution which by its terms is to become available only if the beneficiary enters into a contract to teach doctrines subversive of the Constitution is clearly bad. An affirmance of the authority of Congress so to condition the expenditure of an appropriation would tend to nullify all constitutional limitations upon legislative power. . . .

Congress has no power to enforce its commands on the farmer to the ends sought by the Agricultural Adjustment Act. It must follow that it may not indirectly accomplish those ends by taxing and spending to purchase compliance. The Constitution and the entire plan of our government negative any such use of the power to tax and to spend as the act undertakes to authorize. It does not help to declare that local conditions throughout the nation have created a situation of national concern; for this is but to say that whenever there is a widespread similarity of local conditions, Congress may ignore constitutional limitations upon its own powers and usurp those reserved to the states. . . .

Hamilton himself, the leading advocate of broad interpretation of the power to tax and to appropriate for the general welfare, never suggested that any power granted by the Constitution could be used for the destruction of local self-government in the states. Story countenances no such doctrine. It seems never to have occurred to them, or to those who have agreed with them, that the general welfare of the United States, (which has aptly been termed "an indestructible Union, composed of indestructible States,") might be served by obliterating the constituent members of the Union. But to this fatal conclusion the doctrine contended for would inevitably lead. And its sole premise is that, though the makers of the Constitution, in erecting the federal government, intended sedulously to limit and define its powers, so as to reserve to the states and the people sovereign power, to be wielded by the states and their citizens and not to be invaded by the United States, they nevertheless by a single clause gave power to the Congress to tear down the barriers, to invade the states' jurisdiction, and to become a parliament of the whole people, subject to no restrictions save such as are self-imposed. The argument when seen in its true character and in the light of its inevitable results must be rejected. . . .

Affirmed.

Mr. Justice STONE, dissenting.* . . .

1. The power of courts to declare a statute unconstitutional is subject to two guiding principles of decision which ought never to be absent from judicial consciousness. One is that courts are concerned only with the power to enact statutes, not with their wisdom. The other is that while unconstitutional exercise of power by the executive and legislative branches of the government is subject to judicial restraint, the only check upon our own exercise of power is our own sense of self-restraint. For the removal of

---

* The opening and closing passages in this dissent are of special historical interest: it was passages like these that President Roosevelt relied on in his attacks on the Court at the time of the Court-packing plan. See, e. g., his radio address of March 9, 1937, quoted in chap. 3 above: "[T]he Court has been assuming the power to pass on the wisdom of these acts of the Congress . . . . That is not only my accusation. It is the accusation of most distinguished Justices of the present Supreme Court."

unwise laws from the statute books appeal lies not to the courts but to the ballot and to the processes of democratic government.

2. The constitutional power of Congress to levy an excise tax upon the processing of agricultural products is not questioned. The present levy is held invalid, not for any want of power in Congress to lay such a tax to defray public expenditures, including those for the general welfare, but because the use to which its proceeds are put is disapproved.

3. As the present depressed state of agriculture is nation wide in its extent and effects, there is no basis for saying that the expenditure of public money in aid of farmers is not within the specifically granted power of Congress to levy taxes to "provide for the . . . general welfare." The opinion of the Court does not declare otherwise. . . .

Of the assertion that the payments to farmers are coercive, it is enough to say that no such contention is pressed by the taxpayer, and no such consequences were to be anticipated or appear to have resulted from the administration of the act. The suggestion of coercion finds no support in the record or in any data showing the actual operation of the act. Threat of loss, not hope of gain, is the essence of economic coercion. . . .

It is upon the contention that state power is infringed by purchased regulation of agricultural production that chief reliance is placed. . . . The Constitution requires that public funds shall be spent for a defined purpose, the promotion of the general welfare. Their expenditure usually involves payment on terms which will insure use by the selected recipients within the limits of the constitutional purpose. Expenditures would fail of their purpose and thus lose their constitutional sanction if the terms of payment were not such that by their influence on the action of the recipients the permitted end would be attained. The power of Congress to spend is inseparable from persuasion to action over which Congress has no legislative control. Congress may not command that the science of agriculture be taught in state universities. But if it would aid the teaching of that science by grants to state institutions, it is appropriate, if not necessary, that the grant be on the condition, incorporated in the Morrill Act, 12 Stat. 503, 26 Stat. 417, that it be used for the intended purpose. Similarly it would seem to be compliance with the Constitution, not violation of of it, for the government to take and the university to give a contract that the grant would be so used. It makes no difference that there is a promise to do an act which the condition is calculated to induce. Condition and promise are alike valid since both are in furtherance of the national purpose for which the money is appropriated.

These effects upon individual action, which are but incidents of the authorized expenditure of government money, are pronounced to be themselves a limitation upon the granted power . . . .. Such a limitation is contradictory and destructive of the power to appropriate for the public welfare, and is incapable of practical application. . . . It is a contradiction in terms to say that there is power to spend for the national welfare, while rejecting any power to impose conditions reasonably adapted to the attainment of the end which alone would justify the expenditure.

The limitation now sanctioned must lead to absurd consequences. The government may give seeds to farmers, but may not condition the gift upon their being planted in places where they are most needed or even planted at all. The government may give money to the unemployed, but may not ask that those who get it shall give labor in return, or even use it to support their families. . . . It may support rural schools, [but] may not condition its grant by the requirement that certain standards be maintained. [Do] all its activities collapse because, in order to effect the permissible purpose, in myriad ways the money is paid out upon terms and conditions which influence action of the recipients within the states, which Congress cannot command? The answer would seem plain. If the expenditure is for a national public purpose, that purpose will not be thwarted because payment is on condition which will advance that purpose. The action which Congress induces by payments of money to promote the general welfare, but which it does not command or coerce, is but an incident to a specifically granted power, but a permissible means to a legitimate end. If appropriation in aid of a program of curtailment of agricultural production is constitutional, and it is not denied that it is, payment to farmers on condition that they reduce their crop acreage is constitutional. It is not any the less so because the farmer at his own option promises to fulfill the condition.

That the governmental power of the purse is a great one is not now for the first time announced. . . . The suggestion that it must now be curtailed by judicial fiat because it may be abused by unwise use hardly rises to the dignity of argument. So may judicial power be abused. . . . The power to tax and spend is not without constitutional restraints. One restriction is that the purpose must be truly national. Another is that it may not be used to coerce action left to state control. Another is the conscience and patriotism of Congress and the Executive. . . .

A tortured construction of the Constitution is not to be justified by recourse to extreme examples of reckless congressional spending which might occur if courts could not prevent—expenditures which, even if they could be thought to effect any national purpose, would be possible only by action of a legislature lost to all sense of public responsibility. Such suppositions are addressed to the mind accustomed to believe that it is the business of courts to sit in judgment on the wisdom of legislative action. Courts are not the only agency of government that must be assumed to have capacity to govern. Congress and the courts both unhappily may falter or be mistaken in the performance of their constitutional duty. But interpretation of our great charter of government which proceeds on any assumption that the responsibility for the preservation of our institutions is the exclusive concern of any one of the three branches of government, or that it alone can save them from destruction is far more likely, in the long run, "to obliterate the constituent members" of "an indestructible union of indestructible states" than the frank recognition that language, even of a constitution, may mean what it says: that the power to tax and spend includes the power to relieve a nationwide economic maladjustment by conditional gifts of money.

Mr. Justice BRANDEIS and Mr. Justice CARDOZO join in this opinion.

CONDITIONAL SPENDING AND THE BUTLER CASE

1. *The majority opinion.* What was the significance of the Butler majority's endorsement of the Hamilton-Story position on the spending power? Was that endorsement consistent with the result? Did the majority in effect adopt the Madison position after all? If this power to spend for the "general Welfare" is not limited by the other grants of power in Art. I, § 8, why was it unconstitutional to spend for the purpose of reducing agricultural production, even though that production could not then be regulated directly under the other powers? If, as the majority apparently concedes, "conditional appropriation of money" is permissible—including "appropriations in aid of education" with stipulations of "the sort of education for which money shall be expended"—why is conditional spending to aid farmers unconstitutional? Was the problem of agricultural production less "general" than that of education? Could the Government have given money to farmers who voluntarily cut agricultural production, with provisions that grants would not be renewed if productive acreage were not reduced? What difference did it make that the Agricultural Adjustment Act involved contractual arrangements? Should that have been viewed as a difference of constitutional dimensions? What were the permissible purposes of—and permissible conditions on—spending after Butler? Can the result in Butler be reconciled with the 1937 Social Security cases, which follow?

2. *The dissent.* Was Justice Stone persuasive in asserting in his dissent: "Threat of loss, not hope of gain, is the essence of economic coercion"? What restrictions on the spending power would the dissenters recognize? Justice Stone states that "the purpose must be truly national." Is the Court competent to identify "non-national" purposes in the face of a judgment by the national legislature that a spending program serves the national interest? Justice Stone also asserts that the spending power "may not be used to coerce action left to state control." Does he not effectively sanction economic coercion of farmers? Would there nevertheless be a barrier in Justice Stone's view if the national program sought to compel state governments rather than individuals to take affirmative action? Compare Steward Machine Co. v. Davis, below.

What constitutional standards must conditions on spending meet under Justice Stone's view? Is it enough that the conditions are relevant to the general welfare? Is there a more focused requirement that the condition be related to the purpose of the particular spending program? Note Justice Stone's comment: "If the expenditure is for a national public purpose, that purpose will not be thwarted because payment is on condition which will advance that purpose." Note also his earlier reference to "conditions reasonably adapted to the attainment of the end which alone would justify the expenditure." What "purpose," what "end," did Justice Stone have in mind? What criteria for judicial scrutiny of conditional spending remained after the 1937 Social Security cases, which follow? After Flemming v. Nestor, the 1960 decision below?

THE 1937 SOCIAL SECURITY CASES

After the Butler case, New Dealers feared that the Social Security Act of 1935 was in danger of judicial invalidation. But in companion cases in 1937, during the Court-packing controversy, the Court sustained the unemployment compensation and old age benefits schemes of the Social Security Act. Were these decisions consistent with Butler? What restraints on congressional power under Art. I, § 8, cl. 1, remain after these decisions?

1. The 5 to 4 decision in STEWARD MACHINE CO. v. DAVIS, 301 U.S. 548 (1937), sustained the unemployment compensation provisions of the Social Security Act. Title IX of the Act imposed a payroll tax on employers of eight or more. Unlike the tax in the Butler case, this tax was not earmarked but went into general funds like other revenue collections. Under the scheme an employer was entitled to a credit of up to 90% of the federal tax for any contributions to a state unemployment fund certified by a federal agency as meeting the requirements of the Act. As described by the Court, some of the federal requirements were "designed to give assurance that the state unemployment compensation law shall be one in substance as well as name." Others were "designed to give assurance that the contributions shall be protected against loss after payment to the state." Among the latter was a provision requiring that state funds be paid over immediately to the Secretary of the Treasury to the credit of the "Unemployment Trust Fund," to be managed by the Secretary, with payments made to state authorities upon proper requisitions.

Justice Cardozo's majority opinion concluded that the scheme was "not void as involving the coercion of the States in contravention of the Tenth Amendment or of restrictions implicit in our federal form of government." He insisted that it had not been shown that "the tax and the credit in combination are weapons of coercion, destroying or impairing the autonomy of the states." Passages from his opinion follow:

"To draw the line intelligently between duress and inducement there is no need to remind ourselves of facts as to the problem of unemployment that are now matters of common knowledge. . . . During the years 1929 to 1936, when the country was passing through a cyclical depression, the number of the unemployed mounted to unprecedented heights. Often the average was more than 10 million; at times a peak was attained of 16 million or more. Disaster to the breadwinner meant disaster to dependents. Accordingly the roll of the unemployed, itself formidable enough, was only a partial roll of the destitute or needy. The fact developed quickly that the states were unable to give the requisite relief. The problem had become national in area and dimensions. There was need of help from the nation if the people were not to starve. It is too late today for the argument to be heard with tolerance that in a crisis so extreme the use of the moneys of the nation to relieve the unemployed and their dependents is a use for any purpose narrower than the promotion of the general welfare. Cf. United States v. Butler, 297 U.S. 1, 65, 66. . . .

"In the presence of this urgent need for some remedial expedient, the question is to be answered whether the expedient adopted has overlept the bounds of power. The assailants of the statute say that its dominant end

and aim is to drive the state legislatures under the whip of economic pressure into the enactment of unemployment compensation laws at the bidding of the central government. Supporters of the statute say that its operation is not constraint, but the creation of a larger freedom, the states and the nation joining in a cooperative endeavor to avert a common evil. Before Congress acted, unemployment compensation insurance was still, for the most part, a project and no more. Wisconsin was the pioneer. Her statute was adopted in 1931. At times bills for such insurance were introduced elsewhere, but they did not reach the stage of law. [I]f states had been holding back before the passage of the federal law, inaction was not owing, for the most part, to the lack of sympathetic interest. Many held back through alarm lest, in laying such a toll upon their industries, they would place themselves in a position of economic disadvantage as compared with neighbors or competitors. . . . Two consequences ensued. One was that the freedom of a state to contribute its fair share to the solution of a national problem was paralyzed by fear. The other was that in so far as there was failure by the states to contribute relief according to the measure of their capacity, a disproportionate burden, and a mountainous one, was laid upon the resources of the Government of the nation.

"The Social Security Act is an attempt to find a method by which all these public agencies may work together to a common end. Every dollar of the new taxes will continue in all likelihood to be used and needed by the nation as long as states are unwilling, whether through timidity or for other motives, to do what can be done at home. At least the inference is permissible that Congress so believed, though retaining undiminished freedom to spend the money as it pleased. On the other hand fulfilment of the home duty will be lightened and encouraged by crediting the taxpayer upon his account with the Treasury of the nation to the extent that his contributions under the laws of the locality have simplified or diminished the problem of relief and the probable demand upon the resources of the fisc. Duplicated taxes, or burdens that approach them, are recognized hardships that government, state or national, may properly avoid. . . . If Congress believed that the general welfare would be better promoted by relief through local units than by the system then in vogue, the coöperating localities ought not in all fairness to pay a second time.

"Who then is coerced through the operation of this statute? Not the taxpayer. He pays in fulfillment of the mandate of the local legislature. Not the state. Even now [Alabama] does not offer a suggestion that in passing the unemployment law she was affected by duress. . . . The difficulty with petitioner's contention is that it confuses motive with coercion. [E]very rebate from a tax when conditioned upon conduct is in some measure a temptation. But to hold that motive or temptation is equivalent to coercion is to plunge the law in endless difficulties. The outcome of such a doctrine is the acceptance of a philosophical determinism by which choice becomes impossible. Till now the law has been guided by a robust common sense which assumes the freedom of the will as a working hypothesis in the solution of its problems. The wisdom of the hypothesis has illustration in this case. Nothing in the case suggests the exertion of a power akin to undue influence, if we assume that such a concept can ever be applied with fitness to the relations between state and nation. Even on that assumption the loca-

tion of the point at which pressure turns into compulsion, and ceases to be inducement, would be a question of degree,—at times, perhaps, of fact. The point had not been reached when Alabama made her choice. We cannot say that [Alabama] was acting, not of her unfettered will, but under the strain of a persuasion equivalent to undue influence, when she chose to have relief administered under laws of her own making, by agents of her own selection, instead of under federal laws, administered by federal officers, with all the ensuing evils, at least to many minds, of federal patronage and power. There would be a strange irony, indeed, if her choice were now to be annulled on the basis of an assumed duress in the enactment of a statute which her courts have accepted as a true expression of her will. . . .

"In ruling as we do, we leave many questions open. We do not say that a tax is valid, when imposed by act of Congress, if it is laid upon the condition that a state may escape its operation through the adoption of a statute unrelated in subject matter to activities fairly within the scope of national policy and power. No such question is before us. In the tender of this credit Congress does not intrude upon fields foreign to its function. The purpose of its intervention, as we have shown, is to safeguard its own treasury and as an incident to that protection to place the states upon a footing of equal opportunity. Drains upon its own resources are to be checked; obstructions to the freedom of the states are to be leveled. It is one thing to impose a tax dependent upon the conduct of the taxpayers, or of the state in which they live, where the conduct to be stimulated or discouraged is unrelated to the fiscal need subserved by the tax in its normal operation, or to any other end legitimately national. The Child Labor Tax Case, 259 U.S. 20, and Hill v. Wallace, 259 U.S. 44, were decided in the belief that the statutes there condemned were exposed to that reproach. . . . It is quite another thing to say that a tax will be abated upon the doing of an act that will satisfy the fiscal need, the tax and the alternative being approximate equivalents. In such circumstances, if in no others, inducement or persuasion does not go beyond the bounds of power. We do not fix the outermost line. Enough for present purposes that wherever the line may be, this statute is within it. Definition more precise must abide the wisdom of the future. . . .

"United States v. Butler, supra, is cited by petitioner as a decision to the contrary. . . . The decision was by a divided court, a minority taking the view that the objections were untenable. None of them is applicable to the situation here developed.

"(a) The proceeds of the tax in controversy are not earmarked for a special group.

"(b) The unemployment compensation law which is a condition of the credit has had the approval of the state and could not be a law without it.

"(c) The condition is not linked to an irrevocable agreement, for the state at its pleasure may repeal its unemployment law . . . ., terminate the credit, and place itself where it was before the credit was accepted.

"(d) The condition is not directed to the attainment of an unlawful end, but to an end, the relief of unemployment, for which nation and state may lawfully coöperate.

" .   .   .   The statute does not call for a surrender by the states of powers essential to their quasi-sovereign existence. . . . A wide range of judgment is given to the several states as to the particular type of statute to be spread upon their books. . . . What they may not do, if they would earn the credit, is to depart from those standards which in the judgment of Congress are to be ranked as fundamental. . . . In determining essentials Congress must have the benefit of a fair margin of discretion. One cannot say with reason that this margin has been exceeded, or that the basic standards have been determined in any arbitrary fashion." *

2.   In a companion case to Steward Machine Co., HELVERING v. DAVIS, 301 U.S. 619 (1937), Justice Cardozo again wrote for the majority, with only Justices McReynolds and Butler dissenting.   Helvering v. Davis upheld the old age benefits provisions in Titles VIII and II of the Social Security Act of 1935.   Those provisions established an entirely federal program: they laid special taxes on covered employers and employees and provided for the payment of federal old age benefits.   Justice Cardozo's opinion rejected the Tenth Amendment challenge by relying on the endorsement of the Hamilton-Story position on the spending power in the Butler case.   He noted that "difficulties" were left even when the broad view of the power to spend for the general welfare was adopted: "The line must still be drawn between one welfare and another, between particular and general.   Where this shall be placed cannot be known through a formula in advance of the event.   There is a middle ground or certainly a penumbra in which discretion is at large.   The discretion, however, is not confided to the courts.   The discretion belongs to Congress, unless the choice is clearly wrong, a display of arbitrary power, not an exercise of judgment."

Here, it was clear, "Congress did not improvise a judgment when it was found that the award of old age benefits would be conducive to the general welfare."   Justice Cardozo explained: "The problem is plainly national in area and dimensions.   Moreover, laws of the separate states cannot deal with it effectively.   Congress, at least, had a basis for that belief.   States and local governments are often lacking in the resources that are necessary to finance an adequate program of security for the aged.   This is brought out with a wealth of illustration in recent studies of the problem.   Apart from the failure of resources, states and local governments are at times reluctant to increase so heavily the burden of taxation to be borne by their residents for fear of placing themselves in a position of economic disadvantage as compared with neighbors or competitors.   We have seen this in our study of the problem of unemployment compensation.   [Steward Machine Co. v. Davis.] A system of old age pensions has special dangers of its own, if put in force in one state and rejected in another.   The existence of such a system is a bait to the needy and dependent elsewhere, encouraging them to migrate and seek a haven of repose.   Only a power that is national can serve the interests of all."   He concluded: "When money is spent to promote the general wel-

---

* Justices McReynolds, Sutherland, Van Devanter and Butler dissented.   In another 5 to 4 decision on the same day, the Court sustained the Unemploy- ment Compensation Law enacted by Alabama to fit into the scheme of the federal Act.   Carmichael v. Southern Coal & Coke Co., 301 U.S. 495 (1937).

fare, the concept of welfare or the opposite is shaped by Congress, not the states. So the concept be not arbitrary, the locality must yield." †

FEDERAL GRANTS TO STATES AND INDIVIDUALS: SOME MODERN PRACTICES AND PROBLEMS

1. *The practical dimensions of federal grants to states.* The traditional and pervasive nature of federal spending programs was recognized in the Butler opinions. Federal policy guidance via the spending power, especially through conditional grants-in-aid to state and local governments, goes back to the 19th century. The size and range of the programs have increased considerably over the years, and detailed federal conditions have proliferated. For a survey and commentary on mid-20th century dimensions, see two 1955 publications by the Commission on Intergovernmental Relations: Twenty-Five Grant-in-Aid Programs, and A Report to the President.*

During the 1960's, there was growing opposition to narrow categorical grants-in-aid and widespread advocacy of broader unrestricted block grants to states and local governments. See, e. g., Advisory Commission on Intergovernmental Relations, Tenth Annual Report (1969), 6: "Unless state and local governments are permitted 'free,' albeit limited, access to the prime power source—the Federal Income Tax—their positions within our federal system are bound to deteriorate." The drive for "no strings money" instead of "strings money," illustrated by proposals such as the Heller Plan [see Heller, New Dimensions of Political Economy (1966)], finally bore fruit in the 1970's: in October, 1972, President Nixon signed a major general revenue sharing law, the State and Local Fiscal Assistance Act of 1972, 31 U.S.

---

† Note also the Court's broad statements, 23 years later, in recognizing the spending power as a basis for federal land reclamation projects, in United States v. Gerlach Live Stock Co., 339 U.S. 725 (1950): "Congress has a substantive power to tax and appropriate for the general welfare, limited only by the requirement that it shall be exercised for the common benefit as distinguished from some mere local purpose. If any doubt of this power remained, it was laid to rest [in Helvering v. Davis]. Thus the power of Congress to promote the general welfare through large-scale projects for reclamation, irrigation, or other internal improvement, is now as clear and ample as its power to accomplish the same results indirectly through resort to strained interpretation of the power over navigation."

Compare the strained efforts to justify—or avoid adjudication of—federal entrepreneurial activities in earlier litigation. The attempts to challenge the constitutionality of the Tennessee Valley Authority—a flood control, navigation and hydroelectric project—illustrate the common pattern: test cases frequently encountered justiciability barriers; and when the merits were reached, the Court found constitutional justification in a variety of sources other than the spending power. See generally, Freund, On Understanding the Supreme Court (1949), chap. 3. Note, e. g., Ashwander v. TVA, 297 U.S. 288 (1936), where the Court sharply narrowed a broad-scale attack and was able to limit its scrutiny to the constitutionality of one dam, built before the TVA was established; and it found construction and sale of electric power at that dam justified by the war, commerce, and property powers.

* For a discussion of earlier practices, see Elazar, The American Partnership: Intergovernmental Co-operation in the Nineteenth Century United States (1962).

C.A. § 1221 et seq. See generally Stolz, Revenue Sharing: Legal and Policy Analysis (1974).†

2. *The constitutional problems of federal grants to states: State autonomy as a limit?* Recall that in the 1937 unemployment compensation case, Steward Machine Co. v. Davis, above, Justice Cardozo asked whether the Social Security Act involved "the coercion of the States in contravention of the Tenth Amendment or of restrictions implicit in our federal form of government." He found no constitutional violation then. But in the years since, despite the recent movement toward unrestricted block grants, federal requirements in assistance to states have multiplied. When, if ever, may such requirements run counter to "restrictions implicit in our federal form of government"? When may conditions become so pervasive, when may they impinge so much on the structure and operations of state governments, to warrant judicial constraint? (Recall the similar questions about the exercise of the commerce power in chap. 3 above.) So far, the Court has shown little receptivity to challenges to federal spending conditions on state autonomy grounds.* Is greater receptivity warranted?

a. In a rare modern case on the spending power, the Court gave short shrift to a state's claim that federal highway funds could not be conditioned on the state's compliance with a provision of the Hatch Act. The challenged provision states that no state official primarily employed in activities "financed in whole or in part" by federal funds shall "take any active part" in political activities. In OKLAHOMA v. UNITED STATES CIVIL SERVICE COMMISSION, 330 U.S. 127 (1947), the federal agency ordered the removal of a State Highway Commissioner who was also the state chairman of the Democratic Party. Failure by the state to comply with the fed-

---

† See also "Symposium: The New Federalism and the Cities," 52 Jl. Urban Law 55 (1974).

Examination of the impacts of national spending on the federal system is one of the major functions of a permanent agency established in 1959, the Advisory Commission on Intergovernmental Relations, 42 U.S.C. § 4271 et seq. Among its tasks, as stated in the statutory "Declaration of purpose," is to "provide a forum for discussing the administration and coordination of Federal grant and other programs requiring intergovernmental cooperation" ; to "give critical attention to the conditions and controls involved in the administration of Federal grant programs" ; and to "recommend, within the framework of the Constitution, the most desirable allocation of governmental functions, responsibilities and revenues among the several levels of government."

* The modern Court has, however, recognized a state autonomy restraint on federal spending programs in one respect: with regard to the remedies against a state which violates federal conditions. In Edelman v. Jordan, 415 U.S. 651 (1974), the majority reminded that the Eleventh Amendment bars federal court actions by private parties seeking funds in the state treasury, even when the state has violated valid federal regulations under a federal spending program. In that case, beneficiaries under a federal-state program of Aid to the Aged, Blind, and Disabled sought retroactive payments wrongfully withheld by state officials. Justice Rehnquist's majority opinion explained that, though prospective injunctive relief against state officials acting unlawfully is available in the federal courts under Ex parte Young (see chap. 15, sec. 4), a decree ordering retroactive payments is impermissible under the Eleventh Amendment, since the funds "must inevitably come from the general revenues" of the state. Justices Douglas, Brennan, Marshall and Blackmun dissented. Justices Douglas and Marshall argued that the state had waived its constitutional immunity by consenting to participate in a program partly supported by federal funds. (See also the materials on state autonomy in chap. 6 below, and recall the note on 1975 developments at p. 125 above.)

eral requirement risked a federal order cutting off highway grants "in an amount equal to two years compensation" of the Commissioner.

Justice Reed's majority opinion rejected Oklahoma's challenge to the removal order: "While the United States is not concerned with, and has no power to regulate, local political activities as such of state officials, it does have power to fix the terms upon which its money allotments to states shall be disbursed. . . . The end sought by Congress through the Hatch Act is better public service by requiring those who administer funds for national needs to abstain from active political partisanship. So even though the action taken by Congress does have effect upon certain activities within the state, it has never been thought that such effect made the federal act invalid. . . . Oklahoma adopted the 'simple expedient' of not yielding to what she urges is federal coercion. . . . The offer of benefits to a state by the United States dependent upon cooperation by the state with federal plans, assumedly for the general welfare, is not unusual." (Justices Black and Rutledge dissented without opinion.) †

b.   Did the Oklahoma challenge in 1947 deserve a fuller and more concerned answer from the Court? Note Professor Linde's criticism and suggestion in "Justice Douglas on Freedom in the Welfare State," 39 Wash.L. Rev. 4, 28–31 (1964): "[P]robably no one can say today how much state and local tax revenue—the lifeblood of local autonomy—is committed to programs the standards for which are set and controlled under federal law. Yet there must be limits on such conditions if the political values of federalism are to be preserved despite this fiscal centralization. . . . Mr. Justice Reed's easy generalizations about conditioned federal spending prove too much. Even the liberal dissenters in 1936 had found the power to spend not beyond constitutional limitations, 'it may not be used to coerce action left to state control.' [U.S. v. Butler.] If Congress chose to forbid any state officer who spends federal grants to take part in a political campaign, could Oklahoma not choose to have an elected highway commission? [State officers] increasingly administer programs aided by federal funds; may Congress constitutionally decide which may be elected, which others politically appointed, and which must be in a nonpartisan career status? * Surely a line may be perceived between such conditions and conditions that go to the substance of the federally supported project, for instance that it fit a national plan, or be soundly engineered, or meet prescribed standards of hours, wages, or nondiscrimination in employment, or be fairly and honestly administered."

† A companion case to the Oklahoma case, United Public Workers v. Mitchell, 330 U.S. 75 (1947) (see chap. 15, sec. 3), sustained the Hatch Act against a First Amendment challenge. See also the companion cases a generation later rejecting First Amendment challenges to federal and state prohibitions of political activities by public employees, Civil Service Commission v. Letter Carriers and Broadrick v. Oklahoma, the 1973 decisions noted in chaps. 12 and 13, below.

* Professor Linde notes at this point that federal law "does in fact impose such requirements, which may substantially control the administrative organization of state governments, particularly in social welfare programs." And he reminds that the 1961 Governors' Conference deplored "the tendency of federal agencies to dictate the organizational form and structure through which the states carry out federally supported programs." See Council of State Governments, State Government Organization and Federal Grant-in-Aid Program Requirements (1962).

Is there merit in Linde's criticism? It it clear that "a line may be perceived" between conditions which impinge unduly on state autonomy and "conditions that go to the substance of the federally supported project"? Would the recent development of federal revenue sharing, with its "unrestricted" block grants, assure a greater concern for the state interest in its "organizational form and structure"? Not necessarily: though revenue sharing involves fewer "substantive" conditions on federal grants, there have been suggestions for greater "procedural" safeguards to assure local participation in the spending of the federal funds. See, e. g., Stolz, "Revenue Sharing—New American Revolution or Trojan Horse?" 58 Minn.L.Rev. 1 (1973), an extensive commentary on the State and Local Fiscal Assistance Act of 1972. Stolz urges at 117–18: "The single most important aspect in determining the program's future will be the participation of local citizens in the decision making process . . . . A 'New American revolution' of democratic participation in the local decision making process will be required. . . . A requirement of information disclosure and participation at the local level is not inconsistent with the 'no-strings' rhetoric." Does that suggest a sensitivity the reverse of Linde's: a view that conditions as to local governmental processes are less rather than more objectionable than "conditions that go to the substance of the federally supported project"? Does that make sense in terms of the constitutional values of federalism? †

3. *Federal grants to individuals: Constitutional restraints on "substantive" conditions?* In his dissent in the Butler case, Justice Stone suggested that conditions in federal spending programs must be "reasonably adapted to the attainment of the end which alone would justify the expenditure." (Recall the questions after Butler.) Is that a continued requirement of federal conditioned spending programs, even after the 1937 Social Security cases? Consider the final case in this section, which follows: in Flemming v. Nestor, a 1960 decision, the Court divided about the constitutionality of conditions in the Social Security Act. To be sure, the limiting considerations urged in that case did not stem from the nature of the federal system. Rather, they were based on individual rights concerns. But the due process objection considered by the Court has a close similarity to that suggested in Justice Stone's discussion of Art. I, § 8, in Butler: the requirement that the condition be "reasonably adapted" to the end can be viewed either as a derivation from the Necessary and Proper Clause of Art. I, § 8,

---

† Note that federal spending programs are subject to the anti-discrimination provisions of Title VI of the 1964 Civil Rights Act, which authorizes the selective cut-off of funds. Sec. 601 states the general policy: "No person in the United States shall, on the ground of race, color, or national origin, be excluded from participation in, be denied the benefits of, or be subjected to discrimination under any program or activity receiving Federal financial assistance." See Justice Douglas' prevailing opinion in Lau v. Nichols, 414 U.S. 563 (1974), relying on HEW guidelines issued pursuant to Sec. 601: "The Federal Government has power to fix the terms on which its money allotments to the States shall be disbursed. . . . Whatever may be the limits of that power [Steward Machine Co. v. Davis], they have not been reached here." Does § 601 raise less substantial federalistic concerns than the problems considered in text, because states were already subject to the anti-discrimination requirements of the 14th Amendment, so that the statute simply provides added enforcement mechanisms for a pre-existing restraints? (See also chap. 10, sec. 2.)

or as an aspect of the "reasonableness" requirement of due process.* Thus, Justice Harlan's due process discussion in Flemming v. Nestor asked whether the conditions were "relevant" to the purposes of the Social Security system. Consideration of the due process objection in Flemming, then, is an appropriate conclusion to this general examination of potential judicial constraints on legislative selection of conditions in spending programs.

Flemming v. Nestor, moreover, returns to a problem raised at the end of chap. 2: the question of whether the congressional discretion in selecting means is narrower when the limiting considerations stem from individual rights guarantees rather than from federalism concerns. In Flemming v. Nestor, a variety of individual rights guarantees (including due process) are urged as restraints on congressional legislation. Consider the varying attitudes, in the several opinions, about the appropriate intensity of judicial scrutiny; and contrast those positions with the degree of scrutiny in cases involving only federalistic limitations. Finally, Flemming v. Nestor offers an opportunity to return once more to the question of judicial examination of legislative motivation, as developed in the notes following the case.

———

FLEMMING v. NESTOR

363 U.S. 603, 80 S.Ct. 1367, 4 L.Ed.2d 1435 (1960).

Appeal from the United States District Court for the District of Columbia.

Mr. Justice HARLAN delivered the opinion of the Court.

From a decision of the District Court for the District of Columbia holding § 202(n) of the Social Security Act unconstitutional, the Secretary of Health, Education, and Welfare takes this direct appeal. [Sec. 202(n)] provides for the termination of old-age, survivor, and disability insurance benefits payable to, or in certain cases in respect of, an alien individual who, after September 1, 1954 (the date of enactment of the section), is deported under § 241(a) of the Immigration and Nationality Act on any one of certain grounds specified in § 202(n).

Appellee, an alien, immigrated to this country from Bulgaria in 1913, and became eligible for old-age benefits in November 1955. In July 1956 he was deported pursuant to § 241(a) (6) (C) (i) of the Immigration and Nationality Act for having been a member of the Communist Party from 1933 to 1939. This being one of the benefit-termination deportation grounds specified in § 202(n), appellee's benefits were terminated soon thereafter [In this suit under the judicial review provision of the Act, the District Court held] § 202(n) unconstitutional under the Due Process Clause of the Fifth Amendment in that it deprived appellee of an accrued property right.

. . . .

We think that the District Court erred in holding that § 202(n) deprived appellee of an "accrued property right." Appellee's right to Social

---

* See also the modern decisions imposing equal protection "rationality" restraints on conditions in spending programs, as noted in chap. 10, sec. 5, below.

Security benefits cannot properly be considered to have been of that order. . . . To engraft upon the Social Security system a concept of "accrued property rights" would deprive it of the flexibility and boldness in adjustment to ever-changing conditions which it demands. . . .

This is not to say, however, that Congress may exercise its power to modify the statutory scheme free of all constitutional restraint. The interest of a covered employee under the Act is of sufficient substance to fall within the protection from arbitrary governmental action afforded by the Due Process Clause. In judging the permissibility of the cut-off provisions of § 202(n) from this standpoint, it is not within our authority to determine whether the Congressional judgment expressed in that section is sound or equitable, or whether it comports well or ill with the purposes of the Act. . . . [Helvering v. Davis.] Particularly when we deal with a withholding of a non-contractual benefit under a social welfare program such as this, we must recognize that the Due Process Clause can be thought to interpose a bar only if the statute manifests a patently arbitrary classification, utterly lacking in rational justification.

Such is not the case here. The fact of a beneficiary's residence abroad —in the case of a deportee, a presumably permanent residence—can be of obvious relevance to the question of eligibility. One benefit which may be thought to accrue to the economy from the Social Security system is the increased over-all national purchasing power resulting from taxation of productive elements of the economy to provide payments to the retired and disabled, who might otherwise be destitute or nearly so, and who would generally spend a comparatively large percentage of their benefit payments. This advantage would be lost as to payments made to one residing abroad. For these purposes, it is, of course, constitutionally irrelevant whether this reasoning in fact underlay the legislative decision, as it is irrelevant that the section does not extend to all to whom the postulated rationale might in logic apply. See . . . [Steward Machine Co. v. Davis]. Nor, apart from this, can it be deemed irrational for Congress to have concluded that the public purse should not be utilized to contribute to the support of those deported on the grounds specified in the statute.

We need go no further to find support for our conclusion that this provision of the Act cannot be condemned as so lacking in rational justification as to offend due process.

The remaining, and most insistently pressed, constitutional objections rest upon Art. I, § 9, cl. 3, and Art. III, § 2, cl. 3, of the Constitution, and the Sixth Amendment. It is said that the termination of appellee's benefits amounts to punishing him without a judicial trial . . . .; that the termination of benefits constitutes the imposition of punishment by legislative act, rendering § 202(n) a bill of attainder, see [chap. 13, sec. 5, below]; and that the punishment exacted is imposed for past conduct not unlawful when engaged in, thereby violating the constitutional prohibition on ex post facto laws. Essential to the success of each of these contentions is the validity of characterizing as "punishment" in the constitutional sense the termination of benefits under § 202(n).

In determining whether legislation which bases a disqualification on the happening of a certain past event imposes a punishment, the Court has

sought to discern the objects on which the enactment in question was focused. Where the source of legislative concern can be thought to be the activity or status from which the individual is barred, the disqualification is not punishment even though it may bear harshly upon one affected. The contrary is the case where the statute in question is evidently aimed at the person or class of persons disqualified. . . .

Turning, then, to the particular statutory provision before us, appellee cannot successfully contend that the language and structure of § 202(n), or the nature of the deprivation, requires us to recognize a punitive design. . . . Here the sanction is the mere denial of a noncontractual governmental benefit. No affirmative disability or restraint is imposed, and certainly nothing approaching the "infamous punishment" of imprisonment. [Moreover,] it cannot be said [that] the disqualification of certain deportees from receipt of Social Security benefits while they are not lawfully in this country bears no rational connection to the purposes of the legislation of which it is a part, and must without more therefore be taken as evidencing a Congressional desire to punish. Appellee argues, however, that the history and scope of § 202(n) prove that no such postulated purpose can be thought to have motivated the legislature, and that they persuasively show that a punitive purpose in fact lay behind the statute. We do not agree.

We observe initially that only the clearest proof could suffice to establish the unconstitutionality of a statute on such a ground. Judicial inquiries into Congressional motives are at best a hazardous matter, and when that inquiry seeks to go behind objective manifestations it becomes a dubious affair indeed. Moreover, the presumption of constitutionality with which this enactment, like any other, comes to us forbids us lightly to choose that reading of the statute's setting which will invalidate it over that which will save it. . . .

Section 202(n) was enacted as a small part of an extensive revision of the Social Security program. [The House Committee Report states] that the termination of benefits would apply to those persons who were "deported from the United States because of illegal entry, conviction of a crime, or subversive activity . . . .." It was evidently the thought that such was the scope of the statute resulting from its application to deportation under the 14 named paragraphs of § 241(a) of the Immigration and Nationality Act. . . .[1]

Appellee argues that this history demonstrates that Congress was not concerned with the *fact* of a beneficiary's deportation—which it is claimed alone would justify this legislation as being pursuant to a policy relevant to regulation of the Social Security system—but that it sought to reach certain *grounds* for deportation, thus evidencing a punitive intent.[2] It is impos-

1. Paragraphs (1), (2) and (10) of § 241 (a) relate to unlawful entry, or entry not complying with certain conditions; paragraphs (6) and (7) apply to "subversive" and related activities; the remainder of the included paragraphs are concerned with convictions of designated crimes, or the commission of acts related to them, such as narcotics addiction or prostitution. [Footnote by the Court.]

2. . . . In addition, reliance is placed on a letter written to the Senate Finance Committee by appellant's predecessor in office, opposing the enactment of what is now § 202(u) of the Act . . . on the ground that the

sible to find in this meagre history the unmistakable evidence of punitive intent which, under principles already discussed, is required before a Congressional enactment of this kind may be struck down. . . .

Moreover, the grounds for deportation referred to in the Committee Report embrace the great majority of those deported, as is evident from an examination of the four omitted grounds, summarized in the margin.[3] Inferences drawn from the omission of those grounds cannot establish, to the degree of certainty required, that Congressional concern was wholly with the acts leading to deportation, and not with the fact of deportation.[4] . . .

The same answer must be made to arguments drawn from the failure of Congress to apply § 202(n) to beneficiaries voluntarily residing abroad. . . . Congress may have failed to consider such persons; or it may have thought their number too slight, or the permanence of their voluntary residence abroad too uncertain, to warrant application of the statute to them, with its attendant administrative problems of supervision and enforcement. Again, we cannot with confidence reject all those alternatives which imaginativeness can bring to mind, save that one which might require the invalidation of the statute.

Reversed.

Mr. Justice BRENNAN, with whom The Chief Justice [WARREN] and Mr. Justice DOUGLAS join, dissenting. . . .

[The Court] escapes the common-sense conclusion that Congress has imposed punishment by finding the requisite rational nexus to a granted power in the supposed furtherance of the Social Security program "enacted pursuant to Congress' power to 'spend money in aid of the "general welfare."' "
I do not understand the Court to deny that but for that connection, § 202(n) would impose punishment and not only offend the constitutional prohibition on ex post facto laws but also violate the constitutional guarantees against imposition of punishment without a judicial trial.

section was "in the nature of a penalty and based on considerations foreign to the objectives" of the program. . . . The Secretary went on to say that "present law recognizes only three narrowly limited exceptions [of which § 202(n) is one] to the basic principle that benefits are paid without regard to the attitudes, opinions, behavior, or personal characteristics of the individual . . . ." It should be observed, however, that the Secretary did not speak of § 202(n) as a penalty, as he did of the proposed § 202(u). The latter provision is concededly penal, and applies only pursuant to a judgment of a court in a criminal case. [Footnote by the Court.]

3. They are: (1) persons institutionalized at public expense within five years after entry because of "mental disease, defect, or deficiency" not shown to

have arisen subsequent to admission (§ 241(a) (3)) ; (2) persons becoming a public charge within five years after entry from causes not shown to have arisen subsequent to admission (§ 241 (a) (8)): (3) persons admitted as non-immigrants . . . who fail to maintain, or comply with the conditions of, such status (§ 241(a) (9)); (4) persons knowingly and for gain inducing or aiding, prior to or within five years after entry, any other alien to enter or attempt to enter unlawfully (§ 241 (a) (13)). [Footnote by the Court.]

4. Were we to engage in speculation, it would not be difficult to conjecture that Congress may have been led to exclude these four grounds of deportation out of compassionate or *de minimis* considerations. [Footnote by the Court.]

The Court's test of the constitutionality of § 202(n) is whether the legislative concern underlying the statute was to regulate "the activity or status from which the individual is barred" or whether the statute "is evidently aimed at the person or class of persons disqualified." It rejects the inference that the statute is "aimed at the person or class of persons disqualified" by relying upon the presumption of constitutionality. This presumption might be a basis for sustaining the statute if in fact there were two opposing inferences which could reasonably be drawn from the legislation, one that it imposes punishment and the other that it is purposed to further the administration of the Social Security program. The Court, however, does not limit the presumption to that use. Rather the presumption becomes a complete substitute for any supportable finding of a rational connection of § 202(n) with the Social Security program. . . .

It seems to me that the statute itself shows that the sole legislative concern was with "the person or class of persons disqualified." Congress did not disqualify for benefits all beneficiaries residing abroad or even all dependents residing abroad who are aliens. If that had been the case I might agree that Congress' concern would have been with "the activity or status" and not with the "person or class of persons disqualified." . . .

H.R.Rep. No. 1698, 83d Cong., 2d Sess. 25, 77, cited by the Court, describes § 202(n) as including persons who were deported "because of unlawful entry, conviction of a crime, or subversive activity." The section, in addition, covers those deported for such socially condemned acts as narcotic addiction or prostitution. The common element of the 14 grounds is that the alien has been guilty of some blameworthy conduct. In other words Congress worked its will only on aliens deported for conduct displeasing to the lawmakers.

This is plainly demonstrated by the remaining four grounds of deportation, those which do not result in the cancellation of benefits. Two of those four grounds cover persons who become public charges within five years after entry for reasons which predated the entry. A third ground covers the alien who fails to maintain his nonimmigrant status. The fourth ground reaches the alien who, prior to or within five years after entry, aids other aliens to enter the country illegally. . . .

This appraisal of the distinctions drawn by Congress between various kinds of conduct impels the conclusion, beyond peradventure, that the distinctions can be understood only if the purpose of Congress was to strike at "the person or class of persons disqualified." The Court inveighs against invalidating a statute on "implication and vague conjecture." Rather I think the Court has strained to sustain the statute on "implication and vague conjecture," in holding that the congressional concern was "the activity or status from which the individual is barred." Today's decision sanctions the use of the spending power not to further the legitimate objectives of the Social Security program but to inflict hurt upon those who by their conduct have incurred the displeasure of Congress. . . .

[Additional dissenting opinions—by Justices Black and Douglas—are omitted.] †

---

† See generally O'Neil, "Unconstitutional Conditions: Welfare Benefits with Strings Attached," 54 Calif.L.Rev. 443 (1966).

THE SCOPE OF JUDICIAL INQUIRY:
PURPOSE, MOTIVE, AND RATIONALITY

1. *The scope of inquiry in Flemming v. Nestor.* Is Justice Harlan's scrutiny of conditions—purposes (means-ends) relationships consistent with the standards regarding permissible conditions on governmental spending programs as discussed in the spending power cases of the 1930's? The limitations urged in Flemming v. Nestor do not stem from considerations of state autonomy. Does that alter the scope of congressional discretion as to conditions? Is the due process limitation discussed in Justice Harlan's opinion identical with the rational relationship standard under the Necessary and Proper Clause? Is it accurate to say that neither Justice Harlan nor Justice Brennan applies a standard of judicial scrutiny of congressional choices regarding means that is identical with the standard of McCulloch and its progeny? Is it accurate to say that Justice Harlan is even more tolerant of congressional means-ends judgments than the Art. I-federalism cases? And that Justice Brennan is more skeptical of legislative choices than most earlier cases were? Is either deviation from the norm of the Art. I-federalism context (toward greater judicial acquiescence or greater reexamination of legislative premises) justifiable? (Recall the questions on the scope of the Necessary and Proper Clause in the military jurisdiction context, at the end of chap. 2, above.)

2. *The congressional objectives: Legislative actuality or judicial imaginativeness?* Why is it "constitutionally irrelevant whether this reasoning in fact underlay the legislative decision," as Justice Harlan maintains in his opinion? Must the Court sustain legislation if a rational argument for the condition can be imagined, whether or not that argument was in fact considered by Congress? Compare the close of the majority opinion: "Again, we cannot . . . reject all those alternatives which imaginativeness can bring to mind." Do considerations of propriety or feasibility inhibit the Court from demanding an affirmative showing that the legislative deliberations—rather than the Court's or counsel's "imaginativeness"—supply the basis for a finding of rationality? Do these considerations bar the Court from considering evidence in the legislative history that improper grounds were relied on by Congress, even if rational grounds *could* have been given by a hypothetical legislature? Recall the earlier national power cases: To what extent was the need to reach local matters as a means of regulating interstate commerce, for example, justified by arguments in fact considered by Congress, rather than by imaginative afterthoughts by counsel and Court? *

---

* The problems raised by these questions are recurrent ones in judicial review. Note especially the extensive attention to these issues in chaps. 9 and 10 below, in connection with review under the "minimum rationality" model of scrutiny of legislative action under the due process and equal protection guarantees. Should courts test laws on the basis of purposes a hypothetical reasonable legislator *might* have had, or should courts assess "reasonableness" in terms of purposes *articulated* by the state? Should courts hypothesize possible means-ends relationships, or should they demand a showing of how the chosen means might contribute to the achievement of the legislative objectives? See the fuller exploration in the later chapters and in Gunther, "Foreword . . ., A Model for a Newer Equal Protection," 86 Harv.L. Rev. 1 (1972) (considered in chap. 10).

3. *Purpose, motive, and the draft card burning case.* Note the discussion of "purpose" and "motive" in Justice Harlan's opinion in Flemming. Does the Court disavow all inquiry into these, as it did in the Darby case, chap. 3, for example? Is it enough that a rational legislator *might* have had a legitimate purpose? Or is the Court willing to consider the "purpose" manifested in the legislative history? Is it possible to examine "purpose" without improper psychological inquiries into legislative "motive"? Is Justice Brennan's dissent as to purpose based on inferences from the face of the statute, inferences from the effect of the statute, evidence drawn from the record of legislative deliberation, or guesses as to hidden motives of legislators? Would clear-cut statements in the legislative record evidencing an aim to punish those deported on the specified grounds affect the majority's analysis in Flemming?

For a characteristic statement of judicial inhibitions about inquiries into legislative purpose and motive, see United States v. O'Brien, 391 U.S. 367 (1968). In that case the Court rejected a number of constitutional challenges to a conviction under a 1965 amendment to the draft law which prohibited knowing destruction or mutilation of draft certificates. The Court's disposition of most of the First Amendment objections is considered below (chap. 12, sec. 3). The rejection of one of defendant's claims warrants noting here: it was that the amendment was unconstitutional because the "purpose" of Congress was "to suppress freedom of speech." The Court rejected that argument "because under settled principles the purpose of Congress, as O'Brien uses that term, is not a basis for declaring this legislation unconstitutional." Chief Justice Warren's majority opinion elaborated that conclusion as follows:

"Inquiries into congressional motives or purposes are a hazardous matter. When the issue is simply the interpretation of legislation, the Court will look to statements by legislators for guidance as to the purpose of the legislature,[1] because the benefit to sound decision-making in this circumstance is thought sufficient to risk the possibility of misreading Congress' purpose. It is entirely a different matter when we are asked to void a statute that is, under well-settled criteria, constitutional on its face, on the basis of what fewer than a handful of Congressmen said about it. What motivates one legislator to make a speech about a statute is not necessarily what motivates scores of others to enact it, and the stakes are sufficiently high for us to eschew guesswork. We decline to void essentially on the ground that it is unwise [to void] legis-

---

1. "The Court may make the same assumption in a very limited and well-defined class of cases where the very nature of the constitutional question requires an inquiry into legislative purpose. The principal class of cases is readily apparent—those in which statutes have been challenged as bills of attainder. [T]he inquiry into whether the challenged statute contains the necessary element of punishment has on occasion led the Court to examine the legislative motive in enacting the statute. See, e. g., United States v. Lovett, 328 U.S. 303 (1946). Two other decisions not involving a bill of attainder analysis contain an inquiry in-to legislative purpose or motive of the type that O'Brien suggests we engage in in this case. Kennedy v. Mendoza-Martinez, 372 U.S. 144, 169–184 (1963); Trop v. Dulles, 356 U.S. 86, 95–97 (1958). The inquiry into legislative purpose or motive in Kennedy and Trop, however, was for the same limited purpose as in the bill of attainder decisions—i. e., to determine whether the statutes under review were punitive in nature. We face no such inquiry in this case. The 1965 Amendment to § 462(b) was clearly penal in nature, designed to impose criminal punishment for designated acts." [Footnote by the Court.]

lation which Congress had the undoubted power to enact and which could be reenacted in its exact form if the same or another legislator made a 'wiser' speech about it."

Was this passage adequate as a description of judicial practice? Was it persuasive as a statement of the proper scope of judicial scrutiny? What inhibits the Court in examining motivation in this case and in cases such as United States v. Darby, on the commerce-prohibiting power? Is it the *difficulty* of ascertaining legislative motivation? Is it the *futility* of doing so—the sense that judicial invalidation on motivation grounds would not bar the legislature from reenacting a statute with the same operative effect, but without the previously fatal indicia of improper motivation? Is it the sense of *institutional* restraint—the awkwardness of having the judiciary tell the legislators that they acted for improper reasons? Which of these grounds did Chief Justice Warren rely on in O'Brien? Is greater Court examination of actual legislative purposes and motives possible? Wise? Do (and should) the answers depend on the particular constitutional provision invoked? †

SECTION 3. WAR, FOREIGN AFFAIRS, AND FEDERALISM

Scope Note. The commerce, taxing, and spending powers considered in the preceding materials are far the most important national powers with an impact on federalism concerns, but they are by no means the only ones. The limited purpose of this section is to examine briefly what federalistic constraints may exist on two other potentially broad sources of authority: the war power; and the national government's powers to make treaties and deal with foreign affairs. These powers more frequently risk impingement on constitutional concerns other than state autonomy: both the war power and the foreign affairs power often generate controversies involving separation of powers and individual rights concerns. Consideration of the powers in the context of those countervailing interests is postponed to later chapters (see., e. g., chap. 7, on separation of powers); here, the limited sampling of additional national powers focuses on their impacts on federalism. It should be borne in mind that, like all powers of the national government, the powers considered here typically benefit from the broad construction of discretion in the choice of means first articulated in McCulloch v. Maryland.*

† Note the reemergence of these problems in a variety of contexts in later chapters—e. g., the controversy about appropriate judicial inquiry into motive and purpose in Palmer v. Thompson, 403 U.S. 217 (1971) (chap. 10 below), holding constitutional a city's closing of public swimming pools in the face of desegregation; and see generally (and compare) Ely, "Legislative and Administrative Motivation in Constitutional Law," 79 Yale L.J. 1205 (1970), and Brest, "Palmer v. Thompson: An Approach to the Problem of Unconstitutional Legislative Motive," 1971 Sup.Ct.Rev. 95.

Even if a court refuses to scrutinize motives, is a legislator bound to avoid voting on the basis of constitutionally improper motives? See Brest, "The Conscientious Legislator's Guide to Constitutional Interpretation," 27 Stan.L.Rev. 585 (1975).

* The national powers to which the Necessary and Proper Clause is applicable include not only those of Congress in Art. I, but also other powers of the national government, including those in Arts. II and III. Recall that Art. I, § 8, cl. 18, gives Congress the power "To make all Laws which shall be

A. THE WAR POWER

WOODS v. MILLER CO.

333 U.S. 138, 68 S.Ct. 421, 92 L.Ed. 596 (1948).

Appeal from the District Court of the United States for the Northern District of Ohio.

Mr. Justice DOUGLAS delivered the opinion of the Court.

The case is here on a direct appeal [from] a judgment of the District Court holding unconstitutional Title II of the Housing and Rent Act of 1947. . . .

The District Court was of the view that the authority of Congress to regulate rents by virtue of the war power (see Bowles v. Willingham, 321 U.S. 503 [1944]) ended with the Presidential Proclamation terminating hostilities on December 31, 1946,[1] since that proclamation inaugurated "peace-in-fact" though it did not mark termination of the war. It also concluded that, even if the war power continues, Congress did not act under it because it did not say so, and only if Congress says so, or enacts provisions so implying, can it be held that Congress intended to exercise such power. . . .

We conclude, in the first place, that the war power sustains this legislation. The Court said in Hamilton v. Kentucky Distilleries Co., 251 U.S. 146, 161 [1919], that the war power includes the power "to remedy the evils which have arisen from its rise and progress" and continues for the duration of that emergency. Whatever may be the consequences when war is officially terminated, the war power does not necessarily end with the cessation of hostilities. . . . In Hamilton v. Kentucky Distilleries Co., supra, and Ruppert v. Caffey, 251 U.S. 264 [1920], prohibition laws which were enact-

---

necessary and proper for carrying into Execution the foregoing Powers, and *all other Powers* vested by this Constitution in the Government of the United States, or in any Department or Office thereof." (Emphasis added.) Among the other Art. I, § 8, powers is the power to "coin money" and "regulate the Value thereof," see, e. g., one of the "gold clause" cases, Norman v. Baltimore & Ohio R. Co., 294 U.S. 240 (1935). Note also the power over copyrights and patents, see Mazer v. Stein, 347 U.S. 201 (1954). On the impact of the latter on state authority, see Goldstein v. California, 412 U.S. 546 (1973) (copyrights), and Kewanee Oil Co. v. Bicron Corp., 416 U.S. 470 (1974) (patents). Note also the postal power in Art. I, § 8—though it more frequently gives rise to individual rights rather than federalism concerns. See, e. g., Rowan v. Post Office Dept., 397 U.S. 728 (1970) (chap. 12 below). For an example of a source

of national power outside of Art. I, see Art. III, § 2: the federal judicial power over cases in admiralty and maritime jurisdiction was early construed as a source of legislative power as well. See Note, "From Judicial Grant to Legislative Power: The Admiralty Clause in the Nineteenth Century," 67 Harv.L.Rev. 1214 (1954).

1. Proclamation 2714, 12 Fed.Reg. 1. That proclamation recognized that "a state of war still exists." On July 25, 1947, on approving S.J.Res. 123 terminating certain war statutes, the President issued a statement in which he declared that "The emergencies declared by the President on September 8, 1939, and May 27, 1941, and the state of war continue to exist, however, and it is not possible at this time to provide for terminating all war and emergency powers." [Footnote by the Court.]

ed after the Armistice in World War I were sustained as exercises of the war power because they conserved manpower and increased efficiency of production in the critical days during the period of demobilization, and helped to husband the supply of grains and cereals depleted by the war effort. . . .

The constitutional validity of the present legislation follows a fortiori from those cases. The legislative history of the present Act makes abundantly clear that there has not yet been eliminated the deficit in housing which in considerable measure was caused by the heavy demobilization of veterans and by the cessation or reduction in residential construction during the period of hostilities due to the allocation of building materials to military projects. Since the war effort contributed heavily to that deficit, Congress has the power even after the cessation of hostilities to act to control the forces that a short supply of the needed article created. If that were not true, the Necessary and Proper Clause, Art. I, § 8, cl. 18, would be drastically limited in its application to the several war powers. . . .

We recognize the force of the argument that the effects of war under modern conditions may be felt in the economy for years and years, and that if the war power can be used in days of peace to treat all the wounds which war inflicts on our society, it may not only swallow up all other powers of Congress but largely obliterate the Ninth and the Tenth Amendments as well. There are no such implications in today's decision. We deal here with the consequences of a housing deficit greatly intensified during the period of hostilities by the war effort. Any power, of course, can be abused. But we cannot assume that Congress is not alert to its constitutional responsibilities. . . .

The question of the constitutionality of action taken by Congress does not depend on recitals of the power which it undertakes to exercise. Here it is plain from the legislative history that Congress was invoking its war power to cope with a current condition of which the war was a direct and immediate cause. . . .

Reversed.

Mr. Justice JACKSON, concurring.

I agree with the result in this case, but the arguments that have been addressed to us lead me to utter more explicit misgivings about war powers than the Court has done. The Government asserts no constitutional basis for this legislation other than this vague, undefined and undefinable "war power."

No one will question that this power is the most dangerous one to free government in the whole catalogue of powers. It usually is invoked in haste and excitement when calm legislative consideration of constitutional limitation is difficult. It is executed in a time of patriotic fervor that makes moderation unpopular. And, worst of all, it is interpreted by judges under the influence of the same passions and pressures. Always, as in this case, the Government urges hasty decision to forestall some emergency or serve some purpose and pleads that paralysis will result if its claims to power are denied or their confirmation delayed.

Particularly when the war power is invoked to do things to the liberties of people, or to their property or economy that only indirectly affect conduct

of the war and do not relate to the management of the war itself, the constitutional basis should be scrutinized with care.

I think we can hardly deny that the war power is as valid a ground for federal rent control now as it has been at any time. We still are technically in a state of war. I would not be willing to hold that war powers may be indefinitely prolonged merely by keeping legally alive a state of war that had in fact ended. I cannot accept the argument that war powers last as long as the effects and consequences of war, for if so they are permanent—as permanent as the war debts. But I find no reason to conclude that we could find fairly that the present state of war is merely technical. We have armies abroad exercising our war power and have made no peace terms with our allies, not to mention our principal enemies. I think the conclusion that the war power has been applicable during the lifetime of this legislation is unavoidable.

DOMESTIC REGULATION THROUGH THE WAR POWER

As the Woods case illustrates, in its holding and in the prevailing opinion, the war power is available for national regulation of a wide range of problems, of the "police" as well as the economic variety—though not without another expression of misgivings by Justice Jackson.* Note, for example, the rationale for sustaining the post-World War I prohibition law as described in Justice Douglas' opinion in Woods. Was there adequate judicial scrutiny in the Hamilton and Ruppert cases in 1919–20? Or are those decisions additional illustrations of the early 20th century Court's insensitivity to federalism values when Congress moved against such "evils" as immorality and crime? Recall the Court's endorsement of the commerce-prohibiting power in cases beginning with the Lottery Case, chap. 3, sec. 3, above. Compare the Court's statement in the 1919 decision in Hamilton v. Kentucky Distilleries Co., sustaining the post-World War I prohibition law (enacted prior to the adoption of the 18th Amendment): after recognizing that the national government "lacks the police power," the Court insisted "that when the United States exerts any of the powers conferred upon it by the Constitution, no valid objection can be based upon the fact that such exercise may be attended by the same incidents which attend the exercise by a State of its police power, or that it may tend to accomplish a similar purpose." Are there judicially enforceable limits on war power-based regulation, either of the economic or the "police" variety?

---

* Justice Jackson's stance was one he took in a variety of contexts. Recall, for example, his doubts about the taxing power in the Kahriger case, sec. 1 above, and about the commerce power in the Five Gambling Devices case, chap. 3 above. There are similar examples in later chapters: e. g., on the war power and individual rights, in Korematsu v. United States, chap. 10 below, and on equal protection restraints on "economic" regulation, in Railway Express Agency v. New York, also in chap. 10 below.

Justice Frankfurter also concurred separately in Woods.

B. TREATIES, FOREIGN AFFAIRS, AND FEDERALISM

Introduction. Are federalistic constraints irrelevant when the national government engages in the conduct of foreign relations? To what extent does the national government's authority over foreign affairs authorize national regulation of an otherwise local area? That is the central concern of this section; other constitutional problems pertaining to international affairs are left to later chapters.† Most of the materials in this section involve domestic regulatory consequences of national action resting on the treaty power. The final note considers whether there is a foreign affairs power of Congress independent of authority derived from treaties—and what the source of that power is. The central question in this section, then, is: To what extent may a treaty authorize national regulation of local affairs not reachable under other grants of power?

MISSOURI v. HOLLAND

252 U.S. 416, 40 S.Ct. 382, 64 L.Ed. 641 (1920).

Appeal from the District Court of the United States for the Western District of Missouri.

Mr. Justice HOLMES delivered the opinion of the court.

This is a bill in equity brought by the State of Missouri to prevent a game warden of the United States from attempting to enforce the Migratory Bird Treaty Act of July 3, 1918 . . . .. The ground of the bill is that the statute is an unconstitutional interference with the rights reserved to the States by the Tenth Amendment . . . .. A motion to dismiss was sustained by the District Court on the ground that the act of Congress is constitutional. . . .

On December 8, 1916, a treaty between the United States and Great Britain was proclaimed by the President. It recited that many species of birds in their annual migrations traversed certain parts of the United States and of Canada, that they were of great value as a source of food and in destroying insects injurious to vegetation, but were in danger of extermination through lack of adequate protection. It therefore provided for specified closed seasons and protection in other forms, and agreed that the two powers would take or propose to their lawmaking bodies the necessary measures for carrying the treaty out. 39 Stat. 1702. The above mentioned Act of July 3, 1918, entitled an act to give effect to the convention, prohibited the killing, capturing or selling any of the migratory birds included in the terms of the treaty except as permitted by regulations compatible with those terms, to be made by the Secretary of Agriculture. . . . It is unnecessary to go into any details, because, as we have said, the question raised is the general

---

† See, e. g., chap. 7 on separation of powers, for the distinction between executive agreements and treaties and related problems of executive-legislative relations.

one whether the treaty and statute are void as an interference with the rights reserved to the States.

To answer this question it is not enough to refer to the Tenth Amendment, reserving the powers not delegated to the United States, because by Article II, § 2, the power to make treaties is delegated expressly, and by Article VI treaties made under the authority of the United States, along with the Constitution and laws of the United States made in pursuance thereof, are declared the supreme law of the land. If the treaty is valid there can be no dispute about the validity of the statute under Article I, § 8, as a necessary and proper means to execute the powers of the Government. The language of the Constitution as to the supremacy of treaties being general, the question before us is narrowed to an inquiry into the ground upon which the present supposed exception is placed.

It is said that a treaty cannot be valid if it infringes the Constitution, that there are limits, therefore, to the treaty-making power, and that one such limit is that what an act of Congress could not do unaided, in derogation of the powers reserved to the States, a treaty cannot do. An earlier act of Congress that attempted by itself and not in pursuance of a treaty to regulate the killing of migratory birds within the States had been held bad in the District Court. [United States v. Shaurer; United States v. McCullagh.] . . .

Whether the two cases cited were decided rightly or not they cannot be accepted as a test of the treaty power. Acts of Congress are the supreme law of the land only when made in pursuance of the Constitution, while treaties are declared to be so when made under the authority of the United States. It is open to question whether the authority of the United States means more than the formal acts prescribed to make the convention. We do not mean to imply that there are no qualifications to the treaty-making power; but they must be ascertained in a different way. It is obvious that there may be matters of the sharpest exigency for the national well being that an act of Congress could not deal with but that a treaty followed by such an act could, and it is not lightly to be assumed that, in matters requiring national action, "a power which must belong to and somewhere reside in every civilized government" is not to be found. Andrews v. Andrews, 188 U.S. 14, 33. What was said in that case with regard to the powers of the States applies with equal force to the powers of the nation in cases where the States individually are incompetent to act. We are not yet discussing the particular case before us but only are considering the validity of the test proposed. With regard to that we may add that when we are dealing with words that also are a constituent act, like the Constitution of the United States, we must realize that they have called into life a being the development of which could not have been foreseen completely by the most gifted of its begetters. It was enough for them to realize or to hope that they had created an organism; it has taken a century and has cost their successors much sweat and blood to prove that they created a nation. The case before us must be considered in the light of our whole experience and not merely in that of what was said a hundred years ago. The treaty in question does not contravene any prohibitory words to be found in the Constitution. The only question is whether it is forbidden by some invisible radiation from the general terms of the Tenth Amendment.

We must consider what this country has become in deciding what that Amendment has reserved.

The State as we have intimated founds its claim of exclusive authority upon an assertion of title to migratory birds, an assertion that is embodied in statute. No doubt it is true that as between a State and its inhabitants the State may regulate the killing and sale of such birds, but it does not follow that its authority is exclusive of paramount powers. . . .

As most of the laws of the United States are carried out within the States and as many of them deal with matters which in the silence of such laws the State might regulate, such general grounds are not enough to support Missouri's claim. Valid treaties of course "are as binding within the territorial limits of the States as they are elsewhere throughout the dominion of the United States." Baldwin v. Franks, 120 U.S. 678, 683. No doubt the great body of private relations usually fall within the control of the State, but a treaty may override its power. [See note 1 below.] . . .

Here a national interest of very nearly the first magnitude is involved. It can be protected only by national action in concert with that of another power. The subject matter is only transitorily within the State and has no permanent habitat therein. But for the treaty and the statute there soon might be no birds for any powers to deal with. We see nothing in the Constitution that compels the Government to sit by while a food supply is cut off and the protectors of our forests and our crops are destroyed. It is not sufficient to rely upon the States. The reliance is vain, and were it otherwise, the question is whether the United States is forbidden to act. We are of opinion that the treaty and statute must be upheld. . . .

Decree affirmed.

Mr. Justice VAN DEVANTER and Mr. Justice PITNEY dissent.

THE SCOPE AND LIMITS OF THE TREATY POWER

1. *The supremacy of treaties over state law.* As Missouri v. Holland reminds, a treaty made by the President with the required concurrence of two-thirds of the Senate is, under the Supremacy Clause of Art. VI, § 2, part of "the supreme Law of the Land" which takes precedence over contrary state law. Even before the days of the Marshall Court, the Court began to implement the principle that a valid treaty overrides a state law on matters otherwise within state control. For example, in Ware v. Hylton, 3 Dall. 199 (1796), a treaty was held to have overridden a Virginia confiscation law. Recall also the conflict between state confiscations and federal treaties that culminated in Martin v. Hunter's Lessee in 1816, chap. 1 above. Similarly, in Hauenstein v. Lynham, 100 U.S. 483 (1880), a Virginia law providing for the escheat to the state of real estate of aliens dying intestate had to give way to a treaty, with the Court quoting from a treatise stating that "all questions which may arise between us and other powers, be the subject-matter what it may, fall within the treaty-making power."

2. *Limits on the treaty power?—The subject-matter of treaties.* Are there any judicially enforceable limits on the permissible subject-matter of a

treaty? Whenever Art. I powers prove insufficient to reach a local problem, may the national government overcome that obstacle simply by making a treaty with a cooperating foreign government? Are there any traditionally local questions that cannot be "properly the subject of negotiation with a foreign country"? Does not the fact that a treaty exists, that a treaty about a particular matter *has* been negotiated, demonstrate that the matter *is* a proper subject for negotiation? Can the courts scrutinize the good faith of President and Senate in entering into treaties?

The "properly the subject of negotiation" phrase comes from Geofroy v. Riggs, 133 U.S. 258 (1890). Can the statement be considered an effective limit on the treaty power? Justice Field stated: "The treaty power, as expressed in the Constitution, is in terms unlimited except by those restraints which are found in that instrument against the action of the government or of its departments, and those arising from the nature of the government itself and of that of the States. It would not be contended that it extends so far as to authorize what the Constitution forbids, or a change in the character of the government or in that of one of the States, or a cession of any portion of the territory of the latter, without its consent. Fort Leavenworth R. Co. v. Lowe, 114 U.S. 525, 541. But with these exceptions, it is not perceived that there is any limit to the questions which can be adjusted touching any matter which is properly the subject of negotiation with a foreign country." Is this an effective limitation? If not, are there others?* Fear about a potentially unlimited treaty power spawned the Bricker Amendment controversy of the 1950's and the reassurance from the Court in Reid v. Covert, considered in the next notes.

3. *The Bricker Amendment controversy.* In the early 1950's, widely voiced concerns that the treaty power was the Achilles' heel of the Constitution—that any and all constitutional limitations could be overridden via the international agreement route—spurred efforts to amend the Constitution. Justice Holmes' broad statements in Missouri v. Holland proved popular and frequently quoted sources for those anxious to demonstrate the substantiality of the threat to constitutional restrictions. Moreover, the fears that generated popular support for the Bricker Amendment were fed by occasional arguments made in American courts that relied on United Nations provisions.†

---

* Note however that, in terms of domestic effect, congressional legislation is on a par with treaties, so that a later act of Congress may supersede a prior treaty. See the Chinese Exclusion Case, 130 U.S. 581 (1889): "If the treaty operates by its own force, and relates to a subject within the power of Congress, it can be deemed in that particular only the equivalent of a legislative act, to be repealed or modified at the pleasure of Congress. In either case, the last expression of the sovereign will must control."

† The concern was that the UN Charter or resolutions by UN agencies (e.g., the Draft Covenant on Civil and Political Rights) might undercut American constitutional guarantees. For example, Art. 55 of the UN Charter states that the UN shall promote "universal respect for, and observance of, human rights and fundamental freedoms without distinction as to race, sex, language, or religion." In Sei Fujii v. State, 217 P.2d 481 (1950), a California District Court of Appeal held an alien land law invalid on the ground that the UN Charter was self-executing. The California Supreme Court, however, rested its affirmance of the result on the 14th Amendment, 242 P.2d 617 (1952), after finding that the UN Charter provision was "not self-executing."

Those anxieties produced Senator Bricker's constitutional amendment proposal. The version recommended by the Senate Judiciary Committee in 1953 included the statement, as Sec. 1: "A provision of a treaty which conflicts with this Constitution shall not be of any force or effect." And Sec. 2 added: "A treaty shall become effective as internal law in the United States only through legislation which would be valid in the absence of treaty." That second section in particular was directed against the doctrine of enlargement of congressional powers through treaties, as in Missouri v. Holland, as well as against the principle that treaties can be self-executing, as has been true since Ware v. Hylton, note 1 above. After extensive debates in the Senate in 1954, various modifications were offered. A substitute by Senator George of Georgia attracted a majority vote of 60 to 31 in February 1954 —just short of the required two-thirds. The George substitute included the statement: "A provision of a treaty or other international agreement which conflicts with this Constitution shall not be of any force or effect." Similar proposals during the next three years also failed.

4. *The reassurance of Reid v. Covert.* While the Bricker Amendment debate was still alive, the Supreme Court handed down REID v. COVERT, 354 U.S. 1 (1957); and Justice Black's majority opinion contained a passage directly responsive to some of the concerns voiced by the supporters of the Bricker Amendment. Did it give adequate reassurance on all of their concerns? Reid v. Covert, it will be recalled (as noted in chap. 2, above), dealt mainly with congressional power under Art. I, § 8, to provide for military jurisdiction over civilian dependents of American servicemen overseas. But in a passage relevant to the Bricker issue, the Court also rejected an argument that the law might be independently supportable because of the existence of an international agreement. Executive agreements * had been entered into with other countries permitting American military courts to exercise exclusive jurisdiction over offenses by American servicemen or their dependents overseas. The Government argued that the challenged statute could be sustained "as legislation which is necessary and proper to carry out the United States' obligations under the international agreements." Justice Black replied:

"The obvious and decisive answer to this, of course, is that no agreement with a foreign nation can confer power on the Congress, or on any other branch of Government, which is free from the restraints of the Constitution." He found nothing in the history or language of the Supremacy Clause, Art. VI, § 2, "which intimates that treaties and laws enacted pursuant to them do not have to comply with the provisions of the Constitution." Rather, he found it "clear that the reason treaties were not limited to those made in 'pursuance' of the Constitution [see the text of Art. VI] was so that agreements made by the United States under the Articles of Confederation [would] remain in effect." He added: "It would be manifestly contrary to the objectives of those who created the Constitution, as well as those who were responsible for the Bill of Rights—let alone alien to our entire constitutional history and tradition—to construe Article VI as permitting the United States to exercise power under an international agreement without

* On the distinction between executive agreements and treaties, see chap. 7 below.

observing constitutional prohibitions." Moreover, he found nothing contrary in Missouri v. Holland. Justice Black explained: "There the Court carefully noted that the treaty involved was not inconsistent with any specific provision of the Constitution." Missouri v. Holland had been solely concerned with the Tenth Amendment: "To the extent that the United States can validly make treaties, the people and the States have delegated their power to the National Government and the Tenth Amendment is no barrier." Justice Black's comments contributed greatly to putting to rest the concerns that treaties might be the basis for domestic action affecting individual rights beyond the bounds possible under other national powers.

THE FOREIGN AFFAIRS POWER OF CONGRESS: NATURE AND SOURCES

The national government's treaty power is explicitly granted in the Constitution. Is there also a foreign affairs power of Congress independent of authority to implement validly adopted treaties? Where in the Constitution is it found? Is it an inference from granted power? Or does it derive from extra-constitutional sources, as the Court has sometimes suggested? Is the notion of extra-constitutional sources of power consistent with the premises of constitutional government?

a. That there is a power in Congress to regulate foreign affairs has been repeatedly recognized by the Court. The source of the power remains unclear, however. For a modern statement of the power, see Perez v. Brownell, 356 U.S. 44, 57 (1958), sustaining a statutory provision regarding loss of citizenship: "Although there is in the Constitution no specific grant to Congress of power to enact legislation for the effective regulation of foreign affairs, there can be no doubt of the existence of this power in the law-making organ of the Nation. See United States v. Curtiss-Wright Export Corp., 299 U.S. 304, 318; Mackenzie v. Hare, 239 U.S. 299, 311–312. The States that joined together to form a single Nation and to create, through the Constitution, a Federal Government to conduct the affairs of that Nation must be held to have granted that Government the powers indispensable to its functioning effectively in the company of sovereign nations. The Government must be able not only to deal affirmatively with foreign nations, as it does through the maintenance of diplomatic relations with them and the protection of American citizens sojourning within their territories. It must also be able to reduce to a minimum the frictions that are unavoidable in a world of sovereigns sensitive in matters touching their dignity and interests."

b. In the Curtiss-Wright passage cited in Perez, Justice Sutherland's majority opinion had discussed, in 1936, the supposedly "fundamental" differences "between the powers of the federal government in respect to foreign or external affairs and those in respect of domestic or internal affairs." He insisted that the "two classes of power are different, both in respect of their origin and their nature. The broad statement that the federal government can exercise no powers except those specifically enumerated in the Constitution, and such implied powers as are necessary and proper to carry into effect the enumerated powers, is categorically true only in respect of our internal affairs. In that field, the primary purpose of the Constitution was to carve from the general mass of legislative powers *then possessed by*

the states such portions as it was thought desirable to vest in the federal government, leaving those not included in the enumeration still in the states. . . . That this doctrine applies only to powers which the states had, is self-evident. And since the states severally never possessed international powers, such powers could not have been carved from the mass of state powers but obviously were transmitted to the United States from some other source." His review of history led him to conclude that "the investment of the federal government with the powers of external sovereignty did not depend upon the affirmative grants of the Constitution. The powers to declare and wage war, to conclude peace, to make treaties, to maintain diplomatic relations with other sovereignties, if they had never been mentioned in the Constitution, would have vested in the federal government as necessary concomitants of nationality."

Justice Sutherland's Curtiss-Wright dictum is doubtful as history † and certainly represents an approach to national powers notably different from that applied to other powers since the days of McCulloch v. Maryland. Nevertheless, as Perez v. Brownell illustrates, it represents a pervasive thread in Court discussions of foreign affairs matters. See generally Henkin, Foreign Affairs and the Constitution (1972). (The Curtiss-Wright case is considered further in chap. 7 below.)

c. How extensive is the congressional power "to enact legislation for the effective regulation of foreign affairs"? Is it limited to matters that are generally the subject matter of foreign relations? Can the Court reexamine the good faith of—or factual basis for—a congressional assertion that a problem *is* a foreign affairs concern? Is this congressional power subject to any greater federalistic limits than the Geofroy v. Riggs "properly the subject of negotiation" criterion regarding treaties, noted above? See Henkin, "The Treaty Makers and the Law Makers: The Law of the Land and Foreign Relations," 107 U.Pa.L.Rev. 903 (1959).

d. The national concern with foreign affairs is a powerful one even though its bases are not fully spelled out in the Constitution. It supports not only congressional action; its mere existence, though unexercised, may preclude state action as well. (Compare the impact of the unexercised, "dormant" commerce power on state action, chap. 5 below.) The impact of the national power as a restraint on state authority is illustrated by Zschernig v. Miller, 389 U.S. 429 (1968), where the Court barred application of a state alien inheritance law because it intruded "into the field of foreign affairs which the Constitution entrusts to the President and the Congress."

† See Lofgren, "United States v. Curtiss-Wright Corporation: An Historical Reassessment," 83 Yale L.J. 1 (1973).

Chapter 5

STATE REGULATION AND THE NATIONAL ECONOMY: CONSTITUTIONAL LIMITS AND CONGRESSIONAL ORDERING

Scope Note. In accordance with the plan sketched at the outset of Part II, attention now turns to the impact of the federal system's division of powers on the scope of state authority. Chapters 2, 3, and 4 examined the scope of *national* powers as limited by concerns for state autonomy; the next two chapters explore limits on *state* powers that flow from national concerns. Once again, the pervasive questions are the sources and adequacy of constitutional limitations: Do the constraints arise from text? From history? From inferences based on the structure of the Constitution? From society's values—or those of the Justices? Once again, the recurrent concern is the adequacy of the articulations and implementations of constitutional values. On what basis, and to what extent, do the grants of enumerated powers to the national government, and the exercises of those powers, curtail state authority? This chapter explores those problems in the context of the commerce power; but similar restrictions on state authority arise in connection with other national powers as well.*

The commerce barrier to state action arises in two—frequently overlapping—situations. In the first, Congress has been wholly silent: it has taken no action, express or implied, indicating its own policy on a given subject matter. In that situation, the objection to state authority rests entirely on the "dormant" commerce clause of Art. I, § 8—on the unexercised commerce power itself, and on the free trade value it symbolizes. In the second situation, Congress *has* exercised the commerce power, *has* indicated its policy, and the challenge to state action rests on valid, "supreme" national legislation which compels inconsistent state action to give way—by virtue not only of the exercise of the commerce power under Art. I, § 8, but also because of the effect of the Supremacy Clause in Art. VI. These materials are designed to draw attention to the appropriate roles of Court and Congress in furthering commerce clause values; on the source and scope of commerce power-based barriers to state action; and on the extent of—and justifications for—congressional authority to modify and override Court-discovered obstacles to state action.

---

* See, e.g., as to bankruptcy, Sturges v. Crowinshield, 4 Wheat. 122 (1819), and Perez v. Campbell, 402 U.S. 637 (1971); as to foreign affairs, Zschernig v. Miller, 389 U.S. 429 (1968); as to copyright, Goldstein v. California, 412 U.S. 546 (1973); as to patents, Kewanee Oil Co. v. Bicron Corp., 416 U.S. 470 (1974).

SECTION 1. STATE REGULATION AND THE DORMANT COMMERCE CLAUSE

Introduction. 1. *The vision and the achievement.* In the cases in this section, state legislation is challenged on the basis of the dormant commerce power. In these cases, Congress has not acted; instead, the Court has taken it upon itself to implement the values of the grant of power to Congress in the commerce clause by restricting state impingements on interstate commerce. What is the justification for the Court's assumption of that task? How effectively has the Court performed it? Has its performance matched its aspirations?

The Court has not always been articulate, the Justices not always in agreement, about the governing values in the hundreds of cases in which state laws have been challenged as contravening the commerce clause. But the aspirations that have guided the Court are discernible in many of the opinions. And few Justices have stated those aspirations more eloquently than Justice Robert H. Jackson. H. P. Hood & Sons v. DuMond, 336 U.S. 525 (1949) (sec. 1D below), provided the occasion for one of his most notable statements about the free trade goals of the commerce clause. The passages which follow are from Justice Jackson's opinion for the Court in that case: they offer useful introductory comments on the Court's aims in commerce clause litigation; and they help focus on the sources of the Court's elaboration of content for the sparse words of the commerce clause as a restriction on state power. In examining the materials below, then, consider whether Justice Jackson stated the values and the criteria adequately and persuasively: How well do (and can) Court decisions "give reality" to this "vision of the Founders"? Justice Jackson said in Hood:

"The Commerce Clause is one of the most prolific sources of national power and an equally prolific source of conflict with legislation of the state. While the Constitution vests in Congress the power to regulate commerce among the states, it does not say what the states may or may not do in the absence of congressional action, nor how to draw the line between what is and what is not commerce among the states. Perhaps even more than by interpretation of its written word, this Court has advanced the solidarity and prosperity of this Nation by the meaning it has given to these great silences of the Constitution. . . .

"[The] principle that our economic unit is the Nation, which alone has the gamut of powers necessary to control of the economy, including the vital power of erecting customs barriers against foreign competition, has as its corollary that the states are not separable economic units. . . . The material success that has come to inhabitants of the states which make up this federal free trade unit has been the most impressive in the history of commerce, but the established interdependence of the states only emphasizes the necessity of protecting interstate movement of goods against local burdens and repressions. . . .

"[The] distinction between the power of the State to shelter its people from menaces to their health or safety and from fraud, even when those dan-

gers emanate from interstate commerce, and its lack of power to retard, burden or constrict the flow of such commerce for their economic advantage, is one deeply rooted in both our history and our law. . . . This Court consistently has rebuffed attempts of states to advance their own commercial interests by curtailing the movement of articles of commerce, either into or out of the state, while generally supporting their right to impose even burdensome regulations in the interest of local health and safety. . . .

"Our system, fostered by the Commerce Clause, is that every farmer and every craftsman shall be encouraged to produce by the certainty that he will have free access to every market in the Nation, that no home embargoes will withhold his exports, and no foreign state will by customs duties or regulations exclude them. Likewise, every consumer may look to the free competition from every producing area in the Nation to protect him from exploitation by any. Such was the vision of the Founders; such has been the doctrine of this Court which has given it reality. . . ."

2. *The source of the vision.* Justice Jackson states the aims of the commerce clause with force and elegance; and his summary reflects the themes of many other opinions. But what are the sources of the values articulated in Hood? How can the Court justify expending so much of its energy over the last century and a half in implementing values such as these? It is hardly a task explicitly given to the Court by the Constitution. The Constitution does indeed, as in Art. I, § 10, impose limitations on the state— e. g., with respect to imposing duties on imports or exports. But there is no textual barrier to state impingement on interstate commerce. For that limitation, the Court has drawn not an any overt restraint on state power, but rather on the grant of power to Congress in Art. I, § 8, to regulate interstate commerce. Into that affirmative grant of power the Court has read self-executing limits on state legislation when Congress has not acted. To justify these implications from the commerce clause, the Court has relied largely on history—on perceived historical assumptions rather than explicit historical debates—and on inferences from the federal structure established by the Constitution. The additional passages from Justice Jackson's opinion in the Hood case which follow reflect some of these sources of the Court's vision in commerce clause litigation. Do these historical data and this view of structural relationships between nation and state justify the limits on state power announced in the cases that follow? Are the limits adequately responsive to that history and those structural inferences? Justice Jackson summarized the history as follows:

"When victory relieved the Colonies from the pressure for solidarity that war had exerted, a drift toward anarchy and commercial warfare between states began. '. . . each State would legislate according to its estimate of its own interests, the importance of its own products, and the local advantages or disadvantages of its position in a political or commercial view.' This came 'to threaten at once the peace and safety of the Union.' Story, The Constitution, §§ 259, 260. See Fiske, The Critical Period of American History, 144; Warren, The Making of the Constitution, 567. The sole purpose for which Virginia initiated the movement which ultimately produced the Constitution was 'to take into consideration the trade of the United States; to examine the relative situations and trade of the said States;

to consider how far a uniform system in their commercial regulations may be necessary to their common interest and their permanent harmony' and for that purpose the General Assembly of Virginia in January of 1786 named commissioners and proposed their meeting with those from other states. Documents, Formation of the Union, H.R. Doc. No. 398, 12 H. Docs., 69th Cong., 1st Sess., p. 38.

"The desire of the Forefathers to federalize regulation of foreign and interstate commerce stands in sharp contrast to their jealous preservation of the state's power over its internal affairs. No other federal power was so universally assumed to be necessary, no other state power was so readily relinquished. There was no desire to authorize federal interference with social conditions or legal institutions of the states. Even the Bill of Rights amendments were framed only as a limitation upon the powers of Congress. The states were quite content with their several and diverse controls over most matters, but, as Madison has indicated, 'want of a general power over Commerce led to an exercise of this power separately, by the States, wch [sic] not only proved abortive, but engendered rival, conflicting and angry regulations.' 3 Farrand, Records of the Federal Convention, 547.

"The necessity of centralized regulation of commerce among the states was so obvious and so fully recognized that the few words of the Commerce Clause were little illuminated by debate. But the significance of the clause was not lost and its effect was immediate and salutary. We are told by so responsible an authority as Mr. Jefferson's first appointee to this Court [Justice William Johnson] that 'there was not a State in the Union, in which there did not, at that time, exist a variety of commercial regulations; concerning which it is too much to suppose, that the whole ground covered by those regulations was immediately assumed by actual legislation, under the authority of the Union. But where was the existing statute on this subject, that a State attempted to execute? or by what State was it ever thought necessary to repeal those statutes? By common consent, those laws dropped lifeless from their statute books, for want of the sustaining power, that had been relinquished to Congress.' Gibbons v. Ogden, 9 Wheat. 1, concurring opinion at 226."

A. EARLY DEVELOPMENTS

GIBBONS v. OGDEN

9 Wheat. 1, 6 L.Ed. 23 (1824).

[In the first part of his opinion in this case challenging New York's steamboat monopoly grant, Chief Justice Marshall considered the reach of the congressional commerce power into local affairs. (See chap. 3, sec. 1, above.) In the rest of his opinion, printed here, Marshall discussed the impact of the commerce clause, and of national legislation based upon it, on state authority.]

[I]t has been urged with great earnestness, that although the power of Congress to regulate commerce with foreign nations, and among the serv-

eral States, be co-extensive with the subject itself, and have no other limits than are prescribed in the constitution, yet the States may severally exercise the same power, within their respective jurisdictions. In support of this argument, it is said, that they possessed it as an inseparable attribute of sovereignty, before the formation of the constitution, and still retain it, except so far as they have surrendered it by that instrument; that this principle results from the nature of the government, and is secured by the tenth amendment; that an affirmative grant of power is not exclusive, unless in its own nature it be such that the continued exercise of it by the former possessor is inconsistent with the grant, and that this is not of that description.

The appellant, conceding these postulates, except the last, contends that full power to regulate a particular subject, implies the whole power, and leaves no residuum; that a grant of the whole is incompatible with the existence of a right in another to any part of it. . . .

The grant of the power to lay and collect taxes is, like the power to regulate commerce, made in general terms, and has never been understood to interfere with the exercise of the same power by the States; and hence has been drawn an argument which has been applied to the question under consideration. But the two grants are not, it is conceived, similar in their terms or their nature. Although many of the powers formerly exercised by the States, are transferred to the government of the Union, yet the State governments remain, and constitute a most important part of our system. The power of taxation is indispensable to their existence, and is a power which, in its own nature, is capable of residing in, and being exercised by, different authorities at the same time. [A] power in one to take what is necessary for certain purposes, is not, in its nature, incompatible with a power in another to take what is necessary for other purposes. . . . When, then, each government exercises the power of taxation, neither is exercising the power of the other. But, when a State proceeds to regulate commerce with foreign nations, or among the several States, it is exercising the very power that is granted to Congress, and is doing the very thing which Congress, is authorized to do. There is no analogy, then, between the power of taxation and the power of regulating commerce. . . .

But, the inspection laws are said to be regulations of commerce, and are certainly recognized in the constitution, as being passed in the exercise of a power remaining with the States.

That inspection laws may have a remote and considerable influence on commerce, will not be denied; but that a power to regulate commerce is the source from which the right to pass them is derived, cannot be admitted. The object of inspection laws, is to improve the quality of articles produced by the labour of a country; to fit them for exportation; or, it may be, for domestic use. They act upon the subject before it becomes an article of foreign commerce, or of commerce among the States, and prepare it for that purpose. They form a portion of that immense mass of legislation, which embraces every thing within the territory of a State, not surrendered to the general government: all which can be most advantageously exercised by the States themselves. Inspection laws, quarantine laws, health laws of every description, as well as laws for regulating the internal commerce of

a State, and those which respect turnpike roads, ferries, &c., are component parts of this mass.

No direct general power over these objects is granted to Congress; and, consequently, they remain subject to State legislation. If the legislative power of the Union can reach them, it must be for national purposes; it must be where the power is expressly given for a special purpose, or is clearly incidental to some power which is expressly given. It is obvious, that the government of the Union, in the exercise of its express powers, that, for example, of regulating commerce with foreign nations and among the States, may use means that may also be employed by a State, in the exercise of its acknowledged powers; that, for example, of regulating commerce within the State. If Congress license vessels to sail from one port to another, in the same State, the act is supposed to be, necessarily, incidental to the power expressly granted to Congress, and implies no claim of a direct power to regulate the purely internal commerce of a State, or to act directly on its system of police. So, if a State, in passing laws on subjects acknowledged to be within its control, and with a view to those subjects, shall adopt a measure of the same character with one which Congress may adopt, it does not derive its authority from the particular power which has been granted, but from some other, which remains with the State, and may be executed by the same means. All experience shows, that the same measures, or measures scarcely distinguishable from each other, may flow from distinct powers; but this does not prove that the powers themselves are identical. Although the means used in their execution may sometimes approach each other so nearly as to be confounded, there are other situations in which they are sufficiently distinct to establish their individuality.

In our complex system, presenting the rare and difficult scheme of one general government, whose action extends over the whole, but which possesses only certain enumerated powers; and of numerous State governments, which retain and exercise all powers not delegated to the Union, contests respecting power must arise. Were it even otherwise, the measures taken by the respective governments to execute their acknowledged powers, would often be of the same description, and might, sometimes, interfere. This, however, does not prove that the one is exercising, or has a right to exercise, the powers of the other. . . .

It has been contended by counsel for the appellant, that, as the word "to regulate" implies in its nature, full power over the thing to be regulated, it excludes, necessarily, the action of all others that would perform the same operation on the same thing. That regulation is designed for the entire result, applying in those parts which remain as they were, as well as to those which are altered. It produces a uniform whole, which is as much disturbed and deranged by changing what the regulating power designs to leave untouched, as that on which it has operated.

There is great force in this argument, and the Court is not satisfied that it has been refuted.

Since, however, in exercising the power of regulating their own purely internal affairs, whether of trading or police, the States may sometimes enact laws, the validity of which depends on their interfering with, and being contrary to, an act of Congress passed in pursuance of the constitution, the Court

will enter upon the inquiry, whether the laws of New-York . . . have, in their application to this case, come into collision with an act of Congress, and deprived a citizen of a right to which that act entitles him. Should this collision exist, it will be immaterial whether those laws were passed in virtue of a concurrent power "to regulate commerce with foreign nations and among the several States," or in virtue of a power to regulate their domestic trade and police. In one case and the other, the acts of New-York must yield to the law of Congress; and the decision sustaining the privilege they confer, against a right given by a law of the Union, must be erroneous.

[Chief Justice Marshall found the New York steamboat monopoly grant to be in conflict with the federal laws licensing those engaged in the coastal trade. He thus disagreed with Chancellor Kent's view in the state court that the coasting license was merely intended to immunize American ships from the burdens imposed on foreign shipping. The Supreme Court decree accordingly reversed the decision below. As a result, Gibbons, the federal licensee, prevailed, and the injunction proceeding brought by Ogden, the holder of the New York monopoly, was dismissed.*]

[Justice JOHNSON—President Jefferson's first appointee to the Court, see Morgan, Justice William Johnson: The First Dissenter (1954)—submitted a concurring opinion which proved more nationalistic than Marshall's. (Recall Justice Jackson's quotation from the Johnson concurrence in the passages from the Hood case above.) Justice Johnson did not agree with Marshall's reliance on the federal coasting license law. Instead, he rested on the ground suggested but not embraced by Marshall: the exclusiveness of the national commerce power. Note, however, that with Johnson, as with Marshall, denial to the states of any power to regulate interstate commerce, because of limits implied from the dormant commerce clause, did not mean total state inability to enact laws with some effect on commerce. For Johnson, as for Marshall, the "purpose" of state legislation was a critical criterion in distinguishing between permissible and impermissible state laws. On the "exclusive" commerce power, Johnson argued that state power over commerce "amounts to nothing more than a power to limit and restrain it at pleasure. And since the power to prescribe the limits to its freedom, necessarily implies the power to determine what shall remain unrestrained, it follows, that the power must be exclusive; it can reside but in one potentate; and hence, the grant of this power carries with it the whole subject, leaving nothing for the State to act upon." But he also said: "It is no objection to the existence of distinct, substantive powers, that, in their application, they bear upon the same subject. The same bale of goods, the same cask of provisions, or the same ship, that may be the subject of commercial regulation, may also be the vehicle of disease. And the health laws that require them to be stopped and ventilated, are no more intended as regulations on commerce, than the laws which permit their importation, are

---

* See generally, Campbell, "Chancellor Kent, Chief Justice Marshall and the Steamboat Cases," 25 Syracuse L.Rev. 497 (1974); Baxter, The Steamboat Monopoly (1972); and Mann, "The Marshall Court: Nationalization of Private Rights and Personal Liberty from the Authority of the Commerce Clause," 38 Ind.L.J. 117 (1963). See also Abel, "Commercial Regulation Before Gibbons v. Ogden: Interstate Transportation Facilities," 25 N.C.L. Rev. 121 (1947), as well as two related articles by Abel, 14 Brooklyn L.Rev. 215 (1948), and 18 Miss.L.J. 335 (1947).

intended to innoculate the community with disease. Their different purposes mark the distinction between the powers brought into action; and while frankly exercised, they can produce no serious collision. . . . It would be in vain to deny the possibility of a clashing and collision between the measures of the two governments. The line cannot be drawn with sufficient distinctness between the municipal powers of the one, and the commercial powers of the other. In some points they meet and blend so as scarcely to admit of separation. . . . Wherever the powers of the respective governments are frankly exercised, with a distinct view to the ends of such powers, they may act upon the same object, or use the same means, and yet the powers be kept perfectly distinct. A resort to the same means, therefore, is no argument to prove the identity of their respective powers."]

WILLSON v. THE BLACK BIRD CREEK MARSH CO.

2 Pet. 245, 7 L.Ed. 412 (1829).

Error to the High Court of Errors and Appeals of the State of Delaware.

[The Company was authorized by a Delaware law to build a dam in Black Bird Creek—which flowed into the Delaware River—and also to "bank" the adjoining "marsh and low ground." The dam obstructed navigation of the creek. Willson and others were owners of a sloop licensed under the federal navigation laws. The sloop "broke and injured" the Company's dam in order to pass through the creek. The Company successfully sued for damages; the state courts rejected Willson's defense that the law authorizing the dam violated the commerce clause.

[William Wirt—who, with Daniel Webster, had argued against New York's power to establish the steamboat monopoly in Gibbons v. Ogden—was counsel for the Company. He described the creek as "one of those sluggish reptile streams, that do not run but creep, and which, wherever it passes, spreads its venom, and destroys the health of all those who inhabit its marshes." (Wirt wrote poetry and novels as an avocation.) He argued: "[C]an it be asserted, that a law authorising the erection of a dam, and the formation of banks which will draw off the pestilence, and give to those who have before suffered from disease, health and vigour, is unconstitutional? The power given by the constitution to congress to regulate commerce, may not be exercised to prevent such measures; and there has been no legislation by congress under the constitution, with which the proceedings of the defendants under the law of Delaware have interfered."]

Mr. Chief Justice MARSHALL delivered the opinion of the Court.

. . .

The act of assembly by which the plaintiffs were authorized to construct their dam, shows plainly that this is one of those many creeks, passing through a deep level marsh adjoining the Delaware, up which the tide flows for some distance. The value of the property on its banks must be enhanced by excluding the water from the marsh, and the health of the inhabitants probably improved. Measures calculated to produce these objects, provided they do not come into collision with the powers of the general government, are undoubtedly within those which are reserved to the states. But the

measure authorised by this act stops a navigable creek, and must be supposed to abridge the rights of those who have been accustomed to use it.
. . . .

The counsel for the plaintiffs in error insist that it comes in conflict with the power of the United States "to regulate commerce with foreign nations and among the several states."

If congress had passed any act which bore upon the case; any act in execution of the power to regulate commerce, the object of which was to control state legislation over those small navigable creeks into which the tide flows, and which abound throughout the lower country of the middle and southern states; we should feel not much difficulty in saying that a state law coming in conflict with such act would be void. But congress has passed no such act. The repugnancy of the law of Delaware to the constitution is placed entirely on its repugnancy to the power to regulate commerce with foreign nations and among the several states; a power which has not been so exercised as to affect the question.

We do not think that the act empowering the Black Bird Creek Marsh Company to place a dam across the creek, can, under all the circumstances of the case, be considered as repugnant to the power to regulate commerce in its dormant state, or as being in conflict with any law passed on the subject.

There is no error, and the judgment is affirmed.

THE MARSHALL COURT DECISIONS AND THE TANEY COURT GROPINGS BEFORE COOLEY

1. *The Marshall legacy: "Exclusive" commerce power or "tentative idea"?* Gibbons v. Ogden and the Black Bird case were Marshall's only opportunities to write about the impact of the commerce clause on state regulatory authority.* It is sometimes said that Marshall viewed the commerce power as exclusive. Is that borne out by his opinions? To be sure, Marshall in Gibbons v. Ogden noted the "great force" in the argument for exclusiveness and said that he was "not satisfied that it has been refuted." But he rested ultimately on the Supremacy Clause; and his suggestion of a possibly exclusive national commerce power coexisted with a recognition of state power to enact legislation which might affect commerce—"[i]nspection laws, quarantine laws, health laws of every description." The "objects" of legislation were apparently significant to him, as they were to Justice Johnson.

Given Marshall's inclination toward that limited variety of "exclusiveness" in Gibbons, how is his brief opinion in Black Bird explainable? Was it a retreat from exclusiveness? Was it based on the notion that the Delaware law was a "health" law rather than a "commercial" regulation? Was it an unarticulated move toward a variety of "balancing" of state and national interests—a sustaining of the state law because the need for it was great and the burden it imposed on interstate commerce was small? Consider the soundness of Professor Frankfurter's observation, before he was appointed

---

* Between Gibbon v. Ogden and the Black Bird case, Marshall also wrote an extensive opinion on state power to *tax* foreign commerce. Brown v. Maryland, 12 Wheat. 419 (1827).

to the Court: "Had it been given to Marshall to sharpen his coordinate ideas of the exclusive federal commerce power and the reserved state police power through the refining process of litigation, a fruitful analysis might well have eventuated. But employed by minds less sophisticated, less sensitive to the exigencies of government, Marshall's tentative ideas were turned into obscuring formulas whereby issues were confused and evaded." [†] Do the Taney Court's early attempts to formulate criteria in this area, reviewed in the next note, support Professor Frankfurter's assessment that Marshall's "tentative ideas" were turned into "obscuring formulas"?

Marshall's approach has occasionally been deprecated as absorption in "abstract criteria." Consider, in examining the subsequent developments, whether the early Taney Court decisions, the Cooley case, and such modern cases as Southern Pacific Co. v. Arizona (sec. 1B below) substituted improved, more "realistic" standards for Marshall's "abstract criteria." In Gibbons, Marshall emphasized the purpose of state regulation in distinguishing permissible "police" regulations from impermissible "commerce" regulations. Is the "purpose" emphasis used—or useful—in the post-Marshall cases?

2. *The early Taney Court's search.* For a decade and a half after John Marshall's death in 1835—during the first half of the tenure of Marshall's successor, Roger Brooke Taney—the Court groped for formulations with little clarity or agreement. Some of the Justices sought to follow what they perceived to be Marshall's guidance: state regulations of "commerce" were prohibited, but "police" regulations were constitutional. Chief Justice Taney himself took a position at the polar extreme from the exclusiveness of the commerce power. As his opinion in the License Cases, note 2c below, illustrates, *no* implied prohibitions from the dormant commerce clause were acceptable to Taney: to him, state regulations of commerce were valid "unless they come in conflict with a law of Congress." With the Cooley decision in 1851, a new majority approach evolved at last—an approach that the modern Court has frequently asserted to be the still governing one. Before turning to the Cooley case, consider the following sampling of the search for standards in the years preceding Cooley.

a. *The Miln case.* In Mayor of the City of New York v. Miln, 11 Pet. 102 (1837), the Court sustained a New York statute requiring the master of a vessel arriving in the port of New York from any point out of the state to report the names, residences, etc., of the passengers. The Court found the law to be "not a regulation of commerce, but of police," and accordingly found it unnecessary to examine the question whether the power to regulate commerce "be or be not exclusive of the States." Justice Story delivered a dissenting opinion in which he declared the act of New York "unconstitutional and void," and added: "In this opinion I have the consolation to know that I had the entire concurrence, upon the same grounds, of that great constitutional jurist, the late Mr. Chief Justice Marshall. Having heard the former arguments, his deliberate opinion was, that the act of New York was unconstitutional."

[†] Frankfurter, The Commerce Clause
Under Marshall, Taney and Waite
(1937), 31.

b. *The Passenger Cases.* The Passenger Cases, 7 How. 283 (1849), invalidated two state laws. A New York statute imposed on the masters of ships coming from foreign or other state ports a tax for each passenger, the revenue to be used to defray the costs of examination of passengers for contagious diseases and to maintain a hospital for the treatment of those found to be diseased. A similar tax was imposed by a Massachusetts statute applicable to aliens, with the further requirement that the master should post a bond in the amount of $1000 for each alien likely to become a public charge. Both statutes were held "repugnant to the Constitution and laws of the United States, and therefore void." Five Justices concurred in the result and four (including Chief Justice Taney) dissented. There was no opinion by the Court, but a series of individual opinions.*

c. *The License Cases.* In one of the three cases decided together as the License Cases, 5 How. 504 (1847), plaintiffs in error purchased gin in Boston and sold it, in the original cask, in Dover, New Hampshire, in violation of a tate law. On appeal from convictions in the state courts, the judgments were affirmed by a unanimous Court, but without a majority concurring in any of the six opinions. Chief Justice Taney announced the judgments and delivered an opinion in which he said: "It is well known that upon this subject a difference of opinion has existed, and still exists, among the members of this court. But with every respect for the opinion of my brethren with whom I do not agree, it appears to me to be very clear, that the mere grant of power to the general government cannot, upon any just principles of construction, be construed to be an absolute prohibition to the exercise of any power over the same subject by the States. The controlling and supreme power over commerce with foreign nations and the several States is undoubtedly conferred upon Congress. Yet, in my judgment, the State may nevertheless, for the safety or convenience of trade, or for the protection of the health of its citizens, make regulations of commerce for its own ports and harbours, and for its own territory; and such regulations are valid unless they come in conflict with a law of Congress."

---

* A generation later, the problem came again before the Court in Henderson v. Mayor of New York, 92 U.S. 259 (1876). The New York law had been changed so as to require that the carrier provide a bond for each passenger landed to indemnify the local community for any expense for relief, with an option to pay a fixed sum for each passenger. The requirement was held unconstitutional. Justice Miller rejected the argument that the law could be justified under the police power as protection against "pauperism" and "diseases" : "Nothing is gained in the argument by calling it the police power. [W]henever the statute of a State invades the domain of legislation which belongs exclusively to the Congress of the United States, it is void, no matter under what class of powers it may fall, or how closely allied to powers conceded to belong to the States." He argued that "Congress can more appropriately and with more acceptance" regulate the area: "[B]y providing a system of laws in these matters, applicable to all ports and to all vessels, a serious question, which has long been matter of contest and complaint, may be effectually and satisfactorily settled."

COOLEY v. BOARD OF WARDENS OF THE PORT
OF PHILADELPHIA

12 How. 299, 13 L.Ed. 996 (1851).

Error to the Supreme Court of Pennsylvania.

[A Pennsylvania law of 1803 required ships entering or leaving the port of Philadelphia to engage a local pilot to guide them through the harbor. For failure to comply, the law imposed a penalty of half the pilotage fee, payable to the Board for a fund for superannuated pilots and their dependents. Cooley was held liable for the penalty, as consignee of two ships engaged in the coastal trade which had left the port without a local pilot.]

Mr. Justice CURTIS delivered the opinion of the Court. . . .

We think this particular regulation concerning half-pilotage fees, is an appropriate part of a general system of regulations of this subject. [The fitness of such provisions], as part of a system of pilotage, in many places, may be inferred from their existence in so many different States and countries. [The laws] rest upon the propriety of securing lives and property exposed to the perils of a dangerous navigation, by taking on board a person peculiarly skilled to encounter or avoid them; upon the policy of discouraging the commanders of vessels from refusing to receive such persons on board at the proper times and places; and upon the expediency, and even intrinsic justice, of not suffering those who have incurred labor, and expense, and danger, to place themselves in a position to render important service generally necessary, to go unrewarded, because the master of a particular vessel either rashly refuses their proffered assistance, or, contrary to the general experience, does not need it. . . .

[T]he regulation of the qualifications of pilots, of the modes and times of offering and rendering their services, of the responsibilities which shall rest upon them, of the powers they shall possess, of the compensation they may demand, and of the penalties by which their rights and duties may be enforced, do constitute regulations of navigation, and consequently of commerce, within the just meaning of [Art. I, § 8,] of the Constitution. . . .

It becomes necessary, therefore, to consider whether this law of Pennsylvania, being a regulation of commerce, is valid [in view of the grant of the commerce power to Congress].

The act of Congress of the 7th of August, 1789, sect. 4, is as follows:

"That all pilots in the bays, inlets, rivers, harbors, and ports of the United States shall continue to be regulated in conformity with the existing laws of the States, respectively, wherein such pilots may be, or with such laws as the States may respectively hereafter enact for the purpose, until further legislative provision shall be made by Congress."

If the law of Pennsylvania, now in question, had been in existence at the date of this act of Congress, we might hold it to have been adopted by Congress, and thus made a law of the United States, and so valid. Because this act does, in effect, give the force of an act of Congress, to the then existing State laws on this subject, so long as they should continue unrepealed by the State which enacted them.

But the law on which these actions were founded was not enacted till 1803. What effect then can be attributed to so much of the act of 1789, as declares, that pilots shall continue to be regulated in conformity, "with such laws as the States may respectively hereafter enact for the purpose, until further legislative provision shall be made by Congress"?

If the States were divested of the power to legislate on this subject by the grant of the commercial power to Congress, it is plain this act could not confer upon them power thus to legislate. If the Constitution excluded the States from making any law regulating commerce, certainly Congress cannot regrant, or in any manner reconvey to the States that power. And yet this act of 1789 gives its sanction only to laws enacted by the States. This necessarily implies a constitutional power to legislate; for only a rule created by the sovereign power of a State acting in its legislative capacity, can be deemed a law, enacted by a State; and if the State has so limited its sovereign power that it no longer extends to a particular subject, manifestly it cannot, in any proper sense, be said to enact laws thereon. Entertaining these views we are brought directly and unavoidably to the consideration of the question, whether the grant of the commercial power to Congress, did per se deprive the States of all power to regulate pilots. This question has never been decided by this court, nor, in our judgment, has any case depending upon all the considerations which must govern this one, come before this court. . . .

The diversities of opinion, therefore, which have existed on this subject, have arisen from the different views taken of the nature of this power. But when the nature of a power like this is spoken of, when it is said that the nature of the power requires that it should be exercised exclusively by Congress, it must be intended to refer to the subjects of that power, and to say they are of such a nature as to require exclusive legislation by Congress. Now the power to regulate commerce, embraces a vast field, containing not only many, but exceedingly various subjects, quite unlike in their nature; some imperatively demanding a single uniform rule, operating equally on the commerce of the United States in every port; and some, like the subject now in question, as imperatively demanding that diversity, which alone can meet the local necessities of navigation.

Either absolutely to affirm, or deny that the nature of this power requires exclusive legislation by Congress, is to lose sight of the nature of the subjects of this power, and to assert concerning all of them, what is really applicable but to a part. Whatever subjects of this power are in their nature national, or admit only of one uniform system, or plan of regulation, may justly be said to be of such a nature as to require exclusive legislation by Congress. That this cannot be affirmed of laws for the regulation of pilots and pilotage is plain. The act of 1789 contains a clear and authoritative declaration by the first Congress, that the nature of this subject is such, that until Congress should find it necessary to exert its power, it should be left to the legislation of the States; that it is local and not national; that it is likely to be the best provided for, not by one system, or plan of regulations, but by as many as the legislative discretion of the several States should deem applicable to the local peculiarities of the ports within their limits.

Viewed in this light, so much of this act of 1789 as declares that pilots shall continue to be regulated "by such laws as the States may respectively

hereafter enact for that purpose," instead of being held to be inoperative, as an attempt to confer on the States a power to legislate, of which the Constitution had deprived them, is allowed an appropriate and important signification. It manifests the understanding of Congress, at the outset of the government, that the nature of this subject is not such as to require its exclusive legislation. The practice of the States, and of the national government, has been in conformity with this declaration, from the origin of the national government to this time; and the nature of the subject when examined, is such as to leave no doubt of the superior fitness and propriety, not to say the absolute necessity, of different systems of regulation, drawn from local knowledge and experience, and conformed to local wants. How then can we say, that by the mere grant of power to regulate commerce, the States are deprived of all the power to legislate on this subject, because from the nature of the power the legislation of Congress must be exclusive. This would be to affirm that the nature of the power is in any case, something different from the nature of the subject to which, in such case, the power extends, and that the nature of the power necessarily demands, in all cases, exclusive legislation by Congress, while the nature of one of the subjects of that power, not only does not require such exclusive legislation, but may be best provided for by many different systems enacted by the States, in conformity with the circumstances of the ports within their limits. In construing an instrument designed for the formation of a government, and in determining the extent of one of its important grants of power to legislate, we can make no such distinction between the nature of the power and the nature of the subject on which that power was intended practically to operate, nor consider the grant more extensive by affirming of the power, what is not true of its subject now in question.

It is the opinion of a majority of the court that the mere grant to Congress of the power to regulate commerce, did not deprive the States of power to regulate pilots, and that although Congress has legislated on this subject, its legislation manifests an intention, with a single exception, not to regulate this subject, but to leave its regulation to the several states. To these precise questions, which are all we are called on to decide, this opinion must be understood to be confined. . . .

We have not adverted to the practical consequences of holding that the States possess no power to legislate for the regulation of pilots, though in our apprehension these would be of the most serious importance. For more than sixty years this subject has been acted on by the States . . .. Nor would the mischief be limited to the past. If Congress were now to pass a law adopting the existing State laws, if enacted without authority, and in violation of the Constitution, it would seem to us to be a new and questionable mode of legislation. . . .

Affirmed.

Mr. Justice McLEAN [dissenting]. . . .

That a State may regulate foreign commerce, or commerce among the states, is a doctrine which has been advanced by individual judges of this court; but never before, I believe, has such a power been sanctioned by the decision of this court. . . .

I think the charge of half-pilotage is correct under the circumstances, and I only object to the power of the state to pass the law. Congress, to whom the subject peculiarly belongs, should have been applied to, and no doubt it would have adopted the act of the State.

Mr. Justice DANIEL [concurring in the result]. . . . The power and the practice of enacting pilot-laws, which has been exercised by the States from the very origin of their existence, although it is one in some degree connected with commercial intercourse, does not come essentially and regularly within that power of commercial regulation vested by the Constitution in Congress . . . . The true question here is, whether the power to enact pilot laws [is] most appropriate and necessary to the State or the federal governments. It being conceded that this power has been exercised by the States from their very dawn of existence; that it can be practically and beneficially applied by the local authorities only; it being conceded, as it must be, that the power to pass pilot laws, as such, has not been in any express terms delegated to Congress, and does not necessarily conflict with the right to establish commercial regulations, I am forced to conclude that this is an original and inherent power in the States, and not one to be merely tolerated, or held subject to the sanction of the federal government. [Mr. Justice WAYNE also dissented, without opinion.]

COOLEY AND THE MODERN APPROACH

The Cooley decision is frequently cited as an authoritative guide in modern decisions. But what *is* the guidance offered by Cooley? And does the modern Court truly follow that guidance? Note 1 focuses on the first of these questions; note 2 introduces the problems raised by the second—problems which are pursued more fully in the ensuing materials in this section.

1. *The doctrine—and problems—of Cooley.* Cooley steers a middle course between the polar positions suggested in earlier opinions. It rejects the view that the congressional commerce power is exclusive, that the states lack all power to regulate commerce. It also rejects the view that the commerce clause, in the absence of national legislation, imposes no limits on states at all. It recognizes *some* concurrent state regulatory power over commerce. Was the Court justified—by text, history or structure of the Constitution—in rejecting the polar positions and adopting that middle course? And what *was* that middle course?

Cooley purports to focus on the "subject" of regulation as determinative: some subjects are "of such a nature" as to require "a single uniform rule" by Congress; others are local, "imperatively demanding that diversity, which alone can meet the local necessities." But how are the "subjects" to be distinguished? What is the "subject" found to be "local and not national" in Cooley? All pilotage regulation? Pilotage regulation with a certain purpose? Pilotage regulation with a certain effect? Pilotage regulation recognized by Congress to be "local"? And once a subject is recognized as "local," does every variety of state regulation become permissible? Or are there still limitations—e. g., may a state give preference to

local businesses when it regulates a "local" subject? Does a "national subject"-"local subject" approach require that an entire field—e. g., the field
of railroad regulation—be categorized as either "local' or "national"?
Or may some state regulations of railroads be permissible, while others are
invalid? Note the varied results, depending upon the types and impacts of
regulation, in the railroad cases in sec. 1B below.

2. *The modern approach.* Leading modern cases such as Southern
Pacific Co. v. Arizona, sec. 1B below, insist that they are following the (obviously somewhat obscure) Cooley guidance. Are they really? Does the
process of distinguishing "local" and "national" subjects in the modern
cases differ from that engaged in by the Cooley Court? Are "local" and
"national" in the modern cases only conclusionary labels for judgments resting on considerations going far beyond the Cooley Court's emphasis on the
"subject" of the regulation? Cooley purported to abandon the "purpose"
inquiry of the earlier cases—and the distinction between "police" and "commerce" regulations—for a scrutiny of the area regulated, and the effect of
the regulation. Should "purpose" have been rejected as a guide? Has it
been in the later cases? What was the "purpose" of the pilotage law in
Cooley—safety, or economic support of pilots, or both? Is there room for
a "purpose" inquiry in the modern manifestations of the Cooley doctrine?
Does Southern Pacific, while paying lip service to Cooley, really represent
an amalgamation of the Cooley "effect" emphasis with the pre-Cooley
"purpose" concern?

These questions are pursued in the materials which follow. But a
characteristic modern statement may be noted here to illustrate later invocations of Cooley. In California v. Zook, 336 U.S. 725 (1949) (sec.
2 below), the Court commented: "Certain principles are no longer in
doubt. [W]hen Congress has not specifically acted we have accepted the
Cooley cases's broad delineation of the areas of state and national power over
interstate commerce. . . . Absent congressional action, the familiar
test is that of uniformity versus locality: if a case falls within an area in
commerce thought to demand a uniform national rule, state action is struck
down. If the activity is one of predominantly local interest, state action is
sustained. *More accurately,* the question is whether the state interest is
outweighed by a national interest in the unhampered operation of interstate commerce." (Emphasis added.)

Does that "more accurate" restatement of Cooley—more fully developed in Southern Pacific v. Arizona, below—suggest a more complex process
than that of Cooley for drawing the line between permissible and impermissible state regulation? That "more accurate" theme of "balancing"
state and national interests has indeed become the predominant one in the
modern cases. But before it came to crystallize the modern approach in
Southern Pacific v. Arizona, the Court, for nearly a century after Cooley,
experimented with formulations that might serve in lieu of the Cooley doctrine. For example, for some years a distinction between "direct" and "indirect" burdens on commerce was in vogue—a doctrine which coexisted
with other cases emphasizing the purpose of the state regulation and with
still others which focused on the practical impacts of state laws. (See the
materials which follow.) But during all those years of searching, and down

to the present, one message of the Cooley case has retained majority support on the Court: the scope of state power over commerce is not to be determined either by giving the dormant commerce clause a wholly preclusive effect or by giving it no effect at all. Rather, the continuously dominant majority position since Cooley has been that the commerce clause by its its own force bars some, but not all, state regulation.* The remaining, recurrent question has been: When, and why, does state regulation with an impact on interstate commerce become impermissible?

3. *The effect of congressional consent.* In Cooley, what was the effect given to the federal law of 1789 authorizing state pilotage laws? Justice Curtis found "an appropriate and important signification" for it—simply as guidance to the Court in determining whether pilotage was a "local" or "national" subject. But the Court quite clearly refused to consider the congressional declaration as binding: "If the Constitution excluded the States from making any law regulating commerce, certainly Congress cannot regrant or in any manner reconvey to the States that power." Why not? To the Cooley Court, commerce clause restrictions—like other "constitutional" restrictions (but cf. Katzenbach v. Morgan, chap. 11, sec. 4, below)—were untouchable by Congress: once the Court found a constitutional barrier, Congress could not remove it. That aspect of Cooley has been undercut by later developments: after a tortuous course of decisions, the Cooley position was modified to authorize Congress to consent to state regulation of commerce though that regulation would otherwise be barred by the dormant commerce power. See, e. g., Prudential Insurance Co. v. Benjamin, 328 U.S. 408 (1946) (sec. 2 below). The justifications for congressional authority to grant such "consent" are explored more fully in sec. 2B, below.

---

* There have been dissents from that position, to be sure; but some of the dissenters have ultimately come around to the majority view. Justices Black and Douglas, for example, urged early in their judicial careers that the implicit ban of the commerce clause should extend solely to *discriminatory* state laws. But in later years, both voted to invalidate state regulation because it cast an excessive—though not discriminatory—burden on interstate commerce. Compare, e. g., Justice Douglas' dissent in Southern Pacific Co. v. Arizona (1946), printed below ["My view has been that the courts should intervene only where the state legislation discriminated against interstate commerce. . . ."] with Justice Douglas' majority opinion in Bibb v. Navajo Freight Lines, Inc. (1959), printed below ["This is one of those cases . . . where local safety measures that are nondiscriminatory place an unconstitutional burden on interstate commerce."]. See also Morgan v. Virginia, 328 U.S. 373 (1946) (noted below), where Justices Black and Douglas joined in invalidating an "unreasonable" burden on commerce.

B. STATE REGULATION OF TRANSPORTATION

STATE LAWS AFFECTING TRANSPORTATION: THE SEARCH FOR STANDARDS AFTER COOLEY

1. *Railroad rates: The Wabash case.* a. The growth of a nation-wide railroad system stirred widespread demands for legislative controls. (Recall chap. 3, sec. 2, above.) Would pre-Civil War commerce clause doctrine prove adequate when these pressures produced responses from state legislatures? The Cooley doctrine was repeatedly cited by the Court in examining those state laws, and some of the cases are indeed explainable in Cooley terms. But the results did not wholly square with a simplistic application of the "national subject"-"local subject" distinction of Cooley. Certainly, the Court did not engage in a wholesale characterization of "railroad regulation" as either "national" or "local"; instead, it began to supplement its Cooley invocations with other criteria, including references to a "direct"-"indirect" distinction as well as explorations of the practical consequences of a particular variety of regulation. Thus, the Court found commerce clause objections to some state regulations of the rates of interstate railroads; yet many safety regulations were sustained. (Compare notes 1b and 2 below.)

b. In WABASH, ST. L. & P. RY. CO. v. ILLINOIS, 118 U.S. 557 (1886), the Court held that the state's ban on railroad rate discriminations against shippers could not be enforced with regard to interstate shipments. Congress had not acted, but the Court, under the Cooley formula, found that such regulations were of a "national," not "local," character. The Court's inquiry emphasized that there might be "oppressive embarrassments" of interstate transportation if each of the through-states "could fix its own rules for prices, for modes of transit, for times and modes of delivery, and all other incidents to which the word 'regulation' can be applied." A few months after the decision, earlier pressures on Congress bore fruit and the Interstate Commerce Act of 1887 was adopted.

2. *Railroad safety regulations and the evolving Cooley doctrine.* But the Wabash ruling did not cover *all* "incidents of transportation to which the word 'regulation' can be applied"; whatever the Cooley "subject" in Wabash, it was not all that broad. Two years after Wabash, for example, the Court sustained a state examination requirement applied to engineers on interstate trains: the regulation was justified by safety considerations, and the impact on commerce was dismissed as "indirect." Smith v. Alabama, 124 U.S. 465 (1888). Many other "safety" laws were similarly sustained; a number are reviewed—and distinguished—in Southern Pacific Co. v. Arizona, below.*

* Note also Fort Richmond & Bergen Point Ferry Co. v. Board, 234 U.S. 317 (1914), another decision sustaining a state regulation of interstate transportation—and an effort to supplement Cooley with "direct"-"indirect" distinctions. Justice Hughes' opinion in that case found that New Jersey could regulate interstate ferry rates. After paraphrasing the Cooley rule, he elaborated: "It is this principle that is applied in holding that a State may not impose direct burdens upon interstate commerce, for this is to say that the States may not directly regulate or restrain that which from its nature

3. *The attack on the "direct"-"indirect" distinction: Justice Stone's DiSanto dissent.* Citations of Cooley in the transportation cases could not obscure the fact that more particularized analyses underlay the results: the Cooley "subject" apparently varied with the type, and impact, of the regulation challenged. Was the increasingly common talk about "direct" and "indirect" effects on commerce a more helpful tool of analysis? (See, e. g., note * above.) Justice Stone did not think so: in DiSANTO v. PENNSYLVANIA, 273 U.S. 34 (1927), soon after his appointment to the Court, he began a long campaign for more adequate articulation of the applicable criteria—a campaign that produced his majority opinions in Barnwell and Southern Pacific, the next two principal cases. (Compare the attack on "direct"-"indirect" distinctions in the cases on the congressional commerce power, chap. 3.)

In DiSanto, a state statute required a license fee of fifty dollars to be paid by travel agents selling steamship tickets for foreign travel. The license was revocable for misbehavior and was granted only after proof of good character and fitness. A majority of the Court held the statute unconstitutional as a "direct burden" on foreign commerce. The "purpose" of a "direct" regulation was said to be irrelevant. Justice Brandeis, in a dissent concurred in by Justice Holmes, stated that the statute "places no direct burden on such commerce." In a separate dissent, Justice Stone (joined by Justices Holmes and Brandeis) questioned the standard employed in determining the constitutionality of the statute: "In this case the traditional test of the limit of state action by inquiring whether the interference with commerce is direct or indirect seems to me too mechanical, too uncertain in its application, and too remote from actualities, to be of value. In thus making use of the expressions, 'direct' and 'indirect interference' with commerce, we are doing little more than using labels to describe a result rather than any trustworthy formula by which it is reached. [I]t seems clear that those interferences [with interstate commerce which are] not deemed forbidden are to be sustained, not because the effect on commerce is nominally indirect, but because a consideration of all the facts and circumstances, such as the nature of the regulation, its function, the character of the business involved and the actual effect on the flow of commerce, lead to the conclusion that the regulation concerns interests peculiarly local and does not infringe the national interest in maintaining the freedom of commerce across state lines." [The DiSanto decision was overruled in California v. Thompson, 313 U.S. 109 (1941): a law requiring licensing and bonding of travel agents, designed to prevent "fraudulent and unconscionable conduct," was held to deal with a problem "peculiarly a subject of local concern."]

4. *The adequacy of the "direct"-"indirect" approach: The Georgia blow-post law cases.* a. Were the "direct"-"indirect" labels as "remote from actualities," as "mechanical," as Justice Stone insisted? Note that Smith v. Alabama, the railroad safety case in note 2 above, talked of realistic "em-

should be under the control of the one authority and be free from restriction save as it governed by a valid Federal rule." Here, he found, the ferries—not operated in connection with an interstate transportation network—were "a subject of a different character" from railroads. At least where the state regulations were not "burdensome" or "discriminatory," state regulation was permissible, because the problem was "essentially local," and there was no "inherent necessity" for national regulation.

barrassments" while using the "indirect" language; and note that Justice Brandeis, who was always sensitive to economic "actualities," spoke of "direct" burdens in DiSanto—as he did frequently—though he also concurred in Justice Stone's dissent. In examining Justice Stone's later contributions in this area, consider whether his formulations are substantially more helpful than the earlier standards.

b. Litigation regarding a Georgia safety law illustrates the capacity of Justices using mere "labels" to respond to "actualities." The Georgia blow-post law required railroads to erect posts 400 yards from railroad crossings and directed locomotive engineers, when passing the posts, to blow the train whistles and to "simultaneously" check speed "so as to stop in time should any person . . . be crossing" the tracks at the road crossing. Suits for injuries in crossing accidents relied on noncompliance with the law in claiming negligence; the defendants insisted that the law violated the commerce clause. In SOUTHERN RAILWAY CO. v. KING, 217 U.S. 524 (1910), the Court affirmed a judgment against the railroad. The pleadings had alleged that the blow-post law imposed "a direct burden on" interstate traffic. The Court's affirmance noted that the pleadings "set forth no facts which would make the operation of the statute unconstitutional. [For all that appears] the crossing at which this injury happened may have been so located and of such dangerous character as to make the slackening of trains at that point necessary to the safety of those using the public highway, and a statute making such requirement only a reasonable police regulation, and not an unlawful attempt to regulate or hinder interstate commerce." (A trial offer of proof regarding the burden imposed by the law was held properly excluded because of the deficient pleadings.)

Contrast the handling of a second case challenging application of the Georgia law, SEABOARD AIR LINE RY. v. BLACKWELL, 244 U.S. 310 (1917). There, the railroad's answer alleged that along the 123 miles of its track from Atlanta to the South Carolina border, there were 124 grade crossings; that compliance with the law would require "practically a full stop at each of the road crossings"; that each stop would take from three to five minutes; and that compliance by the train involved in the accident would have changed a scheduled 4½ hours' run into one of more than 10½ hours. The state courts held that these pleadings were an inadequate defense: the law was a valid police regulation; any burden on commerce was "indirect." The Supreme Court reversed: the case was distinguishable from the Southern Railway case, above, for the facts that were missing there were alleged here; and the allegations "compel the conclusion that the statute is a direct burden upon interstate commerce, and being such, is unlawful."

5. *State licensing, interstate carriers, and the importance of "purpose": The Buck and Bradley cases.* Do the "direct"-"indirect" or Cooley standards in the foregoing cases articulate the determinative considerations in such cases as BUCK v. KUYKENDALL, 267 U.S. 307 (1925), and BRADLEY v. PUBLIC UTILITIES COMMISSION, 289 U.S. 92 (1933)? Each case involved a state denial of a certificate of convenience and necessity to an applicant seeking to use the highways as an interstate carrier; in each case, Justice Brandeis wrote the Court's opinion; but the denial was set aside in one case and sustained in the other.

a.   Buck, a citizen of Oregon, wanted to operate an "auto stage line" to carry passengers and freight between Portland and Seattle. After obtaining a certificate of convenience and necessity from Oregon, he was denied such a certificate by Washington on the ground that the territory was "already being adequately served" by other carriers. In reversing, Justice Brandeis said: "It may be assumed that . . . the state statute is consistent with the Fourteenth Amendment; and also, that appropriate state regulations adopted primarily to promote safety upon the highways and conservation in their use are not obnoxious to the Commerce Clause, where the indirect burden imposed upon interstate commerce is not unreasonable. . . . The provision here in question is of a different character. Its primary purpose is not regulation with a view to safety or to conservation of the highways, but the prohibition of competition. It determines not the manner of use, but the persons by whom the highways may be used. It prohibits such use to some persons while permitting it to others for the same purpose and in the same manner. Moreover, it determines whether the prohibition shall be applied by resort, through state officials, to a test which is peculiarly within the province of federal action— the existence of adequate facilities for conducting interstate commerce. The vice of the legislation is dramatically exposed by the fact that the State of Oregon had issued its certificate which may be deemed equivalent to a legislative declaration that, despite existing facilities, public convenience and necessity required the establishment by Buck of the auto stage line between Seattle and Portland. Thus, the provision of the Washington statute is a regulation, not of the use of its own highways, but of interstate commerce. Its effect upon such commerce is not merely to burden, but to obstruct it. Such state action is forbidden by the Commerce Clause."

b.   In the Bradley case, eight years later, Ohio denied a certificate to operate between Cleveland, Ohio, and Flint, Michigan, on the ground that the highway to be used "is so badly congested by established motor vehicle operations, that the addition of the applicant's proposed service would create and maintain an excessive and undue hazard to the safety and security of the traveling public, and the property upon such highway." In sustaining the denial, Justice Brandeis noted that in Buck, above, "safety was doubtless promoted when the certificate was denied," but "promotion of safety was merely an incident of the denial" designed "to prevent competition." In Bradley, by contrast, "the purpose of the denial was to promote safety; and the test employed was congestion of the highway. The effect of the denial upon interstate commerce was merely an incident. . . . The Commerce Clause is not violated by denial of the certificate, [if] upon adequate evidence denial is deemed necessary to promote public safety."*

---

* Compare Fry Roofing Co. v. Wood, 344 U.S. 157 (1952), a 5 to 4 decision sustaining an Arkansas statute requiring all contract carriers to obtain a "permit" before using the state's highways. The law listed certain factors to be considered in decisions on permit applications, including the adequacy of transportation services already performed by "any railroad, street railway or contract carrier." The majority stated: "Unlike the situation in the Buck case, Arkansas has not refused to grant a permit for interstate carriage of goods on state highways. It has asked these driver-owners to do nothing except apply for a permit . . . . And the State Commission here expressly disclaims any 'discretionary right to re-

c. What explains the difference between Buck and Bradley? Is the emphasis on "purpose" derivable from the Cooley standard? From the Marshall decisions before Cooley? What was impermissible about the "purpose" in Buck? Why is not the concern with excessive competition a legitimate objective of the police power? Does the regulatory scheme in Buck lend itself more readily to discriminatory burdens on out-of-state interests? Is the Court legitimately concerned with fashioning preventive rules against the *risk* of discrimination? Compare the Barnwell and Southern Pacific cases which follow, and the Dean Milk and Hood cases, secs. 1C and D below.

SOUTH CAROLINA STATE HIGHWAY DEPT. v. BARNWELL BROS., INC.

303 U.S. 177, 58 S.Ct. 510, 82 L.Ed. 734 (1938).

Appeal from the District Court for the Eastern District of South Carolina.

Mr. Justice STONE delivered the opinion of the Court.

Act No. 259 of the General Assembly of South Carolina [1933] prohibits use on the state highways of motor trucks and "semi-trailer motor trucks" whose width exceeds 90 inches, and whose weight including load exceeds 20,000 pounds. . . .

[The three-judge District Court] enjoined the enforcement of the weight provision against interstate motor carriers on the specified highways, and also the width limitation of 90 inches, except in the case of vehicles exceeding 96 inches in width. . . .

The trial court rested its decision that the statute unreasonably burdens interstate commerce, upon findings, not assailed here, that there is a large amount of motor truck traffic passing interstate in the southeastern part of the United States, which would normally pass over the highways of South Carolina, but which will be barred from the state by the challenged restrictions if enforced, and upon its conclusion that when viewed in the light of their effect upon interstate commerce, these restrictions are unreasonable.

To reach this conclusion the court weighed conflicting evidence and made its own determinations as to the weight and width of motor trucks commonly used in interstate traffic and the capacity of the specified highways of the state to accommodate such traffic without injury to them or danger to their users. It found that interstate carriage by motor trucks has become a national industry; that from 85 to 90% of the motor trucks used in interstate transportation are 96 inches wide and of a gross weight, when loaded, of more than ten tons; that only four other states prescribe a gross load weight as low as 20,000 pounds . . . . .

fuse to grant a permit for contract carriage where that carriage is in interstate commerce.' . . . At present we hold only that Arkansas is not powerless to require interstate motor carriers to identify themselves as users of that state's highways." Justice Douglas' dissent insisted that this was "precisely the kind of control which the State of Washington tried to exercise over motor carriers and which was denied her in Buck v. Kuykendall." Cf. Castle v. Hayes Freight Lines, 348 U.S. 61 (1954), sec. 2A, below.

It also found that the gross weight of vehicles is not a factor to be considered in the preservation of concrete highways, but that the appropriate factor to be considered is wheel or axle weight; the vehicles engaged in interstate commerce are so designed and the pressure of their weight is so distributed by their wheels and axles that gross loads of more than 20,000 pounds can be carried over concrete roads without damage to the surface; that a gross weight limitation of that amount, especially as applied to semi-trailer motor trucks, is unreasonable as a means of preserving the highways; that it has no reasonable relation to safety of the public using the highways; and that the width limitation of 90 inches is unreasonable when applied to standard concrete highways of the state, in view of the fact that all other states permit a width of 96 inches, which is the standard width of trucks engaged in interstate commerce.

In reaching these conclusions, and at the same time holding that the weight and width limitations do not infringe the Fourteenth Amendment, the court proceeded upon the assumption that the commerce clause imposes upon state regulations to secure the safe and economical use of highways a standard of reasonableness which is more exacting when applied to the interstate traffic than that required by the Fourteenth Amendment as to all traffic; that a standard of weight and width of motor vehicles which is an appropriate state regulation when applied to intrastate traffic may be prohibited because of its effect on interstate commerce, although the conditions attending the two classes of traffic with respect to safety and protection of the highways are the same.

South Carolina has built its highways and owns and maintains them. It has received from the federal government, in aid of its highway improvements, money grants . . . . But appellees do not challenge here the ruling of the district court that Congress has not undertaken to regulate the weight and size of motor vehicles in interstate motor traffic . . . .

While the constitutional grant to Congress of power to regulate interstate commerce has been held to operate of its own force to curtail state power in some measure,[1] it did not forestall all state action affecting interstate commerce. Ever since Willson v. Black Bird Creek Marsh Co., 2 Pet. 245, and Cooley v. Board of Port Wardens, 12 How. 299, it has been recognized that there are matters of local concern, the regulation of which unavoidably involves some regulation of interstate commerce but which, because of their local character and their number and diversity, may never be fully dealt with by Congress. Notwithstanding the commerce clause, such regulation in the absence of Congressional action has for the most part been left to the states . . . .

1. State regulations affecting interstate commerce, whose purpose or effect is to gain for those within the state an advantage at the expense of those without, or to burden those out of the state without any corresponding advantage to those within, have been thought to impinge upon the constitutional prohibition even though Congress has not acted. . . .
Underlying the stated rule has been the thought, often expressed in judicial opinion, that when the regulation is of such a character that its burden falls principally upon those without the state, legislative action is not likely to be subjected to those political restraints which are normally exerted on legislation where it affects adversely some interests within the state. . . . [Footnote by the Court. Compare Justice Stone's Carolene Products footnote, chap. 9, below.]

The commerce clause, by its own force, prohibits discrimination against interstate commerce, whatever its form or method, and the decisions of this Court have recognized that there is scope for its like operation when state legislation nominally of local concern is in point of fact aimed at interstate commerce, or by its necessary operation is a means of gaining a local benefit by throwing the attendant burdens on those without the state. . . . It was to end these practices that the commerce clause was adopted. . . . The commerce clause has also been thought to set its own limitation upon state control of interstate rail carriers so as to preclude the subordination of the efficiency and convenience of interstate traffic to local service requirements.

But the present case affords no occasion for saying that the bare possession of power by Congress to regulate the interstate traffic forces the states to conform to standards which Congress might, but has not adopted, or curtails their power to take measures to insure the safety and conservation of their highways which may be applied to like traffic moving intrastate. Few subjects of state regulation are so peculiarly of local concern as is the use of state highways. There are few, local regulation of which is so inseparable from a substantial effect on interstate commerce. Unlike the railroads, local highways are built, owned and maintained by the state or its municipal subdivisions. The state has a primary and immediate concern in their safe and economical administration. The present regulations, or any others of like purpose, if they are to accomplish their end, must be applied alike to interstate and intrastate traffic both moving in large volume over the highways. The fact that they affect alike shippers in interstate and intrastate commerce in large number within as well as without the state is a safeguard against their abuse. . . .

With respect to the extent and nature of the local interests to be protected and the unavoidable effect upon interstate and intrastate commerce alike, regulations of the use of the highways are akin to local regulation of rivers, harbors, piers and docks, quarantine regulations, and game laws, which, Congress not acting, have been sustained even though they materially interfere with interstate commerce.

. . . This Court has often sustained the exercise of [state power over its own highways] although it has burdened or impeded interstate commerce. It has upheld weight limitations lower than those presently imposed, applied alike to motor traffic moving interstate and intrastate. . . . Restrictions favoring passenger traffic over the carriage of interstate merchandise by truck have been similarly sustained, . . . as has the exaction of a reasonable fee for the use of the highways. . . .

In each of these cases regulation involves a burden on interstate commerce. But so long as the state action does not discriminate, the burden is one which the Constitution permits because it is an inseparable incident of the exercise of a legislative authority, which, under the Constitution, has been left to the states.

Congress, in the exercise of its plenary power to regulate interstate commerce, may determine whether the burdens imposed on it by state regulation, otherwise permissible, are too great, and may, by legislation designed to secure uniformity or in other respects to protect the national interest in

the commerce, curtail to some extent the state's regulatory power. But that is a legislative, not a judicial function . . . . In the absence of such legislation the judicial function, under the commerce clause as well as the Fourteenth Amendment, stops with the inquiry whether the state legislature in adopting regulations such as the present has acted within its province, and whether the means of regulation chosen are reasonably adapted to the end sought.

Here the first inquiry has already been resolved by our decisions that a state may impose non-discriminatory restrictions with respect to the character of motor vehicles moving in interstate commerce as a safety measure and as a means of securing the economical use of its highways. In resolving the second, courts do not sit as legislatures, either state or national. They cannot act as Congress does when, after weighing all the conflicting interests, state and national, it determines when and how much the state regulatory power shall yield to the larger interests of a national commerce. . . . When the action of a legislature is within the scope of its power, fairly debatable questions as to its reasonableness, wisdom and propriety are not for the determination of courts, but for the legislative body . . . . It is not any the less a legislative power committed to the states because it affects interstate commerce, and courts are not any the more entitled, because interstate commerce is affected, to substitute their own for the legislative judgment. . . .

Since the adoption of one weight or width regulation, rather than another, is a legislative not a judicial choice, its constitutionality is not to be determined by weighing in the judicial scales the merits of the legislative choice and rejecting it if the weight of evidence presented in court appears to favor a different standard. . . . Being a legislative judgment it is presumed to be supported by facts known to the legislature unless facts judicially known or proved preclude that possibility. Hence, in reviewing the present determination we examine the record, not to see whether the findings of the court below are supported by evidence, but to ascertain upon the whole record whether it is possible to say that the legislative choice is without rational basis. . . . Not only does the record fail to exclude that possibility, but it shows affirmatively that there is adequate support for the legislative judgment.

At the outset it should be noted that underlying much of the controversy is the relative merit of a gross weight limitation as against an axle or wheel weight limitation. . . . The choice of a weight limitation based on convenience of application and consequent lack of need for rigid supervisory enforcement is for the legislature, and we cannot say that its preference for the one over the other is in any sense arbitrary or unreasonable. . . .

There was testimony before the court to support its conclusion that the highways in question are capable of sustaining without injury a wheel load of 8,000 or 9,000 pounds . . . . Much of this testimony appears to have been based on theoretical strength of concrete highways laid under ideal conditions, and none of it was based on an actual study of the highways of South Carolina . . . . There is uncontradicted testimony that approximately 60% of the South Carolina standard paved highways in question were built without a longitudinal center joint which has since become standard practice

. . . ; and that owing to the distribution of the stresses on concrete roads when in use, those without a center joint have a tendency to develop irregular longitudinal cracks. . . .

These considerations, with the presumption of constitutionality, afford adequate support for the weight limitation without reference to other items of the testimony tending to support it. Furthermore, South Carolina's own experience is not to be ignored. . . . The conditions under which highways must be built in the several states, their construction and the demands made upon them, are not uniform. . . . The legislature, being free to exercise its own judgment, is not bound by that of other legislatures. It would hardly be contended that if all the states had adopted a single standard none, in the light of its own experience and in the exercise of its judgment upon all the complex elements which enter into the problem, could change it.

Only a word need be said as to the width limitation. While a large part of the highways in question are from 18 to 20 feet in width, approximately 100 miles are only 16 feet wide. On all the use of a 96 inch truck leaves but a narrow margin for passing. On the road 16 feet wide it leaves none. The 90 inch limitation has been in force in South Carolina since 1920 and the concrete highways which it has built appear to be adapted to vehicles of that width. The record shows without contradiction that the use of heavy loaded trucks on the highways tends to force other traffic off the concrete surface onto the shoulders of the road adjoining its edges and to increase repair costs materially. It appears also that as the width of trucks is increased it obstructs the view of the highway, causing much inconvenience and increased hazard in its use. It plainly cannot be said that the width of trucks used on the highways in South Carolina is unrelated to their safety and cost of maintenance, or that a 90 inch width limitation adopted to safeguard the highways of the State, is not within the range of the permissible legislative choice.

The regulatory measures taken by South Carolina are within its legislative power. They do not infringe the Fourteenth Amendment, and the resulting burden on interstate commerce is not forbidden.

Reversed.

Mr. Justice CARDOZO and Mr. Justice REED took no part in the consideration or decision of this case.

SOUTHERN PACIFIC CO. v. ARIZONA

325 U.S. 761, 65 S.Ct. 1515, 89 L.Ed. 1915 (1945).

Appeal from the Supreme Court of Arizona.

[The Arizona Train Limit Law of 1912 prohibited operating within the State a railroad train of more than fourteen passenger or seventy freight cars. In 1940, the State sued the Company to recover the statutory penalties for operating within the State two trains exceeding the legal limit. After an extended trial, the trial court found the law to be an unconstitutional burden on commerce. The Arizona Supreme Court reversed, concluding that a state

law enacted in the exercise of the police power, with some reasonable relation to health and safety, could not be overturned despite its adverse affect on interstate commerce. The United States Supreme Court reversed. It rejected a contention that Congress, by authorizing the ICC to regulate train lengths, had superseded state power. The Court then turned to the major challenge to the law, based on the commerce clause.]

Mr. Chief Justice STONE delivered the opinion of the Court. . . .

Although the commerce clause conferred on the national government power to regulate commerce, its possession of the power does not exclude all state power of regulation. Ever since [Willson v. Black-Bird Creek Marsh Co.] and [Cooley v. Board of Wardens], it has been recognized that, in the absence of conflicting legislation by Congress, there is a residuum of power in the state to make laws governing matters of local concern which nevertheless in some measure affect interstate commerce or even, to some extent, regulate it. Thus the states may regulate matters which, because of their number and diversity, may never be adequately dealt with by Congress. When the regulation of matters of local concern is local in character and effect, and its impact on the national commerce does not seriously interfere with its operation, and the consequent incentive to deal with them nationally is slight, such regulation has been generally held to be within state authority.

But ever since [Gibbons v. Ogden], the states have not been deemed to have authority to impede substantially the free flow of commerce from state to state, or to regulate those phases of the national commerce which, because of the need of national uniformity, demand that their regulation, if any, be prescribed by a single authority.[1] [Cooley.] Whether or not this long-recognized distribution of power between the national and the state governments is predicated upon the implications of the commerce clause itself, . . . or upon the presumed intention of Congress, where Congress has not spoken, . . . Dowling, Interstate Commerce and State Power, 27 Va.Law Rev. 1, the result is the same.

In the application of these principles some enactments may be found to be plainly within and others plainly without state power. But between these extremes lies the infinite variety of cases, in which regulation of local matters may also operate as a regulation of commerce, in which reconciliation of the conflicting claims of state and national power is to be attained only by some appraisal and accommodation of the competing demands of the state and national interests involved. . . .

Congress has undoubted power to redefine the distribution of power over interstate commerce. It may either permit the states to regulate the commerce in a manner which would otherwise not be permissible, . . . or exclude state regulation even of matters of peculiarly local concern which nevertheless affect interstate commerce. [See sec. 2 of this chapter, below.]

But in general Congress has left it to the courts to formulate the rules thus interpreting the commerce clause in its application, doubtless because

---

1. In applying this rule the Court has often recognized that to the extent that the burden of state regulation falls on interests outside the state, it is unlikely to be alleviated by the operation of those political restraints normally exerted when interests within the state are affected. . . . [Footnote by the Court.]

it has appreciated the destructive consequences to the commerce of the nation if their protection were withdrawn, and has been aware that in their application state laws will not be invalidated without the support of relevant factual material which will "afford a sure basis" for an informed judgment. Meanwhile, Congress has accommodated its legislation, as have the states, to these rules as an established feature of our constitutional system. There has thus been left to the states wide scope for the regulation of matters of local state concern, even though it in some measure affects the commerce, provided it does not materially restrict the free flow of commerce across state lines, or interfere with it in matters with respect to which uniformity of regulation is of predominant national concern.

Hence the matters for ultimate determination here are the nature and extent of the burden which the state regulation of interstate trains, adopted as a safety measure, imposes on interstate commerce, and whether the relative weights of the state and national interests involved are such as to make inapplicable the rule, generally observed, that the free flow of interstate commerce and its freedom from local restraints in matters requiring uniformity of regulation are interests safeguarded by the commerce clause from state interference. . . .

The findings show that the operation of long trains, that is trains of more than fourteen passengers and more than seventy freight cars, is standard practice over the main lines of the railroads of the United States, and that, if the length of trains is to be regulated at all, national uniformity in the regulation adopted, such as only Congress can prescribe, is practically indispensable to the operation of an efficient and economical national railway system. . . .

In Arizona, approximately 93% of the freight traffic and 95% of the passenger traffic is interstate. Because of the Train Limit Law appellant is required to haul over 30% more trains in Arizona than would otherwise have been necessary. The record shows a definite relationship between operating costs and the length of trains, the increase in length resulting in a reduction of operating costs per car. The additional cost of operation of trains complying with the Train Limit Law in Arizona amounts for the two railroads traversing that state to about $1,000,000 a year. The reduction in train lengths also impedes efficient operation. . . .

The unchallenged findings leave no doubt that the Arizona Train Limit Law imposes a serious burden on the interstate commerce conducted by appellant. . . . Enforcement of the law in Arizona, while train lengths remain unregulated or are regulated by varying standards in other states, must inevitably result in an impairment of uniformity of efficient railroad operation because the railroads are subjected to regulation which is not uniform in its application. Compliance with a state statute limiting train lengths requires interstate trains of a length lawful in other states to be broken up and reconstituted as they enter each state according as it may impose varying limitations upon train lengths. The alternative is for the carrier to conform to the lowest train limit restriction of any of the states through which its trains pass, whose laws thus control the carriers' operations both within and without the regulating state. . . .

At present the seventy freight car laws are enforced only in Arizona and Oklahoma, with a fourteen car passenger car limit in Arizona. The record here shows that the enforcement of the Arizona statute results in freight trains being broken up and reformed at the California border and in New Mexico, some distance from the Arizona line. Frequently it is not feasible to operate a newly assembled train from the New Mexico yard nearest to Arizona, with the result that the Arizona limitation governs the flow of traffic as far east as El Paso, Texas. For similar reasons the Arizona law often controls the length of passenger trains all the way from Los Angeles to El Paso.

If one state may regulate train lengths, so may all the others, and they need not prescribe the same maximum limitation. The practical effect of such regulation is to control train operations beyond the boundaries of the state exacting it because of the necessity of breaking up and reassembling long trains at the nearest terminal points before entering and after leaving the regulating state. The serious impediment to the free flow of commerce by the local regulation of train lengths and the practical necessity that such regulation, if any, must be prescribed by a single body having a nation-wide authority are apparent.

The trial court found that the Arizona law had no reasonable relation to safety, and made train operation more dangerous. Examination of the evidence and the detailed findings makes it clear that this conclusion was rested on facts found which indicate that such increased danger of accident and personal injury as may result from the greater length of trains is more than offset by the increase in the number of accidents resulting from the larger number of trains when train lengths are reduced. In considering the effect of the statute as a safety measure, therefore, the factor of controlling significance for present purposes is not whether there is basis for the conclusion of the Arizona Supreme Court that the increase in length of trains beyond the statutory maximum has an adverse effect upon safety of operation. The decisive question is whether in the circumstances the total effect of the law as a safety measure in reducing accidents and casualties is so slight or problematical as not to outweigh the national interest in keeping interstate commerce free from interferences which seriously impede it and subject it to local regulation which does not have a uniform effect on the interstate train journey which it interrupts.

The principal source of danger of accident from increased length of trains is the resulting increase of "slack action" of the train. Slack action is the amount of free movement of one car before it transmits its motion to an adjoining coupled car. This free movement results from the fact that in railroad practice cars are loosely coupled, and the coupling is often combined with a shock-absorbing device, a "draft gear", which, under stress, substantially increases the free movement as the train is started or stopped. . . .

. . . The amount and severity of slack action, however, are not wholly dependent upon the length of train, as they may be affected by the mode and conditions of operation as to grades, speed, and load. And accidents due to slack action also occur in the operation of short trains. On comparison of the number of slack action accidents in Arizona with those in Nevada, where the length of trains is now unregulated, the trial court found

that with substantially the same amount of traffic in each state the number of accidents was relatively the same in long as in short train operations. . . . As the trial court found, reduction of the length of trains also tends to increase the number of accidents because of the increase in the number of trains. . . .   The record lends support to the trial court's conclusion that the train length limitation increased rather than diminished the number of accidents. . . .

We think, as the trial court found, that the Arizona Train Limit Law, viewed as a safety measure, affords at most slight and dubious advantage, if any, over unregulated train lengths, because it results in an increase in the number of trains and train operations and the consequent increase in train accidents of a character generally more severe than those due to slack action. Its undoubted effect on the commerce is the regulation, without securing uniformity, of the length of trains operated in interstate commerce, which lack is itself a primary cause of preventing the free flow of commerce by delaying it and by substantially increasing its cost and impairing its efficiency. In these respects the case differs from those where a state, by regulatory measures affecting the commerce, has removed or reduced safety hazards without substantial interference with the interstate movement of trains. Such are measures abolishing the car stove; requiring locomotives to be supplied with electric headlights; providing for full train crews; and for the equipment of freight trains with cabooses.

The principle that, without controlling Congressional action, a state may not regulate interstate commerce so as substantially to affect its flow or deprive it of needed uniformity in its regulation is not to be avoided by "simply invoking the convenient apologetics of the police power" . . . . [Numerous cases in which the commerce clause was held to invalidate local "police power" enactments are omitted.]

Here we conclude that the state does go too far. Its regulation of train lengths, admittedly obstructive to interstate train operation, and having a seriously adverse effect on transportation efficiency and economy, passes beyond what is plainly essential for safety since it does not appear that it will lessen rather than increase the danger of accident. Its attempted regulation of the operation of interstate trains cannot establish nation-wide control such as is essential to the maintenance of an efficient transportation system, which Congress alone can prescribe. . . .

Appellees especially rely on the full train crew cases, [e. g., Missouri Pacific R. Co. v. Norwood, 283 U.S. 249], and also on [Barnwell Bros.], as supporting the state's authority to regulate the length of interstate trains. While the full train crew laws undoubtedly placed an added financial burden on the railroads in order to serve a local interest, they did not obstruct interstate transportation or seriously impede it. They had no effects outside the state beyond those of picking up and setting down the extra employees at the state boundaries; they involved no wasted use of facilities or serious impairment of transportation efficiency, which are among the factors of controlling weight here. . . .

[Barnwell] was concerned with the power of the state to regulate the weight and width of motor cars passing interstate over its highways, a legislative field over which the state has a far more extensive control than

over interstate railroads. [There], we were at pains to point out that there are few subjects of state regulation affecting interstate commerce which are so peculiarly of local concern as is the use of the state's highways. Unlike the railroads local highways are built, owned and maintained by the state or its municipal subdivisions. The state is responsible for their safe and economical administration. Regulations affecting the safety of their use must be applied alike to intrastate and interstate traffic. The fact that they affect alike shippers in interstate and intrastate commerce in great numbers, within as well as without the state, is a safeguard against regulatory abuses. Their regulation is akin to quarantine measures, game laws, and like local regulations of rivers, harbors, piers, and docks, with respect to which the state has exceptional scope for the exercise of its regulatory power, and which, Congress not acting, have been sustained even though they materially interfere with interstate commerce.

The contrast between the present regulation and the full train crew laws in point of their effects on the commerce, and the like contrast with the highway safety regulations, in point of the nature of the subject of regulation and the state's interest in it, illustrate and emphasize the considerations which enter into a determination of the relative weights of state and national interests where state regulation affecting interstate commerce is attempted. Here examination of all the relevant factors makes it plain that the state interest is outweighed by the interest of the nation in an adequate economical and efficient railway transportation service, which must prevail.

Reversed.

Mr. Justice RUTLEDGE concurs in the result.

Mr. Justice BLACK, dissenting. . . .

Before the state trial court finally determined that the dangers found by the legislature in 1912 no longer existed, it heard evidence over a period of 5½ months which appears in about 3,000 pages of the printed record before us. It then adopted findings of fact submitted to it by the railroad, which cover 148 printed pages, and conclusions of law which cover 5 pages. . . . This new pattern of trial procedure makes it necessary for a judge to hear all the evidence offered as to why a legislature passed a law and to make findings of fact as to the validity of those reasons. If under today's ruling a court does make findings as to a danger contrary to the findings of the legislature, and the evidence heard "lends support" to those findings, a court can then invalidate the law. In this respect, the Arizona County Court acted, and this Court today is acting, as a "super-legislature." . . .

. . . Congress knew about the Arizona law. It is common knowledge that the Interstate Commerce Committees of the House and the Senate keep in close and intimate touch with the affairs of railroads and other national means of transportation. . . . The history of congressional consideration of this problem leaves little if any room to doubt that the choice of Congress to leave the state free in this field was a deliberate choice, which was taken with a full knowledge of the complexities of the problems and the probable need for diverse regulations in different localities. I am therefore compelled to reach the conclusion that today's decision is the result of the belief of a majority of this Court that both the legislature of Arizona and

the Congress made wrong policy decisions in permitting a law to stand which limits the length of railroad trains. . . .

When we finally get down to the gist of what the Court today actually decides, it is this: [that] running shorter trains would increase the cost of railroad operations. . . .

Mr. Justice DOUGLAS, dissenting.

I have expressed my doubts whether the courts should intervene in situations like the present and strike down state legislation on the grounds that it burdens interstate commerce. McCarroll v. Dixie Greyhound Lines, 309 U.S. 176, 183–189. My view has been that the courts should intervene only where the state legislation discriminated against interstate commerce or was out of harmony with laws which Congress had enacted. It seems to me particularly appropriate that that course be followed here. For Congress has given the Interstate Commerce Commission broad powers of regulation over interstate carriers. . . .

. . . [W]e are dealing here with state legislation in the field of safety where the propriety of local regulation has long been recognized. Whether the question arises under the Commerce Clause or the Fourteenth Amendment, I think the legislation is entitled to a presumption of validity. . . . I am not persuaded that the evidence adduced by the railroads overcomes the presumption of validity to which this train-limit law is entitled. . . .

THE EVOLUTION OF THE MODERN BALANCING APPROACH: STATE SAFETY LAWS FROM BARNWELL TO SOUTHERN PACIFIC AND BEYOND

1. *Southern Pacific and Barnwell: Inconsistent approaches?* Does Chief Justice Stone's opinion in Southern Pacific adequately distinguish his approach in his opinion seven years earlier in Barnwell? To be sure, the Court perceived a greater contribution to safety from South Carolina's law in Barnwell than it did from Arizona's law in Southern Pacific. But could not the Arizona law have passed the constitutional barrier articulated in Barnwell? The Arizona law did not overtly discriminate against interstate commerce; and reasonable legislators could have believed that shortening train lengths would contribute to safety. In short, did not Justice Stone impose a far more substantial commerce clause barrier in Southern Pacific than in Barnwell? Did he not endorse the elaborate trial court proceeding and engage in the quasi-legislative balancing in Southern Pacific that he had condemned in Barnwell? What justified the application of more substantial commerce clause restraints in Southern Pacific? * Were Chief Justice Stone's

-----

* Note the dates of the decisions. Barnwell came in 1938, shortly after the Court-packing controversy, shortly after the Court's retreat from judicial intervention in a number of areas. (Recall the congressional commerce power cases, chap. 3 above; see also the "economic due process" shifts in chap.

9 below.) By the time of Southern Pacific in 1945, the Court's "hands off" attitude in national power and due process cases continued. But there were already signs of a greater— though selective—judicial readiness to intervene (e. g., in First Amendment cases). See chap. 12 below; and note

reasons for distinguishing Barnwell in Southern Pacific persuasive: the "peculiarly local" nature of highways; the local ownership of highways? Was that difference, if any, as persuasive in 1945 as in 1938? Is it today? Is there justification for greater permissiveness towards state regulation of trucks than of railroads? Bibb, the principal case that follows (a 1959 decision involving trucks) applies a standard of judicial scrutiny closer to that of Southern Pacific (the 1945 railroad case) than to that of Barnwell (the 1938 truck case). What explains the changes in approach? The changes in relative degree of state and federal financing of highways from 1938 to 1959? The growth in importance of the trucking industry to national trade from 1938 to 1959? The relative economic conditions of the trucking and railroad industries in 1938 and 1959?

2. *The changing criteria of judicial scrutiny.* Chief Justice Stone's balancing process in Southern Pacific seems quite unlike his approach in Barnwell. What are the ingredients of the new approach? Is it an application of the Cooley standard? Early in his opinion, Chief Justice Stone—in the paragraph beginning: "If one state may regulate train lengths, so may all the others . . . ."—asserts that regulation of train lengths "must be prescribed by a single body having a nation-wide authority." Would that not be enough to hold the subject matter "national" rather than "local" under Cooley? Yet Chief Justice Stone goes on to engage in a lengthy balancing process to evaluate the burdens and benefits of the Arizona legislation. Is this not, then, another example of actual judicial scrutiny involving a good deal more than the Cooley majority had suggested? Under Chief Justice Stone's approach, how clear must the state law's contribution to safety be before the Court will tolerate the burden it imposes on interstate commerce? Compare the Bibb case, which follows.

Chief Justice Stone's opinion in Southern Pacific cites an article by Professor Dowling which appeared between the decisions in Barnwell and Southern Pacific, "Interstate Commerce and State Power," 27 Va.L.Rev. 1 (1940), Selected Essays 1938–62 (1963), 280.† Noel Dowling (who was to become the Harlan Fiske Stone Professor of Law at Columbia) may have influenced Chief Justice Stone's development from Barnwell to Southern Pacific: the approach Dowling articulated in 1940 was very close to the balancing process Stone endorsed in Southern Pacific in 1945. Dowling's article criticized the "direct"-"indirect" test as "far from satisfying"—as indeed Stone had done as early as his dissent in the DiSanto case, noted above. But Dowling evolved another doctrine from the cases: that, in the absence of congressional consent, "a Congressional negative will be presumed" where state regulation produces an "unreasonable interference" with commerce. Adoption of that "unreasonable interference" standard, he explained, would "involve an avowal that the Court is deliberately balancing national and local

Justice Stone's "double standards" footnote in the Carolene Products case (chap. 9 below)—a footnote in 1938 (the year of Barnwell) suggesting a political process rationale for identifying those areas warranting special judicial scrutiny. Southern Pacific indicates that state regulation of commerce had become an "interventionist" rather than a "hands-off" area for Stone by 1945. Why not in 1938, at the time of Barnwell?

† See also a Dowling article after Southern Pacific, "Interstate Commerce and State Power—Revised Version," 47 Colum.L.Rev. 547 (1947).

interests and making a choice as to which of the two *should* prevail." That, he added, would involve "a policy judgment." Moreover, "the test of reasonableness in interstate commerce cases," he emphasized, was "not the same" as in due process cases: "In a sense, a state law must take the hurdle of due process before it comes to the interstate barrier." Moreover, in order to bring all the data relevant to commerce clause "reasonableness" balancing into the judicial forum, Dowling urged "more generous and elastic" rules of evidence to examine the benefits and burdens of state impositions on commerce in the trial courts.

Does the evolution from Barnwell to Southern Pacific reflect such an intensification of judicial scrutiny, from the "mere reasonableness" of a due process, police power standard, to the balancing approach of determining "unreasonable" burdens under the commerce clause? Is the test of "reasonableness" in commerce cases "not the same" as in Barnwell? In Southern Pacific? In Bibb, which follows? Is the greater judicial scrutiny of "reasonableness" in commerce clause cases justified? Contrast Chief Justice Stone's endorsement of balancing in Southern Pacific with his objections to quasi-legislative judgments in Barnwell—and Justice Black's objections to elaborate trials on the benefits and burdens of state legislation in his dissent in Southern Pacific. Are courts institutionally equipped to undertake such balancing inquiries? Are such inquiries worthwhile investments of the courts' institutional energies?

Is Chief Justice Stone's balancing approach a general and valid derivation from commerce clause perceptions? Or is it an approach limited to railroad cases? To transportation cases? (See the Bibb case, which follows.) Is balancing the appropriate approach in all situations in which an unconstitutional burden on interstate commerce is alleged? Or is that intensive and time-consuming balancing ordinarily beyond institutional capacities of the courts? Note the cases which follow; and see especially the Oregon Bottle Law Case, sec. 1E below.

3. *State full crew laws after Southern Pacific: Justice Black's Firemen opinion.* In invalidating the train length law in Southern Pacific, Chief Justice Stone explicitly distinguished cases such as Missouri Pac. R. Co. v. Norwood, 283 U.S. 249 (1931), which had sustained state full train crew laws. Yet there was considerable doubt whether full crew laws could on reexamination survive the rigid judicial scrutiny authorized by Southern Pacific. Nevertheless, a renewed challenge to the Arkansas full train crew laws proved unsuccessful. In Engineers v. Chicago, R. I. & P. R. Co., 382 U.S. 423 (1966), the Court rejected a preemption claim resting on a 1963 congressional act compelling arbitration of certain crew disputes. On remand for consideration of the constitutional challenges, the District Court found after a full hearing that the crew laws had "no substantial effect on safety of operations," placed "substantial financial burdens" on the carriers, and interfered with the continuity of railroad operations. Accordingly, the trial court held the laws unconstitutional, in part on the basis of the Southern Pacific approach.

The Supreme Court reversed. FIREMEN v. CHICAGO, R. I. & P. R. CO., 393 U.S. 129 (1968). Justice Black's majority opinion concluded: "We

think it plain that in striking down the full-crew laws on this basis, the District Court indulged in a legislative judgment wholly beyond its limited authority to review state legislation under the Commerce Clause." For example, the evidence regarding the need for additional crewmen was "conflicting" and "inconclusive." And it was "difficult at best to say that financial losses should be balanced against the loss of lives and limbs of workers"; the Court "certainly cannot do so on this showing." Moreover, Justice Black found no unconstitutional discrimination in mileage exemptions in the laws that had the effect of freeing all of Arkansas' 17 intrastate railroads from coverage, while leaving most of the 11 interstate railroads subject to them. The Court found evidence in the record suggesting "a number of legitimate reasons for the mileage exemption"—e. g., the "apparent use of much slower trains over the short lines." Accordingly, "we see no reason to depart from this Court's previous decisions holding that the Arkansas full-crew laws do not unduly burden interstate commerce or otherwise violate the Constitution." Disputes about the laws "will continue to be worked out in the legislatures and in various forms of collective bargaining."

What explains the Supreme Court's hostility to the District Court's indulgence in "legislative judgment" in the Firemen case? Was not the District Court's type of inquiry justified by Southern Pacific? Did the Court repudiate that in Firemen because it felt bound by the pre-Southern Pacific precedents on full crew laws? Was Firemen a triumph for Justice Black's dissenting position in Southern Pacific? Do not the cases which follow indicate that the post-Southern Pacific Court continues to endorse judicial scrutinies beyond those that would be required under standards of "reasonableness" under the due process clause? Does not the modern Court continue to demand, in most cases, a greater showing of justification for the state law when it encounters a commerce clause barrier than the standards of Barnwell or of due process would demand?

BIBB v. NAVAJO FREIGHT LINES, INC.

359 U.S. 520, 79 S.Ct. 962, 3 L.Ed.2d 1003 (1959).

Appeal from the United States District Court for the Southern District of Illinois.

Mr. Justice DOUGLAS delivered the opinion of the Court.

We are asked in this case to hold that an Illinois statute requiring the use of a certain type of rear fender mudguard on trucks and trailers operated on the highways of that State conflicts with the Commerce Clause of the Constitution. The statutory specification for this type of mudguard provides that the guard shall contour the rear wheel, with the inside surface being relatively parallel to the top 90 degrees of the rear 180 degrees of the whole surface. The surface of the guard must extend downward to within 10 inches from the ground when the truck is loaded to its maximum legal capacity. The guards must be wide enough to cover the width of the protected tire, must be installed not more than 6 inches from the tire surface when the vehicle is loaded to maximum capacity, and must have a lip or flange on its outer edge of not less than 2 inches.

Appellees, interstate motor carriers holding certificates from the Interstate Commerce Commission, challenged the constitutionality of the Illinois Act. A specially constituted three-judge District Court concluded that it unduly and unreasonably burdened and obstructed interstate commerce, because it made the conventional or straight mudflap, which is legal in at least 45 States, illegal in Illinois, and because the statute, taken together with a Rule of the Arkansas Commerce Commission requiring straight mudflaps, rendered the use of the same motor vehicle equipment in both States impossible.

. . . .

The power of the State to regulate the use of its highways is broad and pervasive. We have recognized the peculiarly local nature of this subject of safety, and have upheld state statutes applicable alike to interstate and intrastate commerce, despite the fact that they may have an impact on interstate commerce. South Carolina Highway Dept. v. Barnwell Bros. . . .

These safety measures carry a strong presumption of validity when challenged in court. If there are alternative ways of solving a problem, we do not sit to determine which of them is best suited to achieve a valid state objective. Policy decisions are for the state legislature, absent federal entry into the field.[1] Unless we can conclude on the whole record that "the total effect of the law as a safety measure in reducing accidents and casualties is so slight or problematical as not to outweigh the national interest in keeping interstate commerce free from interferences which seriously impede it" (Southern Pacific Co. v. Arizona), we must uphold the statute.

The District Court found that "since it is impossible for a carrier operating in interstate commerce to determine which of its equipment will be used in a particular area, or on a particular day, or days, carriers operating into or through Illinois . . . will be required to equip all of their trailers in accordance with the requirements of the Illinois Splash Guard statute." With two possible exceptions the mudflaps required in those States which have mudguard regulations would not meet the standards required by the Illinois statute. The cost of installing the contour mudguards is $30 or more per vehicle. The District Court found that the initial cost of installing those mudguards on all the trucks owned by the appellees ranged from $4,500 to $45,840. There was also evidence in the record to indicate that the cost of maintenance and replacement of these guards is substantial.

Illinois introduced evidence seeking to establish that contour mudguards had a decided safety factor in that they prevented the throwing of debris into the faces of drivers of passing cars and into the windshields of a following vehicle. But the District Court in its opinion stated that it was "conclusively shown that the contour mud flap possesses no advantages over the conventional or straight mud flap previously required in Illinois and presently required in most of the states," (159 F.Supp., at 388) and that "there is rather convincing testimony that use of the contour flap creates hazards previously

1. It is not argued that there has been a pre-emption of the field by federal regulation. While the Interstate Commerce Commission [has] promulgated its Motor Carrier Safety Regulations to govern vehicles operating in interstate or foreign commerce, it has expressly declined to establish any requirements concerning wheel flaps, and has disclaimed any intention to occupy the field or abrogate state regulations not inconsistent with its standards. [Footnote by the Court. Compare sec. 2A, below.]

unknown to those using the highways." Id., at 390. These hazards were found to be occasioned by the fact that this new type of mudguard tended to cause an accumulation of heat in the brake drum, thus decreasing the effectiveness of brakes, and by the fact that they were susceptible of being hit and bumped when the trucks were backed up and of falling off on the highway.

These findings on cost and on safety are not the end of our problem. . . . Cost taken into consideration with other factors might be relevant in some cases to the issue of burden on commerce. But it has assumed no such proportions here. If we had here only a question whether the cost of adjusting an interstate operation to these new local safety regulations prescribed by Illinois unduly burdened interstate commerce, we would have to sustain the law . . . . . The same result would obtain if we had to resolve the much discussed issues of safety presented in this case.

This case presents a different issue. The equipment in [earlier] cases could pass muster in any State, so far as the records in those cases reveal. We were not faced there with the question whether one State could prescribe standards for interstate carriers that would conflict with the standards of another State, making it necessary, say, for an interstate carrier to shift its cargo to differently designed vehicles once another state line was reached. We had a related problem in Southern Pacific Co. v. Arizona, supra . . . . . More closely in point is Morgan v. Virginia, 328 U.S. 373, where a local law required a reseating of passengers on interstate busses entering Virginia in order to comply with a local segregation law. Diverse seating arrangements for people of different races imposed by several States interfered, we concluded, with "the need for national uniformity in the regulations for interstate travel." [2] . . .

An order of the Arkansas Commerce Commission, already mentioned, requires that trailers operating in that State be equipped with straight or conventional mudflaps. Vehicles equipped to meet the standards of the Illinois

2. In Morgan v. Virginia, in 1946, the Court noted that "related statutes of other states are important to show whether there are cumulative effects which make local regulation impracticable." The Morgan case came one year after Southern Pacific, where Justices Black and Douglas had opposed the majority's approach. Justice Douglas did not explain his vote with the majority in Morgan. In a concurrence, Justice Black recalled his protests against the "undue burdens" doctrine, stated that he still believed that it led the Court to act as a "super-legislature," but concluded that in view "of the Court's present disposition to apply that formula, I acquiesce." Morgan relied on Hall v. DeCuir, 95 U.S. 485 (1878), which had invalidated as an unconstitutional burden on commerce a Louisiana anti-segregation law of 1869 as applied to steamboats.
Note the more recent cases involving application of state civil rights laws to transportation. in Bob-Lo Excursion Co. v. Michigan, 333 U.S. 28 (1948), the Court sustained a state law barring racial discrimination as applied to an amusement park company's vessel operating from Detroit to the park, on an island in the Detroit River in Canadian waters. Though the Court found that the state was regulating foreign commerce, it upheld the law because of the company's "highly localized business." And in Colorado Anti-Discrimination Comm'n v. Continental Airlines, 372 U.S. 714 (1963), the Court reversed the state court's holding that the state civil rights law could not be applied to the hiring of flight personnel by an interstate air carrier. The Morgan-DeCuir kind of burden, Justice Black stated, "simply cannot exist here." Moreover, hiring of employees is "a much more localized matter" than transporting passengers. [On the current impact of the Fourteenth Amendment and federal legislation on segregation in transportation facilities, see chap. 3, above, and chap. 10, below.]

statute would not comply with Arkansas standards, and vice versa. Thus if a trailer is to be operated in both States, mudguards would have to be interchanged, causing a significant delay in an operation where prompt movement may be of the essence. It was found that from two to four hours of labor are required to install or remove a contour mudguard. Moreover, the contour guard is attached to the trailer by welding and if the trailer is conveying a cargo of explosives (e. g., for the United States Government) it would be exceedingly dangerous to attempt to weld on a contour mudguard without unloading the trailer.

It was also found that the Illinois statute seriously interferes with the "interline" operations of motor carriers—that is to say, with the interchanging of trailers between an originating carrier and another carrier when the latter serves an area not served by the former. These "interline" operations provide a speedy through-service for the shipper. Interlining contemplates the physical transfer of the entire trailer; there is no unloading and reloading of the cargo. The interlining process is particularly vital in connection with shipment of perishables, which would spoil if unloaded before reaching their destination, or with the movement of explosives carried under seal. Of course, if the originating carrier never operated in Illinois, it would not be expected to equip its trailers with contour mudguards. Yet if an interchanged trailer of that carrier were hauled to or through Illinois, the statute would require that it contain contour guards. Since carriers which operate in and through Illinois cannot compel the originating carriers to equip their trailers with contour guards, they may be forced to cease interlining with those who do not meet the Illinois requirements. Over 60 percent of the business of 5 of the 6 plaintiffs is interline traffic. For the other it constitutes 30 percent. All of the plaintiffs operate extensively in interstate commerce, and the annual mileage in Illinois of none of them exceeds 7 percent of total mileage.

This in summary is the rather massive showing of burden on interstate commerce which appellees made at the hearing.

Appellants did not attempt to rebut the appellees' showing that the statute in question severely burdens interstate commerce. Appellants' showing was aimed at establishing that contour mudguards prevented the throwing of debris into the faces of drivers of passing cars and into the windshields of a following vehicle. They concluded that, because the Illinois statute is a reasonable exercise of the police power, a federal court is precluded from weighing the relative merits of the contour mudguard against any other kind of mudguard and must sustain the validity of the statute notwithstanding the extent of the burden it imposes on interstate commerce. They rely in the main on South Carolina Highway Dept. v. Barnwell Bros., supra. There is language in that opinion which, read in isolation from such later decisions as Southern Pacific Co. v. Arizona, supra, and Morgan v. Virginia, supra, would suggest that no showing of burden on interstate commerce is sufficient to invalidate local safety regulations in absence of some element of discrimination against interstate commerce.

The various exercises by the States of their police power stand, however, on an equal footing. All are entitled to the same presumption of validity when challenged under the Due Process Clause of the Fourteenth Amendment. . . . Similarly the various state regulatory statutes are of equal dig-

nity when measured against the Commerce Clause. Local regulations which would pass muster under the Due Process Clause might nonetheless fail to survive other challenges to constitutionality that bring the Supremacy Clause into play. Like any local law that conflicts with federal regulatory measures . . ., state regulations that run afoul of the policy of free trade reflected in the Commerce Clause must also bow.

This is one of those cases—few in number—where local safety measures that are nondiscriminatory place an unconstitutional burden on interstate commerce. This conclusion is especially underlined by the deleterious effect which the Illinois law will have on the "interline" operation of interstate motor carriers. The conflict between the Arkansas regulation and the Illinois regulation also suggests that this regulation of mudguards is not one of those matters "admitting of diversity of treatment, according to the special requirements of local conditions" . . . . A State which insists on a design out of line with the requirements of almost all the other States may sometimes place a great burden of delay and inconvenience on those interstate motor carriers entering or crossing its territory. Such a new safety device—out of line with the requirements of the other States—may be so compelling that the innovating State need not be the one to give way. But the present showing—balanced against the clear burden on commerce—is far too inconclusive to make this mudguard meet that test.

We deal not with absolutes but with questions of degree. The state legislatures plainly have great leeway in providing safety regulations for all vehicles—interstate as well as local. Our decisions so hold. Yet the heavy burden which the Illinois mudguard law places on the interstate movement of trucks and trailers seems to us to pass the permissible limits even for safety regulations.

Affirmed.

Mr. Justice HARLAN, whom Mr. Justice STEWART joins, concurring.

The opinion of the Court clearly demonstrates the heavy burden, in terms of cost and interference with "interlining," which the Illinois statute here involved imposes on interstate commerce. In view of the findings of the District Court . . . . to the effect that the contour mudflap "possesses no advantages" in terms of safety over the conventional flap permitted in all other States, and indeed creates certain safety hazards, this heavy burden cannot be justified on the theory that the Illinois statute is a necessary, appropriate, or helpful local safety measure. Accordingly, I concur in the judgment of the Court.

————

BIBB AND BALANCING IN HIGHWAY CASES

What is the standard of review in Bibb? Apparently, it is more intensive than in Barnwell. Is it as intensive as in Southern Pacific? Or is it somewhere in between? Why should there be a difference between cases such as Southern Pacific and Bibb? What explains Justice Harlan's concurrence? Is it closer to the Southern Pacific approach than Justice Douglas' majority opinion? Is Bibb as unusual a case as Justice Douglas suggests? Are the Illinois and Arkansas standards any more "inconsistent" than the "conflicting" standards in the Southern Pacific case?

Can it be argued that, if the Illinois law is unconstitutional, mudguard regulation must be a subject requiring "uniform" rather than permitting "diverse" regulation under Cooley? Does it then follow that *no* state regulation of mudguards is permissible, so that the Arkansas straight mudguard requirement falls as a result of Bibb? Only if the Arkansas requirement is no more effective than the Illinois one? Does the fate of other mudguard standards turn not on the question of which requirement is more effective, but which is the more common? Or which came first?

Should the Bibb approach be applied only when there are in fact "inconsistent" regulations in different states? Or should it be available when there is merely a *risk* of inconsistent regulations? Recall Chief Justice Stone's comment in Southern Pacific: "If one state may regulate train lengths, so may all the others, and they need not prescribe the same . . . ." On the unsettled problem of whether it is the actuality or the mere risk of multiple inconsistent regulations that is determinative, note also the comments in the next group of notes.

THE HURON PORTLAND CEMENT CASE: COMMERCE CLAUSE OBJECTIONS AGAINST A BACKGROUND OF CONGRESSIONAL POLICY

1. *The commerce clause criteria: The Huron standards in the light of Bibb and Pike.* a. A year after the extensive attention to the commerce clause claim in Bibb, the Court disposed of a seemingly substantial commerce objection almost summarily, in HURON PORTLAND CEMENT CO. v. CITY OF DETROIT, 362 U.S. 440 (1960). Is the apparent difference in the articulated standards explainable? Justifiable? In Huron, Justice Stewart's majority opinion held that Detroit's Smoke Abatement Code could constitutionally be applied to the company's ships. The ships' boilers emitted smoke exceeding Detroit's maximum standard; compliance would require structural alterations in the boilers. Most of the Court's discussion was devoted to the claim that federal laws had preempted the field (see sec. 2A below). The Court found no bar either in the "extensive and comprehensive" federal boiler inspection provisions or in the federal licensing of the vessels. The main purpose of federal inspection was to assure safety; the Detroit ordinance was directed solely at air pollution. And possession of the federal license "does not immunize a ship from the . . . local police power, not constituting a direct regulation of commerce." Justice Stewart's opinion for the Court relied heavily on evidence of "Congressional recognition that the problem of air pollution is peculiarly a matter of state and local concern."

Justice Stewart disposed of the commerce clause objection in two paragraphs: "The claim that the Detroit ordinance, quite apart from the effect of federal legislation, imposes as to the appellant's ships an undue burden on interstate commerce needs no extended discussion. State regulation, based on the police power, which does not discriminate against interstate commerce or operate to disrupt its required uniformity, may constitutionally stand.
. . . .

"It has not been suggested that the local ordinance, applicable alike to 'any person, firm or corporation' within the city, discriminates against interstate commerce as such. It is a regulation of general application, designed

to better the health and welfare of the community. And while the appellant argues that other local governments might impose differing requirements as to air pollution, it has pointed to none. The record contains nothing to suggest the existence of any such competing or conflicting local regulations. Cf. [Bibb]. We conclude that no impermissible burden on commerce has been shown." Justice Douglas, joined by Justice Frankfurter, dissented on the ground of federal preemption.

b. Was Justice Stewart's summary a comprehensive statement of all available bases for commerce clause objections? Is a commerce clause attack available only if "discrimination" is shown, or if the existence of "differing requirements" in other jurisdictions is demonstrated? What about the *risk* that other jurisdictions *might* impose "competing or conflicting" requirements? What about the general balancing approach of Southern Pacific? Another opinion by Justice Stewart a decade later indicates that he does indeed find a greater bite in the commerce clause than his statement in Huron suggested. He once again wrote for the Court in PIKE v. BRUCE CHURCH, INC., 397 U.S. 137 (1970) (considered further below, sec. 1D), striking down an Arizona requirement barring the shipment of local cantaloupes out of the state if they were uncrated. In Pike, in "rephrasing" the "general rule" of the commerce clause for a unanimous Court, Justice Stewart stated: "Where the statute regulates evenhandedly to effectuate a legitimate local public interest, and its effects on interstate commerce are only incidental, it will be upheld unless the burden imposed on such commerce is clearly excessive in relation to the putative local benefits. [Huron.] If a legitimate local purpose is found, then the question becomes one of degree. And the extent of the burden that will be tolerated will of course depend on the nature of the local interest involved, and on whether it could be promoted as well with a lesser impact on interstate activities. Occasionally the Court has candidly undertaken a balancing approach in resolving these issues [Southern Pacific], but more frequently it has spoken in terms of 'direct' and 'indirect' effects and burdens." (On the relevance to the balancing approach of inquiry into means "with a lesser impact on interstate activities," see the Dean Milk case, sec. 1C below; and compare the Oregon Bottle Case, sec. 1E below.)

2. *Multiple inconsistent burdens: Actuality or risk?* When does the problem of multiple inconsistent burdens become significant in commerce clause litigation? The Court has been ambivalent about whether it is the *actuality* or the *risk* of multiple inconsistent burdens that is the evil. In Bibb, there were conflicting regulations in fact. In Huron, the Court dismissed the burden argument by noting that no "differing requirements" had been shown. Yet in Southern Pacific, the Court seemed to be concerned with the *potential* of multiple inconsistent burdens: "If one state may regulate train lengths, so may all the others . . . ." What if Chicago and Cleveland were in the future to impose "competing and conflicting regulations" on Huron's ships? Would that cause the Detroit ordinance to fall? Chicago's and Cleveland's? All three? Compare also the approaches to the multiple burdens argument in the Morgan and DeCuir cases, footnote 2 to Bibb: in the Morgan case in 1946, in striking down a local segregation law, the Court noted other state statutes to demonstrate "cumulative effects." But in invalidating a local anti-segregation requirement in DeCuir in 1878,

the Court emphasized the risk: "If each State was at liberty to regulate the conduct of carriers while within its jurisdiction, the confusion likely to follow could not but be productive of great inconvenience and unnecessary hardship." *

3. *The role of Congress.* May the real explanation of the Court's curt treatment of the commerce clause issue in Huron lie in the Court's perception of a congressional "recognition" of air pollution as a "local" matter? Might the Court have examined the commerce clause claim more carefully if there had been no such congressional "recognition"? Determination of congressional policy was clearly essential to the evaluation of the preemption challenge. But should congressional policy have influenced the statements about commerce clause doctrine as well? Could the decision have been explained as an example of congressional consent to what might otherwise be unconstitutionally burdensome local regulation (see sec. 2B below)? On the influence of congressional policy in the disposition of "constitutional" commerce clause objections, see also Parker v. Brown, sec. 1D below. On potential impacts in the other direction—"constitutional" commerce clause considerations influencing the decision as to congressional "intent" regarding preemption—see sec. 2A below and especially Campbell v. Hussey.

C. ACCESS OF FOREIGN SELLERS TO LOCAL MARKETS: STATE BARRIERS TO INCOMING TRADE

Introduction: State regulation of interstate trade. In most of the cases in sec. 1B above, the impact of the challenged state regulation fell on an interstate transportation facility, and the typical state objective was the promotion of local safety and health. In most of the cases in this section and the next, secs. 1C and 1D, the impact of the state regulation falls on interstate trade, on an interstate seller or buyer; and the objectives of state regulation at times extend beyond concern with local health and safety to "economic" purposes. What guidance can be derived from the commerce clause and the structure of the federal system to resolve conflicts between local regulation and interstate trade? Are the criteria developed in the inter-

---

* For a recent consideration of the risk of multiple burdens, see Burbank v. Lockheed Air Terminal, 411 U.S. 624 (1973) (further noted below, sec. 2A). In a 5 to 4 decision, the Court invalidated a local airport noise curfew. Justice Douglas' majority opinion, which purported to rely solely on preemption grounds, nevertheless stated: "If we were to uphold the Burbank ordinance and a significant number of municipalities followed suit, it is obvious that fractionalized control of the timing of takeoffs and landings would severely limit the flexibility of the FAA in controlling air traffic flow." (The District Court decision invalidating the ordinance had relied on the commerce clause as well.) Contrast with Justice Douglas' majority opinion the comment on that issue in Justice Rehnquists's dissent, joined by Justices Stewart, White and Marshall: "The District Court's conclusion appears to be based, at least in part, on a consideration of the effect on interstate commerce that would result if all municipal airports in the country enacted ordinances such as that of Burbank. Since the proper determination of the question turns on an evaluation of the facts of each case, see, e.g., [Bibb], and not on a predicted proliferation of possibilities, the District Court's conclusion is of doubtful validity."

state transportation cases wholly applicable to those involving interstate trade? Or do the latter involve added variables and warrant variations in the analytical tools? Should interstate trade be more readily reachable by the state than interstate transportation? Because interstate buyers and sellers are likely to engage in more separable "local" activities than interstate carriers? Should "economic" purposes be more suspect than health and safety objectives?

As the transportation cases indicate, state concerns with health and safety are legitimate; yet when regulations resting on those proper state concerns fall on interstate carriers, the Court frequently engages in the process of balancing the state's interest in achieving the legitimate objectives against the burdens imposed on interstate commerce. Is balancing any less appropriate when state health and safety laws fall on interstate trade? The opinions in the transportation cases also indicate that state objectives become more questionable when they are "economic" in nature. No doubt, hostility to state efforts to give a competitive advantage to local economic interests is one of the core values of the commerce clause. But does that justify judicial suspicion of all "economic" legislation? Does Buck v. Kuykendall, sec. 1B above, suggest special scrutiny of *all* "economic" laws? Is not concern with the local economy as legitimate an ingredient of the police power as the protection of health and safety? Modern due process cases leave no doubt that a state regulating within its own borders may establish a scheme of price regulation for example. May the state apply that legitimate local scheme to interstate trade transactions, in the interest of preserving the integrity of the local regulatory system? Or must a state accept the risk of undercutting its system of economic regulation by immunizing interstate sales from its reach? May a state preserve its own natural resources for its own inhabitants?

Questions such as these are recurrent ones in the materials that follow. How well has the Court articulated the national commerce concerns to be protected? What state justifications are recognized as legitimate? How does the Court determine state purposes? How does it identify effects on interstate commerce? Is it concerned with actualities or risks? What of mixed state objectives and uncertain effects on commerce? Are the Court's perceptions adequate? Or are its attributions of purposes and assertions of effects too often question-begging?

In assessing the Court's performance in the cases that follow, recall Justice Jackson's summary of "the vision of the Founders" in the Hood case, quoted at the beginning of this chapter, above. He insisted that "our economic unit is the Nation," that "the States are not separable economic units." He asserted: "This Court consistently has rebuffed attempts of states to advance their own commercial interests by curtailing the movement of articles of commerce, either into or out of the state, while generally supporting their right to impose even burdensome regulations in the interest of local health and safety." And he stated as the governing ideal: "Our system, fostered by the Commerce Clause, is that every farmer and every craftsman shall be encouraged to produce by the certainty that he will have free access to every market in the Nation, that no home embargoes will withhold his exports, and no foreign state will by customs duties or regulations exclude them. Likewise, every consumer may look to the free competition from every producing area in the Nation to protect him from exploitation

by any. Such was the vision of the Founders; such has been the doctrine of this Court which has given it reality." Once again, and with even more immediate application, that quotation poses the underlying questions relevant to the ensuing materials: Is that "free access" vision a justifiable one? A realistic one? Have Court doctrine and implementation indeed given "reality" to that "vision"? *

BALDWIN v. SEELIG, "HOSTILE" ECONOMIC BARRIERS— AND "CATCH WORDS AND LABELS"

1. *The Baldwin decision.* BALDWIN v. G. A. F. SEELIG, INC., 294 U.S. 511 (1935), dealt with the impact on interstate trade of a state effort to regulate milk prices. The New York Milk Control Act of 1933 set the minimum prices to be paid by New York dealers to milk producers. In a decision prior to Baldwin, the Court recognized that the state's price control law was well within New York's police power so far as its wholly intrastate impact was concerned: in Nebbia v. New York, 291 U.S. 502 (1934) (chap. 9 below), the Court sustained the law as applied to New York's domestic economy, against a challenge that price regulation constituted a deprivation of liberty and property without the due process of law required by the 14th Amendment. In Nebbia, the Court had taken note of the "desperate" situation of dairy producers because of the fall in prices for milk during the Depression. But in the Baldwin case a year later, the commerce clause was held to prohibit some applications of the New York price control law. Seelig, a New York milk dealer, bought milk in Vermont at prices lower than the New York minimum. The New York law prohibited New York sales of out-of-state milk if the milk had been purchased below the price set for similar purchases within New York. New York refused to license Seelig to sell milk unless there was an agreement to conform to the state's price regulation regarding the sale of imported milk. Seelig sued to enjoin enforcement of the Act. The Supreme Court unanimously held the application of the Act unconstitutional.

Justice Cardozo stated that New York's regulation "set a barrier to traffic between one state and another as effective as if customs duties, equal to the price differential, had been laid upon the thing transported. . . . Nice distinctions have been made at times between direct and indirect burdens. They are irrelevant when the avowed purpose of the obstruction, as well as its necessary tendency, is to suppress or mitigate the consequences of competition between the states. Such an obstruction is direct by the very terms of the hypothesis. We are reminded in the opinion below that a chief occasion of the commerce clause was 'the mutual jealousies and aggressions of the States, taking form in customs barriers and other economic retaliation.' . . . If New York, in order to promote the economic welfare of her

---

* Most of the leading cases in secs. 1C and 1D—Baldwin, Dean Milk, Eisenberg, Hood—involve regulations of the dairy industry. That is not of course the only context that has given rise to problems of state regulations of incoming or outgoing commerce; but the unity of context of these decisions aids analysis of the Court's efforts to articulate protected values and constitutional limitations.

farmers, may guard them against competition with the cheaper prices of Vermont, the door has been opened to rivalries and reprisals that were meant to be averted by subjecting commerce between the states to the power of the nation."

The Court rejected the argument that the Act was justified by the state's aim to assure "a regular and adequate supply of pure and wholesome milk." Supply was jeopardized, it was claimed, when farmers cannot earn a living income: "the economic motive is secondary and subordinate; the state intervenes to make its inhabitants healthy, and not to make them rich." Justice Cardozo stated that these contentions could not justify the Act as a valid "police" measure with only "incidental" impact on commerce: "This would be to eat up the rule under the guise of an exception. Economic welfare is always related to health .   .   . . Let such an exception be admitted, and all that a state will have to do in times of stress and strain is to say that its farmers and merchants and workmen must be protected against competition from without, lest they go upon the poor relief lists or perish altogether. To give entrance to that excuse would be to invite a speedy end of our national solidarity. The Constitution was framed under the dominion of a political philosophy less parochial in range. It was framed upon the theory that the peoples of the several states must sink or swim together, and that in the long run prosperity and salvation are in union and not division. .   .   . The line of division between direct and indirect restraints of commerce involves in its marking a reference to considerations of degree. Even so, the borderland is wide between the restraints upheld as incidental and those attempted here. Subject to the paramount power of the Congress, a state may regulate the importation of unhealthy swine or cattle [Mintz v. Baldwin] * or decayed or noxious foods. [Savage v. Jones, 225 U.S. 501.] So a state may protect its inhabitants against the fraudulent substitution, by deceptive coloring or otherwise, of one article for another. Plumley v. Massachusetts, 155 U.S. 461. .   .   . . It may give protection to travelers against the dangers of overcrowded highways .   .   . . None of these statutes—inspection laws, game laws, laws intended to curb fraud or exterminate disease—approaches in drastic quality the statute here in controversy which would neutralize the economic consequences of free trade among the states.

".   .   . Neither the power to tax nor the police power may be used by the state of destination with the aim and effect of establishing an economic barrier against competition with the products of another state .   .   . .. Restrictions so contrived are an unreasonable clog on the mobility of Com-

---

* Mintz v. Baldwin, 289 U.S. 346 (1933), sustained New York's law barring the importation of cattle unless they were from herds certified as being free from Bang's disease. (Note the comment on the genuineness of that purpose, below.) But not all state laws assertedly based on health concerns survive commerce clause scrutiny, as the interstate transportation cases have already indicated. For invalidated state laws regarding interstate trade, see e. g., Dean Milk, printed below, and Minnesota v. Barber, noted below.

And compare with the Mintz decision, Hannibal & St. Joseph R. v. Husen, 95 U.S. 465 (1877) (invalidating a Missouri statute prohibiting bringing certain cattle into the state for three-fourths of the year; the Court, while recognizing the state's interest in preventing disease, insisted that a state may not interfere with interstate commerce "beyond what is absolutely necessary for its self-protection. It may not, under the cover of exerting its police powers, substantially prohibit or burden" interstate commerce.)

merce. They set up what is the equivalent of a rampart of customs duties designed to neutralize advantages belonging to the place of origin. They are thus hostile in conception as well as burdensome in result."

2. *Economic barriers and judicial competence.* Are all state economic barriers affecting an out-of-state supplier unconstitutional? Only those with certain effects? Only those with certain purposes? The New York regulation did not discriminate against the Vermont producer in the sense of imposing a ban on imports or singling out that seller for regulations not imposed on local producers. Was the effect nevertheless excessively burdensome because it tended "to neutralize advantages belonging to the place of origin"? Does Baldwin condemn economic burdens too broadly? When are such burdens permitted? When they are very light? Is the Court competent to assess the relative economic impacts of various "burdens"?

3. *State purpose and judicial "psychoanalysis."* Does the permissibility of an economic burden turn on the state's purpose? Is the Court more competent to assess purpose than economic effect? Is Justice Cardozo's emphasis on purpose reconcilable with his objection to purpose inquiries involving the federal taxing power? In 1935, the year of the Baldwin decisions, he dissented from a decision in which the Court struck down a federal tax because "the purpose is to usurp" state police powers. Justice Cardozo countered: "Thus the process of psychoanalysis has spread to unaccustomed fields." United States v. Constantine, 296 U.S. 287 (1935) (noted in chap. 4, sec. 1, above). Does inquiry into "purpose" when state laws are challenged under the commerce clause, as in Baldwin, involve less difficult "psychoanalysis"? Is "psychoanalysis" a more appropriate Court function there?

4. *State purpose and interstate commerce.* What was the forbidden purpose in Baldwin, and why was it forbidden? Was hostility to Vermont producers New York's primary concern? The Court recognized that some state laws with "pure" police purposes—e. g., bans on "noxious foods"— were permissible barriers to imports. At the other extreme, obviously discriminatory laws to protect the local producers against foreign competitors are illegitimate. Did Justice Cardozo deny New York's contention that its law in Baldwin lay between those extremes? Is his analysis adequate to deal with this gray borderline area? Would it have been better to articulate the values and conflicting indicia and engage in a form of the "balancing" of the Southern Pacific case?

New York had argued in Baldwin that application of the law to distributors in Seelig's position was essential to protect the domestic operation of the law, and that the effect on interstate commerce was incidental to the aim of achieving its domestic objectives. Justice Cardozo's opinion rejected that argument. Was greater attention warranted for the claim that application of the law to interstate transactions was necessary to protect the integrity of the state's system of economic regulation—a system concededly resting on valid internal state objectives? Did the inability to apply the New York law to milk originating in Vermont undermine legitimate domestic objectives? Would application of the law to Seelig's milk purchase have constituted undue New York economic self-interest to the disadvantage of out-of-staters? If that state need in Baldwin was not sufficient justification,

would it not have been preferable to explain why commerce clause values outweighed that need, rather than portraying the state's concern so unsympathetically? Did the Court recognize the justifiability of the state's interest in preserving the integrity of its economic regulatory system four years later, in the Eisenberg case, sec. 1D below? Are Baldwin and Eisenberg distinguishable?

5. *Hostile "economic barriers" and benign "equalization": The relevance of Justice Cardozo's Silas Mason opinion.* Compare, with Justice Cardozo's broad-gauged condemnation of New York's economic barrier in Baldwin v. Seelig, his rejection of a similar attack, on a tax barrier, in HENNEFORD v. SILAS MASON CO., 300 U.S. 577 (1937). That decision upheld a Washington use tax on goods bought in other states. Washington law placed a 2% tax on retail sales within Washington; another section imposed a "compensating tax" on the price of goods (including transportation costs) for the "privilege of using" in Washington goods bought at retail out of the state. (The use tax was inapplicable to any article which had already been subjected to a sales or use tax of at least 2%; for articles previously taxed at less than 2%, there was a prorated exemption from the use tax.) The point of that scheme was clear to the Court: as Justice Cardozo put it in his opinion for a unanimous Court, local retail sellers "will be helped to compete upon terms of equality with retail dealers in other states who are exempt from a sales tax"; local buyers will "no longer [be] tempted to place their orders in other states" to escape the local sales tax.

Nevertheless, this was not a forbidden economic barrier to Justice Cardozo: "Equality is the theme that runs through all sections of the statute. . . . When the account is made up, the stranger from afar is subject to no greater burdens as a consequence of ownership than the dweller within the gates. . . . In each situation the burden borne by the owner is balanced by an equal burden where the sale is strictly local." Nor were the reasons for the use tax fatal. The challengers attacked it as "equivalent to a protective tariff." Justice Cardozo was not impressed: "[M]otives alone will seldom, if ever, invalidate a tax that apart from its motives would be recognized as lawful. . . . Least of all will they be permitted to accomplish that result when equality and not preference is the end to be achieved. Catch words and labels, such as the words 'protective tariff,' are subject to the dangers that lurk in metaphors and symbols, and must be watched with circumspection lest they put us off our guard. [A] tax upon use [unlike a tariff] is not a clog on the process of importation at all."

Justice Cardozo insisted, moreover, that Baldwin v. Seelig was distinguishable. That case, he stated "is far apart from this one. . . . New York was attempting to project its legislation within the borders of another state by regulating the price to be paid in that state for milk acquired there. She said in effect to farmers in Vermont: your milk cannot be sold by dealers to whom you ship it in New York unless you sell it to them in Vermont at a price determined here. What Washington is saying to sellers beyond her borders is something very different. In substance what she says is this: You may ship your goods in such amounts and at such prices as you please, but the goods when used in Washington after the transit is completed, will share an equal burden with goods that have been purchased here."

Are Baldwin and Silas Mason truly reconcilable? In result? In reasoning? Was Justice Cardozo's characterization of the Baldwin regulation—as a hostile "customs barrier"—unduly harsh? Was his characterization of the Silas Mason tax—as an "equality measure"—unduly benign? Was he, too, "put off guard" by the "catch words and labels" he warned against? Are the cases really distinguishable because of the "extraterritorial" impact of Baldwin? In Baldwin, the immediate sanction was imposed on the New York distributor. To be sure, that sanction discouraged buying from the Vermont producer. But did not the intrastate sanction in the Washington use tax also discourage buying from the out-of-state seller? Could New York have achieved its price control objective by imposing an appropriately scaled tax on low-cost milk purchased elsewhere for sale in New York? Are Baldwin and Silas Mason more persuasively distinguishable because Washington's use tax cancelled only the advantage the out-of-state seller had because he was not subject to a sales tax, while New York's scheme in Baldwin cancelled all the advantages the Vermont seller had because of lower costs of production—taxes as well as all other costs? Washington's plan, in other words, still permitted some price competition; New York's did not. But is the free trade ideal—so eloquently described by Justice Cardozo in Baldwin—adequately satisfied by a finding that at least *some* price competition remains in the consuming market? Should Baldwin and Silas Mason have been subjected to a balancing analysis, rather than "customs barrier" and "equality" characterizations? Do the cases since the 1930's move toward such a balancing approach?

6. *The vitality of Baldwin: The Polar Ice Cream case.* In its most recent encounter with "the recurring question of the validity of a State's attempt to regulate the supply and distribution of milk," a unanimous Court relied on the dairy industry decisions in these materials, especially Baldwin, in invalidating a Florida regulatory scheme which had the effect of reserving to local producers "a substantial share of the Florida milk market." POLAR ICE CREAM & CREAMERY CO. v. ANDREWS, 375 U.S. 361 (1964). Florida attempted to compel a local distributor to accept his total supply of certain milk from designated local producers at a fixed price and obligated the distributor to take all milk which the local producers offered. Justice White stated: "The principles of Baldwin are as sound today as they were when announced. [T]he exclusion of foreign milk from a major portion of the Florida market cannot be justified as an economic measure to protect the welfare of Florida dairy farmers or as a health measure designed to insure the existence of a wholesome supply of milk. This much Baldwin and Dean [which follows] made clear." Justice White distinguished cases such as Eisenberg, sec. 1D, below, because they did not involve "any attempt to reserve a local market for local producers or to protect local producers from out-of-state competition by means of purchase and allocation requirements imposed upon milk distributors."

7. *Personal mobility, hostile state barriers, and the commerce clause: Edwards v. California.* a. *Edwards and commerce.* In most commerce clause cases, it is interstate businesses that seek protection against state action. But the commerce clause is also one of several constitutional provisions that has been invoked to safeguard the individual's ability to move from state to

state. Baldwin v. Seelig was relied on for that purpose in EDWARDS v. CALIFORNIA, 314 U.S. 160 (1941), which struck down a law making it a misdemeanor to bring into California "any indigent person who is not a resident of the State, knowing him to be an indigent person." Justice Byrnes' opinion found this to be an unconstitutional burden on commerce. He quoted the Baldwin v. Seelig statement that the Constitution "was framed upon the theory that the peoples of the several states must sink or swim together" and commented: "It is difficult to conceive of a statute more squarely in conflict with this theory [than the California 'Okie' law]." It might well be true, as the state asserted, that "the huge influx of migrants into California in recent years has resulted in problems of health, morals and especially finance, the proportions of which are staggering." But no state could "isolate itself from difficulties common to all of them by restraining the transportation of persons and property across its borders."

b. *The Edwards concurrence.* The commerce clause has not been the only source of increasingly frequent arguments to support a right of personal mobility. In Edwards itself, for example, four of the Justices concurred on the basis of the rarely invoked privileges and immunities clause of the 14th Amendment (see chap. 8, sec. 2, below). Note, e. g., the concurrence of Justice Jackson: "[T]he migrations of a human being . . . do not fit easily into my notions as to what is commerce."

c. *Other constitutional supports for personal mobility.* The debate over the appropriateness of looking to the commerce clause as a source for a right to interstate mobility has not prevented the Court from asserting the existence of such a right, despite the uncertainty about its basis. Suggestions as to the source have ranged from the commerce clause and the privileges and immunities clause of the 14th Amendment (see chap. 8 below) to a structural inference from the Constitution. See, e. g., Justice Stewart's majority opinion in United States v. Guest, 383 U.S. 745 (1966) (civil rights violence; chap. 11 below): "Although the Articles of Confederation provided that 'the people of each State shall have free ingress and regress to and from any other State,' that right finds no explicit mention in the Constitution. The reason, it has been suggested, is that a right so elementary was conceived from the beginning to be a necessary concomitant of the stronger Union the Constitution created. In any event, freedom to travel throughout the United States has long been recognized as a basic right under the Constitution." See also Crandall v. Nevada, 6 Wall. 35 (1868) (invalidating a tax on passengers leaving the state via common carrier, and noting the citizen's "right to come to the seat of government"—see the discussion in the Slaughter-House Cases, chap. 8 below).*

* As to more specific sources in the Constitution for the right, see, in addition to the commerce clause and the privileges and immunities clause of the 14th Amendment, the interstate privileges and immunities clause in the Constitution—that referring to state citizenship, in Art. IV, see chap. 6 below. Moreover, a right to travel may be an aspect of the "liberty" protected by due process guarantees, see Kent v. Dulles, 357 U.S. 116 (1958) (passport restrictions and foreign travel). Is there a difference between a right to pass through a state and a right to settle in another state? Which variety of right was involved in Edwards? Note the considerations of the right to move into and settle in another state in the consideration of durational residence requirements challenged as penalties on the right to travel in later materials. See, e. g., Shapiro v. Thompson, 394 U.S. 618 (1969) (chap.

DEAN MILK CO. v. CITY OF MADISON

340 U.S. 349, 71 S.Ct. 295, 95 L.Ed. 329 (1951).

Appeal from the Supreme Court of Wisconsin.

Mr. Justice CLARK delivered the opinion of the Court.

This appeal challenges the constitutional validity of two sections of an ordinance of the City of Madison, Wisconsin, regulating the sale of milk and milk products within the municipality's jurisdiction. One section in issue makes it unlawful to sell any milk as pasteurized unless it has been processed and bottled at an approved pasteurization plant within a radius of five miles from the central square of Madison. Another section which prohibits the sale of milk . . . in Madison unless from a source of supply possessing a permit issued after inspection by Madison officials, is attacked insofar as it expressly relieves municipal authorities from any duty to inspect farms located beyond twenty-five miles from the center of the city.

Appellant is an Illinois corporation engaged in distributing milk and milk products in Illinois and Wisconsin. . . . The Supreme Court of Wisconsin upheld the five-mile limit on pasteurization. As to the twenty-five-mile limitation the court ordered the complaint dismissed for want of a justiciable controversy. . . .

The City of Madison is the county seat of Dane County. Within the county are some 5,600 dairy farms with total raw milk production in excess of 600,000,000 pounds annually and more than ten times the requirements of Madison. Aside from the milk supplied to Madison, fluid milk produced in the county moves in large quantities to Chicago and more distant consuming areas, and the remainder is used in making cheese, butter and other products. At the time of trial the Madison milkshed was not of "Grade A" quality by the standards recommended by the United States Public Health Service, and no milk labeled "Grade A" was distributed in Madison.

The area defined by the ordinance with respect to milk sources encompasses practically all of Dane County and includes some 500 farms which supply milk for Madison. Within the five-mile area for pasteurization are plants of five processors, only three of which are engaged in the general wholesale and retail trade in Madison. Inspection of these farms and plants is scheduled once every thirty days and is performed by two municipal inspectors, one of whom is full-time. The courts below found that the ordinance in question promotes convenient, economical and efficient plant inspection.

Appellant purchases and gathers milk from approximately 950 farms in northern Illinois and southern Wisconsin, none being within twenty-five miles of Madison. Its pasteurization plants are located at Chemung and Huntley, Illinois, about 65 and 85 miles respectively from Madison. Appellant was denied a license to sell its products within Madison solely because its pasteurization plants were more than five miles away.

10 below) (one year residence requirement for welfare assistance invalidated as discriminatory burden on interstate mobility).

It is conceded that the milk which appellant seeks to sell in Madison is supplied from farms and processed in plants licensed and inspected by public health authorities of Chicago, and is labeled "Grade A" under the Chicago ordinance which adopts the rating standards recommended by the United States Public Health Service. . . . Madison contends and we assume that in some particulars its ordinance is more rigorous than that of Chicago. . . . [W]e agree with appellant that the ordinance imposes an undue burden on interstate commerce.

This is not an instance in which an enactment falls because of federal legislation . . . . There is no pertinent national regulation by the Congress . . . . Nor can there be objection to the avowed purpose of this enactment. We assume that difficulties in sanitary regulation of milk and milk products originating in remote areas may present a situation in which "it appears that the matter is one which may appropriately be regulated in the interest of the safety, health and well-being of local communities" . . . .

But this regulation, like the provision invalidated in Baldwin v. Seelig, Inc., supra, in practical effect excludes from distribution in Madison wholesome milk produced and pasteurized in Illinois. "The importer . . . may keep his milk or drink it, but sell it he may not." Id., at 521. In thus erecting an economic barrier protecting a major local industry against competition from without the State, Madison plainly discriminates against interstate commerce.[1] This it cannot do, even in the exercise of its unquestioned power to protect the health and safety of its people, if reasonable nondiscriminatory alternatives, adequate to conserve legitimate local interests, are available. Cf. Baldwin v. G. A. F. Seelig, Inc., supra; Minnesota v. Barber . . . . A different view, that the ordinance is valid simply because it professes to be a health measure, would mean that the Commerce Clause of itself imposes no limitations on state action other than those laid down by the Due Process Clause, save for the rare instance where a state artlessly discloses an avowed purpose to discriminate against interstate goods. . . . Our issue then is whether the discrimination inherent in the Madison ordinance can be justified in view of the character of the local interests and the available methods of protecting them. . . .

It appears that reasonable and adequate alternatives are available. If the City of Madison prefers to rely upon its own officials for inspection of distant milk sources, such inspection is readily open to it without hardship for it could charge the actual and reasonable cost of such inspection to the importing producers and processors. . . . Moreover, appellee Health Commissioner of Madison testified that as proponent of the local milk ordinance he had submitted the provisions here in controversy and an alternative proposal based on § 11 of the Model Milk Ordinance recommended by the United States Public Health Service. The model provision imposes no geographical limitation on location of milk sources and processing plans but excludes from the municipality milk not produced and pasteurized conformably to standards as high as those enforced by the receiving city. . . . The Commissioner

1. It is immaterial that Wisconsin milk from outside the Madison area is subjected to the same proscription as that moving in interstate commerce. . . . [Footnote by the Court].

testified that Madison consumers "would be safeguarded adequately" under either proposal and that he had expressed no preference. . . .

To permit Madison to adopt a regulation not essential for the protection of local health interests and placing a discriminatory burden on interstate commerce would invite a multiplication of preferential trade areas destructive of the very purpose of the Commerce Clause. Under the circumstances here presented, the regulation must yield to the principle that "one state in its dealings with another may not place itself in a position of economic isolation." Baldwin v. Seelig, Inc., supra, at 527.

For these reasons we conclude that the judgment below sustaining the five-mile provision as to pasteurization must be reversed.

The Supreme Court of Wisconsin thought it unnecessary to pass upon the validity of the twenty-five-mile limitation, apparently in part for the reason that this issue was made academic by its decision upholding the five-mile section. In view of our conclusion as to the latter provision, a determination of appellant's contention as to the other section is now necessary. As to this issue, therefore, we vacate the judgment below and remand for further proceedings not inconsistent with the principles announced in this opinion.

It is so ordered.

Mr. Justice BLACK, with whom Mr. Justice DOUGLAS and Mr. Justice MINTON concur, dissenting.

. . . I disagree with the Court's premises, reasoning, and judgment.

(1) This ordinance does not exclude wholesome milk coming from Illinois or anywhere else. It does require that all milk sold in Madison must be pasteurized within five miles of the center of the city. But there was no finding in the state courts [that] Dean Milk Company is unable to have its milk pasteurized within the defined geographical area. . . . Dean's personal preference to pasteurize in Illinois, not the ordinance, keeps Dean's milk out of Madison.

(2) Characterization of § 7.21 as a "discriminatory burden" on interstate commerce is merely a statement of the Court's result, which I think incorrect. . . . [B]oth state courts below found that § 7.21 represents a good-faith attempt to safeguard public health by making adequate sanitation inspections possible. . . .

(3) This health regulation should not be invalidated merely because the Court believes that alternative milk-inspection methods might insure the cleanliness and healthfulness of Dean's Illinois milk. . . . No case is cited, and I have found none, in which a bona fide health law was struck down on the ground that some other method of safeguarding health would be as good as, or better than, the one the Court was called on to review.
. . . .

If, however, the principle announced today is to be followed, the Court should not strike down local health regulations unless satisfied beyond a reasonable doubt that the substitutes it proposes would not lower health standards. I do not think that the Court can so satisfy itself on the basis of its

judicial knowledge.   And the evidence in the record leads me to the conclusion that the substitute health measures suggested by the Court do not insure milk as safe as the Madison ordinance requires.

One of the Court's proposals is that Madison require milk processors to pay reasonable inspection fees at the milk supply "sources."   Experience shows, however, that the fee method gives rise to prolonged litigation over the calculation and collection of the charges.   .   .   .   Moreover, nothing in the record before us indicates that the fee system might not be as costly to Dean as having its milk pasteurized in Madison.   .   .   .

The Court's second proposal is that Madison adopt § 11 of the "Model Milk Ordinance."   .   .   .   The evidence indicates to me that enforcement of the Madison law would assure a more healthful quality of milk than that which is entitled to use the label of "Grade A" under the Model Ordinance. .   .   .   [M]oreover, Madison would be required to depend on the Chicago inspection system   .   .   .   .   But there is direct and positive evidence in the record that milk produced under Chicago standards did not meet the Madison requirements.

Furthermore, the Model Ordinance would force the Madison health authorities to rely on "spot checks" by the United States Public Health Service to determine whether Chicago enforced its milk regulations.   The evidence shows that these "spot checks" are based on random inspection of farms and pasteurization plants.   .   .   .   .   There was evidence that neither the farms supplying Dean with milk nor Dean's pasteurization plants were necessarily inspected in the last "spot check" of the Chicago milkshed made two years before the present case was tried.   .   .   .   On this record I would uphold the Madison law.   At the very least, however, I would not invalidate it without giving the parties a chance to present evidence and get findings on the ultimate issues the Court thinks crucial—namely, the relative merits of the Madison ordinance and the alternatives suggested by the Court today.

DEAN MILK, "DISCRIMINATION," AND LESS BURDENSOME ALTERNATIVES

1. *"Discrimination."*   a.   Explicit discrimination against out-of-state interest—singling out interstate commerce for hostile treatment—has traditionally been condemned in commerce clause litigation.*   Even Justices who opposed most judicial restraints based on the dormant commerce clause have joined in the condemnation of patent discrimination.   But "discrimination" is not a self-defining term, and once the problem goes beyond the overtly preferential provision, there is much room for dispute about hidden and potential discriminations.   The Dean Milk opinion, for example, asserts that "Madison plainly discriminates against interstate commerce," yet im-

---

* For an early example, see Welton v. Missouri, 91 U.S. 275 (1876). It invalidated a Missouri license requirement for peddlers—itinerant sellers. The statute applied only to peddlers of merchandise "not the growth, produce or manufacture of this State" ; peddlers of Missouri goods did not need a license. Justice Field stated for the Court that the "very object" of the commerce clause was to protect "against discriminating State legislation."

mediately adds, in footnote 1 to the opinion, that it is "immaterial" that intrastate milk from outside the Madison area was subject to the same prohibition as that moving in interstate commerce. Should it be relevant that a local regulation burdens some intrastate as well as out-of-state producers? Does the impact on intrastate businesses assure political safeguards against risk of abuse against interstate commerce? Note also Minnesota v. Barber, 136 U.S. 313 (1890), relied on in Dean Milk. The Barber case invalidated a law forbidding the sale of meat unless there had been an inspection by a Minnesota official within a day of slaughter. The Court held that the law could not be applied to meat from animals slaughtered in Illinois: "[T]he enactment of a similar statute by each one of the states . . . would result in the destruction of commerce among the states"; the "obvious and necessary" result of the law was to create "discrimination against the products and business of other states."

What is the meaning of "discrimination" in Dean Milk? In Barber? Is it useful to invoke the "discrimination" label in situations where interstate commerce is not singled out on the face of the law or in its application? In talking of discrimination, is the Court characterizing legislative purpose? Is it talking only about effect? Despite the avowed recognition of local health interests in Dean Milk, is Justice Clark skeptical of that purpose because milk production is a "major local industry" in the Madison area? Is the attribution of hostile purpose aided by his reference to the fact, near the beginning of his opinion, that no "Grade A" milk was sold in the Madison area? † If the Court is using the "discrimination" label simply to describe effects rather than to attribute purposes, is it doing anything that could not be done more satisfyingly by balancing legitimate local justifications such as health against the burdens on commerce—and perhaps including in that balancing the "alternatives" examination of Dean Milk? In short, is anything gained by speaking of "discrimination" in situations not involving explicit singling out of interstate commerce for hostile purposes?

2. *Adequate, less burdensome alternatives.* The Dean Milk inquiry into the availability of less "discriminatory" or less burdensome alternatives has become a prominent feature of individual rights litigation, as the materials in Part III will show. See, e. g., the reliance on Dean Milk in applying an alternatives approach in the First Amendment context in Shelton v. Tucker, 364 U.S. 479 (1960) (chap. 13 below): "[E]ven though the governmental purpose be legitimate and substantial, that purpose cannot be pursued by means that broadly stifle fundamental personal liberties when the end can be more narrowly achieved."

† Compare Mintz v. Baldwin, 289 U.S. 346 (1933), upholding a New York law prohibiting the importation of cattle unless they were from herds certified to be free from Bang's disease. Justice Cardozo cited that case with approval in Baldwin v. Seelig, even while condemning the law challenged in Baldwin as "hostile in conception." Should and would Mintz have been decided differently if the Court had known that Bang's disease was "widespread" in New York and "no steps were being taken to see that the incoming cattle were placed in clean herds"? See Freund, "Review and Federalism," in Supreme Court and Supreme Law (Cahn ed., 1954), 86, 99. [On identifying unconstitutional "discrimination" under the equal protection clause, see chap. 10 below.)

Is judicial inquiry into possible available alternative methods of regulation appropriate? Feasible? When a "mere rationality" standard of scrutiny prevails, courts do not speculate about alternatives; they sustain the legislative choice if it is *a* reasonable or plausible method of promoting the objective. That is so, for example, in modern applications of the 14th Amendment to state economic regulation (see chap. 9 below), as it typically has been with respect to congressional implementation of Art. I, § 8, powers since the days of McCulloch v. Maryland. Is more intensive scrutiny, including consideration of "alternatives," justified to protect commerce clause values? To protect civil liberties? Or is concern with alternatives, as in Dean Milk, a haphazard, uninformed judicial intrusion into legislative spheres?

Has concern with available alternatives become a standard ingredient of commerce clause balancing? Is the Dean Milk approach implicit in earlier balancing cases? Is it implicit, for example, in Chief Justice Stone's comment in Southern Pacific v. Arizona, sec. 1B above, that the Arizona train length law went beyond "what is plainly essential for safety"? Is concern with alternatives in any event understandable when the Court engages in as elaborate a quasi-legislative inquiry as has been commonplace in commerce clause cases? Has the Court consistently invoked the alternatives approach? * Compare with Dean Milk the majority's approach in a case decided later in the same year, the Breard case considered in the following note.

3. *Alternatives and the Breard case.* a. Consider the relevance, and actual use, of consideration of alternatives in BREARD v. CITY OF ALEXANDRIA, 341 U.S. 622 (1951). Should the Dean Milk variety of "alternatives" analysis have been applied? What investigation of alternatives did the Court in fact undertake? The majority in Breard, a few months after Dean Milk, sustained the application of a "Green River type of ordinance" † —an ordinance prohibiting door-to-door solicitation of orders to sell goods unless there were requests by the occupants. The Alexandria, La., ordinance in Breard prohibited "the practice of going in and upon private residences . . . by solicitors, peddlers, hawkers, itinerant merchants or transient vendors of merchandise not having been requested or invited so to do by the [occupant] for the purpose of soliciting orders for the sale of goods, wares and merchandise." Breard, a Texan, led a crew of salesmen who solicited subscriptions for national magazines in a Louisiana city on behalf of a Pennsylvania corporation. Justice Reed's majority opinion rejected all constitutional objections—under the First Amendment as well as the commerce clause. He commented that "opportunists, for private gain, cannot be permitted to arm themselves with an acceptable principle, such as that of a right to work, a privilege to engage in interstate commerce, or a free

---

* See, in addition to Dean Milk, Justice Stewart's statement of commerce clause standards in Pike v. Bruce Church, Inc., 397 U.S. 137 (1970) (quoted in sec. 1B above), identifying as one criterion for determining the permissibility of a burden on commerce whether the "local interest involved . . . could be promoted as well with a lesser impact on interstate activities."

† The "Green River type of ordinance" derives its name from the town of Green River, Wyoming, which, as the Court explained, "undertook in 1931 to remedy by ordinance the irritating incidents of house-to-house canvassing for sales." The Alexandria ordinance was similar to the Green River model.

press, and proceed to use it as an iron standard to smooth their path by crushing the living rights of others to privacy and repose." He noted that door-to-door canvassing had "flourished increasingly in recent years," and he commented: "Unwanted knocks on the door by day or night are a nuisance, or worse, to peace and quiet. The local retail merchant, too, has not been unmindful of the effect of competition furnished by house-to-house selling in many lines." And he added: "The idea of barring classified salesmen from homes by means of notices posted by individual householders was rejected early as less practical than an ordinance regulating solicitors."

Against that background, Justice Reed examined Breard's claim that the "practical operation of the ordinance" imposed "an undue and discriminatory burden upon interstate commerce" and was "tantamount to a prohibition of such commerce." Breard claimed that obtaining the resident's consent would be "too costly and the results negligible." A large interstate business was concededly involved: more than 50% of annual subscription sales of magazines came from "solicitation of subscriptions in the field." Breard argued that Dean Milk demonstrated "that this Court will not permit local interests to protect themselves against out-of-state competition by curtailing interstate business."

Justice Reed did not find that invocation of Dean Milk persuasive. He commented: "It was partly because the regulation in Dean Milk Co. discriminated against interstate commerce that it was struck down." And he added: "Nor does the clause as to alternatives [in Dean Milk] apply to the Alexandria ordinance. Interstate commerce itself knocks on the local door. It is only by regulating that knock that the interests of the home may be protected by public as distinct from private action." He concluded: "When there is a reasonable basis for legislation to protect the social, as distinguished from the economic, welfare of a community, it is not for this Court because of the Commerce Clause to deny the exercise locally of the sovereign power of Louisiana. Changing living conditions or variations in the experiences and habits of different communities may well call for different legislative regulations as to methods and manners of doing business. . . . We cannot say that this ordinance of Alexandria so burdens or impedes interstate commerce as to exceed the regulatory powers of that city."

Chief Justice Vinson's dissent joined by Justice Douglas, concluded: "I would apply to this case the principles so recently announced in [Dean Milk]." Chief Justice Vinson emphasized the traditional protection of solicitors from local regulations which "in their practical operation discriminate against or unduly burden interstate commerce." He pointed out that the majority had conceded the "severe economic impact" of the regulation on subscription sales and he added: "That this ordinance, on its face, professes to protect the home does not relieve us of our duty to weigh the practical effect of the ordinance upon interstate commerce. Lack of discrimination on its face has not heretofore been regarded as sufficient to sustain an ordinance without inquiry into its practical effects upon interstate commerce. E. g., [Dean Milk; Minnesota v. Barber.]" Moreover, in passing on other restraints on solicitors, Chief Justice Vinson noted, "this Court has not hesitated in noting the economic fact that 'the "real competitors" of [solicitors] are, among others, the local retail merchants.' " He concluded: "I

think it plain that a 'blanket prohibition' upon appellant's solicitation discriminates against and unduly burdens interstate commerce in favoring local retail merchants. 'Whether or not it was so intended, those are its necessary effects.' . . . No one doubts that protection of the home is a proper subject of legislation, but that end can be served without prohibiting interstate commerce." (In another dissent, Justices Black and Douglas objected to the ordinance on First Amendment grounds as well.)

b. Should the Court have inquired whether there were less burdensome alternatives to achieve the city's objectives? Was that not the variety of alternatives inquiry undertaken in Dean Milk? Were there less burdensome, less "discriminatory," alternatives in the Breard situation? The majority in Breard did not undertake that kind of inquiry. But it did consider alternatives briefly in another sense—not to determine whether the locality could have achieved its objectives via less burdensome means, but whether the burdened interstate commerce operation had alternative methods to operate. Justice Reed commented that "the usual methods of seeking business are left open by the ordinance. That such methods do not produce as much business as house-to-house canvassing is, constitutionally, immaterial and a matter for adjustment at the local level in the absence of federal legislation."

Was there justification for considering alternatives in assessing the burden on the interstate business, rather than in determining the weight of the justification for the ordinance? Was it justifiable to dismiss as "constitutionally immaterial" the impact of the ban on solicitation—even if alternative ways of doing business were left open? As Chief Justice Vinson's dissent emphasized, in the state taxation context the Court has traditionally protected door-to-door solicitation from local fees and taxes because of the risk of discriminatory impacts. What explains the Court's unwillingness to extend its usual protection to interstate solicitors to the Breard situation? Note Justice Reed's comment for the majority: "The general use of the Green River type of ordinance shows its adaptation to the needs of the many communities that have enacted it. We are not willing even to appraise the suggestion, unsupported in the record, that such wide use springs predominantly from the selfish influence of local merchants."

c. Does Breard disavow balancing and return to the deferential reasonableness scrutiny of the Barnwell case? Or is Breard explainable as a variety of balancing, with unusually heavy weight given to the local interest in protecting the privacy of homeowners? Note that Justice Reed's majority opinion quoted at length from a leading libertarian commentary, Zechariah Chafee, Jr.'s Free Speech in the United States (1941): "House to house canvassing raises more serious problems. Of all the methods of spreading unpopular ideas, this seems the least entitled to extensive protection. The possibilities of persuasion are slight compared with the certainties of annoyance. . . . Freedom of the home is as important as freedom of speech. I cannot help wondering whether the Justices of the Supreme Court are quite aware of the effect of organized front-door intrusions upon people who are not sheltered from zealots and impostors by a staff of servants or the locked entrance of an apartment house." (Compare the increasing recognition of privacy as an aspect of protected constitutional liberty in the materials in Part III below.)

D. ACCESS OF FOREIGN BUYERS TO LOCAL RESOURCES: STATE BARRIERS TO OUTGOING TRADE

THE EISENBERG AND PARKER CASES: LEGITIMATE ECONOMIC PURPOSES?

In the Eisenberg and Parker cases in the notes that follow, local "economic" regulations were held applicable to out-of-state buyers of local products, despite commerce clause objections. Yet in the next principal case, Hood, the majority invalidated the application of a local regulation to an out-of-state purchaser. Consider, in examining these cases, whether they contain distinguishing features that justify the results. Consider, too, whether these cases are distinguishable from Baldwin v. Seelig, sec. 1C above. And consider, finally, whether the Court's articulations adequately delineate the distinctions. (A comparison of the cases is pursued in the notes following the Hood case, below.)

1. *Eisenberg.* In MILK CONTROL BOARD v. EISENBERG FARM PRODUCTS, 306 U.S. 346 (1939), a New York milk dealer who bought milk from Pennsylvania producers for shipment out-of-state challenged Pennsylvania's minimum price regulation. The dealer operated a milk receiving plant in Pennsylvania. The milk he bought from Pennsylvania farmers was cooled at the plant for less than 24 hours; then, all of it was shipped to New York. Pennsylvania law set the minimum price to be paid by dealers to milk producers and required dealers to obtain a license. The Pennsylvania Milk Control Act of 1935 was similar to the New York law involved in Baldwin v. Seelig, above; Eisenberg claimed the application of the law to him similarly violated the commerce clause. The state courts agreed with him, but the Supreme Court reversed.

Justice Roberts' majority opinion explained: "The purpose of the statute under review obviously is to reach a domestic situation in the interest of the welfare of the producers and consumers of milk in Pennsylvania. Its provisions with respect to license, bond, and regulation of prices to be paid to producers are appropriate means to the ends in view. The question is whether the prescription of prices to be paid producers in the effort to accomplish these ends constitutes a prohibited burden on interstate commerce, or an incidental burden which is permissible until superseded by Congressional enactment. That question can be answered only by weighing the nature of the respondent's activities, and the propriety of local regulation of them, as disclosed by the record."

He insisted that the state did not attempt to regulate shipment to or sale in New York. The "activity affected" was "essentially local in Pennsylvania." "If dealers conducting receiving stations in various localities in Pennsylvania were free to ignore the requirements of the statute on the ground that all or a part of the milk they purchase is destined to another state the uniform operation of the statute locally would be crippled and might be impracticable. Only a small fraction of the milk produced by farmers in Pennsylvania is shipped out of the Commonwealth. There is, therefore, a comparatively large field remotely affecting and wholly unrelated to interstate

commerce within which the statute operates.   [The opinion noted that, in 1934, "approximately 4,500,000,000 pounds of milk were produced in Pennsylvania of which approximately 470,000,000 pounds were shipped out of the state."]   These considerations we think justify the conclusion that the effect of the law on interstate commerce is incidental and not forbidden by the Constitution, in the absence of regulation by Congress."   Baldwin v. Seelig was not controlling.   According to Justice Roberts, that decision "condemned an enactment aimed solely at interstate commerce attempting to affect and regulate the price to be paid for milk in a sister state, and we indicated that the attempt amounted in effect to a tariff barrier set up against milk imported into the enacting state."   Is Eisenberg consistent with the Baldwin case, above?   With the Hood case, the next principal case?   See the questions following Hood.

2.   *Parker.*   Note also the rejection of a commerce clause challenge to another law designed to promote a local economic concern, in PARKER v. BROWN, 317 U.S. 341 (1943).   A California raisin producer attacked a marketing scheme established pursuant to the state Agricultural Prorate Act. That law compelled each producer to put most of his raisin crop under the marketing control of a program committee, for the purpose of eliminating price competition among producers.   As the Court noted, "since 95 per cent of the crop is marketed in interstate commerce, the program may be taken to have a substantial effect on the commerce, in placing restrictions on the sale and marketing of a product to buyers who eventually sell and ship it in interstate commerce."   Nevertheless, the Court sustained the program.   Chief Justice Stone explained:

"Such regulations by the state are to be sustained, not because they are 'indirect' rather than 'direct,' [but] because upon a consideration of all the relevant facts and circumstances it appears that the matter is one which may appropriately be regulated in the interest of the safety, health and well-being of local communities, and which, because of its local character, and the practical difficulties involved, may never be adequately dealt with by Congress. .   .   .   There may also be, as in the present case, local regulations whose effect upon the national commerce is such as not to conflict but to coincide with a policy which Congress has established with respect to it.

"Examination of the evidence in this case and of available data of the raisin industry in California, of which we may take judicial notice, leaves no doubt that the evils attending the production and marketing of raisins in that state present a problem local in character and urgently demanding state action for the economic protection of those engaged in one of its important industries.   .   .   .   The history of the industry, at least since 1929, is a record of a continuous search for expedients which would stabilize the marketing of the raisin crop and maintain a price standard which would bring fair return to the producers.   It is significant of the relation of the local interest in maintaining this program to the national interest in interstate commerce, that throughout the period from 1929 until the adoption of the prorate program for the 1940 raisin crop, the national government has contributed to these efforts either by its establishment of marketing programs pursuant to Act of Congress or by aiding programs sponsored by the state. .   .   .   .

"This history shows clearly enough that the adoption of legislative measures to prevent the demoralization of the industry by stabilizing the marketing of the raisin crop is a matter of state as well as national concern and, in the absence of inconsistent Congressional action, is a problem whose solution is peculiarly within the province of the state. . . . The program was not aimed at nor did it discriminate against interstate commerce, although it undoubtedly affected the commerce by increasing the interstate price of raisins and curtailing interstate shipments to some undetermined extent. . . .

"In comparing the relative weights of the conflicting local and national interests involved, it is significant that Congress, by its agricultural legislation, has recognized the distressed condition of much of the agricultural production of the United States . . . . It thus appears that whatever effect the operation of the California program may have on interstate commerce, it is one which it has been the policy of Congress to aid and encourage through federal agencies in conformity to the Agricultural Marketing Agreement Act, and § 302 of the Agricultural Adjustment Act. Nor is the effect on the commerce greater than or substantially different in kind from that contemplated by the stabilization programs authorized by federal statutes. . . ."

H. P. HOOD & SONS v. DuMOND

336 U.S. 525, 69 S.Ct. 657, 93 L.Ed. 865 (1949).

Certiorari to the Supreme Court of New York, Albany County.

[Hood distributed milk in Boston. The city obtained 90% of its milk supply from outside of Massachusetts. Hood had long obtained milk from New York producers and had maintained three receiving depots there. Hood sought a New York license to establish a fourth depot in New York, in the area that had been developed as a major source of milk for Boston. Hood's new, fourth depot was to be at Greenwich, N.Y., ten miles from its Salem, N.Y., depot and twelve miles from its Eagle Bridge, N.Y., depot. Under the New York law, a license for a new plant could not be issued unless the Commissioner of Agriculture and Markets was satisfied that "issuance of the license will not tend to a destructive competition in a market already adequately served, and that the issuance of the license is in the public interest." The Commissioner denied the license for the fourth depot on the basis of this provision. Hood had complied with all other conditions of the law.]

Mr. Justice JACKSON delivered the opinion of the Court.

This case concerns the power of the State of New York to deny additional facilities to acquire and ship milk in interstate commerce where the grounds of denial are that such limitation upon interstate business will protect and advance local economic interests. . . .

The Commissioner found that Hood, if licensed at Greenwich, would permit its present suppliers, at their option, to deliver at the new plant rather than the old ones and for a substantial number this would mean shorter hauls and savings in delivery costs. The new plant also would attract twenty to thirty producers, some of whose milk Hood anticipates will or may be diverted from other buyers. Other large milk distributors have

plants within the general area and dealers serving Troy obtain milk in the locality. He found that Troy was inadequately supplied during the preceding short season.

In denying the application for expanded facilities, the Commissioner states his grounds as follows:

"If applicant is permitted to equip and operate another milk plant in this territory, and to take on producers now delivering to plants other than those which it operates, it will tend to reduce the volume of milk received at the plants which lose those producers, and will tend to increase the cost of handling milk in those plants.

"If applicant takes producers now delivering milk to local markets such as Troy, it will have a tendency to deprive such markets of a supply needed during the short season.

"There is no evidence that any producer is without a market for his milk. There is no evidence that any producers not now delivering milk to applicant would receive any higher price, were they to deliver their milk to applicant's proposed plant.

"The issuance of a license to applicant which would permit it to operate an additional plant, would tend to a destructive competition in a market already adequately served, and would not be in the public interest."

Denial of the license was sustained by the Court of Appeals over constitutional objections duly urged under the Commerce Clause . . . .

Production and distribution of milk are so intimately related to public health and welfare that the need for regulation to protect those interests has long been recognized and is, from a constitutional standpoint, hardly controversial. . . . As the states extended their efforts to control various phases of export and import also, questions were raised as to limitations on state power under the Commerce Clause of the Constitution. . . .

The present controversy begins where the Eisenberg decision [above] left off. New York's regulations, designed to assure producers a fair price and a responsible purchaser, and consumers a sanitary and modernly equipped handler, are not challenged here but have been complied with. It is only additional restrictions, imposed for the avowed purpose and with the practical effect of curtailing the volume of interstate commerce to aid local economic interests, that are in question here, and no such measures were attempted or such ends sought to be served in the Act before the Court in the Eisenberg case.

Our decision in a milk litigation most relevant to the present controversy deals with the converse of the present situation. Baldwin v. Seelig. [The discussion of the case is omitted.]

This distinction between the power of the State to shelter its people from menaces to their health or safety and from fraud, even when those dangers emanate from interstate commerce, and its lack of power to retard, burden or constrict the flow of such commerce for their economic advantage, is one deeply rooted in both our history and our law. [See the passages on commerce clause history quoted at the beginning of this chapter.]

[Baldwin v. Seelig] is an explicit, impressive, recent and unanimous condemnation by this Court of economic restraints on interstate commerce for local economic advantage, but it does not stand alone. This Court con-

sistently has rebuffed attempts of states to advance their own commercial interests by curtailing the movement of articles of commerce, either into or out of the state, while generally supporting their right to impose even burdensome regulations in the interest of local health and safety. As most states serve their own interests best by sending their produce to market, the cases in which this Court has been obliged to deal with prohibitions or limitations by states upon exports of articles of commerce are not numerous. [The Court reviewed a number of decisions in which states had not been permitted to bar the export of local resources for the benefit of local consumers—e. g., Pennsylvania v. West Virginia and the Foster-Fountain Packing Co. case, noted below, and Toomer v. Witsell, in chap. 6.]

This principle that our economic unit is the Nation, which alone has the gamut of powers necessary to control of the economy, including the vital power of erecting customs barriers against foreign competition, has as its corollary that the states are not separable economic units. [In Baldwin v. Seelig, the Court] but followed the principle that the state may not use its admitted powers to protect the health and safety of its people as a basis for suppressing competition. [Buck v. Kuykendall.] . . .

The material success that has come to inhabitants of the states which make up this federal free trade unit has been the most impressive in the history of commerce, but the established interdependence of the states only emphasizes the necessity of protecting interstate movement of goods against local burdens and repressions. We need only consider the consequences if each of the few states that produce copper, lead, high-grade iron ore, timber, cotton, oil or gas should decree that industries located in that state shall have priority. What fantastic rivalries and dislocations and reprisals would ensue if such practices were begun! Or suppose that the field of discrimination and retaliation be industry. May Michigan provide that automobiles cannot be taken out of that State until local dealers' demands are fully met? Would she not have every argument in the favor of such a statute that can be offered in support of New York's limiting sales of milk for out-of-state shipment to protect the economic interests of her competing dealers and local consumers? Could Ohio then pounce upon the rubber-tire industry, on which she has a substantial grip, to retaliate for Michigan's auto monopoly?

Our system, fostered by the Commerce Clause, is that every farmer and every craftsman shall be encouraged to produce by the certainty that he will have free access to every market in the Nation, that no home embargoes will withhold his exports, and no foreign state will by customs duties or regulations exclude them. Likewise, every consumer may look to the free competition from every producing area in the Nation to protect him from exploitation by any. Such was the vision of the Founders; such has been the doctrine of this Court which has given it reality.

The State, however, insists that denial of the license for a new plant does not restrict or obstruct interstate commerce, because petitioner has been licensed at its other plants without condition or limitation as to the quantities it may purchase. . . .   In the face of affirmative findings that the proposed plant would increase petitioner's supply, we can hardly be asked to assume that denial of the license will not deny petitioner access to such added supplies. While the state power is applied in this case to limit expansion by

a handler of milk who already has been allowed some purchasing facilities, the argument of doing so, if sustained, would be equally effective to exclude an entirely new foreign handler from coming into the State to purchase.

. . . .

Since the statute as applied violates the Commerce Clause, [it] cannot stand. . . .

Reversed and remanded.†

Mr. Justice BLACK, dissenting. . . .

Had a dealer supplying New York customers applied for a license to operate a new plant, the commissioner would have been compelled under the Act to protect petitioner's plants supplying Boston consumers in the same manner that this order would have protected New York consumers. In protecting inter- or intra-state dealers from destructive competition which would endanger the milk farmers' price structure or the continued supply of healthful milk to the customers of existing dealers, the commissioner would be faithful to the Act's avowed purposes. The commerce clause should not be stretched to forbid New York's fair attempt to protect the healthful milk supply of consumers, even though some of the consumers in this case happen to live in Troy, New York. And unless this Court is willing to charge an unfairness to the commissioner that has not been charged by petitioner or shown by the evidence, the Court cannot attribute to the commissioner an invidious purpose to discriminate against petitioner's interstate business in order to benefit local intrastate competitors and their local consumers. . . .

The language of this state Act is not discriminatory, the legislative history shows it was not so intended, and the commissioner has not administered it with a hostile eye. The Act must stand or fall on this basis notwithstanding the overtones of the Court's opinion. If petitioner and other interstate milk dealers are to be placed above and beyond this law, it must be done solely on this Court's new constitutional formula which bars a state from protecting itself against local destructive competitive practices so far as they are indulged in by dealers who ship their milk into other states. . . .

. . . The basic principles of the Cooley rule have been entangled and sometimes obscured with much language. In the main, however, those ["balance-of-interests"] principles have been the asserted grounds for determination of all commerce cases decided by this Court from 1852 until today.

. . .

In this Court, challenges to the Cooley rule on the ground that the rule was an ineffective protector of interstate commerce from state regulations have been confined to dissents and concurring opinions. Duckworth v.

---

† For a recent approving quotation from Hood, see Allenberg Cotton Co. v. Pittman, 419 U.S. 20 (1974). The majority found an unconstitutional burden on commerce in the Mississippi courts' refusal to entertain a suit on a cotton delivery contract. The state courts relied on appellant's failure to qualify to do business in the state.

The Supreme Court majority concluded that appellant could not be required to obtain a certificate to do business in the state: though it stored cotton in Mississippi, the goods were there only temporarily and already in the stream of commerce. Compare Eli Lilly & Co. v. Sav-On-Drugs, Inc., 366 U.S. 276 (1961).

Arkansas, 314 U.S. 390, 400–401. [In Duckworth, a] concurring opinion expressed the view that the Court's opinion written by Chief Justice Stone, rooted as it was in the Cooley principle, "let commerce struggle for Congressional action to make it free," and expressed the writer's unwillingness to follow the Court's "trend" beyond the "plain requirements" of existing cases.*

The Cooley balancing-of-interests principle which the Court accepted and applied in the Duckworth case is today supplanted by the philosophy of the Duckworth concurring opinion . . . . For the New York statute is killed by a mere automatic application of a new mechanistic formula. The Court appraises nothing, unless its stretching of the old commerce clause interpretation results from a reappraisal of the power and duty of this Court under the commerce clause. . . .

Both the commerce and due process clauses serve high purposes when confined within their proper scope. But a stretching of either outside its sphere can paralyze the legislative process, rendering the people's legislative representatives impotent to perform their duty of providing appropriate rules to govern this dynamic civilization. Both clauses easily lend themselves to inordinate expansions of this Court's power at the expense of legislative power. . . .

The basic question here is not the greatness of the commerce clause concept, but whether all local phases of interstate business are to be judicially immunized from state laws against destructive competitive business practices such as those prohibited by New York's law. Of course, there remains the bare possibility Congress might attempt to federalize all such local business activities in the forty-eight states. While I have doubt about the wisdom of this New York law, I do not conceive it to be the function of this Court to revise that state's economic judgments. Any doubt I may have concerning the wisdom of New York's law is far less, however, than is my skepticism concerning the ability of the Federal Government to reach out and effectively regulate all the local business activities in the forty-eight states.

I would leave New York's law alone.

Mr. Justice MURPHY joins in this opinion.

Mr. Justice FRANKFURTER, with whom Mr. Justice RUTLEDGE joins, dissenting.

If the Court's opinion has meaning beyond deciding this case in isolation, its effect is to hold that no matter how important to the internal economy of a State may be the prevention of destructive competition, and no matter how unimportant the interstate commerce affected, a State cannot as a means of

---

* The reference is to the concurring opinion by Justice Jackson in Duckworth v. Arkansas, 314 U.S. 390 (1941). The case sustained a statute requiring a permit for the transportation of intoxicating liquor through the State. Justice Jackson agreed with the result on the basis of the Twenty-first Amendment but urged that, absent that provision, the result should have been the opposite. In his view the inertia of government made it unlikely that Congress, hard-pressed with more urgent matters, would correct minor obstructions to interstate commerce: "The practical result is that in default of action by us, [the States] will go on suffocating and retarding and Balkanizing American commerce, trade and industry."

preventing such competition deny an applicant access to a market within the State if that applicant happens to intend the out-of-state shipment of the product that he buys. I feel constrained to dissent because I cannot agree in treating what is essentially a problem of striking a balance between competing interests as an exercise in absolutes. Nor does it seem to me that such a problem should be disposed of on a record from which we cannot tell what weights to put in which side of the scales. . . .

The Court's opinion deems the decision in [Baldwin v. Seelig] as most relevant to the present controversy. But it is the essential teaching of that case that "considerations of degree" determine the line of decision between what a State may and what a State may not regulate . . . . But guarding against out-of-state competition is a very different thing from curbing competition from whatever source. A tariff barrier between States, moreover, presupposes a purpose to prefer those who are within the barrier; where no such preference appears there can be no justification for reprisals and there is consequently little probability of them. In the determination that an extension of petitioner's license would tend to destructive competition, the fact that petitioner intended the out-of-state shipment of what it bought was, so far as the records tells us, wholly irrelevant; under the circumstances, any other applicant, no matter where he meant to send his milk, would presumably also have been refused a license. . . .

This case falls somewhere between [the] most nearly decisive authorities. It is closer to [Buck v. Kuykendall] than to the Eisenberg case in that the denial of a license to enter a market because the market is "adequately served" imposes a disqualification beyond the power of the applicant to remove. In that respect the effect upon the free flow of commerce is more enduring than is the case where all that is required is compliance with a local regulation. The State's interest in restricting competition, moreover, is less obvious than its interest in preserving health or insuring probity in business dealings. Yet the commerce involved [in Buck] was exclusively interstate. Here, however, it does not appear that any of Hood's competitors sent milk out of the State, and, in fact, only about 8% of New York's entire production of milk is sent out. In this respect the case resembles the Eisenberg case, in which it appeared that only slightly more than 10% of the milk produced in Pennsylvania was exported. . . . But comparison could be carried further and still the similarities and dissimilarities of the facts in the record before us to the Eisenberg case and [the Buck case] would be inconclusive. In an area where differences of degree depend on slight differences of fact, precedent alone is an inadequate guide.

It is argued, however, that New York can have no interest in the restriction of competition great enough to warrant shutting its doors to one who would buy its products for shipment to another State. This must mean that the protection of health and the promotion of fair dealing are of a different order, somehow, than the prevention of destructive competition. But the fixing of prices was a main object of the regulation upheld in the Eisenberg case, and it is obvious that one of the most effective ways of maintaining a price structure is to control competition. The milk industry is peculiarly subject to internecine warfare, as this Court recognized in sustaining against due-process attack the precursor of New York's present milk-control law. . . .

As matters now stand, however, it is impossible to say whether or not the restriction of competition among dealers in milk does in fact contribute to their economic well-being and, through them, to that of the entire industry. And if we assume that some contribution is made, we cannot guess how much. Why, when the State has fixed a minimum price for producers, does it take steps to keep competing dealers from increasing the price by bidding against each other for the existing supply? Is it concerned with protecting consumers from excessive prices? Or is it concerned with seeing that marginal dealers, forced by competition to pay more and charge less, are not driven either to cut corners in the maintenance of their plants or to close them down entirely? Might these consequences follow from operation at less than capacity? What proportion of capacity is necessary to enable the marginal dealer to stay in business? Could Hood's potential competitors in the Greenwich area maintain efficient and sanitary standards of operation on a lower margin of profit? How would their closing down affect producers? Would the competition of Hood affect dealers other than those in that area? How many of those dealers are also engaged in interstate commerce? How much of a strain would be put on the price structure maintained by the State by a holding that it cannot regulate the competition of dealers buying for an out-of-state market? Is this a situation in which State regulation, by supplementing federal regulation, is of benefit to interstate as well as to intrastate commerce?

We should, I submit, have answers at least to some of these questions before we can say either how seriously interstate commerce is burdened by New York's licensing power or how necessary to New York is that power.

. . .

Nor should we now dispose of the case upon the claim that New York cannot discriminate against interstate commerce by keeping its milk for absorption by "local markets such as Troy." [T]here is much force in the argument that if a State cannot keep for its own use a natural resource like gas, as it can keep its wild game, Geer v. Connecticut, 161 U.S. 519 [below], then a fortiori it cannot prefer its own inhabitants in the consumption of a product that would not have come into existence but for its commercial value. . . . Broadly stated, the question is whether a State can withhold from interstate commerce a product derived from local raw materials upon a determination by an administrative agency that there is a local need for it. For me it has not been put to rest by Pennsylvania v. West Virginia [below]. More narrowly, the question is whether the State can prefer the consumers of one community to consumers in other States as well as to consumers in other parts of its own territory. It is arguable, moreover, that the Commissioner was actuated not by preference for New York consumers, but by the aim of stabilizing the supply of all the local markets, including Boston as well as Troy, served by the New York milkshed. . . .

My conclusion [is] that the case should be remanded . . . . .

THE HOOD CASE, FORBIDDEN ECONOMIC PURPOSES, AND CONTROL OF LOCAL RESOURCES

1.   *Economic purposes and balancing: The Hood, Eisenberg and Parker cases.*   a.   Does Hood abandon the Cooley-Southern Pacific balancing approach to establish a per se rule when economic interests (rather than interests in health and safety, for example) underlie the state regulation?   Or does Hood assert that balancing continues, but that economic objectives tend to tip the scale against the state regulation?   How broad is Hood?   Does Hood bar all state economic concerns?   Does it bar primarily any state protectionist interest to shield local industry against out-of-state competition—the kind of protectionism the Court perceived in Baldwin v. Seelig?   Does it bar any state interest in encouraging local economic well-being by limiting competition?   Is that the proper lesson to be drawn from Buck v. Kuykendall, sec. 1B above?   Even if economic well-being plainly affects health, safety, etc.?   Again, how broad is Hood: Does it deprecate all economic concerns?   All economic concerns relating to the curtailment of competition?   Or only economic concerns designed to protect local economic interests against out-of-state competitors?

b.   What *was* New York's economic concern in Hood?   Was Justice Jackson right to say that the restrictions were "imposed for the avowed purpose and with the practical affect of curtailing the volume of interstate commerce to aid local economic interests"?   Was there a protectionist purpose inherent in a law denying a license if it "would tend to destructive competition in a market already adequately served"?   Even if *any* applicant for a new license would have been unsuccessful—applicants from New York as well as from Massachusetts?   Was it enough that as applied in Hood the unsuccessful applicant was from out-of-state: was this a situation where the law, as applied, preferred domestic needs to out-of-state ones?

c.   Much of Justice Jackson's opinion in Hood emphasizes the condemnation of "economic restraints" for "local economic advantage."   Can that broad condemnation be reconciled with Eisenberg and with Parker?   Recall that the Eisenberg Court characterized the Pennsylvania price regulation found validly applicable there to an out-of-stater as one "in the interest of the welfare of the producers and consumers of milk in Pennsylvania."   Was the critical element in Eisenberg the need to protect the integrity of Pennsylvania's scheme of economic regulation?   But if that interest in the viability of the domestic regulatory scheme is a valid one, is not Hood overbroad in suggesting that all curtailments of interstate commerce "to aid local economic interests" violate the commerce clause?   Was the subjection of Hood to the New York law less critical to the viability of the New York scheme than the subjection of Eisenberg to the Pennsylvania law?

Can Justice Jackson's condemnation of "economic restraints" for "local economic advantage" be reconciled with the Parker Court's statement that California's marketing regulation "for the economic protection" of the important California raisin industry served "a legitimate state end"?   Was it critical in Parker that Justice Stone was able to find that the local regulation's effect upon interstate commerce was "such as not to conflict but to coincide with a policy which Congress has established with respect to it"?

(On the influence of perceptions of congressional policy, recall the Huron Portland Cement case, sec. 1B above. But note that in Parker the United States argued as amicus curiae "that the state program, though not inconsistent with Federal agricultural legislation, was invalid" under the Sherman Act as well as the commerce clause.)

d. Justice Jackson's opinion in Hood reemphasizes the distinction between a state's power to protect its people against dangers to "health or safety and from fraud" and its lack of power to impede commerce for local "economic advantage." Was that distinction persuasively applied by Justice Jackson? Was economic self-interest all that supported the state regulation? Compare Justice Frankfurter's questions and Justice Black's reference to "New York's fair attempt to protect the healthful milk supply of consumers."

The Hood opinion states that the commerce clause assures that every producer will have "free access to every market in the Nation, that no home embargoes will withhold its exports." Does Hood simply stand for a flat constitutional ban on all such embargoes? Or does it merely speak against preferences for local consumers? Was there such a preference in the Hood case? How broad an anti-embargo principle emerges from the natural resources cases prior to Hood? Do the more recent cases suggest a broader anti-embargo principle than the earlier ones? The cases are reviewed in note 3 below.

2. *The Cities Service case: A narrowing of Hood?* Before turning to the pre-Hood natural resources case, consider the decision a year after Hood, in CITIES SERVICE CO. v. PEERLESS CO., 340 U.S. 179 (1950). There, the Court rejected a commerce clause attack on a state regulation of natural gas prices to conserve local resources. Was that decision consistent with the broad statements in Hood? Can it be reconciled with narrower readings of Hood? Cities Service sustained an Oklahoma order fixing a minimum wellhead price of natural gas. Most of the gas was exported from the state. Justice Clark's opinion noted the consumers' interest in inexpensive gas, but emphasized that a state is "justifiably concerned with preventing rapid and uneconomic dissipation of one of its chief natural resources." He stated that the applicable commerce clause requirements were "that the regulation not discriminate against or place an embargo on interstate commerce, that it safeguard an obvious state interest, and that the local interest at stake outweigh whatever national interest there might be in the prevention of state restrictions." Here, the "legitimate local interest" was "clear." And, "in a field of this complexity, [we] cannot say that there is a clear national interest so harmed that the state price-fixing orders here employed fall within the ban of the Commerce Clause. [Eisenberg]."

Note the Court's basis for saying that the Hood case was "not inconsistent" with the Cities Service holding: "The vice in the regulation [in Hood] was solely that it denied facilities to a company in interstate commerce on the articulated ground that such facilities would divert milk supplies needed by local consumers; in other words, the regulation discriminated against interstate commerce. There is no such problem here. The price regulation applies to all gas taken from the field, whether destined for interstate or intrastate consumers." Was that an adequate basis for distinguishing Hood? Does Cities Service in effect narrow Hood? Was the analysis akin

to Parker in its suggestion that state and national policies might be harmonious? In Cities Service, the Court noted that "it is far from clear that on balance [the national] interest is harmed by the state regulations under attack here." (Justice Jackson was among those who joined Justice Clark's opinion in Cities Service.)

3. *State control of local resources.* a. Hood suggested that a state may not hold on to its economic resources to meet local needs. How broad and how well supported is that principle? The Court has increasingly curtailed state control over its natural resources: some early cases sustained state embargoes, often drawing on notions of state property interests; but in more recent cases, the Court has typically barred state efforts to keep local resources at home for local benefit. Justice Jackson's opinion in Hood relied on three of those more recent cases in which local restrictions were invalidated. In Pennsylvania v. West Virginia, 262 U.S. 553 (1923), West Virginia had required that all local needs for natural gas be met before any gas could be transported out of the state. The majority found that requirement "a prohibited interference" with interstate commerce. But Justice Holmes, joined by Justice Brandeis, dissented, saying that he could "see nothing in the commerce clause to prevent a State from giving a preference to its inhabitants in the enjoyment of its natural advantages." (Note Justice Frankfurter's statement on that problem of state power in Hood: "For me it has not been put to rest by Pennsylvania v. West Virginia." Why not, in view of that case and related decisions which follow?) In Foster-Fountain Packing Co. v. Haydel, 278 U.S. 1 (1928), the Court invalidated a Louisiana ban on shipping shrimp out of the state until shells and heads supposedly needed for fertilizer had been removed. The Court suggested that the real purpose of the requirement was "to bring about the removal of the packing and canning industry from Mississippi to Louisiana." More recently, the Court invalidated South Carolina's discriminatory license fee on non-residents trawling for shrimp in its waters. The majority relied not on the commerce clause but on the privileges and immunities clause of Art. IV. Toomer v. Witsell, 334 U.S. 385 (1948) (printed in chap. 6 below). See also the Pike case, note 3c below.

b. But an earlier line of cases had sustained a variety of local controls over natural resources. For example, Geer v. Connecticut, 161 U.S. 519 (1896), upheld a statute prohibiting the killing of certain game birds for the purpose of shipment out of the state, even though sale of the game birds within the state was permitted. The Court emphasized property rights: the birds were collectively owned by the people of the state. And Hudson County Water Co. v. McCarter, 209 U.S. 349 (1908), sustained a New Jersey law prohibiting the transportation of water from that state's rivers and lakes to any other state. Justice Holmes for the Court noted that the state as "guardian of the public welfare" had a strong interest in maintaining local rivers "substantially undiminished." Can the water case be reconciled with the natural gas case? The game bird case with the shrimp case? Are Geer and McCarter in effect undercut by the later cases starting with Pennsylvania v. West Virginia? In any event, are they undercut by the balancing analysis and by the Hood case? (Note that Foster-Fountain involved not a total ban on exports but an effort to assure local processing before export. Does that

make it justifiably more vulnerable under the commerce clause? Note, however, that Geer and Pennsylvania v. West Virginia were both flat embargoes.)

c. Note also the Court's unanimous invalidation of a state regulation of its domestic produce in Pike v. Bruce Church, Inc., 397 U.S. 137 (1970). Justice Stewart's formulation of commerce clause criteria in that case has been noted earlier, sec. 1B above. In Pike, Arizona prohibited the company from shipping uncrated cantaloupes from its Arizona ranch to its nearby California packing plant. Compliance with the requirement that the cantaloupes be packed in Arizona would have required a capital outlay of $200,000 by the company. The cantaloupes were of very high quality; when packed in California, they were not identified as Arizona-grown. Justice Stewart noted that the state's purpose here was not to keep the reputation of its own growers unsullied, "but to enhance their reputation through the reflected goodwill of the company's superior produce." That state interest was found "legitimate" but "tenuous" and inadequate to justify the state-imposed burden: "The nature of that burden is, constitutionally, more significant than its extent. For the Court has viewed with particular suspicion state statutes requiring business operations to be performed in the home State that could more efficiently be performed elsewhere. Even where the State is pursuing a clearly legitimate local interest, this particular burden on commerce has been declared to be virtually per se illegal. [Foster-Fountain Packing Co.] If the Commerce Clause forbids a State to require work to be done within its jurisdiction to promote local employment, then surely it cannot permit a State to require a person to go into the local packing business solely for the sake of enhancing the reputation of other producers within its borders."

E. SOME CONCLUDING OBSERVATIONS ON COMMERCE CLAUSE CRITERIA: ENVIRONMENTAL PROTECTION LAWS; STATE TAXES

ENVIRONMENTAL LAWS AND THE COMMERCE CLAUSE: THE OREGON BOTTLE CASE

The growing interest in protecting the environment in recent years has produced a variety of state laws. Some of these environmental protection laws have been challenged as impinging on interstate commerce concerns. What are the appropriate standards when environmental legislation is attacked under the commerce clause? Is the balancing approach of Southern Pacific applicable? Is the "alternatives" analysis of Dean Milk applicable? Or may courts avoid balancing in the environmental context? Why? Because the interest in the environment is so powerful as to outweigh any conceivable burden on commerce? More powerful than the interest in health and safety? Because it would impose an intolerable institutional burden on courts to weigh the costs and benefits of environmental legislation? Even though costs and benefits are examined in detail in other commerce clause litigation? An examination of the Oregon courts' recent encounter with

a widely publicized environmental protection effort, the so-called Oregon Bottle Bill, serves not only to pursue those questions but also to review and reconsider the range of commerce clause criteria examined in the preceding materials. The Oregon courts considered and rejected the relevance of most of the cases in the preceding materials and found a balancing analysis inappropriate. Was the state courts' approach justifiable? Would it have been possible to sustain the Oregon law if a balancing analysis had been applied?

AMERICAN CAN CO. v. OREGON LIQUOR CONTROL COMMISSION

517 P.2d 691 (Or.App.1973)

[This decision rejected a constitutional attack on the so-called Oregon Bottle Bill enacted in 1971.* The primary purpose of the law—as described by the court—was "to cause bottlers of carbonated soft drinks and brewers to package their products for distribution in Oregon in returnable, multiple-use deposit bottles toward the goals of reducing litter and solid waste in Oregon and reducing the injuries to people and animals due to discarded 'pull tops.' " The law requires every retailer of soft drinks or beer to "accept from a consumer any empty beverage containers of the kind, common size, and brand sold by the dealer" and to pay the consumer the prescribed refund. The usual refund is 5 cents per container; but a reduced "refund value" of 2 cents was set for "certified" containers usable by more than one manufacturer. The law also requires distributors and manufacturers to accept empty containers from retailers and pay them the "refund value." In addition, the law prohibits the sale of "pull top" cans in Oregon.

[The challengers included out-of-state brewers, soft drink companies, and manufacturers of bottles and cans. The commerce clause was the main basis of their effort to enjoin enforcement of the law.† The attackers claimed that the law would affect not only the container manufacturers but would have severe impact upon the "entire distribution chain." Their evidence showed that the great increase in the consumption of beer and soft drinks in recent years was largely attributable "to the use of convenient 'one-way' packages, including both cans and non-returnable bottles." They asserted "that non-returnable containers are essential to the existence of national and regional [beverage] markets." The law, they claimed, would impair the ability of distant producers to compete in the Oregon market and would "necessitate substantial changes in the structure of the industries involved." The trial court rejected the constitutional challenge. (Excerpts from the trial court's opinion appear in the notes following this case.)]

* The Oregon Supreme Court denied review of this decision by the Oregon Court of Appeals. The challengers did not seek review in the United States Supreme Court.

† Professors Philip Kurland of Chicago, Alexander Bickel of Yale, and Gerald Gunther of Stanford submitted a brief in the Oregon Court of Appeals advocating a balancing analysis and an invalidation of the law; Professors Hans Linde of Oregon and Thomas Grey of Stanford were on briefs disagreeing with that approach and urging upholding of the law.

TANZER, Judge.   .   .   .

The development of the one-way container provided a great technological opportunity for the beverage industry to turn logistical advantages into economic advantages.   By obviating the expensive necessity of reshipping empty bottles back to the plant for refilling, the new containers enabled manufacturers to produce in a few centralized plants to serve more distant markets.   The industry organized its manufacturing and distribution systems to capitalize maximally on the new technology.

The Oregon legislature was persuaded that the economic benefit to the beverage industry brought with it deleterious consequences to the environment and additional cost to the public.   The aggravation of the problems of litter in public places and solid waste disposal and the attendant economic and esthetic burden to the public outweighed the narrower economic benefit to the industry.   Thus the legislature enacted the bottle bill over the articulate opposition of the industries represented by plaintiffs.   .   .   .

The purpose of the Commerce Clause, following the intolerable experience of the economic Balkanization of America which existed in the colonial period and under the Articles of Confederation, was to assure to the commercial enterprises in every state substantial equality of access to a free national market.   It was not meant to usurp the police power of the states which was reserved under the Tenth Amendment.   Therefore, although most exercises of the police power affect interstate commerce to some degree, not every such exercise is invalid under the Commerce Clause.

Plaintiffs [assert] that the state exercise of its police power must yield to federal authority over interstate commerce because, they claim, the impact on interstate commerce in this case outweighs the putative benefit to the state and because alternative methods exist to achieve the state goal with a less deleterious impact on interstate commerce.   They urge us [to] perform for ourselves the weighing process already performed by the Legislative Assembly, relying largely upon Pike v. Bruce Church, Inc. (1970).   [The court quoted Justice Stewart's statement of criteria printed in sec. 1B above.]

The language of the United States Supreme Court is not always consistent in analyzing the application of the Commerce Clause to varying facts and it is difficult to rationalize it into one harmonious jurisprudential whole. On their facts, however, the cases cluster around certain basic concepts and the treatment accorded to state action is consistent within each grouping.   The cases consistently hold that the Commerce Clause bars state police action only where:

(1) federal action has pre-empted regulation of the activity;

(2) the state action impedes the free physical flow of commerce from one state to another; or

(3) protectionist state action, even though under the guise of police power, discriminates against interstate commerce.

In this case there is no claim of federal preemption, so we are concerned only with the latter two concepts, interstate transportation and economic protectionism.   No party cited and we were unable to find any case striking down state action under the Commerce Clause which did not come within one of these two categories.

The language of [Pike] does not mechanically compel a weighing process in every case. The language is instructive in appropriate cases rather than mandatory in all cases. The blight of the landscape, the appropriation of lands for solid waste disposal, and the injury to children's feet caused by pull tops discarded in the sands of our ocean shores are concerns not divisible by the same units of measurement as is economic loss to elements of the beverage industry and we are unable to weigh them, one against the other. The United States Supreme Court recognized the inappropriateness of a weighing process in cases of non-comparable benefit and injury when it chastised the District Court for having done so in [the Firemen case on "full crew" laws (1968), sec. 1B above].

The court has weighed comparables such as the relative effectiveness of safety measures in transportation cases, see, e. g., [Bibb and Southern Pacific], or health inspection cases [Dean Milk; Minnesota v. Barber], or economic benefit and injury in economic discrimination cases such as [Pike], but it does not weigh non-comparables such as cost to the railroads against arms and legs of the workers in [Firemen] because the result would be wholly subjective. That process becomes political and is constitutionally assigned to the legislative branch as the determiner of policy.

Where the putative state benefit and the impact upon interstate commerce are grossly disproportionate, the disparity is apparent without going through the motions of a judicial weighing process. The question then becomes one of equal protection and we [reject that attack] below. . . .

The United States Supreme Court has also made clear that it will not only recognize the authority of the state to exercise the police power, but also its right to do so in such manner as it deems most appropriate to local conditions, free from the homogenizing constraints of federal dictation [—quoting from Breard v. Alexandria]. The Oregon legislature is thus constitutionally authorized to enact laws which address the economic, esthetic and environmental consequences of the problems of litter in public places and solid waste disposal which suit the particular conditions of Oregon even though it may, in doing so, affect interstate commerce.

The enactment of the bottle bill is clearly a legislative act in harmony with federal law. Congress has directed that the states take primary responsibility for action in this field.* . . .

While it is clear that the Oregon legislature was authorized to act in this area, plaintiffs assert that the means incorporated in the bottle bill are not effective to accomplish its intended purpose and that alternative means are available which will have a lesser impact upon interstate commerce. Particularly, they offered evidence to show: (1) that the deposit system is inadequate to motivate the consuming public to return containers; (2) that

---

* The court referred mainly to the Federal Solid Waste Disposal Act. Its comment on that Act stated: "It disclaimed federal preemption and assigned to local government the task of coping with the problem with limited federal fiscal assistance." In support of that statement, the court quoted portions of the congressional findings, including: "(6) that while the collection and disposal of solid wastes should continue to be primarily the function of State, regional, and local agencies, the problems of waste disposal set forth above have become a matter national in scope and in concern and necessitate Federal action through financial and technical assistance . . . ."

mechanical means are being developed for improved collection of highway litter; and (3) that public education, such as the "Pitch In To Clean Up America" campaign, is a desirable means of dealing with container litter.

Selection of a reasonable means to accomplish a state purpose is clearly a legislative, not a judicial, function . . .. In particular, the courts may not invalidate legislation upon the speculation that machines may be developed or because additional and complementary means of accomplishing the same goal may also exist. The legislature may look to its imagination rather than to traditional methods such as those which plaintiffs suggest, to develop suitable means of dealing with state problems, even though their methods may be unique. Each state is a laboratory for innovation and experimentation in a healthy federal system. What fails may be abandoned and what succeeds may be emulated by other states. The bottle bill is now unique; it may later be regarded as seminal.

We conclude, therefore, that the bottle bill was properly enacted within the police power of the state of Oregon and that it is imaginatively, but reasonably, calculated to cope with problems of legitimate state concern.

Plaintiffs next assert that "Oregon's 'Bottle Bill' would not merely 'impede substantially the free flow of commerce' [Southern Pacific] but in many cases totally destroy and eliminate it . . .." The law surrounding the concept of impediments to the flow of interstate commerce relates consistently to the actual instrumentalities of interstate commerce, i. e., railroad, truck, air and other of the actual means of transportation of goods across state lines, not to the goods being transported. . . .

Plaintiffs argue persuasively that this case involves more than the transportation of bottles and cans, that it involves an interstate system of distribution for a national industry. Accepting that, the distribution system is still subject to the reasonable exercise of state police power. [Breard v. Alexandria.] . . .

In summary, the "free flow of commerce" cases are of no help to plaintiffs because they protect only the physical means of interstate transportation from unauthorized intrusion. The protection of the goods in that flow is found in the next cluster of cases, those that bar economic discrimination against interstate commerce.

Plaintiffs seek the benefit of the latter cases by asserting that the bottle bill burdens interstate commerce by economic discrimination against out-of-state interests. If that were indeed the design of the legislature,[1] then the

---

1. Plaintiffs base their claim of intentional economic protectionism on a statement of Attorney General Lee Johnson in his testimony before a legislative committee that the bottle bill would result in more jobs for Oregonians because Oregon producers would have a competitive advantage. They quote the statement out of context. The Attorney General was not asserting competitive advantage as a reason for the legislation. Rather, he was merely answering the anticipated argument from the bill's opponents that the legislation would cost Oregon business sales and jobs. The paragraph of his testimony, with the portion quoted by plaintiffs emphasized, reads as follows:

"We recognize that this bill will face heavy sledding in the Oregon Legislature. In the State of Washington a citizens' group tried to pass a similar bill by way of referendum. Powerful vested interests, particularly large national bottle and can manufacturers, mounted a well-financed campaign and defeated the measure. These same vested interests, most of whom are not located in the State of Oregon, will be mounting the same campaign here.

burden would likely be intolerable, despite a claim of lofty purpose under the police power. The United States Supreme Court has invalidated milk quota preferences for in-state milk, [Baldwin v. Seelig], preferential inspection laws which inhibit non-state distributors, [Minnesota v. Barber; Dean Milk], and, in a recent case relied on heavily by plaintiffs, a requirement that Arizona cantaloupes be packed in Arizona, [Pike], but even there the court carefully limited its weighing process to economic considerations and specifically distinguished safety or consumer protection legislation. The purpose of the legislation in each case was protectionist, despite the invocation of the police power.

On the other hand, legislation which has negative economic consequences for non-state business is not necessarily discriminatory against interstate commerce. In particular, the Pike case notes and distinguishes Pacific States Co. v. White, 296 U.S. 176 (1935), in which an Oregon regulation of containers for berries packed in Oregon was upheld despite the diminution of the ability of California box makers to compete with Oregon interests. It also noted the California raisin marketing system which was upheld in [Parker v. Brown], although the express design of that law was to give the California raisin industry an economic tactical advantage.

Lower courts have recently upheld the state's authority to ban products altogether from the state's market for legitimate state police purposes as against Commerce Clause claims. A New York law prohibiting sale of products made from the skins of endangered species, none of which are indigenous to New York, was upheld in Palladio, Inc. v. Diamond, 321 F. Supp. 630 (S.D.N.Y.1970), and [a] ban on the sale of phosphate detergents was upheld in Soap and Detergent Association v. Clark, 330 F.Supp. 1218 (S.D.Fla.1971), although not in Soap and Detergent Association v. City of Chicago, 357 F.Supp. 44 (N.D.Ill.1973) [reversed on appeal, 7th Cir., Jan. 1975]. . . .

The bottle bill is not discriminatory against interstate commerce and is not intended to operate to give Oregon industry a competitive advantage against outside firms. The ban on pull tops and the deposit-and-return provisions apply equally to all distributors and manufacturers whether Oregon-based or from out of state. . . .

Plaintiffs assert particularly that the reduction in the refund value of standardized containers from five cents to two cents each operates to discriminate against out-of-state manufacturers. They argue that they cannot produce the container for two cents and that an Oregon producer enjoys a competitive advantage by being able to buy the out-of-state producer's bottles at the lower cost and without the additional expense of shipping them to a distant plant. In effect, they claim, distant shippers must sell bottles to Oregon firms at below cost.

They will contend that the bill will increase the price of soft drinks and beer, but I believe that this is simply not true. Any price increase should be offset by the refund. They will also contend that the bill will destroy Oregon businesses and lead to a loss of jobs. This likewise is not true. Many small bottle distributors in Oregon who are now being forced out of business will be able to survive and provide new jobs. *Many Oregon concerns will indeed be given a competitive advantage over outside firms who have inadequate distribution facilities to handle re-cycled bottles."* [Footnote by the Court.]

We do not agree that the device of a reduced refund for standardized containers is discriminatory against out-of-state interests. The purpose of the provision is clearly to provide an incentive to make bottles as fungible as possible in order to ease the burden upon the distribution system by eliminating the need for sorting, facilitating industry-wide redemption and obviating the cost of reshipment. The firm which attempts to compete at a great distance from its market suffers a natural disadvantage, whatever container is allowed. Just as use of the non-returnable container reduced the inherent disadvantage of a distant competitor, the refund provisions tend to partially restore the former degree of disadvantage. The disadvantage does not relate to the state borders. A bottler in southern Oregon, for example, would be at a disadvantage competing to recapture used bottles in the Portland market relative to a competing bottler from Vancouver, Washington. The competitive disadvantage is one of distance, not one of state boundaries. While the state is under an obligation not to discriminate against out-of-state business interests, it is under no obligation to maintain equal levels of competitive advantage for all producers regardless of their distance from the market. We hold that the refund provisions of the bottle bill neither operate nor are designed to operate as devices of protectionism for Oregon interests or discrimination against non-Oregon interests.

Because the bottle bill is a legitimate exercise of the police power, consistent with federal policy legislation, which does not impede the flow of interstate commerce and which does not discriminate against non-Oregon interests, we hold that it is valid legislation under the Commerce Clause. . .

Affirmed.

SOME FURTHER COMMENTS
ON THE OREGON BOTTLE CASE

1. *Balancing.* Recall the questions posed in the note preceding this case. Were the state courts justified in refusing to engage in a balancing analysis? Do they adequately distinguish the Supreme Court cases engaging in such balancing? Would it have been possible to sustain the Bottle Bill if a balancing analysis had been applied? Compare the analysis of the case in Note, "State Environmental Protection Legislation and the Commerce Clause," 87 Harv.L.Rev. 1762 (1974). That Note comments: "[T]he concept of the dormant commerce power allows the judiciary to arbitrate the competing state and federal interests. The courts fulfill this role by applying a balancing test to the effects of the statute: the burden on interstate commerce must be outweighed by the state interest in the regulation. By refusing to engage in this balancing analysis, the Oregon trial and appellate courts in American Can failed to recognize this vital judicial function. [I]t appears to be the duty of the courts to balance the harms and benefits of the state's environmental legislation." However, after engaging in balancing, the Note concludes that "the Oregon statute should be upheld despite the lack of an obvious tipping of the scales in favor of its validity. The benefits are demonstrable, the burden is so tailored that it seeks to shift to the manufacturers no more than the cost to the state of the pollution they create, and the state is not attempting to achieve for itself an unreasonably high standard

of living.   [Earlier, the Note had stated that: "[T]here is little reason to restrict one state's attempts to 'raise the quality of life' to some conception of the national mean."]   Nevertheless, even though interstate commerce regulation by a state survives a test which balances its effect, the likelihood of conflicting commands by different states in the future may demand recognition at the outset that only uniform regulation is permissible."   At the time of the Oregon case, at least one other state had enacted similar legislation and other state legislatures had such bills under consideration.   Would a multiple burdens approach have been appropriate in the case? †

2.   *Alternatives.*   Did the Oregon Court of Appeals take adequate account of the Dean Milk "alternatives" analysis?   Would—and should—the Oregon court's attitude toward that aspect of the problem have changed if recent reports about experiences in the neighboring state of Washington had been available?   Washington, instead of following Oregon's approach, adopted a Model Litter Control Act in 1972.   That law emphasizes education and citizen participation programs, imposes fines for littering, and raises funds for the programs through a .015% tax on the gross sales of industries that contribute to litter.   According to a report in Time of December 23, 1974, the Washington law, like the Oregon one, "works": in Oregon, the volume of bottles and cans in roadside litter "has dropped by as much as 92% in the past three years"; in Washington, there has been "a reduction of more than 90%" in roadside litter.

3.   *The trial court.*   Compare, with the Oregon Court of Appeals statement of the available bases for commerce clause attacks, the trial court's view.*   The trial judge concluded that the Bottle Bill did not violate the commerce clause because it "does not regulate any instrumentalities of interstate commerce" and "does not discriminate in favor of local commerce."   Was the law "discriminatory" in the sense of some of the earlier cases?   And do those grounds exhaust the appropriate bases of commerce clause attacks?

The trial court commented, moreover, that it "would be ill-advised to interfere in any manner in this timely and necessary endeavor," in this "bold and forceful action," by the Oregon legislature.   And, near the end of his opinion, the trial judge stated: "What could be more appropriate and perhaps anticipated that the State of Oregon . . . the State which has demonstrated in many ways its concern for its environment and the happiness and well-being of its citizens; the State which has the largest area percentage-wise of its beaches in the public domain; the State which has recognized the dangers of esthetic pollution, and is a leader in the removal of bill-boards from our highway system; the State which has demonstrated its concern for a way of life by enacting laws preventing air pollution and protecting our water supply, would be the first State to enact major legislation

† In examining the balancing problems of this case, consider the relevance of a recommendation in January, 1975, by the Presidential Citizens Advisory Committee on Environmental Quality. The Committee recommended—largely as an energy-saving measure—the enactment of federal legislation mandating a refundable deposit on beer and soft-drink containers. The Committee called for national legislation "because it would be less disruptive than state-by-state laws"; federal legislation, the Committee stated, would "make for less economic disruption in the long run." See The New York Times, Jan. 24, 1975.

* The trial court opinion is unreported. The decision was by the Oregon Circuit Court for the Third Judicial District.

directed at the litter and solid waste disposal problems. While Oregon may be considered to be first in this field, it is no longer a lonely voice crying out in the wilderness of pollution, waste and litter, because many other states have embarked on their own perilous journey through these troubled waters as is evidenced by the [challengers'] Exhibits." Does that passage strengthen the argument for the law? Or for a cumulative burdens attack on the law? Or both?

———

STATE TAXATION AND FREE TRADE

The preceding materials have examined at length the problems of state regulatory statutes challenged under the commerce clause. But state regulation is not the only variety of state legislative activity subject to commerce clause restraints. A similarly prolific source of litigation has been state taxation challenged as impinging upon interstate commerce. States need tax revenues, and the Court has recognize that state tax bases would be unjustifiably curtailed if all interstate business were immunized from state tax obligations: "Even interstate business must pay its way, by bearing its share of local tax burdens." Yet, with respect to taxes as with regulations, the commerce clause "by its own force" creates "an area of trade free from interference by the State." States may not impose discriminatory or unduly burdensome taxes: without commerce clause restraints, the Court has feared, interstate business would be subject to the risk of multiple taxation, with most or all of a company's property or income being subjected to the tax scheme of each state in which it does business.

The Court from the beginning has sought to draw lines distinguishing between the permissible and the impermissible state tax. As in the regulatory area, it has sought accommodation of legitimate local needs and the interest in a national economy. The decisions are numerous, difficult to organize, and even more difficult to comprehend in their totality. As the Court noted in a 1959 decision: "This Court alone has handed down some three hundred full-dress opinions spread through slightly more than that number of our reports." And as the Court added in an understatement: "The decisions have been 'not always clear . . . consistent or reconcilable.' " [1] Or as Justice Frankfurter had said thirteen years earlier: "The history of this problem is spread over hundreds of volumes of our Reports. To attempt to harmonize all that has been said in the past would neither clarify what has gone before nor guide the future." [2]

The cases have been what Justices have called a "tangled underbrush" and a "quagmire" because in the area of state taxation the variables are even more numerous and complex and the tools of analysis even more uncertain than in the field of state regulation of commerce. Types of taxes and types of taxed activities vary widely. The most commonly litigated taxes have been property taxes, sales and use taxes, net and gross receipts taxes, and license and franchise taxes. The subjects of taxation in most of the cases

———

1. Justice Clark in Northwestern States Portland Cement Co. v. Minnesota, 358 U.S. 450 (1959).

2. Freeman v. Hewit, 329 U.S. 249 (1946).

have been interstate transportation and interstate sales, and various segments thereof.[3] Moreover, far more than in the state regulatory area, the Court has had great difficulty in assessing the reasonableness or necessity of a particular tax scheme: a state's need for revenue is always an available justification for a tax.

The special complexity of state tax problems has prompted some Justices to voice their frustrations and perceptions of judicial incompetence for the task. Advocacy of a substantial Court withdrawal from the tax area has been more common than in the regulatory area. A well-known statement is that in a dissent by Justice Black, joined by Justices Frankfurter and Douglas, in McCarroll v. Dixie Greyhound Lines, 309 U.S. 176 (1940): "Judicial control of national commerce—unlike legislative regulation— must from inherent limitations of the judicial process treat the subject by the hit-and-miss method of deciding single local controversies upon evidence and information limited by the narrow rules of litigation. Spasmodic and unrelated instances of litigation cannot afford an adequate basis for the creation of integrated national rules which alone can afford that full protection for interstate commerce intended by the Constitution. [The problems faced by the challenged tax should accordingly be left] for consideration of Congress in a nation-wide survey of the constantly increasing barriers to trade among the States." Yet, assuming that Congress *is* more competent to solve the problem, what should the Court do in the absence of congressional guidance: let the challenged tax stand, or invalidate it? The characteristic majority stance has been to exercise continued commerce clause scrutiny while hoping for, and urging, legislative assistance.[4]

But congressional legislation has been sparse and of narrow range.[5] A congressional committee did indeed at last undertake a comprehensive empirical study of state taxes in the early 1960's; and in 1965 the House Judiciary Committee recommended a comprehensive legislative solution. But the proposed Interstate Taxation Act failed of enactment after extensive hearings—and after widespread opposition, especially from state tax authorities adversely affected by particular recommendations. Accordingly,

3. Among the pervasive problems that have confronted the Court—some parallel to, some in addition to, those in the state regulation area—are: To what extent does constitutionality of a tax turn on the "subject" of the tax? To what extent on the "measure" of the tax? To what extent do the Court's standards rest on "formal" bases? To what extent do they reflect "economic realities"—the "actual" extent of the tax burden? To what extent do the decisions rest wholly on the commerce clause? To what extent do due process limits on state legislative jurisdiction join with—or become confused with—commerce clause restraints?

4. See, e. g., Justice Frankfurter's dissent in Northwestern States Portland Cement Co. v. Minnesota, 358 U.S. 450 (1959), voting to invalidate a tax even while articulating the need for legisla-

tive solutions: "[A] determination of who is to get how much out of the common fund can hardly be made wisely and smoothly through the adjudicatory process." The Court "can only act negatively," on the basis of "rough and ready legal concepts," without "detailed inquiry into the incidence of diverse economic burdens." "The problem calls for solution by devising a congressional policy. . . . The solution to these problems ought not to rest on the self-serving determination of the States of what they are entitled to out of the Nation's resources." Recall also Justice Jackson's comment in the Duckworth case, noted above (in a footnote to Justice Black's dissent in Hood, sec. 1D).

5. See, e. g., the stop-gap law on state net income taxes enacted after the Northwestern States case in 1959, 15 U.S.C. § 381.

the problems of restraints on state taxes in the interest of the national economy continue to be of considerable practical importance. However, they have not given rise to much significant constitutional litigation in recent years.[6] To pursue the intricacies of state taxation here would require more time and space than the undertaking warrants. There is accordingly no effort at detailed consideration of state taxation in this edition.[7]

SECTION 2. CONGRESSIONAL ORDERING OF FEDERAL–STATE RELATIONSHIPS

Scope Note. The materials in sec. 1 of this chapter emphasized limits on state regulatory power derived from the commerce clause itself. But in many cases the commerce clause is not entirely "dormant"; with increasing frequency, objections based on the *exercise* of the congressional power are joined with those resting on the constitutional *grant* of the power. That, indeed, was so as early as Gibbons v. Ogden; it is even more common in the context of proliferating national legislation of the 20th century.* This section, then, briefly examines the impact of congressional exercises of power. The major concern is with federal legislation (a) imposing new limits on state action, and (b) removing pre-existing barriers to state control. Most of the materials continue to deal with commerce regulations, but congressional action is of course significant with regard to a wide range of other delegated powers as well. Moreover, the techniques of imposing new and removing old obstacles to state legislation should be viewed in a broader context, as a small sampling of the wide variety of devices available in the congressional ordering of federal-state relations. (See the concluding note in this section.) This section, in short, seeks to highlight what has been a pervasive but somewhat obscured phenomenon in the earlier materials: that the Court in fact operates as an important yet limited partner of Congress in articulating federalism

6. For rare recent examples of Supreme Court decisions on state taxation, see Evansville-Vanderburgh Airport v. Delta Airlines, 405 U.S. 707 (1972); United Air Lines v. Mahin, 410 U.S. 623 (1973); Standard Pressed Steel Co. v. Wash. Revenue Dept., 419 U.S. 560 (1975); and Colonial Pipeline Co. v. Traigle, 421 U.S. —— (1975).

7. For fuller analyses of the field, see— in addition to chap. 9 of Gunther and Dowling, Constitutional Law (8th ed. 1970)—Note, "Developments in the Law: Federal Limitations on State Taxation of Interstate Business," 75 Harv.L.Rev. 953 (1962); Hartman, State Taxation of Interstate Commerce (1953); Barrett, "State Taxation of Interstate Commerce—'Direct Burdens,' 'Multiple Burdens' or What Have You?" 4 Vand.L.Rev. 496 (1951),

Selected Essays 1938–62 (1963), 324; and Brown, "The Open Economy: Justice Frankfurter and the Position of the Judiciary," 67 Yale L.J. 219 (1957), Selected Essays 1938–62 (1963), 371.

* Recall how frequently in the cases in the preceding section preemption claims were joined with commerce clause objections. Repeatedly, the challengers to state regulation launched two-pronged attacks, arguing that the state law was barred by congressional action as well as by the commerce clause. In those situations, the cases produced commerce clause discussions only after the Court had rejected the preemption argument. That was true, for example, in the Barnwell, Southern Pacific, and Huron Portland Cement cases in sec. 1B.

limits on state power; that Congress plays a decisive role in determining the relations between state and federal power, and in defining the operative scope of state and federal substantive law; and that the interrelationships between state and federal law present problems of subtlety and complexity for Congress and Court.

A. PREEMPTION OF STATE AUTHORITY

Introduction. When Congress exercises a granted power, the federal legislation may displace state law under the supremacy clause of Art. VI. But Congress does not typically act on a wholesale basis, and congressional entry into a field does not necessarily end all state authority. In considering the preemption cases, as with the entire area of congressional ordering, it is vital to bear in mind an observation in Hart and Wechsler, The Federal Courts and the Federal System (1953), 435: "Federal law is generally interstitial in nature. It rarely occupies a legal field completely . . . . Federal legislation, on the whole, has been conceived and drafted on an *ad hoc* basis to accomplish limited objectives. It builds upon legal relationships established by the states, altering or supplanting them only so far as necessary for the special purpose. Congress acts, in short, against the background of the total *corpus juris* of the states in much the way that a state legislature acts against the background of the common law, assumed to govern unless changed by legislation." See also Hart, "The Relations Between State and Federal Law," 54 Colum.L.Rev. 489 (1954), and the note on political safeguards of federalism, chap. 2 above.

Preemption as a preferential ground. What, then, is the function of the Court in examining claims that federal legislation has displaced state authority? In form, the problem is one of statutory interpretation: state regulation falls not because of the commerce clause but because, under the supremacy clause of Art. VI, the "supreme" congressional law supersedes state law. But preemption occurs not only when there is an outright conflict between the federal scheme and the state requirement. State authority is barred as well when congressional action is an *implicit* barrier: when state regulation would interfere unduly with the accomplishment of congressional objectives. Determination of congressional requirements and purposes must start of course with the congressional statute itself, and the cases accordingly require a particularized examination of the specific regulatory scheme. Examination of the varied statutory contexts is not the aim of these materials. Rather, this section examines preemption problems for the purpose of suggesting some general themes and examining some considerations (going beyond those of traditional statutory interpretation) that may enter the Court's decisions in preemption controversies.

The fact that Congress has spoken in the area of state regulation does not necessarily preclude state regulation; and the fact that there is no explicit federal-state conflict or no explicit congressional statement of intent to bar state authority does not bar a finding of preemption. How, then, does the Court determine when state authority has been preempted, and when it has

not? Consider the preemption criteria articulated and applied in the materials that follow: to what extent do they resemble the "constitutional" standards evolved in the state regulation cases above? In the sec. 1 materials above, congressional declarations of policy occasionally affected the adjudication of the constitutional claim. Recall, e. g., the Huron Portland Cement case and Parker v. Brown. Conversely, a number of the cases in these preemption materials indicate that "constitutional" criteria influence the adjudication of what in form purport to be determinations of congressional preemptive purpose. Before turning to specific illustrations, consider the general observations in the law review note which follows; and note especially the italicized passage. [Note, "Pre-emption as a Preferential Ground: A New Canon of Construction," 12 Stan.L.Rev. 208 (1959), Selected Essays 1938–62 (1963), 310]: *

"Many of the Supreme Court's recent pre-emption decisions have been condemned [as] unwarranted substitution of judicial wisdom for that of Congress. [E. g., Pennsylvania v. Nelson, noted below.] Much of the criticism appears to have been misdirected. The critics have focused discussion on whether there was a specific congressional intent to supersede state law rather than whether the coexistence of state law is compatible with the general purpose of the federal legislation involved. Moreover, the critics have failed to appreciate that in many instances the same results might easily have been reached on other constitutional grounds had the Court not chosen to articulate them in terms of pre-emption.

"By framing the pre-emption question in terms of specific congressional intent the Supreme Court has manufactured difficulties for itself. Apart from the difficult problem of defining which Congress' and which congressman's intent is relevant, this manner of stating the issue suggests that the pre-emption question was consciously resolved and that only diligent effort is needed to reveal the intended solution. But Congress, embroiled in controversy over policy issues, rarely anticipates the possible ramifications of its acts upon state law. [P]re-emption questions are implicit in many federal statutes but remain for the courts to answer. . . .

"In the great majority of cases the pre-emptive implications of the federal statute must be derived without the aid of specific legislative guidance, and even when such guidance is offered, it does not represent the whole solution in many instances. Thus several writers have suggested that the proper approach is to determine whether the continued existence of the state law is consistent with the general purpose of the federal statute by seeking to define the evil Congress sought to remedy and the method chosen to effectuate its cure. And, to understand the evil and the remedy the court should look to the entire text of the statute, to its history, and to administrative interpretations, when available.

"Most of the cases appear to have adopted this approach, although lip service is still paid to the specific intent inquiry. In some cases, however, the Court has precluded state action despite the fact that none of the interpretative sources revealed a federal policy which required the invalidation of the state law in question. Just as the Court construes a statute in such a

---

way as to avoid a constitutional question whenever possible, it may be that the Court bases its decision on the pre-emption ground in order to avoid reaching some other constitutional question. . . . At times the Court has precluded state action despite the fact that the process of interpretation failed to reveal a conflict of the strength that appears to be required to invoke the supremacy clause. Rather than treat this group of cases merely as another example of 'judicial legislation,' these decisions will be examined for signs that the Court is in actuality implementing constitutional principles external to the supremacy clause, while nominally deciding the case on the pre-emption ground.

[After discussing Pennsylvania v. Nelson and Hines v. Davidowitz, below, the Note continued:] "Recently . . . the Court has relied increasingly on the pre-emption doctrine in cases which would have been decided under the commerce clause only a short time ago. It is now frequently argued (1) that the states lack concurrent power under the doctrine of Cooley v. Board of Wardens, and (2) that if the states possess such power, the field has been pre-empted by federal legislation. Almost all of the cases so argued which result in the preclusion of state action have rested on the pre-emption ground without reaching the commerce clause issue. The Court, however, appears to use essentially the same reasoning process in a case nominally hinging on pre-emption as it has in past cases in which the question was whether the state law regulated or burdened interstate commerce. . . .

"*[T]he Court has adopted the same weighing of interests approach in pre-emption cases that it uses to determine whether a state law unjustifiably burdens interstate commerce. In a number of situations the Court has invalidated statutes on the pre-emption ground when it appeared that the state laws sought to favor local economic interests at the expense of the interstate market. On the other hand, when the Court has been satisfied that valid local interests, such as those in safety or in the reputable operation of local business, outweigh the restrictive effect on interstate commerce, the Court has rejected the pre-emption argument and allowed state regulation to stand.* . . . [Emphasis added.]

"The critics of the Court have discerned correctly that the pre-emption decisions do not uniformly represent the product of sound statutory construction, much less a supportable finding of specific congressional intent. Pre-emption can never be the product of statutory construction alone, since the Court and only the Court can make the final judgment of incompatibility required by the supremacy clause.

"As a practical matter, it is understandable that the Court has relied increasingly upon the pre-emption ground. By so doing, the Court in some measure shifts to Congress the odium for invalidating state law. But when the discrepancy between the judicial finding of congressional intent and the known temper of the Congress on the subject becomes too great, this attempt to shift responsibility backfires upon the Court in the form of accusations of 'judicial legislation.' If the Court continues to rationalize its pre-emption decisions in terms of spurious specific intent, or even if it speaks in terms of congressional purpose when it is actually motivated by other constitutional considerations, the Court can only earn the disrespect of the legal profession and the public. In order to use pre-emption validly as a substitute ground

the Court must both make clear that it is invoking an overriding principle of decision and justify the use of such a principle. . . .

"Flexibility is gained by deciding a case on the pre-emption ground rather than on some other constitutional basis because pre-emption decisions invite congressional reconsideration and adjustment. It might seem, however, that even if Congress subsequently enacts a statute to remove the pre-emption barrier, the Court will be forced to invalidate the state law when next it is challenged, since the premise for employing pre-emption was that the Court believed the state law to be invalid on substantive constitutional grounds. In those situations where the alternative constitutional ground is an independent standard, such as due process or equal protection, congressional approval of the state law is not likely to alter the Court's hostile view of the state law, and the only effect of relying preferentially on pre-emption would be to postpone the eventual showdown. [But cf. Katzenbach v. Morgan, chap. 11 below.] But when the question is one of the negative implications of some affirmative constitutional grant of power, such as that over commerce, the view Congress takes of the permissible limits of state action is of proper concern to the Court. Used as a method of allowing Congress a greater share in the elaboration of the areas constitutionally reserved for its own action, the pre-emption doctrine can thus become a valuable device in the give and take between branches of the government which is the ultimate guarantee of sound constitutional government."

TRENDS IN PREEMPTION CASES: THE IMPACT OF COMMERCE CLAUSE DOCTRINES IN ASCERTAINING CONGRESSIONAL PURPOSES

Does the course of decisions suggest a growing influence of doctrines familiar from state regulation of commerce cases in determining whether Congress has preempted state authority? Does the course of decisions suggest an increasing readiness to find that Congress has preempted a field? A sampling of cases of past generations, and a contrast with more recent decisions, provides clues—though it bears renewed warning that general statements may be less important to particular results than the specific statutory contexts.

1. *The typical formulas: The Rice and Hines cases.* In modern cases, the Court has frequently recited the standards articulated a generation ago. Are the standards applied similarly, however? Probably the most widely quoted passages are from RICE v. SANTA FE ELEVATOR CORP., 331 U.S. 218, 229–30 (1947), and HINES v. DAVIDOWITZ, 312 U.S. 52, 67 (1941).* In Rice, Justice Douglas stated: "The question in each case is

---

* See, e. g., Pennsylvania v. Nelson, 350 U.S. 497 (1956), quoting both the Rice and Hines passages. Note also the Court's reiteration of its adherence to the Hines "articulation of the meaning of the Supremacy Clause" in Perez v. Campbell, 402 U.S. 637 (1971), involving a state conflict with federal legislation resting on the bankruptcy rather than the commerce power. And see the discussion of preemption principles in still another context outside the commerce area, in Goldstein v. California, 412 U.S. 546 (1973) (copyright).

what the purpose of Congress was. . . . Such a purpose may be evidenced in several ways. The scheme of federal regulation may be so pervasive as to make reasonable the inference that Congress left no room for the State to supplement it. . . . Or the Act of Congress may touch a field in which the federal interest is so dominant that the federal system will be assumed to preclude enforcement of state laws on the same subject. . . . Likewise, the object sought to be obtained by the federal law and the character of obligations imposed by it may reveal the same purpose. . . . Or the state policy may produce a result inconsistent with the objective of the federal statute." In the Hines case, Justice Black stated that, in considering the validity of state laws in the light of federal laws touching the same subject, the Court "has made use of the following expressions: conflicting; contrary to; occupying the field; repugnance; difference; irreconcilability; inconsistency; violation; curtailment; and interference. But none of these expressions provides an infallible constitutional test or an exclusive constitutional yardstick. In the final analysis, there can be no one crystal clear distinctly marked formula." †

Are the Rice criteria similar to those used when state laws are challenged as conflicting with the commerce power rather than with federal legislation— with the constitutional *grant* of power to Congress, rather than with its *exercise?* Note especially the similarity between Justice Douglas' second criterion in Rice and the Cooley standard in commerce clause litigation. Compare Justice Douglas' formulation a quarter of a century later, in BURBANK v. LOCKHEED AIR TERMINAL, 411 U.S. 624 (1973). In Burbank, has the role of Cooley changed to confusing rather than influencing preemption standards? Or is that growing intermingling of commerce clause and preemption doctrines an understandable and desirable development?

The 5 to 4 decision in Burbank sustained a preemption attack on a local effort to curb airport noise. The Burbank ordinance had prohibited jet airplanes from taking off from the local, privately owned airport between 11:00 p. m. and 7:00 a. m. Justice Douglas began his majority opinion with the statement: "The Court [in Cooley] first stated the rule of pre-emption which is the critical issue in the present case." He quoted the Rice criteria, considered in detail the statutory roles of the Federal Aviation Administration and the Environmental Protection Agency, and concluded that "the pervasive nature of the scheme of federal regulation of aircraft noise . . .

---

† In the Hines case, the Court held that enforcement of Pennsylvania's Alien Registration Act of 1939 was barred by the federal Alien Registration Act of 1940. Much of the opinion —characteristically (see the student Note quoted above)—dealt with the broad national power over aliens, rather than its specific exercise. The Court concluded that, "whether or not registration of aliens is of such a nature that the Constitution permits only of one uniform national system," Congress had enacted a uniform system. Justice Stone's dissent concluded that a congressional ban on state registration laws was "not to be inferred from the silence of Congress [regarding state authority] in enacting a law which at no point conflicts with the state legislation and is harmonious with it." Note also an earlier statement in the dissent: "Little aid can be derived from the vague and illusory but often repeated formula that Congress 'by occupying the field' has excluded from it all state legislation. Every Act of Congress occupies some field, but we must know the boundaries of that field before we can say that it has precluded [state legislation]. To discover the boundaries we look to the federal statute itself, read in the light of its constitutional setting and its legislative history."

leads us to conclude that there is pre-emption." Yet in elaborating his pre-emption conclusion, he also drew on multiple burdens considerations commonplace in commerce clause litigation. He recognized that noise control "is of course deepseated in the police power of the States," but he added: "If we were to uphold the Burbank ordinance and a significant number of municipalities followed suit, it is obvious that fractionalized control of the timing of take-offs and landings would severely limit the flexibility of the FAA in controlling air traffic flow."

Justice Rehnquist's dissent, joined by Justices Stewart, White and Marshall, strongly disagreed with Justice Douglas' interpretation of congressional considerations of the problem. Yet he, too, invoked guidelines akin to those found in commerce clause litigation: "Because noise regulation has traditionally been an area of local, not national, concern, in determining whether congressional legislation has, by implication, foreclosed remedial local enactments 'we start with the assumption that the historic police powers of the States were not to be superseded by the Federal Act unless that was the clear and manifest purpose of Congress.' [Rice]. This assumption derives from our basic constitutional division of legislative competence between the States and Congress; from 'due regard for the presuppositions of our embracing federal system, *including the principle of diffusion of power not as a matter of doctrinaire localism but as a promoter of democracy* . . . .' (emphasis added)." *

2. *Preemption in last generation's commerce cases: Kelly, Maurer, and related decisions.* a. In Kelly v. Washington, 302 U.S. 1 (1937), the Court held that enforcement of a state law requiring safety inspections of tugs was not barred by enactment of the federal Motor Boat Act of 1910. Chief Justice Hughes' opinion was typical of preemption cases of the period: "States are thus enabled to deal with local exigencies and to exert in the absence of conflict with federal legislation an essential protective power [although interstate commerce may be affected]. And when Congress does exercise its paramount authority, it is obvious that Congress may determine how far its regulation shall go. There is no constitutional rule which compels Congress to occupy the whole field. Congress may circumscribe its regulation and occupy only a limited field. When it does so, state regulation outside that limited field and otherwise admissible is not forbidden or displaced. The principle is thoroughly established that the exercise by the State of its police power, which would be valid if not superseded by federal action, is superseded only where the repugnance or conflict is so 'direct and positive' that the two acts cannot 'be reconciled or consistently stand together.' A few illustrations will suffice. . . . ."

Chief Justice Hughes' "illustrations" in Kelly were substantially repeated by Justice Black four years later, in a footnote to his opinion in Hines v. Davidowitz, above. In the Hines text, Justice Black emphasized the "broad national authority" in the international field and stated that the preemption effect of a federal alien registration law, dealing with "the rights, liberties

---

* The District Court in Burbank had invalidated the ordinance both on commerce clause and supremacy clause grounds, but the Supreme Court purported not to reach the commerce clause issue. See the earlier comment on the case, sec. 1B above.

emption claims? Or must decisions in this field inevitably turn on the particular statutory context and the specific field (and purpose) of regulation? After the decision in Pennsylvania v. Nelson, 350 U.S. 497 (1956), a proposal for a general statute was introduced in several Congresses by Congressman Smith of Virginia. The Nelson case, applying the standards of the Rice and Hines cases, note 1 above, held that a conviction for "sedition against the United States" under the Pennsylvania Sedition Act was barred by the Smith Act and other federal laws. (Cf. Uphaus v. Wyman, 364 U.S. 388 (1960), chap. 13 below.) The Court concluded: "Since we find that Congress has occupied the field to the exclusion of parallel state legislation, that the dominant interest of the Federal Government precludes state intervention, and that administration of state Acts would conflict with the operation of the federal plan, we are convinced that the decision of the Supreme Court of Pennsylvania [reversing Nelson's conviction on the ground of 'supersession of the state law' by federal law] is unassailable."

Congressman Smith's proposal (see, e. g., H.R. 3, 85th Cong., 2d Sess. (1958), which was passed by the House) provided: "No Act of Congress shall be construed as indicating an intent on the part of Congress to occupy the field in which such Act operates, to the exclusion of all State laws on the same subject matter, unless such Act contains an express provision to that effect, or unless there is a direct and positive conflict between such Act and a State law so that the two cannot be reconciled or consistently stand together."

B. CONSENT TO STATE LAWS

Introduction. May Congress, instead of precluding state action through preemption, validate state laws regulating commerce—laws which, in the absence of the federal consent, would violate the commerce clause? In the Cooley case, the Court indicated that Congress could not validate laws which were "unconstitutional" under the commerce clause; yet a century later, it seemed clear to Justice Stone in the Southern Pacific case that the "undoubted" congressional "power to redefine the distribution of power over interstate commerce" included the authority "to permit the states to regulate the commerce in a manner which would otherwise not be permissible." What is the justification for that congressional authority? What is its scope? The examples of congressional "consent" in this section are designed to explore those problems.*

1. *The Wilson Act of 1890 and the Rahrer case.* a. In LEISY v. HARDIN, 135 U.S. 100 (1890), the Court invalidated an Iowa law prohibiting the sale of intoxicating liquors as applied to beer brewed in Illinois and offered for sale in the "original package" in Iowa. Chief Justice Fuller, after reviewing the Cooley doctrine, tied it to congressional intent and

---

* On the problems of congressional "consent," see generally Biklé, "The Silence of Congress," 41 Harv.L.Rev. 200 (1927); Dowling, "Interstate Commerce and State Power," 27 Va.L.Rev. 1 (1940), Selected Essays 1938–62 (1963), 280, and "Interstate Commerce and State Power—Revised Version," 47 Colum.L.Rev. 547 (1947); and Note, "Congressional Consent to Discriminatory State Legislation," 45 Colum.L. Rev. 927 (1945).

stated that "inasmuch as interstate commerce, consisting in the transportation, purchase, sale and exchange of commodities, is national in its character, and must be governed by a uniform system, so long as Congress does not pass any law to regulate it, or allowing the States so to do, it thereby indicates its will that such commerce shall be free and untrammeled." He insisted that Peirce v. New Hampshire (one of the License Cases, sec. 1A above), "in so far as it rests on the view that the law of New Hampshire was valid because Congress had made no regulation on the subject, must be regarded as having been distinctly overthrown by numerous cases." Accordingly, he concluded that Leisy "had the right to import this beer into that State, [and] had the right to sell it, by which act alone it would become mingled in the common mass of property within the State. Up to that point of time, we hold that, *in the absence of congressional permission to do so,* the State had no power to interfere by seizure." [Emphasis added.]†

b.   In August, 1890, only a few months after the decision in Leisy v. Hardin, Congress passed the Wilson Act which provided that "all . . . intoxicating liquors . . . transported into any state or territory, or remaining therein, for use, consumption, sale, or storage therein, shall upon arrival in such state or territory be subject to the operation and effect of the laws of such state or territory enacted in the exercise of its police powers, to the same extent and in the same manner as though such . . . liquors had been produced in such state or territory, and shall not be exempt therefrom by reason of being introduced therein in original packages or otherwise." Thereafter it was held that by virtue of this Act a state may apply its prohibition laws to sales of intoxicating liquors in the original packages.   IN RE RAHRER, 140 U.S. 545 (1891). According to the Rahrer opinion, "Congress has not attempted to delegate the power to regulate commerce, or to exercise any power reserved to the States, or to grant a power not possessed by the States, or to adopt state laws. . . . It imparted no power to the State not then possessed, but allowed imported property to fall at once upon arrival within the local jurisdiction."   The Court added: "No reason is perceived why, if Congress chooses to provide that certain designated subjects of interstate commerce shall be governed by a rule which divests them of that character at an earlier period of time than would otherwise be the case, it is not within its competency to do so."

2.   *The Webb-Kenyon Act of 1913 and the Clark Distilling case.*   In March 1913, Congress passed the Webb-Kenyon Act, "An Act divesting intoxicating liquors of their interstate character in certain cases"—a reliance on the "divesting" language of In re Rahrer, above.   The 1913 law provided that "the shipment or transportation of any . . . intoxicating liquor of any kind, from one State . . . into any other State, . . . which said . . . liquor is intended by any person interested therein, to be received, possessed, sold, or in any manner used either in the original package or otherwise, in violation of any law of such State, . . . is hereby prohibited."

† But see Plumley v. Massachusetts, decided four years after Leisy, 155 U.S. 461 (1894). The Plumley decision sustained application of a state ban on sale of oleomargarine colored to resemble butter, even though the oleo involved was imported from another age. state and sold in the original pack-

An action was begun in a federal court in Maryland to compel a railway to accept a consignment of liquor tendered for shipment to West Virginia. To the defense that such shipment was illegal under the Webb-Kenyon Act, because the laws of West Virginia barred shipments of liquor into the State, it was countered that the federal law was unconstitutional. The Supreme Court stated that "if [the 1913 Act] was within the power of Congress to adopt, there is no possible reason for holding that to enforce the prohibitions of the state law would conflict with the commerce clause." The Act was adjudged a valid exercise of the commerce power by Congress. CLARK DISTILLING CO. v. WESTERN MARYLAND R. CO., 242 U.S. 311 (1917). On the constitutional point, the Court accepted the Webb-Kenyon Act as "but a larger degree of exertion of the identical power which was brought into play in the [Wilson Act]." *

3. *The McCarran Act of 1945 and the Prudential case.* a. In 1944, the Supreme Court found that the Sherman Anti-Trust Act of 1890 applied to the insurance business, even though the Court had held in 1868 that insurance was not commerce. United States v. South-Eastern Underwriters Ass'n, 322 U.S. 533 (1944). The Court concluded that "a nationwide business" like insurance "is not deprived of its interstate character merely because it is built upon . . . contracts which are local in nature." In response, Congress enacted the McCarran Act of 1945, 59 Stat. 33, 15 U.S.C. § 1011 et seq., which not only deferred and limited the applicability of anti-trust laws to the business, but also sought to assure continued state authority over insurance. The Act contained a declaration "that the continued regulation and taxation by the several States of the business of insurance is in the public interest, and that silence on the part of the Congress shall not be construed to impose any barrier to the regulation or taxation of such business by the several States."

---

* The substance and much of the language of the Webb-Kenyon Act was written into the Twenty-first Amendment, which also repealed the Eighteenth. Does the broad recognition of state power over liquor, in the Twenty-first Amendment, make commerce clause concerns wholly inapplicable in that area of regulation? Justice Brandeis, once so suggested for a unanimous Court: "Since that amendment, the right of a State to prohibit or regulate the importation of intoxicating liquor is not limited by the commerce clause." Finch Co. v. McKittrick, 305 U.S. 395 (1939). But in 1964, the Court held that the Twenty-first Amendment did not leave absolute control of liquor traffic to the states. See especially Hostetter v. Idlewild Bon Voyage Liquor Corp., 377 U.S. 324 (1964), where the Court described the basic issue as "whether the Twenty-first Amendment so far obliterates the Commerce Clause as to empower New York to prohibit absolutely the passage of liquor through its territory, under the supervision of the United States Bureau of Customs acting under federal law, for delivery to consumers in foreign countries." The Court held that New York could not prohibit the sale of tax-free liquor to departing international airline travelers for delivery upon arrival at foreign destinations. Compare Seagram & Sons v. Hostetter, 384 U.S. 35 (1966), sustaining a 1964 amendment of New York's Alcoholic Beverage Control Law requiring that liquor prices to domestic wholesalers and retailers be "no higher than the lowest" prices offered elsewhere in the country. The Court emphasized that this case, unlike the Idlewild one, concerned liquor destined for use, distribution, or consumption in New York: "In that situation, the Twenty-first Amendment demands wide latitude for regulation by the State. We need not now decide whether the mode of liquor regulation chosen by a State in such circumstances could ever constitute so grave an interference with a company's operations elsewhere as to make the regulation invalid under the Commerce Clause."

Section 2 of the law provided: "(a) The business of insurance . . . shall be subject to the laws of the several States which relate to the regulation or taxation of such business. (b) No Act of Congress shall be construed to invalidate, impair, or supersede any law enacted by any State for the purpose of regulating the business of insurance, or which imposes a fee or tax upon such business, unless such Act specifically relates to the business of insurance."

b. In PRUDENTIAL INSURANCE CO. v. BENJAMIN, 328 U.S. 408 (1946), the Company, a New Jersey corporation, objected to the continued collection of a long-standing tax of 3% of the premiums received from all business done in South Carolina. No similar tax was required of South Carolina corporations. The Court assumed that the tax was "discriminatory" and hence invalid under the Court's commerce clause decisions. Nevertheless the Court rejected the Company's challenge and held that the McCarran Act validated the tax. Justice Rutledge disagreed with the Company's contention that "Congress' declaration of policy adds nothing to the validity of what the states have done within the area covered by the declaration." To accept the claim "would ignore the very basis on which [the] Clark Distilling case [has] set the pattern of the law for governing situations like that now presented." He explained:

"Not yet has this Court held such a disclaimer [of a commerce clause prohibition] invalid . . . . On the contrary, in each instance it has given effect to the congressional judgment contradicting its own previous one. It is true that rationalizations have differed concerning those decisions . . . . But the results have been lasting and are at least as important, for the direction given to the process of accommodating federal and state authority, as the reasons stated for reaching them. [A]part from [the] function of defining the outer boundary of its power, whenever Congress' judgment has been uttered affirmatively to contradict the Court's previously expressed view that specific action taken by the states in Congress' silence was forbidden by the commerce clause, this body has accommodated its previous judgment to Congress' expressed approval. Some part of this readjustment may be explained in ways acceptable on any theory of the commerce clause and the relations of Congress and the courts toward its functioning. Such explanations, however, hardly go to the root of the matter. For the fact remain that, in these instances, the sustaining of Congress' overriding action has involved something beyond correction of erroneous factual judgment in deference to Congress' presumably better-informed view of the facts, and also beyond giving due deference to its conception of the scope of its powers, when it repudiates, just as when its silence is thought to support, the inference that it has forbidden state action."

"[W]e would be going very far to rule that South Carolina no longer may collect her tax. To do so would flout the expressly declared policies of both Congress and the state. Moreover it would establish a ruling never heretofore made and in doing this would depart from the whole trend of decision in a great variety of situations most analogous to the one now presented. . . . The power of Congress over commerce exercised entirely without reference to coordinated action of the states is not restricted, except as the Constitution expressly provides, by any limitation which forbids it to discriminate against interstate commerce and in favor of local trade. . . .

"This broad authority Congress may exercise alone, subject to those limitations, or in conjunction with coordinated action by the states, in which case limitations imposed for the preservation of their powers become inoperative and only those designed to forbid action altogether by any power or combination of powers in our governmental system remain effective. Here both Congress and South Carolina have acted, and in complete co-ordination, to sustain the tax. It is therefore reinforced by the exercise of all the power of government residing in our scheme. Clear and gross must be the evil which would nullify such an exertion, one which could arise only by exceeding beyond cavil some explicit and compelling limitation imposed by a constitutional provision or provisions designed and intended to outlaw the action taken entirely from our constitutional framework."

c. Justice Rutledge's conclusion regarding congressional power is obviously easier to understand than his reasoning. Congress can clearly "consent" to any variety of state legislation impinging on commerce: in the exercise of the national commerce power, it can permit state laws the Court would otherwise consider "unconstitutional" under the dormant commerce clause. To the Cooley Court, congressional "consent" authority was unthinkable; to Justice Rutledge a century later, the authority was clear. Why? What explanations *do* go "to the root of the matter," in Justice Rutledge's phrase? What "something beyond" justifies congressional authority today?

After exploring the Rutledge opinion, Noel Dowling confessed that "I was still not sure that my vision had caught the 'something beyond.' " Dowling, "Interstate Commerce and State Power—Revised Version," 47 Colum.L.Rev. 547 (1947). In his earlier "State Power" article, 27 Va.L. Rev. 1 (1940), Dowling had suggested rationalizing congressional "consent" by viewing commerce clause restraints as resting on implied congressional policy: "[I]n the absence of affirmative consent a Congressional negative will be presumed [against] state action [unreasonably interfering with interstate commerce], the presumption being rebuttable at the pleasure of Congress." Is that explanation preferable to Justice Rutledge's effort to explain the "consent" power? Does this congressional power to consent to otherwise "unconstitutional" state laws support arguments for a similar congressional power *outside* the commerce area to modify constitutional restraints on state authority? Does congressional power under § 5 of the 14th Amendment, for example, authorize Congress to validate state laws otherwise unconstitutional under the due process and equal protection clauses of § 1 of that Amendment? That 14th Amendment problem has become a widely debated one as a result of such decision as Katzenbach v. Morgan, 384 U.S. 641 (1966) (chap. 11 below); it will be explored at length in chap. 11, sec. 4.

As noted at the outset, congressional preemption and consent are examples of a far wider range of techniques Congress may employ in the ordering of the complex relations between federal and state law. Additional devices illustrating the central role of Congress should be noted in other chapters of this volume. For example: the congressional role in determining the scope of intergovernmental immunities, chap. 6, sec. 1, below; federal incorporation or adoption of state law—expressly, as in the Federal Assimi-

lative Crimes Act, also in chap. 6 below, and in the Federal Tort Claims Act, or by implication, as in a wide area of tax, copyright and bankruptcy law; and state administration of federal law, as in the unemployment compensation scheme of the Social Security Act, chap. 4, sec. 2, above, or in the varied exercises of the federal spending power through conditional grants-in-aid to the states, ibid, or in the utilization of state courts for federal law enforcement, cf. Testa v. Katt, in the note on state autonomy, chap. 6, sec. 1, below. See generally Hart, "The Relations Between State and Federal Law," 54 Colum.L.Rev. 489 (1954).

Chapter 6

INTERGOVERNMENTAL IMMUNITIES AND
INTERSTATE RELATIONSHIPS

Introduction. To complete the examination of problems of the federal system, this chapter focuses first on relations between federal and state governments and then turns to the relationships of the states with each other. The federal-state problems of sec. 1 are particularly fertile sources for structural analysis by the Court. To what extent may states tax the federal government's operations? To what extent may the federal government tax the states and those in close relationships with state governments? To what extent may state and nation claim constitutional immunity from each other's regulatory schemes? Constitutional text and history are not wholly without guidance on these issues. But in resolving these problems the Court has turned to an unusually great degree to inferences from structures and relationships inherent in the federal system. That was so as early as McCulloch v. Maryland, the first case below. What sources did Marshall turn to in answering the second question in that case—in determining whether the operations of the Bank of the United States were immune from Maryland's tax? Is Professor Charles L. Black, Jr. correct in viewing that portion of the McCulloch opinion as a prime example of structural analysis? See Black, Structure and Relationship in Constitutional Law (1969), 15: "Marshall's reasoning on this branch of the case is, as I read it, essentially structural. It has to do in great part with what he conceives to be the warranted relational proprieties between the national government and the government of the states, with the structural corollaries of national supremacy—and, at one point, of the mode of formation of the Union. . . . In this, perhaps the greatest of our constitutional cases, judgment is reached not fundamentally on the basis of that kind of textual exegesis which we tend to regard as normal, but on the basis of reasoning from the total structure which the text has created." To what extent is that mode of reasoning at the heart of most of the remaining materials in this chapter as well?

SECTION 1. INTERGOVERNMENTAL IMMUNITIES:
TAXATION AND REGULATION

McCULLOCH v. MARYLAND

4 Wheat. 316, 4 L.Ed. 579 (1819).

[This case—sustaining the constitutionality of the Bank of the United States and holding unconstitutional Maryland's tax on the operations of the Bank—is printed in chap. 2 above. The second part of Chief Justice Marshall's opinion, explaining the Bank's immunity from state taxation, should be reexamined at this point. See also the consideration of the tax immunity of modern national banks, with the majority resting the immunity on statu-

373

tory grounds and the dissenters finding no constitutionally required immunity, in First Agric. Nat. Bank v. State Tax Comm'n, 392 U.S. 339 (1968), noted below.]

THE GROWTH AND DECLINE OF TAX IMMUNITIES

Introduction. McCulloch v. Maryland invalidated a state tax on the operations of the federally incorporated Bank. Ten years later, the Marshall Court held unconstitutional the application of a city's general property tax on a taxpayer's federal bonds. Weston v. Charleston, 2 Pet. 449 (1829). From these beginnings, and for over a century, constitutional tax immunities expanded in a number of directions. Marshall, for example, had suggested that his views of federal immunity from state taxation did not imply a reciprocal immunity of state operations from federal taxes. Recall his passage in McCulloch which ends: "The difference is that which always exists, and always must exist, between the action of the whole on a part, and the action of a part on the whole." Nevertheless, the post-Civil War Court held that state activities enjoyed a reciprocal immunity from federal taxation. See note 1 below. Moreover, the Court steadily expanded the circle of immunities, from the primary immunity of the governmental activity itself to the derivative immunity of third persons—employees, lessees, patentees—in some way related to the governmental activities. See note 2 below.

Since the late 1930's, that circle has contracted sharply.[1] Yet intergovernmental immunities doctrines continue to have vitality, through statutory recognition as well as by constitutional mandate. This section briefly traces the growth and shrinking of the immunities from Marshall's day to Stone's, and then samples some of the contemporary dimensions of the doctrine.

1. *State immunity from federal taxation: Justice Nelson in Collector v. Day.* In COLLECTOR v. DAY, 11 Wall. 113 (1871), the Court held the salary of a state judge immune from the national income tax. Justice Nelson's majority opinion, after noting that the Taney Court had held that a state could not tax a federal officer's salary (in Dobbins v. Erie County, 16 Pet. 435 (1842)), rejected the suggestion in McCulloch that federal taxation might not be subject to a similar limitation. With regard to reserved powers, "the State is as sovereign and independent as the general government." And "if the means and instrumentalities employed by [the national] government to carry into operation the powers granted to it are, necessarily, and, for the sake of self-preservation, exempt from taxation by the States, why are not those of the States depending upon their reserved powers, for like reasons, equally exempt from Federal taxation?"

2. *The expansion and contraction of intergovernmental immunities to private taxpayers: From Justice Nelson to Justice Stone.* In the last third of

---

1. See generally Powell, "The Waning of Intergovernmental Tax Immunities," 58 Harv.L.Rev. 633 (1945); Powell, "The Remnant of Intergovernmental Tax Immunities," 58 Harv.L.Rev. 757 (1945), Selected Essays 1938–62 (1963), 403; Konefsky, Chief Justice Stone and the Supreme Court (1945), chap. 1; Powell, Vagaries and Varieties in Constitutional Interpretation (1956), chap. 4.

the nineteenth century and the first third of the twentieth, many cases sustained private taxpayers' claims that their relationship to government entitled them to tax immunity. For example, state sales taxes could not be applied to sales made to the federal government, Panhandle Oil Co. v. Mississippi, 277 U.S. 218 (1928), and a federal tax could not be collected on sales by a private business to a state, Indian Motorcycle Co. v. United States, 283 U.S. 570 (1931). On the same premise—that the tax burden on the individual would ultimately fall on government—a private lessee of state lands did not have to pay federal income taxes on profits from the lease, Burnet v. Coronado Oil & Gas Co., 285 U.S. 393 (1932), reciprocating the immunity from state income taxes that had been granted to a lessee of Indian lands in Gillespie v. Oklahoma, 257 U.S. 501 (1922). And, for a few years, even patent royalties were free from state income taxes. Long v. Rockwood, 277 U.S. 142 (1928), overruled in a copyright royalties case four years later, Fox Film Corp. v. Doyal, 286 U.S. 123 (1932).[2]

By the late 1930's, the repeated protests by Justice Stone and others finally produced a halt—and, soon, a retreat—in that trend. In a 5 to 4 decision, the Court held that proceeds from a construction contract with the United States were subject to a state gross receipts tax. James v. Dravo Contracting Co., 302 U.S. 134 (1937). And in Helvering v. Mountain Producers Corp., 303 U.S. 376 (1938), the Burnet and Gillespie cases, above, were overruled and a lessee of state lands was held subject to the federal income tax. Shortly thereafter, Justice Stone had the opportunity to reexamine the scope of tax immunities: his opinions in Helvering v. Gerhardt and Graves v. O'Keefe mark the virtual abandonment of derivative intergovernmental immunities.[3] Employees of state and federal governments can no longer claim immunities from income taxes simply because of their relationship to government. However, the direct, primary immunity of government itself from the sanctions imposed by the other government continues; and the scope of that tax immunity remains an area of controversy, as New York v. United States, below, and the notes following that case illustrate.

In examining the employees' income tax cases which follow, consider whether Stone's approach was a return to Marshall's position or a new one. Note Stone's statement of the holding of McCulloch, at the beginning of Helvering v. Gerhardt. Is that an accurate statement? Was Marshall truly speaking of congressional intent? Or was he speaking of constitutional

2. Compare Metcalf & Eddy v. Mitchell, 269 U.S. 514 (1926) (sustaining a state tax on the net income received for engineering work for the federal government).

3. See also the recent rejection, by a divided Court, of a claim that federal law rendered an Indian tribe's off-reservation ski resort "a federal instrumentality constitutionally immune from state taxes of all sorts." Mescalero Apache Tribe v. Jones, 411 U.S. 145 (1973). Justice White's majority opinion refused "to resurrect the expansive version of the intergovernmental-immunity doctrine that has been so consistently rejected in mod-

ern times." Justice Douglas' dissent, joined by Justices Brennan and Stewart, insisted that the tribal ski enterprise was "plainly a federal instrumentality—authorized and financed by Congress with the aim of starting the tribe on commercial ventures." Compare McClanahan v. Arizona State Tax Comm'n, 411 U.S. 164 (1973), a companion case in which a unanimous Court barred a state tax on income earned by reservation Indians from reservation sources. Justice Marshall relied on the applicable treaties and statutes "read with this tradition of [Indian] sovereignty in mind."

implications from the federal structure? Compare Stone's own emphasis on constitutional structure rather than congressional intent in the state immunity context, in New York v. United States, below. In examining the primary governmental tax immunity cases beginning with the New York case, consider not only what degree of *tax* immunity is constitutionally justifiable, but bear in mind as well the parallel problem of intergovernmental *regulatory* immunities, considered in the materials following the tax cases.

HELVERING v. GERHARDT

304 U.S. 405, 58 S.Ct. 969, 82 L.Ed. 1427 (1938).

Certiorari to the Circuit Court of Appeals for the Second Circuit.

Mr. Justice STONE delivered the opinion of the Court. . . .

[Employees of the Port of New York Authority resisted the federal income tax on their salaries, as an unconstitutional burden on New York and New Jersey. The Authority, a bi-state corporation, was created pursuant to an interstate compact, see sec. 2B below, to improve the port and operate bridges, tunnels, terminals and other facilities. The Court of Appeals held that the salaries were exempt from the federal tax.]

The Constitution contains no express limitation on the power of either a state or the national government to tax the other, or its instrumentalities. The doctrine that there is an implied limitation stems from McCulloch v. Maryland, 4 Wheat. 316, in which it was held that a state tax laid specifically upon the privilege of issuing bank notes, and in fact applicable alone to the notes of national banks, was invalid since it impeded the national government in the exercise of its power to establish and maintain a bank . . . . . It was held that Congress, having power to establish a bank by laws which . . . are supreme, also had power to protect the bank by striking down state action impeding its operations; and it was thought that the state tax in question was so inconsistent with Congress's constitutional action in establishing the bank as to compel the conclusion that Congress intended to forbid application of the tax to the federal bank notes.[1] . . .

We need not stop to inquire how far, as indicated in [McCulloch], the immunity of federal instrumentalities from state taxation rests on a different basis from that of state instrumentalities; or whether or to what degree it is more extensive. . . . It is enough for present purposes that the state immunity from the national taxing power, when recognized in Collector v. Day, supra, was narrowly limited to a state judicial officer

---

1. It follows that in considering the immunity of federal instrumentalities from state taxation two factors may be of importance which are lacking in the case of a claimed immunity of state instrumentalities from federal taxation. Since the acts of Congress within its constitutional power are supreme, the validity of state taxation of federal instrumentalities must depend (a) on the power of Congress to create the instrumentality and (b) its intent to protect it from state taxation. Congress may curtail an immunity which might otherwise be implied, . . . or enlarge it beyond the point where, Congress being silent, the Court would set its limits. . . . [Footnote by the Court.]

engaged in the performance of a function which pertained to state governments at the time the Constitution was adopted, without which no state "could long preserve its existence."

There are cogent reasons why any constitutional restriction upon the taxing power granted to Congress, so far as it can be properly raised by implication, should be narrowly limited. One, as was pointed out by Chief Justice Marshall . . ., is that the people of all the states have created the national government and are represented in Congress. Through that representation they exercise the national taxing power. The very fact that when they are exercising it they are taxing themselves, serves to guard against its abuse through the possibility of resort to the usual processes of political action which provides a readier and more adaptable means than any which courts can afford, for securing accommodation of the competing demands for national revenue, on the one hand, and for reasonable scope for the independence of state action, on the other.[2]

Another reason rests upon the fact that any allowance of a tax immunity for the protection of state sovereignty is at the expense of the sovereign power of the nation to tax. Enlargement of the one involves diminution of the other. When enlargement proceeds beyond the necessity of protecting the state, the burden of the immunity is thrown upon the national government with benefit only to a privileged class of taxpayers. . . . Once impaired by the recognition of a state immunity found to be excessive, restoration of [the national taxing] power is not likely to be secured through the action of state legislatures; for they are without the inducements to act which have often persuaded Congress to waive immunities thought to be excessive. . . .

In a period marked by a constant expansion of government activities and the steady multiplication of the complexities of taxing systems, it is perhaps too much to expect that the judicial pronouncements marking the boundaries of state immunity should present a completely logical pattern. But they disclose no purposeful departure from, and indeed definitely establish, two guiding principles of limitation for holding the tax immunity of state instrumentalities to its proper function. The one, dependent upon the nature of the function being performed by the state or in its behalf, excludes from the immunity activities thought not to be essential to the preservation of state governments even though the tax be collected from the state treasury. [T]he other principle, exemplified by those cases where the tax laid upon individuals affects the state only as the burden is passed on to it by the taxpayer, forbids recognition of the immunity when the burden on the state is so speculative and uncertain that if allowed it would restrict the federal taxing power without affording any corresponding tangible protection to the state government . . . .

With these controlling principles in mind we turn to their application in the circumstances of the present case. The challenged taxes . . . are

---

2. Compare Justice Stone's emphasis on the operation of the political processes in two cases decided shortly before Gerhardt: South Carolina State Highway Dep't v. Barnwell Bros., 303 U.S. 177 (1938), chap. 5 above, and United States v. Carolene Prod. Co., 304 U.S. 144 (1938), chap. 9 below.

upon the net income of respondents, derived from their employment in common occupations not shown to be different in their methods or duties from those of similar employees in private industry. . . . Even though, to some unascertainable extent, the tax deprives the state of the advantage of paying less than the standard rate for the services which they engage, it does not curtail any of those functions which have been thought hitherto to be essential to their continued existence as states. . . . The effect of the immunity if allowed would be to relieve respondents of their duty of financial support to the national government, in order to secure to the state a theoretical advantage so speculative in its character and measurement as to be unsubstantial. A tax immunity devised for protection of the states as governmental entities cannot be pressed so far. . . .

Reversed.

[A concurring opinion by Justice BLACK, and a dissenting opinion by Justice BUTLER, joined by Justice McREYNOLDS, are omitted.]

GRAVES v. O'KEEFE:
FEDERAL EMPLOYEES AND STATE TAXES

In a second major Stone decision, GRAVES v. NEW YORK EX REL. O'KEEFE, 306 U.S. 466 (1939), an employee of the Home Owners' Loan Corporation—established by Congress as an "instrumentality of the United States" and wholly government-owned—resisted the New York income tax on his salary. The state courts sustained his claim, in reliance on New York ex rel. Rogers v. Graves, 299 U.S. 401 (1937), which had held that New York could not tax the salary of an employee of the Panama Railroad Company, another wholly-owned corporate instrumentality of the United States. The Supreme Court, one year after Gerhardt, reversed, again in a majority opinion by Justice Stone:

"The conclusion reached in [Gerhardt] makes it imperative that we should consider anew the immunity here claimed for the salary of an employee of a federal instrumentality. [S]uch differences as there may be between the implied tax immunity of a state and the corresponding immunity of the national government and its instrumentalities may be traced to the fact that the national government is one of delegated powers, in the exercise of which it is supreme. Whatever scope this may give to the national government to claim immunity from state taxation of all instrumentalities which it may constitutionally create, and whatever authority Congress may possess as incidental to the exercise of its delegated powers to grant or withhold immunity from state taxation, Congress has not sought in this case to exercise such power. Hence these distinctions between the two types of immunity cannot affect the question with which we are now concerned. The burden on government of a non-discriminatory income tax applied to the salary of the employee of a government or its instrumentality is the same, whether a state or national government is concerned. . . .

"Assuming, as we do, that the Home Owners' Loan Corporation is clothed with the same immunity from state taxation as the government itself, we cannot say that the present tax on the income of its employees lays any

unconstitutional burden upon it. All the reasons for refusing to imply a constitutional prohibition of federal income taxation of salaries of state employees, stated at length in the Gerhardt case, are of equal force when immunity is claimed from state income tax on salaries paid by the national government or its agencies. . . . Collector v. Day, supra, and New York ex rel. Rogers v. Graves, supra, are overruled so far as they recognize an implied constitutional immunity from income taxation of the salaries of officers or employees of the national or a state government or their instrumentalities."

NEW YORK v. UNITED STATES

326 U.S. 572, 66 S.Ct. 310, 90 L.Ed. 326 (1946).

Certiorari to the Circuit Court of Appeals for the Second Circuit.

Mr. Justice FRANKFURTER announced the judgment of the Court and delivered an opinion in which Mr. Justice RUTLEDGE joined.

Section 615(a)(5) of the 1932 Revenue Act imposed a tax on mineral waters. The United States brought this suit to recover taxes assessed against the State of New York on the sale of mineral waters taken from Saratoga Springs, New York. The State claims immunity from this tax on the ground that "in the bottling and sale of the said waters the defendant State of New York was engaged in the exercise of a usual, traditional and essential governmental function." [The lower federal courts rejected New York's claim.]

On the basis of authority the case is quickly disposed of. When States sought to control the liquor traffic by going into the liquor business, they were denied immunity from federal taxes upon the liquor business. South Carolina v. United States, 199 U.S. 437; Ohio v. Helvering, 292 U.S. 360. And in rejecting a claim of immunity from federal taxation when Massachusetts took over the street railways of Boston, this Court a decade ago said: "We see no reason for putting the operation of a street railway [by a State] in a different category from the sale of liquors." Helvering v. Powers, 293 U.S. 214, 227. We certainly see no reason for putting soft drinks in a different constitutional category from hard drinks. . . .

But the fear that one government may cripple or obstruct the operations of the other early led to the assumption that there was a reciprocal immunity of the instrumentalities of each from taxation by the other. . . . The considerations bearing upon taxation by the States of activities or agencies of the federal government are not correlative with the considerations bearing upon federal taxation of State agencies or activities. The federal government is the government of all the States, and all the States share in the legislative process by which a tax of general applicability is laid. . . .

In the older cases, the emphasis was on immunity from taxation. The whole tendency of recent cases reveals a shift in emphasis to that of limitation upon immunity. They also indicate an awareness of the limited role of courts in assessing the relative weight of the factors upon which immunity is based. Any implied limitation upon the supremacy of the federal power to levy a tax like that now before us, in the absence of discrimination against State

activities, brings fiscal and political factors into play. The problem cannot escape issues that do not lend themselves to judgment by criteria and methods of reasoning that are within the professional training and special competence of judges. . . .

We have already held that by engaging in the railroad business a State cannot withdraw the railroad from the power of the federal government to regulate commerce. United States v. California, 297 U.S. 175 (noted below). Surely the power of Congress to lay taxes has impliedly no less a reach than the power of Congress to regulate commerce. There are, of course, State activities and State-owned property that partake of uniqueness from the point of view of intergovernmental relations. These inherently constitute a class by themselves. Only a State can own a Statehouse; only a State can get income by taxing. These could not be included for purposes of federal taxation in any abstract category of taxpayers without taxing the State as a State. But so long as Congress generally taps a source of revenue by whomsoever earned and not uniquely capable of being earned only by a State, the Constitution of the United States does not forbid it merely because its incidence falls also on a State. . . .

The process of Constitutional adjudication does not thrive on conjuring up horrible possibilities that never happen in the real world and devising doctrines sufficiently comprehensive in detail to cover the remotest contingency. . . . So we decide enough when we reject limitations upon the taxing power of Congress derived from such untenable criteria as "proprietary" against "governmental" activities of the States, or historically sanctioned activities of government, or activities conducted merely for profit, and find no restriction upon Congress to include the States in levying a tax exacted equally from private persons upon the same subject matter.

Affirmed.

Mr. Justice JACKSON took no part in the consideration or decision of this case. [A concurring opinion by Justice RUTLEDGE is omitted.]

Mr. Chief Justice STONE, [joined by Justices REED, MURPHY and BURTON, concurring in the result]. . . .

In view of our decisions . . . ., we would find it difficult not to sustain the tax in this case, even though we regard as untenable the distinction between "governmental" and "proprietary" interests on which those cases rest to some extent. But we are not prepared to say that the national government may constitutionally lay a nondiscriminatory tax on every class of property and activities of States and individuals alike.

Concededly a federal tax discriminating against a State would be an unconstitutional exertion of power over a coexisting sovereignty within the same framework of government. But our difficulty with the formula, now first suggested as offering a new solution for an old problem, is that a federal tax which is not discriminatory as to the subject matter may nevertheless so affect the State, merely because it is a State that is being taxed, as to interfere unduly with the State's performance of its sovereign functions of government. The counterpart of such undue interference has been recognized since Marshall's day as the implied immunity of each of the dual sovereignties of our constitutional system from taxation by the other. [McCulloch.] We add

nothing to this formula by saying, in a new form of words, that a tax which Congress applies generally to the property and activities of private citizens may not be in some instances constitutionally extended to the States, merely because the States are included among those who pay taxes on a like subject of taxation.

If the phrase "non-discriminatory tax" is to be taken in its long accepted meaning as referring to a tax laid on a like subject matter, without regard to the personality of the taxpayer, whether a State, a corporation or a private individual, it is plain that there may be non-discriminatory taxes which, when laid on a State, would nevertheless impair the sovereign status of the State quite as much as a like tax imposed by a State on property or activities of the national government. . . . This is not because the tax can be regarded as discriminatory but because a sovereign government is the taxpayer, and the tax, even though non-discriminatory, may be regarded as infringing its sovereignty.

A State may, like a private individual, own real property and receive income. But in view of our former decisions we could hardly say that a general non-discriminatory real estate tax (apportioned), or an income tax laid upon citizens and States alike could be constitutionally applied to the State's capitol, its State-house, its public school houses, public parks, or its revenues from taxes or school lands, even though all real property and all income of the citizen is taxed. . . .

It is enough for present purposes that the immunity of the State from federal taxation would, in this case, accomplish a withdrawal from the taxing power of the nation a subject of taxation of a nature which has been traditionally within that power from the beginning. Its exercise now, by a non-discriminatory tax, does not curtail the business of the state government more than it does the like business of the citizen. It gives merely an accustomed and reasonable scope to the federal taxing power. [This] taxation does not unduly impair the State's functions of government. . . .

The problem is not one to be solved by a formula, but we may look to the structure of the Constitution as our guide to decision. "In a broad sense, the taxing power of either government, even when exercised in a manner admittedly necessary and proper, unavoidably has some effect upon the other. . . . Taxation by either the state or the federal government affects in some measure the cost of operation of the other.

"But neither government may destroy the other nor curtail in any substantial manner the exercise of its powers. Hence the limitation upon the taxing power of each, so far as it affects the other, must receive a practical construction which permits both to function with the minimum of interference each with the other; and that limitation cannot be so varied or extended as seriously to impair either the taxing power of the government imposing the tax . . . or the appropriate exercise of the functions of the government affected by it." [Metcalf & Eddy v. Mitchell, 269 U.S. 514 (1926).]

Since all taxes must be laid by general, that is, workable, rules, the effect of the immunity on the national taxing power is to be determined not quantitatively but by its operation and tendency in withdrawing taxable property

or activities from the reach of federal taxation. Not the extent to which a particular State engages in the activity, but the nature and extent of the activity by whomsoever performed is the relevant consideration.

Regarded in this light we cannot say that the Constitution either requires immunity of the State's mineral water business from federal taxation, or denies to the federal government power to lay the tax.

Mr. Justice DOUGLAS, with whom Mr. Justice BLACK concurs, dissenting. . . .

I do not believe South Carolina v. United States states the correct rule. A State's project is as much a legitimate governmental activity whether it is traditional, or akin to private enterprise, or conducted for profit. . . . What might have been viewed as an inprovident or even dangerous extension of state activities may today be deemed indispensable. [A]ny activity in which a State engages within the limits of its police power is a legitimate governmental activity. . . . Must it pay the federal government for the privilege of exercising that inherent power? . . .

The notion that the sovereign position of the States must find its protection in the will of a transient majority of Congress is foreign to and a negation of our constitutional system. . . .

The immunity of the States from federal taxation is no less clear because it is implied. . . . The Constitution is a compact between sovereigns. The power of one sovereign to tax another is an innovation so startling as to require explicit authority if it is to be allowed. If the power of the federal government to tax the States is conceded, the reserved power of the States guaranteed by the Tenth Amendment does not give them the independence which they have always been assumed to have. They are relegated to a more servile status. They become subject to interference and control both in the functions which they exercise and the methods which they employ. They must pay the federal government for the privilege of exercising the powers of sovereignty guaranteed them by the Constitution,[1] whether, as here, they are disposing of their natural resources, or tomorrow they issue securities or perform any other acts within the scope of their police power. . . .

PROBLEMS OF TAX IMMUNITIES: SOME MODERN DIMENSIONS

1. *Sales taxes on government contractors.* The argument that taxes on private activities impose immediate economic burdens on government is at its strongest where a contractor performs work for the government on a cost-plus-fixed-fee basis. Nevertheless, in Alabama v. King & Boozer, 314 U.S. 1 (1941), the Court sustained a sales tax on a contractor's purchases of materials to be used in constructing an army camp under such a contract. The

---

1. That fact distinguishes those cases where a citizen seeks tax immunity because his income was derived from a State or the federal government. Recognition of such a claim would create a "privileged class of taxpay- ers" [Helvering v. Gerhardt] and extend the tax immunity of the States or the federal government to private citizens. . . . [Footnote by Justice Douglas.]

Court noted that the Gerhardt and O'Keefe cases, above, precluded any immunity argument based simply on the passing on of the economic burden to the Government. Moreover, the Court rejected the argument that, because the contractor "in a loose and general sense" acted for the Government, the "legal incidence" of the tax was on the United States. But Kern-Limerick, Inc. v. Scurlock, 347 U.S. 110 (1954), invalidated a similar tax in a similar situation, where the contract specifically authorized the contractor to "act as the purchasing agent of the Government" and where the Government was directly liable to the seller. The Court recognized that the economic impact of the tax on the Government was the same here as in King & Boozer, but emphasized that the "legal incidence" differed.

2. *Taxes on users of government property.* United States v. Allegheny County, 322 U.S. 174 (1944), held invalid a state ad valorem property tax on a mill, where the valuation included machinery leased from the United States and used in performing a federal contract. Compare S.R.A., Inc. v. Minnesota, 327 U.S. 558 (1946), upholding a tax on realty where legal title was in the United States with possession in a private party holding under an executory sales contract. Taxes on users of government property came before the Court in three companion cases in 1958; in each, the state tax was sustained by a divided Court. United States and Borg-Warner Corp. v. Detroit, 355 U.S. 466; United States v. Muskegon, 355 U.S. 484; Detroit v. Murray Corp., 355 U.S. 489. In the first Detroit case, for example, the taxpayer was lessee of a government-owned plant used in his private manufacturing business; the tax was based on the value of the leased property. The Supreme Court sustained the tax as neither discriminatory nor on the property of the United States, but as on the lessee's privilege of using the property in a private business. In the Muskegon case, the same tax statute was sustained as applied to an industrial plant furnished by the Government to a contractor, rent-free, for use in performing federal contracts. A comment in the first Detroit case reflects the Court's theme in all three cases: "Today the United States does business with a vast number of private parties. In this Court the trend has been to reject immunizing these private parties from non-discriminatory state taxes as a matter of constitutional law." For an analysis of these cases, see Whelan, "Government Contract Privileges: A Fertile Ground for State Taxation," 44 Va.L.Rev. 1099 (1958), Selected Essays 1938–62 (1963), 436. Compare Rohr Aircraft Corp. v. San Diego County, 362 U.S. 628 (1960), invalidating a real property tax on federal property leased to a private company. The Court was primarily concerned with interpreting the scope of a federal statute waiving immunity on certain federal property; there was no difficulty with the situation in the absence of a waiver: "[T]he general rule is 'that the lands owned by the United States of America or its instruments are immune from state and local taxation.' "

3. *Congressional ordering and tax immunities.* a. *The role of Congress.* As in the Rohr Aircraft case, the scope of federal immunities often turns on congressional statements recognizing or waiving immunities. See, e. g., the statutory recognition of the rule of Weston v. Charleston, 2 Pet. 449 (1829), above, exempting federal obligations from local taxation. 31 U.S.C. § 742.[1] See also the statutes granting immunities to federal instru-

---

1. Compare Society for Savings v. Bowers, 349 U.S. 143 (1955) (property tax on mutual savings bank invalid because federal bonds in bank portfolio

mentalities, as in Pittman v. Home Owners Loan Corp., 308 U.S. 21 (1939), and Federal Land Bank v. Bismarck Lumber Co., 314 U.S. 95 (1941); cf. Carson v. Roane-Anderson Co., 342 U.S. 232 (1952) (company managing town and producing materials for Atomic Energy Commission). Would some of these federal activities be subject to state taxation, cf. New York v. United States, above, in the absence of the statutory immunities?

b. *The modern tax immunity of national banks: Statutory rather than constitutional?* Note the emphasis on the statutory grant of immunity when a divided Court reaffirmed the immunity of national banks from state taxation in FIRST AGRIC. NAT. BANK v. STATE TAX COMM'N, 392 U.S. 339 (1968). The highest Massachusetts court had sustained the application of state sales and use taxes to purchases of personal property by a national bank. The state court had thought that "the status of national banks has been so changed by the establishment of the Federal Reserve System that they should no longer be considered nontaxable by the States as instrumentalities of the United States." In the Supreme Court, Justice Black's majority opinion sustaining the tax immunity did not reach the constitutional question. It found that federal legislation—12 U.S.C. § 548, derived from an 1864 law—"was intended to prescribe the only ways in which the States can tax national banks"; that since the decision in Owensboro Nat'l. Bank v. Owensboro, 173 U.S. 664 (1899), it had been "abundantly clear" that this provision marked "the outer limit" of taxability; and that, accordingly, "if a change is to be made in state taxation of national banks, it must come from the Congress, which has established the present limits."

Justice Marshall, in an extensive dissent joined by Justices Harlan and Stewart, concluded: "I think that in light of the present functions and role of national banks that they should not in this day and age be considered constitutionally immune from nondiscriminatory state taxation, and that § 548 should not be construed as giving them a statutory immunity from the taxes here involved." He insisted that the "hoary cases"—McCulloch, Osborn and Owensboro—could be given a limited reading. (See the notes following McCulloch, chap. 2 above.) That would "require a re-evaluation of the validity of the doctrine of intergovernmental tax immunities—a doctrine which does not rest upon any specific provisions of the Constitution, but rather upon this Court's concepts of federalism." Since Congress may provide statutory immunities, "there is little reason for this Court to cling to the view that the Constitution itself makes federal instrumentalities immune from state taxation in the absence of authorizing legislation. The disparate kinds of instrumentalities and forms of state taxation create difficulties for ad hoc resolution of the immunity issue by this Court based only upon abstract concepts of federalism."

included in tax base), with Werner Machine Co. v. Director of Taxation, 350 U.S. 492 (1956) (franchise tax on corporations measured by "net worth" valid, though net worth includes investments in federal bonds).

Pollock v. Farmers' Loan & Trust Co., 157 U.S. 429 (1895), held income from state and local bonds constitutionally immune from Federal taxation. Does that case still represent valid constitutional doctrine? The Internal Revenue Code specifically exempts interest from such bonds. There has been considerable controversy about this provision and tax reform advocates unsuccessfully urged its repeal or modification in the major tax law revision of 1969.

Though the Court had not indicated "any great desire to reconsider in toto" the constitutional immunity, there had been a wise trend to restrict the scope of the tax immunity of "private persons seeking to clothe themselves with governmental character." In view of that trend, a modern national bank "cannot be considered a tax-immune federal instrumentality." Developments since the creation of the Federal Reserve System in 1913 had produced radical changes. National banks no longer issue currency; the Federal Reserve banks and the System are now the monetary and fiscal agents of the United States. National banks, to be sure, are required to be members of the System. But that did not make them "sufficiently quasi-public to enjoy the tax-immune status of federal instrumentalities. [T]here is little difference today between a national bank and its state-chartered competitor."

c. *Congressional waivers and in-lieu payments.* On congressional responses to state tax losses due to federal immunities, see the survey of federal statutory devices for making contributions to localities containing United States property, in Study Committee Report for the Commission on Intergovernmental Relations, Payments in Lieu of Taxes and Shared Revenues (1955). The Report considers examples of revenue sharing provisions, payments in lieu of taxes, and consents to property tax liability. The Report recommended additional waivers of immunity and payments in lieu of taxes. See also Commission on Intergovernmental Relations, A Report to the President (1955).

INTERGOVERNMENTAL IMMUNITIES AND REGULATORY STATUTES

1. *Federal immunity from state regulation.* In JOHNSON v. MARYLAND, 254 U.S. 51 (1920), Justice Holmes' opinion for the Court relied on the principle of McCulloch v. Maryland in reversing the conviction of a post office employee for driving a truck without a state license. As Justice Holmes posed the question, it was "whether the State can interrupt the acts of the general government itself." He concluded: "It seems to us that the immunity of the instruments of the United States from state control in the performance of their duties extends to a requirement that they desist from performance until they satisfy a state officer upon examination that they are competent for a necessary part of them and pay a fee for permission to go on. Such a requirement does not merely touch the Government servants remotely by a general rule of conduct; it lays hold of them in their specific attempt to obey orders and requires qualifications in addition to those that the Government has pronounced sufficient. It is the duty of the Department to employ persons competent for their work and that duty it must be presumed has been performed." But the Court left the scope of the immunity somewhat unclear. Justice Holmes stated: "Of course an employee of the United States does not secure a general immunity from state law while acting in the course of his employment. . . . It very well may be that, when the United States has not spoken, the subjection to local law would extend to general rules that might affect incidentally the mode of carrying out the employment—as, for instance, a statute or ordinance regulating the mode of turning at the corners of streets."

That federal immunity from state regulation may at times be claimed by those in a close relationship with the government. For example, Leslie Miller, Inc. v. Arkansas, 352 U.S. 187 (1956), barred application of a state licensing scheme to a federal contractor. The Court found a "conflict" between the Arkansas requirement and federal regulations designed to ensure the reliability of contractors. Similarly, Public Utilities Comm'n of California v. United States, 355 U.S. 534 (1958), barred application of state rate regulations to carriers transporting goods under contracts with the federal government. Compare Paul v. United States, 371 U.S. 245 (1963), holding that California could not apply its minimum milk price regulations to sales to United States military posts: "The collision between the federal policy of [competitive bidding] and the state policy of regulated prices is as clear and acute here as was the conflict between federal negotiated rates and state regulated rates" in the Public Utilities Comm'n case, above.*

2. *State immunity from federal regulation.* In cases noted in earlier chapters, state autonomy restraints on national powers were repeatedly urged with special force when national regulation impinged directly on state operations; but the Court typically has not been receptive to those objections. Recall, e. g., on the commerce power, Maryland v. Wirtz, chap. 3 above, and on the spending power, Oklahoma v. United States Civil Service Comm'n, chap. 4 above. A leading decision rejecting a state immunity claim is UNITED STATES v. CALIFORNIA, 297 U.S. 175 (1936), upholding a statutory penalty imposed on the state for violation of the Federal Safety Appliance Act by a state-owned railroad. Justice Stone's opinion for a unanimous Court stated: "[W]e think it unimportant to say whether the state conducts its railroad in its 'sovereign' or in its 'private' capacity. That in operating its railroad it is acting within a power reserved to the states cannot be doubted. The only question we need consider is whether the exercise of that power, in whatever capacity, must be in subordination to the power to regulate interstate commerce . . . . The sovereign power of the states is necessarily diminished to the extent of the grants of power to the federal government in the Constitution. . . . The analogy of the constitutional immunity of state instrumentalities from federal taxation [is] not illuminating. That immunity is implied from the nature of our federal system and the relationship within it of state and national governments, and is equally a restriction on taxation by either of the instrumentalities of the other. . . . But there is no such limitation upon the plenary power to regulate commerce. The state can no more deny the power if its exercise has been authorized by Congress than can an individual. California, by engaging in interstate commerce by rail, has subjected itself to the commerce

* The Court relied on Paul v. United States in United States v. Mississippi Tax Comm'n, 412 U.S. 363 (1973), holding that the exclusive congressional jurisdiction over federal enclaves barred state regulation of liquor sales by out-of-state wholesalers to military bases. The majority rejected the State's reliance on the Twenty-first Amendment, holding that that provision "confers no power on a State to regulate—whether by licensing, taxation, or otherwise—the importation of distilled spirits into territory over which the United States exercises exclusive jurisdiction." Justice Douglas' dissent, joined by Justice Rehnquist, stated: "This is an amazing decision doing irreparable harm to the cause of states rights under the Twenty-first Amendment." (See also the material curtailed. (See also p. 125 above.)

† But see the May 1975 developments noted at p. 125 above, suggesting a revived sensitivity to state autonomy concerns.

power . . . . The danger to be apprehended [from violations of the Act] is as great and commerce may be equally impeded whether the defective appliance is used on a railroad which is state-owned or privately-owned."

Recall the questions about the Court's rejection of state autonomy objections in earlier chapters. Was Justice Stone persuasive in rejecting the analogy of state immunity from federal taxation? Can no immunity from regulation be "implied from the nature of our federal system"? Speaking of the tax immunity, Justice Stone stated in United States v. California: "Its nature requires that it be so construed as to allow to each government reasonable scope for its taxing power, which would be unduly curtailed if either by extending its activities could withdraw from the taxing power of the other subjects of taxation traditionally within it. Hence we look to the activities in which the states have traditionally engaged as marking the boundary of the restriction upon the federal taxing power." (But see New York v. United States, above.) Does that reference to a *limited* tax immunity for the state support a conclusion that the state should have *no* regulatory immunity?

For later cases applying federal regulatory statutes to state operations, see California v. Taylor, 353 U.S. 553 (1957); Parden v. Terminal Railway, 377 U.S. 184 (1964); and Maryland v. Wirtz, 392 U.S. 183 (1968). Recall especially the discussion of the state autonomy problem in the note (in chap. 3, sec. 5, above) on Maryland v. Wirtz, the 1968 decision relying on United States v. California in rejecting a challenge to the extension of the Fair Labor Standards Act to employees of state schools and hospitals.* Recall, too, Justice Douglas' dissent in that case, joined by Justice Stewart, insisting that intergovernmental tax immunities principles such as those in New York v. United States, rather than standard commerce power analyses, should provide the guide. He found cases such as United States v. California distinguishable because federal regulation there did not "overwhelm state fiscal policy." And he concluded: "In this case the State as a sovereign power is being seriously tampered with, potentially crippled." †

---

* In April 1975, the Supreme Court heard argument in a case challenging regulations issued under the 1974 Amendments to the Fair Labor Standards Act. The regulations sought to bring employees of state and local fire protection and law enforcement agencies under the coverage of the Act. A three-judge District Court denied relief because it deemed itself bound by Maryland v. Wirtz, even though it thought the case raised "a difficult and substantial question of law." Chief Justice Burger, as Circuit Justice, stayed enforcement of the regulations because of their "pervasive impact" on "every state and municipal government," "the novelty of the legal questions presented," and "the expressed concern of the District Court as to the substantiality of the constitutional questions raised." See National League of Cities v. Brennan, 419 U.S. —— (1974) (argued sub nom. National League of Cities v. Dunlop). The challengers argued, inter alia, that Maryland v. Wirtz was distguish-

able because state activities covered there were in competition with private hospitals and schools, and that the national government lacked power to control essential state and city governmental services by increasing the cost of providing some services so greatly that they must be altered or curtailed.

† Although Maryland v. Wirtz sustained the extension of the Fair Labor Standards Act to some state employees, the employees are not permitted to sue their governmental employers in federal courts, according to Employees of Dept. of Public Health & Welfare v. Missouri, 411 U.S. 279 (1973). Justice Douglas, who had dissented in Maryland v. Wirtz, wrote the majority opinion in the Missouri case. In pursuing the question "whether Congress has brought the States to heel, in the sense of lifting their immunity from suit in a federal court," Justice Douglas concluded: "It is not easy to infer that Congress in legislating pursuant to the

3. *Congressional ordering, "static conformity" and "dynamic conformity": State law on federal enclaves.* a. *The inapplicability of state law by its own force.* Under Art. I, § 8, clause 17, Congress has power of "exclusive Legislation" not only over the District of Columbia but also "over all Places purchased by the Consent of the Legislature of the State . . . for the Erection of Forts, Magazines, Arsenals, dock-Yards, and other needful Buildings." A California milk price regulation was accordingly held inapplicable to sales on a military installation: even though there was no conflicting federal regulation, the constitutional grant of power barred state regulation. Pacific Coast Dairy v. Department of Agriculture, 318 U.S. 285 (1943). State law is effective of its own force on federal enclaves only when a state conditions its "Consent" on its retention of jurisdiction over land acquired by the United States.

b. *Static conformity.* But what law governs federal enclaves where the State has not reserved jurisdiction and Congress has not supplied legislation? Ordinarily, only state law existing at the time of the acquisition remains enforceable; laws enacted subsequently are not effective on the enclave. See Stewart & Co. v. Sadrakula, 309 U.S. 94 (1940), applying a pre-acquisition state law requiring certain safeguards for workers in the case of the death of a workman engaged in constructing a post office: "The Constitution does not command that every vestige of the laws of the former sovereignty must vanish. On the contrary its language has long been interpreted so as to permit the continuance until abrogated of those rules existing at the time of the surrender of sovereignty which govern the rights of the occupants of the territory transferred. This assures that no area however small will be left without a developed legal system for private rights."

Is a "developed legal system" adequate? Development of legal systems is a continuing process. The "static conformity" of the quoted passage may produce a federal enclave where the applicable law is that of another day, while the surrounding state land is governed by a less obsolescent legal system. Is congressional enactment of substantive federal law the only way to achieve law reform on the enclave? Or may Congress enact "dynamic conformity," making state law changes after acquisition enforceable on the enclave?

c. *Dynamic conformity and the Assimilative Crimes Act.* In the Assimilative Crimes Act of 1948, Congress provided for such "dynamic conformity" by making the changing body of state criminal law applicable to federal enclaves. In United States v. Sharpnack, 355 U.S. 286 (1958), a divided Court sustained the constitutionality of the Act. [Cf. Wayman v. Southard, 10 Wheat. 1 (1825), and United States v. Paul, 6 Pet. 141 (1832).] In Sharpnack, appellee was charged with a sex crime on an Air Force Base in Texas. The Texas criminal statute "assimilated" was enacted two years after the 1948 Act. Justice Burton's majority opinion reviewed the long congressional experience with "static conformity" in assimilative crime laws for federal enclaves, and noted a number of examples of "dynamic conformity" in other areas of federal regulation. The 1948 Act, Justice Burton stated, "thus

Commerce Clause, which has grown to vast proportions in its applications, desired silently to deprive the States of an immunity they have long enjoyed under another part of the Constitution [the Eleventh Amendment]." Note also the application of the Eleventh Amendment barrier in Edelman v. Jordan, 415 U.S. 651 (1974) (chap. 3, sec. 5, above).

at last provided that within each federal enclave, to the extent that offenses are not pre-empted by congressional enactments, there shall be complete current conformity with the criminal laws of the respective States in which the enclaves are situated." He added: "Having the power to assimilate the state laws, Congress obviously has like power to renew such assimilation annually or daily in order to keep the laws in the enclaves current with those in the States. That being so, we conclude that Congress is within its constitutional powers and legislative discretion when, after 123 years of experience with the policy of conformity, it enacts that policy in its most complete and accurate form. Rather than being a delegation by Congress of its legislative authority to the States, it is a deliberate continuing adoption by Congress for federal enclaves of such unpreempted offenses and punishments as shall have been already put in effect by the respective States for their own government."

Justice Douglas, joined by Justice Black, dissented: "It [is] the Congress, and the Congress alone, that has the power to make rules governing federal enclaves. . . . The power to make laws under which men are punished for crimes calls for as serious a deliberation as the fashioning of rules for the seizure of the industrial plants involved in the Youngstown case. [The Steel Seizure Case, chap. 7, sec. 1, below.] Both call for the exercise of legislative judgment; and I do not see how that requirement can be satisfied by delegating the authority to the President, the Department of the Interior, or, as in this case, to the States."

SOME ADDITIONAL COMMENTS ON STATE AUTONOMY

1. *Territorial integrity.* Cases such as New York v. United States, United States v. California, and Maryland v. Wirtz, above—which recognize some federal authority to tax and regulate state activities—suggest a somewhat broader inquiry into the present status of state autonomy. The Constitution contains a number of safeguards. In addition to the implications from the allocation of power between nation and states and from the Tenth Amendment considered earlier, note especially the assurance of territorial integrity of states in Art. IV, § 3: "[N]o new State shall be formed or erected within the Jurisdiction of any other State; nor any State be formed by the Junction of two or more States, or parts of States, without the Consent of the Legislatures of the States concerned as well as of the Congress." Note also the restriction on the amending power in Art. V: "[N]o State, without its Consent, shall be deprived of its equal Suffrage in the Senate."

2. *Conditions on the admission of new states.* May Congress restrict state autonomy by conditioning the admission of a state into the Union? The problem has been a prolific source of controversy, especially in extrajudicial debates, as those from 1819 to 1821 regarding the Missouri Compromise. Coyle v. Smith, 221 U.S. 559 (1911), involved the federal law providing for the admission of Oklahoma. It stipulated that the state capital should be temporarily located at Guthrie and not changed prior to 1913, and that meanwhile no public money should be appropriated for building a capitol. In 1910 Oklahoma passed an act removing the capital to Oklahoma City and appropriating money for buildings. Affirming a judgment which sustained the state act, Justice Lurton said: "The power to locate its own seat of govern-

ment and to determine when and how it shall be changed from one place to another, and to appropriate its own public funds for that purpose, are essentially and peculiarly state powers. That one of the original thirteen States could now be shorn of such powers by an act of Congress would not be for a moment entertained. [C]onstitutional equality of the States is essential to the harmonious operation of the scheme upon which the Republic was organized." See Hanna, "Equal Footing in the Admission of States," 3 Baylor L.Rev. 519 (1951).

3. *State courts and the enforcement of federal law.* It is part of the basic constitutional scheme that state courts are not only competent but obligated to consider federal claims raised there. And Congress may give federal courts exclusive jurisdiction to hear federal claims. See chap. 1, above. But may Congress create new statutory rights and compel the states to make their judicial machinery available for enforcement proceedings? The Emergency Price Control Act of 1942 permitted treble damage suits for violations of federal price regulations to be brought in state as well as federal courts. Rhode Island's highest court held that the Act was a "penal" statute of a foreign sovereign which the state courts would not enforce. In Testa v. Katt, 330 U.S. 386 (1947), the Court reversed: even assuming the statute was penal, the Supremacy Clause does not permit state courts to decline enforcement of federal statutory rights on local policy grounds—at least where the state courts "have jurisdiction adequate and appropriate under established local law to adjudicate this action." The qualifying phrase is, of course, significant, though much of Justice Black's opinion speaks more broadly than that. Compare Chief Justice Taney's language in Kentucky v. Dennison, 24 How. 66 (1861), in the note on Interstate Rendition, sec. 2A, below. See Note, "Utilization of State Courts to Enforce Federal Penal and Criminal Statutes: Development in Judicial Federalism," 60 Harv.L.Rev. 966 (1947).

4. *State courts and "interference" with federal action.* a. Federal courts have broad authority to grant habeas corpus where persons are in state custody. See 28 U.S.C. § 2254. Do state courts have any similar authority with regard to those in federal custody? In Tarble's Case, 13 Wall. 397 (1872), a Wisconsin court had issued habeas corpus to discharge a soldier from the custody of a federal recruiting officer, on the ground that the soldier had enlisted while under age and without parental consent. The Supreme Court held that the state lacked authority, relying heavily on broad language in Ableman v. Booth, 21 How. 506 (1859), where the Wisconsin courts had ordered release of a person held under a federal charge. In the Booth litigation, Chief Justice Taney had said that "no State can authorize one of its judges . . . to exercise judicial power, by habeas corpus or otherwise, within the jurisdiction of another and independent Government. [A]fter the return is made, and the State judge or court judicially apprized that the party is in custody under the authority of the United States, they can proceed no further." Accordingly, in Tarble's Case, Justice Field stated: "Such being the distinct and independent character of the two governments . . ., it follows that neither can intrude with its judicial process into the domain of the other, except so far as such intrusion may be necessary on the part of the National government to preserve its rightful supremacy in cases of conflict of authority."

b. If the federal courts' statutory jurisdiction on habeas corpus for state prisoners were repealed, would those cases be decided the same way? Perhaps Tarble's Case can be justified as resting on an exclusive federal jurisdiction implied from acts of Congress, though ordinarily concurrent state jurisdiction is assumed unless exclusive jurisdiction is fairly clear in the federal statutes. See Claflin v. Houseman, 93 U.S. 130 (1876). Unless Tarble's Case is so limited, does it not undercut the role of the state courts "as the primary guarantors of constitutional rights, and in many cases"—in view of the congressional authority over the jurisdiction of federal courts—perhaps "the ultimate" guarantors? See Hart and Wechsler, The Federal Courts and the Federal System (2d ed. 1973), 330, 427.

SECTION 2.   INTERSTATE RELATIONSHIPS

A.   INTERSTATE OBLIGATIONS

Introduction. The major constitutional source of interstate obligations is Art. IV. The most important and most litigated provision has been § 1 of that Article, the Full Faith and Credit Clause. Full Faith and Credit problems are usually considered in conflict of laws courses and are not developed here. Two additional limitations—both in Art. IV, § 2—warrant notice, however: the interstate privileges and immunities clause, and the obligation regarding rendition of fugitives from justice.

THE PRIVILEGES AND IMMUNITIES CLAUSE OF ARTICLE IV

The injunction that the "Citizens of each State shall be entitled to all Privileges and Immunities of Citizens in the several States" was a briefer version of—but had the same purpose as [1]—a similar provision in the Articles of Confederation. In the first significant judicial interpretation of the clause, Corfield v. Coryell, 4 Wash.C.C. 371, Fed.Cas.No.3,230 (Cir.Ct.E.D.Pa., 1823), Justice Bushrod Washington described the scope of the clause broadly.[2] But in the Corfield case itself, a state statute was held not to violate Art. IV, § 2, and the clause has had a rather limited function over the years: it serves as a barrier against certain state discriminations against citizens of other states. See, e. g., Paul v. Virginia, 8 Wall. 168 (1869): "[I]t inhibits discriminating legislation . . . . Indeed, without some provision of the kind removing from the citizens of each State the disabilities of alienage in the other States, and giving them equality of privilege with citizens of those States, the Re-

---

1. See the discussion in Justice Miller's opinion in the Slaughter-House Cases, 16 Wall. 36 (1873), chap. 8 below.

2. For excerpts from the Corfield opinion, see the Slaughter-House Cases, chap. 8 below.

public would have constituted little more than a league of States; it would not have constituted the Union which now exists." [3]

Moreover, the functions of several other provisions of the Constitution overlap those of the interstate privileges and immunities clause—as has already been seen with regard to the anti-discrimination, nationalizing impact of the commerce clause, chap. 5 above, and as will be seen in the interpretations of the equal protection clause of the Fourteenth Amendment, chap. 10 below. (The Fourteenth Amendment contains a privileges and immunities clause as well. It prohibits state infringements on the privileges of *national,* not state, citizenship, and the Court's interpretations have made it the least significant of the protections in § 1 of the 14th Amendment.)

The next principal case illustrates one of the Court's rare modern reliances on the interstate privileges and immunities clause. It deals with a statute somewhat similar to that sustained in the first judicial consideration of the clause, Corfield v. Coryell, above; and it raises questions related to those that have arisen under the commerce clause with respect to a state's authority to control the use of its natural resources, see chap. 5, sec. 1D, above. (Recall also the materials on the sources of the right to interstate mobility, chap. 5 above.) In Corfield, Justice Washington sustained a New Jersey law prohibiting nonresidents from gathering clams, oysters, or shells in the state's waters. The Circuit Court rejected the claim that Art. IV, § 2, compelled New Jersey, in "regulating the use of the common property" of its citizens, "to extend to the citizens of all the other states the same advantages as are secured to their own citizens." Compare the discussion in the case which follows.

TOOMER v. WITSELL

334 U.S. 385, 68 S.Ct. 1156, 92 L.Ed. 1460 (1948).

Appeal from the District Court for the Eastern District of South Carolina.

Mr. Chief Justice VINSON delivered the opinion of the Court.

This is a suit to enjoin as unconstitutional the enforcement of several South Carolina statutes governing commercial shrimp fishing in the three-mile maritime belt off the coast of that State. Appellants, who initiated the action, are five individual fishermen, all citizens and residents of Georgia,

---

3. In Paul v. Virginia, a Virginia statute required foreign—but not domestic—insurance companies, as a condition of doing business in the State, to deposit with the State Treasurer bonds of a specified amount and character. The agent of a New York corporation unsuccessfully challenged the statute under Art. IV, § 2. The Court held that a corporation is not a citizen for purposes of the clause, and that a state may therefore exclude it except upon such conditions as it sees fit. Other constitutional provisions, however, limit the types of conditions a state may impose. For examples of "unconstitutional conditions," see, e. g., Western Union Telegraph Co. v. Kansas, 216 U.S. 1 (1910) (attempt to oust foreign corporation for failure to pay franchise tax measured by total capital; invalid under due process and commerce clauses); Terral v. Burke Construction Co., 257 U.S. 529 (1922) (corporation cannot be compelled to "waive" right to resort to federal courts); and Hale, "Unconstitutional Conditions and Constitutional Rights," 35 Colum.L.Rev. 321 (1935).

and a non-profit fish dealers' organization incorporated in Florida. [The three-judge District Court upheld the statutes.]

[South Carolina's regulations applied to a part of a large shrimp fishery extending from North Carolina to Florida. The shrimp are migratory. There are no federal regulations and attempts at uniform legislation by the adjoining states failed. Commercial shrimpers wanted to start trawling off the Carolinas in the summer and follow the shrimp down to Florida. They encountered state restrictions—some based on a desire to channel business derived from local waters to local residents. "Restrictions on non-resident fishing in the marginal sea . . . invited retaliation to the point that the fishery [was] effectively partitioned at the state lines." One of the statutes challenged— Section 3379—imposed license fees on shrimp boats: $25 on those owned by residents; $2500 on those belonging to non-residents.]

. . . Appellants' most vigorous attack is directed at § 3379 [which] requires non-residents of South Carolina to pay license fees one hundred times as great as those which residents must pay. The purpose and effect of this statute, they contend, is not to conserve shrimp, but to exclude non-residents and thereby create a commercial monopoly for South Carolina residents. As such, the statute is said to violate the privileges and immunities clause of Art. IV, § 2, of the Constitution . . . .

The primary purpose of this clause, like the clauses between which it is located—those relating to full faith and credit and to interstate extradition of fugitives from justice—was to help fuse into one Nation a collection of independent, sovereign States. It was designed to insure to a citizen of State A who ventures into State B the same privileges which the citizens of State B enjoy.[1] . . .

In line with this underlying purpose, it was long ago decided that one of the privileges which the clause guarantees to citizens of State A is that of doing business in State B on terms of substantial equality with the citizens of that State.

Like many other constitutional provisions, the privileges and immunities clause is not an absolute. It does bar discrimination against citizens of other States where there is no substantial reason for the discrimination beyond the mere fact that they are citizens of other States. But it does not preclude dis-

---

1. See Paul v. Virginia, 8 Wall. 168, 180–81 (1868); Travis v. Yale & Towne Mfg. Co., 252 U.S. 60, 78 (1920). [Footnote by the Court.]

The Travis case invalidated a New York income tax law as applied to Connecticut and New Jersey residents employed in New York, because the law granted to residents exemptions denied to nonresidents. Under the law, nonresidents were allowed credits against the New York tax if their home state imposed an income tax and granted reciprocal credits to New Yorkers working there. Connecticut and New Jersey had no income tax. The Court found no "adequate ground" for the discrimination" and rejected a defense based on the reciprocity provision: New York's discrimination "would not be cured" by "like discriminations" in adjoining states; nor can "discrimination be corrected by retaliation," for "to prevent this was one of the chief ends" of the Constitution.

In Austin v. New Hampshire, 420 U.S. —— (1975), the Court relied on Art. IV, § 2, and the Travis case to sustain a challenge by Maine residents to New Hampshire's Commuters Income Tax. The Court emphasized that "the tax falls exclusively on the incomes of nonresidents" and "is not offset even approximately by other taxes imposed on residents alone."

parity of treatment in the many situations where there are perfectly valid independent reasons for it. Thus the inquiry in each case must be concerned with whether such reasons do exist and whether the degree of discrimination bears a close relaion to them. . . .

As justification for the statute, appellees urge that the State's obvious purpose was to conserve its shrimp supply, and they suggest that it was designed to head off an impending threat of excessive trawling. The record casts some doubt on these statements. But in any event, appellees' argument assumes that any means adopted to attain valid objectives necessarily squares with the privileges and immunities clause. It overlooks the purpose of that clause, which [is] to outlaw classifications based on the fact of non-citizenship unless there is something to indicate that non-citizens constitute a peculiar source of the evil at which the statute is aimed.

. . . Nothing in the record indicates that non-residents use larger boats or different fishing methods than residents, that the cost of enforcing the laws against them is appreciably greater, or that any substantial amount of the State's general funds is devoted to shrimp conservation. But assuming such were the facts, they would not necessarily support a remedy so drastic as to be a near equivalent of total exclusion. The State is not without power, for example, to restrict the type of equipment used in its fisheries, to graduate license fees according to the size of the boats, or even to charge non-residents a differential which would merely compensate the State for any added enforcement burden they may impose . . . . We would be closing our eyes to reality, we believe, if we concluded that there was a reasonable relationship between the danger represented by non-citizens, as a class, and the severe discrimination practiced upon them.

Thus, § 3379 must be held unconstitutional unless commercial shrimp fishing in the maritime belt falls within some unexpressed exception to the privileges and immunities clause.

Appellees strenuously urge that there is such an exception. Their argument runs as follows: Ever since Roman times, animals *ferae naturae* [have been] subject to control by the sovereign or other governmental authority. More recently this thought has been expressed by saying that fish and game are the common property of all citizens of the governmental unit and that the government, as a sort of trustee, exercises this "ownership" for the benefit of its citizens. . . . Language frequently repeated by this Court appears to lend some support to this analysis.[2] [McCready v. Virginia, 94 U.S. 391 (1876)] . . .

The whole ownership theory, in fact, is now generally regarded as but a fiction expressive in legal shorthand of the importance to its people that a State have power to preserve and regulate the exploitation of an important resource. And there is no necessary conflict between that vital policy consideration and the constitutional command that the State exercise that power, like its other powers, so as not to discriminate without reason against citizens of other States.

2. The most extended exposition appears in the majority opinion in Geer v. Connecticut, 161 U.S. 519 (1896). [Footnote by the Court. The Geer case is noted in chap. 5, sec. 1D, above.]

These considerations lead us to the conclusion that the McCready exception to the privileges and immunities clause, if such it be, should not be expanded to cover this case.

Thus we hold that commercial shrimping in the marginal sea, like other common callings, is within the purview of the privileges and immunities clause. And since we have previously concluded that the reasons advanced in support of the statute do not bear a reasonable relationship to the high degree of discrimination practiced upon citizens of other States, it follows that § 3379 violates Art. IV, § 2, of the Constitution.

Appellants maintain that by a parity of reasoning the statute also contravenes the equal protection clause of the Fourteenth Amendment. That may well be true, but we do not pass on this argument since it is unnecessary to disposition of the present case. . . .

Reversed.

Mr. Justice FRANKFURTER, whom Mr. Justice JACKSON joins, concurring. . . .

[A] State cannot project its powers over its own resources by seeking to control the channels of commerce among the States. It is one thing to say that a food supply that may be reduced to control by a State for feeding its own people should be only locally consumed. The State has that power and the Privileges-and-Immunities Clause is no restriction upon its exercise. It is a wholly different thing for the State to provide that only its citizens shall be engaged in commerce among the States, even though based on a locally available food supply. That is not the exercise of the basic right of a State to feed and maintain and give enjoyment to its own people. When a State regulates the sending of products across State lines we have commerce among the States as to which State intervention is subordinate to the Commerce Clause. That is the nub of the decision in Foster Fountain Packing Co. v. Haydel, 278 U.S. 1 [chap. 5, sec. 1D]. South Carolina has attempted such regulation of commerce in shrimp among the States. In doing so she has exceeded the restrictions of the Commerce Clause.

[A concurring opinion by Justice RUTLEDGE is omitted.]

INTERSTATE RENDITION

a. The rendition clause of Art. IV, § 2, speaks in mandatory terms: A fugitive from justice "shall . . . be delivered up" on "demand of the executive Authority of the State from which he fled." And in 1793, Congress prescribed the procedure to be followed in making the "demand." But the duty is not enforceable against a governor: in Kentucky v. Dennison, 24 How. 66 (1861), the Court denied Kentucky's mandamus petition to compel the Governor of Ohio to deliver a fugitive. The Court held that it had original jurisdiction to consider the application under Art. III —see New Jersey v. New York, 5 Pet. 284 (1831)—but refused to issue the writ. Chief Justice Taney stated: "[L]ooking to the subject-matter [of the 1793 law], and the relations which the United States and the several States bear to each other, the court is of opinion, the words 'it shall be the

duty' were not used as mandatory and compulsory, but as declaratory of the moral duty [which the Constitution created]. [S]uch a power would place every State under the control and dominion of the General Government, even in . . . its internal concerns and reserved rights. And we think it clear, that the Federal Government . . . has no power to impose on a State officer, as such, any duty whatever, and compel him to perform it." But cf. Testa v. Katt, 330 U.S. 386 (1947), sec. 1 above.

b. Congress has enacted legislation under the commerce clause to deal with interstate fugitives from justice. See the Fugitive Felon and Witness Act of 1934, 18 U.S.C. § 1073. Moreover, many states have adopted the Uniform Law to Secure the Attendance of Witnesses from Within or Without a State in Criminal Proceedings. In New York v. O'Neill, 359 U.S. 1 (1959), a divided Court rejected a claim that the Act as adopted by Florida was unconstitutional.

B. INTERSTATE COLLABORATION

WEST VIRGINIA ex rel. DYER v. SIMS

341 U.S. 22, 71 S.Ct. 557, 95 L.Ed. 713 (1951).

Certiorari to the Supreme Court of Appeals of West Virginia.

Mr. Justice FRANKFURTER delivered the opinion of the Court.

After extended negotiations eight States entered into a Compact to control pollution in the Ohio River system. See Ohio River Valley Water Sanitation Compact, 54 Stat. 752. Illinois, Indiana, Kentucky, New York, Ohio, Pennsylvania, Virginia and West Virginia recognized that they were faced with one of the problems of government that are defined by natural rather than political boundaries. Accordingly, they pledged themselves to cooperate in maintaining waters in the Ohio River basin in a sanitary condition through the administrative mechanism of the Ohio River Valley Water Sanitation Commission, consisting of three members from each State and three representing the United States.

The heart of the Compact is Article VI. This provides that sewage discharged into boundary streams or streams flowing from one State into another "shall be so treated . . . as to provide for substantially complete removal of settleable solids, and the removal of not less than forty-five per cent (45%) of the total suspended solids." . . .

By Article X the States also agree "to appropriate for the salaries, office and other administrative expenses, their proper proportion of the annual budget as determined by the Commission and approved by the Governors of the signatory States . . . ."

The present controversy arose because of conflicting views between officials of West Virginia regarding the responsibility of West Virginia under the Compact.

The Legislature of that State ratified and approved the Compact on March 11, 1939. . . . Congress gave its consent on July 11, 1940, . . . and upon adoption by all the signatory States the Compact was formally executed by the Governor of West Virginia on June 30, 1948. At its 1949 session the West Virginia Legislature appropriated $12,250 as the State's contribution to the expenses of the Commission for the fiscal year beginning July 1, 1949. . . . Respondent Sims, the auditor of the State, refused to issue a warrant upon its treasury for payment of this appropriation. To compel him to issue it, the West Virginia Commissioners to the Compact Commission and the members of the West Virginia State Water Commission instituted this original mandamus proceeding in the Supreme Court of Appeals of West Virginia. The court denied relief on the merits . . . .

The West Virginia court found that the "sole question" before it was the validity of the Act of 1939 approving West Virginia's adherence to the Compact. It found that Act invalid in that . . . the Compact was deemed to delegate West Virginia's police power to other States and to the Federal Government . . . .

Control of pollution in interstate streams might, on occasion, be an appropriate subject for national legislation. . . . But, with prescience, the Framers left the States free to settle regional controversies in diverse ways. Solution of the problem underlying this case may be attempted directly by the affected States through contentious litigation before this Court. . . .

[But] so awkward and unsatisfactory is the available litigious solution for these problems that this Court deemed it appropriate to emphasize the practical constitutional alternative provided by the Compact Clause. Experience led us to suggest that a problem such as that involved here is "more likely to be wisely solved by coöperative study and by conference and mutual concession on the part of representatives of the States so vitally interested in it than by proceedings in any court however constituted." New York v. New Jersey, [256 U.S. 296]. The suggestion has had fruitful response.

The growing interdependence of regional interests, calling for regional adjustments, has brought extensive use of compacts. A compact is more than a supple device for dealing with interests confined within a region. That it is also a means of safeguarding the national interest is well illustrated in the Compact now under review. Not only was congressional consent required, as for all compacts; direct participation by the Federal Government was provided in the President's appointment of three members of the Compact Commission. . . .

But a compact is after all a legal document. Though the circumstances of its drafting are likely to assure great care and deliberation, all avoidance of disputes as to scope and meaning is not within human gift. Just as this Court has power to settle disputes between States where there is no compact, it must have final power to pass upon the meaning and validity of compacts. It requires no elaborate argument to reject the suggestion that an agreement solemnly entered into between States by those who alone have political authority to speak for a State can be unilaterally nullified, or given final meaning by an organ of one of the contracting States. A State cannot be its own ultimate judge in a controversy with a sister State. To determine the nature and scope of obligations as between States, whether they arise through the leg-

islative means of compact or the "federal common law" governing interstate controversies (Hinderlider v. La Plata Co., 304 U.S. 92, 110), is the function and duty of the Supreme Court of the Nation. Of course every deference will be shown to what the highest court of a State deems to be the law and policy of its State, particularly when recondite or unique features of local law are urged. Deference is one thing; submission to a State's own determination of whether it has undertaken an obligation, what that obligation is, and whether it conflicts with a disability of the State to undertake it is quite another. . . .

That a legislature may delegate to an administrative body the power to make rules and decide particular cases is one of the axioms of modern government. The West Virginia court does not challenge the general proposition but objects to the delegation here involved because it is to a body outside the State and because its Legislature may not be free, at any time, to withdraw the power delegated. We are not here concerned, and so need not deal, with specific language in a State constitution requiring that the State settle its problems with other States without delegating power to an interstate agency. What is involved is the conventional grant of legislative power. We find nothing in that to indicate that West Virginia may not solve a problem such as the control of river pollution by compact and by the delegation, if such it be, necessary to effectuate such solution by compact. If this Court, in the exercise of its original jurisdiction, were to enter a decree requiring West Virginia to abate pollution of interstate streams, that decree would bind the State. The West Virginia Legislature would have no part in determining the State's obligation. The State Legislature could not alter it; it could not disregard it, as West Virginia on another occasion so creditably recognized.* The obligation would be fixed by this Court on the basis of a master's report. Here, the State has bound itself to control pollution by the more effective means of an agreement with other States. The Compact involves a reasonable and carefully limited delegation of power to an interstate agency. Nothing in its Constitution suggests that, in dealing with the problem dealt with by the Compact, West Virginia must wait for the answer to be dictated by this Court after harassing and unsatisfactory litigation. . . .

Reversed and remanded.

Mr. Justice REED, concurring.

---

* Justice Frankfurter's reference was presumably to the extensive litigation between Virginia and West Virginia to enforce West Virginia's obligation to assume a share of Virginia's public debt, upon the separation of the two states. The Court handed down nine opinions or orders in the case, from Virginia v. West Virginia, 206 U.S. 290 (1907), to Virginia v. West Virginia, 246 U.S. 565 (1918). The litigation raised major issues about the enforceability of a money judgment against a state. In one of the opinions, Justice Holmes used a phrase that found its way into the implementation decision in the School Segregation Cases, Brown v. Board of Education, 349 U.S. 294 (1955) (chap. 10 below). Justice Holmes said, in Virginia v. West Virginia, 222 U.S. 17, 19–20 (1911): "A question like the present should be disposed of without undue delay. But a State cannot be expected to move with the celerity of a private business man; it is enough if it proceeds, in the language of the English chancery, *with all deliberate speed*." [Emphasis added.] The controversy was finally resolved in 1919, when West Virginia enacted a law providing for payment of the Supreme Court's judgment. See Powell, "Coercing a State to Pay a Judgment: Virginia v. West Virginia," 17 Mich. L.Rev. 1 (1918).

I concur in the judgment of the Court but disagree with the assertion of power by this Court to interpret the meaning of the West Virginia Constitution. . . .   The interpretation of the meaning of the compact controls over a state's application of its own law through the Supremacy Clause and not by any implied federal power to construe state law. . . . †

INTERSTATE COMPACTS

1. *The utility of compacts.* The interstate compact device, illustrated by the principal case, has been used to deal with a wide variety of interstate and regional problems, including boundaries, natural resources regulation and allocation, flood control, transportation, taxation, and crime control. Compacts, like other devices, are not always effective. Recall, for example, the shrimp fishery problem, Toomer v. Witsell, sec. 2A above, where the affected states engaged in retaliatory legislation despite the existence of a compact.[1]

2. *Congressional consent.* Interstate compacts require the consent of Congress, in view of the constitutional prohibition, Art. I, § 10, of any state "Agreement or Compact" with other states or foreign nations "without the Consent of Congress." Congress has at times encouraged compacts by giving advance consent, as with crime and flood control. Do all interstate agreements require congressional consent? See Virginia v. Tennessee, 148 U.S. 503 (1893), stating that the Clause "is directed to the formation of any combination tending to the increase of political power in the States, which may encroach upon . . . the just supremacy of the United States," and that there are "many matters upon which different States may agree that can in no respect concern the United States." See Engdahl, "Characterization of Interstate Arrangements: When Is a Compact Not a Compact?" 64 Mich.L. Rev. 63 (1965).

---

† Justice Jackson submitted a separate concurrence. Justice Black concurred in the result.

1. See generally Zimmerman and Wendell, The Interstate Compact Since 1925 (1951); Thursby, Interstate Cooperation—A Study of the Interstate Compact (1953); Comm'n on Intergovernmental Relations, A Report to the President (1955); Leach and Sugg, The Administration of Interstate Compacts (1959); Ridgeway, Interstate Compacts: A Question of Federalism (1971); and Frankfurter and Landis, "The Compact Clause of the Constitution—A Study in Interstate Adjustments," 34 Yale L.J. 685 (1925).

Chapter 7

SEPARATION OF POWERS:
THE PRESIDENT, CONGRESS, AND THE COURT

Introduction. This final chapter of Part II, like the five preceding ones, deals with problems of structure and relationships among units of government. The preceding chapters focused on allocations of power between nation and states. This chapter turns to another set of constitutional arrangements for limiting power through diffusion of authority among various units of government: the allocation of powers among the three branches of the national government. The Framers diffused power on a horizontal as well as a vertical plane: chapters 2 through 6 examined the vertical dimension, the division of powers between national and state governments; this chapter samples problems of the horizontal plane, the separation of powers between President, Congress, and Court.

The makers of the Constitution, influenced not only by their own experiences but also by theorists such as Montesquieu, consciously provided for allocation of national authority among the executive, legislative and judicial branches. That separation is symbolized by the discrete delineations of structure and powers for each branch in Articles I, II, and III of the Constitution. But, as an examination of the constitutional provisions readily reveals, separation was not intended to be total and airtight. Repeatedly, powers are intermixed, as with the participation of the President in the legislative process through the veto power. And repeatedly, restraints by one branch upon another are authorized, as with the impeachment power. Beyond the explicit restraints and overlaps, moreover, lie boundary lines indistinct in the original document and additionally blurred by historical practice. Those areas of uncertainty have left ample room for competitions and jealousies among the branches—conflicts most often resolved by tests of political strengths in particular periods of our history. Those conflict-producing ambiguities may themselves have contributed to furthering the Framers' purpose of combatting excessive concentration of power; but they also yield an area of constitutional law with special disappointments for those yearning for clear and authoritative lines. In the area of separation of powers, far more so than with problems of federalism and individual rights, judicial resolutions have been relatively sparse and temporary political accommodations have predominated. As Justice Jackson commented early in his concurring opinion in the Steel Seizure Case, which follows: "A century and a half of partisan debate and scholarly speculation yields no net result but only supplies more or less apt quotations from respected sources on each side of any question."

Yet lack of Court decisions does not make separation of powers any less important and challenging an area of constitutional interpretation. The raw materials for study here, more than in other areas, lie in executive documents and legislative assertions as well as Court opinions. But as in

other areas, text and history and inferences from structure and relationships warrant search for appropriate guidelines.

Sampling of separation of powers problems here begins with some examples of competition between President and Congress over the authority to make policy governing national affairs. To what extent does the constitutional grant of executive powers authorize the President to fashion policy in the absence of, or in the face of, congressional decisionmaking? Sec. 1A examines the boundaries between presidential and congressional policy-making authority in the domestic sphere; Sec. 1B considers the lines between executive and legislative authority with regard to external affairs, with particular emphasis on conflicts regarding the making of foreign policy and the use of military forces.

Sec. 2 turns to problems concerning the integrity and autonomy of each of the branches vis-à-vis interferences by the others. To what extent does the separation of powers protect each branch against intervention in its internal processes? To what degree are the legislative and executive branches amenable to judicial process? To what extent may their decisions be re-examined in the courts? To what extent does the Constitution grant final, nonreviewable authority to decide some constitutional issues to organs of government other than the courts? Sec. 2 culminates with an examination of the Watergate Tapes litigation and the 1974 decision in United States v. Nixon as a case study presenting several of the interrelated problems in this section: the amenability of the President to judicial process; the claimed finality of his judgment regarding the scope of executive privilege; and the contents of a judicially delineated executive privilege for confidential communications.

SECTION 1. THE AUTHORITY TO MAKE NATIONAL POLICY: THE CONFLICT BETWEEN LEGISLATIVE POWERS AND EXECUTIVE AUTHORITY

A. DOMESTIC AFFAIRS

Presidential leadership and congressional lawmaking. The actual influence of the President, as the elected official with a national constituency and as party leader, is obviously great. What of his constitutional authority to devise and implement policy to deal with domestic problems in the private sector? Does the Chief Executive have residual emergency power to regulate private conduct? Do the specified executive powers in Art. II or the inherent powers of the Presidency authorize the President to act when Congress has been silent? Are there any circumstances in which his powers take precedence even over conflicting congressional directives? Or is the President limited to the specific tasks assigned by Art. II and to the execution of laws Congress enacts? The executive power to make "law" has evoked frequent and intense battles, most commonly over abstractions, with Presidents as well as commentators on opposing sides. But the operative and most help-

ful answers may lie less in embracive absolutes than in discriminating distinctions and practical adjustments: compare, for example, the broad assertions of Justice Black with the more detailed analysis of Justice Jackson in the Steel Seizure Case, below.

YOUNGSTOWN SHEET & TUBE CO. v. SAWYER
[THE STEEL SEIZURE CASE]

343 U.S. 579, 72 S.Ct. 863, 96 L.Ed. 1153 (1952).

Certiorari to the United States Court of Appeals for the District of Columbia Circuit.

Mr. Justice BLACK delivered the opinion of the Court.

We are asked to decide whether the President was acting within his constitutional power when he issued an order directing the Secretary of Commerce to take possession of and operate most of the Nation's steel mills. The mill owners argue that the President's order amounts to lawmaking, a legislative function which the Constitution has expressly confided to the Congress and not to the President. The Government's position is that the order was made on findings of the President that his action was necessary to avert a national catastrophe which would inevitably result from a stoppage of steel production, and that in meeting this grave emergency the President was acting within the aggregate of his constitutional powers as the Nation's Chief Executive and the Commander in Chief of the Armed Forces of the United States. The issue emerges here from the following series of events:

In the latter part of 1951 [during the Korean War], a dispute arose between the steel companies and their employees over terms and conditions that should be included in new collective bargaining agreements. [Efforts to settle the dispute—including reference to the Federal Wage Stabilization Board—failed.] On April 4, 1952, the Union [the United Steelworkers of America] gave notice of a nation-wide strike called to begin at 12:01 a. m. April 9. The indispensability of steel as a component of substantially all weapons and other war materials led the President to believe that the proposed work stoppage would immediately jeopardize our national defense and that governmental seizure of the steel mills was necessary in order to assure the continued availability of steel. Reciting these considerations for his action, the President, a few hours before the strike was to begin, issued Executive Order 10340 [directing] the Secretary of Commerce [Sawyer] to take possession of most of the steel mills and keep them running. The Secretary immediately issued his own possessory orders, calling upon the presidents of the various seized companies to serve as operating managers for the United States. . . . The next morning the President sent a message to Congress reporting his action. . . . Congress has taken no action.

Obeying the Secretary's orders under protest, the companies brought proceedings against him in the District Court, [which] on April 30 issued a preliminary injunction restraining the Secretary from "continuing the seizure and possession of the plants [and] from acting under the purported

authority of Executive Order No. 10340."* On the same day the Court of Appeals stayed the District Court's injunction. Deeming it best that the issues raised be promptly decided by this Court, we granted certiorari on May 3 and set the cause for argument on May 12. [This decision was announced on June 2, 1952.]

The President's power, if any, to issue the order must stem either from an act of Congress or from the Constitution itself. There is no statute that expressly authorizes the President to take possession of property as he did here. Nor is there any act of Congress to which our attention has been directed from which such a power can fairly be implied. . . . There are two statutes which do authorize the President to take both personal and real property under certain conditions. [The Selective Service Act of 1948 and the Defense Production Act of 1950.] However, the Government admits that these conditions were not met and that the President's order was not rooted in either of the statutes. The Government refers to the seizure provisions of one of these statutes [the 1950 Act] as "much too cumbersome, involved, and time-consuming for the crisis which was at hand."

Moreover, the use of the seizure technique to solve labor disputes in order to prevent work stoppages was not only unauthorized by any congressional enactment; prior to this controversy, Congress had refused to adopt that method of settling labor disputes. When the Taft-Hartley Act was under consideration in 1947, Congress rejected an amendment which would have authorized such governmental seizures in cases of emergency. . . .

It is clear that if the President had authority to issue the order he did, it must be found in some provision of the Constitution. And it is not claimed that express constitutional language grants this power to the President. The contention is that presidential power should be implied from the aggregate of his powers under the Constitution. Particular reliance is placed on provisions in Article II which say that "The executive Power shall be vested in a President . . ."; that "he shall take Care that the Laws be faithfully executed"; and that he "shall be Commander in Chief of the Army and Navy of the United States."

The order cannot properly be sustained as an exercise of the President's military power as Commander in Chief of the Armed Forces. The Govern-

---

* On the issue of presidential power, the Government argued in the District Court that a strike disrupting steel production would so endanger national safety that the President had "inherent power" to seize the steel mills —a power "supported by the Constitution, by historical precedent, and by court decisions." (See also the comment on the District Court argument in the notes following this case.)

In addition to defending President Truman's authority on the merits, the Government made a procedural argument: it claimed that injunctive relief should be denied because the steel companies had not shown "that their available legal remedies were inadequate or that their injuries from seizure would be irreparable." The Gov-

ernment argued that, if the seizure were ultimately held unlawful, the companies could recover compensation in the Court of Claims for unlawful taking. Justice Black, however, found no reason for delay in reaching the constitutionality of the seizure. Not only was there doubt about the right to sue in the Court of Claims for seizures of this sort, but the seizures "were bound to result in many present and future damages of such nature as to be difficult, if not incapable, of measurement." Were the barriers to equitable relief more substantial than the Court's summary disposition suggested? See Freund, "Foreword: The Year of the Steel Case," 66 Harv.L. Rev. 89 (1952).

ment attempts to do so by citing a number of cases upholding broad powers in military commanders engaged in day-to-day fighting in a theater of war. Such cases need not concern us here. Even though "theater of war" be an expanding concept, we cannot with faithfulness to our constitutional system hold that the Commander in Chief of the Armed Forces has the ultimate power as such to take possession of private property in order to keep labor disputes from stopping production. This is a job for the Nation's lawmakers, not for its military authorities.

Nor can the seizure order be sustained because of the several constitutional provisions that grant executive power to the President. In the framework of our Constitution, the President's power to see that the laws are faithfully executed refutes the idea that he is to be a lawmaker. The Constitution limits his functions in the law-making process to the recommending of laws he thinks wise and the vetoing of laws he thinks bad. And the Constitution is neither silent nor equivocal about who shall make laws which the President is to execute [quoting Art. I, § 1, and Art. I, § 8, cl. 18].

The President's order does not direct that a congressional policy be executed in a manner prescribed by Congress—it directs that a presidential policy be executed in a manner prescribed by the President. The preamble of the order itself, like that of many statutes, sets out reasons why the President believes certain policies should be adopted, proclaims these policies as rules of conduct to be followed, and again, like a statute, authorizes a government official to promulgate additional rules and regulations consistent with the policy proclaimed and needed to carry that policy into execution. The power of Congress to adopt such public policies as those proclaimed by the order is beyond question. It can authorize the taking of private property for public use. It can make laws regulating the relationships between employers and employees, prescribing rules designed to settle labor disputes, and fixing wages and working conditions in certain fields of our economy. The Constitution does not subject this lawmaking power of Congress to presidential or military supervision or control.

It is said that other Presidents without congressional authority have taken possession of private business enterprises in order to settle labor disputes. But even if this be true, Congress has not thereby lost its exclusive constitutional authority to make laws necessary and proper to carry out the powers vested by the Constitution "in the Government of the United States, or any Department or Officer thereof."

The Founders of this Nation entrusted the lawmaking power to the Congress alone in both good and bad times. It would do no good to recall the historical events, the fears of power and the hopes for freedom that lay behind their choice. Such a review would but confirm our holding that this seizure order cannot stand.

Affirmed.†

---

† The decision was 6 to 3. Though all but one of the concurring Justices— Justice Clark—joined the opinion as well as the judgment announced by Justice Black, the separate opinions included important variations on Justice Black's theme.

Mr. Justice FRANKFURTER [concurring].

Although the considerations relevant to the legal enforcement of the principle of separation of powers seem to me more complicated and flexible than may appear from what Mr. Justice Black has written, I join his opinion because I thoroughly agree with the application of the principle to the circumstances of this case. . . .

[The Framers] rested the structure of our central government on the system of checks and balances. For them the doctrine of separation of powers was not mere theory; it was a felt necessity. Not so long ago it was fashionable to find our system of checks and balances obstructive to effective government. It was easy to ridicule that system as outmoded—too easy. The experience through which the world has passed in our own day has made vivid the realization that the Framers of our Constitution were not inexperienced doctrinaires. . . .

The issue before us can be met, and therefore should be, without attempting to define the President's powers comprehensively. I shall not attempt to delineate what belongs to him by virtue of his office beyond the power even of Congress to contract; what authority belongs to him until Congress acts; what kind of problems may be dealt with either by the Congress or by the President or by both; what power must be exercised by the Congress and cannot be delegated to the President. . . .

It cannot be contended that the President would have had power to issue this order had Congress explicitly negated such authority in formal legislation. Congress has expressed its will to withhold this power from the President as though it had said so in so many words. . . .

. . . The powers of the President are not as particularized as are those of Congress. But unenumerated powers do not mean undefined powers. The separation of powers built into our Constitution gives essential content to undefined provisions in the frame of our government.

To be sure, the content of the three authorities of government is not to be derived from an abstract analysis. The areas are partly interacting, not wholly disjointed. The Constitution is a framework for government. Therefore the way the framework has consistently operated fairly establishes that it has operated according to its true nature. Deeply embedded traditional ways of conducting government cannot supplant the Constitution or legislation, but they give meaning to the words of a text or supply them. It is an inadmissibly narrow conception of American constitutional law to confine it to the words of the Constitution and to disregard the gloss which life has written upon them. In short, a systematic, unbroken, executive practice, long pursued to the knowledge of the Congress and never before questioned, engaged in by Presidents who have also sworn to uphold the Constitution, making as it were such exercise of power part of the structure of our government, may be treated as a gloss on "executive Power" vested in the President by § 1 of Art. II. . . .

Down to the World War II period, [the] record is barren of instances comparable to the one before us. Of twelve seizures by President Roosevelt prior to the enactment of the War Labor Disputes Act in June, 1943, three were sanctioned by existing law, and six others were effected after Congress, on December 8, 1941, had declared the existence of a state of war.

In this case, reliance on the powers that flow from declared war has been commendably disclaimed by the Solicitor General. Thus the list of executive assertions of the power of seizure in circumstances comparable to the present reduces to three in the six-month period from June to December of 1941. [I]t suffices to say that these three isolated instances do not add up, either in number, scope, duration or contemporaneous legal justification, to the kind of executive construction of the Constitution [necessary to justify the action here]. Nor do they come to us sanctioned by long-continued acquiescence of Congress giving decisive weight to a construction by the Executive of its powers. . . .

Mr. Justice DOUGLAS, concurring.

There can be no doubt that the emergency which caused the President to seize these steel plants was one that bore heavily on the country. But [the] fact that it was necessary that measures be taken to keep steel in production does not mean that the President, rather than the Congress, had the constitutional authority to act. . . . Legislative action may indeed often be cumbersome, time-consuming, and apparently inefficient. But as Mr. Justice Brandeis stated in his dissent in Myers v. United States, 272 U.S. 52, 293 [below]: "The doctrine of the separation of powers was adopted by the Convention of 1787, not to promote efficiency but to preclude the exercise of arbitrary power. The purpose was, not to avoid friction, but, by means of the inevitable friction incident to the distribution of the governmental powers among three departments to save the people from autocracy." We therefore cannot decide this case by determining which branch of government can deal most expeditiously with the present crisis. The answer must depend on the allocation of powers under the Constitution. . . .

. . . A determination that sanctions should be applied, that the hand of the law should be placed upon the parties, and that the force of the courts should be directed against them, is an exercise of legislative power. . . . The legislative nature of the action taken by the President seems to me to be clear. . . . The seizure of the plant is a taking in the constitutional sense. [But under the Fifth Amendment], there is a duty to pay for all property taken by the Government. . . . The President has no power to raise revenues. . . . The branch of government that has the power to pay compensation for a seizure is the only one able to authorize a seizure or make lawful one that the President has effected. That seems to me to be the necessary result of the condemnation provision in the Fifth Amendment. It squares with the theory of checks and balances expounded by Mr. Justice Black in the opinion of the Court in which I join. . . .

Mr. Justice JACKSON, concurring in the judgment and opinion of the Court. . . .

A judge, like an executive advisor, may be surprised at the poverty of really useful and unambiguous authority applicable to concrete problems of executive power as they actually present themselves. Just what our forefathers did envision, or would have envisioned had they foreseen modern conditions, must be divined from materials almost as enigmatic as the dreams Joseph was called upon to interpret for Pharaoh. A century and a half of partisan debate and scholarly speculation yields no net result but only sup-

plies more or less apt quotations from respected resources on each side of any question. They largely cancel each other. And court decisions are indecisive because of the judicial practice of dealing with the largest questions in the most narrow way.

The actual art of governing under our Constitution does not and cannot conform to judicial definitions of the power of any of its branches based on isolated clauses or even single Articles torn from context. While the Constitution diffuses power the better to secure liberty, it also contemplates that practice will integrate the dispersed powers into a workable government. It enjoins upon its branches separateness but interdependence, autonomy but reciprocity. Presidential powers are not fixed but fluctuate, depending upon their disjunction or conjunction with those of Congress. We may well begin by a somewhat over-simplified grouping of practical situations in which a President may doubt, or others may challenge, his powers, and by distinguishing roughly the legal consequences of this factor of relativity.

1. When the President acts pursuant to an express or implied authorization of Congress, his authority is at its maximum, for it includes all that he possesses in his own right plus all that Congress can delegate.[1] In these circumstances, and in these only, may he be said (for what it may be worth) to personify the federal sovereignty. If his act is held unconstitutional under these circumstances, it usually means that the Federal Government as an undivided whole lacks power. A seizure executed by the President pursuant to an Act of Congress would be supported by the strongest of presumptions and the widest latitude of judicial interpretation, and the burden of persuasion would rest heavily upon any who might attack it.

2. When the President acts in absence of either a congressional grant or denial of authority, he can only rely upon his own independent powers, but there is a zone of twilight in which he and Congress may have concurrent authority, or in which its distribution is uncertain. Therefore, congressional inertia, indifference or quiescence may sometimes, at least as a practical matter, enable, if not invite, measures on independent presidential responsibility. In this area, any actual test of power is likely to depend on the imperatives of events and contemporary imponderables rather than on abstract theories of law.[2]

---

1. It is in this class of cases that we find the broadest recent statements of presidential power, including those relied on here. United States v. Curtiss-Wright Corp., 299 U.S. 304 (below), involved, not the question of the President's power to act without congressional authority, but the question of his right to act under and in accord with an Act of Congress. The constitutionality of the Act under which the President had proceeded was assailed on the ground that it delegated legislative powers to the President. Much of the Court's opinion is dictum . . . .
That case does not solve the present controversy. It recognized internal and external affairs as being in separate categories, and held that the strict limitation upon congressional delegations of power to the President over internal affairs does not apply with respect to delegations of power in external affairs. It was intimated that the President might act in external affairs without congressional authority, but not that he might act contrary to an Act of Congress. . . . [Footnote by Justice Jackson.]

2. Since the Constitution implies that the writ of habeas corpus may be suspended in certain circumstances but does not say by whom, President Lincoln asserted and maintained it as an

3. When the President takes measures incompatible with the expressed or implied will of Congress, his power is at its lowest ebb, for then he can rely only upon his own constitutional powers minus any constitutional powers of Congress over the matter. Courts can sustain exclusive presidential control in such a case only by disabling the Congress from acting upon the subject.[3] Presidential claim to a power at once so conclusive and preclusive must be scrutinized with caution, for what is at stake is the equilibrium established by our constitutional system.

Into which of these classifications does this executive seizure of the steel industry fit? It is eliminated from the first by admission, for it is conceded that no congressional authorization exists for this seizure. That takes away also the support of the many precedents and declarations which were made in relation, and must be confined, to this category. Can it then be defended under flexible tests available to the second category? It seems clearly eliminated from that class because Congress has not left seizure of private property an open field but has covered it by three statutory policies inconsistent with this seizure. . . .

This leaves the current seizure to be justified only by the severe tests under the third grouping, where it can be supported only by any remainder of executive power after subtraction of such powers as Congress may have over the subject. In short, we can sustain the President only by holding that seizure of such strike-bound industries is within his domain and beyond control by Congress. . . .

[H]istory [does not leave] it open to question, at least in the courts, that the executive branch, like the Federal Government as a whole, possesses only delegated powers. [But] because the President does not enjoy unmentioned powers does not mean that the mentioned ones should be narrowed by a niggardly construction. [I give] to the enumerated powers the scope and elasticity afforded by what seem to be reasonable, practical implications instead of the rigidity dictated by a doctrinaire textualism.

The Solicitor General seeks the power of seizure in three clauses of the Executive Article, the first reading, "The executive Power shall be vested in a President of the United States of America." Lest I be thought to exaggerate, I quote the interpretation which his brief puts upon it: "In our view, this clause constitutes a grant of all the executive powers of which the Government is capable." If that be true, it is difficult to see why the forefathers bothered to add several specific items, including some trifling ones.[4] . . .

executive function in the face of judicial challenge and doubt. Ex parte Merryman, 17 Fed.Cas. 144; Ex parte Milligan, 4 Wall. 2, 125 . . . . Congress eventually ratified his action. Habeas Corpus Act of March 3, 1863. . . . [Footnote by Justice Jackson.]

3. President Roosevelt's effort to remove a Federal Trade Commissioner was found to be contrary to the policy of Congress and impinging upon an area of congressional control, and so his removal power was cut down accordingly. Humphrey's Executor v. United States, 295 U.S. 602 (below). However, his exclusive power of removal in executive agencies, affirmed in Myers v. United States, 272 U.S. 52 (below), continued to be asserted and maintained. Morgan v. Tennessee Valley Authority, 115 F.2d 990, cert. denied 312 U.S. 701 . . . . [Footnote by Justice Jackson.]

4. ". . . he may require the Opinion, in writing, of the principal Officer in each of the executive Departments, upon any Subject relating to the Duties of their respective Offices . . . ." U.S.Const., Art. II, § 2.

I cannot accept the view that this clause is a grant in bulk of all conceivable executive power but regard it as an allocation to the presidential office of the generic powers thereafter stated.

The clause on which the Government next relies is that "The President shall be Commander in Chief of the Army and Navy of the United States . . . ." These cryptic words have given rise to some of the most persistent controversies in our constitutional history. Of course, they imply something more than an empty title. But just what authority goes with the name has plagued Presidential advisers who would not waive or narrow it by nonassertion yet cannot say where it begins or ends. It undoubtedly puts the Nation's armed forces under Presidential command. Hence, this loose appellation is sometimes advanced as support for any presidential action, internal or external, involving use of force, the idea being that it vests power to do anything, anywhere, that can be done with an army or navy.

That seems to be the logic of an argument tendered at our bar—that the President having, on his own responsibility, sent American troops abroad derives from that act "affirmative power" to seize the means of producing a supply of steel for them. [N]o doctrine that the Court could promulgate would seem to me more sinister and alarming than that a President whose conduct of foreign affairs is so largely uncontrolled, and often even is unknown, can vastly enlarge his mastery over the internal affairs of the country by his own commitment of the Nation's armed forces to some foreign venture. I do not, however, find it necessary or appropriate to consider the legal status of the Korean enterprise to discountenance argument based on it.

Assuming that we are in a war *de facto*, whether it is or is not a war *de jure*, does that empower the Commander-in-Chief to seize industries he thinks necessary to supply our army? The Constitution expressly places in Congress power "to raise and *support* Armies" and "to *provide* and *maintain* a Navy." (Emphasis supplied.) This certainly lays upon Congress primary responsibility for supplying the armed forces. Congress alone controls the raising of revenues and their appropriation and may determine in what manner and by what means they shall be spent for military and naval procurement. I suppose no one would doubt that Congress can take over war supply as a Government enterprise. . . .

There are indications that the Constitution did not contemplate that the title Commander in Chief *of the Army and Navy* will constitute him also Commander in Chief of the country, its industries and its inhabitants. He has no monopoly of "war powers," whatever they are. While Congress cannot deprive the President of the command of the army and navy, only Congress can provide him an army or navy to command. It is also empowered to make rules for the "Government and Regulation of land and naval Forces," by which it may to some unknown extent impinge upon even command functions.

That military powers of the Commander in Chief were not to supersede representative government of internal affairs seems obvious from the Constitution and from elementary American history. . . . We should

He ". . . shall Commission all the Officers of the United States." U. S.Const., Art. II, § 3. Matters such as those would seem to be inherent in the Executive if anything is. [Footnote by Justice Jackson.]

not use this occasion to circumscribe, much less to contract, the lawful role of the President as Commander in Chief. I should indulge the widest latitude of interpretation to sustain his exclusive function to command the instruments of national force, at least when turned against the outside world for the security of our society. But, when it is turned inward, not because of rebellion but because of a lawful economic struggle between industry and labor, it should have no such indulgence. . . . .

The third clause in which the Solicitor General finds seizure powers is that "he shall take Care that the Laws be faithfully executed . . . . ." That authority must be matched against words of the Fifth Amendment that "No person shall be . . . deprived of life, liberty or property, without due process of law . . . . ." One gives a governmental authority that reaches so far as there is law, the other gives a private right that authority shall go no farther. These signify about all there is of the principle that ours is a government of laws, not of men, and that we submit ourselves to rulers only if under rules.

The Solicitor General lastly grounds support of the seizure upon nebulous, inherent powers never expressly granted but said to have accrued to the office from the customs and claims of preceding administrations. The plea is for a resulting power to deal with a crisis or an emergency according to the necessities of the case, the unarticulated assumption being that necessity knows no law.

Loose and irresponsible use of adjectives colors all nonlegal and much legal discussion of presidential powers. "Inherent" powers, "implied" powers, "incidental" powers, "plenary" powers, "war" powers and "emergency" powers are used, often interchangeably and without fixed or ascertainable meanings.

The vagueness and generality of the clauses that set forth presidential powers afford a plausible basis for pressures within and without an administration for presidential action beyond that supported by those whose responsibility it is to defend his actions in court. The claim of inherent and unrestricted presidential powers has long been a persuasive dialectical weapon in political controversy. While it is not surprising that counsel should grasp support from such unadjudicated claims of power, a judge cannot accept self-serving press statements of the attorney for one of the interested parties as authority in answering a constitutional question, even if the advocate was himself. But prudence has counseled that actual reliance on such nebulous claims stop short of provoking a judicial test. . . .

In view of the ease, expedition and safety with which Congress can grant and has granted large emergency powers, certainly ample to embrace this crisis, I am quite unimpressed with the argument that we should affirm possession of them without statute. Such power either has no beginning or it has no end. If it exists, it need submit to no legal restraint. I am not alarmed that it would plunge us straightway into dictatorship, but it is at least a step in that wrong direction. . . .

Executive power has the advantage of concentration in a single head in whose choice the whole Nation has a part, making him the focus of public hopes and expectations. . . . Moreover, rise of the party system has made a significant extraconstitutional supplement to real executive power.

. . . I cannot be brought to believe that this country will suffer if the Court refuses further to aggrandize the presidential office, already so potent and so relatively immune from judicial review, at the expense of Congress.

But I have no illusion that any decision by this Court can keep power in the hands of Congress if it is not wise and timely in meeting its problems. A crisis that challenges the President equally, or perhaps primarily, challenges Congress. If not good law, there was worldly wisdom in the maxim attributed to Napoleon that "The tools belong to the man who can use them." We may say that power to legislate for emergencies belongs in the hands of Congress, but only Congress itself can prevent power from slipping through its fingers. . . .

Mr. Justice BURTON, concurring in both the opinion and judgment of the Court. . . .

The controlling fact here is that Congress, within its constitutionally delegated power, has prescribed for the President specific procedures, exclusive of seizure, for his use in meeting the present type of emergency. . . . Under these circumstances, the President's order of April 8 invaded the jurisdiction of Congress. . . .

Mr. Justice CLARK, concurring in the judgment of the Court. . . .

I conclude that where Congress has laid down specific procedures to deal with the type of crisis confronting the President, he must follow those procedures in meeting the crisis; but that in the absence of such action by Congress, the President's independent power to act depends upon the gravity of the situation confronting the nation. I cannot sustain the seizure in question because [here] Congress had prescribed methods to be followed by the President in meeting the emergency at hand. . . .

Mr. Chief Justice VINSON, with whom Mr. Justice REED and Mr. Justice MINTON join, dissenting. . . .

One is not here called upon even to consider the possibility of executive seizure of a farm, a corner grocery store or even a single industrial plant. Such considerations arise only when one ignores the central fact of this case—that the Nation's entire basic steel production would have shut down completely if there had been no Government seizure. . . . Accordingly, if the President has any power under the Constitution to meet a critical situation in the absence of express statutory authorization, there is no basis whatever for criticizing the exercise of such power in this case. . . .

. . . [W]e are not called upon today to expand the Constitution to meet a new situation. For, in this case, we need only look to history and time-honored principles of constitutional law—principles that have been applied consistently by all branches of the Government throughout our history. It is those who assert the invalidity of the Executive Order who seek to amend the Constitution in this case.

A review of executive action demonstrates that our Presidents have on many occasions exhibited the leadership contemplated by the Framers when they made the President Commander in Chief, and imposed upon him the trust to "take Care that the Laws be faithfully executed." With or without explicit statutory authorization, Presidents have at such times dealt with na-

tional emergencies by acting promptly and resolutely to enforce legislative programs, at least to save those programs until Congress could act. Congress and the courts have responded to such executive initiative with consistent approval.

Our first President displayed at once the leadership contemplated by the Framers. When the national revenue laws were openly flouted in some sections of Pennsylvania, President Washington, without waiting for a call from the state government, summoned the militia and took decisive steps to secure the faithful execution of the laws. When international disputes engendered by the French revolution threatened to involve this country in war, and while congressional policy remained uncertain, Washington issued his Proclamation of Neutrality. . . .

Jefferson's initiative in the Louisiana Purchase, the Monroe Doctrine, and Jackson's removal of Government deposits from the Bank of the United States further serve to demonstrate by deed what the Framers described by word when they vested the whole of the executive power in the President.

Without declaration of war, President Lincoln took energetic action with the outbreak of the [Civil War]. He summoned troops and paid them out of the Treasury without appropriation therefor. He proclaimed a naval blockade of the Confederacy and seized ships violating that blockade. Congress, far from denying the validity of these acts, gave them express approval. The most striking action of President Lincoln was the Emancipation Proclamation, issued in aid of the successful prosecution of the [Civil War], but wholly without statutory authority.

In an action furnishing a most apt precedent for this case, President Lincoln without statutory authority directed the seizure of rail and telegraph lines leading to Washington. Many months later, Congress recognized and confirmed the power of the President to seize railroads and telegraph lines and provided criminal penalties for interference with Government operation.
.   .   .

In In re Neagle, 135 U.S. 1 (1890), this Court held that a federal officer had acted in line of duty when he was guarding a Justice of this Court riding circuit. It was conceded that there was no specific statute authorizing the President to assign such a guard. In holding that such a statute was not necessary, the Court broadly stated the question as follows:

"[The President] is enabled to fulfil the duty of his great department, expressed in the phrase that 'he shall take care that the laws be faithfully executed.' Is this duty limited to the enforcement of acts of Congress or of treaties of the United States according to their *express terms,* or does it include the rights, duties and obligations growing out of the Constitution itself, our international relations, and all the protection implied by the nature of the government under the Constitution?"

The latter approach was emphatically adopted by the Court.

President Hayes authorized the wide-spread use of federal troops during the Railroad Strike of 1877. President Cleveland also used the troops in the Pullman Strike of 1895 and his action is of special significance. No statute authorized this action. No call for help had issued from the Governor of Illinois; indeed Governor Altgeld disclaimed the need for supplemental forces.

But the President's concern was that federal laws relating to the free flow of interstate commerce and the mails be continuously and faithfully executed without interruption. To further this aim his agents sought and obtained the injunction upheld by this Court in In re Debs, 158 U.S. 564 (1895).
. . .

    Beginning with the Bank Holiday Proclamation and continuing through World War II, executive leadership and initiative were characteristic of President Franklin D. Roosevelt's administration. . . . Some six months before Pearl Harbor, a dispute at a single aviation plant at Inglewood, California, interrupted a segment of the production of military aircraft. . . . President Roosevelt ordered the seizure of the plant "pursuant to the powers vested in [him] by the Constitution and laws of the United States, as President of the United States of America and Commander in Chief of the Army and Navy of the United States." The Attorney General (Jackson) vigorously proclaimed that the President had the moral duty to keep this Nation's defense effort a "going concern." His ringing moral justification was coupled with a legal justification equally well stated: "The Presidential proclamation rests upon the aggregate of the Presidential powers derived from the Constitution itself and from statutes enacted by the Congress. . . ."

    [Before and after Pearl Harbor], industrial concerns were seized to avert interruption of needed production. During the same period, the President directed seizure of the Nation's coal mines to remove an obstruction to the effective prosecution of the war. . . . At the time of the seizure of the coal mines [a] bill to provide a statutory basis for seizures [was] before Congress. As stated by its sponsor, the purpose of the bill was not to augment Presidential power, but to "let the country know that the Congress is squarely behind the President." . . .

    This is but a cursory summary of executive leadership. But it amply demonstrates that Presidents have taken prompt action to enforce the laws and protect the country whether or not Congress happened to provide in advance for the particular method of execution. [T]he fact that Congress and the courts have consistently recognized and given their support to such executive action indicates that such a power of seizure has been accepted throughout our history. . . .

    Much of the argument in this case has been directed at straw men. We do not now have before us the case of a President acting solely on the basis of his own notions of the public welfare. Nor is there any question of unlimited executive power in this case. The President himself closed the door to any such claim when he sent his Message to Congress stating his purpose to abide by any action of Congress, whether approving or disapproving his seizure action. Here, the President immediately made sure that Congress was fully informed of the temporary action he had taken only to preserve the legislative programs from destruction until Congress could act.

    The absence of a specific statute authorizing seizure of the steel mills as a mode of executing the laws—both the military procurement program and the anti-inflation program—has not until today been thought to prevent the President from executing the laws. Unlike an administrative commis-

sion confined to the enforcement of the statute under which it was created, or the head of a department when administering a particular statute, the President is a constitutional officer charged with taking care that a "mass of legislation" be executed. Flexibility as to mode of execution to meet critical situations is a matter of practical necessity. . . .

In this case, there is no statute prohibiting the action taken by the President in a matter not merely important but threatening the very safety of the Nation. Executive inaction in such a situation, courting national disaster, is foreign to the concept of energy and initiative in the Executive as created by the Founding Fathers. . . .

The broad executive power granted by Article II to an officer on duty 365 days a year cannot, it is said, be invoked to avert disaster. Instead, the President must confine himself to sending a message to Congress recommending action. Under this messenger-boy concept of the Office, the President cannot even act to preserve legislative programs from destruction so that Congress will have something left to act upon. . . .

THE STEEL SEIZURE CASE AND THE JACKSON ANALYSIS

1. *Dicta and holding.* Does Justice Black recognize *any* "emergency powers" of the President? Does the majority of the Court? Is Justice Black's opinion unduly broad? Is the problem "more complicated," as Justice Frankfurter suggests? What holding does the majority truly agree upon? Does it go beyond the third category described by Justice Jackson? Does the case stand for any principle other than that the President may not establish domestic policy "incompatible with the expressed or implied will of Congress"? Do the broader statements in Justice Black's opinion suggest that the Court was unwise to speak about the merits? Should the Court have delayed the decision for longer than the three weeks between argument and decision in this case?*

2. *The broad statements: Provocation and impact.* Were Justice Black's broad statements provoked by the broad arguments of the Government? In addition to the Government's contentions noted above, note the arguments in the District Court hearing, printed in Westin, The Anatomy of a Constitutional Law Case (1958), 56–65. For example, note the exchange between District Judge Pine and Assistant Attorney General Baldridge, id. at 64: *"The Court:* So [the Constitution] limited the powers of the Congress and limited the powers of the judiciary, but did not limit the powers of the Executive. Is that what you say? *Mr. Baldridge:* That is the way we read Article II of the Constitution. *The Court:* I see . . . ." A few days after the argument, President Truman issued a statement: "The powers of the President are derived from the Constitution, and they are

---

* For a sampling of the extensive commentary provoked by the case, see Kauper, "The Steel Seizure Case: Congress, the President, and the Supreme Court," 51 Mich.L.Rev. 141 (1952), Selected Essays 1938–62 (1963), 129, and Corwin, "The Steel Seizure Case: A Judicial Brick Without Straw," 53 Colum.L.Rev. 53 (1953).

limited, of course, by the provisions of the Constitution." Moreover, the Government submitted a supplemental brief in the District Court because of the "misunderstandings which may have arisen during the course of the oral argument." For President Truman's subsequent reflections, see Truman, II Memoirs: Years of Trial and Hope (1956), 475–78, concluding: "Whatever the six justices of the Supreme Court meant by their differing opinions, [the President] must always act in a national emergency."

3. *The Jackson distinctions and their applicability.* a. *Domestic affairs.* Does Justice Jackson's distinction among three types of situations provide a useful general framework for the analysis of presidential power problems? To what extent do the other opinions accept that framework? To what extent do the various opinions accept Justice Frankfurter's view that unquestioned and continuous "executive practice" "may be treated as a gloss on 'Executive power'" granted by Art. II? How persuasive should such "practice" be in constitutional interpretation? How persuasive was the evidence of historical practice relied on by the Justices in the Steel Seizure Case?

Justice Jackson's first category—presidential action pursuant to congressional authority—refers to the most common variety of executive action. Justice Jackson's second category—presidential action in the context of congressional silence—presents greater difficulty. Justice Jackson suggests "a zone of twilight" in which President and Congress "may have concurrent authority." Congressional authority in that zone typically stems from Art. I, § 8, powers. But what is the source of executive power in that twilight zone? Is it in any event a presidential authority subject to being overridden by congressional action? Are there any situations in the domestic sphere which fall within Justice Jackson's third category: a presidential power to act even in the face of contrary congressional directions? Are any such powers granted by Art. II? Note, e. g., the controversy over the power to impound funds, in the next group of notes.†

b. *External affairs.* Can Justice Jackson's tripartite distinction be applied outside the domestic sphere? Did Justice Jackson have doubts about its applicability to the conduct of foreign relations and to the use of military forces? Are there more explicit constitutional grants of autonomous presidential authority as to external affairs? See the materials in sec. 1B below. Note especially the controversy over the War Powers Resolution of 1973, a congressional effort to delineate guidelines for the use of armed forces in

† For an example of an analysis akin to that of Justice Jackson, note the Pentagon Papers case, New York Times Co. v. United States, 403 U.S. 713 (1971), chap. 13 below. In finding no governmental authority to enjoin newspapers from further publication of the Pentagon Papers, the majority relied not only on First Amendment principles. Several of the Justices emphasized separation of powers. See especially the opinions of Justices Stewart, White and Marshall. Justice Marshall, for example, stated: "The Constitution provides that Congress shall make laws, the President execute laws, and courts interpret law. [Youngstown Sheet & Tube Co. v. Sawyer.] It did not provide for government by injunction in which the courts and the Executive can 'make law' without regard to the action of Congress." Analogously to the Steel Seizure Case, Justice Marshall and others emphasized that on "at least two occasions Congress has refused to enact legislation that would have made the conduct engaged in here unlawful and given the President the power that he seeks in this case."

hostilities. Is that Resolution an exercise of congressional authority in Justice Jackson's second category—a congressional effort to speak where there had been congressional silence in "a zone of twilight"? Or is it an exercise of congressional power in Justice Jackson's third category—a legislative-executive confrontation requiring determination whether congressional action improperly treads upon autonomous executive power?

THE IMPOUNDMENT CONTROVERSY: PRESIDENTIAL CLAIMS AND CONGRESSIONAL GUIDELINES

Introduction. Does the President have inherent constitutional power to refuse to spend funds appropriated by Congress? A claimed executive authority to impound was one of the executive-legislative conflicts which reached new levels of intensity and scope in the 1970's. The "power of the purse" is traditionally associated with Congress and is reflected in several provisions of Art. I. Yet Presidents have repeatedly refused to spend money appropriated by Congress. Most of those refusals rested on express or implied grants of executive discretion in the legislation. Exercise of executive power in that situation, then, readily falls within the first of Justice Jackson's three categories in the Steel Seizure case. Early in President Nixon's second term, in the face of mounting legislative criticism and court challenges to executive impoundment, the President turned to constitutional justifications, asserting an inherent discretion to impound even in the face of a mandatory spending directive from Congress. President Nixon stated the new position in a press conference on January 31, 1973. He claimed that there was an "absolutely clear" "constitutional right" of the President to "impound" funds when the spending "would mean either increasing prices or increasing taxes for all the people." [1] That position moved the impoundment controversy from one in Justice Jackson's first category to one in his third category.

1. *The Impounding Control Act of 1974.* Increasingly broad executive claims were matched by increasingly firm proposals for congressional countermeasures. Efforts initiated by Senator Ervin ultimately culminated in the enactment, in June, 1974, of the Congressional Budget and Impounding Control Act of 1974.[2] That Act—like the War Powers Resolution of 1973, sec. 1B below—represents congressional action of an unusual and especially important nature. Instead of congressional directives regarding substantive governmental policies, it delineates structures and processes. It is legislation that can be viewed as quasi-constitutional in nature, for it seeks to clarify and define basic relationships among the branches of government.

---

1. Note also a statement by President Nixon in vetoing legislation mandating the spending of certain funds the President had previously impounded: a veto of April 5, 1973, relied on an opinion by Attorney General Kleindienst, stating that the congressional attempt to reverse the impoundment was an unconstitutional interference "with the allocation of executive power to the President made by Article II of the Constitution."

2. P.L. 93–344, 88 Stat. 297, 31 U.S.C. § 1301 et seq. President Nixon signed the Act on July 12, 1974, while impeachment proceedings against him were pending. Senator Ervin called the Act "one of the most important pieces of legislation Congress has ever considered." And in signing it, President Nixon stated: "This bill is the most significant reform of budget procedures since Congress began."

The 1974 Act attempts to impose substantial restraints on presidential authority to impound, requiring legislative approval of executive decisions to end or reduce programs for which funds are authorized. The Act distinguishes between two types of impoundment. Where the President proposes simply to *defer* the expenditure of appropriated funds, the initiative to curb falls on Congress: either house may disapprove the deferral by adopting a simple resolution. But for proposed presidential impoundments that *terminate* programs or cut total spending, explicit congressional authorization is necessary: the Act permits such impoundments only if Congress enacts new legislation rescinding the previous appropriation. If Congress fails to adopt such a rescission measure within 45 days, the President must spend the money. To enable Congress to exercise these controls, the Act requires the President to report all impoundment actions. The Comptroller General is obligated to report to Congress any impoundments made without presidential reports, and he is also empowered to bring civil suits to enforce the Act's impoundment provisions.

The 1974 Act is not limited to curbing presidential authority, however. It also includes important affirmative measures to increase the capability of Congress to make comprehensive judgments on budget matters. That reinvigoration of the congressional budget role is of special importance in view of one of the arguments occasionally urged by Nixon Administration defenders of inherent executive impoundment authority. The claim was that Congress was institutionally incapable of making comprehensive judgments in view of the fragmented manner in which Congress had typically reacted to specific items in executive budgets, as a result of the compartmentalized committee structure in Congress, lacking centralized guidance and coordination. Under the 1974 Act, however, new budget committees were established in each house to prepare tentative budget recommendations to be adopted as concurrent resolutions in May. A Congressional Budget Office was created to give Congress the kind of staff assistance and coordinating capacity that the President had long received from the Office of Management and Budget. Other congressional committees are to be guided by the targets established in the concurrent resolutions. The Act requires that committee actions on spending bills ordinarily be completed by early September; at that time, Congress is to take another overall look at budget problems and may pass a second concurrent resolution adjusting the targets established earlier.[3]

2. *Constitutional problems?* Do the impoundment control provisions of the 1974 Act raise any constitutional problems? As applied to domestic spending programs? As applied to foreign programs—cf. sec. 1B below? Can any plausible constitutional arguments be made that executive discretion to impound is an inherent power untouchable by Congress? Does the congressional spending power in Art. I, § 8, resolve any conflicts in favor of the legislative branch, in the situations in Justice Jackson's third category?

In the only modern impoundment case to reach the Supreme Court, a unanimous Court rejected the Government's argument that Congress intended to grant wide discretion to the Executive to control the rate of spending

---

3. To accommodate the new procedures, the Act shifts the beginning of the fiscal year from July 1 to October 1.

under the Federal Water Pollution Control Act Amendments of 1972. Train v. City of New York, 420 U.S. —— (1975). The impoundment in that case occurred before the adoption of the 1974 Impoundment Act; the Executive based its claim of discretionary power entirely on the statute and did not rely on inherent constitutional authority. In the lower federal courts in the years immediately preceding the adoption of the 1974 Act, most executive claims did not fare well. For a rejection of a rare claim of executive discretion under the Constitution, see Local 2677 v. Phillips, 358 F.Supp. 60 (D.D.C. 1973).[4]

The constititutional arguments regarding inherent executive impoundment authority have been aired at length in recent congressional hearings, however.[5] Note especially Deputy Attorney General Sneed's remarks early in 1973, while proposed congressional restraints on impoundment were under consideration, claiming that a "mandatory spending statute" would "raise substantial constitutional questions." He claimed that there was "doubt whether Congress could legislate against impoundment even in the domestic area when to do so results in substantially increasing the rate of inflation." He elaborated: "To admit the existence of such power deprives the President of a substantial portion of the 'executive power' vested in him by the Constitution . . . . The President, as part of his executive power, has a duty to administer the national budget which, in turn, inescapably imposes on him a heavy responsibility to avoid fiscal instability. . . . I question whether Congress has the power to convert the Chief Executive into a 'Chief Clerk.'"[6]

---

4. More commonly, the impoundment claims rejected in the lower courts rested solely on statutory grounds. See, e. g., State Highway Commission v. Volpe, 347 F.Supp. 950 (W.D.Mo. 1972), aff'd, 479 F.2d 1099 (8th Cir. 1973). See generally Note, "Presidential Impoundment: Constitutional Theories and Political Realities," 61 Georgetown L.J. 1295 (1973), and Note, "Impoundment of Funds," 86 Harv.L. Rev. 1505 (1973). See also Mikva and Hertz, "Impoundment of Funds—The Courts, the Congress and the President: A Constitutional Triangle," 69 Northwestern L.Rev. 335 (1974).

5. See especially Joint Hearings Before the Senate Ad Hoc Subcommittee on Impoundment of Funds of the Committee on Government Operations and the Subcommittee on the Separation of Powers of the Committee of the Judiciary on S. 373, 93d Cong., 1st Sess. (1973), and Hearings on the Executive Impoundment of Appropriated Funds Before the Subcommittee on Separation of Powers of the Senate Committee on the Judiciary, 92d Cong., 1st Sess. 279 (1971).

6. Deputy Attorney General (now Judge) Sneed thought that Kendall v. United States, 12 Pet. 524 (1838), was "distinguishable in several respects." In Kendall, the Court sustained jurisdiction to compel the Postmaster General to pay a government contractor monies appropriated by Congress. The Court rejected the defense based on the Executive's constitutional discretion: "To contend that the obligation imposed on the President to see the laws safely executed, implies a power to forbid their execution, is a novel construction of the Constitution, and entirely inadmissible." Mr. Sneed's response emphasized that Kendall involved "ministerial" rather than "discretionary" executive action. And he argued that the modern context was different from Kendall's day: "Today's context is one in which the powers of Congress and the President must be accommodated to the inexorable necessities of national fiscal policy. Expenditures must be linked to taxes in a manner that avoids ruinous inflation. If Congress insists on raising expenditures without raising taxes, the President must serve the commitment [to restrain inflation] by impounding."

Mr. Sneed added: "Constitutional questions under the bill would perhaps be greatest in the areas of national defense and foreign relations. [There], the President's constitutional powers and responsibilities find their source not only in his duty to take care that the laws shall be faithfully executed, but also in his powers and responsibilities derived from his express status as Commander-in-Chief of the Nation's Armed Forces, and as the sole organ of the Nation and of its foreign affairs. I do not believe that Congress is constitutionally empowered in those areas to compel the President to spend willy-nilly." Emphasizing the President's "broad constitutional authority in the field of foreign affairs" and citing the Curtiss-Wright case, sec. 1B below, he stated: "In those areas, Congressional directives to spend may intrude impermissibly into matters reserved by the Constitution for the President. It is noteworthy that Congress has never successfully challenged an impounding action in the foreign relations and national defense fields."

Compare an executive position more typical in earlier years, expressed by Assistant Attorney General Rehnquist in a memorandum in December, 1969: "With respect to the suggestion that the President has a constitutional power to decline to spend appropriated funds, we must conclude that existence of such a broad power is supported by neither reason nor precedent. . . . It is in our view extremely difficult to formulate a constitutional theory to justify a refusal by the President to comply with a Congressional directive to spend. It may be argued that the spending of money is inherently an executive function, but the execution of any law is, by definition, an executive function, and it seems an anomalous proposition that because the Executive branch is bound to execute the laws, it is free to decline to execute them. Of course, if the Congressional directives to spend would interfere with the President's authority in any area confided by the Constitution to his substantive direction and control, such as his authority as Commander-in-Chief of the Armed Forces and his authority over foreign affairs [Curtiss-Wright], a situation would be presented very different from the one before us. But the President has no mandate under the Constitution to determine national policy on assistance to education independent from his duty to execute such laws on the subject as Congress chooses to pass." [7]

---

7. Assistant Attorney General Rehnquist thought Kendall v. United States to be an "authority against the asserted Presidential power." Mr. Rehnquist also took note of the argument that the President's "duty to take care that the laws be faithfully executed" might justify refusals to spend, "in the interest of preserving the fiscal integrity of the government or the stability of the economy." He found some weight in that argument "in a situation in which the President is faced with conflicting statutory demands." But the conflict would have to be "real and imminent for this argument to have validity; it would not be enough that the President disagreed with spending priorities established by Congress." [Compare the Sneed position, at footnote 6. The Sneed statement is from the 1973 Hearings cited above. The 1969 Rehnquist position—Memorandum re Presidential Authority to Impound Funds Appropriated for Assistance to Federally Impacted Schools—is reprinted in those Hearings; it also appears in the 1971 Hearings cited above.]

B. FOREIGN AFFAIRS AND USE OF ARMED FORCES

Introduction. Are the limits on presidential policy-making authority in the domestic sphere, considered in sec. 1A, substantially attenuated when the context is international affairs and the use of armed forces? Is the inherent executive power denied by the Steel Seizure Case available to the President when the action is external rather than domestic? What are the President's powers as Chief Executive and "Commander in Chief"? Curtiss-Wright, which follows, contains broad statements about the special responsibility of the President in foreign relations. Does that special role include any constitutional authority other than the specific functions allocated in Art. II, and in addition to powers granted by Congress?

These questions, suggested by the Curtiss-Wright opinion, introduce the problems of executive-legislative competition in the materials that follow. Does the President have autonomous authority to make foreign policy via executive agreements and thereby bypass the treaty route in which the Senate participates? Concern about executive agreements was one of the fears that fueled the Bricker Amendment campaign in the 1950's. More recently, warnings of risks of congressional subservience to the President have come from different sources: many of those who deprecated the anxieties of Bricker Amendment proponents demanded, in the context of the Vietnam controversy, that Congress assert greater control.

The Vietnam debate also attracted special attention to the President's authority regarding the use of armed forces. Art. II designates the President as "Commander in Chief." Art. I grants Congress the authority to "declare War." To what extent do these powers conflict? How can they be accommodated? To what extent may military forces be used without a formal declaration of war? To what extent must and can Congress participate in the decisionmaking process? Constitutional questions such as these seldom come to the courts, though they were discussed in the Civil War Prize Cases, below. Growing congressional concern with these issues culminated in 1973 in the enactment of several measures to curtail presidential authority to commit American combat forces—commitments that had grown over the years, through executive practice and congressional acquiescence. Most importantly, the War Powers Resolution of 1973 seeks to delineate more explicit guidelines for presidential action and to assure greater participation by Congress. That Resolution was objected to by President Nixon on constitutional grounds. Do the efforts to restrain presidential authority in the War Powers Resolution (printed below) raise questions of unconstitutional interference with Art. II powers? The materials in this section are in a large part designed to provide background for consideration of that question.

UNITED STATES v. CURTISS–WRIGHT EXPORT CORP.

299 U.S. 304, 57 S.Ct. 216, 81 L.Ed. 255 (1936).

Appeal from the United States District Court for the Southern District of New York.

[A Joint Resolution of Congress in 1934 provided that "if the President finds that the prohibition of the sale of arms and munitions of war in the United States to those countries now engaged in armed conflict in the Chaco may contribute to the re-establishment of peace between those countries, and [if] he makes proclamation to that effect," then it shall be unlawful to make such a sale "except under such limitations and exceptions as the President prescribes." Penalties were prescribed. Appellee was indicted for conspiracy to sell arms to Bolivia—a country then engaged in armed conflict in the Chaco—in violation of the Joint Resolution and Proclamation. The District Court sustained appellee's demurrer on the ground that the Resolution contained an unconstitutional delegation of legislative power to the President.]

Mr. Justice SUTHERLAND delivered the opinion of the Court. . . .

Whether, if the Joint Resolution had related solely to internal affairs, it would be open to the challenge that it constituted an unlawful delegation of legislative power to the Executive, we find it unnecessary to determine. The whole aim of the resolution is to affect a situation entirely external to the United States, and falling within the category of foreign affairs. The determination which we are called to make, therefore, is whether the Joint Resolution, as applied to that situation, is vulnerable to attack under the rule that forbids a delegation of the law-making power. In other words, assuming (but not deciding) that the challenged delegation, if it were confined to internal affairs, would be invalid, may it nevertheless be sustained on the ground that its exclusive aim is to afford a remedy for a hurtful condition within foreign territory? [The Court first considered the differences between national powers regarding external and domestic affairs, "both in respect of their origin and their nature." Excerpts from those passages, asserting that national foreign affairs powers "did not depend upon the affirmative grants of the Constitution," are printed in chap. 4, sec. 3, above. The Court then turned to the special role of the President in the conduct of foreign affairs:]

Not only, as we have shown, is the federal power over external affairs in origin and essential character different from that over internal affairs, but participation in the exercise of the power is significantly limited. In this vast external realm, with its important, complicated, delicate and manifold problems, the President alone has the power to speak or listen as a representative of the nation. He *makes* treaties with the advice and consent of the Senate; but he alone negotiates. Into the field of negotiation the Senate cannot intrude; and Congress itself is powerless to invade it. As Marshall said in his great argument of March 7, 1800, in the House of Representatives, "The President is the sole organ of the nation in its external relations, and its sole representative with foreign nations." . . .

It is important to bear in mind that we are here dealing not alone with an authority vested in the President by an exertion of legislative power, but

with such an authority plus the very delicate, plenary and exclusive power of the President as the sole organ of the federal government in the field of international relations—a power which does not require as a basis for its exercise an act of Congress, but which, of course, like every other governmental power, must be exercised in subordination to the applicable provisions of the Constitution.   It is quite apparent that if, in the maintenance of our international relations, embarrassment—perhaps serious embarrassment—is to be avoided and success for our aims achieved, congressional legislation which is to be made effective through negotiation and inquiry within the international field must often accord to the President a degree of discretion and freedom from statutory restriction which would not be admissible were domestic affairs alone involved.   Moreover, he, not Congress, has the better opportunity of knowing the conditions which prevail in foreign countries, and especially is this true in time of war.   He has his confidential sources of information.   He has his agents in the form of diplomatic, consular and other officials.   Secrecy in respect of information gathered by them may be highly necessary, and the premature disclosure of it productive of harmful results. . . .

When the President is to be authorized by legislation to act in respect of a matter intended to affect a situation in foreign territory, the legislator properly bears in mind the important consideration that the form of the President's action—or, indeed, whether he shall act at all—may well depend, among other things, upon the nature of the confidential information which he has or may thereafter receive, or upon the effect which his action may have upon our foreign relations.   This consideration [discloses] the unwisdom of requiring Congress in this field of governmental power to lay down narrowly definite standards by which the President is to be governed. . . .

In the light of the foregoing observations, it is evident that this court should not be in haste to apply a general rule which will have the effect of condemning legislation like that under review as constituting an unlawful delegation of legislative power.   The principles which justify such legislation find overwhelming support in the unbroken legislative practice which has prevailed almost from the inception of the national government to the present day. . . .

. . . [B]oth upon principle and in accordance with precedent, we conclude there is sufficient warrant for the broad discretion vested in the President to determine whether the enforcement of the statute will have a beneficial effect upon the re-establishment of peace in the affected countries; whether he shall make proclamation to bring the resolution into operation; whether and when the resolution shall cease to operate and to make proclamation accordingly; and to prescribe limitations and exceptions to which the enforcement of the resolution shall be subject. . . .

Reversed.

Mr. Justice McREYNOLDS does not agree. . . .

SOME PROBLEMS SUGGESTED BY CURTISS–WRIGHT

1. *The special presidential role in foreign affairs.* As already noted in chap. 4, sec. 3B, the national government's power over foreign affairs, while widely recognized as broad, is largely based on historical and structural inferences rather than explicit constitutional delegations. And the contours of that national power remain uncertain in a number of respects, for adjudications are sparse and assertions and practices in political contexts are numerous and at times inconsistent. The Curtiss-Wright case has already been noted in chap. 4 for its broad readings of *national* foreign affairs authority. Some of Justice Sutherland's broad statements on that problem have been questioned. Is there also reason to question some of the Curtiss-Wright assertions about *presidential* authority?

a. *Justifications.* Even assuming a broad national authority has been established, uncertainty remains about the allocation of powers between President and Congress in the exercise of that authority. Did Curtiss-Wright contain excessively broad dicta not only about the extra-constitutional source of a national foreign affairs power, but also regarding the presidential predominance in external relations? Recall footnote 1 in Justice Jackson's opinion in the Steel Seizure case, noting, inter alia, that "[m]uch of the Court's opinion [in Curtiss-Wright] is dictum"; that Curtiss-Wright did not involve a question of presidential power to act in a twilight zone, without congressional authority (Justice Jackson's second category), "but the question of his right to act under and in accord with an Act of Congress"; and that, though Curtiss-Wright "intimated that the President might act in external affairs without Congressional authority," it did not state "that he might act contrary to an Act of Congress" (Justice Jackson's third category).

What external affairs power does the President have in the absence of congressional action? What may the President do in the face of congressional efforts to control executive actions? [1] In addition to the broad statements in Curtiss-Wright, note the comment in Chicago & Southern Airlines v. Waterman Steamship Corp., 333 U.S. 103 (1948), stating that the President, "both as Commander-in-Chief and as the Nation's organ for foreign affairs, has available intelligence services whose reports are not and ought not be published to the world." The Waterman case speaks largely to the undesirability of judicial review of some presidential decisions, a problem pursued further in sec. 2 below. It was relied on in Justice Harlan's dissent in the Pentagon Papers case, New York Times v. United States, 403 U.S. 713 (1971), chap. 13 below. Curtiss-Wright similarly noted the importance of "confidential information" to the President's conduct of foreign relations. How valid is that confidentiality concern with respect to, e. g., delineating the appropriate scope of executive privilege? See United States v. Nixon, the Watergate Tapes case, sec. 2 below.

b. *Presidential wiretapping.* What bearing should that special presidential role have on presidential authority to conduct foreign intelligence wiretapping without court order as an exercise of inherent authority? In

---

1. See, in addition to this note, the materials on executive agreements which follow and, generally, Henkin, Foreign Affairs and the Constitution (1972).

the Keith case, United States v. United States District Court, 407 U.S. 297 (1972), the Court, without dissent, rejected the executive's claim that warrantless electronic surveillance in domestic security cases was an inherent presidential authority. (The Court relied on First as well as Fourth Amendment principles.) But Justice Powell's opinion for the Court was carefully limited to "the domestic aspects of national security" and expressed no opinion on "the issues which may be involved with respect to activities of foreign powers or their agents." Is inherent executive power justifiable in the foreign intelligence area? Such an authority was sustained by a court of appeals in United States v. Brown, 484 F.2d 418 (5th Cir. 1973), citing the Waterman case and concluding that "because of the President's constitutional duty to act for the United States [in] the field of foreign relations, and his inherent power to protect national security in the context of foreign affairs, we reaffirm [that] the President may constitutionally authorize warrantless wiretaps for the purpose of gathering foreign intelligence." What if the problem arose in the context of Justice Jackson's third category in the Steel Seizure case: what if Congress sought specifically to curtail the claimed presidential authority in the foreign field? Is presidential power sufficiently strong and clear to supersede a contrary congressional directive?

2. *Delegation of legislative powers to the executive.* In its most immediate aspect, Curtiss-Wright is a case about delegation of legislative powers. Delegation problems involve not conflicts between President and Congress but, if anything, excessive harmony: the charge is not that Congress has usurped presidential powers but rather that Congress has sought to give to the executive too much of its own powers. Curtiss-Wright holds that limits on delegation of powers are less restrictive in the foreign affairs field than in the domestic area. What are those limits? How valid is the distinction between the two spheres?

a. *Domestic sphere.* In the domestic area, the Court had imposed substantial restraints on delegation of legislative powers in the years immediately preceding Curtiss-Wright. Recall Schechter Poultry Corp. v. United States, 295 U.S. 495 (1935), chap. 3 above, one of the controversial early New Deal cases, in which the Court had unanimously invalidated the provision of the National Industrial Recovery Act which authorized the President to approve "codes of fair competition." Even those Justices who in most New Deal cases took a generous view of the congressional commerce power objected here. (Recall that Justice Cardozo in Schechter commented: "This is delegation running riot.") See also Panama Ref. Co. v. Ryan, 293 U.S. 388 (1935), the "hot oil" case, striking down another provision of the NIRA as excessive delegation. But in subsequent cases of domestic economic regulation, the Court did not find the delegation barrier a substantial one. See, e. g., Yakus v. United States, 321 U.S. 414 (1944).

In recent years, however, approving references to Schechter's delegation point have occasionally surfaced in the opinions, to the surprise of some observers. In National Cable Television Ass'n v. United States, 415 U.S. 336 (1974), Justice Douglas' majority opinion construed the fee-setting authority of federal agencies narrowly to avoid constitutional problems of delegation. Justice Marshall's dissent, joined by Justice Brennan, thought the alleged constitutional problems "nonexistent": "The notion that the Con-

stitution narrowly confines the power of Congress to delegate authority to administrative agencies, which was briefly in vogue in the 1930's, has been virtually abandoned by the Court for all practical purposes, at least in the absence of a delegation creating 'the danger of overbroad, unauthorized, and arbitrary application of criminal sanctions in the area of [constitutionally] protected freedoms.' This doctrine is surely as moribund as the substantive due process approach of the same era—for which the Court is fond of writing an obituary [see chap. 9 below]—if not more so. It is hardly surprising that, until today's decision, the Court has not relied upon [Schechter] almost since the day it was decided."

b. *Foreign sphere.* Does the Schechter doctrine have even less vitality in the foreign affairs sphere, as Curtiss-Wright suggests? Note Kent v. Dulles, 357 U.S. 116 (1958), reading a passport control statute narrowly to avoid constitutional problems and denying to the Secretary of State the authority to withhold passports on the basis of beliefs and associations. The opinion emphasized the right-to-travel aspect of "liberty" as the major lurking constitutional problem. But it also contained a passage stating that, if the "right to exit" is to be regulated, "it must be pursuant to the lawmaking functions of the Congress. [Steel Seizure Case.] And if that power is delegated, standards must be adequate to pass scrutiny by the accepted test. See Panama Refining Co. v. Ryan." Was that 1958 citation of Panama Refining, the domestic regulation "hot oil" case of 1935, surprising? Was the failure to cite Curtiss-Wright in a foreign travel case surprising? Does Kent v. Dulles provide another basis for some skepticism about the broad statements in Curtiss-Wright, not only about delegation but also about national authority in foreign affairs and about special presidential authority? On presidential authority, note also the executive agreement problems which follow.

THE PRESIDENT, CONGRESS, AND EXECUTIVE AGREEMENTS

Introduction. Over the years, the executive branch has frequently resorted to executive agreements rather than treaties in its dealings. Concerns have recurrently been voiced that the executive agreements route may unduly intrude upon the Senate's role by bypassing treaty-making. Fears have also been voiced that executive agreements may be on a par with treaties and may thus be able to supersede prior legislation. To a large extent, the magnitude of those risks turns on when such agreements are constitutionally justified. Are they supportable simply on the basis of a special inherent presidential authority in the foreign affairs sphere? To what extent may executive agreements be justified as incidental to specified Art. II powers? Must all executive agreements be made in pursuance of a statute? And may Congress bar or overturn executive agreements? The following materials sample that range of problems raised by the executive agreements device.

1. *The Belmont case.* In UNITED STATES v. BELMONT, 301 U.S. 324 (1937), the Court sustained the validity of an executive agreement and held that it took precedence over conflicting state policy. Justice Sutherland, who had written Curtiss-Wright a year earlier, wrote for the majority in Belmont. The agreement arose out of the American diplomatic recog-

nition of the Soviet Union in 1933. At the same time as President Roosevelt recognized the Soviet Union, an exchange of diplomatic correspondence between the President and Maxim Litvinov effected an assignment to the United States of all Soviet claims against Americans who held funds of Russian companies seized after the Revolution. The Belmont suit was brought by the United States in reliance upon that assignment, to recover funds deposited by a Russian corporation with a private New York banker. The lower courts dismissed the action on the ground that implementing the U.S.S.R.'s confiscation would violate the public policy of New York.

Justice Sutherland's majority opinion emphasized that the recognition, the establishment of diplomatic relations, and the assignment "were all parts of one transaction, resulting in an international compact between the two governments." He had no doubt that the negotiations and the agreements "were within the competence of the President": "in respect of what was done here, the Executive had authority to speak as the sole organ." And the assignment and agreements, unlike treaties, did not require senatorial participation. He noted that "an international compact, as this was, is not always a treaty which requires the participation of the Senate. There are many such compacts, of which a protocol, a modus vivendi, a postal convention, and agreements like that now under consideration are illustrations." And the Supremacy Clause's assurance that contrary state policies must give way applied here: "In respect of all international negotiations and compacts, and in respect of our foreign relations generally, state lines disappear." [1]

2. *Sources of authority for executive agreements.* Does Belmont, against the background of Curtiss-Wright, support a broad autonomous presidential authority to enter into executive agreements? Or is it important to distinguish among sources for particular agreements? Is it useful to invoke the three-pronged analysis of Justice Jackson's opinion in the Steel Seizure Case? Many executive agreements fall within his first category: they are adopted pursuant to statutory authority, as in the Trade Agreements Act, authorizing modification of tariffs through presidential agreements. The Litvinov agreement involved in Belmont, by contrast, rested on the specifically delegated presidential authority regarding diplomatic "recognition," in Art. II, § 3. As to such agreements, it is arguable that Congress possesses no authority to interfere with executive power. Could Congress enact guidelines for the negotiation of executive agreements under the Necessary and Proper Clause?

Is there a broader inherent executive power such as that suggested in Curtiss-Wright which may justify executive agreements? Even in the face of contrary congressional directives? Note that in the Belmont case, the argued limits on executive agreements stemmed from conflicting policies of the state, not from inconsistent policies of Congress. On conflicts between federal legislation and executive agreements, see United States v.

1. Note also the reappearance of the Litvinov Assignment before the Court in United States v. Pink, 315 U.S. 203 (1942). Justice Douglas' opinion for the Court stated that the President "has the power to determine the policy [to] govern the question of recogni-tion" and that such "international compacts and agreements as the Litvinov Assignment have a similar dignity" as treaties under the Supremacy Clause. See Note, "United States v. Pink: A Reappraisal," 48 Colum.L. Rev. 890 (1948).

Capps, 204 F.2d 655 (1953), where the Fourth Circuit held that an agreement with Canada regarding the importation of potatoes was invalid because it conflicted with a prior law enacted by Congress under its power over foreign commerce. The Supreme Court affirmed that judgment without reaching the important issue of the validity of the executive agreement. 348 U.S. 296 (1955). Does the court of appeals decision in Capp suggest need for care in reading the broad approval of executive agreements in cases such as Belmont?

Contrast with the reliance on the recognition authority in the Litvinov agreement President Roosevelt's pre-World War II lend-lease agreement. In September, 1940, the President announced the signing of an executive agreement between the United States and Great Britain, providing for the lease of certain military bases to the United States in return for 50 destroyers turned over to Britain. The President accompanied his message to Congress with an opinion by Attorney General Jackson upholding the agreement. 39 Op.A.G. 484 (1940). What presidential powers justified the lend-lease agreement?

3. *Executive agreements as alternatives to treaties.* To what extent may the Senate's role in international relations be curtailed by using executive agreements rather than treaties?[2] One of the purposes of the Bricker Amendment proposals (chap. 4, sec. 3B, above) was to block the executive agreement bypass. For example, sec. 2 of the version that failed narrowly in 1954 stated: "An international agreement other than a treaty shall become effective as internal law in the United States only by an act of Congress." To what extent could such a result be achieved by legislation? Compare § 8 (a)(2) of the War Powers Resolution of 1973, below, a congressional effort to curb the impact of treaties on the use of American military forces. On the inability of executive agreements and treaties to override non-federalistic constitutional guarantees, recall Reid v. Covert, chap. 4, sec. 3B, above.

THE PRESIDENT, CONGRESS, AND THE USE OF ARMED FORCES

Introduction. The mounting controversy in the late 1960's about American military involvement in Southeast Asia produced unprecedented debate and action regarding the competing spheres of authority of President and Congress in the commitment of military force overseas. Increasingly, the White House claimed autonomous authority under the constitutional powers of the President, especially as Commander in Chief. Increasingly, Congress sought to interpose its judgment, relying especially on its power to "declare War" and its power to "raise and support Armies." The materials in these notes sample some of the historical and legal data relevant to an analysis of the constitutional debate during and after the American engagement in Viet-

---

2. For contrasting views, compare Borchard, "Shall the Executive Agreement Replace the Treaty?" 53 Yale L.J. 664 (1944), with McDougal and Lans, "Treaties and Congressional-Executive or Presidential Agreements: Interchangeable Instruments of National Policy," 54 Yale L.J. 181 (1945). See also Mathews, "The Constitutional Power of the President to Conclude International Agreements," 64 Yale L. J. 345 (1955), and Henkin, Foreign Affairs and the Constitution (1972).

nam. These materials are intended to throw light on two pervasive problems: Was there legal justification for the use of military forces in Vietnam without a formal declaration of war? Does Congress have power to enact guidelines for the use of armed forces in overseas hostilities short of a declaration of war?

Two documents are printed at the outset to symbolize those problems and to help focus consideration of the materials which follow. The first document asks some of the questions about the legality of American military involvement in Southeast Asia. It is a dissent by Justice Stewart from a denial of certiorari—a rare contribution from the Supreme Court to the Vietnam debate, for the majority repeatedly refused to grant review in cases raising those issues. The second document raises questions about the respective authorities of Congress and President to determine policy for any future use of armed forces in foreign hostilities. It is the War Powers Resolution of 1973, a joint resolution enacted by Congress after President Nixon had vetoed it on constitutional grounds. These documents, then, raise the problems to be examined in considering the materials which follow: Was there adequate constitutional basis for the use of American troops in Vietnam? Is Congress acting within its constitutional powers, or is it intruding into exclusive executive authority, in its effort to assure greater legislative participation in future decisionmaking about the use of armed forces?

1. *The constitutionality of the Vietnam conflict: Justice Stewart's dissent.* The questions Justice Stewart raises below came in one of a considerable number of cases in which efforts were made to bring the constitutional controversy over Vietnam to the Supreme Court.[1] Justice Stewart's dissent came in Mora v. McNamara, 389 U.S. 934 (1967). That was a challenge by army draftees who had been ordered to a West Coast base for shipment to Vietnam. They brought suit to prevent the carrying out of the orders and to obtain a declaratory judgment that American military activity in Vietnam was "illegal." The lower federal courts dismissed their action. Justice Stewart's dissent from the denial of certiorari, joined by Justice Douglas, stated:

"There exist in this case questions of great magnitude. . . . :

"I. Is the present United States military activity in Vietnam a 'war' within the meaning of Article I, Section 8, Clause 11 of the Constitution?

"II. If so, may the Executive constitutionally order the petitioners to participate in that military activity, when no war has been declared by the Congress?

"III. Of what relevance to Question II are the present treaty obligations of the United States?

---

1. There were recurrent dissents from the Court's denials of review, especially by Justice Douglas. In addition to the case noted in the text (where Justice Douglas added a dissent to that of Justice Stewart), see, e. g., McArthur v. Clifford, 393 U.S. 1002 (1968), Holmes v. United States, 391 U.S. 936 (1968), Velvel v. Nixon, 396 U.S. 1042 (1970), Massachusetts v. Laird, 400 U. S. 886 (1970), and DaCosta v. Laird, 405 U.S. 979 (1972). The final round of judicial encounters with the war in Southeast Asia came in the summer of 1973, in Holtzman v. Schlesinger, an effort to enjoin continued American air operations over Cambodia. Justice Marshall refused to vacate a court of appeals stay of a district court injunction; Justice Douglas then vacated the stay; but later on the same day, Justice Marshall, after communi-

"IV. Of what relevance to Question II is the Joint Congressional ('Tonkin Gulf') Resolution of August 10, 1964?

"(a) Do present United States military operations fall within the terms of the Joint Resolution?

"(b) If the Joint Resolution purports to give the Chief Executive authority to commit United States forces to armed conflict limited in scope only by his own absolute discretion, is the Resolution a constitutionally impermissible delegation of all or part of Congress' power to declare war?" [2]

"These are large and deeply troubling questions. Whether the Court would ultimately reach them depends, of course, upon the resolution of serious preliminary issues of justiciability. We cannot make these problems go away simply by refusing to hear the case of three obscure Army privates. I intimate not even tentative views upon any of these matters, but I think the Court should squarely face them by granting certiorari."

2. *The War Powers Resolution of 1973.* [Consider the constitutional problems about allocation of authority between President and Congress raised by the following joint resolution adopted over a presidential veto in 1973:] [3]

SHORT TITLE

Section 1. This joint resolution may be cited as the "War Powers Resolution."

cating with the other Justices, reinstated the stay. See 414 U.S. 1304, 1316, 1321 (1973).

A recurrent problem in obtaining access to courts was that of justiciability—the contention that the claims presented "political questions" not for the courts. The justiciability issues are considered further below, in sec. 2 of this chapter and in chap. 15. Most lower courts found most issues nonjusticiable; some found challenges partly justiciable but typically rejected attacks on the war on the merits. See, e. g., Orlando v. Laird, 443 F.2d 1039 (2d Cir. 1971).

For an extensive discussion of the justiciability issue, see the 2 to 1 decision by a three-judge District Court dismissing a challenge to the constitutionality of the war in Southeast Asia on political question grounds. Atlee v. Laird, 347 F.Supp. 689 (E.D.Pa.1972). The Supreme Court, in a unique indication of views on the issue, summarily affirmed, over the dissents of Justices Douglas, Brennan and Stewart. 411 U.S. 911 (1973).

2. Some of these questions are further explored, and the text of the Tonkin Gulf Resolution is printed, below.

3. 87 Stat. 555, Public Law 93–148, 93d Cong. (H.J.Res. 542, adopted over a presidential veto on Nov. 7, 1973). The Resolution—like the Impounding Control Act of 1974, sec. 1A above— is an unusual, quasi-constitutional variety of congressional action, delineating not substantive policy but processes and relationships.

Some of the questions raised by the Resolution are pursued after the historical background materials below. Note the books by two senators who played an active role in efforts to curb presidential powers, Javits, Who Makes War? (1973), and Eagleton, War and Presidential Power (1974). And, among the voluminous writing on the problems raised by this group of notes, see especially Note, "Congress, The President, and the Power to Commit Forces to Combat," 81 Harv.L.Rev. 1771 (1968); Van Alstyne, "Congress, the President, and the Power to Declare War . . . .," 121 U.Pa.L.Rev. 1 (1972); Berger, "War-Making and the President," 121 U.Pa.L.Rev. 29 (1972); and Bickel, "Congress, the President, and the Power to Wage War," 48 Chicago-Kent L.Rev. 131 (1971).

PURPOSE AND POLICY

Sec. 2. (a) It is the purpose of this joint resolution to fulfill the intent of the framers of the Constitution of the United States and insure that the collective judgment of both the Congress and the President will apply to the introduction of United States Armed Forces into hostilities, or into situations where imminent involvement in hostilities is clearly indicated by the circumstances, and to the continued use of such forces in hostilities or in such situations.

(b) Under article I, section 8, of the Constitution, it is specifically provided that the Congress shall have the power to make all laws necessary and proper for carrying into execution, not only its own powers but also all other powers vested by the Constitution in the Government of the United States, or in any department or officer thereof.

(c) The constitutional powers of the President as Commander-in-Chief to introduce United States Armed Forces into hostilities, or into situations where imminent involvement in hostilities is clearly indicated by the circumstances, are exercised only pursuant to (1) a declaration of war, (2) specific statutory authorization, or (3) a national emergency created by attack upon the United States, its territories or possessions, or its armed forces.

CONSULTATION

Sec. 3. The President in every possible instance shall consult with Congress before introducing United States Armed Forces into hostilities or into situations where imminent involvement in hostilities is clearly indicated by the circumstances, and after every such introduction shall consult regularly with the Congress until United States Armed Forces are no longer engaged in hostilities or have been removed from such situations.

REPORTING

Sec. 4. (a) In the absence of a declaration of war, in any case in which United States Armed Forces are introduced—

(1) into hostilities or into situations where imminent involvement in hostilities is clearly indicated by the circumstances;

(2) into the territory, airspace or waters of a foreign nation, while equipped for combat, except for deployments which relate solely to supply, replacement, repair, or training of such forces; or

(3) in numbers which substantially enlarge United States Armed Forces equipped for combat already located in a foreign nation;
the President shall submit within 48 hours to the Speaker of the House of Representatives and to the President pro tempore of the Senate a report, in writing, setting forth—

(A) the circumstances necessitating the introduction of United States Armed Forces;

(B) the constitutional and legislative authority under which such introduction took place; and

(C) the estimated scope and duration of the hostilities or involve-ment. . . .

CONGRESSIONAL ACTION

Sec. 5 . . . (b) Within sixty calendar days after a report is sub-mitted or is required to be submitted pursuant to section 4(a)(1), whichever is earlier, the President shall terminate any use of United States Armed Forces with respect to which such report was submitted (or required to be submitted), unless the Congress (1) has declared war or has enacted a specific authorization for such use of United States Armed Forces, (2) has extended by law such sixty-day period, or (3) is physically unable to meet as a result of an armed attack upon the United States. Such sixty-day period shall be extended for not more than an additional thirty days if the President determines and certifies to the Congress in writing that unavoidable military necessity respecting the safety of United States Armed Forces requires the continued use of such armed forces in the course of bringing about a prompt removal of such forces.

(c) Notwithstanding subsection (b), at any time that United States Armed Forces are engaged in hostilities outside the territory of the United States, its possessions and territories without a declaration of war or specific statutory authorization, such forces shall be removed by the President if the Congress so directs by concurrent resolution. . . .

INTERPRETATION OF JOINT RESOLUTION

Sec. 8. (a) Authority to introduce United States Armed Forces into hos-tilities or into situations wherein involvement in hostilities is clearly indicated by the circumstances shall not be inferred—

(1) from any provision of law (whether or not in effect before the date of the enactment of this joint resolution), including any pro-vision contained in any appropriation Act, unless such provision specifically authorizes the introduction of United States Armed Forces into hostilities or into such situations and states that it is intended to con-stitute specific statutory authorization within the meaning of this joint resolution; or

(2) from any treaty heretofore or hereafter ratified unless such treaty is implemented by legislation specifically authorizing the introduc-tion of United States Armed Forces into hostilities or into such situa-tions and stating that it is intended to constitute specific statutory au-thorization within the meaning of this joint resolution. . . .

(d) Nothing in this joint resolution—

(1) is intended to alter the constitutional authority of the Con-gress or of the President, or the provisions of existing treaties; or

(2) shall be construed as granting any authority to the President with respect to the introduction of United States Armed Forces into hostilities or into situations wherein involvement in hostilities is clearly indicated by the circumstances which authority he would not have had in the absence of this joint resolution. . . .

PRESIDENT, CONGRESS, AND MILITARY FORCE:
SOME BACKGROUND MATERIALS

1. *The Prize Cases.* a. *The opinions.* A rare, and limited, Court consideration of presidential powers to commit armed forces came during the Civil War. In the PRIZE CASES, 2 Black 635 (1863), ships carrying goods to the Confederate States were seized by Union ships, pursuant to President Lincoln's April 1861 order declaring a blockade of Southern ports. The Supreme Court sustained most of the seizures challenged in these cases in a 5 to 4 decision, even though there had been no congressional declaration of war. Justice Grier's majority opinion, in considering "whether, at the time this blockade was instituted, a state of war existed which would justify a resort to these means of subduing the hostile force," included the following passages:

"By the Constitution, Congress alone has the power to declare a national or foreign war. It cannot declare war against a State, or any number of States, by virtue of any clause in the Constitution. The Constitution confers on the President the whole Executive power. He is bound to take care that the laws be faithfully executed. He is Commander-in-chief of the Army and Navy of the United States, and of the militia of the several States when called into the actual service of the United States. He has no power to initiate or declare a war either against a foreign nation or a domestic State. But by the Acts of Congress of February 28th, 1795, and 3d of March, 1807, he is authorized to call out the militia and use the military and naval forces of the United States in case of invasion by foreign nations, and to suppress insurrection against the government of a State or of the United States.

"If a war be made by invasion of a foreign nation, the President is not only authorized but bound to resist force, by force. He does not initiate the war, but is bound to accept the challenge without waiting for any special legislative authority. And whether the hostile party be a foreign invader, or States organized in rebellion, it is none the less a war, although the declaration of it be 'unilateral.' . . .

" . . . The President was bound to meet [the Civil War] in the shape it presented itself, without waiting for Congress to baptize it with a name. . . .

"Whether the President in fulfilling his duties, as Commander-in-chief, in suppressing an insurrection, has met with such armed hostile resistance, and a civil war of such alarming proportions as will compel him to accord to them the character of belligerents, is a question to be decided *by him,* and this Court must be governed by the decisions and acts of the political department of the Government to which this power was entrusted. . . .

"If it were necessary to the technical existence of a war, that it should have a legislative sanction, we find it in almost every act passed at the extraordinary session of the Legislature of 1861, which was wholly employed in enacting laws to enable the Government to prosecute the war with vigor and efficiency. And finally, in 1861, we find Congress [passing] an act approving, legalizing, and making valid all the acts, proclamations, and orders of the President, &c., as if they had been *issued and done under the*

previous express authority and direction of the Congress of the United States.'

"Without admitting that such an act was necessary under the circumstances, it is plain that if the President had in any manner assumed powers which it was necessary should have the authority or sanction of Congress, . . . this ratification has operated to perfectly cure the defect. . . .

"[W]e are of the opinion that the President had a right, *jure belli*, to institute a blockade of ports in possession of the States in rebellion, which neutrals are bound to regard."

Justice Nelson's dissent, joined by Chief Justice Taney and Justices Catron and Clifford, included the following passages: "[Before an] insurrection against the established Government can be dealt with on the footing of a civil war, [it] must be recognized or declared by the war-making power of the Government. . . . There is no difference in this respect between a civil or a public war. . . .

"Now, in one sense, no doubt this is war, and may be a war of the most extensive and threatening dimensions and effects, but it is a statement simply of its existence in a material sense, and has no relevancy or weight when the question is what constitutes war in a legal sense. [T]o constitute a civil war [in] contemplation of law, it must be recognized or declared by the sovereign power of the State, and which sovereign power by our Constitution is lodged in the Congress of the United States—civil war, therefore, under our system of government, can exist only by an act of Congress . . . .

"We have thus far been speaking of the war power and of the Constitution of the United States, and as known and recognized by the law of nations. But we are asked, what would become of the peace and integrity of the Union in case of an insurrection at home or invasion from abroad if this power could not be exercised by the President in the recess of Congress, and until that body could be assembled?

"The framers of the Constitution fully comprehended this question, and provided for the contingency [by giving Congress the power "to provide for calling forth the militia to execute the laws of the Union, suppress insurrections, and repel invasions"]. . . .

"The Acts of 1795 and 1807 did not, and could not, under the Constitution, confer on the President the power of declaring war against a State of this Union, or of deciding that war existed, and upon that ground authorize the capture and confiscation of the property of every citizen of the State whenever it was found on the waters. The laws of war, whether the war be civil or *inter gentes,* as we have seen, convert every citizen of the hostile State into a public enemy, and treat him accordingly, whatever may have been his previous conduct. This great power over the business and property of the citizen is reserved to the legislative department by the express words of the Constitution. It cannot be delegated or surrendered to the Executive. Congress alone can determine whether war exists or should be declared; and until they have acted, no citizen of the State can be punished in his person or property, unless he has committed some offense against a law of Congress passed before the act was committed, which made it a crime and defined the punishment. The penalty of confiscation for the acts of others with which

he had no concern cannot lawfully be inflicted." [Congressional ratification of the seizures was found ineffective as an ex post facto law.]

b. *The bearing of the Prize Cases on modern problems.* What light do the opinions in the Prize Cases throw on the constitutionality of the Vietnam conflict and on the constitutionality of the War Powers Resolution of 1973? As to the former question, Justice Douglas' dissents from denials of certiorari in cases challenging the Vietnam involvement several times referred to the Prize Cases. For example, in dissenting in McArthur v. Clifford, 393 U.S. 1002 (1968), he commented that the Prize Cases involved "an internal insurrection which would perhaps be analogous here if the Vietnamese were invading the United States": "Would [the decision] have been the same if Lincoln had had an expeditionary force fighting a 'war' overseas?" Note also Justice Douglas' dissent from the denial of certiorari in Mora v. McNamara, 389 U.S. 934 (1967), reviewing the ongoing constitutional debate about respective presidential and congressional powers to commit military forces and adding: "These opposed views are reflected in the [Prize Cases]. During all subsequent periods in our history—through the Spanish-American War, the Boxer Rebellion, two World Wars, Korea, and now Vietnam—the two points of view urged in the Prize Cases have continued to be voiced. A host of problems is raised. Does the President's authority to repel invasions and quiet insurrections, do his powers in foreign relations and his duty to execute faithfully the laws of the United States, including its treaties, justify [sending American soldiers overseas absent a declaration of war]? What is the relevancy of the Gulf of Tonkin Resolution and the yearly appropriations in support of the Vietnam effort?" Note the further examination of the alleged authorizations for the Vietnam engagement in the materials in the next note.

Does the majority position in the Prize Cases cast constitutional doubt on some of the restrictions on executive authority in the War Powers Resolution of 1973? Note that the Resolution recognizes presidential Commander-in-Chief authority to react to national emergencies caused by threatened attacks, a power acknowledged by the Framers and in the Prize Cases. Is the description of national emergencies in the Resolution sufficiently broad to encompass traditionally recognized executive powers? [1] Is the time limitation on executive authority in the War Powers Resolution a valid restraint on presidential emergency powers to respond to attacks?

1. The Senate version of the Resolution, rejected in conference in 1973, included among situations where presidential use of armed forces was permitted a reference to the necessity to protect and evacuate American citizens and nationals abroad whose lives are threatened. Does the omission of that situation in the enacted version limit presidential authority?

That problem of presidential authority engendered renewed controversy when President Ford used armed forces to evacuate Americans and South Vietnamese from Saigon on April 29, 1975. Earlier in that month, the President had asked for congressional "clarification" of his authority to use military force to evacuate Americans and foreign nationals. Though most legislators took the view that the President had inherent authority to evacuate endangered Americans (despite the silence in the War Powers Resolution), there was considerable doubt about the evacuation of foreign nationals. Legislation to grant limited authority to use force to evacuate South Vietnamese in the course of evacuating Americans passed the Senate and was pending before the House when the President ordered troops into action shortly before the end of the war in Vietnam. (In response to ques-

2. *The constitutional and historical background regarding authority to direct the use of armed forces: The Senate Committee Report of 1967.* [The major early forum for constitutional debates during the growing Vietnam controversy of the late 1960's was the Senate Committee on Foreign Relations under the chairmanship of Senator J. William Fulbright. As a part of the Committee's search for better methods of reasserting congressional control of the use of military force, the Committee produced a Report, "National Commitments." That Report contained an extensive review of constitutional groundrules and historical developments in the expanding role of the executive in committing armed forces to overseas actions. Excerpts from that 1967 Report follow.*]

Our country has come far toward the concentration in its national executive of unchecked power over foreign relations, particularly over the disposition and use of the armed forces. So far has this process advanced that, in the committee's view, it is no longer accurate to characterize our government, in matters of foreign relations, as one of separated powers checked and balanced against each other. For causes to be detailed in the following pages, the executive has acquired virtual supremacy over the making as well as the conduct of the foreign relations of the United States.

The principal cause of the constitutional imbalance has been the circumstance of American involvement and responsibility in a violent and unstable world. . . . The committee believes that changed conditions, though the principal cause of the present constitutional imbalance, are not its sole cause. . . . Both the executive and the Congress have been periodically unmindful of constitutional requirements and proscriptions, the

tions about the President's legal authority to evacuate foreign nationals, the White House stated that the President had acted on "moral" grounds.) Two days later, the House voted to reject the pending legislation, partly on the ground that the evacuation issue had become moot. See 33 Cong. Quar. Weekly Report (May 3, 1975), 904–907. For a sharp criticism of the House decision, see Senator Eagleton's comment, "Congress's 'Inaction' on War," The New York Times (Op-Ed page), May 6, 1975: "This unfortunate decision raises grave questions about the willingness of Congress to fulfill its constitutional responsibilities. . . . Future Presidents might now conclude that the Commander in Chief had an inherent right to do what Mr. Ford did. . . . Congress fumbled the ball." Senator Eagleton suggested that liberals in Congress were so fearful of authorizing limited use of force that they "unintentionally threw their considerable weight in the direction of Presidential omnipotence" and "chose to leave a precedent for unilateral and unrestricted Presidential rescue authority." (Consider also the Cambodian funds cut-off provision of 1973, p. 444 below.)

In another crisis two weeks later, the President used military force to rescue the American merchant ship S.S. Mayagüez and its crew. The ship had been seized by Cambodia. In a letter to the Speaker of the House on May 15, 1975—reporting to Congress in accordance with § 4 of the War Powers Resolution—President Ford described the action after it had been successfully concluded. Some congressional leaders complained because they had not been "consulted" and had only been "notified" while the action was under way. The President concluded his May 15 "report" letter with the statement: "The operation was ordered and conducted pursuant to the President's constitutional executive power and his authority as Commander in Chief of the United States Armed Forces."

* National Commitments, Sen.Rep.No. 797, 90th Cong., 1st Sess. (Nov. 20, 1967). See also, Sen.Rep.No.91–129, 91st Cong., 1st Sess. (Apr. 16, 1969). For the evolution of congressional techniques to assert greater control, from the Fulbright Committee's deliberations to the War Powers Resolution of 1973, see the next group of notes.

executive by its incursions upon Congressional prerogative at moments when action seemed more important than the means of its initiation, the Congress by its uncritical and sometimes unconscious acquiescence in these incursions. If blame is to be apportioned, the greater share probably belongs to the Congress. It is understandable, though not acceptable, that in times of real or seeming emergency the executive will be tempted to take shortcuts around constitutional procedure. It is less understandable that the Congress should acquiesce in these shortcuts, giving away that which is not its to give, notably the war power, which the framers of the Constitution vested not in the executive but, deliberately and almost exclusively, in the Congress.

More important than the allocation of blame, of which there is a fair share for all concerned, is the identification of causes and the prescription of correctives for the existing constitutional imbalance. The committee believes that the basic cause has been the unfamiliarity of world involvement and recurrent crisis to the American people and their government. Prior to 1940 foreign crises were infrequent and therefore put no lasting strain on our institutions. Since 1940 crisis has been chronic and, coming as something new in our experience, has given rise to a tendency toward anxious expediency in our response to it. The natural expedient—natural because of the real or seeming need for speed—has been executive action. . . .

1. THE INTENT OF THE FRAMERS

There is no uncertainty or ambiguity about the intent of the framers of the Constitution with respect to the war power. . . . It was understood by the framers—and subsequent usage confirmed their understanding —that the President in his capacity as commander in chief of the armed forces would have the right, indeed the duty, to use the armed forces to repel sudden attacks on the United States, even in advance of Congressional authorization to do so. It was further understood that he would direct and lead the armed forces and put them to any use specified by Congress but that this did not extend to the initiation of hostilities. . . .

The Constitutional Convention had at first proposed to give Congress the power to "*make war*" but changed this to "*declare war.*" The purpose of the change was not to enlarge Presidential power in any significant degree . . ., but to permit him to take action to repel sudden attacks. Madison's notes on the proceedings of the convention report the change of wording as follows:

> Mr. Madison and Mr. Gerry *moved* to insert "*declare,*" striking out "*make*" war; leaving to the Executive the power to repel sudden attacks. . . .

The evidence is abundant that the framers did not intend the executive to have the power to initiate war. In a letter to Madison in 1789 Thomas Jefferson wrote:

> We have already given in example one effectual check to the Dog of war by transferring the power of letting him loose from the Executive to the Legislative body, from those who are to spend to those who are to pay.

2. THE WAR POWER FROM 1789 TO 1900

The early Presidents carefully respected Congress's authority to initiate war. President Adams took action to protect American ships from French attacks on the Atlantic only to the extent that Congress authorized him to do so; even in the case of this "limited war" between the United States and revolutionary France the President did not regard himself as free to use the armed forces without authorization by Congress.

Early in his term of office President Jefferson sent a naval squadron to the Mediterranean to protect American commerce against piracy, but it was not permitted to engage in offensive action against the Barbary pirates. Later such action was taken after having been authorized by Congress. On December 8, 1801, President Jefferson sent [a] message to Congress [and in] referring to the capture of one of the American ships by the pirates, [stated]:

> . . . Unauthorized by the Constitution, without the sanction of Congress, to go beyond the line of defense, the vessel, being disabled from committing further hostilities, was liberated with its crew. The Legislature will doubtless consider whether, by authorizing measures of offense also, they will place our force on an equal footing with that of its adversaries. . . .

During the 19th century American armed forces were used by the President on his own authority for such purposes as suppressing piracy, suppressing the slave trade by American ships, "hot pursuit" of criminals across frontiers, and protecting American lives and property in backward areas or areas where government had broken down. Such limited uses of force without authorization by Congress, not involving the initiation of hostilities against foreign governments, came to be accepted practice, sanctioned by usage though not explicitly by the Constitution.

Some Presidents, notably Polk, Grant, and McKinley, interpreted their powers as commander in chief broadly, while others, such as the early Presidents and Buchanan and Cleveland, were scrupulously deferential to the war power of Congress. Summarizing the war power in the 19th century, Robert William Russell writes: [1]

> It is not a simple matter to arrive at conclusions concerning this period in which the constitutional interpretation was far from consistent, where Grant's extreme view is sandwiched between the conservative views of Buchanan and Cleveland. But there was one opinion that enjoyed wide acceptance: the President could constitutionally employ American military force outside the nation as long as he did not use it to commit "acts of war." While the term was never precisely defined, an "act of war" in this context usually meant *the use of military force against a sovereign nation* without that nation's *consent* and without that nation's having declared war upon or used force against the United States. To perform acts of war the President needed the authorization of Congress. . . .

1. Russell, The United States Congress and the Power to Use Military Force Abroad (Ph.D. Thesis, Fletcher School of Law and Diplomacy, 1967).

This dividing line between the proper spheres of legislative and executive authority was sufficiently flexible to permit the President to use military force in the unimportant cases, while preserving the role of Congress in important decisions. The acts of war doctrine was probably a step beyond what the framers intended when they changed the congressional power from "make" war to "declare" war, and was certainly a move in the direction of Presidential power compared to the cautious stance of Washington, Adams, Jefferson, and Madison. The central objective which the Constitution sought—congressional authority to approve the initiation of major conflicts—was undamaged, but a certain fraying of the edges had occurred. This slight deterioration was greatly accelerated during the following 50 years.

3. THE EXPANSION OF EXECUTIVE POWER IN THE 20TH CENTURY, 1900–1941

The use of the armed forces against sovereign nations without authorization by Congress became common practice in the 20th century. President Theodore Roosevelt used the Navy to prevent Colombian forces from suppressing insurrection in their province of Panama and intervened militarily in Cuba and the Dominican Republic. Presidents Taft and Wilson also sent armed forces to the Carribbean and Central America without Congressional authorization. In Haiti, the Dominican Republic, and Nicaragua these interventions resulted in the establishment of American military governments.

President Wilson seized the Mexican port of Vera Cruz in 1914 as an act of reprisal, in order, he said, to "enforce respect" for the government of the United States. The two Houses of Congress adopted separate resolutions in support of President Wilson's action but the Senate did not complete action on its resolution until after the seizure of Vera Cruz. . . .

The military powers which had been acquired by Presidents in the 19th century—for purposes of "hot pursuit" and the protection of American lives and property, and under treaties which conferred rights and obligations on the United States—were not serious infringements on Congress' war power because they had been used for the most part against individuals or bands of pirates or bandits and not against sovereign states. Roosevelt, Taft, and Wilson used these powers to engage in military action against sovereign states, thereby greatly expanding the scope of executive power over the use of the armed forces and setting precedents for the greater expansions of executive power which were to follow. The Congresses of that era did not see fit to resist or oppose these incursions of their constitutional authority . . . .

President Franklin Roosevelt expanded executive power over the use of the armed forces to an unprecedented degree. The exchange of overaged American destroyers for British bases in the Western Hemisphere was accomplished by executive agreement, in violation of the Senate's treaty power, and was also a violation of the international law of neutrality, giving Germany legal cause, had she chosen to take it, to declare war on the United States. The transaction was an *emergency* use of Presidential power, taken in the belief that it might be essential to save Great Britain from invasion.

In 1941 President Roosevelt, on his own authority, committed American forces to the defense of Greenland and Iceland and authorized American naval vessels to escort convoys to Iceland provided that at least one ship in each convoy flew the American or Icelandic flag. When the American destroyer *Greer* was fired on by a German submarine, after having radioed the submarine's position to the British who then sent planes to attack it, President Roosevelt utilized the occasion to announce that thereafter American naval vessels would shoot on sight against German and Italian ships west of the 26th meridian. By the time Germany and Italy declared war on the United States, in the wake of the Japanese attack on Pearl Harbor, the United States had already been committed by its President, acting on his own authority, to an undeclared naval war in the Atlantic. Roosevelt, however, achieved his objective without asserting a general or "inherent" Presidential power to commit the armed forces abroad.

4. THE PASSING OF THE WAR POWER FROM CONGRESS TO THE EXECUTIVE AFTER WORLD WAR II

The trend initiated by Theodore Roosevelt, Taft, and Wilson, and accelerated by Franklin Roosevelt, continued at a rapid rate under Presidents Truman, Eisenhower, Kennedy, and Johnson, bringing the country to the point at which the real power to commit the country to war is now in the hands of the President. . . .

By the late 1940's there had developed a kind of ambivalence as to the war power in the minds of officials in the executive branch, Members of Congress and, presumably, the country at large. On the one hand, it was and still is said that Congress alone has the power to declare war; on the other hand it was widely believed, or at least conceded, that the President in his capacity as commander in chief had the authority to use the armed forces in any way he saw fit. . . .

President Truman committed American Armed Forces to Korea in 1950 without Congressional authorization. . . . President Truman himself made no public explanation of his use of the war power but an article in the Department of State Bulletin asserted that "the President, as Commander in Chief of the Armed Forces of the United States, has full control over the use thereof." The article pointed to past instances in which the President had used the Armed Forces in what was said to be "the broad interests of American foreign policy" and also asserted that there was a "traditional power of the President to use the armed forces of the United States without consulting Congress." Here, clearly expostulated, is a doctrine of general or "inherent" Presidential power—something which had not been claimed by previous Presidents.

Voices of dissent were raised in Congress, but not at the time of Truman's action. . . .

In 1951 the Senate Committees on Foreign Relations and Armed Services held joint hearings to discuss President Truman's plan for sending six divisions of American soldiers to Europe. Secretary of State Acheson gave the committees the following interpretation of the President's powers:

Not only has the President the authority to use the Armed Forces in carrying out the broad foreign policy of the United States and im-

plementing treaties, but it is equally clear that this authority may not be interfered with by the Congress in the exercise of powers which it has under the Constitution. . . .

President Eisenhower exhibited some ambivalence as to his authority to use the armed forces. . . . It is significant that in the case of the Formosa resolution [in 1954] President Eisenhower asked for *authority* rather than mere approval or support and that under the resolution adopted by Congress the President was "*authorized* to employ the Armed Forces." . . . Although the word *authorize* was used, [the] authorization was an extremely broad one, empowering the President to employ the armed forces to defend Formosa and the Pescadores "as he determines necessary." It can be argued that an authorization so general and imprecise amounts to an unconstitutional alienation of its war power on the part of the Congress.

. . .

Subsequent resolutions involving the possible use of armed force abandoned the principle of *authorization*, demonstrating not only ambivalence as to extent of the President's authority but a lack of attention to the underlying constitutional question. The Middle East resolution of 1957, the Cuba resolution of 1962, and the Gulf of Tonkin resolution of 1964 dropped the vital concept of Congressional authorization and instead used terminology which, by failing to express a grant of power by Congress, implied acceptance of the view that the President already had the power to use the armed forces in the ways proposed and that, the resolutions were no more than expressions of Congressional support and national unity. The prevailing attitude in each instance seems to have been one of concern not with constitutional questions but with the problem at hand and with the need for a method of dealing with it, heightened in all three cases by a sense of urgency. Nonetheless, precedents were set.

The debate on the Middle East resolution of 1957 revealed two dominant attitudes on the war power; first, a reluctance to define it with precision, and, second, growing senatorial acceptance of the view that the President, in his capacity as Commander in Chief, could commit the armed forces to defend what he might regard as the "vital interest" of the nation. In testimony before the Committees on Foreign Relations and Armed Services, Secretary of State Dulles refused to express an opinion as to whether or not the President could commit the armed forces in the absence of the resolution. Senator Fulbright, whose view has changed with time and experience, thought at the time that the President had power as Commander in Chief to use the armed forces to defend the "vital interests" of the country and that the resolution would have the effect of limiting that power.[2] This viewpoint was widely shared at the time. In their report the two

2. On Senator Fulbright's earlier position—a position which illustrates the shift in views between the time of the Bricker Amendment controversy in the 1950's and the Vietnam debate—see also the Senator's statements in a 1961 lecture, Fulbright, "American Foreign Policy in the 20th Century Under an 18th-Century Constitution," 47 Cornell L.Q. 1 (1961). There, Senator Fulbright had stated that the President's considerable authority in the foreign affairs area "falls short of his responsibilities." He added: "As Commander-in-Chief of the armed forces, the President has full responsibility, which cannot be shared, for military decisions in a world in which the difference between safety and cataclysm can be a matter of hours or even minutes." In 1961, the Senator saw the "checks and balances" of con-

committees struck out the word "authorize" and expressed satisfaction at having avoided the necessity of defining the relative powers of Congress and the President. . . .

In September 1962 Congress adopted a joint resolution pertaining to Cuba. The Kennedy Administration favored a concurrent resolution expressing the sense of Congress that the President "possesses all necessary authority" to prevent Cuba, "by whatever means may be necessary, including the use of arms," from "exporting its aggressive purposes" in the hemisphere, to prevent the establishment of a foreign, i. e., Soviet, military base in Cuba, and to support Cuban aspirations for self-determination. Senator Russell opposed the concurrent resolution favored by the Administration. "I do not believe," he said, "that the Armed Services Committee is going to make a constitutional assertion that the President of the United States has the right to declare war, and that is what this does." The resolution as finally adopted was a joint resolution, stating that "the United States is determined" to do those things spelled out in the abandoned concurrent resolution.

The Cuban missile crisis occurred 1 month later. Two hours before he went on television on October 22, 1962, to announce the "quarantine" on shipments of offensive missiles to Cuba, President Kennedy met with the Congressional leadership and briefed them on the decisions which had, of course, already been made. In the belief that they had a *duty* to give the President their best judgment, certain Senators expressed opinions as to possible wise courses of action. This was the extent of Congressional participation in the greatest crisis of the postwar era, the one crisis which brought the world to the brink of nuclear war. Finding the Congressional advice in some cases "captious and inconsistent," Theodore Sorensen later wrote that the President's meeting with the Congressional leadership was the "only sour note of the day." . . .

The Gulf of Tonkin resolution represents the extreme point in the process of constitutional erosion that began in the first years of this century. Couched in broad terms, the resolution constitutes an acknowledgment of virtually unlimited Presidential control of the armed forces.[3] . . . The present Administration has not been entirely consistent in its interpretations

gressional control, dispersed as it was among autonomous committees, as a serious obstacle to effective presidential leadership: "The question I put [is] whether in the face of the harsh necessities of the 1960's we can afford the luxury of 18th century procedures for measured deliberation." He questioned whether the nation could successfully execute long-range programs by leaving important decisionmaking power "in the hands of a decentralized, independent-minded, and largely parochial-minded body of legislators." He added: "I submit that the price of democratic survival in a world of aggressive totalitarianism is to give up some of the democratic luxuries of the past."

3. The text of the Resolution, H.J.Res. 1145, 73 Stat. 384 (1964):

Whereas naval units of the Communist regime in Vietnam, in violation of the principles of the Charter of the United Nations and of international law, have deliberately and repeatedly attacked United States naval vessels lawfully present in international waters, and have thereby created a serious threat to international peace; and

Whereas these attacks are part of a deliberate and systematic campaign of aggression that the Communist regime in North Vietnam has been waging against its neighbors and the nations joined with them in the collective defense of their freedom; and

of the Gulf of Tonkin resolution, but on a number of occasions it has been asserted that the President would have full authority to conduct the war in Vietnam on its present scale even in the absence of the resolution. In March 1966, for example, the Legal Adviser to the Department of State wrote:

> There can be no question in present circumstances of the President's authority to commit U. S. forces to the defense of South Vietnam. The grant of authority to the President in Article II of the Constitution extends to the actions of the United States currently undertaken in Vietnam.

Speaking of the Gulf of Tonkin resolution in his news conference on August 18, 1967, President Johnson said:

> . . . We stated then, and we repeat now, we did not think the resolution was necessary to do what we did and what we're doing. But we thought it was desirable and we thought if we were going to ask them [Congress] to stay the whole route and if we expected them to be there on the landing we ought to ask them to be there on the takeoff.

The exact view of the executive as to the meaning of Congress's constitutional power to "declare war" remains somewhat obscure. In his testimony before the Foreign Relations Committee on August 17, 1967, Under Secretary Katzenbach referred to a declaration of war as something which is "outmoded in the international arena" and also as something that would not "correctly reflect the limited objectives of the United States with respect to Vietnam." The Under Secretary thought that, in any case, the

Whereas the United States is assisting the peoples of southeast Asia to protect their freedom and has no territorial, military or political ambitions in that area, but desires only that these peoples should be left in peace to work out their own destinies in their own way: Now, therefore, be it *Resolved by the Senate and House of Representatives of the United States of America in Congress assembled,*

Sec. 1. The Congress approves and supports the determination of the President, as Commander in Chief, to take all necessary measures to repel any armed attack against the forces of the United States and to prevent further aggression.

Sec. 2. The United States regards as vital to its national interest and to world peace the maintenance of international peace and security in southeast Asia. Consonant with the Constitution of the United States and the Charter of the United Nations and in accordance with its obligations under the Southeast Asia Collective Defense Treaty, the United States is, therefore, prepared, as the President determines, to take all necessary steps, including the use of armed force, to assist any member or protocol state of the Southeast Asia Collective Defense Treaty requesting assistance in defense of its freedom.

Sec. 3. This resolution shall expire when the President shall determine that the peace and security of the area is reasonably assured by international conditions created by action of the United Nations or otherwise, except that it may be terminated earlier by concurrent resolution of the Congress.

[The Gulf of Tonkin Resolution was repealed in January 1971. See 84 Stat. 2053. In the months of debate preceding repeal, the Administration abandoned reliance on the Resolution to justify the Vietnam hostilities, explaining that it was relying instead largely on the President's Commander-in-Chief authority, and accordingly took a neutral position on repeal. See also the Conference Committee comment on the repeal: "Recent legislation and Executive statements make the 1964 resolution unnecessary for the prosecution of U. S. foreign policy."]

SEATO Treaty and the Gulf of Tonkin resolution, taken together, were the "functional equivalent" of a declaration of war, and he asked: "What could a declaration of war have done that would have given the President more authority and a clearer voice of the Congress of the United States than that did?" The Gulf of Tonkin resolution, he said, was "as broad an authorization for the use of armed forces for a purpose as any declaration of war so-called could be in terms of our internal constitutional process." Mr. Katzenbach also said, however, that he did not wish to be understood as having said that the Gulf of Tonkin resolution was tantamount to a declaration of war. "We did not declare war," he said. "Our objectives are limited. We are there for a limited purpose." . . .

The last four Presidents—Eisenhower a shade less than the others—have all asserted unrestricted executive authority to commit the armed forces without the consent of Congress, and Congress, for the most part, has acquiesced in the transfer of its war power to the executive. . . . Claims to unlimited executive authority over the use of armed force are made on grounds of both legitimacy and necessity. The committee finds both sets of contentions unsound. . . .

[T]he committee rejects the contention that the war powers as spelled out in the Constitution are obsolete and strongly recommends that the Congress reassert its constitutional authority over the use of the armed forces. No constitutional amendment or legislative enactment is required for this purpose; all that is required is the restoration of constitutional procedures which have been permitted to atrophy. . . .

The committee does not believe that formal declarations of war are the only available means by which Congress can authorize the President to initiate limited or general hostilities. Joint resolutions such as those pertaining to Formosa, the Middle East, and the Gulf of Tonkin are a proper method of granting authority, provided that they are precise as to what is to be done and for what period of time, and provided that they do in fact *grant authority* and not merely express approval of undefined action to be taken by the President. . . .

CONGRESSIONAL EFFORTS TO LIMIT THE PRESIDENT'S USE OF THE ARMED FORCES: FROM THE FULBRIGHT COMMITTEE'S DELIBERATIONS TO THE WAR POWERS RESOLUTION OF 1973

Introduction. The Senate Foreign Relations Committee Hearings and Report of 1967 initiated a new era of congressional searches for more effective techniques to curtail presidential authority to commit armed forces to hostilities, from "sense to Senate" resolutions to funds cut-offs and, ultimately, to the War Powers Resolution of 1973. Early in that era, a law review comment concluded: "[A]ny attempt to brand particular conflicts as constitutional or unconstitutional is likely to be of little consequence. The constitutional analysis is better viewed as yielding a working directive to the executive and legislative branches that the commitment of country to war be accomplished only through the closest collaboration possible, rather than an automatic formula for condemning or approving particular

presidential action. The question should be: what concrete steps should the two branches take to assure that the policies behind the constitutional scheme are served?" [1]

Was that the proper question? Was the debate about the constitutionality of the Vietnam conflict "of little consequence"? Were the progressively more "concrete steps" by Congress to delineate the boundaries of constitutional power and practice appropriate, useful, and constitutional ones?

1. *Congressional policy statements.* As a result of the Fulbright Committee's deliberations, the Senate in June 1969 enacted S.Res. 85, expressing the "sense of the Senate" that "a national commitment by the United States results only from affirmative action taken by the executive and legislative branches of the United States government by means of a treaty, statute, or concurrent resolution of both Houses of Congress, specifically providing for such commitment." Did that change constitutional doctrine? Did that alter actual practice? Were the problems susceptible to solution via congressional policy statements?

2. *Funds cut-offs.* After unsuccessful earlier efforts to cut off Vietnam appropriations,[2] congressional efforts to control military activities in Southeast Asia through the appropriations route bore fruit in 1973—after the Vietnam cease-fire had been negotiated. The strongest language was in the Case-Church Amendment stating that no appropriations, past or future, could be used to finance the "involvement" of American forces in Indochina "unless specifically authorized" by Congress. That amendment was adopted by the Senate in June 1973. In the same month, Congress took final action on an amendment cutting off all funds for American combat activities in Cambodia and Laos, in response to ongoing American bombing in Cambodia. After President Nixon successfully vetoed that provision, he signed a "compromise" on July 1, 1973, with a funds cut-off provision carrying an August 15 date. President Nixon agreed to seek congressional authorization for any military action in Indochina after that date. See 87 Stat. 99.

3. *Congressional guidelines: The War Powers Resolution of 1973.* The guidelines technique to limit presidential war-making powers for the future first met partial success in 1972, when the Senate adopted a version of a proposal by Senator Javits to "make rules governing the use of the Armed Forces in the absence of a declaration of war by the Congress." The efforts by Senator Javits and others culminated in the adoption by the entire Congress of the War Powers Resolution of 1973, printed above. Reconsider the congressional guidelines enacted in 1973 in the light of the preceding materials. Does the 1973 Resolution present constitutional problems?

The Resolution was enacted after a veto by President Nixon. In his October, 1973, veto message,[3] President Nixon insisted that the Resolution

1. Note, "Congress, the President, and the Power to Commit Forces to Combat," 81 Harv.L.Rev. 1771 (1968).

2. E. g., in June, 1970, the Senate—after more than a month of debate—adopted the Cooper-Church Amendment, but that provision was dropped in conference.

3. See Message of October 23, 1973, H. Doc.No.93–171, 119 Cong.Rec. H 9400 (daily ed. Oct. 25, 1973). See also Ehrlich, "The Legal Process in Foreign Affairs: Military Intervention—A Testing Case," 27 Stan.L.Rev. 637, 648 (1975).

was not only "dangerous to the best interests of our nation" but also "unconstitutional." He argued that the Framers had wisely chosen "not to draw a precise and detailed line of demarcation" between the powers of the two branches, because of "the impossibility of foreseeing every contingency that might arise in this complex area."

The President especially objected to two provisions which "would attempt to take away, by a mere legislative act, authorities which the President has properly exercised under the Constitution for almost 200 years." He singled out § 5(b), requiring the president to withdraw American forces from foreign hostilities within 60 or 90 days unless Congress grants authorization, and § 5(c), requiring immediate withdrawal of forces if Congress so directs by concurrent resolution—a resolution not subject to presidential veto. President Nixon stated: "I believe that both these provisions are unconstitutional. The only way in which the constitutional powers of a branch of the Government can be altered is by amending the Constitution—and any attempt to make such alterations by legislation alone is clearly without force." [4] The President explained that he was "particularly disturbed by the fact that certain of the President's constitutional powers as Commander-in-Chief of the Armed Forces would terminate automatically" after 60 days without "overt congressional action." In effect, the President added, "the Congress is here attempting to increase its policy-making role through a provision which requires it to take absolutely no action at all. In my view, the proper way for the Congress to make known its will [is] through a positive action. [O]ne cannot become a responsible partner unless one is prepared to take responsible action." [5]

Note one respect in which the Resolution may be weaker than earlier proposals: the Resolution relegates the description of the exclusive circumstances under which the President can introduce American forces into hostilities without a declaration of war to a section entitled "Purpose and Policy"; Senator Eagleton and others who criticized the Resolution as too weak argued that the "Purpose and Policy" section has no statutory effect. Critics of the measure also urged that, rather than imposing a restraint on the President, the Resolution actually licenses the President to engage in brief military actions, since Congress is unlikely, once American forces are engaged, to terminate such actions before the 60 or 90 day periods expire.

In addition to the constitutional questions raised in the President's veto message, does the Resolution present other constitutional difficulties? Note that the Resolution does not limit the use of armed forces to formal declarations of war; it also includes "specific statutory authorization," though it excludes mere congressional appropriations for military expenditures. Recall the arguments about implicit authorizations of the Vietnam conflict, in the 1967 Fulbright Committee Report above. Are the congressional "au-

4. Did that statement imply that the President would ignore the provisions if circumstances arose where the War Powers Resolutions would be applicable? After Congress enacted the Resolution over the President's veto, the White House refused to make any statement as to whether the Resolu-

tion would be obeyed. See the Ehrlich article, footnote 4 above.

5. The President conceded, however, that the Resolution included "certain constructive measures" furthering "cooperation" between the branches—e. g., § 3 on "consultation."

thorizations" recognized by the 1973 Resolution constitutionally adequate alternatives for formal declarations of war? Recall also the questions about the scope of "national emergency" under § 2 of the Resolution and about the time limits, in light of the traditional recognition of presidential power to repel attacks. (See the questions after the Prize Cases, above). Note also the recognition of traditional presidential authority to use armed forces to protect the lives and property of Americans abroad, in the Fulbright Committee's 1967 Report. The statement of circumstances under which the President may use force in § 2(c) of the 1973 Resolution does not include any such authority. Does that improperly curtail constitutional powers of the President? [6]

SECTION 2. THE INTEGRITY AND AUTONOMY OF THE THREE BRANCHES: INTERFERENCES WITH THE INTERNAL AFFAIRS OF ANOTHER BRANCH; COMMITMENT OF CONSTITUTIONAL ISSUES FOR FINAL DECISIONS BY NONJUDICIAL BRANCHES

Introduction. The preceding section considered problems of competition between President and Congress in making policy for the domestic and foreign spheres. This section samples a range of problems pertaining to the integrity and autonomy of the executive and legislative branches from interferences by each other and by the judiciary. To what extent may Congress control the removal of executive personnel? To what extent may it intrude into the internal processes of the executive branch? To what extent are the President and members of Congress amenable to judicial process? To what extent are constitutional issues committed for final decision to Congress or the President rather than Court?

The sampling of these interrelated issues of executive and legislative autonomy and judicial authority begins with an examination of the removal of executive officials. When may Congress restrain the President's power to remove subordinates? On what grounds may Congress exercise its power to impeach and remove the President? Attention then turns to problems of amenability to the judicial process. The central focus of the section is the Watergate Tapes litigation culminating with the decision in United States v. Nixon in 1974. That case raises several questions: Can the President be brought to court? What are the contours of executive privilege? Who has the authority to determine those contours? A study of that litigation accord-

---

6. Recall the references to the evacuation of Americans and South Vietnamese from Saigon and to the S.S. Mayagüez incident in April and May, 1975, p. 434 above. Note also the provision of § 8(2) requiring implementing legislation to permit use of American forces in accordance with treaty obligations. Recall that the existence of the SEATO Treaty was one of the justifications for use of American forces in Vietnam. Can congressional action such as the War Powers Resolution curtail whatever independent authority may exist under treaty obligations? Recall the consideration of the treaty power in Missouri v. Holland and Reid v. Covert, chap. 4, sec. 3, above; and of the problems of executive agreements and congressional control, above.

ingly draws together several of the strands in this section: amenability to judicial process; scope of executive privilege; authority to delineate that scope.   And the last of these issues offers an opportunity for an exploration of one of the ingredients of the "political questions" concept: what issues are constitutionally committed for final decisions to branches other than the courts?

A. CONGRESS AND THE CONTROL OF EXECUTIVE PERSONNEL AND PROCESSES: PRESIDENTIAL POWER TO REMOVE SUBORDINATES; IMPEACHING THE PRESIDENT; OTHER PROBLEMS

---

1. *Congress and the President's power to remove subordinates.* The only explicit constitutional reference to the removal of executive personnel is in the impeachment provisions, considered below.   But from the outset, a power to remove subordinate executive officials by routes other than impeachment has been assumed.   Where is that power lodged?   Is it solely in the President?   Or may Congress limit presidential removal authority?   The first modern judicial answer was a broad endorsement of executive autonomy, but subsequent decisions have found considerable room for congressional participation.[1]

a. *The Myers case.* In MYERS v. UNITED STATES, 272 U.S. 52 (1926), the Court held unconstitutional a legislative provision that certain groups of postmasters could not be removed by the President without the consent of the Senate.   Chief Justice Taft's opinion for the Court rested on an expansive reading of executive powers under Art. II and found the statute an unconstitutional restriction on the President's control over executive personnel.   The Chief Justice found that it was a "reasonable implication" from the President's power to execute the laws that "he should select those who were to act for him under his direction in the execution of the laws." And it was an additional plausible implication that "as his selection of administrative officers is essential to the execution of the laws by him, so must be his power of removing those for whom he can not continue to be responsible."

b. *Humphrey's Executor.* Less than a decade after Myers, the Court curtailed some of its implications and distinguished the decision in holding that the President could not remove a member of an independent regulatory agency in defiance of restrictions in the statutory framework.   HUMPHREY'S EXECUTOR v. UNITED STATES, 295 U.S. 602 (1935).   Justice Sutherland's opinion for the Court found that the Federal Trade Commission Act specified the causes for removal of Commissioners and held that,

---

1. See generally Corwin, The President: Office and Powers (4th ed. 1957).

A 19th century congressional effort to restrict presidential removal power did not reach the courts.   In the Tenure of Office Act of 1867, Congress required Senate consent to the removal of Cabinet members.   A central charge in President Andrew Johnson's impeachment was that he had removed a department head without that consent. President Johnson claimed that the legislative restraints on his power were unconstitutional.

in view of the functions of the agency, Congress could limit the President's power of removal. The Court found the Myers principle limited to "purely executive officers." The FTC, by contrast, "cannot in any proper sense be characterized as an arm or an eye of the executive." Under the statute, its duties were to be "free from executive control." Instead, the Commission acted "in part quasi-legislatively and in part quasi-judicially." The Myers rule, then, stands simply for "the unrestrictable power of the President to remove purely executive officers."

c. *Wiener.* The Court applied the Humphrey's rather than the Myers rule in WIENER v. UNITED STATES, 357 U.S. 349 (1958), involving the removal of a member of the War Claims Commission. The statute establishing that Commission, unlike the one in Humphrey's Executor, was silent on removal and did not specify permissible grounds to remove. But the Court emphasized that the Commission's function was of an "intrinsic judicial character" and held the removal illegal. As to officers who were not purely executive, power to remove existed "only if Congress may fairly be said to have conferred it." The Court noted: "This sharp differentiation derives from the difference in functions between those who are part of the Executive establishment and those whose tasks require absolute freedom from Executive interference." [2]

d. *An independent national prosecutor?* Consider the bearing of these principles on the proposals in the wake of the Watergate controversy to establish an independent national prosecutor by congressional action, with safeguards against presidential removal. Some of the proposals went so far as to suggest that the Attorney General's entire prosecutorial functions should be made independent of presidential control. Other proposals—e. g., for a national Counsel General—would create an independent prosecutor solely for the purpose of policing misconduct in the executive branch. Do those pro-

---

2. For another area in which presidential powers and congressional legislation may produce conflicts, consider the President's power to grant reprieves and pardons, Art. II, § 2. Recall United States v. Klein, 13 Wall. 128 (1871), considered in the notes after the McCardle case in chap. 1 above: In Klein, the congressional act on the effect to be given to pardons was found unconstitutional because it violated separation of powers in two respects—it not only interfered with the judicial power, but also with the presidential power to pardon. The Court has repeatedly stated in dictum, moreover, that the presidential pardon power is not subject to legislative control. See, e. g., Ex parte Garland, 4 Wall. 333 (1866). However, the presidential pardoning power "has never been held to take from Congress the power to pass acts of general amnesty." See Brown v. Walker, 161 U.S. 591, 601 (1896). For a modern reiteration of the breadth of the presidential pardoning power, see Schick v. Reed, 419 U.S. 256 (1974), a 6 to 3 decision rejecting a constitutional attack by one who had been sentenced to death by a court-marital and whose sentence had been commuted by the President to life imprisonment subject to the condition that he would not thereafter be eligible for parole. Chief Justice Burger's majority opinion found the condition within presidential power. Note the statement in the opinion that "the power flows from the Constitution alone, not from any legislative enactments, and [it] cannot be modified, abridged, or diminished by the Congress." The Court found that the President may attach "any condition which does not otherwise offend the Constitution." Justice Marshall's dissent, joined by Justices Douglas and Brennan, insisted that the President's condition had imposed a sentence not authorized by the statute and argued that in commuting a sentence, "the Chief Executive is not imbued with the constitutional power to create unauthorized punishments."

posals raise constitutional difficulties? Recall also the proposals after the firing of Special Prosecutor Cox in 1973, for congressional establishment of a special prosecutor who would be outside of executive control with respect to appointment as well as removal. Some of those proposals relied for constitutional justification on the language in Art. II, § 2, cl. 2, stating that Congress may in some instances vest the appointment of inferior officers "in the Courts of Law," as well as on general checks and balances principles. Would such proposals be subject to serious constitutional objection on the basis of an argument that prosecutorial activities are "purely executive"?

2. *Impeaching the President.* The proceedings of the House Committee on the Judiciary during the spring and summer of 1974 provoked the most intense national attention to problems of impeachment in more than a century. The most important constitutional problem aired in the debates which culminated in the Committee approval of three Articles of Impeachment against President Nixon pertained to the scope of impeachable offenses.[1] In the course of those debates, seldom examined provisions of the constitutional text—especially Art. II, § 4, and Art. I, §§ 2 and 3—were pored over, and relevant historical precedents and policy considerations were probed. American experience with the impeachment weapon has been sparse: Andrew Johnson is the only President who was impeached, escaping conviction and removal by the Senate by only one vote; most impeachments voted by the House involved federal judges; the Senate has voted to convict in only four instances, all involving judges.

Art. II, § 4, states: "The President, Vice President and all civil Officers of the United States, shall be removed from Office on Impeachment for, and Conviction of, Treason, Bribery, or other high Crimes and Misdemeanors." What is the scope of the phrase "other high Crimes and Misdemeanors"? What presidential misconduct is properly the subject of impeachment proceedings? Must the conduct constitute a criminal offense? Criminal under what law? If the scope of impeachable offenses is not coextensive with criminality, what acceptable criteria can be stated? What criminal behavior may not be impeachable? What noncriminal conduct may be impeachable? Consider the appropriate criteria in light of the considerations aired during the course of the proceedings before the House Judiciary Committee (note 2a below) and in light of the Articles of Impeachment against President Nixon adopted by the Committee (excerpted in note 2b).

a. *The scope of impeachable offenses.* The modern debate about impeachable offenses focused on two contending views: President Nixon's counsel claimed that "other high Crimes and Misdemeanors" is limited to serious acts which would be indictable as criminal offenses; the staff of the Judiciary Committee insisted that the scope of impeachable offenses and of criminality are not synonymous, and that the impeachment route may reach serious abuses of office or breaches of trust not constituting criminal acts.

1. This group of notes is limited to that problem. A range of other constitutional problems were brought to the fore during the consideration of the Nixon impeachment—e. g., whether judgments of conviction in the Senate after votes of impeachment in the House are judicially reviewable, and the extent to which a President may assert claims of executive privilege in the course of impeachment inquiries. Those questions are considered in later materials in this section.

The main support for the President's position came from the terminology used in the Constitution, though the text is not unambiguous. The main reliance of the defenders of the broader position was on history—both English historical background and the evidence as to the intent of the Framers. Moreover, both sides marshalled policy arguments on their behalf.

Thus, Presidential counsel James D. St.Clair and his colleagues asserted: [2] "Impeachment of a President should be resorted to only for cases of the gravest kind—the commission of a crime named in the Constitution or a criminal offense against the laws of the United States." Impeachment, they contended, "was designed to deal exclusively with indictable criminal conduct." Broader views asserted in the context of judicial impeachment are irrelevant: the reference to "good Behavior" in Art. III justifies broader grounds against judges; but in the President's case, the impeachment provision is "limited solely to indictable crimes and cannot extend to misbehavior." They argued: "Those who seek to broaden the impeachment power invite the use of power 'as a means of crushing political adversaries or ejecting them from office.' The acceptance of such an invitation would be destructive to our system of government and to the fundamental principle of separation of powers. The Framers never intended that the impeachment clause serve to dominate or destroy the executive branch of the government." Constitutional text and history, they concluded, required as a basis for impeachment not merely "a criminal offense, but one of a very serious nature committed in one's governmental capacity." They found the "use of a predetermined criminal standard for the impeachment of a President" supported "by history, logic, legal precedent and a sound and sensible public policy which demands stability in our form of government."

Contrast the view of the legal staff of the impeachment inquiry,[3] concluding: "Impeachment is a constitutional remedy addressed to serious offenses against the system of government. . . . Because impeachment of a President is a grave step for the nation, it is to be predicated only upon conduct seriously incompatible with either the constitutional form and principles of our government or the proper performance of constitutional duties of the presidential office." Criminality is not the central issue: the reason treason and bribery are specifically named is not because they are crimes but because "they are constitutional wrongs that subvert the structure of government, or undermine the integrity of office and even the Constitution itself, and thus are 'high' offenses in the sense that word was used in English impeachments." The Framers were concerned that "the executive would not become the creature of the legislature, dismissable at its will," to be sure; but they "also recognized that some means would be needed to deal with excesses by the executive." Typically, in the English practice and in several of the American impeachments, "the criminality issue was not raised at all. The emphasis has been on the significant effects of the conduct—undermining the integrity of office, disregard of constitutional duties and oath of office, ar-

2. St. Clair et al., Summary of an Analysis of the Constitutional Standard for Presidential Impeachment (released February 28, 1974).

3. Staff Report (by the staff headed by Special Committee Counsel John Doar and Special Minority Counsel Albert E. Jenner, Jr.), Constitutional Grounds for Presidential Impeachment (released February 22, 1974).

rogation of power, abuse of the governmental process, adverse impact on the system of government. Clearly, these effects can be brought about in ways not anticipated by the criminal law. Criminal standards and criminal courts were established to control individual conduct. Impeachment was evolved by Parliament to cope with both the inadequacy of criminal standards and the impotence of courts to deal with the conduct of great public figures." [4]

Compare a brief, thoughtful study prepared by a committee of the Association of the Bar of the City of New York shortly before the House impeachment inquiry began.[5] That committee concluded "that the grounds for impeachment are not limited to or synonymous with crimes (indeed, acts constituting a crime may not be sufficient for the impeachment of an office-holder in all circumstances). Rather, we believe that acts which undermine the integrity of government are appropriate grounds whether or not they happen to constitute offenses under the general criminal law. In our view, the essential nexus to damaging the integrity of government may be found in acts which constitute corruption in, or flagrant abuse of the powers of, official position. It may also be found in acts which, without directly affecting governmental processes, undermine that degree of public confidence in the probity of executive and judicial officers that is essential to the effectiveness of government in a free society. . . . At the heart of the matter is the determination [that] the officeholder has demonstrated by his actions that he is unfit to continue in the office in question."

The committee continued: "The constitutional intention that impeachment not be treated as a partisan political weapon cannot be effectuated by attempting to limit to specific categories the range of presidential misconduct which would justify impeachment. The seriousness with which the Constitution impresses resort to these procedures should be respected in a different way. Congress should not impeach and remove a President except for conduct for which it would be prepared to impeach and remove any President. We emphatically disagree with the casual view of impeachment recently put forth by then-Congressman Gerald Ford, that 'an impeachable offense is what-

---

4. Contrast the conflicting inferences drawn from the Constitutional Convention debates by these two studies. After George Mason objected to language limited to "treason or bribery" as too narrow, he moved to add the word "maladministration" as a ground for impeachment. Madison objected that "so vague a term will be equivalent to a tenure during pleasure of the Senate." Mason then withdrew "maladministration" and successfully substituted "high crimes and misdemeanors agst. the State." Mason in objecting to the "treason and bribery" limitation argued that so narrow a phrase would "not reach many great and dangerous offences" including "[a]ttempts to subvert the Constitution."
The inquiry staff concluded from this that Mason believed "high Crimes and Misdemeanors" would "cover the offenses about which he was concern-

ed." The staff found added support in Hamilton's Federalist No. 65, which refers to impeachment for "the abuse or violation of some public trust"— for offenses which are "POLITICAL, as they relate chiefly to injuries done immediately to the society itself." In light of the historical context, then, the staff concluded that impeachment was viewed "as a remedy for usurpation or abuse of power or serious breach of trust." The study by President Nixon's counsel, by contrast, emphasized the rejection of "maladministration" as a standard for impeachment at the Constitutional Convention. That study concluded that the "debates clearly indicate a purely criminal meaning" for the constitutional phrase.

5. Committee on Federal Legislation, The Law of Presidential Impeachment (released January 21, 1974).

ever a majority of the House of Representatives considers it to be . . . .'
[That statement was made in 1970, in the context of efforts to impeach Justice Douglas.] And we likewise reject the view of impeachment suggested in the challenge of former Attorney General Kleindienst, testifying before a Senate committee, that 'you don't need facts, you don't need evidence' to impeach the President, 'all you need is votes.' . . . That the grounds for impeachment may not be limited to criminal acts, or otherwise defined by predetermined categories of conduct, does not mean that Congress should ignore its responsibility to principle in exercising its quasi-judicial powers of impeachment and removal." Note also the Committee's earlier summary of its position: "We submit that Congress may properly impeach and remove a President only for conduct amounting to a gross breach of trust or serious abuse of power, and only if it would be prepared to take the same action against any President who engaged in comparable conduct in similar circumstances." [6]

  b. *The Articles of Impeachment against President Nixon.* [On July 27, 29 and 30, 1974, the House Judiciary Committee adopted three Articles of Impeachment. The most general Articles—Articles I and II, dealing with the Watergate cover-up and with other abuses of power—are excerpted below. Article III, on defiance of House subpoenas, appears later in these materials, with other problems of executive privilege. Consider whether the charges in these Articles reflect appropriate criteria of impeachable offenses.[7]]

RESOLUTION

  Impeaching Richard M. Nixon, President of the United States, of high crimes and misdemeanors.

  Resolved, That Richard M. Nixon, President of the United States, is impeached for high crimes and misdemeanors, and that the following articles of impeachment be exhibited to the Senate:

  Articles of impeachment exhibited by the House of Representatives of the United States of America in the name of itself and of all of the people

6. For recent compilations of historical materials on impeachment, see, e. g., the several volumes of reports compiled by the staff of the House Judiciary Committee, including "Impeachment—Selected Materials" (October 1973) and "Impeachment—Selected Materials on Procedure" (January 1974), and "The Legal Aspects of Impeachment: An Overview," prepared by the Office of Legal Counsel of the Department of Justice (February 1974). See also Berger, "Impeachment: The Constitutional Problems" (1973); Black, "Impeachment: A Handbook" (1974); and, of course, the airing of these issues in the historic public deliberations of the House Judiciary Committee in the summer of 1974, and in the Committee's final report, Report on the Impeachment of Richard M. Nixon, President of the United States, H.R.Rep.No.1035, 93d Cong., 2d Sess. [For an especially thoughtful account of the impeachment debate by a journalist, see Elizabeth Drew's Washington Journal (1975), originally published in The New Yorker.]

7. See the House Committee's Report on Impeachment, cited in the preceding footnote, and reprinted in 120 Cong. Rec. (daily ed. August 22, 1974). Articles I and II were adopted by Committee votes of 27 to 11 and 28 to 10 respectively. The majority on Article III shrank to 21 to 17. Further proceedings on the Impeachment Articles were abandoned when President Nixon resigned on August 9, 1974, after the release of Watergate tapes in the wake of the Supreme Court's decision in United States v. Nixon, below.

of the United States of America, against Richard M. Nixon, President of the United States of America, in maintenance and support of its impeachment against him for high crimes and misdemeanors.

Article I

In his conduct of the office of President of the United States, Richard M. Nixon, in violation of his constitutional oath faithfully to execute the office of President of the United States and, to the best of his ability, preserve, protect, and defend the Constitution of the United States, and in violation of his constitutional duty to take care that the laws be faithfully executed, has prevented, obstructed, and impeded the administration of justice, in that:

On June 17, 1972, and prior thereto, agents of the Committee for the Re-election of the President committed unlawful entry of the headquarters of the Democratic National Committee in Washington, District of Columbia, for the purpose of securing political intelligence. Subsequent thereto, Richard M. Nixon, using the powers of his high office, engaged personally and through his subordinates and agents, in a course of conduct or plan designed to delay, impede, and obstruct the investigation of such unlawful entry; to cover up, conceal, and protect those responsible; and to conceal the existence and scope of other unlawful covert activities.

The means used to implement this course of conduct or plan included one or more of the following:

(1) making or causing to be made false or misleading statements to lawfully authorized investigative officers and employees of the United States;

(2) withholding relevant and material evidence or information from lawfully authorized investigative officers and employees of the United States;

(3) approving, condoning, acquiescing in, and counseling witnesses with respect to the giving of false or misleading statements . . . .;

(4) interfering or endeavoring to interfere with the conduct of investigations by the Department of Justice of the United States, the Federal Bureau of Investigation, the Office of Watergate Special Prosecution Force, and Congressional Committees;

(5) approving, condoning, and acquiescing in, the surreptitious payment of substantial sums of money for the purpose of obtaining the silence or influencing the testimony of witnesses, potential witnesses or individuals who participated in such unlawful entry and other illegal activities;

(6) endeavoring to misuse the Central Intelligence Agency, an agency of the United States;

(7) disseminating information received from officers to the Department of Justice of the United States to subjects of investigations . . . for the purpose of aiding and assisting such subjects in their attempts to avoid criminal liability;

(8) making false or misleading public statements for the purpose of deceiving the people of the United States into believing that a thorough and complete investigation had been conducted with respect to allegations of misconduct on the part of personnel of the executive branch of the United

States and personnel of the Committee for the Re-election of the President, and that there was no involvement of such personnel in such misconduct; or

(9) endeavoring to cause prospective defendants, and individuals duly tried and convicted, to expect favored treatment and consideration in return for their silence or false testimony, or rewarding individuals for their silence or false testimony.

In all of this, Richard M. Nixon has acted in a manner contrary to his trust as President and subversive of constitutional government, to the great prejudice of the cause of law and justice and to the manifest injury of the people of the United States.

Wherefore Richard M. Nixon, by such conduct, warrants impeachment and trial, and removal from office.

Article II

Using the powers of the office of President of the United States, Richard M. Nixon, in violation of his constitutional oath faithfully to execute the office of President of the United States and, to the best of his ability, preserve, protect, and defend the Constitution of the United States, and in disregard of his constitutional duty to take care that the laws be faithfully executed, has repeatedly engaged in conduct violating the constitutional rights of citizens, impairing the due and proper administration of justice and the conduct of lawful inquiries, or contravening the laws governing agencies of the executive branch and the purposes of these agencies.

This conduct has included one or more of the following:

(1) He has, acting personally and through his subordinates and agents, endeavored to obtain from the Internal Revenue Service, in violation of the constitutional rights of citizens, confidential information contained in income tax returns for purposes not authorized by law, and to cause, in violation of the constitutional rights of citizens, income tax audits or other income tax investigations to be initiated or conducted in a discriminatory manner.

(2) He misused the Federal Bureau of Investigation, the Secret Service, and other executive personnel, in violation or disregard of the constitutional rights of citizens, by directing or authorizing such agencies or personnel to conduct or continue electronic surveillance or other investigations for purposes unrelated to national security, the enforcement of laws, or any other lawful function of his office; he did direct, authorize, or permit the use of information obtained thereby for purposes unrelated to national security, the enforcement of laws, or any other lawful function of his office; and he did direct the concealment of certain records made by the Federal Bureau of Investigation of electronic surveillance.

(3) He has, acting personally and through his subordinates and agents, in violation or disregard of the constitutional rights of citizens, authorized and permitted to be maintained a secret investigative unit within the office of the President, financed in part with money derived from campaign contributions, which unlawfully utilized the resources of the Central Intelligence Agency, engaged in covert and unlawful activities, and attempted to prejudice the constitutional right of an accused to a fair trial.

(4) He has failed to take care that the laws were faithfully executed by failing to act when he knew or had reason to know that his close subordinates endeavored to impede and frustrate lawful inquiries by duly constituted executive, judicial, and legislative entities concerning the unlawful entry into the headquarters of the Democratic National Committee, and the cover-up thereof, and concerning other unlawful activities, including those relating to the confirmation of Richard Kleindienst as Attorney General of the United States, the electronic surveillance of private citizens, the break-in into the offices of Dr. Lewis Fielding, and the campaign financing practices of the Committee to Re-elect the President.

(5) In disregard of the rule of law, he knowingly misused the executive power by interfering with agencies of the executive branch, including the Federal Bureau of Investigation, the Criminal Division, and the Office of Watergate Special Prosecution Force, of the Department of Justice, and the Central Intelligence Agency, in violation of his duty to take care that the laws be faithfully executed.

In all of this, Richard M. Nixon has acted in a manner contrary to his trust as President and subversive of constitutional government, to the great prejudice of the cause of law and justice and to the manifest injury of the people of the United States.

Wherefore Richard M. Nixon, by such conduct, warrants impeachment and trial, and removal from office.

B.   AMENABILITY TO JUDICIAL PROCESS: LEGISLATIVE AND EXECUTIVE IMMUNITIES

1. *Legislative immunity and the Speech and Debate Clause.* Art. I, § 6, states that Senators and Representatives "shall not be questioned in any other Place" for "any Speech or Debate in either House." [1] In recent years, the Court has had repeated occasion to construe the scope of that immunity of national legislators. Note, for example, Powell v. McCormack, 395 U.S. 486 (1969) (below), where an action challenging an exclusion from the House was dismissed against those defendants who were members of Congress on the basis of that Clause; but the Clause did not preclude the Court's review of the merits of the challenged congressional action "since congressional employees were also sued," and they were retained as defendants. A more extensive consideration of the Clause became necessary in UNITED STATES v. BREWSTER, 408 U.S. 501 (1972), a 6 to 3 decision holding that the Clause did not bar prosecution of a former Senator for accepting a bribe relating to his actions on postage rate legislation. Chief Justice Burger's majority opinion concluded that the Clause did not protect all conduct "*relating* to the legislative process"; it only "protects against inquiry into acts which occur in the regular course of the legislative process and the motivation for those acts." Here, he explained, the prosecution could succeed simply by showing acceptance of the bribe, without getting into the question whether the illegal promise was performed. Justices Brennan, White and Douglas dissented. But Justice White spoke for the majority in the 5 to 4 decision in Gravel v. United States, 408 U.S. 606 (1972), a case growing out of a

1. Note also a different congressional immunity granted by the preceding phrase in the same sentence of the Constitution: a privilege "from Arrest during their Attendance at the Session" in most cases.

grand jury investigation into the disclosure of the Pentagon Papers.   The Court held that a Senator could invoke the protection of the Clause to block questioning of his assistant, but that the immunity covered only legislative acts and did not bar investigation of alleged arrangements for private publication of the Pentagon Papers.   Justices Douglas, Brennan and Marshall dissented, and Justice Stewart dissented in part.   The case is noted further below, in chap. 13.

The Court continued divided about the scope of the Clause a year later, in DOE v. McMILLAN, 412 U.S. 306 (1973).   Petitioners were parents of District of Columbia students seeking relief for alleged invasion of privacy in the dissemination of a congressional committee report on the D.C. school system.   The 6 to 3 decision found the Clause to be a partial but not a total barrier to suit.   According to Justice White's majority opinion, Congressmen and staff members are absolutely immune from suit for introducing the allegedly derogatory material at committee hearings and for voting for publication of the committee report.   But there is no absolute immunity for legislative functionaries "who, with authorization from Congress, distribute materials which allegedly infringe upon the rights of individuals."   Despite the conceded "importance of informing the public of the business of Congress," participants in "distributions of actionable material beyond the reasonable bounds of the legislative task enjoy no Speech or Debate Clause immunity."   In short, distributing objectionable materials becomes actionable, despite congressional authorization, where the dissemination of information is "beyond the reasonable requirements of the legislative function."   Justice Rehnquist's dissent, joined by Chief Justice Burger and Justice Blackmun (and, in part, by Justice Stewart), insisted that the majority's endorsement of liability for public dissemination—as distinguished from dissemination within Congress—contravened not only the Clause but also general principles of separation of powers.[*]

2. *Executive immunity.*   a.   *Judicial process.*   Unlike legislators, executive officials are not granted any express immunity in the Constitution. And the Court long ago rejected any inference from separation of power principles that executive officers are wholly immune from court orders.   Indeed, Thomas Jefferson's irritation about Marbury v. Madison stemmed largely from John Marshall's assertion that courts could issue mandamus against Cabinet members in proper cases.   And Cabinet members have repeatedly been defendants before courts, as in the Steel Seizure Case.   However, the development of judicial remedies against executive action has been a slow one.   The Marbury v. Madison dicta about mandamus to compel performance of ministerial acts bore fruit in Kendall v. United States, 12 Pet. 524 (1838).   But that holding by no means assured easy access to courts.   The difficulties of asserting claims against the United States and its officials have stemmed particularly from uncertainties in the law of remedies and from the occasional availability of the defense of sovereign immunity.   For a survey of the evolution since the Marbury and Kendall cases, see "Developments in the Law—Remedies Against the United States and Its Officials," 70 Harv. L.Rev. 827 (1957).

---

[*] See also the reliance on the Clause to bar an action to enjoin a congressional investigating committee's subpoena of an organization's bank records, in Eastland v. U. S. Servicemen's Fund, 421 U.S. —— (1975) (also noted in chap. 13, sec. 6, below).

b. *Criminal liability.* Can an executive immunity from criminal prosecution nevertheless be implied from the existence of the impeachment provisions? The last clause in Art. I, § 3, states that "the Party convicted" in an impeachment proceeding "shall nevertheless be liable and subject to Indictment, Trial, Judgment, and Punishment, according to Law." Does that mean that an official must be removed and convicted through the impeachment route before he can be tried criminally? Vice President Agnew raised that contention prior to his resignation, in response to the grand jury proceedings against him. The Justice Department's response was that only the President, not the Vice President, was immune from criminal prosecution while in office.

The Justice Department's memorandum argued that the constitutional language was merely intended to foreclose any argument that double jeopardy notions bar prosecution of any impeached and removed official. The fact that Art. I, § 3, *mentions* impeachment and removal from office before mentioning criminal prosecution, it was argued, should not be read as a requirement that impeachment *precede* criminal prosecution.[2] Was the Justice Department's distinction between the President and the Vice President persuasive? There are some statements in the Convention Debates and in the Federalist Papers reflecting an assumption that impeachment and removal of the President would precede any criminal trial. See, e. g., Hamilton's Federalist Essays Nos. 65 and 69. But the major argument made on behalf of presidential immunity from criminal prosecution rested on inferences from the unique and important nature of the office.[3] (On additional problems of special presidential immunity, see the next note.)

3. *Presidential immunity.* The President's unique position raises special problems of amenability to judicial process, even though the President, like other executive officials, cannot rely on an explicit grant of immunity in the Constitution. While the courts have reviewed presidential actions through the device of suits against Cabinet members since the Kendall case, above, suits naming the President as a defendant have been extremely rare. Recall Mississippi v. (President Andrew) Johnson, 4 Wall. 475 (1867) (noted after the McCardle case, chap. 1 above). There, the Court refused to enjoin President Johnson from executing the Reconstruction Acts, and used language which suggested that the President—like members of Congress—was ordinarily not reachable directly by judicial process. The Court emphasized enforcement problems: If the President disobeyed an injunction, "it is needless to observe that the court is without power to enforce its process. If, on the other hand, the President complies with the order of the

2. Resolution of that issue in the Agnew case was avoided when the Vice President pleaded nolo contendere to a tax charge and resigned.

3. Compare Bickel, "The Constitutional Tangle," The New Republic (Oct. 6, 1973), with Berger, "The President, Congress, and the Courts," 83 Yale L.J. 1111 (1974).
An aspect of that problem was raised but not decided in United States v. Nixon, below. In the criminal proceedings against former Attorney General Mitchell et al., the grand jury had named President Nixon as an unindicted coconspirator. Initially, the Court's grant of certiorari included "the issue whether the Grand Jury acted within its authority in naming the President as an unindicted coconspirator." But in its decision, below, the Court found "resolution of this issue unnecessary to resolution of the question whether the claim of privilege is to prevail," and certiorari on that aspect of the case was accordingly "dismissed as improvidently granted."

court and refuses to execute the acts of Congress, is it not clear that a collision may occur between the executive and legislative departments of the government? May not the House of Representatives impeach the President for such refusal? And in that case could this court interfere, in behalf of the President?" Attorney General Stanbery had made additional arguments, emotionally and forcefully, in his jurisdictional plea in Mississippi v. Johnson. To issue an order against the President, he suggested, implied the power to enforce the order; and even if the physical power existed, punishing a President for contempt would in effect remove him from office—and would accordingly usurp the impeachment route.

The claim that the President is not amenable to judicial process was renewed in the course of the Watergate Tapes litigation. Mississippi v. Johnson, as well as the implications of the Burr trial and its subpoena to Thomas Jefferson, were repeatedly aired in the Nixon case arguments. Presidential Counsel St. Clair, for example, recalled the Johnson case and the Stanbery argument in his presentation to the Supreme Court.[4] The issue was considered at some length in the lower court proceedings in the Watergate Tapes litigation. The Supreme Court's result in United States v. Nixon is clear: a court order directed to the President did issue. But did the court adequately consider the separable issue of amenability? That problem is considered with other aspects of United States v. Nixon, below.

THE WATERGATE TAPES LITIGATION: AMENABILITY TO JUDICIAL PROCESS; EXECUTIVE AUTONOMY; THE SCOPE OF EXECUTIVE PRIVILEGE

Introduction. The Supreme Court's decision in United States v. Nixon follows. The Court's discussion bears on some of the issues already considered and raises additional ones. Examination of the various strands of the Nixon case is postponed to the notes following the case. But at the outset, it may be useful to note that there are indeed several issues intertwined in the litigation, and that the issues may be more separable than the Court's treatment suggests. The Nixon decision stemmed from an effort by Special Prosecutor Jaworski to obtain access to tape recordings and other documents pertaining to presidential conversations and allegedly necessary to press criminal proceedings against several defendants other than the President for conspiracy to obstruct justice and other charges. President Nixon raised several defenses, not always sharply distinguished in the Court's opinion. The constitutional defenses pertaining to separation of powers involved at least three different strands. First, there was the claim introduced in the preceding group of notes, that the President was not amenable to judicial process, that he was wholly immune, that impeachment and removal was a precondition to judicial proceedings. Second, there was the argument that, even if he were subject to court order, the scope of executive privilege was a constitutional issue committed to the executive branch for final decision under the constitutional scheme. That was an argument, in short, that "executive

---

4. For a convenient compilation of the briefs and oral arguments in the Supreme Court in United States v. Nixon, see United States v. Nixon—The President Before the Supreme Court (Friedman ed., 1974).

privilege" was one of those constitutional issues not justiciable, one to be finally decided by a branch of the government other than the courts. (See the further discusion of that aspect of the "political questions" doctrine below.) Third, there was the argument on the merits of the executive privilege issue: even if the President was amenable to judicial process, even if the scope of executive privilege was not wholly a matter of presidential judgment and was an issue to which courts could speak, the Court should find the subpoenaed tapes within the appropriate scope of executive privilege, in view of the needs for confidentiality in the executive branch. Did the Court adequately distinguish among, and adequately respond to, each of these contentions: (1) presidential immunity; (2) presidential autonomy and finality; (3) generous construction of the scope of executive privilege?

UNITED STATES v. NIXON

418 U.S. 683, 94 S.Ct. 3090, 41 L.Ed.2d 1039 (1974).

Certiorari to the United States Court of Appeals for the District of Columbia Circuit before judgment.*

Mr. Chief Justice BURGER delivered the opinion of the Court.

This litigation presents for review the denial of a motion, filed [on] behalf of the President of the United States, in the case of United States v. Mitchell et al., to quash a third-party subpoena *duces tecum* issued by the United States District Court for the District of Columbia, pursuant to Fed.Rule Crim. Proc. 17(c). The subpoena directed the President to produce certain tape recordings and documents relating to his conversations with aides and advisers. The court rejected the President's claims of absolute executive privilege, of lack of jurisdiction, and of failure to satisfy the requirements of Rule 17(c). The President appealed to the Court of Appeals. We granted the United States' petition for certiorari before judgment, and also the President's cross-petition for certiorari before judgment, because of the public importance of the issues presented and the need for their prompt resolution.[1]

On March 1, 1974, a grand jury of the United States District Court for the District of Columbia returned an indictment charging seven named individuals[2] with various offenses, including conspiracy to defraud the United

---

* Together with Nixon v. United States, also on certiorari before judgment to the same court.

other contributors to the Symposium supported the Court's decision to grant speedy review.

1. For a criticism of the Court's decision to bypass full consideration in the Court of Appeals and to grant extraordinarily speedy review in the case —a criticism noting the effect of that judgment as to timing in aborting full development of the impeachment process—see Gunther, "Judicial Hegemony and Legislative Autonomy: The Nixon Case and the Impeachment Process," 22 UCLA L.Rev. 30 (1974). That comment was part of a Symposium on United States v. Nixon. Some of the

2. The seven defendants were John N. Mitchell, H. R. Haldeman, John D. Ehrlichman, Charles W. Colson, Robert C. Mardian, Kenneth W. Parkinson, and Gordon Strachan. Each had occupied either a position of responsibility on the White House staff or a position with the Committee for the Re-election of the President. Colson entered a guilty plea on another charge and is no longer a defendant. [Footnote by the Court.]

States and to obstruct justice. Although he was not designated as such in the indictment, the grand jury named the President, among others, as an unindicted co-conspirator. On April 18, 1974, upon motion of the Special Prosecutor, a subpoena *duces tecum* was issued pursuant to Rule 17(c) to the President by the United States District Court and made returnable on May 2, 1974. This subpoena required the production, in advance of the September 9 trial date, of certain tapes, memoranda, papers, transcripts, or other writings relating to certain precisely identified meetings between the President and others. The Special Prosecutor was able to fix the time, place and persons present at these discussions because the White House daily logs and appointment records had been delivered to him. On April 30, the President publicly released edited transcripts of 43 conversations; portions of 20 conversations subject to subpoena in the present case were included. On May 1, 1974, the President's counsel filed a "special appearance" and a motion to quash the subpoena, under Rule 17(c). This motion was accompanied by a formal claim of privilege. . . .

On May 20, 1974, the District Court denied the motion to quash. [It] further ordered "the President or any subordinate officer, official or employee with custody or control of the documents or objects subpoenaed" to deliver to the District Court, on or before May 31, 1974, the originals of all subpoenaed items, as well as an index and analysis of those items, together with tape copies of those portions of the subpoenaed recordings for which transcripts had been released to the public by the President on April 30. The District Court rejected [the] contention that the judiciary was without authority to review an assertion of executive privilege by the President. [That] second challenge was held to be foreclosed by the decision in Nixon v. Sirica, 487 F.2d 700 (1973).

The District Court held that the judiciary, not the President, was the final arbiter of a claim of executive privilege. The court concluded that, under the circumstances of this case, the presumptive privilege was overcome by the Special Prosecutor's prima facie "demonstration of need sufficiently compelling to warrant judicial examination in chambers . . . ."

On May 24, 1974, the President filed a timely notice of appeal from the District Court order, and the certified record from the District Court was docketed in the United States Court of Appeals for the District of Columbia Circuit. . . . Later on May 24, the Special Prosecutor also filed, in this Court, a petition for a writ of certiorari before judgment. On May 31, the petition was granted with an expedited briefing schedule. [T]he case was set for argument on July 8, 1974.[3]

---

3. This case was decided on July 24, 1974.

Before the decision in the case, the President and his representatives had left it unclear whether he would obey an adverse Court decision. In the oral argument before the Supreme Court, for example, Presidential Counsel St. Clair had emphasized that the President "has his obligations under the Constitution." But eight hours after the Court decision was announced, President Nixon's office issued a statement reporting that he would comply. Among the 64 tape recordings to be turned over to Judge Sirica as a result of the decision was a particularly damaging one of conversations on June 23, 1972, six days after the Watergate burglary. On August 5, President Nixon released transcripts of those conversations. On August 8, President Nixon announced that he would resign on the next day.

[Before turning to the major issues in the case, the Court held that (1) the District Court order was an appealable order and that the case was properly "in" the Court of Appeals when the Supreme Court granted certiorari; (2) the Special Prosecutor's subpoena duces tecum satisfied the requirements of Fed.R.Crim.Proc. 17(c)—i. e., the requisite relevancy, admissibility, and specificity were shown; and (3) that the case was not a nonjusticiable intra-branch dispute. The Court then turned to the central portion of its opinion, entitled "The Claim of Privilege," and proceeded as follows:]

A

[W]e turn to the claim that the subpoena should be quashed because it demands "confidential conversations between a President and his close advisors that it would be inconsistent with the public interest to produce." The first contention is a broad claim that the separation of powers doctrine precludes judicial review of a President's claim of privilege. The second contention is that if he does not prevail on the claim of absolute privilege, the court should hold as a matter of constitutional law that the privilege prevails over the subpoena duces tecum.

In the performance of assigned constitutional duties each branch of the Government must initially interpret the Constitution, and the interpretation of its powers by any branch is due great respect from the others. The President's counsel, as we have noted, reads the Constitution as providing an absolute privilege of confidentiality for all Presidential communications. Many decisions of this Court, however, have unequivocally reaffirmed the holding of [Marbury v. Madison] that "it is emphatically the province and duty of the judicial department to say what the law is."

No holding of the Court has defined the scope of judicial power specifically relating to the enforcement of a subpoena for confidential Presidential communications for use in a criminal prosecution, but other exercises of powers by the Executive Branch and the Legislative Branch have been found invalid as in conflict with the Constitution. [Powell v. McCormack, below; Steel Seizure.] In a series of cases, the Court interpreted the explicit immunity conferred by express provisions of the Constitution on Members of the House and Senate by the Speech or Debate Clause. (E. g., Doe v. McMillan; United States v. Brewster.] Since this Court has consistently exercised the power to construe and delineate claims arising under express powers, it must follow that the Court has authority to interpret claims with respect to powers alleged to derive from enumerated powers.

Our system of government "requires that federal courts on occasion interpret the Constitution in a manner at variance with the construction given the document by another branch." [Powell v. McCormack.] And in [Baker v. Carr, below and chap. 15], the Court stated:

"Deciding whether a matter has in any measure been committed by the Constitution to another branch of government, or whether the action of that branch exceeds whatever authority has been committed, is itself a delicate exercise in constitutional interpretation, and is a responsibility of this Court as ultimate interpreter of the Constitution."

Notwithstanding the deference each branch must accord the others, the "judicial Power of the United States" vested in the federal courts by Art. III, § 1, of the Constitution can no more be shared with the Executive Branch than the Chief Executive, for example, can share with the Judiciary the veto power, or the Congress share with the Judiciary the power to override a Presidential veto. Any other conclusion would be contrary to the basic concept of separation of powers and the checks and balances that flow from the scheme of a tripartite government. [The Federalist, No. 47.] We therefore reaffirm that it is the province and the duty of this Court "to say what the law is" with respect to the claim of privilege presented in this case. [Marbury v. Madison.]

B

In support of his claim of absolute privilege, the President's counsel urges two grounds, one of which is common to all governments and one of which is peculiar to our system of separation of powers. The first ground is the valid need for protection of communications between high Government officials and those who advise and assist them in the performance of their manifold duties; the importance of this confidentiality is too plain to require further discussion. Human experience teaches that those who expect public dissemination of their remarks may well temper candor with a concern for appearances and for their own interests to the detriment of the decision-making process.[4] Whatever the nature of the privilege of confidentiality of Presidential communications in the exercise of Art. II powers, the privilege can be said to derive from the supremacy of each branch within its own assigned area of constitutional duties. Certain powers and privileges flow from the nature of enumerated powers;[5] the protection of the confidentiality of Presidential communications has similar constitutional underpinnings.

The second ground asserted by the President's counsel in support of the claim of absolute privilege rests on the doctrine of separation of powers. Here it is argued that the independence of the Executive Branch within its own sphere insulates a President from a judicial subpoena in an ongoing criminal prosecution, and thereby protects confidential Presidential communications.

However, neither the doctrine of separation of powers, nor the need for confidentiality of high level communications, without more, can sustain an absolute, unqualified Presidential privilege of immunity from judicial

---

4. There is nothing novel about governmental confidentiality. The meetings of the Constitutional Convention in 1787 were conducted in complete privacy. Moreover, all records of those meetings were sealed for more than 30 years after the Convention. Most of the Framers acknowledged that without secrecy no constitution of the kind that was developed could have been written. [Footnote by the Court.]

5. The Special Prosecutor argues that there is no provision in the Constitution for a presidential privilege as to his communications corresponding to the privilege of Members of Congress under the Speech or Debate Clause. But the silence of the Constitution on this score is not dispositive. "The rule of constitutional interpretation announced in McCulloch v. Maryland, that that which was reasonably appropriate and relevant to the exercise of a granted power was to be considered as accompanying the grant, has been so universally applied that it suffices merely to state it." Marshall v. Gordon, 243 U.S. 521, 537 (1917). [Footnote by the Court.]

process under all circumstances. The President's need for complete candor and objectivity from advisers calls for great deference from the courts. However, when the privilege depends solely on the broad, undifferentiated claim of public interest in the confidentiality of such conversations, a confrontation with other values arises. Absent a claim of need to protect military, diplomatic, or sensitive national security secrets, we find it difficult to accept the argument that even the very important interest in confidentiality of Presidential communications is significantly diminished by production of such material for in camera inspection with all the protection that a district court will be obliged to provide.

The impediment that an absolute, unqualified privilege would place in the way of the primary constitutional duty of the Judicial Branch to do justice in criminal prosecutions would plainly conflict with the function of the courts under Art. III. In designing the structure of our Government and dividing and allocating the sovereign power among three co-equal branches, the Framers of the Constitution sought to provide a comprehensive system, but the separate powers were not intended to operate with absolute independence. .   .   .   To read the Art. II powers of the President as providing an absolute privilege as against a subpoena essential to enforcement of criminal statutes on no more than a generalized claim of the public interest in confidentiality of nonmilitary and nondiplomatic discussions would upset the constitutional balance of "a workable government" and gravely impair the role of the courts under Art. III.

C

Since we conclude that the legitimate needs of the judicial process may outweigh Presidential privilege, it is necessary to resolve those competing interests in a manner that preserves the essential functions of each branch. The right and indeed the duty to resolve that question does not free the judiciary from according high respect to the representations made on behalf of the President.

The expectation of a President to the confidentiality of his conversations and correspondence, like the claim of confidentiality of judicial deliberations, for example, has all the values to which we accord deference for the privacy of all citizens and added to those values the necessity for protection of the public interest in candid, objective, and even blunt or harsh opinions in Presidential decision-making. A President and those who assist him must be free to explore alternatives in the process of shaping policies and making decisions and to do so in a way many would be unwilling to express except privately. These are the considerations justifying a presumptive privilege for Presidential communications. The privilege is fundamental to the operation of government and inextricably rooted in the separation of powers under the Constitution. In Nixon v. Sirica, 487 F.2d 700 (1973), the Court of Appeals held that such Presidential communications are "presumptively privileged," and this position is accepted by both parties in the present litigation. .   .   .

But this presumptive privilege must be considered in light of our historic commitment to the rule of law. This is nowhere more profoundly manifest than in our view that "the twofold aim [of criminal justice] is

that guilt shall not escape or innocence suffer." We have elected to employ an adversary system of criminal justice in which the parties contest all issues before a court of law. The need to develop all relevant facts in the adversary system is both fundamental and comprehensive. The ends of criminal justice would be defeated if judgments were to be founded on a partial or speculative presentation of the facts. The very integrity of the judicial system and public confidence in the system depend on full disclosure of all the facts, within the framework of the rules of evidence. To ensure that justice is done, it is imperative to the function of courts that compulsory process be available for the production of evidence needed either by the prosecution or by the defense.

Only recently the Court restated the ancient proposition of law, albeit in the context of a grand jury inquiry rather than a trial, "that 'the public . . . has a right to every man's evidence,' except for those persons protected by a constitutional, common law, or statutory privilege . . . ." Branzburg v. United States, 408 U.S. 665, 688 (1973) [chap. 13, below]. The privileges referred to by the Court are designed to protect weighty and legitimate competing interests [e. g., self-incrimination, attorney, and priest privileges] [and] are not lightly created nor expansively construed, for they are in derogation of the search for truth.

In this case the President challenges a subpoena served on him as a third party requiring the production of materials for use in a criminal prosecution; he does so on the claim that he has a privilege against disclosure of confidential communications. He does not place his claim of privilege on the ground they are military or diplomatic secrets. As to these areas of Art. II duties the courts have traditionally shown the utmost deference to presidential responsibilities. [E. g., C. & S. Air Lines v. Waterman Steamship Corp., 333 U.S. 103, 111 (1948); United States v. Reynolds, 345 U.S. 1 (1952).] . . .

No case of the Court, however, has extended his high degree of deference to a President's generalized interest in confidentiality. . . .

In this case we must weigh the importance of the general privilege of confidentiality of Presidential communications in performance of his responsibilities against the inroads of such a privilege on the fair administration of criminal justice.[6] The interest in preserving confidentiality is weighty indeed and entitled to great respect. However, we cannot conclude that advisers will be moved to temper the candor of their remarks by the infrequent occasions of disclosure because of the possibility that such conversations will be called for in the context of a criminal prosecution.

On the other hand, the allowance of the privilege to withhold evidence that is demonstrably relevant in a criminal trial would cut deeply into the guarantee of due process of law and gravely impair the basic function of

6. We are not here concerned with the balance between the President's generalized interest in confidentiality and the need for relevant evidence in civil litigation, nor with that between the confidentiality interest and congressional demands for information, nor with the President's interest in preserving state secrets. We address only the conflict between the President's assertion of a generalized privilege of confidentiality against the constitutional need for relevant evidence in criminal trials. [Footnote by the Court.]

the courts. A President's acknowledged need for confidentiality in the communications of his office is general in nature, whereas the constitutional need for production of relevant evidence in a criminal proceeding is specific and central to the fair adjudication of a particular criminal case in the administration of justice. . . .

We conclude that when the ground for asserting privilege as to subpoenaed materials sought for use in a criminal trial is based only on the generalized interest in confidentiality, it cannot prevail over the fundamental demands of due process of law in the fair administration of criminal justice. The generalized assertion of privilege must yield to the demonstrated, specific need for evidence in a pending criminal trial.

D

We have earlier determined that the District Court did not err in authorizing the issuance of the subpoena. If a President concludes that compliance with a subpoena would be injurious to the public interest he may properly, as was done here, invoke a claim of privilege on the return of the subpoena. Upon receiving a claim of privilege from the Chief Executive, it became the further duty of the District Court to treat the subpoenaed material as presumptively privileged and to require the Special Prosecutor to demonstrate that the Presidential material was "essential to the justice of the [pending criminal] case." [United States v. Burr.] [W]e affirm the order of the District Court that subpoenaed materials be transmitted to that court. We now turn to the important question of the District Court's responsibilities in conducting the in camera examination of Presidential materials or communications delivered under the compulsion of the subpoena duces tecum.

E

Enforcement of the subpoena duces tecum was stayed pending this Court's resolution of the issues raised by the petitions for certiorari. Those issues now having been disposed of, the matter of implementation will rest with the District Court. "[T]he guard, furnished to [the President] to protect him from being harassed by vexatious and unnecessary subpoenas, is to be looked for in the conduct of the [district] court after the subpoenas have issued; not in any circumstances which is to precede their being issued." [United States v. Burr.] Statements that meet the test of admissibility and relevance must be isolated; all other material must be excised. [I]t is obvious that the District Court has a very heavy responsibility to see to it that Presidential conversations, which are either not relevant or not admissible, are accorded that high degree of respect due the President of the United States. Mr. Chief Justice Marshall sitting as a trial judge in [Burr] was extraordinarily careful to point out that:

> "[i]n no case of this kind would a Court be required to proceed against the president as against an ordinary individual."

Marshall's statement cannot be read to mean in any sense that a President is above the law, but relates to the singularly unique role under Art. II of a President's communications and activities, related to the performance of duties under that Article. Moreover, a President's communications and

activities encompass a vastly wider range of sensitive material than would be true of any "ordinary individual." It is therefore necessary [7] in the public interest to afford Presidential confidentiality the greatest protection consistent with the fair administration of justice. The need for confidentiality even as to idle conversations with associates in which casual reference might be made concerning political leaders within the country or foreign statesmen is too obvious to call for further treatment. We have no doubt that the District Judge will at all times accord to Presidential records that high degree of deference suggested in [Burr]. . . .

Affirmed.*

Mr. Justice REHNQUIST took no part in the consideration or decision of these cases.

A transitional note. Recall the distinction in the notes introducing United States v. Nixon among three varieties of problems presented by that case: the amenability of the President to judicial process; the arguable constitutional autonomy of the executive branch to make final decisions about executive privilege; and the scope of executive privilege. Further examination of those three strands of the Nixon problem is the purpose of the remaining materials in this chapter. After a brief reexamination of the amenability problem, the last of the strands—the scope of executive privilege—will be examined before turning to the second of the themes, the autonomy problem. The autonomy issue is postponed to the end of this group of notes to permit further pursuit of a broader problem—the "commitment to other branches" aspect of the political questions concept.

PRESIDENTIAL AMENABILITY TO JUDICIAL PROCESS AFTER THE NIXON CASE

In result, United States v. Nixon clearly answered the unresolved question as to whether the President is wholly immune from judicial process. But did the Court adequately justify that aspect of its result? Did it adequately respond to the doubts that had been voiced by the post-Civil War Court in Mississippi v. Johnson, as recounted in the earlier notes on amenability to judicial process? And does the Nixon opinion, holding the President subject to a subpoena for evidence needed in a criminal case, throw light on the problem of the amenability of a President to criminal prosecution?

7. When the subpoenaed material is delivered to the District Judge in camera questions may arise as to the excising of parts and it lies within the discretion of that court to seek the aid of the Special Prosecutor and the President's counsel for in camera consideration of the validity of particular excisions, whether the basis of excision is relevancy or admissibility or under such cases as Reynolds, supra, or Waterman Steamship, supra. [Footnote by the Court.]

* For early comments on the Nixon case, see the articles in "Symposium: United States v. Nixon," 22 UCLA L.Rev. 1 (1974), and Freund, "Foreword: On Presidential Privilege," 88 Harv.L. Rev. 13 (1974).

The amenability of President Nixon to the Special Prosecutor's subpoena was confronted more squarely in the earlier rounds of the Watergate Tapes litigation. Judge Sirica ruled in 1973 that the President was not immune from compulsory process when he granted Special Prosecutor Cox's demand for materials sought by the grand jury investigating Watergate matters. In In re Grand Jury Subpoena Duces Tecum Issued to Richard M. Nixon, 360 F.Supp. 1 (D.D.C.1973), Judge Sirica found the separation of powers argument against issuance of compulsory court process an "unpersuasive" contention that "overlooks history." He conceded that earlier decisions directing members of the executive branch to perform nondiscretionary acts had involved "officials other than the President." But he found no reason to treat the President differently: that argument "tends to set the White House apart as a fourth branch of government." He added: "It is true that [Mississippi v. Johnson] left open the question whether the President can be required by court process to perform a purely ministerial act, but to persist in the opinion, after 1952, that he cannot would seem to exalt the form of the Youngstown Sheet & Tube Co. case over its substance. Though the Court's order there went to the Secretary of Commerce, it was the direct order of President Truman that was reversed."

Judge Sirica stated, moreover: "That the Court has not the physical power to enforce its order to the President is immaterial to a resolution of the issues. [T]he Court has a duty to issue appropriate orders. [I]t would tarnish the Court's reputation to fail to do what it could in pursuit of justice. In any case, the courts have always enjoyed the good faith of the Executive Branch, [and] there is no reason to suppose that the courts in this instance cannot again rely on the same good faith."

The Court of Appeals 5 to 2 decision affirming Judge Sirica's position in the grand jury subpoena case also commented on the amenability issue. Nixon v. Sirica, 487 F.2d 700 (D.C.Cir.1973). The Court of Appeals majority insisted that the President was "legally" bound by an order enforcing a subpoena even though a court might lack physical power to enforce its judgment. (Compare the discussion in Powell v. McCormack, below.) The per curiam opinion contended that, "to find the President immune from judicial process, we must read out of Burr and Youngstown the underlying principles that the eminent jurists in each case thought they were establishing." The Court of Appeals majority proceeded to reject every argument for executive immunity: "Lacking textual support, counsel for the President nonetheless would have us infer immunity from the President's political mandate, or from his vulnerability to impeachment, or from his broad discretionary powers. These are invitations to refashion the Constitution, and we reject them. . . . That the Impeachment Clause may qualify the court's power to sanction non-compliance with judicial orders is immaterial. Whatever the qualifications, they were equally present in [Youngstown]. The legality of judicial orders should not be confused with the legal consequences of their breach; for the courts in this country always assume that their orders will be obeyed, especially when addressed to responsible government officials."

The two lengthy dissenting opinions in the Court of Appeals, by Judges MacKinnon and Wilkey, were largely devoted to the executive autonomy is-

sue—the President's right to have the final say on the scope of executive privilege. But Judge Wilkey's dissent commented briefly on the amenability problem, noting that if "the court has no physical power to enforce its subpoena should the President refuse to comply, [then] what purpose is served by determining whether the President is 'immune' from process? It can hardly be questioned that in any direct confrontation between the Judiciary and the Executive, the latter must prevail. Therefore, the 'issue' of whether the President is amenable to court process is an illusory one. No one questions that the court can issue to the President a piece of paper captioned 'Subpoena' and that the President owes some obligation at least to inform the court of how he intends to respond. But our history is full of examples of situations in which direct confrontations between two or more of the co-equal Branches were avoided by one of the Branches deciding not to push its position to the limit."

In the second round of the Watergate Tapes litigation—the Jaworski subpoena culminating in United States v. Nixon—Judge Sirica relied simply on his position in the 1973 case. Should the Supreme Court have addressed the amenability issue more fully? Were the lower courts' references to the Steel Seizure Case and the Burr trial persuasive? Were the Supreme Court's repeated citations of Marbury v. Madison helpful on the amenability issue?

THE PROPER SCOPE OF EXECUTIVE PRIVILEGE

1. *Executive privilege and the Nixon case.* Assuming that the judiciary was the proper department to define the scope of executive privilege—the question that is postponed to the next group of notes—did the Court give the right answer in the Nixon case? What were the arguments supporting such a privilege? What were the Court's reasons for rejecting "an absolute, unqualified, presidential privilege" stemming from "the very important interest in confidentiality of presidential communications" pertaining to "non-military and nondiplomatic discussions"? [1] What considerations outweigh the qualified confidentiality privilege which the Court does recognize? Note the Court's footnote 6, as to the potential competing considerations not reached in this case. What about claims of privilege based on the "need to protect military, diplomatic, or sensitive national security secrets"? Are they to be scrutinized by balancing as well? Or are they absolute privileges—like the self-incrimination privilege of the Fifth Amendment—rather than qualified ones? [2]

1. For a view that the confidentiality privilege should be absolute rather than qualified, see Judge MacKinnon's dissent in Nixon v. Sirica, 487 F.2d 700 (D.C.Cir.1973).

2. Does the qualified confidentiality privilege recognized for the executive branch in Nixon apply to the other branches as well? Note the Pentagon Papers Case, New York Times Co. v. United States, 403 U.S. 713 (1971) (chap. 13 below), where Chief Justice Burger's dissent commented in a footnote: "No statute gives this Court express power to establish and enforce the utmost security measures for the secrecy of our deliberations and records. Yet I have little doubt as to the inherent power of the Court to protect the confidentiality of its internal operations by whatever judicial measures may be required." Is the judiciary's right to protect confidentiality an absolute or a qualified one?

The confidentiality privilege recognized in the Nixon case is found to rest on a constitutional basis.[3] If the privilege is constitutionally based, to what extent may Congress legislate guidelines about the scope of the privilege? Note the comment in Justice White's majority opinion in EPA v. Mink, 410 U.S. 73 (1973), construing the executive secrecy exemption in the Freedom of Information Act of 1966, 5 U.S.C. § 552. Justice White commented: "Congress could certainly have provided that the Executive Branch adopt new procedures or it could have established its own procedures— subject only to whatever limitations the Executive privilege may be held to impose upon such congressional ordering." What are those "limitations"? Proposals for such "guideline" legislation surfaced in Congress in the wake of Watergate.[4]

2. *Congressional inquiries and executive privilege.* There have been frequent conflicts between legislative demands for information and executive officials' refusals to comply, on instructions from the President, on grounds of interference with confidential deliberations.[5] Is the broad congressional power to investigate—see chap. 13, sec. 5, below—entitled to less weight in the balancing process than the interest in the "fair administration of criminal justice," the interest that outweighed the privilege claimed in the Nixon case? Note the footnote in the Nixon case stating that the Court was not passing on the balance "between the confidentiality interest and congressional demands for information." That issue arose repeatedly in the course of the investigation by Senator Ervin's Senate Select Committee. (See the proceedings of that Committee—as well as the tapes of the White House conversations about planning strategy for invocations of executive privilege.) In the fall of 1973, at about the time that Special Prosecutor Cox proved successful in obtaining access to some tapes to aid in the grand jury investigation in the Nixon v. Sirica litigation, the Senate Select Committee made an effort to enforce its subpoena for tapes in the courts. But the Committee proved unsuccessful. After its initial effort was rejected because of the lack of a jurisdictional statute authorizing Committee access to the courts, Congress enacted authorizing legislation. But when the case finally reached a decision on the merits, District Judge Gesell rejected the claim after application of the balancing criteria first elaborated in Nixon v. Sirica. He concluded that the Committee's need to know did not outweigh the interest in executive confidentiality. But by the time that case was decided, the Special Prosecutor had already obtained the material involved, and there was a special risk of publication of data needed in forthcoming criminal trials. See Senate Select Committee on Presidential Campaign Activities v. Nixon, 370 F.Supp. 521

3. Compare Berger, Executive Privilege: A Constitutional Myth (1974), with a Book Review of that attack on executive privilege, Sofaer, 88 Harv.L. Rev. 281 (1974). See generally Dorsen and Shattuck, "Executive Privilege, the Congress and the Courts," 35 Ohio St.L.J. 1 (1974).

4. See also the recommendations for such legislation in a report by the Committee on Civil Rights of the Association of the Bar of the City of New York, "Executive Privilege: Analysis and Recommendations for Congressional Legislation" (1974), printed in 29 Record of N.Y.C.B.A. 177.

5. See generally Younger, "Congressional Investigations and Executive Secrecy: A Study in the Separation of Powers," 20 U.Pitt.L.Rev. 755 (1959), and Berger, "Executive Privilege v. Congressional Inquiry," 12 UCLA L.Rev. 1044 (1965).

(D.D.C.1974). What should be the result in an investigation such as that of the Ervin Committee, in the absence of the risk of prejudicial trial publicity?

3. *Executive privilege and impeachment inquiries.* Do the needs of an impeachment inquiry or trial present a stronger claim for outweighing executive confidentiality needs than the needs of an ordinary congressional committee? In the late spring and early summer of 1974, President Nixon repeatedly refused to honor subpoenas issued by the House Judiciary Committee; and that refusal ultimately produced Article III of the Impeachment Articles. Earlier Presidents, in invoking executive privilege against ordinary congressional inquiries, had recognized the special strength of congressional demands in the course of an impeachment proceeding.[6] The President's growing resistance to House Committee demands culminated in a letter from President Nixon to Chairman Rodino on June 10, 1974. After an earlier letter by the Chairman had characterized the President's refusal to comply with the prior subpoena as "a grave matter," the President wrote: "The question at issue is not who conducts the inquiry, but where the line is to be drawn on an apparently endlessly escalating spiral of demands for confidential presidential tapes and documents. The Committee asserts that it should be the sole judge of presidential confidentiality. I cannot accept such a doctrine . . . . What is commonly referred to now as 'executive privilege' is part and parcel of the basic doctrine of separation of powers. . . . If the institution of an impeachment inquiry against a President were permitted to override all restraints of separation of powers this would spell the end of the doctrine of separation of powers; it would be an open invitation to future Congresses to use an impeachment inquiry, however frivolously, as a device to assert their own supremacy over the executive, and to reduce executive confidentiality to a nullity." He concluded: "[T]he executive must remain the final arbiter of demands on its confidentiality, just as the legislative and judicial branches must remain the final arbiters of demands on their confidentiality." The President accordingly continued to refuse to comply with impeachment inquiry subpoenas. It was that refusal that produced the final Article of the charges adopted by the Committee:

Article III

In his conduct of the office of President of the United States, Richard M. Nixon, contrary to his oath faithfully to execute the office of President of the United States and, to the best of his ability, preserve, protect, and defend the Constitution of the United States, and in violation of his constitutional duty to take care that the laws be faithfully executed, has failed without lawful cause or excuse to produce papers and things as directed by duly authorized subpoenas issued by the Committee on the Judiciary of the House of Representatives on April 11, 1974, May 15, 1974, May 30, 1974,

---

6. The earlier statements are summarized in House Committee on the Judiciary, Report on the Impeachment of Richard M. Nixon, President of the United States, H.Rep. No. 1305, 93rd Cong., 2d Sess. See in particular 120 Cong.Rec. at H 925 (daily ed. August 22, 1974). For example, President Polk had stated in 1846, in rejecting a congressional demand for information, that in the context of an impeachment inquiry, the congressional power "would penetrate into the most secret recesses of the Executive department."

and June 24, 1974, and willfully disobeyed such subpoenas. The subpoenaed papers and things were deemed necessary by the Committee in order to resolve by direct evidence fundamental, factual questions relating to Presidential direction, knowledge, or approval of actions demonstrated by other evidence to be substantial grounds for impeachment of the President. In refusing to produce these papers and things, Richard M. Nixon, substituting his judgment as to what materials were necessary for the inquiry, interposed the powers of the Presidency against the lawful subpoenas of the House of Representatives, thereby assuming to himself functions and judgments necessary to the exercise of the sole power of impeachment vested by the Constitution in the House of Representatives.

In all of this, Richard M. Nixon has acted in a manner contrary to his trust as President and subversive of constitutional government, to the great prejudice of the cause of law and justice, and to the manifest injury of the people of the United States.

Wherefore Richard M. Nixon, by such conduct, warrants impeachment and trial, and removal from office.

———

That Article was adopted by a smaller majority than the first two Articles, printed earlier. (The majority on Article III was 21 rather than 28 and 27 respectively.) As the statements during the debates and in the final report of the House Judiciary Committee indicate, a number of the Committee members who opposed Article III did so on the basis of perceived implications of United States v. Nixon. See, e. g., the statement by Congressman Railsback: "You have two contesting political, separate but co-equal branches. What could be more natural but than to ask the third branch, which has been the traditional arbiter in disputes, to arbitrate this dispute . . . .?" In elaborating that statement, he emphasized the Supreme Court's assertion that it was the "ultimate interpreter of the Constitution" in United States v. Nixon, and the Court's repeated quotations from Marbury v. Madison in that case.[7] Some Congressmen, moreover, thought Article III in any event inappropriate because the Committee, on May 30, 1974, had voted 32 to 6 not to go to court to enforce its subpoenas.

Did Article III state an impeachable offense? Did United States v. Nixon and its invocations of Marbury v. Madison make Article III an improper impeachment charge? Did the Court use overbroad language about its special role in resolving constitutional disputes? Should the Committee have gone to court to enforce its subpoenas? Could it have? Assuming that impeachment convictions and the proper scope of impeachable offenses are matters finally for the Senate rather than the Court—a problem pursued in the next group of notes—could courts nevertheless adjudicate whether an impeachment committee subpoena sought "relevant" information? Could relevance be determined without stating at least a tentative judicial position regarding the controversy over the scope of impeachable offenses? Note the majority's view in the final Report on the Nixon impeachment by the House Judiciary Committee, concluding on this point: "Inevitably, there would be a serious impairment of the confidence of the people in the legitimacy

7. See The New York Times, July 31, 1974, and the final Report on the Nixon impeachment by the House Committee, in 120 Cong.Rec. at H 9103 (daily ed. Aug. 22, 1974).

of the impeachment process if the court's definition varied from those adopted by the House or the Senate in any significant respect." [8]

C. WHO DECIDES?
EXECUTIVE AND LEGISLATIVE AUTONOMY: THE "COMMITMENT TO OTHER BRANCHES" STRAND OF THE POLITICAL QUESTIONS DOCTRINE

Introduction. United States v. Nixon primarily focuses on the substantive content of executive privilege. But was that constitutional issue one properly decided by the courts? In United States v. Nixon, the question of substantive content and authority to decide were closely connected; and the Court's treatment of the case may have made the issues overlap even more than necessary. But analytically they are separate problems. It was possible to argue that the content and application of executive privilege doctrine should be viewed as one of those constitutional issues committed to another branch for final decision: that it was a nonjusticiable issue in the sense that the executive rather than the courts should have the final authority to decide it. The Court has long recognized that the Constitution does contain such nonjusticiable issues. This group of notes will examine that aspect of justiciability first in the context of the Nixon case and then more generally.

1. *Executive autonomy, justiciability, and the Nixon case.* Did the Court adequately distinguish the issue of autonomy and substantive content of executive privilege in its handling of the Nixon case? Should the executive privilege for confidential communications have been viewed as an issue committed for final decision to the executive branch because of the implications of the Constitution? Did the Court jump too quickly from its view that the President was amenable to judicial process to a conclusion that it was for the Court to decide the content of executive privilege? Note the comment in Gunther, "Judicial Hegemony and Legislative Autonomy: The Nixon Case and the Impeachment Process," 22 UCLA L.Rev. 30 (1974), arguing that "it was possible to decide against President Nixon's claim" as to amenability "and yet support his argument as to autonomy": "it was possible to say that in subpoena efforts incident to a criminal case there is no presidential immunity from judicial process and yet conclude that the President, as a matter of constitutional interpretation of Article II powers, had absolute discretion to determine the scope of executive privilege. Mar-

---

8. For a defense of Article III of the Impeachment Articles, a criticism of the Court for overbroad statements casting a shadow over the congressional debate on that Article, and the view that "the House Committee was wise in deciding by a large margin in May to avoid going to court to enforce its subpoenas," see Gunther, "Judicial Hegemony and Legislative Autonomy: The Nixon Case and the Impeachment Process," 22 UCLA L.Rev. 30 (1974). For arguments that the Committee should have taken the judicial enforcement route, see Bickel, "Should Rodino Go to Court?" The New Republic, June 8, 1974. See also Professor Bickel's comments in Watergate, Politics, and the Legal Process (1974) (American Enterprise Institute Round Table). For a criticism of Article III of the Impeachment Articles, see Van Alstyne, "The Third Impeachment Article: Congressional Bootstrapping," 60 A.B.A.J. 1199 (1974).

bury v. Madison is an especially relevant source in deciding the first issue. It is far more tenuously related to the second. Respectable arguments after all have been made,[1] and not only by President Nixon's counsel, that absolute executive immunity [and absolute scope of executive privilege] is a legitimate constitutional inference. The opinion in United States v. Nixon tended to merge and blur those separate issues. And the linchpin in intertwining them was the excessive use of Marbury v. Madison."[2]

In Marbury, John Marshall did say that it is "the province and duty of the judicial department to say what the law is." But does that statement answer the executive autonomy-finality claim in a case such as Nixon? Recall the comments about the ambiguity of that Marshall statement in chap. 1, above. If it is taken to imply that the courts have a special guardianship role in constitutional interpretation, then it can indeed be argued that the Court must have the final say as to all constitutional problems. But more commonly, that Marshall statement and the entire Marbury v. Madison argument for judicial review is taken to mean a good deal less than that: it is taken to mean only that courts have authority to adjudicate constitutional issues when those are relevant in cases properly within their jurisdiction. That does leave it to the courts to determine their jurisdiction; but it does not preclude a constitutional interpretation which finds some issues committed to final decision by another branch. If the Marbury statement were taken at its broadest, there could be no such issues. But over most of its history, the Court has recognized that some issues are nonjusticiable because they are committed to other branches for final decision. The rest of these notes consider that ingredient of the political questions doctrine. Do Court approaches such as those in United States v. Nixon and in Powell v. McCormack, below, throw doubt on the continued vitality of that strand of the political questions doctrine?

2. *Questions nonjusticiable because they are "committed by the Constitution to another branch of government."* The arguments for executive

1. See, e. g., Charles L. Black, Jr., "Mr. Nixon, the Tapes, and Common Sense," The New York Times, Aug. 3, 1973. See also Judge Wilkey's dissent in Nixon v. Sirica, 400 F.2d 200 (D.C. Cir. 1973), beginning: "The critical issue on which I part company with my five colleagues is, in the shortest terms, *Who Decides?* [T]he Judicial Branch or Executive Branch?"

2. After noting that the Nixon ruling relied heavily on Marbury v. Madison in response to the President's claim, the comment argues that "there is nothing in [Marbury] that precludes a constitutional interpretation which gives final authority to another branch." The comment continues: "I do not believe that the Court intended to announce that every constitutional issue requires final adjudication on the merits by the judiciary. As in the past, there are likely to be issues in the future which the Court will find to have been 'committed by the Constitution to another branch of government . . . .' [Baker v. Carr, below.] For example, I would think (and hope) that a conviction on impeachment would be found unreviewable in the courts. Nor do I mean to suggest that the Court's result was wrong on the merits: I think checks and balances arguments make a nonabsolute view of executive privilege [and a rejection of the presidential autonomy argument] appropriate. I simply suggest that the argument for absolute executive privilege [and autonomy] deserved a more focused, careful, separable answer than the Court's invocation of Marbury v. Madison provides." [On the impact of "the Court's overbroad reliance on Marbury" on the Judiciary Committee debate on Article III, see the earlier comments, at the end of the preceding group of notes.]

autonomy as to executive privilege illustrate one strand of the political questions doctrine. That aspect of United States v. Nixon makes a preliminary exploration of that strand appropriate here. (Additional inquiry into the problem will be found in chap. 15.) The concept that some constitutional issues are nonjusticiable or "political" is well established; but what the ingredients of that concept are has produced considerable uncertainty and controversy. The ingredient examined here is the most solid and confined one—and in some commentators' views, the only legitimate one: that the Constitution commits the final determination of some constitutional questions to agencies other than courts. But the Court's political questions decisions cannot all be explained on that constitutional "commitment" ground. Some decisions on political question nonjusticiability emphasize the nature of the question and its aptness for judicial resolution in view of judicial competence: that strand of the political questions doctrine finds some issues nonjusticiable because they cannot be resolved by judicially manageable standards, or on the basis of data available to the courts. Still another, even more openended, strand of the concept suggests that the political questions notion is essentially a problem of judicial discretion, of prudential judgments that some issues ought not to be decided by the courts because they are too controversial or could produce enforcement problems or other institutional difficulties. Those last two strands—judicially unmanageable standards and data and prudential considerations—are more fully explored in chap. 15. The first, most clearly "constitutional interpretation" strand of political questions doctrine is introduced in these notes.

Consider one of the best known modern statements as to the ingredients of political questions nonjusticiability, in Baker v. Carr, 369 U.S. 186 (1962). The divided decision in that case held that equal protection challenges to legislative districting schemes were justiciable and not "political." Though fuller consideration of reapportionment controversies is postponed to chap. 15, consider Baker v. Carr here for the light it throws on the various, intertwined, strands of the political question concept. Justice Brennan's majority opinion stated:

"It is apparent that several formulations which vary slightly according to the settings in which the questions arise may describe a political question, although each has one or more elements which identifies it as essentially a function of the separation of powers. Prominent on the surface of any case held to involve a political question is found a textually demonstrable constitutional commitment of the issue to a coordinate political department; or a lack of judicially discoverable and manageable standards for resolving it; or the impossibility of deciding without an initial policy determination of a kind clearly for nonjudicial discretion; or the impossibility of a court's undertaking independent resolution without expressing lack of the respect due coordinate branches of government; or an unusual need for unquestioning adherence to a political decision already made; or the potentiality of embarrassment from multifarious pronouncements by various departments on one question."

To what extent are Justice Brennan's grounds all "essentially a function of the separation of powers"? To what extent are they considerations of prudence? Of concern with "manageable standards"? Here, the empha-

sis is on the first of his ingredients: "a textually demonstrable constitutional commitment of the issue to a coordinate political department." Herbert Wechsler has argued that that is the only legitimate ingredient of the political questions concept. He recognizes that the line between political and justiciable questions "is thin, indeed," but he adds that "it is thinner than it needs to be or ought to be": "I submit that in [political question cases], the only proper judgment that may lead to an abstention from decision is that the Constitution has committed the determination of the issue to another agency of government than the courts. Difficult as it may be to make that judgment wisely, whatever factors may be rightly weighed in situations where the answer is not clear, what is involved is in itself an act of constitutional interpretation, to be made and judged by standards that should govern the interpretive process generally. That, I submit, is *toto caelo* different from a broad discretion to abstain or intervene." [1] Contrast Alexander Bickel's view: "[O]nly by means of a play on words can the broad discretion that the courts have in fact exercised be turned into an act of constitutional interpretation. The political-question doctrine simply resists being domesticated in this fashion. There is something different about it, in kind, not in degree, from the general 'interpretive process'; something greatly more flexible, something of prudence, not construction and principle." [2]

But whatever the outer edges of the political questions doctrine, can some decisions of nonjusticiability be justified on the "commitment to other branches" ground of constitutional interpretation? Does United States v. Nixon adequately explain why the issue of executive privilege is not such an issue, for final decision by the executive? Consider the Court's fuller discussion of such a "constitutional commitment" claim a few years before the Nixon case, in a suit calling upon the Court to reexamine a congressional rather than a presidential contention, in Powell v. McCormack, which follows. The notes after the Powell case will examine additional aspects of the "commitment to other branches" strand of the political questions concept.

POWELL v. McCORMACK

395 U.S. 486, 81 S.Ct. 1944, 23 L.Ed.2d 491 (1969).

Certiorari to the United States Court of Appeals for the District of Columbia Circuit.

Mr. Chief Justice WARREN delivered the opinion of the Court.

In November 1966, Petitioner Adam Clayton Powell, Jr., was duly elected from the 18th Congressional District of New York to serve in the United States House of Representatives for the 90th Congress. However, pursuant to a House resolution, he was not permitted to take his seat. Powell (and some of the voters of his district) then filed suit in Federal District

---

1. Wechsler, "Toward Neutral Principles of Constitutional Law," 73 Harv. L.Rev. 1, 7, 9, Selected Essays 1938–62 (1963), 463, 468. See also the reprinting of the "Neutral Principles" lecture in Wechsler, Principles, Politics, and Fundamental Law (1961).

2. Bickel, "Foreword: The Passive Virtues," 75 Harv.L.Rev. 40, 46, Selected Essays 1938–62 (1963), 24, 29. See also Bickel, The Least Dangerous Branch (1962), and chap. 15, sec. 5, below.

Court, claiming that the House could exclude him only if it found he failed to meet the standing requirements of age, citizenship, and residence contained in Art. I, § 2, of the Constitution—requirements the House specifically found Powell met—and thus had excluded him unconstitutionally. The District Court dismissed petitioners' complaint "for want of jurisdiction of the subject matter." The Court of Appeals affirmed the dismissal . . . . We have determined that it was error to dismiss the complaint and that Petitioner Powell is entitled to a declaratory judgment that he was unlawfully excluded from the 90th Congress.

I.—FACTS

During the 89th Congress, a Special Subcommittee on Contracts of the Committee on House Administration conducted an investigation into the expenditures of the Committee on Education and Labor, of which petitioner Adam Clayton Powell, Jr., was chairman. The Special Subcommittee issued a report concluding that Powell and certain staff employees had deceived the House authorities as to travel expenses. The report also indicated there was strong evidence that certain illegal salary payments had been made to Powell's wife at his direction. . . .

When the 90th Congress met to organize in January 1967, Powell was asked to step aside while the oath was administered to the other members-elect. [After debate], the House adopted House Resolution 1, which provided that the Speaker appoint a Select Committee to determine Powell's eligibility. . . . [O]n February 23, 1967, the Committee issued its report, finding that Powell met the standing qualifications of Art. I, § 2. . . . However, the Committee further reported that Powell had asserted an unwarranted privilege and immunity from the processes of the courts of New York; that he had wrongfully diverted House funds for the use of others and himself; and that he had made false reports on expenditures of foreign currency to the Committee on House Administration. . . . The Committee recommended that Powell be sworn and seated as a member of the 90th Congress but that he be censured by the House, fined $40,000 and be deprived of his seniority. . . .

The report was presented to the House on March 1, 1967, and the House debated the Select Committee's proposed resolution. At the conclusion of the debate, by a vote of 222 to 202 the House rejected a motion to bring the resolution to a vote. An amendment to the resolution was then offered; it called for the exclusion of Powell and a declaration that his seat was vacant. The Speaker ruled that a majority vote of the House would be sufficient to pass the resolution if it were so amended. After further debate, the amendment was adopted by a vote of 248 to 176. Then the House adopted by a vote of 307 to 116 House Resolution No. 278 in its amended form, thereby excluding Powell . . . .

Powell and 13 voters of the 18th Congressional District of New York subsequently instituted this suit in the United States District Court for the District of Columbia. Five members of the House of Representatives were named as defendants individually and "as representatives of a class of citizens who are presently serving . . . as members of the House of Representatives." John W. McCormack was named in his official capacity as

Speaker, and the Clerk of the House of Representatives, the Sergeant at Arms and the Doorkeeper were named individually and in their official capacities. The complaint alleged that House Resolution No. 278 violated the Constitution, specifically Art. I, § 2, cl. 1, because the resolution was inconsistent with the mandate that the members of the House shall be elected by the people of each State, and Art. I, § 2, cl. 2, which, petitioners alleged, sets forth the exclusive qualifications for membership. . . .

    Petitioners [sought] a permanent injunction restraining respondents from executing the House Resolution, and enjoining the Speaker from refusing to administer the oath, the Clerk from refusing to perform the duties due a Representative, the Sergeant at Arms from refusing to pay Powell his salary, and the Doorkeeper from refusing to admit Powell to the Chamber. [Petitioners also sought mandamus.] The complaint also requested a declaratory judgment that Powell's exclusion was unconstitutional. . . .

    [In its Part II, "Mootness," the Court concluded that the case had not become moot even though Representative Powell had been elected to and seated by the 91st Congress, since his "claim for back salary remains viable." In its Part III, "Speech or Debate Clause," the Court found that the Clause, Art. I, § 6, justified dismissal of the action against members of Congress but did not bar proceeding against the congressional employees. Though the employees were "acting pursuant to express orders of the House," that did not "bar judicial review of the constitutionality of the underlying legislative decision."]

IV.—EXCLUSION OR EXPULSION

    The resolution excluding petitioner Powell was adopted by a vote in excess of two-thirds of the 434 Members of Congress—307 to 116. . . . Article I, § 5, grants the House authority to expel a member "with the Concurrence of two thirds." [1] Respondents assert that the House may expel a member for any reason whatsoever and that, since a two-thirds vote was obtained, the procedure by which Powell was denied his seat in the 90th Congress should be regarded as an expulsion not an exclusion. . . .

    . . . The Speaker ruled that the House was voting to exclude Powell [and accordingly that only a majority vote was necessary to adopt the resolution], and we will not speculate what the result might have been if Powell had been seated and expulsion proceedings subsequently instituted. Nor is the distinction between exclusion and expulsion merely one of form. The misconduct for which Powell was charged occurred prior to the convening of the 90th Congress. On several occasions the House has debated whether a member can be expelled for actions taken during a prior Congress. [W]e will not assume that two-thirds of its members would have expelled

---

1. Powell was "excluded" from the 90th Congress, i. e., he was not administered the oath of office and was prevented from taking his seat. If he had been allowed to take the oath and subsequently had been required to surrender his seat, the House's action would have constituted an "expulsion."

Since we conclude that Powell was excluded from the 90th Congress, we express no view on what limitations may exist on Congress' power to expel or otherwise punish a member once he has been seated. [Footnote by the Court.]

Powell for his prior conduct had the Speaker announced that House Resolution 278 was for expulsion rather than exclusion.   .   .   .

V.—SUBJECT MATTER JURISDICTION

As we pointed out in Baker v. Carr, 369 U.S. 186, 198 (1962), there is a significant difference between determining whether a federal court has "jurisdiction of the subject matter" and determining whether a cause over which a court has subject matter jurisdiction is "justiciable." The District Court determined that "to decide this case on the merits   .   .   .   would constitute a clear violation of the doctrine of separation of powers" and then dismissed the complaint "for want of jurisdiction of the subject matter." However, as the Court of Appeals correctly recognized, the doctrine of separation of powers is more properly considered in determining whether the case is "justiciable." We agree with the unanimous conclusion of the Court of Appeals that the District Court had jurisdiction over the subject matter of this case. However, for reasons set forth in Part VI, infra, we disagree with the Court of Appeals' conclusion that this case is not justiciable.

In Baker v. Carr, we noted that a federal district court lacks jurisdiction over the subject matter (1) if the cause does not "arise under" the Federal Constitution, laws or treaties (or fall within one of the other enumerated categories of Article III); or (2) if it is not a "case or controversy" within the meaning of that phrase in Article III; or (3) if the cause is not one described by any jurisdictional statute. [Our] determination [Part VI, § B, below] that this cause presents no nonjusticiable "political question" disposes of respondents' contentions that this cause is not a "case or controversy."   .   .   .

Respondents   .   .   .   contend that this is not a case "arising under" the Constitution within the meaning of Article III. They emphasize that Art. I, § 5, assigns to each House of Congress the power to judge the elections and qualifications of its own members and to punish its members for disorderly behavior. Respondents also note that under Art. I, § 3, the Senate has the "sole power" to try all impeachments. Respondents argue that these delegations (to "judge," to "punish," and to "try") to the Legislative Branch are explicit grants of "judicial power" to the Congress and constitute specific exceptions to the general mandate of Article III that the "judicial power" shall be vested in the federal courts. Thus, respondents maintain, the "power conferred on the courts by article III does not authorize this Court to do anything more than declare its lack of jurisdiction to proceed."

We reject this contention.   .   .   .   It has long been held that a suit "arises under" the Constitution if a petitioner's claims "will be sustained if the Constitution   .   .   .   [is] given one construction and will be defeated if it [is] given another." Bell v. Hood, 327 U.S. 678, 685 (1946). Thus, this case clearly is one "arising under" the Constitution as the Court has interpreted that phrase. Any bar to federal courts reviewing the judgments made by the House or Senate in excluding a member arises from the allocation of powers between the two branches of the Federal Government (a question of justiciability), and not from the petitioners' failure to state a claim based on federal law.   .   .   .

VI.—JUSTICIABILITY

. . . Two determinations must be made in this regard. First, we must decide whether the claim presented and the relief sought are of the type which admit of judicial resolution. Second, we must determine whether the structure of the Federal Government renders the issue presented a "political question"—that is, a question which is not justiciable in federal court because of the separation of powers provided by the Constitution.

A. *General Considerations.*

In deciding generally whether a claim is justiciable, a court must determine whether "the duty asserted can be judicially identified and its breach judicially determined, and whether protection for the right asserted can be judicially molded." [Baker v. Carr.] Respondents do not seriously contend that the duty asserted and its alleged breach cannot be judicially determined. If petitioners are correct, the House had a duty to seat Powell once it determined he met the standing requirements set forth in the Constitution. It is undisputed that he met those requirements and that he was nevertheless excluded.

Respondents do maintain, however, that this case is not justiciable because, they assert, it is impossible for a federal court to "mold effective relief for resolving this case." . . .

We need express no opinion about the appropriateness of coercive relief in this case, for petitioners sought a declaratory judgment, a form of relief the District Court could have issued. [I]n terms of the general criteria of justiciability, this case is justiciable.

B. *Political Question Doctrine.*

1. Textually Demonstrable Constitutional Commitment.

Respondents maintain that even if this case is otherwise justiciable, it presents only a political question. It is well-established that the federal courts will not adjudicate political questions. In Baker v. Carr, we noted that political questions are not justiciable primarily because of the separation of powers within the Federal Government. [The Court quoted the political questions criteria noted above.]

In order to determine whether there has been a textual commitment to a co-ordinate department of the Government, we must interpret the Constitution. In other words, we must first determine what power the Constitution confers upon the House through Art. I, § 5, before we can determine to what extent, if any, the exercise of that power is subject to judicial review. Respondents maintain that the House has broad power under § 5, and, they argue, the House may determine which are the qualifications necessary for membership. On the other hand, petitioners allege that the Constitution provides that an elected representative may be denied his seat only if the House finds he does not meet one of the standing qualifications expressly prescribed by the Constitution.

If examination of § 5 disclosed that the Constitution gives the House judicially unreviewable power to set qualifications for membership and

to judge whether prospective members meet those qualifications, further review of the House determination might well be barred by the political question doctrine. On the other hand, if the Constitution gives the House power to judge only whether elected members possess the three standing qualifications set forth in the Constitution, further consideration would be necessary to determine whether any of the other formulations of the political question doctrine are "inextricable from the case at bar." [2] Baker v. Carr. In other words, whether there is a "textually demonstrable constitutional commitment of the issue to a coordinate political department" of government and what is the scope of such commitment are questions we must resolve for the first time in this case. . . .

In order to determine the scope of any "textual commitment" under Art. I, § 5, we necessarily must determine the meaning of the phrase to "be the Judge of the Qualifications of its own Members." Petitioners argue that the records of the debates during the Constitutional Convention; available commentary from the post-Convention, pre-ratification period; and early congressional applications of Art. I, § 5, support their construction of the section. Respondents insist, however, that a careful examination of the pre-Convention practices of the English Parliament and American colonial assemblies demonstrates that by 1787, a legislature's power to judge the qualifications of its members was generally understood to encompass exclusion or expulsion on the ground that an individual's character or past conduct rendered him unfit to serve. When the Constitution and the debates over its adoption are thus viewed in historical perspective, argue respondents, it becomes clear that the "qualifications" expressly set forth in the Constitution were not meant to limit the long-recognized legislative power to exclude or expel at will, but merely to establish "standing incapacities," which could be altered only by a constitutional amendment. Our examination of the relevant historical materials leads us to the conclusion that petitioners are correct and that the Constitution leaves the House without authority to *exclude* any person, duly elected by his constituents, who meets all the requirements for membership expressly prescribed in the Constitution. [The review of the history is omitted.]

Had the intent of the Framers emerged from these materials with less clarity, we would nevertheless have been compelled to resolve any ambiguity in favor of a narrow construction of the scope of Congress' power to exclude members-elect. A fundamental principle of our representative democracy is, in Hamilton's words, "that the people should choose whom they please to govern them." 2 Elliot's Debates 257. As Madison pointed out at the Convention, this principle is undermined as much by limiting whom the people can select as by limiting the franchise itself. In apparent agreement with this basic philosophy, the Convention adopted his suggestion limiting the power to expel. To allow essentially that same power to be exercised under the guise of judging qualifications would be to ignore Madison's warning, borne out in the Wilkes case and some of Congress' own post-Civil War exclusion

2. Consistent with this interpretation, federal courts might still be barred by the political question doctrine from reviewing the House's factual determination that a member did not meet one of the standing qualifications. This is an issue not presented in this case and we express no view as to its resolution. [Footnote by the Court.]

cases, against "vesting an improper & dangerous power in the Legislature."
2 Farrand 249. Moreover, it would effectively nullify the Convention's decision to require a two-third vote for expulsion. Unquestionably, Congress has an interest in preserving its institutional integrity, but in most cases that interest can be sufficiently safeguarded by the exercise of its power to punish its members for disorderly behavior and, in extreme cases, to expel a member with the concurrence of two-thirds. . . .

For these reasons, we have concluded that Art. I, § 5, is at most a "textually demonstrable commitment" to Congress to judge only the qualifications expressly set forth in the Constitution. Therefore, the "textual commitment" formulation of the political question doctrine does not bar federal courts from adjudicating petitioners' claims.

2.   Other Considerations.

Respondents' alternate contention is that the case presents a political question because judicial resolution of petitioners' claim would produce a "potentially embarrassing confrontation between coordinate branches" of the Federal Government. But, as our interpretation of Art. I, § 5, discloses, a determination of petitioner Powell's right to sit would require no more than an interpretation of the Constitution. Such a determination falls within the traditional role accorded courts to interpret the law, and does not involve a "lack of respect due [a] coordinate [branch] of government," nor does it involve an "initial policy determination of a kind clearly for nonjudicial discretion." Baker v. Carr. Our system of government requires that federal courts on occasion interpret the Constitution in a manner at variance with the construction given the document by another branch. The alleged conflict[3] that such an adjudication may cause cannot justify the courts' avoiding their constitutional responsibility. . . .

Nor are any of the other formulations of a political question "inextricable from the case at bar." Baker v. Carr. Petitioners seek a determination that the House was without power to exclude Powell from the 90th Congress, which, we have seen, requires an interpretation of the Constitution—a determination for which clearly there are "judicially manageable standards." Finally, a judicial resolution of petitioners' claim will not result in "multifarious pronouncements by various departments on one question." For, as we noted in Baker v. Carr, it is the responsibility of this Court to act as the ultimate interpreter of the Constitution. Marbury v. Madison, 1 Cranch 137 (1803). Thus, we conclude that petitioners' claim is not barred by the political question doctrine, and, having determined that the claim is otherwise generally justiciable, we hold that the case is justiciable. . . .

. . . [W]e hold that [the] House was without power to exclude [Powell] from its membership. . . .

Reversed and remanded.†

---

3. In fact, the Court has noted that it is an "inadmissible suggestion" that action might be taken in disregard of a judicial determination. McPherson v. Blacker, 146 U.S. 1, 24 (1892). [Footnote by the Court.]

† A concurring opinion by Justice Douglas, omitted here, included the statement: "If this were an expulsion case I would think that no justiciable controversy would be presented, the vote of the House being two-thirds or

COMMITMENT OF CONSTITUTIONAL ISSUES TO OTHER BRANCHES AFTER POWELL

1. *The impact of the Powell and Nixon cases on the "commitment" strand of the political questions concept.* Given the approach of the Powell case, do any constitutional questions remain which the Court is likely to find committed to other branches for final decision? Writing several years before Powell, Herbert Wechsler's discussion of the political questions doctrine —quoted in the notes preceding the Powell case—had given two examples of issues in which the commitment to other branches was "explicit" in the Constitution: convictions after impeachment, in Art. I, § 3 (Senate's "sole Power to try"); and the seating or expulsion of members of Congress in view of Art. I, § 5 (each House shall judge "Qualifications" of its own Members and may "expel a Member"). The Powell decision on exclusions from Congress obviously undercuts a portion of Wechsler's statement. Is that because, on a proper reading of the Constitution, the commitment of the exclusion issue to the House is simply not as clear as Wechsler thought? Or is it because the Court's approach makes it difficult to conceive of any issue the Court will find committed to another branch?

What was determinative in the Court's reading of the constitutional provisions? Note the Court's statement, in Part VI.B.2, that "it is the responsibility of this Court to act as the ultimate interpreter of the Constitution." The Court cites Marbury v. Madison for that position. Recall the questions about the reliance on Marbury v. Madison in United States v. Nixon, above. Does that Court view of its own powers rest on a fair reading of Marbury? Does that reading govern the result not only in Powell but in Nixon and in most if not all other cases of arguable commitments of constitutional issues to other branches? † Note the criticism in Sandalow, "Comments on Powell v. McCormack," 17 UCLA L.Rev. 172 (1969), arguing that the Court confused the questions of jurisdiction to decide and the merits, and suggesting that the source of the confusion was the Court's assumption about its role as "the ultimate interpreter of the Constitution." He adds: "On that premise, it is but a short step to the conclusion that the Court is obligated to intervene when another branch of government acts in a manner prohibited by the Constitution." If Powell is correct, he suggests, "it is difficult to see [why the Court] may not similarly review expulsions from the Congress or the removal of judges or other officers upon conviction after impeachment." Is that a persuasive criticism? Compare Justice Douglas' concurring opinion in Powell, suggesting an expulsion decision would not be reviewable, and note the Court's footnote 2 in Powell, suggesting that "the

more." A dissent by Justice Stewart, on grounds of mootness, is also omitted. He argued that, because the case was moot, the Court should refrain "from deciding the novel, difficult, and delicate constitutional questions which the case presented at its inception."

† For recent recognitions of commitments of constitutional issues to other branches, see Roudebush v. Hartke, 405 U.S. 15 (1972) (Art. I, § 5, commits to the Senate the final decision of which candidate "received more lawful votes" in an election for a Senate seat), and Gilligan v. Morgan, 413 U.S. 1 (1973) (Art. I, § 8, cl. 16, commits to Congress the authority to provide for "organizing, arming and disciplining the Militia"—now the National Guard).

House's factual determination that a member did not meet one of the standing qualifications" might be nonreviewable. How do those issues differ from the ones the Court did examine in the Powell and Nixon cases? [1]

2. *Judicial review and impeachment.* Does the approach of the Powell case throw significant doubt on the general assumption that Senate convictions after impeachment are not reviewable? Or does at least that Wechsler example of "explicit" commitments to another branch retain vitality? [2] Recall the earlier discussion about Article III of the impeachment charges against President Nixon, and the debate as to whether the Judiciary Committee should have sought court assistance in enforcing its subpoenas. If the impeachment process had continued and a conviction in the Senate had resulted, could judicial review have been sought on the ground that Article III or the other Articles did not charge "high Crimes and Misdemeanors" and hence were not within the constitutional scope of impeachable offenses? The majority of commentators who addressed that issue during the impeachment proceedings against President Nixon concluded that convictions after impeachment are not reviewable. They relied primarily on the constitutional language and on historical understandings. Those who asserted that impeachment issues are reviewable relied primarily on the implications of Powell v. McCormack. See, for example, a study noted earlier, by a Committee of the Association of the Bar for the City of New York. [3] A large majority of that Committee argued against reviewability. [4] Reexamine the data relied on in the Powell case: can a plausible case for the reviewability of impeachment issues be developed on the basis of that approach?

1. The Powell case—particularly its concluding passages—also raises questions as to whether the "prudential considerations" strand of the political questions doctrine retains substantial vitality. The Court in Powell was not inhibited by any concerns about problems of enforceability or potential conflict with other branches. That aspect of Powell is pursued further in chap. 15 below, where the political questions ingredients not directly related to constitutional "commitments to other branches" are considered.

2. For contrasting views on reviewability of convictions in impeachment proceedings, compare Berger, Impeachment: The Constitutional Problems (1973), with Black, Impeachment: A Handbook (1974).

3. Committee on Federal Legislation, The Law of Presidential Impeachment (1974).

4. Note that at the Constitutional Convention, the function of conducting trials on impeachment charges was transferred from the Supreme Court to the Senate.

Part III

INDIVIDUAL RIGHTS

Scope Note. The Federal Constitution's protections of individual freedoms are central in this final Part. Like most of Part II, these materials are concerned with limitations on governmental power. In the preceding chapters, the argued limits stemmed from the allocations of power among governmental units—the division of powers between nation and states, and the separation of powers among the three branches of the national government. In the remaining chapters, the constitutional guarantees of individual rights—guarantees primarily directed against interferences by state and federal governments—are at the forefront.

As with the earlier materials, the concern here goes well beyond the delineation of the past and present contours of constitutional doctrines. It extends to the recurrent problems of the process of constitutional interpretation. How can one give content to the constitutional guarantees? What are the sources of interpretation? Are there legitimate sources beyond text and history and structural inferences? Those problems are difficult enough in efforts to interpret the relatively "specific" guarantees such as those pertaining to speech and religion in the First Amendment. But the challenge is especially acute when the task is that of pouring content into such vague assurances as the due process and equal protection clauses of the 14th Amendment. Due process and equal protection, central in the next few chapters, have proved particularly controversial: Are those broad phrases appropriate vessels for judicial infusions of values drawn from sources other than constitutional text, history and structure? Do those phrases irresistibly tempt the Justices to read social and personal values into constitutional law?

To pursue the twin goals of examining the development of doctrine and the nature of the interpretive process, this Part begins with a sketch of the constitutional framework and an initial venture into the problems of interpretation in a relatively uncomplicated context: chap. 8 emphasizes the nationalizing impact of the 14th Amendment's due process guarantee on state criminal procedures. It contrasts the scope of constitutional guarantees in the original and the post-Civil War Constitution; and it begins the exploration of the judicial function in the articulation and enforcement of individual rights. A review of the "incorporation" controversy provides the vehicle for that initial exploration. Did the 14th Amendment's due process clause make all of the Bill of Rights—originally applicable only to the federal government—applicable to the states as well? Or does the due process clause leave the Court with a more open-ended task of ascertaining what is "fundamental" to fair procedure? Are the Justices limited to enforcement of rights explicitly listed in the Constitution, or does that document authorize a broader Court function of elaborating the general values of fundamental liberties?

That tension, reflected in part in the "incorporation" controversy pursued in chap. 8, echoes throughout the remaining materials. It emerges

most controversially in chap. 9, on "substantive due process." The due process guarantee has a concern with procedure as its most obvious ingredient; and the Court's preoccupation with criminal procedure problems in chap. 8 is accordingly the most understandable impact of the due process clause. But the Court has not limited itself to a consideration of the fairness of the procedures by which personal rights and duties are delineated: since the late 19th century, the Court has also found in due process constitutional restraints on the substantive ordering of those rights and duties, a restraint on the content as well as the methods of governmental action. The Court of another generation found in substantive due process special protection of economic and property rights, and the rise and decline of that emphasis is traced in sec. 1 of chap. 9. The modern Court, even while repudiating that variety of substantive due process, has apparently revived a variation of its own: a constitutional protection of individual rights that are hardly explicit in the basic document—especially the right of privacy. That development is the focus of sec. 3 of chap. 9.

Chap. 10 turns to the occasionally parallel developments in the interpretation of the equal protection clause of the 14th Amendment. From an initial concern with racial discrimination and a limited early impact on the means of governmental regulation, that clause grew in the Warren years to have a far broader sweep. The "new" equal protection found constitutional safeguards for a variety of "fundamental interests"—interests which, though again not explicitly guaranteed in the Constitution, were nevertheless protected against legislation with differential impacts. That value-oriented process of equal protection interpretation—e. g., in the area of voting—bears considerable kinship to substantive due process; indeed, some have referred to it as "substantive equal protection." Chap. 11 turns to two problems of 14th Amendment reach that have been most commonly raised in equal protection contexts: the applicability of the 14th Amendment guarantees to certain varieties of "private" rather than "state" action; and the authority of Congress, under its enforcement power under § 5 of the Amendment, to give a scope to 14th Amendment guarantees different from that the Court may have delineated on its own in its interpretations of the self-executing first section of the Amendment.

Chaps. 12 and 13 examine the free speech guarantee of the First Amendment, made applicable to the states as a result of the interpretations of the 14th Amendment. On its face the First Amendment's free speech guarantee is far more specific and certainly more explicit than the constitutional "rights" and "interests" that have emerged in the interpretations of substantive due process and the "new" equal protection. But specificity and explicitness have left ample room for controversy about the proper analysis and scope of the free speech guarantee, as those chapters will illustrate. Chap. 14 turns to another controversial aspect of First Amendment interpretation, that Amendment's religion clauses, purporting both to assure the "free exercise" of religion and to safeguard against the "establishment" of religion. Chap. 15, finally, returns to "procedural" and "jurisdictional" problems of judicial review in operation—a theme first taken up in Part I, and postponed for additional exploration to this point because the substantive contents of constitutional rights often affect the Court's dispositions of justiciability issues.

Chapter 8

THE BILL OF RIGHTS AND THE STATES:
THE PROCEDURAL CONTENTS OF DUE PROCESS

Introduction. The major theme of this chapter, developed at length in sec. 3 below, is the way in which the 14th Amendment's due process clause has been read to make applicable to state criminal proceedings virtually all of the procedural requirements that govern federal criminal law enforcement as a result of the Bill of Rights. That process of "incorporating" Bill of Rights guarantees into the 14th Amendment illustrates two larger themes. First, it provides a reminder of the federalism aspects of individual rights concerns. State constitutions typically have bills of rights of their own; but the concern here is with the restraints imposed on the states by the *federal* Constitution. Those restraints were very few before the Civil War. The post-Civil War Amendments signified a major escalation in the national concern with the protection of individual rights against state governments. It was the 14th Amendment's due process clause that became the major vehicle for that nationalization of individual rights; and that Amendment looks to implementation of the new guarantees through the mechanism of a *national* Supreme Court and Congress. As the opinions bearing on the "incorporation" controversy illustrate, federalism and individual rights concerns are frequently intertwined in the process of interpreting the scope of those new national guarantees.

Second, this exploration of the *procedures* due process requires of the states introduces the larger problems of the appropriate ingredients of due process interpretation. It is easier to infer a procedural content from the face of the due process clause than to derive substantive due process doctrines from it; but even the procedural due process materials reflect the tensions that permeate all due process litigation—the tensions between "objective" standards and judicial subjectivity; between the specific and the vague; between the fixed and the flexible; between historical meaning and contemporary values; between ingredients readily traceable to constitutional text and structure and those resting ultimately on extra-constitutional values. To set the backdrop for the nationalizing impact of the post-Civil War Amendments, this chapter begins with a brief sketch of the pre-Civil War situation (sec. 1) and reviews the Court's earliest interpretation of the Amendments (sec. 2) before turning to the details of the "incorporation" dispute (sec. 3).

SECTION 1. THE PRE–CIVIL WAR SITUATION

The 1787 document. There were relatively few references to individual rights in the original Constitution: its major concern was with governmental structures and relationships.* The most important limitation on state power protective of individual rights—certainly in terms of litigation—was the con-

---

* Though the explicit guarantees of individual rights were sparse, the basic

document's concerns with diffusion of power—the concerns of Part II of this

tract clause. See chap. 9, sec. 2, below. Moreover, prohibitions of state bills of attainder and ex post facto laws were coupled with the contract clause in Art. I, § 10; and Art. IV, § 4, announced that the "Citizens of each State shall be entitled to all Privileges and Immunities of Citizens in the several States." See chap. 6, sec. 2, above. Nor was there a significantly broader spectrum of individual rights restrictions on the national government. Art. I, § 9, stated that the "privilege of the Writ of Habeas Corpus" could not be "suspended" and, paralleling restrictions on states, prohibited ex post facto laws and bills of attainder. And Art. III defined treason narrowly and assured jury trials in criminal cases.

The Bill of Rights. The ratification debates soon revealed that there was widespread demand for additional constitutional protection of individual—as well as states'—rights. In response to these pressures, Madison introduced proposals for constitutional amendments at the first session of Congress, and the first ten amendments were ratified in 1791. The Marshall Court held that the Bill of Rights restricted only the national government and did not limit state authority, in the Barron case which follows. There was relatively little occasion for Court interpretation of the Bill of Rights before the Civil War—in part because federal criminal decisions were not ordinarily reviewable by the Supreme Court.†

BARRON v. THE MAYOR AND CITY COUNCIL OF BALTIMORE

7 Pet. 243, 8 L.Ed. 672 (1833).

Error to the Court of Appeals of Maryland.

[Barron sued the City for making his wharf in Baltimore harbor useless. He claimed that the City had diverted the flow of streams in the course of street construction work; that this diversion had deposited "large masses of sand and earth" near the wharf; and that the water had become too shallow for most vessels. The trial court awarded Barron $45,000, but the state appellate court reversed. Barron claimed that the state's action violated the guarantee in the last phrase of the Fifth Amendment, that private property shall not be "taken for public use, without just compensation." The Supreme Court decided the issue of the applicability of the Fifth Amendment to state action in a jurisdictional context: under the jurisdictional statute, it could not review the case unless a federal right was involved; since in the Court's view, the Fifth Amendment did not apply to relations between an individual and a state, there was no jurisdiction. The Court rejected Barron's argument that the Fifth Amendment provision, "being in favour

book—do of course have an impact on personal autonomy, often indirectly and sometimes directly: recall, e. g., the argument that a right to interstate mobility can be derived from the commerce clause, chap. 5 above.

† However, there was considerable extrajudicial debate about the First Amendment, particularly during the controversy over the Alien and Sedition Acts of 1798. That debate proved of considerable importance in later litigation regarding freedom of expression. See chap. 12 below.

of the liberty of the citizen, ought to be so construed as to restrain the legislative power of a state, as well as that of the United States." The Court's reasoning follows.]

Mr. Chief Justice MARSHALL delivered the opinion of the Court.

. . .

The question [is], we think, of great importance, but not of much difficulty. The constitution was ordained and established by the people of the United States for themselves, for their own government, and not for the government of the individual states. Each state established a constitution for itself, and, in that constitution, provided such limitations and restrictions on the powers of its particular government as its judgment dictated. The people of the United States framed such a government for the United States as they supposed best adapted to their situation, and best calculated to promote their interests. The powers they conferred on this government were to be exercised by itself; and the limitations on power, if expressed in general terms, are naturally, and, we think, necessarily applicable to the government created by the instrument. They are limitations of power, granted in the instrument itself; not of distinct governments, framed by different persons and for different purposes. . . .

If these propositions be correct, the fifth amendment must be understood as restraining the power of the general government, not as applicable to the states. In their several constitutions they have imposed such restrictions on their respective governments as their own wisdom suggested; such as they deemed most proper for themselves. . . .

The ninth section [of Art. I] having enumerated, in the nature of a bill of rights, the limitations intended to be imposed on the powers of the general government, the tenth proceeds to enumerate those which were to operate on the state legislatures. These restrictions are brought together in the same section, and are by express words applied to the states. "No state shall enter into any treaty," &c. Perceiving that in a constitution framed by the people of the United States for the government of all, no limitation of the action of government on the people would apply to the state government, unless expressed in terms; the restrictions contained in the tenth section are in direct words so applied to the states. . . .

If the original constitution, in the ninth and tenth sections of the first article, draws this plain and marked line of discrimination between the limitations it imposes on the powers of the general government, and on those of the states; if in every inhibition intended to act on state power, words are employed which directly express that intent; some strong reason must be assigned for departing from this safe and judicious course in framing the amendments, before that departure can be assumed.

We search in vain for that reason.

Had the people of the several states, or any of them, required changes in their constitutions; had they required additional safeguards to liberty from the apprehended encroachments of their particular governments: the remedy was in their own hands, and would have been applied by themselves. A convention would have been assembled by the discontented state, and the

required improvements would have been made by itself.   The unwieldy and cumbrous machinery of procuring a recommendation from two-thirds of congress, and the assent of three-fourths of their sister states, could never have occurred to any human being as a mode of doing that which might be effected by the state itself.   Had the framers of these amendments intended them to be limitations on the powers of the state governments, they would have imitated the framers of the original constitution, and have expressed that intention.   Had congress engaged in the extraordinary occupation of improving the constitutions of the several states by affording the people additional protection from the exercise of power by their own governments in matters which concerned themselves alone, they would have declared this purpose in plain and intelligible language.

But it is universally understood, it is a part of the history of the day, that the great revolution which established the constitution of the United States, was not effected without immense opposition.   Serious fears were extensively entertained that those powers which the patriot statesmen, who then watched over the interests of our country, deemed essential to union, and to the attainment of those invaluable objects for which union was sought, might be exercised in a manner dangerous to liberty.   In almost every convention by which the constitution was adopted, amendments to guard against the abuse of power were recommended.   These amendments demanded security against the apprehended encroachments of the general government—not against those of the local governments.

In compliance with a sentiment thus generally expressed, to quiet fears thus extensively entertained, amendments were proposed by the required majority in congress, and adopted by the states.   These amendments contain no expression indicating an intention to apply them to the state governments. This court cannot so apply them.

We are of opinion that the provision in the fifth amendment to the constitution, declaring that private property shall not be taken for public use without just compensation, is intended solely as a limitation on the exercise of power by the government of the United States, and is not applicable to the legislation of the states.   We are therefore of opinion that there is no repugnancy between the several acts of the general assembly of Maryland, given in evidence by the defendants at the trial of this cause, in the court of that state, and the constitution of the United States.   This court, therefore, has no jurisdiction of the cause;   and it is dismissed.

THE MARSHALL COURT'S POSITION

The Marshall Court's position that the Bill of Rights guarantees applied only to the national government and not to the states seemed a self-evident proposition to the Justices in 1833.   Marshall described the question as "not of much difficulty";   indeed, counsel for the Baltimore officials —including soon-to-become Chief Justice Roger Brooke Taney—were "stopped by the Court" before they could complete their oral argument.   But was the question all that easy?   Note that a different inference might be drawn from the text of the Bill of Rights: the First Amendment explicitly inhibits

"Congress" (but has been read to apply to the entire national government);
the Seventh Amendment is explicitly addressed to "any Court of the United
States"; but all of the other Bill of Rights provisions speak in general terms.
And a few courts, before Barron, thought those provisions generally applicable. See 2 Crosskey, Politics and the Constitution in the History of the United States (1953), 1050. Yet Marshall—ordinarily not averse to nationalistic interpretations—refused to find the amendments applicable to the states;
and his position prevailed. What were the bases of his position, and how
persuasive were they? To what extent does he rely on constitutional text?
On structure? On history—"a part of the history of the day"?

SECTION 2. THE PURPOSE AND IMPACT OF THE POST–CIVIL WAR AMENDMENTS

Before the Civil War, Barron v. Baltimore makes clear, the Constitution had a very narrow impact on the relationships between state governments
and individuals. Did the post-Civil War Amendments dramatically change
that picture? With the hindsight of more than a century, it is clear that
they did: those amendments, and particularly the 14th, have spawned national protection of a wide range of individual rights, procedural and substantive. But that far-reaching impact was not immediately apparent. The
immediate provocation for the amendments was the Civil War concern with
problems of slavery and emancipation. And the Court's first interpretation
of the Amendments, in the Slaughter-House Cases below, resisted the effort
to give the Amendments a content going beyond the problems which immediately gave rise to them. Justice Miller's majority opinion, like Marshall's in
Barron, relied strongly on historical memory: paralleling Marshall's reference
to "the history of the day," Miller spoke of the history "fresh within the
memory of us all"—the "history of the times" which showed the "one pervading purpose" of the Amendments to be "the freedom of the slave race,
the security and firm establishment of that freedom, and the protection of
the newly-made freeman and citizen from the oppressions of those who had
formerly exercised unlimited dominion over him." To Miller and his brethren
in the majority, the Amendments were not to be given a reading which "radically changes the whole theory of the relations of the State and Federal governments to each other and of both these governments to the people"; they
were not to be read to "constitute this court a perpetual censor upon all legislation of the States, on the civil rights of their own citizens." But Miller's
position did not prove to be a lasting one. The broad language of the
Amendment, and especially of the first section of the 14th, has not been
confined to problems of racial discrimination; the scope of the Amendments
has not been read so as to make only a minimal impact on allocations of
power within the federal system. Within a generation, the essence of the
position of the dissenters in the Slaughter-House Cases prevailed, and a vast
increase in national, and especially judicial, power was assured.

The Slaughter-House Cases themselves were immediately concerned
with an effort to read substantive rather than procedural content into the

Amendments: the effort was to use the Amendments as a weapon against state monopoly legislation. The ultimate vindication of the dissenting position in the Slaughter-House Cases appears in the next chapter, in the materials tracing the rise of substantive due process. But the Slaughter-House Cases warrant attention at this point as well, for the decision implicitly speaks to the issue of the applicability to the states of the procedural guarantees of the Bill of Rights. The Slaughter-House majority's narrow reading of the Amendments meant defeat for the time being for any claim that the Amendments amounted to a de facto overturning of Barron v. Baltimore. That narrow reading of the Amendments, tying them closely to the immediate historical background, meant that, for the time being, the procedural guarantees of the Bill of Rights would not be nationally enforceable safeguards in state criminal proceedings. It would be left to later generations and their broader readings of the Amendments to realize the full nationalizing potential of the post-Civil War changes. One realization came through the growth of substantive due process traced in the next chapter. The other came in the selective but virtually total incorporation of Bill of Rights guarantees into the 14th, traced in sec. 3 of this chapter.

The Slaughter-House Cases warrant attention at this point for reasons going beyond their doctrinal contributions. They also serve as a useful summary of a nearly contemporaneous perception of the historical background of the post-Civil War Amendments. As Justice Miller develops more fully, the 13th Amendment, in 1865, gave constitutional sanction to President Lincoln's wartime Emancipation Proclamation. But that anti-slavery amendment did not end the problems of ex-slaves: their rights continued to be severely limited by the "black codes" of several states. Congress accordingly adopted the Civil Rights Act of 1866—over President Andrew Johnson's veto, based on constitutional grounds—and immediately set the amendment process in motion to assure the constitutional validity of that law. The 14th Amendment was ratified in 1868. (For the provisions of the post-Civil War Civil Rights Acts and their interrelationships with the amendments, see chap. 11 below.) The 14th Amendment used even more sweeping, general terms than the Act it was designed to sustain: the Amendment's language was not limited to discrimination based on race, color, or previous condition of servitude. The last of the post-Civil War Amendments came two years later, in 1870; and that 15th Amendment did speak specifically about racial discrimination, in voting. For generations, delineation of the scope of the Amendments was left almost entirely to the Court. But each of the three post-Civil War Amendments ended with a section authorizing Congress to enact legislation to enforce its provisions. Those congressional enforcement provisions, too, contained a vast nationalizing potential—a potential not realized until the abandonment of restrictive judicial interpretations and the revival of legislative interest in the 1960's, as the materials in chap. 11 will demonstrate.

SLAUGHTER–HOUSE CASES

16 Wall. 36, 21 L.Ed. 394 (1873).

Error to the Supreme Court of Louisiana.

[A Louisiana law of 1869 chartered a corporation—the Crescent City Live-Stock Landing and Slaughter-House Company—and granted to it a 25-year monopoly "to maintain slaughterhouses, landings for cattle and stock-yards" in three parishes. The parishes covered an area of 1154 square miles with a population of over 200,000, including the city of New Orleans. The statute also prescribed the rates to be charged at the company's facilities. Butchers not included in the monopoly challenged the statute under the 13th and 14th Amendments. The Supreme Court of Louisiana sustained the law.]

Mr. Justice MILLER delivered the opinion of the Court. . . .

[The police] power is, and must be from its very nature, incapable of any very exact definition or limitation. Upon it depends the security of social order, the life and health of the citizen, the comfort of an existence in a thickly populated community, the enjoyment of private and social life, and the beneficial use of property. . . . The regulation of the place and manner of conducting the slaughtering of animals, and the business of butchering within a city, [are] among the most necessary and frequent exercises of this power. . . .

It cannot be denied that the statute under consideration is aptly framed to remove from the more densely populated part of the city, the noxious slaughter-houses, and large and offensive collections of animals necessarily incident to the slaughtering business of a large city, and to locate them where the convenience, health, and comfort of the people require they shall be located. And it must be conceded that the means adopted by the act for this purpose are appropriate, are stringent, and effectual. But it is said that in creating a corporation for this purpose, and conferring upon it exclusive privileges—privileges which it is said constitute a monopoly—the legislature has exceeded its power. [The only arguable constraints are those arising from the federal Constitution. The challengers claim that the law created an "involuntary servitude" in violation of the 13th Amendment, and that it violated the 14th Amendment by abridging the "privileges and immunities" of citizens of the United States, denying the challengers "the equal protection of the laws," and depriving them "of their property without due process of law."]

This Court is thus called upon for the first time to give construction to these [Amendments].

The most cursory glance at [the three post-Civil War Amendments—the 13th, 14th and 15th] discloses a unity of purpose, when taken in connection with the history of the times, which cannot fail to have an important bearing on any question of doubt concerning their true meaning. Nor can such doubts, when any reasonably exist, be safely and rationally solved without a reference to that history. . . . Fortunately that history is fresh within the memory of us all, and its leading features, as they bear upon the matter before us, free from doubt.

The institution of African slavery, as it existed in about half the States of the Union, and the contests pervading the public mind for many years, between those who desired its curtailment and ultimate extinction and those who desired additional safeguards for its security and perpetuation, culminated in the effort, on the part of most of the States in which slavery existed, to separate from the Federal government, and to resist its authority. This constituted the war of the rebellion, and whatever auxiliary causes may have contributed to bring about this war, undoubtedly the overshadowing and efficient cause was African slavery.

In that struggle slavery, as a legalized social relation, perished. It perished as a necessity of the bitterness and force of the conflict. . . . The [emancipation] proclamation of President Lincoln expressed an accomplished fact as to a large portion of the insurrectionary districts, when he declared slavery abolished in them all. But the war being over, those who had succeeded in re-establishing the authority of the Federal government were not content to permit this great act of emancipation to rest on the actual results of the contest or the proclamation of the Executive, both of which might have been questioned in after times, and they determined to place this main and most valuable result in the Constitution of the restored Union as one of its fundamental articles. Hence the thirteenth article of amendment of that instrument. . . .

To withdraw the mind from the contemplation of this grand yet simple declaration of the personal freedom of all the human race within the jurisdiction of this government—a declaration designed to establish the freedom of four millions of slaves—and with a microscopic search endeavor to find in it a reference to servitudes, which may have been attached to property in certain localities, requires an effort, to say the least of it.

That a personal servitude was meant is proved by the use of the word "involuntary," which can only apply to human beings. . . . The word servitude is of larger meaning than slavery, as the latter is popularly understood in this country, and the obvious purpose was to forbid all shades and conditions of African slavery. It was very well understood that in the form of apprenticeship for long terms, as it had been practiced in the West India Islands, on the abolition of slavery by the English government, or by reducing the slaves to the condition of serfs attached to the plantation, the purpose of the article might have been evaded, if only the word slavery had been used. . . . . And it is all that we deem necessary to say on the application [of the 13th Amendment to the Louisiana monopoly law].*

* The scope of the 13th Amendment—especially as a source of congressional power "rationally to determine what are the badges and the incidents of slavery" and to "translate that determination into effective legislation," against private as well as state action—is examined in Jones v. Alfred H. Mayer Co., 392 U.S. 409 (1968), chap. 11, sec. 3, below.
For Court encounters with applications of the 13th Amendment to problems other than racial discrimination, see Bailey v. Alabama, 219 U.S. 219 (1911), invalidating state laws which sought "to compel . . . service of labor" under contracts "by making it a crime to refuse or fail to perform it." See also Pollock v. Williams, 322 U.S. 4 (1944). But the Amendment does not bar all compulsory service—e. g., by seamen, Robertson v. Baldwin, 165 U.S. 275 (1897), or by soldiers, Selective Service Draft Law Cases, 245 U.S. 366 (1918). See generally tenBroek, "Thirteenth Amendment . . .—Consummation to Abolition and Key to the Fourteenth Amendment," 39 Calif.L.

The process of restoring to their proper relations with the Federal government and with the other States those which had sided with the rebellion . . . developed the fact that, notwithstanding the formal recognition by those States of the abolition of slavery, the condition of the slave race would, without further protection of the Federal government, be almost as bad as it was before. Among the first acts of legislation adopted by several of the States . . . were laws which imposed upon the colored race onerous disabilities and burdens, and curtailed their rights in the pursuit of life, liberty, and property to such an extent that their freedom was of little value, while they had lost the protection which they had received from their former owners from motives both of interest and humanity.

They were in some States forbidden to appear in the towns in any other character than menial servants. They were required to reside on and cultivate the soil without the right to purchase or own it. They were excluded from many occupations of gain, and were not permitted to give testimony in the courts in any case where a white man was a party. It was said that their lives were at the mercy of bad men, either because the laws for their protection were insufficient or were not enforced.

These circumstances, whatever of falsehood or misconception may have been mingled with their presentation, forced upon the statesmen who had conducted the Federal government in safety through the crisis of the rebellion, and who supposed that by the thirteenth article of amendment they had secured the result of their labors, the conviction that something more was necessary in the way of constitutional protection to the unfortunate race who had suffered so much. They accordingly passed through Congress the proposition for the fourteenth amendment, and they declined to treat as restored to their full participation in the government of the Union the States which had been in insurrection, until they ratified that article by a formal vote of their legislative bodies.

Before we proceed to examine more critically the provisions of this amendment, on which the plaintiffs in error rely, let us complete and dismiss the history of the recent amendments, as that history relates to the general purpose which pervades them all. A few years' experience satisfied the thoughtful men who had been the authors of the other two amendments that, notwithstanding the restraints of those articles on the States, and the laws passed under the additional powers granted to Congress, these were inadequate for the protection of life, liberty, and property, without which freedom to the slave was no boon. They were in all those States denied the right of suffrage. The laws were administered by the white man alone. It was urged that a race of men distinctively marked as was the negro, living in the midst of another and dominant race, could never be fully secured in their person and the property without the right of suffrage.

Hence the fifteenth amendment . . . .. The negro having, by the fourteenth amendment, been declared to be a citizen of the United States, is thus made a voter in every State of the Union.

Rev. 171 (1951); Brodie, "The Federally-Secured Right to be Free from Bondage," 40 Geo.L.J. 367 (1952); and, on the enforcement of federal anti-peonage statutes, Shapiro, "Involuntary Servitude: The Need for a More Flexible Approach," 19 Rutgers L.Rev. 65 (1964).

We repeat, then, in the light of this recapitulation of events, almost too recent to be called history, but which are familiar to us all; and on the most casual examination of the language of these amendments, no one can fail to be impressed with the one pervading purpose found in them all, lying at the foundation of each, and without which none of them would have been even suggested; we mean the freedom of the slave race, the security and firm establishment of that freedom, and the protection of the newly-made freeman and citizen from the oppressions of those who had formerly exercised unlimited dominion over him. It is true that only the fifteenth amendment, in terms, mentions the negro by speaking of his color and his slavery. But it is just as true that each of the other articles was addressed to the grievances of that race, and designed to remedy them as the fifteenth.

We do not say that no one else but the negro can share in this protection. Both the language and spirit of these articles are to have their fair and just weight in any question of construction. Undoubtedly while negro slavery alone was in the mind of the Congress which proposed the thirteenth article, it forbids any other kind of slavery, now or hereafter. If Mexican peonage or the Chinese coolie labor system shall develop slavery of the Mexican or Chinese race within our territory, this amendment may safely be trusted to make it void. And so if other rights are assailed by the States which properly and necessarily fall within the protection of these articles, that protection will apply, though the party interested may not be of African descent. But what we do say, and what we wish to be understood is, that in any fair and just construction of any section or phrase of these amendments, it is necessary to look to the purpose which we have said was the pervading spirit of them all, the evil which they were designed to remedy, and the process of continued addition to the Constitution, until that purpose was supposed to be accomplished, as far as constitutional law can accomplish it.

The first section of the [14th Amendment], to which our attention is more specially invited, opens with a definition of citizenship—not only citizenship of the United States, but citizenship of the States. ["All persons born or naturalized in the United States, and subject to the jurisdiction thereof, are citizens of the United States and of the State wherein they reside."] . . . . [I]t overturns the Dred Scott decision by making *all persons* born within the United States and subject to its jurisdiction citizens of the United States. That its main purpose was to establish the citizenship of the negro can admit of no doubt. . . .

The next observation is more important in view of the arguments of counsel in the present case. It is, that the distinction between citizenship of the United States and citizenship of a State is clearly recognized and established. Not only may a man be a citizen of the United States without being a citizen of a State, but an important element is necessary to convert the former into the latter. He must reside within the State to make him a citizen of it, but it is only necessary that he should be born or naturalized in the United States to be a citizen of the Union.

It is quite clear, then, that there is a citizenship of the United States, and a citizenship of a State, which are distinct from each other, and which depend upon different characteristics or circumstances in the individual.

We think this distinction and its explicit recognition in this amendment of great weight in this argument, because the next paragraph of this same section, which is the one mainly relied on by the plaintiffs in error, speaks only of privileges and immunities of citizens of the United States, and does not speak of those of citizens of the several States. The argument, however, in favor of the plaintiffs rests wholly on the assumption that the citizenship is the same, and the privileges and immunities guaranteed by the clause are the same.

The language is, "No State shall make or enforce any law which shall abridge the privileges or immunities of citizens of *the United States.*" It is a little remarkable, if this clause was intended as a protection to the citizen of a State against the legislative power of his own State, that the word citizen of the State should be left out when it is so carefully used, and used in contradistinction to citizens of the United States, in the very sentence which precedes it. It is too clear for argument that the change in phraseology was adopted understandingly and with a purpose.

Of the privileges and immunities of the citizen of the United States, and of the privileges and immunities of the citizen of the State, and what they respectively are, we will presently consider; but we wish to state here that it is only the former which are placed by this clause under the protection of the Federal Constitution, and that the latter, whatever they may be, are not intended to have any additional protection by this paragraph of the amendment. . . .

In the Constitution of the United States, [Art. IV, Sec. 2—the inter-state privileges and immunities clause, see chap. 6, sec. 2, above—states]: "The citizens of each State shall be entitled to all the privileges and immunities of citizens of the several States." . . . Fortunately we are not without judicial construction of this clause of the Constitution. The first and the leading case on the subject is that of Corfield v. Coryell, decided by Mr. Justice Washington in the Circuit Court for the District of Pennsylvania in 1823. [See chap. 6 above.] "The inquiry," he says, "is, what are the privileges and immunities of citizens of the several States? We feel no hesitation in confining these expressions to those privileges and immunities which are *fundamental*; which belong of right to the citizens of all free governments, and which have at all times been enjoyed by citizens of the several States which compose this Union, from the time of their becoming free, independent, and sovereign. What these fundamental principles are, it would be more tedious than difficult to enumerate. They may all, however, be comprehended under the following general heads: protection by the government, with the right to acquire and possess property of every kind, and to pursue and obtain happiness and safety, subject, nevertheless, to such restraints as the government may prescribe for the general good of the whole."

. . . The description, when taken to include others not named, but which are of the same general character, embraces nearly every civil right for the establishment and protection of which organized government is instituted. They are, in the language of Judge Washington, those rights which are fundamental. Throughout his opinion, they are spoken of as rights belonging to the individual as a citizen of a State. They are so spoken of in the con-

stitutional provision which he was construing. And they have always been held to be the class of rights which the State governments were created to establish and secure. . . .

[Art. IV] did not create those rights, which it called privileges and immunities of citizens of the States. It threw around them in that clause no security for the citizen of the State in which they were claimed or exercised. Nor did it profess to control the power of the State governments over the rights of its own citizens. Its sole purpose was to declare to the several States, that whatever those rights, as you grant or establish them to your own citizens, or as you limit or qualify, or impose restrictions on their exercise, the same, neither more nor less, shall be the measure of the rights of citizens of other States within your jurisdiction.

It would be the vainest show of learning to attempt to prove by citations of authority, that up to the adoption of the recent amendments, no claim or pretence was set up that those rights depended on the Federal government for their existence or protection, beyond the very few express limitations which the Federal Constitution imposed upon the States—such, for instance, as the prohibition against ex post facto laws, bills of attainder, and laws impairing the obligation of contracts. But with the exception of these and a few other restrictions, the entire domain of the privileges and immunities of citizens of the States, as above defined, lay within the constitutional and legislative power of the States, and without that of the Federal government. Was it the purpose of the fourteenth amendment, by the simple declaration that no State should make or enforce any law which shall abridge the privileges and immunities of *citizens of the United States*, to transfer the security and protection of all the civil rights which we have mentioned, from the States to the Federal government? And where it is declared that Congress shall have the power to enforce that article, was it intended to bring within the power of Congress the entire domain of civil rights heretofore belonging exclusively to the States?

All this and more must follow, if the proposition of the plaintiffs in error be sound. For not only are these rights subject to the control of Congress whenever in its discretion any of them are supposed to be abridged by State legislation, but that body may also pass laws in advance, limiting and restricting the exercise of legislative power by the States, in their most ordinary and usual functions, as in its judgment it may think proper on all such subjects. And still further, such a construction followed by a reversal of the judgments of the Supreme Court of Louisiana in these cases, would constitute this court a perpetual censor upon all legislation of the States, on the civil rights of their own citizens, with authority to nullify such as it did not approve as consistent with those rights, as they existed at the time of the adoption of this amendment. The argument we admit is not always the most conclusive which is drawn from the consequences urged against the adoption of a particular construction of an instrument. But when, as in the case before us, these consequences are so serious, so far-reaching and pervading, so great a departure from the structure and spirit of our institutions; when the effect is to fetter and degrade the State governments by subjecting them to the control of Congress, in the exercise of powers heretofore universally conceded to them of the most ordinary and fundamental

character; when in fact it radically changes the whole theory of the relations of the State and Federal governments to each other and of both these governments to the people; the argument has a force that is irresistible, in the absence of language which expresses such a purpose too clearly to admit of doubt.

We are convinced that no such results were intended by the Congress which proposed these amendments, nor by the legislatures of the States which ratified them.

Having shown that the privileges and immunities relied on in the argument are those which belong to citizens of the States as such, and that they are left to the State governments for security and protection, and not by this article placed under the special care of the Federal government, we may hold ourselves excused from defining the privileges and immunities of citizens of the United States which no State can abridge, until some case involving those privileges may make it necessary to do so.

But lest it should be said that no such privileges and immunities are to be found if those we have been considering are excluded, we venture to suggest some which owe their existence to the Federal government, its National character, its Constitution, or its laws.

One of these is well described in the case of Crandall v. Nevada [6 Wall. 36 (1868) (chap. 5 above)]. It is said to be the right of the citizen of this great country, protected by implied guarantees of its Constitution, "to come to the seat of government to assert any claim he may have upon that government, to transact any business he may have with it, to seek its protection, to share its offices, to engage in administering its functions. He has the right of free access to its seaports, through which all operations of foreign commerce are conducted, to the subtreasuries, land offices, and courts of justice in the several States." . . .

Another privilege of a citizen of the United States is to demand the care and protection of the Federal government over his life, liberty, and property when on the high seas or within the jurisdiction of a foreign government. . . . The right to peaceably assemble and petition for redress of grievances, the privilege of the writ of *habeas corpus,* are rights of the citizen guaranteed by the Federal Constitution. The right to use the navigable waters of the United States, however they may penetrate the territory of the several States, all rights secured to our citizens by treaties with foreign nations, are dependent upon citizenship of the United States, and not citizenship of a State. One of these privileges is conferred by the very article under consideration. It is that a citizen of the United States can, of his own volition, become a citizen of any State of the Union by a *bona fide* residence therein, with the same rights as other citizens of that State. To these may be added the rights secured by the thirteenth and fifteenth articles of amendment, and by the other clause of the fourteenth, next to be considered. . .

The argument has not been much pressed in these cases that the defendant's charter deprives the plaintiffs of their property without due process of law, or that it denies to them the equal protection of the law. The first of these paragraphs has been in the Constitution since the adoption of the fifth amendment, as a restraint upon the Federal power. It is also to be

found in some form of expression in the constitutions of nearly all the States, as a restraint upon the power of the States. This law then, has practically been the same as it now is during the existence of the government, except so far as the present amendment may place the restraining power over the States in this matter in the hands of the Federal government.

We are not without judicial interpretation, therefore, both State and National, of the meaning of this clause. And it is sufficient to say that under no construction of that provision that we have ever seen, or any that we deem admissible, can the restraint imposed by the State of Louisiana upon the exercise of their trade by the butchers of New Orleans be held to be a deprivation of property within the meaning of that provision.

"Nor shall any State deny to any person within its jurisdiction the equal protection of the laws."

In the light of the history of these amendments, and the pervading purpose of them, which we have already discussed, it is not difficult to give a meaning to this clause. The existence of laws in the States where the newly emancipated negroes resided, which discriminated with gross injustice and hardship against them as a class, was the evil to be remedied by this clause, and by it such laws are forbidden.

If, however, the States did not conform their laws to its requirements, then by the fifth section of the article of amendment Congress was authorized to enforce it by suitable legislation. We doubt very much whether any action of a State not directed by way of discrimination against the negroes as a class, or on account of their race, will ever be held to come within the purview of this provision. It is so clearly a provision for that race and that emergency, that a strong case would be necessary for its application to any other. But as it is a State that is to be dealt with, and not alone the validity of its laws, we may safely leave that matter until Congress shall have exercised its power, or some case of State oppression, by denial of equal justice in its courts, shall have claimed a decision at our hands. We find no such case in the one before us, and do not deem it necessary to go over the argument again, as it may have relation to this particular clause of the amendment. . . .

Unquestionably [the "late civil war"] added largely to the number of those who believe in the necessity of a strong National government.

But, however prevading this sentiment, and however it may have contributed to the adoption of the amendments we have been considering, we do not see in those amendments any purpose to destroy the main features of the general system. Under the pressure of all the excited feeling growing out of the war, our statesmen have still believed that the existence of the States with powers for domestic and local government, including the regulation of civil rights—the rights of person and of property—was essential to the perfect working of our complex form of government, though they have thought proper to impose additional limitations on the States, and to confer additional power on that of the Nation.

But whatever fluctuations may be seen in the history of public opinion on this subject during the period of our national existence, we think it will be found that this court, so far as its functions required, has always held with a steady and an even hand the balance between State and Federal pow-

er, and we trust that such may continue to be the history of its relation to that subject so long as it shall have duties to perform which demand of it a construction of the Constitution, or of any of its parts.

Affirmed.

Mr. Justice FIELD, dissenting: . . .

The act of Louisiana presents the naked case, unaccompanied by any public considerations, where a right to pursue a lawful and necessary calling, previously enjoyed by every citizen, and in connection with which a thousand persons were daily employed, is taken away and vested exclusively for twenty-five years, for an extensive district and a large population, in a single corporation . . . . [U]pon the theory on which the exclusive privileges granted by the act in question are sustained, there is no monopoly, in the most odious form, which may not be upheld.

The question presented is, therefore, one of the gravest importance, not merely to the parties here, but to the whole country. It is nothing less than the question whether the recent amendments to the Federal Constitution protect the citizens of the United States against the deprivation of their common rights by State legislation. In my judgment the fourteenth amendment does afford such protection, and was so intended by the Congress which framed and the States which adopted it. . . .

The terms, privileges and immunities, are not new in the amendment; they were in the Constitution before the amendment was adopted. [Justice Field, as had Justice Miller, quoted Justice Bushrod Washington's elaboration of Art. IV, § 2, in Corfield v. Coryell.] This appears to me to be a sound construction of the clause in question. The privileges and immunities designated are those *which of right belong to the citizens of all free governments.* Clearly among these must be placed the right to pursue a lawful employment in a lawful manner, without other restraint than such as equally affects all persons. In the discussions in Congress upon the passage of the Civil Rights Act [of 1866] repeated reference was made to this language of Mr. Justice Washington. . . .

What [Art. IV, § 2] did for the protection of the citizens of one State against hostile and discriminating legislation of other States, the fourteenth amendment does for the protection of every citizen of the United States against hostile and discriminating legislation against him in favor of others, whether they reside in the same or in different States. If under the fourth article of the Constitution equality of privileges and immunities is secured between citizens of different States, under the fourteenth amendment the same equality is secured between citizens of the United States. . . .

This equality of right, with exemption from all disparaging and partial enactments, in the lawful pursuits of life, throughout the whole country, is the distinguishing privilege of citizens of the United States. To them, everywhere, all pursuits, all professions, all avocations are open without other restrictions than such as are imposed equally upon all others of the same age, sex, and condition. The State may prescribe such regulations for every pursuit and calling of life as will promote the public health, secure the good order and advance the general prosperity of society, but when once prescribed, the pursuit or calling must be free to be followed by every citizen

who is within the conditions designated, and will conform to the regulations. This is the fundamental idea upon which our institutions rest, and unless adhered to in the legislation of the country our government will be a republic only in name.   The fourteenth amendment, in my judgment, makes it essential to the validity of the legislation of every State that this equality of right should be respected.   How widely this equality has been departed from, how entirely rejected and trampled upon by the act of Louisiana, I have already shown.   And it is to me a matter of profound regret that its validity is recognized by a majority of this court, for by it the right of free labor, one of the most sacred and imprescriptible rights of man, is violated.[1] [G]rants of exclusive privileges [are] opposed to the whole theory of free government, and it requires no aid from any bill of rights to render them void. That only is a free government, in the American sense of the term, under which the inalienable right of every citizen to pursue his happiness is unrestrained, except by just, equal, and impartial laws.[2]

I am authorized by the Chief Justice [CHASE], Mr. Justice SWAYNE, and Mr. Justice BRADLEY, to state that they concur with me in this dissenting opinion.

Mr. Justice BRADLEY, also dissenting: .   .   .

.   .   .   In this free country, the people of which inherited certain traditionary rights and privileges from their ancestors, citizenship means something.   It has certain privileges and immunities attached to it which the government, whether restricted by express or implied limitations, cannot take away or impair.   It may do so temporarily by force, but it cannot do so by right.   And these privileges and immunities attach as well to citizenship of the United States as to citizenship of the States.

The people of this country brought with them to its shores the rights of Englishmen; the rights which had been wrested from English sovereigns at various periods of the nation's history.   One of these fundamental rights was expressed in these words, found in Magna Charta: "No freeman shall be taken or imprisoned, or be disseized of his freehold or liberties or free customs, or be outlawed or exiled, or any otherwise destroyed; nor will we pass upon him or condemn him but by lawful judgment of his peers or by the law of the land."   English constitutional writers expound this article as rendering life, liberty, and property inviolable, except by due process of law. This is the very right which the plaintiffs in error claim in this case.   .   .   .

---

1.   "The property which every man has in his own labor," says Adam Smith, "as it is the original foundation of all other property, so it is the most sacred and inviolable.   The patrimony of the poor man lies in the strength and dexterity of his own hands; and to hinder him from employing this strength and dexterity in what manner he thinks proper, without injury to his neighbor, is a plain violation of this most sacred property.   It is a manifest encroachment upon the just liberty both of the workman and of those who might be disposed to employ him.   As it hinders the one from working at what he thinks proper, so it hinders the others from employing whom they think proper."   (Smith's Wealth of Nations, b. 1, ch. 10, part 2.)   [Footnote by Justice Field.]

2.   "Civil liberty, the great end of all human society and government, is that state in which each individual has the power to pursue his own happiness according to his own views of his interest, and the dictates of his conscience, unrestrained, except by equal, just, and impartial laws."   (1 Sharswood's Blackstone, 127, note 8.) [Footnote by Justice Field.]

Blackstone classifies these fundamental rights under three heads, as the absolute rights of individuals, to wit: the right of personal security, the right of personal liberty, and the right of private property. . . . Rights to life, liberty, and the pursuit of happiness are equivalent to the rights of life, liberty, and property. These are the fundamental rights which can only be taken away by due process of law, and which can only be interfered with, or the enjoyment of which can only be modified, by lawful regulations necessary or proper for the mutual good of all; and these rights, I contend, belong to the citizens of every free government.

For the preservation, exercise, and enjoyment of these rights the individual citizen, as a necessity, must be left free to adopt such calling, profession, or trade as may seem to him most conducive to that end. Without this right he cannot be a freeman. This right to choose one's calling is an essential part of that liberty which it is the object of government to protect; and a calling, when chosen, is a man's property and right. Liberty and property are not protected where these rights are arbitrarily assailed. . . .

But we are not bound to resort to implication, or to the constitutional history of England, to find an authoritative declaration of some of the most important privileges and immunities of citizens of the United States. It is in the Constitution itself. The Constitution, it is true, as it stood prior to the recent amendments, specifies, in terms, only a few of the personal privileges and immunities of citizens, but they are very comprehensive in their character. The States were merely prohibited from passing bills of attainder, ex post facto laws, laws impairing the obligation of contracts, and perhaps one or two more. But others of the greatest consequence were enumerated, although they were only secured, in express terms, from invasion by the Federal government; such as the right of habeas corpus, the right of trial by jury, of free exercise of religious worship, the right of free speech and a free press, the right peaceably to assemble for the discussion of public measures, the right to be secure against unreasonable searches and seizures, and above all, and including almost all the rest, the right of *not being deprived of life, liberty, or property, without due process of law.* These, and still others are specified in the original Constitution, or in the early amendments of it, as among the privileges and immunities of citizens of the United States, or, what is still stronger for the force of the argument, the rights of all persons, whether citizens or not. . . .

Admitting [that] formerly the States were not prohibited from infringing any of the fundamental privileges and immunities of citizens of the United States, except in a few specified cases, that cannot be said now, since the adoption of the fourteenth amendment. In my judgment, it was the intention of the people of this country in adopting that amendment to provide National security against violation by the States of the fundamental rights of the citizen. . . . [A]ny law which establishes a sheer monopoly, depriving a large class of citizens of the privilege of pursuing a lawful employment, does abridge the privileges of those citizens. . . .

In my view, a law which prohibits a large class of citizens from adopting a lawful employment, or from following a lawful employment previously adopted, does deprive them of liberty as well as property, without due process of law. Their right of choice is a portion of their liberty; their occupation

is their property.   Such a law also deprives those citizens of the equal protection of the laws, contrary to the last clause of the section.   .   .   .

It is futile to argue that none but persons of the African race are intended to be benefited by this amendment.   They may have been the primary cause of the amendment, but its language is general, embracing all citizens, and I think it was purposely so expressed.

The mischief to be remedied was not merely slavery and its incidents and consequences; but that spirit of insubordination and disloyalty to the National government which had troubled the country for so many years in some of the States, and that intolerance of free speech and free discussion which often rendered life and property insecure, and led to much unequal legislation.   .   .   .

But great fears are expressed that this construction of the amendment will lead to enactments by Congress interfering with the internal affairs of the States   .   .   .   ; or else, that it will lead the Federal courts to draw to their cognizance the supervision of State tribunals on every subject of judicial inquiry   .   .   .   .   In my judgment no such practical inconveniences would arise.   Very little, if any, legislation on the part of Congress would be required to carry the amendment into effect.   Like the prohibition against passing a law impairing the obligation of a contract, it would execute itself. The point would be regularly raised, in a suit at law, and settled by final reference to the Federal court.   As the privileges and immunities protected are only those fundamental ones which belong to every citizen, they would soon become so far defined as to cause but a slight accumulation of business in the Federal courts.   Besides, the recognized existence of the law would prevent its frequent violation.   But even if the business of the National courts should be increased, Congress could easily supply the remedy by increasing their number and efficiency.   The great question is, What is the true construction of the amendment?   When once we find that, we shall find the means of giving it effect.   The argument from inconvenience ought not to have a very controlling influence in questions of this sort.   The National will and National interest are of far greater importance.   .   .   .

[Mr. Justice SWAYNE also submitted a separate dissenting opinion.]

THE AFTERMATH OF THE SLAUGHTER-HOUSE CASES: PRIVILEGES AND IMMUNITIES; DUE PROCESS

1. *Privileges and immunities of national citizenship.*   The framers of the 14th Amendment had great difficulty in articulating any specific content for the broad phrases—"due process," "equal protection," "privileges and immunities"—of its first section.   In no part of the congressional debates on the Amendment is there greater evidence of vagueness and inconsistencies than in the discussions of "privileges and immunities." *   The Justices of the

* Note a contemporary recollection that the clause "came from [Congressman] Bingham of Ohio.   Its euphony and indefiniteness of meaning were a charm to him."   Fairman, "Does the Fourteenth Amendment Incorporate the Bill of Rights?   The Original Understanding," 2 Stan.L.Rev. 5 (1949).

See also Fairman, Reconstruction and Reunion, 1864–88 (Part One) (6 History of the Supreme Court of the United States) (1971).   Compare Justice Black's comments on Professor Fairman and on Congressman Bingham in Duncan v. Louisiana, sec. 3 below, and in In re Winship, sec. 3 below.

Supreme Court have not been able to be much more concrete so far. There have been only sporadic attempts to give the clause a more expansive scope than that found by Justice Miller in 1873. His majority position in the Slaughter-House Cases has so far prevailed: the clause is limited to rights of national as distinct from state citizenship; and those rights are few. Even though the language of the clause speaks more explicitly to substantive matters than the companion clauses in the first section of the 14th Amendment, the development of privileges and immunities has been overshadowed by expanding views of due process and equal protection, as the remaining materials in this volume illustrate.

The privileges and immunities clause has been relied on only once for a majority invalidation of a state law, in Colgate v. Harvey, 296 U.S. 404 (1935), striking down a Vermont tax provision. But that interpretation of the clause was short-lived: the Colgate case was overruled in Madden v. Kentucky, 309 U.S. 83 (1940), where the Court reiterated that the clause "protects all citizens against abridgement by states of rights of national citizenship as distinct from the fundamental or natural rights inherent in state citizenship." For examples of reliances on the clause by individual Justices, see Edwards v. California, 314 U.S. 160 (1941) (chap. 5 above) (concurring opinion of Justice Douglas joined by Justices Black and Murphy—"[t]he right to move freely from State to State"); Hague v. CIO, 307 U.S. 496 (1939) (concurring opinion by Justice Roberts, joined by Justice Black—right to assemble and "discuss national legislation").[†]

For an early 20th century attempt to catalogue national privileges and immunities, see Twining v. New Jersey, 211 U.S. 78 (1908), which lists the right to travel from state to state, to petition Congress, to vote for national offices, to enter the public lands, the right to be "protected against violence while in the lawful custody of a United States marshal," and "the right to inform the United States authorities of violation of its laws." Consider this list, and recall also Justice Miller's potpourri of rights "which owe their existence to the Federal government, its National character, its Constitution, or its laws." Was the privileges and immunities clause necessary to give constitutional protection to any of those rights? Were they not protected by the structural limitations implied under the approach of McCulloch v. Maryland? Did not Congress have power to safeguard all of them even without the 14th Amendment? (See also chap. 11, sec. 3, below.)

What explains the Court's reluctance to give a broader content to the 14th Amendment's privileges and immunities clause? Because pressure for the broad reading rejected in the Slaughter-House Cases became no longer necessary when later Courts read the due process and equal protection clauses expansively? Because the privileges and immunities clause is limited to the "citizen," while the due process and equal protection clauses apply to any "person" (and "person" was soon read to include corporations)? Is it possible that the virtually dead privileges and immunities clause may yet be revived, as a last resort shelter for expansive judicial interpretation when the elastic capacities of due process and equal protection come to be perceived as

---

† Note also Justice Black's partial reliance on the clause in explaining his "incorporationist" position—e. g., in his dissent in Duncan v. Louisiana, sec. 3 below.

exhausted? Note the "prognosis" based "on the existent and potential needs that the privileges or immunities clause may be able to meet"—a "prognosis" by an articulate critic of many of the Warren Court's expansions of the equal protection and due process guarantees, Professor Philip B. Kurland. Kurland suggests, in "The Privileges or Immunities Clause: 'Its Hour Come Round at Last'?" 1972 Wash.U.L.Q. 405: "With government in control of so many essentials of our life, where in the Constitution can we turn for haven against the impositions of *1984*? . . . [I]f the legislative and executive discretion is to be limited by the Constitution on such matters as public education, public welfare, and public housing; police, fire, and sanitation; ecology; and, to repeat, most importantly, with reference to the right of privacy, I expect it will come as an attempt to define the privileges or immunities of American citizenship."

2. *Due Process.* Though the efforts to turn the privileges and immunities clause into a significant national instrument for protection of individual rights have failed so far, many of the arguments of the dissenters in the Slaughter-House Cases have found their way into majority opinions through the channels of the due process and equal protection clauses. Thus, the insistence of dissenting Justices Bradley and Swayne that the due process clause imposed substantive limits on state economic regulation was echoed by other dissenters for the next generation. By the end of the 19th century, a majority of the Court embraced substantive due process; and in the first three decades of the 20th century, the Court applied that doctrine frequently. Since the mid-1930's, the Court has followed a "hands-off" policy towards state regulation of commercial affairs; but a substantive due process approach has reemerged more recently on behalf of such personal rights as privacy. Those developments are traced in the next chapter. Moreover, a range of fundamental interests have found protection in the recent emergence of the "new" equal protection. See chap. 10 below. A review of the Slaughter-House Cases will be appropriate when those later developments are examined.

Among the broad interpretations of the 14th Amendment implicitly rejected by the Slaughter-House Cases was the position that all the Bill of Rights guarantees had been made applicable to the states as a result of the post-Civil War constitutional changes. What criminal procedure protections *were* made available in state cases as a result of the 14th Amendment's due process clause? The majority's narrow reading in the Slaughter-House Cases did not mark the end of the development of procedural due process any more than it signified a permanent halt to the evolution of substantive guarantees via the 14th Amendment. But the course of development of procedural rights has differed from that respecting substantive ones. Wholesale incorporation of Bill of Rights guarantees into the 14th Amendment continues to be rejected by the Court; but the modern Court's technique of "selective incorporation" has achieved virtually the same result—virtually all of the procedural protections in the first eight Amendments now apply to the states in the same way in which they restrict federal criminal proceedings. The tracing of that development is the theme of the next, major section of this chapter.

SECTION 3. THE MEANING OF DUE PROCESS: CRIMINAL PROCEDURE AND THE "INCORPORATION" CONTROVERSY

Introduction. Due process speaks most obviously to problems of procedure. What aspects of procedure—especially of criminal procedure—are required of the states because of the 14th Amendment due process guarantee? * That issue has provoked some of the most heated debates on the Court; and pursuit of that question provides a useful introductory vehicle for exploring the difficulties of defining the meaning of due process. The Court's battles over issues of state criminal procedure have taken place in the larger arena of the "incorporation" controversy: Did the 14th Amendment "incorporate" or "absorb" all of the Bill of Rights guarantees and make them applicable to the states? For decades after the Slaughter-House Cases, the Court continued to reject any such expansive reading. It was very reluctant to impose federal constitutional requirements on state procedures; but it clothed that reluctance in formulas which proved ultimately expansive after all.

The traditional Court position was that only "fundamental" matters—rights essential to "fundamental principles of liberty and justice," rights "essential to a fair trial"—were constitutionally required in state proceedings. Those broad formulations, which have their origins in late 19th century cases, have been most articulately elaborated in the 20th century by Justices Cardozo, Frankfurter, and Harlan. Beginning in the post-World War II years, however, a forceful counterposition began to be voiced, especially by Justice Black. He insisted that the 14th Amendment *did* incorporate the "specific" guarantees of the Bill of Rights; he objected to the vague, "natural law" formulations of the majority that spoke in terms of "fundamentals." That pitched battle over the meaning and historical intent of due process is traced in the series of decisions beginning with Palko and Adamson below. Are at least some of the guarantees of the Bill of Rights applicable to the states as a result of the 14th Amendment? If so, do those guarantees limit the states in precisely the same way that they restrain the national government?

As the concluding cases in this chapter (beginning with Duncan v. Louisiana) illustrate, the outcome of the incorporation battle is fairly well settled: as to doctrine, the majority has adhered to the "fundamental rights" approach and has refused to accept Justice Black's wholesale incorporation

---

* Criminal procedure, the focus of this section, does not exhaust the range of procedural due process concerns. The due process clause also imposes restraints on the conduct of civil proceedings, with an especially important impact in recent years on the administrative process. Those developments are considered in detail in administrative law courses; but some of them are touched on later in these materials. See chap. 10, sec. 6, below.

This section's emphasis on procedural guarantees in the administration of criminal law is not intended as an exhaustive survey of all constitutional aspects of criminal procedure; that task is left to other courses. The purpose of these materials from the criminal context is simply to illustrate recurrent controversies about giving content to the procedural dimensions of the 14th Amendment's due process guarantee.

notion; in practice, most of the procedural guarantees of the Bill of Rights have been incorporated into the 14th Amendment, and the incorporated guarantees apply to the states in precisely the same way that they restrain national law enforcement.   As Justice Black stated in his concurring opinion in Duncan, sec. 3C below: "I am very happy to support this selective process through which our Court has since the Adamson case held most of the specific Bill of Rights' protections applicable to the States to the same extent they are applicable to the Federal Government."   Nevertheless, that battle of the last generation is worth examining, especially for the light it throws on due process methodology.   As the cases below demonstrate, the controversy over the procedural content of due process echoes as well as anticipates some of the continuing disputes about the open-endedness of substantive due process notions.   When Justice Black attacks the majority's Palko-Adamson approach for its "natural law" characteristics, he reflects the fears of judicial subjectivity long associated with substantive due process.

What are the guidelines available to the Court in giving content to due process—guidelines that will promote adjudication on bases going beyond ad hoc reactions of the judges, beyond injection of personal value schemes into the Constitution?   Before turning to the modern manifestations of the "incorporation" dispute in which those questions have been at the forefront, consider the potential guidance available from text, early interpretations, and English history surveyed in the following preliminary notes.

1.   *Due process and procedure before the Civil War.*   The procedural content of due process was not a wholly blank slate when the clause was put into the 14th Amendment.   The Supreme Court had already had occasion to speak about the history and scope of due process in the course of interpreting the due process clause of the Fifth Amendment.   The best known statement was that by Justice Curtis in the course of considering the constitutionality of a distress warrant procedure in MURRAY'S LESSEE v. HOBOKEN LAND & IMPROVEMENT CO., 18 How. 272 (1856): "The words, 'due process of law,' were undoubtedly intended to convey the same meaning as the words, 'by the law of the land,' in Magna Charta.   Lord Coke, in his commentary on those words, (2 Inst. 50) says they mean due process of law. The constitutions which had been adopted by the several States before the formation of the federal constitution, following the language of the great charter more closely, generally contained the words, 'but by the judgment of his peers, or the law of the land.' . . .   The constitution contains no description of those processes which it was intended to allow or forbid.   It does not even declare what principles are to be applied to ascertain whether it be due process.   It is manifest that it was not left to the legislative power to enact any process which might be devised.   The article is a restraint on the legislative as well as on the executive and judicial powers of the government, and cannot be so construed as to leave congress free to make any process 'due process of law,' by its mere will.   To what principles, then, are we to resort to ascertain whether this process, enacted by congress, is due process? To this the answer must be twofold.   We must examine the constitution itself, to see whether this process be in conflict with any of its provisions.   If not found to be so, we must look to those settled usages and modes of proceeding existing in the common and statute law of England, before the

emigration of our ancestors, and which are shown not to have been unsuited to their civil and political condition by having been acted on by them after the settlement of this country. . . . [T]hough 'due process of law' generally implies and includes actor, reus, judex, regular allegations, opportunity to answer, and a trial according to some settled course of judicial proceedings, . . . yet, this is not universally true."

As Justice Curtis' last sentence indicates, concepts of notice and hearing have been at the core of due process from the beginning; and adaptation of those concepts to varied circumstances has contributed greatly to the flexibility of procedural due process. (See, e. g., Powell v. Alabama, note 3 below.) But Justice Curtis' major emphasis is not on flexibility but on a more confining, static reference, to English history. English history has indeed proved useful in giving content to due process, but the Court has not limited itself to that source, as the next notes illustrate.

2. *The utility of history.* The "settled usages and modes of proceeding" in English law may indeed be persuasive in some cases, as Ownbey v. Morgan, 256 U.S. 94 (1921), demonstrates. There the Court sustained the validity of a Delaware statute under which, in foreign attachment proceedings, special bail was required of defendant as a condition of being heard on the merits. The statute in question had been modeled on the Custom of London and had been on the statute books of Delaware from early colonial days.

3. *The inadequacy of English history.* But English legal history may be silent on many of the issues arising under due process; and even where it speaks, the Court has not felt compelled to listen. A good example is Powell v. Alabama, 287 U.S. 45 (1932), where the Court for the first time found a limited right to counsel essential to due process in some criminal cases, despite the lack of a corresponding guarantee in English practice of the late 18th century. In England, a full right to representation by counsel in felony cases was not granted until 1836, after the adoption of the federal Constitution. But that did not stop the Court from requiring the appointment of counsel in a capital case such as Powell. Instead of the contrary English practice, the Court relied on the "unanimous accord" in the American states regarding appointment of counsel in capital cases: it was the American practice that lent "convincing support to the conclusion we have reached as to the fundamental nature of that right." And in deriving that right, the Court reached back to the core meaning of due process articulated by Justice Curtis in the excerpt in note 1 above: the Powell Court emphasized that "notice and hearing" were "basic elements of the constitutional requirement of due process of law"; and the concept of a "hearing," in turn, was the basis for inferences as to legal representation: "The right to be heard would be, in many cases, of little avail if it did not comprehend the right to be heard by counsel."

Moreover, while references to English history have been useful in upholding some challenged procedures, the Court has not attempted to tie American lawmakers to the models of the English tradition. For example, Hurtado v. California, 110 U.S. 516 (1884), sustained a California statute which permitted criminal proceedings to be instituted by information rather than by grand jury indictment. In explaining that conclusion, the Hurtado

Court used a phrase—"principles of liberty and justice"—characteristic of the flexible, open-ended majority view during much of the 20th century incorporation controversy, beginning with Palko and Adamson below. The Hurtado opinion stated: "There is nothing in Magna Charta . . . which ought to exclude the best ideas of all systems and of every age. . . [A]ny legal proceeding enforced by public authority, whether sanctioned by age and custom, or newly devised in the discretion of the legislative power, in furtherance of the general public good, which regards and preserves . . . principles of liberty and justice, must be held to be due process of law."

Not the details of English practice, then, but "principles of liberty and justice" became the dominant confines of due process. As used in cases such as Hurtado, that broad formula tended to minimize federal intervention in state criminal procedures. That, too, was the thrust of later variations on the Hurtado theme, in cases such as Palko and Adamson. But as the more recent cases below show, references to vague standards such as "fundamental justice" could also provide the Supreme Court the bases for an increasing nationalization of standards of state criminal procedure.

A. THE PALKO–ADAMSON DISPUTE

PALKO v. CONNECTICUT

302 U.S. 319, 58 S.Ct. 149, 82 L.Ed. 288 (1937).

Appeal from the Supreme Court of Errors of Connecticut.

Mr. Justice CARDOZO delivered the opinion of the Court. . . .

Appellant was indicted in Fairfield County, Connecticut, for the crime of murder in the first degree. A jury found him guilty of murder in the second degree, and he was sentenced to confinement in the state prison for life. Thereafter the State of Connecticut, with the permission of the judge presiding at the trial, gave notice of appeal to the Supreme Court of Errors. This it did pursuant to an act adopted in 1886. [T]he Supreme Court of Errors reversed the judgment [because of errors of law] and ordered a new trial. . . .

[D]efendant was brought to trial again. [H]e made the objection that the effect of the new trial was to place him twice in jeopardy for the same offense, and in so doing to violate the [14th Amendment]. Upon the overruling of the objection the trial proceeded. The jury returned a verdict of murder in the first degree, and the court sentenced the defendant to the punishment of death. The Supreme Court of Errors affirmed. . . .

1. The execution of the sentence will not deprive appellant of his life without the process of law assured to him by the Fourteenth Amendment of the Federal Constitution.

The argument for appellant is that whatever is forbidden by the Fifth Amendment is forbidden by the Fourteenth also. . . . To retry a de-

fendant, though under one indictment and only one, subjects him, it is said, to double jeopardy in violation of the Fifth Amendment, if the prosecution is one on behalf of the United States. From this the consequence is said to follow that there is a denial of life or liberty without due process of law, if the prosecution is one on behalf of the People of a State. . . .

[Appellant's] thesis is even broader. Whatever would be a violation of the original bill of rights (Amendments I to VIII) if done by the federal government is now equally unlawful by force of the Fourteenth Amendment if done by a state. There is no such general rule.

The Fifth Amendment provides, among other things, that no person shall be held to answer for a capital or otherwise infamous crime unless on presentment or indictment of a grand jury. This court has held that, in prosecutions by a state, presentment or indictment by a grand jury may give way to informations at the instance of a public officer. Hurtado v. California, 110 U.S. 516 [1884]. The Fifth Amendment provides also that no person shall be compelled in any criminal case to be a witness against himself. This court has said that, in prosecutions by a state, the exemption will fail if the state elects to end it. Twining v. New Jersey, 211 U.S. 78 [1908]. The Sixth Amendment calls for a jury trial in criminal cases and the Seventh for a jury trial in civil cases at common law where the value in controversy shall exceed twenty dollars. This court has ruled that consistently with those amendments trial by jury may be modified by a state or abolished altogether. . . .

On the other hand, the due process clause of the Fourteenth Amendment may make it unlawful for a state to abridge by its statutes the freedom of speech which the First Amendment safeguards against encroachment by the Congress . . . ; or the like freedom of the press . . . ; or the free exercise of religion . . . ; or the right of peaceable assembly, without which speech would be unduly trammeled . . . ; or the right of one accused of crime to the benefit of counsel. Powell v. Alabama, 287 U.S. 45 [1932]. In these and other situations immunities that are valid as against the federal government by force of the specific pledges of particular amendments have been found to be implicit in the concept of ordered liberty, and thus, through the Fourteenth Amendment, become valid as against the states.

The line of division may seem to be wavering and broken if there is a hasty catalogue of the cases on the one side and the other. Reflection and analysis will induce a different view. There emerges the perception of a rationalizing principle which gives to discrete instances a proper order and coherence. The right to trial by jury and the immunity from prosecution except as the result of an indictment may have value and importance. Even so, they are not of the very essence of a scheme of ordered liberty. To abolish them is not to violate a "principle of justice so rooted in the traditions and conscience of our people as to be ranked as fundamental." Snyder v. Massachusetts, [291 U.S. 97 (1934)]. Few would be so narrow or provincial as to maintain that a fair and enlightened system of justice would be impossible without them. What is true of jury trials and indictments is true also, as the cases show, of the immunity from compulsory self-incrimination. . . . This too might be lost, and justice still be done. [E]xclusion of these immunities

and privileges from the privileges and immunities protected against the action of the states has not been arbitrary or casual. It has been dictated by a study and appreciation of the meaning, the essential implications, of liberty itself.

We reach a different plane of social and moral values when we pass to the privileges and immunities that have been taken over from the earlier articles of the federal bill of rights and brought within the Fourteenth Amendment by a process of absorption. These in their origin were effective against the federal government alone. If the Fourteenth Amendment has absorbed them, the process of absorption has had its source in the belief that neither liberty nor justice would exist if they were sacrificed. . . .[1] This is true, for illustration, of freedom of thought, and speech. Of that freedom one may say that it is the matrix, the indispensable condition, of nearly every other form of freedom. With rare aberrations a pervasive recognition of that truth can be traced in our history, political and legal. So it has come about that the domain of liberty, withdrawn by the Fourteenth Amendment from encroachment by the states, has been enlarged by latter-day judgments to include liberty of the mind as well as liberty of action. The extension became, indeed, a logical imperative when once it was recognized, as long ago it was, that liberty is something more than exemption from physical restraint, and that even in the field of substantive rights and duties the legislative judgment, if oppressive and arbitrary, may be overridden by the courts.[2] . . . Fundamental too in the concept of due process, and so in that of liberty, is the thought that condemnation shall be rendered only after trial. . . . The hearing, moreover, must be a real one, not a sham or a pretense. Moore v. Dempsey, 261 U.S. 86 [1923]. For that reason, ignorant defendants in a capital case were held to have been condemned unlawfully when in truth, though not in form, they were refused the aid of counsel. [Powell v. Alabama, above.] The decision did not turn upon the fact that the benefit of counsel would have been guaranteed to the defendants by the provisions of the Sixth Amendment if they had been prosecuted in a federal court. The decision turned upon the fact that in the particular situation laid before us in the evidence the benefit of counsel was essential to the substance of a hearing.

Our survey of the cases serves, we think, to justify the statement that the dividing line between them, if not unfaltering throughout its course, has been true for the most part to a unifying principle. On which side of the line the case made out by the appellant has appropriate location must be the next inquiry and the final one. Is that kind of double jeopardy to which

---

1. " . . . it is possible that some of the personal rights safeguarded by the first eight Amendments against National action may also be safeguarded against state action, because a denial of them would be a denial of due process of law. Chicago, Burlington & Quincy Railroad v. Chicago, 166 U.S. 226. If this is so, it is not because those rights are enumerated in the first eight Amendments, but because they are of such a nature that they are included in the conception of due process of law." [Footnote by the Court. The quotation is from Twining v. New Jersey, above.]

2. The First Amendment's free speech guarantee was first held applicable to the states via the 14th in Gitlow v. New York, 268 U.S. 652 (1925). First Amendment limitations are examined in chaps. 12 through 14 below. The development of substantive due process limits on economic regulations is traced in chap. 9 below.

the statute has subjected him a hardship so acute and shocking that our polity will not endure it? Does it violate those "fundamental principles of liberty and justice which lie at the base of all our civil and political institutions"? Hebert v. Louisiana, [272 U.S. 312 (1926)]. The answer surely must be "no." What the answer would have to be if the state were permitted after a trial free from error to try the accused over again or to bring another case against him, we have no occasion to consider. We deal with the statute before us and no other. The state is not attempting to wear the accused out by a multitude of cases with accumulated trials. It asks no more than this, that the case against him shall go on until there shall be a trial free from the corrosion of substantial legal error. . . . This is not cruelty at all, nor even vexation in any immoderate degree. If the trial had been infected with error adverse to the accused, there might have been review at his instance, and as often as necessary to purge the vicious taint. A reciprocal privilege, subject at all times to the discretion of the presiding judge, has now been granted to the state. There is here no seismic innovation. The edifice of justice stands, its symmetry, to many, greater than before.

2. The conviction of appellant is not in derogation of any privileges or immunities that belong to him as a citizen of the United States. . . .

Affirmed.[3]

Mr. Justice BUTLER dissents.

ADAMSON v. CALIFORNIA

332 U.S. 46, 67 S.Ct. 1672, 91 L.Ed. 1903 (1947).

Appeal from the Supreme Court of California.

Mr. Justice REED delivered the opinion of the Court.

[Adamson was convicted in a California court] of murder in the first degree [and sentenced to death.] The provisions of California law which were challenged in the state proceedings as invalid under the Fourteenth Amendment . . . permit the failure of a defendant to explain or to deny evidence against him to be commented upon by court and by counsel and to be considered by court and jury. . . .

We shall assume, but without any intention thereby of ruling upon the issue, that permission by law to the court, counsel and jury to comment upon and consider the failure of defendant "to explain or to deny by his testimony any evidence or facts in the case against him" would infringe defendant's privilege against self-incrimination under the Fifth Amendment if this were a trial in a court of the United States under a similar law. Such an assumption does not determine appellant's rights under the Fourteenth Amendment. [After rejecting a privileges and immunities clause claim, the Court continued:]

3. In Benton v. Maryland, 395 U.S. 784 (1969) (one of the modern "selective incorporation" cases, sec. 3C below), the Court held that the Fifth Amendment's double jeopardy guarantee "should apply to the States through the Fourteenth." The Court added: "Insofar as it is inconsistent with this holding, Palko v. Connecticut is overruled."

[Appellant contends that] the privilege against self-incrimination, [to] its full scope under the Fifth Amendment, inheres in the right to a fair trial. A right to a fair trial is a right admittedly protected by the due process clause of the Fourteenth Amendment. . . .   The due process clause of the Fourteenth Amendment, however, does not draw all the rights of the federal Bill of Rights under its protection. That contention was made and rejected in Palko v. Connecticut . . . . Nothing has been called to our attention that either the framers of the Fourteenth Amendment or the states that adopted intended its due process clause to draw within its scope the earlier amendments to the Constitution. Palko held that such provisions of the Bill of Rights as were "implicit in the concept of ordered liberty" . . . became secure from state interference by the clause. But it held nothing more.

. . . For a state to require testimony from an accused is not necessarily a breach of a state's obligation to give a fair trial. Therefore, we must examine the effect of the California law applied in this trial to see whether the comment on failure to testify violates the protection against state action that the due process clause does grant to an accused. The due process clause forbids compulsion to testify by fear of hurt, torture or exhaustion. It forbids any other type of coercion that falls within the scope of due process. . . . So our inquiry is directed, not at the broad question of the constitutionality of compulsory testimony from the accused under the due process clause, but to the constitutionality of the provision of the California law that permits comment upon his failure to testify. . . .

It is true that if comment were forbidden, an accused in this situation could remain silent and avoid evidence of former crimes and comment upon his failure to testify. We are of the view, however, that a state may control such a situation in accordance with its own ideas of the most efficient administration of criminal justice. The purpose of due process is not to protect an accused against a proper conviction but against an unfair conviction. When evidence is before a jury that threatens conviction, it does not seem unfair to require him to choose between leaving the adverse evidence unexplained and subjecting himself to impeachment through disclosure of former crimes. . . .

Affirmed.

Mr. Justice FRANKFURTER, concurring. . . .

For historical reasons a limited immunity from the common duty to testify was written into the Federal Bill of Rights, and I am prepared to agree that, as part of that immunity, comment on the failure of an accused to take the witness stand is forbidden in federal prosecutions. . . . But to suggest that such a limitation can be drawn out of "due process" in its protection of ultimate decency in a civilized society is to suggest that the Due Process Clause fastened fetters of unreason upon the States. . . .

Between the incorporation of the Fourteenth Amendment into the Constitution and the beginning of the present membership of the Court—a period of seventy years—the scope of that Amendment was passed upon by forty-three judges. Of all these judges, only one, who may respectfully be called an eccentric exception, ever indicated the belief that the Fourteenth Amendment was a shorthand summary of the first eight Amendments . . . . .

The short answer to the suggestion that the [due process clause] was a way of saying that every State must thereafter initiate prosecutions through indictment by a grand jury, must have a trial by a jury of twelve in criminal cases, and must have trial by such a jury in common law suits where the amount in controversy exceeds twenty dollars, is that it is a strange way of saying it. It would be extraordinarily strange for a Constitution to convey such specific commands in such a roundabout and inexplicit way. . . . Those reading the English language with the meaning which it ordinarily conveys, those conversant with the political and legal history of the concept of due process, those sensitive to the relations of the States to the central government as well as the relation of some of the provisions of the Bill of Rights to the process of justice, would hardly recognize the Fourteenth Amendment as a cover for the various explicit provisions of the first eight Amendments. Some of these are enduring reflections of experience with human nature, while some express the restricted views of Eighteenth-Century England regarding the best methods for the ascertainment of facts. The notion that the Fourteenth Amendment was a covert way of imposing upon the States all the rules which it seemed important to Eighteenth Century statesmen to write into the Federal Amendments, was rejected by judges who were themselves witnesses of the process by which the Fourteenth Amendment became part of the Constitution. . . . [A]t the time of the ratification of the Fourteenth Amendment the constitutions of nearly half of the ratifying States did not have the rigorous requirements of the Fifth Amendment for instituting criminal proceedings through a grand jury. It could hardly have occurred to these States that by ratifying the Amendment they uprooted their established methods for prosecuting crime and fastened upon themselves a new prosecutorial system.

Indeed, the suggestion that the Fourteenth Amendment incorporates the first eight Amendments as such is not unambiguously urged. . . . There is suggested merely a selective incorporation of the first eight Amendments into the Fourteenth Amendment. Some are in and some are out, but we are left in the dark as to which are in and which are out. Nor are we given the calculus for determining which go in and which stay out. If the basis of selection is merely that those provisions of the first eight Amendments are incorporated which commend themselves to individual justices as indispensable to the dignity and happiness of a free man, we are thrown back to a merely subjective test. The protection against unreasonable search and seizure might have primacy for one judge, while trial by a jury of 12 for every claim above $20 might appear to another as an ultimate need in a free society. In the history of thought "natural law" has a much longer and much better founded meaning and justification than such subjective selection of the first eight Amendments for incorporation into the Fourteenth. If all that is meant is that due process contains within itself certain minimal standards which are "of the very essence of a scheme of ordered liberty" [Palko v. Connecticut], putting upon this Court the duty of applying these standards from time to time, then we have merely arrived at the insight which our predecessors long ago expressed. . . .

. . . . The Amendment neither comprehends the specific provisions by which the founders deemed it appropriate to restrict the federal government nor is it confined to them. The Due Process Clause of the Fourteenth

Amendment has an independent potency, precisely as does the Due Process Clause of the Fifth Amendment in relation to the Federal Government. It ought not to require argument to reject the notion that due process of law meant one thing in the Fifth Amendment and another in the Fourteenth. The Fifth Amendment specifically prohibits prosecution of an "infamous crime" except upon indictment; it forbids double jeopardy; it bars compelling a person to be a witness against himself in any criminal case; it precludes deprivation of "life, liberty, or property, without due process of law." Are Madison and his contemporaries in the framing of the Bill of Rights to be charged with writing into it a meaningless clause? . . .

A construction which gives to due process no independent function but turns it into a summary of the specific provisions of the Bill of Rights . . . would deprive the States of opportunity for reforms in legal process designed for extending the area of freedom. It would assume that no other abuses would reveal themselves in the course of time than those which had become manifest in 1791. Such a view not only disregards the historic meaning of "due process." It leads inevitably to a warped construction of specific provisions of the Bill of Rights to bring within their scope conduct clearly condemned by due process but not easily fitting into the pigeon-holes of the specific provisions. It seems pretty late in the day to suggest that a phrase so laden with historic meaning should be given an improvised content consisting of some but not all of the provisions of the first eight Amendments, selected on an undefined basis, with improvisation of content for the provisions so selected.

And so, when, as in a case like the present, a conviction in a State court is here for review under a claim that a right protected by the Due Process Clause of the Fourteenth Amendment has been denied, the issue is not whether an infraction of one of the specific provisions of the first eight Amendments is disclosed by the record. The relevant question is whether the criminal proceedings which resulted in conviction deprived the accused of the due process of law to which the United States Constitution entitled him. Judicial review of that guaranty of the Fourteenth Amendment inescapably imposes upon this Court an exercise of judgment upon the whole course of the proceedings in order to ascertain whether they offend those canons of decency and fairness which express the notions of justice of English-speaking peoples even toward those charged with the most heinous offenses. These standards of justice are not authoritatively formulated anywhere as though they were prescriptions in a pharmacopoeia. But neither does the application of the Due Process Clause imply that judges are wholly at large. The judicial judgment in applying the Due Process Clause must move within the limits of accepted notions of justice and is not to be based upon the idiosyncrasies of a merely personal judgment. The fact that judges among themselves may differ whether in a particular case a trial offends accepted notions of justice is not disproof that general rather than idiosyncratic standards are applied. An important safeguard against such merely individual judgment is an alert deference to the judgment of the State court under review.

Mr. Justice BLACK, dissenting.   .   .   .

This decision reasserts a constitutional theory spelled out in Twining v. New Jersey, 211 U.S. 78, that this Court is endowed by the Constitution

with boundless power under "natural law" periodically to expand and contract constitutional standards to conform to the Court's conception of what at a particular time constitutes "civilized decency" and "fundamental liberty and justice." . . . I would not reaffirm the Twining decision. I think that decision and the "natural law" theory of the Constitution upon which it relies degrade the constitutional safeguards of the Bill of Rights and simultaneously appropriate for this Court a broad power which we are not authorized by the Constitution to exercise. My reasons for believing that the Twining decision should not be revitalized can best be understood by reference to the constitutional, judicial and general history that preceded and followed the case. . . .

. . . I am attaching to this dissent an appendix which contains a résumé, by no means complete, of the Amendment's history.* In my judgment that history conclusively demonstrates that the language of the first section of the Fourteenth Amendment, taken as a whole, was thought by those responsible for its submission to the people, and by those who opposed its submission, sufficiently explicit to guarantee that thereafter no state could deprive its citizens of the privileges and protections of the Bill of Rights. Whether this Court ever will, or whether it now should, in the light of past decisions, give full effect to what the Amendment was intended to accomplish is not necessarily essential to a decision here. However that may be, our prior decisions, including Twining, do not prevent our carrying out that purpose, at least to the extent of making applicable to the states, not a mere part, as the Court has, but the full protection of the Fifth Amendment's provision against compelling evidence from an accused to convict him of crime. And I further contend that the "natural law" formula which the Court uses to reach its conclusion in this case should be abandoned as an incongruous excrescence on our Constitution. . . .

. . . I fear to see the consequences of the Court's practice of substituting its own concepts of decency and fundamental justice for the language of the Bill of Rights as its point of departure in interpreting and enforcing that Bill of Rights. If the choice must be between the selective process of the Palko decision applying some of the Bill of Rights to the States, or the Twining rule applying none of them, I would choose the Palko selective process. But rather than accept either of these choices, I would follow what I believe was the original purpose of the Fourteenth Amendment— to extend to all the people of the nation the complete protection of the Bill of Rights. . . .

Conceding the possibility that this Court is now wise enough to improve on the Bill of Rights by substituting natural law concepts for the Bill of Rights, I think the possibility is entirely too speculative to agree to take that course. I would therefore hold in this case that the full protection of the Fifth Amendment's proscription against compelled testimony must be afforded by California. This I would do because of reliance upon the original purpose of the Fourteenth Amendment.

---

* The appendix is omitted. For an historical examination disagreeing with Justice Black's conclusion, see Fairman, "Does the Fourteenth Amendment Incorporate the Bill of Rights? The Original Understanding," 2 Stan. L.Rev. 5 (1949). For Justice Black's review of the historical dispute and a reply to Fairman, see the 1968 decision in Duncan, sec. 3C below.

It is an illusory apprehension that literal application of some or all of the provisions of the Bill of Rights to the States would unwisely increase the sum total of the powers of this Court to invalidate state legislation. . . . It must be conceded, of course, that the natural-law-due-process formula, which the Court today reaffirms, has been interpreted to limit substantially this Court's power to prevent state violations of the individual civil liberties guaranteed by the Bill of Rights. But this formula also has been used in the past, and can be used in the future, to license this Court in considering regulatory legislation, to roam at large in the broad expanses of policy and morals and to trespass, all too freely, on the legislative domain of the States as well as the Federal Government.

Since [Marbury v. Madison] was decided, the practice has been firmly established for better or worse, that courts can strike down legislative enactments which violate the Constitution. This process, of course, involves interpretation, and since words can have many meanings, interpretation obviously may result in contraction or extension of the original purpose of a constitutional provision thereby affecting policy. But to pass upon the constitutionality of statutes by looking to the particular standards enumerated in the Bill of Rights and other parts of the Constitution is one thing; to invalidate statutes because of application of "natural law" deemed to be above and undefined by the Constitution is another. "In the one instance, courts proceeding within clearly marked constitutional boundaries seek to execute policies written into the Constitution; in the other, they roam at will in the limitless area of their own beliefs as to reasonableness and actually select policies, a responsibility which the Constitution entrusts to the legislative representatives of the people." Federal Power Commission v. Natural Gas Pipeline Co., 315 U.S. 575, 599, 601, n. 4 [1942].

Mr. Justice DOUGLAS joins in this opinion.

Mr. Justice MURPHY, with whom Mr. Justice RUTLEDGE concurs, dissenting.

While in substantial agreement with the views of Mr. Justice Black, I have one reservation and one addition to make.

I agree that the specific guarantees of the Bill of Rights should be carried over intact into the first section of the Fourteenth Amendment. But I am not prepared to say that the latter is entirely and necessarily limited by the Bill of Rights. Occasions may arise where a proceeding falls so far short of conforming to fundamental standards of procedure as to warrant constitutional condemnation in terms of a lack of due process despite the absence of a specific provision in the Bill of Rights.

That point, however, need not be pursued here inasmuch as the Fifth Amendment . . . guarantee against self-incrimination has been violated in this case. . . . *

---

* In Malloy v. Hogan, 378 U.S. 1 (1964), the Court held that the Fifth Amendment's privilege against self-incrimination was applicable to the states under the Fourteenth: "Decisions of the Court since Twining and Adamson have departed from the contrary view expressed in those cases." A year later, the Court overruled the specific holding in Adamson and found unconstitutional the California rule permitting comment on the defendant's failure to testify. Griffin v. California, 380 U.S. 609 (1965). Note the discussion of "incorporation" developments after Adamson in the

B. SOME CASE STUDIES IN DUE PROCESS METHODOLOGY

THE WOLF–ROCHIN–IRVINE SEQUENCE, FOURTH AMENDMENT VIOLATIONS, AND "CONDUCT THAT SHOCKS THE CONSCIENCE"

Consider the process and problems of articulating due process criteria as reflected in the series of cases that follow. The majority in each case was committed to the Palko-Adamson approach. Does the course of the decisions suggest the inadequacy of that approach? Because it is too unpredictable? Because it is too idiosyncratic and personal? Were the failings—particularly of Justice Frankfurter—in the application rather than the statement of the approach? Should there have been greater emphasis on the facts—in Wolf, for example? But would not such greater emphasis have added to the unpredictability of the approach? Does the "incorporation" of "specific" rights approach offer more satisfactory analyses of these cases? How "specific" is the 4th Amendment? And what "specific" rights of the Bill of Rights are directly involved in stomach-pumping and blood-testing? (See also the questions following this group of notes.)

1. *Wolf.* In Wolf v. Colorado, 338 U.S. 25 (1949), the Court, in an opinion by Justice Frankfurter reaffirming the Palko approach, stated that the "security of one's privacy against arbitrary intrusion by the police—which is at the core of the Fourth Amendment—is basic to a free society. It is therefore implicit in 'the concept of ordered liberty' and as such enforceable against the States through the Due Process Clause." Accordingly, "were a State affirmatively to sanction such police incursion into privacy," it would violate the 14th Amendment. The Court added, however, that "the ways of enforcing such a basic right raise questions of a different order"; the problem of remedies was susceptible of "varying solutions." And the Court therefore concluded that the federal exclusionary rule—the rule that "the Fourth Amendment [bars] the use of evidence secured through an illegal search and seizure" in federal prosecutions—was not applicable to the states by way of the 14th Amendment. The state court conviction under review was therefore affirmed though it rested on evidence illegally obtained.

Justice Frankfurter once again insisted that defining due process was a "gradual and empiric process of 'inclusion and exclusion' "; yet his opinion in Wolf did not state the specific facts in the case. Rather, he described the question presented in the abstract. (From the state reports, it appears that the illegal police conduct consisted of seizing a doctor's records without a warrant, at the time of an arrest; there was no brutality.) Justice Black, adhering to his Adamson position, nevertheless concurred in the Wolf affirmance, on the ground that "the federal exclusionary rule is not a command of the Fourth Amendment but is a judicially created rule of evidence which Congress might negate." Justices Douglas, Murphy and Rutledge dissented,

1968 decision in Duncan v. Louisiana, sec. 3C below. And for another round in the battle between Justices Black and Frankfurter, see the 1952 decision in Rochin v. California, sec. 3B, below.

with Justice Murphy stating that the exclusionary rule was the only effective sanction for violations of the search and seizure guarantee: "[T]here is but one alternative to the rule of exclusion. That is no sanction at all."

2. *Rochin.* Three years after Wolf, the Court decided Rochin v. California, 342 U.S. 165 (1952). Justice Frankfurter again wrote the majority opinion. The Court reversed the state court conviction—without mentioning Wolf. In Rochin (unlike Wolf) Justice Frankfurter stated the facts in detail: three detectives broke into petitioner's room and saw two capsules on a night table next to his bed; he put the capsules in his mouth; the detectives "jumped upon him" to extract the capsules, were unsuccessful, and took him to a hospital; and in the hospital, a doctor, under police direction, "forced an emetic solution through a tube into Rochin's stomach." Petitioner vomited as a result of the "stomach-pumping"; the vomited matter contained two morphine capsules; and the capsules were used in evidence to convict Rochin.

Justice Frankfurter's opinion concluded "that the proceedings by which invoked by the Court in Rochin, so of course the Wolf case was not menness or private sentimentalism about combatting crime too energetically. This is conduct that shocks the conscience. Illegally breaking into the privacy of the petitioner, the struggle to open his mouth and remove what was there, the forcible extraction of his stomach's contents—this course of proceeding by agents of government to obtain evidence is bound to offend even hardened sensibilities. They are methods too close to the rack and the screw to permit of constitutional differentiation."

The Court relied in part on decisions reversing convictions based on coerced confessions; these showed, Justice Frankfurter insisted, that state law enforcement must "respect certain decencies of civilized conduct." Coerced confessions are constitutionally excluded from trials "not only because of their unreliability" but also because, even if independently verifiable, they "offend the community's sense of fair play and decency." Similarly, to permit admission of the capsules in Rochin's case "would be to afford brutality the cloak of law"; it would be "a stultification" of the Court's responsibility to hold "that in order to convict a man the police cannot extract by force what is in his mind but can extract what is in his stomach." Accordingly, "on the facts" here, petitioner had been convicted "by methods that offend the Due Process Clause."

In the course of his Rochin opinion, Justice Frankfurter once again defended the Palko-Adamson approach at length; and Justice Black, in dissent, once again attacked it. Justice Frankfurter stated: "The vague contours of the Due Process Clause do not leave judges at large. We may not draw on our merely personal and private notions and disregard the limits that bind judges in their judicial function. Even though the concept of due process of law is not final and fixed, these limits are derived from considerations that are fused in the whole nature of our judicial process. These are considerations deeply rooted in reason and in the compelling traditions of the legal profession. . . . Due process of law thus conceived is not to be derided as resort to a revival of 'natural law.' To believe that this judicial exercise of judgment could be avoided by freezing 'due process of law' at some fixed stage of time or thought is to suggest that the most important aspect of con-

stitutional adjudication is a function for inanimate machines and not for judges . . . . Even cybernetics has not yet made that haughty claim. To practice the requisite detachment and to achieve sufficient objectivity no doubt demands of judges the habit of self-discipline and self-criticism, incertitude that one's own views are incontestable and alert tolerance toward views not shared. . . . The faculties of the Due Process Clause may be indefinite and vague, but the mode of their ascertainment is not self-willed. In each case 'due process of law' requires an evaluation based on a disinterested inquiry pursued in the spirit of science, on a balanced order of facts exactly and fairly stated, on the detached consideration of conflicting claims, on a judgment not ad hoc and episodic but duly mindful of reconciling the needs both of continuity and of change in a progressive society."

Justice Black retorted: "I believe that faithful adherence to the specific guarantees in the Bill of Rights insures a more permanent protection of individual liberty than that which can be afforded by the nebulous standards stated by the majority. What the majority hold is that the Due Process Clause empowers this Court to nullify any state law if its application 'shocks the conscience,' offends 'a sense of justice' or runs counter to the 'decencies of civilized conduct.' The majority emphasize that these statements do not refer to their own consciences or to their senses of justice and decency. . . . We are further admonished to measure the validity of state practices, not by our reason, or by the traditions of the legal profession, but by 'the community's sense of fair play and decency'; by the 'traditions and conscience of our people'; or by 'those canons of decency and fairness which express the notions of justice of English-speaking peoples.' . . .

"If the Due Process Clause does vest this Court with such unlimited power to invalidate laws, I am still in doubt as to why we should consider only the notions of English-speaking peoples to determine what are immutable and fundamental principles of justice. Moreover, one may well ask what avenues of investigation are open to discover 'canons' of conduct so universally favored that this Court should write them into the Constitution?

"Some constitutional provisions are stated in absolute and unqualified language such, for illustration, as the First Amendment stating that no law shall be passed prohibiting the free exercise of religion or abridging the freedom of speech or press. Other constitutional provisions do require courts to choose between competing policies, such as the Fourth Amendment which, by its terms, necessitates a judicial decision as to what is an 'unreasonable' search or seizure. There is, however, no express constitutional language granting judicial power to invalidate *every* state law of *every* kind deemed 'unreasonable' or contrary to the Court's notion of civilized decencies. [Past cases] show the extent to which the evanescent standards of the majority's philosophy have been used to nullify state legislative programs passed to suppress evil economic practices. What paralyzing role this same philosophy will play in the future economic affairs of this country is impossible to predict. Of even graver concern, however, is the use of the philosophy to nullify the Bill of Rights. I long ago concluded that the accordion-like qualities of this philosophy must inevitably imperil all the individual liberty safeguards specifically enumerated in the Bill of Rights." (Justice Black—as did Justice Douglas—joined in the vote to reverse Rochin's

conviction on the basis of the Adamson dissent, insisting that petitioner's Fifth Amendment privilege against self-incrimination had been violated.) [1]

3. *Irvine.* Two years after Rochin and five years after Wolf, the Court was faced with the task of reconciling divergent implications of the decisions. In Irvine v. California, 347 U.S. 128 (1954), petitioner was convicted of gambling offenses in part on the basis of incriminating statements overheard by police officers by means of a listening apparatus installed in petitioner's home. While petitioner and his wife were absent from their home, the police arranged to have a locksmith make a door key. Two days later, officers used the key to enter the home and installed a concealed microphone in the hall. A hole was bored in the roof of the house to string wires to a neighboring garage containing a receiver. On two subsequent occasions, officers again used the key to enter the house and move the microphone to more favorable locations—first to the bedroom, then to the bedroom closet.

Justice Jackson announced the judgment of the Court affirming the conviction and delivered an opinion in which Chief Justice Warren and Justices Reed and Minton joined. He stated that each of the repeated entries of petitioner's home without a warrant was "a trespass, and probably a burglary"; that the police practices would be "almost incredible" if they had not been admitted; and that "few police measures have come to our attention that more flagrantly, deliberately and persistently violated the fundamental principle declared by the Fourth Amendment." But, he concluded, the holding of Wolf "would seem to control here." Moreover, he rejected petitioner's reliance on Rochin: "That case involved, among other things, an illegal search of the defendant's person. But it also presented an element totally lacking here—coercion . . ., applied by a physical assault. . . . This was the feature which led to a result in Rochin contrary to that in Wolf. Although Rochin raised the search-and-seizure question, this Court studiously avoided it and never once mentioned the Wolf case. [H]owever obnoxious are the facts in the case before us, they do not involve coercion, violence or brutality to the person, but rather a trespass to property, plus eavesdropping." (Justice Jackson added a suggestion, for himself and the Chief Justice, that the police conduct might constitute a federal crime and that a copy of the record and the opinion should be forwarded "for attention of the Attorney General of the United States.") Justice Clark, concurring, said that he would have opposed the result in Wolf had he been on the Court then, but felt compelled to apply it here: "In light of the 'incredible' activity of the police here, it is with great reluctance that I follow Wolf. Perhaps strict adherence to the tenor of that decision may produce needed converts for its extinction."

Justice Frankfurter dissented, insisting that his opinions in Wolf and Rochin had been misunderstood by Justice Jackson here: "The comprehend-

---

1. The dissent by Justice Douglas stated that "words taken from [an accused's] lips, capsules taken from his stomach, blood taken from his veins are all inadmissible . . . because of the command of the Fifth Amendment," where the accused has not consented. He pointedly noted that evidence taken from Rochin's stomach would be admissible "in the majority of states where the question has been raised." [In Wolf, Justice Frankfurter (in arguing that the exclusionary rule was not required by the due process clause) had emphasized that "most of the English-speaking world"—including 30 states—did not regard the rule as "vital" to "the protection of the right of privacy."]

ing principle of [Wolf and Rochin] is at the heart of 'due process.' The judicial enforcement of the Due Process Clause is the very antithesis of a Procrustean rule. . . . In the Wolf case, the Court rejected one absolute. In Rochin, it rejected another. [Wolf] did not change prior applications of the requirements of due process, whereby this Court considered the whole course of events by which conviction was obtained. . . . Neither of these concepts [search and seizure and self-incrimination] was invoked by the Court in Rochin, so of course the Wolf case was not mentioned. While there is in the case before us, as [in] Rochin, an element of unreasonable search and seizure, what is decisive here, as in Rochin, is additional aggravating conduct which the Court finds repulsive. . . . There was lacking here physical violence. . . . We have here, however, a more powerful and offensive control over the Irvines' life than a single, limited physical trespass. Certainly the conduct of the police here went far beyond a bare search and seizure." Justice Burton joined Justice Frankfurter's dissent. Justices Black and Douglas also dissented, relying mainly on the asserted violation of the Fifth Amendment, made applicable to the states under their view in Adamson.

4. *The aftermath.* As a result of Wolf, then, evidence obtained through "ordinary" violations of Fourth Amendment rights was admissible in state courts; but, in view of Rochin, evidence could not be used if the methods used in obtaining it involved "additional aggravating conduct." But in 1961, Mapp v. Ohio, which follows, overruled Wolf and held the products of *all* state searches in violation of "incorporated" Fourth Amendment rights inadmissible. There have been additional chapters in the doctrinal saga illustrated by the Wolf et al. sequence, and those—involving a variety of arguably "aggravated conduct"—are worth brief notation here.

Rochin did not mean that the exclusionary rule was appropriate for all bodily evasions of an accused. Thus, Breithaupt v. Abram, 352 U.S. 432 (1957), affirmed a manslaughter conviction growing out of an auto accident and permitted the use of a blood test taken in a hospital after the accident, while petitioner was unconscious. The test showed that he had been drinking. Justice Frankfurter joined Justice Clark's majority opinion finding "nothing comparable here to the facts in Rochin." Though "indiscriminate taking of blood" might violate due process, the test here, by a doctor, was not "offensive"; such tests had "become routine." Chief Justice Warren, joined by Justices Black and Douglas, urged reversal on the basis of Rochin: "Only personal reaction to the stomach pump and the blood test can distinguish them."

The most recent installment of the sequence came in Schmerber v. California, 384 U.S. 757 (1966), a 5 to 4 ruling adhering to the Breithaupt result. Schmerber was decided after Mapp v. Ohio, below, had overruled Wolf, and after Malloy v. Hogan, 378 U.S. 1 (1964), had held the Fifth Amendment self-incrimination privilege applicable to the states. All relevant "specific" Bill of Rights guarantees—the Fourth and Fifth Amendments—were thus applicable to the states by the time of Schmerber. Nevertheless, the post-incorporation result in Schmerber was the same as that in the pre-incorporation Breithaupt case. In Schmerber, Justice Brennan's majority opinion found no violation of the Rochin standard in the taking

of blood tests from a conscious person being treated in a hospital after an
auto accident.   The newly incorporated self-incrimination privilege was
held inapplicable because it covered only "evidence of a testimonial or
communicative nature."   And the search and seizure guarantee, now fully
applicable to the states, was not violated either.   Justice Black's dissent,
joined by Justice Douglas, found a violation of the Fifth Amendment privilege.   Chief Justice Warren and Justice Fortas also dissented.   Consider
the bearing of the Breithaupt-Schmerber sequence on Justice Black's insistence in Adamson that incorporation of "specific" Bill of Rights provision increases certainty, reduces judicial subjectivity—and presumably expands protection of individual rights.   (See also the questions in note 3
below.)

THE BLACK–FRANKFURTER DEBATE: "SPECIFIC" RIGHTS, VAGUE GUARANTEES, AND IMPERSONAL STANDARDS

   1. *Impersonality and the Frankfurter position.*   Justice Frankfurter's
flexible due process approach in Adamson and Rochin—a position echoing
that of Justice Cardozo in Palko and in turn echoed by Justices Harlan and
Powell in later cases—insists that judges "may not draw on our merely personal and private notions" and asserts that due process interpretation "is not
to be based upon the idiosyncrasies of merely personal judgment."   Yet can
that approach be truly impersonal?   What external criteria are available to
give content to procedural due process?   As Justice Black asked in Rochin,
if "canons of decency and fairness which express the notions of justice of
English-speaking peoples" are to govern, "one may well ask what avenues
of investigation are open to discover 'canons' of conduct so universally favored that this Court should write them into the Constitution."

   As the introductory notes in this section indicate, English legal history
can be helpful, but it is hardly conclusive.   Where else can the Court turn?
Note the comments in a careful analysis of the Palko-Adamson technique,
in Kadish, "Methodology and Criteria in Due Process Adjudication—A Survey and Criticism," 66 Yale L.J. 319 (1957), Selected Essays, 1938–1962
(1963), 522.   Kadish traces the two main routes by which the majority in
the post-Adamson years sought "to eliminate the purely personal preference
from flexible due process decision making": the first was "a respectful deference to the judgment of the state court or the act of the legislature under
review"; the second was to rely on external evidence of judgments already
made by others, to appear to be "discovering and applying preformed moral
judgments, rather than of making new moral choices."   Kadish notes the
Court's reliance on four varieties of such external data: "the opinions of
the progenitors and architects of American institutions"; "the implicit opinions of the policy-making organs of state governments"; "the explicit opinions of other American courts that have evaluated the fundamentality of a
given mode of procedure"; and "the opinions of other countries in the
Anglo-Saxon tradition."

   To what extent were any or all of these truly determinative in the samples of the Palko-Adamson technique in these materials?   Kadish views due
process as ultimately "more a moral command than a strictly jural precept,"

but suggests that there are "possibilities of reason and pragmatic inquiry" in such morally-centered due process decisionmaking. He also explores the primary values underlying procedural due process decisions: "insuring the reliability of the guilt-determining process," and "insuring respect for the dignity of the individual" (and curbing law enforcement practices which inadequately respect that dignity?). Consider the extent to which rationality and pragmatic data justify the cases above and below; and consider the due process values furthered by these cases. Note especially the emphasis on individual dignity and civilized law enforcement standards, rather than reliability, in the search and seizure decisions from Wolf through Mapp (below) and beyond.

2. *Federalism and the Frankfurter position.* Consciousness of federalism consideration and respect for state policy-makers permeate the majority positions of the Palko-Adamson tradition. Are there elements in that tradition, however, that contravene state interests? Is the unpredictability of the flexible due process approach arguably more harmful to state autonomy concerns than a more rigid—possibly more interventionist, yet also more certain—due process interpretation? In the right to counsel area, even Justice Harlan, an adherent of the Cardozo-Frankfurter position, ultimately came to support fixed rather than flexible rules. Powell v. Alabama in 1932 had required appointment of counsel in capital cases; but for years it was the Court's position in non-capital cases that appointment of counsel was required only if lack of counsel produced unfairness in a particular case—the "special circumstances" rule of Betts v. Brady, 316 U.S. 455 (1942). In the two decades of experience under that rule, many state convictions were reversed by applying that case-by-case approach. Finally, in Gideon v. Wainwright, 372 U.S. 335 (1963), Betts was overruled and a flat requirement of counsel in *all* felony cases was substituted. In a concurring opinion in Gideon, Justice Harlan commented that, in application, "the Betts v. Brady rule is no longer a reality," for the Court for years had found "special circumstances" justifying reversal for lack of counsel in virtually every case decided by it on the merits. Justice Harlan added: "This evolution, however, appears not to have been fully recognized by many state courts . . . .. To continue a rule which is honored by this Court only with lip service is not a healthy thing and in the long run will do disservice to the federal system." (See generally Israel, "Gideon v. Wainwright: The 'Art' of Overruling," 1963 Sup.Ct.Rev. 211.)

3. *Justice Black's position.* Does Justice Black's position really avoid the problem of judicial subjectivity? Does incorporation of a "specific" Bill of Rights provision significantly curtail the range of judicial judgment? *

---

* The degree to which "vague" due process standards akin to due process can continue to plague the Court even when "specific" guarantees are incorporated is most dramatically illustrated by the interpretations of the Eighth Amendment's prohibition of "cruel and unusual punishments." Note especially the Death Penalty Case, Furman v. Georgia, 408 U.S. 238 (1972). Though in form the nine opinions in that case focused on the "specific" Eighth Amendment provision, the issues considered were very similar to those encountered in giving content to the "vague contours" of due process. Indeed, several of the opinions in Furman—especially those of Justices Marshall and Powell—explicitly recognized the kinship between the Palko-Adamson variety of due process and Eighth Amendment problems. See, e. g., Justice Powell's comment that "it seems clear that the tests for applying these

How "specific" are those guarantees? Contrast the guarantee of jury trial in civil cases involving more than $20—one of the few guarantees that has not been "incorporated" in recent years—with the considerably more open-ended dimensions of the protections against "unreasonable" searches and seizures and the assurance of "the Assistance of Counsel." Note the comment in the Kadish article cited above: "The consequence of requiring due process to be measured precisely by the provisions of the Bill of Rights is not to eliminate broad judicial inquiry, but rather to change its focus from due process to freedom of speech or freedom from double jeopardy, and the rest, and to disguise its essential character." For example, there have been recurrent disputes—some traced below—about whether the exclusionary rule is part of the Fourth Amendment guarantee, whether compulsory blood samples violate the Fifth Amendment's self-incrimination provision, and whether the Sixth Amendment right to counsel extends to pre-trial proceedings. Does emphasis on the "specific" Bill of Rights guarantees breed "a warped construction" of the specifics—"to bring within their scope conduct clearly condemned by due process but not easily fitting into the pigeon-holes of the specific provisions," as Justice Frankfurter argued in Adamson? May that emphasis on "specifics" also have a restrictive rather than expansive impact: may it breed the dilution of Bill of Rights guarantees in order to escape from the incorporationist "straitjacket," as Justice Harlan charged in some of the modern "selective incorporation" cases? See the Black-Harlan debate in Duncan v. Louisiana, sec. 3C below, and the Harlan dissent in Williams v. Florida, also in sec. 3C below.†

4. *The reign and aftermath of the Palko-Adamson standard.* For a decade and a half after Adamson, the Court continued its efforts to apply the flexible due process approach Justice Frankfurter had defended in that case. The material on the Wolf-Rochin-Irvine sequence above illustrates some of the difficulties of that approach. The case-by-case inquiries as to counsel under the Betts v. Brady rule, note 2 above, illustrates another difficulty. Beginning in the early 1960's, the Warren Court—without ever formally abandoning the "fundamental fairness" standard—began to incorporate more and more Bill of Rights guarantees into the 14th Amendment. And in that process, the Court insisted that, once incorporated, the scope of

two provisions are fundamentally identical." And most of the opinions in Furman relied on the earlier statement in Trop v. Dulles, 356 U.S. 86 (1958), that the Eighth Amendment standard is one of "evolving standards of decency"—a common phrase in Court elaborations of procedural due process as well.

† On the historical support for Justice Black's "incorporation" thesis, see especially the Black-Harlan confrontation in Duncan v. Louisiana, sec. 3C below. Searches in the obscure origins of the 14th Amendment have been inconclusive. Compare the criticism of the Black position by Fairman, as noted with Adamson, above, with Crosskey, "Charles Fairman, 'Legislative History,' and the Constitutional Limitations on State Authority," 22 U.Chi.L.Rev. 1 (1954).

The implications of the "incorporation" controversy have engendered an even wider range of commentary than the historical debate. In addition to the Kadish article quoted above, see, e. g., Schaefer, "Federalism and State Criminal Procedures," 70 Harv.L.Rev. 1 (1956); Note, "The Adamson Case: A Study in Constitutional Technique," 58 Yale L.J. 268 (249), Selected Essays 1938–62 (1963), 506; Allen, "Due Process and State Criminal Procedures: Another Look," 48 Nw.U.L.Rev. 16 (1953); Henkin, "'Selective Incorporation' in the 14th Amendment," 73 Yale L.J. 74 (1963); and Friendly, "The Bill of Rights as a Code of Criminal Procedure," 53 Calif.L.Rev. 929 (1965).

the guarantee would be exactly the same in state as in federal proceedings. The Wolf v. Colorado notion that the "core" of a federal right could be absorbed into due process without incorporating all of the details was abandoned. Instead, the Court has opted for "the 'jot-for-jot and case-for-case' application of the federal right to the States," as Justice Harlan put it in Williams v. Florida, below.

Mapp v. Ohio and its progeny, which follow, mark important steps in the development of the current attitude. Mapp overruled Wolf v. Colorado and applied to the states the exclusionary rule as to evidence obtained in violation of the Fourth Amendment. More recently, that exclusionary rule has come once more under attack, as the materials following Mapp indicate. These search and seizure cases also provide additional examples of modern due process methodology. And Duncan v. Louisiana, which follows the Mapp materials, summarizes the developments of the 1960's and reflects the current approach in criminal due process analysis: de facto incorporation of most procedural guarantees, in exactly the manner in which they apply to the federal government; but incorporation by way of a variation on the "fundamentalness" inquiry of Palko, not through the route of Justice Black's wholesale incorporation argument.

MAPP v. OHIO

367 U.S. 643, 81 S.Ct. 1684, 6 L.Ed.2d 1081 (1961).

Appeal from the Supreme Court of Ohio.

Mr. Justice CLARK delivered the opinion of the Court.

Appellant stands convicted of knowingly having had in her possession and under her control certain lewd and lascivious books, pictures, and photographs [in violation of Ohio law]. [T]he Supreme Court of Ohio found that her conviction was valid though "based primarily upon the introduction in evidence of lewd and lascivious books and pictures unlawfully seized during an unlawful search of defendant's home." . . .

The State says that even if the search were made without authority, or otherwise unreasonably, it is not prevented from using the unconstitutionally seized evidence at trial, citing [Wolf v. Colorado]. [I]t is urged once again that we review that holding.

. . . [I]n the year 1914, in [Weeks v. United States, 232 U.S. 383], this Court "for the first time" held that "in a federal prosecution the Fourth Amendment barred the use of evidence secured through an illegal search and seizure." . . . This Court has ever since required of federal law officers a strict adherence to that command which this Court has held to be a clear, specific, and constitutionally required—even if judicially implied—deterrent safeguard without insistence upon which the Fourth Amendment would have been reduced to "a form of words." . . .

. . . The Court's reasons [in Wolf] for not considering essential to the right to privacy, as a curb imposed upon the States by the Due Process Clause, that which decades before had been posited as part and parcel of

the Fourth Amendment's limitation upon federal encroachment of individual privacy, were bottomed on factual considerations.

While they are not basically relevant to a decision that the exclusionary rule is an essential ingredient of the Fourth Amendment as the right it embodies is vouchsafed against the States by the Due Process Clause, we will consider the current validity of the factual grounds upon which Wolf was based.

The Court in Wolf first stated that "[t]he contrariety of views of the States" on the adoption of the exclusionary rule of Weeks was "particularly impressive" . . . . While in 1949, prior to the Wolf case, almost two-thirds of the States were opposed to the use of the exclusionary rule, now, despite the Wolf case, more than half of those since passing upon it, by their own legislative or judicial decision, have wholly or partly adopted or adhered to the Weeks rule. . . . [T]he second basis elaborated in Wolf [was] that "other means of protection" have been afforded "the right to privacy." . . . The experience of California that such other remedies have been worthless and futile is buttressed by the experience of other States. . . .

Likewise, time has set its face against what Wolf called the "weighty testimony" of People v. Defore, 242 N.Y. 13, 150 N.E. 585 (1926). There Justice (then Judge) Cardozo, rejecting adoption of the Weeks exclusionary rule in New York, had said that "[t]he Federal rule as it stands is either too strict or too lax." . . . However, the force of that reasoning has been largely vitiated by later decisions of this Court. . . .

Some five years after Wolf, in answer to a plea made here Term after Term that we overturn [it], this Court indicated that such should not be done until the States had "adequate opportunity to adopt or reject the [Weeks] rule." [Irvine v. California.] Today we once again examine Wolf's constitutional documentation of the right to privacy free from unreasonable state intrusion, and, after its dozen years on our books, are led by it to close the only courtroom door remaining open to evidence secured by official lawlessness in flagrant abuse of that basic right, reserved to all persons as a specific guarantee against that very same unlawful conduct. We hold that all evidence obtained by searches and seizures in violation of the Constitution is, by that same authority, inadmissible in a state court.

Since the Fourth Amendment's right of privacy has been declared enforceable against the States through the Due Process Clause of the Fourteenth, it is enforceable against them by the same sanction of exclusion as is used against the Federal Government. Were it otherwise, [the] freedom from state invasions of privacy would be so ephemeral and so neatly severed from its conceptual nexus with the freedom from all brutish means of coercing evidence as not to merit this Court's high regard as a freedom "implicit in the concept of ordered liberty." . . . The right to privacy, when conceded operatively enforceable against the States, was not susceptible of destruction by avulsion of the sanction upon which its protection and enjoyment had always been deemed dependent [in the federal courts]. Therefore, in extending the substantive protections of due process to all constitutionally unreasonable searches—state or federal—it was logically and constitutionally necessary that the exclusion doctrine—an essential part of the

right to privacy—be also insisted upon as an essential ingredient of the right newly recognized by the Wolf case. In short, the admission of the new constitutional right by Wolf could not consistently tolerate denial of its most important constitutional privilege, namely, the exclusion of the evidence which an accused had been forced to give by reason of the unlawful seizure. To hold otherwise is to grant the right but in reality to withhold its privilege and enjoyment. . . .

[Our holding is] not only the logical dictate of prior cases, but it also makes very good sense. . . .   Presently, a federal prosecutor may make no use of evidence illegally seized, but a State's attorney across the street may, although he supposedly is operating under the enforceable prohibitions of the same Amendment. Thus the State, by admitting evidence unlawfully seized, serves to encourage disobedience to the Federal Constitution which it is bound to uphold. [Under] the double standard recognized until today, [in] nonexclusionary States, federal officers, being human, were by it invited to and did, as our cases indicate, step across the street to the State's attorney with their unconstitutionally seized evidence. Prosecution on the basis of that evidence was then had in a state court in utter disregard of the enforceable Fourth Amendment. If the fruits of an unconstitutional search had been inadmissible in both state and federal courts, this inducement to evasion would have been sooner eliminated. . . .

There are those who say, as did Justice (then Judge) Cardozo, that under our constitutional exclusionary doctrine "[t]he criminal is to go free because the constable has blundered." People v. Defore, 242 N.Y., at 21, 150 N.E., at 587. In some cases this will undoubtedly be the result. But, as [has been said], "there is another consideration—the imperative of judicial integrity." . . .   Nor can it lightly be assumed that, as a practical matter, adoption of the exclusionary rule fetters law enforcement. . . . .

The ignoble shortcut to conviction left open to the State tends to destroy the entire system of constitutional restraints on which the liberties of the people rest. Having once recognized that the right to privacy embodied in the Fourth Amendment is enforceable against the States, . . . we can no longer permit that right to remain an empty promise. . . .

Reversed and remanded.

Mr. Justice BLACK, concurring. . . .

I am still not persuaded that the Fourth Amendment, standing alone, would be enough to bar the introduction into evidence against an accused of papers and effects seized from him in violation of its commands. . . . Reflection on the problem, however, in the light of cases coming before the Court since Wolf, has led me to conclude that when the Fourth Amendment's ban against unreasonable searches and seizures is considered together with the Fifth Amendment's ban against compelled self-incrimination, a constitutional basis emerges which not only justifies but actually requires the exclusionary rule.

. . . .   As I understand the Court's opinion in this case, we again reject the confusing "shock-the-conscience" standard of the Wolf and Rochin

cases and, instead, set aside this state conviction in reliance upon the precise, intelligible and more predictable constitutional doctrine [under the Fourth and Fifth Amendments].†

Mr. Justice HARLAN, whom Mr. Justice FRANKFURTER and Mr. Justice WHITTAKER join, dissenting. . . .

I would not impose upon the States this federal exclusionary remedy. The reasons given by the majority for now suddenly turning its back on Wolf seem to me notably unconvincing.

First, it is said that "the factual grounds upon which Wolf was based" have since changed, in that more States now follow the Weeks exclusionary rule than was so at the time Wolf was decided. While that is true, a recent survey indicates that at present one-half of the States still adhere to the common-law non-exclusionary rule . . . . But in any case surely all this is beside the point, as the majority itself indeed seems to recognize. . . . Moreover, the very fact on which the majority relies, instead of lending support to what is now being done, points away from the need of replacing voluntary state action with federal compulsion. . . .

. . . I do not see how it can be said that a trial becomes unfair simply because a State determines that evidence may be considered by the trier of fact, regardless of how it was obtained, if it is relevant to the one issue with which the trial is concerned, the guilt or innocence of the accused. Of course, a court may use its procedures as an incidental means of pursuing other ends than the correct resolution of the controversies before it. Such indeed is the Weeks rule, but if a State does not choose to use its courts in this way, I do not believe that this Court is empowered to impose this much-debated procedure on local courts . . . .*

† Justice Douglas also concurred separately. Justice Stewart concurred in the result without reaching the search and seizure issue.

* The aftermath of Mapp once again illustrates that the full incorporation of a "specific" Bill of Rights guarantee does not necessarily make for certainty and clarity. (See also the aftermath of Duncan v. Louisiana, below.) The post-Mapp difficulty is illustrated by Ker v. California, 374 U.S. 23 (1963), the Court's first "suitable opportunity for further explication" of Mapp: Though the Court held that the constitutional limits imposed on the states by Mapp were identical with those the Fourth Amendment placed on federal law enforcement, that "uniformity" ruling did not make all preexisting federal search and seizure law available to guide state officers; rather, since prior federal law rested in part on rules and statutes instead of the Constitution itself, it became necessary to determine whether a particular federal requirement is compelled by the Fourth Amendment before it can be imposed on the states via Mapp.

In the Ker case, for example, Justice Clark's discussion of "the standard by which state searches" must be evaluated had the support of all but Justice Harlan. But the eight Justices agreeing on the "standard" divided 4 to 4 on its application. Thus, Justice Harlan's vote, based on a different standard, was necessary for the 5 to 4 affirmance of the convictions. On the general standard, Justice Clark emphasized that "reasonableness is the same under the Fourth and Fourteenth Amendments," but he added that "the demands of our federal system compel us to distinguish between evidence held inadmissible because of our supervisory powers over federal courts and that held inadmissible because prohibited by the United States Constitution." Justice Harlan objected to the application of the "same constitutional standards" to federal and state searches and seizures; he thought that searches should be subject to "the more flexible concept of 'fundamental' fairness."

MAPP AND THE BURGER COURT:
THE EXCLUSIONARY RULE UNDER ATTACK

1. *The criticisms of the 1970's.* Ten years after Mapp v. Ohio, its exclusionary rule came under attack to a degree unprecedented on the modern Court. In a dissent in Bivens v. Six Unknown Named Agents, 403 U. S. 388 (1971), Chief Justice Burger set forth his views about the deficiencies of the exclusionary rule, urged an alternative remedy via legislation, and outlined his own model for congressional consideration. And in a number of separate opinions in another case decided on the same day, Coolidge v. New Hampshire, 403 U.S. 443(1971), there were additional criticisms of the exclusionary rule: Justice Black reiterated his view that it could not rest on the Fourth Amendment alone and that the Fifth Amendment was necessary to support it; Justice Blackmun specifically joined that part of Justice Black's opinion "which is to the effect that the Fourth Amendment supports no exclusionary rule"; and Chief Justice Burger commented once again on "the monstrous price we pay for the exclusionary rule in which we seem to have imprisoned ourselves."

The attack that began in Bivens has continued. Two years later, an elaborate opinion by Justice Powell, joined by Chief Justice Burger and Justice Rehnquist, reviewed the criticisms of the exclusionary rule in urging that Fourth Amendment violations should not be challengeable in collateral attacks on criminal convictions: "Whatever the [exclusionary] rule's merits on an initial trial and appeal—a question not in issue here—the case for collateral application of the rule is an anemic one." Schneckloth v. Bustamonte, 412 U.S. 218 (1973). And in 1974, in United States v. Calandra, 414 U.S. 338, the dissenters feared that the decision marked a "long step toward abandonment of the exclusionary rule." Justice Powell's majority opinion held that a grand jury witness may not refuse to answer questions on the ground that they are based on evidence obtained from an unlawful search and seizure.

2. *Chief Justice Burger's critique in Bivens.* The specific issue in the Bivens case—the 1971 case in which the modern attacks began—was the creation of a new remedy for Fourth Amendment violations by federal officials. Justice Brennan's majority opinion concluded that "violation of that command by a federal agent acting under color of his authority gives rise to a [judicially created] cause of action for damages consequent upon his unconstitutional conduct." There were dissents by Justices Black and Blackmun as well as by Chief Justice Burger, primarily objecting to the creation of such a remedy by the Court rather than by Congress. But the Chief Justice took the occasion to go far beyond the immediate issue. Rather than having the Court create a remedy not enacted by Congress, he thought the Justices could "more surely preserve the important values of the doctrine of separation of powers" by "recommending a solution to the Congress as the branch of government in which the Constitution has vested the legislative power." Before spelling out his own recommendation, he traced the evolution, criticisms, and weaknesses of the exclusionary rule. The Chief Justice stated: "Some clear demonstration of the benefits and effectiveness of the exclusionary rule is required to justify it in view of the high price it extracts from society—the release of countless guilty criminals. But there

is no empirical evidence to support the claim that the rule actually deters illegal conduct of law enforcement officials. Oaks, Studying the Exclusionary Rule in Search and Seizure, 37 U.Chi.L.Rev. 665, 667 (1970)." There were "several reasons for this failure." The rule applies no "direct sanction" to the individual official. The prosecutor who loses his case because of police misconduct is not a police official and does not usually control police procedures. And the rule's deterrent impact "is diluted by the fact that there are large areas of police activity which do not result in criminal prosecutions—hence the rule has virtually no applicability and no effect in such situations."

From these criticisms, he proceeded to develop "better ways" to handle the problem. The rest of his opinion included the following passages: "I do not propose, however, that we abandon the suppression doctrine until some meaningful alternative can be developed. . . . I see no insuperable obstacle to the elimination of the suppression doctrine if Congress would provide some meaningful and effective remedy against unlawful conduct by government officials.

"Private damage actions against individual police officers concededly have not adequately met this requirement . . . . I conclude, therefore, that an entirely different remedy is necessary but it is one that in my view is as much beyond judicial power as the step the Court takes today. Congress should develop an administrative or quasi-judicial remedy against the government itself to afford compensation and restitution for persons whose Fourth Amendment rights have been violated. . . .

"A simple structure would suffice. [The Chief Justice then outlined possible federal legislation, including the following provisions: "the creation of a cause of action for damages sustained by any person aggrieved by conduct of governmental agents in violation of the Fourth Amendment or statutes regulating official conduct"; "a provision that this statutory remedy is in lieu of the exclusion of evidence secured for use in criminal cases in violation of the Fourth Amendment."]

"Once the constitutional validity of such a statute is established,* it can reasonably be assumed that the States would develop their own remedial systems on the federal model. . . . Independent of the alternative embraced in this dissenting opinion, I believe the time has come to re-examine the scope of the exclusionary rule and consider at least some narrowing of its thrust so as to eliminate the anomalies it has produced."

---

* "Any such legislation should emphasize the interdependence between the waiver of sovereign immunity and the elimination of the judicially created exclusionary rule so that if the legislative determination to repudiate the exclusionary rule falls, the entire statutory scheme would fall." [Footnote by Chief Justice Burger.] Note the legislative proposal (S. 881, 93rd Cong., 1st Sess.) to limit the exclusionary rule to situations of "substantial" constitutional violations. The bill also provides for actual and punitive damages against the United States, with a $25,000 maximum. [On the power of Congress to modify the Court's "constitutional" rulings, see the notes after Katzenbach v. Morgan, chap. 11, sec. 4, below.]

C. THE CURRENT APPROACH

DUNCAN v. LOUISIANA

391 U.S. 145, 88 S.Ct. 1444, 20 L.Ed.2d 491 (1968).

Appeal from the Supreme Court of Louisiana.

Mr. Justice WHITE delivered the opinion of the Court.

Appellant, Gary Duncan, was convicted of simple battery [a misdemeanor under Louisiana law], punishable by a maximum of two years' imprisonment and a $300 fine. Appellant sought trial by jury, but because the Louisiana Constitution grants jury trials only in cases in which capital punishment or imprisonment at hard labor may be imposed, the trial judge denied the request. Appellant was convicted and sentenced to serve 60 days in the parish prison and pay a fine of $150. Appellant [alleges] that the Sixth and Fourteenth Amendments to the United States Constitution secure the right to jury trial in state criminal prosecutions where a sentence as long as two years may be imposed. . . .

. . . In resolving conflicting claims concerning the meaning of this spacious language [of due process], the Court has looked increasingly to the Bill of Rights for guidance; many of the rights guaranteed by the first eight Amendments to the Constitution have been held to be protected against state action by the Due Process Clause of the Fourteenth Amendment. That clause now protects the right to compensation for property taken by the State;[1] the rights of speech, press, and religion covered by the First Amendment;[2] the Fourth Amendment rights to be free from unreasonable searches and seizures and to have excluded from criminal trials any evidence illegally seized;[3] the right guaranteed by the Fifth Amendment to be free of compelled self-incrimination;[4] and the Sixth Amendment rights to counsel,[5] to a speedy[6] and public[7] trial, to confrontation of opposing witnesses,[8] and to compulsory process for obtaining witnesses.[9]

The test for determining whether a right extended by the Fifth and Sixth Amendments with respect to federal criminal proceedings is also protected against state action by the Fourteenth Amendment has been phrased in a variety of ways in the opinions of this Court. The question has been asked whether a right is among those " 'fundamental principles of liberty and justice which lie at the base of all our civil and political institutions,' "

1. Chicago, B. & Q. R. Co. v. Chicago, 166 U.S. 226 (1897). [All footnotes to this opinion are by the Court.]

2. See, e. g., Fiske v. Kansas, 274 U.S. 380 (1927).

3. See Mapp v. Ohio, 367 U.S. 643 (1961).

4. Malloy v. Hogan, 378 U.S. 1 (1964).

5. Gideon v. Wainwright, 372 U.S. 335 (1963).

6. Klopfer v. North Carolina, 386 U.S. 213 (1967).

7. In re Oliver, 333 U.S. 257 (1948).

8. Pointer v. Texas, 380 U.S. 400 (1965).

9. Washington v. Texas, 388 U.S. 14 (1967).

Powell v. Alabama, 287 U.S. 45, 67 (1932); [10] whether it is "basic in our system of jurisprudence," In re Oliver, 333 U.S. 257, 273 (1948); and whether it is "a fundamental right, essential to a fair trial," Gideon v. Wainwright, 372 U.S. 335, 343–344 (1963); Malloy v. Hogan, 378 U.S. 1, 6 (1964); Pointer v. Texas, 380 U.S. 400, 403 (1965). [The majority opinions in Gideon and Pointer were written by Justice Black. Justice Brennan wrote Malloy.] The claim before us is that the right to trial by jury guaranteed by the Sixth Amendment meets these tests. The position of Louisiana, on the other hand, is that the Constitution imposes upon the States no duty to give a jury trial in any criminal case, regardless of the seriousness of the crime or the size of the punishment which may be imposed. Because we believe that trial by jury in criminal cases is fundamental to the American scheme of justice, we hold that the Fourteenth Amendment guarantees a right of jury trial in all criminal cases which—were they to be tried in a federal court—would come within the Sixth Amendment's guarantee. [11] Since

---

10. Quoting from Hebert v. Louisiana, 272 U.S. 312, 316 (1926).

11. In one sense recent cases applying provisions of the first eight Amendments to the States represent a new approach to the "incorporation" debate. Earlier the Court can be seen as having asked, when inquiring into whether some particular procedural safeguard was required of a State, if a civilized system could be imagined that would not accord the particular protection. For example, Palko v. Connecticut, 302 U.S. 319, 325 (1937), stated: "The right to trial by jury and the immunity from prosecution except as the result of an indictment may have value and importance. Even so, they are not of the very essence of a scheme of ordered liberty . . . . Few would be so narrow or provincial as to maintain that a fair and enlightened system of justice would be impossible without them." The recent cases, on the other hand, have proceeded upon the valid assumption that state criminal processes are not imaginary and theoretical schemes but actual systems bearing virtually every characteristic of the common-law system that has been developing contemporaneously in England and in this country. The question thus is whether given this kind of system a particular procedure is fundamental—whether, that is, a procedure is necessary to an Anglo-American regime of ordered liberty. It is this sort of inquiry that can justify the conclusions that state courts must exclude evidence seized in violation of the Fourth Amendment, Mapp v. Ohio, 367 U.S. 643 (1961); that state prosecutors may not comment on a defendant's failure to testify, Griffin v. California, 380 U.S. 609 (1965); and that criminal punishment may not be imposed for the status of narcotics addiction, Robinson v. California, 370 U.S. 660 (1962). Of immediate relevance for this case are the Court's holdings that the States must comply with certain provisions of the Sixth Amendment, specifically that the States may not refuse a speedy trial, confrontation of witnesses, and the assistance, at state expense if necessary, of counsel. See cases cited in nn. [5–9], above. Of each of these determinations that a constitutional provision originally written to bind the Federal Government should bind the States as well it might be said that the limitation in question is not necessarily fundamental to fairness in every criminal system that might be imagined but is fundamental in the context of the criminal processes maintained by the American States. When the inquiry is approached in this way the question whether the States can impose criminal punishment without granting a jury trial appears quite different from the way it appeared in the older cases opining that States might abolish jury trial. See, e. g., Maxwell v. Dow, 176 U.S. 581 (1900). A criminal process which was fair and equitable but used no juries is easy to imagine. It would make use of alternative guarantees and protections which would serve the purposes that the jury serves in the English and American systems. Yet no American State has undertaken to construct such a system. Instead, every American State, including Louisiana, uses the jury extensively, and imposes very serious punishments only after a trial at which the defendant has a right to a jury's verdict.

we consider the appeal before us to be such a case, we hold that the Constitution was violated when appellant's demand for jury trial was refused.

The history of trial by jury in criminal cases has been frequently told. It is sufficient for present purposes to say that by the time our Constitution was written, jury trial in criminal cases had been in existence in England for several centuries and carried impressive credentials traced by many to Magna Carta. . . .

Jury trial continues to receive strong support. The laws of every State guarantee a right to jury trial in serious criminal cases; no State has dispensed with it; nor are there significant movements underway to do so. . . .

We are aware of prior cases in this Court in which the prevailing opinion contains statements contrary to our holding today that the right to jury trial in serious criminal cases is a fundamental right and hence must be recognized by the States as part of their obligation to extend due process of law to all persons within their jurisdiction. Louisiana relies especially on Maxwell v. Dow, 176 U.S. 581 (1900); Palko v. Connecticut, 302 U.S. 319 (1937); and Snyder v. Massachusetts, 291 U.S. 97 (1934). None of these cases, however, dealt with a State which had purported to dispense entirely with a jury trial in serious criminal cases. Maxwell held that no provision of the Bill of Rights applied to the States—a position long since repudiated—and that the Due Process Clause of the Fourteenth Amendment did not prevent a State from trying a defendant for a noncapital offense with fewer than 12 men on the jury. . . . Perhaps because the right to jury trial was not directly at stake, the Court's remarks about the jury in Palko and Snyder took no note of past or current developments regarding jury trials, did not consider its purposes and functions, attempted no inquiry into how well it was performing its job, and did not discuss possible distinctions between civil and criminal cases. In Malloy v. Hogan, supra, the Court rejected Palko's discussion of the self-incrimination clause. Respectfully, we reject the prior dicta regarding jury trial in criminal cases.

The guarantees of jury trial in the Federal and State Constitutions reflect a profound judgment about the way in which law should be enforced and justice administered. A right to jury trial is granted to criminal defendants in order to prevent oppression by the Government. . . . Providing an accused with the right to be tried by a jury of his peers gave him an inestimable safeguard against the corrupt or overzealous prosecutor and against the compliant, biased, or eccentric judge. If the defendant preferred the common-sense judgment of a jury to the more tutored but perhaps less sympathetic reaction of the single judge, he was to have it. Beyond this, the jury trial provisions in the Federal and State Constitutions reflect a fundamental decision about the exercise of official power—a reluctance to entrust plenary powers over the life and liberty of the citizen to one judge or to a group of judges. . . . The deep commitment of the Nation to the right of jury trial in serious criminal cases as a defense against arbitrary law enforcement qualifies for protection under the Due Process Clause of the Fourteenth Amendment, and must therefore be respected by the States.

In every State, including Louisiana, the structure and style of the criminal process—the supporting framework and the subsidiary procedures— are of the sort that naturally complement jury trial, and have developed in connection with and in reliance upon jury trial.

Of course jury trial has "its weaknesses and the potential for misuse." We are aware of the long debate, especially in this century, among those who write about the administration of justice, as to the wisdom of permitting untrained laymen to determine the facts in civil and criminal proceedings. Although the debate has been intense, with powerful voices on either side, most of the controversy has centered on the jury in civil cases. [Louisiana] urges that holding that the Fourteenth Amendment assures a right to jury trial will cast doubt on the integrity of every trial conducted without a jury. Plainly, this is not the import of our holding. Our conclusion is that in the American States, as in the federal judicial system, a general grant of jury trial for serious offenses is a fundamental right, essential for preventing miscarriages of justice and for assuring that fair trials are provided for all defendants. We would not assert, however, that every criminal trial—or any particular trial—held before a judge alone is unfair or that a defendant may never be as fairly treated by a judge as he would be by a jury. Thus we hold no constitutional doubts about the practices, common in both federal and state courts, of accepting waivers of jury trial and prosecuting petty crimes without extending a right to jury trial. .   .   .[12]

Reversed and remanded.

Mr. Justice BLACK, with whom Mr. Justice DOUGLAS joins, concurring.

.   .   . I agree [with the holding] for reasons given by the Court. I also agree because of reasons given in my dissent in [Adamson v. California]. I am very happy to support this selective process through which our Court has since the Adamson case held most of the specific Bill of Rights' protections applicable to the States to the same extent they are applicable to the Federal Government. .   .   .

12. Louisiana also asserts that if due process is deemed to include the right to jury trial, States will be obligated to comply with all past interpretations of the Sixth Amendment, an amendment which in its inception was designed to control only the federal courts and which throughout its history has operated in this limited environment where uniformity is a more obvious and immediate consideration. In particular, Louisiana objects to application of the decisions of this Court interpreting the Sixth Amendment as guaranteeing a 12-man jury in serious criminal cases, Thompson v. Utah, 170 U.S. 343 (1898); as requiring a unanimous verdict before guilt can be found, Maxwell v. Dow, 176 U.S. 581, 586 (1900); and as barring procedures by which crimes subject to the Sixth Amendment jury trial provision are tried in the first instance without a jury but at the first appellate stage by de novo trial with a jury, Callan v. Wilson, 127 U.S. 540, 557 (1888). It seems very unlikely to us that our decision today will require widespread changes in state criminal processes.

First, our decisions interpreting the Sixth Amendment are always subject to reconsideration, a fact amply demonstrated by the instant decision. In addition, most of the States have provisions for jury trials equal in breadth to the Sixth Amendment, if that amendment is construed, as it has been, to permit the trial of petty crimes and offenses without a jury. Indeed, there appear to be only four States in which juries of fewer than 12 can be used without the defendant's consent for offenses carrying a maximum penalty of greater than one year. Only in Oregon and Louisiana can a less-than-unanimous jury convict for an offense with a maximum penalty greater than one year. However 10 States authorize first-stage trials without juries for crimes carrying lengthy penalties; these States give a convicted defendant the right to a de novo trial before a jury in a different court. The statutory provisions are listed in the briefs filed in this case. [See the notes following this case.]

All of these holdings making Bill of Rights' provisions applicable as such to the States mark, of course, a departure from the Twining doctrine holding that none of those provisions were enforceable as such against the States. The dissent in this case, however, makes a spirited and forceful defense of that now discredited doctrine. I do not believe that it is necessary for me to repeat the historical and logical reasons for my challenge to the Twining holding contained in my Adamson dissent and Appendix to it. What I wrote there in 1947 was the product of years of study and research. My appraisal of the legislative history followed 10 years of legislative experience as a Senator of the United States, not a bad way, I suspect, to learn the value of what is said in legislative debates, committee discussions, committee reports, and various other steps taken in the course of passage of bills, resolutions, and proposed constitutional amendments. My Brother Harlan's objections to my Adamson dissent history, like that of most of the objectors, relies most heavily on a criticism written by Professor Charles Fairman and published in the Stanford Law Review. 2 Stan.L.Rev. 5 (1949). I have read and studied this article extensively, including the historical references, but am compelled to add that in my view it has completely failed to refute the inferences and arguments that I suggested in my Adamson dissent. Professor Fairman's "history" relies very heavily on what was *not* said in the state legislatures that passed on the Fourteenth Amendment. Instead of relying on this kind of negative pregnant, my legislative experience has convinced me that it is far wiser to rely on what *was* said, and most importantly, said by the men who actually sponsored the Amendment in the Congress. I know from my years in the United States Senate that it is to men like Congressman Bingham, who steered the Amendment through the House, and Senator Howard, who introduced it in the Senate, that members of Congress look when they seek the real meaning of what is being offered. . . .

In addition to the adoption of Professor Fairman's "history," the dissent states that "the great words of the four clauses of the first section of the Fourteenth Amendment would have been an exceedingly peculiar way to say that 'The rights heretofore guaranteed against federal intrusion by the first eight Amendments are henceforth guaranteed against state intrusion as well.' " In response to this I can say only that the words "No State shall make or enforce any law which shall abridge the privileges or immunities of citizens of the United States" seem to me an eminently reasonable way of expressing the idea that henceforth the Bill of Rights shall apply to the States.[1] What more precious "privilege" of American citizenship could there be than that privilege to claim the protections of our great Bill of Rights? I suggest that any reading of "privileges or immunities of citizens of the United States" which excludes the Bill of Rights' safeguards renders the words of this section of the Fourteenth Amendment meaningless. [I]f anything, it is "exceedingly peculiar" to read the Fourteenth Amendment differently from the way I do.

While I do not wish at this time to discuss at length my disagreement with Brother Harlan's forthright and frank restatement of the now dis-

---

1. My view has been and is that the Fourteenth Amendment, *as a whole*, makes the Bill of Rights applicable to the States. This would certainly include the language of the Privileges and Immunities Clause, as well as the Due Process Clause. [Footnote by Justice Black.]

credited Twining doctrine, I do want to point out what appears to me to be the basic difference between us. [D]ue process, according to my Brother Harlan, is to be a phrase with no permanent meaning, but one which is found to shift from time to time in accordance with judges' predilections and understandings of what is best for the country. [It] is impossible for me to believe that such unconfined power is given to judges in our Constitution that is a written one in order to limit governmental power.

Another tenet of the Twining doctrine as restated by my Brother Harlan is that "due process of law requires only fundamental fairness." But the "fundamental fairness" test is one on a par with that of shocking the conscience of the Court. Each of such tests depends entirely on the particular judge's idea of ethics and morals instead of requiring him to depend on the boundaries fixed by the written words of the Constitution. . . .

Finally I want to add that I am not bothered by the argument that applying the Bill of Rights to the States, "according to the same standards that protect those personal rights against federal encroachment," interferes with our concept of federalism in that it may prevent States from trying novel social and economic experiments. I have never believed that under the guise of federalism the States should be able to experiment with the protections afforded our citizens through the Bill of Rights. . . .

In closing I want to emphasize that I believe as strongly as ever that the Fourteenth Amendment was intended to make the Bill of Rights applicable to the States. I have been willing to support the selective incorporation doctrine, however, as an alternative, although perhaps less historically supportable than complete incorporation. The selective incorporation process, if used properly, does limit the Supreme Court in the Fourteenth Amendment field to specific Bill of Rights' protections only and keeps judges from roaming at will in their own notions of what policies outside the Bill of Rights are desirable and what are not. And, most importantly for me, the selective incorporation process has the virtue of having already worked to make most of the Bill of Rights' protections applicable to the States.

Mr. Justice FORTAS, concurring [in an opinion also applicable to a companion case, Bloom v. Illinois, 391 U.S. 194 (1968)]. . . .

[A]lthough I agree with the decision of the Court, I cannot agree with the implication that the tail must go with the hide: that when we hold, influenced by the Sixth Amendment, that "due process" requires that the States accord the right of jury trial for all but petty offenses, we automatically import all of the ancillary rules which have been or may hereafter be developed incidental to the right to jury trial in the federal courts. I see no reason whatever, for example, to assume that our decision today should require us to impose federal requirements such as unanimous verdicts or a jury of 12 upon the States. We may well conclude that these and other features of federal jury practice are by no means fundamental—that they are not essential to due process of law—and that they are not obligatory on the States. . . .

Mr. Justice HARLAN, whom Mr. Justice STEWART joins, dissenting.

. . . The Due Process Clause of the Fourteenth Amendment requires that [state] procedures be fundamentally fair in all respects. It does not, in

my view, impose or encourage nationwide uniformity for its own sake; it does not command adherence to forms that happen to be old; and it does not impose on the States the rules that may be in force in the federal courts except where such rules are also found to be essential to basic fairness.

The Court's approach to this case is an uneasy and illogical compromise among the views of various Justices on how the Due Process Clause should be interpreted. The Court does not say that those who framed the Fourteenth Amendment intended to make the Sixth Amendment applicable to the States. And the Court concedes that it finds nothing unfair about the procedure by which the present appellant was tried. Nevertheless, the Court reverses his conviction: it holds, for some reason not apparent to me, that the Due Process Clause incorporates the particular clause of the Sixth Amendment that requires trial by jury in federal criminal cases—including, as I read its opinion, the sometimes trivial accompanying baggage of judicial interpretation in federal contexts. I have raised my voice many times before against the Court's continuing undiscriminating insistence upon fastening on the States federal notions of criminal justice,[1] and I must do so again in this instance. With all respect, the Court's approach and its reading of history are altogether topsy-turvy. . . .

[The 14th Amendment's] restrictions are couched in very broad and general terms . . . . Consequently, for 100 years this Court has been engaged in the difficult process Professor Jaffe has well called "the search for intermediate premises."[2] The question has been, Where does the Court properly look to find the specific rules that define and give content to such terms as "life, liberty, or property" and "due process of law"?

A few members of the Court have taken the position that the intention of those who drafted the first section of the Fourteenth Amendment was simply, and exclusively, to make the provisions of the first eight Amendments applicable to state action.[3] This view has never been accepted by this Court. In my view, often expressed elsewhere, the first section of the Fourteenth Amendment was meant neither to incorporate, nor to be limited to, the specific guarantees of the first eight Amendments. The overwhelming historical evidence marshalled by Professor Fairman demonstrates, to me conclusively, that the Congressmen and state legislators who wrote, debated, and ratified the Fourteenth Amendment did not think they were "incorporating" the Bill of Rights[4] and the very breadth and generality of the Amendment's provisions suggest that its authors did not suppose that the Nation would always

1. See, e. g., my opinions in Mapp v. Ohio, 367 U.S. 643, 672 (dissenting); Ker v. California, 374 U.S. 23, 44 (concurring); Malloy v. Hogan, 378 U.S. 1, 14 (dissenting); Pointer v. Texas, 380 U.S. 400, 408 (concurring); Griffin v. California, 380 U.S. 609, 615 (concurring); Klopfer v. North Carolina, 386 U.S. 213, 226 (concurring). [All footnotes to this opinion are by Justice Harlan.]

2. Jaffe, Was Brandeis an Activist? The Search for Intermediate Premises, 80 Harv.L.Rev. 986 (1967).

3. See Adamson v. California, 332 U.S. 46, 71 (dissenting opinion of Black, J.); O'Neil v. Vermont, 144 U.S. 323, 366, 370 (dissenting opinion of Harlan, J.) (1892); H. Black, "Due Process of Law," in A Constitutional Faith 23 (1968).

4. Fairman, Does the Fourteenth Amendment Incorporate the Bill of Rights? The Original Understanding, 2 Stan.L.Rev. 5 (1949). Professor Fairman was not content to rest upon the overwhelming fact that the great words of the four clauses of the first

be limited to mid-19th century conceptions of "liberty" and "due process of law" but that the increasing experience and evolving conscience of the American people would add new "intermediate premises." In short, neither history, nor sense, supports using the Fourteenth Amendment to put the States in a constitutional straitjacket with respect to their own development in the administration of criminal or civil law.

Although I therefore fundamentally disagree with the total incorporation view of the Fourteenth Amendment, it seems to me that such a position does at least have the virtue, lacking in the Court's selective incorporation approach, of internal consistency: we look to the Bill of Rights, word for word, clause for clause, precedent for precedent because, it is said, the men who wrote the Amendment wanted it that way. For those who do not accept this "history," a different source of "intermediate premises" must be found. The Bill of Rights is not necessarily irrelevant to the search for guidance in interpreting the Fourteenth Amendment, but the reason for and the nature of its relevance must be articulated.

Apart from the approach taken by the absolute incorporationists, I can see only one method of analysis that has any internal logic. That is to start with the words "liberty" and "due process of law" and attempt to define them in a way that accords with American traditions and our system of government. This approach, involving a much more discriminating process of adjudication than does "incorporation," is, albeit difficult, the one that was followed throughout the 19th and most of the present century. It entails a "gradual process of judicial inclusion and exclusion," seeking, with due recognition of constitutional tolerance for state experimentation and disparity, to ascertain those "immutable principles . . . of free government which no member of the Union may disregard." Due process was not restricted to rules fixed in the past . . . . Nor did it impose nationwide uniformity in details . . . .

section of the Fourteenth Amendment would have been an exceedingly peculiar way to say that "The rights heretofore guaranteed against federal intrusion by the first eight Amendments are henceforth guaranteed against state intrusion as well." He therefore sifted the mountain of material comprising the debates and committee reports relating to the Amendment in both Houses of Congress and in the state legislatures that passed upon it. He found that in the immense corpus of comments on the purpose and effects of the proposed amendment, and on its virtues and defects, there is almost no evidence whatever for "incorporation." The first eight Amendments are so much as mentioned by only two members of Congress, one of whom effectively demonstrated (a) that he did not understand Barron v. Baltimore, 7 Pet. 243, and therefore did not understand the question of incorporation, and (b) that he was not himself understood by his colleagues. One state legislative committee report, rejected by the legislature as a whole, found § 1 of the Fourteenth Amendment superfluous because it duplicated the Bill of Rights: the committee obviously did not understand Barron v. Baltimore either. That is all Professor Fairman could find, in hundreds of pages of legislative discussion prior to passage of the Amendment, that even suggests incorporation.

To this negative evidence the judicial history of the Amendment could be added. For example, it proved possible for a Court whose members had lived through Reconstruction to reiterate the doctrine of Barron v. Baltimore, that the Bill of Rights did not apply to the States, without so much as questioning whether the Fourteenth Amendment had any effect on the continued validity of that principle. E. g., Walker v. Sauvinet, 92 U.S. 90; see generally Morrison, Does the Fourteenth Amendment Incorporate the Bill of Rights? The Judicial Interpretation, 2 Stan.L.Rev. 140 (1949).

The relationship of the Bill of Rights to this "gradual process" seems to me to be twofold. In the first place it has long been clear that the Due Process Clause imposes some restrictions on state action that parallel Bill of Rights restrictions on federal action. Second, and more important than this accidental overlap, is the fact that the Bill of Rights is evidence, at various points, of the content Americans find in the term "liberty" and of American standards of fundamental fairness. . . .

Today's Court still remains unwilling to accept the total incorporationists' view of the history of the Fourteenth Amendment. This, if accepted, would afford a cogent reason for applying the Sixth Amendment to the States. The Court is also, apparently, unwilling to face the task of determining whether denial of trial by jury in the situation before us, or in other situations, is fundamentally unfair. Consequently, the Court has compromised on the ease of the incorporationist position, without its internal logic. It has simply assumed that the question before us is whether the Jury Trial Clause of the Sixth Amendment should be incorporated into the Fourteenth, jot-for-jot and case-for-case, or ignored. Then the Court merely declares that the clause in question is "in" rather than "out." [5]

The Court has justified neither its starting place nor its conclusion. If the problem is to discover and articulate the rules of fundamental fairness in criminal proceedings, there is no reason to assume that the whole body of rules developed in this Court constituting Sixth Amendment jury trial must be regarded as a unit. The requirement of trial by jury in federal criminal cases has given rise to numerous subsidiary questions respecting the exact scope and content of the right. It surely cannot be that every answer the Court has given, or will give, to such a question is attributable to the Founders; or even that every rule announced carries equal conviction of this Court; still less can it be that every such subprinciple is equally fundamental to ordered liberty.

Examples abound. I should suppose it obviously fundamental to fairness that a "jury" means an "impartial jury." I should think it equally obvious that the rule, imposed long ago in the federal courts, that "jury" means "jury of exactly twelve," is not fundamental to anything: there is no significance except to mystics in the number 12. Again, trial by jury has been held to require a unanimous verdict of jurors in the federal courts, although unanimity has not been found essential to liberty in Britain, where the requirement has been abandoned. . . .

Even if I could agree that the question before us is whether Sixth Amendment jury trial is totally "in" or totally "out," I can find in the Court's opinion no real reasons for concluding that it should be "in." The basis for differentiating among clauses in the Bill of Rights cannot be that only some

---

5. The same illogical way of dealing with a Fourteenth Amendment problem was employed in Malloy v. Hogan, 378 U.S. 1, which held that the Due Process Clause guaranteed the protection of the Self-Incrimination Clause of the Fifth Amendment against state action. I disagreed at that time both with the way the question was framed and with the result the Court reached. See my dissenting opinion, id., at

14. I consider myself bound by the Court's holding in Malloy with respect to self-incrimination. See my concurring opinion in Griffin v. California, 380 U.S. 609, 615. I do not think that Malloy held, nor would I consider myself bound by a holding, that every question arising under the Due Process Clause shall be settled by an arbitrary decision whether a clause in the Bill of Rights is "in" or "out."

clauses are in the Bill of Rights, or that only some are old and much praised, or that only some have played an important role in the development of federal law. These things are true of all. The Court says that some clauses are more "fundamental" than others, but it turns out to be using this word in a sense that would have astonished Mr. Justice Cardozo and which, in addition, is of no help. The word does not mean "analytically critical to procedural fairness" for no real analysis of the role of the jury in making procedures fair is even attempted. Instead, the word turns out to mean "old," "much praised," and "found in the Bill of Rights." The definition of "fundamental" thus turns out to be circular. . . .

The argument that jury trial is not a requisite of due process is quite simple. . . . If due process of law requires only fundamental fairness, then the inquiry in each case must be whether a state trial process was a fair one. The Court has held, properly I think, that in an adversary process it is a requisite of fairness, for which there is no adequate substitute, that a criminal defendant be afforded a right to counsel and to cross-examine opposing witnesses. But it simply has not been demonstrated, nor, I think, can it be demonstrated, that trial by jury is the only fair means of resolving issues of fact.

The jury is of course not without virtues. . . . The jury system can also be said to have some inherent defects, which are multiplied by the emergence of the criminal law from the relative simplicity that existed when the jury system was devised. . . . That trial by jury is not the only fair way of adjudicating criminal guilt is well attested by the fact that it is not the prevailing way, either in England or in this country. . . .

In the United States, [two] experts have estimated that, of all prosecutions for crimes triable to a jury, 75% are settled by guilty plea and 40% of the remainder are tried to the court.[6] [I] see no reason why this Court should reverse the conviction of appellant, absent any suggestion that his particular trial was in fact unfair, or compel the State of Louisiana to afford jury trial in an as yet unbounded category of cases that can, without unfairness, be tried to a court. . . .

[T]he Court has chosen to impose upon every State one means of trying criminal cases; it is a good means, but it is not the only fair means, and it is not demonstrably better than the alternatives States might devise. . . .

THE MODERN APPROACH: INCORPORATION TRIUMPHANT? CERTAINTY ASSURED?

Introduction. Reexamine the battle over due process criteria in light of Duncan v. Louisiana and the post-Duncan cases below. Does the "fundamental rights" approach survive in name only, with "incorporation" providing the spirit? Has "selective incorporation" proceeded so far as to "select" all of the Bill of Rights for "incorporation" in fact? Note the 1960's decisions reviewed in Duncan and see note 1 below. Virtually all of the "specific" procedural guarantees of the Bill of Rights have now been

6. Kalven & Zeisel, [The American Jury], at 12–32.

held applicable to the states to the same extent that they apply to federal law enforcement: only the grand jury indictment requirement of the Fifth Amendment and the civil cases jury trial guarantee of the Seventh have not been incorporated into the 14th. And—as the Winship case in note 1 below shows—due process may require protections beyond those specified in the Bill of Rights.*

Does the current approach afford defenses against the charges of subjectivity and idiosyncrasy and unpredictability long levied against the Palko-Adamson approach? How predictable and coherent are the interpretations of the "specific" rights now incorporated into the 14th? Have the recent Court decisions vindicated the warning that emphasis on "specific" rights produces distortion of those rights? See note 2 below. What values are promoted by applying the incorporated guarantees to the states in exactly the same way in which they apply to the federal government? What goals are furthered by making all interpretations of the specific guarantees applicable to the states, "bag and baggage"? Federalism? Individual rights? The economy of judicial labors? Predictability? Certainty?

1. *Incorporation since Duncan.* a. The process of incorporation has continued since Duncan. The majority in BENTON v. MARYLAND, 395 U.S. 784 (1969), held "that the double jeopardy prohibition of the Fifth Amendment represents a fundamental ideal in our constitutional heritage, and that it should apply to the States through the Fourteenth Amendment." At his first trial, petitioner had been found not guilty of larceny but convicted of burglary. Because of improper jury selection, he was able to elect reindictment and retrial. At his second trial, he was convicted of both offenses. After "incorporating" the double jeopardy guarantee, Justice Marshall's majority opinion concluded that "petitioner's larceny conviction cannot stand once federal double jeopardy standards are applied." He added: "Insofar as it is inconsistent with this holding, Palko v. Connecticut is overruled."

Justice Marshall explained: "Our recent cases have thoroughly rejected the Palko notion that basic constitutional rights can be denied by the States as long as the totality of the circumstances does not disclose a denial of 'fundamental fairness.' Once it is decided that a particular Bill of Rights guarantee is 'fundamental to the American scheme of justice,' Duncan v. Louisiana [above], the same constitutional standards apply against both the State and Federal Governments." Justice Harlan, joined by Justice Stewart, dissented from the reversal of the conviction because he did not think that the Court should have "reached out" to decide the merits of the case. But if those were reached, he made clear, he too would have been prepared to reverse on constitutional grounds—but via the "traditional due process approach" of Palko rather than the majority's route of "incorporating" all of the details of the federal double jeopardy guarantee.

b. But the selective incorporation technique is not the sole source of 14th Amendment restraints on state procedures in the post-Duncan era. Due

---

* As to substantive guarantees in the Bill of Rights, recall that the First Amendment guarantees had been found "fundamental" and "implicit in the concept of ordered liberty" by the time of Palko v. Connecticut. The rarely litigated Second and Third Amendments have not been formally incorporated.

process is a reservoir for added limits when no relevant "specific" rights are available. (Recall the Murphy-Rutledge dissent in Adamson, above.) Thus, IN RE WINSHIP, 397 U.S. 358 (1970), held that "proof beyond a reasonable doubt is among the 'essentials of due process and fair treatment' required during the adjudicatory stage when a juvenile is charged with an act which would constitute a crime if committed by an adult." In the course of the majority opinion finding that a "preponderance of the evidence" standard was inadequate, Justice Brennan stated: "Lest there remain any doubt about the constitutional stature of the reasonable-doubt standard, we explicitly hold that the Due Process Clause protects the accused against conviction except upon proof beyond a reasonable doubt of every fact necessary to constitute the crime with which he is charged."

The Winship case provided the final occasion for a debate between Justices Harlan and Black about due process standards, during the year before each retired from the Court and died. But in this instance, Justice Harlan found himself on the side of imposing restraints on state procedures, with Justice Black dissenting. Justice Harlan's concurrence emphasized the "fundamental fairness" approach to due process. Justice Black's dissent rested on the fact that "nowhere in [the Constitution] is there any statement that conviction of crime requires proof of guilt beyond a reasonable doubt." *

2. *The jury trial guarantee after Duncan: Dilution of federal rights as an escape from the incorporationist "straitjacket"?* Before the Duncan decision, Court comments on the Sixth Amendment jury requirement in federal trials had repeatedly indicated that the Constitution contemplated a twelve-person jury and required unanimous verdicts. After Duncan, claimants sought to rely on its incorporation of the Sixth Amendment to impose a jury with those traditional common law features on state proceedings; but the majority rejected their claims. Were Justices Harlan and Powell persuasive in asserting that these post-Duncan decisions illustrate the distorting impact of the incorporationist approach?

a. *Williams v. Florida.* In the first of these cases, WILLIAMS v. FLORIDA, 399 U.S. 78 (1970), the petitioner seeking reversal of a robbery conviction claimed that he should have been tried by a twelve-person jury rather than the six-person panel provided by Florida law in all but capital cases. Justice White's majority opinion concluded, however, that "the twelve-man panel is not a necessary ingredient of 'trial by jury.'" Though earlier decisions had "assumed" the twelve-person panel to be constitutionally necessary, Justice White explained, "that particular feature of the jury sys-

---

* In this final major encounter between Justices Black and Harlan, Justice Harlan expressed his "continued bafflement" at Justice Black's incorporation thesis. Justice Black replied with another comment on Professor Fairman's scholarly research (see also Duncan v. Louisiana, above). To rebut Fairman, Justice Black cited Flack, The Adoption of the Fourteenth Amendment (1908), "at least an equally 'scholarly' writing" surveying "substantially the same documents relied upon by Mr. Fairman and [concluding] that a prime objective of Congress in proposing the adoption of the Fourteenth Amendment was '[t]o make the Bill of Rights (the first eight Amendments) binding upon, or applicable to, the States.'" Justice Black added: "It is, of course, significant that since the adoption of the Fourteenth Amendment this Court has held almost all the provisions of the Bill of Rights applicable to the States . . . . To me this history indicates that in the end Mr. Flack's thesis has fared much better than Mr. Fairman's 'uncontroverted' scholarship."

tem appears to have been a historical accident, unrelated to the great purposes which gave rise to the jury in the first place." He conceded that a twelve-person jury might well have been "the usual expectation" of the Framers, but "there is absolutely no indication in 'the intent of the Framers' of an explicit decision to equate the constitutional and common-law characteristics of the jury." The constitutionally required features of a jury system turned on "other than purely historical considerations": "The relevant inquiry [must] be the function that the particular feature performs and its relation to the purposes of the jury trial." Justice White found a critical purpose of a jury to be "the interposition between the accused and his accuser of the common sense judgment of a group of laymen"; and that did not require any particular number on the jury. Moreover, "neither currently available evidence nor theory suggests that the twelve-man jury is necessarily more advantageous to the defendant than a jury composed of fewer members."

In an extensive opinion concurring in the result, Justice Harlan reiterated his adherence to the Palko-Adamson approach, restated his opposition to Duncan, and objected to the majority's "dilution" of Sixth Amendment guarantees: "The necessary consequence of this decision is that twelve-member juries are not constitutionally required in *federal* criminal trials either. . . . The decision evinces, I think, a recognition that the 'incorporationist' view [of due process] must be tempered to allow the States more elbow room in ordering their own criminal systems. With that much I agree. But to accomplish this by diluting constitutional protections within the federal system itself is something to which I cannot possibly subscribe. Tempering the rigor of Duncan should be done forthrightly, by facing up to the fact that at least in this area the 'incorporation' doctrine does not fit well with our federal structure." He added: "I consider that before today it would have been unthinkable to suggest that the Sixth Amendment's right to a trial by jury is satisfied by a jury of six, or less, [or] by less than a unanimous verdict. [The] Court's elaboration of what is required provides no standard and vexes the meaning of the right to a jury trial in federal courts, as well as state courts, by uncertainty. Can it be doubted that a unanimous jury of 12 provides a greater safeguard than a majority vote of six?"

Justice Harlan added: "These decisions demonstrate that the difference between a 'due process' approach, that considers each particular case on its own bottom to see whether the right alleged is one 'implicit in the concept of ordered liberty' [Palko], and 'selective incorporation' is not an abstract one whereby different verbal formulae achieve the same results. The internal logic of the selective incorporation doctrine cannot be respected if the Court is both committed to interpreting faithfully the meaning of the federal Bill of Rights and recognizing the governmental diversity that exists in this country. The 'backlash' in Williams exposes the malaise, for there the Court dilutes a federal guarantee in order to reconcile the logic of 'incorporation,' the 'jot-for-jot and case-for-case' application of the federal right to the States, with the reality of federalism. Can one doubt that had Congress tried to undermine the common-law right to trial by jury before Duncan came on the books the history today recited would have barred such action? Can we expect repeat performances when this Court is called upon to give definition and meaning to other federal guarantees that have been 'incorporated'?" He

reminded that in his concurrence in the result in Ker v. California in 1963 (noted above), he had viewed incorporation as "unwise because the States, with their differing law enforcement problems, should not be put in a constitutional straitjacket . . . . And if the Court is prepared to relax [federal] standards in order to avoid unduly fettering the States, this would be in derogation of law enforcement standards in the federal system." [Note also his "constitutional straitjacket" reference in his Duncan dissent.] He referred to the Williams decision as a demonstration of "a constitutional schizophrenia born of the need to cope with national diversity under the constraints of the incorporation doctrine," and he concluded by urging the Court "to face up to the reality implicit" in the decision and "reconsider the 'incorporation' doctrine before its leveling tendencies further retard development in the field of criminal procedure by stifling flexibility in the States and by discarding the possibility of federal leadership by example." [Note the echoing of these views in Justice Powell's 1972 opinion in Apodaca, below.]

An opinion by Justice Black, joined by Justice Douglas, concurred with the majority on the jury aspect of Williams and took issue with some of Justice Harlan's assertions: "Today's decision is in no way attributable to any desire to dilute the Sixth Amendment in order more easily to apply it to the States, but follows solely as a necessary consequence of our duty to reexamine prior decisions to reach the correct constitutional meaning in each case." Justice Black insisted that, had the same question been presented to the Court in a federal case before Duncan, "this Court would still, in my view, have reached the result announced today." In another opinion, Justice Stewart joined most of Justice Harlan's objections to the "mechanistic 'incorporation' approach." Justice Marshall, finally, dissented from the jury trial holding in Williams, stating that he was "convinced that the requirement of 12 should be applied to the States."

b.   *Apodaca v. Oregon.*   Another issue left open by Duncan—the question whether a *unanimous* jury verdict is required in state courts after the incorporation of the Sixth Amendment—came before the Court in APODACA v. OREGON, 406 U.S. 404 (1972). As in Williams, the Court ruled that what had formerly been thought to be an ingredient of the Sixth Amendment guarantee was not constitutionally required after all and accordingly sustained the constitutionality of a state nonunanimous jury verdict. This time, however, the division on the Court was particularly sharp and unusual. The nonunanimous jury verdict was approved though only eight of the Justices adhered to the Duncan position that each element of the Sixth Amendment jury trial guarantee is fully applicable to the states via the 14th, and even though five of the Justices read the Sixth Amendment as requiring unanimous jury verdicts. The result nevertheless sustaining the nonunanimous verdict was made possible by the decisive concurring position of Justice Powell, following in the footsteps of Justice Harlan: Justice Powell found that the Sixth Amendment required the traditional jury unanimity in federal trials, but he did not think that all of the elements of the federal guarantee should be imposed on the states as a requirement of due process.

The Oregon system sustained in Apodaca requires the vote of at least ten out of twelve jurors for conviction in noncapital cases. Justice White's plurality opinion, joined by Chief Justice Burger and Justices Blackmun and

Rehnquist, adhered to the Williams approach: unanimity was not constitutionally required because it "does not materially contribute to" the central function "served by the jury in contemporary society," to interpose "the common sense judgment of a group of laymen" between accused and accuser. Justices Douglas, Brennan, Stewart, and Marshall each submitted dissenting opinions. Justice Douglas distinguished his approval of the six-person jury in Williams by noting that "neither evidence nor theory suggested that 12 was more favorable to the accused than six." Justice Stewart urged that "settled Sixth Amendment precedents" regarding unanimity be followed.

Justice Powell's opinion explaining his decisive vote for the result rejected the plurality's "major premise" that "the concept of jury trial, as applicable to the States under the Fourteenth Amendment, must be identical in every detail to the concept required in federal courts by the Sixth Amendment." In federal proceedings, he explained, he would require unanimity, "not because unanimity is necessarily fundamental to the function performed by the jury, but because that result is mandated by history." But as to state proceedings, due process simply required that states adhere to "what is fundamental in jury trial"; and the Oregon system adequately respected the fundamentals. To impose upon the state every detail of incorporated federal guarantees would derogate basic principles of federalism and would deprive the states of "freedom to experiment with adjudicatory processes different from the federal model." Moreover, under the prevailing approach, the Court ended up, here as in Williams, with "the dilution of federal rights which were, until these decisions, never seriously questioned."

3. *Incorporation and the retroactivity problem.* Ordinarily, newly announced doctrines are given fully retroactive effect by American courts: the new standard is applicable to all cases pending in the judicial system. That general principle was perceived as a substantial brake on the incorporation of new constitutional rights into the due process clause: especially in light of the availability of collateral challenges via habeas corpus, the concern was that expansion of federal rights applicable in state criminal proceedings would flood the federal courts and open the prison gates by permitting the invocation of the new rules by prisoners whose convictions had long become final for direct review purposes. Those pragmatic considerations no doubt played a major role in inducing the Court to announce a major exception to the normal retroactivity rule in the midst of the rapid growth of selective incorporation during the 1960's. The legitimacy of those exceptions, and the appropriate contours of permissible prospectivity, have produced sharp divisions on and off the Court.

a. A majority endorsed departures from the ordinary retroactivity rule in Linkletter v. Walker, 381 U.S. 618 (1965). The Court announced that "the Constitution neither prohibits nor requires retrospective effect" for new rulings. The proper approach was to "weigh the merits and demerits" of retroactivity in each case "by looking to the prior history of the rule in question, its purpose and effect, and whether retrospective operation will further or retard its operation." (Justice Black's dissent, joined by Justice Douglas, insisted, in this case and many later ones, that departures from full retroactivity were discriminatory and unjustified.) Two years later, Stovall v. Denno, 388 U.S. 293 (1967), articulated more fully the criteria which

have since governed the Court's choice between retroactivity and prospectivity: "The criteria guiding resolution of the question implicate (a) the purpose to be served by the new standards, (b) the extent of the reliance by law enforcement authorities on the old standards, and (c) the effect on the administration of justice of a retroactive application of the new standards." *

b.   In Linkletter and other early decisions rejecting full retroactivity, the Court did not require "pure prospectivity": the new constitutional requirements were applied to all cases still pending on direct review at the time the new rule was announced. That was so in Linkletter, for example, involving the new exclusionary rule of Mapp v. Ohio. In later cases, the Court moved closer to "pure prospectivity." By the time of Stovall v. Denno, some new rulings were found purely prospective except with respect to the parties in the immediate cases before the Court. The fact that the Supreme Court challengers were the only retroactive beneficiaries of the new rules was described in Stovall as "an unavoidable consequence of the necessity that constitutional adjudications not stand as mere dictum." The Stovall majority recognized that such a cut-off point made the challengers "chance beneficiaries" of the new rules, but thought the "anomalies" justified by the desirability of the prospectivity technique—a technique facilitating "the implementation of long-overdue reforms, which otherwise could not be practicably effected."

Do the Court's frequent denials of retroactivity properly expose it to the charge of acting more like a legislative than a judicial body? Are the differing treatments of defendants under the varying cut-off rules arbitrary and discriminatory? What are the benefits and costs of the prospective overruling technique? Is its widespread invocation in the course of incorporation developments consistent with basic premises about the judicial function? †

* Compare Justice Marshall's comment on the considerations underlying the application of the Linkletter-Stovall criteria, in dissenting in Michigan v. Payne, 412 U.S. 47 (1973). Justice Marshall characterized the process of "carefully balancing countervailing considerations when deciding the question of retroactivity" under those criteria as a "charade." He thought most cases fell into two categories. Where the new constitutional requirement "was central to the process of determining guilt or innocence," the holdings had been given retroactive effect; in all other cases, the new rules were made prospective in varying degrees. Thus, rules going to the reliability of the guilt-determining process, such as the right to counsel or the barrier to coerced confessions, were made retroactive; rules promulgated to safeguard the integrity of the courts and the dignity of individuals, such as the exclusion of illegally seized evidence, were denied fully retroactive effect.

† The retroactivity-prospectivity controversy has produced voluminous scholarly commentary. Compare, e. g., Mishkin, "The High Court, the Great Writ, and the Due Process of Time and Law," 79 Harv.L.Rev. 56 (1965), with Schwartz, "Retroactivity, Reliability, and Due Process: A Reply to Professor Mishkin," 33 U.Chi.L.Rev. 719 (1966). See also Wellington, "Common Law Rules and Constitutional Double Standards," 83 Yale L.J. 221 (1973), and Comment, "Prospective Overruling and Retroactive Application in the Federal Courts," 71 Yale L.J. 907 (1962).

Chapter 9

SUBSTANTIVE DUE PROCESS: RISE, DECLINE, REVIVAL

Introduction. In no part of constitutional law has the search for legitimate ingredients of constitutional interpretation been more difficult and more controversial than in the turbulent history of substantive due process. To what extent does the due process clause do more than limit governmental procedures affecting individual rights and restrain as well governmental ordering of those rights? To what extent does the due process clause concern itself not simply with the methods of governmental action but also with its substance? To what extent does the due process clause authorize the Court to articulate fundamental values—values not explicitly designated for special protection by the Constitution, yet values which government may not impinge upon, at least not without meeting an unusually high standard of justification?

That the due process clause can serve as a springboard for judicial articulation of "fundamentals" has already been demonstrated in the preceding materials on the Palko-Adamson incorporation controversy. But that course of decisions led the Court to search merely for the fundamentals of *procedure*—for example, the essentials of a fair trial. In its first interpretation of the 14th Amendment in the Slaughter-House Cases, it will be recalled, the majority rejected any notion of *substantive* due process. But the dissenters' plea for the protection of fundamental values prevailed by the end of the 19th century.

The 1905 decision in Lochner v. New York (sec. 1B below), striking down New York's maximum hours law for bakers, symbolizes the rise of substantive due process as a protection of economic and property rights. For three decades thereafter, the Court engaged in "Lochnerizing"—scrutinizing economic regulation with care and frequently striking down governmental efforts at economic regulation (sec. 1B). In the mid-1930's, judicial intervention in economic legislation began a gradual decline, and the use of substantive due process to protect economic and property rights is now discredited (sec. 1C). Yet in recent years, substantive due process has once again flourished, as a haven for fundamental values other than economic and property rights; and that development is illustrated in modern decisions protecting autonomy and privacy by striking down laws banning abortions and the use of contraceptives (sec. 3).

These substantive due process cases, old and new, raise common issues: Are these decisions, from Lochner v. New York to Griswold v. Connecticut and Roe v. Wade, justifiable as interpretations of the Constitution? Are they plausible extrapolations from constitutional text, history, or structure? Or are they ultimately extra-constitutional, non-interpretive judicial infusions of fundamental values? And what, if any, fundamental values *may* the Court properly impose? Are there basic values—moral, social, or economic—that truly reflect a national consensus? Even if there are such wide-

ly shared values, does the existence of a consensus justify reading it into the Constitution? Do the Court's fundamental values adjudications in fact rest on an adequately widespread consensus? Or do they reflect values shared by only a segment of the society? Or do the Court articulations of fundamental values ultimately reflect nothing more than the beliefs of a majority of Justices at a particular time? And are fundamental value adjudications in any event acceptable if the Court cannot demonstrate an adequate link to constitutional text, history, or structure?

As this suggestion of pervasive themes indicates, there is reason to examine the cases of the Lochner era even though substantive due process does not impose serious restraints on economic regulation today. The economic regulation cases bear directly on the judicial function in the protection of those individual liberties that receive greater attention from the modern Court. Are the abortion and contraception decisions essentially modern examples of Lochnerizing, or are those recent judicial interventions more justifiable than the earlier ones? The resemblances between Lochner and Roe and Griswold are most evident, but the linkage between the Lochner era cases and modern Court developments extends beyond. For example, the source of the Court's interventions in the Lochner era was most commonly the "liberty" protected by the due process clauses; it is that same "liberty" that is the major textual basis of the Court's active enforcement of personal rights today—not only "fundamental" rights not explicitly listed in the Constitution (such as privacy), but also the "specific" First Amendment guarantees of freedom of speech, press and religion long "incorporated" into the 14th Amendment. Is there justification for the sharp decline in judicial protection of some varieties of "liberty" and the equally dramatic rise in judicial intervention on behalf of other kinds of "liberty"? That problem of a "double standard" pervades the rest of this book, but it is raised with special force by the contrast between the old and new varieties of substantive due process in secs. 1 and 3 of this chapter.

The Court's encounters with substantive due process in the economic sphere in sec. 1, then, not only influenced its responses to personal rights claims such as those in sec. 3 and later chapters, but also provide essential background for a critical assessment of those recent responses. Substantive due process is the major vehicle for the protection of economic interests examined in sec. 1, but it has not been the only vehicle. Sec. 1A notes some historical antecedents of economic due process developments, some early efforts to find constitutional safeguards for fundamental values. And sec. 2 surveys two themes tangential to the development of substantive due process as a protection of economic and property rights: the role of the contract clause; and the protection of property against "taking" without just compensation.

SECTION 1. SUBSTANTIVE DUE PROCESS AND ECONOMIC REGULATION: THE RISE AND DECLINE OF JUDICIAL INTERVENTION

A. ANTECEDENTS

Introduction. Substantive due process as a protection of fundamental economic rights did not receive wholehearted support from a Supreme Court majority until the end of the 19th century. But arguments that property and economic rights were basic had long been in the air: the notion that there *were* fundamental rights, and that they were entitled to judicial protection, had considerable earlier support. Some of that support, it will be recalled, was voiced by the dissenters in the Slaughter-House Cases. And the fundamental values those dissenters sought to enshrine in the post-Civil War constitutional changes were values in turn rooted in the thinking of earlier generations: the legacy of Blackstone and Magna Charta—as well as Adam Smith—is explicit in those dissents. As Justice Bradley noted, for example, Blackstone had emphasized property, together with personal security and liberty, as one of the three basic rights of individuals. So, too, had John Locke's social compact philosophy. There was, then, a respectable natural law tradition which, drawing on English antecedents, viewed a written constitution not as the initial source but as a reaffirmation of a social compact preserving preexisting fundamental rights—rights entitled to protection whether or not they were explicitly stated in the basic document.[1]

1. *Calder v. Bull.* Some of those natural law ideas surfaced sporadically in early Supreme Court opinions: during the pre-Marshall years, some Justices were tempted to read the Constitution as a whole as a guarantor of fundamental rights—rights that stemmed from the social compact and did not need any explicit textual support. The prime example is Justice Chase's opinion in 1798, in CALDER v. BULL, 3 Dall. 386. There, the Court rejected an attack on a Connecticut legislative act setting aside a probate court decree which had refused to approve a will. The legislation required a new hearing; and at that second hearing, the will was approved. The challenge to the legislative act came from the heirs who would have taken the property if the will had been ineffective. The Court rejected their claim that the ex post facto clause barred the Connecticut act: that clause was construed as being limited to criminal legislation. But more important for present purposes is the willingness of some Justices to entertain arguments on natural law grounds. Calder v. Bull was handed down in the years before John Marshall persuaded his colleagues to abandon seriatim opinions. And of the several opinions, Justice Chase's most elaborately announced an early inclination to invalidate legislation quite apart from specific constitu-

---

1. See generally, Corwin, "The Basic Doctrine of American Constitutional Law," 12 Mich.L.Rev. 247 (1914); Corwin, "The 'Higher Law' Background of American Constitutional Law," 42 Harv.L.Rev. 149, 365 (1928–29); Corwin, Liberty Against Government (1948). See also Grey, "Do We Have an Unwritten Constitution?" 27 Stan.L.Rev. 703 (1975).

tional limitations. Justice Chase stated (with the emphases—but not the typeface that makes s's look like f's—as they appear in the original Reports):

"I cannot subscribe to the *omnipotence* of a *State Legislature*, or that it is *absolute* and *without controul;* although its authority should not be *expressly* restrained by the *Constitution*, or *fundamental law*, of the State. The people of the *United States* erected their Constitutions, or forms of governments, to establish justice, to promote the general welfare, to secure the blessings of liberty; and to protect their *persons* and *property* from violence. The purposes for which men enter into society will determine the *nature* and *terms* of the *social* compact; and as *they* are the foundation of the *legislative* power, *they* will decide what are the *proper* objects of it: The *nature*, and *ends* of *legislative* power will limit the *exercise* of it. This *fundamental* principle flows from the very nature of our free *Republican* governments, that no man should be compelled to do what the laws do *not* require; *nor to refrain from acts which the laws permit.* There are acts which the *Federal*, or *State*, Legislature cannot do, *without exceeding their authority.* There are certain *vital* principles in our *free Republican governments*, which will determine and over-rule an *apparent and flagrant* abuse of *legislative* power; as to authorize *manifest injustice by positive law*; or to take away that security for *personal liberty*, or *private property*, for the protection whereof the government was established. An ACT of the Legislature (for I cannot call it a *law*) contrary to the *great first principles* of the *social compact,* cannot be considered a *rightful exercise* of *legislative authority.* The obligation of a law in governments established on *express compact, and on republican principles,* must be determined by the *nature* of the *power,* on which it is founded. A few instances will suffice to explain what I mean. A law that punished a citizen for an *innocent* action, or, in other words, for an act, which, when done, was in violation of no *existing* law; a law that destroys, or impairs, the *lawful private* contracts of citizens; a law that makes a man *a Judge in his own cause;* or a law that takes *property* from A. and gives it to B: It is against all reason and justice, for a people to entrust a Legislature with SUCH powers; and, therefore, it cannot be presumed that they have done it. The *genius*, the *nature*, and the *spirit*, of our State Governments, amount to a prohibition of *such acts of legislation;* and the *general principles of law and reason* forbid them. The Legislature may enjoin, permit, forbid, and punish; they may declare *new* crimes; and establish rules of conduct for *all* its citizens in *future* cases; they may *command* what is right, and *prohibit* what is wrong; but they cannot change *innocence* into *guilt*; or punish *innocence* as a *crime;* or violate the right of an *antecedent lawful private contract;* or the *right of private property.* To maintain that our Federal, or State, Legislature possesses *such powers,* if they had not been *expressly* restrained; would, in my opinion, be a *political heresy,* altogether inadmissible in our *free republican governments.*" [2]

Justice Iredell's opinion was a direct challenge to Justice Chase's natural law-social compact-vested rights approach. He stated: "[S]ome specu-

---

2. Justice Chase concluded that legislative powers had not been exceeded by the Connecticut act, because the initial invalidation of the will had not created any "vested" property rights in the heirs.

lative jurists have held, that a legislative act against natural justice must, in itself, be void; but I cannot think that, under [a constitutional scheme allocating powers without explicit limitations], any Court of Justice would possess a power to declare it so. Sir *William Blackstone*, having put the strong case of an act of Parliament, which should authorize a man to try his own cause, explicitly adds, that even in that case, 'there is no court that has power to defeat the intent of the Legislature . . .' In order, therefore, to guard against so great an evil, it has been the policy of all the *American* states, which have, individually, framed their state constitutions since the revolution, and of the people of the *United States,* when they framed the Federal Constitution, to define with precision the objects of the legislative power, and to restrain its exercise within marked and settled boundaries. If any act of Congress, or of the Legislature of a state, violates those constitutional provisions, it is unquestionably void; though, I admit, that as the authority to declare it void is of a delicate and awful nature, the Court will never resort to that authority, but in a clear and urgent case. If, on the other hand, the Legislature of the Union, or the Legislature of any member of the Union, shall pass a law, within the general scope of their constitutional power, the Court cannot pronounce it to be void, merely because it is, in their judgment, contrary to the principles of natural justice. The ideas of natural justice are regulated by no fixed standard: the ablest and the purest men have differed upon the subject; and all that the Court could properly say, in such an event, would be, that the Legislature (possessed of an equal right of opinion) had passed an act which, in the opinion of the judges, was inconsistent with the abstract principles of natural justice."

2. *The early Marshall Court.* In the early years of the Marshall Court, there were occasional echoes of Chase's natural law-vested rights approach. For example, in Fletcher v. Peck, 6 Cranch 87 (1810), Chief Justice Marshall flirted with such a notion as an alternative ground for invalidating a Georgia effort to revoke a land grant. He thought the result justified "either by general principles which are common to our free institutions, or by the particular provisions of the constitution of the United States." Justice Johnson's concurrence went even further in that direction. He repudiated any reliance on the contract clause of the Constitution; instead, he relied on "general principle, on the reason and nature of things." But passages such as these vanished from the opinions in the later Marshall Court years. Instead, the Court linked all of its protections of economic rights to specific constitutional provisions—most often, the contract clause. (See sec. 2B below.) In short, Justice Iredell's insistence that only explicit constitutional limits on legislative power were judicially enforceable ultimately prevailed. Marshall's rationale for judicial authority in Marbury v. Madison helped assure that Iredell's formal position, not Chase's, would emerge as the dominant one: a justification for judicial review that relied so heavily on the implications of a written constitution no doubt found it more congenial to justify any invalidations ultimately by reference to an explicit constitutional restraint. Nevertheless, notions of natural law and vested rights such as Justice Chase's remained useful and influential, not as an adequate formal basis for invalidation as such, but as a source of values for giving content to the explicit guarantees such as the contract clause—and, later, substantive due process.

3. *Due process before the Civil War.* Though most pre-Civil War discussion of due process clauses in state constitutions and in the Fifth Amendment spoke of the more obvious procedural implications of due process—recall Justice Curtis' comments in the Murray's Lessee case, chap. 8 above—there were a few intimations that due process might also impose substantive restraints on legislation, might serve as the vehicle for the infusion of fundamental values-vested rights notions into a written constitution. One of those intimations came from the Supreme Court, in the controversial Dred Scott decision [Dred Scott v. Sandford, 19 How. 393 (1857)]. There, Chief Justice Taney's opinion—explaining why Congress could not bar slavery from the territories and why the Missouri Compromise was therefore unconstitutional—commented, without elaboration, that "An Act of Congress which deprives a citizen of the United States of his liberty or property, merely because he came himself or brought his property into a particular Territory of the United States, and who had committed no offense against the laws, could hardly be dignified with the name of due process of law."

On the state level, the best-known suggestion of substantive due process came in an opinion in Wynehamer v. People, 13 N.Y. 378 (1856), invalidating a liquor prohibition law. As the most prolific student of due process has written, Wynehamer reads due process to "prohibit, regardless of the matter of procedure, a certain kind or degree of exertion of legislative power altogether": due process, rather than merely protecting the "mode of procedure," was made to reach "the substantive content of legislation." [3]

4. *The slow movement toward substantive due process in the generation after the Slaughter-House Cases.* The Slaughter-House Cases in 1873 (chap. 8, sec. 2, above)—which should be reexamined at this point—temporarily blocked the utilization of the 14th Amendment as a substantive restraint on state legislation. In 1873, a bare majority resisted the dissenters' appeal to social compact and natural law and vested rights ideology; but a generation later, a new majority embraced substantive due process. It was not a sudden change: in retrospect, one can perceive a variety of pressures, on and off the Court, that contributed to the conversion of due process into a more interventionist tool. For one, lawyers kept pressing the Court to restrain economic regulation despite the rebuff of the Slaughter-House Cases. As Justice Miller noted five years later, "the docket of this court is crowded with cases in which we are asked to hold that state courts and state legislatures have deprived their own citizens of life, liberty, or property without due process of law. There is here abundant evidence that there exists some strange misconception of the scope of this provision as found in the Fourteenth Amendment. In fact, it would seem, from the character of many of the cases before us, and the arguments made in them, that the clause under consideration is looked upon as a means of bringing to the test of the decision of this court the abstract opinions of every unsuccessful litigant in a State court of the justice of the decision against

3. Corwin, Liberty Against Government (1948). See also Corwin, "The Doctrine of Due Process of Law Before the Civil War," 24 Harv.L.Rev. 366, 460 (1911).

him, and of the merits of the legislation on which such a decision may be founded." Davidson v. New Orleans, 96 U.S. 97 (1877).[4]

And those lawyers' arguments that seemed a "misconception" of due process to Justice Miller in turn reflected deeper social developments and ideological movements.[5] The growth of industrialization and corporate power in the post-Civil War years stirred popular demands and legislative responses. And the new regulatory laws, opponents argued, contravened not only the economic laissez faire theories of Adam Smith—theories explicitly invoked in Justice Bradley's dissent in the Slaughter-House Cases— but also the social views of 19th century writers such as Herbert Spencer. In his Lochner dissent (sec. 1B below), Justice Holmes was to insist that the 14th Amendment "does not enact Mr. Herbert Spencer's Social Statics." But Spencer's emphasis on the survival of the fittest in his 1850 volume, and the echoes of Social Darwinism in the writings of American defenders of economic inequalities and a governmental hands-off policy, found their way into legal treatises and briefs. And, increasingly, there were responsive listeners on the bench. As Justice Brewer stated in Budd v. New York, 143 U.S. 517 (1892): "The paternal theory of government is to me odious. The utmost possible liberty to the individual, and the fullest possible protection to him and his property, is both the limitation and duty of government." (Dissenting opinion.)

Substantive due process flourished in some state courts before it found majority support in the Supreme Court. The leading case was In the Matter of Jacobs, 98 N.Y. 98 (1885), holding unconstitutional a law prohibiting the manufacture of cigars in a tenement house. To the New York court, the public health justification was unpersuasive, and the law interfered not only with "the profitable and free use" of property but also with "personal liberty." And even while a Supreme Court majority refused for a while longer to take a similar path, the seeds of substantive due process began to be visible in its opinions.

     a. *Rate regulation and the Munn case.* A leading case of the 1870's, for example, is commonly viewed as a symbol of judicial deference to legislative judgments; yet it at the same time suggested potential limits on legislative power. In MUNN v. ILLINOIS, 94 U.S. 113 (1877), the Court rejected an attack on a state law regulating the rates of grain elevators. Chief Justice Waite's majority opinion emphasized that the police power

---

4. Even Justice Miller, in the years between his majority opinion in Slaughter-House and his continued rejection of substantive due process in Davidson, proved not wholly immune to fundamental values arguments via other routes. For example, in 1875 he wrote for the Court in holding invalid an ordinance authorizing the issuance of municipal bonds for the benefit of private enterprise. Without tying his analysis to any particular constitutional provision, Justice Miller echoed Chase's sentiments in Calder v. Bull by writing in a well-known passage that there are "rights in every free government beyond the con-

trol of the State. . . . There are limitations on such power which grow out of the essential nature of all free governments. Implied reservations of individual rights, without which the social compact could not exist, and which are respected by all governments entitled to the name." Loan Association v. City of Topeka, 20 Wall. 655 (1874).

5. See generally Paul, Conservative Crisis and the Rule of Law: Attitudes of Bar and Bench 1887–1896 (1960), and Twiss, Lawyers and the Constitution: How Laissez Faire Came to the Supreme Court (1942).

included regulation of individual use of property "when such regulation becomes necessary for the public good." He relied in part on 17th century English writings to conclude that private property may be regulated when it is "affected with a public interest" and that property becomes "clothed with a public interest when used in a manner to make it of public consequence, and affect the community at large." The business owners regulated here easily fell within that category: they had a near monopoly on grain storage; regulation of their rates was similar to traditional price regulation of utilities and monopolies. The majority refused to scrutinize the reasonableness of the rates: since there was power to regulate, the legislative right to establish maximum rates was implied. Chief Justice Waite added: "We know that this is a power which may be abused; but that is no argument against its existence. For protection against abuses by legislatures the people must resort to the polls." Yet the Chief Justice prefaced that passage with a statement which could later be relied on to justify judicial control of rate regulation in other contexts: "Undoubtedly, in mere private contracts, relating to matters in which the public has no interest, what is reasonable must be ascertained judicially." [Justice Field dissented in Munn, as he had in the Slaughter-House Cases. Note the reexamination of Munn and its legacy in Nebbia v. New York, sec. 1C below.]

Chief Justice Waite took a similar noninterventionist stance in The Railroad Commission Cases, 116 U.S. 307 (1886), sustaining state regulation of railroad rates. But, again, the deference to legislative judgments was joined with a passage which left the door open for greater judicial control in the future. He warned that "it is not to be inferred that this power of limitation or regulation is itself without limit. This power to regulate is not a power to destroy, and limitation is not the equivalent of confiscation. Under pretence of regulating fares and freights, the State cannot require a railroad corporation to carry persons or property without reward; neither can it do that which in law amounts to a taking of private property for public use without just compensation, or without due process of law."[6] In the same year, in Santa Clara County v. Southern Pac. R. R., 118 U.S. 394 (1886), the Court held, without discussion, that corporations were "persons" within the meaning of the 14th Amendment.[7] The early resist-

6. In the further development of judicial control of rate making, Chicago, M. & St. P. R. Co. v. Minnesota, 134 U.S. 418 (1890), was a significant turning point. That decision invalidated a state law authorizing administrative rate making without providing for judicial review. The immediate vice of the statute was the lack of adequate procedural protection for the railroads—the lack of judicial review. But the majority explanation suggested Court concern with substance as well as procedure: reasonableness of rates was found to be "eminently a question for judicial investigation"; depriving the railroad of the power to charge reasonable rates by administrative order would be, "in substance and effect," a deprivation of property without due process of law. Justice Bradley's dissent viewed the decision as a virtual overruling of Munn v. Illinois. By the end of the decade, the Court was wholeheartedly in the business of scrutinizing the reasonableness of rates. Smyth v. Ames, 169 U.S. 466 (1898), provided the governing rate making formulas for decades. For a review of rate regulation developments after the 1890's and a repudiation of the reign of Smyth v. Ames, see FPC v. Hope Natural Gas Co., 320 U.S. 591 (1944).

7. See Graham, "The 'Conspiracy Theory' of the Fourteenth Amendment," 47 Yale L.J. 371 and 48 Yale L.J. 171 (1938). Justices Black and Douglas objected to this interpretation. See the dissents in Con-

ance to judicial intervention was weakening; dicta even in nonintervention-ist cases were leaving the door slightly ajar; and soon it swung wide open to substantive due process.

b. *Mugler v. Kansas.* Before long, substantive due process review ranging well beyond rate regulation and encompassing a wide variety of police power exercises was fully launched. MUGLER v. KANSAS, 123 U.S. 623 (1887), signaled the impending receptivity of the Court to sub-stantive due process challenges. Mugler sustained a law prohibiting in-toxicating beverages, but the Court announced that it was prepared to ex-amine the substantive reasonableness of state legislation. The first Justice Harlan spoke for a Court whose composition had changed almost totally since the Slaughter-House Cases. He stated that not "every statute enacted ostensibly for the promotion" of "the public morals, the public health, or the public safety" would be accepted "as a legitimate exertion of the police powers of the State." The courts would not be "misled by mere pretences": they were obligated, he insisted, "to look at the substance of things." Accord-ingly, if a purported exercise of the police powers "has no real or substantial relation to those objects, or is a palpable invasion of rights secured by the fun-damental law, it is the duty of the courts to so adjudge." And facts "within the knowledge of all" would be relied on in making that determination.

c. *The Allgeyer case and liberty of contract.* Ten years later, in ALL-GEYER v. LOUISIANA, 165 U.S. 578 (1897), the slow movement to substantive due process was completed: the Court for the first time invali-dated a state law on substantive due process grounds—a judgment that was to be frequently repeated in the first three decades of the 20th century. Allgeyer involved a Louisiana statute prohibiting anyone from doing any act in the State to effect insurance on any Louisiana property "from any marine insurance company which has not complied in all respects" with Louisiana law. Allgeyer was convicted for mailing a letter advising an insurance company in New York of the shipment of goods, in accordance with a marine policy. The company was not licensed to do business in Louisiana. The Supreme Court re-versed, holding the statute violated the 14th Amendment "in that it deprives the defendants of their liberty without due process of law."

Justice Peckham's opinion contained an extensive discussion of the power of the state in respect of foreign corporations and emphasized the fact that the insurance contract was made outside Louisiana. But it was the Court's articu-lation of the liberty of contract that gave the case its special significance in the development of substantive due process: "The liberty mentioned in that amendment means not only the right of the citizen to be free from the mere physical restraint of his person, as by incarceration, but the term is deemed to embrace the right of the citizen to be free in the enjoyment of all his faculties; to be free to use them in all lawful ways; to live and work where he will; to earn his livelihood by any lawful calling; to pursue any livelihood or avocation, and for that purpose to enter into all contracts which may be proper, necessary and essential to his carrying out to a successful conclusion the purposes above mentioned. . . . When we speak of the liberty to contract for insurance, [we] refer to and have in mind the facts of this case. [The] act done

necticut General Life Ins. Co. v. John-son, 303 U.S. 77 (1938), and Wheeling   Steel Corp. v. Glander, 337 U.S. 562 (1949).

within the limits of the State [we] hold a proper act, one which the defendants were at liberty to perform and which the state legislature had no right to prevent, at least with reference to the Federal Constitution. . . .

"In the privilege of pursuing an ordinary calling or trade and of acquiring, holding and selling property must be embraced the right to make all proper contracts in relation thereto, and although it may be conceded that this right to contract in relation to persons or property or to do business within the jurisdiction of the State may be regulated and sometimes prohibited when the contracts or business conflict with the policy of the State as contained in its statutes, yet the power does not and cannot extend to prohibiting a citizen from making contracts of the nature involved in this case outside of the limits and jurisdiction of the State, and which are also to be performed outside of such jurisdiction."

Allgeyer involved insurance regulation. Soon after the turn of the century, its expansive conception of "liberty" bore fruit in more controversial contexts, exemplified by the Lochner case, which follows.[8] When the modern Court looks back to the discredited "Allgeyer-Lochner-Adair-Coppage constitutional doctrine" (the phrase is from the Lincoln Federal Labor Union case in 1949, sec. 1C below), the Allgeyer reference is not to its specific setting but to its significance in opening the door to substitution of the Justices' notions of public policy and fundamental values for legislative choices regarding economic and social regulation, as assertedly took place in Lochner. Is that what happened in Lochner and its progeny? Has that due process philosophy been wholly rejected by the modern Court?

B. THE LOCHNER ERA: JUDICIAL INTERVENTION AND ECONOMIC REGULATION

LOCHNER v. NEW YORK

198 U.S. 45, 25 S.Ct. 539, 49 L.Ed. 937 (1905).

Error to the County Court of Oneida County, State of New York.

[A New York labor law prohibited the employment of bakery employees for more than 10 hours a day or 60 hours a week. Lochner was convicted and fined for permitting an employee to work in his Utica, N. Y., bakery for more than 60 hours in one week.]

Mr. Justice PECKHAM . . . delivered the opinion of the court.

. . . The employé may desire to earn the extra money, which would arise from his working more than the prescribed time, but this statute forbids the employer from permitting the employé to earn it. . . . The statute necessarily interferes with the right of contract between the employer and employés . . . .. The general right to make a contract in

8. In the period between Allgeyer and Lochner, in 1898, the Court decided Holden v. Hardy, 169 U.S. 366, sustaining a Utah law limiting the employment of workers "in all underground mines" to eight hours a day. Note the effort to distinguish Holden v. Hardy in the Lochner majority opinion, which follows.

relation to his business is part of the liberty of the individual protected by the Fourteenth Amendment of the Federal Constitution. [Allgeyer v. Louisiana.] The right to purchase or to sell labor is part of the liberty protected by this amendment, unless there are circumstances which exclude the right. There are, however, certain powers, existing in the sovereignty of each State in the Union, somewhat vaguely termed police powers, the exact description and limitation of which have not been attempted by the courts. Those powers, broadly stated and without, at present, any attempt at a more specific limitation, relate to the safety, health, morals and general welfare of the public. Both property and liberty are held on such reasonable conditions as may be imposed by the governing power of the State in the exercise of those powers, and with such conditions the Fourteenth Amendment was not designed to interfere.

The State, therefore, has power to prevent the individual from making certain kinds of contracts, and in regard to them the Federal Constitution offers no protection. If the contract be one which the State, in the legitimate exercise of its police power, has the right to prohibit, it is not prevented from prohibiting it by the Fourteenth Amendment. Contracts in violation of a statute, either of the Federal or state government, or a contract to let one's property for immoral purposes, or to do any other unlawful act, could obtain no protection from the Federal Constitution, as coming under the liberty of person or of free contract. Therefore, when the State, by its legislature, in the assumed exercise of its police powers, has passed an act which seriously limits the right to labor or the right of contract in regard to their means of livelihood between persons who are *sui juris* (both employer and employé), it becomes of great importance to determine which shall prevail—the right of the individual to labor for such time as he may choose, or the right of the State to prevent the individual from laboring [beyond] a certain time prescribed by the State.

This court has recognized the existence and upheld the exercise of the police powers of the States in many cases which might fairly be considered as border ones, and it [has] been guided by rules of a very liberal nature, the application of which has resulted, in numerous instances, in upholding the validity of state statutes thus assailed. Among the later cases where the state law has been upheld by this court is that of Holden v. Hardy, 169 U.S. 366. [I]t was held that the kind of employment, mining, smelting, etc., and the character of the employés in such kinds of labor, were such as to make it reasonable and proper for the State to interfere to prevent the employés from being constrained by the rules laid down by the proprietors in regard to labor. . . . There is nothing in Holden v. Hardy which covers the case now before us. . . .

It must, of course, be conceded that there is a limit to the valid exercise of the police power by the State. . . . Otherwise the Fourteenth Amendment would have no efficacy and the legislatures of the States would have unbounded power, and it would be enough to say that any piece of legislation was enacted to conserve the morals, the health or the safety of the people; such legislation would be valid, no matter how absolutely without foundation the claim might be. The claim of the police power would be a mere pretext—become another and delusive name for the supreme sov-

ereignty of the State to be exercised free from constitutional restraint. This is not contended for. In every case that comes before this court, therefore, where legislation of this character is concerned   .   .   ., the question necessarily arises: Is this a fair, reasonable and appropriate exercise of the police power of the State, or is it an unreasonable, unnecessary and arbitrary interference with the right of the individual to his personal liberty or to enter into those contracts in relation to labor which may seem to him appropriate or necessary for the support of himself and his family? Of course the liberty of contract relating to labor includes both parties to it. The one has as much right to purchase as the other to sell labor.

This is not a question of substituting the judgment of the court for that of the legislature. If the act be within the power of the State it is valid, although the judgment of the court might be totally opposed to the enactment of such a law. But the question would still remain: Is it within the police power of the State? and that question must be answered by the court.

The question whether this act is valid as a labor law, pure and simple, may be dismissed in a few words. There is no reasonable ground for interfering with the liberty of person or the right of free contract, by determining the hours of labor, in the occupation of a baker. There is no contention that bakers as a class are not equal in intelligence and capacity to men in other trades or manual occupations, or that they are not able to assert their rights and care for themselves without the protecting arm of the State, interfering with their independence of judgment and of action. They are in no sense wards of the State. Viewed in the light of a purely labor law, with no reference whatever to the question of health, we think that a law like the one before us involves neither the safety, the morals nor the welfare of the public, and that the interest of the public is not in the slightest degree affected by such an act. The law must be upheld, if at all, as a law pertaining to the health of the individual engaged in the occupation of a baker. It does not affect any other portion of the public than those who are engaged in that occupation. Clean and wholesome bread does not depend upon whether the baker works but ten hours per day or only sixty hours a week. The limitation of the hours of labor does not come within the police power on that ground.

.   .   .   The mere assertion that the subject relates though but in a remote degree to the public health does not necessarily render the enactment valid. The act must have a more direct relation, as a means to an end, and the end itself must be appropriate and legitimate, before an act can be held to be valid which interferes with the general right of an individual to be free in his person and in his power to contract in relation to his own labor.   .   .   .

We think the limit of the police power has been reached and passed in this case. There is, in our judgment, no reasonable foundation for holding this to be necessary or appropriate as a health law to safeguard the public health or the health of the individuals who are following the trade of a baker. If this statute be valid,   .   .   .   there would seem to be no length to which legislation of this nature might not go.   .   .   .

We think that there can be no fair doubt that the trade of a baker, in and of itself, is not an unhealthy one to that degree which would authorize

the legislature to interfere with the right to labor, and with the right of free contract on the part of the individual, either as employer or employé. In looking through statistics regarding all trades and occupations, it may be true that the trade of a baker does not appear to be as healthy as some other trades, and is also vastly more healthy than still others. To the common understanding the trade of a baker has never been regarded as an unhealthy one. . . . It might be safely affirmed that almost all occupations more or less affect the health. There must be more than the mere fact of the possible existence of some small amount of unhealthiness to warrant legislative interference with liberty. It is unfortunately true that labor, even in any department, may possibly carry with it the seeds of unhealthiness. But are we all, on that account, at the mercy of legislative majorities? . . .

It is also urged, pursuing the same line of argument, that it is to the interest of the State that its population should be strong and robust, and therefore any legislation which may be said to tend to make people healthy must be valid as health laws, enacted under the police power. If this be a valid argument and a justification for this kind of legislation, it follows that the protection of the Federal Constitution from undue interference with liberty of person and freedom of contract is visionary, wherever the law is sought to be justified as a valid exercise of the police power. Scarcely any law but might find shelter under such assumptions, and conduct, properly so called, as well as contract, would come under the restrictive sway of the legislature. Not only the hours of employés, but the hours of employers, could be regulated, and doctors, lawyers, scientists, all professional men, as well as athletes and artisans, could be forbidden to fatigue their brains and bodies by prolonged hours of exercise, lest the fighting strength of the State be impaired. We mention these extreme cases because the contention is extreme. We do not believe in the soundness of the views which uphold this law. On the contrary, we think that such a law as this, although passed in the assumed exercise of the police power, and as relating to the public health, or the health of the employés named, is not within that power, and is invalid. The act is not, within any fair meaning of the term, a health law, but is an illegal interference with the rights of individuals, both employers and employés, to make contracts regarding labor upon such terms as they may think best, or which they may agree upon with the other parties to such contracts. Statutes of the nature of that under review, limiting the hours in which grown and intelligent men may labor to earn their living, are mere meddlesome interferences with the rights of the individual, and they are not saved from condemnation by the claim that they are passed in the exercise of the police power and upon the subject of the health of the individual whose rights are interfered with, unless there be some fair ground, reasonable in and of itself, to say that there is material danger to the public health or to the health of the employés, if the hours of labor are not curtailed. [All that the State] could properly do has been done by it with regard to the conduct of bakeries, as provided for in the other sections of the act, [which] provide for the inspection of the premises where the bakery is carried on, with regard to furnishing proper wash-rooms and water-closets, apart from the bake-room, also with regard to providing proper drainage, plumbing and painting [and] for other things of that nature. . . .

It was further urged [that] restricting the hours of labor in the case of bakers was valid because it tended to cleanliness on the part of the workers, as a man was more apt to be cleanly when not overworked, and if cleanly then his "output" was also more likely to be so. In our judgment it is not possible in fact to discover the connection between the number of hours a baker may work in the bakery and the healthful quality of the bread made by the workman. The connection, if any exists, is too shadowy and thin to build any argument for the interference of the legislature. If the man works ten hours a day it is all right, but if ten and a half or eleven his health is in danger and his bread may be unhealthful, and, therefore, he shall not be permitted to do it. This, we think, is unreasonable and entirely arbitrary. When assertions such as we have adverted to become necessary in order to give, if possible, a plausible foundation for the contention that the law is a "health law," it gives rise to at least a suspicion that there was some other motive dominating the legislature than the purpose to subserve the public health or welfare.

This interference on the part of the legislatures of the several States with the ordinary trades and occupations of the people seems to be on the increase. . . .

It is impossible for us to shut our eyes to the fact that many of the laws of this character, while passed under what is claimed to be the police power for the purpose of protecting the public health or welfare, are, in reality, passed from other motives. We are justified in saying so when, from the character of the law and the subject upon which it legislates, it is apparent that the public health or welfare bears but the most remote relation to the law. The purpose of a statute must be determined from the natural and legal effect of the language employed; and whether it is or is not repugnant to the Constitution of the United States must be determined from the natural effect of such statutes when put into operation, and not from their proclaimed purpose. The court looks beyond the mere letter of the law in such cases. [Yick Wo v. Hopkins, 118 U.S. 356 (chap. 10 below).]

It is manifest to us that the [law here] has no such direct relation to and no such substantial effect upon the health of the employé as to justify us in regarding the section as really a health law. It seems to us that the real object and purpose were simply to regulate the hours of labor between the master and his employés (all being men, *sui juris*), in a private business, not dangerous in any degree to morals or in any real and substantial degree, to the health of the employés. Under such circumstances the freedom of master and employé to contract with each other in relation to their employment, and in defining the same, cannot be prohibited or interfered with, without violating the Federal Constitution.

Reversed.

Mr. Justice HARLAN, with whom Mr. Justice WHITE and Mr. Justice DAY concurred, dissenting. . . .

Speaking generally, the State in the exercise of its powers may not unduly interfere with the right of the citizen to enter into contracts that may be necessary and essential in the enjoyment of the inherent rights belonging to every one, among which rights is the right "to be free in the enjoyment

of all his faculties; to be free to use them in all lawful ways; to live and work where he will; to earn his livelihood by any lawful calling; to pursue any livelihood or avocation." This was decided in [Allgeyer]. . . .

Granting then that there is a liberty of contract which cannot be violated even under the sanction of direct legislative enactment, but assuming, as according to settled law we may assume, that such liberty of contract is subject to such regulations as the State may reasonably prescribe for the common good and the well-being of society, what are the conditions under which the judiciary may declare such regulations to be in excess of legislative authority and void? Upon this point there is no room for dispute; for, the rule is universal [that] the power of the courts to review legislative action in respect of a matter affecting the general welfare exists *only* "[if] a statute purporting to have been enacted to protect the public health, the public morals or the public safety, has no real or substantial relation to those objects, or is, beyond all question, a plain, palpable invasion of rights secured by the fundamental law." . . .

Let these principles be applied to the present case. . . .

It is plain that this statute was enacted in order to protect the physical well-being of those who work in bakery and confectionery establishments. It may be that the statute had its origin, in part, in the belief that employers and employés in such establishments were not upon an equal footing, and that the necessities of the latter often compelled them to submit to such exactions as unduly taxed their strength. Be this as it may, the statute must be taken as expressing the belief of the people of New York that, as a general rule, and in the case of the average man, labor in excess of sixty hours during a week in such establishments may endanger the health of those who thus labor. Whether or not this be wise legislation, it is not the province of the court to inquire. . . . I find it impossible, in view of common experience, to say that there is here no real or substantial relation between the means employed by the State and the end sought to be accomplished by its legislation. . . . It must be remembered that this statute does not apply to all kinds of business. It applies only to work in bakery and confectionery establishments, in which, as all know, the air constantly breathed by workmen is not as pure and healthful as that to be found in some other establishments or out of doors.

Professor Hirt in his treatise on the "Diseases of the Workers" has said: "The labor of the bakers is among the hardest and most laborious imaginable, because it has to be performed under conditions injurious to the health of those engaged in it. It is hard, very hard work, not only because it requires a great deal of physical exertion in an overheated workshop and during unreasonably long hours, but more so because of the erratic demands of the public, compelling the baker to perform the greater part of his work at night, thus depriving him of an opportunity to enjoy the necessary rest and sleep, a fact which is highly injurious to his health." Another writer says: "The constant inhaling of flour dust causes inflammation of the lungs and of the bronchial tubes. The eyes also suffer through this dust, which is responsible for the many cases of running eyes among the bakers. The long hours of toil to which all bakers are subjected produce rheumatism, cramps and swollen legs. The intense heat in the workshops

induces the workers to resort to cooling drinks, which together with their habit of exposing the greater part of their bodies to the change in the atmosphere, is another source of a number of diseases of various organs. Nearly all bakers are pale-faced and of more delicate health than the workers of other crafts, which is chiefly due to their hard work and their irregular and unnatural mode of living, whereby the power of resistance against disease is greatly diminished. The average age of a baker is below that of other workmen; they seldom live over their fiftieth year, most of them dying between the ages of forty and fifty. During periods of epidemic diseases the bakers are generally the first to succumb to the disease . . . ." [Summaries of additional data are omitted.]

We judicially know that the question of the number of hours during which a workman should continuously labor has been, for a long period, and is yet, a subject of serious consideration among civilized peoples, and by those having special knowledge of the laws of health. . . . We also judicially know that the number of hours that should constitute a day's labor in particular occupations involving the physical strength and safety of workmen has been the subject of enactments by Congress and by nearly all of the States. Many, if not most, of those enactments fix eight hours as the proper basis of a day's labor.

I do not stop to consider whether any particular view of this economic question presents the sounder theory. What the precise facts are it may be difficult to say. It is enough for the determination of this case, and it is enough for this court to know, that the question is one about which there is room for debate and for an honest difference of opinion. There are many reasons of a weighty, substantial character, based upon the experience of mankind, in support of the theory that, all things considered, more than ten hours' steady work each day, from week to week, in a bakery or confectionery establishment, may endanger the health, and shorten the lives of the workmen, thereby diminishing their physical and mental capacity to serve the State, and to provide for those dependent upon them.

If such reasons exist that ought to be the end of this case, for the State is not amenable to the judiciary, in respect of its legislative enactments, unless such enactments are plainly, palpably, beyond all question, inconsistent with the Constitution of the United States. . . . A decision that the New York statute is void under the Fourteenth Amendment will, in my opinion, involve consequences of a far-reaching and mischievous character; for such a decision would seriously cripple the inherent power of the States to care for the lives, health and well-being of their citizens. Those are matters which can be best controlled by the States. . . .

Mr. Justice HOLMES, dissenting. . . .

This case is decided upon an economic theory which a large part of the country does not entertain. If it were a question whether I agreed with that theory, I should desire to study it further and long before making up my mind. But I do not conceive that to be my duty, because I strongly believe that my agreement or disagreement has nothing to do with the right of a majority to embody their opinions in law. It is settled by various decisions of this court that state constitutions and state laws may regulate life in many ways which we

as legislators might think as injudicious or if you like as tyrannical as this, and which equally with this interfere with the liberty to contract. Sunday laws and usury laws are ancient examples. A more modern one is the prohibition of lotteries. The liberty of the citizen to do as he likes so long as he does not interfere with the liberty of others to do the same, which has been a shibboleth for some well-known writers, is interfered with by school laws, by the Post Office, by every state or municipal institution which takes his money for purposes thought desirable, whether he likes it or not. The Fourteenth Amendment does not enact Mr. Herbert Spencer's Social Statics. The other day we sustained the Massachusetts vaccination law. Jacobson v. Massachusetts, 197 U.S. 11. United States and state statutes and decisions cutting down the liberty to contract by way of combination are familiar to this court. . . . The decision sustaining an eight hour law for miners is still recent. [Holden v. Hardy.] Some of these laws embody convictions or prejudices which judges are likely to share. Some may not. But a constitution is not intended to embody a particular economic theory, whether of paternalism and the organic relation of the citizen to the State or of *laissez faire*. It is made for people of fundamentally differing views, and the accident of our finding certain opinions natural and familiar or novel and even shocking ought not to conclude our judgment upon the question whether statutes embodying them conflict with the Constitution of the United States.

General propositions do not decide concrete cases. The decision will depend on a judgment or intuition more subtle than any articulate major premise. But I think that the proposition just stated, if it is accepted, will carry us far toward the end. Every opinion tends to become a law. I think that the word liberty in the Fourteenth Amendment is perverted when it is held to prevent the natural outcome of a dominant opinion, unless it can be said that a rational and fair man necessarily would admit that the statute proposed would infringe fundamental principles as they have been understood by the traditions of our people and our law. It does not need research to show that no such sweeping condemnation can be passed upon the statute before us. A reasonable man might think it a proper measure on the score of health. Men whom I certainly could not pronounce unreasonable would uphold it as a first instalment of a general regulation of the hours of work. Whether in the latter aspect it would be open to the charge of inequality I think it unnecessary to discuss.

THE DISCREDITED PERIOD OF JUDICIAL INTERVENTION: WHAT WAS WRONG WITH LOCHNER?

Introduction. From the Lochner decision in 1905 to the mid-1930's, the Court invalidated a considerable number of laws on substantive due process grounds. Regulations of prices, labor relations, and conditions for entry into business were especially vulnerable. As the Court recalled in the Lincoln Federal Labor Union Case (sec. 1C below), the Allgeyer-Lochner doctrine "was used to strike down laws fixing minimum wages and maximum hours of employment, laws fixing prices, and laws regulating business activities." Typically, as in Lochner, the invalidations pro-

voked dissents, most often by Holmes and, later, Brandeis, Stone and Cardozo.[1]

Though free-wheeling judicial invalidation of economic regulations is the characteristic most commonly associated with the Lochner era, that feature should not be exaggerated. Even during those years, most challenged laws withstood attack. Nearly 200 regulations were struck down, to be sure; but an even larger group survived scrutiny. The Court sustained a maximum hours law for women only three years after Lochner, in Muller v. Oregon, below; and it upheld a 10-hour day for factory workers in Bunting v. Oregon in 1917, below.[2] Yet the extent of judicial intervention during the Lochner era was no doubt substantial; and the modern Court has repeatedly insisted that it has turned its back on the evils of the Lochner philosophy.

What were those evils? The giving of substantive content to due process? The expansive view of "liberty" and "property" to include values not specifically stated in the Constitution? The selection of the "wrong" fundamental values for special judicial protection? The failure to state general standards? The inadequacy of the articulated standards? The failure to apply the standards with adequate receptiveness to factual data? The failure to apply the general standards with adequate receptiveness to the society's hierarchy of values? The failure to apply the general standards with adequate consistency and neutrality? Excessive preoccupation with the permissibility of legislative ends? Excessive preoccupation with the "reasonableness" of legislative means—the extent to which the means contributed to the achievement of permissible ends?

Examining the cases of the Lochner era in light of questions such as these—and the related questions below—is of more than historical interest. Rejection of the Lochner heritage is a common starting point for modern Justices; reaction against the excessive intervention of the "Old Men" of the pre-1937 Court has strongly influenced the judicial philosophies of their successors. Yet the modern Court has *not* drawn from Lochner the lesson that *all* judicial intervention via substantive due process is improper. Rather, it has withdrawn from careful scrutiny in most economic areas but has maintained and increased intervention with respect to a variety of noneconomic personal interests. Identifying the evils of the Lochner era is especially relevant, then, to determine (a) whether the modern Court's interventions avoid those evils, and (b) whether those evils warranted as substantial a withdrawal from the economic area as has taken place.

1. *Lochner and the language of the 14th Amendment. a. "Liberty" and economic rights.* Did the basic vice of Lochner lie in its expansive

---

1. Substantive due process was far and away the most important judicial tool, but it was not the only basis for restraints on economic regulation during this period. On the role of the 14th Amendment's equal protection clause as a source of limits on economic regulation—a role which paralleled but was less significant than that of substantive due process—see chap. 10 below. Recall also the restrictive interpretations of national regulatory powers considered in earlier chapters, and the continued reliances on the contract clause even after the advent of substantive due process, sec. 2B below.

2. For a comprehensive summary of the decisions of the period, see The Constitution of the United States (Gov't Printing Office, 1972 ed.). See also Wright, The Growth of American Constitutional Law (1942).

reading of "liberty"? Justice Peckham read "liberty" broadly to include freedom of contract. That was in the tradition of Allgeyer, where he had stated that liberty included more than "the right of the citizen to be free from the mere physical restraint of his person." Some critics have insisted that that was the basic flaw of the Lochner philosophy: that liberty at common law meant no more than freedom from physical restraint, and that it should have meant no more in the due process clause. See, e. g., Warren, "The New 'Liberty' Under the Fourteenth Amendment," 39 Harv.L.Rev. 431 (1926). But even if that view of common law is correct, should that control the limits of "liberty" under the Constitution? Is the difficulty with excessively interventionist uses of due process the readings of "liberty" that go beyond the narrowest common law connotations? Or does the real difficulty lie elsewhere? See the notes below.

Is one ingredient of the underlying difficulty not the generous reading of "liberty" but rather the selection of some aspects of liberty, some rights, for *special* protection? Simply reading liberty broadly need not be an interventionist doctrine: if a "mere rationality" standard is used—if legislative restraints on liberty are permissible so long as reasonable persons might think that the restraints plausibly promote broadly conceived legislative objectives—an expansive reading of liberty does not produce frequent judicial invalidations. It is only when the "liberty" allegedly infringed is thought to be "fundamental," deserving of special protection, and thus imposing on the state especially high burdens of justification for the infringement, that due process turns into an interventionist tool. Thus, the retreat from interventionist uses of due process in the economic area on the modern Court has not taken place by way of a shrinking of the reading of liberty; instead, it has taken the form of an extremely deferential "minimum rationality" standard in testing whether alleged infringements of economic interest are justifiable.

    b. *"Liberty" and noneconomic rights.* Note, too, that it is the reading of "liberty" beyond the narrowest common law confines that has made possible the protection of a wide range of noneconomic interests under the 14th Amendment. Protection of personal liberties beyond freedom from bodily restraint, not only liberty of contract, is one of the consequences of the Lochner era. Not only economic regulations fell victim to substantive due process attacks in the three decades beginning with Lochner. That period, it is often forgotten, also saw the early development of 14th Amendment protections of civil liberties (and of the rights of the accused considered in the previous chapter). Thus, the Allgeyer-Lochner philosophy formed the basis for absorbing rights such as those in the First Amendment into the 14th Amendment's concept of liberty, as chap. 12 shows. Justice Brandeis' eloquent defense of free speech in Whitney v. California, 274 U.S. 357 (1927) (chap. 12 below), included a reluctant acceptance of the triumph of substantive due process—a triumph that supported the speech protection he advocated there: "Despite arguments to the contrary which had seemed to me persuasive, it is settled that the due process clause of the 14th Amendment applies to matters of substantive law as well as to matters of procedure." [3]

3. Indeed, Charles Warren's article cited above—attacking the reading of   "liberty" beyond common law confines —had as its main target Gitlow v.

Moreover, that aspect of the Lochner philosophy that refused to limit liberty to its narrowest reading helped justify intervention on behalf of personal, noneconomic rights other than those that had counterparts in the First Amendment. Note, for example, the noneconomic personal liberties recognized in Meyer v. Nebraska, 262 U.S. 390 (1923) (sec. 3 below), reversing a conviction of a parochial school teacher under a law prohibiting teaching "in any language other than" English. Justice McReynolds' majority opinion, squarely within the Lochner tradition, contained a broad reading of liberty that has been of renewed significance in the modern revival of substantive due process on behalf of noneconomic fundamental rights. He stated that "liberty" denotes "not merely freedom from bodily restraint but also the right of the individual to contract, to engage in any of the common occupations of life, to acquire useful knowledge, to marry, to establish a home and bring up children, to worship God according to the dictates of his own conscience, and generally to enjoy those privileges long recognized at common law as essential to the orderly pursuit of happiness by free men." [4]

c. *"Property" and "due process".* Does criticism of the broad readings of "property" and "due process" get any closer to the roots of the Court's difficulties in the Lochner era than the questioning of the expansive view of "liberty"? A good many of the cases of the Lochner era involved restrictions on the use of property even under the narrowest reading of that term. But the Court's penchant for broad interpretations extended to "property" as well: the much-invoked right to contract, for example, was not traced solely to "liberty," as in Lochner, but was also viewed as a derivation from notions of "property." See, e. g., Coppage v. Kansas, 236 U.S. 1 (1915), in the next group of notes. Perhaps the strongest textual criticism of the Court's substantive due process development comes back to the phrase "due process" itself: How does a legitimate method of interpretation move from a phrase with evident procedural connotations to a basis for scrutiny of the substance of legislation? What, if any, "process" is the Court concerned with in substantive due process cases?

2. *Lochner and legislative ends.* Justice Peckham's opinion in Lochner does not consider liberty of contract an absolute. He, and all the other Justices, recognize that liberty of contract is subject to reasonable restraints under the police power. But what governmental objectives are legitimately within the police power? Does the real vice of the Lochner philosophy lie in its unduly narrow conception of those objectives? Justice Peckham recognizes that "health" is a legitimate end of the police power, and most of his opinion considers whether New York's regulation can be justified as a

New York, 268 U.S. 652 (1925), where the Court for the first time assumed that the First Amendment freedoms of speech and press were "among the fundamental personal rights and liberties" protected by the 14th Amendment.

4. See also Pierce v. Society of Sisters, 268 U.S. 510 (1925), another broad reading of "liberty" during that period to include noneconomic rights. See the additional comments on Meyer and Pierce and their impact on the modern revival of substantive due process, in sec. 3 below. And note the reliance on the Meyer and Pierce cases in the 1965 decision on the Connecticut birth control law, Griswold v. Connecticut, sec. 3 below; and Justice Black's rejection of those cases, as products of the Lochner philosophy, in his dissent in Griswold.

health law—as a law to promote the health of bakers or of the consuming public. With respect to health, he is not satisfied that the means adequately promote that legitimate state end. But there was another arguable end of the law—one that received short shrift from Justice Peckham. That justification stressed the unequal bargaining position of bakery workers and argued that a state may, within its police powers, redress perceived economic inequalities. That is what Justice Peckham calls "a labor law, pure and simple"; and a "purely labor law" is not within the objectives contemplated by the police power: "There is no contention that bakers as a class are not equal in intelligence and capacity to men in other trades or manual occupations . . . .. They are in no sense wards of the State." (Miners and women, by contrast, were among those perceived by the Lochner era Court to be "unequal" and hence, presumably, legitimate "wards." See Holden v. Hardy, noted in Lochner, and Muller v. Oregon, below.)

That refusal of the Court to accept the redressing of inequalities as a legitimate ingredient of the police power lay at the base of many of the Lochner era invalidations. Coppage v. Kansas, 236 U.S. 1 (1915), in the next group of notes, makes the point very clearly: in striking down a law designed to protect labor organizing efforts, the majority stated that the police power may not be invoked to remove "those inequalities that are but the normal and inevitable result" of the exercise of rights of contract and property. "[I]t is from the nature of things impossible to uphold freedom of contract and the right of private property without at the same time recognizing as legitimate those inequalities of fortune that are the necessary result of the exercise of those rights." Justice Holmes' dissent in Coppage, as in Lochner, was squarely directed at that narrow view of legislative ends: the police power, he insisted in Coppage, may be used "to establish the equality of position between the parties in which liberty of contract begins." And as he said in the Lochner dissent, a constitution "is not intended to embody a particular economic theory, whether of paternalism and the organic relation of the citizen to the State or of *laissez faire*." [5]

Is there any basis for the Lochner majority's view of impermissible ends other than an improper reading of a particular economic philosophy into the Constitution? Is there a better basis for the modern Court's perceptions of new impermissible ends, other than an acceptance of a particular variety of social philosophy? See the notes following the abortion case, Roe v. Wade, sec. 3 below. Even if the Lochner Court's view of impremissible ends is justifiable, were the applications of that position defensible? Can Lochner be squared with Holden v. Hardy, the miners case, above, or Muller v. Oregon and Bunting v. Oregon in the next group of notes?

3. *Lochner and means-ends relationships.* a. *Minimum rationality.* The Lochner majority's objection to the New York law goes not merely to ends but also to means. Is concern with means as questionable a judicial intervention as a narrow view of police power objectives? Does repudiation of the "evils" of the Lochner philosophy warrant judicial withdrawal from means scrutiny as well as from ends scrutiny? Viewed as a "labor law," a

5. Consider the comment in Gunther, "Foreword: In Search of Evolving Doctrine on a Changing Court: A Model for a Newer Equal Protection," 86 Harv.L.Rev. 1, 42 (1972): "[T]he primary evil of the discredited [Loch-

law designed to protect bakery workers in an unequal bargaining position, the Lochner majority rejects the legitimacy of the legislative end out of hand. But the majority concedes the validity of health objectives. In its scrutiny of the legislation as a health law, the Court purports to be concerned only with the means invoked to promote a legitimate objective. Justice Peckham concedes that a valid health law may restrict liberty of contract: his test is that there must be "some fair ground, reasonable in and of itself, to say that there is material danger to the public health or to the health of the employés, if the hours of labor are not curtailed." How is that test satisfied? Why was it not satisfied in Lochner?

Justice Harlan's dissent, unlike Justice Holmes,' is directed at the means rather than the ends analysis in the majority opinion.[6] Does the majority's standard as to means-ends relationships differ from Justice Harlan's insistence that there be a "real or substantial relation between the means employed by the State and the end sought to be accomplished by its legislation"? Is the difference between the majority and Justice Harlan one in application rather than in statement of the rule? Is the Court better equipped to scrutinize means than to interpose objections as to ends? What are the relevant data to which the Court may turn in determining whether the requisite means-ends relationship exists? Its own sense of desirable legislation? Judicial notice? Data considered by the legislature? Data put forth by the defenders of the law in court?

Note Justice Harlan's recital of data regarding the health of bakers. Does the majority disagree with those data? Note Justice Harlan's statement that it is enough that "the question is one about which there is room for debate and for an honest difference of opinion." Does the majority demand more than that? Why do not those data demonstrate a "fair" and "reasonable" basis for the relationship between working hours and health? Note the majority's statement that the bakers' trade "is not an unhealthy one to that degree which would authorize the legislature to interfere." Is the majority in effect imposing a greater burden of justification on the defenders of the law than "minimum rationality"? Is it demanding more than a showing that reasonable men might think that the means would promote the end, that a relationship between means and ends is plausible?

b. *Stricter scrutiny*. Is it defensible to impose a burden of justification requirement higher than "mere rationality," to apply a stricter judicial standard than minimum scrutiny? Is a higher standard of justification ap-

ner] doctrine was the dogmatic judicial intervention regarding ends, not means. Although the Court of the early twentieth century would occasionally—as in the case of maximum hours for women workers—permit protective legislation designed to redress inequality and to 'secure a real equality of right,' the majority's devotion to liberty of contract typically led it to deny the legitimacy of paternalistic legislation. Such laws were 'disturbing of equality of right' ; most 'inequalities of fortune' were 'legitimate' consequences of the economic system, beyond the legislature's reach. Justice Holmes' classic dissents properly identified the dominant evil of that approach."

6. Would Justice Harlan have sustained the law as "a labor law, pure and simple" ? Would he have disagreed with the majority on the illegitimacy of the "labor law" end? Note Justice Harlan's opinion for a majority, three years later, in Adair v. United States, 208 U.S. 161 (1908), in the next group of notes.

propriate only when specially cherished constitutional rights are involved? Does the Lochner majority's approach rest on an implicit assumption that liberty of contract is such a fundamental value warranting special judicial protection? Is that, then, one of the "evils" of Lochner: not the recognition that liberty of contract can be viewed as an aspect of "liberty," but rather that it is such a fundamental aspect that "mere reasonableness" in means-ends relationships will not justify restraints on liberty of contract? In other words, is it one of the "evils" that the Lochner Court paid only lip service to a reasonableness standard and applied stricter scrutiny of the means in fact? When such stricter scrutiny is applied, does it inevitably rest on a value judgment: not only a judgment selecting some values for special judicial protection, but also implementing that protection by "balancing" the competing public and private interests?

Court insistence on scrutiny stricter than "mere rationality" has become a commonplace modern technique in areas other than economic regulation challenged under due process. One way of stating a pervasive problem in the exercise of judicial review is to ask what—in constitutional text, history, structure or justifiable value choices—legitimates judicial applications of stricter scrutiny requirements in some contexts. The Court frequently exercises greater than minimal scrutiny and "balances" when it examines state regulations of commerce, it will be recalled. (See, e. g., the Southern Pacific case, and the Dean Milk insistence that a state must resort to less restrictive alternatives and may not choose "merely reasonable" means to accomplish legitimate objectives, in chap. 5 above.) Higher standards of justification and stricter degrees of scrutiny also surface in later materials: e. g., with respect to the "fundamental right" of privacy, sec. 3 below, and "fundamental" First Amendment rights, chaps. 12 and 13 below. Note also the strict scrutiny exercised when "fundamental interests" are impinged, under the doctrine of the "new" equal protection, chap. 10 below. Was it, then, an evil of Lochner that the majority imposed a scrutiny stricter than "mere rationality" without adequately justifying that special protection of liberty of contract? Why, if at all, was that special scrutiny less justified than some of the currently accepted areas of stricter scrutiny?

If that de facto stricter scrutiny of Lochner is rejected as an evil of that discredited era, does it follow that even "mere rationality" means scrutiny—means scrutiny according to the standard stated but not followed by Justice Peckham, or that stated and followed by Justice Harlan—should be abandoned? Has the modern Court abandoned even "mere rationality" scrutiny of means in the economic area? See sec. 1C below. Is abandonment a justifiable response to the evils of Lochner? The conferral of an especially high value on liberty of contract without adequate justifications for that cherished status permeated the Lochner era, both in the narrow conception of legislative goals and the stricter scrutiny applied to legislative means. Can a genuine means scrutiny "with bite" avoid the problems of value-laden adjudication?[7]

---

7. That question is pursued briefly in sec. 3 and more fully in the next chapter, on equal protection. Note the advocacy of a "rational means" scrutiny "with bite" in the context of equal protection in the Gunther article cited in footnote 5 above. See also chap. 10, sec. 1, below). That means-focused inquiry would have the Court "assess the means in terms of legislative purposes that have substantial basis in actuality, not merely in conjecture," and "it would have the Justices gauge the reasonableness of ques-

JUDICIAL SCRUTINY OF ECONOMIC REGULATIONS DURING THE LOCHNER ERA—SOME EXAMPLES

1. *Muller, Bunting, maximum hours, and the Brandeis brief.* a. MULLER v. OREGON, 208 U.S. 412 (1908), sustained an Oregon law of 1903 which provided that "no female" shall be employed in any factory or laundry "more than ten hours during any one day." The conviction of Muller, a laundry operator, was affirmed by the Supreme Court, "without questioning in any respect the decision" in Lochner. Justice Brewer's opinion emphasized that the liberty of contract "is not absolute," that it was obvious that "woman's physical structure" placed her "at a disadvantage in the struggle for subsistence," and that, "as healthy mothers are essential to vigorous offspring, the physical well-being of woman becomes an object of public interest." Moreover, "woman has always been dependent upon man." Legislation to protect women "seems necessary to secure a real equality of right"; goals and the stricter scrutiny applied to legislative means. Can a genuine necessary for men and could not be sustained." The "inherent difference between the two sexes" justified "a difference in legislation" and "upholds that which is designed to compensate for some of the burdens which rest upon her." (Cf. the sex discrimination materials in chap. 10, sec. 3C.)

b. At the beginning of the Muller opinion, the Court made these observations: "In patent cases counsel are apt to open the argument with a discussion of the state of the art. It may not be amiss, in the present case, before examining the constitutional question, to notice the course of legislation, as well as expressions of opinion from other than judicial sources. In the brief filed by Mr. Louis D. Brandeis for the defendant in error is a very copious collection of all these matters, an epitome of which is found in the margin. . . .

"The legislation and opinions referred to in the margin may not be, technically speaking, authorities, and in them is little or no discussion of the constitutional question presented to us for determination, yet they are significant of a widespread belief that woman's physical structure, and the functions she performs in consequence thereof, justify special legislation . . .. Constitutional questions, it is true, are not settled by even a consensus of present public opinion, for it is the peculiar value of a written constitution that it places in unchanging form limitations upon legislative action . . .. At the same time, when a question of fact is debated and debatable, and the extent to which a special constitutional limitation goes is affected by the truth in respect to that fact, a widespread and long continued belief concerning it is

tionable means on the basis of materials that are offered to the Court, rather than resorting to rationalizations created by perfunctory judicial hypothesizing." Though that article speaks of the equal protection context, the means-oriented analysis is relevant to due process as well: "In principle, the means-focused inquiry is as legitimate an ingredient of due process as of equal protection. . . . A narrower due process inquiry focusing on *means* and deferring to legislative ends might have been far less subject to the risks of legislative paralysis through dogmatically imposed judicial values. But preoccupation with the ghost of the old due process produced a judicial overreaction and continues to cast a shadow on due process scrutiny of means as well as ends. [Evolution of greater means-oriented scrutiny] is likely to fare better along the equal protection route than on the haunted paths of due process."

worthy of consideration. We take judicial cognizance of all matters of general knowledge."

c. Louis D. Brandeis, with the assistance of Felix Frankfurter, prepared a similar brief in the litigation which led to the decision in BUNTING v. OREGON, 243 U.S. 426 (1917). Brandeis was appointed to the Court before the argument, and Mr. Frankfurter submitted the brief. A divided Court—with Justice Brandeis not participating—sustained a law establishing a 10-hour day for manufacturing work, but permitting up to three hours overtime at a time-and-a-half rate. The conviction was for not paying the overtime rate in a flour mill. The Court did not mention the Lochner decision.*

2. *"Yellow dog" contracts, Coppage, and Adair.* a. The modern Court has referred to the discredited line of cases of the Lochner era as "the Allgeyer-Lochner-Adair-Coppage constitutional doctrine." The first two are noted above. Coppage and Adair involved laws protecting employees' rights to organize unions. In COPPAGE v. KANSAS, 236 U.S. 1 (1915), Coppage had been convicted under a Kansas law of 1903 directed against "yellow dog" contracts: it prohibited employers from requiring that employees agree as a condition of employment "not to join or become or remain a member of any labor organization." The Supreme Court, in an opinion by Justice Pitney, held the law unconstitutional under the due process clause: "Included in the right of personal liberty and the right of private property [is] the right to make contracts. [An] interference with this liberty so serious as that now under consideration, and so disturbing of equality of right, must be deemed to be arbitrary, unless it be supportable as a reasonable exercise of the police power of the State. . . . Conceding the full right of the individual to join the union, he has no inherent right to do this and still remain in the employ of one who is unwilling to employ a union man, any more than the same individual has a right to join the union without the consent of that organization. . . .

"[I]t is said by the [state court] to be a matter of common knowledge that 'employés, as a rule, are not financially able to be as independent in making contracts for the sale of their labor as are employers in making contracts of purchase thereof.' No doubt, wherever the right of private property exists, there must and will be inequalities of fortune; and thus it naturally happens that parties negotiating about a contract are not equally unhampered by circumstances. This applies to all contracts, and not merely to that between employer and employé. [I]t is from the nature of things impossible to uphold freedom of contract and the right of private property without at the same time recognizing as legitimate those inequalities of fortune that are the necessary result of the exercise of those rights. But the [14th Amendment] recognizes 'liberty' and 'property' as co-existent human rights, and debars the States from any unwarranted interference with either.

---

* Is the "Brandeis brief" technique as useful in attacking legislation as in sustaining it? See Freund, On Understanding the Supreme Court (1949), 86–91, and Karst, "Legislative Facts in Constitutional Litigation," 1960 Sup. Ct.Rev. 75. On the utility of the "Brandeis brief" and the presentation of "constitutional facts," see also Biklé, "Judicial Determination of Questions of Fact Affecting the Constitutional Validity of Legislative Action," 38 Harv.L.Rev. 6 (1924).

"And since a State may not strike them down directly it is clear that it may not do so indirectly, as by declaring in effect that the public good requires the removal of those inequalities that are but the normal and inevitable result of their exercise, and then invoking the police power in order to remove the inequalities, without other object in view."

Justice Day, joined by Justice Hughes, dissented. In another dissenting opinion, Justice Holmes stated: "In present conditions a workman not unnaturally may believe that only by belonging to a union can he secure a contract that shall be fair to him. . . . If that belief, whether right or wrong, may be held by a reasonable man, it seems to me that it may be enforced by law in order to establish the equality of position between the parties in which liberty of contract begins. Whether in the long run it is wise for the workingmen to enact legislation of this sort is not my concern, but I am strongly of opinion that there is nothing in the Constitution of the United States to prevent it . . .."

b. The Court in Coppage relied on ADAIR v. UNITED STATES, 208 U.S. 161 (1908), which had held unconstitutional, under the due process clause of the Fifth Amendment, a federal law against "yellow dog" contracts on interstate railroads. The opinion in Adair was written by Justice Harlan, one of the dissenters in Lochner. Justice Harlan stated that "it is not within the function of government [to] compel any person in the course of his business [to] retain the personal services of another . . .. The right of a person to sell his labor upon such terms as he deems proper [is] the same as the right of the purchaser of labor to prescribe the conditions. [T]he employer and the employé have equality of right, and any legislation that disturbs that equality is an arbitrary interference with the liberty of contract." What about the "disturbing of equality" in Muller v. Oregon, note 1 above, decided in the same year as Adair? Compare the Adkins case in 1923, note 3 below. Justices Holmes and McKenna dissented in Adair. Note the repudiation of Coppage and Adair, in the Lincoln Federal Labor Union case in 1949, sec. 1C below.

3. *Minimum wages and the Adkins case.* Though Bunting v. Oregon in 1917, note 1 above, had sustained regulation of *hours*—including a requirement of overtime wages—(and though Muller v. Oregon in 1908, also in note 1, had sustained regulation of women's working hours), the Court held in 1923 that the District of Columbia law prescribing minimum *wages* for women was unconstitutional under the due process clause of the Fifth Amendment. ADKINS v. CHILDREN'S HOSPITAL, 261 U.S. 525. Justice Sutherland emphasized that freedom of contract was "the general rule, and restraint the exception." Since Muller, he noted, the 19th Amendment had been adopted, and the civil inferiority of women was almost at a "vanishing point." Hence, the liberty of contract could not be subjected to greater restriction in the case of women than of men. The chief objection was that the law compelled payment of wages without regard to the employment contract, the business involved, or the work done: this was "a naked, arbitrary exercise" of legislative power. Chief Justice Taft and Justice Sanford dissented; Justice Brandeis did not participate.

In another dissent, Justice Holmes stated: "I confess that I do not understand the principle on which the power to fix a minimum for the wages

of women can be denied by those who admit the power to fix a maximum for their hours of work. . . . The bargain is equally affected whichever half you regulate. . . . It will need more than the Nineteenth Amendment to convince me that there are no differences between men and women, or that legislation cannot take those differences into account."

Was the 19th Amendment sufficient to explain the difference between Muller and Adkins? Or was regulation of hours more acceptable than regulation of wages because (despite the Lochner result) control of the hours worked could be seen as promoting health, a legitimate legislative end, while control of wages paid looked more like redressing inequalities in bargaining power in the market, a generally impermissible objective? Does that laissez faire attitude toward "equalizing" legislation even more clearly explain the majority's hostility to price regulations, in the next note? [The Adkins decision was adhered to in the Morehead case in 1936, but was overruled in the West Coast Hotel case in 1937. See sec. 1C below.]

4. *Price regulations.* The Court of the Lochner era imposed a variety of restraints on laws that interfered with the free market by controlling prices. The noninterventionist decision of the 1870's, in Munn v. Illinois (sec. 1A above), was read narrowly: the rate regulation authority there recognized, it was emphasized, was limited to businesses "affected with a public interest." Thus, public utility rate regulation was permitted, but the Court reviewed the substantive reasonableness of the rates. And in the areas of the economy not deemed to be "affected with a public interest," price regulations were barred altogether. The Court stated the general rule applied during this period to price (as well as wage) regulations as follows: "[A] state legislature is without constitutional power to fix prices at which commodities may be sold, services rendered, or property used, unless the business or property involved is 'affected with a public interest.' " Williams v. Standard Oil Co., 278 U.S. 235 (1929). Compare the more generous attitude toward price regulation in Nebbia v. New York, 291 U.S. 502 (1934), which follows. The Williams case involved gasoline prices; see also Tyson & Brother v. Banton, 273 U.S. 418 (1927) (resale price of theatre tickets); Ribnik v. McBride, 277 U.S. 350 (1928) (employment agency fees). [The Tyson decision was explicitly overruled (in a per curiam decision, without argument) in Gold v. DiCarlo, 380 U.S. 520 (1965). Ribnik had been overruled earlier, in Olsen v. Nebraska, 313 U.S. 236 (1941) (sec. 1C below).]

5. *Restrictions on business entry and other economic regulations.* a. *Business entry.* In a number of cases, the Court invalidated restraints on competition that curtailed entry into a particular line of business. For example, in NEW STATE ICE CO. v. LIEBMANN, 285 U.S. 262 (1932), the Court invalidated an Oklahoma law which treated the manufacture of ice like a public utility, requiring a certificate of convenience and necessity as a prerequisite to entry into the business. Under the scheme, a state agency had to find that existing facilities were not "sufficient to meet the public needs" before issuing new certificates. See also ADAMS v. TANNER, 244 U.S. 590 (1917), striking down a law prohibiting employment agencies from collecting fees from workers. The majority called that law an "arbitrary and oppressive" ban on a "useful business." Justice Brandeis

submitted extensive, data-laden dissents in both cases to demonstrate why reasonable legislators might think the restraints necessary. Note, moreover, Liggett Co. v. Baldridge, 278 U.S. 105 (1928), invalidating a law barring corporate ownership of pharmacies unless all stockholders were pharmacists. Decisions such as these have been undermined if not explicitly overruled by the developments since the 1930's. [See sec. 1C below and, e. g., North Dakota Bd. of Pharmacy v. Snyder's Drug Stores, 414 U.S. 156 (1973), reversing a state court decision relying on Liggett in invalidating a similar law. Justice Douglas stated for a unanimous Court that Liggett "belongs to that vintage of decisions which exalted substantive due process by striking down state legislation which a majority of the Court deemed unwise. . . . The Liggett case, being a derelict in the stream of the law, is hereby overruled."]

b. *Scrutiny of means.* Nevertheless, the police power proved broad enough during the Lochner era to justify a range of restraints on business practices that might defraud consumers or injure their health. When cases of that variety were invalidated, the Court criticized the means rather than the ends of the legislation. A good example is WEAVER v. PALMER BROS. CO., 270 U.S. 402 (1926). There, the majority invalidated a total prohibition of the use, in the manufacture of bedding materials such as mattresses and quilts, of shoddy (cut up or torn up fabrics). Other secondhand materials could be used so long as they were sterilized and the finished product carried a label showing the materials used. The Court found the absolute prohibition of shoddy "purely arbitrary": protection of health and against consumer deception did not justify so drastic a remedy. As to health, the Court emphasized that the parties had agreed that "shoddy may be rendered harmless by disinfection or sterilization," even where the shoddy had been made from "filthy rags." As to public deception, the Court noted the tagging and inspection requirements applicable to other bedding and stated: "Obviously, these regulations or others that are adequate may be effectively applied to shoddy-filled articles." Justice Holmes' dissent, joined by Justices Brandeis and Stone, argued that the lawmakers "may have been of opinion" that "the actual practice of filling comfortables with unsterilized shoddy gathered from filthy floors was wide spread"—an opinion "we must assume to be true." Moreover, it was impossible "to distinguish the innocent from the infected [final] product in any practicable way." Thus, the total ban was justifiable for health reasons, for the legislature might have "regarded the danger as very great and inspection and tagging as inadequate remedies."

See also JAY BURNS BAKING CO. v. BRYAN, 264 U.S. 504 (1924), invalidating a law requiring standardized weights for loaves of bread. The majority noted that the law in effect made it impossible to sell bread without wrappers, even though there was "a strong demand by consumers" for unwrapped bread. (Sale of unwrapped bread was not feasible under the law because of the difficulty of controlling evaporation from unwrapped bread.) The majority found the restrictions "essentially unreasonable and arbitrary," because they were "not necessary for the protection of purchasers against imposition and fraud by short weights" and "not calculated to effectuate that purpose." The problem of "short weights," the Court noted, "readily could have been dealt with in a direct and effective

way." Justice Brandeis' dissent, joined by Justice Holmes, contained another extensive summary of data largely based on judicial notice, to show the reasonableness of the legislation—particularly to show why "legislators, bent only on preventing short weights, prohibit, also, excessive weights." He insisted that the majority's views of the reasonableness and necessity of the legislation was "an exercise of the powers of a super-legislature."

Would a means-oriented inquiry be appropriate in the shoddy and bread cases under the principles of the more recent decisions, below? Would there be any scrutiny of the means in fact by the modern Court, in view of the summary manner the Court has applied those principles? Should there be? Is the degree of scrutiny exercised by the majority in the shoddy and bread cases more intense than is justified by the statements of the "mere reasonableness" standard? Is it similar to the "less restrictive alternatives" analysis of the Dean Milk case, chap. 5, sec. 1C, above? † Is concern with alternatives appropriate when there is no claim of impingement on a specially cherished constitutional value? If the majority's scrutiny is too strict for a "mere reasonableness" standard, is Justice Brandeis's scrutiny too deferential? Should it be enough to speculate, partly on the basis of judicial notice, about the opinions legislators *might* have had regarding the contributions of the means to the end? Or should there be some requirement that the defenders of the law present data to the Court—data which explain the way in which the means contribute to the achievement of the end? (Note Justice Brandeis' comment near the end of his long dissent in the bread case: "Much evidence referred to by me is not in the record." He added, however, that evidence in the record was "ample to sustain the validity of the statute." And he emphasized that the central question was "whether the provision as applied is so clearly arbitrary or capricious that legislators acting reasonably could not have believed it to be necessary or appropriate for the public welfare.")

C. THE MODERN ERA: THE DECLINE—AND DISAPPEARANCE?—OF JUDICIAL SCRUTINY OF ECONOMIC REGULATION

NEBBIA v. NEW YORK

291 U.S. 502, 54 S.Ct. 505, 78 L.Ed. 940 (1934).

Appeal from the County Court of Monroe County, New York.

Mr. Justice ROBERTS delivered the opinion of the Court.

The Legislature of New York established [in 1933] a Milk Control Board with power . . . to "fix minimum and maximum . . . retail prices to be charged by . . . stores to consumers for consumption off the premises where sold." The Board fixed nine cents as the price to be charged by a store for a quart of milk. Nebbia, the proprietor of a grocery store in Rochester, sold two quarts and a five cent loaf of bread for eighteen

† Compare Struve, "The Less-Restrictive-Alternative Principle and Economic Due Process," 80 Harv.L.Rev. 1463 (1967).

cents; and was convicted for violating the Board's order. . . . The question for decision is whether the Federal Constitution prohibits a state from so fixing the selling price of milk. We first inquire as to the occasion for the legislation and its history.

During 1932 the prices received by farmers for milk were much below the cost of production. . . . The situation of the families of dairy producers had become desperate and called for state aid similar to that afforded the unemployed, if conditions should not improve.

[The Court summarized the conclusions reached after an extensive study by a legislative committee:] Milk is an essential item of diet. . . . Failure of producers to receive a reasonable return [threatens] a relaxation of vigilance against contamination. The production and distribution of milk is a paramount industry of the state, and largely affects the health and prosperity of its people. . . . The fluid milk industry is affected by factors of [price] instability peculiar to itself which call for special methods of control. . . .

The legislature adopted [this law] as a method of correcting the evils, which the report of the committee showed could not be expected to right themselves through the ordinary play of the forces of supply and demand, owing to the peculiar and uncontrollable factors affecting the industry. [The Court then turned to the due process objection:]

Under our form of government the use of property and the making of contracts are normally matters of private and not a public concern. The general rule is that both shall be free of governmental interference. But neither property rights nor contract rights are absolute; for government cannot exist if the citizen may at will use his property to the detriment of his fellows, or exercise his freedom of contract to work them harm. Equally fundamental with the private right is that of the public to regulate it in the common interest. . . .

[The 5th and 14th Amendments] do not prohibit governmental regulation for the public welfare. They merely condition the exertion of the admitted power, by securing that the end shall be accomplished by methods consistent with due process. And the guaranty of due process, as has often been held, demands only that the law shall not be unreasonable, arbitrary or capricious, and that the means selected shall have a real and substantial relation to the object sought to be attained. It results that a regulation valid for one sort of business, or in given circumstances, may be invalid for another sort, or for the same business under other circumstances, because the reasonableness of each regulation depends upon the relevant fact. [The Court reviewed cases sustaining regulations against due process attacks—including laws "concerning sales of goods, and incidentally affecting prices."]

The legislative investigation of 1932 was persuasive of the fact [that] unrestricted competition aggravated existing evils, and the normal law of supply and demand was insufficient to correct maladjustments detrimental to the community. The inquiry disclosed destructive and demoralizing competitive conditions and unfair trade practices which resulted in retail price cutting and reduced the income of the farmer below the cost of production. [The legislature] believed conditions could be improved by preventing destructive pricecutting by stores which, due to the flood of surplus milk, were able to buy

at much lower prices than the larger distributors and to sell without incurring the delivery costs of the latter. . . .

But we are told that because the law essays to control prices it denies due process. Notwithstanding the admitted power to correct existing economic ills by appropriate regulation of business, [the] appellant urges that the direct fixation of prices is a type of regulation absolutely forbidden. . . . The argument runs that the public control of rates or prices is per se unreasonable and unconstitutional, save as applied to business affected with a public interest; that a business so affected is [one] such as is commonly called a public utility; or a business in its nature a monopoly. The milk industry, it is said, possesses none of these characteristics. . . .

[The Court conceded that the dairy industry was not, "in the accepted sense of the phrase, a public utility," nor a "monopoly."] But if, as must be conceded, the industry is subject to regulation in the public interest, what constitutional principle bars the state from correcting existing maladjustments by legislation touching prices? We think there is no such principle. The due process clause makes no mention of sales or of prices any more than it speaks of business or contracts or buildings or other incidents of property. The thought seems nevertheless to have persisted that there is something peculiarly sacrosanct about the price one may charge for what he makes or sells, and that, however able to regulate other elements of manufacture or trade, with incidental effect upon price, the state is incapable of directly controlling the price itself. This view was negatived many years ago. Munn v. Illinois, 94 U.S. 113 [1877; sec. 1A above]. [Appellant claims that this Court there] limited permissible [price regulation] to businesses affected with a public interest [—primarily, public utilities or monopolies]. But this is a misconception. [The Court in Munn] concluded the circumstances justified the legislation as an exercise of the governmental right to control the business in the public interest; that is, as an exercise of the police power. It is true that the court [in Munn] cited a statement from Lord Hale's De Portibus Maris, to the effect that when private property is "affected with a public interest, it ceases to be juris privati only"; but the court proceeded at once to define what it understood by the expression, saying: "Property does become clothed with a public interest when used in a manner to make it of public consequence, and affect the community at large." Thus understood, "affected with a public interest" is the equivalent of "subject to the exercise of the police power" . . . .

It is clear that there is no closed class or category of businesses affected with a public interest, and the function of courts in the application of the Fifth and Fourteenth Amendments is to determine in each case whether circumstances vindicate the challenged regulation as a reasonable exertion of governmental authority or condemn it as arbitrary or discriminatory. . . . The phrase "affected with a public interest" can, in the nature of things, mean no more than that an industry, for adequate reason, is subject to control for the public good. [T]here can be no doubt that upon proper occasion and by appropriate measures the state may regulate a business in any of its aspects, including the prices to be charged for the products or commodities it sells.

So far as the requirement of due process is concerned, and in the absence of other constitutional restriction, a state is free to adopt whatever economic

policy may reasonably be deemed to promote public welfare, and to enforce that policy by legislation adapted to its purpose. The courts are without authority either to declare such policy, or, when it is declared by the legislature, to override it. If the laws passed are seen to have a reasonable relation to a proper legislative purpose, and are neither arbitrary nor discriminatory, the requirements of due process are satisfied, and judicial determination to that effect renders a court functus officio. . . . And it is equally clear that if the legislative policy be to curb unrestrained and harmful competition by measures which are not arbitrary or discriminatory it does not lie with the courts to determine that the rule is unwise. With the wisdom of the policy adopted, with the adequacy or practicability of the law enacted to forward it, the courts are both incompetent and unauthorized to deal. . . . Times without number we have said that the legislature is primarily the judge of the necessity of such an enactment, that every possible presumption is in favor of its validity, and that though the court may hold views inconsistent with the wisdom of the law, it may not be annulled unless palpably in excess of legislative power. . . . Price control, like any other form of regulation, is unconstitutional only if arbitrary, discriminatory, or demonstrably irrelevant to the policy the legislature is free to adopt, and hence an unnecessary and unwarranted interference with individual liberty.

Tested by these considerations we find no basis in the due process clause of the Fourteenth Amendment for condemning the provisions of the Agriculture and Markets Law here drawn into question. [Recall the upholding of a commerce clause challenge to an application of the law a year after Nebbia, in Baldwin v. Seelig, chap. 5, sec. 1C, above.]

[Affirmed.]

Separate opinion of Mr. Justice McREYNOLDS [dissenting]. . . .

Regulation to prevent recognized evils in business has long been upheld as permissible legislative action. But fixation of the price at which "A," engaged in an ordinary business, may sell, in order to enable "B," a producer, to improve his condition, has not been regarded as within legislative power. This is not regulation, but management, control, dictation—it amounts to the deprivation of the fundamental right which one has to conduct his own affairs honestly and along customary lines. This Court has declared that [a] State may not by legislative fiat convert a private business into a public utility. . . .

[P]lainly, I think, this Court must have regard to the wisdom of the enactment. At least, we must inquire concerning its purpose and decide whether the means proposed have reasonable relation to something within legislative power—whether the end is legitimate, and the means appropriate. . . . Here, we find direct interference with guaranteed rights defended upon the ground that the purpose was to promote the public welfare by increasing milk prices at the farm. . . .

The court below has not definitely affirmed this necessary relation; it has not attempted to indicate how higher charges at stores to impoverished customers when the output is excessive and sale prices of producers are unrestrained, can possibly increase receipts at the farm. The Legislative Committee pointed out as the obvious cause of decreased consumption notwith-

standing low prices, the consumers' reduced buying power. Higher store prices will not enlarge this power; nor will they decrease production. . . . It is not true as stated that "the State seeks to protect the producer by fixing a minimum price for his milk." She carefully refrained from doing this; but did undertake to fix the price after the milk had passed to other owners. Assuming that the views and facts reported by the Legislative Committee are correct, it appears to me wholly unreasonable to expect this legislation to accomplish the proposed end—increase of prices at the farm. . . . Not only does the statute interfere arbitrarily with the rights of the little grocer to conduct his business according to standards long accepted . . . ; but it takes away the liberty of twelve million consumers to buy a necessity of life in an open market. . . .

Mr. Justice VAN DEVANTER, Mr. Justice SUTHERLAND and Mr. Justice BUTLER authorize me to say that they concur in this opinion.*

WEST COAST HOTEL CO. v. PARRISH

300 U.S. 379, 57 S.Ct. 578, 81 L.Ed. 703 (1937).

Appeal from the Supreme Court of Washington.

Mr. Chief Justice HUGHES delivered the opinion of the Court.

This case presents the question of the constitutional validity of the minimum wage law [for women] of the State of Washington. . . .

The appellant conducts a hotel. The appellee Elsie Parrish was employed as a chambermaid [and sued to recover her minimum wage, which was] $14.50 per week of 48 hours. . . . [Appellant's due process attack relied on the Adkins decision in 1923, sec. 1B above.]

[T]he violation [of due process] alleged by those attacking minimum wage regulation for women is deprivation of freedom of contract. What is this freedom? The Constitution does not speak of freedom of contract. It speaks of liberty and prohibits the deprivation of liberty without due process of law. In prohibiting that deprivation the Constitution does not recognize an absolute and uncontrollable liberty. [T]he liberty safeguarded is liberty in a social organization which requires the protection of law against the evils which menace the health, safety, morals and welfare of the people. Liberty under the Constitution is thus necessarily subject to the restraints of due process, and regulation which is reasonable in relation to its subject and is adopted in the interests of the community is due process. This essential limitation of liberty in general governs freedom of contract in particular. [The Court reviewed decisions sustaining restrictions on freedom of contract, including "contracts between employer and employee."]

We think that [the Adkins decision] was a departure from the true application of the principles governing the regulation by the State of the

---

relation of employer and employed. . . . What can be closer to the public interest than the health of women and their protection from unscrupulous and overreaching employers? And if the protection of women is a legitimate end of the exercise of state power, how can it be said that the requirement of the payment of a minimum wage fairly fixed in order to meet the very necessities of existence is not an admissible means to that end? The legislature of the State was clearly entitled to consider the situation of women in employment, the fact that they are in the class receiving the least pay, that their bargaining power is relatively weak, and that they are the ready victims of those who would take advantage of their necessitous circumstances. The legislature was entitled to adopt measures to reduce the evils of the "sweating system," the exploiting of workers at wages so low as to be insufficient to meet the bare cost of living, thus making their very helplessness the occasion of a most injurious competition. The legislature had the right to consider that its minimum wage requirements would be an important aid in carrying out its policy of protection. The adoption of similar requirements by many States evidences a deep-seated conviction both as to the presence of the evil and as to the means adapted to check it. Legislative response to that conviction cannot be regarded as arbitrary or capricious, and that is all we have to decide. . . .

There is an additional and compelling consideration which recent economic experience has brought into a strong light. The exploitation of a class of workers who are in an unequal position with respect to bargaining power and are thus relatively defenceless against the denial of a living wage is not only detrimental to their health and well being but casts a direct burden for their support upon the community. What these workers lose in wages the taxpayers are called upon to pay. The bare cost of living must be met. We may take judicial notice of the unparalleled demands for relief which arose during the recent period of depression and still continue to an alarming extent despite the degree of economic recovery which has been achieved. It is unnecessary to cite official statistics to establish what is of common knowledge through the length and breadth of the land. While in the instant case no factual brief has been presented, there is no reason to doubt that the State of Washington has encountered the same social problem that is present elsewhere. The community is not bound to provide what is in effect a subsidy for unconscionable employers. The community may direct its law-making power to correct the abuse which springs from their selfish disregard of the public interest. . . .

Our conclusion is that the case of Adkins v. Children's Hospital, supra, should be, and it is, overruled.

Affirmed.

Mr. Justice SUTHERLAND.—Mr. Justice VAN DEVANTER, Mr. Justice McREYNOLDS, Mr. Justice BUTLER and I think the judgment of the court below should be reversed.

[T]he meaning of the Constitution does not change with the ebb and flow of economic events. . . . Neither the statute involved in the Adkins case nor the Washington statute . . . has the slightest relation to the capacity or earning power of the employee, to the number of hours which constitute the day's work, the character of the place where the work is to be done, or the circumstances or surroundings of the employment. The sole basis upon which the question of validity rests is the assumption that the employee is

entitled to receive a sum of money sufficient to provide a living for her, keep her in health and preserve her morals. [What we said in Adkins] is equally applicable here:

"The law takes account of the necessities of only one party to the contract. It ignores the necessities of the employer by compelling him to pay not less than a certain sum, not only whether the employee is capable of earning it, but irrespective of the ability of his business to sustain the burden . . .. To the extent that the sum fixed exceeds the fair value of the services rendered, it amounts to a compulsory exaction from the employer for the support of a partially indigent person, for whose condition there rests upon him no peculiar responsibility, and therefore . . . arbitrarily shifts to his shoulders a burden which, if it belongs to anybody, belongs to society as a whole." . . .

THE IMPACT OF NEBBIA AND WEST COAST HOTEL

1. *The standards of the mid-1930's.* The Nebbia and West Coast decisions obviously marked a significant shift from the Lochner era: they curtailed judicial intervention in economic regulation. But in what way did they reduce judicial intervention, and how far? Do the later decisions, which follow, simply apply the Nebbia and West Coast Hotel approaches? Or do they carry the rejection of the Lochner philosophy even further, to an even greater "hands off" position? Nebbia and West Coast Hotel obviously mark a sharp retreat from the Lochner era's restrictive attitude toward permissible legislative ends. Price control is no longer limited to the narrow category of businesses "affected with a public interest"; wage control for women is authorized, with an explicit endorsement not only of the health objective but also the objective of redressing "unequal position with respect to bargaining power."

Is there a similarly great retreat with respect to scrutiny of means-ends relationships? Note that Nebbia insists that the means must have "a real and substantial relation to the object sought to be attained." And note that both majority opinions contain elaborate explanations of the background and rationales for the laws sustained. Compare the curt statements (or assumptions) about legislative justifications in the later decisions which follow. Were the justifications in those later cases so obvious, the "real and substantial" relations between means and ends so evident, so that no more detailed statements were needed in the later cases? For example, was the Day-Brite case (printed below) so similar to plainly valid regulations of working conditions as to warrant so brief a judicial examination?* In Day-

* Note also United States v. Darby, 312 U.S. 100 (1941), sustaining the Fair Labor Standards Act of 1938, and considered earlier with respect to the commerce power challenge (chap. 3, sec. 5, above). Justice Stone's rejection of a due process attack on wage and hour laws (for men as well as women) was very brief indeed. He cited West Coast Hotel as justifying minimum wage laws. And he added: "Similarly the statute is not objectionable because applied alike to both men and women." Recall the rationale of West Coast Hotel: Was no greater justification warranted for the extension of such laws to men as well? Or does Justice Stone's summary rejection of the due process claim suggest abdication rather than limitation of judicial intervention?

Brite, the Court stated: "We could strike down this law only if we returned to the philosophy of the Lochner, Coppage and Adkins cases." Was there truly no middle ground? Or was greater scrutiny in some of the later cases possible (and desirable) without risking the central evils of the excessive judicial intervention of the Lochner era? (See also the later questions in this section.)

2. *The context of Nebbia and West Coast Hotel.* Note that Nebbia's deference to the legislature came in 1934, just before the Supreme Court rendered its major decisions striking down a variety of New Deal laws as exceeding national powers, just before Schechter in 1935 and Carter and Butler in 1936. (See chaps. 3 and 4 above.) And the course with respect to due process restraints, from Nebbia to West Coast Hotel, was not smooth: Court critics thought that due process restraints, too, were hardening when —two years after Nebbia—the Court adhered to the Adkins decision in Morehead v. New York ex rel. Tipaldo, 298 U.S. 587 (1936), invalidating New York's minimum wage law for women. A few months after Morehead, President Roosevelt announced his Court-Packing Plan; and while that controversy was raging, West Coast Hotel came down. Justice Roberts was with the majority in each case.

Some have viewed Justice Roberts' West Coast Hotel vote as "the switch in time that saved the Nine" from the Court-Packing Plan that failed in the Senate soon after. But recall Justice Roberts' own explanation of his votes in Morehead and West Coast Hotel, in a memorandum left with Justice Frankfurter and noted in chap. 3, sec. 4, above. Justice Roberts made clear that the Court's conference vote in West Coast Hotel came weeks before the Court-Packing Plan was announced, so that he was not responding directly to that threat. Moreover, he claimed that his Morehead vote to adhere to Adkins rested on the fact that the Court in Morehead, unlike West Coast Hotel, was not explicitly asked to overrule Adkins. Chief Justice Hughes gave a similar explanation in his majority opinion in West Coast Hotel: he stated that the Morehead decision rested on the fact that the Court "considered that the only question before it was whether the Adkins case was distinguishable and that reconsideration of that decision had not been sought." He went on to say in West Coast Hotel: "We think that the question which was not deemed to be open in the Morehead case is open and is necessarily presented here"; and the overruling of Adkins followed. It is nevertheless clear that constitutional doctrine changed significantly beginning in 1937. But pinpointing that shift as of the time of the Court-Packing Plan is easiest with respect to national powers doctrines; with respect to due process, West Coast Hotel is certainly of a deferential piece with the pre-Court-Packing decision in 1934 (written by Justice Roberts) in the Nebbia case.

THE MODERN ERA: REDUCED JUDICIAL SCRUTINY OR ABDICATION?

Justice Roberts' opinion in Nebbia suggested a continuing, though reduced, judicial role in scrutinizing the means employed in economic regulations challenged under the due process clause—both in its announced standard that "the means selected shall have a real and substantial relation to the object sought to be attained" and in its detailed examination of the background of the legislation. Have the due process decisions since the mid-1930's reduced the judicial role even further? Have they, in formulation or in exercise, eliminated it altogether?

1. *Economic regulation and the Carolene Products case.* In 1938, in UNITED STATES v. CAROLENE PRODUCTS CO., 304 U.S. 144, the Court rejected a Fifth Amendment due process challenge to a federal prohibition of the interstate shipment of "filled milk"—skimmed milk mixed with non-milk fats. (The attack on the statute was on its face—on its purported broad reach—rather than on the prohibition as applied to particular circumstances.) Justice Stone's majority opinion stated: "We may assume for present purposes [that] a statute would deny due process which precluded the disproof in judicial proceedings of all facts which would show or tend to show that a statute depriving the suitor of life, liberty, or property had a rational basis." Here, the congressional declarations that filled milk was injurious to health and a fraud upon the public did not bar such "disproof"; but challenging the "rational basis" of economic legislation, he made clear, would be a difficult task. The legislative findings, like reports of legislative committees, were simply aids to "informed judicial review," "by revealing the rationale of the legislation." But they were not essential: "Even in the absence of such aids, the existence of facts supporting the legislative judgment is to be presumed, for regulatory legislation affecting ordinary commercial transactions is not to be pronounced unconstitutional unless in the light of the facts made known or generally assumed it is of such a character as to preclude the assumption that it rests upon some rational basis within the knowledge and experience of the legislators." † Justice Stone added:

"Where the existence of a rational basis for legislation whose constitutionality is attacked depends upon facts beyond the sphere of judicial notice, such facts may properly be made the subject of judicial inquiry, and the constitutionality of a statute predicated upon the existence of a particular state of facts may be challenged by showing to the court that those facts have ceased to exist. Similarly we recognize that the constitutionality of a statute, valid on its face, may be assailed by proof of facts tending to

† At this point, Justice Stone added his famous footnote 4, suggesting that there may be a stronger case for judicial intervention—a "narrower scope for operation of the presumption of constitutionality"—in regulations of matters other than "commercial transactions." That footnote 4 has been widely relied on to explain the Court's growing interventionism regarding "legislation which restricts . . . political processes," even while it has retreated from review of economic regulation. The Carolene Products footnote is printed at p. 592 below. And the question whether that footnote adequately justifies the "double standard" of judicial review recurs frequently throughout the rest of these materials.

show that the statute as applied to a particular article is without support in reason because the article, although within the prohibited class, is so different from others of the class as to be without the reason for the prohibition, though the effect of such proof depends on the relevant circumstances of each case, as for example the administrative difficulty of excluding the article from the regulated class. But by their very nature such inquiries, where the legislative judgment is drawn in question, must be restricted to the issue whether any state of facts either known or which could reasonably be assumed, affords support for it. Here the demurrer challenges the validity of the statute on its face and it is evident from all the considerations presented to Congress, and those of which we may take judicial notice, that the question is at least debatable whether commerce in filled milk should be left unregulated, or in some measure restricted, or wholly prohibited.''

2. *Total withdrawal from review?* Carolene Products indicated some continued willingness to consider the ''rational basis'' of economic legislation. The cases in this note—and Day-Brite, which follows—disclose the Court rejecting due process attacks even more summarily. Do these ''hands off'' decisions indicate an even greater withdrawal from judicial scrutiny than that suggested by the standards of the 1930's decisions? Or are these cases explainable on the ground that their central concerns were the legitimacy of legislative objectives, not the reasonableness of the means? Is a somewhat greater scrutiny suggested by the 1955 decision in Williamson v. Lee Optical Co., printed below?

a. *Olsen v. Nebraska.* An early example of the extreme ''hands off'' attitude was OLSEN v. NEBRASKA, 313 U.S. 236 (1941), where the state courts had held unconstitutional a law fixing maximum employment agency fees, in reliance on the 1928 decision in Ribnik v. McBride (sec. 1B above). The Supreme Court unanimously reversed, in an opinion by Justice Douglas: ''We are not concerned [with] the wisdom, need, or appropriateness of the legislation. . . . There is no necessity for the state to demonstrate before us that evils persist despite the competition which attends the bargaining in this field. In final analysis, the only constitutional prohibitions or restraints which respondents have suggested for the invalidation of this legislation are those notions of public policy embedded in earlier decision of this Court but which, as Mr. Justice Holmes long admonished, should not be read into the Constitution. . . . Since they do not find expression in the Constitution, we cannot give them continuing validity as standards by which the constitutionality of the economic and social programs of the states is to be determined.'' [See also the summary rejection of the due process challenge to minimum wage laws for men as well as women, in United States v. Darby, noted above.]

b. *The Lincoln Federal Labor Union case.* In LINCOLN FEDERAL LABOR UNION v. NORTHWESTERN IRON & METAL CO., 335 U.S. 525 (1949), the Court was again unanimous in sustaining state ''right to work'' laws requiring that employment decisions not be based on union membership. Justice Black's opinion recalled the Lochner era, when the Adair and Coppage decisions had struck down pro-union laws banning ''yellow-dog contracts,'' and emphasized the change in doctrine since then. The ''Allgeyer-Lochner-Adair-Coppage constitutional doctrine'' had been reject-

ed; ever since Nebbia, the Court had "steadily rejected the due process philosophy enunciated in the Adair-Coppage line of cases." He added: "In doing so it has consciously returned closer and closer to the earlier constitutional principle that states have power to legislate against what are found to be injurious practices in their internal commercial and business affairs, so long as their laws do not run afoul of some specific federal constitutional prohibition, or of some valid federal law." He rejected a return "to the due process philosophy that has been deliberately discarded" and concluded: "Just as we have held that the due process clause erects no obstacle to block legislative protection of union members, we now hold that legislative protection can be afforded non-union workers."

c. *Ferguson v. Skrupa.* A more recent example of broad deference to legislative judgments is FERGUSON v. SKRUPA, 372 U.S. 726 (1963), sustaining a Kansas law prohibiting anyone from engaging "in the business of debt adjusting" except as an incident to "the lawful practice of law." Justice Black's opinion concluded that Kansas "was free to decide for itself that legislation was needed to deal with the business of debt adjusting." He reiterated that the Court had abandoned "the use of the 'vague contours' of the Due Process Clause to nullify laws which a majority of the Court believed to be economically unwise." And he added: "Unquestionably, there are arguments showing that the business of debt adjusting has social utility, but such arguments are properly addressed to the legislature, not to us. We refuse to sit as a 'super legislature to weigh the wisdom of legislation' . . . . Whether the legislature takes for its textbook Adam Smith, Herbert Spencer, Lord Keynes or some other is no concern of ours."

Justice Harlan concurred in a brief separate notation, "on the ground that this state measure bears a rational relation to a constitutionally permissible objective. See Williamson v. Lee Optical Co. [below]." What is the significance of Justice Harlan's separate notation? Does his "rational relation" standard indicate greater judicial scrutiny than Justice Black's approach? Recall Justice Black's statement in the Lincoln case above, rejecting any judicial intervention in "commercial and business" regulation so long as state laws "do not run afoul of some specific federal constitutional prohibition." Does that indicate the total inapplicability of due process in that area? Has the majority of the Court committed itself to so complete a withdrawal from review? Or does the Lee Optical case, cited in Justice Harlan's concurrence, suggest that some judicial scrutiny remains? Does the variety of scrutiny exercised in Lee Optical, below, have any teeth in fact, or is it the functional equivalent of total withdrawal, with only lip service to a judicially enforceable "rational relation" standard as to scrutiny of means? Is the "rational relation" approach of Lee Optical more deferential than the "real and substantial relation" requirement of Nebbia? Is Justice Black correct in suggesting that there is no constitutional basis for requiring more of legislatures than compliance with specific constitutional prohibitions? (See Linde, "Without 'Due Process' . . . .," 49 Ore.L. Rev. 125 (1970).) Or can the due process clause properly be read to impose a judicially enforceable requirement that legislatures have some reason for impinging on economic interests? May the Court legitimately demand some showing of the "real and substantial" relation between means and

ends?   Are courts competent to exercise means scrutiny?   Was adequate scrutiny exercised in the two additional examples of modern due process cases which follow? *

DAY-BRITE LIGHTING, INC. v. MISSOURI

342 U.S. 421, 72 S.Ct. 405, 96 L.Ed. 469 (1952).

Appeal from the Supreme Court of Missouri.

Mr. Justice DOUGLAS delivered the opinion of the Court.

Missouri has a statute,   . . .   first enacted in 1897, which was designed to end the coercion of employees by employers in the exercise of the franchise.   It provides that an employee may absent himself from his employment for four hours between the opening and closing of the polls without penalty, and that any employer who among other things deducts wages for that absence is guilty of a misdemeanor.

. . .   November 5, 1946, was a day for general elections in Missouri, the polls being open from 6 A.M. to 7 P.M.   One Grotemeyer, an employee of appellant, was on a shift that worked from 8 A.M. to 4:30 P.M. each day, with thirty minutes for lunch.   His rate of pay was $1.60 an hour.   He requested four hours from the scheduled work day to vote on November 5, 1946.   That request was refused; but Grotemeyer and all other employees on his shift were allowed to leave at 3 P.M. that day, which gave them four consecutive hours to vote before the polls closed.

Grotemeyer left his work at 3 P.M. in order to vote and did not return to work that day.   He was not paid for the hour and a half between 3 P.M. and 4:30 P.M.   Appellant was found guilty and fined for penalizing Grotemeyer in violation of the statute.   [The state courts rejected due process and equal protection challenges.]

The liberty of contract argument pressed on us is reminiscent of the philosophy of [Lochner, Coppage, and Adkins] and others of that vintage.   Our recent decisions make plain that we do not sit as a super-legislature to weigh the wisdom of legislation.   [T]he state legislatures have constitutional authority to experiment with new techniques; [they] may within extremely broad limits control practices in the business-labor field . . . .

[West Coast Hotel] held constitutional a state law fixing minimum wages for women.   The present statute contains in form a minimum wage requirement.   There is a difference in the purpose of the legislation.   Here it is not the protection of the health and morals of the citizen.   Missouri by this legislation has sought to safeguard the right of suffrage by taking from employers the incentive and power to use their leverage over employees to influence the vote.   But the police power is not confined to a narrow category . . . .   The protection of the right of suffrage under our scheme of things is basic and fundamental.

---

* These cases, like many challenges to economic regulation, involved equal protection as well as due process claims.   In the equal protection area, there has been a withdrawal from scrutiny generally parallel to that under due process.   The equal protection developments are pursued in the next chapter.

The only semblance of substance in the constitutional objection to Missouri's law is that the employer must pay wages for a period in which the employee performs no services. . . . Most regulations of business necessarily impose financial burdens on the enterprise for which no compensation is paid. Those are part of the costs of our civilization. Extreme cases are conjured up where an employer is required to pay wages for a period that has no relation to the legitimate end. Those cases can await decision as and when they arise. The present law has no such infirmity. It is designed to eliminate any penalty for exercising the right of suffrage and to remove a practical obstacle to getting out the vote. The public welfare is a broad and inclusive concept. . . . The judgment of the legislature that time out for voting should cost the employee nothing may be a debatable one. . . . But if our recent cases mean anything, they leave debatable issues as respects business, economic, and social affairs to legislative decision. We could strike down this law only if we returned to the philosophy of the Lochner, Coppage, and Adkins cases. . . .

Affirmed.

Mr. Justice FRANKFURTER concurs in the result.

Mr. Justice JACKSON, dissenting. . . .

To sustain this statute by resort to the analogy of minimum wage laws seems so farfetched and unconvincing as to demonstrate its weakness rather than its strength. Because a State may require payment of a minimum wage for hours that are worked it does not follow that it may compel payment for time that is not worked. To overlook a distinction so fundamental is to confuse the point in issue.

The Court, by speaking of the statute as though it applies only to industry, sinister and big, further obscures the real principle involved. The statute plainly requires farmers, small service enterprises, professional offices, housewives with domestic help, and all other employers, not only to allow their employees time to vote, but to pay them for time to do so. It does not, however, require the employee to use any part of such time for that purpose. Such legislation stands in a class by itself and should not be uncritically commended as a mere regulation of "practices in the business-labor field." . . .

[T]here must be some limit to the power to shift the whole voting burden from the voter to someone else who happens to stand in some economic relationship to him. [D]oes the success of an enticement to vote justify putting its cost on some other citizen? . . . *

---

* Note the reliance on the Day-Brite decision in a unanimous per curiam decision in Dean v. Gadsden Times Publ. Corp., 412 U.S. 543 (1973). The Alabama court had held unconstitutional a law providing that an employee excused for jury duty "shall be entitled to his usual compensation received from such employment less the fee or compensation he received for serving" as a juror. In reversing that due process decision, the Court concluded that the Alabama law "stands on no less sturdy a footing" as the statute sustained in Day-Brite.

WILLIAMSON v. LEE OPTICAL CO.

348 U.S. 483, 75 S.Ct. 461, 99 L.Ed. 563 (1955).

Appeal from the District Court for the Western District of Oklahoma.

Mr. Justice DOUGLAS delivered the opinion of the Court. . . .

The District Court held unconstitutional portions of three sections of [an Oklahoma law of 1953]. First, it held invalid under the Due Process Clause of the Fourteenth Amendment the portions of § 2 which make it unlawful for any person not a licensed optometrist or ophthalmologist to fit lenses to a face or to duplicate or replace into frames lenses or other optical appliances, except upon written prescriptive authority of an Oklahoma licensed ophthalmologist or optometrist.

An ophthalmologist is a duly licensed physician who specializes in the care of the eyes. An optometrist examines eyes for refractive error, recognizes (but does not treat) diseases of the eye, and fills prescriptions for eyeglasses. The optician is an artisan qualified to grind lenses, fill prescriptions, and fit frames.

The effect of § 2 is to forbid the optician from fitting or duplicating lenses without a prescription from an ophthalmologist or optometrist. In practical effect, it means that no optician can fit old glasses into new frames or supply a lens, whether it be a new lens or one to duplicate a lost or broken lens, without a prescription. The District Court . . . rebelled at the notion that a State could require a prescription . . . "to take old lenses and place them in new frames and then fit the completed spectacles to the *face* of the eyeglass wearer." . . . The court found that through mechanical devices and ordinary skills the optician could take a broken lens or a fragment thereof, measure its power, and reduce it to prescriptive terms. The court held that "Although on this precise issue of duplication, the legislature . . . was dealing with a matter of public interest, the particular means chosen are neither reasonably necessary nor reasonably related to the end sought to be achieved." . . .

The Oklahoma law may exact a needless, wasteful requirement in many cases. But it is for the legislature, not the courts, to balance the advantages and disadvantages of the new requirement. It appears that in many cases the optician can easily supply the new frames or new lenses without reference to the old written prescription. It also appears that many written prescriptions contain no directive data in regard to fitting spectacles to the face. But in some cases the directions contained in the prescription are essential, if the glasses are to be fitted so as to correct the particular defects of vision or alleviate the eye condition. The legislature might have concluded that the frequency of occasions when a prescription is necessary was sufficient to justify this regulation of the fitting of eyeglasses. Likewise, when it is necessary to duplicate a lens, a written prescription may or may not be necessary. But the legislature might have concluded that one was needed often enough to require one in every case. Or the legislature may have concluded that eye examinations were so critical, not only for correction of vision but also for detection of latent ailments or diseases, that every change in frames and every

duplication of a lens should be accompanied by a prescription from a medical expert. To be sure, the present law does not require a new examination of the eyes every time the frames are changed or the lenses duplicated. For if the old prescription is on file with the optician, he can go ahead and make the new fitting or duplicate the lenses. But the law need not be in every respect logically consistent with its aims to be constitutional. It is enough that there is an evil at hand for correction, and that it might be thought that the particular legislative measure was a rational way to correct it.

The day is gone when this Court uses the Due Process Clause of the Fourteenth Amendment to strike down state laws, regulatory of business and industrial conditions, because they may be unwise, improvident, or out of harmony with a particular school of thought. . . .

Secondly, the District Court held that it violated the Equal Protection Clause of the Fourteenth Amendment to subject opticians to this regulatory system and to exempt, as § 3 of the Act does, all sellers of ready-to-wear glasses. [The passage rejecting this claim is noted in chap. 10, sec. 1, below.]

Third, the District Court held unconstitutional, as violative of the Due Process Clause . . . , that portion of § 3 which makes it unlawful "to solicit the sale of . . . frames, mountings, . . . or any other optical appliances." [R]egulation of the advertising of eyeglass frames was said to intrude "into a mercantile field only casually related to the visual care of the public" and restrict "an activity which in no way can detrimentally affect the people. . . ."

An eyeglass frame, considered in isolation, is only a piece of merchandise. But an eyeglass frame is not used in isolation . . . ; it is used with lenses; and lenses, pertaining as they do to the human eye, enter the field of health. Therefore, the legislature might conclude that to regulate one effectively it would have to regulate the other. Or it might conclude that both the sellers of frames and the sellers of lenses were in a business where advertising should be limited or even abolished in the public interest. . . . The advertiser of frames may be using his ads to bring in customers who will buy lenses. If the advertisement of lenses is to be abolished or controlled, the advertising of frames must come under the same restraints; or so the legislature might think. We see no constitutional reason why a State may not treat all who deal with the human eye as members of a profession who should use no merchandising methods for obtaining customers.

Fourth, the District Court held unconstitutional, as violative of the Due Process Clause of the Fourteenth Amendment, the provision of § 4 of the Oklahoma Act which reads as follows:

> "No person, firm, or corporation engaged in the business of retailing merchandise to the general public shall rent space, sublease departments, or otherwise permit any person purporting to do eye examination or visual care to occupy space in such retail store."

It seems to us that this regulation is on the same constitutional footing as the denial to corporations of the right to practice dentistry. Semler v. Dental Examiners [294 U.S. 608]. It is an attempt to free the profession, to as great an extent as possible, from all taints of commercialism. It certainly might be

easy for an optometrist with space in a retail store to be merely a front for the retail establishment.   In any case, the opportunity for that nexus may be too great for safety, if the eye doctor is allowed inside the retail store.   Moreover, it may be deemed important to effective regulation that the eye doctor be restricted to geographical locations that reduce the temptations of commercialism.   Geographical location may be an important consideration in a legislative program which aims to raise the treatment of the human eye to a strictly professional level.   We cannot say that the regulation has no rational relation to that objective and therefore is beyond constitutional bounds. . . .

[Reversed.]

THE "HANDS OFF" APPROACH TO ECONOMIC LEGISLATION: EXCESSIVE WITHDRAWAL? JUSTIFIABLE DOUBLE STANDARD?

Introduction.   The modern Court has turned away due process challenges to economic regulation with a broad "hands off" approach.   No such law has been invalidated on substantive due process grounds since 1937. Moreover, the Court struck down only one such law on equal protection grounds before the 1970's—in 1957, in Morey v. Doud (chap. 10 below). Equal protection, like economic due process, has typically meant "minimal scrutiny in theory and virtually none in fact." [1]   Indeed, opinions from the Court are rare, for most appeals raising substantive due process challenges are dismissed for want of a substantial federal question; and argument is ordinarily heard only when a lower court has enjoined enforcement of a statute. Only on a few occasions have some Justices expressed doubts about the Court's stance of extreme deference to economic regulation.

That Court withdrawal from intervention raises two basic questions. First, has the Court gone too far in its withdrawal?   Would it be possible, and justifiable, to exercise a level of review which would have more content than the modern "hands off" attitude and yet avoid the vices of the Lochner era?   Second, is the substantial withdrawal from review in the economic area reconcilable with the modern Court's considerable degree of interventionism when noneconomic rights and interests are affected?   Is there justification for such a double standard, for a two-tier level of scrutiny, intense in some areas, minimal or virtually nonexistent in others?   And the two problems are related: Even if some "double standard" is justifiable, is the wide gap between levels of review justifiable?   Or should, and can, the two levels of review draw closer together?

1.   *The possibility of more substantial scrutiny of economic regulation.* Are the summary dispositions of the Court in many modern due process cases consistent with the Court's own articulated requirements?   Can the

---

1.   Gunther, "Foreword: . . . A Model for a Newer Equal Protection," 86 Harv.L.Rev. 1, 8 (1972).

Some state courts, applying state constitutional provisions similar to due process, scrutinize legislation in this area with greater care and invalidate laws more frequently. See Heth-erington, "State Economic Regulation and Substantive Due Process of Law," 53 Nw.U.L.Rev. 13, 226 (1958), Selected Essays 1938–62 (1963), 487, and Paulsen, "The Persistence of Substantive Due Process in the States," 34 Minn. L.Rev. 91 (1950).

theoretically still operative Nebbia standard—"that the means selected shall have a real and substantial relation to the object sought to be attained"—be translated into genuine practice? Recall the suggestions about more intense means-oriented scrutiny, noted in sec. 1B above: Can the minimal rationality standard be applied with greater "bite"? By a reduced willingness of the Court to hypothesize legislative objectives—by testing the reasonableness of the means in terms of purposes put forth by the defenders of the law, rather than the Court's attribution of purposes a legislature *might* have had? And by requiring the defenders of the law to come forth with some data to show how the means promote the legislative purposes? Can such means scrutiny avoid the dangers of judicial value infusions and implicit balancing of the Lochner era? The possibilities of a more genuine means scrutiny are further explored below, in the context of equal protection standards, in chap. 10, sec. 1.

Note the comment in McCloskey, "Economic Due Process and the Supreme Court: An Exhumation and Reburial," 1962 Sup.Ct.Rev. 34: "Why did the Court move all the way from the inflexible negativism of the old majority to the all-out tolerance of the new? Why did it not establish a halfway house between the extremes, retaining a measure of control over economic legislation but exercising that control with discrimination and self-restraint?" McCloskey suggested as one explanation that the "intransigence" of the majority of the Lochner era "tended to discredit the whole concept of judicial supervision"—that "extremism had bred extremism": that excessive intervention in the Lochner years bred the arguably excessive modern abdication.[2] Would an intensified means scrutiny represent such a halfway house? And may the time now be ripe to move in that direction, under the banner of equal protection if not due process? Note McCloskey's suggested "halfway house": The Court would "not strike down an arguably rational law, but it would require some showing by the State that there was a basis for believing it to be rational and would consider evidence to the contrary presented by the affected business. Laws like those involved in the Lee Optical case . . . might be invalidated, or at any rate more sharply queried." In 1962 McCloskey did not expect such a change to come about. Is there greater basis to anticipate such a change today, under the banner of equal protection if not due process? (See chap. 10 below.)

2. *The new interventionism: The Carolene Products footnote.* Is the withdrawal from review of economic regulations consistent with the increased scrutiny that has marked the Court's activities in other areas? That the Court would not abandon interventionism across the board when it turned its back on the Lochner era was suggested in a famous footnote by Justice Stone in the Carolene Products case in 1938. While describing in the text of his opinion some guidelines for the deferential "some rational basis" review of economic legislation challenged under due process (as noted above),[3] Chief

2. See also Gunther, above, at 43: "[P]reoccupation with the ghost of the old due process produced a judicial overreaction and continues to cast a shadow on due process scrutiny of means as well as ends."

3. Recall that in the same year Justice Stone also wrote the Barnwell Bros.

opinion, suggesting a virtually complete withdrawal from review of state regulations challenged under the commerce clause (5, sec. 1, above); but his opinion in the Southern Pacific case a few years later made clear that a more intense, "balancing" mode of review was appropriate in implementing the dormant commerce clause

Justice Stone added a footnote 4 [United States v. Carolene Products Co., 304 U.S. 144 (1938)]:

"There may be narrower scope for operation of the presumption of constitutionality when legislation appears on its face to be within a specific prohibition of the Constitution, such as those of the first ten Amendments, which are deemed equally specific when held to be embraced within the Fourteenth. See Stromberg v. California, 283 U.S. 359, 369–370; Lovell v. Griffin, 303 U.S. 444, 452.

"It is unnecessary to consider now whether legislation which restricts those political processes which can ordinarily be expected to bring about repeal of undesirable legislation, is to be subjected to more exacting judicial scrutiny under the general prohibitions of the Fourteenth Amendment than are most other types of legislation. On restrictions upon the right to vote, see Nixon v. Herndon, 273 U.S. 536; Nixon v. Condon, 286 U.S. 73; on restraints upon the dissemination of information, see Near v. Minnesota, 283 U.S. 697, 713–714, 718–720, 722; Grosjean v. American Press Co., 297 U. S. 233; Lovell v. Griffin, supra; on interferences with political organizations, see Stromberg v. California, supra, 369; Fiske v. Kansas, 274 U.S. 380; Whitney v. California, 274 U.S. 357, 373–378; Herndon v. Lowry, 301 U.S. 242; and see Holmes, J., in Gitlow v. New York, 268 U.S. 652, 673; as to prohibition of peaceable assembly, see De Jonge v. Oregon, 299 U.S. 353, 365.

"Nor need we enquire whether similar considerations enter into the review of statutes directed at particular religious, Pierce v. Society of Sisters, 268 U.S. 510, or national, Meyer v. Nebraska, 262 U.S. 390; Bartels v. Iowa, 262 U.S. 404; Farrington v. Tokushige, 273 U.S. 284, or racial minorities, Nixon v. Herndon, supra; Nixon v. Condon, supra; whether prejudice against discrete and insular minorities may be a special condition, which tends seriously to curtail the operation of those political processes ordinarily to be relied upon to protect minorities, and which may call for a correspondingly more searching judicial inquiry. Compare McCulloch v. Maryland, 4 Wheat. (17 U.S.) 316, 428; South Carolina v. Barnwell Bros., 303 U.S. 177, 184, n. 2, and cases cited." [Most of the cited cases are considered in the chapters which follow.]

The "double standard" suggested by that footnote—an interventionist stance in some areas, a deferential one in others—has had a pervasive influence. As a justification for the varieties of scrutiny by the modern Court at levels higher than minimal rationality, the footnote raises a number of difficulties. (See, e. g., sec. 3 below.) But there can be no doubt that the modern Court, particularly during the Warren years, has been characterized by a notable activism on behalf of fundamental rights and interests outside the economic sphere. In addition to the selective incorporation of Bill of Rights guarantees of criminal procedure noted in the preceding chapter, the use of the 14th Amendment has burgeoned with respect to First Amendment rights, discrimination against racial and other minorities, fundamental rights such as privacy, and fundamental interests such as voting,

barrier (chap. 5 above). Recall also the variations on the political processes theme so prominent in the Carolene Products footnote in those commerce clause opinions by Justice Stone.

all to be explored below. Should, and can, judicial scrutiny in the economic due process sphere remain as deferential as in the modern cases, given that sharp intensification of review in so many other areas? Are the spheres sufficiently distinguishable?

    3. *Property and economic rights and the contrast with fundamental personal liberties.* Can the different standards of review be justified because of an inherent difference in the "fundamentalness" of economic rights and other personal rights? Can they be justified because of differences in judicial competence regarding economic and noneconomic rights? In the modern due process cases, the Court repeatedly states its determination to keep hands off the economic sphere. That is a recurrent theme: for example, in refusing to extend the strict scrutiny of the "new" equal protection to state welfare programs, Justice Stewart announced for the Court in Dandridge v. Williams, 397 U.S. 471 (1970) (chap. 10 below), that nonintervention was appropriate in "the area of economic and social welfare" and commented that "the intractable economic, social, and even philosophical problems presented by public welfare assistance programs are not the business of this Court." But are the "social, and even philosophical" problems truly less intractable in the modern areas of intervention? Does protection of property and economic interests have less textual and historical basis than protection of other interests? Compare the recent comment (in another prevailing opinion) on the frequent modern efforts to explain the "double standard" of judicial intervention in terms of an allegedly sharp difference between property and noneconomic rights. Justice Stewart stated in Lynch v. Household Finance Corp., 405 U.S. 538 (1972) [4]:

    "[T]he dichotomy between personal liberties and property rights is a false one. Property does not have rights. People have rights. The right to enjoy property without unlawful deprivation, no less than the right to speak or the right to travel, is, in truth, a 'personal' right, whether the 'property' in question be a welfare check, a home or a savings account. In fact, a fundamental interdependence exists between the personal right to liberty and the personal right in property. Neither could have meaning without the other. That rights in property are basic civil rights has long been recognized. J. Locke, Of Civil Government . . . ; J. Adams, A Defence of the Constitutions of the Government of the United States of America . . . ; 1 W. Blackstone, Commentaries *138–140." [5]

4. Justice Stewart's opinion in the 4 to 3 decision in Lynch was joined by Justices Douglas, Brennan and Marshall, usually viewed as the most "liberal," interventionist Justices. Lynch interpreted 28 U.S.C. § 1343(3), the jurisdictional counterpart to the basic statute giving remedies for violations of civil rights, 42 U.S.C. § 1983. (See chap. 11 below). The lawsuit was a procedural due process attack on a state law authorizing summary pre-judgment garnishments. The lower court had dismissed the case because it thought § 1343(3) applied only to "personal" rights and not to "property" rights. The Supreme Court rejected that distinction. One of Justice Stewart's reasons for doing so was "the virtual impossibility of applying" such a distinction.

5. Recall the influence of John Locke's social compact philosophy and Blackstone's Commentaries in early natural law jurisprudential thinking, and in the early, abortive efforts by the dissenters in the Slaughter-House Cases to read a substantive due process protection of economic rights into the 14th Amendment.

4. *Economic rights and the contrast with First Amendment liberties.* In the area of First Amendment liberties, the modern Court has imposed very substantial restraints on state action. Is the distinction between "economic" and "civil liberties" cases sufficiently clear to justify the differences in judicial scrutiny? (On First Amendment developments, see chaps. 12 and 13 below, especially the return to the double standard problem at the beginning of chap. 12.) Is the "liberty" of the individual who is denied a master electrician's license under a guild-type state law all that different from the kind of "liberty" protected in the free speech cases? [6] Is it to be expected that a Court engaged in invalidating a considerable number of laws under the First Amendment will be able to adhere consistently, and to quite the present extent, to nonintervention in the economic and social sphere? Is there any constitutional justification for the present degree of difference in judicial scrutiny of the two types of legislation? Is the difference adequately explainable by the fact that First Amendment rights are "specific" and "explicit"? Note that they are not "specific" and "explicit" vis-á-vis the states: they apply to states only because they have been "incorporated" into the "liberty" protected by the due process clause of the 14th Amendment.

5. *The contrast with non-"specific," noneconomic fundamental rights and interests.* Is the Court's "hands off" stance in the economic regulation cases made substantially more untenable by the recent protection of a range of fundamental values no more explicit in the Constitution than such economic rights as freedom of contract? If fundamental values other than those explicitly safeguarded in the Bill of Rights can claim substantive due process protection, can the modern Court justify in principle its summary rejection of economic claims? During the 1960's, during the last years of the Warren era, the Court's "new" equal protection exercised strict scrutiny under the equal protection clause when a variety of "fundamental interests" were affected—fundamental interests such as voting and the fair administration of justice. And litigants as well as some Justices urged extension of that fundamental interest analysis into additional areas as well—education, housing, relief against poverty, for example (see chap. 10 below). Do those developments and arguments signify a breakdown of the economic-personal rights double standard in the equal protection area? Do those developments and arguments make it even more difficult to maintain the double standard with respect to economic due process, at least at the level of the extremes of difference in judicial attitudes revealed when the cases in this section are compared with the interventionist ones in the following chapters?

But the questions raised by the virtual demise of economic due process scrutiny are most acute when contrasted with the recent invigorations of the due process clause itself. In the cases in sec. 3 below, fundamental rights of "privacy" are enforced in the contraception and abortion contexts. Does the "privacy" of Griswold v. Connecticut and Roe v. Wade have any better

---

6. See, e. g., chap. 3, "The Right to Make a Living," in Gellhorn, Individual Freedom and Governmental Restraints (1956), 105–151, on "the significant interference with the traditional freedom to work" by "the occupational license." See generally Reich, "The New 'Property,'" 73 Yale L.J. 733 (1964). Compare also the Court's growing solicitude for procedural protections of property rights in modern administrative hearings cases, chap. 10, sec. 6, below.

textual or historical basis than economic rights? Do the Griswold and Roe decisions have any greater justification than Lochner? Do they avoid the vices of Lochner? Does the revival of substantive due process in those recent cases cast added doubt on the virtual abandonment of scrutiny—even of means scrutiny—in the economic area? Even if the Court may legitimately enforce its own, or society's, scale of values, is the present hierarchy justifiable? Perhaps economic liberties should rank lower than speech and privacy on such a scale. But should they rank so low as to justify the decline of judicial scrutiny to the level manifested in the modern economic due process cases?

Transitional note. The comparison between the Lochner era and the modern revival of substantive due process is pursued in sec. 3 below. Those materials can usefully be considered at this point. But before turning to them, the next section completes the coverage of constitutional protections of economic rights with a review of (a) the "taking-regulation" distinction in due process adjudication, and (b) the role of the contract clause as a restraint on state legislative authority.

SECTION 2. OTHER CONSTITUTIONAL SAFEGUARDS OF ECONOMIC RIGHTS: THE "TAKING–REGULATION" DISTINCTION; THE CONTRACT CLAUSE

A. EMINENT DOMAIN AND THE "TAKING–REGULATION" DISTINCTION

Introduction. Among the earliest "specific" Bill of Rights guarantees absorbed into the 14th Amendment's due process guarantee was the Fifth Amendment command that private property shall not "be taken for public use, without just compensation." [1] State and federal resorts to the power of eminent domain are common, and a prolific source of constitutional litigation: when government seeks to "take" private land for a new schoolhouse or a park or an airport or an urban redevelopment project, the property is "taken" through condemnation, and the owner is entitled to "just compensation." The specialized bodies of doctrine as to the meaning of "just compensation" and "public use" are beyond the scope of these materials. But one area of eminent domain law touches so closely on substantive due process restraints on economic regulation that it warrants brief mention here, though its ramifications are also left to other courses.

Suppose government, rather than condemning property and formally transferring title to itself, merely "regulates" its use and substantially diminishes its value? Can such governmental action ever give rise to an obligation to afford the property owner "just compensation" for his loss? The answer

---

1. See Chicago, B. & Q. R. R. v. Chicago, 166 U.S. 226 (1897), (just compensation), and Missouri Pac. Ry. v. Nebraska, 164 U.S. 403 (1896) (even if compensation is paid, property may not be taken for "private" rather than "public" use).

is clear: it can.   What has been unclear and continues to be perplexing is the
question of when.   Justice Holmes, in the Pennsylvania Coal case, which follows, stated the "general rule": "[W]hile property may be regulated to
a certain extent, if regulation goes too far it will be recognized as a taking."
Government need not compensate the property owner for losses that are
incidental consequences of valid regulation; it must compensate when regulation is tantamount to "taking."   When does governmental action give rise
to a duty to compensate?   When may government impose property losses
without paying compensation, through "the petty larceny of the police power"? [2]

Can adequate criteria be articulated to distinguish between compensable
and noncompensable impositions of property losses by government?   The
two cases which follow are decisions of the 1920's, but they serve to raise
the problem.   Can the Court do better than Justice Holmes' effort in the
Pennsylvania Coal case?   With the modern Court's expansive reading of
the police power and its retreat from careful scrutiny of economic regulations, successful "taking" challenges to regulatory schemes are understandably rare.   Nevertheless, the Court continues to recognize the possibility
of compensation in some circumstances, and the taking-regulation problem
is addressed in some of the modern cases noted at the end of this section,
in a less summary manner than in the economic due process decisions of the
modern era.   Consider, in examining these materials, what criteria might
serve to draw the taking-regulation distinction: The magnitude of the harm
to the private interest?   The manner of imposing the harm?   The degree to
which the imposition interferes with legitimate private expectations?   The
nature and the magnitude of the public interest?   Or must decision turn
inevitably on a vague balancing of public need and private cost? [3]

2. The phrase was used by Justice
Holmes in a draft opinion he prepared in a case, Jackman v. Rosenbaum Co., 260 U.S. 22 (1922), decided
shortly before the Pennsylvania Coal
case, below. He deleted the phrase in
the final version: "my brethren, as
usual and as I expected, corrected my
taste . . . . It is done—our effort is to please." Holmes to Laski,
October 22, 1922, I Holmes-Laski Letters (Howe ed. 1953), 457.

3. For the most valiant modern effort
to articulate standards, see Michel-
man, "Property, Utility, and Fairness:
Comments on the Ethical Foundations
of 'Just Compensation' Law," 80 Harv.
L.Rev. 1165 (1967). See also Sax,
"Takings and the Police Power," 74
Yale L.J. 36 (1964), Sax, "Takings,
Private Property and Public Rights,"
81 Yale L.J. 149 (1971), and Dunham,
"Griggs v. Allegheny County in Per-
spective: Thirty Years of Supreme
Court Expropriation Law," 1962 Sup.
Ct.Rev. 63.

PENNSYLVANIA COAL CO. v. MAHON

260 U.S. 393, 43 S.Ct. 158, 67 L.Ed. 322 (1922).

Error to the Supreme Court of Pennsylvania.

Mr. Justice HOLMES delivered the opinion of the Court.

This is a bill in equity brought by the defendants in error to prevent the Pennsylvania Coal Company from mining under their property in such way as to remove the supports and cause a subsidence of the surface and of their house. The bill sets out a deed executed by the Coal Company in 1878, under which the plaintiffs claim. The deed conveys the surface, but in express terms reserves the right to remove all the coal under the same, and the grantee takes the premises with the risk, and waives all claim for damages that may arise from mining out the coal. But the plaintiffs say that whatever may have been the Coal Company's rights, they were taken away by an Act of Pennsylvania [of 1921] commonly known there as the Kohler Act. The [trial court] denied an injunction, holding that the statute if applied to this case would be unconstitutional. On appeal the [highest state court] held that the statute was a legitimate exercise of the police power and directed a decree for the plaintiffs. . . .

The statute forbids the mining of anthracite coal in such way as to cause the subsidence of, among other things, any structure used as a human habitation, with certain exceptions, including among them land where the surface is owned by the owner of the underlying coal and is distant more than one hundred and fifty feet from any improved property belonging to any other person. As applied to this case the statute is admitted to destroy previously existing rights of property and contract. The question is whether the police power can be stretched so far.

Government hardly could go on if to some extent values incident to property could not be diminished without paying for every such change in the general law. As long recognized, some values are enjoyed under an implied limitation and must yield to the police power. But obviously the implied limitation must have its limits, or the contract and due process clauses are gone. One fact for consideration in determining such limits is the extent of the diminution. When it reaches a certain magnitude, in most if not in all cases there must be an exercise of eminent domain and compensation to sustain the act. So the question depends upon the particular facts. The greatest weight is given to the judgment of the legislature, but it always is open to interested parties to contend that the legislature had gone beyond its constitutional power.

This is the case of a single private house. No doubt there is a public interest even in this, as there is in every purchase and sale and in all that happens within the commonwealth. Some existing rights may be modified even in such a case. . . . But usually in ordinary private affairs the public interest does not warrant much of this kind of interference. A source of damage to such a house is not a public nuisance even if similar damage is inflicted on others in different places. The damage is not common or public. . . . The extent of the public interest is shown by the statute to be limited, since the statute ordinarily does not apply to land when the surface is owned by the owner of the coal. Furthermore, it is not justified as a protec-

tion of personal safety. That could be provided for by notice. Indeed the very foundation of this bill is that the defendant gave timely notice of its intent to mine under the house. On the other hand the extent of the taking is great. It purports to abolish what is recognized in Pennsylvania as an estate in land —a very valuable estate—and what is declared by the Court below to be a contract hitherto binding the plaintiffs. If we were called upon to deal with the plaintiffs' position alone, we should think it clear that the statute does not disclose a public interest sufficient to warrant so extensive a destruction of the defendant's constitutionally protected rights.

But the case has been treated as one in which the general validity of the act should be discussed. . . . It seems, therefore, to be our duty to go farther in the statement of our opinion, in order that it may be known at once, and that further suits should not be brought in vain.

It is our opinion that the act cannot be sustained as an exercise of the police power, so far as it affects the mining of coal under streets or cities in places where the right to mine such coal has been reserved. As said in a Pennsylvania case, "For practical purposes, the right to coal consists in the right to mine it." What makes the right to mine coal valuable is that it can be exercised with profit. To make it commercially impracticable to mine certain coal has very nearly the same effect for constitutional purposes as appropriating or destroying it. This we think that we are warranted in assuming that the statute does.

It is true that in Plymouth Coal Co. v. Pennsylvania, 232 U.S. 531, it was held competent for the legislature to require a pillar of coal to be left along the line of adjoining property, that with the pillar on the other side of the line would be a barrier sufficient for the safety of the employees of either mine in case the other should be abandoned and allowed to fill with water. But that was a requirement for the safety of employees invited into the mine, and secured an average reciprocity of advantage that has been recognized as a justification of various laws.

The rights of the public in a street purchased or laid out by eminent domain are those that it has paid for. If in any case its representatives have been so short sighted as to acquire only surface rights without the right of support, we see no more authority for supplying the latter without compensation than there was for taking the right of way in the first place and refusing to pay for it because the public wanted it very much. The protection of private property in the Fifth Amendment presupposes that it is wanted for public use, but provides that it shall not be taken for such use without compensation. A similar assumption is made in the decisions upon the Fourteenth Amendment. . . . When this seemingly absolute protection is found to be qualified by the police power, the natural tendency of human nature is to extend the qualification more and more until at last private property disappears. But that cannot be accomplished in this way under the Constitution . . . .

The general rule at least is, that while property may be regulated to a certain extent, if regulation goes too far it will be recognized as a taking. It may be doubted how far exceptional cases, like the blowing up of a house to stop a conflagration, go—and if they go beyond the general rule, whether they do not stand as much upon tradition as upon principle. Bowditch v. Boston, 101 U.S.

16. In general it is not plain that a man's misfortunes or necessities will justify his shifting the damages to his neighbor's shoulders. . . . We are in danger of forgetting that a strong public desire to improve the public condition is not enough to warrant achieving the desire by a shorter cut than the constitutional way of paying for the change. . . .

Decree reversed.

Mr. Justice BRANDEIS, dissenting. . . .

Every restriction upon the use of property imposed in the exercise of the police power deprives the owner of some right theretofore enjoyed, and is, in that sense, an abridgment by the State of rights in property without making compensation. But restriction imposed to protect the public health, safety or morals from dangers threatened is not a taking. The restriction here in question is merely the prohibition of a noxious use. The property so restricted remains in the possession of its owner. The State does not appropriate it or make any use of it. The State merely prevents the owner from making a use which interferes with paramount rights of the public. . . .

The restriction upon the use of this property can not, of course, be lawfully imposed, unless its purpose is to protect the public. But the purpose of a restriction does not cease to be public, because incidentally some private persons may thereby receive gratuitously valuable special benefits. Thus, owners of low buidings may obtain, through statutory restrictions upon the height of neighboring structures, benefits equivalent to an easement of light and air. . . . Furthermore, a restriction, though imposed for a public purpose, will not be lawful, unless the restriction is an appropriate means to the public end. But to keep coal in place is surely an appropriate means of preventing subsidence of the surface; and ordinarily it is the only available means. Restriction upon use does not become inappropriate as a means, merely because it deprives the owner of the only use to which the property can then be profitably put. The liquor and the oleomargarine cases settled that. . . .

. . . [I]t is said that these provisions . . . cannot be sustained as an exercise of the police power where the right to mine such coal has been reserved. The conclusion seems to rest upon the assumption that in order to justify such exercise of the police power there must be "an average reciprocity of advantage" as between the owner of the property restricted and the rest of the community; and that here such reciprocity is absent. Reciprocity of advantage is an important consideration, and may even be essential, where the State's power is exercised for the purpose of conferring benefits upon the property of a neighborhood, as in drainage projects . . . or upon adjoining owners, as by party wall provisions, Jackman v. Rosenbaum Co., [260 U.S. 22]. But where the police power is exercised, not to confer benefits upon property owners but to protect the public from detriment and danger, there is in my opinion, no room for considering reciprocity of advantage. There was no reciprocal advantage to the owner prohibited from using his oil tanks, in [Pierce Oil Corp. v. City of Hope,] 248 U.S. 498; his brickyard, in [Hadacheck v. Sebastian,] 239 U.S. 394; his livery stable, in [Reinman v. City of Little Rock,] 237 U.S. 171; his billiard hall, in [Murphy v. California,] 225 U.S. 623; his oleomargarine factory, in [Powell v. Pennsylvania,] 127 U.S. 678; his brewery, in [Mugler v. Kansas,] 123

U.S. 623; unless it be the advantage of living and doing business in a civilized community. That reciprocal advantage is given by the act to the coal operators.

MILLER v. SCHOENE

276 U.S. 272, 48 S.Ct. 246, 72 L.Ed. 568 (1928).

Error to the Supreme Court of Appeals of Virginia.

Mr. Justice STONE delivered the opinion of the Court.

Acting under the Cedar Rust Act of Virginia . . ., defendant in error, the state entomologist, ordered the plaintiffs in error to cut down a large number of ornamental red cedar trees growing on their property, as a means of preventing the communication of a rust or plant disease with which they were infected to the apple orchards in the vicinity. The plaintiffs in error appealed from the order to the [trial court, which] affirmed the order and allowed to plaintiffs in error $100 to cover the expense of removal of the cedars. Neither the judgment of the court nor the statute as interpreted allows compensation for the value of the standing cedars or the decrease in the market value of the realty caused by their destruction whether considered as ornamental trees or otherwise. But they save to plaintiffs in error the privilege of using the trees when felled. [The statute was challenged under the due process clause of the 14th Amendment.]

The Virginia statute presents a comprehensive scheme for the condemnation and destruction of red cedar trees infected by cedar rust. By § 1 it is declared to be unlawful for any person to "own, plant or keep alive and standing" on his premises any red cedar tree which is or may be the source or "host plant" of the communicable plant disease known as cedar rust, and any such tree growing within a certain radius of any apple orchard is declared to be a public nuisance, subject to destruction. Section 2 makes it the duty of the state entomologist "[to] ascertain if any cedar tree or trees [constitute] a menace to the health of any apple orchard in said locality." If affirmative findings are so made, he is required to direct the owner in writing to destroy the trees . . . . Section 5 authorizes the state entomologist to destroy the trees if the owner, after being notified, fails to do so. . . .

As shown by the evidence . . ., cedar rust is an infectious plant disease in the form of a fungoid organism which is destructive of the fruit and foliage of the apple, but without effect on the value of the cedar. Its life cycle has two phases which are passed alternately as a growth on red cedar and on apple trees. It is communicated by spores from one to the other over a radius of at least two miles. It appears not to be communicable between trees of the same species, but only from one species to the other, and other plants seem not to be appreciably affected by it. The only practicable method of controlling the disease and protecting apple trees from its ravages is the destruction of all red cedar trees, subject to the infection, located within two miles of apple orchards.

The red cedar, aside from its ornamental use, has occasional use and value as lumber. It is indigenous to Virginia, is not cultivated or dealt in commer-

cially on any substantial scale, and its value throughout the state is shown to be small as compared with that of the apple orchards of the state. Apple growing is one of the principal agricultural pursuits in Virginia. The apple is used there and exported in large quantities. Many millions of dollars are invested in the orchards, which furnish employment for a large portion of the population . . . .

On the evidence we may accept the conclusion of the Supreme Court of Appeals that the state was under the necessity of making a choice between the preservation of one class of property and that of the other wherever both existed in dangerous proximity. It would have been none the less a choice if, instead of enacting the present statute, the state, by doing nothing, had permitted serious injury to the apple orchards within its borders to go on unchecked. When forced to such a choice the state does not exceed its constitutional powers by deciding upon the destruction of one class of property in order to save another which, in the judgment of the legislature, is of greater value to the public. It will not do to say that the case is merely one of a conflict of two private interests and that the misfortune of apple growers may not be shifted to cedar owners by ordering the destruction of their property; for it is obvious that there may be, and that here there is, a preponderant public concern in the preservation of the one interest over the other. . . . And where the public interest is involved preferment of that interest over the property interest of the individual, to the extent even of its destruction, is one of the distinguishing characteristics of every exercise of the police power which affects property. . . .

Affirmed.

THE "TAKING–REGULATION" DISTINCTION AND THE MODERN COURT

1. *Zoning, "safety regulations," and Goldblatt v. Hempstead.* During the heyday of economic due process, a divided Court sustained a general zoning ordinance as a valid "police regulation," in Euclid v. Ambler Realty Co., 272 U.S. 365 (1926). But the Euclid Court emphasized that it was not passing on specific applications of zoning ordinances; and two years later, in Nectow v. Cambridge, 277 U.S. 183 (1928), a particular application of a zoning law was invalidated. Property owners' challenges to zoning laws have produced much litigation in state and lower federal courts. See generally Symposium, 20 Law & Contemp.Prob. (1955). But property rights challenges to modern zoning laws have rarely come to the Supreme Court.

A rare recent example is GOLDBLATT v. HEMPSTEAD, 369 U.S. 590 (1962), where, after a state court had blocked an effort to reach a local problem via zoning, the town resorted to a "safety regulation"—and prevailed in the Supreme Court. Goldblatt owned a sand and gravel pit in a suburban area; the town had expanded rapidly. In the latest of a series of local regulations of excavations, the town banned some types of mining and imposed a duty to refill some pits. Goldblatt claimed that the latest ordinance was "not regulatory" but rather amounted to confiscation of property

without compensation. Justice Clark's opinion for the Court conceded that the regulation "completely prohibits a beneficial use to which the property has previously been devoted," but nevertheless found it justified as a "reasonable" exercise of the police power. It is noteworthy, however, that Justice Clark's discussion of "reasonableness" was more extensive than is typical in the modern economic due process cases in the previous section. Moreover, he cited the Pennsylvania Coal case and recognized "that governmental action in the form of regulation cannot be so onerous as to constitute a taking." He added: "There is no set formula to determine where regulation ends and taking begins. Although a comparison of values before and after is relevant, [it] is by no means conclusive . . . . How far regulation may go before it becomes a taking we need not now decide, for there is no evidence in the present record which even remotely suggests that prohibition of further mining will reduce the value of the lot in question."

2. *Taxation and "taking."* In PITTSBURGH v. ALCO PARKING CORP., 417 U.S. 369 (1974), operators of commercial parking lots claimed that a 20% tax on their gross receipts amounted to an unconstitutional "taking" in view of the competitive advantage it gave municipal lots. The highest state court sustained the attack, but Justice White's opinion for the Court reversed. He recalled that the size of a tax traditionally was not a ground for invalidation; and the competition by public parking facilities proved no more persuasive—that would involve the courts in the improper task of "judicial oversight of the terms and circumstances" of public competition with the private sector. Justice White commented: "The city was constitutionally entitled to put the automobile parker to the choice of using other transportation or paying the increased tax." But Justice Powell noted in a concurrence that the decision "does not foreclose the possibility that some combination of unreasonably burdensome taxation and direct competition by the taxing authority might amount to a taking of property without just compensation": such a combination "would be the functional equivalent of a governmental taking of private property for public use." *

B. THE CONTRACT CLAUSE

Introduction. During the first century of government under the Constitution, the prohibition of any state "Law impairing the Obligation of Contracts," Art. I, § 10, was the major restraint on state economic regulation. Since the late 19th century, when the Court began to interpret the due process clause of the 14th Amendment as a limitation on the content of state legislation, the contract clause has played a less prominent role in constitu-

---

* For other confrontations with the "taking" problem by the post-Lochner era Court, note the decisions sustaining compensation for "takings" by low-flying airplanes and rejecting arguments that the injuries were "merely incidental" consequences of authorized air navigation. United States v. Causby, 328 U.S. 256 (1946), and Griggs v. Allegheny County, 369 U.S. 84 (1962). Compare the series of modern cases in which losses from wars and riots have been held noncompensable: United States v. Caltex, 344 U.S. 149 (1952); United States v. Central Eureka Mining Co., 357 U.S. 155 (1958); and National Board of YMCA v. United States, 395 U.S. 85 (1969).

tional litigation. And as substantive due process restrictions on the police power diminished, as they have most markedly since the 1930's, contract clause barriers were lowered as well. Indeed, it has been suggested that interpretations of the contract and due process clauses have merged to such an extent that the "results might be the same if the contract clause were dropped out of the Constitution, and the challenged statutes all judged as reasonable or unreasonable deprivations of property" under the due process clause. Hale, "The Supreme Court and the Contract Clause," 57 Harv.L. Rev. 852, 890 (1944). Yet the contract clause deserves brief separate attention here. It *was*, after all, the major textual basis for judicial protection of "fundamental" economic rights, not only in the pre-Civil War era (see sec. 1A above) but throughout the entire 19th century and into the 20th. It *is*, unlike some of the fundamental values of the Lochner era, an explicit constitutional guarantee. In short, the contract clause, as distinguished from substantive due process, has an importance of its own, in present-day as well as historical terms. The opening note below reviews the developments in the 19th century. The principal case that follows, the Blaisdell case, came in 1934, the same year as Nebbia v. New York (sec. 1C above), and suggests a loosening of contract clause restraints paralleling those respecting substantive due process. But, as the later cases indicate, the contract clause may retain greater, distinguishable bite than economic due process in some contexts: certainly it did for Justice Black, as his dissent in the El Paso case below illustrates.

THE CONTRACT CLAUSE IN THE 19TH CENTURY

The major purpose of the contract clause was to restrain state laws affecting private contracts. It was aimed mainly at debtor relief laws—for example, laws staying or postponing payments of debts and laws authorizing payments in installments or in commodities. Yet the Court first interpreted the contract clause in cases involving public grants rather than private contracts. Fletcher v. Peck, 6 Cranch 87 (1810)[1]; New Jersey v. Wilson, 7 Cranch 164 (1812)[2]; Dartmouth College v. Woodward, 4 Wheat. 518 (1819). As Marshall said in Dartmouth College—in holding that New Hampshire could not "pack" the College board of trustees by legislation increasing the size of the board, since the 1769 royal charter of the College had given the trustees the right to fill all vacancies on the board—: "It is more than possible that the preservation of rights of this description was not particularly in the view of the framers of the Constitution. [It] is probable that interferences of more frequent recurrence, [of] which the mischief was more extensive, constituted

---

1. In 1795, several companies had obtained a huge grant of land from the Georgia legislature. There were charges of bribery, and a new legislature annulled the grant. The grantees had in the meanwhile sold their lands to investors. The Court held the 1796 law invalid: according to Marshall, the law was barred "either by general principles which are common to our free institutions, or by the particular provisions" of the Constitution. (See sec. 1A above.) On the background of the controversy, see Magrath, Yazoo: Law and Politics in the New Republic (1966).

2. The Court invalidated a New Jersey law of 1804 repealing a tax exemption which the colonial legislature had given for certain lands in 1758.

the great motive for imposing this restriction on the State legislatures." But that was no reason for limiting the scope of the clause.[3]   And the fact that a state was a party to the contract made no difference.

A few weeks after the Dartmouth College decision, the Marshall Court applied the contract clause to a law closer to the "mischief" which supplied the Framers with the "great motive for imposing this restriction on the State legislatures": in Sturges v. Crowninshield, 4 Wheat. 122 (1819), the Court held unconstitutional a New York insolvency law discharging debtors of their obligations upon surrender of their property.   And in Green v. Biddle, 8 Wheat. 1 (1823), the Court invalidated Kentucky's Occupying Claimants Law, designed to make it more difficult for landowners to eject those who in good faith had settled and made improvements on Western lands.

Historians have probably exaggerated the impact of the early contract clause decisions on American economic and legal developments.   The cases did indeed restrict; but they did not compel legislative paralysis, they were not the keystone of American corporate development, they did not establish an inflexible safeguard for all vested rights.[4]   The lack of statutory restrictions on corporations in the 19th century, for example, was probably more attributable to the legislators' unwillingness to enact them than to any constitutionally imposed incapacities.   Indeed, in the Dartmouth College Case itself, Justice Story's concurring opinion had pointed out what the political leaders in New Hampshire and elsewhere already well knew: "If the legislature mean to claim such an authority" to alter or amend corporate charters, "it must be reserved in the grant.   The charter of Dartmouth College contains no such reservation."   After the Dartmouth decision, the Court later said, "many a State of the Union   .   .   .   inserted, either in its statutes or in its constitutions, a provision that charters thenceforth granted should be subject to alteration, amendment or repeal at the pleasure of the legislature."[5]   Indeed, some legislatures had done so before the Dartmouth College decision.   But many states gave special corporate privileges and failed to include adequate reservations of amending powers in corporate charters even after the Dartmouth decision.   The relatively protected position of corporations later in the 19th century, in short, was due less to any shield supplied by the Court than it was to the legislatures' own unwillingness to impose restraints—an unwillingness reflecting the *laissez faire* philosophy of the day.

Moreover, the Court's interpretations from the beginning assured that the contract clause would not be an inflexible barrier to public regulation.   Space does not permit a detailed charting of the doctrinal developments; only a few

---

3.   For a succinct analysis of this much-discussed case, see Baxter, Daniel Webster & the Supreme Court (1966).

4.   For an extreme example of the recurrent hyperbole in comments on the early cases, see Sir Henry Maine's statement that the contract clause "secured full play to the economical forces by which the achievement of cultivating the soil of the American continent has been performed; it is the bulwark of American individualism against democratic impatience

and socialistic fantasy." Popular Government (1885), 247–48.

5.   Looker v. Maynard, 179 U.S. 46 (1900), sustaining a stockholders' cumulative voting statute enacted pursuant to a reserved power clause in the Michigan constitution.   In its opinion, the Court said that such a clause gave "at least" the power to make "any alteration   .   .   .   which will not defeat or substantially impair the object of the grant."

of the bases for sustaining legislative authority can be noted here. See also the opinion in Home Building & Loan Ass'n v. Blaisdell, 290 U.S. 398 (1934) (the next principal case); Hale, "The Supreme Court and the Contract Clause," 57 Harv.L.Rev. 512, 621, 852 (1944); and Wright, The Contract Clause of the Constitution (1938).

The Dartmouth College Case, as noted, recognized the legislature's authority to reserve the power to amend corporate charters. A few years later, a closely divided Court—with Marshall in dissent—stated that the contract clause did not prohibit all state insolvency laws. Ogden v. Saunders, 12 Wheat. 213 (1827), held that such laws could be validly applied to contracts made *after* the law was enacted; the earlier decision in Sturges v. Crowninshield, above, the Court made clear, applied only to retroactive insolvency laws.[6] Moreover, the Court soon elaborated on a distinction stated in Sturges and other early cases: that the constitutional ban on the impairment of contract "obligations" did not prohibit legislative changes in "remedies": "The distinction between the obligation [and] the remedy . . . exists in the nature of things. Without impairing the obligation of the contract, the remedy may certainly be modified as the wisdom of the nation shall direct," the Court had said in Sturges. And in Bronson v. Kinzie, 1 How. 311 (1843), the Court stated that the permissible scope of remedial changes depended on their "reasonableness," provided "no substantial right" was impaired.[7] Justice Cardozo was guilty of something of an understatement when he said that the "dividing line" between remedy and obligation "is at times obscure." Worthen Co. v. Kavanaugh, 295 U.S. 56 (1935).[8] Yet the allowance of remedial changes provided some flexibility: it authorized extensions of time, for example—so long as extensions were not "so piled up as to make the remedy a shadow," as Cardozo put it.

The early Court safeguarded against excessively broad interpretations of publicly granted privileges as well. In Dartmouth College, the Marshall Court had to strain somewhat to find in the royal charter an implied inviolability of the trustees' rights. In later years, the Court tended to be less charitable in construing the grantees' privileges. In Providence Bank v. Billings, 4 Pet. 514 (1830), for example, Marshall refused to read an implied immunity from taxation into a bank's charter. Roger Brooke Taney, Marshall's successor, quickly developed the Providence Bank approach, in the better-known Charles River Bridge Case in 1837.[9] The Charles River Bridge Company's charter to operate a toll bridge did not prevent the state from authorizing the construction of the competing, free Warren Bridge: "[A]ny ambiguity in the terms of the contract, must operate against the adventurers, and in favour of the public."

6. In Ogden, the Court justified the prospective operation of the insolvency law on the ground that laws in existence at the time of the making of a contract "enter into and form a part of" the contract.

7. In Bronson, the Court invalidated a state law restricting the mortgagee's rights on foreclosure.

8. See "Contract Clause Cases after Blaisdell," below.

9. Charles River Bridge v. Warren Bridge, 11 Pet. 420 (1837).

Moreover, the states were not left entirely powerless even where they had failed to reserve authority to amend charters and where strict construction of corporate privileges found a granted immunity. Certain powers of the state were held to be inalienable. No legislative assurance that the power of eminent domain would not be exercised could prevent subsequent action taking corporate property upon the payment of just compensation.[10] So, still more important, with at least some exercises of the police power: a Mississippi grant of a charter to operate a lottery did not bar the application of a later law prohibiting lotteries. "All agree that the legislature cannot bargain away the police power," Chief Justice Waite said in Stone v. Mississippi, 101 U.S. 814 (1880).[11] "No legislature can bargain away the public health or the public morals." But, he added, "we have held, not, however, without strong opposition at times, that [the contract clause] protected a corporation in its charter exemptions from taxation."[12] As a later Court put it broadly: "It is settled that neither the 'contract' clause nor the 'due process' clause has the effect of overriding the power of the State to establish all regulations that are reasonably necessary to secure the health, safety, good order, comfort, or general welfare of the community; that this power can neither be abdicated nor bargained away, and is inalienable even by express grant; and that all contract and property rights are held subject to its fair exercise."[13] And so with private contracts: "[P]arties by entering into contracts may not estop the legislature from enacting laws intended for the public good."[14]

In the late 19th century, the Court used broad language of that sort primarily in cases involving prohibitions of matters widely regarded as "evil": for example, lotteries and intoxicating beverages.[15] Compare the early development of the congressional commerce-prohibiting power, in the Lottery Case and related decisions, chap. 3 above. Would the Court also sustain legislation provoked by 20th century economic crises—the modern versions of the debtor relief laws that had motivated the adoption of the contract clause in 1787? The materials that follow focus on the interpretations of the contract clause in the contemporary economic context.

10. See, e. g., West River Bridge Co. v. Dix, 6 How. 507 (1848), and Pennsylvania Hospital v. Philadelphia, 245 U.S. 20 (1917).

11. Compare New Orleans Gas Co. v. Louisiana Light Co., 115 U.S. 650 (1885), holding that the police power argument did not justify elimination of the gas company's 50-year exclusive franchise by a subsequent anti-monopoly amendment to the state constitution. The Court added: "The right and franchises . . . can be taken by the public, upon just compensation to the company."

12. For recent litigation on 19th century state grants of tax exemptions to railroads, see Georgia R. Co. v. Redwine, 342 U.S. 299 (1952), and Atlantic Coast Line R. Co. v. Phillips, 332 U.S. 168 (1947).

13. Atlantic Coast Line R. Co. v. Goldsboro, 232 U.S. 548 (1914).

14. Manigault v. Springs, 199 U.S. 473 (1905).

15. See, e. g., Stone v. Mississippi, 101 U.S. 814 (1880); Beer Co. v. Massachusetts, 97 U.S. 25 (1878). During the same period, it should be noted, Court invalidation of state laws impairing corporate charter privileges reached its highest frequency in our history. Between 1865 and 1888, there were 49 cases in which state laws were held invalid under the contract clause—and 36 of these involved public grants rather than contracts between private parties. The Constitution of the United States of America (Gov't Printing Off., 1972 ed.).

HOME BUILDING & LOAN ASS'N v. BLAISDELL

290 U.S. 398, 54 S.Ct. 231, 78 L.Ed. 413 (1934).

Appeal from the Supreme Court of Minnesota.

[The Minnesota Mortgage Moratorium Law of 1933, enacted during the depression emergency, authorized relief against mortgage foreclosures and execution sales of real property. County courts were permitted to extend the period of redemption from foreclosure sales "for such additional time as the court may deem just and equitable," but not beyond May 1, 1935. Such extensions were to be conditioned upon an order requiring the mortgagor to "pay all or a reasonable part" of the income or rental value of the property toward the payment of taxes, insurance, interest and principal. No action for a deficiency judgment could be brought during such a court-extended period of redemption. John H. Blaisdell and his wife secured an order under the law extending the period of redemption on condition that they pay the Association $40 per month. The highest state court sustained the law as an "emergency" measure.]

Mr. Chief Justice HUGHES delivered the opinion of the Court. . . .

In determining whether the provision for this temporary and conditional relief exceeds the power of the State by reason of the [contract clause], we must consider the relation of emergency to constitutional power, the historical setting of the contract clause, the development of the jurisprudence of this Court in the construction of that clause, and the principles of construction which we may consider to be established.

Emergency does not create power. Emergency does not increase granted power or remove or diminish the restrictions imposed upon power granted or reserved. . . .

While emergency does not create power, emergency may furnish the occasion for the exercise of power. . . . The constitutional question presented in the light of an emergency is whether the power possessed embraces the particular exercise of it in response to particular conditions. . . .

[T]he reasons which led to the adoption of that clause [have] frequently been described with eloquent emphasis. The widespread distress following the revolutionary period, and the plight of debtors, had called forth in the States an ignoble array of legislative schemes for the defeat of creditors and the invasion of contractual obligations. Legislative interferences had been so numerous and extreme that the confidence essential to prosperous trade had been undermined and the utter destruction of credit was threatened. . . . It was necessary to interpose the restraining power of a central authority in order to secure the foundations even of "private faith." . . .

. . . To ascertain the scope of the constitutional prohibition we examine the course of judicial decisions in its application. These put it beyond question that the prohibition is not an absolute one and is not to be read with literal exactness like a mathematical formula. . . . The inescapable

problems of construction have been: What is a contract? What are the obligations of contracts? What constitutes impairment of these obligations? What residuum of power is there still in the States, in relation to the operation of contracts, to protect the vital interests of the community? . . .

Not only is the [contract clause] qualified by the measure of control which the State retains over remedial processes, but the State also continues to possess authority to safeguard the vital interests of its people. . . . Not only are existing laws read into contracts in order to fix obligations as between the parties, but the reservation of essential attributes of sovereign power is also read into contracts as a postulate of the legal order. The policy of protecting contracts against impairment presupposes the maintenance of a government by virtue of which contractual relations are worth while,—a government which retains adequate authority to secure the peace and good order of society. This principle of harmonizing the constitutional prohibition with the necessary residuum of state power has had progressive recognition in the decisions of this Court. . . . Whatever doubt there may have been that the protective power of the State, its police power, may be exercised—without violating the true intent of the provision of the Federal Constitution—in directly preventing the immediate and literal enforcement of contractual obligations by a temporary and conditional restraint, where vital public interests would otherwise suffer, was removed by our decisions relating to the enforcement of provisions of leases during a period of scarcity of housing [after World War I]. . . .

Undoubtedly, whatever is reserved of state power must be consistent with the fair intent of the constitutional limitation of that power. The reserved power cannot be construed so as to destroy the limitation, nor is the limitation to be construed to destroy the reserved power in its essential aspects. They must be construed in harmony with each other. This principle precludes a construction which would permit the State to adopt as its policy the repudiation of debts or the destruction of contracts or the denial of means to enforce them. But it does not follow that conditions may not arise in which a temporary restraint of enforcement may be consistent with the spirit and purpose of the constitutional provision and thus be found to be within the range of the reserved power of the state to protect the vital interests of the community. . . . [I]f state power exists to give temporary relief from the enforcement of contracts in the presence of disasters due to physical causes such as fire, flood, or earthquake, that power cannot be said to be nonexistent when the urgent public need demanding such relief is produced by other and economic causes. . . .

It is manifest from this review of our decisions that there has been a growing appreciation of public needs and of the necessity of finding ground for a rational compromise between individual rights and public welfare. The settlement and consequent contraction of the public domain, the pressure of a constantly increasing density of population, the interrelation of the activities of our people and the complexity of our economic interests, have inevitably led to an increased use of the organization of society in order to protect the very bases of individual opportunity. . . . [T]he question is no longer merely that of one party to a contract as against another, but of the use of reasonable means to safeguard the economic structure upon which the good of all depends.

It is no answer to say that this public need was not apprehended a century ago, or to insist that what the provision of the Constitution meant to the vision of that day it must mean to the vision of our time. If by the statement that what the Constitution meant at the time of its adoption it means today, it is intended to say that the great clauses of the Constitution must be confined to the interpretation which the framers, with the conditions and outlook of their time, would have placed upon them, the statement carries its own refutation. It was to guard against such a narrow conception that Chief Justice Marshall uttered the memorable warning—"We must never forget, that it is *a constitution* we are expounding" [McCulloch v. Maryland]; "a constitution intended for ages to come, and, consequently, to be adapted to the various *crises* of human affairs." . . .

. . . When we consider the contract clause and the decisions which have expounded it in harmony with the essential reserved power of the States to protect the security of their peoples, we find no warrant for the conclusion that the clause has been warped by these decisions from its proper significance . . . . With a growing recognition of public needs and the relation of individual right to public security, the Court has sought to prevent the perversion of the clause through its use as an instrument to throttle the capacity of the States to protect their fundamental interests. This development is a growth from the seeds which the fathers planted. . . . The principle of this development is, as we have seen, that the reservation of the reasonable exercise of the protective power of the State is read into all contracts . . . .

Applying the criteria established by our decisions, we conclude [inter alia]: The conditions upon which the period of redemption is extended do not appear to be unreasonable. . . . As already noted, the integrity of the mortgage indebtedness is not impaired; interest continues to run; the validity of the sale and the right of a mortgagee-purchaser to title or to obtain a deficiency judgment, if the mortgagor fails to redeem within the extended period, are maintained; and the conditions of redemption, if redemption there be, stand as they were under the prior law. If it be determined, as it must be, that the contract clause is not an absolute and utterly unqualified restriction of the State's protective power, this legislation is clearly so reasonable as to be within the legislative competency. . . .

The legislation is temporary in operation. It is limited to the exigency which called it forth. [T]he operation of the statute itself could not validly outlast the emergency or be so extended as virtually to destroy the contracts.

We are of the opinion that the Minnesota statute as here applied does not violate the contract clause of the Federal Constitution. . . .

Judgment affirmed.

Mr. Justice SUTHERLAND, dissenting. . . .

If it be possible by resort to the testimony of history to put any question of constitutional intent beyond the domain of uncertainty, the foregoing leaves no reasonable ground upon which to base a denial that the clause of the Constitution now under consideration was meant to foreclose state action impairing the obligation of contracts *primarily and especially* in respect of such action

aimed at giving relief to debtors *in time of emergency*. And if further proof be required to strengthen what already is inexpungable, such proof will be found in the previous decisions of this court. . . .

The Minnesota statute either impairs the obligation of contracts or it does not. If it does not, the occasion to which it relates becomes immaterial, since then the passage of the statute is the exercise of a normal, unrestricted, state power and requires no special occasion to render it effective. If it does, the emergency no more furnishes a proper occasion for its exercise than if the emergency were nonexistent. . . .

A statute which materially delays enforcement of the mortgagee's contractual right of ownership and possession does not modify the remedy merely; it destroys, for the period of delay, *all* remedy so far as the enforcement of that right is concerned. . . .

I am authorized to say that Mr. Justice VAN DEVANTER, Mr. Justice McREYNOLDS, and Mr. Justice BUTLER concur in this opinion.

CONTRACT CLAUSE CASES AFTER BLAISDELL

Most modern decisions have sustained state laws against contract clause challenges. They are noted in Justice Black's dissent in the El Paso case below, the most recent major rejection of a contract clause attack. But Blaisdell did not assure the validity of all state measures affecting contracts: laws were held to violate the contract clause in several cases in the decade after Chief Justice Hughes' opinion in 1934. In Worthen Co. v. Thomas, 292 U.S. 426 (1934), an Arkansas law exempted payments on life insurance policies from garnishment. Though an emergency existed, the law was invalid, according to the opinion by Chief Justice Hughes, because it contained no time limitation and because the amount of exemption was not limited to the necessities of the particular case. In Worthen Co. v. Kavanaugh, 295 U.S. 56 (1935), a municipal improvement district issued bonds and pledged benefit assessments as security. A subsequent Arkansas law changed the procedures for enforcing the payment of benefit assessments, to protect property owners. Justice Cardozo's opinion for the Court concluded that the procedural changes were "an oppressive and unnecessary destruction of nearly all the incidents that give attractiveness and value to collateral security. . . . Not even changes of the remedy may be pressed so far as to cut down the security of a mortgage without moderation or reason." And Wood v. Lovett, 313 U.S. 362 (1941), involved an Arkansas repeal in 1937 of a 1935 law protecting purchasers at state tax sales from state attempts to set aside the transaction on the basis of certain irregularities. The Court held that the 1937 repeal could not be applied to a 1936 sale; under the contract clause, the purchaser in 1936 was entitled to rely on the 1935 law designed to make "the land saleable." Justice Black, joined by Justices Douglas and Murphy dissented, insisting that, under Blaisdell, Arkansas had not acted "unreasonably, unjustly, oppressively, or counter to sound policy." Compare Justice Black's comment on this dissent in his 1965 dissent in El Paso v. Simmons, which follows.

EL PASO v. SIMMONS

379 U.S. 497, 85 S.Ct. 577, 13 L.Ed.2d 446 (1965).

Certiorari to the Court of Appeals for the Fifth Circuit.

[In 1910, Texas sold some public land by contract calling for a small down payment. State law provided for forfeiture of the purchaser's rights for nonpayment of interest; but, in case of forfeiture, the purchaser or his vendee could reinstate his claim at any time upon payment of delinquent interest, provided no rights of third parties had intervened. In 1941, Texas amended its laws to limit this reinstatement right to five years from the forfeiture date.

[The land contracts in issue in this case were declared forfeited for nonpayment of interest in 1947—37 years after the contracts were made. Subsequently, Simmons purchased the contract rights to the land. In 1952, five years and two days after the forfeiture, Simmons tendered payment of back interest and filed for reinstatement. The State, relying on the 5-year limitation enacted in 1941, refused to reinstate the claims. In 1955, the State sold the land to the City of El Paso. Simmons, a citizen of Kentucky, brought a federal court action against the City to determine title to the land. The District Court granted the City's motion for summary judgment on the basis of the 1941 law. The Court of Appeals reversed, holding the 1941 law unconstitutional: the 1910 reinstatement provision conferred a vested contractual right; the 1941 statute "was not a mere modification of remedy but a change in the obligation of a contract." The Court of Appeals remanded for a trial on the City's additional defenses of laches and adverse possession. The Supreme Court reversed.]

Mr. Justice WHITE delivered the opinion of the Court. . . .

We do not pause [to] chart again the dividing line [between] "remedy" and "obligation" . . . .. For it is not every modification of a contractual promise that impairs the obligation of contract under federal law, any more than it is every alteration of existing remedies that violates the Contract Clause. . . . Assuming the provision for reinstatement after default to be part of the State's obligation, we do not think its modification by a five-year statute of repose contravenes the Contract Clause. [The Blaisdell case] makes it quite clear that "the State . . . continues to possess authority to safeguard the vital interests of its people. . . ."

Of course, the power of a State to modify or affect the obligation of contract is not without limit. . . . But we think the objects of the Texas statute make abundantly clear that it impairs no protected right under the Contract Clause. . . .

Texas, upon entering the Union, reserved its entire public domain, one-half of which was set aside under the 1876 Constitution to finance a universal system of free public education. These lands, over 42,000,000 acres, were to be sold as quickly as practicable in order to provide revenues for the public school system and to encourage the settlement of the vast public domain. The terms of sale were undemanding and designed to accomplish the widespread sale and development of the public domain. . . . But eventually the evolution of a frontier society to a modern State, attended by the discovery of

oil and gas deposits which led to speculation and exploitation of the changes in the use and value of the lands, called forth amendments to the Texas land laws modifying the conditions of sale in favor of the State. . . .

. . . The general purpose of the legislation enacted in 1941 was to restore confidence in the stability and integrity of land titles and to enable the State to protect and administer its property in a businesslike manner. "[T]he records [of the land office] show that through the years many thousands of purchase contracts . . . have been forfeited by failure of the purchasers to meet the small annual interest payments requisite to the maintenance of the contracts." . . . This state of affairs was principally attributable to the opportunity for speculation to which unlimited reinstatement rights gave rise. Forfeited purchaser contracts which had remained dormant for years could be reinstated if and when the land became potentially productive of gas and oil. . . . .

No less significant was the imbroglio over land titles in Texas. The long shadow cast by perpetual reinstatement gave rise to a spate of litigation between forfeiting purchasers and the State or between one or more forfeiting purchasers and other forfeiting purchasers. . . .

The Contract Clause of the Constitution does not render Texas powerless to take effective and necessary measures to deal with the above. We note at the outset that the promise of reinstatement . . . was not the central undertaking of the seller nor the primary consideration for the buyer's undertaking. [T]he right of reinstatement [was] conditioned on the State's refusal or failure to dispose of the land by sale or lease. . . . We do not believe that it can seriously be contended that the buyer was substantially induced to enter into these contracts on the basis of a defeasible right to reinstatement in case of his failure to perform, or that he interpreted that right to be of everlasting effect. . . .

The State's policy of quick resale of forfeited lands did not prove entirely successful . . . . These developments, hardly to be expected or foreseen, operated to confer considerable advantages on the purchaser and his successors and a costly and difficult burden on the State. . . . Laws which restrict a party to those gains reasonably to be expected from the contract are not subject to attack under the Contract Clause, notwithstanding that they technically alter an obligation of a contract. . . .

Reversed.

Mr. Justice BLACK, dissenting.

I have previously had a number of occasions to dissent from judgments of this Court balancing away the First Amendment's unequivocally guaranteed rights [see chap. 12 below]. In this case I am compelled to dissent from the Court's balancing away the plain guarantee of [the contract clause].

. . . If the hope and realization of profit to a contract breaker are hereafter to be given either partial or sufficient weight to cancel out the unequivocal constitutional command against impairing the obligations of contracts, that command will be nullified by what is the most common cause for breaking contracts. I cannot subscribe to such a devitalizing constitutional doctrine.

.   .   .   The Court carefully does not deny that this promise by Texas is the kind of "obligation" which the Contract Clause was written to protect. The Court does not [treat] this as a mere change in court remedies for enforcement. [Instead,] the Court says that since the State acts out of what this Court thinks are good motives, and has not repudiated its contract except in a way which this Court thinks is "reasonable," therefore the State will be allowed to ignore the Contract Clause of the Constitution.   .   .   .

[T]he Court's discussion of the Contract Clause and this Court's past decisions applying it is brief.   [T]he first thing it is important to point out is that there is no support whatever in history or in this Court's prior holdings for the decision reached in this case.   .   .   .

The cases the Court mentions do not support its reasoning.   [Blaisdell], which the Court seems to think practically read the Contract Clause out of the Constitution, actually did no such thing, as the Blaisdell opinion read in its entirety shows and as subsequent decisions of this Court were careful to point out.   [T]he Blaisdell Court relied on [the] established distinction between an invalid impairment of a contract's obligation and a valid change in the remedy to enforce it.   .   .   .   Other state laws which did not meet the constitutional standard applied in Blaisdell were subsequently struck down.   .   .   .[1]

None of the other cases which the Court quotes or mentions in passing altered in any way the rule [that] a State may not pass a law repudiating contractual obligations without compensating the injured parties.[2]   .   .   .

.   .   .   On the side of the purchasers the Court finds nothing that weighs much   .   .   .   The Court tries to downgrade the importance of the reinstatement obligation in the contract by volunteering the opinion that this obligation "was not the central undertaking of the seller [Texas] nor the primary consideration for the buyer's undertaking."   Why the Court guesses this we are not told.   My guess is different.   .   .   .   To my way of thinking it demonstrates a striking lack of knowledge of credit buying and selling even to imply that these express contractual provisions safeguarding credit purchasers against forfeitures were not one of the greatest, if not the greatest, selling arguments Texas had to promote purchase of its great surfeit of lands.   The

---

1. I dissented in Wood v. Lovett, [as noted above], because [I] believed that the state law in that case, which protected purchasers of land against loss even though their titles were based only on quitclaim deeds, should have been upheld under Blaisdell. Even had my dissent prevailed, however, that case would not have supported the Court's holding in the case before us. [Footnote by Justice Black.]

2. None of the cases mentioned by the Court involved legislation by which a State attempted to repudiate its own contractual obligation without giving compensation, nor did any of them come near suggesting or implying that a State might do so. Honeyman v. Jacobs, 306 U.S. 539, . . . upheld a state statute providing that a mortgagee who bid at a foreclosure sale could not obtain a deficiency judgment if the value of the property equaled or exceeded the amount of the debt plus costs and interest; the Court said that the mortgagee under this law received all the compensation to which his contract entitled him, and that the statute "merely restricted the exercise of the contractual remedy." . . . Veix v. Sixth Ward Building & Loan Assn., 310 U.S. 32, held only that by issuing shares of stock at a time when state law permitted shareholders to withdraw their shares in exchange for a cash refund a private company regulated by the State could not prevent the State from applying later general legislation forbidding shareholders to

Court's factual inference is all the more puzzling since its opinion emphasizes that many people entered these contracts for speculative purposes which without the redemption provision would not have been nearly so attractive. . . .

Let us now look at some of the weights the Court throws on the scales on the side of Texas. . . . I do not believe that any or all of the things [on] which the Court relies are reasons for relieving Texas of the unconditional duty of keeping its contractual obligations. . . . It is a commonplace that land values steadily rise when population increases and rise sharply when valuable minerals are discovered, and that many sellers would be much richer and happier if when lands go up in value they were able to welch on their sales. No plethora of words about state school funds can conceal the fact that to get money easily without having to tax the whole public Texas took the easy way out and violated the Contract Clause of the Constitution as written and as applied up to now. . . .

All this for me is just another example of the delusiveness of calling "balancing" a "test." With its deprecatory view of the equities on the side of Simmons and other claimants and its remarkable sympathy for the State, the Court through its balancing process states the case in a way inevitably destined to bypass the Contract Clause and let Texas break its solemn obligation. . . .

RETROACTIVITY AND REGULATORY LAWS

Retroactivity is a pervasive concern in the cases in this section: attention to the extent to which reasonable private expectations are defeated by governmental action is an ingredient of many of the opinions. That is so not only with respect to the contract clause, which on its face purports to safeguard prior contractual arrangements, but also in such "taking" opinions as Justice Holmes' in the Pennsylvania Coal case. Is there a more general constitutional safeguard against retroactivity? The contract clause applies only to state, not federal, action; and retroactive legislation may affect private rights other than contractual ones. And despite occasional arguments to the contrary, the ex post facto clauses have been held to apply only to criminal, not civil, legislation, ever since Calder v. Bull in 1798 (sec. 1A above). Is there, then, any other, more general, constitutional safeguard against retroactive legislation? Some additional restraint on retroactivity has been found, through interpretations of the due process clause, particularly in challenges to federal legislation. But, like the contract clause and "taking" barriers, the due process limit does not help if there is a sufficently overriding public interest to be served.*

sue for the withdrawal value; this rule of course had been recognized in Blaisdell . . . . Gelfert v. National City Bank, 313 U.S. 221, upheld a New York law which redefined fair market value of property purchased by mortgagees at foreclosure sales; . . . the Court held that this law was merely a regulation of the remedy, and did not affect any substantial right given by the contract. . . . East New York Savings Bank v. Hahn, 326 U.S. 230, upheld a mortgage moratorium law much like that in Blaisdell . . . . [Footnote by Justice Black.]

* See generally Hochman, "The Supreme Court and the Constitutionality of Retroactive Legislation," 73 Harv.L.

With respect to federal legislation, the due process retroactivity barrier has been found greater when the government seeks to modify its own contractual obligations than when it regulates private contracts. For an example of the first situation, see Lynch v. United States, 292 U.S. 571 (1934), where the Court held that Congress could not cancel government war risk life insurance policies, as it had attempted to do in 1933 because of the economic crisis of the Depression. Justice Brandeis said for the Court that rights against the federal government "arising out of contract with it are protected by the Fifth Amendment" and that the government could not annul them "unless, indeed, the action taken falls within the federal police power or some other paramount power." See also Perry v. United States, 294 U.S. 330 (1935), the "gold clause" case dealing with the government's own obligation on its bonds. Contrast Norman v. B. & O. R. Co., 294 U.S. 240 (1935), another "gold clause" case, recognizing a wider power to affect private obligations.

For an example of a retroactive change in United States obligations "within the federal police power or some other paramount power," see Lichter v. United States, 334 U.S. 742 (1948) (renegotiation and recapture of excess profits on government contracts). Cf. FHA v. Darlington, 358 U.S. 84 (1958) (sustaining 1954 "clarifying" amendment restricting use of housing constructed under FHA-insured mortgage in 1949; Justices Harlan, Frankfurter and Whittaker dissented on the basis of Lynch); and note Flemming v. Nestor, on termination of social security benefits, chap. 4, sec. 2, above. See also Battaglia v. General Motors, 169 F.2d 254 (2d Cir.), cert. denied, 335 U.S. 887 (1948), sustaining the Portal-to-Portal Pay Act of 1947, which had relieved employers of overtime pay liability created by an unanticipated Supreme Court interpretation of the Fair Labor Standards Act. On due process challenges to retroactive state legislation, see, e. g., Chase Securities Corp. v. Donaldson, 325 U.S. 304 (1945), upholding a Minnesota law which lifted the bar of the statute of limitations in pending suits.

SECTION 3. THE REVIVAL OF SUBSTANTIVE DUE PROCESS, FOR NONECONOMIC RIGHTS: PRIVACY AND AUTONOMY

Introduction. Attention now returns to the theme of sec. 1, substantive due process. The question here, as there, is whether due process authorizes the Court to resort to what some have called natural law or noninterpretive modes of constitutional interpretation: to pour into the due process clause fundamental values not readily traceable to constitutional text or history or structure. The modern cases in sec. 1C contain frequent assertions that Lochner is dead, that the approach which Lochner symbolizes is dis-

Rev. 692 (1960); Slawson, "Constitutional and Legislative Considerations in Retroactive Lawmaking," 48 Calif. L.Rev. 216 (1960); Greenblatt, "Judicial Limitations on Retroactive Civil Legislation," 51 Nw.U.L.Rev. 540 (1956). Hochman identifies "three major factors" in retroactivity cases: "the nature and strength of the public interest served"; "the extent to which the statute modifies or abrogates the asserted preenactment right"; and "the nature of the right which the statute alters."

credited. But is it? This section focuses on two modern decisions which dissenters and other critics have characterized as indistinguishable from the Lochner philosophy: Griswold v. Connecticut in 1965, striking down Connecticut's ban on the use of contraceptives; and Roe v. Wade in 1973, invalidating most abortion laws. Do these decisions constitute "Lochnerizing," or are they distinguishable? Or do they suggest that "Lochnerizing" is justifiable after all?

Before turning to the decisions, a brief historical reminder is appropriate. Griswold and Roe v. Wade cannot be viewed as a sudden revival of substantive due process: in one sense, they built on an aspect of the Lochner tradition that never wholly died. To be sure, the aspect of Lochner that curtailed economic regulation has clearly waned since the 1930's, as sec. 1C demonstrates. But the Lochner era's protection of "fundamentals" was not wholly limited to economic rights: to the Court of that era, there was no sharp distinction between economic and noneconomic, "personal" liberties; some of the Lochner era decisions protected personal rights; and the modern Court had no qualms about citing those decisions in Griswold v. Connecticut.

MEYER v. NEBRASKA, 262 U.S. 390 (1923), is the outstanding example. Its broad reading of "liberty" (see also sec. 1B above) came from the pen of Justice McReynolds, supposedly one of the most opinionated and reactionary of the "Old Men" of the majority that provoked the Court-Packing crisis of the 1930's; and that "libertarian" Meyer decision came over the dissent of Justice Holmes. In Meyer, the Court reversed the conviction of a teacher for teaching German and thus violating a state law prohibiting the teaching of foreign languages to young children. Recall Justice McReynolds' broad view of "liberty" in the 14th Amendment, a view encompassing the personal as well as the economic: "Without doubt, it denotes not merely freedom from bodily restraint but also the right of the individual to contract, to engage in any of the common occupations of life, to acquire useful knowledge, to marry, establish a home and bring up children, to worship God according to the dictates of his own conscience, and generally to enjoy those privileges long recognized at common law as essential to the orderly pursuit of happiness by free men." Justice McReynolds found that the Nebraska law "materially" interfered "with the calling of modern language teachers, with the opportunities of pupils to acquire knowledge, and with the power of parents to control the education of their own." A legislative interest "to foster a homogeneous people with American ideals" was understandable, particularly in view of the "[u]nfortunate experiences during the late war." But now it was a "time of peace and domestic tranquility," and there was accordingly "no adequate justification" for the restraints on liberty. Justice McReynolds concluded: "No emergency has arisen which renders knowledge by a child of some language other than English so clearly harmful as to justify its inhibition with a consequent infringement of rights long freely enjoyed. [T]he statute as applied is arbitrary and without reasonable relation to any end within the competency of the State."

Justice McReynolds wrote in a similar vein for a unanimous Court two years later, in PIERCE v. SOCIETY OF SISTERS, 268 U.S. 510 (1925),

sustaining a challenge by parochial and private schools to an Oregon law requiring children to attend public schools. Again, there were "no peculiar circumstances or present emergencies which demand extraordinary measures relative to primary education." Under the view of protected rights of Meyer, the law interfered "with the liberty of parents and guardians to direct the upbringing and education of children under their control." There was no "general power of the State to standardize its children by forcing them to accept instruction from public teachers only. The child is not the mere creature of the State; those who nurture him and direct his destiny have the right, coupled with the high duty, to recognize and prepare him for additional obligations."

In the years before Griswold, the Warren Court, too, occasionally protected aspects of liberty even though they were not explicitly designated in the Constitution. For example, APTHEKER v. SECRETARY OF STATE, 378 U.S. 500 (1964) (chap. 12, sec. 1, below), invalidated a provision denying passports to Communist Party members because it "too broadly and indiscriminately restricts the right to travel and thereby abridges the liberty guaranteed by the Fifth Amendment." The Court relied on a dictum six years earlier, in Kent v. Dulles, 357 U.S. 116 (1958): "The right to travel is a part of the 'liberty' of which the citizen cannot be deprived without due process of law under the Fifth Amendment."

In light of modern First Amendment doctrine (see chaps. 12 and 13 below), cases such as those may be explainable on the bases of freedom of speech, association, and religion, though they did not rest on them explicitly.* But another decision only a few years after the supposed withdrawal from the Lochner doctrine is not so readily explainable by reference to specific constitutional guarantees. SKINNER v. OKLAHOMA, 316 U.S. 535 (1942), was a forerunner of the special protection of some "fundamental interests" under the "new" equal protection, traced in the next chapter. It was an equal protection case in form, but it rested in part on language akin to substantive due process. Justice Douglas' opinion in Skinner invalidated Oklahoma's Habitual Criminal Sterilization Act, providing for compulsory sterilization after a third conviction for a felony "involving moral turpitude," but excluding such felonies as embezzlement. Though state classifications of crimes would not ordinarily be overturned, Justice Douglas explained, that usual deference to state police power legislation was not warranted here: "We are dealing here with legislation which involves one of the basic civil rights of man. Marriage and procreation are fundamental to the very existence and survival of the race. . . . There is no redemption for the individual whom the law touches. Any experiment which the State conducts is to his irreparable injury. He is forever deprived of a basic liberty. We mention these matters not to reexamine the scope of the police power of the States. We advert to them merely in emphasis of our view that *strict scrutiny* of the classification which a State makes in a sterilization law is essential, lest unwittingly, or otherwise, invidious discriminations are made against groups or types of individuals in

---

* Justice Douglas so explains them in the Griswold case, below: he views Meyer and Pierce as enforcing "peripheral rights" stemming from the First Amendment.

violation of the constitutional guaranty of just and equal laws. . . . Sterilization of those who have thrice committed grand larceny, with immunity for those who are embezzlers, is a clear, pointed, unmistakable discrimination." (Emphasis added.) *

But the 1942 reference in Skinner to "fundamental," "basic" liberties in the area of marriage and procreation was extraordinary: that decision mixing due process and equal protection considerations was virtually the only one in that period from the demise of Lochner to Griswold to exercise special scrutiny in favor of a "basic liberty" not tied to or justifiable by a specific constitutional guarantee. In short, between the Lochner era and Griswold, the methodology of substantive due process review on behalf of fundamental, judicially defined values was, if not wholly discarded, largely dormant. With Griswold and Roe v. Wade, which follow, it may have regained greater vitality than it has had in more than a generation.

GRISWOLD v. CONNECTICUT

381 U.S. 479, 85 S.Ct. 1678, 14 L.Ed.2d 510 (1965).

On appeal from the Supreme Court of Errors of Connecticut.

Mr. Justice DOUGLAS delivered the opinion of the Court.

Appellant Griswold is Executive Director of the Planned Parenthood League of Connecticut. Appellant Buxton is a licensed physician and a professor at the Yale Medical School who served as Medical Director for the League at its Center in New Haven—a center open and operating from November 1 to November 10, 1961, when appellants were arrested.†

They gave information, instruction, and medical advice to *married persons* as to the means of preventing conception. They examined the wife and prescribed the best contraceptive device or material for her use. Fees were usually charged, although some couples were serviced free.

The statutes whose constitutionality is involved in this appeal are §§ 53–32 and 54–196 of the General Statutes of Connecticut (1958 rev.). The former provides:

"Any person who uses any drug, medicinal article or instrument for the purpose of preventing conception shall be fined not less than fifty dollars or imprisoned not less than sixty days nor more than one year or [both]." Section 54–196 provides:

---

* The case is further considered in chap. 10 below. Compare Buck v. Bell, 274 U.S. 200 (1927), sustaining a state law for the sterilization of mentally defectives in institutions. Justice Holmes—in a much criticized opinion, though characteristic of his stance on substantive due process—rejected the due process claims summarily, saying that "three generations of imbeciles are enough." See Rogat, "The Judge As Spectator," 31 U.Chi.L.Rev. 213 (1964).

† Earlier efforts to test the constitutionality of the Connecticut contraception law had been turned away by the Court on justiciability grounds. See Tileston v. Ullman, 318 U.S. 44 (1943), and Poe v. Ullman, 367 U.S. 497 (1961), both in chap. 15, below.

"Any person who assists, abets, counsels, causes, hires or commands another to commit any offense may be prosecuted and punished as if he were the principal offender."

The appellants were found guilty as accessories and fined $100 each, against the claim that the accessory statute as so applied violated the Fourteenth Amendment. . . . The Court of Errors affirmed that judgment. [The Court's reasons for holding "that appellants have standing to raise the constitutional rights of the married people with whom they had a professional relationship" are noted in chap. 15, sec. 2, below.]

Coming to the merits, we are met with a wide range of questions that implicate the Due Process Clause of the Fourteenth Amendment. Overtones of some arguments suggest that [Lochner v. New York] should be our guide. But we decline that invitation as we did in [the West Coast Hotel, Olsen v. Nebraska, Lincoln Union, and Lee Optical cases, all in sec. 1C above]. We do not sit as a super-legislature to determine the wisdom, need, and propriety of laws that touch economic problems, business affairs, or social conditions. This law, however, operates directly on an intimate relation of husband and wife and their physician's role in one aspect of that relation.

The association of people is not mentioned in the Constitution nor in the Bill of Rights. The right to educate a child in a school of the parents' choice—whether public or private or parochial—is also not mentioned. Nor is the right to study any particular subject or any foreign language. Yet the First Amendment has been construed to include certain of those rights.

By [Pierce v. Society of Sisters], the right to educate one's children as one chooses is made applicable to the States by the force of the First and Fourteenth Amendments. By [Meyer v. Nebraska], the same dignity is given the right to study the German language in a private school. In other words, the State may not, consistently with the spirit of the First Amendment, contract the spectrum of available knowledge. The right of freedom of speech and press includes not only the right to utter or to print, but the right to distribute, the right to receive, the right to read [and] freedom of inquiry, freedom of thought, and freedom to teach . . .—indeed the freedom of the entire university community. . . . Without those peripheral rights the specific rights would be less secure. And so we reaffirm the principle of the Pierce and the Meyer cases.

In NAACP v. Alabama, 357 U.S. 449, 462 [1958], we protected the "freedom to associate and privacy in one's association," noting that freedom of association was a peripheral First Amendment right. Disclosure of membership lists of a constitutionally valid association, we held, was invalid [chap. 13, below]. In other words, the First Amendment has a penumbra where privacy is protected from governmental intrusion. In like context, we have protected forms of "association" that are not political in the customary sense but pertain to the social, legal, and economic benefit of the members. . . . [The right to association,] while it is not expressly included in the First Amendment, [is] necessary in making the express guarantees fully meaningful.

The foregoing cases suggest that specific guarantees in the Bill of Rights have penumbras, formed by emanations from those guarantees that help give them life and substance. See Poe v. Ullman, 367 U.S. 497, 516–522

(dissenting opinion).   Various guarantees create zones of privacy.   The right of association contained in the penumbra of the First Amendment is one, as we have seen.   The Third Amendment in its prohibition against the quartering of soldiers "in any house" in time of peace without the consent of the owner is another facet of that privacy.   The Fourth Amendment explicitly affirms the "right of the people to be secure in their persons, houses, papers, and effects against unreasonable searches and seizures."   The Fifth Amendment in its Self-Incrimination Clause enables the citizen to create a zone of privacy which government may not force him to surrender to his detriment.   The Ninth Amendment provides: "The enumeration in the Constitution, of certain rights, shall not be construed to deny or disparage others retained by the people." . . .

The Fourth and Fifth Amendments were described in Boyd v. United States, 116 U.S. 616 [1886], as protection against all governmental invasions "of the sanctity of a man's home and the privacies of life."   We recently referred in [Mapp v. Ohio] to the Fourth Amendment as creating a "right to privacy, no less important than any other right carefully and particularly reserved to the people." . . .   We have had many controversies over these penumbral rights of "privacy and repose." . . .   These cases bear witness that the right of privacy which presses for recognition here is a legitimate one.

The present case, then, concerns a relationship lying within the zone of privacy created by several fundamental constitutional guarantees.   And it concerns a law which, in forbidding the *use* of contraceptives rather than regulating their manufacture or sale, seeks to achieve its goals by means having a maximum destructive impact upon that relationship.   Such a law cannot stand in light of the familiar principle, so often applied by this Court, that a "governmental purpose to control or prevent activities constitutionally subject to state regulation may not be achieved by means which sweep unnecessarily broadly and thereby invade the area of protected freedoms." NAACP v. Alabama, 377 U.S. 288, 307.   Would we allow the police to search the sacred precincts of marital bedrooms for telltale signs of the use of contraceptives?   The very idea is repulsive to the notions of privacy surrounding the marriage relationship.

We deal with a right of privacy older than the Bill of Rights—older than our political parties, older than our school system.   Marriage is a coming together for better or for worse, hopefully enduring, and intimate to the degree of being sacred.   The association promotes a way of life, not causes; a harmony in living, not political faiths; a bilateral loyalty, not commercial or social projects.   Yet it is an association for as noble a purpose as any involved in our prior decisions.

Reversed.

Mr. Justice GOLDBERG, whom The Chief Justice [WARREN] and Mr. Justice BRENNAN join, concurring.

I agree with the Court that Connecticut's birth-control law unconstitutionally intrudes upon the right of marital privacy, and I join in its opinion and judgment.   Although I have not accepted the view that "due process" as used in the Fourteenth Amendment incorporates all of the first eight

Amendments, . . . I do agree that the concept of liberty protects those personal rights that are fundamental, and is not confined to the specific terms of the Bill of Rights. My conclusion that the concept of liberty is not so restricted and that it embraces the right of marital privacy though that right is not mentioned explicitly in the Constitution is supported both by numerous decisions of this Court, referred to in the Court's opinion, and by the language and history of the Ninth Amendment. [I] add these words to emphasize the relevance of that Amendment to the Court's holding. . . .

This Court [has] held that the Fourteenth Amendment absorbs and applies to the States those specifics of the first eight amendments which express fundamental personal rights. The language and history of the Ninth Amendment reveal that the Framers of the Constitution believed that there are additional fundamental rights, protected from governmental infringement, which exist alongside those fundamental rights specifically mentioned in the first eight constitutional amendments.

The Ninth Amendment reads, "The enumeration in the Constitution, of certain rights, shall not be construed to deny or disparage others retained by the people." The amendment is almost entirely the work of James Madison. . . . It was proffered to quiet expressed fears that a bill of specifically enumerated rights could not be sufficiently broad to cover all essential rights and that the specific mention of certain rights would be interpreted as a denial that others were protected. . . .

While this Court has had little occasion to interpret the Ninth Amendment,[1] "[i]t cannot be presumed that any clause in the constitution is intended to be without effect." [Marbury v. Madison.] The Ninth Amendment to the Constitution may be regarded by some as a recent discovery, but since 1791 it has been a basic part of the Constitution which we are sworn to uphold. To hold that a right so basic and fundamental and so deeprooted in our society as the right of privacy in marriage may be infringed because that right is not guaranteed in so many words by the first eight amendments to the Constitution is to ignore the Ninth Amendment and to give it no effect whatsoever. . . .

A dissenting opinion suggests that my interpretation of the Ninth Amendment somehow "broaden[s] the powers of this Court." . . . With all due respect, I believe that it misses the import of what I am saying. [I] do not mean to imply that the Ninth Amendment is applied against the States by the Fourteenth. Nor do I mean to state that the Ninth Amendment constitutes an independent source of rights protected from infringement by either the States or Federal Government. Rather, the Ninth Amendment

---

1. This Amendment has been referred to as "The Forgotten Ninth Amendment," in a book with that title by Bennet B. Patterson (1955). Other commentary on the Ninth Amendment includes Redlich, "Are There Certain Rights . . . Retained by the People"? 37 N.Y.U.L.Rev. 787 (1962), and Kelsey, The Ninth Amendment of the Federal Constitution, 11 Ind.L.J. 309 (1936). As far as I am aware, until today this Court has referred to the Ninth Amendment only in United Public Workers v. Mitchell, 330 U.S. 75, 94–95; Tennessee Electric Power Co. v. TVA, 306 U.S. 118, 143–144; and Ashwander v. TVA, 297 U.S. 288, 330–331. See also **Calder v.** Bull, 3 Dall. 386, 388; Loan Assn. v. Topeka, 20 Wall. 655, 662–663. . . . [Footnote by Justice Goldberg.]

shows a belief of the Constitution's authors that fundamental rights exist that are not expressly enumerated in the first eight amendments and an intent that the list of rights included there not be exhaustive. As any student of this Court's opinions knows, this Court has held, often unanimously, that the Fifth and Fourteenth Amendments protect certain fundamental personal liberties from abridgment by the Federal Government or the States. . . . The Ninth Amendment simply shows the intent of the Constitution's authors that other fundamental personal rights should not be denied such protection or disparaged in any other way simply because they are not specifically listed in the first eight constitutional amendments. I do not see how this broadens the authority of the court; rather it serves to support what this Court has been doing in protecting fundamental rights.

Nor am I turning somersaults with history in arguing that the Ninth Amendment is relevant in a case dealing with a *State's* infringement of a fundamental right. While the Ninth Amendment—and indeed the entire Bill of Rights—originally concerned restrictions upon *federal* power, the subsequently enacted Fourteenth Amendment prohibits the States as well from abridging fundamental personal liberties. And, the Ninth Amendment, in indicating that not all such liberties are specifically mentioned in the first eight amendments, is surely relevant in showing the existence of other fundamental personal rights, now protected from state, as well as federal, infringement. . . .

In determining which rights are fundamental, judges are not left at large to decide cases in light of their personal and private notions. Rather, they must look to the "traditions and [collective] conscience of our people" to determine whether a principle is "so rooted [there] . . . as to be ranked as fundamental." . . . The inquiry is whether a right involved "is of such a character that it cannot be denied without violating those 'fundamental principles of liberty and justice which lie at the base of all our civil and political institutions.'" [Powell v. Alabama.] . . . I agree fully with the Court that, applying these tests, the right of privacy is a fundamental personal right, emanating "from the totality of the constitutional scheme under which we live." . . .

The logic of the dissents would sanction federal or state legislation that seems to me even more plainly unconstitutional than the statute before us. Surely the Government, absent a showing of a compelling subordinating state interest, could not decree that all husbands and wives must be sterilized after two children have been born to them. Yet by their reasoning such an invasion of marital privacy would not be subject to constitutional challenge because, while it might be "silly," no provision of the Constitution specifically prevents the Government from curtailing the marital right to bear children and raise a family. [I]f upon a showing of a slender basis of rationality, a law outlawing voluntary birth control by married persons is valid, then, by the same reasoning, a law requiring compulsory birth control also would seem to be valid. In my view, however, both types of law would unjustifiably intrude upon rights of marital privacy which are constitutionally protected.

In a long series of cases this Court has held that where fundamental personal liberties are involved, they may not be abridged by the States simply on a showing that a regulatory statute has some rational relationship to the

effectuation of a proper state purpose. "Where there is a significant encroachment upon personal liberty, the State may prevail only upon showing a subordinating interest which is compelling " [Bates v. Little Rock, chap. 13 below]. The law must be shown "necessary, and not merely rationally related, to the accomplishment of a permissible state policy." [McLaughlin v. Florida, chap. 10 below.] The State, at most, argues that there is some rational relation between this statute and what is admittedly a legitimate subject of state concern—the discouraging of extra-marital relations. It says that preventing the use of birth-control devices by married persons helps prevent the indulgence by some in such extra-marital relations. The rationality of this justification is dubious, particularly in light of the admitted widespread availability to all persons in the State of Connecticut, unmarried as well as married, of birth-control devices for the prevention of disease, as distinguished from the prevention of conception. But, in any event, it is clear that the state interest in safeguarding marital fidelity can be served by a more discriminately tailored statute, which does not, like the present one, sweep unnecessarily broadly, reaching far beyond the evil sought to be dealt with and intruding upon the privacy of all married couples. . . . Connecticut does have statutes, the constitutionality of which is beyond doubt, which prohibit adultery and fornication. These statutes demonstrate that means for achieving the same basic purpose of protecting marital fidelity are available to Connecticut without the need to "invade the area of protected freedoms." . . .

Finally, it should be said of the Court's holding today that it in no way interferes with a State's proper regulation of sexual promiscuity or misconduct. [A passage from Justice Harlan's dissent in Poe v. Ullman is omitted. See Justice Harlan's opinion, which follows.] . . .

Mr. Justice HARLAN, concurring in the judgment.

I fully agree with the judgment of reversal, but find myself unable to join the Court's opinion. The reason is that it seems to me to evince an approach to this case very much like that taken by my Brothers Black and Stewart in dissent, namely: the Due Process Clause of the Fourteenth Amendment does not touch this Connecticut statute unless the enactment is found to violate some right assured by the letter or penumbra of the Bill of Rights. . . .

In my view, the proper constitutional inquiry in this case is whether this Connecticut statute infringes the Due Process Clause of the Fourteenth Amendment because the enactment violates basic values "implicit in the concept of ordered liberty," [Palko v. Connecticut]. For reasons stated at length in my dissenting opinion in Poe v. Ullman [see the excerpts below], I believe that it does. While the relevant inquiry may be aided by resort to one or more of the provisions of the Bill of Rights, it is not dependent on them or any of their radiations. The Due Process Clause of the Fourteenth Amendment stands, in my opinion, on its own bottom. . . .

While I could not more heartily agree that judicial "self-restraint" is an indispensable ingredient of sound constitutional adjudication, I do submit that the formula suggested for achieving it is more hollow than real. "Specific" provisions of the Constitution, no less than "due process," lend them-

selves as readily to "personal" interpretations by judges whose constitutional outlook is simply to keep the Constitution in supposed "tune with the times."

. . .

[Justice Harlan relied on his dissent in Poe v. Ullman, 367 U.S. 497 (1961), where he had elaborated his due process approach. The majority in Poe (see chap. 15 below) had failed to reach the merits of a challenge to the Connecticut law; it had dismissed the appeal on justiciability grounds. Excerpts from Justice Harlan's dissent in POE v. ULLMAN follow:]

. . . I believe that a statute making it a criminal offense for *married couples* to use contraceptives is an intolerable and unjustifiable invasion of privacy in the conduct of the most intimate concerns of an individual's personal life. I reach this conclusion, even though I find it difficult and unnecessary at this juncture to accept appellants' other argument that the judgment of policy behind the statute, so applied, is so arbitrary and unreasonable as to render the enactment invalid for that reason alone. Since both the contentions draw their basis from no explicit language of the Constitution, and have yet to find expression in any decision of this Court, I feel it desirable at the outset to state the framework of Constitutional principles in which I think the issue must be judged. . . .

It is but a truism to say that [due process] is not self-explanatory. . . . Were due process merely a procedural safeguard it would fail to reach those situations where the deprivation of life, liberty or property was accomplished by legislation which by operating in the future could, given even the fairest possible procedure in application to individuals, nevertheless destroy the enjoyment of all three. . . . However it is not the particular enumeration of rights in the first eight Amendments which spells out the reach of Fourteenth Amendment due process, but rather, as was suggested in another context long before the adoption of that Amendment, those concepts which are considered to embrace those rights "which are . . . *fundamental*; which belong . . . to the citizens of all free governments" [Corfield v. Coryell], for "the purposes [of securing] which men enter into society," [Calder v. Bull]. [See sec. 1A above.]

Due process has not been reduced to any formula; its content cannot be determined by reference to any code. The best that can be said is that through the course of this Court's decisions it has represented the balance which our Nation, built upon postulates of respect for the liberty of the individual, has struck between that liberty and the demands of organized society. If the supplying of content to this Constitutional concept has of necessity been a rational process, it certainly has not been one where judges have felt free to roam where unguided speculation might take them. The balance of which I speak is the balance struck by this country, having regard to what history teaches are the traditions from which it developed as well as the traditions from which it broke. That tradition is a living thing. A decision of this Court which radically departs from it could not long survive, while a decision which builds on what has survived is likely to be sound. No formula could serve as a substitute, in this area, for judgment and restraint.

It is this outlook which has led the Court continuingly to perceive distinctions in the imperative character of Constitutional provisions, since that

character must be discerned from a particular provision's larger context. And inasmuch as this context is one not of words, but of history and purposes, the full scope of the liberty guaranteed by the Due Process Clause cannot be found in or limited by the precise terms of the specific guarantees elsewhere provided in the Constitution. This "liberty" is not a series of isolated points pricked out in terms of the taking of property; the freedom of speech, press, and religion; the right to keep and bear arms; the freedom from unreasonable searches and seizures; and so on. It is a rational continuum which, broadly speaking, includes a freedom from all substantial arbitrary impositions and purposeless restraints, see [e. g., Allgeyer v. Louisiana; Nebbia v. New York], and which also recognizes, what a reasonable and sensitive judgment must, that certain interests require particularly careful scrutiny of the state needs asserted to justify their abridgment. . .

Appellants contend that the Connecticut statute deprives them, as it unquestionably does, of a substantial measure of liberty in carrying on the most intimate of all personal relationships, and that it does so arbitrarily and without any rational, justifying purpose. The State, on the other hand, asserts that it is acting to protect the moral welfare of its citizenry, both directly, in that it considers the practice of contraception immoral in itself, and instrumentally, in that the availability of contraceptive materials tends to minimize "the disastrous consequence of dissolute action," that is fornication and adultery.

It is argued by appellants that the judgment, implicit in this statute— that the use of contraceptives by married couples is immoral—is an irrational one, that in effect it subjects them in a very important matter to the arbitrary whim of the legislature, and that it does so for no good purpose. . . . Yet the very inclusion of the category of morality among state concerns indicates that society is not limited in its objects only to the physical well-being of the community, but has traditionally concerned itself with the moral soundness of its people as well. Indeed to attempt a line between public behavior and that which is purely consensual or solitary would be to withdraw from community concern a range of subjects with which every society in civilized times has found it necessary to deal. The laws regarding marriage which provide both when the sexual powers may be used and the legal and societal context in which children are born and brought up, as well as laws forbidding adultery, fornication and homosexual practices which express the negative of the proposition, confining sexuality to lawful marriage, form a pattern so deeply pressed into the substance of our social life that any Constitutional doctrine in this area must build upon that basis. . . .

It is in this area of sexual morality, which contains many proscriptions of consensual behavior having little or no direct impact on others, that the State of Connecticut has expressed its moral judgment that all use of contraceptives is improper. . . . Certainly, Connecticut's judgment is no more demonstrably correct or incorrect than are the varieties of judgment, expressed in law, on marriage and divorce, on adult consensual homosexuality, abortion, and sterilization, or euthanasia and suicide. If we had a case before us which required us to decide simply, and in abstraction, whether the moral judgment implicit in the application of the present statute to married couples was a sound one, the very controversial nature of these

questions would, I think, require us to hesitate long before concluding that the Constitution precluded Connecticut from choosing as it has among these various views. . . . *

But [we] are not presented simply with this moral judgment to be passed on as an abstract proposition. The secular state is not an examiner of consciences: it must operate in the realm of behavior, of overt actions, and where it does so operate, not only the underlying, moral purpose of its operations, but also the *choice of means* becomes relevant to any Constitutional judgment on what is done. . . .

Precisely what is involved here is this: the State is asserting the right to enforce its moral judgment by intruding upon the most intimate details of the marital relation with the full power of the criminal law. Potentially, this could allow the deployment of all the incidental machinery of the criminal law, arrests, searches and seizures; inevitably, it must mean at the very least the lodging of criminal charges, a public trial, and testimony as to the *corpus delicti.* Nor could any imaginable elaboration of presumptions, testimonial privileges, or other safeguards, alleviate the necessity for testimony as to the mode and manner of the married couples' sexual relations, or at least the opportunity for the accused to make denial of the charges. In sum, the statute allows the State to enquire into, prove and punish married people for the private use of their marital intimacy.

The statute must pass a more rigorous Constitutional test than that going merely to the plausibility of its underlying rationale. This enactment involves what, by common understanding throughout the English-speaking world, must be granted to be a most fundamental aspect of "liberty," the privacy of the home in its most basic sense, and it is this which requires that the statute be subjected to "strict scrutiny." [Skinner v. Oklahoma.]

That aspect of liberty which embraces the concept of the privacy of the home receives explicit Constitutional protection at two places only [—the Third and Fourth Amendments]. [T]his Court has held in the strongest terms [that] the concept of "privacy" embodied in the Fourth Amendment is part of the "ordered liberty" assured against state action by the Fourteenth Amendment. . . .

It is clear, of course, that this Connecticut statute does not invade the privacy of the home in the usual sense, since the invasion involved here may, and doubtless usually would, be accomplished without any physical intrusion whatever into the home. What the statute undertakes to do, however, is to create a crime which is grossly offensive to this privacy, while the Constitution refers only to methods of ferreting out substantive wrongs, and the procedure it requires presupposes that substantive offenses may be committed and sought out in the privacy of the home. But such an analysis forecloses any claim to Constitutional protection against this form of deprivation of privacy, only if due process in this respect is limited to what is explicitly provided in the Constitution, divorced from the rational purposes, historical roots, and subsequent developments of the relevant provisions. . . .

---

* Note the consideration of these passages in Justice Harlan's opinion in note 6 following Roe v. Wade, below.

It would surely be an extreme instance of sacrificing substance to form were it to be held that the Constitutional principle of privacy against arbitrary official intrusion comprehends only physical invasions by the police. . . . [I]f the physical curtilage of the home is protected, it is surely as a result of solicitude to protect the privacies of the life within. Certainly the safeguarding of the home does not follow merely from the sanctity of property rights. The home derives its pre-eminence as the seat of family life. And the integrity of that life is something so fundamental that it has been found to draw to its protection the principles of more than one explicitly granted Constitutional right. [See, e. g., Meyer; Pierce.] Of [the] whole "private realm of family life" it is difficult to imagine what is more private or more intimate than a husband and wife's marital relations. . . .

Of course, [there] are countervailing considerations. [I]t would be an absurdity to suggest either that offenses may not be committed in the bosom of the family or that the home can be made a sanctuary for crime. The right of privacy most manifestly is not an absolute. Thus, I would not suggest that adultery, homosexuality, fornication and incest are immune from criminal enquiry, however privately practiced. So much has been explicitly recognized in acknowledging the State's rightful concern for its people's moral welfare. [See above.] But not to discriminate between what is involed in this case and either the traditional offenses against good morals or crimes which, though they may be committed anywhere, happen to have been committed or concealed in the home, would entirely misconceive the argument that is being made.

Adultery, homosexuality and the like are sexual intimacies which the State forbids altogether, but the intimacy of husband and wife is necessarily an essential and accepted feature of the institution of marriage, an institution which the State not only must allow, but which always and in every age it has fostered and protected. It is one thing when the State exerts its power either to forbid extra-marital sexuality altogether, or to say who may marry, but it is quite another when, having acknowledged a marriage and the intimacies inherent in it, it undertakes to regulate by means of the criminal law the details of that intimacy.

In sum, even though the State has determined that the use of contraceptives is as iniquitous as any act of extra-marital sexual immorality, the intrusion of the whole machinery of the criminal law into the very heart of marital privacy, requiring husband and wife to render account before a criminal tribunal of their uses of that intimacy, is surely a very different thing indeed from punishing those who establish intimacies which the law has always forbidden and which can have no claim to social protection.

In my view the appellants have presented a very pressing claim for Constitutional protection. . . . Since [the] statute marks an abridgment of important fundamental liberties protected by the Fourteenth Amendment, it will not do to urge in justification of that abridgment simply that the statute is rationally related to the effectuation of a proper state purpose. A closer scrutiny and stronger justification than that are required.

Though the State has argued the Constitutional permissibility of the moral judgment underlying this statute, neither its brief, nor its argument,

nor anything in any of the opinions of its highest court in these or other cases even remotely suggests a justification for the obnoxiously intrusive means it has chosen to effectuate that policy. . . .

But conclusive, in my view, is the utter novelty of this enactment. Although the Federal Government and many States have at one time or other had on their books statutes forbidding or regulating the distribution of contraceptives, none, so far as I can find, has made the *use* of contraceptives a crime. . . .

Though undoubtedly the States are and should be left free to reflect a wide variety of policies, and should be allowed broad scope in experimenting with various means of promoting those policies, I must agree with Mr. Justice Jackson that "There are limits to the extent to which a legislatively represented majority may conduct . . . experiments at the expense of the dignity and personality" of the individual. [Skinner v. Oklahoma, concurring opinion.] In this instance these limits are, in my view, reached and passed. . . .

Mr. Justice WHITE, concurring in the judgment. . . .

. . . [T]his is not the first time this Court has had occasion to articulate that the liberty entitled to protection under the Fourteenth Amendment includes the right "to marry, establish a home and bring up children," [Meyer v. Nebraska] and "the liberty . . . to direct the upbringing and education of children," [Pierce v. Society of Sisters], and that these are among "the basic civil rights of man." [Skinner v. Oklahoma.] These decisions affirm that there is a "realm of family life which the state cannot enter" without substantial justification. Prince v. Massachusetts, 321 U.S. 158, 166. Surely the right invoked in this case, to be free of regulation of the intimacies of the marriage relationship, "come[s] to this Court with a momentum for respect lacking when appeal is made to liberties which derive merely from shifting economic arrangements." Kovacs v. Cooper, 336 U.S. 77, 95 (opinion of Frankfurter, J.) [chap. 12 below].

The Connecticut anti-contraceptive statute deals rather substantially with this relationship. . . . In my view, a statute with these effects bears a substantial burden of justification when attacked under the Fourteenth Amendment. . . .

An examination of the justification offered, however, cannot be avoided by saying that the Connecticut anti-use statute invades a protected area of privacy and association or that it demeans the marriage relationship. The nature of the right invaded is pertinent, to be sure, for statutes regulating sensitive areas of liberty do, under the cases of this Court, require "strict scrutiny," [Skinner v. Oklahoma] and "must be viewed in light of less drastic means for achieving the same basic purpose." . . . But such statutes, if reasonably necessary for the effectuation of a legitimate and substantial state interest, and not arbitrary or capricious in application, are not invalid under the Due Process Clause. . . .

As I read the opinions of the Connecticut courts and the argument of Connecticut in this Court, the State claims but one justification for its anti-use statute. . . . There is no serious contention that Connecticut thinks the use of artificial or external methods of contraception immoral or unwise

in itself, or that the anti-use statute is founded upon any policy of promoting population expansion. Rather, the statute is said to serve the State's policy against all forms of promiscuous or illicit sexual relationships, be they pre-marital or extramarital, concededly a permissible and legitimate legislative goal.

Without taking issue with the premise that the fear of conception op-erates as a deterrent to such relationships in addition to the criminal proscriptions Connecticut has against such conduct, I wholly fail to see how the ban on the use of contraceptives by married couples in any way reinforces the State's ban on illicit sexual relationships. . . .

. . . It is purely fanciful to believe that the broad proscription on use facilitates discovery of use by persons engaging in a prohibited relationship or for some other reason makes such use more unlikely and thus can be sup-ported by any sort of administrative consideration. Perhaps the theory is that the flat ban on use prevents married people from possessing contra-ceptives and without the ready availability of such devices for use in the marital relationship, there will be no or less temptation to use them in extra-marital ones. This reasoning rests on the premise that married people will comply with the anti-use ban in regard to their marital relationship, notwith-standing total nonenforcement in this context and apparent nonenforcibility, but will not comply with criminal statutes prohibiting extramarital affairs and the anti-use statute in respect to illicit sexual relationships, a premise whose validity has not been demonstrated and whose intrinsic validity is not very evident. At most the broad ban is of marginal utility to the declared ob-jective. A statute limiting its prohibition on use to persons engaging in the prohibited relationship would serve the end posited by Connecticut in the same way, and with the same effectiveness, or ineffectiveness, as the broad anti-use statute under attack in this case. I find nothing in this record justi-fying the sweeping scope of this statute, with its telling effect on the freedoms of married persons, and therefore conclude that it deprives such persons of liberty without due process of law.

Mr. Justice BLACK, with whom Mr. Justice STEWART joins, dis-senting.

. . . [T]he law is every bit as offensive to me as it is to my Breth-ren . . . who, reciting reasons why it is offensive to them, hold it un-constitutional. There is no single one of the graphic and eloquent strictures and criticisms fired at the policy of this Connecticut law either by the Court's opinion or by those of my concurring Brethren to which I cannot subscribe—except their conclusion that the evil qualities they see in the law make it unconstitutional. . . .

The Court talks about a constitutional "right of privacy" as though there is some constitutional [provision] forbidding any law ever to be passed which might abridge the "privacy" of individuals. But there is not. There are, of course, guarantees in certain specific constitutional provisions which are designed in part to protect privacy at certain times and places with re-spect to certain activities. Such, for example, is the [Fourth Amendment]. But I think it belittles that Amendment to talk about it as though it protects nothing but "privacy." . . .

One of the most effective ways of diluting or expanding a constitutionally guaranteed right is to substitute for the crucial word or words of a constitutional guarantee another word or words, more or less flexible and more or less restricted in meaning. This fact is well illustrated by the use of the term "right of privacy" as a comprehensive substitute for the Fourth Amendment's guarantee against "unreasonable searches and seizures." "Privacy" is a broad, abstract and ambiguous concept which can easily be shrunken in meaning but which can [also] easily be interpreted as a constitutional ban against many things other than searches and seizures. . . . I get nowhere in this case by talk about a constitutional "right of privacy" as an emanation from one or more constitutional provisions.[1] I like my privacy as well as the next one, but I am nevertheless compelled to admit that government has a right to invade it unless prohibited by some specific constitutional provision. . . .

This brings me to the arguments made by my Brothers Harlan, White and Goldberg for invalidating the Connecticut law. . . . I discuss the due process and Ninth Amendment arguments together because on analysis they turn out to be the same thing—merely using different words to claim for this Court and the federal judiciary power to invalidate any legislative act which the judges find irrational, unreasonable or offensive.

The due process argument which my Brothers Harlan and White adopt here is based, as their opinions indicate, on the premise that this Court is vested with power to invalidate all state laws that it considers to be arbitrary, capricious, unreasonable, or oppressive, or on this Court's belief that a particular state law under scrutiny has no "rational or justifying" purpose, or is offensive to a "sense of fairness and justice." If these formulas based on "natural justice," or others which mean the same thing,[2] are to prevail, they require judges to determine what is or is not constitutional on the basis of their own appraisal of what laws are unwise or unnecessary.[3] The power to make such decisions is of course that of a legis-

---

1. The phrase "right to privacy" appears first to have gained currency from an article written by Messrs. Warren and (later Mr. Justice) Brandeis in 1890 which urged that States should give some form of tort relief to persons whose private affairs were exploited by others. The Right to Privacy, 4 Harv.L.Rev. 193. [T]oday this Court, which I did not understand to have power to sit as a court of common law, now appears to be exalting a phrase which Warren and Brandeis used in discussing grounds for tort relief, to the level of a constitutional rule which prevents state legislatures from passing any law deemed by this Court to interfere with "privacy." [Footnote by Justice Black.]

2. A collection of the catchwords and catch phrases invoked by judges who would strike down under the Fourteenth Amendment laws which offend their notions of natural justice would fill many pages. [Quotations from, inter alia, Rochin v. California, Irvine v. California [both in chap. 8], and Lochner v. New York are omitted.] [Footnote by Justice Black.]

3. See Hand, The Bill of Rights (1958) 70:
"[J]udges are seldom content merely to annul the particular solution before them; they do not, indeed they may not, say that taking all things into consideration, the legislators' solution is too strong for the judicial stomach. On the contrary they wrap up their veto in a protective veil of adjectives such as 'arbitrary,' 'artificial,' 'normal,' 'reasonable,' 'inherent,' 'fundamental,' or 'essential,' whose office usually, though quite innocently, is to disguise what they are doing and impute to it a derivation far more im-

lative body. Surely it has to be admitted that no provision of the Constitution specifically gives such blanket power to courts to exercise such a supervisory veto over the wisdom and value of legislative policies and to hold unconstitutional those laws which they believe unwise or dangerous. . . .

Of the cases on which my Brothers White and Goldberg rely so heavily, undoubtedly the reasoning of two of them supports their result here —as would that of a number of others which they do not bother to name, e. g., [Lochner v. New York, Coppage v. Kansas, Jay Burns Baking Co. v. Bryan, and Adkins v. Children's Hospital]. The two they do cite and quote from, [Meyer v. Nebraska] and [Pierce v. Society of Sisters], were both decided in opinions by Mr. Justice McReynolds which elaborated the same natural law due process philosophy found in [Lochner], one of the cases on which he relied in Meyer, along with such other long-discredited decisions as, e. g., [Adams v. Tanner] and [Adkins v. Children's Hospital]. . . . Without expressing an opinion as to whether either of those cases reached a correct result in light of our later decisions applying the First Amendment to the States through the Fourteenth, I merely point out that the reasoning stated in Meyer and Pierce was the same natural law due process philosophy which many later opinions repudiated, and which I cannot accept. . . .

My Brother Goldberg has adopted the recent discovery [4] that the Ninth Amendment as well as the Due Process Clause can be used by this Court as authority to strike down all state legislation which this Court thinks violates "fundamental principles of liberty and justice," or is contrary to the "traditions and collective conscience of our people." He also states, without proof satisfactory to me, that in making decisions on this basis judges will not consider "their personal and private notions." One may ask how they can avoid considering them. [The Framers did not give this Court] veto powers over lawmaking, either by the States or by the Congress. Nor does anything in the history of the Amendment offer any support for such a shocking doctrine. The whole history of the adoption of the Constitution and Bill of Rights points the other way . . . . . That Amendment was passed, not to broaden the powers of this Court or any other department of "the General Government," but, as every student of history knows, to assure

---

pressive than their personal preferences, which are all that in fact lie behind the decision." . . . [Footnote by Justice Black.]

4. See Patterson, The Forgotten Ninth Amendment (1955). Mr. Patterson urges that the Ninth Amendment be used to protect unspecified "natural and inalienable rights." P. 4. The Introduction by Roscoe Pound states that "there is a marked revival of natural law ideas throughout the world. Interest in the Ninth Amendment is a symptom of that revival."

In Redlich, Are There "Certain Rights . . . Retained by the People"?, 37 N.Y.U.L.Rev. 787, Professor Redlich, in advocating reliance on the Ninth and Tenth Amendments to in-

validate the Connecticut law before us, frankly states:

"But for one who feels that the marriage relationship should be beyond the reach of a state law forbidding the use of contraceptives, the birth control case poses a troublesome and challenging problem of constitutional interpretation. He may find himself saying, 'The law is unconstitutional—but why?' There are two possible paths to travel in finding the answer. One is to revert to a frankly flexible due process concept even on matters that do not involve specific constitutional prohibitions. The other is to attempt to evolve a new constitutional framework within which to meet this and similar problems which are likely to arise." Id., at 798. [Footnote by Justice Black.]

the people that the Constitution in all its provisions was intended to limit the Federal Government to the powers granted expressly or by necessary implication. . . .

. . . The adoption of . . . a loose, flexible, uncontrolled standard for holding laws unconstitutional, if ever it is achieved, will amount to a great unconstitutional shift of power to the courts which I believe and am constrained to say will be bad for the courts and worse for the country. Subjecting federal and state laws to such an unrestrained and unrestrainable judicial control as to the wisdom of legislative enactments would, I fear, jeopardize the separation of governmental powers . . . .[5]

I realize that many good and able men have eloquently spoken and written, sometimes in rhapsodical strains, about the duty of this Court to keep the Constitution in tune with the times. [I] must with all deference reject that philosophy. The Constitution makers knew the need for change and provided for it. Amendments suggested by the people's elected representatives can be submitted to the people or their selected agents for ratification. That method of change was good for our Fathers, and being somewhat old-fashioned I must add it is good enough for me. And so, I cannot rely on the Due Process Clause or the Ninth Amendment or any mysterious and uncertain natural law concept as a reason for striking down this state law. The Due Process Clause with an "arbitrary and capricious" or "shocking to the conscience" formula was liberally used by this Court to strike down economic legislation in the early decades of this century, threatening, many people thought, the tranquility and stability of the Nation. See, e. g., [Lochner]. That formula, based on subjective considerations of "natural justice," is no less dangerous when used to enforce this Court's views about personal rights than those about economic rights. I had thought that we had laid that formula, as a means for striking down state legislation, to rest . . . . Apparently my Brethren have less quarrel with state economic regulations than former Justices of their persuasion had. But any limitation upon their using the natural law due process philosophy to strike down any state law, dealing with any activity whatever, will obviously be only self-imposed. . . .

. . . The late Judge Learned Hand, after emphasizing his view that judges should not use the due process formula suggested in the con-

5. Justice Holmes in one of his last dissents, Baldwin v. Missouri, 281 U. S. 586, 595, warned:
"I have not yet adequately expressed the more than anxiety that I feel at the ever increasing scope given to the Fourteenth Amendment in cutting down what I believe to be the constitutional rights of the States. As the decisions now stand, I see hardly any limit but the sky to the invalidating of those rights if they happen to strike a majority of this Court as for any reason undesirable. I cannot believe that the Amendment was intended to give us *carte blanche* to embody our economic or moral beliefs in its prohibitions. Yet I can think of no narrower reason that seems to me to justify the present and the earlier decisions to which I have referred. . . ." [Footnote by Justice Black.] and while it is too late to deny that they have been given a much more extended and artificial signification, still we ought to remember the great caution shown by the Constitution in limiting the power of the States, and should be slow to construe the clause in the Fourteenth Amendment as committing to the Court, with no guide but the Court's own discretion, the validity of whatever laws the States may pass." [Footnote by Justice Black.]

curring opinions today or any other formula like it to invalidate legislation offensive to their "personal preferences," made the statement, with which I fully agree, that:

> "For myself it would be most irksome to be ruled by a bevy of Platonic Guardians, even if I knew how to choose them, which I assuredly do not." [6]

So far as I am concerned, Connecticut's law as applied here is not forbidden by any provision of the Federal Constitution as that Constitution was written, and I am therefore to affirm.

Mr. Justice STEWART, whom Mr. Justice BLACK joins, dissenting.

Since 1879 Connecticut has had on its books a law which forbids the use of contraceptives by anyone. I think this is an uncommonly silly law. . . . But we are not asked in this case to say whether we think this law is unwise, or even asinine. We are asked to hold that it violates the United States Constitution. And that I cannot do.

In the course of its opinion the Court refers to no less than six Amendments to the Constitution: the First, the Third, the Fourth, the Fifth, the Ninth, and the Fourteenth. But the Court does not say which of these Amendments, if any, it thinks is infringed by this Connecticut law.

We *are* told that the Due Process Clause of the Fourteenth Amendment is not, as such, the "guide" in this case. With that much I agree. There is no claim that this law, duly enacted by the Connecticut Legislature, is unconstitutionally vague. There is no claim that the appellants were denied any of the elements of procedural due process at their trial. [And] the day has long passed since the Due Process Clause was regarded as a proper instrument for determining "the wisdom, need, and propriety" of state laws. . . .

As to the First, Third, Fourth, and Fifth Amendments, I can find nothing in any of them to invalidate this Connecticut law, even assuming that all those Amendments are fully applicable against the States. [T]o say that the Ninth Amendment has anything to do with this case is to turn somersaults with history. The Ninth Amendment, like its companion the Tenth, . . . was framed by James Madison and adopted by the States simply to make clear that the adoption of the Bill of Rights did not alter the plan that the *Federal* Government was to be a government of express and limited powers. . . .

What provision of the Constitution, then, does make this state law invalid? The Court says it is the right of privacy "created by several fundamental constitutional guarantees." With all deference, I can find no such

---

6. [Hand, The Bill of Rights (1958)], at 73. While Judge Hand condemned as unjustified the invalidation of state laws under the natural law due process formula, see id., at 35–45, he also expressed the view that this Court in a number of cases had gone too far in holding legislation to be in violation of specific guarantees of the Bill of Rights. Although I agree with his criticism of use of the due process formula, I do not agree with all the views he expressed about construing the specific guarantees of the Bill of Rights. [Footnote by Justice Black. See the comments on Justice Black's reliance on Judge Hand in the notes following this case.]

general right of privacy in the Bill of Rights, in any other part of the Constitution, or in any case ever before decided by this Court.[1]

At the oral argument in this case we were told that the Connecticut law does not "conform to current community standards." But it is not the function of this Court to decide cases on the basis of community standards. We are here to decide cases "agreeably to the Constitution and laws of the United States." It is the essence of judicial duty to subordinate our own personal views, our own ideas of what legislation is wise and what is not. If, as I should surely hope, the law before us does not reflect the standards of the people of Connecticut, the people of Connecticut can freely exercise their true Ninth and Tenth Amendment rights to persuade their elected representatives to repeal it. That is the constitutional way to take this law off the books.[2]

GRISWOLD, PENUMBRAS, AND DOUBLE STANDARDS

1. *The constitutional basis of the decision.* Consider the range of modes of constitutional adjudication disclosed by the opinions in Griswold. Is Justice Black right in charging that Griswold is of a piece with the free-wheeling, subjective variety of substantive due process adjudication long discredited in the economic regulation area? Or is Griswold distinguishable? How? Justice Douglas disavows Lochner as a guide. He relies instead on the "penumbras" and "emanations" of several specific guarantees in the Bill of Rights. Is the "right of privacy" he finds a legitimate derivation from the constitutional text? Does that depend on what the content of that "right of privacy" is? See note 2 below.

Does Justice Douglas' "penumbras-emanations" approach avoid subjective, idiosyncratic, extra-constitutional, "natural law" adjudication more effectively than the Lochner approach or the other opinions on the majority side in Griswold? Is it genuinely different from the Lochner approach? Does Justice Douglas' approach channel judicial power more rigorously than the analyses of the other opinions? Than Justice Harlan's "basic values 'implicit in the concept of ordered liberty' " approach? Than Justice Goldberg's Ninth Amendment—"fundamental rights" approach? Compare Justice Stewart's comment on Griswold, eight years after he dissented in that case, when he concurred in Roe v. Wade, the abortion decision which follows: "[T]he Griswold decision can be rationally understood only as a holding that the Connecticut statute substantively invaded the 'liberty' that is protected by the Due Process Clause of the Fourteenth Amendment. As so understood Griswold stands as one in a long line of pre-Skrupa [Ferguson v. Skrupa, sec. 1C

---

1. . . . . The Court does not say how far the new constitutional right of privacy announced today extends. See, e. g., Mueller, Legal Regulation of Sexual Conduct, at 127; Ploscowe, Sex and the Law, at 189. I suppose, however, that even after today a State can constitutionally still punish at least some offenses which are not committed in public. [Footnote by Justice Stewart.]

2. See Reynolds v. Sims, 377 U.S. 533, 562. The Connecticut House of Representatives recently passed a bill (House Bill No. 2462) repealing the birth control law. The State Senate has apparently not yet acted on the measure, and today is relieved of that responsibility by the Court. [Footnote by Justice Stewart.]

above] cases decided under the doctrine of substantive due process, and I now accept it as such."

Does Justice Douglas' approach help distinguish "economic" and "personal" rights and justify the double standard? Are liberty of contract and the right to use property, the favored rights of the Lochner era, distinguishable because they are not specifically mentioned in the Constitution? But could not liberty of contract be seen as an emanation, or within the penumbra, of the contract clause—not to speak of the "liberty" specified in the 14th Amendment? And could not a general protection of property be seen as within the penumbra of the specific mention of "property" in the condemnation clause of the Fifth Amendment—not to speak of the historical importance of property rights (see sec. 1A) and the "specific" reference to property in the 14th Amendment itself? See Kauper, "Penumbras, Peripheries, Emanations, Things Fundamental and Things Forgotten: The Griswold Case," 64 Mich.L.Rev. 235 (1965).

2. *The scope of Griswold.* What is the scope of the "right of privacy" recognized in Griswold? What is the fundamental personal interest protected? Is it the interest in preventing intrusions into the home? The interest in avoiding disclosure of personal information? The interest in the protection of the "intimacies of the marriage relationship"? A broader interest in personal autonomy—in freedom from governmental regulation of some range of personal activities that do not harm others? Consider the emphases of the various opinions in Griswold, and their implications for laws other than that banning the use of contraceptives in Griswold. And consider the distinction suggested in Note, "Roe and Paris*: Does Privacy Have a Principle?" 26 Stan.L.Rev. 1161 (1974)—a distinction between two meanings of privacy: (1) a "right of selective disclosure," or interest in control of information; and (2) a private "autonomy" of choice about performing acts or undergoing experiences. Consider what added light on the scope as well as source of the right of privacy is shed by Roe v. Wade, which follows; and note the further examination of "privacy" and "autonomy" in the notes following that case.

The Court has decided one other case involving control of contraceptives since Griswold: Eisenstadt v. Baird, 405 U.S. 438 (1972) (chap. 10, sec. 6). Does Baird clarify the nature of the right of privacy recognized in Griswold? Griswold involved the *use* of contraceptives. Justice Douglas there distinguished the regulation of "their manufacture or sale." But Baird overturned a conviction under a law banning the distribution of contraceptives: Baird had distributed contraceptive foam. The Court managed to avoid deciding the question of whether Griswold extended beyond use to distribution. Instead, it purported to decide the case on a minimum rationality-equal protection ground (though in fact the degree of scrutiny exercised seemed stricter than the extremely deferential one of the post-Lochner era, see Gunther, "Foreword: . . . A Model for a Newer Equal Protection," 86 Harv.L.Rev. 1 (1972)). Yet despite Justice Brennan's great care in avoiding decision of the question of whether distribution of contra-

---

* The reference is to Paris Adult Theater I v. Slaton, one of the Burger Court's major opinions on the problem of obscenity control, chap. 13, sec. 2, below.

ceptives can be prohibited, even to married persons, after Griswold, he managed to make some comments on Griswold in his Baird opinion: "It is true that in Griswold the right of privacy in question inhered in the marital relationship. Yet the marital couple is not an independent entity with a mind and heart of its own, but an association of two individuals each with a separate intellectual and emotional make-up. If the right of privacy means anything, it is the right of the *individual,* married or single, to be free from unwarranted governmental intrusion into matters so fundamentally affecting a person as the decision whether to bear or beget a child. See Stanley v. Georgia, 394 U.S. 557 (1969) [banning prosecution for possessing obscene materials in the home—see chap. 13, sec. 2, below]. See also [Skinner v. Oklahoma]."   And Justice White's concurrence in Baird (joined by Justice Blackmun) commented: "Just as in Griswold, where the right of married persons to use contraceptives was 'diluted or adversely affected' by permitting a conviction for giving advice as to its exercise, . . . so here to sanction a medical restriction upon distribution of a contraceptive not proved hazardous to health would impair the exercise of the constitutional right."

3. *Griswold and the double standard.* There is one common theme to all of the opinions supporting the majority result in Griswold, whatever the differences in the modes of constitutional interpretation and whatever the differences in the scope of the fundamental right perceived: all agree that Griswold involves an individual interest sufficiently special, sufficiently cherished, to warrant review at something beyond the "reasonable relation"- minimum rationality-deferential stance of judicial scrutiny. And once a stricter degree of scrutiny is justified and applied, invalidation of the law becomes quite predictable. That common theme provokes once again the recurrent question: What justifies that "double standard"—of strict scrutiny in some situations, hands off in others? The frequently invoked justification suggested by Justice Stone's footnote in the Carolene Products Case (printed above) is least helpful in a situation like Griswold. Stone suggested that greater scrutiny was justified when legislation conflicts with values expressed in the "specific" prohibitions of the Constitution or when it "restricts" the "political processes." That justification has created some difficulty even where First Amendment freedoms are involved. But the value protected in the Griswold decision does not fit those descriptions: even the Justices to whom the core of the penumbra is most visible would not call privacy a "specific" guarantee, or one central to the "political processes." Justice Stone also suggested special judicial solicitude for some "discrete and insular minorities." Is there anything in the Griswold context that satisfies that criterion? Or is there nothing more to be said for Griswold than could have been said for any of the Court's invalidations in the Lochner era?

Justice Black in his dissent obviously thought there was not. But ironically, he repeatedly quotes Judge Learned Hand. As Justice Black's footnote 8 hints, Judge Hand repudiated any double standard and was profoundly skeptical of the judicial enforceability of the due process clause in any context, whether of civil liberties or of economic regulation: he disapproved of Justice Black's variety of "absolute" enforcement of free speech (see chap. 12 below), as he did of the Lochner case. As he said of the shift in the Court after the 1937 Court crisis: "It began to seem as though,

when 'personal rights' were in issue, something strangely akin to the discredited attitude toward the Bill of Rights of the old apostles of the institution of property was regaining recognition." Judge Hand apparently thought that this was "an opportunistic reversion." To him, the principle of nonintervention via the due process clause of the 14th Amendment could not mean "that, when concerned with interests other than property, the Court should have a wider latitude for enforcing their own predilections." Does Griswold, then, illustrate the validity of Hand's critique? Even Justice Frankfurter, who spoke most frequently against the double standard on the modern Court, and was thus closest to Judge Hand's position, did not truly escape the difficulty. He, too, found some values more important than others. As Justice White's quotation in Griswold from Justice Frankfurter's opinion in Kovacs v. Cooper shows, Justice Frankfurter thought some rights "come to this Court with a momentum for respect lacking when appeal is made to liberties which derive merely from shifting economic arrangements." Justice Harlan, too, obviously thought some ordering of constitutional values necessary and justified. How then does the Court determine the proper place of a particular right on this scale of values? How does Justice White, for example, defend placing the right invoked in Griswold at a different place in the hierarchy than "mere" economic rights? Consider these problems in light of Roe v. Wade, the abortion case, and the notes which follow it, for Roe v. Wade raises even more acutely the twin pervasive issues: What justifies a double standard in degrees of scrutiny? What are the proper sources of "fundamental" values in constitutional adjudication?

ROE v. WADE

410 U.S. 113, 93 S.Ct. 705, 35 L.Ed.2d 147 (1973).

Appeal from the United States District Court for the Northern District of Texas.

[This was an attack on the Texas abortion laws—typical of those adopted by most states—making it a crime to "procure an abortion" except "by medical advice for the purpose of saving the life of the mother." * The challengers here were a pregnant single woman (Jane Roe), a childless couple, with the wife not pregnant (John and Mary Doe), and a licensed physician (Dr. Hallford). The suits by the Roes and the Does were class actions. The three-judge District Court ruled the Does' complaint nonjusticiable, but granted declaratory relief to Roe and Dr. Hallford, holding the law unconstitutional under the Ninth Amendment. On the Supreme Court's handling of the problems of justiciability and standing, see chap. 15 below.]

Mr. Justice BLACKMUN delivered the opinion of the Court. . . .

We forthwith acknowledge our awareness of the sensitive and emotional nature of the abortion controversy, of the vigorous opposing views, even

---

* In a companion case, Doe v. Bolton, 410 U.S. 179 (1973), which follows, the Court examined the constitutionality of the Georgia abortion laws, statutes with "a modern cast," reflecting "the influences of recent attitudinal change, of advancing medical knowledge and techniques and of new thinking about an old issue."

among physicians, and of the deep and seemingly absolute convictions that the subject inspires. One's philosophy, one's experiences, one's exposure to the raw edges of human existence, one's religious training, one's attitudes toward life and family and their values, and the moral standards one establishes and seeks to observe, are all likely to influence and to color one's thinking and conclusions about abortion. In addition, population growth, pollution, poverty, and racial overtones tend to complicate and not to simplify the problem.

Our task, of course, is to resolve the issue by constitutional measurement, free of emotion and of predilection. We seek earnestly to do this, and, because we do, we have inquired into, and in this opinion place some emphasis upon, medical and medical-legal history and what that history reveals about man's attitudes toward the abortion procedure over the centuries. We bear in mind, too, Mr. Justice Holmes' admonition in his now-vindicated dissent in [Lochner v. New York. The quotation from that dissent is omitted.] . . .

The principal thrust of appellant's attack on the Texas statutes is that they improperly invade a right, said to be possessed by the pregnant woman, to choose to terminate her pregnancy. . . . Before addressing this claim, we feel it desirable briefly to survey, in several aspects, the history of abortion, for such insight as that history may afford us . . . . [Justice Blackmun's review of that history is omitted. His survey began with "ancient attitudes"—starting with "Persian Empire abortifacients"—and continued through "the Hippocratic Oath," "the common law," "English statutory law," and "American law," to the positions of the American Medical, Public Health and Bar Associations. After stating the possible state interests—summarized below—Justice Blackmun continued:]

The Constitution does not explicitly mention any right of privacy. [However], the Court has recognized that a right of personal privacy, or a guarantee of certain areas or zones of privacy, does exist under the Constitution. In varying contexts, the Court or individual Justices have, indeed, found at least the roots of that right in the First Amendment [Stanley v. Georgia]; in the Fourth and Fifth Amendments [e. g., Terry v. Ohio]; in the penumbras of the Bill of Rights [Griswold v. Connecticut]; in the Ninth Amendment [id.]; or in the concept of liberty guaranteed by the first section of the Fourteenth Amendment, see [Meyer v. Nebraska]. These decisions make it clear that only personal rights that can be deemed "fundamental" or "implicit in the concept of ordered liberty" [Palko v. Connecticut] are included in this guarantee of personal privacy. They also make it clear that the right has some extension to activities relating to marriage [Loving v. Virginia], procreation [Skinner v. Oklahoma], contraception [Eisenstadt v. Baird], family relationships [Prince v. Massachusetts], and child rearing and education [Pierce v. Society of Sisters; Meyer v. Nebraska].

This right of privacy, whether it be founded in the Fourteenth Amendment's concept of personal liberty and restrictions upon state action, as we feel it is, or, as the District Court determined, in the Ninth Amendment's reservation of rights to the people, is broad enough to encompass a woman's decision whether or not to terminate her pregnancy. The detriment that the State would impose upon the pregnant woman by denying this choice

altogether is apparent. Specific and direct harm medically diagnosable even in early pregnancy may be involved. Maternity, or additional offspring, may force upon the woman a distressful life and future. Psychological harm may be imminent. Mental and physical health may be taxed by child care. There is also the distress, for all concerned, associated with the unwanted child, and there is the problem of bringing a child into a family already unable, psychologically and otherwise, to care for it. In other cases, as in this one, the additional difficulties and continuing stigma of unwed mother-hood may be involved. All these are factors the woman and her responsible physician necessarily will consider in consultation.

On the basis of elements such as these, appellants and some amici argue that the woman's right is absolute and that she is entitled to terminate her pregnancy at whatever time, in whatever way, and for whatever reason she alone chooses. With this we do not agree. . . . The Court's decisions recognizing a right of privacy also acknowledge that some state regulation in areas protected by that right is appropriate. [A] State may properly as-sert important interests in safeguarding health, in maintaining medical stand-ards, and in protecting potential life. At some point in pregnancy, these respective interests become sufficiently compelling to sustain regulation of the factors that govern the abortion decision. The privacy right involved, therefore, cannot be said to be absolute. In fact, it is not clear to us that the claim asserted by some amici that one has an unlimited right to do with one's body as one pleases bears a close relationship to the right of privacy previous-ly articulated in the Court's decisions. The Court has refused to recognize an unlimited right of this kind in the past. [Jacobson v. Massachusetts] (vaccination); [Buck v. Bell] (sterilization).

We, therefore, conclude that the right of personal privacy includes the abortion decision, but that this right is not unqualified and must be con-sidered against important state interests in regulation. . . .

Where certain "fundamental rights" are involved, the Court has held that regulation limiting these rights may be justified only by a "compelling state interest" . . . and that legislative enactments must be narrowly drawn to express only the legitimate state interests at stake. . . .

A. The appellee and certain amici argue that the fetus is a "person" within the language and meaning of the Fourteenth Amendment. In sup-port of this, they outline at length and in detail the well-known facts of fetal development. If this suggestion of personhood is established, the appel-lant's case, of course, collapses, for the fetus' right to life is then guaranteed specifically by the Amendment. . . . On the other hand, the appellee conceded on reargument that no case could be cited that holds that a fetus is a person within the meaning of the Fourteenth Amendment.

The Constitution does not define "person" in so many words. Section 1 of the Fourteenth Amendment contains three references to "person." The first, in defining "citizens," speaks of "persons born or naturalized in the United States." The word also appears both in the Due Process Clause and in the Equal Protection Clause. "Person" is used in other places in the Constitution: in the listing of qualifications for Representatives and Sena-tors, Art. I, § 2, cl. 2, and § 3, cl. 3; in the Apportionment Clause, Art. I, § 2, cl. 3; [1] in the Migration and Importation provision, Art. I, § 9, cl. 1;

in the Emolument Clause, Art. I, § 9, cl. 8; in the Electors provisions, Art. II, § 1, cl. 2, and the superseded cl. 3; in the provision outlining qualifications for the office of President, Art. II, § 1, cl. 5; in the Extradition provisions, Art. IV, § 2, cl. 2, and the superseded Fugitive Slave Clause 3; and in the Fifth, Twelfth, and Twenty-second Amendments, as well as in §§ 2 and 3 of the Fourteenth Amendment. But in nearly all these instances, the use of the word is such that it has application only postnatally. None indicates, with any assurance, that it has any possible pre-natal application.[2]

All this, together with our observation . . . that throughout the major portion of the 19th century prevailing legal abortion practices were far freer than they are today, persuades us that the word "person," as used in the Fourteenth Amendment, does not include the unborn. . . . This conclusion, however, does not of itself fully answer the contentions raised by Texas, and we pass on to other considerations.

B. The pregnant woman cannot be isolated in her privacy. She carries an embryo and, later, a fetus . . . .. The situation therefore is inherently different from marital intimacy, or bedroom possession of obscene material, or marriage, or procreation, or education, with which Eisenstadt, Griswold, Stanley, Loving, Skinner, Pierce, and Meyer were respectively concerned. [I]t is reasonable and appropriate for a State to decide that at some point in time another interest, that of health of the mother or that of potential human life, becomes significantly involved. The woman's privacy is no longer sole and any right of privacy she possesses must be measured accordingly.

Texas urges that, apart from the Fourteenth Amendment, life begins at conception and is present throughout pregnancy, and that, therefore, the State has a compelling interest in protecting that life from and after conception. We need not resolve the difficult question of when life begins. When those trained in the respective disciplines of medicine, philosophy, and theology are unable to arrive at any concensus, the judiciary, at this point in the development of man's knowledge, is not in a position to speculate as to the answer.

It should be sufficient to note briefly the wide divergence of thinking on this most sensitive and difficult question. There has always been strong support for the view that life does not begin until live birth. This was the belief of the Stoics. It appears to be the predominant, though not the unanimous, attitude of the Jewish faith. It may be taken to represent also the position of a large segment of the Protestant community, insofar as that can be ascertained . . . .. As we have noted, the common law found

---

1. We are not aware that in the taking of any census under this clause, a fetus has ever been counted. [Footnote by Justice Blackmun.]

2. When Texas urges that a fetus is entitled to Fourteenth Amendment protection as a person, it faces a dilemma. Neither in Texas nor in any other State are all abortions prohibited. Despite broad proscription, an exception always exists. The exception [in the Texas law] for an abortion procured or attempted by medical advice for the purpose of saving the life of the mother, is typical. But if the fetus is a person who is not to be deprived of life without due process of law, and if the mother's condition is the sole determinant, does not the Texas exception appear to be out of line with the Amendment's command? . . . [Footnote by Justice Blackmun.]

greater significance in quickening.* Physicians and their scientific colleagues have regarded that event with less interest and have tended to focus either upon conception, upon live birth, or upon the interim point at which the fetus becomes "viable," that is, potentially able to live outside the mother's womb, albeit with artificial aid. Viability is usually placed at about seven months (28 weeks) but may occur earlier, even at 24 weeks. The Aristotelian theory of "mediate animation," that held sway throughout the Middle Ages and the Renaissance in Europe, continued to be official Roman Catholic dogma until the 19th century, despite opposition to this "ensoulment" theory from those in the Church who would recognize the existence of life from the moment of conception. The latter is now, of course, the official belief of the Catholic Church. [T]his is a view strongly held by many non-Catholics as well, and by many physicians. Substantial problems for precise definition of this view are posed, however, by new embryological data that purport to indicate that conception is a "process" over time, rather than an event, and by new medical techniques such as menstrual extraction, the "morning-after" pill, implantation of embryos, artificial insemination, and even artificial wombs.

In areas other than criminal abortion, the law has been reluctant to endorse any theory that life, as we recognize it, begins before live birth or to accord legal rights to the unborn except in narrowly defined situations and except when the rights are contingent upon live birth. [Justice Blackmun noted illustrations in the law of torts and of inheritance.] In short, the unborn have never been recognized in the law as persons in the whole sense.

In view of all this, we do not agree that, by adopting one theory of life, Texas may override the rights of the pregnant woman that are at stake. We repeat, however, that the State does have an important and legitimate interest in preserving and protecting the health of the pregnant woman, whether she be a resident of the State or a nonresident who seeks medical consultation and treatment there, and that it has still *another* important and legitimate interest in protecting the potentiality of human life. These interests are separate and distinct. Each grows in substantiality as the woman approaches term and, at a point during pregnancy, each becomes "compelling."

With respect to the State's important and legitimate interest in the health of the mother, the "compelling" point, in the light of present medical knowledge, is at approximately the end of the first trimester. This is so because of the now established medical fact . . . that until the end of the first trimester mortality in abortion is less than mortality in normal childbirth. It follows that, from and after this point, a State may regulate the abortion procedure to the extent that the regulation reasonably relates to the preservation and protection of maternal health. Examples of permissible state regulation in this area are requirements as to the qualifications of the person who is to perform the abortion; as to the licensure of that person; as to the facility in which the procedure is to be performed, that is, whether it must be a hospital or may be a clinic or some other place of less-than-hospital status; as to the licensing of the facility; and the like.

---

* Earlier in his opinion, Justice Blackmun had stated: "It is undisputed that at common law, abortion performed *before* 'quickening'—the first recognizable movement of the fetus *in utero*, appearing usually from the 16th to the 18th week of pregnancy—was not an indictable offense."

This means, on the other hand, that, for the period of pregnancy prior to this "compelling" point, the attending physician, in consultation with his patient, is free to determine, without regulation by the State, that, in his medical judgment, the patient's pregnancy should be terminated. If that decision is reached, the judgment may be effectuated by an abortion free of interference by the State.

With respect to the State's important and legitimate interest in potential life, the "compelling" point is at viability. This is so because the fetus then presumably has the capability of meaningful life outside the mother's womb. State regulation protective of fetal life after viability thus has both logical and biological justifications. If the State is interested in protecting fetal life after viability, it may go so far as to proscribe abortion during that period, except when it is necessary to preserve the life or health of the mother.

Measured against these standards, [Texas law] sweeps too broadly. The statute makes no distinction between abortions performed early in pregnancy and those performed later, and it limits to a single reason, "saving" the mother's life, the legal justification for the procedure. . . .

To summarize and to repeat:

1. A state criminal abortion statute of the current Texas type, that excepts from criminality only a *life saving* procedure on behalf of the mother, without regard to pregnancy stage and without recognition of the other interests involved, is violative of the Due Process Clause of the Fourteenth Amendment.

(a) For the stage prior to approximately the end of the first trimester, the abortion decision and its effectuation must be left to the medical judgment of the pregnant woman's attending physician.

(b) For the stage subsequent to approximately the end of the first trimester, the State, in promoting its interest in the health of the mother, may, if it chooses, regulate the abortion procedure in ways that are reasonably related to maternal health.

(c) For the stage subsequent to viability, the State in promoting its interest in the potentiality of human life may, if it chooses, regulate, and even proscribe, abortion except where it is necessary, in appropriate medical judgment, for the preservation of the life or health of the mother.

2. The State may define the term "physician" . . . to mean only a physician currently licensed by the State, and may proscribe any abortion by a person who is not a physician as so defined.

In Doe v. Bolton, post, procedural requirements contained in one of the modern abortion statutes are considered. That opinion and this one, of course, are to be read together.[1]

1. Neither in this opinion nor in Doe v. Bolton, post, do we discuss the father's rights, if any exist in the constitutional context, in the abortion decision. No paternal right has been asserted in either of the cases, and the Texas and the Georgia statutes on their face take no cognizance of the father. We are aware that some statutes recognize the father under certain circumstances. North Carolina, for example, . . . requires written permission for the abortion from the husband when the woman is a married minor, that is,

This holding, we feel, is consistent with the relative weights of the respective interests involved, with the lessons and examples of medical and legal history, with the lenity of the common law, and with the demands of the profound problems of the present day. The decision leaves the State free to place increasing restrictions on abortion as the period of pregnancy lengthens, so long as those restrictions are tailored to the recognized state interests. The decision vindicates the right of the physician to administer medical treatment according to his professional judgment up to the points where important state interests provide compelling justifications for intervention. Up to those points, the abortion decision in all its aspects is inherently, and primarily, a medical decision, and basic responsibility for it must rest with the physician. If an individual practitioner abuses the privilege of exercising proper medical judgment, the usual remedies, judicial and intraprofessional, are available. . . .

It is so ordered.

Mr. Justice STEWART, concurring.

In 1963, this Court, in [Ferguson v. Skrupa], purported to sound the death knell for the doctrine of substantive due process . . . . Barely two years later, in [Griswold v. Connecticut], the Court held a Connecticut birth control law unconstitutional. In view of what had been so recently said in Skrupa, the Court's opinion in Griswold understandably did its best to avoid reliance on the Due Process Clause . . . . Yet, the Connecticut law did not violate [any] specific provision of the Constitution. So it was clear to me then, and it is equally clear to me now, that the Griswold decision can be rationally understood only as a holding that the Connecticut statute substantively invaded the "liberty" that is protected by the Due Process Clause of the Fourteenth Amendment. As so understood Griswold stands as one in a long line of pre-Skrupa cases decided under the doctrine of substantive due process, and I now accept it as such.

[T]he "liberty" protected by the Due Process Clause of the Fourteenth Amendment covers more than those freedoms explicitly named in the Bill of Rights. . . . Several decisions of this Court make clear that freedom of personal choice in matters of marriage and family life is one of the liberties protected by the Due Process Clause of the Fourteenth Amendment. . . . As recently as last Term, in [Eisenstadt v. Baird], we recognized "the right of the *individual,* married or single, to be free from unwarranted governmental intrusion into matters so fundamentally affecting a person as the decision whether to bear or beget a child." That right necessarily includes the right of a woman to decide whether or not to terminate her pregnancy. . . .

It is evident that the Texas abortion statute infringes that right directly. . . . The question then becomes whether the state interests advanced

when she is less than 18 years of age . . . ; if the woman is an unmarried minor, written permission from the parents is required. We need not now decide whether provisions of this kind are constitutional. [Footnote by Justice Blackmun.]

[In August 1973, a Florida "permission" statute similar to North Carolina's was held unconstitutional by a three-judge District Court; the Supreme Court dismissed an appeal from that declaratory judgment on jurisdictional grounds. Gerstein v. Coe, 417 U.S. 279 (1974).]

to justify this abridgment can survive the "particularly careful scrutiny" that the Fourteenth Amendment here requires.

The asserted state interests . . . are legitimate objectives, amply sufficient to permit a State to regulate abortions as it does other surgical procedures, and perhaps sufficient to permit a State to regulate abortions more stringently or even to prohibit them in the late stages of pregnancy. But such legislation is not before us, and I think the Court today has thoroughly demonstrated that these state interests cannot constitutionally support the broad abridgment of personal liberty worked by the existing Texas law. Accordingly, I join the Court's opinion holding that that law is invalid under the Due Process Clause of the Fourteenth Amendment.

Mr. Justice DOUGLAS, concurring [in Doe v. Bolton, the Georgia abortion case noted below, as well as in Roe v. Wade.* . . .

The Ninth Amendment obviously does not create federally enforceable rights. It merely says, "The enumeration in the Constitution, of certain rights, shall not be construed to deny or disparage others retained by the people." But a catalogue of these rights includes customary, traditional, and time-honored rights, amenities, privileges, and immunities that come within the sweep of "the Blessings of Liberty" mentioned in the preamble to the Constitution. Many of them in my view come within the meaning of the term "liberty" as used in the Fourteenth Amendment.

First is the autonomous control over the development and expression of one's intellect, interests, tastes, and personality.

These are rights protected by the First Amendment and in my view they are absolute, permitting of no exceptions. . . .

Second is freedom of choice in the basic decisions of one's life respecting marriage, divorce, procreation, contraception, and the education and upbringing of children.

These ["fundamental"] rights, unlike those protected by the First Amendment, are subject to some control by the police power. . . . [1]

* Another concurring opinion applicable to both cases, by Chief Justice Burger, is omitted. He ended his brief concurrence with the comment: "Plainly, the Court today rejects any claim that the Constitution requires abortion on demand."

1. My Brother Stewart [says] that our decision in Griswold reintroduced substantive due process that had been rejected in Ferguson v. Skrupa. Skrupa involved legislation governing a business enterprise; and the Court [there] rejected the idea that "liberty" within the meaning of the Due Process Clause of the Fourteenth Amendment was a vessel to be filled with one's personal choices of values, whether drawn from the laissez faire school, from the socialistic school, or from the technocrats. Griswold involved legislation touching on the marital relation . . . .

There is nothing specific in the Bill of Rights that covers that item. Nor is there anything in the Bill of Rights that in terms protects the right of association or the privacy in one's association. . . . Other peripheral rights are the right to educate one's children as one chooses, and the right to study the German language. . . . These decisions, with all respect, have nothing to do with substantive due process. One may think they are not peripheral rights to other rights that are expressed in the Bill of Rights. But that is not enough to bring into play the protection of substantive due process.

There are of course those who have believed that the reach of due process in the Fourteenth Amendment included all of the Bill of Rights but went further. Such was the view of Mr. Justice Murphy and Mr. Justice Rutledge.

Third is the freedom to care for one's health and person, freedom from bodily restraint or compulsion, freedom to walk, stroll, or loaf.

These rights, though fundamental, are likewise subject to regulation on a showing of "compelling state interest." . . .

[A] woman is free to make the basic decision whether to bear an unwanted child. Elaborate argument is hardly necessary to demonstrate that childbirth may deprive a woman of her preferred life style and force upon her a radically different and undesired future. . . . Such reasoning is, however, only the beginning of the problem. The State has interests to protect. . . . While childbirth endangers the lives of some women, voluntary abortion at any time and place regardless of medical standards would impinge on a rightful concern of society. The woman's health is part of that concern; as is the life of the fetus after quickening. These concerns justify the State in treating the procedure as a medical one. . . . †

Mr. Justice WHITE, with whom Mr. Justice REHNQUIST joins, dissenting [in Doe v. Bolton as well as in Roe v. Wade].

At the heart of the controversy in these cases are those recurring pregnancies that pose no danger whatsoever to the life or health of the mother but are nevertheless unwanted for any one or more of a variety of reasons—convenience, family planning, economics, dislike of children, the embarrassment of illegitimacy, etc. The common claim before us is that for any one of such reasons, or for no reason at all, and without asserting or claiming any threat to life or health, any woman is entitled to an abortion at her request if she is able to find a medical advisor willing to undertake the procedure.

The Court for the most part sustains this position: During the period prior to the time the fetus becomes viable, the Constitution of the United States values the convenience, whim or caprice of the putative mother more than the life or potential life of the fetus; the Constitution, therefore, guarantees the right to an abortion as against any state law or policy seeking to protect the fetus from an abortion not prompted by more compelling reasons of the mother.

With all due respect, I dissent. I find nothing in the language or history of the Constitution to support the Court's judgment. The Court simply fashions and announces a new constitutional right for pregnant mothers and, with scarcely any reason or authority for its action, invests that right with sufficient substance to override most existing state abortion statutes. The upshot is that the people and the legislatures of the 50 States are constitutionally disentitled to weigh the relative importance of the continued existence and development of the fetus on the one hand against a spectrum of possible impacts on the mother on the other hand. As an exercise of raw judicial power, the Court perhaps has authority to do what it does today; but in my view its

---

See [Adamson v. California]. Perhaps they were right; but it is a bridge that neither I nor those who joined the Court's opinion in Griswold crossed. [Footnote by Justice Douglas.]

† Later in his opinion, in commenting on the Georgia statute, Justice Doug-las stated that a legislature may not equate "all phases of maturation preceding birth." One of the reasons for the law's overbreadth was accordingly that "it equates the value of embryonic life immediately after conception with the worth of life immediately before birth."

judgment is an improvident and extravagant exercise of the power of judicial review that the Constitution extends to this Court.

The Court apparently values the convenience of the pregnant mother more than the continued existence and development of the life or potential life that she carries. Whether or not I might agree with that marshaling of values, I can in no event join the Court's judgment because I find no constitutional warrant for imposing such an order of priorities on the people and legislatures of the States. In a sensitive area such as this, involving as it does issues over which reasonable men may easily and heatedly differ, I cannot accept the Court's exercise of its clear power of choice by interposing a constitutional barrier to state efforts to protect human life and by investing mothers and doctors with the constitutionally protected right to exterminate it. This issue, for the most part, should be left with the people and to the political processes the people have devised to govern their affairs.

It is my view, therefore, that the Texas statute is not constitutionally infirm because it denies abortions to those who seek to serve only their convenience rather than to protect their life or health. . . .

Mr Justice REHNQUIST, dissenting. . . . *

I have difficulty in concluding, as the Court does, that the right of "privacy" is involved in this case. [Texas] bars the performance of a medical abortion by a licensed physician on a plaintiff such as Roe. A transaction resulting in an operation such as this is not "private" in the ordinary usage of that word. Nor is the "privacy" which the Court finds here even a distant relative of the freedom from searches and seizures . . . .

If the Court means by the term "privacy" no more than that the claim of a person to be free from unwanted state regulation of consensual transactions may be a form of "liberty" protected by the Fourteenth Amendment, there is no doubt that similar claims have been upheld in our earlier decisions on the basis of that liberty. I agree [that "liberty"] embraces more than the rights found in the Bill of Rights. But that liberty is not guaranteed absolutely against deprivation, but only against deprivation without due process of law. The test traditionally applied in the area of social and economic legislation is whether or not a law such as that challenged has a rational relation to a valid state objective. [Williamson v. Lee Optical Co.] The Due Process Clause of the Fourteenth Amendment undoubtedly does place a limit, albeit a broad one, on legislative power to enact laws such as this. If the Texas statute were to prohibit an abortion even where the mother's life is in jeopardy, I have little doubt that such a statute would lack a rational relation to a valid state objective under the test stated in [Williamson]. But the Court's sweeping invalidation of any restrictions on abortion during the first trimester is impossible to justify under that standard, and the conscious weighing of competing factors which the Court's opinion apparently substitutes for the established test is far more appropriate to a legislative judgment than to a judicial one.

* Justice Rehnquist also submitted a separate, brief dissent in Doe v. Bolton, the Georgia case below.

The Court eschews the history of the Fourteenth Amendment in its reliance on the "compelling state interest" test. . . . But the Court adds a new wrinkle to this test by transposing it from the legal considerations associated with the Equal Protection Clause of the Fourteenth Amendment to this case arising under the Due Process Clause of the Fourteenth Amendment. Unless I misapprehend the consequences of this transplanting of the "compelling state interest test," the Court's opinion will accomplish the seemingly impossible feat of leaving this area of the law more confused than it found it.

While the Court's opinion quotes from the dissent of Mr. Justice Holmes in [Lochner v. New York], the result it reaches is more closely attuned to the majority opinion of Mr. Justice Peckham in that case. As in Lochner and similar cases applying substantive due process standards to economic and social welfare legislation, the adoption of the compelling state interest standard will inevitably require this Court to examine the legislative policies and pass on the wisdom of these policies in the very process of deciding whether a particular state interest put forward may or may not be "compelling." The decision here to break the term of pregnancy into three distinct terms and to outline the permissible restrictions the State may impose in each one, for example, partakes more of judicial legislation than it does of a determination of the intent of the drafters of the Fourteenth Amendment.

The fact that a majority of the States, reflecting after all the majority sentiment in those States, have had restrictions on abortions for at least a century is a strong indication, it seems to me, that the asserted right to an abortion is not "so rooted in the traditions and conscience of our people as to be ranked as fundamental" [Snyder v. Massachusetts]. Even today, when society's views on abortion are changing, the very existence of the debate is evidence that the "right" to an abortion is not so universally accepted as the appellants would have us believe.

To reach its result the Court necessarily has had to find within the scope of the Fourteenth Amendment a right that was apparently completely unknown to the drafters of the Amendment. As early as 1821, the first state law dealing directly with abortion was enacted by the Connecticut Legislature. By the time of the adoption of the Fourteenth Amendment in 1868, there were at least 36 laws enacted by state or territorial legislatures limiting abortion. While many States have amended or updated their laws, 21 of the laws on the books in 1868 remain in effect today. . . .

The only conclusion possible from this history is that the drafters did not intend to have the Fourteenth Amendment withdraw from the States the power to legislate with respect to this matter. . . .

DOE v. BOLTON, 410 U.S. 179 (1973), was the companion case to Roe v. Wade. The Georgia abortion laws attacked in Doe—unlike the traditional ones invalidated in Roe—were statutes with "a modern cast," enacted in 1968, patterned after the American Law Institute's Model Penal Code, and similar to laws enacted by about one-fourth of the states. Nevertheless, the Court invalidated substantial portions of the Georgia statute. Georgia law made noncriminal an abortion performed by a licensed physician when, "based

upon his best clinical judgment," an abortion was necessary because continued pregnancy would endanger the life or seriously injure the health of a pregnant woman; or the fetus would likely be born with serious defects; or if the pregnancy had resulted from rape. In addition to a requirement that the patient must be a Georgia resident, the scheme imposed procedural conditions regarding hospital accreditation and medical judgments beyond that of the performing physician. The three-judge District Court invalidated the statutory reference to the three situations in which the attending physician might undertake an abortion, leaving only the bare reference to "his best clinical judgment." But the District Court sustained the procedural requirements regarding "manner of performance" of an abortion, relying partly on the state interest in the protection of a "*potential* of independent human existence." On appeal, Justice Blackmun's majority opinion upheld the "best clinical judgment" provision but struck down the procedural conditions as well as the residence requirement.

The Court rejected the argument that the District Court's surgery on the provisions governing the physician's judgment had rendered the statute unconstitutionally vague. As the Court read the remaining reference to "best clinical judgment," it required the exercise of professional judgment "in the light of *all* the attendant circumstances. He is not now restricted to the three situations originally specified: judgment "may be exercised in light of all factors—physical, emotional, psychological, familial, and the woman's age— relevant to the well-being of the patient."

The three challenged procedural requirements ran into a variety of constitutional obstacles. (1) In striking down the requirement that abortion be performed in a hospital accredited by JCAH (Joint Commission on Accreditation of Hospitals), the Court invoked the 1957 equal protection ruling in Morey v. Doud (chap. 10 below). It insisted that "the State must show more than it has in order to prove that only the full resources of a licensed hospital, rather than those of some other appropriately licensed institution, satisfy [the] health interests."

(2) The second requirement, requiring prior approval for an abortion by the hospital staff abortion committee, was also struck down. The Court could find "no constitutionally justifiable pertinence" for that requirement. Committee review after the physician's approval would be review "once removed from diagnosis" and "basically redundant." No other surgical procedure required a similar review. Accordingly, the requirement was "unduly restrictive of the patient's rights and needs." *

(3) The final invalid procedural condition required "confirmation [of the abortion judgment] by two Georgia-licensed physicians in addition to the

---

* Note, however, Justice Blackmun's reference to the discretion that remains with hospitals and hospital personnel: A hospital is "free not to admit a patient for an abortion." Moreover, "a physician or any other employee has the right to refrain, for moral or religious reasons, from participating in the abortion procedure." Justice Blackmun added: "These provisions obviously are in the statute to afford appropriate protection for the individual and the denominational hospital." But the Georgia provision incorporating those safeguards and sustained by the Court here, § 26–1202(e), does not limit that hospital discretion to "denominational" hospitals. Moreover, the provision in the same subsection regarding objecting staff members refers to those who object "on moral or religious grounds."

recommendation of the pregnant woman's own consultant (making under the statute, a total of six physicians involved, including the three on the hospital's abortion committee).'' The Court concluded that the attending physician's "best clinical judgment" "should be sufficient." Though the reasons for the confirmation step were "perhaps apparent," "they are insufficient to withstand constitutional challenge." No other surgical procedure required similar confirmation. "Required acquiescence by co-practitioners has no rational connection with a patient's needs and unduly infringes on the physician's right to practice."

Finally, the Court struck down the requirement that the patient must be a Georgia resident. That provison had been attacked as violative of the right to travel discussed in Shapiro v. Thompson (chap. 10 below), but the Court took a somewhat different route in striking it down. Justice Blackmun recognized that the requirement "could be deemed to have some relationship to the availability of post-procedure medical care for the aborted patient," but it could not survive the obstacle of Privileges and Immunities Clause of Art. IV, § 2. Justice Blackmun stated that the requirement was not based "on any policy of preserving state-supported facilities for Georgia residents," since the bar also applied to private hospitals and doctors. Moreover, it had not been shown that Georgia facilities were being used to capacity. Accordingly, just as the Clause "protects persons who enter other States to ply their trade, . . . so must it protect persons who enter Georgia seeking the medical services that are available there. . . . A contrary holding would mean that a State could limit to its own residents the general medical care available within its borders." (Recall chap. 6, sec. 2.)

ROE v. WADE, PERSONAL AUTONOMY, AND THE LEGITIMATE SOURCES OF CONSTITUTIONAL VALUES *

1. *The protected personal interest: "Privacy" and Roe.* Recall the questions above, after Griswold, about the content of a due process right of privacy. What is the privacy right recognized in Roe? Justice Blackmun finds the right of privacy "broad enough to encompass a woman's decision whether or not to terminate her pregnancy." It is not an "absolute" right, but neither is it one that can be overridden simply by merely "rational" state legislation. Rather, it is a prima facie, specially protected, qualified right to have an abortion that is subject to regulation only on the showing of a "compelling" state interest. What aspect of "privacy" explains this powerful interest? The interests in protecting the home against intrusions or in the marital relationship or in avoiding disclosures of information seem in-

---

* There has been extensive commentary on Roe v. Wade and on the broader problems of constitutional interpretation it raises. For a particularly powerful criticism, more elaborate than those in the dissenting opinions in Roe, see Ely, "The Wages of Crying Wolf: A Comment on Roe v. Wade," 82 Yale L.J. 920 (1973). For a defense of the decision and its approach, see Heymann and Barzelay, "The Forest and the Trees: Roe v. Wade and Its Critics," 53 B.U.L.Rev. 765 (1973). For a defense of the result on other grounds, see Tribe, "Foreword: Toward a Model of Roles in the Due Process of Life and Law," 87 Harv.L.Rev. 1 (1973). See also Grey, "Do We Have an Unwritten Constitution?" 27 Stan.L.Rev. 703 (1975).

applicable here: as the Court recognizes, the situation here "is inherently different from marital intimacy, or bedroom possession of obscene material [see chap. 13 below], or marriage, or procreation, or education," with which cases from Meyer v. Nebraska to Eisenstadt v. Baird were concerned.

Is the relevant interest then that in personal "autonomy" of choice about performing acts or undergoing experiences? Yet Justice Blackmun expressed doubt that the claim "that one has an unlimited right to do with one's body as one pleases bears a close relationship to the right of privacy previously articulated in the Court's decisions." But do not the autonomy aspects of privacy have added force after Roe? Roe involves not only the interest of the woman but some concern for the fetus—what the Court calls the state's "important and legitimate interest in protecting the potentiality of human life." Does that suggest that an autonomy claim may be even stronger when no other competing personal interest, actual or potential, is involved—when only the claimant's body or life style, or only private consensual conduct, is involved? See note 6 below.

2. *"Balancing" the competing interests.* The Court finds that the woman's strong prima facie right to abort her pregnancy can be defeated only by "compelling" state interests. The Court notes two relevant state interests: that in protecting the woman's health; and that in "protecting the potentiality of human life" of the fetus. At various points, those interests become sufficiently "compelling" to justify state restraints. How does the Court determine when these interests become "compelling"? Is it helpful to discuss whether the fetus is a "person" within the 14th Amendment—or within any other provision of the Constitution? Is it accurate to say: "We need not resolve the difficult question of when life begins"? Must not the Court at least determine when "the potentiality of human life" represents a sufficiently strong moral claim to justify curtailment of the woman's interest in autonomy? Justice Blackmun states that Texas may not, "by adopting one theory of life," "override the rights of the pregnant woman that are at stake." Yet Justice Blackmun also notes that there is wide disagreement, in medicine and philosophy and law, about when life begins. Why should not that lack of consensus lead the Court to defer to, rather than invalidate, the state's judgment? Can the Court's judgment be supported by anything other than a judicial authority to infuse one set of moral values into the Constitution?

Compare Laurence Tribe's suggestion that the result of Roe v. Wade may be supportable on other grounds. In "Foreword: Toward a Model of Roles in the Due Process of Life and Law," 87 Harv.L.Rev. 1 (1973), he argued there that "some types of choices ought to be remanded, on principle, to private decision-makers unchecked by substantive governmental control." As he viewed Roe in his 1973 article, the Court was not choosing simply between abortion and continued pregnancy, but "instead *choosing among alternative allocations of decisionmaking authority.*" And he suggested that the religion clauses of the First Amendment (see chap. 14 below) bar legislators from making judgments about potential life because, given the nature of the problem, "views of organized religious groups have come to play a pervasive role" in legislative considerations of that issue. Does Tribe's general "role allocation" approach help justify substantive due process adjudication? Does it distinguish Lochner?

More recently, Tribe has said that he is not satisfied with that explanation of Roe. He has suggested another one: the right of the judiciary to intervene when moral consensus is in flux, to permit a new moral consensus to evolve. (Cf. the Tribe view noted in chap. 10, sec. 6.) Is principled justification for such judicial intervention possible? Can the existence of instability in society's consensus argue for rather than against judicial intervention? Recall the Holmesian arguments for withdrawal from the interventionism of the Lochner era.

3. *Is Roe distinguishable from Lochner?* Is Roe v. Wade more justifiable than the value-laden interventions of the Lochner era? Are the judicially articulated values of Roe more defensible? Can it be argued that Roe—rather than being more defensible than Lochner, or at least as defensible—is even less defensible? John Ely makes such an argument in "The Wages of Crying Wolf: A Comment on Roe v. Wade," 82 Yale L.J. 920 (1973). He insists that the "general philosophy of constitutional adjudication" is the same as in Roe as in Lochner. To argue that noneconomic rights such as the right to abort a pregnancy accord more closely with "this generation's idealization of America" [1] does not help to distinguish Lochner: it was "precisely" the point of the Lochner philosophy, Ely argues, to "grant unusual protection to those 'rights' that somehow *seem* most pressing, regardless of whether the Constitution suggests any special solicitude for them." Ely goes on to argue, moreover, that Roe may be a "more dangerous precedent" than Lochner. At least the cases of the Lochner era "did us the favor of sowing the seeds of their destruction." Lochner era invalidations rested either on the illegitimacy of the legislative goal or the lack of a "plausible argument" that legislative means furthered the permissible end. By contrast, Roe's rejection of the legislative judgment "takes neither of these forms." The state interest in protecting potential life is not denied, and the efficacy of the means is not questioned. Instead, Roe simply announces that the "goal is not important enough to sustain the restriction." Unlike the Lochner era cases, "Roe's 'refutation' of the legislative judgment [is] *not* obviously wrong, for the substitution of one nonrational judgment for another [can] be labeled neither wrong nor right. The problem with Roe is not so much that it bungles the question it sets itself, but rather that it sets itself a question the Constitution has not made the Court's business." Is that a fair description of the Lochner era cases? Is that a persuasive criticism of Roe?

4. *The difference between Roe and Griswold (and other Warren Court decisions).* Is Roe less defensible than Griswold? Ely so argues. Does that depend upon how Griswold is read? Ely reads it as being a case "about likely invasions of the privacy of the bedroom," not one "directly enshrining a right to contraception." He finds "a general right of privacy" a legitimate constitutional inference, *"so long as some care is taken in defining the sort of right the inference will support."* In Griswold, the contraceptives use law was invalid because its enforcement ordinarily required "prying into the privacy of the home." According to Ely, in short, a general right of privacy regarding "governmental snooping" is justifiable; a general

---

1. That phrase is from Karst and Horo-witz, "Reitman v. Mulkey, A Teleo-　　　　phase of Substantive Equal Protection," 1967 Sup.Ct.Rev. 39.

right of autonomy—"the freedom to live one's life without governmental interference"—is not, and was not asserted in Griswold. Does that reading of Griswold adequately take account of what Ely concedes to be "vague and openended" passages in Griswold?

Can Roe v. Wade be criticized without calling into question many of the interventionist decisions of the Warren Court? See especially the "new" equal protection decisions in the next chapter. Ely insists that, despite the problems of some Warren Court opinions, the results can all be rationalized more persuasively than Roe: "What is frightening about Roe is that this super-protected right is not inferable from the language of the Constitution, the framers' thinking respecting the specific problem in issue, any general value derivable from the provisions they included, or the nation's governmental structure. Nor is it explainable in terms of the unusual political impotence of the group judicially protected vis-a-vis the interest that legislatively prevailed over it.[2] And that, I believe [is] a charge than can responsibly be leveled at no other decision of the past twenty years. At times the inferences the Court has drawn from the values the Constitution marks for special protection have been controversial, even shaky, but never before has its sense of an obligation to draw one been so obviously lacking."[3]

5. *Roe and "non-interpretive" modes of adjudication.* Ely's criteria in criticizing Roe and distinguishing it from interventionist Warren era decisions once again suggests a pervasive problem of judicial review—a problem most acutely raised by the substantive due process cases in this chapter. Are those criteria the right ones? Must the Court limit itself to the sources of values Ely lists: is the Court's authority limited to values derived from text, history, structure, and, perhaps, Stone's political process rationale? Or does it confine the Court unduly to limit it to "interpretation" of that sort?

For an argument that "non-interpretive" modes of adjudication are also legitimate, see Grey, "Do We Have an Unwritten Constitution?" 27 Stan.L.Rev. 703 (1975). Grey disagrees with Ely's type of criticism and with the Marbury v. Madison-Justice Black heritage of the "pure interpretive model" on which it rests.[4] Grey suggests that the Court is not limited

---

2. The reference here is to the rationale of Stone's Carolene Products footnote, printed above, justifying special protection for "discrete and insular minorities" that do not receive adequate consideration in the political process. Ely argues that, "even assuming that that approach can be given principled content," it is only applicable to "those interests which, *as compared with the interest to which they have been subordinated*, constitute minorities unusually incapable of protecting themselves." He adds: "Compared with men, women may constitute such a 'minority'; compared with the unborn, they do not. I'm not sure I'd know a discrete and insular minority if I saw one, but confronted with a multiple choice question requiring me to designate (a) women or (b) fetuses as one, I'd expect no credit for the former answer."

3. See also Ely's comment that Roe is "a very bad decision. Not because it will perceptively weaken the Court—it won't; and not because it conflicts with either my idea of progress or what the evidence suggests is society's—it doesn't. It is bad because it is bad constitutional law, or rather because it is *not* constitutional law and gives almost no sense of an obligation to try to be."

4. For example, Grey takes issue with Ely's statement: "A neutral and dur-

to enforcing "norms derived from the written Constitution": it may "also enforce principles of liberty and justice when the normative content of those principles is not to be found within the four corners of our founding document." He argues that "there was an original understanding, both implicit and textually expressed [in the Ninth Amendment], that unwritten higher law principles had constitutional status" [recall sec. 1A above]; and he claims that the courts have "enforced unwritten constitutional principles" from the beginning. He adds that an "extraordinarily radical purge of established constitutional doctrine would be required if we candidly and consistently applied the pure interpretive model." He recognizes a number of difficulties with the open avowal of the "noninterpretive" approach, especially: "Conceding the natural-rights origins of our Constitution, does not the erosion and abandonment of the 18th century ethics and epistemology on which the natural rights theory was founded require the abandonment of the mode of judicial review flowing from that theory? Is a 'fundamental law' judicially enforced in a climate of historical and cultural relativism the legitimate offspring of a fundamental law which its exponents felt expressed rationally demonstrable, universal and immutable human rights?"

Is is possible to develop a "legitimate pedigree of non-interpretive judicial review"? Can the Court's judicial review authority be defended on grounds other than the interpretive approach of Marbury v. Madison? Would a modern "natural rights" authority for the Court be within its institutional competence? Can a "higher law-natural rights" approach be reconciled with democratic theory? Is there a sufficient basis for finding a natural rights approach incorporated in the Constitution as a whole, or in the Ninth Amendment, or in the 14th Amendment? What guidance for judicial judgment can be articulated if a natural rights approach is openly adopted?

6. *The implications of Roe and Griswold: Private autonomy and public morality.* a. *The individual interest in autonomy.* Recall the questions at the end of note 1. Has the basis for a due process interest in personal autonomy now been established? Griswold may involve less than that, especially if it is limited to the intrusion-into-the-home rationale; Roe involves more than that—not only the woman's interest, but also that of the potential life of the fetus. But do the Griswold and Roe opinions and

able principle may be a thing of beauty and a joy forever. But if it lacks connection with any value the Constitution marks as special, it is not a constitutional principle and the Court has no business imposing it." Grey cites as other examples of "interpretive" criticism Bork, "Neutral Principles and Some First Amendment Problems," 47 Ind.L.J. 1 (1971) ("[T]he choice of 'fundamental values' by the Court cannot be justified. . . . The judge must stick close to the text and the history, and their implications, and not construct new rights") and Linde, "Judges, Critics, and the Realist Tradition," 82 Yale L.J. 227 (1972) ("The judicial responsibility begins and ends with determining the present scope and meaning of a decision that the nation, at an earlier time, articulated and enacted into constitutional text"). Grey does, however, distinguish the "interpretive" model from "literalism." For example, he includes inferences from structures and relationships within the "interpretive model." But the common denominator of all "unduly narrow," "purely interpretive" models, he finds, is the insistence "that the only norms used in constitutional adjudication must be those inferable from the text"; the interpretive model does not authorize courts "to articulate and apply contemporary norms not demonstrably expressed or implied by the Framers."

their general statements suggest the basis for a constitutionally recognized right of private autonomy—of private choice in performing acts or undergoing experiences—so long as there is no demonstrable harm to others? What varieties of laws would be threatened by recognition of such a right?

A claim to autonomy has been argued not only in Roe but in a number of other contexts. For example, should such a right apply to regulations of consensual sexual behavior, see, e. g., Note, "The Constitutionality of Laws Forbidding Private Homosexual Conduct," 72 Mich.L.Rev. 1613 (1974)? Regulations of dress and hair style? Requirements that motorcyclists wear helmets, see Note, "Motorcycle Helmets and the Constitutionality of Self-Protective Legislation," 30 Ohio St.L.J. 355 (1969)? Prohibitions of the possession or use of marijuana, see Comment, "The California Marijuana Possession Statute: An Infringement on the Right of Privacy or Other Peripheral Constitutional Rights?" 19 Hast.L.J. 758 (1968)? See generally Packer, "The Aims of the Criminal Law Revisited: A Plea for a New Look at 'Substantive Due Process,' " 44 So.Cal.L.Rev. 490 (1971), and Henkin, "Privacy and Autonomy," 74 Colum.L.Rev. 1410 (1974).[5]

b. *The state interest in morality.* What legitimate countervailing governmental interests justify such laws? Are they constitutionally legitimate state interests? Is there a legitimate interest in preventing an individual from doing harm to himself or herself, or in regulating private consensual conduct deemed to be "immoral"? What, if anything, justifies the regulation of "morality"? Recall Justice Harlan's discussion above [printed with his concurrence in Griswold] of Connecticut's claim that use of contraceptives could be banned "to protect the moral welfare of its citizenry": though Justice Harlan found Connecticut's means impermissible, he suggested that the "morality" end was legitimate. He noted that the police power traditionally included the "morality objective": "Indeed to attempt a line between public behavior and that which is purely consensual or solitary would be to withdraw from community concern a range of subjects with which every society in civilized times has found it necessary to deal. . . . Connecticut's judgment is no more demonstrably correct or incorrect than are the varieties of judgment, expressed in law, on marriage and divorce, on adult consensual homosexuality, abortion, and sterilization, or euthanasia and suicide." Can the traditional state interest in private morality nevertheless be found noncompelling under the modes of adjudication reflected in Griswold and Roe? Note the question in Brest, Processes of Constitutional Decisionmaking (1975), chap. 7: "If the Constitution does not enact Her-

---

5. Compare Village of Belle Terre v. Boraas, 416 U.S. 1 (1974), where Justice Douglas' majority opinion, over Justice Marshall's dissent, found no privacy rights involved in a family-oriented zoning restriction excluding most unrelated groups from a village. Justice Douglas insisted the ordinance represented "economic and social legislation" and invoked the deferential judicial stance characteristic of zoning cases, see sec. 2A above. Justice Marshall argued that strict scrutiny was appropriate: "The choice of household companions—of whether a person's 'intellectual and emotional' needs are best met by living with family, friends, professional associates or others—involves deeply personal considerations as to the kind and quality of intimate relationships within the home. That decision surely falls within the ambit of the right to privacy protected by the Constitution. See [Roe v. Wade; Eisenstadt; Griswold]." (See also chap. 10 below.)

bert Spencer's Social Statics, does it enact John Stuart Mill's *On Liberty* (1859)?" [6]   (Compare the 1973 obscenity cases, chap. 13, sec. 2.)

7. *The reaction to Roe: Proposed constitutional amendments.*   In the wake of Roe v. Wade, well-publicized efforts to amend the Constitution were launched and several proposals were introduced in Congress.   For one echoing Justice Rehnquist's stance in his dissent, see the amendment introduced in the House providing that nothing in the Constitution shall bar any State "from allowing, regulating, or prohibiting the practice of abortion."   (H.J.Res. 527.)   Contrast with this "neutral" proposal two amendments proposed in the Senate in 1973 which are clearly anti-abortion in tendency.   S.J.Res. 130, introduced by Senator Helms, seeks to protect life "from the moment of conception."   And S.J.Res. 119, introduced by Senator Buckley, protects unborn children "at every stage of their biological development," but is inapplicable "in an emergency when a reasonable medical certainty exists that continuation of the pregnancy will cause the death of the mother."

Note that neither the Helms nor the Buckley proposals mentions "abortion" explicitly.   Rather, each seeks to extend the guarantees of due process and equal protection clauses to unborn children.   The reason for this "indirect" approach to the abortion issue was that both Senators claimed to oppose the Court's decision in Roe v. Wade on grounds that went beyond "the special concern that many of us have with the matter of abortion itself."   For example, in introducing his amendment, Senator Helms asserted: "[I]f an innocent human being can be defined as a nonperson [and therefore not entitled to constitutional rights] because he is too young   .   .   ., there is no reason in principle why he cannot be defined as a nonperson because he is too old, or too retarded, or too disabled." [7] Is it clear that the approach embodied in the two Senate amendments would have the intended effect of prohibiting abortions?   Would it erect a per se barrier to state legislation authorizing abortion, or would it simply require the application of a heightened degree of scrutiny to such legislation?

---

6. Mill's well-known argument elaborated "one very simple principle": "That the sole end to which mankind are warranted, individually or collectively, in interfering with the liberty of action of any of their number is self-protection"; that government may control the individual only "to prevent harm to others"; "His own good, either physical or moral, is not a sufficient warrant.   .   .   .   Over himself, over his own body and mind, the individual is sovereign." See also the bearing of Mill's On Liberty on First Amendment theory, noted in chap. 12 below.

chap. 12 below—and the rejection of the J. S. Mill view by the majority in the 1973 obscenity cases, chap. 13, sec. 2, below.

7. Senator Bayh's Judiciary Subcommittee on Constitutional Amendments conducted a series of hearings on the anti-abortion amendments in 1974 and 1975.   Sizable "right-to-life" rallies were also staged by supporters of the amendments.   (Compare a decision by the German Constitutional Court in the spring of 1975, striking down a law making abortions more readily available: the German Court relied on the protection of "life" in the German Constitution.)

For a review of the debates as well as the constitutional and statutory proposals in the wake of Roe v. Wade, see 33 Cong.Quar. Weekly Report (May 3, 1975), 917–922.

May Congress modify the impact of Roe v. Wade through the statutory rather than the amendment route, by invoking its powers under § 5 of the 14th Amendment? See Katzenbach v. Morgan, chap. 11, sec. 4, below.

Chapter 10

EQUAL PROTECTION

EQUAL PROTECTION, "OLD," "NEW," AND "NEWER": AN INTRODUCTORY OVERVIEW

1. *Modest origins: The "old" equal protection in the pre-Warren years.* The equal protection clause of the 14th Amendment has undergone rapid and dramatic transformation in recent years. Traditionally, it supported only minimal judicial intervention in most contexts. Ordinarily, the command of equal protection was only that government must not impose differences in treatment "except upon some reasonable differentiation fairly related to the object of regulation," as Justice Jackson put it in the Railway Express case, sec. 1 below. That "old" variety of equal protection scrutiny focused solely on the means used by the legislature: it insisted merely that the classification in the statute reasonably relate to the legislative purpose. Unlike substantive due process, equal protection scrutiny was not typically concerned with second-guessing and restraining legislative ends. And usually that rational classification requirement was satisfied fairly readily: the courts did not demand a close fit between classification and purpose; perfect congruence between means and ends was not required; judges were prepared to allow legislators considerable flexibility to act on the basis of broadly accurate generalizations and were prepared to tolerate some over-inclusiveness and underinclusiveness in classification schemes. Only in special, limited contexts was equal protection found to have a deeper bite during most of its history—most notably in racial discrimination cases. The historical background of the 14th Amendment persuaded judges at an early point to apply a stricter scrutiny and to adopt a less deferential stance when racial classifications were challenged. But in most contexts, the impact of equal protection was very limited, both in frequency of invocation and in scope of intervention.

During the decades of extensive Court interference with state economic legislation under the 14th Amendment, it was usually due process, not equal protection, that provided the cutting edge. (Recall chap. 9, sec. 1B.) At the height of the Lochner era, for example, Justice Holmes could refer to equal protection as "the usual last resort of constitutional arguments." Buck v. Bell, 274 U.S. 200 (1927). Another comment, by Justice Jackson in the Railway Express case, sec. 1 below, reflects the relatively narrow intrusion into the legislative domain traditionally associated with equal protection: "Invalidation of a statute or an ordinance on due process grounds leaves ungoverned and ungovernable conduct which many people find objectionable. Invocation of the equal protection clause, on the other hand, does not disable any governmental body from dealing with the subject at hand. It merely means that the prohibition or regulation must have a broader impact." What Justice Jackson there emphasized is that the "old" equal

protection ordinarily focused solely on legislative means, on the rationality of classifications, not on legislative objectives. Though due process, too, has a means ingredient, as noted in the preceding chapter, it is more commonly associated with restraints on legislative ends, in the era of Roe v. Wade as in the Lochner era.

2. *From marginal intervention to major cutting edge: The Warren Court's "new" equal protection and the two-tier approach.* From that long-maintained modest role, equal protection burgeoned into a major interventionist tool during the Warren era, especially in the 1960's. The Warren Court did not abandon the deferential ingredients of the old equal protection: in most areas of economic and social legislation, the demands imposed by equal protection remained as minimal as ever—indeed, the Warren Court's hands-off stance was more permissive than that of its predecessors. The equal protection revolution of the Warren years took the form of finding large new areas where strict rather than deferential scrutiny was applied. A sharply differentiated two-tier approach evolved by the late 1960's: in addition to the deferential "old" equal protection, there was the mounting phenomenon of a "new" equal protection connoting strict scrutiny. It was a sharply differentiated two-level approach: "The Warren Court embraced a rigid two-tier attitude. Some situations evoked the aggressive 'new' equal protection, with scrutiny that was 'strict' in theory and fatal in fact; in other contexts, the deferential 'old' equal protection reigned, with minimal scrutiny in theory and virtually none in fact." [1] The intensive review associated with the strict scrutiny of the new equal protection imposed two demands— a demand not only as to means but also one as to ends. Legislation qualifying for new equal protection strict scrutiny required a far closer fit between classification and statutory purpose, a far closer congruence between means and ends, than the rough and ready flexibility traditionally tolerated by the old equal protection. Moreover, equal protection became a source of ends scrutiny as well: legislation in the areas of the new equal protection had to be justified by "compelling" state interests.

The Warren Court identified the areas appropriate for the strict scrutiny of the new equal protection by searching for two characteristics: the presence of "suspect" classifications; or an impact on "fundamental" rights or interests.[2] In the category of "suspect classifications," the Warren Court's major contribution was to intensify the strict scrutiny in the traditionally interventionist area of racial classifications. (Sec. 2 below.) But there were also tantalizing statements suggesting that there were other suspect cate-

---

1. Gunther, "Foreword: In Search of Evolving Doctrine on a Changing Court: A Model for a Newer Equal Protection," 86 Harv.L.Rev. 1 (1972) (hereinafter cited as Gunther, "Newer Equal Protection"). (All quotations in this introductory overview, unless otherwise attributed, are from that article.)
For a comprehensive review of the state of equal protection doctrine near the end of the Warren years, distinguishing the "restrained review" and "active review" spheres, see "Developments in the Law—Equal Protection,"

82 Harv.L.Rev. 1065 (1969) (hereinafter cited as "Developments").

2. Whether suspect classifications and fundamental interests were separate or interrelated categories was not always clear. Consider that question in the context of the new equal protection cases below, especially in secs. 4 and 5; and note the commentaries cited in Gunther, "Newer Equal Protection," at 9, n. 36, speculating that the two categories might be related gradients or intersecting variables or intertwined helices.

gories as well: illegitimacy, for example; and dicta hinting that wealth classifications might be suspect. (Secs. 3 and 5 below.) But it was the "fundamental interests" ingredient of the new equal protection that proved particularly dynamic, open-ended, and amorphous: "It was the element which bore the closest resemblance to freewheeling substantive due process, for it circumscribed legislative choices in the name of newly articulated values that lacked clear support in constitutional text and history. The list of interests identified as fundamental by the Warren Court was in fact quite modest: voting, criminal appeals, and the right of interstate travel were the prime examples. But in the extraordinary amount of commentary that followed, analysts searching for justifications for those enshrinements were understandably tempted to ponder analogous spheres that might similarly qualify. Welfare benefits, exclusionary zoning, municipal services and school financing came to be the most inviting frontiers." [3]

3. *The Burger Court and equal protection.* The Warren Court's equal protection legacy, then, was an "amalgam of deeds and spurred hopes." What has been the Burger Court's response to that legacy? There has been neither undiminished carrying forward nor wholesale turning back of the Warren Court approach. The response has been more complex than that.

---

3. Gunther, "Newer Equal Protection," at 8–9. See the materials below, especially secs. 4 and 5.

For a critical evaluation of new equal protection developments at the end of the Warren era, see Justice Harlan's dissent in Shapiro v. Thompson, 394 U.S. 618 (1969) (sec. 4 below). In dissenting from a decision holding durational residency requirements in welfare laws unconstitutional, Justice Harlan especially objected to the ends scrutiny of the new equal protection, to the "expansion of the comparatively new constitutional doctrine that some state statutes will be deemed to deny equal protection of the laws unless justified by a 'compelling' governmental interest." He saw that approach as an "increasingly significant exception to the long-established rule that a statute does not deny equal protection if it is rationally related to a legitimate governmental objective." He noted the "two branches" of the new doctrine, the triggering of strict scrutiny either because of the presence of "certain 'suspect' criteria" or because "fundamental rights" were affected. He thought the first of these branches "sound when applied to racial classifications, for historically the Equal Protection Clause was largely a product of the desire to eradicate legal distinctions founded upon race." But he opposed extensions of the "suspect" category. And he found "even more troublesome" the "second branch of the 'compelling interest' principle," the "fundamental" rights or interests

strand. That branch was "unfortunate because it creates an exception which threatens to swallow the standard equal protection rule. Virtually every state statute affects important rights." And he found that strand "unnecessary as well": "When the right affected is one assured by the Federal Constitution, any infringement can be dealt with under the Due Process Clause. But when a statute affects only matters not mentioned in the Federal Constitution and is not arbitrary or irrational," the Court had no justification to pick out "particular human activities, characterize them as 'fundamental,' and give them added protection under an unusually stringent equal protection test."

For a more sympathetic view of new equal protection developments, see Karst and Horowitz, "Reitman v. Mulkey: A Telophase of Substantive Equal Protection," 1967 Sup.Ct.Rev. 39, noting that "some classifications although far from irrational [are] nonetheless unconstitutional because they produce inequities that are unacceptable in this generation's idealization of America," and praising the "egalitarian revolution" supported by the Warren Court's new equal protection. Note the additional comment by one of the co-authors of that article, in Karst, "Invidious Discrimination: Justice Douglas and the Return to the 'Natural-Law-Due-Process Formula,'" 16 UCLA L.Rev. 716 (1969), at a time when "the law of substantive equal protection continue[d] to grow." Karst

In form, the two-tier new equal protection-old equal protection distinction persists. In fact, the modern exercises of scrutiny in equal protection cases do not conform to so simple a bifurcated pattern. An attempt to summarize the early years of the Burger Court's work stated the pattern as follows: "(1) The Burger Court is reluctant to expand the scope of the new equal protection, although its best established ingredients retain vitality. (2) There is mounting discontent with the rigid two-tier formulations of the Warren Court's equal protection doctrine. (3) The Court is prepared to use the clause as an interventionist tool without resorting to the strict scrutiny language of the new equal protection." [4]

a. *Blocking the expansion of the new equal protection.* The Burger Court's "thus far and no further" approach to the new equal protection has been especially marked with respect to the most amorphous aspect of Warren Court doctrine, that employing strict scrutiny where "fundamental interests" were affected. Those inclined to read Warren Court decisions most broadly (including dissenters like Justice Harlan) had perceived in equal protection a potential tool on a wide front: even if not all "wealth" classifications were suspect, there were suggestions that all legislation impinging on "necessities" (welfare, housing, education, etc.) might be subjected to strict scrutiny.[5] Those hopes (or fears) did not materialize, perhaps in part because the Warren Court's doctrinal heritage was least well-fixed in those areas. Thus, Dandridge v. Williams, sec. 5 below, made clear during the first years of Chief Justice Burger's tenure that equal protection would not be employed with respect to welfare legislation generally, that equal protection would not be read as imposing substantial new affirmative obligations on government and as assuring equality of condition. And the series of cases rejecting efforts to invoke equal protection as an affirmative, broad-gauged weapon on behalf of the poor culminated in Rodriguez, the School Financing Case, in 1973, where the majority rejected a claim that education was a "fundamental interest" and refused to find wealth a "suspect" classification (sec. 5 below). But refusal to expand has not meant that the Burger Court has scuttled the new equal protection. Its relatively well-established strands survive, as in the area of voting rights (sec. 4 below). With respect to suspect classifications, indeed, the Burger Court has not only maintained strict scrutiny of racial classifications, but has added to the list of "suspect" classifications those based on alienage and has struck down a number of gender-based classifications, even though a majority has not formally found sex to be a suspect classification (sec. 3 below).

b. *Mounting discontent with two-tier formulations.* Yet even while the new-old equal protection distinction has been adhered to in form, there has also been an increasingly noticeable undercurrent of resistance to the sharp difference between deferential old and interventionist new equal protection. A number of Justices, from all segments of the Court, have sought

there acknowledged: "The doctrine of invidious discrimination [as used in the new equal protection cases] does not permit an escape from the problems associated with substantive due process."

4. Gunther, "Newer Equal Protection," at 12.

5. See, e. g., the fears voiced in Justice Harlan's dissent, footnote 3 above, and the hopes advanced in some of the commentaries cited in Gunther, "Newer Equal Protection," at 9.

formulations that would blur the sharp distinctions of the two-tiered approach or that would narrow the gap between the levels of scrutiny. That mounting discontent with the two-tier approach has sometimes been manifested in efforts to formulate a single standard applicable to "all" equal protection cases;[6] at other times, the effort has been to decide equal protection cases without articulating any standard of review.[7] But the most elaborate attacks on the two-tier notion have come from members of the Warren Court rather than new appointees. Justice Marshall has been at the forefront of that development. His position was stated most elaborately in his dissent in San Antonio Ind. School Dist. v. Rodriguez, 411 U.S. 1 (1973):[8] "I must once more voice my disagreement with the Court's rigidified approach to equal protection analysis. The Court apparently seeks to establish today that equal protection cases fall into one of two neat categories which dictate the appropriate standard of review—strict scrutiny or mere rationality. But this Court's decisions in the field of equal protection defy such easy categorization. A principled reading of what this Court has done reveals that it has applied a spectrum of standards in reviewing discrimination allegedly violative of the Equal Protection Clause. This spectrum clearly comprehends variations in the degree of care with which the Court will scrutinize particular classifications, depending, I believe, on the constitutional and societal importance of the interest adversely affected and the recognized invidiousness of the basis upon which the particular classification is drawn."[9]

c. *The gropings for new standards: "Minimum scrutiny with bite" as a "newer equal protection"?* Justice Marshall's "sliding scale" approach may explain many of the Burger Court's decisions, as his Rodriguez dissent argues, but it is a formulation that the majority has refused to embrace. But the Burger Court's results indicate that at least one significant shift has taken place in the operation of equal protection law. Invocation of the formulations of the "old" equal protection no longer signals, as it did with the Warren Court, an extreme deference to legislative classifications and a virtually automatic validation of challenged statutes. Instead, there has been a significant number of cases in which the majority, even while voicing the traditional "mere rationality," "hands-off" standards of the old equal protection, proceeds to find the statute unconstitutional: for the first time in years, old equal protection standards occasionally mean something other than perfunctory opinions sustaining the law under attack. *Milwaukee*

Increasingly, too, formulations of "mere rationality" standards by some of the Justices have hinted at increased bite to the scrutiny. Contrast, for example, an extremely deferential statement from the Warren Court with

6. See Justice Powell's opinion for the Court in Weber v. Aetna Casualty & Surety Co., 406 U.S. 164 (1972) (sec. 3 below).

7. See, e. g., Chief Justice Burger's opinion in Jimenez v. Weinberger, 417 U.S. 628 (1974) (sec. 5 below).

8. For earlier reflections of Justice Marshall's growing discontent with the two-tier approach, see Chicago Police Dept. v. Mosley, 408 U.S. 92 (1972), and Dandridge v. Williams, 397 U.S. 471 (1970).

9. Justice White has endorsed much of Justice Marshall's analysis. See his concurring opinion in Vlandis v. Kline, 412 U.S. 441 (1973) (sec. 6 below), commenting that "it is clear that we employ not just one, or two, but, as my Brother Marshall has so ably demonstrated, a 'spectrum of standards.'"

somewhat more demanding versions in more recent years. Thus, Chief Justice Warren conveyed the deferential mood applied to the old equal protection category during the 1960's when he said that the equal protection clause was violated "only if the classification rests on grounds wholly irrelevant to the achievement of the State's objective," that a "statutory discrimination will not be set aside if any state of facts reasonably may be conceived to justify it." [10]   By contrast, Burger Court Justices have sporadically articulated somewhat more demanding criteria, in two respects: first, they have suggested that the means, the classification, must *substantially* further the statutory objective; [11] second, there has been the suggestion that the Court will no longer regularly hypothesize *conceivable* state purposes against which to test the rationality of the means—the hypothesizing so familiar in the economic due process area (chap. 9, sec. 1) and a concomitant of the Warren Court's old equal protection approach as well.   Instead, there have been statements such as Justice Powell's opinion for the Court in McGinnis v. Royster, 410 U.S. 263 (1973), asking "whether the challenged distinction rationally furthers some legitimate, *articulated* state purpose"; insisting that the state objective be "nonillusory"; and claiming that the Court supplied "no imaginary basis or purpose" in sustaining the statutory scheme. [12]

---

10.   McGowan v. Maryland, 366 U.S. 420 (1961). For an, if anything, even more deferential restatement of the old equal protection standard, see the Chief Justice's opinion shortly before his retirement in McDonald v. Board of Election, 394 U.S. 802 (1969). (Both cases are further noted in sec. 1 below.)

11.   See, e. g., Chief Justice Burger's statement in invalidating a challenged sex discrimination while purporting to apply minimum rationality criteria: he quoted from a 1920 decision, F. S. Royster Guano Co. v. Virginia, 253 U.S. 412 (1920) (noted in sec. 1 below), insisting that the classification "must rest upon some ground of difference having a fair and substantial relation to the object of the legislation." Reed v. Reed, 404 U.S. 71 (1971) (sec. 3C).

12.   For a review of some examples of the modern Court's increasing—albeit sporadic—emphasis on articulated or actual purposes rather than hypothesized ones, see Justice Brennan's comment in dissenting in Schlesinger v. Ballard, 419 U.S. 498 (1975) (further considered in sec. 3C below): "While we have in the past exercised our imaginations to conceive of possible rational justifications for statutory classifications, see [McGowan v. Maryland], we have recently declined to manufacture justifications in order to save an apparently invalid statutory classification. Cf. James v. Strange, 407 U.S. 128 (1972); Weber v. Aetna Casualty and Surety Co., 406 U.S. 164 (1972) (sec. 3B below). Moreover, we have analyzed asserted governmental interests to determine whether they were in fact the legislative purpose of a statutory classification, Eisenstadt v. Baird, 405 U.S. 438 (1972) (sec. 6 below) [see also Weinberger v. Wiesenfeld, 420 U.S. —— (1975), sec. 3C below], and we have limited our inquiry to the legislature's stated purposes when these purposes are clearly set out in the statute or its legislative history. Johnson v. Robison, 415 U.S. 361 (1974). Never, to my knowledge, have we endeavored to sustain a statute upon a supposition about the legislature's purpose in enacting it when the asserted justification can be shown conclusively *not* to have underlain the classification in any way." [Justice Brennan added in a footnote: "Indeed, to do so is to undermine the very premises of deference to legislative determination. If a legislature, considering the competing factors, determines that it is wise policy to treat two groups of people differently in pursuit of a certain goal, courts often defer to that legislative determination. But when a legislature has decided *not* to pursue a certain goal, upholding a statute on the basis of that goal is not properly deference to a legislative decision at all; it is deference to a decision which the legislature could have made but did not. See Gunther, [Newer Equal Protection], 86 Harv.L.Rev. 1, 44–45 (1972).")

What emerges clearly from the Burger Court's invocations of "rationality" scrutiny is that the reliance on that old equal protection standard sometimes carries new bite. While most laws subjected to "mere rationality" scrutiny continue to be upheld, a significant number have been invalidated. The meaning of that development is less clear. To Justice Marshall, in his Rodriguez dissent, the emerging pattern shows that the Court is in fact applying a multi-variable sliding scale approach. Some Burger Court decisions do indeed suggest that questions going beyond minimum rationality are being asked, even if not always voiced in the opinions.[13] Yet the emerging tendency of a "new bite for the old equal protection" may offer the basis for a coherent, principled approach, though the Court's performance so far has been understandably criticized as erratic. A model for a "newer equal protection" that may justify less perfunctory scrutiny under the "mere rationality" standard would view equal protection "as a means-focused, relatively narrow, preferred ground of decision in a broad range of cases." It would have the Court "less willing to supply justifying rationales by exercising its imagination. It would have the Court assess the means in terms of legislative purposes that have substantial basis in actuality, not merely in conjecture. Moreover, it would have the Justices gauge the reasonableness of questionable means on the basis of materials that are offered to the Court, rather than resorting to rationalizations created by perfunctory judicial hypothesizing."[14] The problems of that "newer equal protection" model, and the modern cases raising the question whether the Court is moving in the direction of that model, are considered further below.[15]

4. *Modern equal protection developments: Summary and challenge.* What is clear from the history of equal protection over the last decade and a half—and what is suggested by this brief overview—is that equal protection has come a very long way indeed from being the "last resort of constitutional arguments." Instead, it has become perhaps the most prolific source of constitutional litigation. Expanding interventionism under the "fundamental interests" strand of the Warren Court's new equal protection has been brought to a halt, to be sure. But the proportion of equal protection cases on the Burger Court's docket has not substantially diminished. Equal protection remains a body of doctrine influx. The Warren Court created a relatively clear, if not always adequately explained and justified, two-tiered approach. The gropings for new formulations by all wings of the Burger Court make for less neat doctrine, even though two-tier analysis has not been formally abandoned. Is the Burger Court's variety of equal protection simply an accumulation of ad hoc interventions? Is it best explainable by Justice Marshall's sliding scale analysis? Does it offer promise for evolution toward a different variety of two-tier analysis, retaining the well-established ingredients of the new equal protection and its strict scrutiny, but raising the

13. Most notably, a number of recent sex discrimination cases, while purporting to rest simply on mere rationality grounds for the invalidations, may mean that the Court in fact is scrutinizing gender-based classifications with greater care even while eschewing the adoption of a sex-is-a-suspect-classification position. (See sec. 3C below.)

14. Gunther, "Newer Equal Protection," at 20–21.

15. For elaborations of—and questions about—that model, see the final group of notes in sec. 1 below. For modern cases invalidating laws on the alleged basis of the traditional "mere rationality" standard, see secs. 3–6 below.

level of scrutiny appropriate for the old equal protection area, by applying the greater bite, the diminished deference toward legislative selection of means, of the "newer equal protection"?

The search for coherence in emerging equal protection law is the challenge, then—not only for the Court, but also in the examination of the materials which follow. Those materials reveal a doctrinal landscape strewn with not always reconcilable fragments: the fundamental interests and suspect classifications of the strict scrutiny new equal protection; the very deferential rationality review of the Warren Court's old equal protection; the occasional greater scrutiny under the umbrella of rationality formulations in the Burger Court's variations on minimum rationality with bite; sliding scale analyses; and so forth. The doctrinal strands touched on in these introductory materials will be examined at greater length in a variety of settings below. The recurrent questions are: Do the individual strands make sense? Do they provide ingredients for a coherent whole? Or is equal protection doctrine simply the modern Justices' garb for judicially selected value infusions, for Lochnerizing without wearing the partly discredited mantle of substantive due process? [16]

5. *A note on organization.* The aim of this chapter is to look at the roots, contents, and implications of equal protection—"old," "new," and "newer"; two-tier and multi-variable and sliding scale theories—to see where we are, how we got here, and where we may be going. A body of decisions and dicta this volatile and diffuse is difficult to organize: one cannot simultaneously bring to bear all of the relevant perspectives—chronological, functional, variations in modes of review, subgroups of substantive doctrine. In pursuing the multiple strands of equal protection, this chapter will proceed as follows:

Sec. 1 examines the "classic," means-oriented focus of traditional equal protection: it pursues the ingredients of the requisite classification-purpose congruence in the context of modern economic and social legislation, and it introduces the question whether the Court can impose more demanding requirements regarding the requisite fit between means and ends under the "newer" equal protection model without unduly hampering flexibility in legislative generalizations. Sec. 2 turns to an examination of the historically best established, most justified area of strict scrutiny, the area of racial discrimination. Sec. 3 examines a number of other bases for classifications that have been sought to be brought into the circle of "suspect" ones triggering strict scrutiny. The central concerns of that section are the arguably "suspect" classifications based on alienage, illegitimacy, and gender. Sec. 4 turns from the suspect classifications strand of stricter scrutiny to that turning on the presence of "fundamental interests," emphasizing the develop-

16. On the similarity between the "fundamental interests" strand of the new equal protection and the problems of value choices in substantive due process, see, in addition to Karst, footnote 3 above, "Developments," 82 Harv.L. Rev. 1065, 1131 (1969): "The resurrection of a wider-ranging review when fundamental personal interests are at stake has come under the guise of equal protection rather than substantive due process. This development is not surprising in light of the discredit which had attached to the use of substantive due process in the field of business regulation." See also Michelman, "Foreword: On Protecting the Poor Through the Fourteenth Amendment," 83 Harv.L.Rev. 7 (1969).

ments in the areas of voting, criminal procedure, and restraints on travel. Sec. 5 turns to a group of problems pertaining to equal protection and the poor. Strict scrutiny where "necessities" are affected—and constitutional bases for some affirmative governmental obligations to equalize economic conditions—was the amorphous and potentially most embracive frontier of the new equal protection at the end of the Warren era. The Burger Court decisions have called a halt to further expansion of that variety of "substantive equal protection"; yet occasional invocations of minimum rationality with bite indicate that equal protection has not become wholly toothless in the welfare area. Sec. 6, finally, brings together some examples of Burger Court departures from the Warren Court's rigid two-tier approach to equal protection—examples in addition to those that surface repeatedly in the materials in the preceding sections. Equal protection invalidations while voicing minimum rationality formulas—the "newer equal protection"—illustrate one such departure. "Irrebuttable presumptions" analysis, a recent, occasionally puzzling and frequently criticized phenomenon that purports to analyze classification problems without resort to the equal protection clause, is another such example.[17]

These sectional divisions are not separated by bright lines: the groupings overlap; the materials abound with historical, doctrinal, and functional interrelations. At first glance, the intertwined strands of equal protection law are bound to appear inchoate if not chaotic. The organization of this chapter seeks to aid understanding of the separate strands and to encourage efforts to integrate them into a coherent whole.

SECTION 1. THE "OLD" EQUAL PROTECTION: LIMITED SCRUTINY OF MEANS UNDER THE TRADITIONAL STANDARDS

THE "RATIONAL RELATION" REQUIREMENT: WHEN ARE CLASSIFICATIONS EXCESSIVELY "UNDERINCLUSIVE" OR "OVERINCLUSIVE"?

Introduction. Racial discrimination was plainly the central purpose of the post-Civil War Amendments, including the equal protection clause of the 14th. As the Court's virtually contemporaneous review of the history in the Slaughter House Cases, 16 Wall. 36 (1873) (chap. 8 above), concluded, there was "one pervading purpose": "we mean the freedom of the slave race, the security and firm establishment of that freedom, and the protection of the newly-made freeman and citizen from the oppressions of those who had formally exercised unlimited dominion over him." But only the language of the 15th Amendment was limited to racial considerations. The equal protection clause is one of those post-Civil War provisions not explicitly limited to racial problems. And that broader language of equal protection has long been read to impose some restraint on the use of classi-

---

17. Because "irrebuttable presumptions" analysis purports to be an aspect of procedural due process, that section also provides occasion for a brief sur-vey of recent developments in more traditional areas of procedural due process.

fications in state legislation generally, whatever the area regulated, whatever the classification criterion used.[1] What restraints are placed on legislatures under that traditional standard in differentiating among persons and activities regulated?

In a sense, the equal protection command is an aspect of the broader constitutional requirement that there must be a "rational" connection between legislative means and ends—a requirement already examined, as an aspect of due process, in chap. 9, sec. 1. The added thrust provided by equal protection for that general requirement of rationality focuses on legislative *classifications*: laws do not apply universally; they characteristically classify; equal protection demands that there be some "rational" connection between classifications and objectives. There must be a minimal "fit" or "congruence" between the classifying means and the legislative ends. But the traditional, "old" equal protection standard does not demand a perfect fit: legislatures must often act on the basis of generalizations; perfect congruence would often make such action impossible and would demand individualized hearings in every case. The deferential old equal protection, then, leaves considerable flexibility to the legislature. (And one characteristic of the new equal protection, of the area of "strict scrutiny," is that the Court tolerates far fewer deviations from congruence, insists on a far closer fit.)

The materials in this section stem from areas of economic and social legislation which do not evoke the strict scrutiny associated with "suspect classifications" and "fundamental interests." What restraints on classifications-ends relationships can and does the Court impose in this area? What limits on legislative flexibility exist, what demands of congruence? Even in the days when the Court was using economic due process as a significant restraint on legislative choices, equal protection was not a major interventionist tool. A frequently quoted formulation of the basic standard came in a 1920 decision, already quoted in part: "[T]he classification must be reasonable, not arbitrary, and must rest upon some ground of difference having a fair and substantial relation to the object of the legislation, so that all persons similarly circumstanced shall be treated alike." [2]

---

1. As noted earlier, consideration of the equal protection clause in the context of its central historical purpose, racial discrimination, is postponed to sec. 2 of this chapter.

2. F. S. Royster Guano Co. v. Virginia, 253 U.S. 412, 415 (1920). Compare a frequently cited "minimum rationality" standard as to economic due process, insisting that "the means selected shall have a real and substantial relation to the object sought to be attained." Nebbia v. New York, 291 U.S. 502 (1934) (chap. 9, sec. 1C, above).

Is a lesser degree of scrutiny suggested by another frequently cited case from the early years of the 20th century, Lindsley v. Natural Carbonic Gas Co., 220 U.S. 61 (1911)? In that case, the Court set forth the rules for testing discrimination under the equal protection clause as follows: "1. The equal protection clause of the Fourteenth Amendment does not take from the State the power to classify in the adoption of police laws, but admits of the exercise of a wide scope of discretion in that regard, and avoids what is done only when it is without any reasonable basis and therefore is purely arbitrary. 2. A classification having some reasonable basis does not offend against that clause merely because it is not made with mathematical nicety or because in practice it results in some inequality. 3. When the classification in such a law is called in question, if any state of facts reasonably can be conceived that would sustain it, the existence of that state of facts at the time the law was enacted must be assumed. 4. One who assails the classification in such a law must carry

That was a formulation by the old Court of pre-New Deal days. Does it still express the general standard? In a fair number of modern cases, from the 1940's through the 1960's, the Court sounded as if it was demanding less than that. (Recall the parallel development of an increasingly "hands-off" attitude as to the demands of economic due process, in chap. 9 above.) See, e. g., Williamson v. Lee Optical Co., already noted in chap. 9, and examined once more later in this section. See also the Court's opinion in Dandridge v. Williams, 397 U.S. 471 (1970), sec. 5 below.[3] Yet the Royster formulation demanding a "fair and substantial relation" between classification and legislative objective persists. Indeed, it has once again become a favorite citation, in the Burger Court's invalidations of statutory classifications while voicing traditional equal protection criteria. See, e. g., the examples of the "newer equal protection"—at least in form—in Reed v. Reed, sec. 3 below, and in Eisenstadt v. Baird, sec. 6 below. During the Warren years, there was only one major example of invalidation on the basis of traditional equal protection criteria: Morey v. Doud, below. During the 1970's, there have been more such invalidations.

In short, the Warren Court was consistently more deferential to state social and economic legislation challenged under the equal protection clause under traditional standards; the Burger Court seems willing to put somewhat more bite into those traditional standards. But those variations in practice and those varying nuances in articulation cannot obscure the basic fact that traditional equal protection imposes a constitutional requirement that the Court has never formally abandoned: that legislative means must substantially further legislative ends. In short, some examination of traditional equal protection criteria and their meaning in theory and practice is justified by more than historical reasons. What, then, is signified by the "old" equal protection's demand for some but not perfect congruence between classifications and objectives?

1. *Classifications and adequate congruence: The Tussman-tenBroek analysis.* Consider the analysis of the requisite relationship between classifications and legislative objectives called for by traditional equal protection standards, in the classic discussion by Tussman and tenBroek, "The Equal Protection of the Laws," 37 Calif.L.Rev. 341 (1949), Selected Essays 1938–62 (1963), 789:[4]

the burden of showing that it does not rest upon any reasonable basis, but is essentially arbitrary." Ironically, the Court quoted that deferential passage in the one case during the Warren era to strike down a business regulation on equal protection grounds, Morey v. Doud, 354 U.S. 457 (1957), below.

3. Justice Stewart's majority opinion stated there that "[i]n the area of economics and social welfare," equal protection tolerated "imperfect" classifications: "If the classification has some 'reasonable basis,' it does not offend the Constitution simply because the classification 'is not made with mathematical nicety or because in practice it results in some inequality.' . . . 'The problems of government are practical ones and may justify, if they do not require, rough accommodations—illogical, it may be, and unscientific.' " So long as "any state of facts reasonably may be conceived to justify it," the statutory classification was to be sustained. See also the formulations in such Warren Court opinions as McGowan v. Maryland and McDonald v. Board of Election, later in this section.

4. Reprinted with the permission of the publisher, © 1949, California Law Review, Inc.

"The equal protection of the laws is a 'pledge of the protection of equal laws.' But laws may classify. And 'the very idea of classification is that of inequality.' In tackling this paradox the Court has neither abandoned the demand for equality nor denied the legislative right to classify. It has taken a middle course. It has resolved the contradictory demands of legislative specialization and constitutional generality by a doctrine of reasonable classification.

"The essence of that doctrine can be stated with deceptive simplicity. The Constitution does not require that things different in fact be treated in law as though they were the same. But it does require, in its concern for equality, that those who are similarly situated be similarly treated. The measure of the reasonableness of a classification is the degree of its success in treating similarly those similarly situated.

"[W]here are we to look for the test of similarity of situation which determines the reasonableness of a classification? The inescapable answer is that we must look beyond the classification to the purpose of the law. A reasonable classification is one which includes all persons who are similarly situated with respect to the purpose of the law. . . .

"The purpose of a law may be either the elimination of a public 'mischief' or the achievement of some positive public good. To simplify the discussion we shall refer to the purpose of a law in terms of the elimination of mischief, since the same argument holds in either case. We shall speak of the defining character or characteristics of the legislative classification as the trait. We can thus speak of the relation of the classification to the purpose of the law as the relation of the Trait to the Mischief.

"A problem arises at all because the classification in a law usually does not have as its defining Trait the possession of or involvement with the Mischief at which the law aims.[5] [In the usual problem], we are really dealing with the relation of two classes to each other. The first class consists of all individuals possessing the defining Trait; the second class consists of all individuals possessing, or rather, tainted by, the Mischief at which the law aims. The former is the legislative classification; the latter is the class of those similarly situated with respect to the purpose of the law. We shall refer to these two classes as T and M respectively.

---

5. As an example at this point, the authors use the situation involved in Skinner v. Oklahoma, 316 U.S. 527 (1942), noted below. They state: "For example, let us suppose that a legislature proposes to combat hereditary criminality—an admitted Mischief—and that the sterilization of transmitters of hereditary criminality is a permissible means to that end. Now if the legislature were to pass a law declaring that for the purpose of eliminating hereditary criminality, all individuals who are tainted with inheritable criminal tendencies are to be sterilized, and if it provided for proper administrative identification of transmitters of hereditary criminality, our problem would largely disappear. The class, being defined directly in terms of the Mischief, automatically includes all who are similarly situated with respect to the purpose of the law. This procedure requires, however, delegation of considerable discretion to administrators to determine which individuals to sterilize. Legislators, reluctant to confer such discretion, tend to classify by Traits which limit the range of administrative freedom. Suppose then, that they pass a law providing for the sterilization of all persons convicted of three felonies. The 'reasonableness' of this classification depends upon the relation between the class of three-time felons and the class of hereditary criminals."

"Now, since the reasonableness of any class T depends entirely upon its relation to a class M, it is obvious that it is impossible to pass judgment on the reasonableness of a classification without taking into consideration, or identifying, the purpose of the law. . . .

"There are five possible relationships between the class defined by the Trait and the class defined by the Mischief. These relationships can be indicated by the following diagrams:

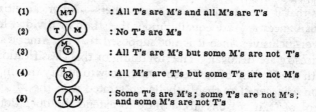

(1)   : All T's are M's and all M's are T's

(2)   : No T's are M's

(3)   : All T's are M's but some M's are not T's

(4)   : All M's are T's but some T's are not M's

(5)   : Some T's are M's; some T's are not M's; and some M's are not T's

One of these five relationships holds in fact in any case of legislative classification, and we will consider each from the point of view of its 'reasonableness.'

"The first two situations represent respectively the ideal limits of reasonableness and unreasonableness. In the first case, the classification in the law coincides completely with the class of those similarly situated with respect to the purpose of the law. It is perfectly reasonable. In the second case, no member of the class defined in the law is tainted with the mischief at which the law aims. The classification is, therefore, perfectly unreasonable. These two situations need not detain us.

"Classification of the third type may be called 'under-inclusive.' All who are included in the class are tainted with the mischief, but there are others also tainted whom the classification does not include. Since the classification does not include all who are similarly situated with respect to the purpose of the law, there is a prima facie violation of the equal protection requirement of reasonable classification.

"But the Court has recognized the very real difficulties under which legislatures operate—difficulties arising out of both the nature of the legislative process and of the society which legislation attempts perennially to reshape—and it has refused to strike down indiscriminately all legislation embodying the classificatory inequality here under consideration.

"In justifying this refusal, the Court has defended under-inclusive classifications on such grounds as: the legislature may attack a general problem in a piecemeal fashion; 'some play must be allowed for the joints of the machine'; . . . 'the law does all that is needed when it does all that it can' . . . .

"The fourth type of classification imposes a burden upon a wider range of individuals than are included in the class of those tainted with the mischief at which the law aims. It can thus be called 'over-inclusive.' . . . It is exemplified by the quarantine and the dragnet. The wartime treatment of American citizens of Japanese ancestry is a striking recent instance of the imposition of burdens upon a large class of individuals because some of them were believed to be disloyal. . . .

"The final situation to be considered is one in which the previously discussed factors of under-inclusiveness and over-inclusiveness are both present. While it may seem paradoxical to assert that a classification can be at once over-inclusive and under-inclusive, many classifications do, in fact, fall into this category, that is, they can be challenged separately on both grounds.

"For example, in the Hirabayashi case [Hirabayashi v. United States, 320 U.S. 81 (1943)] the classification of 'American citizens of Japanese ancestry' for the purpose of meeting the dangers of sabotage can be challenged both on the grounds that it is under-inclusive, since others—American citizens of German or Italian ancestry—are equally under the strain of divided loyalties, and that it is over-inclusive, since it is not supposed that all American citizens of Japanese ancestry are disloyal. The sustaining of this classification, therefore, requires both the finding of sufficient emergency to justify the imposition of a burden upon a larger class than is believed tainted with the Mischief and the establishment of 'fair reasons' for failure to extend the operation of the law to a wider class of potential saboteurs. . . . ."

2. *Some preliminary observations on the requirements of congruence and the modern economic regulation cases.* Consider the congruence demands of the traditional standard as applied in the modern economic and social regulation cases from the Vinson and Warren Courts which follow. To what extent were the classifications involved in the cases "overinclusive" or "underinclusive"? Should they have survived scrutiny under the traditional criteria? Most in fact did so survive. As Tussman and tenBroek recognized, the Court does not demand perfect congruence; the critical issue in the cases, then, is the degree to which a legislature shall be permitted to generalize or to deal with portions of a problem at a time, and thus to fall short of perfect congruence. What were the reasons offered by the Court for the failures to invalidate the noncongruence situations in the cases which follow? Are they persuasive reasons? Do those reasons, does that degree of deference to legislative discretion, ultimately remove all bite from the traditional equal protection standard? Could the Court have demanded more? Could it have done so by limiting itself simply to the question of legislative "means," without getting into the more difficult sphere of curtailing legislative discretion as to ends?

In considering the applications of the traditional approach in the cases below, note also the observation that the typical formulations—e. g., that a classification must include "all [and only those] persons who are similarly situated with respect to the purpose of the law"—are "outwardly simple" but entail "some complex judgments": "First, how is the 'purpose of the law' to be determined with respect to each separate statutory classification? Second, what does 'similarly situated' mean and to what extent will the state be allowed to group together persons who are not quite similarly situated? The decisions dealing with economic regulation indicate that in this context the courts have used concepts of 'purpose' and 'similar situation' which give considerable leeway to the legislature. However, when 'suspect classifications' or fundamental interests are involved, this leeway has been severely narrowed." "Developments," 82 Harv.L.Rev. 1065, 1076 (1969).

RAILWAY EXPRESS AGENCY v. NEW YORK

336 U.S. 106, 69 S.Ct. 463, 93 L.Ed. 533 (1949).

Appeal from the Court of Appeals of New York.

Mr. Justice DOUGLAS delivered the opinion of the Court.

Section 124 of the Traffic Regulations of the City of New York promulgated by the Police Commissioner provides:

> "No person shall operate, or cause to be operated, in or upon any street an advertising vehicle; provided that nothing herein contained shall prevent the putting of business notices upon business delivery vehicles, so long as such vehicles are engaged in the usual business or regular work of the owner and not used merely or mainly for advertising."

Appellant is engaged in a nation-wide express business. It operates about 1,900 trucks in New York City and sells the space on the exterior sides of these trucks for advertising. That advertising is for the most part unconnected with its own business. It was convicted [and] fined. . . .

The Court of Special Sessions concluded that advertising on vehicles using the streets of New York City constitutes a distraction to vehicle drivers and to pedestrians alike and therefore affects the safety of the public in the use of the streets. We do not sit to weigh evidence on the due process issue in order to determine whether the regulation is sound or appropriate; nor is it our function to pass judgment on its wisdom. [See chap. 9, sec. 1.] . . . .

The question of equal protection of the laws is pressed more strenuously on us. It is pointed out that the regulation draws the line between advertisements of products sold by the owner of the truck and general advertisements. It is argued that unequal treatment on the basis of such a distinction is not justified by the aim and purpose of the regulation. It is said, for example, that one of appellant's trucks carrying the advertisement of a commercial house would not cause any greater distraction of pedestrians and vehicle drivers than if the commercial house carried the same advertisement on its own truck. Yet the regulation allows the latter to do what the former is forbidden from doing. It is therefore contended that the classification which the regulation makes has no relation to the traffic problem since a violation turns not on what kind of advertisements are carried on trucks but on whose trucks they are carried.

That, however, is a superficial way of analyzing the problem . . . .. The local authorities may well have concluded that those who advertise their own wares on their trucks do not present the same traffic problem in view of the nature or extent of the advertising which they use. It would take a degree of omniscience which we lack to say that such is not the case. If that judgment is correct, the advertising displays that are exempt have less incidence on traffic than those of appellants.

We cannot say that that judgment is not an allowable one. Yet if it is, the classification has relation to the purpose for which it is made and does not contain the kind of discrimination against which the Equal Protection Clause affords protection. It is by such practical considerations based on experience rather than by theoretical inconsistencies that the question of equal protection is to be answered. . . . And the fact that New York City sees fit to

eliminate from traffic this kind of distraction but does not touch what may be even greater ones in a different category, such as the vivid displays on Times Square, is immaterial. It is no requirement of equal protection that all evils of the same genus be eradicated or none at all.   .   .   .

Affirmed.

Mr. Justice RUTLEDGE acquiesces in the Court's opinion and judgment, *dubitante* on the question of equal protection of the laws.

Mr. Justice JACKSON, concurring.   .   .   .

My philosophy as to the relative readiness with which we should resort to [the due process and equal protection] clauses is almost diametrically opposed to the philosophy which prevails on this Court. While claims of denial of equal protection are frequently asserted, they are rarely sustained. But the Court frequently uses the due process clause to strike down measures taken by municipalities to deal with activities in their streets and public places which the local authorities consider as creating hazards, annoyances or discomforts to their inhabitants. And I have frequently dissented when I thought local power was improperly denied. See, for example, [Saia v. New York, chap. 12].

The burden should rest heavily upon one who would persuade us to use the due process clause to strike down a substantive law or ordinance. Even its provident use against municipal regulations frequently disables all government —state, municipal and federal—from dealing with the conduct in question because the requirement of due process is also applicable to State and Federal Governments. Invalidation of a statute or an ordinance on due process grounds leaves ungoverned and ungovernable conduct which many people find objectionable.

Invocation of the equal protection clause, on the other hand, does not disable any governmental body from dealing with the subject at hand. It merely means that the prohibition or regulation must have a broader impact. I regard it as a salutary doctrine that cities, states and the Federal Government must exercise their powers so as not to discriminate between their inhabitants except upon some reasonable differentiation fairly related to the object of regulation. [T]here is no more effective practical guaranty against arbitrary and unreasonable government than to require that the principles of law which officials would impose upon a minority must be imposed generally. Conversely, nothing opens the door to arbitrary action so effectively as to allow those officials to pick and choose only a few to whom they will apply legislation and thus to escape the political retribution that might be visited upon them if larger numbers were affected. Courts can take no better measure to assure that laws will be just than to require that laws be equal in operation.

This case affords an illustration. Even casual observations from the sidewalks of New York will show that an ordinance which would forbid all advertising on vehicles would run into conflict with many interests, including some, if not all, of the great metropolitan newspapers, which use that advertising extensively. Their blandishment of the latest sensations is not less a cause of diverted attention and traffic hazard than the commonplace cigarette advertisement which this truckowner is forbidden to display. But any regulation applicable to all such advertising would require much clearer justification in local conditions to enable its enactment than does some regu-

lation applicable to a few.   I do not mention this to criticize the motives of those who enacted this ordinance, but it dramatizes the point that we are much more likely to find arbitrariness in the regulation of the few than of the many. . . .

In this case, if the City of New York should assume that display of any advertising on vehicles tends and intends to distract the attention of persons using the highways and to increase the dangers of its traffic, I should think it fully within its constitutional powers to forbid it all. . . . . Instead of such general regulation of advertising, however, the City seeks to reduce the hazard only by saying that while some may, others may not exhibit such appeals. The same display, for example, advertising cigarettes, which this appellant is forbidden to carry on its trucks, may be carried on the trucks of a cigarette dealer . . . .

The City urges that this applies equally to all persons of a permissible classification, because, [while it] does not eliminate vehicular advertising, it does eliminate such advertising for hire and to this extent cuts down the hazard sought to be controlled.

That the difference between carrying on any business for hire and engaging in the same activity on one's own is a sufficient one to sustain some types of regulations of the one that is not applied to the other, is almost elementary. But it is usual to find such regulations applied to the very incidents wherein the two classes present different problems, such as in charges, liability and quality of service.

The difference, however, is invoked here to sustain a discrimination in a problem in which the two classes present identical dangers. The courts of New York have declared that the sole nature and purpose of the regulation before us is to reduce traffic hazards. There is not even a pretense here that the traffic hazard created by the advertising which is forbidden is in any manner or degree more hazardous than that which is permitted. It is urged with considerable force that this local regulation does not comply with the equal protection clause because it applies unequally upon classes whose differentiation is in no way relevant to the objects of the regulation.

As a matter of principle and in view of my attitude toward the equal protection clause, I do not think differences of treatment under law should be approved on classification because of differences unrelated to the legislative purpose. The equal protection clause ceases to assure either equality or protection if it is avoided by any conceivable difference that can be pointed out between those bound and those left free. This Court has often announced the principle that the differentiation must have an appropriate relation to the object of the legislation or ordinance. . . .

The question in my mind comes to this. Where individuals contribute to an evil or danger in the same way and to the same degree, may those who do so for hire be prohibited, while those who do so for their own commercial ends but not for hire be allowed to continue? I think the answer has to be that the hireling may be put in a class by himself and may be dealt with differently than those who act on their own. But this is not merely because such a discrimination will enable the lawmaker to diminish the evil. That might be done by many classifications, which I should think wholly unsustainable. It is

rather because there is a real difference between doing in self-interest and doing for hire, so that it is one thing to tolerate action from those who act on their own and it is another thing to permit the same action to be promoted for a price. . . .

Of course, this appellant did not hold itself out to carry or display everybody's advertising, and its rental of space on the sides of its trucks was only incidental to the main business which brought its trucks into the streets. But it is not difficult to see that, in a day of extravagant advertising more or less subsidized by tax deduction, the rental of truck space could become an obnoxious enterprise. While I do not think highly of this type of regulation, that is not my business, and in view of the control I would concede to cities to protect citizens in quiet and orderly use for their proper purposes of the highways and public places, I think the judgment below must be affirmed.

THE TRADITIONAL APPROACH IN OPERATION: RESTRICTIONS ON BUSINESS ENTRY

Some introductory questions. In all but one of the cases that follow, as in Railway Express, the Court rejected equal protection challenges to statutes charged with being "underinclusive" protections of a favored interest group.[1] Were these situations in which Justice Jackson's Railway Express suggestion should have been heeded: Should the Court have insisted that the regulations "must have a broader impact," to safeguard against arbitrary action? Should the Court have demanded a greater congruence between classifications and purposes? Should the Court have used less imaginativeness to think of conceivable rationales that *might* have influenced a hypothetical legislature? Should it have used less imaginativeness in suggesting how the classifications *might* have furthered the legislative purposes? Should it have used less imaginativeness in determining what the legislative purpose *might* have been? Should it have tested the fit between means and ends on the basis of actual rather than conceivable purposes, and on the basis of demonstrated rather than imagined contributions of classifications to purposes? Should it have probed further to assess "real" purposes and motives? Could greater scrutiny of rationality of means or actuality of purposes have been undertaken without resuming the discredited substantive due process practice of unduly curtailing legislative ends in the economic regulation area? Should some of the classifications employed in these cases have been viewed as "suspect"? Should some of the interests affected have been considered "fundamental," warranting the exercise of stricter judicial scrutiny?[2]

1. In one sense, the cases in this section are atypical: in the cases noted here, the Court did write an opinion; and in most, several modern Justices did dissent. In far the greater number of "old" equal protection cases involving economic regulation during the Vinson and Warren eras, the challenges were rejected summarily—for example, by dismissing appeals for want of a substantial federal question. The cases in which the Court undertook plenary review were usually ones in which a lower court had invalidated a statute. Recall also the usually unanimous deferential positions of the Courts of those eras in the economic due process cases (chap. 9, sec. 1C).

2. In addition to the cases in these notes, see also Goesaert v. Cleary, 335 U.S. 464 (1948), decided a few weeks before Railway Express and sustaining a Michigan statute which provided that no woman could obtain a bartender's license unless she was "the wife or

1. *Daniel and funeral insurance.* In DANIEL v. FAMILY SECURITY LIFE INS. CO., 336 U.S. 220 (1949), a unanimous Court rejected equal protection and due process challenges to a South Carolina law prohibiting life insurance companies and their agents from operating an undertaking business, and undertakers from serving as agents for life insurance companies. The challenger was the only company selling "funeral insurance" in South Carolina; most of its agents were undertakers. Justice Murphy's opinion stated: "The South Carolina legislature might well have concluded that funeral insurance, although paid in cash, carries the same evils that are present in policies payable in merchandise or services: the beneficiary's tendency to deliver the policy's proceeds to the agent-undertaker for whatever funeral the money will buy, whether or not an expensive ceremony is consistent with the needs of the survivors. Considerations which might have been influential include the likelihood of overreach on the part of insurance companies, and the possibilities of monopoly control . . .. We cannot say that South Carolina is not entitled to call the funeral insurance business an evil. Nor can we say that the statute has no relation to the elimination of those evils. There our inquiry must stop."

The Court summarily rejected the argument "that the 'insurance lobby' obtained this statute" from the legislature: the Court "must judge by results. [We] cannot undertake a search for motive in testing constitutionality." Any further scrutiny would involve the Court improperly in examining "the desirability of the legislation."

2. *Kotch and river pilots.* In KOTCH v. BOARD OF RIVER PILOT COMM'RS, 330 U.S. 552 (1947), Louisiana's pilotage laws required that state pilots guide all ships going through the Mississippi River approaches to New Orleans. New pilots were appointed by the governor upon certification of names by a board composed of pilots. Only those with six months apprenticeship under an incumbent pilot were eligible for certification. Administration of the system was attacked on the ground that the board certified only relatives and friends of the incumbents.

The Supreme Court, in a 5 to 4 decision, rejected the equal protection challenge. Justice Black relied on the "entirely unique" nature of pilotage "in the light of its history in Louisiana": The object of the system "is to secure [the] safest and most efficiently operated pilotage system practicable. We cannot say that the method adopted [is] unrelated to this objective." He mentioned "the benefits to morale and esprit de corps which family and neighborly tradition might contribute" as one of the useful functions "a closely knit pilotage system may serve." Justice Rutledge, joined by Justices Reed, Douglas and Murphy, dissented: "Blood is, in effect, made the crux of selection." Even if the classification was related to the purpose of the system—even if family ties made the system more efficient—a standard of

daughter of the male owner" of a licensed liquor establishment. Justice Frankfurter wrote for the majority; Justice Rutledge's dissent, joined by Justices Douglas and Murphy, thought the law "arbitrarily discriminates between male and female owners of liquor establishments." Would that law survive scrutiny under the Burger Court decisions involving gender-based classifications? The case is considered further with the examination of sex-based classifications in sec. 3 below.

."race or consanguinity" was impermissible. Accordingly, the system was invalid for "unconstitutional administration," though valid on its face.

Would the law sustained in Kotch survive challenge under the modern expansions of the "suspect classifications" categories triggering strict scrutiny, see sec. 3 below? Should consanguinity be considered a suspect classification? Would the Kotch law survive scrutiny under the standards of the "newer equal protection," the "minimal scrutiny with bite," that has occasionally surfaced on the Burger Court? Should it have survived scrutiny under the traditional equal protection standards assertedly applied in the 1940's?

3. *Lee Optical and opticians.* Recall that in WILLIAMSON v. LEE OPTICAL CO., 348 U.S. 483 (1955) (chap. 9, sec. 1C), the challenge to Oklahoma's scheme for the regulation of opticians rested not only on due process but also on equal protection. But the Lee Optical Court, at the height of the deferential stance toward business regulation, rejected the equal protection claim even more summarily than the due process ones. Justice Douglas stated for a unanimous Court:

"[T]he District Court held that it violated the Equal Protection Clause of the Fourteenth Amendment to subject opticians to this regulatory system and to exempt [all] sellers of ready-to-wear glasses. The problem of legislative classification is a perennial one, admitting of no doctrinaire definition. Evils in the same field may be of different dimensions and proportions, requiring different remedies. Or so the legislature may think. Or the reform may take one step at a time, addressing itself to the phase of the problem which seems most acute to the legislative mind. The legislature may select one phase of one field and apply a remedy there, neglecting the others. The prohibition of the Equal Protection Clause goes no further than the invidious discrimination. We cannot say that that point has been reached here. For all this record shows, the ready-to-wear branch of this business may not loom large in Oklahoma or may present problems of regulation distinct from the other branch."

Was Justice Douglas' standard of review even more deferential than the "fair and substantial relation" criterion purportedly governing traditional equal protection scrutiny, as noted at the beginning of this section? Would adherence to Justice Douglas' approach assure validation of virtually all departures from congruence in the business regulation area? Recall the questions about the due process aspects of the case in chap. 9, sec. 1C and note the additional questions in the next group of notes.

4. *McGowan and McDonald: The deferential approach at the extreme.* Judicial unwillingness to put any teeth into traditional "old" equal protection standards in the scrutiny of business regulations may have reached its most extreme form in two opinions written by Chief Justice Warren in the 1960's. Contrast Chief Justice Warren's criteria with the Royster standard, noted at the beginning of this section—a standard reiterated in more recent Burger Court decisions. Does Chief Justice Warren's approach in these cases—even more than Justice Douglas' in Lee Optical—reduce scrutiny under the old equal protection to a variety characterized by "minimal scrutiny in theory and virtually none in fact"?

a. *McGowan.* In a group of cases in 1961, state Sunday closing laws were sustained against challenges based not only on the religion clauses of the First Amendment (see chap. 14) but also on equal protection. The Court rejected the latter attack by applying traditional, permissive standards.[3] In McGOWAN v. MARYLAND, 366 U.S. 420 (1961), Chief Justice Warren spoke for a unanimous Court in rejecting the claim that the exemptions of certain businesses from the Maryland Sunday closing law violated equal protection. One of the provisions, for example, banned the Sunday "sale of all merchandise except the retail sale of tobacco products, confectioneries, milk, bread, fruits, gasoline, greases, drugs and medicines, and newspapers and periodicals." Chief Justice Warren stated:

"Although no precise formula has been developed, the Court has held that the Fourteenth Amendment permits the States a wide scope of discretion in enacting laws which affect some groups of citizens differently than others. The constitutional safeguard is offended only if the classification rests on grounds wholly irrelevant to the achievement of the State's objective. State legislatures are presumed to have acted within their constitutional power despite the fact that, in practice, their laws result in some inequality. A statutory discrimination will not be set aside if any state of facts reasonably may be conceived to justify it.

"It would seem that a legislature could reasonably find that the Sunday sale of the exempted commodities was necessary either for the health of the populace or for the enhancement of the recreational atmosphere of the day . . . .. The record is barren of any indication that this apparently reasonable basis does not exist, that the statutory distinctions are invidious, that local tradition and custom might not rationally call for this legislative treatment."

b. *McDonald.* Perhaps the most extremely deferential restatement of traditional equal protection criteria on the Warren Court—and one of the most graphic statements of the sharp difference between the strict scrutiny of new equal protection and the leniency of the old—came in McDONALD v. BOARD OF ELECTION, 394 U.S. 802 (1969). That was a claim by qualified Cook County, Illinois, voters imprisoned in a County jail while awaiting trial that the state could not deny them absentee ballots when they were provided to other classes of persons.[4] Chief Justice Warren's opinion for a unanimous Court first disposed of the claim that this was a case for the Warren Court's new equal protection criteria because the fundamental interest in voting was involved. Here, the Chief Justice replied, only a right to an absentee ballot, not an impact on "the fundamental right to vote," was in issue; conceivably, there were other opportunities for the challengers to vote. (See the further note on the case in the materials on voting, sec. 4 below.) Hence, the very demanding criteria of the new equal protection were found inapplicable.

3. Why, in the context of First Amendment claims, was not a stricter judicial scrutiny appropriate, akin to that in the "fundamental interest" areas of the new equal protection, below?

4. The four classes who were entitled to absentee ballots were persons absent from their county of residency for any reason whatever, the "physically incapacitated," those kept from the polls because of observance of a religious holiday, and those serving as poll watchers in precincts other than their own.

Accordingly, the lower level of the two-tier approach was invoked. And the Chief Justice stated the "basic guidelines" governing the "more traditional standards for evaluating" equal protection claims as follows: "The distinctions drawn by a challenged statute must bear some rational relationship to a legitimate state end and will be set aside as violative of the Equal Protection Clause only if based on reasons totally unrelated to the pursuit of that goal. Legislatures are presumed to have acted constitutionally even if source materials normally resorted to for ascertaining their grounds for action are otherwise silent, and their statutory classifications will be set aside only if no grounds can be conceived to justify them. With this much discretion, a legislature traditionally has been allowed to take reform 'one step at a time . . . .' [Lee Optical]; and a legislature need not run the risk of losing an entire remedial scheme simply because it failed, through inadvertence or otherwise, to cover every evil that might conceivably have been attacked." [5]

Does even a commitment to a basic stance of deference in the sphere of the old equal protection require or justify leaning over backwards to quite the degree manifested by Chief Justice Warren's McDonald approach? (a) Is there significance to the Chief Justice's phrasing of the requisite means-ends nexus not in terms of "fair and substantial" relation but as "some rational relationship," with a reference to "reasons totally unrelated to the pursuit of [the] goal"? (b) Need judicial hypothesizing about the requisite relationship go so far as to say that invalidation will result "only if no grounds can be conceived to justify" classifications? (c) Is the "one step at a time" rationale ultimately subversive of *any* scrutiny under traditional standards? Some deference to legislative realities may be appropriate: legislators may want to experiment, or to respond to immediate needs or political pressures. But judicial blessing of every effort at piecemeal legislation would block all challenges based on underinclusiveness. What limits can and should the Court impose on justifying laws on the "one step at a time" ground? (Note also the "remedial legislation" rationale, considered in footnote 5.)

5. *The unique exception to Warren Court deference: Morey v. Doud.* Only one business regulation fell afoul of traditional equal protection standards during the Warren years: an exemption by name of a company from a general regulatory scheme. MOREY v. DOUD, 354 U.S. 457 (1957). The

5. In searching for conceivable rationales to explain the "different treatment accorded unsentenced inmates incarcerated within and those incarcerated without their resident counties," the Chief Justice suggested that the difference "may reflect a legislative determination that without the protection of the voting booth, local officials might be too tempted to try to influence the local voter in-county inmates." But his justification for the law placed special reliance on the fact that this was "remedial legislation," the result of "a consistent and laudable state policy of adding, over a 50-year period, groups to the absentee coverage as their existence comes to the attention of the legislature." That "Illinois has not gone still further, as perhaps it might," was justified by the "one step at a time" rationale. Some classes of voters were entitled to absentee ballots, to be sure; but the challengers' class was not the only one excluded. (He noted that among the others excluded were "mothers with children who cannot afford a babysitter" and "persons attending ill relations within their own county.")

Can the "remedial" purpose of legislation justify deferential scrutiny even in the context of suspect classifications and fundamental interests? For a similar reliance on the "remedial legislation" rationale to justify minimal scrutiny, see the last part of Justice Brennan's opinion in Katzenbach v. Morgan, chap. 11. sec. 4, below.

Illinois Community Currency Exchanges Act imposed strict financial responsibility requirements on businesses issuing money orders but explicitly exempted the American Express Company and several others.[6] The American Express exemption was challenged by a local partnership which sought to sell money orders largely through drug and grocery store agencies. In the 6 to 3 decision, the Court held the exemption unconstitutional. Justice Burton's majority opinion, after noting that American Express sold money orders in substantially the same manner planned by the challengers, stated:

"The Act creates a statutory class of sellers of money orders. The money orders sold by one company, American Express, are excepted from that class. There is but one 'American Express Company.' If the exception is to be upheld, it must be on the basis on which it is cast—an exception of a particular business entity and not of a generic category.

"The purpose of the Act's licensing and regulatory provisions clearly is to protect the public when dealing with currency exchanges. Because the American Express Company is a world-wide enterprise of unquestioned solvency and high financial standing, the State argues that the legislative classification is reasonable. It contends that the special characteristics of the American Express Company justify excepting its money orders from the requirements of an Act aimed at local companies doing local business . . . .

"That the Equal Protection Clause does not require that every state regulatory statute apply to all in the same business is a truism. For example, where size is an index to the evil at which the law is directed, discriminations between the large and the small are permissible. Moreover, we have repeatedly recognized that 'reform may take one step at a time.' [Lee Optical.] On the other hand, a statutory discrimination must be based on differences that are reasonably related to the purposes of the Act in which it is found. Smith v. Cahoon, 283 U.S. 553 [1931; noted further below]. Of course, distinctions in the treatment of business entities engaged in the same business activity may be justified by genuinely different characteristics of the business involved. This is so even where the discrimination is by name. But distinctions cannot be so justified if the 'discrimination has no reasonable relation to these differences.'

". . . The provisions in the Illinois Act, such as those requiring an annual inspection of licensed community currency exchanges by the State Auditor, make it clear that the statute was intended to afford the public *continuing* protection. The discrimination in favor of the American Express Company does not conform to this purpose. The exception of its money orders apparently rests on the legislative hypothesis that the characteristics of the American Express Company make it unnecessary to regulate their sales. Yet these sales, by virtue of the exception, will continue to be unregulated whether or not the American Express Company retains its present characteristics. On the other hand, sellers of competing money orders are subject to the Act even though

6. The other explicit exemptions were not challenged. They covered the U. S. Post Office, the Postal Telegraph Company and the Western Union Telegraph Company. In a footnote, the Court referred to an earlier lower court case challenging similar exemptions in a Wisconsin statute. Post Office money orders, it was explained there, could not be regulated by a state; and the Western Union exemption (and that of Postal Telegraph, which had merged with Western Union) was reasonable because the company was regulated by the FCC and by a state commission.

their characteristics are, or become, substantially identical with those the American Express Company now has. . . .

"The effect of the discrimination is to create a closed class by singling out American Express money orders. . . . Taking all of these factors in conjunction—the remote relationship of the statutory classification to the Act's purpose or to business characteristics, and the creation of a closed class by the singling out of the money orders of a named company, with accompanying economic advantages—we hold that the application of the Act to appellees deprives them of equal protection of the laws."

Justice Black's dissent stated that, "whatever one may think of the merits of this legislation, its exemption of a company of known solvency from a solvency test applied to others of unknown financial responsibility can hardly be called 'invidious.'" In another dissent, Justice Frankfurter, joined by Justice Harlan, insisted that equal protection analysis must emphasize "the actualities," not the "abstractions," of legislation. He thought the exemption justified: American Express "contains within itself, in the judgment of Illinois, the necessary safeguards for solvency and reliability," unlike those subject to the Act. He stated: "Surely this is a distinction of significance in fact that the law cannot view with a glass eye." To argue that American Express might not retain its present characteristics was "to deny a State the right to legislate on the basis of circumstances that exist because a State may not in speculatively different circumstances that may never come to pass have such a right. Surely there is time enough to strike down legislation when its constitutional justification is gone."

    6. *Some concluding comments on the Warren Court's old equal protection—and on Justice Douglas' "selective intervention" on behalf of minorities.* a. *The Morey case.* As the cases in this section illustrate, the Vinson and Warren Courts applied traditional equal protection standards with great deference to legislative classifications. By the 1960's the avowed deference of the old equal protection was greater than ever—even while the strict scrutiny of the new equal protection flourished. Was there truly greater justification for the exceptional invalidation in Morey v. Doud than in the previous cases? Was the Court in Morey demanding more of legislatures than a fair reading of traditional standards should? Was it demanding less than that in the other cases? Was the interventionism of the Morey case limited to *named* exemptions such as that for the American Express Company? Was there room for greater "selective intervention" even under the standards of the old equal protection?

    b. *"Selective intervention" and economic minorities.* Note that Justice Douglas, the author of the deferential opinion in the Lee Optical case, voted to invalidate several economic regulations noted in this section—not only in Morey but also in Kotch, the river pilots case.[7] Consider the effort to explain Justice Douglas' move "from abdication to selective intervention" in Karst, "Invidious Discrimination: Justice Douglas and the Return of the 'Natural-Law-Due-Process Formula,'" 16 UCLA L.Rev. 716 (1969). Karst notes that in each case the state was perpetuating "economic advantages

---

7. He also voted to invalidate in the Goesaert case on women bartenders, briefly noted above and further considered in sec. 3 below.

for a favored group, at the expense of those who claimed to be relatively disadvantaged. The appeal of such an argument to a Justice with strong egalitarian views is great, great enough in these cases to overcome the inclination to keep the judiciary aloof from decisions about economic regulation."

But what about Justice Douglas' opinion in Lee Optical? That, Karst suggests, is distinguishable because there "the losers in the legislature were not permanently disadvantaged minorities. The opticians might well have anticipated new legislative alliances" [though, he concedes in a footnote, "the opticians are still looking for such an alliance"]. There were no such legislative alliance prospects for the excluded groups in Kotch and Goesaert, according to Karst. (But on that criterion, he adds, the "unfortunate" vote in Morey "is out of line.") In short, "consciously or not," the Douglas record accords with "a principle of activism in the cause of economic opportunity"—a principle which is "the equal protection analogue of the double standard of judicial review under the due process clauses, enunciated in Justice Stone's footnote 4 [in the Carolene Products case], which made the legitimacy of judicial protection of the losers in the legislative process turn on the losers' long-term chances of becoming winners."

c. *The relevance of the Carolene Products footnote.* Recall Justice Stone's footnote 4, printed in chap. 9, sec. 1C, above. It is the third paragraph of that footnote, the "protecting losing minorities" aspect, that is arguably relevant here. Recall that Justice Stone suggested a greater basis for judicial scrutiny where there was "prejudice against discrete and insular minorities"—prejudice which "tends seriously to curtail the operation of those political processes ordinarily to be relied upon to protect minorities." That consideration may well underlie some of the expansions of strict scrutiny for suspect classifications, see sec. 3 below. But can that rationale apply to losing *economic* minorities as well? Can economic minorities be protected without a return to the ad hoc interventionism of the Lochner era? [8] Is the "minorities" rationale in any event as persuasive as the other portions of Justice Stone's footnote? Is not the majoritarian political process a *generally* unreliable protector of minorities? Restrictions of the political process through curtailment of political debate or voting—Justice Stone's second category in his footnote—is a clear enough concept. Can the same be said of restrictions on the "process"—though all may speak and vote—because the *results* bear harshly on certain minorities? If that is a valid justification for "more searching judicial inquiry," did some of the due process as well as the equal protection claims summarily dismissed in the modern economic regulation cases—see, in addition to this section, chap. 9, sec. 1C, above— deserve more careful scrutiny? [9]

---

8. Note Karst's comment, in the article on Justice Douglas above: "Perhaps . . . activism offers no particular risk to a judiciary's independence unless it is directed at the wrong substantive ends."

9. Compare the critical comments by Justice Rehnquist on the "minorities" aspect of the Carolene Products footnote, in objecting to the elevation of

alienage into the category of "suspect classifications" triggering strict scrutiny. (See sec. 3 below.) In his dissent in In re Griffiths, 413 U.S. 717 (1973), Justice Rehnquist stated:

"The mere recitation of the words 'insular and discrete minority' is hardly a *constitutional* reason for prohibiting state legislative classifications such as are involved here, and is not

Rather than attempting that difficult justification for sporadic "selective intervention" on behalf of some economic as well as other minorities on the basis of traditional equal protection criteria, would a more fruitful approach be to try to apply those criteria more seriously across the board?   Is there some basis for such a development in the growing number of Burger Court decisions invalidating laws while reciting traditional equal protection criteria?   See the examples which surface repeatedly in secs. 3 to 6 below, and consider the suggestion for a "newer equal protection" examined in the next group of notes.

A POSSIBILITY OF APPLYING TRADITIONAL EQUAL PROTECTION STANDARDS WITH GREATER BITE?—THE "NEWER EQUAL PROTECTION" MODEL

1. *The proposed model.* [Can and should courts demand more of legislative classifications than they require under the characteristically deferential stance reflected in the materials above?   Consider the suggestions for "a new bite for the old equal protection" in the "newer equal protection" model sketched below.   Is the approach of that model legitimate?   Feasible?   Would any of the cases in this section have been decided differently under that model?   To what extent do the Burger Court decisions in secs. 3 to 6 below purport to apply standards consistent with the model?   To what extent do those Burger Court decisions invalidating laws on traditional equal protection grounds truly conform to that model?] [10]

necessarily consistent with the theory propounded in that footnote.   The approach taken in [these cases] appears to be that whenever the Court feels that a societal group is 'discrete and insular,' it has the constitutional mandate to prohibit legislation that somehow treats the group differently from some other group.

"Our society, consisting of over 200 million individuals of multitudinous origins, customs, tongues, beliefs, and cultures, is, to say the least, diverse. It would hardly take extraordinary ingenuity for a lawyer to find 'insular and discrete' minorities at every turn in the road. Yet, unless the Court can precisely define and constitutionally justify both the terms and analysis it uses, these decisions today stand for the proposition that the Court can choose a 'minority' it 'feels' deserves 'solicitude' and thereafter prohibit the States from classifying that 'minority' differently from the 'majority.' I cannot find, and the Court does not cite, any constitutional authority for such a 'ward of the Court' approach to equal protection."

Note the comment in Ely, "The Wages of Crying Wolf . . .," 82 Yale L.J. 920, 934: "[I]t is at least arguable that, constitutional directive or not, the Court should throw *its* weight on the side of the minority demanding in court more than it was able to achieve politically.   But even assuming this suggestion can be given principled content, it was clearly intended [by Stone] and should be reserved for those interests which, *as compared with the interests to which they have been subordinated,* constitute minorities unusually incapable of protecting themselves."

For a defense and elaboration of this aspect of Justice Stone's footnote, see Ball, "Judicial Protection of Powerless Minorities," 59 Iowa L.Rev. 1059 (1974).

10. The excerpts which follow are from Gunther, "Foreword: In Search of Evolving Doctrine on a Changing Court: A Model for a Newer Equal Protection," 86 Harv.L.Rev. 1, 20–24, 44–48 (1972), reprinted with the permission of the publisher, © copyright 1972 by the Harvard Law Review Association.

The "newer equal protection" model was prompted by an unusual phenomenon which first emerged during the 1971 Term: in seven cases during that

The model [would] view equal protection as a means-focused, relatively narrow, preferred ground of decision in a broad range of cases. [I]t would have the Court take seriously a constitutional requirement that has never been formally abandoned: that legislative means must substantially further legislative ends. The equal protection requirement that legislative classifications must have a substantial relationship to legislative purposes is, after all, essentially a more specific formulation of that general principle. The core of that principle survived the constitutional revolution of 1937. In reality, however, it has received little more than lip service: extreme deference to imaginable supporting facts and conceivable legislative purposes was characteristic of the "hands off" attitude of the old equal protection. Putting consistent new bite into the old equal protection would mean that the Court would be less willing to supply justifying rationales by exercising its imagination. It would have the Court assess the means in terms of legislative purposes that have substantial basis in actuality, not merely in conjecture. Moreover, it would have the Justices gauge the reasonableness of questionable means on the basis of materials that are offered to the Court, rather than resorting to rationalizations created by perfunctory judicial hypothesizing.

This relatively vigorous scrutiny would be more interventionist than the Warren Court's applications of old equal protection formulas. But it would be considerably less strict than the new equal protection. First, it would concern itself solely with means, not with ends. . . .　Moreover, the strengthened "rationality" scrutiny would curtail the state's choice of means far less severely than the new equal protection approach. The Warren Court's strict scrutiny repeatedly asked whether the means were "necessary" and whether "less drastic means" were available to achieve the statutory purpose. . . .　The more modest interventionism, by contrast, would permit the state to select any means that substantially furthered the legislative purpose. . . .

Term, the Court found substantial bases for constitutional challenges even though the traditional equal protection criteria were recited. See, e. g., Reed v. Reed, 404 U.S. 71 (1971), and Eisenstadt v. Baird, 405 U.S. 438 (1972), both below. Since then, the Burger Court has continued to find constitutional flaws on old equal protection grounds. See, e. g., Weinberger v. Wiesenfeld, 420 U.S. — (1975), sec. 3. It should be noted here that the 1972 article did not claim that the Burger Court decisions relying on old equal protection criteria in fact conformed to the model: "Closer examination of the cases reveals [that] Court adherence to the model of intensified rationality scrutiny is inchoate and fragmentary at present. Old equal protection formulations, with applications that show new bite, abound. . . . But the actual exercise of the scrutiny leaves considerable doubt that a disciplined technique of consistent intensity has as yet emerged." The excerpts from the "Newer Equal Protection" discussion are printed here largely to prompt inquiry into the potential of that approach. At the same time, these excerpts can serve as a basis for added reflection on the preceding cases in this section and, especially, for a critical examination of the Burger Court invalidations on the bases of criteria avowedly less interventionist than the strict scrutiny of the new equal protection, in secs. 3 to 6 below.

For a review of some efforts by lower courts to apply the "newer equal protection" model, see, e. g., Comment, " 'Newer' Equal Protection: The Impact of the Means-Focused Model," 23 Buffalo L.Rev. 665 (1974). For an effort at a somewhat different model to accommodate recent developments in equal protection, see Nowak, "Realigning the Standards of Review Under the Equal Protection Guarantee—Prohibited, Neutral, and Permissive Classifications," 62 Georgetown L.J. 1071 (1974). For a skeptical view of the possibilities of means-oriented rationality scrutiny, see Note, "Legislative Purpose, Rationality, and Equal Protection," 82 Yale L.J. 123 (1972).

The means-oriented scrutiny of this model would be applicable to a wide range of statutes, including the social and economic regulatory legislation that has been the most characteristic context for expressions of the hands off attitude of the last generation. The major limitation on the exercise of that scrutiny would stem from particularized considerations of judicial competence, not from broad a priori categorizations of the "social and economic" variety. That competence parameter to judicial intervention might be elaborated by refining an observation in Justice Stewart's majority opinion in Dandridge v. Williams [sec. 5 below]:

> [T]he intractable economic, social, and even philosophical problems presented by public welfare assistance programs are not the business of this Court. [The] Constitution does not empower this Court to second-guess state officials charged with the difficult responsibility of allocating limited public welfare funds among the myriad of potential recipients.

Justice Stewart's is a justifiable concern when problems are truly "intractable": when the Court cannot confidently assess whether the means contribute to the end because the data are exceedingly technical and complex; or when a "myriad" of claimants upon the legislature permits a wide range of responses, with any one as "reasonable" an allocation decision as any other. But the rationality of means used in solving *many* "economic and social" problems is a judicially manageable question; and the model would have the Court "apply a modest but real version of the rational-basis standard in economic fields that are not intrinsically inaccessible to the judicial power." *

That expanded reasonable means inquiry would not mean the end of strict scrutiny. In the context of fundamental interests or suspect classifications, the Court would continue to demand that the means be more than reasonable . . . . Under the means-focused model, however, there would be constraints in other legislative spheres as well. The intensified means scrutiny would, in short, close the wide gap between the strict scrutiny of the new equal protection and the minimal scrutiny of the old not by abandoning the strict but by raising the level of the minimal from virtual abdication to genuine judicial inquiry. . . .

Modest interventionism would certainly differ from the "all-out tolerance" of the old equal protection and from the attitude of the hands off due process era. It would place a greater burden on the state to come forth with explanations about the contributions of its means to its ends. But that demand would reinforce, not conflict with, one of the most pervasively articulated themes in the thinking about the Court's modern role: safeguarding the structure of the political process has been acknowledged as a major judicial obligation since the 1930's.† The Court's special sensitivity to interferences with debate on public issues and with the right to vote is a familiar manifestation of that emphasis. But the widespread abdication from means scrutiny is not a compelling inference from that view of the Court's appropriate role. It does indeed follow from the political process theme that legislative value choices warrant judicial deference so long as the people can have their say in the public forum and at the ballot box. It does not follow,

---

* McCloskey, "Economic Due Process and the Supreme Court: An Exhumation and Reburial," 1962 Sup.Ct.Rev. 34, 60.

† See, e. g., Justice Stone's Carolene Products footnote 4.

however, that the Court should eschew all concern with the relationship of the means adopted to the legislatively chosen ends. Means scrutiny, to the contrary, can improve the quality of the political process—without second-guessing the substantive validity of its results—by encouraging a fuller airing in the political arena of the grounds for legislative action. Examination of means in light of asserted state purposes would directly promote public consideration of the benefits assertedly sought by the proposed legislation; indirectly, it would stimulate fuller political examination, in relation to those benefits, of the costs that would be incurred if the proposed means were adopted.

A common defense of extreme judicial abdication is that the state has considered the contending considerations. Too often the only assurance that the state has thought about the issues is the judicial presumption that it has. Means scrutiny would provide greater safeguards that the presumed process corresponds to reality—and would thereby give greater content to the underlying premise for deferring to the state's resolution of the competing issues.
. . .

[A demand for] greater state articulation of legislative rationales seems an appropriate ingredient of means scrutiny . . . . There is no inherent lack of judicial capacity to demand more of the state than the Court required in Williamson v. Lee Optical Co., for example. . . .

The model concededly would provide only limited assurance that competing considerations had been aired. First of all, a legislature could comply with the model without specifying the *costs* of the means adopted in relation to the ends achieved. But in any public debate encouraged by requiring the legislature to explain the benefits sought, the costs would be likely to emerge. Second, and more serious, the model would not have the Court inquire into the motivations of legislatures. But under the model, a legislature wanting simply to give optometrists a guild advantage over opticians could do so in only two ways: first, by articulating the guild purpose; second, by stating plausible health reasons as a credible façade. Under the first route, the acceptability of the legislative objective would be exposed at once to critical public debate. And even under the second route, in addition to the indirect encouragement of debate on costs, the public scrutiny of the proposed legislation would ultimately pierce any *fragile* façade obscuring real objectives. Either route seems a healthier one for the political process than the Court's approach in Lee Optical. There, legislative silence was sufficient to legitimate possible arbitrariness; the Court supplied the "conceivable" rationale. Making the state address itself to supporting arguments in the first instance would serve the function Justice Jackson advocated in Railway Express for means-focused equal protection: not a total denial of legislative power, but a narrow, intermediate safeguard against arbitrariness. . . .

The model sketched here has the vices, if also the virtues, of a model: it is relatively simple to describe, but the description may obscure difficulties in its application. . . .

The identification of state purposes illustrates the complex problems likely to be encountered in the task of elaborating techniques capable of disciplined and consistent application. The model asks that the Court assess the rationality of the means in terms of the *state's* purposes, rather than hy-

pothesizing conceivable justifications on its own initiative. But identifying the purposes against which the means are to be measured is not a simple undertaking. What are the relevant data regarding purpose? The model would not call for a delving into actual legislative motivation. The obstacles to judicial inquiry into motivation are as formidable here as elsewhere. Nor, at the other extreme, would the only judicially cognizable purpose be one explicitly set forth in a statutory preamble or the legislative history. A state court's or attorney general office's description of purpose should be acceptable. If the Court were to require an articulation of purpose from an authoritative state source, rather than hypothesizing one on its own, there would at least be indirect pressure on the legislature to state its own reasons for selecting particular means and classifications. And that pressure would further the political process aims of the moderate intervention model.

The call for testing the rationality of means on the basis of state-articulated purposes raises other complications as well. A legislature may legitimately have a multiplicity of purposes, especially in carving exceptions from the scope of a general statute. Court inquiry should not be limited to a primary purpose; subsidiary purposes may also support the rationality of a means. The model would call on the Court to be receptive to all purposes, few or many, articulated by the state. It would not, for example, have the Court disbelieve some asserted state purposes and artificially test the means in the context of a single purpose chosen by the Court, in the manner of Eisenstadt v. Baird [sec. 6 below]. Although this approach obviously will encourage imagination in the defenders of legislation to articulate a range of legitimating purposes, that need not imply that the model encourages futile judicial gestures. Articulation of legitimating purposes would avoid judicial invalidation, to be sure. But it would do so at the cost of greater explicitness as to the reasons justifying the legislative means; and it would encourage the airing and critique of those reasons in the state's political process.

Nor are the difficulties ended once the articulated purposes are identified. The model requires that there be an affirmative relation between means and ends—or, in more traditional equal protection terms, that there be a genuine difference in terms of the state's objective between the group within the classification and those without. To a large extent, that is an empirical inquiry. The model would have the Court assess the justification for the classification largely in terms of information presented by the defenders of the law rather than hypothesizing data of its own. But such an inquiry would be neither mechanical nor value-free. Requiring compulsively neat logical correlations between classification and objective would ignore legitimate demands for legislative flexibility. The inquiry, like others entrusted to the Court, would involve questions of degree, turning on sensitivity to legislative realities and not on purely abstract considerations of fairness. Still, the value judgments involved in that inquiry would be of drastically narrower dimension than efforts to identify new fundamental interests and to proscribe varieties of legislative objectives. Indeed, perhaps the greatest difficulty in applying the model will be to delineate the boundary between the narrow value judgments required in evaluating means and the broad ones implicit in choosing among ends—in short, to avoid a disguised examination of legislative ends, such as Baird's excessively intense concentration on actual state objectives. The line between means and ends will be drawn

primarily in such terms of breadth of value judgments; it will present the most difficult questions of degree.

The model is, in sum, not a simple formula capable of automatic, problem-free application. It is a suggestion of a direction for modest interventionism with substantial promise of feasibility as well as substantial attractiveness for the changing Court. The challenge of developing disciplined techniques for the evolving means inquiry does not seem to be an insurmountable one. At least the effort, begun in last term's gropings, seems worth pursuing, to the end that the Jacksonian theme will indeed prevail over the Holmesian one: instead of equal protection being the "usual last resort of constitutional arguments," it will become the preferred ground for intervention by a less interventionist Court.

2. *Problems of the "newer equal protection" model.* The "newer equal protection" model is obviously an attempt to move somewhat away from the deferential stance by which courts uphold laws in terms of conceivable rather than actual objectives, and on the basis of means-ends relationships resting on hypothesized facts that may never have been considered by the legislators. But can that model be applied without unduly scrutinizing the actualities of legislative processes or the difficult areas of legislative motivation? Would application of the model unduly intrude into legislative value choices? What are the problems of the model, in addition to those suggested in the excerpts above? And does the model go far enough if it is to achieve the objectives it states?

a. *The requisite means-ends relationship.* The "newer equal protection" model argues that a demonstrable, "affirmative relation between means and ends" must be shown, and that the Court should assess the relationship "largely in terms of information presented by the defenders of the law rather than hypothesizing data of its own." Is that a practicable standard? Is it a legitimate one? What kinds of data may be presented, and how strong must they be? Can the Court examine the data under this version of the traditional equal protection standard without intruding unduly into legislative choices as to ends and values? Consider the adequacy of the means-ends relationship data in the preceding cases in this section. The article argues that more can be demanded of the defenders of the law than was done in Lee Optical. But how much more? Consider, too, the Burger Court decisions in secs. 3 to 6 below, in which the Court invalidates legislation on the ground that the classification is not adequately related to the legislative objective. Are those cases persuasive applications of a theory akin to the "newer equal protection" model? Or do those cases in fact impose higher demands than the model would, on the basis of unarticulated perceptions of factors justifying more than the traditional scrutiny—e. g., the presence of semi-suspect gender-based classifications? Compare, in this respect, Reed v. Reed with Weinberger v. Wiesenfeld, decisions invalidating sex classifications on the basis of traditional equal protection standards, in sec. 3 below.

b. *Legislative purpose.* (i) Does the model demand too little by stating that a judicially cognizable purpose need not be one "explicitly set forth in a statutory preamble or the legislative history"? Preambles are typically vague, and state legislative history is more difficult to come by than congressional materials. Would it nevertheless be legitimate for a court to

exert greater pressure on state legislatures by invalidating when such data as to legislative purposes are lacking? Could the Court in effect "remand" to a legislature for a more adequate record regarding purposes? Note the comment in the "Newer Equal Protection" article: "Means scrutiny would thus resemble the judicial technique of remanding to the legislature, familiar in other areas of constitutional law." [1]

(ii) If, as the model suggests, "a state court's or attorney general office's description of purpose should be acceptable," would that in fact impose "indirect pressure on the legislature to state its own reasons for selecting particular means and classifications"? Can those spokesmen be relied upon to state legislative purposes accurately? Or does such an approach simply encourage the spokesmen to put forth all conceivable legitimate state purposes? Would that simply shift "the locus of requisite imagination from the judge's chambers to the attorney general's office"? [2]

(iii) So long as courts are willing to use their imaginativeness in searching for all *conceivable* purposes, means scrutiny is likely to be meaningless: if an adequate number of specific purposes are imagined, or if an adequately overarching purpose such as the general welfare is hypothesized, it will virtually always be possible to find a sufficient relationship between the challenged classification and the supposed objectives. Is there any way to limit the purposes against which classifications are tested other than the "newer equal protection" model? Should classifications at least be tested in terms of plausible rather than conceivable objectives? Should the judicially accepted purpose at least be limited by the context of the legislation?

Consider the Court's handling of such a problem in SMITH v. CAHOON, 283 U.S. 553 (1931) (cited in Morey v. Doud, above). That decision invalidated a Florida law which required commercial motor vehicles to post liability bonds or furnish insurance policies for the protection of those injured through the carriers' negligence. Among the exemptions in the law was one for "any transportation company engaged exclusively in the transporting [of] agricultural, horticultural, dairy or other farm products" as well as fish and other seafood products. Chief Justice Hughes' opinion for a unanimous Court found a violation of equal protection. He explained:

"In determining what is within the range of discretion and what is arbitrary, regard must be had to the particular subject of the State's action. In the present instance, the regulation as to the giving of a bond or insur-

---

1. The article referred to Justice Harlan's concurrence in Garner v. Louisiana, 368 U.S. 157, 185 (1961), a First Amendment case where the Justice refused to permit the hypothesized possibility of a legitimate state interest to prevail without greater assurance that the state had in fact focused on the competing considerations with sufficient explicitness. See also the argument for a "remanding function" in Bickel and Wellington, "Legislative Purpose and the Judicial Function: The Lincoln Mills Case," 71 Harv.L. Rev. 1 (1957).

2. See Brest, Processes of Constitutional Decisionmaking, chap. 10.

Does the model adequately handle the common situation of a legislature acting on the basis of a *variety* of purposes? The "Newer Equal Protection" article criticizes the Court's handling of that problem in Eisenstadt v. Baird, sec. 6 below. There, Justice Brennan's opinion may be faulted for taking inadequate account of some preferred purposes, as well as for considering the several purposes in isolation rather than jointly. Consider, too, the existence of multiple and partly inconsistent objectives that may in fact have prompted some of the legislation challenged in the cases considered in this section.

ance policy, [in] order to be sustained, must be deemed to relate to the public safety. This is a matter of grave concern as the highways become increasingly crowded with motor vehicles . . . . But in establishing such a regulation, there does not appear to be the slightest justification for making a distinction between those who carry for hire farm products, or milk or butter, or fish or oysters, and those who carry for hire bread or sugar, or tea or coffee, or groceries in general, or other useful commodities. So far as the statute was designed to safeguard the public with respect to the use of the highways, we think that the discrimination it makes between the private carriers which are relieved of the necessity of obtaining certificates and giving security, and a carrier such as the appellant, was wholly arbitrary and constituted a violation of the appellant's constitutional rights. 'Such a classification is not based on anything having relation to the purpose for which it is made.' "

Was that a justifiable application of traditional equal protection standards? Note that the Court did not test the classifications by all *conceivable* purposes. Indeed, a fairly obvious basis for the exemptions had nothing to do with the highway risks caused by the exempted carriers: "[I]t was obviously motivated by a desire to foster the production of farm and seafood products. Although this is a goal which can properly be served by classifications made in other statutory settings, and it plainly was the goal the legislators had in mind, the Court refused to refer to it in order to uphold the classification." Ely, "Legislative and Administrative Motivation in Constitutional Law," 79 Yale L.J. 1205 (1970). Ely suggests that Cahoon in effect rejects the position that "government officials should be privileged to pursue in any context any goal they may acceptably pursue in any other context." He adds: "In cases like Cahoon—which subsequent developments made clear is not simply a derelict surviving from the 'overactive' early 1930's [3]—the Court is supplying a sort of 'consensus' theory, asking not what motivation underlay the specific distinction in question, but rather what such laws are generally concerned with, what most legislators intend to accomplish by most such laws considered in their entirety. Where the law has generally to do with traffic safety, the Court is saying, classifications must—regardless of the motivation underlying the specific classification in issue—be justifiable in terms of traffic safety. . . . A subsidy program or a tax may constitute an appropriate vehicle for legislative promotion of whatever activity is deemed to advance the general welfare, but a motor vehicle code does not."

Is there justification for that contextual limitation on the legislative purposes courts may consider in adjudicating compliance with traditional

---

3. Ely points out in a footnote that in the Railway Express case, above, "the Court declined to rest its decision on the theory that since owner operation can obviously be encouraged in other ways, it can be encouraged this way. . . . Instead it chose the vastly more tortured route of attempting, not altogether successfully, to postulate a rational relation between the challenged distinction and something it was willing to credit as an acceptable goal, increased traffic safety." He gives as other examples of "the Court's having to strain to find a distinction rationally defensible because of its unwillingness to credit as acceptable the goal the legislature plainly had intended to serve in making the challenged distinction, even though that goal could properly have been served by distinctions in other statutory settings," the Lee Optical case as well as Daniel, the funeral insurance case above.

equal protection criteria? Should the Court have sustained the Cahoon regulation if the Florida legislature had explicitly stated its subsidy purpose? Recall the discussion of the Lee Optical case in the excerpts from the "Newer Equal Protection" article, above.

SECTION 2. RACE

Introduction. Racial discrimination was the major target of the 14th Amendment; racial classifications are ordinarily "suspect": these are among the few clear and continuously voiced themes in equal protection doctrine. But agreement on those themes does not answer all troublesome questions. What is necessary to demonstrate unconstitutional racial discrimination? Must purposeful racial bias be expressed in formal statements of state policy, on the face of a statute? May bias be inferred from the administration of laws? Is purposeful, de jure discrimination an essential ingredient of a constitutional claim, or does the Constitution protect as well against de facto, adventitious discrimination—i. e., against state action which has a disproportionate disadvantageous impact on a particular racial group, even though the law is neutral on its face and its administration is not grounded on a hostile racial purpose?

When, if ever, may racial criteria be relied on in state action? Are all racial classifications forbidden: must government be truly "color blind"? Are racial classifications always at least "suspect"? Are they impermissible unless the state can advance a strong justification? What justifications will do? Are racial criteria acceptable if their purpose is "benign" rather than hostile? Does a benign purpose provide the compelling justification required under strict scrutiny standards? Or does rationality replace strict scrutiny when the purpose is shown to be benign? When is a purpose benign? When may race be used for remedial purposes? Only to remedy past de jure discrimination? To remedy de facto discrimination as well? To serve other goals?

Questions such as these are raised by the materials that follow. Sec. 2A examines some general, pervasive problems: the forms in which racial discrimination may manifest itself; the problems of proof of discrimination; the appropriate standard of judicial scrutiny in examining discriminatory action shown to be based on racial factors. Sec. 2B turns to the special problem of—and explores the methods of implementing—the modern command that racial segregation of schools is impermissible. Sec. 2C considers the question whether racial criteria may be relied upon for benign purposes, as in the context of preferential admissions programs.

A. PURPOSEFUL RACIAL DISCRIMINATION AND THE SCRUTINY OF RACIAL CLASSIFICATIONS

SOME FORMS OF PURPOSEFUL DISCRIMINATION

1. *Discrimination on the face of the law: The Strauder case.* Seven years after the Slaughter-House Cases (chap. 8 above) had emphasized the racial concerns central in the adoption of the 14th Amendment, the Court recalled and applied that background in STRAUDER v. WEST VIRGINIA, 100 U.S. 303 (1880). Strauder, a Black, was convicted of murder by a jury from which Blacks had been barred as a result of a state law providing: "All white male persons who are twenty-one years of age and who are citizens of this State shall be eligible to serve as jurors." Before trial, he had unsuccessfully sought to remove his case to a federal court. (See 28 U.S.C. § 1443.) After conviction in the state courts, the Supreme Court held that removal should have been granted. Justice Strong's majority opinion noted that the controlling question was not whether a Black had a right to a jury "composed in whole or in part of persons of his own race or color" but whether in selecting a jury, "all persons of his race or color may be excluded by law, solely because of their race or color, so that by no possibility can any colored man sit upon the jury." Justice Strong continued:

"[The 14th Amendment] is one of a series of constitutional provisions having a common purpose; namely, securing to a race recently emancipated, a race that through many generations had been held in slavery, all the civil rights the superior race enjoy. The true spirit and meaning of the amendments, as we said in the Slaughter-House Cases, cannot be understood without keeping in view the history of the times when they were adopted, and the general objects they plainly sought to accomplish. At the time when they were incorporated into the Constitution, it required little knowledge of human nature to anticipate that those who had long been regarded as an inferior and subject race would, when suddenly raised to the rank of citizenship, be looked upon with jealousy and positive dislike, and that State laws might be enacted or enforced to perpetuate the distinctions that had before existed. Discriminations against them had been habitual. It was well known that in some States laws making such discriminations then existed, and others might well be expected. The colored race, as a race, was abject and ignorant, and in that condition was unfitted to command the respect of those who had superior intelligence. Their training had left them mere children, and as such they needed the protection which a wise government extends to those who are unable to protect themselves. They especially needed protection against unfriendly action in the States where they were resident. It was in view of these considerations the Fourteenth Amendment was framed and adopted. It was designed to assure to the colored race the enjoyment of all the civil rights that under the law are enjoyed by white persons, and to give to that race the protection of the general government, in that enjoyment, whenever it should be denied by the States. . . .

"If this is the spirit and meaning of the amendment, whether it means more or not, it is to be construed liberally, to carry out the purposes of its

framers. . . . What is [the equal protection clause] but declaring
that the law in the States shall be the same for the black as for the white;
that all persons, whether colored or white, shall stand equal before the laws
of the States, and, in regard to the colored race, for whose protection the
amendment was primarily designed, that no discrimination shall be made
against them by law because of their color? The words of the amendment,
it is true, are prohibitory, but they contain a necessary implication of a positive immunity, or right, most valuable to the colored race,—the right to exemption from unfriendly legislation against them distinctively as colored,—
exemption from legal discriminations, implying inferiority in civil society,
lessening the security of their enjoyment of the rights which others enjoy,
and discriminations which are steps towards reducing them to the condition
of a subject race.

"That the West Virginia statute respecting juries—the statute that controlled the selection of the grand and petit jury in the case of the plaintiff
in error—is such a discrimination ought not to be doubted. Nor would it be
if the persons excluded by it were white men. If in those States where the
colored people constitute a majority of the entire population a law should be
enacted excluding all white men from jury service, thus denying to them the
privilege of participating equally with the blacks in the administration of
justice, we apprehend no one would be heard to claim that it would not be a
denial to white men of the equal protection of the laws. Nor if a law
should be passed excluding all naturalized Celtic Irishmen, would there be
any doubt of its inconsistency with the spirit of the amendment. The very
fact that colored people are singled out and expressly denied by a statute all
right to participate in the administration of the law, as jurors, because of
their color, though they are citizens, and may be in other respects fully qualified, is practically a brand upon them, affixed by the law, an assertion of
their inferiority, and a stimulant to that race prejudice which is an impediment to securing to individuals of the race that equal justice which the law
aims to secure to all others."

"The right to a trial by jury is guaranteed to every citizen of West
Virginia by the Constitution of that State, and the constitution of juries is a
very essential part of the protection such a mode of trial is intended to secure. The very idea of a jury is a body of men composed of the peers or
equals of the persons whose rights it is selected or summoned to determine;
that is, of his neighbors, fellows, associates, persons having the same legal
status in society as that which he holds. . . . It is well known that
prejudices often exist against particular classes in the community, which
sway the judgment of jurors, and, which, therefore, operate in some cases
to deny to persons of those classes the full enjoyment of that protection
which others enjoy. . . . The framers of the constitutional amendment must have known full well the existence of such prejudice and its likelihood to continue against the manumitted slaves and their race, and that
knowledge was doubtless a motive that led to the amendment. . . . It
is not easy to comprehend how it can be said that while every white man is
entitled to a trial by a jury selected from persons of his own race or color, or,
rather, selected without discrimination against his color, and a negro is not,
the latter is equally protected by the law with the former. [H]ow can it be
maintained that compelling a colored man to submit to a trial for his life

by a jury drawn from a panel from which the State has expressly excluded every man of his race, because of color alone, however well qualified in other respects, is not a denial to him of equal legal protection?

"We do not say that within the limits from which it is not excluded by the amendment a State may not prescribe the qualifications of its jurors, and in so doing make discriminations. It may confine the selection to males,[1] to freeholders, to citizens, to persons within certain ages, or to persons having educational qualifications. We do not believe the Fourteenth Amendment was ever intended to prohibit this. Looking at its history, it is clear it had no such purpose. Its aim was against discrimination because of race or color. [I]ts design was to protect an emancipated race, and to strike down all possible legal discriminations against those who belong to it. . . . We are not now called upon to affirm or deny that it had other purposes."[2]

2. *Discrimination in the administration of law.* a. *Yick Wo.* A San Francisco ordinance prohibited operating a laundry without the consent of the Board of Supervisors except in a brick or stone building. The Board granted permits to operate laundries in wooden buildings to all but one of the non-Chinese applicants, but to none of about 200 Chinese applicants. Yick Wo, a Chinese alien who had operated a laundry for many years, was refused a permit and was convicted under the ordinance. In YICK WO v. HOPKINS, 118 U.S. 356 (1886), the Court reversed the conviction. Justice Matthews' opinion found discrimination in the *administration* of the law:

"[T]he cases present the ordinances in actual operation, and the facts shown establish an administration directed so exclusively against a particular class of persons as to warrant and require the conclusion, that, whatever may have been the intent of the ordinances as adopted, they are applied by the public authorities charged with their administration, and thus representing the State itself, with a mind so unequal and oppressive as to amount to a practical denial by the State of that equal protection of the laws which is secured to the petitioners, as to all other persons, by the broad and benign provisions of [the 14th Amendment]. Though the law itself be fair on its face and impartial in appearance, yet, if it is applied and administered by public authority with an evil eye and an unequal hand, so as practically to make un-

1. Nearly a century later, the Court held that the systematic exclusion of women from jury panels was unconstitutional—relying on the Sixth Amendment's jury trial guarantee ("incorporated" into the 14th) rather than the equal protection clause. See Taylor v. Louisiana, 419 U.S. 522 (1975), sec. 3C below.

2. Note that in Strauder, the claim of racial discrimination was raised by a member of the excluded class. (Note, too, that it was enough that there was a *risk* of prejudice, and that no actual prejudice needed to be shown.) The law as to challenging discrimination in jury selection has changed since Strauder. For example, in Peters v. Kiff, 407 U.S. 493 (1972), a white defendant successfully challenged a conviction on the ground that Blacks had been systematically excluded from jury service. And in Taylor v. Louisiana, footnote 1 above, a male defendant was permitted to raise the exclusion of women. That change in the jury selection context stems from the change in emphasis regarding the relevant "right" involved: the focus has shifted from equal protection to an aspect of the jury trial guarantee. In the Taylor case, Justice White's majority opinion stated "that the selection of a petit jury from a representative cross section of the community is an essential component of the Sixth Amendment right to a jury trial" (made applicable to the states via the Fourteenth).

just and illegal discriminations between persons in similar circumstances, material to their rights, the denial of equal justice is still within the prohibition of the Constitution.

"The present cases, as shown by the facts disclosed in the record, are within this class. It appears that both petitioners have complied with every requisite, deemed by the law or by the public officers charged with its administration, necessary for the protection of neighboring property from fire, or as a precaution against injury to the public health. No reason whatever, except the will of the supervisors, is assigned why they should not be permitted to carry on, in the accustomed manner, their harmless and useful occupation, on which they depend for a livelihood. And while this consent of the supervisors is withheld from them and from two hundred others who have also petitioned, all of whom happened to be Chinese subjects, eighty others, not Chinese subjects, are permitted to carry on the same business under similar conditions. The fact of this discrimination is admitted. No reason for it is shown, and the conclusion cannot be resisted, that no reason for it exists except hostility to the race and nationality to which the petitioners belong, and which in the eye of the law is not justified."

b. *Proof of purposeful discrimination.* In Strauder, the racial basis for the disadvantaging governmental action was explicit on the face of the statute. Most of the cases that follow similarly involve racial classifications on the face of the law. But impermissible racial criteria may enter governmental decisionmaking through other routes as well. Yick Wo illustrates a common problem: purposeful, hostile discrimination is inferred from data regarding administration of a facially neutral law. Reliance on statistical data showing a racially discriminatory pattern of administration has become commonplace in modern cases. Discrimination in jury selection was the earliest area; the practices spread to other fields as well, such as discrimination in voting and employment. See, e. g., the Court's comment in Mayor of Philadelphia v. Educational Equality League, 415 U.S. 605 (1974): "Statistical analyses have served and will continue to serve an important role as one indirect indicator of racial discrimination in access to service on governmental bodies, particularly where, as in the case of jury service, the duty to serve falls equally on all citizens."[3] In that 1974 case, however, the Court found that the claimed discrimination in mayoral appointments to a nominating panel for the city school board had not been established.

May a defendant, in cases claiming racial discrimination or other violations of equal protection, assert that individual variations in administration of law were not deliberate discriminations? See Snowden v. Hughes, 321 U.S. 1 (1944), stating that "unequal application" of statutes fair on their face is not a violation of equal protection "unless there is shown an element of intentional or purposeful discrimination." See also Oyler v. Boles, 368

---

3. As examples of jury discrimination cases, the Court cited Carter v. Jury Comm'n, 396 U.S. 320 (1970), Hernandez v. Texas, 347 U.S. 475 (1954), and Avery v. Georgia, 345 U.S. 559 (1953). It also cited McDonnell Douglas Corp. v. Green, 411 U.S. 792 (1973), an employment discrimination case under Title VII of the Civil Rights Act of 1964, where the Court had commented that "statistics as to petitioner's employment policy and practice may be helpful to a determination of whether petitioner's refusal to rehire respondent in this case conformed to a general pattern of discrimination against blacks."

U.S. 448 (1962), where the Court rejected a challenge to sentencing under a habitual criminal statute. The challenger claimed that there had been failure to prosecute other habitual offenders. Justice Clark noted that the allegations did not state whether the failure to prosecute was due to a deliberate policy or to lack of knowledge. If there was lack of knowledge, there would clearly be no equal protection violation, he insisted. And he added: "Moreover, the conscious exercise of some selectivity in enforcement is not in itself a federal constitutional violation. Even though the statistics in this case might imply a policy of selective enforcement, it was not stated that the selection was deliberately based upon an unjustifiable standard such as race, religion, or other arbitrary classification. Therefore grounds supporting a finding of denial of equal protection were not alleged."[4]

3. *Discriminatory motivation.* What if the law reveals no purposeful racial discrimination either on its face or in the pattern of its administration: may courts invalidate otherwise valid official action because it was adopted for racial motives? Pleas for judicial scrutiny in this area encounter the courts' institutional inhibitions regarding inquiries into improper motive.[5] See, e. g., the 5 to 4 decision in PALMER v. THOMPSON, 403 U.S. 217 (1971), holding that the city of Jackson, Mississippi, had not acted unconstitutionally in closing its public swimming pools after they had been ordered desegregated. Justice Black's majority opinion, after noting that there was no "affirmative duty" to operate swimming pools, rejected the argument that the closing was unconstitutional because it "was motivated by a desire to avoid integration." He asserted that "no case in this Court had held that a legislative act may violate equal protection solely because of the motivations of the men who voted for it." Ascertaining motivation was "extremely difficult." Though there was some evidence here that the city had acted in part because of "ideological opposition to racial integration," there was also substantial evidence that the city had thought that the pools "could not be operated safely and economically on an integrated basis." Justice Black added that it was "difficult or impossible for any court to determine the 'sole' or 'dominant' motivation behind the choices of a group of legislators. Furthermore, there is an element of futility in a judicial attempt to invalidate a law because of the bad motives of its supporters. If the law is struck down for this reason, rather than because of its facial content or effect, it would presumably be valid as soon as the legislature or relevant governing body repassed it for different reasons." Justice Black conceded that there was "language in some of our cases" suggesting "that the motive or purpose behind a law is relevant to its constitutionality." "But," he added, "the focus in those cases was on the actual effect of the enactments, not upon the motivation which led the States to behave as they did." The record here showed "no state action affecting blacks different from whites."

Justice White's lengthy dissent insisted that whites and Blacks were not being treated alike when both were denied use of public services: "The

---

4. See, e. g., Comment, "The Right to Nondiscriminatory Enforcement of State Penal Laws," 61 Colum.L.Rev. 1103 (1961).

5. See generally Brest, "Palmer v. Thompson: An Approach to the Problem of Unconstitutional Legislative Motive," 1971 Sup.Ct.Rev. 95, and Ely, "Legislative and Administrative Motivation in Constitutional Law," 79 Yale L.J. 1205 (1970). (Recall the discussion of legislative motivation in chap. 2 above.)

fact is that closing the pools is an expression of official policy that Negroes are unfit to associate with whites." He asserted that forbidden "racial motive or animus" was a common focus of judicial inquiry—in the context of federal civil rights legislation, for example. He found that here "desegregation, and desegregation alone," was the cause of the closing.

Compare Griffin v. County School Board of Prince Edward County, 377 U.S. 218 (1964), where the Court found the closing of public schools unconstitutional in one of the counties involved in the first group of school desegregation cases decided together with Brown v. Board of Education, sec. 2B below. The public school closing scheme was accompanied by grants of public funds to white children to attend private schools. Justice Black there emphasized that "public schools were closed and private schools operated in their place with state and county assistance, for one reason, and one reason only: to ensure [that] white and colored children in Prince Edward County would not, under any circumstances, go to the same school. Whatever nonracial grounds might support a State's allowing a county to abandon public schools, the object must be a constitutional one, and grounds of race and opposition to desegregation do not qualify as constitutional." In Palmer, Justice Black distinguished Griffin because, "unlike the 'private schools' in Prince Edward County there is nothing here to show the city is directly or indirectly involved in the funding or operation" of the swimming pools. Compare also Gomillion v. Lightfoot, 364 U.S. 339 (1960), finding that an Alabama law redefining the city boundaries of Tuskegee was a device to disenfranchise Blacks in violation of the 15th Amendment. The statute, which altered "the shape of Tuskegee from a square to an uncouth twenty-eight-sided figure" was alleged to result in removing from the city "all save only four or five of its 400 Negro voters while not removing a single white voter or resident." Justice Frankfurter's opinion found that the allegations, if proved, would "abundantly establish" that the law "was not an ordinary geographic redistricting measure even within familiar abuses of gerrymandering." If the claims were proved, "the conclusion would be irresistible, tantamount for all practical purposes to a mathematical demonstration, that the legislation is solely concerned with segregating white and colored voters by fencing Negro citizens out of town so as to deprive them of their pre-existing municipal vote."[6]

4. *De facto discrimination: Is differential effect sufficient?* Suppose that no purposeful discrimination appears on the face of a statute, and that none can be inferred from the manner in which it is administered. Suppose, moreover, that the action, taken for reasons independent of racial factors, has a differential and disadvantaging effect on racial minorities. Is such

---

6. Compare Wright v. Rockefeller, 376 U.S. 52 (1964), rejecting a claim that congressional districts in Manhattan were racially gerrymandered: appellants failed to prove that the legislature "was either motivated by racial considerations or in fact drew the districts on racial lines." For later Court considerations of claims that redistricting schemes—especially multimember districting—discriminated unfairly against racial minorities, compare

Whitcomb v. Chavis, 403 U.S. 124 (1971), with White v. Regester, 412 U.S. 755 (1973). The latter case for the first time sustained a claim that a multimember district unconstitutionally tended "to cancel out or minimize the voting strength of racial groups." See the additional consideration of these cases with the reapportionment materials in chap. 15, sec. 5.

action unconstitutional?　Should de facto discrimination be treated like de jure discrimination?　A wide range of laws not carrying racial classifications and not resting on racially discriminatory purposes have disproportionate harmful impacts on racial minorities.　That problem is more fully considered in the context of de facto segregation issues, sec. 2B below.　But consider preliminarily a modern Court response to a de facto discrimination claim in the welfare legislation context.　JEFFERSON v. HACKNEY, 406 U.S. 535 (1972) (further noted in sec. 5 below), was an attack on a Texas scheme for computing AFDC benefits in allocating the state's fixed amount of welfare money.　A lower percentage of "need" was granted to AFDC recipients than to beneficiaries of other categorical assistance programs.　One of the grounds for attacking that scheme was that "there is a larger percentage of Negroes and Mexican-Americans in AFDC than in other programs."　Justice Rehnquist's majority opinion was not moved by that "naked statistical argument."　He noted that "the number of minority members in all categories is substantial" and added that, "given the heterogeneity of the Nation's population, it would be only an infrequent coincidence that the racial composition of each grant class was identical to that of the others."　But he went on to state a broader ground: "The acceptance of appellants' constitutional theory would render suspect each difference in treatment among the grant classes, however lacking in racial motivation and however otherwise rational the treatment might be.　Few legislative efforts to deal with the difficult problems posed by current welfare programs could survive such scrutiny, and we do not find it required by the Fourteenth Amendment."

Compare the Court's handling of a *statutory* discrimination claim a few years earlier, in GRIGGS v. DUKE POWER CO., 401 U.S. 424 (1971).　That was a case arising under Title VII, the employment discrimination provisions of the Civil Rights Act of 1964.　Chief Justice Burger's unanimous opinion read the Act to prohibit an employer from subjecting job applicants to a general intelligence test and from requiring high school diplomas, where the effect was to disadvantage Black applicants and where the criteria had not been shown to predict job performance.　He stated: "What is required by Congress is the removal of artificial, arbitrary, and unnecessary barriers to employment where the barriers operate invidiously to discriminate on the basis of racial or other impermissible classification. . . . The Act proscribes not only overt discrimination but also practices that are fair in form, but discriminatory in operation.　The touchstone is business necessity. If an employment practice which operates to exclude Negroes cannot be shown to be related to job performance, the practice is prohibited."

Here, he emphasized, the requirements had been adopted "without meaningful study of their relationship to job-performance ability."　Yet employees who had not been subjected to those standards were shown to have performed satisfactorily.　The lower court, to be sure, had found that the diploma and test requirements had been adopted without any "intention to discriminate against Negro employees."　But Chief Justice Burger replied that "good intent or absence of discriminatory intent does not redeem employment procedures or testing mechanisms that operate as 'built-in headwinds' for minority groups and are unrelated to measuring job capability. . . . Congress directed the thrust of the Act to the *consequences*

of employment practices, not simply the motivation. More than that, Congress has placed on the employer the burden of showing that any given requirement must have a manifest relationship to the employment in question." [7]

In the Griggs case, the employer had discriminated openly prior to the adoption of the 1964 Act. But that prior discrimination apparently was not a central factor in the Court's opinion, though the Court noted: "Under the Act, practices, procedures, or tests neutral on their face, and even neutral in terms of intent, cannot be maintained if they operate to 'freeze' the status quo of prior discriminatory employment practices." Is the Griggs standard the appropriate one in the absence of prior discrimination by the employer? Is the standard limited to claims resting on violations of statutes barring discrimination? Or is the Griggs approach applicable to claims of 14th Amendment violations as well? [8] Is the Griggs principle a proper inference from the constitutional command? In the absence of purposeful discrimination, is differential effect sufficient to require the state to demonstrate that qualifications are job-related?

THE SCRUTINY OF RACIAL CLASSIFICATIONS

Race as a "suspect" classification: The Korematsu case. Though, as Strauder and Yick Wo illustrate, the Court has long perceived special bite in the equal protection clause when it is invoked as a weapon against racial discrimination, explicit reference to race as a "suspect" criterion did not come until well into the 20th century, in KOREMATSU v. UNITED STATES, 323 U.S. 214 (1944). Ironically, Korematsu is one of the very rare cases in which a classification based on race or ancestry survived Court scrutiny. The majority sustained the conviction of an American of Japanese descent for violating a military order during World War II excluding all persons of Japanese ancestry from designated West Coast areas. Shortly after the outbreak of war with Japan, President Roosevelt issued an Executive Order, designed to protect "against espionage and against sabotage," and providing that certain military commanders might designate "military areas" in the United States "from which any or all persons may be excluded, and with respect to which the right of any person to enter, remain in, or leave shall be subject to whatever restrictions" the "Military Commander may impose in his discretion." The program established for the West Coast for persons of

---

7. See Blumrosen, "Strangers in Paradise: Griggs v. Duke Power Co. and the Concept of Employment Discrimination," 71 Mich.L.Rev. 59 (1972).

8. For reliance on the Griggs approach in 14th Amendment cases in the lower courts, see, e. g., Castro v. Beecher, 459 F.2d 725 (1st Cir. 1972) (intelligence tests cannot be applied in screening applicants for the police force absent validation).

Note also Lau v. Nichols, 414 U.S. 563 (1974), sustaining an HEW guideline under Title VI of the Civil Rights Act of 1964 and requiring the school district to provide special assistance to non-English speaking Chinese students. Justice Douglas' opinion found that HEW was authorized to prohibit discriminatory *"effect*, even though no purposeful design is present." Several of the Justices concurred only in the result. Would failure to provide special instruction to non-English speaking students be open to a successful constitutional challenge if there had been no statute and implementing HEW regulations? In Lau, the Court did not reach the equal protection issue.

Japanese ancestry included curfews, detention in relocation centers, and exclusion from the West Coast area. After unanimously upholding the curfew orders in 1943,[1] the Court in the following year, in the Korematsu case, sustained the exclusion aspect of the program.

Early in his majority opinion, Justice Black stated the governing standard: "[A]ll legal restrictions which curtail the civil rights of a single racial group are immediately suspect. That is not to say that all such restrictions are unconstitutional. It is to say that courts must subject them to the most rigid scrutiny. Pressing public necessity may sometimes justify the existence of such restrictions; racial antagonism never can." But here, the requisite "pressing public necessity" was found. He explained:

"Like curfew, exclusion of those of Japanese origin was deemed necessary [by the military authorities] because of the presence of an unascertained number of disloyal members of the group, most of whom we have no doubt were loyal to this country." The military authorities had found "that it was impossible to bring about an immediate segregation of the disloyal from the loyal." Accordingly, the judgment that "exclusion of the whole group [was] a military imperative answers the contention that the exclusion was in the nature of group punishment based on antagonism to those of Japanese origin."[2] Justice Black added: "Compulsory exclusion of large groups of citizens from their homes, except under circumstances of direst emergency and peril, is inconsistent with our basic governmental institutions. But when under conditions of modern warfare our shores are threatened by hostile forces, the power to protect must be commensurate with the threatened danger."

In a closing passage, Justice Black reiterated that the Court was not endorsing racial discrimination: "Our task would be simple, our duty clear, were this a case involving the imprisonment of a loyal citizen in a concentration camp because of racial prejudice." Only the exclusion order was involved here, and to "cast this case into outlines of racial prejudice, without reference to the real military dangers which were presented, merely confuses the issue." Korematsu was excluded, he insisted, "because we are at war with the Japanese Empire, because the properly constituted military authorities feared an invasion of our West Coast and felt constrained to take proper security measures, because they decided that the military urgency of the situa-

1. Hirabayashi v. United States, 320 U.S. 81 (1943).

2. Justice Black added: "That there were members of the group who retained loyalties to Japan has been confirmed by investigations made subsequent to the exclusion. Approximately five thousand American citizens of Japanese ancestry refused to swear unqualified allegiance to the United States and to renounce allegiance to the Japanese Emperor, and several thousand evacuees requested repatriation to Japan." Compare the comments on this issue in Justice Murphy's dissent.

The Court did not in this case—or any other—pass on the constitutionality of the detention and confinement programs. But see Ex parte Endo, 323 U.S. 283 (1944), decided on the same day as Korematsu, holding continued detention under the relocation program invalid for lack of statutory authority, without reaching the constitutional issues.

On these cases and on the evacuation program generally, see, e. g., Rostow, "The Japanese American Cases—A Disaster," 54 Yale L.J. 489 (1945); Dembitz, "Racial Discrimination and the Military Judgment," 45 Colum.L. Rev. 175 (1945); and Grodzins, Americans Betrayed: Politics and the Japanese Evacuation (1949).

tion demanded that all citizens of Japanese ancestry be segregated from the West Coast temporarily, and finally, because Congress, reposing its confidence in this time of war in our military leaders—as inevitably it must—determined that they should have the power to do just this.   There was evidence of disloyalty on the part of some, the military authorities considered that the need for action was great, and time was short.   We cannot—by availing ourselves of the calm perspective of hindsight—now say that at that time these actions were unjustified." [3]

Justice Murphy wrote the strongest dissent—even though he did not invoke the "suspect classification"-"strict scrutiny" test and purported to apply simply standards of "reasonableness."   He acknowledged that "great respect" for military judgment in wartime was "appropriate."   But "the military claim must subject itself to the judicial process of having its reasonableness determined."   He was not persuaded that the deprivation of individual rights here was "reasonably related to a public danger that is so 'immediate, imminent, and impending' as not to admit of delay and not to permit the intervention of ordinary constitutional processes to alleviate the danger."   The exclusion order applicable to "all persons of Japanese ancestry" seemed to him "an obvious racial discrimination" and hence a denial of equal protection.[4]

Justice Murphy conceded that there was "a very real fear of invasion of the Pacific Coast," and fears of sabotage and espionage, on the Pacific Coast in 1942.   But he insisted that "the exclusion, either temporarily or permanently, of all persons with Japanese blood in their veins has [no] reasonable relation" to the "removal of the dangers."   He explained: "[T]hat relation is lacking because the exclusion order necessarily must rely for its reasonableness upon the assumption that *all* persons of Japanese ancestry may have a dangerous tendency to commit sabotage and espionage."   He found it "difficult to believe that treason, logic or experience could be marshalled in support of such an assumption."   He argued that the "forced exclusion was the result in good measure of [an] erroneous assumption of racial guilt rather than bona fide military necessity."   The justification for exclusion rested "mainly upon questionable racial and sociological grounds" not charged or proved—"an accumulation of much of the misinformation, half-truths and

---

3. Note a comment on Korematsu 30 years after that decision, by Justice Douglas, a member of the Korematsu majority. He stated in DeFunis v. Odegaard, 416 U.S. 312 (1974) (sec. 2C below): "The decisions [on wartime restrictions imposed upon Japanese-Americans] were extreme and went to the verge of wartime power; and they have been severely criticized. It is, however, easy in retrospect to denounce what was done, as there actually was no attempted Japanese invasion of our country. . . . But those making plans for defense of the Nation had no such knowledge and were planning for the worst."

4. Justice Murphy stated that equal protection was "guaranteed by the Fifth Amendment."   That the equal protection guarantee is in effect a part of the due process assurance of the Fifth Amendment has been accepted by the modern Court. See, e. g., Chief Justice Warren's opinion in Bolling v. Sharpe, 347 U.S. 497 (1954) (sec. 2B), a companion case to Brown v. Board of Education, holding public school segregation in states violative of the equal protection clause. In applying that ruling to the District of Columbia in Bolling, the Chief Justice stated that "it would be unthinkable that the same Constitution would impose a lesser duty on the Federal Government."   Is it so unthinkable? Was the "incorporation" of equal protection into due process adequately heedful of text and history?

insinuations that for years have been directed against Japanese Americans by people with racial and economic prejudices—the same people who have been among the foremost advocates of the evacuation. A military judgment based upon such racial and sociological considerations is not entitled to the great weight ordinarily given the judgments based upon strictly military considerations."

"[E]xamples of individual disloyalty" did not "prove group disloyalty and justify discriminatory action against the entire group." Moreover, there was no adequate proof that the FBI and other intelligence services did not have the espionage problem well in hand. He noted, too, that "not one person of Japanese ancestry was accused or convicted of espionage or sabotage after Pearl Harbor while they were still free, a fact which is some evidence of the loyalty of the vast majority of these individuals and of the effectiveness of the established methods of combating these evils." He added: "It seems incredible that under these circumstancs it would have been impossible to hold loyalty hearings for the mere 112,000 persons involved—or at least for the 70,000 American citizens." [5] He accordingly dissented from "this legalization of racism."

In a separate dissent, Justice Jackson stated that he would hold "that a civil court cannot be made to enforce an order which violates constitutional limitations even if it is a reasonable exercise of military authority." Judicial review of questions of military necessity was inappropriate: "I do not suggest that the Court should have attempted to interfere with the army in carrying out its task. But I do not think they may be asked to execute a military expedient that has no place in law or under the Constitution." He elaborated: "[A] judicial construction of the due process clause that will sustain this order is a far more subtle blow to liberty than the promulgation of the order itself. A military order, however unconstitutional, is not apt to last longer than the military emergency. . . . But once a judicial opinion rationalizes such an order to show that it conforms to the Constitution, or rather rationalizes the Constitution to show that the Constitution sanctions such an order, the Court for all time has validated the principle of racial discrimination in criminal procedure and of transplanting American citizens. The principle then lies about like a loaded weapon ready for the hand of any authority that can bring forward a plausible claim of an urgent need. . . . A military commander may overstep the bounds of constitutionality, and it is an incident. But if we review and approve, that passing incident becomes a doctrine of the Constitution." Earlier he had noted: "[I]f we cannot confine military expedients by the Constitution, neither would I distort the Constitution to approve all that the military may deem expedient. That is what the Court appears to be doing, whether consciously or not." The military orders may or may not have been "expedient military precautions"; but they should not be enforced by civil courts committed to the Constitution.[6]

5. He added in a footnote that the British government had been able to determine through individualized hearings whether 74,000 German and Austrian aliens were genuine risks or only "friendly enemies." The British had accomplished that task in a six months period after the outbreak of war, and only 2,000 were ultimately interned.

6. Justice Roberts also submitted a dissent; Justice Frankfurter delivered a concurring opinion.

LOVING v. VIRGINIA

388 U.S. 1, 87 S.Ct. 1817, 18 L.Ed.2d 1010 (1967).

Appeal from the Supreme Court of Appeals of Virginia.

Mr. Chief Justice WARREN delivered the opinion of the Court.

This case presents a constitutional question never addressed by this Court: whether a statutory scheme adopted by the State of Virginia to prevent marriages between persons solely on the basis of racial classifications violates the Equal Protection and Due Process Clauses of the Fourteenth Amendment. For reasons which seem to us to reflect the central meaning of those constitutional commands, we conclude that these statutes cannot stand consistently with the Fourteenth Amendment.

In June 1958, two residents of Virginia, Mildred Jeter, a Negro woman, and Richard Loving, a white man, were married in the District of Columbia pursuant to its laws. Shortly after their marriage, the Lovings returned to Virginia. [They were indicted for] violating Virginia's ban on interracial marriages . . ., pleaded guilty [and] were sentenced to one year in jail; however, the trial judge suspended the sentence for a period of 25 years on the condition that the Lovings leave the State and not return to Virginia together for 25 years. . . . After their convictions, the Lovings took up residence in the District of Columbia. On November 6, 1963, they filed a motion in the state trial court to vacate the judgment and set aside the sentence on the ground that the statutes which they had violated were repugnant to the Fourteenth Amendment. [The trial court denied that motion and the highest state court, after modifying the sentence, "affirmed the convictions."]

Virginia is now one of 16 States which prohibit and punish marriages on the basis of racial classifications. Penalties for miscegenation arose as an incident to slavery and have been common in Virginia since the colonial period. The present statutory scheme dates from the adoption of the Racial Integrity Act of 1924, passed during the period of extreme nativism which followed the end of the First World War.

In upholding the constitutionality of these provisions in the decision below, the Supreme Court of Appeals of Virginia referred to its 1955 decision in Naim v. Naim [see chap. 15, below, on the Supreme Court's dismissal of the Naim appeal], as stating the reasons supporting the validity of these laws. In Naim, the state court concluded that the State's legitimate purposes were "to preserve the racial integrity of its citizens," and to prevent "the corruption of blood," "a mongrel breed of citizens," and "the obliteration of racial pride," obviously an endorsement of the doctrine of White Supremacy. . . .

[T]he State does not contend in its argument before this Court that its powers to regulate marriage are unlimited notwithstanding the commands of

---

For Court considerations of alleged racial discriminations against Oriental aliens—at a time when federal laws made certain non-white racial groups ineligible for citizenship—see Takahashi v. Fish and Game Commission, 334 U.S. 410 (1948), and Oyama v. California, 332 U.S. 633 (1948). For modern Court decisions considering state restrictions on aliens and finding alienage to be a "suspect" classification in those contexts, see sec. 3A below.

the Fourteenth Amendment. . . . Instead, the State argues that the meaning of the Equal Protection Clause, as illuminated by the statements of the Framers, is only that state penal laws containing an interracial element as part of the definition of the offense must apply equally to whites and Negroes in the sense that members of each race are punished to the same degree. Thus, the State contends that, because its miscegenation statutes punish equally both the white and the Negro participants in an interracial marriage, these statutes, despite their reliance on racial classifications, do not constitute an invidious discrimination based upon race. . . .

Because we reject the notion that the mere "equal application" of a statute containing racial classifications is enough to remove the classifications from the Fourteenth Amendment's proscription of all invidious racial discriminations, we do not accept the State's contention that these statutes should be upheld if there is any possible basis for concluding that they serve a rational purpose. [W]e deal with statutes containing racial classifications, and the fact of equal application does not immunize the statute from the very heavy burden of justification which the Fourteenth Amendment has traditionally required of state statutes drawn according to race.

The State argues that statements in the Thirty-ninth Congress about the time of the passage of the Fourteenth Amendment indicate that the Framers did not intend the Amendment to make unconstitutional state miscegenation laws. [W]e have said in connection with a related problem that although these historical sources "cast some light" they are not sufficient to resolve the problem; "[a]t best, they are inconclusive. . . ." Brown v. Board of Education [1954; sec. 2B below]. We have rejected the proposition that the debates in the Thirty-ninth Congress or in the state legislatures which ratified the Fourteenth Amendment supported the theory advanced by the State, that the requirement of equal protection of the laws is satisfied by penal laws defining offenses based on racial classifications so long as white and Negro participants in the offense were similarly punished. McLaughlin v. Florida.[1]

---

1. McLaughlin v. Florida, 379 U.S. 184 (1964), invalidated a criminal statute prohibiting cohabitation by interracial married couples. Justice White's majority opinion emphasized: "Normally, the widest discretion is allowed the legislative judgment [under the equal protection clause]. But we deal here with a classification based upon the race of the participants, which must be viewed in light of the historical fact that the central purpose of the Fourteenth Amendment was to eliminate racial discrimination emanating from official sources in the States. This strong policy renders racial classifications 'constitutionally suspect' [Bolling v. Sharpe], and subject to the 'most rigid scrutiny' [Korematsu], and 'in most circumstances irrelevant' to any constitutionally acceptable legislative purpose [Hirabayashi]. Thus it is that racial classifications have been held invalid in a variety of contexts. We deal here with a racial classification embodied in a criminal statute. . . . Our inquiry, therefore, is whether there clearly appears in the relevant materials some overriding statutory purpose requiring the proscription of the specified conduct when engaged in by a white person and a Negro, but not otherwise. Without such justification the racial classification [here] is reduced to an invidious discrimination forbidden by the Equal Protection Clause."

Compare a statement later in Justice White's opinion: "There is involved here an exercise of the state police power which trenches upon the constitutionally protected freedom from invidious official discrimination based on race. Such a law, even though enacted pursuant to a valid state interest, bears a heavy burden of justification, as we have said, and will be upheld only if it is necessary, and not

The State finds support for its "equal application" theory in the decision of the Court in Pace v. Alabama, 106 U.S. 583 (1883). In that case, the Court upheld a conviction under an Alabama statute forbidding adultery or fornication between a white person and a Negro which imposed a greater penalty than that of a statute proscribing similar conduct by members of the same race. The Court reasoned that the statute could not be said to discriminate against Negroes because the punishment for each participant in the offense was the same. However, as recently as the 1964 Term, in rejecting the reasoning of that case, we stated: "Pace represents a limited view of the Equal Protection Clause which has not withstood analysis in the subsequent decisions of this Court." McLaughlin v. Florida. . . .

There can be no question but that Virginia's miscegenation statutes rest solely upon distinctions drawn according to race. The statutes proscribe generally accepted conduct if engaged in by members of different races. . . . At the very least, the Equal Protection Clause demands that racial classifications, especially suspect in criminal statutes, be subjected to the "most rigid scrutiny" [Korematsu], and, if they are ever to be upheld, they must be shown to be necessary to the accomplishment of some permissible state objective, independent of the racial discrimination which it was the object of the Fourteenth Amendment to eliminate. . . .

There is patently no legitimate overriding purpose independent of invidious racial discrimination which justifies this classification. The fact that Virginia prohibits only interracial marriages involving white persons demonstrates that the racial classifications must stand on their own justification, as measures designed to maintain White Supremacy.[2] We have consistently de-

---

merely rationally related, to the accomplishment of a permissible state policy." Is there a significant shift in emphasis in that second passage? Most of the strict scrutiny formulations speak of legislative ends and require that there be compelling, overriding justification. But the second passage emphasizes means—"necessary" rather than merely rational means—to the accomplishment of a "permissible" state end. Compare the other areas of a strict scrutiny under the equal protection clause below, secs. 3–5, suggesting that strict scrutiny requires both a "compelling" end and carefully tailored, "necessary" means. Is strict scrutiny in the racial area similarly concerned with both ends and means?

Justice Stewart's concurrence in McLaughlin, joined by Justice Douglas, stated: "[T]he Court implies that a criminal law of the kind here involved might be constitutionally valid if a State could show 'some overriding statutory purpose.' This is an implication in which I cannot join, because I cannot conceive of a valid legislative purpose under our Constitution for a state law which makes the color of a person's skin the test of whether his conduct is a criminal offense. . . . There might be limited room under the Equal Protection Clause for a civil law requiring the keeping of racially segregated public records for statistical or other valid public purposes. Cf. Tancil v. Woolls [below]. But we deal here with a criminal law which imposes criminal punishment. And I think it is simply not possible for a state law to be valid under our Constitution which makes the criminality of an act depend upon the race of the actor. Discrimination of that kind is invidious per se."

2. Appellants point out that the State's concern in these statutes, as expressed in the words of the 1924 Act's title, "An Act to Preserve Racial Integrity," extends only to the integrity of the white race. While Virginia prohibits whites from marrying any nonwhite (subject to the exception for the descendants of Pocahontas), Negroes, Orientals, and any other racial class may intermarry without statutory interference. Appellants contend that this distinction renders Virginia's miscegenation statutes arbitrary and un-

nied the constitutionality of measures which restrict the rights of citizens on account of race. There can be no doubt that restricting the freedom to marry solely because of racial classifications violates the central meaning of the Equal Protection Clause.

These statutes also deprive the Lovings of liberty without due process of law in violation of the Due Process Clause of the Fourteenth Amendment. . . . Marriage is one of the "basic civil rights of man," fundamental to our very existence and survival. [Skinner v. Oklahoma.] To deny this fundamental freedom on so unsupportable a basis as the racial classifications embodied in these statutes, classifications so directly subversive of the principle of equality at the heart of the Fourteenth Amendment, is surely to deprive all the State's citizens of liberty without due process of law. . . .

Reversed.

Mr. Justice STEWART, concurring.

I have previously expressed the belief that "it is simply not possible for a state law to be valid under our Constitution which makes the criminality of an act depend upon the race of the actor." McLaughlin v. Florida (concurring opinion). Because I adhere to that belief, I concur in the judgment of the Court.

OTHER RACIAL CLASSIFICATIONS: SOME EXAMPLES AND QUESTIONS

Introduction. "Our Constitution is color-blind," insisted the first Justice Harlan's dissent in Plessy v. Ferguson (sec. 2B below). Over the years, some Justices have suggested a per se rule invalidating all governmental distinctions among individuals because of race. And some commentators have argued that such a total ban on racial classifications is the most persuasive justification for a number of Court decisions—e. g., the invalidation of racial segregation in public facilities generally after the 1954 decision in the School Segregation Case (sec. 2B below). But, as the preceding cases illustrate, the Court has not stated so comprehensive a prohibition; rather, racial classifications are ordinarily "suspect," must be subjected to "the most rigid scrutiny," and bear a "very heavy burden of justification." Consider, in light of the foregoing cases and the materials which follow, when—if ever—racial criteria are or should be constitutionally permissible. What justification is strong enough to survive the strict scrutiny avowed by the Court in these cases? [1] Were the following cases proper applications of the "suspect classification"-strict scrutiny approach?

reasonable even assuming the constitutional validity of an official purpose to preserve "racial integrity." We need not reach this contention because we find the racial classifications in these statutes repugnant to the Fourteenth Amendment, even assuming an even-handed state purpose to protect the "integrity" of all races. [Footnote by the Court.]

1. Do strict scrutiny criteria or results change when racial criteria are used for "benign" purposes? May (or must) a state use racial classifications when the purpose or effect of the law is remedial or compensatory? Does benignness of purpose provide the strong justification demanded by the strict scrutiny standard? Or does benignness of purpose justify substituting a rea-

1. *Identification of political candidates.* ANDERSON v. MARTIN, 375 U.S. 399 (1964), invalidated a state law requiring that every candidate's race appear on the ballot. The Court rejected the defense that the requirement was nondiscriminatory because it applied to candidates of all races. Justice Clark's opinion for a unanimous Court stated that "by directing the citizen's attention to the single consideration of race or color, the State indicated that a candidate's race or color is an important—perhaps paramount—consideration in the citizen's choice, which may decisively influence the citizen to cast his ballot along racial lines. . . . The vice lies [in] the placing of the power of the State behind a racial classification that induces racial prejudice at the polls."

What if it were argued that racial designations helped elect more minority candidates—that, while making most voters more race conscious and inducing majority race voters to reject minority candidates, it induced minority voters to vote for more candidates of their own race? Should that argument satisfy the "very heavy burden of justification"?

2. *Public security as justification.* To what extent may arguments emphasizing national emergencies or local order justify racial ingredients in regulatory controls? Recall the Korematsu case, above, and note LEE v. WASHINGTON, 390 U.S. 333 (1968), a per curiam approval of a federal court order holding unconstitutional Alabama statutes requiring racial segregation in prisons and jails and establishing a schedule for desegregation. The one paragraph affirmance noted Alabama's argument "that the specific orders directing desegregation of prisons and jails make no allowance for the necessities of prison security and discipline" and commented that "we do not so read" the District Court order, "which when read as a whole we find unexceptionable." A separate concurring paragraph, by Justices Black, Harlan, and Stewart, elaborated: "[W]e wish to make explicit [that] prison authorities have the right, acting in good faith and in particularized circumstances, to take into account racial tensions in maintaining security, discipline, and good order in prisons and jails. We are unwilling to assume that state or local prison authorities might mistakenly regard such an explicit pronouncement as evincing any dilution of this Court's firm commitment to the Fourteenth Amendment's prohibition of racial discrimination."

3. *Official records.* In per curiam orders in Tancil v. Woolls and Virginia Board of Elections v. Hamm, 379 U.S. 19 (1964), the Court summarily affirmed decisions (a) invalidating laws requiring separate lists of whites and Blacks in voting, tax and property records, but (b) sustaining a law requiring that every divorce decree indicate the race of the husband and wife. The District Judge stated that "the designation of race [may] in certain records serve a useful purpose"—for example, "for identification or statistical use." He found no such purpose in the separate records law: it served "no other purpose than to classify and distinguish official records on the basis of race." The divorce law requirement, on the other hand, aided "vital statistics."

---

sonableness standard for that of strict scrutiny? Questions such as these are not pursued in this group of notes; they are postponed to the concluding notes in sec. 2B and to sec. 2C.

4. *Special traits.* Consider the comment by Justice Douglas in his book, We the Judges (1956), at 399: "Experience shows that liquor has a devastating effect on the North American Indian and Eskimo. It is, therefore, commonly provided in the United States and Canada that no liquor should be sold to those races. Other regulations based on race may likewise be justified by reason of the special traits of those races, such, for example, as their susceptibility to particular diseases. [W]hat at first blush may seem to be an invidious discrimination may on analysis be found to have plausible grounds justifying it." Is the justification sufficient if the grounds are "plausible"? Are the traits possessed by every member of the race? If not, can such regulations be challenged for overinclusiveness under the strict scrutiny appropriate to racial classifications?

5. *Racial classifications and lawmaking processes.* Under the Akron City Charter, most City Council measures became effective after a short time period, subject to repeal by referendum initiated by 10 percent of the voters. After the City Council had adopted a fair housing ordinance, the City Charter was amended by popular vote to provide for an automatic referendum procedure in certain cases: the amendment, § 137, provided that any ordinance regulating real estate transactions "on the basis of race, color, religion, national origin or ancestry must first be approved by a majority of the electors voting on the question at a regular or general election before said ordinance shall be effective." That charter amendment was held unconstitutional in HUNTER v. ERICKSON, 393 U.S. 385 (1969). Justice White's majority opinion stated that § 137 "makes an explicitly racial classification" which "obviously made it substantially more difficult to secure enactment of ordinances subject to § 137." Was there truly a "suspect" classification properly triggering strict scrutiny? Consider Justice White's explanation:

"It is true that the section draws no distinctions among racial and religious groups. Negroes and whites, Jews and Catholics are all subject to the same requirements if there is housing discrimination against them which they wish to end." Nevertheless, the amendment "disadvantages those who would benefit from laws barring racial, religious, or ancestral discriminations as against those who would bar other discriminations or who would otherwise regulate the real estate market in their favor. The automatic referendum system does not reach housing discrimination on sexual or political grounds, or against those with children or dogs, nor does it affect tenants seeking more heat or better maintenance from landlords, nor those seeking rent control, urban renewal, public housing, or new building codes. Moreover, although the law on its face treats Negro and white, Jew and gentile in an identical manner, the reality is that the law's impact falls on the minority. The majority needs no protection against discrimination and if it did, a referendum might be bothersome but no more than that. Like the law requiring specification of candidates' race on the ballot" [see note 1 above], the amendment "places special burdens on racial minorities within the governmental process."

In a concurring opinion, Justice Harlan, joined by Justice Stewart, agreed that § 137 was "discriminatory on its face" and could not meet the heavy burden of justification. He emphasized that the charter amendment did not attempt to allocate governmental power on the basis of any general, neutral principle. But he pointed out that the 10 percent referendum provision, by

contrast, was valid, even though it "might occasionally operate to disadvantage Negro political interests." That was a "neutral" provision, and the mere fact that a minority group might lose an important political battle did not constitute a denial of equal protection. Justice Black dissented.

Suppose § 137 had included a number of other "delicate areas" in which the city had decided "to move slowly." Would such a broadened provision be invalid under the Hunter reasoning? Compare the Court's disposition of a "neutral" state constitutional amendment in effect barring fair housing laws, in Reitman v. Mulkey, 387 U.S. 369 (1967), chap. 11, sec. 2, below.[2]

B. RACIAL SEGREGATION

THE "SEPARATE BUT EQUAL" DOCTRINE

1. *Plessy v. Ferguson.* In PLESSY v. FERGUSON, 163 U.S. 537 (1896), the Court sustained a Louisiana law of 1890 requiring "equal but separate accommodations" for white and Black railroad passengers.[1] Justice Brown's majority opinion, after finding the 13th Amendment inapplicable, stated: "The object of the [14th] Amendment was undoubtedly to enforce the absolute equality of the two races before the law, but in the nature of things it could not have been intended to abolish distinctions based upon color, or to enforce social, as distinguished from political equality, or a commingling of the two races upon terms unsatisfactory to either. Laws permitting, and even requiring, their separation in places where they are liable to be brought into contact do not necessarily imply the inferiority of either race to the other, and have been generally, if not universally, recognized as within the competency of the state legislatures in the exercise of their police power. The most common instance of this is connected with the establishment of separate schools for white and colored children, which have been [upheld] even by courts of States where the political rights of the colored race have been longest and most earnestly enforced.[2] . . . Laws forbidding the intermarriage of the two races may be said in a technical sense to interfere with the freedom of contract, and yet have been universally recognized as within the police power of the state. . . . The distinction between laws interfering with the political equality of the negro and those requiring the separation of the two races in schools, theaters, and railway carriages has been frequently drawn by this Court. [E. g., Strauder.] . . .

---

2. For additional consideration of why racial classifications are ordinarily "suspect," when classifications are "racial," and whether all racial classifications should be "suspect," see sec. 2C below.

For an unsuccessful effort to rely on Hunter in the context of "wealth" rather than race classifications, see James v. Valtierra, sec. 5 below.

1. Plessy, the challenger, alleged that he was "seven-eighths Caucasian and one-eighth African blood; that the mixture of colored blood was not discernible in him; and that he was entitled to every right [of] the white race." He was arrested for refusing to leave a seat in a coach for whites.

2. See, e. g., Roberts v. City of Boston, 5 Cush. 198 (Mass.1850).

"[It is suggested] that the same argument that will justify the state legislature in requiring railways to provide separate accommodations for the two races will also authorize them to require separate cars to be provided for people whose hair is of a certain color, or who are aliens, or who belong to certain nationalities, or to enact laws requiring colored people to walk upon one side of the street, and white people upon the other, or requiring white men's houses to be painted white, and colored men's black, or their vehicles or business signs to be of different colors, upon the theory that one side of the street is as good as the other, or that a house or vehicle of one color is as good as one of another color. The reply to all this is that every exercise of the police power must be reasonable, and extend only to such laws as are enacted in good faith for the promotion of the public good, and not for the annoyance or oppression of a particular class. [E. g., Yick Wo.] . . .

"So far, then, as a conflict with the Fourteenth Amendment is concerned, the case reduces itself to the question whether the statute of Louisiana is a reasonable regulation, and with respect to this there must necessarily be a large discretion on the part of the legislature. In determining the question of reasonableness it is at liberty to act with reference to the established usages, customs, and traditions of the people, and with a view to the promotion of their comfort, and the preservation of the public peace and good order. Gauged by this standard, we cannot say that a law which authorizes or even requires the separation of the two races in public conveyances is unreasonable, or more obnoxious to the Fourteenth Amendment than the acts of Congress requiring separate schools for colored children in the District of Columbia, the constitutionality of which does not seem to have been questioned, or the corresponding acts of state legislatures.

"We consider the underlying fallacy of the plaintiff's argument to consist in the assumption that the enforced separation of the two races stamps the colored race with a badge of inferiority. If this be so, it is not by reason of anything found in the act, but solely because the colored race chooses to put that construction upon it. The argument necessarily assumes that if, as has been more than once the case, and is not unlikely to be so again, the colored race should become the dominant power in the state legislature, and should enact a law in precisely similar terms, it would thereby relegate the white race to an inferior position. We imagine that the white race, at least, would not acquiesce in this assumption. The argument also assumes that social prejudices may be overcome by legislation, and that equal rights cannot be secured to the negro except by an enforced commingling of the two races. We cannot accept this proposition. If the two races are to meet upon terms of social equality, it must be the result of natural affinities, a mutual appreciation of each other's merits, and a voluntary consent of individuals. . . . Legislation is powerless to eradicate racial instincts or to abolish distinctions based upon physical differences, and the attempt to do so can only result in accentuating the difficulties of the present situation. If the civil and political rights of both races be equal one cannot be inferior to the other civilly or politically. If one race be inferior to the other socially, the Constitution of the United States cannot put them upon the same plane."

The first Justice Harlan dissented: "In respect of civil rights, common to all citizens, the Constitution of the United States does not, I think, permit any public authority to know the race of those entitled to be protected in the

enjoyment of such rights. Every true man has pride of race, and under appropriate circumstances when the rights of others, his equals before the law, are not to be affected, it is his privilege to express such pride and to take such action based upon it as to him seems proper. But I deny that any legislative body or judicial tribunal may have regard to the race of citizens when the civil rights of those citizens are involved. . . .

"It was said in argument that the statute of Louisiana does not discriminate against either race, but prescribes a rule applicable alike to white and colored citizens. But this argument does not meet the difficulty. Every one knows that [the law] had its origin in the purpose, not so much to exclude white persons from railroad cars occupied by blacks, as to exclude colored people from coaches occupied by or assigned to white persons. . . The thing to accomplish was, under the guise of giving equal accommodation for whites and blacks, to compel the latter to keep to themselves while travelling in railroad passenger coaches. No one would be so wanting in candor as to assert the contrary. The fundamental objection, therefore, to the statute is that it interferes with the personal freedom of citizens. . . .

"The white race deems itself to be the dominant race in this country. And so it is, in prestige, in achievements, in education, in wealth and in power. So, I doubt not, it will continue to be for all time, if it remains true to its great heritage and holds fast to the principles of constitutional liberty. But in view of the Constitution, in the eye of the law, there is in this country no superior, dominant, ruling class of citizens. There is no caste here. Our Constitution is color-blind, and neither knows nor tolerates classes among citizens. . . . It is, therefore, to be regretted that this high tribunal, the final expositor of the fundamental law of the land, has reached the conclusion that it is competent for a State to regulate the enjoyment by citizens of their civil rights solely upon the basis of race. In my opinion, the judgment this day rendered will, in time, prove to be quite as pernicious as the decision made by this tribunal in the Dred Scott case. . . .

"The present decision [will] encourage the belief that it is possible, by means of state enactments, to defeat the beneficent purposes which the people of the United States had in view when they adopted the recent amendments of the Constitution . . . . Sixty millions of whites are in no danger from the presence here of eight millions of blacks. The destinies of the two races, in this country, are indissolubly linked together, and the interests of both require that the common government of all shall not permit the seeds of race hate to be planted under the sanction of law. What can more certainly arouse race hate, what more certainly create and perpetuate a feeling of distrust between these races, than state enactments, which, in fact, proceed on the ground that colored citizens are so inferior and degraded that they cannot be allowed to sit in public coaches occupied by white citizens? That, as all will admit, is the real meaning of such legislation as was enacted in Louisiana. . . .

"If evils will result from the commingling of the two races upon public highways established for the benefit of all, they will be infinitely less than those that will surely come from state legislation regulating the enjoyment of civil rights upon the basis of race. We boast of the freedom enjoyed by our

people above all other peoples. But it is difficult to reconcile that boast with a state of the law which, practically, puts the brand of servitude and degradation upon a large class of our fellow citizens,—our equals before the law. The thin disguise of 'equal' accommodations for passengers in railroad coaches will not mislead any one, nor atone for the wrong this day done."

2. *The 20th century attack on de jure segregation.* The modern legal attack on officially mandated segregation, led by the NAACP, began with efforts to show that the "separate but equal" doctrine of Plessy was vulnerable in the education provided for Black students seeking graduate and professional school education. The first in the sequence of modern school segregation cases that culminated in Brown v. Board of Education was Missouri ex rel. Gaines v. Canada, 305 U.S. 337 (1938). Gaines, a Black applicant, had been refused admission to the University of Missouri Law School because of his race. Missouri's defense to his suit for admission was that, pending the establishment of a Black law school in the state, it would pay Gaines' tuition in an out-of-state school. Chief Justice Hughes' opinion concluded that the State was obligated to furnish Gaines "within its borders facilities for legal education substantially equal to those which the State there offered for persons of the white race, whether or not other negroes sought the same opportunity." In the absence of such facilities, Gaines was entitled to be admitted to the existing state law school. Justices McReynolds and Butler dissented. Subsequent decisions dealing with segregated facilities in graduate and professional education are described in the Court's opinion in Brown, which follows.

BROWN v. BOARD OF EDUCATION

347 U.S. 483, 74 S.Ct. 686, 98 L.Ed. 873 (1954).

Appeal from the United States District Court for the District of Kansas.

Mr. Chief Justice WARREN delivered the opinion of the Court.

These cases come to us from the States of Kansas, South Carolina, Virginia, and Delaware.* They are premised on different facts and different local conditions, but a common legal question justifies their consideration together in this consolidated opinion.

In each of the cases, minors of the Negro race, through their legal representatives, seek the aid of the courts in obtaining admission to the public schools of their community on a nonsegregated basis. In each instance, they had been denied admission to schools attended by white children under laws requiring or permitting segregation according to race. This segregation was alleged to deprive the plaintiffs of the equal protection of the laws under the Fourteenth Amendment. In each of the cases, [the court below relied on]

---

* The cases decided together with Brown v. Board of Education of Topeka were Briggs v. Elliott (South Carolina); Davis v. County School Board of Prince Edward County, Virginia; and Gebhart v. Belton (Delaware). See also Bolling v. Sharpe, the companion case from the District of Columbia, below.

the so-called "separate but equal" doctrine announced by this Court in Plessy v. Ferguson. . . .

The plaintiffs contend that segregated public schools are not "equal" and cannot be made "equal," and that hence they are deprived of the equal protection of the laws. Because of the obvious importance of the question presented, the Court took jurisdiction. Argument was heard in the 1952 Term, and reargument was heard this Term on certain questions propounded by the Court.†

Reargument was largely devoted to the circumstances surrounding the adoption of the Fourteenth Amendment in 1868. It covered exhaustively consideration of the Amendment in Congress, ratification by the states, then existing practices in racial segregation, and the views of proponents and opponents of the Amendment. This discussion and our own investigation convince us that, although these sources cast some light, it is not enough to resolve the problem with which we are faced. At best, they are inconclusive. The most avid proponents of the post-War Amendments undoubtedly intended them to remove all legal distinctions among "all persons born or naturalized in the United States." Their opponents, just as certainly, were antagonistic to both the letter and the spirit of the Amendments and wished them to have the most limited effect. What others in Congress and the state legislatures had in mind cannot be determined with any degree of certainty.

An additional reason for the inconclusive nature of the Amendment's history, with respect to segregated schools, is the status of public education at that time. In the South, the movement toward free common schools, supported by general taxation, had not yet taken hold. Education of white children was largely in the hands of private groups. Education of Negroes was almost nonexistent, and practically all of the race were illiterate. In fact, any education of Negroes was forbidden by law in some states. Today, in contrast, many Negroes have achieved outstanding success in the arts and sciences as well as in the business and professional world. It is true that public school education [had] advanced further in the North, but the effect of the Amendment on Northern States was generally ignored in

† The first three questions propounded by the Court in its order at the end of the 1952 Term follow. [The 1952 Term was Chief Justice Vinson's last Term; Chief Justice Warren's tenure began with the 1953 Term.]

"1. What evidence is there that the Congress which submitted and the State legislatures and conventions which ratified the Fourteenth Amendment contemplated or did not contemplate, understood or did not understand, that it would abolish segregation in public schools?

"2. If neither the Congress in submitting nor the States in ratifying the Fourteenth Amendment understood that compliance with it would require the immediate abolition of segregation in public schools, was it nevertheless the understanding of the framers of the Amendment

"(a) that future Congresses might, in the exercise of their power under section 5 of the Amendment, abolish such segregation, or

"(b) that it would be within the judicial power, in light of future conditions, to construe the Amendment as abolishing such segregation of its own force?

"3. On the assumption that the answers to questions 2(a) and (b) do not dispose of the issue, is it within the judicial power, in construing the Amendment, to abolish segregation in public schools?" [Questions 4 and 5 were set for further argument in the Court's disposition of this case. Those questions appear in the footnote to the second Brown case, below.]

the congressional debates. Even in the North, the conditions of public education did not approximate those existing today. The curriculum was usually rudimentary; ungraded schools were common in rural areas; the school term was but three months a year in many states; and compulsory school attendance was virtually unknown. As a consequence, it is not surprising that there should be so little in the history of the Fourteenth Amendment relating to its intended effect on public education.

In the first cases in this Court construing the Fourteenth Amendment, decided shortly after its adoption, the Court interpreted it as proscribing all state-imposed discriminations against the Negro race.[1] The doctrine of "separate but equal" did not make its appearance in this Court until 1896 in the case of Plessy v. Ferguson, involving not education but transportation.[2] American courts have since labored with the doctrine for over half a century. In this Court, there have been six cases involving the "separate but equal" doctrine in the field of public education. In Cumming v. County Board of Education, 175 U.S. 528, and Gong Lum v. Rice, 275 U.S. 78, the validity of the doctrine itself was not challenged.[3] In more recent cases, all on the graduate school level, inequality was found in that specific benefits enjoyed by white students were denied to Negro students of the same educational qualifications. Missouri ex rel. Gaines v. Canada, 305 U.S. 337; Sipuel v. Oklahoma, 332 U.S. 631; Sweatt v. Painter, 339 U.S. 629; McLaurin v. Oklahoma State Regents, 339 U.S. 637.* In none of these cases was it necessary to reex-

1. Slaughter-House Cases, 16 Wall. 36, 67–72 (1873); Strauder v. West Virginia, 100 U.S. 303, 307–308 (1880) . . . . [Footnote by the Court.]

2. The doctrine apparently originated in Roberts v. City of Boston, 59 Mass. 198, 206 (1850), upholding school segregation against attack as being violative of a state constitutional guarantee of equality. Segregation in Boston public schools was eliminated in 1855. But elsewhere in the North segregation in public education has persisted until recent years. It is apparent that such segregation has long been a nationwide problem, not merely one of sectional concern. [Footnote by the Court.]

3. In the Cumming case, Negro taxpayers sought an injunction requiring the defendant school board to discontinue the operation of a high school for white children until the board resumed operation of a high school for Negro children. Similarly, in the Gong Lum case, the plaintiff, a child of Chinese descent, contended only that state authorities had misapplied the doctrine by classifying him with Negro children and requiring him to attend a Negro school. [Footnote by the Court.]

* The Sipuel case in 1948 reaffirmed the principles of the Gaines case, note 2 preceding this case. The Sweatt case in 1950 required the admission of Blacks to the University of Texas Law School even though the state had recently established a law school for Blacks. Chief Justice Vinson's opinion for the Court found no "substantial equality in the educational opportunities offered white and Negro law students by the State. In terms of number of the faculty, variety of courses and opportunity for specialization, size of the student body, scope of the library, availability of law review and similar activities, the University of Texas Law School is superior. What is more important, the University of Texas Law School possesses to a far greater degree those qualities which are incapable of objective measurement but which make for greatness in a law school. Such qualities, to name but a few, include reputation of the faculty, experience of the administration, position and influence of the alumni, standing in the community, traditions and prestige." He added that a law school "cannot be effective in isolation from the individuals and institutions with which the law interacts," and he noted that the newly established Black law school "excludes from its student body members of the racial groups which number 85% of the population of the state and include most of the lawyers, witnesses, jurors,

amine the doctrine to grant relief to the Negro plaintiff. And in Sweatt v. Painter, the Court expressly reserved decision on the question whether Plessy v. Ferguson should be held inapplicable to public education.

In the instant cases, that question is directly presented. Here, unlike Sweatt v. Painter, there are findings below that the Negro and white schools involved have been equalized or are being equalized, with respect to buildings, curricula, qualifications and salaries of teachers, and other "tangible" factors. Our decision, therefore, cannot turn on merely a comparison of these tangible factors in the Negro and white schools involved in each of the cases. We must look instead to the effect of segregation itself on public education.

In approaching this problem, we cannot turn the clock back to 1868 when the Amendment was adopted, or even to 1896 when Plessy v. Ferguson was written. We must consider public education in the light of its full development and its present place in American life throughout the Nation. Only in this way can it be determined if segregation in public schools deprives these plaintiffs of the equal protection of the laws.

Today, education is perhaps the most important function of state and local governments. Compulsory school attendance laws and the great expenditures for education both demonstrate our recognition of the importance of education to our democratic society. It is required in the performance of our most basic public responsibilities, even service in the armed forces. It is the very foundation of good citizenship. Today it is a principal instrument in awakening the child to cultural values, in preparing him for later professional training, and in helping him to adjust normally to his environment. In these days, it is doubtful that any child may reasonably be expected to succeed in life if he is denied the opportunity of an education. Such an opportunity, where the state has undertaken to provide it, is a right which must be made available to all on equal terms.

We come then to the question presented: Does segregation of children in public schools solely on the basis of race, even though the physical facilities and other "tangible" factors may be equal, deprive the children of the minority group of equal educational opportunities? We believe that it does.

In Sweatt v. Painter, in finding that a segregated law school for Negroes could not provide them equal educational opportunities, this Court relied in large part on "those qualities which are incapable of objective measurement but which make for greatness in a law school." In McLaurin v. Oklahoma State Regents, the Court, in requiring that a Negro admitted to a white graduate school be treated like all other students, again resorted to intangible con-

---

judges and other officials with whom petitioner would inevitably be dealing when he becomes a member of the Texas Bar."

The McLaurin case in 1950, finally, involved a Black student who had been admitted to a state university's graduate program not offered at the state's Black school, but had been required to sit in separate sections in or adjoining the classrooms, library and cafeteria facilities. Chief Justice Vinson's opinion for a unanimous Court found that the restrictions impaired the "ability to study, to engage in discussions and exchange views with other students and, in general, to learn his profession." In rejecting the argument that petitioner might in any event be ostracized by his fellow students, the Chief Justice stated that "there is a vast difference—a Constitutional difference —between restrictions imposed by the state [and] the refusal of individuals to commingle."

siderations: ". . . his ability to study, to engage in discussions and exchange views with other students, and, in general, to learn his profession." Such considerations apply with added force to children in grade and high schools. To separate them from others of similar age and qualifications solely because of their race generates a feeling of inferiority as to their status in the community that may affect their hearts and minds in a way unlikely ever to be undone. The effect of this separation on their educational opportunities was well stated by a finding in the Kansas case by a court which nevertheless felt compelled to rule against the Negro plaintiffs:

"Segregation of white and colored children in public schools has a detrimental effect upon the colored children. The impact is greater when it has the sanction of the law; for the policy of separating the races is usually interpreted as denoting the inferiority of the negro group. A sense of inferiority affects the motivation of a child to learn. Segregation with the sanction of law, therefore, has a tendency to [retard] the educational and mental development of negro children and to deprive them of some of the benefits they would receive in a racial[ly] integrated school system." [4] Whatever may have been the extent of psychological knowledge at the time of Plessy v. Ferguson, this finding is amply supported by modern authority.[5] Any language in Plessy v. Ferguson contrary to this finding is rejected.

We conclude that in the field of public education the doctrine of "separate but equal" has no place. Separate educational facilities are inherently unequal. Therefore, we hold that the plaintiffs and others similarly situated for whom the actions have been brought are, by reason of the segregation complained of, deprived of the equal protection of the laws guaranteed by the Fourteenth Amendment. This disposition makes unnecessary any discussion whether such segregation also violates the Due Process Clause of the Fourteenth Amendment.

Because these are class actions, because of the wide applicability of this decision, and because of the great variety of local conditions, the formulation of decrees in these cases presents problems of considerable complexity. On reargument, the consideration of appropriate relief was necessarily subordinated to the primary question—the constitutionality of segregation in public education. We have now announced that such segregation is a denial of the equal protection of the laws. In order that we may have the full assistance of the parties in formulating decrees, the cases will be restored to the docket, and the parties are requested to present further argument on

---

4. A similar finding was made in the Delaware case: "I conclude from the testimony that in our Delaware society, State-imposed segregation in education itself results in the Negro children, as a class, receiving educational opportunities which are substantially inferior to those available to white children otherwise similarly situated." [Footnote by the Court.]

5. K. B. Clark, Effect of Prejudice and Discrimination on Personality Development (Midcentury White House Conference on Children and Youth, 1950); Witmer and Kotinsky, Personality in the Making (1952), c. VI; Deutscher and Chein, The Psychological Effects of Enforced Segregation: A Survey of Social Science Opinion, 26 J.Psychol. 259 (1948); Chein, What are the Psychological Effects of Segregation Under Conditions of Equal Facilities?, 3 Int.J.Opinion and Attitude Res. 229 (1949); Brameld, Educational Costs, in Discrimination and National Welfare (McIver, ed., 1949), 44–48; Frazier, The Negro in the United States (1949), 674–681. And see generally Myrdal, An American Dilemma (1944). [Footnote by the Court.]

Questions 4 and 5 previously propounded by the Court for the reargument of this Term. [The questions appear in the footnote to the second Brown case, below.] . . .

It is so ordered.

————

BOLLING v. SHARPE, 347 U.S. 497 (1954): In this case, decided on the same day as Brown, the Court held that racial segregation in the District of Columbia public schools violated the due process clause of the Fifth Amendment. Chief Justice Warren's opinion stated: "The Fifth Amendment [does] not contain an equal protection clause. [But] the concepts of equal protection and due process, both stemming from our American ideal of fairness, are not mutually exclusive. The 'equal protection of the laws' is a more explicit safeguard of prohibited unfairness than 'due process of law,' and, therefore, we do not imply that the two are always interchangeable phrases. But, as this Court has recognized, discrimination may be so unjustifiable as to be violative of due process. Classifications based solely upon race must be scrutinized with particular care, since they are contrary to our traditions and hence constitutionally suspect. [E. g., Korematsu.] . . .

"Although the Court has not assumed to define 'liberty' with any great precision, that term is not confined to mere freedom from bodily restraint. Liberty under law extends to the full range of conduct which the individual is free to pursue, and it cannot be restricted except for a proper governmental objective. Segregation in public education is not reasonably related to any proper governmental objective, and thus it imposes on Negro children of the District of Columbia a burden that constitutes an arbitrary deprivation of their liberty in violation of the Due Process Clause. In view of our decision that the Constitution prohibits the states from maintaining racially segregated public schools, it would be unthinkable that the same Constitution would impose a lesser duty on the Federal Government."

————

SEGREGATION AND THE BROWN PRINCIPLE

1. *Legally compelled segregation in other public facilities.* After the 1954 decision in Brown v. Board of Education, the Court found segregation unconstitutional in other public facilities as well. Despite the emphasis on the school context in Brown, the results in the later cases were reached in curt per curiam orders, most simply citing Brown. See, e. g., Mayor of Baltimore v. Dawson, 350 U.S. 877 (1955) (beaches); Gayle v. Browder, 352 U.S. 903 (1956) (buses); Holmes v. City of Atlanta, 350 U.S. 879 (1955) (golf courses); New Orleans City Park Imp. Ass'n v. Detiege, 358 U.S. 54 (1958) (parks). Cf. Turner v. City of Memphis, 369 U.S. 350 (1962). In Johnson v. Virginia, 373 U.S. 61 (1963), petitioner had been convicted of contempt for refusal to comply with a state judge's order to move to a section of a courtroom reserved for Blacks. In reversing, the Supreme Court said: "Such a conviction cannot stand, for it is no longer open to question that a State may not constitutionally require segregation of public

facilities." See also Lee v. Washington, 390 U.S. 333 (1968), prohibiting segregated prison facilities, noted in sec. 2A above.

2. *The Brown rationale.* In light of the school segregation opinion, and the public facilities cases in note 1, what are the bases and justifications for Brown? [1] What is its scope?

a. *History.* Do the history and "central purpose" of the 14th Amendment justify the decision? Was the Court's treatment of the historical understanding adequate? Consider Professor Bickel's [2] observation that the ban on segregation might well have been an improper implication if the 14th Amendment were a statute but adding: "[W]e are dealing with a constitutional amendment, not a statute." He noted that the history of the 14th Amendment "rather clearly" demonstrates "that it was not expected in 1866 to apply to segregation." But his historical survey found "an awareness on the part of [the framers of the 14th Amendment] that it was *a constitution* they were writing, which led to a choice of language capable of growth," and he concluded that "the record of history, properly understood, left the way open to, in fact invited, a decision based on the moral and material state of the nation in 1954, not 1866."

b. *Impact on educational and psychological development.* Was the critical element in Brown the Court's endorsement of the finding that state-imposed segregation "has a tendency to retard the educational and mental development of Negro children"? Were empirical data central to the Court's holding? The reliance on social science evidence—and the quality of those data, then and now [3]—have been criticized. See, e. g., Professor Cahn's comment that "I would not have the constitutional rights of Negroes —or of other Americans—rest on any such flimsy foundation as some of the scientific demonstrations in these records. [Behavioral science findings] have an uncertain expectancy of life."

Was the critical element in the Court's decision the statement that segregation "generates a feeling of inferiority"? What are the critical elements in establishing such a conclusion? Social science data? Judicial notice? History? The intent of the legislators enacting segregation laws? The stereotypical assumption of Black inferiority—the assumption which supposedly provided the underpinnings for the general system of segregation?

1. For a sampling of the extensive commentary on the Brown opinion, see the articles reprinted in Selected Essays 1938–62 (1963), 463, 819, 844: Wechsler, "Toward Neutral Principles of Constitutional Law," 73 Harv.L.Rev. 1 (1959); Pollak, "Racial Discrimination and Judicial Integrity: A Reply to Professor Wechsler," 108 U.Pa.L. Rev. 1 (1959); C. L. Black, Jr., "The Lawfulness of the Segregation Decisions," 69 Yale L.J. 421 (1960). See also Bickel, "The Original Understanding and the Segregation Decision," 69 Harv.L.Rev. 1 (1955), Selected Essays 1938–62 (1963), 853.
For comments on the social science evidence in Brown, see Cahn, "Jurisprudence," 30 N.Y.U.L.Rev. 150 (1955);

K. B. Clark, "The Desegregation Cases," 5 Vill.L.Rev. 224 (1959); and K. B. Clark, "The Social Scientists, the Brown Decision, and Contemporary Confusion," in Argument (Friedman ed. 1969). See also Stell v. Chatham Bd. of Ed., 220 F.Supp. 667 (S.D.Ga. 1963, rev'd, 333 F.2d 55 (5th Cir. 1964).

2. The sources of all of the comments referred to in this note are cited in footnote 1.

3. For a recent review of the available (and controversial) data, see Goodman, "De Facto School Segregation: A Constitutional and Empirical Analysis," 70 Calif.L.Rev. 275 (1972).

The Black community's perception of the stigma imposed by segregation? Note Cahn's emphasis on "the most familiar and universally accepted standards of right and wrong" as demonstrating that "racial segregation under government auspices inevitably inflicts humiliation" and that "official humiliation of innocent, law-abiding citizens is psychologically injurious and morally evil." Can the Court properly rest a decision on "universal" moral standards without added support in empirical data or history?

Compare Professor Black's defense of the "lawfulness" of Brown, emphasizing that the southern cultural tradition during the period of enforced segregation makes it clear that "segregation is a massive intentional disadvantaging of the Negro race, as such, by state law." He commented: "[I]f a whole race of people finds itself confined within a system which is set up and continued for the very purpose of keeping it in an inferior station, and if the question is then solemnly propounded whether such a race is being treated 'equally,' I think we ought to exercise one of the sovereign prerogatives of philosophers—that of laughter." And the segregation system, he insisted, clearly answered that description. He noted: "Segregation is historically and contemporaneously associated in a functioning complex with practices which are indisputably and grossly discriminatory." "The purpose and impact of segregation in the southern regional culture," he added, were "matters of common notoriety, matters not so much for judicial notice as for the background knowledge of educated men who live in the world." Southern segregation at the time of Brown, he emphasized, was not "mutual separation of whites and Negroes," but rather "one in-group enjoying full normal communal life and one out-group that is barred from this life and forced into an inferior life of its own." That "regional culture" was properly determinative, he concluded: the question was not whether segregation is inevitably discriminatory, but whether "discrimination inheres in that segregation which is imposed by law in the twentieth century in certain specific states in the American Union. And that question has meaning and can find an answer only on the ground of history and of common knowledge about the facts of life."

Are positions such as Professor Cahn's or Professor Black's an adequate answer to Professor Wechsler's argument: "For me, assuming equal facilities, the question posed by state-enforced segregation is not one of discrimination at all. Its human and its constitutional dimensions lie entirely elsewhere, in the denial by the state of freedom to associate, a denial that impinges in the same way on any groups or races that may be involved." He asked: "Given a situation where the state must practically choose between denying the association to those individuals who wish it or imposing it on those who would avoid it, is there a basis in neutral principles for holding that the Constitution demands that the claims for association should prevail?"

c. *The scope of the holding.* In view of the emphasis on the impact of segregation on *educational* opportunity in Brown, should the Court have explained more fully the basis for its ultimate general principle "that a State may not constitutionally require segregation of public facilities," rather than resting that development largely on the per curiam orders noted in note 1, above? Do the considerations articulated in Brown, or the reasons that may justify its result, support a claim that de facto as well as de jure segregation in public schools is unconstitutional? Do they support the im-

position of an affirmative duty on school officials to achieve racial balance where schools are segregated because of residential patterns not compelled by law? Those problems of de facto segregation are considered further below, after a tracing of the developments in implementing the Brown decision.

BROWN v. BOARD OF EDUCATION
[BROWN II—THE IMPLEMENTATION DECISION]

349 U.S. 294, 75 S.Ct. 753, 99 L.Ed. 1083 (1955).

Mr. Chief Justice WARREN delivered the opinion of the Court.

These cases were decided on May 17, 1954. The opinions of that date, declaring the fundamental principle that racial discrimination in public education is unconstitutional, are incorporated herein by reference. All provisions of federal, state, or local law requiring or permitting such discrimination must yield to this principle. There remains for consideration the manner in which relief is to be accorded.

Because these cases arose under different local conditions and their disposition will involve a variety of local problems, we requested further argument on the question of relief.[1] In view of the nationwide importance of the decision, we invited the Attorney General of the United States and the Attorneys General of all states requiring or permitting racial discrimination in public education to present their views on that question. The parties, the United States, and the States of Florida, North Carolina, Arkansas, Oklahoma, Maryland, and Texas filed briefs and participated in the oral argument.

These presentations were informative and helpful to the Court in its consideration of the complexities arising from the transition to a system of public education freed of racial discrimination. The presentations also demonstrated that substantial steps to eliminate racial discrimination in public schools have already been taken, not only in some of the communities in which these cases arose, but in some of the states appearing as amici curiae, and in other states as well. . . .

---

1. Further argument was requested on the following questions, . . . previously propounded by the Court:

"4. Assuming it is decided that segregation in public schools violates the Fourteenth Amendment

"(a) would a decree necessarily follow providing that, within the limits set by normal geographic school districting, Negro children should forthwith be admitted to schools of their choice, or

"(b) may this Court, in the exercise of its equity powers, permit an effective gradual adjustment to be brought about from existing segregated systems to a system not based on color distinctions?

"5. On the assumption on which questions 4(a) and (b) are based, and assuming further that this Court will exercise its equity powers to the end described in question 4(b),

"(a) should this Court formulate detailed decrees in these cases;

"(b) if so, what specific issues should the decrees reach;

"(c) should this Court appoint a special master to hear evidence with a view to recommending specific terms for such decrees;

"(d) should this Court remand to the courts of first instance with directions to frame decrees in these cases, and if so what general directions should the decrees of this Court include and what procedures should the courts of first instance follow in arriving at the specific terms of more detailed decrees?" [Footnote by the Court.]

Full implementation of these constitutional principles may require solution of varied local school problems. School authorities have the primary responsibility for elucidating, assessing, and solving these problems; courts will have to consider whether the action of school authorities constitutes good faith implementation of the governing constitutional principles. Because of their proximity to local conditions and the possible need for further hearings, the courts which originally heard these cases can best perform this judicial appraisal. Accordingly, we believe it appropriate to remand the cases to those courts.

In fashioning and effectuating the decrees, the courts will be guided by equitable principles. Traditionally, equity has been characterized by a practical flexibility in shaping its remedies and by a facility for adjusting and reconciling public and private needs. These cases call for the exercise of these traditional attributes of equity power. At stake is the personal interest of the plaintiffs in admission to public schools as soon as practicable on a nondiscriminatory basis. To effectuate this interest may call for elimination of a variety of obstacles in making the transition to school systems operated in accordance with the constitutional principles set forth in our May 17, 1954, decision. Courts of equity may properly take into account the public interest in the elimination of such obstacles in a systematic and effective manner. But it should go without saying that the vitality of these constitutional principles cannot be allowed to yield simply because of disagreement with them.

While giving weight to these public and private considerations, the courts will require that the defendants make a prompt and reasonable start toward full compliance with our May 17, 1954, ruling. Once such a start has been made, the courts may find that additional time is necessary to carry out the ruling in an effective manner. The burden rests upon the defendants to establish that such time is necessary in the public interest and is consistent with good faith compliance at the earliest practicable date. To that end, the courts may consider problems related to administration, arising from the physical condition of the school plant, the school transportation system, personnel, revision of school districts and attendance areas into compact units to achieve a system of determining admission to the public schools on a nonracial basis, and revision of local laws and regulations which may be necessary in solving the foregoing problems. They will also consider the adequacy of any plans the defendants may propose to meet these problems and to effectuate a transition to a racially nondiscriminatory school system. During this period of transition, the courts will retain jurisdiction of these cases.

The [cases are accordingly remanded to the lower courts] to take such proceedings and enter such orders and decrees consistent with this opinion as are necessary and proper to admit to public schools on a racially nondiscriminatory basis with all deliberate speed the parties to these cases.   .   .   .

THE IMPLEMENTATION OF BROWN: FROM DESEGREGATION TO INTEGRATION

Introduction. After its promulgation of general guidelines in Brown II, with the insistence on "a prompt and reasonable start" and the demand for full transition to nondiscriminatory school admissions "with all deliberate speed," the Court maintained silence about implementation for several years. Enforcement of the desegregation requirement was left largely to lower court litigation—and to the political arena. During the early post-Brown years of "massive resistance" in the South, the Court broke its silence only rarely, though firmly: in Cooper v. Aaron, 358 U.S. 1 (1958) (chap. 1 above), all of the Justices signed an opinion reaffirming the Brown principle in the face of the official resistance in Little Rock, Arkansas. And in Griffin v. Prince Edward County School Board, 377 U.S. 218 (1964) (noted in sec. 2A above), the Court held unconstitutional an effort to avoid desegregation "by a combination of closed public schools and county grants to white children" to attend private schools. (Prince Edward County, a county involved in one of the companion cases to Brown, had closed its public schools in 1959.)

During the sixties (after the doctrine of the Brown decision had been adopted by the other branches of the national government through the Civil Rights Act of 1964), Court rulings on implementation came with greater frequency, specificity, and urgency. Court actions during the early sixties were limited to invalidations of impermissible student transfer plans and expressions of mounting impatience with the pace of desegregation (note 1 below). But that pace remained slow during most of the sixties: widely used and officially approved "freedom of choice" plans had relatively little impact on the racial composition of schools. The first major reentry by the Court into implementation problems came in 1968, in the Green case (note 2 below), which rejected freedom of choice plans where they failed to produce a "unitary, nonracial system of public education." And beginning with the Swann case in 1971, the Court has repeatedly spoken in detail about remedial requirements.

In all of these cases—even the 1970's ones involving northern communities—the Court has purported to speak solely about remedies for prior purposeful discrimination: dismantling the dual school systems established by state-wide de jure segregation in the South; undoing the effects of localized hostile racial action in the North. But the Court has been willing to pursue the consequences of past de jure discriminations very far, both in time and in areas of impact. And the Court has put an increasing emphasis on *results* in measuring success of efforts to eliminate past discriminations. In examining those developments, consider whether the purportedly "remedial" decisions in fact rest on changing perceptions of substantive rights. Do the far-reaching demands for eliminating past discrimination make the distinction between de jure and de facto segregation increasingly unjustifiable, as Justice Powell suggested in his dissent in the Keyes case, below? Or is the continued insistence on finding some formal evidence of past de jure discrimination an indication that condemnation of purposeful discrimination exhausts the command of the 14th Amendment? [1]

1. For an early examination of potential evasion and delaying devices, see Leflar and Davis, "Segregation in the Public Schools—1953," 67 Harv.L.Rev.

In the 1950's, a lower court stated that the Constitution "does not require integration. It merely forbids [segregation]." Was that true at the time of the Brown decisions? Is it still true, in view of the condemnation of freedom of choice plans in the Green case, note 2 below, and the emphasis there on producing a "unitary" system? Note the distinction between "process-oriented" and "result-oriented" antidiscrimination remedies by Professor Fiss:[2] the process orientation "emphasizes the purification of the decisional process," banning decisions based on racial criteria; the result-oriented approach "emphasizes the achievement of certain results"—for example, achieving racial integration rather than merely refraining from racially-based pupil assignments. Do the implementation decisions which follow indicate a shift from process orientation to result orientation? Does the Constitution justify an exclusive emphasis on result, whether or not there was a past impurity in the process—the impurity of purposeful discrimination?

     1. *Unacceptable transfer plans.* Those southern school districts who sought to comply with the mandate to abolish dual school systems by adopting rezoning plans typically tried to soften the impact of rezoning by permitting students in a school in which their race was in the minority to transfer to schools in which they would be in the majority. The Court unanimously struck down minority-to-majority transfer plans in GOSS v. BOARD OF EDUCATION, 373 U.S. 683 (1963). Justice Clark's opinion held that "transfer plans being based solely on racial factors which, under their terms, inevitably lead towards segregation of the students by race," were unconstitutional under the standards of Brown II. Racial classifications, he reminded, are "obviously irrelevant and invidious." That first Court reinvolvement with the details of desegregation came in the context of mounting impatience with the pace. As the Goss Court said, Brown II had been decided eight years earlier and "the context in which we must interpret and apply [its] language to plans for desegregation has been significantly altered."[3]

377 (1954), Selected Essays 1938–62 (1963), 897. For a survey of the experience in the lower courts in the years immediately after Brown, see McKay. "With All Deliberate Speed," 31 N.Y. U.L.Rev. 991 (1956) and 43 Va.L.Rev. 1205 (1957), and Note, "Implementation of Desegregation by the Lower Courts," 71 Harv.L.Rev. 486 (1958). For a review of the problems in the years before the Court reentered the picture, see Bickel, "A Decade of School Desegregation," 64 Colum.L. Rev. 193 (1964). For a subsequent evaluation by that observer, see The Supreme Court and the Idea of Progress (1970). See also the Fiss articles, footnote 2 below, and Kirp and Youdof, Educational Policy and the Law (1974).

2. Fiss, "The Fate of an Idea Whose Time Has Come: Antidiscrimination Law in the Second Decade After Brown v. Board of Education," 41 U.

Chi.L.Rev. 742 (1974). See also Fiss, "School Desegregation: The Uncertain Path of the Law," 4 Philosophy & Public Affairs 3 (1974).

3. For a fuller expression of that impatience, the Goss Court referred to a case decided a week earlier, Watson v. City of Memphis, 373 U.S. 526 (1963). In holding that Memphis could not rely on Brown II to justify delay in desegregating municipal recreational facilities, Justice Goldberg commented in Watson: "Given the extended time which has elapsed, it is far from clear that the mandate of the second Brown decision requiring that desegregation proceed with 'all deliberate speed' would today be fully satisfied by types of plans or programs for desegregation of public educational facilities which eight years ago might have been deemed sufficient. Brown never contemplated that the concept of 'deliberate

2.　*"Freedom of choice" and the Green case.*　The decision in GREEN v. COUNTY SCHOOL BOARD, 391 U.S. 430 (1968), marked a major turning point in the Court's role in—and requirements for—desegregation. For the first time since Brown II, the Court issued a detailed opinion on the question of remedies.　And that opinion, in focusing on the effects rather than the purpose and good faith of desegregation efforts, raised important new questions about underlying substantive doctrine as well as remedies. At the time of Green, freedom of choice plans had become commonplace in the South.　School districts argued that good faith plans of that variety, employing no improper pressures on students and parents, adequately complied with the Brown mandate, since students were able to attend schools of their own choice without encountering racial barriers.　The opponents of the plans emphasized that desegregation under "freedom of choice" had not significantly changed the racial composition of the formerly dual school system: most formerly Black and white schools were still identifiable as such. The opponents insisted that the constitutional mandate was not merely the elimination of formal racial barriers but the abolition of racially identifiable schools.　In short, in the context of formerly de jure segregated schools, the freedom of choice issue sharply presented the question of whether the 14th Amendment merely prohibited segregation—the elimination of formal racial barriers—or compelled integration—the creation of racially mixed schools. In that context, the Court's answer was clear: its emphasis shifted from "purification of the decisional process" to "achievement of a certain result," [4] albeit on the theory that achieving results was the only acceptable evidence that the process had been purified.

The Green case involved a small school district with two schools, in a county where about half the population was Black and where there was no significant residential segregation.　The district had adopted a freedom of choice plan in 1965 to remain eligible for federal financial aid—a plan which had not resulted in any significant change in the racial composition of the schools.　After three years of operation, no white child had chosen to attend a former Black school and about 85% of the Black children remained in all-Black schools.　Under these circumstances, the unanimous Court found the plan to be an inadequate compliance with desegregation requirements. Justice Brennan's majority opinion emphasized that "[r]acial identification of the system's schools" remained "complete" : "The pattern of separate 'white' and 'Negro' schools in the New Kent County school system [is] precisely the pattern of segregation to which Brown I and Brown II were particularly addressed."　In effect, state officials "operated a dual system, part 'white' and part 'Negro.' "　He proceeded to review the evolution of implementation

---

speed' would countenance indefinite delay in elimination of racial barriers in schools . . . ."

4.　See Fiss, 41 U.Chi.L.Rev. 742 (1974) (footnote 2 above).　The increasing emphasis on affirmative obligations to overcome past de jure segregation, on results rather than process, had come somewhat earlier in lower courts and in HEW guidelines issued under the 1964 Civil Rights Act.　See, e. g., the extensive discussion of the "duty to desegregate"-"duty to integrate" distinction in United States v. Jefferson County Board of Education, 372 F.2d 836 (5th Cir. 1966), aff'd en banc, 380 F.2d 385, cert. denied, 389 U.S. 840 (1967).　See also Dunn, "Title VI, the Guidelines, and School Desegregation in the South," 53 Va.L.Rev. 42 (1967), and Note, "The Courts, HEW, and Southern School Desegregation," 77 Yale L.J. 321 (1967).

requirements since Brown II—and suggested a change in emphasis: "It was such dual systems that 14 years ago Brown I held unconstitutional and a year later Brown II held must be abolished; school boards operating such school systems were *required* by Brown II 'to effectuate a transition to a racially nondiscriminatory school system.' It is of course true that for the time immediately after Brown II the concern was with making the initial break in a long-established pattern of excluding Negro children from schools attended by white children. The principal focus was on obtaining for those Negro children courageous enough to break with tradition a place in the 'white' schools. Under Brown II that immediate goal was only the first step, however. The transition to a unitary, nonracial system of public education was and is the ultimate end to be brought about . . . .

"It is against this background [that] we must measure the effectiveness of respondent School Board's 'freedom-of-choice' plan to achieve that end. The School Board contends that it has fully discharged its obligation by adopting a plan by which every student, regardless of race, may 'freely' choose the school he will attend. The Board attempts to cast the issue in its broadest form by arguing that its 'freedom-of-choice' plan may be faulted only by reading the Fourteenth Amendment as universally requiring 'compulsory integration,' a reading it insists the wording of the Amendment will not support. But that argument ignores the thrust of Brown II. In the light of the command of that case, what is involved here is the question whether the Board has achieved the 'racially nondiscriminatory school system' Brown II held must be effectuated in order to remedy the established unconstitutional deficiencies of its segregated system. In the context of the state-imposed segregated pattern of long standing, the fact that in 1965 the Board opened the doors of the former 'white' school to Negro children and of the 'Negro' school to white children merely begins, not ends, our inquiry whether the Board has taken steps adequate to abolish its dual, segregated system. Brown II was a call for dismantling of well-entrenched dual systems tempered by an awareness that complex and multifaceted problems would arise which would require time and flexibility for their successful resolution. School boards such as the respondent then operating state-compelled dual systems were nevertheless clearly charged with the affirmative duty to take whatever steps might be necessary to convert to a unitary system in which racial discrimination would be eliminated root and branch. The constitutional rights of Negro school children articulated in Brown I permit no less than this; and it was to this end that Brown II commanded school boards to bend their efforts.[5]

"In determining whether respondent School Board met that command by adopting its 'freedom-of-choice' plan, it is relevant that this first step did not come until some 11 years after Brown I was decided and 10 years after Brown II directed the making of a 'prompt and reasonable start.' This deliberate perpetuation of the unconstitutional dual system can only have compounded the harm of such a system. Such delays are no longer tolerable. . . . Moreover, a plan that at this late date fails to provide meaningful assurance

5. " 'We bear in mind that the court has not merely the power but the duty to render a decree which will so far as possible eliminate the discriminatory effects of the past as well as bar like discrimination in the future.' Louisiana v. United States, 380 U.S. 145, 154 . . .." [Footnote by the Court.]

of prompt and effective disestablishment of a dual system is also intolerable.
. . . The burden on a school board today is to come forward with a plan
that promises realistically to work, and promises realistically to work *now*.

"We do not hold that 'freedom of choice' can have no place in [a
desegregation] plan. We do not hold that a 'freedom-of-choice' plan might
of itself be unconstitutional, although that argument has been urged upon us.
Rather, all we decide today is that in desegregating a dual system a plan
utilizing 'freedom of choice' is not an end in itself. As Judge Sobeloff has
put it, ' "Freedom of choice" is not a sacred talisman; it is only a means
to a constitutionally required end—the abolition of the system of segregation
and its effects. If the means prove effective, it is acceptable, but if it fails
to undo segregation, other means must be used to achieve this end. The
school officials have the continuing duty to take whatever action may be
necessary to create a "unitary, nonracial system." ' . . . Although the
general experience under 'freedom of choice' to date has been such as to
indicate its ineffectiveness as a tool of desegregation, there may well be
instances in which it can serve as an effective device. [But] if there are
reasonably available other ways, such for illustration as zoning, promising
speedier and more effective conversion to a unitary, nonracial school system,
'freedom of choice' must be held unacceptable." Given the results in New
Kent County, with "a dual system" still in existence and the availability of
other courses "such as zoning," the school officials were required to "fashion
steps which promise realistically to convert promptly to a system without a
'white' school and a 'Negro' school, but just schools." [6]

In rural and small town areas with no significant residential segregation, the elimination of "freedom of choice" plans and their variants and
the adoption of geographic zoning largely eliminated racially identifiable
schools. But in large southern cities with substantial residential segregation—as in the North—geographic zoning alone could not substantially alter
the racial composition of schools. The Court turned to the problem of
metropolitan areas in the South in the Swann case in 1971, which follows.

---

6. In several other decisions from 1968
to 1970, the Court reemphasized the
implications of Green and its "at once"
requirement. On the opposition to any
further delay, see Alexander v. Holmes
County Bd. of Educ., 396 U.S. 19
(1969), Carter v. West Feliciana Parish
School Board, 396 U.S. 290 (1970), and
Northcross v. Board of Ed. of Memphis, 397 U.S. 323 (1970). Some of
these cases produced the first divisions
on the Court in the post-Brown II sequence. See also Monroe v. Board of
Commissioners, 391 U.S. 450 (1968), a
companion case to Green, invalidating
a "free transfer" plan in a geographically zoned system. Though the plan
was not limited to minority-to-majority
transfers, it permitted students to return, "at the implicit invitation of the
Board," to "the comfortable security of
the old, established discriminatory pattern." The Court was unpersuaded by
the school officials' argument that
without the "free transfer" choice,
"white students will flee the school
system altogether." On the problem
of "white flight" and resegregation,
note the comments in Bickel, The Supreme Court and the Idea of Progress
(1970) as well as the results of empirical studies of the 1970's.

SWANN v. CHARLOTTE-MECKLENBURG BOARD OF EDUCATION

402 U.S. 1, 91 S.Ct. 1267, 28 L.Ed.2d 554 (1971).

Certiorari to the United States Court of Appeals for the Fourth Circuit.
Mr. Chief Justice BURGER delivered the opinion of the Court. . . .

This case and those argued with it [1] arose in states having a long history of maintaining two sets of schools in a single school system deliberately operated to carry out a governmental policy to separate pupils in schools solely on the basis of race. That was what Brown v. Board of Education was all about. These cases present us with the problem of defining in more precise terms than heretofore the scope of the duty of school authorities and district courts in implementing Brown I. . . .

[This case involved desegregation in the school district covering the Charlotte, North Carolina, metropolitan area. Nearly 30% of the students were Black. By 1969, after several years of operation under a court-approved desegregation plan, about half of the Black students were in formerly white schools; the others remained in virtually all-Black schools. After Green, the District Court ordered that the school authorities prepare a more effective desegregation plan. After rejecting several of the proposed plans, that court appointed its own expert and accepted his plan, which involved some grouping of outlying white schools with inner city Black schools, and some busing of elementary school students in both directions. The Court of Appeals set aside that provision on the ground that "pairing and grouping of elementary schools would place an unreasonable burden on the board and the system's pupils."]

The problems encountered by the [lower courts] make plain that we should now try to amplify guidelines, however incomplete and imperfect, for the assistance of school authorities and courts. The failure of local authorities to meet their constitutional obligations aggravated the massive problem of converting from the state-enforced discrimination of racially separate school systems. This process has been rendered more difficult by changes since 1954 in the structure and patterns of communities, the growth of student population, movement of families, and other changes, some of which had marked impact on school planning, sometimes neutralizing or negating remedial action before it was fully implemented. Rural areas accustomed for half a century to the consolidated school systems implemented by bus transportation could make adjustments more readily than metropolitan areas . . . .

The objective today remains to eliminate from the public schools all vestiges of state-imposed segregation. . . . If school authorities fail in their affirmative obligations under [Brown and later] holdings, judicial authority may be invoked. Once a right and a violation have been shown, the scope of a district court's equitable powers to remedy past wrongs is broad, for breadth and flexibility are inherent in equitable remedies. . . .

1. McDaniel v. Barresi, 402 U.S. 39; Davis v. Board of School Comm'rs of Mobile County, 402 U.S. 33; Moore v. Charlotte-Mecklenburg Board of Education, 402 U.S. 47; North Carolina State Board of Education v. Swann, 402 U.S. 43. The Court's opinion in the last of these is noted below.

School authorities are traditionally charged with broad power to formulate and implement educational policy and might well conclude, for example, that in order to prepare students to live in a pluralistic society each school should have a prescribed ratio of Negro to white students reflecting the proportion for the district as a whole.   To do this as an educational policy is within the broad discretionary powers of school authorities;   absent a finding of a constitutional violation, however, that would not be within the authority of a federal court. . . .[2]

The central issue in this case is that of student assignment, and there are essentially four problem areas:

(1) to what extent racial balance or racial quotas may be used as an implement in a remedial order to correct a previously segregated system;

(2) whether every all-Negro and all-white school must be eliminated as an indispensable part of a remedial process of desegregation;

(3) what are the limits, if any, on the rearrangement of school districts and attendance zones, as a remedial measure; and

(4) what are the limits, if any, on the use of transportation facilities to correct state-enforced racial school segregation.

(1) *Racial Balances or Racial Quotas.* . . .

We are concerned in these cases with the elimination of the discrimination inherent in the dual school systems, not with myriad factors of human existence which can cause discrimination in a multitude of ways on racial, religious, or ethnic grounds.   The target of the cases from Brown I to the present was the dual school system.   The elimination of racial discrimination in public schools is a large task and one that should not be retarded by efforts to achieve broader purposes lying beyond the jurisdiction of school authorities. One vehicle can carry only a limited amount of baggage.   It would not serve the important objective of Brown I to seek to use school desegregation cases for purposes beyond their scope, although desegregation of schools ultimately will have impact on other forms of discrimination.   We do not reach in this case the question whether a showing that school segregation is a consequence of other types of state action, without any discriminatory action by the school authorities, is a constitutional violation requiring remedial action by a school desegregation decree. . . .

In this case it is urged that the District Court has imposed a racial balance requirement of 71%–29% on individual schools.   [The District Court opin-

---

2. The Court rejected the argument that federal judicial authority had been limited by Title IV of the Civil Rights Act of 1964.   For example, that Title had defined "desegregation" as "the assignment of students to public schools and within such schools without regard to their race, color, religion, or national origin, but 'desegregation' shall not mean the assignment of students to public schools in order to overcome racial imbalance."   The Court read the statutory provisions as simply intended "to foreclose any interpretation of the Act as expanding the *existing* powers of federal courts to enforce the Equal Protection Clause.

There is no suggestion of an intention to restrict those powers."   Chief Justice Burger found in the legislative history a concern that the Act "might be read as creating a right of action under the Fourteenth Amendment in the situation of so-called 'de facto segregation,' where racial imbalance exists in the schools but with no showing that this was brought about by discriminatory action of state authorities."   In that view, the Act provided no "material assistance in answering the question of remedy for state-imposed segregation in violation of Brown I."

ion] contains intimations that the "norm" is a fixed mathematical racial balance reflecting the pupil constituency of the system.   If we were to read the holding of the District Court to require, as a matter of substantive constitutional right, any particular degree of racial balance or mixing, that approach would be disapproved and we would be obliged to reverse.   The constitutional command to desegregate schools does not mean that every school in every community must always reflect the racial composition of the school system as a whole.

[But] the use made of mathematical ratios was no more than a starting point in the process of shaping a remedy, rather than an inflexible requirement.   .   .   .   As we said in Green, a school authority's remedial plan or a district court's remedial decree is to be judged by its effectiveness. Awareness of the racial composition of the whole school system is likely to be a useful starting point in shaping a remedy to correct past constitutional violations.   In sum, the very limited use made of mathematical ratios was within the equitable remedial discretion of the District Court.

(2) One-Race Schools.

The record in this case reveals the familiar phenomenon that in metropolitan areas minority groups are often found concentrated in one part of the city.   In some circumstances certain schools may remain all or largely of one race until new schools can be provided or neighborhood patterns change. Schools all or predominantly of one race in a district of mixed population will require close scrutiny to determine that school assignments are not part of state-enforced segregation.

In light of the above, it should be clear that the existence of some small number of one-race, or virtually one-race, schools within a district is not in and of itself the mark of a system which still practices segregation by law. [But the] court should scrutinize such schools, and the burden upon the school authorities will be to satisfy the court that their racial composition is not the result of present or past discriminatory action on their part.   .   .   .

(3) Remedial Altering of Attendance Zones.

The maps submitted in these cases graphically demonstrate that one of the principal tools employed by school planners and by courts to break up the dual school system has been a frank—and sometimes drastic—gerrymandering of school districts and attendance zones.   An additional step was pairing, "clustering," or "grouping" of schools with attendance assignments made deliberately to accomplish the transfer of Negro students out of formerly segregated Negro schools and transfer of white students to formerly all-Negro schools.   More often than not, these zones are neither compact [3] nor contiguous; indeed they may be on opposite ends of the city.   As an interim corrective measure, this cannot be said to be beyond the broad remedial powers of a court.

3.   The reliance of school authorities on the reference to the "revision of .   .   .   attendance areas into *compact* units," Brown II, at 300, is misplaced. The enumeration in that opinion of considerations to be taken into account by district courts was patently intended to be suggestive rather than exhaustive.   The decision in Brown II to remand the cases decided in Brown I to local courts for the framing of specific decrees was premised on a recognition that this Court could not at that time foresee the particular means which would be required to implement the constitutional principles announced.   .   .   .   [Footnote by Chief Justice Burger.]

Absent a constitutional violation there would be no basis for judicially ordering assignment of students on a racial basis. All things being equal, with no history of discrimination, it might well be desirable to assign pupils to schools nearest their homes. But all things are not equal in a system that has been deliberately constructed and maintained to enforce racial segregation. The remedy for such segregation may be administratively awkward, inconvenient, and even bizarre in some situations and may impose burdens on some; but all awkwardness and inconvenience cannot be avoided in the interim period when remedial adjustments are being made to eliminate the dual school systems.

No fixed or even substantially fixed guidelines can be established as to how far a court can go, but it must be recognized that there are limits. The objective is to dismantle the dual school system. "Racially neutral" assignment plans proposed by school authorities to a district court may be inadequate; such plans may fail to counteract the continuing effects of past school segregation resulting from discriminatory location of school sites or distortion of school size in order to achieve or maintain an artificial racial separation. When school authorities present a district court with a "loaded game board," affirmative action in the form of remedial altering of attendance zones is proper to achieve truly nondiscriminatory assignments. . . . We hold that the pairing and grouping of non-contiguous school zones is a permissible tool and such action is to be considered in light of the objectives sought. . . .

(4) Transportation of Students.

[No rigid guidelines are possible about the scope] of permissible transportation of students as an implement of a remedial decree . . . . Bus transportation has been an integral part of the public education system for years . . . . Eighteen million of the Nation's public school children, approximately 39%, were transported to their schools by bus in 1969–1970 in all parts of the country.

The importance of bus transportation as a normal and accepted tool of educational policy is readily discernible in this and the companion case. . . . The decree provided that the . . . trips for elementary school pupils average about seven miles and the District Court found that they would take "not over 35 minutes at the most." This system compares favorably with the transportation plan previously operated in Charlotte under which each day 23,600 students on all grade levels were transported an average of 15 miles one way for an average trip requiring over an hour. In these circumstances, we find no basis for holding that the local school authorities may not be required to employ bus transportation as one tool of school desegregation. Desegregation plans cannot be limited to the walk-in school.

An objection to transportation of students may have validity when the time or distance of travel is so great as to risk either the health of the children or significantly impinge on the educational process. District courts must weigh the soundness of any transportation plan in light of what is said in subdivisions (1), (2), and (3) above. . . . The reconciliation of competing values in a desegregation case is, of course, a difficult task with many sensitive facets but fundamentally no more so than remedial measures courts of equity have traditionally employed. . . .

At some point, these school authorities and others like them should have achieved full compliance with this Court's decision in Brown I. The systems will then be "unitary" in the sense required by our decisions in Green and Alexander.

It does not follow that the communities served by such systems will remain demographically stable, for in a growing, mobile society, few will do so. Neither school authorities nor district courts are constitutionally required to make year-by-year adjustments of the racial composition of student bodies once the affirmative duty to desegregate has been accomplished and racial discrimination through official action is eliminated from the system. This does not mean that federal courts are without power to deal with future problems; but in the absence of a showing that either the school authorities or some other agency of the State has deliberately attempted to fix or alter demographic patterns to affect the racial composition of the schools, further intervention by a district court should not be necessary.

[So ordered.] *

CONGRESS AND ANTI–BUSING LEGISLATION

In the wake of Swann, proposals for congressional curbs on busing proliferated. The several years of debate, summarized below, culminated in the enactment of anti-busing provisions in 1974. Are the proposed and enacted provisions within the constitutional power of Congress? On the basis of Article III? On the basis of § 5 of the 14th Amendment, under the rationale of Katzenbach v. Morgan, chap. 11, sec. 4, below?

1. *The efforts from 1972 to 1974.* The first major effort to curb busing came from Senator Griffin of Michigan, early in 1972. His proposed amendment to the Higher Education Act provided: "No court of the United States shall have jurisdiction to make any decision, enter any judgment or issue any order the effect of which would be to require that pupils be transported to or from school on the basis of their race, color, religion, or national origin." That effort failed by a very narrow margin.[1]

* In a companion case noted further below (sec. 2C), the Court held unconstitutional North Carolina's Anti-Busing Law prohibiting school assignments on the basis of race: that purportedly "color blind" directive was an impermissible restraint on the implementation of Brown. North Carolina State Board of Education v. Swann, 402 U.S. 43 (1971).

Note also the opinion by Chief Justice Burger as Circuit Justice denying a stay in another Southern busing case, handed down in the summer following the Swann decision. Winston-Salem/Forsyth County Bd. of Education v. Scott, 404 U.S. 1221 (1971). The Chief Justice commented on "the possibility" that the lower courts had misread the Swann opinion: If they "read this Court's opinions as requiring a fixed racial balance or quota, they would appear to have overlooked specific language [in Swann] to the contrary." The Chief Justice reproduced selected passages from the Swann case throughout this opinion written in his capacity as Circuit Justice.

1. The Griffin Amendment was defeated by a 50 to 47 vote on February 29, 1972. A similar amendment, by Senator Dole, lost the next day by an even narrower margin, 48 to 47. And on February 29, the Senate adopted the much milder Mansfield-Scott Amendment.

After the failure of his statutory route, Senator Griffin turned to the constitutional amendment technique. In the spring of 1973, hearings were held on

Soon after the defeat of the Griffin Amendment, President Nixon began a series of efforts to persuade Congress to adopt anti-busing proposals framed by the Administration. In a message to Congress in March 1972, he urged the legislators to use their powers under the 14th Amendment "to clear up the confusion which contradictory court orders had created, and to establish reasonable national standards." He elaborated his constitutional rationale in a news conference soon after: "The Constitution under the 14th Amendment provides for equal protection of the law. The Constitution does not provide, as a remedy, busing or any other device. The Constitution in the 14th Amendment explicitly grants power to the Congress to set up the remedies to accomplish the right of equal protection of the law." He emphasized the "fundamental difference" between "a remedy" and "a right." See Bork, The Constitutionality of the President's Busing Proposals (1972).

The Nixon Administration's proposals contained, in addition to a brief moratorium on busing orders, a long-run proposal to have Congress establish a priority of remedies to be used by federal courts and agencies, with specific limits on the use of busing in implementation plans. But the Nixon proposals were temporarily sidetracked in Congress. Instead, Congress adopted milder provisions as amendments to the Higher Education Act in June, 1972—including a moratorium on court orders adopted "for the purpose of achieving a balance among students with respect to race, sex, religion, or socioeconomic status." As President Nixon's critical comments in signing that law predicted, the stay provision of the 1972 Act did not prove a significant obstacle to busing orders. In Drummond v. Acree, 409 U.S. 1228 (1972), Justice Powell as Circuit Justice refused to stay a desegregation decree "entered to accomplish desegregation of the school system in accordance with the mandate of Swann and not for the purpose of achieving a racial balance." He viewed the statutory provision as limited to "desegregation plans that seek to achieve racial balance." If Congress had decided to stay all busing orders, he noted, "it could have used clear and explicit language appropriate to that result."

Before the end of the congressional session in 1972, the Administration proposals were revived and were adopted by the House in revised form. But the anti-busing provision was killed in the Senate in October, 1972, because its supporters could not muster the necessary votes to impose cloture on a filibuster. However, President Nixon renewed his appeals for anti-busing laws in 1973, and the provisions blocked in 1972 became law in modified form in 1974.

2. *The anti-busing provisions of 1974.* The anti-busing provisions of the Education Amendments of 1974, P.L. 93–380, 88 Stat. 484, became law in late August, 1974, after bitter legislative wrangling over a period of several months. The version adopted includes most of the harsher language initially approved by the House rather than the milder form originally approved by the Senate. But the law contains significant introductory statements demanded by the Senate conferees that the provisions "are not intended to modify or diminish the authority of the courts of the United States to enforce fully the fifth and fourteenth amendments." Does that

an amendment with language similar to Senator Griffin's 1972 statutory proposal. However, the primary congressional focus remained on legislative proposals, as noted in the text.

proviso significantly undercut the remaining provisions, summarized below? Without that proviso, would the statute be within congressional powers under § 5 of the 14th Amendment? (The problem of congressional powers under that Amendment, as noted, is pursued in chap. 11 below.)

The congressional findings in the 1974 Act repeatedly condemn "excessive transportation of students" and state a purpose to provide "appropriate remedies for the elimination of the vestiges of dual school systems." Moreover, a general declaration of congressional policy states not only that "all children enrolled in public schools are entitled to equal educational opportunity without regard to race, color, sex, or national origin," but also that "the neighborhood is the appropriate basis for determining public school assignments." The most important operative provisions follow. Sec. 205 states: "The failure of an educational agency to attain a balance, on the basis of race, color, sex, or national origin, of students among its schools shall not constitute a denial of equal educational opportunity, or equal protection of the laws." Sec. 206 states that ordinarily assignment of students to neighborhood schools is permissible. Sec. 214 lists a "priority of remedies" to be resorted to by federal courts and agencies in implementing desegregation. The final section in this sequence is the most important one: Sec. 215, "Transportation of Students," explicitly states that no federal court or agency shall "order the implementation of a plan that would require the transportation of any student to a school other than the school closest or next closest to his place of residence."

DESEGREGATION IN THE NORTH: THE DENVER AND DETROIT CASES

1. *Broad intradistrict remedies for de jure segregation: The Keyes case.* The Denver case, KEYES v. SCHOOL DISTRICT NO. 1, DENVER, COLO., 413 U.S. 189 (1973), was the Court's first decision on school desegregation in the North. Justice Brennan's majority opinion did not question the de jure-de facto distinction. Instead, he set forth criteria that would facilitate a finding of de jure discrimination in northern areas without a background of state-mandated segregation. Moreover, he announced standards that would permit court orders for district-wide remedies to rest on findings of intentional discrimination in only part of the district.[1]

The immediate charges of purposeful discrimination were limited to one portion of the city-wide Denver school district. The claim was that school officials had intentionally discriminated with respect to that Park Hill area

---

1. An elaborate separate opinion by Justice Powell went considerably further, on the issue of rights as well as on remedies. As to the former, he advocated abandonment of the de jure-de facto distinction and urged recognition of a uniform, nationwide right to have local school boards operate "integrated school systems." Consideration of that aspect of his opinion is postponed until the next group of notes. And as to the question of remedies, Justice Powell's proposals would mean greatly reduced use of massive busing as a desegregation tool. In a separate opinion, Justice Douglas agreed with Justice Powell on the issue of rights: he, too, advocated scrapping the de jure-de facto distinction. Chief Justice Burger concurred only in the majority's result. Justice Rehnquist dissented. And Justice White did not participate.

"by use of various techniques such as the manipulation of student attendance zones, schoolsite selection and a neighborhood school policy." More than one-third of the Black students were in the Park Hill area. There was also a heavy concentration of Black students in the core city area. Justice Brennan's opinion provided guidelines that would permit city-wide desegregation on the basis of the finding regarding the Park Hill area. He sketched two routes to such a result. First, "where plaintiffs prove that the school authorities have carried out a systematic program of segregation affecting a substantial proportion of the students, schools, teachers and facilities," a finding that the entire district is a dual, segregated one is authorized, absent a showing that the district is divided into clearly unrelated units. And once such a city-wide finding is made, the usual remedies evolved in the southern context, from Brown II to Swann, are applicable. He explained that "common sense dictates the conclusion that racially inspired school board actions have an impact beyond the particular schools that are the subjects of those actions." Second, even if the areas within a district are treated separately, showing of intentional segregation in one area may be probative as to intentional segregation in other areas. Accordingly, the finding as to Park Hill was usable in the efforts to prove segregative intent in the core city area. He added: "We have no occasion to consider [here] whether a 'neighborhood school policy' of itself will justify racial or ethnic concentrations in the absence of a finding that school authorities have committed acts constituting de jure segregation." (Earlier, he had stated: "We emphasize that the differentiating factor between de jure segregation and so-called de facto segregation" is "*purpose* or *intent* to segregate.")

Justice Powell's separate opinion was largely devoted to arguing that the de jure-de facto distinction was no longer tenable, as pursued in the next group of notes. But he also examined the question of remedies and spoke favorably of the neighborhood school norm. He expressed misgivings about "requiring so far-reaching a remedy as student transportation solely to maximize integration." He urged viewing Swann as announcing "a broad rule of reason under which desegregation remedies must remain flexible and other values and interests be considered." He suggested that many affirmative steps are possible "without damaging state and parental interests in having children attend schools within a reasonable vicinity of home." He insisted that particular schools "may be all white or all black and still not infringe constitutional rights if the *system* is genuinely integrated and school authorities are pursuing integrative steps short of extensive and disruptive transportation." He suggested, moreover, that "courts may have overlooked the fact that the rights and interests of children affected by a desegregation program also are entitled to consideration." Compelling children to leave their neighborhoods impaired "liberty" and "privacy." And there were also "broader considerations" for questioning "any remedial requirement of extensive student transportation solely to further integration." Such remedies imposed the remedial burden on "children and parents who did not participate in any constitutional violation" and risked "setting in motion unpredictable and unmanageable social consequences." For example, dismantling neighborhood education "might hasten an exodus to private schools" and "the movement from inner city to suburb," and might diminish support for public schools and quality education. He emphasized that he would not

prohibit all court-ordered busing; but he would require "that the legitimate community interests in neighborhood school systems be accorded far greater respect."

Justice Rehnquist was the only member of the Court in total disagreement with the majority. He concluded: "The Court has taken a long leap [in] equating the district-wide consequences of gerrymandering individual attendance zones in a district where separation of the races was never required by law with statutes or ordinances in other jurisdictions which did so require. It then adds to this potpourri a confusing enunciation of evidentiary rules in order to make it more likely that the trial court will on remand reach the result which the Court apparently wants it to reach." He thought "neither of these steps" justified by prior decisions. He also took occasion to criticize the "drastic extension" of Brown in the Green case—an extension which "was barely, if at all, explicated in the latter opinion." He elaborated: "To require that a genuinely 'dual' system be disestablished, in the sense of the assignment of a child to a particular school is not made to depend on his race, is one thing. To require that school boards affirmatively undertake to achieve racial mixing in schools where such mixing is not achieved in sufficient degree by neutrally drawn boundary lines is quite obviously something else." (See also the additional materials below, on Justice Powell's opinion in Keyes.)

2. *The limits on remedies for de jure segregation: Interdistrict remedies and the Detroit case.* In 1974, a sharply divided Court at last addressed the question of the permissible extent of multidistrict remedies for situations in which de jure segregation had been found to exist in only one of the districts.[2] MILLIKEN v. BRADLEY, 418 U.S. 717 (1974). The Milliken decision reversed lower court orders that had directed interdistrict remedies in the Detroit metropolitan area after a finding of de jure segregation in the city of Detroit: the majority concluded "that absent an inter-district violation there is no basis for an inter-district remedy." Chief Justice Burger wrote for the majority in the 5 to 4 decision.[3]

In the Detroit area, the city constituted one school district and there were separate districts for the suburban areas. Blacks were concentrated in the city. The District Court found that there was de jure segregation in the Detroit school system because of acts of state and city officials, and the Supreme Court saw no reason to disturb that finding in view of the 1973 standards of Keyes, above. But the District Court, in fashioning remedies, concluded that desegregation could not be effective if it were limited to the city boundaries and accordingly issued an order including 53 surrounding school districts. The lower court, in justifying its multidistrict remedy, pointed

---

2. Discussion of that problem had been averted a year earlier when the Court divided 4 to 4 (with Justice Powell not participating) in an interdistrict remedy case involving the Richmond, Virginia, metropolitan area. School Board of Richmond v. State Board of Educ., 412 U.S. 92 (1973).

3. Justice Stewart submitted a concurring opinion. The dissenters were Justices Douglas, Brennan, White and Marshall. There were lengthy dissents by Justices White and Marshall; each of those opinions was joined by all of the other dissenters. There was also a brief separate dissent by Justice Douglas.

not only to the practical obstacles to a narrower order,[4] but also to other considerations as well: the Detroit district was an agent of the state; the state had power to prevent segregation there—by changing district boundaries, for example. Moreover, the state had contributed to segregation in the city— e. g., by prohibiting the use of state funds for busing in the city. Concluding that "district lines are simply matters of political convenience and may not be used to deny constitutional rights," the District Judge designated 53 of the 85 suburban school districts and Detroit as the "desegregation area" and, without any finding that there had been de jure segregation in any of the suburban districts, directed the preparation of "an effective desegregation plan" for the entire area. The Court of Appeals agreed that crossing boundary lines was "the only feasible desegregation plan," but the Supreme Court majority insisted that the remedy exceeded the scope of the constitutional wrong.

Chief Justice Burger's majority opinion concluded: "Boundary lines may be bridged where there has been a constitutional violation calling for inter-district relief, but, the notion that school district lines may be casually ignored or treated as a mere administrative convenience is contrary to the history of public education in our country. No single tradition in public education is more deeply rooted than local control over the operation of schools." And in delineating the limited circumstances in which inter-district remedies were permissible, he stated:

"The controlling principle consistently expounded in our holdings is that the scope of the remedy is determined by the nature and extent of the constitutional violation. [Swann.] Before the boundaries of separate and autonomous school districts may be set aside by consolidating the separate units for remedial purposes or by imposing a cross-district remedy, it must first be shown that there has been a constitutional violation within one district that produces a significant segregative effect in another district. Specifically it must be shown that racially discriminatory acts of the state or local school districts, or of a single school district, have been a substantial cause of inter-district segregation. Thus an inter-district remedy might be in order where the racially discriminatory acts of one or more school districts caused racial segregation in an adjacent district, or where district lines have been deliberately drawn on the basis of race. In such circumstances an inter-district remedy would be appropriate to eliminate the inter-district segregation directly caused by the constitutional violation. Conversely, without an inter-district violation and inter-district effect, there is no constitutional wrong calling for an inter-district remedy."

In reaching these conclusions, the Chief Justice scrutinized the lower courts' performance and characterized it in ways sharply challenged in Justice Marshall's dissent. The Chief Justice found indications in the lower court opinions that they had "shifted the primary focus from a Detroit remedy to the metropolitan area only because of their conclusion that total desegregation of Detroit would not produce the racial balance which they perceived as desirable. Both courts proceeded on an assumption that the Detroit schools

4. The lower court noted that the most promising Detroit-only remedy would "leave many of its schools 75 to 90 per cent Black." In 1970, the Detroit public school enrollment was approximately 64% Black, amid a metropolitan school population that was 81% white. By 1973, the percentage of Black students in Detroit schools had risen to about 70%.

could not be truly desegregated—in their view of what constituted desegregation—unless the racial composition of the student body of each school substantially reflected the racial composition of the population of the metropolitan area as a whole." But under the Swann case, he insisted, "desegregation, in the sense of dismantling a dual school system, does not require any particular racial balance in each 'school, grade or classroom.' " [5]

In criticizing the interdistrict remedy adopted here, the Chief Justice emphasized that it "could disrupt and alter the structure of public education in Michigan. The metropolitan remedy would require, in effect, consolidation of 54 independent school districts historically administered as separate units into a vast new super school district. Entirely apart from the logistical and other serious problems attending large-scale transportation of students, the consolidation would give rise to an array of other problems in financing and operating this new school system." [6] The Chief Justice emphasized, more-

5. The Chief Justice elaborated in a footnote: "Disparity in the racial composition of pupils within a single district may well constitute a 'signal' to a district court at the outset, leading to inquiry into the causes accounting for a pronounced racial identifiability of schools within one school system. . . . However, the use of significant racial imbalance in schools within an autonomous school district as a signal which operates simply to shift the burden of proof, is a very different matter from equating racial imbalance with a constitutional violation calling for a remedy."

6. The Chief Justice noted, however, that school district lines "are not sacrosanct" if they violate 14th Amendment rights. He cited Wright v. Council of City of Emporia, 407 U.S. 451 (1972), and United States v. Scotland Neck Board of Education, 407 U.S. 484 (1972), where state or local officials were prevented from carving out a new school district from an existing district that was in the process of dismantling a dual school system. In the Emporia case, for example, the city had tried to withdraw from a county system under court-ordered desegregation in order to establish a separate school district. Withdrawal of the city would have resulted in a slight increase in the percentage of Black students in the county system. Justice Stewart's majority opinion in the 5 to 4 decision thought the lower court "justified in its conclusion that Emporia's establishment of a separate system would actually impede the process of dismantling the existing dual system." The majority emphasized the effect of Emporia's separation and frowned upon inquiry into "dominant purpose." But in the similar Scotland Neck case, the four dis-

senters in Emporia concurred on the ground that separation would result in racially identifiable schools "in a very real sense" and that "severance was substantially motivated by a desire to create a predominantly white system" in the city schools, leaving the county ones largely Black.

Note also Gilmore v. City of Montgomery, 417 U.S. 556 (1974) (chap. 11, sec. 2, below), affirming a judgment enjoining a city from permitting exclusive access to its recreational facilities by segregated private schools. The Court emphasized that "the city's action significantly enhanced the attractiveness of segregated private schools, formed in reaction against the federal court's school order, by enabling them to offer complete athletic programs." The city's assistance "significantly tended to undermine the federal court order mandating the establishment and maintenance of a unitary school system in Montgomery." See also Norwood v. Harrison, 413 U.S. 455 (1973), holding unconstitutional a Mississippi program in which textbooks were purchased by the State and loaned to students in both public and private schools, without reference to whether any participating private school had racially discriminatory policies. Chief Justice Burger's opinion concluded: "A State's constitutional obligation requires it to steer clear not only of operating the old dual system of racially segregated schools but also of giving significant aid to institutions that practice racial or other invidious discrimination." (The Mississippi program was adopted in 1940, long before Brown, but "good intentions" could not save it. Relying on the Emporia case, he commented that "impermissible effect" could not be saved by "permissible purpose.")

over, that de jure segregation existed only in the Detroit schools: "With no showing of significant violation by the 53 outlying school districts and no evidence of any inter-district violation or effect, the court went beyond the original theory of the case as framed by the pleadings and mandated a metropolitan area remedy. To approve the remedy ordered by the court would impose on the outlying districts, not shown to have committed any constitutional violation, a wholly impermissible remedy based on a standard not hinted at in Brown I and II or any holding of this Court."

The Chief Justice was not persuaded by the dissenters' argument that the participation in state officials in maintaining de jure segregation in Detroit justified interdistrict relief. Even assuming that there was significant state participation,[7] "established doctrine" required focusing on particular districts. He continued: "The constitutional right of the Negro respondents residing in Detroit is to attend a unitary school system in that district. Unless [the officials] drew the district lines in a discriminatory fashion, or arranged for White students residing in the Detroit district to attend schools in [adjacent counties], they were under no constitutional duty to make provisions for Negro students to do so. The view of the dissenters, that the existence of a dual system *in Detroit* can be made the basis for a decree requiring cross-district transportation of pupils cannot be supported on the grounds that it represents merely the devising of a suitably flexible remedy for the violation of rights already established by our prior decisions. It can be supported only by drastic expansion of the constitutional right itself, an expansion without any support in either constitutional principle or precedent."

Justice Stewart joined the opinion of the Court with a separate opinion expressing his understanding of the decision. His opinion was prompted by "some of the extravagant language of the dissenting opinions." He emphasized that since the Court had accepted the de jure segregation finding below, the decision did not deal with "questions of substantive constitutional law," but only with the problem of "the appropriate exercise of federal equity jurisdiction." The lower courts were properly found in error "for the simple reason that the remedy they thought necessary was not commensurate with the constitutional violation found." Justice Stewart's concurrence included a significant passage elaborating his understanding of the situations in which inter-district remedies *would* be permissible: "Were it to be shown, for example, that state officials had contributed to the separation of the races by drawing or redrawing school district lines . . . .; by transfer of school units between districts . . . .; or by purposeful, racially discriminatory use of state housing or zoning laws, then a decree calling for transfer of pupils across district lines or for restructuring of district lines might well be appropriate."

The most extensive and strongest dissent came from Justice Marshall. He protested that "public opposition, no matter how strident, cannot be permitted to divert this Court from the enforcement of the constitutional

---

7. Though the Chief Justice assumed, arguendo, that the State shared responsibility for the segregated conditions within the city of Detroit, another part of his opinion emphasized that there was very little evidence that either the state or the adjacent districts "engaged in activity that had a cross-district effect."

principles at issue in this case. Today's holding, I fear, is more a reflection of a perceived public mood that we have gone far enough in enforcing the Constitution's guarantee of equal justice than it is the product of neutral principles of law. In the short run, it may seem to be the easier course to allow our great metropolitan areas to be divided up each into two cities—one white, the other black—but it is a course, I predict, our people will ultimately regret." He thought the decision "a giant step backwards" and an "emasculation" of the equal protection guarantee. He insisted that "where, as here, state-imposed segregation has been demonstrated, it becomes the duty of the State to eliminate root and branch all vestiges of racial discrimination and to achieve the greatest possible degree of actual desegregation." And here, the lower courts had been right in finding that "this duty cannot be fulfilled unless the State of Michigan involves outlying metropolitan area school districts in its desegregation remedy." He added that he saw "no basis either in law or in the practicalities of the situation justifying the State's interposition of school district boundaries as absolute barriers to the implementation of an effective desegregation remedy."

In criticizing the majority's approach at length, Justice Marshall objected to its "totally inaccurate" characterization of the District Court's approach. The trial court had not, he insisted, shifted to a "racial imbalance" analysis. The majority's "largely fictional account" of the trial court's objectives could not becloud the fact that "inter-district relief was seen as a necessary part of any meaningful effort by the State of Michigan to remedy the state-caused segregation within the city of Detroit." There was ample support for the conclusions that the State "was ultimately responsible" for curing segregation and "that a Detroit-only remedy would not accomplish this task."

Justice White's dissent explained: "The core of my disagreement is that deliberate acts of segregation and their consequences will go unremedied, not because a remedy will be infeasible or unreasonable in terms of the usual criteria governing school desegregation cases, but because an effective remedy would cause what the Court considers to be undue administrative inconvenience to the State. The result is that the State of Michigan, the entity at which the Fourteenth Amendment is directed, has successfully insulated itself from its duty to provide effective desegregation remedies by vesting sufficient power over its public schools in its local school districts. If this is the case in Michigan, it will be the case in most States." He insisted that the Court had fashioned "out of whole cloth an arbitrary rule that remedies for constitutional violations occurring in a single Michigan school district must stop at the school district line. Apparently, no matter how much less burdensome or more effective and efficient in many respects, such as transportation, the metropolitan plan might be, the school district line may not be crossed."

Justice White added that "the talismanic invocation of the desirability of local control over education" could not justify the Court's result. He concluded that the majority had compelled "an intracity desegregation plan more expensive to the district, more burdensome for many of Detroit's Negro students and surely more conducive to white flight than a metropolitan plan would be—all of this merely to avoid what the [lower courts] considered to be the very manageable and quite surmountable difficulties that

would be involved in extending the desegregation remedy to the suburban school districts." [8]

THE CONSTITUTIONALITY OF DE FACTO SCHOOL SEGREGATION

1. *Justice Powell's attack on the de jure-de facto distinction.* [Have the modern desegregation cases, since the Green decision in 1968, undercut the justifications for maintaining a constitutional distinction between de jure and de facto school segregation? Consider Justice Powell's arguments in his separate opinion in KEYES v. SCHOOL DISTRICT NO. 1, DENVER, COLO., 413 U.S. 189 (1973):]

The situation in Denver is generally comparable to that in other large cities across the country in which there is a substantial minority population and where desegregation has not been ordered by the federal courts. There is segregation in the schools of many of these cities fully as pervasive as that in southern cities prior to the desegregation decrees of the past decade and a half. The focus of the school desegregation problem has now shifted from the South to the country as a whole. Unwilling and footdragging as the process was in most places, substantial progress toward achieving integration has been made in southern States.[1] No comparable progress has been made in many nonsouthern cities with large minority populations,[2] primarily because of the de facto/de jure distinction nurtured by the courts and accepted complacently by many of the same voices which denounced the evils of segregated schools in the South. But if our national concern is for those who attend such schools, rather than for perpetuating a legalism rooted in history rather than present reality, we must recognize that the evil of operating separate schools is no less in Denver than in Atlanta.

I. In my view we should abandon a distinction which long since has outlived its time, and formulate constitutional principles of national rather than merely regional application. When Brown I was decided, the distinction between de jure and de facto segregation was consistent with the limited constitutional rationale of that case. . . . Although some of the language was more expansive, the holding in Brown I was essentially negative: It was impermissible under the Constitution for the States, or their instru-

---

8. In a separate dissent, Justice Douglas insisted that the lower courts had acted "responsibly" and argued that the prohibition of a metropolitan remedy would "put the problems of the Blacks in our society back to the period that antedated the 'separate but equal' regime of Plessy v. Ferguson."

1. According to the 1971 Department of Health, Education, and Welfare (HEW) estimate, 43.9% of Negro pupils attended majority white schools in the South as opposed to only 27.8% who attended such schools in the North and West. Fifty-seven percent of all Negro pupils in the North and West attend schools with over 80% minority population as opposed to

32.2% who do so in the South. [Footnote by Justice Powell.]

2. The 1971 HEW Enrollment Survey dramatized the segregated character of public school systems in many nonsouthern cities. The percentage of Negro pupils which attended schools more than 80% black was 91.3 in Cleveland, Ohio; 97.8 in Compton, California; 78.1 in Dayton, Ohio; 78.6 in Detroit, Michigan; 95.7 in Gary, Indiana; 86.4 in Kansas City, Missouri; 86.6 in Los Angeles, California; 78.8 in Milwaukee, Wisconsin; 91.3 in Newark, New Jersey; 89.8 in St. Louis, Missouri. [Footnote by Justice Powell.]

mentalities, to force children to attend segregated schools. The forbidden action was de jure, and the opinion in Brown I was construed—for some years and by many courts—as requiring only state neutrality, allowing "freedom of choice" as to schools to be attended so long as the State itself assured that the choice was genuinely free of official restraint.

But the doctrine of Brown I, as amplified by Brown II, did not retain its original meaning. In a series of decisions extending from 1954 to 1971 the concept of state neutrality was transformed into the present constitutional doctrine requiring affirmative state action to desegregate school systems. The keystone case was [Green]. . . . The Court properly identified the freedom-of-choice program there as a subterfuge, and the language in Green imposing an affirmative duty to convert to a unitary system was appropriate on the facts before the Court. There was, however, reason to question to what extent this duty would apply in the vastly different factual setting of a large city with extensive areas of residential segregation, presenting problems and calling for solutions quite different from those in the rural setting of New Kent County, Virginia.

But the doubt as to whether the affirmative-duty concept would flower into a new constitutional principle of general application was laid to rest by [Swann]. . . . [Swann] refrained from even considering whether the evolution of constitutional doctrine from Brown I to Green/Swann undercut whatever logic once supported the de facto/de jure distinction. In imposing on metropolitan southern school districts an affirmative duty, entailing large-scale transportation of pupils, to eliminate segregation in the schools, the Court required these districts to alleviate conditions which in large part did *not* result from historic, state-imposed de jure segregation. Rather, the familiar root cause of segregated schools in *all* the biracial metropolitan areas of our country is essentially the same: one of segregated residential and migratory patterns the impact of which on the racial composition of the schools was often perpetuated and rarely ameliorated by action of public school authorities. This is a national, not a southern, phenomenon. And it is largely unrelated to whether a particular State had or did not have segregative school laws.

Whereas Brown I rightly decreed the elimination of state-imposed segregation in that particular section of the country where it did exist, Swann imposed obligations on southern school districts to eliminate conditions which are not regionally unique but are similar both in origin and effect to conditions in the rest of the country. As the remedial obligations of Swann extend far beyond the elimination of the outgrowths of the state-imposed segregation outlawed in Brown, the rationale of Swann points inevitably toward a uniform, constitutional approach to our national problem of school segregation.

II. The Court's decision today, while adhering to the de jure/de facto distinction, will require the application of the Green/Swann doctrine of "affirmative duty" to the Denver School Board despite the absence of any history of state-mandated school segregation. The only evidence of a constitutional violation was found in various decisions of the School Board. I concur in the Court's position that the public school authorities are the responsible agency of the State, and that if the affirmative-duty doctrine is

sound constitutional law for Charlotte, it is equally so for Denver. I would not, however, perpetuate the de jure/de facto distinction nor would I leave to petitioners the initial tortuous effort of identifying "segregative acts" and deducing "segregative intent." I would hold, quite simply, that where segregated public schools exist within a school district to a substantial degree, there is a prima facie case that the duly constituted public authorities (I will usually refer to them collectively as the "school board") are sufficiently responsible [3] to warrant imposing upon them a nationally applicable burden to demonstrate they nevertheless are operating a genuinely integrated school system.

A. The principal reason for abandonment of the de jure/de facto distinction is that, in view of the evolution of the holding in Brown I into the affirmative-duty doctrine, the distinction no longer can be justified on a principled basis. [And], as the Court's opinion today abundantly demonstrates, the facts deemed necessary to establish de jure discrimination present problems of subjective intent which the courts cannot fairly resolve.

At the outset, one must try to identify the constitutional right which is being enforced. This is not easy, as the precedents have been far from explicit. [Brown means at least] that one has the right not to be compelled by state action to attend a segregated school system. In the evolutionary process since 1954, decisions of this Court have added a significant gloss to this original right. Although nowhere expressly articulated in these terms, I would now define it as the right, derived from the Equal Protection Clause, to expect that once the State has assumed responsibility for education, local school boards will operate *integrated school systems* within their respective districts. This means that school authorities, consistent with the generally accepted educational goal of attaining quality education for all pupils, must make and implement their customary decisions with a view toward enhancing integrated school opportunities.

The term "integrated school system" presupposes, of course, a total absence of any laws, regulations, or policies supportive of the type of "legalized" segregation condemned in Brown. A system would be integrated in accord with constitutional standards if the responsible authorities had taken appropriate steps to (i) integrate faculties and administration; (ii) scrupulously assure equality of facilities, instruction, and curriculum opportunities throughout the district; (iii) utilize their authority to draw attendance zones to promote integration; and (iv) locate new schools, close old ones, and determine the size and grade categories with this same objective in mind. Where school authorities decide to undertake the transportation of students, this also must be with integrative opportunities in mind. . . .

Having school boards operate an integrated school system provides the best assurance of meeting the constitutional requirement that racial discrimination, subtle or otherwise, will find no place in the decisions of public

---

3. A prima facie case of constitutional violation exists when segregation is found to a substantial degree in the schools of a particular district. It is recognized, of course, that this term is relative and provides no precise standards. But circumstances, demographic and otherwise, vary from district to district and hard-and-fast rules should not be formulated. The existence of a substantial percentage of schools populated by students from one race only or predominantly so populated, should trigger the inquiry. [Footnote by Justice Powell.]

school officials. Courts judging past school board actions with a view to their *general integrative effect* will be best able to assure an absence of such discrimination while avoiding the murky, subjective judgments inherent in the Court's search for "segregative intent." Any test resting on so nebulous and elusive an element as a school board's segregative "intent" provides inadequate assurance that minority children will not be short-changed in the decisions of those entrusted with the nondiscriminatory operation of our public schools.

Public schools are creatures of the State, and whether the segregation is state-created or state-assisted or merely state-perpetuated should be irrelevant to constitutional principle. The school board exercises pervasive and continuing responsibility over the long-range planning as well as the daily operations of the public school system. It sets policies on attendance zones, faculty employment and assignments, school construction, closings and consolidations, and myriad other matters. School board decisions obviously are not the sole cause of segregated school conditions. But if, after such detailed and complete public supervision, substantial school segregation still persists, the presumption is strong that the school board, by its acts or omissions, is in some part responsible. Where state action and supervision are so pervasive and where, after years of such action, segregated schools continue to exist within the district to a substantial degree, this Court is justified in finding a prima facie case of a constitutional violation. The burden then must fall on the school board to demonstrate it is operating an "integrated school system."

It makes little sense to find prima facie violations and the consequent affirmative duty to desegregate solely in those States with state-imposed segregation at the time of the Brown decision. The history of state-imposed segregation is more widespread in our country than the de jure/de facto distinction has traditionally cared to recognize.[4] . . .

Not only does the de jure/de facto distinction operate inequitably on communities in different sections of the country, more importantly, it disadvantages minority children as well. As the Fifth Circuit stated:

" 'The Negro children in Cleveland, Chicago, Los Angeles, Boston, New York, or any other area of the nation which the opinion classifies under de facto segregation, would receive little comfort from the assertion that the racial make-up of their school system does not violate their constitutional rights because they were born into a de facto society, while the exact same racial make-up of the school system in the 17 Southern and border states violates the constitutional rights of their counterparts, or even their blood brothers, because they were born into a de jure society. All children everywhere in the nation are protected by the Constitution, and treatment which violates their constitutional rights in one area of the country, also violates such constitutional rights in another area.' " Cisneros v. Corpus Christi Independent School District, 467 F.2d 142, 148 (CA5 1972) (en banc). . . .

---

4. Indeed, if one goes back far enough, it is probable that all racial segregation, wherever occurring and whether or not confined to the schools, has at some time been supported or maintained by government action. . . . [Footnote by Justice Powell.]

B.   There is thus no reason as a matter of constitutional principle to adhere to the de jure/de facto distinction in school desegregation cases.   In addition, there are reasons of policy and prudent judicial administration which point strongly toward the adoption of a uniform national rule.   The litigation heretofore centered in the South already is surfacing in other regions.   The decision of the Court today, emphasizing as it does the elusive element of segregative intent, will invite numerous desegregation suits in which there can be little hope of uniformity of result.

The issue in these cases will not be whether segregated education exists. This will be conceded in most of them.   The litigation will focus as a consequence of the Court's decision on whether segregation has resulted in any "meaningful or significant" portion of a school system from a school board's "segregative intent."   The intractable problems involved in litigating this issue are obvious to any lawyer.   .   .   .

C.   Rather than continue to prop up a distinction no longer grounded in principle, and contributing to the consequences indicated above, we should acknowledge that whenever public school segregation exists to a substantial degree there is prima facie evidence of a constitutional violation by the responsible school board.   .   .   .[5]

2.   *The survival of the de jure-de facto distinction.*   Despite the criticisms of the rationale of the cases since Green, the Court in all the modern cases has reiterated the premise that de jure and de facto segregation *are* constitutionally different.   Recall, for example, Justice Brennan's emphasis in Keyes on the difference between "purposeful" and "adventitious" discrimination, between deliberate discrimination and discrimination in effect. Moreover, the lower courts have virtually unanimously rejected claims that "mere" de facto segregation gives rise to a constitutional claim.[6]   Justice Powell's argument rests largely on the Court's increasing emphasis, since Green, on *results* in communities in which formal de jure segregation once existed—and on the increasingly tenuous search for evidence of deliberate discrimination in the North.   But an argument resting on those premises may simply show, as Justice Rehnquist argues, that the Court has gone too far in imposing affirmative obligations and in focusing on results in the de jure context since Green.   Does the argument also demonstrate that de facto

---

5.   Recall also Justice Rehnquist's dissent in Keyes, summarized earlier, claiming that the Court decisions since Green were a "marked extension of the principles of Brown."

6.   See, e. g., Bell v. School City of Gary, 324 F.2d 209 (7th Cir. 1963), cert. denied, 377 U.S. 924 (1964), and Deal v. Cincinnati Board of Education, 369 F.2d 55 (6th Cir. 1966), cert. denied, 389 U.S. 847 (1967).   Compare Judge J. Skelly Wright's extensive discussion in the District of Columbia school segregation case, Hobson v. Hansen, 269 F.Supp. 401 (D.D.C.1967), aff'd sub nom. Smuck v. Hobson, 408 F.2d 175 (D.C.Cir. 1969).   See generally, Fiss, "Racial Imbalance in the Public Schools: The Constitutional Concepts,"

78 Harv.L.Rev. 564 (1965), and Kaplan, "Segregation Litigation and the Schools," 58 Nw.U.L.Rev. 1, 157 (1963). Compare with Justice Powell's opinion, note 1 above, the sporadic efforts in Congress to eliminate de facto segregation.   In 1970, for example, there was extensive debate on a proposed amendment to a school aid bill by Senator Stennis of Mississippi—an amendment which would have denied federal aid to segregated schools "in all regions of the United States [without] regard to the origin or cause of such segregation."   Senator Ribicoff of Connecticut, after criticizing the "monumental hypocrisy" of the North, supported the effort to treat de facto and de jure segregation alike.

segregation is independently a constitutional wrong? To what extent do the factors relied on in Brown I to demonstrate the discrimination and harm inherent in school segregation apply to the de facto situation? Is there similar stigma? Is there similar impairment of educational opportunity and quality? Is the condemnation of de facto segregation justified by the purposes of the 14th Amendment? Recall the rejection of the claim, in the welfare legislation context, that differential impact of welfare programs on races amounts to unconstitutional discrimination. Jefferson v. Hackney, sec. 2A above. Can de facto school segregation be considered unconstitutional without bringing all de facto "discriminations," all differential impacts of governmental action, within the constitutional ban? Can the 14th Amendment be read as safeguarding not only the purity of the process—the elimination of racial factors in decisionmaking—but also the quality of results, the assurance of equality of condition? [7] Has school segregation law moved fully, and justifiably, from concern with elimination of racial factors in student assignments to achievement of racial integration as the constitutionally mandated result?

C. RACIAL CRITERIA AND "BENIGN" PURPOSES

Introduction. May racial classifications be used for "benign" purposes? May the state single out racial minorities for favorable treatment, for remedial, compensatory, or similar purposes? The earlier materials in this section, especially in sec. 2A, frequently reiterate that racial classifications are at least "suspect," and are permissible only for "compelling" state justifications. Does that general rule apply to "benign" classifications as well? Is benignness of purpose a compelling justification? Or does the strict scrutiny for suspect classifications become inapplicable when the objective is benign? Are benign racial classifications subject only to a "mere rationality" standard, rather than a strict scrutiny one? When *may* government be color conscious rather than color blind? When *must* it be color conscious? Can courts adequately distinguish between truly benign purposes and hostile ones masquerading behind a "benign" facade?

1. *Color consciousness and school desegregation.* The materials in the preceding sec. 2B demonstrate that there is at least one area where government need not be color blind and indeed must be color conscious. The Court's requirements for eliminating the effects of de jure segregation, particularly in cases since the Green decision in 1968, have emphasized the *results* of desegregation efforts—results measured by the racial identification of schools. That a state may not be color blind when it is under a duty to eliminate past de jure discrimination was especially emphasized in the Swann litigation.

a. In a companion case to the Swann decision in sec. 2B, the Court unanimously struck down a state law mandating color blindness as an undue

7. For thoughtful recent discussions, see the two articles by Professor Fiss cited earlier, 4 Philosophy & Public Affairs 3 (1974), and 41 U.Chi.L.Rev. 742 (1974). And for an extensive examination of modern developments and problems, see Goodman, "De Facto School Segregation: A Constitutional and Empirical Analysis," 60 Calif.L. Rev. 275 (1972).

interference with desegregation requirements. In NORTH CAROLINA STATE BOARD OF EDUCATION v. SWANN, 402 U.S. 43 (1971), the Court held unconstitutional North Carolina's Anti-Busing Law [1] prohibiting student assignments on the basis of race. Chief Justice Burger stated that "if a state-imposed limitation on a school authority's discretion operates to inhibit or obstruct the operation of a unitary school system or impede the disestablishing of a [dual] system, it must fall; state policy must give way when it operates to hinder vindication of federal constitutional guarantees." He commented that "the statute exploits an apparently neutral form to control school assignment plans by directing that they be 'color blind'; that requirement, against the background of segregation, would render illusory the promise" of Brown I. He elaborated: "Just as the race of students must be considered in determining whether a constitutional violation has occurred, so also must race be considered in formulating a remedy. To forbid, at this stage, all assignments made on the basis of race would deprive school authorities of the one tool absolutely essential to fulfillment of their constitutional obligation to eliminate existing dual school systems." [2]

b. Is that endorsement of color consciousness limited to the remedying of de jure segregation? Or may school authorities also consider racial factors in efforts to eliminate de facto segregation—efforts not mandated under present interpretations of the Constitution? In dicta in the Swann cases, Chief Justice Burger suggested that such voluntary use of racial criteria in the discretion of school officials was permissible. Recall that in the major Swann case, 402 U.S. 1 (1971) (sec. 2B above), the Chief Justice stated: "School authorities are traditionally charged with broad power to formulate and implement educational policy and might well conclude, for example, that in order to prepare students to live in a pluralistic society each school should have a prescribed ratio of Negro to white students reflecting the proportion for the district as a whole. To do this as an educational policy is within the broad discretionary powers of school authorities." And in the companion Swann case, 402 U.S. 43 (1971), he reiterated that theme. What justifies those dicta? Is administrative use of race in the elimination of de facto segregation "suspect," with the "educational policy" providing the "compelling" justification? Or is the use of race in that context not subject to strict scrutiny and sustainable on "mere rationality" grounds? [3]

1. The Law provided: "No student shall be assigned or compelled to attend any school on account of race, creed, color or national origin, or for the purpose of creating a balance or ratio of race, religion or national origins. Involuntary bussing of students in contravention of this article is prohibited, and public funds shall not be used for any such bussing."

2. The statute prohibited not only assignment of students on the basis of race but also assignment for the purpose of creating a racial balance. The latter provision, too, was found to conflict with desegregation duties. Though, as the major Swann case had

indicated, no "particular degree of racial balance" was required, "when past and continuing constitutional violations are found, some ratios are likely to be useful starting points in shaping a remedy."

3. For earlier decisions rejecting attacks on "color conscious" voluntary school integration programs, see Balaban v. Rubin, 14 N.Y.2d 193, cert. denied, 379 U.S. 881 (1964); School Comm. v. Board of Educ., 352 Mass. 693 (1967), appeal dismissed, 389 U.S. 572 (1968); and Tometz v. Board of Educ., 39 Ill.2d 593, 237 N.E.2d 493 (1968). Some of these cases explicitly applied a permissive, "mere rationality" standard of scrutiny. What

Do the arguments for color consciousness in public school desegregation efforts apply to other "benign" classifications as well? Do they justify preferential admissions programs in law schools, for example? Preferential, "affirmative action" employment programs? "Benign" quotas to promote integrated housing? Those questions are pursued in the following notes.[4]

2. *Preferential admissions programs: The DeFunis case.* The De-Funis litigation promised to produce a Court ruling on the "benign" use of racial criteria in minority admissions programs, but adjudication on the merits was averted when the Court found the controversy moot. DeFunis claimed that he had been unconstitutionally denied admission to the University of Washington Law School because of a program which gave preference to minority applicants over better qualified white applicants. The lower state court agreed with his claim, but the Washington Supreme Court reversed. DeFUNIS v. ODEGAARD, 82 Wash. 11, 507 P.2d 1169 (1973). After hearing oral argument, the Supreme Court, in a 5 to 4 decision, found the case moot, on the ground that DeFunis, who had attended the school while the case was in the courts, was about to graduate. 416 U.S. 312 (1974). (On mootness, see chap. 15 below.) Justice Douglas, one of the dissenters from the finding of mootness, was the only Justice moved to produce an opinion on the merits. As the dissenters on the mootness issue pointed out in DeFunis: "The constitutional issues which are avoided today concern vast numbers of people, organizations, and colleges and universities, as evidenced by the filing of twenty-six amicus curiae briefs. Few constitutional questions in recent history have stirred as much debate, and they will not disappear."[5] A summary of the highest state court's position and of Justice Douglas' comments accordingly follows.

a. *The state court decision.* Under the University of Washington Law School admissions program involved in DeFunis, the decision on most applications were based on Predicted First Year Averages, a composite of LSAT scores and undergraduate records. Most admitted applicants had PFYA's above 74.5. But PFYA's were less important in assessing applicants for the minority admissions program—Black, Chicano, Native American and Filipino applicants. Most of the minority applicants admitted to the School had PFYA's below 74.5, and all but one of them had PFYA's lower than DeFunis' 76.2. DeFunis was rejected for admission and claimed that the

justification was there for abandoning the strict scrutiny of "suspect" classifications? Because race is "relevant" here? Because the aim is to "help"? Should "relevance" and "helpfulness" go to the issue of whether justification is adequate and compelling rather than reducing the high justification requirement to a "reasonable" one? Should courts ask whether nonracial alternatives exist? Recall the McDonald case, at the end of sec. 1 above, applying permissive rather than strict review standards in the context of "remedial" legislation. Even if that permissiveness for "remedial" laws is a justifiable standard generally, does it justify diminished scrutiny when racial classifications are used?

4. See generally Kaplan, "Equal Justice in an Unequal World: Equality for the Negro—The Problem of Special Treatment," 61 Nw.U.L.Rev. 363 (1966); "Developments," 82 Harv.L. Rev. 1065 (1969); Ely, "The Constitutionality of Reverse Racial Discrimination," 41 U.Chi.L.Rev. 723 (1974).

5. Compare with the state courts' disposition of the DeFunis case a spring 1975 ruling by a lower court in California holding a preferential admissions program at one of the medical schools of the University of California unconstitutional.

minority program discriminated against him on the basis of race. The majority of the Washington Supreme Court overturned a lower court ruling on behalf of DeFunis. The majority rejected the argument that a "mere rationality" standard applied, but held that the program satisfied "strict scrutiny" requirements as to both ends and means.

In examining the applicable criteria, the state court majority insisted that the Brown principle was not a total barrier to racial classifications but simply a holding "that invidious racial classifications—i. e., those that stigmatize a racial group with the stamp of inferiority—are unconstitutional." Here, the admissions program was not "invidious discrimination" vis-à-vis whites. The majority noted, moreover, that the U. S. Supreme Court had not only permitted but required racial criteria in some cases—in disestablishing de jure segregation, as in Swann and Green. DeFunis argued that those cases were inapposite since no students were deprived of an education by a plan to achieve a unitary school system. The Washington court, accepting "arguendo" DeFunis' contention that he had been denied a "benefit" on the basis of race, insisted that such action was not "a per se violation of the Fourteenth Amendment, if the racial classification is used in a compensatory way to promote integration." (The court relied in part on employment discrimination cases, note 3 below.)

After finding that racial factors in admissions were not invalid per se, the court turned to a consideration of the appropriate standard of review. It rejected the argument that a "rational basis" test should apply because the purpose of the program was "benign": "[T]he minority admissions policy is certainly not benign with respect to nonminority students who are displaced by it." Accordingly, strict scrutiny standards applied. The court found several "compelling state interests" justifying the policy. "The serious underrepresentation of minority groups in the law schools" justified "eliminating racial imbalance within public legal education," even though there might not have been de jure segregation in the past and "the law school itself may have previously been neutral in the matter." Moreover lawyers need to be "cognizant" of the views and demands or all segments of society: in view of that need, the "educational interest of the state in producing a racially balanced student body" was "compelling." Finally, "the shortage of minority attorneys" constituted "an undeniably compelling state interest. If minorities are to live within the rule of law, they must enjoy equal representation within our legal system."

The court also found the "necessary means" ingredient of strict scrutiny readily satisfied: correcting racial imbalance required racial factors; no "less restrictive means" were available to cure "underrepresentation"; the preferential admissions policy was "the only feasible 'plan that promises realistically to work, and promises realistically to work *now*.' [Green]." And, finally, the classification was permissible even though it did not include all racial minorities, since the purpose of the program was "to give special consideration to those racial minority groups which are underrepresented in the law schools and legal profession, and which cannot secure proportionate representation if strictly subjected to the standardized mathematical criteria for admission to the law school."

A dissent by the Chief Justice of the state court insisted that the "color blind" criterion was appropriate and had been violated. Special assistance to disadvantaged groups was permissible in many areas, but not when it deprived an applicant of admission on the basis of race. The fact that the state court had sustained a local program of busing to promote integration in public schools was not persuasive here: "Providing one child with a better, i. e., integrated, education did not operate to deprive another of an equal, integrated education. The benefit to one would not be at the expense of another."

     b. *Justice Douglas' views on the merits.* Justice Douglas' opinion in DeFunis—the only one in the Supreme Court to reach the merits—contained strong passages condemning racial factors in admissions programs but also suggested possible cultural bias in the ordinary admissions criteria and urged that the case be remanded for a new trial, in part to consider whether reliance on LSAT scores was inappropriate for minority applicants.[6] On the broad constitutional question, however, he opposed racial criteria in selections, even when used for "benign" purposes. He repeatedly insisted that decisions must be made "on the basis of individual attributes, rather than according a preference solely on the basis of race." Admissions committees might handle minority applications differently on the basis of a finding that LSAT scores were culturally biased; but the ultimate constitutional requirement was "the consideration of each application *in a racially neutral way.*" Admissions programs might dispense with LSAT scores or undergraduate grades and could consider the applicants' background, but any such program of evaluating potential would not be limited to the minority groups singled out here, though "these may in practice be the principal beneficiaries of it. But a poor Appalachian white, or a second generation Chinese in San Francisco, or some other American whose lineage is so diverse as to defy ethnic labels, may demonstrate similar potential and thus be accorded favorable consideration by the committee." Here, he insisted, the program—without "becoming embroiled in a semantic debate over whether this practice constitutes a 'quota' "—reduced the total number of places for which DeFunis could compete, "solely on account of his race." And the use of racial classifications in selecting students was subject "to the strictest scrutiny under the Equal Protection Clause." [7]

6. Justice Douglas read the limited record in DeFunis as involving a program which "admitted minority students who, by the tests given, seemed less qualified than some white students who were not accepted, in order to achieve a 'reasonable representation.'" Though the school might have been acting in order to rectify cultural bias in the LSAT and undergraduate records, "the record in this case is devoid of any evidence of such bias, and the school has not sought to justify its procedures on this basis."

7. Compare Justice Douglas' majority opinion one day after DeFunis, in Kahn v. Shevin, 416 U.S. 351 (1974) (sec. 3C below), sustaining with minimal scrutiny a property tax exemption for widows against a widower's charge of sex discrimination—even though Justice Douglas had joined Justice Brennan's opinion in Frontiero v. Richardson, sec. 3C below, urging that sex be considered a suspect classification. In dissent in Kahn, Justice Brennan, joined by Justice Marshall, thought the strict scrutiny standard applied, found the benign purpose of the tax exemption a compelling justification, but concluded that the means were overinclusive.

Justice Douglas commented: "There is no constitutional right for any race to be preferred. . . . There is no superior person by constitutional standards. A DeFunis who is white is entitled to no advantage by reason of that fact; nor is he subject to any disability, no matter his race or color. Whatever his race, he had a constitutional right to have his application considered on its individual merits in a racially neutral manner." And on the problem of alleged quotas, he noted: "The reservation of a proportion of a law school class for members of selected minority groups is fraught with [dangers], for one must immediately determine which groups are to receive such favored treatment and which are to be excluded, the proportions of the class that are to be allocated to each, and even the criteria by which to determine whether an individual is a member of the favored group. . . . Once the Court sanctioned racial preferences such as these, it could not then wash its hands of the matter. [For example], the Court could attempt to assess how grievously each group has suffered from discrimination, and allocate proportions accordingly; if that were the standard the current University of Washington policy would almost surely fall, for there is no western State which can claim that it has always treated Japanese and Chinese in a fair and evenhanded manner." The only solution to these unacceptable problems of race-consciousness, he concluded, was "the consideration of such applications *in a racially neutral way.*"

Near the end of his opinion, Justice Douglas turned to—and rejected—the argument that the benign aims of a program could justify racial preferences: "The argument is that a 'compelling' state interest can easily justify the racial discrimination that is practiced here. To many 'compelling' would give members of one race even more than pro rata representation. [For example], large quotas of blacks or browns could be added to the Bar, waiving examinations required of other groups, so that it would be better racially balanced. The State, however, may not proceed by racial classification to force strict population equivalencies for every group in every occupation, overriding individual preferences. The Equal Protection Clause commands the elimination of racial barriers, not their creation in order to satisfy our theory as to how society ought to be organized. The purpose of the University of Washington cannot be to produce Black lawyers for Blacks, Polish lawyers for Poles, Jewish lawyers for Jews, Irish lawyers for Irish. It should be to produce good lawyers for Americans . . . . A segregated admissions process creates suggestions of stigma and caste no less than a segregated classroom, and in the end it may produce that result despite its contrary intentions. One other assumption must be clearly disapproved, that Blacks or Browns cannot make it on their individual merit. That is a stamp of inferiority that a State is not permitted to place on any lawyer. If discrimination based on race is constitutionally permissible when those who hold the reins can come up with 'compelling' reasons to justify it, then constitutional guarantees acquire an accordionlike quality. . . . It may well be that racial strains, racial susceptibility to certain diseases, racial sensitiveness to environmental conditions that other races do not experience, may in an extreme situation justify differences in racial treatment that no fairminded person would call 'invidious' discrimination. Mental ability is not in that category. All races can compete fairly at all professional levels. So far as race is concerned, any state-sponsored preference to one race over

another in that competition is in my view 'invidious' and violative of the Equal Protection Clause."[8]

    c. *Some questions.* What *should* be the appropriate standard in determining the constitutionality of preferential admissions programs: "strict scrutiny" or "mere rationality"? Consider the suggestions in Ely, "The Constitutionality of Reverse Racial Discrimination," 41 U.Chi.L.Rev. 723 (1974): "When the group that controls the decision making process classifies so as to advantage a minority and disadvantage itself, the reasons for being unusually suspicious, and, consequently, employing a stringent brand of review, are lacking. A White majority is unlikely to disadvantage itself for reasons of racial prejudice . . .. Of course, there will be cases in which it will not be clear whether the legislative majority or the allegedly benefitted minority has ended up, on balance, with the comparative advantage —or, more to the point, whether the decision makers intended a greater benefit to the 'we's or the 'they's. In these cases we should be suspicious. Furthermore, preoccupation with a majority-minority analytic framework should not obscure the fundamental premise that racial and related prejudices can properly give rise to suspicion. Such prejudice could obviously generate a 'they-they' classification, and for that matter a classification that facially disadvantages the legislative majority but was intended, and will function, as a de facto they-they classification. Thus, there might be reason to believe that a law that apparently favors Blacks over Whites was specifically intended to disadvantage a subset of Whites that is both inadequately represented in the decision making body and the object of unusual prejudice. But where there is no reason to suspect that the comparative disadvantage will not be distributed evenly throughout the 'we' class, a we-they classification that favors the 'they's' does not merit 'special scrutiny'—though obviously the court should take a careful look to make sure that the case presented fits this description. Whether or not it is more blessed to give than to receive, it is surely less suspicious."

    Is that approach persuasive? Feasible? Does it take adequate account of the argument that "any legal classification by race weakens the government as an educative force"? See Kaplan, "Equal Justice in an Unequal World: Equality for the Negro—The Problem of Special Treatment," 61 Nw.U.L.Rev. 363 (1966). He notes that a major theme of anti-discrimination laws is to require "that a man is entitled to be judged on his own individual merit alone" and "that race is irrelevant to the worth of the individual." He adds: "Whatever the formulation, however, a statute specifically granting Negroes a benefit tends to undermine the principle we are working so hard to establish. Preference for Negroes can thus be expected to be a major factor in preventing the education [toward color blindness] we are trying to bring about through a host of other laws."

    If preferential programs are subject to strict scrutiny rather than the "mere rationality" test, can they survive constitutional attack, with respect to

---

8. In a footnote, Justice Douglas rejected reliance on the dictum in Swann indicating that school authorities could use racial factors to promote integration: "[T]here is a crucial difference between the policy suggested in Swann and that under consideration here: the Swann policy would impinge on no person's constitutional rights, because no one would be excluded from a public school and no one has a right to attend a segregated public school."

means and ends? Does that depend on the justification for the particular program? Is aid to a minority historically injured by discrimination a sufficiently "compelling" justification? Is a program like that in DeFunis justified by compensatory reasons—even if the harm was not directly inflicted by the State of Washington or its University or its Law School? Is it justified by social goals such as assuring more adequate legal representation for minorities? By a desire to enrich the education of nonminority students? [9]

3. *Preferences and "quotas" in employment.* Several courts have recently considered "affirmative action" employment programs attacked as unconstitutional racial quotas. See, e. g., Contractors Ass'n of Eastern Pa. v. Secretary of Labor, 442 F.2d 159, cert. denied, 404 U.S. 854 (1971), sustaining the so-called Philadelphia Plan established by Executive Order. That plan requires contractors bidding on federally assisted construction projects to include in their bids "affirmative action" programs "which shall include specific goals of minority manpower utilization." See also the division on the Court of Appeals on the question of the appropriate remedy for past discrimination in the hiring of firemen, in Carter v. Gallagher, 452 F.2d 315 (8th Cir. 1972), cert. denied, 406 U.S. 950 (1972): that court set aside an absolute preference for minority applicants but directed that one out of three new employees be a minority member until at least 20 minority persons were hired.

Is there a factual—and constitutionally relevant—difference between "goals" and "quotas"? Between judicially ordered remedies and programs established by the executive and legislative branches? Between remedies for past discrimination and programs in the absence of such findings? Between the employment programs and the school programs considered in note 2? [10]

4. *Benign programs and objecting members of the minority group.* a. What if the doubts about the benignness of a program arise because of harm to individual members of the supposedly aided minority? That problem has been discussed most commonly in connection with quota and "tipping point" programs designed to promote integrated housing: e. g., may racial exclusion of a Negro from a housing project be justified on the ground that the exclusion is pursuant to a quota designed to provide integrated housing for Negroes generally? Cf. Hughes v. Superior Court, 339 U.S. 460 (1950) (permitting enforcement of state policy against picketing to induce employment of workers in proportion to racial origin of customers). Do the harsh impacts of such quotas, precluding individuals solely because of race, and the risks of abuse of quota systems, compel their rejection? Should they be permitted if, after strict scrutiny, the Court is satisfied that no adequate

9. For a sampling of the extensive commentary on the constitutionality of color conscious admissions programs, see O'Neil, "Preferential Admissions: Equalizing the Access of Minority Groups to Higher Education," 80 Yale L.J. 699 (1971); Graglia, "Special Admission of the 'Culturally Deprived' to Law School," 119 U.Pa.L.Rev. 351 (1970); Bell, "In Defense of Minority Admissions Programs: A Response to Professor Graglia," 119 U.Pa.L.Rev. 364 (1970); Ely, "The Constitutionality of Reverse Discrimination," 41 U.

Chi.L.Rev. 723 (1974). See also the symposia on DeFunis in 60 U.Va.L. Rev. (1974) and in 75 Colum.L.Rev. (1975).

10. Recall also the comments in sec. 1 on the problem of whether employment qualifications are adequately job-related, in cases such as Griggs v. Duke Power Co., 401 U.S. 424 (1971), and the applications of that approach to litigation under the 14th Amendment in some lower court cases.

alternative means exist? See generally Bittker, "The Case of the Checker-Board Ordinance: An Experiment in Race Relations," 71 Yale L.J. 1387 (1962), and Navasky, "The Benevolent Housing Quota," 6 Howard L.J. 30 (1960).

b. More generally, may courts view integration programs that are clearly pro-integration in purpose and effect as "benign" even if some segments of the "benefited" minority assert that separation is desirable in the long run or at least needed temporarily to develop the group's cohesiveness, power and pride? See "Developments," 82 Harv.L.Rev. 1065, 1114 (1969): "A state program permitting or encouraging racial separatism could also be used to create a system of segregation." That comment proposes a middle course between permissive and strict review, suggesting careful scrutiny to determine the actual "predominant purpose" of the program. The racial classification would be permissible if "truly benign"—i. e., if used in a program "designed to achieve an equal position in society for all races."

Would that approach help with the problems created by the "division of opinion within the Black community itself"? Do the school segregation cases in sec. 2B commit the Court to adhering to integration as the only legitimate goal, and to opposing separateness as an ideal, whether it is called "separatism" or "segregation"? May a state university establish minority group residence halls on the ground that most members of the minority prefer separate residences? Could the university compel all members of the minority to live there? May a school system that has practiced de jure segregation permit some segregation to continue, in response to an expressed desire by a majority of the Black community for control of its own schools? May a de facto segregated system voluntarily undertaking an integration program exempt minority schools where the majority of parents prefer control of the school by the minority community?

5. *Preferential treatment for Native Americans.* In MORTON v. MANCARI, 417 U.S. 535 (1974), a unanimous Court rejected a constitutional attack on the federal program for employment preferences for qualified Native Americans in the Bureau of Indian Affairs. Justice Blackmun insisted that this "long standing Indian preference" was not a "racial" preference, but rather "an employment criterion reasonably designed to further the cause of Indian self-government and to make the BIA more responsive to the needs of its constituent groups." Since the preference only applies to Indians who are members of "federally recognized" tribes, he added, "the preference is political rather than racial in nature." He noted, moreover, that the "legal status of the BIA is truly sui generis." The preference was limited to BIA employment, "and we need not consider the obviously more difficult question that would be presented by a blanket exemption for Indians from all civil service examinations. Here the preference is reasonably and directly related to a legitimate, nonracially based goal" —a characteristic generally "absent from proscribed forms of racial discrimination." He concluded: "As long as the special treatment can be rationally tied to the fulfillment of Congress' unique obligation toward the Indians, such legislative judgments will not be disturbed." He emphasized the "unique legal status of Indian tribes under federal law" and "the plenary power of Congress, based on a history of treaties and the assumption of a

'guardian-ward' status, to legislate on behalf of federally-recognized Indian tribes."

SECTION 3. OTHER SUSPECT CLASSIFICATIONS?— ALIENAGE; ILLEGITIMACY; GENDER

Introduction. Are there classifications beyond race that are "suspect" and trigger strict scrutiny as to ends and means? Efforts to expand the category of suspect classifications beyond race is one of the strands of the "new" equal protection, as noted in the introduction to this chapter. To what extent are those efforts persuasive? To what extent have they succeeded? Sec. 3A considers classifications involving alienage: with respect to these, the Court has most clearly applied a "suspect" label. Secs. 3B and 3C turn to classifications involving illegitimacy and gender: with respect to these, the Court has repeatedly exercised greater scrutiny than that of the traditional, deferential "rationality" stance, though a majority has not clearly announced an elevation of either to the circle of the "suspect." [1] In examining the materials in this section, consider especially the extent to which the reasons which justify strict scrutiny of most racial classifications are properly applicable to governmental action based on alienage, illegitimacy and gender.

If the history and immediate purpose of the 14th Amendment were all that counted, only racial classifications directed against Blacks would be suspect. Recall the Slaughter-House Cases, chap. 8. But, as we have seen, the Court has readily found that *all* classifications resting on race and ancestry are ordinarily suspect. As long ago as the Strauder case, sec. 2A above, the Court had no doubt that a law "excluding all white men from jury service" would violate equal protection as well. Indeed, in that case the Court had no greater doubt that there would be a violation of equal protection "if a law should be passed excluding all naturalized Celtic Irishmen." Accordingly, the Court—and anti-discrimination legislation generally—have assimilated without much discussion governmental action based on national origin or ethnic criteria to that resting on racial factors. [2]

But is it possible to generalize more broadly? To what extent can one justify additional suspect classifications by extrapolating from the character-

---

1. One other criterion has elicited much litigation and commentary as a possibly "suspect" one: "wealth" or economic status. Consideration of wealth classifications is postponed to a separate section on equal protection and poverty, sec. 5 below, since the poverty area is an especially good example of the intertwining of "fundamental interests" and "suspect classification" analysis in equal protection developments.

2. See Hernandez v. Texas, 347 U.S. 475 (1954), involving discrimination against Mexican-Americans in selection for jury service. Where "persons of Mexican descent" constituted a separate class from whites in the community, an equal protection challenge was maintainable. Chief Justice Warren stated that "community prejudices are not static, and from time to time other differences [than "differences in race and color"] from the community norm may define other groups which need the same protection. Whether such a group exists within a community is a question of fact. [The 14th Amendment] is not directed solely against discrimination due to a 'two-class theory'—that is, based upon differences between 'white' and 'Negro.'"

istics that have elicited special scrutiny of racial criteria? Is a critical element the possession of an unalterable trait? A trait distinguishing the possessor from the majority? A trait relied on by the classifier for the purpose—or with the effect—of stigmatizing those possessing it? A trait frequently relied upon by the majority to signify its superiority vis-à-vis those possessing the trait? A trait rarely relevant to legitimate governmental objectives yet traditionally used to disadvantage those who possess it? A trait traditionally used and readily usable for "we-they" generalizations as opposed to "they-they" generalizations?[3]

Compare the brief comment in Justice Powell's majority opinion in San Antonio Ind. School Dist. v. Rodriguez, 411 U.S. 1 (1973) (sec. 5 below), characterizing "the traditional indices of suspectness" as follows: "The class [is] saddled with such disabilities, or subjected to such a history of purposeful unequal treatment, or relegated to such a position of political powerlessness as to command extraordinary protection from the majoritarian political process."[4] Note the references in that passage to "political power-lessness" and "protection from the majoritarian political process": it calls to mind the last paragraph of Justice Stone's Carolene Products footnote, considered in chap. 9 above.[5] Recall the earlier questions about the justifi-

---

3. See Ely, "The Wages of Crying Wolf: A Comment on Roe v. Wade," 82 Yale L.J. 920 (1973), suggesting special suspicion for classifications in which the decision makers (the "we"s) are particularly apt to resort to stereotypes resting on superiority-inferiority judgments when the "we"s resort to classifications disadvantaging the "they"s: "A decision to distinguish blacks from whites (or women from men) will therefore have its roots in a comparison between a 'we' stereotype and a 'they' stereotype, *viz.* They [blacks or women] are generally inferior to or not so well qualified as *we* [whites or men] are in the following respect(s), which we find sufficient to justify the classification: . . ." Ely adds: "The danger is therefore greater in we-they situations that we will overestimate the validity of the proposed stereotypical classification by seizing upon the positive myths about our own class and the negative myths about theirs—or indeed the realities respecting some or most members of the two classes—and too readily assuming that virtually the entire membership of the two classes fit the stereotypes and therefore that not many of 'them' will be unfairly deprived, nor many of 'us' unfairly benefitted, by the proposed classification. In short, I trust your generalizations about the differences between my gang and Wilfred's more than I do your generalizations about the differences between my gang and yours"—i. e.,

"there is less justification for special scrutiny of 'they-they' generalizations than for 'we-they' generalizations."

4. That case involved an unsuccessful claim that a variety of "wealth" discrimination should be viewed as suspect. Compare Justice Marshall's identification of "suspect" factors in his dissent in that case: "That wealth classifications alone have not necessarily been considered to bear the same high degree of suspectness as have classifications based on, for instance, race or alienage may be explainable on a number of grounds. The 'poor' may not be seen as politically powerless as certain discrete and insular minority groups. Personal poverty may entail much the same social stigma as historically attached to certain racial or ethnic groups. But personal poverty is not a permanent disability; its shackles may be escaped. Perhaps, most importantly, though, personal wealth may not necessarily share the general irrelevance as basis for legislative action that race or nationality is recognized to have."

5. Note also the explicit reliance on the Carolene Products footnote in elevating alienage to the list of suspect classifications in Graham v. Richardson, the next case below—and the criticism of that approach in Justice Rehnquist's dissent in Sugarman v. Dougall, also in sec. 3A below.

cations for that aspect of the footnote. Would "political powerlessness" alone justify a conclusion of "suspectness"?

What if the classifier relies on a trait which has some but not all of the characteristics that have made race traditionally suspect? Would a partial similarity to race justify a strict scrutiny similar to that usually afforded for racial classifications? Would a partial resemblance to racial criteria justify at least greater than minimal, if not strict, scrutiny? In short, are varying degrees of scrutiny warranted, depending upon the degree of suspectness of the classifying criterion? Is the Court implicitly applying such a sliding scale in some of the cases which follow? Is such a sliding scale approach, such a departure from two-tier analysis, justifiable? Or does it create too great a risk of ad hoc, unprincipled judicial intervention?

A. ALIENAGE

---

1. *Graham v. Richardson and welfare benefits.* The formal announcement that state classifications based on alienage are "suspect" came in 1971, from the Burger Court rather than the Warren Court, in GRAHAM v. RICHARDSON (decided together with Sailer v. Leger), 403 U.S. 365 (1971). That case involved challenges by aliens to state laws denying welfare benefits (a) to all noncitizens and (b) to aliens who had not resided in the United States for a total of 15 years. The Court held those eligibility restrictions unconstitutional.

Justice Blackmun stated: "[T]he Court's decisions have established that classifications based on alienage, like those based on nationality or race, are inherently suspect and subject to close judicial scrutiny. Aliens as a class are a prime example of a 'discrete and insular' minority (see United States v. Carolene Products Co., 304 U.S. 144, 152–153 n. 4 (1938)) for whom such heightened judicial solicitude is appropriate. Accordingly, it was said in [Takahashi v. Fish & Game Comm'n, 334 U.S. 410 (1948) that] 'the power of a state to apply its laws exclusively to its alien inhabitants as a class is confined within narrow limits.' " The Court accordingly rejected the argument that—since the states were not "discriminating with respect to race or nationality"—the favoring of American citizens over aliens in distributing welfare benefits involved no "invidious discrimination."

The Court was also unpersuaded by the states' efforts to justify the restrictions "on the basis of a State's 'special public interest' in favoring its own citizens over aliens in the distribution of limited resources such as welfare benefits." Justice Blackmun recognized that there were references to such a "special public interest" in prior opinions. For example, Crane v. New York, 239 U.S. 195 (1915), had affirmed a New York decision written by Justice Cardozo sustaining a New York prohibition on the employment of aliens in public works projects. Then-Judge Cardozo had said: "To disqualify aliens is discrimination indeed, but not arbitrary discrimination, for the principle of exclusion is the restriction of the resources of the state to the advancement and profit of the members of the state. . . . The state in determining what use shall be made for its own moneys, may legitimately consult

the welfare of its own citizens . . . . Whatever is a privilege rather than a right, may be made dependent upon citizenship." Justice Blackmun replied: "Whatever may be the contemporary vitality of the special public-interest doctrine in other contexts, [we] conclude that a State's desire to preserve limited welfare benefits for its own citizens is inadequate to justify" the restrictions challenged here. He noted that the "special public interest" doctrine was "heavily grounded" on the "privilege-right" distinction and added: "But this Court now has rejected the concept that constitutional rights turn upon whether a governmental benefit is characterized as a 'right' or as a 'privilege.' " Moreover, since "an alien as well as a citizen is a 'person' for equal protection purposes, a concern for fiscal integrity is no more compelling a justification for the questioned classification in these cases than it was in [Shapiro v. Thompson, sec. 4C below]." [1]

2. *Bar admission and public employment.* Three years later, a divided Court applied the strict scrutiny of Graham v. Richardson to invalidate Connecticut's exclusion of resident aliens from law practice—IN RE GRIFFITHS, 413 U.S. 717 (1973)—and New York's law providing that only American citizens may hold permanent positions in the competitive class of the state civil service—SUGARMAN v. DOUGALL, 413 U.S. 634 (1973). Chief Justice Burger and Justice Rehnquist dissented in Griffiths; Justice Rehnquist was the sole dissenter in Sugarman.

Justice Powell's majority opinion in Griffiths stated the appropriate scrutiny as follows: "In order to justify the use of a suspect classification, a State must show that its purpose or interest is both constitutionally permissible and substantial, and that its use of the classification is 'necessary [to] the accomplishment' of its purpose or the safeguarding of its interest." None of the asserted state interests was sufficiently substantial. The "undoubted interest in high professional standards" did not justify exclusion of all aliens. And the Court was unimpressed by the State's emphasis on lawyers as "officers of the Court" and "office holders." Justice Powell replied: "[T]hey are not officials of government by virtue of being lawyers. Nor does the status of holding a license to practice law place one so close to the core of the political process as to make him a formulator of government policy." [2]

In Sugarman, Justice Blackmun's majority opinion focused the strict scrutiny more on the State's means than on its ends. The state interest in assuring loyalty and defining the members of "its political community" could not justify a ban as broad and imprecise as New York's. The restriction was overinclusive and underinclusive: it applied, for example, to the "sanitation man" and the office worker, as well as to those directly participating in making important state policy. And it did not apply to high level positions not filled by competitive examinations. The Court concluded

---

1. In a separate part of his opinion, Justice Blackmun found "an additional reason" for unconstitutionality in federalism principles: the state laws conflicted with "overriding national policies in an area constitutionally entrusted to the Federal Government"; control over "entrance and abode" of aliens was an "exclusive federal power." Justice Harlan's concurrence did not join the equal protection passages of Justice Blackmun's opinion.

2. In a footnote, Justice Powell noted that appellant was eligible for naturalization—in part by reason of marriage to an American citizen—, had not filed a declaration of intention to become a citizen, "and has no present intention of doing so. In order

that state legislation treating "aliens differently from citizens requires a greater degree of precision." Moreover, Justice Blackmun found the "special public interest" argument no more persuasive here than in the welfare benefits context in Graham v. Richardson. And the claim that "aliens are more likely to leave their work than citizens" was not an adequate justification. Justice Blackmun noted, however, that alien restrictions were permissible in the exercise of "a State's constitutional prerogatives" to "preserve the basic conception of a political community": "This Court has never held that aliens have a constitutional right to vote or to hold high public office under the Equal Protection Clause. Indeed, implicit in many of this Court's voting rights decisions [sec. 4A below] is the notion that citizenship is a permissible criterion for limiting such rights." [3]

Justice Rehnquist's lengthy dissent, applicable to both cases, questioned any extension of the "suspect classification" notion beyond the race area. He insisted that "there is no language [or] any historical evidence as to the intent of the Framers [of the 14th Amendment], which would suggest in the slightest degree that it was intended to render alienage a 'suspect' classification, that it was designed in any way to protect 'discrete and insular minorities' other than racial minorities, or that it would in any way justify" the result reached here. He noted that in numerous cases "the Constitution itself recognizes a basic difference between citizens and aliens." The 14th Amendment itself, he noted, begins with a definition of citizenship: "That a 'citizen' was considered [to] be a rationally distinct subclass of all 'persons' is obvious from the language of the Amendment."

Moreover, Justice Rehnquist objected to the reliance on the Carolene Products footnote rationale in Graham v. Richardson to include alienage within the suspect classifications category.[4] Nor could he agree with the

---

to become a citizen, appellant would be required to renounce her citizenship of the Netherlands."

3. See also the Court's summary affirmance of a decision invalidating Indiana's requirement of citizenship for licensed real estate salesmen. Indiana Real Estate Comm'n v. Satoskar, 417 U.S. 938 (1974). The order simply cited Griffiths. Justice Rehnquist dissented.

Compare Espinoza v. Farah Mfg. Co., 414 U.S. 86 (1973), an 8 to 1 decision holding that a private employer's refusal to hire aliens did not constitute employment discrimination on the basis of "national origin" in violation of Title VII of the Civil Rights Act of 1964. Justice Douglas commented at the outset of his dissent: "It is odd that the Court which holds that a State may not bar an alien from the practice of law or deny employment to aliens can read a federal statute that prohibits discrimination in employment on account of 'national origin' as to permit discrimination against aliens." Justice Marshall's

majority opinion insisted, however, that an attribution of such a congressional intent to protect aliens would be inconsistent with "the historical practice of requiring citizenship as a condition" of federal employment. (He added that it was not necessary here to reach the question of the constitutionality of that "historical practice." See note 3 below.) Justice Marshall refused to defer to a contrary EEOC guideline—broadly condemning alienage restrictions as violations of the statute—since Farah's general hiring practices did not discriminate against persons of Mexican national origin.

4. Portions of Justice Rehnquist's critique of that rationale have been quoted earlier, in chap. 9. Recall his comment: "It would hardly take extraordinary ingenuity for a lawyer to find 'insular and discrete' minorities at every turn in the road. . . . I cannot find [any] constitutional authority for such a 'ward of the Court' approach to equal protection."

Court's suggestion that it was inappropriate to classify on the basis of alienage because it is a "status": "[T]here is a marked difference between a status or condition such as illegitimacy, national origin, or race, which cannot be altered by an individual, and the 'status' of the [challengers here]." He insisted that the traditional rationality test was applicable and readily satisfied here.

3. *Some questions.* Is the extension of the suspect classifications category to aliens justifiable? Even though alienage is not an "unalterable" trait? Does the extension rest primarily on the "political powerlessness" rationale? Note the indication in Sugarman that the exclusion of aliens from voting and holding public office is justifiable.

What other restrictions on aliens can survive strict scrutiny? Is it permissible to ban aliens from positions where undivided allegiance to this country is important? Is the strict scrutiny approach applicable to the restrictions on employment of aliens by the federal government? Note the traditionally recognized exclusive and broad power of the national government over aliens—a power which provided an alternative ground for decision in Graham v. Richardson, indeed. (See also Kleindienst v. Mandel, 408 U.S. 753 (1972), where Justice Blackmun found the ordinary bite of the First Amendment very much softened in the context of excluding aliens on political grounds.) At the end of the 1973 Term, the Court granted review—in Hampton v. Mow Sun Wong—of a decision holding unconstitutional U.S. Civil Service regulations excluding resident aliens from employment in the federal civil service. During the 1974 Term, the Court set that case for reargument in the fall of 1975. Do the equal protection ingredients read into the due process clause of the Fifth Amendment since Bolling v. Sharpe, sec. 2B above, invalidate that ban? [5]

B. ILLEGITIMACY

Introduction. What is the meaning of the modern Court's wavering course in the review of classifications based on illegitimacy? What is clear from the cases which follow is that the Court *has* invalidated some illegitimacy classifications that would seem capable of surviving the deferential standards of the old equal protection. Description and explanation of that phenomenon is more difficult. What is the Court's standard of review? Has illegitimacy become a "suspect" classification? Should it be? Is the standard something short of strict scrutiny but greater than "mere rationality"— even "rationality with bite"? Do the cases turn in part on the "fundamental interests" strand of the new equal protection, sec. 4 below? If so, what is the "fundamental interest" involved?

1. *Levy and Glona.* In companion cases near the end of the Warren era, a divided Court held unconstitutional provisions of the Louisiana wrongful death statute that barred unacknowledged illegitimate children from re-

---

5. Recall Justice Marshall's reference to the "historical practice of requiring citizenship as a condition" of federal employment, in the Espinoza case, footnote 3 above.

covering for the death of the mother, and barred a mother from recovering for the death of her unacknowledged illegitimate child. (Under Louisiana law, an illegitimate child can be "acknowledged"—and treated as legitimate for many purposes—by a declaration formally executed by at least one of the parents.) Justice Douglas wrote for the majority in each case. LEVY v. LOUISIANA, 391 U.S. 68 (1968); GLONA v. AMERICAN GUARANTEE & LIABILITY INS. CO., 391 U.S. 73 (1968).

Justice Douglas' brief opinion in Levy stated: "We start from the premise that illegitimate children are not 'nonpersons.' They are humans, live and have their being. They are clearly 'persons' within the meaning of [the equal protection clause]. While a State has broad power when it comes to making classifications, it may not draw a line which constitutes an invidious discrimination against a particular class. Though the test has been variously stated, the end result is whether the line drawn is a rational one. See [Morey v. Doud].

"In applying the Equal Protection Clause to social and economic legislation, we give great latitude to the legislature in making classifications. [Williamson v. Lee Optical]. [But] we have been extremely sensitive when it comes to basic civil rights [e. g., Harper v. Board of Elections (voting—sec. 4 below)] and have not hesitated to strike down an invidious classification even though it had history and tradition on its side. [Brown v. Board of Education]. The rights asserted here involve the intimate, familial relationship between a child and his own mother. When the child's claim of damage for loss of his mother is in issue, why, in terms of 'equal protection,' should the tortfeasors go free merely because the child is illegitimate? Why should the illegitimate child be denied rights merely because of his birth out of wedlock? He certainly is subject to all the responsibilities of a citizen, including the payment of taxes and conscription under the Selective Service Act. How under our constitutional regime can he be denied correlative rights which other citizens enjoy?

"Legitimacy or illegitimacy of birth has no relation to the nature of the wrong allegedly inflicted on the mother. These children, though illegitimate, were dependent on her; she cared for them and nurtured them; they were indeed hers in the biological and in the spiritual sense; in her death they suffered wrong in the sense that any dependent would. We conclude that it is invidious to discriminate against them when no action, conduct, or demeanor of theirs [1] is possibly relevant to the harm that was done the mother."

In Glona, the companion case, Justice Douglas' majority opinion concluded that "we see no possible rational basis (Morey v. Doud) for assuming that if the natural mother is allowed recovery for the wrongful death of her illegitimate child, the cause of illegitimacy will be served. It would, indeed,

---

1. We can say with Shakespeare: "Why bastard, wherefore base? When my dimensions are as well compact, My mind as generous, and my shape as true, As honest madam's issue? Why brand they us With base? with baseness? bastardy? base, base?" King Lear, Act I, Scene 2. [Footnote by the Court.]

[Compare the response in Justice Harlan's dissent: "Supposing that the Bard had any views on the law of legitimacy, they might more easily be discerned from Edmund's character than from the words he utters in defense of the only thing he cares for, himself."]

be farfetched to assume that women have illegitimate children so that they can be compensated in damages for their death. . . . To say that the test of equal protection should be the 'legal' rather than the biological relationship is to avoid the issue." [2]

Justice Harlan's dissent, joined by Justices Black and Stewart and applicable to both cases, called the decisions "constitutional curiosities." He noted: "One important reason why recovery for wrongful death had everywhere to await statutory delineation is that the interest one person has in the life of another is inherently intractable." Louisiana's statute was part of a typical pattern: legislatures, responding to the "diffuseness of interests, generally defined classes of proper plaintiffs by highly arbitrary lines based on family relationships, excluding issues concerning the actual effect of the death on the plaintiff." Accordingly, the Louisiana scheme, like that in such statutes generally, "makes everything the Court says about affection and nurture and dependence altogether irrelevant." He insisted that states could properly define eligible classes "in terms of their legal rather than their biological relation to the deceased." He could not understand how the Court's insistence on biological rather than legal relationships would make a statutory scheme "even marginally more 'rational,' [for] neither a biological relationship nor legal acknowledgment is indicative of the love or economic dependence that may exist between two persons." He thought it "preposterous to suggest" that Louisiana had made illegitimates into "nonpersons."

Moreover, denying recovery to unacknowledged illegitimates had "obvious justification": "If it be conceded, as I assume it is, that the State has power to provide that people who choose to live together should go through the formalities of marriage and, in default, that people who bear children should acknowledge them, it is logical to enforce these requirements by declaring that the general class of rights that are dependent upon family relationships shall be accorded only when the formalities as well as the biology of those relationships are present. Moreover, and for many of the same reasons why a State is empowered to require formalities in the first place, a State may choose to simplify a particular proceeding by reliance on formal papers rather than a contest of proof. That suits for wrongful death, actions to determine the heirs of intestates, and the like, must as a constitutional matter deal with every claim of biological paternity or maternity on its merits is an exceedingly odd proposition."

2. *Labine.* Three years later, LABINE v. VINCENT, 401 U.S. 532 (1971), suggested to many a substantial Court withdrawal from the greater scrutiny of state impositions of disadvantages on illegitimates indicated in Levy-Glona. In Labine, the dissenters in Levy joined with the two new appointees (Chief Justice Burger and Justice Blackmun) in distinguishing Levy and sustaining an illegitimacy classification. Labine involved a Louisiana intestate succession provision which subordinated rights of *acknowledged* illegitimate children to those of legitimates and other relatives of the parent.

---

2. Note also King v. Smith, 392 U.S. 309 (1968), a welfare benefits case decided by the majority on statutory grounds, with Justice Douglas' concurrence citing Levy and invoking the equal protection clause to conclude: "I would say that the immorality of the mother has no rational connection with the need of her children under any welfare program."

Levy and Glona were distinguished in part by general references to the traditional state interest in succession laws and in part by a more specific statement that here, unlike Levy, the state had not "created an insurmountable barrier to this illegitimate child," since the father could have left a portion of his estate to the acknowledged illegitimate "had he bothered to follow the simple formalities of executing a will."

Justice Black's brief opinion found remarkably little federal constitutional basis for review. One passage suggested that there might not even be minimum rationality review: Justice Black emphasized that "the power to make rules to establish, protect, and strengthen family life as well as to regulate the disposition of property left in Louisiana by a man dying there is committed [to] the legislature of that State. Absent a specific constitutional guarantee, it is for that legislature, not the life-tenure judges of this Court, to select from among possible laws." In only one brief passage, in a footnote, did Justice Black suggest any greater scrutiny than that: "Even if we were to apply the 'rational basis' test, [the] statute clearly has a rational basis in view of Louisiana's interest in promoting family life and of directing the disposition of property left within the State."

Justice Brennan's dissent, joined by Justices Douglas, White and Marshall, thought the decision unprincipled: he viewed it as excluding illegitimates entirely from the protection of the equal protection clause, "in order to uphold the untenable and discredited moral prejudice of bygone centuries which vindictively punished not only the illegitimates' parents, but also the hapless, and innocent, children." The attempted distinction of Levy, he insisted, was inadequate: Levy involved no "insurmountable barrier," since recovery would have been allowed if the mother had formally acknowledged the child. Accordingly, the law was plainly unconstitutional, even under minimum rationality standards.[3]

3. *Weber.* The comments on the demise of Levy in view of Labine proved exaggerated. In WEBER v. AETNA CASUALTY & SURETY CO., 406 U.S. 164 (1972), Justice Powell's majority opinion felt bound to follow Levy and distinguish Labine. The Court held that the claims of dependent unacknowledged illegitimate children to death benefits under Louisiana's workmen's compensation law could not be subordinated to the claims of legitimate children. This "denial of equal recovery rights" was found to be a violation of equal protection.

In explaining why Levy rather than Labine was the governing precedent, Justice Powell described Labine as reflecting primarily "the traditional deference to a State's prerogative to regulate the disposition at death of property within its borders." In Labine, moreover, the father "might easily have modified his daughter's disfavored position"; here, by contrast, the father could not have acknowledged his illegitimate children even if he had wished to do so (because he remained formally married to the mother of his legiti-

---

3. In a footnote, Justice Brennan added: "In view of my conclusion that the present discrimination cannot stand even under the 'some rational basis' standard, I need not reach the questions whether illegitimacy is a 'suspect' classification that the State could not adopt in any circumstances without showing a compelling state interest." He commented, however: "This Court has generally treated as suspect a classification that discriminates against an individual on the basis of factors over which he has no control."

mate children). Here, in short, there was an "insurmountable barrier." Accordingly, Justice Powell concluded, "it would require a disregard of precedent and the principles of stare decisis to hold that Levy did not control the facts of the case before us."

Justice Powell proceeded, moreover, to "reaffirm" and elaborate the reasoning of Levy. He stated: "The tests to determine the validity of state statutes under the Equal Protection Clause have been variously expressed, but this Court requires, at a minimum, that a statutory classification bear some rational relationship to a legitimate state purpose. [Morey v. Doud; Lee Optical.] Though the latitude given state economic and social regulation is necessarily broad, when state statutory classifications approach sensitive and fundamental personal rights, this Court exercises a stricter scrutiny [e. g., Brown v. Board of Education]. The essential inquiry in all the foregoing cases is, however, inevitably a dual one: What legitimate state interest does the classification promote? What fundamental personal rights might the classification endanger?"

Justice Powell recognized the important state interest in the "protection of the family unit," but questioned that the statute would promote that interest: e. g., as in Glona, denial of recovery would not lead persons to "shun illicit relations." Justice Powell was also "mindful that States have frequently drawn arbitrary lines in workmen's compensation and wrongful-death statutes to facilitate potentially difficult problems of proof." But that state interest, he found, would not be "significantly disturbed by our decision."

In a more general concluding paragraph, Justice Powell added: "The status of illegitimacy has expressed through the ages society's condemnation of irresponsible liaisons beyond the bonds of marriage. But visiting this condemnation on the head of an infant is illogical and unjust." Moreover, it was "contrary to the basic concept of our system that legal burdens should bear some relationship to individual responsibility or wrongdoing. [P]enalizing the illegitimate child is an ineffectual—as well as an unjust—way of deterring the parent. Courts are powerless to prevent the social opprobrium suffered by these hapless children, but the Equal Protection Clause does enable us to strike down discriminatory laws relating to status of birth [citing "suspect" classification cases involving alienage and race] where—as in this case—the classification is justified by no legitimate state interest, compelling or otherwise." [4]

Justice Rehnquist was the sole dissenter. He thought that the case might be closer to Labine than to Levy, though he "would not feel impelled to dissent if I regarded Levy as rightly decided." But he thought Levy wrong and insisted that "rational relation" was the appropriate standard—a standard he thought satisfied in Levy and here. He added: "Since Levy was a constitutional holding, its doctrine is open to later re-examination to a greater extent than if it had decided a [nonconstitutional issue]." He proceeded to review the history of equal protection litigation and to disagree

---

4. Justice Blackmun concurred in the result, placing "far more emphasis than does the Court" on the statutory barrier to acknowledgment by the father. Without that barrier, "the case might be a different one."

with the recent emergence of the two-tier approach. He characterized the Weber majority's "two-pronged" standard as a "hybrid" version of "old" and "new" equal protection and concluded: "While the Court's opinion today is by no means a sharp departure from the precedents on which it relies, it is an extraordinary departure from what I conceive to be the intent of the framers of the [14th Amendment]. The relationship of the 'legitimate' state interest and 'fundamental personal right' analysis to the constitutional guarantee of equal protection of the law is approximately the same as that of 'freedom of contract' to the constitutional guarantee [of due process]. [See chap. 9 above.] It is an invitation for judicial exegesis over and above the commands of the Constitution, in which values that cannot possibly have their source in that instrument are invoked to either validate or condemn the countless laws enacted by the various States." Equal protection does not require state laws to be "logical" or "just"; it "requires only that there be some conceivable set of facts that may justify the classification involved"; and that requirement was met here.[5]

C. GENDER–BASED CLASSIFICATIONS

Introduction. Should gender-based classifications be considered "suspect"? Does legislation differentiating on the basis of sex warrant stricter scrutiny? While the battle for ratification of the proposed 27th Amendment, the Equal Rights Amendment, was being waged in the state legislatures in the early 1970's, the Court considered a growing number of cases challenging gender-based classifications under the equal protection clause. Majority support for considering sex a suspect classification did not develop; but in a considerable number of cases, the Court sustained the challenges without formally invoking strict scrutiny. Consider the standards of review applied in the cases which follow. To what extent do they rest on minimum rationality standards? To what extent do they illustrate the "newer" equal protection? Do the Court's actual exercises of review conform with its articulated standards? Is gender sufficiently like other traits which have been considered "suspect" to warrant strict scrutiny? The materials begin with a 1973 decision—Frontiero v. Richardson—in which four of the Justices found gender to be a suspect classification. Consider the arguments

---

5. The Levy-Weber approach was solidified and applied in a series of subsequent cases. Thus, the per curiam decision in Gomez v. Perez, 409 U.S. 535 (1973), invalidated Texas laws denying illegitimate children a judicially enforceable right to support from their natural fathers. The Court concluded that, under Levy and Weber, "a State may not invidiously discriminate against illegitimate children by denying them substantial benefits accorded children generally. . . . For a State to do so is 'illogical and unjust.'" See also New Jersey Welfare Rights Organization v. Cahill, 411 U.S. 619 (1973).

Compare Jimenez v. Weinberger, 417 U.S. 629 (1974) (sec. 5 below), where the Court found it unnecessary to decide whether illegitimacy is a "suspect classification" and thought it sufficient to quote Weber's "illogical and unjust" language in striking down a Social Security Act provision affecting some illegitimates adversely. The Court's emphasis was on discrimination *among* classes of illegitimates rather than on distinctions between legitimates and illegitimates.

marshalled there to show the suspectness of sex classifications in light of the later materials—cases both before and after Frontiero examining sex classifications without formally adopting strict scrutiny.

FRONTIERO v. RICHARDSON

411 U.S. 677, 93 S.Ct. 1764, 36 L.Ed.2d 583 (1973).

Appeal from the United States District Court for the Middle District of Alabama.

Mr. Justice BRENNAN announced the judgment of the Court in an opinion in which Mr. Justice DOUGLAS, Mr. Justice WHITE, and Mr. Justice MARSHALL join.

The question before us concerns the right of a female member of the uniformed services to claim her spouse as a "dependent" for the purposes of obtaining increased quarters allowances and medical and dental benefits [on] an equal footing with male members. Under [the] statutes, a serviceman may claim his wife as a "dependent" without regard to whether she is in fact dependent upon him for any part of her support. A servicewoman, on the other hand, may not claim her husband as a "dependent" under these programs unless he is in fact dependent upon her for over one-half of his support. Thus, the question for decision is whether this difference in treatment constitutes an unconstitutional discrimination against servicewomen in violation of the Due Process Clause of the Fifth Amendment. A three-judge [court] rejected this contention .   .   ..

I.   In an effort to attract career personnel through reenlistment, Congress established [a] scheme for the provision of fringe benefits to members of the uniformed services on a competitive basis with business and industry. Thus, [a] member of the uniformed services with dependents is entitled to an increased "basic allowance for quarters" and [a] members' dependents are provided comprehensive medical and dental care.

Appellant Sharron Frontiero, a lieutenant in the United States Air Force, sought increased quarters allowances, and housing and medical benefits for her husband, appellant Joseph Frontiero, on the ground that he was her "dependent." Although such benefits would automatically have been granted with respect to the wife of a male member of the uniformed services, appellant's application was denied because she failed to demonstrate that her husband was dependent on her for more than one-half of his support.[1] Appellants then commenced this suit, contending that, by making this distinction, the statutes unreasonably discriminate on the basis of sex in violation of the Due Process Clause of the Fifth Amendment.[2] In essence, appellants asserted

---

1. Appellant Joseph Frontiero is a full-time student at Huntingdon College in Montgomery, Alabama. According to the agreed stipulation of facts, his living expenses, including his share of the household expenses, total approximately $354 per month. Since he receives $205 per month in veterans' benefits, it is clear that he is not dependent upon appellant Sharron Fron-tiero for more than one-half of his support. [Footnote by Justice Brennan.]

2. "[W]hile the Fifth Amendment contains no equal protection clause, it does forbid discrimination that is 'so unjustifiable as to be violative of due process.'" Schneider v. Rusk, 377 U. S. 163, 168 (1964); see Shapiro v.

that the discriminatory impact of the statutes is two fold: first, as a procedural matter, a female member is required to demonstrate her spouse's dependency, while no such burden is imposed upon male members; and second, as a substantive matter, a male member who does not provide more than one-half of his wife's support receives benefits, while a similarly situated female member is denied such benefits. . . . .

Although the legislative history of these statutes sheds virtually no light on the purposes underlying the differential treatment accorded male and female members, a majority of the three-judge District Court surmised that Congress might reasonably have concluded that, since the husband in our society is generally the "breadwinner" in the family—and the wife typically the "dependent" partner—"it would be more economical to require married female members claiming husbands to prove actual dependency than to extend the presumption of dependency to such members." Indeed, given the fact that approximately 99% of all members of the uniformed services are male, the District Court speculated that such differential treatment might conceivably lead to a "considerable saving of administrative expense and manpower."

II.   At the outset, appellants contend that classifications based upon sex, like classifications based upon race, alienage, and national origin, are inherently suspect and must therefore be subjected to close judicial scrutiny. We agree and, indeed, find at least implicit support for such an approach in our unanimous decision only last Term in Reed v. Reed, 404 U.S. 71 (1971).

In Reed, the Court considered the constitutionality of an Idaho statute providing that, when two individuals are otherwise equally entitled to appointment as administrator of an estate, the male applicant must be preferred to the female.   Appellant, the mother of the deceased, and appellee, the father, filed competing petitions for appointment as administrator of their son's estate.   Since the parties, as parents of the deceased, were members of the same entitlement class, the statutory preference was invoked and the father's petition was therefore granted.   Appellant claimed that this statute, by giving a mandatory preference to males over females without regard to their individual qualifications, violated the Equal Protection Clause of the Fourteenth Amendment.

The Court noted that the Idaho statute "provides that different treatment be accorded to the applicants on the basis of their sex; it thus establishes a classification subject to scrutiny under the Equal Protection Clause." Under "traditional" equal protection analysis, a legislative classification must be sustained unless it is "patently arbitrary" and bears no rational relationship to a legitimate governmental interest.

In an effort to meet this standard, appellee contended that the statutory scheme was a reasonable measure designed to reduce the workload on probate courts by eliminating one class of contests.   Moreover, appellee argued that

Thompson, 394 U.S. 618, 641–642 (1969); Bolling v. Sharpe, 347 U.S. 497 (1954). [Footnote by Justice Brennan.]

[Note Justice Brennan's stronger statement in the 1975 decision in Wein-

berger v. Wiesenfeld, below: "This Court's approach to Fifth Amendment equal protection claims has always been precisely the same as to equal protection claims under the Fourteenth Amendment."]

the mandatory preference for male applicants was in itself reasonable since "men [are] as a rule more conversant with business affairs than . . . women." Indeed, appellee maintained that "it is a matter of common knowledge, that women still are not engaged in politics, the professions, business or industry to the extent that men are." And the Idaho Supreme Court, in upholding the constitutionality of this statute, suggested that the Idaho Legislature might reasonably have "concluded that in general men are better qualified to act as an administrator than are women."

Despite these contentions, however, the Court held the statutory preference for male applicants unconstitutional. In reaching this result, the Court implicitly rejected appellee's apparently rational explanation of the statutory scheme, and concluded that, by ignoring the individual qualifications of particular applicants, the challenged statute provided "dissimilar treatment for men and women who are . . . similarly situated." The Court therefore held that, even though the State's interest in achieving administrative efficiency "is not without some legitimacy," "[t]o give a mandatory preference to members of either sex over members of the other, merely to accomplish the elimination of hearings on the merits, is to make the very kind of arbitrary legislative choice forbidden by the [Constitution] . . . ." This departure from "traditional" rational-basis analysis with respect to sex-based classifications is clearly justified.

There can be no doubt that our Nation has had a long and unfortunate history of sex discrimination.[3] Traditionally, such discrimination was rationalized by an attitude of "romantic paternalism" which, in practical effect, put women, not on a pedestal, but in a cage. Indeed, this paternalistic attitude became so firmly rooted in our national consciousness that, 100 years ago, a distinguished Member of this Court was able to proclaim:

> "Man is, or should be, woman's protector and defender. The natural and proper timidity and delicacy which belongs to the female sex evidently unfits it for many of the occupations of civil life. The constitution of the family organization, which is founded in the divine ordinance, as well as in the nature of things, indicates the domestic sphere as that which properly belongs to the domain and functions of womanhood. The harmony, not to say identity, of interests and views which belong, or should belong, to the family institution is repugnant to the idea of a woman adopting a distinct and independent career from that of her husband. . . .
>
> " . . . The paramount destiny and mission of woman are to fulfil the noble and benign offices of wife and mother. This is the law of the Creator." Bradwell v. State, 16 Wall. 130, 141 (1873) (Bradley, J., concurring).[4]

3. Indeed, the position of women in this country at its inception is reflected in the view expressed by Thomas Jefferson that women should be neither seen nor heard in society's decision-making councils. [Footnote by Justice Brennan.]

4. The Bradwell decision sustained a statute denying to women the right to practice law. After the reference to "the law of the Creator" in his concurrence, Justice Bradley added: "And the rules of civil society must be adapted to the general constitution of things, and cannot be based upon exceptional cases."

As a result of notions such as these, our statute books gradually became laden with gross, stereotyped distinctions between the sexes and, indeed, throughout much of the 19th century the position of women in our society was, in many respects, comparable to that of blacks under the pre-Civil War slave codes. Neither slaves nor women could hold office, serve on juries, or bring suit in their own names, and married women traditionally were denied the legal capacity to hold or convey property or to serve as legal guardians of their own children. And although blacks were guaranteed the right to vote in 1870, women were denied even that right—which is itself "preservative of other basic civil and political rights"—until adoption of the Nineteenth Amendment half a century later.

It is true, of course, that the position of women in America has improved markedly in recent decades. Nevertheless, it can hardly be doubted that, in part because of the high visibility of the sex characteristic, women still face pervasive, although at times more subtle, discrimination in our educational institutions, in the job market and, perhaps most conspicuously, in the political arena.[5]

Moreover, since sex, like race and national origin, is an immutable characteristic determined solely by the accident of birth, the imposition of special disabilities upon the members of a particular sex because of their sex would seem to violate "the basic concept of our system that legal burdens should bear some relationship to individual responsibility . . .." [Weber, sec. 2B above.] And what differentiates sex from such nonsuspect statuses as intelligence or physical disability, and aligns it with the recognized suspect criteria, is that the sex characteristic frequently bears no relation to ability to perform or contribute to society. As a result, statutory distinctions between the sexes often have the effect of invidiously relegating the entire class of females to inferior legal status without regard to the actual capabilities of its individual members.

 . . . Congress has itself concluded that classifications based upon sex are inherently invidious [in submitting the Equal Rights Amendment and in enacting laws against sex discrimination], and this conclusion of a coequal branch of Government is not without significance to the question presently under consideration. Cf. [Oregon v. Mitchell; Katzenbach v. Morgan (both chap. 11, sec. 4, below)].

With these considerations in mind, we can only conclude that classifications based upon sex, like classifications based upon race, alienage, or national origin, are inherently suspect, and must therefore be subjected to strict judicial scrutiny. Applying the analysis mandated by that stricter standard of review, it is clear that the statutory scheme now before us is constitutionally invalid.

---

5. It is true, of course, that when viewed in the abstract, women do not constitute a small and powerless minority. Nevertheless, in part because of past discrimination, women are vastly underrepresented in this Nation's decisionmaking councils. There has never been a female President, nor a female member of this Court. Not a single woman presently sits in the United States Senate, and only 14 women hold seats in the House of Representatives. And, as appellants point out, this underrepresentation is present throughout all levels of our State and Federal Government. [Footnote by Justice Brennan.]

III.   The sole basis of the classification established in the challenged statutes is the sex of the individuals involved. [T]he statute operates so as to deny benefits to a female [while] at the same time granting such benefits to a [male] who likewise provides less than one-half of his spouse's support. [Moreover], the Government concedes that the differential treatment accorded men and women under these statutes serves no purpose other than mere "administrative convenience." In essence, the Government maintains that, as an empirical matter, wives in our society frequently are dependent upon their husbands, while husbands rarely are dependent upon their wives. Thus, the Government argues that Congress might reasonably have concluded that it would be both cheaper and easier simply conclusively to presume that wives of male members are financially dependent upon their husbands, while burdening female members with the task of establishing dependency in fact.[6]

The Government offers no concrete evidence, however, tending to support its view that such differential treatment in fact saves the Government any money. In order to satisfy the demands of strict judicial scrutiny, the Government must demonstrate, for example, that it is actually cheaper to grant increased benefits with respect to *all* male members, than it is to determine which male members are in fact entitled to such benefits and to grant increased benefits only to those members whose wives actually meet the dependency requirement. Here, however, there is substantial evidence that, if put to the test, many of the wives of male members would fail to qualify for benefits. And in light of the fact that the dependency determination with respect to the husbands of female members is presently made solely on the basis of affidavits, rather than through the more costly hearing process, the Government's explanation of the statutory scheme is, to say the least, questionable.

In any case, our prior decisions make clear that, although efficacious administration of governmental programs is not without some importance, "the Constitution recognizes higher values than speed and efficiency." And when we enter the realm of "strict judicial scrutiny," there can be no doubt that "administrative convenience" is not a shibboleth, the mere recitation of which dictates constitutionality. On the contrary, any statutory scheme which draws a sharp line between the sexes, *solely* for the purpose of achieving administrative convenience, necessarily commands "dissimilar treatment for men and women who are . . . similarly situated," and therefore involves the "very kind of arbitrary legislative choice forbidden by the [Constitution] . . .." [Reed v. Reed.] We therefore conclude that, by according differential treatment to male and female members of the uniformed services for the sole purpose of achieving administrative convenience, the challenged statutes violate the Due Process Clause of the Fifth Amendment insofar as they require a female member to prove the dependency of her husband.[7]

Reversed.

6. It should be noted that these statutes are not in any sense designed to rectify the effects of past discrimination against women. On the contrary, these statutes seize upon a group—women—who have historically suffered discrimination in employment, and rely on the effects of this past discrimination as a justification for heaping on additional economic disadvantages. [Footnote by Justice Brennan. Cf. Kahn v. Shevin, below.]

7. As noted earlier, the basic purpose of these statutes was to provide fringe benefits to members of the uniformed

Mr. Justice STEWART concurs in the judgment, agreeing that the statutes before us work an invidious discrimination in violation of the Constitution. Reed v. Reed.

Mr. Justice POWELL, with whom The Chief Justice [BURGER] and Mr. Justice BLACKMUN join, concurring in the judgment.

I agree that the challenged statutes constitute an unconstitutional discrimination against servicewomen in violation of the Due Process Clause of the Fifth Amendment, but I cannot join the opinion of Mr. Justice Brennan . . . .. It is unnecessary for the Court in this case to characterize sex as a suspect classification, with all of the far-reaching implications of such a holding. Reed v. Reed, which abundantly supports our decision today, did not add sex to the narrowly limited group of classifications which are inherently suspect. In my view, we can and should decide this case on the authority of Reed and reserve for the future any expansion of its rationale.

There is another, and I find compelling, reason for deferring a general categorizing of sex classifications as invoking the strictest test of judicial scrutiny. The Equal Rights Amendment, which if adopted will resolve the substance of this precise question, has been approved by the Congress and submitted for ratification by the States. If this Amendment is duly adopted, it will represent the will of the people accomplished in the manner prescribed by the Constitution. By acting prematurely and unnecessarily, as I view it, the Court has assumed a decisional responsibility at the very time when state legislatures, functioning within the traditional democratic process, are debating the proposed Amendment. It seems to me that this reaching out to pre-empt by judicial action a major political decision which is currently in process of resolution does not reflect appropriate respect for duly prescribed legislative processes. . . .

Mr. Justice REHNQUIST dissents for the reasons stated by Judge Rives in his opinion for the District Court, Frontiero v. Laird, 341 F.Supp. 201 (1972).*

GENDER–BASED CLASSIFICATIONS AND THE APPROPRIATE STANDARD OF REVIEW

1. *Reed v. Reed: Traditional or stricter scrutiny?* a. In REED v. REED, 404 U.S. 71 (1971), the appellant's elaborate brief strenuously urged the Court to find sex a suspect classification and accordingly to subject gender-based laws to strict scrutiny. The Court declined that invitation. Yet,

services in order to establish a compensation pattern which would attract career personnel through re-enlistment. Our conclusion in no wise invalidates the statutory schemes except insofar as they require a female member to prove the dependency of her spouse. [Footnote by Justice Brennan.]

* Judge Rives, after doubting that the statute classified according to sex, insisted that the law was valid even if it contained a sex classification. Sex, in his view, was not "suspect," and the classification satisfied the standard articulated in Reed v. Reed because it was a rational means to the legislative end—administrative convenience in the disbursement of dependency benefits. (In any event, Judge Rives added, Reed was distinguishable because qualified females in Frontiero were not *totally* excluded, but merely had to overcome a greater burden in order to qualify for benefits.)

in the opinion discussed at length in Frontiero, above, the unanimous Reed Court sustained the discrimination claim, purporting to apply a traditional "rationality" standard of review. Chief Justice Burger stated the question as being "whether a difference in the sex of competing applicants for letters of administration bears a rational relationship to a state objective that is sought to be advanced by the operation of [the Idaho law]." And he quoted as the applicable standard the statement in Royster Guano Co. v. Virginia, 253 U.S. 412 (1920), noted at the beginning of this chapter: a classification "must be reasonable, not arbitrary, and must rest upon some ground of difference having a fair and substantial relation to the object of the legislation, so that all persons similarly circumstanced shall be treated alike." In Reed, the state courts had sustained the preference for men over women in the appointment of administrators as a rational method "to resolve an issue that would otherwise require a hearing as to the relative merits" of the petitioning relatives. The Supreme Court disagreed: "Clearly the objective of reducing the work load on probate courts by eliminating one class of contests is not without some legitimacy." Nevertheless, there was a denial of equal protection: giving "a mandatory preference to members of either sex over members of the other, merely to accomplish the elimination of hearings on the merits, is to make the very kind of arbitrary legislative choice forbidden by [equal protection]; and whatever may be said as to the positive values of avoiding intrafamily controversy, the choice in this contest may not lawfully be mandated solely on the basis of sex."

b. Was the exercise of scrutiny in Reed truly in accord with the articulated, traditional rationality standard of the old equal protection? In Frontiero, Justice Brennan described Reed as a justified "departure from 'traditional' rational-basis analysis." Was it? Compare the reliances on Reed by Justices Stewart and Powell in Frontiero. Was the state's justification in Reed in fact so weak as to be vulnerable to the scrutiny associated with the deferential old equal protection? Was it an example of the "newer" equal protection, of minimal scrutiny "with bite," see sec. 1 above? Or was the Court in fact applying a greater degree of scrutiny than that authorized under the "old" or even the "newer" equal protection? [1] Is the Court in fact applying an intensified scrutiny stricter than that justified by traditional standards but less severe than that associated with the "new" equal protection? Is that the significance of Justice Stewart's concurring notation? Similar questions are raised by a number of post-Frontiero decisions noted below, invalidating challenged sex discriminations while purporting to apply "rationality" standards, as in Reed.

c. Is strict—or at least stricter than traditional—scrutiny justified for gender-based classifications? Are Justice Brennan's reasons in Frontiero

---

1. See Gunther, "Newer Equal Protection," 86 Harv.L.Rev. 1, 34 (1972): "It is difficult to understand [the result in Reed] without an assumption that some special sensitivity to sex as a classifying factor entered into the analysis. . . . Only by importing some special suspicion of sex-related means from the new equal protection area can the result be made entirely persuasive. Yet application of new equal protection criteria is precisely what Reed v. Reed purported to avoid." See also Justice Marshall's dissent in Rodriguez, sec. 5 below: "[Reed] can only be understood as [an instance] in which the particularly invidious character of the classification caused the Court to pause and scrutinize with more than traditional care the rationality of state discrimination."

persuasive? Are the reasons that make racial classifications suspect fully applicable to the use of sex criteria? [2] Even if they are not fully applicable, are the problems sufficiently analogous to warrant some variety of strict scrutiny for sex classifications? Are the situations analogous in terms of the typical classifier's intent? Do sex classifications typically imply a sense of superiority by the classifier? Are the classifications properly suspect because they are "we-they" classifications? [3] For example, if statistical data show that an overwhelming percentage of women cannot meet a job qualification—e. g., lifting very heavy weights—is a general ban on women nevertheless impermissible so long as some women can meet the qualifications? Are individualized hearings required in every such case? May a court consider the cost in inefficiency of individualized hearings in particular contexts? [4] Questions such as these are raised by the Court's uncertain course in scrutinizing sex discrimination challenges in the post-Frontiero cases below.

2. *The deferential old equal protection in action: Goesaert v. Cleary.* Compare the purported application of traditional equal protection standards in Reed v. Reed with an equal protection case a generation earlier, at the height of deferential equal protection scrutiny on the Vinson Court (recall sec. 1 above), GOESAERT v. CLEARY, 335 U.S. 464 (1948). Does Goesaert retain vitality today? In Goesaert, the majority sustained a Michigan statute which provided that no woman could obtain a bartender's license unless she was "the wife or daughter of the male owner" of a licensed liquor establishment. In rejecting the equal protection challenge, Justice Frankfurter stated: "Michigan could, beyond question, forbid all women from working behind a bar. This is so despite the vast changes in the social and legal position of women. The fact that women may now have achieved the virtues that men have long claimed as their prerogatives and now indulge in vices that men have long practiced, does not preclude the States from drawing a sharp line between the sexes, certainly in such matters as the regulation of the liquor traffic. [The] Constitution does not require legislatures to reflect sociological insight, or shifting social standards, any more than it requires them to keep abreast of the latest scientific standards.

2. Note the comment by Professor Ruth Bader Ginsburg (who had prime responsibility for appellant's brief in Reed v. Reed and in other sex discrimination cases) urging "recognition that generators of race and sex discrimination are often *different*." She states: "Neither ghettoized minorities nor women are well served by lumping their problems together for *all* purposes, by pretending that all are oppressed in the same way and for the same reasons. Prime among the differences: women are found in every economic class and in every neighborhood; they generally live and work in close physical contact with the men who, under traditional arrangements, held a control rein over them." Ginsburg, "Realizing the Equality Principle" (Keynote Address, 6th National Conference on Women and the Law, 1975).

3. See Ely, "The Wages of Crying Wolf: A Comment on Roe v. Wade," 82 Yale L.J. 920 (1973) (noted in sec. 2 above): "[L]egislators traditionally have not only not been black (or female); they have been white (and male). A decision to distinguish blacks from whites (or women from men) will therefore have its roots in a comparison between a 'we' stereotype and a 'they' stereotype."

4. See, e. g., the employment cases such as Phillips Marietta and LaFleur, below. See also the discussion of permissible generalizations in several of the other cases below—e. g., Weinberger v. Wiesenfeld. And note the "irrebuttable presumptions" cases in sec. 6 below.

"While Michigan may deny to all women opportunities for bartending, Michigan cannot play favorites among women without rhyme or reason. . . . Since bartending by women may, in the allowable legislative judgment, give rise to moral and social problems against which it may devise preventive measures, the legislature need not go to the full length of the prohibition if it believes that as to a defined group of females other factors are operating which either eliminate or reduce the moral and social problems otherwise calling for prohibition. Michigan evidently believes that the oversight assured through ownership of a bar by a barmaid's husband or father minimizes hazards that may confront a barmaid without such protecting oversight. This Court is certainly not in a position to gainsay such belief by the Michigan legislature. If it is entertainable, as we think it is, Michigan has not violated its duty to afford equal protection of its laws. We cannot cross-examine either actually or argumentatively the mind of Michigan legislators nor question their motives. Since the line they have drawn is not without a basis in reason, we cannot give ear to the suggestion that the real impulse behind this legislation was an unchivalrous desire of male bartenders to try to monopolize the calling."

Justice Rutledge, joined by Justices Douglas and Murphy, dissented. The dissent did not challenge the basic assumptions expressed by Justice Frankfurter; instead, it focused on the inadequate "fit" between means and ends. Justice Rutledge noted: "A male owner although he himself is always absent from his bar, may employ his wife and daughter as barmaids. A female owner may neither work as a barmaid herself nor employ her daughter in that position, even if a man is always present in the establishment to keep order. This inevitable result of the classification belies the assumption that the statute was motivated by a legislative solicitude for the moral and physical well-being of women who, but for the law, would be employed as barmaids. Since there could be no other conceivable justification for such discrimination against women owners of liquor establishments, the statute should be held invalid." (In more recent cases, state and lower federal courts have explicitly abandoned the equal protection approach of Goesaert.[5] Would Goesaert survive the Reed v. Reed intensity of scrutiny? The level of scrutiny of the post-Frontiero decisions which follow?)

5. See, e. g., Seidenberg v. McSorleys' Old Ale House, Inc., 317 F.Supp. 593 (S.D.N.Y.1970), which found no merit "in the argument that the presence of the argument that the presence of women in bars gives rise to 'moral and social problems' against which McSorleys' can reasonably protect itself by excluding women from the premises. Social mores have not stood still since that argument was used in 1948 to convince a 6–3 majority of the Supreme Court," in the Goesaert case.

Note also the California Supreme Court's decision invalidating a state law forbidding women to tend bar unless they were licensees or wives of licensees. The Court relied on the 1964 Civil Rights Act and the California Constitution as well as the federal equal protection clause. The Court found the "compelling state interest" standard applicable because "classifications based upon sex should be treated as suspect." Sail'er Inn, Inc. v. Kirby, 485 P.2d 529 (1971).

SUCCESSFUL CHALLENGES AFTER FRONTIERO

1. *Mandatory pregnancy leaves.* In CLEVELAND BOARD OF EDUCATION v. LaFLEUR, 414 U.S. 632 (1974), pregnant teachers successfully attacked school board rules requiring unpaid maternity leaves several months before expected childbirth. In this first major case after Frontiero, equal protection was the main basis for the challenge—a challenge apparently strengthened by the fact that the EEOC had promulgated guidelines stating that mandatory pregnancy leaves presumptively violated the sex discrimination provisions of Title VII of the 1964 Civil Rights Act. But the majority decision sustaining the challenge managed to do so without reaching the equal protection issue. Instead, Justice Stewart found the school rules invalid on the basis of the newly fashionable "procedural due process" approach of hostility to "irrebuttable presumptions." (That alleged alternative to equal protection analysis, and its use in the LaFleur case, is considered more fully in sec. 6, below.)

In LaFleur, only Justice Powell's concurrence was prepared to invalidate on the basis of equal protection, and he found the rules invalid as "irrational classifications" under traditional standards without reaching the question of whether sex classifications are suspect, or indeed whether the regulations here involved sex classifications at all: "Whether the challenged aspects of the regulations constitute sex classifications or disability classifications,"—cf. Geduldig v. Aiello in the next group of notes—they fail to "rationally serve" legitimate state interests.

2. *Barriers to jury service by women.* In 1961, in Hoyt v. Florida, 368 U.S. 57, the Court rejected due process and equal protection attacks on a Florida jury selection system under which women were not called unless they registered for jury service. Fourteen years later, a similar barrier to jury service by women was held unconstitutional—but on the basis of the Sixth Amendment's jury trial guarantee incorporated into the 14th rather than the equal protection clause. TAYLOR v. LOUISIANA, 419 U.S. 522 (1975).[1] The Louisiana scheme invalidated in Taylor provided that a woman should not be selected for a jury unless she had previously filed a written declaration of her desire to be subject to jury service. Justice White's majority opinion found "that the selection of a petit jury from a representative cross section of the community is an essential component of the Sixth Amendment right to a jury trial."[2] The state scheme had the effect of excluding a large "identifiable class of citizens" from jury service, and the male defendant was able to challenge his conviction because of the exclusion of women. Justice White noted that "women are sufficiently numerous and distinct from men that if they are systematically eliminated from jury panels, the Sixth Amendment's fair cross section requirement cannot be satisfied."[3]

1. Note also an intervening case, Alexander v. Louisiana, 405 U.S. 625 (1972), where the majority reversed a conviction for discrimination in jury selection on racial grounds, without reaching a sex discrimination claim. In an elaborate separate opinion, Justice Douglas urged a finding of sex discrimination as well.

2. Recall the "selective incorporation" developments—especially Duncan v. Louisiana in 1968—in chap. 8 above.

3. He quoted from a 1946 decision, Ballard v. United States, 329 U.S. 187, which had held exclusion of women from *federal* juries illegal without resting on constitutional grounds:

Justice White rejected the argument "that women as a class serve a distinctive role in society and that jury service would so substantially interfere with that function that the State has ample justification for excluding women from service unless they volunteer, even though the result is that almost all jurors are men." He conceded that Hoyt v. Florida had held that such a system was "sufficiently rational" to satisfy due process and equal protection standards in 1961. But here, the newly recognized Sixth Amendment "fair cross section" right was involved, and that right "cannot be overcome on merely rational grounds"; "weightier reasons" were needed to justify such jury exclusion, and none existed here.[4]

Justice Rehnquist was the sole dissenter.[5] He thought the "complete swing of the judicial pendulum" since Hoyt v. Florida was not justified by any intervening changes of constitutional significance. He commented that one of the changes that appeared "to undergird the Court's turnabout is societal in nature, encompassing both our higher degree of sensitivity to distinctions based on sex, and the 'evolving nature of the structure of the family unit in American society.'" He conceded that the Louisiana system might in fact be "an anachronism, inappropriate at this 'time or place'" but added: "[S]urely constitutional adjudication is a more canalized function than enforcing as against the States this Court's perception of modern life."

3. *Social security benefits to the surviving spouse.* Two years after Frontiero, the Court at last sustained a sex discrimination claim on equal protection grounds rather than resorting to other constitutional rationales. WEINBERGER v. WIESENFELD, 420 U.S. —— (1975). The Court was unanimous as to result, and the prevailing opinion was written by Justice Brennan, the author of the Frontiero opinion which had viewed sex as a suspect classification. But the Brennan opinion in Wiesenfeld did not invoke that strict scrutiny; instead, it rested on the "rationality" approach of Reed v. Reed. However, Wiesenfeld, unlike Reed, may be a genuine example of rationality scrutiny without covertly applying a stricter standard of review: its analysis may be the best example so far of the type of scrutiny suggested by the model for a "newer" equal protection, sec. 1 above.

The challenge in Wiesenfeld was to 42 U.S.C. § 402(g), a provision of the Social Security Act awarding survivors' benefits when a covered wage earner dies. In the case of a deceased husband and father, benefits are pay-

"The truth is that the two sexes are not fungible; a community made up exclusively of one is different from a community composed of both; the subtle interplay of influence one on the other is among the imponderables. To insulate the courtroom from either may not in a given case make an iota of difference. Yet a flavor, a distinct quality is lost if either sex is excluded. The exclusion of one may indeed make the jury less representative of the community than would be true if an economic or racial group were excluded." that "woman is still regarded as the center of home and family life." But he cited 1974 statistics showing the very large percentage of women now in the labor force and commented: "While these statistics perhaps speak more to the evolving nature of the structure of the family unit in American society than to the nature of the role played by women who happen to be members of a family unit, they certainly put to rest the suggestion that all women should be exempt from jury service based solely on their sex and the presumed role in the home."

4. In a footnote, Justice White noted that in Hoyt, in 1961, the Court had placed some emphasis on the notion

5. Chief Justice Burger did not join Justice White's opinion but concurred in the result.

able both to the widow and to the couple's minor children in her care. But in a case of a deceased wife and mother, benefits are payable only to the minor children and not to the widower. That provision was challenged by a widower. The wife's earnings had been the couple's principal source of support during the marriage; after her death, Mr. Wiesenfeld was left with the sole responsibility for the care of their infant son. Under the statutory scheme, he received survivor's benefits for his son, but not for himself. The Court found that scheme an unjustifiable discrimination against covered women wage earners by affording them less protection for their survivors than that provided for men wage earners. That "gender-based distinction" violated the Fifth Amendment's due process clause.[6]

Justice Brennan's opinion thought the sex distinction here "indistinguishable" from that invalidated in Frontiero. Quoting from Schlesinger v. Ballard (below), he found the statutory distinction based on an "archaic and overbroad" generalization not "tolerated under the Constitution": the generalization "that male workers' earnings are vital to the support of their families, while the earnings of female wage-earners do not significantly contribute to their families' support."[7] He conceded that "the notion that men are more likely than women to be the primary supporters of their spouses and children is not entirely without empirical support." But, he added, "such a gender-based generalization cannot suffice to justify the denigration of the efforts of women who do work and whose earnings contribute significantly to their families' support." Like the statute in Frontiero, this provision deprived "women of protection for their families which men receive as a result of their employment." Indeed, the classification here was "more pernicious": in Frontiero, at least, the servicewoman had an opportunity to prove that her husband was in fact dependent upon her; here, moreover, the wife had paid Social Security taxes and thus "was deprived of a portion of her own earnings in order to contribute to the fund out of which benefits would be paid to others." And the Constitution did not permit a "gender-based differentiation that results in the efforts of women workers required to pay social security taxes producing less protection for their families than is produced by the efforts of men."

It was in Justice Brennan's handling of the Government's asserted justifications that an approach similar to the "newer" equal protection model most clearly emerged. Both in considering whether the classification could be characterized as a "benign" one and in determining whether the means were rationally related to the legislative ends, Justice Brennan rejected hypothesized purposes and rested his scrutiny on the "articulated" purpose as it emerged "from the statutory scheme itself and from the legislative history."[8]

6. Note the unusually strong statement of the applicability of equal protection standards to federal action via the due process clause, in a footnote to Justice Brennan's opinion: "This Court's approach to Fifth Amendment equal protection claims has always been precisely the same as to equal protection claims under the Fourteenth Amendment."

7. He noted that § 402(g), added to the Social Security Act in 1939, was designed to meet the "probable needs" of beneficiaries and dependents, and that Congress had acted on the "then generally accepted presumption that a man is responsible for the support of his wife and child."

8. The Government also argued that, since Social Security benefits "are not

As he stated in a footnote: "This Court need not in equal protection cases accept at face value assertions of legislative purposes, when an examination of the legislative scheme and its history demonstrates that the asserted purpose could not have been a goal of the legislation." [9]

The Government's effort to justify the classification as "benign"—"to compensate women beneficiaries as a group for the economic difficulties which still confront women who seek to support themselves and their families"—relied on the "benign justification" rationale of Kahn v. Shevin, 416 U.S. 351 (1974) (considered further below). But that rationale was unpersuasive here, given the Court's independent inquiry into "actual purposes." Justice Brennan stated: "[T]he mere recitation of a benign, compensatory purpose is not an automatic shield which protects against any inquiry into the actual purposes underlying a statutory scheme. Here, it is apparent both from the statutory scheme itself and from the legislative history of § 402(g) that Congress' purpose in providing benefits to young widows with children was not to provide an income to women who were, because of economic discrimination, unable to provide for themselves. Rather, § 402(g), linked as it is directly to responsibility for minor children, was intended to permit women to elect not to work and to devote themselves to the care of children. Since this purpose in no way is premised upon any special disadvantages of women, it cannot serve to justify a gender-based distinction which diminishes the protection afforded to women who do work."

Emphasis on "actual" and "articulated" purposes—rather than hypothesized or "conceivable" ones—once again predominated when Justice Brennan turned to the question of whether the classification met the "rationality" standard. In examining the relationship between means and legislative ends, Justice Brennan stated: "That the purpose behind § 402(g) is to provide children deprived of one parent with the opportunity for the personal attention of the other could not be more clear in the legislative history. [E. g., the] Advisory Council on Social Security, which developed the 1939 amendments, said explicitly that '[s]uch benefits [§ 402(g)] are intended as supplements to the orphans' benefits *with the purpose of enabling the widow to remain at home and care for the children.'* . . . Indeed, consideration was given in 1939 to extending benefits to all widows regardless of whether or not there were children. [But] Congress decided *not* to provide benefits to all widows even though it was recognized that some of them would have serious problems in the job market. Instead, it provided benefits only to those women who had responsibility for minor children, because it believed that they should not be required to work.

compensation for work done, Congress is not obliged to provide a covered female employee with the same benefits as it provides to a male." Justice Brennan replied that, even though Social Security benefits were "noncontractual,"—see Flemming v. Nestor, 363 U.S. 603 (1960) (chap. 4, sec. 2, above)—"benefits must be distributed according to classifications which do not without sufficient justification differentiate among covered employees solely on the basis of sex."

9. For this statement, he cited Eisenstadt v. Baird, 405 U.S. 438 (1972), Jimenez v. Weinberger, 417 U.S. 628 (1974), and Dept. of Agriculture v. Moreno, 413 U.S. 528 (1973), all further noted below, in secs. 5 and 6. See also Justice Brennan's emphasis on nonhypothesized purposes in his dissent in Schlesinger v. Ballard, below.

"The whole structure of survivors' benefits conforms to this articulated purpose. Widows without children obtain no benefits on the basis of their husband's earnings until they reach age 60 or, in certain instances of disability, age 50. Further, benefits under § 402(g) cease when all children of a beneficiary are no longer eligible for children's benefits. If Congress were concerned with providing women with benefits because of economic discrimination, it would be entirely irrational to except those women who had spent many years at home rearing children, since those women are most likely to be without the skills required to succeed in the job market. . . .

"Given the purpose of enabling the surviving parent to remain at home to care for a child, the gender-based distinction of § 402(g) is entirely irrational. The classification discriminates among surviving children solely on the basis of the sex of the surviving parent. Even in the typical family hypothesized by the Act, in which the husband is supporting the family and the mother is caring for the children, this result makes no sense. The fact that a man is working while there is a wife at home does not mean that he would, or should be required to, continue to work if his wife dies. It is no less important for a child to be cared for by its sole surviving parent when that parent is male rather than female. And a father, no less than a mother, has a constitutionally protected right to the 'companionship, care, custody, and management' of 'the children he has sired and raised, [which] undeniably warrants deference and, absent a powerful countervailing interest, protection.' Stanley v. Illinois, 405 U.S. 645, 651 (1972). Further, to the extent that women who work when they have sole responsibility for children encounter special problems, it would seem that men with sole responsibility for children will encounter the same child-care related problems. Stephen Wiesenfeld, for example, found that providing adequate care for his infant son impeded his ability to work."

There were two concurring opinions.[10] Justice Powell, joined by Chief Justice Burger, stated that he agreed "generally" with Justice Brennan's opinion, but "would identify the impermissible discrimination [involved] somewhat more narrowly than the Court does." He emphasized that social security was a contributory scheme designed for the "protection of the *family*." He noted that a surviving father may have the same need for benefits as a surviving mother and concluded that the scheme "impermissibly discriminates against a female wage earner because it provides her family less protection than it provides that of a male wage earner, even though the family needs may be identical. I find no legitimate governmental interest that supports this gender classification." [11]

A separate opinion by Justice Rehnquist concurring in the result stated that Justice Brennan's examination of the legislative history "convincingly demonstrates that the only purpose of § 402(g) is to make it possible for

10. Justice Douglas did not participate in the case.

11. In a footnote he noted: "I attach less significance to the view emphasized by the Court that a purpose of the statute is to enable the surviving parent to remain at home to care for a child. In light of the long experience to the contrary, one may doubt that fathers generally will forgo work and remain at home to care for children to the same extent that mothers may make this choice. Under the current statutory program, however, the payment of benefits is not conditioned on the surviving parent's decision to remain at home."

children of deceased contributing workers to have the personal care and attention of the surviving parent, should that parent desire to remain in the home with the child. Moreover, the Court's opinion establishes that the Government's proffered legislative purpose is so totally at odds with the context and history of § 402(g) that it cannot serve as a basis for judging whether the statutory distinction between men and women rationally serves a valid legislative objective." He added: "This being the case, I see no necessity for reaching the issue of whether the statute's purported discrimination against female workers violates [the Frontiero principles]. I would simply conclude [that] the restriction of § 402(g) benefits to surviving mothers does not rationally serve any valid legislative purpose, including that for which § 402(g) was obviously designed. This is so because it is irrational to distinguish between mothers and fathers when the sole question is whether a child of a deceased contributing worker should have the opportunity to receive the full time attention of the only parent remaining it. To my mind, that should be the end of the matter."

4. *Age of majority in the child support context.* In striking down a gender classification in STANTON v. STANTON, 421 U.S. —— (1975), the Court once again relied on the Reed v. Reed approach and found it "unnecessary" "to decide whether a classification based on sex is inherently suspect." Stanton was a suit on a child support agreement incorporated in a divorce decree. Appellant, the divorced wife, sued for support payments when the divorced husband stopped support payments for the daughter who had turned 18. The agreement did not specify the age at which the child support obligation ceased. The state courts found that the obligation ended when the daughter became 18, relying on a Utah law providing that males attain majority at 21 but females at 18. Justice Blackmun's opinion, after finding the Reed approach "controlling here," concluded "that under any test—compelling state interest, or rational basis, or something in between—[the Utah statute], in the context of child support, does not survive an equal protection attack. In that context, no valid distinction between male and female may be drawn."

In explaining why the gender distinction was unjustified here, Justice Blackmun stated: "It may be true [as the Utah court observed] that it is the man's primary responsibility to provide a home and that it is salutary for him to have education and training before he assumes that responsibility; that girls tend to mature earlier than boys; and that females tend to marry earlier than males. . . . Notwithstanding the 'old notions' to which the Utah court referred, we perceive nothing rational in the distinction drawn by [the law] which, when related to the divorce decree, results in the appellee's liability for support for [the daughter] only to age 18 but for [the son] to age 21. This imposes 'criteria wholly unrelated to the objective of that statute.' [Reed.] A child, male or female, is still a child. No longer is the female destined solely for the home and the rearing of the family, and only the male for the marketplace and the world of ideas. Women's activities and responsibilities are increasing and expanding. Coeducation is a fact, not a rarity. The presence of women in business, in the professions, in government and, indeed, in all walks of life where education is a desirable, if not always a necessary antecedent, is apparent and a proper subject of judicial notice. If a specified age of minority is required for the boy

in order to assure him parental support while he attains his education and training, so, too, it is for the girl. To distinguish between the two on educational grounds is to be self-serving: if the female is not to be supported so long as the male, she hardly can be expected to attend school as long as he does, and bringing her education to an end earlier coincides with the role-typing society has long imposed. And if any weight remains in this day in the claim of earlier maturity of the female, with a concomitant inference of absence of need for support beyond 18, we fail to perceive its unquestioned truth or its significance, particularly when marriage, as the statute provides, terminates minority for a person of either sex." [12]

UNSUCCESSFUL CHALLENGES AFTER FRONTIERO

1. *What is adequate justification for gender-based classifications?*— *Schlesinger v. Ballard.* The 5 to 4 decision in SCHLESINGER v. BALLARD, 419 U.S. 498 (1975), rejected a male naval officer's attack on gender-based distinctions in a military promotion system. Justice Stewart's majority opinion applied rationality standards of review, and found that here, unlike Reed and Frontiero, there were rational justifications for the distinction. Justice Brennan's dissent, joined by Justices Douglas and Marshall, insisted that strict scrutiny was applicable, but also argued that the scheme could not even meet the rational basis test.[1]

The challenged system accorded to women officers a 13-year tenure before mandatory discharge for want of promotion; male officers were required to be discharged after they had been twice passed over for promotion, even though they might have had less than 13 years of commissioned service. That scheme was challenged by a male officer who was subject to discharge after nine years of service. Justice Stewart's examination of the legislative structure persuaded him that "Congress may thus quite rationally have believed that women line officers had less opportunity for promotion than did their male counterparts, and that a longer period of tenure for women officers would, therefore, be consistent with the goal to provide women officers with 'fair and equitable career advancement programs.' Cf. Kahn v. Shevin [below]." (The Navy restricts women officers' participation in combat and in most sea duty. That restriction was not challenged in this case.) Reed and Frontiero were accordingly found distinguishable: "[There], the challenged classifications based on sex were premised on overbroad generalizations that could not be tolerated. [I]n contrast, the different treatment of men and women naval officers [here] reflects, not archaic and overbroad generalizations, but, instead, the demonstrable fact that male and

12. Justice Blackmun noted, however, that the appellant "although prevailing here on the federal constitutional issue, may or may not ultimately win her law suit." All the Court held was that the age differential was invalid. It was for the state courts to decide, as a matter of state law, how to eliminate the inequality: by choosing 21 or 18 as the age of majority for males and females.

Justice Rehnquist was the sole dissenter, urging that the appeal be dismissed on the quasi-jurisdictional grounds of the Rescue Army case, chap. 15 below.

1. Justice White also dissented, stating that he agreed "for the most part with" Justice Brennan's opinion.

female line officers in the Navy are *not* similarly situated with respect to opportunities for professional service." Moreover, in both Reed and Frontiero only "administrative convenience" was offered as justification for the classification; here, by contrast, the distinctions promoted the Navy's needs for promotions and incentives.[2]

Justice Brennan's dissent insisted that gender-based classifications must be subjected "to close judicial scrutiny" and could be sustained only if they served "compelling interests that cannot be otherwise achieved." He objected, moreover, because the majority had gone "far to conjure up a legislative purpose which *may* have underlain the gender-based distinction here attacked. I find nothing in the statutory scheme or the legislative history to support the supposition that Congress intended [to] compensate women for other forms of disadvantage visited upon them by the Navy.[3] Thus, the gender-based classification [here] is not related, rationally or otherwise, to any legitimate legislative purpose fairly to be inferred from the statutory scheme or its history, and cannot be sustained."

Justice Brennan reiterated that, in his view, a benign, compensatory purpose could justify a sex classification even under his strict scrutiny. (See his opinion in Kahn v. Shevin, below.) But the alleged compensatory goal, he found, was "not in fact" the purpose of the statute. Moreover, even if it had been the purpose, the distinction would still fail under the "means" ingredient of his strict scrutiny approach, because longer tenure for women was not "necessary" to compensate for other disadvantages.[4]

2. *What constitutes a sex-based classification?—Exclusion of normal pregnancies from state disability insurance.* To what extent is any stricter scrutiny that may be appropriate for gender-based classifications applicable to statutes where the sex distinction is a de facto rather than a de jure one? That problem is raised by GEDULDIG v. AIELLO, 417 U.S. 484 (1974). California's disability insurance, funded entirely from employee contributions, pays benefits for most but not all disabilities stemming from "mental or physical" illnesses and injuries. Among the exclusions from coverage are disabilities that accompany normal pregnancy and childbirth. In a 6 to 3 decision, the Court rejected the sex discrimination claim by insisting that the challenged classification was not "based upon gender as such" and sustained the statute by applying the lenient standard of review appropriate to social welfare programs under cases such as Dandridge v. Williams, sec. 5 below.

Justice Stewart's majority opinion concluded that the pregnancy exclusion did not amount to "invidious discrimination under the Equal Pro-

---

2. Note also Forbush v. Wallace, 405 U.S. 970 (1972), a unanimous summary affirmance of a decision sustaining an Alabama regulation requiring that a married woman seeking a driver's license use her husband's surname.

3. He added in a footnote: "Indeed, I find quite troublesome the notion that a gender-based difference in treatment can be justified by another, broader, gender-based difference in treatment imposed directly and currently by the Navy itself."

4. Note also the excerpt from Justice Brennan's opinion printed with the discussion of the "newer" equal protection in sec. 1 above, beginning with the statement: "While we have in the past exercised our imaginations to conceive of possible rational justifications for statutory classifications, we have recently declined to manufacture justifications in order to save an apparently invalid statutory classification."

tection Clause." As he described the challenge, it alleged "underinclusiveness of the set of risks that the State has elected to insure." He commented: "This Court has held that, consistently with the Equal Protection Clause, a State 'may take one step at a time' [Williamson v. Lee Optical Co]." He argued, moreover: "It is evident that a totally comprehensive program would be substantially more costly than the present program and would inevitably require state subsidy, a higher rate of employee contribution, a lower scale of benefits for those suffering insured disabilities, or some combination of these measures. There is nothing in the Constitution, however, that requires the State to subordinate or compromise its legitimate interests solely to create a more comprehensive social insurance program than it already has." He found a number of "legitimate interests," including the maintenance of the self-supporting nature of the program and of "the contribution rate at a level that will not unduly burden participating employees, particularly low-income employees." He added: "These policies provide an objective and wholly non-invidious basis for the State's decision." Moreover, he found "no risk from which men are protected and women are not. Likewise, there is no risk from which women are protected and men are not."

It was only at this point that Justice Stewart took specific cognizance of the dissenters' sex discrimination argument; and his observations were limited to a footnote. This case, Justice Stewart insisted, was "a far cry from cases like [Reed] and [Frontiero], involving discrimination based upon gender as such. The California insurance program does not exclude anyone from benefit eligibility because of gender but merely removes one physical condition—pregnancy—from the list of compensable disabilities. While it is true that only women can become pregnant, it does not follow that every legislative classification concerning pregnancy is a sex-based classification like those considered in [Reed] and [Frontiero]. Normal pregnancy is an objectively identifiable physical condition with unique characteristics. Absent a showing that distinctions involving pregnancy are mere pretexts designed to effect an invidious discrimination against the members of one sex or the other, lawmakers are constitutionally free to include or exclude pregnancy from the coverage of legislation such as this on any reasonable basis, just as with respect to any other physical condition. The lack of identity between the excluded disability and gender as such under this insurance program becomes clear upon the most cursory analysis. The program divides potential recipients into two groups—pregnant women and nonpregnant persons. While the first group is exclusively female, the second includes members of both sexes. The fiscal and actuarial benefits of the program thus accrue to members of both sexes."

Justice Brennan, joined by Justices Douglas and Marshall, dissented because "I believe that [Reed] and [Frontiero] mandate a stricter standard of scrutiny which the State's classification fails to satisfy." He noted that under the program, "compensation is paid for virtually all disabling conditions without regard to cost, voluntariness, uniqueness, predictability, or 'normalcy' of the disability." Yet, "compensation is denied for disabilities suffered in connection with a 'normal' pregnancy—disabilities suffered only by women." He argued that "the economic effects caused by pregnancy-related disabilities are functionally indistinguishable from the effects caused by any other disability," and he concluded: "In my view, by singling out

for less favorable treatment a gender-linked disability peculiar to women, the State has created a double standard for disability compensation: a limitation is imposed upon the disabilities for which women workers may recover, while men receive full compensation for all disabilities suffered, including those that affect only or primarily their sex, such as prostatectomies, circumcision, hemophilia and gout. In effect, one set of rules is applied to females and another to males. Such dissimilar treatment of men and women, on the basis of physical characteristics inextricably linked to one sex, inevitably constitutes sex discrimination." He noted that EEOC guidelines on sex discrimination "prohibit the disparate treatment of pregnancy disabilities in the employment context."

Applying the strict scrutiny standard of his Frontiero opinion, he concluded that "the State's interest in preserving the fiscal integrity of its disability insurance program simply cannot render the State's use of a suspect classification constitutional." Moreover, he added: "California's legitimate interest in fiscal integrity could have been achieved through a variety of less drastic, sexually neutral means." He referred to the lower court's suggestion that "increased costs could be accommodated quite easily by making reasonable changes in the contribution rate, the maximum benefits allowable, and the other variables affecting the solvency of the program."

"BENIGN" GENDER–BASED CLASSIFICATIONS

Introduction. Sec. 2C considered the question of appropriate judicial scrutiny of racial classifications employed for allegedly benign purposes. For those Justices who view sex classifications as suspect, allegedly "benign" uses of gender-based classifications present similar problems. Does benignness of purpose provide compelling state justification for an otherwise questionable classification criterion? Or should rationality standards replace strict scrutiny when the purpose is to help rather than to injure a traditionally disadvantaged class?

1. *The modern Court and benign sex classifications: Kahn v. Shevin.* The Court confronted the problem of the constitutionality of preferential treatment of women in a tax context in KAHN v. SHEVIN, 416 U.S. 351 (1974). The attack was on a Florida provision granting widows, but not widowers, an annual property tax exemption of $500. The attack was brought by a widower—and supported by women's rights groups. Justice Douglas—who had joined Justice Brennan's opinion in Frontiero finding sex to be a suspect classification—sustained this "benign" classification in a brief, deferential opinion applying "mere rationality" standards. The other supporters of the Frontiero opinion advocating strict scrutiny for sex classifications—Justices Brennan, Marshall and White—dissented, with Justice Brennan finding benignness of purpose a compelling justification, but insisting that the means were not "necessary" to the achievement of that acceptable objective.

Justice Douglas, instead of invoking the strict scrutiny of the plurality opinion which he had joined in Frontiero, recited the "fair and substantial relation" standard of Reed v. Reed. That standard was readily satisfied:

"There can be no dispute that the financial difficulties confronting the lone woman in Florida or in any other State exceed those facing the man. Whether from overt discrimination or from the socialization process of a male-dominated culture, the job market is inhospitable to the woman seeking any but the lowest paid jobs. . . . The disparity is likely to be exacerbated for the widow." Frontiero was distinguishable: there the justification for the sex distinction rested solely on "administrative convenience"; here, "[w]e deal [with] a state tax law reasonably designed to further the state policy of cushioning the financial impact of spousal loss upon the sex for which that loss imposes a disproportionately heavy burden." [1] He emphasized the equal protection tradition permitting the states "large leeway in making classifications and drawing lines" in tax statutes.

Kahn v. Shevin was decided the day after the DeFunis case, sec. 2C. Recall that in DeFunis Justice Douglas had exercised strict scrutiny and generally condemned racial classifications in "benign" preferential admissions programs to law schools. And in Frontiero, Justice Douglas had joined in finding sex, like race, a suspect classification. Can his positions in DeFunis and Kahn be reconciled? Does emphasis on the fact that Kahn was a tax case provide adequate distinction? Note another footnote by Justice Douglas in Kahn: "Gender has never been rejected as an impermissible classification in all instances. Congress has not so far drafted women into the Armed Services. The famous Brandeis Brief in Muller v. Oregon, 208 U.S. 412, on which the Court specifically relied, emphasized that the special physical structure of women has a bearing on the 'conditions under which she should be permitted to toil.' These instances are pertinent to the problem in the tax field which is presented by this present case." (On Muller and "protective" laws, see note 2 below.)

Justice Brennan's dissent, joined by Justice Marshall, stated: "In my view, [a] legislative classification that distinguishes potential beneficiaries solely by reference to their gender-based status as widows or widowers [must] be subjected to close judicial scrutiny. . . . While, in my view, the statute serves a compelling governmental interest by 'cushioning the financial impact of spousal loss upon the sex for which that loss imposes a disproportionately heavy burden,' I think that the statute is invalid because the State's interest can be served equally well by a more narrowly drafted statute.

"I agree that, in providing special benefits for a needy segment of society long the victim of purposeful discrimination and neglect, the statute serves the compelling state interest of achieving equality for such groups. No one familiar with this country's history of pervasive sex discrimination against women can doubt the need for remedial measures to correct the resulting economic imbalances. [In the circumstances here], the purpose and effect of the suspect classification are ameliorative; the statute neither stigmatizes nor denigrates widowers not also benefited by the legislation. Moreover, inclusion of needy widowers within the class of beneficiaries would not further the State's overriding interest in remedying the economic effects of past sex discrimination for needy victims of that discrimination. While

1. In a footnote, Justice Douglas recalled that the Frontiero plurality opinion had noted that the statutes there were "not in any sense designed to rectify the effects of past discrimination against women."

doubtless some widowers are in financial need, no one suggests that such need results from sex discrimination as in the case of widows.

"The statute nevertheless fails to satisfy the requirements of equal protection, since the State has not borne its burden of proving that its compelling interest could not be achieved by a more precisely tailored statute or by use of feasible, less drastic means. Section 196.191(7) is plainly over-inclusive, for the $500 property tax exemption may be obtained by a financially independent heiress as well as by an unemployed widow with dependent children. The State has offered nothing to explain why inclusion of widows of substantial economic means was necessary to advance the State's interest in ameliorating the effects of past economic discrimination against women.

"Moreover, alternative means of classification, narrowing the class of widow beneficiaries, appear readily available. The exemption is granted only to widows who complete and file with the tax assessor a form application establishing their status as widows. By merely redrafting that form to exclude widows who earn annual incomes, or possess assets, in excess of specified amounts, the State could readily narrow the class of beneficiaries to those widows for whom the effects of past economic discrimination against women have been a practical reality."

Justice White's dissent, instead of emphasizing the overinclusiveness of the class of widows, focused primarily on the fact that the tax exemption is available "to all widows but not to widowers": "The presumption is that all widows are financially more needy and less trained or less ready for the job market than men. It may be that most widows have been occupied as housewife, mother, and homemaker and are not immediately prepared for employment. But there are many rich widows who need no largess from the State; many others are highly trained and have held lucrative positions long before the death of their husbands. At the same time, there are many widowers who are needy and who are in more desperate financial straits and have less access to the job market than many widows. Yet none of them qualifies for the exemption. . . .

"It may be suggested that the State is entitled to prefer widows over widowers because their assumed need is rooted in past and present economic discrimination against women. But this is not a credible explanation of Florida's tax exemption; for if the State's purpose was to compensate for past discrimination against females, surely it would not have limited the exemption to women who are widows. Moreover, even if past discrimination is considered to be the criterion for current tax exemption, the State nevertheless ignores all those widowers who have felt the effects of economic discrimination, whether as a member of a racial group or as one of the many who cannot escape the cycle of poverty. It seems to me that the State in this case is merely conferring an economic benefit in the form of a tax exemption and has not adequately explained why women should be treated differently from men."[1]

---

1. Note the post-Kahn cases attempting to rely on its "benign purpose" rationale to justify sex distinctions. Weinberger v. Wiesenfeld, 420 U.S. —— (1975) (above), rejected such an effort: Justice Brennan's majority opinion there stated that "the mere recitation of a benign, compensatory purpose is

2. *Women's "protective" laws.* Recall that, during the Lochner era, one of the few types of laws regulating working conditions readily sustained by the Court was the setting of maximum working hours for women. Muller v. Oregon, 208 U.S. 412 (1908) (chap. 9, sec. 1, above) relied on women's "dependence" and "physical weakness" to justify protective legislation. Would legislation of the Muller variety survive judicial scrutiny under the standards of modern cases such as Kahn and Frontiero? Recall the approving reference to Muller and its Brandeis Brief in Justice Douglas' majority opinion in Kahn v. Shevin, above. Compare a regulation issued by the EEOC to implement Title VII of the 1964 Civil Rights Act, 29 CFR 1604.1(b): "Many states have enacted laws or promulgated administrative regulations with respect to the employment of females. Among those laws are those which prohibit or limit the employment of females, e. g., the employment of females in certain occupations, in jobs requiring the lifting or carrying of weights exceeding certain prescribed limits, during certain hours of the night, or for more than a specified number of hours per day or per week.

"(2) The Commission believes that such State laws and regulations, although originally promulgated for the purpose of protecting females, have ceased to be relevant to our technology or to the expanding role of the female worker in our economy. The Commission has found that such laws and regulations do not take into account the capacities, preferences, and abilities of individual females and tend to discriminate rather than protect. Accordingly, the Commission has concluded that such laws and regulations conflict with Title VII of the Civil Rights Act of 1964 and will not be considered a defense to an otherwise established unlawful employment practice or as a basis for the application of the bona fide occupational qualification exception." For a judicial interpretation in accordance with this view, see Rosenfeld v. Southern Pacific Co., 444 F.2d 1219 (9th Cir. 1971). Should the equal protection rule be the same as that adopted by EEOC under the statute? Would the Equal Rights Amendment compel such a rule? [The EEOC guidelines were expanded in April 1972, 37 Fed.Reg. 6835.]

COMBATING SEX DISCRIMINATION THROUGH STATUTORY AND CONSTITUTIONAL CHANGES

Would the battle against gender-based discrimination proceed more usefully through statutory or constitutional changes rather than through equal protection litigation? To what extent should recent statutory enactments and the pending 27th Amendment affect Court interpretations of the equal protection clause?

1. *The proposed Equal Rights Amendment.* The pending 27th Amendment would provide that "[e]quality of rights under the law shall not be denied or abridged by the United States or by any State on account of sex," and would authorize Congress to enact implementing legislation.

not an automatic shield which protects against any inquiry into the actual purposes underlying a statutory scheme." Compare Schlesinger v. Ballard, 419 U.S. 498 (1975) (above), where the majority found rational basis for the sex distinction in the Navy promotion scheme.

Final action in Congress on the Amendment was completed early in 1972; by the summer of 1972, about half of the necessary number of states had ratified it; but the drive for the Amendment ran into greater obstacles thereafter. By spring 1975, 34 of the necessary 38 states had ratified it, but two of those states had sought to withdraw their ratifications.

What would be the impact of the Amendment?[1] Would it clearly make sex a suspect classification? To what extent would it change the result in the equal protection cases considered above? For example, would it clearly invalidate the provision sustained in Geduldig, denying disability payments for pregnancy? Would it do more than that: Would it bar all sexual classifications? Would it permit laws limited to physical sex differences? Classifications in the interest of privacy?[2] Has the pendency of the Amendment inhibited Court recognition of sex as a suspect classification under the equal protection clause? Recall Justice Powell's opinion in Frontiero.[3]

1. On the impact and desirability of the Amendment, see generally Brown, Emerson, Falk and Freedman, "The Equal Rights Amendment: A Constitutional Basis for Equal Rights for Women," 80 Yale L.J. 871 (1971), and "Equal Rights for Women: A Symposium on the Proposed Constitutional Amendment," 6 Harv.Civ.Rts.Civ. Libs.L.Rev. 125 (1971).

On the Amendment and on the problems of sec. 3C generally, see Davidson, Ginsburg and Kay, Cases and Materials on Sex-Based Discrimination (1974); Babcock, Freedman, Norton and Ross, Sex Discrimination and the Law—Causes and Remedies (1975).

2. See, e. g., Note, "The Sexual Segregation of American Prisons," 82 Yale L.J. 1229 (1973), and Note, "The Equal Rights Amendment and the Military," 82 Yale L.J. 1533 (1973).

Note the responses to the "parade of horribles" raised against the Amendment, in Ginsburg, "The Fear of the Equal Rights Amendment" (The Washington Post, April 7, 1975). One of the allegedly baseless "horribles" Professor Ginsburg mentions is: "ERA will require unisex restrooms in public places." Her answer: "Again, emphatically not so. Separate places to disrobe, sleep, perform personal bodily functions are permitted, in some situations required, by regard for individual privacy. Individual privacy, a right of constitutional dimension, is appropriately harmonized with the equality principle. But the 'potty issue' is likely to remain one of those ultimate questions never pressed to final solution. . . . What the amendment would proscribe is extension of separation from an area where it protects privacy without implying inferiority, to an area where the privacy principle is not in point, but equal opportunity is." See also the Brown et al. article on the Amendment cited in footnote 1 above, also invoking the privacy principle of Griswold v. Connecticut (chap. 9) and stating "that the scope of the right of privacy in this area of equal rights is dependent upon the current mores of the community. Existing attitudes toward relations between the sexes could change over time [and] in that event the impact of the right of privacy would change too."

The "potty issue" may never be tested, and may not be important. But is invocation of Griswold v. Connecticut and the privacy principle really an adequate answer? Does privacy turn on prevailing attitudes? "Existing attitudes" would not be recognized as a justification for race segregation rather than sex segregation, would they?

3. Compare with Justice Powell's suggestion that the pendency of the Amendment made Court recognition of sex as a suspect classification premature and unnecessary, Justice Brennan's plurality opinion in Frontiero, referring to congressional condemnation of sex discrimination (in legislation as well as in the submission of the Amendment) as added support for his position: "Congress itself has concluded that classifications based upon sex are inherently invidious, and this conclusion of a coequal branch of Government is not without significance to the question presently under consideration."

2. *Statutory prohibitions of sex discrimination.* The first modern Supreme Court encounter with the sex discrimination problem occurred in a statutory rather than a constitutional context. Title VII of the Civil Rights Act of 1964 prohibits employment discrimination on the basis of "sex" as well as "race, color, religion" or "national origin." The statute adds, however, that sex (like religion and national origin) is a legitimate criterion where it "is a bona fide occupational qualification reasonably necessary to the normal operation of that particular business or enterprise." The per curiam decision in PHILLIPS v. MARTIN MARIETTA CORP., 400 U.S. 542 (1971), held illegal an employer's refusal to hire women with preschool-age children while hiring men with such children. The Court added, however, that the "existence of such conflicting family obligations, if demonstrably more relevant to job performance for a woman than for a man, could arguably be a basis for distinction" under the "bona fide occupational qualification" provision. But the record in this case was inadequate to resolve that issue.

Justice Marshall's concurrence objected to the Court's suggestion that the "occupational qualification" provision could be met by a showing "that some women, even the vast majority, with pre-school-age children have family responsibilities that interfere with job performance and that men do not usually have such responsibilities." Such a reading would fall into the trap "of assuming that the Act permits ancient canards about the proper role of women to be a basis for discrimination. Congress, however, sought just the opposite result. . . . Even characterizations of the proper domestic roles of the sexes were not to serve as predicates for restricting employment opportunity. The exception for a 'bona fide occupational qualification' was not intended to swallow the rule."

Justice Marshall pointed out that the EEOC had found the "bona fide occupational qualification" exception "to be applicable only to job situations that require specific physical characteristics necessarily possessed by only one sex. Thus the exception would apply where necessary for the 'purpose of authenticity or genuineness' in the employment of actors or actresses, fashion models, and the like. If the exception is to be limited as Congress intended, the Commission has given it the only possible construction. When performance characteristics of an individual are involved, even when parental roles are concerned, employment opportunity may be limited only by employment criteria that are neutral as to the sex of the applicant."

Are statistically valid generalizations ever permissible under the statute? Under the equal protection clause? Suppose it were shown that 95% of women could not meet the physical strength requirements for a particular job, and that all men could. Would an employer be able to frame a general gender-based rule on the basis of those data? Or would individualized testing be required in the case of each applicant? Under the statute? Under the Constitution? Under the Equal Rights Amendment? (See also the LaFleur case in sec. 6 below.) [4]

---

4. Note also the Court's first interpretation of the Equal Pay Act of 1963, in Corning Glassworks v. Brennan, 417 U.S. 188 (1974). As the Court described it, the Act "added to the Fair Labor Standards Act the principle of equal pay for equal work regardless of sex." And note the ban on discrimination against women in school admission, curriculum and employ-

SECTION 4. THE "FUNDAMENTAL RIGHTS AND INTERESTS" STRAND OF THE "NEW" EQUAL PROTECTION:

VOTING AND THE BALLOT; ACCESS TO THE JUDICIAL PROCESS; TRAVEL AND RESIDENCY REQUIREMENTS

Introduction. As noted in the Introductory Overview to this chapter, the Warren Court "identified the areas appropriate for the strict scrutiny of the new equal protection by searching for two characteristics: the presence of 'suspect' classifications; or an impact on 'fundamental rights or interests.'" The preceding two sections traced the evolution of the suspect classifications strand of stricter scrutiny. This section and the next explore the fundamental interests strand. This section examines the reasonably well established ingredients of that strand: the fundamental interests in voting and access to the ballot; the fundamental interest in access to the judicial process; and the fundamental right to travel.[1]

Recall Justice Harlan's critical comment on this strand of the new equal protection, quoted in the Introductory Overview. He thought this branch of the doctrine not only unfortunate, because "it creates an exception which threatens to swallow the standard equal protection rule," but also "unnecessary": "When the right affected is one assured by the Federal Constitution, any infringement can be dealt with under the Due Process Clause. But when a statute affects only matters not mentioned in the Federal Constitution and is not arbitrary or irrational," the Court had no justification to pick out "particular human activities, characterize them as 'fundamental,' and give them added protection under an unusually stringent equal protection test." Is that persuasive criticism? Consider, in examining the materials below, to what extent these areas of stricter scrutiny involve "rights" found in the Constitution, and to what extent the cases rest on "fundamental" human activities or interests eliciting special scrutiny even though they do not amount to constitutional "rights."

Consider, for example, the voting and judicial process cases in secs. 4A and 4B. According to the Court, there is no constitutional "right" to vote in state elections or to appeal criminal convictions. Yet when a state decides to make an office an elective one, restrictions on the franchise elicit strict scrutiny.[2] Similarly, once the state creates an appellate process, some differential impacts of the appeal structure trigger intensive review. By con-

---

ment policies, in the Higher Education Act of 1972.

1. The most amorphous and controversial aspect of fundamental interests analysis is considered in the next section, sec. 5, on poverty and equal protection. The Warren Court had hinted that there might be a fundamental interest in "necessities," and advocates had urged special scrutiny of legislation in areas such as welfare benefits and housing and education. But the Burger Court has re-

fused to expand the new equal protection in those directions. See especially the Rodriguez case, sec. 5 below.

2. See especially the Harper and Kramer cases, sec. 4A. In Harper, the majority said: "[O]nce the franchise is granted to the electorate, lines may not be drawn which are inconsistent with [equal protection]." Kramer explained "the need for exacting judicial scrutiny of statutes distributing the franchise."

trast, the stricter scrutiny in the cases in sec. 4C purports to rest on the constitutional "right" to travel. Does that "right" rest on firmer constitutional foundation than the "interest" involved in the voting and court access cases? Is the process of identifying "interests" and "rights" in the new equal protection area distinguishable from the problem of identifying "fundamental" rights eliciting special scrutiny in the substantive due process context? Is "substantive equal protection" [3]—the identification of fundamental interests for special scrutiny under equal protection—"Lochnerizing" by another name?

Note the review of the developments in fundamental interests analysis in the Rodriguez case, sec. 5 below. In Rodriguez, the Burger Court majority found further expansion of the fundamental interests category an unjustifiable judicial venture; yet earlier in the same year, in 1973, a majority expanded the scope of substantive due process by striking down abortion laws as impingements on the "right of privacy" in Roe v. Wade, chap. 9 above. Do the differing directions of "substantive due process" and "substantive equal protection" make sense? And now that an expanded "right of privacy" has been found to be an aspect of "liberty" in the due process clause, will it in turn trigger stricter scrutiny under equal protection when there are differential impacts on exercises of that right? Finally, is Justice Harlan correct in saying that stricter equal protection scrutiny for "fundamental rights" is "unnecessary"? At least when the Court is dealing with reasonably explicit constitutional rights, such as those in the First Amendment, what is added by resorting to the equal protection clause in applying strict scrutiny to impingements on such rights?

A. VOTING AND ACCESS TO THE BALLOT

HARPER v. VIRGINIA BOARD OF ELECTIONS

383 U.S. 663, 86 S.Ct. 1079, 16 L.Ed.2d 169 (1966).

Appeal from the United States District Court for the Eastern District of Virginia.

[Virginia imposed an annual $1.50 poll tax on all residents over twenty-one. The state made payment of the poll taxes a precondition for voting. The tax proceeds supported local governmental activities, including schools. Appellants' suit to have the poll tax declared unconstitutional was dismissed by a three-judge district court on the authority of Breedlove v. Suttles, 302 U.S. 277 (1937), where the Court had unanimously rejected an equal protection attack on the Georgia poll tax.]

Mr. Justice DOUGLAS delivered the opinion of the Court. . . .

While the right to vote in federal elections is conferred by Art. I, § 2, of the Constitution, the right to vote in state elections is nowhere expressly mentioned. It is argued that the right to vote in state elections is implicit,

------

3. See Karst and Horowitz, "Reitman v. Mulkey: A Telophase of Substantive Equal Protection," 1967 Sup.Ct. Rev. 39.

particularly by reason of the First Amendment, and that it may not constitutionally be conditioned upon the payment of a tax or fee. We do not stop to canvass the relation between voting and political expression. For it is enough to say that once the franchise is granted to the electorate, lines may not be drawn which are inconsistent with the Equal Protection Clause of the Fourteenth Amendment. . . . [1]

We conclude that a State violates [equal protection] whenever it makes the affluence of the voter or payment of any fee an electoral standard. Voter qualifications have no relation to wealth nor to paying or not paying this or any other tax. Our cases demonstrate that [equal protection] restrains the States from fixing voter qualifications which invidiously discriminate. Thus without questioning the power of a State to impose reasonable residence restrictions on the availability of the ballot, we held in Carrington v. Rash, 380 U.S. 89 [1965], that a State may not deny the opportunity to vote to a bona fide resident merely because he is a member of the armed services. "By forbidding a soldier ever to controvert the presumption of non-residence, the Texas Constitution imposes an invidious discrimination in violation of the Fourteenth Amendment." [2] Previously we had said that neither homesite nor occupation "affords a permissible basis for distinguishing between qualified voters within the State." Gray v. Sanders, 372 U.S. 368, 380. We think the same must be true of requirements of wealth or affluence or payment of a fee.

Long ago in [Yick Wo v. Hopkins], the Court referred to "the political franchise of voting" as a "fundamental political right, because preservative of all rights." Recently in Reynolds v. Sims, 377 U.S. 533 [1964—the "one person-one vote" reapportionment case, chap. 15 below], we said, "Undoubtedly, the right of suffrage is a fundamental matter in a free and democratic society. Especially since the right to exercise the franchise in a free and unimpaired manner is preservative of other basic civil and political rights, any alleged infringement of the right of citizens to vote must be carefully and meticulously scrutinized." There we were considering charges

---

1. . . . While the "Virginia poll tax was born of a desire to disenfranchise the Negro" (Harman v. Forssenius, 380 U.S. 528, 543) we do not stop to determine whether on this record the Virginia tax in its modern setting serves the same end. [Footnote by the Court.]

2. Carrington v. Rash invalidated a Texas bar on voting by members of the armed forces who had moved into the state on military service. Justice Stewart's majority opinion rejected the argument that the restriction was justified by the fear of a "takeover" of voting in local communities by large numbers of military personnel nearby: fear of "political views" could not justify disenfranchising bona fide residents. And to the state's claim that the provision sought to limit voting to bona fide

residents rather than transients, the Court found the legitimate end pursued by overbroad means: "We deal here with matters close to the core of our constitutional system." [Note Justice Harlan's comment on Carrington in his dissent in Shapiro v. Thompson (sec. 4C below), three years later: "I recognize that in my dissenting opinion in [Harper] I characterized the test applied in Carrington as the traditional equal protection standard. I am now satisfied that this was too generous a reading of the Court's opinion. [A]s I now see that case, the Court applied an abnormally severe equal protection standard." In Carrington, Justice Harlan had dissented, arguing that, even assuming that the equal protection clause applied to voting restrictions, the Texas one surely met "rational basis" requirements.]

that voters in one part of the State had greater representation per person in the State Legislature than voters in another part of the State. We concluded:

"A citizen, a qualified voter, is no more nor no less so because he lives in the city or on the farm. This is the clear and strong command of our Constitution's Equal Protection Clause. This is an essential part of the concept of a government of laws and not men. This is at the heart of Lincoln's vision of 'government of the people, by the people, [and] for the people.' The Equal Protection Clause demands no less than substantially equal state legislative representation for all citizens, of all places as well as of all races."

We say the same whether the citizen, otherwise qualified to vote, has $1.50 in his pocket or nothing at all, pays the fee or fails to pay it. The principle that denies the State the right to dilute a citizen's vote on account of his economic status or other such factors by analogy bars a system which excludes those unable to pay a fee to vote or who fail to pay.

It is argued that a State may exact fees from citizens for many different kinds of licenses; that if it can demand from all an equal fee for a driver's license,[3] it can demand from all an equal poll tax for voting. But we must remember that the interest of the State, when it comes to voting, is limited to the power to fix qualifications. Wealth, like race, creed, or color, is not germane to one's ability to participate intelligently in the electoral process. Lines drawn on the basis of wealth or property, like those of race, are traditionally disfavored. See Edwards v. California, 314 U.S. 160, 184–185 (Jackson, J., concurring) [chap. 5 above]; Griffin v. Illinois, 351 U.S. 12; Douglas v. California, 372 U.S. 353 [both sec. 4B below]. To introduce wealth or payment of a fee as a measure of a voter's qualifications is to introduce a capricious or irrelevant factor. The degree of the discrimination is irrelevant. In this context—that is, as a condition of obtaining a ballot—the requirement of fee paying causes an "invidious" discrimination (Skinner v. Oklahoma),[4] that runs afoul of the Equal Protection Clause. Levy "by

---

3. Maine has a poll tax . . . which is not made a condition of voting; instead, its payment is a condition of obtaining a motor vehicle license or a motor vehicle operator's license. [Footnote by the Court.]

4. Skinner v. Oklahoma, 316 U.S. 535 (1942), has been noted earlier, at the beginning of chap. 9, sec. 3. Skinner was a forerunner of the "fundamental interests" strand of the new equal protection which did not flourish until two decades later, in the 1960's. Skinner invalidated Oklahoma's Habitual Criminal Sterilization Act, providing for compulsory sterilization after a third conviction for a felony "involving moral turpitude," but excluding such felonies as embezzlement. The formal invalidation rested on equal protection grounds: though ordinarily there was great deference to state classifications of crimes, Justice Douglas explained, this case dealt with

"legislation which involves one of the basic civil rights of man. Marriage and procreation are fundamental to the very existence and survival of the race. [S]trict scrutiny of the classification which a State makes in a sterilization law is essential, lest unwittingly, or otherwise, invidious discriminations are made."

Note the praise of Skinner in Karst, "Invidious Discrimination: Justice Douglas and the Return of the 'Natural-Law-Due-Process Formula,'" 16 UCLA L.Rev. 716 (1969), viewing Skinner as laying "a *doctrinal* foundation" for "the most significant constitutional development of our time." If the strict scrutiny in Harper seems an "improvised innovation," Karst comments, it is only because insufficient attention was paid to what Skinner had in effect said: "a classification that discriminates with respect to a right of very great importance is not to be sustained merely because the

the poll," as stated in Breedlove v. Suttles, is an old familiar form of taxation; and we say nothing to impair its validity so long as it is not made a condition to the exercise of the franchise. Breedlove v. Suttles sanctioned its use as "a prerequisite of voting." To that extent the Breedlove case is overruled.

We agree, of course, with Mr. Justice Holmes that the Due Process Clause of the Fourteenth Amendment "does not enact Mr. Herbert Spencer's Social Statics" (Lochner v. New York). Likewise, the Equal Protection Clause is not shackled to the political theory of a particular era. In determining what lines are unconstitutionally discriminatory, we have never been confined to historic notions of equality, any more than we have restricted due process to a fixed catalogue of what was at a given time deemed to be the limits of fundamental rights. Notions of what constitutes equal treatment for purposes of the Equal Protection Clause *do* change. [When, in 1954,] we repudiated the "separate-but-equal" doctrine of Plessy as respects public education we stated: "In approaching this problem, we cannot turn the clock back to 1868 when the Amendment was adopted, or even to 1896 when Plessy v. Ferguson was written." Brown v. Board of Education.

In a recent searching re-examination of the Equal Protection Clause, we held, as already noted, that "the opportunity for equal participation by all voters in the election of state legislators" is required. [Reynolds v. Sims.] We decline to qualify that principle by sustaining this poll tax. Our conclusion, like that in Reynolds v. Sims, is founded not on what we think governmental policy should be, but on what the Equal Protection Clause requires.

We have long been mindful that where fundamental rights and liberties are asserted under the Equal Protection Clause, classifications which might invade or restrain them must be closely scrutinized and carefully confined. See [e. g., Skinner v. Oklahoma; Reynolds v. Sims; Carrington v. Rash].

Those principles apply here. For to repeat, wealth or fee paying has, in our view, no relation to voting qualifications; the right to vote is too precious, too fundamental to be so burdened or conditioned.

Reversed.

Mr. Justice BLACK, dissenting. . . .

The equal protection cases carefully analyzed boil down to the principle that distinctions drawn and even discriminations imposed by state laws do not violate the Equal Protection Clause so long as these distinctions and discriminations are not "irrational," "irrelevant," "unreasonable," "arbitrary,"

classification has a rational basis; if a state fails to supply a substantial justification, its discrimination is invidious and unconstitutional."
Should Skinner have rested on substantive due process rather than equal protection grounds? For a suggestion that Skinner was an "abdication of the Court's responsibility" not to consider the "biological evidence" that was "overwhelmingly against the reasonableness of the statute"—and for a criticism of the Court's failure to help the "thousands of institutional inmates" subject to sterilization laws who would have been aided by a substantive due process ruling, but who would not benefit from the "vague Skinner formulation"—see [Foote], "The Proper Role of the United States Supreme Court in Civil Liberties Cases," 10 Wayne L.Rev. 457 (1964). For the development of the "fundamental interest" recognized in Skinner, under the aegis of substantive due process, recall chap. 9, sec. 3, above.

or "invidious." The restrictive connotations of these terms [are] a plain recognition of the fact that under a proper interpretation of the Equal Protection Clause States are to have the broadest kind of leeway in areas where they have a general constitutional competence to act. [I]t would be difficult to say that the poll tax requirement is "irrational" or "arbitrary" or works "invidious discriminations." State poll tax legislation can "reasonably," "rationally" and without an "invidious" or evil purpose to injure anyone be found to rest on a number of state policies including (1) the State's desire to collect its revenue, and (2) its belief that voters who pay a poll tax will be interested in furthering the State's welfare when they vote. Certainly it is rational to believe that people may be more likely to pay taxes if payment is a prerequisite to voting. And [whatever] may be our personal opinion, history is on the side of "rationality" of the State's poll tax policy. Property qualifications existed in the Colonies and were continued by many States after the Constitution was adopted. Although I join the Court in disliking the policy of the poll tax, this is not in my judgment a justifiable reason for holding this poll tax law unconstitutional. . . .

Another reason for my dissent from the Court's judgment and opinion is that it seems to be using the old "natural-law-due-process formula" to justify striking down state laws as violations of [equal protection]. I have heretofore had many occasions to express my strong belief that there is no constitutional support whatever for this Court to use [due process] as though it provided a blank check to alter the meaning of the Constitution as written so as to add to it substantive constitutional changes which a majority of the Court at any given time believes are needed to meet present-day problems. [See, e. g., Justice Black's dissent in Griswold v. Connecticut, chap. 9 above.] Nor is there in my opinion any more constitutional support for this Court to use [equal protection], as it has today, to write into the Constitution its notions of what it thinks is good governmental policy. . . .

Mr. Justice HARLAN, whom Mr. Justice STEWART joins, dissenting.

The final demise of state poll taxes, already totally proscribed by the Twenty-Fourth Amendment with respect to federal elections and abolished by the States themselves in all but four States with respect to state elections, is perhaps in itself not of great moment. But the fact that the *coup de grace* has been administered by this Court instead of being left to the affected States or to the federal political process should be a matter of continuing concern to all interested in maintaining the proper role of this tribunal under our scheme of government.

I do not propose to retread ground covered in my dissents in [Reynolds v. Sims] and [Carrington v. Rash] and will proceed on the premise that the Equal Protection Clause of the [14th] Amendment now reaches both state apportionment (Reynolds) and voter-qualification (Carrington) cases.[1] My disagreement with the present decision is that in holding the Virginia poll tax violative of [equal protection] the Court has departed from long-established standards governing the application of that clause.

1. Justice Harlan had argued in those cases that the legislative history of the 14th Amendment, and the text of its § 2, demonstrated that the Amendment was not intended to apply to voting qualifications. See also his opinion once again exploring that history in Oregon v. Mitchell, 400 U.S. 112 (1970) (chap. 11, sec. 4, below).

The Equal Protection Clause prevents States from arbitrarily treating people differently under their laws. [The test] for determining whether an asserted justifying classification exists is whether such a classification can be deemed to be founded on some rational and otherwise constitutionally permissible state policy. . . .[2]

Reynolds v. Sims, among its other breaks with the past, also marked a departure from these traditional and wise principles. [Today] the Court reverts to the highly subjective judicial approach manifested by Reynolds. [The Court uses] captivating phrases, but they are wholly inadequate to satisfy the standard governing adjudication of the equal protection issue: Is there a rational basis for Virginia's poll tax as a voting qualification? I think the answer to that question is undoubtedly "yes."

Property qualifications and poll taxes have been a traditional part of our political structure. [W]ith property qualifications, it is only by fiat that it can be said, especially in the context of American history, that there can be no rational debate as to their advisability. Most of the early Colonies had them; many of the States have had them during much of their histories; and, whether one agrees or not, arguments have been and still can be made in favor of them. For example, it is certainly a rational argument that payment of some minimal poll tax promotes civic responsibility, weeding out those who do not care enough about public affairs to pay $1.50 or thereabouts a year for the exercise of the franchise. It is also arguable, indeed it was probably accepted as sound political theory by a large percentage of Americans through most of our history, that people with some property have a deeper stake in community affairs, and are consequently more responsible, more educated, more knowledgeable, more worthy of confidence, than those without means, and that the community and Nation would be better managed if the franchise were restricted to such citizens. Nondiscriminatory and fairly applied literacy tests, upheld by this Court in Lassiter v. Northampton Election Board, 360 U.S. 45 [see chap. 11, sec. 4, below], find justification on very similar grounds.

These viewpoints, to be sure, ring hollow on most contemporary ears. Their lack of acceptance today is evidenced by the fact that nearly all of the States, left to their own devices, have eliminated property or poll-tax qualifications; by the cognate fact that Congress and three-quarters of the States quickly ratified the Twenty-Fourth Amendment . . .. Property and poll-tax qualifications, very simply, are not in accord with current egalitarian notions of how a modern democracy should be organized. It is of course entirely fitting that legislatures should modify the law to reflect such changes in popular attitudes. However, it is all wrong, in my view, for the Court to adopt the political doctrines popularly accepted at a particular moment of our history and to declare all others to be irrational and invidious, barring them from the range of choice by reasonably minded people acting through the political process. It was not too long ago that Mr. Justice Holmes felt im-

2. I think the somewhat different application of the Equal Protection Clause to racial discrimination cases finds justification in the fact that insofar as that clause may embody a particular value in addition to rationality, the historical origins of the Civil War Amendments might attribute to racial equality this special status. . . . [Footnote by Justice Harlan.]

pelled to remind the Court that the Due Process Clause of the Fourteenth Amendment does not enact the *laissez-faire* theory of society [Lochner v. New York]. The times have changed, and perhaps it is appropriate to observe that neither does the Equal Protection Clause of that Amendment rigidly impose upon America an ideology of unrestrained egalitarianism. . . .

THE BASES AND IMPLICATIONS OF HARPER

1. *A voting case or a poverty case?* Should the poll tax survive traditional "rationality" scrutiny? The dissents in Harper, and the decision in Breedlove v. Suttles, so suggest: legitimate state interests that might plausibly be promoted by the classification can be identified. Though the majority opinion in Harper contained no elaborate passages of the modern "strict scrutiny" variety, it indicates a more interventionist stance than courts undertake pursuant to the "old" equal protection. Why? Because "fundamental interests" in voting are affected—because state restrictions on voting carry an especially heavy burden of justification? Or because of the classification criterion rather than the interest affected—because "lines drawn on the basis of wealth or poverty, like those of race," are "traditionally disfavored"? Were both features—effect on "fundamental interests" *and* classification by wealth—necessary to justify the high level of judicial scrutiny exercised in Harper? Should Harper be viewed as a decision "about the interest in voting" rather than "as a statement about poverty and special judicial protection linked with that status"? [1]

"Fundamental interests" and "suspect classifications" analysis evidently *both* play a role in the Harper opinion. The former theme has proved a sturdier one than the latter. The major emphasis of this section is on the further development of strict scrutiny for laws affecting participation in the electoral process. Most of the discussion of the subsequent history of the "wealth as a suspect classification" theme is postponed to sec. 5 below. But it warrants noting here that the Court has not adopted the principle that laws marked by either a de jure or a de facto wealth classification are for that reason alone subject to strict scrutiny. Neither formal classification in wealth terms nor differential economic impact is alone sufficient to evoke the judicial review standards of the new equal protection.

To be sure, Warren Court dicta occasionally suggested that wealth criteria might be independent bases for strict scrutiny. See, e. g., Chief Justice Warren's opinion in McDonald v. Board of Election Comm'rs, 394 U.S. 802 (1969), stating that "careful examination" was "especially warranted where lines are drawn on the basis of wealth or race [citing Harper], two factors which would independently render a classification highly suspect and thereby demand a more exacting judicial scrutiny." But James v. Valtierra, 402 U.S. 137 (1971) (sec. 5 below), indicated that not even a de jure wealth classification would without more trigger intensive review. And by the time of the Rodriguez case in 1973, also in sec. 5, all members of the Court appeared to agree that differential impacts in terms of economic status did not warrant the intensity of judicial scrutiny long associated with racial

1. That is a suggestion in Michelman, "Foreword: On Protecting the Poor   Through the Fourteenth Amendment," 83 Harv.L.Rev. 7 (1969).

classifications. By contrast, the electoral process-"fundamental interest" theme of Harper has flourished vigorously since that decision, as the materials which follow illustrate.

2. *Financial barriers and the electoral process.* Several years after Harper, the Court considered financial barriers to participation in the electoral process different from those involved in Harper. BULLOCK v. CARTER, 405 U.S. 134 (1972), and LUBIN v. PANISH, 415 U.S. 709 (1974), involved not financial barriers to participation by voters but financial barriers to candidates' access to primary ballots. In each case, the Court was unanimous in invalidating the filing fee requirements for candidates. Chief Justice Burger wrote the prevailing opinion in each case. And each opinion was marked by some obscurity about the appropriate standards of review: though there were several references to the strict scrutiny suggested by Harper, there were also invocations of traditional "rationality" standards. The results, in any event, are clear: the Harper approach implies Court reluctance to sustain financial barriers not only to voters but also to candidates.

The Texas scheme invalidated in Bullock required candidates for local office to pay fees as high as $8900 to get on the primary ballot. Chief Justice Burger emphasized that "the very size of the fees" indicated a "patently exclusionary system" with an obviously immediate impact on voters. He concluded that the state had not established the "requisite justification" either in its concern about regulating the size of the ballot or in its interest in financing the election. Lubin v. Panish invalidated a California requirement of a fee fixed at a percentage of the salary for the office sought. Petitioner, an indigent, was unable to get on the primary ballot for County Supervisor because he was unable to pay a filing fee of about $700. The Chief Justice identified the critical problem as the accommodation of "the desire for increased ballot access with the imperative of protecting the integrity of the electoral system from the recognized dangers of ballots listing so many candidates as to undermine the process of giving expression to the will of the majority." He concluded that California had "chosen to achieve the important and legitimate interest of maintaining the integrity of elections by means which can operate to exclude some potentially serious candidates from the ballot without providing them with any alternative means of coming before the voters." The Court accordingly held "that in the absence of reasonable alternative means of valid access, a State may not, consistent with constitutional standards, require from an indigent candidate filing fees he cannot pay."

The Bullock and Lubin cases are of special interest, however, for their wavering course in attempting to articulate the appropriate standard of review. Do they represent "strict scrutiny"? Traditional scrutiny? Minimum scrutiny "with bite"? A "sliding scale" approach? Note the varying formulations employed by Chief Justice Burger. He began his Bullock opinion by stating: "The threshold question to be resolved is whether the filing-fee system should be sustained if it can be shown to have some rational basis [citing Dandridge v. Williams and McGowan v. Maryland], or whether it must withstand a more rigid standard of review. [W]e must determine whether the strict standard of review of the Harper case should be applied." And at the end of that discussion, he stated that "we conclude, as in Harper,

that the laws must be 'closely scrutinized' and found reasonably necessary to the accomplishment of legitimate state objectives in order to pass constitutional muster." Yet in applying that "more rigid standard of review," that "close scrutiny," the Chief Justice pursued an uncertain path. In testing the state law against the interest in relieving the state treasury of the cost of conducting primary elections, the Chief Justice acknowledged "a legitimate state objective" and added that "it cannot be said that the fee system lacks a rational basis." But he went on to say that "under the standard of review we consider applicable to this case, there must be a showing of necessity"; and that showing was not made. Yet in measuring the state's scheme against the state interest in regulating the number of candidates on the ballot, he explained that though the filing fee clearly tended to limit the number of candidates, "even under conventional standards of review, a State cannot achieve its objectives by totally arbitrary means; the criterion for differing treatment must bear some relevance to the object of the legislation." He went on to say that there "may well be some relationship" between willingness to pay a fee and seriousness of a candidacy; but he struck down the fee requirement because it "is extraordinarily ill-fitted" to the State's goal: "other means to protect those valid interests are available."

Compare, however, the Chief Justice's description of Bullock v. Carter two years later, in a footnote to his opinion in Lubin ⋅v. Panish: "Bullock, of course, does not completely resolve the present attack [because] it involved filing fees that were so patently exclusionary as to violate traditional equal protection concepts." In striking down the fee requirement in Lubin, the Chief Justice did not explore the level of scrutiny issue at length. At one point, he noted that the legitimate state interest in controlling ballot length "must be achieved by a means that does not unfairly or unnecessarily burden either a minority party's or an individual candidate's equally important interest in the continued availability of political opportunity." And later he concluded: "Selection of candidates solely on the basis of ability to pay a fixed fee without providing any alternative means is not reasonably necessary to the accomplishment of the State's legitimate election interests." Compare Justice Douglas' concurrence in Lubin, which began: "While I join the Court's opinion I wish to add a few words, since in my view this case is clearly controlled by prior decisions applying the Equal Protection Clause to wealth discriminations." He began his recital of the cases with Harper— a decision the Chief Justice had invoked in Bullock but did not mention in Lubin.

3. *Nonfinancial barriers and the "fundamental interest" in voting.* The "fundamental interest" theme of Harper clearly is not limited to economic barriers. Harper itself did involve a financial restriction on voting, and the Bullock and Lubin cases in note 2 dealt with economic barriers to ballot access. But the Harper opinion's view that participation in the electoral process is "fundamental" drew on sources not involving economic barriers; and the implications of Harper have spread far beyond the financial barriers sphere. Note that in Harper, the Court relied on Reynolds v. Sims, the reapportionment case, and on Carrington v. Rash, involving voting restrictions on members of the armed forces. And a few years after Harper, at the end of the Warren era, the Court made clear that the "fundamental interest" approach justified strict scrutiny of restrictions on the franchise

generally, not merely of economic barriers.[2] The clarification came in the Kramer case, which follows.

KRAMER v. UNION FREE SCHOOL DISTRICT NO. 15

395 U.S. 621, 89 S.Ct. 1886, 23 L.Ed.2d 583 (1969).

Appeal from the United States District Court for the Eastern District of New York.

Mr. Chief Justice WARREN delivered the opinion of the Court.

In this case we are called on to determine whether § 2012 of the New York Education Law is constitutional. The legislation provides that in certain New York school districts residents who are otherwise eligible to vote in state and federal elections may vote in the school district election only if they (1) own (or lease) taxable real property within the district, or (2) are parents (or have custody of) children enrolled in the local public schools.[1]

. . .

[W]e must give the statute a close and exacting examination. "[S]ince the right to exercise the franchise in a free and unimpaired manner is preservative of other basic civil and political rights, any alleged infringement of the right of citizens to vote must be carefully and meticulously scrutinized." [Reynolds v. Sims.] This careful examination is necessary because statutes distributing the franchise constitute the foundation of our representative society. Any unjustified discrimination in determining who may participate in political affairs or in the selection of public officials undermines the legitimacy of representative government.

2. If strict scrutiny of franchise restrictions is the norm, what restrictions on voting remain permissible? In addition to the cases noted below, consider the pre-Harper decision rejecting an on-the-face equal protection challenge to literacy tests, Lassiter v. Northampton County Board of Elections, 360 U.S. 45 (1959). Justice Douglas wrote for a unanimous Court that "residence requirements, age, previous criminal record" were "obvious examples" of valid state voting qualifications. Literacy had "some relation to standards designed to promote intelligent use of the ballot" and was "neutral on race, creed, color and sex." Literacy tests were temporarily suspended on a nationwide basis by the Voting Rights Act Amendments of 1970, and that congressional enactment was sustained in Oregon v. Mitchell, chap. 11, sec. 4, below. In the absence of congressional legislation, could literacy tests survive strict scrutiny? See also Cardona v. Power, 384 U.S. 672 (1966), considered together with Katzenbach v. Morgan, chap. 11, sec. 4 below, an equal protection challenge to New York's English literacy requirement as applied to Spanish-speaking voters. In Cardona, the majority did not reach the constitutional challenge, since § 4(e) of the Voting Rights Act of 1965 barred application of literacy tests to some voters educated in Spanish language schools. Sec. 4(e) was sustained in Katzenbach v. Morgan. Note also the discussion in Oregon v. Mitchell, below, of age restrictions on voting in light of equal protection developments. (The 5 to 4 decision in Oregon v. Mitchell held unconstitutional a congressional effort to authorize eighteen-year-olds to vote in state elections.)

1. The law was unsuccessfully challenged in the lower court by "a bachelor who neither owns nor leases taxable real property": appellant was "a thirty-one-year-old college-educated stockbroker who lives in his parents' home" in the district.

[Rigid] examination is applicable to statutes *denying* the franchise to citizens who are otherwise qualified by residence and age.[2] Statutes granting the franchise to residents on a selective basis always pose the danger of denying some citizens any effective voice in the governmental affairs which substantially affect their lives. Therefore, if a challenged state statute grants the right to vote to some bona fide residents of requisite age and citizenship and denies the franchise to others, the Court must determine whether the exclusions are necessary to promote a compelling state interest. See [Carrington v. Rash].

And, for these reasons, the deference usually given to the judgment of legislators does not extend to decisions concerning which resident citizens may participate in the election of legislators and other public officials. Those decisions must be carefully scrutinized by the Court to determine whether each resident citizen has, as far as is possible, an equal voice in the selections. Accordingly, when we are reviewing statutes which deny some residents the right to vote, the general presumption of constitutionality afforded state statutes and the traditional approval given state classifications if the Court can conceive of a "rational basis" for the distinctions made are not applicable. See [Harper]. The presumption of constitutionality and the approval given "rational" classifications in other types of enactments are based on an assumption that the institutions of state government are structured so as to represent fairly all the people. However, when the challenge to the statute is in effect a challenge of this basic assumption, the assumption can no longer serve as the basis for presuming constitutionality. . . .

The need for exacting judicial scrutiny of statutes distributing the franchise is undiminished simply because, under a different statutory scheme, the offices subject to election might have been filled through appointment.[3] "[O]nce the franchise is granted to the electorate, lines may not be drawn which are inconsistent with the Equal Protection Clause." [Harper.] . . .

Besides appellant and others who similarly live in their parents' homes, the statute also disenfranchises the following persons (unless they are parents or guardians of children enrolled in the district public school): senior citizens and others living with children or relatives; clergy, military personnel, and others who live on tax-exempt property; boarders and lodgers; parents who neither own nor lease qualifying property and whose children are too young to attend school; parents who neither own nor lease qualifying property and whose children attend private schools. . . .

---

2. This case presents an issue different from the one we faced in McDonald v. Board of Election Comm'rs of Chicago, 394 U.S. 802 (1969). The present appeal involves an absolute denial of the franchise. In McDonald, on the other hand, we were reviewing a statute which made casting a ballot easier for some who were unable to come to the polls. As we noted, there was no evidence that the statute absolutely prohibited anyone from exercising the franchise; at issue was not a claimed right to vote but a claimed right to an absentee ballot. [Footnote by the Court. McDonald applied traditional, deferential review standards to a law allegedly "remedial" in nature and not clearly denying the vote. Recall the comments on the case in sec. 1 above.]

3. Similarly, no less a showing of a compelling justification for disenfranchising residents is required merely because the questions scheduled for the election need not have been submitted to the voters. [Footnote by the Court.]

We turn therefore to question whether the exclusion is necessary to promote a compelling state interest. First, appellees argue that the State has a legitimate interest in limiting the franchise in school district elections to "members of the community of interest"—those "primarily interested in such elections." Second, appellees urge that the State may reasonably and permissibly conclude that "property taxpayers" (including lessees of taxable property who share the tax burden through rent payments) and parents of the children enrolled in the district's schools are those "primarily interested" in school affairs. . . .

We need express no opinion as to whether the State in some circumstances might limit the exercise of the franchise to those "primarily interested" or "primarily affected." . . . For, assuming, arguendo, that New York legitimately might limit the franchise in these school district elections to those "primarily interested in school affairs," close scrutiny of the § 2012 classifications demonstrates that they do not accomplish this purpose with sufficient precision to justify denying appellant the franchise.

Whether classifications allegedly limiting the franchise to those resident citizens "primarily interested" deny those excluded equal protection of the laws depends, inter alia, on whether all those excluded are in fact substantially less interested or affected than those the statute includes. In other words, the classifications must be tailored so that the exclusion of appellant and members of his class is necessary to achieve the articulated state goal.[4] Section 2012 does not meet the exacting standard of precision we require of statutes which selectively distribute the franchise. The classifications in § 2012 permit inclusion of many persons who have, at best, a remote and indirect interest in school affairs and, on the other hand, exclude others who have a distinct and direct interest in the school meeting decisions.[5]

. . . [T]he issue is not whether the legislative judgments are rational. A more exacting standard obtains. The issue is whether the § 2012 requirements do in fact sufficiently further a compelling state interest to justify denying the franchise to appellant and members of his class. The requirements of § 2012 are not sufficiently tailored to limiting the franchise to those "primarily interested" in school affairs to justify the denial of the franchise to appellant and members of his class. . . .

Reversed.

Mr. Justice STEWART, with whom Mr. Justice BLACK and Mr. Justice HARLAN join, dissenting. . . .

[Appellant concedes] the validity of voting requirements relating to residence, literacy, and age. Yet he argues—and the Court accepts the argu-

---

4. Of course, if the exclusions are necessary to promote the articulated state interest, we must then determine whether the interest promoted by limiting the franchise constitutes a compelling state interest. We do not reach that issue in this case. [Footnote by the Court.]

5. For example, appellant resides with his parents in the school district, pays state and federal taxes and is interested in and affected by school board decisions; however, he has no vote. On the other hand, an uninterested unemployed young man who pays no state or federal taxes, but who rents an apartment in the district, can participate in the election. [Footnote by the Court.]

ment—that the voting qualifications involved here somehow have a different constitutional status. I am unable to see the distinction.

Clearly a State may reasonably assume that its residents have a greater stake in the outcome of elections held within its boundaries than do other persons. Likewise, it is entirely rational for a state legislature to suppose that residents, being generally better informed regarding state affairs than are nonresidents, will be more likely than nonresidents to vote responsibly. And the same may be said of legislative assumptions regarding the electoral competence of adults and literate persons on the one hand, and of minors and illiterates on the other. It is clear, of course, that lines thus drawn cannot infallibly perform their intended legislative function. Just as "[i]l-literate people may be intelligent voters," nonresidents or minors might also in some instances be interested, informed, and intelligent participants in the electoral process. Persons who commute across a state line to work may well have a great stake in the affairs of the State in which they are employed; some college students under 21 may be both better informed and more passionately interested in political affairs than many adults. But such discrepancies are the inevitable concomitant of the line drawing that is essential to law making. So long as the classification is rationally related to a permissible legislative end, therefore—as are residence, literacy, and age requirements imposed with respect to voting—there is no denial of equal protection.

Thus judged, the statutory classification involved here seems to me clearly to be valid. New York has made the judgment that local educational policy is best left to those persons who have certain direct and definable interests in that policy: those who are either immediately involved as parents of school children or who, as owners or lessees of taxable property, are burdened with the local cost of funding school district operations. True, persons outside those classes may be genuinely interested in the conduct of a school district's business—just as commuters from New Jeresy may be genuinely interested in the outcome of a New York City election. But unless this Court is to claim a monopoly of wisdom regarding the sound operation of school systems in the 50 States, I see no way to justify the conclusion that the legislative classification involved here is not rationally related to a legitimate legislative purpose. .   .   .

With good reason, the Court does not really argue the contrary. Instead, it strikes down New York's statute by asserting that the traditional equal protection standard is inapt in this case, and that a considerably stricter standard—under which classifications relating to "the franchise" are to be subjected to "exacting judicial scrutiny"—should be applied. But the asserted justification for applying such a standard cannot withstand analysis.

.   .   .   The voting qualifications at issue have been promulgated, not by Union Free School Ditrict No. 15, but by the New York State Legislature, and the appellant is of course fully able to participate in the election of representatives in that body. [And the law] does not involve racial classifications [nor impinge] upon a constitutionally protected right. [For] "the Constitution of the United States does not confer the right of suffrage upon any one." Minor v. Happersett, 21 Wall. 162, 178.

In any event, it seems to me that under *any* equal protection standard, short of a doctrinaire insistence that universal suffrage is somehow mandated by the Constitution, the appellant's claim must be rejected. . . .

KRAMER AND ITS AFTERMATH

1. *The Kramer rationale.* Does Kramer explain more adequately than Harper why participation in the electoral process is a "fundamental interest," even though there is no constitutional "right" to vote? Are there persuasive reasons for imposing a heavy burden on the state to justify restrictions on voting and ballot access? Are they legitimate derivations from text, history or structure of the Constitution? Note the explanation of the Harper-Kramer line of "fundamental interest" decisions in the Rodriguez case, sec. 5 below, where the majority refused to extend fundamental interests analysis into such new areas as education. Justice Powell's majority opinion there insisted the "fundamental interests" strand of the new equal protection was limited to rights "explicitly or implicitly guaranteed by the Constitution." He included voting rights cases within that category, quoting Dunn v. Blumstein, below, as making clear that "a citizen has a *constitutionally protected right* to participate in elections on an equal basis with other citizens in the jurisdiction." Justice Powell added: "The constitutional underpinning of the right to equal treatment in the voting process can no longer be doubted even though, as the Court noted in [Harper], 'the right to vote in state elections is nowhere expressedly mentioned.'" Justice Powell recognized however that "the right to vote, per se, is not a constitutionally protected right"; what is the "protected right, implicit in our constitutional system," is the "right" to "participate in state elections on an equal basis with other qualified voters whenever the State has adopted an elective process for determining who will represent any segment of the State's population."

Compare Justice Stewart's concurrence in Rodriguez: he insisted that "the equal protection clause confers no substantive rights and creates no substantive liberties." But he added in a footnote: "There is one notable exception to the above statement: It has been established in recent years that the Equal Protection Clause confers the substantive right to participate on an equal basis with other qualified voters whenever the state has adopted an electoral process for determining who will represent any segment of the State's population. . . . But there is no constitutional right to vote, as such."

Consider the post-Kramer electoral process cases which follow. To what extent could the challenged restrictions survive the standards of the old equal protection? What state interests are sufficiently "compelling" to sustain restrictions under strict scrutiny? How narrowly tailored must the means be? What standards of review is the Court in fact applying in these cases: Is there a consistent exercise of strict scrutiny? Are some cases examples of minimum scrutiny "with bite"? Is the Court applying a "sliding scale" approach? See especially Dunn v. Blumstein, below; and recall the Bullock and Lubin cases, in the notes preceding Kramer.

2. *Other efforts to limit limited purpose elections to taxpayers and property owners.* a. *Cipriano.* In CIPRIANO v. CITY OF HOUMA, 395 U.S. 701 (1969), decided on the same day as Kramer, the Court was unanimous in invalidating provisions of Louisiana law granting only property taxpayers the right to vote in elections called to approve the issuance of revenue bonds by a municipal utility. A per curiam opinion noted that the revenue bonds were to be financed from the operations of the utilities, not from property taxes, and concluded: "The challenged statute contains a classification which excludes otherwise qualified voters who are as substantially affected and directly interested in the matter voted upon as are those who are permitted to vote." In a concurring notation, Justices Black and Stewart stated that this case, unlike Kramer, "involves a voting classification 'wholly irrelevant to achievement' of the State's objective. [Kotch.]"

b. *Kolodziejski.* In CITY OF PHOENIX v. KOLODZIEJSKI, 399 U.S. 204 (1970), the majority extended the Cipriano ruling, holding that the restriction of the franchise to real property taxpayers was no more valid in elections on general obligation bonds (which looked only to property tax revenues for servicing) than in elections to approve the issuance of revenue bonds. Justice White's majority opinion concluded that the differences between the interests of property owners and of nonproperty owners were not "sufficiently substantial to justify excluding the latter from the franchise." Justice Stewart, joined by Chief Justice Burger and Justice Harlan, dissented.*

c. *Salyer.* Three years later, the majority found the Kramer-Cipriano-Kolodziejski line of cases inapplicable to an election scheme for a water storage district under which only landowners were permitted to vote and in which votes were proportioned according to the assessed valuation of the land. SALYER LAND CO. v. TULARE LAKE BASIN WATER STORAGE DISTRICT, 410 U.S. 719 (1973). Justice Rehnquist's majority opinion noted that the district's main purpose was to assure water for farming, and that project costs were assessed against the land in proportion to benefits received. He found the demanding popular election requirements of the line of cases emanating from Kramer and Reynolds v. Sims inapplicable to the district "by reason of its special limited purpose and of the disproportionate effect of its activities on landowners as a group." Accordingly, the details of the election scheme were subjected only to the minimal scrutiny of the old equal protection, and those details—the exclusion of mere residents and lessees, and weighting the votes according to the value of the land —easily survived that scrutiny. There was a vigorous dissent by Justice Douglas, joined by Justices Brennan and Marshall. Justice Douglas emphasized that all residents had an interest in the district's flood control activity. He especially objected to voting by the large land-owning corporations which farmed 85% of the land in the district: "The result is a corporate political kingdom undreamed of by those who wrote our Constitution." [1]

* Note also the reliance on the "compelling state interests" test of Kramer-Cipriano-Kolodziejski in Hill v. Stone, 421 U.S. —— (1975).

1. See also Gordon v. Lance, 403 U.S. 1 (1971), noted further in chap. 15. West Virginia's highest court had relied on Cipriano in part in finding a denial of equal protection in a state requirement of 60% approval of local bond issues in referendum elections. In reversing, Chief Justice Burger found the reliance on Cipriano "misplaced."

3. *Durational residence requirements: Dunn v. Blumstein.* a. The 6 to 1 decision in DUNN v. BLUMSTEIN, 405 U.S. 330 (1972), invalidated Tennessee's durational residence requirements for voters. Tennessee required one year residence in the state and three months in the county as a condition of voting. Justice Marshall's majority opinion—while recognizing the state's strong interest in limiting voting to residents—held that durational residence requirements were subject to strict scrutiny because they curtailed the interest in voting and because they burdened the right to travel (see sec. 4C below), and found the length of the residence requirements unjustifiable.

Justice Marshall's discussion of the appropriate standard of review afforded him his first opportunity to articulate the "sliding scale" approach which he has reiterated and elaborated frequently. (See the Introductory Overview, above.) He stated: "To decide whether a law violates [equal protection] we look, in essence, to three things: the character of the classification in question; the individual interests affected by the classification; and the governmental interests asserted in support of the classification. [The] Court has evolved more than one test, depending on the interest affected or the classification involved. [Here], whether we look to the benefit withheld by the classification (the opportunity to vote) of the basis for the classification (recent interstate travel) we conclude that the state must show a substantial and compelling reason for imposing durational residence requirements." Such requirements could not stand "unless the State can demonstrate that such laws are '*necessary* to promote a *compelling* government interest.' [Shapiro v. Thompson, sec. 4C; Kramer.]" That "strict equal protection test," Justice Marshall explained, was not mathematically precise, but rather one "of degree." It meant "that a heavy burden of justification is on the State, and that the statute will be closely scrutinized in light of its asserted purposes." It meant, too, that the means must be carefully tailored to the end and that "if there are other, reasonable ways to achieve those goals with a lesser burden on constitutionally protected activity, a State may not choose the way of greater interference." And that "less drastic means" ingredient proved decisive in the invalidation of the Tennessee laws.

Tennessee asserted two basic justifications: insuring "purity of the ballot box" and furthering the goal of having "knowledgeable voters." Neither proved sufficient. With respect to preventing fraud, "30 days appears to be an ample period of time for the State . . . —and a year, or three months, too much." (The State closed its registration books 30 days before election.) And with regard to knowledgeability, "the conclusive presumptions of durational residence requirements are much too crude." Justice Marshall added: "By requiring classifications to be tailored to their purpose, we do not secretly require the impossible." Here, the relationship between method and purpose was "simply too attenuated." Justice Blackmun concurred in the result. Chief Justice Burger was the only dissenter: "Some lines must be drawn. To challenge such lines by the 'compelling state interest' standard is to condemn them all. So far as I am aware, no state law has ever satisfied this seemingly insurmountable standard, and I doubt one ever will."

b. Compare two more recent decisions in which the Court found 50-day residency requirements constitutional. Marston v. Lewis, 410 U.S. 679

(1973); Burns v. Fortson, 410 U.S. 686 (1973). The per curiam decisions in those cases accepted the states' judgments that the 50-day period was "necessary" to serve the states' "important interest in accurate voter lists." Justice Marshall's dissents, joined by Justices Douglas and Brennan, insisted that 30 days gave the states ample time to achieve their objectives.

4. *Disenfranchisement of felons.* California, like many of the states, disenfranchises convicted felons who have served their sentences and completed their parole. In RICHARDSON v. RAMIREZ, 418 U.S. 24 (1974), the highest state court had struck down that barrier under the assumed compulsion of the higher decree of scrutiny demanded by modern voting cases. But the Supreme Court majority reversed: It found an exception to the equal protection standards usual in the voting area in the recognition of ex-felons' disenfranchisement in the rarely invoked § 2 of the 14th Amendment.

The reduced representation sanction of § 2 is specifically inapplicable to denials of the vote "for participation in rebellion, or other crime." Justice Rehnquist's majority opinion drew on the language and history of that provision to conclude that "the exclusion of felons from the vote has an affirmative sanction in § 2 of the Fourteenth Amendment." He found textually and historically "persuasive" the argument "that those who framed and adopted the Fourteenth Amendment could not have intended to prohibit outright in § 1 of that Amendment that which was expressly exempted from the lesser sanction of reduced representation imposed by § 2 of the Amendment." He accordingly concluded that "the exclusion of felons from the vote has an affirmative sanction [which] was not present in the case of the other restrictions on the franchise" invalidated in the Harper-Kramer line of cases.

Justice Marshall, joined by Justice Brennan, dissented on the merits. (Justice Douglas dissented on jurisdictional grounds.) Justice Marshall viewed § 2 of the 14th Amendment as a provision of limited purpose which should not be viewed as "the exclusive remedy for all forms of electoral discrimination" and should not be invoked to avoid the strict scrutiny compelled by § 1 of the Amendment. Applying the 14th Amendment standards he had articulated in Dunn v. Blumstein, he readily concluded that the burden of showing that the restriction was *necessary* to promote a *compelling* state interest" had not been met.[2]

5. *Anti-"raiding" cutoff requirements for party enrollment: The appropriate level of scrutiny.* a. The 5 to 4 decision in ROSARIO v.

---

2. Compare the Court's repeated encounters with claims to absentee ballots by persons in jail. Recall that in McDonald v. Board of Election Comm'rs, 394 U.S. 802 (1969), Chief Justice Warren applied deferential equal protection standards to a "remedial law" which failed to provide absentee ballots to jail inmates awaiting trial in their county of residence. (See sec. 1 above.) But later lower court efforts to rely on McDonald in rejecting absentee ballot claims were unsuccessful. For example,

O'Brien v. Skinner, 414 U.S. 524 (1974), held unconstitutional a New York system which failed to provide absentee registration or voting for pre-trial detainees and convicted misdemeanants confined in the county of their residence. Chief Justice Burger's majority opinion found the scheme "wholly arbitrary." A concurrence by Justice Marshall, joined by Justices Douglas and Brennan, emphasized the strict scrutiny standard. See also Goosby v. Osser, 409 U.S. 512 (1973).

ROCKEFELLER, 410 U.S. 752 (1973), sustained New York's unusually lengthy enrollment time prerequisite for voting in party primaries. The provisions required a voter to register affiliation 30 days before a general election in order to be eligible to vote in the following year's party primary. That scheme in effect prevented a change in party affiliation for up to eleven months to retain eligibility to vote in primaries. In rejecting the constitutional attack, Justice Stewart's majority opinion insisted that the challengers' reliance on cases such as Dunn v. Blumstein was not "apposite," since the New York scheme "did not absolutely disenfranchise the class to which the petitioners belong." Rather, it "merely imposed a time deadline": "if their plight can be characterized as disenfranchisement at all, it was not caused by [the statute], but by their own failure to take timely steps to effect their enrollment." And here, the requirement was not "unreasonably long" and did not unduly burden the exercise of rights of voting and free association. Though the period was "lengthy," it was "not an arbitrary time limit unconnected to any important state goal." The justifiable purpose of the system was "to inhibit party 'raiding' whereby voters in sympathy with one party designate themselves as voters of another party so as to influence or determine the results of the other party's primary."

Justice Powell's dissent, joined by Justices Douglas, Brennan and Marshall, objected especially to the majority's lack of clarity about applicable standards and insisted that the strict scrutiny of Dunn v. Blumstein was appropriate here. He concluded that the law imposed "substantial and unnecessary restrictions" on voting and associational rights. More than a mere "time deadline" was involved: "Deferment of a right [can] be tantamount to its denial." He added: "The Court's formulation, though the terminology is somewhat stronger, resembles the traditional equal protection 'rational basis' test." And that was an inappropriate standard: under Dunn v. Blumstein, the test was whether "the exclusions are *necessary* to promote a *compelling* state interest." Yet the requirements of that "strict judicial scrutiny" were not met here. The lower court, to be sure, had found the state interest in deterring "raiding" a "compelling" one. But that was not enough. The "less restrictive alternatives" inquiry was not satisfied: the majority had failed "to address the critical question of whether [the state] interest may be protected adequately by lesser measures."

b. Justice Powell's advocacy of a clear-cut strict scrutiny approach bore fruit in the following Term. In KUSPER v. PONTIKES, 414 U.S. 51 (1973), Justice Stewart's majority opinion distinguished Rosario and invalidated an Illinois scheme prohibiting a person from voting in the primary election of a political party if he had voted in the primary of any other party within the preceding 23 months. The Court emphasized that the provision "substantially restricts an Illinois voter's freedom to change his political party affiliation" and thus significantly encroached upon First Amendment associational freedoms. The Illinois system was found to differ from the New York delayed-enrollment law sustained in Rosario in a number of respects. In New York, disenfranchisement was caused by the voters' own failure to take timely measures to enroll; the Illinois law, by contrast, " 'locks' voters into a preexisting party affiliation from one primary to the next, and the only way to break the 'lock' is to forego voting in *any* primary for a period of almost two years." The Court concluded that "the legitimate interest of

Illinois in preventing 'raiding' cannot justify the device it has chosen to effect its goal"; Rosario itself indicated that "the asserted state interest can be attained by 'less drastic means,' which do not unnecessarily burden the exercise of constitutionally protected activity." Chief Justice Burger concurred in the result. Justices Blackmun and Rehnquist dissented.

6. *Access to the ballot: Williams v. Rhodes and its progeny.* a. *The Williams decision.* In WILLIAMS v. RHODES, 393 U.S. 23 (1968), the Court held that Ohio's election laws created unduly burdensome obstacles to third party candidates seeking a place on presidential election ballots. And since that decision, the Court has had repeated occasion to delineate the states' authority to curtail access to ballots by independent candidates and third parties.

The challenge in Williams came from a new party, the American Independent Party supporting George Wallace, as well as from an established minor party. Under the Ohio system, the major parties retained their positions on the ballot simply by obtaining 10% of the votes in the last gubernatorial election. Parties newly seeking access to the presidential election ballot, by contrast, faced formidable obstacles: early in the presidential election year, they were required to file petitions signed by 15% of the number of ballots cast in the last gubernatorial election; they had to erect an elaborate party structure; and they had to conduct primaries. Justice Black's majority opinion stated that these requirements "made it virtually impossible for a new political party, even though it has hundreds of thousands of members, or an old party, which has a very small number of members," to gain a place on the ballot. As a result, the two established major parties had "a decided advantage over any new parties struggling for existence." Justice Black found strict scrutiny appropriate. He explained: "In determining whether or not a state law violates [equal protection], we must consider the facts and circumstances behind the law, the interests which the state claims to be protecting, and the interests of those who are disadvantaged by the classification." Here the state scheme placed "unequal burdens" on "two different, although overlapping, kinds of rights—the right of individuals to associate for the advancement of political beliefs, and the right of qualified voters [to] cast their votes effectively." He found that the state had "failed to show any 'compelling interest' which justifies imposing such heavy burdens" on such "precious freedoms."

None of the state interests asserted proved adequate justifications. Encouraging a two party system to promote compromise and political stability could not support giving the two major parties a permanent monopoly. And the interest in avoiding run-off elections and preventing voter confusion could not support the crippling restrictions here: those dangers were too remote; and the experience of other states showed that "no more than a handful of parties attempts to qualify for ballot positions even where a very low number of signatures, such as 1% of the electorate, is required." There were dissents by Justices Stewart and White and by Chief Justice Warren.[3]

3. A concurrence by Justice Harlan stated that he would rest "entirely" on First Amendment associational rights and insisted that reliance on equal protection was "unnecessary."

How far-reaching is the Williams principle? What was the "voting" interest protected? The right to "vote effectively"—i. e., for a particular candidate—rather than simply access

b. *Jenness v. Fortson.* Three years after Williams, a unanimous Court found that decision distinguishable in rejecting challenges to Georgia's nominating procedures in JENNESS v. FORTSON, 403 U.S. 431 (1971). Unlike Ohio, Georgia permits write-in votes and allows independent candidates to appear on the ballots without third party endorsement if they have filed nominating petitions signed by at least 5% of those eligible to vote in the last election for the office. Petitions can be filed as late as June of the election year, and there are no requirements for establishing an elaborate primary election machinery.

Justice Stewart found that scheme "vastly different" from that in Williams. The Georgia system did not unduly "freeze the political status quo." And the different treatment of established large parties and new small parties was justifiable: "There is surely an important state interest in requiring some preliminary showing of a significant modicum of support before printing the name of a political organization and its candidates on the ballot—the interest, if no other, in avoiding confusion, deception, and even frustration of the democratic process at the general election." [4]

c. *The 1974 decisions.* In two 1974 decisions, the Court reexamined ballot access barriers to independent candidates and small political parties, found them of a magnitude somewhere between Williams v. Rhodes and Jenness v. Fortson, and rejected most of the challenges. STORER v. BROWN, 415 U.S. 724 (1974); AMERICAN PARTY OF TEXAS v. WHITE, 415 U.S. 767 (1974). The majority acknowledged, however, that a strict scrutiny standard was applicable: as the Court put it in the Texas case, "whether the qualifications for ballot positions are viewed as substantial burdens on the right to associate or as discriminations against [small parties], their validity depends upon whether they are necessary to further compelling state interests."

In Storer, the Court sustained a California provision denying a ballot position to an independent candidate if he had registered with a political party within a year prior to the immediately preceding primary election or if he had voted in that election. That barrier was not found discriminatory against independents. The one-year disaffiliation provision furthered the state's "compelling" interest in the "stability of its political system." [5] In the Texas case, the Court sustained most of that state's provisions regarding independents and minor parties, but invalidated a provision under which only names of major parties were included on absentee ballots. Justice

to the ballot or equality of votes? Does that suggest a constitutional "right to write-in space," see Note, 83 Harv.L.Rev. 96 (1969)? Is the basic concern in Williams with *groups* rather than with *individuals*? Should the elaborations of the new principles move in the direction of encouraging third parties, or in the direction of encouraging the major parties to represent divergent viewpoints more effectively? Consider these questions in light of the cases elaborating the Williams principle, below, and see generally Barton, "The General-Election Ballot: More Nominees or More Representative Nominees?" 22 Stan.L.Rev. 165 (1970).

4. Note also the Court's rejection, by a 5 to 4 vote, of a Williams v. Rhodes-based challenge to an Ohio provision barring a person's candidacy in a party primary "if he voted as a member of a different political party in any primary election within the next preceding four calendar years." Lippitt v. Cipollone, 405 U.S. 1032 (1972).

5. The Court had greater difficulty with a challenge to the requirement that independents file a petition signed

White's majority opinion noted that the Texas scheme "affords minority political parties a real and substantially equal opportunity for ballot qualification" and found most of the regulations were "valid measures, reasonably taken in pursuit of vital state objectives that cannot be served equally well in significantly less burdensome ways." Justices Douglas, Brennan and Marshall dissented in the California case; Justice Douglas was the sole dissenter in the Texas case.

B. THE FAIR ADMINISTRATION OF JUSTICE: ACCESS AND EQUALITY IN CRIMINAL AND CIVIL CASES

Introduction. In the cases which follow, the Court carefully scrutinizes and frequently invalidates economic barriers impeding adequate access to and participation in the criminal and civil processes. What is the reach of the principles of these cases? What are the constitutional bases? The Court has repeatedly divided on the issue of whether due process or equal protection provides the appropriate framework for analysis. Justice Harlan was the leading advocate of the due process approach. The majority has most commonly emphasized the relevance of equal protection; and that reasonably well-established strand of the new equal protection has retained vitality on the Burger Court, at least in the criminal area.

Which provision *does* provide the most appropriate basis for the developments traced below: due process or equal protection? Does either clause provide adequate basis? The core of procedural due process notions is adequate notice and opportunity to be heard. (Recall chap. 8, sec. 2.) Do the results in the cases which follow flow plausibly from those core concepts? In a number of the cases, the Court holds that a state may not impose fee requirements and must provide counsel when defendants seek to appeal criminal convictions. Yet the Court continues to maintain that there is no constitutional *right* to appeal a conviction: no such right has been found "fundamental" in the evolution of criminal procedure guarantees. (Recall chap. 8.) Does a due process right to access and participation nevertheless arise once the state chooses to establish an appellate structure? Do access and participation rights then flow from the "opportunity to be heard" ingredient of due process? Even though, on appeal and unlike at trial, the initiative to invoke the judicial process comes from the defendant rather than the state?

Does equal protection provide a more plausible rationale? What justifies the Court's interventionism in this area? Do such economic barriers as fee requirements in filing appeals contravene traditional equal protection standards? Note Justice Black's statement in Griffin, which follows, that there is "no rational relationship" between "the ability to pay costs" and "a defendant's guilt or innocence." But are there not other legitimate state objectives to which fee requirements do bear a rational relationship? If

by 5% of the total number of votes cast in California in the last general election. That issue was remanded with guidelines "to assess realistically

whether the law imposes excessively burdensome requirements" on independents' access to the ballot.

wealth were a "suspect classification," strict scrutiny of economic barriers—
and perhaps imposition of affirmative state obligations to eliminate inequalities—would be justified in a wide range of areas. But, as sec. 5 below
makes clear, the Court has not accepted any such principle across the board.
Something more than the mere existence of economic barriers must be involved to explain the Court interventions with respect to participation in the
judicial process. What is that "something more"? Is the stricter scrutiny
triggered by the existence of a "fundamental interest" in these cases? What
is that "fundamental interest"? What is its source? Is there a "fundamental
interest," for example, in effective participation in the criminal appellate
process—even though there is no constitutional "right" to a criminal appeal? What are the plausible limits on the principles implicit in these cases?

The Griffin case. The evolution of this strand of the new equal protection had its origin in GRIFFIN v. ILLINOIS, 351 U.S. 12 (1956). Griffin held that a state must provide a trial transcript or its equivalent to an
indigent criminal defendant appealing his conviction on nonfederal grounds,
even though the state ordinarily required that, in order to obtain review,
appellants must furnish transcripts to the appellate court. The challengers
in Griffin attacked the failure to provide them the free transcripts they
sought and claimed that the resulting "refusal to afford appellate reviews
solely because of poverty" was unconstitutional.[1]

Justice Black's opinion, joined by Chief Justice Warren and Justices
Douglas and Clark, stated: "Providing equal justice for poor and rich, weak
and powerful alike is an age-old problem. [D]ue process and equal protection both call for procedures in criminal trials which allow no invidious
discriminations between persons and different groups of persons. Both
equal protection and due process emphasize the central aim of our entire
judicial system—all people charged with crime must, so far as the law is
concerned, 'stand on an equality before the bar of justice in every American
court.' . . . In criminal trials a State can no more discriminate on account of poverty than on account of religion, race, or color. Plainly the
ability to pay costs in advance bears no rational relationship to a defendant's
guilt or innocence and could not be used as an excuse to deprive a defendant
of a fair trial. . . .

"There is no meaningful distinction between a rule which would deny
the poor the right to defend themselves in a trial court and one which effectively denies the poor an adequate appellate review accorded to all who have
money enough to pay the costs in advance. It is true that a State is not required by the Federal Constitution to provide appellate courts or a right to
appellate review at all. See, e. g., McKane v. Durston, 153 U.S. 684, 687–
688. But that is not to say that a State that does grant appellate review can do
so in a way that discriminates against some convicted defendants on account
of their poverty. Appellate review has now become an integral part of the
Illinois trial system for finally adjudicating the guilt or innocence of a

1. In denying their request for a free
transcript, Illinois stated that it provided free transcripts only to indigent
defendants sentenced to death. The
petitioners in Griffin had been sentenced to prison for armed robbery.

Originally, their discrimination claim
focused primarily on the distinction
between capital and noncapital cases;
but the Supreme Court's approach
rested on broader grounds.

defendant. Consequently at all stages of the proceedings the Due Process and Equal Protection Clauses protect persons like petitioners from invidious discriminations. . . .

"All of the States now provide some method of appeal from criminal convictions, recognizing the importance of appellate review to a correct adjudication of guilt or innocence. Statistics show that a substantial proportion of criminal convictions are reversed by state appellate courts. Thus to deny adequate review to the poor means that many of them may lose their life, liberty or property because of unjust convictions which appellate courts would set aside. Many States have recognized this and provided aid for convicted defendants who have a right to appeal and need a transcript but are unable to pay for it. A few have not. Such a denial is a misfit in a country dedicated to affording equal justice to all and special privileges to none in the administration of its criminal law. There can be no equal justice where the kind of trial a man gets depends on the amount of money he has. Destitute defendants must be afforded as adequate appellate review as defendants who have money enough to buy transcripts." [2]

Justice Frankfurter concurred in the result: "[N]either the fact that a State may deny the right of appeal altogether nor the right of a State to make an appropriate classification, based on differences in crimes and their punishment, nor the right of a State to lay down conditions it deems appropriate for criminal appeals, sanctions differentiations by a State that have no relation to a rational policy of criminal appeal or authorize the imposition of conditions that offend the deepest presuppositions of our society." Justices Reed, Burton, Minton, and Harlan dissented.[3] Justice Harlan's dissent sketched an approach he was to reiterate and elaborate in a number of later cases. He thought the equal protection emphasis misplaced and found no violation of due process guarantees.

On equal protection, Justice Harlan noted: "All that Illinois has done is to fail to alleviate the consequences of differences in economic circumstances that exist wholly apart from any state action. The Court thus holds that, at least in this area of criminal appeals, the Equal Protection Clause imposes on the States an affirmative duty to lift the handicaps flowing from differences in economic circumstances. That holding produces the anomolous result that a constitutional admonition to the States to treat all persons equally means in this instance that Illinois must give to some what it requires others to pay for. [T]he real issue in this case is not whether Illinois *has* discriminated but whether it has a duty *to* discriminate. [T]he issue here is not the typical equal protection question of the reasonableness of a 'classification' on the basis of which the State has imposed legal disabilities, but rather the reasonableness of the State's failure to remove natural disabilities.

---

2. Justice Black added, however, that the transcript might not be necessary in every case: the state courts "may find other means of affording adequate and effective appellate review to indigent defendants. For example, it may be that bystanders' bills of exceptions or other methods of reporting trial proceedings could be used in some cases."

3. The dissent by Justices Burton and Minton, joined by Justices Reed and Harlan, commented: "We think the distinction [between] capital cases and noncapital cases is a reasonable and valid one. [Illinois] is not bound to make the defendants economically equal before its bar of justice."

[I] submit that the basis for that holding is simply an unarticulated conclusion that it violates 'fundamental fairness' for a State which provides for appellate review [not] to see to it that such appeals are in fact available to those it would imprison for serious crimes. That of course is the traditional language of due process."

Turning to the due process issue, he asked: "Can it be that, while it was not unconstitutional for Illinois to afford no appeals, its steady progress in increasing the safeguards against erroneous convictions has resulted in a constitutional decline?" [4] He noted that "there is no 'right' to an appeal in the same sense that there is a right to a trial." The only due process guarantee was "simply the right not to be denied an appeal for arbitrary or capricious reasons," and "[n]othing of that kind" appeared here. (The divisions in approaches and assessments which first surfaced in Griffin were more fully developed seven years later, in the Douglas case which follows.)

DOUGLAS v. CALIFORNIA

372 U.S. 353, 83 S.Ct. 814, 9 L.Ed.2d 811 (1963).

Certiorari to the District Court of Appeal of California, Second Appellate District.

[Petitioners, indigent criminal defendants, unsuccessfully sought appointed counsel to represent them in their direct appeal as of right to the California District Court of Appeal. In denying their requests, the appellate court relied on the state procedure under which the appellate court made "an independent investigation of the record" to "determine whether it would be of advantage to the defendant or helpful to the appellate court to have counsel appointed." The appellate court stated that it had "gone through" the record and had come to the conclusion that "no good whatever would be served by appointment of counsel." The Supreme Court reversed.]

Mr. Justice DOUGLAS delivered the opinion of the Court. .   .   .

We agree [with] Justice Traynor of the California Supreme Court, who said that the "[d]enial of counsel on appeal [to an indigent] would seem to be a discrimination at least as invidious as that condemned in Griffin v. Illinois." [In Griffin], the right to a free transcript on appeal was an issue. Here the issue is whether or not an indigent shall be denied the assistance of counsel on appeal. In either case the evil is the same: discrimination against the indigent. For there can be no equal justice where the kind of an appeal a man enjoys "depends on the amount of money he has." [Griffin.]

In spite of California's forward treatment of indigents, under its present practice the type of an appeal a person is afforded in the District Court of Appeal hinges upon whether or not he can pay for the assistance of counsel. If he can the appellate court passes on the merits of his case only after having the full benefit of written briefs and oral argument by counsel. If he cannot the appellate court is forced to prejudge the merits before it can even determine whether counsel should be provided. At this stage in the proceedings only the

---

4. Compare the Court's deferential stance toward "remedial" legislation in other contexts. Recall, e. g., the McDonald case, in sec. 1 above.

barren record speaks for the indigent, and, unless the printed pages show that an injustice has been committed, he is forced to go without a champion on appeal. Any real chance he may have had of showing that his appeal has hidden merit is deprived him when the court decides on an ex parte examination of the record that the assistance of counsel is not required.

We are not here concerned with problems that might arise from the denial of counsel for the preparation of a petition for discretionary or mandatory review beyond the stage in the appellate process at which the claims have once been presented by a lawyer and passed upon by an appellate court. We are dealing only with the *first appeal*, granted [by state law] as a matter of right to rich and poor alike, from a criminal conviction. We need not now decide whether California would have to provide counsel for an indigent seeking a discretionary hearing from the California Supreme Court after the District Court of Appeal had sustained his conviction, or whether counsel must be appointed for an indigent seeking review of an appellate affirmance of his conviction in this Court by appeal as of right or by petition for a writ of certiorari which lies within the Court's discretion.* But it is appropriate to observe that a State can, consistently with the Fourteenth Amendment, provide for differences so long as the result does not amount to a denial of due process or an "invidious discrimination." [Williamson v. Lee Optical Co.; Griffin.] Absolute equality is not required; lines can be and are drawn and we often sustain them. But where the merits of *the one and only appeal* an indigent has as of right are decided without benefit of counsel, we think an unconstitutional line has been drawn between rich and poor.

When an indigent is forced to run this gantlet of a preliminary showing of merit, the right to appeal does not comport with fair procedure. [This] case, where counsel was denied petitioners on appeal, shows that the discrimination is not between "possibly good and obviously bad cases," but between cases where the rich man can require the court to listen to argument of counsel before deciding on the merits, but a poor man cannot. There is lacking that equality demanded by the Fourteenth Amendment where the rich man, who appeals as of right, enjoys the benefit of counsel's examination into the record, research of the law, and marshalling of arguments on his behalf, while the indigent, already burdened by a preliminary determination that his case is without merit, is forced to shift for himself. The indigent, where the record is unclear or the errors are hidden, has only the right to a meaningless ritual, while the rich man has a meaningful appeal.

Reversed and remanded.

Mr. Justice HARLAN, whom Mr. Justice STEWART joins, dissenting.

In holding that an indigent has an absolute right to appointed counsel on appeal of a state criminal conviction, the Court appears to rely both on the Equal Protection Clause and on the guarantees of fair procedure inherent in the Due Process Clause of the Fourteenth Amendment, with obvious emphasis on "equal protection." In my view the Equal Protection Clause is not apposite, and its application to cases like the present one can lead only to mischie-

---

* Eleven years later, a divided Court held that the considerations underlying Douglas v. California did not require appointment of counsel in discretionary appeals. Ross v. Moffit, 417 U.S. 600 (1974) (noted further below).

vous results. This case should be judged solely under the Due Process Clause, and I do not believe that the California procedure violates that provision.

EQUAL PROTECTION.

To approach the present problem in terms of the Equal Protection Clause is, I submit, but to substitute resounding phrases for analysis. I dissented from this approach in [Griffin v. Illinois],[1] and I am constrained to dissent from the implicit extension of the equal protection approach here—to a case in which the State denies no one an appeal, but seeks only to keep within reasonable bounds the instances in which appellate counsel will be assigned to indigents.

The States, of course, are prohibited by the Equal Protection Clause from discriminating between "rich" and "poor" *as such* in the formulation and application of their laws. But it is a far different thing to suggest that this provision prevents the State from adopting a law of general applicability that may affect the poor more harshly than it does the rich, or, on the other hand, from making some effort to redress economic imbalances while not eliminating them entirely.

Every financial exaction which the State imposes on a uniform basis is more easily satisfied by the well-to-do than by the indigent. Yet I take it that no one would dispute the constitutional power of the State to levy a uniform sales tax, to charge tuition at a state university, to fix rates for the purchase of water from a municipal corporation, to impose a standard fine for criminal violations, or to establish minimum bail for various categories of offenses. Nor could it be contended that the State may not classify as crimes acts which the poor are more likely to commit than are the rich. And surely, there would be no basis for attacking a state law which provided benefits for the needy simply because those benefits fell short of the goods or services that others could purchase for themselves.

Laws such as these do not deny equal protection to the less fortunate for one essential reason: the Equal Protection Clause does not impose on the States "an affirmative duty to lift the handicaps flowing from differences in economic circumstances." To so construe it would be to read into the Constitution a philosophy of leveling that would be foreign to many of our basic concepts of the proper relations between government and society. The State may have a moral obligation to eliminate the evils of poverty, but it is not required by the Equal Protection Clause to give to some whatever others can afford.

Thus it should be apparent that the present case [is] not one properly regarded as arising under this clause. California does not discriminate between rich and poor in having a uniform policy permitting everyone to appeal and to retain counsel, and in having a separate rule dealing *only* with the standards for the appointment of counsel for those unable to retain their own attorneys. The sole classification established by this rule is between those cases that are believed to have merit and those regarded as frivolous. And, of course, no matter how far the state rule might go in providing counsel for indigents, it could never be expected to satisfy an affirmative duty—if one existed

---

1. The majority in Griffin appeared to rely, as here, on a blend of the Equal Protection and Due Process Clauses in arriving at the result. So far as the result in that case rested on due process grounds, I fully accept the authority of Griffin. [Footnote by Justice Harlan.]

—to place the poor on the same level as those who can afford the best legal talent available. . . .

The real question in this case, I submit, and the only one that permits of satisfactory analysis, is whether or not the state rule, as applied in this case, is consistent with the requirements of fair procedure guaranteed by the Due Process Clause. Of course, in considering this question, it must not be lost sight of that the State's responsibility under the Due Process Clause is to provide justice for all. Refusal to furnish criminal indigents with some things that others can afford may fall short of constitutional standards of fairness. The problem before us is whether this is such a case.

DUE PROCESS. . . .

We have today held that in a case such as the one before us, there is an absolute right to the services of counsel at trial. [Gideon v. Wainwright, 372 U.S. 335 (1963).] But the appellate procedures involved here stand on an entirely different constitutional footing. [E. g.,] appellate review is in itself not required by the Fourteenth Amendment, [and] thus the question presented is the narrow one whether the State's rules with respect to the appointment of counsel are so arbitrary or unreasonable, *in the context of the particular appellate procedure that it has established,* as to require their invalidation. . . .

What the Court finds constitutionally offensive in California's procedure bears a striking resemblance to the rules of this Court and many state courts of last resort on petitions for certiorari or for leave to appeal filed by indigent defendants pro se. Under the practice of this Court, only if it appears from the petition for certiorari that a case merits review is leave to proceed in forma pauperis granted [and] counsel appointed. [But this Court] has never deemed itself constitutionally required to appoint counsel to assist in the preparation of each of the more than 1,000 pro se petitions for certiorari currently being filed each Term. . . .

The Court distinguishes our review from the present case on the grounds that the California rule relates to "the *first appeal,* granted as a matter of right." But I fail to see the significance of this difference. Surely, it cannot be contended that the requirements of fair procedure are exhausted once an indigent has been given one appellate review. Nor can it well be suggested that having appointed counsel is more necessary to the fair administration of justice in an initial appeal taken as a matter of right, which the reviewing court on the full record has already determined to be frivolous, than in a petition asking a higher appellate court to exercise its discretion to consider what may be a substantial constitutional claim. . . .

I cannot agree that the Constitution prohibits a State, in seeking to redress economic imbalances at its bar of justice and to provide indigents with full review, from taking reasonable steps to guard against needless expense. This is all that California has done. . . .†

† Justice Clark also submitted a dissenting opinion.

ECONOMIC DIFFERENTIATIONS AND THE CRIMINAL PROCESS: THE REACH OF THE GRIFFIN–DOUGLAS PRINCIPLES

1. *Transcripts and filing fees.* The Court has had little difficulty in extending the free transcript claim recognized in Griffin to a variety of other settings. In a large number of decisions since Griffin—many of them per curiam ones—the Court has found financial barriers to the obtaining of transcripts unconstitutional. For example, Lane v. Brown, 372 U.S. 477 (1963), held that an indigent defendant was entitled to a free transcript in a state post-conviction proceeding where the filing of a transcript was necessary to give the reviewing court appellate jurisdiction. Accordingly, a public defender's "unreviewable discretion" as to obtaining free transcripts for indigent defendants was found constitutionally impermissible. Long v. District Court, 385 U.S. 192 (1966), extended that holding to require free transcripts in post-conviction proceedings even where the filing of transcripts was not necessary to give the appellate court jurisdiction. And Roberts v. LaVallee, 389 U.S. 40 (1967), found an indigent prisoner entitled to a free transcript of a portion of the preliminary hearing, to aid him in preparing a challenge to his conviction. In Roberts, the Court stated the emerging constitutional requirement in very broad terms: "Our decisions for more than a decade now have made clear that differences in access to the instruments needed to vindicate legal rights, when based upon the financial situation of the defendant, are repugnant to the Constitution." Do all the decisions which follow reflect such a broad principle? What are the limits on the "instruments" to which the indigent defendant is entitled? [1]

2. *Counsel.* Efforts to extend the Griffin-Douglas principles in the Douglas context of right to appointed counsel for appeals have encountered far greater difficulty. ROSS v. MOFFIT, 417 U.S. 600 (1974), refused to extend Douglas v. California to discretionary appeals. Justice Rehnquist's majority opinion emphasized that Douglas was limited to the "appointment of counsel for indigent state defendants on their first appeal as of right" and found no constitutional mandate "to require counsel for discretionary state appeals and for applications for review in this Court." He reviewed the Griffin-Douglas line of cases and noted that their "precise rationale" had "never been explicitly stated, some support being derived from [equal protection], and some from [due process]." He added: "Neither clause by itself provides an entirely satisfactory basis for the result reached."

Turning to the clauses separately, he disposed of the due process contention in a brief passage. He emphasized the "significant differences between the trial and appellate stages," noting that "it is ordinarily the defendant, rather than the State, who initiates the appellate process, seeking not to fend off the efforts of the State's prosecutor but rather to overturn a finding

---

1. See also Mayer v. City of Chicago, 404 U.S. 189 (1971), holding the Griffin requirement of a transcript or an adequate alternative applicable to non-felony cases as well. For a consideration of what constitutes an adequate alternative, see Britt v. North Carolina, 404 U.S. 226 (1971).

One easy extension of the free transcript context of Griffin proved to be the invalidation of filing fee requirements. See, e. g., Burns v. Ohio, 360 U.S. 252 (1959) (appeals); Smith v. Bennett, 365 U.S. 708 (1961) (post-conviction proceedings).

of guilt made by a judge or a jury below. The defendant needs an attorney on appeal not as a shield to protect him against being 'haled into court' by the State and stripped of his presumption of innocence, but rather as a sword to upset the prior determination of guilt." This was a "significant" difference. Defendants were entitled to a trial, but there was no right to an appeal: "The fact that an appeal *has* been provided does not automatically mean that a State then acts unfairly by refusing to provide counsel to indigent defendants at every stage of the way. Unfairness results only if indigents are singled out by the State and denied meaningful access to the appellate system because of their poverty. That question is more profitably considered under an equal protection analysis."

Turning to equal protection, Justice Rehnquist emphasized that equal protection "does not require absolute equality" but merely appellate systems "free of unreasoned distinctions" and assurance that "indigents have an adequate opportunity to present their claims fairly within the adversarial system." States could not deprive indigents of a "meaningful appeal," but that question was "not one of absolutes, but one of degrees." And here, where there had been one appeal as of right in the state structure, providing counsel to assist in seeking discretionary review did not deny indigents "meaningful access" to the highest state court. Justice Rehnquist conceded that a skilled lawyer would "prove helpful to any litigant able to employ him" so that an indigent was "somewhat handicapped in comparison with a wealthy defendant who has counsel assisting him in every conceivable manner at every stage in the proceeding." But this was only a "relative handicap," one "far less than the handicap borne by the indigent defendant denied counsel on his initial appeal as of right in Douglas. And the fact that a particular service might be of benefit to an indigent defendant does not mean that the service is constitutionally required. The duty of the State under our cases is not to duplicate the legal arsenal that may be privately retained by a criminal defendant, [but] only to assure the indigent defendant an adequate opportunity to present his claims fairly in the context of the State's appellate process." And Justice Rehnquist found even less basis for the claim to appointed counsel to aid in seeking discretionary review in the U.S. Supreme Court.

Justice Douglas' dissent, joined by Justices Brennan and Marshall, drew on due process as well as equal protection, stated that "Douglas v. California was grounded on concepts of fairness and equality," and insisted that the "same concepts of fairness and equality, which require counsel in a first appeal of right, require counsel in other and subsequent discretionary appeals." He added: "The right to discretionary review is a substantial one, and one where a lawyer can be of significant assistance to an indigent defendant." [2]

2. Douglas v. California has not been extended to require provision of counsel to aid prisoners in applying for collateral post-conviction relief. But note Johnson v. Avery, 393 U.S. 483 (1969), where the majority struck down a state prison regulation that barred inmates—"jailhouse lawyers"—from assisting other prisoners in preparing legal documents. That rule could not be applied "unless and until the State provides some reasonable alternative to assist inmates in the preparation of petitions for post-conviction relief." See also the elaborations of the Johnson requirements—and their application to prisoners' efforts to seek relief under the federal civil rights laws—in Wolff v. McDonnell, 418 U.S. 539 (1974).

3. *State recoupment of funds expended for indigents.* When a state expends funds to assist indigents in the criminal process—e. g., as a result of the constitutional mandate of the Griffin-Douglas line of cases or of the "incorporated" Sixth Amendment guarantee of counsel, Gideon v. Wainwright—may it claim reimbursement of those expenditures? As Ross v. Moffit made clear, "absolute equality" independent of economic status is not required by the equal protection clause; an equal protection challenge to a recoupment law accordingly failed in FULLER v. OREGON, 417 U.S. 40 (1974). Justice Stewart's majority opinion sustained a scheme under which the state sought recoupment of legal expenses to the extent a convicted defendant became able to repay, and conditioned a solvent defendant's probation on his reimbursement of the county's legal and investigatory expenses incurred because of his indigency. The Court rejected the claim that that obligation to repay might impel the defendant "to decline the services of an appointed attorney and thus 'chill' his constitutional right to counsel." Justice Stewart responded:

"We live in a society where the distribution of legal assistance, like the distribution of all goods and services, is generally regulated by the dynamics of private enterprise. A defendant in a criminal case who is just above the line separating the indigent from the nonindigent must borrow money, sell off his meager assets, or call upon his family or friends in order to hire a lawyer. We cannot say that the Constitution requires that those only slightly poorer must remain forever immune from any obligation to shoulder the expenses of their legal defense, even when they are able to pay without hardship." [3]

Though a direct challenge to recoupment provisions does not lie under the Griffin-Douglas principles, traditional equal protection principles—especially the application of minimum scrutiny "with bite"—make the classifications in some recoupment statutes vulnerable. Though such an attack failed in Fuller v. Oregon, it succeeded with respect to another recoupment law in James v. Strange, 407 U.S. 128 (1972). (James v. Strange is discussed in Gunther, "Newer Equal Protection," 86 Harv.L.Rev. 1 (1972).)[4]

4. *Jail sentences to "work off" fines.* In WILLIAMS v. ILLINOIS, 399 U.S. 235 (1970), appellant had been given the maximum sentence for

3. Note also Justice Stewart's summary rejection of the challengers' wealth discrimination claim: "[T]he imposition of a repayment requirement upon those for whom counsel was appointed but not upon those who hired their own counsel simply does not constitute invidious discrimination against the poor. Indeed, the entire thrust of Oregon's appointment-of-counsel plan is to insure an indigent effective representation of counsel at all significant steps of the criminal process. Those who are indigent may be conditionally required to repay because only they, in contrast to nonindigents, were provided counsel by the State in the first place."

4. Under the Kansas recoupment law invalidated in James v. Strange, indigent criminal defendants were not accorded most of the exemptions afforded civil judgment debtors—e. g., exemptions of personal necessities. Justice Powell's opinion for a unanimous Court recognized that recoupment laws furthered a legitimate state interest, but objected to the "punitiveness and discrimination" in the law, insisted that equal protection required "more even treatment of indigent criminal defendants with other classes of debtors," and concluded that the state could not "blight in such discriminatory fashion the hopes of indigents for self-sufficiency and self-respect." See

petty theft: one year's imprisonment and a $500 fine, plus $5 in court costs. The judgment provided that if appellant was in default of payments at the expiration of his sentence, he would remain in jail to "work off" his obligations at the rate of $5 per day. That judgment exposed the indigent appellant to confinement for 101 days beyond the statutory maximum sentence for the crime. Chief Justice Burger's majority opinion concluded, on the basis of the Griffin equal protection emphasis, "that an indigent criminal defendant may not be imprisoned in default of payment of a fine beyond the maximum authorized by the statute regulating the substantive offense. [O]nce the State has defined the outer limits of incarceration necessary to satisfy its penological interests and policies, it may not then subject a certain class of convicted defendants to a period of imprisonment beyond the statutory maximum solely by reason of their indigency." To imprison beyond the maximum statutory term solely because of "involuntary nonpayment of a fine or court cost" constituted "an impermissible discrimination that rests on ability to pay." And there were no adequate state justifications for such discriminations: the statutory term satisfied the state's penological policies, and the state had "numerous alternatives" for recouping the money, including use of installment plans. Justice Harlan concurred in the result, but wrote a separate opinion in order "to dissociate myself from the 'equal protection' rationale" and once again to urge a due process analysis. He noted that a "basic liberty"—the "right to remain free"—was involved which authorized the court to "squint hard" at restrictive legislation. "Administrative convenience" could not justify the restraint in view of the existence of "less restrictive alternatives." And he found no "considered legislative judgment" that the state's penological interest would be served by the statutory scheme.[5]

5. *Noneconomic distinctions and the criminal process.* Does the unusual degree of scrutiny manifested by the Court in Griffin, Douglas and its progeny stem from the impact of the challenged state practices on a "fundamental interest"? Is there a "fundamental interest" analogous to that con-

also Rinaldi v. Yeager, 384 U.S. 305 (1966). But a similar challenge to classifications failed in Fuller v. Oregon. The Fuller majority distinguished James v. Strange because Oregon's scheme retained all of the exemptions available to other judgment debtors. And it found no equal protection violation in the fact that the recoupment obligations applied only to *convicted* defendants, not to those who were not convicted or to those whose convictions were reversed. Justice Stewart's majority opinion applied a "some rationality" standard and found "objective rationality" in Oregon's distinction. Justice Marshall's dissent, joined by Justice Brennan, found an equal protection flaw in Oregon's different treatment of indigent criminal defendants and civil judgment debtors who could not be imprisoned for failing to pay their debts.

5. In Tate v. Short, 401 U.S. 395 (1971), Williams was extended to cover the case of an indigent who was unable to pay fines of $425 for traffic offenses and was ordered to a prison farm for a period to "work off" the fines at $5 a day. Justice Brennan's opinion stated: "Although the instant case involves offenses punishable by fines only, petitioner's imprisonment for nonpayment constitutes precisely the same unconstitutional discrimination [as in Williams, since] petitioner was subjected to imprisonment solely because of his indigency." The Court noted, however, that Williams might not bar imprisonment "as an enforcement method when alternative means are unsuccessful despite the defendant's reasonable efforts to satisfy the fines by those means." And Williams left open the question whether imprisonment for nonpayment of fines is permissible when the total jail sentence was no greater than the statutory maximum.

sidered in sec. 2A above—the interest in participation in the electoral process? In the cases in sec. 2A, the presence of the fundamental interest triggered strict scrutiny whether or not economic distinctions were present: It served to invalidate not only poll taxes and fee barriers to ballot access but also restrictions turning on party allegiance and length of residence, for example. The thrust of the Griffin-Douglas principles, by contrast, has been more limited. Intense scrutiny has been exercised only where the interest in access to the criminal process was combined with differential economic impacts.

Yet the modern Court has not treated noneconomic classifications in the criminal area with the extreme deference of the old equal protection. Rather, it has steered a somewhat uncertain course, occasionally invalidating classifications by announcing traditional equal protection standards but applying them "with bite." More commonly, the Court has sustained challenged classifications, yet with occasional restatements of old equal protection criteria in the direction of the "newer" equal protection. For an example of an invalidation pursuant to traditional criteria applied "with bite," see Jackson v. Indiana, 406 U.S. 715 (1972), invalidating provisions for the pretrial commitment of incompetent criminal defendants. The equal protection violation was uncovered by comparing the laws applicable to petitioner with those governing commitment of persons not charged with offenses: criminal defendants were subject to more lenient commitment standards and to a more stringent standard of release. See also Humphrey v. Cady, 405 U.S. 504 (1972), finding an equal protection challenge to commitment procedures under Wisconsin's Sex Crimes Act sufficiently persuasive to warrant an evidentiary hearing on remand. Justice Marshall's opinion devoted most attention to the fact that jury determinations preceded commitments under the Mental Health Act but were not afforded under the Sex Crimes Act.[6]

Since 1972, equal protection challenges have proved less successful, even though standards somewhat more interventionist than those of the old equal protection have sometimes been voiced. For example, in McGINNIS v. ROYSTER, 410 U.S. 263 (1973), the majority rejected a challenge to a New York scheme under which a prisoner receives "good time" credit toward parole eligibility for the time spent in state prison after sentencing, but not for time spent in a county jail before sentencing. The challengers claimed discrimination against those not out on bail before trial and sentencing, because the presentence detainees were subject to a longer period of incarceration. Justice Powell's majority opinion found justification for the scheme: good time credit reflected an inmate's performance under rehabilitation programs, and such programs were offered only in state prisons and not in county jails. The lower court had found the scheme irrational because good time credit was primarily designed to foster prisoners' discipline. Justice

---

6. These decisions are discussed in Gunther, "Newer Equal Protection," 86 Harv.L.Rev. 1 (1972).

Compare Schilb v. Kuebel, 404 U.S. 357 (1971), sustaining a state bail reform law against an attack claiming that it discriminated against the poor.

The Court refused to apply strict scrutiny, noted that the legislation was remedial, and commented that no fundamental right or suspect criterion was involved: "This smacks of administrative detail and of procedure." (Recall the leniency as to "remedial" laws in McDonald, sec. 1 above.)

Powell insisted, however, that a state's purpose need not be the primary one to serve as justification for a distinction.

But in sustaining the scheme, Justice Powell used language (noted in the Introductory Overview to this chapter) which insisted on testing a state scheme by actual purposes rather than the hypothesized ones frequently invoked in the deferential review of the old equal protection. He insisted that the test was "whether the challenged distinction rationally furthers some legitimate, *articulated* state purpose. . . . So long as the state purpose upholding the statutory class is legitimate and *nonillusory,* its lack of primacy is not disqualifying. . . . We have supplied *no imaginary basis or purpose* for this statutory scheme, but we likewise refuse to discard a clear and legitimate purpose because the court below perceived another to be primary." [Emphasis added.] Justice Douglas, joined by Justice Marshall, dissented, questioning the alleged rehabilitative purpose and emphasizing the differential impact of the scheme on those too poor to afford bail.

Compare MARSHALL v. UNITED STATES, 414 U.S. 417 (1974), where the majority's avowed standards as well as actual exercise of scrutiny appeared to retreat to the "rational basis" deference of the old equal protection—and where Justice Marshall found occasion to renew his attack on the two-tier approach. In the Marshall case, the Court found no violation of the equal protection ingredients of Fifth Amendment due process in the federal Narcotic Addict Rehabilitation Act. That Act allows some convicted addicts to participate in drug rehabilitative commitment programs in lieu of penal incarceration, but excludes those with two or more prior felony convictions. In response to Chief Justice Burger's "rational basis" defense of the classification, Justice Marshall's dissent, joined by Justices Douglas and Brennan, argued that the majority's "analysis is so deferential as to confirm an earlier observation that, except in cases where the Court chooses to invoke strict scrutiny, the Equal Protection Clause has been all but emasculated." He added:

"I must once again take issue with the Court's apparently rigid approach to equal protection issues.[7] True, . . . this case does not fit into any neat 'fundamental interest' or 'suspect classification' mold. Notwithstanding, I find it hard to understand why a statute which sends a man to prison and deprives him of the opportunity even to be considered for treatment for his disease of narcotics addiction, while providing treatment and suspension of prison sentence to others similarly situated, should be tested under the same minimial standards of rationality that we apply to statutes regulating who can sell eyeglasses or who can own pharmacies. This case does not involve discrimination against business interests more than powerful enough to protect themselves in the legislative halls, but the very life and health of a man caught up in the spiralling web of addiction and crime. I press my disagreement no further here, for a careful analysis of the two felony exclusion and the ends Congress sought to achieve shows that the exclusion is a totally irrational means toward those ends. If deferential scrutiny under the Equal Protection Clause is to mean more than total deference and no scrutiny, surely it must reach the statutory exclusion involved in this case."

7. He cited his earlier dissents in Dandridge v. Williams, Richardson v. Belcher, and San Antonio School Dist. v. Rodriguez, all in sec. 5 below. Recall also Dunn v. Blumstein, sec. 4A above, and the references to Justice Marshall's "sliding scale" in the Introductory Overview.

ECONOMIC BARRIERS AND CIVIL LITIGATION: THE BASES—AND LIMITS—OF BODDIE

1. *The Boddie case.* The appellants in BODDIE v. CONNECTI-CUT, 401 U.S. 371 (1971), were indigent welfare recipients who sought to file divorce actions in the state courts but claimed to be unable to pay the required court fees and costs for services of process. The payment requirement amounted to $60. The state refused to waive payment, and appellants claimed that this financial barrier unconstitutionally restricted their access to the courts. Justice Harlan's majority opinion sustained that claim, relying entirely on due process rather than equal protection. He concluded "that, given the basic position of the marriage relationship in this society's hierarchy of values and the concomitant state monopolization of the means for legally dissolving this relationship, due process does prohibit a State from denying, solely because of inability to pay, access to its courts to individuals who seek judicial dissolution of their marriages."

In reaching this conclusion, Justice Harlan noted that "this Court has seldom been asked to view access to the courts as an element of due process." But that was because "resort to the courts is not usually the only available, legitimate means of resolving private disputes." Here, however, the claims asserted by "would-be plaintiffs" were "akin to that of defendants faced with exclusion from the only forum effectively empowered to settle their disputes." Accordingly, the applicable principles were those stated "in our due process decisions that delimit rights of defendants compelled to litigate their differences in the judicial forum."

Justice Harlan emphasized one of these settled principles: "due process requires, at a minimum, that absent a countervailing state interest of overriding significance, persons forced to settle their claims of right and duty through the judicial process must be given a meaningful opportunity to be heard." Here, "the State's refusal to admit these appellants to its courts, the sole means in Connecticut for obtaining a divorce, must be regarded as the equivalent of denying them an opportunity to be heard upon their claimed right to a dissolution of their marriages, and, in the absence of a sufficient countervailing justification for the State's action, a denial of due process." Justice Harlan concluded with an attempt to limit the scope of the decision: "We do not decide that access for all individuals to the courts is a right that is, in all circumstances, guaranteed [by due process, for] in the case before us this right is the exclusive precondition to the adjustment of the fundamental human relationship. The requirement that these appellants resort to the judicial process is entirely a state-created matter."

Justice Douglas' concurring opinion insisted that the equal protection principles of the Griffin line of cases, not due process, were the appropriate grounds of decision: "An invidious discrimination based on poverty is adequate for this case." The elastic notions of substantive due process should not be revived. The majority's approach was too uncertain: "I do not see the length of the road we must follow if we accept my Brother Harlan's invitation." In another concurring opinion, Justice Brennan joined the Court's opinion to the extent that it rested on "procedural due process"

grounds. Justice Black was the only dissenter. He emphasized that his opinion in Griffin did not suggest that its requirements for criminal defendants were applicable to "the quite different field of civil cases."

2. *The Kras and Ortwein decisions.* Two months after the Boddie decision in 1971, Justice Black, who had dissented in Boddie, was prepared to find broad implications in it. In disagreeing with the Court's disposition of eight other cases "in which indigents were denied access to civil courts because of their poverty," Justice Black argued that if Boddie were to continue to be the law, it should be "expanded to all civil cases." Relying on equal protection, he insisted: "Persons seeking a divorce are no different from other members of society who must resort to the judicial process for resolution of their disputes." Meltzer v. LeCraw, 402 U.S. 954 (1971). Justice Black argued that Boddie "can safely rest on only one crucial foundation—that the civil courts [in this country] belong to the people of this country and that no person can be denied access to those courts, either for a trial or an appeal, because he cannot pay a fee, finance a bond, risk a penalty, or afford to hire an attorney." Lower courts, too, read Boddie broadly. But when the issue of the applicability of Boddie in other civil contexts finally reached the Court, the majority called a halt to that trend and read Boddie narrowly. Were those narrow readings persuasive? Are the distinctions between Boddie and the later cases justifiable?

a. *Kras.* In the first post-Boddie ruling, the Court refused to extend "the principle of Boddie to the no-asset bankruptcy proceeding." UNITED STATES v. KRAS, 409 U.S. 434 (1973). An indigent had challenged the $50 filing fee requirement in voluntary bankruptcy proceedings. The District Court sustained his attack: relying primarily on Boddie, it found a violation of the "Fifth Amendment right of due process, including equal protection." But Justice Blackmun's majority opinion disagreed. Boddie, he emphasized, "obviously stopped short of an unlimited rule that an indigent at all times and in all cases has the right to relief without the payment of fees." And the bankruptcy situation was sufficiently distinguishable from divorce. Reliance on Boddie was "misplaced": Boddie involved the "fundamental" marital relationship and related associational interests. The interest in discharge in bankruptcy, by contrast, "does not rise to the same constitutional level." Moreover, Boddie had emphasized the "utter exclusiveness" of a court remedy; governmental control over debts is not "nearly so exclusive." And like the due process challenge, an equal protection attack was inadequate: "bankruptcy legislation is in the area of economics and social welfare"; accordingly, "rational justification," rather than a demonstration of "a compelling governmental interest," sufficed.

Justice Stewart's dissent, joined by Justices Douglas, Brennan, and Marshall, thought the Boddie due process rationale "equally" applicable here. He argued that, "in the unique situation of the indigent bankrupt, the Government provides the only effective means of his ever being free of these Government-imposed obligations" of "legally enforceable debts." He concluded: "The Court today holds that Congress may say that some of the poor are too poor even to go bankrupt. I cannot agree." In a separate dissent, Justice Marshall was prepared to go further: "I view the case as involving the right of access to the courts, the opportunity to be heard when

one claims a legal right, and not just the right to a discharge in bankruptcy. When a person raises a claim of right or entitlement under the laws, the only forum in our legal system empowered to determine that claim is a court." In another dissent, Justice Douglas, joined by Justice Brennan, emphasized that "discrimination based on wealth" is "particularly 'invidious.'"

b. *Ortwein.* Two months later, the same 5 to 4 majority found Kras rather than Boddie applicable in rejecting an attack by indigents on Oregon's $25 filing fee prerequisite to judicial review of administrative denials of welfare benefits. ORTWEIN v. SCHWAB, 410 U.S. 656 (1973). In a per curiam summary reversal, the Court noted that the interest in welfare payments, like that in a bankruptcy discharge, "has far less constitutional significance than the interest of the Boddie appellants." Moreover, the claim of discrimination against the poor must fail because welfare payments are "in the area of economics and social welfare" and no suspect classification, "such as race, nationality, or alienage," was involved. There were separate dissents by Justices Douglas, Brennan, Marshall and Stewart. Most of the dissenters insisted that the case was closer to Boddie than to Kras.

C. DURATIONAL RESIDENCE REQUIREMENTS "PENALIZING" THE RIGHT OF INTERSTATE MIGRATION

SHAPIRO v. THOMPSON

394 U.S. 618, 89 S.Ct. 1322, 22 L.Ed.2d 600 (1969).

Appeal from the United States District Court for the District of Connecticut.[*]

Mr. Justice BRENNAN delivered the opinion of the Court.

[Each of these appeals is] from a decision of a three-judge District Court holding unconstitutional a State or District of Columbia statutory provision which denies welfare assistance to residents of the State or District who have not resided within their jurisdictions for at least one year immediately preceding their applications for such assistance.[1] We affirm the judgments of the District Courts in the three cases. · · ·

II.

There is no dispute that the effect of the waiting-period requirement in each case is to create two classes of needy resident families indistinguishable

---

[*] Together with Washington v. Legrant, on appeal from the United States District Court for the District of Columbia, and Reynolds v. Smith, on appeal from the United States District Court for the Eastern District of Pennsylvania.

[1] All but one of the appellees herein applied for assistance under the Aid to Families with Dependent Children Program (AFDC) which was established by the Social Security Act of 1935. The program provides partial federal funding of state assistance plans

from each other except that one is composed of residents who have resided a year or more, and the second of residents who have resided less than a year, in the jurisdiction. One the basis of this sole difference the first class is granted and the second class is denied welfare aid upon which may depend the ability of the families to obtain the very means to subsist—food, shelter, and other necessities of life. [A]ppellees' central contention is that the statutory prohibition of benefits to residents of less than a year creates a classification which constitutes an invidious discrimination denying them equal protection of the laws. We agree. The interests which appellants assert are promoted by the classification either may not constitutionally be promoted by government or are not compelling governmental interests.

III.

Primarily, appellants justify the waiting-period requirement as a protective device to preserve the fiscal integrity of state public assistance programs. It is asserted that people who require welfare assistance during their first year of residence in a State are likely to become continuing burdens on state welfare programs. Therefore, the argument runs, if such people can be deterred from entering the jurisdiction by denying them welfare benefits during the first year, state programs to assist long-time residents will not be impaired by a substantial influx of indigent newcomers. . . .

We do not doubt that the one-year waiting period device is well suited to discourage the influx of poor families in need of assistance. An indigent who desires to migrate, resettle, find a new job, start a new life will doubtless hesitate if he knows that he must risk making the move without the possibility of falling back on state welfare assistance during his first year of residence, when his need may be most acute. But the purpose of inhibiting migration by needy persons into the State is constitutionally impermissible.

This Court long ago recognized that the nature of our Federal Union and our constitutional concepts of personal liberty unite to require that all citizens be free to travel throughout the length and breadth of our land uninhibited by statutes, rules, or regulations which unreasonably burden or restrict this movement. . . .

We have no occasion to ascribe the source of this right to travel interstate to a particular constitutional provision.[2] It suffices that, as Mr. Jus-

which meet certain specifications. One appellee applied for Aid to the Permanently and Totally Disabled which is also jointly funded by the States and the Federal Government. [Footnote by the Court.]

2. In Corfield v. Coryell, 6 F.Cas. 546, 552 (No. 3230) (C.C.E.D.Pa.1823), Paul v. Virginia, 8 Wall. 168, 180 (1808), and Ward v. Maryland, 12 Wall. 418, 430 (1870), the right to travel interstate was grounded upon the Privileges and Immunities Clause of Art. IV, § 2. See also Slaughter-House Cases, 16 Wall. 36, 79 (1872); Twining v. New Jersey, 211 U.S. 78, 97 (1908). In Edwards v. California, 314 U.S. 160, 181, 183–185 (Douglas and Jackson, JJ., concurring), and Twining v. New Jersey, supra, reliance was placed on the Privileges and Immunities Clause of the Fourteenth Amendment. See also Crandall v. Nevada, 6 Wall. 35 (1868). In Edwards v. California, supra, and Passenger Cases, 7 How. 283 (1849), a Commerce Clause approach was employed.

See also Kent v. Dulles, 357 U.S. 116, 125 (1958); Aptheker v. Rusk, 378 U. S. 500, 505–506 (1964); Zemel v. Rusk, 381 U.S. 1, 14 (1966), where the freedom of Americans to travel outside the country was grounded upon the due process clause of the Fifth Amendment. [Footnote by the Court.]

tice Stewart said for the Court in United States v. Guest, 383 U.S. 745 (1966) [printed in chap. 11, sec. 3, below]: "The constitutional right to travel from one State to another . . . occupies a position fundamental to the concept of our Federal Union. It is a right that has been firmly established and repeatedly recognized . . . [T]he right finds no explicit mention in the Constitution. The reason, it has been suggested, is that a right so elementary was conceived from the beginning to be a necessary concomitant of the stronger Union the Constitution created. . . ."

Thus, the purpose of deterring the in-migration of indigents cannot serve as justification for the classification created by the one-year waiting period, since that purpose is constitutionally impermissible. . . .

Alternatively, appellants argue that even if it is impermissible for a State to attempt to deter the entry of all indigents, the challenged classification may be justified as a permissible state attempt to discourage those indigents who would enter the State solely to obtain larger benefits. We observe first that none of the statutes before us is tailored to serve that objective. . . . More fundamentally, a State may no more try to fence out those indigents who seek higher welfare benefits than it may try to fence out indigents generally. Implicit in any such distinction is the notion that indigents who enter a State with the hope of securing higher welfare benefits are somehow less deserving than indigents who do not take this consideration into account. But we do not perceive why a mother who is seeking to make a new life for herself and her children should be regarded as less deserving because she considers, among other factors, the level of a State's public assistance. . . .

Appellants argue further that the challenged classification may be sustained as an attempt to distinguish between new and old residents on the basis of the contribution they have made to the community through the payment of taxes. . . . Appellants' reasoning would logically permit the State to bar new residents from schools, parks, and libraries or deprive them of police and fire protection. Indeed it would permit the State to apportion all benefits and services according to the past tax contributions of its citizens. The Equal Protection Clause prohibits such an apportionment of state services.[3]

We recognize that a State has a valid interest in preserving the fiscal integrity of its programs. It may legitimately attempt to limit its expenditures, whether for public assistance, public education, or any other program. But a State may not accomplish such a purpose by invidious distinctions between classes of its citizens. It could not, for example, reduce expenditures for education by barring indigent children from its schools. Similarly, in the cases before us, appellants must do more than show that denying welfare benefits to new residents saves money. The saving of welfare costs cannot justify an otherwise invidious classification. . . .

IV.

Appellants next advance as justification certain administrative and related governmental objectives allegedly served by the waiting-period require-

---

3. We are not dealing here with state insurance programs which may legitimately tie the amount of benefits to the individual's contributions. [Footnote by the Court.]

ment. They argue that the requirement (1) facilitates the planning of the welfare budget; (2) provides an objective test of residency; (3) minimizes the opportunity for recipients fraudulently to receive payments from more than one jurisdiction; and (4) encourages early entry of new residents into the labor force.

At the outset, we reject appellants' argument that a mere showing of a rational relationship between the waiting period and these four admittedly permissible state objectives will suffice to justify the classification. [E. g., McGowan v. Maryland.] The waiting-period provision denies welfare benefits to otherwise eligible applicants solely because they have recently moved into the jurisdiction. But in moving from State to State or to the District of Columbia appellees were exercising a constitutional right, and any classification which serves to penalize the exercise of that right, unless shown to be necessary to promote a *compelling* governmental interest, is unconstitutional. [Cf., e. g., Skinner v. Oklahoma; Korematsu.]

The argument that the waiting-period requirement facilitates budget predictability is wholly unfounded. The records in all three cases are utterly devoid of evidence that either State or the District of Columbia in fact uses the one-year requirement as a means to predict the number of people who will require assistance in the budget year. . . . The argument that the waiting period serves as an administratively efficient rule of thumb for determining residency similarly will not withstand scrutiny. . . . Similarly, there is no need for a State to use the one-year waiting period as a safeguard against fraudulent receipt of benefits; for less drastic means are available, and are employed, to minimize that hazard. . . . A state purpose to encourage employment provides no rational basis for imposing a one-year waiting-period restriction on new residents only.

We conclude therefore that appellants in these cases do not use and have no need to use the one-year requirement for the governmental purposes suggested. Thus, even under traditional equal protection tests a classification of welfare applicants according to whether they have lived in the State for one year would seem irrational and unconstitutional. But, of course, the traditional criteria do not apply in these cases. Since the classification here touches on the fundamental right of interstate movement, its constitutionality must be judged by the stricter standard of whether it promotes a *compelling* state interest. Under this standard, the waiting period requirement clearly violates the Equal Protection Clause.[4]

V.

[The Court also rejected the states' argument "that the constitutional challenge to the waiting-period requirement must fail because Congress expressly approved the imposition of the requirement by the State" as part of the jointly funded benefit programs. The Court found no such approval and added that, "even if we were to assume, arguendo, that Congress did ap-

4. We imply no view of the validity of waiting-period *or* residence requirements determining eligibility to vote, eligibility for tuition-free education, to obtain a license to practice a profession, to hunt or fish, and so forth. Such requirements may promote compelling state interests on the one hand, or, on the other, may not be penalties upon the exercise of the constitutional right of interstate travel. [Footnote by the Court. See the cases which follow.]

prove the imposition of a one-year waiting period," such an approval "would be unconstitutional. Congress may not authorize the States to violate the Equal Protection Clause . . . Congress is without power to enlist state cooperation in a joint federal-state program by legislation which authorizes the States to violate the Equal Protection Clause."] [5]

Affirmed.

Mr. Justice STEWART, concurring.

In joining the opinion of the Court, I add a word in response to the dissent of my Brother Harlan, who I think, has quite misapprehended what the Court's opinion says. The Court today does *not* "pick out particular human activities, characterize them as 'fundamental,' and give them added protection . . . ." To the contrary, the Court simply recognizes, as it must, an established constitutional right, and gives to that right no less protection than the Constitution itself demands. "The constitutional right to travel from one State to another [has] been firmly established and repeatedly recognized." . . .

The Court today, therefore, is not "contriving new constitutional principles." It is deciding these cases under the aegis of established constitutional law.

Mr. Chief Justice WARREN, with whom Mr. Justice BLACK joins, dissenting. . . .

Congress has imposed a residence requirement in the District of Columbia and authorized the States to impose similar requirements. The issue before us must therefore be framed in terms of whether Congress may create minimal residence requirements, not whether the States, acting alone, may do so. See [Prudential Insurance Co. v. Benjamin; In re Rahrer, both in chap. 5, sec. 2, above]. Appellees insist that a congressionally mandated residence requirement would violate their right to travel. The import of their contention is that Congress, even under its "plenary" power to control interstate commerce, is constitutionally prohibited from imposing residence requirements. I reach a contrary conclusion for I am convinced that the extent of the burden on interstate travel when compared with the justification for its imposition requires the Court to uphold this exertion of federal power.

Congress, pursuant to its commerce power, has enacted a variety of restrictions upon interstate travel. [Recall chap. 3.] Although these restrictions operate as a limitation upon free interstate movement of persons, their constitutionality appears well settled. . . .

The Court's right-to-travel cases lend little support to the view that congressional action is invalid merely because it burdens the right to travel.

5. Justice Brennan cited Katzenbach v. Morgan, 384 U.S. 641 (1966), and his controversial footnote in that case. That problem—the power of Congress to determine the substantive content of the equal protection guarantee—is fully considered in chap. 11, sec. 4, below.

In the final section of the Shapiro opinion, the Court found the District of Columbia waiting-period requirement similarly unconstitutional because of the equal protection ingredients of the Fifth Amendment's due process clause.

[Here], travel itself is not prohibited. Any burden inheres solely in the fact that a potential welfare recipient might take into consideration the loss of welfare benefits for a limited period of time if he changes his residence. Not only is this burden of uncertain degree, but appellees themselves assert there is evidence that few welfare recipients have in fact been deterred by residence requirements. . . .

The insubstantiality of the restriction imposed by residence requirements must then be evaluated in light of the possible congressional reasons for such requirements. Our cases require only that Congress have a rational basis for finding that a chosen regulatory scheme is necessary to the furtherance of interstate commerce. Certainly, a congressional finding that residence requirements allowed each State to concentrate its resources upon new and increased programs of rehabilitation ultimately resulting in an enhanced flow of commerce as the economic condition of welfare recipients progressively improved is rational and would justify imposition of residence requirements under the Commerce Clause. . . . Although the Court dismisses [the federal permission] with the remark that Congress cannot authorize the States to violate equal protection, I believe that the dispositive issue is whether under its commerce power Congress can impose residence requirements. . . .

. . . The Court's decision reveals only the top of the iceberg. Lurking beneath are the multitude of situations in which States have imposed residence requirements including eligibility to vote, to engage in certain professions or occupations or to attend a state-supported university. Although the Court takes pains to avoid acknowledging the ramifications of its decision, its implications cannot be ignored. I dissent.

Mr. Justice HARLAN, dissenting. . . .

In upholding the equal protection argument, the Court has applied an equal protection doctrine of relatively recent vintage: the rule that statutory classifications which either are based upon certain "suspect" criteria or affect "fundamental rights" will be held to deny equal protection unless justified by a "compelling" governmental interest. [See also the excerpts from Justice Harlan's opinion printed in the Introductory Overview to this chapter.]

The "compelling interest" doctrine, which today is articulated more explicitly than ever before, constitutes an increasingly significant exception to the long-established rule that a statute does not deny equal protection if it is rationally related to a legitimate governmental objective. The "compelling interest" doctrine has two branches. The branch which requires that classifications based upon "suspect" criteria be supported by a compelling interest apparently had its genesis in cases involving racial classifications . . . .. Today the list [of "suspect" criteria] apparently has been further enlarged to include classifications based upon recent interstate movement, and perhaps those based upon the exercise of *any* constitutional right . . . ..

I think that this branch of the "compelling interest" doctrine is sound when applied to racial classifications [because of the historical purpose of equal protection]. However, I believe that the more recent extensions have been unwise. [I] do not consider wealth a "suspect" statutory criterion.

And when, as in Williams v. Rhodes and the present case, a classification is based upon the exercise of rights guaranteed against state infringement by the Federal Constitution, then there is no need for any resort to the Equal Protection Clause; in such instances, this Court may properly and straightforwardly invalidate any undue burden upon those rights under the Fourteenth Amendment's Due Process Clause.

The second branch of the "compelling interest" principle is even more troublesome. For it has been held that a statutory classification is subject to the "compelling interest" test if the result of the classification may be to affect a "fundamental right," regardless of the basis of the classification. This rule was foreshadowed in [Skinner v. Oklahoma] and reemerged in Reynolds v. Sims. [See also Carrington v. Rash; Harper; Williams v. Rhodes.] [1] It has reappeared today in the Court's cryptic suggestion that the "compelling interest" test is applicable merely because the result of the classification may be to deny the appellees "food, shelter, and other necessities of life," as well as in the Court's statement that "[s]ince the classification here touches on the fundamental right of interstate movement, its constitutionality must be judged by the stricter standard of whether it promotes a *compelling* state interest."

I think this branch of the "compelling interest" doctrine particularly unfortunate and unnecessary. It is unfortunate because it creates an exception which threatens to swallow the standard equal protection rule. Virtually every state statute affects important rights. This Court has repeatedly held, for example, that the traditional equal protection standard is applicable to statutory classifications affecting such fundamental matters as the right to pursue a particular occupation, the right to receive greater or smaller wages or to work more or less hours, and the right to inherit property. Rights such as these are in principle indistinguishable from those involved here, and to extend the "compelling interest" rule to all cases in which such rights are affected would go far toward making this Court a "super-legislature." This branch of the doctrine is also unnecessary. When the right affected is one assured by the federal Constitution, any infringement can be dealt with under the Due Process Clause. But when a statute affects only matters not mentioned in the Federal Constitution and is not arbitrary or irrational, I must reiterate that I know of nothing which entitles this Court to pick out particular human activities, characterize them as "fundamental," and give them added protection under an unusually stringent equal protection test.

. . . If the issue is regarded purely as one of equal protection, then, for the reasons just set forth, this nonracial classification should be

1. Analysis is complicated when the statutory classification is grounded upon the exercise of a "fundamental" right. For then the statute may come within the first branch of the "compelling interest" doctrine because exercise of the right is deemed a "suspect" criterion and also within the second because the statute is considered to affect the right by deterring its exercise. Williams v. Rhodes [sec. 4A above], is such a case insofar as the statutes involved both inhibited exercise of the right of political association and drew distinctions based upon the way the right was exercised. The present case is another instance, insofar as welfare residence statutes both deter interstate movement and distinguish among welfare applicants on the basis of such movement. Consequently, I have not attempted to specify the branch of the doctrine upon which these decisions rest. [Footnote by Justice Harlan.]

judged by ordinary equal protection standards. The applicable criteria are familiar and well-established. . . . For reasons hereafter set forth, a legislature might rationally find that the imposition of a welfare residence requirement would aid in the accomplishment of at least four valid governmental objectives. It might also find that residence requirements have advantages not shared by other methods of achieving the same goals. In light of this undeniable relation of residence requirements to valid legislative aims, it cannot be said that the requirements are "arbitrary" or "lacking in rational justification." Hence, I can find no objection to these residence requirements under the Equal Protection Clause . . . .

The next issue, which I think requires fuller analysis than that deemed necessary by the Court under its equal protection rationale, is whether a one-year welfare residence requirement amounts to an undue burden upon the right of interstate travel. Four considerations are relevant: *First,* what is the constitutional source and nature of the right to travel which is relied upon? *Second,* what is the extent of the interference with that right? *Third,* what governmental interests are served by welfare residence requirements? *Fourth,* how should the balance of the competing considerations be struck?

[I conclude] that the right to travel interstate is a "fundamental" right which, for present purposes, should be regarded as having its source in the Due Process Clause of the Fifth Amendment. . . .

[On "the extent of the interference" with that right, Justice Harlan noted: "The number or proportion of persons who are actually deterred from changing residence by the existence of these provisions is unknown."]

[Turning to the "governmental interests" served by the requirements, Justice Harlan stated:] There appear to be four such interests. First, it is evident that a primary concern [of the legislatures] was to deny welfare benefits to persons who moved into the jurisdiction primarily in order to collect those benefits. This seems to me an entirely legitimate objective. . . .

A second possible purpose of residence requirements is the prevention of fraud. A residence requirement provides an objective and workable means of determining that an applicant intends to remain indefinitely within the jurisdiction. . . . Third, the requirement of a fixed period of residence may help in predicting the budgetary amount which will be needed for public assistance in the future. . . . Fourth, the residence requirements conceivably may have been predicated upon a legislative desire to restrict welfare payments financed in part by state tax funds to persons who have recently made some contribution to the State's economy . . . . This too would appear to be a legitimate purpose.

The next question is the decisive one: whether the governmental interests served by residence requirements outweigh the burden imposed upon the right to travel. In my view, a number of considerations militate in favor of constitutionality. [He noted the four "legitimate governmental interests" above; the "indirect" and "insubstantial" impact on travel; the state-federal cooperation; and the "mature deliberation" on the competing arguments by the legislatures. He added:] Fifth, and of longer-range im-

portance, the field of welfare assistance is one in which there is a widely recognized need for fresh solutions and consequently for experimentation. Invalidation of welfare residence requirements might have the unfortunate consequence of discouraging the Federal and State Governments from establishing unusually generous welfare programs in particular areas on an experimental basis, because of fears that the program would cause an influx of persons seeking higher welfare payments. Sixth and finally, a strong presumption of constitutionality attaches to statutes of the types now before us.

. . .

Taking all of these competing considerations into account, I believe that the balance definitely favors constitutionality. [A]lthough the appellees assert that the same objectives could have been achieved by less restrictive means, this is an area in which the judiciary should be especially slow to fetter the judgment of Congress and of some 46 states legislatures in the choice of methods. Residence requirements have advantages, such as administrative simplicity and relative certainty, which are not shared by the alternative solutions proposed by the appellees. In these circumstances, I cannot find that the burden imposed by residence requirements upon ability to travel outweighs the governmental interests in their continued employment.

. . .

I conclude with the following observations. Today's decision, it seems to me, reflects to an unusual degree the current notion that this Court possesses a peculiar wisdom all its own whose capacity to lead this Nation out of its present troubles is contained only by the limits of judicial ingenuity in contriving new constitutional principles to meet each problem as it arises. For anyone who, like myself, believes that it is an essential function of this Court to maintain the constitutional divisions between state and federal authority and among the three branches of the Federal Government, today's decision is a step in the wrong direction. This resurgence of the expansive view of "equal protection" carries the seeds of more judicial interference with the state and federal legislative process, much more indeed than does the judicial application of "due process" according to traditional concepts, about which some members of this Court have expressed fears as to its potentialities for setting us judges "at large." . . .

SHAPIRO AND RESIDENCE REQUIREMENTS

Introduction. Shapiro v. Thompson was an important step in the Warren eras development of the "fundamental rights and interests" strand of the new equal protection in two respects. First, it launched strict scrutiny of durational residence requirements "penalizing" the "right" of interstate mobility. That strand proved a quite sturdy one, and its evolution is traced in this group of notes. Second, Shapiro hinted at an amorphous, new fundamental interest with potentially far-reaching implications in imposing affirmative governmental obligations to redress economic inequalities—the hint Justice Harlan's dissent referred to as the "cryptic suggestion that the 'compelling interest' test is applicable merely because the result of the classification may be to deny appellees food, shelter, and other necessities of

life." That strand proved far less sturdy: a year after Shapiro, Dandridge v. Williams indicated—and later decisions confirmed—that the Burger Court would not extend the strict scrutiny of the new equal protection to a broad range of "necessities." Further consideration of that aspect of Shapiro is postponed to sec. 5 below.

Consider, then, the impact of Shapiro on durational residence requirements, as examined in the following notes. Shapiro applies the strict scrutiny variety of equal protection to "penalties" on the right of interstate mobility. Note that the Court considers interstate travel a constitutional "right," though it is somewhat unclear about the source of that right. Unlike the "fundamental interests" considered in secs. 4A and 4B, interstate mobility has independent constitutional basis, according to the Court. Why, then, was it necessary or justifiable to resort to an equal protection analysis? Recall Justice Harlan's comment that that extension of the new equal protection was "unnecessary": "When the right affected is one assured by the Federal Constitution, any infringement can be dealt with under the Due Process Clause." Is there any explanation for the Court's resort to equal protection? Any justification? [1] And assuming the equal protection analysis is appropriate, when are restraints on interstate mobility permissible? And what are the criteria for determining whether an asserted state justification is adequately "compelling"?

One case considered earlier throws light on the implications of Shapiro. Recall that in Dunn v. Blumstein, 405 U.S. 330 (1972) (sec. 4A above), the strict scrutiny invalidation of a state one-year residence requirement for voting rested not only on the interference with the "fundamental interest" in participation in the electoral process, but also on the "right" to travel. In Dunn, Justice Marshall noted that the state sought to avoid "the clear command of Shapiro" by claiming "that durational residence requirements for voting neither seek to nor actually do deter such travel." He insisted that that argument reflected "a fundamental misunderstanding": "Shapiro did not rest upon a finding that denial of welfare actually deterred travel." Rather, Shapiro found strict scrutiny triggered by "any classification which serves to *penalize* the exercise" of the right to travel. Justice Marshall explained that, though the Shapiro majority had noted "the frank legislative purpose to deter migration by the poor" and had speculated about the effect on migration, it had "found no need to dispute the 'evidence that few welfare recipients have in fact been deterred [from moving] by residence requirements.'"

Justice Marshall continued: "Indeed, none of the litigants [in Shapiro] had themselves been deterred. Only last Term, it was specifically noted that because a durational residence requirement for voting 'operates to *penalize* those persons, and only those persons, who have exercised their constitutional right of interstate migration . . ., [it] may withstand constitutional scrutiny only upon a clear showing that the burden imposed

---

1. Note also the similar analysis in Police Department of Chicago v. Mosley, 408 U.S. 92 (1972) (chap. 13 below), invalidating an ordinance prohibiting picketing near a school but excepting labor picketing. Justice Marshall's opinion relied on equal protection, though he noted that "the equal protection claim in this case is closely intertwined with First Amendment interests."

is necessary to protect a compelling and substantial governmental interest.' "
[That quotation was from the separate opinion of Justices Brennan, White
and Marshall in Oregon v. Mitchell, 400 U.S. 112 (1970) (chap. 11, sec.
4, below).]

If the suspiciously viewed residence requirements are those that "serve
to *penalize*," and if the notion of "penalty" does not necessarily rest on legislative purpose or effect, how are the occasions for strict scrutiny to be
identified? Justice Marshall elaborated on that theme in the Maricopa case,
which follows. Ironically, in the context of distinguishing permissible from
impermissible residence requirements as to eligibility for state benefits, the
"necessities of life" concept of Shapiro continues to play a role. "Necessities of life" did not become a full-blown new "fundamental interest," as
Justice Harlan in Shapiro had feared, and as others had hoped. Shapiro's
major impact has been confined to the context of residence requirements;
but in the evolution of that impact, requirements barring eligibility for
"necessities" have proved to be particularly vulnerable.

1. *Medical care for indigents: The Maricopa County case.* Justice
Marshall's majority opinion in MEMORIAL HOSPITAL v. MARICOPA
COUNTY, 415 U.S. 250 (1974), reexamined and relied on Shapiro in invalidating an Arizona requirement of a year's residence in a county as a condition to an indigent's receiving nonemergency hospitalization or medical care
at the county's expense. In that reexamination of Shapiro, it emerged that
not all residence requirements were impermissible: Shapiro had cautioned that
some "waiting periods . . . may not be penalties"; in other cases, the
Court had sustained durational residence requirements as a condition to lower
tuition at state universities. (See note 3 below.) The critical ingredient for
triggering strict scrutiny and probable invalidation proved to be the existence
of a "penalty"; and whether there was a "penalty" apparently turned largely
on whether there was an effect on a "necessity of life."

Justice Marshall's reexamination of Shapiro noted that the constitutional
right of interstate travel "was involved in only a limited sense in Shapiro."
Both Shapiro and Dunn v. Blumstein had endorsed "bona fide residence requirements"; yet even those requirements "would burden the right to travel,
if travel meant merely movement." Not mere travel but the right to "migrate
with intent to settle and abide" had been central in Shapiro, according to
Justice Marshall. And though any durational residence requirement "impinges to some extent" on that right, Shapiro had not condemned all of those
requirements. Shapiro required them to be found "penalties" to justify intensive review. And whether a durational residence requirement was a "penalty" giving rise to strict scrutiny depended on the impact of the requirement.
He acknowledged that the "amount of impact required to give rise to the com-
pelling-state-interest test was not made clear" in Shapiro. Shapiro had suggested two criteria: first, "whether the waiting period would deter migration"; second, "the extent to which the residency requirement served to
penalize the exercise of the right to travel." In Justice Marshall's view,
it was the second, not the first, criterion that was central: actual deterrence
need not be shown; the "penalty" characterization was critical. And whether a residence requirement is a "penalty" depends on the nature of the
benefits affected: in Shapiro "the Court found denial of the basic 'neces-

sities of life' to be a penalty"; on the other hand, state college tuition differentials between residents and nonresidents had not been invalidated. Accordingly, Justice Marshall found: "Whatever the ultimate parameters of the Shapiro penalty analysis, it is at least clear that medical care is as much 'a basic necessity of life' to an indigent as welfare assistance. And, governmental privileges or benefits necessary to basic sustenance have often been viewed as being of greater constitutional significance than less essential forms of governmental entitlements." That analysis led Justice Marshall to his ultimate conclusion about the appropriate standard of scrutiny:

"Not unlike the admonition of the Bible that, 'Ye shall have one manner of law, as well for the stranger as for one of your country,' Leviticus, 24:22, the right of interstate travel must be seen as insuring new residents the same right to vital government benefits and privileges in the States to which they migrate as are enjoyed by other residents. The State of Arizona's durational residency requirement for free medical care penalizes indigents for exercising their right to migrate to and settle in that State. Accordingly, the classification created by the residence requirement, 'unless shown to be necessary to promote a *compelling* [state] interest, is unconstitutional.' Shapiro."

Justice Marshall had little difficulty in concluding that the Arizona scheme could not survive the strict scrutiny demanded by that standard. All of the proffered state justifications were found either inadequate or pursued via unnecessarily burdensome means. In the course of that scrutiny, Justice Marshall canvassed state claims regarding fiscal savings, inhibiting the immigration of indigents generally, deterring indigents from moving into the county solely to use the medical facilities, protecting long-time residents who had contributed to the community, and maintaining political support for county medical facilities. The Court also rejected a range of administrative concerns, from preventing fraud and determining bona fide residence to budgetary planning. Accordingly, the defenders of the durational residence requirement had not "met their heavy burden of justification, or demonstrated that the State, in pursuing legitimate objectives, has chosen means which do not unnecessarily impinge on constitutionally protected interests."

Justice Rehnquist was the sole dissenter.[2] Justice Rehnquist criticized the majority's inadequate exploration of the travel rationale and offered his own alternative. He stated: "Since the Court concedes that 'some waiting period[s] . . . may not be penalties,' one would expect to learn from the opinion how to distinguish a waiting period which is a penalty from one which is not. Any expense imposed on citizens crossing state lines but not imposed on those staying put could theoretically be deemed a penalty on travel; the toll exacted from persons crossing from Delaware to New Jersey by the Delaware Memorial Bridge is a 'penalty' on interstate travel in the most literal sense of

---

2. However, other Justices also withheld full support from Justice Marshall's rationale. Chief Justice Burger and Justice Blackmun simply noted their concurrence in the result. And Justice Douglas' concurrence stated that he shared Justice Rehnquist's doubts about "interstate travel per se." He concluded: "The political processes rather than equal protection litigation are the ultimate solution of the present problem. But in the setting of this case the invidious discrimination against the poor [Harper], not the right to travel interstate is in my view the critical issue."

all. But such charges, as well as other fees for use of transportation facilities such as taxes on airport users,[3] have been upheld by this Court against attacks based upon the right to travel. It seems to me that the line to be derived from our prior cases is that some financial impositions on interstate travelers have such indirect or inconsequential impact on travel that they simply do not constitute the type of direct purposeful barrier struck down in [Edwards v. California, the decision invalidating California's anti-Okie law, chap. 5] and Shapiro. Where the impact is that remote, a State can reasonably require that the citizen bear some proportion of the State's cost in its facilities. I would think that this standard is not only supported by this Court's decisions, but would be eminently sensible and workable. But the Court not only rejects this approach, but leaves it entirely without guidance as to the proper standard to be applied."

Justice Rehnquist added: "The solicitude which the Court has shown in cases involving the right to vote, and the virtual denial of entry inherent in denial of welfare benefits, ought not to be so casually extended to the alleged deprivation here. Rather, the Court should examine, as it has done in the past, whether the challenged requirement erects a real and purposeful barrier to movement, or the threat of such a barrier, or whether the effects on travel, viewed realistically, are merely incidental and remote. [T]he barrier here is hardly a counterpart to the barriers condemned in earlier cases. That being so, the Court should observe its traditional respect for the State's allocation of its limited financial resources rather than unjustifiedly imposing its own preferences." Justice Rehnquist also objected to the majority's rejection of the state justifications "virtually out of hand." He concluded that the holding was "a substantial broadening of, and departure from," prior decisions "all the more remarkable for the lack of explanation which accompanies the result. Since I can subscribe neither to the method nor the result, I dissent."

2. *Divorce laws.* A year later, in rejecting another attack on a state residence requirement, Justice Rehnquist wrote for the majority and Justice Marshall was in dissent. In SOSNA v. IOWA, 419 U.S. —— (1975), the Court upheld a requirement that a party reside in the state for one year before bringing a divorce action against a nonresident. In rejecting the attack based on the line of cases from Shapiro to Maricopa, Justice Rehnquist noted that most states had "durational residency requirements for divorce," and that the area of domestic relations "has long been regarded as a virtually exclusive province of the States." None of the earlier cases, he reminded, had "intimated that the States might never impose durational residency requirements." And he found ample justification for the requirement here.

He explained: "What [the earlier] cases had in common was that the durational residency requirements they struck down were justified on the basis of budgetary or record-keeping considerations which were held insufficient to outweigh the constitutional claims of the individuals. But Iowa's divorce residency requirement is of a different stripe. Appellant was

---

3. See Evansville-Vanderburg Airport v. Delta Airlines, 405 U.S. 707 (1972), distinguishing Shapiro v. Thompson in sustaining airport use fees based on the number of enplaning passengers. Justice Brennan explained that the Shapiro standard of review was not applicable because the airport facility "aids rather than hinders the right to travel" and a charge to help defray its costs "is therefore not a burden in the constitutional sense."

not irretrievably foreclosed from obtaining some part of what she sought, as was the case with the welfare recipients in Shapiro, the voters in Dunn, or the indigent patient in Maricopa County. She would eventually qualify for the same sort of adjudication which she demanded virtually upon her arrival in the State. Iowa's requirement delayed her access to the courts, but, by fulfilling it, a plaintiff could ultimately obtain the same opportunity for adjudication which she asserts ought to be hers at an earlier point in time.

"Iowa's residency requirement may reasonably be justified on grounds other than purely budgetary considerations or administrative convenience. A decree of divorce is not a matter in which the only interested parties are the State as a sort of 'grantor,' and a plaintiff such as appellant in the role of 'grantee.' Both spouses are obviously interested in the proceedings, since it will affect their marital status and very likely their property rights. Where a married couple has minor children, a decree of divorce would usually include provisions for their custody and support. With consequences of such moment riding on a divorce decree issued by its courts, Iowa may insist that one seeking to initiate such a proceeding have the modicum of attachment to the State required here.

"Such a requirement additionally furthers the State's parallel interests in both avoiding officious intermeddling in matters in which another State has a paramount interest, and in minimizing the susceptibility of its own divorce decrees to collateral attack. A State such as Iowa may quite reasonably decide that it does not wish to become a divorce mill for unhappy spouses who have lived there as short a time as appellant had when she commenced her action in the state court after having long resided elsewhere." He accordingly concluded "that the state interest in requiring that those who seek a divorce from its courts be genuinely attached to the State, as well as a desire to insulate divorce decrees from the likelihood of collateral attack, requires a different resolution of the constitutional issue presented than was the case in Shapiro, Dunn, and Maricopa County." [4]

Justice Marshall, joined by Justice Brennan, dissented on the merits,[5] insisting that the decision "departs sharply from the course we have followed in analyzing durational residency requirements since Shapiro v. Thompson." He thought the majority's approach suggested "a new distaste for the mode of analysis we have applied to this corner of equal protection law." The majority, he stated, had substituted "an ad hoc balancing test, under which the State's putative interest in ensuring that its divorce plaintiffs establish some roots in Iowa is said to justify the one-year residency requirement." He was especially critical of the majority's failure to make what "should be the first inquiry: whether the right to obtain a divorce is of sufficient importance that its denial to recent immigrants constitutes a penalty on inter-

4. Justice Rehnquist also rejected the claim that the residence requirement "denies a litigant the opportunity to make an individualized showing of bona fide residence and therefore denies such residents access to the only method of legally dissolving their marriage." In part, that claim rested on Vlandis v. Klein, 412 U.S. 441 (1973), considered in sec. 6 below. In part it rested on Boddie v. Connecticut, sec. 4B above. In distinguishing Boddie, Justice Rehnquist noted that the claim here was "not total deprivation, as in Boddie, but only delay."

5. Justice White also dissented, on grounds of mootness. See chap. 15 below.

state travel." He added: "In my view, it clearly meets that standard." And since "the interest in obtaining a divorce is of substantial social importance," he continued, "I would scrutinize Iowa's durational residency requirement to determine whether it constitutes a reasonable means of furthering important interests asserted by the State." The majority, by contrast, had not only declined to apply the "compelling interest" test, but had also "conjured up possible justifications for the State's restriction in a manner much more akin to the lenient standard we have in the past applied in analyzing equal protection challenges to business regulations."

In exercising the strict scrutiny he thought appropriate, Justice Marshall found only one argument on behalf of the state law of "any real force": the claim that "the State has interests both in protecting itself from use as a 'divorce mill' and in protecting its judgments from possible collateral attack in other States." But he found that those interests "would adequately be protected by a simple requirement of domicile—physical presence plus intent to remain—which would remove the rigid one-year barrier while permitting the State to restrict the availability of its divorce process to citizens who are genuinely its own." [6]

3. *Other state benefits.* What is the constitutional status of other state durational residence requirements in light of the preceding cases? All Justices agree that Shapiro and its progeny do not invalidate all residence requirements; yet the cases also indicate that some may be vulnerable to constitutional challenge—if they affect "important interests," under Justice Marshall's approach, or if they lack adequate justification, under Justice Rehnquist's analysis. One of the barriers to nonresidents frequently mentioned as a permissible one is state tuition preference for local students at state universities. In 1971, a summary affirmance suggested the futility of a direct Shapiro-based attack on such preference schemes: the Court sustained Minnesota's one-year durational residence requirement for receipt of in-state tuition benefits. Starns v. Malkerson, 326 F.Supp. 234, aff'd, 401 U.S. 985 (1971). Yet implementation of such a scheme proved vulnerable via another route, in Vlandis v. Kline, 412 U.S. 441 (1973). There, most of the Justices reaffirmed their adherence to Starns, yet found the Connecticut scheme for implementing in-state students' tuition preferences invalid by purporting to resort to procedural due process principles, finding in the scheme a reliance on forbidden "irrebuttable presumptions." The dissenters charged that the majority's position was inconsistent with Starns, that its approach amounted to a resurrection of substantive due process, that its analysis was tantamount to importing the strict scrutiny of the new equal protection into the procedural due process area, and that it in any event amounted to adjudicating what was in substance an equal protection claim by resorting to another label. The majority's "irrebuttable presumptions" approach in Vlandis and a number of other recent cases is more fully examined in sec. 6 below.

6. Justice Marshall thought the argument that the requirement merely meant "delay" rather than "total deprivation" rested on a "specious" distinction. It ignored "the severity of the deprivation suffered by the divorce petitioner who is forced to wait a year for relief." Nor was he impressed by the emphasis on "the magnitude of the interests affected and resolved by a divorce proceeding." Such an amorphous justification and mere recital of the State's traditional control over family law matters was inadequate: "Some tangible interference with the State's regulatory scheme must be shown."

SECTION 5.　DIFFERENTIAL ECONOMIC IMPACTS, POVERTY, AND "NECESSITIES": REFUSALS TO EXTEND THE NEW EQUAL PROTECTION

Introduction. At the end of the Warren era, one could find in Court opinions suggestions that equal protection might serve as a broad-ranging tool to redress economic inequalities, impose affirmative obligations on government, and impel redistribution of wealth. Both strands of the new equal protection appeared to be moving in those directions: there were dicta that "wealth" was a "suspect" classification; there were references to "necessities"—welfare benefits, housing, education—as possible "fundamental interests" triggering strict scrutiny. The Burger Court has stopped the evolution of the new equal protection in those directions. But legislation with special impact on the poor has not become wholly immune from serious judicial review: there are sporadic indications that the "newer equal protection" and other variations on traditional approaches may afford some genuine scrutiny of welfare legislation. This section reviews those developments. Note, in addition to the brief survey in the Introductory Overview to this chapter, the following summary of equal protection trends in this area: [1]

"The Warren Court left a legacy of anticipations as well as accomplishments. Its new equal protection was a dynamic concept, and the radiations encouraged hopes of further steps toward egalitarianism. 'Once loosed, the idea of Equality is not easily cabined,' Archibald Cox noted in the mid-sixties. The commentators' speculations, even more than the Court's results, confirmed the validity of that observation. The fundamental interests ingredient of the new equal protection was particularly open-ended. It was the element which bore the closest resemblance to freewheeling substantive due process, for it circumscribed legislative choices in the name of newly articulated values that lacked clear support in constitutional text and history. The list of interests identified as fundamental by the Warren Court was in fact quite modest: voting, criminal appeals and the right of interstate travel were the prime examples. But in the extraordinary amount of commentary that followed, analysts searching for justifications for those enshrinements were understandably tempted to ponder analogous spheres that might similarly qualify. Welfare benefits, exclusionary zoning, municipal services and school financing came to be the most inviting frontiers. . . .

"Even with regard to suspect classifications, tantalizing statements from the Warren Court beckoned the searchers into the inner circle of strict scrutiny. For example, dicta suggested that wealth classifications were suspect—even though no case had actually invalidated a law solely because of differential impact on the poor, and even though it was difficult to believe that the Court seriously intended to impose broad affirmative equalizing obligations on government. But it was the fundamental interest analysis that es-

---

1. Gunther, "Newer Equal Protection," 86 Harv.L.Rev. 1 (1972). Reprinted with the permission of the publisher,

pecially invited the spinning of analogies to justify strict scrutiny of one area after another.   Some strategists recognized that the open-endedness of fundamental interests might prove a fatal flaw: if the claims extended beyond schools and housing to golf courses and sewers, the sheer magnitude of the enterprise might stifle the Court's egalitarian zeal.   .   .   .

"How has the Burger Court responded to the amalgam of deeds and spurred hopes that constitutes the Warren Court's equal protection legacy? [T]entative conclusions emerge from the opinions: (1) The Burger Court is reluctant to expand the scope of the new equal protection, although its best established ingredients retain vitality.   (2) There is mounting discontent with the rigid two-tier formulations of the Warren Court's equal protection doctrine.   (3) The Court is prepared to use the clause as an interventionist tool without resorting to the strict scrutiny language of the new equal protection.   .   .   .   [In a section entitled "Thus Far and No Further," the survey considers the "blocking [of] the expansion of the new equal protection," noting:] The anticipations spurred by the Warren Court have not fared well. The new Justices are disinclined to add to the list of fundamental interests unearthed by their predecessors.   .   .   .   Those failures to fulfill hopes kindled by the Warren Court's approach are not surprising.   Judicial hesitancy in articulating values not clearly rooted in the Constitution is, after all, the clearest element of the elusive 'strict construction' theme so prominent in the selection of the new appointees.   .   .   ."   [But cf. Roe v. Wade, chap. 9, sec. 3.]

THE REFUSAL TO FIND WEALTH A "SUSPECT" CLASSIFICATION

Do classifications based on wealth sufficiently share the characteristics that have made criteria such as race "suspect"?   Should de jure wealth classifications trigger strict scrutiny?   What constitutes a de jure wealth classification?   Should de facto wealth classifications—governmental action that has a differential impact dependent upon economic condition—trigger strict scrutiny?   Dicta in Warren Court opinions suggested an affirmative answer to these questions, though commentators were skeptical that the Court was prepared to apply that approach across the board.   Burger Court developments make clear that the mere presence of wealth classifications or the mere existence of differential economic impact will not alone evoke extraordinary judicial intervention.

1.   *The Warren Court dicta.*   Recall that in the Harper case in 1966, invalidating poll tax payment requirements as conditions on voting, Justice Douglas stated: "Lines drawn on the basis of wealth or property, like those of race, are traditionally disfavored."   (See the questions about that aspect of Harper in sec. 4A above.)   Three years later, in McDonald v. Board of Election Commissioners, 394 U.S. 802 (1969), Chief Justice Warren stated in dictum that "a careful examination on our part is especially warranted where lines are drawn on the basis of wealth or race, two factors which independently render a classification highly suspect and thereby demand a more

exacting judicial scrutiny." [2]   Yet Harper was also a case which involved the "fundamental interest" in voting. Similarly, the Court's special concern with economic barriers in the Griffin-Douglas line of cases (sec. 4B) came in a context involving a "fundamental interest" in access to the criminal process.

The suspectness of "wealth" classifications, then, was not clearly established by the Warren Court decisions, though there were those who feared or hoped that it was. Recall Justice Harlan's dissent in Douglas v. California, sec. 4B: "The States, of course, are prohibited by the Equal Protection Clause from discriminating between 'rich' and 'poor' *as such* in the formulation and application of their laws. But it is a far different thing to suggest that this provision prevents the State from adopting a law of general applicability that may affect the poor more harshly than it does the rich." If the scheme invalidated in Douglas v. California had truly "classified" in a suspect manner, and if that had been the sole reason for invalidation, payment requirements generally would indeed have come under a constitutional cloud. Was there justification for finding such a far-reaching implication in the equal protection clause? Would it be justifiable to treat all differential economic impacts as suspect in a society which relies so heavily on a system of markets and prices? [3]

2. See also the earlier statement in Justice Jackson's concurrence in Edwards v. California, 314 U.S. 160 (1941), invalidating the California anti-Okie law barring the bringing of nonresident indigents into the state. Justice Jackson remarked that "mere property status, without more," cannot be used to limit the rights of citizens. He added: " 'Indigence' in itself [is] a neutral fact—constitutionally an irrelevance, like race, creed, or color."

3. Note the comment that such a broad principle is "endemically troublesome as a matter of principle," in Michelman, "Foreword: On Protecting the Poor Through the Fourteenth Amendment," 83 Harv.L.Rev. 7 (1969). Michelman elaborated: "The trouble is that, unlike a de facto racial classification which usually must seek its justifications in purposes completely distinct from its race-related impacts, a de facto pecuniary classification typically carries a highly persuasive justification inseparable from the very effect which excites antipathy—i. e., the hard choices it forces upon the financially straitened. For the typical form assumed by such a classification is simply the charging of a price, reasonably approximating cost, for some good or service which the complaining person may freely choose to purchase or not to purchase. A de facto pecuniary classification, that is, is usually nothing more or less than the

making of a market (e. g., in trial transcripts) or the failure to relieve someone of the vicissitudes of market pricing (e. g., for appellate legal services). But the risk of exposure to markets and their 'decisions' is not normally deemed objectionable, to say the least, in our society. Not only do we not inveigh generally against unequal distribution of income or full-cost pricing for most goods. We usually regard it as both the fairest and most efficient arrangement to require each consumer to pay the full market price of what he consumes, limiting his consumption to what his income permits. Exceptions, of course, exist. The point is precisely that such 'commodities' as a vote, an effective defense to criminal prosecution, perhaps education, conceivably some others, *are* exceptional, and that the exceptions depend on the special qualities of the excepted commodities. It is uninformative at best, and very likely misleading as well, to defend such exceptional holdings through formulas of disparagement [invidious or suspect classification; lines . . . drawn on the basis of wealth; discrimination against the indigent] which apply nonselectively to the pricing practice and refer not at all to any exceptional attributes in the excepted commodities." (For elaboration of Michelman's "minimum protection" approach, see the additional note on his analysis, below.)

2. *The Burger Court and wealth classifications.* That wealth classifications alone—even arguably de jure ones—would not be sufficient to trigger strict scrutiny became clear in JAMES v. VALTIERRA, 402 U.S. 137 (1971). There, Justice Black's majority opinion rejected an equal protection challenge to a California constitutional requirement that "[n]o low rent housing project shall hereafter be developed [by] any state public body" without prior approval in a local referendum. The provision defined "low rent housing project" as any development "for persons of low income"— "persons or families who lack the amount of income which is necessary [to] enable them, without financial assistance, to live in decent, safe and sanitary dwellings, without overcrowding." Justice Black's opinion emphasized that the provision did not involve "distinctions based on race," [4] and he noted: "Provisions for referendums demonstrate devotion to democracy, not to bias, discrimination, or prejudice."

Justice Black also rejected the contention that the provision "singled out" advocates of low-income housing by requiring a referendum while many other referendums only take place upon citizen initiative. Justice Black replied that "a law making procedure that 'disadvantages' a particular group does not always deny equal protection." The Court should not undertake analysis of a variety of governmental structures to determine which "is likely to 'disadvantage' any of the diverse and shifting groups that make up the American people." Moreover, low-income housing advocates were not in fact singled out: mandatory referendums were required in a variety of areas —e. g., the issuance of long-term local bonds.

Justice Marshall's dissent, joined by Justices Brennan and Blackmun, insisted that the provision "on its face constitutes invidious discrimination" : it was "an explicit classification on the basis of poverty—a suspect classification which demands exacting judicial scrutiny." He argued that the provision "explicitly" burdened low-income persons: "Publicly assisted housing developments designed to accommodate the aged, veterans, state employees, persons of moderate income, or any class of citizens other than the poor, need not be approved by prior referenda." The majority, he argued, had applied "no scrutiny whatsoever" and had treated the provision "as if it contained a totally benign, technical economic classification." The reach of equal protection went beyond racial discrimination, and "singling out the poor to bear a burden not placed on any other class of citizens tramples the values the Fourteenth Amendment was designed to protect."

That the Court would not exercise strict scrutiny simply because of the presence of wealth classifications or economic differentiations was confirmed in San Antonio Ind. School Dist. v. Rodriguez, 411 U.S. 1 (1973) (below), rejecting a challenge to interdistrict inequalities in school financing. Justice Powell's majority opinion noted "that this Court has never heretofore held that wealth discrimination alone provides an adequate basis for invoking strict scrutiny." And even Justice Marshall's dissent agreed with that observation, though noting that "we have generally gauged the invidiousness of wealth classifications with an awareness of the importance of the interests

---

4. That proved the basis for distinguishing the decision heavily relied on by the lower court in invalidating the California provision: Hunter v. Erickson, 393 U.S. 385 (1969) (sec. 2 above), invalidating an Akron, Ohio, referendum provision.

being affected and the relevance of personal wealth to those interests." [5] It is that "fundamental interests" analysis that has provided the strongest basis for arguments invoking equal protection to redress economic inequalities; and developments pertaining to that theme are the concern of the rest of this section.

REFUSALS TO EXPAND "FUNDAMENTAL INTERESTS" ANALYSIS TO REDRESS ECONOMIC INEQUALITIES

Introduction: The potentials and problems at the end of the Warren era. As noted earlier, the hopes and fears that the "fundamental interests" strand of the new equal protection might serve as a basis for redressing economic inequalities on a wide front were spurred by Shapiro v. Thompson, 394 U.S. 618 (1969) (sec. 4C above). Justice Brennan's majority opinion had noted in dictum that the case involved denial of "welfare aid upon which may depend the ability of the families to obtain the very means to subsist— food, shelter, and other necessities of life." And Justice Harlan's dissent had assured special attention to that dictum by criticizing "the Court's cryptic suggestion [that] the 'compelling interest' test is applicable merely because the result of the classification may be to deny the appellees 'food, shelter, and other necessities of life.' "

Shapiro v. Thompson, as well as the concern with economic barriers in the Harper-Kramer line of voting cases (sec. 4A) and the Griffin-Douglas line of criminal process cases (sec. 4B), prompted wide-ranging speculation and advocacy. What interests might be found to be "fundamental" ? What were the limits, in principle and in institutional capabilities, to judicial expansion of the new equal protection? Much of the commentary supported further expansion. See, e. g., Karst, "Invidious Discrimination: Justice Douglas and the Return of the 'Natural-Law-Due-Process Formula,' " 16 UCLA L.Rev. 716 (1969), suggesting a three-part formulation for identifying whether a classification is an unconstitutional "invidious discrimination" : (1) Does it "discriminate" against a "disadvantaged group" ; (2) does that discrimination relate to an interest that is "basic" or "fundamental" or "critical"; if so, (3) is the state's justification " 'compelling' enough to overcome the presumptive invalidity implied in a phrase like 'strict scrutiny.' " (Compare Justice Marshall's "sliding scale" approach, most fully developed in his dissent in Rodriguez, below.)

But reservations and doubts were also voiced. Note, e. g., the comment in "Developments," 82 Harv.L.Rev. 1065, 1192 (1969): "But the suggestion that government has an affirmative duty to raise everyone to a minimum acceptable standard of living has not yet assumed the dignity of a constitutional proposition. Three major reasons for this lack of development may be suggested. The first is the conceptual difficulty of finding support for the proposition in the Constitution. [T]he guarantee of a minimum standard of living appears to be on a completely different level from the

---

5. The Rodriguez opinions are printed below; excerpts from Justice Marshall's comparison of "wealth" and   traditionally "suspect" classifications have been noted earlier, with the Harper case in sec. 4A.

guarantee of effectively equal access to the criminal process, to the political process, to education, or even to other state activities. The latter find their sources primarily, if not exclusively, in the state. One seeking income, housing, or a job, on the other hand, is remitted primarily to the private sector for satisfaction of his needs. Extending the equal protection clause from a guarantee of equal participation in fundamental state benefits to a guarantee of similar equality in these areas seems improper precisely because the latter are not benefits we customarily think the state is in the habit of distributing at all. Second, the practical problems in reallocating resources according to an infinite variety of needs, and in establishing acceptable minimum norms, would be far greater than those which have already attended judicial efforts to impose precise standards of equality on the states. Finally, state and federal legislatures themselves have taken significant, if as yet small, strides through social security and other welfare measures to provide minimum standards for selected groups of people." [1]

Perhaps the most imaginative analysis of new equal protection frontiers at the end of the Warren era came in Michelman, "Foreword: On Protecting the Poor Through the Fourteenth Amendment," 83 Harv.L.Rev. 7 (1969). As noted earlier, he criticized language suggesting that wealth was a suspect classification on the ground that that was an unacceptable principle in a society generally committed to a market pricing system. But he drew from the fundamental interests analysis a somewhat different approach, arguing that even in a market economy persons were entitled to "minimum protection" against economic deprivations in certain areas. He urged a formulation which avoids treating "the pricing practice rather than nonsatisfaction of a particular want as chiefly constituting the evil to be curbed." He suggested as an appropriate doctrinal statement regarding payment requirements: "It is no justification for deprivation of a fundamental right (i. e., involuntary nonfulfillment of a just want) that the deprivation results from a general practice of requiring persons to pay for what they get." And he added: "Such a construction forces the inquiry on the crucial variable—the nature and quality of the deprivation—and thereby avoids the distractions, false stirring of hopes, and tunneling of vision which results from a rhetorical emphasis on acts of discrimination that consist of nothing more than charging a price." Michelman's "minimum protection" approach would emphasize "severe deprivations" rather than "inequalities." It would identify "instances

1. Note also Cox, "Foreword: Constitutional Adjudication and the Promotion of Human Rights," 80 Harv.L. Rev. 91 (1966), commenting on cases expanding equal protection to "require the state to make changes in the status quo [and] impose affirmative obligations upon the states," noting that "ability to rationalize a constitutional judgment in terms of principles referrable to accepted sources of law is an essential, major element of constitutional adjudication," and suggesting that, as "a staple diet," "political perceptions without roots in objective standards are an inadequate basis for law, and to accept them would give judges unacceptably dangerous powers." See also Sager, "Tight Little Islands: Exclusionary Zoning, Equal Protection, and the Indigent," 21 Stan. L.Rev. 767 (1969): "Any move away from race as such, away from purposeful discrimination, and away from criminal defense and the franchise, stretches thin the fabric of judicial restraint. It would not be surprising if the Court were to assimilate a single area at a time into the new equal protection fold, and were to do so rather cautiously." See, in addition, Winter, "Poverty, Economic Equality, and the Equal Protection Clause," 1972 Sup.Ct.Rev. 51.

in which persons have important needs or interests which they are prevented from satisfying because of traits or predicaments not adopted by free and proximate choice"; it would then seek to determine which of these instances are intolerable ones by asking which risks of deprivation would be consensually deemed unacceptable in a "just society." [2]

Michelman recognized that the notion of "minimum protection is more readily assimilated to the due process than to the equal protection clause." Nevertheless, courts might decide to invoke "the verbiage of inequality and discrimination" in developing a "minimum protection" analysis, because, for example, "detecting a failure to provide the required minimum may nonetheless depend in part upon the detection of inequalities; and elimination or reduction of inequality may be entailed in rectifying such a failure, insofar as the just minimum is understood to be a function (in part) of the existing maximum. [W]idening inequalities become increasingly suggestive of failure to furnish the just minimum." (Do the Burger Court developments traced below leave any room for adoption of Michelman's "minimum protection against economic hazards" approach? Note especially Justice Powell's majority opinion in the Rodriguez case, including its reference to the possibility "that some identifiable quantum of education is a constitutionally protected prerequisite to the meaningful exercise" of other rights.)

1. *Welfare benefits.* a. *Dandridge v. Williams.* The first indication that the Court would not build on the Shapiro v. Thompson suggestion of special scrutiny of classifications affecting "necessities" came a year later, in DANDRIDGE v. WILLIAMS, 397 U.S. 471 (1970). In scrutinizing the classifications in a welfare benefits program, Justice Stewart recognized that welfare assistance "involves the most basic economic needs of impoverished human beings," but nevertheless applied a very deferential standard of review. Dandridge was a challenge to Maryland's AFDC (Aid to Families with Dependent Children) program which imposed a "maximum grant" limit of $250 per month per family, regardless of the family's size or computed standards of needs. That limitation was attacked as discriminating among welfare recipients merely on the basis of the size of the families.[3] The lower court had invalidated the Maryland scheme as "overreaching" because "it cuts too broad a swath on an indiscriminate basis as applied to the entire group of AFDC eligibles." Justice Stewart's majority opinion found that too stringent a standard of review. He elaborated:

"If this were a case involving government action claimed to violate the First Amendment guarantee of free speech, a finding of 'overreaching' would be significant and might be crucial. . . . But the concept of 'overreaching' has no place in this case. For here we deal with state regula-

2. Cf. Rawls, A Theory of Justice (1971). Professor Rawls' earlier writings heavily influenced Michelman's "just wants" analysis. [But see Nozic, Anarchy, State, and Utopia (1975).]

3. Justice Marshall's dissent stated the flaw of the scheme as follows: "[T]he maximum grant regulation produces a basic denial of equitable treatment. Persons who are concededly similarly situated (dependent children and their families), are not afforded [equal] treatment under the maximum grant regulation. Subsistence benefits are paid with respect to some needy dependent children; nothing is paid with respect to others. Some needy families receive full [assistance] as calculated by the State; the assistance paid to other families is grossly below their similarly calculated needs."

tion in the social and economic field, not affecting freedoms guaranteed by the Bill of Rights, and claimed to violate the Fourteenth Amendment only because the regulation results in some disparity in grants of welfare payments to the largest AFDC families. For this Court to approve the invalidation of state economic or social regulation as 'overreaching' would be far too reminiscent of an era when the Court thought the Fourteenth Amendment gave it power to strike down state laws "because they may be unwise, improvident, or out of harmony with a particular school of thought." [Williamson v. Lee Optical Co.]. That era long ago passed into history. [Ferguson v. Skrupa].

"In the area of economics and social welfare, a State does not violate the Equal Protection Clause merely because the classifications made by its laws are imperfect. If the classification has some 'reasonable basis,' it does not offend the Constitution. [Lindsley v. Natural Carbonic Gas Co.; McGowan v. Maryland]. To be sure, [the cases] enunciating this fundamental standard under the Equal Protection Clause have in the main involved state regulation of business or industry. The administration of public welfare assistance, by contrast, involves the most basic economic needs of impoverished human beings. We recognize the dramatically real factual difference between the cited cases and this one, but we can find no basis for applying a different constitutional standard. It is a standard that has consistently been applied to state legislation restricting the availability of employment opportunities. [Goesaert v. Cleary; Kotch]. And it is a standard that is true to the principle that the Fourteenth Amendment gives the federal courts no power to impose upon the States their views of what constitutes wise economic or social policy.

" . . . Conflicting claims of morality and intelligence are raised by opponents and proponents of almost every measure, certainly including the one before us. But the intractable economic, social, and even philosophical problems presented by public welfare assistance programs are not the business of this Court. The Constitution may impose certain procedural safeguards upon systems of welfare administration. But the Constitution does not empower this Court to second-guess state officials charged with the difficult responsibility of allocating limited public welfare funds among the myriad of potential recipients."

And the majority readily found a "reasonable basis" for the challenged regulation "in the State's legitimate interest in encouraging employment and in avoiding discrimination between welfare families and the families of the working poor." Justice Stewart added: "It is true that in some AFDC families there may be no person who is employable. It is also true that with respect to AFDC families whose determined standard of need is below the regulatory maximum, [the] employment incentive is absent. But the Equal Protection Clause does not require that a State must choose between attacking every aspect of a problem or not attacking the problem at all. It is enough that the State's action be rationally based and free from invidious discrimination. The regulation before us meets that test." [4]

4. Justices Harlan and Black (joined by Chief Justice Burger) joined the Court's opinion with separate nota-tions. Justice Douglas dissented, solely on the basis of "the inconsistency of the Maryland maximum grant regu-

Justice Marshall's dissent, joined by Justice Brennan, insisted that the Maryland regulation could not be sustained even under the majority's "reasonableness" test. But he devoted most of his opinion to advocating a stricter standard of review, even while finding the Warren Court's rigid two-tier analysis inappropriate here. Justice Marshall's dissent, then, marked another important step in the evolution of his "sliding scale" approach more fully elaborated in his Rodriguez dissent, below. In Dandridge, he criticized the majority for "focusing upon the abstract dichotomy between two different approaches to equal protection problems that have been utilized by this Court":

"This case simply defies easy characterization in terms of one or the other of these 'tests.' The cases relied on by the Court, in which a 'mere rationality' [rather than 'compelling' interest] test was actually used, are most accurately described as involving the application of equal protection reasoning to the regulation of business interests. . . . This case, involving the literally vital interests of a powerless minority—poor families without bread-winners—is far removed from the area of business regulation, as the Court concedes. Why then is the standard used in those cases imposed here? . . .

"In my view, equal protection analysis of this case is not appreciably advanced by the a priori definition of a 'right,' fundamental or otherwise.[5] Rather, concentration must be placed upon the character of the classification in question, the relative importance to individuals in the class discriminated against of the governmental benefits that they do not receive, and the asserted state interests in support of the classification. . . . [6]

"It is the individual interests here at stake that, as the Court concedes, most clearly distinguish this case from the 'business regulation' equal protection cases. AFDC support to needy dependent children provides the stuff that sustains those children's lives: food, clothing, shelter. And this Court has already recognized several times that when a benefit, even a 'gratuitous'

lation with the Social Security Act." Justice Marshall's opinion, endorsed that statutory argument before moving on to the constitutional discussion noted in the text.

5. See generally Van Alstyne, The Demise of the Right-Privilege Distinction in Constitutional Law, 81 Harv. L.Rev. 1439 (1968). Appellees do argue that their "fundamental rights" are infringed by the maximum grant regulation. They cite, for example, Skinner v. Oklahoma for the proposition that the "right of procreation" is fundamental. This statement is no doubt accurate as far as it goes, but the effect of the maximum grant regulation upon the right of procreation is marginal and indirect at best, totally unlike the compulsory sterilization law that was at issue in Skinner.

At the same time the Court's insistence that equal protection analysis turns on the basis of a closed category of "fundamental rights" involves a curious value judgment. It is certainly difficult to believe that a person whose very survival is at stake would be comforted by the knowledge that his "fundamental" rights are preserved intact. . . . [Footnote by Justice Marshall.]

6. This is essentially what this Court has done in applying equal protection concepts in numerous cases, though the various aspects of the approach appear with a greater or lesser degree of clarity in particular cases. . . . [Footnote by Justice Marshall.]

benefit, is necessary to sustain life, stricter constitutional standards, both procedural [7] and substantive,[8] are applied to the deprivation of that benefit."

Justice Marshall found none of the asserted rationales for the State's scheme persuasive. For example, with respect to the work incentive objective, he thought the regulation both "drastically *overinclusive*" and "grossly *underinclusive*." He concluded: "[I]t cannot suffice merely to invoke the spectre of the past and to recite from [Lindsley] and [Lee Optical] to decide the case. Appellees are not a gas company or an optical dispenser. They are needy dependent children and families who are discriminated against by the State. The basis of that discrimination—the classification of individuals into large and small families—is too arbitrary and too unconnected to the asserted rationale, the impact on those discriminated against—the denial of even a subsistence existence—too great, and the supposed interests served too contrived and attenuated to meet the requirements of the Constitution."

b. *Richardson v. Belcher.* The approach to "necessities"—and the divisions on the Court—manifested in Dandridge have surfaced repeatedly in later cases, culminating with Rodriguez, below. For example, the 4 to 3 decision in RICHARDSON v. BELCHER, 404 U.S. 78 (1971), applied the minimum rationality standards of Dandridge to sustain provisions of the Social Security Act requiring a reduction in disability benefits to reflect workmen's compensation receipts, although persons receiving other kinds of disability compensation (e. g., private insurance benefits or tort damages) do not have their social security payments reduced. In that case, the majority found "a rational basis" for the offset in the judgment that workmen's compensation and social security programs served a common purpose, and that "the workmen's compensation programs should take precedence in the area of overlap." Accordingly, "Congress could rationally conclude [that] a federal program which began to duplicate the efforts of the States might lead to the gradual weakening or atrophy of the state programs," and that it was not for the Court to say whether the congressional purposes "might have been better served by applying the same offset to recipients of private insurance."

A dissent by Justice Marshall, joined by Justice Brennan, to some extent restated his dissenting views in Dandridge v. Williams: He urged special attention to "the individual interests at stake": "Judges should not ignore what everyone knows, namely that legislation regulating business cannot

---

7. See Sniadach v. Family Finance Corp., 395 U.S. 337, 340–342 (1969) (relying on devastating impact of wage garnishment to require prior hearing as a matter of due process); Goldberg v. Kelly, [397 U.S. 179 (1970).] [Footnote by Justice Marshall. See sec. 6 below.]

8. Compare Shapiro v. Thompson, . . noting that the benefits in question are "the very means to subsist—food, shelter, and other necessities of life," with Kirk v. Board of Regents, 78 Cal. Rptr. 260 (1969), appeal dismissed, 396 U.S. 554 (1970), upholding one-year residency requirement for tuition-free graduate education at state universi-

ty, and distinguishing Shapiro on the ground that it "involved the immediate and pressing need for preservation of life and health of persons unable to live without public assistance, and their dependent children."

These cases and those cited in n. [7], supra, suggest that whether or not there is a constitutional "right" to subsistence . . . ., deprivations of benefits necessary for subsistence will receive closer constitutional scrutiny, under both the Due Process and Equal Protection Clauses, than will deprivations of less essential forms of governmental entitlements. [Footnote by Justice Marshall.]

be equated to legislation dealing with destitute, disabled or elderly individuals." But even under the majority's test, he insisted, there "simply is no reasonable basis" to treat workmen's compensation recipients differently from those receiving other kinds of disability compensation. The concern that duplicate benefits might "erode" state programs was neither supported by the legislative history nor "in fact rational." Justice Douglas also dissented.

c. *Jefferson v. Hackney.* The deferential approach of Dandridge was once again invoked in JEFFERSON v. HACKNEY, 406 U.S. 535 (1972), a 5 to 4 decision upholding a scheme whereby Texas granted a lower percentage of "need" to AFDC recipients than to beneficiaries of other categorical assistance programs. Justice Rehnquist's majority opinion, applying the "traditional standard of review," found that "the variation in percentages is rationally related to the purposes of the separate welfare programs." For example, it was "not irrational for the State to believe that the young are more adaptable than the sick and elderly, especially because the latter have less hope of improving their situation in the years remaining to them." [9]

Dandridge and its progeny have not meant, however, that all welfare programs survive scrutiny by the Court. As the cases noted after Rodriguez, below, indicate, applications of traditional equal protection standards "with bite" or resort to unarticulated standards of review, or to alternatives to equal protection, have produced rulings of unconstitutionality in several instances. See, e. g., Dept. of Agriculture v. Moreno, 413 U.S. 528 (1973) (below), and Dept. of Agriculture v. Murry, 413 U.S. 528 (1973) (sec. 6 below), invalidating provisions of the Federal Food Stamp Act.

2. *Housing: Lindsey v. Normet.* An effort to establish a "fundamental interest" in "decent shelter" and "possession of one's home" failed in LINDSEY v. NORMET, 405 U.S. 56 (1972). That 5 to 2 decision sustained provisions of Oregon's Forcible Entry and Wrongful Detainer statute prescribing judicial procedures for eviction of tenants after alleged nonpayment of rent. Justice White's majority opinion rejected the appellants' argument "that a more stringent standard than mere rationality should be applied both to the challenged classification and its stated purpose." One of the rejected contentions was that "the 'need for decent shelter' and the 'right to retain peaceful possession of one's home' are fundamental interests which are particularly important to the poor and which may be trenched upon only after the State demonstrates some superior interest." The Court replied:

"We do not denigrate the importance of decent, safe and sanitary housing. But the Constitution does not provide judicial remedies for every social and economic ill. We are unable to perceive in that document any constitutional guarantee of access to dwellings of a particular quality or any recognition of the right of a tenant to occupy the real property of his land-

---

9. Recall also the excerpt from Justice Rehnquist's opinion in sec. 2 above, rejecting the "naked statistical argument [that] there is a larger percentage of Negroes and Mexican-Americans in AFDC than in other programs." Such an approach would render unacceptably suspect "each difference in treatment among the grant classes, however lacking in racial motivation

and however otherwise rational the treatment might be."
Justices Douglas, Brennan, Marshall and Stewart dissented, largely on statutory grounds. But Justice Marshall's dissent, joined by Justice Brennan, made it clear that he did not "subscribe in any way to the manner in which the Court treats" the equal protection issue.

lord beyond the term of his lease, without the payment of rent . . ..
Absent constitutional mandate, the assurance of adequate housing and the
definition of landlord-tenant relationships is a legislative not a judicial function. Nor should we forget that the Constitution expressly protects against
confiscation of private property or the income therefrom."

Applying deferential standards of review, the majority found no constitutional flaw in the fact that eviction actions "differ substantially from
other litigation, where the time between complaint and trial is substantially
longer, and where a broader range of issues may be considered." Here, there
were "unique factual and legal characteristics of the landlord-tenant relationship that justify special statutory treatment inapplicable to other litigants."
Accordingly, such features as limiting the issue at trial to that of the tenant's
default and barring such defenses as the landlord's failure to maintain the
premises were found rational.[10]

SAN ANTONIO IND. SCHOOL DIST. v. RODRIGUEZ

411 U.S. 1, 93 S.Ct. 1278, 36 L.Ed.2d 16 (1973).

Appeal from the United States District Court for the Western District
of Texas.

[This was an attack on the Texas system of financing public education,
with its heavy reliance on local property taxes. The targets of the attack were
the substantial interdistrict disparities in per-pupil expenditures resulting
primarily from differences in taxable property values among the districts.
The appellees who brought the class action were Mexican-American parents
of children attending schools in the Edgewood Independent School District
in San Antonio, suing on behalf of children of poor families residing in districts having a low property tax base.

[Though there is some federal aid, Texas public schools, like those in
most states, are financed through a combination of state and local funds.
And though a statewide Minimum Foundation School Program serves to
reduced disparities among district tax bases, district spending varies considerably on the basis of local property wealth. For example, as the Court's

---

10. One feature of the Oregon system
was invalidated, however: a requirement that a tenant desiring to appeal
a decision post a bond of twice the
rent that would accrue pending decision, with the bond to be forfeited if
a tenant lost the appeal. Relying on
the Griffin v. Illinois strain of equal
protection doctrine, Justice White
found that special burden on appeals
unconstitutional and unjustified by
any desire to eliminate frivolous appeals. The only disagreement on the
merits in Lindsey came in a partial
dissent from Justice Douglas, resting
on due process grounds. He stated
that "where the right is so fundamental as the tenant's claim to his
home, the requirements of due process

should be more embracing" than in the
ordinary case.

Justice Douglas wrote for the majority, however, when the Court rejected an effort to apply stricter equal
protection scrutiny to a village zoning
ordinance restricting land use to one-
family dwellings, with the definition
of "family" limited to the traditional,
related, family and to groups of not
more than two unrelated persons. Justice Marshall's dissent insisted that
strict scrutiny was required because
the classification burdened "fundamental rights of association and privacy."
Village of Belle Terre v. Boraas, 416
U.S. 1 (1974) (considered further below, after the Rodriguez case).

opinion pointed out, a spending comparison between appellees' Edgewood district and the Alamo Heights district—the "most affluent district in the San Antonio area"—indicated "the extent to which substantial disparities exist despite the State's impressive progress in recent years." During the 1967–68 school year, Edgewood had an average assessed property value per pupil of $5960. By taxing itself at about 1%—the highest rate in the metropolitan area—the district raised $26 for the education of each child, after paying its share to the statewide Foundation Program. State and federal support brought Edgewood per pupil expenditures to $356. By contrast, the Alamo Heights district had a property tax base of more than $49,000 per pupil. By taxing itself at only .85%, it raised $333 per pupil over and above its contribution to the Foundation Program. State and federal support brought Alamo Heights spending to $594 per pupil.]

Mr. Justice POWELL delivered the opinion of the Court. . . .

I . . .

. . . We must decide, first, whether the Texas system of financing public education operates to the disadvantage of some suspect class or impinges upon a fundamental right explicitly or implicitly protected by the Constitution, thereby requiring strict judicial scrutiny. If so, the judgment of the District Court should be affirmed. If not, the Texas scheme must still be examined to determine whether it rationally furthers some legitimate, articulated state purpose and therefore does not constitute an invidious discrimination in violation of the Equal Protection Clause of the Fourteenth Amendment.

II

The District Court's opinion does not reflect the novelty and complexity of the constitutional questions posed by appellees' challenge to Texas' system of school financing. In concluding that strict judicial scrutiny was required, that court relied on decisions dealing with the rights of indigents to equal treatment in the criminal trial and appellate processes, and on cases disapproving wealth restrictions on the right to vote. Those cases, the District Court concluded, established wealth as a suspect classification. Finding that the local property tax system discriminated on the basis of wealth, it regarded those precedents as controlling. It then reasoned, based on decisions of this Court, affirming the undeniable importance of education, that there is a fundamental right to education and that, absent some compelling state justification, the Texas system could not stand.

We are unable to agree that this case, which in significant aspects is sui generis, may be so neatly fitted into the conventional mosaic of constitutional analysis under the Equal Protection Clause. Indeed, for the several reasons that follow, we find neither the suspect-classification nor the fundamental-interest analysis persuasive.

A

The wealth discrimination discovered by the District Court in this case, and by several other courts that have recently struck down school financing

laws in other States,[1] is quite unlike any of the forms of wealth discrimination heretofore reviewed by this Court. Rather than focusing on the unique features of the alleged discrimination, the courts in these cases have virtually assumed their findings of a suspect classification through a simplistic process of analysis: since, under the traditional systems of financing public schools, some poorer people receive less expensive educations than other more affluent people, these systems discriminate on the basis of wealth. This approach largely ignores the hard threshold questions, including whether it makes a difference for purposes of consideration under the Constitution that the class of disadvantaged "poor" cannot be identified or defined in customary equal protection terms, and whether the relative—rather than absolute—nature of the asserted deprivation is of significant consequence. Before a State's laws and the justifications for the classifications they create are subjected to strict judicial scrutiny, we think these threshold considerations must be analyzed more closely than they were in the court below.

[There are] at least three ways in which the discrimination claimed here might be described. The Texas system of school finance might be regarded as discriminating (1) against "poor" persons whose incomes fall below some identifiable level of poverty or who might be characterized as functionally "indigent," or (2) against those who are relatively poorer than others, or (3) against all those who, irrespective of their personal incomes, happen to reside in relatively poorer school districts. Our task must be to ascertain whether, in fact, the Texas system has been shown to discriminate on any of these possible bases and, if so, whether the resulting classification may be regarded as suspect.

The precedents of this Court provide the proper starting point. The individuals or groups of individuals who constituted the class discriminated against in our prior cases shared two distinguishing characteristics: because of their impecunity they were completely unable to pay for some desired benefit, and as a consequence, they sustained an absolute deprivation of a meaningful opportunity to enjoy that benefit. * . . .

Only appellees' first possible basis for describing the class disadvantaged by the Texas school finance system—discrimination against a class of definably "poor" persons—might arguably meet the criteria established in these prior cases. Even a cursory examination, however, demonstrates that neither of the two distinguishing characteristics of wealth classifications can be found here. First, in support of their charge that the system discriminates against the "poor," appellees have made no effort to demonstrate that it operates to the peculiar disadvantage of any class fairly definable as indigent, or as composed of persons whose incomes are beneath any designated poverty level. Indeed, there is reason to believe that the poorest families are not necessarily clustered in the poorest property districts. [A recent] Connecticut study found, not surprisingly, that the poor were clustered around commercial and industrial

---

1. Serrano v. Priest, 96 Cal.Rptr. 601, 487 P.2d 1241, 5 Cal.3d 584 (1971); Van Dusartz v. Hatfield, 334 F.Supp. 870 (Minn.1971); Robinson v. Cahill, 118 N.J.Super. 223, 287 A.2d 187 (1972); Milliken v. Green, 203 N.W.2d 457 (Mich.1972), rehearing granted,

Jan. 1973. [Footnote by Justice Powell.]

* At this point, Justice Powell discussed Griffin v. Illinois, Douglas v. California, Williams v. Illinois, Tate v. Short and Bullock v. Carter, all in sec. 4 above.

areas—those same areas that provide the most attractive sources of property tax income for school districts. [T]here is no basis on the record in this case for assuming that the poorest people—defined by reference to any level of absolute impecunity—are concentrated in the poorest districts.

Second, neither appellees nor the District Court addressed the fact that, unlike each of the foregoing cases, lack of personal resources has not occasioned an absolute deprivation of the desired benefit. The argument here is not that the children in districts having relatively low assessable property values are receiving no public education; rather, it is that they are receiving a poorer quality education than that available to children in districts having more assessable wealth. Apart from the unsettled and disputed question whether the quality of education may be determined by the amount of money expended for it,[2] a sufficient answer to appellees' argument is that, at least where wealth is involved, the Equal Protection Clause does not require absolute equality or precisely equal advantages. Nor, indeed, in view of the infinite variables affecting the educational process, can any system assure equal quality of education except in the most relative sense. . . .

For these two reasons—the absence of any evidence that the financing system discriminates against any definable category of "poor" people or that it results in the absolute deprivation of education—the disadvantaged class is not susceptible of identification in traditional terms.[3]

As suggested above, appellees and the District Court may have embraced a second or third approach, the second of which might be characterized as a theory of relative or comparative discrimination based on family income. Appellees sought to prove that a direct correlation exists between the wealth of families within each district and the expenditures therein for education. That is, along a continuum, the poorer the family the lower the dollar amount of education received by the family's children.

[If the facts supported this theory, it] would still face serious unanswered questions, including whether a bare positive correlation or some higher degree of correlation is necessary to provide a basis for concluding that the financing system is designed to operate to the peculiar disadvantage of the comparatively poor, and whether a class of this size and diversity

2. Each of appellees' possible theories of wealth discrimination is founded on the assumption that the quality of education varies directly with the amount of funds expended on it and that, therefore, the difference in quality between two schools can be determined simplistically by looking at the difference in per-pupil expenditures. This is a matter of considerable dispute among educators and commentators. [Footnote by Justice Powell.]

3. An educational financing system might be hypothesized, however, in which the analogy to the wealth discrimination cases would be considerably closer. If elementary and secondary education were made available by the State only to those able to pay a tuition assessed against each pupil, there would be a clearly defined class of "poor" people—definable in terms of their inability to pay the prescribed sum—who would be absolutely precluded from receiving an education. That case would present a far more compelling set of circumstances for judicial assistance than the case before us today. After all, Texas has undertaken to do a good deal more than provide an education to those who can afford it. It has provided what it considers to be an adequate base education for all children and has attempted, though imperfectly, to ameliorate by state funding and by the local assessment program the disparities in local tax resources. [Footnote by Justice Powell.]

could ever claim the special protection accorded "suspect" classes. These questions need not be addressed in this case, however, since appellees' proof fails to support their allegations or the District Court's conclusions. . . .

This brings us, then, to the third way in which the classification scheme might be defined—*district* wealth discrimination. Since the only correlation indicated by the evidence is between district property wealth and expenditures, it may be argued that discrimination might be found without regard to the individual income characteristics of district residents. Assuming a perfect correlation between district property wealth and expenditures from top to bottom, the disadvantaged class might be viewed as encompassing every child in every district except the district that has the most assessable wealth and spends the most on education. Alternatively, [the] class might be defined more restrictively to include children in districts with assessable property which falls below the statewide average, or median, or below some other artificially defined level.

However described, it is clear that appellees' suit asks this Court to extend its most exacting scrutiny to review a system that allegedly discriminates against a large, diverse, and amorphous class, unified only by the common factor of residence in districts that happen to have less taxable wealth than other districts. The system of alleged discrimination and the class it defines have none of the traditional indicia of suspectness: the class is not saddled with such disabilities, or subjected to such a history of purposeful unequal treatment, or relegated to such a position of political powerlessness as to command extraordinary protection from the majoritarian political process.

We thus conclude that the Texas system does not operate to the peculiar disadvantage of any suspect class. But in recognition of the fact that this Court has never heretofore held that wealth discrimination alone provides an adequate basis for invoking strict scrutiny, appellees have not relied solely on this contention. They also assert that the State's system impermissibly interferes with the exercise of a "fundamental" right and that accordingly the prior decisions of this Court require the application of the strict standard of judicial review. . . . It is this question—whether education is a fundamental right, in the sense that it is among the rights and liberties protected by the Constitution—which has so consumed the attention of courts and commentators in recent years.

B

In [Brown v. Board of Education] a unanimous Court recognized that "education is perhaps the most important function of state and local governments." . . . Nothing this Court holds today in any way detracts from our historic dedication to public education. . . . But the importance of a service performed by the State does not determine whether it must be regarded as fundamental for purposes of examination under the Equal Protection Clause. [After discussing Shapiro v. Thompson, Lindsey v. Normet, and Dandridge v. Williams—and noting Jefferson v. Hackney and Richardson v. Belcher—,† Justice Powell continued:]

† In the course of his review of the cases, Justice Powell recalled Justice   Harlan's dissent in Shapiro v. Thompson: "[I]f the degree of judicial scru-

The lesson of these cases in addressing the question now before the Court is plain. It is not the province of this Court to create substantive constitutional rights in the name of guaranteeing equal protection of the laws. Thus the key to discovering whether education is "fundamental" is not to be found in comparisons of the relative societal significance of education as opposed to subsistence or housing. Nor is it to be found by weighing whether education is as important as the right to travel. Rather, the answer lies in assessing whether there is a right to education explicitly or implicitly guaranteed by the Constitution. [Eisenstadt v. Baird; Dunn v. Blumstein; [4] Chicago Police Dept. v. Mosley; [5] Skinner v. Oklahoma.[6]]

Education, of course, is not among the rights afforded explicit protection under our Federal Constitution. Nor do we find any basis for saying it is implicitly so protected. As we have said, the undisputed importance of education will not alone cause this Court to depart from the usual standard for reviewing a State's social and economic legislation. It is appellees' contention, however, that education is distinguishable from other services and benefits provided by the State because it bears a peculiarly close relationship to other rights and liberties accorded protection under the Constitution. Specifically, they insist that education is itself a fundamental personal right because it is essential to the effective exercise of First Amendment freedoms and to intelligent utilization of the right to vote. In asserting a nexus between speech and education, appellees urge that the right to speak is meaningless unless the speaker is capable of articulating his thoughts intelligently and persuasively. The "marketplace of ideas" is an empty forum for those lacking basic communicative tools. Likewise, they argue that the corollary right to receive information becomes little more than a hollow privilege when the recipient has not been taught to read, assimilate, and utilize available knowledge. A similar line of reasoning is pursued with respect to the right

tiny of state legislation fluctuated depending on a majority's view of the importance of the interest affected, we would have gone 'far toward making this Court a "super-legislature." ' " Justice Powell added: "We would, indeed, then be assuming a legislative role and one for which the Court lacks both authority and competence."

4. Dunn fully canvasses this Court's voting rights cases and explains that "this Court has made clear that a citizen has a *constitutionally protected right* to participate in elections on an equal basis with other citizens in the jurisdiction." [Emphasis supplied.] The constitutional underpinnings of the right to equal treatment in the voting process can no longer be doubted even though, as the Court noted in [Harper], "the right to vote in state elections is nowhere expressly mentioned." . . . [Footnote by Justice Powell.]

5. In Mosley, the Court struck down a Chicago antipicketing ordinance that exempted labor picketing from its prohibitions. The ordinance was held invalid under the Equal Protection Clause after subjecting it to careful scrutiny and finding that the ordinance was not narrowly drawn. The stricter standard of review was appropriately applied since the ordinance was one "affecting First Amendment interests." [Footnote by Justice Powell.]

6. Skinner applied the standard of close scrutiny to a state law permitting forced sterilization of "habitual criminals." Implicit in the Court's opinion is the recognition that the right of procreation is among the rights of personal privacy protected under the Constitution. See [Roe v. Wade]. [Footnote by Justice Powell.]

to vote.[7] Exercise of the franchise, it is contended, cannot be divorced from the educational foundation of the voter. . . .

We need not dispute any of these propositions. The Court has long afforded zealous protection against unjustifiable governmental interference with the individual's rights to speak and to vote. Yet we have never presumed to possess either the ability or the authority to guarantee to the citizenry the most *effective* speech or the most *informed* electoral choice. That these may be desirable goals of a system of freedom of expression and of a representative form of government is not to be doubted. . . . But they are not values to be implemented by judicial intrusion into otherwise legitimate state activities.

Even if it were conceded that some identifiable quantum of education is a constitutionally protected prerequisite to the meaningful exercise of either right, we have no indication that the present level of educational expenditure in Texas provide an education that falls short. Whatever merits appellees' argument might have if a State's financing system occasioned an absolute denial of education opportunities to any of its children, that argument provides no basis for finding an interference with fundamental rights where only relative differences in spending levels are involved and where—as is true in the present case—no charge fairly could be made that the system fails to provide each child with an opportunity to acquire the basic minimal skills necessary for the enjoyment of the rights of speech and of full participation in the political process.

Furthermore, the logical limitations on appellees' nexus theory are difficult to perceive. How, for instance, is education to be distinguished from the significant personal interests in the basics of decent food and shelter? Empirical examination might well buttress an assumption that the ill-fed, ill-clothed, and ill-housed are among the most ineffective participants in the political process and that they derive the least enjoyment from the benefits of the First Amendment. If so appellees' thesis would cast serious doubt on the authority of Dandridge v. Williams and Lindsey v. Normet.

. . . In one further respect we find this a particularly inappropriate case in which to subject state action to strict judicial scrutiny. . . . Each of our prior [strict scrutiny-"protected rights"] cases involved legislation which "deprived," "infringed," or "interfered" with the free exercise of some such fundamental personal right or liberty. [See Skinner; Shapiro; Dunn.] A critical distinction between those cases and the one now before us lies in what Texas is endeavoring to do with respect to education. . . . The Texas system of school finance is not unlike the federal legislation involved in [Katzenbach v. Morgan, chap. 11, sec. 4, below]. Every step leading to the establishment of the system Texas utilizes today—including the decisions permitting localities to tax and expend locally, and creating and continuously expanding state aid—was implemented in an effort to *extend*

---

7. Since the right to vote, per se, is not a constitutionally protected right, we assume that appellees' references to that right are simply shorthand references to the protected right, implicit in our constitutional system, to participate in state elections on an equal basis with other qualified voters whenever the State has adopted an elective process for determining who will represent any segment of the State's population. See n. [4] supra. [Footnote by Justice Powell.]

public education and to improve its quality. Of course, every reform that benefits some more than others may be criticized for what it fails to accomplish. But we think it plain that, in substance, the thrust of the Texas system is affirmative and reformatory and, therefore, should be scrutinized under judicial principles sensitive to the nature of the State's efforts and to the rights reserved to the States under the Constitution.

C . . .

We need not rest our decision, however, solely on the inappropriateness of the strict scrutiny test. A century of Supreme Court adjudication under the Equal Protection Clause affirmatively supports the application of the traditional standard of review, which requires only that the State's system be shown to bear some rational relationship to legitimate state purposes. . . . We have here nothing less than a direct attack on the way in which Texas has chosen to raise and disburse state and local tax revenues. [A]ppellees would have the Court intrude in an area in which it has traditionally deferred to state legislatures. This Court has often admonished against such interferences with the State's fiscal policies under the Equal Protection Clause. . . .

Thus we stand on familiar ground when we continue to acknowledge that the Justices of this Court lack both the expertise and the familiarity with local problems so necessary to the making of wise decisions with respect to the raising and disposition of public revenues. . . . In such a complex arena in which no perfect alternatives exist, the Court does well not to impose too rigorous a standard of scrutiny lest all local fiscal schemes become subjects of criticism under the Equal Protection Clause.[8] In addition to matters of fiscal policy, this case also involves the most persistent and difficult questions of educational policy, another area in which this Court's lack of specialized knowledge and experience counsels against premature interference with the informed judgments made at the state and local levels. . . .

The foregoing considerations buttress our conclusion that Texas' system of public school finance is an inappropriate candidate for strict judicial scrutiny. These same considerations are relevant to the determination whether that system, with its conceded imperfections, nevertheless bears some rational relationship to a legitimate state purpose. It is to this question that we next turn our attention.

---

8. Those who urge that the present system be invalidated offer little guidance as to what type of school financing should replace it. The most likely result of rejection of the existing system would be statewide financing of all public education with funds derived from taxation of property or from the adoption or expansion of sales and income taxes. . . . The authors of Private Wealth and Public Education, [Coons, Clune and Sugarman], suggest an alternative scheme, known as "district power equalizing." In simplest terms, the State would guarantee that at any particular rate of property taxation the district would receive a stated number of dollars regardless of the district's tax base. To finance the subsidies to "poorer" districts, funds would be taken away from the "wealthier" districts that, because of their higher property values, collect more than the stated amount at any given rate. This is not the place to weigh the arguments for and against "district power equalizing," beyond noting that commentators are in disagreement as to whether it is feasible, how it would work, and indeed whether it would violate the equal protection theory underlying appellees' case. . . . [Footnote by Justice Powell.]

III . . .

.   .   .   The District Court found that the State had failed even "to establish a reasonable basis" for a system that results in different levels of per pupil expenditure. We disagree. . . .

The Texas system of school finance, [w]hile assuring a basic education for every child in the State, [permits] and encourages a large measure of participation in and control of each district's schools at the local level. In an era that has witnessed a consistent trend toward centralization of the functions of government, local sharing of responsibility for public education has survived. . . . In part, local control means [the] freedom to devote more money to the education of one's children. Equally important, however, is the opportunity it offers for participation in the decisionmaking process that determines how those local tax dollars will be spent. Each locality is free to tailor local programs to local needs. Pluralism also affords some opportunity for experimentation, innovation, and a healthy competition for educational excellence. . . .

Appellees do not question the propriety of Texas' dedication to local control of education. To the contrary, they attack the school finance system precisely because, in their view, it does not provide the same level of local control and fiscal flexibility in all districts. Appellees suggest that local control could be preserved and promoted under other financing systems that resulted in more equality in educational expenditures. While it is no doubt true that reliance on local property taxation for school revenues provides less freedom of choice with respect to expenditures for some districts than for others,[9] the existence of "some inequality" in the manner in which the State's rationale is achieved is not alone a sufficient basis for striking down the entire system. . . . Nor must the financing system fail because, as appellees suggest, other methods of satisfying the State's interest, which occasion "less drastic" disparities in expenditures, might be conceived. Only where state action impinges on the exercise of fundamental constitutional rights or liberties must it be found to have chosen the least restrictive alternative. . . . It is also well to remember that even those districts that have reduced ability to make free decisions with respect to how much they spend on education still retain under the present system a large measure of authority as to how available funds will be allocated. They further enjoy the power to make numerous other decisions with respect to the operation of the schools.[10]   The people of Texas may be justified in believing that other

9. Mr. Justice White suggests in his dissent that the Texas system violates the Equal Protection Clause because the means it has selected to effectuate its interest in local autonomy fail to guarantee complete freedom of choice to every district. He places special emphasis on the statutory provision that establishes a maximum rate of $1.50 per $100 valuation at which a local school district may tax for school maintenance. The maintenance rate in Edgewood when this case was litigated in the District Court was $.55 per $100, barely one-third of the allowable rate. . . .

Appellees do not claim that the ceiling presently bars desired tax increases in Edgewood or in any other Texas district. Therefore, the constitutionality of that statutory provision is not before us and must await litigation in a case in which it is properly presented. . . . [Footnote by Justice Powell.]

10. Mr. Justice Marshall states in his dissenting opinion that the State's asserted interest in local control is a "mere sham," and that it has been offered not as a legitimate justification but "as an excuse . . . for

systems of school financing, which place more of the financial responsibility in the hands of the State, will result in a comparable lessening of desired local autonomy. That is, they may believe that along with increased control of the purse strings at the State level will go increased control over local policies.

Appellees further urge that the Texas system is unconstitutionally arbitrary because it allows the availability of local taxable resources to turn on "happenstance." They see no justification for a system that allows, as they contend, the quality of education to fluctuate on the basis of the fortuitous positioning of the boundary lines of political subdivisions and the location of valuable commercial and industrial property. But any scheme of local taxation—indeed the very existence of identifiable local governmental units—requires the establishment of jurisdictional boundaries that are inevitably arbitrary. It is equally inevitable that some localities are going to be blessed with more taxable assets than others. Nor is local wealth a static quantity. . . .

Moreover, if local taxation for local expenditure is an unconstitutional method of providing for education then it may be an equally impermissible means of providing other necessary services customarily financed largely from local property taxes, including local police and fire protection, public health and hospitals, and public utility facilities of various kinds. We perceive no justification for such a severe denigration of local property taxation and control as would follow from appellees' contentions. . . .

In sum, to the extent that the Texas system of school finance results in unequal expenditures between children who happen to reside in different districts, we cannot say that such disparities are the product of a system that is so irrational as to be invidiously discriminatory. . . . The constitutional standard under the Equal Protection Clause is whether the challenged state action rationally furthers a legitimate state purpose or interest. . . . We hold that the Texas plan abundantly satisfies this standard.

IV

In light of the considerable attention that has focused on the District Court opinion in this case and on its California predecessor [Serrano v. Priest], a cautionary postscript seems appropriate. [Affirmance here] would occasion in Texas and elsewhere an unprecedented upheaval in public education. Some commentators have concluded that, whatever the contours of the alternative financing programs that might be devised and approved, the result could not avoid being a beneficial one. But [those] who have devoted the most thoughtful attention to the practical ramifications of these cases have found no clear or dependable answers and their scholarship reflects no such

interdistrict inequality." [T]he dissent suggests that Texas' lack of good faith may be demonstrated by examining the extent to which the State already maintains considerable control. [T]he assertion, that genuine local control does not exist in Texas, simply cannot be supported. It is abundantly refuted by the elaborate statutory division of responsibilities set out in the Texas Education Code. Although policy decision-making and supervision in certain areas are reserved to the State, the day-to-day authority over the "management and control" of all public elementary and secondary schools is squarely placed on the local school boards. . . . [Footnote by Justice Powell.]

unqualified confidence in the desirability of completely uprooting the existing system.

The complexity of these problems is demonstrated by the lack of consensus with respect to whether it may be said with any assurance that the poor, the racial minorities, or the children in overburdened core-city school districts would be benefitted by abrogation of traditional modes of financing education. Unless there is to be a substantial increase in state expenditures on education across the board—an event the likelihood of which is open to considerable question—these groups stand to realize gains in terms of increased per pupil expenditures only if they reside in districts that presently spend at relatively low levels, i. e., in those districts that would benefit from the redistribution of existing resources. Yet recent studies have indicated that the poorest families are not invariably clustered in the most impecunious school districts. Nor does it now appear that there is any more than a random chance that racial minorities are concentrated in property-poor districts. Additionally, several research projects have concluded that any financing alternative designed to achieve a greater equality of expenditures is likely to lead to higher taxation and lower educational expenditures in the major urban centers, a result that would exacerbate rather than ameliorate existing conditions in those areas.

These practical considerations, of course, play no role in the adjudication of the constitutional issues presented here. But they serve to highlight the wisdom of the traditional limitations on this Court's function. . . . We hardly need add that this Court's action today is not to be viewed as placing its judicial imprimatur on the status quo. The need is apparent for reform in tax systems which may well have relied too long and too heavily on the local property tax. And certainly innovative new thinking as to public education, its methods and its funding, is necessary to assure both a higher level of quality and greater uniformity of opportunity. . . . But the ultimate solutions must come from the lawmakers and from the democratic pressures of those who elect them.

Reversed.

Mr. Justice STEWART, concurring.

. . . I join the opinion and judgment of the Court because I am convinced that any other course would mark an extraordinary departure from principled adjudication under the Equal Protection Clause of the Fourteenth Amendment. The uncharted directions of such a departure are suggested, I think, by the imaginative dissenting opinion my Brother Marshall has filed today.

Unlike other provisions of the Constitution, the Equal Protection Clause confers no substantive rights and creates no substantive liberties.[1] The func-

---

1. There is one notable exception to the above statement: It has been established in recent years that the Equal Protection Clause confers the substantive right to participate on an equal basis with other qualified voters whenever the State has adopted an electoral process for determining who will represent any segment of the State's population. See, e. g., Reynolds v. Sims, 377 U.S. 533 . . . . But there is no constitutional right to vote, as such. . . . [Footnote by Justice Stewart.]

tion of the Equal Protection Clause, rather, is simply to measure the validity of *classifications* created by state laws. . . .

[Q]uite apart from the Equal Protection Clause, a state law that impinges upon a substantive right or liberty created or conferred by the Constitution is, of course, presumptively invalid, whether or not the law's purpose or effect is to create any classifications. . . . Numerous cases in this Court illustrate this principle.[2] In refusing to invalidate the Texas system of financing its public schools, the Court today applies with thoughtfulness and understanding the basic principles [of equal protection].[*]

Mr. Justice WHITE, with whom Mr. Justice DOUGLAS and Mr. Justice BRENNAN join, dissenting. . . .

[T]his case would be quite different if it were true that the Texas system, while insuring minimum educational expenditures in every district through state funding, extended a meaningful option to all local districts to increase their per-pupil expenditures and so to improve their children's education to the extent that increased funding would achieve that goal. The system would then arguably provide a rational and sensible method of achieving the stated aim of preserving an area for local initiative and decision.

The difficulty with the Texas system, however, is that it provides a meaningful option to Alamo Heights and like school districts but almost none to Edgewood and those other districts with a low per-pupil real estate tax base. In these latter districts, no matter how desirous parents are of supporting their schools with greater revenues, it is impossible to do so through the use of the real estate property tax. In these districts, the Texas system utterly fails to extend a realistic choice to parents because the property tax, which is the only revenue-raising mechanism extended to school districts, is practically and legally unavailable. That this is the situation may be readily demonstrated.

. . . . Requiring the State to establish only that unequal treatment is in furtherance of a permissible goal, without also requiring the State to show that the means chosen to effectuate that goal are rationally related to its achievement, makes equal protection analysis no more than an empty gesture.[1] . . .

2. See, e. g., Mosley v. Police Dept. of City of Chicago, 408 U.S. 92 (free speech); Shapiro v. Thompson, 394 U.S. 618 (freedom of interstate travel); Williams v. Rhodes, 393 U.S. 23 (freedom of association); Skinner v. Oklahoma, 316 U.S. 535 ("liberty" conditionally protected by Due Process Clause of Fourteenth Amendment). [Footnote by Justice Stewart.]

[*] A brief dissenting notation by Justice Brennan is omitted.

1. . . . . [The State] insists that districts have a choice and that the people in each district have exercised that choice by providing some real property tax money over and above the minimum funds guaranteed by the State. Like the majority, however, the State fails to explain why the Equal Protection Clause is not violated or how its goal of providing local government with realistic choices as to how much money should be expended on education is implemented where the system makes it much more difficult for some than for others to provide additional educational funds and where as a practical and legal matter it is impossible for some districts to provide the educational budgets that other districts can make available from real property tax revenues. [Footnote by Justice White.]

Mr. Justice MARSHALL, with whom Mr. Justice DOUGLAS concurs, dissenting. . . .

I . . .

Despite the evident discriminatory effect of the Texas financing scheme, both the appellants and the majority raise substantial questions concerning the precise character of the disadvantaged class in this case. [T]he conclusion that the school children of property poor districts constitute a sufficient class for our purposes seems indisputable to me. . . .

I believe it is sufficient that the overarching form of discrimination in this case is between the schoolchildren of Texas on the basis of the taxable property wealth of the districts in which they happen to live. To understand both the precise nature of this discrimination and the parameters of the disadvantaged class it is sufficient to consider the constitutional principle which appellees contend is controlling in the context of educational financing. In their complaint appellees asserted that the Constitution does not permit local district wealth to be determinative of educational opportunity. This is simply another way of saying, as the District Court concluded, that consistent with the guarantee of equal protection of the laws, "the quality of public education may not be a function of wealth, other than the wealth of the state as a whole." Under such a principle, the children of a district are excessively advantaged if that district has more taxable property per pupil than the average amount of taxable property per pupil considering the State as a whole. By contrast, the children of a district are disadvantaged if that district has less taxable property per pupil than the state average. . . .

II . . .

[The majority's conclusion that a "lenient standard of rationality" rather than a "strict standard of review" applies] avoids the telling task of searching for a substantial state interest which the Texas financing scheme, with its variations in taxable district property wealth, is necessary to further. I cannot accept such an emasculation of the Equal Protection Clause in the context of this case.

A

To begin, I must once more voice my disagreement with the Court's rigidified approach to equal protection analysis. . . . The Court apparently seeks to establish today that equal protection cases fall into one of two neat categories which dictate the appropriate standard of review—strict scrutiny or mere rationality. But this Court's decisions in the field of equal protection defy such easy categorization. A principled reading of what this Court has done reveals that it has applied a spectrum of standards in reviewing discrimination allegedly violative of the Equal Protection Clause. This spectrum clearly comprehends variations in the degree of care with which the Court will scrutinize particular classifications, depending, I believe, on the constitutional and societal importance of the interest adversely affected and the recognized invidiousness of the basis upon which the particular classification is drawn. I find in fact that many of the Court's recent decisions embody the very sort of reasoned approach to equal protection

analysis for which I previously argued [in the "sliding scale" Dandridge v. Williams dissent].

I therefore cannot accept the majority's labored efforts to demonstrate that fundamental interests, which call for strict scrutiny of the challenged classification, encompass only established rights which we are somehow bound to recognize from the text of the Constitution itself. To be sure, some interests which the Court has deemed to be fundamental for purposes of equal protection analysis are themselves constitutionally protected rights. [E. g., Shapiro v. Thompson.] But it will not do to suggest that the "answer" to whether an interest is fundamental for purposes of equal protection analysis is *always* determined by whether that interest "is a right . . . explicitly or implicitly guaranteed by the Constitution." [1]

I would like to know where the Constitution guarantees the right to procreate [Skinner v. Oklahoma], or the right to vote in state elections [e. g., Reynolds v. Sims], [2] or the right to an appeal from a criminal conviction, [e. g., Griffin v. Illinois]. [3] These are instances in which, due to the importance of the interests at stake, the Court has displayed a strong concern with the existence of discriminatory state treatment. But the Court has never said or indicated that these are interests which independently enjoy full-blown constitutional protection. . . .

The majority is, of course, correct when it suggests that the process of determining which interests are fundamental is a difficult one. But I do not think the problem is insurmountable. And I certainly do not accept the view that the process need necessarily degenerate into an unprincipled, subjective "picking-and-choosing" between various interests or that it must involve this Court in creating "substantive constitutional rights in the name of guaranteeing equal protection of the laws." Although not all fundamental interests are constitutionally guaranteed, the determination of which interests are fundamental should be firmly rooted in the text of the Constitution. The task in every case should be to determine the extent to which constitutionally guaranteed rights are dependent on interests not mentioned in the Constitution.

1. Indeed, the Court's theory would render the established concept of fundamental interests in the context of equal protection analysis superfluous, for the substantive constitutional right itself requires that this Court strictly scrutinize any asserted state interest for restricting or denying access to any particular guaranteed right . . . . [Footnote by Justice Marshall.]

2. It is interesting that in its effort to reconcile the state voting rights cases with its theory of fundamentality the majority can muster nothing more than the contention that "[t]he constitutional underpinnings of the right to equal treatment in the voting *process* can no longer be doubted . . . ." (emphasis added). If, by this, the Court intends to recognize a substantive constitutional "right to equal treatment in the voting process"

independent of the Equal Protection Clause, the source of such a right is certainly a mystery to me. [Footnote by Justice Marshall—later in the opinion.]

3. It is true that Griffin [also] involved discrimination against indigents, that is, wealth discrimination. But, as the majority points out, [the] Court has never deemed wealth discrimination alone to be sufficient to require strict judicial scrutiny; rather, such review of wealth classifications has been applied only where the discrimination affects an important individual interest, see, e. g., [Harper]. Thus, I believe Griffin [can] only be understood as premised on a recognition of the fundamental importance of the criminal appellate process. [Footnote by Justice Marshall—later in the opinion.]

As the nexus between the specific constitutional guarantee and the nonconstitutional interest draws closer, the nonconstitutional interest becomes more fundamental and the degree of judicial scrutiny applied when the interest is infringed on a discriminatory basis must be adjusted accordingly. Thus, it cannot be denied that interests such as procreation, the exercise of the state franchise, and access to criminal appellate processes are not fully guaranteed to the citizen by our Constitution. But these interests have nonetheless been afforded special judicial consideration in the face of discrimination because they are, to some extent, interrelated with constitutional guarantees. Procreation is now understood to be important because of its interaction with the established constitutional right of privacy. The exercise of the state franchise is closely tied to basic civil and political rights inherent in the First Amendment. And access to criminal appellate processes enhances the integrity of the range of rights implicit in the Fourteenth Amendment guarantee of due process of law. Only if we closely protect the related interests from state discrimination do we ultimately ensure the integrity of the constitutional guarantee itself. This is the real lesson that must be taken from our previous decisions involving interests deemed to be fundamental.

The effect of the interaction of individual interests with established constitutional guarantees upon the degree of care exercised by this Court in reviewing state discrimination affecting such interests is amply illustrated [by recent decisions]. [Justice Marshall discussed Eisenstadt v. Baird, 405 U.S. 438 (1972) (sec. 6 below; see his Rodriguez comments on Baird, quoted in sec. 6); James v. Strange, 407 U.S. 128 (1972) (sec. 4B above) (on state recoupment statutes; Justice Marshall stated that, though the Court purported to apply the traditional "some rationality" requirement, it scrutinized the law "with less than the traditional deference and restraint"); and Reed v. Reed, 404 U.S. 71 (1971) (sec. 3C above) (Justice Marshall commented that the Court, despite its statement of the rationality standard, was "unwilling to consider a theoretical and unsubstantiated basis for distinction—however reasonable it might appear—sufficient to sustain a statute discriminating on the basis of sex").]

James and Reed can only be understood as instances in which the particularly invidious character of the classification caused the Court to pause and scrutinize with more than traditional care the rationality of state discrimination. Discrimination on the basis of past criminality and on the basis of sex posed for the Court the spectre of forms of discrimination which it implicitly recognized to have deep social and legal roots without necessarily having any basis in actual differences. Still, the Court's sensitivity to the invidiousness of the basis for discrimination is perhaps most apparent in its decisions protecting the interests of children born out of wedlock from discriminatory state action. See [Levy and Weber, sec. 3A above]. . . .

In summary, it seems to me inescapably clear that this Court has consistently adjusted the care with which it will review state discrimination in light of the constitutional significance of the interests affected and the invidiousness of the particular classification. In the context of economic interests, we find that discriminatory state action is almost always sustained, for such interests are generally far removed from constitutional guarantees. . . .
But the situation differs markedly when discrimination against important in-

dividual interests with constitutional implications and against particularly disadvantaged or powerless classes is involved. The majority suggests, however, that a variable standard of review would give this Court the appearance of a "super-legislature." I cannot agree. Such an approach seems to me a part of the guarantees of our Constitution and of the historic experiences with oppression of and discrimination against discrete, powerless minorities which underlie that document. In truth, the Court itself will be open to the criticism raised by the majority so long as it continues on its present course of effectively selecting in private which cases will be afforded special consideration without acknowledging the true basis of its action.[4] Opinions such as those in Reed and James seem drawn more as efforts to shield rather than to reveal the true basis of the Court's decisions. Such obfuscated action may be appropriate to a political body such as a legislature, but it is not appropriate to this Court. Open debate of the bases for the Court's action is essential to the rationality and consistency of our decisionmaking process. Only in this way can we avoid the label of legislature and ensure the integrity of the judicial process.

Nevertheless, the majority today attempts to force this case into the same category for purposes of equal protection analysis as decisions involving discrimination affecting commercial interests. By so doing, the majority singles this case out for analytic treatment at odds with what seems to me to be the clear trend of recent decisions in this Court, and thereby ignores the constitutional importance of the interest at stake and the invidiousness of the particular classification, factors that call for far more than the lenient scrutiny of the Texas financing scheme which the majority pursues. Yet if the discrimination inherent in the Texas scheme is scrutinized with the care demanded by the interest and classification present in this case, the unconstitutionality of that scheme is unmistakable.

B

. . . It is true that this Court has never deemed the provision of free public education to be required by the Constitution. Nevertheless, the fundamental importance of education is amply indicated by the prior decisions of this Court, by the unique status accorded public education by our society, and by the close relationship between education and some of our most basic constitutional values. . . . [E]ducation bears [a "substantial relationship"] to guarantees of our Constitution.

Education directly affects the ability of a child to exercise his First Amendment interests both as a source and as a receiver of information and ideas, whatever interests he may pursue in life. . . . Of particular importance is the relationship between education and the political process. . . . [O]f most immediate and direct concern must be the demonstrated effect of education on the exercise of the franchise by the electorate. . . . It is this very sort of intimate relationship between a particular personal interest and specific constitutional guarantees that has heretofore caused the Court

---

4. See generally Gunther, The Supreme Court, 1971 Term: Foreword, In Search of Evolving Doctrine on a Changing Court: A Model for a Newer Equal Protection, 86 Harv.L.Rev. 1 (1972). [Footnote by Justice Marshall. See also his footnote [7] below.]

to attach special significance, for purposes of equal protection analysis, to individual interests such as procreation and the exercise of the state franchise.[5]

[These factors] compel us to recognize the fundamentality of education and to scrutinize with appropriate care the bases for state discrimination affecting equality of educational opportunity in Texas, school districts—a conclusion which is only strengthened when we consider the character of the classification in this case.   .   .   .

C

The District Court found that in discriminating between Texas schoolchildren on the basis of the amount of taxable property wealth located in the district in which they live, the Texas financing scheme created a form of wealth discrimination.   .   .   .   The majority, however, considers any wealth classification in this case to lack certain essential characteristics which it contends are common to the instances of wealth discrimination that this Court has heretofore recognized. We are told that in every prior case involving a wealth classification, the members of the disadvantaged class have "shared two distinguishing characteristics: because of their impecunity they were completely unable to pay for some desired benefit, and as a consequence, they sustained an absolute deprivation of a meaningful opportunity to enjoy that benefit." I cannot agree.   .   .   .   [Harper, Griffin and Douglas—secs. 4A and 4B above] refute the majority's contention that we have in the past required an absolute deprivation before subjecting wealth classifications to strict scrutiny.   .   .   .

This is not to say that the form of wealth classification in this case does not differ significantly from those recognized in the previous decisions of this Court. Our prior cases have dealt essentially with discrimination on the basis of personal wealth. Here, by contrast, the children of the disadvantaged Texas school districts are being discriminated against not necessarily because of their personal wealth or the wealth of their families, but because of the taxable property wealth of the residents of the district in which they happen to live. The appropriate question, then, is whether the same degree of judicial solicitude and scrutiny that has previously been afforded wealth classifications is warranted here.

---

5. I believe that the close nexus between education and our established constitutional values with respect to freedom of speech and participation in the political process makes this a different case than our prior decisions concerning discrimination affecting public welfare, see, e. g., [Dandridge v. Williams], or housing, see, e. g., [Lindsey v. Normet]. There can be no question that, as the majority suggests, constitutional rights may be less meaningful for someone without enough to eat or without decent housing. But the crucial difference lies in the closeness of the relationship. Whatever the severity of the impact of insufficient food or inadequate housing on a person's life, they have never been considered to bear the same direct and immediate relationship to constitutional concerns for free speech and for our political processes as education has long been recognized to bear. Perhaps the best evidence of this fact is the unique status which has been accorded public education as the single public service nearly unanimously guaranteed in the constitutions of our States. Education, in terms of constitutional values, is much more analogous, in my judgment, to the right to vote in state elections than to public welfare or public housing. Indeed, it is not without significance that we have long recognized education as an essential step in providing the disadvantaged with the tools necessary to achieve economic self-sufficiency. [Footnote by Justice Marshall.]

As the Court points out, no previous decision has deemed the presence of just a wealth classification to be sufficient basis to call forth "rigorous judicial scrutiny" of allegedly discriminatory state action. That wealth classifications alone have not necessarily been considered to bear the same high degree of suspectness as have classifications based on, for instance, race or alienage may be explainable on a number of grounds. The "poor" may not be seen as politically powerless as certain discrete and insular minority groups. Personal poverty may entail much the same social stigma as historically attached to certain racial or ethnic groups. But personal poverty is not a permanent disability; its shackles may be escaped. Perhaps, most importantly, though, personal wealth may not necessarily share the general irrelevance as basis for legislative action that race or nationality is recognized to have. While the "poor" have frequently been a legally disadvantaged group, it cannot be ignored that social legislation must frequently take cognizance of the economic status of our citizens. Thus, we have generally gauged the invidiousness of wealth classifications with an awareness of the importance of the interests being affected and the relevance of personal wealth to those interests. [See Harper.]

When evaluated with these considerations in mind, it seems to me that discrimination on the basis of group wealth in this case likewise calls for careful judicial scrutiny. First, it must be recognized that while local district wealth may serve other interests, it bears no relationship whatsoever to the interest of Texas school children in the educational opportunity afforded them by the State of Texas. Given the importance of that interest, we must be particularly sensitive to the invidious characteristics of any form of discrimination that is not clearly intended to serve it, as opposed to some other distinct state interest. Discrimination on the basis of group wealth may not, to be sure, reflect the social stigma frequently attached to personal poverty. Nevertheless, insofar as group wealth discrimination involves wealth over which the disadvantaged individual has no significant control,[6] it represents in fact a more serious basis of discrimination than does personal wealth. For such discrimination is no reflection of the individual's characteristics or his abilities. And thus—particularly in the context of a disadvantaged class composed of children—we have previously treated discrimination on a basis which the individual cannot control as constitutionally disfavored. Cf. [Weber; Levy].

The disability of the disadvantaged class in this case extends as well into the political processes upon which we ordinarily rely as adequate for the protection and promotion of all interests. . . . Nor can we ignore the extent to which, in contrast to our prior decisions, the State is responsible for the wealth discrimination in this instance. Griffin, Douglas, Williams, Tate, and our other prior cases have dealt with discrimination on the basis of indigency which was attributable to the operation of the private sector. But we have no such simple de facto wealth discrimination here. The means for financing public education in Texas are selected and specified by the

6. True, a family may move to escape a property-poor school district, assuming it has the means to do so. But such a view would itself raise a serious constitutional question concerning an impermissible burdening of the right to travel, or, more precisely, the concomitant right to remain where one is. Cf. Shapiro v. Thompson. [Footnote by Justice Marshall.]

State. It is the State that has created local school districts, and tied educational funding to the local property tax and thereby to local district wealth. At the same time, governmentally imposed land use controls have undoubtedly encouraged and rigidified natural trends in the allocation of particular areas for residential or commercial use, and thus determined each district's amount of taxable property wealth. In short, this case, in contrast to the Court's previous wealth discrimination decisions, can only be seen as "unusual in the extent to which governmental action *is* the cause of the wealth classifications."

In the final analysis, then, the invidious characteristics of the group wealth classification present in this case merely serves to emphasize the need for careful judicial scrutiny of the State's justifications for the resulting interdistrict discrimination in the educational opportunity afforded to the school children of Texas.

D

The nature of our inquiry into the justifications for state discrimination is essentially the same in all equal protection cases: We must consider the substantiality of the state interests sought to be served, and we must scrutinize the reasonableness of the means by which the State has sought to advance its interests. Differences in the application of this test are, in my view, a function of the constitutional importance of the interests at stake and the invidiousness of the particular classification. In terms of the asserted state interests, the Court has indicated that it will require, for instance, a "compelling" or a "substantial" or "important" state interest to justify discrimination affecting individual interests of constitutional significance. Whatever the differences, if any, in these descriptions of the character of the state interest necessary to sustain such discrimination, basic to each is, I believe, a concern with the legitimacy and the reality of the asserted state interests. Thus, when interests of constitutional importance are at stake, the Court does not stand ready to credit the State's classification with any conceivable legitimate purpose, but demands a clear showing that there are legitimate state interests which the classification was in fact intended to serve. Beyond the question of the adequacy of the state's purpose for the classification, the Court traditionally has become increasingly sensitive to the means by which a State chooses to act as its action affects more directly interests of constitutional significance. . . . Thus, by now, "less restrictive alternatives" analysis is firmly established in equal protection jurisprudence. . . . It seems to me that the range of choice we are willing to accord the State in selecting the means by which it will act, and the care with which we scrutinize the effectiveness of the means which the State selects, also must reflect the constitutional importance of the interest affected and the invidiousness of the particular classification. Here both the nature of the interest and the classification dictate close judicial scrutiny of the purposes which Texas seeks to serve with its present educational financing scheme and of the means it has selected to serve that purpose.

The only justification offered by appellants to sustain the discrimination in educational opportunity caused by the Texas financing scheme is local educational control. [T]rue state dedication to local control would present, I think, a substantial justification to weigh against simply interdistrict variations

in the treatment of a State's school children. But I need not now decide how I might ultimately strike the balance were we confronted with a situation where the State's sincere concern for local control inevitably produced educational inequality. For on this record, it is apparent that the State's purported concern with local control is offered primarily as an excuse rather than as a justification for interdistrict inequality.

In Texas statewide laws regulate in fact the most minute details of local public education. . . . Moreover, even if we accept Texas' general dedication to local control in educational matters, it is difficult to find any evidence of such dedication with respect to fiscal matters. . . . If Texas had a system truly dedicated to local fiscal control one would expect the quality of the educational opportunity provided in each district to vary with the decision of the voters in that district as to the level of sacrifice they wish to make for public education. In fact, the Texas scheme produces precisely the opposite result. Local school districts cannot choose to have the best education in the State by imposing the highest tax rate. Instead, the quality of the educational opportunity offered by any particular district is largely determined by the amount of taxable property located in the district—a factor over which local voters can exercise no control. . . .

In my judgment, any substantial degree of scrutiny of the operation of the Texas financing scheme reveals that the State has selected means wholly inappropriate to secure its purported interest in assuring its school districts local fiscal control.[7] At the same time, appellees have pointed out a variety of alternative financing schemes which may serve the State's purported interest in local control as well as, if not better than, the present scheme without the current impairment of the educational opportunity of vast numbers of Texas schoolchildren.[8] I see no need, however, to explore

7. My Brother White, in concluding that the Texas financing scheme runs afoul of the Equal Protection Clause, likewise finds on analysis that the means chosen by Texas—local property taxation dependent upon local taxable wealth—is completely unsuited in its present form to the achievement of the asserted goal of providing local fiscal control. Although my Brother White purports to reach this result by application of that lenient standard of mere rationality traditionally applied in the context of commercial interests, it seem to me that the care with which he scrutinizes the practical effectiveness of the present local property tax as a device for affording local fiscal control reflects the application of a more stringent standard of review, a standard which at the least is influenced by the constitutional significance of the process of public education. [Footnote by Justice Marshall.]

8. Centralized educational financing is, to be sure, one alternative. On analysis, though, it is clear that even centralized financing would leave in local hands the entire gamut of local educational policymaking—teachers, curriculum, school sites, the whole process of allocating resources among alternative educational objectives.

A second possibility is the much discussed theory of district power equalization put forth by Professors Coons, Clune, and Sugarman in their seminal work, Private Wealth and Public Education 201–242 (1970). Such a scheme would truly reflect a dedication to local fiscal control. Under their system, each school district would receive a fixed amount of revenue per pupil for any particular level of tax effort regardless of the level of local property tax base. . . .

District wealth reapportionment is yet another alternative which would accomplish directly essentially what district power equalization would seek to do artificially. . . .

A fourth possibility would be to remove commercial, industrial, and mineral property from local tax rolls, to tax this property on a state-wide basis, and to return the resulting revenues to the local districts in a fashion that

the practical or constitutional merits of those suggested alternatives at this time for, whatever their positive or negative features, experience with the present financing scheme impugns any suggestion that it constitutes a serious effort to provide local fiscal control. If, for the sake of local education control, this Court is to sustain interdistrict discrimination in the educational opportunity afforded Texas school children, it should require that the State present something more than the mere sham now before us. . . .

INTENSIFIED SCRUTINY OF WELFARE LAWS UNDER TRADITIONAL STANDARDS

Introduction. a. *A retrospective view.* The extensive and thoughtful debate between Justices Powell and Marshall in Rodriguez affords a useful vantage point for reexamination of the modern controversies about the meaning of the equal protection clause. Is Justice Powell persuasive in claiming that it is "not the province of this Court to create substantive constitutional rights in the name of guaranteeing equal protection"? Even though he accepts not only such constitutional "rights" cases as Shapiro v. Thompson but also such "fundamental interests" cases as Griffin and Harper and Skinner v. Oklahoma? Do voting and access to the criminal process have a closer tie to the Constitution than the interests not considered "fundamental" in the cases from Dandridge v. Williams to Rodriguez? Has the "fundamental interests" strand of equal protection truly been limited to "rights" "explicitly or implicitly guaranteed by the Constitution"? Has the Court truly avoided subjectivity in choosing particular interests for special protection? * Has it truly limited itself to interests with adequate roots in constitutional text, history, or structure? Are substantive equal protection developments, even as curtailed by cases such as Rodriguez, truly distinguishable from substantive due process doctrines from Lochner to Roe v. Wade (chap. 9 above)? Was the right recognized by the Burger Court in Roe v. Wade any more explicitly or implicitly created by the Constitution than the unsuccessfully asserted fundamental interest in Rodriguez? Does Justice Marshall's "nexus" approach offer adequate restraints on judicial discretion? Is Justice Marshall persuasive in his criticism of the Court's applications of the "two-tier" approach? Do the modern cases support his view that the Court is in fact applying a "sliding scale" or "multi-variable" approach to equal protection problems—an approach turning on assessments of the interests affected and the classification criteria used?

b. *Scrutiny without expanding the new equal protection.* Despite the Court's refusal to find "fundamental interests" in welfare benefits and other "necessities" in cases from Dandridge v. Williams through Rodriguez, the modern scrutiny of welfare legislation has not in fact been as extremely deferential as the repeated references to Williamson v. Lee Optical Co. would

would compensate for remaining variations in the local tax bases.
None of these particular alternatives [is] necessarily constitutionally compelled; rather, they indicate the breadth of choice which remains to the State if the present interdistrict disparities were eliminated. [Footnote by Justice Marshall—elsewhere in the opinion.]

* Recall footnote † to Justice Powell's opinion in Rodriguez.

suggest. In a number of cases, the Court, while purporting to apply traditional rationality standards, has invalidated legislation. Are these cases, which follow, examples of a consistently exercised "newer" equal protection "with bite," or do they support Justice Marshall's Rodriguez critique that the Court is in fact applying a variable standard of review despite its formal adherence to the two-tier approach? †

1. *Dept. of Agriculture v. Moreno.* The Court invalidated one aspect of a federal welfare program on the avowed basis of traditional equal protection criteria in DEPT. OF AGRICULTURE v. MORENO, 413 U.S. 528 (1973). That 7 to 2 decision held unconstitutional a provision of the federal food stamp program of assistance to "households." A 1971 amendment had redefined "households" to be limited to groups of *related* persons, so that any household containing an unrelated person was excluded from eligibility. Justice Brennan's majority opinion held that "unrelated person" provision "an irrational classification in violation of the equal protection component of the Due Process Clause of the Fifth Amendment." He agreed that under the "traditional" equal protection analysis of Dandridge v. Williams, a classification need not be drawn with "precise mathematical nicety." But here, he insisted, the classification "is not only 'imprecise'; it is wholly without any rational basis."

The classification was "clearly irrelevant" to the purposes stated in the statutory preamble—satisfying nutritional needs and helping the agricultural economy. The legislative history also suggested a purpose of excluding "hippie communes" from the food stamp program. But that was not a permissible purpose: "a bare congressional desire to harm a politically unpopular group cannot constitute a *legitimate* governmental interest." Continuing his search for governmental justifications, he turned to the government's argument that the classification could be upheld as "rationally related" to the "interest in minimizing fraud"—and rejected that as well. Justice Brennan pointed to other statutory provisions on fraud as casting "considerable doubt" on the argument that the 1971 amendment "could rationally have been intended to prevent those very same abuses." [He cited Eisenstadt v. Baird, sec. 6 below, in justifying that aspect of his analysis.]

Justice Douglas' concurrence rested on a strict scrutiny rather than minimum rationality analysis. He thought the challenged provision had a " 'rational' relation to control of fraud." But here, standards higher than Dandridge v. Williams applied because the classification touched on "associational rights that lie in the penumbra of the First Amendment." He viewed the case as involving "desperately poor people with acute problems who, though unrelated, come together for mutual help and assistance," and this "banding together" of the poor was "an expression of the right of freedom of association." [1] Justice Rehnquist's dissent joined by Chief Justice Burger,

---

† Recall also the reliance on a "newer" equal protection approach in invalidating benefit laws challenged as sex discriminations, in sec. 3C above—e. g., Weinberger v. Wiesenfeld, 420 U.S. ⸺ (1975).

1. But compare Justice Douglas' very deferential majority opinion in Village

of Belle Terre v. Boraas, 416 U.S. 1 (1974), rejecting an attack on a village zoning ordinance restricting land use to one-family dwellings, with the definition of "family" limited to the traditional, related family and to groups of not more than two unrelated persons. The ordinance was challenged by six students who had rented a

thought the classification, though "rather blunt," rational to further the fraud objective.[2]

2. *Jimenez v. Weinberger.* A year after Moreno, the Court once again found an equal protection flaw in a federal welfare program. Chief Justice Burger wrote for the 8 to 1 majority. He eschewed "strict scrutiny," but found Dandridge v. Williams distinguishable and apparently applied an intermediate level of scrutiny in an opinion which Justice Rehnquist's dissent understandably termed "puzzling." JIMENEZ v. WEINBERGER, 417 U.S. 628 (1974). Can Jimenez be viewed as an application of traditional standards "with bite"? Compare the advocacy in Justice Rehnquist's dissent of the extreme deference of the old equal protection of the 1960's.

The challenge in Jimenez was to a provision of the Social Security Act which denied disability benefits to some but not all illegitimate children born after the onset of their wage earner parent's disability.[3] Chief Justice

house in the village and who claimed that strict scrutiny was applicable because of impingement on their rights of association, privacy and travel. A lower court sustained their challenge without exercising "strict scrutiny," by exercising a variety of rationality scrutiny "with bite"—the "newer" equal protection. But Justice Douglas' brief majority opinion sustained the ordinance via a level of scrutiny which was, if anything, even more deferential than the Lee Optical variety. He emphasized that the case was essentially a zoning case and that this was "economic and social legislation." He found no impingement on fundamental interests and dismissed the attack on the exclusion of most groups of unrelated persons with the curt comment: "But every line drawn by a legislature leaves some out that might well have been included." His Moreno opinion of a year earlier proved worthy of no more than a one-sentence footnote: Moreno was "inapt as there a household containing anyone unrelated to the rest was denied food stamps." Justice Marshall's dissent insisted that strict scrutiny was required because the classification burdened "the students' fundamental rights of association and privacy." He thought the means chosen to accomplish such goals as controlling population density and preventing traffic problems "both over- and under-inclusive."

Note also the 8 to 1 decision in Johnson v. Robison, 415 U.S. 361 (1974), rejecting the claim that Congress, in limiting the class of draftees entitled to veterans' educational benefits to those who served on active duty in the armed forces, had denied equal protection to those who performed alternate civilian service as conscientious objectors. The lower court, applying a variety of the "newer" equal protection, had characterized the major legislative purpose as eliminating "the educational gaps between persons who served their country and those who did not" and accordingly found the distinction irrational. Justice Brennan, however, thought the overriding purpose was better stated as one "to compensate for the disruption that military service causes," and that justified the distinction under the "fair and substantial relation" standard of Reed v. Reed. Strict scrutiny was inappropriate because no fundamental interest was involved. Justice Douglas' dissent concluded that the legislative scheme was "an invidious discrimination and a penalty on those who served their religious scruples." (See also the additional comment on the case in chap. 14, sec. 2, below.)

2. See also a companion case striking down another provision of the Food Stamp Act, but purporting to rely on procedural due process-"irrebuttable presumptions" analysis rather than on equal protection grounds. Dept. of Agriculture v. Murry, 413 U.S. 528 1973) (sec. 6 below). To the extent that "irrebuttable presumptions" analysis has vitality if not plausibility— and especially to the extent that it constitutes equal protection review under another name—it provides an additional basis for challenging classifications in the area of "necessities" despite the Dandridge-Rodriguez line of cases. See also the Jimenez case in the next note.

3. As described by the Court, the scheme divided after-born illegitimate children "into two sub-classifications": "One sub-class is made up of those

Burger found it unnecessary to reach the argument that the scheme should be carefully scrutinized as a suspect classification directed at illegitimates; instead, he emphasized the discrimination *among* classes of illegitimate children. Yet after rejecting that plea to apply strict scrutiny, the Chief Justice also found the deferential standard of review of Dandridge v. Williams "not controlling." The "special deference" in Dandridge, he explained, was necessary because of the problem of the State's "finite resources" for welfare benefits. Here, by contrast, "there is no evidence supporting the contention that to allow illegitimates in the classification of appellants to receive benefits would significantly impair the federal Social Security trust fund and necessitate a reduction in the scope of persons benefited by the Act." Rather, the Government had "persistently maintained" that the general purpose of the scheme was to provide support for dependents of disabled wage earners, and that the exclusion of some after-born illegitimates was "designed only to prevent spurious claims."

Proceeding to examine the statute under his unarticulated standard of review, the Chief Justice rejected the Government's claim that the excluded illegitimate children were those "likely," "as a class," not to "possess the requisite economic dependency on the wage earner." The Chief Justice replied: "We do not read the statute as supporting that view of its purpose." Testing the law's rationality solely in terms of a purpose of preventing spurious claims, the Chief Justice found "a legitimate governmental interest," but criticized its implementation. He noted that the government "maintains that the possibility that evidence of parentage or support may be fabricated is greater when the child is not born until after the wage earner has become entitled to benefits." But the Chief Justice replied: "It does not follow, however, that the blanket and conclusive exclusion of appellants' subclass of illegitimates is reasonably related to the prevention of spurious claims. Assuming that the appellants are in fact dependent on the claimant, it would not serve the purposes of the Act to conclusively deny them an opportunity to establish their dependency and their right to insurance benefits, and it would discriminate between the two subclasses of after-born illegitimates without any basis for the distinction since the potential for spurious claims is exactly the same as to both subclasses." He added: "Even if children might rationally be classified on the basis of whether they are dependent upon their disabled parents, the Act's definition of these two subclasses of illegitimates is 'over-inclusive' in that it benefits some children who are legitimated, or entitled to inherit, or illegitimate solely because of a defect in the marriage of their parents, but who are not dependent on their disabled parents. Conversely, the Act is 'under-inclusive' in that it conclusively excludes some illegitimates in appellants' subclass who are, in fact, dependent upon their disabled parents." He accordingly concluded: "Thus, for all that is shown in this record, the two subclasses of illegitimates stand on equal

(a) who can inherit under state intestacy law, or (b) who are legitimated under state law, or (c) who are illegitimate only because of some formal defect in their parents' ceremony of marriage. These children are deemed entitled to receive benefits under the Act without any showing that they are in fact dependent upon their disabled parent. The second subclassification of after-born illegitimate children" was "those who are conclusively denied benefits." (Illegitimate children who were not after-born were entitled to benefits if the disabled wage earner parent had contributed to the child's support or had lived with the child prior to the disability.)

footing, and the potential for spurious claims is the same as to both; hence to conclusively deny one subclass benefits presumptively available to the other denies the former the equal protection of the law guaranteed by the due process provisions of the Fifth Amendment." The case was remanded to provide appellants an opportunity "to establish their claim to eligibility as 'children' of the claimant" under the Act.

Justice Rehnquist's dissent found the opinion "a perplexing three-legged stool": though the holding was "clearly founded in notions of equal protection," the opinion "has strong due process overtones as well, at times appearing to play homage to the still-novel, and I think unsupportable, theory that 'irrebuttable presumptions' violate due process [see sec. 6 below]. At other times the opinion seems to suggest that the real problem in this case is the Government's failure to build an adequate evidentiary record in support of a challenged legislation. The result is a rather impressionistic determination that Congress' efforts to cope with spurious claims of entitlement, while preserving maximum benefits for those persons most likely to be deserving, are simply not satisfactory to the members of this Court. I agree with neither the Court's approach nor its decision."

He found the Court's equal protection analysis "most difficult to understand." He commented: "Whatever may be the rationale for giving some form of stricter scrutiny to classifications between legitimates and illegitimates, that rationale simply vanishes when the alleged discrimination is between classes of illegitimates." He insisted that the Dandridge deference was appropriate here. He thought the emphasis on further hearings represented "simply an attack on 'irrebuttable presumptions' in another guise." Nor was he satisfied with the distinction of Dandridge: "I should think it obvious that any increase in the number of eligible recipients would serve to additionally deplete a fixed fund, but I find even stranger the notion that the Government must present evidence to justify each and every classification that a legislature chooses to make. If I read the Court's opinion correctly, it would seem to require, for example, that the Government compile evidence to support Congress' determination that Social Security benefits begin at a specified age, perhaps even requiring statistics to show that need is greater (in all cases?) at that age than at lesser ages. This proposition is certainly far removed from traditional principles of deference to legislative judgment. As we stated in McGowan v. Maryland [1961—sec. 1 above]: 'A statutory discrimination will not be set aside if any state of facts reasonably may be conceived to justify it.' There is nothing in that language that suggests to me that courtrooms should become forums for a second round of legislative hearings whenever a legislative determination is later challenged." He accordingly concluded that the lower court had been correct in finding "that the classifications at issue rest upon a rational basis."

SECTION 6. SOME VARIATIONS ON EQUAL PROTECTION THEMES—ESPECIALLY THE "IRREBUTTABLE PRESUMPTIONS" ANALYSIS

Introduction. The preceding sections have traced the rapidly moving developments in equal protection analysis, especially since the early 1960's. This section not only provides an occasion for reflection on the meaning of Burger Court deviations from Warren Court patterns, but also introduces one more variation that achieved considerable popularity during the early 1970's—a procedural due process-"irrebuttable presumptions" analysis that purports to avoid the equal protection route.

a. *The "newer" equal protection.* Materials for pursuit of the first theme—reflections on recent developments that avowedly rest on the equal protection clause—abound in the preceding materials. The doctrinal framework during the 1960's was relatively clear, even though the proferred justifications were not always persuasive: intensity of scrutiny on the Warren Court followed a rigid two-tier approach, with strict and typically fatal scrutiny for the new equal protection and deferential, very undemanding scrutiny for areas within the old equal protection. Though the Burger Court has not abandoned formal allegiance to that two-tier structure, exercises of scrutiny have obviously changed and the standards are evidently in flux. Reconsider the recent equal protection cases which depart from the two-tier pattern, and recall the questions and suggestions in the Introductory Overview and in sec. 1. Are the modern variations on the "old"-"new" equal protection dichotomy best described by Justice Marshall's "sliding scale"-"multi-variables" analysis? [1] Is that analysis a justifiable, adequately principled one? Is the "newer" equal protection model justifiable in principle? [2] Do the modern cases exercising minimum rationality review "with bite" adequately conform to that model? [3] Are there alternative explanations and justifications for modern variations on equal protection themes? In addition to the examples considered in the preceding sections, consider one more case invalidating a law while purporting to apply traditional rationality standards: Eisenstadt v. Baird, the next principal case. Note especially the Court's technique for ascertaining legislative "purposes" in that case.

b. *"Irrebuttable presumptions."* The second theme—the Court's recent, sporadic penchant for "irrebuttable presumptions" analysis—is a new

---

1. See especially the fullest articulation of Justice Marshall's position, in his dissent in the Rodriguez case, sec. 5 above.

2. See the description of that model in the excerpts from Gunther, "Newer Equal Protection," 86 Harv.L.Rev. 1 (1972), sec. 1 above.

3. See especially the sex discrimination cases from Reed v. Reed to Weinberger v. Wiesenfeld and Stanton v. Stanton in sec. 3C above. See also the samples of the recent invalidations

purporting to rest on invocations of the "rationality" standards of the old equal protection in other areas—e. g., Dept. of Agriculture v. Moreno, sec. 5 above—as well as the statements of traditional standards with greater emphasis on articulated or actual rather than hypothesized purposes in such opinions as Justice Powell's majority opinion in McGinnis v. Royster, sec. 4B, and in Justice Brennan's dissent in Schlesinger v. Ballard, sec. 3C. Note, in addition, the "purpose" scrutiny in Eisenstadt v. Baird, below.

one. The opinions that rest on "irrebuttable presumptions" analysis claim to draw on procedural due process principles and purport to avoid the equal protection challenge. Instead of overtly confronting the equal protection claim, the Court in these cases invalidates the classifications on alleged procedural due process grounds: the Court's scrutiny purports to uncover the vice of arbitrary "conclusive" or "irrebuttable" presumptions inherent in the legislative scheme. Increasingly sharp dissents have claimed that the Court is really deciding equal protection issues without saying so, that it is unduly inhibiting legislative ability to classify, and that it is applying the new technique in an ad hoc and unpredictable manner. Does' the new technique make sense? Is it truly an analysis that rests on grounds other than equal protection? Or is it in fact a treatment of equal protection issues under a different, obscuring guise? Those are the issues raised by the LaFleur case—the second principal case below—and the other "irrebuttable presumptions" cases discussed in LaFleur and in the notes following it.

EISENSTADT v. BAIRD

405 U.S. 438, 92 S.Ct. 1029, 31 L.Ed.2d 349 (1972).

Appeal from the United States Court of Appeals for the First Circuit.

Mr. Justice BRENNAN delivered the opinion of the Court.

[William Baird was convicted in a Massachusetts court] first, for exhibiting contraceptive articles in the course of delivering a lecture on contraception to a group of students at Boston University and, second, for giving a young woman a package of Emko vaginal foam at the close of his address.[1] The Massachusetts Supreme Judicial Court unanimously set aside the conviction for exhibiting contraceptives on the ground that it violated Baird's First Amendment rights, but by a four-to-three vote sustained the conviction for giving away the foam. [Commonwealth v. Baird.] [On federal habeas corpus, the Court of Appeals directed that the writ be granted.] We affirm.

[The state law, § 21, applies to] "whoever . . . gives away . . . any drug, medicine, instrument or article whatever for the prevention of conception," except as authorized in § 21A. Under § 21A, "[a] registered physician may administer to or prescribe for any married person drugs or articles intended for the prevention of pregnancy or conception." [There is a similar exception for registered pharmacists.] The statutory scheme distinguishes among three distinct classes of distributees—*first*, married persons may obtain contraceptives to prevent pregnancy, but only from doctors or druggists on prescription; *second*, single persons may not obtain contraceptives from anyone to prevent pregnancy; and, *third*, married or single persons may obtain contraceptives from anyone to prevent, not pregnancy, but the spread of disease. . . .

The legislative purposes that the statute is meant to serve are not altogether clear. In Commonwealth v. Baird, the Supreme Judicial Court noted

---

1. The Court of Appeals below described the recipient of the foam as "an unmarried adult woman." However, there is no evidence in the record about her marital status. [Footnote by the Court.]

only the State's interest in protecting the health of its citizens . . . . In a [later] decision, the court, however, found "a second and more compelling ground for upholding the statute"—namely, to protect morals through "regulating the private sexual lives of single persons." . . . We agree [with the U.S. Court of Appeals] that the goals of deterring premarital sex and regulating the distribution of potentially harmful articles cannot reasonably be regarded as legislative aims of §§ 21 and 21A. And we hold that the statute, viewed as a prohibition on contraception per se, violates the rights of single persons under the Equal Protection Clause of the Fourteenth Amendment. [After finding that Baird had standing "to assert the rights of unmarried persons denied access to contraceptives" (see chap. 15 below), the Court turned to the merits.]

The basic principles governing application of the Equal Protection Clause of the Fourteenth Amendment are familiar. [The Court quoted the minimum rationality criteria of the "old" equal protection stated in Reed v. Reed, sec. 3C above.] The question for our determination in this case is whether there is some ground of difference that rationally explains the different treatment accorded married and unmarried persons under Massachusetts General Laws c. 272, §§ 21 and 21A.[2] For the reasons that follow, we conclude that no such ground exists.

First [as to the alleged "deterrent to fornication" purpose]. . . . Conceding that the State could, consistently with the Equal Protection Clause, regard the problems of extramarital and premarital sexual relations as "[e]vils [of] different dimensions and proportions, requiring different remedies" [Williamson v. Lee Optical Co.], we cannot agree that the deterrence of premarital sex may reasonably be regarded as the purpose of the Massachusetts law.

It would be plainly unreasonable to assume that Massachusetts has prescribed pregnancy and the birth of an unwanted child as punishment for fornication, [a misdemeanor]. [And it is] abundantly clear that the effect of the ban on distribution of contraceptives to unmarried persons has at best a marginal relation to the proferred objective. . . . The very terms of the State's criminal statutes, coupled with the de minimis effect of §§ 21 and 21A in deterring fornication, [compel] the conclusion that such deterrence cannot reasonably be taken as the purpose of the ban on distribution of contraceptives to unmarried persons.

Second [as to the alleged "health" purpose]. If health were the rationale of § 21A, the statute would be both discriminatory and overbroad. [Two dissenting Justices of the state court stated:] "If there is need to have a physician prescribe (and a pharmacist dispense) contraceptives, that need is as great for unmarried persons as for married persons." . . . Furthermore, we must join the Court of Appeals in noting that not all contraceptives are potentially dangerous. As a result, if the Massachusetts statute were

---

2. Of course, if we were to conclude that the Massachusetts statute impinges upon fundamental freedoms under Griswold, the statutory classification would have to be not merely *rationally related* to a valid public purpose but *necessary* to the achievement of a *compelling* state interest. But just as in [Reed v. Reed], we do not have to address the statute's validity under that test because the law fails to satisfy even the more lenient equal protection standard. [Footnote by the Court.]

a health measure, it would not only invidiously discriminate against the unmarried, but also be overbroad with respect to the married .   .   . .

But if further proof that the Massachusetts statute is not a health measure is necessary, the argument of [another state court dissenter] is conclusive: "It is at best a strained conception to say that the Legislature intended to prevent the distribution of articles 'which may have undesirable, if not dangerous, physical consequences.' If that was the Legislature's goal, § 21 is not required" in view of the federal and state laws *already* regulating the distribution of harmful drugs. We conclude, accordingly, that, despite the statute's superficial earmarks as a health measure, health, on the face of the statute, may no more reasonably be regarded as its purpose than the deterrence of premarital sexual relations.

Third. If the Massachusetts statute cannot be upheld as a deterrent to fornication or as a health measure, may it, nevertheless, be sustained simply as a prohibition on contraception? The Court of Appeals [relied on Griswold and held that the State could not "say that contraceptives are immoral as such": "In the absence of demonstrated harm, we hold it is beyond the competency of the state"; it "conflicts with fundamental human rights."] We need not and do not, however, decide that important question in this case because, whatever the rights of the individual to access to contraceptives may be, the rights must be the same for the unmarried and the married alike.

If under Griswold the distribution of contraceptives to married persons cannot be prohibited, a ban on distribution to unmarried persons would be equally impermissible. It is true that in Griswold the right of privacy in question inhered in the marital relationship. Yet the marital couple is not an independent entity with a mind and heart of its own, but an association of two individuals each with a separate intellectual and emotional make-up. If the right of privacy means anything, it is the right of the *individual*, married or single, to be free from unwarranted governmental intrusion into matters so fundamentally affecting a person as the decision whether to bear or beget a child. See Stanley v. Georgia, 394 U.S. 557 (1969) [chap. 13, sec. 2, below]. See also [Skinner v. Oklahoma].

On the other hand, if Griswold is no bar to a prohibition on the distribution of contraceptives, the State could not, consistently with the Equal Protection Clause, outlaw distribution to unmarried but not to married persons. In each case the evil, as perceived by the State, would be identical, and the underinclusion would be invidious. Mr. Justice Jackson, concurring in [Railway Express Agency v. New York, sec. 1 above], made the point .   .   . . We hold that by providing dissimilar treatment for married and unmarried persons who are similarly situated, [§§ 21 and 21A] violate the Equal Protection Clause.

Affirmed.*

Mr. Justice WHITE, with whom Mr. Justice BLACKMUN joins, concurring in the result. .   .   .

I assume that a State's interest in the health of its citizens empowers it to restrict to medical channels the distribution of products whose use should be

---

* Justice Douglas' concurrence also noted a "narrower ground" for the decision: he thought this "a simple First Amendment case." Justices Powell and Rehnquist did not participate in the decision.

accompanied by medical advice. I also do not doubt that various contraceptive medicines and articles are properly available only on prescription, and I therefore have no difficulty with the Massachusetts court's characterization of the statute at issue here as expressing "a legitimate [health] interest . . . ." Had Baird distributed a supply of the so-called "pill," I would sustain his conviction under this statute. . . .

Baird, however, was found guilty of giving away vaginal foam. . . . Our general reluctance to question a State's judgment on matters of public health must give way where, as here, the restriction at issue burdens the constitutional rights of married persons to use contraceptives. In these circumstances we may not accept on faith the State's classification of a particular contraceptive as dangerous to health. Due regard for protecting constitutional rights requires that the record contain evidence that a restriction on distribution of vaginal foam is essential to achieve the statutory purpose, or the relevant facts concerning the product must be such as to fall within the range of judicial notice. Neither requirement is met here. . . .

[Just as in Griswold] so here to sanction a medical restriction upon distribution [to married persons] of a contraceptive not proved hazardous to health would impair the exercise of the constitutional right.

That Baird could not be convicted for distributing Emko to a married person disposes of this case. Assuming, arguendo, that the result would be otherwise had the recipient been unmarried, nothing has been placed in the record to indicate her marital status. . . .

Mr. Chief Justice BURGER, dissenting. . . .

In affirming appellee's conviction, the highest tribunal in Massachusetts held that the statutory requirement that contraceptives be dispensed only through medical channels served the legitimate interest of the State in protecting the health of its citizens. The Court today blithely hurdles this authoritative [statement of purpose]. [The Court's second argument] confuses the validity of the restriction on distributors with the validity of the further restriction on distributees, a part of the statute not properly before the Court. Assuming the legislature too broadly restricted the class of persons who could obtain contraceptives, it hardly follows that it saw no need to protect the health of all persons to whom they are made available. Third, the Court sees no health purpose underlying the restriction on distributors because other state and federal laws regulate the distribution of harmful drugs. I know of no rule that all enactments relating to a particular purpose must be neatly consolidated in one package in the statute books . . . .

The actual hazards of introducing a particular foreign substance into the human body are frequently controverted, and I cannot believe that unanimity of expert opinion is a prerequisite to a State's exercise of its police power, no matter what the subject matter of the regulation. . . . Even if it were conclusively established once and for all that the product dispensed by appellee is not actually or potentially dangerous in the somatic sense, I would still be unable to agree that the restriction on dispensing it falls outside the State's power to regulate in the area of health. The choice of a means of birth control, although a highly personal matter, is also a health matter in a very real sense, and I see nothing arbitrary in a requirement of medical supervision. It is generally acknowledged that contraceptives vary in

degree of effectiveness and potential harmfulness. There may be compelling health reasons for certain women to choose the most effective means of birth control available, no matter how harmless the less effective alternatives. Others might be advised not to use a highly effective means of contraception because of their peculiar susceptibility to an adverse side effect. Moreover, there may be information known to the medical profession that a particular brand of contraceptive is to be preferred or avoided, or that it has not been adequately tested. Nonetheless, the concurring opinion would hold, as a constitutional matter, that a State must allow someone without medical training the same power to distribute this medicinal substance as is enjoyed by a physician.

    . . . I see nothing in the Fourteenth Amendment or any other part of the Constitution which even vaguely suggests that these medicinal forms of contraceptives must be available in the open market. I do not challenge Griswold v. Connecticut, supra, despite its tenuous moorings to the text of the Constitution, but I cannot view it as controlling authority for this case. . . . I simply cannot believe that the limitation on the class of lawful distributors has significantly impaired the right to use contraceptives in Massachusetts. By relying on Griswold in the present context, the Court has passed beyond the penumbras of the specific guarantees into the uncircumscribed area of personal predilections. . . .

A FINAL NOTE ON "PURPOSE" INQUIRY UNDER THE "NEWER" EQUAL PROTECTION

On its face, Eisenstadt purports to apply traditional rationality standards. Is it a persuasive application of the deferential rationality scrutiny of the old equal protection? Is it a justifiable example of traditional standards "with bite"? On the conformity of Eisenstadt with the "newer" equal protection model, note the comment in Gunther, "Newer Equal Protection," 86 Harv.L. Rev. 1 (1972): "The actual scrutiny exercised in [Eisenstadt seems] more intense than that appropriate under the model of means-focused inquiry or under Justice Brennan's articulated standard. The deviation between articulation and execution of the inquiry probably reflects the considerable pressure to strain for grounds of invalidation which would avoid the Griswold v. Connecticut issue. [Justice Brennan sought to uncover the "actual purpose" of the Massachusetts legislature.] Avoiding the deferential approach and concentrating on actual state purposes is of course an indication of conformity to the model of means-oriented scrutiny. But Justice Brennan's movement in the direction of the model overshot the mark. . . . Justice Brennan's rejection of the antifornication and health purposes carried concentration on actual state objectives much further than the model would suggest. Indeed, it undercuts the model in a fundamental way. A peremptory rejection of proffered state purposes strongly suggests a value-laden appraisal of the legitimacy of ends. The two disbelieved purposes had been offered by the State and explained by the state courts. Intensified rationality scrutiny justifies focus on actual purposes rather than court-conceived ones; it does not justify rejecting several properly offered state objectives in the interest of molding the controversy into an equal protection violation. . . . Justice

Brennan, in his eagerness to sidestep the Griswold issue, produced an opinion in which the actual intensity of scrutiny was at variance with the articulated standard." *   (Recall also the questions at the end of sec. 1 above, about the difficulties of the "purpose"-focused aspect of the "newer" equal protection model.) †

CLEVELAND BOARD OF EDUCATION v. LaFLEUR

414 U.S. 632, 94 S.Ct. 791, 39 L.Ed.2d 52 (1974).

Certiorari to the United States Court of Appeals for the Sixth Circuit.**

Mr. Justice STEWART delivered the opinion of the Court.

The respondents in No. 72–777 and the petitioner in No. 72–1129 are female public school teachers. During the 1970–1971 school year, each informed her local school board that she was pregnant; each was compelled by a mandatory maternity leave rule to quit her job without pay several months before the expected birth of her child. These cases call upon us to decide the constitutionality of the school boards' rules.

I. Jo Carol LaFleur and Ann Elizabeth Nelson, the respondents in No. 72–777, are junior high school teachers employed by the Board of Education of Cleveland, Ohio. Pursuant to a rule first adopted in 1952, the school board requires every pregnant school teacher to take maternity leave without pay, beginning five months before the expected birth of her child. Application for such leave must be made no later than two weeks prior to the date of departure. A teacher on maternity leave is not allowed to return to work until the begnning of the next regular school semester which follows the date when her child attains the age of three months. A doctor's certificate

---

* Note also the later comment in the Gunther article: "The model would call on the Court to be receptive to all purposes, few or many, articulated by the state. It would not, for example, have the Court disbelieve some asserted state purposes and artificially test the means in the context of a single purpose chosen by the Court, in the manner of Eisenstadt v. Baird."

† Note also the comments on Eisenstadt v. Baird in Justice Marshall's dissent in the Rodriguez case, sec. 5 above: "The effect of the interaction of individual interests with established constitutional guarantees upon the degree of care exercised by this Court in reviewing state discrimination affecting such interests is amply illustrated by our decision [in Eisenstadt v. Baird]. [I]n Baird the Court clearly did not adhere to [the standards it purported to apply—the] highly tolerant standards of traditional rational review.

For although there were conceivable state interests intended to be advanced by the statute—e. g., deterrence of premarital sexual activity; regulation of the dissemination of potentially dangerous articles—the Court was not prepared to accept these interests on their face, but instead proceeded to test their substantiality by independent analysis. Such close scrutiny of the State's interests was hardly characteristic of the deference shown state classifications in the context of economic interests. [Yet] I think the Court's action was entirely appropriate, for access to and use of contraceptives bears a close relationship to the individual's constitutional right of privacy."

** Together with No. 72–1129, Cohen v. Chesterfield County School Board, on certiorari to the United States Court of Appeals for the Fourth Circuit. (LaFleur was No. 72–777.)

attesting to the health of the teacher is a prerequisite to return; an additional physical examination may be required. . . .

Neither Mrs. LaFleur nor Mrs. Nelson wished to take an unpaid maternity leave; each wanted to continue teaching until the end of the school year. Because of the mandatory maternity leave rule, however, each was required to leave her job in March 1971. . . .

The petitioner in No. 72–1129, Susan Cohen, was employed by the School Board of Chesterfield County, Virginia. That school board's maternity leave regulation requires that a pregnant teacher leave work at least four months prior to the expected birth of her child. Notice in writing must be given to the school board at least six months prior to the expected birth date. A teacher on maternity leave is declared re-eligible for employment when she submits written notice from a physician that she is physically fit for re-employment, and when she can give assurance that care of the child will cause only minimal interference with her job responsibilities. [Mrs. Cohen] informed the Chesterfield County School Board in November 1970, that she was pregnant and expected the birth of her child about April 28, 1971. The school board [rejected her request] that she be allowed to teach until January 21, 1971, the end of the first school semester. Instead, she was required to leave her teaching job on December 18, 1970. . . .[1]

II.   This Court has long recognized that freedom of personal choice in matters of marriage and family life is one of the liberties protected by the Due Process Clause of the Fourteenth Amendment. [E. g., Roe v. Wade; Skinner v. Oklahoma. See also Eisenstadt v. Baird.] . . .

By acting to penalize the pregnant teacher for deciding to bear a child, overly restrictive maternity leave regulations can constitute a heavy burden on the exercise of these protected freedoms. [Due process] requires that such rules must not needlessly, arbitrarily, or capriciously impinge upon this vital area of a teacher's constitutional liberty. The question before us [is] whether the interests advanced in support of the rules [can] justify the particular procedures they have adopted.

The school boards in these cases have offered two essentially overlapping explanations for their mandatory maternity leave rules. First, they contend that the firm cutoff dates are necessary to maintain continuity of classroom instruction, since advance knowledge of when a pregnant teacher must leave facilitates the finding and hiring of a qualified substitute. Secondly, the school boards seek to justify their maternity rules by arguing that at least

---

1. . . . The practical impact of our decision in the present cases may have been somewhat lessened by several recent developments. At the time that the teachers in these cases were placed on maternity leave, Title VII of the Civil Rights Act of 1964, did not apply to state agencies and educational institutions. On March 24, 1972, however, the Equal Employment Opportunity Act of 1972 amended Title VII to withdraw those exemptions. Shortly thereafter, the Equal Employment Opportunity Commission promulgated guidelines providing that a mandatory leave or termination policy for pregnant women presumptively violates Title VII. While the statutory amendments and the administrative regulations are, of course, inapplicable to the cases now before us, they will affect like suits in the future. In addition, a number of other federal agencies have promulgated regulations similar to those of the Equal Employment Opportunity Commission, forbidding discrimination against pregnant workers with regard to sick leave policies. . . . [Footnote by the Court.]

some teachers become physically incapable of adequately performing certain of their duties during the latter part of pregnancy. . . .[2]

It cannot be denied that continuity of instruction is a significant and legitimate educational goal. [W]hile the advance-notice provisions [are] wholly rational and may well be necessary to serve the objective of continuity of instruction, the absolute requirements of termination at the end of the fourth or fifth month of pregnancy are not. Were continuity the only goal, cutoff dates much later during pregnancy would serve as well as or better than the challenged rules, providing that ample advance notice requirements were retained. Indeed, continuity would seem just as well attained if the teacher herself were allowed to choose the date upon which to commence her leave, at least so long as the decision were required to be made and notice given of it well in advance of the date selected.[3] . . .

We thus conclude that the arbitrary cutoff dates embodied in the mandatory leave rules before us have no rational relationship to the valid state interest of preserving continuity of instruction. [With advance notice], the choice of firm dates later in pregnancy would serve the boards' objectives just as well, while imposing a far lesser burden on the women's exercise of constitutionally protected freedom.

The question remains as to whether the cutoff dates at the beginning of the fifth and sixth months can be justified on the other ground advanced by the school boards—the necessity of keeping physically unfit teachers out of the classroom. There can be no doubt that such an objective is perfectly legitimate, both on educational and safety grounds. And, despite the plethora of conflicting medical testimony in these cases, we can assume, arguendo, that at least some teachers become physically disabled from effectively performing their duties during the latter stages of pregnancy.

The mandatory termination provisions of the Cleveland and Chesterfield County rules surely operate to insulate the classroom from the presence of

2. The records in these cases suggest that the maternity leave regulations may have originally been inspired by other, less weighty, considerations. For example, Dr. Mark C. Schinnerer, who served as Superintendent of Schools in Cleveland at the time the leave rule was adopted, testified in the District Court that the rule had been adopted in part to save pregnant teachers from embarrassment at the hands of giggling schoolchildren; the cutoff date at the end of the fourth month was chosen because this was when the teacher "began to show." Similarly, at least several members of the Chesterfield County School Board thought a mandatory leave rule was justified in order to insulate schoolchildren from the sight of conspicuously pregnant women. One member of the school board thought that it was "not good for the school system" for students to view pregnant teachers, "because some of the kids say, my teacher swallowed a water melon, things like that."

The school boards have not contended in this Court that these considerations can serve as a legitimate basis for a rule requiring pregnant women to leave work; we thus note the comments only to illustrate the possible role of outmoded taboos in the adoption of the rules. Cf. Green v. Waterford Board of Education, 473 F.2d, at 635 ("Whatever may have been the reaction in Queen Victoria's time, pregnancy is no longer a dirty word"). [Footnote by the Court.]

3. It is, of course, possible that either premature childbirth or complications in the later stages of pregnancy might upset even the most careful plans of the teacher, the substitute, and the school board. But there is nothing in these records to indicate that such emergencies could not be handled, as are all others, through the normal use of the emergency substitute teacher process. [Footnote by the Court.]

potentially incapacitated pregnant teachers. But the question is whether the rules sweep too broadly. See Shelton v. Tucker, 364 U.S. 479 [chap. 13, below]. That question must be answered in the affirmative, for the provisions amount to a conclusive presumption that every pregnant teacher who reaches the fifth or sixth month of pregnancy is physically incapable of continuing. There is no individualized determination by the teacher's doctor—or the school board's—as to any particular teacher's ability to continue at her job. The rules contain an irrebuttable presumption of physical incompetency, and that presumption applies even when the medical evidence as to an individual woman's physical status might be wholly to the contrary.

As the Court noted last Term in Vlandis v. Kline [below], "permanent irrebuttable presumptions have long been disfavored under the Due Process Clauses of the Fifth and Fourteenth Amendments." In Vlandis, the Court declared unconstitutional, under the Due Process Clause of the Fourteenth Amendment, a Connecticut statute mandating an irrebuttable presumption of nonresidency for the purposes of qualifying for reduced tuition rates at a state university. We said in that case: "[I]t is forbidden by the Due Process Clause to deny an individual the resident rates on the basis of a permanent and irrebuttable presumption of nonresidence, when that presumption is not necessarily or universally true in fact, and when the State has reasonable alternative means of making the crucial determination."

Similarly, in Stanley v. Illinois [below], the Court held that an Illinois statute containing an irrebuttable presumption that unmarried fathers are incompetent to raise their children violated the Due Process Clause. . . . [T]he Due Process Clause required a more individualized determination. See also United States Dept. of Agriculture v. Murry; Bell v. Burson; Carrington v. Rash. [All below.]

These principles control our decision in the cases before us. While the medical experts in these cases differed on many points, they unanimously agreed on one—the ability of any particular pregnant woman to continue at work past any fixed time in her pregnancy is very much an individual matter. Even assuming, arguendo, that there are some women who would be physically unable to work past the particular cutoff dates embodied in the challenged rules, it is evident that there are large numbers of teachers who are fully capable of continuing work for longer than the Cleveland and Chesterfield County regulations will allow. Thus, the conclusive presumption embodied in these rules, like that in Vlandis, is neither "necessarily [nor] universally true," and is violative of the Due Process Clause.

The school boards have argued that the mandatory termination dates serve the interest of administrative convenience, since there are many instances of teacher pregnancy, and the rules obviate the necessity for case-by-case determinations. Certainly, the boards have an interest in devising prompt and efficient procedures to achieve their legitimate objectives in this area. But, as the Court stated in Stanley v. Illinois: "[T]he Constitution recognizes higher values than speed and efficiency. . . ."

While it might be easier for the school boards to conclusively presume that all pregnant women are unfit to teach past the fourth or fifth month or even the first month, of pregnancy, administrative convenience alone is insufficient to make valid what otherwise is a violation of due process of

law.[4] The Fourteenth Amendment requires the school boards to employ alternative administrative means, which do not so broadly infringe upon basic constitutional liberty, in support of their legitimate goals.[5]

We conclude, therefore, that neither the necessity for continuity of instruction nor the state interest in keeping physically unfit teachers out of the classroom can justify the sweeping mandatory leave regulations that the Cleveland and Chesterfield County School Boards have adopted. While the regulations no doubt represent a good-faith attempt to achieve a laudable goal, they cannot pass muster under the Due Process Clause of the Fourteenth Amendment, because they employ irrebuttable presumptions that unduly penalize a female teacher for deciding to bear a child. . . .[*]

So ordered.

Mr. Justice DOUGLAS concurs in the result.

Mr. Justice POWELL, concurring in the result.

I concur in the Court's result, but I am unable to join its opinion. In my view these cases should not be decided on the ground that the mandatory maternity leave regulations impair any right to bear children or create an "irrebuttable presumption." It seems to me that equal protection analysis is the appropriate frame of reference.

These regulations undoubtedly add to the burdens of childbearing. But certainly not every government policy that burdens childbearing violates the Constitution. [See Dandridge v. Williams.] . . .

I am also troubled by the Court's return to the "irrebuttable presumption" line of analysis of [Stanley and Vlandis]. Although I joined the opinion of the Court in Vlandis and continue fully to support the result

4. This is not to say that the only means for providing appropriate protection for the rights of pregnant teachers is an individualized determination in each case and in every circumstance. We are not dealing in these cases with maternity leave regulations requiring a termination of employment at some firm date during the last few weeks of pregnancy. We therefore have no occasion to decide whether such regulations might be justified by considerations not presented in these records—for example, widespead medical consensus about the "disabling" effect of pregnancy on a teacher's job performance during these latter days, or evidence showing that such firm cutoffs were the only reasonable method of avoiding the possibility of labor beginning while some teacher was in the classroom, or proof that adequate substitutes could not be procured without at least some minimal lead time and certainty as to the dates upon which their employment was to begin. [Footnote by the Court.]

5. The school boards have available to them reasonable alternative methods of keeping physically unfit teachers out of the classroom. For example, they could require the pregnant teacher to submit to medical examination by a school board physician, or simply require each teacher to submit a current certification from her obstetrician as to her ability to continue work. Indeed, when evaluating the physical ability of a teacher to *return* to work, each school board in this case relies upon precisely such procedures. [Footnote by the Court.]

* The majority also invalidated Cleveland's three-month return-to-work rule. Justice Stewart stated that to the extent this provision "reflects the school board's thinking that no mother is fit to return until that point in time, it suffers from the same constitutional deficiencies that plague the irrebuttable presumption in the termination rules," since "the factual hypothesis of such a presumption [is] neither necessarily nor universally true." (The other return-to-work provisions were found valid.)

reached there, the present cases have caused me to re-examine the "irrebuttable presumption" rationale. This has led me to the conclusion that the Court should approach that doctrine with extreme care. There is much to what Mr. Justice Rehnquist says in his dissenting opinion about the implications of the doctrine for the traditional legislative power to operate by classification. As a matter of logic, it is difficult to see the terminus of the road upon which the Court has embarked under the banner of "irrebuttable presumptions." If the Court nevertheless uses "irrebuttable presumption" reasoning selectively, the concept at root often will be something else masquerading as a due process doctrine. That something else, of course, is the Equal Protection Clause.

These cases present precisely the kind of problem susceptible to treatment by classification. Most school teachers are women, a certain percentage of them are pregnant at any given time, and pregnancy is a normal biological function possessing, in the great majority of cases, a fairly well defined term. The constitutional difficulty is not that the boards attempted to deal with this problem by classification. Rather, it is that the boards chose irrational classifications. . . .

To be sure, the boards have a legitimate and important interest in fostering continuity of teaching. And, even a normal pregnancy may at some point jeopardize that interest. But the classifications chosen by these boards, so far as we have been shown, are either counterproductive or irrationally overinclusive even with regard to this significant, nonillusory goal. Accordingly, in my opinion these regulations are invalid under rational-basis standards of equal protection review.[1] . . .

. . . I believe the linkage between the boards' legitimate ends and their chosen means is too attenuated to support those portions of the regulations overturned by the Court. Thus, I concur in the Court's result. But I think it important to emphasize the degree of latitude the Court, as I read it, has left the boards for dealing with the real and recurrent problems presented by teacher pregnancies. [E.g.], they may require all pregnant teachers to cease teaching "at some firm date during the last few weeks of pregnancy."[2] . . .

1. I do not reach the question whether sex-based classifications invoke strict judicial scrutiny, e. g., Frontiero v. Richardson (sec. 3C), or whether these regulations involve sex classifications at all. Whether the challenged aspects of the regulations constitute sex classifications or disability classifications, they must at least rationally serve some legitimate articulated or obvious state interest. While there are indeed some legitimate state interests at stake here, it has not been shown that they are rationally furthered by the challenged portions of these regulations. [Footnote by Justice Powell.]

2. The Court's language does not specify a particular prebirth cutoff point, and we need not decide that issue, as these boards have attempted to support only four- and five-month dates. In light of the Court's language, however, I would think that a four-week prebirth period would be acceptable. I do not agree with the Court's view of the stringent standards a board must meet to justify a reasonable prebirth cutoff date. Nothing in the Constitution mandates the heavy burden of justification the Court has imposed on the boards in this regard. If school boards must base their policies on a "widespread medical consensus . . .," the "only reasonable method . . ." for accomplishing a goal, or a demonstration that needed services will otherwise be impossible to obtain, they may be seriously handicapped in the performance of their duties. [Footnote by Justice Powell.]

In my opinion, such class-wide rules for pregnant teachers are constitutional under traditional equal protection standards. School boards, confronted with sensitive and widely variable problems of public education, must be accorded latitude in the operation of school systems and in the adoption of rules and regulations of general application. [Rodriguez.] My concern with the Court's opinion is that, if carried to logical extremes, the emphasis on individualized treatment is at war with [the] need for discretion. Indeed, stringent insistence on individualized treatment may be quite impractical in a large school district with thousands of teachers. But despite my reservations as to the rationale of the majority, I nevertheless conclude that in these cases the gap between the legitimate interests of the boards and the particular means chosen to attain them is too wide. . . .

Mr. Justice REHNQUIST, with whom the Chief Justice [BURGER] joins, dissenting.

The Court rests its invalidation of the school regulations involved in these cases on the Due Process Clause of the Fourteenth Amendment, rather than on any claim of sexual discrimination under the Equal Protection Clause of that Amendment. My Brother Stewart thereby enlists the Court in another quixotic engagement in his apparently unending war on irrebuttable presumptions. In these cases we are told that although a regulation "requiring a termination of employment at some firm date during the last few weeks of pregnancy" might pass muster, the regulations here challenged requiring termination at the end of the fourth or fifth month of pregnancy violate due process of law.

As the Chief Justice pointed out in his dissent last year in [Vlandis], "literally thousands of state statutes create classifications permanent in duration, which are less than perfect, as all legislative classifications are, and might be improved on by individualized determinations . . . ." Hundreds of years ago in England, before Parliament came to be thought of as a body having general lawmaking power, controversies were determined on an individualized basis without benefit of any general law. Most students of government consider the shift from this sort of determination, made on an ad hoc basis by the king's representative, to a relatively uniform body of rules enacted by a body exercising legislative authority, to have been a significant step forward in the achievement of a civilized political society. It seems to me a little late in the day for this Court to weigh in against such an established consensus.

Countless state and federal statutes draw lines such as those drawn by the regulations here which, under the Court's analysis, might well prove to be arbitrary in individual cases. The District of Columbia Code, for example, draws lines with respect to age for several purposes. The Code requires that a person to be eligible to vote be 18 years of age, that a male be 18 and a female be 16 before a valid marriage may be contracted,* that alcoholic beverages not be sold to a person under age 21 years, or beer or light wines to any person under the age of 18 years. A resident of the District of Columbia must be 16 years of age to obtain a permit to operate a motor vehicle, and the District of Columbia delegate to the United States

---

* Cf. Stanton v. Stanton, 421 U.S. —— (1975) (sec. 3C above).

Congress must be 25 years old. Nothing in the Court's opinion clearly demonstrates why its logic would not equally well sustain a challenge to these laws from a 17-year-old who insists that he is just as well informed for voting purposes as an 18-year-old, from a 20-year-old who insists that he is just as able to carry his liquor as a 21-year-old, or from the numerous other persons who fall on the outside of lines drawn by these and similar statutes.

More closely in point is the jeopardy in which the Court's opinion places longstanding statutes providing for mandatory retirement of government employees. 5 U.S.C. § 8335 provides with respect to Civil Service employees: "(a) Except as otherwise provided by this section, an employee who becomes 70 years of age and completes 15 years of service shall be automatically separated from the service. . . ." Since [the] right to pursue an occupation is presumably on the same lofty footing as the right of choice in matters of family life [cf. Roe v. Wade], the Court will have to strain valiantly in order to avoid having today's opinion lead to the invalidation of mandatory retirement statutes for governmental employees. In that event federal, state, and local governmental bodies will be remitted to the task, thankless both for them and for the employees involved, of individual determinations of physical impairment and senility.

It has been said before, Williamson v. Lee Optical Co., but it bears repeating here: All legislation involves the drawing of lines, and the drawing of lines necessarily results in particular individuals who are disadvantaged by the line drawn being virtually indistinguishable for many purposes from those individuals who benefit from the legislative classification. The Court's disenchantment with "irrebuttable presumptions," and its preference for "individualized determination," is in the last analysis nothing less than an attack upon the very notion of lawmaking itself.

The lines drawn by the school boards in the city of Cleveland and Chesterfield County in these cases require pregnant teachers to take forced leave at a stage of their pregnancy when medical evidence seems to suggest that a majority of them might well be able to continue teaching without any significant possibility of physical impairment. But, so far as I am aware, the medical evidence also suggests that in some cases there may be physical impairment at the stage of pregnancy fastened on by the regulations in question, and that the probability of physical impairment increases as the pregnancy advances. If legislative bodies are to be permitted to draw a general line anywhere short of the delivery room, I can find no judicial standard of measurement which says the ones drawn here were invalid. I therefore dissent.

"IRREBUTTABLE PRESUMPTIONS"—A VIABLE ALTERNATIVE TO EQUAL PROTECTION ANALYSIS?

1. *Other examples of resort to the "irrebuttable presumptions" technique.* a. *The tax cases of the 1920's and 1930's.* Though the modern Court's "irrebuttable presumptions" cases rarely mention ancient antecedents, the technique flourished briefly in the 1920's and 1930's. At that time, it encountered the dissents of Justices such as Brandeis, Stone, and Holmes;

and, prior to its modern revival, the technique had been thought to be discredited and moribund. The leading example of the earlier era of "irrebuttable presumptions" popularity is HEINER v. DONNAN, 285 U.S. 312 (1932), invalidating a provision of the Internal Revenue Act of 1926 stating that a gift made within two years prior to the donor's death was to be "deemed and held to have been made in contemplation of death" and included in the donor's estate. Justice Sutherland's majority opinion stated that, whether viewed "as a rule of evidence or of substantive law," the provisions "constitutes an attempt, by legislative fiat, to enact into existence a fact which here does not, and cannot be made to, exist in actuality." He added that a law "creating a presumption which operates to deny a fair opportunity to rebut it violates the due process clause." [1]

b. *Modern antecedents.* The majority opinion in LaFleur cites as support two modern cases decided by the Court before the formal reemergence of "irrebuttable presumptions" analysis. Carrington v. Rash, 380 U.S. 89 (1965) (sec. 4A above), was an opinion by Justice Stewart stating that the Texas ban on voting by certain service personnel was unconstitutional: by "forbidding a soldier ever to controvert the presumption of nonresidence, the Texas Constitution imposes an invidious discrimination in violation of the Fourteenth Amendment." Though the Carrington decision rested ultimately on equal protection, Justice Stewart did cite Heiner v. Donnan. The other early case cited in LaFleur, BELL v. BURSON, 402 U.S. 535 (1971), was more clearly an antecedent of the modern "irrebuttable presumption" cases, though it did not articulate that approach. Bell invalidated a Georgia law which required that the driver's license of an uninsured motorist involved in an accident be suspended unless security was posted to cover the amount of damages claimed by aggrieved parties. The administrative hearing conducted prior to the suspension excluded consideration of the motorist's fault. Justice Brennan's opinion held that the denial of a hearing on that issue prior to license suspension violated procedural due process. As the Court later explained the case (see the Vlandis case, below), the decision ultimately rested on the ground "that since the State purported to be concerned with fault in suspending a driver's license, it could not, consistent with procedural due process, conclusively presume fault from the fact than an uninsured motorist was involved in an accident, and could not, therefore, suspend his driver's license without a hearing on that crucial factor." [2]

---

1. In Heiner, Justices Stone and Brandeis dissented; Justice Holmes had retired from the Court. Justice Holmes was among the dissenters, however, in two other cases of that period invalidating tax provisions on similar grounds. Hoeper v. Tax Commission, 284 U.S. 206 (1931); Schlesinger v. Wisconsin, 270 U.S. 230 (1926). For a modern variation on the approach of those cases, purporting to be inspired by Burger Court decisions, see In re Estate of Cavill, 329 A.2d 503 (Pa.1974), a Pennsylvania decision invalidating a "Mortmain statute" generally invalidating bequests to religious and charitable organizations made within 30 days of the testator's death. The trial court had invalidated the law on both equal protection and "irrebuttable presumptions"-procedural due process grounds. The majority of the Pennsylvania Supreme Court rested entirely on equal protection grounds, finding the provision irrationally overinclusive as well as underinclusive.

2. Another antecedent of the "irrebuttable presumptions" approach, Stanley v. Illinois, 405 U.S. 645 (1972), is noted in the LaFleur opinion.

c. *The Vlandis case.* The "irrebuttable presumptions" analysis surfaced in its full-blown modern form a year before LaFleur, in VLANDIS v. KLINE, 412 U.S. 441 (1973). Vlandis arose in the controversial equal protection context of durational residence requirements allegedly impinging on the right to interstate mobility. (Recall sec. 4C above). More immediately, the problem involved tuition preferences for in-state students at a state university. Though, as noted in sec. 4C, the Court had earlier held that those tuition preferences did not "penalize" the right to travel—and reiterated that holding in Vlandis—the method of implementing the preference was struck down on "irrebuttable presumption" grounds.

Under the Connecticut scheme invalidated in Vlandis, students were "non-residents" for tuition purposes for the entire period of the student's attendence at the state university if, "at the time of application for admission, the student if married, was living outside of Connecticut, or, if single, had lived outside the State at some point during the preceding year." Justice Stewart's majority opinion stated: "[S]ince Connecticut purports to be concerned with residency in allocating the rates for tuition, [it] is forbidden by the Due Process Clause to deny an individual the resident rates on the basis of a permanent and irrebuttable presumption of non-residence, when the presumption is not *necessarily or universally true in fact,* and when the State has reasonable alternative means of making the crucial determination. Rather, standards of due process require that the State allow such an individual to present evidence showing that he is a bona fide resident entitled to the in-state rates." (Emphasis added.) The italicized passage represents the strongest and most extreme statement of the requirements of the "irrebuttable presumptions" doctrine. (Note that it is quoted in LaFleur.)

Did Connecticut truly enact a "conclusive and unchangeable presumption," as Justice Stewart claimed? Or was it simply a "classification" which, even under strict scrutiny equal protection standards, need not constitute an absolutely perfect "fit"? Could any legislative classification—any legislative effort to generalize—satisfy a "necessarily or universally true in fact" standard?

Justice White concurred in the judgment on a different ground: he found an equal protection violation in the different treatment of "at least three classes of bona fide Connecticut residents." A dissent by Justice Rehnquist, joined by Chief Justice Burger and Justice Douglas, objected to the majority's "highly abstract and theoretical analysis" and found in it a heavy reliance on "notions of substantive due process." He found ample justification for distinguishing between residents and nonresidents and, citing the Lee Optical case, commented that "the fact that a generally valid rule may have rough edges around its perimeter does not make it unconstitutional under the Due Process Clause." In another dissent, Chief Justice Burger, joined by Justice Rehnquist, charged the majority with transferring the strict scrutiny of the new equal protection into the due process sphere and added: "The doctrinal difficulties of the Equal Protection Clause are indeed trying, but today the Court makes an uncharted drift towards complications for the Due Process Clause comparable in scope and seriousness with those we are encountering in the equal protection area. Can this be what we are headed for?"

d. *Dept. of Agriculture v. Murry.* A few months after Vlandis, "irrebuttable presumption" principles once again provided the basis for the invalidation of a statutory scheme. DEPT. OF AGRICULTURE v. MURRY, 413 U.S. 508 (1973), struck down a 1971 amendment to the federal Food Stamp Act. The challenged amendment was one of several prompted by concern about non-needy households participating in the program.[3] Under the challenged provision, "any household which includes a member who has reached his eighteenth birthday and who is claimed as a dependent child for Federal income tax purposes by a taxpayer who is not a member of an eligible household, shall be ineligible to participate in any food stamp program [during] the tax period such dependency is claimed and for a period of one year after expiration of such tax period." In short, such a "tax dependent" in a household made the entire household ineligible for food stamps. Justice Douglas' majority opinion found an inadequate relationship between that provision and the statutory purpose of preventing abuses of the Food Stamp Program by children of well-to-do parents. He concluded "that the deduction taken for the benefit of the parent in the prior year is not a rational measure of the need of a different household with which the child of the tax-deducting parent lives and rests on an irrebuttable presumption often contrary to fact. It therefore lacks critical ingredients of due process found wanting in [Vlandis, Stanley v. Illinois, and Bell v. Burson]." Similarly, Justice Stewart's concurrence criticized Congress for relying on a "conclusive presumption" rather than "individualized determination" and noted that "Congress has alternative means available to it by which its purpose can be achieved."[4]

Justice Rehnquist's dissent, joined by Chief Justice Burger and Justice Powell, stated that the classification was plainly rational under traditional equal protection principles and insisted that the cases relied on by the Court were not in point: "There is a qualitative difference between, on the one hand, holding unconstitutional on procedural due process grounds presumptions which conclude factual inquiries without a hearing on such questions as fault [Bell v. Burson], the fitness of an unwed father to be a parent [Stanley v. Illinois], [or] residency [Vlandis v. Kline], and on the other hand, holding unconstitutional a duly enacted prophylactic limitation on the dispensation of funds which is designed to cure systematic abuses."[5]

e. *Rejections of the "irrebuttable presumptions" approach.* Despite that substantial group of recent cases relying on the new approach, "irrebuttable presumptions" analysis has not been invoked consistently. Thus, a number of the modern equal protection cases considered earlier could have been phrased in "irrebuttable presumptions" terms, but were not. And in several other cases, "irrebuttable presumptions" challenges were explicitly re-

---

3. Recall that another amendment was struck down on traditional equal protection grounds, in Dept. of Agriculture v. Moreno, 413 U.S. 528 (1973) (sec. 5 above).

4. Justice Marshall also submitted a concurrence, summarized in note 2 below.

5. Recall also Justice Rehnquist's dissent in Jimenez v. Weinberger, 417 U. S. 628 (1974) (sec. 5 above). Though Chief Justice Burger's majority opinion there ultimately relied on equal protection, Justice Rehnquist found in it "strong due process overtones as well, at times appearing to pay homage to the still novel, and I think unsupportable, theory that 'irrebuttable presumptions' violate due process."

jected. For example, MOURNING v. FAMILY PUBLICATIONS SERV-ICE, 411 U.S. 356 (1973), unanimously rejected an attack on an "imprecise" classification in the disclosure requirements regarding credit transactions in the Truth in Lending Act. The Act requires disclosures by those extending consumer credit and imposing a finance charge. A regulation requires disclosure when credit is extended and either a finance charge is imposed or the loan is payable in more than four installments. A magazine subscription service which imposed no finance charge but permitted payments in more than four installments claimed that the regulation created an "irrebuttable presumption" that credit payments involving more than four installments include a finance charge. Chief Justice Burger emphasized that the regulation was designed to prevent evasion by concealing finance charges in installment payments and concluded: "The rule was intended as a prophylactic measure; it does not presume that all creditors who are within its ambit assess finance charges, but, rather, imposes a disclosure requirement on all members of a defined class in order to discourage evasion by a substantial portion of that class." [6]

2. *The justifiability of the "irrebuttable presumptions" analysis.* a. *Some questions.* The opinions relying on the "irrebuttable presumptions" analysis claim that it is something different than equal protection analysis—indeed, the newly popular technique has frequently been relied on to avoid reaching an equal protection claim. But is there a genuine difference? Note that in the cases relying on "irrebuttable presumptions" grounds, the law scrutinized actually spoke in substantive regulatory terms, and the Court recast it in "presumption" terms. Does that not suggest that most substantive classifications can be recast as irrebuttable presumptions, and vice versa? When the Court finds an unconstitutional "irrebuttable presumption" in these cases, is it not essentially finding an overbroad classification? And is it not applying extraordinarily strict standards to classification requirements? Under equal protection standards—even under most examples of the new equal protection—an absolutely perfect fit between classification and purpose is not demanded. But is that not just what *is* demanded by a statement such as the Vlandis complaint that the "presumption" there was "not necessarily or universally true in fact"? In short, is "irrebuttable presumptions" analysis the equivalent of an extraordinarily strict variety of "means" scrutiny? In the equal protection cases, strict scrutiny is evoked only when "fundamental interests" or "suspect classifications" are involved. Has the Court adequately explained what triggers the "irrebuttable presumptions" variety of strict scrutiny? Do LaFleur and the cases in note 1 involve the typical ingredients triggering strict scrutiny? Does "irrebuttable presumptions" analysis afford the Court a technique for applying strict scrutiny on

---

6. See also Marshall v. United States, 414 U.S. 417 (1974) (sec. 4B above), sustaining provisions of the Narcotic Addict Rehabilitation Act of 1966 excluding from rehabilitative commitments, in lieu of penal incarceration, addicts with two or more prior felony convictions. Chief Justice Burger's majority opinion emphasized a traditional, deferential equal protection approach. Justice Marshall's dissent, joined by Justices Douglas and Brennan, thought the "two felony exclusion, to the extent it is justified by reference to [the rehabilitative] policy, amounts to a conclusive and irrebuttable presumption that a person with two or more felony convictions is not likely to be rehabilitated through treatment."

an ad hoc basis, without feeling the usual obligation to explain why strict scrutiny is appropriate?

b. *Justice Marshall's explanation.* Compare Justice Marshall's effort to explain his support of the Murry decision, note 1d above. In a concurring opinion there, he introduced elements of his "sliding scale" equal protection analysis in determining whether due process permitted Congress to proceed by general rule or required individualized hearings. He stated that "we must decide whether, considering the private interest affected and the governmental interest sought to be advanced, a hearing must be provided to one who claims that the application of some general provision of the law aimed at certain abuses will not in fact lower the incidence of those abuses but will instead needlessly harm him. In short, where the private interests affected are every important and the governmental interest can be promoted without much difficulty by a well-designed hearing procedure, the Due Process Clause requires the Government to act on an individualized basis, with general propositions serving only as rebuttable presumptions or other burden-shifting devices. That, I think, is the import of Stanley v. Illinois." In Murry, the food stamp case, he emphasized that the impact of the general rule on needy persons was great, and that there were "readily available alternatives that might prevent abuse of the program." (To what extent is it generally true of legislative classifications that the same governmental interest "can be promoted without much difficulty" through individualized hearings?) Justice Marshall conceded in Murry: "This analysis of course combines elements traditionally invoked in what are usually treated as distinct classes of cases, involving due process and equal protection. But the elements of fairness should not be so rigidly cabined." [7]

c. *Some comments.* The recent resorts to "irrebuttable presumptions" analysis have evoked puzzlement and criticism, on the Court and off.[8] For example, Note, "The Irrebuttable Presumption Doctrine in the Supreme Court," 87 Harv.L.Rev. 1534 (1974), finds "no justification" for the approach. It concludes: "The Court's analysis manifests a misunderstanding of the nature of such presumptions. It has treated them as evidentiary rules involved in the process of fact-finding, failing to recognize that irrebuttable presumptions are nothing more than statutory classifications." The "exacting standard of precision" imposed on classifications by this approach "reflects a fundamental confusion between legislative prescription and adjudica-

---

7. Justice Marshall added: "Sometimes fairness will require a hearing to determine whether a statutory classification would advance the legislature's purposes in a particular case so that the classification can properly be used only as a burden-shifting device, while at other times the fact that a litigant falls within the classification will be enough to justify its application. There is no reason, I believe, to categorize inflexibly the rudiments of fairness."

Note one significant difference between resort to the "irrebuttable presumptions" and the equal protection modes of analysis. Typically, when a classification is struck down as overbroad, the statute falls. Under the "irrebuttable presumptions" analysis, individualized hearings are required. But the Court has not prohibited all generalizations in its "irrebuttable presumptions" cases. See, e. g., footnote 4 to Justice Stewart's opinion in LaFleur, above.

8. My colleague William Cohen has called the new technique the "New Old Equally Protective Substantively Procedural Due Process."

tory application of statutory classification." [9]   The Note calls the doctrine a "strange hybrid"—"if not simply a confusion"—of equal protection and due process scrutiny.

See also Note, "Irrebuttable Presumptions: An Illusory Analysis," 27 Stan.L.Rev. 449 (1975), viewing the doctrine as "fundamentally misconceived," seeing the irrebuttable presumption technique as "logically equivalent to an equal protection argument," and finding it a "standardless, illusory" approach.   For a rare comment viewing the technique with approval, see Tribe, "From Environmental Foundations to Constitutional Structures: Learning from Nature's Future," 84 Yale L.J. 545 (1975).   Professor Tribe sees such "little-understood cases" as LaFleur and Stanley as involving substantive rules resting on attitudes which were once broadly held but which "no longer command general assent."   Court invalidations demanding more individualized determinations serve a useful purpose in that view: they unfreeze the status quo and contribute to "an evolving moral consensus": "perhaps only personalized justice can be acceptable in settling disputes about broadly agreed-upon rights when such disputes arise in settings of widely perceived moral flux."   Professor Tribe notes that "the agencies affected by the Court's decisions had been in a position to prevent the emergence of an alternative consensus if not to prevent the erosion of the old agreement." [10]

d.   *Statutory presumptions in criminal statutes.*   The "irrebuttable presumptions" cases purport to draw on well-established "procedural due process" lines of cases.   In Vlandis, for example, the Court referred to such statutory presumption cases as Tot v. United States, 319 U.S. 463 (1943), and Leary v. United States, 395 U.S. 6 (1969).   Leary, for example, held unconstitutional a provision deeming possession of marijuana to be sufficient evidence to show the defendant knew of its illegal importation, unless "the defendant explains his possession to the satisfaction of a jury." Justice Harlan's opinion finding this an unconstitutional presumption stated the governing principle as follows: "[A] criminal statutory presumption must be regarded as 'irrational' or 'arbitrary' and hence unconstitutional, unless it can at least be said with substantial assurance that the presumed fact is more likely than not to flow from the proved fact on which it is made to depend."   But the Tot-Leary principle as to presumptions in criminal statutes is usually thought to be justified by the special concern for fair criminal processes and by the constitutional requirement of proof beyond a reasonable doubt in criminal cases.   Those considerations of course do not apply to the modern "irrebuttable presumptions" cases noted above.

9.   The Note finds Justice Marshall's explanation in Murry, above, "somewhat more coherent," although reducing the doctrine to a veiled "adoption of a rigorous equal protection scrutiny."   Although Justice Marshall's approach "does not rest upon a misunderstanding of the nature of legislative classifications, it too fails to provide an adequate justification for this ill-founded doctrine."

10.   Professor Tribe develops this "moral flux" justification—the argument justifying intervention to facilitate "the emergence of an alternative consensus" where the setting is one of "widely perceived moral flux"—in two more elaborate articles, "Childhood, Suspect Classifications, and Conclusive Presumptions: Three Linked Riddles," [forthcoming, 39 Law & Contemp.Prob. (1975)], and "Structural Due Process," 10 Harv.Civ.Rights-Civ. Lib.L.Rev. 269 (1975).

More generally, the Court's references to "procedural due process" in these "irrebuttable presumptions" cases have sought to invoke echoes of an established line of due process cases requiring individualized hearings in certain contexts. Those hearings cases, too, seem quite distinguishable from the modern "irrebuttable presumptions" analysis, despite the superficial similarity in remedies. Because of the apparent similarity, the "right to hearing"-procedural due process cases of recent years are briefly reviewed in the next note.

3. *The well-established "right to hearing"-procedural due process cases.* Since the impact of "irrebuttable presumptions" invalidation is to require government to proceed via individualized hearings, they bear a superficial resemblance to a well-established line of procedural due process-right to hearing cases. Consider briefly that latter line of cases, and note the analytical distinctions between the issues there and the problems in such cases as LaFleur. In the established procedural due process cases the challenge is not to the legislator's or rulemaker's general classification, but to the application of the general rule to a particular individual. That line of cases has applied fair hearing requirements to the process of determining whether an individual falls within the class delineated by the general rule. If application of the general rule deprives an individual of interest in "liberty" or "property," the individual must be afforded an appropriate hearing. GOLDBERG v. KELLY, 397 U.S. 254 (1970), is the first important modern case of that variety. Goldberg stated that welfare benefits were an "entitlement"; and, in order to safeguard against eligible recipients being denied benefits, the Court held that due process required a pre-termination hearing to afford the claimants an opportunity to show that they fell within the class entitled to the welfare benefits. Justice Brennan's majority opinion in Goldberg found the governmental interest in "conserving fiscal and administrative resources" not "overriding in the welfare context" so as to justify denials of pre-termination hearings.[11]

Decisions since Goldberg v. Kelly have required hearings in a wide variety of administrative process and civil litigation contexts. The pervasive issues have been when—at what stage in a proceeding—a hearing is required, and what type of hearing is mandated. Though Goldberg v. Kelly was at first read by some as placing special emphasis on the importance of welfare benefits as "necessities" (recall sec. 5 above),[12] the Court soon applied its hearing requirements to a wide range of "property" and "liberty" entitlements. What constitutes a protected "property" interest has given the

---

11. Justice Black's dissent objected to the majority's "balancing act": weighing "the recipient's interest in avoiding" the termination of welfare benefits against "the governmental interest in summary adjudication." Recall Justice Black's dissents from the due process balancing approach in the other well-established area of procedural due process guarantees—the guarantees of "fundamental fairness" in the criminal procedure context. Recall, e. g., his dissent in Adamson v. California, with the criminal procedure-procedural due process devel-opments traced in chap. 8, sec. 2, above.

12. Justice Brennan in Goldberg stated, for example, that public welfare assistance "is not mere charity, but a means to 'promote the general Welfare, and secure the Blessings of Liberty to ourselves and our Posterity.'" He noted, too, "that termination of aid pending resolution of a controversy over eligibility may deprive an *eligible* recipient of the very means by which to live while he waits."

Court considerable difficulty. Note the discussion in Justice Stewart's majority opinion in BOARD OF REGENTS v. ROTH, 408 U.S. 564 (1972), recalling that the Court has "rejected the wooden distinction between 'rights' and 'privileges' that once seemed to govern the applicability of procedural due process rights. The Court has also made clear that the property interests protected by procedural due process extend well beyond actual ownership of real estate, chattels, or money." Yet "property" is not an unlimited concept: "To have a property interest in a benefit, a person clearly must have more than an abstract need or desire for it. He must have more than a unilateral expectation of it. He must, instead, have a legitimate claim of entitlement to it. . . . Property interests, of course, are not created by the Constitution. Rather, they are created and their dimensions are defined by existing rules or understandings that stem from an independent source such as state law— rules or understandings that secure certain benefits and that support claims of entitlement to those benefits." [13]

The difficulties of applying that approach are illustrated by Roth and its companion case, PERRY v. SINDERMANN, 408 U.S. 593 (1972). Both cases involved state college teachers whose appointments had not been renewed and who had not received a hearing. In Roth, where a non-tenured teacher was not rehired for a second year, the one year appointment "secured absolutely no interest in re-employment for the next year." In Sindermann, by contrast, there was a "property interest" giving rise to a procedural due process hearing claim, even though there the appointment carried no formal tenure guarantee either. But Sindermann had been employed in the state college system for ten years and alleged that the college had a de facto tenure program. Accordingly, he was entitled on remand to "an opportunity to prove the legitimacy of his claim of such entitlement in light of 'the policies and practices of the institution.' "

The need for or scope of procedural due process hearings were central issues in a number of modern cases in other areas as well. Note, for example, the holdings that at least informal hearings are required in parole

---

13. To what extent may the statutory background of "understandings" that are looked to as to the existence of a "property interest" themselves include binding provisions barring a hearing? Note the approach of Justice Rehnquist in Arnett v. Kennedy, 416 U.S. 134 (1974), a decision rejecting a non-probationary civil service employee's claim to a full trial-type hearing prior to dismissal. The governing federal statute prescribed not only the grounds for removal but also set forth removal procedures. In Justice Rehnquist's view, those procedural provisions were dispositive of the procedural due process claim. Though the law created a constitutionally protected property interest—an expectancy of employment—"where the grant of a substantive right is inextricably intertwined with the limitations on the procedures which are to be employed in determining that right, a litigant [must] take the bitter with the sweet. . . . Here the property interest which appellee had in his employment was itself conditioned by the procedural limitations which had accompanied the grant of that interest." Justice Rehnquist's approach was not, however, that of the majority. His opinion was joined only by Chief Justice Burger and Justice Stewart. Though a majority rejected the procedural due process claim, the remaining Justices dissociated themselves from Justice Rehnquist's approach. For example, Justice Powell's concurrence found that approach incompatible with Roth and Sindermann and stated: "While the legislature may elect not to confer a property interest in federal employment, it may not constitutionally authorize a deprivation of such an interest, once conferred, without appropriate procedural safeguards."

revocation proceedings, Morrissey v. Brewer, 408 U.S. 471 (1972), in probation revocation proceedings, Gagnon v. Scarpelli, 411 U.S. 778 (1973), and in in-prison disciplinary proceedings which might result in the imposition of serious punishment, Wolff v. McDonnell, 418 U.S. 539 (1974). Note also the concern for aspects of students' "liberty" that prompted the decision in Goss v. Lopez, 419 U.S. 565 (1975), requiring informal hearings before high school students may be suspended. Procedural due process principles have also been central in a long and wavering line of cases challenging summary prejudgment remedies in civil litigation. See, e. g., Sniadach v. Family Finance Corp., 395 U.S. 337 (1969) (garnishment); Fuentes v. Shevin, 407 U.S. 67 (1972) (repossession remedies), Mitchell v. W.T. Grant Co., 416 U.S. 600 (1974) (another summary repossession action under an installment sales contract); and North Georgia Finishing, Inc. v. Di-Chem, Inc., 419 U.S. 601 (1975) (garnishment).

Chapter 11

THE POST–CIVIL WAR AMENDMENTS AND CIVIL RIGHTS LEGISLATION: CONSTITUTIONAL RESTRAINTS ON PRIVATE CONDUCT; CONGRESSIONAL POWER TO IMPLEMENT THE AMENDMENTS

AN INTRODUCTORY OVERVIEW

In the preceding chapters on due process and equal protection, the actions challenged as violating the constitutional restraints have clearly been actions by an arm of *state government;* and the virtually exclusive focus has been on the role of the *Court* in elaborating constitutional guarantees. This chapter broadens the focus to add two significant dimensions. First, the concern here extends beyond the applicability of constitutional guarantees to *state* action to the restraints effective against seemingly *private* conduct. Second, concern here is with the role of *Congress,* not merely the Court, in enforcing and elaborating the provisions of the post-Civil War Amendments.

    1.   *"State action" limits and private actors.*   The first new theme—the applicability of constitutional guarantees to seemingly private conduct—reflects the fact that the 14th and 15th Amendments, like most limits of the Constitution, are addressed to government, not to private behavior. For example, the prohibitions of § 1 of the 14th Amendment begin with "No State shall . . . ." From the beginning, the Court's interpretations of that Amendment have emphasized "the essential dichotomy set forth in that Amendment between deprivation by the State, subject to scrutiny under its provisions, and private conduct, 'however discriminatory and wrongful,' against which the Fourteenth Amendment offers no shield." [1] But the much repeated state-private distinction is deceptively simple in statement. As government involvement in the private sector has become more pervasive, traditional notions as to what activity constitutes "state" action subject to the 14th and 15th Amendments have become blurred. How far do the constitutional guarantees reach? Under what circumstances is arguably private behavior subject to restraints such as those in the 14th Amendment? When may a challenger relying on the 14th Amendment insist that a seemingly "private" actor be governed by constitutional limitations—or at least insist that government withdraw from its involvement with private conduct? The materials in sec. 2 below elaborate a theme the Court acknowledged (and probably understated) in a recent case: "While the principle that private action is immune from the restrictions of the Fourteenth Amendment is well-established and easily stated, the question whether particular conduct is 'private,' on the one hand, or 'state action,' on the other, frequently admits of no easy answer."

---

1.   The recent reiterations of the state action-private action distinction quoted in this paragraph are from Jack-   son v. Metropolitan Edison Co., 419 U.S. 345 (1974), considered in sec. 2B below.

2. *Congress and the Amendments.* The second theme—the role of Congress—reflects the fact that each of the three post-Civil War amendments grants the national legislature authority to protect civil rights: the final sections of the 13th, 14th, and 15th Amendments give "power to enforce" each amendment :"by appropriate legislation." These are of course not the only sources of congressional power to enact civil rights laws: the commerce power as well as other grants in the 1787 document have been invoked on behalf of civil rights. (Recall, e. g., chap. 3 above.) But the post-Civil War additions, unlike the original grants, were born of a special concern with racial discrimination; and the civil rights powers they confer are potentially the most far-reaching.

3. *Court-Congress interactions.* The second theme, then, focuses on Congress; the development of the first—the reach of the constitutional guarantees to private action—has been largely in the Court's keeping. The two themes are combined in this chapter because they historically have been intertwined and, especially, because the evolution of the post-Civil War Amendments has evoked a pattern of institutional interactions unlike any under the Art. I powers traced in earlier chapters. Early congressional action under the post-Civil War Amendments stimulated Court responses which helped inhibit further legislative enforcement; subsequent Court elaborations of the self-executing aspects of the Amendments in turn influenced a new, modern cycle of congressional action. Congressional resort to the post-Civil War Amendments has been energetic during only two periods of our history: there was a spurt of activity at the very beginning, soon after the adoption of the Amendments, and then again in the most recent years; for the near-century intervening, the Amendments were effectively in the Court's sole keeping. After a series of civil rights laws during the Reconstruction era, between 1866 and 1875 (many of which foundered in the courts), there was no further significant congressional activity until the late 1950's. In the interval, decisions about the Amendments consisted mainly of judicial delineations of their self-executing aspects: delineations of the substantive rights in the Amendments such as those considered in the preceding chapters; and delineations about the reach of the Amendments, considered in the "state action" materials in sec. 2 below. And the most recent spurt of legislative activity in turn provoked new, broader Court statements of the scope of congressional powers.

That historical sequence of Court-Congress interactions yielded the institutional collaborations and tensions pursued in this chapter. How far-reaching is the power to enact "appropriate legislation" under the Amendments? Is congressional discretion to be interpreted with the same breadth here as that characteristic of the McCulloch v. Maryland tradition regarding Art. I, § 8, powers? Do the Court's interpretations of the self-executing impacts of the Amendments mark the outermost limits of the congressional power? Is congressional enforcement power under the post-Civil War Amendments limited to enacting remedial legislation, to provide enforcement mechanisms for substantive rights defined by the Court? Or may Congress extend the reach and amplify the substantive contents of the Amendments beyond the boundaries set by Court interpretations of such phrases as equal protection and due process?

4. *A note on organization.* To explore these interrelated themes of Court determinations of reach and content and congressional authority to amplify, this chapter is organized to focus on two specific, climactic problems. The first deals with the reach of the Amendments and the state action-private action dichotomy: Does Congress have power to expand the reach of the Amendments, to reach private rather than governmental invasions of individual rights? May it, for example, expand the 14th Amendment's state action boundaries to reach private conduct? May it reach private behavior through its power to implement federal constitutional rights other than those rooted in the 14th Amendment? That inquiry culminates in cases such as United States v. Guest, sec. 3 below.

The second is the problem of the congressional power to modify the substantive content of the Amendments. Is congressional enforcement power limited to providing remedies for substantive rights perceived by the Court —rights such as those traced in the independent judicial interpretations of equal protection and due process in the preceding chapter, interpretations largely arrived at without the aid of Congress? Or may Congress add substantive rights beyond those found to exist through judicial interpretation? May it use its enforcement power to "reinterpret" constitutional rights? That inquiry culminates in Katzenbach v. Morgan and Oregon v. Mitchell, sec. 4 below.

Secs. 3 and 4, then, test the outer limits of congressional power, both with respect to reach as to private action and as to substantive content of rights. As background for those inquiries, sec. 1 sketches the statutory framework of the post-Civil War laws and their modern counterparts. And as further background—and because of its independent significance as a problem of continuing vitality—sec. 2 examines the evolution of the "state action" concept in the Court's autonomous hands. Sec. 2A contains the restrictive readings regarding the reach of the post-Civil War Amendments that blocked much of the civil rights legislation in the 19th century. Sec. 2B considers the amorphously expanding modern readings, in cases involving the scope of the 14th Amendment when it operates of its own force.

Those materials set the stage for the examination, in sec. 3, of the modern efforts to apply the remnants of the post-Civil War laws to private action. That section concludes with the late sixties' varieties of congressional action (prompted in part by suggestions in the Guest case), and with the rediscovery in the Jones case of the 13th Amendment (which is not saddled with a state action limitation) as a far-reaching source of congressional power over private racial discrimination. Sec. 4, finally, focuses on the question of congressional power to provide remedies for, and perhaps to add to, the substantive rights unearthed by the Court in its interpretations, especially of the equal protection and due process clauses of the 14th Amendment. The major context for that examination is voting rights legislation—legislation in 1965 and 1970 which went beyond prior, Court-imposed restrictions on voting discrimination in several respects. The broad potential of the enforcement sections of the Amendments to modify the substantive contours of constitutional rights—uses especially suggested by Katzenbach v. Morgan —are potentially even more far-reaching than the congressional authority suggested by United States v. Guest to modify the Court-announced bounda-

ries between state and private action. These materials, then, are not only an essential supplement to the understanding of the due process and equal protection guarantees considered in the preceding chapters, but also a provocative and novel manifestation of Court-Congress interactions raising questions reaching back all the way to those considered in connection with Marbury v. Madison in chap. 1—questions about institutional autonomy and ultimate authority in the interpretation of constitutional rights.

SECTION 1.　THE STATUTORY FRAMEWORK

THE LAWS OF THE RECONSTRUCTION ERA

Introduction: The historical background and the Slaughter-House Cases. There was an intimate interrelationship among the emancipation aspect of the Civil War, the adoption of the 13th, 14th, and 15th Amendments, and the enactment of the Civil Rights Acts of 1866, 1870, 1871, and 1875. The central purpose of the Amendments was articulated in the course of the Court's first encounter with them, in 1873. Recall the passages in Justice Miller's majority opinion in the Slaughter-House Cases, 16 Wall. 36 (1873) (chap. 8 above), tracing the interaction between racially discriminatory laws and practices and the several Amendments and summarizing, on the basis of "the history of the times," the "one pervading purpose" underlying all of the Amendments: "[W]e mean the freedom of the slave race, the security and firm establishment of that freedom, and the protection of the newly-made freeman and citizen from the oppressions of those who had formerly exercised unlimited dominion over him."

1. *The 1866 Act.* The 13th Amendment, in 1865, gave constitutional support to the wartime Emancipation Proclamation, as Justice Miller's review noted. Congress considered additional protection of the newly freed Black necessary, however—especially in view of the "black codes" enacted in several states, imposing severe legal restrictions just short of formal slavery. The Civil Rights Act of 1866 sought to end these restrictions. Section 1 stated that all persons born in the United States were "citizens of the United States" and proceeded to list certain rights of "such citizens, of every race and color, without regard to any previous condition of slavery": they were to "have the same right [to] make and enforce contracts, to sue, be parties, and give evidence, to inherit, purchase, lease, sell, hold, and convey real and personal property, and to full and equal benefit of all laws [for] the security of persons and property, as is enjoyed by white citizens, and shall be subject to like punishment, [and] to none other, any law, statute, ordinance, regulation, or custom, to the contrary notwithstanding." [See the modern counterparts, 42 U.S.C. §§ 1981, 1982. § 1982 was the basis for the Jones decision, sec. 3 below.]

The "declaration" of rights in Section 1 was followed by a criminal enforcement provision, Section 2: "That any person who, under color of any law, statute, ordinance, regulation, or custom, shall subject or cause to be subjected, any inhabitant of any State or Territory to the deprivation of any right

secured or protected by this act, or to different punishment [on] account of [former slavery] or by reason of his color or race, than is prescribed for punishment of white persons, shall be deemed guilty of a misdemeanor." The punishment provided was a maximum fine of $1000, a one year sentence, or both. [For the current version of this provision, see 18 U.S.C. § 242, below, considered in a companion case to United States v. Guest, the Price case, sec. 3 below, among others.]

During the debates on the 1866 Act, constitutional doubts were raised about the adequacy of the 13th Amendment to support the constitutionality of the law. The doubts were reflected in President Johnson's veto: "[W]here can we find a Federal prohibition against the power of any State to discriminate . . .?" Congress overrode the veto, but the amendment machinery was immediately put in motion, and the 14th Amendment— designed at least in part to validate the 1866 Act—was ratified in 1868.

2. *The 1870 Act.* In 1870, the 15th Amendment was ratified. It prohibited denial of the franchise "on account of race, color, or previous condition of servitude"; unlike the 14th Amendment, it spoke explicitly about the race-slavery problem which provoked all of the post-Civil War Amendments. Congress promptly passed enforcement legislation. The 1870 Enforcement Act, 16 Stat. 140, dealt primarily with denials of voting rights. [The development of voting rights laws is traced in sec. 4 below.] Section 6, however, contained broader terms: it made it a felony "if two or more persons shall band or conspire together, or go in disguise upon the public highway, or upon the premises of another, with intent to violate any provision of this act, or to injure, oppress, threaten or intimidate any citizen with intent to prevent or hinder his free exercise and enjoyment of any right or privilege granted or secured to him by the Constitution or laws of the United States, or because of his having exercised the same." [For the current version of this provision, see 18 U.S.C. § 241, below. It was the basis for the indictment in the Guest case, sec. 3 below.]

3. *The 1871 and 1875 Acts.* In 1871, Congress not only made amendments to the 1870 law, but enacted a new law, the Civil Rights Act of 1871. The 1871 Act "to enforce . . . the Fourteenth Amendment," known as the Ku Klux Klan Act, was "among the last of the reconstruction legislation to be based on the 'conquered province' theory which prevailed in Congress for a period following the Civil War. This statute [established] civil liabilities, together with parallel criminal liabilities." Collins v. Hardyman, 341 U.S. 651, 656 (1951) (sec. 3 below). The substance of these civil provisions has been preserved *—and has been involved in important

---

* Another provision of the 1871 Act, subsequently repealed, dealt with private criminal conspiracies directed against government operations or intended to deprive persons of the equal protection of laws. The latter provision was found beyond the reach of the 14th Amendment in United States v. Harris, 106 U.S. 629 (1882), noted further below.

For a useful brief review of the post-Civil War laws, and their fate in later decades, see Gressman, "The Unhappy History of Civil Rights Legislation," 50 Mich.L.Rev. 1323 (1952). See also Carr, Federal Protection of Civil Rights (1947).

cases. For example, 42 U.S.C. § 1983 creates a cause of action for deprivations, under color of state law, of rights secured by the Constitution and federal laws. See, e. g., Monroe v. Pape, sec. 3 below. And 42 U.S.C. § 1985(3) provides for civil actions for certain anti-civil rights conspiracies. That civil conspiracy provision contains no "under color of state law" limitation and thus raises the problem of congressional authority to reach private action. Constitutional doubts about that power led to a narrow construction of the provision in Collins v. Hardyman, but that narrow statutory reading was abandoned in Griffin v. Breckenridge, 403 U.S. 88 (1971) (sec. 3 below); and that expansive reading raises a host of still unsettled constitutional issues. Finally, the Civil Rights Act of 1875, 18 Stat. 335, contained, inter alia, "public accommodations" provisions. These and other sections of the 1875 Act are discussed in the opinions in the 1883 Civil Rights Cases (sec. 2 below), holding the provisions unconstitutional.

THE SURVIVING REMNANTS OF THE POST–CIVIL WAR LAWS: THE MODERN COUNTERPARTS

1. Criminal provisions:

18 U.S.C. § 241.[1] *"Conspiracy against rights of citizens.* If two or more persons conspire to injure, oppress, threaten, or intimidate any citizen in the free exercise or enjoyment of any right or privilege secured to him by the Constitution or laws of the United States, or because of his having so exercised the same; or

"If two or more persons go in disguise on the highway, or on the premises of another, with intent to prevent or hinder his free exercise or enjoyment of any right or privilege so secured—

"They shall be fined not more than $10,000 or imprisoned not more than ten years, or both; and if death results, they shall be subject to imprisonment for any term of years or for life."

18 U.S.C. § 242.[2] *"Deprivation of rights under color of law.* Whoever, under color of any law, statute, ordinance, regulation, or custom, willfully subjects any inhabitant of any State, Territory, or District to the deprivation of any rights, privileges, or immunities secured or protected by the Constitution or laws of the United States, or to different punishments, pains, or penalties, on account of such inhabitant being an alien, or by reason of his

---

[1]. Derived from § 6 of the 1870 Act, above. Before being designated 18 U.S.C. § 241, it was § 5508 of Rev. Stats., 1874–78; § 19 of the Criminal Code of 1909; and § 51 of the 1946 edition of 18 U.S.C. It is referred to by the earlier designations in some of the cases below. The concluding portions of the penalty provisions in §§ 241 and 242 were added by the 1968 Civil Rights Act. For modern applications of § 241, see the Guest and Price cases sec. 3, below.
The Guest case helped provoke the first criminal law to protect civil rights

that departed from the post-Civil War models. See the new 18 U.S.C. § 245, "Federally protected activities," added by Title I of the Civil Rights Act of 1968. Excerpts are printed in sec. 3 below.

[2]. Derived from § 2 of the 1866 Act, above, as amended by § 17 of the 1870 Act. The section was § 5510 of Rev.Stats., 1874–78; § 20 of the 1909 Criminal Code; and § 52 of the 1946 edition of 18 U.S.C. The section is discussed and applied in the Price case, sec. 3, below.

color, or race, than are prescribed for the punishment of citizens, shall be fined not more than $1,000 or imprisoned not more than one year, or both; and if death results shall be subject to imprisonment for any term of years or for life."

2. Civil provisions:

42 U.S.C. § 1981.[3] *"Equal rights under the law.* All persons within the jurisdiction of the United States shall have the same right in every State and Territory to make and enforce contracts, to sue, be parties, give evidence, and to the full and equal benefit of all laws and proceedings for the security of persons and property as is enjoyed by white citizens, and shall be subject to like punishment, pains, penalties, taxes, licenses, and exactions of every kind, and to no other."

42 U.S.C. § 1982.[4] *"Property rights of citizens.* All citizens of the United States shall have the same right, in every State and Territory, as is enjoyed by white citizens thereof to inherit, purchase, lease, sell, hold, and convey real and personal property."

42 U.S.C. § 1983.[5] *"Civil action for deprivation of rights.* Every person who, under color of any statute, ordinance, regulation, custom, or usage, of any State or Territory, subjects, or causes to be subjected, any citizen of the United States or other persons within the jurisdiction thereof to the deprivation of any rights, privileges or immunities secured by the Constitution and laws, shall be liable to the person injured in an action of law, suit in equity, or other proper proceedings for redress."

42 U.S.C. § 1985(3).[6] *Conspiracy to interfere with civil rights.* . . . If two or more persons in any State or Territory conspire or go in disguise on the highway or on the premises of another, for the purpose of depriving, either directly or indirectly, any person or class of persons of the equal protection of the laws, or of equal privileges and immunities under the laws; . . . the party so injured or deprived may have an action for the recovery of damages, occasioned by such injury or deprivation, against any one or more of the conspirators."[7]

3. Derived from the 1866 and 1870 Acts. It was § 1977 of Rev.Stats., 1874–78.

4. Derived from the 1866 Act. It was § 1978 of Rev.Stats., 1874–78. This section was found to have a broad sweep and a solid constitutional base (in the 13th Amendment) in the Jones case, Jones v. Alfred H. Mayer Co., 392 U.S. 409 (1968), sec. 3 below.

5. Derived from § 1 of the Civil Rights Act of 1871, Rev.Stats. § 1979 (1875). See the discussion in Monroe v. Pape, sec. 3 below. Note also the discussion of the "custom, or usage, of any State" phrase, in the Adickes case, sec. 3 below.

6. Derived from Civil Rights Act of 1871, Rev.Stats. § 1980. After a narrow reading in Collins v. Hardyman

in 1951, the Court found a broader reach to the statute in Griffin v. Breckenridge in 1971. See sec. 3 below.

7. See also the following, less frequently litigated, provisions of 42 U.S.C.: § 1986 (derived from the 1871 Act) (neglecting to prevent acts wrongful under § 1985); § 1994 (the anti-peonage law of 1867). The provisions specifically dealing with voting are considered in sec. 4, below. See also the broad jurisdictional provision, 28 U.S.C. § 1343, giving federal district courts original jurisdiction in civil actions for violations of civil rights. And note 28 U.S.C. § 1443, authorizing defendants to remove certain civil rights cases from state to federal courts.

MODERN CIVIL RIGHTS LEGISLATION

The modern revival of congressional civil rights activity began with the Civil Rights Act of 1957; that law, like the Civil Rights Act of 1960, was primarily designed to improve remedies against racial discrimination in voting. The voting aspects of those laws, as well as the broader voting provisions adopted in 1965 and 1970, are considered further in sec. 4, below.[1] The 1957 Act also established the Civil Rights Commission, whose studies have been important in the consideration of subsequent legislation, as well as in litigation.

The Civil Rights Act of 1964 was the first comprehensive modern civil rights law—the first to move substantially beyond the area of voting rights. The 1964 provisions based primarily on Art. I powers of Congress have already been considered. (Recall, e. g., the Public Accommodations Title, based mainly on the commerce clause, chap. 3 above.) In addition, the 1964 Act included several provisions primarily rooted in the post-Civil War Amendments: Titles I and VIII contain new voting rights provisions; Titles III and IV dealt with desegregation of schools and other public facilities; Title X established a Community Relations Service; and Title IX authorized federal intervention in suits claiming denial of equal protection.

After the adoption of the 1965 Voting Rights Act (sec. 4 below),[2] Johnson Administration proposals for additional omnibus civil rights laws were repeatedly blocked in the Senate. In 1968, however—after the assassination of Dr. Martin Luther King in April 1968—new legislation was enacted. The provisions of the 1968 Act of special concern in this chapter are the elaborate additions to federal criminal laws dealing with civil rights violence in the new 18 U.S.C. § 245 (printed in sec. 3 below). Title VIII of the 1968 Act was a comprehensive fair housing law; it, too, is noted further below, in sec. 3. The 1968 Act also contained extensive provisions on Indian rights (Titles II–VII), a "Civil Obedience Act of 1968" (Title X—see chap. 3 above), and provisions on rioting (§ 104 of Title I, see chap. 3 above).

1. The 1960 Act also included a criminal prohibition of interstate travel to avoid state prosecution for "damaging or destroying by fire or explosive" any structure, including schools and churches. See 18 U.S.C. § 1074. Another provision, 18 U.S.C. § 837(b), prohibited interstate transportation of explosives with knowledge that they will be used to damage certain buildings. Recall also related commerce clause-based criminal provisions considered in chap. 3 above.

2. The major provisions of the Voting Rights Act of 1965 are examined in South Carolina v. Katzenbach and Katzenbach v. Morgan, sec. 4 below. The Voting Rights Act Amendments of 1970 extended and elaborated the congressional protections of suffrage. The major provisions are considered in Oregon v. Mitchell, sec. 4 below.

SECTION 2.   THE PROBLEM OF STATE ACTION

A. STATE ACTION IN THE 19TH CENTURY: THE COLLAPSE OF EARLY CONGRESSIONAL EFFORTS TO REACH PRIVATE CONDUCT

CIVIL RIGHTS CASES

109 U.S. 3, 3 S.Ct. 18, 27 L.Ed. 835 (1883).

On certificates of division from and writs of error to various Circuit Courts of the United States.

[Section 1 of the Civil Rights Act of 1875 provided: "That all persons within the jurisdiction of the United States shall be entitled to the full and equal enjoyment of the accommodations, advantages, facilities, and privileges of inns, public conveyances on land or water, theatres, and other places of public amusement; subject only to the conditions and limitations established by law, and applicable alike to citizens of every race and color, regardless of any previous condition of servitude." Section 2 made violation of § 1 a misdemeanor and also authorized aggrieved persons to recover $500 "for every such offense."

[The decision involved five cases, from Kansas, California, Missouri, New York and Tennessee. Four of the cases were criminal indictments; the fifth, an action for the civil penalty. The cases grew out of exclusions of Blacks from hotels, theaters and railroads.]

Mr. Justice BRADLEY delivered the opinion of the Court. .   .   .

It is obvious that the primary and important question in all the cases is the constitutionality of the law [the "essence" of which] is to declare, [that] colored citizens, whether formerly slaves or not, and citizens of other races, shall have the same accommodations and privileges in all inns, public conveyances, and places of amusement as are enjoyed by white citizens; and vice versa. .   .   .

Has Congress constitutional power to make such a law? Of course, no one will contend that the power to pass it was contained in the Constitution before the adoption of the last three amendments. The power is sought, first, in the Fourteenth Amendment. .   .   .

It is State action of a particular character that is prohibited [by the first section of the 14th Amendment]. Individual invasion of individual rights is not the subject-matter of the amendment. [It] nullifies and makes void all State legislation, and State action of every kind, which impairs the privileges and immunities of citizens of the United States, or which injures them in life, liberty or property without due process of law, or which denies to any of them the equal protection of the laws. [The] last section of the amendments invests Congress with power to enforce it by appropriate legislation. To enforce what? To enforce the prohibition. To adopt appropriate legislation for correcting the effects of such prohibited State laws and State acts, and thus to render them effectually null, void, and innocuous. This is the

legislative power conferred upon Congress, and this is the whole of it. It does not invest Congress with power to legislate upon subjects which are within the domain of State legislation; but to provide modes of relief against State legislation, or State action, of the kind referred to. It does not authorize Congress to create a code of municipal law for the regulation of private rights; but to provide modes of redress against the operation of State laws, and the action of State officers executive or judicial, when these are subversive of the fundamental rights specified in the amendment. . . .

And so in the present case, until some State law has been passed, or some State action through its officers or agents has been taken, adverse to the rights of citizens sought to be protected by the [14th] Amendment, no legislation of the United States under said amendment, nor any proceeding under such legislation, can be called into activity: for the prohibitions of the amendment are against State laws and acts done under State authority. . . . .

An inspection of the law shows that it makes no reference whatever to any supposed or apprehended violation of the Fourteenth Amendment on the part of the States. It is not predicated on any such view. It proceeds *ex directo* to declare that certain acts committed by individuals shall be deemed offences, and shall be prosecuted and punished by proceedings in the courts of the United States. It does not profess to be corrective of any constitutional wrong committed by the States; it does not make its operation to depend upon any such wrong committed. It applies equally to cases arising in States which have the justest laws respecting the personal rights of citizens, and whose authorities are ever ready to enforce such laws, as to those which arise in States that may have violated the prohibition of the amendment. In other words, it steps into the domain of local jurisprudence, and lays down rules for the conduct of individuals in society towards each other, and imposes sanctions for the enforcement of those rules, without referring in any manner to any supposed action of the State or its authorities.

If this legislation is appropriate for enforcing the prohibitions of the amendment, it is difficult to see where it is to stop. Why may not Congress with equal show of authority enact a code of laws for the enforcement and vindication of all rights of life, liberty, and property? . . .

[C]ivil rights, such as are guaranteed by the Constitution against State aggression, cannot be impaired by the wrongful acts of individuals, unsupported by State authority in the shape of laws, customs, or judicial or executive proceedings. The wrongful act of an individual, unsupported by any such authority, is simply a private wrong, or a crime of that individual; an invasion of the rights of the injured party, it is true, whether they affect his person, his property, or his reputation; but if not sanctioned in some way by the State, or not done under State authority, his rights remain in full force, and may presumably be vindicated by resort to the laws of the State for redress. An individual cannot deprive a man of his right to vote, to hold property, to buy and sell, to sue in the courts, or to be a witness or a juror; he may, by force or fraud, interfere with the enjoyment of the right in a particular case; he may commit an assault against the person, or commit murder, or use ruffian violence at the polls, or slander the good name of a fellow citizen; but, unless protected in these wrongful acts by some shield

of State law or State authority, he cannot destroy or injure the right; he will only render himself amenable to satisfaction or punishment; and amenable therefor to the laws of the State where the wrongful acts are committed. [I]t is not individual offences, but abrogation and denial of rights, which [the amendment] denounces, and for which it clothes the Congress with power to provide a remedy. This abrogation and denial of rights, for which the States alone were or could be responsible, was the great seminal and fundamental wrong which was intended to be remedied. And the remedy to be provided must necessarily be predicated upon that wrong. It must assume that in the cases provided for, the evil or wrong actually committed rests upon some State law or State authority for its excuse and perpetration.

Of course, these remarks do not apply to those cases in which Congress is clothed with direct and plenary powers of legislation over the whole subject, accompanied with an express or implied denial of such power to the States, as in the regulation of commerce, [the] coining of money, the establishment of post offices and post roads, the declaring of war, etc. In these cases Congress has power to pass laws for regulating the subjects specified in every detail, and the conduct and transactions of individuals in respect thereof. . . .

[I]t is clear that the law in question cannot be sustained by any grant of legislative power made to Congress by the Fourteenth Amendment. . . . This is not corrective legislation; it is primary and direct; it takes immediate and absolute possession of the subject of the right of admission to inns, public conveyances, and places of amusement. [It] assumes that the matter is one that belongs to the domain of national regulation.* [W]hether Congress, in the exercise of its power to regulate commerce amongst the several States, might or might not pass a law regulating rights in public conveyances passing from one State to another, [is] a question which is not now before us, as the sections in question are not conceived in any such view.

But the power of Congress to adopt direct and primary, as distinguished from corrective legislation on the subject in hand, is sought, in the second place, from the Thirteenth Amendment, [which] declares "that neither slavery, nor involuntary servitude, except as a punishment for crime, whereof the party shall have been duly convicted, shall exist within the United States, or any place subject to their jurisdiction;" and it gives Congress power to enforce the amendment by appropriate legislation. [S]uch legislation may be primary and direct in its character; for the amendment is not a mere prohibition of State laws establishing or upholding slavery, but an absolute declaration that slavery or involuntary servitude shall not exist in any part of the United States.

. . . [I]t is assumed, that the power vested in Congress to enforce the article by appropriate legislation, clothes Congress with power to pass

---

* Justice Bradley added the following comment: "We have discussed the question presented by the law on the assumption that a right to enjoy equal accommodation and privileges in all inns, public conveyances, and places of public amusement, is one of the essential rights of the citizen which no State can abridge or interfere with. Whether it is such a right, or not, is a different question which, in the view we have taken of the validity of the law on the ground already stated, it is not necessary to examine." Recall chap. 8 above.

all laws necessary and proper for abolishing all badges and incidents of slavery in the United States: and upon this assumption it is claimed, that this is sufficient authority for declaring by law that all persons shall have equal accommodations and privileges in all inns, public conveyances, and places of amusement; the argument being, that the denial of such equal accommodations and privileges is, in itself, a subjection to a species of servitude within the meaning of the amendment. Conceding the major proposition to be true, that Congress has a right to enact all necessary and proper laws for the obliteration and prevention of slavery with all its badges and incidents, is the minor proposition also true, that the denial to any person of admission to the accommodations and privileges of an inn, a public conveyance, or a theatre, does subject that person to any form of servitude, or tend to fasten upon him any badge of slavery? . . .

Can the act of a mere individual, the owner of the inn, the public conveyance or place of amusement, refusing the accommodation, be justly regarded as imposing any badge of slavery or servitude upon the applicant, or only as inflicting an ordinary civil injury, properly cognizable by the laws of the State, and presumably subject to redress by those laws until the contrary appears?

[W]e are forced to the conclusion that such an act of refusal has nothing to do with slavery or involuntary servitude, and that if it is violative of any right of the party, his redress is to be sought under the laws of the State; or if those laws are adverse to his rights and do not protect him, his remedy will be found in the corrective legislation which Congress has adopted, or may adopt, for counteracting the effect of State laws, or State action, prohibited by the Fourteenth Amendment. It would be running the slavery argument into the ground to make it apply to every act of discrimination which a person may see fit to make as to the guests he will entertain, or as to the people he will take into his coach or cab or car, or admit to his concert or theatre, or deal with in other matters of intercourse or business. Innkeepers and public carriers, by the laws of all the States, so far as we are aware, are bound, to the extent of their facilities, to furnish proper accommodation to all unobjectionable persons who in good faith apply for them. If the laws themselves make any unjust discrimination, amenable to the prohibitions of the Fourteenth Amendment, Congress has full power to afford a remedy under that amendment and in accordance with it.

When a man has emerged from slavery, and by the aid of beneficent legislation has shaken off the inseparable concomitants of that state, there must be some stage in the progress of his elevation when he takes the rank of a mere citizen, and ceases to be the special favorite of the laws . . . . . . There were thousands of free colored people in this country before the abolition of slavery . . . . . Mere discriminations on account of race or color were not regarded as badges of slavery. If, since that time, the enjoyment of equal rights in all these respects has become established by constitutional enactment, it is not by force of the Thirteenth Amendment (which merely abolishes slavery), but by force of the [Fourteenth] and Fifteenth Amendments.

On the whole we are of opinion, that no countenance of authority for the passage of the law in question can be found in either the Thirteenth or

Fourteenth Amendment of the Constitution; and no other ground of authority for its passage being suggested, it must necessarily be declared void. . . .

So ordered.

Mr. Justice HARLAN dissenting.

The opinion in these cases proceeds, it seems to me, upon grounds entirely too narrow and artificial. I cannot resist the conclusion that the substance and spirit of the recent amendments of the Constitution have been sacrificed by a subtle and ingenious verbal criticism. . . .

The Thirteenth Amendment, it is conceded, did something more than to prohibit slavery as an *institution*, resting upon distinctions of race, and upheld by positive law. . . . Was it the purpose of the nation simply to destroy the institution, and then remit the race, theretofore held in bondage, to the several States for such protection, in their civil rights, necessarily growing out of freedom, as those States, in their discretion, might choose to provide? Were the States against whose protest the institution was destroyed, to be left free, so far as national interference was concerned, to make or allow discriminations against that race, as such, in the enjoyment of those fundamental rights which by universal concession, inhere in a state of freedom? . . .

That there are burdens and disabilities which constitute badges of slavery and servitude, and that the power to enforce by appropriate legislation the Thirteenth Amendment may be exerted by legislation of a direct and primary character, for the eradication, not simply of the institution, but of its badges and incidents, are propositions which ought to be deemed indisputable. . . . I do not contend that the Thirteenth Amendment invests Congress with authority, by legislation, to define and regulate the entire body of the civil rights which citizens enjoy, or may enjoy, in the several States. But I hold that since slavery [was] the moving or principal cause of the adoption of that amendment, and since that institution rested wholly upon the inferiority, as a race, of those held in bondage, their freedom necessarily involved immunity from, and protection against, all discrimination against them, because of their race, in respect of such civil rights as belong to freemen of other races. Congress, therefore, under its express power to enforce that amendment, by appropriate legislation, may enact laws to protect that people against the deprivation, *because of their race,* of any civil rights granted to other freemen in the same State; and such legislation may be of a direct and primary character operating upon States, their officers and agents, and, also, upon, at least, such individuals and corporations as exercise public functions and wield power and authority under the State. . . .

It remains now to inquire what are the legal rights of colored persons in respect of the accommodations, privileges and facilities of public conveyances, inns and places of public amusement?

First, as to public conveyances on land and water. In New Jersey Steam Navigation Co. v. Merchants' Bank, 6 How. 344, this court [said] that a common carrier is "in the exercise of a sort of public office, and has public duties to perform, from which he should not be permitted to ex-

onerate himself without the assent of the parties concerned." . . . In Olcott v. Supervisors, 16 Wall. 678, it was ruled that railroads are public highways, established by authority of the State for the public use; that they are none the less public highways, because controlled and owned by private corporations; that it is a part of the function of government to make and maintain highways for the convenience of the public; that no matter who is the agent, or what is the agency, the function performed is *that of the State;* that although the owners may be private companies, they may be compelled to permit the public to use these works in the manner in which they can be used; that, upon these grounds alone, have the courts sustained the investiture of railroad corporations with the State's right of eminent domain, or the right of municipal corporations, under legislative authority, to assess, levy and collect taxes to aid in the construction of railroads. . . . The sum of the adjudged cases is that a railroad corporation is a governmental agency, created primarily for public purposes, and subject to be controlled for the public benefit. . . . Such being the relations these corporations hold to the public, it would seem that the right of a colored person to use an improved public highway, upon the terms accorded to freemen of other races, is as fundamental, in the state of freedom established in this country, as are any of the rights which my brethren concede to be so far fundamental as to be deemed the essence of civil freedom. "Personal liberty consists," says Blackstone, "in the power of locomotion, of changing situation, or removing one's person to whatever places one's own inclination may direct, without restraint, unless by due course of law." But of what value is this right of locomotion, if it may be clogged by such burdens as Congress intended by the act of 1875 to remove? They are burdens which lay at the very foundation of the institution of slavery as it once existed. . . .

Second, as to inns. The same general observations which have been made as to railroads are applicable to inns. [A] keeper of an inn is in the exercise of a quasi-public employment. The law gives him special privileges and he is charged with certain duties and responsibilities to the public. The public nature of his employment forbids him from discriminating against any person asking admission as a guest on account of the race or color of that person.

Third. As to places of public amusement. [P]laces of public amusement, within the meaning of the act of 1875, are such as are established and maintained under direct license of the law. The authority to establish and maintain them comes from the public. The colored race is a part of that public. The local government granting the license represents them as well as all other races within its jurisdiction. A license from the public to establish a place of public amusement, imports, in law, equality of right, at such places, among all the members of that public. . . .

I am of the opinion that [racial] discrimination practised by corporations and individuals in the exercise of their public or quasi-public functions is a badge of servitude the imposition of which Congress may prevent under its power, by appropriate legislation, to enforce the [13th Amendment].

It remains now to consider these cases with reference to the power Congress has possessed since the adoption of the Fourteenth Amendment.

Much that has been said as to the power of Congress under the Thirteenth Amendment is applicable to this branch of the discussion, and will not be repeated. . . .

The assumption that this amendment consists wholly of prohibitions upon State laws and State proceedings in hostility to its provisions, is unauthorized by its language. The first clause of the first section—"All persons born or naturalized in the United States, and subject to the jurisdiction thereof, are citizens of the United States, and of the State wherein they reside"—is of a distinctly affirmative character. . . . The citizenship thus acquired, by that race, in virtue of an affirmative grant from the nation, may be protected, not alone by the judicial branch of the government, but by congressional legislation of a primary direct character; this, because the power of Congress is not restricted to the enforcement of prohibitions upon State laws or State action. It is, in terms distinct and positive, to enforce "the *provisions* of *this article*" of amendment; not simply those of a prohibitive character, but the provisions—*all* of the provisions—affirmative and prohibitive, of the amendment. . . .

But what was secured to colored citizens of the United States—as between them and their respective States—by the national grant to them of State citizenship? With what rights, privileges, or immunities did this grant invest them? There is one, if there be no other—exemption from race discrimination in respect of any civil right belonging to citizens of the white race in the same State. That, surely, is their constitutional privilege when within the jurisdiction of other States. And such must be their constitutional right, in their own State, unless the recent amendments be splendid baubles, thrown out to delude those who deserved fair and generous treatment at the hands of the nation. Citizenship in this country necessarily imports at least equality of civil rights among citizens of every race in the same State. . . . If the grant to colored citizens of the United States of citizenship in their respective States, imports exemption from race discrimination, in their States, in respect of such civil rights as belong to citizenship, then, to hold that the amendment remits that right to the States for their protection, primarily, and stays the hands of the nation, until it is assailed by State laws or State proceedings, is to adjudge that the amendment, so far from enlarging the powers of Congress—as we have heretofore said it did—not only curtails them, but reverses the policy which the general government has pursued from its very organization. . . .

But if it were conceded that the power of Congress could not be brought into activity until the rights specified in the act of 1875 had been abridged or denied by some State law or State action, I maintain that the decision of the court is erroneous. There has been adverse State action within the Fourteenth Amendment as heretofore interpreted by this court. . . .

In every material sense applicable to the practical enforcement of the Fourteenth Amendment, railroad corporations, keepers of inns, and managers of place of public amusement are agents or instrumentalities of the State, because they are charged with duties to the public, and are amenable, in respect of their duties and functions, to governmental regulation. It seems to me [that] a denial, by these instrumentalities of the State, to the citizen, because of his race, of that equality of civil rights secured to him by law, is a

denial by the State, within the meaning of the Fourteenth Amendment. If it be not, then that race is left, in respect of the civil rights in question, practically at the mercy of corporations and individuals wielding power under the States.

.   .   .   It is, I submit, scarcely just to say that the colored race has been the special favorite of the laws. The statute of 1875, now adjudged to be unconstitutional, is for the benefit of citizens of every race and color.   .   .   .   Today, it is the colored race which is denied, by corporations and individuals wielding public authority, rights fundmental in their freedom and citizenship. At some future time, it may be that some other race will fall under the ban of race discrimination. If the constitutional amendments be enforced, according to the intent with which, as I conceive, they were adopted, there cannot be, in this republic, any class of human beings in practical subjection to another class, with power in the latter to dole out to the former just such privileges as they may choose to grant.   .   .   .

CONGRESSIONAL INCAPACITY TO REACH PRIVATE ACTS UNDER THE 14TH AMENDMENT: SOME ADDITIONAL EARLY EXAMPLES

1. *Cruikshank, the 14th Amendment limitation to state action—and the recognition of other rights against private action.* a. UNITED STATES v. CRUIKSHANK, 92 U.S. 542 (1875), involved an indictment under Section 6 of the 1870 Act, the predecessor of 18 U.S.C. § 241. Three persons were convicted of participating in a lynching of two Blacks, under charges of conspiring to interfere with rights and privileges "granted and secured" by the Constitution. One of the charges referred to the "right and privilege peaceably to assemble together." The Court affirmed the trial court's grant of a motion in arrest of judgment. Chief Justice Waite stated that the indictment would have been adequate if it had charged interference with the right to assemble "for the purpose of petitioning Congress for a redress of grievances," an "attribute of national citizenship"; but the charge was merely a conspiracy "to prevent a meeting for any lawful purpose whatever."

Another charge—depriving citizens of "lives and liberty of person without due process of law"—was found "even more objectionable": "It is no more the duty or within the power of the United States to punish for a conspiracy to falsely imprison or murder within a State, than it would be to punish for false imprisonment or murder itself. The fourteenth amendment prohibits a State from depriving any person of life, liberty, or property, without due process of law; but this adds nothing to the rights of one citizen as against another." A final charge—to "injure" for having voted at an election—was also insufficient: the election might have been a state election, and there was no claim of a conspiracy based on race; the charge, then, "is really of nothing more than a conspiracy to commit a breach of the peace within a State. Certainly it will not be claimed that the United States have the power or are required to do mere police duty in the States."

b. Cruikshank, like other cases of that era, emphasized that 14th Amendment rights were enforceable only against state action, not individual behavior.   Yet, private misconduct was not wholly outside congressional reach under the Cruikshank view: Cruikshank also recognized that there might be constitutional rights derived from sources not subject to the state action limitation, and that those might accordingly be protected against private as well as state interferences.   That distinction—between constitutional rights against the state and constitutional rights not limited by the state action concept—remains an important one in the search for bases of congressional action against private misconduct.   As the materials in sec. 3 will show, congressional power to reach private conduct under the 14th Amendment still presents substantial difficulties, though the power is not so tightly confined today as it was at the time of Cruikshank and the Civil Rights Cases. That continuing state action difficulty under the 14th and 15th Amendments makes the Court's efforts to articulate constitutional rights not based on those Amendments and hence not subject to the state action limitation of special importance.   That problem is pursued more fully in sec. 3 below: see especially United States v. Guest and the accompanying notes.[1]

2. *Harris.* UNITED STATES v. HARRIS, 106 U.S. 629 (1882), held unconstitutional a criminal provision of the 1875 Act prohibiting conspiracies to deprive any persons of "the equal protection of the laws or of equal privileges and immunities under the law."   (That provision was repealed in 1909.   Compare the civil counterpart, derived from the 1871 Act and still on the books, 42 U.S.C. § 1985(3), considered in Collins v. Hardyman and Griffin v. Breckenridge, sec. 3 below.)   Harris, a private person, was charged with participating in a lynching—killing one person as well as beating three others while they were in the custody of a Tennessee sheriff. The Supreme Court held the statute unconstitutional: "When the State has been guilty of no violation of its provisions; when it has not made or enforced any law abridging the privileges or immunities of citizens of the United States; when no one of its departments has deprived any person of life, liberty, or property without due process of law, or denied to any person within its jurisdiction the equal protection of the laws; when, on the contrary, the laws of the State, as enacted by its legislative, and construed by its judicial, and administered by its executive departments, recognize and protect the rights of all persons, the amendment imposes no duty and confers no power upon Congress."[2]

3. *The legacy of the Civil Rights Cases era: A transitional note.* What is the contemporary vitality of the majority's position in the Civil Rights Cases?   Most of the remaining materials in this chapter will pursue that question.   In examining it, bear in mind the varied ingredients of the ma-

---

1. Note also the modern congressional efforts to reach private interferences with civil rights, in the provisions of the Civil Rights Act of 1968 which added 18 U.S.C. § 245.   In examining those provisions, in sec. 3 below, consider especially which of the rights delineated there are traceable to sources other than the 14th and 15th Amendments.

2. See also, e. g., Virginia v. Rives, 100 U.S. 313 (1879), stating that the 14th Amendment's provisions "all have reference to State action exclusively, and not to any action of private individuals."   See also Baldwin v. Franks, 120 U.S. 678 (1887).   There were parallel difficulties in reaching private action under the 15th Amendment. See, e. g., James v. Bowman, 190 U.S. 127 (1903).

jority's position. First, it insisted that the 14th Amendment's self-executing impact did not reach private discrimination: by its own force, the Amendment covers only state action. As noted in the introduction to this chapter, the Court continues to reiterate that position—and continues to cite the Civil Rights Cases for it. Yet notions of what discrimination may fairly be attributed to the state have expanded considerably in recent decades. The ingredients of modern state action concepts—the extent to which the Amendment by its own force may reach arguably private action—is the theme of the next group of materials, sec. 2B.

Second, the Civil Rights Cases insisted that congressional enforcement powers under § 5 of the 14th Amendment could not reach beyond the state action limits of § 1 of the Amendment: Congress did not have power to forbid private discrimination. The extent to which that position is valid today is in doubt. Modern cases, considered in secs. 3 and 4 below, have taken a more expansive view of congressional powers under § 5 of the 14th Amendment. And in the 1966 decision in United States v. Guest, most of the Justices indicated that congressional power under the 14th Amendment could reach at least some private activity, though the issue was not fully explored and though the Court's holding did not rest on that ground. That problem is further pursued in sec. 3 below.

Third, the majority in the Civil Rights Cases recognized that the 13th Amendment is not limited to state action and extends to private actors as well. But that majority limited congressional enforcement power to problems of involuntary servitude; it refused to find in § 2 of the 13th Amendment a general congressional power to deal with private racial discrimination as "badges of servitude." That view has in effect been overruled by the 1968 decision in Jones v. Alfred H. Mayer Co.; and that ingredient of the Civil Rights Cases themes is pursued more fully in connection with the Jones case, in sec. 3 below.

B. COURT ELABORATIONS OF THE STATE ACTION CONCEPT IN THE 20TH CENTURY

Introduction. Beginning in the 1940's, while congressional power under the 14th Amendment lay dormant (at least as much for political reasons as because of constitutional obstacles), the Supreme Court began to expand the boundaries of the state action concept. The results were often clearer than the contents and limits of the principles. What was obvious was that, in many cases before the Court, arguably private conduct was being treated as state action, with the result either that the private actor was subjected to constitutional prohibitions or that the state was required to disengage itself from the private activity. What was often obscure was the extent to which additional seemingly private activities would be reachable on the basis of those holdings. Yet it was clear enough that none of the Court's principles was intended to be limitless: as the Court has made increasingly clear in some of the most recent cases, a state action limit persists and not every claim for extension of the state action concept will receive judicial support.*

---

* The literature on this problem is extensive. See generally Lewis, "The Meaning of State Action," 60 Colum. L.Rev. 1083 (1960), Selected Essays

What must be shown to bring seemingly private actors within the confines of constitutional guarantees ordinarily applicable only to government? An examination of the cases of the last three decades is necessary to identify the varied strands. But that examination may be aided by noting at the outset some recurrent themes. Consider, for example, the relative emphasis in the cases on two distinguishable lines of inquiry: first, whether the private actor is sufficiently entangled with or sufficiently like the state to consider the private conduct "state action"; second, whether applicability of constitutional guarantees to the private actor unduly impinges on the private interest in being free to discriminate or behave in other ways constitutionally barred to the state.

The second inquiry rests on the assumption that there is a sphere of private behavior in which individuals are free to discriminate. That there are such areas, and that some legitimate freedom in the private sector acts as a limit to expansions of the applicability of 14th Amendment guarantees, is recognized even by those Justices who have advocated the broadest extensions of the state action concept. See, e. g., Justice Douglas' dissent, joined by Justice Marshall, in the Moose Lodge case in 1972, below: "The associational rights which our system honors permit all white, all black, all brown, and all yellow clubs to be formed. . . . Government may not tell a man or woman who his or her associates must be. The individual can be as selective as he desires." Freedoms of association, rights of privacy, perhaps interests in personal property, all have some claim to constitutional recognition, as the preceding chapters illustrate. But what is the relevance of those competing individual interests to the delineation of the boundaries of the state action concept? Is the individual freedom to associate or to privacy the central ingredient in determining what behavior is not state action for 14th Amendment purposes? Or does the emphasis on individual interests suggest that affirmative state action is irrelevant, or is to be found everywhere, and that the underlying question about the reach of constitutional guarantees is always one of balancing the impacts on the aggrieved against the proper area of unrestrained choice and privacy of the discriminator? †

1938–62 (1963), 915. Compare Wechsler, "Toward Neutral Principles of Constitutional Law," 73 Harv.L.Rev. 1 (1959), Selected Essays 1938–62 (1963), 463, with Pollak, "Racial Discrimination and Judicial Integrity: A Reply to Professor Wechsler," 108 U. Pa.L.Rev. 1 (1959). Selected Essays 1938–62 (1963), 819. See also, e. g., Williams, "The Twilight of State Action," 41 Texas L.Rev. 347 (1963); Van Alstyne and Karst, "State Action," 14 Stan.L.Rev. 3 (1961); Horowitz, "The Misleading Search for 'State Action' Under the Fourteenth Amendment," 30 So.Cal.L.Rev. 208 (1957); and Henkin, "Shelley v. Kraemer: Notes for a Revised Opinion," 110 U.Pa.L.Rev. 473 (1962). For a critical review of the literature as well as of the entire state action concept (urging that it go into "honored retirement as an innocuous truism"), see C. L. Black, Jr., "Fore-

word: 'State Action,' Equal Protection, and California's Proposition 14," 81 Harv.L.Rev. 69 (1967). Despite that plea for "retirement," the state action concept remains in active service, as the recent cases below illustrate.

† The term "discriminator" is used here as shorthand for the private actor engaging in allegedly unconstitutional behavior. Bear in mind, however, that discrimination is not the only focus of the 14th Amendment. Though racial discrimination cases predominate in the "state action" materials which follow, due process and equal protection restraints have wide application outside the racial context. See, e. g., Marsh v. Alabama (free speech), which follows, and Jackson v. Metropolitan Edison Co. (procedural due process and termination of electric utility service), the 1974 decision at

Though many of the results in the cases can be explained via that "balancing" route, and though explicit consideration of the privacy interests of the private actor occasionally surfaces in the opinions, most of the cases are preoccupied with the search for adequate elements of the "state." That search for indicia of the state follows two distinguishable routes. One may be called the "nexus" approach: it seeks to identify points of contact between the private actor and the state—contacts adequate to justify imposing constitutional restraints on the private actor or commanding state disentanglement. That approach is exemplified by Burton v. Wilmington Parking Authority, 365 U.S. 715 (1961), below, stating "that private conduct abridging individual rights does no violence to the Equal Protection Clause unless to some significant extent the State in any of its manifestations has been found to have become involved in it." That search for "significant state involvements" permeates most of the cases below—and raises numerous problems. The Burton approach assumes that a total state "hands-off" approach vis-à-vis the private discriminator does not bring the 14th Amendment into play— that genuinely neutral state tolerance of private discrimination is permissible. But how much active, affirmative engagement of the state is necessary under that approach? Is it enough that the state "authorize" the private discrimination? Can authorization be distinguished from mere tolerance, where the state has power to forbid private discrimination and does not exercise that power? What varieties of more active state involvement satisfy the state action requirement? Must the state be shown to approve discrimination? To encourage discrimination? Is it enough that the state confers some benefits on the private discriminator? Must there be special benefits, such as a grant of a monopoly? Is state regulation of the discriminator enough? State licensing? State leasing or sale of property? Is it enough that the state judicial system enforces the private discriminator's wishes, as part of a general system of property and contract law? Questions such as these are characteristic of the "significant state involvements" approach.

An alternative to that "nexus" approach is one that searches not for formal contacts between the state and the private discriminator but rather examines the nature of the activity the private discriminator engages in. That alternative analysis is the "public function" approach; and Marsh v. Alabama, the company town case below, is a major representative of that approach. The "public function" analysis insists that private enterprises whose "operation is essentially a public function" are sufficiently state-like to be treated as a state for purposes of the applicability of constitutional guarantees. That public function approach is one of the earliest, most amorphous, and potentially most far-reaching themes in the expansion of the state action concept. When may "private" action be subjected to the 14th and 15th Amendments because it constitutes exercise of a "public function"? An examination of that problem follows, as the first group of the materials exploring the varying strands of state action analysis.

the end of this section. Should the ingredients of the state action requirement vary with the variety of constitutional claim involved?

THE "PUBLIC FUNCTION" STRAND
OF STATE ACTION ANALYSIS

1. *Marsh v. Alabama and the development of modern "public function" analysis.* a. *The decision.* One of the major sources of the view that the private performance of "public functions" can make 14th Amendment guarantees applicable was Justice Black's majority opinion in MARSH v. ALABAMA, 326 U.S. 501 (1946).[1] Marsh arose in the context of First Amendment rights rather than in a racial discrimination setting. The Court held that a state cannot "impose criminal punishment on a person who undertakes to distribute religious literature on the premises of a company-owned town contrary to the wishes of the town's management."

The town of Chickasaw, a suburb of Mobile, Alabama, was owned by the Gulf Shipbuilding Corporation. Except for that private ownership, "it has all the characteristics of any other American town." Marsh, a Jehovah's Witness, was convicted under the state criminal trespass law because she distributed religious literature without permission. Justice Black noted that an ordinary town could not have prohibited her activities, in view of cases such as Lovell v. Griffin, chap. 12, sec. 2A, below. The fact that a corporation owned title to the town could not justify impairing the public's interest "in the functioning of the community in such a manner that the channels of communication remain free." Accordingly, Justice Black rejected the argument that "the corporation's right to control the inhabitants of Chickasaw is coextensive with the right of a homeowner to regulate the conduct of his guests." He stated: "Ownership does not always mean absolute dominion. The more an owner, for his advantage, opens up his property for use by the public in general, the more do his rights become circumscribed by the statutory and constitutional rights of those who use it Thus, the owners of privately held bridges, ferries, turnpikes and railroads may not operate them as freely as a farmer does his farm. Since these facilities are built and operated primarily to benefit the public and *since their operation is essentially a public function,* it is subject to state regulation." (Emphasis added.)

Justice Black also noted that many Americans "live in company-owned towns," and that to act "as good citizens, they must be informed." He added: "When we balance the Constitutional rights of owners of property against those of the people to enjoy freedom of press and religion, as we must here, we remain mindful of the fact that the latter occupy a preferred position." Justice Black noted, moreover, that "the town and its shopping district are accessible to and freely used by the public in general and there is nothing to distinguish them from any other town and shopping center except the fact that the title to the property belongs to a private corporation." And that property interest could not justify impingement on First Amendment rights: "The 'business block' serves as the community shopping center and is freely accessible and open to the people in the area and those passing through. The managers appointed by the corporation cannot

---

1. Recall also the "public function" discussion in Justice Harlan's dissent in the Civil Rights Cases, above, and compare the evolution of "public function" analysis—an evolution paralleling that in the Marsh line of cases—in the white primary cases, noted below.

curtail the liberty of press and religion of these people consistently with the purposes of the Constitutional guarantees, and a state statute, as the one here involved, which enforces such action by criminally punishing those who attempt to distribute religious literature clearly violates the First and Fourteenth Amendments to the Constitution." [2]

Justice Reed's dissent, joined by Chief Justice Stone and Justice Burton, noted that this was "the first case to extend by law the privilege of religious exercises beyond public places or to private places without the assent of the owner," and disagreed with this "novel Constitutional doctrine." He added: "The rights of the owner, which the Constitution protects as well as the right of free speech, are not outweighed by the interests of the trespasser, even though he trespasses in behalf of religion or free speech."

b. *Some questions.* What satisfied the state action requirement in Marsh? Was the invocation of state trespass law important to the finding of state action? That feature received little emphasis from Justice Black. Should that state "nexus" have played a more prominent role? Compare Shelley v. Kraemer, below, where, two years later, the Court placed great emphasis on state judicial enforcement of a private restrictive covenant. Shelley, viewed as a far-reaching and novel approach to state action, barely mentioned Marsh. Did Marsh, then, rest on the nature of the private activity—the exercise of a "public function," the fact that Chickasaw was "a town" which in "its community aspects [did] not differ from other towns"? What is the relevance of the "public function" discussion? Is that the way of showing an adequate relationship with the state? Does it rest on an implicit view that the state has "delegated" a non-delegable function to the private entity? If the "delegation" concept is the nexus, does it rest on any real delegation in fact? Or is the "public function" discussion simply a substitute for the search for formal state involvement: Does it merely substitute a balancing of competing interests—those of the First Amendment claimant and those of the private property owner? Was it a balancing which gave great weight to the claimant's First Amendment interests (and the great power wielded by the defendant in restraining them), and little weight to the defendant's property and privacy concerns? Compare the relative emphases on the existence of a formal state nexus and a competing interests-balancing analysis in the evolution of the public function approach in the notes which follow.[3]

2. *The Marsh problem revisited: The modern shopping center cases.*
a. *Logan Valley Plaza.* More than twenty years later, the Court relied extensively on—and extended—Marsh (over Justice Black's dissent) in sustaining constitutional objections to a state court injunction banning peaceful picketing of a store in a privately owned shopping center. AMALGAMATED

2. Justice Frankfurter submitted a concurring opinion stating that, in view of First Amendment rights in ordinary municipalities, "I am unable to find legal significance in the fact that a town in which the Constitutional freedoms of religion and speech are invoked happens to be company-owned." He added: "Title to property as defined by State law controls property relations; it cannot control issues of civil liberties which arise precisely because a company town is a town as well as a congeries of property relations."

3. Compare the evolution of First Amendment principles of rights of access to the "private forum"—the right to express views on privately owned property—in chap. 12, sec. 2, below.

FOOD EMPLOYEES UNION v. LOGAN VALLEY PLAZA, 391 U.S. 308 (1968). Justice Marshall's majority opinion concluded that the injunction could not be justified on the ground that the picketing constituted an unconsented invasion of private property rights: "The shopping center here is clearly the functional equivalent to the business district of Chickasaw involved in Marsh. It is true that, unlike the corporation in Marsh, the respondents here do not own the surrounding residential property and do not provide municipal services therefor. [U]nlike the situation in Marsh, there is no power on respondents' part to have petitioners totally denied access to the community for which the mall serves as a business district. This fact, however, is not determinative. [We] see no reason why access to a business district in a company town for the purpose of exercising First Amendment rights should be constitutionally required, while access for the same purpose to property functioning as a business district should be limited simply because the property surrounding the 'business district' is not under the same ownership."

Since "the shopping center serves as the community business block," Justice Marshall explained, "the State may not delegate the power, through the use of its trespass laws, wholly to exclude those members of the public wishing to exercise their First Amendment rights on the premises in a manner and for a purpose generally consonant with the use to which the property is actually put." He noted that, "unlike a situation involving a person's home, no meaningful claim to protection of a right of privacy can be advanced by respondents here." He added: "The economic development of the United States in the last 20 years reinforces our opinion of the correctness of the approach taken in Marsh. The large-scale movement of this country's population from the cities to the suburbs has been accompanied by the advent of the suburban shopping center. [The data] illustrate the substantial consequences for workers seeking to challenge substandard working conditions, consumers protesting shoddy or overpriced merchandise, and minority groups seeking nondiscriminatory hiring policies that a contrary decision here would have. Business enterprises located in downtown areas would be subject to on-the-spot public criticism for their practices, but businesses situated in the suburbs could largerly immunize themselves from similar criticism by creating a *cordon sanitaire* of parking lots around their stores. Neither precedent nor policy compels a result so at variance with the goal of free expression and communication that is the heart of the First Amendment." Justice Douglas concurred.

The author of Marsh v. Alabama, Justice Black, dissented. The majority, he insisted, had misread Marsh: "The question is, Under what circumstances can private property be treated as though it were public? The answer that Marsh gives is when that property has taken on *all* the attributes of a town, i. e., 'residential buildings, streets, a system of sewers, a sewage disposal plant and a "business block" on which business places are situated.' I can find nothing in Marsh which indicates that if one of these features is present, e. g., a business district, this is sufficient for the Court to confiscate a part of an owner's private property and give its use to people who want to picket on it." There were also dissenting opinions by Justices Harlan and White. Justice White elaborated on the differences between the Marsh and Logan Valley contexts: "Logan Valley Plaza is not a town but only a collection of stores. . . . The public is invited to the premises but only in order to

do business with those who maintain establishments there. . . . Even if the Plaza has some aspects of 'public' property, it is nevertheless true that some public property is available for some uses and not for others; some public property is neither designed nor dedicated for use by pickets or for other communicative activities." (Compare the similar emphasis in Justice Powell's majority opinion in Lloyd, which follows.)

b. *Lloyd.* Four years after the Logan Valley case, its implications were sharply curtailed in LLOYD CORP. v. TANNER, 407 U.S. 551 (1972). The lower federal courts had relied on Marsh and Logan Valley in holding unconstitutional the application to anti-war leafletters of a shopping center ban on the distribution of handbills. In a 5 to 4 decision, the Supreme Court reversed, finding the facts in its earlier cases "significantly different." Justice Powell's majority opinion emphasized that here, unlike the Logan Valley picketing, the handbilling "had no relation to any purpose for which the center was built and being used"; the leafletters' message was "directed to all members of the public, not solely to patrons of Lloyd Center." [4] Moreover, Justice Powell noted that the store in Logan Valley was "in the center of a large private enclave with the consequence that no other reasonable opportunities" to convey the picketers' message existed. Here, by contrast, the enclosed shopping mall was surrounded by public streets, so that adequate alternative means of communication were available: "Handbills may be distributed conveniently to pedestrians, and also to occupants of automobiles, from these public sidewalks and streets."

Justice Powell also noted that Marsh had involved "an economic anomaly of the past, 'the company town,' " where private enterprise had assumed "all of the attributes of a state-created municipality." And he did not find reliance on the "functional equivalent of a public business district" language in Logan Valley justifiable. The "business district" language in Logan Valley, he commented, was "unnecessary to the decision." The fact that the shopping center was "open to the public" was not sufficient to apply constitutional restrictions. That argument "misapprehends the scope of the invitation extended to the public": it was simply an invitation "to come to the Center to do business with the tenants," not an "open-ended invitation" to use it "for any and all purposes." (Recall Justice White's dissent in Logan Valley.)

More generally, Justice Powell commented that the free speech guarantees are "limitations on *state* action, not on action by the owner of private property used nondiscriminatorily for private purposes only." And, like Justice Black's Logan Valley dissent, he emphasized that the protection of property in the due process clauses were "also relevant": "Although accommodations between [speech and property values] are sometimes necessary, and the courts properly have shown a special solicitude for the [First Amendment], this Court has never held that a trespasser or an uninvited guest may exercise general rights of free speech on property privately owned . . . .." The argument stressing the functional similarity of a center to a town business district "reaches too far": "The Constitution by no means requires such an attenuated doctrine of dedication of private property to public use. . . .

---

4. Justice Marshall had stated in Logan Valley that the Court was not deciding whether picketing could be banned if it was not "directly related in its purpose to the use to which the shopping center property was being put."

Nor does property lose its private character merely because the public is generally invited to use it for designated purposes. Few would argue that a free-standing store, with abutting parking space for customers, assumes significant public attributes merely because the public is invited to shop there." [5] And "size alone" did not change the "essentially private character" of business property. He concluded: "Fifth and Fourteenth Amendment rights of private property owners, as well as the First Amendment rights of all citizens, must be respected and protected." Here, there had been "no such dedication of Lloyd's privately owned and operated shopping center to public use as to entitle respondents to exercise therein the asserted First Amendment rights."

Justice Marshall's sharp dissent, joined by Justices Douglas, Brennan and Stewart, insisted that Logan Valley was not truly distinguishable, that the majority opinion was "an attack" on the rationale of Marsh as well as Logan Valley, and that "one may suspect from reading the [majority opinion] that it is Logan Valley itself that the Court finds bothersome." He added: "I am aware that composition of this Court has radically changed in four years"; but Logan Valley should be "binding unless and until it is overruled." The dissent insisted that the shopping center here *was* "the equivalent of a public 'business district'" within the meaning of the earlier cases: "In fact, the Lloyd Center is much more analogous to the company town in Marsh than was the Logan Valley Plaza." All the operational differences between Lloyd Center and Logan Valley Plaza cut against the majority's approach: Lloyd Center was larger, contained a wider range of services, was more intertwined with public streets, and, unlike Logan Valley, had private guards that were given full police power by the city. Justice Marshall conceded that the Logan Valley case had explicitly left open the question whether speech activity could be barred where it was not "directly related in its purpose to the use to which the shopping center was being put." But that issue need not be faced here because Lloyd Center had in fact been opened to First Amendment activities—e. g., Veterans Day parades, speeches by presidential candidates, and American Legion poppy sales. Accordingly, the activities here "were directly related in purpose to the use to which the shopping center was being put."

But even if the Center had not been open to other First Amendment activity, Justice Marshall argued, the handbill ban should not stand. Under Logan Valley, handbills criticizing the stores would clearly be protected: "I cannot see any logical reason to treat differently speech that is related to subjects other than the Center and its member stores." He explained: "We must remember that it is a balance that we are striking—a balance between the freedom to speak, a freedom that is given a preferred place in our

---

5. Such a "free standing store" was involved in a companion case, Central Hardware Co. v. NLRB, 407 U.S. 539 (1972). The NLRB and the lower court had relied on Logan Valley in holding that the company's no-solicitation rule barring union organizers from the store's parking lots constituted an unfair labor practice. In a 6 to 3 decision, with the majority opinion again written by Justice Powell, the Court found the Logan Valley principle inapplicable and remanded to the lower court for reconsideration in light of the statute—the NLRA. Justice Marshall's dissent, joined by Justices Douglas and Brennan, agreed that the case should have been handled as a statutory rather than a constitutional one, but urged a remand to the Board rather than the lower court. Justice Marshall conceded that the constitutional issue was a "difficult" one.

hierarchy of values, and the freedom of a private property owner to control his property. When the competing interests are fairly weighed, the balance can only be struck in favor of speech." Many residents could do all their shopping in the Center: "If speech is to reach these people, it must reach them in Lloyd Center." [6]

3. *The reach of the "public function" rationale: Evans v. Newton and the parks context.* How far-reaching is the "public function" analysis? Efforts to rely on it in areas beyond company towns and shopping centers have encountered considerable difficulties. But the public function theme was relied on as an alternative ground in Justice Douglas' majority opinion in EVANS v. NEWTON, 382 U.S. 296 (1966). That case involved a park created in Macon, Ga., pursuant to a trust established in the 1911 will of Senator Bacon. The trust provided that the park, Baconsfield, be used by white people only. The city originally acted as trustee and enforced the racial exclusion, but decided after the racial segregation decisions beginning with Brown v. Board of Education (chap. 10 above) that it could no longer participate in discrimination. In the Newton litigation, the state court accepted the city's resignation as trustee and appointed private trustees instead. The Supreme Court held that Baconsfield could nevertheless not be operated on a racially restrictive basis. In explaining why the 14th Amendment prohibition continued to apply to the park despite the substitution of private trustees, Justice Douglas' majority opinion in Evans v. Newton relied in part on the ground that, so far as the record showed, "there has been no change in municipal maintenance and concern over this facility. [W]here the tradition of municipal control had become firmly established, we cannot take judicial notice that the mere substitution of trustees instantly transferred this park from the public to the private sector."

But Justice Douglas suggested a "public function" ground as additional support: "This conclusion is buttressed by the nature of the service rendered the community by a park. The service rendered even by a private park of this character is municipal in nature. It is open to every white person, there being no selective element other than race. Golf clubs, social centers, luncheon clubs, schools such as Tuskegee was at least in origin, and other like organizations in the private sector are often racially oriented. A park, on the other hand, is more like a fire department or police department that traditionally serves the community. Mass recreation through the use of parks is plainly in the public domain; and state courts that aid private parties to perform that public function on a segregated basis implicate the State in conduct proscribed by the Fourteenth Amendment. Like the streets of the company town in Marsh v. Alabama, supra, the elective process of Terry v. Adams [below], and the transit system of Public Utilities Comm'n v. Pollak [343 U.S. 451 (1951) (chap. 12, sec. 2)], the predominant character and purpose of this park are municipal." [7]

6. See also the additional discussion of the First Amendment aspects of these shopping center cases in chap. 12, sec. 2E, below.

7. Note also Justice Douglas' comment: "There are two complementary principles to be reconciled in this case. One is the right of the individual to pick his own associates so as to express his preferences and dislikes, and to fashion his private life by joining such clubs and groups as he chooses. The other is the constitutional ban [against] state-sponsored racial inequality."

That passage evoked special criticism in Justice Harlan's dissent, joined by Justice Stewart: [8] "More serious than the absence of any firm doctrinal support for this theory of state action are its potentialities for the future. Its failing as a principle of decision in the realm of Fourteenth Amendment concerns can be shown by comparing—among other examples that might be drawn from the still unfolding sweep of governmental functions—the 'public function' of privately established schools with that of privately owned parks. Like parks, the purpose schools serve is important to the public. Like parks, private control exists, but there is also a very strong tradition of public control in this field. Like parks, schools may be available to almost anyone of one race or religion but to no others. Like parks, there are normally alternatives for those shut out but there may also be inconveniences and disadvantages caused by the restriction. Like parks, the extent of school intimacy varies greatly depending on the size and character of the institution.

"For all the resemblance, the majority assumes that its decision leaves unaffected the traditional view that the Fourteenth Amendment does not compel private schools to adapt their admission policies to its requirements, but that such matters are left to the States acting within constitutional bounds. I find it difficult, however, to avoid the conclusion that this decision opens the door to reversal of these basic constitutional concepts, and, at least in logic, jeopardizes the existence of denominationally restricted schools while making of every college entrance rejection letter a potential Fourteenth Amendment question.

"While this process of analogy might be spun out to reach privately owned orphanages, libraries, garbage collection companies, detective agencies, and a host of other functions commonly regarded as nongovernmental though paralleling fields of governmental activity, the example of schools is, I think, sufficient to indicate the pervasive potentialities of this 'public function' theory of state action. It substitutes for the comparatively clear and concrete tests of state action a catch-phrase approach as vague and amorphous as it is far-reaching."

[After the reversal in Evans v. Newton, the state courts held that the trust had failed because the Senator's intention had become impossible to fulfill and that the property had accordingly reverted to the heirs. A divided Supreme Court (Justices Brennan and Douglas dissenting) affirmed that decision. Evans v. Abney, 396 U.S. 435 (1970), further noted below.]

4. *Public function and private power.* Does the reliance on the public function analysis in the foregoing cases rest ultimately on the notion that 14th Amendment restraints become applicable whenever private action has substantial impact on important interests of individuals? How does that "private government" emphasis satisfy the "state action" requirement? Does it rest simply on a balancing of competing interests, with the power and impact of the challenged enterprise playing a large role? Or is the requisite formal state involvement provided by the probability that the "private government" is chartered by the state? Compare the licensing and regulation cases below. Is an adequate involvement with the state shown simply by the

---

8. The dissenters also rejected Justice Douglas' first ground of decision as based on unsupportable speculation.

fact that the state has tolerated the challenged practice? Compare Shelley v. Kramer and later cases, below. If mere state tolerance, mere state failure to prohibit, suffices, is the approach inconsistent with any genuine effort to preserve a "state action"-"private action" or "public sector"-"private sector" distinction? Is any such effort necessary or worthwhile? See C. L. Black, Jr., "Foreword: 'State Action,' Equal Protection, and California's Proposition 14," 81 Harv.L.Rev. 69 (1967). Would expansion of a "public function" or "private government" approach unduly constitutionalize all operations of the "private" group found subject to the Amendments? See Wellington, "The Constitution, the Labor Union, and 'Governmental Action,'" 70 Yale L.J. 345 (1961).[9]

Consider the assertion of an "emerging principle" in Berle, "Constitutional Limitations on Corporate Activity—Protection of Personal Rights from Invasion through Economic Power," 100 U.Pa.L.Rev. 933 (1952). Berle suggests that "principle" to be that a corporation may be "as subject to constitutional limitations as is the state itself." He notes two prerequisites: the "undeniable fact" of the state's action in chartering the corporation, and "the existence of sufficient economic power [to] invade the constitutional rights of the individual to a material degree." Berle offers as one of the justifications the fact that the state relies upon "the corporate system to carry out functions for which in modern life by community demand the government is held ultimately responsible." See also Hale, "Force and the State: A Comparison of 'Political' and 'Economic' Compulsion," 35 Colum. L.Rev. 149 (1935). To what extent is Berle's "emerging principle" supported by the cases above? By those which follow?

5. *The contemporary vitality of public function analysis: The Metropolitan Edison case.* Consider the current vigor of public function analyses in view of the decision in JACKSON v. METROPOLITAN EDISON CO., 419 U.S. 345 (1974). That decision (considered at greater length at the end of this section) involved a federal suit against a privately owned utility licensed and regulated by a state public utilities commission. Petitioner sought relief against the company's termination of her electric service for nonpayment. She claimed that the company was bound by the 14th Amendment and that her procedural due process rights had been denied by the failure to give adequate notice and a hearing. Among the various state action grounds argued (and noted further below) was one urging that "state action is present because respondent provides an essential public service required to be supplied on a reasonably continuous basis by [state law] and hence performs a 'public function.'"

---

9. On the obligation of a union designated as exclusive bargaining representative under federal labor legislation to avoid racial discrimination, see, e. g., Steele v. Louisville & Nashville R. Co., 323 U.S. 192 (1944), and Oliphant v. Brotherhood of Locomotive Firemen, 262 F.2d 359 (6th Cir. 1958), cert. denied, 359 U.S. 935 (1959). In Steele, the Court stated: "We think that the Railway Labor Act imposes upon the statutory representative of a craft at least as exacting a duty to protect equally the interests of the members of the craft as the Constitution imposes upon a legislature to give equal protection . . . . Congress has seen fit to clothe the bargaining representative with powers comparable to those possessed by a legislative body [but] it has also imposed [a] corresponding duty." See generally Sovern, "The NLRA and Racial Discrimination," 62 Colum.L.Rev. 563 (1962). (See also the licensing cases, below.)

Justice Rehnquist's majority opinion rejected this as well as all other state action claims. As to public function, he stated: "We have of course found state action present in the exercise by private entity of powers traditionally exclusively reserved to the State. [He cited Marsh v. Alabama, Evans v. Newton, as well as the white primary cases, below.] If we were dealing with the exercise by [the company] of some power delegated to it by the State which is traditionally associated with sovereignty, such as eminent domain, our case would be quite a different one. But while [state law] imposes an obligation to furnish service on regulated utilities, it imposes no such obligation on the State. The [state courts] have rejected the contention that the furnishing of utility services are either state functions or municipal duties.

"Perhaps in recognition of the fact that the supplying of utility service is not traditionally the exclusive prerogative of the State, petitioner invites the expansion of a doctrine of this limited line of cases into a broad principle that all businesses 'affected with a public interest' are state actors in all their actions.

"We decline the invitation for reasons stated long ago in Nebbia v. New York [chap. 9 above], in the course of rejecting a substantive due process attack on state legislation: 'It is clear that there is no closed class or category of businesses affected with a public interest. . . . The phrase "affected with a public interest" can, in the nature of things, mean no more than that an industry, for adequate reason, is subject to control for the public good.'

"Doctors, optometrists, lawyers, Metropolitan [the utility here], and Nebbia's upstate New York grocery selling a quart of milk are all in regulated businesses, providing arguably essential goods and services, 'affected with a public interest.' We do not believe that such a status converts their every action, absent more, into that of the State." In a footnote, Justice Rehnquist added that the argument had been "impliedly rejected by this Court on a number of occasions." He cited the Civil Rights Cases and the disavowal of intruding into the maintenance of parochial schools, despite the "public interest" nature of schools, in a dictum in Evans v. Newton.

Justice Marshall's dissent included a passage disagreeing with that approach and emphasizing that presence of "a service uniquely public in nature" had been important in past state action cases. He stated that the fact that the utility "supplies an essential public service that is in many communities supplied by the government weighs more heavily for me than for the majority." He elaborated: "The Court concedes that state action might be present if the activity in question were 'traditionally associated with sovereignty,' but it then undercuts that point by suggesting that a particular service is not a public function if the State in question has not required that it be governmentally operated. This reads the 'public function' argument too narrowly. The whole point of the 'public function' cases is to look behind the State's decision to provide public services through private parties. See [Evans v. Newton; Terry v. Adams [below]; Marsh v. Alabama]. In my view, utility service is traditionally identified with the State through universal public regulation or ownership to a degree sufficient to render it a 'public function.'

"I agree with the majority that it requires more than a finding that a particular business is 'affected with the public interest' before constitutional burdens can be imposed on that business. But when the activity in question is of such public importance that the State invariably either provides the service itself or permits private companies to act as state surrogates in providing it, much more is involved than just a matter of public interest. In those cases, the State has determined that if private companies wish to enter the field, they will have to surrender many of the prerogatives normally associated with private enterprise and behave in many ways like a governmental body. And when the State's regulatory scheme has gone that far, it seems entirely consistent to impose on the public utility the constitutional burdens normally reserved for the State.

"Private parties performing functions affecting the public interest can often make a persuasive claim to be free of the constitutional requirements applicable to governmental institutions because of the value of preserving a private sector in which the opportunity for individual choice is maximized. See [Evans v. Newton]; Friendly, The Dartmouth College Case and the Private-Public Penumbra (1969). Maintaining the private status of parochial schools, cited by the majority, advances just this value. In the due process area, a similar value of diversity may often be furthered by allowing various private institutions the flexibility to select procedures that fit their particular needs. See Wahba v. New York University, 492 F.2d 96, 102 (C.A.2), cert. denied, 419 U.S. 874 (1974). But it is hard to imagine any such interests that are furthered by protecting public utility companies from meeting the constitutional standards that would apply if the companies were state-owned. The values of pluralism and diversity are simply not relevant when the private company is the only electric company in town." [10] (See also the additional portions of the opinions printed at the end of sec. 2B, below.)

THE WHITE PRIMARY CASES

The white primary cases were a series of decisions in the forties and fifties holding that the Democratic Party groups in southern one-party states could not exclude Blacks from the pre-general election candidate selection process, despite the repeated efforts to eliminate all formal indicia of state involvement in the primary schemes. To what extent did these white primary cases support a general "public function" theory? To what extent did those cases rest on their special context of voting and elections? To what extent were they supportable on the basis of the 15th rather than the 14th Amendment? To what extent were they explainable on the basis of the fact or tradition of state regulation of primaries?

10. In another dissent, Justice Douglas commented more briefly on the majority's rejection of the public function argument. He stated: "It is said that the fact that respondent's services are 'affected with the public interest' is not determinative. I agree that doctors, lawyers, and grocers are not transformed into state actors simply because they provide arguably essential goods and services and are regulated by the State. In the present case, however, respondent is not just one person among many; it is the only public utility furnishing electric power to the town. When power is denied a householder, the home, under modern conditions, is likely to become unlivable."

The sequence began with Nixon v. Herndon, 273 U.S. 536 (1927), where the exclusion of Blacks from Democratic primaries was expressed on the face of a state law. That was held to be state racial discrimination in violation of the 14th Amendment. Texas responded by giving the executive committee of a party the power to prescribe membership qualifications. A resultant racial exclusion was again found unconstitutional under the 14th Amendment, in Nixon v. Condon, 286 U.S. 73 (1932), on the ground that the statute had made the committee an agent of the state. This time, Texas enacted no new law. Instead, a third round of racial exclusions stemmed from action of the state party convention. That exclusion survived constitutional attack in Grovey v. Townsend, 295 U.S. 45 (1935): the convention was found to be an organ of a voluntary, private group, not of the state; the state was no longer unconstitutionally involved.

But Grovey v. Townsend was overruled nine years later, in SMITH v. ALLWRIGHT, 321 U.S. 649 (1944). Where the Nixon cases had relied on the 14th Amendment, Smith found the white primary established by the state convention to be a violation of the 15th Amendment. The Smith Court pointed to an intervening decision, United States v. Classic, 313 U.S. 299 (1941), which held that Art. I, § 4, of the Constitution authorized congressional control of primaries "where the primary is by law made part of the election machinery." The Smith Court found Classic relevant, according to Justice Reed's majority opinion, "not because exclusion of Negroes from primaries is any more or less state action by reason of the unitary character of the electoral process but because the recognition of the place of the primary in the electoral scheme makes clear that state delegation to a party of the power to fix the qualifications of primary elections is delegation of a state function that may make the party's action the action of the State. [O]ur ruling in Classic as to the unitary character of the electoral process calls for a re-examination as to whether or not the exclusion of Negroes from a Texas party primary was state action." The Court examined the Texas statutes and concluded: "We think that this statutory system for the selection of party nominees for inclusion on the general election ballot makes the party which is required to follow these legislative directions an agency of the State in so far as it determines the participants in a primary election."

After Smith v. Allwright, several efforts to preserve "private" white primaries by abandoning much of the state statutory framework of the primary election process were thwarted in the lower courts. Note especially the language in Rice v. Ellmore, 165 F.2d 387 (4th Cir. 1947), cert. denied, 333 U.S. 875 (1948), where South Carolina had repealed all primary laws. The Court of Appeals concluded: "Having undertaken to perform an important function relating to the exercise of sovereignty by the people, [a political party] may not violate the fundamental principles laid down by the Constitution for its exercise."

In 1953, the issue came to the Supreme Court for the last time, in its most extreme "private" form. TERRY v. ADAMS, 345 U.S. 461, involved racial exclusion in the "pre-primary" elections of the Jaybird Democratic Association, a "voluntary club" of white Democrats. Candidates winning the Jaybird elections typically ran unopposed in the Democratic primaries. The trial court found a "complete absence" of state involvement in the Jaybirds'

operations. The Supreme Court nevertheless found the 15th Amendment violated by the exclusion of Black voters from the pre-primary. There was no opinion on which a majority could agree, but only one Justice dissented from the result.

Justice Black, joined by Justices Douglas and Burton, found that, as in the Rice case above, "the combined Jaybird-Democratic-general election machinery" was unconstitutional. He stated that though the Amendment "excludes social or business clubs," it "includes any election" in which public officials are elected. Any election machinery with the "purpose or effect" of denying "Negroes on account of their race an effective voice in governmental affairs" was barred: "For a State to permit such a duplication of its election processes" as the Jaybird pre-primary was unconstitutional. In a separate opinion, Justice Frankfurter stated that the "vital requirement is State responsibility—that somewhere, somehow, to some extent, there be an infusion by conduct by officials [into] any scheme" denying the franchise because of race. Nevertheless, he found a constitutional violation here: he thought that county election officials were in effect "participants in the scheme." They had participated by voting in the primary, and that indicated that they "condone" the effectiveness of the exclusionary pre-primary; the "action and abdication" of state officials had in effect permitted a procedure "which predetermines the legally devised primary."

Justice Clark, joined by Chief Justice Vinson and Justices Reed and Jackson, concurred on the ground that the Jaybirds operated "as an auxiliary of the local Party," and that they were therefore subject to the principles of Smith v. Allwright. He emphasized the Jaybirds' "decisive power" in the county's electoral process and concluded that "when a state structures its electoral apparatus in a form which devolves upon a political organization the uncontested choice of public officials, that organization itself, in whatever disguise, takes on those attributes of government which draw the Constitution's safeguards into play." Justice Minton was the only dissenter: he thought that the Jaybirds' activities, like those of other pressure groups, were protected private "attempts to influence or obtain state action."

"STATE ACTION" THROUGH STATE INVOLVEMENT: THE "NEXUS" APPROACH FROM SHELLEY v. KRAEMER TO JACKSON v. METROPOLITAN EDISON CO.

SHELLEY v. KRAEMER

334 U.S. 1, 68 S.Ct. 836, 92 L.Ed. 1161 (1948).

Certiorari to the Supreme Court of Missouri.*

[These cases were successful challenges to judicial enforcement of the once widely used practice of restrictive covenants—agreements among property owners to exclude persons of designated races. In the Missouri case, for example, a 1911 agreement signed by 30 out of 39 property owners in the

---

* Together with McGhee v. Sipes, on certiorari to the Supreme Court of Michigan.

area restricted use and occupancy for 50 years to persons of "the Caucasian race" and excluded "people of the Negro or Mongolian race." The petitioners in these cases were Blacks who had purchased houses from white owners despite the fact that the properties were subject to racially restricted covenants signed by most of the owners in the area. Respondents, owners of other properties subject to the terms of the covenants, sued to enjoin Black purchasers from taking possession of the property and to divest them of title. The state courts granted the relief.]

Mr. Chief Justice VINSON delivered the opinion of the Court. . . .

Whether the equal protection clause of the Fourteenth Amendment inhibits judicial enforcement by state courts of restrictive covenants based on race or color is a question which this Court has not heretofore been called upon to consider. . . .

It cannot be doubted that among the civil rights intended to be protected from discriminatory state action by the Fourteenth Amendment are the rights to acquire, enjoy, own and dispose of property. Equality in the enjoyment of property rights was regarded by the framers of that Amendment as an essential pre-condition to the realization of other basic civil rights and liberties which the Amendment was intended to guarantee. Thus, § 1978 of the Revised Statutes [now 42 U.S.C. § 1982 [1]], derived from § 1 of the Civil Rights Act of 1866 which was enacted by Congress while the Fourteenth Amendment was also under consideration, provides:

"All citizens of the United States shall have the same right, in every State and Territory, as is enjoyed by white citizens thereof to inherit, purchase, lease, sell, hold, and convey real and personal property." This Court has given specific recognition to the same principle. Buchanan v. Warley, 245 U.S. 60 (1917).[2]

It is likewise clear that restrictions on the right of occupancy of the sort sought to be created by the private agreements in these cases could not be squared with the requirements of the Fourteenth Amendment if imposed by state statute or local ordinance. . . .

But the present cases [do] not involve action by state legislatures or city councils. Here the particular patterns of discrimination and the areas in which the restrictions are to operate, are determined, in the first instance, by the terms of agreements among private individuals. Participation of the State consists in the enforcement of the restrictions so defined. The crucial issue with which we are here confronted is whether this distinction removes these cases from the operation of the prohibitory provisions of the Fourteenth Amendment.

1. On the modern interpretation (and reinvigoration) of 42 U.S.C. § 1982, see Jones v. Alfred H. Mayer, Co., 392 U.S. 409 (1968), printed in sec. 3 below.

2. Buchanan v. Warley held unconstitutional a city ordinance making it unlawful for any "colored person" to move in and occupy a house on a block where the majority of residents were whites. The ordinance was held to violate due process of law as an interference with "the civil right of a white man to dispose of his property if he saw fit to do so to a person of color." The issue arose in an action for specific performance of a contract for the sale of land. The vendee set up as a defense that he was a colored person and that the purchase of the land would violate the ordinance.

Since the decision of this Court in the Civil Rights Cases, the principle has become firmly embedded in our constitutional law that the action inhibited by the first section of the Fourteenth Amendment is only such action as may fairly be said to be that of the States. That Amendment erects no shield against merely private conduct, however discriminatory or wrongful.

We conclude, therefore, that the restrictive agreements standing alone cannot be regarded as violative of any rights guaranteed to petitioners by the Fourteenth Amendment. So long as the purposes of those agreements are effectuated by voluntary adherence to their terms, it would appear clear that there has been no action by the State and the provisions of the Amendment have not been violated.

But here there was more. These are cases in which the purposes of the agreements were secured only by judicial enforcement by state courts of the restrictive terms of the agreements. The respondents urge that judicial enforcement of private agreements does not amount to state action; or, in any event, the participation of the State is so attenuated in character as not to amount to state action within the meaning of the Fourteenth Amendment. Finally, it is suggested, even if the States in these cases may be deemed to have acted in the constitutional sense, their action did not deprive petitioners of rights guaranteed by the Fourteenth Amendment. . . .

That the action of state courts and judicial officers in their official capacities is to be regarded as action of the State within the meaning of the Fourteenth Amendment, is a proposition which has long been established by decisions of this Court. . . .

[T]he examples of state judicial action which have been held by this Court to violate the Amendment's commands are not restricted to situations in which the judicial proceedings were found in some manner to be procedurally unfair. It has been recognized that the action of state courts in enforcing a substantive common-law rule formulated by those courts, may result in the denial of rights guaranteed by the Fourteenth Amendment.

[Thus, in] Cantwell v. Connecticut, 310 U.S. 296 (1940), a conviction in a state court of the common-law crime of breach of the peace was, under the circumstances of the case, found to be a violation of the Amendment's commands relating to freedom of religion. In Bridges v. California, 314 U.S. 252 (1941), enforcement of the state's common-law rule relating to contempts by publication was held to be state action inconsistent with the prohibitions of the Fourteenth Amendment. . . . [All of these cases are considered in chaps. 12 and 13, below.]

The short of the matter is that from the time of the adoption of the Fourteenth Amendment until the present, it has been the consistent ruling of this Court that the action of the States to which the Amendment has reference includes actions of state courts and state judicial officials. . . .

We have no doubt that there has been state action in these cases in the full and complete sense of the phrase. The undisputed facts disclose that petitioners were willing purchasers of properties upon which they desired to establish homes. The owners of the properties were willing sellers; and contracts of sale were accordingly consummated. It is clear that but for the active intervention of the state courts, supported by the full panoply

of state power, petitioners would have been free to occupy the properties in question without restraint.

These are not cases, as has been suggested, in which the States have merely abstained from action, leaving private individuals free to impose such discriminations as they see fit. Rather, these are cases in which the States have made available to such individuals the full coercive power of government to deny to petitioners, on the grounds of race or color, the enjoyment of property rights in premises which petitioners are willing and financially able to acquire and which the grantors are willing to sell. The difference between judicial enforcement and non-enforcement of the restrictive covenants is the difference to petitioners between being denied rights of property available to other members of the community and being accorded full enjoyment of those rights on an equal footing.

The enforcement of the restrictive agreements by the state courts in these cases was directed pursuant to the common-law policy of the States as formulated by those courts in earlier decisions. [The] judicial action in each case bears the clear and unmistakable imprimatur of the State. We have noted that previous decisions of this Court have established the proposition that judicial action is not immunized from the operation of the Fourteenth Amendment simply because it is taken pursuant to the state's common-law policy. Nor is the Amendment ineffective simply because the particular pattern of discrimination, which the State has enforced, was defined initially by the terms of a private agreement. State action, as that phrase is understood for the purposes of the Fourteenth Amendment, refers to exertions of state power in all forms. And when the effect of that action is to deny rights subject to the protection of the Fourteenth Amendment, it is the obligation of this Court to enforce the constitutional commands.

We hold that in granting judicial enforcement of the restrictive agreements in these cases, the States have denied petitioners the equal protection of the laws and that, therefore, the action of the state courts cannot stand. We have noted that freedom from discrimination by the States in the enjoyment of property rights was among the basic objectives sought to be effectuated by the framers of the Fourteenth Amendment. That such discrimination has occurred in these cases is clear. . . .

Respondents urge, however, that since the state courts stand ready to enforce restrictive covenants excluding white persons from the ownership or occupancy of property covered by such agreements, enforcement of covenants excluding colored persons may not be deemed a denial of equal protection of the laws to the colored persons who are thereby affected. This contention does not bear scrutiny. The parties have directed our attention to no case in which a court, state or federal, has been called upon to enforce a covenant excluding members of the white majority from ownership or occupancy of real property on grounds of race or color. But there are more fundamental considerations. The rights created by the first section of the Fourteenth Amendment are, by its terms, guaranteed to the individual. The rights established are personal rights. It is, therefore, no answer to these petitioners to say that the courts may also be induced to deny white persons rights of ownership and occupancy on grounds of race or color.

Equal protection of the laws is not achieved through indiscriminate imposition of inequalities. . . .

Reversed.*

Mr. Justice REED, Mr. Justice JACKSON, and Mr. Justice RUTLEDGE took no part in the consideration or decision of these cases.

SHELLEY v. KRAEMER: THE APPLICATIONS AND THE SEARCH FOR LIMITS

Introduction. Does Shelley make 14th Amendment restrictions applicable whenever private choices are enabled to be carried out because of the backing of the state? Even if the decision to discriminate originates wholly with the individual and the state aid is extended neutrally, to enforce whatever private choice is made? Is private action converted into state action whenever the individual seeks court or police aid to enforce contract or property rights? Is there state aid whenever the state fails to forbid an individual choice which it has power to control? Given the pervasive state regulatory power—indeed, the pervasiveness of law as an ultimate backstop that makes private choices possible—does so broad a reading not convert virtually all private decisions into state action and obliterate the state-private distinction?

Is Chief Justice Vinson persuasive in his emphasis on the role of the state in the restrictive covenant cases? Is "neutral" judicial enforcement a more significant benefit to the private actor than "neutral" provision of police and fire services? Is it as significant a benefit as a grant of governmental funds or a monopoly status, considered in some of the cases below? Does the denial of "neutral" judicial enforcement promote self-help by the private actor? Suppose there is violent resistance to that self-help: may the private property owner call on the state's resources for help? Or is the private actor liable to civil and criminal sanctions if he resorts to self-help?

Are narrower readings of Shelley v. Kraemer possible? Is Shelley limited to situations where the state intervention has the effect of blocking a transaction between a willing seller and buyer? Can Shelley be explained on the basis of 42 U.S.C. § 1982, cited by the Court? Cf. Jones v. Alfred H. Mayer Co., sec. 3 below. Can it be explained via a "public function" rationale, on the ground that restrictive covenants applying to a large area are equivalent to impermissible racial zoning laws? [1] Does the Shelley v. Kraemer approach give adequate weight to competing interests in privacy and association and property? Compare Henkin, "Shelley v. Kraemer: Notes for a

---

* In a companion case to Shelley, Hurd v. Hodge, 334 U.S. 24 (1948), the Court held that courts in the District of Columbia could not enforce restrictive covenants even though the 14th Amendment is not applicable to the federal government. Chief Justice Vinson stated that such action would deny "rights . . . protected by the Civil Rights Act"; moreover, it would be contrary to the public policy of the United States to allow a federal court to enforce an agreement constitutionally unenforceable in state courts.

1. Note the comment in Justice Douglas' concurring opinion in Reitman v. Mulkey, below: "Leaving the zoning function to groups [e. g., real estate brokers] which practice discrimination and are licensed by the States constitutes state action in the narrowest sense in which Shelley can be construed."

Revised Opinion," 110 U.Pa.L.Rev. 473 (1962): "If the competing claims of liberty and the possibility that they may sometimes prevail are recognized, Shelley v. Kraemer must be given [a] limited reading." Henkin suggests that "there are circumstances where the discriminator can invoke a protected liberty which is not constitutionally inferior to the claim of equal protection. There, the Constitution requires or permits the state to favor the right to discriminate over the victim's claim to equal protection; the state, then, is not in violation of the fourteenth amendment when it legislates or affords a remedy in support of the discrimination." He suggests as those "special cases" where the discriminator should prevail "those few where the state supports that basic liberty, privacy, autonomy, which outweighs even the equal protection of the laws." Are the only competing interests which limit the application of the Shelley principle those that are themselves of constitutional dimensions? In other words, is the Shelley principle applicable, and must state action be found, in any situation in which state or federal legislatures have the *power* to outlaw racial discrimination without impinging on constitutional guarantees? Or is Shelley's reach narrower than that?

If Shelley were read at its broadest, a simple citation of the case would have disposed of most subsequent state action controversies—and would have provided a simple answer to most of the problems in the preceding materials. Some seemingly "neutral" state nexus with the private actor could typically be found: at least by way of state backdrop for exercises of private choice; usually, more concrete state participation than that. But, as the cases that follow illustrate, the Court has rejected so embracive a reading and has taken seriously the Shelley assurance that, despite some of its language, a state-private distinction was to be retained. The efforts to find limiting principles on the broadest implications of Shelley have produced extensive commentary on and off the Court.

1. *Restrictive covenants and damage actions.* Chief Justice Vinson, the author of the Shelley opinion, dissented five years later when the Court held the Shelley principle applicable to an enforcement of a restrictive covenant by a damage suit against a co-covenantor. BARROWS v. JACKSON, 346 U.S. 249 (1953). The Court noted that permitting damage judgments would induce prospective sellers of restricted land either to refuse to sell to non-Caucasians or to "require non-Caucasians to pay a higher price to meet the damages which the seller may incur." The Court "will not permit or require" the state "to coerce respondent to respond in damages for failure to observe a restrictive covenant that this Court would deny [the state] the right to enforce in equity." [2]

2. *Reverter provisions in deeds.* The Court's 5 to 2 decision in its second encounter with the litigation over Baconsfield park in Macon, Ga., in EVANS v. ABNEY, 396 U.S. 435 (1970), illustrated that Shelley had not barred all state involvement in enforcing private restrictions on property. Senator Bacon's will had conveyed property in trust to the city for use as a

2. Do Shelley and Barrows bar recognition of a restrictive covenant as a defense in actions for damages for breach of contract? See Rice v. Sioux City Memorial Park Cemetery, 245 Iowa 147, 60 N.W.2d 110 (1953), aff'd by an equally divided Court, 348 U.S. 880 (1954), vacated and cert. dismissed as improvidently granted, 349 U.S. 70 (1955). Cf. Black v. Cutter Laboratories, 351 U.S. 292 (1956).

park "for white people only."   After Evans v. Newton, 382 U.S. 296 (1966), had held that Baconsfield could not be operated on a racially discriminatory basis (as noted in the "public function" materials above), the state court ruled that "Senator Bacon's intention to provide a park for whites only had become impossible to fulfill and that accordingly the trust had failed and the parkland and other trust property had reverted by operation of Georgia law to the heirs of the Senator."   The Supreme Court, in a majority opinion by Justice Black, held that this ruling did not constitute state discrimination under the 14th Amendment.

The state court had rejected arguments that it should save the trust by applying the *cy pres* doctrine to amend the will by striking the racial restriction. The state court "concluded, in effect, that Senator Bacon would have rather had the whole trust fail than have Baconsfield integrated."   Justice Black concluded that the termination of the trust and the enforcement of the reverter violated no federal rights: "[A]ny harshness that may have resulted from the State court's decision can be attributed solely to its intention to effectuate as nearly as possible the explicit terms of Senator Bacon's will."

Justice Black insisted that "the situation presented in this case [is] easily distinguishable from that presented in Shelley v. Kraemer, 334 U.S. 1 (1948), where we held unconstitutional state judicial action which had affirmatively enforced a private scheme of discrimination against Negroes.   Here the effect of the Georgia decision eliminated all discrimination against Negroes in the park by eliminating the park itself, and the termination of the park was a loss shared equally by the white and Negro citizens of Macon."

Petitioners insisted, moreover, that the state court had not really given effect to a clear-cut private intent, but had exercised choice in interpreting that intent as requiring a reverter.   Justice Black rejected "the idea that the Georgia courts had a constitutional obligation in this case to resolve any doubt about the testator's intent in favor of preserving the trust.   [T]he Constitution imposes no requirement upon the Georgia court to approach Bacon's will any differently than it would approach any will creating any charitable trust of any kind."

There were dissents by Justices Douglas and Brennan;   Justice Marshall did not participate.   Only Justice Brennan's dissent mentioned Shelley v. Kraemer: "[Shelley] stands at least for the proposition that where parties of different races are willing to deal with one another a state court cannot keep them from doing so by enforcing a privately authored racial restriction." But Justice Brennan placed greater emphasis on other, albeit related, arguments: "The exculpation of the State and city from responsibility for the closing of the park is simply indefensible on this record.   This discriminatory closing is permeated with state action: at the time Senator Bacon wrote his will Georgia statutes expressly authorized and supported the precise kind of discrimination provided for by him;   in accepting title to the park, public officials of the City of Macon entered into an arrangement vesting in private persons the power to enforce a reversion if the city should ever incur a constitutional obligation to desegregate the park;   it is a *public* park that is being closed for a discriminatory reason after having been operated for nearly half a century as a segregated *public* facility.   [T]here is state action whenever a State enters into an arrangement which creates a private right to compel or en-

force the reversion of a public facility. Whether the right is a possibility of reverter, a right of entry, an executory interest, or a contractual right, it can be created only with the consent of a public body or official."

3. *Other testamentary provisions: The Girard College litigation.* Does Evans v. Abney end the two decades of speculation about the impact of Shelley on the enforcement of restrictive provisions in wills? For example, may a court enforce a testamentary provision to cut off a beneficiary if he marries someone of another religion or race? See Gordon v. Gordon, 332 Mass. 197, 124 N.E.2d 228, cert. denied, 349 U.S. 947 (1955), where the state court enforced such a will and summarily rejected Shelley and similar cases as involving "quite different considerations from the right to dispose of property by will."

Does Evans v. Abney cast doubt on the ultimate outcome of the lengthy Girard College litigation? In PENNSYLVANIA v. BOARD OF TRUSTS, 353 U.S. 230 (1957), petitioners were denied admission to the school on the basis of race, pursuant to Stephen Girard's will, probated in 1831, setting up a trust for a school for "poor white male orphans." The will named the City of Philadelphia as trustee; subsequently, a "Board of Directors of City Trusts," composed of city officials and persons named by local courts, was established to administer the trust and the college. The state court refused to order admission. The Supreme Court reversed per curiam: "The Board which operates Girard College is an agency of the State. . . . Therefore, even though the Board was acting as trustee, its refusal to admit [petitioners] was discrimination by the State." After the Court's reversal, the state courts substituted private persons as trustees to carry out Girard's will. The Supreme Court denied certiorari. In re Girard College Trusteeship, 391 Pa. 434, 138 A.2d 844, cert. denied, 357 U.S. 570 (1958). Ten years after that denial of certiorari, however, the Court of Appeals for the Third Circuit held that the state courts' substitution of private trustees was unconstitutional state action. Pennsylvania v. Brown, 392 F.2d 120 (1968), cert. denied, 391 U.S. 921 (1968). See Clark, "Charitable Trusts, the Fourteenth Amendment and the Will of Stephen Girard," 66 Yale L.J. 979 (1957).

4. *Trespass actions and the sit-in cases.* Does Shelley v. Kraemer bar the enforcement of state trespass laws against persons excluded from private property on racial grounds? Is the state's enforcement of the property owner's restrictions sufficient state action to make the 14th Amendment applicable? That was the broadest issue inherent in a number of sit-in convictions of demonstrators who had protested discrimination by restaurants and other businesses prior to the enactment of the public accommodations provisions of the 1964 Civil Rights Act. In a series of decisions in the early sixties, the Court set aside all of the convictions—yet all of the decisions managed to avoid reliance on the Shelley principle. The broadest reading of Shelley would have covered these cases with ease; the failure to rely on Shelley and the statements in some of the cases suggested that more state involvement than even-handed enforcement of private biases was necessary to find unconstitutional state action.

For example, in Peterson v. Greenville, 373 U.S. 244 (1963)—one of five sit-in cases reversed at that time—the Court found official segregation policies in the background and refused to inquire whether the restaurant

manager would have excluded the demonstrators if the state had been wholly silent: the unconstitutional ingredients "cannot be saved by attempting to separate the mental urges of the discriminators." Justice Harlan's separate opinion asserted that the "ultimate substantive question" was whether "the character of the State's involvement in an arbitrary discrimination is such that it should be held *responsible* for the discrimination."

In another 1963 sit-in case resting on narrow grounds, Lombard v. Louisiana, 373 U.S. 267 (1963), Justice Douglas argued that state courts cannot "put criminal sanctions behind racial discrimination in public places." He distinguished the restaurant situation from "an intrusion of a man's home or yard or farm or garden," where "the property owner could seek and obtain the aid of the State against the intruder." But the restaurant had "no aura of constitutionally protected privacy about it." Compare Justice Harlan's dissent in Peterson, insisting that the sit-in problem involved "a clash of competing constitutional claims of a high order: liberty and equality." He emphasized the restaurant proprietor's freedom to "use and dispose of his property as he sees fit."

Another group of five sit-in cases reached the Court in 1964. The trespass convictions were once again reversed on narrow grounds; but this time six of the Justices reached the broader issues—and divided 3 to 3. BELL v. MARYLAND, 378 U.S. 226 (1964). None of the opinions took a "simple" view of Shelley. For example, Justice Douglas, joined by Justice Goldberg, reiterated his approach in Lombard and emphasized that restaurant discrimination "did not reflect 'personal' prejudices but business reasons." This was not property associated with privacy interests, but "property that is serving the public." And he argued that Shelley v. Kraemer should govern here: "The preferences involved in [Shelley] were far more personal than the motivations of the corporate managers in the present case."

Justice Black's dissent in Bell, joined by Justices Harlan and White, viewed Shelley and the reach of § 1 of the 14th Amendment more narrowly.[3] Justice Black insisted that § 1 of the 14th Amendment "does not of itself, standing alone, in the absence of some cooperative state action or compulsion, forbid property holders, including restaurant owners, to ban people from entering or remaining upon their premises, even if the owners act out of racial prejudice." He elaborated:

"The Amendment does not forbid a State to prosecute for crimes committed against a person or his property, however prejudiced or narrow the victim's views may be. Nor can whatever prejudice and bigotry the victim of a crime may have be automatically attributed to the State that prosecutes. Such a doctrine would not only be based on a fiction; it would also severely handicap a State's efforts to maintain a peaceful and orderly society. . . . It would betray our whole plan for a tranquil and orderly society to say that a citizen, because of his personal prejudices, habits, attitudes, or beliefs, is cast outside the law's protection . . . . .

3. Justice Black's opinion also included an important suggestion of a congressional power to reach further into the private sphere under § 5 of the 14th Amendment than the Court itself could properly go in its interpretations of § 1. He stated that § 1 "un- like other sections [citing the congressional enforcement power under § 5] is a prohibition against certain conduct only when done by a State." See the consideration of that congressional power under § 5 in sec. 3 of this chapter.

"[R]eliance [on Shelley] is misplaced. . . . It seems pretty clear that the reason judicial enforcement of the restrictive covenants in Shelley was deemed state action was not merely the fact that a state court had acted, but rather that state enforcement of the covenants had the effect of denying to the parties their federally guaranteed right to own, occupy, enjoy, and use their property without regard to race or color. Thus, the line of cases from [Buchanan v. Warley, the racial zoning ordinance case,] through Shelley establishes these propositions: (1) When an owner of property is willing to sell and a would-be purchaser is willing to buy, then the Civil Rights Act of 1866, which gives all persons the same right to "inherit, lease, sell, hold and convey' property, prohibits a State [from] preventing the sale on the grounds of the race or color of one of the parties. . . . (2) Once a person has become a property owner, then he acquires all the rights that go with ownership. [When] *both* parties are willing parties, then the principles stated in Buchanan and Shelley protect this right. But equally, when one party is unwilling, as when the property owner chooses *not* to sell to a particular person or *not* to admit that person, then [he] is entitled to rely on the guarantee of due process of law [to] protect his free use and enjoyment of property." [4]

5. *Transitional note.* Recall the questions raised at the beginning of this group of notes about the possible explanations for, and limits upon, the Shelley principle. What are the limitations on Shelley suggested by the materials in these notes? Do the cases below indicate additional limits on broad readings of Shelley and suggest different directions for delineating the scope of the state action concept? The Burton case, which follows, requires state involvement "to some significant extent" to convert private action into unconstitutional discrimination. What constitutes the requisite state involvement? What is the relevance of the use of state property? Of state regulation? Of licensing? Of conferral of other state benefits? Does Reitman v. Mulkey, below, indicate that state "encouragement" is enough? When does the state "encourage" private discrimination? Is state authorization enough? Can state "authorization" be distinguished from mere failure to prohibit private discrimination when the state has the power to do so?

BURTON v. WILMINGTON PARKING AUTHORITY

365 U.S. 715, 81 S.Ct. 856, 6 L.Ed.2d 45 (1961).

Certiorari to the Supreme Court of Delaware.

Mr. Justice CLARK delivered the opinion of the Court.

In this action for declaratory and injunctive relief it is admitted that the Eagle Coffee Shoppe, Inc., a restaurant located within an off-street automobile parking building in Wilmington, Delaware, has refused to serve appellant food or drink solely because he is a Negro. The parking building is owned and operated by the Wilmington Parking Authority, an agency of the State of Delaware, and the restaurant is the Authority's lessee. . . . The Supreme Court of Delaware has held that Eagle was acting in "a purely private capacity"

---

4. Soon after this decision, the Court held in Hamm v. City of Rock Hill, 379 U.S. 306 (1964), that the enactment of the 1964 Civil Rights Act abated prosecutions against persons who would have been entitled to service under its public accommodations provisions if the Act had been in force.

under its lease; that its action was not that of the Authority and was not, therefore, state action . . . . . It also held that under 24 Del.Code § 1501,[1] Eagle was a restaurant, not an inn, and that as such it "is not required [under Delaware law] to serve any and all persons entering its place of business." . . . On the merits we have concluded that the exclusion of appellant under the circumstances shown to be present here was discriminatory state action in violation of the Equal Protection Clause.

The Authority was created [to] provide adequate parking facilities for the convenience of the public . . . . . The first project undertaken by the Authority was the erection of a parking facility. [T]he Authority was advised by its retained experts that the anticipated revenue from the parking of cars and proceeds from sale of its bonds would not be sufficient to finance the construction costs of the facility. . . . . To secure additional capital needed for its "debt-service" requirements, and thereby to make bond financing practicable, the Authority decided it was necessary to enter long-term leases with responsible tenants for commercial use of some of the space available in the projected "garage building." The public was invited to bid for these leases.

In April 1957 such a private lease, for 20 years, [was] made with Eagle Coffee Shoppe, Inc., for use as a "restaurant." [The lease] contains no requirement that its restaurant services be made available to the general public on a nondiscriminatory basis, in spite of the fact that the Authority has power to adopt rules and regulations respecting the use of its facilities . . . . .

. . . It is clear, as it always has been since the Civil Rights Cases, that "Individual invasion of individual rights is not the subject-matter of the amendment," and that private conduct abridging individual rights does no violence to the Equal Protection Clause unless to some significant extent the State in any of its manifestations has been found to have become involved in it. [T]o fashion and apply a precise formula for recognition of state responsibility under the Equal Protection Clause is "an impossible task" which "this Court has never attempted." Only by sifting facts and weighing circumstances can the nonobvious involvement of the State in private conduct be attributed its true significance.

[T]he Delaware Supreme Court seems to have placed controlling emphasis on its conclusion, as to the accuracy of which there is doubt, that only some 15% of the total cost of the facility was "advanced" from public funds; that the cost of the entire facility was allocated three-fifths to the space for commercial leasing and two-fifths to parking space; that anticipated revenue from parking was only some 30.5% of the total income, the balance of which was expected to be earned by the leasing; . . . that Eagle expended considerable moneys on furnishings; that the restaurant's main and marked public entrance is on Ninth Street without any public entrance direct from the parking area; and that "the only connection Eagle has with the public facility [is] the furnishing of the sum of $28,700 annually in the form of rent

1. The statute provides that: "No keeper of an inn, tavern, hotel, or restaurant, or other place of public entertainment or refreshment of travelers, guests, or customers shall be obliged, by law, to furnish entertainment or refreshment to persons whose reception or entertainment by him would be offensive to the major part of his customers, and would injure his business. . . . ." [Footnote by the Court. Cf. the concurrences, below.]

which is used by the Authority to defray a portion of the operating expense of an otherwise unprofitable enterprise." While these factual considerations are indeed validly accountable aspects of the enterprise upon which the State has embarked, we cannot say that they lead inescapably to the conclusion that state action is not present. Their persuasiveness is diminished when evaluated in the context of other factors which must be acknowledged.

The land and building were publicly owned. As an entity, the building was dedicated to "public uses" in performance of the Authority's "essential governmental functions." The costs of land acquisition, construction, and maintenance are defrayed entirely from donations by the City of Wilmington, from loans and revenue bonds and from the proceeds of rentals and parking services out of which the loans and bonds were payable. Assuming that the distinction would be significant, cf. Derrington v. Plummer, 5 Cir., 240 F.2d 922, 925, the commercially leased areas were not surplus state property, but constituted a physically and financially integral and, indeed, indispensable part of the State's plan to operate its project as a self-sustaining unit. . . It cannot be doubted that the peculiar relationship of the restaurant to the parking facility in which it is located confers on each an incidental variety of mutual benefits. . . . Neither can it be ignored, especially in view of Eagle's affirmative allegation that for it to serve Negroes would injure its business, that profits earned by discrimination not only contribute to, but are indispensable elements in, the financial success of a governmental agency.

Addition of all these activities, obligations and responsibilities of the Authority, the benefits mutually conferred, together with the obvious fact that the restaurant is operated as an integral part of a public building devoted to a public parking service, indicates that degree of state participation and involvement in discriminatory action which it was the design of the Fourteenth Amendment to condemn. It is irony amounting to grave injustice that in one part of a single building, erected and maintained with public funds by an agency of the State to serve a public purpose, all persons have equal rights, while in another portion, also serving the public, a Negro is a second-class citizen. [I]n its lease with Eagle the Authority could have affirmatively required Eagle to discharge the responsibilities under the Fourteenth Amendment imposed upon the private enterprise as a consequence of state participation. But no State may effectively abdicate its responsibilities by either ignoring them or by merely failing to discharge them whatever the motive may be. It is of no consolation to an individual denied the equal protection of the laws that it was done in good faith. . . . By its inaction, the Authority, and through it the State, has not only made itself a party to the refusal of service, but has elected to place its power, property and prestige behind the admitted discrimination. The State has so far insinuated itself into a position of interdependence with Eagle that it must be recognized as a joint participant in the challenged activity, which, on that account, cannot be considered to have been so "purely private" as to fall without the scope of the Fourteenth Amendment.

Because readily applicable formulae may not be fashioned, the conclusions drawn from the facts and circumstances of this record are by no means declared as universal truths on the basis of which every state leasing agreement is to be tested. Owing to the very "largeness" of government, a multi-

tude of relationships might appear to some to fall within the Amendment's embrace, but that, it must be remembered, can be determined only in the framework of the peculiar facts or circumstances present. Therefore respondents' prophecy of nigh universal application of a constitutional precept so peculiarly dependent for its invocation upon appropriate facts fails to take into account "Differences in circumstances [which] beget appropriate differences in law" . . . . Specifically defining the limits of our inquiry, what we hold today is that when a State leases public property in the manner and for the purpose shown to have been the case here, the proscriptions of the Fourteenth Amendment must be complied with by the lessee as certainly as though they were binding covenants written into the agreement iself. . . .

Reversed and remanded.

Mr. Justice STEWART, concurring.

I agree that the judgment must be reversed, but I reach that conclusion by a route much more direct than the one traveled by the Court. In upholding Eagle's right to deny service to the appellant solely because of his race, the Supreme Court of Delaware relied upon a statute of that State which permits the proprietor of a restaurant to refuse to serve "persons whose reception or entertainment by him would be offensive to the major part of his customers . . . ." There is no suggestion in the record that the appellant as an individual was such a person. The highest court of Delaware has thus construed this legislative enactment as authorizing discriminatory classification based exclusively on color. Such a law seems to me clearly violative of the Fourteenth Amendment. I think, therefore, [that] the statute, as authoritatively construed, [is] constitutionally invalid.

Mr. Justice HARLAN, whom Mr. Justice WHITTAKER joins, dissenting.

The Court's opinion, by a process of first undiscriminatingly throwing together various factual bits and pieces and then undermining the resulting structure by an equally vague disclaimer, seems to me to leave completely at sea just what it is in this record that satisfies the requirement of "state action."

I find it unnecessary, however, to inquire into the matter at this stage, for it seems to me apparent that before passing on the far-reaching constitutional questions that may, or may not, be lurking in this judgment, the case should first be sent back to the state court for clarification as to the precise basis of its decision. . . .

If [the] Delaware court construed this state statute "as authorizing discriminatory classification based exclusively on color," I would certainly agree, without more, that the enactment is offensive to the Fourteenth Amendment. It would then be quite unnecessary to reach the much broader questions dealt with in the Court's opinion. If, on the other hand, the state court meant no more than that under the statute, as at common law, Eagle was free to serve only those whom it pleased, then, and only then, would the question of "state action" be presented in full-blown form. . . . *

* Justice Frankfurter also dissented.

STATE INVOLVEMENT IN PRIVATE ACTION—"TO SOME SIGNIFICANT EXTENT"

Does the majority approach in Burton retreat from the broadest implications of Shelley, by suggesting that finding some nexus of the state with the private discrimination is not enough and by insisting that the state must be involved "to some significant extent" to bring the private conduct under the 14th Amendment? [1] What *was* "significant" in Burton? Does Burton give any guidance for evaluating "significance"? Cf. Lewis, "Burton v. Wilmington Parking Authority—A Case Without Precedent," 61 Colum. L.Rev. 1458 (1961).

1. *Leases and sales of public property.* Was the critical factor in Burton the involvement of public property? The majority opinion in Burton cited Derrington v. Plummer, 240 F.2d 922 (5th Cir. 1956), cert. denied, 353 U.S. 924 (1957). There, a county had equipped a courthouse basement as a cafeteria and leased it to a private party who refused to serve Blacks. The lease required that the cafeteria be open while the courthouse was open, and that the operator give a discount to county employees. The court held that an injunction against renewal of the lease should be granted. It explained that, though "a county may in good faith lawfully sell and dispose of its surplus property," the property here was not surplus and emphasized that the purpose of the lease was to furnish service to users of the courthouse. The court concluded that the county was providing services "through the instrumentality" of the lease, and that in rendering such service, "the lessee stands in the place of the County." Compare Tonkins v. City of Greensboro, 276 F.2d 890 (4th Cir. 1960), holding that a bona fide sale of a public swimming pool to private parties did not constitute unconstitutional state involvement in discrimination by the private owners. But Hampton v. City of Jacksonville, 304 F.2d 320 (5th Cir. 1962), barred the exclusion of Blacks from a golf course sold by the city to a private owner, where the sale included a provision that the property would revert to the city if it was not used as a golf course. The court found the case closer to Derrington than to Tonkins.

2. *Use of city property by private groups.* The question before the Court in GILMORE v. CITY OF MONTGOMERY, 417 U.S. 556 (1974), was the propriety of a federal court injunction barring a city from permitting the use of its recreational facilities by private segregated school groups and by other non-school groups that were racially discriminatory. The Court had little difficulty in sustaining that portion of the injunction that barred *exclusive* temporary use of public recreational facilities by segregated private schools. That use was clearly a significant interference with an outstanding federal court public school desegregation order, as noted in chap. 10 above.[2]

1. For further consideration of the "state authorization" approach of the separate opinions in Burton, see the notes following Reitman v. Mulkey, below.

2. Does that suggest that a governmental body under a duty to undo the effects of past de jure segregation is less free to make public property available to private discriminatory groups than bodies which have not practiced de jure segregation? See also chap. 10 above and Norwood v. Harrison, 413 U.S. 455 (1973), holding that Mississippi could not lend text-

But the Court had greater difficulty about *nonexclusive* use of recreational facilities by private schools and other segregated groups. Justice Blackmun's prevailing opinion remanded that problem for further consideration: "Upon this record, we are unable to draw a conclusion as to whether the use of zoos, museums, parks, and other recreational facilities by private school groups in common with others, and by private nonschool organizations, involves government so directly in the actions of those users as to warrant court intervention on constitutional grounds." In giving guidance for consideration on remand, the Court emphasized the need for a particularized examination of the circumstances in accordance with the approach of Burton. If the uses could be identified as underminings of outstanding desegregation orders for public schools and parks, the case would be relatively easy. But the "problem of private group use is much more complex" if the decision had to turn solely on state action principles. He elaborated:

"Because the city makes city property available for use by private entities, this case is more like Burton than Moose Lodge [below]. Traditional state monopolies, such as electricity, water, and police and fire protection—all generalized governmental services—do not by their mere provision constitute a showing of state involvement in invidious discrimination. The same is true of a broad spectrum of municipal recreational facilities: parks, playgrounds, athletic facilities, amphitheaters, museums, zoos, and the like. Cf. [Evans v. Newton]. It follows, therefore, that the portion of the District Court's order prohibiting the mere use of such facilities by *any* segregated 'private group, club or organization' is invalid because it was not predicated upon a proper finding of state action.

"If, however, the city or other governmental entity rations otherwise freely accessible recreational facilities, the case for state action will naturally be stronger than if the facilities are simply available to all comers without condition or reservation. Here, for example, petitioners allege that the city engages in scheduling softball games for an all-white church league and provides balls, equipment, fields and lighting. The city's role in that situation would be dangerously close to what was found to exist in Burton." But the task for the trial court on remand was to engage in the "case-by-case" examination of "nonobvious involvement of the State in private conduct" in accordance with the Burton analysis.

There were several concurring opinions. Note especially the comments on the Burton problem in Justice White's concurrence, joined by Justice Douglas: "It may be useful also to emphasize that there is very plainly state action of some sort involved in the leasing, rental or extending the use

books to students in private segregated schools under a long-established program for providing books to all public and private school students. Compare McGlotten v. Connally, 338 F.Supp. 448 (D.D.C.1972), holding that the Government could not allow charitable deductions and gifts to discriminating fraternal orders and could not grant federal tax exemptions to such groups. Though every tax deduction confers benefits, that is not enough to impose constitutional restraints on the beneficiary; here, however, the government was "sufficiently entwined with private parties" to make the Constitution applicable, in part because of the extensive control by the government over the purposes of exempt organizations and "the aura of government approval inherent in an exempt ruling." See Bittker and Kaufman, "Taxes and Civil Rights: 'Constitutionalizing' the Internal Revenue Code," 82 Yale L.J. 51 (1972).

of scarce city-owned recreation facilities to private schools or other private
groups. [T]he question is not whether there is state action but whether the
conceded state action [is] such that the State must be deemed to have denied
the equal protection of the laws. [H]as the State furnished such aid to the
group's segregated policies or become so involved in them that the State itself
may fairly be said to have denied equal protection? Under [Burton], it is
perfectly clear that to violate the Equal Protection Clause the State itself need
not make, advise or authorize the private decision to discriminate that involves
the State in the pracice of segregation or would appear to do so in the minds
of ordinary citizens."

    3. *Governmental involvement through licensing.* Does governmental
licensing of a private actor constitute sufficient governmental involvement,
or sufficient grant of governmental benefits, to warrant the application of
constitutional restraints? Does the nature of the licensing scheme make
a difference: are licenses that simply certify qualifications of the licensee,
for example, distinguishable from licenses that grant special rights to use
scarce resources? In one of the sit-in cases, Garner v. Louisiana, 368 U.S.
157 (1961), Justice Douglas' separate opinion suggested that licensing and
regulation of a restaurant made it a "public facility" and constituted adequate
state action. The majority disposed of that sit-in case, as it did all others,
on narrower grounds.

    a. *Liquor licenses.* The full Court confronted the relevance of li-
censing a decade later, in MOOSE LODGE NO. 107 v. IRVIS, 407 U.S.
163 (1972). That 6 to 3 decision rejected a claim that a private club's
racial discrimination was unconstitutional because the club held a state liquor
license. In the Moose Lodge case, the club had refused service in its dining
room and bar to a Black guest of a Lodge member. The lower federal
court sustained Irvis' state action claim and declared the Lodge's liquor
license invalid. Justice Rehnquist's majority opinion for the Court, however,
rejected most of the attacks on the Lodge's guest restrictions.

    The Court concluded that, with one exception, the operation of the
state liquor regulation scheme did "not sufficiently implicate the State in
the discriminatory guest policies of Moose Lodge so as to make the latter
'State action.'" After recalling the "essential dichotomy" between state
and private action, Justice Rehnquist conceded that "the impetus for the
forbidden discrimination need not originate with the State if it is state action
that enforces privately originated discrimination," citing the Shelley case.
But that did not mean, he emphasized, "that discrimination by an otherwise
private entity would be violative of the Equal Protection Clause if the private
entity receives any sort of benefit or service at all from the state, or if it is
subject to state regulation in any degree whatever. Since state-furnished
services include such necessities of life as electricity, water, and police
and fire protection, such a holding would utterly emasculate the distinction between private as distinguished from State conduct." To find unconstitutional state action in situations "where the impetus for the discrimination is private, the State must have 'significantly involved itself with invidious
discriminations.'" And the Court found no such involvement here. Justice Rehnquist took special care to note the distinctions between the Lodge
situation and that in the Burton case. Here, for example, there was "nothing

approaching the symbiotic relationship between lessor and lessee" in Burton. That was "a public restaurant in a public building"; this was "a private social club in a private building."

The Court insisted that the liquor regulations did not demonstrate the requisite state involvement. The lower court had emphasized that these regulations were "pervasive." Justice Rehnquist responded: "However detailed this type of regulation may be in some particulars, it cannot be said to in any way foster or encourage racial discrimination." And that conclusion was not undercut by the fact that Pennsylvania limited the number of liquor licenses in each city, since that fell "far short of conferring upon club licensees a monopoly in the dispensing of liquor." [3]

Justice Douglas' dissent explained that he would *not* apply constitutional restrictions to private clubs simply because they had a state license of one sort or another. He noted that First Amendment and related guarantees create "a zone of privacy": "The associational rights which our system honors permit all white, all black, all brown, and all yellow clubs to be formed." Accordingly, the mere fact that the Lodge had a racially restrictive policy was "constitutionally irrelevant." Moreover, earlier cases in which he had emphasized a state nexus because of licensing (see, e. g., Garner v. Louisiana, above) were not apposite, because a private club "is not in the public domain." "And the fact that a private club gets some kind of permit from the [state] does not make it ipso facto a public enterprise or undertaking, any more than the grant to a householder of a permit to operate an incinerator puts the householder in the public domain." But here, there was ample reason to distinguish "the liquor license possessed by Moose Lodge from the incinerator permit"; here, there were "special circumstances" distinguishable from the ordinary licensing situation.

Here, Justice Douglas emphasized, the State was "putting the weight of its liquor license, concededly a valued and important adjunct to a private club, behind racial discrimination." If the specific regulation invalidated by the majority had been the only problem, he might have agreed with the Court's narrow injunction. But he found "another flaw in the scheme not so easily cured": a result of the complex restrictive licensing system was that the Harrisburg quota had been full for many years. And this "state-enforced scarcity of licenses restricts the ability of blacks to obtain liquor." A group desiring to form a nondiscriminatory club would have to "purchase a license held by an existing club, which can exact a monopoly price for the transfer." And "without a liquor license a fraternal organization would be hard-pressed to survive." [4] Justice Marshall joined Justice Douglas' dissent as well as another

3. The Court found a constitutional defect in only one respect: An administrative regulation required that "every club licensee shall adhere to all the provisions of its constitution and by-laws." That regulation was defended as a means to prevent the subterfuge of a place of public accommodation masquerading as a private club. But the Court found the regulation unconstitutional though "neutral in its terms," because "the result of its application" in a case such as this "would be to invoke the sanctions of the State to enforce a concededly discriminatory private rule," and that was barred by Shelley v. Kraemer. The Court accordingly directed an injunction against the enforcement of that regulation; but appellee "was entitled to no more."

4. Soon after the Irvis decision, in July 1972, Mr. Irvis won his battle on

dissent by Justice Brennan. The latter stressed the "pervasive regulatory schemes under which the State dictates and continually supervises virtually every detail of the operation of the licensee's business." Justice Brennan thought the state involvement sufficient to fall within the principle banning all state efforts "to authorize, encourage, or otherwise support racial discrimination in a particular facet of life."

b. *Broadcasting licenses.* In COLUMBIA BROADCASTING SYSTEM v. DEMOCRATIC NAT. COMM., 412 U.S. 94 (1973), the majority sustained the FCC's refusal to compel broadcasters to accept editorial advertisements. The Court's analysis of the First Amendment issues is considered in chap. 12, sec. 2E, below. In the course of the disposition, several of the Justices also considered the "novel question" whether "the action of a broadcast licensee such as that challenged here is 'governmental action' for purposes of the First Amendment." Chief Justice Burger concluded "that the policies complained of do not constitute governmental action violative of the First Amendment"; but the Chief Justice was joined only by Justices Stewart and Rehnquist in that conclusion. The other Justices who supported the Chief Justice in his discussion of the statutory and First Amendment issues withheld approval of the "governmental action" part of his opinion. The dissenting opinion by Justice Brennan, joined by Justice Marshall, found ample "governmental involvement" to justify application of the First Amendment.

Chief Justice Burger's discussion of the state action issue noted that the FCC "has not fostered the licensee policy challenged here; it has simply declined to command particular action because it fell within the area of journalistic discretion." He concluded: "Thus, it cannot be said that the government is a 'partner' to the action of the broadcast licensee complained of here, nor is it engaged in a 'symbiotic relationship' with the licensee, profiting from the invidious discrimination of its proxy. Compare [Moose Lodge] with [Burton]. The First Amendment does not reach acts of private parties in every instance where the Congress or the Commission has merely permitted or failed to prohibit such acts." In supporting that position in his concurrence, Justice Stewart explained his reasons for rejecting the suggested analogies to such cases as Logan Valley, Marsh and Public Utilities Comm'n v. Pollak, 343 U.S. 451 (1952), "where a policy of a privately owned but publicly regulated bus company that had been approved by the regulatory commission was held to activate First Amendment review." [5]

---

the basis of state law. The Pennsylvania Supreme Court sustained an administrative ruling under the state public accommodations law ordering the Harrisburg Moose Lodge to end its ban on Black guests.

5. In the Pollak case, the Court held that a private bus company did not violate the First Amendment by subjecting its captive audiences to radio broadcasts. See chap. 12, sec. 2, below. However, the Court apparently did find the company subject to constitutional limits. The Court noted

that it was not simply relying on the fact that the company operated a public utility or that it enjoyed a substantial monopoly of transit in the District of Columbia. Rather, the emphasis was placed on the regulatory supervision by the Public Utilities Commission and "particularly upon the fact that that agency, pursuant to protests against the radio program, ordered an investigation of it, and after formal public hearings, ordered its investigation dismissed on the ground that the public safety, comfort, and convenience were not impaired there-

Justice Brennan justified his state action conclusion by reciting the "myriad indicia" of "governmental involvement." He concluded: "[G]iven the confluence of these various indicia of 'governmental action'—including the public nature of the airwaves, the governmentally created preferred status of broadcasters, the extensive Government regulation of broadcast programming, and the specific governmental approval of the challenged policy—I can only conclude that the Government 'has so far insinuated itself into a position' of participation in this policy" that the restraints of the First Amendment are applicable.

   c. *Transitional Note: The relevance of governmental licensing, regulation, and benefits.* Reexamine, in the lights of these cases, what the appropriate impact of governmental licensing and regulation should be in finding constitutional guarantees applicable to private actors. Should licensing be sufficient only when special benefits, such as monopolies, are conferred? Should regulation or grants of benefits be adequate only when the regulation or benefits are immediately relevant to the particular challenged practices of the private actor? [6] The Court reexamined those problems at the end of 1974, in Jackson v. Metropolitan Edison Co., 419 U.S. 345. Consideration of that case is postponed until after Reitman v. Mulkey, which follows. Reitman examines the problem of state "encouragement" of private discrimination, and raises again an issue suggested by the separate opinions in Burton, above: the extent to which state failure to prohibit private discrimination constitutes "authorization." The Reitman issues, too, are reexamined in Jackson v. Metropolitan Edison Co., below.

REITMAN v. MULKEY

387 U.S. 369, 87 S.Ct. 1627, 18 L.Ed.2d 830 (1967).

Certiorari to the Supreme Court of California.

Mr. Justice WHITE delivered the opinion of the Court.

The question here is whether Art. I, § 26 of the California Constitution denies "to any person . . . the equal protection of the laws" within the

---

by." See the further consideration of Pollak in Jackson v. Metropolitan Edison Co., below.

6. Cf. Judge Duniway's concurrence in Ascherman v. Presbyterian Hospital, 507 F.2d 1103 (9th Cir. 1974). The court held that a private hospital's receipt of federal funds, coupled with federal and state tax exemptions, did not constitute "state action." The case involved a doctor's complaint that his staff privileges were terminated in violation of procedural due process guarantees. Judge Duniway commented: "There are many 'private' charitable organizations that receive subventions of various kinds from the state or its political subdivisions. I think that it would be most unfortunate to adopt a rule that receipt of such subventions automatically transforms everything that these organizations do into 'state action.' The proposition could produce startling results. For example, if a private tax exempt university received state moneys to build and used them to build a library, would that mean that the librarian's action in ejecting a noisy student from that library is 'state action'? I cannot believe that the state action notion goes so far. . . . What I believe to be the correct rule is stated by Judge Friendly in Powe v. Miles [407 F.2d 73 (2d Cir. 1968)]: '[T]he state must be involved not simply with some activity of the institution . . . but with the activity that caused the injury.' No such involvement is shown here."

meaning of the Fourteenth Amendment of the Constitution of the United States. Section 26 of Art. I, an initiated measure submitted to the people as Proposition 14 in a statewide ballot in 1964, provides in part as follows:

> "Neither the State nor any subdivision or agency thereof shall deny, limit or abridge, directly or indirectly, the right of any person, who is willing or desires to sell, lease or rent any part or all of his real property, to decline to sell, lease or rent such property to such person or persons as he, in his absolute discretion, chooses."

The real property covered by § 26 is limited to residential property and contains an exception for state-owned real estate.

[Respondents] sued under §§ 51 and 52 of the California Civil Code [prohibiting racial and certain other discrimination "in all business establishments"] alleging that petitioners had refused to rent them an apartment solely on account of their race. An injunction and damages were demanded. Petitioners moved for summary judgment on the ground that §§ 51 and 52, insofar as they were the basis for the Mulkeys' action, had been rendered null and void by the adoption of Proposition 14 after the filing of the complaint. The trial court granted the motion [but] the California Supreme Court [held] that Art. I, § 26, was invalid as denying [equal protection].

We affirm [that] judgment of the California Supreme Court, [which] quite properly undertook to examine the constitutionality of § 26 in terms of its "immediate objective," its "ultimate effect" and its "historical context and the conditions existing prior to its enactment." Judgments such as these we have frequently undertaken ourselves. But here the California Supreme Court has addressed itself to these matters and we should give careful consideration to its views because they concern the purpose, scope, and operative effect of a provision of the California Constitution.

First, the court considered whether § 26 was concerned at all with private discriminations in residential housing. This involved a review of past efforts by the California Legislature to regulate such discriminations. The Unruh Act, Civ.Code §§ 51–52, on which respondents based their cases, was passed in 1959. [I]n 1963, came the Rumford Fair Housing Act, [prohibiting] racial discriminations in the sale or rental of any private dwelling containing more than four units. . . .

It was against this background that Proposition 14 was enacted. Its immediate design and intent, the California court said, was "to overturn state laws that bore on the right of private sellers and lessors to discriminate," the Unruh and Rumford Acts, and "to forestall future state action that might circumscribe this right." This aim was successfully achieved . . . .

Second, the court conceded that the State was permitted a neutral position with respect to private racial discriminations and that the State was not bound by the Federal Constitution to forbid them. But [the] court deemed it necessary to determine whether Proposition 14 invalidly involved the State in racial discriminations in the housing market. Its conclusion was that it did.

To reach this result, the state court examined certain prior decisions in this Court in which discriminatory state action was identified. Based on these cases, it concluded that a prohibited state involvement could be found "even where the State can be charged only with encouraging," rather than commanding discrimination. Also of particular interest to the court was Mr.

Justice Stewart's concurrence in [Burton], where it was said that the Delaware courts had construed an existing Delaware statute as "authorizing" racial discrimination in restaurants and that the statute was therefore invalid. To the California court "the instant case presents an undeniably analogous situation" wherein the State had taken affirmative action designed to make private discriminations legally possible. Section 26 was said to have changed the situation from one in which discriminatory practices were restricted "to one where it is encouraged, within the meaning of the cited decisions"; § 26 was legislative action "which authorized private discrimination" and made the State "at least a partner in the instant act of discrimination . . . ." The court could "conceive of no other purpose for an application of § 26 aside from authorizing the perpetration of a purported private discrimination . . . ." The judgment of the California court was that § 26 unconstitutionally involves the State in racial discriminations . . . ."

There is no sound reason for rejecting this judgment. Petitioners contend that the California court has misconstrued the Fourteenth Amendment since the repeal of any statute prohibiting racial discrimination, which is constitutionally permissible, may be said to "authorize" and "encourage" discrimination because it makes legally permissible that which was formerly proscribed. But [the California court] did not read either our cases or the Fourteenth Amendment as establishing an automatic constitutional barrier to the repeal of an existing law prohibiting racial discriminations in housing; nor did the court rule that a State may never put in statutory form an existing policy of neutrality with respect to private discriminations. [It] held the purpose and intent of § 26 was to authorize private racial discriminations in the housing market, to repeal the Unruh and Rumford Acts and to create a constitutional right to discriminate on racial grounds in the sale and leasing of real property. Hence, the court dealt with § 26 as though it expressly authorized and constitutionalized the private right to discriminate. [And] the court assessed the ultimate impact of § 26 in the California environment and concluded that the section would encourage and significantly involve the State in private racial discrimination contrary to the Fourteenth Amendment.

The California court could very reasonably conclude that § 26 would and did have wider impact than a mere repeal of existing statutes. . . . Private discriminations in housing were now not only free from Rumford and Unruh but they also enjoyed a far different status than was true before the passage of those statutes. The right to discriminate, including the right to discriminate on racial grounds, was now embodied in the State's basic charter, immune from legislative, executive, or judicial regulation at any level of the state government. Those practicing racial discriminations need no longer rely solely on their personal choice. They could now invoke express constitutional authority, free from censure or interference of any kind from official sources. . . .

This Court has never attempted the "impossible task" of formulating an infallible test for determining whether the State "in any of its manifestations" has become significantly involved in private discriminations. [Burton.] Here the California court, armed as it was with the knowledge of the facts and circumstances concerning the passage and potential impact of § 26, and familiar with the milieu in which that provision would operate, has determin-

ed that the provision would involve the State in private racial discriminations to an unconstitutional degree. We accept this holding of the California court. The assessment of § 26 by the California court is similar to what this Court has done in appraising state statutes or other official actions in other contexts. . . .

None of these cases squarely controls the case we now have before us. But they do illustrate the range of situations in which discriminatory state action has been identified. They do exemplify the necessity for a court to assess the potential impact of official action in determining whether the State has significantly involved itself with invidious discriminations. Here we are dealing with a provision which does not just repeal an existing law forbidding private racial discriminations. Section 26 was intended to authorize, and does authorize, racial discrimination in the housing market. The right to discriminate is now one of the basic policies of the State. The California Supreme Court believes that the section will significantly encourage and involve the State in private discriminations. We have been presented with no persuasive considerations indicating that this judgment should be overturned.

Affirmed.*

Mr. Justice DOUGLAS, concurring [joining the Court's opinion but adding a comment "to indicate the dimensions of our problem"]. . . .

Real estate brokers and mortgage lenders are largely dedicated to the maintenance of segregated communities. . . . Zoning is a state and municipal function. . . . When the State leaves that function to private agencies or institutions which are licensees and who practice racial discrimination and zone our cities into white and black belts or white and black ghettoes, it suffers a governmental function to be performed under private auspices in a way the State itself may not act. The present case is therefore kin to [Terry v. Adams]. Leaving the zoning function to groups which practice discrimination and are licensed by the States constitutes State action in the narrowest sense in which [Shelley v. Kraemer] can be construed. . . .

If we were in a domain exclusively private, we would have different problems. But urban housing is in the public domain [and] is clearly marked with the public interest. . . . Since the real estate brokerage business is one that can be and is state-regulated and since it is state-licensed, it must be dedicated, like the telephone companies and the carriers and the hotels and motels, to the requirements of service to all without discrimina-

---

* Compare Hunter v. Erickson, 393 U.S. 385 (1969), invalidating a city charter amendment requiring that any city council ordinance regulating real property transactions "on the basis of race, color, religion, national origin or ancestry must first be approved by a majority of the electors voting on the question at a regular or general election before said ordinance shall be effective." That amendment superseded an earlier fair housing ordinance adopted by the city council. The city sought to distinguish Reitman v. Mulkey "in that here the city charter declares no right to discriminate in housing, authorizes and encourages no housing discrimination, and places no ban on the enactment of fair housing ordinances." Justice White did not pursue that argument: elaboration of Reitman was unnecessary here because in this case, unlike Reitman, "there was an explicitly racial classification treating racial housing matters differently from other racial and housing matters." (Recall the consideration of this case in chap. 10 above.)

tion—a standard that in its modern setting is conditioned by the demands of the Equal Protection Clause . . . .

Mr. Justice HARLAN, whom Mr. Justice BLACK, Mr. Justice CLARK, and Mr. Justice STEWART join, dissenting. . . .

[California] has decided to remain "neutral" in the realm of private discrimination affecting the sale or rental of private residential property . . . . In short, all that has happened is that California has effected a *pro tanto* repeal of its prior statutes forbidding private discrimination. This runs no more afoul of the Fourteenth Amendment than would have California's failure to pass any such antidiscrimination statutes in the first instance. The fact that such repeal was also accompanied by a constitutional prohibition against future enactment of such laws [cannot] well be thought to affect, from a federal constitutional standpoint, the validity of what California has done. . . .

The Court attempts to fit § 26 within the coverage of the Equal Protection Clause by characterizing it as in effect an affirmative call to residents of California to discriminate. The main difficulty with this viewpoint is that it depends upon a characterization of § 26 that cannot fairly be made. The provision is neutral on its face, and it is only by in effect asserting that this requirement of passive official neutrality is camouflage that the Court is able to reach its conclusion. In depicting the provision as tantamount to active state encouragement of discrimination the Court essentially relies on the fact that the California Supreme Court so concluded. . . . I agree of course, that *findings of fact* by a state court should be given great weight, but this familiar proposition hardly aids the Court's holding in this case. . . .

. . . There were no disputed issues of fact at all . . . . There was no finding, for example, that the defendants' actions were anything but the product of their own private choice. . . . There were no findings as to the general effect of § 26. The Court declares that the California court "held the purpose and intent of § 26 was to authorize private racial discriminations in the housing market . . . ," but there is no supporting fact in the record for this characterization. Moreover, the grounds which prompt legislators or state voters to repeal a law do not determine its constitutional validity. . . . The only "factual" matter relied on by the majority of the California Supreme Court was the context in which Proposition 14 was adopted, namely, that several strong antidiscrimination acts had been passed by the legislature, and opposed by many of those who successfully led the movement for adoption of Proposition 14 by popular referendum. These circumstances, and these alone, the California court held, made § 26 unlawful under this Court's cases interpreting the Equal Protection Clause. This, of course, is nothing but a legal conclusion as to federal constitutional law . . . . Accepting all the suppositions under which the state court acted, I cannot see that its conclusion is entitled to any special weight in the discharge of our own responsibilities. Put in another way, I cannot transform the California court's conclusion of law into a finding of fact that the State through the adoption of § 26 is actively promoting racial discrimination. It seems to me manifest that the state court decision rested

entirely on what that court conceived to be the compulsion of the Fourteenth Amendment, not on any fact-finding by the state courts.

There is no question that the adoption of § 26, repealing the former state antidiscrimination laws and prohibiting the enactment of such state laws in the future, constituted "state action" within the meaning of the Fourteenth Amendment. The only issue is whether this provision impermissibly deprives any person of equal protection of the laws. . . . The core of the Court's opinion is that § 26 is offensive to the Fourteenth Amendment because it effectively *encourages* private discrimination. By focusing on "encouragement" the Court, I fear, is forging a slippery and unfortunate criterion by which to measure the constitutionality of a statute simply permissive in purpose and effect, and inoffensive on its face.

It is true that standards in this area have not been definitely formulated, and that acts of discrimination have been included within the compass of the Equal Protection Clause not merely when they were compelled by a state statute or other governmental pressures, but also when they were said to be "induced" or "authorized" by the State. Most of these cases, however, can be approached in terms of the impact and extent of affirmative state governmental activities, e. g., the action of a sheriff [Lombard v. Louisiana]; the official supervision over a park [Evans v. Newton]; a joint venture with a lessee in a municipally owned building [Burton]. In situations such as these the focus has been on positive state cooperation or partnership in affirmatively promoted activities, an involvement that could have been avoided. Here, in contrast, we have only the straightforward adoption of a neutral provision restoring to the sphere of free choice, left untouched by the Fourteenth Amendment, private behavior within a limited area of the racial problem. The denial of equal protection emerges only from the conclusion reached by the Court that the implementation of a new policy of governmental neutrality, embodied in a constitutional provision and replacing a former policy of antidiscrimination, has the effect of lending encouragement to those who wish to discriminate. In the context of the actual facts of the case, this conclusion appears to me to state only a truism: people who want to discriminate but were previously forbidden to do so by state law are now left free because the State has chosen to have no law on the subject at all. Obviously whenever there is a change in the law it will have resulted from the concerted activity of those who desire the change, and its enactment will allow those supporting the legislation to pursue their private goals.

A moment of thought will reveal the far-reaching possibilities of the Court's new doctrine, which I am sure the Court does not intend. Every act of private discrimination is either forbidden by state law or permitted by it. There can be little doubt that such permissiveness—whether by express constitutional or statutory provision, or implicit in the common law—to some extent "encourages" those who wish to discriminate to do so. Under this theory "state action" in the form of laws that do nothing more than passively permit private discrimination could be said to tinge *all* private discrimination with the taint of unconstitutional state encouragement.

. . . I believe the state action required to bring the Fourteenth Amendment into operation must be affirmative and purposeful, actively fostering discrimination. Only in such a case is ostensibly "private" action more

properly labeled "official." I do not believe that the mere enactment of § 26, on the showing made here, falls within this class of cases.

I think that this decision is not only constitutionally unsound, but in its practical potentialities short-sighted. Opponents of state antidiscrimination statutes are now in a position to argue that such legislation should be defeated because, if enacted, it may be unrepealable. More fundamentally, the doctrine underlying this decision may hamper, if not preclude, attempts to deal with the delicate and troublesome problems of race relations through the legislative process. . . .

STATE ACTION THROUGH STATE "ENCOURAGEMENT" AND "AUTHORIZATION"

1. *State "encouragement."* What is the reach of the "encouragement" theme of Reitman v. Mulkey? Can a state provision which keeps hands off private discrimination, or "authorizes"—by failing to forbid—private discrimination, be deemed an "encouragement"? Was Proposition 14 truly distinguishable from a mere repeal of an anti-discrimination law? Because of its purpose? Because of its effect? Did either the California Supreme Court or the United States Supreme Court make such findings as a matter of fact? Was there a significant difference here because California did not merely repeal anti-discrimination laws but incorporated that repeal in a constitutional provision? Because a state may not disable its subdivisions from combating racial discrimination? Even though the constitutional provision is adopted by a popular initiative route? Was the flaw the effect of the provision in disadvantaging racial minorities, and the lack of the heavy justification required to support such an impact? (Recall the equal protection principles in the racial discrimination area, in chap. 10.) Or does Reitman ultimately rest on the notion that a state may not "authorize" racial discrimination? See the next note.

2. *"Authorization" of racial discrimination.* Recall the separate opinions in the Burton case above, all indicating that a finding of a state "authorization" of private discrimination would be a "more direct," "easy road to decision." Was that truly an easier route? Justice Stewart in Burton was willing to find "authorization." And Justice Harlan in Burton suggested that a finding of "authorization," if the state statute could be construed that way, would indeed be a narrower ground. Yet both Justices dissented in Reitman. What kind of "authorization" did they have in mind in Burton? Is "authorization" really any different from failure to prohibit where the state has power to prohibit? Is the "authorization" rationale truly any different from imposing an affirmative duty on the state to prevent private discrimination? Is such "authorization" of unrestrained private choices, by constitutional provision, statute, or common law, "significant involvement" by the state?

Why was the enforcement of the reverter in the Baconsfield Park litigation, above, not "authorization" in this sense? Was the 1970 decision in the Baconsfield Park litigation, Evans v. Abney, above, a retreat from Burton and Reitman? Were not the "significant" state involvements recited in Justice Brennan's dissent there as substantial as those in Burton and Reit-

man? After Reitman and before Evans v. Abney, some commentators, noting that no modern Court decision had rejected a discrimination claim because of the state action barrier, had suggested that the concept was moribund.[1] Did Evans v. Abney make it clear that the state action barrier was not moribund? And do the more recent Burger Court decisions, such as the Moose Lodge case above, make it even clearer that the state action barrier continues to have substantial vitality?

Reexamine the present state of the various, often inchoate, strands in the expansions of the state action principle in light of the December 1974 decision in Jackson v. Metropolitan Edison Co., which follows. Note that the rejection of the state action claims in that case occurred in a context of trying to enforce a procedural due process claim, not a racial discrimination-equal protection claim. Would and should state action criteria be interpreted differently depending on the claims involved? For example, should the Metropolitan Edison Co. have been found subject to constitutional restraints if the charge had been racial discrimination in cutting off services?

Is the Court's recent general unwillingness to intrude further into the private sphere under § 1 of the 14th Amendment related to the increasing scope and exercise of congressional power to reach private activities under § 5 of the 14th Amendment? Is the Court's direction related as well to the even broader congressional power to deal with private racial discrimination under § 2 of the 13th Amendment?[2] The scope of congressional power to go beyond where the Court has gone in its interpretations of the first sections of the Amendments is pursued in sec. 3, below.

JACKSON v. METROPOLITAN EDISON CO.

419 U.S. 345, 95 S.Ct. 449, 42 L.Ed.2d 477 (1974).

Certiorari to the United States Court of Appeals for the Third Circuit.

[Petitioner Catherine Jackson brought a federal civil rights action under 42 U.S.C. § 1983 against respondent Metropolitan Edison Co., a privately owned and operated corporation holding a certificate of public convenience issued by the Pennsylvania Public Utilities Commission empowering it to deliver electricity to a specific service area. Petitioner sought injunctive and damages relief against the Company for terminating electric service to her residence for nonpayment, claiming that she had not been afforded notice, hearing, and opportunity to pay any amounts found due. She claimed that under state law she was entitled to reasonably continuous electrical service to her home, and that Metropolitan's termination of this service constituted "state action" depriving her of property in violation of procedural due process guarantees. The lower federal courts dismissed her complaint, finding that the termination did not constitute state action.]

---

1. See e. g., C. L. Black, Jr., "Foreword: 'State Action,' Equal Protection and California's Proposition 14," 81 Harv. L.Rev. 69 (1967); and note Karst and Horowitz, "Reitman v. Mulkey: A Telophase of Substantive Equal Protection," 1967 Sup.Ct.Rev. 39.

2. See especially Jones v. Alfred H. Mayer Co., sec. 3C below, decided under the 13th Amendment-based 1866 Civil Rights Act, 42 U.S.C. § 1982, rather than on the basis of state action analysis.

Mr. Justice REHNQUIST delivered the opinion of the Court. . . .

. . . While the principle that private action is immune from the restrictions of the Fourteenth Amendment is well established and easily stated, the question whether particular conduct is "private," on the one hand, or "state action," on the other, frequently admits of no easy answer.

Here the action complained of was taken by a utility company which is privately owned and operated, but which in many particulars of its business is subject to extensive state regulation. The mere fact that a business is subject to state regulation does not by itself convert its action into that of the State for purposes of the Fourteenth Amendment.[1] Nor does the fact that the regulation is extensive and detailed, as in the case of most public utilities, do so. Public Utilities Comm'n v. Pollak, 343 U.S. 451, 462 (1952). It may well be that acts of a heavily regulated utility with at least something of a governmentally protected monopoly will more readily be found to be "state" acts than will the acts of an entity lacking these characteristics. But the inquiry must be whether there is a sufficiently close nexus between the State and the challenged action of the regulated entity so that the action of the latter may be fairly treated as that of the State itself. [Moose Lodge.] The true nature of the State's involvement may not be immediately obvious, and detailed inquiry may be required in order to determine whether the test is met. [Burton.]

Petitioner advances a series of contentions which, in her view, lead to the conclusion that this case should fall on the Burton side of the line drawn in the Civil Rights Cases, rather than on the Moose Lodge side of that line. We find none of them persuasive.

Petitioner first argues that "state action" is present because of the monopoly status allegedly conferred upon Metropolitan by the State of Pennsylvania. As a factual matter, it may well be doubted that the State ever granted or guaranteed Metropolitan a monopoly.[2] But assuming that it had,

---

1. Enterprises subject to the same regulatory system as Metropolitan are enumerated in the definition of "public utility" contained in 66 Pa.Stat. § 1102(17). Included in this definition are all companies engaged in providing gas, power, or water, all common carriers, pipeline companies, telephone and telegraph companies, sewage collection and disposal companies, and corporations affiliated with any company engaging in such activities. Among some of the enterprises held subject to this regulatory scheme are freight forwarding and storage companies, real estate developers who, incident to their business, provide water services, and individually owned taxicabs. In [a 1932 case, the state court] estimated that there were 26 distinct types of enterprises subject to this regulatory system and a fair reading of Pennsylvania law indicates a substantial expansion of included enterprises since that case. The incidents of regulation do not appear materially different between enterprises. If the mere existence of this regulatory scheme made Metropolitan's action that of the State, then presumably the actions of a lone Philadelphia cab driver could also be fairly treated as those of the State of Pennsylvania. [Footnote by the Court.]

2. . . . . [S]uch public utility companies are natural monopolies created by the economic forces of high threshold capital requirements and virtually unlimited economy of scale. Regulation was superimposed on such natural monopolies as a substitute for competition and not to eliminate it . . . .. [Footnote by the Court.]

this fact is not determinative in considering whether Metropolitan's termination of service to petitioner was "state action" for purposes of the Fourteenth Amendment. In Pollak, where the Court dealt with the activities of the District of Columbia Transit Company, a congressionally established monopoly, we expressed disclaimed reliance on the monopoly status of the transit authority. Similarly, although certain monopoly aspects were presented in [Moose Lodge], we found that the lodge's action was not subject to the provisions of the Fourteenth Amendment. In each of those cases, there was insufficient relationship between the challenged actions of the entities involved and their monopoly status. There is no indication of any greater connection here.

Petitioner next urges that state action is present because respondent provides an essential public service [and] hence performs a "public function." [The portion of the opinion rejecting the "public function" argument is printed earlier in this section, at p. 925.]

We also reject the notion that Metropolitan's termination is state action because the State "has specifically authorized and approved" the termination practice. In the instant case, Metropolitan filed with the Public Utilities Commission a general tariff—a provision of which states Metropolitan's right to terminate service for nonpayment.[3] This provision has appeared in Metropolitan's previously filed tariffs for many years and has never been the subject of a hearing or other scrutiny by the Commission.[4] Although the Commission did hold hearings on portions of Metropolitan's general tariff relating to a general rate increase, it never even considered the reinsertion of this provision in the newly filed general tariff. . . .

The case most heavily relied on by petitioner is Public Utilities Comm'n v. Pollak. There the Court dealt with the contention that Capital Transit's installation of a piped music system on its buses violated the First Amendment rights of the bus riders. [T]he nature of the state involvement there was quite different than it is here. The District of Columbia Public Utilities Commission, on its own motion, commenced an investigation of the effects of the piped music, and after a full hearing concluded not only that Capital Transit's practices were "not inconsistent with public convenience, comfort, and safety," but that the practice "in fact through the creation of better will among passengers, . . . tends to improve the conditions under which the public rides." Here, on the other hand, there was no such *imprimatur* placed on the practice of Metropolitan about which petitioner complains. The nature of governmental regulation of private utilities is such that a utility may frequently be required by the state regulatory scheme to obtain approval for practices a business regulated in less detail would be free to

3. The same provision appeared in all of Metropolitan's prior general tariffs. The sole reason for substituting the new general tariff, which contains all the terms and conditions of Metropolitan's service, was to procure a rate increase. This was the sole change between Metropolitan's Electrical Tariff No. 41 and its predecessor. [Footnote by the Court. The termination provision of the Tariff stated: "Rule

15. Cause for discontinuance of service. Company reserves the right to discontinue its service on reasonable notice and to remove its equipment in the case of nonpayment of bill."]

4. Petitioner concedes that Metropolitan had this right, before the advent of regulation, at common law. [Footnote by the Court.]

institute without any approval from a regulatory body. Approval by a state utility commission of such a request from a regulated utility, where the Commission has not put its own weight on the side of the proposed practice by ordering it, does not transmute a practice initiated by the utility and approved by the Commission into "state action." At most, the Commission's failure to overturn this practice amounted to no more than a determination that a Pennsylvania utility was authorized to employ such a practice if it so desired. Respondent's exercise of the choice allowed by state law where the initiative comes from it and not from the State, does not make its action in doing so "state action" for purposes of the Fourteenth Amendment.

We also find absent in the instant case the symbiotic relationship presented in [Burton.] There [the Court] cautioned [that] differences in circumstances beget differences in law, limiting the actual holding to lessees of public property.

Metropolitan is a privately owned corporation, and it does not lease its facilities from the State of Pennsylvania. It [is] subject to a form of extensive regulation by the State in a way that most other business enterprises are not. But this was likewise true of the appellant club in [Moose Lodge], where we said: "However detailed this type of regulation may be in some particulars, it cannot be said to in any way foster or encourage racial discrimination. Nor can it be said to make the state in any realistic sense a partner or even a joint venturer in the club's enterprise."

All of petitioner's arguments taken together show no more than that Metropolitan was a heavily regulated private utility, enjoying at least a partial monopoly in the providing of electrical service within its territory, and that it elected to terminate service to petitioner in a manner which the Pennsylvania Public Utilities Commission found permissible under state law. Under our decision this is not sufficient to connect the State of Pennsylvania with respondent's action so as to make the latter's conduct attributable to the State for purposes of the Fourteenth Amendment. . . .

Affirmed.

Mr. Justice DOUGLAS, dissenting.

. . . May a State allow a utility—which in this case has no competitor—to exploit its monopoly in violation of its own tariff? May a utility have complete immunity under federal law when the State allows its regulatory agency to become the prisoner of the utility or, by a listless attitude of no concern, to permit the utility to use its monopoly power in a lawless way?

. . . [As Burton] made clear, the dispositive question in any state action case is not whether any single fact or relationship presents a sufficient degree of state involvement, but rather whether the aggregate of all relevant factors compels a finding of state responsibility. It is not enough to examine seriatim each of the factors upon which a claimant relies and to dismiss each individually as being insufficient to support a finding of state action. It is the aggregate that is controlling.

It is said that the mere fact of respondent's monopoly status, assuming *arguendo* that that status is state-conferred or state-protected,[1] "is not deter-

_____

1. It seems irrelevant that Metropolitan was organized prior to the inauguration of utility regulation in Pennsylvania, and that a utility of this sort is,

minative . . . ." Even so, a state-protected monopoly status is highly relevant in assessing the aggregate weight of a private entity's ties to the State. [See also Justice Douglas' comment on the "public function" argument, quoted earlier, at p. 927 above.]

Respondent's procedures for termination of service may never have been subjected to the same degree of state scrutiny and approval, whether explicit or implicit, that was present in [Pollak]. Yet in the present case the State is heavily involved in respondent's termination procedures, getting into the approved tariff a requirement of "reasonable notice." Pennsylvania has undertaken to regulate numerous aspects of respondent's operations in some detail, and a "hands-off" attitude of permissiveness or neutrality towards the operations in this case is at war with the state agency's functions of supervision over respondent's conduct in the area of servicing householders, particularly where (as here) the State would presumably lend its weight and authority to facilitate the enforcement of respondent's published procedures. Cf. . . . [Shelley v. Kraemer].

In the aggregate, these factors depict a monopolist providing essential public services as a licensee of the State and within a framework of extensive state supervision and control. The particular regulations at issue, promulgated by the monopolist, were authorized by state law and were made enforceable by the weight and authority of the State. Moreover, the State retains the power of oversight to review and amend the regulations if the public interest so requires. Respondent's actions are sufficiently intertwined with those of the State, and its termination-of-service provisions are sufficiently buttressed by state law, to warrant a holding that respondent's actions in terminating this householder's service were "state action" . . . . Though the Court pays lip service to the need for assessing the totality of the State's involvement in this enterprise, its underlying analysis is fundamentally sequential rather than cumulative. In that perspective, what the Court does today is to make a significant departure from our previous treatment of state action issues. . . . *

Mr. Justice MARSHALL, dissenting. . . .

I. Our state action cases have repeatedly relied on several factors clearly presented by this case: a state-sanctioned monopoly; an extensive pattern of cooperation between the "private" entity and the state; and a service uniquely public in nature. Today the Court takes a major step in repudiating this line of authority and adopts a stance that is bound to lead to mischief when applied to problems beyond the narrow sphere of due process objections to utility terminations.

for all practical purposes, a natural monopoly. Whatever its origins, the existing situation presents a monopoly enterprise subject to detailed state regulation; the nature and extent of that regulation take on particular significance in light of the lack of any alternative source of service available to Metropolitan's customers. . . . [Footnote by Justice Douglas.]

* A dissent by Justice Brennan, finding that on the facts of this case "no controversy existed between petitioner and respondent," is omitted. Justice Marshall thought those factual complexities were such that certiorari should be dismissed as improvidently granted. But, since the majority had reached the state action issue, he submitted a dissent on that problem, which follows.

A.   When the State confers a monopoly on a group or organization, this Court has held that the organization assumes many of the obligations of the State.   .   .   .   The majority distinguishes this line of cases with a cryptic assertion that public utility companies are "natural monopolies."   The theory behind the distinction appears to be that since the State's purpose in regulating a natural monopoly is not to aid the company but to prevent its charging monopoly prices, the State's involvement is somehow less significant for state action purposes.   I cannot agree that so much should turn on so narrow a distinction.   Initially, it is far from obvious that an electric company would not be subject to competition if the market were unimpeded by governmental restrictions.   Certainly the "start-up" costs of initiating electric service are substantial, but the rewards available in a relatively inelastic market might well be sufficient under the right circumstances to attract competitive investment.   Instead, the State has chosen to forbid the high profit margins that might invite private competition or increase pressure for state ownership and operation of electric power facilities.

The difficulty inherent in this kind of economic analysis counsels against excusing natural monopolies from the reach of state action principles.   To invite inquiry into whether a particular state-sanctioned monopoly might have survived without the State's express approval grounds the analysis in hopeless speculation.   Worse, this approach ignores important implications of the State's policy of utilizing private monopolies to provide electric service. Encompassed within this policy is the State's determination not to permit governmental competition with the selected private company, but to cooperate with and regulate the company in a multitude of ways to ensure that the company's service will be the functional equivalent of service provided by the State.

B.   The pattern of cooperation between Metropolitan Edison and the State has led to significant state involvement in virtually every phase of the company's business.   The majority, however, accepts the relevance of the State's regulatory scheme only to the extent that it demonstrates state support for the challenged termination procedure.   Moreover, after concluding that the State in this case had not approved the company's termination procedures, the majority suggests that even state authorization and approval would not be sufficient: the State would apparently have to *order* the termination practice in question to satisfy the majority's state action test.

I disagree with the majority's position on three separate grounds.   First, the suggestion that the State would have to "put its own weight on the side of the proposed practice by ordering it" seems to me to mark a sharp departure from our previous state action cases.   From the Civil Rights Cases to Moose Lodge, we have consistently indicated that state authorization and approval of "private" conduct would support a finding of state action.[1]

---

1. In the Civil Rights Cases, the Court suggested that state action might be found if the conduct in question were "sanctioned in some way by the State." Later cases made it clear that the State's sanction did not need to be in the form of an affirmative command.   In Burton, the Court noted that by its inaction, the State had "elected to place its power, property, and prestige behind the admitted discrimination," although the State did not actually order the discrimination. See id., (Stewart, J., concurring).   And in Reitman v. Mulkey, the Court based its "state action" ruling on the fact

Second, I question the wisdom of giving such short shrift to the extensive interaction between the company and the State, and focusing solely on the extent of state support for the particular activity under challenge. In cases where the State's only significant involvement is through financial support or limited regulation of the private entity, it may be well to inquire whether the State's involvement suggests state approval of the objectionable conduct. See Powe v. Miles, 407 F.2d 73, 81 (C.A.2 1968); Grossner v. Trustees of Columbia University, 287 F.Supp. 535, 547–548 (S.D.N.Y. 1968). But where the State has so thoroughly insinuated itself into the operations of the enterprise, it should not be fatal if the State has not affirmatively sanctioned the particular practice in question.

Finally, it seems to me in any event that the State *has* given its approval to Metropolitan Edison's termination procedures. The state utility commission approved a tariff provision under which the company reserved the right to discontinue its service on reasonable notice for nonpayment of bills. . . . That [the provision] was not seriously questioned before approval does not mean that it was not approved. It suggests, instead, that the commission was satisfied to permit the company to proceed in the termination area as it had done in the past. . . . Apparently, authorization and approval would require the kind of hearing that was held in Pollak . . . . I am afraid that the majority has in effect restricted Pollak to its facts if it has not discarded it altogether.

C. [The portion of Justice Marshall's dissent finding the "public function" argument persuasive is printed at p. 926 above.]

II. The majority's conclusion that there is no state action in this case is likely guided in part by its reluctance to impose on a utility company burdens that might ultimately hurt consumers more than they would help them. Elaborate hearings prior to termination might be quite expensive, and for a responsible company there might be relatively few cases in which such hearings would do any good. The solution to this problem, however, is to require only abbreviated pretermination procedures for all utility companies, not to free the "private" companies to behave however they see fit. . . .

III. What is perhaps most troubling about the Court's opinion is that it would appear to apply to a broad range of claimed constitutional violations by the company. The Court has not adopted the notion, accepted elsewhere, that different standards should apply to state action analysis when different constitutional claims are presented. Thus, the majority's analysis would seemingly apply as well to a company that refused to extend service to Negroes, welfare recipients, or any other group that the company preferred, for its own reasons, not to serve. I cannot believe that this Court would hold that the State's involvement with the utility company was not sufficient to impose upon the company an obligation to meet the constitutional mandate

that the California constitutional provision "was intended to authorize, and does authorize, racial discrimination in the housing market." Even in Moose Lodge the Court suggested that if the State's regulation had in any way fostered or encouraged racial discrimination, a state action finding might have been justified. Certainly this is a less rigid standard than the Court's requirement in this case that the public utility commission be shown to have ordered the challenged conduct, not merely to have approved it. [Footnote by Justice Marshall.]

of nondiscrimination.   Yet nothing in the analysis of the majority opinion suggests otherwise.   I dissent.

SECTION 3.   CONGRESSIONAL POWER TO REACH PRIVATE INTERFERENCES WITH CONSTITUTIONAL RIGHTS: MODERN SCOPE AND PROBLEMS

IDENTIFYING THE INGREDIENTS OF THE PROBLEM: AN INTRODUCTORY SKETCH

To what extent may Congress provide criminal and civil sanctions against private interferences with constitutional rights?   That question is a complex one, and the answer is unclear.   It is a question that is pursued here by focusing on two modern cases and tracing their background and implications.   The cases are United States v. Guest, 383 U.S. 745 (1966) (sec. 3A), and Griffin v. Breckenridge, 403 U.S. 88 (1971) (sec. 3B).   A careful examination of those cases suggests answers to some ingredients of the problem, and highlights the substantial additional ingredients that are yet unresolved.   Before turning to those cases and their predecessors, it may be useful to sketch the recurrent clusters of problems presented by cases of this nature, to aid in disentangling the often interwined strands of constitutional and statutory issues.

At the outset, it should be noted that a central question presented by these materials is the statutory and constitutional reaches of the modern counterparts of the post-Civil War civil rights laws summarized in sec. 1 above. Recall that those modern counterparts contain both criminal and civil provisions.   Recall, moreover, that those statutes fall into two groups: one purports to reach only action "under color" of law; the other purports to reach private conspiracies, without any state nexus on the face of the statutes. Thus, on the criminal side, 18 U.S.C. § 242 is entitled "Deprivation of rights under color of law," while 18 U.S.C. § 241 applies "[i]f two or more persons conspire" and thus appears directed at private conspiracies. There is a similar distinction with the major civil provisions: 42 U.S.C. § 1983 is the state action-related statute, applying to "[e]very person who, under color of any statute," engages in the forbidden conduct; 42 U.S.C. § 1985(3) is the civil conspiracy provision applying to "two or more persons."   What persons are covered by these provisions?   What rights are protected by them?   What is the statutory and constitutional reach of the provisions?   A number of variables need to be borne in mind in exploring those issues.

1.   *The sources of the protected rights.*   In the analysis of the scope of congressional power to reach private interferences with constitutional rights, the most important pervasive theme is the problem of identifying the sources of the covered rights.   Note especially three types of rights, with quite different implications as to content and potential reach to private action.

a.   *14th and 15th Amendment rights against the "state."*   First, there are the rights presenting problems introduced in sec. 2 above: the rights under the 14th (and 15th) Amendments which, in terms of Court interpretations of their self-executing impacts, are rights against *state* interference. Under the Court's expansions of the state action concept, some seemingly private behavior is reachable under the 14th and 15th Amendments.   But may Congress go beyond the Court's view of state action and reach additional private actors, under § 5 of the 14th Amendment (and § 2 of the 15th Amendment)?   For example, can the private conspiracies provisions, 18 U.S.C. § 241 and 42 U.S.C. § 1985(3), be applied to private actors who interfere with 14th Amendment rights?   That problem is suggested, but not resolved, by United States v. Guest, sec. 3A below.

b.   *13th Amendment rights.*   The other post-Civil War Amendment, the 13th Amendment, is not limited by the state action requirement;   it applies generally to private interferences.   And under Jones v. Alfred H. Mayer Co., sec. 3C below, Congress may under its enforcement power under that Amendment deal broadly with private acts of racial discrimination.   The 13th Amendment, then, provides an independent constitutional basis for congressional sanctions against private interferences with rights (see, e. g., Griffin v. Breckenridge, sec. 3B below);   but its scope is limited by its racial discrimination emphasis, and it does not help with non-racial interferences with rights such as the free speech guarantee and the protection against unreasonable searches and seizures.

c.   *Rights stemming from sources other than the post-Civil War Amendments.*   Third, the Court has recognized some constitutional rights arising from sources other than the post-Civil War Amendments and not subject to the state action limitation.*   To the extent that those rights can be identified, they provide another source of congressional power to reach private conduct.   As the cases below illustrate, the rights involved are largely rights derived from structures and relationships found implicit in the Constitution (recall McCulloch v. Maryland).   Note, for example, the reliance on the right to travel in United States v. Guest.   And note the recognition of the existence of some such constitutional rights applicable to private action in an opinion by a Justice not inclined to assert such rights loosely—Justice Harlan's 1966 opinion in the Guest case.   After expressing his doubt that the Constitution was generally intended to create "rights of private individuals as against other private individuals," he conceded: "It is true that there is a very narrow range of rights against individuals which have been read into the Constitution.   In Ex parte Yarbrough, 110 U.S. 651 [1884], the Court held that implicit in the Constitution is the right of citizens to be free of private interference in federal elections.   United States v. Classic, 313 U.S. 299 [1941], extended this coverage to primaries.   Logan v. United States, 144 U.S. 263 [1892], applied the predecessor of § 241 to a conspiracy to injure someone in the custody of a United States marshal;   the case has been read as dealing with a privilege and immunity of citizenship, but it would seem to have depended as well on extrapolations from statutory provisions providing for supervision of prisoners.   The Court in In re

---

* That there might be such rights was recognized as early as United States v. Cruikshank, 92 U.S. 542 (1875) (right to assemble "for the purpose of petitioning Congress for a redress of grievances"), as noted in sec. 2A above.

Quarles, 158 U.S. 532 [1895], extending Logan, declared that there was a right of federal citizenship to inform federal officials of violations of federal law. See also United States v. Cruikshank, 92 U.S. 542, 552 [1875], which announced in dicta a federal right to assemble to petition the Congress for a redress of grievances." †

2. *Other variables.* a. *Specificity and vagueness.* Provisions such as 18 U.S.C. § 242 speak in very general terms: they contain broad references to "rights, privileges, or immunities" under the "Constitution or laws." Even assuming that there is congressional power to reach private interferences with at least some constitutional rights, are those statutory references sufficiently specific to give adequate notice to those subjected to them? To the extent that such phrases appear in criminal provisions, do they risk invalidation for vagueness? That concern may inhibit the Court in searching out new varieties of rights to read into those broadly phrased remnants of the post-Civil War laws, as some of the cases below illustrate. And cases such as Screws v. United States, sec. 3A, reflect the Court's difficulties in finding adequate specificity in such broad formulations. Suggestions in an opinion in United States v. Guest, urging greater specificity in congressional formulations, in turn helped produce the new 1968 civil rights provisions, 18 U.S.C. § 245, sec. 3A below. That more specific enumeration of protected rights—rights Congress explicitly sought to protect against private interferences—raises anew the problems of congressional powers, and invites reference back to the distinctions among the constitutional sources of protected rights summarized in note 1.

b. *Statutory interpretation.* Another pervasive theme in the materials below—a theme related to those noted in the preceding paragraphs—is that of statutory construction: in construing the general civil rights statutes, what varieties of constitutional rights can be read into such phrases as "rights, privileges, or immunities secured or protected by the Constitution"? Thus, when Congress purports to reach private actors in a statute originally enacted soon after adoption of the 14th Amendment, should the Court read a state action limitation into the statute, or should the statute be read in accordance with its apparent terms—and thus include in it constitutional rights not subject to the state action limitation, as well as 14th Amendment rights made applicable to private interferences because of an arguable congressional power to reach beyond Court-announced state action limits? Note in the materials which follow that in the cases of the early 1950's—e. g., the Williams cases on the criminal side and Collins v. Hardyman on the civil side—there was strong support on the Court for narrow readings of the statutes to avoid constitutional doubts. More recent cases, by contrast—e. g., Griffin v. Breckenridge and United States v. Price—take a broader view of the meaning of the statutes, in part because of diminished constitutional doubts.

† The text emphasizes the range of federal *constitutional* rights relevant to an analysis of these problems. But note that the relevant statutes typically speak of not only rights under the Constitution but also of rights under the "laws of the United States." To the extent that Congress acts under powers applicable to private individuals as well as state actors—e. g., the commerce power—Congress may create statutory rights enforceable against private interferences. Recall, e. g., the public accommodations provisions of the 1964 Civil Rights Act, in chap. 3.

Sensitivity to this intertwined trilogy of concerns—-sources of constitutional rights, vagueness, and statutory construction—may help clarify the discussions in some of the opinions below. But bear in mind that the primary emphasis here is on the issue foreshadowed by the materials in sec. 2: the congressional protection of 14th Amendment rights against seemingly private actors, either by drawing on the Court's expansions of the state action concept traced in sec. 2, or by relying on the arguable power of Congress under § 5 of the 14th Amendment to reach private actors the Court would not reach on its own.

A. PRIVATE INTERFERENCES WITH FEDERAL RIGHTS: CRIMINAL SANCTIONS

UNITED STATES v. GUEST

383 U.S. 745, 86 S.Ct. 1170, 16 L.Ed.2d 239 (1966).

Appeal from the United States District Court for the Middle District of Georgia.

Mr. Justice STEWART delivered the opinion of the Court.

The six defendants in this case were indicted by a United States grand jury in the Middle District of Georgia for criminal conspiracy in violation of 18 U.S.C. § 241. . . . In five numbered paragraphs, the indictment alleged a single conspiracy by the defendants to deprive Negro citizens of the free exercise and enjoyment of several specified rights secured by the Constitution and laws of the United States.[1] The defendants moved

---

1. The indictment, filed on October 16, 1964, was as follows:
"THE GRAND JURY CHARGES:
"Commencing on or about January 1, 1964, and continuing to the date of this indictment, HERBERT GUEST, JAMES SPERGEON LACKEY, CECIL WILLIAM MYERS, DENVER WILLIS PHILLIPS, JOSEPH HOWARD SIMS, and GEORGE HAMPTON TURNER, did, within the Middle District of Georgia, Athens Division, conspire together, with each other, and with other persons to the Grand Jury unknown, to injure, oppress, threaten, and intimidate Negro citizens of the United States in the vicinity of Athens, Georgia, in the free exercise and enjoyment by said Negro citizens of the following rights and privileges secured to them by the Constitution and laws of the United States:
"1. The right to the full and equal enjoyment of the goods, services, facilities, privileges, advantages, and accommodations of motion picture theaters, restaurants, and other places of public accommodation;
"2. The right to the equal utilization, without discrimination upon the basis of

race, of public facilities in the vicinity of Athens, Georgia, owned, operated or managed by or on behalf of the State of Georgia or any subdivision thereof;
"3. The right to the full and equal use on the same terms as white citizens of the public streets and highways in the vicinity of Athens, Georgia;
"4. The right to travel freely to and from the State of Georgia and to use highway facilities and other instrumentalities of interstate commerce within the State of Georgia;
"5. Other rights exercised and enjoyed by white citizens in the vicinity of Athens, Georgia.
"It was a part of the plan and purpose of the conspiracy that its objects be achieved by various means, including the following:
"1. By shooting Negroes;
"2. By beating Negroes;
"3. By killing Negroes;
"4. By damaging and destroying property of Negroes;
"5. By pursuing Negroes in automobiles and threatening them with guns;

to dismiss the indictment on the ground that it did not charge an offense under the laws of the United States. The District Court sustained the motion . . . .

The United States appealed directly to this Court under the Criminal Appeals Act, 18 U.S.C. § 3731.[2] [As to all issues over which we have appellate jurisdiction under that statute], we reverse the judgment of the District Court. [W]e deal here with issues of statutory construction, not with issues of constitutional power.

I. [As to the] first numbered paragraph of the indictment, reflecting a portion of the language of § 201(a) of the Civil Rights Act of 1964, [the] District Court [found] a fatal flaw in the failure [to] include an allegation that the acts of the defendants were motivated by racial discrimination. [That ruling was] based, at least alternatively, upon [the] determination that this paragraph was defective as a matter of pleading. [T]he Criminal Appeals Act therefore preclude[s] our review [of that part of the lower court's judgment].

II. The second numbered paragraph of the indictment alleged that the defendants conspired to injure, oppress, threaten, and intimidate Negro citizens of the United States in the free exercise and enjoyment of:

> "The right to the equal utilization, without discrimination upon the basis of race, of public facilities in the vicinity of Athens, Georgia, owned, operated or managed by or on behalf of the State of Georgia or any subdivision thereof."

Correctly characterizing this paragraph as embracing rights protected by the Equal Protection Clause of the Fourteenth Amendment, the District Court held as a matter of statutory construction that 18 U.S.C. § 241 does not encompass any Fourteenth Amendment rights, and further held as a matter of constitutional law that "any broader construction of § 241 [would] render it void for indefiniteness." In so holding, the District Court was in error, as our opinion in United States v. Price [which follows], decided today, makes abundantly clear. . . .

[I]nclusion of Fourteenth Amendment rights within the compass of 18 U.S.C. § 241 does not render the statute unconstitutionally vague. Since the gravamen of the offense is conspiracy, the requirement that the offender must act with a specific intent to interfere with the federal rights in

---

"6. By making telephone calls to Negroes to threaten their lives, property, and persons, and by making such threats in person;

"7. By going in disguise on the highway and on the premises of other persons;

"8. By causing the arrest of Negroes by means of false reports that such Negroes had committed criminal acts; and

"9. By burning crosses at night in public view.

"All in violation of Section 241, Title 18, United States Code."

The only additional indication in the record concerning the factual details of the conduct with which the defendants

were charged is the statement of the District Court that: "It is common knowledge that two of the defendants, Sims and Myers, have already been prosecuted in the Superior Court of Madison County, Georgia, for the murder of Lemuel A. Penn and by a jury found not guilty." 246 F.Supp. 475, 487. [All footnotes by the Court.]

2. This appeal concerns only the first four numbered paragraphs of the indictment. The Government conceded in the District Court that the fifth paragraph added nothing to the indictment, and no question is raised here as to the dismissal of that paragraph.

question is satisfied. [Screws v. United States; United States v. Williams (dissenting opinion) [both below]. And the rights under the Equal Protection Clause described by this paragraph of the indictment have been so firmly and precisely established by a consistent line of decisions in this Court, that the lack of specification of these rights in the language of § 241 itself can raise no serious constitutional question on the ground of vagueness or indefiniteness.

Unlike the indictment in Price, however, the indictment in the present case names no person alleged to have acted in any way under the color of state law. The argument is therefore made that, since there exist no Equal Protection Clause rights against wholly private action, the judgment of the District Court on this branch of the case must be affirmed. On its face, the argument is unexceptionable. The Equal Protection Clause speaks to the State or to those acting under the color of its authority.

In this connection, we emphasize that § 241 by its clear language incorporates no more than the Equal Protection Clause itself; the statute does not purport to give substantive, as opposed to remedial, implementation to any rights secured by that Clause. Since we therefore deal here only with the bare terms of the Equal Protection Clause itself, nothing said in this opinion goes to the question of what kinds of other and broader legislation Congress might constitutionally enact under § 5 of the Fourteenth Amendment to implement that Clause or any other provision of the Amendment.[3]

. . . .

It is a commonplace that rights under the Equal Protection Clause itself arise only where there has been involvement of the State or of one acting under the color of its authority. . . . This is not to say, however, that the involvement of the State need be either exclusive or direct. In a variety of situations the Court has found state action of a nature sufficient to create rights under the Equal Protection Clause even though the participation of the State was peripheral, or its action was only one of several co-operative forces leading to the constitutional violation.

This case, however, requires no determination of the threshold level that state action must attain in order to create rights under the Equal Protection Clause. This is so because, contrary to the argument of the litigants, the indictment in fact contains an express allegation of state involvement sufficient at least to require the denial of a motion to dismiss. One of the means of accomplishing the object of the conspiracy, according to the indictment, was "By causing the arrest of Negroes by means of false reports that such Negroes had committed criminal acts." [T]he extent of official involvement [alleged here] is not clear. [T]he allegation is broad enough to cover a charge of active connivance by agents of the State in the making of the "false reports," or other conduct amounting to official discrimination clearly sufficient to constitute denial of rights protected by the Equal Protection Clause. Although it is possible that a bill of particulars, or the proof if the case goes to trial, would disclose no co-operative action of that kind by officials of the State, the allegation is enough to prevent dismissal of this branch of the indictment.

3. Thus, contrary to the suggestion in Mr. Justice Brennan's separate opinion, nothing said in this opinion has the slightest bearing on the validity or construction of Title III or Title IV of the Civil Rights Act of 1964.

III. The fourth numbered paragraph of the indictment alleged that the defendants conspired to injure, oppress, threaten, and intimidate Negro citizens of the United States in the free exercise and enjoyment of:

> "The right to travel freely to and from the State of Georgia and to use highway facilities and other instrumentalities of interstate commerce within the State of Georgia." 4

The District Court was in error in dismissing the indictment as to this paragraph. The constitutional right to travel from one State to another, and necessarily to use the highways and other instrumentalities of interstate commerce in doing so, occupies a position fundamental to the concept of our Federal Union. It is a right that has been firmly established and repeatedly recognized. [Recall chap. 10, sec. 4A, above.]

Although the Articles of Confederation provided that "the people of each State shall have free ingress and regress to and from any other State," that right finds no explicit mention in the Constitution. The reason, it has been suggested, is that a right so elementary was conceived from the beginning to be a necessary concomitant of the stronger Union the Constitution created. . . .

In Edwards v. California, 314 U.S. 160, invalidating a California law which impeded the free interstate passage of the indigent, the Court based its reaffirmation of the federal right of interstate travel upon the Commerce Clause. . . . It [is] well settled in our decisions that the federal commerce power authorizes Congress to legislate for the protection of individuals from violations of civil rights that impinge on their free movement in interstate commerce. . . .

Although there have been recurring differences in emphasis within the Court as to the source of the constitutional right of interstate travel, there is no need here to canvass those differences further. All have agreed that the right exists. Its explicit recognition as one of the federal rights protected by what is now 18 U.S.C. § 241 goes back at least as far as 1904. United States v. Moore, 129 F. 630, 633. We reaffirm it now.[5]

This does not mean, of course, that every criminal conspiracy affecting an individual's right of free interstate passage is within the sanction

---

4. The third numbered paragraph alleged that the defendants conspired to injure, oppress, threaten, and intimidate Negro citizens of the United States in the free exercise and enjoyment of:

"The right to the full and equal use on the same terms as white citizens of the public streets and highways in the vicinity of Athens, Georgia."

Insofar as the third paragraph refers to the use of local public facilities, it is covered by the discussion of the second numbered paragraph of the indictment in Part II of this opinion. Insofar as the third paragraph refers to the use of streets or highways in interstate commerce, it is covered by the present discussion of the fourth numbered paragraph of the indictment.

5. As emphasized in Mr. Justice Harlan's separate opinion, § 241 protects only against interference with rights secured by other federal laws or by the Constitution itself. The right to interstate travel is a right that the Constitution itself guarantees, as the cases cited in the text make clear. Although these cases in fact involved governmental interference with the right of free interstate travel, their reasoning fully supports the conclusion that the constitutional right of interstate travel is a right secured against interference from any source whatever, whether governmental or private. In this connection, it is important to reiterate that the right to travel freely from State to State finds constitutional protection that is quite independent of the Fourteenth Amendment. . . .

of 18 U.S.C. § 241. A specific intent to interfere with the federal right must be proved, and at a trial the defendants are entitled to a jury instruction phrased in those terms. [Screws v. United States.] Thus, for example, a conspiracy to rob an interstate traveler would not, of itself, violate § 241. But if the predominant purpose of the conspiracy is to impede or prevent the exercise of the right of interstate travel, or to oppress a person because of his exercise of that right, then, whether or not motivated by racial discrimination, the conspiracy becomes a proper object of the federal law under which the indictment in this case was brought. Accordingly, it was error to grant the motion to dismiss on this branch of the indictment.

Reversed and remanded.

Mr. Justice CLARK, with whom Mr. Justice BLACK and Mr. Justice FORTAS join, concurring.

I join the opinion of the Court in this case, but believe it worthwhile to comment on its Part II . . . . .

The Court carves out of its opinion the question of the power of Congress, under § 5 of the Fourteenth Amendment, to enact legislation implementing the Equal Protection Clause or any other provision of the Fourteenth Amendment. The Court's interpretation of the indictment clearly avoids the question whether Congress, by appropriate legislation, has the power to punish private conspiracies that interfere with Fourteenth Amendment rights, such as the right to utilize public facilities. My Brother Brennan, however, says that the Court's disposition constitutes an acceptance of appellees' aforesaid contention as to § 241. Some of his language further suggests that the Court indicates sub silentio that Congress does not have the power to outlaw such conspiracies. Although the Court specifically rejects any such connotation, it is, I believe, both appropriate and necessary under the circumstances here to say that there now can be no doubt that the specific language of § 5 empowers the Congress to enact laws punishing all conspiracies—with or without state action—that interfere with Fourteenth Amendment rights.

Mr. Justice HARLAN, concurring in part and dissenting in part.

I join Parts I and II [1] of the Court's opinion, but I cannot subscribe to Part III in its full sweep. To the extent that it is there held that 18 U.S.C. § 241 reaches conspiracies, embracing only the action of private persons, to obstruct or otherwise interfere with the right of citizens freely to engage in interstate travel, I am constrained to dissent. On the other hand, I agree that § 241 does embrace state interference with such interstate travel, and I therefore consider that this aspect of the indictment is sustainable on the reasoning of Part II of the Court's opinion.

This right to travel must be found in the Constitution itself. This is so because [no] "right to travel" can be found in § 241 or in any other law of the United States. My disagreement with this phase of the Court's opinion lies in this: While past cases do indeed establish that there is a

---

1. The action of three of the Justices who join the Court's opinion in nonetheless cursorily pronouncing themselves on the far-reaching constitutional questions deliberately not reached in Part II seems to me, to say the very least, extraordinary. [Footnote by Justice Harlan.]

constitutional "right to travel" between States free from unreasonable *governmental* interference, today's decision is the first to hold that such movement is also protected against *private* interference, and, depending on the constitutional source of the right, I think it either unwise or impermissible so to read the Constitution. . . .

As a general proposition it seems to me very dubious that the Constitution was intended to create certain rights of private individuals as against other private individuals. The Constitutional Convention was called to establish a nation, not to reform the common law. . . . It is true that there is a very narrow range of rights against individuals which have been read into the Constitution. [See the passage from this opinion quoted in the introduction to this section.] [These cases] are narrow, and are essentially concerned with the vindication of important relationships with the Federal Government—voting in federal elections, involvement in federal law enforcement, communicating with the Federal Government. The present case stands on a considerably different footing.

It is arguable that the same considerations which led the Court on numerous occasions to find a right of free movement against oppressive state action now justify a similar result with respect to private impediments. . . . Although this argument is not without force, I do not think it is particularly persuasive. There is a difference in power between States and private groups so great that analogies between the two tend to be misleading. If the State obstructs free intercourse of goods, people, or ideas, the bonds of the union are threatened; if a private group effectively stops such communication, there is at most a temporary breakdown of law and order, to be remedied by the exercise of state authority or by appropriate federal legislation. . . .

I do not gainsay that the immunities and commerce provisions of the Constitution leave the way open for the finding of this "private" constitutional right, since they do not speak solely in terms of governmental action. Nevertheless, I think it wrong to sustain a criminal indictment on such an uncertain ground. To do so subjects § 241 to serious challenge on the score of vagueness and serves in effect to place this Court in the position of making criminal law under the name of constitutional interpretation. It is difficult to subdue misgivings about the potentialities of this decision. . . .

Mr. Justice BRENNAN, with whom The Chief Justice [WARREN] and Mr. Justice DOUGLAS join, concurring in part and dissenting in part.

I join Part I of the Court's opinion. I reach the same result as the Court on that branch of the indictment discussed in Part III of its opinion but for other reasons. See footnote [1], infra. And I agree with so much of Part II as construes 18 U.S.C. § 241 to encompass conspiracies to injure, oppress, threaten or intimidate citizens in the free exercise or enjoyment of Fourteenth Amendment rights and holds that, as so construed, § 241 is not void for indefiniteness. I do not agree, however, with the remainder of Part II which holds, as I read the opinion, that a conspiracy to interfere with the exercise of the right to equal utilization of state facilities is not, within the meaning of § 241, a conspiracy to interfere with the exercise of a "right . . . secured . . . by the Constitution" unless discriminatory conduct by state officers is involved in the alleged conspiracy.

I. . . . [W]hile the order dismissing the second numbered paragraph of the indictment is reversed, severe limitations on the prosecution of that branch of the indictment are implicitly imposed. These limitations could only stem from an acceptance of appellees' contention . . . .

. . . I am of the opinion that a conspiracy to interfere with the right to equal utilization of state facilities described in the second numbered paragraph of the indictment is a conspiracy to interfere with a "right . . secured . . . . by the Constitution" within the meaning of § 241—without regard to whether state officers participated in the alleged conspiracy. I believe that § 241 reaches such a private conspiracy, not because the Fourteenth Amendment of its own force prohibits such a conspiracy, but because § 241, as an exercise of congressional power under § 5 of that Amendment, prohibits *all* conspiracies to interfere with the exercise of a "right . . . secured . . . . by the Constitution" and because the right to equal utilization of state facilities is a "right . . . secured . . . by the Constitution" within the meaning of that phrase as used in § 241.[1]

My difference with the Court stems from its construction of the term "secured" as used in § 241 . . .. The Court tacitly construes the term "secured" so as to restrict the coverage of § 241 to those rights that are "fully protected" by the Constitution or another federal law. Unless private interferences with the exercise of the right in question are prohibited by the Constitution itself or another federal law, the right cannot, in the Court's view, be deemed "secured . . . by the Constitution or laws of the United States" so as to make § 241 applicable to a private conspiracy to interfere with the exercise of that right. The Court then premises that neither the Fourteenth Amendment nor any other federal law prohibits private interferences with the exercise of the right to equal utilization of state facilities.

In my view, however, a right can be deemed "secured . . . by the Constitution or laws of the United States," within the meaning of § 241, even though only governmental interferences with the exercise of the right are prohibited by the Constitution itself (or another federal law). The term "secured" means "created by, arising under or dependent upon," rather than "fully protected." A right is "secured . . . by the Constitution" within the meaning of § 241 if it emanates from the Constitution, if it finds its source in the Constitution. Section 241 must thus be viewed, in this context, as an exercise of congressional power to amplify prohibitions of the Constitution addressed, as is invariably the case, to government officers; contrary to the view of the Court, I think we are dealing here with a statute that seeks to implement the Constitution, not with the "bare terms" of the Constitution. Section 241 is not confined to protecting rights against private conspiracies that the Constitution or another federal law also protects against private interferences. No such duplicative function was envisioned in its enactment. . . . Nor has this Court construed § 241 in such a restric-

---

1. Similarly, I believe that § 241 reaches a private conspiracy to interfere with the right to travel from State to State. I therefore need not reach the question whether the Constitution of its own force prohibits private interferences with that right; for I construe § 241 to prohibit such interferences, and as so construed I am of the opinion that § 241 is a valid exercise of congressional power. [All footnotes to this opinion by Justice Brennan.]

tive manner in other contexts.   Many of the rights that have been held to be encompassed within § 241 are not additionally the subject of protection of specific federal legislation or of any provision of the Constitution addressed to private individuals.   For example, the prohibitions and remedies of § 241 have been declared to apply, without regard to whether the alleged violator was a government officer, to interferences with the right to vote in a federal election, Ex parte Yarbrough, 110 U.S. 651, or primary, United States v. Classic, 313 U.S. 299; the right to discuss public affairs or petition for redress of grievances, [United States v. Cruikshank; cf. Collins v. Hardyman (dissenting opinion)]; the right to be protected against violence while in the lawful custody of a federal officer, Logan v. United States, 144 U.S. 63; and the right to inform of violations of federal law [In re Quarles], 158 U.S. 532.   The full import of our decision in United States v. Price [below] regarding § 241 is to treat the rights purportedly arising from the Fourteenth Amendment in parity with those rights just enumerated, arising from other constitutional provisions.   The reach of § 241 should not vary with the particular constitutional provision that is the source of the right.   .   .   .

For me, the right to use state facilities without discrimination on the basis of race is, within the meaning of § 241, a right created by, arising under and dependent upon the Fourteenth Amendment and hence is a right "secured" by that Amendment.   It finds its source in that Amendment.   .   .   . The Fourteenth Amendment commands the State to provide the members of all races with equal access to the public facilities it owns or manages, and the right of a citizen to use those facilities without discrimination on the basis of race is a basic corollary of this command.   Cf. Brewer v. Hoxie School District No. 46, 238 F.2d 91 (C.A.8th Cir. 1956).   Whatever may be the status of the right to equal utilization of *privately owned facilities*, see generally Bell v. Maryland, 378 U.S. 226, it must be emphasized that we are here concerned with the right to equal utilization of *public facilities owned or operated by or on behalf of the State*.   To deny the existence of this right or its constitutional stature is to deny the history of the last decade, or to ignore the role of federal power, predicated on the Fourteenth Amendment, in obtaining nondiscriminatory access to such facilities.   It is to do violence to the common understanding, an understanding that found expression in Titles III and IV of the Civil Rights Act of 1964, dealing with state facilities.   Those provisions reflect the view that the Fourteenth Amendment creates the right to equal utilization of state facilities.   Congress did not preface those Titles with a provision comparable to that in Title II explicitly creating the right to equal utilization of certain privately owned facilities.   Congress rightly assumed that a specific legislative declaration of the right was unnecessary, that the right arose from the Fourteenth Amendment itself.

In reversing the District Court's dismissal of the second numbered paragraph, I would therefore hold that proof at the trial of the conspiracy charged to the defendants in that paragraph will establish a violation of § 241 without regard to whether there is also proof that state law enforcement officers actively connived in causing the arrests of Negroes by means of false reports.

II.   My view as to the scope of § 241 requires that I reach the question of constitutional power—whether § 241 or legislation indubitably designed

to punish entirely private conspiracies to interfere with the exercise of Fourteenth Amendment rights constitutes a permissible exercise of the power granted to Congress by § 5 of the Fourteenth Amendment "to enforce by appropriate legislation, the provisions of" the Amendment.

A majority of the members of the Court[2] expresses the view today that § 5 empowers Congress to enact laws punishing *all* conspiracies to interfere with the exercise of Fourteenth Amendment rights, whether or not state officers or others acting under the color of state law are implicated in the conspiracy. Although the Fourteenth Amendment itself, according to established doctrine, "speaks to the State or to those acting under the color of its authority," legislation protecting rights created by that Amendment, such as the right to equal utilization of state facilities, need not be confined to punishing conspiracies in which state officers participate. Rather, § 5 authorizes Congress to make laws that it concludes are reasonably necessary to protect a right created by and arising under that Amendment; and Congress is thus fully empowered to determine that punishment of private conspiracies interfering with the exercise of such a right is necessary to its full protection. It made that determination in enacting § 241, [and], therefore § 241 is constitutional legislation as applied to reach the private conspiracy alleged in the second numbered paragraph of the indictment.

I acknowledge that some of the decisions of this Court, most notably an aspect of the Civil Rights Cases, have declared that Congress' power under § 5 is confined to the adoption of "appropriate legislation for correcting the effects of . . . prohibited State laws and State acts, and thus to render them effectually null, void, and innocuous." I do not accept—and a majority of the Court today rejects—this interpretation of § 5. It reduces the legislative power to enforce the provisions of the Amendment to that of the judiciary; and it attributes a far too limited objective to the Amendment's sponsors. Moreover, the language of § 5 of the Fourteenth Amendment and § 2 of the Fifteenth Amendment are virtually the same, and we recently held in South Carolina v. Katzenbach [sec. 4 below] that "[t]he basic test to be applied in a case involving § 2 of the Fifteenth Amendment is the same as in all cases concerning the express powers of Congress with relation to the reserved powers of the States." The classic formulation of that test by Chief Justice Marshall in McCulloch v. Maryland was there adopted . . . . It seems to me that this is also the standard that defines the scope of congressional authority under § 5 of the Fourteenth Amendment. . . .

Viewed in its proper perspective, § 5 of the Fourteenth Amendment appears as a positive grant of legislative power, authorizing Congress to exercise its discretion in fashioning remedies to achieve civil and political equality for all citizens. No one would deny that Congress could enact legislation directing state officials to provide Negroes with equal access to state schools, parks and other facilities owned or operated by the State. Nor could it be denied that Congress has the power to punish state officers who, in excess of their

2. The majority consists of the Justices joining my Brother Clark's opinion and the Justices joining this opinion. The opinion of Mr. Justice Stewart construes § 241 as applied to the second numbered paragraph to require proof of active participation by state officers in the alleged conspiracy and that opinion does not purport to deal with this question. [Footnote by Justice Brennan.]

authority and in violation of state law, conspire to threaten, harass and murder Negroes for attempting to use these facilities. And I can find no principle of federalism nor word of the Constitution that denies Congress power to determine that in order adequately to protect the right to equal utilization of state facilities, it is also appropriate to punish other individuals—not state officers themselves and not acting in concert with state officers—who engage in the same brutal conduct for the same misguided purpose.

III. Section 241 is certainly not model legislation for punishing private conspiracies to interfere with the exercise of the right of equal utilization of state facilities. It deals in only general language "with Federal rights and with all Federal rights" and protects them "in the lump"; it protects in most general terms "any right or privilege secured . . . by the Constitution or laws of the United States." Congress has left it to the courts to mark the bounds of those words, to determine on a case-by-case basis whether the right purportedly threatened is a federal right. That determination may occur after the conduct charged has taken place or it may not have been anticipated in prior decisions . . . . Reliance on such wording plainly brings § 241 close to the danger line of being void for vagueness.

But, as the Court holds, a stringent scienter requirement saves § 241 from condemnation as a criminal statute failing to provide adequate notice of the proscribed conduct. The gravamen of the offense is conspiracy, and therefore, like a statute making certain conduct criminal only if it is done "willfully," § 241 requires proof of a specific intent for conviction. We have construed § 241 to require proof that the persons charged conspired to act in defiance, or in reckless disregard, of an announced rule making the federal right specific and definite. . . . Since this case reaches us on the pleadings, there is no occasion to decide now whether the Government will be able on trial to sustain the burden of proving the requisite specific intent *vis-à-vis* the right to travel freely from State to State or the right to equal utilization of state facilities. . . . In any event, we may well agree that the necessity to discharge that burden can imperil the effectiveness of § 241 where, as is often the case, the pertinent constitutional right must be implied from a grant of congressional power or a prohibition upon the exercise of governmental power. But since the limitation on the statute's effectiveness derives from Congress' failure to define—with any measure of specificity —the rights encompassed, the remedy is for Congress to write a law without this defect. . . . [See 18 U.S.C. § 245, below, enacted by Congress two years after the decision in this case.]

SOME PROBLEMS OF APPLYING CRIMINAL SANCTIONS TO STATE–INVOLVED DEFENDANTS INTERFERING WITH 14TH AMENDMENT RIGHTS

Introduction. This group of notes focus on one cluster of problems among the range of issues raised by the Guest case. Recall Part II of Justice Stewart's opinion in Guest: that part of the opinion finds a possibility of sustaining a portion of the indictment (covering interference with 14th Amendment rights) without reaching the question whether § 5 of the 14th

Amendment may reach purely private actors; it does so by finding the allegation "broad enough to cover a charge of active connivance by agents of the State" or "other conduct amounting to official discrimination." Under that theory, in short, nominally private defendants may be reached if they are sufficiently involved with state officials, by building directly on the Court interpretations of § 1 of the 14th Amendment considered in sec. 2B above, without attributing any independent power to Congress in expanding the reach of the 14th Amendment. But even the rationale of reaching private actors because of state involvement is not without difficulty, as this group of notes illustrates. There is, first, the problem of how much state involvement with the private actors needs to be shown—a problem akin to those considered in sec. 2B. There is, moreover, the question of construing 18 U.S.C. §§ 241 and 242 as reaching 14th Amendment rights and state-involved private actors. There is, finally, the concern—voiced in Guest— about vagueness problems raised by broad constructions of those general sections. *

1. *The Price case.* UNITED STATES v. PRICE, 383 U.S. 787 (1966), arose out of a widely publicized murder of three civil rights workers near Philadelphia, Mississippi, in 1964. The defendants were three local law enforcement officials (Deputy Sheriff Price of Neshoba County, the Sheriff, and a policeman) and fifteen private individuals, all allegedly involved in the killing of Schwerner, Chaney and Goodman. There were two indictments against the 18 defendants: one based on 18 U.S.C. § 242; the other on § 241. The alleged conspiracy involved releasing the victims from jail at night, intercepting and killing them, and disposing of their bodies—all with the purpose to "punish" the victims summarily and thus to deprive them of their 14th Amendment right "not to be summarily punished without due process of law by persons acting under color of the laws of the State of Mississippi." The District Court dismissed most of the charges. On direct appeal, the Supreme Court reversed all of the dismissals. Justice Fortas wrote for the Court, stating (like Justice Stewart in Guest) that the case involved only issues "of construction, not of constitutional power."

a. The first indictment charged substantive violations of 18 U.S.C. § 242 (the "under color" of law provision) as well as a conspiracy to violate that Section. The District Court sustained the conspiracy count against all of the defendants: as to the private defendants, the lower court found it "immaterial" that they were "not acting under color of law" because the charge was "that they were conspiring with persons who were so acting." But the trial court sustained the substantive counts against the three official defendants only; it dismissed these counts against the private defendants since they were not "officers in fact."

The Supreme Court reversed the dismissal of the substantive charges against the private defendants. § 242 concededly required that the "person indicted has acted 'under color' of law," and "under color" of law should

---

* The Guest case of course raises additional, more far-reaching problems as well: e. g., congressional authority to reach purely private actors under § 5 of the 14th Amendment, and congressional authority to reach private actors by drawing upon federal rights not limited by the state action concept. Those additional problems are considered in the next group of notes.

be treated, as it had been under its civil counterpart (sec. 3B below), "as the same thing as the 'state action' required under the 14th Amendment." But that did not bar reaching private individuals in view of the expanding readings by the Court of the state action coverage of the 14th Amendment: "Private persons, jointly engaged with state officials in the prohibited action, are acting 'under color' of law for purposes of the statute. To act 'under color' of law does not require that the accused be an officer of the State. It is enough that he is a willful participant in joint activity with the State or its agents." Justice Fortas particularly emphasized the relevance of the Burton case analysis, sec. 2 above.

Here, he noted, "the brutal joint adventure was made possible by state detention and calculated release of the prisoners by an officer of the State. This action, clearly attributable to the State, was part of the monstrous design described by the indictment. State officers participated in every phase of the alleged venture: the release from jail, the interception, assault and murder. It was a joint activity, from start to finish. Those who took advantage of participation by state officers in accomplishment of the foul purpose alleged must suffer the consequences of that participation. In effect, if the allegations are true, they were participants in official lawlessness, acting in willful concert with state officers and hence under color of law."

b. The second indictment in Price charged all 18 defendants with a conspiracy under 18 U.S.C. § 241, the "private conspiracy" section. Fifteen years earlier, the Court, in one of the Williams cases (note 2 below) had left in doubt the question whether that provision applied to interferences with 14th Amendment rights. But in Price, the Court had no difficulty in resolving that question: it held that § 241 did apply, and that its reach in this context presented no constitutional difficulty because of the presence of state action. The district court had dismissed the indictment against all the defendants, holding that the section did not apply to rights under the 14th Amendment, relying on Justice Frankfurter's opinion in one of the Williams cases. But in Price, the Court, noting that the 4 to 4 division in 1951 had left the construction of § 241 "an open question," adopted Justice Douglas' position in that Williams case: "[Section 241] includes rights or privileges protected by the Fourteenth Amendment; [and] whatever the ultimate coverage of the section may be, it extends to conspiracies otherwise within the scope of the section, participated in by officials alone or in collaboration with private persons. [The] present application of the statutes does not raise fundamental questions of federal-state relationships. We are here concerned with allegations which squarely and undisputably involve state action in direct violation of the mandate of the Fourteenth Amendment." *

2. *The Williams cases.* The 1951 decisions in the Williams cases, referred to in Price, throw light on two problems: first, they provide another example of using Court-developed state action analyses of § 1 of the 14th Amendment to reach private individuals; second, they raise the problem of statutory construction resolved in Price.

---

* See also the expansive modern statutory interpretation of 18 U.S.C. § 1985(3), a civil provision reaching certain private conspiracies, in Griffin v. Breckenridge, sec. 3B below.

a. One of the cases, WILLIAMS v. UNITED STATES, 341 U.S. 97 (1951), was a prosecution under the predecessor of 18 U.S.C. § 242, the "under color" of law provision. Defendant, a private detective who had been issued a special police officer's badge, was employed by a lumber company to investigate thefts of its property. Flashing his badge and accompanied by a regular police officer detailed to assist him in the investigation, he took four suspects to a shack on the company's premises and beat them until they confessed to the thefts. Indicted for depriving his victims, under color of law, of the right to be tried by due process of law, he was found guilty. The Court affirmed. Justice Douglas' majority opinion concluded that the jury could find that defendant was acting "under color" of state law. Defendant was "no mere interloper but had a semblance of policeman's power," and "the manner of his conduct of the interrogations makes clear that he was asserting the authority granted him and not acting in the role of a private person." Justices Frankfurter, Jackson and Minton dissented for the reasons set forth in the dissent in the Screws case, note 3 below. Justice Black also dissented.

b. In a companion case, UNITED STATES v. WILLIAMS, 341 U.S. 70 (1951), the same defendant, two of his employees who participated in the beatings, and the police officer detailed to assist him, were convicted of conspiracy under the predecessor of 18 U.S.C. § 241, the private conspiracy provision. The Court found that the convictions should be reversed; but only eight of the Justices reached the critical issue of statutory construction, and they divided 4 to 4, leaving the uncertainty that was clarified by the Price case. (Justice Black cast the decisive vote for the result, relying on res judicata grounds.) Justice Frankfurter's opinion, joined by Chief Justice Vinson and Justices Jackson and Minton, argued that § 241 should not be read as covering 14th Amendment rights: § 241 covered conspiracies by private persons without an explicit requirement of state action; § 242 was apparently intended to deal fully with conspiracies under color of state law to deprive persons of 14th Amendment rights; accordingly, § 241 should be construed as protecting only those rights "which Congress can beyond doubt constitutionally secure against interference by private individuals." Justice Frankfurter added: "Decisions of this Court have established that this category includes rights which arise from the relationship of the individual and the Federal Government,"—e. g., "the right of citizens to vote in congressional elections"—and not "those rights which the Constitution merely guarantees from interference by a State." He emphasized the "familiar" distinction "between rights that flow from the substantive powers of the Federal Government and may clearly be protected from private interference, and interests which the Constitution only guarantees from interference by States." †

The other four Justices in that Williams case—Justice Douglas, joined by Justices Reed, Burton and Clark—took a broader view of § 242, and their view was adopted by the Court in the Price case. They insisted that § 241, like § 242, was applicable to 14th Amendment rights as well as others.

---

† Note the increasing importance of that distinction in developing bases for federal action against private interferences with constitutional rights. For additional illustrations of those rights, see the opinions of Justices Stewart and Brennan in Guest and the excerpt from Justice Harlan's opinion in the introduction to this section.

They thought it was "strange to hear it said that though [§ 242] extends to rights guaranteed against state action by the 14th Amendment [§ 241] is limited to rights which the Federal Government can secure against invasion by private persons." [Note that Justice Douglas' emphasis was solely on the question of statutory construction: he insisted that conspiracies to deny 14th Amendment rights were reachable under § 241; but he recognized that the constitutionality of reaching such conspiracies depended on satisfying the state action requirement in each case. Compare the broader reach of § 241 suggested by Justice Brennan's opinion in Guest.]

3. *The Screws case.*   a. *Vagueness and civil rights laws.* The broad references in 18 U.S.C. §§ 241 and 242 to "rights . . . secured" by the Constitution have stimulated recurrent challenges by defendants that the statutes do not give adequate notice of what is prohibited and are therefore void for vagueness. The Court has repeatedly rejected those challenges by reading what Justice Brennan in Guest called "a strict scienter requirement" into the criminal provisions. As Justice Stewart's opinion in Guest noted, "the offender must act with a specific intent to interfere with the federal rights in question" to be punishable under the broad criminal provisions. That reading stems from one of the earliest of the modern cases under the civil rights laws, SCREWS v. UNITED STATES, 321 U.S. 91 (1945). That case involved a "shocking and revolting episode in law enforcement." The defendants were police officers (Screws was sheriff of Baker County, Ga.) who arrested the Black victim for theft and beat him "with their fists and with a solid-bar blackjack" after he allegedly reached for a gun and used insulting language. The victim was knocked on the ground and beaten until he was unconscious. He died soon after. "There was evidence that Screws held a grudge against [the victim] and had threatened to 'get' him."

The defendants were convicted under 18 U.S.C. § 242 for "willfully" and "under color of law" depriving the victim of his 14th Amendment rights, including "the right not to be deprived of life without due process of law" and "the right to be tried, upon the charge on which he was arrested, by due process of law." Justice Douglas' opinion, joined by Chief Justice Stone, Justice Black and Justice Reed, found that the law could be interpreted to avoid the vagueness challenge—the claim that "there is no ascertainable standard of guilt" because the Court had given "broad and fluid definitions of due process." Justice Douglas conceded that that would be a serious challenge if "the customary standard of guilt for statutory crimes" were adopted: "If a man intentionally adopts certain conduct in certain circumstances known to him, and that conduct is forbidden by the law under those circumstances, he intentionally breaks the law." Under such a test, "a local law enforcement officer violates [§ 242] if he does an act which some court later holds deprives a person of due process of law. And he is a criminal though his motive was pure and though his purpose was unrelated to the disregard of any constitutional guarantee." Under such a view, state officials would indeed walk on "treacherous ground," given the "character and closeness of decisions of this Court interpreting the due process clause." But Justice Douglas found it possible to read § 242 "more narrowly" to avoid the constitutional difficulty of vagueness. He explained: "[I]f we construe 'willfully' in [§ 242] as connoting a purpose to deprive a person of a specific constitutional right, we would introduce no innovation. The Court, indeed,

has recognized that the requirement of a specific intent to do a prohibited act may avoid those consequences to the accused which may otherwise render a vague or indefinite statute invalid. [W]here the punishment imposed is only for an act knowingly done with the purpose of doing that which the statute prohibits, the accused cannot be said to suffer from lack of warning or knowledge that the act which he does is a violation of law. [T]he presence of a bad purpose or evil intent alone may not be sufficient. [But] a requirement of a specific intent to deprive a person of a federal right made definite by decision or other rule of law saves the Act from any charge of unconstitutionality on the grounds of vagueness. . . .

"It is said, however, that this construction of the Act will not save it from the infirmity of vagueness since neither a law enforcement official nor a trial judge can know with sufficient definiteness the range of rights that are constitutional. But that criticism is wide of the mark. For the specific intent required by the Act is an intent to deprive a person of a right which has been made specific either by the express terms of the Constitution or laws of the United States or by decisions interpreting them. Take the case of a local officer who persists in enforcing a type of ordinance which the Court has held invalid as violative of the guarantees of free speech or freedom of worship. Or a local official continues to select juries in a manner which flies in the teeth of decisions of the Court. If those acts are done willfully, how can the officer possibly claim that he had no fair warning that his acts were prohibited by the statute? He violates the statute not merely because he has a bad purpose but because he acts in defiance of announced rules of law. He who defies a decision interpreting the Constitution knows precisely what he is doing. If sane, he hardly may be heard to say that he knew not what he did. [W]illful violators of constitutional requirements, which have been defined, certainly are in no position to say that they had no adequate advance notice that they would be visited with punishment. When they act willfully in the sense in which we use the word, they act in open defiance or in reckless disregard of a constitutional requirement which has been made specific and definite. When they are convicted for so acting, they are not punished for violating an unknowable something. . . .

" . . . The fact that the defendants may not have been thinking in constitutional terms is not material where their aim was not to enforce local law but to deprive a citizen of a right and that right was protected by the Constitution. When they so act they at least act in reckless disregard of constitutional prohibitions or guarantees. Likewise, it is plain that basic to the concept of due process of law in a criminal case is a trial—a trial in a court of law, not a 'trial by ordeal.' . . . It could hardly be doubted that they who 'under color of any law, statute, ordinance, regulation, or custom,' act with that evil motive violate [§ 242]. Those who decide to take the law into their own hands and act as prosecutor, jury, judge, and executioner plainly act to deprive a prisoner of the trial which due process of law guarantees him. And such a purpose need not be expressed; it may at times be reasonably inferred from all the circumstances attendant on the act."

But in this case, the trial judge had not instructed the jury properly on the question of intent, and the conviction was accordingly reversed.* Justice

---

* At the second trial, Screws was acquitted. See also the 18 U.S.C. § 242 prosecutions in Koehler v. United States, 189 F.2d 711 (5th Cir.), cert. denied, 342

Rutledge cast the decisive vote to make that disposition possible: though he agreed with Justice Murphy that the trial judge's instructions were adequate and that the conviction should be affirmed, he noted that the case "cannot have disposition" if each Justice adhered to his belief; he accordingly voted to remand for disposition in accordance with Justice Douglas' views. Justices Roberts, Frankfurter, and Jackson dissented, insisting that the "intrinsic vagueness" of the statute "surely cannot be removed by making the statute applicable only where the defendant has the 'requisite bad purpose.' Does that not amount to saying that the black heart of the defendant enables him to know what are the constitutional rights deprivation of which the statute forbids, although we as judges are not able to define their classes or their limits, or, at least, are not prepared to state what they are unless it be to say that [§ 242] protects whatever rights the Constitution protects? "

b. *Action in violation of state law as action "under color" of law.* The Screws case also involved a second issue—one which no longer gives the Court real difficulty. That issue was whether a defendant could be treated as acting "under color" of state law when the action was in violation of state law. The Court rejected that contention by a 6 to 3 vote. Justice Douglas' opinion stated of the Screws defendants: "They were officers of the law who made the arrest. By their own admission they assaulted [the victim] in order to protect themselves and to keep their prisoner from escaping. It was their duty under Georgia law to make the arrest effective. Hence, their conduct comes within the statute." He relied on the Court's statement in United States v. Classic, 313 U.S. 299 (1941): "Misuse of power, possessed by virtue of state law and made possible only because the wrongdoer is clothed with the authority of state law, is action taken 'under color of' state law." And he noted, too, that as early as Ex parte Virginia, 100 U.S. 339 (1879), a state judge had been found punishable under federal law for discriminating against Blacks in jury selection, though his action violated state law as well. There, "the Court in deciding what was state action within the meaning of the Fourteenth Amendment held that it was immaterial that the state officer exceeded the limits of his authority"; since the state officer "acts in the name and for the State, and is clothed with the State's power, his act is that of the State. This must be so, or the constitutional prohibition has no meaning. Then the State has clothed one of its agents with power to annul or to evade it." Justice Douglas added: "It is clear that under 'color' of law means under 'pretense' of law. Thus acts of officers in the ambit of their personal pursuits are plainly excluded. Acts of officers who undertake to perform their official duties are included whether they hew to the line of their authority or overstep it."

The dissent of Justices Roberts, Frankfurter and Jackson was willing to assume that the officers' action "in flagrant defiance of State law" could amount to state action under the 14th Amendment; but "this does not make it action under 'color of any law.' " They insisted that § 242 "is much narrower than the power of Congress." They argued that it was the congressional purpose "to leave undisturbed the power and the duty of the States to enforce their criminal law by restricting federal authority to the punish-

U.S. 852 (1951), and Crews v. United
States, 160 F.2d 746 (5th Cir. 1947).
See Alfange, " 'Under Color of Law':   Classic and Screws Revisited," 47 Cornell L.Q. 395 (1962).

ment only of those persons who violate federal rights under claim of State authority and not by exerting federal authority against offenders of State authority."

THE REACH OF CONGRESSIONAL POWER, THE GUEST CASE, AND THE NEW LAW

1. *Congressional power under § 5 of the 14th Amendment.* The cases in the preceding group of notes all involved applications of the criminal sanctions of the civil rights laws to actors reachable under the Court's own interpretations of the state action concept under § 1 of the 14th Amendment. But Justice Brennan's opinion in Guest (and presumably Justice Clark's endorsing comment) suggested that Congress under § 5 of the Amendment may go further in reaching private behavior than the Court would under § 1. How far-reaching is that suggested congressional power? Justice Clark's opinion stated that "the specific language of § 5 empowers the Congress to enact laws punishing all conspiracies—with or without state action—that interfere with Fourteenth Amendment rights." And Justice Brennan insisted that "legislation protecting rights created by [the 14th] Amendment, such as the right to equal utilization of state facilities, need not be confined to punishing conspiracies in which state officers participate"; Congress is "fully empowered to determine that punishment of private conspiracies interfering with the exercise of such a right is necessary to its full protection."

Note that the Brennan and Clark opinions in Guest continue to assume that 14th Amendment rights are rights against the state. Thus, Justice Brennan notes that the 14th Amendment "commands the State to provide the members of all races with equal access" to public facilities. He draws from this obligation a "basic corollary": "the right of a citizen to use those facilities without discrimination on the basis of race." What kinds of private interferences with the relationship between the state and the individual are reachable under the broad view of § 5 of the 14th Amendment? Are the private interferences limited to those that are directed at state officials, in order to hamper them from carrying out their 14th Amendment obligations? Or may Congress also reach private interferences with the private citizen who has a "corollary" right against the state? May Congress go even further than that?

The theory is most readily applicable to situations where the private interference is directed against the state officials themselves. That was the situation in a case cited by Justice Brennan in Guest, Brewer v. Hoxie School District No. 46, 238 F.2d 91 (8th Cir. 1956). That case sustained federal power to reach private actors who intimidate state officials in the performance of their 14th Amendment obligations. It upheld an injunction restraining private persons from intimidating school officials who were trying to carry out a plan to desegregate schools that had been operated under a system of de jure segregation. The court noted that the school officials were trying to apply the Constitution as interpreted in Brown v. Board of Education, and that it followed "as a necessary corollary that they have a federal

right to be free from direct and deliberate interference with the performance of the constitutionally imposed duty. The right arises by necessary implication from the imposition of the duty."

But Justice Brennan in Guest was clearly willing to give that theory a broader reach: he was prepared to sustain the application of 18 U.S.C. § 241 to a private interference with the private citizen who had a right of access to public facilities. In short, he found power to reach the private actor interfering with the state-victim relationship by intimidations directed not against the state official but against the victim. Under that theory, is it essential that the defendant intends to interfere with the victim's access to state facilities? Is it enough that murder of the victim, for example, has the effect of interfering with the victim's use of state facilities? Is that a limitless concept?

Is the theory even more far-reaching than that? Is a special relationship between the victim and the state an essential ingredient for invoking § 5? Or may Congress act directly under § 5 to prevent private interference with access to *private* facilities as well? May Congress, for example, move directly to reach private interferences with access to private housing, on the ground that that is appropriate legislation to protect access to public housing? If the Guest rationale does not support such power, can justification for it be found in the approach of Katzenbach v. Morgan, sec. 4 below—an approach that gives Congress some power to "reinterpret" the content of 14th Amendment guarantees, and arguably some power to redraw the lines between state action and private action under the 14th Amendment? (Recall also the justifications for regulation of intrastate commerce in the interest of protecting interstate commerce, in chap. 3.) *

2. *Criminal sanctions against private conduct: Sources outside the 14th Amendment.* Recall again that the Guest case and related materials point to sources of congressional authority beyond 14th Amendment rights. There are, for example, the constitutional provisions running against private behavior as well as state conduct, such as the 13th Amendment (sec. 3C below), and the constitutional rights implied from the relation of the individual to the national government. Thus, 18 U.S.C. § 241 has been repeatedly applied to prevent private interferences with the victim's relationship with the national government, such as voting in national elections and petitioning the national government for redress of grievances. (Recall the listing of such rights in Guest and in the introductory materials to this chapter.) Moreover, private interferences may be reached when Congress establishes new rights by statute under powers that clearly reach private activity—e. g., the commerce power, used as the basis for the public accommodations provisions of the Civil Rights Act of 1964.

Against that background as to sources of congressional power to reach private interferences, consider the 1968 provisions affording criminal sanc-

---

* See generally Cox, "Foreword—Constitutional Adjudication and the Promotion of Human Rights," 80 Harv.L. Rev. 91 (1966), Feuerstein, "Civil Rights Crimes . . .," 19 Vand. L.Rev. 641 (1966), and Brest, "The Federal Government's Power to Protect Negroes and Civil Rights Workers Against Privately Inflicted Harm," 1 Harv.Civ.Rts.—Civ.Libs.L.Rev. 1 (1966). See also the notes following Katzenbach v. Morgan and Oregon v. Mitchell, sec. 4 below.

tions against private actors, 18 U.S.C. § 245. The text of that new law follows. Can the new provisions be viewed as a response to Justice Brennan's suggestion of more specific legislation in Guest? Do the specifications in 18 U.S.C. § 245 cure the vagueness concerns aroused by 18 U.S.C. §§ 241 and 242? What explains the differences in intent requirements for (b)(1) violations and (b)(2) acts? What explains the grouping of § 245(b) into two subsections? What are the sources of the various rights specified? Which are 14th Amendment rights? Which stem from other sources? Does 18 U.S.C. § 245 raise any constitutional questions? †

THE CRIMINAL PROVISIONS ADDED BY THE
CIVIL RIGHTS ACT OF 1968:
18 U.S.C. § 245

§ 245. *Federally protected activities.* . . .

(b) Whoever, whether or not acting under color of law, by force or threat of force willfully injures, intimidates or interferes with, or attempts to injure, intimidate or interfere with—

(1) any person because he is or has been, or in order to intimidate such person or any other person or any class of persons from—

(A) voting or qualifying to vote, qualifying or campaigning as a candidate for elective office, or qualifying or acting as a poll watcher, or any legally authorized election official, in any primary, special, or general election;

(B) participating in or enjoying any benefit, service, privilege, program, facility or activity provided or administered by the United States;

(C) applying for or enjoying employment, or any perquisite thereof, by any agency of the United States;

(D) serving, or attending upon any court in connection with possible service, as a grand or petit juror in any court of the United States;

(E) participating in or enjoying the benefits of any program or activity receiving Federal financial assistance; or

(2) any person because of his race, color, religion or national origin and because he is or has been—

(A) enrolling in or attending any public school or public college;

(B) participating in or enjoying any benefit, service, privilege, program, facility or activity provided or administered by any State or subdivision thereof;

(C) applying for or enjoying employment, or any perquisite thereof, by any private employer or any agency of any State or subdivision thereof, or joining or using the services or advantages of any labor organization, hiring hall, or employment agency;

(D) serving, or attending upon any court of any State in connection with possible service, as a grand or petit juror;

---

† The background of 18 U.S.C. § 245 reveals the interactions between the Court and the other branches with special vividness. Thus, President Johnson in January 1966 asked for new laws "to try those who murder, attack, or intimidate either civil rights workers or others exercising federal rights." But implementation of that Administration proposal was delayed, in part to await the Court's decisions in Guest and Price. Those cases came down on March 28, 1966. Exactly a month later, the President submitted a special Civil Rights Message to Congress, accompanied by detailed proposals to prescribe "penalties for certain acts of violence or intimidation." The 1966 legislative efforts ended in a Senate filibuster. A slightly revised version of the 1966 proposal was included in the Johnson Administration's 1967 civil rights bill. That bill, as substantially amended, became the Civil Rights Act of 1968, and included 18 U.S.C. § 245.

(E) traveling in or using any facility of interstate commerce, or using any vehicle, terminal, or facility of any common carrier by motor, rail, water, or air;

(F) enjoying the goods, services, facilities, privileges, advantages, or accommodations of any inn, hotel, motel, or other establishment which provides lodging to transient guests, or of any restaurant, cafeteria, lunchroom, lunch counter, soda fountain, or other facility which serves the public and which is principally engaged in selling food or beverages for consumption on the premises, or of any gasoline station, or of any motion picture house, theater, concert hall, sports arena, stadium, or any other place of exhibition or entertainment which serves the public, or of any other establishment which serves the public and (i) which is located within the premises of any of the aforesaid establishments or within the premises of which is physically located any of the aforesaid establishments, and (ii) which holds itself out as serving patrons of such establishments; or

(3) during or incident to a riot or civil disorder, any person engaged in a business in commerce or affecting commerce, including, but not limited to, any person engaged in a business which sells or offers for sale to interstate travelers a substantial portion of the articles, commodities, or services which it sells or where a substantial portion of the articles or commodities which it sells or offers for sale have moved in commerce; or

(4) any person because he is or has been, or in order to intimidate such person or any other person or any class of persons from—

(A) participating, without discrimination on account of race, color, religion or national origin, in any of the benefits or activities described in subparagraphs (1) (A) through (1) (E) or subparagraphs (2) (A) through (2) (F); or

(B) affording another person or class of persons opportunity or protection to so participate; or

(5) any citizen because he is or has been, or in order to intimidate such citizen or any other citizen from lawfully aiding or encouraging other persons to participate, without discrimination on account of race, color, religion or national origin, in any of the benefits or activities described in subparagraphs (1) (A) through (1) (E) or subparagraphs (2) (A) through (2) (F), or participating lawfully in speech or peaceful assembly opposing any denial of the opportunity to so participate—

shall be fined not more than $1,000, or imprisoned not more than one year, or both; and if bodily injury results shall be fined not more than $10,000, or imprisoned not more than ten years, or both; and if death results shall be subject to imprisonment for any term of years or for life. As used in this section, the term "participating lawfully in speech or peaceful assembly" shall not mean the aiding, abetting, or inciting of other persons to riot . . . . .

B. PRIVATE INTERFERENCES WITH FEDERAL RIGHTS: CIVIL SANCTIONS

Introduction. As the statutory survey in sec. 1 of this chapter indicates, several of the laws of the 1860's and 1870's afforded civil rather than criminal sanctions; and the modern remnants of those civil sanction laws give rise to problems of statutory scope and constitutional authority analogous to those considered in sec. 3A in connection with the criminal provisions. Thus, 42 U.S.C. § 1983 is the civil counterpart of 18 U.S.C. § 242: it provides civil remedies for deprivations of rights "under color" of law. And 42 U.S.C. § 1985(3) grants civil remedies for certain private conspiracies, as 18 U.S.C. § 241 does in the criminal sphere. The notes which follow will first consider the more difficult statutory and constitutional problems raised by that civil private conspiracy provision—problems analo-

gous to those raised by the Guest case—before examining some issues raised by the "under color" of law provision.

PRIVATE CONSPIRACIES AND GRIFFIN v. BRECKENRIDGE

1. *The Griffin interpretation of § 1985(3).* In 1951, the Court, beset by constitutional doubts, gave a narrow interpretation to the conspiracy provision in 42 U.S.C. § 1985—the provision granting a civil remedy for conspiracies to deny "the equal protection of the laws, or of equal privileges and immunities under the laws." Collins v. Hardyman, 341 U.S. 651 (1951),[1] in effect construed § 1985(3) as reaching only conspiracies under color of state law. Twenty years later, however, in GRIFFIN v. BRECKENRIDGE, 403 U.S. 88 (1971), a unanimous Court discarded that interpretation, found that "many of the constitutional problems" perceived in Collins "simply do not exist," and held § 1985(3) applicable to certain private conspiracies. On the congressional power issue, the Court found it unnecessary to reach the 14th Amendment question. Instead, Justice Stewart relied on the power to reach private conduct under the 13th Amendment and in protection of the right of interstate travel.[2]

1. In Collins, plaintiffs, members of a political club, stated that defendants broke up their meeting—planned to adopt a resolution opposing the Marshall Plan—and thus interfered with their rights to petition the national government for redress of grievances and to equal privileges under the laws. There was no allegation that defendants acted under color of law. Justice Jackson's majority opinion concluded that no cause of action under § 1985(3) had been stated. A conspiracy to deprive "of the equal protection of the laws, or of equal privileges and immunities under the laws," was a statutory requirement, and was not shown here. He noted: "The only inequality suggested is that the defendants broke up plaintiffs' meetings and did not break up meetings of others with whose sentiments they agreed. . . . Such private discrimination is not inequality before the law unless there is some manipulation of the law or its agencies to give sanction or sanctuary for doing so." He added: "We do not say that no conspiracy by private individuals could be of such magnitude and effect as to work a deprivation of [equal protection]. Indeed, the post-Civil War Ku Klux Klan [may have] done so. . . . It may well be that a conspiracy, so far-flung and embracing such numbers, [was] able effectively to deprive Negroes of their equal rights and to close all avenues [of] redress or vindication. [H]ere nothing of that sort appears. We have a case of a lawless political brawl, precipitated by a handful of white citizens against other white citizens. California courts are open to plaintiffs . . . ." Justice Burton, joined by Justices Black and Douglas, dissented. The right to petition the federal government for a redress of grievances, he noted, was a constitutional right, under the dictum in United States v. Cruikshank; and it was not a right limited to state interferences. He added that cases holding that the 14th Amendment was directed only at state action "are not authority for the contention that Congress may not pass laws supporting rights which exist apart from [the 14th Amendment]."

2. Justice Harlan's concurrence dissociated himself from the reliance on the right to travel rationale.

Note the parallels in the evolution of the civil and criminal conspiracy provisions: Collins v. Hardyman was decided in the same year as the United States v. Williams cases, sec. 3A above. In Williams, Justice Frankfurter's opinion had read 18 U.S.C. § 241 narrowly; that statutory interpretation was repudiated in the Price case in 1966. Similarly, Justice Jackson's narrow reading of § 1985(3) was overturned in Griffin in 1971.

The petitioners in Griffin were Mississippi Blacks who were passengers in an automobile operated by a Tennessean in Mississippi, near the Mississippi-Alabama border. They charged that respondents, white Mississippians, had conspired to detain, assault and beat them for the purpose of preventing them and other Blacks "from seeking the equal protection of the laws and from enjoying the equal rights, privileges and immunities of citizens," including their rights to free speech, movement, association, assembly, and "their rights not to be enslaved nor deprived of life and liberty other than by due process of law." The complaint in their damage action charged that the respondents, mistakenly believing the driver to be a civil rights worker, blocked the car, forced the inhabitants to get out of it, and threatened and clubbed them. The lower federal courts dismissed the complaint on the authority of Collins v. Hardyman.

Justice Stewart's opinion concluded, without deciding whether Collins was decided correctly "on its own facts," that, "in the light of the evolution of decisional law," the statute should now be given its "apparent meaning." Not only the text but "companion provisions, and legislative history" pointed "unwaveringly to § 1985(3)'s coverage of private conspiracies." [3] Reading the law to cover private action did not, however, mean that it would apply "to all tortious, conspiratorial interferences with the rights of others." Justice Stewart explained: "The constitutional shoals that would lie in the path of interpreting § 1985(3) as a general federal tort law can be avoided by giving full effect to the congressional purpose—by requiring, as an element of the cause of action," an "invidiously discriminatory motivation." He added: "The language requiring intent to deprive of *equal* protection, or *equal* privileges and immunities, means that there must be some racial, or perhaps otherwise class-based, invidiously discriminatory animus behind the conspirators' action." [4]

3. In rejecting a state action limitation on § 1985(3), Justice Stewart found that all possible state action-related interpretations were covered by companion statutes. Note his description of the "three possible forms for this state action limitation": "that there must be action under color of state law, that there must be interference with or influence upon state authorities, or that there must be a private conspiracy so massive and effective that it supplants those authorities and thus satisfies the state action requirement."

Note also Justice Stewart's recognition that the similarity of the statutory language to § 1 of the Fourteenth Amendment had channeled past "judicial thinking about what can constitute an equal protection deprivation" to focus almost entirely on the state action problem. But there could be "a deprivation of the equal protection of the laws by private persons," he insisted: "[T]here is nothing inherent in the phrase that requires the action working the deprivation to come from the State." But the congressional power to reach these private deprivations of equal protection, the opinion found, was adequately supportable on non-Fourteenth Amendment grounds.

4. Justice Stewart added in a footnote: "We need not decide, given the facts of this case, whether a conspiracy motivated by invidiously discriminatory intent other than racial bias would be actionable under the portion of § 1985 (3) before us." He noted, too, that the motivation requirement stemming from the reference to "equal" in the statute "must not be confused with" the scienter test of Screws v. United States. "Willfulness" was not an element of § 1985(3), unlike 18 U.S.C. § 242. (Cf. Monroe v. Pape, below.) Justice Stewart added: "The motivation aspect of § 1985(3) focuses not on scienter in relation to deprivation of rights but on invidiously discriminatory animus."

After finding that petitioners' complaint easily fell within that new construction of § 1985(3)—"[i]ndeed, the conduct here alleged lies so close to the care of the coverage intended by Congress that it is hard to conceive of wholly private conduct that would come within the statute if this does not"—, Justice Stewart turned to the question of congressional power to reach this private conspiracy. He noted: "That § 1985(3) reaches private conspiracies to deprive others of legal rights can, of itself, cause no doubts of its constitutionality. It has long been settled that 18 U.S.C. § 241, a criminal statute of far broader phrasing, reaches wholly private conspiracies and is constitutional. Our inquiry, therefore, need go only to identifying a source of congressional power to reach the private conspiracy alleged by the complaint in this case." He found one adequate constitutional basis in the 13th Amendment, explaining that the varieties of private conduct which Congress may reach under it "extend far beyond the actual imposition of slavery or involuntary servitude." He concluded "that Congress was wholly within its powers under § 2 of the Thirteenth Amendment in creating a statutory cause of action for Negro citizens who have been the victims of conspiratorial, racially discriminatory private action aimed at depriving them of the basic rights that the law secures to all free men." (See the Jones case, sec. 3C.) Justice Stewart also found an independent basis in "the right of interstate travel," relying, inter alia, on his opinion in United States v. Guest. In a concluding passage, Justice Stewart stated: "In identifying these two constitutional sources of congressional power, we do not imply the absence of any other. More specifically, the allegations of the complaint in this case have not required consideration of the scope of the power of Congress under § 5 of the Fourteenth Amendment.[5] By the same token, since the allegations of the complaint bring this cause of action so close to the constitutionally authorized core of the statute, there has been no occasion here to trace out its constitutionally permissible periphery."

2. *The implications of Griffin.* What *is* the "constitutionally permissible periphery" of 42 U.S.C. § 1985(3)? To what extent may Congress reach "invidiously discriminatory intent other than racial bias"? To what extent may Congress reach private interferences with 14th Amendment rights—an issue not reached in Griffin? Recall the analogous questions about the implications of the Guest case, sec. 3A above.

a. *Action v. Gannon.* Is there constitutional justification for the application of § 1985(3) in Action v. Gannon, 450 F.2d 1227 (8th Cir. 1971)? In Gannon, the District Court had enjoined civil rights groups from disrupting services at the Roman Catholic Cathedral in St. Louis. In affirming that injunction, the Court of Appeals relied on § 1985(3) and on what it saw as the implications of Griffin and Guest, and accordingly affirmed the injunction against interfering with parishioners' "rights to exercise freedom of religion, freedom of speech, freedom of assembly and the same right, as enjoyed by other citizens of the United States, to hold and use the parish property for religious purposes." The court noted that the defendants were acting on behalf of Black citizens, and that their demands "to a predominantly white parish" were based on "racial and economic

5. At this point, Justice Stewart cited the Clark and Brennan opinions in United States v. Guest, as well as two cases in sec. 4 below: Katzenbach v. Morgan, and two of the opinions in Oregon v. Mitchell.

motives." (The demands "would have required the church to devote substantial portions of its income to programs dedicated to Black advancement.") The court found plaintiffs' First Amendment rights "of freedom of assembly and worship" covered by the 14th Amendment, and insisted "that Congress was given the power in § 5 of the Fourteenth Amendment to enforce the rights guaranteed by the Amendment against private conspiracies." The court thought that view justified by the Clark and Brennan opinions in Guest.[1]

    b. *Other Courts of Appeals decisions.* Compare the more recent division in the Courts of Appeals in other attempts to apply § 1985(3) to private interferences with 14th Amendment rights. In Westberry v. Gilman Paper Co., 507 F.2d 206 (1975), a divided Fifth Circuit found § 1985(3) applicable against private parties who allegedly conspired to kill a "white environmental activist" in violation of the plaintiff's equal protection and due process rights. (One defendant was the plaintiff's former private employer.) The court recognized that the constitutional rationales of Griffin— e. g., the 13th Amendment—were not applicable here; but the majority concluded that congressional power under § 5 of the 14th Amendment was adequate: "There are three reasons for believing that private discriminatory acts come within the purview of [§ 5] should Congress believe that a preclusion of such acts is helpful in insuring the effectuation of Section 1. First, we find such indication in the legislative history behind the Act. Second, we find such a conclusion expressed by a majority of the members of the Supreme Court [in United States v. Guest]. Third, decisions in previous cases, allowing a cause of action, are difficult to distinguish from the case before us." Those earlier cases, to be sure, were situations in which courts had restrained individual activities aimed at preventing the state from performing its 14th Amendment duties. Here, such immediacy of relationship between the state and the injured person could not be found, but no constitutional distinction could rest upon the mere presence or absence of a non-injuring state representative. The court found in the 14th Amendment a focus on protection of the victim. The court concluded: "Here, we do not erect a new structure for a constitutional law of torts but rather enter a door which Griffin left ajar."

    Are Westberry and Gannon persuasive readings of the implications of Griffin and Guest? Contrast another Court of Appeals decision, a month before Westberry: the Fourth Circuit's decision in Bellamy v. Mason's Stores, Inc., 508 F.2d 504 (1974). That decision refused to find § 1985(3) jurisdiction for a suit by an employee discharged by a private employer because of membership in the Ku Klux Klan: "[W]e think the language of equal protection chosen by the 1871 Congress cannot be interpreted to mean that persons who conspire without involvement of government to deny another person the right of free association are liable under this statute. This is so because the right of association derives from the First Amend-

---

1. The Court endorsed the conclusion in Flack, The Adoption of the Fourteenth Amendment (1908), that "Congress had the constitutional power to enact direct legislation to secure the rights of citizens against violation by individuals as well as by States." See also Frantz, "Congressional Power to Enforce the Fourteenth Amendment Against Private Acts," 73 Yale L.J. 1353 (1964).

ment—itself framed as a prohibition against the federal Government and not against private persons." The court added that any holding that the 14th Amendment "speaks to private persons" would be "an innovation that must come from the Congress or the Supreme Court." The court suggested, however, that Congress has the power to punish private conspiracies to violate 14th Amendment guarantees. One of the judges, concurring in the result, rejected that suggestion: "Congress does not have such authority [to punish purely private conspiracies] under the Fourteenth Amendment."

CIVIL REMEDIES AGAINST ACTIONS "UNDER COLOR" OF LAW

Introduction. 42 U.S.C. § 1983—like its criminal counterpart, 18 U. S.C. § 242—provides remedies against actions "under color" of law, and has given rise to problems similar to those presented by 18 U.S.C. § 242, considered in sec. 2A above.

1. *The scope of § 1983.* a. *"Under color" of law.* MONROE v. PAPE, 365 U.S. 167 (1961), was a damage action against Chicago police officers for unlawful invasion of petitioners' home and for illegal search, seizure and detention. Justice Douglas' majority opinion found a deprivation of a constitutional "right" (the Fourth Amendment guarantee "incorporated" into the 14th) and rejected a contention similar to that made in the Screws case: that police action could not be "under color" of state law if it violated state law. He stated: "We conclude that the meaning given 'under color of' law in the Classic case and in the Screws and Williams cases was the correct one, and we adhere to it." With regard to the intent required to impose civil liability, the Court stated that the "specific intent" requirement for criminal cases in Screws was not applicable here: "Section [1983] should be read against the background of tort liability that makes a man responsible for the natural consequences of his actions." *

b. *"Custom or usage."* 42 U.S.C. § 1983 also contains language referring to "custom, or usage, of any State." That language received its first extensive consideration by the Court in ADICKES v. KRESS & CO., 398 U. S. 144 (1970). Justice Harlan's majority opinion concluded that this phrase "requires state involvement and is not simply a practice that reflects longstanding social habits." "Custom," he insisted, "must have the force of law by virtue of the persistent practices of state officials." Justices Brennan and Douglas dissented. Justice Brennan urged that "custom" means "custom of the people of a State, not custom of state officials"—"a widespread and longstanding practice," not necessarily "backed by the force of the State." His analysis did not require him to reach the question whether the "custom" he described would itself constitute state action under the Fourteenth Amend-

---

* See generally Klitgaard, "The Civil Rights Acts and Mr. Monroe," 49 Calif.L.Rev. 144 (1961), Selected Essays 1938–62 (1963), 949, and Note, "The Proper Scope of the Civil Rights Acts," 66 Harv.L.Rev. 1285 (1953). Note also the *judicially created* civil damages remedy for Fourth Amendment violations by *federal* law enforcement officials (who are not covered by § 1983), in Bivens v. Six Unknown Named Agents, 403 U.S. 388 (1971) (see chap. 8 above).

ment. Justice Douglas, who supported a similar view of the statute, relied on the 13th Amendment for constitutional authority.

2. *Defenses under § 1983.* In a number of decisions before and after Monroe v. Pape, the Court has found a range of official immunities in § 1983 and has elaborated the standards of liability under that Section. For example, Tenney v. Brandhove, 341 U.S. 367 (1951), announced an absolute immunity for state legislators; and Pierson v. Ray, 386 U.S. 547 (1967), implied an analogous immunity for judges. The Pierson case also announced that, despite the broad language of Monroe v. Pape, police officers may assert "the defense of good faith and probable cause" in § 1983 actions. The Court has rejected absolute executive immunity under the provision, however. For recent discussions of the defenses available to executive officials, see Scheuer v. Rhodes, 416 U.S. 232 (1974), and Wood v. Strickland, 420 U.S. —— (1975).[1] In reading a variety of absolute and qualified defenses into § 1983, the Court has typically relied on "common-law tradition" and "public-policy reasons."

C. CONGRESSIONAL POWER TO REACH PRIVATE CONDUCT UNDER THE 13TH AMENDMENT

JONES v. ALFRED H. MAYER CO.

392 U.S. 409, 88 S.Ct. 2186, 20 L.Ed.2d 1189 (1968).

Certiorari to the United States Court of Appeals for the Eighth Circuit.

Mr. Justice STEWART delivered the opinion of the Court.

In this case we are called upon to determine the scope and the constitutionality of an Act of Congress, 42 U.S.C. § 1982, which provides that:

"All citizens of the United States shall have the same right, in every State and Territory, as is enjoyed by white citizens thereof to inherit, purchase, lease, sell, hold, and convey real and personal property."

On September 2, 1965, the petitioners filed a complaint . . . alleging that the respondents had refused to sell them a home in the Paddock

---

1. Scheuer was a suit arising out of the Kent State killings; the Governor of Ohio and National Guard officers were among the defendants. Chief Justice Burger announced that there was no absolute executive immunity, but that a qualified immunity was appropriate, "in varying scope," the "variation being dependent upon the scope of discretion and responsibilities of the officers and all the circumstances as they reasonably appeared at the time of the action on which liability is sought to be based." Chief Justice Burger was with the dissenters, however, in the Wood case, where Justice Powell's dissent insisted that a considerably more demanding standard of liability was being imposed upon school officials.

The 5 to 4 decision in Wood involved an action by high school students expelled for violating school regulations. Justice White's majority opinion stated that school officials were entitled to a "qualified good-faith immunity" under § 1983, but that "a school board member is not immune from liability for damages under § 1983 if he knew or reasonably should have known that the action he took within his sphere of official responsibility would violate the constitutional rights of the student affected, or if he took the action with a malicious intention to cause a deprivation of constitutional rights or other injury to the student." (On the scope of students' First Amendment rights, see also the materials in chaps. 12 and 13 below.)

Woods community of St. Louis County for the sole reason that petitioner Joseph Lee Jones is a Negro. Relying in part upon § 1982, the petitioners sought injunctive and other relief. The District Court sustained the respondents' motion to dismiss the complaint, and the Court of Appeals for the Eighth Circuit affirmed, concluding that § 1982 applies only to state action and does not reach private refusals to sell. [W]e reverse the judgment of the Court of Appeals. We hold that § 1982 bars *all* racial discrimination, private as well as public, in the sale or rental of property, and that the statute, thus construed, is a valid exercise of the power of Congress to enforce the Thirteenth Amendment.[1]

At the outset, it is important to make clear precisely what this case does *not* involve. Whatever else it may be, 42 U.S.C. § 1982 is not a comprehensive open housing law, [unlike] the Fair Housing Title (Title VIII) of the Civil Rights Act of 1968 [see the excerpts following this case]. . . .

This Court last had occasion to consider the scope of 42 U.S.C. § 1982 in 1948, in Hurd v. Hodge, 334 U.S. 24 [the District of Columbia restrictive covenant case decided on the same day as Shelley v. Kraemer, sec. 2 above.] It is true that a dictum in Hurd said that § 1982 was directed only toward "governmental action," [but] neither Hurd nor any other case before or since has presented that precise issue for adjudication in this Court.[2] . . .

On its face, [the statute] appears to prohibit *all* discrimination against Negroes in the sale or rental of property—discrimination by private owners as well as discrimination by public authorities. . . . Stressing what they consider to be the revolutionary implications of so literal a reading of § 1982, respondents argue that Congress cannot possibly have intended any such result. Our examination of the relevant history, however, persuades us that Congress meant exactly what it said.

In its original form, 42 U.S.C. § 1982 was part of § 1 of the Civil Rights Act of 1866. That section was cast in sweeping terms . . . . The crucial language for our purposes was that which guaranteed all citizens "the same right, in every State and Territory in the United States, . . . to inherit, purchase, lease, sell, hold, and convey real and personal property . . . as is enjoyed by white citizens . . . ." To the Congress that passed the Civil Rights Act of 1866, it was clear that the right to do these things might be infringed not only by "State or local law" but also by "custom, or prejudice." Thus, when Congress provided in § 1 of the Civil Rights Act that the right to purchase and lease property was to be enjoyed equally throughout the United States by Negro and white citizens alike, it plainly meant to secure that right against interference from any source whatever, whether governmental or private.

Indeed, if § 1 had been intended to grant nothing more than an immunity from *governmental* interference, then much of § 2 would have made no sense

1. Because we have concluded that the discrimination alleged in the petitioners' complaint violated a federal statute that Congress had the power to enact under the Thirteenth Amendment, we find it unnecessary to decide whether that discrimination also violated the Equal Protection Clause of the Fourteenth Amendment. [Footnote by the Court.]

2. Two of this Court's early opinions contain dicta to the general effect that § 1982 is limited to state action. Virginia v. Rives, 100 U.S. 313, 317–318; Civil Rights Cases, 109 U.S. 3, 16–17. . . . [Footnote by the Court.]

at all.[3] For that section, which provided fines and prison terms for certain individuals who deprived others of rights "secured or protected" by § 1, was carefully drafted to exempt private violations of § 1 from the criminal sanctions it imposed. There would, of course, have been no private violations to exempt if the only "right" granted by § 1 had been a right to be free of discrimination by public officials. Hence the structure of the 1866 Act, as well as its language, points to the conclusion urged by the petitioners in this case— that § 1 was meant to prohibit *all* racially motivated deprivations of the rights enumerated in the statute, although only those deprivations perpetrated "under color of law" were to be criminally punishable under § 2. . . .

That broad language, we are asked to believe, was a mere slip of the legislative pen. We disagree. For the same Congress that wanted to do away with the Black Codes *also* had before it an imposing body of evidence pointing to the mistreatment of Negroes by private individuals and unofficial groups, mistreatment unrelated to any hostile state legislation. [Extensive excerpts from the legislative debates are omitted.] . . .

Nor was the scope of the 1866 Act altered when it was re-enacted in 1870, some two years after the ratification of the Fourteenth Amendment. It is quite true that some members of Congress supported the Fourteenth Amendment "in order to eliminate doubt as to the constitutional validity of the Civil Rights Act as applied to the States." But it certainly does not follow that the adoption of the Fourteenth Amendment or the subsequent readoption of the Civil Rights Act were meant somehow to *limit* its application to state action. The legislative history furnishes not the slightest factual basis for any such speculation, and the conditions prevailing in 1870 make it highly implausible. . . .

The remaining question is whether Congress has power under the Constitution to do what § 1982 purports to do: to prohibit all racial discrimination, private and public, in the sale and rental of property. Our starting point is the Thirteenth Amendment, for it was pursuant to that constitutional provision that Congress originally enacted what is now § 1982. . . .

As its text reveals, the Thirteenth Amendment "is not a mere prohibition of State laws establishing or upholding slavery, but an absolute declaration that slavery or involuntary servitude shall not exist in any part of the United States." [Civil Rights Cases.] It has never been doubted, therefore, "that the power vested in Congress to enforce the article by appropriate legislation" includes the power to enact laws "direct and primary, operating upon the acts of individuals, whether sanctioned by State legislation or not." Id.

Thus, the fact that § 1982 operates upon the unofficial acts of private individuals, whether or not sanctioned by state law, presents no constitutional problem. . . . The constitutional question in this case, therefore, comes to this: Does the authority of Congress to enforce the Thirteenth Amendment "by appropriate legislation" include the power to eliminate all racial barriers

3. Section 2 provided:
"That any person who, *under color of any law, statute, ordinance, regulation, or custom,* shall subject, or cause to be subjected, any inhabitant of any State or Territory to the deprivation of any right secured or protected by this act . . . shall be deemed guilty of a misdemeanor . . . ." (Emphasis added.)

For the evolution of this provision into 18 U.S.C. § 242, see Screws v. United States, 325 U.S. 91, 98–99; United States v. Price, 383 U.S. 787, 804. [Footnote by the Court.]

to the acquisition of real and personal property?   We think the answer to that question is plainly yes.

"By its own unaided force and effect," the Thirteenth Amendment "abolished slavery, and established universal freedom."   [Civil Rights Cases.] Whether or not the Amendment *itself* did any more than that—a question not involved in this case—it is at least clear that the Enabling Clause of that Amendment empowered Congress to do much more.   For that clause clothed "Congress with power to pass *all laws necessary and proper for abolishing all badges and incidents of slavery in the United States.*"   Ibid.   (Emphasis added.)   . . .

. . . Surely Congress has the power under the Thirteenth Amendment rationally to determine what are the badges and the incidents of slavery, and the authority to translate that determination into effective legislation. Nor can we say that the determination Congress has made is an irrational one.   For this Court recognized long ago that, whatever else they may have encompassed, the badges and incidents of slavery—its "burdens and disabilities"—included restraints upon "those fundamental rights which are the essence of civil freedom, namely, the same right   . . .   to inherit, purchase, lease, sell and convey property, as is enjoyed by white citizens."   [Civil Rights Cases.] [4]   Just as the Black Codes, enacted after the Civil War to restrict the free exercise of those rights, were substitutes for the slave system, so the exclusion of Negroes from white communities became a substitute for the Black Codes.   And when racial discrimination herds men into ghettos and makes their ability to buy property turn on the color of their skin, then it too is a relic of slavery.

Negro citizens North and South, who saw in the Thirteenth Amendment a promise of freedom—freedom to "go and come at pleasure" and to "buy and sell when they please"—would be left with "a mere paper guarantee" if Congress were powerless to assure that a dollar in the hands of a Negro will purchase the same thing as a dollar in the hands of a white man.   At the very least, the freedom that Congress is empowered to secure under the Thirteenth Amendment includes the freedom to buy whatever a white man

---

4.   The Court did conclude in the Civil Rights Cases that "the act of   . . . the owner of the inn, the public conveyance or place of amusement, refusing   . . .   accommodation" cannot be "justly regarded as imposing any badge of slavery or servitude upon the applicant."   . . .

Whatever the present validity of the position taken by the majority on that issue—a question rendered largely academic by Title II of the Civil Rights Act of 1964,—we note that the entire Court agreed upon at least one proposition: The Thirteenth Amendment authorizes Congress not only to outlaw all forms of slavery and involuntary servitude but also to eradicate the last vestiges and incidents of a society half slave and half free, by securing to all citizens, of every race and color, "the same right to make and enforce contracts, to sue, be par-

ties, give evidence, and to inherit, purchase, lease, sell and convey property, as is enjoyed by white citizens." In Hodges v. United States, 203 U.S. 1 [1906], a group of white men had terorized several Negroes to prevent them from working in a sawmill.   The terorizers were convicted under 18 U.S.C. § 241 of conspiring to prevent the Negroes from exercising the right to contract for employment, a right secured by 42 U.S.C. § 1981.   Section 1981 provides, in terms that closely parallel those of § 1982 that all persons in the United States "shall have *the same right   . . .   to make and enforce contracts,* to sue, be parties, give evidence, and 'to the full and equal benefit of all laws and proceedings for the security of persons and property as is enjoyed by white citizens   . . . .*"   (Emphasis added.) This Court reversed the conviction.

can buy, the right to live wherever a white man can live. If Congress cannot say that being a free man means at least this much, then the Thirteenth Amendment made a promise the Nation cannot keep. . . .

Reversed.*

Mr. Justice HARLAN, whom Mr. Justice WHITE joins, dissenting. . . .

The decision in this case appears to me to be most ill-considered and ill-advised. . . . I believe that the Court's construction of § 1982 as applying to purely private action is almost surely wrong, and at the least is open to serious doubt. The issue of the constitutionality of § 1982, as construed by the Court, and of liability under the Fourteenth Amendment alone,[1] also present formidable difficulties. Moreover, the political processes of our own era have, since the date of oral argument in this case, given birth to a civil rights statute embodying "fair housing" provisions which would at the end of this year make available to others, though apparently not to the petitioners themselves, the type of relief which the petitioners now seek. It seems to me that this latter factor so diminishes the public importance of this case that by far the wisest course would be for this Court to refrain from decision and to dismiss the writ as improvidently granted. . . .

Like the Court, I begin analysis of § 1982 by examining its language. . . . The Court finds it "plain and unambiguous" [that] this language forbids purely private as well as state-authorized discrimination. With all respect, I do not find it so. For me, there is an inherent ambiguity in the term "right," as used in § 1982. The "right" referred to may either be a right to equal status under the law, in which case the statute operates only against state-sanctioned discrimination, or it may be an "absolute" right enforceable against private individuals. To me, the words of the statute, taken alone, suggest the former interpretation, not the latter.

. . . It seems to me that [the] original wording indicates even more strongly than the present language that § 1 of the Act (as well as § 2, which is explicitly so limited) was intended to apply only to action taken

---

The majority recognized that "one of the disabilities of slavery, one of the indicia of its existence, was a lack of power to make or perform contracts." And there was no doubt that the defendants had deprived their Negro victims, on racial grounds, of the opportunity to dispose of their labor by contract. Yet the majority said that "no mere personal assault or trespass or appropriation operates to reduce the individual to a condition of slavery," and asserted that only conduct which actually enslaves someone can be subjected to punishment under legislation enacted to enforce the Thirteenth Amendment. . . . Mr. Justice Harlan joined by Mr. Justice Day, dissented. . . .
The conclusion of the majority in Hodges rested upon a concept of congressional power under the Thirteenth

Amendment irreconcilable with the position taken by every member of this Court in the Civil Rights Cases and incompatible with the history and purpose of the Amendment itself. Insofar as Hodges is inconsistent with our holding today, it is hereby overruled. [Footnote by the Court.]

* A concurring opinion by Justice Douglas is omitted.

1. Justice Harlan noted, in a footnote at another point, that the 14th Amendment "state action" argument—not reached by the majority in Jones—had emphasized "the respondents' role as a housing developer who exercised continuing authority over a suburban housing complex with about 1,000 inhabitants."

pursuant to state or community authority, in the form of a "law, statute, ordinance, regulation, or custom." And with deference I suggest that the language of § 2, taken alone, no more implies that § 2 "was carefully drafted to exempt private violations of § 1 from the criminal sanctions it imposed," than it does that § 2 was carefully drafted to enforce all of the rights secured by § 1.

The Court rests its opinion chiefly upon the legislative history of the Civil Rights Act of 1866. I shall endeavor to show that those debates do not, as the Court would have it, overwhelmingly support the result reached by the Court, and in fact that a contrary conclusion may equally well be drawn. [An extensive discussion of the legislative history is omitted.] . . .

The foregoing, I think, amply demonstrates that the Court has chosen to resolve this case by according to a loosely worded statute a meaning which is open to the strongest challenge in light of the statute's legislative history. In holding that the Thirteenth Amendment is sufficient constitutional authority for § 1982 as interpreted, the Court also decides a question of great importance. Even contemporary supporters of the aims of the 1866 Civil Rights Act doubted that those goals could constitutionally be achieved under the Thirteenth Amendment, and this Court has twice expressed similar doubts. Thus, it is plain that the course of decision followed by the Court today entails the resolution of important and difficult issues.

The fact that a case is "hard" does not, of course, relieve a judge of his duty to decide it. Since, the Court did vote to hear this case, I normally would consider myself obligated to decide [it]. After mature reflection, however, I have concluded that this is one of those rare instances in which an event which occurs after the hearing of argument so diminishes a case's public significance, when viewed in light of the difficulty of the questions presented, as to justify this Court in dismissing the writ as improvidently granted.

The occurrence to which I refer is the recent enactment of the Civil Rights Act of 1968 [Title VIII, below]. . . . In effect, this Court, by its construction of § 1982, has extended the coverage of federal "fair housing" laws far beyond that which Congress in its wisdom chose to provide in the Civil Rights Act of 1968. The political process now having taken hold again in this very field, I am at a loss to understand why the Court should have deemed it appropriate or, in the circumstances of this case, necessary to proceed with such precipitous and insecure strides. . . .

———

THIRTEENTH AMENDMENT POWERS AND THE 1866 ACT

1. *The scope of congressional power and the Jones case.* a. How far-reaching is the 13th Amendment power recognized in Jones? Is it an adequate constitutional basis for all conceivable civil rights legislation directed at private conduct? Does it in effect make the public accommodations and employment discrimination provisions of the 1964 Civil Rights Act superfluous? Does it do so especially in view of 42 U.S.C. § 1981, also a legacy of the Civil Rights Act of 1866: As noted in sec. 1, that provision guarantees all persons "the same right [to] make and enforce contracts, to sue, be parties, give evidence, and to the full and equal benefit of all laws

and proceedings for the security of persons and property as is enjoyed by white citizens." *

b.   Is there any action against racial discrimination that Congress may not consider to be a remedy against the "badges of servitude"?   May Congress deal with discrimination against groups other than Blacks under the 13th Amendment?   See Note, 69 Colum.L.Rev. 1019 (1969), suggesting that the Jones reading indicates that "slavery" now includes "the second class citizenship imposed on members of disparate minority groups   .   .   .   . A victim's people need not have been enslaved in order to invoke its protection.   He need only be suffering today under conditions that could reasonably be called symptoms of a slave society."

c.   For an extensive criticism of the Jones majority's reading of history, see Fairman, Reconstruction and Reunion: 1864–1888, Part One (6 History of the Supreme Court of the United States) (1971).†   Compare Levinson, Book Review, 26 Stan.L.Rev. 461 (1974), concluding that Fairman clearly demonstrates the "slipshod" nature of the majority's historical analysis but adding that its conclusion may nevertheless be warranted, "for the Civil Rights Act of 1866 *did* manifest, however imperfectly and ambivalently, a vision of a new order of freedom for the black man."   The real issue, Levinson argues, is not whether the text of the law "dictated" the decision, but "whether the decision was *permitted*."   On that issue, the historical background "need not be conclusive regarding its present application."   Similar arguments have been made about modern interpretations of the equal protection clause.   See Bickel, "The Original Understanding and the Segregation Decision," 69 Harv.L.Rev. 1 (1955).   Assuming such open-ended readings are appropriate for constitutional provisions, are they also appropriate for legislative enactments?

2.   *Sullivan v. Little Hunting Park.*   The Court applied the newly discovered 1866 Act—and expanded its broad interpretation—in SULLI-VAN v. LITTLE HUNTING PARK, INC., 396 U.S. 229 (1969).   There, a "nonstock corporation" operated a community park and playground facilities for the benefit of residents in an area of Fairfax County, Virginia.   Subject to the board's approval, a member who rented his house could assign his share to his tenant.   Sullivan leased his house to Freeman and assigned his membership share to him.   The board "refused to approve the assignment, because Freeman was a Negro."   After protesting that decision, Sullivan was expelled.   The Court found that Sullivan and Freeman could sue under § 1982 for damages and injunctive relief.   Justice Douglas' majority opinion reversing a state court's dismissal of the action found the corporation's refusal an interference with the right to "lease" within the terms of the 1866 Act.   He rejected the state court's finding that the Park was a private social club: "There was no plan or purpose of exclusiveness.   It is open to every white person within the geographic area, there being no selective element other than race."

---

* For a reliance on that provision as basis for an employment discrimination action, see Long v. Ford Motor Co., 496 F.2d 500 (6th Cir. 1974).

† See also Casper, "Jones v. Mayer: Clio, Bemused and Confused Muse," 1968 Sup.Ct.Rev. 89; compare Kohl, "The Civil Rights Act of 1866, Its Hour Come Round at Last," 55 Va. L.Rev. 272 (1969).

Justice Harlan's dissent, joined by Chief Justice Burger and Justice White, urged that certiorari be dismissed as improvidently granted because of the "complexities" under the 1866 Act and the existence of the 1968 fair housing law. He noted that the Court had gone beyond the Jones case, above, "(1) by implying a private right to damages for violations of § 1982; (2) by interpreting § 1982 to prohibit a community recreation association from withholding, on the basis of race, approval of an assignment of a membership that was transferred incident to a lease of real property; and (3) by deciding that a white person who is expelled from a recreation association 'for the advocacy of [a Negro's] cause' has 'standing' to maintain an action for relief under § 1982." He insisted that the majority was "even more unwise than it was in Jones, in precipitately breathing still more life into § 1982, which is both vague and open-ended, when Congress has provided this modern statute, containing various detailed remedial provisions."

Justice Harlan's dissent in Sullivan also commented: "And lurking in the background are grave constitutional issues should § 1982 be extended too far into some types of private discrimination." He cited the Civil Rights Cases. What are those "grave constitutional issues"? Which concerns of the Civil Rights Cases are relevant to 13th Amendment legislation? There is no state action limitation under the 13th Amendment. Is there nevertheless a limitation stemming from the privacy and associational interests of the discriminator? Recall the comments in sec. 2 above on balancing the competing interests of private actor and victim. Is that variety of balancing relevant to 13th Amendment interpretation?

Compare with the scope given to § 1982 by the Court's interpretations the fair housing provisions enacted by Congress in 1968. Excerpts from that law follow.

THE FAIR HOUSING PROVISIONS OF THE
1968 CIVIL RIGHTS ACT

Excerpts from the Coverage Provisions of Title VIII—Fair Housing—of the Civil Rights Act of 1968 (Pub.Law 90–284, 82 Stat. 73):

POLICY

Sec. 801. It is the policy of the United States to provide, within constitutional limitations, for fair housing throughout the United States. . . .

EFFECTIVE DATES OF CERTAIN PROHIBITIONS

Sec. 803. (a) Subject to the provisions of subsection (b) and section 807, the prohibitions against discrimination in the sale or rental of housing set forth in section 804 shall apply:

(1) Upon enactment of this title, to [largely, dwellings owned or financed by the federal government].

(2) After December 31, 1968, to all dwellings covered by paragraph (1) and to all other dwellings except as exempted by subsection (b).

(b) Nothing in section 804 (other than subsection (c)) shall apply to—

(1) any single-family house sold or rented by an owner: *Provided*, That such private individual owner does not own more than three such single-family houses at any one time: *Provided further*, That in the case of the sale of any such single-family house by a private individual owner not residing in such house at the time of such sale or who was not the most recent resident of such house prior to such sale, the exemption granted by this subsection shall apply only with respect to one such sale within any twenty-four

month period: *Provided further*, That such bona fide private individual owner does not own any interest in, nor is there owned or reserved on his behalf, under any express or voluntary agreement, title to or any right to all or a portion of the proceeds from the sale or rental of, more than three such single-family houses at any one time: *Provided further*, That after December 31, 1969, the sale or rental of any such single-family house shall be excepted from the application of this title only if such house is sold or rented (A) without the use in any manner of the sales or rental facilities or the sales or rental services or any real estate broker, agent, or salesman, or of such facilities or services of any person in the business of selling or renting dwellings, or of any employee or agent of any such broker, agent, salesman, or person and (B) without the publication, posting or mailing, after notice, of any advertisement or written notice in violation of section 804(c) of this title; but nothing in this proviso shall prohibit the use of attorneys, escrow agents, abstractors, title companies, and other such professional assistance as necessary to perfect or transfer the title, or

(2) rooms or units in dwellings containing living quarters occupied or intended to be occupied by no more than four families living independently of each other, if the owner actually maintains and occupies one of such living quarters as his residence. . . .

DISCRIMINATION IN THE SALE OR RENTAL OF HOUSING

Sec. 804. As made applicable by section 803 and except as exempted by sections 803(b) and 807, it shall be unlawful—

(a) To refuse to sell or rent after the making of a bona fide offer, or to refuse to negotiate for the sale or rental of, or otherwise make unavailable or deny, a dwelling to any person because of race, color, religion, or national origin.

(b) To discriminate against any person in the terms, conditions, or privileges of sale or rental of a dwelling, or in the provision of services or facilities in connection therewith, because of race, color, religion, or national origin.

(c) To make, print or publish, or cause to be made, printed, or published any notice, statement, or advertisement, with respect to the sale or rental of a dwelling that indicates any preference, limitation, or discrimination based on race, color, religion, or national origin, or an intention to make any such preference, limitation, or discrimination.

(d) To represent to any person because of race, color, religion, or national origin that any dwelling is not available for inspection, sale, or rental when such dwelling is in fact so available.

(e) For profit, to induce or attempt to induce any person to sell or rent any dwelling by representations regarding the entry or prospective entry into the neighborhood of a person or persons of a particular race, color, religion, or national origin. . . .

[Secs. 805 and 806 cover discrimination in financing and in brokerage services.]

EXEMPTION

Sec. 807. Nothing in this title shall prohibit a religious organization, association, or society, or any nonprofit institution or organization operated, supervised or controlled by or in conjunction with a religious organization, association or society, from limiting the sale, rental or occupancy of dwellings which it owns or operates for other than a commercial purpose to persons of the same religion, or from giving preference to such persons, unless membership in such religion is restricted on account of race, color, or national origin. Nor shall anything in this title prohibit a private club not in fact open to the public, which as an incident to its primary purpose or purposes provides lodgings which it owns or operates for other than a commercial purpose, from limiting the rental or occupancy of such lodgings to its members or from giving preference to its members. . . .

SECTION 4. CONGRESSIONAL POWER TO MODIFY THE SUBSTANTIVE CONTENT OF CONSTITUTIONAL RIGHTS

Introduction. Most of the legislation enacted by Congress under its powers to "enforce" the post-Civil War Amendments has been clearly remedial and procedural: in the statutes considered in the preceding sections, Congress has ordinarily undertaken simply to provide enforcement mechanisms to implement judicially declared rights. For example, the "under color of law" criminal and civil provisions, 18 U.S.C. § 242 and 42 U.S.C. § 1983, afforded remedies for the deprivation of rights as secured by the Constitution and interpreted by the Court. The Guest case in the preceding section raised questions of a potentially broader congressional authority: the authority to extend the reach of the 14th and 15th Amendments to cover private behavior not within the state action limit delineated by the Court. But even in that context, Congress does not directly purport to modify the *content* of the right it protects: typically, the right protected continues to be the right as established in the Constitution and interpreted by the Court. The materials in this section focus on the question of congressional authority to go beyond that: not merely to provide remedies for practices independently held unconstitutional under court-announced doctrine, but also to determine on its own that some practices are unconstitutional even though a court has not said so.

That novel variety of congressional action has arisen largely in the voting rights context; it began with the Voting Rights Act of 1965. Thus, in South Carolina v. Katzenbach, 383 U.S. 301 (1966), the Court sustained a provision, applicable largely to the South, suspending literacy tests—even though a 1959 decision, Lassiter v. Northampton County Board of Elections, 360 U.S. 45 (1959), had unanimously rejected an on-the-face equal protection attack on literacy tests. And Katzenbach v. Morgan, 384 U.S. 641 (1966), upheld another provision of the 1965 Act, giving the vote to certain Puerto Ricans educated in Spanish-language schools—even though, in a companion case, Cardona v. Power, 384 U.S. 672 (1966), the Court avoided deciding whether the equal protection clause by itself barred the application of New York's English literacy requirement to a challenger literate in Spanish but arguably not covered by the Act. In the South Carolina v. Katzenbach situation, Congress acted against the background of a Court-endorsed principle that racially discriminatory literacy tests are unconstitutional—even though the Court had not been willing to find that all literacy tests were racially discriminatory. The basic holding in South Carolina v. Katzenbach was unanimous: the Court was able to approve the suspension of literacy tests as "remedial" legislation. Such a rationale was more difficult to support in Katzenbach v. Morgan. In sustaining the ban on English literacy tests there, the Court was divided, and controversial language in the majority opinion suggested great judicial deference not only to congressional creation of remedies but also to congressional refashioning of the substantive content of constitutional rights. Four years later, however, the Katzenbach v. Morgan rationale did not prove adequate to sustain a congressional lowering of the minimum voting age in state elections to eighteen: the congressional effort to do so, in the Voting Rights Act Amendments of 1970, was rejected

by a 5 to 4 vote in Oregon v. Mitchell, 400 U.S. 112 (1970). But another provision of the 1970 Act, applying the suspension of literacy tests on a nationwide basis, was sustained unanimously in Oregon v. Mitchell: that was not seen as a significant extension of South Carolina v. Katzenbach.

It is that series of cases that provides the focus of this section. How far-reaching is the congressional "enforcement" power? To what extent does it go beyond the providing of remedies for judicially-declared rights? Can the provisions sustained in South Carolina v. Katzenbach be justified as merely "remedial," as earlier enactments undoubtedly were? Are cases like Morgan and Oregon v. Mitchell truly distinguishable as "substantive" congressional actions? When may congressional action move beyond the merely remedial to the reinterpretation, expansion, and perhaps dilution, of constitutional rights? Does extreme judicial deference to congressional "reinterpretations" run counter to the views of judicial autonomy in Marbury v. Madison and Cooper v. Aaron, chap. 1 above? In what contexts outside the voting rights area may Congress resort to the broad power of the Morgan case? Does Oregon v. Mitchell curtail the scope of the power suggested by Morgan?

Before turning to the most controversial modern cases on the congressional power to modify the content of constitutional rights, this section examines the background of court and congressional action in the voting rights field culminating in the statutory provisions sustained in South Carolina v. Katzenbach.

PROTECTION OF VOTING RIGHTS: THE BACKGROUND AND SOUTH CAROLINA v. KATZENBACH

1. *Chief Justice Warren's summary of the background.* [Prior to the Voting Rights Act of 1965, congressional legislation directed against racial discrimination in voting was quite clearly procedural and remedial. Congress typically provided enforcement mechanisms; but the rights guaranteed were stated in very general terms—essentially in the terms of the Constitution, and especially the 15th Amendment.* Detailed delineation of the content of the rights was accordingly left to the courts; and implementation was left to litigation. It was frustration with that case-by-case approach that led to the enactment of the 1965 Act. Chief Justice Warren's opinion in South Carolina v. Katzenbach, 383 U.S. 301 (1966), contained a summary of the "historical experience" which led Congress to two basic conclusions, summarized by the Chief Justice: "First: Congress felt itself confronted by an insidious and pervasive evil which had been perpetuated in certain parts of our country through unremitting and ingenious defiance of the Constitution. Second: Congress concluded that the unsuccessful remedies which it had

---

* See, e. g., the only remnant of the post-Civil War voting laws that remained on the books as of 1957. 42 U.S.C. § 1971(a), derived from the 1870 Act, provided:

"All citizens of the United States who are otherwise qualified to vote at any election by the people in any State . . . . shall be entitled and allowed to vote at all such elections, without distinction of race, color, or previous condition of servitude; any constitution, law, custom, usage, or regulation of any State . . . ., or by or under its authority, to the contrary notwithstanding."

prescribed in the past would have to be replaced by sterner and more elaborate measures in order to satisfy the clear commands of the Fifteenth Amendment." Chief Justice Warren's summary of the historical background follows:]

The Fifteenth Amendment to the Constitution was ratified in 1870. Promptly thereafter Congress passed the Enforcement Act of 1870, which made it a crime for public officers and private persons to obstruct exercise of the right to vote. The statute was amended in the following year to provide for detailed federal supervision of the electoral process, from registration to the certification of returns. As the years passed and fervor for racial equality waned, enforcement of the laws became spotty and ineffective, and most of their provisions were repealed in 1894. The remnants have had little significance in the recently renewed battle against voting discrimination.

Meanwhile, beginning in 1890, the States of Alabama, Georgia, Louisiana, Mississippi, North Carolina, South Carolina, and Virginia enacted tests still in use which were specifically designed to prevent Negroes from voting. Typically, they made the ability to read and write a registration qualification and also required completion of a registration form. These laws were based on the fact that as of 1890 in each of the named States, more than two-thirds of the adult Negroes were illiterate while less than one-quarter of the adult whites were unable to read or write. At the same time, alternate tests were prescribed in all of the named States to assure that white illiterates would not be deprived of the franchise. These included grandfather clauses, property qualifications, "good character" tests, and the requirement that registrants "understand" or "interpret" certain matter.

The course of subsequent Fifteenth Amendment litigation in this Court demonstrates the variety and persistence of these and similar institutions designed to deprive Negroes of the right to vote. Grandfather clauses were invalidated in Guinn v. United States, 238 U.S. 347, and Myers v. Anderson, 238 U.S. 368. Procedural hurdles were struck down in Lane v. Wilson, 307 U.S. 268. The white primary was outlawed in Smith v. Allwright, 321 U.S. 649, and Terry v. Adams, 345 U.S. 461. Improper challenges were nullified in United States v. Thomas, 362 U.S. 58. Racial gerrymandering was forbidden by Gomillion v. Lightfoot, 364 U.S. 339. Finally, discriminatory application of voting tests was condemned in Schnell v. Davis, 336 U.S. 933; Alabama v. United States, 371 U.S. 37; and Louisiana v. United States, 380 U.S. 145.

According to the evidence in recent Justice Department voting suits, the latter stratagem is now the principal method used to bar Negroes from the polls. Discriminatory administration of voting qualifications has been found in all eight Alabama cases, in all nine Louisiana cases, and in all nine Mississippi cases which have gone to final judgment. Moreover, in almost all of these cases, the courts have held that the discrimination was pursuant to a widespread "pattern or practice." White applicants for registration have often been excused altogether from the literacy and understanding tests or have been given easy versions, have received extensive help from voting officials, and have been registered despite serious errors in their answers. Negroes, on the other hand, have typically been required to pass difficult versions of all the tests, without any outside assistance and without the slight-

est error. The good-morals requirement is so vague and subjective that it has constituted an open invitation to abuse at the hands of voting officials. Negroes obliged to obtain vouchers from registered voters have found it virtually impossible to comply in areas where almost no Negroes are on the rolls.

In recent years, Congress has repeatedly tried to cope with the problem by facilitating case-by-case litigation against voting discrimination. The Civil Rights Act of 1957 authorized the Attorney General to seek injunctions against public and private interference with the right to vote on racial grounds. Perfecting amendments in the Civil Rights Act of 1960 permitted the joinder of States as parties defendant, gave the Attorney General access to local voting records, and authorized courts to register voters in areas of systematic discrimination. Title I of the Civil Rights Act of 1964 expedited the hearing of voting cases before three-judge courts and outlawed some of the tactics used to disqualify Negroes from voting in federal elections. . . .

The previous legislation has proved ineffective for a number of reasons. Voting suits are unusually onerous to prepare, sometimes requiring as many as 6,000 man-hours spent combing through registration records in preparation for trial. Litigation has been exceedingly slow, in part because of the ample opportunities for delay afforded voting officials and others involved in the proceedings. Even when favorable decisions have finally been obtained, some of the States affected have merely switched to discriminatory devices not covered by the federal decrees or have enacted difficult new tests designed to prolong the existing disparity between white and Negro registration. Alternatively, certain local officials have defied and evaded court orders or have simply closed their registration offices to freeze the voting rolls. The provision of the 1960 law authorizing registration by federal officers has had little impact on local maladministration because of its procedural complexities.

2. *The Lassiter case.* It was against the background of that history that Congress enacted the Voting Rights Act of 1965 "to rid the country of racial discrimination in voting." The most controversial provision of that "complex scheme of stringent remedies aimed at areas where voting discrimination has been most flagrant" was one suspending literacy tests in covered localities without a prior judicial finding of discriminatory practices. In that sense, then, Congress was moving beyond where the courts had gone on their own. As noted, the Supreme Court had refused six years earlier to strike down literacy tests on their face. In LASSITER v. NORTH-AMPTON COUNTY BOARD OF ELECTIONS, 360 U.S. 45 (1959), Justice Douglas, for a unanimous Court, rejected a Black citizen's attack on the North Carolina literacy test. He emphasized that the states had a wide discretion in setting voting qualifications: "Residence requirements, age, previous criminal record [are] obvious examples indicating factors which a State may take into consideration in determining the qualifications of voters. The ability to read and write likewise has some relation to standards designed to promote intelligent use of the ballot. Literacy and illiteracy are neutral on race, creed, color, and sex. [I]n our society where newspapers, periodicals, books, and other printed matter canvass and debate campaign issues, a

State might conclude that only those who are literate should exercise the franchise."

Justice Douglas added: "Of course a literacy test, fair on its face, may be employed to perpetuate that discrimination which the Fifteenth Amendment was designed to uproot. No such influence is charged here. On the other hand, a literacy test may be unconstitutional on its face. In Davis v. Schnell, 81 F.Supp. 872, aff'd 336 U.S. 933, the test was the citizen's ability to 'understand and explain' an Article of the federal Constitution. The legislative setting of that provision and the great discretion it vested in the registrar made clear that a literacy requirement was merely a device to make racial discrimination easy. We cannot make the same inference here. [The North Carolina requirement—requiring an ability "to read and write any section of the Constitution of North Carolina in the English language"—] seems to us to be one fair way of determining whether a person is literate, not a calculated scheme to lay springes for the citizen. Certainly we cannot condemn it on its face as a device unrelated to the desire of North Carolina to raise the standards for people of all races who cast the ballot." * But the Lassiter decision proved no obstacle to Congress' broad-gauged move against literacy tests in 1965.

3.   *South Carolina v. Katzenbach.*   The Court sustained the most controversial provisions of the Voting Rights Act of 1965, directed at racial discrimination largely in the South, as a proper exercise of congressional power under § 2 of the 15th Amendment.   SOUTH CAROLINA v. KATZENBACH, 383 U.S. 301 (1966).   In the general passages of his opinion examining the scope of the congressional power, Chief Justice Warren rejected South Carolina's claim that the Act's provisions "exceed the powers of Congress and encroach on an area reserved to the States by the Constitution" by delineating the "groundrules" for resolving the "basic question": "Has Congress exercised its powers under the Fifteenth Amendment in an appropriate manner with relation to the States?"   The Chief Justice emphasized: "The language and purpose of the Fifteenth Amendment, the prior decisions construing its several provisions, and the general doctrines of constitutional interpretation, all point to one fundamental principle.   As against the reserved powers of the States, Congress may use any rational means to effectuate the constitutional prohibition of racial discrimination in voting. . . .   The basic test to be applied in a case involving § 2 of the Fifteenth Amendment is the same as in all cases concerning the express powers of Congress with relation to the reserved powers of the States.   Chief Justice Marshall laid down the classic formulation, 50 years before the Fifteenth Amendment was ratified [quoting the "Let the end be legitimate . . . ." statement from McCulloch v. Maryland].   The Court has subsequently echoed his language in describing each of the Civil War Amendments: 'Whatever legislation is appropriate, that is, adapted to carry out the objects the amendments have in view, whatever tends to enforce submission to the prohibitions they contain, and to secure to all persons the enjoyment of perfect equality of civil rights and the equal protection of the laws against

---

* On the Court's later "strict scrutiny"
of state restrictions on voting, recall
chap. 10, sec. 4A.

State denial or invasion, if not prohibited, is brought within the domain of congressional power.' [Ex parte Virginia.]" Those premises led the Chief Justice to conclude:

"We therefore reject South Carolina's argument that Congress may appropriately do no more than to forbid violations of the Fifteenth Amendment in general terms—that the task of fashioning specific remedies or of applying them to particular localities must necessarily be left entirely to the courts. Congress is not circumscribed by any such artificial rules under § 2 of the Fifteenth Amendment. In the oft-repeated words of Chief Justice Marshall, referring to another specific legislative authorization in the Constitution, 'This power, like all others vested in Congress, is complete in itself, may be exercised to its utmost extent, and acknowledges no limitations, other than are prescribed in the constitution.' [Gibbons v. Ogden.]"

That broad discretion validated the "inventive" use of congressional powers here. Prescribing remedies for voting discrimination "which go into effect without any need for prior adjudication" was "clearly a legitimate response to the problem, for which there is ample precedent under other constitutional provisions." (Chief Justice Warren cited Katzenbach v. McClung and United States v. Darby, the commerce clause cases in chap. 3 above.) Congress "had found that case-by-case litigation was inadequate to combat widespread and persistent discrimination in voting"; accordingly, it "might well decide to shift the advantage of time and inertia from the perpetrators of the evil to its victims." And the "specific remedies" in the Act were "appropriate means of combatting the evil."

Turning to those specific remedies, the Court focused on the coverage formula for determining the localities in which literacy tests and similar voting qualifications were to be suspended for a period of five years. Under that formula, the Act was applicable to any state or political subdivision "for which two findings have been made: (1) the Attorney General has determined that on November 1, 1964, it maintained a 'test or device' [1] and (2) the Director of the Census has determined that less than 50 percent of its voting-age residents were registered on November 1, 1964, or voted in the presidential election of November, 1964." These findings were not reviewable. Statutory coverage could be terminated if the covered area obtained a declaratory judgment from the District Court of the District of Columbia, "determining that tests and devices have not been used during the preceding five years to abridge the franchise on racial grounds." [2]

Pursuant to administrative determinations, a number of areas were promptly brought under the coverage of the Act.[3] The Chief Justice found

1. Under the Act, a "test or device" was any requirement that a registrant or voter must "(1) demonstrate the ability to read, write, understand, or interpret any matter, (2) demonstrate any educational achievement of his knowledge of any particular subject, (3) possess good moral character, or (4) prove his qualifications by the voucher of registered voters or members of any other class."

2. However, no locality could obtain such a declaratory judgment if a federal court had found discrimination through "tests or devices" anywhere in the state during that period.

3. The areas brought under the Act by the time this case reached the Supreme Court were South Carolina, Alabama, Alaska, Georgia, Louisiana, Mississippi, Virginia, 26 counties in North Carolina, and three counties in Arizona, one county in Hawaii, and one county in Idaho.

that the areas covered by the Act "were an appropriate target for the new remedies." He noted that the law "intentionally confines these remedies to a small number of States and political subdivisions which in most instances were familiar to Congress by name." Congress had properly chosen "to limit its attention to the geographic areas where immediate action seemed necessary." The Court was not persuaded by South Carolina's argument "that the coverage formula is awkwardly designed in a number of respects and that it disregards various local conditions which have nothing to do with racial discrimination." The Chief Justice replied: "Congress began work with reliable evidence of actual voting discrimination in a great majority of the States and political subdivisions affected by the new remedies of the Act. The formula eventually evolved to describe these areas was relevant to the problem of voting discrimination, and Congress was therefore entitled to infer a significant danger of the evil in the few remaining States and political subdivisions covered" by the Act. Thus, in three of the states covered—Alabama, Louisiana and Mississippi—federal courts had "repeatedly found substantial voting discrimination." In Georgia and South Carolina and large portions of North Carolina, "there was more fragmentary evidence of recent voting discrimination mainly adduced by the Justice Department and the Civil Rights Commission." The Court noted: "All of these areas were appropriately subjected to the new remedies. In identifying past evils, Congress obviously may avail itself of information from any probative source."

All of those areas for which there was evidence of actual voting discrimination, Chief Justice Warren noted, shared the "two characteristics incorporated by Congress into the coverage formula." He elaborated: "Tests and devices are relevant to voting discrimination because of their long history as a tool for perpetrating the evil; a low voting rate is pertinent for the obvious reason that widespread disenfranchisement must inevitably affect the number of actual voters. Accordingly, the coverage formula is rational in both practice and theory. It was therefore permissible to impose the new remedies on the few remaining States and political subdivisions covered by the formula, at least in the absence of proof that they have been free of substantial voting discrimination in recent years." And it was "irrelevant that the coverage formula excludes certain localities which do not employ voting tests and devices but for which there is evidence of voting discrimination by other means": "Legislation need not deal with all phases of a problem in the same way, so long as the distinctions drawn have some basis in practical experience." Moreover, the existence of the termination procedure was an adequate safeguard against overbreadth of the Act. And South Carolina's argument "that these termination procedures are a nullity because they impose an impossible burden of proof" were not persuasive.

The rejection of the constitutional attack on literacy tests in the Lassiter case (note 2 above) did not bar these legislative remedies. Lassiter itself had recognized that literacy tests could be used as discriminatory devices. And the record here showed "that in most of the States covered by the Act, including South Carolina, various tests and devices have been instituted with the purpose of disenfranchising Negroes, have been framed in such a way as to facilitate this aim, and have been administered in a discriminatory fashion for many years. Under these circumstances, the Fifteenth Amendment has clearly been violated."

In areas covered, the Act suspended literacy tests and similar devices for five years from the last occurrence of substantial voting discrimination, and suspended all new voting regulations pending scrutiny by federal authorities—the Attorney General or a three-judge court in the District of Columbia —to determine whether their use would violate the Fifteenth Amendment. These were "legitimate" responses to the problem, since continuance of the tests "would freeze the effect of past discrimination in favor of unqualified white registrants" and since Congress knew that some of the covered states "had resorted to the extraordinary strategem of contriving new rules of various kinds for the sole purpose of perpetuating voting discrimination in the face of adverse federal court decrees." [4]

Other provisions of the Act authorized the appointment of federal examiners to list qualified applicants as "eligible voters." The examiners were to be appointed by the Civil Service Commission whenever the Attorney General certified either that he had received written complaints from at least twenty residents alleging that they had been disenfranchised on racial grounds or that the appointment of examiners was otherwise necessary to effectuate the guarantees of the 15th Amendment. The examiners were authorized to place on a list of "eligible voters" any person meeting the voting requirements of state law. The listing procedures could be terminated either on notice by the Attorney General to the Civil Service Commission that there was no longer reasonable cause to fear racial discrimination in voting or if the area had obtained a declaratory judgment in the District of Columbia determining the facts justifying termination and the Director of the Census had determined "that more than fifty percent of the non-white residents of voting age are registered to vote." This system, too, was sustained as "an

---

4. For an attempt by a county to reinstate a literacy test suspended pursuant to the Act, see Gaston County v. United States, 395 U.S. 285 (1969). Though the Court did not question the county's claim that it had administered its tests in a fair and impartial manner, it rejected the county's reinstatement effort in view of past unequal educational opportunities. Justice Harlan's opinion noted "the sad truth that throughout the years, Gaston County systematically deprived its Black citizens of the educational opportunities it granted to its white citizens. 'Impartial' administration of the literacy test today would serve only to perpetuate these inequities in a different form." The Court noted, too, that "it would seem a matter of no legal significance that [the Black voters] may have been educated in other counties or states also maintaining segregated and unequal school systems." See Fiss, "Gaston County v. United States: Fruition of the Freezing Principle," 1969 Sup.Ct. Rev. 379.

As to changes in state election laws subject to the federal approval requirement of the Act, see Allen v. State Board of Elections, 393 U.S. 544 (1969), giving a broad reading to the types of changes subject to the Act. The Allen case concluded that "any State enactment which altered the election law of a covered State in even a minor way" was subject to federal approval—including "State rules relating to the qualification of candidates" and "State decisions as to which offices shall be elective." Justice Harlan's dissent urged that the Act should be read to require federal approval "only of those state laws that change either voting qualifications or the manner in which elections are conducted." See also Georgia v. United States, 411 U.S. 526 (1973), holding that the federal approval provisions were applicable to state reapportionment plans as well. But note the indication that Chief Justice Burger and Justices Blackmun and Rehnquist are prepared to reexamine the Allen interpretation on "an appropriate occasion." See the concurrence in Holt v. Richmond, 406 U.S. 903 (1972).

appropriate response to the problem, closely related to remedies authorized in prior cases." In short, all of the remedies considered by the Court were found to be "valid means for carrying out the commands of the Fifteenth Amendment." [5]

A separate opinion by Justice Black agreed with most of the Chief Justice's opinion—for example, as to the constitutionality of the provisions "dealing with the suspension of state voting tests that have been used as notorious means to deny and abridge voting rights on racial grounds." But Justice Black dissented with regard to the provision prohibiting an area from changing its voting rules without prior federal approval. That remedy, he insisted, utilized means "that conflict with the most basic principles of the Constitution": requiring states "to beg federal authorities to approve their policies" before changing their voting laws "so distorts our constitutional structure of government as to render any distinction drawn in the Constitution between state and federal power almost meaningless." Under the Constitution, he insisted, "States have power to pass laws and amend their constitutions without first sending their officials hundreds of miles away to beg federal authorities to approve them." Moreover, the federal approval requirement conflicted with the "Republican Form of Government" guarantee. It was a system which created the impression that states were treated as "little more than conquered provinces."

4. *Some questions about the "remedial" provisions in the 1965 and 1970 Acts.* Can the exercise of congressional power sustained in the South Carolina case be justified as "remedial," or did Congress in fact change the substantive content of rights? Do the "enforcement" provisions of the 1965 Voting Rights Act sustained in South Carolina v. Katzenbach differ substantially from those in earlier civil rights laws? Was Congress acting "remedially" because it acted on the basis of the Court-endorsed rule that discriminatory "tests and devices" are unconstitutional? Even though the Court in Lassiter had not found literacy tests unconstitutional per se? Recall Chief Justice Warren's statement in the South Carolina case: "Under these circumstances, the Fifteenth Amendment has clearly been violated." Can the South Carolina decision be viewed as an implicit overruling of Lassiter in view of the new information gathered by Congress? Or was it an endorsement of congressional action independent of the Court's view as to the constitutionality of literacy tests? Is the Court's analogy to congressional discretion in the exercise of Art. I powers under McCulloch v. Maryland apt?

What light is thrown on the South Carolina v. Katzenbach rationale by the sustaining of the literacy test provisions of the Voting Rights Act Amendments of 1970? In the 1970 Act, the provisions of the 1965 Act were extended for five years—and expanded. As to literacy tests, Congress suspended the use of literacy tests on a nationwide basis, not just in the areas covered by the 1965 Act. Constitutionality of that provision was one of the issues considered in Oregon v. Mitchell, 400 U.S. 112 (1970), below.

5. Several other provisions of the Act were found not properly before the Court in South Carolina v. Katzenbach: e. g., the provision authorizing the appointment of federal poll watchers in places to which federal examiners have already been assigned, and a provision providing for balloting by persons denied access to the polls in areas where federal examiners had been appointed.

Although the Court divided on all other provisions of the 1970 Act—and held the 18-year-old vote provision for state elections unconstitutional—it was unanimous in upholding the nationwide literacy test suspension. Note the rationales in the several opinions in Oregon v. Mitchell for justifying that provision. Do they substantially extend South Carolina v. Katzenbach? Note also the distinction of South Carolina v. Katzenbach in the dissent in Katzenbach v. Morgan, which follows. Justice Harlan emphasized in Morgan that the South Carolina case involved merely "remedial" provisions, while the section challenged in Morgan was "significantly different": it was not "appropriate remedial legislation to cure an established violation of a constitutional command"; rather, the Morgan legislation sought to determine "whether there has in fact been an infringement of that constitutional command, that is, whether a particular practice" violated the equal protection clause. Is that persuasive? Was there "an established violation of a constitutional command" in the South Carolina case? Is the congressional power sustained in the Morgan case substantially more far-reaching than that in the South Carolina case? Did the South Carolina case involve mere implementation of constitutional rights, while the Morgan case involved virtually autonomous congressional reinterpretation of constitutional rights? †

KATZENBACH v. MORGAN

384 U.S. 641, 86 S.Ct. 1717, 16 L.Ed.2d 828 (1966).

Appeal from the United States District Court for the District of Columbia.*

Mr. Justice BRENNAN delivered the opinion of the Court.

These cases concern the constitutionality of § 4(e) of the Voting Rights Act of 1965. That law, in the respects pertinent in these cases, provides that no person who has successfully completed the sixth primary grade in a public school in, or a private school accredited by, the Commonwealth of Puerto Rico in which the language of instruction was other than English shall be denied the right to vote in any election because of his inability to read or write English. Appellees, registered voters in New York City, brought this suit to challenge the constitutionality of § 4(e) insofar as it pro tanto prohibits the enforcement of the election laws of New York requiring an ability to read

---

† Consider also the adequacy of the principles of the South Carolina, Morgan, and Oregon cases to sustain the proposals pending before Congress in the spring of 1975 to extend and broaden the Voting Rights Act. Among the proposals approved by the House Judiciary Committee by May 1975 were the following: extending the Act for 10 years, to 1985; making permanent the nationwide ban on literacy tests; and broadening the provisions to cover many Mexican-Americans and other minorities. For example, the proposal would make applicable to new areas the special restrictions imposed primarily on several southern states by the 1965 Act. The Committee bill would broaden the coverage formula to include areas whose populations are at least 5% non-English speaking and where voter registration had been less than 50% among minorities. It would require bilingual election materials for certain native Alaskans, Asian-Americans, Indians as well as Spanish-speaking Americans. Among the major new areas to be covered would be Texas and Alaska.

* Together with New York City Board of Elections v. Morgan, on appeal from the same court.

and write English as a condition of voting. Under these laws many of the several hundred thousand New York City residents who have migrated there from the Commonwealth of Puerto Rico had previously been denied the right to vote, and appellees attack § 4(e) insofar as it would enable many of these citizens to vote. [A three-judge court] held that in enacting § 4(e) Congress exceeded the powers granted to it by the Constitution and therefore usurped powers reserved to the States by the Tenth Amendment. . . . We reverse. We hold that, in the application challenged in these cases, § 4(e) is a proper exercise of the powers granted to Congress by § 5 of the Fourteenth Amendment and that by force of the Supremacy Clause, Article VI, the New York English literacy requirement cannot be enforced to the extent that it is inconsistent with § 4(e).

Under the distribution of powers effected by the Constitution, the States establish qualifications for voting for state officers, and the qualifications established by the States for voting for members of the most numerous branch of the state legislature also determine who may vote for United States Representatives and Senators, Art. I, § 2; Seventeenth Amendment. But, of course, the States have no power to grant or withhold the franchise on conditions that are forbidden by the Fourteenth Amendment . . . . .

The Attorney General of the State of New York argues that an exercise of congressional power under § 5 of the Fourteenth Amendment that prohibits the enforcement of a state law can only be sustained if the judicial branch determines that the state law is prohibited by the provisions of the Amendment that Congress sought to enforce. More specifically, he urges that § 4(e) cannot be sustained as appropriate legislation to enforce the Equal Protection Clause unless the judiciary decides—even with the guidance of a congressional judgment—that the application of the English literacy requirement prohibited by § 4(e) is forbidden by the Equal Protection Clause itself. We disagree. Neither the language nor history of § 5 supports such a construction. As was said with regard to § 5 in Ex parte Virginia, 100 U.S. 339, 345, "It is the power of Congress which has been enlarged. Congress is authorized to *enforce* the prohibitions by appropriate legislation. Some legislation is contemplated to make the amendments fully effective." A construction of § 5 that would require a judicial determination that the enforcement of the state law precluded by Congress violated the Amendment, as a condition of sustaining the congressional enactment, would depreciate both congressional resourcefulness and congressional responsibility for implementing the Amendment. It would confine the legislative power in this context to the insignificant role of abrogating only those state laws that the judicial branch was prepared to adjudge unconstitutional, or of merely informing the judgment of the judiciary by particularizing the "majestic generalities" of § 1 of the Amendment.

Thus our task in this case is not to determine whether the New York English literacy requirement as applied to deny the right to vote to a person who successfully completed the sixth grade in a Puerto Rican school violates the Equal Protection Clause. Accordingly, our decision in Lassiter v. Northampton Election Bd., sustaining the North Carolina English literacy requirement as not in all circumstances prohibited by the first sections of the Fourteenth and Fifteenth Amendments, is inapposite. Lassiter did not present the question before us here: Without regard to whether the judiciary would

find that the Equal Protection Clause itself nullifies New York's English literacy requirement as so applied, could Congress prohibit the enforcement of the state law by legislating under § 5 of the Fourteenth Amendment? In answering this question, our task is limited to determining whether such legislation is, as required by § 5, appropriate legislation to enforce the Equal Protection Clause.

By including § 5 the draftsmen sought to grant to Congress, by a specific provision applicable to the Fourteenth Amendment, the same broad powers expressed in the Necessary and Proper Clause, Art. I, § 8, cl. 18. The classic formulation of the reach of those powers was established by Chief Justice Marshall in McCulloch v. Maryland . . .. Ex parte Virginia, decided 12 years after the adoption of the Fourteenth Amendment, held that congressional power under § 5 had this same broad scope . . . . Correctly viewed, § 5 is a positive grant of legislative power authorizing Congress to exercise its discretion in determining whether and what legislation is needed to secure the guarantees of the Fourteenth Amendment.

We therefore proceed to the consideration whether § 4(e) is "appropriate legislation" to enforce the Equal Protection Clause, that is, under the Mc-Culloch v. Maryland standard, whether § 4(e) may be regarded as an enactment to enforce the Equal Protection Clause, whether it is "plainly adapted to that end" and whether it is not prohibited by but is consistent with "the letter and spirit of the Constitution." [1]

There can be no doubt that § 4(e) may be regarded as an enactment to enforce the Equal Protection Clause. Congress explicitly declared that it enacted § 4(e) "to secure the rights under the fourteenth amendment of persons educated in American-flag schools in which the predominant classroom language was other than English." The persons referred to include those who have migrated from the Commonwealth of Puerto Rico to New York and who have been denied the right to vote because of their inability to read and write English, and the Fourteenth Amendment rights referred to include those emanating from the Equal Protection Clause. More specifically, § 4(e) may be viewed as a measure to secure for the Puerto Rican community residing in New York nondiscriminatory treatment by government—both in the imposition of voting qualifications and the provision or administration of governmental services, such as public schools, public housing and law enforcement.

Section 4(e) may be readily seen as "plainly adapted" to furthering these aims of the Equal Protection Clause. The practical effect of § 4(e) is to prohibit New York from denying the right to vote to large segments of its Puerto Rican community. Congress has thus prohibited the State from denying to that community the right that is "preservative of all rights."

1. Contrary to the suggestion of the dissent, § 5 does not grant Congress power to exercise discretion in the other direction and to enact "statutes so as in effect to dilute equal protection and due process decisions of this Court." We emphasize that Congress' power under § 5 is limited to adopting measures to enforce the guarantees of the Amendment; § 5 grants Congress no power to restrict, abrogate, or dilute these guarantees. Thus, for example, an enactment authorizing the States to establish racially segregated systems of education would not be—as required by § 5—a measure "to enforce" the Equal Protection Clause since that clause of its own force prohibits such state laws. [Footnote by the Court.]

This enhanced political power will be helpful in gaining nondiscriminatory treatment in public services for the entire Puerto Rican community.[2] Section 4(e) thereby enables the Puerto Rican minority better to obtain "perfect equality of civil rights and equal protection of the laws." It was well within congressional authority to say that this need of the Puerto Rican minority for the vote warranted federal intrusion upon any state interests served by the English literacy requirement. It was for Congress, as the branch that made this judgment, to assess and weigh the various conflicting considerations—the risk or pervasiveness of the discrimination in governmental services, the effectiveness of eliminating the state restriction on the right to vote as a means of dealing with the evil, the adequacy or availability of alternative remedies, and the nature and significance of the state interest that would be affected by the nullification of the English literacy requirement as applied to residents who have successfully completed the sixth grade in a Puerto Rican school. It is not for us to review the congressional resolution of these factors. It is enough that we be able to perceive a basis upon which the Congress might resolve the conflict as it did. There plainly was such a basis to support § 4(e) in the application in question in this case. Any contrary conclusion would require us to be blind to the realities familiar to the legislators.

The result is no different if we confine our inquiry to the question whether § 4(e) was merely legislation aimed at the elimination of an invidious discrimination in establishing voter qualifications. We are told that New York's English literacy requirement originated in the desire to provide an incentive for non-English speaking immigrants to learn the English language and in order to assure the intelligent exercise of the franchise. Yet Congress might well have questioned, in light of the many exemptions provided,[3] and some evidence suggesting that prejudice played a prominent role in the enactment of the requirement [4] whether these were actually the interests being served. Congress might have also questioned whether de-

---

2. Cf. James Everards' Breweries v. Day [265 U.S. 545 (1924)], which held that, under the Enforcement Clause of the Eighteenth Amendment, Congress could prohibit the prescription of intoxicating malt liquor for medicinal purposes even though the Amendment itself only prohibited the manufacture and sale of intoxicating liquors for beverage purposes. Cf. also the settled principle applied in the Shreveport Case (Houston, E. & W. T. R. Co. v. United States, 234 U.S. 342), and expressed in United States v. Darby, 312 U.S. 100, 118, that the power of Congress to regulate interstate commerce "extends to those activities intrastate which so affect interstate commerce or the exercise of the power of Congress over it as to make regulation of them appropriate means to the attainment of a legitimate end . . . ." Accord, Atlanta Motel v. United States, 379 U.S. 241, 258. [Footnote by the Court.]

3. The principal exemption complained of is that for persons who had been eligible to vote before January 1, 1922. [Footnote by the Court.]

4. This evidence consists in part of statements made in the Constitutional Convention first considering the English literacy requirement, such as the following made by the sponsor of the measure: "More precious even than the forms of government are the mental qualities of our race. While those stand unimpaired, all is safe. They are exposed to a single danger, and that is that by constantly changing our voting citizenship through the wholesale, but valuable and necessary infusion of Southern and Eastern European races . . . . The danger has begun. . . . We should check it." This evidence was reinforced by an understanding of the cultural milieu at the time of proposal and enactment, spanning a period

nial of a right deemed so precious and fundamental in our society was a necessary or appropriate means of encouraging persons to learn English, or of furthering the goal of an intelligent exercise of the franchise.[5] Finally, Congress might well have concluded that as a means of furthering the intelligent exercise of the franchise, an ability to read or understand Spanish is as effective as ability to read English for those to whom Spanish-language newspapers and Spanish-language radio and television programs are available to inform them of election issues and governmental affairs. Since Congress undertook to legislate so as to preclude the enforcement of the state law, and did so in the context of a general appraisal of literacy requirements for voting, see South Carolina v. Katzenbach, to which it brought a specially informed legislative competence,[6] it was Congress' prerogative to weigh these competing considerations. Here again, it is enough that we perceive a basis upon which Congress might predicate a judgment that the application of New York's English literacy requirement . . . constituted an invidious discrimination in violation of the Equal Protection Clause.

There remains the question whether the congressional remedies adopted in § 4(e) constitute means which are not prohibited by, but are consistent "with the letter and spirit of the constitution." The only respect in which appellees contend that § 4(e) fails in this regard is that the section itself works an invidious discrimination in violation of the Fifth Amendment by prohibiting the enforcement of the English literacy requirement only for those educated in American-flag schools (schools located within United States jurisdiction) in which the language of instruction was other than English, and not for those educated in schools beyond the territorial limits of the United States in which the language of instruction was also other than English. This is not a complaint that Congress, in enacting § 4(e), has unconstitutionally denied or diluted anyone's right to vote but rather that

from 1915 to 1921—not one of the enlightened eras of our history. Congress was aware of this evidence. . . . [Footnote by the Court.]

5. Other States have found ways of assuring an intelligent exercise of the franchise short of total disenfranchisement of persons not literate in English. For example, in Hawaii, where literacy in either English or Hawaiian suffices, candidates' names may be printed in both languages; New York itself already provides assistance for those exempt from the literacy requirement and are literate in no language; and, of course, the problem of assuring the intelligent exercise of the franchise has been met by those States, more than 30 in number, that have no literacy requirement at all. Section 4(e) does not preclude resort to these alternative methods of assuring the intelligent exercise of the franchise. True, the statute precludes, for a certain class, disenfranchisement and thus limits the States' choice of means of satisfying a purported state

interest. But our cases have held that the States can be required to tailor carefully the means of satisfying a legitimate state interest when fundamental liberties and rights are threatened, and Congress is free to apply the same principle in the exercise of its powers. [Footnote by the Court.]

6. See, e. g., 111 Cong.Rec. 11061 (Senator Long of Louisiana and Senator Young), 11064 (Senator Holland), drawing on their experience with voters literate in a language other than English. See also an affidavit from Representative Willis of Louisiana expressing the view that on the basis of his thirty years' personal experience in politics he has "formed a definite opinion that French-speaking voters who are illiterate in English generally have as clear a grasp of the issues and an understanding of the candidates, as do people who read and write the English language." [Footnote by the Court.]

Congress violated the Constitution by not extending the relief effected in § 4(e) to those educated in non-American-flag schools. We need not pause to determine whether appellees have a sufficient personal interest to have § 4 (e) invalidated on this ground, see generally United States v. Raines, 362 U.S. 17, since the argument, in our view, falls on the merits.

Section 4(e) does not restrict or deny the franchise but in effect extends the franchise to persons who otherwise would be denied it by state law. Thus we need not decide whether a state literacy law conditioning the right to vote on achieving a certain level of education in an American-flag school (regardless of the language of instruction) discriminates invidiously against those educated in non-American-flag schools. We need only decide whether the challenged limitation on the relief effected in § 4(e) was permissible. In deciding that question, the principle that calls for the closest scrutiny of distinctions in laws *denying* fundamental rights . . . is inapplicable; for the distinction challenged by appellees is presented only as a limitation on a reform measure aimed at eliminating an existing barrier to the exercise of the franchise. Rather, in deciding the constitutional propriety of the limitations in such a reform measure we are guided by the familiar principles that . . . "reform may take one step at a time, addressing itself to the phase of the problem which seems most acute to the legislative mind," Williamson v. Lee Optical Co. [chap. 9, above].

Guided by these principles, we are satisfied that appellees' challenge to this limitation in § 4(e) is without merit. In the context of the case before us, the congressional choice to limit the relief effected in § 4(e) may, for example, reflect Congress' greater familiarity with the quality of instruction in American-flag schools, a recognition of the unique historic relationship between the Congress and the Commonwealth of Puerto Rico, an awareness of the Federal Government's acceptance of the desirability of the use of Spanish as the language of instruction in Commonwealth schools, and the fact that Congress has fostered policies encouraging migration from the Commonwealth to the States. We have no occasion to determine in this case whether such factors would justify a similar distinction embodied in a voting-qualification law that denied the franchise to persons educated in non-American-flag schools. We hold only that the limitation on relief effected in § 4(e) does not constitute a forbidden discrimination since these factors might well have been the basis for the decision of Congress to go "no farther than it did." . . .

Reversed.

Mr. Justice DOUGLAS joins the Court's opinion except for the discussion of the question whether the congressional remedies adopted in § 4(e) constitute means which are not prohibited by, but are consistent with "the letter and spirit of the Constitution." On that question, he reserves judgment until such time as it is presented by a member of the class against which that particular discrimination is directed.

[CARDONA v. POWER, 384 U.S. 672 (1962), decided on the same day as Morgan, was an appeal from an unsuccessful state court equal protection challenge to the New York literacy requirement. That challenge was brought by a New York resident educated in Puerto Rico who did not allege that she had completed sixth grade education—the minimum under

§ 4(e) of the Voting Rights Act of 1965. The state courts, prior to the enactment of § 4(e), rejected her attack. Justice Brennan's majority opinion vacated the judgment and remanded the case to the highest state court: Appellant might be covered by § 4(e), and this case "might therefore be moot"; even if she were not so covered, the state courts should determine whether "in light of this federal enactment, those applications of the New York English literacy requirement not in terms prohibited by § 4(e) have continuing validity." Justice Douglas, joined by Justice Fortas, dissented, arguing that the requirement could not survive the strict equal protection scrutiny mandated in voting cases by Harper v. Virginia Board of Elections, 383 U.S. 663 (1966) (chap. 10, sec. 4A). Justice Harlan, joined by Justice Stewart, dissented in both Cardona and Morgan. That dissenting opinion follows.]

Mr. Justice HARLAN, whom Mr. Justice STEWART joins, dissenting.

Worthy as its purposes may be thought by many, I do not see how § 4 (e) of the Voting Rights Act of 1965 can be sustained except at the sacrifice of fundamentals in the American constitutional system—the separation between the legislative and judicial function and the boundaries between federal and state political authority. By the same token I think that the validity of New York's literacy test, a question which the Court considers *only* in the context of the federal statute, must be upheld. It will conduce to analytical clarity if I discuss the second issue first.

I.   [The Cardona Case.]

.   .   .   [A]pplying the basic equal protection standard, the issue in this case is whether New York has shown that its English-language literacy test is reasonably designed to serve a legitimate state interest. I think that it has.

I believe the same interests recounted in [Lassiter, above,] indubitably point toward upholding the rationality of the New York voting test. It is true that the issue here is not so simply drawn between literacy per se and illiteracy. Appellant [maintains] that whatever may be the validity of literacy tests per se as a condition of voting, application of such a test to one literate in Spanish, in the context of the large and politically significant Spanish-speaking community in New York, serves no legitimate state interest   .   .   .   .

.   .   .   I do not believe that this added factor vitiates the constitutionality of the New York statute. Accepting appellant's allegations as true, it is nevertheless also true that the range of material available to a resident of New York literate only in Spanish is much more limited than what is available to an English-speaking resident, that the business of national, state, and local government is conducted in English, and that propositions, amendments, and offices for which candidates are running listed on the ballot are likewise in English. It is also true that most candidates, certainly those campaigning on a national or statewide level, make their speeches in English. New York may justifiably want its voters to be able to understand candidates directly, rather than through possibly imprecise translations or summaries reported in a limited number of Spanish news media.   .   .   .   Given the State's legitimate concern with promoting and safeguarding the intelligent

use of the ballot, and given also New York's long experience with the process of integrating non-English-speaking residents into the mainstream of American life, I do not see how it can be said that this qualification for suffrage is unconstitutional. I would uphold the validity of the New York statute, unless the federal statute prevents that result, the question to which I now turn.

II. [The Morgan Case.] . . .

The pivotal question in this instance is what effect the added factor of a congressional enactment has on the straight equal protection argument dealt with above. The Court declares that since § 5 of the Fourteenth Amendment gives to the Congress power to "enforce" the prohibitions of the Amendment by "appropriate" legislation, the test for judicial review of any congressional determination in this area is simply one of rationality; that is, in effect, was Congress acting rationally in declaring that the New York statute is irrational? . . . I believe the Court has confused the issue of how much enforcement power Congress possesses under § 5 with the distinct issue of what questions are appropriate for congressional determination and what questions are essentially judicial in nature.

When recognized state violations of federal constitutional standards have occurred, Congress is of course empowered by § 5 to take appropriate remedial measures to redress and prevent the wrongs. But it is a judicial question whether the condition with which Congress has thus sought to deal is in truth an infringement of the Constitution, something that is the necessary prerequisite to bringing the § 5 power into play at all. Thus, in Ex parte Virginia, [100 U.S. 339 (1879)], involving a federal statute making it a federal crime to disqualify anyone from jury service because of race, the Court first held as a matter of constitutional law that "the Fourteenth Amendment secures, among other civil rights, to colored men, when charged with criminal offences against a State, an impartial jury trial, by jurors indifferently selected or chosen without discrimination against such jurors because of their color." Only then did the Court hold that to enforce this prohibition upon state discrimination, Congress could enact a criminal statute of the type under consideration. . . .

A more recent Fifteenth Amendment case also serves to illustrate this distinction. In South Carolina v. Katzenbach, decided earlier this Term, we held certain remedial sections of this Voting Rights Act of 1965 constitutional . . . . In enacting those sections of the Voting Rights Act the Congress made a detailed investigation of various state practices that had been used to deprive Negroes of the franchise. In passing upon the remedial provisions, we reviewed first the "voluminous legislative history" as well as judicial precedents supporting the basic congressional finding that the clear commands of the Fifteenth Amendment had been infringed by various state subterfuges. Given the existence of the evil, we held the remedial steps taken by the legislature under the Enforcement Clause of the Fifteenth Amendment to be a justifiable exercise of congressional initiative.

Section 4(e), however, presents a significantly different type of congressional enactment. The question here is not whether the statute is appropriate remedial legislation to cure an established violation of a constitutional command, but whether there has in fact been an infringement of that con-

stitutional command, that is, whether a particular state practice or, as here, a statute is so arbitrary or irrational as to offend the command of the Equal Protection Clause of the Fourteenth Amendment. That question is one for the judicial branch ultimately to determine. Were the rule otherwise, Congress would be able to qualify this Court's constitutional decisions under the Fourteenth and Fifteenth Amendments, let alone those under other provisions of the Constitution, by resorting to congressional power under the Necessary and Proper Clause. In view of this Court's holding in Lassiter, supra, that an English literacy test is a permissible exercise of state supervision over its franchise, I do not think it is open to Congress to limit the effect of that decision as it has undertaken to do by § 4(e). In effect the Court reads § 5 of the Fourteenth Amendment as giving Congress the power to define the *substantive* scope of the Amendment. If that indeed be the true reach of § 5, then I do not see why Congress should not be able as well to exercise its § 5 "discretion" by enacting statutes so as in effect to dilute equal protection and due process decisions of this Court. In all such cases there is room for reasonable men to differ as to whether or not a denial of equal protection or due process has occurred, and the final decision is one of judgment. Until today this judgment has always been one for the judiciary to resolve.

I do not mean to suggest in what has been said that a legislative judgment of the type incorporated in § 4(e) is without any force whatsoever. Decisions on questions of equal protection and due process are based not on abstract logic, but on empirical foundations. To the extent "legislative facts" are relevant to a judicial determination, Congress is well equipped to investigate them, and such determinations are of course entitled to due respect. In South Carolina v. Katzenbach, supra, such legislative findings were made to show that racial discrimination in voting was actually occurring. Similarly, in Heart of Atlanta Motel, Inc. v. United States and Katzenbach v. McClung, [chap. 3 above], the congressional determination that racial discrimination in a clearly defined group of public accommodations did effectively impede interstate commerce was based on "voluminous testimony," which had been put before the Congress and in the context of which it passed remedial legislation.

But no such factual data provide a legislative record supporting § 4(e) [1] by way of showing that Spanish-speaking citizens are fully as capable of making informed decisions in a New York election as are English-speaking citizens. Nor was there any showing whatever to support the Court's alternative argument that § 4(e) should be viewed as but a remedial measure designed to cure or assure against unconstitutional discrimination of other varieties, e. g., in "public schools, public housing and law enforcement," to which Puerto Rican minorities might be subject in such communities as New York. There is simply no legislative record supporting such hypothesized discrimination of the sort we have hitherto insisted upon when congressional power is brought to bear on constitutionally reserved state concerns. . . .

Thus, we have here not a matter of giving deference to a congressional estimate, based on its determination of legislative facts, bearing upon the

---

1. There were no committee hearings or reports referring to this section, which was introduced from the floor during debate on the full Voting Rights Act. . . . [Footnote by Justice Harlan.]

validity *vel non* of a statute, but rather what can at most be called a legislative announcement that Congress believes a state law to entail an unconstitutional deprivation of equal protection. Although this kind of declaration is of course entitled to the most respectful consideration, coming as it does from a concurrent branch and one that is knowledgeable in matters of popular political participation, I do not believe it lessens our responsibility to decide the fundamental issue of whether in fact the state enactment violates federal constitutional rights.

In assessing the deference we should give to this kind of congressional expression of policy, it is relevant that the judiciary has always given to congressional enactments a presumption of validity. However, it is also a canon of judicial review that state statutes are given a similar presumption. Whichever way this case is decided, one statute will be rendered inoperative in whole or in part, and although it has been suggested that this Court should give somewhat more deference to Congress than to a state legislature,[2] such a simple weighing of presumptions is hardly a satisfying way of resolving a matter that touches the distribution of state and federal power in an area so sensitive as that of the regulation of the franchise. Rather it should be recognized that while the Fourteenth Amendment is a "brooding omnipresence" over all state legislation, the substantive matters which it touches are all within the primary legislative competence of the States. Federal authority, legislative no less than judicial, does not intrude unless there has been a denial by state action of Fourteenth Amendment limitations, in this instance a denial of equal protection. At least in the area of primary state concern a state statute that passes constitutional muster under the judicial standard of rationality should not be permitted to be set at naught by a mere contrary congressional pronouncement unsupported by a legislative record justifying that conclusion.

. . . To hold, on this record, that § 4(e) overrides the New York literacy requirement seems to me tantamount to allowing the Fourteenth Amendment to swallow the State's constitutionally ordained primary authority in this field. For if Congress by what, as here, amounts to mere *ipse dixit* can set that otherwise permissible requirement partially at naught I see no reason why it could not also substitute its judgment for that of the States in other fields of their exclusive primary competence as well. . . .

CONGRESSIONAL POWER AND THE MORGAN CASE

How far-reaching is the § 5 power recognized in Morgan? Though most problems about the scope of the Morgan rationale are most usefully postponed until after considering its reexamination in Oregon v. Mitchell, which follows, some preliminary questions should be noted here. Is there merit in the assessment of Morgan in Burt, "Miranda and Title II: A Morganatic Marriage," 1969 Sup.Ct.Rev. 81: "In effect, the Court is saying that—at least in some circumstances—where Congress and the Court disagree about the meaning of the Fourteenth Amendment, the Court will defer to

---

2. See Thayer, The Origin and Scope of the American Doctrine of Constitutional Law, 7 Harv.L.Rev. 129, 154– 155 (1893). [Footnote by Justice Harlan.]

Congress' version. The Court is suggesting that, to some extent at least, § 5 exempts the Fourteenth Amendment from the principle of Court-Congress relationships expressed by Marbury v. Madison, that the judiciary is the final arbiter of the meaning of the Constitution." To what "extent"? Under what "circumstances"?

Note that Justice Brennan's majority opinion in Morgan rests on alternative rationales. One theory views § 4(e) as a measure to secure for Puerto Ricans in New York nondiscriminatory treatment in "the provision or administration of governmental services, such as public schools, public housing and law enforcement." The second theory views § 4(e) as assuring the elimination "of an invidious discrimination in establishing voter qualifications." Under that second theory, Congress is permitted to find, because the Court can perceive "a basis" for such a finding, that application of New York's English literacy requirement to covered Puerto Ricans itself constitutes "an invidious discrimination in violation of the Equal Protection Clause."

Which of these theories is more far-reaching? Note that discrimination against Puerto Ricans in providing public services is clearly unconstitutional under Court-developed interpretations of equal protection; under the first theory, then, Congress can be viewed as implementing judicially-determined constitutional rights. Even under that theory, Congress is making the factual determination that New York is discriminating in public services, and that Puerto Rican voting is an appropriate remedy for such discrimination. Under the second theory, Congress does more than that. The Court has not held that application of an English literacy test to those literate in Spanish is itself unconstitutional discrimination in voting. And the Court did not so hold in Morgan or in Cardona v. Power. Under that theory, then, it is *Congress* that is making the initial determination that an English literacy test in these circumstances is unconstitutional.

Can that determination be rested simply on congressional findings of fact? Or is it a determination which involves a resolution of competing values and a delineation of substantive constitutional rights by Congress rather than by the Court? Is Justice Brennan endorsing virtually autonomous congressional application of the strict scrutiny-"compelling interest" standard of modern equal protection doctrine in the voting area (recall chap. 10)? Does Morgan authorize Congress to make the value choices typically involved in judicial interpretations of equal protection? Note that Justice Brennan stated that it "was for Congress" to "assess and weigh the various conflicting considerations," including such considerations as the "significance of the state interest." And Morgan adds that it is "not for us to review the congressional resolution of these factors," so long as the Justices can "perceive a basis upon which the Congress might resolve the conflict as it did." Does that rationale authorize Congress to resolve the value conflicts in constitutional interpretation with a result different from that the Court might reach—or has reached? May Congress utilize that rationale to dilute as well as expand constitutional rights? Is that value choice-substantive constitutional decisionmaking rationale endorsed by any of the opinions in Oregon v. Mitchell, which follows? Is Justice Brennan's rationale in Oregon v. Mitchell different from his position in Morgan? Does Justice Stewart

describe the Morgan rationale accurately in Oregon v. Mitchell? (Note also the additional questions on the implications of Morgan after the Oregon v. Mitchell opinions, which follow.)*

OREGON v. MITCHELL

400 U.S. 112, 91 S.Ct. 260, 27 L.Ed.2d 272 (1970).

On Bill of Complaint.†

[These cases—in the Supreme Court's original jurisdiction—involved challenges by several states to three provisions of the Voting Rights Act Amendments of 1970. (1) One provision attempted to lower the voting age to eighteen: § 302 prohibited denying to any citizen the right to vote in any election "on account of age if such citizen is eighteen years of age or older." [1] By a 5 to 4 vote, that provision was upheld as applied to federal elections; but by another 5 to 4 division, the eighteen-year-old vote provision was held unconstitutional as applied to state elections. Justices Douglas, Brennan, White and Marshall found it valid as applied to any election; Chief Justice Burger and Justices Harlan, Stewart and Blackmun thought it entirely invalid; Justice Black cast the deciding vote, holding it constitutional as applied to federal elections but unconstitutional as to state elections. [2]

[(2) Section 201 was a nationwide suspension for a period of five years of the use of literacy tests in any election, state or national. That provision was upheld unanimously. (3) Section 202 prohibited the application

---

* The major constitutional controversy in Oregon v. Mitchell was provoked by the 1970 Act provision lowering the voting age to eighteen in state elections. Enactment came after an extensive constitutional debate in Congress. In Congress, the proponents of the 18-year-old vote provision relied heavily on a statement by Archibald Cox resting on Morgan for the proposition that "Congress has constitutional power to determine what the Equal Protection Clause requires," though cautioning that "some constitutional scholars would not share my view . . . . Possibly, my reasoning runs the logic of Katzenbach v. Morgan into the ground." Opponents of the lowering of the voting age by statute rather than by constitutional amendment introduced a statement by Louis H. Pollak noting that Morgan "provides the basis for a modestly plausible, but not for an ultimately persuasive, case for the constitutionality of the statute."

† Together with Texas v. Mitchell, United States v. Arizona, and United States v. Idaho, also on bills of complaint in the original jurisdiction of the Supreme Court.

1. The congressional findings accompanying that provision stated that a requirement that a voter be 21 years old "(1) denies and abridges the inherent constitutional rights of citizens eighteen years of age but not yet twenty-one years of age to vote—a particularly unfair treatment of such citizens in view of the national defence responsibilities imposed upon such citizens; (2) has the effect of denying to citizens eighteen years of age . . . the due process and equal protection of the laws . . . ; and (3) does not bear a reasonable relationship to any compelling State interest." 42 U.S.C. § 1973bb.

2. This decision was handed down on Dec. 21, 1970. On March 23, 1971, Congress submitted the 26th Amendment to the States for ratification. Three months later, on June 30, 1971, the ratification process was completed. The Amendment provides that the federal and state governments may not deny the vote "on account of age" to citizens "eighteen years of age or older."

of state durational residency requirements in presidential elections and established uniform standards for registration and absentee balloting. It included a provision that voters could register within thirty days of a presidential election.[3] Those provisions were sustained by an 8 to 1 vote, with Justice Harlan the only dissenter.]

Mr. Justice BLACK announcing the judgments of the Court in an opinion expressing his own view of the cases. . . .

I. [T]he responsibility of the States for setting the qualifications of voters in congressional elections was made subject to the power of Congress to make or alter such regulations if it deemed it advisable to do so. This was done in Art. I, § 4 . . . . . Moreover, the power of Congress to make election regulations in national elections is augmented by the Necessary and Proper Clause. See McCulloch v. Maryland. . . .

The breadth of power granted to Congress to make or alter election regulations in national elections, including the qualifications of voters, is demonstrated by the fact that the Framers of the Constitution and the state legislatures which ratified it intended to grant to Congress the power to lay out or alter the boundaries of the congressional districts. . . . Surely no voter *qualification* was more important to the Framers than the *geographical qualification* embodied in the concept of congressional districts. . . . There can be no doubt that the power to alter congressional district lines is vastly more significant in its effect than the power to permit 18-year-old citizens to go to the polls and vote in all federal elections.

In short, the Constitution allotted to the States the power to make laws regarding national elections, but provided that if Congress became dissatisfied with the state laws, Congress could alter them. . . . The Voting Rights Act Amendments of 1970 now before this Court evidence dissatisfaction of Congress with the voting age set by many of the States for national elections. I would hold, as have a long line of decisions in this Court, that Congress has ultimate supervisory power over congressional elections. Similarly, it is the prerogative of Congress to oversee the conduct of presidential and vice-presidential elections and to set the qualifications for voters for electors for those offices. It cannot be seriously contended that Congress has less power over the conduct of presidential elections than it has over congressional elections.[4]

---

3. That section was preceded by congressional findings that the imposition of durational residency requirements and the lack of sufficient opportunities for absentee registration and voting in presidential elections "(1) denies or abridges the inherent constitutional right of citizens to vote for their President and Vice President; (2) denies or abridges the inherent constitutional right of citizens to enjoy their free movement across State lines; (3) denies or abridges the privileges and immunities guaranteed to citizens of each State under [Art. IV, § 2]; (4) in some instances has the impermissible purpose or effect of denying citizens the right to vote for such officers because of the way they may vote; (5) has the effect of denying to citizens the equality of civil rights, and due process and equal protection of the laws . . . ; and (6) does not bear a reasonable relationship to any compelling State interest in the conduct of presidential elections."

4. With reference to the selection of the President and Vice President, Art. II, § 1, provides: "Each State shall appoint, in such Manner as the Legislature thereof may direct, a Number of Electors, equal to the whole Number of Senators and Representatives to which the State may be entitled in the Congress . . . ." But this Court

On the other hand, the Constitution was also intended to preserve to the States the power that even the Colonies had to establish and maintain their own separate and independent governments, except insofar as the Constitution itself commands otherwise. . . . No function is more essential to the separate and independent existence of the States and their governments than the power to determine within the limits of the Constitution the qualifications of their own voters for state, county, and municipal offices and the nature of their own machinery for filling local public offices. Moreover, Art. I, § 2, is a clear indication that the Framers intended the States to determine the qualifications of their own voters for state offices . . . . My Brother Brennan's opinion, if carried to its logical conclusion, would, under the guise of insuring equal protection, blot out all state power, leaving the 50 States little more than impotent figureheads. . . .

Of course, we have upheld congressional legislation under the Enforcement Clauses in some cases where Congress has interfered with state regulation of the local electoral process. [Katzenbach v. Morgan; South Carolina v. Katzenbach.] But division of power between state and national governments, like every provision of the Constitution, was expressly qualified by the Civil War Amendments' ban on racial discrimination. Where Congress attempts to remedy racial discrimination under its enforcement powers, its authority is enhanced by the avowed intention of the Framers of the Thirteenth, Fourteenth, and Fifteenth Amendments.

In enacting the 18-year-old vote provisions of the Act now before the Court, Congress made no legislative findings that the 21-year-old vote requirement was used by the States to disenfranchise voters on account of race. I seriously doubt that such a finding, if made, could be supported by substantial evidence. Since Congress has attempted to invade an area preserved to the States by the Constitution without a foundation for enforcing the Civil War Amendments' ban on racial discrimination, I would hold that Congress has exceeded its powers in attempting to lower the voting age in state and local elections. On the other hand, where Congress legislates in a domain not exclusively reserved by the Constitution to the States, its enforcement power need not be tied so closely to the goal of eliminating discrimination on account of race. . . .

II. . . . In enacting the literacy test ban of Title II Congress had before it a long history of the discriminatory use of literacy tests to disfranchise voters on account of their race. [A]s to the Nation as a whole, Congress had before it statistics which demonstrate that voter registration and voter participation are consistently greater in States without literacy tests.

Congress also had before it this country's history of discriminatory educational opportunities in both the North and the South. . . . There is substantial, if not overwhelming, evidence from which Congress could have con-

in Burroughs v. United States, 290 U. S. 534 (1934), [rejected] a construction of Art. II, § 1, that would have curtailed the power of Congress to regulate such elections. Finally, and most important, inherent in the very concept of a supreme national government with national officers is a residual power in Congress to insure that those officers represent their national constituency as responsively as possible. This power arises from the nature of our constitutional system of government and from the Necessary and Proper Clause. [Footnote by Justice Black.]

cluded that it is a denial of equal protection to condition the political participation of children educated in a dual school system upon their educational achievement. . . . Faced with this and other evidence that literacy tests reduce voter participation in a discriminatory manner not only in the South but throughout the Nation, Congress was supported by substantial evidence in concluding that a nationwide ban on literacy tests was appropriate to enforce the Civil War amendments. . . .

III. . . . In enacting [the residency and absentee voting provisions], Congress was attempting to insure a fully effective voice to all citizens in national elections. What I said in Part I of this opinion applies with equal force here. Acting under its broad authority to create and maintain a national government, Congress unquestionably has power under the Constitution to regulate federal elections. . . .

Mr. Justice DOUGLAS.*

I dissent from the judgments of the Court insofar as they declare [§ 302] unconstitutional as applied to state elections and concur in the judgments as they affect federal elections, but for different reasons. I rely on the Equal Protection Clause and on the Privileges and Immunities Clause of the Fourteenth Amendment.

The grant of the franchise to 18-year-olds by Congress is in my view valid across the board. . . . Congress might well conclude that a reduction in the voting age from 21 to 18 was needed in the interest of equal protection. . . . Certainly there is not a word of limitation in § 5 which would restrict its applicability to matters of race alone. . . . I likewise find the objections [to] the literacy and residence requirements of the 1970 Act to be insubstantial. [Congress found] that a durational residency requirement denies citizens their privileges and immunities. [That judgment] is plainly a permissible one in its efforts under § 5 to "enforce" the Fourteenth Amendment.

Mr. Justice BRENNAN, Mr. Justice WHITE, and Mr. Justice MARSHALL dissent from the judgments insofar as they declare § 302 unconstitutional as applied to state and local elections, and concur in the judgments in all other respects, for the following reasons. [I]n our view, congressional power to enact the challenged Amendments is found in the enforcement clauses of the Fourteenth and Fifteenth Amendments, and [we] easily perceive a rational basis for the congressional judgments underlying each of them . . . . .

I. [Literacy.] . . . The legislative history of the 1970 Amendments contains substantial information upon which Congress could have based a finding that the use of literacy tests in Arizona and in other States where their use was not proscribed by the 1965 Act has the effect of denying the vote to racial minorities whose illiteracy is the consequence of a previous, governmentally sponsored denial of equal educational opportunity. . . .†

---

* The additional opinions in Oregon v. Mitchell are printed here in an order somewhat different from the seniority sequence in the United States Reports. As printed here, opinions supporting the constitutionality of all of the provisions precede those finding some provisions unconstitutional.

† Justice Brennan rejected Arizona's argument "that to the extent that any citizens of Arizona have been denied

II.   [Residency.]   .   .   .   [W]e believe there is an adequate constitutional basis for § 202 in § 5 of the Fourteenth Amendment. For more than a century, this Court has recognized the constitutional right of all citizens to unhindered interstate travel and settlement.   .   .   .   By definition, the imposition of a durational residence requirement operates to penalize those persons, and only those persons, who have exercised their constitutional right of interstate migration. Of course, governmental action that has the incidental effect of burdening the exercise of the constitutional right is not ipso facto unconstitutional. But in such a case, governmental action may withstand constitutional scrutiny only upon a clear showing that the burden imposed is necessary to protect a compelling and substantial governmental interest. [Shapiro v. Thompson.] In the present case, Congress has explicitly found that the imposition of durational residence requirements abridges the right of free interstate migration and that such requirements are not reasonably related to any compelling state interests. [W]e find ample justification for the congressional conclusion that § 202 is a reasonable means for eliminating an unnecessary burden on the right of interstate migration. United States v. Guest.

III.   [18-year-old vote.]   .   .   .   We believe there is serious question whether a statute granting the franchise to citizens over 21 while denying it to those between the ages of 18 and 21 could, in any event, withstand present scrutiny under the Equal Protection Clause. Regardless of the answer to this question, however, it is clear to us that proper regard for the special function of Congress in making determinations of legislative fact compels this Court to respect those determinations unless they are contradicted by evidence far stronger than anything that has been adduced in these cases. We would uphold § 302 as a valid exercise of congressional power under § 5 of the Fourteenth Amendment.

A.   All parties to these cases are agreed that the States are given power, under the Constitution, to determine the qualifications for voting in state elections. But it is now settled that exercise of this power, like all other exercises of state power, is subject to the Equal Protection Clause. [W]hen exclusions from the franchise are challenged as violating the Equal Protection Clause,   .   .   .   "the Court must determine whether the exclusions are necessary to promote a compelling state interest."

In the present cases, the States justify exclusion of 18- to 21-year-olds from the voting rolls solely on the basis of the States' interests in promoting intelligent and responsible exercise of the franchise. [We must] examine with particular care the asserted connection between age limitations and the admittedly laudable state purpose to further intelligent and responsible voting.   .   .   .   Every State in the Union has concluded for itself that citizens 21 years of age and over are capable of responsible and intelligent voting. Accepting this judgment, there remains the question whether citizens 18 to 21 years of age may fairly be said to be less able.

the right to vote because of illiteracy resulting from discriminatory governmental practices, the unlawful discrimination has been by governments other than the State of Arizona or it political subdivisions." He responded in part that "congressional power to remedy the evils resulting from state-sponsored racial discrimination does not end when the subject of that discrimination removes himself from the jurisdiction in which the injury occurred."

State practice itself in other areas casts doubt upon any such proposition. Each of the 50 States has provided special mechanisms for dealing with persons who are deemed insufficiently mature and intelligent to understand, and to conform their behavior to, the criminal laws of the State. Forty-nine of the States have concluded that, in this regard, 18-year-olds are invariably to be dealt with according to precisely the same standards prescribed for their elders. This at the very least is evidence of a nearly unanimous legislative judgment on the part of the States themselves that differences in maturity and intelligence between 18-year-olds and persons over the age of 21 are too trivial to warrant specialized treatment for *any* of the former class in the critically important matter of criminal responsibility. Similarly, every State permits 18-year-olds to marry . . . . . No State in the Union requires attendance at school beyond the age of 18. . . . [T]hat 18-year-olds as a class may be less educated than some of their elders cannot justify restriction of the franchise, for the States themselves have determined that this incremental education is irrelevant to voting qualifications. And finally, we have been cited to no material whatsoever that would support the proposition that intelligence, as opposed to educational attainment, increases between the ages of 18 and 21.

One final point remains. No State seeking to uphold its denial of the franchise to 18-year-olds has adduced anything beyond the mere difference in age. We have already indicated that the relevance of this difference is contradicted by nearly uniform state practice in other areas. But perhaps more important is the uniform experience of those States—Georgia since 1943, and Kentucky since 1955—that have permitted 18-year-olds to vote. [E]very person who spoke to the issue in either the House or Senate was agreed that 18-year-olds in both States were at least as interested, able, and responsible in voting as were their elders.

In short, we are faced with an admitted restriction upon the franchise, supported only by bare assertions and long practice, in the face of strong indications that the States themselves do not credit the factual propositions upon which the restriction is asserted to rest. But there is no reason for us to decide whether, in a proper case, we would be compelled to hold this restriction a violation of the Equal Protection Clause. [For] the question we face today [is] the scope of congressional power under § 5 of the Fourteenth Amendment. To that question we now turn.

B. As we have often indicated, questions of constitutional power frequently turn in the last analysis on questions of fact. This is particularly the case when an assertion of state power is challenged under the Equal Protection Clause of the Fourteenth Amendment. For although equal protection requires that all persons "under like circumstances and conditions" be treated alike, such a formulation merely raises, but does not answer the question whether a legislative classification has resulted in different treatment of persons who are in fact "under like circumstances and conditions."

. . . . When a state legislative classification is subjected to judicial challenge as violating the Equal Protection Clause, it comes before the courts cloaked by the presumption that the legislature has, as it should, acted within constitutional limitations. Accordingly, "[a] statutory discrimination will

not be set aside as the denial of equal protection of the laws if any state of facts reasonably may be conceived to justify it."

But, as we have consistently held, this limitation on judicial review of state legislative classifications is a limitation stemming, not from the Fourteenth Amendment itself, but from the nature of judicial review. . . . The nature of the judicial process makes it an inappropriate forum for the determination of complex factual questions of the kind so often involved in constitutional adjudication. Courts, therefore, will overturn a legislative determination of a factual question only if the legislature's finding is so clearly wrong that it may be characterized as "arbitrary," "irrational," or "unreasonable."

Limitations stemming from the nature of the judicial process, however, have no application to Congress. . . . Should Congress, pursuant to [§ 5] undertake an investigation in order to determine whether the factual basis necessary to support a state legislative discrimination actually exists, it need not stop once it determines that some reasonable men could believe the factual basis exists. Section 5 empowers Congress to make its own determination on the matter. [Katzenbach v. Morgan.] It should hardly be necessary to add that if the asserted factual basis necessary to support a given state discrimination does not exist, § 5 of the Fourteenth Amendment vests Congress with power to remove the discrimination by appropriate means. Id. The scope of our review in such matters has been established by a long line of consistent decisions. "[W]here we find that the legislators, in light of the facts and testimony before them, have a rational basis for finding a chosen regulatory scheme necessary [our] investigation is at an end." [E. g., Katzenbach v. McClung; Katzenbach v. Morgan.] [1]

This scheme is consistent with our prior decisions in related areas. The core of dispute [here] is a conflict between state and federal legislative determinations of the factual issues upon which depends decision of a federal constitutional question—the legitimacy, under the Equal Protection Clause, of state discrimination against persons between the ages of 18 and 21. Our cases have repeatedly emphasized that, when state and federal claims come into conflict, the primacy of federal power requires that the federal finding of fact control. The Supremacy Clause requires an identical result when the conflict is one of legislative, not judicial, findings.

Finally, it is no answer to say that Title III intrudes upon a domain reserved to the States—the power to set qualifications for voting. It is no longer open to question that the Fourteenth Amendment applies to this, as to any other, exercise of state power. . . .

1. As we emphasized in Katzenbach v. Morgan, supra, "§ 5 does not grant Congress power to . . . enact 'statutes so as in effect to dilute equal protection and due process decisions of this Court.'" 384 U.S., at 651 n. [1]. As indicated above, a decision of this Court striking down a state statute expresses, among other things, our conclusion that the legislative findings upon which the statute is based are so far wrong as to be unreasonable. Unless Congress were to unearth new evidence in its investigation, its identical findings on the identical issue would be no more reasonable than those of the state legislature. [Footnote by Justice Brennan et al.]

C. [A lengthy discussion rejected Justice Harlan's historical argument that the 14th Amendment "was never intended to restrict the authority of the States to allocate their political power as they see fit." It concluded:] We could not accept [Justice Harlan's] thesis even if it were supported by historical evidence far stronger than anything adduced today. But in our view, [his] historical analysis is flawed by his ascription of 20th-century meanings to the words of 19th-century legislators. In consequence, his analysis imposes an artificial simplicity upon a complex era, and presents, as universal, beliefs that were held by merely one of several groups competing for political power. . . . The historical record left by the framers of the Fourteenth Amendment, because it is a product of differing and conflicting political pressures and conceptions of federalism, is thus too vague and imprecise to provide us with sure guidance in deciding the pending cases. We must therefore conclude that its framers understood their Amendment to be a broadly worded injunction capable of being interpreted by future generations in accordance with the vision and needs of those generations. We would be remiss in our duty if, in an attempt to find certainty amidst uncertainty, we were to misread the historical record and cease to interpret the Amendment as this Court has always interpreted it.

D. There remains only the question whether Congress could rationally have concluded that denial of the franchise to citizens between the ages of 18 and 21 was unnecessary to promote any legitimate interests of the States in assuring intelligent and responsible voting. . . . Congress was aware, of course, of the facts and state practices already discussed. [E. g., it] was aware that 18-year-olds today make up a not insubstantial proportion of the adult work force . . . . As Congress recognized, its judgment that 18-year-olds are capable of voting is consistent with its practice of entrusting them with the heavy responsibilities of military service. Finally, Congress was presented with evidence that the age of social and biological maturity in modern society has been consistently decreasing. . . . Finally, and perhaps more important, Congress had before it information on the experience of two States, Georgia and Kentucky, which have allowed 18-year-olds to vote since 1943 and 1955, respectively. . . .

In sum, Congress had ample evidence upon which it could have based the conclusion that exclusion of citizens 18 to 21 years of age from the franchise is wholly unnecessary to promote any legitimate interest the States may have in assuring intelligent and responsible voting. [Katzenbach v. Morgan.] If discrimination is unnecessary to promote any legitimate state interest, it is plainly unconstitutional under the Equal Protection Clause, and Congress has ample power to forbid it under § 5 of the Fourteenth Amendment. . . .

Mr. Justice STEWART, with whom The Chief Justice [BURGER] and Mr. Justice BLACKMUN join, concurring in part and dissenting in part.

. . . I agree with the Court in sustaining the congressional ban on state literacy tests, for substantially the same reasons relied upon by Mr. Justice Black. I also agree that the action of Congress in removing the restrictions of state residency requirements in presidential elections is constitutionally valid, but I base this judgment upon grounds quite different from those relied upon by Mr. Justice Black. And finally, I disagree with the

Court's conclusion that Congress could constitutionally reduce the voting age to 18 for federal elections, since I am convinced that Congress was wholly without constitutional power to alter—for the purpose of *any* elections—the voting age qualifications now determined by the several States. . . .

I. [Literacy.] . . . Because the justification for extending the ban on literacy tests to the entire Nation need not turn on whether literacy tests unfairly discriminate against Negroes in every State in the Union, Congress was not required to make state-by-state findings concerning either the equality of educational opportunity or actual impact of literacy requirements on the Negro citizen's access to the ballot box. In the interests of uniformity, Congress may paint with a much broader brush than may this Court, which must confine itself to the judicial function of deciding individual cases and controversies upon individual records. The findings that Congress made when it enacted the Voting Rights Act of 1965 would have supported a nationwide ban on literacy tests. Experience gained under the 1965 Act has now led Congress to conclude that it should go the whole distance. This approach to the problem is a rational one; consequently it is within the constitutional power of Congress under § 2 of the Fifteenth Amendment.

II. [Residency.] Congress, in my view, has the power under the Constitution to eradicate political and civil disabilities that arise by operation of state law following a change in residence from one State to another. Freedom to travel from State to State—freedom to enter and abide in any State in the Union—is a privilege of United States citizenship. [Although § 5 of the 14th Amendment confers power to enforce that Amendment's provisions], this Court has sustained the power of Congress to protect and facilitate the exercise of privileges of United States citizenship without reference to § 5. [E. g., United States v. Guest.] Congress brings to the protection and facilitation of the exercise of privileges of United States citizenship all of its power under the Necessary and Proper Clause. . . . Congress could rationally conclude that the imposition of durational residency requirements unreasonably burdens and sanctions the privilege of taking up residence in another State. . . . Congress has acted to protect a constitutional privilege that finds its protection in the Federal Government and is national in character.

But even though general constitutional power clearly exists, Congress may not overstep the letter or spirit of any constitutional restriction in the exercise of that power. . . . I have concluded that, while § 202 applies only to presidential elections, nothing in the Constitution prevents Congress from protecting those who have moved from one State to another from disenfranchisement in any federal election, whether congressional or presidential.

The Constitution withholds from Congress any general authority to change by legislation the qualifications for voters in federal elections. [Art. I, § 2, and the 17th Amendment adopt] as the federal standard the standard which each State has chosen for itself. Accordingly, a state law that purported to establish distinct qualifications for congressional elections would be invalid as repugnant to Article I, § 2, and the Seventeenth Amendment. By the same token, it cannot be gainsaid that federal legislation that

had no objective other than to alter the qualifications to vote in congressional elections would be invalid for the same reasons. . . .

Contrary to the submission of my Brother Black, Article I, § 4, does not create in the Federal Legislature the power to alter the constitutionally established qualifications to vote in congressional elections. . . . The "manner" of holding elections can hardly be read to mean the *qualifications* for voters, when it is remembered that § 2 of the same Article I explicitly speaks of the "qualifications" for voters in elections to choose Representatives. It is plain, in short, that when the Framers meant qualifications they said "qualifications." That word does not appear in Article I, § 4. Moreover, § 4 does not give Congress the power to do anything that a State might not have done, and, as pointed out above, no State may establish distinct qualifications for congressional elections. . . .

Different provisions of the Constitution govern the selection of the President and the Vice President. . . . Because the Constitution does not require the popular election of members of the electoral college, it does not specify the qualifications that voters must have when this election of electors is by popular election. This is left to the States in the exercise of their power to "direct" the manner of choosing presidential electors.

The issue then is whether, despite the intentional withholding from the Federal Government of a general authority to establish qualifications to vote in either congressional or presidential elections, there exists congressional power to do so when Congress acts with the objective of protecting a citizen's privilege to move his residence from one State to another. Although the matter is not entirely free from doubt, I am persuaded that the constitutional provisions discussed above are not sufficient to prevent Congress from protecting a person who exercises his constitutional right to enter and abide in any State in the Union from losing his opportunity to vote, when Congress may protect the right of interstate travel from other less fundamental disabilities. . . . The power that Congress has exercised in enacting § 202 is not a general power to prescribe qualifications for voters in either federal or state elections. It is confined to federal action against a particular problem clearly within the purview of congressional authority. . . . We should strive to avoid an interpretation of the Constitution that would withhold from Congress the power to legislate for the protection of those constitutional rights that the States are unable effectively to secure. For all these reasons, I conclude that it was within the power of Congress to enact § 202.

III. [18-year-old vote.] . . . Although it was found necessary to amend the Constitution in order to confer a federal right to vote upon Negroes and upon females, the Government asserts that a federal right to vote can be conferred upon people between 18 and 21 years of age simply by this Act of Congress. Our decision in Katzenbach v. Morgan, it is said, established the power of Congress, under § 5 of the Fourteenth Amendment, to nullify state laws requiring voters to be 21 years of age or older if Congress could rationally have concluded that such laws are not supported by a "compelling state interest."

In my view, neither the Morgan case, nor any other case upon which the Government relies, establishes such congressional power, even assuming that

all those cases were rightly decided. Mr. Justice Black is surely correct when he writes, " . . . It is obvious that the whole Constitution reserves to the States the power to set voter qualifications in state and local elections, except to the limited extent that the people through constitutional amendments have specifically narrowed the powers of the States." For the reasons that I have set out in Part II of this opinion, it is equally plain to me that the Constitution just as completely withholds from Congress the power to alter by legislation qualifications for voters in federal elections, in view of the explicit provisions of Article I, Article II, and the Seventeenth Amendment.

To be sure, recent decisions have established that state action regulating suffrage is not immune from the impact of the Equal Protection Clause. But we have been careful in those decisions to note the undoubted power of a State to establish a qualification for voting based on age. Indeed, none of the opinions filed today suggest that the States have anything but a constitutionally unimpeachable interest in establishing some age qualification as such. Yet to test the power to establish an age qualification by the "compelling interest" standard is really to deny a State any choice at all, because no State could demonstrate a "compelling interest" in drawing the line with respect to age at one point rather than another. Obviously, the power to establish an age qualification must carry with it the power to choose 21 as a reasonable voting age, as the vast majority of the States have done.[1]

Katzenbach v. Morgan does not hold that Congress has the power to determine what are and what are not "compelling state interests" for equal protection purposes. In Morgan the Court [upheld] the statute on two grounds: that Congress could conclude that enhancing the political power of the Puerto Rican community by conferring the right to vote was an appropriate means of remedying discriminatory treatment in public services; and that Congress could conclude that the New York statute was tainted by the impermissible purpose of denying the right to vote to Puerto Ricans, an undoubted invidious discrimination under the Equal Protection Clause. Both of these decisional grounds were farreaching. The Court's opinion made clear that Congress could impose on the States a remedy for the denial of equal protection that elaborated upon the direct command of the Constitution, and that it could override state laws on the ground that they were in fact used as instruments of invidious discrimination even though a court in an individual lawsuit might not have reached that factual conclusion.

1. If the Government is correct in its submission that a particular age requirement must meet the "compelling interest" standard, then, of course, a substantial question would exist whether a 21-year-old voter qualification is constitutional even in the absence of congressional action, as my Brothers point out. Yet it is inconceivable to me that this Court would ever hold that the denial of the vote to those between the ages of 18 and 21 constitutes such an invidious discrimination as to be a denial of the equal protection of the laws. The establishment of an age qualification is not state action aimed at any discrete and insular minority. Cf. United States v. Carolene Products Co., 304 U.S. 144, 152 n. 4. Moreover, so long as a State does not set the voting age higher than 21, the reasonableness of its choice is confirmed by the very Fourteenth Amendment upon which the Government relies. Section 2 of that Amendment provides for sanctions when the right to vote "is denied to any of the male inhabitants of such State, *being twenty-one years of age*, and citizens of the United States . . . ." (Emphasis added.) [Footnote by Justice Stewart.]

But it is necessary to go much further to sustain § 302. The state laws that it invalidates do not invidiously discriminate against any discrete and insular minority. Unlike the statute considered in Morgan, § 302 is valid only if Congress has the power not only to provide the means of eradicating situations that amount to a violation of the Equal Protection Clause, but also to determine as a matter of substantive constitutional law what situations fall within the ambit of the clause, and what state interests are "compelling." I concurred in Mr. Justice Harlan's dissent in Morgan. That case, as I now read it, gave congressional power under § 5 the furthest possible legitimate reach. Yet to sustain the constitutionality of § 302 would require an enormous extension of that decision's rationale. I cannot but conclude that § 302 was beyond the constitutional power of Congress to enact.

Mr. Justice HARLAN, concurring in part and dissenting in part. . . .

I am of the opinion that the Fourteenth Amendment was never intended to restrict the authority of the States to allocate their political power as they see fit and therefore that it does not authorize Congress to set voter qualifications, in either state or federal elections. I find no other source of congressional power to lower the voting age as fixed by state laws, or to alter state laws on residency, registration, and absentee voting, with respect to either state or federal elections. The suspension of Arizona's literacy requirement, however, can be deemed an appropriate means of enforcing the Fifteenth Amendment, and I would sustain it on that basis.

I and II. . . . I think that the history of the Fourteenth Amendment makes it clear beyond any reasonable doubt that no part of the legislation now under review can be upheld as a legitimate exercise of congressional power under that Amendment. [Justice Harlan's extensive examination of the historical data is omitted.*]

I must confess to complete astonishment at the position of some of my Brethren that the history of the Fourteenth Amendment has become irrelevant. . . . [T]he very fact that constitutional amendments were deemed necessary to bring about federal abolition of state restrictions on voting by reason of race (amdt. XV), sex (amdt. XIX), and, even with respect to federal elections the failure to pay state poll taxes (amdt. XXIV), is itself forceful evidence of the common understanding in 1869, 1919, and 1962, respectively, that the Fourteenth Amendment did not empower Congress to legislate in these respects.

It must be recognized, of course, that the amending process is not the only way in which constitutional understanding alters with time. The judiciary has long been entrusted with the task of applying the Constitution in changing circumstances, and as conditions change the Constitution in a sense changes as well. But when the Court gives the language of the Constitution an unforeseen application, it does so, whether explicitly or implicitly, in the

---

* Justice Harlan argued that history made it clear that § 1 of the 14th Amendment was not intended to "reach discriminatory voting qualifications." He emphasized § 2 of the 14th Amendment—see footnote 1 to Justice Stewart's opinion, above. He concluded: "The only sensible explanation of § 2 [is] that the racial voter qualifications it was designed to penalize were understood to be permitted by § 1 of the Fourteenth Amendment." [Recall also Justice Harlan's dissents in the voting cases in chap. 10, sec. 4A, above.]

name of some underlying purpose of the Framers. . . . When the Court disregards the express intent and understanding of the Framers, it has invaded the realm of the political process to which the amending power was committed, and it has violated the constitutional structure which it is its highest duty to protect.

As the Court is not justified in substituting its own views of wise policy for the commands of the Constitution, still less is it justified in allowing Congress to disregard those commands as the Court understands them. Although Congress' expression of the view that it does have power to alter state suffrage qualifications is entitled to the most respectful consideration by the judiciary, coming as it does from a coordinate branch of government, this cannot displace the duty of this Court to make an independent determination whether Congress has exceeded its powers. The reason for this goes beyond Marshall's assertion that: "It is emphatically the province and duty of the judicial department to say what the law is." Marbury v. Madison.[1] It inheres in the structure of the constitutional system itself. Congress is subject to none of the institutional restraints imposed on judicial decisionmaking; it is controlled only by the political process. In Article V, the Framers expressed the view that the political restraints on Congress alone were an insufficient control over the process of constitution making. The concurrence of two-thirds of each House and of three-fourths of the States was needed for the political check to be adequate. To allow a simple majority of Congress to have final say on matters of constitutional interpretation is therefore fundamentally out of keeping with the constitutional structure. Nor is that structure adequately protected by a requirement that the judiciary be able to perceive a basis for the congressional interpretation, the only restriction laid down in Katzenbach v. Morgan.

It is suggested that the proper basis for the doctrine enunciated in Morgan lies in the relative factfinding competence of Court, Congress, and state legislatures. In this view, as I understand it, since Congress is at least as well qualified as a state legislature to determine factual issues, and far better qualified than this Court, where a dispute is basically factual in nature the congressional finding of fact should control, subject only to review by this Court for reasonableness.

In the first place, this argument has little or no force as applied to the issue whether the Fourteenth Amendment covers voter qualifications. Indeed, I do not understand the adherents of Morgan to maintain the contrary. But even on the assumption that the Fourteenth Amendment does place a limit on the sorts of voter qualifications which a State may adopt, I still do not see any real force in the reasoning.

When my Brothers refer to "complex factual questions," they call to mind disputes about primary, objective facts dealing with such issues as the

1. In fact, however, I do not understand how the doctrine of deference to rational constitutional interpretation by Congress espoused by the majority in Katzenbach v. Morgan, is consistent with this statement of Chief Justice Marshall or with our reaffirmation of it in Cooper v. Aaron, 358 U. S. 1, 18 (1958) (chap. 1 above): "[Marbury] declared the basic principle that the federal judiciary is supreme in the exposition of the law of the Constitution, and that principle has ever since been respected by this Court and the Country as a permanent and indispensable feature of our constitutional system." [Footnote by Justice Harlan.]

number of persons between the ages of 18 and 21, the extent of their education, and so forth. [But the] disagreement in these cases revolves around the evaluation [of] largely uncontested factual material. On the assumption that maturity and experience are relevant to intelligent and responsible exercise of the elective franchise, are the immaturity and inexperience of the average 18-, 19-, or 20-year-old sufficiently serious to justify denying such a person a direct voice in decisions affecting his or her life? Whether or not this judgment is characterized as "factual," it calls for striking a balance between incommensurate interests. Where the balance is to be struck depends ultimately on the values and the perspective of the decisionmaker. It is a matter as to which men of good will can and do reasonably differ.

I fully agree that judgments of the sort involved here are beyond the institutional competence and constitutional authority of the judiciary. They are pre-eminently matters for legislative discretion, with judicial review, if it exists at all, narrowly limited. But the same reasons which in my view would require the judiciary to sustain a reasonable state resolution of the issue also require Congress to abstain from entering the picture.

Judicial deference is based, not on relative factfinding competence, but on due regard for the decision of the body constitutionally appointed to decide. Establishment of voting qualifications is a matter for state legislatures. Assuming any authority at all, only when the Court can say with some confidence that the legislature has demonstrably erred in adjusting the competing interests is it justified in striking down the legislative judgment. . . .

The same considerations apply, and with almost equal force, to Congress' displacement of state decisions with its own ideas of wise policy. The sole distinction between Congress and the Court in this regard is that Congress, being an elective body, presumptively has popular authority for the value judgment it makes. But since the state legislature has a like authority, this distinction between Congress and the judiciary falls short of justifying a congressional veto on the state judgment. The perspectives and values of national legislators on the issue of voting qualifications are likely to differ from those of state legislators, but I see no reason a priori to prefer those of the national figures, whose collective decision, applying nationwide, is necessarily less able to take account of peculiar local conditions. Whether one agrees with this judgment or not, it is the one expressed by the Framers in leaving voter qualifications to the States. The Supremacy Clause does not, as my colleagues seem to argue, represent a judgment that federal decisions are superior to those of the States whenever the two may differ. . . .

It seems to me that the notion of deference to congressional interpretation of the Constitution, which the Court promulgated in Morgan, is directly related to this higher standard of constitutionality which the Court intimated in Harper v. Virginia Board of Elections and brought to fruition in Kramer [chap. 10, sec. 4A]. When the scope of federal review of state determinations became so broad as to be judicially unmanageable, it was natural for the Court to seek assistance from the national legislature. If the federal role were restricted to its traditional and appropriate scope, review for the sort of "plain error" which is variously described as "arbitrary and capricious," "irrational," or "invidious," there would be no call for the Court to defer to a congressional judgment on this score that it did not find convincing. Whether a state

judgment has so exceeded the bounds of reason as to authorize federal intervention is not a matter as to which the political process is intrinsically likely to produce a sounder or more acceptable result. It is a matter of the delicate adjustment of the federal system. In this area, to rely on Congress would make that body a judge in its own cause. The role of final arbiter belongs to this Court.

III. Since I cannot agree that the Fourteenth Amendment empowered Congress, or the federal judiciary, to control voter qualifications, I turn to other asserted sources of congressional power. My Brother Black would find that such power exists with respect to *federal* elections . . . . Surely nothing in [Art. I, §§ 2 and 4, and the XVII Amendment] lends itself to the view that voting qualifications in federal elections are to be set by Congress. . . . Even the power to control the "Manner" of holding elections, given with respect to congressional elections by Article I, § 4, is absent with respect to the selection of presidential electors. . . . Any shadow of a justification for congressional power with respect to congressional elections therefore disappears utterly in presidential elections.

IV. With these major contentions resolved, it is convenient to consider the three sections of the Act individually to determine whether they can be supported by any other basis of congressional power.

A. Voting Age. The only constitutional basis advanced in support of the lowering of the voting age is the power to enforce the Equal Protection Clause . . . . For the reasons already given, it cannot be said that the statutory provision is valid as declaratory of the meaning of that clause. Its validity therefore must rest on congressional power to lower the voting age as a means of preventing invidious discrimination that is within the purview of that clause. . . . I think it fair to say that the suggestion that members of the age group between 18 and 21 are threatened with unconstitutional discrimination, or that any hypothetical discrimination is likely to be affected by lowering the voting age, is little short of fanciful. I see no justification for stretching to find any such possibility when all the evidence indicates that Congress—led on by recent decisions of this Court— thought simply that 18-year-olds were fairly entitled to the vote and that Congress could give it to them by legislation. . . .

B. Residency. For reasons already stated, neither the power to regulate voting qualifications in presidential elections, asserted by my Brother Black, nor the power to declare the meaning of § 1 of the Fourteenth Amendment, relied on by my Brother Douglas, can support § 202 of the Act. . . . With no specific clause of the Constitution empowering Congress to enact § 202, I fail to see how that nebulous judicial construct, the right to travel, can do so.

C. Literacy. . . . Although the issue is not free from difficulty, I am of the opinion that this provision can be sustained as a valid means of enforcing the *Fifteenth* Amendment. Despite the lack of evidence of specific instances of discriminatory application or effect, Congress could have determined that racial prejudice is prevalent throughout the Nation, and that literacy tests unduly lend themselves to discriminatory application, either conscious or unconscious. This danger of violation of § 1 of the

Fifteenth Amendment was sufficient to authorize the exercise of congressional power under § 2. . . . While a less sweeping approach in this delicate area might well have been appropriate, the choice which Congress made was within the range of the reasonable. . . .

CONGRESSIONAL POWER AND CONSTITUTIONAL RIGHTS AFTER MORGAN AND OREGON v. MITCHELL

What is the scope of congressional power to modify the content of constitutional rights via § 5 of the 14th Amendment after Oregon v. Mitchell? Recall the questions about the two alternative theories in Morgan, in the notes after the Morgan case. Do both of those theories retain vitality after Oregon v. Mitchell? To what extent does the congressional action considered in Oregon v. Mitchell rest on Justice Brennan's first theory in Morgan—congressional judgments about remedies that might in fact be appropriate to implement judicially-declared rights? To what extent do the various provisions of the 1970 Act rest on Justice Brennan's second theory—congressional determinations of the substantive content of constitutional rights? In Morgan, Justice Brennan was willing to support § 4(e) on the basis of a congressional determination that the English literacy requirement applied to Puerto Ricans was itself unconstitutional under equal protection standards governing voting. In Oregon v. Mitchell, does Justice Brennan support a congressional determination that denial of the vote to 18-year-olds is itself a denial of equal protection? Only if such a determination rested on "facts"? Even if such a determination rested on resolution of conflicting "values"? Are equal protection determinations ever wholly "factual" ones, or do they always involve some resolution of value choices? May Congress make such determinations, or are they primarily or exclusively for the courts?

If Congress is permitted to make determinations that state practices are "unconstitutional," should the Court accord them the kind of deference associated with McCulloch v. Maryland? The even greater deference suggested by the "perceive a basis" test in Morgan? Can Court deference to congressional decisions of "constitutionality" be squared with Marbury v. Madison and Cooper v. Aaron? What limits on congressional authority (and judicial deference) can be articulated? Is congressional modification of constitutional rights permissible only in special circumstances—circumstances taking proper account of congressional competence and judicial authority? Is it permissible only if it rests primarily on determinations of facts? Only if it is ultimately in accord with judicial value preferences? Only if it resolves problems of federalism rather than individual rights? Consider the suggestions of such justifications for, and limits upon, congressional authority by several commentators on the recent decisions, in note 2 below. Compare Justice Brennan's suggestions, in the next note.

1. *Limits on (and justifications for) congressional power to "interpret" constitutional rights: Justice Brennan's footnotes.* a. Can the Court recognize a congressional power to reinterpret constitutional provisions, as the second theory in Morgan seems to do, without deferring to congressional judgments contracting or diluting as well as expanding rights? Justice Brennan's footnote [1] in Morgan tried to safeguard against that possibility:

Justice Brennan insisted that the dissent was wrong in suggesting that the Court's broad view of § 5 granted Congress power to exercise discretion "in the other direction" and "in effect to dilute equal protection and due process decisions of this Court." Section 5, he insisted, "grants Congress no power to restrict, abrogate, or dilute these guarantees." Thus, if Congress were to try to authorize the states to establish racial segregation in schools, justification could not be found in § 5 in the power "to enforce" equal protection "since that clause of its own force prohibits such state laws." Is that footnote a justifiable and substantial barrier to "restrictive" invocations of the Morgan power? Can that footnote be squared with Justice Brennan's rationale in the Morgan text, deferring to congressional resolution of "the various conflicting considerations" if the Court can "perceive a basis upon which the Congress might resolve the conflict as it did"? What does equal protection prohibit "by its own force"? What does that mean: that the Court has ruled, and that no different evaluation of competing considerations is possible? Is that true of most due process and equal protection interpretations?

    In Oregon v. Mitchell, the opinion joined by Justice Brennan contained another footnote [1], once again trying to safeguard against uses of the § 5 power to contract constitutional rights. The new footnote purported to reiterate the Morgan footnote's limit on congressional power. Did it in fact restate it? The Oregon v. Mitchell footnote emphasized fact-finding capacity in Congress as the critical element in § 5 power. Was that a retreat from deference to Congress in resolving value conflicts? The new footnote stated that "a decision of this Court striking down a state statute expresses, among other things, our conclusion that the legislative findings upon which the statute is based are so wrong as to be unreasonable. Unless Congress were to unearth new evidence in its investigation, its identical findings on the identical issue would be no more reasonable than those of the state legislature." In the text, Justice Brennan emphasized Congress' superior capacity to "determine whether the factual basis necessary to support a state legislative discrimination actually exists."

    Are fact-findings in fact critical in typical equal protection controversies? Note the criticism of Justice Brennan's "modified ratchet theory" in Cohen, "Congressional Power to Interpret Due Process and Equal Protection," 27 Stan.L.Rev. 603: "This new rationale for the ratchet theory is as unpersuasive as the first [in the Morgan footnote]. If Congress is a more appropriate forum than the courts for determining issues of legislative fact, it is hard to understand why a congressional determination that there exists a sufficient 'factual' basis to [justify] discrimination by the state should, in the absence of new evidence, be entitled to no weight at all." Moreover, Cohen notes that the new footnote in fact recognizes "that the ratchet may be released—that in some cases Congress can turn back the clock on equal protection and due process on the basis of new evidence."

    b. Even if Justice Brennan's distinction between "dilution" and "expansion" in the Morgan footnote is persuasive, how is it to be applied? Recall the Court's disposition, in the last part of the Morgan opinion, of the claim that § 4(e) of the 1965 Act unfairly discriminated against those literate in foreign languages who were not covered by § 4(e). Justice

Brennan's scrutiny of that claim was very deferential, supposedly because § 4(e) was "a reform measure" rather than a restriction on existing rights. Is that "reform" rationale, permitting a legislature to "take one step at a time," persuasive? Compare MacDonald v. Board of Elections with O'Brien v. Skinner, noted in chap. 10, sec. 4, above.[1]

c. Can Congress use the Morgan rationale to readjust the balance when constitutional claims compete? Are such readjustments "expansions" or "dilutions" of constitutional guarantees? For example, may Congress redefine the boundaries between the rights of the free press and the accused? Consider the reliance on the Morgan rationale in an opinion in Welsh v. United States, 398 U.S. 333 (1970) (chap. 14 below). In the Welsh case, Justice White, joined by Chief Justice Burger and Justice Stewart, thought the "religious training and belief" limitation on the conscientious objector exemption in the /draft law constitutional on the ground that the Court, by analogy to Morgan, "should respect congressional judgment accommodating the Free Exercise Clause and the power to raise armies."[2]

d. Would the Morgan rationale justify the anti-busing legislative proposals that followed in the wake of the 1971 Swann decisions, chap. 10 above? Recall that President Nixon based his 1972 proposals to limit busing in the desegregation of schools on the ground that the proposed legislation "deals with a remedy and not a right." Is the remedial-interpretation distinction of South Carolina v. Katzenbach and the Morgan case adequate to support anti-busing laws? If busing is not viewed as a mere remedy, is congressional action nevertheless supportable on the basis of the second part of the Morgan rationale? Note that the Equal Educational Opportunities Act of 1974 includes a provision prohibiting any court to require "the transportation of any student to a school other than the school closest or next closest to his place of residence which provides an appropriate grade level and type of education for such student." Yet the Court in the Swann case, 402 U.S. 1 (1971), chap. 10 above, suggested that busing at a greater distance is justifiable as a remedy for de jure segregation. And in a companion case, North Carolina Board of Education v. Swann, 402 U.S. 43 (1971), the Court struck down a state law prohibiting assignment of students by race: the state prohibition impeded "the operation of a unified school system" and hindered "vindication of federal constitutional guarantees." Is a congressionally established barrier to dismantling de jure

1. Note the criticism of the Morgan "ratchet theory" in the Cohen article cited above: He finds two problems—"it does not satisfactorily explain why Congress may move the due process and equal protection handle in only one direction"; and there is "difficulty in determining the direction in which the handle is turning."

2. Note also another unusual reliance on the Morgan rationale by Justice White, in Trafficante v. Metropolitan Life Ins. Co., 409 U.S. 205 (1972). In a concurring opinion joined by Justices Blackmun and Powell, he cited Morgan as well as Oregon v. Mitchell in explaining his agreement with the Court's "generous construction" of the standing provisions regarding housing discrimination complaints under the Civil Rights Act of 1968. Absent the statute, he explained, he would have had serious constitutional doubts because of the Art. III case or controversy requirement, chap. 15 below. But he concluded—invoking the Morgan analogy—that the statute was adequate to overcome those doubts.

For additional Court comments on the Morgan rationale and its limits, see the passages in Shapiro v. Thompson and Graham v. Richardson, chap. 10 above.

school systems entitled to greater deference than the North Carolina law, either as an exercise of congressional authority to readjust "remedies" for the violation of constitutional rights or as an exercise of congressional authority to "weigh competing considerations" in determining the content of constitutional rights?

What other congressional legislation might find support in Morgan? The civil rights violence provisions of the 1968 Act (sec. 3 above)? Applying to private conduct all restrictions governing "state action" under § 1 of the 14th Amendment? Prohibitions of de facto segregation in public education? Modifications of the Court's criminal procedure due process decisions (chap. 8 above)? Varying the "one person"-"one vote" theme of the Court's reapportionment decisions (chap. 15 below)? Readjusting the competing constitutional interests in the Court's interpretations of the Constitution's religion provisions—e. g., the decision banning Bible reading in schools, the Schempp case (chap. 14 below)? The 1975 proposals to broaden the scope of federal voting rights laws (p. 1007 above)? (See also the additional examples noted below.)

2. *Limits on (and justifications for) congressional power to "interpret" constitutional rights: Some alternative views.* Most commentators on Morgan and Oregon v. Mitchell have found Justice Brennan's footnotes unpersuasive efforts to articulate limits on congressional power under § 5 of the 14th Amendment. In addition to William Cohen's comments noted earlier, see, e. g., Cox, "Foreword: Constitutional Adjudication and the Promotion of Human Rights," 80 Harv.L.Rev. 91 (1966): "It is hard to see how the Court can persistently give weight to the congressional judgment in expanding the definition of equal protection in the area of human rights and refuse to give it weight in narrowing the definition where the definition depends upon appraisal of facts. The footnote, therefore, may not be the end of the argument." See also Burt, "Miranda and Title II: A Morganatic Marriage," 1969 Sup.Ct.Rev. 81, suggesting that "the Court was wrong to erect its apparently rigid footnote [1] limitation on § 5 legislation." But those commentators have also tried their hands at justifying some congressional authority to determine the content of constitutional rights, and at suggesting limits other than those in Justice Brennan's footnotes. Consider the alternative justifications and limits they suggest: Are they more persuasive? Are they adequate?

a. *"Line-drawing" capacities and congressional power "around the edges" of Court doctrine—consistent with judicial "value preferences."* Professor Burt, in "Miranda and Title II: A Morganatic Marriage," 1969 Sup.Ct.Rev. 81, after recognizing that the Morgan rationale "to some extent" exempts the 14th Amendment from "the principle of Court-Congress relationships expressed by Marbury v. Madison" (as noted in the comments after Morgan, above), endorses some congressional autonomy in situations where principled lines to accommodate competing interests are difficult to draw. He notes that "Congress is less burdened by the principled constraints under which courts labor," and suggests that Congress may impose restrictions on states "where the Court does not feel able to do so itself" because of line-drawing difficulties—so long as Congress does not simply impose its own value preferences on the states, "but rather that Congress

'enforces' the Court's value preferences." Thus, he supports a congressional "revisory authority" that "would be 'around the edges' of the Court's proclaimed doctrine"—i. e., a congressional power to redefine doctrine, but not too much: "As in Morgan, the Court would independently characterize the measure as a 'reform' that it approved or a 'restriction' that it did not." [1]

Burt suggests as an example of potential congressional authority the difficulties of delineating the reach of the 14th Amendment to private discrimination: The Court "could not independently proscribe some private discrimination without its proclaimed principle extending to proscribe all discrimination." That would unduly sacrifice competing values such as privacy. Congress, by contrast, could "arbitrarily" exempt some private choice, as it did in the Fair Housing Act of 1968. Thus, he endorses a congressional role where "the legislative mechanism is greatly superior to the Court's."

Is that an appropriate rationale to justify congressional power to apply 14th Amendment guarantees to private actors in situations where the Court would not find state action (see the problems considered in connection with the Guest case in sec. 3 above)? Has the Court in fact been hampered in extending the 14th Amendment reach to seemingly private behavior by the difficulties in line-drawing? Would Burt's criterion significantly limit congressional opportunity to resolve conflicts among competing interests in constitutional interpretation? How would the Court determine whether the congressional resolution was in accord with its "value preferences"? Would that approach authorize Congress to "reinterpret" due process by curtailing the situations in which abortions are permissible after Roe v. Wade? Would it permit Congress to "interpret" due process to ban all state legislation regulating consensual sexual conduct? Would it authorize federal legislation to define the scope of a newsman's privilege in state courts, after the Court's rejection of such a privilege under the First Amendment in Branzburg v. Hayes, 408 U.S. 665 (1972), chap. 13 below? [2]

b. *Fact-finding capacities and the Morgan power.* Rather than endorsing a congressional power to resolve contests among competing interests, so long as they are in accord with the Court's "value preferences," would it be preferable to emphasize congressional power to elaborate constitutional guarantees in terms of its superior fact-finding capacity? The latter emphasis is increasingly prominent in Archibald Cox's comments on the § 5 power. In commenting on the second part of the Morgan rationale in 1966, he drew from it "the generalization that Congress, in the field of state activities except as confined by the Bill of Rights, has the power to enact any

---

1. Note however that Burt recognizes the "substantial risk for the Court" in such a view of Morgan: Though the Court "retains ample doctrinal handles to disapprove congressional action, nonetheless its presentational rhetoric —that Congress has, to whatever degree, an 'independent' role in interpreting the Constitution—is likely to remove an important restraint on Congress which has, in the past, counseled great wariness in trespassing on the Court's prerogatives."

2. In Branzburg, Justice White's majority opinion commented that Congress had freedom at the federal level "to determine whether a statutory newsman's privilege is necessary and desirable and to fashion standards and rules as narrow or broad as deemed necessary [and] to refashion those rules as experience from time to time may dictate." See generally Dixon, "Newsmen's Privilege by Federal Legislation: Within Congressional Power?" 1 Hastings L.Q. 39 (1974).

law which may be viewed as a measure for correction of any condition which Congress might believe involves a denial of equality or other Fourteenth Amendment rights." Cox, "Foreword: Constitutional Adjudication and the Promotion of Human Rights," 80 Harv.L.Rev. 91 (1966). In 1971, in "The Role of Congress in Constitutional Determinations," 40 U.Cinn. L.Rev. 199, Cox argued that "the Morgan decision follows logically from the basic principles determining the respective functions of the legislative and judicial branches outside the field of preferred constitutional rights. Whether a state law denies equal protection depends to a large extent upon the finding and appraisal of the practical importance of relevant facts." He emphasized the "presumption that facts exist which sustain federal legislation" and the "principle of deference to congressional judgment upon questions of proportion and degree, as illustrated by the Due Process and Commerce Clause cases."

Are the actual and potential uses of the Morgan rationale in fact limited to determinations resting on factual grounds? Or may they involve congressional value choices as well? Even if they rest solely on factual bases, why should there be greater deference to congressional rather than to state legislative judgments? And if there should be greater deference to congressional assessments, should the Court hypothesize facts that might justify congressional resolutions, or should it insist on a factual record in Congress? Was there such a factual record for § 4(e) in the Morgan case? Was there for the provisions involved in Oregon v. Mitchell? Are congressional findings such as those introducing the provisions in the 1970 Act considered in Oregon v. Mitchell adequate? Should judicial deference, in short, turn on the degree to which the congressional findings truly involve issues of fact, and on the degree to which those factual issues are spelled out in the legislative record?

What legislation under § 5 would be permissible if the special competence of—or deference to—congressional fact determinations is emphasized? Would it justify "a comprehensive code of criminal procedure applicable to prosecutions in state courts," as Cox suggested in 80 Harv.L.Rev. 91: "Congress would seem to have the power, under the second branch of the Morgan decision, not only to enforce the specifics but also to make its own findings of fact and evaluation of the competing considerations in determining what constitutes due process and what measures are necessary to secure it in practice." Recall Chief Justice Burger's suggestions for congressional elimination of the exclusionary rule for Fourth Amendment violations (and for legislative provision of an alternative remedy) in Bivens v. Six Unknown Named Agents, 403 U.S. 388 (1971) (chap. 8 above).[3]

c. *A distinction between "federalism" and "liberty" issues?* Professor William Cohen's search for limits on congressional power under § 5 of the 14th Amendment looks in a different direction. In "Congressional Power to Interpret Due Process and Equal Protection," 27 Stan.L.Rev. 603

---

3. See also Title II of the Omnibus Crime Control Act of 1968, including a partial overturning of the Court's requirements of safeguards in the questioning of suspects, established in Miranda v. Arizona, 384 U.S. 436 (1966). The Burt article noted above sees the statute supportable under Morgan because the differences between Miranda and Title II "are limited in scope, and do not entrench upon the basic purposes which the Court was pursuing."

(1975), he finds Justice Brennan's efforts to articulate limits in Morgan and Oregon v. Mitchell unpersuasive: under the Brennan approach, "the Congress does have an ill-defined power to dilute judicially declared protections of section 1 of the 14th Amendment." But Cohen adds: "A viable theory concerning the limits of Congress' enforcement power under section 5 of the 14th Amendment—one that realistically assesses the different strengths of Congress and the courts—can be formulated. . . . The theory turns partly on considerations of federalism, distinguishing the relative capacity of Congress to draw the lines between national and state power from the courts' sensitivity to the rights of racial, religious, and political minorities." In short, he "distinguishes between congressional competence to make 'liberty' and 'federalism' judgments." Drawing on Herbert Wechsler's emphasis on the "political safeguards of federalism" (recall chap. 2 above), he argues that "a congressional judgment resolving at the national level an issue that could—without constitutional objection—be decided in the same way at the state level, ought normally to be binding on the courts, since Congress presumably reflects a balance between both national and state interests and hence is better able to adjust such conflicts." But a "congressional judgment rejecting a judicial interpretation of the due process or equal protection clauses—an interpretation that had given the individual procedural or substantive protection from state and federal government alike—is entitled to no more deference than the identical decision of the state legislature."

Is that approach persuasive? Is it different from Justice Brennan's "ratchet" theory?[4] Is the "political safeguards" factor the only one that explains judicial deference to congressional judgments when the exercise of Art. I powers allegedly impinges on federalism concerns? Or is there a special breadth to those powers—a breadth not necessarily applicable to congressional "interpretations" of 14th Amendment rights? And even under Art. I powers, does Congress have the power to determine what is interstate commerce, rather than merely deciding what is appropriate to regulate that commerce?

Is such legislation nevertheless barred by footnote [1] in Morgan?

Could modifications of the Fourth Amendment exclusionary rule, or of the Miranda requirements, be justified simply as congressional variation of remedies rather than redefinition of constitutional rights? Note that even the dissenters in Morgan—and the unanimous Court in Oregon v. Mitchell, with respect to the nationwide suspension of literacy tests—endorsed congressional remedial measures. See the questions raised about the remedy-interpretation distinction in Cohen, "Congressional Power to Interpret Due Process and Equal Protection," 27 Stan.L.Rev. 603 (1975).

4. William Cohen recognizes that the two theories will typically produce the same results: Congressional "extensions" of due process and equal protection would usually involve "federalism" decisions; congressional "dilutions" will ordinarily raise "liberty" decisions. But he insists that the outcomes under the two approaches would not always be the same.

Chapter 12

FREEDOM OF EXPRESSION: BASIC THEMES

Introduction. The history of Supreme Court litigation regarding First Amendment freedoms is short in years but heavy in volume. The Court's first major encounter with freedom of speech claims did not come until after World War I; yet in the little more than 50 years since, claimed infringements of freedoms of expression and association have become a staple of Supreme Court business—and a frequent source of controversy.

What are the ingredients and dimensions of the constitutionally protected values? What analyses are helpful, what techniques useful? An extensive and at times bewildering array of phrases, slogans and standards abounds in the cases. What is the meaning and scope of the "clear and present danger" test? What are the alternative judicial approaches and doctrinal tools? Is it meaningful to talk about "preferred positions" of certain freedoms? Of presumptions of unconstitutionality? How significant is the clash between judicial positions of "balancing" and of "absolute" guarantees?

The problems of freedom of expression are too varied and multifaceted to lend themselves to solution by any single, simple, all-embracing formula. Most cases involve more than one value of constitutional dimensions, and the resolution of value clashes cannot be a mechanical process. But, after a half century of First Amendment litigation, there is special justification for an effort to examine the complex and diffuse materials in an orderly manner. Aiding that effort is the purpose of the next two chapters.

Chap. 12 explores the most pervasive doctrines at the core of First Amendment analysis; chap. 13 tests and elaborates those core concepts in additional settings. To introduce the core ingredients, this chapter focuses on two recurrent contexts: the first is criminal legislation directed at the content of speech critical of national policies (sec. 1); the second is the local regulation of the manner of expression in public places (sec. 2). In these cases, restraints on expression are typically sought to be justified by the state's concern with the risks of crime, disorder and revolution. An initial understanding of the judicial techniques for interpreting the First Amendment can best be obtained in connection with these problems, as the text materials below will repeatedly note.

Sec. 3 of this chapter reviews the strengths and weaknesses of the basic analyses developed in the opening sections and illustrates their interaction in several modern "symbolic expression" cases. Chap. 16 continues the critical testing of the core doctrines and introduces a variety of elaborations by examining a series of special problems of free expression.

This grouping of the materials makes possible the exploration of the central ideas through a study of a limited number of materials, gathered in this chapter. More intensive investigation can then be pursued by selecting additional problems in chap. 13.

FIRST AMENDMENT FREEDOMS AND JUDICIAL RESPONSIBILITY—SOME RECURRENT THEMES: ARE FREE SPEECH VALUES SPECIAL? WHAT ARE THOSE VALUES?

The First Amendment bars "abridging the freedom of speech." The complexities inherent in those few words are best explored in the particularized contexts of the cases that follow. What is "the freedom of speech"? What action amounts to an "abridging" of that freedom? What competing governmental and individual interests warrant recognition in the delineation of the scope of that freedom? Questions such as these cannot be answered through an abstract, generalized discussion of text or history or philosophy or judicial attitudes. But two related problems recur so frequently in these materials that they warrant introductory attention here. First, what justifies special judicial solicitude toward the protection of freedom of expression? Second, assuming a special judicial role is warranted, what are the appropriate sources for the elaboration of free speech values?

The first question underlies the controversies over double standards, presumptive unconstitutionality, preferred positions, the "absoluteness" of the First Amendment and the legitimacy of "balancing" First Amendment interests against competing concerns. Are First Amendment values truly special, preferred ones? Is special judicial scrutiny warranted when those values are allegedly infringed? Is it useful to speak of the appropriate judicial stance in general terms? The second, related question speaks to the roots of the values governing the scope of protected expression: To what extent can and should the values of history and philosophy and society guide the judicial implementation of the First Amendment guarantee? These introductory materials are not adequate for full exploration of those problems; rather, they are designed to note recurrent themes in the materials that follow, to call attention to undercurrents often obscured in the Court opinions, and to signal themes to be borne in mind in the examination of the particularized contexts.

Is there a special judicial responsibility to safeguard First Amendment rights? In one sense, that first pervasive problem is an aspect of a larger one, the problem of "double standards" explored especially in chap. 9, on substantive due process: Is there a case for more careful judicial scrutiny of alleged infringements of personal, noneconomic liberties than of restrictions on economic and property rights? In the First Amendment setting, Court attention to that double standard issue has been more continuous and rigorous, judicial articulation of rationales has been less amorphous, than, for example, in the Lochner to Griswold to Roe v. Wade sequence in chap. 9; and the Court's efforts to justify its special solicitude for First Amendment interests help illuminate the nature and sources of the values the Court has undertaken to protect.

1. *Justifying the special protection of speech: The Carolene Products footnote.* One of the most influential statements of the modern Court's double standard—of its justifications for intervening in some areas while keeping "hands off" others—came in footnote 4 in Justice Stone's opinion in United States v. Carolene Products Co., 304 U.S. 144 (1938). Recall

the contents of that footnote, chap. 9, sec. 3, above: though that rationale extends beyond the First Amendment area, two of its three paragraphs suggest justifications for special scrutiny of restraints on freedom of expression. In his first paragraph, Justice Stone spoke of a "narrower scope for operation of the presumption of constitutionality when legislation appears on its face to be within a specific prohibition of the Constitution, such as those of the first ten amendments, which are deemed equally specific when held to be embraced within the Fourteenth." And in his second paragraph, he suggested, somewhat more tentatively, a "more exacting judicial scrutiny" of legislation restricting the "political processes"; and he listed "restraints upon the dissemination of information" among his examples under that head.

How persuasive are those rationales? And what are their implications? Are First Amendment rights truly more "specific" than constitutional guarantees that do not elicit special judicial solicitude from the modern Court— e. g., the contract clause and protections of "property"? Are they still "specific" when they are "incorporated" into the "liberty" of the 14th Amendment? Is the scope of First Amendment rights narrowed when primary reliance is placed on the "political processes" rationale: does that rationale suggest a greater protection for "political" than for "nonpolitical" speech —e. g., obscenity or "commercial speech" or "private" defamations? Is it helpful in analyses of First Amendment problems to think of a core area of "political" speech, with less protection for nonpolitical expressions at the penumbras? Note Alexander Meiklejohn's argument suggesting that "public" speech—speech on public issues, speech connected with "self-government"—must be wholly immune from regulation, while "private" speech is entitled to less complete protection. See Meiklejohn, Free Speech and Its Relation to Self-Government (1948). Compare the majority's statement in New York Times Co. v. Sullivan, 376 U.S. 254 (1964) (chap. 13, sec. 1, below), discussing the "central meaning of the First Amendment" and emphasizing the "broad consensus" that the Sedition Act of 1798 was unconstitutional "because of the restraint it imposed upon criticism of government and public officials."

2. *Justifying special protection for speech: The uses of history.* In Palko v. Connecticut (chap. 8), Justice Cardozo justified protection of speech as a "fundamental" liberty in part on the ground that "our history, political and legal," recognized "freedom of thought and speech" as "the indispensable condition of nearly every other form of freedom." Does history in fact support special protection of First Amendment rights? And what is the scope of "the freedom of speech" enshrined by the Framers of the Bill of Rights? When the Court has sought to justify special protection for criticism of government on historical grounds, the Justices have typically turned *not* to the thinking of the time the First Amendment was ratified in 1791, but rather to an episode a decade later—the Jeffersonian response to the Sedition Act of 1798. See, e. g., New York Times Co. v. Sullivan, note 1 above, and Justice Holmes' dissent in Abrams v. United States, sec. 1 below. But what of the intent of the Framers?

a. *The Framers' intent:* i. *Prior restraints.* The scope of "the freedom of speech" the adopters of the First Amendment intended to protect is a good deal more uncertain. What evils of pre-Constitution history was

the Amendment designed to avert? In the realm of political speech, the most prominent technique of restraint in English law had been the licensing of printers and the prosecutions for seditious libel. But prior restraint through licensing was abandoned in England a century before the adoption of the American Bill of Rights. Nevertheless, a barrier to licensing was at one time viewed as the major thrust of the First Amendment. See, e. g., Justice Holmes' opinion in Patterson v. Colorado, 205 U.S. 454 (1907), embracing the Blackstonian view that freedom of expression was protected solely against prior restraint. Compare his grudging recognition in Schenck, 12 years later, sec. 1 below, that "[i]t well may be that the prohibition of laws abridging the freedom of speech is not confined to previous restraints, although to prevent them may have been the main purpose, as intimated in Patterson v. Colorado."

ii. *Seditious libel.* Zechariah Chafee, Jr.'s influential work on free speech [see Free Speech in the United States (1941), a revision of Freedom of Speech (1920)] argued that the Framers of the First Amendment had more in mind than the banning of the long-gone censorship through licensing: he insisted that they "intended to wipe out the common law of sedition and make further prosecutions for criticism of the government, without any incitement to law-breaking, forever impossible in the United States of America." There had been frequent prosecutions in pre-Revolutionary England for seditious libel—"the intentional publication, without lawful excuse or justification, of written blame of any public man, or of the law, or of any institution established by law." Compare, however, Leonard Levy's careful historical study—Legacy of Suppression: Freedom of Speech and Press in Early American History (1960)—denying that the First Amendment was "intended to wipe out the common law of sedition." His "revisionist interpretation" claims that 18th century Americans "did not believe in a broad scope for freedom of expression, particularly in the realm of politics." [1] He concludes that "libertarian theory from the time of Milton to the ratification of the First Amendment substantially accepted the right of the state to suppress seditious libel," and he argues that a "broad libertarian theory of freedom of speech and press did not emerge in the United States" until the Jeffersonian battle against the Sedition Act of 1798.[2] Levy adds that "[n]o one can say for certain what the Framers had in mind . . . .. It is not even certain that the Framers themselves knew what they had in mind . . . .. The traditional libertarian interpretation of the original meaning of the First Amendment is surely subject to the Scottish verdict: not proven."

3. *Justifying special protection for—and identifying the content of— free speech: Values from philosophy.* The efforts to justify the primacy and delineate the contents of freedom of speech cannot rely on history alone. What values does the free speech guarantee reflect? What are the functions of free speech? Some assumptions about the answers to those questions typically enter into the resolution of the concrete problems raised by the

1. Note also that obscenity and blasphemy laws and civil actions for defamations were in existence during that period.

2. Levy adds that the Jeffersonians in power "were not much more tolerant of their political critics than the Federalists had been." For an effective elaboration of that thesis, see his Jefferson and Civil Liberties: The Darker Side (1963).

materials below—even though most of the Court opinions do not fully articulate those assumptions. Two themes are most prominent in the judicial and philosophical justifications for free speech: one emphasizes the function of freedom of speech in individual self-expression and development of individual potential; the other stresses the value of freedom of expression for a system of self-government and representative democracy. Another frequent argument for speech—relevant to both of these themes—is the utility of free expression in the search for "truth." Which function of speech plays the major role in the justifications sampled in this note? What is the consequence of one emphasis or another for the implementation of First Amendment values in the materials that follow? Consider, e. g., the implications of the varying emphases for a position that would extend greater protection to political than to nonpolitical speech.[3]

    a. *Articulating the values and functions of speech: Some judicial efforts.* Though efforts to state the special values and functions of speech are relatively rare in the Court's opinions, Justice Stone's Carolene Products footnote is by no means the only one. Some explanations have already surfaced in earlier materials. Recall, for example, Justice Cardozo on "freedom of thought and speech" in Palko v. Connecticut, chap. 8 above: "Of that freedom one may say that it is the matrix, the indispensable condition, of nearly every other form of freedom." Probably the most eloquent defense of free speech in the Reports is that by Justice Brandeis in his concurrence in Whitney v. California, 274 U.S. 357 (1927) (sec. 1 below). Note, for example, his passage explaining "why a State is, ordinarily, denied the power to prohibit dissemination of social, economic and political doctrine which a vast majority of its citizens believes to be false and fraught with evil consequence":

    "Those who won our independence believed that the final end of the State was to make men free to develop their faculties; and that in its government the deliberative forces should prevail over the arbitrary. They valued liberty both as an end and as a means. They believed liberty to be the secret of happiness and courage to be the secret of liberty. They believed that freedom to think as you will and to speak as you think are means indispensable to the discovery and spread of political truth; that without free speech and assembly discussion would be futile; that with them, discussion affords ordinarily adequate protection against the dissemination of noxious

---

3. For a modern effort to summarize the values and functions of freedom of expression, see Emerson, The System of Freedom of Expression (1970), 6: "First, freedom of expression is essential as a means of assuring individual self-fulfillment. . . . Second, freedom of expression is an essential process for advancing knowledge and discovering truth. . . . Third, freedom of expression is essential to provide for participation in decision making by all members of society. This is particularly significant for political decisions. . . . Finally, freedom of expression [is] an essential mechanism for maintaining the balance between stability and change." Compare the varying emphases on the several strands in the selections below from judges' and philosophers' efforts to articulate the values of speech. What are the operational consequences of the varying emphases?

    Emerson draws from his articulation a "fundamental distinction between belief, opinion, and communication of ideas on the one hand, and different forms of conduct on the other"—a distinction between specially protected "expression" and regulatable "action." Compare the competing distinctions that emerge in the opinions below.

doctrine; that the greatest menace to freedom is an inert people; that public discussion is a political duty; and that this should be a fundamental principle of the American government. They recognized the risks to which all human institutions are subject. But they knew that order cannot be secured merely through fear of punishment for its infraction; that it is hazardous to discourage thought, hope and imagination; that fear breeds repression; that repression breeds hate; that hate menaces stable government; that the path of safety lies in the opportunity to discuss freely supposed grievances and proposed remedies; and that the fitting remedy for evil counsels is good ones. Believing in the power of reason as applied through public discussion, they eschewed silence coerced by law—the argument of force in its worst form. Recognizing the occasional tyrannies of governing majorities, they amended the Constitution so that free speech and assembly should be guaranteed."

Ranking with Justice Brandeis' among the best known articulations of the values of speech is Justice Holmes' dissent in Abrams v. United States, 250 U.S. 616 (1919) (sec. 1 below): "[W]hen men have realized that time has upset many fighting faiths, they may come to believe even more than they believe the very foundations of their own conduct that the ultimate good desired is better reached by free trade in ideas—that the best test of truth is the power of the thought to get itself accepted in the competition of the market, and that truth is the only ground upon which their wishes safely can be carried out. That at any rate is the theory of our Constitution." [4] See also Judge Learned Hand in Masses Publishing Co. v. Patten, 244 Fed. 535 (S.D.N.Y.1917) (sec. 1 below), insisting that the "right to criticise either by temperate reasoning, or by immoderate and indecent invective [is] normally the privilege of the individual in countries dependent upon the free expression of opinion as the ultimate source of authority."

For more recent statements, see, e. g., Justice Jackson's opinion in the second Flag Salute Case, West Virginia State Bd. of Education v. Barnette, 319 U.S. 624 (1943) (chap. 14, sec. 2, below): "If there is any fixed star in our constitutional constellation, it is that no official, high or petty, can prescribe what shall be orthodox in politics, nationalism, religion, or other matters of opinion or force citizens to confess by word or act their faith therein." See also Justice Brennan's reference to "a profound national commitment to the principle that debate on public issues should be uninhibited, robust, and wide-open, and that it may well include vehement, caustic, and sometimes unpleasantly sharp attacks on government and public officials," in New York Times Co. v. Sullivan, 376 U.S. 254 (1964) (chap. 13 below).

b. *Articulating the values and functions of speech: Some philosophers' comments.* Though the Court opinions rarely refer to nonjudicial writings explicitly, some of the Justices' articulations obviously echo the themes of many philosophers and political theorists. The classic speech-protective

4. See also Holmes' dissent in Gitlow v. New York, 268 U.S. 652 (1925) (sec. 1 below), and his dissent in United States v. Schwimmer, 279 U.S. 644 (1929), defending the right of a pacifist to become a naturalized citizen: "[I]f there is any principle of the Consti- tution that more imperatively calls for attachment than any other it is the principle of free thought—not free thought for those who agree with us but freedom for the thought that we hate."

statements are those of John Milton and John Stuart Mill. John Milton said—in the course of a speech in Parliament in 1643 protesting a licensing scheme for books—: "And though all the winds of doctrine were let loose to play upon the earth, so Truth be in the field, we do injuriously, by licensing and prohibiting, to misdoubt her strength. Let her and Falsehood grapple; who ever knew Truth put to the worst, in a free and open encounter?" [5] (Compare Milton's battle metaphor with Holmes' references to the "free trade in ideas" and "the competition of the market," in the Abrams case.)

Compare John Stuart Mill's classic libertarian argument two centuries later, in On Liberty (1859). Mill's central argument was that the suppression of opinion is wrong, whether or not the opinion is true: if it is true, society is denied the truth; if it is false, society is denied the fuller understanding of truth which comes from its conflict with error; and when the received opinion is part truth and part error, society can know the whole truth only by allowing the airing of competing views. As he summarized his argument in chapter II of On Liberty: "First, if any opinion is compelled to silence, that opinion may, for aught we can certainly know, be true. To deny this is to assume our own infallibility. Secondly, though the silenced opinion be in error, it may, and very commonly does, contain a portion of the truth; and since the general or prevailing opinion on any subject is rarely or never the whole truth, it is only by the collision of adverse opinions that the remainder of the truth had any chance of being supplied. Thirdly, even if the received opinion be not only true, but the whole truth; unless it is suffered to be, and actually is, vigorously and earnestly contested, it will, by most of those who receive it, be held in the manner of a prejudice, with little comprehension or feeling of its rational grounds. And not only this, but, fourthly, the meaning of the doctrine itself will be in danger of being lost, or enfeebled . . . .''

What are the implications of Mill's classic defense of freedom of opinion? Does it bar all restraints on speech? Even incitement to violation of law—the problem pursued in sec. 1 below? Compare Mill's own elaboration a few pages later in On Liberty, in Chapter III: "No one pretends that actions should be as free as opinions. On the contrary, even opinions lose their immunity, when the circumstances in which they are expressed are such as to constitute their expression a positive instigation to some mischievous act. An opinion that corn-dealers are starvers of the poor, or that private property is robbery, ought to be unmolested when simply circulated through the press, but may justly incur punishment when delivered orally to an excited mob assembled before the house of a corn-dealer, or when handed about among the same mob in the form of a placard. Acts of whatever kind, which, without justifiable cause, do harm to others, may be, and in the more important cases absolutely require to be, controlled by the unfavorable sentiments, and, when needful, by the active interference of mankind. The liberty of the individual must be thus far limited; he must not make himself a nuisance to other people." Compare Learned Hand's "incitement" standard

---

5. Milton, Areopagitica—A Speech for the Liberty of Unlicensed Printing (1644).

in the Masses case, and Oliver Wendell Holmes' "clear and present danger" test in Schenck, sec. 1 below.

Assuming that freedom of expression is valuable to the individual and to society, what is the appropriate judicial responsibility in protecting it? The detailed doctrinal developments in a variety of particularized contexts are the subject of this chapter and the next. But is it also useful to speak more generally in terms of an appropriate judicial stance—e. g., of speech as a "preferred" freedom, or of a presumptive unconstitutionality of laws impinging on speech? Is it useful to speak generally about whether the First Amendment guarantee is an "absolute" one, or one that requires the "balancing" of competing interests? Those problems have produced recurrent disputes on the Court; introducing them is the purpose of the next two notes.

4. *The appropriate judicial stance: The "preferred position" talk and Justice Frankfurter's critique.* Is the "preferred position" debate a meaningful one? A helpful one? Consider Justice Frankfurter's well-known review of (and attack on) "preferred position" statements in Court opinions. Do the passages he quotes demonstrate that use of "preferred position" language is the equivalent of a presumption of unconstitutionality? What does it mean to say that a law is "presumptively unconstitutional"? Is such a "presumption" justifiable? Is Justice Frankfurter's rejection of "preferred position" the equivalent of Judge Hand's repudiation of any double standard? [6] Does Frankfurter suggest that First Amendment commands ought to be judicially unenforceable? Or does Justice Frankfurter, too, recognize a hierarchy of values, with free speech values near or at the apex? In short, does he, too, agree that First Amendment rights are specially protected ones? Justice Frankfurter said in a concurring opinion in KOVACS v. COOPER, 336 U.S. 77 (1949) (one of the Loudspeaker Cases, sec. 2 below):

". . . My brother Reed speaks of 'the preferred position of freedom of speech' . . . . This is a phrase that has uncritically crept into some recent opinions of this Court. I deem it a mischievous phrase, if it carries the thought, which it may subtly imply, that any law touching communication is infected with presumptive invalidity. . . . I say the phrase is mischievous because it radiates a constitutional doctrine without avowing it. Clarity and candor in these matters, so as to avoid gliding unwittingly into error, make it appropriate to trace the history of the phrase 'preferred position.' The following is a chronological account of the evolution of talk about 'preferred position' except where the thread of derivation is plain enough to be indicated. [Justice Frankfurter's review of the cases included the following:]

"United States v. Carolene Products Co., 304 U.S. 144, 152, n. 4. A footnote hardly seems to be an appropriate way of announcing a new constitutional doctrine, and the Carolene footnote did not purport to

---

6. For Judge Hand's rejection of a double standard between "personal rights" and "property," see his essay, "Chief Justice Stone's Concept of the Judicial Function," in The Spirit of Liberty (3d ed. Dilliard 1960). In his last years, Judge Hand went even beyond that deferential attitude: he viewed the Bill of Rights primarily as "admonitory or hortatory, not definite enough to be guides on concrete occasions." See Hand, The Bill of Rights (1958). Compare his opinion in the Masses case, sec. 1 below.

announce any new doctrine; incidentally, it did not have the concurrence of a majority of the Court.   . . .

"Thomas v. Collins, 323 U.S. 516, 530: 'For these reasons any attempt to restrict those liberties must be justified by clear public interest, threatened not doubtfully or remotely, but by clear and present danger. The rational connection between the remedy provided and the evil to be curbed, which in other contexts might support legislation against attack on due process grounds, will not suffice. These rights rest on firmer foundation. Accordingly, whatever occasion would restrain orderly discussion and persuasion, at appropriate time and place must have clear support in public danger, actual or impending. Only the gravest abuses, endangering paramount interests, give occasion for permissible limitation.' This is perhaps the strongest language dealing with the constitutional aspect of legislation touching utterance. But it was the opinion of only four members of the Court. [After reviewing the cases, the Justice added:]

"In short, the claim that any legislation is presumptively unconstitutional which touches the field of the First Amendment and the Fourteenth Amendment, insofar as the latter's concept of 'liberty' contains what is specifically protected by the First, has never commended itself to a majority of this Court.

"Behind the notion sought to be expressed by the formula as to 'the preferred position of freedom of speech' lies a relevant consideration in determining whether an enactment relating to the liberties protected by the Due Process Clause of the Fourteenth Amendment is violative of it. In law also, doctrine is illuminated by history. The ideas now governing the constitutional protection of freedom of speech derive essentially from the opinions of Mr. Justice Holmes.

"The philosophy of his opinions on that subject arose from a deep awareness of the extent to which sociological conclusions are conditioned by time and circumstance. Because of this awareness Mr. Justice Holmes seldom felt justified in opposing his own opinion to economic views which the legislature embodied in law. But since he also realized that the progress of civilization is to a considerable extent the displacement of error which once held sway as official truth by beliefs which in turn have yielded to other beliefs, for him the right to search for truth was of a different order than some transient economic dogma. And without freedom of expression, thought becomes checked and atrophied. Therefore, in considering what interests are so fundamental as to be enshrined in the Due Process Clause, those liberties of the individual which history has attested as the indispensable conditions of an open as against a closed society come to this Court with a momentum for respect lacking when appeal is made to liberties which derive merely from shifting economic arrangements. Accordingly, Mr. Justice Holmes was far more ready to find legislative invasion where free inquiry was involved than in the debatable area of economics. See my Mr. Justice Holmes and the Supreme Court, 58 et seq.

"The objection to summarizing this line of thought by the phrase 'the preferred position of freedom of speech' is that it expresses a complicated process of constitutional adjudication by a deceptive formula. And it was

Mr. Justice Holmes who admonished us that 'To rest upon a formula is a slumber that, prolonged, means death.' Collected Legal Papers, 306. Such a formula makes for mechanical jurisprudence. . . . ."

5. *The appropriate judicial stance: "Absolutes" or "balancing"?* A recurrent theme in modern First Amendment adjudication has been the debate as to whether First Amendment rights are "absolute," or whether First Amendment interpretation requires the "balancing" of competing interests. Justice Black was the most eloquent advocate of the former position; Justices Frankfurter, Harlan and Powell have been especially identified with the latter.[7] One of the classic confrontations between Justices Black and Harlan came in KONIGSBERG v. STATE BAR OF CALIFORNIA, 366 U.S. 36 (1961) (chap. 13, sec. 5, below). Justice Harlan's majority opinion sustained the State's denial of bar admission to an applicant who had refused to answer questions as to Communist Party membership. Justice Black dissented from that 5 to 4 decision. Justice HARLAN'S opinion included the following passage: "[W]e reject the view that freedom of speech and association as protected by the First and Fourteenth Amendments are 'absolutes,' not only in the undoubted sense that where the constitutional protection exists it must prevail, but also in the sense that the scope of that protection must be gathered solely from a literal reading of the First Amendment.[1] Throughout its history this Court has consistently recognized at least two ways in which constitutionally protected freedom of speech is narrower than an unlimited license to talk. On the one hand, certain forms of speech, or speech in certain contexts, has been considered

7. For elaboration of Justice Black's view of "absolutes" and "balancing"— in addition to his other opinions, below—see his lectures, "The Bill of Rights," 35 N.Y.U.L.Rev. 865 (1960), and A Constitutional Faith (1968). See also Cahn, "Justice Black and First Amendment 'Absolutes': A Public Interview," 37 N.Y.U.L.Rev. 549 (1962). For elaborations of the "balancing" analysis, in addition to the materials below, see, e. g., Gunther, "In Search of Judicial Quality on a Changing Court: The Case of Justice Powell," 24 Stan.L.Rev. 1001 (1972), including a discussion of "First Amendment balancing in the Harlan manner," and concluding: "In the finest manifestations of Justice Harlan's approach to First Amendment problems, then, he viewed balancing not as an escape from judicial responsibility, but as a mandate to perceive every free speech interest in a situation and to scrutinize every justification for a restriction of individual liberty. Moreover, after the closest possible analysis had isolated the crucial conflicts of values, Justice Harlan strove for unifying principles that might guide future decisions." Consider which, if any, "balancing" opinions below support that appraisal. See also note 6 below.

1. "That view, which of course cannot be reconciled with the law relating to libel, slander, misrepresentation, obscenity, perjury, false advertising, solicitation of crime, complicity by encouragement, conspiracy, and the like, is said to be compelled by the fact that the commands of the First Amendment are stated in unqualified terms: 'Congress shall make no law . . . abridging the freedom of speech, or of the press; or the right of the people peaceably to assemble . . . .' But as Mr. Justice Holmes once said: '[T]he provisions of the Constitution are not mathematical formulas having their essence in their form; they are organic living institutions transplanted from English soil. Their significance is vital not formal; it is to be gathered not simply by taking the words and a dictionary, but by considering their origin and the line of their growth.' . . . ." Gompers v. United States, 233 U.S. 604, 610. [Footnote by Justice Harlan.]

outside the scope of constitutional protection.[2]   See, e. g., Schenck v. United States, 249 U.S. 47; Chaplinsky v. New Hampshire, 315 U.S. 568; Dennis v. United States, 341 U.S. 494; Beauharnais v. Illinois, 343 U.S. 250; Yates v. United States, 354 U.S. 298; Roth v. United States, 354 U.S. 476.   On the other hand, general regulatory statutes, not intended to control the content of speech but incidentally limiting its unfettered exercise, have not been regarded as the type of law the First or Fourteenth Amendment forbade Congress or the States to pass, when they have been found justified by subordinating valid governmental interests, a prerequisite to constitutionality which has necessarily involved a weighing of the governmental interest involved.   See, e. g., Schneider v. State, 308 U.S. 147, 161; Cox v. New Hampshire, 312 U.S. 569; Prince v. Massachusetts, 321 U.S. 158; Kovacs v. Cooper, 336 U.S. 77; American Communications Assn. v. Douds, 339 U.S. 382; Breard v. Alexandria, 341 U.S. 622.   It is in the latter class of cases that this Court has always placed rules compelling disclosure of prior association as an incident of the informed exercise of a valid governmental function.   Bates v. Little Rock, 361 U.S. 516, 524.   Whenever, in such a context, these constitutional protections are asserted against the exercise of valid governmental powers a reconciliation must be effected, and that perforce requires an appropriate weighing of the respective interests involved. . . . ."

Justice BLACK'S dissent countered: "I do not subscribe to ['the doctrine that permits constitutionally protected rights to be "balanced" away when a majority of the Court thinks that a State might have interest sufficient to justify abridgment of those freedoms'] for I believe that the First Amendment's unequivocal command that there shall be no abridgment of the rights of free speech and assembly shows that the men who drafted our Bill of Rights did all the 'balancing' that was to be done . . . .

"I recognize [that] the 'clear and present danger test,' though itself a great advance toward individual liberty over some previous notions of the protections afforded by the First Amendment, does not go as far as my own views as to the protection that should be accorded these freedoms. I agree with Justices Holmes and Brandeis, however, that a primary purpose of the First Amendment was to insure that all ideas would be allowed to enter the 'competition of the market.'   But I fear that the creation of 'tests' by which speech is left unprotected under certain circumstances is a standing invitation to abridge it. . . .

"The Court suggests that a 'literal reading of the First Amendment' would be totally unreasonable because it would invalidate many widely ac-

---

2. "That the First Amendment immunity for speech, press and assembly has to be reconciled with valid but conflicting governmental interests was clear to Holmes, J. ('I do not doubt for a moment that by the same reasoning that would justify punishing persuasion to murder, the United States constitutionally may punish speech that produces or is intended to produce a clear and imminent danger that it will bring about forthwith certain substantive evils that the United States constitutionally may seek to prevent.' Abrams v. United States, 250 U.S. 616, 627); to Brandeis, J. ('But, although the rights of free speech and assembly are fundamental, they are not in their nature absolute.' Whitney v. California, 274 U.S. 357, 373); and to Hughes, C. J. ('[T]he protection [of free speech] even as to previous restraint is not absolutely unlimited.' Near v. Minnesota, 283 U.S. 697, 716.)" [Footnote by Justice Harlan.]

cepted laws. I do not know to what extent this is true. I do not believe, for example, that it would invalidate laws resting upon the premise that where speech is an integral part of unlawful conduct that is going on at the time, the speech can be used to illustrate, emphasize and establish the unlawful conduct.[1] On the other hand, it certainly would invalidate all laws that abridge the right of the people to discuss matters of religious or public interest, in the broadest meaning of those terms, for it is clear that a desire to protect this right was the primary purpose of the First Amendment. Some people have argued with much force, that the freedoms guaranteed by the First Amendment are limited to somewhat broad areas like those.[2] But I believe this Nation's security and tranquility can best be served by giving the First Amendment the same broad construction that all Bill of Rights guarantees deserve. . . .

"Whatever may be the wisdom [of] an approach that would reject exceptions to the plain language of the First Amendment based upon such things as 'libel,' 'obscenity'[3] or 'fighting words,'[4] such is not the issue in this case. [T]he only issue presently before us is whether speech that must be well within the protection of the Amendment should be given complete protection or whether it is entitled only to such protection as is consistent in the minds of a majority of this Court with whatever interest the Government may be asserting to justify its abridgment. The Court, by stating unequivocally that there are no 'absolutes' under the First Amendment, necessarily takes the position that even speech that is admittedly protected by the First Amendment is subject to the 'balancing test' and that therefore no kind of speech is to be protected if the Government can assert an interest of sufficient weight to induce this Court to uphold its abridgment. In my judgment, such a sweeping denial of the existence of any inalienable right to speak undermines the very foundation upon which the First Amendment, the Bill of Rights, and, indeed, our entire structure of government rest. . . .

"I cannot believe that this Court would adhere to the 'balancing test' to the limit of its logic. Since that 'test' denies that any speech, publication or petition has an 'absolute' right to protection under the First Amendment, strict adherence to it would necessarily mean that there would be only a conditional right, not a complete right, for any American to express his views to his neighbors—or for his neighbors to hear those views. In other words, not even a candidate for public office, high or low, would have an 'absolute' right to speak in behalf of his candidacy, no newspaper would have an 'absolute' right to print its opinion on public governmental affairs, and the American people would have no 'absolute' right to hear such discussions. All of these rights would be dependent upon the accuracy of the

1. "Roth v. United States, 354 U.S. 476, 514 (dissenting opinion). See also Labor Board v. Virginia Electric & Power Co., 314 U.S. 469; Giboney v. Empire Storage Co., 336 U.S. 490." [Footnote by Justice Black.]

2. "See, e. g., Meiklejohn, What Does the First Amendment Mean? 20 U. of Chi.L.Rev. 461, 464." [Footnote by Justice Black.]

3. "See, e. g., Roth v. United States, 354 U.S. 476." [Footnote by Justice Black.]

4. "See, e. g., Chaplinsky v. New Hampshire, 315 U.S. 568." [Footnote by Justice Black.]

scales upon which this Court weighs the respective interests of the Government and the people. It therefore seems to me that the Court's 'absolute' statement that there are no 'absolutes' under the First Amendment must be an exaggeration of its own views.

"These examples also serve to illustrate the difference between the sort of 'balancing' that the majority has been doing and the sort of 'balancing' that was intended when that concept was first accepted as a method for insuring the complete protection of First Amendment freedoms even against purely incidental or inadvertent consequences. The term came into use chiefly as a result of cases in which the power of municipalities to keep their streets open for normal traffic was attacked by groups wishing to use those streets for religious or political purposes.[5] When those cases came before this Court, we did not treat the issue posed by them as one primarily involving First Amendment rights. Recognizing instead that public streets are avenues of travel which must be kept open for that purpose, we upheld various city ordinances designed to prevent unnecessary noises and congestions that disrupt the normal and necessary flow of traffic. In doing so, however, we recognized that the enforcement of even these ordinances, which attempted no regulation at all of the content of speech and which were neither openly nor surreptitiously aimed at speech, could bring about an 'incidental' abridgment of speech. So we went on to point out that even ordinances directed at and regulating only conduct might be invalidated if, after 'weighing' the reasons for regulating the particular conduct, we found them insufficient to justify diminishing 'the exercise of rights so vital to the maintenance of democratic institutions' as those of the First Amendment.[6]

"But those cases never intimated that we would uphold as constitutional an ordinance which purported to rest upon the power of a city to regulate traffic but which was aimed at speech or attempted to regulate the content of speech. None of them held, nor could they constitutionally have held, that a person rightfully walking or riding along the streets and talking in a normal way could have his views controlled, licensed or penalized in any way by the city—for that would be a direct abridgment of speech itself. Those cases have only begun to take on that meaning by being relied upon, again and again as they are here, to justify the application of the 'balancing test' to governmental action that is aimed at speech and depends for its application upon the content of speech. . . ."

6. *A concluding note on the appropriate judicial stance, "attitudes," and analyses.* How useful are the debates about the appropriate judicial stance in First Amendment cases, when the debate is at the level of generality of these controversies about the "preferred position" talk and the "absolutes"-"balancing" issue? Consider, for example, Justice Frankfurter's criticism of the "preferred position" language, note 4 above. Justice Frankfurter's position on the First Amendment is often represented as one of extreme deference to legislative judgments and of emphatic disavowal

---

5. "Typical of such cases are those referred to by the majority in its opinion here: Schneider v. State, 308 U.S. 147; Cox v. New Hampshire, 312 U.S. 569; Prince v. Massachusetts, 321 U.S.

158; Kovacs v. Cooper, 336 U.S. 77." [Footnote by Justice Black.]

6. "Schneider v. State, 308 U.S. 147, 161." [Footnote by Justice Black.]

of double standards. Yet his Kovacs attack on "preferred position" recognized that freedom of expression is a liberty that comes to the Court "with a momentum for respect lacking when appeal is made to liberties which derive merely from shifting economic arrangements." What, then, is the fighting all about? All modern Justices have agreed that the First Amendment is "special" in some senses; the disputes have been over the implementations of that "specialness."

Similarly, there may be less to the general "absolutes"-"balancing" debate than meets the eye. See, e. g., Kalven, "Upon Rereading Mr. Justice Black on the First Amendment," 14 UCLA L.Rev. 428 (1967): The "absolutes"-"balancing" controversy "seems to me on the whole to have been an unfortunate, misleading, and unnecessary one." Justice Black, for example, did not support every freedom of expression claim, as the passage from Konigsberg and some of his opinions below illustrate. He urged protection for "direct" infringements of those aspects of expression he considered to be within "the freedom of speech." Justice Harlan's "balancing," on the other hand, was not necessarily deferential. In one of the flag burning cases, Street v. New York, sec. 3 below, for example, he wrote the majority opinion sustaining the First Amendment challenge while Justice Black dissented on the ground that the prosecution was not for "spoken words," but for speech "used as an integral part of conduct" in burning the flag in public. See also, e. g., Cohen v. California, sec. 2 below.

Are the "preferred position" and "absolutes"-"balancing" debates nevertheless important for what they say about judicial "attitudes"? That has been repeatedly suggested. See, for example, McKay, "The Preference for Freedom," 34 N.Y.U.L.Rev. 1182 (1959), urging that the notion of a "preferred position" for speech is a useful concept because it suggests an attitude, "a whole manner of approaching" free speech. Similarly as to "absolutes": Professor Charles L. Black, Jr., while conceding that Justice Black's "absolutes" position cannot be taken literally, has suggested: "Attitude is what is at stake between Mr. Justice Black and his adversaries." (See "Mr. Justice Black, the Supreme Court, and the Bill of Rights," in The Occasions of Justice (1963).)* Is it fruitful to engage in extended discussions of general "attitudes"? Though the "preferred position" and "balancing"-"absolutes" controversies surface repeatedly in the following materials, does evaluation of the competing positions not require examination of concrete conflicts and disparate judicial techniques? For example, if (as the McKay article above suggests) "preferred position" consists of "a variety of devices" to protect speech—including "the clear and present danger test" and

---

* Compare Mendelson, "The First Amendment and the Judicial Process: A Reply to Mr. Frantz," 17 Vand.L. Rev. 479 (1964): "Balancing seems to me the essence of the judicial process —the nexus between abstract law and concrete life . . . .. Surely the choice is simply this: shall the balancing be done 'intuitively' or rationally; covertly or out in the open?" That comment is part of an extended debate between Mendelson and Frantz on the "absolutes"-"balancing" con-troversy. See also Frantz, 71 Yale L.J. 1424 (1962), Mendelson, 50 Calif.L. Rev. 821 (1962), and Frantz, 51 Calif. L.Rev. 729 (1963). There is an extensive literature on the "balancing"-"absolutes" dispute. See, e. g., Bickel, The Least Dangerous Branch (1962); Emerson, "Toward a General Theory of the First Amendment," 72 Yale L.J. 877 (1963); and Shapiro, Freedom of Speech: The Supreme Court and Judicial Review (1966). See also the closing notes in this chapter.

"prohibitions against prior restraint and subsequent punishment"—is it not more important to examine those varied "devices" in detail, in the context of recurrent problems, than to debate moods and attitudes? A more particularistic exploration of these devices and problems is the aim of the two chapters that follow.

SECTION 1. REGULATION OF POLITICAL SPEECH BECAUSE OF ITS CONTENT:

THE PROBLEM OF SUBVERSIVE ADVOCACY

A. THE WORLD WAR I CASES: CLEAR AND PRESENT DANGER—ORIGINS, WEAKNESSES, ALTERNATIVES

Introduction. The Court's first significant encounter with the problem of articulating the scope of constitutionally protected speech came in a series of cases involving agitation against the war and the draft during World War I. The "clear and present danger" language stems from the first of these cases, Justice Holmes' opinion for the Court in Schenck v. United States.

"Clear and present danger" has been a prominent and controversial ingredient of First Amendment law. When is restriction on speech permissible? "Clear and present danger" has been hailed as an answer that avoids extremes yet draws the line on the libertarian side of the spectrum. At one extreme, it can be argued that restriction on speech, at least political speech, is *never* legitimate—that punishment must be limited to illegal action, even if the speech directly "incites" that action. Holmes rejected that "perfect immunity" for speech. But Holmes also, as one of the strongest defenders of "clear and present danger" emphasized, rejected a far more restrictive, far more widely supported, alternative: that "any tendency in speech to produce bad acts, no matter how remote, would suffice to validate a repressive statute." See Chafee, Book Review, 62 Harv.L.Rev. 891 (1949), Selected Essays 1938–62 (1963), 618. "Clear and present danger" purports to draw the line somewhere in-between, but with a strong leaning toward protection of speech.

But what is the meaning of "clear and present danger"? What are its uses, what its weaknesses? The test has been criticized as too simplistic. It has been charged with being insensitive to legitimate state interests for curtailing speech. It has been criticized from another direction as too flexible, as permitting too much incursion on speech, as a shield too likely to collapse under stress. It has been employed far outside its original context. It has had periods of disfavor as well as of popularity with Justices and commentators. See generally Strong, "Fifty Years of 'Clear and Present Danger': From Schenck to Brandenburg—and Beyond," 1969 Sup.Ct.Rev. 41. It is

less widely invoked today than it once was; yet it remains an important strain at the core of Court efforts to protect expression; and from it later doctrinal variations have grown.

Attention to the origins and meaning of clear and present danger is one of the justifications for beginning this chapter with an examination of the post-World War I cases. The Schenck case gave birth to the language; but Schenck was followed within a week by two other Holmes decisions, Frohwerk and Debs, which purported to follow Schenck, and those opinions are important to an understanding of the original Schenck criterion. Later in the same year came Holmes' dissent in Abrams. Did the Abrams dissent simply apply the Schenck standard, or did it give new meaning to clear and present danger? To pursue the critical examination of the Schenck-Abrams criterion, District Judge Learned Hand's opinion in the Masses case is printed: does Hand's analysis, dealing with the same World War I statute about two years before Schenck, suggest a useful alternative to that of Holmes? And doctrinal significance is not the only justification for beginning with these cases: their factual context—of agitation against war and the draft—is obviously of more than historical interest.*

SCHENCK v. UNITED STATES

249 U.S. 47, 39 S.Ct. 247, 63 L.Ed. 470 (1919).

Error to the District Court of the United States for the Eastern District of Pennsylvania.

Mr. Justice HOLMES delivered the opinion of the court.

This is an indictment in three counts. The first charges a conspiracy to violate the Espionage Act of June 15, 1917, c. 30, § 3, 40 Stat. 217, 219, by causing and attempting to cause insubordination, &c., in the military and naval forces of the United States, and to obstruct the recruiting and enlistment service of the United States, when the United States was at war with the German Empire, to-wit, that the defendants wilfully conspired to have printed and circulated to men who had been called and accepted for military service under the Act of May 18, 1917, a document set forth and alleged to be calculated to cause such insubordination and obstruction. The count alleges overt acts in pursuance of the conspiracy, ending in the dis-

---

* Most of the cases below arose under section 3 of Title I of the 1917 Espionage Act. (The Abrams case involved 1918 amendments to the law.) The 1917 Act created three new offenses: "[1] Whoever, when the United States is at war, shall wilfully make or convey false reports or false statements with intent to interfere with the operation or success of the military or naval forces of the United States or to promote the success of its enemies, [2] and whoever, when the United States is at war, shall wilfully cause or attempt to cause insubordination, disloyalty, mutiny, or refusal of duty, in the military or naval forces of the United States, [3] or shall wilfully obstruct the recruiting or enlistment service of the United States, to the injury of the service or of the United States, shall be punished by a fine of not more than $10,000 or imprisonment for not more than twenty years, or both."

tribution of the document set forth. The second count alleges a conspiracy to commit an offence against the United States, to-wit, to use the mails for the transmission of matter declared to be non-mailable by Title XII, § 2 of the Act of June 15, 1917, to-wit, the above mentioned document, with an averment of the same overt acts. The third count charges an unlawful use of the mails for the transmission of the same matter and otherwise as above. The defendants were found guilty on all the counts. They set up the First Amendment to the Constitution forbidding Congress to make any law abridging the freedom of speech, or of the press, and bringing the case here on that ground have argued some other points also   .   .   . .

The document in question upon its first printed side recited the first section of the Thirteenth Amendment, said that the idea embodied in it was violated by the Conscription Act and that a conscript is little better than a convict. In impassioned language it intimated that conscription was despotism in its worst form and a monstrous wrong against humanity in the interest of Wall Street's chosen few. It said "Do not submit to intimidation," but in form at least confined itself to peaceful measures such as a petition for the repeal of the act. The other and later printed side of the sheet was headed "Assert Your Rights." It stated reasons for alleging that any one violated the Constitution when he refused to recognize "your right to assert your opposition to the draft," and went on "If you do not assert and support your rights, you are helping to deny or disparage rights which it is the solemn duty of all citizens and residents of the United States to retain." It described the arguments on the other side as coming from cunning politicians and a mercenary capitalist press, and even silent consent to the conscription law as helping to support an infamous conspiracy. It denied the power to send our citizens away to foreign shores to shoot up the people of other lands, and added that words could not express the condemnation such cold-blooded ruthlessness deserves, &c., &c., winding up "You must do your share to maintain, support and uphold the rights of the people of this country." Of course the document would not have been sent unless it had been intended to have some effect, and we do not see what effect it could be expected to have upon persons subject to the draft except to influence them to obstruct the carrying of it out. The defendants do not deny that the jury might find against them on this point.

But it is said, suppose that that was the tendency of this circular, it is protected by the First Amendment to the Constitution. Two of the strongest expressions are said to be quoted respectively from well-known public men. It well may be that the prohibition of laws abridging the freedom of speech is not confined to previous restraints, although to prevent them may have been the main purpose, as intimated in Patterson v. Colorado, 205 U.S. 454, 462. We admit that in many places and in ordinary times the defendants in saying all that was said in the circular would have been within their constitutional rights. But the character of every act depends upon the circumstances in which it is done. Aikens v. Wisconsin, 195 U.S. 194, 205, 206. The most stringent protection of free speech would not protect a man in falsely shouting fire in a theatre and causing a panic. It does not even protect a man from an injunction against uttering words that may have all the effect of force. Gompers v. Bucks Stove & Range Co., 221 U.S. 418, 439.

The question in every case is whether the words used are used in such circumstances and are of such a nature as to create a clear and present danger that they will bring about the substantive evils that Congress has a right to prevent. It is a question of proximity and degree. When a nation is at war many things that might be said in time of peace are such a hindrance to its effort that their utterance will not be endured so long as men fight, and that no Court could regard them as protected by any constitutional right. It seems to be admitted that if an actual obstruction of the recruiting service were proved, liability for words that produced that effect might be enforced. The statute of 1917 in § 4 punishes conspiracies to obstruct as well as actual obstruction. If the act (speaking, or circulating a paper), its tendency and the intent with which it is done are the same, we perceive no ground for saying that success alone warrants making the act a crime. Goldman v. United States, 245 U.S. 474, 477. Indeed that case might be said to dispose of the present contention if the precedent covers all *media concludendi.* But as the right to free speech was not referred to specially, we have thought fit to add a few words. . . .

Judgments affirmed.

FROHWERK v. UNITED STATES

249 U.S. 204, 39 S.Ct. 249, 63 L.Ed. 561 (1919).

Error to the District Court of the United States for the Western District of Missouri.

Mr. Justice HOLMES delivered the opinion of the court.

This is an indictment in thirteen counts. The first alleges a conspiracy between the plaintiff in error and one Carl Gleeser, they then being engaged in the preparation and publication of a newspaper, the Missouri Staats Zeitung, to violate the Espionage Act of June 15, 1917 c. 30, § 3, 40 Stat. 217, 219. It alleges as overt acts the preparation and circulation of twelve articles, &c. in the said newspaper at different dates from July 6, 1917, to December 7 of the same year. The other counts allege attempts to cause disloyalty, mutiny and refusal of duty in the military and naval forces of the United States, by the same publications, each count being confined to the publication of a single date. Motion to dismiss and a demurrer on constitutional and other grounds, especially that of the First Amendment as to free speech, were overruled . . . .. Frohwerk was found guilty [and] was sentenced to a fine and to ten years imprisonment on each count, the imprisonment on the later counts to run concurrently with that on the first.

. . . With regard to [the constitutional] argument we think it necessary to add to what has been said in [Schenck] only that the First Amendment while prohibiting legislation against free speech as such cannot have been, and obviously was not, intended to give immunity for every possible use of language. . . . We venture to believe that neither Hamilton nor Madi-

son, nor any other competent person then or later, ever supposed that to make criminal the counselling of a murder within the jurisdiction of Congress would be an unconstitutional interference with free speech.

Whatever might be thought of the other counts on the evidence, if it were before us, we have decided in Schenck v. United States, that a person may be convicted of a conspiracy to obstruct recruiting by words of persuasion. [S]o far as the language of the articles goes there is not much to choose between expressions to be found in them and those before us in Schenck v. United States.

The first begins by declaring it a monumental and inexcusable mistake to send our soldiers to France, says that it comes no doubt from the great trusts, and later that it appears to be outright murder without serving anything practical; speaks of the unconquerable spirit and undiminished strength of the German nation, and characterizes its own discourse as words of warning to the American people. [A]fter deploring "the draft riots in Oklahoma and elsewhere" in language that might be taken to convey an innuendo of a different sort, it is said that the previous talk about legal remedies is all very well for those who are past the draft age and have no boys to be drafted . . . .. Who then, it is asked, will pronounce a verdict of guilty upon him if he stops reasoning and follows the first impulse of nature: self-preservation; and further, whether, while technically he is wrong in his resistance, he is not more sinned against than sinning; and yet again whether the guilt of those who voted the unnatural sacrifice is not greater than the wrong of those who now seek to escape by ill-advised resistance. . . . There is much more to the general effect that we are in the wrong and are giving false and hypocritical reasons for our course, but the foregoing is enough to indicate the kind of matter with which we have to deal.

It may be that all this might be said or written even in time of war in circumstances that would not make it a crime. We do not lose our right to condemn either measures or men because the Country is at war. It does not appear that there was any special effort to reach men who were subject to the draft; and if the evidence should show that the defendant was a poor man, turning out copy for Gleeser, his employer, at less than a day laborer's pay, for Gleeser to use or reject as he saw fit, in a newspaper of small circulation, there would be a natural inclination to test every question of law to be found in the record very thoroughly before upholding the very severe penalty imposed. But we must take the case on the record as it is, and on that record it is impossible to say that it might not have been found that the circulation of the paper was in quarters where a little breath would be enough to kindle a flame and that the fact was known and relied upon by those who sent the paper out. Small compensation would not exonerate the defendant if it were found that he expected the result, even if pay were his chief desire. When we consider that we do not know how strong the Government's evidence may have been we find ourselves unable to say that the articles could not furnish a basis for a conviction upon the first count at least. We pass therefore to the other points that are raised.

It is said that the first count is bad because it does not allege the means by which the conspiracy was to be carried out. But a conspiracy to obstruct

recruiting would be criminal even if no means were agreed upon specifically by which to accomplish the intent. It is enough if the parties agreed to set to work for that common purpose. That purpose could be accomplished or aided by persuasion as well as by false statements, and there was no need to allege that false reports were intended to be made or made. It is argued that there is no sufficient allegation of intent, but intent to accomplish an object cannot be alleged more clearly than by stating that parties conspired to accomplish it. . . .

Affirmed.

DEBS v. UNITED STATES

249 U.S. 211, 39 S.Ct. 252, 63 L.Ed. 566 (1919).

Error to the District Court of the United States for the Northern District of Ohio.

Mr. Justice HOLMES delivered the opinion of the court.

This is an indictment under the Espionage Act of June 15, 1917 . . . It has been cut down to two counts, originally the third and fourth. The former of these alleges that on or about June 16, 1918, at Canton, Ohio, the defendant caused and incited and attempted to cause and incite insubordination, disloyalty, mutiny and refusal of duty in the military and naval forces of the United States and with intent so to do delivered, to an assembly of people, a public speech, set forth. The fourth count alleges that he obstructed and attempted to obstruct the recruiting and enlistment service of the United States and to that end and with that intent delivered the same speech, again set forth. The defendant was found guilty and was sentenced to ten years' imprisonment on each of the two counts, the punishment to run concurrently on both.

The main theme of the speech was socialism, its growth, and a prophecy of its ultimate success. With that we have nothing to do, but if a part or the manifest intent of the more general utterances was to encourage those present to obstruct the recruiting service and if in passages such encouragement was directly given, the immunity of the general theme may not be enough to protect the speech. The speaker began by saying that he had just returned from a visit to the workhouse in the neighborhood where three of their most loyal comrades were paying the penalty for their devotion to the working class—these being Wagenknecht, Baker and Ruthenberg, who had been convicted of aiding and abetting another in failing to register for the draft. Ruthenberg v. United States, 245 U.S. 480. He said that he had to be prudent and might not be able to say all that he thought, thus intimating to his hearers that they might infer that he meant more, but he did say that those persons were paying the penalty for standing erect and for seeking to pave the way to better conditions for all mankind. Later he added further eulogies and said that he was proud of them. . . .

There followed personal experiences and illustrations of the growth of socialism, a glorification of minorities, and a prophecy of the success of the international socialist crusade, with the interjection that "you need to know that you are fit for something better than slavery and cannon fodder." The rest of the discourse had only the indirect though not necessarily ineffective bearing on the offences alleged that is to be found in the usual contrasts between capitalists and laboring men, sneers at the advice to cultivate war gardens, attribution to plutocrats of the high price of coal, &c. . . . The defendant addressed the jury himself, and while contending that his speech did not warrant the charges said "I have been accused of obstructing the war. I admit it. Gentlemen, I abhor war. I would oppose the war if I stood alone." The statement was not necessary to warrant the jury in finding that one purpose of the speech, whether incidental or not does not matter, was to oppose not only war in general but this war, and that the opposition was so expressed that its natural and intended effect would be to obstruct recruiting. If that was intended and if, in all the circumstances, that would be its probable effect, it would not be protected by reason of its being part of a general program and expressions of a general and conscientious belief.

[The chief defense is] that based upon the First Amendment to the Constitution, disposed of in Schenck v. United States. . . .

There was introduced [in evidence] an "Anti-war Proclamation and Program" adopted at St. Louis in April, 1917, coupled with testimony that about an hour before his speech the defendant had stated that he approved of that platform in spirit and in substance. [Counsel] argued against its admissibility, at some length. This document contained the usual suggestion that capitalism was the cause of the war and that our entrance into it "was instigated by the predatory capitalists in the United States." . . . Its first recommendation was, "continuous, active, and public opposition to the war, through demonstrations, mass petitions, and all other means within our power." Evidence that the defendant accepted this view and this declaration of his duties at the time that he made his speech is evidence that if in that speech he used words tending to obstruct the recruiting service he meant that they should have that effect. The principle is too well established and too manifestly good sense to need citation of the books. We should add that the jury were most carefully instructed that they could not find the defendant guilty for advocacy of any of his opinions unless the words used had as their natural tendency and reasonably probable effect to obstruct the recruiting service, &c., and unless the defendant had the specific intent to do so in his mind.

Without going into further particulars we are of opinion that the verdict on the fourth count, for obstructing and attempting to obstruct the recruiting service of the United States, must be sustained. Therefore it is less important to consider whether that upon the third count, for causing and attempting to cause insubordination, &c., in the military and naval forces, is equally impregnable. The jury were instructed that for the purposes of the statute the persons designated by the Act of May 18, 1917, registered and enrolled under it, and thus subject to be called into the active service, were a part of the military forces of the United States. The Government presents a strong argument from the history of the statutes that the instruction was correct and in accordance with established legislative usage. We see no sufficient reason

for differing from the conclusion but think it unnecessary to discuss the question in detail.

Affirmed.

THE ABRAMS CASE AND THE BEGINNING OF THE CLEAR AND PRESENT DANGER DISSENTS

1. *The Abrams case.* In 1918, the Espionage Act was amended to add to the provisions relied on in the Schenck group of cases a new series of offenses, including urging any curtailment of production of materials necessary to the prosecution of the war against Germany with intent to hinder its prosecution. The convictions of the defendants in ABRAMS v. UNITED STATES, 250 U.S. 616 (1919), rested in part on that amendment; they were found guilty of unlawfully writing and publishing language "intended to incite, provoke and encourage resistance to the United States" during World War I, and of conspiring "to urge, incite and advocate curtailment of production of . . . ordnance and ammunition, necessary . . . to the prosecution of the war." The Court sustained the convictions: it rejected the constitutional attack summarily on the basis of Schenck and found the proof sufficient to sustain the charges.

Justice Clarke's majority opinion noted that it was part of the charge "that the defendants would attempt to accomplish their unlawful purpose by printing, writing and distributing in the City of New York many copies of a leaflet or circular, printed in the English language, and of another printed in the Yiddish language." He added: "All of the five defendants were born in Russia. They were intelligent, had considerable schooling, and at the time they were arrested they had lived in the United States terms varying from five to ten years, but none of them had applied for naturalization. Four of them testified as witnesses in their own behalf and of these, three frankly avowed that they were 'rebels,' 'revolutionists,' 'anarchists' . . . . It was admitted on the trial that the defendants had united to print and distribute the described circulars and that five thousand of them had been printed and distributed about the 22d day of August, 1918. . . . The circulars were distributed some by throwing them from a window of a building where one of the defendants was employed and others secretly, in New York City." The contents of the circulars are summarized in Justice Holmes' dissenting opinion, note 2 below; see also the additional excerpts from the majority opinion in note 3 below.

2. *The Holmes dissent in Abrams.* [The Abrams affirmance provoked one of the most famous Holmes dissents, joined by Brandeis. Justice Holmes stated:]

This indictment is founded wholly upon the publication of two leaflets which I shall describe in a moment. [There were four counts; the majority found sufficient evidence to justify conviction under the third and

fourth.] The third count alleges a conspiracy to encourage resistance to the United States in the [war with Germany] and to attempt to effectuate the purpose by publishing the [two] leaflets. The fourth count lays a conspiracy to incite curtailment of production of things necessary to the prosecution of the war and to attempt to accomplish it by publishing the second leaflet. . . .

The first of these leaflets says that the President's cowardly silence about the intervention in Russia reveals the hypocrisy of the plutocratic gang in Washington. It intimates that "German militarism combined with allied capitalism to crush the Russian revolution"—goes on that the tyrants of the world fight each other until they see a common enemy—working class enlightenment, when they combine to crush it; and that now militarism and capitalism combined, though not openly, to crush the Russian revolution. It says that there is only one enemy of the workers of the world and that is capitalism; that it is a crime for workers of America, &c., to fight the the workers' republic of Russia, and ends "Awake! Awake, you Workers of the World! Revolutionists." A note adds "It is absurd to call us pro-German. We hate and despise German militarism more than do you hypocritical tyrants. We have more reasons for denouncing German militarism than has the coward of the White House."

The other leaflet, headed "Workers—Wake Up," with abusive language says that America together with the Allies will march for Russia to help the Czecko-Slovaks in their struggle against the Bolsheviki, and that this time the hypocrites shall not fool the Russian emigrants and friends of Russia in America. It tells the Russian emigrants that they now must spit in the face of the false military propaganda by which their sympathy and help to the prosecution of the war have been called forth and says that with the money they have lent or are going to lend "they will make bullets not only for the Germans but also for the Workers Soviets of Russia," and further, "Workers in the ammunition factories, you are producing bullets, bayonets, cannon, to murder not only the Germans, but also your dearest, best, who are in Russia and are fighting for freedom." It then appeals to the same Russian emigrants at some length not to consent to the "inquisitionary expedition to Russia," and says that the destruction of the Russian revolution is "the politics of the march to Russia." The leaflet winds up by saying "Workers, our reply to this barbaric intervention has to be a general strike!," and after a few words on the spirit of revolution, exhortations not to be afraid, and some usual tall talk ends "Woe unto those who will be in the way of progress. Let solidarity live! The Rebels."

[With regard to the fourth count] it seems too plain to be denied that the suggestion to workers in the ammunition factories that they are producing bullets to murder their dearest, and the further advocacy of a general strike, both in the second leaflet, do urge curtailment of production of things necessary to the prosecution of the war within the meaning of the Act of May 16, 1918, amending § 3 of the earlier Act of 1917. But to make the conduct criminal that statute requires that it should be "with intent by such curtailment to cripple or hinder the United States in the prosecution of the war." It seems to me that no such intent is proved.

I am aware of course that the word intent as vaguely used in ordinary legal discussion means no more than knowledge at the time of the act that the consequences said to be intended will ensue. Even less than that will satisfy the general principle of civil and criminal liability. A man may have to pay damages, may be sent to prison, at common law might be hanged, if at the time of his act he knew facts from which common experience showed that the consequences would follow, whether he individually could foresee them or not. But, when words are used exactly, a deed is not done with intent to produce a consequence unless that consequence is the aim of the deed. It may be obvious, and obvious to the actor, that the consequence will follow, and he may be liable for it even if he regrets it, but he does not do the act with intent to produce it unless the aim to produce it is the proximate motive of the specific act, although there may be some deeper motive behind.

It seems to me that this statute must be taken to use its words in a strict and accurate sense. They would be absurd in any other. A patriot might think that we were wasting money on aeroplanes, or making more cannon of a certain kind than we needed, and might advocate curtailment with success, yet even if it turned out that the curtailment hindered and was thought by other minds to have been obviously likely to hinder the United States in the prosecution of the war, no one would hold such conduct a crime. I admit that my illustration does not answer all that might be said but it is enough to show what I think and to let me pass to a more important aspect of the case. I refer to the First Amendment to the Constitution that Congress shall make no law abridging the freedom of speech.

I never have seen any reason to doubt that the questions of law that alone were before this Court in the cases of [Schenck, Frohwerk and Debs] were rightly decided. I do not doubt for a moment that by the same reasoning that would justify punishing persuasion to murder, the United States constitutionally may punish speech that produces or is intended to produce a clear and imminent danger that it will bring about forthwith certain substantive evils that the United States constitutionally may seek to prevent. The power undoubtedly is greater in time of war than in time of peace because war opens dangers that do not exist at other times.

But as against dangers peculiar to war, as against others, the principle of the right to free speech is always the same. It is only the present danger of immediate evil or an intent to bring it about that warrants Congress in setting a limit to the expression of opinion where private rights are not concerned. Congress certainly cannot forbid all effort to change the mind of the country. Now nobody can suppose that the surreptitious publishing of a silly leaflet by an unknown man, without more, would present any immediate danger that its opinions would hinder the success of the government arms or have any appreciable tendency to do so. Publishing those opinions for the very purpose of obstructing however, might indicate a greater danger and at any rate would have the quality of an attempt. So I assume that the second leaflet if published for the purposes alleged in the fourth count might be punishable. But it seems pretty clear to me that nothing less than that would bring these papers within the scope of this law. An actual intent in the sense that I have explained is necessary to constitute an attempt,

where a further act of the same individual is required to complete the substantive crime, for reasons given in Swift & Co. v. United States, 196 U.S. 375, 396. It is necessary where the success of the attempt depends upon others because if that intent is not present the actor's aim may be accomplished without bringing about the evils sought to be checked. An intent to prevent interference with the revolution in Russia might have been satisfied without any hindrance to carrying on the war in which we were engaged.

I do not see how anyone can find the intent required by the statute in any of the defendants' words. The second leaflet is the only one that affords even a foundation for the charge, and there, without invoking the hatred of German militarism expressed in the former one, it is evident from the beginning to the end that the only object of the paper is to help Russia and stop American intervention there against the popular government—not to impede the United States in the war that it was carrying on. To say that two phrases taken literally might import a suggestion of conduct that would have interference with the war as an indirect and probably undesired effect seems to me by no means enough to show an attempt to produce that effect.

I [turn] for a moment to the third count. That charges an intent to provoke resistance to the United States in its war with Germany. Taking the clause in the statute that deals with that in connection with the other elaborate provisions of the act, I think that resistance to the United States means some forcible act of opposition to some proceeding of the United States in pursuance of the war. I think the intent must be the specific intent that I have described and for the reasons that I have given I think that no such intent was proved or existed in fact. I also think that there is no hint at resistance to the United States as I construe the phrase.

In this case sentences of twenty years imprisonment have been imposed for the publishing of two leaflets that I believe the defendants had as much right to publish as the Government has to publish the Constitution of the United States now vainly invoked by them. Even if I am technically wrong and enough can be squeezed from these poor and puny anonymities to turn the color of legal litmus paper; I will add, even if what I think the necessary intent were shown; the most nominal punishment seems to me all that possibly could be inflicted, unless the defendants are to be made to suffer not for what the indictment alleges but for the creed that they avow—a creed that I believe to be the creed of ignorance and immaturity when honestly held, as I see no reason to doubt that it was held here, but which, although made the subject of examination at the trial, no one has a right even to consider in dealing with the charges before the Court.

Persecution for the expression of opinions seems to me perfectly logical. If you have no doubt of your premises or your power and want a certain result with all your heart you naturally express your wishes in law and sweep away all opposition. To allow opposition by speech seems to indicate that you think the speech impotent, as when a man says that he has squared the circle, or that you do not care whole-heartedly for the result, or that you doubt either your power or your premises. But when men have realized that time has upset many fighting faiths, they may come to believe even more than they believe the very foundations of their own conduct that the ultimate good

desired is better reached by free trade in ideas—that the best test of truth is the power of the thought to get itself accepted in the competition of the market, and that truth is the only ground upon which their wishes safely can be carried out. That at any rate is the theory of our Constitution. It is an experiment, as all life is an experiment. Every year if not every day we have to wager our salvation upon some prophecy based upon imperfect knowledge. While that experiment is part of our system I think that we should be eternally vigilant against attempts to check the expression of opinions that we loathe and believe to be fraught with death, unless they so imminently threaten immediate interference with the lawful and pressing purposes of the law that an immediate check is required to save the country. I wholly disagree with the argument of the Government that the First Amendment left the common law as to seditious libel in force. History seems to me against the notion. I had conceived that the United States through many years had shown its repentance for the Sedition Act of 1798, by repaying fines that it imposed. Only the emergency that makes it immediately dangerous to leave the correction of evil counsels to time warrants making any exception to the sweeping command, "Congress shall make no law . . . abridging the freedom of speech." Of course I am speaking only of expressions of opinion and exhortations, which were all that were uttered here, but I regret that I cannot put into more impressive words my belief that in their conviction upon this indictment the defendants were deprived of their rights under the Constitution of the United States.

3. *The majority's evaluation of the evidence in Abrams.* Compare with Justice Holmes' evaluation of the circulars in Abrams, the following comments in the majority opinion's review of the evidence. Which estimate seems closer to the approach of Schenck-Frohwerk-Debs: the majority's or the dissent's? Justice Clarke's majority opinion stated:

"It will not do to say, as is now argued, that the only intent of these defendants was to prevent injury to the Russian cause. Men must be held to have intended, and to be accountable for, the effects which their acts were likely to produce. Even if their primary purpose and intent was to aid the cause of the Russian Revolution, the plan of action which they adopted necessarily involved, before it could be realized, defeat of the war program of the United States, for the obvious effect of this appeal, if it should become effective, as they hoped it might, would be to persuade persons of character such as those whom they regarded themselves as addressing, not to aid government loans and not to work in ammunition factories, where their work would produce 'bullets, bayonets, cannon' and other munitions of war, the use of which would cause the 'murder' of Germans and Russians. . . .

"That the interpretation we have put upon these articles, circulated in the greatest port of our land, from which great numbers of soldiers were at the time taking ship daily, and in which great quantities of war supplies of every kind were at the time being manufactured for transportation overseas, is not only the fair interpretation of them, but that it is the meaning which their authors consciously intended should be conveyed by them to others is further shown by the additional writings found in the meeting place of the defendant group and on the person of one of them. One of these circulars is headed: 'Revolutionists! Unite for Action!' . . .

"These excerpts sufficiently show, that while the immediate occasion for this particular outbreak of lawlessness, on the part of the defendant alien anarchists, may have been resentment caused by our Government sending troops into Russia as a strategic operation against the Germans on the eastern battle front, yet the plain purpose of their propaganda was to excite, at the supreme crisis of the war, disaffection, sedition, riots, and, as they hoped, revolution, in this country for the purpose of embarrassing and if possible defeating the military plans of the Government in Europe."

4. *The Schaefer case.* Soon after Abrams, Justice Holmes also joined in dissents from other decisions affirming convictions under the 1917 Act. See Pierce v. United States, 252 U.S. 239 (1920), and Schaefer v. United States, 251 U.S. 466 (1920). In his Schaefer dissent, Justice Brandeis said of the Schenck standard: "This is a rule of reason. Correctly applied, it will preserve the right of free speech both from suppression by tyrannous, well-meaning majorities and from abuse by irresponsible, fanatical minorities. Like many other rules for human conduct, it can be applied correctly only by the exercise of good judgment; and to the exercise of good judgment, calmness is, in times of deep feeling and on subjects which excite passion, as essential as fearlessness and honesty. The question whether in a particular instance the words spoken or written fall within the permissible curtailment of free speech is, under the rule enunciated by this court, one of degree. And because it is a question of degree the field in which the jury may exercise its judgment is, necessarily, a wide one. But its field is not unlimited. . . . In my opinion, no jury acting in calmness could reasonably say that any of the publications set forth in the indictment was of such a character or was made under such circumstances as to create a clear and present danger either that they would obstruct recruiting or that they would promote the success of the enemies of the United States."

CLEAR AND PRESENT DANGER FROM SCHENCK TO ABRAMS—EVOLUTION OR REBIRTH?

1. *Some questions about the Schenck-Frohwerk-Debs approach.* Clear and present danger supposedly assures special attention to the time dimension: speech may not be curtailed until there is an immediate risk of an evil; speech with a remote tendency to cause danger cannot be curtailed. Is that sense conveyed by the language of the Schenck group of cases? By the facts?

a. *Schenck.* What showing was there that the substantive evil had come about, or that the words would "bring about" the evils? Does Schenck clearly reject a "tendency" criterion and replace it with one of "clear and present" immediacy? Note the reference to "the act, . . . its tendency and the intent" at the end of the opinion. What is the relevance of "intent" to immediate risk of harm? "Tendency"? Is the "shouting fire" analogy apt? To political speech? Are truth and falsity relevant? What if the speaker thought there was a fire?

b. *Frohwerk.* Was the Frohwerk "counselling of a murder" reference helpful in delineating the requisite "proximity and degree"? Was the language in Frohwerk indistinguishable from that in Schenck? Frohwerk refers to "language that might be taken to convey an innuendo of a different sort." Is talk of risks of "innuendos" consistent with a sensitive regard for speech? Is talk of the possibility of evidence about "a little breath" that might "kindle a flame"? Does that suggest insistence on showing a high probability of harm? Is that talk more protective of speech than "bad tendency"?

c. *Debs.* Did Holmes demonstrate the "clear and present danger" of Eugene V. Debs' speeches? Did he deprecate the "general theme" unduly? Did he unduly emphasize what "his hearers   .   .   .   might infer"? Does the talk of "natural tendency and reasonably probable effect" sound like an immediacy-emphasizing alternative to a "bad tendency" approach?

2. *The impact of Abrams.* Does Abrams give new content to "clear and present danger"? Can it be said that the Schenck phrase was not turned into an effective safeguard of speech until the Abrams dissent? A great admirer of Holmes has suggested about the Schenck-Abrams sequence that the Justice "was biding his time until the Court should have before it a conviction so clearly wrong as to let him speak out his deepest thoughts about the First Amendment." Chafee, Free Speech in the United States (1941), 86. Is that persuasive? *Were* the Abrams convictions more "clearly wrong" than those in the Schenck group of cases? Was the Abrams majority fairly following the Schenck approach? Does the Holmes dissent indicate a change of views since Schenck? (See also note 3 below.)

How useful is the approach of the Abrams dissent? It emphasizes immediacy more than the predecessors. Does it concentrate adequately on immediate proximity of speech to danger? Note the comment about a "silly leaflet" that would not present "any immediate danger" *or* "have any appreciable tendency to do so." Is "tendency" enough? Note also the reference to "the present danger of immediate evil" *or* "an intent to bring it about." Is "intent" enough? Are "tendency" and "intent" reliable indicia of immediacy of danger?

Is the Abrams approach applicable only in contexts where the law is mainly directed at an evil other than speech (e. g., obstruction of military recruitment), and where speech is evidence of the risk of that evil? Is it also useful when the legislature proscribes speech directly, as in Gitlow and Whitney, below? Does Holmes accept the legislative statement of the evil? Must speech cause immediate risk of causing the legislatively determined evil —e. g., interference with recruiting? Or does the Court define the evil? Note the reference to "an immediate check   .   .   .   required to save the country," in Holmes' last paragraph. Is Holmes concerned with the gravity of the evil? Do immediacy requirements vary with gravity? What light is cast on these questions by the elaborations of clear and present danger in Gitlow and Whitney? Before turning to those cases, consider the historical data on the Schenck-Abrams evolution in note 3 below and the alternative analysis suggested by Judge Learned Hand's Masses opinion, which follows that note.

3. *From Schenck to Abrams: Some data from history.* That Justice Holmes' thinking underwent considerable change in the period between the Schenck trilogy of cases in the spring of 1919 and the Abrams dissent in the fall of that year is suggested by some of Justice Holmes' correspondence. See Gunther, "Learned Hand and the Origins of Modern First Amendment Doctrine: Some Fragments of History," 27 Stan.L.Rev. 719 (1975), concluding "that Holmes was [at the time of Schenck] quite insensitive to any claim for special judicial protection of free speech; that the Schenck standard was not truly speech-protective; and that it was not until the fall of 1919, with his famous dissent in Abrams v. United States, that Holmes put some teeth into the clear and present danger formula, at least partly as a result of probing criticism by acquaintances such as Learned Hand." *

In the summer of 1918, for example, Holmes, in a letter to Hand, espoused the "natural right" to silence "the other fellow when he disagrees": free speech, he insisted, "stands no differently than freedom from vaccination"—a freedom that the state could legitimately curtail, as demonstrated in Jacobson v. Massachusetts, 197 U.S. 11 (1905), and as consistent with Justice Holmes' general deferential due process philosophy. (Recall chap. 9 above.) In 1918, Holmes seemed impervious to Hand's arguments that the "natural right" to silence dissenters must be curbed by the law in the interest of the search for truth. In the spring of 1919, after Debs, Hand insisted to Holmes that responsibility for speech should not rest on guesses about the future impact of the words: "in nature the causal sequence is perfect, but responsibility does not go pari passu"; the liability of the speaker should not turn "upon reasonable forecast"; the punishability of speech should begin only "when the words [are] directly an incitement." But, again, Holmes was impervious to the criticism. As Hand wrote to another critic of the Debs decision, "I have so far been unable to make [Holmes] see that he and we have any real differences." Holmes' insensitivity to free speech values and lack of concern for tailoring doctrine to implement those values as of the spring of 1919 is supported by Holmes' own letters: as Holmes began his letter in response to Hand's critique of the Debs approach, "I don't quite get your point." But by the fall of 1919, with the Abrams dissent and the infusion of a genuine immediacy element, the clear and present danger test was launched as a truly speech-protective doctrine. Was it an adequate doctrine in that refurbished form? Compare Learned Hand's continued criticism, in the notes following the Masses opinion below.

---

* See also Kalven, "Professor Ernst Freund and Debs v. United States," 40 U.Chi.L.Rev. 235 (1973); Ginsburg, "Afterword to Ernst Freund and the First Amendment Tradition," 40 U. Chi.L.Rev. 243 (1973); and Ragan, "Justice Oliver Wendell Holmes, Jr., Zechariah Chafee, Jr., and the Clear and Present Danger Test for Free Speech: The First Year, 1919," 58 J. Am.Hist. 24 (1971).

LEARNED HAND AND THE MASSES CASE: DIFFERENT FROM, AND PREFERABLE TO, CLEAR AND PRESENT DANGER?

Introduction. Two years before Schenck, the problem of interpreting the Espionage Act of 1917 arose in a case before Learned Hand, then a District Judge. The Hand opinion plainly reveals considerable solicitude for speech, and it does so without mentioning clear and present danger. Consider the advantages and disadvantages of Hand's approach in the World War I context. How would Schenck, Debs, or Abrams have gone under that standard? Would Hand's approach have avoided some of the difficulties clear and present danger encountered in later years? Has Hand's approach surfaced in substance in some of the later Supreme Court cases—e. g., in the Yates and Scales cases under the Smith Act and in the 1969 decision in Brandenburg v. Ohio, below? See also the notes following the Masses case.

MASSES PUBLISHING CO. v. PATTEN

244 Fed. 535 (1917).

United States District Court, Southern District of New York.

LEARNED HAND, District Judge. The plaintiff applies for a preliminary injunction against the postmaster of New York to forbid his refusal to accept its magazine in the mails under the following circumstances: The plaintiff is a publishing company in the city of New York engaged in the production of a monthly revolutionary journal called "The Masses," containing both text and cartoons . . .. In July, 1917, the postmaster of New York, acting upon the direction of the Postmaster General, advised the plaintiff that the August number to which he had had access would be denied the mails under the Espionage Act of June 15, 1917. [T]he defendant, while objecting generally that the whole purport of the number was in violation of the law, since it tended to produce a violation of the law, to encourage the enemies of the United States, and to hamper the government in the conduct of the war, specified four cartoons and four pieces of text as especially falling within sections 1 and 2 of title 12 of the act and by the reference of section 1 as within section 3 of title 1. These sections are quoted in the margin.[1]

---

1. Title I. Espionage.

Sec. 3. Whoever, when the United States is at war, shall willfully make or convey false reports or false statements with intent to interfere with the operation or success of the military or naval forces of the United States or to promote the success of its enemies and whoever when the United States is at war, shall willfully cause or attempt to cause insubordination, disloyalty, mutiny, or refusal of duty, in the military or naval forces of the United States, or shall willfully obstruct the recruiting or enlistment service of the United States, to the injury of the service or of the United States, shall be punished by a fine of not more than $10,000 or imprisonment for not more than twenty years, or both.

Title XII. Use of Mails.

Section 1. Every letter, writing, circular, postal card, picture, print, engraving, photograph, newspaper, pamphlet, book, or other publication, matter or thing, of any kind, in violation of any of the provisions of this act is hereby declared to be nonmail-

. . . In this case there is no dispute of fact which the plaintiff can successfully challenge except the meaning of the words and pictures in the magazine. As to these the query must be: What is the extreme latitude of the interpretation which must be placed upon them, and whether that extremity certainly falls outside any of the provisions of the act of June 15, 1917. Unless this be true, the decision of the postmaster must stand. It will be necessary, first, to interpret the law, and, next, the words and pictures.

[N]o question arises touching the war powers of Congress. . . . Here is presented solely the question of how far Congress after much discussion has up to the present time seen fit to exercise a power which may extend to measures not yet even considered, but necessary to the existence of the state as such. . . .

Coming to the act itself, [I] turn directly to section 3 of title 1, which the plaintiff is said to violate. That section contains three provisions. The first is, in substance, that no one shall make any false statements with intent to interfere with the operation or success of the military or naval forces of the United States or to promote the success of its enemies. The defendant says that the cartoons and text of the magazine, constituting, as they certainly do, a virulent attack upon the war . . ., may interfere with the success of the military forces of the United States. That such utterances may have the effect so ascribed to them is unhappily true . . .. Dissension within a country is a high source of comfort and assistance to its enemies. . . .

All this, however, is beside the question whether such an attack is a willfully false statement. That phrase properly includes only a statement of fact which the utterer knows to be false, and it cannot be maintained that any of these statements are of fact, or that the plaintiff believes them to be false. They are all within the range of opinion and of criticism; they are all certainly believed to be true by the utterer. As such they fall within the scope of that right to criticise either by temperate reasoning, or by immoderate and indecent invective, which is normally the privilege of the individual in countries dependent upon the free expression of opinion as the ultimate source of authority. The argument may be trivial in substance, and violent and perverse in manner, but so long as it is confined to abuse of existing policies or laws, it is impossible to class it as a false statement of facts of the kind here in question. To modify this provision, so clearly intended to prevent the spreading of false rumors which may embarrass the military, into the prohibition of any kind of propaganda, honest or vicious, is to disregard the meaning of the language, established by legal construction and common use, and to raise it into a means of suppressing intemperate and inflammatory public discussion, which was surely not its purpose.

able matter and shall not be conveyed in the mails or delivered from any post office or by any letter carrier: Provided, that nothing in this act shall be so construed as to authorize any person other than an employé of the dead letter office, duly authorized there to, or other person upon a search warrant authorized by law, to open any letter not addressed to himself.

Sec. 2. Every letter, writing, circular, postal card, picture, print, engraving, photograph, newspaper, pamphlet, book, or other publication, matter or thing, of any kind, containing any matter advocating or urging treason, insurrection, or forcible resistance to any law of the United States, is hereby declared to be nonmailable. [Footnote by the Court.]

The next phrase relied upon is that which forbids any one from willfully causing insubordination, disloyalty, mutiny, or refusal of duty in the military or naval forces of the United States. The defendant's position is that to arouse discontent and disaffection among the people with the prosecution of the war and with the draft tends to promote a mutinous and insubordinate temper among the troops. This, too, is true; men who become satisfied that they are engaged in an enterprise dictated by the unconscionable selfishness of the rich, and effectuated by a tyrannous disregard for the will of those who must suffer and die, will be more prone to insubordination than those who have faith in the cause and acquiesce in the means. Yet to interpret the word "cause" so broadly would, as before, involve necessarily as a consequence the suppression of all hostile criticism, and of all opinion except what encouraged and supported the existing policies, or which fell within the range of temperate argument. It would contradict the normal assumption of democratic government that the suppression of hostile criticism does not turn upon the justice of its substance or the decency and propriety of its temper. Assuming that the power to repress such opinion may rest in Congress in the throes of a struggle for the very existence of the state, its exercise is so contrary to the use and wont of our people that only the clearest expression of such a power justifies the conclusion that it was intended.

The defendant's position, therefore, in so far as it involves the suppression of the free utterance of abuse and criticism of the existing law, or of the policies of the war, is not, in my judgment, supported by the language of the statute. Yet there has always been a recognized limit to such expressions, incident indeed to the existence of any compulsive power of the state itself. One may not counsel or advise others to violate the law as it stands. Words are not only the keys of persuasion, but the triggers of action, and those which have no purport but to counsel the violation of law cannot by any latitude of interpretation be a part of that public opinion which is the final source of government in a democratic state. The defendant asserts not only that the magazine indirectly through its propaganda leads to a disintegration of loyalty and a disobedience of law, but that in addition it counsels and advises resistance to existing law, especially to the draft. The consideration of this aspect of the case more properly arises under the third phrase of section 3, which forbids any willful obstruction of the recruiting or enlistment service of the United States, but, as the defendant urges that the magazine falls within each phrase, it is as well to take it up now. To counsel or advise a man to an act is to urge upon him either that it is his interest or his duty to do it. While, of course, this may be accomplished as well by indirection as expressly, since words carry the meaning that they impart, the definition is exhaustive, I think, and I shall use it. Political agitation, by the passions it arouses or the convictions it engenders, may in fact stimulate men to the violation of law. Detestation of existing policies is easily transformed into forcible resistance of the authority which puts them in execution, and it would be folly to disregard the causal relation between the two. Yet to assimilate agitation, legitimate as such, with direct incitement to violent resistance, is to disregard the tolerance of all methods of political agitation which in normal times is a safeguard of free government. The distinction is not a scholastic subterfuge, but a hard-bought acquisition in the fight for freedom, and the purpose to disregard it

must be evident when the power exists. If one stops short of urging upon others that it is their duty or their interest to resist the law, it seems to me one should not be held to have attempted to cause its violation. If that be not the test, I can see no escape from the conclusion that under this section every political agitation which can be shown to be apt to create a seditious temper is illegal. I am confident that by such language Congress had no such revolutionary purpose in view.

It seems to me, however, quite plain that none of the language and none of the cartoons in this paper can be thought directly to counsel or advise insubordination or mutiny, without a violation of their meaning quite beyond any tolerable understanding. I come, therefore, to the third phrase of the section, which forbids any one from willfully obstructing the recruiting or enlistment service of the United States. I am not prepared to assent to the plaintiff's position that this only refers to acts other than words, nor that the act thus defined must be shown to have been successful. One may obstruct without preventing, and the mere obstruction is an injury to the service; for it throws impediments in its way. Here again, however, since the question is of the expression of opinion, I construe the sentence, so far as it restrains public utterance, as I have construed the other two, and as therefore limited to the direct advocacy of resistance to the recruiting and enlistment service. If so, the inquiry is narrowed to the question whether any of the challenged matter may be said to advocate resistance to the draft, taking the meaning of the words with the utmost latitude which they can bear.

As to the cartoons it seems to me quite clear that they do not fall within such a test. Certainly the nearest is that entitled "Conscription," and the most that can be said of that is that it may breed such animosity to the draft as will promote resistance and strengthen the determination of those disposed to be recalcitrant. There is no intimation that, however hateful the draft may be, one is in duty bound to resist it, certainly none that such resistance is to one's interest.   .   .   .

The text offers more embarrassment. The poem to Emma Goldman and Alexander Berkman, at most, goes no further than to say that they are martyrs in the cause of love among nations. Such a sentiment holds them up to admiration, and hence their conduct to possible emulation.   .   .   .   The paragraphs upon conscientious objectors are of the same kind.   .   .   . It is plain enough that the paper has the fullest sympathy for these people, that it admires their courage, and that it presumptively approves their conduct. .   .   .

Moreover, these passages, it must be remembered, occur in a magazine which attacks with the utmost violence the draft and the war. That such comments have a tendency to arouse emulation in others is clear enough, but that they counsel others to follow these examples is not so plain. Literally at least they do not, and while, as I have said, the words are to be taken, not literally, but according to their full import, the literal meaning is the starting point for interpretation. One may admire and approve the course of a hero without feeling any duty to follow him. There is not the least implied intimation in these words that others are under a duty to follow. The most that can be said is that, if others do follow, they will get the same admiration and the same approval. Now, there is surely an appreciable distance between esteem

and emulation; and unless there is here some advocacy of such emulation, I cannot see how the passages can be said to fall within the law.   .   .   .

The question before me is quite the same as what would arise upon a motion to dismiss an indictment at the close of the proof: Could any reasonable man say, not that the indirect result of the language might be to arouse a seditious disposition, for that would not be enough, but that the language directly advocated resistance to the draft?   I cannot think that upon such language any verdict would stand.   .   .   . *

COMPARING THE HOLMES AND HAND APPROACHES: SOME QUESTIONS AND COMMENTS

1. *The differences between Hand and Holmes: Some questions.* Is the Masses standard distinctively different from the clear and present danger test?   How does it differ?   How would Eugene Debs have fared under the Masses approach?   Is Hand more sensitive than Holmes to the risk of sustaining convictions based on the "natural tendency" and "probable effect" of words?   Is he more sensitive because he focuses less on the proximity of danger (e. g., of draft obstruction) and more on the speaker and the value of speech—on the protection that must be afforded if widespread critical debate of governmental policy is to be maintained?

Is the shift in focus from proximity of danger to content of speech an assurance of greater protection of speech?   Is it an inquiry courts are more competent to conduct?   Does it involve less concern about "circumstances" and variable degrees of dangers?   Does it draw on more traditional, more manageable judicial tools?   Are courts better at concentrating on what the defendant said than on how near (and serious) the danger is?   More competent to define "counselling" than to assess risks?   Or are these simply different ways to state the same question?   Does Masses articulate speech values more effectively than Schenck?   Than Abrams?   Does Masses foreshadow emphasis on articulating the nature of protected debate in a free society, as in the New York Times case, chap. 13 below?   Is the Masses approach usable in situations where the legislature has described prohibited speech, as in Gitlow and Whitney which follow?   Does it avoid a judicial second-guessing of the legislative determination of danger?

2. *The differences between Hand and Holmes: Some historical data.* Learned Hand's correspondence reveals that he himself perceived a considerable difference between his Masses approach and Holmes' clear and pres-

---

* District Judge Hand's decision was reversed on appeal. Masses Publishing Co. v. Patten, 246 Fed. 24 (2d Cir. 1917). The Circuit Court not only emphasized the broad administrative discretion of the Postmaster General, but also disagreed with Hand's incitement test: "This court does not agree that such is the law. If the natural and reasonable effect of what is said is to encourage resistance to a law, and the words are used in an endeavor to persuade to resistance, it is immaterial that the duty to resist is not mentioned, or the interest of the persons addressed in resistance is not suggested." As Learned Hand wrote in one of his letters, his Masses opinion "seemed to meet with practically no professional approval whatever."

ent danger test, even as refined in the Abrams dissent.[1] Though Hand welcomed Holmes' greater sensitivity to free speech values in the Abrams dissent, he questioned Holmes' doctrinal implementation. In a series of letters from 1919 to 1921 to Professor Zechariah Chafee, Jr.,[2] Hand elaborated the differences between the Masses analysis and the alternatives. As Hand wrote to Chafee, soon after Abrams: "I do not altogether like the way Justice Holmes put the limitation. I myself think it is a little more manageable and quite adequate a distinction to say that there is an absolute and objective test to language. [I] still prefer that which I attempted to state in my first 'Masses' opinion, rather than to say that the connection between the words used and the evil aimed at should be 'immediate and direct.' " And as he elaborated later, "I prefer a test based upon the nature of the utterance itself. If, taken in its setting, the effect upon the hearers is only to counsel them to violate the law, it is unconditionally illegal. . . . As to other utterances, it appears to me that regardless of their tendency they should be permitted."

Hand's major objection to formulations such as "clear and present danger" or "natural and reasonable tendency" was that they were too slippery in "practical administration": "I think it is precisely at those times when alone the freedom of speech becomes important as an institution, that the protection of a jury on such an issue is illusory." And, as he said in still another letter, "I am not wholly in love with Holmesy's test and the reason is this. Once you admit that the matter is one of degree, while you may put it where it genuinely belongs, [you] so obviously make it a matter of administration . . . . I should prefer a qualitative formula, hard, conventional, difficult to evade." His "incitement" test was intended to be such a formula.[3]

After 1921, Hand gave up on his advocacy of the Masses approach: he no longer had any real hope that that standard "would ever be recognized

1. See the documents and commentary in Gunther, "Learned Hand and the Origins of Modern First Amendment Doctrine: Some Fragments of History," 27 Stan.L.Rev. 719 (1975).

2. Professor Chafee, for more than three decades after Schenck and Abrams, was the most prominent commentator on First Amendment problems. See especially his Freedom of Speech (1920) and the revisions of that volume in Free Speech in the United States (1941). Though the 1920 volume was dedicated to Judge Learned Hand, Chafee's writings tended to minimize the differences between Hand and Holmes and were the single most important academic source for the widely held view that clear and present danger was the best possible libertarian doctrine.

3. See also the evaluation of the Hand letters to Chafee in Gunther, note 1 above: "These letters make clear what has long been doubted or ignored:

that the Masses approach was indeed a distinctive, carefully considered alternative to the prevalent analyses of free speech issues. According to the usual arguments, the punishability of speech turned on an evaluation of its likelihood to cause forbidden consequences. [All of the prevalent approaches] shared the common characteristic of requiring factfinders—typically, juries—to assess circumstances and to guess about the risks created by the challenged speech. Learned Hand thought this [characteristic] too slippery, too dangerous to free expression, too much at the mercy of factfinders reflecting majoritarian sentiments hostile to dissent. Instead, he urged, in Masses and for several years thereafter, the adoption of a strict, 'hard,' 'objective' test focusing on the speaker's words: if the language used was solely that of direct incitement to illegal action, speech could be proscribed; otherwise, it was protected."

as law." Compare that prophecy with the evolution of doctrine in the cases that follow, especially the Yates, Scales, and Brandenburg decisions below. Compare the evaluation in Gunther, note 1 above, that that course of decisions represents "a belated adoption by the Supreme Court of aspects of the Masses approach—long after Hand himself had lost confidence in it, after the rise and decline of Schenck's clear and present danger standard, after Hand had contributed to Schenck's disintegration [in his Court of Appeals opinion in the Dennis case, below]." Note also the comment that the 1969 decision in Brandenburg v. Ohio "combines the most protective ingredients of the Masses incitement emphasis with the most useful elements of the clear and present danger heritage."

What *were* the most useful elements of the clear and present danger heritage? What *were* the most protective ingredients of the Masses approach? What *were* the weaknesses of the Masses approach? Was it a weakness that "it could not easily deal with the indirect but purposeful incitement of Marc Anthony's oration over the body of Caesar"? [4] Was it a weakness that Hand did not "fully deal with the problem of the harmless inciter, the speaker explicitly urging law violation but with little realistic hope of success"?

B. LEGISLATION AGAINST FORBIDDEN ADVOCACY IN THE TWENTIES AND THIRTIES

GITLOW, WHITNEY, AND THE INCREASING PROTECTION OF SPEECH

GITLOW v. NEW YORK

268 U.S. 652, 45 S.Ct. 625, 69 L.Ed. 1138 (1925).

Error to the Supreme Court of New York.

Mr. Justice SANFORD delivered the opinion of the Court.

Benjamin Gitlow was indicted [and convicted] for the statutory crime of criminal anarchy. New York Penal Law, §§ 160, 161.* . . . The

---

4. Compare a comment in one of the Chafee letters to Hand, in Gunther, note 1 above: "Your test is surely easier to apply although our old friend Marc Anthony's speech is continually thrown at me in discussion."

* The New York statute—enacted in 1902, after the assassination of President McKinley—provided:
"§ 160. *Criminal anarchy defined.* Criminal anarchy is the doctrine that organized government should be overthrown by force or violence, or by

assassination of the executive head or of any of the executive officials of government, or by any unlawful means. The advocacy of such doctrine either by word of mouth or writing is a felony.

"§ 161. *Advocacy of criminal anarchy.* Any person who:
"1. By word of mouth or writing advocates, advises or teaches the duty, necessity or propriety of overthrowing or overturning organized government by force or violence, or by assassination of the executive head or of any

contention here is that the statute, by its terms and as applied in this case, is repugnant to the due process clause of the Fourteen Amendment. . . .

The indictment was in two counts. The first charged that the defendant had advocated, advised and taught the duty, necessity and propriety of overthrowing and overturning organized government by force, violence and unlawful means, by certain writings therein set forth entitled "The Left Wing Manifesto"; the second that he had printed, published and knowingly circulated and distributed a certain paper called "The Revolutionary Age," containing the writings set forth in the first count . . . . .

The following facts were established on the trial by undisputed evidence and admissions: The defendant is a member of the Left Wing Section of the Socialist Party, a dissenting branch or faction of that party formed in opposition to its dominant policy of "moderate Socialism." Membership in both is open to aliens as well as citizens. The Left Wing Section was organized nationally at a conference in New York City in June, 1919 . . . . The conference elected a National Council, of which the defendant was a member, and left to it the adoption of a "Manifesto." This was published in The Revolutionary Age, the official organ of the Left Wing. The defendant was on the board of managers of the paper and was its business manager. He arranged for the printing of the paper and took to the printer the manuscript of the first issue which contained the Left Wing Manifesto, and also a Communist Program and a Program of the Left Wing that had been adopted by the conference. Sixteen thousand copies were printed, which were delivered at the premises in New York City used as the office of the Revolutionary Age and the headquarters of the Left Wing, and occupied by the defendant and other officials. . . . It was admitted that the defendant signed a card subscribing to the Manifesto and Program of the Left Wing, which all applicants were required to sign before being admitted to membership; that he went to different parts of the State to speak to branches of the Socialist Party about the principles of the Left Wing and advocated their adoption; and that he was responsible for the Manifesto as it appeared, that "he knew of the publication, in a general way and he knew of its publications afterwards, and is responsible for its circulation."

There was no evidence of any effect resulting from the publication and circulation of the Manifesto.

No witnesses were offered in behalf of the defendant. . . . Coupled with a review of the rise of Socialism, [the Manifesto] condemned the dominant "moderate Socialism" for its recognition of the necessity of the democratic parliamentary state . . . and advocated, in plain and unequivocal language, the necessity of accomplishing the "Communist Revolution" by a militant and "revolutionary Socialism," based on "the class struggle" and mobilizing the "power of the proletariat in action," through mass industrial revolts developing into mass political strikes and "revolutionary

of the executive officials of government, or by any unlawful means; or,
"2. Prints, publishes, edits, issues or knowingly circulates, sells, distributes or publicly displays any book, paper, document, or written or printed matter in any form, containing or

advocating, advising or teaching the doctrine that organized government should be overthrown by force, violence or any unlawful means . . .,
"Is guilty of a felony and punishable" by imprisonment or fine, or both.

mass action," for the purpose of conquering and destroying the parliamentary state and establishing in its place, through a "revolutionary dictatorship of the proletariat," the system of Communist Socialism. [R]evolutionary Socialism, it was urged, must [use] mass industrial revolts to broaden the strike, make it general and militant, and develop it into mass political strikes and revolutionary mass action for the annihilation of the parliamentary state. . . .

The court, among other things, charged the jury, in substance, that they must determine what was the intent, purpose and fair meaning of the Manifesto; [that] a mere statement or analysis of social and economic facts and historical incidents, in the nature of an essay, accompanied by prophecy as to the future course of events, but with no teaching, advice or advocacy of action, would not constitute the advocacy, advice or teaching of a doctrine for the overthrow of government within the meaning of the statute; that a mere statement that unlawful acts might accomplish such a purpose would be insufficient, unless there was a teaching, advising and advocacy of employing such unlawful acts for the purpose of overthrowing government . . . .

The defendant's counsel submitted two requests to charge which embodied in substance the statement that to constitute criminal anarchy within the meaning of the statute it was necessary that the language used or published should advocate, teach or advise the duty, necessity or propriety of doing "some definite or immediate act or acts" of force, violence or unlawfulness directed toward the overthrowing of organized government. These were denied further than had been charged. . . .

. . . The sole contention here is, essentially, that as there was no evidence of any concrete result flowing from the publication of the Manifesto or of circumstances showing the likelihood of such result, the statute as construed and applied by the trial court penalizes the mere utterance, as such, of "doctrine" having no quality of incitement, without regard either to the circumstances of its utterance or to the likelihood of unlawful consequences; and that, as the exercise of the right of free expression with relation to government is only punishable "in circumstances involving likelihood of substantive evil," the statute contravenes the due process clause of the Fourteenth Amendment. The argument in support of this contention rests primarily upon the following propositions: 1st, That the "liberty" protected by the Fourteenth Amendment includes the liberty of speech and of the press; and 2d, That while liberty of expression "is not absolute," it may be restrained "only in circumstances where its exercise bears a causal relation with some substantive evil, consummated, attempted or likely," and as the statute "takes no account of circumstances," it unduly restrains this liberty and is therefore unconstitutional. . . .

The statute does not penalize the utterance or publication of abstract "doctrine" or academic discussion having no quality of incitement to any concrete action. It is not aimed against mere historical or philosophical essays. It does not restrain the advocacy of changes in the form of government by constitutional and lawful means. What it prohibits is language advocating, advising or teaching the overthrow of organized government by unlawful means. These words imply urging to action. . . .

The Manifesto, plainly, is neither the statement of abstract doctrine nor, as suggested by counsel, mere prediction that industrial disturbances and revolutionary mass strikes will result spontaneously in an inevitable process of evolution in the economic system. It advocates and urges in fervent language mass action which shall progressively foment industrial disturbances and through political mass strikes and revolutionary mass action overthrow and destroy organized parliamentary government. It concludes with a call to action in these words: "The proletarian revolution and the Communist reconstruction of society—*the struggle for these*—is now indispensable. . . . The Communist International calls the proletariat of the world to the final struggle!" This is not the expression of philosophical abstraction, the mere prediction of future events; it is the language of direct incitement.

The means advocated for bringing about the destruction of organized parliamentary government, namely, mass industrial revolts usurping the functions of municipal government, political mass strikes directed against the parliamentary state, and revolutionary mass action for its final destruction, necessarily imply the use of force and violence, and in their essential nature are inherently unlawful in a constitutional government of law and order. That the jury were warranted in finding that the Manifesto advocated not merely the abstract doctrine of overthrowing organized government by force, violence and unlawful means, but action to that end, is clear.

For present purposes we may and do assume that freedom of speech and of the press—which are protected by the First Amendment from abridgment by Congress—are among the fundamental personal rights and "liberties" protected by the due process clause of the Fourteenth Amendment from impairment by the States. . . .

It is a fundamental principle, long established, that the freedom of speech and of the press which is secured by the Constitution, does not confer an absolute right to speak or publish, without responsibility, whatever one may choose . . . . That a State in the exercise of its police power may punish those who abuse this freedom by utterances inimical to the public welfare, tending to corrupt public morals, incite to crime, or disturb the public peace, is not open to question. . . . And, for yet more imperative reasons, a State may punish utterances endangering the foundations of organized government and threatening its overthrow by unlawful means. . . . In short this freedom does not deprive a State of the primary and essential right of self preservation . . . .

By enacting the present statute the State has determined, through its legislative body, that utterances advocating the overthrow of organized government by force, violence and unlawful means, are so inimical to the general welfare and involve such danger of substantive evil that they may be penalized in the exercise of its police power. That determination must be given great weight. Every presumption is to be indulged in favor of the validity of the statute. Mugler v. Kansas, 123 U.S. 623, 661. [Chap. 9, above.] That utterances inciting to the overthrow of organized government by unlawful means, present a sufficient danger of substantive evil to bring their punishment within the range of legislative discretion, is clear. Such utterances, by their very nature, involve danger to the public peace and to the security of

the State. They threaten breaches of the peace and ultimate revolution. And the immediate danger is none the less real and substantial, because the effect of a given utterance cannot be accurately foreseen. The State cannot reasonably be required to measure the danger from every such utterance in the nice balance of a jeweler's scale. A single revolutionary spark may kindle a fire that, smouldering for a time, may burst into a sweeping and destructive conflagration. It cannot be said that the State is acting arbitrarily or unreasonably when in the exercise of its judgment as to the measures necessary to protect the public peace and safety, it seeks to extinguish the spark without waiting until it has enkindled the flame or blazed into the conflagration. It cannot reasonably be required to defer the adoption of measures for its own peace and safety until the revolutionary utterances lead to actual disturbances of the public peace or imminent and immediate danger of its own destruction; but it may, in the exercise of its judgment, suppress the threatened danger in its incipiency. .   .   .

We cannot hold that the present statute is an arbitrary or unreasonable exercise of the police power of the State unwarrantably infringing the freedom of speech or press; and we must and do sustain its constitutionality.

This being so it may be applied to every utterance—not too trivial to be beneath the notice of the law—which is of such a character and used with such intent and purpose as to bring it within the prohibition of the statute. .   .   .   In other words, when the legislative body has determined generally, in the constitutional exercise of its discretion, that utterances of a certain kind involve such danger of substantive evil that they may be punished, the question whether any specific utterance coming within the prohibited class is likely, in and of itself, to bring about the substantive evil, is not open to consideration. It is sufficient that the statute itself be constitutional and that the use of the language comes within its prohibition.

It is clear that the question in such cases is entirely different from that involved in those cases where the statute merely prohibits certain acts involving the danger of substantive evil, without any reference to language itself, and it is sought to apply its provisions to language used by the defendant for the purpose of bringing about the prohibited results. There, if it be contended that the statute cannot be applied to the language used by the defendant because of its protection by the freedom of speech or press, it must necessarily be found, as an original question, without any previous determination by the legislative body, whether the specific language used involved such likelihood of bringing about the substantive evil as to deprive it of the constitutional protection. In such cases it has been held that the general provisions of the statute may be constitutionally applied to the specific utterance of the defendant if its natural tendency and probable effect was to bring about the substantive evil which the legislative body might prevent. [Schenck; Debs.]   And the general statement in [Schenck] that the "question in every case is whether the words are used in such circumstances and are of such a nature as to create a clear and present danger that they will bring about the substantive evils,"—upon which great reliance is placed in the defendant's argument—was manifestly intended, as shown by the context, to apply only in cases of this class, and has no application to those like the present, where the legislative body itself has previously deter-

mined the danger of substantive evil arising from utterances of a specified character.

. . . It was not necessary, within the meaning of the statute, that the defendant should have advocated "some definite or immediate act or acts" of force, violence or unlawfulness. It was sufficient if such acts were advocated in general terms; and it was not essential that their immediate execution should have been advocated. Nor was it necessary that the language should have been "reasonably and ordinarily calculated to incite certain persons" to acts of force, violence or unlawfulness. The advocacy need not be addressed to specific persons. Thus, the publication and circulation of a newspaper article may be an encouragement or endeavor to persuade to murder, although not addressed to any person in particular. . . .

We need not enter upon a consideration of the English common law rule of seditious libel or the Federal Sedition Act of 1798, to which reference is made in the defendant's brief. These are so unlike the present statute, that we think the decisions under them cast no helpful light upon the questions here. . . .

Affirmed.

Mr. Justice HOLMES (dissenting). Mr. Justice BRANDEIS and I are of opinion that this judgment should be reversed. The general principle of free speech, it seems to me, must be taken to be included in the Fourteenth Amendment, in view of the scope that has been given to the word "liberty" as there used, although perhaps it may be accepted with a somewhat larger latitude of interpretation than is allowed to Congress by the sweeping language that governs or ought to govern the laws of the United States. If I am right, then I think that the criterion sanctioned by the full Court in [Schenck] applies. . . . It is true that in my opinion this criterion was departed from in [Abrams], but the convictions that I expressed in that case are too deep for it to be possible for me as yet to believe that it and Schaefer v. United States, 251 U.S. 466, have settled the law. If what I think the correct test is applied, it is manifest that there was no present danger of an attempt to overthrow the government by force on the part of the admittedly small minority who shared the defendant's views. It is said that this manifesto was more than a theory, that it was an incitement. Every idea is an incitement. It offers itself for belief and if believed it is acted on unless some other belief outweighs it or some failure of energy stifles the movement at its birth. The only difference between the expression of an opinion and an incitement in the narrower sense is the speaker's enthusiasm for the result. Eloquence may set fire to reason. But whatever may be thought of the redundant discourse before us it had no chance of starting a present conflagration. If in the long run the beliefs expressed in proletarian dictatorship are destined to be accepted by the dominant forces of the community, the only meaning of free speech is that they should be given their chance and have their way.

If the publication of this document had been laid as an attempt to induce an uprising against government at once and not at some indefinite time in the future it would have presented a different question. The object would have been one with which the law might deal, subject to the doubt whether

there was any danger that the publication could produce any result, or in other words, whether it was not futile and too remote from possible consequences. But the indictment alleges the publication and nothing more.

THE GITLOW PROBLEM AND THE HOLMES DISSENT

Was the majority right in claiming that the question in a case such as Gitlow "is entirely different from that involved in those cases where the statute merely prohibits certain acts involving the danger of substantive evil, without any reference to language itself, and it is sought to apply its provisions to language used by the defendant for the purpose of bringing about the prohibited results"? Was it accurate to say that the Schenck standard only applied to such cases, "and has no application to those like the present, where the legislative body itself has previously determined the danger of substantive evil arising from utterances of a specified character"? Or *did* the clear and present danger test, as it had been formulated in Schenck, apply —explicitly or implicitly—to the Gitlow (and Whitney, below) problem?

How does Justice Holmes answer the majority's assertion? Does he answer? What is his view in the Gitlow dissent regarding the weight to be given the legislative judgment? Does he have any view? Is the question of the weight appropriate for the legislative judgment irrelevant here? Compare Justice Holmes' emphasis on deference to legislative judgments in his substantive due process dissents in cases beginning with Lochner, chap. 9, above.

Consider the following comment: "In Gitlow, Holmes was confronted by, and evaded, the difficulty of applying his Schenck remark without modification to this different kind of problem." Rogat, "The Judge as Spectator," 31 U.Chi.L.Rev. 213 (1964). Do you agree? What is "evaded"? Does Brandeis' opinion in Whitney, which follows, adequately confront what Holmes "evaded"? Professor Rogat argues that when the legislature prohibits advocacy of a specific doctrine, the question is no longer "proximity" to a specified act: "Here a court may have to establish . . . the importance (or the legitimacy) of forbidding the completed act." The important question, he argues, may well not be "proximity," but "which 'evils' a legislature may prohibit." What does Whitney say about that question? Would that be the important question if Masses provided the constitutional approach? Would Masses emphasize instead what speech is protected? Is that simply another way of putting the same "important question"? Compare the responses to the problem of prior legislative judgments focusing on prohibited speech in Dennis and subsequent cases below.

WHITNEY v. CALIFORNIA

274 U.S. 357, 47 S.Ct. 641, 71 L.Ed. 1095 (1927).

Error to the District Court of Appeal, First Appellate District, Division One, of California.

Mr. Justice SANFORD delivered the opinion of the Court.

By a criminal information filed in the Superior Court of Alameda County, California, the plaintiff in error was charged, in five counts, with violations of the Criminal Syndicalism Act of that State. Statutes 1919, c. 188, p. 281.* She was tried, convicted on the first count, and sentenced to imprisonment. . . .

The first count of the information, on which the conviction was had, charged that on or about November 28, 1919, in Alameda County, the defendant, in violation of the Criminal Syndicalism Act, "did then and there unlawfully, wilfully, wrongfully, deliberately and feloniously organize and assist in organizing, and was, is, and knowingly became a member of an organization, society, group and assemblage of persons organized and assembled to advocate, teach, aid and abet criminal syndicalism." . . .

[In its summary of the facts, the Court stated that Miss Whitney had attended the 1919 national convention of the Socialist Party as a delegate from the Oakland branch. The convention split, and the "radicals"—including Miss Whitney—went to another hall and formed the Communist Labor Party. Later in 1919, she was a branch delegate to a convention called to organize a California unit of the new Party. As a member of that convention's resolutions committee, she supported a resolution endorsing "the value of political action" and urging workers "to cast their votes for the party which represents their immediate and final interest—the C. L. P.—at all elections." The proposed resolution was defeated on the floor of the convention and a more extreme program was adopted. Miss Whitney remained a member of the Party and testified at the trial "that it was not her intention that the Communist Labor Party of California should be an instrument of terrorism or violence."]

1. While it is not denied that the evidence warranted the jury in finding that the defendant became a member of and assisted in organizing the Communist Labor Party of California, and that this was organized to advocate, teach, aid or abet criminal syndicalism as defined by the Act, it is urged

---

* The pertinent provisions of the Criminal Syndicalism Act stated:

"Section 1. The term 'criminal syndicalism' as used in this act is hereby defined as any doctrine or precept advocating, teaching or aiding and abetting the commission of crime, sabotage (which word is hereby defined as meaning willful and malicious physical damage or injury to physical property), or unlawful acts of force and violence or unlawful methods of terrorism as a means of accomplishing a change in industrial ownership or control, or effecting any political change.

"Sec. 2. Any person who: . . .
4. Organizes or assists in organizing, or is or knowingly becomes a member of, any organization, society, group or assemblage of persons organized or assembled to advocate, teach or aid and abet criminal syndicalism; . . .

"Is guilty of a felony and punishable by imprisonment."

that the Act, as here construed and applied, deprived the defendant of her liberty without due process of law . . . . . The argument is, in effect, that the character of the state organization could not be forecast when she attended the convention; that she had no purpose of helping to create an instrument of terrorism and violence; that she "took part in formulating and presenting to the convention a resolution which, if adopted, would have committed the new organization to a legitimate policy of political reform by the use of the ballot"; that it was not until after the majority of the convention turned out to be "contrary-minded, and other less temperate policies prevailed" that the convention could have taken on the character of criminal syndicalism; and that as this was done over her protest, her mere presence in the convention, however violent the opinions expressed therein, could not thereby become a crime. This contention, while advanced in the form of a constitutional objection to the Act, is in effect nothing more than an effort to review the weight of the evidence for the purpose of showing that the defendant did not join and assist in organizing the Communist Labor Party of California with a knowledge of its unlawful character and purpose. This question, which is foreclosed by the verdict of the jury, . . is one of fact merely which is not open to review in this Court, involving as it does no constitutional question whatever. . . .

2. It is clear that the Syndicalism Act is not repugnant to the due process clause by reason of vagueness and uncertainty of definition. . . .

4. Nor is the Syndicalism Act as applied in this case repugnant to the due process clause as a restraint of the rights of free speech, assembly, and association.

That the freedom of speech which is secured by the Constitution does not confer an absolute right to speak, without responsibility, whatever one may choose . . . .; and that a State in the exercise of its police power may punish those who abuse this freedom by utterances inimical to the public welfare, tending to incite to crime, disturb the public peace, or endanger the foundations of organized government and threaten its overthrow by unlawful means, is not open to question. [Gitlow v. New York.]

By enacting the provisions of the Syndicalism Act the State has declared, through its legislative body, that to knowingly be or become a member of or assist in organizing an association to advocate, teach or aid and abet the commission of crimes or unlawful acts of force, violence or terrorism . . . involves such danger to the public peace and the security of the State, that these acts should be penalized in the exercise of its police power. That determination must be given great weight. . . .

The essence of the offense denounced by the Act is the combining with others in an association for the accomplishment of the desired ends through the advocacy and use of criminal and unlawful methods. It partakes of the nature of a criminal conspiracy. . . . That such united and joint action involves even greater danger to the public peace and security than the isolated utterances and acts of individuals, is clear. We cannot hold that, as here applied, the Act is an unreasonable or arbitrary exercise of the police power of the State, unwarrantably infringing any right of free speech, assembly or association, or that those persons are protected from punishment by the

due process clause who abuse such rights by joining and furthering an organization thus menacing the peace and welfare of the State.   .   .   .

Affirmed.

Mr. Justice BRANDEIS, concurring.   .   .   .

The felony which the statute created is a crime very unlike the old felony of conspiracy or the old misdemeanor of unlawful assembly. The mere act of assisting in forming a society for teaching syndicalism, of becoming a member of it, or of assembling with others for that purpose is given the dynamic quality of crime. There is guilt although the society may not contemplate immediate promulgation of the doctrine. Thus the accused is to be punished, not for contempt, incitement or conspiracy, but for a step in preparation, which, if it threatens the public order at all, does so only remotely. The novelty in the prohibition introduced is that the statute aims, not at the practice of criminal syndicalism, nor even directly at the preaching of it, but at association with those who propose to preach it.

Despite arguments to the contrary which had seemed to me persuasive, it is settled that the due process clause of the Fourteenth Amendment applies to matters of substantive law as well as to matters of procedure. Thus all fundamental rights comprised within the term liberty are protected by the Federal Constitution from invasion by the States. The right of free speech, the right to teach and the right of assembly are, of course, fundamental rights. See [Meyer v. Nebraska; Gitlow v. New York]. These may not be denied or abridged. But, although the rights of free speech and assembly are fundamental, they are not in their nature absolute. Their exercise is subject to restriction, if the particular restriction proposed is required in order to protect the State from destruction or from serious injury, political, economic or moral. That the necessity which is essential to a valid restriction does not exist unless speech would produce, or is intended to produce, a clear and imminent danger of some substantive evil which the State constitutionally may seek to prevent has been settled. See [Schenck].

It is said to be the function of the legislature to determine whether at a particular time and under the particular circumstances the formation of, or assembly with, a society organized to advocate criminal syndicalism constitutes a clear and present danger of substantive evil; and that by enacting the law here in question the legislature of California determined that question in the affirmative. Compare [Gitlow v. New York]. The legislature must obviously decide, in the first instance, whether a danger exists which calls for a particular protective measure. But where a statute is valid only in case certain conditions exist, the enactment of the statute cannot alone establish the facts which are essential to its validity. Prohibitory legislation has repeatedly been held invalid, because unnecessary, where the denial of liberty involved was that of engaging in a particular business. The power of the courts to strike down an offending law is no less when the interests involved are not property rights, but the fundamental personal rights of free speech and assembly.

This Court has not yet fixed the standard by which to determine when a danger shall be deemed clear; how remote the danger may be and yet be deemed present; and what degree of evil shall be deemed sufficiently sub-

stantial to justify resort to abridgement of free speech and assembly as the means of protection. To reach sound conclusions on these matters, we must bear in mind why a State is, ordinarily, denied the power to prohibit dissemination of social, economic and political doctrine which a vast majority of its citizens believes to be false and fraught with evil consequence.

Those who won our independence believed that the final end of the State was to make men free to develop their faculties; and that in its government the deliberative forces should prevail over the arbitrary. They valued liberty both as an end and as a means. They believed liberty to be the secret of happiness and courage to be the secret of liberty. They believed that freedom to think as you will and to speak as you think are means indispensable to the discovery and spread of political truth; that without free speech and assembly discussion would be futile; that with them, discussion affords ordinarily adequate protection against the dissemination of noxious doctrine; that the greatest menace to freedom is an inert people; that public discussion is a political duty; and that this should be a fundamental principle of the American government. They recognized the risks to which all human institutions are subject. But they knew that order cannot be secured merely through fear of punishment for its infraction; that it is hazardous to discourage thought, hope and imagination; that fear breeds repression; that repression breeds hate; that hate menaces stable government; that the path of safety lies in the opportunity to discuss freely supposed grievances and proposed remedies; and that the fitting remedy for evil counsels is good ones. Believing in the power of reason as applied through public discussion, they eschewed silence coerced by law—the argument of force in its worst form. Recognizing the occasional tyrannies of governing majorities, they amended the Constitution so that free speech and assembly should be guaranteed.

Fear of serious injury cannot alone justify suppression of free speech and assembly. Men feared witches and burnt women. It is the function of speech to free men from the bondage of irrational fears. To justify suppression of free speech there must be reasonable ground to fear that serious evil will result if free speech is practiced. There must be reasonable ground to believe that the danger apprehended is imminent. There must be reasonable ground to believe that the evil to be prevented is a serious one. Every denunciation of existing law tends in some measure to increase the probability that there will be violation of it. Condonation of a breach enhances the probability. Expressions of approval add to the probability. Propagation of the criminal state of mind by teaching syndicalism increases it. Advocacy of lawbreaking heightens it still further. But even advocacy of violation, however reprehensible morally, is not a justification for denying free speech where the advocacy falls short of incitement and there is nothing to indicate that the advocacy would be immediately acted on. The wide difference between advocacy and incitement, between preparation and attempt, between assembling and conspiracy, must be borne in mind. In order to support a finding of clear and present danger it must be shown either that immediate serious violence was to be expected or was advocated, or that the past conduct furnished reason to believe that such advocacy was then contemplated.

Those who won our independence by revolution were not cowards. They did not fear political change. They did not exalt order at the cost of

liberty. To courageous, self-reliant men, with confidence in the power of free and fearless reasoning applied through the processes of popular government, no danger flowing from speech can be deemed clear and present, unless the incidence of the evil apprehended is so imminent that it may befall before there is opportunity for full discussion. If there be time to expose through discussion the falsehood and fallacies, to avert the evil by the processes of education, the remedy to be applied is more speech, not enforced silence. Only an emergency can justify repression. Such must be the rule if authority is to be reconciled with freedom. Such, in my opinion, is the command of the Constitution. It is therefore always open to Americans to challenge a law abridging free speech and assembly by showing that there was no emergency justifying it.

Moreover, even imminent danger cannot justify resort to prohibition of these functions essential to effective democracy, unless the evil apprehended is relatively serious. Prohibition of free speech and assembly is a measure so stringent that it would be inappropriate as the means for averting a relatively trivial harm to society. A police measure may be unconstitutional merely because the remedy, although effective as a means of protection, is unduly harsh or oppressive. Thus, a State might, in the exercise of its police power, make any trespass upon the land of another a crime, regardless of the results or of the intent or purpose of the trespasser. It might, also, punish an attempt, a conspiracy, or an incitement to commit the trespass. But it is hardly conceivable that this Court would hold constitutional a statute which punished as a felony the mere voluntary assembly with a society formed to teach that pedestrians had the moral right to cross unenclosed, unposted, waste lands and to advocate their doing so, even if there was imminent danger that advocacy would lead to a trespass. The fact that speech is likely to result in some violence or in destruction of property is not enough to justify its suppression. There must be the probability of serious injury to the State. Among free men, the deterrents ordinarily to be applied to prevent crime are education and punishment for violations of the law, not abridgment of the rights of free speech and assembly.

[The California] legislative declaration satisfies the requirement of the constitution of the State concerning emergency legislation. . . . But it does not preclude enquiry into the question whether, at the time and under the circumstances, the conditions existed which are essential to validity under the Federal Constitution. As a statute, even if not void on its face, may be challenged because invalid as applied, Dahnke-Walker Milling Co. v. Bondurant, 257 U.S. 282, the result of such an enquiry may depend upon the specific facts of the particular case. Whenever the fundamental rights of free speech and assembly are alleged to have been invaded, it must remain open to a defendant to present the issue whether there actually did exist at the time a clear danger; whether the danger, if any, was imminent; and whether the evil apprehended was one so substantial as to justify the stringent restriction interposed by the legislature. The legislative declaration, like the fact that the statute was passed and was sustained by the highest court of the State, creates merely a rebuttable presumption that these conditions have been satisfied.

Whether in 1919, when Miss Whitney did the things complained of, there was in California such clear and present danger of serious evil, might have been made the important issue in the case. She might have required that the issue be determined either by the court or the jury. She claimed below that the statute as applied to her violated the Federal Constitution; but she did not claim that it was void because there was no clear and present danger of serious evil, nor did she request that the existence of these conditions of a valid measure thus restricting the rights of free speech and assembly be passed upon by the court or a jury. On the other hand, there was evidence on which the court or jury might have found that such danger existed. I am unable to assent to the suggestion in the opinion of the Court that assembling with a political party, formed to advocate the desirability of a proletarian revolution by mass action at some date necessarily far in the future, is not a right within the protection of the Fourteenth Amendment. In the present case, however, there was other testimony which tended to establish the existence of a conspiracy, on the part of members of the International Workers of the World, to commit present serious crimes; and likewise to show that such a conspiracy would be furthered by the activity of the society of which Miss Whitney was a member. Under these circumstances the judgment of the state court cannot be disturbed.

Our power of review in this case is limited not only to the question whether a right guaranteed by the Federal Constitution was denied, but to the particular claims duly made below, and denied. . . . We lack here the power occasionally exercised on review of judgments of lower federal courts to correct in criminal cases vital errors, although the objection was not taken in the trial court. . . . This is a writ of error to a state court. Because we may not enquire into the errors now alleged, I concur in affirming the judgment of the state court.

Mr. Justice HOLMES joins in this opinion.

OTHER CASES OF THE TWENTIES AND THIRTIES: THE GROWING PROTECTION OF SPEECH

Introduction. Most states enacted anti-sedition laws in the immediate post-World War I years—some patterned on the New York and California ones in Gitlow and Whitney, some going off in different and often more extreme directions. See generally Chafee, Free Speech in the United States (1941). In a number of cases in the 1920's and 1930's, the Court set aside convictions under such laws.*

* In addition to the three decisions considered here (Fiske, DeJonge, and Herndon v. Lowry), note also Stromberg v. California, 283 U.S. 359 (1931) (holding unconstitutional a version of a widely adopted red flag law; Stromberg is noted with the materials on symbolic expression, sec. 3 below), and two cases not directly involving "Red scare," antisubversion concerns: Near v. Minnesota, 283 U.S. 697 (1931) (invalidating injunctive remedies against "malicious, scandalous and defamatory" periodicals, see chap. 13, sec. 3, below); and Hague v. CIO, 307 U.S. 496 (1939) (invalidating a licensing requirement for meetings on public property, see sec. 2 below).

Did the protection of freedom of speech in the cases that follow rest on the Schenck standard? On the minority views in Abrams, Gitlow, or Whitney? Or do these decisions represent new doctrinal developments? Is Herndon in effect a Court acceptance of the temporal, immediacy ingredient of clear and present danger—an ingredient not emphasized in the Court decisions in Gitlow and Whitney? Do these cases begin to articulate the contours of political discussion and agitation required by First Amendment values (at some point short of "incitement" or "counselling") in much the same manner as Learned Hand had in the Masses case? Compare the analytical process in Yates and Scales, below, and in New York Times v. Sullivan, chap. 13, sec. 1: is the effort to define the protected area of debate at the core of the First Amendment more productive than the immediacy-of-danger preoccupation of the clear and present danger test? Do the cases which follow speak to the Gitlow or Whitney problem (of the weight to be given to prior legislative judgments regarding the danger of specified speech) more directly than the Gitlow dissent had? Do the cases which follow provide clear guidance regarding the constitutionality of the post-World War II Smith Act prosecutions of Communists, in cases such as Dennis, below? To what extent do the cases from Fiske to Herndon represent substantive First Amendment adjudications, delineating the scope of protected "speech"? To what extent do they rest on grounds only peripherally related to the First Amendment? Note, e. g., the discussion of "vagueness" in Herndon, and the comments on improper "inferences" in Fiske.

1. FISKE v. KANSAS. The Fiske case, 274 U.S. 380 (1927), decided on the same day as Whitney, held unconstitutional an application of the Kansas version of criminal syndicalism legislation. Fiske was convicted for soliciting new members for a branch of the IWW (Industrial Workers of the World). The only trial evidence of IWW doctrine was the preamble to its constitution, containing such statements as: "Between [the working and employing] classes a struggle must go on until the workers of the World organize as a class, take possession of the earth, and the machinery of production and abolish the wage system." Fiske insisted that the preamble taught "peaceful," not "criminal or unlawful," action, and that he had not advocated criminal syndicalism or sabotage.

In affirming the conviction, the highest state court said: "The language quoted from the I.W.W. preamble need not—in order to sustain the judgment—be held, necessarily and as a matter of law, to advocate, teach or even affirmatively suggest physical violence as a means of accomplishing industrial or political ends. It is open to that interpretation and is capable of use to convey that meaning. . . . The jury were not required to accept the defendant's testimony as a candid and accurate statement. There was room for them to find [that] the equivocal language of the preamble and of the defendant in explaining it to his prospects was employed to convey and did convey the sinister meaning attributed to it by the state." The United States Supreme Court unanimously reversed, in an opinion by Justice Sanford:

"[T]his Court will review the finding of facts by a State court where a federal right has been denied as the result of a finding shown by the record to be without evidence to support it; or where a conclusion of law as to

a Federal right and a finding of fact are so intermingled as to make it necessary, in order to pass upon the Federal question, to analyze the facts. . . .

". . . No substantial inference can, in our judgment, be drawn from the language of this preamble, that the organization taught, advocated or suggested the duty, necessity, propriety, or expediency of crime, criminal syndicalism, sabotage, or other unlawful acts or methods. . . . And standing alone, as it did in this case, there was nothing which warranted the court or jury in ascribing to this language, either as an inference of law or fact, 'the sinister meaning attributed to it by the state.' In this respect the language of the preamble is essentially different from that of the manifesto involved in [Gitlow v. New York]. And it is not as if the preamble were shown to have been followed by further statements or declarations indicating that it was intended to mean, and to be understood as advocating, that the ends outlined therein would be accomplished or brought about by violence or other related unlawful acts or methods. . . .

"The result is that the Syndicalism Act has been applied in this case to sustain the conviction of the defendant, without any charge or evidence that the organization in which he secured members advocated any crime, violence or other unlawful acts or methods as a means of effecting industrial or political changes or revolution. Thus applied the Act is an arbitrary and unreasonable exercise of the police power of the State, unwarrantably infringing the liberty of the defendant in violation of the due process clause of the Fourteenth Amendment."

[Note that Fiske was written by Justice Sanford, the author of the majority opinion in Gitlow. Was Fiske an early example of a double standard—of special protection for personal liberties? Or was it simply one more example of the Lochner-substantive due process approach? Was Fiske truly a First Amendment decision? Or did it rest on "procedural due process" grounds: the impermissibility of drawing conclusory inferences from inadequate facts, rather than the constitutionally protected nature of the defendant's conduct? Cf. the Thompson v. Louisville "principle." *]

* In Thompson v. Louisville, 362 U.S. 199 (1960), Justice Black's opinion for the Court reversed a conviction for loitering and disorderly conduct on the ground that the charges "were so totally devoid of evidentiary support as to render [petitioner's] conviction unconstitutional under the Due Process Clause of the Fourteenth Amendment." He insisted that the decision turned "not on the sufficiency of the evidence, but on whether this conviction rests upon any evidence at all." And he concluded: "We find no evidence whatever in the record to support these convictions. Just as 'Conviction upon a charge not made would be sheer denial of due process,' so is it a violation of due process to convict and punish a man without evidence of his guilt."

Note that Thompson v. Louisville purports to be a "procedural due proc-ess" decision. It does not say that petitioner's conduct was constitutionally protected or could not be made a crime. Instead, it claims that the state could not infer from the evidence shown that he had committed the crime charged. In principle, that due process defense is available whether or not the conduct is constitutionally protected: in theory, for example, it would be as bad to convict someone of murder on evidence showing only drunken driving, even though drunken driving could be made a crime.

The Thompson v. Louisville principle was applied by the Warren Court in a variety of contexts, especially as a procedural technique for the indirect protection of substantive rights. In a number of instances, it was relied on to reverse convictions without the necessity of reaching underlying First

2. DeJONGE v. OREGON. Ten years later, the DeJonge case, 299 U.S. 353 (1937), set aside a conviction under Oregon's criminal syndicalism act. The statute defined criminal syndicalism as "the doctrine which advocates crime, physical violence, sabotage, or any unlawful acts or methods as a means of accomplishing or effecting industrial or political change or revolution." DeJonge was charged with assisting in the conduct of a meeting "which was called under the auspices of the Communist Party, an organization advocating criminal syndicalism." At the trial, he moved for acquittal on the ground "that the meeting was public and orderly and was held for a lawful purpose; that while it was held under the auspices of the Communist Party, neither criminal syndicalism nor any unlawful conduct was taught or advocated at the meeting either by appellant or by others." The motion was denied. The highest state court affirmed this ruling, holding that there was no charge that criminal syndicalism was advocated at the meeting; rather, the court construed the indictment as simply charging that DeJonge conducted a meeting called by the Party, and that the Party advocated criminal syndicalism. Accordingly, lack of proof of illegal advocacy at the meeting itself was immaterial. The Supreme Court unanimously reversed. Chief Justice Hughes' opinion included the following passages:

"We must take the indictment as thus construed. Conviction upon a charge not made would be sheer denial of due process. It thus appears that, while defendant was a member of the Communist Party, he was not indicted for participating in its organization, or for joining it, or for soliciting members or for distributing its literature. He was not charged with teaching or advocating criminal syndicalism or sabotage or any unlawful acts, either at the meeting or elsewhere. . . . His sole offense . . . was that he had assisted in the conduct of a public meeting, albeit otherwise lawful, which was held under the auspices of the Communist Party.

"The broad reach of the statute as thus applied is plain. While defendant was a member of the Communist Party, that membership was not necessary to conviction on such a charge. A like fate might have attended any speaker, although not a member who 'assisted in the conduct' of the meeting. However innocuous the object of the meeting, however lawful the subjects and tenor of the addresses, however reasonable and timely the discussion, all those assisting in the conduct of the meeting would be subject to imprisonment as felons if the meeting were held by the Communist Party. . . .

"The right of peaceable assembly is a right cognate to those of free speech and free press and is equally fundamental. . . . These rights may be abused by using speech or press or assembly in order to incite to violence and crime. . . . But the legislative intervention can find constitutional justification only by dealing with the abuse. The rights themselves must not be curtailed. . . .

"It follows from these considerations that, consistently with the Federal Constitution, peaceable assembly for lawful discussion cannot be made a crime. The holding of meetings for peaceable political action cannot be pro-

Amendment issues. See, e. g., Gregory v. Chicago, 394 U.S. 111 (1969), and Shuttlesworth v. Birmingham, 382 U. S. 87 (1965), sec. 2 below. Compare the due process doctrine limiting the creating of statutory presumptions, as in Tot v. United States (chap. 10, sec. 6, above), cited in Thompson.

scribed. Those who assist in the conduct of such meetings cannot be branded as criminals on that score. The question, if the rights of free speech and peaceable assembly are to be preserved, is not as to the auspices under which the meeting is held but as to its purpose; not as to the relations of the speakers, but whether their utterances transcend the bounds of the freedom of speech which the Constitution protects. . . .

"We are not called upon to review the findings of the state court as to the objectives of the Communist Party. Notwithstanding those objectives, the defendant still enjoyed his personal right of free speech and to take part in a peaceable assembly having a lawful purpose, although called by that Party. . . . We hold that the Oregon statute as applied to the particular charge as defined by the state court is repugnant to the due process clause of the Fourteenth Amendment."

HERNDON v. LOWRY

301 U.S. 242, 57 S.Ct. 732, 81 L.Ed. 1066 (1937).

Appeal from the Supreme Court of Georgia.

Mr. Justice ROBERTS delivered the opinion of the Court. . . .

The charge ["attempt to incite insurrection"] was founded on § 56 of the [Georgia] Penal Code, one of four related sections. . . . [1] The evidence on which the judgment rests consists of appellant's admissions and certain documents found in his possession. The appellant told the state's officers that [he] came to Atlanta as a paid organizer for the [Communist Party], his duties being to call meetings, to educate and disseminate information respecting the party, to distribute literature, to secure members, and to work up an organization of the party in Atlanta, and that he had held or attended three meetings called by him. . . .

Certain documents in his possession when he was arrested were placed in evidence [including membership blanks. These] indicate more specific aims for which members of the Communist Party are to vote. They are to vote Communist for:

"1. Unemployment and Social Insurance at the expense of the State and employers. 2. Against Hoover's wage-cutting policy. 3. Emergency relief for the poor farmers without restrictions by the government and banks; exemption of poor farmers from taxes and from forced collection of rents or debts. 4. Equal rights for the Negroes and self-determination for the Black Belt. 5. Against capitalistic terror: against all forms of suppression of the political rights of the workers. 6. Against imperialist war; for the defense of the Chinese people and of the Soviet Union."

None of these aims is criminal upon its face. As to one, the fourth, the claim is that criminality may be found because of extrinsic facts. [T]he state

---

[1]. "55. Insurrection shall consist in any combined resistance to the lawful authority of the State, with intent to the denial thereof, when the same is manifested or intended to be manifested by acts of violence.

"56. Any attempt, by persuasion or otherwise, to induce others to join in any combined resistance to the lawful authority of the State shall constitute an attempt to incite insurrection. . . . ." [Footnote by the Court.]

especially relies upon a booklet entitled "The Communist Position on the Negro Question," on the cover of which appears a map of the United States having a dark belt across certain Southern states and the phrase "Self-Determination for the Black Belt." The booklet affirms that the source of the Communist slogan "Right of Self-Determination of the Negroes in the Black Belt" is a resolution of the Communist International on the Negro question in the United States adopted in 1930, which states that the Communist Party in the United States has been actively attempting to win increasing sympathy among the negro population, that certain things have been advocated for the benefit of the Negroes in the Northern states, but that in the Southern portion of the United States the Communist slogan must be "The Right of Self-Determination of the Negroes in the Black Belt." . . .

There is no evidence the appellant distributed any writings or printed matter found in the box he carried when arrested, or any other advocating forcible subversion of governmental authority. There is no evidence the appellant advocated, by speech or written word, at meetings or elsewhere, any doctrine or action implying such forcible subversion. . . . Appellant's intent to incite insurrection, if it is to be found, must rest upon his procuring members of the Communist Party and his possession of that party's literature when he was arrested. . . .

To ascertain how the Act is held to apply to the appellant's conduct we turn to the rulings of the state courts in his case. [The Georgia Supreme Court] sustained the conviction by construing the statute thus: "Force must have been contemplated, but, as said above, the statute does not include either its occurrence or its imminence as an ingredient of the particular offense charged." . . . The affirmance of conviction upon the trial record necessarily gives § 56 the construction that one who seeks members for or attempts to organize a local unit of a party which has the purposes and objects disclosed by the documents in evidence may be found guilty of an attempt to incite insurrection.

The questions are whether this construction and application of the statute deprives the accused of the right of freedom of speech and of assembly guaranteed by the Fourteenth Amendment, and whether the statute so construed and applied furnishes a reasonably definite and ascertainable standard of guilt.

The appellant [insists] that legislative regulation may not go beyond measures forefending against "clear and present danger" of the use of force against the state. For this position he relies upon [e. g., Schenck]. The legislation under review differs radically from the Espionage Acts in that it does not deal with a wilful attempt to obstruct a described and defined activity of the government.

The State, on the other hand, insists that our decisions uphold state statutes making criminal utterances which have a "dangerous tendency" towards the subversion of government. It relies particularly upon Gitlow v. New York, 268 U.S. 652. There, however, we dealt with a statute which, quite unlike § 56 of the Georgia Criminal Code, denounced as criminal certain acts carefully and adequately described.

It is evident that [Gitlow, permitting the penalizing of "utterances which openly advocate" overthrow by unlawful means,] furnishes no warrant

for the appellee's contention that under a law general in its description of
the mischief to be remedied and equally general in respect of the intent of
the actor, the standard of guilt may be made the "dangerous tendency" of his
words.

The power of a state to abridge freedom of speech and of assembly is
the exception rather than the rule and the penalizing even of utterances of a
defined character must find its justification in a reasonable apprehension of
danger to organized government. The judgment of the legislature is not
unfettered. The limitation upon individual liberty must have appropriate
relation to the safety of the state. Legislation which goes beyond this need
violates the principle of the Constitution. [See DeJonge.]　. . .

1. The appellant had a constitutional right to address meetings and organize parties unless in so doing he violated some prohibition of a valid
statute. The only prohibition he is said to have violated is that of § 56 forbidding incitement or attempted incitement to insurrection by violence. If
the evidence fails to show that he did so incite, then, as applied to him, the
statute unreasonably limits freedom of speech and freedom of assembly and
violates the Fourteenth Amendment. We are of opinion that the requisite
proof is lacking. From what has been said above with respect to the evidence
offered at the trial it is apparent that the documents found upon the appellant's person were certainly, as to some of the aims stated therein, innocent
and consistent with peaceful action for a change in the laws or the constitution.
The proof wholly fails to show that the appellant had read these documents;
that he had distributed any of them; that he believed and advocated any or
all of the principles and aims set forth in them, or that those he had procured
to become members of the party knew or approved of [them].

Thus, the crucial question is not the formal interpretation of the statute
by the Supreme Court of Georgia but the application given it. In its application the offense made criminal is that of soliciting members for a political
party and conducting meetings of a local unit of that party when one of the
doctrines of the party, established by reference to a document not shown to
have been exhibited to anyone by the accused, may be said to be ultimate resort to violence at some indefinite future time against organized government.
It is to be borne in mind that the legislature of Georgia has not made membership in the Communist Party unlawful by reason of its supposed dangerous
tendency even in the remote future. The question is not whether Georgia
might, in analogy to what other states have done, so declare.[2] The appellant
induced others to become members of the Communist Party. Did he thus
incite to insurrection by reason of the fact that they agreed to abide by the
tenets of the party, some of them lawful, others, as may be assumed, unlawful,
in the absence of proof that he brought the unlawful aims to their notice, that
he approved them, or that the fantastic program they envisaged was conceived
of by anyone as more than an ultimate ideal? Doubtless circumstantial evidence might affect the answer to the question if appellant had been shown
to have said that the Black Belt should be organized at once as a separate
state and that that objective was one of his principal aims. But here circum-

---

2. See the statutes drawn in question
in Gitlow v. New York, 268 U.S. 652,
at 654, and in Whitney v. California,
274 U.S. 357, 359. [Footnote by the
Court.]

stantial evidence is all to the opposite effect. [His] membership in the Communist Party and his solicitation of a few members wholly fail to establish an attempt to incite others to insurrection. [T]o make membership in the party and solicitation of members for that party a criminal offense, punishable by death, in the discretion of a jury, is an unwarranted invasion of the right of freedom of speech [in the circumstances of this case].

2. The statute, as construed and applied in the appellant's trial, does not furnish a sufficiently ascertainable standard of guilt. The Act does not prohibit incitement to violent interference with any given activity or operation of the state. By force of it, as construed, the judge and jury trying an alleged offender cannot appraise the circumstances and character of the defendant's utterances or activities as begetting a clear and present danger of forcible obstruction of a particular state function. Nor is any specified conduct or utterance of the accused made an offense.

. . . If the jury conclude that the defendant should have contemplated that any act or utterance of his in opposition to the established order or advocating a change in that order, might, in the distant future, eventuate in a combination to offer forcible resistance to the State, or as the State says, if the jury believe he should have known that his words would have "a dangerous tendency" then he may be convicted. To be guilty under the law, as construed, a defendant need not advocate resort to force. . . . If, by the exercise of prophecy, he can forecast that, as a result of a chain of causation, following his proposed action a group may arise at some future date which will resort to force, he is bound to make the prophesy and abstain, under pain of punishment, possibly of execution. Every person who attacks existing conditions, who agitates for a change in the form of government, must take the risk that if a jury should be of opinion he ought to have foreseen that his utterances might contribute in any measure to some future forcible resistance to the existing government he may be convicted of the [incitement] offense. [It] would be sufficient if the jury thought he reasonably might foretell that those he persuaded to join the party might, at some time in the indefinite future, resort to forcible resistance of government. The question thus proposed to a jury involves pure speculation as to future trends of thought and action. Within what time might one reasonably expect that an attempted organization of the Communist Party in the United States would result in violent action by that party? If a jury returned a special verdict saying twenty years or even fifty years the verdict could not be shown to be wrong. The law, as thus construed, licenses the jury to create its own standard in each case. . . .

The statute, as construed and applied, amounts merely to a dragnet which may enmesh anyone who agitates for a change of government if a jury can be persuaded that he ought to have foreseen his words would have some effect in the future conduct of others. . . . So vague and indeterminate are the boundaries thus set to the freedom of speech and assembly that the law necessarily violates the guaranties of liberty embodied in the Fourteenth Amendment. . . .

Reversed.

Mr. Justice VAN DEVANTER, dissenting. . . .

It should not be overlooked that Herndon was a negro member and organizer in the Communist Party and was engaged actively in inducing others, chiefly southern negroes, to become members of the party and participate in effecting its purposes and program. The literature placed in his hands by the party for that purpose was particularly adapted to appeal to negroes in that section, for it pictured their condition as an unhappy one resulting from asserted wrongs on the part of white landlords and employers, and sought by alluring statements of resulting advantages to induce them to join in an effort to carry into effect the measures which the literature proposed. These measures included a revolutionary uprooting of the existing capitalist state, as it was termed; confiscation of the landed property of white landowners and capitalists for the benefit of negroes; establishment in the black belt of an independent State, possibly followed by secession from the United States; organization of mass demonstrations, strikes and tax boycotts in aid of this measure; adoption of a fighting alliance with the revolutionary white proletariat; revolutionary overthrow of capitalism and establishment of Communism through effective physical struggles against the class enemy. Proposing these measures was nothing short of advising a resort to force and violence, for all know that such measures could not be effected otherwise. Not only so, but the literature makes such repelling use of the terms "revolution," "national rebellion," "revolutionary struggle," "revolutionary overthrow," "effective physical struggle," "smash the National Guard," "mass strikes," and "violence," as to leave no doubt that the use of force in an unlawful sense is intended.

The purpose and probable effect of such literature, when under consideration in a prosecution like that against Herndon, are to be tested and determined with appropriate regard to the capacity and circumstances of those who are sought to be influenced. In this instance the literature is largely directed to a people whose past and present circumstances would lead them to give unusual credence to its inflaming and inciting features. . . .

[Justices McREYNOLDS, SUTHERLAND and BUTLER joined this dissent.]

C. THE SMITH ACT PROSECUTIONS

CLEAR AND PRESENT DANGER IN THE FORTIES: WIDENING USE; RISING DISSATISFACTION

Introduction. The post-World War II prosecutions of Communist Party leaders were brought under the Smith Act of 1940, a law quite similar to the New York statute sustained in Gitlow. When the first group of defendants brought their appeals to the Supreme Court, in the 1951 Dennis case which follows, they relied extensively on clear and present danger; and the opinions in Dennis reexamine that standard at length.

The defendants' reliance on the test was understandable: the Court had spoken of it with increasing frequency. But the appearances had often

been in contexts far removed from subversive advocacy. For example, an early use in a majority opinion was Schneider v. State, 308 U.S. 147 (1939), involving an ordinance against littering streets. And the most consistent use of the test had been to strike down contempt of court penalties imposed for newspaper comments allegedly interfering with the administration of justice. See, e. g., Craig v. Harney, 331 U.S. 367 (1947) (chap. 13, sec. 4, below.)

Moreover, there had been increasing criticism of the standard itself. Some critics, then and later, thought clear and present danger afforded either too much or too little protection to free speech: the Vinson plurality opinion in Dennis, for example, finds the immediacy emphasis too restrictive on government; [1] the Douglas opinion in Brandenburg v. Ohio, the 1969 decision below, illustrates the dissatisfaction with the use of the standard to "balance away" liberties.[2]

But much of the criticism dealt less with the scope of protection afforded by the Schenck phrase than with its suitability: it was argued that the standard was used in inappropriate contexts, that it was too simplistic, that in any event it did not deal adequately with the type of problem presented by Gitlow and Dennis.

1. *Clear and present danger and legislative balancing.* For example, as early as 1941—a few months after the Smith Act was enacted, eight years before the Dennis trial—Herbert Wechsler suggested not only that the Smith Act variety of statute had "little positive merit" as a legislative formula but also that the clear and present danger judicial formula urged as a protection of speech had "little positive content" and "prescribes no rigid limitation on legislative action." Symposium on Civil Liberties, 9 Am.L.Sch.Rev. 881 (1941), Selected Essays 1938–62 (1963), 628. As a legislative approach, the Smith Act, an "advocacy of violent overthrow" statute, was unresponsive to current dangers: it was "an uncritical acceptance of a formula devised during the days when the Communist manifesto represented the technique of revolution; when revolutionaries operated by declaring rather than disguising their principles." And as a judicial technique, clear and present danger was of limited utility: what it "can do, and all that it can do, is to require an extended judicial review in the fullest legislative sense of the competing values which the particular situation presents"; but that review "may be limited" by a "deference to legislative judgment, at least where the legislation condemns specific doctrine."

2. *Clear and present danger as oversimplification.* Compare an evaluation of clear and present danger near the end of the decade, just before Dennis (an evaluation quoted by Justice Frankfurter in Dennis): "The truth is that the clear-and-present-danger test is an oversimplified judgment unless it takes account also of a number of other factors: the relative seriousness of the danger in comparison with the value of the occasion for speech or political activity; the availability of more moderate controls than those which the state has imposed; and perhaps the specific intent with which the speech or activity is launched. No matter how rapidly we utter the phrase 'clear and

---

1. See also the comments on the Schenck-Gitlow heritage in the Frankfurter and Jackson concurrences in Dennis.

2. Recall also Justice Black's comments in Konigsberg v. State Bar of California, in the introductory materials to this chapter.

present danger,' or how closely we hyphenate the words, they are not a substitute for the weighing of values. They tend to convey a delusion of certitude when what is most certain is the complexity of the strands in the web of freedoms which the judge must disentangle." Freund, On Understanding the Supreme Court (1949), 27.

3. *Clear and present danger and Learned Hand.* Among the critics of clear and present danger was Judge Learned Hand. His "Bill of Rights" lectures in 1958 included a skeptical aside on Holmes' Schenck formulation: "Homer nodded." More generally, those lectures revealed deep skepticism that substantive constitutional guarantees were judicially enforceable at all. Yet as District Judge in Masses, above, Hand had tried to articulate judicial criteria of his own. And it fell to him on the Circuit Court of Appeals to pass on the Dennis defendants' clear and present danger defense—and reformulate it in words adopted by the majority opinion in the Supreme Court.

Note Judge Hand's puzzled comment on the variety of clear and present danger invocations [in the course of his effort to restate the test in the Dennis case, 183 F.2d 201 (2d Cir. 1950)]: "[Cases such as Gitlow] concerned the validity of statutes which had made it unlawful to stir up opposition to the Government or a state in the discharge of some vital function. There followed several which held that an ordinance or statute might not trench upon freedom of speech in order to promote minor public convenience: e. g., preventing the streets from being littered by broadsides, Schneider v. State, 308 U.S. 147 (1939); requiring a license to solicit contributions for societies, Cantwell v. Connecticut, 310 U.S. 296 (1940); requiring a union leader to register his name and union affiliation with the Secretary of State, Thomas v. Collins, 323 U.S. 516 (1945). The opinions in all these cases [all below] did however repeat the rubric of Schenck v. United States [clear and present danger], though none of them attempted to define how grave, or how imminent the danger must be, or whether the two factors are mutually interdependent. Moreover, the situation in all was wholly different from that in the preceding decisions. It is one thing to say that the public interest in keeping streets clean, or in keeping a register of union leaders, or in requiring solicitors to take out licenses, will not justify interference with freedom of utterance . . .; but it is quite another matter to say that an organized effort to inculcate the duty of revolution may not be repressed. It does not seem to us therefore that these decisions help towards a solution here."

4. *Clear and present danger and Dennis.* Consider the use of clear and present danger in Dennis, below, against the background of these criticisms. Does Dennis give inadequate protection to speech? If so, is that because it failed to apply clear and present danger? Or because of problems inherent in clear and present danger? Was a greater emphasis on immediacy in Dennis compelled by the earlier cases? What different approach to speech would have been preferable in Dennis?

5. *Clear and present danger as inadequate protection of Meiklejohn's "public" speech.* While the clarity and applicability of clear and present danger were being questioned during the forties, another—and increasingly influential—challenge attacked it for protecting speech insufficiently. In 1948, philosopher Alexander Meiklejohn took direct issue with Schenck

because its standard authorized some suppression of speech that should be wholly immune. (Recall the introductory materials to this chapter.) The First Amendment, he insisted, "means that certain substantive evils which, in principle, Congress has a right to prevent, must be endured if the only way of avoiding them is by the abridging of that freedom of speech upon which the entire structure of our free institutions rests." Meiklejohn, Free Speech and Its Relation to Self-Government (1948), 48. Meiklejohn would distinguish among varieties of speech: only "public" speech—speech on public issues, speech connected with "self-government"—must be immune from regulation; "private" speech is entitled to less complete protection. Note the criticism in Chafee's Book Review, 62 Harv.L.Rev. 891 (1949), Selected Essays 1938–62 (1963), 618.

Would the Meiklejohn approach have been preferable in Dennis? Has it had greater acceptance in the cases since Dennis? See Brennan, "The Supreme Court and the Meiklejohn Interpretation of the First Amendment," 79 Harv.L.Rev. 1 (1965). In New York Times v. Sullivan, 376 U.S. 254 (1964) (chap. 13, sec. 1, below)? In Brandenburg v. Ohio, 395 U.S. 444 (1969), below?

DENNIS v. UNITED STATES

341 U.S. 494, 71 S.Ct. 857, 95 L.Ed. 1137 (1951).

Certiorari to the Court of Appeals for the Second Circuit.

Mr. Chief Justice VINSON announced the judgment of the Court and an opinion in which Mr. Justice REED, Mr. Justice BURTON and Mr. Justice MINTON join.

Petitioners were indicted in July, 1948, for violation of the conspiracy provisions of the Smith Act during the period of April, 1945, to July, 1948. . . . A verdict of guilty as to all petitioners was returned by the jury on October 14, 1949. The Court of Appeals affirmed . . . . We granted certiorari, 340 U.S. 863, limited to the following two questions: (1) Whether either § 2 or § 3 of the Smith Act, inherently or as construed and applied in the instant case, violates the First Amendment and other provisions of the Bill of Rights; (2) whether either § 2 or § 3 of the Act inherently or as construed and applied in the instant case, violates the First and Fifth Amendments because of indefiniteness.

Sections 2 and 3 of the Smith Act (see present 18 U.S.C. § 2385) provide as follows:

"Sec. 2. (a) It shall be unlawful for any person—

"(1) to knowingly or willfully advocate, abet, advise, or teach the duty, necessity, desirability, or propriety of overthrowing or destroying any government in the United States by force or violence, or by the assassination of any officer of any such government; . . .

"(3) to organize or help to organize any society, group, or assembly of persons who teach, advocate, or encourage the overthrow or destruction of any government in the United States by force or violence; or to be or be-

come a member of, or affiliate with, any such society, group, or assembly of persons, knowing the purposes thereof. . . .

"Sec. 3. It shall be unlawful for any person to attempt to commit, or to conspire to commit, any of the acts prohibited by . . . this title."

The indictment charged the petitioners with wilfully and knowingly conspiring (1) to organize as the Communist Party of the United States of America a society, group and assembly of persons who teach and advocate the overthrow and destruction of the Government of the United States by force and violence, and (2) knowingly and wilfully to advocate and teach the duty and necessity of overthrowing and destroying the Government of the United States by force and violence. The indictment further alleged that § 2 of the Smith Act proscribes these acts and that any conspiracy to take such action is a violation of § 3 of the Act.

The trial of the case extended over nine months, six of which were devoted to the taking of evidence, resulting in a record of 16,000 pages. Our limited grant of the writ of certiorari has removed from our consideration any question as to the sufficiency of the evidence to support the jury's determination that petitioners are guilty of the offense charged. Whether on this record petitioners did in fact advocate the overthrow of the Government by force and violence is not before us, and we must base any discussion of this point upon the conclusions stated in the opinion of the Court of Appeals, which treated the issue in great detail. [T]he Court of Appeals held that the record supports the following broad conclusions: By virtue of their control over the political apparatus of the Communist Political Association, petitioners were able to transform that organization into the Communist Party; that the policies of the Association were changed from peaceful cooperation with the United States and its economic and political structure to a policy which had existed before the United States and the Soviet Union were fighting a common enemy, namely, a policy which worked for the overthrow of the Government by force and violence; that the Communist Party is a highly disciplined organization, adept at infiltration into strategic positions, use of aliases, and double-meaning language; that the Party is rigidly controlled; that Communists, unlike other political parties, tolerate no dissension from the policy laid down by the guiding forces . . . ; that the literature of the Party and the statements and activities of its leaders, petitioners here, advocate, and the general goal of the Party was, during the period in question, to achieve a successful overthrow of the existing order by force and violence. . . . [After finding that the statute required a showing of "intent as an element of the crime," Chief Justice Vinson continued:]

The obvious purpose of the statute is to protect existing Government, not from change by peaceable, lawful and constitutional means, but from change by violence, revolution and terrorism. That it is within the *power* of the Congress to protect the Government of the United States from armed rebellion is a proposition which requires little discussion. Whatever theoretical merit there may be to the argument that there is a "right" to rebellion against dictatorial governments is without force where the existing structure of the government provides for peaceful and orderly change. We reject any principle of governmental helplessness in the face of preparation for

revolution, which principle, carried to its logical conclusion, must lead to anarchy. No one could conceive that it is not within the power of Congress to prohibit acts intended to overthrow the Government by force and violence. The question with which we are concerned here is not whether Congress has such *power*, but whether the *means* which it has employed conflict with the First and Fifth Amendments to the Constitution.

One of the bases for the contention that the means which Congress has employed are invalid takes the form of an attack on the face of the statute on the grounds that by its terms it prohibits academic discussion of the merits of Marxism-Leninism, that it stifles ideas and is contrary to all concepts of a free speech and a free press. . . .

The very language of the Smith Act negates the interpretation which petitioners would have us impose on that Act. It is directed at advocacy, not discussion. Thus, the trial judge properly charged the jury that they could not convict if they found that petitioners did "no more than pursue peaceful studies and discussions or teaching and advocacy in the realm of ideas." . . .

But although the statute is not directed at the hypothetical cases which petitioners have conjured, its application in this case has resulted in convictions for the teaching and advocacy of the overthrow of the Government by force and violence, which, even though coupled with the intent to accomplish that overthrow, contains an element of speech. For this reason, we must pay special heed to the demands of the First Amendment marking out the boundaries of speech.

[T]he basis of the First Amendment is the hypothesis that speech can rebut speech, propaganda will answer propaganda, free debate of ideas will result in the wisest governmental policies. . . . An analysis of the leading cases in this Court which have involved direct limitations on speech, however, will demonstrate that both the majority of the Court and the dissenters in particular cases have recognized that this is not an unlimited, unqualified right, but that the societal value of speech must, on occasion, be subordinated to other values and considerations. . . .

The rule we deduce from the World War I Espionage Act cases [such as Schenck and Abrams] is that where an offense is specified by a statute in nonspeech or nonpress terms, a conviction relying upon speech or press as evidence of violation may be sustained only when the speech or publication created a "clear and present danger" of attempting or accomplishing the prohibited crime, e. g., interference with enlistment. The dissents, [in] emphasizing the value of speech, were addressed to the argument of the sufficiency of the evidence. . . .

Although no case subsequent to Whitney and Gitlow has expressly overruled the majority opinions in those cases, there is little doubt that subsequent opinions have inclined toward the Holmes-Brandeis rationale. [N]either Justice Holmes nor Justice Brandeis ever envisioned that a shorthand phrase should be crystallized into a rigid rule to be applied inflexibly without regard to the circumstances of each case. Speech is not an absolute, above and beyond control by the legislature when its judgment, subject to review here, is that certain kinds of speech are so undesirable as to warrant

criminal sanction. Nothing is more certain in modern society than the principle that there are no absolutes, that a name, a phrase, a standard has meaning only when associated with the considerations which gave birth to the nomenclature. . . . To those who would paralyze our Government in the face of impending threat by encasing it in a semantic strait-jacket we must reply that all concepts are relative.

In this case we are squarely presented with the application of the "clear and present danger" test, and must decide what that phrase imports. We first note that many of the cases in which this Court has reversed convictions by use of this or similar tests have been based on the fact that the interest which the State was attempting to protect was itself too insubstantial to warrant restriction of speech. . . . Overthrow of the Government by force and violence is certainly a substantial enough interest for the Government to limit speech. Indeed, this is the ultimate value of any society, for if a society cannot protect its very structure from armed internal attack, it must follow that no subordinate value can be protected. If, then, this interest may be protected, the literal problem which is presented is what has been meant by the use of the phrase "clear and present danger" of the utterances bringing about the evil within the power of Congress to punish.

Obviously, the words cannot mean that before the Government may act, it must wait until the *putsch* is about to be executed, the plans have been laid and the signal is awaited. If Government is aware that a group aiming at its overthrow is attempting to indoctrinate its members and to commit them to a course whereby they will strike when the leaders feel the circumstances permit, action by the Government is required. The argument that there is no need for Government to concern itself, for Government is strong, it possesses ample powers to put down a rebellion, it may defeat the revolution with ease needs no answer. For that is not the question. Certainly an attempt to overthrow the Government by force, even though doomed from the outset because of inadequate numbers or power of the revolutionists, is a sufficient evil for Congress to prevent. The damage which such attempts create both physically and politically to a nation makes it impossible to measure the validity in terms of the probability of success, or the immediacy of a successful attempt. In the instant case the trial judge charged the jury that they could not convict unless they found that petitioners intended to overthrow the Government "as speedily as circumstances would permit." This does not mean, and could not properly mean, that they would not strike until there was certainty of success. What was meant was that the revolutionists would strike when they thought the time was ripe. We must therefore reject the contention that success or probability of success is the criterion.

The situation with which Justices Holmes and Brandeis were concerned in Gitlow was a comparatively isolated event, bearing little relation in their minds to any substantial threat to the safety of the community. . . . They were not confronted with any situation comparable to the instant one— the development of an apparatus designed and dedicated to the overthrow of the Government, in the context of world crisis after crisis.

Chief Judge Learned Hand, writing for the majority below, interpreted the phrase as follows: "In each case [courts] must ask whether the gravity

of the 'evil,' discounted by its improbability, justifies such invasion of free speech as is necessary to avoid the danger." 183 F.2d at 212. We adopt this statement of the rule. As articulated by Chief Judge Hand, it is as succinct and inclusive as any other we might devise at this time. It takes into consideration those factors which we deem relevant, and relates their significances. More we cannot expect from words.

Likewise, we are in accord with the court below, which affirmed the trial court's finding that the requisite danger existed. The mere fact that from the period 1945 to 1948 petitioners' activities did not result in an attempt to overthrow the Government by force and violence is of course no answer to the fact that there was a group that was ready to make the attempt. The formation by petitioners of such a highly organized conspiracy, with rigidly disciplined members subject to call when the leaders, these petitioners, felt that the time had come for action, coupled with the inflammable nature of world conditions, similar uprisings in other countries, and the touch-and-go nature of our relations with countries with whom petitioners were in the very least ideologically attuned, convince us that their convictions were justified on this score. And this analysis disposes of the contention that a conspiracy to advocate, as distinguished from the advocacy itself, cannot be constitutionally restrained, because it comprises only the preparation. It is the existence of the conspiracy which creates the danger. . . . If the ingredients of the reaction are present, we cannot bind the Government to wait until the catalyst is added.

Although we have concluded that the finding that there was a sufficient danger to warrant the application of the statute was justified on the merits, there remains the problem of whether the trial judge's treatment of the issue was correct. . . .

The first paragraph of [the] instructions calls for the jury to find the facts essential to establish the substantive crime, violation of §§ 2(a)(1) and 2(a)(3) of the Smith Act, involved in the conspiracy charge. There can be no doubt that if the jury found those facts against the petitioners violation of the Act would be established. The argument that the action of the trial court is erroneous, in declaring as a matter of law that such violation shows sufficient danger to justify the punishment despite the First Amendment, rests on the theory that a jury must decide a question of the application of the First Amendment. We do not agree.

When facts are found that establish the violation of a statute, the protection against conviction afforded by the First Amendment is a matter of law. The doctrine that there must be a clear and present danger of a substantive evil that Congress has a right to prevent is a judicial rule to be applied as a matter of law by the courts. The guilt is established by proof of facts. Whether the First Amendment protects the activity which constitutes the violation of the statute must depend upon a judicial determination of the scope of the First Amendment applied to the circumstances of the case. . . .

There remains to be discussed the question of vagueness—whether the statute as we have interpreted it is too vague, not sufficiently advising those

who would speak of the limitations upon their activity.   [The contention was rejected.]

We hold that §§ 2(a) (1), 2(a) (3) and 3 of the Smith Act do not inherently, or as construed or applied in the instant case, violate the First Amendment and other provisions of the Bill of Rights, or the First and Fifth Amendments because of indefiniteness.   Petitioners intended to overthrow the Government of the United States as speedily as the circumstances would permit.   Their conspiracy to organize the Communist Party and to teach and advocate the overthrow of the Government of the United States by force and violence created a "clear and present danger" of an attempt to overthrow the Government by force and violence. . . .

Affirmed.

Mr. Justice CLARK took no part [in the decision].

Mr. Justice FRANKFURTER, concurring in affirmance of the judgment.

. . . The historic antecedents of the First Amendment preclude the notion that its purpose was to give unqualified immunity to every expression that touched on matters within the range of political interest.
. . . Absolute rules would inevitably lead to absolute exceptions, and such exceptions would eventually corrode the rules.   The demands of free speech in a democratic society as well as the interest in national security are better served by candid and informed weighing of the competing interests, within the confines of the judicial process, than by announcing dogmas too inflexible for the non-Euclidian problems to be solved.

But how are competing interests to be assessed?   Since they are not subject to quantitative ascertainment, the issue necessarily resolves itself into asking, who is to make the adjustments? . . . . Full responsibility for the choice cannot be given to the courts.   Courts are not representative bodies. . . . Their judgment is best informed, and therefore most dependable, within narrow limits.   Their essential quality is detachment, founded on independence.   History teaches that the independence of the judiciary is jeopardized when courts become embroiled in the passions of the day and assume primary responsibility in choosing between competing political, economic and social pressures.

Primary responsibility for adjusting the interests which compete in the situation before us of necessity belongs to the Congress. . . . We are to set aside the judgment [of legislators] only if there is no reasonable basis for it. . . .

. . . In reviewing statutes which restrict freedoms protected by the First Amendment, we have emphasized the close relation which those freedoms bear to maintenance of a free society.   See Kovacs v. Cooper [Frankfurter concurrence, in the introduction to this chapter].   Some members of the Court—and at times a majority—have done more.   They have suggested that our function in reviewing statutes restricting freedom of expression differs sharply from our normal duty in sitting in judgment on legislation. . . . It has been suggested, with the casualness of a footnote, that such legislation is not presumptively valid [Carolene Prod-

ucts] and it has been weightily reiterated that freedom of speech has a "preferred position" among constitutional safeguards. [Kovacs v. Cooper.]

[The] cumulative force [of such phrases] has, not without justification, engendered belief that there is a constitutional principle [prohibiting] restriction upon utterance unless it creates a situation of "imminent" peril against which legislation may guard. It is on this body of the Court's pronouncements that the defendants' argument here is based.

In all fairness, the argument cannot be met by reinterpreting the Court's frequent use of "clear" and "present" to mean an entertainable "probability." In giving this meaning to the phrase "clear and present danger," the Court of Appeals was fastidiously confining the rhetoric of opinions to the exact scope of what was decided by them. We have greater responsibility for having given constitutional support, over repeated protests, to uncritical libertarian generalities. . . . If [past] decisions are to be used as a guide and not as an argument, it is important to view them as a whole and to distrust the easy generalizations to which some of them lend themselves.

We have recognized and resolved conflicts between speech and competing interests in six different types of cases. . . . I must leave to others the ungrateful task of trying to reconcile all these decisions. In some instances we have too readily permitted juries to infer deception from error, or intention from argumentative or critical statements. [E. g., the Abrams case.] In other instances we weighted the interest in free speech so heavily that we permitted essential conflicting values to be destroyed. Bridges v. California; Craig v. Harney. [Both decisions applied the clear and present danger test to set aside contempt rulings against press interference with the administration of justice. See chap. 13.] Viewed as a whole, however, the decisions express an attitude toward the judicial function and a standard of values which for me are decisive of the case before us.

First.—Free-speech cases are not an exception to the principle that we are not legislators, that direct policy-making is not our province. . . . In Gitlow v. New York, we put our respect for the legislative judgment in terms which, if they were accepted here, would make decision easy. . . . It has not been explicitly overruled. But it would be disingenuous to deny that the dissent in Gitlow has been treated with the respect usually accorded to a decision. . . . It requires excessive tolerance of the legislative judgment to suppose that the Gitlow publication in the circumstances could justify serious concern.

In contrast, there is ample justification for a legislative judgment that the conspiracy now before us is a substantial threat to national order and security. . . .

Second.—A survey of the relevant decisions indicates that the results which we have reached are on the whole those that would ensue from careful weighing of conflicting interests. The complex issues presented by regulation of speech in public places, by picketing, and by legislation prohibiting advocacy of crime have been resolved by scrutiny of many factors besides the imminence and gravity of the evil threatened. . . .

It is a familiar experience in the law that new situations do not fit neatly into legal conceptions that arose under different circumstances to satisfy different needs. . . . So it is with the attempt to use the direction of

thought lying behind the criterion of "clear and present danger" wholly out of the context in which it originated, and to make of it an absolute dogma and definitive measuring rod for the power of Congress to deal with assaults against security through devices other than overt physical attempts.

Bearing in mind that Mr. Justice Holmes regarded questions under the First Amendment as questions of "proximity and degree" [Schenck], it would be a distortion, indeed a mockery, of his reasoning to compare the "puny anonymities" [to] which he was addressing himself in the Abrams case in 1919 or the publication that was "futile and too remote from possible consequences" [in] the Gitlow case in 1925 with the setting of events in this case in 1950.   .   .   .

Third.—Not every type of speech occupies the same position on the scale of values. There is no substantial public interest in permitting certain kinds of utterances: "the lewd and obscene, the profane, the libelous, and the insulting or 'fighting' words—those which by their very utterance inflict injury or tend to incite an immediate breach of the peace." [Chaplinsky v. New Hampshire, sec. 2 below.]   On any scale of values which we have hitherto recognized, speech of this sort ranks low.

Throughout our decisions there has recurred a distinction between the statement of an idea which may prompt its hearers to take unlawful action, and advocacy that such action be taken.   .   .   .   The object of the conspiracy before us is so clear that the chance of error in saying that the defendants conspired to advocate rather than to express ideas is slight.   Mr. Justice Douglas quite properly points out that the conspiracy before us is not a conspiracy to overthrow the Government.   But it would be equally wrong to treat it as a seminar in political theory.

These general considerations underlie decision of the case before us.

On the one hand is the interest in security.   The Communist Party was not designed by these defendants as an ordinary political party.   For the circumstances of its organization, its aims and methods, and the relation of the defendants to its organization and aims we are concluded by the jury's verdict.   .   .   .

In finding that the defendants violated the statute, we may not treat as established fact that the Communist Party in this country is of significant size, well-organized, well-disciplined, conditioned to embark on unlawful activity when given the command.   But in determining whether application of the statute to the defendants is within the constitutional powers of Congress, we are not limited to the facts found by the jury.   We must view such a question in the light of whatever is relevant to a legislative judgment.   We may take judicial notice that the Communist doctrines which these defendants have conspired to advocate are in the ascendency in powerful nations who cannot be acquitted of unfriendliness to the institutions of this country. We may take account of evidence brought forward at this trial and elsewhere, much of which has long been common knowledge.   In sum, it would amply justify a legislature in concluding that recruitment of additional members for the Party would create a substantial danger to national security.

In 1947, it has been reliably reported, at least 60,000 members were enrolled in the Party [citing congressional testimony by the FBI Director].

Evidence was introduced in this case that the membership was organized in small units [protected] by elaborate precautions designed to prevent disclosure of individual identity. There are no reliable data tracing acts of sabotage or espionage directly to these defendants. But a Canadian Royal Commission [reported in 1946] that "the Communist movement was the principal base in which the espionage network was recruited." The most notorious spy within recent history [Klaus Fuchs] was led into the service of the Soviet Union through Communist indoctrination. Evidence supports the conclusion that members of the Party seek and occupy positions of importance in political and labor organizations. Congress was not barred by the Constitution from believing that indifference to such experience would be an exercise not of freedom but of irresponsibility.

On the other hand is the interest in free speech. The right to exert all governmental powers in aid of maintaining our institutions and resisting their physical overthrow does not include intolerance of opinions and speech that cannot do harm although opposed and perhaps alien to dominant, traditional opinion. . . . It is better for those who have almost unlimited power of government in their hands to err on the side of freedom. . . .

. . . No matter how clear we may be that the defendants now before us are preparing to overthrow our Government at the propitious moment, it is self-delusion to think that we can punish them for their advocacy without adding to the risks run by loyal citizens who honestly believe in some of the reforms these defendants advance. It is a sobering fact that in sustaining the convictions before us we can hardly escape restriction on the interchange of ideas. . . .

It is not for us to decide how we would adjust the clash of interests which this case presents were the primary responsibility for reconciling it ours. Congress has determined that the danger created by advocacy of overthrow justifies the ensuing restriction on freedom of speech. The determination was made after due deliberation, and the seriousness of the congressional purpose is attested by the volume of legislation passed to effectuate the same ends. . . . Can we hold that the First Amendment deprives Congress of what it deemed necessary for the Government's protection?

To make validity of legislation depend on judicial reading of events still in the womb of time—a forecast, that is, of the outcome of forces at best appreciated only with knowledge of the topmost secrets of nations—is to charge the judiciary with duties beyond its equipment. . . .

[I]t is relevant to remind that in sustaining the power of Congress in a case like this nothing irrevocable is done. The democratic process at all events is not impaired or restricted. Power and responsibility remain with the people and immediately with their representatives. All the Court says is that Congress was not forbidden by the Constitution to pass this enactment and that a prosecution under it may be brought against a conspiracy such as the one before us. . . .

Mr. Justice JACKSON, concurring. . . .

. . . [E]ither by accident or design, the Communist stratagem outwits the anti-anarchist pattern of statute aimed against "overthrow by

force and violence" if qualified by the doctrine that only "clear and present danger" of accomplishing that result will sustain the prosecution.

The "clear and present danger" test was an innovation by Mr. Justice Holmes in the Schenck case, reiterated and refined by him and Mr. Justice Brandeis in later cases, all arising before the era of World War II revealed the subtlety and efficacy of modernized revolutionary techniques used by totalitarian parties. . . .

I would save it, unmodified, for application as a "rule of reason" in the kind of case for which it was devised. When the issue is criminality of a hot-headed speech on a street corner, or circulation of a few incendiary pamphlets, or parading by some zealots behind a red flag, or refusal of a handful of school children to salute our flag, it is not beyond the capacity of the judicial process to gather, comprehend, and weigh the necessary materials for decision whether it is a clear and present danger of substantive evil or a harmless letting off of steam. It is not a prophecy, for the danger in such cases has matured by the time of trial or it was never present. The test applies and has meaning where a conviction is sought to be based on a speech or writing which does not directly or explicitly advocate a crime but to which such tendency is sought to be attributed by construction or by implication from external circumstances. The formula in such cases favors freedoms that are vital to our society, and, even if sometimes applied too generously, the consequences cannot be grave. But its recent expansion has extended, in particular to Communists, unprecedented immunities. Unless we are to hold our Government captive in a judge-made verbal trap, we must approach the problem of a well-organized, nation-wide conspiracy, such as I have described, as realistically as our predecessors faced the trivialities that were being prosecuted until they were checked with a rule of reason.

I think reason is lacking for applying that test to this case.

If we must decide that this Act and its application are constitutional only if we are convinced that petitioner's conduct creates a "clear and present danger" of violent overthrow, we must appraise imponderables, including international and national phenomena which baffle the best informed foreign offices and our most experienced politicians. . . . No doctrine can be sound whose application requires us to make a prophecy of that sort in the guise of a legal decision. The judicial process simply is not adequate to a trial of such far-flung issues. The answers given would reflect our own political predilections and nothing more.

The authors of the clear and present danger test never applied it to a case like this, nor would I. If applied as it is proposed here, it means that the Communist plotting is protected during its period of incubation; its preliminary stages of organization and preparation are immune from the law; the Government can move only after imminent action is manifest, when it would, of course, be too late. . . .

The highest degree of constitutional protection is due to the individual acting without conspiracy. But even an individual cannot claim that the Constitution protects him in advocating or teaching overthrow of government by force or violence. I should suppose no one would doubt that Congress has power to make such attempted overthrow a crime. But the con-

tention is that one has the constitutional right to work up a public desire and will to do what it is a crime to attempt. I think direct incitement by speech or writing can be made a crime, and I think there can be a conviction without also proving that the odds favored its success by 99 to 1, or some other extremely high ratio. . . .

Of course, it is not always easy to distinguish teaching or advocacy in the sense of incitement from teaching or advocacy in the sense of exposition or explanation. It is a question of fact in each case.

What really is under review here is a conviction of conspiracy, after a trial for conspiracy, on an indictment charging conspiracy, brought under a statute outlawing conspiracy. With due respect to my colleagues, they seem to me to discuss anything under the sun except the law of conspiracy. . . .

The Constitution does not make conspiracy a civil right. . . . While I consider criminal conspiracy a dragnet device capable of perversion into an instrument of injustice in the hands of a partisan or complacent judiciary, it has an established place in our system of law, and no reason appears for applying it only to concerted action claimed to disturb interstate commerce and withholding it from those claimed to undermine our whole Government. . . .

I do not suggest that Congress could punish conspiracy to advocate something, the doing of which it may not punish. Advocacy or exposition of the doctrine of communal property ownership, or any political philosophy unassociated with advocacy of its imposition by force or seizure of government by unlawful means could not be reached through conspiracy prosecution. But it is not forbidden to put down force or violence, it is not forbidden to punish its teaching or advocacy, and the end being punishable, there is no doubt of the power to punish conspiracy for the purpose. . . .

Mr. Justice BLACK, dissenting. . . .

So long as this Court exercises the power of judicial review of legislation, I cannot agree that the First Amendment permits us to sustain laws suppressing freedom of speech and press on the basis of Congress' or our own notions of mere "reasonableness." Such a doctrine waters down the First Amendment so that it amounts to little more than an admonition to Congress. The Amendment as so construed is not likely to protect any but those "safe" or orthodox views which rarely need its protection. I must also express my objection to the holding because, as Mr. Justice Douglas' dissent shows, it sanctions the determination of a crucial issue of fact by the judge rather than by the jury. . . .

Public opinion being what it now is, few will protest the conviction of these Communist petitioners. There is hope, however, that in calmer times, when present pressures, passions and fears subside, this or some later Court will restore the First Amendment liberties to the high preferred place where they belong in a free society.

Mr. Justice DOUGLAS, dissenting.

If this were a case where those who claimed protection under the First Amendment were teaching the techniques of sabotage, the assassination of

the President, the filching of documents from public files, the planting of bombs, the art of street warfare, and the like, I would have no doubts. The freedom to speak is not absolute; the teaching of methods of terror and other seditious conduct should be beyond the pale along with obscenity and immorality. This case was argued as if those were the facts. The argument imported much seditious conduct into the record. That is easy and it has popular appeal, for the activities of Communists in plotting and scheming against the free world are common knowledge. But the fact is that no such evidence was introduced at the trial. There is a statute which makes a seditious conspiracy unlawful. Petitioners, however, were not charged with a "conspiracy to overthrow" the Government. They were charged with a conspiracy to form a party and groups and assemblies of people who teach and advocate the overthrow of our Government by force or violence and with a conspiracy to advocate and teach its overthrow by force and violence. It may well be that indoctrination in the techniques of terror to destroy the Government would be indictable under either statute. But the teaching which is condemned here is of a different character.

So far as the present record is concerned, what petitioners did was to organize people to teach and themselves teach the Marxist-Leninist doctrine contained chiefly in four books: Foundations of Leninism by Stalin (1924), The Communist Manifesto by Marx and Engels (1848), State and Revolution by Lenin (1917), History of the Communist Party of the Soviet Union (B) (1939).

Those books are to Soviet Communism what Mein Kampf was to Nazism. If they are understood, the ugliness of Communism is revealed, its deceit and cunning are exposed, the nature of its activities becomes apparent, and the chances of its success less likely. That is not, of course, the reason why petitioners chose these books for their classrooms. They are fervent Communists to whom these volumes are gospel. They preached the creed with the hope that some day it would be acted upon.

The opinion of the Court does not outlaw these texts nor condemn them to the fire, as the Communists do literature offensive to their creed. But if the books themselves are not outlawed, if they can lawfully remain on library shelves, by what reasoning does their use in a classroom become a crime? . . . The Act, as construed, requires the element of intent— that those who teach the creed believe in it. The crime then depends not on what is taught but on who the teacher is. That is to make freedom of speech turn not on *what is said,* but on the *intent* with which it is said. Once we start down that road we enter territory dangerous to the liberties of every citizen. . . .

There comes a time when even speech loses its constitutional immunity. Speech innocuous one year may at another time fan such destructive flames that it must be halted in the interests of the safety of the Republic. That is the meaning of the clear and present danger test. When conditions are so critical that there will be no time to avoid the evil that the speech threatens, it is time to call a halt. Otherwise, free speech which is the strength of the Nation will be the cause of its destruction.

Yet free speech is the rule, not the exception. The restraint to be constitutional must be based on more than fear, on more than passionate opposi-

tion against the speech, on more than a revolted dislike for its contents. There must be some immediate injury to society that is likely if speech is allowed. . . .

I had assumed that the question of the clear and present danger, being so critical an issue in the case, would be a matter for submission to the jury. . . . The Court, I think, errs when it treats the question as one of law.

Yet, whether the question is one for the Court or the jury, there should be evidence of record on the issue. This record, however, contains no evidence whatsoever showing that the acts charged, *viz.*, the teaching of the Soviet theory of revolution with the hope that it will be realized, have created any clear and present danger to the Nation. The Court, however, rules to the contrary. . . .

That ruling is in my view not responsive to the issue in the case. We might as well say that the speech of petitioners is outlawed because Soviet Russia and her Red Army are a threat to world peace.

The nature of Communism as a force on the world scene would, of course, be relevant to the issue of clear and present danger of petitioners' advocacy within the United States. But the primary consideration is the strength and tactical position of petitioners and their converts in this country. On that there is no evidence in the record. If we are to take judicial notice of the threat of Communists within the nation, it should not be difficult to conclude that *as a political party* they are of little consequence. . . . Communism in the world scene is no bogeyman; but Communism as a political faction or party in this country plainly is. Communism has been so thoroughly exposed in this country that it has been crippled as a political force. Free speech has destroyed it as an effective political party. It is inconceivable that those who went up and down this country preaching the doctrine of revolution which petitioners espouse would have any success. . . . How it can be said that there is a clear and present danger that this advocacy will succeed is, therefore, a mystery. [I]n America [Communists] are miserable merchants of unwanted ideas; their wares remain unsold. The fact that their ideas are abhorrent does not make them powerful.

The political impotence of the Communists in this country does not, of course, dispose of the problem. Their numbers; their positions in industry and government; the extent to which they have in fact infiltrated the police, the armed services, transportation, stevedoring, power plants, munitions works, and other critical places—these facts all bear on the likelihood that their advocacy of the Soviet theory of revolution will endanger the Republic. But the record is silent on these facts. If we are to proceed on the basis of judicial notice, it is impossible for me to say that the Communists in this country are so potent or so strategically deployed that they must be suppressed for their speech. . . . To believe that petitioners and their following are placed in such critical positions as to endanger the Nation is to believe the incredible. . . .

This is my view if we are to act on the basis of judicial notice. But the mere statement of the opposing views indicates how important it is that we know the facts before we act. Neither prejudice nor hate nor senseless fear

should be the basis of this solemn act. Free speech—the glory of our system of government—should not be sacrificed on anything less than plain and objective proof of danger that the evil advocated is imminent. . . .

SMITH ACT CASES AFTER DENNIS: DEFINING SPEECH RATHER THAN GUESSING ABOUT DANGERS?

1. *The problems of Dennis.* Recall the questions immediately preceding Dennis. Did Dennis ignore clear and present danger? Distort clear and present danger? What did the Holmes standard say about the Dennis problem? What "substantive evil" was relevant? Actual overthrow? Risk of overthrow? Conspiracy to overthrow? Conspiracy to advocate overthrow?

What weight did the legislative judgment deserve? Should it have been weighed in terms of the 1940 circumstances, when the Smith Act became law? 1948? Should the Court have insisted on greater record evidence of the 1948 situation? Should it have ignored the world situation? Did the Court deemphasize the temporal dimension—i. e., the *immediacy* of the risk —unduly? Did it consider risks more remote than the Abrams dissent would permit? Than the Whitney concurrence? Than Herndon v. Lowry?

What alternative approaches would have been preferable in Dennis? Consider the subsequent Smith Act cases "clarifying" Dennis—and, in the view of many, assuring greater protection of speech (notes 2 and 3 below). Does the emphasis in Yates, Scales, and Noto on the distinction between advocacy of abstract doctrine and advocacy of action, and on the need for scrutiny of the evidence, repudiate Dennis? Do these cases shift to an earlier clear and present danger approach? Do they apply the Masses approach—of defining the contours of protected speech and of using traditional judicial techniques of construing statutes and scrutinizing evidence? Do these post-Dennis cases suggest that courts should concentrate on defining protected speech rather than on second-guessing legislatures about the risks of dangerous consequences? *

2. *The Yates case.* After Dennis, the Government brought Smith Act cases against a number of Communists who were "lower echelon" rather than "first string" leaders. In YATES v. UNITED STATES, 354 U.S. 298 (1957), the Court reversed the convictions of fourteen defendants. In "explaining" the requirements of Dennis, the Court made it clear that Smith Act convictions would not be easy to sustain. Justice Harlan wrote the majority opinion. Justices Burton and Black, joined by Justice Douglas, submitted separate opinions. Justice Clark dissented. On an examination of the record, Justice Harlan concluded that the lower courts had given too

---

* For a sampling of the extensive commentary on Dennis, see Richardson, "Freedom of Expression and the Function of Courts," 65 Harv.L.Rev. 1 (1951), Mendelson, "Clear and Present Danger—From Schenck to Dennis," 52 Colum.L.Rev. 313 (1952), Gorfinkel and Mack, "Dennis v. United States and the Clear and Present Danger Rule," 39 Calif.L.Rev. 475 (1951), and Konefsky, The Legacy of Holmes and Brandeis (1956). And see generally "Developments in the Law: The National Security Interest and Civil Liberties," 85 Harv.L.Rev. 1130 (1972).

broad a meaning to the term "organize" in the Smith Act; that the trial court's instructions to the jury gave inadequate guidance on the distinction between advocacy of abstract doctrine and advocacy of action; and that the evidence was insufficient to support conviction. Some excerpts from his opinion follow:

"Petitioners contend that the instructions to the jury were fatally defective in that the trial court refused to charge that, in order to convict, the jury must find that the advocacy which the defendants conspired to promote was of a kind calculated to 'incite' persons to action for the forcible overthrow of the Government. . . . The Government [argues] that the true constitutional dividing line is not between inciting and abstract advocacy of forcible overthrow, but rather between advocacy as such, irrespective of its inciting qualities, and the mere discussion or exposition of violent overthrow as an abstract theory. [The trial court charged:]

" 'Any advocacy or teaching which does not include the urging of force and violence as the means of overthrowing and destroying the Government of the United States is not within the issue of the indictment here and can constitute no basis for any finding against the defendants.

" 'The kind of advocacy and teaching which is charged and upon which your verdict must be reached is not merely a desirability but a necessity that the Government of the United States be overthrown and destroyed by force and violence and not merely a propriety but a duty to overthrow and destroy the Government of the United States by force and violence.'

"There can be no doubt from the record that in so instructing the jury the court regarded as immaterial, and intended to withdraw from the jury's consideration, any issue as to the character of the advocacy in terms of its capacity to stir listeners to forcible action. . . . We are thus faced with the question whether the Smith Act prohibits advocacy and teaching of forcible overthrow as an abstract principle, divorced from any effort to instigate action to that end, so long as such advocacy or teaching is engaged in with evil intent. We hold that it does not.

"The distinction between advocacy of abstract doctrine and advocacy directed at promoting unlawful action is one that has been consistently recognized in the opinions of this Court . . . . We need not, however, decide the issue before us in terms of constitutional compulsion, for our first duty is to construe this statute. [Recall Judge Hand's approach in Masses; and compare the "restatement" of Yates in later cases such as Brandenburg v. Ohio, below.] In doing so we should not assume that Congress chose to disregard a constitutional danger zone so clearly marked, or that it used the words 'advocate' and 'teach' in their ordinary dictionary meanings when they had already been construed as terms of art carrying a special and limited connotation. . . .

"In failing to distinguish between advocacy of forcible overthrow as an abstract doctrine and advocacy of action to that end, the District Court appears to have been led astray by the holding in Dennis that advocacy of violent action to be taken at some future time was enough. It seems to have considered that, since 'inciting' speech is usually thought of as something calculated to induce immediate action, and since Dennis held advocacy of ac-

tion for future overthrow sufficient, this meant that advocacy, irrespective of its tendency to generate action, is punishable, provided only that it is uttered with a specific intent to accomplish overthrow. In other words, the District Court apparently thought that Dennis obliterated the traditional dividing line between advocacy of abstract doctrine and advocacy of action.

"This misconceives the situation confronting the Court in Dennis and what was held there. Although the jury's verdict, interpreted in light of the trial court's instructions, did not justify the conclusion that the defendants' advocacy was directed at, or created any danger of, immediate overthrow, it did establish that the advocacy was aimed at building up a seditious group and maintaining it in readiness for action at a propitious time. In such circumstances, said Chief Justice Vinson, the Government need not hold its hand 'until the *putsch* is about to be executed, the plans have been laid and the signal is awaited.' . . . The essence of the Dennis holding was that indoctrination of a group in preparation for future violent action, as well as exhortation to immediate action, by advocacy found to be directed to 'action for the accomplishment' of forcible overthrow, to violence as 'a rule or principle of action,' and employing 'language of incitement,' . . . is not constitutionally protected when the group is of sufficient size and cohesiveness, is sufficiently oriented towards action, and other circumstances are such as reasonably to justify apprehension that action will occur. This is quite a different thing from the view of the District Court here that mere doctrinal justification of forcible overthrow, if engaged in with the intent to accomplish overthrow, is punishable *per se* under the Smith Act. That sort of advocacy, even though uttered with the hope that it may ultimately lead to violent revolution, is too remote from concrete action to be regarded as the kind of indoctrination preparatory to action which was condemned in Dennis. [Dennis was] not concerned with a conspiracy to engage at some future time in seditious advocacy, but rather with a conspiracy to advocate presently the taking of forcible action in the future. It was action, not advocacy, that was to be postponed until 'circumstances' would 'permit.' . . .

"In light of the foregoing we are unable to regard the District Court's charge upon this aspect of the case as adequate. The jury was never told that the Smith Act does not denounce advocacy in the sense of preaching abstractly the forcible overthrow of the Government. We think that the trial court's statement that the proscribed advocacy must include the 'urging,' 'necessity,' and 'duty' of forcible overthrow, and not merely its 'desirability' and 'propriety,' may not be regarded as a sufficient substitute for charging that the Smith Act reaches only advocacy of action for the overthrow of government by force and violence. The essential distinction is that those to whom the advocacy is addressed must be urged to *do* something, now or in the future, rather than merely to *believe* in something. . . .

"We recognize that distinctions between advocacy or teaching of abstract doctrines, with evil intent, and that which is directed to stirring people to action, are often subtle and difficult to grasp, for in a broad sense, as Mr. Justice Holmes said in his dissenting opinion in Gitlow, 268 U.S., at 673: 'Every idea is an incitement.' But the very subtlety of these distinctions required the most clear and explicit instructions with reference to them, for they concerned an issue which went to the very heart of the charges against

these petitioners. The need for precise and understandable instructions on this issue is further emphasized by the equivocal character of the evidence in this record .   .   .. Instances of speech that could be considered to amount to 'advocacy of action' are so few and far between as to be almost completely overshadowed by the hundreds of instances in the record in which overthrow, if mentioned at all, occurs in the course of doctrinal disputation so remote from action as to be almost wholly lacking in probative value. Vague references to 'revolutionary' or 'militant' action of an unspecified character, which are found in the evidence, might in addition be given too great weight by the jury in the absence of more precise instructions. Particularly in light of this record, we must regard the trial court's charge in this respect as furnishing wholly inadequate guidance to the jury on this central point in the case." [The Court ordered acquittals of five of the defendants and remanded the indictments of the remaining nine for new trials. On remand, those indictments were dismissed at the Government's request, because of expected inability to meet the Yates requirements. See the comments in Scales, which follows, on the evaluation of the evidence in Yates.]

3. *The Scales and Noto cases.* a. In SCALES v. UNITED STATES, 367 U.S. 203 (1961), the Court sustained the membership clause of the Smith Act and clarified the evidentiary requirements of Yates. The challenged clause, as described in Justice Harlan's majority opinion, "makes a felony the acquisition or holding of knowing membership in any organization which advocates the overthrow of the Government of the United States by force or violence." Petitioner was charged with having been a member of the Communist Party "with knowledge of the Party's illegal purpose and a specific intent to accomplish overthrow 'as speedily as circumstances would permit.'" The Court found that the trial judge had properly construed the statute to require "specific intent" and "active" rather than merely "nominal" membership. As so construed, the Court rejected the claim that the statute violated the Fifth Amendment "in that it impermissibly imputes guilt to an individual merely on the basis of his associations and sympathies, rather than because of some concrete personal involvement in criminal conduct." Moreover, the majority refused to find a First Amendment violation:

"It was settled in Dennis that the advocacy with which we are here concerned is not constitutionally protected speech, and it was further established that a combination to promote such advocacy, albeit under the aegis of what purports to be a political party, is not such association as is protected by the First Amendment. We can discern no reason why membership, when it constitutes a purposeful form of complicity in a group engaging in this same forbidden advocacy, should receive any greater degree of protection from the guarantees of that Amendment.

"If it is said that the mere existence of such an enactment tends to inhibit the exercise of constitutionally protected rights, in that it engenders an unhealthy fear that one may find himself unwittingly embroiled in criminal liability, the answer surely is that the statute provides that a defendant must be proven to have knowledge of the proscribed advocacy before he may be convicted. .   .   .   The clause does not make criminal all association with an organization which has been shown to engage in illegal advocacy. There

must be clear proof that a defendant 'specifically intend[s] to accomplish [the aims of the organization] by resort to violence.' Noto v. United States [below]. Thus the member for whom the organization is a vehicle for the advancement of legitimate aims and policies does not fall within the ban of the statute: he lacks the requisite specific intent 'to bring about the overthrow of the government as speedily as circumstances would permit.' Such a person may be foolish, deluded, or perhaps merely optimistic, but he is not by this statute made a criminal."

The Court then proceeded to examine the sufficiency of the evidence in considerable detail, "to make sure that substantive constitutional standards have not been thwarted." Justice Harlan stated that the evidentiary question was "controlled in large part by Yates" and explained at some length the Yates criteria for the evaluation of evidence. He noted: "The decision in Yates rested on the view (not articulated in the opinion, though perhaps it should have been) that the Smith Act offenses, involving as they do subtler elements than are present in most other crimes, call for strict standards in assessing the adequacy of the proof needed to make out a case of illegal advocacy. This premise is as applicable to prosecutions under the membership clause of the Smith Act as it is to conspiracy prosecutions under that statute as we had in Yates."

Justice Harlan continued: "The impact of Yates with respect to this petitioner's evidentiary challenge is not limited, however, to that decision's requirement of strict standards of proof. Yates also articulates general criteria for the evaluation of evidence in determining whether this requirement is met. The Yates opinion, through its characterizations of large portions of the evidence which were either described in detail or referred to by reference to the record, indicates what type of evidence is needed to permit a jury to find that (a) there was 'advocacy of action' and (b) the Party was responsible for such advocacy.

"First, Yates makes clear what type of evidence is not *in itself* sufficient to show illegal advocacy. This category includes evidence of the following: the teaching of Marxism-Leninism and the connected use of Marxist 'classics' as textbooks; the official general resolutions and pronouncements of the Party at past conventions; dissemination of the Party's general literature, including the standard outlines on Marxism; the Party's history and organizational structure; the secrecy of meetings and the clandestine nature of the Party generally; statements by officials evidencing sympathy for and alliance with the U.S.S.R. It was the predominance of evidence of this type which led the Court to order the acquittal of several Yates defendants, with the comment that they had not themselves 'made a single remark or been present when someone else made a remark which would tend to prove the charges against them.' However, this kind of evidence, while insufficient in itself to sustain a conviction, is not irrelevant. Such evidence, in the context of other evidence, may be of value in showing illegal advocacy.

"Second, the Yates opinion also indicates what kind of evidence is sufficient. There the Court pointed to two series of events which justified the denial of directed acquittals as to nine of the Yates defendants. The Court noted that with respect to seven of the defendants, meetings in San Francisco might be considered to be 'the systematic teaching and advocacy of illegal

action which is condemned by the statute.' In those meetings, a small group of members were not only taught that violent revolution was inevitable, but they were also taught techniques for achieving that end. For example, the Yates record reveals that members were directed to be prepared to convert a general strike into a revolution and deal with Negroes so as to prepare them specifically for revolution. In addition to the San Francisco meetings, the Court referred to certain activities in the Los Angeles area 'which might be considered to amount to "advocacy of action" ' and with which two Yates defendants were linked. Here again, the participants did not stop with teaching of the inevitability of eventual revolution, but went on to explain techniques, both legal and illegal, to be employed in preparation for or in connection with the revolution. [Viewed together], these events described in Yates indicate at least two patterns of evidence sufficient to show illegal advocacy: (a) the teaching of forceful overthrow, accompanied by directions as to the type of illegal action which must be taken when the time for the revolution is reached; and (b) the teaching of forceful overthrow, accompanied by a contemporary, though legal, course of conduct clearly undertaken for the specific purpose of rendering effective the later illegal activity which is advocated."

Justice Harlan found these evidentiary criteria satisfied in the Scales record: "[T]his evidence sufficed to make a case for the jury on the issue of illegal Party advocacy. Dennis and Yates have definitely laid at rest any doubt that present advocacy of *future* actions for violent overthrow satisfies statutory and constitutional requirements equally with advocacy of *immediate* action to that end. Hence this record cannot be considered deficient because it contains no evidence of advocacy for immediate overthrow."

The Scales decision elicited dissenting opinions from Justices Black, Douglas and Brennan (joined by Chief Justice Warren and Justice Douglas). Justice Black once again objected to the "balancing test." Justice Douglas emphasized that the "membership" clause of the Smith Act did not require a finding of conspiracy and added: "The case is not saved by showing that petitioner was an active member. None of the activity constitutes a crime. . . . Not one single illegal act is charged to petitioner. That is why the essence of the crime covered by the indictment is merely belief—belief in the proletarian revolution, belief in Communist creed." Justice Brennan's dissent insisted that Congress had legislated immunity from prosecution under the membership clause of the Smith Act by enacting the Internal Security Act of 1950. See sec. 1E below.

b. Though the Court found the evidentiary criteria of Yates satisfied in the conviction of Scales, it reversed a conviction under the membership clause in a companion case because "the evidence of illegal Party advocacy was insufficient." NOTO v. UNITED STATES, 367 U.S. 290 (1961). With Justice Harlan once again writing for the Court, the opinion noted that the evidence of "advocacy of action" was "sparse indeed," was not "broadly based" geographically, and "lacked the compelling quality which in Scales was supplied by the petitioner's own utterances and systematic course of conduct as a high Party official." He added: "It need hardly be said that it is upon the particular evidence in a particular record that a particular

defendant must be judged, and not upon the evidence in some other record or upon what may be supposed to be the tenets of the Communist Party." The Noto record, he emphasized, "bears much of the infirmity that we found in the Yates record." There were a number of separate concurring opinions in Noto.

4. *The impact of Yates and Scales.* Were the Yates and Scales decisions truly restatements of Dennis, or did they mark a significant shift in emphasis? Can Justice Harlan's opinions be viewed as a "long-delayed vindication of Masses"? Note the contending arguments by the parties in Yates, as summarized by Justice Harlan. Consider the validity of the following comment: "[Harlan] reinvigorated free speech protection in the post-Dennis years by exhibiting the best qualities of judicial craftsmanship so long associated with Learned Hand. Harlan found a way to curtail prosecutions under the Smith Act even though the constitutionality of the Act had been sustained in Dennis. He did it by invoking techniques very similar to those applied by Hand in Masses to the World War I Espionage Act: he read the statute in terms of constitutional presuppositions; and he strove to find standards 'manageable' by judges and capable of curbing jury discretion. He insisted on strict statutory standards of proof emphasizing the actual speech of the defendants—a variation on the 'hard,' 'objective,' words-oriented focus of Masses. Harlan claimed to be interpreting Dennis. In fact, Yates and Scales represented doctrinal evolution in a new direction, a direction in the Masses tradition." Gunther, "Learned Hand and the Origins of Modern First Amendment Doctrine: Some Fragments of History," 27 Stan.L.Rev. 719 (1975).* (On the evolution of Yates and Scales from statutory to constitutional standards, and on the elaboration of those standards, see Brandenburg v. Ohio, below.)

Transitional note. The modern Court's variations on the contending techniques traced in the cases from Schenck and Abrams and Masses to Yates and Scales appear in sec. 1E below, especially in Brandenburg v. Ohio. Those recent cases can usefully be considered at this point. But before turning to them, these materials briefly consider the Court's responses, in the early and mid-sixties, to the largely ineffectual congressional laws of the fifties. The federal anti-Communist legislation of the fifties, unlike the Smith Act of 1940, did not follow the traditional pattern of the Gitlow-

---

* To what extent does Yates return to Hand's incitement test? Note Justice Harlan's comment: "We recognize that distinctions between advocacy or teaching of abstract doctrines, with evil intent, and that which is directed to stirring people to action, are often subtle and difficult to grasp . . . . But the very subtlety of these distinctions required the most clear and explicit instructions with reference to them." Recall Justice Holmes' comment in Gitlow: "Every idea is an incitement." Contrast Justice Brandeis' greater sensitivity to the potential utility of the incitement concept in his concurrence in Whitney: "The wide difference between advocacy and incitement, between preparation and attempt, between assembling and conspiracy, must be borne in mind." Is the incitement ingredient in Brandenburg, below, more speech-protective than Harlan's emphasis in Yates? More so than Hand's in Masses?

Whitney sedition-syndicalism statutes. For example, the major law, the Subversive Activities Control Act of 1950, aimed largely at registration and disclosure rather than direct "prohibition of speech because of its content." Although examination of most cases on disclosure requirements is postponed to chap. 13, sec. 5, below, the anti-Communist laws of the fifties are noted here to bring together the major federal criminal legislation on Communism and to provide background for the examination of the modern approaches to First Amendment issues in sec. 1E.

D. THE COURT AND ANTI–COMMUNIST LAWS OF THE FIFTIES

Introduction. The major federal anti-Communist law of the fifties was the Subversive Activities Control Act (Title I of the Internal Security Act of 1950). It established what the Court was to call an "extended and intricate regulatory" scheme for registration and disclosure, to be administered in part by a Subversive Activities Control Board. After the Board's registration orders to "Communist-action" organizations became final, a variety of sanctions were to be imposed on the organizations and their members, including passport denials and prohibitions of employment in defense facilities. In its first encounter with the statute, a divided Court sustained the basic legislative scheme (note 1 below). But, as the subsequent notes indicate, the registration provisions were never implemented, the Court found most of the sanctions unconstitutional, and, after extensive litigation, the Subversive Activities Control Board was disbanded a few years ago.* Another law of the fifties, the Communist Control Act of 1954, proved even more ineffectual. (See note 4 below.) The laws of the fifties may be more important for their doctrinal than their practical consequences: e. g., challenges to some of the sanctions in the 1950 Act provided the Warren Court with the opportunity to elaborate and apply the relatively new judicial technique of "overbreadth." See the Aptheker and Robel cases, note 3 below, and the discussion of "overbreadth," sec. 1E below.

1. *The 1961 decision sustaining the registration requirement.* In COMMUNIST PARTY v. SUBVERSIVE ACTIVITIES CONTROL BOARD, 367 U.S. 1 (1961), the majority sustained an SACB order requiring the Communist Party to register as a "Communist-action organization" under the Subversive Activities Control Act of 1950.† Justice Frankfurter rejected the claim that the First Amendment barred the SACB or-

---

* See also the repeal of the registration provisions in 81 Stat. 765.

† The statute included extensive legislative findings, concluding: "The Communist movement in the United States is an organization numbering thousands of adherents, rigidly and ruthlessly disciplined. . . . The Communist organization in the United States, pursuing its stated objectives, the recent successes of Communist methods in other countries, and the nature and control of the world Communist movement itself, present a clear and present danger to the security of the United States and to the existence of free American institutions, and make it necessary that Congress [enact] appropriate legislation recognizing the existence of such world-wide conspiracy and designed to prevent it from accomplishing its purpose in the United States."

der requiring the Party to register with the Attorney General. He insisted that the guarantees of freedom of speech and of association did not prevent Congress "from requiring the registration and filing of information, including membership lists, by organizations substantially dominated or controlled by the foreign powers controlling the world Communist movement." Though requirements of registration "as a condition upon the exercise of speech may in some circumstances" violate the First Amendment (see chap. 13 below), the majority noted that here the requirement did not attach "to the incident of speech, but to the incidents of foreign domination and of operation to advance the objectives of the world Communist movement— operation which, the Board has found here, includes extensive, long-continuing organizational as well as 'speech,' activity." Similarly, rights of association were not violated: cases such as NAACP v. Alabama [chap. 13, sec. 5, below] were distinguishable as involving situations where "the required making public of an organization's membership lists bears no rational relation to the interest which is asserted by the State to justify disclosure." Here, by contrast, the disclosure provisions were relevant to public interests of "magnitude."

Justice Frankfurter emphasized the detailed legislative findings: "We certainly cannot dismiss them as unfounded or irrational imaginings"; they reflected a permissible "appraisal by Congress of the threat which Communist organizations pose." Though "[i]ndividual liberties fundamental to American institutions are not to be destroyed under pretext of preserving those institutions, even from the gravest external dangers," "where the problems of accommodating the exigencies of self-preservation and the values of liberty are as complex and intricate [as here], the legislative judgment as to how that threat may best be met consistently with the safeguarding of personal freedom is not to be set aside merely because the judgment of judges would, in the first instance, have chosen other methods."

Justice Frankfurter insisted that the decision did not imply that "Congress may impose similar requirements upon any group which pursues unpopular political objectives": the Act applied "only to *foreign-dominated* organizations which work primarily to advance the objectives of a world movement controlled by the government of a *foreign* country. . . . There is no attempt here to impose stifling obligations upon the proponents of a particular political creed as such, or even to check the importation of particular political ideas from abroad for propogation here." The majority also held that the Act was not a bill of attainder. It found most other constitutional challenges premature—including a claim that compelling Party officials to file registration statements would violate the privilege against self-incrimination.

There were dissenting opinions by Chief Justice Warren and Justices Black, Douglas and Brennan. They all found merit in the self-incrimination claim. Justice Black, moreover, insisted that the Act was a bill of attainder by inflicting "pains, penalties and punishments in a number of ways without a judicial trial." A passage on the First Amendment issue in Justice Douglas' dissent is of special interest: though he was persuaded by the Fifth Amendment challenge, he conceded that "the bare requirement that the Communist Party register and disclose the names of its officers and directors

is in line with the most exacting adjudications touching First Amendment activities." He explained: "When an organization is used by a foreign power to make advances here, questions of security are raised beyond the ken of disputation and debate between the people resident here. Espionage, business activities, formation of cells for subversion, as well as the exercise of First Amendment rights, are then used to pry open our society and make intrusions of a foreign power easy. These machinations of a foreign power add additional elements to free speech just as marching up and down adds something to picketing that goes beyond free speech." (Justice Black was the only dissenter who found the First Amendment challenge persuasive.)

2. *The aftermath: Subsequent efforts to implement registration requirements of the 1950 Act.* As a result of the 1961 decision above, the SACB order finding the Party to be a "Communist-action organization" became final. Under the Act, the Party was accordingly under duty to register. But, as a result of several subsequent decisions, this and other registration orders were never implemented. (However, a final order to register, even without actual registration, triggered additional sanctions under the Act, considered in note 3 below.) The Party's refusal to register on self-incrimination grounds was sustained: in Communist Party v. United States, 331 F.2d 807 (D.C.Cir. 1963), cert. denied, 377 U.S. 968 (1964), the Court of Appeals set aside the conviction of the Party for failure to register.

After the Party's successful resistance to registration, Albertson v. SACB, 332 F.2d 317 (D.C.Cir. 1964), sustained a Board order directing two members of the Party to register. That decision was unanimously reversed by the Supreme Court, 382 U.S. 70 (1965). Justice Brennan's opinion found that the Board orders violated the privilege against self-incrimination, and that the challenge was no longer one that could be rejected as "premature." The Court noted that an admission of Party membership "may be used to prosecute the registrant under the membership clause of the Smith Act" as well as other provisions.

3. *The invalidation of other sanctions under the 1950 Act: The Aptheker and Robel cases.* a. *Aptheker.* One of the sanctions triggered by the existence of a final registration order was § 6 of the 1950 Act prohibiting any "member" of a "Communist organization" to use a passport with "knowledge or notice" that a registration order had become final. The State Department tried to revoke the passports of two Party leaders because it "believed that their use of the passports would violate § 6." In APTHEKER v. SECRETARY OF STATE, 378 U.S. 500 (1964), the Court held § 6 "unconstitutional on its face" because it "too broadly and indiscriminately restricts the right to travel and thereby abridges the liberty guaranteed by the Fifth Amendment." [1] Justice Goldberg's majority opinion rejected the Government's argument that "surely Section 6 was reasonable as applied to the top-ranking Party leaders involved here" [2]: "The clarity and precise-

1. In relying on the "right to travel abroad" aspect of "liberty," rather than free speech, Justice Goldberg's majority opinion cited Kent v. Dulles, 357 U.S. 116 (1958). See the discussion of "non-specific" constitutional rights, chap. 9 above.

2. A dissent by Justice Clark, joined by Justices Harlan and White, would have accepted the argument that the statute was valid as applied to the top-ranking Party members involved here. Justices Clark and Harlan would also have sustained the statute

ness of the provision in question make it impossible to narrow its indiscriminately cast and overly broad scope without substantial rewriting."

Justice Goldberg explained that the Section "sweeps within its prohibition both knowing and unknowing members" and "renders irrelevant the
member's degree of activity in the organization and his commitment to
its purpose." He insisted that § 6 could not be saved by an interpretation analogous to the reading of the membership clause of the Smith Act
in Scales v. United States (sec. 1C above)—the reading limiting the Smith
Act's prohibition to "active" members having a "guilty knowledge and intent." He explained that in Scales, the membership clause "explicitly required 'that a defendant must have knowledge of the organization's illegal
advocacy.' That requirement was intimately connected with the construction limiting membership to 'active' members. With regard to the [1950]
Act, however, as the Government concedes, 'neither the words nor history
of Section 6 suggests limiting its application to active members.' " [3]

The Court's conclusion that § 6 "too broadly" restricted the right to
travel has been of special significance in the free speech area: the emphasis
on "overbreadth" in Aptheker and other cases provided an increasingly
popular basis for decision in the Warren era. See, e. g., the Robel case,
which follows; and note the commentary on developments in the "overbreadth" doctrine in sec. 1E below.

b. *Robel.* Another consequence of a final registration order under
the 1950 Control Act was that specified in § 5(a)(1)(D): it made it a
crime for any member of a Communist-action organization "to engage in
any employment in any defense facility," with knowledge or notice that
there was in effect a final order requiring the organization to register. In
UNITED STATES v. ROBEL, 389 U.S. 258 (1967), as in Aptheker, the
majority invalidated that sanction on "overbreadth" grounds; but unlike
Aptheker, Robel emphasized the infringement of First Amendment rights
rather than the impairment of the "liberty" guaranteed by the due process
clause. Chief Justice Warren found the provision to be "an unconstitutional
abridgment of the right of association protected by the First Amendment."
The Chief Justice noted that it was irrelevant under the section "that an
individual may be a passive or inactive member of a designated organization,
that he may be unaware of the organization's unlawful aims, or that he may
disagree with those unlawful aims." Moreover, the statute made it irrelevant that an individual subject to it "may occupy a nonsensitive position in
a defense facility." He concluded that the provision "contains the fatal

on its face, as a restriction reasonably related to national security.

3. Note also the Aptheker opinion's argument that "Congress has within its
power 'less drastic' means of achieving the congressional objective of safeguarding our national security." Justice Goldberg added that the "broad
and enveloping prohibition" applying
to all members "indiscriminately excludes plainly relevant considerations
such as the individual's knowledge, ac-

tivity, commitment, and purposes in
and places for travel."

Does the Aptheker approach suggest
that the statutory interpretation views
regarding membership in Scales had
become constitutional requirements by
the time of Aptheker? Note also the
evolution of Scales and Yates statutory requirements into constitutional
limits in government employees' security cases such as Keyishian v.
Board of Regents, 385 U.S. 589 (1967)
(chap. 13, sec. 5, below).

defect of overbreadth because it seeks to bar employment both for association which may be proscribed and for association which may not be proscribed consistently with First Amendment rights." Justices White and Harlan dissented, emphasizing the "public interest in national security." On the majority's technique in Robel, see Gunther, "Reflections on Robel . . .," 20 Stan.L.Rev. 1140 (1968).

4. *The Communist Control Act of 1954.* Federal legislation directed at the Communist Party culminated with the 1954 Communist Control Act, a law with sweeping provisions but with fewer practical and legal consequences than the 1950 Act. The congressional "findings" included a statement that the Communist Party, "although purportedly a political party, is in fact an instrumentality of a conspiracy to overthrow the Government of the United States," and concluded: "Therefore, the Communist Party should be outlawed." [4] One section of the law stated that the Party was "not entitled to any of the rights, privileges, and immunities attendant upon legal bodies created under [the] laws of the United States or [any] subdivision thereof," but it added that this section was not to be construed as amending the 1950 Act. Another provision stated that "knowingly and willfully" becoming or remaining a Party member was to subject the individual to the 1950 Act as a member of a "Communist-action" organization. Still another section listed thirteen types of evidence a jury "shall consider" in "determining membership or participation" in the Party, including evidence as to whether the accused had "indicated by word, action, conduct, writing or in any other way a willingness to carry out in any manner and to any degree the plans, designs, objectives, or purposes of the organization." [5]

In the only case involving the 1954 Act to reach the Supreme Court, the Court avoided decision on any constitutional challenges. In Communist Party v. Catherwood, 367 U.S. 389 (1961), New York courts had relied on the "rights, privileges, and immunities" provision of the Act in upholding the termination of the Party's registration and liability to state taxation as an employer under the State Unemployment Insurance Law. Justice Harlan's opinion in Catherwood held that the state courts' reliance had been erroneous: constitutional challenges to the 1954 Act did not have to be reached because the state interpretation, "raising as it does novel constitutional questions, the answers to which are not necessarily controlled by decisions of this Court in connection with other legislation dealing with the Communist Party, must, we think, be rejected."

5. *Communist propaganda, foreign mail, and aliens: The Lamont and Mandel cases.* Under a 1962 law, the Post Office screened foreign unsealed mail, detained "communist political propaganda," and notified the addressee that the mail would be destroyed unless the addressee requested delivery

---

4. The law stemmed from a Democratic proposal that membership in the Party be made a crime—a proposal introduced by Senator Humphrey with the statement: "I am tired of reading headlines about being 'soft' toward communism." President Eisenhower opposed the proposal because it might obstruct enforcement of the Smith Act and the 1950 law. The final version of the 1954 Act was a compromise substituted by Republicans. See generally, Chase, "The Libertarian Case for Making it a Crime to Be a Communist," 29 Temp.L.Q. 121 (1956).

5. See Note, "The Communist Control Act of 1954," 64 Yale L.J. 712 (1955).

by returning a reply card within 20 days. That statute was found inconsistent with the First Amendment in Lamont v. Postmaster General, 381 U.S. 301 (1965). The Court rested on the First Amendment right to "receive information and ideas": Justice Douglas' majority opinion thought the reply card scheme "carries an affirmative obligation which we do not think the government may impose"; that requirement was "almost certain to have a deterrent effect."

But the right to "receive information and ideas" recognized in Lamont was not sufficient to curtail the government's broad power over the exclusion of aliens. A 6 to 3 decision in Kleindienst v. Mandel, 408 U.S. 753 (1972), sustained a statutory provision of the Internal Security Act of 1950 making foreign Communists "ineligible" to receive visas. In Mandel's case, the Attorney General refused to exercise his statutory discretion to waive ineligibility. Though Justice Blackmun's majority opinion recognized "that First Amendment rights are implicated," he emphasized the traditional recognition of Congress' "plenary power" over the exclusion of aliens. Justice Douglas dissented on statutory grounds. Another dissent, by Justice Marshall, joined by Justice Brennan, rested on the First Amendment. He noted that the statute excluded aliens "solely because they have advocated communist doctrine," and he insisted that there was no reason to depart from "the established First Amendment law" simply because the power of excluding aliens was involved.

E. SUBVERSIVE ADVOCACY AND THE COURT AFTER A HALF CENTURY: OLD PRECEDENTS AND NEW TOOLS

Introduction. This section returns to the statutory and factual context of the Schenck-Gitlow-Whitney era. What do evolving free speech doctrines say about the modern counterparts of those problems? The Brandenburg case is the Warren Court's response to a Whitney-type statute. And the anti-Vietnam protests considered in the materials after Brandenburg involve modern variations on the setting of the World War I Espionage Act prosecutions.

What is the role of clear and present danger in the handling of these questions? What of the Masses approach? What of the impact of Dennis and the later Smith Act cases, Yates and Scales? Are alternative analyses of free speech problems now available—and preferable? In order to explore the last of these questions, the final portion of this section offers a preliminary sampling of some additional speech-protective techniques that flourished in the last years of the Warren Court—especially the "overbreadth" approach.

BRANDENBURG v. OHIO

395 U.S. 444, 89 S.Ct. 1827, 23 L.Ed.2d 430 (1969).

Appeal from the Supreme Court of Ohio.

PER CURIAM.

The appellant, a leader of a Ku Klux Klan group, was convicted under the Ohio Criminal Syndicalism statute for "advocat[ing] . . . the duty, necessity, or propriety of crime, sabotage, violence, or unlawful methods of terrorism as a means of accomplishing industrial or political reform" and for "voluntarily assembl[ing] with any society, group, or assemblage of persons formed to teach or advocate the doctrines of criminal syndicalism." He was fined $1,000 and sentenced to one to 10 years' imprisonment. The appellant challenged the constitutionality of the criminal syndicalism statute [under the First and 14th Amendments], but the intermediate appellate court [affirmed without opinion]. The Supreme Court of Ohio dismissed his appeal, *sua sponte*, "for the reason that no substantial constitutional question exists herein." . . . We reverse.

The record shows that a man, identified at trial as the appellant, telephoned an announcer-reporter on the staff of a Cincinnati television station and invited him to come to a Ku Klux Klan "rally" to be held at a farm in Hamilton County. With the cooperation of the organizers, the reporter and a cameraman attended the meeting and filmed the events. Portions of the films were later broadcast on the local station and on a national network.

The prosecution's case rested on the films and on testimony identifying the appellant as the person who communicated with the reporter and who spoke at the rally. The State also introduced into evidence several articles appearing in the film, including a pistol, a rifle, a shotgun, ammunition, a Bible, and a red hood worn by the speaker in the films.

One film showed 12 hooded figures, some of whom carried firearms. They were gathered around a large wooden cross, which they burned. No one was present other than the participants and the newsmen who made the film. Most of the words uttered during the scene were incomprehensible when the film was projected, but scattered phrases could be understood that were derogatory of Negroes and, in one instance, of Jews.[1] Another scene on the same film showed the appellant, in Klan regalia, making a speech. The speech, in full, was as follows:

"This is an organizers' meeting. We have had quite a few members here today which are—we have hundreds, hundreds of members

---

1. The significant portions that could be understood were:

"How far is the nigger going to—yeah."
"This is what we are going to do to the niggers."
"A dirty nigger."
"Send the Jews back to Israel."
"Let's give them back to the dark garden."
"Save America."
"Let's go back to constitutional betterment."
"Bury the niggers."
"We intend to do our part."
"Give us our state rights."
"Freedom for the whites."
"Nigger will have to fight for every inch he gets from now on." [All footnotes to this opinion by the Court.]

throughout the State of Ohio. I can quote from a newspaper clipping from the Columbus, Ohio Dispatch, five weeks ago Sunday morning. The Klan has more members in the State of Ohio than does any other organization. We're not a revengent organization, but if our President, our Congress, our Supreme Court, continues to suppress the white, Caucasian race, it's possible that there might have to be some revengeance taken.

"We are marching on Congress July the Fourth, four hundred thousand strong. From there we are dividing into two groups, one group to march on St. Augustine, Florida, the other group to march into Mississippi. Thank you."

The second film showed six hooded figures one of whom, later identified as the appellant, repeated a speech very similar to that recorded on the first film. The reference to the possibility of "revengeance" was omitted, and one sentence was added: "Personally, I believe the nigger should be returned to Africa, the Jew returned to Israel." Though some of the figures in the films carried weapons, the speaker did not.

The Ohio Criminal Syndicalism Statute was enacted in 1919. From 1917 to 1920, identical or quite similar laws were adopted by 20 States and two territories. [In 1927,] this Court sustained the constitutionality of California's Criminal Syndicalism Act, the text of which is quite similar to that of the laws of Ohio [Whitney v. California]. The Court upheld the statute on the ground that, without more, "advocating" violent means to effect political and economic change involves such danger to the security of the State that the State may outlaw it. Cf. [Fiske v. Kansas]. But Whitney has been thoroughly discredited by later decisions. See [Dennis]. These later decisions have fashioned the principle that the constitutional guarantees of free speech and free press do not permit a State to forbid or proscribe advocacy of the use of force or of law violation except where such advocacy is directed to inciting or producing imminent lawless action and is likely to incite or produce such action.[2] As we said in [Noto], "the mere abstract teaching . . . of the moral propriety or even moral necessity for a resort to force and violence, is not the same as preparing a group for violent action and steeling it to such action." See also [Herndon v. Lowry; Bond v. Floyd (which follows)]. A statute which fails to draw this distinction impermissibly intrudes upon the freedoms guaranteed by the First and Fourteenth Amendments. It sweeps within its condemnation speech which our Constitution has immunized from governmental control. Cf. [Yates; DeJonge; Stromberg v. California].

Measured by this test, Ohio's Criminal Syndicalism Act cannot be sustained. The Act punishes persons who "advocate or teach the duty, necessity,

---

2. It was on the theory that the Smith Act embodied such a principle and that it had been applied only in conformity with it that this Court sustained the Act's constitutionality. [Dennis]. That this was the basis for Dennis was emphasized in [Yates], in which the Court overturned convictions for advocacy of the forcible overthrow of the Government under the Smith Act, because the trial judge's instructions had allowed conviction for mere advocacy, unrelated to its tendency to produce forcible action.

or propriety" of violence "as a means of accomplishing industrial or political reform"; or who publish or circulate or display any book or paper containing such advocacy; or who "justify" the commission of violent acts "with intent to exemplify, spread or advocate the propriety of the doctrines of criminal syndicalism"; or who "voluntarily assemble" with a group formed "to teach or advocate the doctrines of criminal syndicalism." Neither the indictment nor the trial judge's instructions to the jury in any way refined the statute's bald definition of the crime in terms of mere advocacy not distinguished from incitement to imminent lawless action.[3]

Accordingly, we are here confronted with a statute which, by its own words and as applied, purports to punish mere advocacy and to forbid, on pain of criminal punishment, assembly with others merely to advocate the described type of action.[4] Such a statute falls within the condemnation of the First and Fourteenth Amendments. The contrary teaching of [Whitney v. California] cannot be supported, and that decision is therefore overruled.

Reversed.[*]

Mr. Justice BLACK, concurring.

I agree with the views expressed by Mr. Justice Douglas in his concurring opinion in this case that the "clear and present danger" doctrine should have no place in the interpretation of the First Amendment. I join the Court's opinion, which, as I understand it, simply cites [Dennis], but does not indicate any agreement on the Court's part with the "clear and present danger" doctrine on which Dennis purported to rely.

Mr. Justice DOUGLAS, concurring.

While I join the opinion of the Court, I desire to enter a *caveat*.

[Schenck and the other post-World War I cases] put the gloss of "clear and present danger" on the First Amendment. Whether the war power— the greatest leveler of them all—is adequate to sustain that doctrine is debatable. The dissents in Abrams, Schaefer, and Pierce show how easily "clear and present danger" is manipulated to crush what Brandeis [in Pierce] call-

---

3. The first count of the indictment charged that appellant "did unlawfully by word of mouth advocate the necessity, or propriety of crime, violence, or unlawful methods of terrorism as a means of accomplishing political reform. . . ." The second count charged that appellant "did unlawfully voluntarily assemble with a group or assemblage of persons formed to advocate the doctrines of criminal syndicalism. . . ." The trial judge's charge merely followed the language of the indictment. No construction of the statute by the Ohio courts has brought it within constitutionally permissible limits. . . .

4. Statutes affecting the right of assembly, like those touching on freedom of speech, must observe the established distinctions between mere advocacy and incitement to imminent lawless action, for as Chief Justice Hughes wrote in [DeJonge]: "The right of peaceable assembly is a right cognate to those of free speech and free press and is equally fundamental."

* Direct challenges to the New York law sustained in Gitlow and the California law sustained in Whitney produced the litigation in Younger v. Harris, 401 U.S. 37 (1971), and Samuels v. Mackell, 401 U.S. 66 (1971). But the Court did not reach the First Amendment issues and rested instead on jurisdictional grounds relating to the appropriateness of federal injunctive relief. The cases are discussed in chap. 15 below. However, a state court later held unconstitutional the California law that had been sustained in Whitney. In re Harris, 97 Cal. Rptr. 844 (1971).

ed "[t]he fundamental right of free men to strive for better conditions through new legislation and new institutions" by argument and discourse even in time of war. Though I doubt if the "clear and present danger" test is congenial to the First Amendment in time of a declared war, I am certain it is not reconcilable with the First Amendment in days of peace.

The Court quite properly overrules [Whitney], which involved advocacy of ideas which the majority of the Court deemed unsound and dangerous.

Mr. Justice Holmes, though never formally abandoning the "clear and present danger" test, moved closer to the First Amendment ideal when he said in dissent in Gitlow [quoting the passage beginning "Every idea is an incitement"]. We have never been faithful to the philosophy of that dissent.

The Court in Herndon v. Lowry overturned a conviction for exercising First Amendment rights to incite insurrection because of lack of evidence of incitement. In Bridges v. California, we approved the "clear and present danger" test in an elaborate dictum that tightened it and confined it to a narrow category. But in Dennis v. United States, we opened wide the door, distorting the "clear and present danger" test beyond recognition. . . . Out of the "clear and present danger" test came other offspring. [See Yates; Scales; Noto; Barenblatt (chap. 13, sec. 6, below)].

My own view is quite different. I see no place in the regime of the First Amendment for any "clear and present danger" test, whether strict and tight as some would make it, or free-wheeling as the Court in Dennis rephrased it.

When one reads the opinions closely and sees when and how the "clear and present danger" test has been applied, great misgivings are aroused. First, the threats were often loud but always puny and made serious only by judges so wedded to the status quo that critical analysis made them nervous. Second, the test was so twisted and perverted in Dennis as to make the trial of those teachers of Marxism an all-out political trial which was part and parcel of the cold war that has eroded substantial parts of the First Amendment.

Action is often a method of expression and within the protection of the First Amendment. Suppose one tears up his own copy of the Constitution in eloquent protest to a decision of this Court. May he be indicted? Suppose one rips his own Bible to shreds to celebrate his departure from one "faith" and his embrace of atheism. May he be indicted?

Last Term the Court held in United States v. O'Brien, 391 U.S. 367, 382 [sec. 3 below], that a registrant under Selective Service who burned his draft card in protest of the war in Vietnam could be prosecuted. The First Amendment was tendered as a defense and rejected . . . .. But O'Brien was not prosecuted for not having his draft card available when asked for by a federal agent. He was indicted, tried, and convicted for burning the card. And this Court's affirmance of that conviction was not, with all respect, consistent with the First Amendment. . . .

The line between what is permissible and not subject to control and what may be made impermissible and subject to regulation is the line between ideas and overt acts.

The example usually given by those who would punish speech is the case of one who falsely shouts fire in a crowded theatre. This is, however, a

classic case where speech is brigaded with action. . . . They are indeed inseparable and a prosecution can be launched for the overt acts actually caused. Apart from rare instances of that kind, speech is, I think, immune from prosecution. Certainly there is no constitutional line between advocacy of abstract ideas as in Yates and advocacy of political action as in Scales. The quality of advocacy turns on the depth of the conviction; and government has no power to invade that sanctuary of belief and conscience.

THE IMPACT OF BRANDENBURG

1. *The implications of Brandenburg.* To what extent does Brandenburg change rather that restate First Amendment doctrine? Recall the question raised earlier: Can Brandenburg be viewed as combining "the most protective ingredients of the Masses incitement emphasis with the most useful elements of the clear and present danger heritage"? * Can Brandenburg be viewed as building on Yates and Scales "to produce [the Warren Court's] clearest and most protective standard under the first amendment"? Can Brandenburg be viewed as resting "ultimately on the insight Learned Hand urged without success at the end of World War I"? Are the Brandenburg Court's descriptions of the prior cases accurate? See, e. g., the reference in footnote 4 to "the established distinctions between mere advocacy and incitement to imminent lawless action." Where was that distinction "established"? Consider the comment in Gunther, above: "An incitement-nonincitement distinction had only fragmentary and ambiguous antecedents in the pre-Brandenburg era; it was Brandenburg that really 'established' it; and, it was essentially an establishment of the legacy of Learned Hand."

2. *The vitality of Brandenburg.* The Brandenburg decision came during the last Term of Chief Justice Warren's tenure, but the case has several times been cited with approval in the Burger era. For a modern reliance on the Brandenburg incitement standard, note its invocation as the primary ground for reversal of a disorderly conduct conviction in HESS v. INDIANA, 414 U.S. 105 (1973). After a campus anti-war demonstration during which there had been arrests, over 100 demonstrators blocked the street until they were moved to the curb by the police. Appellant, standing off the street, said: "We'll take the fucking street later (or again)." The state court relied primarily on a finding that this statement was "intended to incite further lawless action on the part of the crowd in the vicinity of appellant and was likely to produce such action." The Supreme Court reversed in a per curiam opinion, without oral argument. And it chose to

---

* Consider Gunther, "Learned Hand and the Origins of Modern First Amendment Doctrine: Some Fragments of History," 27 Stan.L.Rev. 719 (1975): "The incitement emphasis is Hand's; the reference to 'imminent' reflects a limited influence of Holmes, combined with later experience; and 'the likely to incite or produce such action' addition in the Brandenburg standard is the only reference to the need to guess about future consequences of speech, so central to the Schenck approach. Under Brandenburg, probability of harm is no longer the central criterion for speech limitations. The inciting language of the speaker—the Hand focus on 'objective' words—is the major consideration. And punishment of the harmless inciter is prevented by the Schenck-derived requirement of a likelihood of dangerous consequences."

rely on "as applied" grounds rather than to reach overbreadth and vagueness claims—claims particularly popular in the later Warren years, as noted in the concluding materials in this section.†

The Supreme Court's majority opinion in Hess emphasized that the Brandenburg standard governed and disagreed with the state court's evaluation of appellant's speech: "At best, [the] statement could be taken as counsel for present moderation; at worst, it amounted to nothing more than advocacy of illegal action at some indefinite future time." The majority added that "since there was no evidence, or rational inference from the import of the language, that his words were intended to produce, and likely to produce, *imminent* disorder, those words could not be punished by the State on the ground that they had 'a tendency to lead to violence.' "

Justice Rehnquist's dissent, joined by Chief Justice Burger and Justice Blackmun, thought the majority had improperly substituted "a different complex of factual inferences for the inferences reached by the courts below" and had accordingly "exceeded the proper scope of our review." He thought appellant's words were "susceptible of characterization as an exhortation, particularly when uttered in a loud voice while facing a crowd." Perhaps, he added, Hess had simply expressed his views "to the world at large, but that is surely not the only rational explanation."

OPPOSITION TO VIETNAM POLICY AND TO THE DRAFT: SOME CASES IN THE YEARS IMMEDIATELY PRECEDING BRANDENBURG

Consider the scope given to freedom of expression (and the criteria applied) in the following modern cases decided in the years just before Brandenburg—all war and draft protest counterparts to the milieu of the Espionage Act cases.

1. *Criticism of governmental policy and state legislators' oaths: The Julian Bond case.* In BOND v. FLOYD, 385 U.S. 116 (1966), the Court held that a Georgia House of Representatives resolution excluding Julian Bond from membership violated the First Amendment. The State's justification was that Bond could not conscientiously take the required oath to "support the Constitution of this State and of the United States." The House relied on Bond's endorsement of a SNCC statement and his supplementary remarks critical of the draft and of Vietnam policy. Chief Justice Warren's opinion for a unanimous Court is of special interest for the problems considered in this section because of its discussion of the question whether Bond's statements would have been protected by the First Amendment if they had been made by a private citizen. The Chief Justice was emphatic in explaining that the statements *were* protected criticism of Vietnam policy and the draft:

"Bond could not have been constitutionally convicted under 50 U.S.C. § 462(a), which punishes any person who 'counsels, aids, or abets another to

---

† Before reaching the Brandenburg issue, the majority noted briefly that it was clear that appellant's words were not punishable as a public nuisance invading private interests or as "fighting words" or as offensive language. See sec. 2 below.

refuse or evade registration.' Bond's statements were at worst unclear on the question of the means to be adopted to avoid the draft. While the SNCC statements said 'We are in sympathy with, and support, the men in this country who are unwilling to respond to a military draft,' this statement alone cannot be interpreted as a call to unlawful refusal to be drafted. Moreover, Bond's supplementary statements tend to resolve the opaqueness in favor of legal alternatives to the draft, and there is no evidence to the contrary. On the day the statement was issued, Bond explained that he endorsed it 'because I like to think of myself as a pacifist and one who opposes that war and any other war and eager and anxious to encourage people not to participate in it for any reason that they choose.' [He] further stated 'I oppose the Viet Cong fighting in Viet Nam as much as I oppose the United States fighting in Viet Nam.' At the hearing before the Special Committee of the Georgia House, when asked his position on persons who burned their draft cards, Bond replied that he admired the courage of persons who 'feel strongly enough about their convictions to take an action like that knowing the consequences that they will face.' When pressed as to whether his admiration was based on the violation of federal law, Bond stated:

> 'I have never suggested or counseled or advocated that any one other person burn their draft card. In fact, I have mine in my pocket and will produce it if you wish. I do not advocate that people should break laws. What I simply try to say was that I admired the courage of someone who could act on his convictions knowing that he faces pretty stiff consequences.'

"Certainly this clarification does not demonstrate any incitement to violation of law. No useful purpose would be served by discussing the many decisions of this Court which establish that Bond could not have been convicted for these statements consistently with the First Amendment. . . .

Nor did Bond's position as an elected legislator change the situation: "The State attempts to circumvent the protection the First Amendment would afford to these statements if made by a private citizen by arguing that a State is constitutionally justified in exacting a higher standard of *loyalty* from its legislators than from its citizens. [W]hile the State has an interest in requiring its legislators to swear to a belief in constitutional processes of government, surely the oath gives it no interest in limiting its legislators' capacity to discuss their views of local or national policy."

2. *Counselling draft evasion and the Bond case.* Consider the First Amendment comments in Bond in light of the Spock-Coffin prosecution, see 416 F.2d 165 (1st Cir. 1969); and compare United States v. O'Brien, the 1968 draft-card burning case, sec. 3 below. Compare the Bond opinion with the "counselling" and "admiration" approaches in Hand's Masses opinion and Holmes' Debs opinion, respectively.*

---

* Also compare Bond's statements with the statements found punishable in the Schenck-Frohwerk-Debs trilogy. Note one commentator's reaction to such a comparison: "[T]he distance traversed in First Amendment interpretation is quite apparent." Emerson, "Freedom of Expression in Wartime," 116 U.Pa. L.Rev. 975 (1968).

3. *Threats against the President and the Watts case.* For a per curiam decision considering anti-draft comments in an unusual context, note the Court's reversal without argument in WATTS v. UNITED STATES, 394 U.S. 705 (1969). Petitioner had been convicted under a 1917 statute making it a felony "knowingly and willfully" to make "any threat to take the life" of the President. Petitioner had said at a public rally (after it had been urged that young people get more education before speaking): "They always holler at us to get an education. And now I have already received my draft classification as 1–A and I have got to report for my physical this Monday coming. I am not going. If they ever make me carry a rifle, the first man I want to get in my sights is L.B.J. They are not going to make me kill my black brothers."

The Court stated: "Certainly the statute [is] constitutional on its face. The Nation undoubtedly has a valid, even an overwhelming, interest in protecting the safety of its Chief Executive and in allowing him to perform his duties without interference from threats of physical violence. Nevertheless, a statute such as this one, which makes criminal a form of pure speech, must be interpreted with the commands of the First Amendment clearly in mind. What is a threat must be distinguished from what is constitutionally protected speech.

"[W]hatever the 'willfulness' requirement implies,† the statute initially requires the Government to prove a true 'threat.' We do not believe that the kind of political hyperbole indulged in by petitioner fits within that statutory term. For we must interpret the language Congress chose 'against the background of a profound national commitment to the principle that debate on public issues should be uninhibited, robust, and wide-open, and that it may well include vehement, caustic, and sometimes unpleasantly sharp attacks on government and public officials.' New York Times Co. v. Sullivan, 376 U.S. 254, 270 (1964) [chap. 13, sec. 1, below]. The language of the political arena, like the language used in labor disputes, [is] often vituperative, abusive, and inexact. We agree with petitioner that his only offense [was] 'a kind of very crude offensive method of stating a political opposition to the President.' Taken in context, and regarding the expressly conditional nature of the statement and the reaction of the listeners [there had been laughter after the statement], we do not see how it could be interpreted otherwise."

4. *Protests through symbols rather than words: A transitional note.* Do the applicable judicial criteria change when anti-war, anti-draft protest

---

† In the Court of Appeals, the majority opinion (by then-Court of Appeals Judge Burger) thought it adequate that the threat was made "knowingly and willfully," that there was "an apparent determination" to carry it out; the dissenter insisted that a defendant must intend to carry out his threat. The Supreme Court did not resolve that issue, but commented that it had "grave doubts" about the majority position in the Court of Appeals. Does the Watts case comply with the incitement or clear and present danger standards? Does it authorize greater restrictions on speech than those standards would permit? Why? Because of the "overwhelming" national interest in protecting the President? In protecting the President from threats as well as actual harm? Because threats against the President are not "speech" ? Compare the cases in chap. 13 below holding "obscenity" not to be "speech" within the First Amendment. Is such a definitional approach a persuasive one?

is expressed symbolically, through behavior rather than words? How? Is the First Amendment inapplicable because "conduct" rather than "speech" is involved? Is less First Amendment protection appropriate? Issues such as these have repeatedly come before the modern Court. See, e. g., United States v. O'Brien, 391 U.S. 367 (1968), sustaining a conviction for burning a draft card against a First Amendment symbolic expression defense, and Tinker v. Des Moines Comm. School Dist., 393 U.S. 503 (1969), protecting the wearing of black armbands by school children as a war protest symbol. See also the protests involving the mutilation of the American flag, considered after O'Brien and Tinker, in sec. 3 below.

ALTERNATIVE TECHNIQUES TO PROTECT SPEECH: THE "OVERBREADTH" DOCTRINE

Introduction. The preceding materials have considered a variety of analytical approaches prominent in the Court's protection of political speech critical of government. The major emphasis has been on the evolutions of the clear and present danger and incitement standards. But that emphasis should not obscure the fact that those are not the only judicial techniques available in the adjudication of First Amendment claims. Others have already surfaced sporadically in the preceding cases, and additional ones will appear in the materials which follow. Recall, for example, the Court's quotation, in the Watts case on threats to the President (note 3 above), from the 1964 decision in New York Times Co. v. Sullivan, emphasizing the "profound national commitment to the principle that debate on public issues should be uninhibited, robust, and wide-open." That New York Times case sustained a First Amendment defense to a libel action brought by a public official against a newspaper, and its analysis and implications in the defamation context are considered at length in chap. 13, sec. 1, below. But the New York Times theme of uninhibited debate on public issues has served the modern Court in a variety of other contexts as well. Does the articulation of that theme add anything to the preceding cases? Does it suggest greater protection for "public" rather than "private" speech? Does it reinforce the Masses focus on what is most valued by democratic presuppositions, rather than on "dangers"? Does it stress defining protected speech, rather than assessing risks?

The language of the New York Times case, though echoed in a number of modern cases, is at best an aid to the articulation of First Amendment values, not by itself an elaborate alternative technique. But there is another frequent theme in modern cases which warrants somewhat greater preliminary attention here: the "overbreadth" analysis in the First Amendment area. It, too, has already surfaced briefly, in the Aptheker and Robel cases, sec. 1D above. The fullest development of overbreadth has taken place in contexts not fully explored until later in these materials. Nevertheless, a preliminary sampling of the important modern doctrinal tool of overbreadth is useful here, for it offers a related, alternative, possibly more effective technique for the protection of freedom of expression. It is a technique that proved increasingly popular with the Warren Court, though it has encountered mount-

ing criticism and some curtailment in the Burger era. It is surveyed here to invite comparison with the approaches central in the doctrinal evolution from Schenck and Masses to Brandenburg.

1. *The distinctive features of overbreadth.* The modern Court—particularly in the last decade of the Warren era—repeatedly, and in a variety of circumstances, invoked the principle that "a governmental purpose to control or prevent activities constitutionally subject [to] regulation may not be achieved by *means which sweep unnecessarily broadly and thereby invade the area of protected freedoms.*" (Emphasis added.)[1] That overbreadth approach differs significantly from the "as applied" inquiry most commonly encountered in the preceding cases. In the usual "as applied" case, the Court asks whether the challenger's activities are protected by the First Amendment. In the typical "as applied" case, the holding is that the challenger's speech *is* constitutionally protected and that he cannot be punished under any statute. The overbreadth technique, by contrast, does not reach the question whether the *challenger's* speech is constitutionally protected; instead it strikes the statute down entirely because it *might* be applied to others not before the Court whose activities *are* constitutionally protected. In other words, the law is invalidated at the behest of a litigant whose conduct may or may not be constitutionally protected—though the Court often assumes that the challenger's behavior is not protected by the First Amendment and *is* reachable by the state under a more "narrowly drawn" law. The challenged statute is struck down because the challenger is permitted to argue that *other* conceivable statutory applications *might* constitutionally burden protected activity. One of the pervasive problems in the application of the doctrine is how far the Court should seek out *possible* unconstitutional applications of the law as a basis for reversing a conviction of someone whose behavior could presumably be punished by a more narrowly drawn law. It is that difficulty that has contributed to the Burger Court's "substantial overbreadth" limitation on the technique. See notes 4 and 5 below.

The reason the Court has at times been willing to invalidate laws which on their face fairly suggest potential unconstitutional applications to others is to protect First Amendment interests: the Court assumes that an overbroad law's "very existence may cause others not before the Court to refrain from constitutionally protected speech or expression"; the Court strikes down the statute to defuse the deterrent or "chilling" effect of the overbroad statute.[2] When the Court finds a legitimate state interest in curtailing the challenger's conduct, yet the means chosen too "broad," should it be under an obligation to explain what narrower means to achieve the state's objective are available? In a considerable number of overbreadth decisions, the Court has been largely silent about such alternatives.[3] May that help explain the attractiveness of

1. The quotation is from Justice Harlan's opinion for the Court in NAACP v. Alabama ex rel. Flowers, 377 U.S. 288 (1964).

2. See generally, Note, "The First Amendment Overbreadth Doctrine," 83 Harv.L.Rev. 844 (1970); cf. Note, "The Chilling Effect in Constitutional

Law," 69 Colum.L.Rev. 808 (1969), and Note, "Standing to Assert Constitutional Jus Tertii," 88 Harv.L.Rev. 423 (1974).

3. Note, e. g., an early example of the overbreadth approach, Shelton v. Tucker, 364 U.S. 479 (1960) (chap. 13, sec. 5, below), invalidating a law com-

overbreadth to some Justices: Is overbreadth analysis more palatable because it gives the appearance of leaving alternatives open to the legislature—of intervening in the legislative choices more marginally than outright "balancing" would?   See also note 2.

2.   *The attractiveness of the overbreadth technique.* What else accounts for the considerable popularity of the overbreadth doctrine, particularly in the late Warren years?   Its attractiveness may be attributable to its relatively technical, tentative appearance.   It strikes down the law at the behest of challenger A without saying much about the First Amendment dimensions of A's behavior; it strikes down the law because of a possible application to B not before the Court, an application that is often only briefly discussed rather than fully explored.   Unlike many of the techniques considered earlier, overbreadth opinions frequently do not deal explicitly and elaborately with the substantive dimensions of protected speech; they purport to be concerned with *means* to legitimate ends, not ultimate quasi-legislative choices; they avoid explicit "balancing"; they do not pursue the constitutionality of government regulation of A's behavior.[4]

Yet an overbreadth opinion necessarily involves some delineation of protected expression under the First Amendment, albeit more obliquely and less explicitly than do many other techniques.   To strike down an excessively broad "means" because it impinges on an "area of protected freedom" presupposes, after all, at least an implicit judgment about what the contours of that "area" are.   To strike down a law at A's behest because of its potential invalid application to B involves at least implicit assumptions about *why* B is protected by the First Amendment.   Some of the popularity of the overbreadth technique to the Court may stem, then, from its usefulness in deciding speech problems somewhat more indirectly, often more sketchily, than the more open confrontations of ultimate speech issues noted earlier— even though the Court's overbreadth opinions often emphasize that it is not denying legislative power to reach challenger A's behavior through more "narrowly drawn" legislation.[5]   (The popularity of the technique to the chal-

---

pelling a teacher to list every organization with which he was affiliated over a five-year period.   The Court explained: "[E]ven though the governmental purpose be legitimate and substantial, that purpose cannot be pursued by means that broadly stifle fundamental personal liberties when the end can be more narrowly achieved.   The breadth of legislative abridgment must be viewed in the light of less drastic means for achieving the same basic purpose."   (A footnote suggested an analogy to the less-drastic-alternatives rationale of Dean Milk Co. v. Madison, 340 U.S. 349, the state regulation of commerce case in chap. 5 above.   See the additional comments on Shelton in chap. 13 below.)

4.   See, e. g., Chief Justice Warren's opinion for the Court in United States

v. Robel, sec. 1D above, and note Gunther, "Reflections on Robel . . . ," 20 Stan.L.Rev. 1140 (1968).

5.   An "overbreadth" challenge should not be confused with one on grounds of "vagueness," though a challenger will often assert both grounds of invalidity.   An unconstitutionally vague statute, like an overbroad one, creates "chilling effect" risks to protected speech.   But a statute can be quite specific—i. e., not "vague"—and yet be overbroad.   The vagueness challenge rests ultimately on the procedural due process requirement of notice, though it is a challenge with special bite in the First Amendment area.   The due process requirement of a minimum degree of definiteness in the statutory prescription of standards demands language which conveys "sufficiently definite warning as to the

lenger is evident: when successfully invoked, it produces not a limited holding that the law is invalid "as applied" to the particular challenger, but rather that it is void "on its face" and hence unenforceable against anyone.)

3.   *The mounting criticisms of the overbreadth technique.*   The overbreadth technique finding statutes invalid on their face was resorted to with considerable frequency during the sixties.   In addition to its use in striking down provisions of the Subversive Activities Control Act of 1950, in the Aptheker and Robel cases above, other prominent examples include Keyishian v. Board of Regents, 385 U.S. 589 (1967) (government employees' security program, chap. 13, sec. 5, below), and Gooding v. Wilson, 405 U.S. 518 (1972) (law prohibiting "opprobrious words or abusive language," sec. 2 below).   But in recent years, there has been increasing criticism of invocations of overbreadth.   See, e. g., Justice Black's opinion in Younger v. Harris, 401 U.S. 37 (1971) (chap. 15 below), including the comment that "the existence of a 'chilling effect' even in the area of First Amendment rights has never been considered a sufficient basis, in and of itself, for prohibiting state action."   In curtailing federal injunctive relief against a law claimed to be "on its face" vague or overly broad, Justice Black also emphasized a "more basic consideration": "the function of the federal courts in our constitutional plan."   The federal judicial power to resolve "concrete disputes," he noted, "does not amount to an unlimited power to survey the statute books and pass judgment on laws before the courts are called upon to enforce them."   Implicitly attacking a characteristic of overbreadth review —the consideration of *potential* applications of a statute, to parties not before the Court—he commented: "The combination of the relative remoteness of the controversy, the impact on the legislative process of the relief sought, and above all the speculative and amorphous nature of the required line-by-line analysis of detailed statutes ordinarily results in a kind of case that is wholly unsatisfactory for deciding constitutional questions."

Note also Justice White's dissent from an invalidation for vagueness and overbreadth in Coates v. Cincinnati, 402 U.S. 611 (1971), and Chief Justice Burger's dissent from the overbreadth invalidation in Gooding v. Wilson, 405 U.S. 518 (1972) (both in sec. 2 below).   Building on Justice Black's comments in Younger v. Harris, Chief Justice Burger in Gooding

proscribed conduct when measured by common understanding and practices." Jordan v. DeGeorge, 341 U.S. 223 (1951). But, as the most astute commentator on "vagueness" has remarked, the doctrine is "most frequently employed as an implement for curbing legislative invasion of constitutional rights *other* than that of fair notice," though there is "an actual vagueness component in the vagueness decisions." Amsterdam, "The Void-for-Vagueness Doctrine in the Supreme Court," 109 U.Pa.L.Rev. 67 (1960), Selected Essays 1938–62 (1963), 560.

Note the emphasis on the distinction between "overbreadth" and "vagueness" in Zwickler v. Koota, 389 U.S. 241 (1967), a challenge to a ban on the distribution of anonymous handbills. Justice Brennan noted that the attack was not on grounds of vagueness, "that is, that it is a statute 'which either forbids or requires the doing of an act in terms so vague that men of common intelligence must necessarily guess at its meaning and differ as to its application,'" but rather an attack "that the statute, although lacking neither clarity nor precision, is void for 'overbreadth,' that is, that it offends the constitutional principle that 'a governmental purpose to control or prevent activities constitutionally subject to state regulation may not be achieved by means which sweep unnecessarily broadly and thereby invade the area of protected freedoms.'"

advocated "restrained" rather than "insensitive" applications of the over-breadth doctrine. He objected to the majority's reliance "on certain sweeping language contained in a few opinions for the proposition that, without regard to the nature of appellee's conduct, the statute in question must be invalidated on its face unless 'it is not susceptible of application' to [protected] speech." And he argued that the more proper, narrower approach would be to invalidate only for "*substantial* overbreadth." The only legitimate purpose of the overbreadth doctrine, he insisted, was "to allow the Court to invalidate statutes because their language demonstrates their potential for sweeping improper applications posing a significant likelihood of deterring important First Amendment speech—not because of some insubstantial or imagined potential for occasional and isolated applications that go beyond constitutional bounds."

4. *The curtailment of overbreadth attacks: Broadrick and "substantial overbreadth."* Criticisms such as those bore fruit by 1973, when a new majority apparently endorsed a curtailment of the overbreadth technique, though not its elimination. In BROADRICK v. OKLAHOMA, 413 U.S. 601 (1973), Justice White—who dissented from some earlier overbreadth invalidations—wrote for the majority, and Justice Brennan—who had written some of the major overbreadth opinions of the Warren era, including Keyishian—wrote for most of the dissenters. Justice White emphasized a "substantial overbreadth" theme, and he suggested that overbreadth invalidations were generally inappropriate when the allegedly impermissible applications of the challenged statute affected "conduct" rather than "speech." Though Broadrick arose in the context of government employees' conduct to be examined more fully below (chap. 13, sec. 5), a look at the overbreadth discussion in the Broadrick opinions is appropriate here to round out this preliminary survey of the nature, attractions, problems and status of the overbreadth technique.

The Broadrick case was a challenge to § 818 of Oklahoma's Merit System Act restricting political activities by classified civil servants. Among the challenged provisions was one prohibiting employees from "tak[ing] part in the management or affairs of any political party or in any political campaign, except to exercise his right as a citizen privately to express his opinion and to cast his vote." Other provisions more specifically prohibited soliciting for campaign contributions. Appellants, who had campaigned for a superior, challenged § 818 on vagueness and overbreadth grounds. The Court's 5 to 4 decision rejected that challenge.[6] Justice White's majority opinion, after rejecting the vagueness attack in a brief passage, devoted most attention to the overbreadth challenge:

"Appellants assert that § 818 has been construed as applying to such allegedly protected political expression as the wearing of political buttons or the displaying of bumper stickers. But appellants did not engage in any such activity. They are charged with actively engaging in partisan political

6. In a companion case, the Court upheld § 9(a) of the Hatch Act, which prohibits federal employees from taking an "active part in political management or in political campaigns," in a 6 to 3 decision in Civil Service Comm'n v. Letter Carriers, 413 U.S. 548 (1973). See also the earlier rejection of a challenge to the Hatch Act in United Public Workers v. Mitchell, 330 U.S. 75 (1947) (chap. 15 below).

activities—including the solicitation of money—among their co-workers for the benefit of their superior. Appellants concede [that] § 818 would be constitutional as applied to this type of conduct. They nevertheless maintain that the statute is overbroad and purports to reach protected, as well as unprotected conduct, and must therefore be struck down on its face and held to be incapable of any constitutional application. We do not believe that the overbreadth doctrine may appropriately be invoked in this manner here."

Justice White then proceeded to justify and delineate a "substantial overbreadth" approach at some length: "Embedded in the traditional rules governing constitutional adjudication is the principle that a person to whom a statute may constitutionally be applied will not be heard to challenge that statute on the ground that it may conceivably be applied unconstitutionally to others, in other situations not before the Court. [A] closely related principle is that constitutional rights are personal and may not be asserted vicariously. [See the materials on "standing," chap. 15 below.] These principles rest on more than the fussiness of judges. They reflect the conviction that under our constitutional system courts are not roving commissions assigned to pass judgment on the validity of the Nation's laws. See [Younger v. Harris]. Constitutional judgments, as [Marbury v. Madison] recognized, are justified only out of the necessity of adjudicating rights in particular cases between the litigants brought before the Court . . ..

"In the past, the Court has recognized some limited exceptions to these principles, but only because of the most 'weighty countervailing policies.' [One such exception] has been carved out in the area of the First Amendment. It has long been recognized that the First Amendment needs breathing space and that statutes attempting to restrict or burden the exercise of First Amendment rights must be narrowly drawn and represent a considered legislative judgment that a particular mode of expression has to give way to other compelling needs of society. [E. g., Herndon v. Lowry; Shelton v. Tucker.] As a corollary, the Court has altered its traditional rules of standing to permit—in the First Amendment area—'attacks on overly broad statutes with no requirement that the person making the attack demonstrate that his own conduct could not be regulated by a statute drawn with the requisitie narrow specificity.' [Dombrowski v. Pfister, 380 U.S. 479 (1965) (chap. 15 below).] Litigants, therefore, are permitted to challenge a statute not because their own rights of free expression are violated, but because of a judicial prediction or assumption that the statute's very existence may cause others not before the court to refrain from constitutionally protected speech or expression.

"Such claims of facial overbreadth have been entertained in cases involving statutes which, by their terms, seek to regulate 'only spoken words.' [Gooding v. Wilson.] In such cases, it has been the judgment of this Court that the possible harm to society in permitting some unprotected speech to go unpunished is outweighed by the possibility that protected speech of others may be muted and perceived grievances left to fester because of the possible inhibitory effects of overly broad statutes. Overbreadth attacks have also been allowed where the Court thought rights of association were ensnared in statutes which, by their broad sweep, might result in burdening

innocent associations. [See Keyishian; Robel; Aptheker; Shelton v. Tucker.] Facial overbreadth claims have also been entertained where statutes, by their terms, purport to regulate the time, place, and manner of expressive or communicative conduct, see [e. g., Grayned v. City of Rockford, (sec. 2 below)], and where such conduct has required official approval under laws that delegated standardless discretionary power to local functionaries, resulting in virtually unreviewable prior restraints on First Amendment rights. See [e. g., Shuttlesworth; Cox I; Kunz; Lovell v. Griffin][7].

"The consequence of our departure from traditional rules of standing in the First Amendment area is that any enforcement of a statute thus placed at issue is totally forbidden until and unless a limiting construction or partial invalidation so narrows it as to remove the seeming threat or deterrence to constitutionally protected expression. Application of the overbreadth doctrine in this manner is, manifestly, strong medicine. It has been employed by the Court sparingly and only as a last resort. Facial overbreadth has not been invoked when a limiting construction has been or could be placed on the challenged statute. See, [e. g., Cox v. New Hampshire]. Equally important, overbreadth claims, if entertained at all, have been curtailed when invoked against ordinary criminal laws that are sought to be applied to protected conduct. In Cantwell v. Connecticut, [we] did not hold that the offense 'known as breach-of-the-peace' must fall in toto because it was capable of some unconstitutional application. In [Edwards v. South Carolina] and [Cox v. Louisiana I, we] concluded that the conduct at issue could not itself be punished under a breach of the peace statute. On that basis, the convictions were reversed.[8] . . . Additionally, overbreadth scrutiny has generally been somewhat less rigid in the context of statutes regulating conduct in the shadow of the First Amendment, but doing so in a neutral, noncensorial manner. See, [e. g., United States v. Harriss, 347 U.S. 612 (1954)].

"It remains a 'matter of no little difficulty' to determine when a law may properly be held void on its face and when 'such summary action' is inappropriate. . . . But the plain import of our cases is, at the very least, that facial overbreadth adjudication is an exception to our traditional rules of practice and that its function, a limited one at the outset, attenuates as the otherwise unprotected behavior that it forbids the State to sanction moves from 'pure speech' towards conduct and that conduct—even if expressive—falls within the scope of otherwise valid criminal laws that reflect legitimate state interests in maintaining comprehensive controls over harmful, constitutionally unprotected conduct. Although such laws, if too broadly worded, may deter protected speech to some unknown extent, there comes a point where that effect—at best a prediction—cannot, with confidence,

7. The cases cited by Justice White in this and the following passages—cases regulating "time, place and manner" of expression—are considered at length in sec. 2 below.

8. "In both Edwards and Cox I, at the very end of the discussions, the Court also noted that the statutes would be facially unconstitutional for overbreadth. In Cox I, the Court termed this discussion an 'additional reason' for its reversal. These 'additional' holdings were unnecessary to the dispositions of the cases, so much so that only one Member of this Court relied on Cox's 'additional' holding in [Brown v. Louisiana], which involved convictions under the very same breach-of-the-peace statute. See id., at 143–150 (Brennan, J., concurring)." [Footnote by Justice White.]

justify invalidating a statute on its face and so prohibiting a State from enforcing the statute against conduct that is admittedly within its power to proscribe. . . . To put the matter another way, particularly where conduct and not merely speech is involved, we believe that the overbreadth of a statute must not only be real, but substantial as well, judged in relation to the statute's plainly legitimate sweep. It is our view that § 818 is not substantially overbroad and that whatever overbreadth may exist should be cured through case-by-case analysis of the fact situations to which its sanctions, assertedly, may not be applied.[9]

"Unlike ordinary breach-of-the-peace statutes or other broad regulatory acts, § 818 is directed, by its terms, at political expression which if engaged in by private persons would plainly be protected by the First and Fourteenth Amendments. But at the same time, § 818 is not a censorial statute, directed at particular groups or viewpoints. Cf. [Keyishian]. The statute, rather, seeks to regulate political activity in an even-handed and neutral manner. As indicated, such statutes have in the past been subject to a less exacting overbreadth scrutiny. Moreover, the fact remains that § 818 regulates a substantial spectrum of conduct that is as manifestly subject to state regulation as the public peace or criminal trespass. . . .[10] Without question, the conduct appellants have been charged with falls squarely within those proscriptions.

"Appellants assert that § 818 goes much farther. [They point to] interpretive rules purporting to restrict such allegedly protected activities as the wearing of political buttons or the use of bumper stickers. It may be that such restrictions are impermissible and that § 818 may be susceptible of some other improper applications. But, as presently construed, we do not believe that § 818 must be discarded in toto because some persons' arguably protected conduct may or may not be caught or chilled by the statute. Section 818 is not substantially overbroad and is not, therefore, unconstitutional on its face."

9. "My Brother Brennan asserts that in some sense a requirement of substantial overbreadth is already implicit in the doctrine. This is a welcome observation. It perhaps reduces our differences to our differing views of whether the Oklahoma statute is substantially overbroad. The dissent also insists that [Coates v. Cincinnati] must be taken as overruled. But we are unpersuaded that Coates stands as a barrier to a rule that would invalidate statutes for overbreadth only when the flaw is a substantial concern in the context of the statute as a whole. Our judgment is that the Oklahoma statute, when authoritative administrative constructions are accepted, is not invalid under such a rule." [Footnote by Justice White.]

10. Justice White described that "substantial spectrum of conduct" as follows: "Under the decision in Letter Carriers, there is no question that § 818 is valid at least insofar as it forbids classified employees from: soliciting contributions for partisan candidates, political parties, or other partisan political purposes; becoming members of national, state, or local committees of political parties, or officers or committee members in partisan political clubs, or candidates for any paid public office; taking part in the management or affairs of any political party's partisan political campaign; serving as delegates or alternates to caucuses or conventions of political parties; addressing or taking an active part in partisan political rallies or meetings; soliciting votes or assisting voters at the polls or helping in a partisan effort to get voters to the polls; participating in the distribution of partisan campaign literature; initiating or circulating partisan nominating petitions; or riding in caravans for any political party or partisan political candidate."

The major dissent was by Justice Brennan, joined by Justices Stewart and Marshall. (Justice Douglas dissented separately.) Justice Brennan thought the decision a "wholly unjustified retreat from fundamental and previously well-established" principles. The "substantial overbreadth" approach, he insisted, was unsupported by prior decisions and "effectively overrules" the 1971 decision in Coates v. City of Cincinnati (sec. 2 below). The majority had conceded the possibility of some "improper applications." "[T]hat assumption requires a finding that the statute is unconstitutional on its face."

Justice Brennan summarized the majority's curtailment of overbreadth challenges as follows: "Where conduct is involved, a statute's overbreadth must henceforth be 'substantial' before the statute can properly be found invalid on its face." And he objected to that approach in the following passage: "I cannot accept the validity of [the majority's overbreadth] analysis. In the first place, the Court makes no effort to define what it means by 'substantial overbreadth.' We have never held that a statute should be held invalid on its face merely because it is possible to conceive of a single impermissible application, and in that sense a requirement of substantial overbreadth is already implicit in the doctrine. . . . Whether the Court means to require some different or greater showing of substantiality is left obscure by today's opinion, in large part because the Court makes no effort to explain why the overbreadth of the Oklahoma Act, while real, is somehow not quite substantial. . . .

"More fundamentally, the Court offers no rationale to explain its conclusion that, for purposes of overbreadth analysis, deterrence of conduct should be viewed differently from deterrence of speech, even where both are equally protected by the First Amendment. Indeed, in the case before us it is hard to know whether the protected activity falling within the Act should be considered speech or conduct. In any case, the conclusion that a distinction should be drawn was the premise of Mr. Justice White's dissenting opinion in [Coates v. Cincinnati], and that conclusion—although squarely rejected in Coates—has now been adopted by the Court. [Coates] stood, until today, for the proposition that where a statute is 'unconstitutionally broad because it authorizes the punishment of constitutionally protected conduct,' it must be held invalid on its face whether or not the person raising the challenge could have been prosecuted under a properly narrowed statute.[11] . . .

"At this stage, it is obviously difficult to estimate the probable impact of today's decision. If the requirement of 'substantial' overbreadth is construed to mean only that facial review is inappropriate where the likelihood of an impermissible application of the statute is too small to generate a 'chilling effect' on protected speech or conduct, then the impact is likely to be small. On the other hand, if today's decision necessitates the drawing of artificial distinctions between protected speech and protected conduct, and if the 'chill' on protected conduct is rarely, if ever, found sufficient to require the

11. "The Court has applied overbreadth review to many other statutes that assertedly had a 'chilling effect' on protected conduct, rather than on 'pure speech.' See, e. g., [Robel; Aptheker]. . . ." [Footnote by Justice Brennan.]

facial invalidation of an overbroad statute, then the effect could be very grave indeed."

5. *The impact of the modern skepticism about overbreadth.* To what extent does the skepticism about overbreadth manifested in Broadrick curtail the availability of that technique? Since Broadrick, the Court has indicated that overbreadth continues available in certain circumstances—e. g., in challenging some regulations of "speech" rather than "conduct." [12] For example, the divided Court's 1972 decision in Gooding v. Wilson, noted above, invalidating a ban on "opprobrious words or abusive language," retains vitality, at least in its "fighting words" context. See Lewis v. New Orleans, 415 U.S. 130 (1974) (sec. 2 below). But in other contexts, a divided Court has rejected several overbreadth attacks since Broadrick. Note especially Arnett v. Kennedy, 416 U.S. 134 (1974), rejecting overbreadth and vagueness challenges to the Lloyd-LaFollette Act providing for the discharge of federal civil service employees for "such cause as will promote the efficiency of the service." Kennedy, an OEO employee, had been removed for making allegedly false and defamatory statements about fellow employees—e. g., that they had attempted bribery. Justice Rehnquist's majority opinion conceded, on the overbreadth aspect of the case, that the law "without doubt intended to authorize dismissal for speech as well as other conduct." But not all speech of public employees is immune from regulation. And as he construed the Act, Congress "did not intend to authorize discharge [for] speech which is constitutionally protected." Moreover, he noted that "the Act is not directed at speech as such, but at employee behavior, including speech, which is detrimental to the efficiency of the employing agency." He concluded that the Act "excludes constitutionally protected speech, and that the statute is therefore not overbroad."

Justice Marshall's dissent, joined by Justice Douglas and Brennan, thought the Court's answer to the overbreadth attack "no answer at all": "To accept this response is functionally to eliminate overbreadth from the First Amendment lexicon. No statute can reach and punish constitutionally protected speech. The majority has not given the statute a limiting construction but merely repeated the obvious." He insisted that the majority had misunderstood the overbreadth principle by overlooking the "potential deterrent effect on constitutionally protected speech of a statute that is overbroad or vague on its face." He added that, by "the uncertainty of its scope, the standard here creates the very danger of a chilling effect that concerned the Court in Keyishian." He argued that the dismissal standard "hangs over [employees'] heads like a sword of Damocles," and he concluded: "That this Court will ultimately vindicate an employee if his speech is constitutionally protected is of little consequence—for the value of a sword of Damocles is that it hangs—not that it drops. For every employee who risks his job by testing the limits of the statute, many more will choose the cautious path and not speak at all." And commenting more generally on the overbreadth doctrine, he noted that its focus "is not on the individual actor before the court but on others who may forgo protected activity rather than run afoul of the

12. On the difficulties of the "speech"- "conduct" distinction, see the materi- als below, especially sec. 3 of this chapter.

statute's proscriptions." He insisted: "The danger of that chilling effect upon the exercise of vital First Amendment rights must be guarded against by sensitive tools which clearly inform [employees] of what is being proscribed." [13]

SECTION 2. EXPRESSION IN PUBLIC PLACES AND THE MAINTENANCE OF LOCAL PEACE AND ORDER: REGULATING THE "TIME, PLACE AND MANNER" RATHER THAN THE CONTENT OF SPEECH IN THE "PUBLIC FORUM"?

A. DOCTRINAL FOUNDATIONS AND RECURRENT QUESTIONS

PROBLEMS AND CONTOURS OF THE PUBLIC FORUM: AN OVERVIEW

Introduction. To what extent may government regulate those who want to march in city streets or ring doorbells or meet in the parks to publicize their views? To what extent does concern with such values as order and quiet and traffic control and audience sensitivities justify the curbing of expression? Questions of governmental stability raised by subversive speech problems (sec. 1 above) had been coming to the Court for 20 years before these issues of municipal tranquility spawned massive constitutional litigation. But the problems of the public forum have produced a constant flow of judicial business since the late 1930's, as a variety of minorities, from the Jehovah's Witnesses at the beginning to anti-war and civil rights demon-

---

13. Note also the rejection of vagueness and overbreadth attacks in a challenge to a court-martial conviction in Parker v. Levy, 417 U.S. 733 (1974), sustaining Uniform Code of Military Justice provisions proscribing "conduct unbecoming an officer and a gentleman" and prohibiting "all disorders and neglects to the prejudice of good order and discipline in the armed forces." Captain Levy had made public statements urging Black enlisted men to refuse to obey orders to go to Vietnam. The Court's 5 to 3 decision rejecting the challenge relied on the special needs of the military as well as on the alleged adequate clarity of the standards vis-á-vis Levy and on the constitutionally unprotected nature of his statements. Justice Rehnquist's majority opinion stated that the reasons for permitting First Amendment overbreadth attacks in the civilian sector "must be accorded a good deal less weight in the military context." In any event, as cases such as Broadrick showed, the Court was reluctant "to strike down a statute on its face where there were a substantial number of situations to which it might be validly applied." Here, though some constitutionally protected conduct might be reachable "at the fringes" of the provisions, that was insufficient to invalidate, for Levy's statements were "unprotected under the most expansive notions of the First Amendment." Justices Stewart, Douglas and Brennan dissented; Justice Marshall did not participate. See also the additional confrontations with the overbreadth problem in the materials which follow.

strators more recently, have sought access to streets, parks, and other public places to change ideas and induce action. To what degree are these recurrent problems distinguishable from those considered in the preceding section? To what extent are the values and doctrines articulated there useful here? To what extent do these problems require new analyses?

1. *Justice Frankfurter's survey of contexts and problems.* [Consider, for an initial overview of the range of problems presented by regulations of expression in public places, the following suggestions for classification and analysis. They are from a survey of the background written by Justice Frankfurter in 1951, after only a little more than a decade of Court experience with these questions. Justice Frankfurter undertook this review in a concurring opinion (in Niemotko v. Maryland, 340 U.S. 268, 273) reexamining the problem of "how to reconcile the interest in allowing free expression of ideas in public places with the protection of the public peace and of the primary uses of streets and parks." * Justice Frankfurter stated in Niemotko:]

[Previous decisions primarily] concerned with restrictions upon expression in its divers forms in public places have answered problems varying greatly in content and difficulty.

The easiest cases have been those in which the only interest opposing free communication was that of keeping the streets of the community clean. This could scarcely justify prohibiting the dissemination of information by handbills or censoring their contents. [See Lovell v. Griffin, 303 U.S. 444 (1938), on inadequate licensing standards.†] In Schneider v. State, 308 U.S. 147 [1938], three of the four ordinances declared invalid by the Court prohibited the distribution of pamphlets. . . .

In a group of related cases, regulation of solicitation has been the issue. Here the opposing interest is more substantial—protection of the public from fraud and from criminals who use solicitation as a device to enter homes. The fourth ordinance considered in Schneider v. State, supra, allowed the chief of police to refuse a permit if he found, in his discretion, that the canvasser was not of good character or was canvassing for a project not free from fraud. The ordinance was found invalid because the officer who could, in his discretion, make the determinations concerning "good character" and "project not free from fraud" in effect held the power of censorship. . . .

Control of speeches made in streets and parks draws on still different considerations—protection of the public peace and of the primary uses of travel and recreation for which streets and parks exist. [An attempt to assert] the right of a city to exercise any power over its parks, however arbitrary or discriminatory, was rejected in Hague v. C. I. O. [307 U.S. 496 (1939)]. The ordinance presented in the Hague case required a permit for meetings on public ground, the permit to be refused by the licensing official only "for the purpose of preventing riots, disturbances or disorderly as-

---

* Justice Frankfurter's opinion was one concurring in the result in three cases (all considered further below): Feiner v. New York, 340 U.S. 315, and Kunz v. New York, 340 U.S. 290, as well as Niemotko v. Maryland, 340 U.S. 268.

† This decision, and the others cited by Justice Frankfurter, are considered more fully below.

semblage." The facts of the case, however, left no doubt that the licensing power had been made an "instrument of arbitrary suppression of free expression of views on national affairs." And the construction given the ordinance in the State courts gave the licensing officials wide discretion. The holding of the Hague case was not that a city could not subject the use of its streets and parks to reasonable regulation. The holding was that the licensing officials could not be given power arbitrarily to suppress free expression, no matter under what cover of law they purported to act. Cox v. New Hampshire, 312 U.S. 569 [1941], made it clear that the United States Constitution does not deny localities the power to devise a licensing system if the exercise of discretion by the licensing officials is appropriately confined.

Two cases have involved the additional considerations incident to the use of sound trucks. [See the Saia and Kovacs cases, below.] . . .

The results in these multifarious cases have been expressed in language looking in two directions. While the Court has emphasized the importance of "free speech," it has recognized that "free speech" is not in itself a touchstone. The Constitution is not unmindful of other important interests, such as public order, if interference with free expression of ideas is not found to be the overbalancing consideration. More important than the phrasing of the opinions are the questions on which the decisions appear to have turned.

(1) What is the interest deemed to require the regulation of speech? The State cannot of course forbid public proselyting or religious argument merely because public officials disapprove the speaker's views. It must act in patent good faith to maintain the public peace, to assure the availability of the streets for their primary purposes of passenger and vehicular traffic, or for equally indispensable ends of modern community life.

(2) What is the method used to achieve such ends as a consequence of which public speech is constrained or barred? A licensing standard which gives an official authority to censor the content of a speech differs *toto cælo* from one limited by its terms, or by nondiscriminatory practice, to considerations of public safety and the like. Again, a sanction applied after the event assures consideration of the particular circumstances of a situation. The net of control must not be cast too broadly.

(3) What mode of speech is regulated? A sound truck may be found to affect the public peace as normal speech does not. A man who is calling names or using the kind of language which would reasonably stir another to violence does not have the same claim to protection as one whose speech is an appeal to reason.

(4) Where does the speaking which is regulated take place? Not only the general classifications—streets, parks, private buildings—are relevant. The location and size of a park; its customary use for the recreational, esthetic and contemplative needs of a community; the facilities, other than a park or street corner, readily available in a community for airing views, are all pertinent considerations in assessing the limitations the Fourteenth Amendment puts on State power in a particular situation. . . .

2. *The utility of familiar doctrinal tools in the analysis of public forum problems.* To what extent are the problems surveyed by Justice

Frankfurter susceptible to useful analysis and solution via the doctrines encountered in the materials in sec. 1 of this chapter? For example, does the clear and present danger test offer substantial help in the solution of public forum problems? That test is mentioned in a number of the opinions in this section—several early ones (e. g., Schneider v. State) as well as a few subsequent ones (e. g., Edwards v. South Carolina, 372 U.S. 229 (1963), below). But *proximity* of the challenged expression to the "substantive evil" is not the major problem here, is it? Is not the often more difficult issue the assessment of the *gravity* of the evil, as well as the legitimacy and scope of the First Amendment entitlements of the claimant? For example, if street-littering is the feared "substantive evil," is not a more significant question whether that risk is sufficiently substantial to warrant a ban on leafleting, rather than whether leafleting creates an "immediate" risk of littering? And is not another significant question whether the leafleter has some legitimate claim of access to public places to distribute his message? Are the problems more susceptible to a less-restrictive alternatives, overbreadth analysis? To other analyses? Consider the suggestions in the following note.

3. *The First Amendment "right" to a public forum: Mere assurance of equal access, or* guarantee *of access to some public places?* In considering the varieties of contexts, competing interests, and regulatory techniques presented by the cases in this section, it is useful to bear in mind a pervasive underlying theme frequently obscured in the Court opinions. What *are* the plausible dimensions of a First Amendment claim to use streets, parks and other public places? A broad public forum position would argue that government *must* permit access to some forms of public property: that government has an affirmative obligation to make some public places available for the expression of ideas; that access to places such as streets and parks is of special importance as the "poor man's printing press," for those who cannot afford to resort to other means of communication, or who cannot effectively reach audiences through alternative means. A narrower public forum theory would limit government's obligation to that of providing *equal* access to public places: it would recognize First Amendment aspects of public forum problems, but would limit scrutiny to assurance that government was not using its power over public places to control the content of speech and to discriminate among competing views. In short, the broad "guaranteed access" issue arises when a city decides that *no one* can use the streets or parks for meetings; the narrower, "equal access" view would concentrate scrutiny on situations when a city allows some groups but not others to use public property for meetings.

Under the narrower view, flat bans on the use of public property by anyone would be permissible: that view would sustain "time, place and manner" regulations so long as they are neutrally framed and applied; it would scrutinize them mainly to assure that they are not devices to exercise control over the content of speech. The broader view would worry not only about the neutrality of "time, place and manner" regulations, but would also strike down evenhanded regulations when they unduly curtailed a "public forum" right of guaranteed access. In considering the public forum cases that follow, note when the Court is primarily or solely concerned with as-

suring merely the evenhandedness of access controls and when it recognizes a broader, guaranteed access claim as inherent in the First Amendment.†

Analysis of the cases in terms of those contending positions is complicated by the fact that the broad "guaranteed access" argument is not advocated by any Justice as one applicable to all public property at all times. For example, some public places—the Senate gallery? courtrooms?—may be so anomalous as places for speeches and meetings as to justify total exclusion of "public forum" uses. And in other public places where the broad view would recognize some guaranteed access, some "time, place and manner" restraints may nevertheless be permissible: e. g., noisy parades in residential areas late at night, or mass gatherings on heavily travelled streets during the rush hour. In short, even the broad, guaranteed access public forum position may require the balancing of competing interests.

Nevertheless, the underlying tensions between the view of the public forum concept as one that supports a guaranteed access claim, as against the narrower view that would simply safeguard against nonneutral, unequal restraints on access, help to explain the emphases and conflicts in many of the cases. Those who urge the broader, guaranteed access view frequently quote a statement in Justice Roberts' opinion in Hague v. CIO, 307 U.S. 496 (1939), one of the cases noted in Justice Frankfurter's survey above: "Wherever the title of streets and parks may rest they have immemorially been held in trust for the use of the public and, time out of mind, have been used for purposes of assembly, communicating thoughts between citizens, and discussing public questions. Such use of the streets and public places has, from ancient times, been a part of the privileges, immunities, rights and liberties of citizens. The privilege [to] use the streets and parks for communication of views on national questions may be regulated in the interest of all; . . . but it must not, in the guise of regulation, be abridged or denied." *

Does Justice Frankfurter's survey (in note 1 above) rest on as broad a view of access to some public places as that suggested in Hague v. CIO? Justice Frankfurter and many of the cases speak of "protection of public peace" and "the primary use of streets and parks" as legitimate interests limiting expression in public places. Does that formulation adequately con-

---

† See generally Note, "The Public Forum: Minimum Access, Equal Access, and the First Amendment," 28 Stan.L.Rev. No. 1 (1975).

* Contrast a narrower view, almost at the polar extreme from that of the Hague case, and articulated by Justice Holmes while sitting on the Massachusetts court. In Hague, the city had relied on Holmes' Davis v. Massachusetts position to justify a scheme to restrict access to public places. Davis v. Massachusetts, 167 U.S. 43 (1897), affirmed the decision in which Justice Holmes had said on the state court: "For the legislature absolutely or conditionally to forbid public speaking in a highway or public park is no more an infringement of the rights of a member of the public than for the owner of a private house to forbid it in his house." No modern Justice views a city's control of its public property as so unrestrained: at the least, under the "narrow" public forum position noted in the text, there is recognition that, because of the First Amendment as well as the equal protection clause, a city may not grant access on a discriminatory basis, may not use its control of public places to regulate the content of speech. The recurrent questions are the contours of that position, and whether a First Amendment public forum claim should imply more than that.

front the importance of a broad right of access to streets and parks if certain views are to be heard? Does that "primary use of streets [traffic?] and parks [recreation?]" emphasis suggest that use of streets and parks for speech is ordinarily a secondary use, to be subordinated whenever traffic or recreation are significantly threatened? Does it suggest that a state can bar the use of public places for expression completely, for the purpose of protecting the "primary" uses? Does it suggest that the Court's primary responsibility ought to be that springing from the narrower, equal access approach to public forum problems: to assure that whatever access the city chooses to permit is delineated and applied evenhandedly? But should not free speech values and public forum claims compel traffic and recreation to give way to speech, sometimes? If the dimensions of that "sometimes" are a central issue in this area, do the Court analyses sufficiently promote inquiry into those dimensions? Does the Roberts statement in Hague v. CIO suggest that "discussing public questions" is also a "primary use" of streets and parks? And does that not suggest that delineation of the contours of the public forum should be a major concern of free speech cases in this area?

For a thoughtful discussion of the public forum problem, and an endorsement of a broad, guaranteed access view, see Kalven, "The Concept of the Public Forum: Cox v. Louisiana," 1965 Sup.Ct.Rev. 1. Kalven suggests three interrelated themes for the examination of public forum problems: "First, that in an open democratic society the streets, the parks, and other public places are an important facility for public discussion and political process. They are in brief a public forum that the citizen can commandeer." (Kalven suggests later, however, that use of some public places for expression would be "anomalous": "Certainly it is easy to think of public places, swimming pools, for example, so clearly dedicated to recreational use that talk of their use as a public forum would in general be totally unpersuasive.") "Second, that only confusion can result from distinguishing sharply between 'speech pure' and 'speech plus.' And, third, that what is required is in effect a set of Robert's Rules of Order for the new uses of the public forum, albeit the designing of such rules poses a problem of formidable practical difficulty."

To what extent do the cases in this section adequately recognize the importance of a right of access to public forums? How useful are distinctions of "speech pure"-"speech plus"? Of "speech"-"conduct"? Of "manner"-"content"? Is the "Robert's Rules" concept a "happy analogy" because, as Kalven suggests, "concern ought not to be with censorship, or with the content of what is said; what is needed is a phasing or timing of the activity, not a ban on it"? What should be the content of a judicially developed set of "Robert's Rules of Order" for the "uses of the public forum"?

Transitional Note. The themes suggested in note 3 are not the only ones that pervade the materials that follow. A variety of additional variables permeate the cases. For example, what are the competing interests allegedly justifying curtailment of the speaker: The interest in preventing outbreaks of violence? In protecting the sensibilities and repose of listeners, willing and unwilling? In safeguarding the "primary uses" of the pub-

lic places? Even if a broad, guaranteed access view of the public forum principle is accepted, interference with other uses may become a substantial restraining factor when the focus of the cases shifts from traditional "forum" areas such as streets and parks to more novel environments such as libraries and courthouses and public transit facilities. Moreover, the appropriate standards, procedural as well as substantive, may vary with the nature of the regulatory scheme: Is licensing legitimately more suspect than subsequent restraint? When may a speaker ignore an apparently invalid licensing scheme, and when must he show compliance with it as a precondition to a court challenge? The materials that follow are designed to aid pursuit of those basic themes and such additional ones as those noted here and in Justice Frankfurter's overview.*

SOME EARLY CASES: WHAT LEGACY?

The cases in this group are among the earliest Court encounters with the problem of regulating access to public places. They continue to be widely cited by the modern Court. What is the legacy of these cases? What do they contribute in the search for answers to the questions posed above? Lovell v. Griffin and Cox v. New Hampshire are early guideposts regarding the impermissible and the permissible in permit schemes; Cantwell v. Connecticut is an early example of the control of street use through a breach of the peace prosecution. Both techniques of control—prior licensing and subsequent punishment—recur in the later materials. What did these early cases contribute to analysis of the validity of the regulatory schemes invoked —and to the delineation of the scope of a justifiable First Amendment public forum claim?

---

* The organizational scheme is partly topical, partly chronological. Both emphases are needed for adequate exploration of the Court's responses to disparate public places problems. The materials below accordingly begin with a group of cases from the period in which the Court first encountered public forum issues—cases on which the modern Court places frequent reliance despite their occasionally ambiguous content. Sec. 2B turns to a largely topical organization, considering a range of competing interests that have been asserted as justifications for curtailing the speaker—from protecting residents from noise to avoiding violence because of hostile audience reactions. Sec. 2C examines the Court's response to the protest demonstrations of the 1960's in the traditional streets setting; sec. 2D surveys access claims to non-traditional public forums—to public places other than parks and streets. Sec. 2E focuses on the modern Court's responses to access claims in contexts other than public property, from the use of private shopping centers as a "forum" to problems of access to the privately owned media.

LOVELL v. GRIFFIN

303 U.S. 444, 58 S.Ct. 666, 82 L.Ed. 949 (1938).

Appeal from the Court of Appeals of Georgia.

Mr. Chief Justice HUGHES delivered the opinion of the Court.

Appellant, Alma Lovell, was convicted in the Recorder's Court of the City of Griffin, Georgia, of the violation of a city ordinance and was sentenced to imprisonment for fifty days in default of the payment of a fine of fifty dollars. . . . The ordinance in question [states in part]:

"Section 1. That the practice of distributing . . . circulars, handbooks, advertising, or literature of any kind, . . . within the limits of the City of Griffin, without first obtaining written permission from the City Manager of the City of Griffin, . . . shall be deemed a nuisance, and punishable as an offense against the City of Griffin. . . ."

The violation, which is not denied, consisted of the distribution without the required permission of a pamphlet and magazine in the nature of religious tracts, setting forth the gospel of the "Kingdom of Jehovah." Appellant did not apply for a permit, as she regarded herself as sent "by Jehovah to do His work" and that such an application would have been "an act of disobedience to His commandment". [At the trial, appellant claimed that the ordinance abridged "freedom of the press" and "the free exercise of (her) religion."]

The ordinance in its broad sweep prohibits the distribution of "circulars, handbooks, advertising, or literature of any kind." It manifestly applies to pamphlets, magazines and periodicals. The evidence against appellant was that she distributed a certain pamphlet and a magazine called the "Golden Age". Whether in actual administration the ordinance is applied, as apparently it could be, to newspapers does not appear. The City Manager testified that "every one applied to me for a license to distribute literature in this City. None of these people (including defendant) secured a permit from me to distribute literature in the City of Griffin." The ordinance is not limited to "literature" that is obscene or offensive to public morals or that advocates unlawful conduct. There is no suggestion that the pamphlet and magazine distributed in the instant case were of that character. The ordinance embraces "literature" in the widest sense.

The ordinance is comprehensive with respect to the method of distribution. It covers every sort of circulation "either by hand or otherwise." There is thus no restriction in its application with respect to time or place. It is not limited to ways which might be regarded as inconsistent with the maintenance of public order or as involving disorderly conduct, the molestation of the inhabitants, or the misuse or littering of the streets. The ordinance prohibits the distribution of literature of any kind at any time, at any place, and in any manner without a permit from the City Manager.

We think that the ordinance is invalid on its face. Whatever the motive which induced its adoption, its character is such that it strikes at the very foundation of the freedom of the press by subjecting it to license and censorship. The struggle for the freedom of the press was primarily directed against the power of the licensor. It was against that power that John Milton

directed his assault by his "Appeal for the Liberty of Unlicensed Printing." And the liberty of the press became initially a right to publish *without* a license what formerly could be published only *with* one." While this freedom from previous restraint upon publication cannot be regarded as exhausting the guaranty of liberty, the prevention of that restraint was a leading purpose in the adoption of the constitutional provision. [Near v. Minnesota, 283 U.S. 697 (1931), chap. 13 below.] . . .

As the ordinance is void on its face, it was not necessary for appellant to seek a permit under it. She was entitled to contest its validity in answer to the charge against her.* . . .

Reversed.

_____

COX v. NEW HAMPSHIRE

312 U.S. 569, 61 S.Ct. 762, 85 L.Ed. 1049 (1941).

Appeal from the Supreme Court of New Hampshire.

Mr. Chief Justice HUGHES delivered the opinion of the Court.

Appellants are five "Jehovah's Witnesses" who, with sixty-three others of the same persuasion, were convicted in the municipal court of Manchester, New Hampshire, for violation of a state statute prohibiting a "parade or procession" upon a public street without a special license.

[A]ppellants raised the questions that the statute was invalid under the [14th Amendment] in that it deprived appellants of their rights of freedom of worship, freedom of speech and press, and freedom of assembly, vested unreasonable and unlimited arbitrary and discriminatory powers in the licensing authority, and was vague and indefinite. These contentions were overruled and the case comes here on appeal.

The statutory prohibition is as follows: "No theatrical or dramatic representation shall be performed or exhibited, and no parade or procession

_____

* The issue considered in the last paragraph of Lovell is a recurrent and difficult one. When may a speaker or leafleter or demonstrator ignore an allegedly unconstitutional permit requirement—or an allegedly improper permit denial—and still challenge it in court (in defense to a prosecution for speaking without a permit)? And when can the requirement be challenged only if there is compliance with the permit scheme? The problem is considered in light of later cases in the note on compliance with permit requirements, sec. 2C below. See also the next case, Cox v. New Hampshire, and compare Poulos v. New Hampshire, 345 U.S. 395 (1953), where a conviction for holding a meeting in a park without a required permit was sustained without considering the argument that the denial had been arbitrary, because the speakers had not gone to court to challenge the denial of the permission. In Poulos, unlike Lovell, the law requiring a permit was valid on its face; it was the administrative denial of the permit that was claimed to be unconstitutional. Under cases like Lovell, then, speakers need not challenge the denial of permission in advance—or even to seek permission—where the claim is that the law is unconstitutional on its face. But if the challenge is that a valid law is unconstitutionally applied, the challengers cannot go ahead and hold their meeting or parade if they want to preserve their constitutional defenses; they must instead challenge the denial immediately to preserve their claims. See also the problem of compliance with court orders restraining parades or meetings, in Walker v. Birmingham, sec. 2C below.

upon any public street or way, and no open-air public meeting upon any ground abutting thereon, shall be permitted, unless a special license therefor shall first be obtained from the selectmen of the town, or from a licensing committee for cities hereinafter provided for." The provisions for licensing are set forth in the margin.[1]

The facts [are] these: The sixty-eight defendants and twenty other persons met at a hall in the City of Manchester on the evening of Saturday, July 8, 1939, "for the purpose of engaging in an information march." The company was divided into four or five groups, each with about fifteen to twenty persons. Each group then proceeded to a different part of the business district of the city and there "would line up in single-file formation and then proceed to march along the sidewalk, 'single-file,' that is, following one another." Each of the defendants carried a small staff with a sign reading "Religion is a Snare and a Racket" and on the reverse "Serve God and Christ the King." Some of the marchers carried placards bearing the statement "Fascism or Freedom. Hear Judge Rutherford and Face the Facts." The marchers also handed out printed leaflets announcing a meeting to be held at a later time in the hall from which they had started, where a talk on government would be given to the public free of charge. Defendants did not apply for a permit and none was issued.

. . . The recital of facts which prefaced the opinion of the state court thus summarizes the effect of the march: "Manchester had a population of over 75,000 in 1930, and there was testimony that on Saturday nights in an hour's time 26,000 persons passed one of the intersections where the defendants marched. The marchers interfered with the normal sidewalk travel, but no technical breach of the peace occurred. The march was a prearranged affair, and no permit for it was sought, although the defendants understood that under the statute one was required." . . .

Civil liberties, as guaranteed by the Constitution, imply the existence of an organized society maintaining public order without which liberty itself would be lost in the excesses of unrestrained abuses. The authority of a municipality to impose regulations in order to assure the safety and convenience of the people in the use of public highways has never been regarded as inconsistent with civil liberties . . . .. The control of travel

1. New Hampshire, P.L., Chap. 145, §§ 3, 4, and 5 are as follows:

"Section 3: Licensing Board. Any city may create a licensing board to consist of the person who is the active head of the police department, the mayor of such city and one other person who shall be appointed by the city government, which board shall have delegated powers to investigate and decide the question of granting licenses under this chapter, and it may grant revocable blanket licenses to fraternal and other like organizations, to theatres and to undertakers.

"Section 4: Licenses: Fees. Every such special license shall be in writing, and shall specify the day and hour of the permit to perform or exhibit or of such parade, procession or open-air public meeting. Every licensee shall pay in advance for such license, for the use of the city or town, a sum not more than three hundred dollars for each day such licensee shall perform or exhibit, or such parade, procession or open-air public meeting shall take place; but the fee for a license to exhibit in any hall shall not exceed fifty dollars.

"Section 5: Penalty. If any person shall violate the provisions of the preceding sections he shall be fined not more than five hundred dollars; and it shall be the duty of the selectmen to prosecute for every violation of this chapter." [Footnote by the Court.]

on the streets of cities is the most familiar illustration of this recognition of social need. Where a restriction of the use of highways in that relation is designed to promote the public convenience in the interest of all, it cannot be disregarded by the attempted exercise of some civil right which in other circumstances would be entitled to protection. One would not be justified in ignoring the familiar red traffic light because he thought it his religious duty to disobey the municipal command or sought by that means to direct public attention to an announcement of his opinions. As regulation of the use of the streets for parades and processions is a traditional exercise of control by local government, the question in a particular case is whether that control is exerted so as not to deny or unwarrantedly abridge the right of assembly and the opportunities for the communication of thought and the discussion of public questions immemorially associated with resort to public places. [Lovell v. Griffin; Hague v. CIO; Schneider v. State; Cantwell.]

In the instant case, we are aided by the opinion of the Supreme Court of the State, which construed the statute and defined the limitations of the authority conferred for the granting of licenses. [T]he court thought that interference with liberty of speech and writing seemed slight; that the distribution of pamphlets and folders by the groups "traveling in unorganized fashion" would have had as large a circulation, and that "signs carried by members of the groups not in marching formation would have been as conspicuous, as published by them while in parade or procession."

It was with this view of the limited objective of the statute that the state court considered and defined the duty of the licensing authority and the rights of the appellants to a license for their parade, with regard only to considerations of time, place and manner so as to conserve the public convenience. The obvious advantage of requiring application for a permit was noted as giving the public authorities notice in advance so as to afford opportunity for proper policing. And the court further observed that, in fixing time and place, the license served "to prevent confusion by overlapping parades or processions, to secure convenient use of the streets by other travelers, and to minimize the risk of disorder." But the court held that the licensing board was not vested with arbitrary power or an unfettered discretion; that its discretion must be exercised with "uniformity of method of treatment upon the facts of each application, free from improper or inappropriate considerations and from unfair discrimination"; that a "systematic, consistent and just order of treatment, with reference to the convenience of public use of the highways, is the statutory mandate." The defendants, said the court, "had a right, under the Act, to a license to march when, where and as they did, if after a required investigation it was found that the convenience of the public in the use of the streets would not thereby be unduly disturbed, upon such conditions or changes in time, place and manner as would avoid disturbance."

If a municipality has authority to control the use of its public streets for parades or processions, as it undoubtedly has, it cannot be denied authority to give consideration, without unfair discrimination, to time, place and manner in relation to the other proper uses of the streets. We find it impossible to say that the limited authority conferred by the licensing provi-

sions of the statute in question as thus construed by the state court contravened any constitutional right.

There remains the question of license fees which [had] a permissible range from $300 to a nominal amount. [The fee was] "not a revenue tax, but one to meet the expense incident to the administration of the Act and to the maintenance of public order in the matter licensed." There is nothing contrary to the Constitution in the charge of a fee limited to the purpose stated. . . .

There is no evidence that the statute has been administered otherwise than in the fair and non-discriminatory manner which the state court has construed it to require.

The decisions upon which appellants rely are not applicable. In [Lovell v. Griffin], the ordinance [struck] at the very foundation of the freedom of the press by subjecting it to license and censorship. In [Hague v. CIO, the ordinance] did not make comfort or convenience in the use of streets the standard of official action but enabled the local official absolutely to refuse a permit on his mere opinion that such refusal would prevent "riots, disturbances or disorderly assemblage." The ordinance thus created [an] instrument of arbitrary suppression of opinions on public questions. . . .

The argument as to freedom of worship is also beside the point. No interference with religious worship or the practice of religion in any proper sense is shown, but only the exercise of local control over the use of streets for parades and processions.

Affirmed.†

CANTWELL v. CONNECTICUT

310 U.S. 296, 60 S.Ct. 900, 84 L.Ed. 1213 (1940).

Appeal from and certiorari to the Supreme Court of Errors of Connecticut.

Mr. Justice ROBERTS delivered the opinion of the Court.

Newton Cantwell and his two sons, Jesse and Russell, members of a group know as Jehovah's Witnesses, and claiming to be ordained ministers, were arrested in New Haven, Connecticut, and each was charged by information in five counts, with statutory and common law offenses. [E]ach of them was convicted on the third count, which charged a violation of [a statute] and on the fifth count, which charged commission of the common law offense of inciting a breach of the peace. On appeal to the Supreme Court

† Why could the appellants in Cox not claim that the statute was void on its face because of the vague standards at the time of their march, and that this vagueness could not be cured as to them by the state court's subsequent construction of the statute? Compare the Court's explanation and distinction of this aspect of Cox in Shuttlesworth v. Birmingham, 394 U.S. 147 (1969), sec. 2C below. Note the Court's frequent reliance on Cox, however, with respect to the state's power to regulate "time, place, or manner" through "properly drawn" licensing statutes. See, e. g., Cox v. Louisiana I, sec. 2C below.

the conviction of all three on the third count was affirmed. The conviction of Jesse Cantwell, on the fifth count, was also affirmed, but the conviction of Newton and Russell on that count was reversed and a new trial ordered as to them. [The third count charged violation of a statute banning solicitation without a permit. Justice Roberts concluded: "[T]o condition the solicitation of aid for the perpetuation of religious views or systems upon a license, the grant of which rests in the exercise of a determination by state authority as to what is a religious cause, is to lay a forbidden burden upon the exercise of liberty protected by the Constitution." See chap. 13, sec. 2.]

We hold that, in the circumstances disclosed the conviction of Jesse Cantwell on the fifth count must [also] be set aside. Decision as to the lawfulness of the conviction demands the weighing of two conflicting interests. . . . We must determine whether the alleged protection of the State's interest [in "peace and good order"] has been pressed, in this instance, to a point where it has come into fatal collision with the overriding interest [in the freedoms of expression and religion] protected by the federal compact.

Conviction on the fifth count was not pursuant to a statute evincing a legislative judgment that street discussion of religious affairs, because of its tendency to provoke disorder, should be regulated, or a judgment that the playing of a phonograph on the streets should in the interest of comfort or privacy be limited or prevented. Violation of an Act exhibiting such a legislative judgment and narrowly drawn to prevent the supposed evil, would pose a question differing from what we must here answer. Such a declaration of the State's policy would weigh heavily in any challenge of the law as infringing constitutional limitations. Here, however, the judgment is based on a common law concept of the most general and undefined nature. . . .

The offense known as breach of the peace embraces a great variety of conduct destroying or menacing public order and tranquility. It includes not only violent acts but acts and words likely to produce violence in others. No one would have the hardihood to suggest that the principle of freedom of speech sanctions incitement to riot or that religious liberty connotes the privilege to exhort others to physical attack upon those belonging to another sect. When clear and present danger of riot, disorder, interference with traffic upon the public streets, or other immediate threat to public safety, peace, or order appears, the power of the State to prevent or punish is obvious. Equally obvious is it that a State may not unduly suppress free communication of views, religious or other, under the guise of conserving desirable conditions. Here we have a situation analogous to a conviction under a statute sweeping in a great variety of conduct under a general and indefinite characterization, and leaving to the executive and judicial branches too wide a discretion in its application.

Having these considerations in mind, we note that Jesse Cantwell, on April 26, 1938, was upon a public street, where he had a right to be, and where he had a right peacefully to impart his views to others. There is no showing that his deportment was noisy, truculent, overbearing or offensive. . . . It is not claimed that he intended to insult or affront the hearers by playing the record. It is plain that he wished only to interest them in his propaganda. The sound of the phonograph is not shown to have disturbed residents of the street, to have drawn a crowd, or to have impeded traf-

fic. Thus far he had invaded no right or interest of the public or of the men accosted.

The record played by Cantwell embodies a general attack on all organized religious systems as instruments of Satan and injurious to man; it then singles out the Roman Catholic Church for strictures couched in terms which natural- ly would offend not only persons of that persuasion, but all others who re- spect the honestly held religious faith of their fellows. The hearers were in fact highly offended. One of them said he felt like hitting Cantwell and the other that he was tempted to throw Cantwell off the street. The one who testified he felt like hitting Cantwell said, in answer to the question "Did you do anything else or have any other reaction?" "No, sir, because he said he would take the victrola and he went." The other witness testified that he told Cantwell he had better get off the street before something happened to him and that was the end of the matter as Cantwell picked up his books and walked up the street.

Cantwell's conduct, in the view of the court below, considered apart from the effect of his communication upon his hearers, did not amount to a breach of the peace. One may, however, be guilty of the offense if he commit acts or make statements likely to provoke violence and disturbance of good order, even though no such eventuality be intended. [But in practically all such cases,] the provocative language which was held to amount to a breach of the peace consisted of profane, indecent, or abusive remarks directed to the per- son of the hearer. Resort to epithets or personal abuse is not in any proper sense communication of information or opinion safeguarded by the Constitu- tion, and its punishment as a criminal act would raise no question under that instrument.

We find in the instant case no assault or threatening of bodily harm, no truculent bearing, no intentional discourtesy, no personal abuse. On the con- trary, we find only an effort to persuade a willing listener to buy a book or to contribute money in the interest of what Cantwell, however misguided others may think him, conceived to be true religion. . . .

Although the contents of the record not unnaturally aroused animosity, we think that, in the absence of a statute narrowly drawn to define and punish specific conduct as constituting a clear and present danger to a substantial in- terest of the State, the petitioner's communication, considered in the light of the constitutional guarantees, raised no such clear and present menace to pub- lic peace and order as to render him liable to conviction of the common law offense in question. . . .

Reversed.

SOME QUESTIONS ON THE EARLY CASES

1. *Lovell, Cox v. New Hampshire, and Cantwell.* What was the cen- tral vice in Lovell? Prior restraint, the risk of abuse of discretion, censor- ship, content control, in the licensing scheme? Or the "broad sweep" of the ordinance: the ban on *all* distribution? Does Lovell reinforce the Hague v. CIO support for a claim of guaranteed access to a public forum (see also note 3 below)? Or is it primarily concerned with the risks to equal access under

the licensing scheme? What is the emphasis of Cox v. New Hampshire? Does it reinforce the guaranteed access claim? Or is it primarily concerned with safeguarding against inequality and censorship risks by assuring adequate standards in the licensing scheme, either on its face or as construed? Does Cox v. New Hampshire suggest that judicial scrutiny will not extend much beyond assurance that the restraints are truly directed at "time, place, and manner," and that they are neutrally framed and administered? [1]

What is the thrust of Cantwell? Does *it* guarantee access to streets? Or does its concern center on restraints that risk content-oriented, unequal applications? What local interests would be sufficiently strong to justify punishment of speakers such as Cantwell under a narrowly drawn statute? Fear of violence? Actual violence? Sensibilities of the audience? What, in short, is the holding in Cantwell? That the First Amendment protected Cantwell's behavior and barred *any* state regulation? Or only that Cantwell's behavior could not be punished without more evidence of violence, or risk of violence, or injury to listeners' sensibilities? Or only that Cantwell's behavior could not be punished in the absence of a narrowly drawn statute?

2. *The Schneider case.* Together with the three cases above, one other decision from the Court's early encounters with public places problems is frequently cited by the modern Court: SCHNEIDER v. STATE, 308 U.S. 147 (1939). As Justice Black summarized that decision in his opinion for the Court in Talley v. California,[2] it invalidated the ordinances of four different cities forbidding distribution of leaflets: "Efforts were made to distinguish these four ordinances from the one held void in the Griffin case. The chief grounds urged for distinction were that the four ordinances had been passed to prevent either frauds, disorder, or littering, according to the records in these cases, and another ground urged was that two of the ordinances applied only to certain city areas. This Court refused to uphold the four ordinances on those grounds pointing out that there were other ways to accomplish these legitimate aims without abridging freedom of speech and press. Frauds, street littering and disorderly conduct could be denounced and punished as offenses, the Court said."

1. Note Kalven's comment on the case, in "The Concept of the Public Forum . . . ," 1965 Sup.Ct.Rev. 1: "Of course, Cox v. New Hampshire did no more than to give a general standard for accommodation of the conflicting interests. It did not tell whether certain congested areas or certain times of the day might not always be held unavailable for parading, nor whether the size of some crowds might always be too large. But it seems to me to symbolize the ideal of Robert's Rules of Order for use of the public forum of the streets."

2. Talley v. California. 362 U.S. 60 (1960), invalidated a Los Angeles ordinance which prohibited the distribution of any handbill "in any place under any circumstances" unless the handbill had printed on it the name and address of the person who prepared, distributed or sponsored it. The ordinance was held "void on its face." The Court noted that the identification requirement itself "would tend to restrict freedom to distribute information and thereby freedom of expression." The Court rejected the argument that the ordinance was a justifiable "way to identify those responsible for fraud, false advertising and libel," stating that "the ordinance is in no manner so limited." Justice Clark, joined by Justices Frankfurter and Whittaker, dissented: "I stand second to none in supporting Talley's right of free speech—but not his freedom of anonymity."

3. *The leaflet cases and the public forum.* For an argument that the early leaflet cases strengthened Justice Roberts' dictum in Hague v. CIO and bolstered the case for a guaranteed access right to the streets as a public forum, see Kalven, "The Concept of the Public Forum: Cox v. Louisiana," 1965 Sup.Ct.Rev. 1. Kalven argues, for example, that Schneider did not involve simply "freedom from arbitrariness in the state's control of public places," but rather "reasonable regulation of the immemorial claim of the free man to use the streets as a forum. The regulation in order to be deemed reasonable, the Court was telling us, must recognize the special nature and value of that claim to be on the street." Kalven suggests the leafleting cases as "the relevant model for analysis of the complex speech issues involved" in the mass demonstration-public forum cases, secs. 2C and 2D below: "The operative theory of the Court, at least for the leaflet situation, is that, although it is a method of communication that interferes with the public use of the streets, the right to the streets as a public forum is such that leaflet distribution cannot be prohibited and can be regulated only for weighty reasons."

In Schneider, the Court also suggested that the city had alternative ways of achieving the objectives—e. g., as to littering, the city could simply arrest the recipient who tossed the leaflets on the street. Was Schneider, then, an overbreadth case emphasizing a less-restrictive-alternatives analysis, cf. Shelton v. Tucker, 364 U.S. 479 (1960) (chap. 13, sec. 5, below)? Note Kalven's comment: "It is difficult to take seriously so impractical an alternative." He sees the alternatives emphasis as an additional flaw in the regulations, not the "decisive flaw." And he emphasizes such language in Justice Roberts' Schneider opinion as: "We are of the opinion that the purpose to keep the streets clean and of good appearance is insufficient to justify an ordinance which prohibits a person rightfully on a public street from handing literature to one willing to receive it. Any burden imposed upon the city authorities in cleaning and caring for the streets as an indirect consequence of such distribution results from the constitutional protection of the freedom of speech and press." †

Note also Kalven's comment: "Mr. Justice Roberts really had it all worked out in Schneider. Since all speech was 'speech plus,' it was subject to regulation of time, place, manner, and circumstance, but to be acceptable the regulation had to weigh heavily the fact that communication was involved." But, Kalven asks, does not the Schneider rationale have "unwanted overtones for free-speech enthusiasts"? "Does it not embrace two hob-

---

† Note also Justice Roberts' response in Schneider to the argument on behalf of some of the ordinances that some public places were left open: "[T]he streets are natural and proper places for the dissemination of information and opinion; and one is not to have the exercise of his liberty of expression in appropriate places abridged on the plea that it may be exercised in some other place." Consider, in the guaranteed access public forum cases below, the relevance of alternative available public places in evaluating a particular forum claim. Compare Justice Frankfurter's comment in the introductory materials above: he lists "the facilities, other than a park or street corner, readily available in a community for airing views," as one of the "pertinent considerations in assessing" public forum claims. (On the applicability to distributions of leaflets with commercial messages, see Valentine v. Chrestensen, 316 U.S. 52 (1942), considered with the materials on "commercial speech," sec. 2D below.)

goblins, a balancing test of First-Amendment interests, and a commitment to prior restraints by licensing?" Kalven answers that the balancing test *is* appropriate, especially "with the Schneider mandate that the thumb of the Court be on the speech side of the scales." He considers the controversy over balancing "fruitless" (see the introductory materials to this chapter above), and he reminds "how awkward for many speech problems the clear-and-present-danger test has proved." Moreover, he notes that in public forum access cases, "Mr. Justice Black has always been willing to balance." See, e. g., Cox v. Louisiana I, sec. 2C below. And as to prior restraint, Kalven argues that "there is little, if anything, left today to the idea that prior licensing is bad per se, regardless of the criteria used. It now appears that the historical reaction was against general licensing with unlimited or unspecified grounds for exercise of discretion." He suggests that Cox v. New Hampshire "stands as a strong and healthy precedent for use of a prior restraint, at least in regulating the public forum." Do the materials which follow support Kalven's observations? Have later Courts perceived the legacy of the leaflet cases and Cox as Kalven did? Did Justice Roberts really have it "all worked out" in Schneider? Have later cases undone that work?

B. EVOLVING DOCTRINES: NOISY, ABRASIVE SPEAKERS; SENSITIVE, HOSTILE AUDIENCES

THE INTRUSIVE SPEAKER AND THE UNWILLING LISTENER: THE LOUDSPEAKER CASES AND THE CAPTIVE AUDIENCE

Introduction. Two decisions in the late 1940's dealing with control of amplified sounds bear not only on the specific loudspeaker question but also suggest evolving approaches to more general problems: the justifications that may support total prohibition of some manifestations of speech; the significance of the city's methods of control as well as the speaker's method of communication; the Justices' varying sensitivities toward a claim that a particular forum is necessary to enable the speaker to reach an audience.

1. *Saia.* In SAIA v. NEW YORK, 334 U.S. 558 (1948), a 5 to 4 decision, the Court held invalid "on its face" a Lockport, N. Y., ordinance prohibiting the use of amplification devices without the permission of the police chief. Justice Douglas' opinion for the majority found that the ordinance established an unconstitutional "previous restraint" on free speech with "no standards prescribed for the exercise of" the administrative discretion. He stated:

"Loud-speakers are today indispensable instruments of effective public speech. The sound truck has become an accepted method of political campaigning. It is the way people are reached. Must a candidate for governor or the Congress depend on the whim or caprice of the Chief of Police in order to use his sound truck for campaigning? Must he prove to the satisfaction of that official that his noise will not be annoying to people?

"The present ordinance would be a dangerous weapon if it were allowed to get a hold on our public life. Noise can be regulated by regulating decibels. The hours and place of public discussion can be controlled. But to allow the police to bar the use of loud-speakers because their use can be abused is like barring radio receivers because they too make a noise. . . .

"Any abuses which loud-speakers create can be controlled by narrowly drawn statutes. When a city allows an official to ban them in his uncontrolled discretion, it sanctions a device for suppression of free communication of ideas. In this case a permit is denied because some persons were said to have found the sound annoying. In the next one a permit may be denied because some people find the ideas annoying. Annoyance at ideas can be cloaked in annoyance at sound. The power of censorship inherent in this type of ordinance reveals its vice."

Justice Frankfurter, joined by Justices Reed and Burton, dissented: "[M]odern devices for amplifying the range and volume of the voice, or its recording, afford easy, too easy, opportunities for aural aggression. If uncontrolled, the result is intrusion into cherished privacy. The refreshment of mere silence, or meditation, or quiet conversation, may be disturbed or precluded by noise beyond one's personal control. . . . Surely there is not a constitutional right to force unwilling people to listen. . . . And so I cannot agree that we must deny the right of a State to control these broadcasting devices so as to safeguard the rights of others not to be assailed by intrusive noise but to be free to put their freedom of mind and attention to uses of their own choice." Justice Jackson also dissented.

2. *Kovacs.* In KOVACS v. COOPER, 336 U.S. 77 (1949), one year after Saia, the Court sustained application of a Trenton, N. J., ordinance designed to regulate loudspeakers. Kovacs was convicted of violating a ban on "any device known as a sound truck, loud speaker or sound amplifier . . . which emits therefrom loud and raucous noises and is attached to and upon any vehicle operated or standing [upon] streets or public places."

Justice Reed's opinion announcing the judgment of the Court was joined only by Chief Justice Vinson and Justice Burton. He rejected the claim that "loud and raucous" were unduly vague terms. He continued: "Unrestrained use throughout a municipality of all sound amplifying devices would be intolerable. Absolute prohibition within municipal limits of all sound amplification, even though reasonably regulated in place, time and volume, is undesirable and probably unconstitutional as an unreasonable interference with normal activities." He found that the ordinance, as construed by the state court, "applies only to vehicles with sound amplifiers emitting loud and raucous noises" and proceeded:

"City streets are recognized as a normal place for the exchange of ideas by speech or paper. But this does not mean the freedom is beyond all control. We think it is a permissible exercise of legislative discretion to bar sound trucks with broadcasts of public interest, amplified to a loud and raucous volume, from the public ways of municipalities. On the business streets of cities like Trenton, with its more than 125,000 people, such distractions would be dangerous to traffic at all hours useful for the dissemination of information, and in the residential thoroughfares the quiet and tran-

quility so desirable for city dwellers would likewise be at the mercy of advocates of particular religious, social or political persuasions. We cannot believe that rights of free speech compel a municipality to allow such mechanical voice amplification on any of its streets.

"The right of free speech is guaranteed every citizen that he may reach the minds of willing listeners and to do so there must be opportunity to win their attention. . . . We do not think the Trenton ordinance abridges that freedom. The preferred position of freedom of speech in a society that cherishes liberty for all does not require legislators to be insensible to claims by citizens to comfort and convenience. [That] more people may be more easily and cheaply reached by sound trucks, perhaps borrowed without cost from some zealous supporter, is not enough to call forth constitutional protection for what those charged with public welfare reasonably think is a nuisance when easy means of publicity are open. . . . There is no restriction upon the communication of ideas or discussion of issues by the human voice, by newspapers, by pamphlets, by dodgers. We think that the need for reasonable protection in the homes or business houses from the distracting noises of vehicles equipped with such sound amplifying devices justifies the ordinance."

Justice Black, joined by Justices Douglas and Rutledge, dissented: "The appellant was neither charged with nor convicted of operating a sound truck that emitted 'loud and raucous noises'. The charge [was] that he violated the city ordinance 'in that he did, on South Stockton Street, in said City, play, use and operate a device known as a sound truck.' The record reflects not even a shadow of evidence to prove that the noise was either 'loud or raucous,' unless these words of the ordinance refer to any noise coming from an amplifier, whatever its volume or tone. [The] ordinance here sustained goes beyond a mere prior censorship of all loud speakers with authority in the censor to prohibit some of them. This Trenton ordinance wholly bars the use of all loud speakers mounted upon any vehicle in any of the city's public streets. In my view this repudiation of the prior *Saia* opinion makes a dangerous and unjustifiable breach in the constitutional barriers designed to insure freedom of expression. . . . The basic premise of the First Amendment is that all present instruments of communication, as well as others that inventive genius may bring into being, shall be free from governmental censorship or prohibition. Laws which hamper the free use of some instruments of communication thereby favor competing channels. [Laws like this] can give an overpowering influence to views of owners of legally favored instruments of communication. [I]t is an obvious fact that public speaking today without sound amplifiers is a wholly inadequate way to reach the people on a large scale. . . .

"A city ordinance that reasonably restricts the volume of sound, or the hours during which an amplifier may be used, does not, in my mind, infringe the constitutionally protected area of free speech. It is because this ordinance does none of these things, but is instead an absolute prohibition of all uses of an amplifier on any of the streets of Trenton at any time that I must dissent." Justices Rutledge and Murphy also dissented.

Justice Jackson concurred on the ground that "operation of mechanical sound-amplifying devices conflicts with quiet enjoyment of home and park

and with safe and legitimate use of street and market place, and that it is constitutionally subject to regulation or prohibition by the state or municipal authority. No violation of the [14th Amendment] arises unless such regulation or prohibition undertakes to censor the contents of the broadcasting. . . . I do not agree that, if we sustain regulations or prohibitions of sound trucks, they must therefore be valid if applied to other methods of 'communication of ideas.' The moving picture screen, the radio, the newspaper, the handbill, the sound truck and the street corner orator have differing natures, values, abuses and dangers. Each, in my view, is a law unto itself, and all we are dealing with now is the sound truck.

"But I agree with Mr. Justice Black that this decision is a repudiation of that in [Saia]. Like him, I am unable to find anything in this record to warrant a distinction because of 'loud and raucous' tones of this machine. The Saia decision struck down a more moderate exercise of the state's police power than the one now sustained. Trenton, as the ordinance reads to me, unconditionally bans all sound trucks from the city streets. Lockport relaxed its prohibition with a proviso to allow their use, even in areas set aside for public recreation, when and where the Chief of Police saw no objection." [1]

3. *The noisy speaker's public forum.* Would a flat ban on all outdoor loudspeakers and sound trucks be constitutional? Should it be? Given the disagreement on the Court about the scope of the ordinance in Kovacs, the impact of the case is unclear. If the Kovacs ordinance is read in accordance with the Jackson and Black views—that it authorized a flat ban—do the results in Saia and Kovacs make sense? What do Saia and Kovacs say about a guaranteed access public forum claim of a loudspeaker user? Is the vice of the administrative censorship risk in a vague licensing ordinance greater than the vice of total silencing of the communication channel? Is a virtually total prohibition of loudspeakers justified because of a legislative judgment that a particular method of communication is obnoxious? Would a specific ban on all speeches or marches in residential neighborhoods be similarly supportable on grounds of deference to legislative judgment? A ban on all street demonstrations? Would it depend on the available alternative communication channels? On those available to the particular speaker? Unless at least some inquiry into the importance of the communication code and the availability of alternative outlets is made, can there be adequate respect for the guaranteed access public forum concept? Was there such an inquiry in Kovacs? Was total prohibition of loudspeakers permissible only because those speakers had other adequate outlets? Or was it enough that a legislative ordinance had decided that this outlet was too annoying?

4. *The captive audience.* a. *The audience interest as a restraint on the public forum access claim.* In his Kovacs opinion, Justice Reed distinguished the loudspeaker problem from other restrictions on expression: "While [the Court] has invalidated an ordinance forbidding a distributor of

---

1. In another concurring opinion, Justice Frankfurter said it would be "an unreality" to dispose of this case on the assumption that Saia was rightly decided and reaffirmed his dissenting views in Saia. Most of his opinion was devoted to "observations" on Justice Reed's reference to "the preferred position of freedom of speech." [Some of these comments are printed in the introductory materials to this chapter.]

pamphlets or handbills from summoning householders to their doors to receive the distributor's writings, this was on the ground that the home owner could protect himself from such intrusion by an appropriate sign 'that he is unwilling to be disturbed.' The Court never intimated that the visitor could insert a foot in the door and insist on a hearing. Martin v. City of Struthers [319 U.S. 141 (1943)]." But "the unwilling listener is not like the passer-by who may be offered a pamphlet in the street but cannot be made to take it. In his home or on the street he is practically helpless to escape this interference with his privacy by loud speakers except through the protection of the municipality." And in dissenting in Saia, Justice Jackson had considered sound truck regulation "not only appropriate," but "a duty of the city." [2]

b. *The audience interest as a basis for an affirmative constitutional claim: The Pollak case.* Can the unwilling listener make a First Amendment or privacy claim to protection from "aural aggression"? See Public Utilities Comm'n v. Pollak, 343 U.S. 451 (1952), where a bus company installed FM radio receivers in its vehicles and broadcast special programs consisting of 90% music, 5% news, and 5% commercial advertising. The District Public Utilities Commission initiated an investigation. Pollak and Martin, two protesting passengers, intervened. The Commission found that the use of the radios was "not inconsistent with public convenience, comfort and, safety." Did the passengers have any basis for a constitutional challenge? The majority found no First Amendment or Fifth Amendment (privacy) flaw. Justice Douglas' dissent emphasized the right to be let alone: he insisted that subjecting the captive audience to the programming violated the constitutional right to privacy. Recall Justice Douglas' position in Saia: Can there be both a constitutional right to reach an unwilling auditor *and* an auditor's right not to listen and be disturbed? How should those rights be accommodated? Note that Justice Douglas' position in Pollak did not rest on the content of the message. He said: "It may be but a short step from a cultural program to a political program." Was the speaker in Saia entitled to special protection because of the importance of the loudspeaker as a "poor man's printing press"? (Justice Frankfurter refused to participate in Pollak because "my feelings are so strongly engaged as a victim of the practice in controversy.") [3]

2. Contrast with Martin v. City of Struthers (involving a distributor of religious literature) the decision in Breard v. City of Alexandria, 341 U.S. 622 (1951), *sustaining* an ordinance barring door-to-door solicitation for magazine subscriptions without the prior consent of the homeowners. The majority emphasized the "householders' desire for privacy" in rejecting First Amendment as well as commerce clause challenges to the ordinance. Recall the excerpts from the case in chap. 5 above. Justice Black, joined by Justice Douglas, dissented on the ground that the majority had not accorded the First Amendment its proper "preferred status." (See also the additional comments on the bear-

ing of Martin and Breard in modern contexts, below.)

3. On the Pollak problem, see Black, "He Cannot Choose But Hear: The Plight of the Captive Auditor," 53 Colum.L.Rev. 960 (1953). For further consideration of efforts to reconcile public forum access claims with the captive auditor's interests, see Lehman v. City of Shaker Heights, 418 U.S. 298 (1974) (sec. 2D below), where Justice Douglas' Pollak-like concern for the audience proved the decisive vote in rejecting an access claim by a political candidate who wanted to advertise in a city bus. Compare the problems considered in the next note.

5. *Modern considerations of the right "to be let alone" as a restriction on the right to communicate: The Rowan and Keefe cases.* a. *Rowan.* In ROWAN v. POST OFFICE DEPT., 397 U.S. 728 (1970), appellants, in the mail order business, unsuccessfully claimed that a federal law violated their right to communicate. The law provides that a person who has received in the mail "a pandering advertisement" which offers for sale "matter which the addressee in his sole discretion believes to be erotically arousing or sexually provocative" may request a post office order requiring the mailer to remove his name from his mailing list and stop all future mailings to the addressee. The law was enacted in response to concern "with use of mail facilities to distribute unsolicited advertisements that recipients found to be offensive because of their lewd and salacious character" and which "was found to be pressed upon minors as well as adults who did not seek and did not want it."

Chief Justice Burger's opinion found the constitutional challenge unpersuasive: "[T]he right of every person 'to be let alone' must be placed in the scales with the right of others to communicate. In today's complex society we are inescapably captive audiences for many purposes, but a sufficient measure of individual autonomy must survive to permit every householder to exercise control over unwanted mail. [Weighing] the highly important right to communicate [against] the very basic right to be free from sights, sounds and tangible matter we do not want, it seems to us that a mailer's right to communicate must stop at the mailbox of an unreceptive addressee. . . . In operative effect the power of a householder under the statute is unlimited; he may prohibit the mailing of a dry goods catalog because he objects to the contents—or indeed the text of the language touting the merchandise. Congress provided the sweeping power not only to protect privacy but to avoid possible constitutional questions that might arise from vesting the power to make any discretionary evaluation of the material in a governmental official." The Chief Justice concluded: "[We] categorically reject the argument that a vendor has a right under the Constitution or otherwise to send unwanted material into the home of another. If this prohibition operates to impede the flow of even valid ideas, the answer is that no one has a right to press even 'good' ideas on an unwilling recipient. That we are often 'captives' outside the sanctuary of the home and subject to objectionable speech and other sound does not mean we must be captives everywhere. See [Pollak]."[4]

b. *Keefe.* Chief Justice Burger had no difficulty distinguishing the Rowan case in ORGANIZATION FOR A BETTER AUSTIN v. KEEFE, 402 U.S. 415 (1971). Respondent, a real estate broker, had obtained from the Illinois courts an injunction enjoining a Chicago racially integrated community organization from distributing its literature criticizing respondent's alleged "blockbusting" and "panic peddling" activities. Respondent's busi-

4. Justice Brennan, joined by Justice Douglas, concurred in a separate opinion expressing concern about the possibility "that parents could prevent their children, even if they are 18 years old, from receiving political, religious or other materials that the parents find offensive." Such an interpretation would give rise to "constitutional difficulties"; but here, he was satisfied, the Court had left open "the question of the right of older children to receive materials through the mail without governmental interference."

ness activities were in Chicago but he resided in a suburb several miles away, and the injunction prevented distribution of the literature in that suburb. The state courts viewed petitioners' activities "as coercive and intimidating, rather than informative," and relied on the state's policy favoring "protection of the privacy of home and family."

Chief Justice Burger found these arguments insufficient to justify the injunction: "The claim that the expressions were intended to exercise a coercive impact on respondent does not remove them from the reach of the First Amendment. . . . Petitioners were engaged openly and vigorously in making the public aware of respondent's real estate practices. Those practices were offensive to them, as the views and practices of petitioners are no doubt offensive to others. But so long as the means are peaceful, the communication need not meet standards of acceptability."

Moreover, the "heavy burden of showing justification" for the imposition of a prior restraint had not been met here: "No prior decisions support the claim that the interest of an individual in being free from public criticism of his business practices in pamphlets or leaflets warrants use of the injunctive power of a court. Designating the conduct as an invasion of privacy [is] not sufficient to support an injunction against peaceful distribution of informational literature of the nature revealed by this record. [Rowan] is not in point; the right of privacy involved in that case is not shown here. Among other important distinctions, respondent is not attempting to stop the flow of information into his own household, but to the public."

PROVOCATIVE SPEECH AND THE HOSTILE AUDIENCE

Introduction. Does hostile audience reaction justify restricting the speaker? Only if the speaker uses extremely provocative words? Even if the audience is very easily provoked by speeches short of "fighting words"? Does the First Amendment impose an obligation on the government to protect the speaker from the angry crowd? Must government attempt to preserve peace by restraining listeners rather than speakers? Or may government stop the speaker simply by showing that his words provoked disorder (or created an immediate danger of disorder)? Does that legitimate a "heckler's veto"? Must some protection of the provocative speaker be assured lest the public forum be blocked by the "heckler's veto"? How effectively have the cases dealt with this Robert's Rules problem?

Recall the Court's comments on this problem in its disposition of Jesse Cantwell's breach of the peace conviction, sec. 2A. Was Cantwell freed because there was not a sufficiently "clear and present danger" of disorder? Would he have been punishable for what he said if a more specific statute had been invoked and disorder had resulted? Or would his speech have been protected by the First Amendment even if it had provoked greater hostility?

The Cantwell opinion suggested that some speech, in any event, might not have been protected—e. g., "personal abuse." A year later, in the much-quoted Chaplinsky case (note 1 below), the Court elaborated that "fight-

ing words" are not entitled to speech protection. But Terminiello (note 2 below) reversed a conviction of a provocative speaker, though without reaching the "fighting words" issue. And the problem of the speaker using words short of the "fighting words" category has recurred in subsequent cases. Feiner v. New York, below was the Court's 1951 response to the hostile audience question. Demonstrations of the 1960's produced similar problems, as the Edwards and Gregory cases below, as well as some of the materials in sec. 1C, show.[1]

1. *Chaplinsky and "fighting words."* In CHAPLINSKY v. NEW HAMPSHIRE, 315 U.S. 568 (1942), the Court unanimously upheld the conviction of a Jehovah's Witness who had gotten into a fight on a sidewalk after calling a policeman "a God damned racketeer" and "a damned Fascist." The statute had enacted the common law "fighting words" doctrine: "No person shall address any offensive, derisive or annoying word to any other person who is lawfully in any street or other public place, nor call him by any offensive or derisive name." The state court had interpreted it to ban "words likely to cause an average addresse to fight," "face-to-face words plainly likely" to cause a breach of the peace by the addressee. The Court thought it obvious that Chaplinsky's words were "likely to provoke the average person to retaliation."

In the course of the opinion, Justice Murphy commented: "There are certain well-defined and narrowly limited classes of speech, the prevention and punishment of which have never been thought to raise any Constitutional problem. These include the lewd and obscene, the profane, the libelous, and the insulting or 'fighting' words—those which by their very utterance inflict injury or tend to incite an immediate breach of the peace. It has been well observed that such utterances are no essential part of any exposition of ideas, and are of such slight social value as a step to truth that any benefit that may be derived from them is clearly outweighed by the social interest in order and morality."

That passage has been widely relied on, even by Justices who profess to support a wide range of speech protection. Does reliance on the passage risk inadequate analysis of speech problems and undue interference with speech? Does the approach of categorizing speech into "classes" and placing some outside the First Amendment? In later years, the "obscene," the "profane," and the "libelous"—other unprotected classes mentioned in Chaplinsky—were found to raise substantial First Amendment problems. See chap. 13, below—e. g., the New York Times case on libel; but compare

1. This group of materials focuses on words allegedy restrainable because of the interest in preventing violence. Note, however, that the "fighting" words doctrine is often stated to include another category of speech as well: offensive speech sought to be restrained not primarily to avert violent audience responses but rather to protect the sensibilities of the audience from shock—or to protect the moral standards of society. That "offensive words" problem is considered in a separate group of materials later in this section. For a linking of the two varieties of "bad" speech, see Justice Murphy's reference in Chaplinsky, note 1 in text, to "insulting or 'fighting' words—those which by their very utterance inflict injury *or* tend to incite an immediate breach of the peace." (Emphasis added.) The fear of breach of the peace predominates in the cases in this group. The concern about words which "by their very utterance inflict injury" is the focus of the "offensive language" materials below.

the "obscenity-is-not-speech" approach of the obscenity cases in chap. 13, sec. 2. Should the "definitional" or "classification" approach be abandoned for "fighting words" as well?

Note Justice Brennan's comment in New York Times Co. v. Sullivan, 376 U.S. 254 (1964): "Like 'insurrection,' contempt, advocacy of unlawful acts, breach of the peace, obscenity, solicitation of legal business, and the various other formulae for the repression of expression that have been challenged in this Court, libel can claim no talismanic immunity from constitutional limitations. It must be measured by standards that satisfy the First Amendment." Should "fighting words" have "talismanic immunity"? Or is it better to recognize explicitly that "fighting words" problems have First Amendment dimensions? Would abandonment of the "fighting words" rubric mean protection for all speech, no matter how obviously provocative to the audience? Would abandonment of the rubric invite more particularized attention to the First Amendment ingredients of the provocative speaker's claim, and the state interests asserted as justifications for restraints? (Note again that Justice Murphy's rubric in Chaplinsky is not limited to "fighting" words which risk "an immediate breach of the peace." It also includes "insulting" words which "by their very utterance inflict injury." Should "offensive" words which shock listeners be placed wholly outside the First Amendment? See the examination of that aspect of concern with audience reactions in the materials on the "offensive language" problem, below.)

2. *Terminiello and "provocative" speech which "invites dispute."* In TERMINIELLO v. CHICAGO, 337 U.S. 1 (1949), the Court reversed the breach of peace conviction of an abrasive speaker, but on the basis of an improper charge to the jury and without directly reaching the "hostile words" issue. The speaker viciously denounced various political and racial groups; outside the auditorium, an angry crowd gathered; the speaker then condemned the crowd as "snakes," "slimy scum," etc. After the disturbance, he was convicted under a breach of the peace statute construed by the trial judge to include speech which "stirs the public to anger, invites dispute, brings about a condition of unrest, or creates a disturbance." Justice Douglas' majority opinion found that standard unconstitutional: "[A] function of free speech under our system of government is to invite dispute. It may indeed best serve its high purpose when it induces a condition of unrest, creates dissatisfaction with conditions as they are, or even stirs people to anger. Speech is often provocative and challenging. It may strike at prejudices and preconceptions and have profound unsettling effects as it presses for acceptance of an idea. That is why freedom of speech, though not absolute [Chaplinsky], is nevertheless protected against censorship or punishment, unless shown likely to produce a clear and present danger of a serious substantive evil that rises far above public inconvenience, annoyance, or unrest."

In Terminiello, Justice Douglas emphasized the constitutional protection of "provocative" speech, even when it "stirs people to anger"; and he insisted that public "annoyance, or unrest" was not an adequate justification for curtailing the speaker. Recall also Justice Brennan's comments, in New York Times Co. v. Sullivan, quoted earlier, that "debate on public issues should be uninhibited, robust, and wide-open," and "that it may well include

vehement, caustic, and sometimes unpleasantly sharp attacks on government and public officials." Do the "heckler's veto" cases in this section give adequate weight to the First Amendment interests of the abrasive speaker in the public forum, or do they give undue weight to audience reactions as justifications for curtailment of speech? What about the First Amendment interests of the heckler? [2] By what standards can the competing interests best be reconciled? By what mechanisms? Subsequent punishment? Permit systems? Protective custody but not punishment of the speaker in violent situations?

3. *Feiner, protected words, and restricting environments.* The Feiner case, which follows, elicited more extensive consideration of problems first encountered in Cantwell, above. To what extent does protection under the First Amendment turn on the content of the speech? To what extent on the audience response? Can the Court delineate the protected area by stating, e. g., that words short of "incitement" are protected, no matter what their actual impact? Or do the boundaries of protection depend on the environment, including the actual response of the audience? Must the state accept responsibility for restraining the sensitive audience, or does the speaker bear the risk of having his provocative words stopped by the hecklers' disorder? Were Feiner's words "incitements" outside the First Amendment? Or were they words made punishable by reason of the audience response? Contrast the Court's response in Feiner with the Edwards case (which follows Feiner), a case growing out of a modern mass demonstration in a hostile environment.

2. See In re Kay, 464 P.2d 142 (Cal. 1970), setting aside a conviction for disturbing a lawful meeting. A small part of a large crowd at a Fourth of July celebration "engaged in rhythmical clapping and some shouting for about five or ten minutes. This demonstration did not affect the program" —the heckled speaker, a Congressman, finished his speech despite the protest, "pausing to assure those protesting that they had a right to do so." The California Supreme Court opinion commented: "Audience activities, such as heckling, interrupting, harsh questioning, and booing, even though they may be impolite and discourteous, can nonetheless advance the goals of the First Amendment." To construe the law within constitutional limits, the Court interpreted it to require "that the defendant substantially impaired the conduct of the meeting by intentionally committing acts in violation of implicit customs or usages or of explicit rules for governance of the meeting, of which he knew, or as a reasonable man should have known." It concluded that "participants at a meeting may express disagreement but must not violate explicit rules or implicit customs and usages, pertaining to the meeting, of which they knew or should have known." (See also Justice Douglas' dissent from the denial of certiorari in Reynolds v. Tennessee, 414 U.S. 1163 (1974).)

FEINER v. NEW YORK

340 U.S. 315, 71 S.Ct. 303, 95 L.Ed. 295 (1951).

Certiorari to the Court of Appeals of New York.

Mr. Chief Justice VINSON delivered the opinion of the Court.

Petitioner was convicted of the offense of disorderly conduct, a misdemeanor under the New York penal laws. [Petitioner claims] that the conviction is in violation of his right of free speech . . . .

In the review of state decisions where First Amendment rights are drawn in question, we of course make an examination of the evidence to ascertain independently whether the right has been violated. . . . Our appraisal of the facts [is] based upon the uncontroverted facts and, where controversy exists, upon that testimony which the trial judge did reasonably conclude to be true.

On the evening of March 8, 1949, petitioner Irving Feiner was addressing an open-air meeting at the corner of South McBride and Harrison Streets in the City of Syracuse. At approximately 6:30 p. m., the police received a telephone complaint concerning the meeting, and two officers were detailed to investigate. [Two policemen] found a crowd of about seventy-five or eighty people, both Negro and white, filling the sidewalk and spreading out into the street. Petitioner, standing on a large wooden box on the sidewalk, was addressing the crowd through a loud-speaker system attached to an automobile. Although the purpose of his speech was to urge his listeners to attend a meeting to be held that night in the Syracuse Hotel, in its course he was making derogatory remarks concerning President Truman, the American Legion, the Mayor of Syracuse, and other local political officials.

The police officers made no effort to interfere with petitioner's speech, but were first concerned with the effect of the crowd on both pedestrian and vehicular traffic. They observed the situation from the opposite side of the street, noting that some pedestrians were forced to walk in the street to avoid the crowd. Since traffic was passing at the time, the officers attempted to get the people listening to petitioner back on the sidewalk. The crowd was restless and there was some pushing, shoving and milling around. . . .

At this time, petitioner was speaking in a "loud, high-pitched voice." He gave the impression that he was endeavoring to arouse the Negro people against the whites, urging that they rise up in arms and fight for equal rights. The statements before such a mixed audience "stirred up a little excitement." Some of the onlookers made remarks to the police about their inability to handle the crowd and at least one threatened violence if the police did not act. There were others who appeared to be favoring petitioner's arguments. Because of the feeling that existed in the crowd both for and against the speaker, the officers finally "stepped in to prevent it from resulting in a fight." . . . Although the officer . . . twice requested petitioner to stop over the course of several minutes, petitioner not only ignored him but continued talking. During all this time, the crowd was press-

ing closer around petitioner and the officer. Finally, the officer told petitioner he was under arrest and ordered him to get down from the box, reaching up to grab him. Petitioner stepped down . . . . In all, the officer had asked petitioner to get down off the box three times over a space of four or five minutes. Petitioner had been speaking for over a half hour.

. . . The bill of particulars [detailed] the facts upon which the prosecution relied to support the charge of disorderly conduct. Paragraph C is particularly pertinent here: "By ignoring and refusing to heed and obey reasonable police orders issued [to] regulate and control said crowd and to prevent a breach or breaches of the peace and to prevent injury to pedestrians attempting to use said walk, [and] prevent injury to the public generally."

We are not faced here with blind condonation by a state court of arbitrary police action. . . . The exercise of the police officers' proper discretionary power to prevent a breach of the peace [was] approved by the trial court and later by two courts on review. The [courts below] found that the officers in making the arrest were motivated solely by a proper concern for the preservation of order and protection of the general welfare, and that there was no evidence which could lend color to a claim that the acts of the police were a cover for suppression of petitioner's views and opinions. Petitioner was thus neither arrested nor convicted for the making or the content of his speech. Rather, it was the reaction which it actually engendered.

The language of [Cantwell v. Connecticut] is appropriate here. ". . . When clear and present danger of riot, disorder, interference with traffic upon the public streets, or other immediate threat to public safety, peace, or order, appears, the power of the State to prevent or punish is obvious." The findings of the New York courts as to the condition of the crowd and the refusal of petitioner to obey the police requests, supported as they are by the record of this case, are persuasive that the conviction of petitioner for violation of public peace, order and authority does not exceed the bounds of proper state police action. This Court respects, as it must, the interests of the community in maintaining peace and order on its streets. . . . We cannot say that the preservation of that interest here encroaches on the constitutional rights of this petitioner.

We are well aware that the ordinary murmurings and objections of a hostile audience cannot be allowed to silence a speaker, and are also mindful of the possible danger of giving overzealous police officials complete discretion to break up otherwise lawful public meetings. . . . But we are not faced here with such a situation. It is one thing to say that the police cannot be used as an instrument for the suppression of unpopular views, and another to say that, when as here the speaker passes the bounds of argument or persuasion and undertakes incitement to riot, they are powerless to prevent a breach of the peace. Nor in this case can we condemn the considered judgment of three New York courts approving the means which the police, faced with a crisis, used in the exercise of their power and duty to preserve peace and order. The findings of the state courts as to the existing situation and the imminence of greater disorder coupled with peti-

tioner's deliberate defiance of the police officers convince us that we should not reverse this conviction in the name of free speech.

Affirmed.

Mr. Justice BLACK, dissenting.

The record before us convinces me that petitioner, a young college student, has been sentenced to the penitentiary for the unpopular views he expressed on matters of public interest while lawfully making a street-corner speech in Syracuse, New York. Today's decision, however, indicates that we must blind ourselves to this fact because the trial judge fully accepted the testimony of the prosecution witnesses on all important points. . . .

But still more has been lost today. Even accepting every "finding of fact" below, I think this conviction makes a mockery of the free speech guarantees. [The end result of the affirmance] is to approve a simple and readily available technique by which cities and states can with impunity subject all speeches, political or otherwise, on streets or elsewhere, to the supervision and censorship of the local police. . . .

[I]t seems far-fetched to suggest that the "facts" show any imminent threat of riot or uncontrollable disorder. It is neither unusual nor unexpected that some people at public street meetings mutter, mill about, push, shove, or disagree, even violently, with the speaker. . . . Nor does one isolated threat to assault the speaker forebode disorder. Especially should the danger be discounted where, as here, the person threatening was a man whose wife and two small children accompanied him and who, so far as the record shows, was never close enough to petitioner to carry out the threat.

Moreover, assuming that the "facts" did indicate a critical situation, I reject the implication of the Court's opinion that the police had no obligation to protect petitioner's constitutional right to talk. The police of course have power to prevent breaches of the peace. But if, in the name of preserving order, they ever can interfere with a lawful public speaker, they first must make all reasonable efforts to protect him. Here the policemen did not even pretend to try to protect petitioner. According to the officers' testimony, the crowd was restless but there is no showing of any attempt to quiet it; pedestrians were forced to walk into the street, but there was no effort to clear a path on the sidewalk; one person threatened to assault petitioner but the officers did nothing to discourage this when even a word might have sufficed. Their duty was to protect petitioner's right to talk, even to the extent of arresting the man who threatened to interfere.[1] Instead, they shirked that duty and acted only to suppress the right to speak.

---

1. In Schneider v. State, 308 U.S. 147, we held that a purpose to prevent littering of the streets was insufficient to justify an ordinance which prohibited a person lawfully on the street from handing literature to one willing to receive it. We said at page 162, "There are obvious methods of preventing littering. Amongst these is the punishment of those who actually throw papers on the streets." In the present case as well, the threat of one person to assault a speaker does not justify suppression of the speech. There are obvious available alternative methods of preserving public order. One of these is to arrest the person who threatens an assault. Cf. Dean Milk Co. v. Madison, 340 U.S. 349 [chap. 5, sec. 1C, above] decided today, in which the Court invalidates a municipal health ordinance under the Commerce Clause because of a belief that the city could have accomplished its purposes by reasonably adequate alternatives. The Court certainly

Finally, I cannot agree with the Court's statement that petitioner's disregard of the policeman's unexplained request amounted to such "deliberate defiance" as would justify an arrest or conviction for disorderly conduct. On the contrary, I think that the policeman's action was a "deliberate defiance" of ordinary official duty as well as of the constitutional right of free speech. For at least where time allows, courtesy and explanation of commands are basic elements of good official conduct in a democratic society. Here petitioner was "asked" then "told" then "commanded" to stop speaking, but a man making a lawful address is certainly not required to be silent merely because an officer directs it. Petitioner was entitled to know why he should cease doing a lawful act. Not once was he told. I understand that people in authoritarian countries must obey arbitrary orders. I had hoped that there was no such duty in the United States.

In my judgment, today's holding means that as a practical matter, minority speakers can be silenced in any city. . . . This is true regardless of the fact that in two other cases decided this day, Kunz v. New York, 340 U.S. 290 [noted below]; Niemotko v. Maryland, 340 U.S. 268,* a majority, in obedience to past decisions of this Court, provides a theoretical safeguard for freedom of speech. For whatever is thought to be guaranteed in Kunz and Niemotko is taken away by what is done here. The three cases read together mean that while previous restraints probably cannot be imposed on an unpopular speaker, the police have discretion to silence him as soon as the customary hostility to his views develops. . . .

Mr. Justice DOUGLAS, with whom Mr. Justice MINTON concurs, dissenting. . . .

A speaker may not, of course, incite a riot . . . .. But this record shows no such extremes. It shows an unsympathetic audience and the threat of one man to haul the speaker from the stage. It is against that kind of threat that speakers need police protection. If they do not receive it and instead the police throw their weight on the side of those who would break up the meetings, the police become the new censors of speech. Police censorship has all the vices of the censorship from city halls which we have repeatedly struck down. . . .

Mr. Justice FRANKFURTER, concurring in the result [in this case, Feiner, as well as in Kunz and Niemotko. Justice Frankfurter's review of the public places cases, printed earlier, came in this opinion.] . . .

. . . It is pertinent [to] note that all members of the New York Court accepted the finding that Feiner was stopped not because the listeners

should not be less alert to protect freedom of speech than it is to protect freedom of trade. [Footnote by Justice Black.]

* In Niemotko v. Maryland, 340 U.S. 268 (1951), members of Jehovah's Witnesses had been found guilty of disorderly conduct because of their attempt to hold a meeting in a municipal park without a permit. There was no evidence of disorder. Appellants had previously applied for and been refused a permit by officials acting pursuant to a local custom of non-statutory character under which permits had been granted to other religious and fraternal organizations. In applying for permits, the Witnesses had been questioned as to their religious beliefs rather than matters related to the orderly use of the park. On appeal the convictions were reversed, the Court concluding that use of the park was denied because of dislike for the appellants and their views.

or police officers disagreed with his views but because these officers were honestly concerned with preventing a breach of the peace. . . . Where conduct is within the allowable limits of free speech, the police are peace officers for the speaker as well as for his hearers. But the power effectively to preserve order cannot be displaced by giving a speaker complete immunity. Here, there were two police officers present for 20 minutes. They interfered only when they apprehended imminence of violence. It is not a constitutional principle that, in acting to preserve order, the police must proceed against the crowd, whatever its size and temper, and not against the speaker.

It is true that breach-of-peace statutes, like most tools of government, may be misused. . . . But the possibility of misuse is not alone a sufficient reason to deny New York the power here asserted or so limit it by constitutional construction as to deny its practical exercise.

EDWARDS v. SOUTH CAROLINA: "A FAR CRY" FROM FEINER?

1. *The decision.* In EDWARDS v. SOUTH CAROLINA, 372 U.S. 229 (1963), the Court reversed breach of peace convictions of 187 Black student demonstrators. Petitioners had walked along the South Carolina State House grounds to protest against racial discrimination. After a large crowd of onlookers gathered, they were ordered to disperse within fifteen minutes; when they did not do so, they were arrested. The Supreme Court, in an opinion by Justice Stewart, held that "South Carolina infringed the petitioners' constitutionally protected rights of free speech, free assembly, and freedom to petition for redress of their grievances." Justice Stewart noted that there had been no violence by the demonstrators or the onlookers; that there was no evidence of "fighting words"; and that the circumstances were "a far cry from the situation" in Feiner v. New York. He noted, too, that the convictions did not arise "from the evenhanded application of a precise and narrowly drawn regulatory statute evincing a legislative judgment that certain specific conduct be limited or proscribed. If, for example, the petitioners had been convicted upon evidence that they had violated a law regulating traffic, or had disobeyed a law reasonably limiting the periods during which the State House grounds were open to the public, this would be a different case." He added: "The Fourteenth Amendment does not permit a State to make criminal the peaceful expression of unpopular views."

Justice Clark's dissent viewed the record differently. To him, this "was by no means the passive demonstration which this Court relates. . . . The question [is] whether a State is constitutionally prohibited from enforcing laws to prevent breach of the peace in a situation where city officials in good faith believe, and the record shows, that disorder and violence are imminent, merely because the activities constituting that breach contain claimed elements of constitutionally protected speech and assembly. To me the answer under our cases is clearly in the negative." The situation in Feiner was "no more dangerous than that found here. . . . It is my belief that anyone conversant with the almost spontaneous combustion in some Southern communities in such a situation will agree that the City Manager's action may well have averted a major catastrophe."

2. *Some questions.* Why was the protest march in Edwards " a far cry" from Feiner? Because here there was "peaceful expression of unpopular views" rather than "incitement to riot," as the Court described Feiner's speech? Were those persuasive descriptions? Have the bounds of provocative speech changed since Feiner? Should the Court have said so? Note the references to Edwards in the cases that follow.

Does the difference lie in the fact that the onlookers in Edwards in fact remained peaceful and that ample police were at hand? What if there had been some disorder: would the speech still have been protected because most onlookers in most cities would remain peaceful? The demonstrators carried placards with such messages as "Down with segregation," and engaged in "chanting," "stamping feet," and "clapping hands"—conduct that created a "much greater danger of riot and disorder" than in Feiner, given the atmosphere in "some Southern communities," according to the dissent. Would an outbreak of disorder in these circumstances simply show police failure to protect "peaceful" speech? Or would it suggest that the speakers had used "fighting words"? Should the Court have spoken further about the hostile audience problem in Edwards? Did the Court clarify the modern Robert's Rules more satisfactorily in the later cases arising from modern street demonstrations (especially Cox I, in sec. 2C below)?

What kind of a "precise and narrowly drawn regulatory statute" would survive judicial scrutiny in light of Edwards? Could the state house grounds be declared off limits to demonstrations entirely, on a legislative finding that the risk of interference with legislative business was too great and that alternative places for demonstrations were available? Or does Edwards imply a guaranteed access to the state house grounds as a public forum at least during some hours? Could a statute such as that sustained with respect to court house picketing in Cox II (sec. 2C below) constitutionally curtail state house demonstrations?

THE GREGORY CASE: STREET DEMONSTRATIONS AND THE UNSOLVED PROBLEM OF THE HOSTILE AUDIENCE

Claims that speakers may be restrained because of the risk of violence in hostile audience responses have come to the Court recurrently. Feiner was the Vinson Court's reaction to the problem. Edwards was a Warren Court effort of the early sixties. The street demonstration cases of the mid-sixties, sec. 2C below, reflect additional encounters with the problem. A brief look at a 1969 decision appears here to illustrate that the hostile audience problem had not been solved by the end of the Warren era. Were the Warren Court analyses more adequate than the prior ones? What problems remain for solution if an adequate set of Robert's Rules is to be achieved?

1. *The decision.* In Gregory v. Chicago, 394 U.S. 111 (1969), petitioners had "marched in a peaceful and orderly procession from city hall to the mayor's residence to press their claims for desegregation of the public schools." When "the number of bystanders increased" and "the onlookers became unruly," Chicago police, "to prevent what they regarded as an im-

pending civil disorder," demanded that the demonstrators disperse. When petitioners refused to do so, they were arrested for disorderly conduct.

Chief Justice Warren's very brief opinion justifying the Court's reversal of the convictions asserted that this was "a simple case": as in Edwards v. South Carolina, petitioners' peaceful conduct was activity protected by the First Amendment; as in Thompson v. Louisville, sec. 1 above, the convictions were "totally devoid of evidentiary support" to show that the conduct was disorderly; and the trial judge's charge permitted the jury to convict for acts clearly entitled to First Amendment protection. Nor could the conviction rest on refusal to follow the dispersal request: petitioners were convicted for the demonstration, "not for a refusal to obey a police officer."

2. *The concurrence.* Justice Black's concurrence, joined by Justice Douglas, found some lurking complexities in the "simple case." After reviewing the facts, he noted that "both police and demonstrators made their best efforts faithfully to discharge their responsibilities as officers and citizens, but they were nevertheless unable to restrain the hostile hecklers within decent and orderly bounds." More generally, he concluded "that when groups with diametrically opposed, deep-seated views are permitted to air their emotional grievances, side by side, on city streets, tranquility and order cannot be maintained even by the joint efforts of the finest and best officers and of those who desire to be the most law-abiding protestors of their grievances." Here, he emphasized, the disorderly conduct convictions were especially vulnerable because the ordinance was not a narrowly drawn law, but rather "a meat-ax ordinance": the Court had repeatedly warned against the "use of sweeping, dragnet statutes that may, because of vagueness, jeopardize" First Amendment freedoms. But, he added, the Court had also been careful to assure that "the Constitution does not bar enactment of laws regulating conduct, even though connected with speech, press, assembly, and petition, if such laws specifically bar only the conduct deemed obnoxious and are carefully and narrowly aimed at that forbidden conduct. The dilemma revealed by this record is a crying example of a need for some such narrowly drawn law."

3. *Some questions, not all rhetorical.* Is Gregory—either in the Warren or Black emphases—a step forward toward evolution of Robert's Rules for the hostile audience problem? Is the Black-Douglas concluding reliance on the speech-conduct distinction helpful? What "specific ban on conduct" would do, in their view? Would a specific ban on marches in all residential areas be a constitutional "narrowly drawn" law? A ban on processions during certain hours? A specific ban on demonstrations near the mayor's residence? A limit on the number of participants? What "conduct," in short, may a "narrowly drawn" ordinance "deem obnoxious"? Anything, so long as it is "conduct," not pure speech, and so long as it is identified in a "narrowly drawn" statute? If so, what of streets as a public forum?

PERMIT REQUIREMENTS AND THE KUNZ CASE

Introduction. The cases from Feiner to Gregory considered efforts to deal with the hostile audience problem through the device of subsequent restraints. But can even "narrowly drawn" laws adequately deal with the problem if those laws must be applied after the fact? Can subsequent punishment laws adequately restrain on-the-spot police discretion? Would it be preferable to use a permit scheme, with prior notice of planned uses of public places, with the aim of providing adequate police protection for the speaker, and with clear standards to govern the issuance of permits? Should it be permissible to deny a permit for a meeting or parade because of anticipated fears of violence and hostile audience reactions? See generally Blasi, "Prior Restraints on Demonstrations," 68 Mich.L.Rev. 1481 (1970).

The recurrent problem of prior restraints and permit requirements, raised as early as Lovell v. Griffin and Cox v. New Hampshire above, reemerged in one of the cases decided together with Feiner. Note especially the last paragraph of the Jackson dissent in the Kunz case which follows, and consider the parallel to the Saia-Kovacs contrast in the Loudspeaker Cases above: Does it make sense to be so suspicious of prior licensing schemes (Saia, Kunz) when the state may penalize the speech by other, after-the-fact punishment routes (Kovacs, Feiner)? The problems raised by Kunz and licensing schemes are reexamined in the modern street demonstration context in the notes in sec. 2C below.

The Kunz case. KUNZ v. NEW YORK, 340 U.S. 290 (1951), reversed a conviction for violating a New York City ordinance which prohibited public worship meetings in the street "without first obtaining a permit" from the police commissioner. The ordinance also made it unlawful "to ridicule or denounce any form of religious belief" or to "expound atheism or agnosticism . . . in any street." Kunz, a Baptist minister, was convicted for holding a meeting in 1948 without a permit. He had obtained a permit in 1946, but that was revoked in the same year after an administrative hearing: there had been complaints that Kunz had engaged in "scurrilous attacks on Catholics and Jews," and the revocation was based on "evidence that he had ridiculed and denounced other religious beliefs in his meetings." Kunz's application for permits in 1947 and 1948 were "disapproved," without stated reason. Chief Justice Vinson's majority opinion included the following passages:

"Disapproval of the 1948 permit application by the police commissioner was justified by the New York courts on the ground that a permit had previously been revoked 'for good reasons.' It is noteworthy that there is no mention in the ordinance of reasons for which such a permit application can be refused. This interpretation allows the police commissioner, an administrative official, to exercise discretion in denying subsequent permit applications on the basis of his interpretation, at that time, of what is deemed to be conduct condemned by the ordinance. We have here, then, an ordinance which gives an administrative official discretionary power to control in advance the right of citizens to speak on religious matters on the streets of

New York. As such, the ordinance is clearly invalid as a prior restraint on the exercise of First Amendment rights. . . .

"The court below has mistakenly derived support for its conclusion from the evidence [that] appellant's religious meetings had, in the past, caused some disorder. There are appropriate public remedies to protect the peace and order of the community if appellant's speeches should result in disorder or violence. . . ." *

Justices Black and Frankfurter concurred in the result. Justice Jackson submitted a lengthy dissent; it included the following passages: "Essential freedoms are today threatened from without and within. It may become difficult to preserve here what a large part of the world has lost—the right to speak, even temperately, on matters vital to spirit and body. In such a setting, to blanket hateful and hate-stirring attacks on races and faiths under the protections for freedom of speech may be a noble innovation. On the other hand, it may be a quixotic tilt at windmills which belittles great principles of liberty. Only time can tell. But I incline to the latter view and cannot assent to the decision. [It] seems hypercritical to strike down local laws on their faces for want of standards when we have no standards.

"[I]f the Court conceives, as Feiner indicates, that upon uttering insulting, provocative or inciting words the policeman on the beat may stop the meeting, then its assurance of free speech in this decision is 'a promise to the ear to be broken to the hope,' if the patrolman on the beat happens to have prejudices of his own. . . . It seems to me that this [permit] procedure better protects freedom of speech than to let everyone speak without leave, but subject to surveillance and to being ordered to stop in the discretion of the police."

OFFENSIVE LANGUAGE AND THE SENSITIVE AUDIENCE

Introduction. In the cases from Chaplinsky, Feiner, and Kunz to Gregory, the state interest invoked to justify curtailment of the speaker was that in preventing violence: the fear was that the provocativeness of the speech would so enrage either the immediate addressee or the audience generally that disorder might result. But the Chaplinsky case above, though it is best known for its "fighting" words emphasis, did not speak about violence-risking words alone. Justice Murphy in Chaplinsky spoke also of a

---

* On the eve of the modern demonstration cases which follow, there was general agreement about the vulnerability of vague licensing requirements. The consensus, based on the decisions since Lovell v. Griffin, was stated in Staub v. City of Baxley, 355 U.S. 313 (1958):

An ordinance prohibited the solicitation of membership in dues-paying organizations without a permit from the Mayor and Council of the City. It was held "invalid on its face": "It is set- tled by a long line of recent decisions of this Court that an ordinance which, like this one, makes the peaceful enjoyment of freedoms which the Constitution guarantees contingent upon the uncontrolled will of an official— as by requiring a permit or license which may be granted or withheld in the discretion of such official—is an unconstitutional censorship or prior restraint upon the enjoyment of those freedoms."

category of words "which by their very utterance inflict injury" and whose suppression was justified not only by the "social interest" in "order" but also by that in "morality." The final group of materials in this section concentrates on that "offensive" rather than "fighting" words problem. The line between the categories is not clear cut: a sensitive audience shocked by the speaker's words may be so outraged as to resort to vigilante tactics. But the primary state interest invoked to justify curtailment of offensive language is not the fear of disorder. Rather, it is the concern with the psychological or emotional injury inflicted on the audience, and the broader and vaguer concern with a minimum level of "morality" in public discourse. Can offensive words be categorized as falling wholly outside the First Amendment, because of their "slight social value as a step to truth," in Justice Murphy's Chaplinsky phrase? Is such a "definitional" approach persuasive, or must some countervailing governmental interest be identified? What precisely are the interests allegedly justifying curtailment of offensive speech? To what extent, if any, do those interests legitimately justify curtailment of offensive speech?

In a series of modern cases, the Court has confronted efforts to bar offensive language. Consider the adequacy of the Court's responses in terms of a viable First Amendment theory—and especially in terms of an adequate assurance of a public forum. Should anything less than threatened violence justify restraint? Does recognition of audience reactions in this context create a "sensitive audience veto" rather than a "heckler's veto"? Can adequate standards be developed if permissibility of speech turns on the sensitivity of a particular audience? Is discourse in the public forum unduly curtailed if general standards of morality are adequate justification for restraint? *

COHEN v. CALIFORNIA

403 U.S. 15, 91 S.Ct. 1780, 29 L.Ed.2d 284 (1971).

Appeal from the Court of Appeal of California, Second Appellate District.

Mr. Justice HARLAN delivered the opinion of the Court.

This case may seem at first blush too inconsequential to find its way into our books, but the issue it presents is of no small constitutional significance.

Appellant Paul Robert Cohen was convicted in the Los Angeles Municipal Court of violating that part of California Penal Code § 415 which prohibits "maliciously and willfully disturb[ing] the peace or quiet of any neighborhood or person [by] offensive conduct." He was given 30 days'

---

* Recall the consideration of "morality" as adequate justification for regulatory action in connection with Roe v. Wade, the abortion case, with the substantive due process materials at the end of chap. 9 above. And note the considerable added attention to the "morality" justification for curbing speech in the obscenity cases, chap. 13, sec. 2, below.

imprisonment. The facts upon which his conviction rests are detailed in the opinion of the Court of Appeal of California:

"On April 26, 1968, the defendant was observed in the Los Angeles County Courthouse in the corridor outside of Division 20 of the Municipal Court wearing a jacket bearing the words 'Fuck the Draft' which were plainly visible. There were women and children present in the corridor. The defendant was arrested. The defendant testified that he wore the jacket as a means of informing the public of the depth of his feelings against the Vietnam War and the draft.

"The defendant did not engage in, nor threaten to engage in, nor did anyone as the result of his conduct in fact commit or threaten to commit any act of violence. The defendant did not make any loud or unusual noise, nor was there any evidence that he uttered any sound prior to his arrest."

In affirming the conviction the Court of Appeal held that "offensive conduct" means "behavior which has a tendency to provoke *others* to acts of violence or to in turn disturb the peace," and that the State had proved this element because, on the facts of this case, "[i]t was certainly reasonably foreseeable that such conduct might cause others to rise up to commit a violent act against the person of the defendant or attempt to forceably remove his jacket." [We reverse.]

I

In order to lay hands on the precise issue which this case involves, it is useful first to canvass various matters which this record does *not* present.

The conviction quite clearly rests upon the asserted offensiveness of the *words* Cohen used to convey his message to the public. The only "conduct" which the State sought to punish is the fact of communication. Thus, we deal here with a conviction resting solely upon "speech," cf. [Stromberg v. California, sec. 3 below], not upon any separately identifiable conduct which allegedly was intended by Cohen to be perceived by others as expressive of particular views but which, on its face, does not necessarily convey any message and hence arguably could be regulated without effectively repressing Cohen's ability to express himself. Cf. [United States v. O'Brien, sec. 3 below.] Further, the State certainly lacks power to punish Cohen for the underlying content of the message the inscription conveyed. At least so long as there is no showing of an intent to incite disobedience to or disruption of the draft, Cohen [could not] be punished for asserting the evident position on the inutility or immorality of the draft his jacket reflected. [Yates v. United States.]

Appellant's conviction, then, rests squarely upon his exercise of the "freedom of speech" [and] can be justified, if at all, only as a valid regulation of the manner in which he exercised that freedom, not as a permissible prohibition on the substantive message it conveys. This does not end the inquiry, of course, for the First and Fourteenth Amendments have never been thought to give absolute protection to every individual to speak whenever or wherever he pleases, or to use any form of address in any circumstances that he chooses. In this vein, too, however, we think it important to note that several issues typically associated with such problems are not presented here.

In the first place, Cohen was tried under a statute applicable throughout the entire State. Any attempt to support this conviction on the ground that the statute seeks to preserve an appropriately decorous atmosphere in the courthouse where Cohen was arrested must fail in the absence of any language in the statute that would have put appellant on notice that certain kinds of otherwise permissible speech or conduct would nevertheless, under California law, not be tolerated in certain places. See [Edwards v. South Carolina; Adderley v. Florida, sec. 2D below.] No fair reading of the phrase "offensive conduct" can be said sufficiently to inform the ordinary person that distinctions between certain locations are thereby created.[1]

In the second place, as it comes to us, this case cannot be said to fall within those relatively few categories of instances where prior decisions have established the power of government to deal more comprehensively with certain forms of individual expression simply upon a showing that such a form was employed. This is not, for example, an obscenity case. Whatever else may be necessary to give rise to the States' broader power to prohibit obscene expression, such expression must be, in some significant way, erotic. [Roth v. United States, chap. 13 below.] It cannot plausibly be maintained that this vulgar allusion to the Selective Service System would conjure up such psychic stimulation in anyone likely to be confronted with Cohen's crudely defaced jacket.

This Court has also held that the States are free to ban the simple use, without a demonstration of additional justifying circumstances, of so-called "fighting words," those personally abusive epithets which, when addressed to the ordinary citizen, are, as a matter of common knowledge, inherently likely to provoke violent reaction. [Chaplinsky v. New Hampshire.] While the four-letter word displayed by Cohen in relation to the draft is not uncommonly employed in a personally provocative fashion, in this instance it was clearly not "directed to the person of the hearer." [Cantwell v. Connecticut.] No individual actually or likely to be present could reasonably have regarded the words on appellant's jacket as a direct personal insult. Nor do we have here an instance of the exercise of the State's police power to prevent a speaker from intentionally provoking a given group to hostile reaction. Cf. [Feiner v. New York; Terminiello v. Chicago]. There is, as noted above, no showing that anyone who saw Cohen was in fact violently aroused or that appellant intended such a result.

Finally, in arguments before this Court much has been made of the claim that Cohen's distasteful mode of expression was thrust upon unwilling or unsuspecting viewers, and that the State might therefore legitimately act as it did in order to protect the sensitive from otherwise unavoidable exposure to appellant's crude form of protest. Of course, the mere presumed presence of unwitting listeners or viewers does not serve automatically to justify curtailing all speech capable of giving offense. See, e. g., [Keefe, noted above]. While this Court has recognized that government may

1. It is illuminating to note what transpired when Cohen entered a courtroom in the building. He removed his jacket and stood with it folded over his arm. Meanwhile, a policeman sent the presiding judge a note suggesting that Cohen be held in contempt of court. The judge declined to do so and Cohen was arrested by the officer only after he emerged from the courtroom. [Footnote by the Court.]

properly act in many situations to prohibit intrusion into the privacy of the home of unwelcome views and ideas which cannot be totally banned from the public dialogue, e. g., [Rowan, noted above], we have at the same time consistently stressed that "we are often 'captives' outside the sanctuary of the home and subject to objectionable speech." Id. The ability of government, consonant with the Constitution, to shut off discourse solely to protect others from hearing it is, in other words, dependent upon a showing that substantial privacy interests are being invaded in an essentially intolerable manner. Any broader view of this authority would effectively empower a majority to silence dissidents simply as a matter of personal predilections.

In this regard, persons confronted with Cohen's jacket were in a quite different posture than, say, those subjected to the raucous emissions of sound trucks blaring outside their residences. Those in the Los Angeles courthouse could effectively avoid further bombardment of their sensibilities simply by averting their eyes. And, while it may be that one has a more substantial claim to a recognizable privacy interest when walking through a courthouse corridor than, for example, strolling through Central Park, surely it is nothing like the interest in being free from unwanted expression in the confines of one's own home. Given the subtlety and complexity of the factors involved, if Cohen's "speech" was otherwise entitled to constitutional protection, we do not think the fact that some unwilling "listeners" in a public building may have been briefly exposed to it can serve to justify this breach of the peace conviction where, as here, there was no evidence that persons powerless to avoid appellant's conduct did in fact object to it, and where [the statute] evinces no concern [with] the special plight of the captive auditor, but, instead, indiscriminately sweeps within its prohibitions all "offensive conduct" that disturbs "any neighborhood or person." [2]

II

Against this background, the issue flushed by this case stands out in bold relief. It is whether California can excise, as "offensive conduct," one particular scurrilous epithet from the public discourse, either upon the theory of the court below that its use is inherently likely to cause violent reaction or upon a more general assertion that the States, acting as guardians of public morality, may properly remove this offensive word from the public vocabulary.

The rationale of the California court is plainly untenable. At most it reflects an "undifferentiated fear or apprehension of disturbance [which] is not enough to overcome the right to freedom of expression." [Tinker, sec. 3 below.] We have been shown no evidence that substantial numbers of cit-

2. In fact, other portions of the same statute do make some such distinctions. For example, the statute also prohibits disturbing "the peace or quiet [by] loud or unusual noise" and using "vulgar, profane or indecent language within the presence or hearing of women or children, in a loud and boisterous manner." This second-quoted provision in particular serves to put the actor on much fairer notice as to what is prohibited. It also buttresses our view that the "offensive conduct" portion, as construed and applied in this case, cannot legitimately be justified in this Court as designed or intended to make fine distinctions between differently situated recipients. [Footnote by Justice Harlan.]

izens are standing ready to strike out physically at whoever may assault their sensibilities with execrations like that uttered by Cohen.　There may be some persons about with such lawless and violent proclivities, but that is an insufficient base upon which to erect, consistently with constitutional values, a governmental power to force persons who wish to ventilate their dissident views into avoiding particular forms of expression.　The argument amounts to little more than the self-defeating proposition that to avoid physical censorship of one who has not sought to provoke such a response by a hypothetical coterie of the violent and lawless, the States may more appropriately effectuate that censorship themselves.

Admittedly, it is not so obvious that the First and Fourteenth Amendments must be taken to disable the States from punishing public utterance of this unseemly expletive in order to maintain what they regard as a suitable level of discourse within the body politic.　We think, however, that examination and reflection will reveal the shortcomings of a contrary viewpoint.

At the outset, we cannot overemphasize that, in our judgment, most situations where the State has a justifiable interest in regulating speech will fall within one or more of the various established exceptions, discussed above but not applicable here, to the usual rule that governmental bodies may not prescribe the form or content of individual expression.　Equally important to our conclusion is the constitutional backdrop against which our decision must be made.　The constitutional right of free expression is powerful medicine in a society as diverse and populous as ours.　It is designed and intended to remove governmental restraints from the arena of public discussion, putting the decision as to what views shall be voiced largely into the hands of each of us, in the hope that use of such freedom will ultimately produce a more capable citizenry and more perfect polity and in the belief that no other approach would comport with the premise of individual dignity and choice upon which our political system rests.　See [Whitney v. California], (concurring opinion of Brandeis, J.).

To many, the immediate consequence of this freedom may often appear to be only verbal tumult, discord, and even offensive utterance.　These are, however, within established limits, in truth necessary side effects of the broader enduring values which the process of open debate permits us to achieve.　That the air may at times seem filled with verbal cacophony is, in this sense, not a sign of weakness but of strength.　We cannot lose sight of the fact that, in what otherwise might seem a trifling and annoying instance of individual distasteful abuse of a privilege, these fundamental societal values are truly implicated.　.　.　.

Against this perception of the constitutional policies involved, we discern certain more particularized considerations that peculiarly call for reversal of this conviction.　First, the principle contended for by the State seems inherently boundless.　How is one to distinguish this from any other offensive word?　Surely the State has no right to cleanse public debate to the point where it is grammatically palatable to the most squeamish among us.　Yet no readily ascertainable general principle exists for stopping short of that result were we to affirm the judgment below.　For, while the particular four-letter word being litigated here is perhaps more distasteful than most others of its genre, it is nevertheless often true that one man's vulgarity is

another's lyric. Indeed, we think it is largely because governmental officials cannot make principled distinctions in this area that the Constitution leaves matters of taste and style so largely to the individual.

Additionally, we cannot overlook the fact, because it is well illustrated by the episode involved here, that much linguistic expression serves a dual communicative function: it conveys not only ideas capable of relatively precise, detached explication, but otherwise inexpressible emotions as well. In fact, words are often chosen as much for their emotive as their cognitive force. We cannot sanction the view that the Constitution, while solicitous of the cognitive content of individual speech, has little or no regard for that emotive function which, practically speaking, may often be the more important element of the overall message sought to be communicated. . . .

Finally, and in the same vein, we cannot indulge the facile assumption that one can forbid particular words without also running a substantial risk of suppressing ideas in the process. Indeed, governments might soon seize upon the censorship of particular words as a convenient guise for banning the expression of unpopular views. . . .

It is, in sum, our judgment that, absent a more particularized and compelling reason for its actions, the State may not, consistently with the First and Fourteenth Amendments, make the simple public display here involved of this single four-letter expletive a criminal offense. . . .

Reversed.*

Mr. Justice BLACKMUN, with whom The Chief Justice [BURGER] and Mr. Justice BLACK join.

I dissent, and I do so for two reasons:

1. Cohen's absurd and immature antic, in my view, was mainly conduct and little speech. See [Street v. New York, sec. 3 below; Cox I; Giboney v. Empire Storage Co.]. Further, the case appears to me to be well within the sphere of [Chaplinsky v. New Hampshire], where Mr. Justice Murphy, a known champion of First Amendment freedoms, wrote for a unanimous bench. As a consequence, this Court's agonizing over First Amendment values seems misplaced and unnecessary.

2. I am not at all certain that the California Court of Appeal's construction of § 415 is now the authoritative California construction. . . . A month [after the ruling below], the State Supreme Court in another case construed § 415, evidently for the first time. In re Bushman. [The Bushman decision stated:] "[The statute] makes punishable only wilful and malicious conduct that is violent and endangers public safety and order

---

* Note the references to Cohen, and the majority's general tracking of Justice Harlan's approach, in the per curiam reversal of a disorderly conduct conviction in Hess v. Indiana, 414 U.S. 105 (1973) (discussed in sec. 1E above). After police had cleared anti-war demonstrators from a street, Hess, standing at the curb, had said: "We'll take the fucking street later (or again)." The Court noted that these words were not punishable as obscene: "Indeed, after [Cohen v. California], such a contention with regard to the language at issue would not be tenable." The Court also cited Cohen in noting that the words were not punishable as "fighting words" or as a public nuisance invading substantial privacy interests. The Brandenburg incitement standard provided the primary ground for reversal.

or that creates a clear and present danger that others will engage in violence of that nature. [It] does not make criminal any nonviolent act unless the act incites or threatens to incite others to violence." Cohen was cited in Bushman, but I am not convinced that its description there and Cohen itself are completely consistent with the "clear and present danger" standard enunciated in Bushman. [This case] ought to be remanded for reconsideration in the light of [Bushman].†

Mr. Justice WHITE concurs in Paragraph 2 of Mr. Justice Blackmun's dissenting opinion.

THE BURGER COURT AND THE PROBLEM OF OFFENSIVE LANGUAGE

1. *Gooding v. Wilson.* In a decision that provoked a major attack on the overbreadth technique (see sec. 1E above), a divided Court reversed a conviction under a Georgia statute providing that any person "who shall, without provocation, use to or of another, and in his presence . . . opprobrious words or abusive language, tending to cause a breach of the peace," was guilty of a misdemeanor. Appellee and others, anti-war picketers at an Army building, refused a police request to stop blocking access to inductees. In the ensuing scuffle, appellee said to a policeman, "white son of a bitch, I'll kill you," "You son of a bitch, I'll choke you to death," and "You son of a bitch, if you ever put your hands on me again, I'll cut you all to pieces." The Court's 4 to 3 decision found that statute void on its face, primarily on overbreadth grounds. GOODING v. WILSON, 405 U.S. 518 (1972).

Justice Brennan's majority opinion rejected the State's argument that the state courts had construed the statute so as to cover only the "fighting words" punishable under Chaplinsky. Justice Brennan replied: "We have [made] our own examination of the Georgia cases [and conclude that] Georgia appellate decisions have not construed [the statute] to be limited in application, as in Chaplinsky, to words that 'have a direct tendency to cause acts of violence by the person to whom, individually, the remark is addressed.'" Accordingly, the statute was overbroad: it was "susceptible of application to protected expression."

The bases for that reading of the Georgia law are illustrated by the following passage in Justice Brennan's opinion: "The dictionary definitions of 'opprobrious' and 'abusive' give them greater reach than 'fighting' words. Webster's Third New International Dictionary (1961) defined 'opprobrious' as 'conveying or intended to convey disgrace,' and 'abusive' as including 'harsh insulting language.' Georgia appellate decisions have construed § 26–6303 to apply to utterances that, although within these definitions, are not 'fighting' words as Chaplinsky defines them. In Lyons v. State, 94 Ga.App. 570, 95 S.E.2d 478 (1956), a conviction under the statute was sustained for

------

† Justice Harlan's majority opinion commented on this passage as follows: "We perceive no difference of substance between the Bushman con-struction and that of the [court below in Cohen], particularly in light of the Bushman court's approving citation of Cohen."

awakening 10 women scout leaders on a camp-out by shouting, 'Boys, this is where we are going to spend the night.' 'Get the G- - d- - - bed rolls out . . . let's see how close we can come to the G- - d- - - tents.' Again, in Fish v. State, 124 Ga. 416, 52 S.E. 737 (1905), the Georgia Supreme Court held that a jury question was presented by the remark, 'You swore a lie.' Again, Jackson v. State, 14 Ga.App. 19, 80 S.E. 20 (1913), held that a jury question was presented by the words addressed to another, 'God damn you, why don't you get out of the road?' Plainly, although 'convey-ing . . . disgrace' or 'harsh insulting language,' these were not words 'which by their very utterance . . . tend to incite an immed-iate breach of the peace.' [Chaplinsky]." *

A dissent by Chief Justice Burger objected to this "bizarre result." He found in the state courts' construction no "significant potential for sweep-ing application" to protected speech: "If words are to bear their common meaning, and are to be considered in context, rather than dissected with surgical precision using a semantic scalpel, this statute has little potential for application outside the realm of 'fighting words.'" In addition to his general attack on excessive use of overbreadth and his advocacy of a *"sub-stantial* overbreadth" approach, noted in sec. 1E above, he objected to the reliance on state court decisions "in a few isolated cases, decided as long ago as 1905 and generally long before" Chaplinsky in 1942. In another dis-sent, Justice Blackmun, joined by Chief Justice Burger, found it "strange, in-deed," that an appellee using language such as that involved here could not be convicted under a statute such as Georgia's.

2. *The 1972 trilogy: Rosenfeld, Lewis, and Brown.* At the end of the Term during which Gooding v. Wilson was decided, the majority sum-marily vacated and remanded three other convictions for use of offensive language; and those cases provided the Gooding dissenters as well as the two new appointees who had just taken their seats—Justices Rehnquist and Powell—an opportunity to voice their concern about the majority's unduly narrow view of the states' power to restrain offensive words. The three de-cisions were ROSENFELD v. NEW JERSEY, LEWIS v. NEW ORLEANS, and BROWN v. OKLAHOMA, reported at 408 U.S. 901, 913, and 914 (1972). Rosenfeld and Brown were remanded for reconsideration in the light of Cohen v. California and Gooding v. Wilson. Lewis was remanded for reconsideration only in light of Gooding, the overbreadth case. Chief Justice Burger and Justices Blackmun and Rehnquist dissented in all three cases. Justice Powell concurred in the results in Lewis and Brown and dis-sented in Rosenfeld.

In Rosenfeld, appellant had addressed a school board meeting attended by about 150 people, including women and children, and had "used the ad-jective 'm- - - f- - - -' [sic] on four occasions, to describe the teachers, the school board, the town and his own country." He was convicted under a

---

* In a footnote, Justice Brennan noted that the dissents "question reliance upon Georgia cases decided more than fifty years ago." He replied that the 1905 and 1913 Georgia decisions had been cited by the highest state court as late as 1967 and accordingly "re-main authoritative interpretations" in Georgia.

"disorderly person" statute prohibiting "indecent" and "offensive" language in public places and interpreted to cover words "of such a nature as to be likely to incite the hearer to an immediate breach of the peace or to be likely, in the light of the gender and age of the listener and the setting of the utterance, to affect the sensibilities of a hearer." In Lewis, appellant addressed police officers who were arresting her son as g- - d- - - m- - - - - f- - - - -. She was convicted under a breach of the peace statute prohibiting anyone from wantonly cursing, reviling, or using "obscene or opprobrious language" toward a policeman on duty. Brown, finally, involved an appellant who, in a meeting at a university chapel, referred to some policemen as "m- - - - - f- - - - - fascist pig cops" and to a particular policeman as that "black m- - - - - f- - - - - - pig." He was convicted under a statute barring "any obscene or lascivious language or word in any public place, or in the presence of females."

Justice Powell's separate opinions explained his differing votes in the three situations. In Rosenfeld, he thought Cohen distinguishable and described the words as a "gross abuse of the respected privilege in this country of allowing every citizen to speak his mind." He conceded that the language "perhaps" did not constitute "fighting words" in the sense of Chaplinsky. Physical retaliation against the speaker was unlikely. Nor were the words directed at a specific individual. But the Chaplinsky principle was not so limited, he insisted: "It also extends to the willful use of scurrilous language calculated to offend the sensibilities of an unwilling audience." [Recall the Court's opinion in Chaplinsky.] He stated that "a verbal assault on an unwilling audience may be so grossly offensive and emotionally disturbing as to be the proper subject of criminal proscription, whether under a statute denominating it [to be] disorderly conduct, or, more accurately, a public nuisance." * In the other two cases, Justice Powell concurred with the majority. In Lewis, he urged reconsideration solely in light of Chaplinsky, not Gooding. [But see his position when the Lewis case returned to the Court two years later, note 3 below.] He explained that he would have no doubt that the words would have been "fighting words" if they "had been addressed by one citizen to another, face to face and in a hostile manner." But he added that "the situation may be different where such words are addressed to a police officer trained to exercise a higher degree of restraint than the average citizen." And in Brown, Justice Powell emphasized that the language had been used in the course of "a political meeting to which appellant had been invited to present the Black Panther viewpoint. In these circum-

---

* More generally, Justice Powell emphasized that there were significant values other than speech: "One of the hallmarks of a civilized society is the level and quality of discourse. We have witnessed in recent years a disquieting deterioration in standards of taste and civility in speech. For the increasing number of persons who derive satisfaction from vocabularies dependent upon filth and obscenities, there are abundant opportunities to gratify their debased tastes. But our free society must be flexible enough to tolerate even such a debasement provided it occurs without subjecting unwilling audiences to the type of verbal nuisance committed in this case. The shock and sense of affront, and sometimes the injury to mind and spirit, can be as great from words as from some physical attacks."

stances language of the character charged might well have been anticipated by the audience." †

The other three dissenters took broader positions. Chief Justice Burger's opinion stated: "When we undermine the general belief that the law will give protection against fighting words and profane and abusive language such as the utterances involved in these cases, we take steps to return to the law of the jungle." In a case like Rosenfeld, there might not be instantaneous retaliation, but it was imaginable that "some justifiably outraged parent whose family were exposed to the foul mouthings of the speaker would 'meet him outside' [and] resort to the 19th Century's vigorous modes of dealing with such people." Justice Rehnquist's dissent stated his agreement with Justice Blackmun's dissent in Cohen and explained that he "would not deny to these States the power to punish language of the sort used here by appropriate legislation." Lewis' words were "fighting words," and the words in the other two cases were "lewd and obscene" and "profane" in the Chaplinsky sense.**

3. *Some 1974 afterthoughts.* a. *Lewis II.* When the Lewis case returned to the Court in 1974, it produced an outright reversal on overbreadth grounds, with Justice Powell joining the support of that technique in this context and with Justice Blackmun, joined by Chief Justice Burger and Justice Rehnquist, objecting to that approach at length. Lewis v. New Orleans, 415 U.S. 130 (1974). Justice Brennan's majority opinion found nothing in the state court's opinion after the remand in Lewis I "that makes any meaningful attempt to limit or properly define—as limited by Chaplinsky and Gooding—'opprobrious,' or indeed any other term" in the statute. In a separate concurrence in Lewis II, Justice Powell, who had objected to the overbreadth remand in Lewis I, now agreed that "the ordinance is facially overbroad." He emphasized that the law "confers on police a virtually unrestrained power" and added: "The present type of ordinance tends to be invoked only where there is no other valid basis for arresting an objectionable or suspicious person. The opportunity for abuse, especially where a statute has received a virtually open-ended interpretation, is self-evident." In a dissent, Justice Blackmun, joined by Chief Justice Burger and Justice Rehnquist, launched another strong attack on the overbreadth technique. He insisted that overbreadth and vagueness in the speech area had "become result-oriented rubberstamps attuned to the easy and imagined self-assurance

---

† Contrast, with Justice Powell's emphasis on the factual setting in Brown and Lewis, his silence about the context in Rosenfeld (involving a White school teacher supporting Black claims at a school board meeting). See Gunther, ". . . The Case of Justice Powell," 24 Stan.L.Rev. 1001 (1972).

** Note also the decision a year later in Papish v. Board of Curators of Univ. of Missouri, 410 U.S. 667 (1973). There, the 6 to 3 majority summarily set aside the expulsion of a graduate student for distributing on campus a publication which, inter alia, used the

"M_____ f_____" language. Justice Rehnquist's dissent, joined by Chief Justice Burger and Justice Blackmun, insisted that even if Rosenfeld were correct, this case, not involving criminal sanctions, was distinguishable. And a separate dissent by the Chief Justice thought the extension of the Cohen-Rosenfeld precedents to the campus situation was "curious—even bizarre." (See the materials on the First Amendment in the school context, chap. 13, sec. 4, below.) He thought publications "which are at the same time obscene and infantile" could be prohibited.

that 'one man's vulgarity is another's lyric.' [Cohen v. California.] If the Court adheres to its present course, no state statute or city ordinance will be acceptable unless it parrots the wording of our opinions."

b. *Eaton.* In the Court's disposition of another offensive language problem, in Eaton v. City of Tulsa, 415 U.S. 697 (1974), the overbreadth technique played no part. Eaton, on trial for violation of a municipal ordinance, had answered a question on cross-examination by referring to an alleged assailant as "chicken shit." He was convicted of criminal contempt for "insolent behavior" in open court. The Court's per curiam reversal stated that this "single isolated usage of street vernacular, not directed at the judge or any officer of the court, cannot constitutionally support the conviction of criminal contempt." The court relied on a 1947 case, Craig v. Harney, one of a number of cases in the next chapter developing the clear and present danger test in the contempt-of-court context. The concurring opinion by Justice Powell emphasized "that petitioner received no prior warning or caution from the trial judge with respect to court etiquette. It may well be, in view of contemporary standards as to the use of vulgar and even profane language, that this particular petitioner had no reason to believe that this expletive would be offensive or in any way disruptive of proper courtroom decorum. Language likely to offend the sensibility of some listeners is now fairly commonplace in many social gatherings as well as in public performances." Justice Rehnquist's dissent, joined by Chief Justice Burger and Justice Blackmun, thought it unclear that the contempt conviction here had rested "solely on the use of the expletive." He added in a footnote, however, that petitioner "could constitutionally be punished for the use of the expletive."

4. *Some questions.* Reconsider, in light of the offensive language cases beginning with Cohen, whether anything other than the risk of violent retaliation justifies restraint on offensive language. Does the majority still endorse restriction on words that, as Chaplinsky put it, "by their very utterance inflict injury"? Does shock, or the sensitivities of the audience, justify restraint? To Justice Harlan in Cohen? Can audience sensitivity be recognized as a basis for restraint without endorsing an undue "sensitive auditor's" veto akin to the "heckler's veto"? Compare the efforts to justify obscenity controls in the interest of protecting the sensibilities of the unwilling audience (chap. 13, sec. 2, below).

Do the majority or the dissenters recognize a more general legitimate interest in "morality"—or, as Justice Harlan put it in Cohen, maintaining a "suitable level of discourse within the body politic"? Compare Justice Harlan's recognition of a legitimate state morality concern in the context of prohibitions of contraceptives (in his Poe v. Ullman dissent, printed together with Griswold v. Connecticut, chap. 9 above); and compare the reemergence of a "morality" or "decency" concern in the obscenity context, chap. 13, sec. 2, below. Is recognition of an audience sensitivity or "privacy" interest as a restraint on offensive language more defensible than a more general social interest in morality or in the "level of discourse"? Should the legitimacy of restraints on offensive language turn on the context of the particular audience, as Justice Powell suggests? Is Justice Powell's effort to pull together the three notions of "nuisance, audience expecta-

tions, and policemen's higher degree of restraint" a useful approach to the offensive language problem? See Gunther, ". . . The Case of Justice Powell," 24 Stan.L.Rev. 1001 (1972).

C. DEMONSTRATIONS IN TRADITIONAL PUBLIC PLACES SUCH AS STREETS: THE MODERN CONTEXT OF THE PUBLIC FORUM

Introduction. How useful are the analyses developed in the public places cases of the thirties and forties for the solution of the street demonstration problems of the sixties and seventies? Most early cases were stimulated by the "robust evangelism" of the Jehovah's Witnesses. During the fifties, as Professor Kalven remarks, "the story of the streets became a bit quaint." But by the sixties, it became clear "that the story is not over": the civil rights movement took to the streets; it was predictable that "the Court's formidable business in the immediate future will require it to confront the issues raised by today's Negro 'evangelism.'" Kalven, "The Concept of the Public Forum: Cox v. Louisiana," 1965 Sup.Ct.Rev. 1.

The Jehovah's Witnesses' evangelism may have been "robust," but it was largely the proselytizing of the single evangelist, selling magazines, ringing doorbells, speaking at street corners. The "evangelism" of the sixties— by the anti-war movement as well as by civil rights groups—was one of numbers, of parades in streets and vigils in parks, of protest meetings in front of and inside public buildings. With a greater need than ever for Robert's Rules, how did the Court respond? The Edwards and Gregory cases above illustrate some Warren Court answers. Are the modern cases which follow more adequate? Are old Rules clarified and adapted to new circumstances? Are the judicial techniques responsive and adequate to the task? The doctrinal tools developed in the preceding pages intertwine in the cases that follow; new techniques emerge; but the problems of principle and practice raised earlier persist as challenges in the examination of the modern cases.

COX v. LOUISIANA

[COX I—No. 24, 1964 Term]

379 U.S. 536, 85 S.Ct. 453, 13 L.Ed.2d 471 (1965).

Appeal from the Supreme Court of Louisiana.

Mr. Justice GOLDBERG delivered the opinion of the Court.

Appellant, the Reverend Mr. B. Elton Cox, the leader of a civil rights demonstration, was arrested and charged with four offenses under Louisiana law—criminal conspiracy, disturbing the peace, obstructing public passages, and picketing before a courthouse. In a consolidated trial before a judge without a jury, and on the same set of facts, he was acquitted of criminal

conspiracy but convicted of the other three offenses. He was sentenced to serve four months in jail and pay a $200 fine for disturbing the peace, to serve five months in jail and pay a $500 fine for obstructing public passages, and to serve one year in jail and pay a $5,000 fine for picketing before a courthouse. The sentences were cumulative.

.   .   .   Appellant filed two separate appeals to this Court [contending] that the three statutes under which he was convicted were unconstitutional on their face and as applied. [This] case, No. 24, involves the convictions for disturbing the peace and obstructing public passages, and No. 49 [Cox II, which follows] concerns the conviction for picketing before a courthouse.

I.—THE FACTS.

On December 14, 1961, 23 students from Southern University, a Negro college, were arrested in downtown Baton Rouge, Louisiana, for picketing stores that maintained segregated lunch counters. This picketing, urging a boycott of those stores, was part of a general protest movement against racial segregation, directed by the local chapter of the Congress of Racial Equality .   .   .. The appellant, an ordained Congregational minister, the Reverend Mr. B. Elton Cox, a Field Secretary of CORE, was an advisor to this movement. On the evening of December 14, [he] spoke at a mass meeting at the college. The students resolved to demonstrate the next day in front of the courthouse in protest of segregation and the arrest and imprisonment of the picketers who were being held in the parish jail located on the upper floor of the courthouse building.

The next morning about 2,000 students left the campus, which was located approximately five miles from downtown Baton Rouge. [Because the student leaders were in jail], Cox felt it his duty to take over the demonstration and see that it was carried out as planned. .   .   .

As Cox, [at] the head of the group, approached the vicinity of the courthouse, he was stopped [and] brought to Police Chief Wingate White. [The Chief] inquired as to the purpose of the demonstration. [Cox] outlined his program to White, stating that it would include a singing of the Star Spangled Banner and a "freedom song," recitation of the Lord's Prayer and the Pledge of Allegiance, and a short speech. White testified that he told Cox that "he must confine" the demonstration "to the west side of the street." White added, "This, of course, was not—I didn't meant it in the import that I was giving him any permission to do it, but I was presented with a situation that was accomplished, and I had to make a decision." Cox testified that the officials agreed to permit the meeting. .   .   .

The students were then directed by Cox to the west sidewalk, across the street from the courthouse, 101 feet from its steps. They were lined up on this sidewalk about five deep and spread almost the entire length of the block. The group did not obstruct the street. It was close to noon and, being lunch time, a small crowd of 100 to 300 curious white people .   .   . gathered on the east sidewalk and courthouse steps, about 100 feet from the demonstrators. Seventy-five to eighty policemen, including city and state patrolmen and members of the Sheriff's staff, as well as members of

the fire department and a fire truck were stationed in the street between the two groups.   .   .   .

[Some students displayed picket signs advocating boycotts of "unfair" stores. The students] then sang "God Bless America," pledged allegiance to the flag, prayed briefly, and sang one or two hymns, including "We Shall Overcome." The 23 students, who were locked in jail cells in the courthouse building out of the sight of the demonstrators, responded by themselves singing; this in turn was greeted with cheers and applause by the demonstrators. Appellant gave a speech, described by a State's witness as follows:

> "He said that in effect that it was a protest against the illegal arrest of some of their members and that other people were allowed to picket .   .   .   and he said that they were not going to commit any violence, that if anyone spit on them, they would not spit back on the person that did it."

Cox then said:

> "All right. It's lunch time. Let's go eat. There are twelve stores we are protesting. A number of these stores have twenty counters; they accept your money from nineteen. They won't accept it from the twentieth counter. This is an act of racial discrimination. These stores are open to the public. You are members of the public. We pay taxes to the Federal Government and you who live here pay taxes to the State."

In apparent reaction to these last remarks, there was what state witnesses described as "muttering" and "grumbling" by the white onlookers.

The Sheriff, deeming, as he testified, Cox's appeal to the students to sit in at the lunch counters to be "inflammatory," then took a power microphone and said, "Now you have been allowed to demonstrate. Up until now your demonstration has been more or less peaceful, but what you are doing now is a direct violation of the law, a disturbance of the peace, and it has got to be broken up immediately." The testimony as to what then happened is disputed. Some of the State's witnesses testified that Cox said, "don't move"; others stated that he made a "gesture of defiance." It is clear from the record, however, that Cox and the demonstrators did not then and there break up the demonstration.   .   .   .

Almost immediately thereafter—within a time estimated variously at two to five minutes—one of the policemen exploded a tear gas shell at the crowd. This was followed by several other shells. The demonstrators quickly dispersed, running back towards the State Capitol and the downtown area.   .   .   .   No Negroes participating in the demonstration were arrested on that day.   .   .   .   The next day appellant was arrested and charged with the four offenses above described.

II.—The Breach of the Peace Conviction.

Appellant was convicted of violating a Louisiana "disturbing the peace" statute, which provides:

> "Whoever with intent to provoke a breach of the peace, or under circumstances such that a breach of the peace may be occasioned thereby

[crowds or congregates with others upon] . . . a public street or public highway, or upon a public sidewalk, or any other public place or building [and] who fails or refuses to disperse and move on, [when] ordered so to do by any law enforcement officer [shall] be guilty of disturbing the peace." . . .

It is clear to us that on the facts of this case, which are strikingly similar to those present in [Edwards v. South Carolina], Louisiana infringed appellant's rights of free speech and free assembly by convicting him under this statute. . . . We hold that Louisiana may not constitutionally punish appellant under this statute for engaging in the type of conduct which this record reveals, and also that the statute as authoritatively interpreted by the Louisiana Supreme Court is unconstitutionally broad in scope.

[O]ur independent examination of the record, which we are required to make, shows no conduct which the State had a right to prohibit as a breach of the peace. [The State argues] that while the demonstrators started out to be orderly, the loud cheering and clapping by the students in response to the singing from the jail converted the peaceful assembly into a riotous one. The record, however, does not support this assertion. . . . Our conclusion that the entire meeting from the beginning until its dispersal by tear gas was orderly and not riotous is confirmed by a film of the events taken by a television news photographer. [We] have viewed the film, and it reveals that the students, though they undoubtedly cheered and clapped, were well-behaved throughout. . . .

Finally, the State contends that the conviction should be sustained because of fear expressed by some of the state witnesses that "violence was about to erupt" because of the demonstration. It is virtually undisputed, however, that the students themselves were not violent and threatened no violence. The fear of violence seems to have been based upon the reaction of the group of white citizens looking on from across the street. . . . There is no indication, however, that any member of the white group threatened violence. And this small crowd estimated at between 100 and 300 were separated from the students by "seventy-five to eighty" armed policemen . . . .. As Inspector Trigg testified, they could have handled the crowd. This situation, like that in Edwards, is "a far cry from the situation in [Feiner]." Nor is there any evidence here of "fighting words." . . . .

There is an additional reason why this conviction cannot be sustained. The statute at issue in this case, as authoritatively interpreted by the Louisiana Supreme Court, is unconstitutionally vague in its overly broad scope. The statutory crime consists of two elements: (1) congregating with others "with intent to provoke a breach of the peace, or under circumstances such that a breach of the peace may be occasioned," and (2) a refusal to move on after having been ordered to do so by a law enforcement officer. While the second part of this offense is narrow and specific, the first element is not. The Louisiana Supreme Court in this case defined ["breach of the peace"] as "to agitate, to arouse from a state of repose, to molest, to interrupt, to hinder, to disquiet." [That] would allow persons to be punished merely for peacefully expressing unpopular views. . . . Therefore, as in Terminiello and Edwards the conviction under this statute must be reversed

as the statute is unconstitutional in that it sweeps within its broad scope activities that are constitutionally protected . . ..

III. THE OBSTRUCTING PUBLIC PASSAGES CONVICTION.

We now turn to the issue of the validity of appellant's conviction for violating the Louisiana statute [which] provides:

"No person shall wilfully obstruct the free, convenient and normal use of any public sidewalk, street, . . . or other passageway, or the entrance, corridor or passage of any public building, . . . by impeding, hindering, stifling, retarding or restraining traffic or passage thereon or therein.

"Providing however nothing herein contained shall apply to a bona fide legitimate labor organization or to any of its legal activities such as picketing . . .."

Appellant was convicted under this statute [for] leading the meeting on the sidewalk across the street from the courthouse. . . .

[Appellant's free speech contention] raises an issue with which this Court has dealt in many decisions. . . . From these decisions certain clear principles emerge. The rights of free speech and assembly, while fundamental in our democratic society, still do not mean that everyone with opinions or beliefs to express may address a group at any public place and at any time. The constitutional guarantee of liberty implies the existence of an organized society maintaining public order, without which liberty itself would be lost in the excesses of anarchy. The control of travel on the streets is a clear example of governmental responsibility to insure this necessary order. A restriction in that relation, designed to promote the public convenience in the interest of all, and not susceptible to abuses of discriminatory application, cannot be disregarded by the attempted exercise of some civil right which, in other circumstances, would be entitled to protection. One would not be justified in ignoring the familiar red light because this was thought to be a means of social protest. Nor could one, contrary to traffic regulations, insist upon a street meeting in the middle of Times Square at the rush hour as a form of freedom of speech or assembly. Governmental authorities have the duty and responsibility to keep their streets open and available for movement. A group of demonstrators could not insist upon the right to cordon off a street, or entrance to a public or private building, and allow no one to pass who did not agree to listen to their exhortations. . . .

We emphatically reject the notion urged by appellant that the First and Fourteenth Amendments afford the same kind of freedom to those who would communicate ideas by conduct such as patrolling, marching, and picketing on streets and highways, as these amendments afford to those who communicate ideas by pure speech. . . . We reaffirm the statement of the Court in Giboney v. Empire Storage & Ice Co. [chap. 13, sec. 4], that "it has never been deemed an abridgment of freedom of speech or press to make a course of conduct illegal merely because the conduct was in part initiated, evidenced, or carried out by means of language, either spoken, written, or printed."

We have no occasion in this case to consider the constitutionality of the uniform, consistent, and nondiscriminatory application of a statute forbidding all access to streets and other public facilities for parades and meetings. Although the statute here involved on its face precludes all street assemblies and parades, it has not been so applied and enforced by the Baton Rouge authorities. City officials who testified for the State clearly indicated that certain meetings and parades are permitted in Baton Rouge, even though they have the effect of obstructing traffic, provided prior approval is obtained. . . . The statute itself provides no standards for the determination of local officials as to which assemblies to permit or which to prohibit. . . . From all the evidence before us it appears that the authorities in Baton Rouge permit or prohibit parades or street meetings in their completely uncontrolled discretion.

The situation is thus the same as if the statute itself expressly provided that there could only be peaceful parades or demonstrations in the unbridled discretion of the local officials. The pervasive restraint on freedom of discussion by the practice of the authorities under the statute is not any less effective than a statute expressly permitting such selective enforcement. . . .

This Court has recognized that the lodging of such broad discretion in a public official allows him to determine which expressions of view will be permitted and which will not. This thus sanctions a device for the suppression of the communication of ideas and permits the official to act as a censor. . . . Also inherent in such a system allowing parades or meetings only with the prior permission of an official is the obvious danger to the right of a person or group not to be denied equal protection of the laws. . . . It is clearly unconstitutional to enable a public official to determine which expressions of view will be permitted and which will not or to engage in invidious discrimination among persons or groups either by use of a statute providing a system of broad discretionary licensing power or, as in this case, the equivalent of such a system by selective enforcement of an extremely broad prohibitory statute. . . . It is, of course, undisputed that appropriate, limited discretion, under properly drawn statutes or ordinances, concerning the time, place, duration, or manner of use of the streets for public assemblies may be vested in administrative officials. [Cox v. New Hampshire.] . . .

Reversed.

[The separate opinions are printed with Cox II, the next principal case.]

COX v. LOUISIANA

[COX II—No. 49, 1964 Term]

379 U.S. 559, 85 S.Ct. 476, 13 L.Ed.2d 487 (1965).

Appeal from the Supreme Court of Louisiana.

Mr. Justice GOLDBERG delivered the opinion of the Court.

Appellant was convicted of violating a Louisiana statute which provides:

"Whoever, with the intent of interfering with, obstructing, or impeding the administration of justice, or with the intent of influencing any judge, juror, witness, or court officer, in the discharge of his duty pickets or parades in or near a building housing a court of the State of Louisiana . . . shall be fined not more than five thousand dollars or imprisoned not more than one year, or both."

This charge was based upon the same set of facts as [the] charges involved and set forth in No. 24 [above]. . . .

We shall first consider appellant's contention that this statute must be declared invalid on its face as an unjustified restriction upon freedoms guaranteed by the First and Fourteenth Amendments to the United States Constitution.

This statute was passed by Louisiana in 1950 and was modeled after a [federal law of 1950] pertaining to the federal judiciary [— a law which] resulted from the picketing of federal courthouses by partisans of the defendants during trials involving leaders of the Communist Party.

This statute, unlike the two previously considered, is a precise, narrowly drawn regulatory statute which proscribes certain specific behavior. . . . It prohibits a particular type of conduct, namely, picketing and parading, in a few specified locations, in or near courthouses.

There can be no question that a State has a legitimate interest in protecting its judicial system from the pressures which picketing near a courthouse might create. Since we are committed to a government of laws and not of men, it is of the utmost importance that the administration of justice be absolutely fair and orderly. This Court has recognized that the unhindered and untrammeled functioning of our courts is part of the very foundation of our constitutional democracy. See Wood v. Georgia, 370 U.S. 375, 383 [chap. 13, sec. 4]. The constitutional safeguards relating to the integrity of the criminal process attend every stage of a criminal proceeding [and] they exclude influence or domination by either a hostile or friendly mob. There is no room at any stage of judicial proceedings for such intervention; mob law is the very antithesis of due process. . . . A State may adopt safeguards necessary and appropriate to assure that the administration of justice at all stages is free from outside control and influence. A narrowly drawn statute such as the one under review is obviously a safeguard both necessary and appropriate to vindicate the State's interest in assuring justice under law.

Nor does such a statute infringe upon the constitutionally protected rights of free speech and free assembly. The conduct which is the subject of this statute—picketing and parading—is subject to regulation even though

intertwined with expression and association. The examples are many of the application by this Court of the principle that certain forms of conduct mixed with speech may be regulated or prohibited. . . .

Bridges v. California, 314 U.S. 252, and Pennekamp v. Florida, 328 U.S. 331 [cases, like Wood above, applying the clear and present danger test in reversing contempt of court convictions—see chap. 13, sec. 4, below] do not hold to the contrary. . . . Here we deal not with the contempt power [but with] a statute narrowly drawn . . . . We are not concerned here with such a pure form of expression as newspaper comment or a telegram by a citizen to a public official. We deal in this case not with free speech alone, but with expression mixed with particular conduct. . . .

We hold that this statute on its face is a valid law dealing with conduct subject to regulation so as to vindicate important interests of society and that the fact that free speech is intermingled with such conduct does not bring with it constitutional protection.

We now deal with the Louisiana statute as applied to the conduct in this case. The group of 2,000, led by appellant, paraded and demonstrated before the courthouse. Judges and court officers were in attendance to discharge their respective functions. It is undisputed that a major purpose of the demonstration was to protest what the demonstrators considered an "illegal" arrest of 23 students the previous day. . . .

It is, of course, true that most judges will be influenced only by what they see and hear in court. However, judges are human; and the legislature has the right to recognize the danger that some judges, jurors, and other court officials, will be consciously or unconsciously influenced by demonstrations in or near their courtrooms both prior to and at the time of the trial. A State may also properly protect the judicial process from being misjudged in the minds of the public. Suppose demonstrators paraded and picketed for weeks with signs asking that indictments be dismissed, and that a judge completely uninfluenced by these demonstrations, dismissed the indictments. A State may protect against the possibility of a conclusion by the public under these circumstances that the judge's action was in part a product of intimidation and did not flow only from the fair and orderly working of the judicial process. . . .

Appellant invokes the clear and present danger doctrine in support of his argument that the statute cannot constitutionally be applied to the conduct involved here [relying upon Pennekamp and Bridges]. He defines the standard to be applied [to] be whether the expression of opinion presents a clear and present danger to the administration of justice.

We have already pointed out the important differences between the contempt cases and the present one . . . . Here we deal not with the contempt power but with a narrowly drafted statute and not with speech in its pristine form but with conduct of a totally different character. Even assuming the applicability of a general clear and present danger test, it is one thing to conclude that the mere publication of a newspaper editorial or a telegram to a Secretary of Labor, however critical of a court, presents no clear and present danger to the administration of justice and quite another thing to conclude that crowds, such as this, demonstrating before a courthouse may not be pro-

hibited by a legislative determination based on experience that such conduct inherently threatens the judicial process. We therefore reject the clear and present danger argument of appellant. . . .

There are, however, more substantial constitutional objections arising from appellant's conviction on the particular facts of this case. Appellant was convicted for demonstrating not "in," but "near" the courthouse. [T]here is some lack of specificity in a word such as "near." While this lack of specificity may not render the statute unconstitutionally vague, at least as applied to a demonstration within the sight and hearing of those in the courthouse, it is clear that the statute, with respect to the determination of how near the courthouse a particular demonstration can be, foresees a degree of on-the-spot administrative interpretation by officials charged with responsibility for administering and enforcing it. [The] administrative discretion to construe the term "near" [is] the type of narrow discretion which this Court has recognized as the proper role of responsible officials in making determinations concerning the time, place, duration, and manner of demonstrations. . . .

The record here clearly shows that the officials present gave permission for the demonstration to take place across the street from the courthouse. In effect, appellant was advised that a demonstration at the place it was held would not be one "near" the courthouse within the terms of the statute. [U]nder all the circumstances of this case, after the public officials acted as they did, to sustain appellant's later conviction for demonstrating where they told him he could "would be to sanction an indefensible sort of entrapment by the State—convicting a citizen for exercising a privilege which the State had clearly told him was available to him." [Raley v. Ohio, 360 U.S. 423.] The Due Process Clause does not permit convictions to be obtained under such circumstances. . . . There remains just one final point: the effect of the Sheriff's order to disperse. The State in effect argues that this order somehow removed the prior grant of permission and reliance on the officials' construction that the demonstration on the far side of the street was not illegal as being "near" the courthouse. This, however, we cannot accept. [I]t is our conclusion from the record that the dispersal order had nothing to do with any time or place limitation, and thus, on this ground alone, it is clear that the dispersal order did not remove the protection accorded appellant by the original grant of permission. . . .

Nothing we have said here or in No. 24, ante, is to be interpreted as sanctioning riotous conduct in any form or demonstrations, however peaceful their conduct or commendable their motives, which conflict with properly drawn statutes and ordinances designed to promote law and order, protect the community against disorder, regulate traffic, safeguard legitimate interests in private and public property, or protect the administration of justice and other essential governmental functions.

. . . We reaffirm the repeated holdings of this Court that our constitutional command of free speech and assembly is basic and fundamental and encompasses peaceful social protest, so important to the preservation of the freedoms treasured in a democratic society. We also reaffirm the repeated decisions of this Court that there is no place for violence in a democratic

society dedicated to liberty under law, and that the right of peaceful protest does not mean that everyone with opinions or beliefs to express may do so at any time and at any place. There is a proper time and place for even the most peaceful protest and a plain duty and responsibility on the part of all citizens to obey all valid laws and regulations. . . .

Reversed.

Mr. Justice BLACK, concurring in No. 24 and dissenting in No. 49.

. . .

The First and Fourteenth Amendments, I think, take away from government, state and federal, all power to restrict freedom of speech, press, and assembly *where people have a right to be for such purposes.* This does not mean, however, that these amendments also grant a constitutional right to engage in the conduct of picketing or patrolling, whether on publicly owned streets or on privately owned property. . . . Were the law otherwise, people on the streets, in their homes and anywhere else could be compelled to listen against their will to speakers they did not want to hear. Picketing, though it may be utilized to communicate ideas, is not speech, and therefore is not of itself protected by the First Amendment. . . . However, because Louisiana's breach-of-peace statute is not narrowly drawn to assure nondiscriminatory application, I think it is constitutionally invalid under our holding in [Edwards v. South Carolina].

[As to the obstructing-public-passages conviction], I believe that the First and Fourteenth Amendments require that if the streets of a town are open to some views, they must be open to all. [B]y specifically permitting picketing for the publication of labor union views, Louisiana is attempting to pick and choose among the views it is willing to have discussed on its streets [in violation of equal protection as well as the First Amendment].

I would sustain the conviction [for picketing near a courthouse]. Certainly the most obvious reason for their protest at the courthouse was to influence the judge and other court officials . . . .. The Court attempts to support its holding by its inference that the Chief of Police gave his consent to picketing the courthouse. But quite apart from the fact that a police chief cannot authorize violations of his State's criminal laws, there was strong, emphatic testimony that if any consent was given it was limited to telling Cox and his group to come no closer to the courthouse than they had already come without the consent of any official, city, state, or federal. And there was also testimony that when told to leave appellant Cox defied the order by telling the crowd not to move. I fail to understand how the Court can justify the reversal of this conviction because of a permission which testimony in the record denies was given, which could not have been authoritatively given anyway, and which even if given was soon afterwards revoked. . . .

. . . Those who encourage minority groups to believe that the United States Constitution and federal laws give them a right to patrol and picket in the streets whenever they choose, in order to advance what they think to be a just and noble end, do no service to those minority groups, their cause, or their country. I am confident from this record that this appellant violated the Louisiana statute because of a mistaken belief that he and his followers had a constitutional right to do so, because of what they believed were just grievan-

ces. But the history of the past 25 years if it shows nothing else shows that his group's constitutional and statutory rights have to be protected by the courts, which must be kept free from intimidation and coercive pressures of any kind. . . . [Justice CLARK also concurred in Cox I and dissented in Cox II.]

Mr. Justice WHITE, with whom Mr. Justice HARLAN joins, concurring in part and dissenting in part.

In No. 49, I agree with the dissent filed by my Brother Black in [the last part] of his opinion. In No. 24, although I do not agree with everything the Court says concerning the breach of peace conviction, particularly its statement concerning the unqualified protection to be extended to Cox's exhortations to engage in sit-ins in restaurants, I agree that the conviction for breach of peace is governed by [Edwards] and must be reversed.

Regretfully, I also dissent from the reversal of the conviction for obstruction of public passages. The Louisiana statute is not invalidated on its face but only in its application. But this remarkable emasculation of a prohibitory statute is based on only very vague evidence that other meetings and parades have been allowed by the authorities. . . . There is no evidence in the record that other meetings of this magnitude had been allowed on the city streets, had been allowed in the vicinity of the courthouse or had been permitted completely to obstruct the sidewalk and to block access to abutting buildings. . . .

Furthermore, even if the obstruction statute, because of prior permission granted to others, could not be applied in this case so as to prevent the demonstration, it does not necessarily follow that the federal license to use the streets is unlimited as to time and circumstance. [A]t some point the authorities were entitled to apply the statute and to clear the streets. That point was reached here. To reverse the conviction under these circumstances makes it only rhetoric to talk of local power to control the streets under a properly drawn ordinance.

DEMONSTRATIONS AND COX: ADEQUATE GUIDELINES FOR THE PUBLIC FORUM? ADEQUATE TECHNIQUE FOR DEVELOPING GUIDELINES?

1. *Cox and the public forum.* Do the Cox cases make significant progress in developing Robert's Rules? Adequate progress? Are the Rules suggested sound? How should the gaps be filled? Is Professor Kalven persuasive in perceiving "a certain scheme of legal results" from the opinions: (1) at one extreme, it is "clear" that "this kind of use" of public places cannot be summarily suppressed as a breach of the peace, though there is some risk of violence; (2) at the other extreme, all picketing of courthouses can be prohibited; (3) "in the middle" is the "obstructing" streets question —a question the Court "colored with dicta but studiously avoided deciding." Kalven, "The Concept of the Public Forum: Cox v. Louisiana," 1965 Sup. Ct.Rev. 1. Is (1) "clear", after Feiner and Edwards? Is (2) sound? How should (3) be decided?

What do the Cox cases contribute to the concept of a public forum? Recall the distinction at the beginning of this section between a "guaranteed access" right to some public places and a narrower "equal access" view. What is the Cox Court's emphasis? Is the preoccupation with overbreadth and abuses of discretion so great that it produces an overwhelming emphasis on the equal access view? Do Justice Goldberg's opinions adequately reflect the legacy of Hague v. CIO and other cases on guaranteed access? Note Justice Goldberg's comment in Cox I: "We have no occasion in this case to consider the constitutionality of the uniform, consistent, and nondiscriminatory application of a statute forbidding all access to streets and other public facilities for parades and meetings." Is that a surprising statement in a 1965 decision by the Warren Court? Was that still an open question, after Hague and its progeny? Does the emphasis on discriminatory application and on the "speech"-"conduct" distinction contribute to an obscuring of the underlying guaranteed access problem? Does the hesitancy about a right of access to streets and parks contribute to the uncertainties of the Court when the issues move to more novel places for public meetings, such as courts in Cox II and libraries and jails in the cases in sec. 2D below?

2. *Cox and the threat to courts.* Was the rejection of clear and present danger regarding (2) sound? Would the clear and present danger test have been relevant here? At least as useful as in the contempt by publication cases distinguished in Cox II? Compare the comments on the contempt cases, chap. 13, sec. 4, below. What *does* justify the ban on courthouse picketing? Is the "speech"-"conduct" distinction helpful? Kalven comments: "[A]ll speech is necessarily 'speech plus.'" He also suggests that the "essential feature" of most civil rights demonstrations in public places is "appeal to public opinion." If that is so, can the Court respond to the communication element by labeling it conduct? If there is justification for restricting these forms of communication, should it not be explicitly stated why this "speech" is controllable, rather than suggesting there is no "speech" at all? Was the Warren Court more sensitive in the Brown and Adderley cases, which follow?

3. *Cox and the "speech"-"conduct" distinction.* Compare the "speech"-"conduct" distinction in the remaining cases in this section, and in the symbolic expression cases in the next section. Does the speech-conduct distinction tend to extend exaggerated protection to the (slim) "pure speech" category—and tend to give inadequate protection to communication outside that category? Does the "conduct" label unduly minimize the speech elements (and exaggerate the permissibility of restrictions)? Does the speech-conduct distinction promote insensitivity to speech ingredients in situations that involve *some* First Amendment elements? Do the draft card burning (O'Brien) and flag burning (Street) cases, sec. 3 below, illustrate that risk? Does the all-or-nothing distinction of two categories artificially separate matters of gradation and degree—and promote inadequate judicial scrutiny of the "conduct" category? And excessive scrutiny in the "speech" category?

USE OF THE STREETS: SOME CASES AFTER COX

Consider the range of judicial techniques employed in scrutinizing restraints on street use, in the following sampling of cases since Cox. Does that mix of overbreadth, vagueness and "as applied" adjudications significantly further the search for guidelines regarding access to traditional public forums?

1. *Bachellar v. Maryland.* Petitioners were convicted under a law which prohibits "acting in a disorderly manner to the disturbance of the public peace, upon any public street." The state courts affirmed their convictions against a challenge that their conduct was constitutionally protected under the First Amendment. The Supreme Court unanimously reversed. BACHELLAR v. MARYLAND, 397 U.S. 564 (1970).

The prosecutions arose out of an antiwar demonstration in front of an Army Recruiting Station in downtown Baltimore. After participating in a march in front of the station, petitioners staged a brief sit-in inside the station, were removed by federal marshals, and ended up on the sidewalk in front of the station. The instructions to the jury offered alternative grounds for conviction under the statute: the jury might find petitioners had engaged in "the doing or saying or both of that which offends, disturbs, incites or tends to incite a number of people gathered in the same area"; or a guilty verdict under the disorderly conduct charge might be based on "refusal to obey a policeman's command to move on when not to do so may endanger the public peace."

Justice Brennan's opinion concluded: "On this record, if the jury believed the State's evidence, petitioners' convictions could constitutionally have rested on a finding that they sat or lay across a public sidewalk with the intent of fully blocking passage along it, or that they refused to obey police commands to stop obstructing the sidewalk in this manner and move on. See, e. g., [Cox I; Shuttlesworth v. Birmingham (which follows)]. It is impossible to say, however, that either of these grounds was the basis for the verdict. On the contrary, so far as we can tell, it is equally likely that the verdict resulted 'merely because [petitioners' views about Vietnam were] themselves offensive to some of their hearers.' [Street v. New York, sec. 3, below.] Thus, since petitioners' convictions may have rested on an unconstitutional ground, they must be set aside."

2. *Coates v. City of Cincinnati.* A Cincinnati ordinance made it illegal for "three or more persons to assemble [on] any of the sidewalks [and] there conduct themselves in a manner annoying to persons passing by." That provision was held unconstitutional on its face on grounds of vagueness and overbreadth in COATES v. CITY OF CINCINNATI, 402 U.S. 611 (1971). Justice Stewart's majority opinion found the ordinance "unconstitutionally vague because it subjects the exercise of the right of assembly to an unascertainable standard, and unconstitutionally broad because it authorizes the punishment of constitutionally protected conduct."

On the vagueness point, Justice Stewart stated that the "annoying" criterion meant that "no standard of conduct is specified at all": "Conduct that

annoys some people does not annoy others."   He added: "[T]he city is free to prevent people from blocking sidewalks, obstructing traffic, littering streets, committing assaults, or engaging in countless other forms of anti-social conduct.   It can do so through the enactment and enforcement of ordinances directed with reasonable specificity toward the conduct to be prohibited.   It cannot constitutionally do so through the enactment and enforcement of an ordinance whose violation may entirely depend upon whether or not a policeman is annoyed."

With respect to overbreadth, Justice Stewart emphasized the rights of free assembly and association.   The right of assembly could not be restricted "simply because its exercise may be 'annoying' to some people."   And such a prohibition "contains an obvious invitation to discriminatory enforcement against those whose association together is 'annoying' because their ideas, their lifestyle or their physical appearance is resented by the majority of their fellow citizens."

The pure "on the face" rather than "as applied" nature of the analysis in Coates was emphasized by the majority's ability to state all of the facts known to the Court in a portion of a single sentence: the record "tells us no more than that the appellant Coates was a student involved in a demonstration and the other appellants were pickets involved in a labor dispute."   To the majority, that dearth of facts was no barrier to reversal of the conviction: "It is the ordinance on its face that sets the standard of conduct and warns against transgression.   The details of the offense could no more serve to validate this ordinance than could the details of an offense charged under an ordinance suspending unconditionally the right of assembly and free speech."

To the four dissenters, by contrast, the lack of record data was the major factor counselling against a ruling of unconstitutionality.   Justice White, joined by Chief Justice Burger and Justice Blackmun, thought that, under the standards applicable to ordinary criminal legislation, there was no basis to find the law vague on its face: "Any man of average comprehension should know that some kinds of conduct, such as assault or blocking passage on the street, will annoy others and are clearly covered by the 'annoying conduct' standard of the ordinance."   That might leave a "vague as applied" challenge, "but ruling on such a challenge obviously requires knowledge of the conduct with which a defendant is charged."   There were decisions suggesting a more receptive attitude toward "on the face" challenges in First Amendment cases, to be sure, but these did not justify reversal here: "Even accepting the overbreadth doctrine with respect to statutes clearly reaching speech, the Cincinnati ordinance does not purport to bar or regulate speech as such."

Justice White concluded: "In the case before us, I would deal with the Cincinnati ordinance as we would with the ordinary criminal statute.   The ordinance clearly reaches certain conduct but may be illegally vague with respect to other conduct.   The statute is not infirm on its face and since we have no information from this record as to what conduct was charged against these defendants we are in no position to judge the statute as applied."   Justice Black also dissented.   [Note the dissenters' claim that Coates has been

"effectively overrule[d]," in Broadrick v. Oklahoma, 413 U.S. 601 (1973), the "substantial overbreadth" case, sec. 1E, above.]

3. *Palmer v. City of Euclid.* Compare with the disposition of the Coates case the Court's handling, a week earlier, of PALMER v. CITY OF EUCLID, 402 U.S. 544 (1971). There, a majority subscribed to a "vague as applied" per curiam reversal of a conviction under a "suspicious person ordinance" applicable to any person "who wanders about the streets or other public ways or who is found abroad at late or unusual hours in the night without any visible or lawful business and who does not give satisfactory account of himself." The majority found that provision so "lacking in ascertainable standards of guilt" that, as applied, it failed to give "fair notice" of the forbidden conduct. Palmer had discharged a female passenger from his car late at night and had then parked with his lights on and used a two-way radio. The Court stated that "the ordinance gave insufficient notice to the average person that discharging a friend at an apartment house and then talking on a car radio while parked on the street was enough to show him to be 'without visible or lawful business.' " Justice Stewart, joined by Justice Douglas, stated that he "would go further" and hold the law vague on its face.

4. *Papachristou v. City of Jacksonville.* The approach advocated by Justices Stewart and Douglas in Palmer prevailed in the following Term: in PAPACHRISTOU v. CITY OF JACKSONVILLE, 405 U.S. 156 (1972), Justice Douglas wrote for a unanimous Court in holding unconstitutional on its face a municipal vagrancy ordinance. The "archaic language" of the law reflected its early English antecedents.* The Court concluded: "This ordinance is void for vagueness, both in the sense that it 'fails to give a person of ordinary intelligence fair notice that his contemplated conduct is forbidden by the statute,' [and] because it encourages arbitrary and erratic arrests and convictions." Justice Douglas commented that the law "makes criminal activities which by modern standards are normally innocent." He added: "Those generally implicated by the imprecise terms of the ordinance—poor people, nonconformists, dissenters, idlers—may be required to comport themselves according to the lifestyle deemed appropriate by the Jacksonville police and the courts. Where, as here, there are no standards governing the exercise of the discretion granted by the ordinance, the scheme permits and encourages an arbitrary and discriminatory enforcement of the law."

5. *Colten v. Kentucky.* In COLTEN v. KENTUCKY, 407 U.S. 104 (1972), the Court, with only Justice Douglas dissenting on this aspect of the case, rejected First Amendment challenges to a disorderly conduct conviction. Appellant was one of a number of college students returning in a group of

---

* The Jacksonville ordinance defined "vagrants" as follows: "Rogues and vagabonds, or dissolute persons who go about begging, common gamblers, persons who use juggling or unlawful games or plays, common drunkards, common night walkers, thieves, pilferers or pickpockets, traders in stolen property, lewd, wanton and lascivious persons, keepers of gambling places, common railers and brawlers, persons wandering or strolling around from place to place without any lawful purpose or object, habitual loafers, disorderly persons, persons neglecting all lawful business and habitually spending their time by frequenting houses of ill fame, gaming houses, or places where alcoholic beverages are sold or served, persons able to work but habitually living upon the earnings of their wives or minor children shall be deemed vagrants."

cars from a political demonstration at an airport. One of appellant's companions was stopped by a policeman for driving with an expired license plate. Appellant and a number of others also pulled off the highway and appellant persisted in efforts to talk to the officer about the traffic ticket despite several requests to leave. He was convicted under a statute stating it to be disorderly conduct "if, with intent to cause public inconvenience, annoyance or alarm, or recklessly creating a risk thereof," a person "congregates with other persons in a public place and refuses to comply with a lawful order of the police to disperse."

Justice White's majority opinion rejected the "as applied" challenge by finding that appellant's conduct was not protected by the First Amendment. Colten's claim that he was "disseminating and receiving information" in observing the issuance of the ticket and in trying to arrange transportation for his companion was dismissed as "a strained, near-frivolous contention." The police order to disperse "was suited to the occasion," to avoid the risk of accidents. Nor did the Court find merit in the vagueness and overbreadth contentions. The statute gave adequately clear notice: "The root of the vagueness doctrine is a rough idea of fairness. It is not a principle designed to convert into a constitutional dilemma the practical difficulties in drawing criminal statutes both general enough to take into account a variety of human conduct and sufficiently specific to provide fair warning that certain kinds of conduct are prohibited." And the state court's construction barred the kind of overbreadth challenge that had prevailed in Cox v. Louisiana. The Kentucky court had made clear that "a crime is committed only where there is no bona fide intention to exercise a constitutional right" or where the individual's interest in expression "is 'minuscule' compared to a particular public interest in preventing that expression or conduct at that time and place." So read, the statute did not permit convictions "merely for expressing unpopular or annoying ideas."

6. *Grayned v. City of Rockford.* One of the challenges rejected in GRAYNED v. CITY OF ROCKFORD, 408 U.S. 104 (1972), was an on the face attack on an anti-noise ordinance on vagueness grounds. Grayned was a participant in a demonstration "promoting a Black cause" in front of a high school. The ordinance provided: "[N]o person, while on public or private grounds adjacent to any building in which a school or any class thereof is in session, shall willfully make or assist in the making of any noise or diversion which disturbs or tends to disturb the peace or good order of such school session or class thereof." Justice Marshall, writing for a unanimous Court, concluded that, though the question was "close," the provision was "not impermissibly vague." He emphasized that this was not "a vague, general 'breach of the peace' ordinance, but a statute written specifically for the school context, where the prohibited disturbances are easily measured by their impact on the normal activities of the school." He thought it sufficiently clear that the ordinance "forbids deliberately noisy or diversionary activity which disrupts or is about to disrupt normal school activities." The phrase "tends to disturb" was troublesome, to be sure. But the Court was satisfied that the state courts would interpret the provision "to prohibit only actual or imminent interference with the 'peace or good order' of the school." Unlike the ordinance in Coates, note 2 above, the ordinance

"does not permit punishment for the expression of an unpopular point of view, and it contains no broad invitation to subjective or discriminatory enforcement."*

COMPLIANCE WITH PERMIT REQUIREMENTS AND INJUNCTIONS IN THE DEMONSTRATIONS CONTEXT

Introduction. A procedural theme of great practical importance has recurrently surfaced in the preceding materials: When may a speaker ignore the existence of a permit requirement, or the refusal of permission under such a scheme, and proceed to make his speech? May a speaker who has spoken or demonstrated without a permit raise constitutional challenges to the permit scheme or the permit denial in a prosecution for speaking without a permit? To what extent do the doctrines of the early licensing cases such as Lovell v. Griffin and Cox v. New Hampshire govern the modern regulations of meetings and parades through permit requirement and other "prior restraints"? The Court considered these questions in connection with two efforts to challenge a Birmingham parade permit ordinance. Both efforts involved the Good Friday civil rights protest march in Birmingham in 1963, led by several Black ministers including Martin Luther King, Jr. The ordinance was ultimately found to be unconstitutional, but the first effort to challenge it failed: in WALKER v. CITY OF BIRMINGHAM, 388 U.S. 307 (1967), the demonstrators had marched in the face of an ex parte injunction directing compliance with the ordinance. The Court held that the demonstrators who had not challenged the injunction in court before marching could not defend contempt charges by asserting the unconstitutionality of the ordinance or the injunction. But two years later, in SHUTTLESWORTH v. BIRMINGHAM, 394 U.S. 147 (1969), one of the demonstrators in the same march was successful in having his constitutional challenge to the ordinance heard and sustained: in Shuttlesworth, the charge was parading without a permit, not disobeying an injunction, and in that context, the Court held the ordinance unconstitutional.

1. *Walker.* In Walker, a 5 to 4 decision sustained a state court's refusal to consider constitutional challenges to the injunction and to the ordinance at the contempt hearing: petitioners had openly flouted the injunction because they considered it "raw tyranny"; Alabama had justifiably relied on the general rule that court orders must be obeyed until "reversed for error by or-

---

* See also the further note on this case in chap. 13, sec. 4, on the unsuccessful overbreadth challenge. But see the invalidation, on the same day, of a ban on picketing near schools but excepting labor picketing: there, the Court relied on equal protection grounds "closely intertwined with First Amendment interests." Police Dept. of Chicago v. Mosley, 408 U.S. 92 (1972). See, moreover, the additional materials on free speech in the school context, chap. 13, sec. 4, below.

Recall also the approach in Hess v. Indiana, 414 U.S. 105 (1973) (sec. 1E above). Though overbreadth and vagueness challenges were made to a disorderly conduct conviction, the majority's per curiam reversal was an "as applied" one. After anti-war demonstrators had been moved to the side of the street by police, appellant had said: "We'll take the fucking street later (or again)." The majority emphasized that these words were not punishable under the standards of Brandenburg v. Ohio and Cohen v. California.

derly review." Justice Stewart concluded: "This Court cannot hold that the petitioners were constitutionally free to ignore all the procedures of the law and carry their battle to the streets." Justice Brennan's dissent, joined by Chief Justice Warren and Justices Douglas and Fortas, insisted that the Court had elevated a "rule of judicial administration above the right of free expression." [Compare the First Amendment limits imposed on ex parte injunctions in a subsequent case in which petitioners obeyed the injunction and then challenged it in court. Carroll v. President & Comm'rs of Princess Anne, 393 U.S. 175 (1968), note 3, below.]

2. *Shuttlesworth.* In Shuttlesworth, however, one of the petitioners in *Walker* was permitted to challenge the parade ordinance in attacking his conviction for marching without a permit. The ordinance directed the city commission to issue a permit "unless in its judgment the public welfare, peace, safety, health, decency, good order, morals, or convenience require that it be refused." Justice Stewart's opinion for the Court had "no doubt" that, as written, the ordinance was unconstitutional: it conferred "virtually unbridled and absolute power" and therefore "fell squarely within the ambit of the many decisions of this Court over the last 30 years, holding that a law subjecting the exercise of First Amendment freedoms to the prior restraint of a license, without narrow, objective, and definite standards to guide the licensing authority," is void.

The state countered that the conviction should nevertheless stand because the highest state court here—following the pattern accepted by the Court in Cox v. New Hampshire, sec. 2A above—had given a narrow construction to the broadly written law in reviewing petitioner's case. The Court conceded that the Alabama judges' "remarkable job of plastic surgery upon the face of the ordinance" had transformed it into one "authorizing no more than the objective and even-handed regulation of traffic." But here, unlike Cox, the narrowing effort came too late. Here, it was difficult to anticipate the subsequent construction: it "would have taken extraordinary clairvoyance for anyone" in 1963 to perceive that the ordinance meant what the highest state court construed it to mean in 1967. Moreover, the city officials had demonstrated in 1963 that they thought "the ordinance meant exactly what it said" on its face: they had given petitioner to understand that "under no circumstances" would he be permitted to demonstrate in Birmingham. In Cox, unlike here, there had been no prior administration different from the state court's subsequent narrowing construction.

3. *Carroll.* Contrast with the impact of the injunction in Walker the restrictions imposed on injunctions in a properly raised challenge, in the Carroll case mentioned at the end of note 1, above. In CARROLL v. PRESIDENT & COMM'RS OF PRINCESS ANNE, 393 U.S. 175 (1968), the Court found unconstitutional the ex parte procedure followed in issuing a 10-day temporary restraining order against holding a public rally. Petitioners had held a meeting at which they made "aggressively and militantly racist" speeches to a crowd of both whites and Blacks. They announced that they would resume the rally the following night. Before that time, local officials obtained the order restraining petitioners and their "white supremacist" National States Rights Party from holding meetings "which will tend to disturb and endanger the citizens of the County." There was no notice

to petitioners prior to the issuance of the order. The rally was cancelled and petitioners (rather than ignoring the injunction as in Walker) challenged the injunction in court.

Justice Fortas' opinion for the Court found no adequate justification for the ex parte nature of the proceedings. In the rare situations where prior restraints were permissible (see Freedman v. Maryland, chap. 13, sec. 3), "the Court has insisted upon careful procedural provisions." "There is a place in our jurisprudence for ex parte issuance, without notice, of temporary restraining orders of short duration; but there is no place within the area of basic freedoms guaranteed by the First Amendment for such orders where no showing is made that it is impossible to serve or to notify the opposing parties and to give them an opportunity to participate." Here, procedural care was even more important than in the obscenity area: "The present case involves a rally and 'political' speech in which the element of timeliness may be important." Moreover, without an adversary hearing, "there is insufficient assurance of the balanced analysis and careful conclusions which are essential in the area of First Amendment adjudication."

4. *Some questions and comments.* Does the distinction between Walker and Shuttlesworth make sense? Does the distinction between Shuttlesworth and Cox v. New Hampshire make sense? What are the operative guidelines in light of the modern cases for demonstrators trying to evaluate the risks of marching without seeking a permit or after denial of a permit: When can they expect to be able to raise constitutional defenses to the permit scheme or permit denial in subsequent prosecutions? See generally Blasi, "Prior Restraints on Demonstrations," 68 Mich.L.Rev. 1481 (1970), and Monaghan, "First Amendment 'Due Process,'" 83 Harv.L.Rev. 518 (1970). Is it still true that, as in Lovell v. Griffin, a facially invalid law may be ignored by the speaker? Is it still true that, as in Cox v. New Hampshire, a speaker takes the risk that a facially questionable law may be construed narrowly and constitutionally by the state courts? Why did that state technique not succeed in Shuttlesworth? Is it still true that a speaker may not ignore a permit scheme where the constitutional objection goes not to the constitutionality of the law but rather to the arbitrariness of its administration? Recall Poulos v. New Hampshire, 345 U.S. 395 (1953) sec. 2A above, where a speaker had been arbitrarily denied a permit under a valid law. The Court rejected the speaker's argument "that he may risk speaking without a license and defeat prosecution by showing the license was arbitrarily withheld." Justice Reed was unpersuaded by the defendant's objection that "his right to preach may be postponed until a case, possibly after years, reaches this Court for final adjudication of constitutional rights." He answered: "Delay is unfortunate, but the expense and annoyance of litigation is a price citizens must pay for life in an orderly society where the rights of the First Amendment have a real and abiding meaning." Is the delay permitted in the Poulos context sharply curtailed by the "careful procedural provisions"—including time requirements—required by the Court in Freedman v. Maryland, 380 U.S. 51 (1965), in the context of prior restraints on film exhibitions, chap. 13, sec. 3, below?

D. ACCESS TO PUBLIC PLACES OTHER THAN THE TRADITIONAL STREETS AND PARKS: EXPANDING CONTOURS OF THE PUBLIC FORUM?

Introduction. In Hague v. CIO, Justice Roberts, in speaking of public places which have "immemorially" and "in time out of mind" been used for "discussing public questions," mentioned only "streets and parks." And most of the preceding materials involved access to and regulation of streets and parks as a public forum. What of other public places? In Cox II, the Court rejected efforts to demonstrate near a court house. Was that because of the special protection of the judicial process? Or was that a signal that places that were not "immemorially" public forums could be kept free of meetings and demonstrations? In a series of modern cases, the Court has confronted claims of speakers seeking access to such nontraditional forums as libraries, jailhouses, and public buses. Should a guaranteed access public forum claim be recognized in those contexts? At least an equal access claim? How adequate are the Court's responses?

BROWN v. LOUISIANA
383 U.S. 131, 86 S.Ct. 719, 15 L.Ed.2d 637 (1966).

Certiorari to the Supreme Court of Louisiana.

Mr. Justice FORTAS announced the judgment of the Court and an opinion in which The Chief Justice [WARREN] and Mr. Justice DOUGLAS join.

This is the fourth time in little more than four years that this Court has reviewed convictions by the Louisiana courts for alleged violations, in a civil rights context, of that State's breach of the peace statute. In the three preceding cases the convictions were reversed. [Garner v. Louisiana, 368 U.S. 157 (1961); Taylor v. Louisiana, 370 U.S. 154 (1962); Cox v. Louisiana, 379 U.S. 536 (1965).] Since the present case was decided under precisely the statute involved in [Cox I] but before our decision in that case was announced, it might well be supposed that, without further ado, we would vacate and remand in light of Cox. But because the incident leading to the present convictions occurred in a public library and might be thought to raise materially different questions, we have heard argument and have considered the case *in extenso.*

The locus of the events was the Audubon Regional Library in the town of Clinton, Louisiana, Parish of East Feliciana. . . . The Audubon Regional Library [has] three branches and two bookmobiles. [Negroes could borrow books, but only from one of the bookmobiles.]

This tidy plan was challenged on Saturday, March 7, 1964, at about 11:30 a.m. Five young Negro males, all residents of East or West Feliciana Parishes, went into the adult reading or service room of the Audubon Regional Library at Clinton. The branch assistant, Mrs. Katie Reeves, was alone in the room. . . . Petitioner Brown requested a book . . . .. Mrs. Reeves checked the card catalogue, ascertained that the Branch did not have the book, so advised Mr. Brown, and told him that she would request the book from the

State Library, that he would be notified upon its receipt and that "he could either pick it up or it would be mailed to him." . . . Mrs. Reeves testified that she expected that the men would then leave; they did not, and she asked them to leave. They did not. Petitioner Brown sat down and the others stood near him. They said nothing; there was no noise or boisterous talking. [I]n "10 to 15 minutes" from the time of the arrival of the men at the library, the sheriff and deputies arrived. The sheriff asked the Negroes to leave. They said they would not. The sheriff then arrested them. . . .

On March 25, 1964, Mr. Brown and his four companions were tried and found guilty. . . . The charge was that they had congregated together in the public library of Clinton, Louisiana, "with the intent to provoke a breach of the peace and under circumstances such that a breach of the peace might be occasioned thereby" and had failed and refused "to leave said premises when ordered to do so" by the librarian and by the sheriff.

The Louisiana breach of peace statute under which they were accused reads as follows: "Whoever with intent to provoke a breach of the peace, or under circumstances such that a breach of the peace may be occasioned thereby: (1) crowds or congregates with others [in a] public place or building [and] who fails or refuses to disperse and move on, or disperse or move on, when ordered so to do by any law enforcement officer [shall] be guilty of disturbing the peace." . . .

We come, then, to the barebones of the problem. Petitioners, five adult Negro men, remained in the library room for a total of ten or fifteen minutes. The first few moments were occupied by a ritualistic request for service and a response. We may assume that the response constituted service, and we need not consider whether it was merely a gambit in the ritual. This ceremony being out of the way, the Negroes proceeded to the business in hand. They sat and stood in the room, quietly, as momuments of protest against the segregation of the library. They were arrested and [convicted].

[T]here is not the slightest evidence which would or could sustain the application of the statute to petitioners. . . . Nor were the circumstances such that a breach of the peace might be "occasioned" by their actions, as the statute alternatively provides. [But the State argues that the issue is "much simpler."] The issue, asserts the State, is simply that petitioners were using the library room "as a place in which to loaf or make a nuisance of themselves." The State argues that the "test"—the permissible civil rights demonstration —was concluded when petitioners entered the library, asked for service and were served. Having satisfied themselves, the argument runs, that they could get service, they should have departed. Instead, they simply sat there, "staring vacantly," and this was "enough to unnerve a woman in the situation Mrs. Reeves was in."

This is a piquant version of the affair, but the matter is hardly to be decided on points. It was not a game. It could not be won so handily by the gesture of service to this particular request. There is no dispute that the library system was segregated, and no possible doubt that these petitioners were there to protest this fact. But even if we were to agree with the State's ingenuous characterization of the events, we would have to reverse. There was no violation of the statute which petitioners are accused of breaching; no disorder, no intent to provoke a breach of the peace and no circumstances indicating

that a breach might be occasioned by petitioners' actions.   The sole statutory provision invoked by the State contains not a word about occupying the reading room of a public library for more than 15 minutes .   .   ..

But there is another and sharper answer which is called for.   We are here dealing with an aspect of a basic constitutional right—the right under the First and Fourteenth Amendments guaranteeing freedom of speech and of assembly, and freedom to petition the Government for a redress of grievances. .   .   .   As this Court has repeatedly stated, these rights are not confined to verbal expression.   They embrace appropriate types of action which certainly include the right in a peaceable and orderly manner to protest by silent and reproachful presence, in a place where the protestant has every right to be, the unconstitutional segregation of public facilities.   Accordingly, even if the accused action were within the scope of the statutory instrument, we would be required to assess the constitutional impact of its application, and we would have to hold that the statute cannot constitutionally be applied to punish petitioners' actions in the circumstances of this case.   See [Edwards v. South Carolina].   The statute was deliberately and purposefully applied solely to terminate the reasonable, orderly, and limited exercise of the right to protest the unconstitutional segregation of a public facility.   Interference with this right, so exercised, by state action is intolerable under our Constitution. .   .   .

It is an unhappy circumstance that the locus of these events was a public library—a place dedicated to quiet, to knowledge, and to beauty.   It is a sad commentary that this hallowed place in the Parish of East Feliciana bore the ugly stamp of racism.   It is sad, too, that it was a public library which, reasonably enough in the circumstances, was the stage for a confrontation between those discriminated against and the representatives of the offending parishes. Fortunately, the circumstances here were such that no claim can be made that use of the library by others was disturbed by the demonstration.   Perhaps the time and method were carefully chosen with this in mind.   Were it otherwise, a factor not present in this case would have to be considered.   Here, there was no disturbance of others, no disruption of library activities, and no violation of any library regulations.

A State or its instrumentality may, of course, regulate the use of its libraries or other public facilities.   But it must do so in a reasonable and non-discriminatory manner, equally applicable to all and administered with equality to all.   It may not do so as to some and not as to all.   It may not provide certain facilities for whites and others for Negroes.   And it may not invoke regulations as to use—whether they are *ad hoc* or general—as a pretext for pursuing those engaged in lawful, constitutionally protected exercise of their fundamental rights. .   .   .

Reversed.

Mr. Justice BRENNAN, concurring in the judgment. .   .   .

Since the overbreadth of § 14:103.1 as construed clearly requires the reversal of these convictions, it is wholly unnecessary to reach, let alone rest reversal, as the prevailing opinion seems to do, on the proposition that even a narrowly drawn "statute cannot constitutionally be applied to punish petitioners' actions in the circumstances of this case."

Mr. Justice WHITE, concurring in the result. . . .

[I]t is difficult to believe that if this group had been white its members would have been asked to leave on such short notice, much less asked to leave by the sheriff and arrested, rather than merely escorted from the building, when reluctance to leave was demonstrated. . . . In my view, the behavior of these petitioners and their use of the library building, even though it was for the purposes of a demonstration, did not depart significantly from what normal library use would contemplate. The conclusion that petitioners were making only a normal and authorized use of this public library requires the reversal of their convictions. . . . On this record, it is difficult to avoid the conclusion that petitioners were asked to leave the library because they were Negroes. If they were, their convictions deny them equal protection of the laws.

Mr. Justice BLACK, with whom Mr. Justice CLARK, Mr. Justice HARLAN, and Mr. Justice STEWART join, dissenting. . . .

. . . The case relied on most heavily by the prevailing opinion and my Brother Brennan is [Cox I]. That case, unlike this one, involved picketing and patrolling in the streets. [T]he phase of the statute under consideration here, relating to congregating in public buildings and refusing to move on when ordered to do so by an authorized person, was in no way involved or discussed in Cox. The problems of state regulation of the streets on the one hand, and public buildings on the other, are quite obviously separate and distinct. Public buildings such as libraries, schoolhouses, fire departments, courthouses, and executive mansions are maintained to perform certain specific and vital functions. Order and tranquillity of a sort entirely unknown to the public streets are essential to their normal operation. Contrary to the implications in the prevailing opinion it is incomprehensible to me that a State must measure disturbances in its libraries and on the streets with identical standards. . . .

[T]here simply was no racial discrimination practiced in this case. These petitioners . . . asked for a book, perhaps as the prevailing opinion suggests more as a ritualistic ceremonial than anything else. The lady in charge nevertheless hunted for the book, found she did not have it, sent for it, and later obtained it from the state library for petitioners' use. . . .

. . . The only factual question which can possibly arise regarding the application of the statute here is whether under Louisiana law petitioners either intended to breach the peace or created circumstances under which a breach might have been occasioned. . . . A tiny parish branch library, staffed by two women, is not a department store as in Garner v. Louisiana, supra, nor a bus terminal as in Taylor v. Louisiana, supra, nor a public thoroughfare as in Edwards v. South Carolina, supra, and Cox. Short of physical violence, petitioners could not have more completely upset the normal, quiet functioning of the Clinton branch of the Audubon Regional Library. The state courts below thought the disturbance created by petitioners constituted a violation of the statute. So far as the reversal here rests on a holding that the Louisiana statute was not violated, the Court simply substitutes its judgment for that of the Louisiana courts as to what conduct satisfies the requirements of that state statute. . . .

. . . Apparently unsatisfied with or unsure of the "no evidence" ground for reversing the convictions, the prevailing opinion goes on to state that the statute was used unconstitutionally in the circumstances of this case because it was "deliberately and purposefully applied solely to terminate the reasonable, orderly, and limited exercise of the right to protest the unconstitutional segregation of a public facility." First, I am constrained to say that this statement is wholly unsupported by the record in this case. . . . Moreover, the conclusion . . . establishes a completely new constitutional doctrine. In this case this new constitutional principle means that even though these petitioners did not want to use the Louisiana public library for library purposes, they had a constitutional right nevertheless to stay there over the protest of the librarians who had lawful authority to keep the library orderly for the use of people who wanted to use its books, its magazines, and its papers. But the principle espoused also has a far broader meaning. It means that the Constitution, the First and the Fourteenth Amendments, requires the custodians and supervisors of the public libraries in this country to stand helplessly by while protesting groups advocating one cause or another, stage "sit-ins" or "stand-ups" to dramatize their particular views on particular issues. And it should be remembered that if one group can take over libraries for one cause, other groups will assert the right to do so for causes which, while wholly legal, may not be so appealing to this Court. The States are thus paralyzed with reference to control of their libraries for library purposes, and I suppose that inevitably the next step will be to paralyze the schools. Efforts to this effect have already been made all over the country. . . .

[The First Amendment] does not guarantee to any person the right to use someone else's property, even that owned by government and dedicated to other purposes, as a stage to express dissident ideas. The novel constitutional doctrine of the prevailing opinion nevertheless exalts the power of private nongovernmental groups to determine what use shall be made of governmental property over the power of the elected governmental officials. . . .

. . . I am deeply troubled with the fear that powerful private groups throughout the Nation will read the Court's action, as I do—that is, as granting them a license to invade the tranquillity and beauty of our libraries whenever they have quarrel with some state policy which may or may not exist. It is an unhappy circumstance in my judgment that the group, which more than any other has needed a government of equal laws and equal justice, is now encouraged to believe that the best way for it to advance its cause, which is a worthy one, is by taking the law into its own hands from place to place and from time to time. Governments like ours were formed to substitute the rule of law for the rule of force. Illustrations may be given where crowds have gathered together peaceably by reason of extraordinarily good discipline reinforced by vigilant officers. "Demonstrations" have taken place without any manifestations of force at the time. But I say once more that the crowd moved by noble ideals today can become the mob ruled by hate and passion and greed and violence tomorrow. . . .*

---

* See Kalven, "Upon Rereading Mr. Justice Black on the First Amendment," 14 UCLA L.Rev. 428 (1967): "[I]t remains something of a puzzle how Justice Black, who has been so sympathetic to the 'poor man's printing press' and so tolerant of noise in Kovacs, the intrusion in [Martin v.

ADDERLEY v. FLORIDA

385 U.S. 39, 87 S.Ct. 242, 17 L.Ed.2d 149 (1966).

Certiorari to the Florida District Court of Appeal.

Mr. Justice BLACK delivered the opinion of the Court.

Petitioners [32 students at Florida A. & M. University in Tallahassee] were convicted [of] "trespass with a malicious and mischievous intent" upon the premises of the county jail contrary to § 821.18 of the Florida statutes.[1] [They] had gone from the school to the jail about a mile away, along with many other students, to "demonstrate" at the jail their protests of arrests of other protesting students the day before, and perhaps to protest more generally against state and local policies and practices of racial segregation, including segregation of the jail. The county sheriff, legal custodian of the jail and jail grounds, tried to persuade [them to leave]. When this did not work he notified them that they must leave, that if they did not leave he would arrest them for trespassing, and that if they resisted he would charge them with that as well. Some of the students left but others, including petitioners, remained and they were arrested. . . .

Petitioners [insist that these cases] are controlled [by Edwards and Cox I]. We cannot agree. . . . In Edwards, the demonstrators went to the South Carolina State Capitol grounds to protest. In this case they went to the jail. Traditionally, state capitol grounds are open to the public. Jails, built for security purposes, are not. [In Edwards, the demonstrators] were told by state officials there that they had a right as citizens to go through the State House grounds as long as they were peaceful. Here the demonstrators entered the jail grounds through a driveway used only for jail purposes and without warning to or permission from the sheriff. More importantly, [the Edwards demonstrators were charged] with the common-law crime of breach of the peace. [The South Carolina law was struck down as too] broad and all-embracing [under the doctrine of Cantwell v. Connecticut]. And it was on this same ground of vagueness that [the] Louisiana breach-of-the-peace law used to prosecute Cox was invalidated.

The Florida trespass statute under which these petitioners were charged cannot be challenged on this ground. It is aimed at conduct of one limited kind, that is, for one person or persons to trespass upon the property of another with a malicious and mischievous intent. There is no lack of notice in this law, nothing to entrap or fool the unwary. . . .

Petitioners here contend that "Petitioners' convictions are based on a total lack of relevant evidence." If true, this would be a denial of due process un-

City of Struthers], the anonymity in [Talley v. California], can be so impatient with this kind of communication. It is as though his strategy of protecting all speech just because it was something other than conduct traps him when he is confronted by conduct which is symbolic." See also the symbolic speech cases in sec. 3 below—especially Justice Black's dissent in Street v. New York, the flag burning case. Compare Justice

Black's majority opinion in Adderley, which follows.

1. "Every trespass upon the property of another, committed wtih a malicious and mischievous intent, the punishment of which is not specially provided for, shall be punished by imprisonment not exceeding three months, or by fine not exceeding one hundred dollars." Fla.Stat. § 821.18, F.S.A. (1965). [Footnote by the Court.]

der [Garner v. Louisiana] and Thompson v. Louisville [362 U.S. 199]. [P]etitioners' summary of facts, as well as that of the Circuit Court, shows an abundance of facts to support the jury's verdict of guilty in this case.

In summary both these statements show testimony ample to prove this: Disturbed and upset by the arrest of their schoolmates the day before, a large number of Florida A. & M. students assembled on the school grounds and decided to march down to the county jail. Some apparently wanted to be put in jail too, along with the students already there. A group of around 200 marched from the school and arrived at the jail singing and clapping. They went directly to the jail-door entrance where they were met by a deputy sheriff, evidently surprised by their arrival. He asked them to move back, claiming they were blocking the entrance to the jail and fearing that they might attempt to enter the jail. They moved back part of the way, where they stood or sat, singing, clapping and dancing, on the jail driveway and on an adjacent grassy area upon the jail premises. This particular jail entrance and driveway were not normally used by the public, but by the sheriff's department for transporting prisoners to and from the courts several blocks away and by commercial concerns for servicing the jail. Even after their partial retreat, the demonstrators continued to block vehicular passage over this driveway up to the entrance of the jail. Someone called the sheriff. [He told two] of the leaders that they were trespassing upon jail property and that he would give them 10 minutes to leave or he would arrest them. Neither of the leaders did anything to disperse the crowd, and one of them told the sheriff that they wanted to get arrested. . . . After about 10 minutes, the sheriff, in a voice loud enough to be heard by all, told the demonstrators that he was the legal custodian of the jail and its premises, that they were trespassing on county property in violation of the law, that they should all leave forthwith or he would arrest them, and that if they attempted to resist arrest, he would charge them with that as a separate offense. Some of the group then left. Others, including all petitioners, did not leave. Some of them sat down. In a few minutes, [the] sheriff ordered his deputies to surround those remaining on jail premises and placed them, 107 demonstrators, under arrest. . . .

Under the foregoing testimony the jury was authorized to find that the State had proven every essential element of the crime, as it was defined by the state court. That [leaves] only the question of whether conviction of the state offense, thus defined, unconstitutionally deprived petitioners of their rights to freedom of speech, press, assembly or petition. We hold it does not. The sheriff, as jail custodian, had power, as the state courts have here held, to direct that this large crowd of people get off the grounds. There is not a shred of evidence in this record that this power was exercised . . . because the sheriff objected to what was being sung or said by the demonstrators or because he disagreed with the objectives of their protest. The record reveals that he objected only to their presence on that part of the jail grounds reserved for jail uses. There is no evidence at all that on any other occasion had similarly large groups of the public been permitted to gather on this portion of the jail grounds for any purpose. Nothing in the Constitution of the United States prevents Florida from even-handed enforcement of its general trespass statute against those refusing to obey the sheriff's order to remove themselves from what amounted to the curtilage of the jailhouse. The State, no less than a pri-

vate owner of property, has power to preserve the property under its control for the use to which it is lawfully dedicated. For this reason there is no merit to the petitioners' argument that they had a constitutional right to stay on the property, over the jail custodian's objections, because this "area chosen for the peaceful civil rights demonstration was not only 'reasonable' but also particularly appropriate . . .." Such an argument has as its major unarticulated premise the assumption that people who want to propagandize protests or views have a constitutional right to do so whenever and however and wherever they please. That concept of constitutional law was vigorously and forthrightfully rejected in two of the cases petitioners rely on, [Cox I and II]. We reject it again. The United States Constitution does not forbid a State to control the use of its own property for its own lawful nondiscriminatory purpose.

Affirmed.

Mr. Justice DOUGLAS, with whom The Chief Justice [WARREN], Mr. Justice BRENNAN, and Mr. Justice FORTAS concur, dissenting. . . .

[T]he Court errs in treating the case as if it were an ordinary trespass case or an ordinary picketing case.

The jailhouse, like an executive mansion, a legislative chamber, a courthouse, or the statehouse itself [Edwards], is one of the seats of government, whether it be the Tower of London, the Bastille, or a small county jail. And when it houses political prisoners or those whom many think are unjustly held, it is an obvious center for protest. The right to petition for the redress of grievances has an ancient history and is not limited to writing a letter or sending a telegram to a congressman; it is not confined to appearing before the local city council, or writing letters to the President or Governor or Mayor. Conventional methods of petitioning may be, and often have been, shut off to large groups of our citizens. Legislators may turn deaf ears; formal complaints may be routed endlessly through a bureaucratic maze; courts may let the wheels of justice grind very slowly. Those who do not control television and radio, those who cannot afford to advertise in newspapers or circulate elaborate pamphlets may have only a more limited type of access to public officials. Their methods should not be condemned as tactics of obstruction and harassment as long as the assembly and petition are peaceable, as these were.

There is no question that petitioners had as their purpose a protest against the arrest of Florida A. & M. students for trying to integrate public theatres. [The] group was protesting the arrests, and state and local policies of segregation, including segregation of the jail. . . . The fact that no one gave a formal speech, that no elaborate handbills were distributed, and that the group was not laden with signs would seem to be immaterial. Such methods are not the sine qua non of petitioning for the redress of grievances. The group did sing "freedom" songs. And history shows that a song can be a powerful tool of protest. . . . There was no violence; no threat of violence; no attempted jail break; no storming of a prison; no plan or plot to do anything but protest. The evidence is uncontradicted that the petitioners' conduct did not upset the jailhouse routine . . . . There was no shoving, no pushing, no disorder or threat of riot. It is said that some of

the group blocked part of the driveway leading to the jail entrance. . . . If there was congestion, the solution was a further request to move to lawns or parking areas, not complete ejection and arrest. . . . Finally, the fact that some of the protestants may have felt their cause so just that they were willing to be arrested for making their protest outside the jail seems wholly irrelevant. A petition is nonetheless a petition, though its futility may make martyrdom attractive.

We do violence to the First Amendment when we permit this "petition for redress of grievances" to be turned into a trespass action. It does not help to analogize this problem to the problem of picketing. Picketing is a form of protest usually directed against private interests. I do not see how rules governing picketing in general are relevant to this express constitutional right to assemble and to petition for redress of grievances. In the first place the jailhouse grounds were not marked with "NO TRESPASSING!" signs, nor does respondent claim that the public was generally excluded from the grounds. Only the sheriff's fiat transformed lawful conduct into an unlawful trespass. To say that a private owner could have done the same if the rally had taken place on private property is to speak of a different case, as an assembly and a petition for redress of grievances run to government, not to private proprietors.

The Court forgets that prior to this day our decisions have drastically limited the application of state statutes inhibiting the right to go peacefully on public property to exercise First Amendment rights [quoting Hague v. CIO]. When we allow Florida to construe her "malicious trespass" statute to bar a person from going on property knowing it is not his own and to apply that prohibition to public property, we discard [Cox v. New Hampshire and Edwards]. Would the case be any different if, as is common, the demonstration took place outside a building which housed both the jail and the legislative body? I think not.

There may be some public places which are so clearly committed to other purposes that their use for the airing of grievances is anomalous. There may be some instances in which assemblies and petitions for redress of grievances are not consistent with other necessary purposes of public property. A noisy meeting may be out of keeping with the serenity of the statehouse or the quiet of the courthouse. No one, for example, would suggest that the Senate gallery is the proper place for a vociferous protest rally. And in other cases it may be necessary to adjust the right to petition for redress of grievances to the other interests inhering in the uses to which the public property is normally put. But this is quite different from saying that all public places are off limits to people with grievances. And it is farther yet from saying that the "custodian" of the public property in his discretion can decide when public places shall be used for the communication of ideas, especially the constitutional right to assemble and petition for redress of grievances. For to place such discretion in any public official, be he the "custodian" of the public property or the local police commissioner (cf. [Kunz]), is to place those who assert their First Amendment rights at his mercy. It gives him the awesome power to decide whose ideas may be expressed and who shall be denied a place to air their claims and petition their government. Such power is out of step with all our decisions prior to to-

day where we have insisted that before a First Amendment right may be curtailed under the guise of a criminal law, any evil that may be collateral to the exercise of the right, must be isolated and defined in a "narrowly drawn" statute [Cantwell] lest the power to control excesses of conduct be used to suppress the constitutional right itself. . . .

Today a trespass law is used to penalize people for exercising a constitutional right. Tomorrow a disorderly conduct statute, a breach-of-the-peace statute, a vagrancy statute will be put to the same end. It is said that the sheriff did not make the arrests because of the views which petitioners espoused. That excuse is usually given, as we know from the many cases involving arrests of minority groups for breaches of the peace, unlawful assemblies, and parading without a permit. [S]uch arrests are usually sought to be justified by some legitimate function of government.[1] Yet by allowing these orderly and civilized protests against injustice to be suppressed, we only increase the forces of frustration which the conditions of second-class citizenship are generating amongst us.

THE WARREN COURT AND THE PUBLIC FORUM IN LIGHT OF BROWN AND ADDERLEY

The claimants in cases such as Cox II and Brown and Adderley sought access to public places beyond the traditional forums of streets and parks. Are these nontraditional public places anomalous areas for speech? And do the Court's responses adequately heed the guaranteed access view of the public forum suggested by Hague v. CIO and other early cases? Do these modern cases of public forum claims in novel contexts retreat entirely to an equal access view of the public forum? Do they retreat even further than that? What does Justice Black mean in Adderley when he says: "The State, no less than a private owner of property, has power to preserve the property under its control for the use to which it is lawfully dedicated." Is that a retreat all the way to Justice Holmes' analogy of the state and the private property owner in Davis v. Massachusetts, sec. 2A above? Does Justice Black at least recognize the equal access notion when he says at the end of the opinion: "The United States Constitution does not forbid a state to control the use of its own property for its own lawful nondiscriminatory purpose." Would Justice Black sustain a blanket prohibition of the use of streets and parks for meetings and parades? Or are his broad comments applicable only to such "novel" forums as jailhouses?

Is it fair to say that Justice Douglas' dissent in Adderley is the first opinion from the Warren Court adequately responsive to guaranteed access public forum claims? Is that surprising? Is it an understandable consequence of the Warren Court's preoccupation with risks of discrimination in administration and with overbreadth and with the "speech"-"conduct"

---

1. See, e. g., [DeJonge; Feiner; Niemotko; Edwards; Cox I; Shuttlesworth]. If the invalidity of regulations and official conduct curtailing First Amendment rights turned on an unequivocal showing that the measure was intended to inhibit the rights, protection would be sorely lacking. It is not the intent or purpose of the measure but its effect on First Amendment rights which is crucial. [Footnote by Justice Douglas.]

distinction? * Is the majority position in Adderley reconcilable with the statehouse case, Edwards v. South Carolina? Does Adderley indicate that guaranteed access public forum claims are minimal whenever the claim goes beyond the traditional streets and parks? Or are nontraditional forums available so long as there is no showing of interference with the functioning of their primary uses? Is that the message of the Brown case? † Can a claim to a nontraditional public forum be adequately analyzed without inquiries as to the availability of adequate alternative forums in which the speaker may reach the desired audience? Should the public forum claimant be required to demonstrate his special interest in the particular location? Was there special justification for the protest near the jailhouse in Adderley, and in the library in Brown? Compare the distinction attempted in the shopping center cases, Logan Valley and Lloyd, sec. 2E below.

LEHMAN v. CITY OF SHAKER HEIGHTS

418 U.S. 298, 94 S.Ct. 2714, 41 L.Ed.2d 770 (1974).

Certiorari to the Supreme Court of Ohio.

[Petitioner Lehman was a candidate for election to the Ohio General Assembly in 1970. He attempted to buy car card space for campaign advertisements on the Shaker Heights city-owned buses. His proposed copy contained his picture and read: "HARRY J. LEHMAN IS OLD-FASHIONED! ABOUT HONESTY, INTEGRITY AND GOOD GOVERNMENT." Advertising space was refused because of the city's rule against political advertising. As the plurality opinion explained, though the transit system "accepted ads from cigarette companies, banks, savings and loan associations, liquor companies, retail and service establishments, churches, and civic and public-service oriented groups," it had always barred "*any* political or public issue advertising" on the buses, "pursuant to city council action." Petitioner unsuccessfully sought relief in the state courts on the basis of the First Amendment and the equal protection clause.]

Mr. Justice BLACKMUN announced the judgment of the Court and an opinion, in which The Chief Justice [BURGER], Mr. Justice WHITE, and Mr. Justice REHNQUIST join.

This case presents the question whether a city which operates a public rapid transit system and sells advertising space for car cards on its vehicles is required by the First and Fourteenth Amendments to accept paid political advertising on behalf of a candidate for public office. . . .

---

* For another articulate public forum opinion in the late years of the Warren Court, see Justice Marshall's opinion in the Logan Valley Plaza case, sec. 2E below.

† For consideration of protests in other "nontraditional" public forums, note also the public school cases, including Tinker, sec. 3 below, and Grayned v. City of Rockford, sec. 2C above. See also chap. 13, sec. 4. Note also the problem of access to military bases, in Flower v. United States, 407 U.S. 197 (1972). There, the Court summarily reversed a conviction for distributing peace leaflets on a street within the boundaries of an Army base in San Antonio: "Whatever power the authorities may have to restrict general access to a military facility, here the fort commander chose not to exclude the public from the street where petitioner was arrested."

It is urged that the car cards here constitute a public forum protected by the First Amendment, and that there is a guarantee of nondiscriminatory access to such publicly owned and controlled areas of communication "regardless of the primary purpose for which the area is dedicated."

We disagree.   In Packer Corp. v. Utah, 285 U.S. 105, 110 (1932), Mr. Justice Brandeis, in speaking for a unanimous Court, recognized that "there is a difference which justifies the classification between display advertising and that in periodicals or newspapers."   In Packer the Court upheld a Utah statute that made it a misdemeanor to advertise cigarettes on " 'any bill board, street car sign, street car, placard,' " but exempted dealers' signs on their places of business and cigarette advertising " 'in any newspaper, magazine, or periodical.' "   The Court found no equal protection violation.   It reasoned that viewers of billboards and streetcar signs had no "choice or volition" to observe such advertising and had the message "thrust upon them by all the arts and devices that skill can produce. . . .   The radio can be turned off, but not so the billboard or street car placard."   "The streetcar audience is a captive audience.   It is there as a matter of necessity, not of choice."   Public Utilities Comm'n v. Pollak, 343 U.S. 451, 468 (1952) (Douglas, J., dissenting). . . .

These situations are different from the traditional settings where First Amendment values inalterably prevail.   Lord Dunedin, in M'Ara v. Magistrates of Edinburgh, [1913] Sess.Cas. 1059, 1073–1074, said, "[T]he truth is that open spaces and public places differ very much in their character, and before you could say whether a certain thing could be done in a certain place you would have to know the history of the particular place."   Although American constitutional jurisprudence, in the light of the First Amendment, has been jealous to preserve access to public places for purposes of free speech, the nature of the forum and the conflicting interests involved have remained important in determining the degree of protection afforded by the Amendment to the speech in question. . . .

Here, we have no open spaces, no meeting hall, park, street corner, or other public thoroughfare.   Instead, the city is engaged in commerce. It must provide rapid, convenient, pleasant, and inexpensive service to the commuters of Shaker Heights.   The car card space, although incidental to the provision of public transportation, is a part of the commercial venture. In much the same way that a newspaper or periodical, or even a radio or television station, need not accept every proffer of advertising from the general public, a city transit system has discretion to develop and make reasonable choices concerning the type of advertising that may be displayed in its vehicles. . . .

Because state action exists, however, the policies and practices governing access to the transit system's advertising space must not be arbitrary, capricious, or invidious.   Here, the city has decided that "[p]urveyors of goods and services saleable in commerce may purchase advertising space on an equal basis, whether they be house builders or butchers."   This decision is little different from deciding to impose a 10-, 25-, or 35-cent fare, or from changing schedules or the location of bus stops.   Revenue earned from long-term commercial advertising could be jeopardized by a requirement that short-term candidacy or issue-oriented advertisements be displayed on car cards.

Users would be subjected to the blare of political propaganda. There could be lurking doubts about favoritism, and sticky administrative problems might arise in parceling out limited space to eager politicians. In these circumstances, the managerial decision to limit car card space to innocuous and less controversial commercial and service oriented advertising does not rise to the dignity of a First Amendment violation. Were we to hold to the contrary, display cases in public hospitals, libraries, office buildings, military compounds, and other public facilities immediately would become Hyde Parks open to every would-be pamphleteer and politician. This the Constitution does not require.

No First Amendment forum is here to be found. The city consciously has limited access to its transit system advertising space in order to minimize chances of abuse, the appearance of favoritism, and the risk of imposing upon a captive audience. These are reasonable legislative objectives advanced by the city in a proprietary capacity. In these circumstances, there is no First or Fourteenth Amendment violation.

[Affirmed.]

Mr. Justice DOUGLAS, concurring in the judgment. . . .

My Brother Brennan would find that "[a] forum for communication was voluntarily established . . .." If the streetcar or bus were a forum for communication akin to that of streets or public parks, considerable problems would be presented. [Hague v. CIO.] But a streetcar or bus is plainly not a park or sidewalk or other meeting place for discussion, any more than is a highway. It is only a way to get to work or back home. The fact that it is owned and operated by the city does not without more make it a forum.

Bus and streetcar placards are in the category of highway billboards which have long been used to display an array of commercial and political messages. But this particular form of communication has been significantly curtailed by state regulation adopted pursuant to the Highway Beautification Act of 1965, which conditions certain federal highway funds upon strict regulation of highway advertising. . . . The fact that land on which a billboard rests is municipal land does not curtail or enhance such regulatory schemes.

If a bus is a forum it is more akin to a newspaper than to a park. Yet if a bus is treated as a newspaper, then, as we hold this date, Miami Herald Publishing Co. v. Tornillo [sec. 2E below], the owner cannot be forced to include in his offerings news or other items which outsiders may desire but which the owner abhors. Newspaper cases are cited to support petitioner's claim. The First Amendment, however, draws no distinction between press privately owned, and press owned otherwise. And if we are to turn a bus or streetcar into either a newspaper or a park, we take great liberties with people who because of necessity become commuters and at the same time captive viewers or listeners.

In asking us to force the system to accept his message as a vindication of his constitutional rights, the petitioner overlooks the constitutional rights of the commuters. While petitioner clearly has a right to express his views to those who wish to listen, he has no right to force his message upon an audience incapable of declining to receive it. In my view the right of the

commuters to be free from forced intrusions on their privacy precludes the city from transforming its vehicles of public transportation into forums for the dissemination of ideas upon this captive audience.

Buses are not recreational vehicles used for Sunday chautauquas as a public park might be used on holidays for such a purpose; they are a practical necessity for millions in our urban centers. I have already stated this view in my dissent in [PUC v. Pollak, sec. 2B above], involving the challenge by some passengers to the practice of broadcasting radio programs over loudspeakers in buses and streetcars: " . . . [T]he man on the streetcar has no choice but to sit and listen, or perhaps to sit and to try *not* to listen." There is no difference when the message is visual, not auricular. In each the viewer or listener is captive. . . .

I do not view the content of the message as relevant either to petitioner's right to express it or to the commuters' right to be free from it. Commercial advertisements may be as offensive and intrusive to captive audiences as any political message. But the validity of the commercial advertising program is not before us since we are not faced with one complaining of an invasion of privacy through forced exposure to commercial ads. Since I do not believe that petitioner has any constitutional right to spread his message before this captive audience, I concur in the Court's judgment.

Mr. Justice BRENNAN, with whom Mr. Justice STEWART, Mr. Justice MARSHALL, and Mr. Justice POWELL join, dissenting. . . .

I would reverse. In my view, the city created a forum for the dissemination of information and expression of ideas when it accepted and displayed commercial and public service advertisements on its rapid transit vehicles. Having opened a forum for communication, the city is barred by the First and Fourteenth Amendments from discriminating among forum users solely on the basis of message content.

The message Lehman sought to convey concerning his candidacy for public office was unquestionably protected by the First Amendment. . . . The fact that the message is proposed as a paid advertisement does not diminish the impregnable shelter afforded by the First Amendment. See [New York Times Co. v. Sullivan, chap. 13, sec. 1.]

Of course, not even the right of political self-expression is completely unfettered. . . . Accordingly, we have repeatedly recognized the constitutionality of reasonable "time, place and manner" regulations which are applied in an evenhanded fashion. . . .

Focusing upon the propriety of regulating "place," the city of Shaker Heights attempts to justify its ban against political advertising by arguing that the interior advertising space of a transit car is an inappropriate forum for political expression and debate. To be sure, there are some public places which are so clearly committed to other purposes that their use as public forums for communication is anomalous. [See Adderley v. Florida, (Douglas, J., dissenting).] The determination of whether a particular type of public property or facility constitutes a "public forum" requires the Court to strike a balance between the competing interests of the government, on the one hand, and the speaker and his audience, on the other. Thus, the Court must assess the importance of the primary use to which the public property

or facility is committed, and the extent to which that use will be disrupted if access for free expression is permitted.

Applying these principles, the Court has long recognized the public's right of access to public streets and parks for expressive activity. [Hague v. CIO.] More recently, the Court has added state capitol grounds to the list of public forums compatible with free speech, free assembly, and the freedom to petition for redress of grievances [Edwards v. South Carolina], but denied similar status to the curtilage of a jailhouse, [Adderley v. Florida].[1]

In the circumstances of this case, however, we need not decide whether public transit cars *must* be made available as forums for the exercise of First Amendment rights. By accepting commercial and public service advertising, the city effectively waived any argument that advertising in its transit cars is incompatible with the rapid transit system's primary function of providing transportation. A forum for communication was voluntarily established when the city installed the physical facilities for the advertisements [and] created the necessary administrative machinery for regulating access to that forum.[2]

The plurality opinion, however, contends that as long as the city limits its advertising space to "innocuous and less controversial commercial and service oriented advertising," no First Amendment forum is created. I find no merit in that position. Certainly, non-commercial public service advertisements convey messages of public concern and are clearly protected by the First Amendment. And while it is possible that commercial advertising may be accorded *less* First Amendment protection than speech concerning political and social issues of public importance, compare [Valentine v. Chrestensen, 316 U.S. 52 (1942), with Schneider v. State, 308 U.S. 147 (1939), and Breard v. City of Alexandria, 341 U.S. 622 (1951), with Martin v. City of Struthers, 319 U.S. 141 (1943)—see the note on "commercial speech," below], it is "speech" nonetheless, often communicating information and ideas found by many persons to be controversial.[3] There can be no question that commercial advertisements, when skillfully employed, are powerful vehicles for the exaltation of commercial values. Once such messages have been accepted and displayed, the existence of a forum for communication cannot be gainsaid. To hold otherwise, and thus sanction the city's preference for bland commercialism and noncontroversial public service messages over "uninhibited, robust, and wide-open" debate on public issues, would reverse the traditional priorities of the First Amendment.

1. Public-forum status has also been extended to municipal bus terminals, see Wolin v. Port of New York Authority, 392 F.2d 83 (C.A.2 1968), and railroad stations, see In re Hoffman, 67 Cal.2d 845, 434 P.2d 353 (1967). [Footnote by Justice Brennan.]

2. My Brother Douglas' analogy to billboard and newspaper advertising is not apropos in the circumstances of this case where the advertising display space is *city* owned and operated. [Footnote by Justice Brennan].

3. There is some doubt whether the "commercial speech" distinction announced in [Valentine v. Chrestensen] retains continuing vitality. [T]he question, however, need not be decided in this case. It is sufficient for the purpose of public forum analysis merely to recognize that commercial speech enjoys at least *some* degree of protection under the First Amendment, without reaching the more difficult question concerning the *amount* of protection afforded. [Footnote by Justice Brennan.]

Once a public forum for communication has been established, both free speech and equal protection principles prohibit discrimination based *solely* upon subject matter or content.[4] "Necessarily, then, under the Equal Protection Clause, not to mention the First Amendment itself, government may not grant the use of a forum to people whose views it finds acceptable, but deny use to those wishing to express less favored or more controversial views. . . ." [Police Dept. of Chicago v. Mosley, 408 U.S. 92 (1972).] That the discrimination is among entire classes of ideas, rather than among points of view within a particular class, does not render it any less odious. Subject matter or content censorship in any form is forbidden.[5]

To insure that subject matter or content is not the sole basis for discrimination among forum users, all selective exclusions from a public forum must be closely scrutinized and countenanced only in cases where the Government makes a clear showing that its action was taken pursuant to neutral "time, place and manner" regulations, narrowly tailored to protect the Government's substantial interest in preserving the viability and utility of the forum itself. . . . The city has failed to discharge that heavy burden in the present case.

The city contends that its ban against political advertising is bottomed upon its solicitous regard for "captive riders" of the rapid transit system . . . . Whatever merit the city's argument might have in other contexts, it has a hollow ring in the present case, where the city has voluntarily opened its rapid transit system as a forum for communication. . . .

The line between ideological and nonideological speech is impossible to draw with accuracy. By accepting commercial and public service advertisements, the city opened the door to "sometimes controversial or unsettling speech" and determined that such speech does not unduly interfere with the rapid transit system's primary purpose of transporting passengers. In the eyes of many passengers, certain commercial or public service messages [6] are as profoundly disturbing as some political advertisements might be to other passengers. . . .

Moreover, even if it were possible to draw a manageable line between controversial and noncontroversial messages, the city's practice of censorship for the benefit of "captive audiences" still would not be justified.[7] This is

4. The plurality opinion's reliance upon [Packer Corp. v. Utah] is misplaced . . . : "In [Packer Corp.] the First Amendment problem was not raised. . . ." [Footnote by Justice Brennan.]

5. The existence of other public forums for the dissemination of political messages is, of course, irrelevant. As the Court said in Schneider v. State, 308 U.S. 147, 163 (1939), "one is not to have the exercise of his liberty of expression in appropriate places abridged on the plea that it may be exercised in some other place." [Footnote by Justice Brennan.]

6. For example, the record indicates that *church advertising* was accepted for display on the Shaker Heights Rapid Transit System. [Footnote by Justice Brennan.]

7. My Brother Douglas' contrary view . . . does not dispose of the First and Fourteenth Amendment issues in this case. The record reveals that the Shaker Heights Rapid Transit System provides advertising space on the *outside* as well as the inside of its cars. Lehman was denied access to both. Whatever applicability a "captive audience" theory may have to interior advertising, it simply cannot justify the city's refusal to rent Lehman *exterior* advertising space. [Footnote by Justice Brennan.]

not a case where an unwilling or unsuspecting rapid transit rider is powerless to avoid messages he deems unsettling. The advertisements [are] not broadcast over loudspeakers in the transit cars. [Pollak; cf. Kovacs v. Cooper.] Rather, all advertisements [are] in *written* form. . . . Should passengers chance to glance at advertisements they find offensive, they can "effectively avoid further bombardment of their sensibilities simply by averting their eyes." [Cohen v. California.] Surely that minor inconvenience is a small price to pay for the continued preservation of so precious a liberty as free speech.

The city's remaining justification is equally unpersuasive. The city argues that acceptance of "political advertisements in the cars of the Shaker Heights rapid transit, would suggest, on the one hand, some political favoritism is being granted to candidates who advertise, or, on the other hand, that the candidate so advertised is being supported or promoted by the government of the City." Clearly, such ephemeral concerns do not provide the city with *carte blanche* authority to exclude an entire category of speech from a public forum. ". . . The endorsement of an opinion expressed in an advertisement on a motor coach is no more attributable to the transit district than the view of a speaker in a public park is to the city administration or the tenets of an organization using school property for meetings is to the local school board." Wirta v. Alameda-Contra Costa Transit District, 68 Cal.2d 51, 61, 434 P.2d 982, 989 (1967). The city has introduced no evidence demonstrating that its rapid transit passengers would naively think otherwise. And though there may be "lurking doubts about favoritism," the Court has held that "[n]o such remote danger can justify the immediate and crippling impact on the basic constitutional rights involved in this case." [Williams v. Rhodes, chap. 10 above.]

Moreover, neutral regulations, which do not distinguish among advertisements on the basis of subject matter, can be narrowly tailored to allay the city's fears. The impression of city endorsement can be dispelled by requiring disclaimers to appear prominently on the face of every advertisement. And while problems of accommodating all potential advertisers may be vexing at times, the appearance of favoritism can be avoided by the even-handed regulation of time, place, and manner for all advertising, irrespective of subject matter. . . .

LEHMAN, THE PUBLIC FORUM, AND THE "COMMERCIAL SPEECH" DOCTRINE

1. *Lehman and the public forum.* Lehman presents primarily an issue of "equal access," not "guaranteed access." As Justice Brennan's dissent notes, it was unnecessary to decide here "whether public transit cars *must* be made available as forums." What if the transit system had excluded all advertising, commercial as well as noncommercial? By what criteria should a guaranteed access claim under such circumstances be decided? Is a city bus an "anomalous" place for messages?*

---

* Cf. Justice Blackmun's majority opinion a few months later, in the Southeastern Promotions case, note 3 below. And on the Lehman problem, see Note,

"The Public Forum: Minimum Access, Equal Access, and the First Amendment," 28 Stan.L.Rev. No. 1 (1975).

Would Justice Douglas' position, building on his Pollak dissent (sec. 2B above), bar all advertising on buses, commercial as well as noncommercial? Can Justice Douglas' solicitude for the "captive audience" be reconciled with his statements in Saia v. New York, the Loudspeaker Case, sec. 2B above? Can the majority's solicitude for the "captive audience"—in Justice Blackmun's opinion as well as Justice Douglas'—be reconciled with the weight accorded to the interests of the audience in the offensive language cases, above? In the hostile audience cases, above?

2. *The "commercial speech" doctrine.* Justice Blackmun's plurality opinion in Lehman places some emphasis on the fact that car card advertising was part of a "commercial venture." As Justice Brennan's dissent notes, there are suggestions in the cases that commercial advertising may be "accorded *less* First Amendment protection than speech concerning political and social issues of public importance." In Lehman, by contrast, the result is that commercial speech is displayed, while political speech is barred.

The "commercial speech" doctrine had its origin in Valentine v. Chrestensen, 316 U.S. 52 (1942), a ruling Justice Douglas was later to call "casual, almost offhand." The brief opinion in Valentine sustained a ban on distribution of handbill advertisements soliciting customers to pay admission to tour a submarine. The entrepreneur in Valentine printed his advertising message on one side of the circular, with a protest on the other against the city's denial of permission to use a city pier for his exhibit. The Court viewed the ban as a regulation of business activity rather than protected speech. Later cases have made it clear however, that speech does not fall wholly outside the First Amendment simply because it is in a commercial context. For example, the "speech" in New York Times Co. v. Sullivan, chap. 13, sec. 1, below, was a paid advertisement containing a political protest; the Court found that the First Amendment barred a libel action based on that advertisement. Nevertheless, the commercial-noncommercial distinction continues to play a role in the cases, as Justice Brennan citations indicate. For example, Martin v. City of Struthers, 319 U.S. 141 (1943), barred the application of a city ordinance prohibiting uninvited solicitors for Jehovah's Witness going door-to-door distributing leaflets about a religious meeting. By contrast, Breard v. Alexandria, 341 U.S. 622 (1951), sustained a conviction of magazine subscription solicitors, emphasizing the householders' interest in privacy and repose.

A year before Lehman, a narrowly divided Court squarely relied on the Valentine v. Chrestensen "commercial speech" doctrine for the first time in many years. The 5 to 4 decision in PITTSBURGH PRESS CO. v. HUMAN RELATIONS COMM'N, 413 U.S. 376 (1973), rejected a First Amendment attack on a local order prohibiting a newspaper from listing advertisements for jobs covered by an anti-sex discrimination ordinance in sex-designated help-wanted columns. Justice Powell wrote for the majority; Chief Justice Burger and Justices Douglas, Stewart and Blackmun were the dissenters. Justice Powell insisted that the "commercial speech" exception limits the ordinary First Amendment immunity of the press. Though he recognized that the First Amendment was not wholly inapplicable to advertisements, the ads were found to "resemble the Chrestensen rather than the [New York Times Co. v. Sullivan] advertisement" and were "classic ex-

amples of commercial speech." He emphasized that the sex-designated column headings used by the newspaper were not "sufficiently dissociated" from the want ads "to make the placement severable for First Amendment purposes from the want ads themselves. The combination, which conveys essentially the same message as an overtly discriminatory want ad, is in practical effect an integrated commercial statement." * He concluded that "the restriction on advertising is incidental to a valid limitation on economic activity."

Chief Justice Burger's dissent perceived "a disturbing enlargement of the 'commercial speech' doctrine" and "a serious encroachment" on the First Amendment. Assuming restrictions on commercial advertisements themselves were permissible, "I would not enlarge that power to reach the layout and organizational decisions of a newspaper." Another dissent, by Justice Douglas, noted that the press "can be regulated on business and economic matters," but that the First Amendment entitles it to "publish what it pleases about any law." A third dissent, by Justice Stewart, insisted that no government "can tell a newspaper in advance what it can print and what it cannot." If government can dictate advertising layout today, "what is there to prevent it from dictating the layout of the news pages tomorrow?" †

3. *The public forum after Lehman: The Southeastern Promotions case.* Contrast Justice Blackmun's reluctance to recognize a public forum claim in Lehman with his majority opinion less than a year later in SOUTHEASTERN PROMOTIONS, LTD. v. CONRAD, 420 U.S. —— (1975). There, the Court found that the challenger's First Amendment rights were violated when the municipal board managing city theaters in Chattanooga refused permission to present "the controversial rock musical 'Hair.'" The refusal was based on the ground that the production would not be "in the best interest of the community." Though the alleged obscenity of "Hair" had been the major issue in the lower courts, Justice Blackmun did not reach that question. Instead, he found that the refusal constituted a prior restraint imposed without affording the "rigorous procedural safeguards" required by Freedman v. Maryland, 380 U.S. 51 (1965) (chap. 13, sec. 3, below).

In the course of reaching that conclusion, Justice Blackmun commented that the municipal theaters were "public forums designed for and dedicated to expressive activities." He added: "None of the circumstances qualifying as an established exception to the doctrine of prior restraint was present. Petitioner was not seeking to use a facility primarily serving a competing use. [E. g., Adderley; Brown.] Nor was rejection of the application based on any regulation of time, place, or manner related to the nature of the facility or applications from other users. [E. g., Cox v. New Hampshire.] No rights of individuals in surrounding areas were violated by noise or any other aspect of the production. [Kovacs v. Cooper.] There was no captive audience. See [Lehman; Pollak]. Whether the petitioner might have used some other, privately owned, theater in the city for the production is of no

---

* Justice Powell added: "Discrimination in employment is not only commercial activity, it is *illegal* commercial activity under the Ordinance. We have no doubt that a newspaper constitutionally could be forbidden to publish a want ad proposing a sale of narcotics or soliciting prostitutes."

† See also the additional materials on restraints on the media, sec. 2E of this chapter, and sec. 3 of the next chapter.

consequence. . . . Even if a privately owned forum had been available, that fact alone would not justify an otherwise impermissible prior restraint. [Schneider.]"

Justice Douglas' dissent thought the "application of a few procedural band-aids" inadequate: he insisted that no prior screening process was permissible. And he added: "A municipal theatre is no less a forum for the expression of ideas than is a public park, or a sidewalk." A dissent by Justice White, joined by Chief Justice Burger, concluded that, whether or not "Hair" is obscene, the city "could constitutionally forbid exhibition of the musical for children" and could "reserve its auditorium for productions suitable for exhibition to all the citizens of the city, adults and children alike." Another dissent, by Justice Rehnquist, argued that a public auditorium should not be equated with public streets and parks. He feared that the majority had given "no constitutionally permissible role in the way of selection to the municipal authorities" and asked: "May a municipal theater devote an entire season to Shakespeare, or is it required to book any potential producer on a first-come, first-served basis?" He concluded that a city policy not to show attractions "of the kind that would offend any substantial number of potential theater goers" was not "arbitrary or unreasonable." He concluded: "A municipal theater may not be run by municipal authorities as if it were a private theater, free to judge on a content basis alone which plays it wished to have performed and which it did not. But, just as surely, that element of it which is 'theater' ought to be accorded some constitutional recognition along with that element of it which is 'municipal.' "

E. PRIVATE PROPERTY AND THE FORUM: A RIGHT OF ACCESS TO SHOPPING CENTERS AND THE MEDIA?

Introduction. The preceding cases considered claimed rights of equal or guaranteed access to public places. Do the principles of those cases aid in developing any claim of access by a speaker who wants to use privately owned property to voice his message? Is there a "private forum" counterpart to the public forum developments? Do the private forum cases throw light on the appropriate ingredients of a public forum doctrine? In recent years, claims of access to privately owned property have been voiced in a variety of contexts. Typically, these cases involve not only First Amendment principles, but also the delineation of the applicability of constitutional norms to the private sector. Recall chap. 11 and its "state action" problem: ordinarily constitutional guarantees limit only government; in several of the private property cases below, accordingly, problems of the applicability of constitutional guarantees are intertwined with the dimensions of First Amendment assurances.

That intertwining is especially reflected in the first group of cases, involving claimed rights of access to privately owned shopping centers as a forum for the airing of messages. The second group of cases presents claims of access to the heavily regulated broadcasting media: May government impose access requirements on the holders of broadcasting licenses? May First

Amendment claimants assert rights against licensees to broadcast messages? And the final case in this group asks whether government may enforce access rights against the privately owned, largely unregulated press media, in the interest of making newspapers the forums for the airing of a wider range of views. In each of these contexts, the public forum principles developed in the preceding materials are reexamined and, occasionally, clarified.

THE FIRST AMENDMENT AND ACCESS TO PRIVATELY OWNED SHOPPING CENTERS: THE LOGAN VALLEY AND LLOYD CASES

1. *Logan Valley.* More than a generation ago, in Marsh v. Alabama, 326 U.S. 501 (1946) (see chap. 11 above), the Court initiated the "state action"-"public function" theory by holding that Jehovah's Witnesses could claim a constitutional right of access to distribute religious literature in a company-owned town. In 1968, the 5 to 4 decision in AMALGAMATED FOOD EMPLOYEES v. LOGAN VALLEY PLAZA, 391 U.S. 308, relied in part on Marsh to hold that a state trespass law could not be applied to enjoin peaceful union picketing of a supermarket in a private shopping center.* Justice Marshall's majority opinion found that the ban on picketing could not be justified on the ground that picketing constituted an unconsented invasion of private property rights: "The shopping center here is clearly the functional equivalent of the business district of Chickasaw involved in Marsh. . . . We see no reason why access to a business district in a company town for the purpose of exercising First Amendment rights should be constitutionally required, while access for the same purpose to property functioning as a business district should be limited simply because the property surrounding the 'business district' is not under the same ownership."

Having established the applicability of constitutional restraints to the shopping center, Justice Marshall proceeded to examine the scope of First Amendment public forum principles in this context: "It is clear that if the shopping center premises were not privately owned but instead constituted the business area of a municipality, which they to a large extent resemble, petitioners could not be barred from exercising their First Amendment rights there on the sole ground that title to the property was in the municipality. The essence of [cases such as Lovell v. Griffin, Hague v. CIO, and Schneider v. State] is that streets, sidewalks, parks, and other similar public places are so historically associated with the exercise of First Amendment rights that access to them for the purpose of exercising such rights cannot constitutionally be denied broadly and absolutely.

"The fact that [decisions such as Lovell and Schneider] were concerned with handbilling rather than picketing is immaterial so far as the question is solely one of right of access for the purpose of expression of views. Handbilling, like picketing, involves conduct other than speech, namely, the physical presence of the person distributing leaflets on municipal property. If title to municipal property is, standing alone, an insufficient basis for pro-

---

* The "state action" aspect of the Logan Valley case is noted in chap. 11 above. Other First Amendment as-pects of union picketing are considered in chap. 13, sec. 4, below.

hibiting all entry onto such property for the purpose of distributing printed matter, it is likewise an insufficient basis for prohibiting all entry for the purpose of carrying an informational placard. While the patrolling involved in picketing may in some cases constitute an interference with the use of public property greater than that produced by handbilling, it is clear that in other cases the converse may be true. .   .   .   That the manner in which handbilling, or picketing, is carried out may be regulated does not mean that either can be barred under all circumstances on publicly owned property simply by recourse to traditional concepts of property law concerning the incidents of ownership of real property."

Justice Marshall distinguished decisions sustaining restrictions on access to public property—such as the jail vicinity in Adderley—by noting that, "where property is not ordinarily open to the public, this Court has held that access to it for the purpose of exercising First Amendment rights may be denied altogether. Even where municipal or state property is open to the public generally, the exercise of First Amendment rights may be regulated so as to prevent interference with the use to which the property is ordinarily put by the State. .   .   .   In addition, the exercise of First Amendment rights may be regulated where such exercise will unduly interfere with the normal use of the public property by other members of the public with an equal right of access to it. Thus it has been held that persons desiring to parade along city streets may be required to secure a permit in order that municipal authorities be able to limit the amount of interference with use of the sidewalks by other members of the public by regulating the time, place, and manner of the parade."

The detailed scope of permissible restrictions was not at issue here, however: "Because the Pennsylvania courts have held that 'picketing and trespassing' can be prohibited absolutely on respondents' premises, we have no occasion to consider the extent to which respondents are entitled to limit the location and manner of the picketing or the number of picketers within the mall in order to prevent interference with either access to the market building or vehicular use of the parcel pickup area and parking lot. Likewise, Adderley furnishes no support for the decision below because it is clear that the public has virtually unrestricted access to the property at issue here. [T]he restraints on picketing and trespassing approved by the Pennsylvania courts here substantially hinder the communication of the ideas which petitioners seek to express . . . . The fact that the nonspeech aspects of petitioners' activity are also rendered less effective is not particularly compelling in light of the absence of any showing [that] the patrolling accompanying the picketing sought to be carried on was significantly interfering with the use to which the mall property was being put by both respondents and the general public. [T]he mere fact that speech is accompanied by conduct does not mean that the speech can be suppressed under the guise of prohibiting the conduct. Here it is perfectly clear that a prohibition against trespass on the mall operates to bar all speech within the shopping center to which respondents object. Yet this Court stated many years ago, '[O]ne is not to have the exercise of his liberty of expression in appropriate places abridged on the plea that it may be exercised in some other place.' [Schneider v. State]."

Justice Black's dissent included the comment: "[O]f course, picketing, that is patrolling, is not free speech and not protected as such." Justice White's

dissent stated, in partial reliance on Adderley: "[S]ome public property is available for some uses and not for others; some public property is neither designed nor dedicated for use by pickets or for other communicative activities. [W]hether Logan Valley Plaza is public or private property, it is a place for shopping and not a place for picketing."

2. *Lloyd.* The Logan Valley decision was "distinguished" four years later, in the 5 to 4 decision in LLOYD CORP. v. TANNER, 407 U.S. 551 (1972). In Lloyd, the lower federal courts had relied on Marsh and Logan Valley in holding unconstitutional the application to anti-war leafleters of a shopping center ban on the distribution of handbills. In a 5 to 4 decision, the Supreme Court reversed, finding the facts in its earlier cases "significantly different." Justice Powell found reliance on the "functional equivalent of a public business district" language in Logan Valley unjustifiable. There, the First Amendment activity—union picketing of a store—"was related to the shopping center's operations." Moreover, the store there was "in the center of a large private enclave with the consequence that no other reasonable opportunities" to convey the picketers' message existed. Here, in contrast to Logan Valley, the handbilling "had no relation to any purpose for which the center was built and being used." Moreover, here, unlike Logan Valley, there were alternative means of communication available. Patrons of the large shopping center had to cross public streets to get into the private areas: "Handbills may be distributed conveniently to pedestrians, and also to occupants of automobiles, from these public sidewalks and streets."

More generally, Justice Powell commented that the free speech guarantees are "limitations on *state* action, not on action by the owner of private property used nondiscriminatorily for private purposes only." And he emphasized that the protections of property in the due process clauses were "also relevant": "Although accommodations between [speech and property values] are sometimes necessary, and the courts properly have shown a special solicitude for the [First Amendment], this Court has never held that a trespasser or an uninvited guest may exercise general rights of free speech on property privately owned."

Justice Marshall's sharp dissent, joined by Justices Douglas, Brennan and Stewart, insisted that Logan Valley was not truly distinguishable, that the majority opinion was "an attack" on the rationale of Marsh as well as Logan Valley, and that "one may suspect from reading the [majority opinion] that it is Logan Valley itself that the Court finds bothersome." [See the excerpts from the Lloyd dissent in chap. 11, sec. 2, above.]

Of special interest to the development of "guaranteed access" public forum principles is Justice Marshall's explanation in Lloyd of the "tremendous need" of the handbillers to have access to the private shopping center: "For many persons who do not have easy access to television, radio, the major newspapers, and the other forms of mass media, the only way they can express themselves to a broad range of citizens on issues of general public concern is to picket, or to handbill, or to utilize other free or relatively inexpensive means of communication. The only hope that these people have to be able to communicate effectively is to be permitted to speak in those areas in which most of their fellow citizens can be found. One such area is the business district of a city or town or its functional equivalent."†

† Note also Justice Marshall's comments on the public forum concept in the public school context, in Grayned v. City of Rockford, 408 U.S. 104 (1972),

A RIGHT OF ACCESS TO THE BROADCASTING MEDIA?

1. *Government regulations to assure a right to reply on the broadcasting media: The Red Lion case.* May government safeguard individual reputations by requiring a broadcaster to afford reply time to the target of an attack? Does that requirement in turn violate the First Amendment rights of the broadcaster? When government has sought to vindicate the interest in private reputation by authorizing defamation actions, the Court has sharply curtailed suits against the press, ever since New York Times Co. v. Sullivan, chap. 13, sec. 1, below. But when the FCC sought to provide rights of access for individuals attacked on the air and imposed requirements that radio and television stations give reply time, the Court sustained the regulations. RED LION BROADCASTING CO. v. FCC, 395 U.S. 367 (1969).

The FCC traditional "fairness doctrine" requires stations to present discussion of public issues, and to assure fair coverage for each side. Later FCC rulings elaborated the personal attack and political editorials aspects of the fairness doctrine by specifying the circumstances in which free reply time had to be made available by licensees. In sustaining those regulations in the Red Lion case, Justice White's opinion supported a limited right of access to the broadcasting media. He found that the FCC's elaborations of the fairness doctrine "enhance rather than abridge the freedoms of speech and press." He emphasized the "scarcity of broadcast frequencies, the Government's role in allocating those frequencies, and the legitimate claims of those unable without governmental assistance to gain access to those frequencies for expression of their views."

In response to the broadcasters' First Amendment claims, the Court stressed the speech interests of the public: "Where there are substantially more individuals who want to broadcast than there are frequencies to allocate, it is idle to posit an unabridgeable First Amendment right to broadcast comparable to the right of every individual to speak, write, or publish. . . . It is the purpose of the First Amendment to preserve an uninhibited marketplace of ideas in which truth will ultimately prevail, rather than to countenance monopolization of that market, whether it be by the Government itself or a private licensee. . . . It is the right of the public to receive suitable access to social, political, esthetic, moral, and other ideas and experiences which is crucial here" and which justified this "enforced sharing of a scarce resource."

in an opinion for the Court rejecting an overbreadth attack on an ordinance prohibiting noise near school buildings. (See also the materials on the First Amendment in the school context in chap. 13, sec. 4.) Justice Marshall said in Grayned: "We would be ignoring reality if we did not recognize that the public schools [are] often the focus of significant grievances. Without interfering wtih normal school activities, daytime picketing and handbilling on public grounds near a school can effectively publicize those grievances . . . . Some picketing to that end will be quiet and peaceful, and will in no way disturb the normal functioning of the school. . . . On the other hand, schools could hardly tolerate boisterous demonstrators who drown out classroom conversation, making studying impossible, block entrances, or incite children to leave the schoolhouse."

The Court commented, moreover: "Although broadcasting is clearly a medium affected by a First Amendment interest, differences in the characteristics of news media justify differences in the First Amendment standards applied to them. Just as the Government may limit the use of sound amplifying equipment potentially so noisy that it drowns out civilized private speech, so may the Government limit the use of broadcast equipment. The right of free speech of a broadcaster, the user of a sound truck, or any other individual does not embrace a right to snuff out the free speech of others."

It would be "a serious matter," to be sure, if the FCC requirements induced self-censorship by licensees and made their coverage of controversial public issues "ineffective." But that was only a speculative possibility. And if licensees "should suddenly prove timorous, the Commission is not powerless to insist that they give adequate and fair attention to public issues. It does not violate the First Amendment to treat licensees given the privilege of using scarce radio frequencies as proxies for the entire community, obligated to give suitable time and attention to matters of great public concern." Rejection of the broadcasters' claim here did not mean that they might not "raise more serious first amendment issues" in other circumstances: here, there was no question, for example, of any FCC "refusal to permit the broadcaster to carry a particular program or to publish his own views," or "of government censorship of a particular program," or "of the official government view dominating public broadcasting."

2. *A First Amendment right of access to the broadcasting media for editorial advertisements?—The Columbia Broadcasting case.* That the right of access to the broadcasting media is a very limited one was made clear three years later, when the Court decided COLUMBIA BROADCASTING SYSTEM v. DEMOCRATIC NAT. COMM., 412 U.S. 94 (1973). The CBS case involved a broadcasting context counterpart to the access claim presented in the city bus advertising situation in Lehman v. City of Shaker Heights, above. The CBS case originated with complaints filed before the FCC in 1970 by the Democratic National Committee and an anti-war group challenging certain broadcasters' policies of refusing all editorial advertisements. The FCC sustained the broadcasters' position, but the Court of Appeals reversed, holding that "a flat ban on paid public issue announcements is in violation of the First Amendment, at least when other sorts of paid announcements are accepted." The divided Court's resolution of that controversy in 1973 produced a series of elaborate opinions. In resolving conflicting emanations from First Amendment values, the majority emphasized the broadcasters' right to control the content of their programs, while the dissenters gave greater weight to the public's right of access to the airwaves.*

Chief Justice Burger's opinion rejected the argument that a broad right of access could be drawn from the Red Lion ruling. Instead, he em-

---

* The majority's position on most issues was stated by Chief Justice Burger. Justice Brennan, joined by Justice Marshall, dissented. Justice Douglas submitted an extensive opinion concurring in the majority's result. Justice Stewart, who concurred with parts of the Chief Justice's opinion, also submitted an extensive concurrence. Moreover, there were brief partial concurring opinions by Justice White and by Justice Blackmun, joined by Justice Powell.

phasized the indications in the statutory background "that Congress intended to permit private broadcasting to develop with the widest journalistic freedom consistent with its public obligations." Chief Justice Burger considered the First Amendment problems despite his earlier conclusion that the broadcasters' policy did not constitute "governmental action" for purposes of the First Amendment. [That "state action" aspect of his opinion, in which only Justices Stewart and Rehnquist joined, is more fully considered in chap. 11 above.] In explaining his justifications for discussing the First Amendment issues—a discussion which the dissenters branded as dicta—the Chief Justice noted that the "public interest" standard of the Federal Communications Act "invites reference to First Amendment principles."

After examining the question "whether the various interests in free expression of the public, the broadcaster, and the individuals require broadcasters to sell commercial time to persons wishing to discuss controversial issues," the Chief Justice concluded: "To agree that debate on public issues should be 'robust, and wide-open' does not mean that we should exchange 'public trustee' broadcasting, with all its limitations, for a system of self-appointed editorial commentators." The Chief Justice emphasized: "The Commission's responsibilities under a right-of-access system would tend to draw it into a continuing case-by-case determination of who should be heard and when." Moreover, he noted "the reality that in a very real sense listeners and viewers constitute a 'captive audience.'"

Justice Douglas' concurrence took a far firmer constitutional position on the side of the broadcasters: "My conclusion is that TV and radio stand in the same protected position under the First Amendment as do newspapers and magazines." The Red Lion case, in which he had not participated, curtailed broadcasters' rights unduly, he insisted, since "the First Amendment puts beyond the reach of government federal regulation of news agencies save only business or financial practices which do not involve First Amendment rights." "The ban of 'no' law that abridges freedom of the press is in my view total and complete." All news media "are entitled to live under the laissez-faire regime which the First Amendment sanctions."

Justice Brennan's extensive dissent, joined by Justice Marshall, concluded, on "balancing" the competing interests, that the broadcasters' "absolute ban on editorial advertising" could "serve only to inhibit, rather than to further" robust public debate. He insisted that the fairness doctrine was "insufficient" to provide that kind of debate. He noted not only the interests of broadcasters and of the listening and viewing public, "but also the independent First Amendment interest of groups and individuals in effective self-expression." Drawing on access principles developed in the public forum context, he commented: "[F]reedom of speech does not exist in the abstract. On the contrary, the right to speak can flourish only if it is allowed to operate in an effective forum—whether it be a public park, a schoolroom, a town meeting hall, a soapbox, or a radio and television frequency. For in the absence of an effective means of communication, the right to speak would ring hollow indeed." Accordingly, "in light of the current dominance of the electronic media as the most effective means of reaching the public, any policy that *absolutely* denies citizens access to the airwaves" was unjustifiable. The majority's emphasis on "the broadcaster's assertedly overriding in-

terest in exercising *absolute* control over 'his' frequency," he insisted, reflected an "absolutist" approach which "wholly disregards" competing First Amendment rights and "ignores" the teachings of the Red Lion decision. "First Amendment values," he concluded, require "that individuals be permitted at least *some* opportunity to express their views on public issues over the electronic media." The majority's fears of excessive governmental interference and administrative "apocalypse" were in his view unjustified.

MAY GOVERNMENT IMPOSE A RIGHT OF ACCESS TO NEWSPAPERS?—"RIGHT OF REPLY" LAWS

Direct enforcement of any First Amendment right of access against privately owned newspapers is presumably barred by the "state action" principle. But is government's interest in protecting "right of access" First Amendment values sufficiently strong to impose upon newspapers an obligation to grant a "right of reply"? In 1974, a unanimous Court found any such interest easily overcome by the powerful protection newspapers enjoy because of the freedom of the press guaranteed by the First Amendment.* The decision in MIAMI HERALD PUB. CO. v. TORNILLO, 418 U.S. 241 (1974), held unconstitutional Florida's "right of reply" law and rejected efforts to justify it on the basis of a First Amendment right of access. The statute granted a political candidate a right to equal space to reply to criticism and attacks on his record by a newspaper. The Florida Supreme Court had sustained the law because it furthered the "broad societal interest in the free flow of information to the public." Chief Justice Burger's opinion concluded, however, that the law violated the First Amendment guarantee of a free press.

The Chief Justice reviewed at some length the recent evolution of arguments for "an enforceable right of access to the press" and the concomitant claim "that Government has an obligation to ensure that a wide variety of views reach the public." † He noted that "access advocates" emphasize the concentration of power in the newspaper business and the shrinking number of newspapers; claim that the public has consequently lost its ability to contribute meaningfully to public debate; note the disappearance of real opportunity to form competing newspapers by dissidents; and accordingly urge "that the only effective way to insure fairness and accuracy" is "for government to take affirmative action": "The First Amendment interest of the public in being informed is said to be in peril because the 'marketplace of ideas' is today a monopoly controlled by the owners of the market." But the Chief Justice was not persuaded: "However much validity

---

* For other illustrations of the scope of the press guarantee, recall the Court's division in the Pittsburgh Press case, above, and the protections of newspapers and magazines against prior restraints, in such cases as Near v. Minnesota and New York Times v. United States, chap. 13, sec. 3, below.

† The Chief Justice noted two law review articles on the position of "access advocates": Barron, "Access to the Press—A New First Amendment Right," 80 Harv.L.Rev. 1641 (1967), and Lange, "The Role of the Access Doctrine in the Regulation of the Mass Media: A Critical Review and Assessment," 52 N.Car.L.Rev. 1 (1973). Professor Barron argued for the appellee in the Tornillo case.

may be found in these arguments, at each point the implementation of a remedy such as an enforceable right of access necessarily calls for some mechanism, either governmental or consensual. If it is governmental coercion, this at once brings about a confrontation with the express provisions of the First Amendment and the judicial gloss on that Amendment."

First Amendment principles accordingly barred the Florida remedy. The Court, the Chief Justice noted, had always been sensitive to pressures "on a newspaper to print that which it would not otherwise print." The past Court decisions indicated "that any such a compulsion to publish that which ' "reason" tells them should not be published' is unconstitutional. A responsible press is an undoubtedly desirable goal, but press responsibility is not mandated by the Constitution and like many other virtues it cannot be legislated."

The fact that the newspaper was not being prevented from giving its own views did not help the defenders of the law: "Governmental restraint on publishing need not fall into familiar or traditional patterns to be subject to constitutional limitations on governmental powers. The Florida statute exacts a penalty on the basis of the content of a newspaper." Faced with the statutory compulsion, "editors might well conclude that the safe course is to avoid controversy" and that might induce them to reduce political coverage. The Chief Justice noted: "Government-enforced right of access inescapably 'dampens the vigor and limits the variety of public debate.' " And even if there were no such consequences to the statute, it would nevertheless be invalid "because of its intrusion into the function of editors."

In a brief concurring notation, Justice Brennan, joined by Justice Rehnquist, noted that the Court "implies no view upon the constitutionality of 'retraction' statutes affording plaintiffs able to prove defamatory falsehoods a statutory action to require publication of a retraction." And in another concurring opinion, Justice White agreed that "this law runs afoul of the elementary First Amendment proposition that government may not force a newspaper to print copy which, in its journalistic discretion, it chooses to leave on the newsroom floor." But he urged that the First Amendment permitted "reasonable methods for allowing the average citizen to redeem a falsely tarnished reputation." Freedom of the press, he insisted, "does not carry with it an unrestricted hunting license to prey on the ordinary citizen." He accordingly lamented the restrictions on libel actions against the press announced by the Court on the same day, in the Gertz case (chap. 13, sec. 1).

SECTION 3.   SYMBOLIC EXPRESSION

---

1. *Some introductory questions.* In the modern cases that follow, individuals expressed criticism of public policies in part through symbolic *behavior* rather than words: by burning a draft card; by wearing a black armband in a classroom; by mutilating the flag. In each case, the critic claimed immunity from governmental restraint on the ground that the expression, albeit partly non-verbal, was constitutionally protected "speech." The cases appear in this concluding section of the basic First Amendment chapter not only because of the functional importance of the protest methods and con-

texts. (The symbolic protests stemmed from anti-war and civil rights concerns.) Even stronger reasons for printing the decisions here lie in issues of analysis and doctrine.

In these cases, many of the themes developed in the preceding two sections intertwine and are put to a test; the problems of these cases serve to bring under critical examination the techniques of the earlier cases. How useful, for example, are distinctions between "speech" and "conduct," between "direct" and "indirect" regulations of expression, between regulations of "content" and of "manner"? If threats to First Amendment values warrant a high level of judicial scrutiny, in contrast to the lower level of inquiry appropriate for most areas of social and economic regulation, what are the criteria for invoking that strict as against the "minimum rationality," low level degree of scrutiny? Do the cases that follow involve regulations of "speech," or of "speech plus" or "conduct"? Of "direct," or of "indirect," restraints on communication? What degrees of legislative justification should have been required? What degrees were in fact demanded by the Court? What levels of judicial inquiry were appropriate? What levels were in fact applied? (Note also the questions after Street v. New York, below.)

2. *The background.* The perception that "speech" may be nonverbal did not originate in these modern cases. As the opinions reflect, earlier decisions had given First Amendment protection to some varieties of symbolic expression. For example, as early as 1931, in Stromberg v. California, 283 U.S. 359, the Court held unconstitutional a California prohibition on displaying a red flag "as a sign, symbol or emblem of opposition to organized government." Chief Justice Hughes' majority opinion stated that a law "so vague and indefinite as to permit the punishment of the fair use" of "the opportunity for free political discussion" was "repugnant to the guaranty of liberty" in the 14th Amendment.

In the following decade, moreover, West Virginia State Board of Education v. Barnette, 319 U.S. 624 (1943) (chap. 14, sec. 2, below), held that public school children could not be compelled to salute the flag in violation of their religious scruples. And the prevailing opinion in Brown v. Louisiana, 383 U.S. 131 (1966) (the public library demonstration case, sec. 2D above), emphasized that First Amendment rights "are not confined to verbal expression" and "embrace appropriate types of action." The constitutional claims in the symbolic expression cases which follow sought to build on those premises.

UNITED STATES v. O'BRIEN

391 U.S. 367, 88 S.Ct. 1673, 20 L.Ed.2d 672 (1968).

Certiorari to the United States Court of Appeals for the First Circuit.

Mr. Chief Justice WARREN delivered the opinion of the Court.

On the morning of March 31, 1966, David Paul O'Brien and three companions burned their Selective Service registration certificates on the steps of the South Boston Courthouse. A sizable crowd, including several agents of the Federal Bureau of Investigation, witnessed the event. [O'Brien] stated

to FBI agents that he had burned his registration certificate because of his beliefs, knowing that he was violating federal law. . . .

For this act, O'Brien was [convicted]. He did not contest the fact that he had burned the certificate. He stated in argument to the jury that he burned the certificate publicly to influence others to adopt his antiwar beliefs, as he put it, "so that other people would reevaluate their positions with Selective Service, with the armed forces, and reevaluate their place in the culture of today, to hopefully consider my position."

The indictment upon which he was tried charged that he "willfully and knowingly did mutilate, destroy, and change by burning [his] Registration Certificate in violation of Section 462(b)" [of the Universal Military Training and Service Act of 1948]. Section 462(b)(3), one of six numbered subdivisions of § 462(b), was amended by Congress in 1965 (adding the words italicized below), so that at the time O'Brien burned his certificate an offense was committed by any person "who forges, alters, *knowingly destroys, knowingly mutilates,* or in any manner changes any such certificate . . . ." (Italics supplied.)

[The Court of Appeals] held the 1965 Amendment unconstitutional as a law abridging freedom of speech. At the time the Amendment was enacted, a regulation of the Selective Service System required registrants to keep their registration certificates in their "personal possession at all times." Wilful violations of regulations promulgated pursuant to the Universal Military Training and Service Act were made criminal by statute. The Court of Appeals, therefore, was of the opinion that conduct punishable under the 1965 Amendment was already punishable under the nonpossession regulation, and consequently that the Amendment served no valid purpose; further, that in light of the prior regulation, the Amendment must have been "directed at public as distinguished from private destruction." On this basis, the court concluded that the 1965 Amendment ran afoul of the First Amendment by singling out persons engaged in protests for special treatment. . . . We hold that the 1965 Amendment is constitutional both as enacted and as applied. . . .

When a male reaches the age of 18, he is required by the Universal Military Training and Service Act to register with a local draft board. He is assigned a Selective Service number, and within five days he is issued a registration certificate. Subsequently, and based on a questionnaire completed by the registrant, he is assigned a classification denoting his eligibility for induction, and "[a]s soon as practicable" thereafter he is issued a Notice of Classification. . . .

Congress demonstrated its concern that [registration and classification] certificates issued by the Selective Service System might be abused well before the 1965 Amendment here challenged. The 1948 Act itself prohibited many different abuses involving "any registration certificate, . . . or any other certificate issued pursuant to or prescribed by the provisions of this title, or rules or regulations promulgated hereunder . . . ." Under §§ 12(b) (1)–(5) of the 1948 Act, it was unlawful (1) to transfer a certificate to aid a person in making false identification; (2) to possess a certificate not duly issued with the intent of using it for false identification; (3) to forge, alter, "or in any manner" change a certificate or any notation validly inscribed thereon;

(4) to photograph or make an imitation of a certificate for the purpose of false identification; and (5) to possess a counterfeited or altered certificate. In addition, as previously mentioned, regulations of the Selective Service System required registrants to keep both their registration and classification certificates in their personal possession at all times. . . . And § 12(b) (6) of the Act made knowing violation of any provision of the Act or rules and regulations promulgated pursuant thereto a felony.

By the 1965 Amendment, Congress added to § 12(b) (3) of the 1948 Act the provision here at issue, subjecting to criminal liability not only one who "forges, alters, or in any manner changes" but also one who "knowingly destroys, [or] knowingly mutilates" a certificate. We note at the outset that the 1965 Amendment plainly does not abridge free speech on its face, and we do not understand O'Brien to argue otherwise. Amended § 12(b) (3) on its face deals with conduct having no connection with speech. It prohibits the knowing destruction of certificates issued by the Selective Service System, and there is nothing necessarily expressive about such conduct. The Amendment does not distinguish between public and private destruction, and it does not punish only destruction engaged in for the purpose of expressing views. Compare Stromberg v. California, 283 U.S. 359 (1931). A law prohibiting destruction of Selective Service certificates no more abridges free speech on its face than a motor vehicle law prohibiting the destruction of drivers' licenses, or a tax law prohibiting the destruction of books and records.

O'Brien nonetheless argues that the 1965 Amendment is unconstitutional in its application to him, and is unconstitutional as enacted because what he calls the "purpose" of Congress was "to suppress freedom of speech." We consider these arguments separately.

O'Brien first argues that the 1965 Amendment is unconstitutional as applied to him because his act of burning his registration certificate was protected "symbolic speech" within the First Amendment. His argument is that the freedom of expression which the First Amendment guarantees includes all modes of "communication of ideas by conduct," and that his conduct is within this definition because he did it in "demonstration against the war and against the draft."

We cannot accept the view that an apparently limitless variety of conduct can be labeled "speech" whenever the person engaging in the conduct intends thereby to express an idea. However, even on the assumption that the alleged communicative element in O'Brien's conduct is sufficient to bring into play the First Amendment, it does not necessarily follow that the destruction of a registration certificate is constitutionally protected activity. This Court has held that when "speech" and "nonspeech" elements are combined in the same course of conduct, a sufficiently important governmental interest in regulating the nonspeech element can justify incidental limitations on First Amendment freedoms. To characterize the quality of the governmental interest which must appear, the Court has employed a variety of descriptive terms: compelling; substantial; subordinating; paramount; cogent; strong. Whatever imprecision inheres in these terms, we think it clear that a government regulation is sufficiently justified if it is within the constitutional power of the Government; if it furthers an important or substantial governmental interest; if the governmental interest is unrelated to the suppression of free ex-

pression; and if the incidental restriction on alleged First Amendment freedoms is no greater than is essential to the furtherance of that interest. We find that the 1965 Amendment [meets] all of these requirements, and consequently that O'Brien can be constitutionally convicted for violating it.

The constitutional power of Congress to raise and support armies and to make all laws necessary and proper to that end is broad and sweeping. . . . The power of Congress to classify and conscript manpower for military service is "beyond question." Pursuant to this power, Congress may establish a system of registration for individuals liable for training and service, and may require such individuals within reason to cooperate in the registration system. The issuance of certificates indicating the registration and eligibility classification of individuals is a legitimate and substantial administrative aid in the functioning of this system. And legislation to insure the continuing availability of issued certificates serves a legitimate and substantial purpose in the system's administration.

O'Brien's argument to the contrary is necessarily premised upon his unrealistic characterization of Selective Service certificates. He essentially adopts the position that such certificates are so many pieces of paper designed to notify registrants of their registration or classification, to be retained or tossed in the wastebasket according to the convenience or taste of the registrant. Once the registrant has received notification, according to this view, there is no reason for him to retain the certificates. O'Brien notes that most of the information on a registration certificate serves no notification purpose at all; the registrant hardly needs to be told his address and physical characteristics. We agree that the registration certificate contains much information of which the registrant needs no notification. This circumstance, however, does not lead to the conclusion that the certificate serves no purpose, but that, like the classification certificate, it serves purposes in addition to initial notification. Many of these purposes would be defeated by the certificates' destruction or mutilation. Among these are:

1. . . . Voluntarily displaying the two certificates is an easy and painless way for a young man to dispel a question as to whether he might be delinquent in his Selective Service obligations. Correspondingly, the availability of the certificates for such display relieves the Selective Service System of the administrative burden it would otherwise have in verifying the registration and classification of all suspected delinquents. . . . Additionally, in a time of national crisis, reasonable availability to each registrant of the two small cards assures a rapid and uncomplicated means for determining his fitness for immediate induction . . . .

2. The information supplied on the certificates facilitates communication between registrants and local boards . . . .

3. Both certificates carry continual reminders that the registrant must notify his local board of any change of address, and other specified changes in his status. . . .

4. The regulatory scheme involving Selective Service certificates includes clearly valid prohibitions against the alteration, forgery, or similar deceptive misuse of certificates. The destruction or mutilation of certificates obviously increases the difficulty of detecting and tracing abuses such as these. Further, a mutilated certificate might itself be used for deceptive purposes.

The many functions performed by Selective Service certificates establish beyond doubt that Congress has a legitimate and substantial interest in preventing their wanton and unrestrained destruction and assuring their continuing availability by punishing people who knowingly and wilfully destroy or mutilate them. And we are unpersuaded that the pre-existence of the nonpossession regulations in any way negates this interest. In the absence of a question as to multiple punishment, it has never been suggested that there is anything improper in Congress' providing alternative statutory avenues of prosecution to assure the effective protection of one and the same interest. . . .

Equally important, a comparison of the regulations with the 1965 Amendment indicates that they protect overlapping but not identical governmental interests, and that they reach somewhat different classes of wrongdoers. The gravamen of the offense defined by the statute is the deliberate rendering of certificates unavailable for the various purposes which they may serve. Whether registrants keep their certificates in their personal possession at all times, as required by the regulations, is of no particular concern under the 1965 Amendment, as long as they do not mutilate or destroy the certificates so as to render them unavailable. . . . Finally, the 1965 Amendment, like § 12(b) which it amended, is concerned with abuses involving *any* issued Selective Service certificates, not only with the registrant's own certificates. The knowing destruction or mutilation of someone else's certificates would therefore violate the statute but not the nonpossession regulations.

We think it apparent that the continuing availability to each registrant of his Selective Service certificates substantially furthers the smooth and proper functioning of the system that Congress has established to raise armies. . . .

It is equally clear that the 1965 Amendment specifically protects this substantial governmental interest. We perceive no alternative means that would more precisely and narrowly assure the continuing availability of issued Selective Service certificates than a law which prohibits their wilful mutilation or destruction. The 1965 Amendment prohibits such conduct and does nothing more. In other words, both the governmental interest and the operation of the 1965 Amendment are limited to the noncommunicative aspect of O'Brien's conduct. The governmental interest and the scope of the 1965 Amendment are limited to preventing harm to the smooth and efficient functioning of the Selective Service System. When O'Brien deliberately rendered unavailable his registration certificate, he wilfully frustrated this governmental interest. For this noncommunicative impact of his conduct, and for nothing else, he was convicted.

The case at bar is therefore unlike one where the alleged governmental interest in regulating conduct arises in some measure because the communication allegedly integral to the conduct is itself thought to be harmful. In Stromberg v. California, 283 U.S. 359 (1931) [the "red flag" case, above], for example, the statute was aimed at suppressing communication [and therefore] could not be sustained as a regulation of noncommunicative conduct. . . .

In conclusion, we find that because of the Government's substantial interest in assuring the continuing availability of issued Selective Service certificates, because amended § 462(b) is an appropriately narrow means of protecting this interest and condemns only the independent noncommunicative impact

of conduct within its reach, and because the noncommunicative impact of O'Brien's act of burning his registration certificate frustrated the Government's interest, a sufficient governmental interest has been shown to justify O'Brien's conviction.

O'Brien finally argues that the 1965 Amendment is unconstitutional as enacted because what he calls the "purpose" of Congress was "to suppress freedom of speech." We reject this argument because under settled principles the purpose of Congress, as O'Brien uses that term, is not a basis for declaring this legislation unconstitutional. . . . [See the additional passages from this opinion, on the impropriety of judicial invalidation because "of an alleged illicit legislative motive," printed in chap. 2 above.]

Reversed.

Mr. Justice HARLAN, concurring.

. . . I wish to make explicit my understanding that [the Court's criteria do] not foreclose consideration of First Amendment claims in those rare instances when an "incidental" restriction upon expression, imposed by a regulation which furthers an "important or substantial" governmental interest and satisfies the Court's other criteria, in practice has the effect of entirely preventing a "speaker" from reaching a significant audience with whom he could not otherwise lawfully communicate. This is not such a case, since O'Brien manifestly could have conveyed his message in many ways other than by burning his draft card.

Mr. Justice DOUGLAS, dissenting.

. . . The underlying and basic problem in this case, is whether conscription is permissible in the absence of a declaration of war. That question has not been briefed nor was it presented in oral argument; but it is, I submit, a question upon which the litigants and the country are entitled to a ruling. . . . [See chap. 5 above.] [This case should be restored] to the calendar for reargument on the question of the constitutionality of a peacetime draft. [Note also Justice Douglas' view that O'Brien's conviction violated the First Amendment—expressed not in this case but in a concurring opinion a year later, in Brandenburg v. Ohio, 395 U.S. 444 (1969), sec. 1E above.]

TINKER v. DES MOINES SCHOOL DISTRICT

393 U.S. 503, 89 S.Ct. 733, 21 L.Ed.2d 731 (1969).

Certiorari to the United States Court of Appeals for the Eighth Circuit.

[In December 1965, petitioners—two high school students and one junior high school student—wore black armbands to school to publicize their objections to the Vietnam hostilities and their support for a truce. They were asked to remove the armbands and refused. In accordance with a policy adopted by the school authorities two days earlier in anticipation of such a protest, students were sent home and suspended until they would return without the armbands. Petitioners unsuccessfully sought injunctive relief against the disciplinary action in the lower federal courts.]

Mr. Justice FORTAS delivered the opinion of the Court. . . .

[The District Court] upheld the constitutionality of the school authorities' action on the ground that it was reasonable in order to prevent disturbance of school discipline. The court referred to but expressly declined to follow the Fifth Circuit's holding in a similar case that the wearing of symbols like the armbands cannot be prohibited unless it "materially and substantially interfere[s] with the requirements of appropriate discipline in the operation of the school." Burnside v. Byars, 363 F.2d 744, 749 (1966).[1] [The Court of Appeals, en banc, was equally divided and accordingly affirmed without opinion.]

The District Court recognized that the wearing of an armband for the purpose of expressing certain views is the type of symbolic act that is within the Free Speech Clause of the First Amendment. See [W.Va. State Bd. of Educ. v. Barnette; Stromberg.] As we shall discuss, the wearing of armbands in the circumstances of this case was entirely divorced from actually or potentially disruptive conduct by those participating in it. It was closely akin to "pure speech" which, we have repeatedly held, is entitled to comprehensive protection under the First Amendment. . . .

First Amendment rights, applied in light of the special characteristics of the school environment, are available to teachers and students. It can hardly be argued that either students or teachers shed their constitutional rights to freedom of speech or expression at the schoolhouse gate. This has been the unmistakable holding of this Court for almost 50 years. In Meyer v. Nebraska, 262 U.S. 390 (1923) [chap. 9 above], [the Court] held that the Due Process Clause of the Fourteenth Amendment prevents States from forbidding the teaching of a foreign language. [But we have] repeatedly emphasized the need for affirming the comprehensive authority of the States and of school officials, consistent with fundamental constitutional safeguards, to prescribe and control conduct in the schools. . . . Our problem lies in the area where students in the exercise of First Amendment rights collide with the rules of the school authorities.

The problem posed by the present case does not relate to regulation of the length of skirts or the type of clothing, to hair style, or deportment.* . . . It does not concern aggressive, disruptive action or even group demonstrations. Our problem involves direct, primary First Amendment rights akin to "pure speech."

---

1. In Burnside, the Fifth Circuit ordered that high school authorities be enjoined from enforcing a regulation forbidding students to wear "freedom buttons." It is instructive that in Blackwell v. Issaquena County Board of Education, 363 F.2d 749 (1966), the same panel on the same day reached the opposite result on different facts. It declined to enjoin enforcement of such a regulation in another high school where the students wearing freedom buttons harassed students who did not wear them and created much disturbance. [All numbered footnotes by the Court.]

* In the aftermath of Tinker, a large number of constitutional attacks were launched in the lower federal courts on school rules governing dress and hair style, but the Court has refused to grant review in any of them. See Justice Douglas' dissent from the denial of certiorari in Freeman v. Almon Flake, 405 U.S. 1032 (1972), noting that the eight Circuits that had passed on hair regulation questions had divided four to four. Should such questions be viewed as primarily First Amendment ones, or do they more centrally involve privacy-personal autonomy concerns? Recall sec. 3 of chap. 9, on modern substantive due process, above. [Near the end of the 1974–75 Term, the court granted review of a decision invalidating a regulation of the hair length of policemen. Barry v. Dwen (43 U.S.Law Week 3621 —May 27, 1975).]

The school officials banned and sought to punish petitioners for a silent, passive expression of opinion, unaccompanied by any disorder or disturbance on the part of petitioners. There is here no evidence whatever of petitioners' interference, actual or nascent, with the schools' work or of collision with the rights of other students to be secure and to be let alone. Accordingly, this case does not concern speech or action that intrudes upon the work of the school or the rights of other students. . . . There is no indication that the work of the schools or any class was disrupted. . . .

The District Court concluded that the action of the school authorities was reasonable because it was based upon their fear of a disturbance from the wearing of the armbands. But, in our system, undifferentiated fear or apprehension of disturbance is not enough to overcome the right to freedom of expression. Any departure from absolute regimentation may cause trouble. Any variation from the majority's opinion may inspire fear. Any word spoken, in class, in the lunchroom, or on the campus, that deviates from the views of another person may start an argument or cause a disturbance. But our Constitution says we must take this risk [Terminiello v. Chicago]; and our history says that it is this sort of hazardous freedom—this kind of openness—that is the basis of our national strength and of the independence and vigor of Americans who grow up and live in this relatively permissive, often disputatious, society.

In order for the State in the person of school officials to justify prohibition of a particular expression of opinion, it must be able to show that its action was caused by something more than a mere desire to avoid the discomfort and unpleasantness that always accompany an unpopular viewpoint. Certainly where there is no finding and no showing that engaging in the forbidden conduct would "materially and substantially interfere with the requirements of appropriate discipline in the operation of the school," the prohibition cannot be sustained. Burnside v. Byars, supra, at 749.

In the present case, the District Court made no such finding, and our independent examination of the record fails to yield evidence that the school authorities had reason to anticipate that the wearing of the armbands would substantially interfere with the work of the school or impinge upon the rights of other students. Even an official memorandum prepared after the suspension that listed the reasons for the ban on wearing the armbands made no reference to the anticipation of such disruption.[2]

On the contrary, the action of the school authorities appears to have been based upon an urgent wish to avoid the controversy which might result from

2. The only suggestions of fear of disorder in the report are these:

"A former student of one of our high schools was killed in Viet Nam. Some of his friends are still in school and it was felt that if any kind of a demonstration existed, it might evolve into something which would be difficult to control."

"Students at one of the high schools were heard to say they would wear arm bands of other colors if the black bands prevailed."

Moreover, the testimony of school authorities at trial indicates that it was not fear of disruption that motivated the regulation prohibiting the armbands; the regulation was directed against "the principle of the demonstration" itself. School authorities simply felt that "the schools are no place for demonstrations," and if the students "didn't like the way our elected officials were handling things, it should be handled with the ballot box and not in the halls of our public schools."

the expression, even by the silent symbol of armbands, of opposition to this Nation's part in the conflagration in Vietnam.[3] . . .

It is also relevant that the school authorities did not purport to prohibit the wearing of all symbols of political or controversial significance. The record shows that students in some of the schools wore buttons relating to national political campaigns, and some even wore the Iron Cross, traditionally a symbol of Nazism. The order prohibiting the wearing of armbands did not extend to these. Instead, a particular symbol—black armbands worn to exhibit opposition to this Nation's involvement in Vietnam—was singled out for prohibition. Clearly, the prohibition of expression of one particular opinion, at least without evidence that it is necessary to avoid material and substantial interference with schoolwork or discipline, is not constitutionally permissible.

In our system, state-operated schools may not be enclaves of totalitarianism. School officials do not possess absolute authority over their students. Students in school as well as out of school are "persons" under our Constitution. They are possessed of fundamental rights which the State must respect, just as they themselves must respect their obligations to the State. In our system, students may not be regarded as closed-circuit recipients of only that which the State chooses to communicate. They may not be confined to the expression of those sentiments that are officially approved. In the absence of a specific showing of constitutionally valid reasons to regulate their speech, students are entitled to freedom of expression of their views. . . .

[The] principle of [past] cases is not confined to the supervised and ordained discussion which takes place in the classroom. The principal use to which the schools are dedicated is to accommodate students during prescribed hours for the purpose of certain types of activities. Among those activities is personal intercommunication among the students.[4] This is not only an inevitable part of the process of attending school; it is also an important part of the educational process. A student's rights, therefore, do not embrace merely the classroom hours. When he is in the cafeteria, or on the playing field, or on the campus during the authorized hours, he may express his opinions, even on controversial subjects like the conflict in Vietnam, if he does so without "materially and substantially interfer[ing] with the requirements of appropriate discipline in the operation of the school" and without colliding with the rights of others. Burnside v. Byars, supra, at 749. But conduct by the student, in class or out of it, which for any reason—whether it stems from time, place, or type of behavior—materially disrupts classwork or involves substantial disorder or invasion of the rights of others is, of course, not immunized by the constitutional guarantee of freedom of speech. . . .

3. The District Court found that the school authorities, in prohibiting black armbands, were influenced by the fact that "[t]he Viet Nam war and the involvement of the United States therein has been the subject of a major controversy for some time. . . ."

4. In Hammond v. South Carolina State College, 272 F.Supp. 947 (D.C.S.C.1967), District Judge Hemphill had before him a case involving a meeting on campus of 300 students to express their views on school practices. He pointed out that a school is not like a hospital or a jail enclosure. Cf. [Cox v. Louisiana I; Adderley v. Florida]. It is a public place, and its dedication to specific uses does not imply that the constitutional rights of persons entitled to be there are to be gauged as if the premises were purely private property. Cf. [Edwards v. South Carolina; Brown v. Louisiana].

Reversed and remanded.†

Mr. Justice BLACK, dissenting.

The Court's holding in this case ushers in what I deem to be an entirely new era in which the power to control pupils by the elected "officials of state supported public schools" [is] in ultimate effect transferred to the Supreme Court. . . . Assuming that the Court is correct in holding that the conduct of wearing armbands for the purpose of conveying political ideas is protected by the First Amendment, compare, e. g., Giboney v. Empire Storage & Ice Co., 336 U.S. 490 (1949), the crucial remaining questions are whether students and teachers may use the schools at their whim as a platform for the exercise of free speech—"symbolic" or "pure"—and whether the courts will allocate to themselves the function of deciding how the pupils' school day will be spent. While I have always believed that [under the First Amendment, government has no] authority to regulate or censor the content of speech, I have never believed that any person has a right to give speeches or engage in demonstrations where he pleases and when he pleases. . . .

While the record does not show that any of these armband students shouted, used profane language, or were violent in any manner, detailed testimony by some of them shows their armbands caused comments, warnings by other students, the poking of fun at them, and a warning by an older football player that other, nonprotesting students had better let them alone. There is also evidence that a teacher of mathematics had his lesson period practically "wrecked" chiefly by disputes with Mary Beth Tinker, who wore her armband for her "demonstration." Even a casual reading of the record shows that this armband did divert students' minds from their regular lessons, and that talk, comments, etc., made John Tinker "self-conscious" in attending school with his armband. While the absence of obscene remarks or boisterous and loud disorder perhaps justifies the Court's statement that the few armband students did not actually "disrupt" the classwork, I think the record overwhelmingly shows that the armbands did exactly what the elected school officials and principals foresaw it would, that is, took the students' minds off their classwork and diverted them to thoughts about the highly emotional subject of the Vietnam war. . . .

. . . It was, of course, to distract the attention of other students that some students insisted up to the very point of their own suspension from

† Concurring notations by Justices Stewart and White are omitted.

Compare, with Justice Fortas' standard in the majority opinion, his approach in the dissent in Street, which follows. Can his positions be reconciled? See the comments after Street v. New York, below.

On the specific Tinker problem of students' free speech, compare Justice Fortas' notation—a few weeks after Tinker—concurring in the denial of certiorari in Barker v. Hardway, 394 U.S. 905 (1969):

"I agree that certiorari should be denied. The petitioners were suspended from college *not* for expressing their opinions on a matter of substance, but for violent and destructive interference with the rights of others. An adequate hearing was afforded them on the issue of suspension. The petitioners contend that their conduct was protected by the First Amendment, but the findings of the District Court, which were accepted by the Court of Appeals, establish that the petitioners here engaged in an aggressive and violent demonstration, and not in peaceful, nondisruptive expression, such as was involved in [Tinker]. The petitioners' conduct was therefore clearly not protected by the First and Fourteenth Amendments."

school that they were determined to sit in school with their symbolic arm-bands.

.   .   .   One does not need to be a prophet or the son of a prophet to know that after the Court's holding today some students in Iowa schools and indeed in all schools will be ready, able, and willing to defy their teachers on practically all orders.   This is the more unfortunate for the schools since groups of students all over the land are already running loose, conducting break-ins, sit-ins, lie-ins, and smash-ins.   .   .   .   It is no answer to say that the particular students here have not yet reached such high points in their demands to attend classes in order to exercise their political pressures.   Turn-ed loose with lawsuits for damages and injunctions against their teachers as they are here, it is nothing but wishful thinking to imagine that young, im-mature students will not soon believe it is their right to control the schools rather than the right of the States that collect the taxes to hire the teachers for the benefit of the pupils.   .   .   .

Mr. Justice HARLAN, dissenting.

I certainly agree that state public school authorities in the discharge of their responsibilities are not wholly exempt from the requirements of the Four-teenth Amendment respecting the freedoms of expression and association.   At the same time I am reluctant to believe that there is any disagreement between the majority and myself on the proposition that school officials should be ac-corded the widest authority in maintaining discipline and good order in their institutions.   To translate that proposition into a workable constitutional rule, I would, in cases like this, cast upon those complaining the burden of showing that a particular school measure was motivated by other than legitimate school concerns—for example, a desire to prohibit the expression of an unpopular point of view, while permitting expression of the dominant opinion.

Finding nothing in this record which impugns the good faith of respond-ents in promulgating the armband regulation, I would affirm   .   .   .   .*

STREET v. NEW YORK

394 U.S. 576, 89 S.Ct. 1354, 22 L.Ed.2d 572 (1969).

Appeal from the Court of Appeals of New York.

Mr. Justice HARLAN delivered the opinion of the Court.

Appellant Street has been convicted in the New York courts of violating former § 1425, subd. 16, par. d, of the New York Penal Law, which makes it a misdemeanor "publicly [to] mutilate, deface, defile, or defy, trample upon, or cast contempt upon either by words or act [any flag of the United States]." He was given a suspended sentence.   We must decide whether, in light of all the circumstances, that conviction denied to him rights of free expression pro-tected by the First Amendment.   .   .   .

[T]he events which led to the conviction were these.   [During] the afternoon of June 6, 1966, [appellant] was listening to the radio in his Brooklyn apartment.   He heard a news report that civil rights leader James Meredith had been shot by a sniper in Mississippi.   Saying to himself, "They

---

*For the Court's subsequent considera-tions of the scope of the First Amend-ment in the academic environment, see the materials in chap. 13, sec. 4, below.

didn't protect him," appellant, himself a Negro, took from his drawer a neatly folded, 48-star American flag which he formerly had displayed on national holidays.   Appellant left his apartment and carried the still-folded flag to the nearby intersection of St. James Place and Lafayette Avenue. Appellant stood on the northeast corner of the intersection, lit the flag with a match, and dropped the flag on the pavement when it began to burn.

Soon thereafter, a police officer halted his patrol car and found the burning flag.   The officer testified that he then crossed to the northwest corner of the intersection, where he found appellant "talking out loud" to a small group of persons.   The officer estimated that there were some 30 persons on the corner near the flag and five to 10 on the corner with appellant.   The officer testified that as he approached within 10 or 15 feet of appellant, he heard appellant say, "We don't need no damn flag," and that when he asked appellant whether he had burned the flag appellant replied: "Yes; that is my flag; I burned it.   If they let that happen to Meredith we don't need an American flag." . . .

Street argues that his conviction was unconstitutional for three different reasons.   *First*, he claims that [the provision] is overbroad, both on its face and as applied, because the section makes it a crime "publicly [to] defy [or] cast contempt upon [an American flag] *by words* . . . ." (Emphasis added.)   *Second*, he contends that [it] is vague and imprecise because it does not clearly define the conduct which it forbids.   *Third*, he asserts that New York may not constitutionally punish one who publicly destroys or damages an American flag as a means of protest, because such an act constitutes expression protected by the Fourteenth Amendment.   We deem it unnecessary to consider the latter two arguments, for we hold that [the provision] was unconstitutionally applied in appellant's case because it permitted him to be punished merely for speaking defiant or contemptuous words about the American flag. . . .

In the face of an information explicitly setting forth appellant's words as an element of his alleged crime, and of appellant's subsequent conviction under a statute making it an offense to speak words of that sort, we find this record insufficient to eliminate the possibility either that appellant's words were the sole basis of his conviction or that appellant was convicted for both his words and his deed.

We come finally to the question whether, in the circumstances of this case, New York may constitutionally inflict criminal punishment upon one who ventures "publicly [to] defy [or] cast contempt upon [any American flag] by words" . . . .

In these circumstances, we can think of four governmental interests which might conceivably have been furthered by punishing appellant for his words: (1) an interest in deterring appellant from vocally inciting others to commit unlawful acts; (2) an interest in preventing appellant from uttering words so inflammatory that they would provoke others to retaliate physically against him, thereby causing a breach of the peace; (3) an interest in protecting the sensibilities of passers-by who might be shocked by appellant's words about the American flag; and (4) an interest in assuring that appellant, regardless of the impact of his words upon others, showed proper respect for our national emblem.

In the circumstances of this case, we do not believe that any of these interests may constitutionally justify appellant's conviction [for] speaking as he did. We begin with the interest in preventing incitement. Appellant's words, taken alone, did not urge anyone to do anything unlawful. They amounted only to somewhat excited public advocacy of the idea that the United States should abandon, at least temporarily, one of its national symbols. It is clear that the Fourteenth Amendment prohibits the States from imposing criminal punishment for public advocacy of peaceful change in our institutions. See, e. g., [Cox I, Edwards v. South Carolina, Terminiello; cf. Yates]. Even assuming that appellant's words might be found incitive when considered together with his simultaneous burning of the flag, [the law] does not purport to punish only those defiant or contemptuous words which amount to incitement. [Hence], a conviction for words could not be upheld on this basis. . . .

Nor could such a conviction be justified on the second ground mentioned above: the possible tendency of appellant's words to provoke violent retaliation. Though it is conceivable that some listeners might have been moved to retaliate upon hearing appellant's disrespectful words, we cannot say that appellant's remarks were so inherently inflammatory as to come within that small class of "fighting words" which are "likely to provoke the average person to retaliation, and thereby cause a breach of the peace." [Chaplinsky v. New Hampshire.] And even if appellant's words might be found within that category, [the law] is not narrowly drawn to punish only words of that character, and there is no indication that it was so interpreted by the state courts. Hence, this case is again distinguishable from Chaplinsky, supra, in which the Court emphasized that the statute was "carefully drawn so as not unduly to impair liberty of expression . . ."

Again, such a conviction could not be sustained on the ground that appellant's words were likely to shock passers-by. Except perhaps for appellant's incidental use of the word "damn," upon which no emphasis was placed at trial, any shock effect of appellant's speech must be attributed to the content of the ideas expressed. It is firmly settled that under our Constitution the public expression of ideas may not be prohibited merely because the ideas are themselves offensive to some of their hearers. See, e. g., [Cox I, Edwards, Terminiello; cf. Cantwell v. Connecticut]. And even if such a conviction might be upheld on the ground of "shock," there is again no indication that the state courts regarded the statute as limited to that purpose.

Finally, such a conviction could not be supported on the theory that by making the above-quoted remarks about the flag appellant failed to show the respect for our national symbol which may properly be demanded of every citizen. In Board of Educ. v. Barnette, 319 U.S. 624 (1943) [chap. 14 below], this Court held that to require unwilling schoolchildren to salute the flag would violate rights of free expression assured by the Fourteenth Amendment. In his opinion for the Court, Mr. Justice Jackson wrote words which are especially apposite here:

> "The case is made difficult not because the principles of its decision are obscure but because the flag involved is our own. Nevertheless, we apply the limitations of the Constitution with no fear that freedom to be intellectually and spiritually diverse or even contrary will disintegrate the

social organization. [F]reedom to differ is not limited to things that do not matter much. [The] test of its substance is the right to differ as to things that touch the heart of the existing order.

"If there is any fixed star in our constitutional constellation, it is that no official, high or petty, can prescribe what shall be orthodox in politics, nationalism, religion, or other matters of opinion or force citizens to confess by word or act their faith therein. If there are any circumstances which permit an exception, they do not now occur to us."

We have no doubt that the constitutionally guaranteed "freedom to be intellectually . . . diverse or even contrary," and the "right to differ as to things that touch the heart of the existing order," encompass the freedom to express publicly one's opinions about our flag, including those opinions which are defiant or contemptuous.

Since appellant could not constitutionally be punished under [the statute] for his speech, and since we have found that he may have been so punished, his conviction cannot be permitted to stand. In so holding, we reiterate that we have no occasion to pass upon the validity of this conviction insofar as it was sustained by the state courts on the basis that Street could be punished for his burning of the flag, even though the burning was an act of protest. Nor do we perceive any basis for our Brother White's fears that our decision today may be taken to require reversal whenever a defendant is convicted for burning a flag in protest, following a trial at which his words have been introduced to prove some element of that offense. Assuming that such a conviction would otherwise pass constitutional muster, a matter about which we express no view, nothing in this opinion would render the conviction impermissible merely because an element of the crime was proved by the defendant's words rather than in some other way. See [United States v. O'Brien].

We add that disrespect for our flag is to be deplored no less in these vexed times than in calmer periods of our history. Cf. Halter v. Nebraska, 205 U.S. 34 (1907). Nevertheless, we are unable to sustain a conviction that may have rested on a form of expression, however distasteful, which the Constitution tolerates and protects. . . .

Mr. Chief Justice WARREN, dissenting. . . .

[A]ppellant was convicted for his act not his words. . . .

I believe that the States and the Federal Government do have the power to protect the flag from acts of desecration and disgrace. But because the Court has not met the issue, it would serve no purpose to delineate my reasons for this view. However, it is difficult for me to imagine that, had the Court faced this issue, it would have concluded otherwise. . . .

Mr. Justice BLACK, dissenting.

. . . If I could agree with the Court's interpretation of the record as to the possibility of the conviction's resting on these spoken words, I would firmly and automatically agree that the law is unconstitutional. I would not feel constrained, as the Court seems to be, to search my imagination to see if I could think of interests the State may have in suppressing this freedom of speech. I would not balance away the First Amendment mandate that speech not be abridged in any fashion whatsoever. But I accept the unanimous opinion of the New York Court of Appeals that the conviction

does not and could not have rested merely on the spoken words but that it rested entirely on the fact that the defendant had publicly burned the American flag—against the law of the State of New York.

It passes my belief that anything in the Federal Constitution bars a State from making the deliberate burning of the American flag an offense. It is immaterial to me that words are spoken in connection with the burning. It is the *burning* of the flag that the State has set its face against. "It rarely has been suggested that the constitutional freedom for speech and press extends its immunity to speech or writing used as an integral part of conduct in violation of a valid criminal statute." Giboney v. Empire Storage & Ice Co., 336 U.S. 490, 498 (1949) [chap. 13, sec. 4, below]. In my view this quotation from the Giboney case precisely applies here. The talking that was done took place "as an integral part of conduct in violation of a valid criminal statute" against burning the American flag in public. I would therefore affirm this conviction.

Mr. Justice WHITE, dissenting. . . .

The Court's schema is this: the statute forbids insults to the flag either by act or words; the charge alleged both flag burning and speech; the court rendered a general judgment; since the conviction might logically have been for speech alone or for both words and deeds and since in either event the conviction is invalid, the judgment of the New York courts must be set aside without passing upon the validity of a conviction for burning the flag.[1] I reach precisely the opposite conclusion; before Street's conviction can be either reversed or affirmed, the Court *must* reach and decide the validity of a conviction for flag burning. . . .

The Court is obviously wrong in reversing the judgment below because it believes that Street was unconstitutionally convicted for speaking. Reversal can follow only if the Court reaches the conviction for flag burning and finds that conviction, as well as the assumed conviction for speech, to be violative of the First Amendment.[2] For myself, without the benefit of the majority's thinking if it were to find flag burning protected by the First Amendment, I would sustain such a conviction. I must dissent.

Mr. Justice FORTAS, dissenting.

I agree with the dissenting opinion filed by The Chief Justice, but I believe that it is necessary briefly to set forth the reasons why the States and the Federal Government have the power to protect the flag from acts of desecration committed in public.

1. The Court's theory is not that of unconstitutional overbreadth; it does not argue that New York may not convict for burning because the entire statute is unconstitutional for permitting convictions for insulting speech as well as for the act of flag burning. [Footnote by Justice White.]

2. Arguably, under today's decision any conviction for flag burning where the defendant's words are critical to proving intent or some other element of the crime would be invalid since the conviction would be based in part on speech. The Court disclaims this result, but without explaining why it would not reverse a conviction for burning where words spoken at the time are necessarily used to prove a case and yet reverse burning convictions on precisely the same evidence simply because on that evidence the defendant might also have been convicted for speaking. . . . [Footnote by Justice White.]

If the national flag were nothing more than a chattel, subject only to the rules governing the use of private personalty, its use would nevertheless be subject to certain types of state regulation. For example, regulations concerning the use of chattels which are reasonably designed to avoid danger to life or property, or impingement upon the rights of others to the quiet use of their property and of public facilities, would unquestionably be a valid exercise of police power. They would not necessarily be defeated by a claim that they conflicted with the rights of the owner of the regulated property. See, e. g., Village of Euclid v. Ambler Realty Co., 272 U.S. 365 (1926); Berman v. Parker, 348 U.S. 26 (1954) [—decisions sustaining zoning and eminent domain actions, see chap. 9, sec. 2, above].

If a state statute provided that it is a misdemeanor to burn one's shirt or trousers or shoes on the public thoroughfare, it could hardly be asserted that the citizen's constitutional right is violated. If the arsonist asserted that he was burning his shirt or trousers or shoes as a protest against the Government's fiscal policies, for example, it is hardly possible that his claim to First Amendment shelter would prevail against the State's claim of a right to avert danger to the public and to avoid obstruction to traffic as a result of the fire. This is because action, even if clearly for serious protest purposes, is not entitled to the pervasive protection that is given to speech alone. See [Cantwell v. Connecticut]. It may be subjected to reasonable regulation that appropriately takes into account the competing interests involved.

The test that is applicable in every case where conduct is restricted or prohibited is whether the regulation or prohibition is reasonable, due account being taken of the paramountcy of First Amendment values. If, as I submit, it is permissible to prohibit the burning of personal property on the public sidewalk, there is no basis for applying a different rule to flag burning. And the fact that the law is violated for purposes of protest does not immunize the violator. [United States v. O'Brien; see Giboney v. Empire Storage & Ice Co.]

Beyond this, however, the flag is a special kind of personalty. Its use is traditionally and universally subject to special rules and regulation. As early as 1907, this Court affirmed the constitutionality of a state statute making it a crime to use a representation of the United States flag for purposes of advertising. Halter v. Nebraska, 205 U.S. 34 (1907). Statutes prescribe how the flag may be displayed; how it may lawfully be disposed of; when, how, and for what purposes it may and may not be used. A person may "own" a flag, but ownership is subject to special burdens and responsibilities. A flag may be property, in a sense; but it is property burdened with peculiar obligations and restrictions. Certainly, as Halter v. Nebraska, supra, held, these special conditions are not *per se* arbitrary or beyond governmental power under our Constitution.

One may not justify burning a house, even if it is his own, on the ground, however sincere, that he does so as a protest. One may not justify breaking the windows of a government building on that basis. Protest does not exonerate lawlessness. And the prohibition against flag burning on the public thoroughfare being valid, the misdemeanor is not excused merely because it is an act of flamboyant protest.

O'BRIEN–TINKER–STREET
AS THE CULMINATION OF 50 YEARS OF FIRST
AMENDMENT ADJUDICATION:
SOME ANXIOUS THOUGHTS ABOUT UNSTABLE DOCTRINES
AND UNEVEN RESULTS ON THE WARREN COURT

Introduction. These symbolic expression cases of the late sixties warrant attention not only for their own sake but also as a vantage point for assessment of the accomplishments of the Court's first half-century of First Amendment cases—for evaluation of the basic doctrinal developments in the preceding materials and as framework for the critical examination of the special problems in the next chapter. O'Brien-Tinker-Street came near the close of Chief Justice Warren's tenure. The Warren Court, especially during the sixties, had upheld a large number of First Amendment claims, in a variety of contexts; and it had been almost as prolific in its doctrinal innovations as in its libertarian results. Yet this group of cases suggests not only uncertainty of results but also shakiness of doctrinal foundations. The First Amendment claimant prevailed in two of the three cases, to be sure. But in one of the cases—Street—a tortured reading of the legal posture of the case was necessary to assure reversal of the conviction. And, more important, the range and content of the Justices' doctrinal positions left considerable doubt (despite a half century of talk about "absolute" rights, "preferred" positions, and "immediate" risks) that a coherent, comprehensive, consistent framework for First Amendment protection had yet emerged.

1. *Oversimplifications, evasions, and O'Brien.* Was there not reason to expect a fuller evaluation of the speech ingredients of symbolic draft-card burning protests from the Warren Court than the Chief Justice's opinion in O'Brien provided? Were the criteria suggested in O'Brien adequate? Or did they sidestep the problem of balancing the restriction on expression against the harm caused by the defendant's behavior? Did the justification for the statute spelled out in the opinion approach the high level of governmental need suggested by the "compelling," "substantial," "strong" adjectives as applied in other contexts? Was the Court's scrutiny of the need for the criminal statute, and of possible alternative means, as intensive as it has been in most other First Amendment cases?

Is there justification for describing the Warren Court's disposition of O'Brien's "by no means frivolous" claim as "astonishingly cavalier"? Is there basis for saying that the Court "chose not to deal with the complexities" of the problem, "made no attempt to discuss, let alone to answer, the difficult and disturbing constitutional questions presented," instead "trivialized the issues and handed down an opinion that has all the deceptive simplicity and superficial force that can usually be achieved by begging the question"? Those are among the critical comments in Alfange, Jr., "Free Speech and Symbolic Conduct: The Draft-Card Burning Case," 1968 Sup.Ct.Rev. 1 (which concludes, it should be noted, that "the result in O'Brien is defensible despite the deficiencies of manifest oversimplification in the Court's opinion").

2. *Question-begging distinctions, Tinker, and Justice Fortas.* May the "question-begging" quality of the O'Brien opinion be a reflection of the weaknesses of the doctrinal techniques in vogue, rather than an aberration, or a re-

sponse to the pressures of de facto war? Does the "speech"-"conduct" distinction, especially, tend to avoid subtle judgments and to evoke overstatements? Compare, for example, Justice Fortas in Tinker with Justice Fortas in Barker v. Hardway (the cert. denied concurrence in the footnote to Tinker)—and with Justice Fortas in Street. Does his Tinker opinion convey a sense of greater protection of student behavior than intended because the "akin to 'pure speech'" categorization generates libertarian rhetoric—which promptly requires qualification regarding the "conduct" in Barker? Does the same oversimplified and obscuring "speech"-"conduct" premise in turn give rise to the equally extreme—albeit restrictive rather than libertarian—rhetoric in the Street dissent, which apparently finds a "mere rationality" requirement appropriate via the easy route of an "action"-"speech alone" distinction? How does Justice Fortas' Street dissent give the "due" recognition to the "paramountcy" of First Amendment values that he professes to be necessary? A protest purpose does not "immunize" against law violation, to be sure— but was that the issue? What should be the scope of "symbolic expression" entitled to First Amendment protection? *

    3. *The excessive aversion to "balancing" and Street.* Is the temptation to "solve" hard cases of "indirect" regulation of expression via the simplistic "speech"-"conduct" distinction attributable to the aversion of many of the Justices to "balancing" talk? And yet do not these cases, more than most, demonstrate the necessity of discriminating, sensitive, articulate balancing for many speech problems?

    Justice Fortas and Chief Justice Warren were among those generally identified with the libertarian wing during the closing years of the Warren Court; Justice Harlan, by contrast, was a chief target of those who, like Justice Black, saw in "balancing" a frittering away of First Amendment rights. (Recall the Harlan-Black "balancing"-"absolutes" clash in the Konigsberg excerpts, in the introductory materials to this chapter.) Is it not ironic, then, that Justice Harlan should write the majority opinion in Street—with Chief Justice Warren as well as Justices Fortas and Black finding little difficulty in sustaining the conviction? † Would Justice Harlan have applied his analysis if he had focused on the flag-burning, and not just the words, in Street—i. e., would he have sought to identify the governmental interests and to deter-

---

* Note Henkin, "Foreword: On Drawing Lines," 82 Harv.L.Rev. 63 (1968): "The meaningful constitutional distinction is not between speech and conduct, but between conduct that speaks, communicates, and other kinds of conduct. If it is intended as expression, if in fact it communicates, especially if it becomes a common comprehensible form of expression, it is 'speech.'" See also Note, "Symbolic Conduct," 68 Colum.L.Rev. 1091 (1968).

† See the recognition by Frantz, a critic of "balancing," that "a balancer who attached a very high value to freedom of speech might decide in its favor more often than a definer who applied a narrow definition," in "The First Amendment in the Balance," 71 Yale L.J. 1424 (1962). Recall also Justice Harlan's "balancing" opinion in Cohen v. California, the "Fuck the Draft" jacket case, sec. 2B above. And see generally Gunther, "In Search of Judicial Quality on A Changing Court: The Case of Justice Powell," 24 Stan. L.Rev. 1001 (1972).

Compare the analysis in Ely, "Flag Desecration: A Case Study in the Roles of Categorization and Balancing in First Amendment Analysis," 88 Harv.L.Rev. 1482 (1975). Ely reinterprets and elaborates the standards of O'Brien and finds in them a useful combination of categorization and balancing approaches. (He invokes Cohen v. California as well as Brandenburg v. Ohio as model "categorization" cases. Do you agree?)

mine whether any were sufficiently furthered to justify the conviction? Would a conviction for the act of burning have been sustainable under that approach? Compare the Burger Court confrontations with problems similar to *Street*, in the cases which follow.

SPENCE v. WASHINGTON

418 U.S. 405, 94 S.Ct. 2727, 41 L.Ed.2d 842 (1974).

Appeal from the Supreme Court of Washington.

PER CURIAM. Appellant displayed a United States flag, which he owned, out the window of his apartment. Affixed to both surfaces of the flag was a large peace symbol fashioned of removable tape. Appellant was convicted under a Washington statute forbidding the exhibition of a United States flag to which is attached or superimposed figures, symbols, or other extraneous material. The Supreme Court of Washington affirmed appellant's conviction. [W]e reverse on the ground that as applied to appellant's activity the [law] impermissibly infringed protected expression. . . .

Appellant was not charged under Washington's flag desecration statute.[1] Rather, the State relied on the so-called "improper use" statute.* . . .

[Appellant] testified that he put a peace symbol on the flag and displayed it to public view as a protest to the invasion of Cambodia and the killings at Kent State University, events which occurred a few days prior to his arrest. [He was arrested on May 10, 1970.] He said that his purpose was to associate the American flag with peace instead of war and violence:

> "I felt there had been so much killing and that this was not what America stood for. I felt that the flag stood for America and I wanted people to know that I thought America stood for peace."

Appellant further testified that he chose to fashion the peace symbol from tape so that it could be removed without damaging the flag. [He was convicted and sentenced to 10 days in jail, suspended, and to a $75 fine.]

A number of factors are important in the instant case. First, this was a privately owned flag. In a technical property sense it was not the property of any government. . . . Second, appellant displayed his flag on private property. He engaged in no trespass or disorderly conduct. Nor is this a case that might be analyzed in terms of reasonable time, place, or manner restraints on access to a public area. Third, the record is devoid of proof of any risk of breach of the peace. [Fourth], the State concedes [that] appel-

---

1. This [flag desecration] statute provides in part:
"No person shall knowingly cast contempt upon any flag, standard, color, ensign or shield [by] publicly mutilating, defacing, defiling, burning, or trampling upon said flag, standard, color, ensign or shield." [Footnote by the Court.]

* This statute provides:
"No person shall, in any manner, for exhibition or display : . . .

"(1) Place or cause to be placed any word, figure, mark, picture, design, drawing or advertisement of any nature upon any flag, standard, color, ensign or shield of the United States or of this state . . . or

"(2) Expose to public view any such flag, standard, color, ensign or shield upon which shall have been printed, painted or otherwise produced, or to which shall have been attached, appended, affixed or annexed any such word, figure, mark, picture, design, drawing or advertisement. . . ."

lant engaged in a form of communication. [That] concession is inevitable on this record. The undisputed facts are that appellant "wanted people to know that I thought America stood for peace." To be sure, appellant did not choose to articulate his views through printed or spoken words. It is therefore necessary to determine whether his activity was sufficiently imbued with elements of communication to fall within the scope of the First and Fourteenth Amendments, for as the Court noted in [United States v. O'Brien], "[w]e cannot accept the view that an apparently limitless variety of conduct can be labeled 'speech' whenever the person engaging in the conduct intends thereby to express an idea." But the nature of appellant's activity, combined with the factual context and environment in which it was undertaken, lead to the conclusion that he engaged in a form of protected expression.

Moreover, the context in which a symbol is used for purposes of expression is important, for the context may give meaning to the symbol. See [Tinker]. In this case, appellant's activity was roughly simultaneous with and concededly triggered by the Cambodian incursion and the Kent State tragedy, [issues] of great public moment. A flag bearing a peace symbol and displayed upside down by a student today might be interpreted as nothing more than bizarre behavior, but it would have been difficult for the great majority of citizens to miss the drift of appellant's point at the time that he made it.

It may be noted, further, that this was not an act of mindless nihilism. Rather, it was a pointed expression of anguish by appellant about the then current domestic and foreign affairs of his government. An intent to convey a particularized message was present, and in the surrounding circumstances the likelihood was great that the message would be understood by those who viewed it.

We are confronted then with a case of prosecution for the expression of an idea through activity. Moreover, the activity occurred on private property . . . .. Accordingly, we must examine with particular care [the] range of various state interests that might be thought to support the challenged conviction, drawing upon the arguments before us, the opinions below, and the Court's opinion in Street v. New York.[2] The first interest at issue is prevention of breach of the peace. [It] is totally without support in the record.

We are also unable to affirm the judgment below on the ground that the State may have desired to protect the sensibilities of passersby. "It is firmly settled that under our Constitution the public expression of ideas may not be prohibited merely because the ideas are themselves offensive to some of their hearers." [Street.] Moreover, appellant did not impose his ideas upon a captive audience. Anyone who might have been offended could easily have avoided the display. See [Cohen v. California]. Nor may appellant

2. . . . A subsidiary ground relied on by the Washington Supreme Court must be rejected summarily. It found the inhibition on appellant's freedom of expression "miniscule and trifling" because there are "thousands of other means available to [him] for the dissemination of his personal views . . . ." As the Court noted in, e. g., Schneider v. State, 308 U.S. 147, 163 (1939), "one is not to have the exercise of his liberty of expression in appropriate places abridged on the plea that it may be exercised in some other place." [Footnote by the Court to an earlier passage.]

be punished for failing to show proper respect for our national emblem. [Street; Board of Education v. Barnette.] [3]

We are brought, then, to the state court's thesis that Washington has an interest in preserving the national flag as an unalloyed symbol of our country. The court did not define this interest; it simply asserted it. The dissenting opinion today adopts essentially the same approach. Presumably, this interest might be seen as an effort to prevent the appropriation of a revered national symbol by an individual, interest group, or enterprise where there was a risk that association of the symbol with a particular product or viewpoint might be taken erroneously as evidence of governmental endorsement.[4] Alternatively, it might be argued that the interest asserted by the state court is based on the uniquely universal character of the national flag as a symbol. For the great majority of us, the flag is a symbol of patriotism, of pride in the history of our country, and of the service, sacrifice, and valor of the millions of Americans who in peace and war have joined together to build and to defend a Nation in which self-government and personal liberty endure. It evidences both the unity and diversity which are America. For others the flag carries in varying degrees a different message. "A person gets from a symbol the meaning he puts into it, and what is one man's comfort ar d inspiration is another's jest and scorn." Board of Education v. Barnette. It might be said that we all draw something from our national symbol, for it is capable of conveying simultaneously a spectrum of meanings. If it may be destroyed or permanently disfigured, it could be argued that it will lose its capability of mirroring the sentiments of all who view it.

But we need not decide in this case whether the interest advanced by the court below is valid.[5] We assume, arguendo, that it is. The statute is nonetheless unconstitutional as applied to appellant's activity.[6] There was

---

3. Counsel for the State conceded that promoting respect for the flag is not a legitimate state interest. [Footnote by the Court.]

4. Undoubtedly such a concern underlies that portion of the improper-use statute forbidding the utilization of representations of the flag in a commercial context. . . . There is no occasion in this case to address the application of the challenged statute to commercial behavior. Cf. Halter v. Nebraska, 205 U.S. 34 (1907). The dissent places major reliance on Halter, despite the fact that Halter was decided nearly 20 years before the Court concluded that the First Amendment applies to the States by virtue of the Fourteenth Amendment. See Gitlow v. New York, 268 U.S. 652 (1925). [Footnote by the Court.]

5. If this interest is valid, we note that it is directly related to expression in the context of activity like that undertaken by appellant. For that reason and because no other governmental interest unrelated to expression has been

advanced or can be supported on this record, the four-step analysis of [United States v. O'Brien] is inapplicable. [Footnote by the Court. Cf. Ely, "Flag Desecration . . . .," 88 Harv. L.Rev. 1482 (1975).]

6. Because we agree with appellant's as-applied argument, we do not reach the more comprehensive overbreadth contention he also advances. But it is worth noting the nearly limitless sweep of the Washington improper-use flag statute. Read literally, it forbids a veteran's group from attaching, e. g., battalion commendations to a United States flag. It proscribes photographs of war heroes standing in front of the flag. It outlaws newspaper mastheads composed of the national flag with superimposed print. Other examples could easily be listed.

Statutes of such sweep suggest problems of selective enforcement. We are, however, unable to agree with appellant's void-for-vagueness argument. The statute's application is quite mechanical, particularly when implement-

no risk that appellant's acts would mislead viewers into assuming that the Government endorsed his viewpoint. To the contrary, he was plainly and peacefully [7] protesting the fact that it did not. Appellant was not charged under the desecration statute, nor did he permanently disfigure the flag or destroy it. He displayed it as a flag of his country in a way closely analogous to the manner in which flags have always been used to convey ideas. Moreover, his message was direct, likely to be understood, and within the contours of the First Amendment. Given the protected character of his expression and in light of the fact that no interest the State may have in preserving the physical integrity of a privately-owned flag was significantly impaired on these facts, the conviction must be invalidated. [8]

Reversed.

ed with jury instructions like the ones given in this case. The law in Washington, simply put, is that *nothing* may be affixed to or superimposed on a United States flag or a representation thereof. Thus, if selective enforcement has occurred, it has been a result of prosecutorial discretion, not the language of the statute. Accordingly, this case is unlike Smith v. Goguen, 415 U.S. 566 (1974), where the words of the statute at issue ("publicly . . . treats contemptuously") were themselves sufficiently indefinite to prompt subjective treatment by prosecutorial authorities. [Footnote by the Court.]

[SMITH v. GOGUEN, decided three months before Spence, was a 6 to 3 decision reversing a Massachusetts conviction for wearing a small United States flag sewn to the seat of appellee's trousers. Justice Powell's majority opinion found it unnecessary to reach a variety of First Amendment claims and rested instead on what he called "the due process doctrine of vagueness." (He noted, however, that "a greater degree of specificity" is required in First Amendment contexts than with respect to "purely economic regulation.") Though appellee's behavior seemed to reflect "immaturity" and "silly conduct," Justice Powell observed that "casual treatment of the flag in many contexts has become a widespread contemporary phenomenon." Here, the statutory language "fails to draw reasonably clear lines between the kinds of nonceremonial treatment (of the flag) that are criminal and those that are not." Fair notice standards were not met, given "today's tendencies to treat the flag unceremoniously." Justice Powell added: "Statutory language of such standardless sweep allows policemen, prosecutors, and juries to pursue their personal predilections."

[Justice White disagreed with the majority's reasoning, though not its result. He defended the constitutionality of flag mutilation laws, but objected to the conviction for being contemptuous of the flag: "To convict on this basis is not to protect the physical integrity or to protect against acts interfering with the proper use of the flag, but to punish for communicating ideas about the flag unacceptable to the controlling majority." Justice Rehnquist, joined by Chief Justice Burger, dissented at length, describing the flag as a "unique physical object" and emphasizing the strong state interest in protecting "the physical integrity of a unique national symbol." There was also a second, briefer dissenting opinion, by Justice Blackmun, joined by the Chief Justice.]

7. Appellant's activity occurred at a time of national turmoil over the introduction of United States forces into Cambodia and the deaths at Kent State University. It is difficult now, more than four years later, to recall vividly the depth of emotion that pervaded most colleges and universities at the time, and that was widely shared by young Americans everywhere. A spontaneous outpouring of feeling resulted in widespread action, not all of it rational when viewed in retrospect. This included the closing down of some schools, as well as other disruptions of many centers of education. It was against this highly inflamed background that appellant chose to express his own views in a manner that can fairly be described as gentle and restrained as compared to the actions undertaken by a number of his peers. [Footnote by the Court.]

8. The similarity of our holding to that of the Iowa Supreme Court in State v. Kool, 212 N.W.2d 518 (1973), merits note. In that case, the defendant dis-

Mr. Justice BLACKMUN concurs in the result.

Mr. Justice DOUGLAS [concurred in the result "for substantially the same reasons given by the Iowa Supreme Court in State v. Kool" (see footnote 8 to the per curiam opinion).]

Mr. Justice REHNQUIST, with whom The Chief Justice [BURGER] and Mr. Justice WHITE join, dissenting. . . . *

Since a State concededly may impose some limitations on speech directly, it would seem to follow a fortiori that a State may legislate to protect important state interests even though an incidental limitation on free speech results.   Virtually any law enacted by a State, when viewed with sufficient ingenuity, could be thought to interfere with some citizen's preferred means of expression.   But no one would argue, I presume, that a State could not prevent the painting of public buildings simply because a particular class of protesters believed their message would best be conveyed through that medium. . . .

Yet the Court today holds that the State of Washington cannot limit use of the American flag, at least insofar as its statute prevents appellant from using a privately owned flag to convey his personal message. . . . In my view [the Court] demonstrates a total misunderstanding of the State's interest in the integrity of the American flag, and [places itself] in the position either of ultimately favoring appellant's message because of its [noncommercial] subject matter [or], alternatively, of making the flag available for a limitless succession of political and commercial messages.   I shall treat these issues in reverse order.

The statute under which appellant was convicted is no stranger to this Court, a virtually identical statute having been before the Court in Halter v. Nebraska, 205 U.S. 34 (1907).   In that case the Court held that the State of Nebraska could enforce its statute to prevent use of a flag representation on beer bottles, stating . . . . : "Such an use tends to degrade and cheapen the flag in the estimation of the people, as well as to defeat the object of maintaining it as an emblem of National power and National honor."

The Court todays finds Halter irrelevant to the present case . . . . . Insofar as Halter assesses the State's interest, of course, the Court's argument is simply beside the point. . . .   Yet if the Court is suggesting that Halter would now be decided differently, and that the State's interest in the flag falls before any speech which is "direct, likely to be understood, and within the contours of the First Amendment," that view would mean the flag could be auctioned as a background to anyone willing and able to buy or copy one.   I find it hard to believe the Court intends to presage that result.

played a replica of the United States flag upside down in his window, superimposing a peace symbol to create an effect identical to that achieved by Spence. Recognizing the communicative character of the defendant's activity, the Iowa Supreme Court reversed his conviction for flag misuse and held the statute unconstitutional as applied. The court eschewed an overbreadth analysis, and it rejected a number of the state interests we have found unavailing in the instant case. [Footnote by the Court.]

* Chief Justice Burger also submitted a brief separate dissent.

Turning to the question of the State's interest in the flag, it seems to me that the Court's treatment lacks all substance. The suggestion that the State's interest somehow diminishes when the flag is decorated with *removable* tape trivializes something which is not trivial. The State of Washington is hardly seeking to protect the flag's resale value . . . . Unlike flag-desecration statutes, the Washington statute challenged here seeks to prevent personal *use* of the flag, not simply particular forms of *abuse*. The State of Washington has chosen to set the flag apart for a special purpose, and has directed that it not be turned into a common background for an endless variety of superimposed messages. The physical condition of the flag itself is irrelevant to that purpose.

The true nature of the State's interest in this case is not only one of preserving "the physical integrity of the flag," but also one of preserving the flag as "an important symbol of nationhood and unity." * Although the Court treats this important interest with a studied inattention, it is hardly one of recent invention and has previously been accorded considerable respect by this Court. [Halter v. Nebraska.] There was no question in Halter of physical impairment of a flag since no actual flag was even involved. And it certainly would have made no difference to the Court's discussion of the State's interest if the [challenger] in that case had chosen to advertise his product by decorating the flag with beer bottles fashioned from some removable substance.[1] It is the character, not the cloth, of the flag which the State seeks to protect.

The value of this interest has been emphasized in recent as well as distant times. [After noting Justice Fortas' dissent in Street, Justice Rehnquist quoted Justice White's statement in Smith v. Goguen that "the flag is a national property, and the Nation may regulate those who would make, imitate, sell, possess, or use it."] I agree. What appellant here seeks is simply license to use the flag however he pleases, so long as the activity can be tied to a concept of speech, regardless of any state interest in having the flag used only for more limited purposes. I find no reasoning in the Court's opinion which convinces me that the Constitution requires such license to be given.

The fact that the State has a valid interest in preserving the character of the flag does not mean, of course, that it can employ all conceivable means to enforce it. It certainly could not require all citizens to own the flag or compel citizens to salute one. West Virginia State Board of Education v. Barnette. It presumably cannot punish criticism of the flag, or the principles for which it stands, any more than it could punish criticism of this country's policies or ideas. But the statute in this case demands no such allegiance. Its operation does not depend upon whether the flag is used for communicative or noncommunicative purposes; upon whether a particular message is deemed commercial or political; upon whether the use of the flag is respect-

---

* The quoted phrases are from the opinions of Justices Blackmun and White in Smith v. Goguen, footnote 6 above.

1. It should be noted that Halter makes no mention of the argument that allowing use of the flag for a personal or commercial purpose might suggest endorsement of that purpose by the government. While this might be an *additional* state interest in appropriate cases, it is by no means an indispensable element of the State's concern about the integrity of the flag. [Footnote by Justice Rehnquist.]

ful or contemptuous; or upon whether any particular segment of the State's citizenry might applaud or oppose the intended message.[2] It simply withdraws a unique national symbol from the roster of materials that may be used as a background for communications. Since I do not believe the Constitution prohibits Washington from making that decision, I dissent.

FLAG "MISUSE" AND JUDICIAL TECHNIQUES IN THE BURGER ERA

Consider the Burger Court's encounters with the flag "misuse" problem —in Spence and in Smith v. Goguen (footnote 6 to Spence)—in light of the questions raised after Street. Note the relative roles of overbreadth, vagueness, and "as applied" balancing in the modern cases.

Does the Spence per curiam echo Justice Harlan's approach in Street and in Cohen v. California (sec. 2B above)? Does that variety of balancing lay bare the competing values, including the "speech" ingredients, more effectively than alternative techniques? Does balancing encourage more articulate, less simplistic analyses? Does that make the division in Street not only ironic (see the earlier notes) but also, and more important, a symbol of the weaknesses of "conduct"-"speech" distinctions and "absolutes" emphases as guarantors of First Amendment protections? Do the uncertain courses and vague contours of these techniques at least suggest that "absolutes," "balancing," "speech"-"conduct" distinctions and their offshoots have not yet proved wholly adequate to the task of supplying principled, intellectually respectable, and pragmatically effective tools for the implementation of First Amendment values? The cases in the next chapter apply old doctrines and evolve new variations in a range of additional contexts. Do those materials suggest the ingredients of more satisfactory analytical tools?

2. It is quite apparent that the Court does have considerable sympathy for at least the *form* of appellant's message, describing his use of the flag as "a pointed expression of anguish," and commenting that "appellant chose to express his own views in a manner that can fairly be described as gentle and restrained as compared to the actions undertaken by a number of his peers." One would hope that this last observation does not introduce a doctrine of "comparative" expression, which gives more leeway to certain forms of expression when more destructive methods of expression are being employed by others. [Footnote by Justice Rehnquist.]

Chapter 13

FREEDOM OF EXPRESSION:
ADDITIONAL PROBLEMS

Introduction. The preceding chapter introduced the most pervasive ingredients of First Amendment analysis by exploring two of the most troublesome problems of free speech: criminal penalties directed at speech critical of national policies and local regulation of expression in public places. This chapter pursues the critical testing of the analytical tools developed in those contexts by examining their applications and elaborations in a number of other settings. The division of chapters is not a sharp one: for example, the concern with speech which threatens the administration of justice (sec. 4A below) is foreshadowed in some of the preceding materials; the concern with subversion, manifested in the criminal prosecutions considered in sec. 1 of chap. 15 continues with the government employees security programs and legislative investigations below (secs. 5 and 6). Nevertheless, the arrangement has justification: chap. 12 traces core doctrines in the context of separable functional problems; the problems of chap. 13 contain additional variables that not only test the preceding analyses but require new doctrinal ingredients.

The materials in the opening sections of this chapter, as in the first section of chap. 12, emphasize control of expression because of its content: as with the subversive advocacy problems above, restrictions on defamation, obscenity, and contemptuous comments on courts rest on the allegedly harmful or obnoxious nature of the expression itself. To what extent are the earlier analyses—e. g., as to clear and present danger, First Amendment values, scrutiny of legislative judgments—applicable here? Are the problems manageable by placing some kinds of expression—e. g., obscene speech—wholly outside the First Amendment sphere?

In the later sections of this chapter, the state's main concern purports not to be with the content of speech but with other objectives—e. g., legislative access to information, quality of the professions, and fitness of government employees. As with the public places problems in sec. 2 of chap. 13, can these regulations be distinguished as having only "indirect" impact on speech, or as being concerned with "conduct" rather than "speech"? Do those distinctions justify significantly less judicial scrutiny of state justifications, means, and alternatives than when First Amendment values are "directly" threatened?

SECTION 1. DAMAGE TO REPUTATION AND PRIVACY

THE BACKGROUND AND THE BEAUHARNAIS CASE

Introduction. In 1942, in Chaplinsky v. New Hampshire (chap. 12, sec. 2, above), the unanimous Court was able confidently to list libel and obscenity with "fighting words" as examples of expression plainly not entitled to First Amendment protection. But, as this section and the next indicate, the First Amendment problems of libel and obscenity regulation have absorbed considerable Court attention in recent years. The sustaining of the Illinois criminal libel law in the Beauharnais case in 1952 reflected a more permissive judicial attitude toward libel regulation than toward other laws directed at expression; the New York Times case in the following decade committed the Court to the more intense scrutiny which is manifested in the proliferating modern defamation and privacy cases. The New York Times emphasis on the importance of debate on public issues has had considerable influence outside the libel area as well, as noted earlier (chap. 12, sec. 1). The purpose of this section is to explore the approach of New York Times and its progeny, both for its utility in general First Amendment analysis and for its effectiveness in its immediate context, as a barrier to defamation and privacy actions.

The Beauharnais case and group libel. The 5 to 4 decision in BEAUHARNAIS v. ILLINOIS, 343 U.S. 250 (1952), sustained a state law prohibiting the publishing, selling, or exhibiting in any public place of any publication which "portrays depravity, criminality, unchastity, or lack of virtue of a class of citizens, of any race, color, creed or religion, [or which] exposes the citizens of any race, color, creed or religion to contempt, derision, or obloquy, or which is productive of breach of the peace or riots." Beauharnais, president of the White Circle League, had organized the circulation of a leaflet calling on Chicago officials "to halt the further encroachment, harassment and invasion of white people, their property, neighborhoods and persons, by the Negro." The leaflet called on Chicago's white people to unite and warned that if "persuasion and the need to prevent the white race from becoming mongrelized by the negro will not unite us, then the aggressions, . . . rapes, robberies, knives, guns and marijuana of the negro, surely will." The trial court refused to give a "clear and present danger" charge requested by petitioner. Moreover, it refused offered evidence on the issue of truth, in accordance with its position that the statute was "a form of criminal libel law." Justice Frankfurter's majority opinion recalled the Chaplinsky language and included the following passages:

"No one will gainsay that it is libelous falsely to charge another with being a rapist, robber, carrier of knives and guns, and user of marijuana. The precise question before us, then, is whether [the 14th Amendment] prevents a State from punishing such libels—as criminal libel has been defined, limited and constitutionally recognized time out of mind—directed at designated collectivities and flagrantly disseminated. . . . We cannot say [that] the question is concluded by history and practice. But if an utterance directed at an individual may be the object of criminal sanctions, we cannot deny to a State power to punish the same utterance directed at a defined group, un-

less we can say that this is a wilful and purposeless restriction unrelated to the peace and well-being of the State.

"Illinois did not have to look beyond her own borders or await the tragic experience of the last three decades to conclude that wilful purveyors of falsehood concerning racial and religious groups promote strife and tend powerfully to obstruct the manifold adjustments required for free, ordered life in a metropolitan, polyglot community. From the murder of the abolitionist Lovejoy in 1837 to the Cicero riots of 1951, Illinois has been the scene of exacerbated tension between races, often flaring into violence and destruction. In many of these outbreaks, utterances of the character here in question, so the Illinois legislature could conclude, played a significant part. . . .

"In the face of this history and its frequent obligato of extreme racial and religious propaganda, we would deny experience to say that the Illinois legislature was without reason in seeking ways to curb false or malicious defamation of racial and religious groups, made in public places and by means calculated to have a powerful emotional impact on those to whom it was presented. . . . It may be argued, and weightily, that this legislation will not help matters. [But it] is not within our competence to confirm or deny claims of social scientists as to the dependence of the individual on the position of his racial or religious group in the community. . . . [W]e are precluded from saying that speech concededly punishable when immediately directed at individuals cannot be outlawed if directed at groups with whose position and esteem in society the affiliated individual may be inextricably involved. . . .

"Libelous utterances not being within the area of constitutionally protected speech, it is unnecessary, either for us or for the State courts, to consider the issues behind the phrase 'clear and present danger.' Certainly no one would contend that obscene speech, for example, may be punished only upon a showing of such circumstances. Libel, as we have seen, is in the same class."*

There were four dissenting opinions. Justice Black, joined by Justice Douglas, stated: "[Reliance upon the 'group libel law'] label may make the Court's holding more palatable for those who sustain it, but the sugar-coating does not make the censorship less deadly. However tagged, the Illinois law is not that criminal libel which has been 'defined, limited and constitutionally recognized time out of mind.' For as 'constitutionally recognized' that crime has provided for punishment of false, malicious, scurrilous charges against individuals, not against huge groups. This limited scope of the law of criminal libel is of no small importance. It has confined state punishment of speech and expression to the narrowest of areas involving nothing more than purely private feuds. Every expansion of the law of criminal libel so as to punish discussion of matters of public concern means a corresponding invasion of the area dedicated to free expression by the First Amendment."

Justice Douglas' dissent insisted: "My view is that if in any case other public interests are to override the plain command of the First Amendment,

* See Riesman, "Democracy and Defamation: Control of Group Libel," 42 Colum.L.Rev. 727 (1942), cited by both majority and minority. See also Tanenhaus, "Group Libel," 35 Cornell L.Q. 261 (1950); Beth, "Group Libel and Free Speech," 39 Minn.L.Rev. 167 (1955).

the peril of speech must be clear and present, leaving no room for argument, raising no doubts as to the necessity of curbing speech in order to prevent disaster." Justice Reed's dissent, joined by Justice Douglas, emphasized vagueness: "These words—'virtue,' 'derision,' and 'obloquy'—have neither general nor special meanings well enough known to apprise those within their reach as to limitations on speech."

In still another dissent, Justice Jackson argued at length that the 14th Amendment's restraints on the states were less confining than the First Amendment's limits on Congress: "The history of criminal libel in America convinces me that the [14th Amendment] did not 'incorporate' the First, that the powers of Congress and of the States over the subject are not of the same dimensions, and that because Congress probably could not enact this law it does not follow that the States may not." † Justice Jackson noted the "tolerance of state libel laws by the very authors and partisans" of the 14th Amendment and insisted that the Palko standard (recall chap. 8 above) provided the appropriate standard. But he nevertheless found the Illinois law unconstitutional under that standard: "If one can claim to announce the judgment of legal history on any subject, it is that criminal libel laws are consistent with the concept of ordered liberty only when applied with safe-guards evolved to prevent their invasion of freedom of expression." Under the challenged law, he emphasized, there was no requirement "to find any injury to any person, or group, or to the public peace, nor to find any probability, let alone any clear and present danger, of injury to any of these. . . . The leaflet was simply held punishable as criminal libel per se irrespective of its actual or probable consequences."

NEW YORK TIMES CO. v. SULLIVAN

376 U.S. 254, 84 S.Ct. 710, 11 L.Ed.2d 686 (1964).

Certiorari to the Supreme Court of Alabama.

Mr. Justice BRENNAN delivered the opinion of the Court.

We are required in this case to determine for the first time the extent to which the constitutional protections for speech and press limit a State's power to award damages in a libel action brought by a public official against critics of his official conduct.

Respondent L. B. Sullivan is one of the three elected Commissioners of the City of Montgomery, Alabama. He testified that he was "Commissioner of Public Affairs and the duties are supervision of the Police Department, Fire Department, Department of Cemetery and Department of Scales." He brought this civil libel action against the four individual petitioners, who are Negroes and Alabama clergymen, and against petitioner the New York Times Company. [A state court jury] awarded him damages of $500,000, the full amount claimed, against all the petitioners, and the Supreme Court of Alabama affirmed. . . .

Respondent's complaint alleged that he had been libeled by statements in a full-page advertisement that was carried in the New York Times on March

---

† Note the similar argument in Justice Harlan's separate opinion in the first major obscenity case, Roth v. United States, sec. 2 below.

29, 1960. Entitled "Heed Their Rising Voices," the advertisement [charged that non-violent demonstrations by Southern Negro students to uphold their constitutional rights] "are being met by an unprecedented wave of terror," [which succeeding] paragraphs purported to illustrate [by] describing certain alleged events. The text concluded with an appeal for funds for three purposes: support of the student movement, "the struggle for the right-to-vote," and the legal defense of Dr. Martin Luther King, Jr., leader of the movement, against a perjury indictment then pending in Montgomery. . . .

Of the 10 paragraphs of text in the advertisement, the third and a portion of the sixth were the basis of respondent's claim of libel. They read as follows:

Third paragraph: "In Montgomery, Alabama, after students sang 'My Country, 'Tis of Thee' on the State Capitol steps, their leaders were expelled from school, and truckloads of police armed with shotguns and tear-gas ringed the Alabama State College Campus. When the entire student body protested to state authorities by refusing to re-register, their dining hall was padlocked in an attempt to starve them into submission."

Sixth paragraph: "Again and again the Southern violators have answered Dr. King's peaceful protests with intimidation and violence. They have bombed his home almost killing his wife and child. They have assaulted his person. They have arrested him seven times—for 'speeding,' 'loitering' and similar 'offenses.' And now they have charged him with 'perjury' —a *felony* under which they would imprison him for *ten years.* . . ."

Although neither of these statements mentions respondent by name, he contended that the word "police" in the third paragraph referred to him as the Montgomery Commissioner who supervised the Police Department, so that he was being accused of "ringing" the campus with police. He further claimed that the paragraph would be read as imputing to the police, and hence to him, the padlocking of the dining hall in order to starve the students into submission. As to the sixth paragraph, he contended that since arrests are ordinarily made by the police, the statement "They have arrested [Dr. King] seven times" would be read as referring to him; he further contended that the "They" who did the arresting would be equated with the "They" who committed the other described acts and with the "Southern violators." . . . .

It is uncontroverted that some of the statements contained in the two paragraphs were not accurate descriptions of events which occurred in Montgomery. Although Negro students staged a demonstration on the State Capitol steps, they sang the National Anthem and not "My Country, 'Tis of Thee." Although nine students were expelled by the State Board of Education, this was not for leading the demonstration at the Capitol, but for demanding service at a lunch counter in the Montgomery County Courthouse on another day. Not the entire student body, but most of it, had protested the expulsion, not by refusing to register, but by boycotting classes on a single day; virtually all the students did register for the ensuing semester. The campus dining hall was not padlocked on any occasion, and the only students who may have been barred from eating there were the few who had neither signed a preregistration application nor requested temporary meal tickets. Although the police were deployed near the campus in large numbers on three occasions, they did

not at any time "ring" the campus, and they were not called to the campus in connection with the demonstration on the State Capitol steps, as the third paragraph implied. Dr. King had not been arrested seven times, but only four . . .

[R]espondent was allowed to prove that he had not participated in the events described. . . . Respondent made no effort to prove that he suffered actual pecuniary loss as a result of the alleged libel. . . .

. . . We reverse the judgment. We hold that the rule of law applied by the Alabama courts is constitutionally deficient for failure to provide the safeguards for freedom of speech and of the press that are required by the First and Fourteenth Amendments in a libel action brought by a public official against critics of his official conduct. We further hold that under the proper safeguards the evidence presented in this case is constitutionally insufficient to support the judgment for respondent. . . .

[It is argued] that the constitutional guarantees of freedom of speech and of the press are inapplicable here, at least so far as the Times is concerned, because the allegedly libelous statements were published as part of a paid, "commercial" advertisement. . . . That the Times was paid for publishing the advertisement is as immaterial in this connection as is the fact that newspapers and books are sold. . . . Any other conclusion would discourage newspapers from carrying "editorial advertisements" of this type, and so might shut off an important outlet for the promulgation of information and ideas by persons who do not themselves have access to publishing facilities . . ..

Under Alabama law as applied in this case, a publication is "libelous per se" if the words "tend to injure a person [in] his reputation" or to "bring [him] into public contempt" ; the trial court stated that the standard was met if the words are such as to "injure him in his public office, or impute misconduct to him in his office, or want of official integrity, or want of fidelity to a public trust . . .." The jury must find that the words were published "of and concerning" the plaintiff, but where the plaintiff is a public official his place in the governmental hierarchy is sufficient evidence to support a finding that his reputation has been affected by statements that reflect upon the agency of which he is in charge. Once "libel per se" has been established, the defendant has no defense as to stated facts unless he can persuade the jury that they were true in all their particulars. . . . Unless he can discharge the burden of proving truth, general damages are presumed, and may be awarded without proof of pecuniary injury. A showing of actual malice is apparently a prerequisite to recovery of punitive damages, and the defendant may in any event forestall a punitive award by a retraction meeting the statutory requirements. Good motives and belief in truth do not negate an inference of malice, but are relevant only in mitigation of punitive damages if the jury chooses to accord them weight. . . .

The question before us is whether this rule of liability, as applied to an action brought by a public official against critics of his official conduct, abridges the freedom of speech and of the press . . ..

Respondent relies heavily, as did the Alabama courts, on statements of this Court to the effect that the Constitution does not protect libelous publica-

tions. Those statements do not foreclose our inquiry here. None of the cases sustained the use of libel laws to impose sanctions upon expression critical of the official conduct of public officials. . . . In [Beauharnais] the Court was careful to note that it "retains and exercises authority to nullify action which encroaches on freedom of utterance under the guise of punishing libel" . . . . In deciding the question now, we are compelled by neither precedent nor policy to give any more weight to the epithet "libel" than we have to other "mere labels" of state law. [NAACP v. Button, sec. 4 below.] Like insurrection, contempt, advocacy of unlawful acts, breach of the peace, obscenity, solicitation of legal business, and the various other formulae for the repression of expression that have been challenged in this Court, libel can claim no talismanic immunity from constitutional limitations. It must be measured by standards that satisfy the First Amendment. . . .

[W]e consider this case against the background of a profound national commitment to the principle that debate on public issues should be uninhibited, robust, and wide-open, and that it may well include vehement, caustic, and sometimes unpleasantly sharp attacks on government and public officials. . . . The present advertisement, as an expression of grievance and protest on one of the major public issues of our time, would seem clearly to qualify for the constitutional protection. The question is whether it forfeits that protection by the falsity of some of its factual statements and by its alleged defamation of respondent.

Authoritative interpretations of the First Amendment guarantees have consistently refused to recognize an exception for any test of truth—whether administered by judges, juries, or administrative officials—and especially not one that puts the burden of proving truth on the speaker. "The constitutional protection does not turn upon the truth, popularity, or social utility of the ideas and beliefs which are offered." [E]rroneous statement is inevitable in free debate and [must] be protected if the freedoms of expression are to have the "breathing space" that they "need . . . to survive" [NAACP v. Button]. . . .

Injury to official reputation affords no more warrant for repressing speech that would otherwise be free than does factual error. . . . If judges are to be treated as "men of fortitude, able to thrive in a hardy climate" [Craig v. Harney, see sec. 4 below], surely the same must be true of other government officials, such as elected city commissioners. Criticism of their official conduct does not lose its constitutional protection merely because it is effective criticism and hence diminishes their official reputations.

If neither factual error nor defamatory content suffices to remove the constitutional shield from criticism of official conduct, the combination of the two elements is no less inadequate. This is the lesson to be drawn from the great controversy over the Sedition Act of 1798, 1 Stat. 596, which first crystallized a national awareness of the central meaning of the First Amendment. . . .

Although the Sedition Act was never tested in this Court, the attack upon its validity has carried the day in the court of history. Fines levied in its prose-

cution were repaid by Act of Congress on the ground that it was unconstitutional. . . . Jefferson, as President, pardoned those who had been convicted and sentenced under the Act and remitted their fines . . . . The invalidity of the Act has also been assumed by Justices of this Court. . . . These views reflect a broad consensus that the Act, because of the restraint it imposed upon criticism of government and public officials, was inconsistent with the First Amendment. . . .

What a State may not constitutionally bring about by means of a criminal statute is likewise beyond the reach of its civil law of libel. The fear of damage awards under a rule such as that invoked by the Alabama courts here may be markedly more inhibiting than the fear of prosecution under a criminal statute. . . . The judgment awarded in this case—without the need for any proof of actual pecuniary loss—was one thousand times greater than the maximum fine provided by the Alabama criminal statute, and one hundred times greater than that provided by the Sedition Act. And since there is no double jeopardy limitation applicable to civil lawsuits, this is not the only judgment that may be awarded against petitioners for the same publication. Whether or not a newspaper can survive a succession of such judgments, the pall of fear and timidity imposed upon those who would give voice to public criticism is an atmosphere in which the First Amendment freedoms cannot survive. . . .

The state rule of law is not saved by its allowance of the defense of truth. A defense for erroneous statements honestly made is no less essential here than was the requirement of proof of guilty knowledge which, in [Smith v. California, sec. 3 below], we held indispensable to a valid conviction of a bookseller for possessing obscene writings for sale. . . . Allowance of the defense of truth, with the burden of proving it on the defendant, does not mean that only false speech will be deterred.[1] . . . Under such a rule, would-be critics of official conduct may be deterred from voicing their criticism, even though it is believed to be true and even though it is in fact true, because of doubt whether it can be proved in court or fear of the expense of having to do so. . . . The rule thus dampens the vigor and limits the variety of public debate. . . .

The constitutional guarantees require, we think, a federal rule that prohibits a public official from recovering damages for a defamatory falsehood relating to his official conduct unless he proves that the statement was made with "actual malice"—that is, with knowledge that it was false or with reckless disregard of whether it was false or not. . . .

We hold today that the Constitution delimits a State's power to award damages for libel in actions brought by public officials against critics of their official conduct. Since this is such an action,[2] the rule requiring proof of ac-

---

1. Even a false statement may be deemed to make a valuable contribution to public debate, since it brings about "the clearer perception and livelier impression of truth, produced by its collision with error." Mill, On Liberty . . . . ; see also Milton, Areopagitica . . . . [Footnote by the Court.]

2. We have no occasion here to determine how far down into the lower ranks of government employees the "public official" designation would extend for purposes of this rule, or otherwise to specify categories of persons who would or would not be included. . . . Nor need we here determine the boundaries of the "official con-

tual malice is applicable. While Alabama law apparently requires proof of actual malice for an award of punitive damages, where general damages are concerned malice is "presumed." Such a presumption is inconsistent with the federal rule. . . . Since the trial judge did not instruct the jury to differentiate between general and punitive damages, it may be that the verdict was wholly an award of one or the other. But it is impossible to know, in view of the general verdict returned. Because of this uncertainty, the judgment must be reversed and the case remanded. . . .

Applying these standards, we consider that the proof presented to show actual malice lacks the convincing clarity which the constitutional standard demands, and hence that it would not constitutionally sustain the judgment for respondent under the proper rule of law. . . .

We also think the evidence was constitutionally defective in another respect: it was incapable of supporting the jury's finding that the allegedly libelous statements were made "of and concerning" respondent. . . .

Reversed and remanded.*

Mr. Justice BLACK, with whom Mr. Justice DOUGLAS joins, (concurring).

. . . I base my vote to reverse on the belief that the First and Fourteenth Amendments not merely "delimit" a State's power to award damages to "public officials against critics of their official conduct" but completely prohibit a State from exercising such a power. . . . "Malice," even as defined by the Court, is an elusive, abstract concept, hard to prove and hard to disprove. The requirement that malice be proved provides at best an evanescent protection for the right critically to discuss public affairs and certainly does not measure up to the sturdy safeguard embodied in the First Amendment. Unlike the Court, therefore, I vote to reverse exclusively on the ground that the Times and the individual defendants had an absolute, unconditional constitutional right to publish in the Times advertisement their criticisms of the Montgomery agencies and officials. . . .

Mr. Justice GOLDBERG, with whom Mr. Justice DOUGLAS joins, (concurring in the result). . . .

duct" concept. It is enough for the present case that respondent's position as an elected city commissioner clearly made him a public official, and that the allegations in the advertisement concerned what was allegedly his official conduct as Commissioner in charge of the Police Department. . . . [Footnote by the Court.]

[In Rosenblatt v. Baer, 383 U.S. 75 (1966), Justice Brennan's majority opinion found it unnecessary to draw "precise lines" for determining the content of the "public official" category, but suggested that the designation "applies at the very least to those among the hierarchy of government employees who have, or appear to the public to have, substantial responsibility for or control over the conduct of governmental affairs."]

* Two years after New York Times, the Court had little difficulty in extending its principles to state *criminal* libel cases. Garrison v. Louisiana, 379 U.S. 64 (1964). (Compare the Court's difficulties when added extensions of New York Times were urged, in the notes below.) In Garrison, Justice Brennan's opinion for the Court held that, though criminal libel has a "differing history and purposes" than civil libel, "the New York Times rule also limits state power to impose criminal sanctions for criticism of the official conduct of public officials." Justices Black and Douglas concurred, reiterating their positions in New York Times.

In my view, the First and Fourteenth Amendments to the Constitution afford to the citizen and to the press an absolute, unconditional privilege to criticize official conduct despite the harm which may flow from excesses and abuses. . . .

This is not to say that the Constitution protects defamatory statements directed against the private conduct of a public official or private citizen. Freedom of press and of speech insures that government will respond to the will of the people and that changes may be obtained by peaceful means. Purely private defamation has little to do with the political ends of a self-governing society. The imposition of liability for private defamation does not abridge the freedom of public speech or any other freedom protected by the First Amendment.[1] . . .

The conclusion that the Constitution affords the citizen and the press an absolute privilege for criticism of official conduct does not leave the public official without defenses against unsubstantiated opinions or deliberate misstatements. . . . The public official certainly has equal if not greater access than most private citizens to media of communication. . . .

THE NEW YORK TIMES CASE AND FIRST AMENDMENT ANALYSIS

Does the New York Times opinion utilize the analytical approaches surveyed in chap. 12? Do the various techniques and controversies examined there—"absolutes" versus "balancing," clear and present danger, overbreadth, etc.—play a significant role here? Or does New York Times mark a new departure, with implications beyond the defamation area? Note Harry Kalven's comment, written shortly after the decision, suggesting that the opinion "may prove to be the best and most important [the Court] has ever produced in the realm of freedom of speech." See Kalven, "The New York Times Case: A Note on 'The Central Meaning of the First Amendment,'" 1964 Sup.Ct.Rev. 191. Even if the opinion is among the "best," has it proved the "most important"? Did it play a significant role in the post-New York Times encounters with the problems of subversion and advocacy of illegal action, chap. 12, sec. 1, above? In the encounters with problems of protest demonstrations in the streets, chap. 12, sec. 2, above? With the problems of protest through symbolic speech, chap. 12, sec. 3, above?

Consider, in light of the developments traced in chap. 12 and in the remaining materials in this chapter, the persuasiveness of Kalven's reasons for ascribing great importance to New York Times. His perception of "exciting possibilities" in the Court's opinion stemmed from "its emphasis on

---

1. In most cases, as in the case at bar, there will be little difficulty in distinguishing defamatory speech relating to private conduct from that relating to official conduct. I recognize, of course, that there will be a gray area. The difficulties of applying a public-private standard are, however certainly of a different genre from those attending the differentiation between a malicious and nonmalicious state of mind. If the constitutional standard is to be shaped by a concept of malice, the speaker takes the risk not only that the jury will inaccurately determine his state of mind but also that the injury will fail properly to apply the constitutional standard set by the elusive concept of malice. . . . [Footnote by Justice Goldberg.]

seditious libel and the Sedition Act of 1798 as the key to the meaning of the First Amendment." (Recall the consideration of seditious libel and the reference to the New York Times opinion in chap. 12, sec. 1, above.) Kalven argued that "the importance of the free-speech provision of the Constitution rests on the rejection of seditious libel as an offense," and that that key theme had been ignored in traditional analyses before New York Times. Accordingly, he found the "special virtue of the Times opinion" in "its restoration of seditious libel to its essential role, thus suddenly and dramatically changing the idiom of free-speech analysis." And he added, even more broadly, "that the effect of the Times opinion is necessarily to discard or diminish in importance the clear-and-present danger test, the balancing formula, the two-level speech theory of Beauharnais and Roth [sec. 2 below], and the two-tier theory of different effects of the First Amendment on federal and state action." [1]

Have those tests and formulas and theories been "discarded," have they "diminished in importance," since New York Times? Would free speech analysis be in better shape today if they had? Has New York Times, for example, diminished the importance—or utility—of "balancing"? Kalven noted that "the idiom of balancing was eschewed in the Times case." There was no "ad hoc balancing": no resort to the view "that the court must, in each case, balance the individual and social interest in freedom of expression against the social interest sought by the regulation which restricts expression." [2] But was balancing truly eschewed in New York Times? As Kalven recognizes, there was, "of course, a sense in which the Court did indulge in balancing. It did not go the whole way and give an absolute privilege to the 'citizen-critic.' " It "balanced the two obvious conflicting interests." Is New York Times an example of "definitional balancing"—general rules themselves a product of balancing competing considerations? Note the comment in Nimmer, "The Right to Speak from Times to Time . . . .," 56 Calif.L.Rev. 935 (1968), suggesting that New York Times represents "a third approach which avoids the all or nothing implications of absolutism versus ad hoc balancing. Times points the way to the employment of the balancing process on the definitional rather than the litigation or ad hoc level. That is, the Court employs balancing not for the purpose of determining which litigant deserves to prevail in the particular case, but only for the purpose of defining which forms of speech are to be regarded as 'speech' within the meaning of the First Amendment." Nimmer adds that, by "in effect holding that knowingly and recklessly false speech was not 'speech' within the meaning of the first amendment, the Court must have implicitly (since no explicit explanation was offered) referred to certain competing policy considerations."

1. Kalven urged, moreover, that "analysis of free-speech issues should hereafter begin with the significant issue of seditious libel and defamation of government by its critics rather than with the sterile example of a man falsely yelling fire in a crowded theater." (Recall Justice Holmes in the Schenck case, chap. 12, sec. 1.)

2. That description is from a critic of balancing, Emerson, "Toward a General Theory of the First Amendment," 72 Yale L.J. 877, 912 (1963). Need and should balancing be ad hoc in that sense? Need it deemphasize First Amendment values, as critics charge? Compare Gunther, " . . . The Case of Justice Powell," 24 Stan.L.Rev. 1001 (1972), and recall the comments on balancing in chap. 12.

Is anything gained by this distinction between "definitional" and "ad hoc" balancing? Does "definitional balancing" too readily lend itself to the Chaplinsky v. New Hampshire approach of considering broad categories—at that time, libel and obscenity as well as "fighting words"—as outside the First Amendment? Nimmer suggests that "ad hoc balancing" tends towards "judicial abdication in the weighing process" and excessive deference to the legislature. He argues, moreover, that definitional balancing, unlike ad hoc balancing, produces "a rule [which] can be employed in future cases." Is balancing necessarily deferential to the legislature? Does balancing other than "definitional balancing" fail to produce guidance for future cases? Recall the balancing cases in chap. 12 and note the reliance on that approach in the cases that follow. Contrast e. g., Dennis, in sec. 1 of chap. 12, with Cohen v. California in chap. 12, sec. 2, and Street v. New York in chap. 12, sec. 3.[3] And consider the evolution of the New York Times rule in the cases that follow, in the defamation and privacy contexts: Are those elaborations of New York Times examples of balancing, definitional balancing, or something else? Contrast the positions of Justices Brennan and Harlan, for example, in the following cases: Justice Harlan was avowedly an advocate of balancing; Justice Brennan, according to Nimmer, engaged in definitional balancing in Times. Did one have a distinct advantage over the other in articulating and assessing the competing considerations in the cases which follow?

THE EXTENSION OF NEW YORK TIMES BEYOND DEFAMATION OF PUBLIC OFFICIALS TO "PUBLIC FIGURES"

In his comment on the New York Times case, Professor Kalven wondered whether the Court would view it as covering simply "libel of public officials," or whether the Court would accept "the invitation to follow a dialectic progression from public official to government policy to public policy to matters in the public domain." The invitation seemed to Kalven "overwhelming." But the Court has found that invitation increasingly difficult to follow: as the sequence of cases from the 1967 decisions in this note to the 1974 ruling in Gertz, below, shows, an increasingly divided Court took some steps to extend the applicability of the New York Times rule but ultimately rejected additional expansions.

3. Note Gunther, footnote 2 above, criticizing "case-by-case balancing" without embracing "definitional balancing": "A Supreme Court opinion should strive for more than a 'fair balancing' in the individual case before the Court. It should also provide the maximum possible guidance for lower courts and litigants. An excessively particularized opinion lacks that quality. There must at least be an articulation of the criteria that guide the resolution of the value conflicts in a particular case . . . . Moreover, especially when sensitive First Amendment values are involved, the risks of case-by-case adjudication may be too great and broader prophylactic rules may be appropriate." Effective balancing "must guard against succumbing to excessive particularization and losing sight of the weighty reasons for greater generality. One of Justice Harlan's most admirable qualities was, after all, his 'gift of conjoining the particular *with the general*.'" Cf. Ely, "Flag Desecration: A Case Study in the Roles of Categorization and Balancing in First Amendment Analysis," 88 Harv.L.Rev. 1482 (1975).

The mounting divisions emerged as early as CURTIS PUBLISHING CO. v. BUTTS and ASSOCIATED PRESS v. WALKER, decided together at 388 U.S. 130 (1967). In those cases, the results applied the New York Times rule to libel actions "instituted by persons who are not public officials, but who are 'public figures' and involved in issues in which the public has a justified and important interest." The Butts case grew out of a Saturday Evening Post article which claimed that the University of Georgia football coach had fixed a football game with the University of Alabama. Former General Walker's suit against the AP challenged a report that he had led a violent crowd in opposition to federal enforcement of a court decree ordering the enrollment of James Meredith at the University of Mississippi in 1962. The Court unanimously reversed the $500,000 Walker judgment and, by a 5 to 4 division, affirmed the $460,000 Butts judgment. But the Court was sharply divided in its reasoning: four of the Justices (Harlan, Clark, Stewart and Fortas) opposed extending the New York Times rule and favored curtailing press immunity in this context; three (Chief Justice Warren and Justices Brennan and White) urged application of the New York Times standard of liability; the remaining two (Black and Douglas) urged a broader press immunity, as they had in the earlier cases. For purposes of disposition of cases of this kind, however, the Court agreed that the New York Times rule would govern in "public figures" cases.

In announcing the position of the four Justices who opposed extension of the New York Times rule, Justice Harlan examined the similarities and differences between libel actions by public officials and by other "public figures," "viewed in the light of the principles of liability which are of general applicability in our society"; agreed that "public figures" actions "cannot be left entirely to state libel laws"; but insisted that "the rigorous federal requirements of New York Times are not the only appropriate accommodation of the conflicting interests at stake." He accordingly concluded: "We consider and would hold that a 'public figure' who is not a public official may also recover damages for a defamatory falsehood whose substance makes substantial danger to reputation apparent, on a showing of highly unreasonable conduct constituting an extreme departure from the standards of investigation and reporting ordinarily adhered to by responsible publishers."

Chief Justice Warren stated the position of those who urged application of the New York Times rule here. He found Justice Harlan's "unusual and uncertain" standard inadequate either for guidance to a jury or for protection of First Amendment rights. In his view, the New York Times standard should apply to all "public figures," not merely "public officials": they should not be able to recover without proof of "actual malice"—i. e., proof that the defamatory statement was made "with knowledge that it was false or with reckless disregard of whether it was false or not." *

The third position was stated by Justice Black. He commented that "the Court is getting itself in the same quagmire in the field of libel in which it is now helplessly struggling in the field of obscenity [sec. 2, below]." He sug-

---

* Note also four subsequent cases involving relatively minor elaborations of New York Times: Greenbelt Pub. Ass'n v. Bresler, 398 U.S. 6 (1970); Monitor Patriot Co. v. Roy, 401 U.S. 265 (1971); Ocala Star-Banner Co. v. Damron, 401 U.S. 295 (1971); Time, Inc. v. Pape, 401 U.S. 279 (1971).

gested that the Justices' "various experimental expedients" all "boil down to a determination of how offensive to this Court a particular libel judgment may be" and reiterated his insistence that New York Times be abandoned in favor of full press immunity "from the harassment of libel judgments."

In the Walker case, these three positions led to a common result: unanimous reversal of the libel judgment. But, Justice Harlan emphasized in announcing the judgment of the Court, the governing standard on remand was to be the New York Times rule rather than his new "public figures" proposal, since Justices Black and Douglas had joined the New York Times adherents for the purpose of guidance in further proceedings in this case. In the Butts case, on the other hand, one of the New York Times rule supporters—the Chief Justice—joined the Harlan group to produce a 5 to 4 affirmance of the libel judgment: though the trial judge's charge was not in "strict compliance" with the subsequently announced New York Times standard, Chief Justice Warren found justification for not insisting "on the financial and emotional expenses of retrial" here.†

DEFAMATION ACTIONS BY PRIVATE PLAINTIFFS RATHER THAN PUBLIC FIGURES: THE ROSENBLOOM EXPERIMENT AND THE GERTZ RESOLUTION

As the Butts and Walker decisions indicate, the Court had considerable difficulty coming to the conclusion that the New York Times knowing or reckless falsity standard of liability should apply in libel actions by "public figures" as well as by "public officials." The Court encountered even greater difficulty when it confronted the next major invitation to extend the New York Times libel rule to new areas. The new challenge concerned the delineation of appropriate rules where a publisher is sued by a *private* individual. At first, in the 1971 decision in Rosenbloom, a divided Court decided to extend the New York Times rule to that situation: the focus of New York Times was broadened from the "publicness" of the plaintiff to the "general interest" nature of the publication. But in Gertz, three years later, that experiment was abandoned, a majority for a new approach was gathered at last, and a rule permitting recovery more easily than under the New York Times standard was adopted for situations involving "private" plaintiffs.

In 1971, in ROSENBLOOM v. METROMEDIA, INC., 403 U.S. 29, Justice Brennan's plurality opinion (joined only by Chief Justice Burger and Justice Blackmun) extended the New York Times privilege to a private

---

† Note also the successful invocation of the New York Times standard by a teacher dismissed for writing a letter to a newspaper attacking a school board's handling of financing matters. Pickering v. Board of Education, 391 U.S. 563 (1968). Justice Marshall's majority opinion concluded: "In these circumstances [the] interest of the school administration in limiting teachers' opportunities to contribute to public debate is not significantly greater than its interest in limiting a similar contribution by any member of the general public. [Accordingly,] absent proof of false statements knowingly or recklessly made by him, a teacher's exercise of his right to speak on issues of public importance may not furnish the basis for his dismissal from public employment." There were separate opinions by Justice Douglas, joined by Justice Black, and by Justice White. (See also sec. 5 below.)

plaintiff's action claiming defamation in a report "about the individual's involvement in an event of public or general interest." But in GERTZ v. ROBERT WELCH, INC., 418 U.S. 323 (1974), Justice Powell spoke for a majority taking a different course and holding that state libel law could impose liability in suits by private individuals "on a less demanding showing" than that required by New York Times, "so long as [states] do not impose liability without fault." The Gertz decision, in addition to authorizing such standards of liability as negligence, also imposed restrictions on damages. In lessening the constitutional restraints on standards of liability and in focusing on safeguards regarding damages, the new majority generally followed the approach advocated by the dissents of Justices Marshall and Harlan in the Rosenbloom case.

1. *The Rosenbloom case.* The extension of New York Times in Rosenbloom by a plurality of the Justices came in a case in which a distributor of nudist magazines brought suit for libel because of radio reports about police action against his allegedly obscene books and about his lawsuit against police interference with his business. Some of the news reports referred to "girlie-book peddlers" and the "smut literature racket." Petitioner brought his civil libel action after an acquittal on criminal obscenity charges. He recovered substantial general and punitive damages. But that judgment was found to be wrong because the trial court had not applied the New York Times standard of liability. Justice Brennan's plurality opinion, joined by Chief Justice Burger and Justice Blackmun, argued that the critical criterion should be the subject matter of the report rather than the "public figure" nature of the plaintiff. He insisted that experience since the New York Times decision had "disclosed the artificiality, in terms of the public's interest, of a simple distinction between 'public' and 'private' individuals." He accordingly concluded:

"If a matter is a subject of public or general interest, it cannot suddenly become less so merely because a private individual is involved, or because in some sense the individual did not 'voluntarily' choose to become involved. The public's primary interest is in the event; the public focus is on the conduct of the participant and the content, effect, and significance of the conduct, not the participant's prior anonymity or notoriety. [We] honor the commitment to robust debate on public issues [by] extending constitutional protection to all discussion and communication involving matters of public or general concern, without regard to whether the persons involved are famous or anonymous."

Justice Black's brief concurrence in the judgment reiterated his view that "the First Amendment does not permit the recovery of libel judgments against the news media even when statements are broadcast with knowledge [that] they are false." [Justice Douglas, who was usually in general agreement with Justice Black on this issue, did not participate in Rosenbloom.] Justice White's concurrence in the judgment rejected all other opinions in Rosenbloom because each "decides broader constitutional issues and displaces more state libel law than is necessary for the decision." A "more limited adjudication" seemed adequate: applying the New York Times rule to "discussion of the official actions of public servants such as the police."

Justice Marshall's dissent, joined by Justice Stewart, took a different tack—one that closely resembled the majority position that emerged in

Gertz three years later. He urged that states be left free to articulate whatever fault standard best suited them, subject only to the "constitutional caveat" that "absolute or strict liability, like uncontrolled damages and private fines, cannot be used." He urged focus on the problem of damages rather than that of liability because the "size of the potential judgment that may be rendered against the press must be the most significant factor in producing self censorship." He suggested "restricting the award of damages to proven, actual injuries." Justice Harlan's dissent agreed with many of Justice Marshall's views but reached a different result "with respect to the tolerable limits of punitive damages." Justice Harlan stated that "recoverable damages must be limited to those consequences of a publication which are reasonably foreseeable." But he would not bar punitive damages in all cases: those should be permitted "where actual malice is proved."

2. *The Gertz case.* The surfacing of a majority position different from that of the plurality in Rosenbloom occurred in the Gertz case in 1974. A Chicago policeman had been convicted of murder. The victim's family retained Elmer Gertz, a Chicago lawyer, to represent them in civil litigation against the policeman. Robert Welch, Inc., publishes American Opinion, an "outlet for the views of the John Birch Society." The magazine charged Gertz with being an architect of the "frame-up" of the policeman in the murder trial and called Gertz, inter alia, a "Communist-fronter." Gertz brought a successful libel action with a jury award of $50,000. But the lower courts set aside the verdict: the Court of Appeals relied on Rosenbloom to hold that the New York Times standard applied and that its requirements had not been met. The Supreme Court found that Gertz was not a "public figure" under the pre-Rosenbloom cases * and held that Rosenbloom was wrong and that a private citizen such as Gertz should be able to recover without meeting the New York Times standard.

Justice Powell's majority opinion stated the new standard of liability for private libel actions as follows: "We hold that, so long as they do not impose liability without fault, the States may define for themselves the appropriate standard of liability for a publisher or broadcaster of defamatory falsehood injurious to a private individual. This approach provides a more equitable boundary between the competing concerns involved here. It recognizes the strength of the legitimate state interest in compensating private individuals for wrongful injury to reputation, yet shields the press and broadcast media from the rigors of strict liability for defamation. At least this conclusion obtains where, as here, the substance of the defamatory statement 'makes substantial danger to reputation apparent.' This phrase places

---

* The Court found Gertz not to be a "public figure" even though he had "long been active in community and professional affairs" and was "well-known in some circles." The Court noted that "he had achieved no general fame or notoriety in the community" and added: "We would not lightly assume that a citizen's participation in community and professional affairs rendered him a public figure for all purposes. Absent clear evidence of general fame or notoriety in the community, and pervasive involvement in the affairs of society, an individual should not be deemed a public personality for all aspects of his life. It is preferable to reduce the public figure question to a more meaningful context by looking to the nature and extent of an individual's participation in the particular controversy giving rise to the defamation." And in the course of the policeman's murder trial, Gertz had played only "a minimal role."

in perspective the conclusion we announce today. Our inquiry would involve considerations somewhat different from those discussed above if a State purported to condition civil liability on a factual misstatement whose content did not warn a reasonably prudent editor or broadcaster of its defamatory potential. Cf. Time, Inc. v. Hill [which follows]." And as to the new constitutional restraints on damage awards, Justice Powell announced that states may ordinarily go no further "than compensation for actual injury": "[W]e hold that the States may not permit recovery of presumed or punitive damages, at least when liability is not based on a showing of knowledge of falsity or reckless disregard for the truth."

In justifying the conclusion as to the standard of liability, Justice Powell noted that, though "there is no such thing as a false idea" under the First Amendment, "there is no constitutional value in false statements of fact." Nevertheless, "some falsehood" is protected "in order to protect speech that matters." Strict liability for falsehoods by the news media would risk "intolerable self-censorship." But total immunity for publishers would ignore a competing societal value: "the compensation of individuals for the harm inflicted on them by defamatory falsehoods."

Where the reputation of "public persons" was involved, the state interest in compensation was "limited," and that justified the broad New York Times immunity. But the state interest in compensating injuries to private individuals was stronger and that made a less demanding standard of liability appropriate here. Accordingly, the Court had "no difficulty in distinguishing among defamation plaintiffs." Public figures could use the remedy of "self-help" more effectively because of their "significantly greater access" to the media. Private persons, by contrast, were "more vulnerable to injury." Moreover, there was "a compelling normative consideration" for a stronger defamation remedy by private persons: unlike public figures, they had not "voluntarily exposed themselves to increased risk of injury from defamatory falsehoods concerning them." In short, "private individuals are not only more vulnerable to injury than public officials and public figures; they are also more deserving of recovery." The Rosenbloom plurality rule abridged the legitimate state concern with private plaintiffs' injuries "to a degree that we find unacceptable." Moreover, Rosenbloom unwisely imposed the task on judges of deciding "on an ad hoc basis which publications address issues of 'general or public interest' and which do not." The new Gertz rule of leaving states free to impose any standard of liability short of "liability without fault" accordingly seemed preferable.

The majority's new focus on damage limitations stemmed from the perception that with respect to private plaintiffs the "countervailing state interest extends no further than compensation for actual injury" when the proof fell short of knowledge of falsity or reckless disregard for the truth. "Actual injury," however, "is not limited to out-of-pocket loss." Justice Powell explained: "Indeed, the more customary types of actual harm inflicted by defamatory falsehood include impairment of reputation and standing in the community, personal humiliation, and mental anguish and suffering." But presumed or punitive damages were impermissible: "Like the doctrine of presumed damages, jury discretion to award punitive damages unnecessarily exacerbates the danger of media self-censorship." Moreover,

"punitive damages are wholly irrelevant to the state interest that justifies a negligence standard for private defamation actions. They are not compensation for injury. Instead, they are private fines levied by civil juries to punish reprehensible conduct and to deter its future occurrence. In short, the private defamation plaintiff who establishes liability under a less demanding standard than that stated by New York Times may recover only such damages as are sufficient to compensate him for actual injury."

Justice Blackmun, who had been a member of the Rosenbloom plurality, submitted a brief opinion explaining his vote to make the new Gertz majority. He said that he still thought the Rosenbloom rule "logical and inevitable" and that he saw "some illogic" in the new approach. Nevertheless, he joined this new effort "to strike a balance between competing values where necessarily uncertain assumptions about human behavior color the result." He explained that the new rules' limitations on damages left "what should prove to be sufficient and adequate breathing space for a vigorous press." He concluded: "If my vote were not needed to create a majority, I would adhere to my prior view. A definitive ruling, however, is paramount."

Justice Brennan's dissent was the only one to adhere fully to the Rosenbloom plurality approach.† He reiterated his Rosenbloom arguments as to the unacceptability of the distinction between private defamation plaintiffs and public figures. The argument that public figures had greater access to the media to clear their names was unrealistic: "In the vast majority of libels involving public officials or public figures, the ability to respond through the media will depend on the same complex factor on which the ability of a private individual depends: the unpredictable event of the media's continuing interest in the story." Moreover, "the idea that certain 'public' figures have voluntarily exposed their entire lives to public inspection, while private individuals have kept theirs carefully shrouded from public view is, at best, a legal fiction." The new rule, he insisted, denied "free expression its needed 'breathing space.'" Widespread adoption of a reasonable care standard in private defamations—"the probable result of today's decision"—will "lead to self-censorship."

Justice Douglas' dissent thought the majority's "struggle" to accommodate competing values "a quite hopeless one": under the First Amendment, "no 'accommodation' of its freedoms can be 'proper' except those made by the Framers themselves." He opposed any libel suits "for public discussion of public issues."

An attack on the new majority rule came from a different direction in the final dissent, a lengthy one by Justice White. He objected to "the evisceration of the common law libel remedy for the private citizen" both with respect to standards of liability and as to damages. Traditional libel law should be permitted to stand, particularly in view of "the increasingly prom-

---

† Chief Justice Burger, who had comprised the Rosenbloom plurality together with Justices Brennan and Blackmun, submitted a somewhat puzzling dissent. He explained that he did not like the majority's "new doctrinal theory which has no jurisprudential ancestry," yet he cast his vote to reinstate the jury verdict, which did not satisfy the New York Times standard that Rosenbloom would have required. He emphasized that Gertz was a lawyer and that the right to counsel "would be gravely jeopardized if every lawyer who takes an 'unpopular' case, civil or criminal, would automatically become fair game for irresponsible reporters and editors."

inent role of mass media in our society and the awesome power it has placed in the hands of a select few." He found no adequate reasons "for scuttling the libel laws of the States in such wholesale fashion" and for "deprecating the reputation interest of ordinary citizens and rendering them powerless to protect themselves." The New York Times rule itself was justifiable because "seditious libel—criticism of government and public officials—falls beyond the police power of the State." But traditional standards of liability and the authorization of general and punitive damages should be permitted to stand when private citizens were defamed. He argued that experience showed "that some publications are so inherently capable of injury, and actual injury so difficult to prove, that the risk of falsehood should be borne by the publisher, not the victim." Traditional rules posed "no realistic threat to the press." And the "owners of the press and the stockholders of the communications enterprises can much better bear the burden" of inflicting injury to private reputation. He added: "And if they cannot, the public at large should somehow pay for what is essentially a public benefit derived at private expense." He concluded: "I fail to see how the quality or quantity of public debate will be promoted by further emasculation of state libel laws [protecting nonpublic persons] for the benefit of the news media." **

INVASIONS OF PRIVACY AND THE NEW YORK TIMES RULE

1. *Time, Inc. v. Hill.* The New York Times rule was developed as a limited barrier to defamation actions, designed to vindicate the plaintiff's interest in reputation. Should it also shield against liability when the plaintiff seeks to vindicate an interest in privacy rather than reputation? "True" privacy actions, though widely discussed, are relatively rare: in those actions, the plaintiff does not claim falsity, but simply that true disclosures about the plaintiff's personal life are embarrassing invasions of privacy, not newsworthy, and subject to liability.* More common are "false light" privacy cases, where the claim is that the disclosure not only invaded privacy but was also false—though not necessarily injurious to reputation, the gist of defamation actions. The decision in TIME, INC. v. HILL, 385 U.S. 374 (1967)—a few months before Butts and Walker, above—focused primarily on "false light" privacy actions, and the result from a divided Court was that the New York Times "knowing or reckless falsehood" rule was held applicable to such actions. (Does Hill survive Gertz? See the additional comments below.)

The Hill suit against Time, Inc. was based on a New York "right of privacy" statute generally prohibiting anyone from using "for advertising purposes, or for the purposes of trade, the name, portrait or picture of any living person without having first obtained the written consent of such

---

** Note the disagreement about the implications of Gertz, in the Cox Broadcasting case, noted at the end of this section.

* See the much-discussed article by Warren and Brandeis, "The Right to Privacy," 4 Harv.L.Rev. 193 (1890). Compare Prosser, "Privacy," 48 Calif. L.Rev. 383 (1960).

person."   Under the statute, truth was a defense in actions "based upon newsworthy people or events," but a "newsworthy person" could recover when he or she was the subject of a "fictitious" report—a report involving "material and substantial falsification."   Justice Brennan's "opinion of the Court" † concluded that "the constitutional protections for speech and press preclude the application of the New York statute to redress false reports of matters of public interest in the absence of proof that the defendant published the report with knowledge of its falsity or in reckless disregard of the truth."

The Hill suit arose from the following circumstances: In 1952, the Hill family had been held hostage by three escaped convicts for 19 hours, but was released unharmed.   Three years later, a play—"The Desperate Hours" —based on the incident appeared.   The play portrayed the incident as involving considerable violence, though in fact there had been none.   Life magazine's story on the play posed the actors in the original Hill home and indicated that the play accurately portrayed the actual incident.   The original incident had been widely reported, but the Hills had tried to stay out of the public eye thereafter.   Though the Life magazine report that was the subject of the action did not substantially damage the Hills' reputation—they were portrayed as courageous—, they ultimately recovered a $30,000 judgment under the New York privacy law.

In reversing that judgment, Justice Brennan's opinion not only held that the New York Times barrier applied to "false light" privacy actions but also indicated that newsworthiness would be a complete defense against a "true" privacy action.   He emphasized the media's right to print true, newsworthy stories: "The guarantees for speech and press are not the preserve of political expression or comment upon public affairs, essential as those are to healthy government.   One need only pick up any newspaper or magazine to comprehend the vast range of published matter which exposes persons to public view, both private citizens and public officials.   Exposure of the self to others in varying degrees is a concomitant of life in a civilized community.   The risk of this exposure is an essential incident of life in a society which places a primary value on freedom of speech and of press. .   .   . We have no doubt that the subject of the Life article, the opening of a new play linked to an actual incident, is a matter of public interest. The line between the informing and the entertaining is too elusive for the protection of freedom of the press."   (Does that passage nevertheless permit "true" privacy actions by persons who had once been in the news but who had since faded from public view?)

A separate opinion by Justice Harlan agreed with the reversal because New York had permitted liability upon a "mere showing of substantial falsity."   He thought, however, that the majority had imposed too high a

† Despite that description of the Brennan opinion, the separate opinions revealed that only Justices Stewart and White joined Justice Brennan without reservation.   Justice Black's concurrence, joined by Justice Douglas, made it clear that he supported the Brennan opinion only to enable the Court to dispose of the case on the basis of the prevailing New York Times doctrine.   That did not mean, he emphasized, that he receded from any of his earlier views "about the much wider press and speech freedoms" guaranteed by the Constitution.

standard on remand: "Were the jury on retrial to find negligent rather than, as the Court requires, reckless or knowing 'fictionalization,' I think that federal constitutional requirements would be met." He insisted that the "sweeping extension" of New York Times was unjustified: states should be permitted in situations such as this "to hold the press to a duty of making a reasonable investigation of the underlying facts." He noted that this was not "privacy" litigation "in its truest sense," for there was no claim of any intrusion upon Hill's "solitude or private affairs" nor publication of facts "of such limited public interest and so intimate and potentially embarrassing to an individual" that a state might impose sanctions. He objected to the granting of "'a talismanic immunity' to all unintentional errors." The situation here, he insisted, was sufficiently different to justify "a more limited 'breathing space' than that granted in criticism of public officials."

Justice Fortas' dissent, joined by Chief Justice Warren and Justice Clark, concluded that the jury instructions, although "not a textbook model," adequately satisfied the majority's New York Times standard. He feared that the majority's disposition might place "insuperable obstacles in the way of recovery by persons who are injured by reckless and heedless assault. [I] do not believe that the First Amendment precludes effective protection of the right of privacy—or, for that matter, an effective law of libel."

2. *Some comments.* a. Does the Hill principle (announced in 1967) survive the Court's retreat in Gertz (the 1974 decision above) from Justice Brennan's position that the New York Times principle applies to all "news-worthy" matters? * Is the extension of New York Times to the Hill situation persuasive? See Kalven, "The Reasonable Man and the First Amendment: Hill, Butts, and Walker," 1967 Sup.Ct.Rev. 267. Does Hill move well beyond the seditious libel-political speech emphasis that was seen as the "central meaning" of the First Amendment in the New York Times case?

For a criticism of Hill, see Nimmer, "The Right to Speak from Times to Time: First Amendment Theory Applied to Libel and Misapplied to Privacy," 56 Calif.L.Rev. 935 (1968), suggesting that the Court failed to "pierce the superficial similarity between false light invasion of privacy and defamation" and urging that disclosure of non-defamatory matters interfering with privacy should not be entitled to First Amendment protection. He argues, for example, that, unlike "injury arising from defamation, 'more speech' is irrelevant in mitigating the injury due to an invasion of privacy." Does the Hill approach afford too much immunity to the press, without adequate regard to competing interests? See Kalven, above, suggesting that "the logic of New York Times and Hill taken together grants the press some measure of constitutional protection for anything the press thinks is a matter of public interest."

---

* See Cantrell v. Forest City Publishing Co., 419 U.S. 245 (1974), where the majority found "no occasion to consider whether a State may constitutionally apply a more relaxed standard of liability for a publisher or broadcaster of false statements injurious to a private individual under a false-light theory of invasion of privacy, or whether the constitutional standard announced in Time, Inc. v. Hill applies to all false-light privacy cases. Cf. [Gertz]." See also Justice Powell's concurrence in Cox Broadcasting, note 2b, commenting that Gertz "calls into question the conceptual basis of Time, Inc. v. Hill."

b.   The first "true" privacy case reached the Court in Cox Broadcasting Corp. v. Cohn, 420 U.S. —— (1975). Though the decision rested on narrow grounds, the Court recognized that plaintiffs' interests in "true" privacy cases were especially strong ones. Moreover, the opinions revealed a disagreement on the Court about the implications of Gertz in the defamation context.

In Cox, the Court held that civil liability in a "true" privacy action could not be imposed upon a broadcaster for truthfully publishing information released to the public in official court records. A father had sued because of the broadcast of the fact that his daughter was a rape victim. In barring liability for publishing data in public records, the Court relied especially on "the public interest in a vigorous press." Justice White's majority opinion found it unnecessary to decide "the broader question whether truthful publications may ever be subjected to civil or criminal liability" or "whether the State may ever define and protect an area of privacy free from unwanted publicity in the press." However, he recognized the "impressive credentials for a right of privacy." Moreover, he claimed that earlier cases had "carefully left open the question" whether the Constitution requires "that truth be recognized as a defense in a defamation action brought by a private person," as well as "the question whether truthful publication of very private matters unrelated to public affairs could be constitutionally proscribed."

A concurring opinion by Justice Powell disagreed with that reading of prior opinions. He insisted that "the constitutional necessity of recognizing a defense of truth" in defamation actions by private plaintiffs was "implicit" in Gertz and other cases. He noted, however, that "causes of action grounded in a State's desire to protect privacy generally implicate interests that are distinct from those protected by defamation actions." He added: "But in cases in which the interests sought to be protected are similar to those considered in Gertz, I view that opinion as requiring that the truth be recognized as a complete defense."

SECTION 2.   OBSCENITY: WHAT IS IT?   WHAT JUSTIFIES RESTRICTING IT?

Introduction.   In 1942, in Chaplinsky v. New Hampshire (chap. 12, sec. 2), the Court categorized obscenity, like libel and "fighting words," as expression outside of First Amendment protection. The modern Court's first major encounter with the constitutionality of obscenity control—in the Roth case, 15 years later—purported to preserve that assumption. Yet Roth also made clear that, even if obscenity is not "speech," the regulation and definition of obscenity raise free speech issues. The extraordinary flow of divided decisions and groping opinions in the wake of Roth made obscenity restraints one of the most controversial and troublesome areas of First Amendment litigation. As Justice Harlan commented a little more than a decade after Roth: "The subject of obscenity has produced a variety of views among the members of the Court unmatched in any other course of constitutional adjudication. In the 13 obscenity cases [since Roth, as of 1968] in

which signed opinions were written [for] the Court, there has been a total of 55 separate opinions among the Justices." [1]

This section examines the decisions that have sought to define obscenity and to explain why it may be prohibited. A dominant characteristic of the opinions is that they speak far more fully (though often not clearly) to the first·question than to the second. The usual preoccupation of the Court has been: "What is obscenity?" Only rarely has the Court addressed the question commonplace in other areas of First Amendment litigation: "What justifies restraint?" [2] That silence may be traceable to the "obscenity-is-not-speech" assumption initiated by Roth and adhered to by the majority ever since. Was Roth an example of "definitional balancing"? Does that suggest that that approach obscures the typical First Amendment analysis that involves articulation of state interests? Is it important to confront the justification problem—if only to enable the Court to state the meaning of obscenity more carefully?

After a tortuous course of decisions in the 16 years following Roth, a majority position on the definition of obscenity was at last achieved in 1973, in the Miller and Paris Adult Theatre cases, below. Those decisions were in the tradition of Roth, though they modified the ingredients of obscenity. But in the 1973 cases, the author of the Roth opinion and the Court's leading spokesman on obscenity in ensuing years, Justice Brennan, gave up on that approach. As he noted in his Paris Adult Theatre dissent: "I am convinced that [the Roth approach] cannot bring stability to this area of the law without jeopardizing fundamental First Amendment values, and I have concluded that the time has come to make a significant departure from that approach." It is not the aim of this section to trace in detail every convolution, nuance and byway of the Court's difficult and divided struggles with the obscenity problem in the years between Roth and the announcement of a Burger Court majority position in 1973. The emphasis here, rather, is on those aspects central to a concern with basic First Amendment developments: in addition to surveying the contemporary state of the law, the focus here is on the identification and appropriate weight of the interests allegedly justifying control of obscenity.[3] Obscenity may well be a "foolish and trivial problem" [4] in the universe of free speech concerns; yet the Court's struggles with it have been so continuous and extensive that it warrants some attention,

1. Ginsberg v. New York, 390 U.S. 629 (1968).

2. See, e. g., the complaint in 1966 that no Justice sustaining obscenity controls had yet "explained *why* he thinks obscenity should be regulated." Note, "More Ado About Dirty Books," 75 Yale L.J. 1364 (1966).

3. The developments from Roth to the 1973 decisions will be traced in part by reliance on the summary in Justice Brennan's 1973 dissent, and in part by supplementary materials focusing on those added developments which are particularly useful in the search for state justifications relevant to obscenity control.

4. The phrase is the late Harry Kalven's, in a comment regretting the 1973 decisions below, as indicating that the problem "will be with us for some time to come." Kalven, "A Step Backward," Chicago Tribune, Aug. 31, 1973, quoted in Sunderland, Obscenity —The Court, the Congress and the President's Commission (Amer.Enterprise Inst., 1975). See also his earlier piece, Kalven, "The Metaphysics of the Law of Obscenity," 1960 Sup.Ct.Rev. 1, one of the best of the many commentaries on obscenity decisions.

particularly for the light it throws—or shadows it casts—on the development of a coherent body of First Amendment analysis.

In examining the materials which follow, then, consider especially what objectives may justify obscenity legislation. What state interests are identified by the Court? What additional objectives may be implicit in the various opinions? To protect society's moral standards against erosion? [5] To preserve or improve "the quality of life" and a "decent community environment"? [6] To avoid the "corrupting" of individual morals and character by the "sin of obscenity" [7]—whether or not improper behavior results? To safeguard against the stimulation of—incitement of? creating a clear and present danger of?—illegal or improper behavior? To protect the sensibilities of the audience by safeguarding against the risk of shock from offensive obscene materials? [8] To protect children against exposure to obscene materials, because of the alleged greater susceptibility of the immature to the harmful effects of obscenity? Other justifications? With what level of scrutiny should the Court examine the asserted state justifications? Must the state demonstrate the substantiality—gravity? immediacy? reality?—of the feared harms? Or is a more deferential judicial stance appropriate in the obscenity area, a stance akin to that in the economic due process cases in chap. 9, sec. 1, above? Even though First Amendment concerns exist in this area, at least at the borderline of whatever constitutes obscenity? [9]

ROTH v. UNITED STATES
ALBERTS v. CALIFORNIA

354 U.S. 476, 77 S.Ct. 1304, 1 L.Ed.2d 1498 (1957).

Certiorari to the United States Court of Appeals for the Second Circuit and appeal from the Superior Court of California, Los Angeles County, Appellate Department.

[In these cases, the Court sustained the validity of federal and state obscenity laws without reaching the question of whether any particular materials were obscene. Roth, a New York publisher and seller, was convicted of mailing obscene advertising and an obscene book in violation of the federal obscenity statute. Alberts, engaged in the mail order business, was

5. Recall the materials in sec. 3 of chap. 9 above, on society's interest in maintaining standards of morality and the conflict with claims to personal autonomy; and recall especially Justice Harlan's dissent in Poe v. Ullman, printed with the decision in Griswold v. Connecticut, chap. 9 above.

6. See, e. g., Professor Bickel's comment, quoted in the majority opinion in the Paris Adult Theatre case, below.

7. See Henkin, "Morals and the Constitution: The Sin of Obscenity," 63 Colum.L.Rev. 391 (1963).

8. Recall the concern with the sensibilities of the audience as a justification for restraints on speech in the materials in chap. 12, sec. 2, above, especially the notes on the "offensive language" cases.

9. This section is limited to those "substantive" concerns regarding the definition of obscenity—especially the asserted and implicit justifications for its control. Obscenity regulation has also been an especially prolific source of concern with the *methods* of regulation, particularly in the context of licensing and censorship of motion pictures. Those "procedural" issues are considered in the context of a broader examination of regulatory methods, including "prior restraints," in sec. 3 below.

convicted under a California law for "lewdly keeping for sale obscene and indecent books" and "publishing an obscene advertisement of them." Both convictions were affirmed below.]

Mr. Justice BRENNAN delivered the opinion of the Court. . . .

The dispositive question is whether obscenity is utterance within the area of protected speech and press.[1] Although this is the first time the question has been squarely presented to this Court, either under the First Amendment or under the Fourteenth Amendment, expressions found in numerous opinions indicate that this Court has always assumed that obscenity is not protected by the freedoms of speech and press. . . .

The guaranties of freedom of expression in effect in 10 of the 14 States which by 1792 had ratified the Constitution, gave no absolute protection for every utterance. Thirteen of the 14 States provided for the prosecution of libel, and all of those States made either blasphemy or profanity, or both, statutory crimes. As early as 1712, Massachusetts made it criminal to publish "any filthy, obscene, or profane song, pamphlet, libel or mock sermon" in imitation or mimicking of religious services. . . . Thus, profanity and obscenity were related offenses.

In light of this history, it is apparent that the unconditional phrasing of the First Amendment was not intended to protect every utterance. This phrasing did not prevent this Court from concluding that libelous utterances are not within the area of constitutionally protected speech. [Beauharnais v. Illinois.] At the time of the adoption of the First Amendment, obscenity law was not as fully developed as libel law, but there is sufficiently contemporaneous evidence to show that obscenity, too, was outside the protection intended for speech and press. . . .

All ideas having even the slightest redeeming social importance— unorthodox ideas, controversial ideas, even ideas hateful to the prevailing climate of opinion—have the full protection of the guaranties, unless excludable because they encroach upon the limited area of more important interests. But implicit in the history of the First Amendment is the rejection of obscenity as utterly without redeeming social importance. This rejection for that reason is mirrored in the universal judgment that obscenity should be restrained, reflected in the international agreement of over 50 nations, in the obscenity laws of all of the 48 States, and in the 20 obscenity laws enacted by the Congress from 1842 to 1956. This is the same judgment expressed by this Court in Chaplinsky v. New Hampshire [quoting a passage printed in chap. 12, sec. 2, above]. We hold that obscenity is not within the area of constitutionally protected speech or press.

It is strenuously urged that these obscenity statutes offend the constitutional guaranties because they punish incitation to impure sexual *thoughts,* not shown to be related to any overt antisocial conduct which is or may be incited in the persons stimulated to such *thoughts.* [The Court quoted from the instructions below, which had referred to lustful and lascivious "thoughts."] It is insisted that the constitutional guaranties are violated because convictions may be had without proof either that obscene material

---

1. No issue is presented in either case concerning the obscenity of the material involved. [Footnote by the Court.]

will perceptibly create a clear and present danger of antisocial conduct, or will probably induce its recipients to such conduct. But, in light of our holding that obscenity is not protected speech, the complete answer to this argument is in the holding of this Court in [Beauharnais v. Illinois]:

"Libelous utterances not being within the area of constitutionally protected speech, it is unnecessary, either for us or for the State courts, to consider the issues behind the phrase 'clear and present danger.' Certainly no one would contend that obscene speech, for example, may be punished only upon a showing of such circumstances. Libel, as we have seen, is in the same class."

However, sex and obscenity are not synonymous. Obscene material is material which deals with sex in a manner appealing to prurient interest.[2] The portrayal of sex, e. g., in art, literature and scientific works, is not itself sufficient reason to deny material the constitutional protection of freedom of speech and press. Sex, a great and mysterious motive force in human life, has indisputably been a subject of absorbing interest to mankind through the ages; it is one of the vital problems of human interest and public concern. As to all such problems, this Court said in Thornhill v. Alabama, 310 U.S. 88, 101–102: "The freedom of speech and of the press guaranteed by the Constitution embraces at the least the liberty to discuss publicly and truthfully *all matters of public concern* . . . . Freedom of discussion, if it would fulfill its historic function in this nation, must embrace *all issues about which information is needed or appropriate to enable the members of society to cope with the exigencies of their period.*" (Emphasis added.)

The fundamental freedoms of speech and press have contributed greatly to the development and well-being of our free society and are indispensable to its continued growth. Ceaseless vigilance is the watchword to prevent their erosion by Congress or by the States. The door barring federal and state intrusion into this area cannot be left ajar; it must be kept tightly closed and opened only the slightest crack necessary to prevent encroachment upon more important interests. It is therefore vital that the standards for judging obscenity safeguard the protection of freedom of speech and press for material which does not treat sex in a manner appealing to prurient interest.

The early leading standard of obscenity allowed material to be judged merely by the effect of an isolated excerpt upon particularly susceptible persons. Regina v. Hicklin, [1868] L.R. 3 Q.B. 360. Some American courts

---

2. I. e., material having a tendency to excite lustful thoughts. Webster's New International Dictionary (Unabridged, 2d ed., 1949) defines *prurient*, in pertinent part, as follows:

". . . Itching; longing; uneasy with desire or longing; of persons, having itching, morbid, or lascivious longings; of desire, curiosity or propensity, lewd. . . ."

Pruriency is defined, in pertinent part, as follows:

". . . Quality of being prurient; lascivious desire or thought. . . ."

We perceive no significant difference between the meaning of obscenity developed in the case law and the definition of the A.L.I., Model Penal Code, § 207.10(2) (Tent.Draft No. 6, 1957), viz.:

". . . A thing is obscene if, considered as a whole, its predominant appeal is to prurient interest, i. e., a shameful or morbid interest in nudity, sex, or excretion, and if it goes substantially beyond customary limits of candor in description or representation of such matters. . . ." . . .
[Footnote by the Court.]

adopted this standard but later decisions have rejected it and substituted this test: whether to the average person, applying contemporary community standards, the dominant theme of the material taken as a whole appeals to prurient interest. The Hicklin test, judging obscenity by the effect of isolated passages upon the most susceptible persons, might well encompass material legitimately treating with sex, and so it must be rejected as unconstitutionally restrictive of the freedoms of speech and press. On the other hand, the substituted standard provides safeguards adequate to withstand the charge of constitutional infirmity.

Both trial courts below sufficiently followed the proper standard. Both courts used the proper definition of obscenity. . . .

It is argued that the statutes do not provide reasonably ascertainable standards of guilt and therefore violate the constitutional requirements of due process. Winters v. New York, 333 U.S. 507. The federal [law bars] the mailing of material that is "obscene, lewd, lascivious or filthy . . . or other publication of an indecent character." The California statute makes punishable [the] keeping for sale or advertising material that is "obscene or indecent." The thrust of the argument is that these words are not sufficiently precise because they do not mean the same thing to all people, all the time, everywhere.

Many decisions have recognized that these terms of obscenity statutes are not precise. This Court, however, has consistently held that lack of precision is not itself offensive to the requirements of due process. "[T]he Constitution does not require impossible standards"; all that is required is that the language "conveys sufficiently definite warning as to the proscribed conduct when measured by common understanding and practices." . . .

In summary, then, we hold that these statutes, applied according to the proper standard for judging obscenity, do not offend constitutional safeguards against convictions based upon protected material, or fail to give men in acting adequate notice of what is prohibited. . . .

Affirmed.

Mr. Chief Justice WARREN, concurring in the result. . . .

. . . The defendants in both these cases [were] engaged in the commercial exploitation of the morbid and shameful craving for materials with prurient effect. I believe that the State and Federal Governments can constitutionally punish such conduct. That is all [we] need to decide. . . .

Mr. Justice HARLAN, concurring in the result in [Alberts] and dissenting in [Roth]. . . .

My basic difficulties with the Court's opinion are three-fold. First, the opinion paints with such a broad brush that I fear it may result in a loosening of the tight reins which state and federal courts should hold upon the enforcement of obscenity statutes. Second, the Court fails to discriminate between the different factors which, in my opinion, are involved in the constitutional adjudication of state and federal obscenity cases. Third, relevant distinctions between the two obscenity statutes here involved, and the Court's own definition of "obscenity," are ignored. . . .

.   .   .   The Court seems to assume that "obscenity" is a peculiar *genus* of "speech and press," which is as distinct, recognizable, and classifiable as poison ivy is among other plants.   On this basis the *constitutional* question before us simply becomes, as the Court says, whether "obscenity," as an abstraction, is protected by the First and Fourteenth Amendments, and the question whether a *particular* book may be suppressed becomes a mere matter of classification, of "fact," to be entrusted to a fact-finder and insulated from independent constitutional judgment.   But surely the problem cannot be solved in such a generalized fashion.   Every communication has an individuality and "value" of its own.   The suppression of a particular writing or other tangible form of expression is, therefore, an *individual* matter, and in the nature of things every such suppression raises an individual constitutional problem, in which a reviewing court must determine for *itself* whether the attacked expression is suppressable within constitutional standards.   Since those standards do not readily lend themselves to generalized definitions, the constitutional problem in the last analysis becomes one of particularized judgments which appellate courts must make for themselves.

I do not think that reviewing courts can escape this responsibility by saying that the trier of the facts, be it a jury or a judge, has labeled the questioned matter as "obscene," for, if "obscenity" is to be suppressed, the question whether a particular work is of that character involves not really an issue of fact but a question of constitutional *judgment* of the most sensitive and delicate kind.   Many juries might find that Joyce's "Ulysses" or Bocaccio's "Decameron" was obscene, and yet the conviction of a defendant for selling either book would raise, for me, the gravest constitutional problems, for no such verdict could convince me, without more, that these books are "utterly without redeeming social importance."   In short, I do not understand how the Court can resolve the constitutional problems now before it without making its own independent judgment upon the character of the material upon which these convictions were based.   .   .   .

[T]he Court has not been bothered by the fact that the two cases involve different statutes.   In California the book must have a "tendency to deprave or corrupt its readers"; under the federal statute it must tend "to stir sexual impulses and lead to sexually impure thoughts." [1]   The two statutes do not seem to me to present the same problems.   Yet the Court compounds confusion when it superimposes on these two statutory definitions a third, drawn from the American Law Institute's Model Penal Code, Tentative Draft No. 6: "A thing is obscene if, considered as a whole, its predominant appeal is to prurient interest."   The bland assurance that this definition is the same as the ones with which we deal flies in the face of the authors' express rejection of the "deprave and corrupt" and "sexual thoughts" tests.   [The Court] merely assimilates the various tests into one indiscriminate potpourri.   .   .   .

1.   .   .   .   The two definitions do not seem to me synonymous.   Under the federal definition it is enough if the jury finds that the book as a whole leads to certain thoughts.   In California, the further inference must be drawn that such thoughts will have a substantive "tendency to deprave or corrupt"—i. e., that the thoughts induced by the material will affect character and action.   See American Law Institute, Model Penal Code, Tentative Draft No. 6, § 207.10(2), Comments, p. 10.   [Footnote by Justice Harlan.]

I concur in [Alberts].

. . . We can inquire only whether the state action so subverts the fundamental liberties implicit in the Due Process Clause that it cannot be sustained as a rational exercise of power. . . .

What, then, is the purpose of this California statute? Clearly the state legislature has made the judgment that printed words *can* "deprave or corrupt" the reader—that words can incite to antisocial or immoral action. [The] validity of this assumption is a matter of dispute among critics, sociologists, psychiatrists, and penologists. [I]t is not our function to decide this question. . . . It seems to me clear that it is not irrational, in our present state of knowledge, to consider that pornography can induce a type of sexual conduct which a State may deem obnoxious to the moral fabric of society. In fact the very division of opinion on the subject counsels us to respect the choice made by the State.

Furthermore, even assuming that pornography cannot be deemed ever to cause, in an immediate sense, criminal sexual conduct, other interests within the proper cognizance of the States may be protected by the prohibition placed on such materials. The State can reasonably draw the inference that over a long period of time the indiscriminate dissemination of materials, the essential character of which is to degrade sex, will have an eroding effect on moral standards. And the State has a legitimate interest in protecting the privacy of the home against invasion of unsolicited obscenity.

Above all stands the realization that we deal here with an area where knowledge is small, data are insufficient, and experts are divided. Since the domain of sexual morality is pre-eminently a matter of state concern, this Court should be slow to interfere with state legislation calculated to protect that morality. . . .

What has been said, however, does not dispose of the case. It still remains for us to decide whether the state court's determination that this material should be suppressed is consistent with the Fourteenth Amendment; and that, of course, presents a federal question as to which we, and not the state court, have the ultimate responsibility. And so, in the final analysis, I concur in the judgment because, upon an independent perusal of the material involved, and in light of the considerations discussed above, I cannot say that its suppression would so interfere with the communication of "ideas" in any proper sense of that term that it would offend the Due Process Clause. . . .

I dissent in [Roth].

. . . To me, [the Roth] question is of quite a different order than one where we are dealing with state legislation under the Fourteenth Amendment. [I]n every case where we are called upon to balance the interest in free expression against other interests, it seems to me important that we should keep in the forefront the question of whether those other interests are state or federal. [W]hether a particular limitation on speech or press is to be upheld because it subserves a paramount governmental interest must, to a large extent, I think, depend on whether that government has, under the Constitution, a direct substantive interest, that is, the power to act, in the particular area involved. . . .

.　.　.　[T]he interests which obscenity statutes purportedly protect are primarily entrusted to the care, not of the Federal Government, but of the States.　Congress has no substantive power over sexual morality.　Such powers as the Federal Government has in this field are but incidental to its other powers, here the postal power, and are not of the same nature as those possessed by the States, which bear direct responsibility for the protection of the local moral fabric.　.　.　.

.　.　.　[T]he dangers of federal censorship in this field are far greater than anything the States may do.　.　.　.　The fact that the people of one State cannot read some of the works of D. H. Lawrence seems to me, if not wise or desirable, at least acceptable.　But that no person in the United States should be allowed to do so seems to me to be intolerable, and violative of both the letter and spirit of the First Amendment.

I judge this case, then, in view of what I think is the attenuated federal interest in this field, in view of the very real danger of a deadening uniformity which can result from nation-wide federal censorship, and in view of the fact that the constitutionality of this conviction must be weighed against the First and not the Fourteenth Amendment.　So viewed, I do not think that this conviction can be upheld.　.　.　.　I cannot agree that any book which tends to stir sexual impulses and lead to sexually impure thoughts necessarily is "utterly without redeeming social importance."　Not only did this charge fail to measure up to the standards which I understand the Court to approve, but as far as I can see, much of the great literature of the world could lead to conviction under such a view of the statute.　Moreover, in no event do I think that the limited federal interest in this area can extend to mere "thoughts."　The Federal Government has no business, whether under the postal or commerce power, to bar the sale of books because they might lead to any kind of "thoughts."

It is no answer to say, as the Court does, that obscenity is not protected speech.　The point is that this statute, as here construed, defines obscenity so widely that it encompasses matters which might very well be protected speech. I do not think that the federal statute can be constitutionally construed to reach other than what the Government has termed as "hard-core" pornography.　.　.　.

Mr. Justice DOUGLAS, with whom Mr. Justice BLACK concurs, dissenting.

When we sustain these convictions, we make the legality of a publication turn on the purity of thought which a book or tract instills in the mind of the reader.　I do not think we can approve that standard and be faithful to the command of the First Amendment　.　.　.

The test of obscenity the Court endorses today gives the censor free range over a vast domain.　To allow the State to step in and punish mere speech or publication that the judge or the jury thinks has an *undesirable* impact on thoughts but that is not shown to be a part of unlawful action is drastically to curtail the First Amendment.　.　.　.

I do not think that the problem can be resolved by the Court's statement that "obscenity is not expression protected by the First Amendment." With the exception of [Beauharnais v. Illinois], none of our cases has

resolved problems of free speech and free press by placing any form of expression beyond the pale of the absolute prohibition of the First Amendment. . . . I reject too the implication that problems of freedom of speech and of the press are to be resolved by weighing against the values of free expression, the judgment of the Court that a particular form of that expression has "no redeeming social importance." The First Amendment, its prohibition in terms absolute, was designed to preclude courts as well as legislatures from weighing the values of speech against silence. . . .

THE STRUGGLE TO DEFINE OBSCENITY IN THE YEARS AFTER ROTH

[The Court's tortured and divided efforts to define prohibitable obscenity in the years after Roth were summarized in a dissenting opinion by Justice Brennan, joined by Justices Stewart and Marshall, in one of the 1973 cases, Paris Adult Theatre I v. Slaton, 413 U.S. 49, 73. Justice Brennan did not attempt to mention every case or every variant, but his summary adequately portrays the highlights—and reflects the considerable sense of futility and malaise—that marked the Justices' search. Reliance on Justice Brennan's summary of the efforts at definition during those post-Roth years is especially appropriate because it was Justice Brennan who was the Court's leading spokesman in those efforts—a spokesman who was moved to conclude at last, in 1973, that the task was a hopeless one, as the additional excerpts from his dissent below elaborate. Justice Brennan's summary of the definitional search follows:]

In [Roth], the Court held that obscenity, although expression, falls outside the area of speech or press constitutionally protected under the First and Fourteenth Amendments against state or federal infringement. But at the same time we emphasized in Roth that "sex and obscenity are not synonymous," and that matter which is sexually oriented but not obscene is fully protected by the Constitution. [Roth] rested, in other words, on what has been termed a two-level approach to the question of obscenity. While much criticized, that approach has been endorsed by all but two members of this Court who have addressed the question since Roth. Yet our efforts to implement that approach demonstrate that agreement on the existence of something called "obscenity" is still a long and painful step from agreement on a workable definition of the term.

[W]e have demanded that "sensitive tools" be used to carry out the "separation of legitimate from illegitimate speech." The essence of our problem in the obscenity area is that we have been unable to provide "sensitive tools" to separate obscenity from other sexually oriented but constitutionally protected speech, so that efforts to suppress the former do not spill over into the suppression of the latter. . . .

To be sure, five members of the Court did agree in Roth that obscenity could be determined by asking "whether to the average person, applying contemporary community standards, the dominant theme of the material taken as a whole appeals to prurient interest." But agreement on that test— achieved in the abstract and without reference to the particular material before the Court—was, to say the least, short lived. By 1967 the following

views had emerged: Mr. Justice Black and Mr. Justice Douglas consistently maintained that government is wholly powerless to regulate any sexually oriented matter on the ground of its obscenity. Mr. Justice Harlan, on the other hand, believed that the Federal Government in the exercise of its enumerated powers could control the distribution of "hard core" pornography, while the States were afforded more latitude to "[ban] any material which, taken as a whole, has been reasonably found in state judicial proceedings to treat with sex in a fundamentally offensive manner, under rationally established criteria for judging such material." Jacobellis v. Ohio, [378 U.S. 184 (1964)]. Mr. Justice Stewart regarded "hard core" pornography as the limit of both federal and state power. See, e. g., Ginzburg v. United States, 383 U.S. 463 (1966) (dissenting opinion); [Jacobellis] (concurring opinion).*

The view that, until today, enjoyed the most, but not majority, support was an interpretation of Roth (and not, as the Court suggests [in Miller, below], a veering "sharply away from the Roth concept" and the articulation of "a new test of obscenity") adopted by Mr. Chief Justice Warren, Mr. Justice Fortas, and the author of this opinion in Memoirs v. Massachusetts, 383 U.S. 413 (1966). We expressed the view that Federal or State Governments could control the distribution of material where "three elements . . . coalesce: it must be established that (a) the dominant theme of the material taken as a whole appeals to a prurient interest in sex; (b) the material is patently offensive because it affronts contemporary community standards relating to the description or representation of sexual matters; and (c) the material is utterly without redeeming social value." Even this formulation, however, concealed differences of opinion. Compare Jacobellis v. Ohio, supra, at 192–195 (Brennan, J., joined by Goldberg, J.) (community standards national), with id., at 200–201 (Warren, C. J., joined by Clark, J., dissenting) (community standards local).[1] Moreover, it did not provide a definition covering all situations. See Mishkin v. New York, 383 U.S. 502 (1966) (prurient appeal defined in terms of a deviant

* Justice Stewart's concurrence in Jacobellis said of "hard-core pornography" : "I shall not today attempt further to define the kinds of material I understand to be embraced within that shorthand description; and perhaps I could never succeed in intelligibly doing so. But I know it when I see it, and the motion picture involved in this case is not that." (Jacobellis involved a French film, "The Lovers.") Justice Stewart tried to elaborate that "definition" in his dissent in Ginzburg two years later, using a description in the Solicitor General's brief to explain "the kind of thing to which I have reference" : "Such materials include photographs, both still and motion picture, with no pretense of artistic value, graphically depicting acts of sexual intercourse, including various acts of sodomy and sadism, and sometimes involving several participants in scenes of orgy-like character. They also include strips of drawings in comic-book format grossly depicting similar activities in an exaggerated fashion. There are, in addition, pamphlets and booklets, sometimes with photographic illustrations, verbally describing such activities in a bizarre manner with no attempt whatsoever to afford portrayals of character or situation and with no pretense to literary value."

1. On the question of community standards see also Hoyt v. Minnesota, 399 U.S. 524 (1970) (Blackmun, J., joined by Burger, C. J., and Harlan, J., dissenting) (flexibility for state standards); Cain v. Kentucky, 397 U.S. 319 (1970) (Burger, C. J., dissenting) (same); Manual Enterprises v. Day, 370 U.S. 478, 488 (1962) (Harlan, J., joined by Stewart, J.) (national standards in context of federal prosecution). [Footnote by Justice Brennan.]

sexual group); Ginzburg v. United States, supra ("pandering" probative evidence of obscenity in close cases). See also Ginsberg v. New York, 390 U.S. 629 (1968) (obscenity for juveniles). Nor, finally, did it ever command a majority of the Court. Aside from the other views described above, Mr. Justice Clark believed that "social importance" could only "be considered together with evidence that the material in question appeals to prurient interest and is patently offensive." Memoirs v. Massachusetts, supra, at 445 (dissenting opinion). Similarly, Mr. Justice White regarded "a publication to be obscene if its predominant theme appeals to the prurient interest in a manner exceeding customary limits of candor," id., at 460–461 (dissenting opinion), and regarded " 'social importance' . . . not [as] an independent test of obscenity but [as] relevant only to determining the predominant prurient interest of the material . . .." Id., at 462.

In the face of this divergence of opinion the Court began the practice in Redrup v. New York, 386 U.S. 767 (1967), of per curiam reversals of convictions for the dissemination of materials that at least five members of the Court, applying their separate tests, deemed not to be obscene.[2] This approach capped the attempt in Roth to separate all forms of sexually oriented expression into two categories—the one subject to full governmental suppression and the other beyond the reach of governmental regulation to the same extent as any other protected form of speech or press. Today a majority of the Court offers a slightly altered formulation of the basic Roth test, while leaving entirely unchanged the underlying approach.

[W]e have failed to formulate a standard that sharply distinguishes protected from unprotected speech, and out of necessity, we have resorted to the Redrup approach, which resolves cases as between the parties, but offers only the most obscure guidance to legislation, adjudication by other courts, and primary conduct. By disposing of cases through summary reversal or denial of certiorari we have deliberately and effectively obscured the rationale underlying the decisions. It comes as no surprise that judicial attempts to follow our lead conscientiously have often ended in hopeless confusion.

THE EFFORTS TO ARTICULATE THE JUSTIFICATIONS FOR OBSCENITY CONTROL IN THE YEARS AFTER ROTH

Most of the cases after Roth were conspicuously silent about the interests thought to justify control of obscenity: the preoccupation was almost entirely with definition, as Justice Brennan's summary illustrates. But some articulations of justifications did occasionally surface. An early and rare example was the Kingsley Pictures case, note 1 below: it did not deal directly with an obscenity law; but its examination of "immorality" concerns bore at least a tangential relation to the obscenity area, and made the silence in the obscenity cases themselves even more striking. Finally, in 1969, in Stanley v. Georgia (note 2 below), state justifications were explicitly dis-

2. No fewer than 31 cases have been disposed of in this fashion. [Footnote by Justice Brennan.]

cussed.* Stanley was a case involving possession of obscene materials in the home, resting on rights of privacy as well as the First Amendment. But the expectations of some that Stanley would be the precursor of a new approach to the distribution of obscene materials were ended by the Reidel case two years later (note 3 below). One other important consideration of justifications for obscenity control prior to the 1973 decisions should be noted. In 1970, the Report of the United States Commission on Obscenity and Pornography urged that obscenity restraints be limited to offensive displays to unwilling adults and to the protection of children. (See note 4 below.) Though the Report proved unpersuasive to the executive and legislative branches, its conclusions were similar to those reached by some of the dissenters in 1973.

1. *The Kingsley Pictures case and sexual immorality.* One case in the post-Roth years—though not dealing directly with "obscenity" (and perhaps *because* it was not an obscenity case)—spoke more explicitly than most about the justifications for state regulations of expression pertaining to sex. KINGSLEY INTERNATIONAL PICTURES CORP. v. REGENTS, 360 U.S. 684 (1959), invalidated a New York motion picture licensing law.* The law banned any "immoral" film, defined under a clarifying amendment as a film that "portrays acts of sexual immorality . . . or which expressly or impliedly presents such acts as desirable, acceptable, or proper patterns of behavior." The state denied a license to the film "Lady Chatterley's Lover" under this law because "its subject matter is adultery presented as being right and desirable for certain people under certain circumstances."

The Supreme Court reversed. Justice Stewart's opinion emphasized that "sexual immorality" under the New York scheme was "entirely different from" concepts like "obscenity" or "pornography," and that New York had not claimed that "the film would itself operate as an incitement to illegal action." He concluded that New York had prevented the exhibition of the film "because that picture advocates an idea—that adultery under certain circumstances may be proper behavior. Yet the First Amendment's basic guarantee is of freedom to advocate ideas. The State, quite simply, has thus struck at the very heart of constitutionally protected liberty." It was not adequate state justification that the film "attractively portrays a relationship which is contrary to the moral standards, the religious precepts and the legal code of its citizenry": "This argument misconceives what it is that the Constitution protects. Its guarantee is not confined to the expression of ideas that are conventional or shared by a majority. It protects advocacy of the opinion that adultery may sometimes be proper, no less than advocacy of socialism or the single tax. And in the realm of ideas it protects expression which is eloquent no less than that which is unconvincing." †

---

* Earlier versions of the law had been invalidated because of the vagueness of the criteria. See, e. g., Burstyn v. Wilson, 343 U.S. 495 (1952), sec. 3 below.

† Justices Douglas and Black submitted separate opinions, though they also joined the opinion of the Court. Justice Harlan, joined by Justices Frankfurter and Whittaker, concurred only in the result. He insisted that the state courts had construed the statute as requiring "incitement, not just mere abstract expression of opinion." Nevertheless, he found that the law could

2. *Possession of obscene materials and the Stanley case.* a. *The decision.* In STANLEY v. GEORGIA, 394 U.S. 557 (1969), the Court reversed a conviction for knowing "possession of obscene matter," holding "that the First and Fourteenth Amendments prohibit making the private possession of obscene material a crime." In the Court's opinion by Justice Marshall, asserted state justifications were systematically canvassed, unlike the prior obscenity cases. And some commentators as well as lower courts read Stanley as presaging a new era of greater restraints on laws governing the distribution of obscenity. But in the Reidel case (in the next note), the Court made clear that Stanley would not be read as undercutting the reign of Roth. The Stanley opinion noted privacy as well as First Amendment interests; under the Reidel reading, the privacy interests were emphasized as the dominant if not exclusive ones explaining the result in Stanley.

In Stanley, a search of a home for bookmaking evidence had uncovered obscene films. Georgia had defended its law on the basis of Roth and with the argument: "If the State can protect the body of the citizen, may it [not] protect his mind?" Justice Marshall replied that Roth and its progeny had dealt with the regulation of "certain public actions" taken with respect to obscene material. Though those cases implicitly recognized "a valid governmental interest in dealing with the problem of obscenity," the mere assertion of that interest could not without more dispose of the private possession problem. Justice Marshall continued:

"It is now well established that the Constitution protects the right to receive information and ideas. . . . This right to receive information and ideas, regardless of their social worth, [is] fundamental to our free society. Moreover, in the context of this case—a prosecution for mere possession [in] the privacy of a person's own home—that right takes on an added dimension. For also fundamental is the right to be free, except in very limited circumstances, from unwanted governmental intrusions into one's privacy [see Olmstead v. United States, 277 U.S. 438, 471 (1928) (Brandeis, J., dissenting); Griswold v. Connecticut, chap. 13, sec. 3, above; cf. NAACP v. Alabama, sec. 5A below.]

"These are the rights that appellant is asserting in the case before us. [W]e think that mere categorization of these films as 'obscene' is insufficient justification for such a drastic invasion of personal liberties guaranteed by the First and Fourteenth Amendments. Whatever may be the justifications for other statutes regulating obscenity, we do not think they reach into the privacy of one's own home. If the First Amendment means anything, it means that a State has no business telling a man, sitting alone in his own house, what books he may read or what films he may watch. Our whole constitutional heritage rebels at the thought of giving government the power to control men's minds.

"And yet, in the face of these traditional notions of individual liberty, Georgia asserts the right to protect the individual's mind from the effects of obscenity. We are not certain that this argument amounts to anything more than the assertion that the State has the right to control the moral content

not constitutionally be applied to this film, because it lacked "anything that could properly be deemed obscene or   corruptive of the public morals by inciting the commission of adultery."

of a person's thoughts.[1] To some, this may be a noble purpose, but it is wholly inconsistent with the philosophy of the First Amendment. [Kingsley Pictures.] Whatever the power of the state to control public dissemination of ideas inimical to the public morality, it cannot constitutionally premise legislation on the desirability of controlling a person's private thoughts.

"Perhaps recognizing this, Georgia asserts that exposure to obscenity may lead to deviant sexual behavior or crimes of sexual violence. There appears to be little empirical basis for that assertion. But more importantly, if the State is only concerned about [materials] inducing antisocial conduct, we believe that in the context of private consumption of ideas and information we should adhere to the view that '[a]mong free men, the deterrents ordinarily to be applied to prevent crime are education and punishment for violations of the law . . . .' [Whitney v. California] (Brandeis, J., concurring). Given the present state of knowledge, the State may no more prohibit mere possession of [obscenity] on the ground that it may lead to antisocial conduct than it may prohibit possession of chemistry books on the ground that they may lead to the manufacture of homemade spirits.

"It is true that in Roth this Court rejected the necessity of proving that exposure to obscene material would create a clear and present danger of antisocial conduct or would probably induce its recipients to such conduct. But that case dealt with public distribution of obscene materials and such distribution is subject to different objections. For example, there is always the danger that obscene material might fall into the hands of children or that it might intrude upon the sensibilities or privacy of the general public. No such dangers are present in this case.

"Finally, we are faced with the argument that prohibition of possession of [obscenity] is a necessary incident to statutory schemes prohibiting distribution. That argument is based on alleged difficulties of proving an intent to distribute or in producing evidence of actual distribution. We are not convinced that such difficulties exist, but even if they did we do not think that they would justify infringement of the individual's right to read or observe what he pleases. Because that right is so fundamental to our scheme of individual liberty, its restriction may not be justified by the need to ease the administration of otherwise valid criminal laws."

    b. *Justice Brennan's delayed adherence to Stanley, in 1973.* Despite the Stanley opinion's concern with the evaluation of asserted state interests—a concern strikingly absent from Roth and its progeny—Justice Marshall concluded his opinion by stating that the Roth line of cases was "not impaired" by Stanley: "[T]he States retain broad power to regulate obscenity; that power simply does not extend to mere possession by the individual in the privacy of his own home." Justice Stewart, joined by Justices Brennan

---

1. " 'Communities believe, and act on the belief, that obscenity is immoral, is wrong for the individual, and has no place in a decent society. They believe, too, that adults as well as children are corruptible in morals and character, and that obscenity is a source of corruption that should be eliminated. Obscenity is not suppressed primarily for the protection of others. Much of it is suppressed for the purity of the community and for the salvation and welfare of the 'consumer.' Obscenity, at bottom, is not crime. Obscenity is sin.' Henkin, Morals and the Constitution: The Sin of Obscenity, 63 Col.L.Rev. 391, 395 (1963)." [Footnote in Justice Marshall's opinion for the Court.]

and White, concurred only in the result, on the ground that the films were seized in violation of the Fourth Amendment search and seizure guarantee; they accordingly did not reach the issue of the validity of the obscenity possession law.

Contrast Justice Brennan's comment four years later, in a footnote to his dissent in the Paris Adult Theatre case: "Although I did not join [the Stanley opinion], I am now inclined to agree that 'the Constitution protects the right to receive information and ideas,' and that '[t]his right [is] fundamental to our free society.' This right is closely tied, as Stanley recognized, to 'the right to be free, except in very limited circumstances, from unwarranted governmental intrusions into one's privacy.' See [Griswold v. Connecticut, chap. 9, sec. 3, above]." Justice Brennan also noted the relationship to the right of personal autonomy as to "whether to bear or beget a child," Eisenstadt v. Baird (also in chap. 9 above), as well as to the right to exercise "autonomous control over the development and expression of one's intellect, interests, tastes, and personality." (That quoted passage was from Justice Douglas' concurrence in Doe v. Bolton, one of the 1973 abortion cases, chap. 9, sec. 3, above.) Justice Brennan added in that footnote to his 1973 obscenity dissent: "It seems to me that the recognition of these intertwining rights calls in question the validity of the two-level approach recognized in Roth. After all, if a person has the right to receive information without regard to its social worth—that is, without regard to its obscenity—then it would seem to follow that a State could not constitutionally punish one who undertakes to provide this information to a *willing, adult recipient*." But Justice Brennan added: "I need not rely on this line of analysis or explore all of its possible ramifications, for there is available a narrower basis on which to rest this decision. Whether or not a class of 'obscene' and thus entirely unprotected speech does exist, I am forced to conclude that the class is incapable of definition with sufficient clarity to withstand attack on vagueness grounds. Accordingly, it is on principles of the void-for-vagueness doctrine that this opinion exclusively relies." See the elaboration of this conclusion in Justice Brennan's 1973 dissent in Paris, below.

3. *Roth survives Stanley: The Reidel case.* Two years after Stanley, the Court made clear (over the objections of the author of Stanley) that commentators and lower courts had been wrong in finding reasons in Stanley to question the validity of obscenity distribution laws. In UNITED STATES v. REIDEL, 402 U.S. 351 (1971), a District Court had relied on Stanley to dismiss an indictment under the federal law prohibiting the mailing of obscene materials—the law involved in Roth. The District Court had reasoned that "if a person has the right to receive and possess this material, then someone must have the right to deliver it to him," and had concluded that the federal prohibition could not be applied "where obscene material is not directed at children, or it is not directed at an unwilling public, where the material such as in this case is solicited by adults."

Justice White's majority opinion gave short shrift to that argument: "To extrapolate from Stanley's right to have and peruse obscene material in the privacy of his own home a First Amendment right in Reidel to sell it to him would effectively scuttle Roth, the precise result that the Stanley opinion abjured." As the Reidel Court read Stanley, its "focus" was "on

freedom of mind and thought and on the privacy of one's home." Reidel could not claim infringement of those rights. "Roth has squarely placed obscenity and its distribution outside the reach of the First Amendment and they remain there today. Stanley did not overrule Roth and we decline to do so now." *

Justice Marshall's separate opinion in Reidel disagreed strongly with Justice White's narrow reading of the impact of Stanley. He insisted that "Stanley turned on an assessment of which state interests may legitimately underpin governmental action, and it is disingenuous to contend that Stanley's conviction was reversed because his home, rather than his person or luggage, was the locus of a search." To him, Stanley was a case in which "the Court fully canvassed the range of state interests which might possibly justify a regulation of obscenity. That decision refused to legitimize the argument that obscene materials could be outlawed because the materials might somehow encourage antisocial conduct, and unequivocally rejected the outlandish notion that the State may police the thoughts of its citizenry. The Court did, however, approve the validity of regulatory action taken to protect children and unwilling adults from exposure to materials deemed to be obscene. The need for such protection of course arises when obscenity is distributed or displayed publicly; and the Court reaffirmed the principles of [Roth and its progeny] that involved the commercial distribution of obscene materials." But Stanley, he maintained, made an "assessment of state interests" approach appropriate for distribution cases as well.

Applying that approach, Justice Marshall concurred in Reidel. Mail distribution "poses the danger that obscenity will be sent to children"; though Reidel himself planned to sell only to adults who requested his materials, "the sole safeguard designed to prevent the receipt of his merchandise by minors was his requirement that buyers declare their age." Justice Marshall accordingly concluded "that distributors of purportedly

---

* In a companion case to Reidel, UNITED STATES v. 37 PHOTO-GRAPHS, 402 U.S. 363 (1971), the Court also rejected constitutional challenges to the federal law prohibiting the importation of obscene materials and providing for seizure by customs officials. Though the importation in this case was intended for commercial purposes, the statute covered importation for private use as well. The lower court, relying on Stanley, had held the law overbroad because it reached private-use importation. Justice White's plurality opinion, joined by Chief Justice Burger and Justices Brennan and Blackmun, construed the law more narrowly and held it valid. But Justice White went on to say that Stanley did not in any event immunize private use imports from seizure: "[A] port of entry is not a traveler's home." Congress, in light of Roth, may declare obscenity "a contraband and prohibit its importation."

The plurality opinion's statements about importation for private use did not have majority support in 1971, however. Justice Harlan, who had concurred separately in Reidel, submitted another concurring opinion here, not reaching the private-use importing situation. And in another concurrence, Justice Stewart disagreed with Justice White's approach: "If the government can constitutionally take the book away from [an importer for private use] as he passes through customs, then I do not understand the meaning of Stanley v. Georgia." Justices Marshall, Black and Douglas submitted dissents. On Justice Marshall's position, see the next footnote. [Justice White's position as to private-use importation became the majority position two years later, in one of the companion cases to the major 1973 rulings, below. See United States v. Twelve 200-Ft. Reels, 413 U.S. 123, below.]

obscene merchandise may be required to take more stringent steps to guard against possible receipt by minors." †

4. *The Obscenity Commission's Report, 1970.* On other major—though extrajudicial—consideration of the interests justifying obscenity control should be noted before turning to the Court's major reexamination of the obscenity problem in 1973. The Commission on Obscenity and Pornography was established by Congress in 1967. Its Report, submitted in 1970, rested in part on empirical studies of the impact of sexual literature. It concluded, for example, that patterns of sexual behavior were "not altered substantially by exposure to erotica"; that the available data did not demonstrate that "erotic material is a significant cause of sex crime"; and that exposure to erotica has "little or no effect" on attitudes regarding sexuality or sexual morality.** The Commission majority's legislative recommendations included one urging that laws "prohibiting the sale, exhibition, or distribution of sexual materials to consenting adults should be repealed." The Commission also recommended the adoption of state laws "prohibiting the commercial distribution or display for sale of certain sexual materials to young persons," as well as laws "prohibiting public displays of sexually explicit pictorial materials." The Commission also approved "in principle" federal legislation "regarding the mailing of unsolicited advertisements of a sexually explicit nature." Compare those legislative recommendations with the conclusions in Justice Brennan's dissent in the 1973 cases, which follow. Might the course of obscenity law have been different if Justice Brennan had reached those conclusions a few years earlier, during the Warren era?

† In the importation case, 37 Photographs (in the preceding footnote), Justice Marshall's position led him to dissent, for there the Government had "ample opportunity to protect its valid interests if and when commercial distribution should take place." Justice Black, joined by Justice Douglas, submitted a dissent applicable to both cases. He relied not only on the position announced in many earlier cases that the First Amendment was an absolute bar to obscenity control; he also questioned the consistency of the majority position with the Stanley ruling: "[I]f a citizen had a right to possess 'obscene' material in the privacy of his home he should have the right to receive it voluntarily through the mail. [And the] mere act of importation for private use can hardly be more offensive to others than his private perusal in one's home." He added: "I can only conclude that at least four members of the Court would overrule Stanley."

** The scope and quality of the Commission's empirical studies have been criticized. Did the empirical studies ask the right questions? Are all of the interests allegedly justifying obscenity control susceptible to empirical studies? See generally chap. 3 of Sunderland, Obscenity—The Court, the Congress and the President's Commission (Amer. Enterprise Inst., 1975), summarizing some of the criticisms. Note, e. g., the comment: "The complexities and subtleties of human sexuality within society are extremely difficult to duplicate in the laboratory." Note also Sunderland's discussion of "indirect effect neglected by the Commission"—including "the influence exerted on attitudes by public law, qua law," and "the long-term effects of pornography." See also the comments on the "moral pollution" aspects of obscenity in the majority opinions in the 1973 cases, which follow.

THE 1973 OBSCENITY CASES

MILLER v. CALIFORNIA

413 U.S. 15, 93 S.Ct. 2607, 37 L.Ed.2d 419 (1973).

Appeal from the Appellate Dept., Superior Court of California, County of Orange.

Mr. Chief Justice BURGER delivered the opinion of the Court.

This is one of a group of "obscenity-pornography" cases being reviewed by the Court in a re-examination of standards enunciated in earlier cases involving what Mr. Justice Harlan called "the intractable obscenity problem." *
. . .

This case involves the application of a State's criminal obscenity statute to a situation in which sexually explicit materials have been thrust by aggressive sales action upon unwilling recipients who had in no way indicated any desire to receive such materials. This Court has recognized that the States have a legitimate interest in prohibiting dissemination or exhibition of obscene material when the mode of dissemination carries with it a significant danger of offending the sensibilities of unwilling recipients or of exposure to juveniles. [Stanley.] It is in this context that we are called on to define the standards which must be used to identify obscene material that a State may regulate . . . .

The dissent of Mr. Justice Brennan reviews the background of the obscenity problem, but since the Court now undertakes to formulate standards more concrete than those in the past, it is useful for us to focus on two of the landmark cases in the somewhat tortured history of the Court's obscenity decisions. . . . While Roth presumed "obscenity" to be "utterly without redeeming social value," [Memoirs v. Massachusetts, 383 U.S. 413 (1966)] required that to prove obscenity it must be affirmatively established that the material is "*utterly* without redeeming social value." Thus, even as they repeated the words of Roth, the Memoirs plurality produced a drastically altered test that called on the prosecution to prove a negative, i. e., that the material was "*utterly* without redeeming social value"—a burden virtually impossible to discharge. . . .

Apart from the initial formulation in the Roth case, no majority of the Court has at any given time been able to agree on a standard to determine what constitutes obscene, pornographic material subject to regulation under

---

* As the Chief Justice described the facts, appellant "conducted a mass mailing campaign to advertise the sale of illustrated books, euphemistically called 'adult' material. [H]e was convicted of violating California Penal Code § 311.2(a), a misdemeanor, by knowingly distributing obscene matter. [Appellant had caused] five unsolicited advertising brochures to be sent through the mail . . . . While the brochures contain some descriptive printed material, primarily they consist of pictures and drawings very explicitly depicting men and women in groups of two or more engaging in a variety of sexual activities, with genitals often prominently displayed."

the States' police power. [The variety of views][1] is not remarkable, for in the area of freedom of speech and press the courts must always remain sensitive to any infringement on genuinely serious literary, artistic, political, or scientific expression. This is an area in which there are few eternal verities.

The case we now review was tried on the theory that the California Penal Code § 311 approximately incorporates the three-stage Memoirs test. But now the Memoirs test has been abandoned as unworkable by its author [see Justice Brennan's dissent in the Paris Adult Theatre case, below] and no member of the Court today supports the Memoirs formulation.

This much has been categorically settled by the Court, that obscene material is unprotected by the First Amendment. . . . We acknowledge, however, the inherent dangers of undertaking to regulate any form of expression. State statutes designed to regulate obscene materials must be carefully limited. As a result, we now confine the permissible scope of such regulation to works which depict or describe sexual conduct. That conduct must be specifically defined by the applicable state law, as written or authoritatively construed.[2] A state offense must also be limited to works which, taken as a whole, appeal to the prurient interest in sex, which portray sexual conduct in a patently offensive way, and which, taken as a whole, do not have serious literary, artistic, political, or scientific value.

The basic guidelines for the trier of fact must be: (a) whether "the average person, applying contemporary community standards" would find that the work, taken as a whole, appeals to the prurient interest [Roth], (b) whether the work depicts or describes, in a patently offensive way, sexual conduct specifically defined by the applicable state law, and (c) whether the work, taken as a whole, lacks serious literary, artistic, political, or scientific value. We do not adopt as a constitutional standard the "*utterly* without redeeming social value" test of [Memoirs]; that concept has never commanded the adherence of more than three Justices at one time.[3] If a state law that regulates obscene material is thus limited, as written or construed, [First Amendment values] are adequately protected by the ultimate power of appellate courts to conduct an independent review of constitutional claims when necessary.

1. In the absence of a majority view, this Court was compelled to embark on the practice of summarily reversing convictions for the dissemination of materials that at least five members of the Court, applying their separate tests, found to be protected by the First Amendment. [Redrup v. New York.] Thirty-one cases have been decided in this manner. Beyond the necessity of circumstances, however, no justification has ever been offered in support of the Redrup "policy." . . . The Redrup procedure has cast us in the role of an unreviewable board of censorship for the 50 States, subjectively judging each piece of material brought before us. [Footnote by the Chief Justice.]

2. See, e. g., [Oregon Laws] and [Hawaii Penal Code] as examples of state laws directed at depiction of defined physical conduct, as opposed to expression. . . .
We do not hold, as Mr. Justice Brennan intimates, that all States other than Oregon must now enact new obscenity statutes. Other existing state statutes, as construed heretofore or hereafter, may well be adequate. . . . [Footnote by the Chief Justice.]

3. "A quotation from Voltaire in the flyleaf of a book will not constitutionally redeem an otherwise obscene publication." . . . We also reject, as a constitutional standard, the ambiguous concept of "social importance." [Footnote by the Chief Justice.]

We emphasize that it is not our function to propose regulatory schemes for the States. That must await their concrete legislative efforts. It is possible, however, to give a few plain examples of what a state statute could define for regulation under the second part (b) of the standard announced in this opinion:

(a) Patently offensive representations or descriptions of ultimate sexual acts, normal or perverted, actual or simulated.

(b) Patently offensive representations or descriptions of masturbation, excretory functions, and lewd exhibition of the genitals.

Sex and nudity may not be exploited without limit by films or pictures exhibited or sold in places of public accommodation any more than live sex and nudity can be exhibited or sold without limit in such public places.[4] At a minimum, prurient, patently offensive depiction or description of sexual conduct must have serious literary, artistic, political, or scientific value to merit First Amendment protection. For example, medical books for the education of physicians and related personnel necessarily use graphic illustrations and descriptions of human anatomy. In resolving the inevitably sensitive questions of fact and law, we must continue to rely on the jury system, accompanied by the safeguards that judges, rules of evidence, presumption of innocence and other protective features provide, as we do with rape, murder and a host of other offenses against society and its individual members.[5]

Mr. Justice Brennan, author of the opinions of the Court, or the plurality opinions, in [Roth, Jacobellis, Ginzburg, Mishkin, and Memoirs], has abandoned his former position and now maintains that no formulation of this Court, the Congress, or the States can adequately distinguish obscene material unprotected by the First Amendment from protected expression. [Paris Adult Theatre dissent, below.] Paradoxically, [he] indicates that suppression of unprotected obscene material is permissible to avoid exposure to unconsenting adults, as in this case, and to juveniles, although he gives no indication of how the division between protected and nonprotected materials may be drawn with greater precision for these purposes than for regulation of commercial exposure to consenting adults only. Nor does he indicate where in the Constitution he finds the authority to distinguish between a willing "adult" one month past the state law age of majority and a willing "juvenile" one month younger.

Under the holdings announced today, no one will be subject to prosecution for the sale or exposure of obscene materials unless these materials depict or describe patently offensive "hard core" sexual conduct specifically defined by the regulating state law, as written or construed. We are satisfied that these specific prerequisites will provide fair notice to a dealer in such materials that his public and commercial activities may bring prosecution. If the inability to define regulated materials with ultimate, god-like precision altogether removes the power of the States or the Congress to regulate, then

---

4. Although we are not presented here with the problem of regulating lewd public conduct itself, the States have greater power to regulate nonverbal, physical conduct than to suppress depictions or descriptions of the same behavior. [United States v. O'Brien.] [Footnote by the Chief Justice.]

5. The mere fact juries may reach different conclusions as to the same material does not mean that constitutional rights are abridged. . . . [Footnote by the Chief Justice.]

"hard core" pornography may be exposed without limit to the juvenile, the passerby, and the consenting adult alike, as, indeed, Mr. Justice Douglas contends. . . . In this belief, however, Mr. Justice Douglas now stands alone.

Mr. Justice Brennan also emphasizes "institutional stress" in justification of his change of view. . . . It is certainly true that the absence, since Roth, of a single majority view of this Court as to proper standards for testing obscenity has placed a strain on both state and federal courts. But today, for the first time since Roth was decided in 1957, a majority of this Court has agreed on concrete guidelines to isolate "hard core" pornography from expression protected by the First Amendment. Now we may abandon the casual practice of [Redrup] and attempt to provide positive guidance to the federal and state courts alike.

This may not be an easy road, free from difficulty. But no amount of "fatigue" should lead us to adopt a convenient "institutional" rationale—an absolutist, "anything goes" view of the First Amendment—because it will lighten our burdens. . . .[6] Nor should we remedy "tension between state and federal courts" by arbitrarily depriving the States of a power reserved to them under the Constitution. [Our duty admits of no] "substitute for facing up to the tough individual problems of constitutional judgment involved in every obscenity case." [Roth].

Under a national Constitution, fundamental First Amendment limitations on the powers of the States do not vary from community to community, but this does not mean that there are, or should or can be, fixed, uniform national standards of precisely what appeals to the "prurient interest" or is "patently offensive." These are essentially questions of fact, and our nation is simply too big and too diverse for this Court to reasonably expect that such standards could be articulated for all 50 States in a single formulation, even assuming the prerequisite consensus exists. . . . To require a State to structure obscenity proceedings around evidence of a *national* "community standard" would be an exercise in futility.

As noted before, this case was tried on the theory that the California obscenity statute sought to incorporate the tripartite test of Memoirs. [N]either the State's alleged failure to offer evidence of "national standards," nor the trial court's charge that the jury consider state community standards, were constitutional errors. . . . It is neither realistic nor constitutionally sound to read the First Amendment as requiring that the people of Maine or Mississippi accept public depiction of conduct found tolerable in Las Vegas, or New York City.[7] . . . People in different States vary in their tastes

6. We must note, in addition, that any assumption concerning the relative burdens of the past and the probable burden under the standards now adopted is pure speculation. [Footnote by the Chief Justice.]

7. In [Jacobellis v. Ohio], two Justices argued that application of "local" community standards would run the risk of preventing dissemination of materials in some places because sellers would be unwilling to risk crim-

inal conviction by testing variations in standards from place to place. . . . The use of "national" standards, however, necessarily implies that materials found tolerable in some places, but not under the "national" criteria, will nevertheless be unavailable where they are acceptable. Thus, in terms of danger to free expression, the potential for suppression seems at least as great in the application of a single nationwide standard as in allowing distribu-

and attitudes, and this diversity is not to be strangled by the absolutism of imposed uniformity. . . .

The dissenting Justices sound the alarm of repression. But, in our view, to equate the free and robust exchange of ideas and political debate with commercial exploitation of obscene material demeans the grand conception of the First Amendment and its high purposes in the historic struggle for freedom. . . . The First Amendment protects works which, taken as a whole, have serious literary, artistic, political, or scientific value, regardless of whether the government or a majority of the people approve of the ideas these works represent. "The protection given speech and press was fashioned to assure unfettered interchange of *ideas* for the bringing about of political and social changes desired by the people" [Roth—emphasis added]. But the public portrayal of hard core sexual conduct for its own sake, and for the ensuing commercial gain, is a different matter.

There is no evidence, empirical or historical, that the stern 19th century American censorship of public distribution and display of material relating to sex in any way limited or affected expression of serious literary, artistic, political, or scientific ideas. On the contrary, it is beyond any question that the era following Thomas Jefferson to Theodore Roosevelt was an "extraordinarily vigorous period" not just in economics and politics, but in *belles lettres* and in "the outlying fields of social and political philosophies." We do not see the harsh hand of censorship of ideas—good or bad, sound or unsound—and "repression" of political liberty lurking in every state regulation of commercial exploitation of human interest in sex.

Mr. Justice Brennan [in his Paris dissent, below] finds "it is hard to see how state-ordered regimentation of our minds can ever be forestalled." These doleful anticipations assume that courts cannot distinguish commerce in ideas, protected by the First Amendment, from commercial exploitation of obscene material. . . . One can concede that the "sexual revolution" of recent years may have had useful byproducts in striking layers of prudery from a subject long irrationally kept from needed ventilation. But it does not follow that no regulation of patently offensive "hard core" materials is needed or permissible; civilized people do not allow unregulated access to heroin because it is a derivative of medicinal morphine.

In sum we (a) reaffirm the Roth holding that obscene material is not protected by the First Amendment; (b) hold that such material can be regulated by the States, subject to the specific safeguards enunciated above, without a showing that the material is "*utterly* without redeeming social value"; and (c) hold that obscenity is to be determined by applying "contemporary community standards," not "national standards." . . .

Vacated and remanded.*

Mr. Justice DOUGLAS, dissenting. . . .

[W]e should not allow men to go to prison or be fined when they had no "fair warning" that what they did was criminal conduct. If a

tion in accordance with local tastes. . . . [Footnote by the Chief Justice.]

* The flood of obscenity cases over the years has stimulated not only a large amount of academic commentary but also an extraordinary indulgence in puns and other word games. (See, e. g., the 8th Edition of this casebook, p. 1236.) I cannot resist quoting one reaction to Miller v. California, irre-

specific book, play, paper, or motion picture has in a civil proceeding been condemned as obscene and review of that finding has been completed, and thereafter a person publishes, shows, or displays that particular book or film, then a vague law has been made specific. There would remain the underlying question whether the First Amendment allows an implied exception in the case of obscenity. I do not think it does [1] and my views on the issue have been stated over and over again. But at least a criminal prosecution brought at that juncture would not violate the time-honored void-for-vagueness test.[2]

. . . .

sistible both because it is of high quality, in content as well as form, and because it was a response to a challenge from that most astute of modern First Amendment commentators, the late Professor Harry Kalven, Jr., of the University of Chicago.

The commentary on Miller which follows was made available to me by William Adler-Geller, a student at the University of Chicago Law School. I am grateful to him for permission to publish it here. In the last full course Harry Kalven taught before his death in the fall of 1974, he remarked to his First Amendment class that there really ought to be a third word beginning with the letter "p" to round out the three-part obscenity test in Miller—the test which includes "prurient" and "patent." William Adler-Geller's response to that challenge follows [copyright © William Adler-Geller, 1975]:

PORNOGRAPHY'S PERIL

Miller v. California *and progeny (platitudinously preferring purity, protesting peccancy) perniciously provide pornography parsimonious protection, prohibiting posting prurient, patent, paltry publications; purportedly purifying public places (purging pudenda purveyance, posterior polydipsia); paroxysmally pronouncing panderers putrilage, puerility pollutable, pubic preoccupation perverted; proclaiming particularly palatable platonic Puritanism; protecting palpably private perusal (paradoxically precluding purveyors' practices, perhaps prescribing profitless personal pornography printing); providing prevailing provincial public posture presumptive preeminence, presaging pluralism's paralysis.*

Harry Kalven understandably took delight in this supplement to the Miller "p" criteria. I, who have drawn so heavily on Harry Kalven's commentaries in these materials, am delighted to publish it.

1. It is said that "obscene" publications can be banned on authority of re-

straints on communications incident to decrees restraining unlawful business monopolies or unlawful restraints of trade, or communications respecting the sale of spurious or fraudulent securities. The First Amendment answer is that whenever speech and conduct are brigaded—as they are when one shouts "Fire" in a crowded theater —speech can be outlawed. Mr. Justice Black, writing for a unanimous Court in Giboney v. Empire Storage Co., 336 U.S. 490, stated that labor unions could be restrained from picketing a firm in support of a secondary boycott which a State had validly outlawed. Mr. Justice Black said: "It rarely has been suggested that the constitutional freedom for speech and press extends its immunity to speech or writing used as an integral part of conduct in violation of a valid criminal statute. We reject the contention now." [Footnote by Justice Douglas— presumably in response to comments in the Chief Justice's opinion in Paris, below.]

2. The Commission on Obscenity and Pornography has advocated such a procedure:

"The Commission recommends the enactment, in all jurisdictions which enact or retain provisions prohibiting the dissemination of sexual materials to adults or young persons, of legislation authorizing prosecutors to obtain declaratory judgments as to whether particular materials fall within existing legal prohibitions. . . .

"A declaratory judgment procedure . . . would permit prosecutors to proceed civilly, rather than through the criminal process, against suspected violations of obscenity prohibition. If such civil procedures are utilized, penalties would be imposed for violation of the law only with respect to conduct occurring after a civil declaration is obtained. The Commission believes this course of action to be appropriate whenever there is any existing doubt regarding the legal status of materi-

No such protective procedure has been designed by California in this case. Obscenity—which even we cannot define with precision—is a hodge-podge. To send men to jail for violating standards they cannot under-stand, construe, and apply is a monstrous thing to do in a Nation dedicated to fair trials and due process.

. . . There is no "captive audience" problem in these obscenity cases. No one is being compelled to look or to listen. Those who enter news stands or bookstalls may be offended by what they see. But they are not compelled by the State to frequent those places; and it is only state or governmental action against which [the First Amendment] raises a ban.

The idea that the First Amendment permits government to ban publica-tions that are "offensive" to some people puts an ominous gloss on freedom of the press. That test would make it possible to ban any paper or any journal or magazine in some benighted place. . . . The First Amend-ment was not fashioned as a vehicle for dispensing tranquilizers to the people. Its prime function was to keep debate open to "offensive" as well as to "staid" people. . . .

We deal with highly emotional, not rational, questions. To many the Song of Solomon is obscene. I do not think we, the judges, were ever given the constitutional power to make definitions of obscenity. If it is to be de-fined, let the people debate and decide by a constitutional amendment what they want to ban as obscene and what standards they want the legislatures and the courts to apply. Perhaps the people will decide that the path towards a mature, integrated society requires that all ideas competing for acceptance must have no censor. Perhaps they will decide otherwise. Whatever the choice, the courts will have some guidelines. Now we have none except our own predilections.

Mr. Justice BRENNAN, with whom Mr. Justice STEWART and Mr. Justice MARSHALL join, dissenting.

In my dissent in [Paris Adult Theatre, below], I noted that I had no occasion to consider the extent of state power to regulate the distribution of sexually oriented material to juveniles or the offensive exposure of such ma-terial to unconsenting adults. . . . I need not now decide whether a statute might be drawn to impose, within the requirements of the First Amendment, criminal penalties for the precise conduct at issue here [—mail-ing unsolicited brochures]. For it is clear that under my dissent in [Paris Adult Theatre], the statute under which the prosecution was brought is un-constitutionally overbroad, and therefore invalid on its face. [Since my views on obscenity] represent a substantial departure from the course of our prior decisions, and since the state courts have as yet had no opportunity to con-sider whether a "readily apparent construction suggests itself as a vehicle for rehabilitating the [statute] in a single prosecution" [Dombrowski v. Pfister, chap. 15], I would [reverse and remand].

als; where other alternatives are available, the criminal process should not ordinarily be invoked against per-sons who might have reasonably be-lieved, in good faith, that the books or films they distributed were entitled to constitutional protection, for the threat of criminal sanctions might otherwise deter the free distribution of constitutionally protected material." Report of the Commission on Obsceni-ty and Pornography 63 (1970). [Foot-note by Justice Douglas.]

PARIS ADULT THEATRE I v. SLATON

413 U.S. 49, 93 S.Ct. 2628, 37 L.Ed.2d 446 (1973).

Certiorari to the Supreme Court of Georgia.

Mr. Chief Justice BURGER delivered the opinion of the Court.*

. . .

We categorically disapprove the theory, apparently adopted by the trial judge, that obscene, pornographic films acquire constitutional immunity from state regulation simply because they are exhibited for consenting adults only. . . . The States have a long-recognized legitimate interest in regulating the use of obscene material in local commerce and in all places of public accommodation . . . .

In particular, we hold that there are legitimate state interests at stake in stemming the tide of commercialized obscenity, even assuming it is feasible to enforce effective safeguards against exposure to juveniles and to passers-by.[1] . . . These include the interest of the public in the quality of life and the total community environment, the tone of commerce in the great city centers, and, possibly, the public safety itself. The Hill-Link Minority Report of the Commission on Obscenity and Pornography indicates that there is at least an arguable correlation between obscene material and crime.[2] Quite apart from sex crimes, however, there remains one problem of large proportions aptly described by Professor Bickel:

---

* This was a civil proceeding to enjoin the showing of two allegedly obscene films at two "adult" theaters. At a trial before a judge, the evidence consisted primarily of the films and of photographs of the entrance to the theatres. As described by the Chief Justice, these photographs "show a conventional, inoffensive theatre entrance, without any pictures, but with signs indicating that the theatres exhibit 'Atlanta's Finest Mature Feature Films.' On the door itself is a sign saying: 'Adult Theatre—You must be 21 and able to prove it. If viewing the nude body offends you, Please Do Not Enter.'" (Two state investigators who saw the films testified that the signs did not indicate "the full nature of what was shown. In particular, nothing indicated that the films depicted—as they did—scenes of simulated fellatio, cunnilingus, and group sex intercourse.") The trial judge dismissed the complaint. He held the showing of obscene films permissible where there was "requisite notice to the public" and "reasonable protection against the exposure of these films to minors." The Georgia Supreme Court reversed. Before turning to the issues discussed in the text, the Chief Justice found that it was not error "to fail to re-

quire 'expert' affirmative evidence that the materials were obscene when the materials themselves were placed in evidence." Moreover, he praised the civil injunction procedure because it provides an exhibitor "the best possible notice, prior to any criminal indictments," as to whether the materials are obscene.

1. It is conceivable that an "adult" theatre can—if it really insists—prevent the exposure of its obscene wares to juveniles. An "adult" bookstore, dealing in obscene books, magazines, and pictures, cannot realistically make this claim. . . . The legitimate interest in preventing exposure of juveniles to obscene materials cannot be fully served by simply barring juveniles from the immediate physical premises of "adult" bookstores, when there is a flourishing "outside business" in these materials. [Footnote by the Chief Justice.]

2. The Report of the Commission on Obscenity and Pornography (1970 ed.), 390–412 (Hill-Link Minority Report). For a discussion of earlier studies indicating "a division of thought [among behavioral scientists] on the correlation between obscenity and so-

"It concerns the tone of the society, the mode, or to use terms that have perhaps greater currency, the style and quality of life, now and in the future. A man may be entitled to read an obscene book in his room, or expose himself indecently there. . . . We should protect his privacy. But if he demands a right to obtain the books and pictures he wants in the market, and to foregather in public places—discreet, if you will, but accessible to all—with others who share his tastes, *then to grant him his right is to affect the world about the rest of us, and to impinge on other privacies.* Even supposing that each of us can, if he wishes, effectively avert the eye and stop the ear (which, in truth, we cannot), what is commonly read and seen and heard and done intrudes upon us all, want it or not." 22 The Public Interest 25–26 (Winter, 1971). (Emphasis added.) As Mr. Chief Justice Warren stated, there is a "right of the Nation and of the States to maintain a decent society" [Jacobellis dissent].

But, it is argued, there is no scientific data which conclusively demonstrate that exposure to obscene materials adversely affects men and women or their society. It is [urged] that, absent such a demonstration, any kind of state regulation is "impermissible." We reject this argument. It is not for us to resolve empirical uncertainties underlying state legislation, save in the exceptional case where that legislation plainly impinges upon rights protected by the Constitution itself. . . . Although there is no conclusive proof of a connection between antisocial behavior and obscene material, the legislature of Georgia could quite reasonably determine that such a connection does or might exist. In deciding Roth, this Court implicitly accepted that a legislature could legitimately act on such a conclusion to protect "*the social interest in order and morality.*"

From the beginning of civilized societies, legislators and judges have acted on various unprovable assumptions. Such assumptions underlie much lawful state regulation of commercial and business affairs. See [Ferguson v. Skrupa; Breard v. Alexandria; Lincoln Federal Labor Union]. The same is true of the federal securities and antitrust laws and a host of federal regulations. On the basis of these assumptions both Congress and state legislatures have, for example, drastically restricted associational rights by adopting antitrust laws, and have strictly regulated public expression by issuers of and dealers in securities, profit sharing "coupons," and "trading stamps," commanding what they must and must not publish and announce. Understandably those who entertain an absolutist view of the First Amendment find it uncomfortable to explain why rights of association, speech, and press should be severely restrained in the marketplace of goods and money, but not in the marketplace of pornography.

Likewise, when legislatures and administrators act to protect the physical environment from pollution and to preserve our resources of forests, streams and parks, they must act on such imponderables as the impact of a new highway near or through an existing park or wilderness area. . . . The fact that a congressional directive reflects unprovable assumptions about

cially deleterious behavior" and references to expert opinions that obscene material may induce crime and antisocial conduct, see [Memoirs], (Clark, J., dissenting). . . . [Footnote by the Chief Justice.]

what is good for the people, including imponderable aesthetic assumptions, is not a sufficient reason to find that statute unconstitutional.

If we accept the unprovable assumption that a complete education requires certain books and the well nigh universal belief that good books, plays, and art lift the spirit, improve the mind, enrich the human personality and develop character, can we then say that a state legislature may not act on the corollary assumption that commerce in obscene books, or public exhibitions focused on obscene conduct, have a tendency to exert a corrupting and debasing impact leading to antisocial behavior? . . . The sum of experience, including that of the past two decades, affords an ample basis for legislatures to conclude that a sensitive, key relationship of human existence, central to family life, community welfare, and the development of human personality, can be debased and distorted by crass commercial exploitation of sex. Nothing in the Constitution prohibits a State from reaching such a conclusion and acting on it legislatively simply because there is no conclusive evidence or empirical data.

It is argued that individual "free will" must govern, even in activities beyond the protection of the First Amendment and other constitutional guarantees of privacy, and that government cannot legitimately impede an individual's desire to see or acquire obscene plays, movies, and books. . . . Most exercises of individual free choice—those in politics, religion, and expression of ideas—are explicitly protected by the Constitution. Totally unlimited play for free will, however, is not allowed in ours or any other society. [For example,] neither the First Amendment nor "free will" precludes States from having "blue sky" laws to regulate what sellers of securities may write or publish about their wares. Such laws are to protect the weak, the uninformed, the unsuspecting, and the gullible from the exercise of their own volition. Nor do modern societies leave disposal of garbage and sewage up to the individual "free will" . . . .. States are told by some that they must await a "laissez faire" market solution to the obscenity-pornography problem, paradoxically "by people who have never otherwise had a kind word to say for laissez-faire," particularly in solving urban, commercial, and environmental pollution problems. See I. Kristol, On the Democratic Idea in America 37 (1972).

The States, of course, may follow such a "laissez faire" policy and drop all controls on commercialized obscenity, if that is what they prefer, just as they can ignore consumer protection in the marketplace, but nothing in the Constitution *compels* the States to do so with regard to matters falling within state jurisdiction. "We do not sit as a super-legislature to determine the wisdom, need, and propriety of laws that touch economic problems, business affairs, or social conditions." [Griswold v. Connecticut.]

It is asserted, however, that standards for evaluating state commercial regulations are inapposite in the present context, as state regulation of access by consenting adults to obscene material violates the constitutionally protected right to privacy enjoyed by petitioners' customers. [I]t is unavailing to compare a theater open to the public for a fee, with the private home of [Stanley] and the marital bedroom of [Griswold]. This Court, has, on numerous occasions, refused to hold that commercial ventures such as a mo-

tion-picture house are "private" for the purpose of civil rights litigation and civil rights statutes. . . .

Our prior decisions recognizing a right to privacy [protect] the personal intimacies of the home, the family, marriage, motherhood, procreation, and child rearing. Nothing, however, in this Court's decisions intimates that there is any "fundamental" privacy right "implicit in the concept of ordered liberty" to watch obscene movies in places of public accommodation.

If obscene material unprotected by the First Amendment in itself carried with it a "penumbra" of constitutionally protected privacy, this Court would not have found it necessary to decide Stanley on the narrow basis of the "privacy of the home" . . . .[3] The idea of a "privacy" right and a place of public accommodation are, in this context, mutually exclusive. Conduct or depictions of conduct that the state police power can prohibit on a public street do not become automatically protected by the Constitution merely because the conduct is moved to a bar or a "live" theatre stage, any more than a "live" performance of a man and woman locked in a sexual embrace at high noon in Times Square is protected by the Constitution because they simultaneously engage in a valid political dialogue.

It is also argued that the State has no legitimate interest in "control [of] the moral content of a person's thoughts" [Stanley], and we need not quarrel with this. But we reject the claim that [Georgia] is here attempting to control the minds or thoughts of those who patronize theaters. Preventing unlimited display or distribution of obscene material, which by definition lacks any serious literary, artistic, political, or scientific value as communication [Miller], is distinct from a control of reason and the intellect. . . . Where communication of ideas, protected by the First Amendment, is not involved, or the particular privacy of the home protected by Stanley, or any of the other "areas or zones" of constitutionally protected privacy, the mere fact that, as a consequence, some human "utterances" or "thoughts" may be incidentally affected does not bar the State from acting to protect legitimate state interests. Cf. [Roth; Beauharnais]. The fantasies of a drug addict are his own and beyond the reach of government, but government regulation of drug sales is not prohibited by the Constitution. . . .

Finally, petitioners argue that conduct which directly involves "consenting adults" only has, for that sole reason, a special claim to constitutional protection. [F]or us to say that our Constitution incorporates the proposition that conduct involving consenting adults only is always beyond state regulation,[4] is a step we are unable to take.[5] Commercial exploitation

---

3. The protection afforded by [Stanley] is restricted to a place, the home. In contrast, the constitutionally protected privacy of family, marriage, motherhood, procreation, and child rearing is not just concerned with a particular place, but with a protected intimate relationship. Such protected privacy extends to the doctor's office, the hospital, the hotel room, or as otherwise required to safeguard the right to intimacy involved. Cf. [Roe v. Wade; Griswold]. Obviously, there is no necessary or legitimate expectation of privacy which would extend to marital intercourse on a street corner or a theater stage. [Footnote by the Chief Justice.]

4. Cf. Mill, On Liberty 13. (1955 ed.) [Footnote by the Chief Justice.]

5. The state statute books are replete with constitutionally unchallenged

of depictions, descriptions, or exhibitions of obscene conduct on commercial premises open to the adult public falls within a State's broad power to regulate commerce and protect the public environment. The issue in this context goes beyond whether someone, or even the majority, considers the conduct depicted as "wrong" or "sinful." The States have the power to make a morally neutral judgment that public exhibition of obscene material, or commerce in such material, has a tendency to injure the community as a whole, to endanger the public safety, or to jeopardize, in Chief Justice Warren's words, the States' "right [to] maintain a decent society." . . .

[W]e hold that the States have a legitimate interest in regulating commerce in obscene material and in regulating exhibition of obscene material in places of public accommodation, including so-called "adult" theaters from which minors are excluded. [N]othing precludes the State of Georgia from the regulation [involved here], provided that the applicable Georgia law, as written or authoritatively interpreted by the Georgia courts, meets the First Amendment standards set forth in [Miller]. . . .

Vacated and remanded.*

Mr. Justice BRENNAN, with whom Mr. Justice STEWART and Mr. Justice MARSHALL join, dissenting.

. . . I am convinced that the approach initiated 15 years ago in [Roth], and culminating in the Court's decision today, cannot bring stability to this area of the law without jeopardizing fundamental First Amendment values, and I have concluded that the time has come to make a significant departure from that approach. . . .

The essence of our problem in the obscenity area is that we have been unable to provide "sensitive tools" to separate obscenity from other sexually oriented but constitutionally protected speech, so that efforts to suppress the former do not spill over into the suppression of the latter. [W]e have failed to formulate a standard that sharply distinguishes protected from unprotected speech. [See Justice Brennan's review of the prior cases, above.]

. . .

[A]fter 16 years of experimentation and debate I am reluctantly forced to the conclusion that none of the available formulas, including the one announced today, can reduce the vagueness to a tolerable level . . ..
Any effort to draw a constitutionally acceptable boundary on state power must resort to such indefinite concepts as "prurient interest," "patent of-

laws against prostitution, suicide, voluntary self-mutilation, brutalizing "bare fist" prize fights, and duels, although these crimes may only directly involve "consenting adults." Statutes making bigamy a crime surely cut into an individual's freedom to associate, but few today seriously claim such statutes violate the First Amendment or any other constitutional provision. Consider also the language of this Court [as to] adultery; [as to] fornication; [as to] "white slavery"; [as to] billiard halls; [and] as to gambling. See also the summary of state statutes prohibiting bear baiting, cockfighting, and other brutalizing animal "sports," in Stevens, Fighting and Baiting, in Animals and Their Legal Rights 112–127 (Leavitt ed., 1970 ed.). As Professor Kristol has observed, "Bearbaiting and cockfighting are prohibited only in part out of compassion for the suffering animals; the main reason they were abolished was because it was felt that they debased and brutalized the citizenry who flocked to witness such spectacles." On the Democratic Idea in America, supra. [Footnote by the Chief Justice.]

* A dissent by Justice Douglas is omitted. See his dissent in Miller, above.

fensiveness," "serious literary value," and the like. The meaning of these concepts necessarily varies with the experience, outlook, and even idiosyncracies of the person defining them. . . .

. . . Added to the "perhaps inherent residual vagueness" of each of the current multitude of standards is the further complication that the obscenity of any particular item may depend upon nuances of presentation and the context of its dissemination. . . . *

The vagueness of the standards in the obscenity area produces a number of separate problems, and any improvement must rest on an understanding that the problems are to some extent distinct. First, a vague statute fails to provide adequate notice to persons who are engaged in the type of conduct that the statute could be thought to proscribe. [In addition], a vague statute in the areas of speech and press creates a second level of difficulty [—that of "chilling protected speech"]. [Moreover], a vague statute in this area creates a third, although admittedly more subtle, set of problems. These problems concern the institutional stress that inevitably results where the line separating protected from unprotected speech is excessively vague. [A]lmost every case is "marginal." And since the "margin" marks the point of separation between protected and unprotected speech, we are left with a system in which almost every obscenity case presents a constitutional question of exceptional difficulty. . . .

As a result of our failure to define standards with predictable application to any given piece of material, there is no probability of regularity in obscenity decisions by state and lower federal courts. . . . [O]ne cannot say with certainty that material is obscene until at least five members this Court [have] pronounced it so. . . .

[And] quite apart from the number of cases involved and the need to make a fresh constitutional determination in each case, we are tied to the "absurd business of perusing and viewing the miserable stuff that pours into the Court." . . .

Moreover, we have managed the burden of deciding scores of obscenity cases by relying on per curiam reversals or denials of certiorari—a practice which conceals the rationale of decision and gives at least the appearance of arbitrary action by this Court. [More important,] the practice effectively censors protected expression by leaving lower court determinations of obscenity intact even though the status of the allegedly obscene material is entirely unsettled until final review here. In addition, the uncertainty of the standards creates a continuing source of tension between state and federal courts, since the need for an independent determination by this Court seems to render superfluous even the most conscientious analysis by state tribunals. And our inability to justify our decisions with a persuasive rationale—or indeed, any rationale at all—necessarily creates the impression that we are merely second-guessing state court judges.

The severe problems arising from the lack of fair notice, from the chill on protected expression, and from the stress imposed on the state and federal

* In a footnote at this point, Justice Brennan explained why he was "now inclined to agree" with much of Stanley v. Georgia, even though he had not joined that opinion. His explanation is printed in note 3b of the notes preceding these 1973 decisions.

judicial machinery persuade me that a significant change in direction is urgently required. I turn, therefore, to the alternatives that are now open.

    1. The approach requiring the smallest deviation from our present course would be to draw a new line between protected and unprotected speech, still permitting the States to suppress all material on the unprotected side of the line. In my view, clarity cannot be obtained pursuant to this approach except by drawing a line that resolves all doubt in favor of state power and against the guarantees of the First Amendment. . . .

    2. The alternative adopted by the Court today recognizes that a prohibition against any depiction or description of human sexual organs could not be reconciled with the guarantees of the First Amendment. But the Court does retain the view that certain sexually oriented material can be considered obscene and therefore unprotected by the First and Fourteenth Amendments. To describe that unprotected class of expression, the Court adopts a restatement of the Roth-Memoirs definition of obscenity . . . . .

    The differences between this formulation and the three-pronged Memoirs test are, for the most part, academic.[1] . . . In my view, the restatement leaves unresolved the very difficulties that compel our rejection of the underlying Roth approach, while at the same time contributing substantial difficulties of its own. The modification of the Memoirs test may prove sufficient to jeopardize the analytic underpinnings of the entire scheme. And today's restatement will likely have the effect, whether or not intended, of permitting far more sweeping suppression of sexually oriented expression, including expression that would almost surely be held protected under our current formulation.

    Although the Court's restatement substantially tracks the three-part test [of Memoirs], it does purport to modify the "social value" component of the test. [T]he Court today permits suppression if the government can prove that the materials lack "*serious* literary, artistic, political or scientific value." But the definition of "obscenity" as expression utterly lacking in social importance is the key to the conceptual basis of Roth and our subsequent opinions. In Roth we held that certain expression is obscene, and thus outside the protection of the First Amendment, precisely *because* it lacks even the slightest redeeming social value. The Court's approach necessarily assumes that some works will be deemed obscene—even though they clearly have *some* social value—because the State was able to prove that the value, measured by some unspecified standard, was not sufficiently "serious" to warrant constitutional protection. That result is not merely inconsistent

---

1. While the Court's modification of the Memoirs test is small, it should still prove sufficient to invalidate virtually every state law relating to the suppression of obscenity. For, under the Court's restatement, a statute must specifically enumerate certain forms of sexual conduct, the depiction of which is to be prohibited. It seems highly doubtful to me that state courts will be able to construe state statutes so as to incorporate a carefully itemized list of various forms of sexual conduct, and thus to bring them into conformity with the Court's requirements. . . . The statutes of at least one State should, however, escape the wholesale invalidation. Oregon has recently revised its statute to prohibit only the distribution of obscene materials to juveniles or unconsenting adults. The enactment of this principle is, of course, a choice constitutionally open to every State, even under the Court's decision. . . . [Footnote by Justice Brennan.]

with our holding in Roth; it is nothing less than a rejection of the fundamental First Amendment premises and rationale of the Roth opinion and an invitation to widespread suppression of sexually oriented speech. Before today, the protections of the First Amendment have never been thought limited to expressions of *serious* literary or political value. See [Gooding v. Wilson; Cohen v. California; Terminiello v. Chicago].

.   .   .   One should hardly need to point out that under the third component of the Court's test the prosecution is still required to "prove a negative"   .   .   ..   Whether it will be easier to prove that material lacks "serious" value than to prove that it lacks any value at all remains, of course, to be seen. In any case, even if the Court's approach left undamaged the conceptual framework of Roth, and even if it clearly barred the suppression of works with at least some social value, I would nevertheless be compelled to reject it. For it is beyond dispute that the approach can have no ameliorative impact on the cluster of problems that grow out of the vagueness of our current standards.   .   .   .

Of course, the Court's restated Roth test does limit the definition of obscenity to depictions of physical conduct and explicit sexual acts. And that limitation may seem, at first glance, a welcome and clarifying addition to the Roth-Memoirs formula. [But] the mere formulation of a "physical conduct" test is no assurance that it can be applied with any greater facility. The Court does not indicate how it would apply its test to the materials involved in [Miller]. [E]ven a confirmed optimist could find little realistic comfort in the adoption of such a test. Indeed, the valiant attempt of one lower federal court to draw the constitutional line at depictions of explicit sexual conduct seems to belie any suggestion that this approach marks the road to clarity.[2] The Court surely demonstrates little sensitivity to our own institutional problems, much less the other vagueness-related difficulties, in establishing a system that requires us to consider whether a description of human genitals is sufficiently "lewd" to deprive it of constitutional protection; whether a sexual act is "ultimate"; whether the conduct depicted in materials before us fits within one of the categories of conduct whose depiction the state or federal governments have attempted to suppress; and a host of equally pointless inquiries. In addition, adoption of such a test does not, presumably, obviate the need for consideration of the nuances of presentation of sexually oriented material, yet it hardly clarifies the application of those opaque but important factors.

.   .   .   I am convinced that a definition of obscenity in terms of physical conduct cannot provide sufficient clarity to afford fair notice, to avoid a chill on protected expression, and to minimize the institutional stress, so long as that definition is used to justify the outright suppression of any material that is asserted to fall within its terms.

3.   I have also considered the possibility of reducing our own role, and the role of appellate courts generally, in determining whether particular mat-

2.   Huffman v. United States, 470 F.2d 386 (D.C.Cir. 1971). The test apparently requires an effort to distinguish between "singles" and "duals," between "erect penises" and "semi-erect penises," and between "ongoing sexual activity" and "imminent sexual activity." [Footnote by Justice Brennan.]

ter is obscene. Thus, [we] might adopt the position that where a lower federal or state court has conscientiously applied the constitutional standard, its finding of obscenity will be no more vulnerable to reversal by this Court than any finding of fact. [But] it is implict in [Redrup] that the First Amendment requires an independent review by appellate courts of the constitutional fact of obscenity. [In any event, while this approach would mitigate institutional stress,] it would neither offer or produce any cure for the other vices of vagueness. . . . Plainly, the institutional gain would be more than offset by the unprecedented infringement of First Amendment rights.

4. Finally, I have considered the view, urged so forcefully since 1957 by our Brothers Black and Douglas, that the First Amendment bars the suppression of any sexually oriented expression. [But that would strip] the States of power to an extent that cannot be justified by the commands of the Constitution, at least so long as there is available an alternative approach that strikes a better balance between the guarantee of free expression and the States' legitimate interests.

Our experience since Roth requires us not only to abandon the effort to pick out obscene materials on a case-by-case basis, but also to reconsider a fundamental postulate of Roth: that there exists a definable class of sexually oriented expression that may be totally suppressed by the Federal and State Governments. Assuming that such a class of expression does in fact exist [see p. 1296 above], I am forced to conclude that the concept of "obscenity" cannot be defined with sufficient specificity and clarity to provide fair notice to persons who create and distribute sexually oriented materials, to prevent substantial erosion of protected speech as a byproduct of the attempt to suppress unprotected speech, and to avoid very costly institutional harms. Given these inevitable side-effects of state efforts to suppress what is assumed to be *unprotected* speech, we must scrutinize with care the state interest that is asserted to justify the suppression. For in the absence of some very substantial interest in suppressing such speech, we can hardly condone the ill-effects that seem to flow inevitably from the effort. . . .

Because we assumed—incorrectly, as experience has proven—that obscenity could be separated from other sexually oriented expression without significant costs . . ., we had no occasion in Roth to probe the asserted state interest in curtailing unprotected, sexually oriented speech. Yet, as we have increasingly come to appreciate the vagueness of the concept of obscenity, we have begun to recognize and articulate the state interests at stake. . . .

The opinions in Redrup and [Stanley] reflected our emerging view that the state interests in protecting children and in protecting unconsenting adults may stand on a different footing from the other asserted state interests. It may well be, as one commentator has argued, that "exposure to [erotic material] is for some persons an intense emotional experience. A communication of this nature, imposed upon a person contrary to his wishes, has all the characteristics of a physical assault. [And it] constitutes an invasion of his privacy." [3] But cf. [Cohen v. California]. [Similarly], the

3. T. Emerson, The System of Freedom
of Expression 496 (1970). [Footnote
by Justice Brennan.]

State may have a substantial interest in precluding the flow of obscene materials even to consenting juveniles.

[But whatever the strength of those interests, they] cannot be asserted in defense of the holding of the Georgia Supreme Court. [The justification here] must be found [in] some independent interest in regulating the reading and viewing habits of consenting adults.

At the outset it should be noted that virtually all of [those interests] were also posited in [Stanley]. That decision presages the conclusions I reach here today.[4] [Of course, a State need not] remain utterly indifferent to—and take no action bearing on—the morality of the community. The traditional description of state police power does embrace the regulation of morals as well as health, safety, and general welfare of the citizenry. And much legislation—compulsory public education laws, civil rights laws, even the abolition of capital punishment—is grounded, at least in part, on a concern with the morality of the community. But the State's interest in regulating morality by suppressing obscenity, while often asserted, remains essentially unfocused and ill-defined. And, since the attempt to curtail unprotected speech necessarily spills over into the area of protected speech, the effort to serve this speculative interest through the suppression of obscene material must tread heavily on rights protected by the First Amendment. . . . Like the proscription of abortions [in Roe v. Wade, chap. 9, sec. 3, above], the effort to suppress obscenity is predicated on unprovable, although strongly held, assumptions about human behavior, morality, sex, and religion.[5] The existence of these assumptions cannot validate a statute that substantially undermines the guarantees of the First Amendment, any more than the existence of similar assumptions on the issue of abortion can validate a statute that infringes the constitutionally-protected privacy interests of a pregnant woman.

If, as the Court today assumes, "a state legislature may [act on the assumption that obscenity has] a tendency to exert a corrupting and debasing impact leading to antisocial behavior," then it is hard to see how state-ordered regimentation of our minds can ever be forestalled. For if a State may, in an effort to maintain or create a particular moral tone, prescribe what its citizens cannot read or cannot see, then it would seem to follow that in pursuit of that same objective a State could decree that its citizens must read certain books or must view certain films. . . . However laudable its goal—and that is obviously a question on which reasonable minds may differ—the State cannot proceed by means that violate the Constitution. [Meyer v. Nebraska.] [W]e have held that so-called thematic

4. [Since Stanley] was decided, the President's Commission on Obscenity and Pornography has concluded:
" . . . The Commission cannot conclude that exposure to erotic materials is a factor in the causation of sex crime or sex delinquency." Report of the Commission on Obscenity and Pornography 27 (1970).

To the contrary, the Commission found that "[o]n the positive side, explicit sexual materials are sought as a source of entertainment and information by substantial numbers of American adults. At times, these materials also appear to serve to increase and facilitate constructive communication about sexual matters within marriage." [Footnote by Justice Brennan.]

5. See Henkin, Morals and the Constitution: The Sin of Obscenity, 63 Col. L.Rev. 391, 395 (1963). [Footnote by Justice Brennan.]

obscenity—obscenity which might persuade the viewer or the reader to engage in "obscene" conduct—is not outside the protection of the First Amendment. [Kingsley Pictures.] Even a legitimate, sharply focused state concern for the morality of the community cannot, in other words, justify an assault on the protections of the First Amendment. Cf. [Griswold v. Connecticut; Eisenstadt v. Baird; Loving v. Virginia.] Where the state interest in regulation of morality is vague and ill-defined, interference with the guarantees of the First Amendment is even more difficult to justify.

In short, while I cannot say that the interest of the State—apart from the question of juveniles and unconsenting adults—are trivial or nonexistent, I am compelled to conclude that these interests cannot justify the substantial damage to constitutional rights and to this Nation's judicial machinery that inevitably results from state efforts to bar the distribution even of unprotected material to consenting adults. [NAACP v. Alabama; Cantwell v. Connecticut.] I would hold, therefore, that at least in the absence of distribution to juveniles or obtrusive exposure to unconsenting adults, the First and Fourteenth Amendments prohibit the state and federal governments from attempting wholly to suppress sexually oriented materials on the basis of their allegedly "obscene" contents. Nothing in this approach precludes those governments from taking action to serve what may be strong and legitimate interests through regulation of the manner of distribution of sexually oriented material.

. . . I do not pretend to have found a complete and infallible answer . . ... Difficult questions must still be faced, notably in the areas of distribution to juveniles and offensive exposure to unconsenting adults. Whatever the extent of state power to regulate in those areas,[6] it should be clear that the view I espouse today would introduce a large measure of clarity to this troubled area, would reduce the institutional pressure on this Court and the rest of the State and Federal Judiciary, and would guarantee fuller freedom of expression while leaving room for the protection of legitimate governmental interests. . . .

THE COMPANION CASES TO MILLER AND PARIS

In three additional decisions, handed down together with the preceding cases, the Court sustained obscenity controls in other contexts: it held that federal laws could be applied to prevent the importation and interstate transportation of obscene matters for private use; and it found that a state law could be applied to a book without pictorial contents. Chief Justice Burger again wrote the majority opinions, relying heavily on his analyses in the preceding cases; Justices Douglas, Brennan, Stewart and Marshall again dissented.

6. The Court erroneously states [in Miller] that the author of this opinion "indicates that suppression of unprotected obscene material is permissible to avoid exposure to unconsenting adults . . . and to juveniles . . . ." I defer expression of my views as to the scope of state power in these areas until cases squarely presenting these questions are before the Court. [Footnote by Justice Brennan.]

1. *Importation for private use.* In UNITED STATES v. TWELVE 200-FT. REELS, 413 U.S. 123 (1973), the Court decided the supposedly "narrow" issue about the import ban left open in 37 Photographs (noted above): "Whether the United States may constitutionally prohibit importation of obscene material which the importer claims is for private, personal use and possession only." The Chief Justice noted the "plenary power of Congress to regulate imports" and rejected the argument that, "under Stanley, the right to possess obscene material in the privacy of the home creates a right to acquire it or import it from another country." This, he insisted, "overlooks the explicitly narrow and precisely delineated privacy right on which Stanley rests"—privacy within the home. He added, moreover, that "it would be extremely difficult to control the uses to which obscene materials were put once they entered this country." [He added in a footnote that the Court was prepared to construe the vague terms of the federal obscenity laws "as limiting regulated material to patently offensive representations or descriptions of that specific 'hard-core' sexual conduct given as examples in [Miller]. Of course, Congress could always define other specific 'hard-core' conduct."]

2. *Interstate transportation for private use.* In UNITED STATES v. ORITO, 413 U.S. 139 (1973), the District Court had held the federal ban on interstate transportation overbroad. Cf. Reidel, above. The Chief Justice disagreed: "[W]e cannot say that the Constitution forbids comprehensive federal regulation of interstate transportation of obscene material merely because such transport may be by private carriage, or because material is intended for the private use of the transporter." He explained: "Congress may regulate on the basis of the natural tendency of material in the home being kept private and the contrary tendency once material leaves that area, regardless of a transporter's professed intent. Congress could reasonably determine such a regulation to be necessary to effect permissible federal control of interstate commerce in obscene materials, based as that regulation is on a legislatively determined risk of ultimate exposure to juveniles or to the public and the harm that exposure could cause." He cited commerce and taxing power cases about the immunity of legislative "motive and purpose" from judicial review.

3. *Books without pictures.* Petitioner in KAPLAN v. CALIFORNIA, 413 U.S. 115 (1973), was the owner of "the Peek-A-Boo Bookstore, one of the approximately 200 'adult' stores" in Los Angeles. He had been convicted under a state obscenity law for selling "Suite 69," a book that "has a plain cover and contains no pictures." As the Chief Justice put it, the case "squarely presents the issue of whether expression by words alone can be legally 'obscene.'" The Chief Justice noted: "When the Court declared that obscenity is not a form of expression protected by the First Amendment, no distinction was made as to the medium of the expression. Obscenity can, of course, manifest itself in conduct, in the pictorial representation of conduct, or in the written and oral description of conduct. The Court has applied similarly conceived First Amendment standards to moving pictures, to photographs, and to words in books." And he managed to explain the conclusion as to "words alone" in two simple paragraphs:

"Because of a profound commitment to protecting communication of ideas, any restraint on expression by way of the printed word or in speech

stimulates a traditional and emotional response, unlike the response to obscene pictures of flagrant human conduct. A book seems to have a different and preferred place in our hierarchy of values, and so it should be. But this generalization, like so many, is qualified by the book's content. As with pictures, films, paintings, drawings, and engravings, both oral utterance and the printed word have First Amendment protection until they collide with the long-settled position of this Court that obscenity is not protected by the Constitution. . . .

"For good or ill, a book has a continuing life. It is passed hand to hand, and we can take note of the tendency of widely circulated books of this category to reach the impressionable young and have a continuing impact. A State could reasonably regard the 'hard core' conduct described by Suite 69 as capable of encouraging or causing antisocial behavior, especially in its impact on young people. States need not wait until behavioral experts or educators can provide empirical data before enacting controls of commerce in obscene materials unprotected by the First Amendment or by a constitutional right to privacy."

THE 1974 ELABORATIONS: CONTINUED REVIEW OF "PATENT OFFENSIVENESS"; LOCAL COMMUNITY STANDARDS

1. *Continued Court review.* JENKINS v. GEORGIA, 418 U.S. 153 (1974), demonstrated that the new 1973 standards for obscenity would not wholly extricate the Court from the unwelcome task of case-by-case review in obscenity cases. Jenkins reversed appellant's state conviction for distributing obscene material. Appellant had shown the film "Carnal Knowledge." The highest state court, it turned out, had mistakenly thought that under the new criteria, a jury verdict virtually precluded all further review as to most elements of obscenity. Justice Rehnquist countered: "Even though questions of appeal to the 'prurient interest' or of patent offensiveness are 'essentially questions of fact,' it would be a serious misreading of Miller to conclude that juries have unbridled discretion in determining what is 'patently offensive'." Recalling the examples of "patent offensiveness" in Miller, he noted: "While this did not purport to be an exhaustive catalog of what juries might find patently offensive, it was certainly intended to fix substantive constitutional limitations, deriving from the First Amendment, on the type of material subject to such a determination."

Turning to the specific film at issue, Justice Rehnquist concluded that it "could not be found under the Miller standards to depict sexual conduct in a patently offensive way. Nothing in the movie falls within either of the two examples given in Miller of material which may constitutionally be found to meet the 'patently offensive' element of those standards, nor is there anything sufficiently similar to such material to justify similar treatment. While the subject matter of the picture is, in a broader sense, sex, and there are scenes in which sexual conduct including 'ultimate sexual acts' is to be understood to be taking place, the camera does not focus on the bodies of the actors at such times. There is no exhibition whatever of the actors' genitals,

lewd or otherwise, during these scenes. There are occasional scenes of nudity, but nudity alone is not enough to make material legally obscene under the Miller standards."

Justice Brennan, joined by Justices Stewart and Marshall, concurred in the result in a separate opinion. Justice Brennan commented: "After the Court's decision today, there can be no doubt that Miller requires appellate courts—including this Court—to review independently the constitutional fact of obscenity." He once against objected to the "uncertainty" and "inevitable institutional stress upon the judiciary" of the Miller approach. His preference continued to be to find the statute overbroad. Justice Douglas' concurrence in the result also adhered to his earlier position: "any ban on obscenity is prohibited by the First Amendment."

2. *Local "community standards."* In the pre-1973 cases, there were recurrent divisions about the proper scope of the "community" whose standards governed in obscenity cases. The argument that application of local rather than statewide or national standards would unduly inhibit producers of materials for a national market was rejected in 1974. In the Jenkins case, note 1 above, the Court refused to require that statewide standards be applied in state obscenity prosecutions.* And in a companion case to Jenkins, HAMLING v. UNITED STATES, 418 U.S. 87 (1974), the Court opted for local rather than national standards in prosecutions under the federal ban on mailing obscene materials. In Hamling, the Court affirmed a conviction for mailing an obscene advertising brochure with sexually explicit photographic material relating to an illustrated version of the Report of the Obscenity Commission.

In explaining his "local standards" construction of the national statute, Justice Rehnquist stated that a juror may "draw on knowledge of the community or vicinage from which he comes in deciding what conclusion 'the average person, applying contemporary community standards' would reach in a given case." And that was a constitutionally permissible construction: "The fact that distributors of allegedly obscene materials may be subjected to varying community standards in the various federal judicial districts into which they transmit the materials does not render a federal statute unconstitutional because of the failure of application of uniform national standards of obscenity." In concluding that the relevant community in a federal obscenity case is the federal judicial district from which the jury is drawn, Justice Rehnquist recalled that Miller had viewed uniform nationwide standards as "hypothetical and unascertainable." And the approval of a statewide standard in Miller, the California case, "did not mean that any such precise geographic area is required as a matter of constitutional law."

Justice Brennan's dissent, joined by Justices Stewart and Marshall, found reasons to disagree going beyond those stated in the 1973 cases. He objected

---

* The Jenkins Court held that "the Constitution does not require that juries be instructed in state obscenity cases to apply the standards of a hypothetical statewide community." And in instructions about "community standards," the trial court need not specify what the relevant "community" is. Justice Rehnquist commented: "A State may choose to define an obscenity offense in terms of 'contemporary community standards' as defined in Miller without further specification, as was done here, or it may choose to define the standards in more precise geographic terms, as was done (with respect to the statewide community) by California in Miller."

that the application of local rather than national standards created a construction itself violative of the First Amendment: "National distributors choosing to send their products in interstate travels will be forced to cope with the community standards of every hamlet into which their goods may wander." And if that were a proper and permissible construction, its application here, he insisted, was "a patently indefensible denial" of due process: e. g., after a trial "upon a charge of violating 'national' standards," the "convictions are affirmed as if [there had been a trial] for violating 'local' standards." Justice Douglas also dissented.

SECTION 3. REGULATORY METHODS AND THE FIRST AMENDMENT: PRIOR RESTRAINT, CENSORSHIP, AND RELATED PROBLEMS

Introduction. Efforts at obscenity control have been especially prolific sources for Court considerations of the constitutionality of regulatory methods in the First Amendment context. But obscenity has not been the only area of special preoccupation with procedures. The cases in this section illustrate a wider phenomenon: the concern with substantive free speech values frequently evokes an auxiliary judicial scrutiny of regulatory methods; procedural safeguards often have a special bite in the First Amendment context. As the Court put it in Smith v. California, 361 U.S. 147 (1959) (sec. 3B below): "Our decisions furnish examples of legal devices and doctrines in most applications consistent with the Constitution, which cannot be applied in settings where they have the collateral effect of inhibiting the freedom of expression, by making the individual the more reluctant to exercise it." At times, the safeguards regarding methods have their primary origin in general notions of procedural due process, though those notions apply with special force in the free speech environment; [1] but more commonly, the Court derives special procedural safeguards from the First Amendment itself.[2]

Sec. 3A considers the special judicial scrutiny of prior restraints through two major cases far removed from the obscenity setting. Both cases involved injunctive remedies against the press: Near v. Minnesota in 1931 laid the groundwork; the Pentagon Papers Case in 1971, New York Times Co. v. United States, applied that special hostility to prior restraints in a particularly controversial, national security, context.[3] Sec. 3B turns to problems particularly relevant to the control of obscenity—especially problems of motion

1. Recall, e. g., the special force of the due process-fair notice concept of "void-for-vagueness" in the First Amendment context.

2. See generally Monaghan, "First Amendment 'Due Process,' " 83 Harv. L.Rev. 518 (1970). Professor Monaghan emphasizes two major themes in the First Amendment cases: a requirement of judicial determination of the character of speech; and a requirement that a judicial determination precede or immediately follow governmental intervention.

3. Recall also the earlier illustrations of the Court's solicitude for the press in protecting it against sanctions other than prior restraints—e. g., in the libel context, sec. 1 above, and in the consideration of claims of rights of access to the media, chap. 12, sec. 2. But compare the rejection of a constitutional newsmen's privilege, in sec. 6B below.

picture censorship. But the line between the two groups of cases is not a sharp one: the major modern film censorship case, for example—Freedman v. Maryland, sec. 3B below—set forth guidelines regarding speedy judicial action and burdens of proof which have been influential in controls of political speech as well.[4]

A. PRIOR RESTRAINT AND THE PRESS

NEAR v. MINNESOTA

283 U.S. 697, 51 S.Ct. 625, 75 L.Ed. 1357 (1931).

Appeal from the Supreme Court of Minnesota.

Mr. Chief Justice HUGHES delivered the opinion of the Court.

Chapter 285 of the Session Laws of Minnesota for the year 1925 provides for the abatement, as a public nuisance, of a "malicious, scandalous and defamatory newspaper, magazine or other periodical." Section 1 of the Act is as follows:

"Section 1. Any person who . . . shall be engaged in the business of regularly or customarily producing, publishing or circulating, having in possession, selling or giving away . . .

"(b) a malicious, scandalous and defamatory newspaper, magazine or other periodical,

—is guilty of a nuisance, and all persons guilty of such nuisance may be enjoined, as hereinafter provided. . . .

"In actions brought under (b) above, there shall be available the defense that the truth was published with good motives and for justifiable ends and in such actions the plaintiff shall not have the right to report (sic) to issues or editions of periodicals taking place more than three months before the commencement of the action."

Section two provides that whenever any such nuisance is committed or exists, the County Attorney of any county where any such periodical is published or circulated . . . may maintain an action in the district court of the county in the name of the State to enjoin perpetually the persons committing or maintaining any such nuisance from further committing or maintaining it. . . .

Under this statute, clause (b), the County Attorney of Hennepin County brought this action to enjoin the publication of what was described as a "mali-

---

4. See e. g., the reliance on the Freedman criteria in Carroll v. President & Comm'rs of Princess Anne, 393 U.S. 175 (1968) (chap. 12, sec. 2, above), referring to the "careful procedural provisions" of Freedman in delineating the limits on ex parte restraining orders against demonstrations.

Recall also the earlier encounters with problems of prior restraints—the problems raised by licensing and permit schemes for speech in public places, e. g., Lovell v. Griffin and Cox v. New Hampshire, chap. 12, sec. 2, above. See generally Blasi, "Prior Restraints on Demonstrations," 68 Mich.L.Rev. 1481 (1970).

cious, scandalous and defamatory newspaper, magazine and periodical,"
known as "The Saturday Press," published by the defendants in the city of
Minneapolis. [T]he articles charged in substance that a Jewish gangster was
in control of gambling, bootlegging and racketeering in Minneapolis, and that
law enforcing officers and agencies were not energetically performing their
duties.   .   .   .   There is no question but that the articles made serious
accusations. [The trial court issued a permanent injunction (described in
the opinion below) and the highest state court affirmed.]

This statute, for the suppression as a public nuisance of a newspaper or
periodical, is unusual, if not unique, and raises questions of grave importance
transcending the local interests involved in the particular action. It is no
longer open to doubt that the liberty of the press, and of speech, is within the
liberty safeguarded by the due process clause of the Fourteenth Amendment
from invasion by state action.   .   .   .

First. The statute is not aimed at the redress of individual or private
wrongs. Remedies for libel remain available and unaffected. The statute,
said the state court, "is not directed at threatened libel but at an existing
business which, generally speaking, involves more than libel." It is aimed
at the distribution of scandalous matter as "detrimental to public morals
and to the general welfare," tending "to disturb the peace of the community"
and "to provoke assaults and the commission of crime." In order to obtain an
injunction to suppress the future publication of the newspaper or periodical,
it is not necessary to prove the falsity of the charges that have been made in
the publication condemned. In the present action there was no allegation
that the matter published was not true. It is alleged, and the statute requires
the allegation, that the publication was "malicious." But, as in prosecutions
for libel, there is no requirement of proof by the State of malice in fact
as distinguished from malice inferred from the mere publication of the defamatory matter. The judgment in this case proceeded upon the mere proof
of publication. The statute permits the defense, not of the truth alone, but
only that the truth was published with good motives and for justifiable ends.
.   .   .

Second. The statute is directed not simply at the circulation of scandalous and defamatory statements with regard to private citizens, but at the
continued publication by newspapers and periodicals of charges against public
officers of corruption, malfeasance in office, or serious neglect of duty.
.   .   .

Third. The object of the statute is not punishment, in the ordinary
sense, but suppression of the offending newspaper or periodical. The reason
for the enactment, as the state court has said, is that prosecutions to enforce
penal statutes for libel do not result in "efficient repression or suppression of
the evils of scandal."   .   .   .

Fourth. The statute not only operates to suppress the offending newspaper or periodical but to put the publisher under an effective censorship.
When a newspaper or periodical is found to be "malicious, scandalous and
defamatory," and is suppressed as such, resumption of publication is punishable as a contempt of court by fine or imprisonment. Thus, where a newspaper or periodical has been suppressed because of the circulation of charges

against public officers of official misconduct, it would seem to be clear that the renewal of the publication of such charges would constitute a contempt and that the judgment would lay a permanent restraint upon the publisher, to escape which he must satisfy the court as to the character of a new publication. Whether he would be permitted again to publish matter deemed to be derogatory to the same or other public officers would depend upon the court's ruling. In the present instance the judgment restrained the defendants from "publishing, circulating, having in their possession, selling or giving away any publication whatsoever which is a malicious, scandalous or defamatory newspaper, as defined by law." The law gives no definition except that covered by the words "scandalous and defamatory," and publications charging official misconduct are of that class. While the court, answering the objection that the judgment was too broad, saw no reason for construing it as restraining the defendants "from operating a newspaper in harmony with the public welfare to which all must yield," and said that the defendants had not indicated "any desire to conduct their business in the usual and legitimate manner," the manifest inference is that, at least with respect to a new publication directed against official misconduct, the defendant would be held, under penalty of punishment for contempt as provided in the statute, to a manner of publication which the court considered to be "usual and legitimate" and consistent with the public welfare.

If we cut through mere details of procedure, the operation and effect of the statute in substance is that public authorities may bring the owner or publisher of a newspaper or periodical before a judge upon a charge of conducting a business of publishing scandalous and defamatory matter—in particular that the matter consists of charges against public officers of official dereliction—and unless the owner or publisher is able and disposed to bring competent evidence to satisfy the judge that the charges are true and are published with good motives and for justifiable ends, his newspaper or periodical is suppressed and further publication is made punishable as a contempt. This is of the essence of censorship.

The question is whether a statute authorizing such proceedings in restraint of publication is consistent with the conception of the liberty of the press as historically conceived and guaranteed. In determining the extent of the constitutional protection, it has been generally, if not universally, considered that it is the chief purpose of the guaranty to prevent previous restraints upon publication. The struggle in England, directed against the legislative power of the licenser, resulted in renunciation of the censorship of the press. The liberty deemed to be established was thus described by Blackstone: "The liberty of the press is indeed essential to the nature of a free state; but this consists in laying no *previous* restraints upon publications, and not in freedom from censure for criminal matter when published. Every freeman has an undoubted right to lay what sentiments he pleases before the public; to forbid this, is to destroy the freedom of the press; but if he publishes what is improper, mischievous or illegal, he must take the consequence of his own temerity." . . .

The criticism upon Blackstone's statement has not been because immunity from previous restraint upon publication has not been regarded as deserving of special emphasis, but chiefly because that immunity cannot be

deemed to exhaust the conception of the liberty guaranteed by state and federal constitutions. . . .

The objection has also been made that the principle as to immunity from previous restraint is stated too broadly, if every such restraint is deemed to be prohibited. That is undoubtedly true; the protection even as to previous restraint is not absolutely unlimited. But the limitation has been recognized only in exceptional cases . . . .. No one would question but that a government might prevent actual obstruction to its recruiting service or the publication of the sailing dates of transports or the number and location of troops.* On similar grounds, the primary requirements of decency may be enforced against obscene publications. The security of the community life may be protected against incitements to acts of violence and the overthrow by force of orderly government. The constitutional guaranty of free speech does not "protect a man from an injunction against uttering words that may have all the effect of force." [Schenck.] These limitations are not applicable here. . . .

The exceptional nature of its limitations places in a strong light the general conception that liberty of the press, historically considered and taken up by the Federal Constitution, has meant, principally although not exclusively, immunity from previous restraints or censorship. . . .

The fact that for approximately one hundred and fifty years there has been almost an entire absence of attempts to impose previous restraints upon publications relating to the malfeasance of public officers is significant of the deep-seated conviction that such restraints would violate constitutional right. Public officers, whose character and conduct remain open to debate and free discussion in the press, find their remedies for false accusations in actions under libel laws providing for redress and punishment, and not in proceedings to restrain the publication of newspapers and periodicals. . . .

The importance of this immunity has not lessened. . . . The fact that the liberty of the press may be abused by miscreant purveyors of scandal does not make any the less necessary the immunity of the press from previous restraint in dealing with official misconduct. Subsequent punishment for such abuses as may exist is the appropriate remedy, consistent with constitutional privilege.

The statute in question cannot be justified by reason of the fact that the publisher is permitted to show, before injunction issues, that the matter published is true and is published with good motives and for justifiable ends. If such a statute, authorizing suppression and injunction on such a basis, is constitutionally valid, it would be equally permissible for the legislature to provide that at any time the publisher of any newspaper could be brought before a court, or even an administrative officer (as the constitutional protection may not be regarded as resting on mere procedural details), and required to produce proof of the truth of his publication, or of what he intended to publish and of his motives, or stand enjoined. If this can be done, the legislature may provide machinery for determining in the complete exercise of its discretion what are justifiable ends and restrain publication accord-

---

* Note the attention to this statement
in the Pentagon Papers Case, which
follows.

ingly.   And it would be but a step to a complete system of censorship.
. . .

Equally unavailing is the insistence that the statute is designed to prevent the circulation of scandal which tends to disturb the public peace and to provoke assaults and the commission of crime.   Charges of reprehensible conduct, and in particular of official malfeasance, unquestionably create a public scandal, but the theory of the constitutional guaranty is that even a more serious public evil would be caused by authority to prevent publication.
. . .

For these reasons we hold the statute, so far as it authorized the proceedings in this action under clause (b) of section 1, to be an infringement of the liberty of the press guaranteed by the Fourteenth Amendment.
. . .

Judgment reversed.

Mr. Justice BUTLER, dissenting. . . .

The Minnesota statute does not operate as a *previous* restraint on publication within the proper meaning of that phrase.   It does not authorize administrative control in advance such as was formerly exercised by the licensers and censors but prescribes a remedy to be enforced by a suit in equity. In this case there was previous publication made in the course of the business of regularly producing malicious, scandalous and defamatory periodicals. The business and publications unquestionably constitute an abuse of the right of free press.   The statute denounces the things done as a nuisance on the ground, as stated by the state supreme court, that they threaten morals, peace and good order.   There is no question of the power of the State to denounce such transgressions.   The restraint authorized is only in respect of continuing to do what has been duly adjudged to constitute a nuisance. . . .   There is nothing in the statute purporting to prohibit publications that have not been adjudged to constitute a nuisance.   It is fanciful to suggest similarity between the granting or enforcement of the decree authorized by this statute to prevent *further* publication of malicious, scandalous and defamatory articles and the *previous restraint* upon the press by licensers as referred to by Blackstone and described in the history of the times to which he alludes.
. . .

. . .   The doctrine that measures such as the one before us are invalid because they operate as previous restraints to infringe freedom of press exposes the peace and good order of every community and the business and private affairs of every individual to the constant and protracted false and malicious assaults of any insolvent publisher who may have purpose and sufficient capacity to contrive and put into effect a scheme or program for oppression, blackmail or extortion. . . .

Mr. Justice VAN DEVANTER, Mr. Justice McREYNOLDS, and Mr. Justice SUTHERLAND concur in this opinion.

NEW YORK TIMES CO. v. UNITED STATES
[THE PENTAGON PAPERS CASE]

403 U.S. 713, 91 S.Ct. 2140, 29 L.Ed.2d 822 (1971).

Certiorari to the United States Court of Appeals for the Second Circuit.*

PER CURIAM.

We granted certiorari in these cases in which the United States seeks to enjoin the New York Times and the Washington Post from publishing the contents of a classified study entitled "History of U. S. Decision-Making Process on Viet Nam Policy."†

"Any system of prior restraints of expression comes to this Court bearing a heavy presumption against its constitutional validity." [Bantam Books, Inc. v. Sullivan; see also Near v. Minnesota]. The Government "thus carries a heavy burden of showing justification for the enforcement of such a restraint." Organization for a Better Austin v. Keefe [(1971). See chap. 12, sec. 2.] The [District Court] in the New York Times case and the [District Court] and the [Court of Appeals] in the Washington Post case held that the Government had not met that burden. We agree.

The judgment of the Court of Appeals for the District of Columbia Circuit is therefore affirmed. The order of the Court of Appeals for the Second Circuit is reversed and the case is remanded with directions to enter a judgment affirming the judgment of the District Court for the Southern District of New York. The stays entered June 25, 1971, by the Court are vacated. The mandates shall issue forthwith.

So ordered.

Mr. Justice BLACK, with whom Mr. Justice DOUGLAS joins, concurring.

I adhere to the view that the Government's case against the Washington Post should have been dismissed and that the injunction against the New York Times should have been vacated without oral argument when the cases were first presented to this Court. I believe that every moment's continuance of the injunctions against these newspapers amounts to a flagrant, indefensible, and continuing violation of the First Amendment. Furthermore,

---

* Together with United States v. The Washington Post Co., on certiorari to the United States Court of Appeals for the District of Columbia Circuit.

† On June 13, 1971, the New York Times began publishing portions of that secret Defense Department compilation of the history of the Vietnam involvement, the Pentagon Papers. On June 18, the Washington Post also began publishing portions of the Pentagon Papers, and a separate Government action to restrain publication was brought in the District of Columbia. Between June 15 and June 23, two district courts and two courts of appeals considered the case. On June 25, the Supreme Court granted certiorari in the Times and Post cases. Restraining orders were continued in effect pending decision. (Four Justices—Black, Douglas, Brennan and Marshall—dissented from the grants of certiorari, urged summary action, and stated that they "would not continue the restraint" on the newspapers.) Oral argument was heard on June 26, and the Supreme Court rendered the decision four days later, on June 30, 1971. (See also the further details on the chronology in the Supreme Court, in Justice Harlan's dissent.)

after oral argument, I agree completely [with] my Brothers Douglas and Brennan. In my view it is unfortunate that some of my Brethren are apparently willing to hold that the publication of news may sometimes be enjoined. Such a holding would make a shambles of the First Amendment. . . .

. . . The press was protected [by the First Amendment] so that it could bare the secrets of government and inform the people. Only a free and unrestrained press can effectively expose deception in government. And paramount among the responsibilities of a free press is the duty to prevent any part of the government from deceiving the people and sending them off to distant lands to die of foreign fevers and foreign shot and shell. In my view, far from deserving condemnation for their courageous reporting, the New York Times, the Washington Post, and other newspapers should be commended for serving the purpose that the Founding Fathers saw so clearly.** . . . To find that the President has "inherent power" to halt the publication of news by resort to the courts would wipe out the First Amendment and destroy the fundamental liberty and security of the very people the Government hopes to make "secure." . . . The word "security" is a broad, vague generality whose contours should not be invoked to abrogate the fundamental law embodied in the First Amendment. . . .

Mr. Justice DOUGLAS, with whom Mr. Justice BLACK joins, concurring. . . .

[The First Amendment] leaves, in my view, no room for governmental restraint on the press.

There is, moreover, no statute barring the publication by the press of the material which the Times and Post seek to use. [18 U.S.C. § 793(e), prohibiting "communication" of information relating to the national defense that could be used to the injury of the United States, does not apply to publication.] [I]t is apparent that Congress was capable of and did distinguish between publishing and communication in the various sections of the Espionage Act.

The other evidence that § 793 does not apply to the press is a rejected version of § 793. That version read: "During any national emergency resulting from a war to which the U. S. is a party or from threat of such a war, the President may, by proclamation, [prohibit] the publishing or communicating of, or the attempting to publish or communicate any information relating to the national defense which, in his judgment, is of such character that it is or might be useful to the enemy." During the [1917] debates in the Senate the First Amendment was specifically cited and that provision was defeated. . . .

So any power that the Government possesses must come from its "inherent power." The power to wage war is "the power to wage war successfully." But the war power stems from a declaration of war. The Constitution by Article I, § 8, gives Congress, not the President, power "to declare War." Nowhere are presidential wars authorized. We need not decide therefore what leveling effect the war power of Congress might have.

** In 1972, the New York Times received a Pulitzer Prize for its Pentagon Papers project.

These disclosures [1] may have a serious impact. But that is no basis for sanctioning a previous restraint on the press. [Near.] . . .

The Government says that it has inherent powers to go into court and obtain an injunction to protect that national interest, which in this case is alleged to be national security. [Near] repudiated that expansive doctrine in no uncertain terms. The dominant purpose of the First Amendment was to prohibit the widespread practice of governmental suppression of embarrassing information. . . . A debate of large proportions goes on in the Nation over our posture in Vietnam. . . . Open debate and discussion of public issues are vital to our national health. . . . The stays in these cases that have been in effect for more than a week constitute a flouting of the principles of the First Amendment as interpreted in [Near].

Mr. Justice BRENNAN, concurring.

I write separately in these cases only to emphasize what should be apparent: that our judgment in the present cases may not be taken to indicate the propriety, in the future, of issuing temporary stays and restraining orders to block the publication of material sought to be suppressed by the Government. . . .

The error that has pervaded these cases from the outset was the granting of any injunctive relief whatsoever, interim or otherwise. The entire thrust of the Government's claim throughout these cases has been that publication of the material sought to be enjoined "could," or "might," or "may" prejudice the national interest in various ways. But the First Amendment tolerates absolutely no prior judicial restraints of the press predicated upon surmise or conjecture that untoward consequences may result.[2] Our cases, it is true, have indicated that there is a single, extremely narrow class of cases in which the First Amendment's ban on prior judicial restraint may be overriden. Our cases have thus far indicated that such cases may arise only when the Nation "is at war" [Schenck], during which times "no one would question but that a government might prevent actual obstruction to its recruiting service or the publication of the sailing dates of transports or the number and location of troops." [Near.] Even if the present world situation were assumed to be tantamount to a time of war, or if the

---

1. There are numerous sets of this material in existence and they apparently are not under any controlled custody. Moreover, the President has sent a set to the Congress. We start then with a case where there already is rather wide distribution of the material that is destined for publicity, not secrecy. I have gone over the material listed in the in camera brief of the United States. It is all history, not future events. None of it is more recent than 1968. [Footnote by Justice Douglas.]

2. Freedman v. Maryland [sec. 3B below] and similar cases regarding temporary restraints of allegedly obscene materials are not in point. For those cases rest upon the proposition that "obscenity is not protected by the freedoms of speech and press." [Roth]. Here there is no question but that the material sought to be suppressed is within the protection of the First Amendment; the only question is whether, notwithstanding that fact, its publication may be enjoined for a time because of the presence of an overwhelming national interest. Similarly, copyright cases have no pertinence here: the Government is not asserting an interest in the particular form of words chosen in the documents, but is seeking to suppress the ideas expressed therein. And the copyright laws, of course, protect only the form of expression and not the ideas expressed. [Footnote by Justice Brennan.]

power of presently available armaments would justify even in peacetime the suppression of information that would set in motion a nuclear holocaust, in neither of these actions has the Government presented or even alleged that publication of items from or based upon the material at issue would cause the happening of an event of that nature. "The chief purpose of [the First Amendment's] guarantee [is] to prevent previous restraints upon publication." [Near.] Thus, only governmental allegation and proof that publication must inevitably, directly and immediately cause the occurrence of an event kindred to imperiling the safety of a transport already at sea can support even the issuance of an interim restraining order. . . .

Mr. Justice STEWART, with whom Mr. Justice WHITE joins, concurring.

In the governmental structure created by our Constitution, the Executive is endowed with enormous power in the two related areas of national defense and international relations. . . . In the absence of the governmental checks and balances present in other areas of our national life, the only effective restraint upon executive policy and power in the areas of national defense and international affairs may lie in an enlightened citizenry—in an informed and critical public opinion which alone can here protect the values of democratic government. For this reason, it is perhaps here that a press that is alert, aware, and free most vitally serves the basic purpose of the First Amendment. For without an informed and free press there cannot be an enlightened people.

Yet it is elementary that the successful conduct of international diplomacy and the maintenance of an effective national defense require both confidentiality and secrecy. Other nations can hardly deal with this Nation in an atmosphere of mutual trust unless they can be assured that their confidences will be kept. And within our own executive departments, the development of considered and intelligent international policies would be impossible if those charged with their formulation could not communicate with each other freely, frankly, and in confidence. In the area of basic national defense the frequent need for absolute secrecy is, of course, self-evident.

I think there can be but one answer to this dilemma, if dilemma it be. The responsibility must be where the power is. If the Constitution gives the Executive a large degree of unshared power in the conduct of foreign affairs and the maintenance of our national defense, then under the Constitution the Executive must have the largely unshared duty to determine and preserve the degree of internal security necessary to exercise that power successfully. [I should suppose] that the hallmark of a truly effective internal security system would be the maximum possible disclosure, recognizing that secrecy can best be preserved only when credibility is truly maintained. But be that as it may, it is clear to me that it is the constitutional duty of the Executive— as a matter of sovereign prerogative and not as a matter of law as the courts know law—through the promulgation and enforcement of executive regulations, to protect the confidentiality necessary to carry out its responsibilities in the fields of international relations and national defense.

This is not to say that Congress and the courts have no role to play. Undoubtedly Congress has the power to enact specific and appropriate criminal laws to protect government property and preserve government secrets. [I]f

a criminal prosecution is instituted, it will be the responsibility of the courts to decide the applicability of the criminal law under which the charge is brought. . . . But in the cases before us we are asked neither to construe specific regulations nor to apply specific laws. We are asked, instead, to perform a function that the Constitution gave to the Executive, not the Judiciary. We are asked, quite simply, to prevent the publication by two newspapers of material that the Executive Branch insists should not, in the national interest, be published. I am convinced that the Executive is correct with respect to some of the documents involved. But I cannot say that disclosure of any of them will surely result in direct, immediate, and irreparable damage to our Nation or its people. That being so, there can under the First Amendment be but one judicial resolution of the issues before us. I join the judgments of the Court.

Mr. Justice WHITE, with whom Mr. Justice STEWART joins, concurring.

I concur in today's judgments, but only because of the concededly extraordinary protection against prior restraints enjoyed by the press under our constitutional system. I do not say that in no circumstances would the First Amendment permit an injunction against publishing information about government plans or operations.[1] Nor, after examining the materials the Government characterizes as the most sensitive and destructive, can I deny that revelation of these documents will do substantial damage to public interests. Indeed, I am confident that their disclosure will have that result. But I nevertheless agree that the United States has not satisfied the very heavy burden which it must meet to warrant an injunction against publication in these cases, at least in the absence of express and appropriately limited congressional authorization for prior restraints in circumstances such as these.

The Government's position is simply stated: The responsibility of the Executive for the conduct of the foreign affairs and for the security of the Nation is so basic that the President is entitled to an injunction against publication of a newspaper story whenever he can convince a court that the information to be revealed threatens "grave and irreparable" injury to the public interest;[2] and the injunction should issue whether or not the material to be published is classified, whether or not publication would be lawful under relevant criminal statutes enacted by Congress and regardless of the circumstances by which the newspaper came into possession of the information.

---

1. The Congress has authorized a strain of prior restraints against private parties in certain instances. . . . However, those enjoined under the statutes relating to the National Labor Relations Board and the Federal Trade Commission are private parties, not the press; and when the press is enjoined under the copyright laws the complainant is a private copyright holder enforcing a private right. These situations are quite distinct from the Government's request for an injunction against publishing information about the affairs of government, a request admittedly not based on any statute. [Footnote by Justice White.]

2. The "grave and irreparable danger" standard is that asserted by the Government in this Court. In remanding to Judge Gurfein for further hearings in the Times litigation, five members of the Court of Appeals for the Second Circuit directed him to determine whether disclosure of certain items specified with particularity by the Government would "pose such grave and immediate danger to the security of the United States as to warrant their publication being enjoined." [Footnote by Justice White.]

At least in the absence of legislation by Congress, based on its own investigations and findings, I am quite unable to agree that the inherent powers of the Executive and the courts reach so far as to authorize remedies having such sweeping potential for inhibiting publications by the press. . . . To sustain the Government in these cases would start the courts down a long and hazardous road that I am not willing to travel, at least without congressional guidance and direction.

It is not easy to reject the proposition urged by the United States and to deny relief on its good-faith claims in these cases that publication will work serious damage to the country. But that discomfiture is considerably dispelled by the infrequency of prior-restraint cases. Normally, publication will occur and the damage be done before the Government has either opportunity or grounds for suppression. So here, publication has already begun and a substantial part of the threatened damage has already occurred. . . .

What is more, terminating the ban on publication of the relatively few sensitive documents the Government now seeks to suppress does not mean that the law either requires or invites newspapers or others to publish them or that they will be immune from criminal action if they do. Prior restraints require an unusually heavy justification under the First Amendment; but failure by the Government to justify prior restraints does not measure its constitutional entitlement to a conviction for criminal publication. That the Government mistakenly chose to proceed by injunction does not mean that it could not successfully proceed in another way. [Justice White discussed a number of "potentially relevant" criminal provisions.]

It is thus clear that Congress has addressed itself to the problems of protecting the security of the country and the national defense from unauthorized disclosure of potentially damaging information. Cf. [Youngstown Sheet & Tube Co. v. Sawyer, chap. 7 above.] It has not, however, authorized the injunctive remedy against threatened publication. It has apparently been satisfied to rely on criminal sanctions and their deterrent effect on the responsible as well as the irresponsible press. I am not, of course, saying that either of these newspapers has yet committed a crime or that either would commit a crime if they published all the material now in their possession. That matter must await resolution in the context of a criminal proceeding if one is instituted by the United States. . . . *

---

* On July 1, 1971—the day after the decision in New York Times' Co. v. United States—Attorney General Mitchell commented that the Justice Department "will prosecute all those who have violated federal criminal laws in connection with this matter" and added: "A review of the Court's opinions indicates that there is nothing in them to affect the situation." Daniel Ellsberg and Anthony Russo were subsequently indicted by a grand jury in Los Angeles under provisions of federal espionage, theft and conspiracy laws. Another federal grand jury, in Boston, reportedly investigated the involvement of newspapers and reporters. On May 11, 1973, District Judge Byrne dismissed the Ellsberg-Russo indictment and granted a mistrial because the "totality of the circumstances" of improper government conduct "offends 'a sense of justice.'" [He cited, inter alia, Rochin v. California.] The Judge found that the prosecution had been "incurably infected" by a sequence of "bizarre events" involving several governmental agencies—including undisclosed wiretapping, a break-in at the office of Ellsberg's psychiatrist, and possible other activities by a special White House investigative unit. [Note also the materials on the impeachment of President Nixon, chap. 7 above.]

Mr. Justice MARSHALL, concurring.

.   .   .   I believe the ultimate issue in this case [is] whether this Court or the Congress has the power to make law.

.   .   .   [I]n some situations it may be that under whatever inherent powers the [Executive may have], there is a basis for the invocation of the equity jurisdiction of this Court as an aid to prevent the publication of material damaging to "national security," however that term may be defined. It would, however, be utterly inconsistent with the concept of separation of powers for this Court to use its power of contempt to prevent behavior that Congress has specifically declined to prohibit.   There would be a similar damage to the basic concept of these co-equal branches of Government if when the [executive] has adequate authority granted by Congress to protect "national security" it can choose instead to invoke the contempt power of a court to enjoin the threatened conduct.   The Constitution provides that Congress shall make laws, the President execute laws, and courts interpret laws. [Youngstown case, chap. 7.]   [C]onvenience and political considerations of the moment do not justify a basic departure from the principles of our system of government.   In these cases we are not faced with a situation where Congress has failed to provide the Executive with broad power to protect the Nation from disclosure of damaging state secrets.   [See 18 U.S.C. Chap. 37, Espionage and Censorship.]   .   .   .

Even if it is determined that the Government could not in good faith bring criminal prosecutions against the New York Times and the Washington Post, it is clear that Congress has specifically rejected passing legislation that would have clearly given the President the power he seeks here and made the current activity of the newspapers unlawful.   When Congress specifically declines to make conduct unlawful it is not for this Court to redecide those issues—to overrule Congress.   See [Youngstown case].   On at least two occasions Congress has refused to enact legislation that would have made the conduct engaged in here unlawful and given the President the power that he seeks in this case.   [The first was the 1917 episode noted by Justice Douglas.]   In 1957 the United States Commission on Government Security .   .   .   proposed that "Congress enact legislation making it a crime for any person willfully to disclose without proper authorization, for any purpose whatever, information classified 'secret' or 'top secret,' knowing, or having reasonable grounds to believe, such information to have been so classified."   After substantial floor discussion on the proposal, it was rejected.   If the proposal [had] been enacted, the publication of the docu-

The Boston grand jury investigation gave rise to a 5 to 4 decision turning primarily on the scope of the Speech or Debate Clause, Art. I, § 6, in Gravel v. United States, 408 U.S. 606 (1972) (chap. 7 above).   While the New York Times case was pending in the Supreme Court in June 1971, Senator Gravel convened a midnight meeting of a Senate Subcommittee and placed the full Pentagon Papers in the public record.   Later, there were reports that the Senator had arranged for private publication of the Papers by Beacon Press.   The Boston grand jury called an assistant to the Senator.   The Court held that the Senator could claim the protection of the Clause to bar questioning of his assistant, but that the immunity was limited to legislative conduct and did not include inquiry into such matters as sources of information or arrangements for private publication.   Justice White's majority opinion stated that the Clause "does not privilege either Senator or aide to violate an otherwise valid criminal law in preparing for or implementing legislative acts."

ments involved here would certainly have been a crime. Congress refused, however, to make it a crime. The Government is here asking this Court to remake that decision. This Court has no such power.

Either the Government has the power under statutory grant to use traditional criminal law to protect the country or, if there is no basis for arguing that Congress has made the activity a crime, it is plain that Congress has specifically refused to grant the authority the Government seeks from this Court. In either case this Court does not have authority to grant the requested relief. It is not for this Court to fling itself into every breach perceived by some Government official . . . .

Mr. Chief Justice BURGER, dissenting.

[There is] little variation among the members of the Court in terms of resistance to prior restraints against publication. [In this case], the imperative of a free and unfettered press comes into collision with another imperative, the effective functioning of a complex modern government and specifically the effective exercise of certain constitutional powers of the Executive. Only those who view the First Amendment as an absolute in all circumstances—a view I respect, but reject—can find such a case as this to be simple or easy.

These cases are not simple for another and more immediate reason. We do not know the facts of the cases. . . . Why are we in this posture, in which only those judges to whom the First Amendment is absolute and permits of no restraint in any circumstances or for any reason, are really in a position to act? I suggest we are in this posture because these cases have been conducted in unseemly haste. . . . Here, moreover, the frenetic haste is due in large part to the manner in which the Times proceeded from the date it obtained the purloined documents. It seems reasonably clear now that the haste precluded reasonable and deliberate judicial treatment of these cases and was not warranted. . . .

The newspapers make a derivative claim under the First Amendment; they denominate this right as the public right to know; by implication, the Times asserts a sole trusteeship of that right by virtue of its journalist "scoop." The right is asserted as an absolute. Of course, the First Amendment right itself is not an absolute, as Justice Holmes so long ago pointed out in his aphorism concerning the right to shout fire in a crowded theater if there was no fire. There are other exceptions, some of which Chief Justice Hughes mentioned by way of example in Near v. Minnesota. There are no doubt other exceptions no one has had occasion to describe or discuss. Conceivably such exceptions may be lurking in these cases and would have been flushed had they been properly considered in the trial courts, free from unwarranted deadlines and frenetic pressures. . . .

It is not disputed that the Times has had unauthorized possession of the documents for three to four months, during which it has had its expert analysts studying them, presumably digesting them and preparing the material for publication. During all of this time, the Times, presumably in its capacity as trustee of the public's "right to know," has held up publication for purposes it considered proper and thus public knowledge was delayed. [W]hy should the United States Government, from whom this information

was illegally acquired by someone, along with all the counsel, trial judges, and appellate judges be placed under needless pressure?   . . .

Would it have been unreasonable, since the newspaper could anticipate the Government's objections to release of secret material, to give the Government an opportunity to review the entire collection and determine whether agreement could be reached on publication?   [T]he course followed by the Times, whether so calculated or not, removed any possibility of orderly litigation of the issues.   If the action of the judges up to now has been correct, that result is sheer happenstance.[1]   . . .

The consequence of all this melancholy series of events is that we literally do not know what we are acting on.   .   .   .   I agree generally with [Justices Harlan and Blackmun] but I am not prepared to reach the merits.[2] I would affirm the Court of Appeals for the Second Circuit and allow the District Court to complete the trial aborted by our grant of certiorari meanwhile preserving the status quo in the Post case.   .   .   .   We all crave speedier judicial processes but when judges are pressured as in these cases the result is a parody of the judicial function.

Mr. Justice HARLAN, with whom The Chief Justice [BURGER] and Mr. Justice BLACKMUN join, dissenting.

.   .   .   With all respect, I consider that the Court has been almost irresponsibly feverish in dealing with these cases.

Both the Court of Appeals for the Second Circuit and the Court of Appeals for the District of Columbia Circuit rendered judgment on June 23. The New York Times' petition for certiorari, its motion for accelerated consideration thereof, and its application for interim relief were filed in this Court on June 24, at about 11 a. m.   The application of the United States for interim relief in the Post case was also filed here on June 24, at about 7:15 p. m.   This Court's order setting a hearing before us on June 26 at 11 a. m., a course which I joined only to avoid the possibility of even more peremptory action by the Court, was issued less than 24 hours before.   The record in the Post case was filed with the Clerk shortly before 1 p. m. on June 25; the record in the Times case did not arrive until 7 or 8 o'clock that same night.   The briefs of the parties were received less than two hours before argument on June 26.

This frenzied train of events took place in the name of the presumption against prior restraints created by the First Amendment.   Due regard for the extraordinarily important and difficult questions involved in these liti-

1. Interestingly the Times explained its refusal to allow the Government to examine its own purloined documents by saying in substance this might compromise *its* sources and informants! The Times thus asserts a right to guard the secrecy of its sources while denying that the Government of the United States has that power. [Footnote by Chief Justice Burger.]

2. With respect to the question of inherent power of the Executive to classify papers, records and documents as secret, or otherwise unavailable for public exposure, and to secure aid of the courts for enforcement, there may be an analogy with respect to this Court. No statute gives this Court express power to establish and enforce the utmost security measures for the secrecy of our deliberations and records. Yet I have little doubt as to the inherent power of the Court to protect the confidentiality of its internal operations by whatever judicial measures may be required. [Footnote by Chief Justice Burger. Cf. chap. 7.]

gations should have led the Court to shun such a precipitate timetable. In order to decide the merits of these cases properly, some or all of the following questions should have been faced:

1.　Whether the Attorney General is authorized to bring these suits in the name of the United States. Compare [In re Debs, 158 U.S. 564 (1895)] with [the Youngstown case]. This question involves as well the construction and validity of a singularly opaque statute—the Espionage Act, 18 U.S.C. § 793(e).

2.　Whether the First Amendment permits the federal courts to enjoin publication of stories which would present a serious threat to national security. See [Near] (dictum).

3.　Whether the threat to publish highly secret documents is of itself a sufficient implication of national security to justify an injunction on the theory that regardless of the contents of the documents harm enough results simply from the demonstration of such a breach of secrecy.

4.　Whether the unauthorized disclosure of any of these particular documents would seriously impair the national security.

5.　What weight should be given to the opinion of high officers in the Executive Branch of the Government with respect to questions 3 and 4.

6.　Whether the newspapers are entitled to retain and use the documents notwithstanding the seemingly uncontested facts that the documents, or the originals of which they are duplicates, were purloined from the Government's possession and that the newspapers received them with knowledge that they had been feloniously acquired. Cf. Liberty Lobby, Inc. v. Pearson, 390 F.2d 489 (CADC 1968).

7.　Whether the threatened harm to the national security or the Government's possessory interest in the documents justifies the issuance of an injunction against publication in light of—

　　a.　The strong First Amendment policy against prior restraints on publication;

　　b.　The doctrine against enjoining conduct in violation of criminal statutes; and

　　c.　The extent to which the materials at issue have apparently already been otherwise disseminated.

These are difficult questions of fact, of law, and of judgment; the potential consequences of erroneous decision are enormous. The time which has been available to us, to the lower courts, and to the parties has been wholly inadequate for giving these cases the kind of consideration they deserve. It is a reflection on the stability of the judicial process that these great issues—as important as any that have arisen during my time on the Court—should have been decided under the pressures engendered by the torrent of publicity that has attended these litigations from their inception.

Forced as I am to reach the merits of these cases, I dissent from the opinion and judgments of the Court. Within the severe limitations imposed by the time constraints under which I have been required to operate, I can only state my reasons in telescoped form, even though in different circumstances I would have felt constrained to deal with the cases in the fuller sweep indicated above.

.   .   .   It is plain to me that the scope of the judicial function in passing upon the activities of the Executive Branch of the Government in the field of foreign affairs is very narrowly restricted. This view is, I think, dictated by the concept of separation of powers upon which our constitutional system rests. [The Executive possesses] constitutional primacy in the field of foreign affairs.   .   .   .   The power to evaluate the "pernicious influence" of premature disclosure is not, however, lodged in the Executive alone. I agree that, in performance of its duty to protect the values of the First Amendment against political pressures, the judiciary must review the initial Executive determination to the point of satisfying itself that the subject matter of the dispute does lie within the proper compass of the President's foreign relations power. Constitutional considerations forbid "a complete abandonment of judicial control." Moreover, the judiciary may properly insist that the determination that disclosure of the subject matter would irreparably impair the national security be made by the head of the Executive Department concerned—here the Secretary of State or the Secretary of Defense—after actual personal consideration by that officer.   .   .   .   But in my judgment the judiciary may not properly go beyond these two inquiries and redetermine for itself the probable impact of disclosure on the national security. "[T]he very nature of executive decisions as to foreign policy is political, not judicial. Such decisions are wholly confided by our Constitution to the political departments. [See chaps. 7 and 15.] They are delicate, complex, and involve large elements of prophecy. They are and should be undertaken only by those directly responsible to the people whose welfare they advance or imperil. They are decisions of a kind for which the Judiciary has neither aptitude, facilities nor responsibility and which has long been held to belong in the domain of political power not subject to judicial intrusion or inquiry." Chicago & Southern Air Lines v. Waterman Steamship Corp., 333 U.S. 103, 111 (1948) (Jackson, J.).

Even if there is some room for the judiciary to override the executive determination, it is plain that the scope of review must be exceedingly narrow. I can see no indication in the opinions of [the lower courts] in the Post litigation that the conclusions of the Executive were given even the deference owing to an administrative agency, much less that owing to a co-equal branch of the Government operating within the field of its constitutional prerogative.   .   .   .

Pending further hearings in each case conducted under the appropriate ground rules, I would continue the restraints on publication. I cannot believe that the doctrine prohibiting prior restraints reaches to the point of preventing courts from maintaining the status quo long enough to act responsibly in matters of such national importance as those involved here.

Mr. Justice BLACKMUN.

I join Mr. Justice Harlan in his dissent.   .   .   .

The First Amendment, after all, is only one part of an entire Constitution. [See, e. g., the Executive's power in Art. II.] First Amendment absolutism has never commanded a majority of this Court. [E. g., Near; Schenck.] What is needed here is a weighing, upon properly developed standards, of the broad right of the press to print and of the very narrow right of the Government to prevent. Such standards are not yet de-

veloped. The parties here are in disagreement as to what those standards should be. But even the newspapers concede that there are situations where restraint is in order and is constitutional. . . . I therefore would remand these cases to be developed expeditiously, of course, but on a schedule permitting [orderly presentation of evidence].

[I] add one final comment. . . . Judge Wilkey, dissenting in the District of Columbia case, [concluded] that there were a number of examples of documents that, [if] published, "could clearly result in great harm to the nation," and he defined "harm" to mean "the death of soldiers, the destruction of alliances, the greatly increased difficulty of negotiation with our enemies, the inability of our diplomats to negotiate . . . ." [I] fear that Judge Wilkey's statements have possible foundation. I therefore share his concern. I hope that damage has not already been done. If, however, damage has been done, and if, with the Court's action today, these newspapers proceed to publish the critical documents and there results therefrom "the death of soldiers, the destruction of alliances, the greatly increased difficulty of negotiation with our enemies, the inability of our diplomats to negotiate," to which list I might add the factors of prolongation of the war and of further delay in the freeing of United States prisoners, then the Nation's people will know where the responsibility for these sad consequences rests.*

B.　MOTION PICTURE CENSORSHIP AND OTHER PROCE-DURAL PROBLEMS IN OBSCENITY CONTROL

MOTION PICTURE CENSORSHIP

1.　*The Burstyn case and vague standards in licensing laws.*　The Court's first major encounter with the problem of film censorship did not come in the obscenity context, but rather in a challenge to a law permitting the banning of motion pictures on the ground that they were "sacrilegious." JOSEPH BURSTYN, INC. v. WILSON, 343 U.S. 495 (1952). But the pattern set by Burstyn—finding the film protected by the First Amendment; accepting prior restraints on films; but scrutinizing the statutory standards for adequate specificity—governed the Court's handling of some censorship cases for many years. In Burstyn, New York had rescinded a license to show "The Miracle" after widespread protests about the film. Justice Clark's majority opinion noted that this was the first case to raise the question "whether motion pictures are within the ambit of protection" within the First Amendment. He had no hesitation in finding films a form of "speech": "The importance of motion pictures as an organ of public opinion is not lessened by the fact that they are designed to entertain as well as to inform." Nor did "operation for profit" make the First Amendment inapplicable. And as to the alleged "greater capacity for evil, particularly among the youth of the community," of films, Justice Clark commented: "If there be capacity for evil it may be relevant in determining the permis-

---

* Note also the materials on governmental secrecy (and executive privilege) in chap. 5, on separation of powers, above.

sible scope of community control, but it does not authorize substantially un-bridled censorship such as we have here."

But First Amendment protection did not mean "absolute freedom to exhibit every motion picture of every kind at all times and all places." Nor were the rules applicable to other methods of expression necessarily deter-minative here. But censorship on the basis of the "sacrilegious" character of the film was impermissible. The state had defined that term as mean-ing "that no religion [shall] be treated with contempt, mockery, scorn and ridicule." Under that "broad and all-inclusive definition," Justice Clark stated, "the censor is set adrift upon a boundless sea amid a myriad of con-flicting currents of religious views, with no charts but those provided by the most vocal and powerful orthodoxies. New York cannot vest such un-limited restraining control over motion pictures in a censor." Moreover, such a standard might raise "substantial questions" under the religion clauses of the First Amendment. (See chap. 14 below.) And as to freedom of speech and the press, "the state has no legitimate interest in protecting any or all religions from views distasteful to them which is sufficient to justify prior restraints upon the expression of those views." [1]

2. *Vague standards and film censorship in the wake of Burstyn.* After Burstyn, the Court relied on it in a number of per curiam decisions finding a variety of censorship standards unconstitutionally vague. See, e. g., Gelling v. Texas, 343 U.S. 960 (1952) ("prejudicial to the best interests of the people of said City"), and Commercial Pictures Corp. v. Regents, 346 U.S. 587 (1954) ("immoral" and "tend to corrupt morals"). But the term "ob-scene" was not unduly vague: recall that in Roth the Court found "ob-scenity" a sufficiently specific standard for criminal legislation.[2] After Roth, film censorship cases involving obscenity produced a variety of re-actions from the Justices—most commonly, as with books, a tendency to limit adjudication to the particular publication involved. One exhibitor, how-ever, chose to launch a broad-side attack on film censorship, challenging not the specificity of the standards or the adequacy of the procedures, but rather the basic requirement of pre-exhibition submission of films to a licensing authority. That attack proved unsuccessful, as the next note indicates.

3. *The Times Film case and the validity of prior restraints.* TIMES FILM CORP. v. CHICAGO, 365 U.S. 43 (1961), involved an ordinance

---

1. Justice Reed concurred in the judg-ment. Justice Frankfurter, joined by Justice Jackson, also submitted a separate opinion concurring in the judgment.

For the first case bringing live stage performances within the ambit of the First Amendment, see Southeastern Promotions, Ltd. v. Conrad, 420 U.S. —— (1975) (chap. 12, sec. 2, above).

2. For a rare example of a void-for-vagueness ruling in a context closer to obscenity, see Interstate Circuit, Inc. v. Dallas, 390 U.S. 676 (1968), invali-dating an ordinance authorizing a board to classify films as to whether they were "suitable for young per-sons." Among the suitability stand-ards were references to films portray-ing "sexual promiscuity [in] such a manner as to be, in the judgment of the Board, likely to incite or encourage delinquency or sexual promiscuity on the part of young persons or to appeal to their prurient interest." Even though the ordinance was designed to protect children—an objective given special weight by the Court, see Gins-berg v. New York, 390 U.S. 629 (1968) —that did not save it from the vague-ness attack: "The vices—the lack of guidance to those who seek to adjust their conduct and to those who seek to administer the law, as well as the possible practical curtailing of the ef-fectiveness of judicial review—are the same."

which required submission of all motion pictures for examination by city officials prior to public exhibition. Petitioner refused to submit his film for examination and sued for issuance of the permit, claiming that the submission requirement was invalid on its face as a prior restraint. Justice Clark's majority opinion pointed out that the validity of the Chicago standards for denying a permit and the content of the film were not before the Court. He stated the sole "justiciable issue" to be "whether the ambit of constitutional protection includes complete and absolute freedom to exhibit, at least once, any and every kind of motion picture." The Court refused to hold "that the public exhibition of motion pictures must be allowed under any circumstances," with the state limited to criminal penalties after exhibition. Justice Clark stated that there was no "absolute privilege against prior restraint" and that the submission requirement was accordingly not "void on its face." [3]

A few years after Times Film, however, a more focused challenge to film censorship provisions proved fruitful and produced the most important of the motion picture censorship cases. In Freedman v. Maryland, which follows, the Court announced "procedural safeguards designed to obviate the dangers of a censorship system"—safeguards which have proved important in the protection of First Amendment interests in contexts far beyond the obscenity area.

FREEDMAN v. MARYLAND

380 U.S. 51, 85 S.Ct. 734, 13 L.Ed.2d 649 (1965).

Appeal from the Court of Appeals of Maryland.

Mr. Justice BRENNAN delivered the opinion of the Court.

Appellant sought to challenge the constitutionality of the Maryland motion picture censorship statute and exhibited the film "Revenge at Daybreak" at his Baltimore theatre without first submitting the picture to the State Board of Censors as required by § 2 of the statute. The State concedes that the picture does not violate the statutory standards and would have received a license if properly submitted, but the appellant was convicted of a § 2 violation despite his contention that the statute in its entirety unconstitutionally impaired freedom of expression. . . .

[Appellant] presents a question quite distinct from that passed on in Times Film; accepting the rule in Times Film, he argues that § 2 constitutes an invalid prior restraint because, in the context of the remainder of the statute, it presents a danger of unduly suppressing protected expression. He focuses particularly on the procedure for an initial decision by the censorship board, which, without any judicial participation, effectively bars exhibition of any disapproved film, unless and until the exhibitor undertakes a time-consuming appeal to the Maryland courts and succeeds in having the Board's decision reversed. Under the statute, the exhibitor is required to submit the film to the Board for examination, but no time limit is imposed for completion of Board action, § 17. If the film is disapproved, or any elimination

---

3. Chief Justice Warren and Justices Black, Douglas and Brennan dissented. Chief Justice Warren's dissent insisted that the majority had stated the question too broadly and claimed the issue was whether Chicago could "require all motion picture exhibitors to submit all films" for prior licensing.

ordered, [appellant may obtain "prompt" reexamination by the Board, with right to appeal to the state courts.]

Thus there is no statutory provision for judicial participation in the procedure which bars a film, nor even assurance of prompt judicial review. Risk of delay is built into the Maryland procedure, as is borne out by experience; in the only reported case indicating the length of time required to complete an appeal, the initial judicial determination has taken four months and final vindication of the film on appellate review, six months. . . .

[I]t is as true [of motion pictures] as of other forms of expression that "[a]ny system of prior restraints of expression comes to this Court bearing a heavy presumption against its constitutional validity." . . . The administration of a censorship system for motion pictures presents peculiar dangers to constitutionally protected speech. Unlike a prosecution for obscenity, a censorship proceeding puts the initial burden on the exhibitor or distributor. Because the censor's business is to censor, there inheres the danger that he may well be less responsive than a court—part of an independent branch of government—to the constitutionally protected interests in free expression. And if it is made unduly onerous, by reason of delay or otherwise, to seek judicial review, the censor's determination may in practice be final.

Applying the settled rule of our cases, we hold that a noncriminal process which requires the prior submission of a film to a censor avoids constitutional infirmity only if it takes place under procedural safeguards designed to obviate the dangers of a censorship system. First, the burden of proving that the film is unprotected expression must rest on the censor. As we said in Speiser v. Randall, 357 U.S. 513, 526, "Where the transcendent value of speech is involved, due process certainly requires [that] the State bear the burden of persuasion to show that the appellants engaged in criminal speech." Second, while the State may require advance submission of all films, in order to proceed effectively to bar all showings of unprotected films, the requirement cannot be administered in a manner which would lend an effect of finality to the censor's determination whether a film constitutes protected expression. The teaching of our cases is that, because only a judicial determination in an adversary proceeding ensures the necessary sensitivity to freedom of expression, only a procedure requiring a judicial determination suffices to impose a valid final restraint. To this end, the exhibitor must be assured, by statute or authoritative judicial construction, that the censor will, within a specified brief period, either issue a license or go to court to restrain showing the film. Any restraint imposed in advance of a final judicial determination on the merits must similarly be limited to preservation of the status quo for the shortest fixed period compatible with sound judicial resolution. Moreover, we are well aware that, even after expiration of a temporary restraint, an administrative refusal to license, signifying the censor's view that the film is unprotected, may have a discouraging effect on the exhibitor. Therefore, the procedure must also assure a prompt final judicial decision, to minimize the deterrent effect of an interim and possibly erroneous denial of a license.

Without these safeguards, it may prove too burdensome to seek review of the censor's determination. Particularly in the case of motion pictures, it may take very little to deter exhibition in a given locality. The exhibitor's

stake in any one picture may be insufficient to warrant a protracted and onerous course of litigation. The distributor, on the other hand, may be equally unwilling to accept the burdens and delays of litigation in a particular area when, without such difficulties, he can freely exhibit his film in most of the rest of the country; for we are told that only four States and a handful of municipalities have active censorship laws.

It is readily apparent that the Maryland procedural scheme does not satisfy these criteria. First, once the censor disapproves the film, the exhibitor must assume the burden of instituting judicial proceedings and of persuading the courts that the film is protected expression. Second, once the Board has acted against a film, exhibition is prohibited pending judicial review, however protracted. Under the statute, appellant could have been convicted if he had shown the film after unsuccessfully seeking a license, even though no court had ever ruled on the obscenity of the film. Third, it is abundantly clear that the Maryland statute provides no assurance of prompt judicial determination. We hold, therefore, that appellant's conviction must be reversed. The Maryland scheme fails to provide adequate safeguards against undue inhibition of protected expression, and this renders the § 2 requirement of prior submission of films to the Board an invalid previous restraint. . . .

Reversed.*

Mr. Justice DOUGLAS, whom Mr. Justice BLACK joins, concurring.

On several occasions I have indicated my view that movies are entitled to the same degree and kind of protection under the First Amendment as other forms of expression. . . . I do not believe any form of censorship—no matter how speedy or prolonged it may be—is permissible. As I see it, a pictorial presentation occupies as preferred a position as any other form of expression. . . . I would put an end to all forms and types

---

* In several recent cases, the Freedman criteria have had decisive impact on the consideration of federal obscenity legislation. In Blount v. Rizzi, 400 U.S. 410 (1971), a unanimous Court held unconstitutional the "administrative censorship scheme" created by 39 U.S.C. §§ 4006 and 4007 because it lacked the procedural safeguards essential under Freedman. The Sections authorized the Postmaster General, following administrative hearings, to halt use of the mails and of postal money orders for commerce in allegedly obscene materials and permitted him to obtain a court order detaining the defendant's incoming mail pending the outcome of administrative proceedings. Justice Brennan's opinion restated the Freedman requirements, found lacking here, as follows: "[T]o avoid constitutional infirmity a scheme of administrative censorship must: place the burdens of initiating judicial review and of proving that the material is unprotected expression on the censor; require 'prompt judicial review' [to] prevent the administrative decision of the censor from achieving an effect of finality; and limit to preservation of the status quo for the shortest, fixed period compatible with sound judicial resolution, any restraint imposed in advance of the final judicial determination." [Recall the imposition of the Freedman procedural requirements on a municipal theater's refusal of permission to present the rock musical "Hair," in Southeastern Promotions, Ltd. v. Conrad, 420 U.S. —— (1975) (chap. 12, sec. 2, above).]

Compare with Blount the Court's handling of a Freedman-based challenge to the federal prohibition on the importation of obscene materials, in United States v. 37 Photographs, 402 U.S. 363 (1971) (sec. 2 above). Justice White's majority opinion overcame the lack of explicit procedural safeguards by construing the statute to require "explicit time limits of the sort" demanded by Freedman and Blount. Recall also the impact of Freedman outside the obscenity area, see chap. 12 above.

of censorship and give full literal meaning to the command of the First Amendment.

CAN PRIOR RESTRAINT BE MORE PROTECTIVE THAN SUBSEQUENT PUNISHMENT?—THE KINGSLEY BOOKS CASE

Most of the preceding materials testify to the Court's special hostility to prior restraints. But may not some "prior" screening mechanisms be ultimately more protective of free speech interests than subsequent criminal sanctions? Recall Justice Douglas' dissent in Miller v. California in 1973 (sec. 2 above), including his approving reference to a "prior" declaratory judgment procedure recommended by the Commission on Obscenity and Pornography. Note, moreover, the Court's approval of a limited injunctive remedy in the face of a "prior restraint" attack in KINGSLEY BOOKS, INC. v. BROWN, 354 U.S. 436 (1957).

The Kingsley Books case sustained a New York procedure which authorized an injunction to prevent the sale and distribution of obscene printed matter and an order for its seizure and destruction upon entry of final judgment. Under the statute, § 22–a, an ex parte injunction could be obtained before trial, but the person sought to be enjoined was entitled to trial within one day after joinder of issue, and to a decision within two days of the end of the trial. Kingsley, the publisher of booklets entitled "Nights of Horror," consented to an injunction pendente lite. After trial, the booklets were found obscene, their further distribution was enjoined, and they were ordered destroyed. Kingsley did not challenge the finding of obscenity, but objected to the injunction as a prior restraint. In sustaining the procedure, Justice Frankfurter's opinion stated:

"The phrase 'prior restraint' is not a self-wielding sword. Nor can it serve as a talismanic test. The duty of closer analysis and critical judgment in applying the thought behind the phrase has thus been authoritatively put by one who brings weighty learning to his support of constitutionally protected liberties: 'What is needed,' writes Professor Paul A. Freund, 'is a pragmatic assessment of its operation in the particular circumstances. The generalization that prior restraint is particularly obnoxious in civil liberties cases must yield to more particularistic analysis.' The Supreme Court and Civil Liberties, 4 Vand.L.Rev. 533, 539.

"Wherein does § 22–a differ in its effective operation from the type of statute upheld in Alberts [the California companion case to Roth]? One would be bold to assert that the in terrorem effect of [criminal sanctions] less restrains booksellers in the period before the law strikes than does § 22–a. Instead of requiring the bookseller to dread that the offer for sale of a book may, without prior warning, subject him to a criminal prosecution, [t]he civil procedure assures him that such consequences cannot follow unless he ignores a court order specifically directed to him for a prompt and carefully circumscribed determination of the issue of obscenity. Until then, he may keep the book for sale and sell it on his own judgment rather than steer 'nervously among the treacherous shoals.' . . .

"Criminal enforcement and the proceeding under § 22–a interfere with a book's solicitation of the public precisely at the same stage. In each situation the law moves after publication; the book need not in either case have yet passed into the hands of the public. . . . In each case the bookseller is put on notice by the complaint that sale of the publication charged with obscenity in the period before trial may subject him to penal consequences. In the one case he may suffer fine and imprisonment for violation of the criminal statute, in the other, for disobedience of the temporary injunction. The bookseller may of course stand his ground and confidently believe that in any judicial proceeding the book could not be condemned as obscene, but both modes of procedure provide an effective deterrent against distribution prior to adjudication of the book's content—the threat of subsequent penalization. . . . In each case a judge is the conventional trier of fact; in each, a jury may as a matter of discretion be summoned."

Justice Frankfurter argued that the impact of the New York scheme was a good deal less harsh than the California criminal provision sustained in Alberts: "Not only was [Alberts] completely separated from society for two months but he was also seriously restrained from trafficking in all obscene publications for a considerable time. [The Kingsley appellants], on the other hand, were enjoined from displaying for sale or distributing only the particular booklets theretofore published and adjudged to be obscene. Thus, the restraint upon appellants as merchants in obscenity was narrower than that imposed on Alberts." He added: "It only remains to say that the difference between [Near v. Minnesota] and this case is glaring in fact. The two cases are not less glaringly different when judged by the appropriate criteria of constitutional law. . . . Unlike Near, § 22–a is concerned solely with obscenity and [it] studiously withholds restraint upon matters not already published and not yet found to be offensive." *

OTHER PROCEDURAL SAFEGUARDS IN THE CONTROL OF OBSCENITY

1. *Scienter and Smith v. California.* In SMITH v. CALIFORNIA, 361 U.S. 147 (1959), a bookseller had been convicted of having in his shop an obscene book. The Court reversed because the statutory definition of the crime "included no element of scienter—knowledge by appellant of the contents of the book." In prosecutions in the First Amendment area, Justice Brennan insisted, states could not impose such "strict or absolute criminal responsibility." Though states could impose strict liability in some situations, eliminating the scienter requirement here "may tend to work a substantial restriction on freedom of speech." Justice Brennan relied on analogous situations in which procedural rules ordinarily valid were barred because of the threat to First Amendment rights. For example, states may generally regulate "the allocation of the burden of proof in their courts, and it is a com-

---

* Chief Justice Warren and Justices Black, Douglas and Brennan dissented. Justices Douglas and Black emphasized that the injunction pendente lite provision was "prior restraint and censorship at its worst" and concluded that "the procedure for restraining by equity decree the distribution of all the condemned literature does violence to the First Amendment."

mon procedural device to impose on a taxpayer the burden of proving his entitlement to exemptions from taxation, but where we conceived that this device was being applied in a manner tending to cause even a self-imposed restriction of free expression, we struck down its application. Speiser v. Randall, 357 U.S. 513 [1958]. See Near v. Minnesota."

Here, the "ordinance's strict liability feature would tend seriously" to "restrict the dissemination of books which are not obscene," by "penalizing booksellers, even though they had not the slightest notice of the character of the books they sold." The strict liability feature "tends to impose a severe limitation on the public's access to constitutionally protected matter. For if the bookseller is criminally liable without knowledge of the contents, [he] will tend to restrict the books he sells to those he has inspected." Such a scheme might leave bookshops "depleted indeed": "The bookseller's limitation in the amount of reading material with which he could familiarize himself, and his timidity in the face of his absolute criminal liability, thus would tend to restrict the public's access to forms of the printed word which the State could not constitutionally suppress directly. The bookseller's self-censorship, compelled by the State, would be a censorship affecting the whole public, hardly less virulent for being privately administered. Through it, the distribution of all books, both obscene and not obscene, would be impeded." [1]

2. *Searches and seizures of obscene materials.* In MARCUS v. SEARCH WARRANT, 367 U.S. 717 (1961), the Court, in an opinion by Justice Brennan, found that Missouri's use of "the search and seizure power to suppress obscene publications involved abuses inimical to protected expression" because the "procedures as applied in this case lacked the safeguards which due process demands to assure nonobscene material the constitutional protection to which it is entitled." Acting ex parte, a state judge issued warrants authorizing the seizure of any obscene publications at six places of business. The police seized "approximately 11,000 copies of 280 publications." About two weeks later, a hearing was held at which the owners of the publications appeared. About seven weeks thereafter, the judge ruled that 100 of the publications were obscene and should be held for ultimate burning. The Court emphasized that the warrants were issued "on the strength of the conclusory assertions of a single police officer"; that the officers executing the warrants "made ad hoc decisions on the spot"; and that the officers' task "was simply an impossible one to perform with any realistic expectation that the obscene might be accurately separated from the constitutionally protected." It concluded that "discretion to seize allegedly obscene materials cannot be confided to law enforcement officials without greater safeguards than were here operative."

Three years later, the Court relied heavily on Marcus in A Quantity of Books v. Kansas, 378 U.S. 205 (1964), invalidating another state scheme for the seizure of obscene books "before an adversary determination of their obscenity." Even though the Kansas scheme did not give the police discretion as to the books to be seized and the warrant specifically designated the titles, Justice Brennan's plurality opinion nevertheless held the procedures "consti-

---

1. There were several concurring opinions, and an opinion by Justice Harlan concurring in part and dissenting in part.

tutionally insufficient because they did not adequately safeguard against the suppression of nonobscene books." Justice Harlan's dissent, joined by Justice Clark, thought the case governed by Kingsley Books rather than by Marcus. Note also the discussion of the requirements of the Marcus line of cases in the majority opinions by Chief Justice Burger in Roaden v. Kentucky, 413 U.S. 496 (1973), and Heller v. New York, 413 U.S. 483 (1973). In Roaden, the Court condemned the warrantless seizure of an allegedly obscene film, drawing on both Fourth and First Amendment values. The Chief Justice noted: "The seizure is unreasonable, not simply because it would have been easy to secure a warrant, but rather because prior restraint of the right of expression, whether by books or films, calls for a higher hurdle in the evaluation of reasonableness." [2]

3. *Informal censorship through blacklists.* In BANTAM BOOKS, INC. v. SULLIVAN, 372 U.S. 58 (1963), the Court condemned certain activities of the Rhode Island Commission to Encourage Morality in Youth as unconstitutional "informal censorship." The Commission compiled lists of "objectionable" publications, distributed them to the police, and sought "co-operation" by publishers in order to "eliminate the necessity of our recommending prosecution to the Attorney General's department." Justice Brennan's opinion for the Court characterized that scheme as a "system of prior administrative restraints, since the Commission is not a judicial body and its decisions to list the particular publications as objectionable do not follow judicial determinations that such publications may lawfully be banned." He commented: "It would be naive to credit the State's assertion that these blacklists are in the nature of mere legal advice, when they plainly serve as instruments of regulation independent of the laws against obscenity." In effect, the Commission's activities made resort to the criminal process largely unnecessary, and that was "the vice of the system": "In thus obviating the need to employ criminal sanctions, the State has at the same time eliminated the safeguards of the criminal process." Justice Harlan's dissent objected to the Court's "opaque pronouncements which leave the Commission in the dark as to the permissible constitutional scope of its future activities."

SECTION 4. THE FIRST AMENDMENT IN SOME SPECIAL ENVIRONMENTS

Introduction. In the cases in this section, the state interests put forth as justifications for restraints on expression are often different from those typically encountered in the earlier cases. Moreover, the manner of ex-

2. In Heller, however, a seizure pursuant to an ex parte warrant was sustained. The Court rejected a claim that an adversary hearing prior to the issuance of the warrant was required. The Chief Justice emphasized that this was a seizure of a single copy of the film to preserve it as evidence and that there was no claim that the seizure prevented continuing exhibition of other copies. He contrasted that with "seizing films to destroy them or to block their distribution for exhibition." Justices Douglas, Brennan, Stewart and Marshall dissented in both Roaden and Heller on the basis of their dissents in the major 1973 obscenity decisions, sec. 2 above.

pression of alleged First Amendment rights differs from those most common in the earlier materials. The modes of expression range from labor picketing to prisoners' communications and the conduct of litigation. The state interests range from the special concerns for protecting the administration of justice and assuring prison discipline to the regulation of the legal profession and the setting of economic policy in labor-management relations.

To what extent do and should these variants on the more typical themes affect the applicable First Amendment analyses? Is it any more helpful here to distinguish between "pure speech" and "speech-plus" or "conduct" in the mode of expression? Is it useful to distinguish between "direct" and "indirect" restrictions on expression? Is there less basis for imposing a heavy burden of justification on government when it seeks to restrain expression in the labor or legal profession or academic or prison contexts? Even if the state justification burden remains a heavy one, is the governmental claim entitled to special weight, is it "compelling," when the state relies on an especially "traditional" concern? Are the basic judicial techniques developed and elaborated in the materials in chap. 12 adequate for the solution of problems in these new contexts? Do the materials in this section reveal new judicial tools useful for solution of some of the earlier problems? These are the pervasive questions raised by the following sampling of First Amendment problems in special contexts.

A. INTERFERENCE WITH THE ADMINISTRATION OF JUSTICE

WOOD v. GEORGIA

370 U.S. 375, 82 S.Ct. 1364, 8 L.Ed.2d 569 (1962).

Certiorari to the Court of Appeals of Georgia.

Mr. Chief Justice WARREN delivered the opinion of the Court.

We granted certiorari to consider the scope of the constitutional protection to be enjoyed by persons when the publication of their thoughts and opinions is alleged to be in conflict with the fair administration of justice in state courts. The petitioner, an elected sheriff in Bibb County, Georgia, contends that the Georgia courts, in holding him in contempt of court for expressing his personal ideas on a matter that was presently before the grand jury for its consideration, have abridged his liberty of free speech .   .   ..

On June 6, 1960, a judge of the Bibb Superior Court issued a charge to a regularly impaneled grand jury, giving it special instructions to conduct an investigation into a political situation which had allegedly arisen in the county. The jury was advised that there appeared to be "an inane and inexplicable pattern of Negro bloc voting" in Bibb County, and that "rumors and accusations" had been made which indicated candidates for public office had paid large sums of money in an effort to gain favor and to obtain the Negro vote. The charge explained that certain Negro leaders, after having met and endorsed a candidate, had switched their support to an opposing can-

didate who put up a large sum of money. [The jury was to inquire] into the charges of election law violations. The instructions were given in the midst of a local political campaign and the judge, in order to publicize the investigation, requested reporters for all local news media to be present in the courtroom when the charge was delivered.

The following day, . . . the petitioner issued to the local press a written statement in which he criticized the judges' action and in which he urged the citizenry to take notice when their highest judicial officers threatened political intimidation and persecution of voters in the county under the guise of law enforcement. [This news release] stated:

"Whatever the Judges' intention, the action [ordering the grand jury] to investigate 'negro block voting' will be considered one of the most deplorable examples of race agitation to come out of Middle Georgia in recent years.

"At a time when all thinking people want to preserve the good will and cooperation between the races in Bibb County, this action appears either as a crude attempt at judicial intimidation of negro voters and leaders, or, at best, as agitation for a 'negro vote' issue in local politics.

"Negro people will find little difference in principle between attempted intimidation of their people by judicial summons and inquiry and attempted intimidation by physical demonstration such as used by the K.K.K. . . . It is hoped that the present Grand Jury will not let its high office be a party to any political attempt to intimidate the negro people in this community.

"It seems incredible that all three of our Superior Court Judges, who themselves hold high political office, are so politically nieve [naive] as to actually believe that the negro voters in Bibb County sell their votes in any fashion, either to candidates for office or to some negro leaders.

"If anyone in the community [should] be free of racial prejudice, it should be our Judges. It is shocking to find a Judge charging a Grand Jury in the style and language of a race baiting candidate for political office. . . . However politically popular the judges' action may be at this time, they are employing a practice far more dangerous to free elections than anything they want investigated.

"James I. Wood."

The following day, the petitioner delivered to the bailiff of the court, stationed at the entrance to the grand jury room, "An Open Letter to the Bibb County Grand Jury," which was made available to the grand jury at petitioner's request. This letter, implying that the court's charge was false, asserted that in the petitioner's opinion, the Bibb County Democratic Executive Committee was the organization responsible for corruption in the purchasing of votes, and that the grand jury would be well-advised also to investigate that organization.

A month later, on July 7, 1960, the petitioner was cited in two counts of contempt based on the above statements. The citation charged that the language used by the petitioner was designed and calculated to be contemptuous of the court, to ridicule the investigation ordered by the charge, and "to

hamper, hinder, interfere with and obstruct" the grand jury in its investigation. . . . An amendment to the citation alleged that the statements "in and of [themselves] created [a] clear, present and imminent danger to the investigation being conducted [and] to the proper administration of justice in Bibb Superior Court."

The next day the petitioner issued a further press release in which he repeated substantially the charges he had made in the release on June 7, and in which he asserted that his defense to the contempt citation would be that he had spoken the truth. The contempt citation was thereupon amended by including a third count based on this latter statement. . . . No witnesses were presented at the hearing [before the trial judge] and no evidence was introduced to show that the publications resulted in any actual interference or obstruction of the court or the work of the grand jury. The gravamen of [the] case against the petitioner, was that the mere publishing of the news release and defense statement constituted a contempt of court, and in and of itself was a clear and present danger to the administration of justice.

The trial court, without making any findings and without giving any reasons, adjudged petitioner guilty on all counts and imposed concurrent sentences of 20 days and separate fines of $200 on each. On writ of error to the Court of Appeals the convictions on counts one and three were affirmed and the conviction on count two, based on the open letter to the grand jury, was reversed. . . .

We start with the premise that the right of courts to conduct their business in an untrammeled way lies at the foundation of our system of government and that courts necessarily must possess the means of punishing for contempt when conduct tends directly to prevent the discharge of their functions. While courts have continuously had the authority and power to maintain order in their courtrooms and to assure litigants a fair trial, the exercise of that bare contempt power is not what is questioned in this case. Here it is asserted that the exercise of the contempt power, to commit a person to jail for an utterance out of the presence of the court, has abridged the accused's liberty of free expression. In this situation the burden upon this Court is to define the limitations upon the contempt power according to the terms of the Federal Constitution.

In Bridges v. California, 314 U.S. 252 [1941], this Court for the first time had occasion to review a State's exercise of the contempt power utilized to punish the publisher of an out-of-court statement [and] held that out-of-court publications were to be governed by the clear and present danger standard, described as "a working principle that the substantive evil must be extremely serious and the degree of imminence extremely high before utterances can be punished." [1] Subsequently, in Pennekamp v. Florida, 328 U.S.

---

1. In the Bridges case, a newspaper had editorially asserted that the trial judge should make an example of several union men then awaiting pronouncement of sentence. Moreover, Harry Bridges, a union official, caused the publication of a telegram to the Secretary of Labor stating that the CIO "does not intend to allow state courts to override the majority vote of members in choosing its officers and representatives and to override the National Labor Relations Board." Contempt convictions resting on these publications were reversed by the Court in a 5 to 4 decision. Justice Black's

331, [1946], [the] Court reaffirmed its belief that the "essential right of the courts to be free of intimidation and coercion [is] consonant with a recognition that freedom of the press must be allowed in the broadest scope compatible with the supremacy of order." [2]   The Court's last occasion to consider the application of the clear and present danger principle to a case of the type under review was in Craig v. Harney, 331 U.S. 367 [1947]. There the Court held that to warrant a sanction "[t]he fires which [the expression] kindles must constitute an imminent, not merely a likely, threat to the administration of justice. The danger must not be remote or even probable; it must immediately imperil." [3]

It is with these principles in mind that we consider the case before us. . . .   Despite its conclusion that the petitioner's conduct created [a clear and present danger to the proceedings of the court and grand jury], the Court of Appeals did not cite or discuss the Bridges, Pennekamp or Harney cases, nor did it display an awareness of the standards enunciated in those cases to support a finding of clear and present danger. . . .   The court did not indicate in any manner *how* the publications interfered with the grand jury's investigation, or with the administration of justice. [N]o showing was made that the members of the grand jury, upon reading the petitioner's comments in the newspapers, felt unable or unwilling to complete their assigned task because petitioner "interfered" with its completion. . . .

Thus we have simply been told, as a matter of law without factual support, that if a State is unable to punish persons for expressing their views on matters of great public importance when those matters are being consid-

majority opinion found punishment permissible only when there is a clear and present danger that justice will be obstructed. Justice Frankfurter's dissent stated: "A trial is not 'a free trade in ideas,' nor is the best test of truth in a courtroom 'the power of the thought to get itself accepted in the competition of the market.' "

2. In the Pennekamp case, a newspaper engaged in an anti-vice crusade published editorials and a cartoon implying that the judges were using legal technicalities to hinder the prosecution of several rape and gambling cases. The newspaper and its associate editor, Pennekamp, were held in contempt and fined by the Florida court. The Supreme Court, as in Bridges, applied the clear and present danger test and reversed.

3. Craig v. Harney reversed a contempt conviction for critical news reports and editorials about a judge's handling of a private law suit. Justice Douglas' majority opinion found the "rather sketchy and one-sided" news reports no "imminent or serious threat to a judge of reasonable fortitude."

And editorial comments calling the judge's behavior, e. g., "high handed" and "a travesty on justice" were also found unpunishable: "[T]he law of contempt is not made for the protection of judges who may be sensitive to the winds of public opinion. Judges are supposed to be men of fortitude, able to thrive in a hearty climate." One of the dissenters, Justice Jackson, noted that the judge was one who had been elected for a short term and insisted that the fact that the judge did not yield to the attack "does not prove that the attack was not an effective interference with the administration of justice." He added: "From our sheltered position, fortified by life tenure and other defenses to judicial independence, it is easy to say that this local judge ought to have shown more fortitude in the face of criticism. . . . Of course, the blasts of these little papers in this small community do not jolt us, but I am not so confident that we would be indifferent if a news monopoly in our entire jurisdiction should perpetrate this kind of an attack on us." Note the efforts to distinguish Bridges, Pennekamp, and Craig in Justice Harlan's dissent, below.

ered in an investigation by the grand jury, a clear and present danger to the administration of justice will be created. We find no such danger in the record before us. The type of "danger" evidenced by the record is precisely one of the types of activity envisioned by the Founders in presenting the First Amendment for ratification. . . . Men are entitled to speak as they please on matters vital to them; errors in judgment or unsubstantiated opinions may be exposed, of course, but not through punishment for contempt for the expression. . . . Hence, in the absence of some other showing of a substantive evil actually designed to impede the course of justice in justification of the exercise of the contempt power to silence the petitioner, his utterances are entitled to be protected.

[We find the state court's "clear and present danger" conclusion] unpersuasive. First, it is important to emphasize that this case does not represent a situation where an individual is on trial; there was no "judicial proceeding pending" in the sense that prejudice might result to one litigant or the other by ill-considered misconduct aimed at influencing the outcome of a trial or a grand jury proceeding. Moreover, we need not pause here to consider the variant factors that would be present in a case involving a petit jury. Neither Bridges, Pennekamp nor Harney involved a trial by jury. [O]f course the limitations on free speech assume a different proportion when expression is directed toward a trial as compared to a grand jury investigation. Rather, the grand jury here was conducting a general investigation . . . . .

Historically, this body has been regarded as a primary security to the innocent against hasty, malicious and oppressive persecution . . . . .. Particularly in matters of local political corruption and investigations is it important that freedom of communication be kept open and that the real issues not become obscured to the grand jury. It cannot effectively operate in a vacuum. . . . The necessity to society of an independent and informed grand jury becomes readily apparent in the context of the present case. For here a panel of judges, themselves elected officers and charged under state law with the responsibility of instructing a grand jury to investigate political corruption, have exercised the contempt power to hold in contempt another elected representative of the people for publishing views honestly held and contrary to those contained in the charge. And, an effort by the petitioner to prove the truth of his allegations was rejected, the court holding irrelevant the truth or falsity of the facts and opinions expressed in the publications. If the petitioner could be silenced in this manner, the problem to the people in the State of Georgia and indeed in all the States becomes evident.

The administration of the law is not the problem of the judge or prosecuting attorney alone, but necessitates the active cooperation of an enlightened public. Nothing is to be gained by an attitude on the part of the citizenry of civic irresponsibility and apathy in voicing their sentiments on community problems. The petitioner's attack on the charge to the grand jury would have been likely to have an impeding influence on the outcome of the investigation only if the charge was so manifestly unjust that it could not stand inspection. In this sense discussion serves as a corrective force to

political, economic and other influences which are inevitably present in matters of grave importance. . . .

Moreover, it is difficult to imagine how the voting problem may be alleviated by an abridgment of talk and comment regarding its solution. . . When the grand jury is performing its investigatory function into a general problem area, without specific regard to indicting a particular individual, society's interest is best served by a thorough and extensive investigation, and a greater degree of disinterestedness and impartiality is assured by allowing free expression of contrary opinion. Consistent suppression of discussion likely to affect pending investigations would mean that some continuing public grievances could never be discussed at all, or at least not at the moment when public discussion is most needed. The conviction here produces its "restrictive results at the precise time when public interest in the matters discussed would naturally be at its height," and "[n]o suggestion can be found in the Constitution that the freedom there guaranteed for speech and the press bears an inverse ratio to the timeliness and importance of the ideas seeking expression." [Bridges.] Thus, in the absence of any showing of an actual interference with the undertakings of the grand jury, this record lacks persuasion in illustrating the serious degree of harm to the administration of law necessary to justify exercise of the contempt power. . . .

Finally, we are told by the respondent that, because the petitioner is sheriff of Bibb County and thereby owes a special duty and responsibility to the court and its judges, his right to freedom of expression must be more severely curtailed than that of an average citizen. Under the circumstances of this case, this argument must be rejected. . . .

Our examination of the content of petitioner's statements and the circumstances under which they were published leads us to conclude that they did not present a danger to the administration of justice that should vitiate his freedom to express his opinions in the manner chosen.

Reversed.

Mr. Justice FRANKFURTER and Mr. Justice WHITE took no part in the decision of this case.

Mr. Justice HARLAN, whom Mr. Justice CLARK joins, dissenting. . .

. . . [T]his Court has repeatedly held that a criminal conviction based on the verdict of jurors influenced by extrajudicial statements of the case cannot stand consistently with due process of law. But invalidation of a proceeding so infected is not the only remedy available to combat interference with judicial processes; so to hold would confer a right to frustrate those processes with impunity. And so it is that this Court has uniformly upheld the power of courts to protect themselves by citations for contempt from improper influence upon proceedings before them. . . . The right of free speech, strong though it be, is not absolute; when the right to speak conflicts with the right to an impartial judicial proceeding, an accommodation must be made to preserve the essence of both. . . .

The Court professes to recognize these principles. It holds nevertheless that the contempt sanction cannot be applied in this case, arguing both that "the limitations on free speech assume a different proportion when expression is directed toward a trial as compared to a grand jury investiga-

tion" and that the findings of clear and present danger are unsupported by the record. I cannot agree with either proposition. . . .

[Accepting Bridges for present purposes, the clear and present danger] test is amply met here. Petitioner, a public official connected with the court, accused, from his office in the courthouse, the Superior Court judges of fomenting race hatred; of misusing the criminal law to persecute and to intimidate political and racial minorities; of political naiveté, racial prejudice, and hypocrisy. He compared the calling of the grand jury to the activities of the Ku Klux Klan. He made an undisguised effort to influence the outcome of the investigation by declaring that only the politically naive could believe Bibb County Negroes might be guilty of selling votes. It was stipulated that both of petitioner's formal statements were read by the grand jurors during the course of their investigation.

The Court considers this evidence insufficient because there was no showing of "an actual interference with the undertakings of the jury" . . . . Surely the Court cannot mean that attempts to influence judicial proceedings are punishable only if they are successful. Speech creating sufficient danger of an evil which the State may prevent may certainly be punished regardless of whether that evil materializes. See [Feiner v. New York]. Indeed, the test suggested by the Court is even more stringent than that which it applies in determining whether a conviction should be set aside because of prejudicial "outside" statements reaching a trial jury. In such cases, although the question is whether the rights of the accused have been infringed rather than whether there has been a clear and present danger of their infringement, it is necessary only to show a substantial likelihood that the verdict was affected, and it is no answer that each juror expresses his belief that he remains able to be fair and impartial. The test for punishing attempts to influence a grand or petit jury should be less rather than more stringent.

I cannot agree with the Court that petitioner's statements would have been likely to affect the outcome of the investigation "only if the charge was so manifestly unjust that it could not stand inspection." This is to discredit the persuasiveness of argument, which the Court purports to value so highly. Any expression of opinion on the merits of a pending judicial proceeding is likely to have an impact on deliberations. In this instance that likelihood was increased by two factors which were not present in Bridges, Pennekamp, or Craig, in which the Court held the evidence insufficient to show clear and present danger. None of those cases involved statements by officers of the court; and all concerned statements whose alleged interference was with the deliberations of a judge rather than a jury. . . . Petitioner [was] a law-enforcement officer. [H]is words assumed an overtone of official quality and authority that lent them weight beyond those of an ordinary citizen.

Of equal if not greater importance is the fact that petitioner's statements were calculated to influence, not a judge chosen because of his independence, integrity, and courage and trained by experience and the discipline of law to deal only with evidence properly before him, but a grand jury of laymen chosen to serve for a limited term from the general population of Bibb County. It cannot be assumed with grand jurors, as it has been with judges [Craig v. Harney], that they are all "men of fortitude, able to

thrive in a hardy climate." What may not seriously endanger the independent deliberations of a judge may well jeopardize those of a grand or petit jury.

Moreover, the statements themselves were of such a nature as to distinguish this case from Bridges, Pennekamp, and Craig. It cannot be said here, as it was in Bridges, that petitioner's charges . . . "did no more than threaten future adverse criticism which was reasonably to be expected anyway," or that "if there was electricity in the atmosphere, it was generated by the facts; the charge added by the . . . [petitioner's statement] can be dismissed as negligible." The sheriff's remarks were not, as in Pennekamp, general criticisms with respect to rulings already made, but specific attacks directed toward the disposition of the pending investigation. They cannot be characterized, as in Craig, as merely unfair reports of the activities of others; unlike the editorial in that case, petitioner's criticisms went squarely to the merits of the investigation and impugned as well the motives and honesty of those conducting it. . . .

Finally, petitioner's case is not saved by the fact that both he and the judges he attacked are elected officials, or by the fact that the statement concerned an issue of some political moment. There was ample opportunity to bring the judges' performance to the voters after the investigation was closed. "Political interest" cannot be used as an excuse for affecting the result of a judicial inquiry. . . .*

CONTEMPT BY PUBLICATION, CLEAR AND PRESENT DANGER, AND THE PROBLEM OF IDENTIFYING AND EVALUATING THE "SUBSTANTIVE EVILS"

1. *Clear and present danger of what?* In no other area has the Court more consistently invoked clear and present danger language than in the Bridges-Pennekamp-Craig-Wood line of cases. Recall the questions raised about the test earlier (chap. 12, sec. 1). How useful is emphasis on immediacy of harm in this area? To what extent is the problem that of identifying the "substantive evil," and of assessing its gravity? Is the "evil" that of *any* impact on judicial processes? Is it serious impact, distortion, in-

---

* Compare Mills v. Alabama, 384 U.S. 214 (1966), involving a state restriction on publication threatening to interfere with elections rather than judicial proceedings. The Court held that the free press guarantee prohibited a state from making it a crime "for the editor of a daily newspaper to write and publish an editorial *on election day* urging people to vote a certain way on issues submitted to them." Justice Black's majority opinion stated that the case did not involve the State's power "to regulate conduct in and around the polls in order to maintain peace, order and decorum there" and rejected the highest state court's justification of the statute as one protecting "the public from confusive last-minute charges and countercharges and the distribution of propaganda in an effort to influence voters on an election day; when as a practical matter, because of lack of time, such matters cannot be answered or their truth determined until after the election is over."

terruption? Is it the *appearance* of impact? Which of these are serious or grave enough to justify restricting speech?

2. *The contrast with Cox II.* Compare the contempt cases from Bridges to Wood with Cox v. Louisiana (Cox II, chap. 12, sec. 2), the 1965 decision upholding a ban on courthouse picketing. In Cox II, the Court distinguished these contempt cases: "We are not concerned here with such a pure form of expression as a newspaper comment. [W]e deal in this case not with free speech alone but with expression mixed with particular conduct." Is that persuasive? Moreover, the Cox Court insisted that "even assuming" clear and present danger were the applicable test, "mere publication" in these contempt cases was "quite another thing" from demonstrators barred "by a legislative determination based on experience that such conduct inherently threatens the judicial process." Is that persuasive? Recall, moreover, the Cox Court's statements about "evils" the legislature might legitimately consider: the danger that "some judges [will] be consciously or unconsciously influenced by demonstrations"; the risk of "the judicial process [being] misjudged in the minds of the public" even if the judge was "completely uninfluenced"—the danger, in other words, of "the possibility of a conclusion by the public [that] the judge's action was in part a product of intimidation." Were there such risks in the contempt cases? Were those dangers "clear and present" there? Was the Cox Court persuasive in distinguishing the contempt situations?

B. LABOR PICKETING

TEAMSTERS UNION v. VOGT, INC.

354 U.S. 284, 77 S.Ct. 1166, 1 L.Ed.2d 1347 (1957).

Certiorari to the Supreme Court of Wisconsin.

Mr. Justice FRANKFURTER delivered the opinion of the Court.

This is one more in the long series of cases in which this Court has been required to consider the limits imposed by the Fourteenth Amendment on the power of a State to enjoin picketing. . . . Respondent owns and operates a gravel pit in Oconomowoc, Wisconsin, where it employs 15 to 20 men. Petitioner unions sought unsuccessfully to induce some of respondent's employees to join the unions and commenced to picket the entrance to respondent's place of business with signs reading, "The men on this job are not 100% affiliated with the A.F.L." "In consequence," drivers of several trucking companies refused to deliver and haul goods to and from respondent's plant, causing substantial damage to respondent. Respondent thereupon sought an injunction to restrain the picketing.

The trial court [held that by virtue of a state law] prohibiting picketing in the absence of a "labor dispute," the petitioners must be enjoined from maintaining any pickets near respondent's place of business, from displaying at any place near respondent's place of business signs indicating that there was a labor dispute between respondent and its employees or between respondent and any of the petitioners, and from inducing others to decline

to transport goods to and from respondent's business establishment. [The Wisconsin Supreme Court affirmed on a different ground: drawing its own inferences from the undisputed facts, it found that the picketing had been for the "unlawful purpose" of "coercing the employer" to induce its employees to join the Teamsters Union. Such an employer interference was an "unfair labor practice" under state law.]

[The Court's decisions on 14th Amendment limits on state uses of injunctions in labor controversies] disclose an evolving, not a static, course of decision. [In 1940], in passing on a restrictive instead of a permissive state statute, the Court made sweeping pronouncements about the right to picket in holding unconstitutional a statute that had been applied to ban all picketing, with "no exceptions based upon either the number of persons engaged in the proscribed activity, the peaceful character of their demeanor, the nature of their dispute with an employer, or the restrained character and the accurateness of the terminology used in notifying the public of the facts of the dispute." Thornhill v. Alabama, 310 U.S. 88, 99. As the statute dealt at large with all picketing, so the Court broadly assimilated peaceful picketing in general to freedom of speech, and as such protected against abridgment by the Fourteenth Amendment.

These principles were applied by the Court in A. F. of L. v. Swing, 312 U.S. 321 [1941], to hold unconstitutional an injunction against peaceful picketing, based on a State's common-law policy against picketing when there was no immediate dispute between employer and employee. On the same day, however, the Court upheld a generalized injunction against picketing where there had been violence because "it could justifiably be concluded that the momentum of fear generated by past violence would survive even though future picketing might be wholly peaceful." Milk Wagon Drivers Union v. Meadowmoor Dairies, 312 U.S. 287, 294 [1941].

Soon, however, the Court came to realize that the broad pronouncements, but not the specific holding, of Thornhill had to yield "to the impact of facts unforeseen," or at least not sufficiently appreciated. . . . Cases reached the Court in which a State had designed a remedy to meet a specific situation or to accomplish a particular social policy. These cases made manifest that picketing, even though "peaceful," involved more than just communication of ideas and could not be immune from all state regulation. "Picketing by an organized group is more than free speech, since it involves patrol of a particular locality and since the very presence of a picket line may induce action of one kind or another, quite irrespective of the nature of the ideas which are being disseminated." Bakery Drivers Local v. Wohl, 315 U.S. 769, 776 [1942] (concurring opinion) . . .. [T]he strong reliance on the particular facts in [these cases] demonstrated a growing awareness that these cases involved not so much questions of free speech as review of the balance struck by a State between picketing that involved more than "publicity" and competing interests of state policy. . . .

The implied reassessments of the broad language of the Thornhill case were finally generalized in a series of cases sustaining injunctions against peaceful picketing, even when arising in the course of a labor controversy, when such picketing was counter to valid state policy in a domain open to state regulation. The decisive reconsideration came in Giboney v. Empire

Storage & Ice Co., 336 U.S. 490 [1949]. A union, seeking to organize peddlers, picketed a wholesale dealer to induce it to refrain from selling to nonunion peddlers. The state courts, finding that such an agreement would constitute a conspiracy in restraint of trade in violation of the state antitrust laws, enjoined the picketing. This Court affirmed unanimously. "It is contended that the injunction against picketing adjacent to Empire's place of business is an unconstitutional abridgment of free speech because the picketers were attempting peacefully to publicize truthful facts about a labor dispute. . . . But the record here does not permit this publicizing to be treated in isolation. [For] the sole immediate object of the [picketing and other activities] was to compel Empire to agree to stop selling ice to nonunion peddlers. Thus all of appellants' activities . . . constituted a single and integrated course of conduct, which was in violation of Missouri's valid law. In this situation, the injunction did no more than enjoin an offense against Missouri law, a felony." The Court therefore concluded that it was "clear that appellants were doing more than exercising a right of free speech or press. . . . They were exercising their economic power together with that of their allies to compel Empire to abide by union rather than by state regulation of trade." *

The following Term, the Court decided a group of cases applying and elaborating on the theory of Giboney. In Hughes v. Superior Court, 339 U.S. 460 [1950], the Court held that the Fourteenth Amendment did not bar use of the injunction to prohibit picketing of a place of business solely to secure compliance with a demand that its employees be hired in percentage to the racial origin of its customers. "We cannot construe the Due Process Clause as precluding California from securing respect for its policy against involuntary employment on racial lines by prohibiting systematic picketing that would subvert such policy." [Cf. chap. 10.]

On the same day, the Court decided Teamsters Union v. Hanke, 339 U.S. 470 [1950], holding that a State was not restrained by the Fourteenth Amendment from enjoining picketing of a business, conducted by the owner himself without employees, in order to secure compliance with a demand to become a union shop. . . .

A third case, Building Service Employees v. Gazzam, 339 U.S. 532 [1950], was decided the same day. . . . The State, finding that the object of the picketing was in violation of its statutory policy against employer coercion of employees' choice of bargaining representative, enjoined

---

* The unanimous opinion in Giboney was written by Justice Black. In later cases, Justices Black and Douglas frequently cited Giboney to illustrate their views of regulations not barred by the First Amendment, in the context of their position that "speech" is absolutely protected. Recall, e. g., Justice Black's quotation from Giboney in his dissent in Street v. New York, the flag burning case in chap. 12, sec. 3. The Giboney statement he quoted was: "It rarely has been suggested that the constitutional freedom for speech and press extends its immunity to speech or writing used as an integral part of conduct in violation of a valid criminal statute." Recall also Justice Douglas' concurrence in Brandenburg v. Ohio, chap. 12, sec. 1, stating: "Picketing, as we have said on numerous occasions, is 'free speech plus.' That means it can be regulated when it comes to the 'plus' or 'action' side of the protest." He cited Giboney in that connection, and he added a reference to the false shouting of fire in a crowded theater, explaining that this was "a classic case where speech is brigaded with action." See also Justice Douglas' dissent in this case, below.

picketing for such purpose. This Court affirmed, [distinguishing Swing]. [The Court] struck down the State's restraint on picketing based solely on the absence of an employer-employee relationship. An adequate basis for the instant decree is the unlawful objective of the picketing, namely, coercion by the employer of the employees' selection of a bargaining representative. . . .

This series of cases, then, established a broad field in which a State, in enforcing some public policy, whether of its criminal or its civil law, and whether announced by its legislature or its courts, could constitutionally enjoin peaceful picketing aimed at preventing effectuation of that policy.

In the light of this background, the Maine Supreme Judicial Court in 1955 decided [Pappas v. Stacey]. From the statement, it appeared that three union employees went on strike and picketed a restaurant peacefully "for the sole purpose of seeking to organize other employees of the Plaintiff, ultimately to have the Plaintiff enter into collective bargaining and negotiations with the Union . . .." Maine had a statute providing that workers should have full liberty of self-organization, free from restraint by employers or other persons. The Maine Supreme Judicial Court [noting "the pressure upon the employer to interfere with the free choice of the employees"] enjoined the picketing, and an appeal was taken to this Court. The whole series of cases discussed above allowing, as they did, wide discretion to a State in the formulation of domestic policy, and not involving a curtailment of free speech in its obvious and accepted scope, led this Court, without the need of further argument, to grant appellee's motion to dismiss the appeal in that it no longer presented a substantial federal question. . . . The Stacey case is this case. . . . . As in Stacey, the highest state court drew the inference from the facts that the picketing was to coerce the employer to put pressure on his employees to join the union, in violation of the declared policy of the State. . . . The cases discussed above all hold that, consistent with the Fourteenth Amendment, a State may enjoin such conduct.

Of course, the mere fact that there is "picketing" does not automatically justify its restraint without an investigation into its conduct and purposes. State courts, no more than state legislatures, can enact blanket prohibitions against picketing. [Thornhill; Swing.] The series of cases following Thornhill and Swing demonstrate that the policy of Wisconsin enforced by the prohibition of this picketing is a valid one. In this case, the circumstances set forth in the opinion of the Wisconsin Supreme Court afford a rational basis for the inference it drew concerning the purpose of the picketing. . . .

Affirmed.

Mr. Justice WHITTAKER took no part in the consideration or decision of this case.

Mr. Justice DOUGLAS, with whom The Chief Justice [WARREN] and Mr. Justice BLACK concur, dissenting.

The Court has now come full circle. In [Thornhill] we struck down a state ban on picketing on the ground that "the dissemination of in-

formation concerning the facts of a labor dispute must be regarded as within that area of free discussion that is guaranteed by the Constitution." Less than one year later, we held that the First Amendment protected organizational picketing on a factual record which cannot be distinguished from the one now before us. [Swing.] Of course, we have always recognized that picketing has aspects which make it more than speech. . . . That difference underlies our decision in [Giboney v. Empire Storage & Ice Co.] There, picketing was an essential part of "a single and integrated course of conduct, which was in violation of Missouri's valid law." . . . We emphasized that "there was clear danger, imminent and immediate, that unless restrained, appellants would succeed in making [the state] policy a dead letter . . .." Speech there was enjoined because it was an inseparable part of conduct which the State constitutionally could and did regulate.

But where, as here, there is no rioting, no mass picketing, no violence, no disorder, no fisticuffs, no coercion—indeed nothing but speech—the principles announced in Thornhill and Swing should give the advocacy of one side of a dispute First Amendment protection.

The retreat began when, in [Hanke], four members of the Court announced that all picketing could be prohibited if a state court decided that that picketing violated the State's public policy. The retreat became a rout in [Plumbers Union v. Graham, 345 U.S. 192 (1953)]. It was only the "purpose" of the picketing which was relevant. The state court's characterization of the picketers' "purpose" had been made well-nigh conclusive. Considerations of the proximity of picketing to conduct which the State could control or prevent were abandoned and no longer was it necessary for the state court's decree to be narrowly drawn to proscribe a specific evil. . . .

Today, the Court signs the formal surrender. State courts and state legislatures cannot fashion blanket prohibitions on all picketing. But, for practical purposes, [they] are free to decide whether to permit or suppress any particular picket line for any reason other than a blanket policy against all picketing. I would adhere to the principle announced in Thornhill. I would adhere to the result reached in Swing. I would return to the test enunciated in Giboney—that this form of expression can be regulated or prohibited only to the extent that it forms an essential part of a course of conduct which the State can regulate or prohibit. . . .

LABOR PICKETING AND THE CONSTITUTION

The declining significance of the First Amendment in the labor picketing area, after the broad statements in Thornhill, is traced in Vogt. That decline was not only attributable to the judicial acceptance of limits on picketing; also important was the congressional occupation of the field and the growing displacement of state control of picketing because of preemption principles. See chap. 5, sec. 2A.

Nevertheless, the picketing cases remain an important source of First Amendment doctrine,† especially for the demonstration problems considered

---

† See note * to Vogt above, on the relevance of Giboney for those who, like Justices Black and Douglas, urge "absolute" protection of "speech" but find permissible the restricting of "speech plus" or "conduct."

in chap. 12, sec. 2. And the First Amendment continues to play some direct role in labor picketing as well. See, e. g., the material on Amalgamated Food Employees v. Logan Valley Plaza, 391 U.S. 308 (1968) (chap. 12, sec. 2), where the Court set aside, on the basis of the First Amendment, a state injunction resting simply on trespass grounds and banning all peaceful picketing.

C. THE FIRST AMENDMENT AND THE SCHOOL ENVIRONMENT

Introduction. What should be the proper accommodation of First Amendment values to school concerns? The basic modern case is Tinker v. Des Moines School District, 393 U.S. 503 (1969), the decision protecting the wearing of black armbands by school children as a symbolic protest. That case is printed in chap. 12, sec. 3, and should be reexamined at this point. In the majority opinion there, Justice Fortas stated that "First Amendment rights, applied in light of the special characteristics of the school environment, are available for teachers and students." He insisted that "the prohibition of expression of one particular opinion, at least without evidence that it is necessary to avoid material and substantial interference with schoolwork or discipline, is not constitutionally permissible." But he added that "conduct by the student, in class or out of it, which for any reason—whether it stems from time, place, or type of behavior—materially disrupts classwork or involves substantial disorder or invasion of the rights of others is, of course, not immunized by the constitutional guarantee of freedom of speech." In two 1972 decisions handed down on the same day, the Court elaborated on the Tinker approach and discussed at length the appropriate contours of the First Amendment in the academic environment. In Healy v. James, note 1 below, the Court struck down a state college's denial of official recognition to a local chapter of the Students for a Democratic Society (SDS). And in Grayned v. City of Rockford, note 2 below, the majority rejected an overbreadth attack on an ordinance prohibiting noise near school buildings.

1. *Healy v. James.* a. *The analysis.* In HEALY v. JAMES, 408 U.S. 169 (1972), President James of Central Connecticut State College refused to recognize the local SDS chapter as a campus organization after several hearings. The trial court sustained that refusal in part because the petitioners had failed to meet their burden of showing that they could function free from the National SDS and because the College's denial of recognition of a group found "likely to cause violent acts of disruption" did not violate associational rights. At the outset, Justice Powell's opinion for the Court commented that the precedents "leave no room for the view that, because of the acknowledged need for order, First Amendment protections should apply with less force on college campuses than in the community at large. Quite to the contrary, '[t]he vigilant protection of constitutional freedoms is nowhere more vital than in the community of American schools' [Shelton v. Tucker, sec. 5 below]."

Justice Powell found two "fundamental errors" in the District Court's approach: "discounting the existence of a cognizable First Amendment in-

terest and misplacing the burden of proof." He rejected the argument that the consequences of nonrecognition were too insignificant to constitute interference with associational rights. (Nonrecognition resulted in the denial of use of campus facilities for meetings and news announcements.)

The lower court had been wrong, moreover, in assuming that petitioners had the burden of showing entitlement to recognition: "once petitioners had filed an application in conformity with the requirements, the burden was upon the College administration to justify its decision of rejection. . . . While a college has a legitimate interest in preventing disruption on the campus, which under circumstances requiring the safeguarding of that interest may justify such [prior] restraint, a 'heavy burden' rests on the college to demonstrate the appropriateness of that action."

The Court found a remand of the case appropriate because the "ambiguous" record suggested "at least one potentially acceptable ground for a denial of recognition." And in order to provide guidance on remand, the Court canvassed all four grounds for the College President's decision, including the three inadequate ones. One of President James' reasons had been petitioners' affiliation with the National SDS. Justice Powell responded: "Not only did petitioners proclaim their complete independence from this organization, but they also indicated that they shared only some of the beliefs its leaders have expressed." Accordingly, the affiliation did not justify nonrecognition on this record. More generally, Justice Powell commented that the Court had "consistently disapproved" action based on "a citizen's association with an unpopular organization." [He cited Robel and Scales, in chap. 12; and Keyishian and Elfbrandt, sec. 5 below.] And under the cases, the Government "has the burden of establishing a knowing affiliation with an organization possessing unlawful aims and goals, and a specific intent to further those illegal aims."

President James, in a second, related ground, had emphasized the "philosophy of violence and disruption" of the National SDS and had stated his unwillingness to "sanction an organization that openly advocates the destruction of the very ideals and freedoms upon which the academic life is founded." Justice Powell responded: "The mere disagreement of the President with the group's philosophy affords no reason to deny it recognition. As repugnant as these views may have been, [the] mere expression of them would not justify the denial of First Amendment rights." [He cited Justice Black's dissent in Communist Party v. SACB, chap. 12, sec. 1.]

As a third ground for his decision, President James had relied on the threat that the local chapter would be a "disruptive influence" at the college. Justice Powell stated: "If this reason, directed at the organization's activities rather than its philosophy, were factually supported by the record, this Court's prior decisions would provide a basis for considering the propriety of nonrecognition. The critical line heretofore drawn for determining the permissibility of regulation is [the Brandenburg v. Ohio line]. In the context of the 'special characteristics of the school environment,' the power of the government to prohibit 'lawless action' is not limited to acts of a criminal nature. Also prohibitable are actions which 'materially and substantially disrupt the work and discipline of the school.' [Tinker.] Associational activities need not be tolerated where they infringe reasonable campus rules, interrupt

classes or substantially interfere with the opportunity of other students to obtain an education." But here, the record offered "no substantial basis" for the conclusion that the local chapter "posed a substantial threat of material disruption." On this record, there were only general fears—the sort of "undifferentiated fear or apprehension of disturbance [which] is not enough to overcome the right to freedom of expression." [Tinker.]

Justice Powell turned finally to President James' fourth ground—the one possible ground for nonrecognition which prompted the remand. Petitioners' statements raised "considerable question whether they intend to abide" by campus rules. The campus regulation, "carefully differentiating between advocacy and action, is a reasonable one." Yet petitioners had been equivocal about how they might respond to "issues of violence" and whether they could ever "envision . . . interrupting a class": "These remarks might well have been read as announcing petitioners' unwillingness to be bound by reasonable school rules governing conduct."

Justice Powell explained: "Petitioners may, if they so choose, preach the propriety of amending or even doing away with any or all campus regulations. They may not, however, undertake to flout these rules." He added: "Just as in the community at large, reasonable regulations with respect to the time, the place, and the manner in which student groups conduct their speech-related activities must be respected. A college administration may impose a requirement, such as may have been imposed in this case, that a group seeking official recognition affirm in advance its willingness to adhere to reasonable campus law. [T]his is a minimal requirement, in the interest of the entire academic community, of any group seeking the privilege of official recognition." But here, it was not clear whether the college in fact had such a rule. The existence of the requirement, and petitioners' intent to comply, were accordingly left for remand. "Assuming the existence of a valid rule, however, we do conclude that the benefits of participation in the internal life of the college community may be denied to any group that reserves the right to violate any valid campus rules with which they disagree."

Justice Rehnquist concurred only in the result, explaining: "I find the implication clear from the Court's opinion that the constitutional limitations on the government's acting as administrator of a college differ from the limitations on the government acting as sovereign to enforce its criminal laws." * Justice Rehnquist added: "Because of these acknowledged distinctions of constitutional dimension based upon the role of the government, I have serious doubt as to whether cases dealing with the imposition of criminal sanctions, such as [Brandenburg, Scales and Yates], are properly applicable to this case dealing with the government as college administrator. I also doubt whether cases dealing with the prior restraint imposed by injunctive process of a court, such as [Near v. Minnesota], are precisely comparable to this case . . . . .

---

* Note the Court's consideration, in companion cases decided a few days later, of the First Amendment as well as procedural due process rights of state college teachers whose appointments were not renewed, in Board of Regents v. Roth, 408 U.S. 564 (1972), and Perry v. Sindermann, 408 U.S. 593 (1972), noted in chap. 10, sec. 6. Justice Rehnquist joined in the majority opinions in both cases.

"Prior cases dealing with First Amendment rights are not fungible goods, and I think the doctrine of these cases suggests two important distinctions. The government as employer or school administrator may impose upon employees and students reasonable regulations that would be impermissible if imposed by the government upon all citizens. And there can be a constitutional distinction between the infliction of criminal punishment, on the one hand, and the imposition of milder administrative or disciplinary sanctions, on the other." He added that "some of the language used by the Court tends to obscure these distinctions." †

b. *Some comments.* Does Healy v. James adequately delineate the extent to which off-campus precedents are applicable to the school environment? Note the comment that "Justice Powell generated needless confusion" in answering that question, in Gunther, ". . . The Case of Justice Powell," 24 Stan.L.Rev. 1001 (1972): "In rejecting the first three justifications, he liberally and indiscriminately cited First Amendment precedents from other contexts. But, in finding support for the possible fourth justification, [he] endorsed a requirement that the government presumably could not impose on the public at large—a requirement that was grounded in the special needs of the campus. In short, the opinion's answer to the question of whether First Amendment precedents apply on campus looks in two directions, without adequate reconciliation." Compare the reconciliation suggested in Wright, "The Constitution on the Campus," 22 Vand.L.Rev. 1027 (1969), arguing that the "first amendment applies with full vigor on the campus of a public university," but that "this does *not* mean that precedents about the meaning of the first amendment in other areas of life can be indiscriminately transferred to the university setting." Is that the position suggested by Tinker? Is that the position supported by the result in Healy? By Grayned, which follows?

2. *Grayned v. City of Rockford.* The discussion of overbreadth in Justice Marshall's majority opinion in GRAYNED v. CITY OF ROCK-

---

† A year later, the majority's per curiam opinion relied on Healy v. James in summarily setting aside the expulsion of a graduate student for distributing on campus a newspaper "containing forms of indecent speech." Papish v. Board of Curators of Univ. of Missouri, 410 U.S. 667 (1973). A dissent by Justice Rehnquist, joined by Chief Justice Burger and Justice Blackmun, argued that even if the behavior was immune from criminal prosecution, it should be subject to university sanctions.

Note also the procedural due process limitations imposed on disciplinary suspensions of students in Goss v. Lopez, 419 U.S. 565 (1975). Justice White's majority opinion insisted that students facing temporary suspensions from public schools are entitled to some due process safeguards, including notice of the charges and an opportunity to make an explanation. Justice Powell's dissent, joined by Chief Justice Burger and Justices Blackmun and Rehnquist, objected that the expanded "judicial intervention in the operation of our public schools [may] affect adversely the quality of education." Note especially his comment on Tinker, in a footnote in Goss. He described Tinker as a decision which "extended First Amendment rights under limited circumstances to public school pupils." And he recalled Justice Black's dissent in Tinker, commenting: "There were some who thought Mr. Justice Black was unduly concerned. But the prophesy of Mr. Justice Black is now being fulfilled. In the few years since Tinker there have been literally hundreds of cases by school children alleging violation of their constitutional rights. This flood of litigation [was] triggered by a narrowly written First Amendment case which I could well have joined on its facts." Compare Justice Powell's position on First Amendment rights in the prison context, in sec. 4D, which follows.

FORD, 408 U.S. 104 (1972), threw added light on the scope of the First Amendment in the school context. Grayned was a participant in a demonstration "promoting a Black cause" in front of a high school, as noted in the earlier references to the case in chap. 12 above. A conviction under an anti-noise ordinance applicable to school areas was affirmed. The ordinance stated that no person "adjacent to any building" in which a school is in session "shall willfully make or assist in the making of any noise or diversion which disturbs or tends to disturb the peace or good order of such school session." As understood by the Court, the ordinance prohibited "only actual or imminent interference with the 'peace or good order' of the school." Justice Marshall's opinion rejected the claim that the ordinance reached protected First Amendment activity: the activity reached by the ordinance was expressive activity which could be prohibited under the principles of Tinker.

In rejecting the overbreadth attack, Justice Marshall relied in part on general public forum principles, see chap. 12, sec. 2. It is "the nature of a place" which determines the reasonableness of restrictions, he emphasized: "The crucial question is whether the manner of expression is basically incompatible with the normal activity of a particular place at a particular time." Here, the restraint was appropriate to the school environment. He added:

"We would be ignoring reality if we did not recognize that the public schools [are] often the focus of significant grievances. Without interfering with normal school activities, daytime picketing and handbilling on public grounds near a school can effectively publicize those grievances . . . . Some picketing to that end will be quiet and peaceful, and will in no way disturb the normal functioning of the school. . . . On the other hand, schools could hardly tolerate boisterous demonstrators who drown out classroom conversation, making studying impossible, block entrances, or incite children to leave the schoolhouse. Rockford's anti-noise ordinance goes no further than Tinker says a municipality may go to prevent interference with its schools. It is narrowly tailored to further Rockford's compelling interest in having an undisrupted school session conducive to the students' learning, and does not unnecessarily interfere with First Amendment rights." It was not "an impermissibly broad prophylactic ordinance"; it punished only "conduct which disrupts or is about to disrupt normal school activities."

Note also a further comment by Justice Marshall: "We recognize that the ordinance prohibits some picketing which is neither violent nor physically obstructive. Noisy demonstrations which disrupt or are incompatible with normal school activities are obviously within the ordinance's reach. Such expressive conduct may be constitutionally protected at other places or other times [Edwards v. South Carolina; Cox I], but next to a school, while classes are in session, it may be prohibited.[1] The anti-noise ordinance imposes no such restriction on expressive activity before or after the school session." Justice Douglas dissented.

1. "Different considerations, of course, apply in different circumstances. For example, restrictions appropriate to a single-building high school during class hours would be inappropriate in many open areas on a college campus, just as an assembly that is permitted outside a dormitory would be inappropriate in the middle of a mathematics class." [Footnote by Justice Marshall.]

D. THE FIRST AMENDMENT AND PRISONERS' COMMUNICATIONS

In recent cases, the Court has examined the scope of First Amendment rights as affected by the prison environment. The cases are important not only for the light they throw on the adaptation of free speech principles to new contexts, but also for their occasional, potentially important, general contributions to First Amendment analysis. Note especially Justice Powell's dissent in Saxbe v. Washington Post Co., note 2 below.

1. *Mail censorship.* Note the Court's careful effort to adapt the principles of the Tinker, Healy and O'Brien (chap. 12, sec. 3) cases to the context of prison mail censorship, in PROCUNIER v. MARTINEZ, 416 U.S. 396 (1974). Justice Powell's opinion sustained the prisoners' class action challenge of mail censorship regulations that proscribed, inter alia, statements that "unduly complain" or "magnify grievances," expressions of "inflammatory political, racial, or religious, or other views," and matter deemed "defamatory" or "otherwise inappropriate." He characterized these regulations as fairly inviting prison officials "to apply their own personal prejudices and opinions as standards for prisoner mail censorship."

In exploring the First Amendment issues raised by these regulations, Justice Powell noted the "healthly sense of realism" that ordinarily underlay the courts' sense that they "are ill equipped to deal with the increasingly urgent problems of prison administration and reform." But the ordinary policy of judicial restraint, he added, "cannot encompass any failure to take cognizance of valid constitutional claims" arising in prisons. Lower courts dealing with these problems had unnecessarily viewed them as focusing on "prisoners' rights" and on the question of the "extent to which prisoners may claim First Amendment freedoms." But Justice Powell found "a narrower basis of decision": "In the case of direct personal correspondence between inmates and those who have a particularized interest in communicating with them, mail censorship implicates more than the right of prisoners." He emphasized that "the First Amendment liberties of free citizens are implicated in censorship of prisoner mail. We therefore turn for guidance not to cases involving questions of 'prisoners' rights' but to decisions of this Court dealing with the general problem of incidental restrictions on First Amendment liberties imposed in furtherance of legitimate governmental activities." And cases like Tinker, Healy and O'Brien were accordingly "generally analogous to our present inquiry."

In accordance with that approach, he first identified the governmental interests at stake: "the preservation of internal order and discipline, the maintenance of institutional security against escape or unauthorized entry, and the rehabilitation of the prisoners." In applying a balancing approach, he concluded that "censorship of prisoner mail is justified if the following criteria are met. First, the regulation or practice in question must further an important or substantial governmental interest unrelated to the suppression of expression. . . . Second, the limitation of First Amendment freedoms must be no greater than is necessary or essential to the protection of the

particular governmental interest involved. [A]ny regulation or practice that restricts inmate correspondence must be generally necessary to protect one or more of the legitimate governmental interests identified above." The challenged regulations easily fell before that variety of scrutiny: "Appellants have failed to show that these broad restrictions on prisoner mail were in any way necessary to the furtherance of a governmental interest unrelated to the suppression of expression. Indeed, the heart of appellants' position is not that the regulations are justified by a legitimate governmental interest but that they need not be." *

Justice Marshall, joined by Justice Brennan, added a separate opinion to his concurrence with Justice Powell's view, explaining that he would reach the issue of "the First Amendment rights of inmates" and would hold "that prison authorities may not read inmate mail as a matter of course." He insisted that "prisoners are, in my view, entitled to use the mails as a medium of free expression not as a privilege, but rather as a constitutionally guaranteed right." He explained that the First Amendment "serves not only the needs of the polity but also those of the human spirit—a spirit that demands self-expression." He emphasized that "a prisoner needs a medium for self-expression. It is the role of the First Amendment and this Court to protect those precious personal rights by which we satisfy such basic yearnings of the human spirit." Justice Douglas' concurrence in the judgment was solely based on the prisoners' First Amendment rights.

2. *Press interviews.* Justice Powell proved unsuccessful, however, in his effort to persuade a majority to extend his Procunier v. Martinez approach to cases challenging prison bans on interviews of prisoners. PELL v. PROCUNIER, 417 U.S. 817 (1974), rejected an attack on a California rule providing that "press and other media interviews with specific individual inmates will not be permitted." And a companion case, SAXBE v. WASHINGTON POST CO., 417 U.S. 843 (1974), turned back a challenge to a Federal Bureau of Prisons prohibition on personal interviews between newsmen and individually designated prisoners in most federal prisons. The attack on the federal rule was brought solely by the press; in the California case, there were attacks by prisoners as well as by journalists. The opinions dealt at greater length with rights of the press than with those of the inmates.

Justice Stewart delivered the majority opinion in each case. He insisted that there was no violation of the First Amendment rights of the media because the regulations did not "deny the press access to sources of information available to members of the general public." He noted in the California case that the regulation had been adopted in 1971 "in response to a violent episode" that prison officials felt "was at least partially attributable to the former policy with respect to face-to-face prisoner-press interviews." And he emphasized that the new prohibition "did not impose a discrimination against press access, but merely eliminated a special privilege formerly given to representatives of the press vis-à-vis members of the public generally." Central to his rejection of the journalists' claim was his assertion that "news-

---

* In another part of his opinion, Justice Powell also sustained the invalidation of a ban against the use of law students and legal paraprofessionals to conduct attorney-client interviews with inmates. Those restrictions, he found, unjustifiably burdened the prisoners' due process right of access to the courts.

men have no constitutional right of access to prisons or their inmates beyond that afforded the general public." Though the First Amendment bars "government from interfering in any way with the free press," he insisted, it does not "require government to accord the press special access to information not shared by members of the public generally." He explained: "It is one thing to say that a journalist is free to seek out sources of information not available to members of the general public, that he is entitled to some constitutional protection of the confidentiality of such sources, cf. Branzburg v. Hayes [the newsmen's privilege case, sec. 6 below, where Justice Stewart's dissent arguing for the privilege viewed freedom of the press broadly] and that government cannot restrain the publication of news emanating from such sources. Cf. New York Times v. United States [sec. 3 above]. It is quite another thing to suggest that the Constitution imposes upon government the affirmative duty to make available to journalists sources of information not available to members of the public generally."

Justice Powell found that approach to the right of the press unduly simplistic. He concluded that an absolute ban on interviews "impermissibly restrains the ability of the press to perform its constitutionally established function of informing the people on the conduct of their government." He elaborated these views in the Saxbe case, in a lengthy dissent joined by Justices Brennan and Marshall. He stated: "I cannot follow the Court in concluding that *any* governmental restriction on press access to information, so long as it is nondiscriminatory, falls outside the purview of First Amendment concern." Cases such as Zemel v. Rusk, 381 U.S. 1 (1965) (sustaining area restrictions—here, to Cuba—in passports) and Branzburg v. Hayes should not bar the claim here: "To the extent that Zemel and Branzburg speak to the issue before us, they reflect no more than a sensible disinclination to follow the right-to-access argument as far as dry logic might extend." *
He continued: "It goes too far to suggest that the government must justify under the stringent standards of First Amendment review every regulation that might affect in some tangential way the availability of information to the news media. But to my mind it is equally impermissible to conclude that no governmental inhibition of press access to newsworthy information warrants constitutional scrutiny. At some point official restraints on access to news sources, even though not directed solely at the press, may so undermine the function of the First Amendment that it is both appropriate and necessary to require the Government to justify such regulations in terms

---

* The Pell majority quoted Chief Justice Warren's emphasis on the speech-action distinction in Zemel v. Rusk: "There are few restrictions on action which could not be clothed by ingenious argument in the garb of decreased data flow." Justice Powell's response noted that "the dichotomy between speech and action, while often helpful to analysis, is too uncertain to serve as the dispositive factor in charting the outer boundaries of First Amendment concerns. In the instant case, for example, it may be said with equal facility that the Bureau forbids the *conduct*, at least by newsmen and the public generally, of holding a private meeting with an incarcerated individual or, alternatively, that the Bureau prohibits the direct exchange of *speech* that constitutes an interview with a press representative. In light of the Bureau's willingness to allow lawyers, clergymen, relatives, and friends to meet privately with designated inmates, the latter characterization of the interview ban seems closer to the mark, but in my view the scope and meaning of First Amendment guarantees do not hinge on these semantic distinctions."

more compelling than discretionary authority and administrative convenience." And the claim here, he insisted, was clearly of "constitutional dimensions."

He urged that "this sweeping prohibition of prisoner-press interviews substantially impairs a core value of the First Amendment." He noted that freedom of speech protects two kinds of interests, individual and societal. Here, since government imposed "neither a penalty on speech nor any sanction against publication," the "individualistic values of the First Amendment are not directly implicated." Instead, the "societal function" of the Amendment "in preserving free public discussion of governmental affairs" was critical here. He explained: "For most citizens the prospect of personal familiarity with newsworthy events is hopelessly unrealistic. In seeking out the news the press therefore acts as an agent of the public at large. It is the means by which the people receive that free flow of information and ideas essential to intelligent self-government. By enabling the public to assert meaningful control over the political process, the press performs a crucial function in effecting the societal purpose of the First Amendment."

Justice Powell accordingly concluded his discussion of the appropriate standards of review with the observation that the interview ban "substantially impairs the right of the people to a free flow of information and ideas on the conduct of their Government. The underlying right is the right of the public generally. The press is the necessary representative of the public's interest in this context and the instrumentality which effects the public's right. I therefore conclude that the Bureau's ban against personal interviews must be put to the test of First Amendment review."

In exercising that degree of scrutiny, Justice Powell found that "the First Amendment requires the Bureau to abandon its absolute ban against press interviews." But he did not agree with the District Court's conclusion "that interview requests be evaluated on a case-by-case basis." "Ad hoc balancing of the competing interests involved in each request for an interview" was not necessary. Rather, "a press interview policy that substantially accommodates the public's legitimate interest in a free flow of information and ideas about federal prisons should survive constitutional review."

Justice Powell agreed with the majority, however, when it came to assessing the rights of the prisoners rather than of the press. In that aspect of the California case, he found that "inmates as individuals" do not have "a personal constitutional right to demand interviews with willing reporters." Justice Stewart's majority opinion in the Pell case spelled out that position at greater length. He emphasized "that the regulation cannot be considered in isolation but must be viewed in the light of the alternative means of communication permitted under the regulations with persons outside the prison." Prisoners had such alternative means, such as mail and personal visits from individuals with whom they had special personal or professional relations. And in light of those alternatives, the asserted governmental interests were more persuasive here than in Procunier v. Martinez, the mail censorship case: "When, however, the question involves the entry of people into the prisons for face-to-face communication with inmates, it is obvious that institutional considerations, such as security and related administrative problems, as well as the accepted and legitimate policy objectives of the corrections system itself, require that some limitation be placed on such visita-

tions. So long as reasonable and effective means of communication remain open and no discrimination in terms of content is involved, we believe that, in drawing such lines, 'prison officials must be accorded great latitude.'" Though "a prison inmate retains those First Amendment rights that are not inconsistent with his status as a prisoner or with the legitimate penological objectives of the corrections system," the restriction "on one manner in which prisoners can communicate with persons outside of prison" was not unconstitutional.

Justice Douglas, joined by Justices Brennan and Marshall, supported the rights of the prisoners as well as of the press in a dissent applicable to both cases. As to the inmates' claims, he objected to California's "grossly overbroad restrictions on prisoner speech." He insisted that the state's interest in order and prison discipline could not justify a prohibition as "total" and "coarse" as this. And as to the media claims, he, too, insisted that the right involved was really that "of the people"—the "public's interest in being informed about prisons [is] paramount." Accordingly, the interview ban "is an unconstitutional infringement on the public's right to know protected by the free press guarantee of the First Amendment."

E. THE FURNISHING OF LEGAL SERVICES: LAY GROUPS, SOCIAL GOALS, AND THE LAWYER–CLIENT RELATIONSHIP

NAACP v. BUTTON

371 U.S. 415, 83 S.Ct. 328, 9 L.Ed.2d 405 (1963).

Certiorari to the Supreme Court of Appeals of Virginia.

[This case held unconstitutional the application to the NAACP's litigation activities of a Virginia statutory ban against "the improper solicitation of any legal or professional business." Virginia had long regulated unethical and nonprofessional conduct by attorneys. Among the traditional regulations was a ban on the solicitation of legal business in the form of "running" or "capping." Before 1956, there was no attempt to apply those regulations to curb the NAACP's activities in sponsoring litigation directed at racial segregation. But in 1956, the laws were amended by adding a Chapter 33 to include, in the definition of "runner" or "capper," an agent for any organization which "employs, retains or compensates" any lawyer "in connection with any judicial proceeding in which it has no pecuniary right or liability." Virginia's highest court stated that the amendment's purpose "was to strengthen the existing statutes to further control the evils of solicitation of legal business." It held that the NACCP's Virginia activities violated Chapter 33 as well as Canons 35 and 47 of the ABA's Canons of Professional Ethics, which the court had adopted in 1938.[1]

---

1. As quoted in a footnote by the Court, Canon 35 read in part as follows: "*Intermediaries.*—The professional services of a lawyer should not be controlled or exploited by any lay agency, personal or corporate, which intervene between client and lawyer. A lawyer's responsibilities and qualifica-

[As described by the Court, the Virginia Conference of NAACP branches ordinarily financed only cases in which the assisted litigant retained an NAACP staff lawyer to represent him. The Conference employed 15 lawyers; each lawyer "must agree to abide by the policies of the NAACP, which [limit] the kinds of litigation which the NAACP will assist." The Conference also used some non-staff lawyers in NAACP-assisted cases. In litigation involving public school segregation, cases were typically not initiated by aggrieved persons applying to the Conference for assistance. Rather, a local NAACP branch usually invited a member of the Conference legal staff to explain to a meeting of parents and children the legal steps necessary to achieve desegregation. The staff member would bring printed forms authorizing NAACP attorneys to represent the signers in legal proceedings to achieve desegregation. "In effect, then, the prospective litigant retains not so much a particular attorney as the 'firm' " of NAACP lawyers. The Conference paid for the costs of the litigation, but a litigant was free to withdraw from a suit at any time.]

Mr. Justice BRENNAN delivered the opinion of the Court. . . .

We reverse the judgment of the Virginia Supreme Court of Appeals. We hold that the activities of the NAACP, its affiliates and legal staff shown on this record are modes of expression and association protected by the First and Fourteenth Amendments which Virginia may not prohibit, under its power to regulate the legal profession, as improper solicitation of legal business violative of Chapter 33 and the Canons of Professional Ethics.

We meet at the outset the contention that "solicitation" is wholly outside the area of freedoms protected by the First Amendment. To this contention there are two answers. The first is that a State cannot foreclose the exercise of constitutional rights by mere labels. The second is that abstract discussion is not the only species of communication which the Constitution protects; the First Amendment also protects vigorous advocacy, certainly of lawful ends, against governmental intrusion. . . . In the context of NAACP objectives, litigation is not a technique of resolving private differences; it is a means for achieving the lawful objectives of equality of treatment by all government, federal, state and local, for the members of the Negro community in this country. It is thus a form of political expression. Groups which find themselves unable to achieve their objectives through the ballot frequently turn to the courts. Just as it was true of the opponents of New Deal legislation during the 1930's, for example, no less is it true of the Negro minority today. And under the conditions of modern government, litigation may well be the sole practicable avenue open to a minority to petition for redress of grievances. . . .

The NAACP is not a conventional political party; but the litigation it assists, while serving to vindicate the legal rights of members of the Ameri-

tions are individual. He should avoid all relations which direct the performance of his duties by or in the interest of such intermediary. A lawyer's relation to his client should be personal, and the responsibility should be directed to the client. Charitable societies rendering aid to the indigent are not deemed such intermediaries."

Canon 47 read as follows:

"*Aiding the Unauthorized Practice of Law.*—No lawyer shall permit his professional services, or his name, to be used in aid of, or to make possible, the unauthorized practice of law by any lay agency, personal or corporate."

can Negro community, at the same time and perhaps more importantly, makes possible the distinctive contribution of a minority group to the ideas and beliefs of our society. For such a group, association for litigation may be the most effective form of political association. . . .

We read the decree of the Virginia Supreme Court of Appeals in the instant case as proscribing any arrangement by which prospective litigants are advised to seek the assistance of particular attorneys. No narrower reading is plausible. We cannot accept the reading suggested [that] the Supreme Court of Appeals construed Chapter 33 as proscribing control only of the actual litigation by the NAACP after it is instituted. [S]imple referral to or recommendation of a lawyer may be solicitation within the meaning of Chapter 33. . . .

We conclude that under Chapter 33, as authoritatively construed, a person who advises another that his legal rights have been infringed and refers him to a particular attorney or group of attorneys (for example, to the Virginia Conference's legal staff) for assistance has committed a crime, as has the attorney who knowingly renders assistance under such circumstances. There thus inheres in the statute the gravest danger of smothering all discussion looking to the eventual institution of litigation on behalf of the rights of members of an unpopular minority. Lawyers on the legal staff or even mere NAACP members or sympathizers would understandably hesitate, at an NAACP meeting or on any other occasion, to do what the decree purports to allow, namely, acquaint "persons with what they believe to be their legal rights and [advise] them to assert their rights by commencing or further prosecuting a suit . . . ." For if the lawyers, members or sympathizers also appeared in or had any connection with any litigation supported with NAACP funds contributed under the provision of the decree by which the NAACP is not prohibited "from contributing money to persons to assist them in commencing or further prosecuting such suits," they plainly would risk (if lawyers) disbarment proceedings and, lawyers and nonlawyers alike, criminal prosecution for the offense of "solicitation," to which the Virginia court gave so broad and uncertain a meaning. It makes no difference whether such prosecutions or proceedings would actually be commenced. It is enough that a vague and broad statute lends itself to selective enforcement against unpopular causes. We cannot close our eyes to the fact that the militant Negro civil rights movement has engendered the intense resentment and opposition of the politically dominant white community of Virginia; litigation assisted by the NAACP has been bitterly fought. In such circumstances, a statute broadly curtailing group activity leading to litigation may easily become a weapon of oppression, however evenhanded its terms appear. Its mere existence could well freeze out of existence all such activity on behalf of the civil rights of Negro citizens. . . .

[W]e reject two further contentions of respondents. The first is that the [state court] has guaranteed free expression by expressly confirming petitioner's right to continue its advocacy of civil-rights litigation. But in light of the whole decree of the court, the guarantee is of purely speculative value. As construed by the Court, Chapter 33, at least potentially, prohibits every cooperative activity that would make advocacy of litigation meaningful. . . .

The second contention is that Virginia has a subordinating interest in the regulation of the legal profession [which] justifies limiting petitioner's First Amendment rights. Specifically, Virginia contends that the NAACP's activities [fall] within the traditional purview of state regulation of professional conduct. [But we] have consistently held that only a compelling state interest in the regulation of a subject within [the state's power] can justify limiting First Amendment freedoms.* . . . However valid may be Virginia's interest in regulating the traditionally illegal practices of barratry, maintenance and champerty, that interest does not justify the prohibition of the NAACP activities disclosed by this record. Malicious intent was of the essence of the common-law offenses of fomenting or stirring up litigation. [T]he exercise [of] First Amendment rights to enforce constitutional rights through litigation [cannot] be deemed malicious. . . . [More modern regulations not involving malice] which reflect hostility to stirring up litigation have been aimed chiefly at those who urge recourse to the courts for private gain, serving no public interest. . . .

Objection to the intervention of a lay intermediary, who may control litigation or otherwise interfere with the rendering of legal services in a confidential relationship, also derives from the element of pecuniary gain. Fearful of dangers thought to arise from that element, the courts of several States have sustained regulations aimed at these activities. We intimate no view one way or the other as to the merits of those decisions with respect to the particular arrangements against which they are directed. It is enough that the superficial resemblance in form between those arrangements and that at bar cannot obscure the vital fact that here the entire arrangement employs constitutionally privileged means of expression to secure constitutionally guaranteed civil rights. There has been no showing of a serious danger here of professionally reprehensible conflicts of interest which rules against solicitation frequently seek to prevent. This is so partly because no monetary stakes are involved, and so there is no danger that the attorney will desert or subvert the paramount interests of his client to enrich himself or an outside sponsor. And the aims and interests of NAACP have not been shown to conflict with those of its members and nonmember Negro litigants . . . . . Resort to the courts to seek vindication of constitutional rights is a different matter from the oppressive, malicious, or avaricious use of the legal process for purely private gain. . . .

We conclude that although the petitioner has amply shown that its activities fall within the First Amendment's protections, the State has failed to advance any substantial regulatory interest, in the form of substantive evils flowing from petitioner's activities, which can justify the broad prohibitions which it has imposed. . . .

A final observation is in order. Because our disposition is rested on the First Amendment, [we] do not reach the considerations of race or racial discrimination which are the predicate of petitioner's challenge to the statute under the Equal Protection Clause. That the petitioner happens to be en-

---

* This reference to the "compelling" state interest is often cited in modern cases to express the strict scrutiny required of state regulations in the First Amendment area. See also Justice Harlan's formulation a few years earlier in NAACP v. Alabama, sec. 5A below, and Justice Frankfurter's earlier use of the term in Sweezy v. New Hampshire, sec. 6A below.

gaged in activities of expression and association on behalf of the rights of Negro children to equal opportunity is constitutionally irrelevant to the ground of our decision. The course of our decisions in the First Amendment area makes plain that its protections would apply as fully to those who would arouse our society against the objectives of the petitioner. . . .

Reversed.

Mr. Justice DOUGLAS, concurring.

While I join the opinion of the Court, I add a few words. This Virginia Act is not applied across the board to all groups that use this method of obtaining and managing litigation, but instead reflects a legislative purpose to penalize the N.A.A.C.P. because it promotes desegregation of the races. [The Act] was one of five that Virginia enacted "as parts of the general plan of massive resistance to the integration of schools of the state under the Supreme Court's decrees." . . .

Mr. Justice WHITE, concurring in part and dissenting in part. . . .

If we had before us, which we do not, a narrowly drawn statute proscribing only the actual day-to-day management and dictation of the tactics, strategy and conduct of litigation by a lay entity such as the NAACP, the issue would be considerably different, at least for me; for in my opinion neither the practice of law by such an organization nor its management of the litigation of its members or others is constitutionally protected. Both practices are well within the regulatory power of the State. In this regard I agree with my Brother Harlan. It is not at all clear to me, however, that the opinion of the majority would not also strike down such a narrowly drawn statute. To the extent that it would, I am in disagreement. . . .

Mr. Justice HARLAN, whom Mr. Justice CLARK and Mr. Justice STEWART join, dissenting. . . .

[Justice Harlan's dissent agreed that freedom of expression includes not only the individual right to speak but also "his right to advocate and his right to join with his fellows in an effort to make that advocacy effective." (See, e. g., his opinion for the Court in NAACP v. Alabama, sec. 5 below.) Moreover, it includes "the right to join together for purposes of obtaining judicial redress." But, he added, "to declare that litigation is a form of conduct that may be associated with political expression does not resolve this case." He reminded that the Court had "repeatedly held that certain forms of speech are outside the scope of the protection of [the First Amendment] and that, in addition, 'general regulatory statutes, not intended to control the content of speech but incidentally limiting its unfettered exercise,' are permissible 'when they have been found justified by subordinating valid governmental interests.'" (He quoted from his opinion in Konigsberg v. State Bar, 366 U.S. 36, sec. 5A below.) Accordingly, the problem was "to weigh the legitimate interest of the State against the effect of the regulation on individual rights."

[Justice Harlan suggested an analogy between this case and "the rights of workingmen in labor disputes." See sec. 4B above. He noted that "as we move away from speech alone and into the sphere of conduct—even conduct associated with speech or resulting from it—the area of legitimate governmental interest expands," citing, inter alia, the Giboney case. Here, he agreed, the NAACP members' rights "to associate, to discuss, and to ad-

vocate [must] remain free from frontal attack or suppression," absent "the gravest danger to the community." But he added that "litigation, whether or not associated with the attempt to vindicate constitutional rights, is *conduct.* It is speech *plus.* Although the State surely may not broadly prohibit individuals with a common interest from joining together to petition a court for redress of their grievances, it is equally certain that the State may impose reasonable regulations limiting the permissible form of litigation and the manner of legal representation within its borders." And the "regulation of conduct concerning litigation" challenged here, he concluded, "has a reasonable relation to the furtherance of a proper state interest, and [that] interest outweighs any foreseeable harm to the furtherance of protected freedoms." He explained:]

The interest which Virginia has here asserted is that of maintaining high professional standards among those who practice law within its borders. This Court has consistently recognized the broad range of judgments that a State may properly make in regulating any profession. [The Court's efforts to distinguish this case from the traditional area of state control "are too facile"; they] do not account for the full scope of the State's legitimate interest in regulating professional conduct. [Though] these professional standards may have been born in a desire to curb malice and self-aggrandizement by those who would use clients and the courts for their own pecuniary ends, they have acquired a far broader significance during their long development.

First, with regard to the claimed absence of the pecuniary element. [A] State's felt need for regulation of professional conduct may reasonably extend beyond mere "ambulance chasing." . . . Of particular relevance here is a series of nationwide adjudications culminating in 1958 in In re Brotherhood of Railroad Trainmen, 13 Ill.2d 391, 150 N.E.2d 163. . . . The practices of the Brotherhood, similar in so many respects to those engaged in by the petitioner here, have been condemned by every state court which has considered them.* . . .

Underlying this impressive array of relevant precedent is the widely shared conviction that avoidance of improper pecuniary gain is not the only relevant factor in determining standards of professional conduct. Running perhaps even deeper is the desire of the profession, of courts, and of legislatures to prevent any interference with the uniquely personal relationship between lawyer and client and to maintain untrammeled by outside influences the responsibility which the lawyer owes to the courts he serves.

When an attorney is employed by an association or corporation to represent individual litigants, two problems arise, whether or not the association is organized for profit and no matter how unimpeachable its motives. The lawyer becomes subject to the control of a body that is not itself a litigant and that, unlike the lawyers it employs, is not subject to strict professional discipline as an officer of the court. In addition, the lawyer necessarily finds himself with a divided allegiance—to his employer and to his client— which may prevent full compliance with his basic professional obligations . . .

---

* But see Brotherhood of Railroad Trainmen v. Virginia, 377 U.S. 1 (1964), in the notes which follow.

Second, it is claimed that the interests of petitioner and its members are sufficiently identical to eliminate any "serious danger" of "professionally reprehensible conflicts of interest." . . .

The NAACP may be no more than the sum of the efforts and views infused in it by its members; but the totality of the separate interests of the members and others whose causes the petitioner champions, even in the field of race relations, may far exceed in scope and variety that body's views of policy, as embodied in litigating strategy and tactics. Thus it may be in the interest of the Association in every case to make a frontal attack on segregation, to press for an immediate breaking down of racial barriers, and to sacrifice minor points that may win a given case for the major points that may win other cases too. But in a particular litigation, it is not impossible that after authorizing action in his behalf, a Negro parent, concerned that a continued frontal attack could result in schools closed for years, might prefer to wait with his fellows a longer time for good-faith efforts by the local school board than is permitted by the centrally determined policy of the NAACP. Or he might see a greater prospect of success through discussions with local school authorities than through the litigation deemed necessary by the Association. The parent, of course, is free to withdraw his authorization, but is his lawyer, retained and paid by petitioner and subject to its directions on matters of policy, able to advise the parent with that undivided allegiance that is the hallmark of the attorney-client relation? I am afraid not. . . .

Third, it is said that the practices involved here must stand on a different footing because the litigation that petitioner supports concerns the vindication of constitutionally guaranteed rights. But surely state law is still the source of basic regulation of the legal profession, whether an attorney is pressing a federal or a state claim within its borders. . . . The true question is whether the State has taken action which unreasonably obstructs the assertion of federal rights. Here, it cannot be said that the underlying state policy is inevitably inconsistent with federal interests. . . .

. . . The important function of organizations like petitioner in vindicating constitutional rights is not of course to be minimized, but that function is not, in my opinion, substantially impaired by this statute. [I]t does not, in my view, prevent petitioner from recommending the services of attorneys who are not subject to its directions and control. And since petitioner may contribute to those who need assistance, the prohibition should not significantly discourage anyone with sufficient interest from pressing his claims in litigation or from joining with others similarly situated to press those claims. . . .

––––––––

THE GROUNDS AND APPLICATIONS OF BUTTON

1. *The broad applications of Button.* a. A year after Button, the Court relied on it outside the area of litigation involving racial discrimination or other constitutional rights, to invalidate a Virginia injunction against the union's alleged solicitation and unauthorized practice of law. BROTHERHOOD OF RAILROAD TRAINMEN v. VIRGINIA, 377 U.S. 1 (1964). The Brotherhood admitted that it advised its members to obtain

legal advice before making settlements of their personal injury claims, that it recommended particular attorneys, and that the result of its plan was "to channel legal employment to the particular lawyers approved by the Brotherhood." Justice Black's majority opinion concluded that First and 14th Amendment rights had been violated: "The State can no more keep these workers from using their cooperative plan to advise one another than it could use more direct means to bar them from resorting to the courts to vindicate their legal rights." As in the Button case, "the State again has failed to show any appreciable public interest in preventing the Brotherhood from carrying out its plan to recommend the lawyers it selects to represent injured workers. The Brotherhood's activities fall just as clearly within the protection of the First Amendment. And the Constitution protects the associational rights of the members of the union precisely as it does those of the NAACP."

Justice Clark's dissent, joined by Justice Harlan, claimed that the decision "overthrows state regulation of the legal profession and relegates the practice of law to the level of a commercial enterprise." He insisted that the Button decision was not applicable: "Personal injury litigation is not a form of political expression, but rather a procedure for the settlement of damage claims. No guaranteed civil right is involved. Here, the question involves solely the regulation of the profession, a power long recognized as belonging peculiarly to the State. . . . Finally, no substantive evil would result from the activity permitted in Button. But here the past history of the union indicates the contrary. . . . Virginia has sought only to halt the gross abuses of channeling and soliciting litigation which have been going on here for 30 years. The potential for evil in the union's system is enormous and, in my view, will bring disrepute to the legal profession. The system must also work to the disadvantage of the Brotherhood members by directing their claims into the hands of the 16 approved attorneys who are subject to the control of one man, the president of the union. Finally, it will encourage further departures from the high standards set by canons of ethics as well as by state regulatory procedures and will be a green light to other groups who for years have attempted to engage in similar practices."

b. The Button and Trainmen cases in turn provided the basis for setting aside a state order against another variety of alleged unauthorized practice of law by a union. UNITED MINE WORKERS v. ILLINOIS BAR ASS'N, 389 U.S. 217 (1967). The Union had employed an attorney on a salary basis to assist its members with workmen's compensation claims. Justice Black's majority opinion concluded that the state ban "substantially impairs the associational rights of the Mine Workers and is not needed to protect the State's interest in high standards of legal ethics." Justice Harlan dissented: "Although I agree with the balancing approach employed by the majority, I find the scales tipped differently."

c. The Court relied on the Button, Trainmen, and United Mine Workers cases in UNITED TRANSPORTATION UNION v. STATE BAR OF MICHIGAN, 401 U.S. 576 (1971), setting aside a broad state court injunction against a union's plan purportedly designed to protect union members from excessive fees by incompetent attorneys in FELA actions. In the concluding paragraph of his majority opinion, Justice Black emphasized the general principle upon which he relied: "[T]he basic right to group legal ac-

tion, a right first asserted in this Court by an association of Negroes seeking the protection of freedoms guaranteed by the Constitution." He added: "The common thread running through our decisions in NAACP v. Button, Trainmen, and United Mine Workers is that collective activity undertaken to obtain meaningful access to the courts is a fundamental right within the protection of the First Amendment. However, that right would be a hollow promise if courts could deny associations of workers or others the means of enabling their members to meet the costs of legal representation." Justices Harlan, White and Blackmun dissented in part.*

2. *The grounds of Button and its progeny.* What was the source of the associational rights in Button? Compare the freedom of association discussion when the Court, several years before Button, protected NAACP membership lists from state inquiries. NAACP v. Alabama, 357 U.S. 449 (1958), sec. 5 below. Were those associational rights of the NAACP cases equally applicable in the union cases? Would refusal to apply Button in the subsequent cases have shown Button to be a non-neutral decision (a charge the Court was concerned about in the last paragraph of the Button case)? Would a distinction between "personal injury litigation" and "civil rights litigation" have been non-neutral? Should the Court have inquired further into state motives in Button? May reluctance to characterize motives in cases such as Button lead the Court to give inadequate weight in other cases to "purer" state concerns regarding professional ethics and conflicts of interest? See generally Kalven, The Negro and the First Amendment (1965), Symposium, "Group Legal Services in Perspective," 12 U.C.L.A.L.Rev. 279 (1965), and Birkby and Murphy, "Interest Group Conflict in the Judicial Arena . . .," 42 Tex.L.Rev. 1018 (1964).

SECTION 5. A FIRST AMENDMENT RIGHT OF SILENCE?— GOVERNMENT DEMANDS FOR INFORMATION AND AFFIRMATION: SCOPE OF INQUIRY AND GROUNDS FOR DISQUALIFICATION OF PUBLIC EMPLOYEES AND LICENSEES

Introduction. When may government demand answers from those who work for it or those who (like bar admission applicants, for example) ask for recognition of a special status? To what extent do First Amendment values restrict government with respect to what disclosures or assurances it may seek from employees or licensees? To what extent does the First Amendment permit government to make associations or beliefs a basis for disqualification —a ground for finding an employee or licensee "unfit"? Questions such as these have most commonly arisen in the context of internal security. Criminal legislation against dangerous advocacy, the focus of attention in chap. 12, sec. 1, has not been the only manifestation of the concern with subversion. Security programs and oath requirements have also been a prolific source of litigation, and they are a major concern of this section.

---

* Note also the Court's consideration of the due process interest in "access to courts" in Boddie v. Connecticut, 401 U.S. 371 (1971), chap. 10, sec. 4.

The problems here are obviously related to those of the Gitlow-Dennis-Scales variety: What critical speech is protected? What associations may be forbidden? But these materials differ in important respects. The criminal provisions considered in chap. 12 were immediately concerned with the content of speech. Here, the state's concern purports to be with issues such as fitness of employees and integrity of lawyers. Inquiries related to beliefs and associations affect First Amendment interests, to be sure. Are they constitutionally more tolerable because their impact is not "direct," because their effect on free expression is an indirect consequence of a regulation?

To what extent are questions about beliefs and associations relevant to legitimate governmental concerns regarding public employment and professional qualifications? To what extent may an individual refuse to answer even a "relevant" question, because the effect on First Amendment rights outweighs the public need to know? How strong must state justifications be to make an answer obligatory? What action may the state take on the basis of the answer? Is the last the same question as the earlier ones: May a state ask a question only if an answer might justify dismissal of an employee, for example? Or may the state's right to know be broader than the permissible bases for dismissal? May the state ask a question even though an answer would not by itself be basis for dismissal: may it demand an answer on the ground that the information elicited would be a useful step in the inquiry as to fitness? Consider the extent to which the materials below distinguish between permissible areas of *inquiry* and permissible grounds for *disqualification* of an individual from government employment or from a "privileged" status. See, e. g., the 1971 Bar Admission Cases, below.

The materials that follow explore these and related questions. Section 5A concentrates on the Court responses during the fifties, the first decade of frequent encounters with these problems; section 5B traces the sharply changing analyses since. The First Amendment is the dominant limitation, but other guarantees are also involved—especially the Fifth Amendment privilege against self-incrimination. Internal security provides the most common context, but the materials are not restricted to it: for example, relevant developments have involved demands for information about civil rights activities as well. Indeed, the relationship between inquiry cases involving alleged subversives on the one hand and NAACP activities on the other suggests a series of provocative and illuminating comparisons in this section and the next. See, e. g., the Gibson case, sec. 6A, which involves a legislative committee's demand for information about NAACP membership in the course of an investigation into Communist infiltration.

A.　THE BACKGROUND OF THE FIFTIES

THE GARNER AND WIEMAN CASES:
RELEVANT INQUIRIES; SUSPECT METHODS

Introduction. Demands for information and disavowals regarding subversion are relevant and legitimate so long as the methods of inquiry are clear

and limited: that was the usual theme at the beginning of the modern Court's encounters with these problems. The Garner and Wieman cases illustrate that approach of the early fifties.

1. *Garner.* GARNER v. LOS ANGELES BOARD OF PUBLIC WORKS, 341 U.S. 716 (1951), involved a 1941 state legislative amendment of the Los Angeles City Charter which barred from public employment anyone who (1) within the past 5 years had "advised, advocated or taught," or thereafter should "advise, advocate or teach," the "overthrow by force or violence" of the state or national government; or (2) within the past 5 years had, or thereafter should, become a member of or affiliated with an organization engaging in such advocacy. A 1948 city ordinance implemented that legislation by requiring employees to take an oath (covering the 5 years prior to 1948) regarding the forbidden activities, as well as to execute an affidavit disclosing whether or not he was or had ever been a Communist Party member, and if so, for what period.

The Court sustained both provisions. Justice Clark's majority opinion found the affidavit inquiry relevant: a city may inquire of its employees "as to matters that may prove relevant to their fitness and suitability for the public service. Past conduct may well relate to present fitness; past loyalty may have a reasonable relationship to present and future trust. Both are commonly inquired into in determining fitness for both high and low positions in private industry and are not less relevant in public employment." The Court noted, however, that it was not deciding whether the city could say that disclosure of Party membership by an employee "justifies his discharge"; the category of relevant questions was apparently broader than the category of grounds for disqualification from employment.[1]

The oath requirement was also found valid: it had no retroactive effect, given the 1941 and 1948 dates for state and local provisions; the 1948 oath obligation applied only to those engaging in the forbidden advocacy or association after the 1941 state law: "The provisions operating thus prospectively were a reasonable regulation to protect the municipal service by establishing an employment qualification of loyalty." Finally, the oath was found sufficiently narrow by being read as limited to *knowing* membership: "We have no reason to suppose that the oath [will be] construed [to apply to members of organizations who were] innocent of its purpose. We assume that scienter is implicit in each clause of the oath."[2]

2. *Wieman.* In WIEMAN v. UPDEGRAFF, 344 U.S. 183 (1952), by contrast, the unanimous Court struck down an Oklahoma loyalty oath re-

---

1. Note that, by the time these government employee cases in the subversion area reached the Court, the Court had already decided that the public employment context justified some greater restraints on the speech and association of government workers than on the citizenry generally. See especially the sustaining of the Hatch Act, prohibiting federal employees from taking "any active part in political management or in political campaigns," in United Public Workers v. Mitchell [1947; chap. 15 below]. The Hatch Act and similar state provisions were again sustained against First Amendment attacks in two 1973 decisions, despite the broadening First Amendment protections of the cases of the sixties, below. The two 1973 decisions were Civil Service Comm'n v. Letter Carriers and Broadrick v. Oklahoma, noted in chap. 12, sec. 1.

2. Justice Douglas, joined by Justice Black, dissented in Garner, largely on bill of attainder grounds. Justices Frankfurter and Burton dissented as to the oath requirement.

quiring employees to state that they were not "affiliated directly or indirectly," and for the previous 5 years had "not been a member of," any organization "which has been officially determined by the United States Attorney General or other authorized public agency of the United States to be a communist front or subversive organization." Justice Clark again wrote the opinion. He noted that the state had construed the oath so that here, unlike Garner, "knowledge is not a factor" and continued: "We are thus brought to the question touched on in Garner [note 1 above], Adler[3] and Gerende:[4] whether the Due Process Clause permits a state, in attempting to bar disloyal individuals from its employ, to exclude persons solely on the basis of organizational membership, regardless of their knowledge concerning the organizations to which they had belonged. For, under the statute before us, the fact of membership alone disqualifies. But membership may be innocent. A state servant may have joined a proscribed organization unaware of its activities and purposes. In recent years, many completely loyal persons have severed organizational ties after learning for the first time of the character of groups to which they had belonged. . . . At the time of affiliation, a group itself may be innocent, only later coming under the influence of those who would turn it toward illegitimate ends. Conversely, an organization formerly subversive and therefore designated as such may have subsequently freed itself from the influences which originally led to its listing.

"There can be no dispute about the consequences visited upon a person excluded from public employment on disloyalty grounds. In the view of the community, the stain is a deep one; indeed, it has become a badge of infamy. . . . Yet under the Oklahoma Act, the fact of association alone determines disloyalty and disqualification; it matters not whether association existed innocently or knowingly. To thus inhibit individual freedom of movement is to stifle the flow of democratic expression and controversy at one of its chief sources. We hold that the distinction observed between the case at bar and Garner, Adler and Gerende is decisive. Indiscriminate classification of innocent with knowing activity must fall as an assertion of arbitrary power. The oath offends due process . . . We need not pause to consider whether an abstract right to public employment exists. It is sufficient

3. Adler v. Board of Education, 342 U.S. 485 (1952), sustained the New York Feinberg law directed at subversive teachers and stated that teachers could be barred for "knowing membership" in the Communist Party. Adler is discussed in—and largely overruled by—Keyishian v. Board of Regents, 385 U.S. 589 (1967), sec. 5B below.

4. Gerende v. Board of Supervisors, 341 U.S. 56 (1951), was a per curiam decision sustaining the Maryland Ober Law requirement that any candidate for public office file an affidavit that he was not a "subversive person." In sustaining it, the Court expressed its understanding that the candidate "need only make oath that he is not a person who is engaged 'in one way or another in the attempt to overthrow the government *by force or violence*,' and that he is not knowingly a member of an organization engaged in such an attempt." Compare Whitehill v. Elkins, 389 U.S. 54 (1967), invalidating a teacher's oath —based on the same Law—that the teacher was "not engaged in one way or another in the attempt to overthrow the government [by] force or violence." Justice Douglas' majority opinion, construing the requirement in relation to the Ober Law, found the definition of "subversive person" unconstitutionally vague. Other loyalty oath cases of the sixties are noted in sec. 5B below.

to say that constitutional protection does extend to the public servant whose exclusion pursuant to a statute is patently arbitrary or discriminatory." [5]

THE CONSEQUENCE OF SILENCE IN THE FACE OF RELEVANT INQUIRIES: DISMISSALS FROM EMPLOYMENT AND DENIALS OF BAR ADMISSION FOR FAILURE TO DISCLOSE

Introduction. In a series of cases in the late fifties, the Court considered constitutional claims by state employees and licensees who had refused to answer questions relating to subversion. Typically, the state insisted that the dismissal or license refusal was based on the failure to answer questions "relevant" to a legitimate state interest (in the sense of cases such as Garner, above): the usual claim was that the government's action was a permissible response to the individual's lack of candor vis-à-vis relevant inquiries. The individual, by contrast, characteristically insisted that the real basis for the state's action was hostility to dissident political views and suspicious inferences about the claimant's beliefs. The divisions on the Court were often differences about assessments of the record: there was agreement in principle that penalties for political beliefs would violate First Amendment rights and that inferences of guilt from invocations of the self-incrimination privilege would violate the Fifth; the immediately troublesome issues were problems such as the scope of permissible Court inquiry into "real" state motives and purposes, and the deference appropriate for state judgments in this area. There were other underlying difficulties, to be sure: the contours of relevance, both for inquiries and for grounds of disqualification; the probable cause a state should show to justify questions in a sensitive area; the nature of beliefs and associations that would permit a state to bar or end employment or deny licenses. But questions of that variety were more obscured in the decisions of the fifties than in the subsequent First Amendment cases (considered in sec. 5B below).

Moreover, reliance on the Fifth rather than the First Amendment in many of the refusals to answer added another variable to the early cases; changes in views in the sixties about the "incorporation" of the Fifth into

---

5. In a separate concurring opinion in Wieman, Justice Frankfurter, joined by Justice Douglas, may have been the first to use the "chilling effects" metaphor which played such a prominent role in First Amendment analysis, and especially in the overbreadth technique, in the next two decades. He said: "Such unwarranted inhibition upon the free spirit of teachers affects not only those who, like the appellants, are immediately before the Court. It has an unmistakable tendency to chill that free play of the spirit which all teachers ought especially to cultivate and practice; it makes for caution and timidity in their associations by potential teachers."
Contrast the mounting solicitude for public employees' rights in these cases with a famous comment by Justice Holmes. while he was on the state court, in McAuliffe v. Mayor of New Bedford, 155 Mass. 216, 29 N.E. 517 (1892): "The petitioner may have a constitutional right to talk politics, but he has no constitutional right to be a policeman. There are few employments for hire in which the servant does not agree to suspend his constitutional right of free speech, as well as of idleness, by the implied terms of his contract. The servant cannot complain, as he takes the employment on the terms which are offered him." See generally Van Alstyne, "The Demise of the Right-Privilege Distinction in Constitutional Law," 81 Harv.L.Rev. 1439 (1968).

the 14th accordingly affected the bounds of state inquiries. In Slochower, Lerner, and Beilan (notes 1 and 2), employees were discharged by states after invoking the Fifth Amendment in congressional inquiries of the fifties—during a period when the Fifth was not yet applicable in state inquiries via the 14th. By contrast, in the bar admission cases (Schware and Konigsberg I, below), the refusals to answer rested directly on First Amendment grounds. (A note below considers the impact of the availability since the sixties of a self-incrimination privilege in state inquiries.)

This section concludes with the 1958 decision in NAACP v. Alabama, a case of special importance for the evolving approach of the sixties: it involved a civil rights organization rather than concerns about Communist infiltration; it articulated the competing claims of the state and the individual more explicitly than most; and it is a major example of a Court finding of inadequate justification for a state demand for information though the information was "relevant" to a legitimate state concern. As in Shelton v. Tucker in 1960, the first case in sec. 5B, NAACP v. Alabama found the state need for an answer to a relevant question outweighed by the "indirect" impact a duty to answer would have on First Amendment rights.

1. *Slochower: Improper inference from invocation of Fifth Amendment privilege?* SLOCHOWER v. BOARD OF HIGHER EDUCATION, 350 U.S. 551 (1956), held unconstitutional § 903 of the New York City Charter which provided that whenever an employee of the City utilized the privilege against self-incrimination to avoid answering a question relating to his official conduct, "his term or tenure of office or employment shall terminate." Slochower, a tenured faculty member at a city college, claimed the Fifth Amendment to certain questions at a 1952 hearing of a congressional committee investigating subversion in education. He stated that he was not a Communist, that he was willing to testify about his associations since 1941, but claimed the self-incrimination privilege about inquiries dealing with 1940–41. (He had testified about his affiliations during 1940–41 in earlier state inquiries). He was discharged under § 903, without the usual hearings for tenured faculty members.

The Court concluded in a 5 to 4 decision that the summary dismissal violated due process. As Justice Clark read the record, application of § 903 "falls squarely within the prohibition of Wieman v. Updegraff," above. He explained: "[As applied, § 903] operates to discharge every city employee who invokes the Fifth Amendment. In practical effect the questions asked are taken as confessed and made the basis of the discharge. No consideration is given to such factors as the subject matter of the questions, remoteness of the period to which they are directed, or justification for exercise of the privilege. It matters not whether the plea resulted from mistake, inadvertence or legal advice conscientiously given, whether wisely or unwisely." The section had converted the privilege "into a conclusive presumption of guilt." He noted, moreover: "It is one thing for the city authorities themselves to inquire into Slochower's fitness, but quite another for his discharge to be based entirely on events occurring before a federal committee." He concluded: "The State has broad powers in the selection and discharge of its employees, and it may be that proper inquiry would show Slochower's continued employment to be inconsistent with a real interest of the State. But there has been no such inquiry here."

Justice Reed's dissent, joined by Justices Burton and Minton, insisted: "We disagree with the Court's assumption that § 903 as a practical matter takes the questions asked as confessed. Cities, like other employers, may reasonably conclude that a refusal to furnish appropriate information is enough to justify discharge. . . . The duty to respond may be refused for personal protection against prosecution only, but such avoidance of public duty to furnish information can properly be considered to stamp the employee as a person unfit to hold certain official positions."

Justice Harlan's dissent sketched an approach which was to prove persuasive to the Court in a number of subsequent cases, such as those in the next note. He insisted first of all that the majority had misread the record as to the weight the state had put on the plea of the Fifth Amendment: "[I]t is the exercise of the privilege itself which is the basis for the discharge, quite apart from any inference of guilt." More basically, he insisted that the state scope of inquiry was legitimately broader than the scope of grounds for disqualification—and that refusal to answer a legitimate question was itself a justifiable ground for discharge. As to disqualification, he noted that the Court had already held that a state could bar a teacher for "knowing membership" in the Communist Party. [Adler v. Board of Education, 342 U.S. 485 (1952).] An inquiry as to membership as such was proper because it was "relevant" to that basis for disqualification, though mere membership as such would not be a constitutionally adequate ground for discharge: "A requirement that public school teachers shall furnish information as to their past or present membership in the Communist Party is a relevant step in the implementation of such a state policy [of discharging for "knowing membership"], and a teacher may be discharged for refusing to comply with that requirement. [Garner.]"

2. *Lerner and Beilan: Discharging employees for "lack of candor"?* Two years later, Justice Harlan wrote one of the majority opinions when the Court, in two 5 to 4 decisions, sustained discharges of employees who had refused to answer on self-incrimination grounds questions put by local inquirers about present subversive associations. LERNER v. CASEY, 357 U.S. 468, and BEILAN v. BOARD OF EDUCATION, 357 U.S. 399 (1958). Lerner was a New York City subway conductor dismissed on the stated ground that "reasonable grounds exist for belief that because of his doubtful trust and reliability" he was a "security risk" under state law. Beilan involved a Philadelphia school teacher dismissed for "incompetency" based on refusal to answer school officials' questions.

a. As Justice Harlan's majority opinion in Lerner read the record, Lerner "had been discharged neither because of any inference of Communist Party membership which was drawn from the exercise of the Fifth Amendment privilege, nor because of the assertion of that constitutional protection, but rather because of the doubt created as to his 'reliability' by his refusal to answer a relevant question put by his employer, a doubt which the court held justifiable quite independently of appellant's reasons for his silence. In effect, administrative action was interpreted to rest solely on the refusal to respond. It was this lack of candor which provided the evidence of appellant's doubtful trust and reliability which under the New York statutory scheme constituted him a security risk."

Justice Harlan added: "We think it scarcely debatable that had there been no claim of Fifth Amendment privilege, New York would have been constitutionally entitled to conclude from appellant's refusal to answer what must be conceded to have been a question relevant to the purposes of the statute and his employment, cf. [Garner], that he was of doubtful trust and reliability. The fact that New York has chosen to base its dismissal of employees whom it finds to be of doubtful trust and reliability on the ground that they are in effect 'security risks' hardly requires a different determination. . . . Neither the New York statute nor courts purported to equate this ground for dismissal with 'disloyalty.' " And Lerner's reliance on the Fifth Amendment did not change that outcome: "The federal privilege against self-incrimination was not available to appellant through the Fourteenth Amendment in this state investigation." [Note the impact of the "incorporation" of the Fifth Amendment into the 14th, considered below.]

b. In Beilan, similarly, the majority opinion by Justice Burton emphasized that the Board based dismissal of the teacher upon "refusal to answer any inquiry about his relevant activities—not upon those activities themselves. It took care to charge petitioner with incompetency, and not with disloyalty. It found him insubordinate and lacking in frankness and candor—it made no finding as to his loyalty." He stated further: "By engaging in teaching in the public schools, petitioner did not give up his right to freedom of belief, speech or association. He did, however, undertake obligations of frankness, candor and cooperation in answering inquiries made of him by his employing Board examining into his fitness."

Justice Douglas' dissent, joined by Justice Black, concluded: "[W]e have here only a bare refusal to testify; and the Court holds that sufficient to show these employees are unfit to hold their public posts. That makes qualification for public office turn solely on a matter of belief—a notion very much at war with the Bill of Rights." Earlier, he noted: "I would allow no inference of wrongdoing to flow from the invocation of any constitutional right. If it be said that we deal not with guilt or innocence but with frankness, the answer is the same. There are areas where government may not probe. [G]overnment has no business penalizing a citizen merely for his beliefs or associations. [I]n NAACP v. Alabama, decided this day [see below], [we protected against] governmental probing into political activities and associations of one dissident group of people. We should do the same here."

Separate dissents by Chief Justice Warren and Justice Brennan emphasized that Beilan had lost his job more than 13 months after his refusal to answer the school authorities' questions—and only 5 days after a refusal before a congressional committee. Justice Brennan insisted that Beilan was "actually" discharged because of the latter refusal. More generally, he argued that Lerner and Beilan each had been "branded a disloyal American" and that the record was "wholly devoid of [evidence] to support the ultimate finding of disloyalty."

3. *Other government employee security problems, state and federal.*
a. *State.* Justice Clark, who had written Slochower, note 1 above, also wrote the majority opinion in Nelson v. County of Los Angeles, 362 U.S. 1 (1960), a 5 to 3 decision sustaining a dismissal of an employee for silence.

Nelson involved a temporary County employee who had refused, on First and Fifth Amendment grounds, to answer questions about present Communist membership before a congressional committee after having been ordered to do so by the County. He was discharged for "insubordination."

Justice Clark, writing for the majority, found his opinion in Slochower distinguishable because "the test here, rather than being the invocation of any constitutional privilege, is the failure of the employee to answer. California has not predicated discharge on any 'built-in' inference of guilt in its statute, but solely on employees' insubordination for failure to give information which we have held that the State has a legitimate interest in securing." He accordingly found the case controlled by Beilan and Lerner. Justice Black, joined by Justice Douglas, dissented: "I would hold that no State can put any kind of penalty on any person for claiming a privilege authorized by the Federal Constitution." Justice Brennan, joined by Justice Douglas, also dissented, because he believed "this case to be governed squarely by Slochower."

b. *Federal.* During the fifties, there were several constitutional challenges to federal loyalty-security programs as well, but the Court usually avoided the constitutional issues in the federal program cases by holding that the administrators had violated the applicable regulations and statutes. See, e. g., Peters v. Hobby, 349 U.S. 331 (1955); Service v. Dulles, 354 U.S. 363 (1957); and Vitarelli v. Seaton, 359 U.S. 535 (1959). Compare Bailey v. Richardson, 182 F.2d 46 (D.C.Cir.1950), affirmed by an equally divided Court, 341 U.S. 918 (1951), and Joint Anti-Fascist Refugee Committee v. McGrath, 341 U.S. 123 (1951).*

4. *The 1957 bar admission cases—Schware and Konigsberg I.* a. SCHWARE v. BOARD OF BAR EXAMINERS, 353 U.S. 232 (1957), was one of two decisions in 1957 in which the Court found inadequate support for state refusals to admit applicants to the bar: the state's inferences regarding present moral character were found irrational on the basis of the records adduced and accordingly violated due process.

The New Mexico Board had refused to let Schware take the bar examination because, "taking into consideration the use of aliases by the applicant, his former connection with subversive organizations, and his record of arrests, he has failed to satisfy the Board as to the requisite moral character for admission to the bar of New Mexico." All of these grounds of the 1953 Board decision were based on matters that had occurred during several years up to 1940. Upon his request, the applicant was given a formal hearing at which he offered evidence of his excellent moral character since 1940.

Justice Black noted for the Court: "We need not enter into a discussion whether the practice of law is a 'right' or 'privilege'. Regardless of how the State's grant of permission to engage in this occupation is characterized, it is sufficient to say that a person cannot be prevented from practicing except

* Note also, on the applicability of due process criteria in federal security hearings, Greene v. McElroy, 360 U.S. 474 (1959), chap. 10 above; and for a rejection of a constitutional challenge to dismissal without a hearing (and without giving reasons such as "security risk" for the discharge), see Cafeteria Workers v. McElroy, 367 U.S. 886 (1961). On the pervasiveness of loyalty-security programs during this period, see generally Brown, Loyalty and Security (1958), and Gellhorn, Individual Freedom and Governmental Restraints (1956).

for valid reasons. Certainly the practice of law is not a matter of the State's grace." And here the reasons were insufficient: in light of Schware's "forceful showing of good moral character, the evidence upon which the State relies [including membership in the Communist Party during the 1930's] cannot be said to raise substantial doubts about his present good moral character." In the absence of evidence which "rationally justifies a finding that Schware was morally unfit to practice law," denial of the opportunity to qualify deprived petitioner of due process of law. Justice Frankfurter, joined by Justices Clark and Harlan, delivered a concurring opinion, concluding that the state court's holding "that Communist affiliation for six to seven years up to 1940 [in] and of itself made the petitioner 'a person of questionable character' is so dogmatic an inference as to be wholly unwarranted." †

b. Were the grounds relied on in Schware appropriate for the disposition of Konigsberg I, the companion case? In KONIGSBERG v. STATE BAR, 353 U.S. 252 (1957), petitioner, who had satisfactorily passed the bar examination and who had appeared at hearings before the Committee of Bar Examiners, was denied admission to the California bar because he "failed to demonstrate that he was a person of good moral character" and because he "failed to show that he did not advocate the overthrow of the Government of the United States or California by force, violence, or other unconstitutional means." At the hearings, petitioner refused, on First Amendment grounds, to answer questions about his political associations and beliefs; but the denial of admission was not based on such refusal. Petitioner offered evidence as to his good moral character and in disproof of his advocacy of violent overthrow of Government. (The record contained what the Court in a later case called "some, though weak, independent evidence that petitioner had once been connected with the Communist Party.") Upon an examination of the record, the Supreme Court concluded that the evidence did not rationally support the grounds for denial of admission. The majority treated the case as similar to Schware. Justice Frankfurter dissented on jurisdictional grounds. Justice Harlan, joined by Justice Clark, after joining the views of Justice Frankfurter, dissented on the merits: "The Court decides the case as if the issue were whether the record contains evidence demonstrating [that] Konigsberg had a bad moral character. I do not think this is the issue. The question before us, it seems to me, is whether it violates the Fourteenth Amendment for a state bar committee to decline to certify for admission to the bar an applicant who obstructs a proper investigation into his qualifications by deliberately, and without constitutional justification, refusing to answer questions relevant to his fitness under valid standards, and

† Compare a bar admission case a decade earlier, In re Summers, 325 U.S. 561 (1945)—a 5 to 4 decision sustaining a state refusal to admit to the bar a conscientious objector, on the ground that he could not take the required oath to support the state constitution. The majority emphasized State control "as to the personnel of its bar" and found no religious discrimination. Note also Barsky v. Board of Regents, 347 U.S. 442 (1954), sustaining the license suspension of a physician who had been convicted for failure to produce in a congressional inquiry certain financial records of the Joint Anti-Fascist Refugee Committee. Justices Black, Frankfurter and Douglas delivered dissenting opinions emphasizing that the conduct constituting the crime had no bearing on the appellant's competency to practice medicine.

who is therefore deemed by the State, under its law, to have failed to carry his burden of proof to establish that he is qualified." (The subsequent history of Konigsberg's case appears in the next note.)

5. *Bar admission in 1961: Konigsberg II.* On remand of Konigsberg I, there was another hearing before the bar committee, and Konigsberg was once again denied admission to the bar. But this time, the state explicitly relied on his refusal to answer, and the Supreme Court (as in the employee cases, notes 2 and 3 above), sustained that ban on bar admission in a 5 to 4 decision. KONIGSBERG v. STATE BAR OF CALIFORNIA, 366 U.S. 36 (1961). As Justice Harlan's majority opinion described the second round of bar committee hearings, "Konigsberg introduced further evidence as to his good moral character (none of which was rebutted), reiterated unequivocally his disbelief in violent overthrow, and stated that he had never knowingly been a member of any organization which advocated such action. He persisted, however, in his refusals to answer any questions relating to his membership in the Communist Party. The Committee again declined to certify him, this time on the ground that his refusals to answer had obstructed a full investigation into his qualifications."

Justice Harlan's majority opinion emphasized even more strongly than he had in earlier opinions the distinction between exclusions or dismissals for refusals to answer relevant questions and substantive grounds for denials of employment or a license. The scope of inquiry, he reiterated, was broader than the scope of grounds for disqualification: the state could deny admission for refusing to answer relevant questions even if affirmative answer to the questions would not by themselves have justified exclusion. In short, Justice Harlan insisted that the 14th Amendment permits a state to deny admission to a bar applicant if he refuses to provide unprivileged answers to questions having substantial relevance to his qualifications. He dismissed as "untenable" the claim "that the questions as to Communist Party membership were made irrelevant [by] the fact that bare, innocent membership is not a ground for disqualification." He quoted the bar committee's response as the "entirely correct" answer to that contention: "You see, by failing to answer the initial question there certainly is no basis and no opportunity for us to investigate with respect to the other matters to which the initial question might very well be considered preliminary." [Consider, in examining the later cases, whether that distinction between scope of inquiry and scope of disqualification persists. See, e. g., the Keyishian decision in 1967 and the 1971 Bar Admission Cases, sec. 5B below.]

The rejection of Konigsberg's final claim—that "he was privileged not to respond to questions dealing with Communist Party membership because they unconstitutionally impinged upon rights of free speech and association" —evoked an extensive debate between Justices Harlan and Black on "absolutes" and "balancing." [See the excerpts from that debate printed with the introductory materials to chap. 12, above. See also their similar debate two years earlier, in the congressional investigations context, in Barenblatt v. United States, sec. 6 below.] In rejecting Konigsberg's First Amendment argument, Justice Harlan stated: "As regards the questioning of public employees relative to Communist Party membership it has already been held that the interest in not subjecting speech and association to the deterrence of

subsequent disclosure is outweighed by the State's interest in ascertaining the fitness of the employee for the post he holds. [W]ith respect to this same question of Communist Party membership, we regard the State's interest in having lawyers who are devoted to the law in its broadest sense, including not only its substantive provisions, but also its procedures for orderly change, as clearly sufficient to outweigh the minimal effect upon free association occasioned by compulsory disclosure in the circumstances here presented. There is here no likelihood that deterrence of association may result from foreseeable private action [see NAACP v. Alabama, below], for bar committee interrogations such as this are conducted in private. . . . Nor is there the possibility that the State may be afforded the opportunity for imposing undetectable arbitrary consequences upon protected association [see Shelton v. Tucker, below], for a bar applicant's exclusion by reason of Communist Party membership is subject to judicial review."

Justice Black's dissent, joined by Chief Justice Warren and Justice Douglas, insisted that the record showed, "beyond any shadow of a doubt, that the reason Konigsberg has been rejected is because the Committee suspects that he was at one time a member of the Communist Party. [The] majority avoids the otherwise unavoidable necessity of reversing the judgment below on that ground by simply refusing to look beyond the reason given by the Committee to justify Konigsberg's rejection." He argued, moreover, that the majority's result was indefensible even if its balancing approach were justifiable. He commented: "The interest in free association at stake here is not merely the personal interest of petitioner . . .. It is the interest of all the people in having a society in which no one is intimidated with respect to his beliefs or associations. It seems plain to me that the inevitable effect of the majority's decision is to condone a practice that will have a substantial deterrent effect upon the associations entered into by anyone who may want to become a lawyer in California." He concluded: "The interest of the Committee in satisfying its curiosity with respect to Konigsberg's 'possible' membership in the Communist Party two decades ago has been inflated out of all proportion to its real value—the vast interest of the public in maintaining unabridged the basic freedoms of speech, press and assembly has been paid little if anything more than lip service—and important constitutional rights have once against been 'balanced' away." [Justices Harlan and Black also disagreed about whether California had improperly placed upon the applicant the burden of proof of nonadvocacy of violent overthrow, in violation of Speiser v. Randall, 357 U.S. 513 (1958). Justice Brennan, joined by Chief Justice Warren, submitted a separate dissent emphasizing the burden of proof problem.] *

---

* In a companion case to Konigsberg II, In re Anastaplo, 366 U.S. 82 (1961), the Court upheld Illinois' refusal to admit petitioner to the bar, largely on the authority of Konigsberg. Was the Anastaplo case so clearly governed by Konigsberg II? Did Anastaplo have a stronger case? Did the differences between his case and Konigsberg's warrant more careful treatment?

Justice Harlan's majority opinion in Anastaplo described the proceedings before the bar committee as "a wide-ranging exchange [in] which the Committee sought to explore Anastaplo's ability conscientiously to swear support of the Federal and State Constitutions [and] Anastaplo undertook to expound and defend, on historical and ideological premises, his abstract belief in the 'right of revolution,' and to

PUBLIC DEMANDS FOR INFORMATION: THE IMPACT OF THE EXPANDED SELF-INCRIMINATION PRIVILEGE

In the foregoing cases of the fifties, one of the assumptions supporting the Court's views regarding the permissible scope of state inquiries affecting public employees and the bar was that the federal self-incrimination privilege did not apply to the states. In 1964, in Malloy v. Hogan, 378 U.S. 1, the Court found the privilege applicable via the 14th Amendment. To what extent does that "incorporation" of the Fifth Amendment affect the constitutionally acceptable scope of inquiries—quite apart from modern evolutions in First Amendment doctrine to be considered in sec. 5B below?

1. *Cohen and Spevack.* In COHEN v. HURLEY, 366 U.S. 117 (1961),—decided on the same day as Konigsberg II and Anastaplo—a 5 to 4 decision sustained the disbarment of a lawyer who had refused to produce information relating to alleged "ambulance chasing" in a bar inquiry into his professional fitness. Justice Harlan's opinion noted that no federal self-incrimination privilege was available in state proceedings and found that the state had drawn no "unfavorable inference" from petitioner's assertion of the privilege; rather it had rested "solely upon his refusal to discharge obligations which, as a lawyer, he owed to the court." But in 1964, in Malloy v. Hogan, the Fifth Amendment privilege *was* held applicable to the states. And when the Cohen issue arose again in 1967, in SPEVACK v. KLEIN, 385 U.S. 511, Cohen was overruled in view of the intervening Malloy decision. Justice Douglas' plurality opinion in Spevack, joined by Chief Justice Warren and Justices Black and Brennan, concluded "that the Self-Incrimination Clause [extends] its protection to lawyers as well as to other individuals, and that it should not be watered down by imposing the dishonor of disbarment and the deprivation of a livelihood as a price for asserting it." He insisted that the state may impose no sanction which makes assertion of the Fifth Amendment privilege "costly." Justice Fortas' concurring opinion agreed with the overruling of Cohen but added: "I would

resist, on grounds of asserted constitutional right and scruple, Committee questions which he deemed improper." Justice Harlan insisted that the Konigsberg case was not distinguishable merely because in that case "there was some, though weak, independent evidence that the applicant had once been connected with the Communist Party, while here there was no such evidence as to Anastaplo." Good faith belief in the need for inquiry was enough for Justice Harlan: "Where, as with membership in the bar, the State may withhold a privilege available only to those possessing the requisite qualifications, it is of no constitutional significance whether the state's interrogation of an applicant on matters relevant to these qualifications—in this case Communist Party membership—is prompted by information which it already has about him from other sources, or arises merely from a good faith belief in the need for exploratory or testing questioning of the applicant. Were it otherwise, a bar examining committee such as this, having no resources of its own for independent investigation, might be placed in the untenable position of having to certify an applicant without assurance as to the significant aspect of his qualifications which the applicant himself is best circumstanced to supply. The Constitution does not so unreasonably fetter the states." Justice Black again dissented, joined by Chief Justice Warren and Justices Douglas and Brennan. He saw the case as "a striking illustration of the destruction that can be inflicted upon individual liberty when this Court fails to enforce the First Amendment to the full extent of its express and unequivocal terms."

distinguish between a lawyer's right to remain silent and that of a public employee who is asked questions specifically, directly, and narrowly relating to the performance of his official duties as distinguished from his beliefs or other matters that are not within the scope of the specific duties which he undertook faithfully to perform as part of his employment by the State. [A] lawyer is not an employee of the State." *

2. *Garrity.* In a companion case to Spevack, GARRITY v. NEW JERSEY, 386 U.S. 493 (1967), the appellants were policemen who had answered questions in a state investigation after having been warned that refusals to answer would subject them to removal from office. Their answers were used in a subsequent prosecution for conspiracy to obstruct the administration of the traffic laws. The Supreme Court's 5 to 4 decision held that their statements were "coerced" and that the constitutional ban on coerced confessions "prohibits use in subsequent criminal proceedings of statements obtained under threat of removal from office." Justice Douglas' majority opinion stated that the state could not "use the threat of discharge to secure incriminatory evidence against an employee" and that "policemen, like teachers and lawyers, are not relegated to a watered-down version of constitutional rights."

3. *Gardner v. Broderick.* Spevack and Garrity left in doubt the question whether public employees could be discharged for refusal to testify at hearings on official misconduct. In GARDNER v. BRODERICK, 392 U.S. 273 (1968), the Court made it clear that they could under certain conditions, even though it found appellant's dismissal unconstitutional. Appellant, a policeman, was dismissed because of his failure to sign a "waiver of immunity" from prosecution after being called before a grand jury investigating police misconduct in connection with unlawful gambling operations. Justice Fortas' opinion emphasized that appellant was "discharged from office not for failure to answer relevant questions about his official duties, but for refusal to waive a constitutional right." If he had "refused to answer questions specifically, directly, and narrowly relating to the performance of his official duties, without being required to waive his immunity with respect to the use of his answers or the fruits thereof in a criminal prosecution of himself, Garrity v. New Jersey," Justice Fortas elaborated, "the privilege against self-incrimination would not have been a bar to his dismissal." A policeman, in short, is under a greater duty to respond to inquiries than a lawyer. In reaching that conclusion, Justice Fortas adopted for the Court the distinction he had urged in his concurrence in Spevack: The policeman is "directly, immediately, and entirely responsible to the city or State which is his employer. He owes his entire loyalty to it. . . . Unlike the lawyer who is directly responsible to his client, the policeman is either responsible to the State or to no one." As Justice Fortas put it in a companion case, public employees "subject themselves to dismissal if they refuse to ac-

* Justice Harlan's dissent, joined by Justices Clark and Stewart, insisted that this application of the privilege "serves only to hamper appropriate protection of other fundamental public values." To Justice Harlan, cases like Beilan and Lerner, when read with Slochower, "make plain that so long as state authorities do not derive an imputation of guilt from a claim of the privilege," they may require disclosure of information "in the course of a bona fide assessment" of an employee's or lawyer's fitness. Justice White also dissented.

count for their performance of their public trust, after proper proceedings which do not involve an attempt to coerce them to relinquish their constitutional rights." †

THE EMERGENCE OF THE MODERN APPROACH: SCRUTINIZING THE JUSTIFICATIONS FOR STATE INQUIRIES INTO NAACP MEMBERSHIP LISTS

Introduction. During the late fifties, while most First Amendment defenses to governmental demands for information were proving unsuccessful—typically, in the context of inquiries about subversive associations—, the Court blocked a state effort to obtain access to NAACP membership lists, in NAACP v. Alabama, 357 U.S. 449 (1958), the next principal case. The Court's critical scrutiny of the asserted state justification for the inquiry and its sensitivity to collateral impacts of disclosure on First Amendment areas foreshadowed the broader constitutional restrictions that evolved in the cases of the sixties.

NAACP v. Alabama was followed by a similar ruling in a similar context: BATES v. LITTLE ROCK, 361 U.S. 516 (1960), again protected NAACP membership lists. In Bates, as an aid in the collection of a license tax on any "trade, business, profession, vocation or calling," the city required all organizations to submit certain information, including the names of persons contributing money. Petitioner, custodian of records of a local branch of the organization, was convicted for failing to give this information. The Supreme Court, in an opinion by Justice Stewart, reversed. It found sufficient evidence that the disclosure of the lists "would work a significant interference with the freedom of association" of the members and concluded that there was a "complete failure" in the record "to demonstrate a controlling justification" for such interference. Justice Stewart noted that no plausible claim could be made that the NAACP was subject to the license tax. [See also the NAACP membership list context of a major case of the sixties curtailing legislative investigations, the 1963 decision in Gibson, sec. 6 below.]

In NAACP v. Alabama and in Bates, the Court found the claim that the state was seeking relevant information weak indeed. In Shelton v.

---

† See also the companion case, Uniformed Sanitation Men Ass'n v. Comm'r of Sanitation, 392 U.S. 280 (1968).

Justice Harlan, joined by Justice Stewart, concurred in the result in both cases under the compulsion of Spevack and Garrity. He took comfort, however, in being able to find in these opinions "a procedural formula whereby, for example, public officials may now be discharged and lawyers disciplined for refusing to divulge to appropriate authority information pertinent to the faithful performance of their offices. I add only that this is a welcome breakthrough in what Spevack and Garrity might otherwise have been thought to portend."

Note the restatement of the Garrity-Gardner holdings in Lefkowitz v. Turley, 414 U.S. 70 (1973): "employees of the State do not forfeit their constitutional privilege"; however, "they may be compelled to respond to questions about the performance of their duties but only if their answers cannot be used against them in subsequent criminal prosecutions." Lefkowitz held unconstitutional New York laws providing for cancellation of public contracts and disqualification from state contracts for five years for contractors refusing to waive immunity when called to testify concerning their contracts. Justice White emphasized that the state could not "compel testimony that had not been immunized."

Tucker, 364 U.S. 479 (1960), with NAACP activity once again the context, the relevance of the inquiry into teachers' associations could not be denied. Nevertheless, the Court blocked the questioning. Building on the membership list cases, the Court found "relevance" an inadequate justification for an inquiry so broad. The Shelton case, with which sec. 5B on the modern cases begins, together with the NAACP v. Alabama decision, with which this sec. 5A on the fifties ends, form a bridge between the judicial emphases of the two periods. Shelton, moreover, symbolizes the mounting judicial scrutiny of governmental inquiries and marks the emergence of doctrines (e. g., overbreadth) increasingly prominent in the later cases.

NAACP v. ALABAMA
357 U.S. 449, 78 S.Ct. 1163, 2 L.Ed.2d 1488 (1958).

Certiorari to the Supreme Court of Alabama.

[In this case, the Court held unconstitutional Alabama's demand that the NAACP reveal the names and addresses of all of its Alabama members and agents. The State's demand was made in the course of an injunction action brought in 1956 to stop the NAACP from conducting activities in Alabama, on the ground that it had failed to comply with the requirement that foreign corporations qualify before doing business in the State. The NAACP, a New York membership corporation, operated in Alabama largely through local affiliates which were unincorporated associations. The NAACP considered itself exempt from the State's foreign corporation registration law. While the injunction action was pending, the State moved for the production of a large number of the NAACP's records. The NAACP "produced substantially all the data called for [except] its membership lists, as to which it contended that Alabama could not constitutionally compel disclosure." The trial court adjudged the NAACP in contempt and imposed a $100,000 fine.] *

Mr. Justice HARLAN delivered the opinion of the Court.   .   .   .

Effective advocacy of both public and private points of view, particularly controversial ones, is undeniably enhanced by group association, as this Court has more than once recognized by remarking upon the close nexus between the freedoms of speech and assembly. [E. g., DeJonge v. Oregon, chap. 12, sec. 1.] It is beyond debate that freedom to engage in association for the advancement of beliefs and ideas is an inseparable aspect of the "liberty" assured by the Due Process Clause of the Fourteenth Amendment, which embraces freedom of speech.   .   .   .   Of course, it is immaterial whether the beliefs sought to be advanced by association pertain to political, economic, religious or cultural matters, and state action which may have the effect of curtailing the freedom to associate is subject to the closest scrutiny.

The fact that Alabama [has] taken no direct action [to] restrict the right of petitioner's members to associate freely does not end inquiry into the

---

* Before reaching the merits, the Court rejected two jurisdictional arguments by the state: (1) that the Court had no jurisdiction because the judgment below rested on an independent and adequate state ground; and (2) that the NAACP had no standing to assert the constitutional rights of its members. See chap. 15 below.

effect of the production order. . . . In the domain of these indispensable liberties, whether of speech, press, or association, the decisions of this Court recognize that abridgment of such rights, even though unintended, may inevitably follow from varied forms of governmental action. . . . It is hardly a novel perception that compelled disclosure of affiliation with groups engaged in advocacy may constitute [an effective] restraint on freedom of association. [The] Court has recognized the vital relationship between freedom to associate and privacy in one's associations. . . . Inviolability of privacy in group association may in many circumstances be indispensable to preservation of freedom of association, particularly where a group espouses dissident beliefs. . . .

We think that the production order, in the respects here drawn in question, must be regarded as entailing the likelihood of a substantial restraint upon the exercise by petitioner's members of their right to freedom of association. Petitioner has made an uncontroverted showing that on past occasions revelation of the identity of its rank-and-file members has exposed these members to economic reprisal, loss of employment, threat of physical coercion, and other manifestations of public hostility. Under these circumstances, we think it apparent that compelled disclosure of petitioner's Alabama membership is likely to affect adversely the ability of petitioner and its members to pursue their collective effort to foster beliefs which they admittedly have the right to advocate, in that it may induce members to withdraw from the Association and dissuade others from joining it because of fear of exposure of their beliefs shown through their associations and of the consequences of this exposure. . . .

We turn to the final question whether Alabama has demonstrated an interest in obtaining the disclosures it seeks from petitioner which is sufficient to justify the deterrent effect which we have concluded these disclosures may well have on the free exercise by petitioner's members of their constitutionally protected right of association. [Such a] "subordinating interest of the State must be compelling," [Sweezy v. New Hampshire (concurring opinion), sec. 6 below].

It is important to bear in mind that petitioner asserts no right to absolute immunity from state investigation, and no right to disregard Alabama's laws. As shown by its substantial compliance with the production order, petitioner does not deny Alabama's right to obtain from it such information as the State desires concerning the purposes of the Association and its activities within the State. Petitioner has not objected to divulging the identity of its members who are employed by or hold official positions with it. It has urged the rights solely of its ordinary rank-and-file members. . . .

Whether there was "justification" in this instance turns solely on the substantiality of Alabama's interest in obtaining the membership lists. [The] exclusive purpose [claimed by the state] was to determine whether petitioner was conducting intrastate business in violation of the Alabama foreign corporation registration statute, and the membership lists were expected to help resolve this question. [The critical issues in the litigation were "the character of petitioner and its activities in Alabama."] Without intimating the slightest view upon the merits of these issues, we are unable to perceive that the disclosure of the names of petitioner's rank-and-file members has a sub-

stantial bearing on [them]. As matters stand in the state court, petitioner (1) has admitted its presence and conduct of activities in Alabama since 1918; (2) has offered to comply in all respects with the state qualification statute, although preserving its contention that the statute does not apply to it; and (3) has apparently complied satisfactorily with the production order, except for the membership lists. [W]hatever interest the State may have in obtaining names of ordinary members has not been shown to be sufficient to overcome petitioner's constitutional objections to the production order.

From what has already been said, we think it apparent that Bryant v. Zimmerman, 278 U.S. 63 [1928], cannot be relied on in support of the State's position, for that case involved markedly different considerations in terms of the interest of the State in obtaining disclosure. There, this Court upheld, as applied to a member of a local chapter of the Ku Klux Klan, a New York statute requiring any unincorporated association which demanded an oath as a condition to membership to file with state officials copies of its ". . . constitution, by-laws, rules, regulations and oath of membership, together with a roster of its membership and a list of its officers for the current year." In its opinion, the Court took care to emphasize the nature of the organization which New York sought to regulate. The decision was based on the particular character of the Klan's activities, involving acts of unlawful intimidation and violence, which the Court assumed was before the state legislature when it enacted the statute, and of which the Court itself took judicial notice. Furthermore, the situation before us is significantly different from that in Bryant, because the organization there had made no effort to comply with any of the requirements of New York's statute but rather had refused to furnish the State with *any* information as to its local activities.

We hold that the immunity from state scrutiny of membership lists which the Association claims on behalf of its members is here so related to the right of the members to pursue their lawful private interests privately and to associate freely with others in so doing as to come within the protection of the Fourteenth Amendment. And we conclude that Alabama has fallen short of showing a controlling justification for the deterrent effect on the free enjoyment of the right to associate which disclosure of membership lists is likely to have. . . .

Reversed.*

---

* Is there also a right *not* to associate? Claims to freedom *from* coerced association were argued but not reached by a majority of the Court in several cases challenging union shop and integrated bar arrangements. See, e. g., International Association of Machinists v. Street, 367 U.S. 740 (1961) (claim that dues under union shop agreement were used to support political causes with which members disagreed), and Lathrop v. Donohue, 367 U.S. 820 (1961) (attack on dues requirements under integrated bar system). See also Railway Employees' Department v. Hanson, 351 U.S. 225 (1956), and Brotherhood of Railway Clerks v. Allen, 373 U.S. 113 (1963).

B. THE CHANGES SINCE THE SIXTIES

SHELTON v. TUCKER

364 U.S. 479, 81 S.Ct. 247, 5 L.Ed.2d 231 (1960).

Appeal from the United States District Court for the Eastern District of Arkansas.

[This case held unconstitutional an Arkansas statute—Act 10—which required every teacher, as a condition of employment in a state-supported school or college, to file "annually an affidavit listing without limitation every organization to which he has belonged or regularly contributed within the preceding five years." Shelton, who had taught in the Little Rock Schools for 25 years, refused to file an affidavit pursuant to the Act for the 1959–60 school year, and his teaching contract was not renewed. In his lower federal court proceeding to challenge the Act, the evidence showed that he was not a member of any organization advocating the overthrow of the Government and that he was a member of the NAACP. The trial court upheld Act 10, finding that the information sought was "relevant." (In the same proceeding, however, the lower court held unconstitutional a companion law making it unlawful for any member of the NAACP to be employed by the State or any of its subdivisions.)] †

Mr. Justice STEWART delivered the opinion of the Court. . . .

It is urged [that] Act 10 deprives teachers in Arkansas of their rights to personal, associational, and academic liberty. [I]n considering this contention, we deal with two basic postulates.

First. There can be no doubt of the right of a state to investigate the competence and fitness of those whom it hires to teach in its schools. . . .

This controversy is thus not of a pattern with such cases as [NAACP v. Alabama and Bates v. Little Rock]. In those cases the Court held that there was no substantially relevant correlation between the governmental interest asserted and the state's effort to compel disclosure of the membership lists involved. Here, by contrast, there can be no question of the relevance of a state's inquiry into the fitness and competence of its teachers.[1]

Second. It is not disputed that to compel a teacher to disclose his every associational tie is to impair that teacher's right of free association, a right closely allied to freedom of speech and a right which, like free speech, lies at the foundation of a free society. [DeJonge; Bates.] Such interfer-

---

† In the same case, the Court also sustained a state court challenge to Act 10 —Carr v. Young—brought by a university professor and a high school teacher.

1. The declared purpose of Act 10 is "to provide assistance in the administration and financing of the public schools . . . ." The declared justification for the emergency clause is "to assist in the solution" of problems raised by "the decisions of the United States Supreme Court in the school segregation cases." . . . But neither the breadth and generality of the declared purpose nor the possible irrelevance of the emergency provision detract from the existence of an actual relevant state interest in the inquiry. [Footnote by the Court.]

ence with personal freedom is conspicuously accented when the teacher serves at the absolute will of those to whom the disclosure must be made .   . . .

The statute does not provide that the information it requires be kept confidential. Each school board is left free to deal with the information as it wishes. The record contains evidence to indicate that fear of public disclosure is neither theoretical nor groundless.[2] Even if there were no disclosure to the general public, the pressure upon a teacher to avoid any ties which might displease those who control his professional destiny would be constant and heavy. .   . .

The vigilant protection of constitutional freedoms is nowhere more vital than in the community of American schools. .   . .

The question to be decided here is not whether the State of Arkansas can ask certain of its teachers about all their organizational relationships. It is not whether the State can ask all of its teachers about certain of their associational ties. It is not whether teachers can be asked how many organizations they belong to, or how much time they spend in organizational activity. The question is whether the State can ask every one of its teachers to disclose every single organization with which he has been associated over a five-year period. The scope of the inquiry required by Act 10 is completely unlimited. [The Act] requires a teacher [to] list, without number, every conceivable kind of associational tie—social, professional, political, avocational, or religious. Many such relationships could have no possible bearing upon the teacher's occupational competence or fitness.

In a series of decisions this Court has held that, even though the governmental purpose be legitimate and substantial, that purpose cannot be pursued by means that broadly stifle fundamental personal liberties when the end can be more narrowly achieved.[3] The breadth of legislative abridgment must be viewed in the light of less drastic means for achieving the same basic purpose. .   . .

The unlimited and indiscriminate sweep of the statute now before us brings it within the ban of our prior cases. The statute's comprehensive interference with associational freedom goes far beyond what might be justified in the exercise of the State's legitimate inquiry into the fitness and competency of its teachers.

Reversed.

Mr. Justice FRANKFURTER, dissenting. .   . .

Where state assertions of authority are attacked as impermissibly restrictive upon thought, expression, or association, the existence *vel non* of

2. In the state court proceedings a witness who was a member of the Capital Citizens Council testified that his group intended to gain access to some of the Act 10 affidavits with a view to eliminating from the school system persons who supported organizations unpopular with the group. Among such organizations he named the American Civil Liberties Union, the Urban League, the American Association of University Professors, and the Women's Emergency Committee to Open Our Schools. [Footnote by the Court.]

3. In other areas, involving different constitutional issues, more administrative leeway has been thought allowable in the interest of increased efficiency in accomplishing a clearly constitutional central purpose. See Purity Extract & Tonic Co. v. Lynch, 226 U.S. 192 . . . . . But cf. Dean Milk Co. v. Madison, 340 U.S. 349 [chap. 5, sec. 1]. [Foootnote by the Court.]

other possible less restrictive means of achieving the object which the State seeks is, of course, a constitutionally relevant consideration. This is not because some novel, particular rule of law obtains in cases of this kind. Whenever the reasonableness and fairness of a measure are at issue, [the] availability or unavailability of alternative methods of proceeding is germane. Thus, a State may not prohibit the distribution of literature on its cities' streets as a means of preventing littering, when the same end might be achieved with only slightly greater inconvenience by applying the sanctions of the penal law not to the pamphleteer who distributes the paper but to the recipient who crumples it and throws it away. [E. g., Schneider v. State, chap. 12, sec. 2.] But the consideration of feasible alternative modes of regulation in these cases did not imply that the Court might substitute its own choice among alternatives for that of a state legislature, or that the States were to be restricted to the "narrowest" workable means of accomplishing an end. Consideration of alternatives may focus the precise exercise of state legislative authority which is tested in this Court by the standard of reasonableness, but it does not alter or displace that standard. The issue remains whether, in light of the particular kind of restriction upon individual liberty which a regulation entails, it is reasonable for a legislature to choose that form of regulation rather than others less restrictive. . . .

In the present case the Court strikes down an Arkansas statute requiring that teachers disclose to school officials all of their organizational relationships, on the ground that "many such relationships could have no possible bearing upon the teacher's occupational competence or fitness." Granted that a given teacher's membership in the First Street Congregation is, standing alone, of little relevance to what may rightly be expected of a teacher, is that membership equally irrelevant when it is discovered that the teacher is in fact a member of the First Street Congregation *and* the Second Street Congregation *and* the Third Street Congregation *and* the 4–H Club *and* the 3–H Club *and* half a dozen other groups? Presumably, a teacher may have so many divers associations, so many divers commitments, that they consume his time and energy and interest at the expense of his work or even of his professional dedication. Unlike wholly individual interests, organizational connections—because they involve obligations undertaken with relation to other persons—may become inescapably demanding and distracting. Surely, a school board is entitled to inquire whether any of its teachers has placed himself, or is placing himself, in a condition where his work may suffer. Of course, the State might ask: "To how many organizations do you belong? " or "How much time do you expend at organizational activity? " But the answer to such questions could reasonably be regarded by a state legislature as insufficient, both because the veracity of the answer is more difficult to test, [and] because an estimate of time presently spent in organizational activity reveals nothing as to the quality and nature of that activity, upon the basis of which, necessarily, judgment or prophesy of the extent of future involvement must be based. A teacher's answers to the questions which Arkansas asks, moreover, may serve the purpose of making known to school authorities persons who come into contact with the teacher in all of the phases of his activity in the community, and who can be questioned, if need be, concerning the teacher's conduct in matters which this Court can certainly not now say are lacking in any pertinence to professional fitness. It

is difficult to understand how these particular ends could be achieved by asking "certain of [the State's] teachers about all their organizational relationships," or "all of its teachers about certain of their associational ties," or all of its teachers how many associations currently involve them or during how many hours; and difficult, therefore, to appreciate why the Court deems unreasonable and forbids what Arkansas does ask. . . .

I am authorized to say that Mr. Justice CLARK, Mr. Justice HARLAN and Mr. Justice WHITTAKER agree with this opinion. [A separate dissent by Justice Harlan, joined by the other dissenters, is omitted.]

ALTERNATIVE MEANS AND OVERBREADTH: A FURTHER COMMENT, PROMPTED BY SHELTON v. TUCKER

When the Court finds the state interest legitimate, yet the means chosen too broad, is it under an obligation to explain what narrower means to achieve the state's objective were available? The Court's footnote 4 suggests a 1951 Dean Milk Case as an analogy. See chap. 5, sec. 1, above. But in setting aside the city "health" ordinance on commerce grounds there, the Court did suggest narrower available alternatives. Yet in the increasing resort to the Shelton v. Tucker approach, the Court tends to be silent about alternatives. When the Court does *not* spell out alternatives, is it really using the Dean Milk technique as a facade? Should the Court say simply that state justifications are outweighed by the burdens imposed on First Amendment rights? Is overbreadth talk more palatable to the Court because it gives the appearance of leaving alternatives open to the legislature—of intervening in legislative choices more marginally than outright "balancing" would? Recall the earlier comments on the overbreadth technique, in chap. 12, sec. 1.

Is a decision that fails to spell out more fully in what respect the means are too broad, such as Shelton, a decision that "lacks intellectual coherence"? See Bickel, The Least Dangerous Branch (1962). Would spelling out of alternatives as the Court did in Dean Milk subject the Court to charges of "legislating" without adequate knowledge—as Justice Black's dissent in Dean Milk charged? Is it too much to expect the Court to say more about alternatives than it did in Shelton, even if the degree of detail offered in Dean Milk is not required? Do the later overbreadth cases—e. g., Keyishian, below—do better in achieving a happy medium?

LOYALTY OATHS, EMPLOYEE SECURITY PROGRAMS AND BAR ADMISSIONS SINCE THE SIXTIES

Introduction. Recall the loyalty oath cases of the early fifties—e. g., Wieman v. Updegraff, at the beginning of sec. 5A. Did the Court's encounters with similar problems in the early sixties, in Cramp and Baggett, notes 1 and 2 below, depart sharply from the earlier analyses? Do "void-for-vagueness" decisions like Cramp and Baggett throw adequate light on the underlying problems of the permissible grounds of inquiry and the permissible bases for disqualification? Do bill of attainder analyses, note 3 below,

throw a more adequate light?   Do these cases clarify what constitutes protected expression?   Would explicit balancing have been preferable?

Do vagueness cases such as Cramp and Baggett explain the invalidation of the oath law in Elfbrandt v. Russell, which follows?   Or were the obscurities of Elfbrandt explainable as an implicit repudiation of the approaches of the fifties, including Lerner and Beilan?   Did Elfbrandt suggest the emergence of a new approach: incorporating the standards of criminal cases on subversion (chap. 12, sec. 1) into the government employees and licensees area;   making the scope of inquiry coextensive with the bases for disqualification;   and shrinking the bases for disqualification?   If those were indeed the elements of a new approach, did the Court adequately explain what justified its adoption?   See generally Israel, "Elfbrandt v. Russell: The Demise of the Oath?"   1966 Sup.Ct.Rev. 193.

Did Keyishian, a year after Elfbrandt, provide retroactive explanation of Elfbrandt and make explicit the new directions? [1]   Is Keyishian sound?   In his critique of Elfbrandt, Professor Israel commented: "[O]pinions relying upon the 'overbroadness' rule often provide no more indication of the Court's analysis than a conclusionary statement that a particular aspect of the statutory infringement on speech was overly broad as it applied to the particular interest that the state advanced in that case.   The majority opinion in Elfbrandt fits this pattern and, indeed, is more delinquent, since the Court failed in large part even to identify the state interest against which the legislation was balanced."   Is that comment justified?   Is it less applicable to Keyishian?

Did Keyishian, though an overbreadth case, more fully articulate the range of constitutionally protected activity?   Was it more explicit in delineating the First Amendment limits on inquiries and grounds for disqualification?   Does Keyishian make the strict standards of criminal liability of Scales-Yates-Noto (and Brandenburg) wholly applicable to disqualification of government employees?   Does Keyishian limit questioning of public employees to a scope identical to the grounds for disqualification?   Or does the scope of inquiry still extend somewhat beyond the scope of disqualification grounds?

Do the Burger Court decisions, clarify—or change—the answers suggested by Keyishian?   Has the Burger Court adhered to the—occasionally obscure—developments of the late sixties, or has it retreated from them?   Recall that the Burger Court continues to adhere to the Warren Court criminal standard announced in Brandenburg, chap. 12, sec. 1.   Is there similar adherence to the inquiry and disqualification cases considered in this section?   See the materials after Keyishian, and especially the 1971 Bar Admission Cases below.

1.   *Cramp.*   CRAMP v. BOARD OF PUBLIC INSTRUCTION, 368 U.S. 278 (1961), involved a Florida statute requiring public employees to swear that they had never "knowingly lent their aid, support, advice, counsel or influence to the Communist Party."   Failure to execute the oath resulted in immediate discharge.   The Florida Supreme Court ruled that "the element

---

1.   Recall also United States v. Robel, 389 U.S. 258 (1967), decided soon after Keyishian and holding unconstitutional, on overbreadth grounds, a provision of the Subversive Activities Control Act of 1950 imposing criminal penalties on members of Communist-action organizations engaging "in any employment in any defense facility." The case is considered in chap. 12, sec. 1.

of scienter was implicit [in] the statute." The United States Supreme Court nevertheless sustained a teacher's challenge to the law. Justice Stewart's opinion emphasized the "extraordinary ambiguity of the statutory language" and found it "completely lacking [in] terms susceptible of objective measurement." He noted that the "vice of unconstitutional vagueness is further aggravated where, as here, the statute in question operates to inhibit the exercise of individual freedoms affirmatively protected by the Constitution."

2. *Baggett.* In BAGGETT v. BULLITT, 377 U.S. 360 (1964), the Court relying in part on the Cramp decision, invalidated two loyalty oath requirements imposed by the State of Washington. One required teachers to swear, for example, that they "will by precept and example promote respect for the flag and the institutions of the United States of America and the State of Washington"; the other required all state employees to swear that they were not members of a "subversive organization." In an opinion by Justice White, the Court held the requirements "invalid on their face because their language is unduly vague, uncertain and broad." Justice Clark, joined by Justice Harlan, dissented. As to the first oath, he argued that the state courts should be given an opportunity to construe it. As to the second, he claimed that Cramp was "not apposite"; that the Washington statute was "much more clear than the Smith Act"; and that the Gerende case (at the beginning of sec. 5A above) was in effect being overruled.[2]

3. *Oaths as bills of attainder: A preferable analysis?* Instead of emphasizing void-for-vagueness approaches or First Amendment values, would it have been preferable to analyze oath requirements and other disqualification provisions in terms of the bill of attainder restraints on the national and state governments in Art. I, §§ 9 and 10? Though the bill of attainder provisions have occasionally been mentioned in the cases, reliance has been largely in dissents; and the prohibition has played a relatively small role in the scrutiny of the types of governmental action considered in this section. In one of the major cases of the early fifties, Garner v. Board of Public Works (at the beginning of sec. 5A), Justices Douglas and Black did indeed dissent largely on bill of attainder grounds. But the majority rejected that argument: "Punishment" is not imposed "by a general regulation which merely provides standards of qualifications and eligibility for employment." Compare United States v. Brown, note 3b, below.

a. *The post-Civil War background.* Cases of nearly a century ago did provide a basis for viewing oaths in bill of attainder terms. The Court in the Reconstruction Era relied on that prohibition in invalidating state and federal legislative attempts to exclude former supporters of the Confederacy from certain professions: in Cummings v. Missouri, 4 Wall. 277 (1867), and Ex parte Garland, 4 Wall. 333 (1867), the Court found loyalty oath provisions to be bills of attainder. In Cummings, the Court defined a bill of attainder as "a legislative act which inflicts punishment without a judicial trial." That case held invalid a Missouri provision which required of all priests and clergymen (as well as teachers, lawyers, and corporate officials),

2. See also Whitehill v. Elkins, 389 U.S. 54 (1967), holding the Maryland teachers' oath unconstitutionally vague (as noted together with Gerende, sec. 5A above).

On the Burger Court's consideration of oath problems, see the notes following Keyishian, especially Cole v. Richardson.

as a condition to the continued practice of their professions, an oath that they had not given aid to the enemies of the United States. The Court found no relevant connection between past sympathy for the Confederacy and present professional fitness and concluded that the oath was exacted "not from any notion that the several acts designated indicated unfitness for the callings, but because it was thought that the several acts deserved punishment." In Garland, the companion case to Cummings, the Court held invalid a federal law prohibiting practice in federal courts unless the attorney had taken an oath that he had never engaged in hostility to the United States.[3]

b. *The Brown case.* Despite that background and the references in dissents, only one Warren Court decision relied on the bill of attainder objection to invalidating an employment condition. That case was UNITED STATES v. BROWN, 381 U.S. 437 (1965), holding unconstitutional a federal provision making it a crime for a member of the Communist Party to serve as an officer or an employee of a labor union. Chief Justice Warren's majority opinion emphasized that it was not necessary that a bill of attainder name the parties to be punished. Rather, he found a broader sweep to the prohibition, viewing it "as an implementation of the separation of powers, a general safeguard against legislative exercise of the judicial function, or more simply—trial by legislature." Though he recognized congressional power to protect interstate commerce by barring individuals from positions which might be used "to bring about political strikes," he found the statute invalid because it did not "set forth a generally applicable rule decreeing that any person who commits certain acts or possesses certain characteristics (acts and characteristics which, in Congress' view, make them likely to initiate political strikes) shall not hold union office, and leave to courts and juries the job of deciding what persons had committed the specified acts or possessed the specified characteristics." The fatal flaw was that the provision "designates in no uncertain terms the persons who possess the feared characteristics and therefore cannot hold union office without incurring criminal liability—members of the Communist Party." [4] The dissenters—Justice White, joined by Justices Clark, Harlan and Stewart—insisted that the majority had taken a "too narrow view of the legislative process" and had unduly restricted legislative power to classify and use shorthand phrases.[5] [The Brown principle has not played a central role in the Court's consideration of employment and licensing barriers since that 1965 decision was handed down: none of the subsequent decisions rests on it.]

---

3. Recall also the references to the bill of attainder limitation in Flemming v. Nestor, the loss-of-social-security-benefits-case in chap. 4. And note the reliance on the bill of attainder provision in United States v. Lovett, 328 U.S. 303 (1946), barring payment of compensation to specified government employees whose conduct had been the subject of investigation by a congressional committee.

4. The Court in Brown relied heavily on the analysis advocated in a Note, "The Bounds of Legislative Specification: A Suggested Approach to the Bill of Attainder Clause," 72 Yale L.J. 330 (1962).

5. Recall the somewhat similar problems raised by a more recent development in Supreme Court doctrine— the identification of "irrebuttable presumptions" as a fatal due process-equal protection flaw in legislative classifications. See the materials in chap. 10, sec. 6, above.

ELFBRANDT v. RUSSELL

384 U.S. 11, 86 S.Ct. 1238, 16 L.Ed.2d 321 (1966).

Certiorari to the Supreme Court of Arizona.

Mr. Justice DOUGLAS delivered the opinion of the Court.

This case . . . involves questions concerning the constitutionality of an Arizona Act requiring an oath from state employees. [The] oath reads in conventional fashion as follows:

> "I, (type or print name) do solemnly swear (or affirm) that I will support the Constitution of the United States and the Constitution and laws of the State of Arizona; that I will bear true faith and allegiance to the same, and defend them against all enemies [whatever], and that I will faithfully and impartially discharge the duties of the office of (name of office) according to the best of my ability, so help me God (or so I do affirm)."

The Legislature put a gloss on the oath by subjecting to a prosecution for perjury and for discharge from public office anyone who took the oath and who "knowingly and wilfully becomes or remains a member of the communist party of the United States or its successors or any of its subordinate organizations" or "any other organization" having for "one of its purposes" the overthrow of the government of Arizona or any of its political subdivisions where the employee had knowledge of the unlawful purpose. Petitioner, a teacher and a Quaker, decided she could not in good conscience take the oath, not knowing what it meant and not having any chance to get a hearing at which its precise scope and meaning could be determined. This suit for declaratory relief followed. . . .

We recognized in [Scales, chap. 12, sec. 1] that "quasi-political parties or other groups [may] embrace both legal and illegal aims." We noted that a "blanket prohibition of association with a group having both legal and illegal aims" would pose "a real danger that legitimate political expression or association would be impaired." The statute with which we dealt in Scales, the so-called "membership clause" of the Smith Act, was found not to suffer from this constitutional infirmity because as the Court construed it, the statute reached only "active" membership [with] the "specific intent" of assisting in achieving the unlawful ends of the organization. The importance of this limiting construction from a constitutional standpoint was emphasized in [Noto], decided the same day . . . .

Any lingering doubt that proscription of mere knowing membership, without any showing of "specific intent," would run afoul of the Constitution was set at rest by our decision in [Aptheker, chap. 12, sec. 1.] We dealt there with a statute which provided that no member of a Communist organization ordered by the Subversive Activities Control Board to register shall apply for or use a passport. We concluded that the statute would not permit a narrow reading of the sort we gave § 2385 in Scales. The statute, as we read it, covered membership which was not accompanied by a specific intent to further the unlawful aims of the organization, and we held it unconstitutional.

The oath and accompanying statutory gloss challenged here suffer from an identical constitutional infirmity. One who subscribes to this Arizona oath and who is, or thereafter becomes, a knowing member of an organization which has as "one of its purposes" the violent overthrow of the government, is subject to immediate discharge and criminal penalties. Nothing in the oath, the statutory gloss, or the construction of the oath and statutes given by the Arizona Supreme Court, purports to exclude association by one who does not subscribe to the organization's unlawful ends. Here as in [Baggett] the "hazard of being prosecuted for knowing but guiltless behavior" is a reality. People often label as "communist" ideas which they oppose; and they make up our juries. "[P]rosecutors too are human." [Cramp.] Would a teacher be safe and secure in going to a Pugwash Conference? Would it be legal to join a seminar group predominantly Communist and therefore subject to control by those who are said to believe in the overthrow of the government by force and violence? Juries might convict though the teacher did not subscribe to the wrongful aims of the organization. And there is apparently no machinery provided for getting clearance in advance.

Those who join an organization but do not share its unlawful purposes and who do not participate in its unlawful activities surely pose no threat, either as citizens or as public employees. Laws such as this which are not restricted in scope to those who join with the "specific intent" to further illegal action impose, in effect, a conclusive presumption that the member shares the unlawful aims of the organization. See [Aptheker]. . . .

This Act threatens the cherished freedom of association protected by the First Amendment. [A] statute touching those protected rights must be "narrowly drawn to define and punish specific conduct as constituting a clear and present danger to a substantial interest of the State." [Cantwell v. Connecticut.] Legitimate legislative goals "cannot be pursued by means that broadly stifle fundamental personal liberties when the end can be more narrowly achieved." [Shelton v. Tucker.] . . . A law which applies to membership without the "specific intent" to further the illegal aims of the organization infringes unnecessarily on protected freedoms. It rests on the doctrine of "guilt by association" which has no place here. . . .

Reversed.

Mr. Justice WHITE, with whom Mr. Justice CLARK, Mr. Justice HARLAN and Mr. Justice STEWART concur, dissenting.

According to unequivocal prior holdings of this Court, a state is entitled to condition public employment upon its employees abstaining from knowing membership in the Communist Party and other organizations advocating the violent overthrow of the government which employs them; the state is constitutionally authorized to inquire into such affiliations and it may discharge those who refuse to affirm or deny them. [Gerende; Garner; Adler; Beilan; Lerner; Nelson; see also Wieman; Slochower—all in sec. 5A.] The Court does not mention or purport to overrule these cases; nor does it expressly hold that a state must retain, even in its most sensitive positions, those who lend such support as knowing membership entails to those organizations, such as the Communist Party, whose purposes include the violent destruction of democratic government. Under existing constitutional law, then, Arizona is free to require its teachers to refrain from knowing mem-

bership in the designated organizations and to bar from employment all knowing members as well as those who refuse to establish their qualifications to teach by executing the oath prescribed by the statute.   .   .   .

It would seem, therefore, that the Court's judgment is aimed at the criminal provisions of the Arizona law which expose an employee to a perjury prosecution if he swears falsely about membership when he signs the oath or if he later becomes a knowing member while remaining in public employment. But the State is entitled to condition employment on the absence of knowing membership; and if an employee obtains employment by falsifying his present qualifications, there is no sound constitutional reason for denying the State the power to treat such false swearing as perjury.   By the same token, since knowing membership in specified organizations is a valid disqual-ification, Arizona cannot sensibly be forbidden to make it a crime for a person, while a state employee, to join an organization knowing of its dedica-tion to the forceful overthrow of his employer and knowing that membership disqualifies him for state employment.   The crime provided by the Arizona law is not just the act of becoming a member of an organization but it is that membership plus concurrent public employment.   If a State may disqualify for knowing membership and impose criminal penalties for falsifying em-ployment applications, it is likewise within its powers to move criminally against the employee who knowingly engages in disqualifying acts during his employment.   If a government may remove from office [United Public Workers v. Mitchell, the Hatch Act case], and criminally punish its em-ployees who engage in certain political activities, it is unsound to hold that it may not, on pain of criminal penalties, prevent its employees from affil-iating with the Communist Party or other organizations prepared to employ violent means to overthrow constitutional government.   Our Constitution does not require this kind of protection for the secret proselyting of govern-ment employees into the Communist Party .   .   .   .

There is nothing in [Scales, Noto, or Aptheker] dictating the result reached by the Court.   .   .   .   In any event, [those cases] did not deal with the government employee who is a knowing member of the Communist Party.   They did not suggest that the State or Federal Government should be prohibited from taking elementary precautions against its employees forming knowing and deliberate affiliations with those organizations who conspire to destroy the government by violent means.   .   .   .

Even if Arizona may not take criminal action against its law enforce-ment officers or its teachers who become Communists knowing of the pur-poses of the Party, the Court's judgment overreaches itself in invalidating this Arizona statute.   Whether or not Arizona may make knowing member-ship a crime, it need not retain the member as an employee and is entitled to insist that its employees disclaim, under oath, knowing membership in the designated organizations and to condition future employment upon fu-ture abstention from membership.   It is, therefore, improper to invalidate the entire statute in this declaratory judgment action.   .   .   .

KEYISHIAN v. BOARD OF REGENTS

385 U.S. 589, 87 S.Ct. 675, 17 L.Ed.2d 629 (1967).

Appeal from the United States District Court for the Western District of New York.

Mr. Justice BRENNAN delivered the opinion of the Court.

As faculty members of the State University, [appellants'] continued employment was conditioned upon their compliance with a New York plan, formulated partly in statutes and partly in administrative regulations, which the State utilizes to prevent the appointment or retention of "subversive" persons in state employment. . . .

[Each appellant] refused to sign, as regulations then in effect required, [the "Feinberg Certificate"—] a certificate that he was not a Communist, and that if he had ever been a Communist, he had communicated that fact to the President of the State University of New York. Each was notified that his failure to sign the certificate would require his dismissal. [A lower federal court rejected appellants' constitutional challenges to the program.] We reverse.

We considered some aspects of the constitutionality of the New York plan 15 years ago in Adler v. Board of Education [see chap. 15]. That litigation arose after New York passed the Feinberg Law which added § 3022 to the Education Law. The Feinberg Law was enacted to implement and enforce two earlier statutes. The first was a 1917 law, now § 3021 of the Education Law, under which "the utterance of any treasonable or seditious word or words or the doing of any treasonable or seditious act" is a ground for dismissal from the public school system. The second was a 1939 law [now § 105 of the Civil Service Law]. This law disqualifies from [employment] any person who advocates the overthrow of government by force, violence, or any unlawful means, or publishes material advocating such overthrow or organizes or joins any society or group of persons advocating such doctrine.

The Feinberg Law charged the State Board of Regents with the duty of promulgating rules and regulations providing procedures for the disqualification or removal of persons in the public school system who violate the 1917 law or who are ineligible for appointment to or retention in the public school system under the 1939 law. The Board of Regents was further directed to make a list, after notice and hearing, of "subversive" organizations. [Moreover], the Board was directed to provide in its rules and regulations that membership in any listed organization should constitute prima facie evidence of disqualification for appointment to or retention in any office or position in the public schools of the State. [The Board thereupon issued implementing regulations.]

Adler was a declaratory judgment suit in which the Court held, in effect, that there was no constitutional infirmity in [the predecessor to § 105] or in the Feinberg Law on their faces and that they were capable of constitutional application. But the contention urged in this case that both § 3021 and § 105 are unconstitutionally vague was not heard or decided. [T]hat question is now properly before us for decision. Moreover, to the extent that Adler

sustained the provision of the Feinberg Law constituting membership in an organization advocating forceful overthrow of government a ground for disqualification, pertinent constitutional doctrines have since rejected the premises upon which that conclusion rested. Adler is therefore not dispositive of the constitutional issues we must decide in this case. . . .

Section 3021 requires removal for "treasonable or seditious" utterances or acts. The 1958 amendment to § 105 of the Civil Service Law, now subdivision 3 of that section, added such utterances or acts as a ground for removal under that law also. . . . The difficulty centers upon the meaning of "seditious." Subdivision 3 equates the term "seditious" with "criminal anarchy" as defined in the Penal Law. The teacher cannot know the extent, if any, to which a "seditious" utterance must transcend mere statement about abstract doctrine, the extent to which it must be intended to and tend to indoctrinate or incite to action in furtherance of the defined doctrine. The crucial consideration is that no teacher can know just where the line is drawn between "seditious" and nonseditious utterances and acts. Other provisions of § 105 also have the same defect of vagueness. . . .

We emphasize once again [that] "standards of permissible statutory vagueness are strict in the area of free expression. . . . Because First Amendment freedoms need breathing space to survive, government may regulate in the area only with narrow specificity" [NAACP v. Button.] New York's complicated and intricate scheme plainly violates that standard. . . . The danger of that chilling effect upon the exercise of vital First Amendment rights must be guarded against by sensitive tools which clearly inform teachers what is being proscribed. . . .

The regulatory maze created by New York is wholly lacking in "terms susceptible of objective measurement." [Cramp.] It has the quality of "extraordinary ambiguity" found to be fatal to the oaths considered in Cramp and [Baggett]. Vagueness of wording is aggravated by prolixity and profusion of statutes, regulations, and administrative machinery, and by manifold cross-references to interrelated enactments and rules. We therefore hold that § 3021 of the Education Law and [several subdivisions] of § 105 of the Civil Service Law [are] unconstitutional.

Appellants have also challenged the constitutionality of the discrete provisions of subdivision (1)(c) of § 105 and subdivision 2 of the Feinberg Law, which make Communist Party membership, as such, prima facie evidence of disqualification. . . . Subdivision 2 of the Feinberg Law [was] before the Court in Adler and its constitutionality was sustained. But constitutional doctrine which has emerged since that decision has rejected its major premise. That premise was that public employment, including academic employment, may be conditioned upon the surrender of constitutional rights which could not be abridged by direct government action. [T]hat theory was expressly rejected in a series of decisions following Adler. [Citing, e. g., Wieman; Slochower; Cramp.] In Sherbert v. Verner [chap. 14], we said: "It is too late in the day to doubt that the liberties of religion and expression may be infringed by the denial of or placing of conditions upon a benefit or privilege."

We proceed then to the question of the validity of the provisions of subdivision (c) of § 105 and subdivision 2 of § 3022, barring employment to

members of listed organizations. Here again constitutional doctrine has developed since Adler. Mere knowing membership without a specific intent to further the unlawful aims of an organization is not a constitutionally adequate basis for exclusion from such positions as those held by appellants.

[After reviewing Elfbrandt and Aptheker, the Court continued:] [M]ere Party membership, even with knowledge of the Party's unlawful goals, cannot suffice to justify criminal punishment, see [Scales, Noto, Yates]; nor may it warrant a finding of moral unfitness justifying disbarment. [Schware.]

These limitations clearly apply to a provision, like § 105(1)(c), which blankets all state employees, regardless of the "sensitivity" of their positions. But even the Feinberg Law provision, applicable primarily to activities of teachers, who have captive audiences of young minds, are subject to these limitations in favor of freedom of expression and association; the stifling effect on the academic mind from curtailing freedom of association in such manner is manifest, and has been documented in recent studies. Elfbrandt and Aptheker state the governing standard: legislation which sanctions membership unaccompanied by specific intent to further the unlawful goals of the organization or which is not active membership violates constitutional limitations.

Measured against this standard, both Civil Service Law § 105(1)(c) and Education Law § 3022(2) sweep overbroadly into association which may not be proscribed. The presumption of disqualification arising from proof of mere membership may be rebutted, but only by (a) a denial of membership, (b) a denial that the organization advocates the overthrow of government by force, or (c) a denial that the teacher has knowledge of such advocacy. . . . Thus proof of nonactive membership or a showing of the absence of intent to further unlawful aims will not rebut the presumption . . . .

Thus § 105(1)(c) and § 3022(2) suffer from impermissible "overbreadth." [Elfbrandt; Aptheker; etc.] They seek to bar employment both for association which legitimately may be proscribed and for association which may not be proscribed consistently with First Amendment rights. Where statutes have an overbroad sweep, just as where they are vague, "the hazard of loss or substantial impairment of those precious rights may be critical," [since] those covered by the statute are bound to limit their behavior to that which is unquestionably safe. As we said in [Shelton v. Tucker], "The breadth of legislative abridgment must be viewed in the light of less drastic means for achieving the same basic purpose."

We therefore hold that Civil Service Law § 105(1)(c) and Education Law § 3022(2) are invalid insofar as they proscribe mere knowing membership without any showing of specific intent to further the unlawful aims of the Communist Party of the United States or of the State of New York.

Reversed and remanded.

Mr. Justice CLARK, with whom Mr. Justice HARLAN, Mr. Justice STEWART and Mr. Justice WHITE join, dissenting. . . .

It is clear that the Feinberg Law, in which this Court found "no constitutional infirmity" in 1952, has been given its death blow today. . . . No court has ever reached out so far to destroy so much with so little. . . .

This Court has again and again, since at least 1951, approved procedures either identical or at least similar to the ones [it] condemns today. [Justice Clark quoted from Garner, Adler, Beilan and Lerner.] Since that time the Adler line of cases has been cited gain and again with approval [Shelton v. Tucker; Cramp; Konigsberg II; Anastaplo; cf. Baggett]. In view of this long list of decisions covering over 15 years of this Court's history, in which no opinion of this Court even questioned the validity of the Adler line of cases, it is strange to me that the Court now finds that "the constitutional doctrine which has emerged since [has] rejected [Adler's] major premise." With due respect, as I read them, our cases have done no such thing. [Justice Clark also questioned the majority's view that vagueness challenges had not been passed on in Adler. But he added that "even if Adler did not decide these questions I would be obliged" to reject the challenges. The provisions dealing with "teachers who advocate, advise, or teach the doctrine of overthrow of our Government by force and violence" refer to "the identical conduct that was condemned" in Dennis. That "exact verbiage" was found "not to be unconstitutionally vague" there, "and that finding was of course not affected by [Yates]."]

The majority says that the Feinberg Law is bad because it has an "overbroad sweep." I regret to say—and I do so with deference—that the majority has by its broadside swept away one of our most precious rights, namely, the right of self-preservation. Our public educational system is the genius of our democracy. The minds of our youth are developed there and the character of that development will determine the future of our land. Indeed, our very existence depends upon it. The issue here is a very narrow one. It is not freedom of speech, freedom of thought, freedom of press, freedom of assembly, or of association, even in the Communist Party. It is simply this: May the State provide that one who, after a hearing with full judicial review, is found to have wilfully and deliberately advocated, advised, or taught that our Government should be overthrown by force or violence or other unlawful means; or to have wilfully and deliberately printed, published, etc., any book or paper that so advocated *and who personally* advocated such doctrine himself; or to have wilfully and deliberately become a member of an organization that advocates such doctrine, is prima facie disqualified from teaching in its university? My answer, in keeping with all of our cases up until today, is "Yes"! . . .

LOYALTY OATHS AND THE BURGER COURT

Has the Burger Court significantly modified the guidelines and analyses regarding permissible oaths established by the cases of the late sixties? Have the changes in the composition of the Court produced a change in doctrine in this area? Two employee oath cases are considered in note 1 below. In the major case, Cole v. Richardson, the Court rejected an attack on an oath—unlike the result typical in the Warren era. Yet consider the summary of the applicable doctrine in Chief Justice Burger's opinion in Cole: Does his summary faithfully reflect the principles that emerge from the preceding materials?

1. *Employee loyalty oaths.* a. *Connell.* CONNELL v. HIGGIN-BOTHAM, 403 U.S. 207 (1971), involved two provisions in oaths required of Florida school teachers. In a per curiam opinion, the Court sustained the first of these—"that I will support the Constitution of the United States and of the State of Florida." That demanded no more "than is required of all state and federal officers" under the Constitution: "The validity of this section of the oath would appear settled." *

However, the Court in Connell invalidated the second challenged oath provision—"that I do not believe in the overthrow of the Government of the United States or of the State of Florida by force or violence." That requirement was found to fall "within the ambit of decisions of this Court proscribing summary dismissal from public employment without hearing or inquiry required by due process. [Slochower, sec. 5A above]." In concurring in the result, Justice Marshall, joined by Justices Douglas and Brennan, thought that the Court should strike down this provision on a broader ground: "plainly and simply on the ground that belief as such cannot be the predicate of governmental action." †

b. *Cole.* The 4 to 3 decision in COLE v. RICHARDSON, 405 U.S. 676 (1972), rejected constitutional attacks on a two-part loyalty oath required of all Massachusetts public employees. The first part required a promise to "uphold and defend" the federal and state constitutions; the second, a promise to "oppose the overthrow of the government of the United States of America or of this Commonwealth by force, violence or by any illegal or unconstitutional method." The lower federal court had sustained the first part on the basis of prior decisions (see note 1a), but had found the second provision unconstitutional. The Supreme Court read the "oppose the overthrow" clause as imposing no significantly greater obligation than the "uphold and defend" provision and accordingly concluded that both parts of the oath were constitutional.

Chief Justice Burger's majority opinion found the first "uphold and defend" clause indistinguishable from the traditionally valid "support" oath—an oath "addressed to the future, promising constitutional support in broad terms." And the Chief Justice insisted that the lower court had been "rigidly literal" in not finding in the second, "oppose" clause "the specter of vague, undefinable responsibilities actively to combat a potential overthrow of the government." In the Court's view, the second clause did not "require specific action in some hypothetical or actual situation." As the Chief Justice read the "oppose" clause, "it is a commitment not to use illegal and constitutionally unprotected force to change the constitutional system. [It] does not expand the obligation of the first; it simply makes clear the application of the first clause to a particular issue. . . . That the second clause may be redundant is no ground to strike it down; we are not charged with correcting

---

* The Court cited Knight v. Board of Regents, 269 F.Supp. 339, aff'd per curiam, 390 U.S. 36 (1968), sustaining a New York law requiring that teachers affirm that they "will support" the federal and state constitutions and that they "will faithfully discharge" their duties. See also the further consideration and approval of this variety of "mere support" oath in Wadmond, one of the 1971 Bar Admission Cases, considered after this group of notes.

† Justice Stewart was the only dissenter from the disposition of the "belief" provision. He urged a remand for a state construction of the oath.

grammar but with enforcing a constitution." So read, the oath was not void for vagueness. It was punishable only by a perjury prosecution, and the requirement that there be "a knowing and willful falsehood" removed any fair notice problem. Finally, the Chief Justice saw no requirement that a person refusing to take the oath be granted a hearing. Prior Court decisions requiring a hearing before discharge, he insisted, all involved "impermissible oaths." In a concurring notation, Justice Stewart, joined by Justice White, commented: "[I]f 'uphold' and 'defend' are not words that suffer from vagueness and overbreadth, then surely neither does the word 'oppose' in the second part of the oath."

But the three dissenters read the "oppose" clause more broadly and hence found it unconstitutional. Justice Douglas' dissent charged that the prevailing opinion had "emasculated" the word "oppose": "The tortured route which the majority takes to give this oath a supposedly constitutional interpretation merely emphasizes the unconstitutional effect those words would have were they to be given their natural meaning." In Justice Douglas' view, the "oppose" oath made advocacy of overthrow, protected in cases such as Brandenburg, "a possible offense." The oath required the employee to "oppose" what he has "an indisputable right to advocate."

Justice Marshall's dissent, joined by Justice Brennan, found the "oppose" clause "not only vague, but also overbroad." He could not agree that "the second half of the oath adds nothing to the first." For example, he claimed that the State had contended that the second part imposed a "greater duty" than the first: "While [the State is] unsure as to where and how far that duty extends, [the State never has] suggested that it simply does not exist." "Support" oaths had been tolerated only because the Court had viewed them as affirmations "of minimal loyalty to the Government." He recalled that "each time this Court has been faced with an attempt by government to make the traditional support oath more comprehensive or demanding, it has struck the oath down." More generally, Justice Marshall added: "Perhaps we have become so inundated with a variety of these oaths that we tend to ignore the difficult constitutional issues that they present." Compare Chief Justice Burger's comment, in a footnote: "The time may come when the value of oaths in routine public employment will be thought not 'worth the candle' for all the division of opinion they engender."

A passage in Chief Justice Burger's opinion is of special interest for its effort to summarize the principles established by the prior oath cases. He stated that government may not condition employment on taking oaths which "impinge" First Amendment rights, "as for example those relating to political beliefs." [Here, he cited the 1971 Bar Admission Cases, which follow.] "Nor may employment be conditioned on an oath that one has not engaged, or will not engage, in protected speech activities such as the following: criticizing institutions of government; discussing political doctrine that approves the overthrow of certain forms of government; and supporting candidates for political office. [Keyishian; Baggett v. Bullitt; Cramp.] Employment may not be conditioned on an oath denying past, or abjuring future, associational activities within constitutional protection; such protected activities include membership in organizations having illegal purposes unless one knows of the purpose and shares a specific intent to pro-

mote the illegal purpose. [Whitehill v. Elkins; Keyishian; Elfbrandt; Wieman v. Updegraff.]" And there has been special concern with vagueness in the oath cases "because uncertainty as to an oath's meaning may deter individuals from engaging in constitutionally protected activity conceivably within the scope of the oath. An underlying, seldom articulated concern running throughout these cases is that the oaths under consideration often required individuals to reach back into their pasts to recall minor, sometimes innocent, activities."

2. *Loyalty oaths and ballot access.* Communist Party of Indiana v. Whitcomb, 414 U.S. 441 (1974), held unconstitutional an Indiana requirement conditioning party access to the ballot on the execution of a loyalty oath stating that the party "does not advocate the overthrow of local, state or national government by force or violence." Justice Brennan's prevailing opinion viewed this "broad oath embracing advocacy of abstract doctrine as well as advocacy of action" as unconstitutional under the principles of the Yates-Brandenburg and employee loyalty oaths lines of cases. He rejected the argument that the approach of those cases should not extend to "cases of state regulation of access to the ballot." He noted that "burdening access to the ballot, rights of association in the political party of one's choice, interests in casting an effective vote and in running for office" was "to infringe interests certainly as substantial as those in public employment, tax exemption, or the practice of law." *

THE BURGER COURT ON SCOPE OF INQUIRY AND GROUNDS FOR DISQUALIFICATION: THE 1971 BAR ADMISSION CASES

Introduction. In three 5 to 4 decisions in 1971, the Court returned to the problems of cases such as Konigsberg, sec. 5A: the scope of the State's power to inquire in the course of screening applicants for bar admission. In two of the cases, Baird and Stolar, the petitioner prevailed; in the third, Wadmond, the constitutional challenge failed.† What light do these cases throw on the viability of the Warren court decisions culminating in Keyishian? What light do they throw on the problem of barriers to government employment as well as bar admission? Are the bases of disqualification coextensive with the standards for criminal liability under cases such

---

* Note, however, the doubt suggested in a separate opinion by Justice Powell, joined by Chief Justice Burger and Justices Blackmun and Rehnquist. Justice Powell concurred in the result, but on equal protection rather than First Amendment grounds: he found "discriminatory application" because the challenged oath had not been required of the major parties in the 1972 election. And in a footnote, Justice Powell suggested that "it could be argued" that Yates and its progeny "are not controlling" in situations involving candidates for the Presidency. In the Yates line of cases, he comment-

ed, the constitutional oaths and responsibilities of the President had not been "a relevant issue."

† Justice Stewart's votes were decisive: in all three cases, Justices Black, Douglas, Brennan and Marshall voted against the State; in all three cases, Chief Justice Burger and Justices Harlan, White and Blackmun voted for the State; Justice Stewart submitted concurring opinions in Baird and Stolar to join judgments sustaining the constitutional challenges and wrote the majority opinion in Wadmond sustaining the State's power.

as Scales?　Is the scope of inquiry the same as the scope of disqualification grounds?　Or may government ask questions even though an affirmative answer would not be a ground for disqualification, on the ground that the questions are relevant steps in determining whether grounds for disqualification exist?　Note especially the position of Justice Stewart in these cases: it was Justice Stewart who cast the deciding votes.

1.　*Baird*.　In BAIRD v. STATE BAR OF ARIZONA, 401 U.S. 1 (1971), petitioner was denied admission to the bar because of her refusal to answer one of the questions on the Arizona Bar Committee's questionnaire. The question (No. 27) was whether she had ever been a member of the Communist Party or any organization "that advocates overthrow of the United States Government by force or violence."　Among the questions she answered was one (No. 25) which required her to reveal all organizations with which she had been associated since she reached 16 years of age.　Because of her refusal to answer Question 27, the Committee declined to process her application further, and the highest state court refused to admit her to practice law.

Justice Black's plurality opinion, joined by Justices Douglas, Brennan and Marshall, commented at the outset that the past decisions in this area "contained thousands of pages of confusing formulas, refined reasonings, and puzzling holdings."　He stated that "we have concluded the best way to handle this case is [to relate its facts] to the 45 words that make up the First Amendment."　He concluded that the Amendment protected petitioner "from being subjected to a question potentially so hazardous to her liberty."　He explained: "The First Amendment's protection of association prohibits a State from excluding a person from a profession or punishing him solely because he is a member of a particular political organization or because he holds certain beliefs. [Robel; Keyishian.]　Similarly, when a State attempts to make inquiries about a person's beliefs or associations, its power is limited by the First Amendment.　Broad and sweeping state inquiries into these protected areas, as Arizona has engaged in here, discourage citizens from exercising rights protected by the Constitution. [Shelton v. Tucker; Gibson, sec. 6A.]

"When a State seeks to inquire about an individual's beliefs and associations a heavy burden lies upon it to show that the inquiry is necessary to protect a legitimate state interest. [Gibson.]　Of course Arizona has a legitimate interest in determining whether petitioner has the qualities of character and the professional competence requisite to the practice of law.　But here petitioner has already supplied the Committee with extensive personal and professional information to assist its determination.　By her answers to questions other than No. 25, and her listing of former employers, law school professors, and other references, she has made available to the Committee the information relevant to her fitness to practice law.[1]　And whatever justification may be

---

1.　"Respondent has argued that even when an applicant has answered question 25, listing the organizations to which she has belonged since the age of 16, question 27 still serves a useful and legitimate function.　Respondent urges:

"'Assume an answer including an organization by name such as "The Sons and Daughters of I Will Arise." This could truly be a Christian group with religious objectives.　But it could also be an organization devoted to the objectives of Lenin, Stalin or any

offered, a State may not inquire about a man's views or associations solely for the purpose of withholding a right or benefit because of what he believes."

Justice Stewart concurred in the judgment in an opinion which set forth the reasons for his decisive vote in three paragraphs: "The Court has held that under some circumstances simple inquiry into present or past Communist Party membership of an applicant for admission to the Bar is not as such unconstitutional. [Konigsberg; Anastaplo.]

"Question 27, however, goes further and asks applicants whether they have ever belonged to any organization 'that advocates overthrow of the United States Government by force or violence.' Our decisions have made clear that such inquiry must be confined to knowing membership to satisfy the First and Fourteenth Amendments. See, e. g., [Robel; Wadmond, below]. It follows from these decisions that mere membership in an organization can never, by itself, be sufficient ground for a State's imposition of civil disabilities or criminal punishment. Such membership can be quite different from knowing membership in an organization advocating the overthrow of the Government by force or violence, on the part of one sharing the specific intent to further the organization's illegal goals. See [Scales; Wadmond].

"There is a further constitutional infirmity in Arizona's question 27. The [State Bar's] explanation of its purpose in asking the question makes clear that the question must be treated as an inquiry into political beliefs. For [it] explicitly states that it would recommend denial of admission solely because of an applicant's beliefs that the respondent found objectionable. Cf. Wadmond, post. Yet the First and Fourteenth Amendments bar a State from acting against any person merely because of his beliefs."

There were three dissenting opinions. All of the dissenters joined the first of these—an opinion by Justice Blackmun, joined by Chief Justice Burger and Justices Harlan and White. Justice Blackmun recalled at length the second Konigsberg decision and noted that petitioner had asserted that Konigsberg, "although perhaps distinguishable," warranted "delimiting, and perhaps even overruling in light of the trend since 1961." He added: "In my view, Mrs. Baird has now had striking success in her overruling endeavor despite the majority's seeming recognition of [the case] and the separate concurrence's definite bow in [its] direction." He commented that her refusal to answer Question 27 was "reminiscent of the obstructionist tactics condemned in Konigsberg." He added: "By her refusal to answer Question 27, she would place on [the State] the burden of determining which of the organizations she listed, if any, was an arm of the Communist Party or advocated forceful or violent overthrow of the Government. That, however, is not the task of the Committee or of the Arizona Supreme Court. It is Sara Baird's task. [She] either knew the answer or she did not know it. If

other deceased person whose teachings and objectives were not conducive to the continued security and welfare of our government and way of life.' Brief for Respondent, at 8.

"The organizations petitioner listed in response to question 25 were: Church Choir; Girl Scouts; Girls Athletic Association; Young Republicans; Young Democrats; Stanford Law Association; Law School Civil Rights Research Council. Respondent does not state which of these organizations may threaten the security of the Republic." [Footnote by Justice Black.]

she knew, she coupled her knowledge with an attempt to conceal. If she did not know, she had only to state her lack of knowledge."

Justice Blackmun insisted, moreover, that "a realistic reading of the question discloses that it is directed not at mere belief but at advocacy and at the call to violent action and force in pursuit of that advocacy. . . . I find nothing in this record that indicates that Mrs. Baird automatically would have been denied admission to the Bar had she answered Question 27 in the affirmative." He concluded: "I doubt if this Court is the proper tribunal to judge the sufficiency of materials supplied for legal practice in Arizona. Of course there is a constitutional limit, but that limit is marked by the relevant, by the excesses of unreasonableness and of harassment, and by the otherwise constitutionally forbidden. It should not be marked at an arbitrary point where the applicant, for reasons of convenience or assumed self-protection or contrariness, decides that enough is enough."

Justice White submitted a separate dissent, applicable to Stolar as well as Baird: "It is my view that the Constitution does not require a State to admit to practice a lawyer who believes in violence and intends to implement that belief in his practice of law and advice to clients. I also believe that the State may ask applicants preliminary questions which will permit further investigation and reasoned, articulated judgment as to whether the applicant will or will not advise lawless conduct as a practicing lawyer. Arizona has no intention of barring applicants based on belief alone." Justice Harlan also submitted a separate opinion, applicable to all three cases. He insisted that the records showed "no more than a refusal to certify candidates who deliberately, albeit in good faith, refuse to assist the Bar-admission authorities in their 'fitness' investigations by declining fully to answer the questionnaires." Questionnaires such as these might not be the most efficient or wisest means to weed out those dedicated to overthrowing government by force, but they were not unconstitutional methods: "I do not consider that the 'less drastic means' test which has been applied in some First Amendment cases [see NAACP v. Alabama] suffices to justify this Court in assuming general oversight of state investigatory procedures relating to Bar admissions."

2. *Stolar*. The Justices viewed IN RE STOLAR, 401 U.S. 23 (1971), as raising issues closely akin to Baird. The judgment reversing the State's refusal of bar admission accordingly produced identical divisions on the Court. The applicant, a member of the New York bar, sought admission to practice in Ohio. He made available to Ohio all the information he had furnished New York a year earlier, including his answer to a question about his associational affiliations and his negative reply to a question about membership in any group seeking to effect changes in our form of government or to advance the interest of a foreign country. However, he refused to answer three of the questions on the Ohio application: Question 12(g), which asked about membership in "any organization which advocates the overthrow of the government of the United States by force"; Question 13, which asked for a list of all "organizations of which you are or have been a member"; and Question 7, which sought a list of all organizations "of which you are or have been a member since registering as a law student." He was denied admission to the bar because of his refusal to answer these questions.

The plurality opinion by Justice Black, joined by Justices Douglas, Brennan and Marshall, concluded that the refusals to answer here were, as in Baird, "protected by the First Amendment." Questions 13 and 7 were "impermissible in light of the First Amendment, as was made clear in [Shelton v. Tucker]. Law students who know they must survive this screening process before practicing their profession are encouraged to protect their future by shunning unpopular or controversial organizations. [T]he First Amendment prohibits Ohio from penalizing an applicant by denying him admission to the Bar solely because of his membership in an organization. [Baird; cf. Robel; Keyishian.] Nor may the State penalize petitioner solely because he personally, as the committee suggests, 'espouses illegal aims.' " Justice Black also noted that Stolar had supplied the State with extensive information "to enable it to make the necessary investigation and determination." "Moreover, even though irrelevant to his fitness to practice law, Stolar's answers to questions on the New York application provided Ohio with substantially the information it was seeking." Question 12(g) was found impermissible as well. Since the First Amendment barred the State "from penalizing a man solely because he is a member of a particular organization," there was "no legitimate state interest which is served by a question which sweeps so broadly into areas of belief and association protected against government invasion."

Justice Stewart was able to explain his decisive concurring vote in two sentences: "Ohio's Questions 7 and 13 are plainly unconstitutional under [Shelton v. Tucker]. In addition, Question 12(g) suffers from the same constitutional deficiency as does Arizona's Question 27 in [Baird]." Justice Blackmun again dissented, joined by Chief Justice Burger and Justices Harlan and White. He explained: "I may assume, for present purposes, that the general and broadly phrased list-your-organizations inquiries, that is, Questions 13 and 7, are improper and impermissible under [Shelton v. Tucker], despite the presence of what seems to me to be a somewhat significant difference between nontenured school teachers and about-to-be-licensed attorneys. This assumption, however, does not terminate Stolar's case," and Question 12(g), the inquiry about membership in organizations advocating overthrow by force, was permissible in his view, in accordance with his Baird dissent. Justice Blackmun rejected the suggestion that Stolar's answers to New York should suffice for responses to Ohio: "Time passes and changes can take place even within a few months."

3. *Wadmond.* The challenge in LAW STUDENTS RESEARCH COUNCIL v. WADMOND, 401 U.S. 154 (1971), did not arise from an actual refusal to admit an applicant to the practice of law. Rather, it was "a broad attack, primarily on First Amendment vagueness and overbreadth grounds," on New York's bar admission screening system, brought by individuals and organizations (including the Law Students Civil Rights Research Council) representing a class of law students and graduates "seeking or planning to seek admission to practice law in New York." The "basic thrust" of the attack, as described by the Court, was that the screening system "by its very existence works a 'chilling effect' upon the free exercise of the rights of speech and association of students who must anticipate having to meet its requirements." Several items on the New York questionnaire

were revised as a result of the trial court proceedings, but that court rejected the rest of the challenge. The Supreme Court agreed that the revised New York scheme was constitutional.

Justice Stewart, whose concurrences had been decisive in sustaining the constitutional challenges in Baird and Stolar, now joined the dissenters in those cases and wrote the majority opinion rejecting the constitutional attack. His opinion, joined by Chief Justice Burger and Justices Harlan, White and Blackmun, began by sustaining New York's statutory "character and fitness" requirement: "Long usage [has] given well-defined contours to this requirement, which the appellees have construed narrowly as encompassing no more than 'dishonorable conduct relevant to the legal profession.' "

The Court next turned to Rule 9406 and the implementing questions designed to determine whether an applicant "believes in the form of the government of the United States and is loyal to such government." That Rule was related to a requirement of an oath that an applicant will "support the Constitution of the United States" as well as that of New York. The Court noted that the constitutionality of the actual oath was not under direct attack and added: "In any event, there can be no doubt of its validity." And Rule 9406 was valid as well: though it raised constitutional questions on its face, it was valid as construed by the state authorities. The language of the Rule was troublesome with respect to the burden of proof and the scope of the inquiry. But here, the state authorities had supplied an acceptably narrow interpretation: "There are three key elements to this construction. First, the Rule places upon applicants no burden of proof. Second, 'the form of the government of the United States' and the 'government' refer solely to the Constitution, which is all that the oath mentions. Third, 'belief' and 'loyalty' mean no more than willingness to take the constitutional oath and ability to do so in good faith." Justice Stewart commented: "[A]ccepting this construction, we find no constitutional invalidity in Rule 9406. There is 'no showing of an intent to penalize political beliefs.' [Konigsberg]. At the most, [it] performs only the function of ascertaining that an applicant is not one who 'swears to an oath pro forma while declaring or manifesting his disagreement with or indifference to the oath.' [Bond v. Floyd, chap. 12, sec. 1.]"

The most difficult aspect of this case, as in Baird and Stolar, was the specific questionnaire content under challenge. Justice Stewart's disposition of this aspect of the case follows at length:

"As this case comes to us from the three-judge panel, the questionnaire applicants are asked to complete contains only two numbered questions reflecting the disputed provision of Rule 9406. They are as follows:

" '26. (a) Have you ever organized or helped to organize or become a member of any organization or group of persons which, during the period of your membership or association, you knew was advocating or teaching that the government of the United States or any state or any political subdivision thereof should be overthrown or overturned by force, violence, or any unlawful means? ———— If your answer is in the affirmative, state the facts below.

" '(b) If your answer to (a) is in the affirmative, did you, during the period of such membership or association, have the specific intent to further the aims of such organization or group of persons to overthrow or overturn the government of the United States or any state or any political subdivision thereof by force, violence or any unlawful means?

" '27.   (a) Is there any reason why you cannot take and subscribe to an oath or affirmation that you will support the constitutions of the United States and of the State of New York?   If there is, please explain.

" '(b) Can you conscientiously, and do you, affirm that you are, without any mental reservation, loyal to and ready to support the Constitution of the United States?'   ———.   . . .

"Question 26 is precisely tailored to conform to the relevant decisions of this Court.   Our cases establish that inquiry into associations of the kind referred to is permissible under the limitations carefully observed here.   We have held that knowing membership in an organization advocating the overthrow of the Government by force or violence, on the part of one sharing the specific intent to further the organization's illegal goals, may be made criminally punishable.   [Scales.]   It is also well settled that Bar examiners may ask about Communist affiliations as a preliminary to further inquiry into the nature of the association and may exclude an applicant for refusal to answer.   [Konigsberg.]   See also, e. g., [Robel; Keyishian; Elfbrandt; Beilan; Garner].[1]   Surely a State is constitutionally entitled to make such an inquiry of an applicant for admission to a profession dedicated to the peaceful and reasoned settlement of disputes between men, and between a man and his government.   The very Constitution that the appellants invoke stands as a living embodiment of that ideal.   As to question 27, there can hardly be doubt of its constitutional validity in light of our earlier discussion of Rule 9406 and the appellees' construction of that Rule.   The question is simply supportive of the appellees' task of ascertaining the good faith with which an applicant can take the constitutional oath."

In the concluding passage of his opinion, Justice Stewart turned to "a more fundamental claim" in the challenge: that, apart from the details, there inhered in New York's screening system "so constant a threat to applicants that constitutional deprivations will be inevitable."   He commented: "The implication of this argument is that no screening would be constitutionally permissible beyond academic examination and extremely minimal checking for serious, concrete character deficiencies.   The principal means of policing the Bar would then be the deterrent and punitive effects of such post-admission sanctions as contempt, disbarment, malpractice suits, and criminal prosecutions."   That broad-gauged attack was rejected: "Such an approach

---

1. "Division of question 26 into two parts is wholly permissible under Konigsberg v. State Bar, supra, which approved asking whether an applicant had ever been a member of the Communist Party without asking in the same question whether the applicant shared its illegal goals.   More-over, this division narrows the class of applicants as to whom the Committees are likely to find further investigation appropriate.   For those who answer part (a) in the negative, that is the end of the matter."   [Footnote by Justice Stewart.]

might be wise policy, but decisions based on policy alone are not for us to make. [We] are not persuaded that careful administration of such a system as New York's need result in chilling effects upon the exercise of constitutional freedoms. Consequently, the choice between systems like New York's and approaches like that urged by the appellants rests with the legislatures and other policy-making bodies of the individual States." [2]

There were two dissents in Wadmond: one by Justice Black, joined by Justice Douglas; another by Justice Marshall, joined by Justice Brennan. Justice Black stated: "In my view, the First Amendment absolutely prohibits a State from penalizing a man because of his beliefs. Hence a State cannot require that an applicant's belief in our form of government be established before he can become a lawyer." Moreover, he found the specific questions here "flatly inconsistent with the First Amendment."

Justice Black especially objected to the inquiry into associational activities in Questions 26(a) and (b): "I fail to see how the majority's approval of these questions can be reconciled with [Baird] and [Stolar]." He explained: "In [Baird] and [Stolar], we hold today that States may not require an applicant to the Bar to answer the question 'have you been a member of any organization that advocates overthrow of the government by force?' Ohio recognized in Stolar that it could not exclude an applicant unless he had knowledge of the organization's aims at the time of his membership. However, it argued that its question was appropriate because it was merely a prelude to determining whether petitioner was a 'knowing' member. We rejected that argument, and held that the First Amendment barred Ohio from demanding an answer to that question which required an applicant to supply information about political activities protected by the First Amendment. Here the majority seems to concede that New York could not possibly exclude an applicant unless he had been a member of an organization advocating forcible overthrow, he knew of these aims, and *he had a specific intent to help bring them about.* Since even on the majority's theory New York cannot exclude an applicant unless *all* these requirements are met, why is the State permitted to ask Question 26(a) which makes no reference to 'specific intent'? In Baird and Stolar five members of the Court agreed that questions asked by Bar admissions committees were invalid because they inquired about activities protected by the First Amendment. Why then is the same result not required here?

"It may be argued, of course, that Question 26 is sufficiently specific under the majority's standard because parts (a) and (b) *taken together* do include a 'specific intent' requirement. But the Court's holding permits the knowledge and specific intent elements of Question 26 to be split into two parts. This allows the State to force an applicant to supply information

---

2. Note also Justice Stewart's reliance on—and restatement of—the distinctions he sought to develop in the Bar Admission Cases, in his separate opinion in Connell v. Higginbotham, 403 U.S. 207, a 1971 employee oath case, note 1a in the preceding group of notes. In Connell, in urging state clarification of an oath provision, Justice Stewart explained:

"If the clause embraces the teacher's philosophical or political beliefs, I think it is constitutionally infirm. [Baird.] If on the other hand, the clause does not more than test whether the first clause of the oath [a "support" oath] can be taken 'without mental reservation or purpose of evasion,' I think it is constitutionally valid. [Wadmond.]"

about his associations, which, even under the majority's rationale, are protected by the First Amendment.

"But even if Questions 26(a) and 26(b) were combined into one question, this would not satisfy the standards set by the Court in [Robel] and [Brandenburg]. [Robel] held the Federal Government could not bar a man from private employment in defense facilities unless he had engaged in conduct which could be criminally proscribed. We recognized that banning a man from employment is a form of civil punishment which must meet the requirements of the First Amendment. Cf. [Keyishian]. And [Brandenburg] held that advocacy of violence or the joining with others to do so could not be proscribed 'except where such advocacy is directed to inciting or producing imminent lawless action and is likely to incite or produce such action.' Clearly the New York questions are not nearly so narrowly drawn. [Thus], for their failure to meet the Brandenburg requirements, the New York questions are overbroad. After our decision in Robel, it should make no difference that New York threatens to exclude people from their chosen livelihood rather than putting them in jail."

Justice Marshall, joined by Justice Brennan, agreed with the wide range of the challenges to the New York screening program—not only the specific attacks on the Rule and the Questions but also the "underlying complaint" that the system "focuses impermissibly on the political activities and viewpoints of Bar applicants," and that "this chilling effect is not justified as the necessary impact of a system designed to winnow out those applicants demonstrably unfit to practice law." A general "fitness" inquiry was permissible, but "New York is not content with a politically neutral investigation." Rule 9406 should be struck down on its face: the attempted narrowing construction was not supported by case law or administrative practice; and it was in any event constitutionally defective because the interpretation compounded its vagueness. Justice Marshall then turned to his objections to Question 26, stating:

"Question 26(a) reveals itself as an indiscriminate and highly intrusive device designed to expose an applicant's political affiliations to the scrutiny of screening authorities. As such, it comes into conflict with principles that bar overreaching official inquiry undertaken with a view to predicating the denial of a public benefit on activity protected by the First Amendment.[1]

---

1. "Part (a) of Question 26 is not rendered harmless by reason of the fact that part (b) limits somewhat the breadth of the question as a whole. In the first place, it must be remembered that neither part (a) nor part (b) states the operative criterion for excluding applicants on the basis of political affiliations—the criterion for exclusion, one of impermissible latitude, is given in Rule 9406 itself. Second, if all applicants who answer part (b) in the affirmative were therefore excluded, while those falling within part (a) only were admitted, the result would still be constitutionally problematical. Third, overreaching inquiries are not cured simply by adding narrower follow-up questions. Obviously a State cannot hope to justify the sort of informational demand condemned today in [Stolar] on the theory that the overintrusive inquiry is part of a series that culminates in a sufficiently narrow question. When the questioning is directed at the political activities and affiliations of applicants for a public benefit, the scope of questioning must be carefully limited in light of the permissible criteria for denying the benefit. [E. g., Shelton v. Tucker.]

There is no justification for a requirement of overbroad disclosure that chills the exercise of First Amendment freedoms and is not tail-

Three particular difficulties may be mentioned. First, Question 26(a) is undeniably overbroad in that it covers the affiliations of those who do not adhere to teachings concerning unlawful political change, or are simply indifferent to this aspect of an association's activities. [Elfbrandt v. Russell; Aptheker.] Second, no attempt has been made to limit Question 26(a) to associational advocacy of concrete, specific, and imminent illegal acts, or to associational activity which creates a serious likelihood of harm through imminent illegal conduct. See [Brandenburg; Keyishian]. Third, would-be Bar applicants are left to wonder whether particular political acts amount to 'becoming a member' of a 'group of persons'—law students and others, when embarking on associational activities, must guess whether the association's teachings fall within the nebulous formula of Question 26(a), or more to the point, whether their own assessment of an association's teachings would coincide with that of screening officials. There are penalties for failing to 'state the facts' required by Question 26(a) when the time to make application comes. The indefinite scope of Question 26(a) expectedly operates to induce prospective applicants to resolve doubts by failing to exercise their First Amendment rights. See [e. g., Baggett v. Bullitt]."

SECTION 6.   A FIRST AMENDMENT RIGHT OF SILENCE?— GOVERNMENT DEMANDS FOR INFORMATION: LEGISLATIVE AND GRAND JURY INVESTIGATIONS

A.   LEGISLATIVE INVESTIGATIONS

BACKGROUND AND EARLY CASES

Extensive Supreme Court litigation regarding the permissible scope of legislative investigations is a fairly recent phenomenon. But legislative committees have long conducted investigations. Congress authorized an investigation of a military disaster as early as 1792, for example. In the early years, congressional inquiries dealt mainly with the conduct of the executive department. By the 1820's, however, committees began to summon witnesses to aid in considering proposed legislation.*

What are the sanctions available to Congress when a witness refuses to answer a question claimed to be pertinent to a legislative investigation? Congress has the power to impose direct punishment on its own upon persons in contempt of its authority, without resorting to the courts. See Anderson v. Dunn, 6 Wheat. 204 (1821), a case involving an attempted bribe of a Congressman. But imprisonment for contempt by one of the Houses can-

ored to serve valid governmental interests. See [Gibson; Bates; NAACP v. Alabama]." [Footnote by Justice Marshall.]

* For an excellent study, see Taylor, Grand Inquest—The Story of Congressional Investigations (1955). And on the scope of congressional power to investigate the conduct of the executive departments, see also chap. 7, above, on separation of powers—especially the materials on intrusions by one branch into the internal affairs of another and the discussion of executive privilege.

not extend beyond the adjournment date. Accordingly, since 1857, Congress has provided criminal penalties for refusals to answer pertinent questions. See 2 U.S.C. § 192.

Kilbourn v. Thompson, 103 U.S. 168 (1881), was the first important Supreme Court decision on congressional investigations. The Court set aside the conviction of a recalcitrant witness at an inquiry into Jay Cooke's financial operations. Justice Miller condemned investigations that were "judicial" in nature and stated that Congress cannot constitutionally inquire "into the private affairs of individuals" where the investigation "could result in no valid legislation on the subject to which the inquiry referred." Compare Woodrow Wilson's famous statement, in Congressional Government (1885), 303: "The informing function of Congress should be preferred even to its legislative function." But see Justice Douglas' opinion in Russell v. United States, 369 U.S. 749, 778 (1962): "Wilson was speaking not of a congressional inquiry roaming at large, but of one that inquired into and discussed the functions and operations of government." †

In the 1920's, attempts to punish recalcitrant witnesses fared better than in Kilbourn. In McGrain v. Daugherty, 273 U.S. 135 (1927), the Court, in a case arising out of an investigation of Attorney General Daugherty's conduct of the Justice Department, stated that "the power of inquiry" is "an essential and appropriate auxiliary to the legislative function." And, in order to obtain information needed to exercise the legislative function, Congress may "compel a private individual to appear before it or one of its committees." The McGrain Court noted that the Kilbourn case had not dealt with investigations in aid of "contemplated legislation." Two years later, in Sinclair v. United States, 279 U.S. 263 (1929), the Court reemphasized that it no longer subscribed to the Kilbourn attitude of hostility to congressional inquiries. In Sinclair, the witness in an investigation of federal oil leases refused to answer on the grounds that the questions related to his private affairs and that judicial proceedings were pending. After conceding that "Congress is without authority to compel disclosures for the purpose of aiding the prosecution of pending suits," the Court insisted that the authority "to require pertinent disclosures in aid of its own constitutional power is not abridged because the information sought to be elicited may also be of use in such suits." The Court noted, however, that a witness need not answer "where the bounds of the power are exceeded or where the questions asked are not pertinent to the matter under inquiry."

---

† Compare the laudatory references to the "informing function of Congress" in the dissenting opinions of Justices Douglas and Brennan in Gravel v. United States, 408 U.S. 606 (1972), the case arising out of the questioning of a Senator's assistant by a grand jury investigating the disclosure of the Pentagon Papers, noted in chap. 7 above and sec. 6B below. See, however, Doe v. McMillan, 412 U.S. 306 (1973), rejecting a claim, partly based on the "informing function," that there should be absolute immunity for derogatory statements contained in publicly disseminated congressional committee reports. Compare the 8 to 1 decision in Eastland v. United States Servicemen's Fund, 421 U.S. —— (1975), finding the Speech or Debate Clause, Art. I, § 6, cl. 1 (see chap. 7 above), an absolute bar to a federal injunction action challenging a congressional committee's subpoena of bank records of an organization claiming First Amendment rights.

LEGISLATIVE INVESTIGATIONS IN THE FIFTIES

Introduction. Claims that congressional investigators were unconstitutionally engaging in "exposure for exposure's sake" and were violating First Amendment rights were made in cases involving inquiries into subversion that came to the Court in the early fifties. Typically, however, these challenges were joined with Fifth Amendment objections in those early cases, and the Court was able to dispose of them on the basis of broad interpretations of the protection against self-incrimination, without reaching other constitutional issues. See, e. g., Quinn v. United States, 349 U.S. 155 (1955). Two years later, however, in the Watkins case, no Fifth Amendment claim was raised, and the Court began to address itself to other constitutional issues—albeit mainly in dictum at first. At the same time, state inquiries came under scrutiny, in Sweezy v. New Hampshire. In examining the congressional and state investigating cases of the fifties and thereafter below, note the parallels to the evolution of attitudes considered in sec. 5 above, as well as in sec. 1 of chap. 12. To what extent do legislative inquiries raise distinctive questions? Should the standards of the criminal cases in the subversion area, such as Scales and Yates, define the scope of the legislative investigating power? Are the limits on legislative investigations the same as those on governmental inquiries into the fitness of employees and licensees, as in Keyishian and the 1971 Bar Admission Cases? Are the limits the same as those that confine grand jury investigations, see sec. 6B below?

1. *Watkins.* The petitioner in WATKINS v. UNITED STATES, 354 U.S. 178 (1957), was a labor union official who had been called as a witness before the House Un-American Activities Committee. He testified freely about his own political activities, stating that he had never been a Communist Party member but that he had "cooperated" with the Party. Moreover, he was willing to identify Party members he had known, provided that he thought "they still were members." He refused to answer, however, when asked to tell whether he knew a number of persons to have been members of the Party: "I am not going to plead the fifth amendment, but I refuse to answer certain questions that I believe are outside the proper scope of your committee's activities"; he would not testify about persons "who to my best knowledge and belief have long since removed themselves from the Communist movement." He was convicted of "contempt of Congress," for refusing to answer questions "pertinent to the questions under inquiry," 2 U.S.C. § 192.

The Supreme Court reversed. The specific basis for the holding was that Watkins was not "accorded a fair opportunity to determine whether he was within his rights in refusing to answer, and his conviction is necessarily invalid under the Due Process Clause of the Fifth Amendment." Chief Justice Warren's majority opinion stated that a defendant under 2 U.S. C. § 192 must be accorded "every right which is guaranteed to defendants in all other criminal cases," including the right to have "knowledge of the subject to which the interrogation is deemed pertinent," "with the same degree of explicitness and clarity that the Due Process Clause requires in the expression of any element of a criminal offense." The "vice of vagueness" must be avoided. The Court, after exhausting the several possible indicia of

the question at issue, remained "unenlightened as to the subject to which the questions asked petitioner were pertinent."

Before reaching that due process basis for the reversal, however, Chief Justice Warren spoke at length about "basic premises" regarding the history and constitutional status of legislative investigations. The opinion included the following passages: "The power of the Congress to conduct investigations is inherent in the legislative process. [But], broad as is this power of inquiry, it is not unlimited. There is no general authority to expose the private affairs of individuals without justification in terms of the functions of the Congress. [Nor] is the Congress a law enforcement or trial agency. These are functions of the executive and judicial departments of government. No inquiry is an end in itself; it must be related to, and in furtherance of, a legitimate task of the Congress. Investigations conducted solely for the personal aggrandizement of the investigators or to 'punish' those investigated are indefensible.

"Clearly, an investigation is subject to the command [of the First Amendment]. Accommodation of the congressional need for particular information with the individual and personal interest in privacy is an arduous and delicate task for any court. . . . The critical element is the existence of, and the weight to be ascribed to, the interest of the Congress in demanding disclosures from an unwilling witness. We cannot simply assume, however, that every congressional investigation is justified by a public need that overbalances any private rights affected. To do so would be to abdicate the responsibility placed by the Constitution upon the judiciary to insure that the Congress does not unjustifiably encroach upon an individual's right to privacy nor abridge his liberty of speech, press, religion, or assembly.

"[T]here is no congressional power to expose for the sake of exposure. The public is, of course, entitled to be informed concerning the workings of its government. That cannot be inflated into a general power to expose where the predominant result can only be an invasion of the private rights of individuals. But a solution to our problem is not to be found in testing the motives of committee members for this purpose. Such is not our function. Their motives alone would not vitiate an investigation which had been instituted by a House of Congress if that assembly's legislative purpose is being served. . . .

"It is the responsibility of the Congress, in the first instance, to insure that compulsory process is used only in furtherance of a legislative purpose. That requires that the instructions to an investigating committee spell out that group's jurisdiction and purpose with sufficient particularity. . . . An excessively broad charter, like that of the House Un-American Activities Committee, places the courts in an untenable position if they are to strike a balance between the public need for a particular interrogation and the right of citizens to carry on their affairs free from unnecessary governmental interference. It is impossible in such a situation to ascertain whether any legislative purpose justifies the disclosures sought and, if so, the importance of that information to the Congress in furtherance of its legislative function."

In a concurring opinion, Justice Frankfurter gave his understanding of the Court's holding: "[B]y making the federal judiciary the affirmative agency for enforcing the authority that underlies the congressional power to

punish for contempt, Congress necessarily brings into play the specific provisions of the Constitution relating to the prosecution of offenses and those implied restrictions under which courts function. [T]he actual scope of the inquiry that the Committee was authorized to conduct and the relevance of the questions to that inquiry must be shown to have been luminous at the time when asked and not left, at best, in cloudiness. The circumstances of this case were wanting in these essentials." Justice Clark dissented, objecting to the "mischievous curbing of the informing function of Congress" and finding the Court's requirements for the operation of legislative inquiries "both unnecessary and unworkable."

2. *Sweezy.* SWEEZY v. NEW HAMPSHIRE, 354 U.S. 234 (1957) —decided on the same day as Watkins—was the first of several Court encounters with state rather than congressional investigations; and the first of several coming from New Hampshire. The Court held that a NewHampshire contempt conviction for refusal to answer violated the due process clause of the 14th Amendment. Chief Justice Warren's opinion announcing the judgment of the Court was joined only by Justices Black, Douglas, and Brennan. Justice Frankfurter, joined by Justice Harlan, delivered an opinion concurring in the result. Justice Clark, joined by Justice Burton, dissented.

The New Hampshire legislature had authorized the state Attorney General to act as a one-man investigation committee into subversive activities. Petitioner refused to answer questions about the Progressive Party and about a lecture he had delivered at the University of New Hampshire. He insisted that the questions "were not pertinent to the matter under inquiry" and that they "infringed upon an area protected [by] the First Amendment." At the request of the Attorney General, a lower state court then put the questions to the petitioner. When he persisted in his refusal, he was jailed for contempt.

Chief Justice Warren's opinion, as in Watkins, concluded with a relatively narrow holding after some broad introductory observations: "We do not now conceive of any circumstance wherein a state interest would justify infringement of rights in these fields. But we do not need to reach such fundamental questions of state power to decide this case." Although the highest state court had held that the questions were authorized by the legislature, Chief Justice Warren found that "it cannot be stated authoritatively that the legislature asked the Attorney General to gather the kind of facts comprised in the subjects upon which petitioner was interrogated." He concluded:

"[I]f the Attorney General's interrogation of petitioner were in fact wholly unrelated to the object of the legislature in authorizing the inquiry, the Due Process Clause would preclude the endangering of constitutional liberties. We believe that an equivalent situation is presented in this case. The lack of any indications that the legislature wanted the information the Attorney General attempted to elicit from petitioner must be treated as the absence of authority. It follows that the use of the contempt power, notwithstanding the interference with constitutional rights, was not in accordance with the due process requirements of the Fourteenth Amendment."

Justice Frankfurter's concurrence, joined by Justice Harlan, rested on grounds of substantive due process. He emphasized that, for him, this was "a very different case from Watkins v. United States": "[W]e cannot concern ourselves with the fact that New Hampshire chose to make its Attorney

General in effect a standing committee of its legislature . . . . The case must be judged as though the whole body of the legislature had demanded the information of petitioner. It would make the deepest inroads upon our federal system for this Court now to hold that it can determine the appropriate distribution of powers and their delegation within the forty-eight States."

Justice Frankfurter rested squarely on a substantive "balancing" analysis, a finding of violation of liberty under the 14th Amendment: "For a citizen to be made to forego even a part of so basic a liberty as his political autonomy, the subordinating interest of the State must be compelling.* [T]he inviolability of privacy belonging to a citizen's political loyalties has so overwhelming an importance to the well-being of our kind of society that it cannot be constitutionally encroached upon on the basis of so meagre a countervailing interest of the State as may be argumentatively found in the remote, shadowy threat to the security of New Hampshire allegedly presented in the origins and contributing elements of the Progressive Party and in petitioner's relation to these." He commented: "Whatever, on the basis of massive proof and in the light of history, of which this Court may well take judicial notice, be the justification for not regarding the Communist Party as a conventional political party, no such justification has been afforded in regard to the Progressive Party. A foundation in fact and reason would have to be established far weightier than the intimations that appear in the record to warrant such a view of the Progressive Party." His approach, he insisted, was part of "the inescapable judicial task in giving substantive content" to due process. The conclusion was concededly "based on a judicial judgment in balancing two contending principles—the right of a citizen to political privacy [and] the right of the State to self-protection." Here, he concluded: "When weighed against the grave harm resulting from governmental intrusion into the intellectual life of a university, [the] justification for compelling a witness to discuss the contents of his lecture appears grossly inadequate. Particularly is this so where the witness has sworn that neither in the lecture nor at any other time did he ever advocate overthrowing the Government by force and violence." †

    3. *Uphaus.* Sweezy, note 2, was the state companion decision to Watkins, the congressional inquiry case of 1957, note 1. UPHAUS v. WYMAN, 360 U.S. 72 (1959), was the state case decided on the same day as the congressional Barenblatt case, which follows. Like Sweezy, Uphaus arose

---

* Note the references in later cases to Justice Frankfurter's balancing approach in Sweezy—e. g., NAACP v. Alabama, sec. 5 above. Note also the frequent use in later cases of his formulation that "the subordinating interests of the State must be compelling." Recall also his early use of another term that was to become very popular in Court opinions, the antecedent of the "chilling effects" metaphor in his opinion in Wieman, sec. 5A above.

† The decisions in Watkins and Sweezy —together with several others of the same year bearing on subversion, e. g., Yates, chap. 12, sec. 1, and Konigsberg I, sec. 5A of this chapter—provoked considerable criticism, and were frequently mentioned in congressional debates on the 1958 proposals to curtail the Court's appellate jurisdiction. Recall chap. 1, above.

Compare Barenblatt and Uphaus, the federal and state investigation cases of 1959, which follow. Were those decisions responses to the hostile congressional reaction? Is there basis for the claim that the 1959 decisions were inconsistent with—and marked a retreat from—the 1957 cases? Cf. Murphy, Congress and the Court—A Case Study in the American Political Process (1962), and Pritchett, Congress Versus the Supreme Court, 1957–1960 (1961).

out of an investigation by the New Hampshire Attorney General, acting as a one-man legislative investigating committee. Appellant, Executive Director of World Followship, Inc., was held in contempt for refusal to produce a list of the guests at his organization's summer camp during 1954 and 1955. Justice Clark's majority opinion affirmed the civil contempt order and rejected the 14th Amendment claim:

"[T]he Attorney General had valid reason to believe that the speakers and guests at World Fellowship might be subversive persons within the meaning of the New Hampshire Act. . . . Although the evidence as to the nexus between World Fellowship and subversive activities may not be conclusive, we believe it sufficiently relevant to support the Attorney General's action. . . . The record reveals that appellant had participated in 'Communist front' activities and that '[n]ot less than nineteen speakers invited by Uphaus to talk at World Fellowship had either been members of the Communist Party or had connections or affiliations with it or with one or more of the organizations cited as subversive or Communist controlled in the United States Attorney General's list.' . . . Certainly the investigatory power of the State need not be constricted until sufficient evidence of subversion is gathered to justify the institution of criminal proceedings.

". . . We recognize, of course, that compliance with the subpoena will result in exposing the fact that the persons therein named were guests at World Fellowship. But so long as a committee must report to its legislative parent, exposure—in the sense of disclosure—is an inescapable incident of an investigation into the presence of subversive persons within a State. And the governmental interest in self-preservation is sufficiently compelling to subordinate the interest in associational privacy of persons who, at least to the extent of the guest registration statute, made public at the inception the association they now wish to keep private."

Justice Brennan, joined by Chief Justice Warren, Justice Black, and Justice Douglas, dissented: "I do not agree that a showing of any requisite legislative purpose or other state interest that constitutionally can subordinate appellant's rights is to be found in this record. Exposure purely for the sake of exposure is not such a valid subordinating purpose. [This record] not only fails to reveal any interest of the State sufficient to subordinate appellant's constitutionally protected rights, but affirmatively shows that the investigatory objective was the impermissible one of exposure for exposure's sake. The investigation, as revealed by the report, [was one] in which the processes of law-making and law-evaluating were submerged entirely in exposure of individual behavior—in adjudication, of a sort, however much disclaimed, through the exposure process. . . .

"The Court describes the inquiry we must make in this matter as a balancing of interests. I think I have indicated that there has been no valid legislative interest of the State actually defined and shown in the investigation as it operated, so that there is really nothing against which the appellant's rights of association and expression can be balanced. But if some proper legislative end of the inquiry can be surmised, through what must be a process of speculation, I think it is patent that there is really no subordinating interest in it demonstrated on the part of the State. . . . Here we must demand some initial showing by the State sufficient to counterbalance the interest in

privacy as it relates to freedom of speech and assembly. On any basis that has practical meaning, New Hampshire has not made such a showing here." In a separate notation, Justices Black and Douglas stated that they joined Justice Brennan's dissent "because he makes clear to them that New Hampshire's legislative program" violated the bill of attainder prohibition.

BARENBLATT v. UNITED STATES

360 U.S. 109, 79 S.Ct. 1081, 3 L.Ed.2d 1115 (1959).

Certiorari to the Court of Appeals for the District of Columbia.

Mr. Justice HARLAN delivered the opinion of the Court.

.   .   .   The scope of the power of inquiry [is] as penetrating and far-reaching as the potential power to enact and appropriate under the Constitution. Broad as it is, the power is not, however, without limitations. Since Congress may only investigate into those areas in which it may potentially legislate or appropriate, it cannot inquire into matters which are within the exclusive province of one or the other branches of the Government. .   .   . And the Congress, in common with all branches of the Government, must exercise its powers subject to the limitations placed by the Constitution on governmental action, more particularly in the context of this case the relevant limitations of the Bill of Rights.

.   .   .   In the present case congressional efforts to learn the extent of a nation-wide, indeed world-wide, problem have brought one of its investigating committees into the field of education. Of course, broadly viewed, inquiries cannot be made into the teaching that is pursued in any of our educational institutions. When academic teaching-freedom and its corollary learning-freedom [are] claimed, this Court will always be on the alert against intrusion by Congress into this constitutionally protected domain. But this does not mean that the Congress is precluded from interrogating a witness merely because he is a teacher. An educational institution is not a constitutional sanctuary from inquiry into matters that may otherwise be within the constitutional legislative domain merely for the reason that inquiry is made of someone within its walls. .   .   .

We here review petitioner's conviction under 2 U.S.C. § 192 for contempt of Congress, arising from his refusal to answer certain questions put to him by a Subcommittee of the House Committee on Un-American Activities during the course of an inquiry concerning alleged Communist infiltration into the field of education. .   .   .

Pursuant to a subpoena, and accompanied by counsel, petitioner on June 28, 1954, appeared as a witness before this congressional Subcommittee. After answering a few preliminary questions and testifying that he had been a graduate student and teaching fellow at the University of Michigan from 1947 to 1950 and an instructor in psychology at Vassar College from 1950 to shortly before his appearance before the Subcommittee, petitioner objected generally to the right of the Subcommittee to inquire into his "political" and "religious" beliefs or any "other personal and private affairs" or "associational activities," upon grounds set forth in a previously prepared memorandum

[relying, inter alia, on the First, Ninth and Tenth Amendments and on separation of powers]. Thereafter petitioner specifically declined to answer each of the following five questions:

"Are you now a member of the Communist Party? (Count One.)

"Have you ever been a member of the Communist Party? (Count Two.)

"Now, you have stated that you knew Francis Crowley. Did you know Francis Crowley as a member of the Communist Party? (Count Three.)

"Were you ever a member of the Haldane Club of the Communist Party while at the University of Michigan? (Count Four.)

"Were you a member while a student of the University of Michigan Council of Arts, Sciences, and Professions?" (Count Five.)

In each instance the grounds of refusal were those set forth in the prepared statement. Petitioner expressly disclaimed reliance upon "the Fifth Amendment." [He was convicted on all counts and sentenced to six months' imprisonment and a $250 fine.]

Since this sentence was less than the maximum punishment authorized by the statute for conviction under any one Count, the judgment below must be upheld if the conviction upon any of the Counts is sustainable. . . . As we conceive the ultimate issue in this case to be whether petitioner could properly be convicted of contempt for refusing to answer questions relating to his participation in or knowledge of alleged Communist Party activities at educational institutions in this country, we find it unnecessary to consider the validity of his conviction under the Third and Fifth Counts, the only one involving questions which on their face do not directly relate to such participation or knowledge. . . .

The Court's past cases establish sure guides to decision. Undeniably, the First Amendment in some circumstances protects an individual from being compelled to disclose his associational relationships. However, the protections of the First Amendment, unlike a proper claim of the privilege against self-incrimination under the Fifth Amendment, do not afford a witness the right to resist inquiry in all circumstances. Where First Amendment rights are asserted to bar governmental interrogation resolution of the issue always involves a balancing by the courts of the competing private and public interests at stake in the particular circumstances shown. . . .

The first question is whether this investigation was related to a valid legislative purpose. . . . That Congress has wide power to legislate in the field of Communist activity in this country, and to conduct appropriate investigations in aid thereof, is hardly debatable. The existence of such power has never been questioned by this Court, and it is sufficient to say, without particularization, that Congress has enacted or considered in this field a wide range of legislative measures, not a few of which have stemmed from recommendations of the very Committee whose actions have been drawn in question here. In the last analysis this power rests on the right of self-preservation, "the ultimate value of any society" [Dennis]. Justification for its exercise in turn rests on the long and widely accepted view that the tenets of the Communist Party include the ultimate overthrow of the

Government of the United States by force and violence, a view which has been given final expression by the Congress.

We think that investigatory power in this domain is not to be denied Congress solely because the field of education is involved. . . . Indeed we do not understand petitioner here to suggest that Congress in no circumstances may inquire into Communist activity in the field of education. Rather, his position is in effect that this particular investigation was aimed not at the revolutionary aspects but at the theoretical classroom discussion of communism.

In our opinion this position rests on a too constricted view of the nature of the investigatory process, and is not supported by a fair assessment of the record before us. An investigation of advocacy of or preparation for overthrow certainly embraces the right to identify a witness as a member of the Communist Party and to inquire into the various manifestations of the Party's tenets. The strict requirements of a prosecution under the Smith Act, see [Dennis and Yates], are not the measure of the permissible scope of a congressional investigation into "overthrow," for of necessity the investigatory process must proceed step by step. Nor can it fairly be concluded that this investigation was directed at controlling what is being taught at our universities rather than at overthrow. . . .

Nor can we accept the further contention that this investigation should not be deemed to have been in furtherance of a legislative purpose because the true objective of the Committee and of the Congress was purely "exposure." So long as Congress acts in pursuance of its constitutional power, the Judiciary lacks authority to intervene on the basis of the motives which spurred the exercise of that power. [Watkins.] Having scrutinized this record we cannot say that the unanimous panel of the Court of Appeals which first considered this case was wrong in concluding that "the primary purposes of the inquiry were in aid of legislative processes." . . .

Finally, the record is barren of other factors which in themselves might sometimes lead to the conclusion that the individual interests at stake were not subordinate to those of the state. There is no indication in this record that the Subcommittee was attempting to pillory witnesses. Nor did petitioner's appearance as a witness follow from indiscriminate dragnet procedures, lacking in probable cause for belief that he possessed information which might be helpful to the Subcommittee. And the relevancy of the questions put to him by the Subcommittee is not open to doubt.

We conclude that the balance between the individual and the governmental interests here at stake must be struck in favor of the latter, and that therefore the provisions of the First Amendment have not been offended. . .

Affirmed.

Mr. Justice BLACK, with whom The Chief Justice [WARREN] and Mr. Justice DOUGLAS concur, dissenting. . . .

. . . I do not agree that laws directly abridging First Amendment freedoms can be justified by a congressional or judicial balancing process. There are, of course, cases suggesting that a law which primarily regulates conduct but which might also indirectly affect speech can be upheld if the effect on speech is minor in relation to the need for control of the conduct. With these cases I agree. Typical of them are [Cantwell v. Connecticut and

Schneider v. State, chap. 12, sec. 2]. Both of these involved the right of a city to control its streets.* . . . But even such laws governing conduct, we emphasize, must be tested, though only by a balancing process, if they indirectly affect ideas. . . . But we did not in Schneider, any more than in Cantwell, even remotely suggest that a law directly aimed at curtailing speech and political persuasion could be saved through a balancing process. . . .

But even assuming what I cannot assume, that some balancing is proper in this case, I feel that the Court after stating the test ignores it completely. At most it balances the right of the Government to preserve itself, against Barenblatt's right to refrain from revealing Communist affiliations. Such a balance, however, mistakes the factors to be weighed. In the first place, it completely leaves out the real interest in Barenblatt's silence, the interest of the people as a whole in being able to join organizations, advocate causes and make political "mistakes" without later being subjected to governmental penalties for having dared to think for themselves. It is this right, the right to err politically, which keeps us strong as a Nation. [It] is these interests of society, rather than Barenblatt's own right to silence, which I think the Court should put on the balance . . . . Instead they are not mentioned, while on the other side the demands of the Government are vastly overstated and called "self-preservation." . . . Such a result reduces "balancing" to a mere play on words and is completely inconsistent with the rules this Court has previously given for applying a "balancing test," where it is proper [Schneider].

Finally, I think Barenblatt's conviction violates the Constitution because the chief aim, purpose and practice of the House Un-American Activities Committee, as disclosed by its many reports, is to try witnesses and punish them because they are or have been Communists or because they refuse to admit or deny Communist affiliations. The punishment imposed is generally punishment by humiliation and public shame. . . . It seems to me that the proof that the Un-American Activities Committee is here undertaking a purely judicial function is overwhelming. . . .

Mr. Justice BRENNAN, dissenting.

[I am in] complete agreement with my Brother Black that no purpose for the investigation of Barenblatt is revealed by the record except exposure purely for the sake of exposure. This is not a purpose to which Barenblatt's rights under the First Amendment can validly be subordinated. . . .

LEGISLATIVE INVESTIGATIONS—FROM BARENBLATT TO GIBSON

In a number of congressional investigation cases soon after Barenblatt, the Court adhered to its deferential constitutional stance: it refused to impose strict constitutional restraints on legislative inquiries. Yet during the same period, the Court repeatedly reversed contempt of Congress convic-

---

* Recall the renewal and elaboration of the debate about "balancing" between Justices Black and Harlan in Konigsberg II, the 1961 Bar Admission Case in sec. 5 above. Excerpts from that Konigsberg debate are printed in the introduction to chap. 12.

tions: recalcitrant witnesses were successful in a series of cases decided on narrow grounds. Four years later, in the Gibson case below, a state legislative investigation seeking information about subversive influences in the NAACP came before the Court; and in that 1963 decision, the Court reexamined the constitutional framework governing legislative inquiries. Did Gibson indicate a significant shift from Barenblatt? Compare the contrast between the fifties and the sixties in the government employee and licensee cases in sec. 5 of this chapter and in the criminal cases in the subversion context, in sec. 1 of chap. 12. Gibson illustrates a number of ingredients of the "strict scrutiny" of alleged state impingements upon free expression elaborated by the Warren Court in the sixties. Has the Burger Court followed the Gibson approach? Contrast the interpretations and applications of Gibson and similar cases in the White and Stewart opinions in Branzburg v. Hayes, the 1972 decision rejecting a newsman's privilege in grand jury investigations, in sec. 6B below.

The Court's continued rejection of *constitutional* defenses by congressional committee witnesses in the years immediately after Barenblatt is illustrated by Wilkinson v. United States, 365 U.S. 399 (1961), and Braden v. United States, 365 U.S. 431 (1961). In each case, the Court affirmed convictions for refusal to answer congressional committee inquiries largely on the authority of—and with the same division as in—Barenblatt. A few months later, however, the 5 to 4 decision in Deutch v. United States, 367 U.S. 456 (1961), reversed a contempt conviction. Deutch signalled the emerging tendency: it rested on statutory rather than constitutional grounds. The conviction of Deutch was reversed because "the Government at the trial failed to carry its burden of proving the pertinence of the questions"; pertinence was an element of the offense under 2 U.S.C. § 192. A new basis for challenging contempt of Congress convictions was sanctioned by the decision in six companion cases in the following year, reported as Russell v. United States, 369 U.S. 749 (1962). The convictions were reversed because in each case "the indictment returned by the grand jury failed to identify the subject under congressional subcommittee inquiry at the time the witness was interrogated." Justice Clark's dissent noted that "the Court has now upset 10 convictions under § 192" since the Watkins decision. "This continued frustration [of Congress] indicates to me that the time may have come for Congress to revert to 'its orginal practice of utilizing the coercive sanction of contempt proceedings at the bar of the House [affected].' "

GIBSON v. FLORIDA LEGISLATIVE INVESTIGATION COMMITTEE

372 U.S. 539, 83 S.Ct. 889, 9 L.Ed.2d 929 (1963).

Certiorari to the Supreme Court of Florida.

Mr. Justice GOLDBERG delivered the opinion of the Court.

This case is the culmination of protracted litigation involving legislative investigating committees of the State of Florida and the Miami branch of the National Association for the Advancement of Colored People. . . .

The petitioner, then president of the Miami branch of the NAACP, was ordered to appear before the respondent Committee on November 4, 1959, [and] to bring with him records of the association which were in his possession or custody and which pertained to the identity of members of, and contributors to, the Miami and state NAACP organizations. Prior to interrogation of any witnesses the Committee chairman [stated] that the inquiry would be directed to Communists and Communist activities, including infiltration of Communists into organizations operating in the described fields [including race relations]. . . .

The petitioner told the Committee that he had not brought [the] records with him to the hearing and announced that he would not produce them for the purpose of answering questions concerning membership in the NAACP. He did, however, volunteer to answer such questions on the basis of his own personal knowledge; when given the names and shown photographs of 14 persons previously identified as Communists or members of Communist front or affiliated organizations, the petitioner said that he could associate none of them with the NAACP.

The petitioner's refusal to produce his organization's membership lists was based on the ground that·to bring the lists to the hearing and to utilize them as the basis of his testimony would interfere with the free exercise of Fourteenth Amendment associational rights of members and prospective members of the NAACP.

In accordance with Florida procedure, the petitioner was brought before a state court and, after a hearing, was adjudged in contempt, and sentenced to six months' imprisonment and fined $1,200, or, in default in payment thereof, sentenced to an additional six months' imprisonment. . . .

This Court has repeatedly held that rights of association are within the ambit of the constitutional protections afforded by the First and Fourteenth Amendments. [E. g., NAACP v. Alabama.] And it is equally clear that the guarantee encompasses protection of privacy of association such as [the NAACP—e. g., Bates, NAACP v. Alabama]. At the same time, however, this Court's prior holdings demonstrate that there can be no question that the State has power adequately to inform itself—through legislative investigation, if it so desires—in order to act and protect its legitimate and vital interests. [Watkins; Barenblatt.] It is no less obvious, however, that the legislative power to investigate, broad as it may be, is not without limit. . . . Validation of the broad subject matter under investigation does not necessarily carry with it automatic and wholesale validation of all individual questions, subpoenas, and demands. . . .

Significantly, the parties are in substantial agreement as to the proper test to be applied to reconcile the competing claims of government and individual and to determine the propriety of the Committee's demands. As declared by the respondent Committee in its brief to this Court, "Basically, this case hinges entirely on the question of whether the evidence before the Committee [was] sufficient to show probable cause or nexus between the NAACP Miami Branch, and Communist activities." We understand this to mean—regardless of the label applied, be it "nexus," "foundation," or whatever—that it is an essential prerequisite to the validity of an investigation which intrudes into the area of constitutionally protected rights of speech, press, association and peti-

tion that the State convincingly show a substantial relation between the information sought and a subject of overriding and compelling state interest. Absent such a relation between the NAACP and conduct in which the State may have a compelling regulatory concern, the Committee has not "demonstrated so cogent an interest in obtaining and making public" the membership information sought to be obtained as to "justify the substantial abridgment of associational freedom which such disclosures will effect." [Bates v. Little Rock.]

Applying these principles to the facts of this case, the respondent Committee contends that the prior decisions of this Court in [Uphaus, Barenblatt, Wilkinson, and Braden] compel a result here upholding the legislative right of inquiry. In Barenblatt, Wilkinson, and Braden, however, it was a refusal to answer a question or questions concerning the witness' *own* past or present membership *in the Communist Party* which supported his conviction. It is apparent that the necessary preponderating governmental interest and, in fact, the very result in those cases were founded on the holding that the Communist Party is not an ordinary or legitimate political party, as known in this country, and that, because of its particular nature, membership therein is *itself* a permissible subject of regulation and legislative scrutiny. Assuming the correctness of the premises on which those cases were decided, no further demonstration of compelling governmental interest was deemed necessary, since the direct object of the challenged questions there was discovery of membership in the Communist Party, a matter held pertinent to a proper subject then under inquiry.

Here, however, it is not alleged Communists who are the witnesses before the Committee and it is not discovery of their membership in that party which is the object of the challenged inquiries. Rather, it is the NAACP itself which is the subject of the investigation, and it is its local president [who was] held in contempt . . . . . There is no suggestion that the Miami branch of the NAACP or the national organization with which it is affiliated was, or is, itself a subversive organization. Nor is there any indication that the activities or policies of the NAACP were either Communist dominated or influenced. In fact, this very record indicates that the association was and is against communism and has voluntarily taken steps to keep Communists from being members. . . .

Thus, unlike the situation in Barenblatt, Wilkinson and Braden, supra, the Committee was not here seeking from the petitioner [any] information as to whether he, himself, or even other persons were members of the Communist Party [or other] subversive groups; instead, the entire thrust of the demands on the petitioner was that he disclose whether other persons were members of the NAACP, itself a concededly legitimate and non-subversive organization. Compelling such an organization, engaged in the exercise of First and Fourteenth Amendment rights, to disclose its membership presents, under our cases, a question wholly different from compelling the Communist Party to disclose its own membership. Moreover, even to say, as in Barenblatt, that it is permissible to inquire into the subject of Communist infiltration of educational or other organizations does not mean that it is permissible to demand or require from such other groups disclosure of their membership by inquiry into their records when such disclosure will seri-

ously inhibit or impair the exercise of constitutional rights and has not itself been demonstrated to bear a crucial relation to a proper governmental interest or to be essential to fulfillment of a proper governmental purpose. The prior holdings that governmental interest in controlling subversion and the particular character of the Communist Party and its objectives outweigh the right of individual Communists to conceal party membership or affiliations by no means require the wholly different conclusion that other groups—concededly legitimate—automatically forfeit their rights to privacy of association simply because the general subject matter of the legislative inquiry is Communist subversion or infiltration. The fact that governmental interest was deemed compelling in Barenblatt, Wilkinson, and Braden and held to support the inquiries there made into membership in the Communist Party does not resolve the issues here, where the challenged questions go to membership in an admittedly lawful organization.

Respondent's reliance on [Uphaus v. Wyman] as controlling is similarly misplaced. There, [the] Court found that there was demonstrated a sufficient connection between subversive activity—held there to be a proper subject of governmental concern—and the World Fellowship, itself, to justify discovery of the guest list; no semblance of such a nexus between the NAACP and subversive *activities* has been shown here. . . . Finally, in Uphaus, the State was investigating whether subversive persons were within its boundaries and whether their presence constituted a threat to the State. No such purpose or need is evident here. The Florida Committee is not seeking to identify subversives by questioning the petitioner; apparently it is satisfied that it already knows who they are.

In the absence of directly determinative authority, we turn, then, to consideration of the facts now before us. [W]e rest our result on the fact that the record in this case is insufficient to show a substantial connection between the Miami branch of the NAACP and Communist *activities* which the respondent Committee itself concedes is an essential prerequisite to demonstrating the immediate, substantial, and subordinating state interest necessary to sustain its right of inquiry into the membership lists. . . .

This summary of the evidence discloses the utter failure to demonstrate the existence of any substantial relationship between the NAACP and subversive or Communist activities. In essence, there is here merely indirect, less than unequivocal, and mostly hearsay testimony that in years past some 14 people who were asserted to be, or to have been, Communists or members of Communist front or "affiliated organizations" attended occasional meetings of the Miami branch of the NAACP "and/or" were members of that branch, which had a total membership of about 1,000.

On the other hand, there was no claim made at the hearings, or since, that the NAACP or its Miami branch was engaged in any subversive activities or that its legitimate activities have been dominated or influenced by Communists. [W]ithout any showing of a meaningful relation between the NAACP Miami branch and subversives [we] are asked to find the compelling and subordinating state interest which must exist if essential freedoms are to be curtailed or inhibited. This we cannot do. The respondent Committee has laid no adequate foundation for its direct demands upon the officers and records of a wholly legitimate organization for disclosure of its membership

. . . .. The strong associational interest in maintaining the privacy of membership lists of groups engaged in the constitutionally protected free trade in ideas and beliefs may not be substantially infringed upon such a slender showing as here made by the respondent. While, of course, all legitimate organizations are the beneficiaries of these protections, they are all the more essential here, where the challenged privacy is that of persons espousing beliefs already unpopular with their neighbors and the deterrent and "chilling" effect on the free exercise of constitutionally enshrined rights of free speech, expression, and association is consequently the more immediate and substantial. . . .

Of course, a legislative investigation—as any investigation—must proceed "step by step" [Barenblatt], but step by step or in totality, an adequate foundation for inquiry must be laid. . . . No such foundation has been laid here. . . .

Nothing we say here impairs or denies the existence of the underlying legislative right to investigate or legislate with respect to subversive activities by Communists or anyone else; our decision today deals only with the manner in which such power may be exercised and we hold simply that groups which themselves are neither engaged in subversive or other illegal or improper activities nor demonstrated to have any substantial connections with such activities are to be protected in their rights of free and private association. . . .

To permit legislative inquiry to proceed on less than an adequate foundation would be to sanction unjustified and unwarranted intrusions into the very heart of the constitutional privilege to be secure in associations in legitimate organizations engaged in the exercise of First and Fourteenth Amendment rights; to impose a lesser standard than we here do would be inconsistent with the maintenance of those essential conditions basic to the preservation of our democracy. . . .

Reversed.

Mr. Justice BLACK, concurring.

. . . I would reverse here on the ground that there has been a direct abridgment of the right of association . . . .. But, since the Court assumes for purposes of this case that there was no direct abridgment of First Amendment freedoms, I concur in the Court's opinion . . . ..

Mr. Justice DOUGLAS, concurring. . . .

In my view, government is not only powerless to legislate with respect to membership in a lawful organization; it is also precluded from probing the intimacies of spiritual and intellectual relationships in the myriad of such societies and groups that exist in this country, regardless of the legislative purpose sought to be served. . . .

Mr. Justice HARLAN, whom Mr. Justice CLARK, Mr. Justice STEWART, and Mr. Justice WHITE, join dissenting. . . .

The Court's reasoning is difficult to grasp. I read its opinion as basically proceeding on the premise that the governmental interest in investigating Communist infiltration into admittedly nonsubversive organizations, as distinguished from investigating organizations themselves suspected of subversive activities, is not sufficient to overcome the countervailing right to freedom of

association. On this basis "nexus" is seemingly found lacking because it was never claimed that the NAACP Miami Branch had itself engaged in subversive activity, and because none of the Committee's evidence relating to any of the 52 alleged Communist Party members was sufficient to attribute such activity to the local branch or to show that it was dominated, influenced, or used "by Communists." . . .

But, until today, I had never supposed that any of our decisions relating to state or federal power to investigate in the field of Communist subversion could possibly be taken as suggesting any difference in the degree of governmental investigatory interest as between Communist infiltration *of* organizations and Communist activity *by* organizations. See, e. g., [Barenblatt] (infiltration into education); [Wilkinson] and [Braden] (infiltration into basic industries); Russell v. United States (infiltration of newspaper business). . . .

Given the unsoundness of the basic premise underlying the Court's holding as to the absence of "nexus," this decision surely falls of its own weight. For unless "nexus" requires an investigating agency to prove in advance the very things it is trying to find out, I do not understand how it can be said that the information preliminarily developed by the Committee's investigator was not sufficient to satisfy, under any reasonable test, the requirement of "nexus."

Apart from this, the issue of "nexus" is surely laid at rest by the NAACP's own "Anti-Communism" resolution, first adopted in 1950, which petitioner had voluntarily furnished the Committee before the curtain came down on his examination. [The resolution's recitals included a statement that "there is a well-organized, nationwide conspiracy by Communists either to capture or split and wreck the NAACP" and a direction that the National Board of Directors "take the necessary action to eradicate such *infiltration*."] It hardly meets the point at issue to suggest, as the Court does, that the resolution only serves to show that the Miami Branch was in fact free of any Communist influences—unless self-investigation is deemed constitutionally to block official inquiry.

I also find it difficult to see how this case really presents any serious question as to interference with freedom of association. Given the willingness of the petitioner to testify from recollection as to individual memberships in the local branch of the NAACP, the germaneness of the membership records to the subject matter of the Committee's investigation, and the limited purpose for which their use was sought—as an aid to refreshing the witness' recollection, involving their divulgence only to the petitioner himself—this case of course bears no resemblance whatever to [NAACP v. Alabama] or [Bates v. Little Rock]. In both of those cases the State had sought general divulgence of local NAACP membership lists without any showing of a justifying state interest. In effect what we are asked to hold here is that the petitioner had a constitutional right to give only partial or inaccurate testimony, and that indeed seems to me the true effect of the Court's holding today. . . .

Mr. Justice WHITE, dissenting.

In my view, the opinion of the Court represents a serious limitation upon the Court's previous cases dealing with [the] right of the legislature to

investigate the Communist Party and its activities. Although one of the classic and recurring activities of the Communist Party is the infiltration and subversion of other organizations, either openly or in a clandestine manner, the Court holds that even where a legislature has evidence that a legitimate organization is under assault and even though that organization is itself sounding open and public alarm, an investigating committee is nevertheless forbidden to compel the organization or its members to reveal the fact, or not, of membership in that organization of named Communists assigned to the infiltrating task.

While the Court purports to be saving such a case for later consideration, it is difficult for me to understand how under today's decision a Communist in the process of performing his assigned job could be required to divulge not only his membership in the Communist Party but his membership or activities in the target organization as well. The Court fails to articulate why the State's interest is any the more compelling or the associational rights any the less endangered when a known Communist is asked whether he belongs to a protected association than here when the organization is asked to confirm or deny that membership. As I read the Court's opinion the exposed Communist might well, in the name of the associational freedom of the legitimate organization and of its members including himself, successfully shield his activities from legislative inquiry. Thus to me the decision today represents a marked departure from the principles of [Barenblatt] and like cases.

On the other hand, should a legislature obtain ostensibly reliable information about the penetration of Communists into a particular organization, information which in the course of things would be placed on public record like the testimony here, there could no longer be a weighty interest on the part of that organization to refuse to verify that information or to brand it as false. This is particularly true here where an officer of the association is willing to identify persons from memory and where the organization itself has called upon its own members to root out Communists . . . . Unbending resistance to answering, one way or the other, a legislative committee's limited inquiries in the face of already public information to the same effect reduces the association's interest in secrecy to sterile doctrine. . . .

The net effect of the Court's decision is, of course, to insulate from effective legislative inquiry and preventive legislation the time-proven skills of the Communist Party in subverting and eventually controlling legitimate organizations. Until such a group, chosen as an object of Communist Party action, has been effectively reduced to vassalage, legislative bodies may seek no information from the organization under attack by duty-bound Communists. When the job has been done and the legislative committee can prove it, it then has the hollow privilege of recording another victory for the Communist Party, which both Congress and this Court have found to be an organization under the direction of a foreign power, dedicated to the overthrow of the Government if necessary by force and violence. I respectfully dissent.

THE DeGREGORY CASE:
NEW HAMPSHIRE INVESTIGATIONS REVISITED

DeGREGORY v. NEW HAMPSHIRE ATTORNEY GENERAL, 383 U.S. 825 (1966), like Sweezy and Uphaus, arose out of a New Hampshire subversive activities investigation. Appellant was jailed for contempt for refusal to answer, in 1964, questions relating to Communist activities prior to 1957. The Supreme Court, applying the principles of Gibson and asserting distinctions from Uphaus, reversed in a 6 to 3 decision. Justice Douglas stated for the majority:

"The substantiality of appellant's First Amendment claim can best be seen by considering what he was asked to do. Appellant had already testified that he had not been involved with the Communist Party since 1957 and that he had no knowledge of Communist activities during that period. The Attorney General further sought to have him disclose information relating to his political associations of an earlier day, the meetings he attended, and the views expressed and ideas advocated at any such gatherings. Indeed, the Attorney General here relied entirely upon a 1955 Report on Subversive Activities in New Hampshire to justify renewed investigation of appellant. The Report connects appellant with the Communist Party only until 1953, over 10 years prior to the investigation giving rise to the present contempt.

"On the basis of our prior cases, appellant had every reason to anticipate that the details of his political associations to which he might testify would be reported in a pamphlet purporting to describe the nature of subversion in New Hampshire. (See [Uphaus], Brennan, J., dissenting.) Admittedly, 'exposure—in the sense of disclosure—is an inescapable incident of an investigation into the presence of subversive persons within a State.' [Uphaus.] But whatever justification may have supported such exposure in Uphaus is absent here; the staleness of both the basis for the investigation and its subject matter makes indefensible such exposure of one's associational and political past . . . .

"There is no showing of 'overriding and compelling state interest' [Gibson] that would warrant intrusion into the realm of political and associational privacy protected by the First Amendment. The information being sought was historical, not current. Lawmaking at the investigatory stage may properly probe historic events for any light that may be thrown on present conditions and problems. But the First Amendment prevents [the Government from] using the power to investigate enforced by the contempt power to probe at will and without relation to existing need. [Watkins.] The present record is devoid of any evidence that there is any Communist movement in New Hampshire. The 1955 Report deals primarily with 'world-wide communism' and the Federal Government. There is no showing whatsoever of present danger of sedition against the State itself, the only area to which the authority of the State extends. There is thus absent that 'nexus' between petitioner and subversive activities in New Hampshire which the Court found to exist in [Uphaus]. New Hampshire's interest on this record is too remote and conjectural to override the guarantee of the First Amendment that a person can speak or not, as he chooses, free of all governmental compulsion."

Justice Harlan, joined by Justices Stewart and White, dissented: "New Hampshire in my view should be free to investigate the existence or nonexistence of Communist Party subversion, or any other legitimate subject of concern to the State, without first being asked to produce evidence of the very type to be sought in the course of the inquiry. Then, given that the subject of investigation in this case is a permissible one, the appellant seems to me a witness who could properly be called to testify about it; I cannot say as a constitutional matter that inquiry into the current operations of the local Communist Party could not be advanced by knowledge of its operations a decade ago."

B. GRAND JURY INVESTIGATIONS

BRANZBURG v. HAYES

408 U.S. 665, 92 S.Ct. 2646, 33 L.Ed.2d 626 (1972).

Certiorari to the Court of Appeals of Kentucky.

Opinion of the Court by Mr. Justice WHITE . . . . .

The issue in these cases* is whether requiring newsmen to appear and testify before state or federal grand juries abridges the freedom of speech and press guaranteed by the First Amendment. We hold that it does not.

[The newsmen] press First Amendment claims that may be simply put: that to gather news it is often necessary to agree either not to identify the source of information published or to publish only part of the facts revealed, or both; that if the reporter is nevertheless forced to reveal these confidences

---

* The opinion applied to two other cases in addition to Branzburg: In the Matter of Pappas, on certiorari to the Supreme Judicial Court of Massachusetts; and United States v. Caldwell, on certiorari to the U. S. Court of Appeals for the Ninth Circuit.

Paul Branzburg, a reporter for a Louisville newspaper, had written articles about drug activities he had observed. He refused to testify before a state grand jury regarding his information about possession of marijuana and conversion of marijuana into hashish. Paul Pappas was a newsman for a New Bedford, Mass., television station. While covering "civil disorders" which "involved fires and other turmoil," he was allowed to remain in Black Panther headquarters for three hours on condition that he would not disclose anything he saw or heard except an anticipated police raid. There was no raid, and Pappas wrote no story about what happened at the headquarters. He refused to tell a grand jury about what had taken place inside the headquarters. [The state courts in Branz-

burg and Pappas explicitly rejected the approach of the lower federal courts in Caldwell, below.]

Earl Caldwell was a Black reporter for The New York Times assigned to cover the Black Panthers and other Black militant groups. He had written articles about the Black Panthers and had interviewed their leaders. He objected to testifying before a federal grand jury investigating "possible violations of a number of criminal statutes," including those banning threats against the President and interstate travel to incite to riot. The District Court issued a protective order stating that he "shall not be required to reveal confidential" information unless the government showed "a compelling and overriding national interest" in requiring his testimony "which cannot be served by any alternative means." Subsequently, he refused to appear before a grand jury despite the protective order and was held in contempt. The Court of Appeals reversed, holding that a reporter was not only entitled to a qualified testimonial

to a grand jury, the source so identified and other confidential sources of other reporters will be measurably deterred from furnishing publishable information, all to the detriment of the free flow of information protected by the First Amendment. Although [petitioners] do not claim an absolute privilege against official interrogation in all circumstances, they assert that the reporter should not be forced either to appear or to testify before a grand jury or at trial until and unless sufficient grounds are shown for believing that the reporter possesses information relevant to a crime the grand jury is investigating, that the information the reporter has is unavailable from other sources, and that the need for the information is sufficiently compelling to override the claimed invasion of First Amendment interests occasioned by the disclosure. Principally relied upon are [precedents] requiring that official action with adverse impact on First Amendment rights be justified by a public interest that is "compelling" or "paramount," and those precedents establishing the principle that justifiable governmental goals may not be achieved by unduly broad means having an unnecessary impact on protected rights of speech, press, or association. The heart of the claim is that the burden on news gathering resulting from compelling reporters to disclose confidential information outweighs any public interest in obtaining the information.

We do not [suggest] that news gathering does not qualify for First Amendment protection; without some protection for seeking out the news, freedom of the press could be eviscerated. But this case involves no intrusions upon speech or assembly, [and] no penalty, civil or criminal, related to the content of published material is at issue here. The use of confidential sources by the press is not forbidden or restricted; reporters remain free to seek news from any source by means within the law. No attempt is made to require the press to publish its sources of information or indiscriminately to disclose them on request.

The sole issue before us is the obligation of reporters to respond to grand jury subpoenas as other citizens do and to answer questions relevant to an investigation into the commission of crime. [The Constitution does not protect] the average citizen from disclosing to a grand jury information that he has received in confidence. The claim is, however, that reporters are exempt . . . .

It is clear that the First Amendment does not invalidate every incidental burdening of the press that may result from the enforcement of civil or criminal statutes of general applicability. . . . It has generally been held that the First Amendment does not guarantee the press a constitutional

privilege but also that "absent some special showing of necessity by the Government, attendance by Caldwell at a secret meeting of the grand jury was something he was privileged to refuse because of the potential impact of such an appearance on the flow of news to the public." The Court of Appeals emphasized the special facts of the case: Caldwell had "asserted in affidavit that there is nothing to which he could testify (beyond that which he has already made public and for which, therefore, his appearance is unnecessary) that is not protected by the District Court's order. If this is true—and the Government apparently has not believed it necessary to dispute it—appellant's response to the subpoena would be a barren performance—one of no benefit to the Grand Jury. To destroy appellant's capacity as newsgatherer for such a return **hardly makes sense.**"

right of special access to information not available to the public generally.†
. . . Despite the fact that news gathering may be hampered, the press is
regularly excluded from grand jury proceedings, our own conferences, the
meetings of other official bodies gathered in executive session, and the meetings of private organizations. Newsmen have no constitutional right of access
to the scenes of crime or disaster when the general public is excluded, and they
may be prohibited from attending or publishing information about trials if
such restrictions are necessary to assure a defendant a fair trial before an
impartial tribunal. . . . It is thus not surprising that the great weight
of authority is that newsmen are not exempt from the normal duty of appearing
before a grand jury and answering questions relevant to a criminal investigation. . . .

The prevailing constitutional view of the newsman's privilege is very
much rooted in the ancient role of the grand jury. [I]ts investigative powers are necessarily broad. . . . Although the powers of the grand jury
are not unlimited, [the] longstanding principle that "the public has a right
to every man's evidence," except for those persons protected by a constitutional, common law, or statutory privilege, is particularly applicable to grand
jury proceedings.

A number of States have provided newsmen a statutory privilege of
varying breadth, but the majority have not done so, and none has been provided by federal statute. . . . We are asked to [interpret] the First
Amendment to grant newsmen a testimonial privilege that other citizens do
not enjoy. This we decline to do. . . . On the records now before us,
we perceive no basis for holding that the public interest in law enforcement
and in ensuring effective grand jury proceedings is insufficient to override the
consequential, but uncertain, burden on news gathering which is said to result from insisting that reporters, like other citizens, respond to relevant questions put to them in the course of a valid grand jury investigation or criminal trial.

This conclusion itself involves no restraint on what newspapers may
publish or on the type or quality of information reporters may seek to acquire, nor does it threaten the vast bulk of confidential relationships between reporters and their sources. Grand juries address themselves to the
issues of whether crimes have been committed and who committed them.
Only where news sources themselves are implicated in crime or possess information relevant to the grand jury's task need they or the reporter be concerned about grand jury subpoenas. Nothing before us indicates that a large
number or percentage of *all* confidential news sources fall into either category and would in any way be deterred by our holding . . ..

The preference for anonymity of those confidential informants involved in actual criminal conduct is presumably a product of their desire to
escape criminal prosecution, and this preference, while understandable, is
hardly deserving of constitutional protection. It would be frivolous to assert—and no one does in these cases—that the First Amendment, in the interest of securing news or otherwise, confers a license on either the reporter

---

† Note also the consideration (and majority rejection) of a claimed right of
access by the press, in Procunier v.
Pell and Saxbe v. Washington Post
Co., the 1974 prisoner interview cases
in sec. 4D above.

or his news sources to violate otherwise valid criminal laws. Although stealing documents or private wiretapping could provide newsworthy information, neither reporter nor source is immune from conviction for such conduct, whatever the impact on the flow of news. [W]e cannot seriously entertain the notion that the First Amendment protects a newsman's agreement to conceal the criminal conduct of his source, or evidence thereof, on the theory that it is better to write about crime than to do something about it. . . .

There remain those situations where a source is not engaged in criminal conduct but has information suggesting illegal conduct by others. Newsmen frequently receive information from such sources pursuant to a tacit or express agreement to withhold the source's name and suppress any information that the source wishes not published. . . . The argument that the flow of news will be diminished by compelling reporters to aid the grand jury in a criminal investigation is not irrational, nor are the records before us silent on the matter. But we remain unclear how often and to what extent informers are actually deterred from furnishing information when newsmen are forced to testify before a grand jury. The available data indicate that some newsmen rely a great deal on confidential sources and that some informants are particularly sensitive to the threat of exposure and may be silenced if it is held by this Court that, ordinarily, newmen must testify pursuant to subpoenas,[1] but the evidence fails to demonstrate that there would be a significant constriction of the flow of news to the public if this Court reaffirms the prior common-law and constitutional rule regarding the testimonial obligations of newsmen. Estimates of the inhibiting effect of such subpoenas on the willingness of informants to make disclosures to newsmen are widely divergent and to a great extent speculative. It would be difficult to canvass the views of the informants themselves; surveys of reporters on this topic are chiefly opinions of predicted informant behavior and must be viewed in the light of the professional self-interest of the interviewees.[2] Reliance by the press on confidential informants does not mean that all such sources will in fact dry up because of the later possible appearance of the newsman before a grand jury. The reporter may never be called and if he objects to testifying, the prosecution may not insist. Also, the relationship of many informants to the press is a symbiotic one which is unlikely to be greatly inhibited by the threat of subpoena: quite often, such informants are members of a minority political or cultural group which relies heavily on the media to propagate its views, publicize its aims, and magnify its exposure to the public. Moreover, grand juries characteristically conduct secret proceedings, and law

1. Respondent Caldwell attached a number of affidavits from prominent newsmen to his initial motion to quash, which detail the experiences of such journalists after they have been subpoenaed. [Footnote by the Court.]

2. In his Press Subpoenas: An Empirical and Legal Analysis, Study Report of the Reporters' Committee on Freedom of the Press 6–12, (1971), Prof. Blasi discusses these methodological problems. Prof. Blasi's survey found that slightly more than half of the 975 reporters questioned said that they relied on regular confidential sources for at least 10% of their stories. Of this group of reporters, only 8% were able to say with some certainty that their professional functioning had been adversely affected by the threat of subpoena; another 11% were not certain whether or not they had been adversely affected. [Footnote by the Court.]

enforcement officers are themselves experienced in dealing with informers and have their own methods for protecting them without interference with the effective administration of justice. There is little before us indicating that informants whose interest in avoiding exposure is that it may threaten job security, personal safety, or peace of mind, would in fact be in a worse position, or would think they would be, if they risked placing their trust in public officials as well as reporters. . . .

Accepting the fact, however, that an undetermined number of informants not themselves implicated in crime will nevertheless, for whatever reason, refuse to talk to newsmen if they fear identification by a reporter in an official investigation, we cannot accept the argument that the public interest in possible future news about crime from undisclosed, unverified sources must take precedence over the public interest in pursuing and prosecuting those crimes reported to the press by informants and in thus deterring the commission of such crimes in the future. [C]oncealment of crime and agreements to do so are not looked upon with favor. Such conduct deserves no encomium, and we decline now to afford it First Amendment protection by denigrating the duty of a citizen, whether reporter or informer, to respond to grand jury subpoena and answer relevant questions put to him. . . .

We are admonished that refusal to provide a First Amendment reporter's privilege will undermine the freedom of the press to collect and disseminate news. But this is not the lesson history teaches us. [T]he common law recognized no such privilege, and the constitutional argument was not even asserted until 1958. From the beginning of our country the press has operated without constitutional protection for press informants, and the press has flourished. . . .

It is said that currently press subpoenas have multiplied, that mutual distrust and tension between press and officialdom have increased, that reporting styles have changed, and that there is now more need for confidential sources, particularly where the press seeks news about minority cultural and political groups or dissident organizations suspicious of the law and public officials. These developments, even if true, are treacherous grounds for a far-reaching interpretation of the First Amendment fastening a nationwide rule on courts, grand juries, and prosecuting officials everywhere. . . .

The argument for such a constitutional privilege rests heavily on those cases holding that the infringement of protected First Amendment rights must be no broader than necessary to achieve a permissible governmental purpose. We do not deal, however, with a governmental institution that has abused its proper function, as a legislative committee does when it "expose[s] for the sake of exposure." [Watkins.] Nothing in the record indicates that these grand juries were "prob[ing] at will and without relation to existing need." [DeGregory.] Nor did the grand juries attempt to invade protected First Amendment rights by forcing wholesale disclosure of names and organizational affiliations for a purpose which was not germane to the determination of whether crime has been committed, [cf., e. g., NAACP v. Alabama], and the characteristic secrecy of grand jury proceedings is a further protection against the undue invasion of such rights. . . .

The requirements of those cases [e. g., NAACP v. Alabama] which hold that a State's interest must be "compelling" or "paramount" to justify

even an indirect burden on First Amendment rights, are also met here. As we have indicated, the investigation of crime by the grand jury implements a fundamental governmental role of securing the safety of the person and property of the citizen, and it appears to us that calling reporters to give testimony in the manner and for the reasons that other citizens are called "bears a reasonable relationship to the achievement of the governmental purpose asserted as its justification." [Bates v. Little Rock.] If the test is that the government "convincingly show a substantial relation between the information sought and a subject of overriding and compelling state interest," [Gibson], it is quite apparent (1) that the State has the necessary interest in extirpating the traffic in illegal drugs, in forestalling assassination attempts on the President, and in preventing the community from being disrupted by violent disorders endangering both persons and property; and (2) that, based on the stories Branzburg and Caldwell wrote and Pappas' admitted conduct, the grand jury called these reporters as they would others —because it was likely that they could supply information to help the government determine whether illegal conduct had occurred and, if it had, whether there was sufficient evidence to return an indictment.

Similar considerations dispose of the reporters' claims that preliminary to requiring their grand jury appearance, the State must show that a crime has been committed and that they possess relevant information not available from other sources, for only the grand jury itself can make this determination. The role of the grand jury as an important instrument of effective law enforcement necessarily includes an investigatory function with respect to determining whether a crime has been committed and who committed it. To this end it must call witnesses, in the manner best suited to perform its task. . . . A grand jury investigation "is not fully carried out until every available clue has been run down . . . ." We see no reason to hold that these reporters, any more than other citizens, should be excused from furnishing information that may help the grand jury in arriving at its initial determinations.

The privilege claimed here is conditional, not absolute; given the suggested preliminary showings and compelling need, the reporter would be required to testify. Presumably, such a rule would reduce the instances in which reporters could be required to appear, but predicting in advance when and in what circumstances they could be compelled to do so would be difficult. Such a rule would also have implications for the issuance of compulsory process to reporters at civil and criminal trials and at legislative hearings. If newsmen's confidential sources are as sensitive as they are claimed to be, the prospect of being unmasked whenever a judge determines the situation justifies it is hardly a satisfactory solution to the problem.[3] For them, it would appear that only an absolute privilege would suffice.

---

3. "Under the case-by-case method of developing rules, it will be difficult for potential informants and reporters to predict whether testimony will be compelled since the decision will turn on the judge's ad hoc assessment in different fact settings of 'importance' or 'relevance' in relation to the free press interest. A 'general' deterrent effect is likely to result. This type of effect stems from the vagueness of the tests and from the uncertainty attending their application. . . ." Note, Reporters and Their Sources: The Constitutional Right to a Confidential Relationship, 80 Yale L.J. 317, 341 (1970). [Several cases illustrate] the impact of this ad hoc approach. . . . [Footnote by the Court.]

We are unwilling to embark the judiciary on a long and difficult journey to such an uncertain destination. The administration of a constitutional newsman's privilege would present practical and conceptual difficulties of a high order. Sooner or later, it would be necessary to define those categories of newsmen who qualified for the privilege, a questionable procedure in light of the traditional doctrine that liberty of the press is the right of the lonely pamphleteer who uses carbon paper or a mimeograph just as much as of the large metropolitan publisher who utilitizes the latest photocomposition methods. . . . The informative function asserted by representatives of the organized press in the present cases is also performed by lecturers, political pollsters, novelists, academic researchers, and dramatists. Almost any author may quite accurately assert that he is contributing to the flow of information to the public, that he relies on confidential sources of information, and that these sources will be silenced if he is forced to make disclosures before a grand jury.[4]

In each instance where a reporter is subpoenaed to testify, the courts would also be embroiled in preliminary factual and legal determinations with respect to whether the proper predicate had been laid for the reporter's appearance. [I]n the end, by considering whether enforcement of a particular law served a "compelling" governmental interest, the courts would be inextricably involved in distinguishing between the value of enforcing different criminal laws. [There is merit in leaving legislatures free], within First Amendment limits, to fashion their own standards in light of the conditions and problems with respect to the relations between law enforcement officials and press in their own areas. . . .

In addition, there is much force in the pragmatic view that the press has at its disposal powerful mechanisms of communication and is far from helpless to protect itself from harassment or substantial harm. Furthermore, if what the newsmen urged in these cases is true—that law enforcement cannot hope to gain and may suffer from subpoenaing newsmen before grand juries—prosecutors will be loath to risk so much for so little. Thus, at the federal level the Attorney General has already fashioned a set of rules for federal officials in connection with subpoenaing members of the press to testify before grand juries or at criminal trials.[5] These rules are a major step in the direction the reporters herein desire to move. They may prove wholly sufficient to resolve the bulk of disagreements and controversies between press and federal officials.

---

4. Such a privilege might be claimed by groups that set up newspapers in order to engage in criminal activity and to therefore be insulated from grand jury inquiry, regardless of Fifth Amendment grants of immunity. It might appear that such "sham" newspapers would be easily distinguishable, yet the First Amendment ordinarily prohibits courts from inquiring into the content of expression, except in cases of obscenity or libel, and protects speech and publications regardless of their motivation, orthodoxy, truthfulness, timeliness, or taste. By affording a privilege to some organs of communication but not to others, courts would inevitably be discriminating on the basis of content. [Footnote by the Court.]

5. . . . The Guidelines [Sept. 1970] state that "The Department of Justice recognizes that compulsory process in some circumstances may have a limiting effect on the exercise of First Amendment rights. In determining whether to request issuance of a subpoena to the press, the approach in every case must be to weight that limiting effect against the public interest to be served in the fair administration

[Finally,] grand jury investigations if instituted or conducted other than in good faith, would pose wholly different issues for resolution under the First Amendment. Official harassment of the press undertaken not for purposes of law enforcement but to disrupt a reporter's relationship with his news sources would have no justification. Grand juries are subject to judicial control and subpoenas to motions to quash. We do not expect courts will forget that grand juries must operate within the limits of the First Amendment as well as the Fifth.

We turn, therefore, to the disposition of the cases before us. [The Caldwell decision must be reversed.] If there is no First Amendment privilege to refuse to answer the relevant and material questions asked during a good-faith grand jury investigation, then it is a fortiori true that there is no privilege to refuse to appear before such a grand jury until the Government demonstrates some "compelling need" for a newsman's testimony. [Branzburg] must be affirmed. Here, petitioner refused to answer questions that directly related to criminal conduct which he had observed and written about. [We affirm in Pappas] and hold that petitioner must appear before the grand jury to answer the questions put to him, subject, of course, to the supervision of the presiding judge as to "the propriety, purposes, and scope of the grand jury inquiry and the pertinence of the probable testimony."

So ordered.*

of justice" and that "The Department of Justice does not consider the press 'an investigative arm of the government.' Therefore, all reasonable attempts should be made to obtain information from non-press sources before there is any consideration of subpoenaing the press." The Guidelines provide for negotiations with the press and require the express authorization of the Attorney General for such subpoenas. The principles to be applied in authorizing such subpoenas are stated to be whether there is "sufficient reason to believe that the information sought [from the journalist] is essential to a successful investigation," and whether the Government has unsuccessfully attempted to obtain the information from alternative non-press sources. The Guidelines provide, however, that in "emergencies and other unusual situations," subpoenas may be issued which do not exactly conform to the Guidelines. [Footnote by the Court.]

* Note also another decision handed down on the same day as Branzburg, again rejecting a challenge to a grand jury investigation, with Justice White again writing for the majority. Gravel v. United States, 408 U.S. 606 (1972). The challenge in Gravel relied mainly on the Speech or Debate Clause, Art. I, § 6, cl. 1, rather than the First Amendment. (See the note on the case in chap. 7.) The case arose out of a grand jury investigation into the release of the Pentagon Papers. (See the New York Times Case, sec. 2B above.) Senator Gravel had placed the Pentagon Papers into the public record at a meeting of his subcommittee, and there were reports that he had arranged for private publication with the Beacon Press. The grand jury called an aide to the Senator. The Senator unsuccessfully intervened to quash the subpoena. Justice White's majority opinion concluded, inter alia, that the Speech and Debate Clause did not bar the investigation, because "the Senator's arrangements with Beacon Press were not part and parcel of the legislative process." Justice Douglas' dissent insisted not only that the Clause was a barrier but added: "Alternatively, I would hold that Beacon Press is protected by the First Amendment from prosecution or investigations for publishing or undertaking to publish the Pentagon Papers. [S]urely the First Amendment protects against all inquiry into the dissemination of information which, although once classified, has become part of the public domain." Justice Brennan, joined by Justices Douglas and Marshall, also dissented, relying on the Clause. And a partial dissent by Justice Stewart suggested that a Con-

Mr. Justice POWELL, concurring in the opinion of the Court.

I add this brief statement to emphasize what seems to me to be the limited nature of the Court's holding. The Court does not hold that newsmen, subpoenaed to testify before a grand jury, are without constitutional rights with respect to the gathering of news or in safeguarding their sources. Certainly, we do not hold, as suggested in the [Stewart dissent], that state and federal authorities are free to "annex" the news media as "an investigative arm of government." The solicitude repeatedly shown by this Court for First Amendment freedoms should be sufficient assurance against any such effort, even if one seriously believed that the media—properly free and untrammeled in the fullest sense of these terms—were not able to protect themselves.

As indicated in the concluding portion of the opinion, the Court states that no harassment of newsmen will be tolerated. If a newsman believes that the grand jury investigation is not being conducted in good faith he is not without remedy. Indeed, if the newsman is called upon to give information bearing only a remote and tenuous relationship to the subject of the investigation, or if he has some other reason to believe that his testimony implicates confidential source relationships without a legitimate need of law enforcement, he will have access to the Court on a motion to quash and an appropriate protective order may be entered. The asserted claim to privilege should be judged on its facts by the striking of a proper balance between freedom of the press and the obligation of all citizens to give relevant testimony with respect to criminal conduct. The balance of these vital constitutional and societal interests on a case-by-case basis accords with the tried and traditional way of adjudicating such questions.[1]

In short, the courts will be available to newsmen under circumstances where legitimate First Amendment interests require protection.†

gressman should be protected by the Clause from grand jury inquiries about confidential sources of information "used in preparing for legislative acts."

1. It is to be remembered that Caldwell asserts a constitutional privilege not even to appear before the grand jury unless a court decides that the Government has made a showing that meets the three preconditions specified in the dissenting opinion of Mr. Justice Stewart. To be sure, this would require a "balancing" of interests by the court, but under circumstances and constraints significantly different from the balancing that will be appropriate under the Court's decision. The newsman witness, like all other witnesses, will have to appear; he will not be in a position to litigate at the threshold the State's very authority to subpoena him. Moreover, absent the constitutional preconditions that Caldwell and the dissenting opinion would impose as heavy burdens of proof to be carried by the State, the court—when called upon to protect a newsman from improper or prejudicial questioning—would be free to balance the competing interests on their merits in the particular case. The new constitutional rule endorsed by that dissenting opinion would, as a practical matter, defeat such a fair balancing and the essential societal interest in the detection and prosecution of crime would be heavily subordinated. [Footnote by Justice Powell.]

† Compare Justice Powell's dissent on the rights of the press two years later, in Saxbe v. Washington Post Co., 417 U.S. 843 (1974), involving a ban on press interviews with prisoners, sec. 4D above. In urging recognition of a right of press access to information in Saxbe, Justice Powell distinguished Branzburg as reflecting "no more than a sensible disinclination to follow the right-of-access argument as far as dry logic might extend."

Mr. Justice STEWART, with whom Mr. Justice BRENNAN and Mr. Justice MARSHALL join, dissenting.

The Court's crabbed view of the First Amendment reflects a disturbing insensitivity to the critical role of an independent press in our society. The question whether a reporter has a constitutional right to a confidential relationship with his source is of first impression here, but the principles that should guide our decision are as basic as any to be found in the Constitution. While Mr. Justice Powell's enigmatic concurring opinion gives some hope of a more flexible view in the future, the Court in these cases holds that a newsman has no First Amendment right to protect his sources when called before a grand jury. The Court thus invites state and federal authorities to undermine the historic independence of the press by attempting to annex the journalistic profession as an investigative arm of government. Not only will this decision impair performance of the press' constitutionally protected functions, but it will, I am convinced, in the long run, harm rather than help the administration of justice. . . .

The reporter's constitutional right to a confidential relationship with his source stems from the broad societal interest in a full and free flow of information to the public. It is this basic concern that underlies the Constitution's protection of a free press, because the guarantee is "not for the benefit of the press so much as for the benefit of all of us." . . .

. . . As private and public aggregations of power burgeon in size and the pressures for conformity necessarily mount, there is obviously a continuing need for an independent press to disseminate a robust variety of information and opinion through reportage, investigation and criticism, if we are to preserve our constitutional tradition of maximizing freedom of choice by encouraging diversity of expression. . . .

A corollary of the right to publish must be the right to gather news. [That right] implies, in turn, a right to a confidential relationship between a reporter and his source. [This] follows as a matter of simple logic once three factual predicates are recognized: (1) newsmen require informants to gather news; (2) confidentiality [is] essential to the creation and maintenance of a news-gathering relationship with informants; and (3) the existence of an unbridled subpoena power [will] either deter sources from divulging information or deter reporters from gathering and publishing information. After today's decision, the potential [source must] choose between risking exposure by giving information or avoiding the risk by remaining silent. The reporter must speculate about whether contact with a controversial source or publication of controversial material will lead to a subpoena. . . .

The impairment of the flow of news cannot, of course, be proved with scientific precision, as the Court seems to demand. Obviously, not every news-gathering relationship requires confidentiality. And it is difficult to pinpoint precisely how many relationships do require a promise or understanding of nondisclosure. But we have never before demanded that First Amendment rights rest on elaborate empirical studies demonstrating beyond any conceivable doubt that deterrent effects exist; we have never before required proof of the exact number of people potentially affected by governmental action, who would actually be dissuaded from engaging in First Amendment activity.

Rather, on the basis of common sense and available information, we have asked, often implicitly, (1) whether there was a rational connection between the cause (the governmental action) and the effect (the deterrence or impairment of First Amendment activity) and (2) whether the effect would occur with some regularity, i. e., would not be de minimis. And in making this determination, we have shown a special solicitude towards the "indispensable liberties" protected by the First Amendment. [Once] this threshold inquiry has been satisfied, we have then examined the competing interests in determining whether there is an unconstitutional infringement of First Amendment freedoms. [E. g., NAACP v. Alabama.]

Surely the analogous claim of deterrence here is as securely grounded in evidence and common sense as the claims in [earlier cases], although the Court calls the claim "speculative." The deterrence may not occur in every confidential relationship, [but] it will certainly occur in certain types of relationships involving sensitive and controversial matters. . . . To require any greater burden of proof is to shirk our duty to protect values securely embedded in the Constitution. We cannot await an unequivocal—and therefore unattainable—imprimatur from empirical studies. Thus, we cannot escape the conclusion that when neither the reporter nor his source can rely on the shield of confidentiality against unrestrained use of the grand jury's subpoena power, valuable information will not be published and the public dialogue will inevitably be impoverished.

Posed against the First Amendment's protection of the newsman's confidential relationships in these cases is society's interest in the use of the grand jury to administer justice fairly and effectively. [T]he longstanding rule making every person's evidence available to the grand jury is not absolute. The rule has been limited by the Fifth Amendment, the Fourth Amendment, and the evidentiary privileges of the common law. [The Court has] observed that any exemption from the duty to testify before the grand jury "presupposes a very real interest to be protected." Such an interest must surely be the First Amendment protection of a confidential relationship . . . . .

In striking the proper balance, [we] must begin with the basic proposition [that] First Amendment rights require special safeguards. . . . The established method of "carefully" circumscribing investigative powers is to place a heavy burden of justification on government officials when First Amendment rights are impaired. [NAACP v. Button ("compelling state interest"); Gibson ("a substantial relation between the information sought and a subject of overriding and compelling state interest").] Thus, when an investigation impinges on First Amendment rights, the government must not only show that the inquiry is of "compelling and overriding importance" but it must also "convincingly" demonstrate that the investigation is "substantially related" to the information sought. Governmental officials must, therefore, demonstrate that the information sought is *clearly* relevant to a *precisely* defined subject of governmental inquiry. [Watkins; Sweezy.] They must demonstrate that it is reasonable to think the witness in question has that information. [Sweezy; Gibson.] And they must show that there is not any means of obtaining the information less destructive of First Amendment liberties. [E. g., Shelton v. Tucker.]

I believe [that] the safeguards developed in our decisions involving governmental investigations must apply to the grand jury inquiries in these cases. Surely the function of the grand jury [is] no more important than the function of the legislature. [T]he vices of vagueness and overbreadth which legislative investigations may manifest are also exhibited by grand jury inquiries, [since] standards of materiality and relevance are greatly relaxed.[1] For, as the United States notes in its brief in Caldwell, the grand jury "need establish no factual basis for commencing an investigation, and can pursue rumors which further investigation may prove groundless."

Accordingly, when a reporter is asked to appear before a grand jury and reveal confidences, I would hold that the government must (1) show that there is probable cause to believe that the newsman has information which is clearly relevant to a specific probable violation of law; (2) demonstrate that the information sought cannot be obtained by alternative means less destructive of First Amendment rights; and (3) demonstrate a compelling and overriding interest in the information. . . .

[It] is obviously not true that the only persons about whom reporters will be forced to testify [under the Court's decision] will be those "confidential informants involved in actual criminal conduct" and those having "information suggesting illegal conduct by others." [G]iven the grand jury's extraordinarily broad investigative powers and the weak standards of relevance and materiality that apply during such inquiries, reporters, if they have no testimonial privilege, will be called to give information about informants who have neither committed crimes nor have information about crime. It is to avoid deterrence of such sources and thus to prevent needless injury to First Amendment values that I think the government must be required to show probable cause that the newsman has information which is clearly relevant to a specific probable violation of criminal law.[2] . . .

Both the "probable cause" and "alternative means" requirements [would] serve the vital function of mediating between the public interest in the administration of justice and the constitutional protection of the full flow of information. These requirements would avoid a direct conflict between these competing concerns, and they would generally provide adequate protection for newsmen.[3] No doubt the courts would be required

1. In addition, witnesses customarily are not allowed to object to questions on the grounds of materiality or relevance, since the scope of the grand jury inquiry is deemed to be of no concern to the witness. Nor is counsel permitted to be present to aid a witness. [Footnote by Justice Stewart.]

2. If this requirement is not met, then the government will basically be allowed to undertake a "fishing expedition" at the expense of the press. Such general, exploratory investigations will be most damaging to confidential news-gathering relationships, since they will create great uncertainty in both reporters and their sources. The Court sanctions such explorations, by refusing to apply a meaningful "probable cause" requirement. [Its standard] invites government to try to annex the press as an investigative arm, since any time government wants to probe the relationships between the newsman and his source, it can, on virtually any pretext, convene a grand jury and compel the journalist to testify. . . . [Footnote by Justice Stewart.]

3. We need not, therefore, reach the question of whether government's interest in these cases is "overriding and compelling." I do not, however, believe, as the Court does, that *all* grand jury investigations automatically would override the newsman's tes-

to make some delicate judgments in working out this accommodation. But that, after all, is the function of courts of law. Better such judgments, however difficult, than the simplistic and stultifying absolutism adopted by the Court in denying any force to the First Amendment in these cases.[4]

[I]n the name of advancing the administration of justice, the Court's decision, I think, will only impair the achievement of that goal. People entrusted with law enforcement responsibility, no less than private citizens, need general information relating to controversial social problems. . . .

[In Caldwell, the Ninth Circuit] held that in the circumstances of this case Caldwell need not divulge confidential information. I think this decision was correct. [In addition, the Ninth Circuit] concluded that the very appearance by Caldwell before the grand jury would jeopardize his relationship with his sources. [T]his ruling was also correct in light of the particularized circumstances of the Caldwell case. . . . But *this* aspect of the Caldwell judgment I would confine to its own facts. . . . Accordingly, I would affirm [in Caldwell. In the other two cases, I would remand] for further proceedings . . . .

Mr. Justice DOUGLAS, dissenting [in Caldwell. He dissented in the other two cases on the basis of this dissent.] . . .

It is my view that there is no "compelling need" that can be shown which qualifies the reporter's immunity from appearing or testifying before a grand jury, unless the reporter himself is implicated in a crime. His immunity in my view is therefore quite complete, for, absent his involvement in a crime, the First Amendment protects him against an appearance before a grand jury and if he is involved in a crime, the Fifth Amendment stands as a barrier. Since in my view there is no area of inquiry not protected by a privilege, the reporter need not appear for the futile purpose of invoking one to each question. . . .

Two principles which follow from [Alexander Meiklejohn's view] * of the First Amendment are at stake here. One is that the people, the ultimate governors, must have absolute freedom of, and therefore privacy of, their individual opinions and beliefs regardless of how suspect or strange they may appear to others. Ancillary to that principle is the conclusion that an individual must also have absolute privacy over whatever information he may generate in the course of testing his opinions and beliefs. In this regard, Caldwell's status as a reporter is less relevant than is his status as a student who affirmatively pursued empirical research to enlarge his own intellectual viewpoint. The second principle is that effective self-government cannot succeed unless the people are immersed in a steady, robust, unimpeded, and uncensored flow of opinion and reporting which are continuously subjected to critique, rebuttal, and re-examination. In this respect, Caldwell's status as a news gatherer and an integral part of that process becomes critical. . . .

timonial privilege. [Footnote by Justice Stewart.]

4. The disclaimers in Mr. Justice Powell's concurring opinion leave room for the hope that in some future case the Court may take a less absolute position in this area. [Footnote by Justice Stewart.]

* Justice Douglas quoted from Meiklejohn's "The First Amendment Is An Absolute," 1961 Sup.Ct.Rev. 245. Justice Douglas added that his view was "close to" Meiklejohn's.

Sooner or later, any test which provides less than blanket protection to beliefs and associations will be twisted and relaxed so as to provide virtually no protection at all. . . . A compelling interest test may prove as pliable as did the clear-and-present-danger test. Perceptions of the worth of state objectives will change with the composition of the Court and with the intensity of the politics of the times. . . .

Today's decision will impede the wide open and robust dissemination of ideas and counterthought which a free press both fosters and protects and which is essential to the success of intelligent self-government. Forcing a reporter before a grand jury will have two retarding effects upon the ear and the pen of the press. Fear of exposure will cause dissidents to communicate less openly to trusted reporters. And, fear of accountability will cause editors and critics to write with more restrained pens. I see no way of making mandatory the disclosure of a reporter's confidential source of the information on which he bases his news story. . . . †

---

† In response to Branzburg, numerous bills to establish a newsmen's privilege were introduced not only in state legislatures but also in Congress. Typically, absolute immunity proposals—e.g., S. 158, 93rd Cong., 1st Sess.—did not fare well. Proposals for a qualified privilege attracted more support. See, e.g., H.R. 5928, as amended, which would protect newsmen from demands that they disclose confidential sources or information to federal or state grand juries, legislative committees, or other investigative agencies; however, a trial court could compel a newsman to divulge such information if it was indispensable to the case, could not be obtained in any other way, and if there was strong public interest in the disclosure. Progress of such legislative proposals has been retarded by divisions within the news community: some spokesmen have refused to support any proposals which guarantee less than absolute immunity to newsmen; other critics of the bill, arguing that "what Congress gives, Congress can take away," oppose all so-called "shield" legislation and would "rely on the First Amendment and reasonable conduct by the courts."

Chapter 14

THE CONSTITUTION AND RELIGION: "ESTABLISHMENT" AND "FREE EXERCISE"

Introduction. The First Amendment bars any law "respecting an establishment of religion, or prohibiting the free exercise thereof." Sec. 1 of this chapter focuses on the "establishment" clause, sec. 2 on "free exercise." But this organization of the materials, which reflects the separate treatment typical in the cases, should not obscure the fact that in many contexts both clauses are relevant: the provisions protect overlapping values, yet they may exert conflicting pressures; articulating criteria that will accommodate both provisions is accordingly a recurrent challenge.

One context and two characteristic problems predominate in the establishment materials in sec. 1. The typical context is schools. The most common problems stem from two methods by which the separation between church and state may be threatened: (1) the rendering of governmental aid to activities conducted by religious organizations (e. g., the recurrent battles about financial aid to parochial schools or their students, from Everson in 1947 to Lemon in 1971 and beyond); and (2) the intrusion of religious matters into governmental activities (as in the challenges to religious practices in public schools—practices such as school prayers in Engel and Bible reading in Schempp).

In most "free exercise" problems, in sec. 2, religious scruples are raised as defenses to applications of general state regulations. Is the free exercise guarantee limited to the protection of religious *beliefs*? If so, does that religion provision add anything to the protections already assured by the free speech guarantee? Does the free exercise provision also protect against interference with some *actions* based on or compelled by religious beliefs? The modern Court has indeed found some religion-based conduct protected by the First Amendment; the most difficult contemporary problems turn on the extent of that protection. May the Orthodox Jew refuse to observe a Sunday Closing Law, as claimed in Braunfeld v. Brown? May the Seventh-day Adventist claim unemployment compensation though she is unavailable for work on Saturdays, as in Sherbert v. Verner? May the Amish refuse to comply with compulsory education laws, as in Wisconsin v. Yoder?

In situations such as those, the religious objector in effect claims an exemption from general statutes. Does the free exercise clause compel the exemption? That problem illustrates one of the tensions between the free exercise and establishment guarantees: If a state *must* grant a religious exemption because of "free exercise," is it not granting a preference to religion in violation of the separation assured by "establishment"? Yet if a state *fails* to grant an exemption to the religious objector, is it not interfering with "free exercise"? Even if government is not compelled to exempt, may it, without running afoul of "establishment," afford special treatment because

of an individual's religious scruples (as the conscientious objector exemption from the draft laws purported to do—see the Seeger and Welsh cases)?

Accommodating the two religion clauses. As the division of the materials below indicates, most of the Court opinions deal with the religion clauses separately: they typically discuss either "establishment" or "free exercise." But, as the questions above suggest, the occasionally conflicting emanations of the two guarantees, and the need to strive for reconciling principles, should be borne in mind in examining the Court's controversial struggles to articulate criteria. It has been suggested that accommodation of the two clauses can be furthered by recognizing that "establishment" and "free exercise" serve a single value—the protection of the individual's freedom of religious beliefs and practices, with "free exercise" barring the curbing of that freedom through penalties and "establishment" barring inhibitions on individual choice through governmental aids and rewards to religion. Yet viewing the clauses as protecting that single goal obviously does not eliminate the potential tensions between them. If either the anti-penalties or anti-rewards theme is taken as an absolute, the contending theme may be unduly denigrated: if all penalties are barred, undue benefit to religion may result; if all benefits are barred, undue penalties may be the consequence. Identification of a single "freedom" value, then, does not eliminate the need for accommodation.

Moreover, avoidance of penalties and benefits that impinge on individual religious freedom may not exhaust the values to be served by the establishment clause. The establishment clause barrier to governmental aid to religion may apply even though individual liberties are not significantly affected.[1] If the establishment guarantee serves more than libertarian values, the problem of accommodation becomes all the more difficult. Is the problem susceptible to a simple, embracive principle? Is "neutrality" an adequate reconciling principle? Can the two religion clauses be read as making the Constitution "religion-blind"? That is a suggestion of Professor Kurland.[2] Kurland suggests as the unifying principle for "the proper construction of the religion clauses" that "the freedom and separation clauses should be read as a single precept that government cannot utilize religion as a standard for action or inaction because these clauses prohibit classification in terms of religion either to confer a benefit or to impose a burden."[3] Is the "neutrality" theme adequate for the problems raised by the materials which follow? Is it at least, as Kurland urged, "a starting point for solutions to problems brought before the Court, not a mechanical answer to them"? Or is the search for all-encompassing generalities futile? Does the range of religion problems with constitutional dimensions require more numerous, complex,

1. Note, e. g., the "standing" aspects (cf. chap. 15) of the Schempp case, sec. 1B. In Schempp, the challenge was to the practice of Bible reading in schools. The majority found standing to sue because the challengers were "school children and their parents directly affected" by the practice. The Court stated that "the requirements for standing to challenge state action under the Establishment Clause, unlike those relating to the free exercise clause, do not include proof that particular religious freedoms are infringed." (See also note 1 following Everson, sec. 1A, below.)

2. See Kurland, "Of Church and State and the Supreme Court," 29 U.Chi.L. Rev. 1 (1961), Selected Essays 1938–62 (1963), 699.

3. For a critical comment on Kurland's thesis, see Leo Pfeffer's book review, "Religion-Blind Government," 15 Stan. L.Rev. 389 (1963).

discriminating criteria?   Is "balancing" the most useful approach to achieve the necessary accommodations?   If so, what are the appropriate ingredients for the balancing scale?   And what is the appropriate weight for each ingredient?[4]

SECTION 1. "ESTABLISHMENT":
THE SEPARATION OF CHURCH AND STATE

As noted in the introduction, the "establishment" materials focus on two themes: the intrusion of religious matter into governmental activities, particularly the problem of religious exercises in public schools (sec. 1B); and governmental aid to religious organizations, particularly in the context of financial aid to parochial schools (sec. 1C).   Sec. 1A emphasizes one case, the Everson decision in 1947.   The immediate problem in Everson was financial aid; but Everson appears as sec. 1A rather than in sec. 1C because it serves as the common starting point for all modern establishment controversies.   Everson was the modern Court's first encounter with the establishment clause; its articulation of principles and its review of history is essential background for the consideration of the later issues.

A. THE BACKGROUND: THE EVERSON CASE

EVERSON v. BOARD OF EDUCATION

330 U.S. 1, 67 S.Ct. 504, 91 L.Ed. 711 (1947).

Appeal from the Court of Errors and Appeals of New Jersey.

[A New Jersey statute authorized local school districts to make rules and contracts to transport children to and from school, "including the transportation of school children to and from school other than a public school, except such school as is operated for profit."   Pursuant to that statute, a local board of education authorized reimbursement to parents for money spent by them for the transportation of their children on regular buses operated by the public transportation system.   In this case, a local taxpayer challenged those parts of the district payments that went to parents of Catholic parochial school students.*   The highest state court found no violation of the state or federal constitutions.]

4. These problems have generated much controversy and an extraordinary amount of writing off the Court as well as on. See generally—in addition to the pieces cited in the preceding footnotes—e. g., Pfeffer, Church, State and Freedom (1967); Oaks (ed.), The Wall Between Church and State (1963); Kauper, Religion and the Constitution (1964); Schwarz, "No Imposition of Religion: The Establishment Clause Value," 77 Yale L.J. 692

(1968); and Giannella, "Religious Liberty, Nonestablishment, and Doctrinal Development," 80 Harv.L.Rev. 1381 (1967) and 81 Harv.L.Rev. 513 (1968).

* The dissenting opinions of Justices Jackson and Rutledge took a somewhat different view of the scope of the local school board's reimbursement policy. They noted that the specific resolution authorizing reim-

Mr. Justice BLACK delivered the opinion of the Court.   .   .   .

The only contention here is that the state statute and the resolution, insofar as they authorized reimbursement to parents of children attending parochial schools, violate the Federal Constitution in these two respects, which to some extent overlap. *First.*   They authorize the State to take by taxation the private property of some and bestow it upon others, to be used for their own private purposes.   This, it is alleged, violates the due process clause of the Fourteenth Amendment.   *Second.*   The statute and the resolution forced inhabitants to pay taxes to help support and maintain schools which are dedicated to, and which regularly teach, the Catholic Faith.   This is alleged to be a use of state power to support church schools contrary to the prohibition of the First Amendment which the Fourteenth Amendment made applicable to the states.

First.   .   .   .   It is much too late to argue that legislation intended to facilitate the opportunity of children to get a secular education serves no public purpose.   Cochran v. Louisiana State Board of Education, 281 U.S. 370.[1]   .   .   .   The same thing is no less true of legislation to reimburse needy parents, or all parents, for payment of the fares of their children so that they can ride in public busses to and from schools rather than run the risk of traffic and other hazards incident to walking or "hitchhiking."   .   .   .

Second.   The New Jersey statute is challenged as a "law respecting an establishment of religion."   The First Amendment, as made applicable to the states by the Fourteenth, commands that a state "shall make no law respecting an establishment of religion, or prohibiting the free exercise thereof." Whether this New Jersey law is one respecting an "establishment of religion" requires an understanding of the meaning of that language, particularly with respect to the imposition of taxes.   .   .   .

A large proportion of the early settlers of this country came here from Europe to escape the bondage of laws which compelled them to support and attend government-favored churches.   The centuries immediately before and contemporaneous with the colonization of America had been filled with turmoil, civil strife, and persecutions, generated in large part by established sects determined to maintain their absolute political and religious supremacy. .   .   .   In efforts to force loyalty to whatever religious group happened to be on top and in league with the government of a particular time and place, men and women had been fined, cast in jail, cruelly tortured, and killed. Among the offenses for which these punishments had been inflicted were such things as speaking disrespectfully of the views of ministers of government-es-

---

bursement mentioned only the public high schools and the "Catholic Schools." Justice Rutledge commented that "the resolution by which the statute was applied expressly limits its benefits to students of public and Catholic schools. There is no showing that there are no other private or religious schools in this populous district. I do not think it can be assumed there were none." He added, however, that "in the view I have taken, it is unnecessary to limit grounding to these matters."

1. In the Cochran case, in 1930, the Court sustained the expenditure of state funds for the purchase of books for children attending private and parochial schools, against a challenge that no "public purpose" was involved. The Court said of the legislation: "Its interest is education, broadly; its method, comprehensive." There was no federal "establishment" challenge in the case.

tablished churches, non-attendance at those churches, expressions of non-belief in their doctrines, and failure to pay taxes and tithes to support them.

These practices of the old world were transplanted to and began to thrive in the soil of the new America. The very charters granted by the English Crown to the individuals and companies designated to make the laws which would control the destinies of the colonials authorized these individuals and companies to erect religious establishments which all, whether believers or non-believers, would be required to support and attend. An exercise of this authority was accompanied by a repetition of many of the old-world practices and persecutions. . . . And all of these dissenters were compelled to pay tithes and taxes to support government-sponsored churches whose ministers preached inflammatory sermons designed to strengthen and consolidate the established faith by generating a burning hatred against dissenters.

These practices became so commonplace as to shock the freedom-loving colonials into a feeling of abhorrence. The imposition of taxes to pay ministers' salaries and to build and maintain churches and church property aroused their indignation. It was these feelings which found expression in the First Amendment. . . . Virginia, where the established church had achieved a dominant influence in political affairs and where many excesses attracted wide public attention, provided a great stimulus and able leadership for the movement. The people there, as elsewhere, reached the conviction that individual religious liberty could be achieved best under a government which was stripped of all power to tax, to support, or otherwise to assist any or all religions, or to interfere with the beliefs of any religious individual or group.

The movement toward this end reached its dramatic climax in Virginia in 1785–86 when the Virginia legislative body was about to renew Virginia's tax levy for the support of the established church. Thomas Jefferson and James Madison led the fight against this tax. Madison wrote his great Memorial and Remonstrance against the law. In it, he eloquently argued that a true religion did not need the support of law; that no person, either believer or non-believer, should be taxed to support a religious institution of any kind; that the best interest of a society required that the minds of men always be wholly free; and that cruel persecutions were the inevitable result of government-established religions. Madison's Remonstrance received strong support throughout Virginia, and the Assembly postponed consideration of the proposed tax measure until its next session. When the proposal came up for consideration at that session, it not only died in committee, but the Assembly enacted the famous "Virginia Bill for Religious Liberty" originally written by Thomas Jefferson. The preamble to that Bill stated among other things that

> "Almighty God hath created the mind free; that all attempts to influence it by temporal punishments or burthens, or by civil incapacitations, tend only to beget habits of hypocrisy and meanness . . .; that to compel a man to furnish contributions of money for the propagation of opinions which he disbelieves, is sinful and tyrannical; that even the forcing him to support this or that teacher of his own religious persuasion, is depriving him of the comfortable liberty of giving his contributions to the particular pastor, whose morals he would make his pattern. . . ."

And the statute itself enacted

> "That no man shall be compelled to frequent or support any religious worship, place, or ministry whatsoever, nor shall be enforced, restrained, molested, or burthened in his body or goods, nor shall otherwise suffer on account of his religious opinions or belief .   .   .   ."

This Court has previously recognized that the provisions of the First Amendment, in the drafting and adoption of which Madison and Jefferson played such leading roles, had the same objective and were intended to provide the same protection against governmental intrusion on religious liberty as the Virginia statute.   Prior to the adoption of the Fourteenth Amendment, the First Amendment did not apply as a restraint against the states.   Most of them did soon provide similar constitutional protections for religious liberty. But some states persisted for about half a century in imposing restraints upon the free exercise of religion and in discriminating against particular religious groups.   In recent years, so far as the provision against the establishment of a religion is concerned, the question has most frequently arisen in connection with proposed state aid to church schools and efforts to carry on religious teachings in the public schools in accordance with the tenets of a particular sect.   .   .   .

The meaning and scope of the First Amendment, preventing establishment of religion or prohibiting the free exercise thereof, in the light of its history and the evils it was designed forever to suppress, have been several times elaborated by the decisions of this Court prior to the application of the First Amendment to the states by the Fourteenth.   The broad meaning given the Amendment by these earlier cases has been accepted by this Court in its decisions concerning an individual's religious freedom rendered since the Fourteenth Amendment was interpreted to make the prohibitions of the First applicable to state action abridging religious freedom.   There is every reason to give the same application and broad interpretation to the "establishment of religion" clause.   The interrelation of these complementary clauses was well summarized in [Watson v. Jones, 13 Wall. 679]: "The structure of our government has, for the preservation of civil liberty, rescued the temporal institutions from religious interference.   On the other hand, it has secured religious liberty from the invasion of the civil authority."

The "establishment of religion" clause of the First Amendment means at least this: Neither a state nor the Federal Government can set up a church. Neither can pass laws which aid one religion, aid all religions, or prefer one religion over another.   Neither can force nor influence a person to go to or to remain away from church against his will or force him to profess a belief or disbelief in any religion.   No person can be punished for entertaining or professing religious beliefs or disbeliefs, for church attendance or non-attendance. No tax in any amount, large or small, can be levied to support any religious activities or institutions, whatever they may be called, or whatever form they may adopt to teach or practice religion.   Neither a state nor the Federal Government can, openly or secretly, participate in the affairs of any religious organizations or groups and *vice versa*.   In the words of Jefferson, the clause against establishment of religion by law was intended to erect "a wall of separation between church and State."   .   .   .

We must consider the New Jersey statute in accordance with the foregoing limitations imposed by the First Amendment. But we must not strike that state statute down if it is within the State's constitutional power even though it approaches the verge of that power. New Jersey cannot consistently with the "establishment of religion" clause of the First Amendment contribute tax-raised funds to the support of an institution which teaches the tenets and faith of any church. On the other hand, other language of the amendment commands that New Jersey cannot hamper its citizens in the free exercise of their own religion. Consequently, it cannot exclude individual Catholics, Lutherans, Mohammedans, Baptists, Jews, Methodists, Non-believers, Presbyterians, or the members of any other faith, *because of their faith, or lack of it*, from receiving the benefits of public welfare legislation. While we do not mean to intimate that a state could not provide transportation only to children attending public schools, we must be careful, in protecting the citizens of New Jersey against state-established churches, to be sure that we do not inadvertently prohibit New Jersey from extending its general state law benefits to all its citizens without regard to their religious belief.

Measured by these standards, we cannot say that the First Amendment prohibits New Jersey from spending tax-raised funds to pay the bus fares of parochial school pupils as a part of a general program under which it pays the fares of pupils attending public and other schools. It is undoubtedly true that children are helped to get to church schools. There is even a possibility that some of the children might not be sent to the church schools if the parents were compelled to pay their children's bus fares out of their own pockets when transportation to a public school would have been paid for by the State. The same possibility exists where the state requires a local transit company to provide reduced fares to school children including those attending parochial schools .   . .. Moreover, state-paid policemen, detailed to protect children going to and from church schools from the very real hazards of traffic, would serve much the same purpose and accomplish much the same result as state provisions intended to guarantee free transportation of a kind which the state deems to be best for the school children's welfare. And parents might refuse to risk their children to the serious danger of traffic accidents going to and from parochial schools, the approaches to which were not protected by policemen. Similarly, parents might be reluctant to permit their children to attend schools which the state had cut off from such general government services as ordinary police and fire protection, connections for sewage disposal, public highways and sidewalks. Of course, cutting off church schools from these services, so separate and so indisputably marked off from the religious function, would make it far more difficult for the schools to operate. But such is obviously not the purpose of the First Amendment. That Amendment requires the state to be a neutral in its relations with groups of religious believers and non-believers; it does not require the state to be their adversary. State power is no more to be used so as to handicap religions than it is to favor them.

This Court has said that parents may, in the discharge of their duty under state compulsory education laws, send their children to a religious rather than a public school if the school meets the secular educational requirements which the state has power to impose. See Pierce v. Society of Sisters, 268 U.S. 510. It appears that these parochial schools meet New Jersey's requirements. The

State contributes no money to the schools. It does not support them. Its legislation, as applied, does no more than provide a general program to help parents get their children, regardless of their religion, safely and expeditiously to and from accredited schools.

The First Amendment has erected a wall between church and state. That wall must be kept high and impregnable. We could not approve the slightest breach. New Jersey has not breached it here.

Affirmed.

Mr. Justice JACKSON [joined by Mr. Justice FRANKFURTER], dissenting. . . .

. . . The Court's opinion marshals every argument in favor of state aid and puts the case in its most favorable light, but much of its reasoning confirms my conclusions that there are no good grounds upon which to support the present legislation. In fact, the undertones of the opinion, advocating complete and uncompromising separation of Church from State, seem utterly discordant with its conclusion yielding support to their commingling in educational matters. The case which irresistibly comes to mind as the most fitting precedent is that of Julia who, according to Byron's reports, "whispering 'I will ne'er consent,'—consented." . . .

Mr. Justice RUTLEDGE, with whom Mr. Justice FRANKFURTER, Mr. Justice JACKSON and Mr. Justice BURTON agree, dissenting. . . .

The Amendment's purpose was not to strike merely at the official establishment of a single sect, creed or religion, outlawing only a formal relation such as had prevailed in England and some of the colonies. Necessarily it was to uproot all such relationships. But the object was broader than separating church and state in this narrow sense. It was to create a complete and permanent separation of the spheres of religious activity and civil authority by comprehensively forbidding every form of public aid or support for religion. In proof the Amendment's wording and history unite with this Court's consistent utterances whenever attention has been fixed directly upon the question. . . . [After an extensive historical review, Justice Rutledge continued:]

Does New Jersey's action furnish support for religion by use of the taxing power? Certainly it does, if the test remains undiluted as Jefferson and Madison made it, that money taken by taxation from one is not to be used or given to support another's religious training or belief, or indeed one's own. Today as then the furnishing of "contributions of money for the propagation of opinions which he disbelieves" is the forbidden exaction; and the prohibition is absolute for whatever measure brings that consequence and whatever amount may be sought or given to that end.

The funds used here were raised by taxation. The Court does not dispute, nor could it, that their use does in fact give aid and encouragement to religious instruction. It only concludes that this aid is not "support" in law. But Madison and Jefferson were concerned with aid and support in fact, not as a legal conclusion "entangled in precedents." . . . Here parents pay money to send their children to parochial schools and funds raised by taxation are used to reimburse them. This not only helps the children to get to school and the parents to send them. It aids them in a substantial way to get

the very thing which they are sent to the particular school to secure, namely, religious training and teaching. . . .

[I]t cannot be said that the cost of transportation is no part of the cost of education or of the religious instruction given. That it is a substantial and a necessary element is shown most plainly by the continuing and increasing demand for the state to assume it. Nor is there pretense that it relates only to the secular instruction given in religious schools or that any attempt is or could be made toward allocating proportional shares as between the secular and the religious instruction. It is precisely because the instruction is religious and relates to a particular faith, whether one or another, that parents send their children to religious schools under the Pierce doctrine. And the very purpose of the state's contribution is to defray the cost of conveying the pupil to the place where he will receive not simply secular, but also and primarily religious, teaching and guidance. . . . [T]ransportation where it is needed is as essential to education as any other element. Its cost is as much a part of the total expense, except at times in amount, as the cost of textbooks, of school lunches, of athletic equipment, of writing and other materials; indeed of all other items composing the total burden. . . .

But we are told that the New Jersey statute is valid in its present application because the appropriation is for a public, not a private purpose, namely, the promotion of education, and the majority accept this idea in the conclusion that all we have here is "public welfare legislation." If that is true and the Amendment's force can be thus destroyed, what has been said becomes all the more pertinent. For then there could be no possible objection to more extensive support of religious education by New Jersey. . . .

It is not because religious teaching does not promote the public or the individual's welfare, but because neither is furthered when the state promotes religious education, that the Constitution forbids it to do so. Both legislatures and courts are bound by that distinction. In failure to observe it lies the fallacy of the "public function"-"social legislation" argument, a fallacy facilitated by easy transference of the argument's basing from due process unrelated to any religious aspect to the First Amendment. . . . Legislatures are free to make, and courts to sustain, appropriations only when it can be found that in fact they do not aid, promote, encourage or sustain religious teaching or observances, be the amount large or small. No such finding has been or could be made in this case. The Amendment has removed this form of promoting the public welfare from legislative and judicial competence to make a public function. It is exclusively a private affair. . . .

No one conscious of religious values can be unsympathetic toward the burden which our constitutional separation puts on parents who desire religious instruction mixed with secular for their children. They pay taxes for others' children's education, at the same time the added cost of instruction for their own. Nor can one happily see benefits denied to children which others receive, because in conscience they or their parents for them desire a different kind of training others do not demand.

But if those feelings should prevail, there would be an end to our historic constitutional policy and command. No more unjust or discriminatory in fact is it to deny attendants at religious schools the cost of their transportation than it is to deny them tuitions, sustenance for their teachers, or any other education-

al expense which others receive at public cost.   Hardship in fact there is which none can blink.   But, for assuring to those who undergo it the greater, the most comprehensive freedom, it is one written by design and firm intent into our basic law.   .   .   .

[I]t is only by observing the prohibition rigidly that the state can maintain its neutrality and avoid partisanship in the dissensions inevitable when sect opposes sect over demands for public moneys to further religious education, teaching or training in any form or degree, directly or indirectly.   Like St. Paul's freedom, religious liberty with a great price must be bought.   And for those who exercise it most fully, by insisting upon religious education for their children mixed with secular, by the terms of our Constitution the price is greater than for others.   .   .   .

Nor is the case comparable to one of furnishing fire or police protection, or access to public highways.   These things are matters of common right, part of the general need for safety.[1]   Certainly the fire department must not stand idly by while the church burns.   Nor is this reason why the state should pay the expense of transportation or other items of the cost of religious education.

Two great drives are constantly in motion to abridge, in the name of education, the complete division of religion and civil authority which our forefathers made.   One is to introduce religious education and observances into the public schools.   The other, to obtain public funds for the aid and support of various private religious schools.   .   .   .   In my opinion both avenues were closed by the Constitution.   Neither should be opened by this Court. The matter is not one of quantity, to be measured by the amount of money expended.   Now as in Madison's day it is one of principle, to keep separate the separate spheres as the First Amendment drew them; to prevent the first experiment upon our liberties; and to keep the question from becoming entangled in corrosive precedents.   We should not be less strict to keep strong and untarnished the one side of the shield of religious freedom than we have been of the other.

EVERSON, THE "WALL OF SEPARATION," AND FINANCIAL AID TO RELIGIOUS ACTIVITIES

1.   *Establishment and the states.*   Justice Black in Everson assumed that the applicability of the establishment clause to the states followed from the earlier "incorporation" of the free exercise guarantee into the 14th.   Did that conclusion warrant further explanation?   For example, does the 14th Amendment present any textual barrier to "incorporation" of the establishment clause? [1]   Note Justice Brennan's comment in his concurring opinion in Abington School District v. Schempp, 374 U.S. 203 (1963) (sec. 1B below):

1.   The protections are of a nature which does not require appropriations specially made from the public treasury and earmarked, as is New Jersey's here, particularly for religious institutions or uses.   The First Amendment does not exclude religious property or activities from protection against disorder or the ordinary accidental incidents of community life.   It forbids support, not protection from interference or destruction.   .   .   .   [Footnote by Justice Rutledge.]

1.   Note that the "incorporation" in Everson—of "establishment" as well as "free exercise"—took place without consideration of the textual difficulty of using the "liberty" of the 14th Amendment as the incorporation route.

"It [has] been suggested that the 'liberty' guaranteed by the Fourteenth Amendment logically cannot absorb the Establishment Clause because that clause is not one of the provisions of the Bill of Rights which in terms protects a 'freedom' of the individual. The fallacy in this contention, I think, is that it underestimates the role of the Establishment Clause as a coguarantor, with the Free Exercise Clause, of religious liberty. The Framers did not entrust the liberty of religious beliefs to either clause alone."

Note also Justice Brennan's response in Schempp to other objections to "incorporating" the establishment clause: "It has been suggested, with some support in history, that absorption of the First Amendment's ban against congressional legislation 'respecting an establishment of religion' is conceptually impossible because the Framers meant the Establishment Clause also to foreclose any attempt by Congress to disestablish the existing official state churches. [But] it is clear on the record of history that the last of the formal state establishments was dissolved more than three decades before the Fourteenth Amendment was ratified, and thus the problem of protecting official state churches from federal encroachments could hardly have been any concern of those who framed the post-Civil War Amendments. [The 14th Amendment] created a panoply of new federal rights for the protection of citizens of the various States. And among those rights was freedom from such state governmental involvement in the affairs of religion as the Establishment Clause had originally foreclosed on the part of Congress.

"[It has also been contended] that absorption of the Establishment Clause is precluded by the absence of any intention on the part of the Framers of the Fourteenth Amendment to circumscribe the residual powers of the States to aid religious activities and institutions in ways which fell short of formal establishments. That argument relies in part upon the express terms of the abortive Blaine Amendment—proposed several years after the adoption of the Fourteenth Amendment—which would have added to the First Amendment a provision that '[n]o state shall make any law respecting an establishment of religion. . . .' Such a restriction would have been superfluous, it is said, if the Fourteenth Amendment had already made the Establishment Clause binding upon the States. The argument proves too much, for the Fourteenth Amendment's protection of the free exercise of religion can hardly be questioned; yet the Blaine Amendment would also have added an explicit protection against state laws abridging that liberty." [2]

Note, moreover, that the First Amendment's establishment clause may have been designed primarily as a federalistic limitation: established churches existed in the states when the Bill of Rights was adopted; the main purpose of "establishment" may have been to keep Congress out of that area. Yet incorporation made "establishment"—arguably a "special," "non-libertarian" limitation on the national government—effective against the states. See generally Howe, "Religion and the Free Society: The Constitutional Question" (1960), in Selected Essays 1938–62 (1963), 780, suggesting that "some legislative enactments respecting an establishment of religion affect most remotely, if at all, the personal rights of religious liberty." Should failure to establish impingement upon personal liberty bar a finding of establishment clause violation? Compare the Court's modern standing rule in establishment cases, footnote 1 in the introduction to this chapter, and the discussion of "coercion" of the plaintiff in the notes following Zorach v. Clauson, sec. 1B below.

2. Note that many state constitutions contain prohibitions of aid to religious groups. Some of these provisions have been interpreted to bar practices sustained against federal establishment

2. *The "wall of separation."* Was Justice Black's "wall of separation" metaphor the appropriate derivation from his perceptions of the history and purposes of the establishment clause? Was the "wall of separation" metaphor implemented in Everson? Has it required modification by the Court in its confrontations with later establishment clause challenges, in the materials which follow? Though Everson continues to be the fountainhead of many establishment clause opinions, its "wall of separation" theme—and its result—have to a certain extent become (like the "neutrality" principle) "a starting point for solutions to problems brought before the Court, not a mechanical answer to them." Everson has been criticized by some Justices as not going far enough to assure "separation," and by others as suggesting too rigid a "wall." For an example of the former position, see Justice Douglas' concurrence in Engel v. Vitale, in 1962, sec. 1B: "[The Everson case] seems in retrospect to be out of line with the First Amendment. . . Mr. Justice Rutledge stated in dissent what I think is desirable First Amendment philosophy." (Justice Douglas had been with the majority in Everson.) For an example of the latter position, see Chief Justice Burger's majority opinion in Lemon v. Kurtzman, in 1971, sec. 1C: "[We] must recognize that the line of separation, far from being a 'wall,' is a blurred, indistinct and variable barrier depending on all the circumstances of a particular relationship."

3. *Financial aid.* The Court's attention to financial assistance involving religious groups is long-standing, but it did not become intense and controversial until recently. The first Supreme Court decision on the establishment clause, for example, sustained a federal appropriation for the construction of a public ward to be administered as part of a hospital under the control of sisters of the Roman Catholic Church. Bradfield v. Roberts, 175 U.S. 291 (1899). But the constitutional problem became far more pressing after Everson and with the increasing demands for federal financial aid.[3] Proposals for federal aid to education provoked the most widespread constitutional debate. Court statements in Everson and in subsequent establishment cases not directly involving financing, sec. 1B, were frequently mentioned in that debate, but for years the Justices did not speak directly to the issues. See, e. g., the contrasting interpretations of Court decisions in the 1961 memoranda on the constitutionality of federal aid to parochial schools, by the Department of HEW and the National Catholic Welfare Conference, reprinted in 50 Geo.L.J. 349, 397 (1961).

The enactment of a broad-ranging federal aid to education law in 1965 raised anew the problems of the permissible scope of assistance to parochial schools under Everson and its progeny. The Court assured that it would play a central role with the Flast v. Cohen holding, 392 U.S. 83 (1968) (chap. 15, below), that federal taxpayers had standing to raise establishment chal-

clause attacks. For example, compare with the Everson holding the state constitutional prohibition of transportation for parochial school students in Visser v. Nooksack Valley School Dist., 33 Wash.2d 669, 207 P.2d 198 (1949). See generally Antieau, Carroll and Burke, Religion under the State Constitutions (1965).

3. On the range of potential sources of controversies in direct and indirect financial supports, see the list of "aids" in the footnote to Justice Douglas' concurrence in Engel v. Vitale, sec. 1B below.

lenges to spending. Since the late sixties, the Court has rendered a number of important decisions striving to delineate the limits on federal and state financial support to religious schools and their students. Those decisions are examined in sec. 1C below. Before turning to them, sec. 1B considers the impact of the Everson principles in the intervening years in areas outside of financial aid programs—particularly with respect to religious activities in the public schools.

B. INTRUSION OF RELIGION INTO GOVERNMENTAL ACTIVITIES—ESPECIALLY PUBLIC SCHOOLS

ZORACH v. CLAUSON

343 U.S. 306, 72 S.Ct. 679, 96 L.Ed. 954 (1952).

Appeal from the Court of Appeals of New York.

Mr. Justice DOUGLAS delivered the opinion of the Court.

New York City has a program which permits its public schools to release students during the school day so that they may leave the school buildings and school grounds and go to religious centers for religious instruction or devotional exercises. A student is released on written request of his parents. Those not released stay in the classrooms. The churches make weekly reports to the schools, sending a list of children who have been released from public school but who have not reported for religious instruction.

This "released time" program involves neither religious instruction in public school classrooms nor the expenditure of public funds. All costs, including the application blanks, are paid by the religious organizations. The case is therefore unlike McCollum v. Board of Education, 333 U.S. 203 [1948], which involved a "released time" program from Illinois. In that case the classrooms were turned over to religious instructors. We accordingly held that the program violated the First Amendment . . . .

Appellants, who are taxpayers and residents of New York City and whose children attend its public schools, challenge the present law, contending it is in essence not different from the one involved in the McCollum case. Their argument, stated elaborately in various ways, reduces itself to this: the weight and influence of the school is put behind a program for religious instruction; public school teachers police it, keeping tab on students who are released; the classroom activities come to a halt while the students who are released for religious instruction are on leave; the school is a crutch on which the churches are leaning for support in their religious training; without the cooperation of the schools this "released time" program, like the one in the McCollum case, would be futile and ineffective. The New York Court of Appeals sustained the law against this claim of unconstitutionality. . . .

The briefs and arguments are replete with data bearing on the merits of this type of "released time" program. They largely concern the wisdom of the system . . . . Those matters are of no concern here, since our problem reduces itself to whether New York by this system has either prohibited the "free exercise" of religion or has made a law "respecting an establishment of religion" within the meaning of the First Amendment.

It takes obtuse reasoning to inject any issue of the "free exercise" of religion into the present case. No one is forced to go to the religious classroom and no religious exercise or instruction is brought to the classrooms of the public schools. A student need not take religious instruction. He is left to his own desires as to the manner or time of his religious devotions, if any.

There is a suggestion that the system involves the use of coercion to get public school students into religious classrooms. There is no evidence in the record before us that supports that conclusion.[1] The present record indeed tells us that the school authorities are neutral in this regard and do no more than release students whose parents so request. If in fact coercion were used, if it were established that any one or more teachers were using their office to persuade or force students to take the religious instruction, a wholly different case would be presented.[2] Hence we put aside that claim of coercion both as respects the "free exercise" of religion and "an establishment of religion" within the meaning of the First Amendment.

Moreover, apart from that claim of coercion, we do not see how New York by this type of "released time" program has made a law respecting an establishment of religion within the meaning of the First Amendment. There is much talk of the separation of Church and State in the history of the Bill of Rights and in the decisions clustering around the First Amendment. There cannot be the slightest doubt that the First Amendment reflects the philosophy that Church and State should be separated. And so far as interference with the "free exercise" of religion and an "establishment" of religion are concerned, the separation must be complete and unequivocal. The First Amendment within the scope of its coverage permits no exception; the prohibition is absolute. The First Amendment, however, does not say that in every and all respects there shall be a separation of Church and State. Rather, it studiously defines the manner, the specific ways, in which there shall be no concert or union or dependency one on the other. That is the common sense of the matter. Otherwise the state and religion would be aliens to each other —hostile, suspicious, and even unfriendly. Churches could not be required to pay even property taxes. Municipalities would not be permitted to render police or fire protection to religious groups. Policemen who helped parishioners into their places of worship would violate the Constitution. Prayers in our legislative halls; the appeals to the Almighty in the messages of the Chief Executive; the proclamations making Thanksgiving Day a holiday; "so help me

1. Nor is there any indication that the public schools enforce attendance at religious schools by punishing absentees from the released time programs for truancy. [Footnote by the Court.]

2. Appellants contend that they should have been allowed to prove that the system is in fact administered in a coercive manner. The New York Court of Appeals declined to grant a trial on this issue, noting, inter alia, that appellants had not properly raised their claim in the manner required by state practice. . . . This independent state ground for decision precludes appellants from raising the issue of maladministration in this proceeding. . . .
The only allegation in the complaint that bears on the issue is that the operation of the program "has resulted and inevitably results in the exercise of pressure and coercion upon parents and children to secure attendance by the children for religious instruction." . . . Since the allegation did not implicate the school authorities in the use of coercion, there is no basis for holding that the New York Court of Appeals under the guise of local practice defeated a federal right . . . .. [Footnote by the Court.]

God" in our courtroom oaths—these and all other references to the Almighty that run through our laws, our public rituals, our ceremonies would be flouting the First Amendment. A fastidious atheist or agnostic could even object to the supplication with which the Court opens each session: "God save the United States and this Honorable Court."

We would have to press the concept of separation of Church and State to these extremes to condemn the present law on constitutional grounds. The nullification of this law would have wide and profound effects. A Catholic student applies to his teacher for permission to leave the school during hours on a Holy Day of Obligation to attend a mass. A Jewish student asks his teacher for permission to be excused for Yom Kippur. A Protestant wants the afternoon off for a family baptismal ceremony. In each case the teacher requires parental consent in writing. In each case the teacher, in order to make sure the student is not a truant, goes further and requires a report from the priest, the rabbi, or the minister. The teacher in other words cooperates in a religious program to the extent of making it possible for her students to participate in it. Whether she does it occasionally for a few students, regularly for one, or pursuant to a systematized program designed to further the religious needs of all the students does not alter the character of the act.

We are a religious people whose institutions presuppose a Supreme Being. We guarantee the freedom to worship as one chooses. We make room for as wide a variety of beliefs and creeds as the spiritual needs of man deem necessary. We sponsor an attitude on the part of government that shows no partiality to any one group and that lets each flourish according to the zeal of its adherents and the appeal of its dogma. When the state encourages religious instruction or cooperates with religious authorities by adjusting the schedule of public events to sectarian needs, it follows the best of our traditions. For it then respects the religious nature of our people and accommodates the public service to their spiritual needs. To hold that it may not would be to find in the Constitution a requirement that the government show a callous indifference to religious groups. That would be preferring those who believe in no religion over those who do believe. Government may not finance religious groups nor undertake religious instruction nor blend secular and sectarian education nor use secular institutions to force one or some religion on any person. But we find no constitutional requirement which makes it necessary for government to be hostile to religion and to throw its weight against efforts to widen the effective scope of religious influence. The government must be neutral when it comes to competition between sects. It may not thrust any sect on any person. It may not make a religious observance compulsory. It may not coerce anyone to attend church, to observe a religious holiday, or to take religious instruction. But it can close its doors or suspend its operations as to those who want to repair to their religious sanctuary for worship or instruction. No more than that is undertaken here. . . . The constitutional standard is the separation of Church and State. The problem, like many problems in constitutional law, is one of degree.

In the McCollum case the classrooms were used for religious instruction and the force of the public school was used to promote that instruction. Here, as we have said, the public schools do no more than accommodate their schedules to a program of outside religious instruction. We follow the McCollum

case. But we cannot expand it to cover the present released time program unless separation of Church and State means that public institutions can make no adjustments of their schedules to accommodate the religious needs of the people. We cannot read into the Bill of Rights such a philosophy of hostility to religion.

Affirmed.

Mr. Justice BLACK, dissenting. . . .

I see no significant difference between the invalid Illinois system and that of New York here sustained. Except for the use of the school buildings in Illinois, there is no difference between the systems which I consider even worthy of mention. In the New York program, as in that of Illinois, the school authorities release some of the children on the condition that they attend the religious classes, get reports on whether they attend, and hold the other children in the school building until the religious hour is over. As we attempted to make categorically clear, the McCollum decision would have been the same if the religious classes had not been held in the school buildings. . . .

Difficulty of decision in the hypothetical situations mentioned by the Court, but not now before us, should not confuse the issues in this case. Here the sole question is whether New York can use its compulsory education laws to help religious sects get attendants presumably too unenthusiastic to go unless moved to do so by the pressure of this state machinery. . . . In considering whether a state has entered this forbidden field the question is not whether it has entered too far but whether it has entered at all. New York is manipulating its compulsory education laws to help religious sects get pupils. This is not separation but combination of Church and State. . . .

Mr. Justice FRANKFURTER, dissenting.

By way of emphasizing my agreement with Mr. Justice Jackson's dissent, I add a few words.

. . . Of course, a State may provide that the classes in its schools shall be dismissed, for any reason, or no reason, on fixed days, or for special occasions. The essence of this case is that the school system did not "close its doors" and did not "suspend its operations." There is all the difference in the world between letting the children out of school and letting some of them out of school into religious classes. . . .

The pith of the case is that formalized religious instruction is substituted for other school activity which those who do not participate in the released-time program are compelled to attend. The school system is very much in operation during this kind of released time. If its doors are closed, they are closed upon those students who do not attend the religious instruction in order to keep them within the school. That is the very thing which raises the constitutional issue. It is not met by disregarding it. Failure to discuss this issue does not take it out of the case. . . .

Mr. Justice JACKSON, dissenting.

This released time program is founded upon a use of the State's power of coercion, which, for me, determines its unconstitutionality. Stripped to its es-

sentials, the plan has two stages, first, that the State compel each student to yield a large part of his time for public secular education and, second, that some of it be "released" to him on condition that he devote it to sectarian religious purposes.

No one suggests that the Constitution would permit the State directly to require this "released" time to be spent "under the control of a duly constituted religious body." This program accomplishes that forbidden result by indirection. If public education were taking so much of the pupils' time as to injure the public or the student's welfare by encroaching upon their religious opportunity, simply shortening everyone's school day would facilitate voluntary and optional attendance at Church classes. But that suggestion is rejected upon the ground that if they are made free many students will not go to the Church. Hence, they must be deprived of freedom for this period, with Church attendance put to them as one of the two permissible ways of using it.

The greater effectiveness of this system over voluntary attendance after school hours is due to the truant officer who, if the youngster fails to go to the Church school, dogs him back to the public schoolroom. Here schooling is more or less suspended during the "released time" so the nonreligious attendants will not forge ahead of the churchgoing absentees. But it serves as a temporary jail for a pupil who will not go to Church. It takes more subtlety of mind than I possess to deny that this is governmental constraint in support of religion. It is as unconstitutional, in my view, when exerted by indirection as when exercised forthrightly.

As one whose children, as a matter of free choice, have been sent to privately supported Church schools, I may challenge the Court's suggestion that opposition to this plan can only be antireligious, atheistic, or agnostic. My evangelistic brethren confuse an objection to compulsion with an objection to religion. It is possible to hold a faith with enough confidence to believe that what should be rendered to God does not need to be decided and collected by Caesar.

.   .   .   The same epithetical jurisprudence used by the Court today to beat down those who oppose pressuring children into some religion can devise as good epithets tomorrow against those who object to pressuring them into a favored religion.   .   .   .   We start down a rough road when we begin to mix compulsory public education with compulsory godliness.

A number of Justices just short of a majority of the majority that promulgates today's passionate dialectics joined in answering them in [McCollum]. The distinction attempted between that case and this is trivial, almost to the point of cynicism, magnifying its nonessential details and disparaging compulsion which was the underlying reason for invalidity. A reading of the Court's opinion in that case along with its opinion in this case will show such difference of overtones and undertones as to make clear that the McCollum case has passed like a storm in a teacup. The wall which the Court was professing to erect between Church and State has become even more warped and twisted than I expected. Today's judgment will be more interesting to students of psychology and of the judicial processes than to students of constitutional law.

ZORACH, McCOLLUM, AND "COERCION"

1. *A distinction between Zorach and McCollum?* The Court sustained New York's "dismissed time" program in Zorach 4 years after invalidating the Illinois "released time" program in McCollum. In McCollum (described in the opinions in Zorach), Justice Black had written the majority opinion, a year after Everson. In McCollum, religious teachers held classes on public school premises for those students whose parents had signed request cards. Justice Black had noted that not only were public school buildings used, but that the state afforded "sectarian groups an invaluable aid in that it helps to provide pupils for their religious classes through use of the state's compulsory public school machinery." Is Justice Douglas persuasive in Zorach in distinguishing the McCollum program from that sustained in Zorach? Was Zorach distinguishable because public school space was not used there? Or did Zorach implicitly overrule McCollum? Should Justice Douglas' primary emphasis on governmental financing be determinative, as he suggests in his concurring opinion in Engel, the next case? Was there significant "financing" in Engel, the state-composed prayer case? Was there more financing there than in Zorach, where Justice Douglas wrote the majority opinion?

Note Justice Brennan's comment in his concurrence in the 1963 Schempp case, below. He insisted that Zorach had not overruled McCollum. He said that the cases were not distinguishable in free exercise terms, but that they were consistent with a coherent establishment philosophy. That coherence stemmed not from "the difference in public expenditures involved" —the arguable difference in cost because of the use of school property in McCollum. Rather, the "deeper difference was that the McCollum program placed the religious instructor in the public school classroom in precisely the position of authority held by the regular teachers of secular subjects, while the Zorach program did not." Is that persuasive?

2. *Permissible religious intrusions into school practices and "coercion."* Can a general standard be stated to determine the extent to which state "aid" to religions is permissible? In light of McCollum and Zorach? In light of the later cases in this section? Consider the suggestion in Choper, "Religion in the Schools," 47 Minn.L.Rev. 329 (1963): "The proposed constitutional standard is that for problems concerning religious intrusion in the public schools, the establishment clause of the first amendment is violated when the state engages in what may be fairly characterized as *solely religious activity* that is likely to result in (1) *compromising* the student's religious or conscientious beliefs or (2) *influencing* the student's freedom of religious or conscientious choice." Are the cases in this sec. 1B consistent with that approach? Is that approach justifiable? Why should it not be enough that the school practices are "solely religious"? Why should it also be necessary to demonstrate impact on student beliefs or choice? If that impact is critical, should it turn on whether it is "likely to result," or whether it so results in fact?

What is the relevant "impact" or "coercion" in the preceding cases and those that follow? Is "coercion" a question of judicial assessment of likelihood? Or is it a question of fact in each case, to be proved at trial?

Compare Justice Clark's test in the Schempp case below, emphasizing the "purpose" and the "primary effect" of the practice, and insisting that if "either is the advancement or inhibition of religion then the enactment" is unconstitutional.   Compare Justice Stewart's dissent in Schempp, insisting that it be shown that a particular school exercise is coercive in the particular case before it is struck down.   Would a case-by-case determination of coerciveness produce inadequate guidance as to the permissibility of state practices?   Would it put an undue premium on finding plaintiffs who are both "coerced" enough and strong enough to bring law suits challenging the practice? *

ENGEL v. VITALE

370 U.S. 421, 82 S.Ct. 1261, 8 L.Ed.2d 601 (1962).

Certiorari to the Court of Appeals of New York.

[The New York Board of Regents prepared a "non-denominational" prayer for use in public schools. A local school board directed that the prayer be recited daily by each class. The prayer read: "Almighty God, we acknowledge our dependence upon Thee, and we beg Thy blessings upon us, our parents, our teachers and our Country." The practice of reciting the prayer was challenged by parents of a number of students who claimed that it was "contrary to the beliefs, religions, or religious practices of both themselves and their children." The highest state court upheld the power to use the prayer, so long as the schools did not compel any pupil to join in the prayer over a parent's objection.]

Mr. Justice BLACK delivered the opinion of the Court.   .   .   .

We think that by using its public school system to encourage recitation of the Regents' prayer, the State of New York has adopted a practice wholly inconsistent with the Establishment Clause. There can, of course, be no doubt that New York's program of daily classroom invocation of God's blessings as prescribed in the Regents' prayer is a religious activity. It is a solemn avowal of divine faith and supplication for the blessings of the Almighty. [W]e think that the constitutional prohibition against laws respecting an establishment of religion must at least mean that in this country it is no part of the business of government to compose official prayers for any group of the American people to recite as a part of a religious program carried on by government.

It is a matter of history that this very practice of establishing governmentally composed prayers for religious services was one of the reasons which caused many of our early colonists to leave England and seek religious freedom in America. [The people at the time of the adoption of the Constitution] knew, some of them from bitter personal experience, that one of the greatest dangers to the freedom of the individual to worship in his own way lay in the Government's placing its official stamp of approval upon one particular kind of prayer or one particular form of religious services.   .   .   .   The

---

* Cf. Brown, "Quis Custodiet Ipsos
Custodes?—The School Prayer Cases,"
1963 Sup.Ct.Rev. 1.

First Amendment was added to the Constitution to stand as a guarantee that neither the power nor the prestige of the Federal Government would be used to control, support or influence the kinds of prayer the American people can say   .   .   .   .

.   .   .   Neither the fact that the prayer may be denominationally neutral, nor the fact that its observance on the part of the students is voluntary, can serve to free it from the limitations of the Establishment Clause, as it might from the Free Exercise Clause, of the First Amendment, both of which are operative against the States by virtue of the Fourteenth Amendment. Although these two clauses may in certain instances overlap, they forbid two quite different kinds of governmental encroachment upon religious freedom. The Establishment Clause, unlike the Free Exercise Clause, does not depend upon any showing of direct governmental compulsion and is violated by the enactment of laws which establish an official religion whether those laws operate directly to coerce nonobserving individuals or not. This is not to say, of course, that laws officially prescribing a particular form of religious worship do not involve coercion of such individuals. When the power, prestige and financial support of government is placed behind a particular religious belief, the indirect coercive pressure upon religious minorities to conform to the prevailing officially approved religion is plain. But the purposes underlying the Establishment Clause go much further than that. Its first and most immediate purpose rested on the belief that a union of government and religion tends to destroy government and to degrade religion.   .   .   .   Another purpose of the Establishment Clause rested upon an awareness of the historical fact that governmentally established religions and religious persecutions go hand in hand.   .   .   .

It has been argued that to apply the Constitution in such a way as to prohibit state laws respecting an establishment of religious services in public schools is to indicate a hostility toward religion or toward prayer. Nothing, of course, could be more wrong.   .   .   .   It is neither sacrilegious nor antireligious to say that each separate government in this country should stay out of the business of writing or sanctioning official prayers and leave that purely religious function to the people themselves and to those the people choose to look to for religious guidance.*   .   .   .

Reversed and remanded.†

Mr. Justice DOUGLAS, concurring.

.   .   .   The point for decision is whether the Government can constitutionally finance a religious exercise. Our system at the federal and state

---

* There is of course nothing in the decision reached here that is inconsistent with the fact that school children and others are officially encouraged to express love for our country by reciting historical documents such as the Declaration of Independence which contain references to the Deity or by singing officially espoused anthems which include the composer's professions of faith in a Supreme Being, or with the fact that there are many manifestations in our public life of belief in God. Such patriotic or ceremonial occasions bear no true resemblance to the unquestioned religious exercise that the State of New York has sponsored in this instance. [Footnote by the Court.]

† Justices Frankfurter and White did not participate in the decision.

levels is presently honeycombed with such financing.[1]   Nevertheless, I think it
is an unconstitutional undertaking whatever form it takes.   .   .   .

.   .   .   I cannot say that to authorize this prayer is to establish a religion in the strictly historic meaning of those words.   .   .   .   Yet once
government finances a religious exercise it inserts a divisive influence into
our communities.   .   .   .

"We are a religious people whose institutions presuppose a Supreme
Being."   [Zorach.]   .   .   .   The First Amendment leaves the Government in a position not of hostility to religion but of neutrality.   .   .   .

My problem today would be uncomplicated but for [the Everson case,
which] seems in retrospect to be out of line with the First Amendment.   Its result is appealing, as it allows aid to be given to needy children.   Yet by the
same token, public funds could be used to satisfy other needs of children in parochial schools—lunches, books, and tuition being obvious examples.   Mr.
Justice Rutledge stated in dissent what I think is durable First Amendment
philosophy.   .   .   .

Mr. Justice STEWART, dissenting.   .   .   .

.   .   .   I think that the Court's task, in this as in all areas of constitutional adjudication, is not responsibly aided by the uncritical invocation of
metaphors like the "wall of separation," a phrase nowhere to be found in the
Constitution.   What is relevant to the issue here is not the history of an
established church in sixteenth century England or in eighteenth century
America, but the history of the religious traditions of our people, reflected
in countless practices of the institutions and officials of our government.

At the opening of each day's Session of this Court we stand, while one of
our officials invokes the protection of God.   Since the days of John Marshall
our Crier has said, "God save the United States and this Honorable Court."
Both the Senate and the House of Representatives open their daily Sessions
with prayer.   Each of our Presidents, from George Washington to John F.
Kennedy, has upon assuming his Office asked the protection and help of God.
.   .   .   Countless similar examples could be listed, but there is no need to

---

1. "There are many 'aids' to religion in
    this country at all levels of govern-
    ment.   To mention but a few at the
    federal level, one might begin by ob-
    serving that the very First Congress
    which wrote the First Amendment pro-
    vided for chaplains in both Houses
    and in the armed services.   There is
    compulsory chapel at the service acad-
    emies, and religious services are held
    in federal hospitals and prisons.   The
    President issues religious proclama-
    tions.   The Bible is used for the ad-
    ministration of oaths.   N. Y. A. and
    W. P. A. funds were available to pa-
    rochial schools during the depression.
    Veterans receiving money under the
    'G. I.' Bill of 1944 could attend de-
    nominational schools, to which pay-
    ments were made directly by the gov-
    ernment.   During World War II, fed-
    eral money was contributed to denomi-
    national schools for the training of
    nurses.   The benefits of the National
    School Lunch Act are available to
    students in private as well as public
    schools.   The Hospital Survey and
    Construction Act of 1946 specifically
    made money available to non-public
    hospitals.   The slogan 'In God We
    Trust' is used by the Treasury De-
    partment, and Congress recently added
    God to the pledge of allegiance.   There
    is Bible-reading in the schools of the
    District of Columbia, and religious in-
    struction is given in the District's Na-
    tional Training School for Boys.   Re-
    ligious organizations are exempt from
    the federal income tax and are granted
    postal privileges.   Up to defined lim-
    its   .   .   .   contributions to religious
    organizations are deductible for fed-
    eral income tax purposes.   .   .   .
    This list of federal 'aids' could easily
    be expanded, and of course there is a
    long list in each state."   Fellman,
    The Limits of Freedom (1959), pp. 40–
    41.   [Footnote by Justice Douglas.]

belabor the obvious. It was all summed up by this Court just ten years ago in a single sentence: "We are a religious people whose institutions presuppose a Supreme Being." [Zorach.]*

I do not believe that this Court, or the Congress, or the President has by the actions and practices I have mentioned established an "official religion" in violation of the Constitution. And I do not believe the State of New York has done so in this case. What each has done has been to recognize and to follow the deeply entrenched and highly cherished spiritual traditions of our Nation.

. . .

THE BIBLE READING CASES AND THE SEARCH FOR NEW FORMULATIONS: "PURPOSE" AND "PRIMARY EFFECT"

One year after Engel v. Vitale, the Justices extended its principles beyond state-composed prayers—and in the process tried their hands at reformulating establishment criteria. In ABINGTON SCHOOL DISTRICT v. SCHEMPP and MURRAY v. CURLETT, 374 U.S. 203 (1963), the Court held that the establishment clause prohibits state laws and practices "requiring the selection and reading at the opening of the school day of verses from the Holy Bible and the recitation of the Lord's Prayer by the students in unison."

In the Schempp case a Pennsylvania law provided: "At least ten verses from the Holy Bible shall be read, without comment, at the opening of each public school on each school day. Any child shall be excused from such Bible reading, or attending such Bible reading, upon the written request of his parent or guardian." The Schempp family, members of the Unitarian Church, attacked high school opening exercises involving the recitation of the Lord's Prayer as well as the reading of the Bible verses. In Murray, Mrs. Murray and her son, "both professed atheists," challenged a Baltimore school rule providing for the holding of opening exercises consisting primarily of the "reading, without comment, of a chapter in the Holy Bible and/or the use of the Lord's Prayer." That rule also permitted children to be excused at the request of a parent.

1. *The majority standard.* Justice Clark's opinion for the Court reaffirmed two "basic conclusions of the Court": first, that the First Amendment's religion provisions have "been made wholly applicable to the states by the

---

* Compare, with the use of the Zorach v. Clauson language in the opinions of Justices Stewart and Douglas, the 1961 case of Torcaso v. Watkins, 367 U.S. 488: Appellant had been denied a commission as notary public for his refusal to comply with a state constitutional provision requiring a declaration of belief in God. The Court, in an opinion by Justice Black, concluded: "This Maryland religious test for public office unconstitutionally invades the appellant's freedom of belief and religion and therefore cannot be enforced against him." The Maryland Court of Appeals had thought that the Zorach case had "in part repudiated" statements in Everson and McCollum concerning complete separation between the state and religion. Justice Black answered: "Nothing decided or written in Zorach lends support to the idea that the Court there intended to open up the way for government, state or federal, to restore the historically and constitutionally discredited policy of probing religious beliefs by test oaths or limiting public offices to persons who have, or perhaps more properly, profess to have a belief in some particular kind of religious concept." Justices Frankfurter and Harlan concurred in the result. The Court did not reach the contention that the "no religious test" provision of Article VI applies to state as well as federal offices.

Fourteenth Amendment"; second, that "this Court has rejected unequivocally the contention that the establishment clause forbids only governmental preference of one religion over another." Though these principles had not been questioned in these cases, Justice Clark noted, "others continue to question their history, logic and efficacy. Such contentions [seem] entirely untenable and of value only as academic exercises." After reviewing the decisions through Engel, he concluded that both the establishment clause and the free exercise clause require "neutrality." He explained:

"The wholesome 'neutrality' of which this Court's cases speak thus stems from a recognition of the teachings of history that powerful sects or groups might bring about a fusion of governmental and religious functions or a concert or dependency of one upon the other to the end that official support of the State or Federal Government would be placed behind the tenets of one or of all orthodoxies. This the Establishment Clause prohibits. And a further reason for neutrality is found in the Free Exercise Clause, which recognizes the value of religious training, teaching and observance and, more particularly, the right of every person to freely choose his own course with reference thereto, free of any compulsion from the state. This the Free Exercise Clause guarantees. Thus, as we have seen, the two clauses may overlap. . . . The test may be stated as follows: *what are the purpose and the primary effect of the enactment?* If either is the advancement or inhibition of religion then the enactment exceeds the scope of legislative power as circumscribed by the Constitution. That is to say that to withstand the strictures of the Establishment Clause *there must be a secular legislative purpose and a primary effect that neither advances nor inhibits religion.* [Everson]; McGowan v. Maryland [which follows]. The Free Exercise Clause, likewise considered many times here, withdraws from legislative power, state and federal, the exertion of any restraint on the free exercise of religion. Its purpose is to secure religious liberty in the individual by prohibiting any invasions thereof by civil authority. Hence it is necessary in a free exercise case for one to show the coercive effect of the enactment as it operates against him in the practice of his religion. The distinction between the two clauses is apparent—a violation of the Free Exercise Clause is predicated on coercion while the Establishment Clause violation need not be so attended." [Emphasis added.]

Applying those principles here, Justice Clark emphasized that the exercises were held in school buildings with the participation of teachers and noted that "[n]one of these factors, other than compulsory school attendance, was present in the program upheld" in Zorach. In Schempp, he approved the lower court finding that the exercises were "a religious ceremony." Though there was no such specific finding in Murray, the Court rejected the State's argument that the exercises had "secular purposes"—"the promotion of moral values, the contradiction to the materialistic trends of our times, the perpetuation of our institutions and the teaching of literature." Justice Clark replied: "But even if its purpose is not strictly religious, it is sought to be accomplished through readings, without comment, from the Bible. Surely the place of the Bible as an instrument of religion cannot be gainsaid, and the State's recognition of the pervading religious character of the ceremony is evident from the rule's specific permission" of the Catholic Douay version of the Bible as an alternative to the King James version, "as well as the recent amendment permitting nonattendance at the exercises." He added: "The

conclusion follows that in both cases the laws require religious exercises and such exercises are being conducted in direct violation of the rights of the appellees and petitioners." [1] Permitting individual students to be excused from the exercises "furnishes no defense to the claim of unconstitutionality under the Establishment Clause. [Engel.] Further, it is no defense to urge that the religious practices here may be relatively minor encroachments on the First Amendment. The breach of neutrality that is today a trickling stream may all too soon become a raging torrent."

Justice Clark rejected the argument "that unless these religious exercises are permitted a 'religion of secularism' is established in the schools." Moreover, "we cannot accept that the concept of neutrality, which does not permit a State to require a religious exercise even with the consent of the majority of those affected, collides with the majority's right to free exercise of religion.[2] While the Free Exercise Clause clearly prohibits the use of state action to deny the rights of free exercise to *anyone*, it has never meant that a majority could use the machinery of the State to practice its beliefs." He added that the decision of course did not bar the "study of the Bible or of religion, when presented objectively as part of a secular program of education." But that was not the case here: these were "religious exercises, required by the State in violation of the command of the First Amendment that the Government maintain strict neutrality, neither aiding nor opposing religion." *

Three additional opinions concurred in the opinion and judgment of the Court. Justice Douglas saw two different violations of the establishment clause. The challenged practices were unconstitutional, he insisted, not only because they constituted state-conducted religious exercises in violation of the

1. It goes without saying that the laws and practices involved here can be challenged only by persons having standing to complain. But the requirements for standing to challenge state action under the Establishment Clause, unlike those relating to the Free Exercise Clause, do not include proof that particular religious freedoms are infringed. [McGowan.] The parties here are school children and their parents, who are directly affected by the laws and practices against which their complaints are directed. These interests surely suffice to give the parties standing to complain. See [Engel]. . . . [Footnote by Justice Clark.]

2. We [do] not pass upon a situation such as military service, where the Government regulates the temporal and geographic environment of individuals to a point that, unless it permits voluntary religious services to be conducted with the use of government facilities, military personnel would be unable to engage in the practice of their faiths. [Footnote by Justice Clark.]

* As a result of criticism of the Bible Reading Cases, a large number of constitutional amendments were proposed. Congressional committees held hearings on the proposals in the spring of 1964, and in several sessions in the years since. The most widely discussed suggestion was the proposed Becker Amendment:

"Section 1. Nothing in this Constitution shall be deemed to prohibit the offering, reading from, or listening to prayers or biblical scriptures, if participation therein is on a voluntary basis, in any governmental or public school, institution, or place.

"Section 2. Nothing in this Constitution shall be deemed to prohibit making reference to belief in, reliance upon, or invoking the aid of God or a Supreme Being in any governmental or public document, proceeding, activity, ceremony, school, institution, or place, or upon any coinage, currency, or obligation of the United States.

"Section 3. Nothing in this article shall constitute an establishment of religion." (H.J.Res. 693, 88th Cong., 1st Sess.)

required "neutrality" but also because of "the additional reason that public funds, though small in amount, are being used to promote a religious exercise." Justice Goldberg's separate opinion, joined by Justice Harlan, spoke of the "unavoidable accommodations necessary" to achieve the "fullest realization of true religious liberty." He concluded: "The practices here involved do not fall within any sensible or acceptable concept of compelled or permitted accommodation and involve the state so significantly and directly in the realm of the sectarian as to give rise to those very divisive influences and inhibitions of freedom which both religion clauses of the First Amendment preclude."

2. *The Brennan concurrence.* Justice Brennan's concurrence was far the most extensive. The invalidation of the practices here, he stated, was compelled by the ruling in Engel, for "it is constitutionally irrelevant that the State has not composed the material for the inspirational exercises presently involved." He then proceeded to explore at length the history and interpretations of the religion provisions to explain his conclusion that "not every involvement of religion in public life is unconstitutional." His discussion of "the line we must draw between the permissible and the impermissible" is of particular interest:

"What the Framers meant to foreclose, and what our decisions under the Establishment Clause have forbidden, are those involvements of religious with secular institutions which (a) serve the essentially religious activities of religious institutions; (b) employ the organs of government for essentially religious purposes; or (c) use essentially religious means to serve governmental ends, where secular means would suffice. . . . On the other hand, there may be myriad forms of involvements of government with religion which do not import such dangers and therefore should not, in my judgment, be deemed to violate the Establishment Clause. . . . I think a brief survey of certain of these forms of accommodation will reveal that the First Amendment commands not official hostility toward religion, but only a strict neutrality in matters of religion. . . .

"A. *The Conflict Between Establishment and Free Exercise.*—There are certain practices, conceivably violative of the Establishment Clause, the striking down of which might seriously interfere with certain religious liberties also protected by the First Amendment. . . . In my view, government cannot sponsor religious exercises in the public schools without jeopardizing [neutrality]. On the other hand, hostility, not neutrality, would characterize the refusal to provide chaplains and places of worship for prisoners and soldiers cut off by the State from all civilian opportunities for public communion, the withholding of draft exemptions for ministers and conscientious objectors, or the denial of the temporary use of an empty public building to a congregation whose place of worship has been destroyed by fire or flood. I do not say that government *must* provide chaplains or draft exemptions, or that the courts should intercede if it fails to do so.

"B. *Establishment and Exercises in Legislative Bodies.*—The saying of invocational prayers in legislative chambers, state or federal, and the appointment of legislative chaplains, might well represent no involvements of the kind prohibited by the Establishment Clause. Legislators, federal and state, are mature adults. . . .

"C. *Non-Devotional Use of the Bible In the Public Schools.*—The holding of the Court today plainly does not foreclose teaching *about* the Holy Scriptures .   .   .

"D. *Uniform Tax Exemptions Incidentally Available to Religious Institutions.*—Nothing we hold today questions the propriety of certain tax deductions or exemptions which incidentally benefit churches and religious institutions, along with many secular charities and nonprofit organizations. If religious institutions benefit, it is in spite of rather than because of their religious character. .   .   .

"E. *Religious Considerations in Public Welfare Programs.*—Since government may not support or directly aid religious *activities,* [there] might be some doubt whether non-discriminatory programs of governmental aid may constitutionally include *individuals* who become eligible wholly or partially for religious reasons.   .   .   .   Such a construction would, it seems to me, require government to impose religious discriminations and disabilities, thereby jeopardizing the free exercise of religion, in order to avoid what is thought to constitute an establishment.   .   .   .   The Framers were not concerned with the effects of certain incidental aids to individual worshipers which come about as byproducts of general and non-discriminatory welfare programs.   .   .   .

"F. *Activities Which, Though Religious in Origin, Have Ceased to Have Religious Meaning.*— .   .   .   As we said in McGowan [the Sunday Closing Law case which follows], 'the Establishment clause does not ban federal or state regulation of conduct whose reason or effect merely happens to coincide or harmonize with the tenets of some or all religions.' .   .   .

"This general principle might also serve to insulate the various patriotic exercises and activities used in the public schools and elsewhere which, whatever may have been their origins, no longer have a religious purpose or meaning. The reference to divinity in the revised pledge of allegiance, for example, may merely recognize the historical fact that our Nation was believed to have been founded 'under God.' Thus reciting the pledge may be no more of a religious exercise than the reading aloud of Lincoln's Gettysburg Address, which contains an allusion to the same historical fact."

3. *The Stewart dissent.* Justice Stewart dissented. He insisted that the cases should be remanded for additional evidence. He emphasized that there was no evidence "as to whether there would exist any coercion of any kind upon a student who did not want to participate," and he urged that school authorities be given an opportunity to demonstrate that they could "administer a system of religious exercises during school hours [in] such a way as completely to free from any kind of official coercion those who do not affirmatively want to participate." He remarked that it was "a fallacious oversimplification" to regard the religion clauses "as establishing a single constitutional standard of 'separation of church and state,' which can be mechanically applied in every case." He insisted that "religion and government must necessarily interact in countless ways" and that "there are areas in which a doctrinaire reading of the Establishment Clause leads to irreconcilable conflict with the Free Exercise Clause." He elaborated:

"That the central value embodied in the First Amendment—and, more particularly, in the guarantee of 'liberty' contained in the Fourteenth—is the

safeguarding of an individual's right to free exercise of his religion has been consistently recognized. . . . It is this concept of constitutional protection embodied in our decisions which makes the cases before us such difficult ones for me. For there is involved in these cases a substantial free exercise claim on the part of those who affirmatively desire to have their children's school day open with the reading of passages from the Bible. . . .

"Our decisions make clear that there is no constitutional bar to the use of government property for religious purposes. On the contrary, this Court has consistently held that the discriminatory barring of religious groups from public property is itself a violation of First and Fourteenth Amendment guarantees. [E. g., Niemotko v. Maryland, chap. 12, sec. 2.] A different standard has been applied to public school property, because of the coercive effect which the use by religious sects of a compulsory school system would necessarily have upon the children involved. [McCollum.] But insofar as the McCollum decision rests on the Establishment rather than the Free Exercise Clause, it is clear that its effect is limited to religious instruction—to government support of proselytizing activities of religious sects by throwing the weight of secular authority behind the dissemination of religious tenets. The dangers both to government and to religion inherent in official support of instruction in the tenets of various religious sects are absent in the present cases, which involve only a reading from the Bible unaccompanied by comments which might otherwise constitute instruction. . . .

"In the absence of coercion upon those who do not wish to participate—because they hold less strong beliefs, other beliefs, or no beliefs at all—such provisions cannot, in my view, be held to represent the type of support of religion barred by the Establishment Clause. . . .

"I have said that these provisions authorizing religious exercises are properly to be regarded as measures making possible the free exercise of religion. But it is important to stress [that] the question presented is not whether exercises such as those at issue here are constitutionally compelled, but rather whether they are constitutionally invalid. And that issue, in my view, turns on the question of coercion. . . .

"To be specific, it seems to me clear that certain types of exercises would present situations in which no possibility of coercion on the part of secular officials could be claimed to exist. Thus, if such exercises were held either before or after the official school day, or if the school schedule were such that participation were merely one among a number of desirable alternatives, it could hardly be contended that the exercises did anything more than to provide an opportunity for the voluntary expression of religious belief. On the other hand, a law which provided for religious exercises during the school day and which contained no excusal provision would obviously be unconstitutionally coercive upon those who did not wish to participate. And even under a law containing an excusal provision, if the exercises were held during the school day, and no equally desirable alternative were provided by the school authorities, the likelihood that children might be under at least some psychological compulsion to participate would be great. In a case such as the latter, however, I think we would err if we *assumed* such coercion in the absence of any evidence.

"Viewed in this light, it seems to me clear that the records in both of the cases before us are wholly inadequate to support an informed or responsible decision. Both cases involve provisions which explicitly permit any student who wishes, to be excused from participation in the exercises. There is no evidence in either case as to whether there would exist any coercion of any kind upon a student who did not want to participate. . . ."

SOME OTHER ASPECTS OF SEPARATION

1. *The Sunday Closing Cases.* In elaborating establishment criteria in the Bible Reading cases, the Court relied in part on McGOWAN v. MARYLAND, 366 U.S. 420 (1961). McGowan was one of the few establishment controversies in the Court that did not involve schools. It was one of four 1961 companion cases in which the Court rejected claims that Sunday Closing Laws were "laws respecting an establishment of religion or prohibiting the free exercise thereof." In two of the cases, Two Guys from Harrison-Allentown v. McGinley, 366 U.S. 582, as well as McGowan, the Court held that the establishment claim was the only religion issue which appellants could raise. In the McGowan case, the Court pointed out that "appellants allege only economic injury to themselves; they do not allege any infringement of their own religious freedoms due to Sunday closing."

Chief Justice Warren wrote the opinions for the Court in these cases. He noted in McGowan that there is "no dispute that the original laws which dealt with Sunday labor were motivated by religious forces." He concluded, however: "In light of the evolution of our Sunday Closing Laws through the centuries, and of their more or less recent emphasis upon secular considerations, it is not difficult to discern that as presently written and administered, most of them, at least, are of a secular rather than of a religious character, and that presently they bear no relationship to establishment of religion as those words are used in the Constitution of the United States. . . . The present purpose and effect of most of them is to provide a uniform day of rest for all citizens; the fact that this day is Sunday, a day of particular significance for the dominant Christian sects, does not bar the State from achieving its secular goals. . . . Sunday is a day apart from all others. The cause is irrelevant; the fact exists." [Recall also the rejection of the equal protection claim in McGowan, chap. 10, sec. 1, above.]*

2. *The "Monkey Law" Case.* Arkansas' version of the Tennessee "anti-evolution" law which gained national notoriety in the Scopes trial in 1927 was found to be in conflict with the establishment clause mandate of "governmental neutrality" in EPPERSON v. ARKANSAS, 393 U.S. 97 (1968). The Arkansas statute prohibited teachers in state schools from teaching "the theory or doctrine that mankind ascended or descended from a

---

* Braunfeld v. Brown, 366 U.S. 599, was the major case raising the free exercise contention as well. That case appears in sec. 2 below. Gallagher v. Crown Kosher Market, 366 U.S. 617, involved a "similar, although not as grave," challenge. Justice Frankfurter submitted an extensive separate opinion, joined by Justice Harlan. He substantially agreed with Chief Justice Warren in all four cases. Justice Douglas dissented in all of the cases on establishment and free exercise grounds. The views of Justices Brennan and Stewart, dissenting only on the free exercise issue, appear in Braunfeld, sec. 2 below.

lower order of animals." The highest state court had expressed "no opinion" on "whether the Act prohibits any explanation of the theory of evolution or merely prohibits teaching that the theory is true." On either interpretation, Justice Fortas' majority opinion concluded, the law could not stand: "The overriding fact is that Arkansas' law selects from the body of knowledge a particular segment which it proscribes for the sole reason that it is deemed to conflict with a particular religious doctrine; that is, with a particular interpretation of the Book of Genesis by a particular religious group."

The Court found it unnecessary to rely on broad academic freedom principles (cf. Meyer v. Nebraska, chap. 9) because of the availability of the "narrower terms" of the First Amendment's religion provisions. "The State's undoubted right to prescribe the curriculum for its public schools" did not include the right to bar "the teaching of a scientific theory or doctrine where that prohibition is based upon reasons that violate the First Amendment." Here, clearly, "fundamentalist sectarian conviction was and is the law's reason for existence." This plainly was not the required religious neutrality: "Arkansas did not seek to excise from the curricula of its schools and universities all discussion of the origin of man. The law's effort was confined to an attempt to blot out a particular theory because of its supposed conflict with the Biblical account, literally read."

In separate opinions, Justices Black and Stewart explained that they concurred solely on the ground of vagueness. Justice Black criticized the majority for reaching out to "troublesome" First Amendment questions. He noted, for example, that "a state law prohibiting all teaching of human development or biology is constitutionally quite different from a law that compels a teacher to teach as true only one theory of a given doctrine" and he stated that he was not ready to hold "that a person hired to teach schoolchildren takes with him into the classroom a constitutional right to teach sociological, economic, political, or religious subjects that the school's managers do not want discussed." He questioned, moreover, whether the majority's view achieved "religious neutrality": If some considered evolution anti-religious, was the state constitutionally bound to permit teaching of anti-religious doctrine? Did the Court's holding infringe "the religious freedom of those who consider evolution an anti-religious doctrine?" Since there was no indication that the "literal Biblical doctrine" of evolution was taught, could not the removal of the subject of evolution be justified as leaving the State "in a neutral position toward these supposedly competing religious and anti-religious doctrines?"

3. *Judicial determinations of questions of religious doctrine and belief.* To what extent do the religion clauses prohibit civil courts from adjudicating issues which may involve determinations of the content of religious beliefs? The Court has repeatedly said that inquiry into the "truth" of religious beliefs is foreclosed in the courts; yet courts occasionally adjudicate the "sincerity" of beliefs. See, e. g., conscientious objector draft exemption cases such as United States v. Seeger, sec. 2 below. Can sincerity really be examined without treading on the supposedly forbidden area of the content of the belief? Can free exercise claims of exemption from general laws, on the ground that they intrude unduly into protected areas of belief and conduct, be evaluated without some examination of the content of religious doctrine? See, e. g., the claims of the Orthodox Jew and the Amish parent in Braunfeld and Yoder,

sec. 2 below.   As background to that recurrent problem, note the Court's disavowals of concern with the content and accuracy of belief in the materials in this note.

a.   *Allegedly fraudulent religious claims.*   In UNITED STATES v. BALLARD, 322 U.S. 78 (1944), defendants were indicted under the federal mail fraud laws.   They had solicited funds for the "I Am" movement. Among their representations were the claims that they had been selected as "divine messengers" to communicate the message of the "alleged divine entity, Saint Germain," and that they had, "by reason of supernatural attainments, the power to heal persons of ailments and diseases."   Justice Douglas' majority opinion stated that the First Amendment barred submission to the jury of "the truth or verity of respondents' religious doctrines or beliefs." Justice Douglas commented: "Men may believe what they cannot prove. They may not be put to the proof of their religious doctrines or beliefs. Religious experiences which are as real as life to some may be incomprehensible to others.   Yet the fact that they may be beyond the ken of mortals does not mean that they can be made suspect before the law.   Many take their gospel from the New Testament.   But it would hardly be supposed that they could be tried before a jury charged with a duty of determining whether those teachings contain false representations.   The miracles of the New Testament, the Divinity of Christ, life after death, the power of prayer are deep in the religious convictions of many.   If one could be sent to jail because a jury in a hostile environment found those teachings false, little indeed would be left of religious freedom."   Does that position bar submission to the jury of the question of the defendants' good faith?   Could a jury find that defendants knew that their representations were false and that they therefore solicited funds fraudulently?   Could such a finding be made without some evaluation of the nature of the defendants' representations?

b.   *Internal church disputes.*   Civil courts have traditionally been reluctant to intervene in disputes arising from church schisms.   See, e. g., Kedroff v. St. Nicholas Cathedral, 344 U.S. 94 (1952) (relying on free exercise grounds).   The Supreme Court reaffirmed that tradition in Presbyterian Church v. Mary Elizabeth Blue Hull Memorial Presbyterian Church, 393 U.S. 440 (1969).   The Georgia courts had decided a church property dispute in favor of local dissident churches that had withdrawn from the general church pursuant to state law providing that the property rights at issue turned on "a civil court jury decision as to whether the general church abandoned or departed from the tenets of faith and practice it held at the time the local churches affiliated with it."   The Court held that Georgia could not constitutionally apply this "departure-from-doctrine" element of its law.   Justice Brennan's opinion for the Court emphasized that state law required civil courts "to determine matters at the very core of a religion—the interpretation of particular church doctrines and the importance of those doctrines to religion."   "Marginal judicial involvement" in church disputes was not prohibited.   "Neutral principles of law, developed for use in all property disputes," could be applied to church property without violating the free exercise or establishment guarantees.   But the First Amendment "commands civil courts to decide church property disputes without resolving underlying controversies over religious doctrine."

C.   FINANCIAL AID TO RELIGION: THE CONTEMPORARY DIMENSIONS

BOARD OF EDUCATION v. ALLEN

392 U.S. 236, 88 S.Ct. 1923, 20 L.Ed.2d 1060 (1968).

Appeal from the New York Court of Appeals.

[As the result of a 1965 amendment to the New York Education Law, local school boards were required to lend textbooks without charge "to all children residing in such district who are enrolled in grades seven to twelve of a public or private school which complies with the compulsory education law." The books to be loaned were "text-books which are designated for use in any public, elementary or secondary schools of the state or are approved by any boards of education" and which "a pupil is required to use as a text for a semester or more in a particular class in the school he legally attends." A local school board challenged the statute (§ 701) because it included students attending parochial schools among those to receive text-book loans. The highest state court rejected the attack.]

Mr. Justice WHITE delivered the opinion of the Court. . . .

Everson and later cases have shown that the line between state neutrality to religion and state support of religion is not easy to locate. [Based on prior cases, the Schempp decision (sec. 1B)] fashioned a test subscribed to by eight Justices for distinguishing between forbidden involvements of the State with religion and those contacts which the Establishment Clause permits:

> "The test may be stated as follows: what are the purpose and the primary effect of the enactment? If either is the advancement or inhibition of religion then the enactment exceeds the scope of legislative power as circumscribed by the Constitution. That is to say that to withstand the strictures of the Establishment Clause there must be a secular legislative purpose and a primary effect that neither advances nor inhibits religion. . . ."

This test is not easy to apply, but the citation of Everson by the Schempp Court to support its general standard made clear how the Schempp rule would be applied to the facts of Everson. The statute upheld in Everson would be considered a law having "a secular legislative purpose and a primary effect that neither advances nor inhibits religion." We reach the same result with respect to the New York law requiring school books to be loaned free of charge to all students in specified grades. The express purpose of § 701 was stated by the New York Legislature to be furtherance of the educational opportunities available to the young. Appellants have shown us nothing about the necessary effects of the statute that is contrary to its stated purpose. The law merely makes available to all children the benefits of a general program to lend school books free of charge. Books are furnished at the request of the pupil and ownership remains, at least technically, in the State. Thus no funds or books are furnished to parochial schools, and the financial benefit is to parents and

children, not to schools.[1]　Perhaps free books make it more likely that some children choose to attend a sectarian school, but that was true of the state-paid bus fares in Everson and does not alone demonstrate an unconstitutional degree of support for a religious institution.

Of course books are different from buses.　Most bus rides have no inherent religious significance, while religious books are common.　However, the language of § 701 does not authorize the loan of religious books, and the State claims no right to distribute religious literature.　Although the books loaned are those required by the parochial school for use in specific courses, each book loaned must be approved by the public school authorities; only secular books may receive approval.　.　.　.　Absent evidence, we cannot assume that school authorities [are] unable to distinguish between secular and religious books or that they will not honestly discharge their duties under the law.　In judging the validity of the statute on this record we must proceed on the assumption that books loaned to students are books that are not unsuitable for use in the public schools because of religious content.

The major reason offered by appellants for distinguishing free textbooks from free bus fares is that books, but not buses, are critical to the teaching process, and in a sectarian school that process is employed to teach religion. However this Court has long recognized that religious schools pursue two goals, religious instruction and secular education.　[A] substantial body of case law has confirmed the power of the States to insist that attendance at private schools, if it is to satisfy state compulsory-attendance laws, be at institutions which provide minimum hours of instruction, employ teachers of specified training, and cover prescribed subjects of instruction.[2]　[These] cases were a sensible corollary of Pierce v. Society of Sisters [chap. 9]: if the State must satisfy its interest in secular education through the instrument of private schools, it has a proper interest in the manner in which those schools perform their secular educational function.　.　.　.

Underlying these cases, and underlying also the legislative judgments that have preceded the court decisions, has been a recognition that private education has played and is playing a significant and valuable role in raising national levels of knowledge, competence, and experience.　Americans care about the quality of the secular education available to their children.　.　.　. Considering this attitude, the continued willingness to rely on private school

1.　.　.　.　New York permits private schools to submit to boards of education summaries of the requests for textbooks filed by individual students, and also permits private schools to store on their premises the textbooks being loaned by the Board of Education to the students.　.　.　.　So construing the statute, we find it in conformity with the Constitution, for the books are furnished for the use of individual students and at their request.

It should be noted that the record contains no evidence that any of the private schools in appellants' districts previously provided textbooks for their students.　There is some evidence that at least some of the schools did not. .　.　.　[Footnote by the Court.]

2.　.　.　.　New York State regulates private schools extensively, especially as to attendance and curriculum.　Regents examinations are given to private school students.　The basic requirement is that the instruction given in private schools satisfying the compulsory attendance law be "at least substantially equivalent to the instruction given to minors of like age and attainments at the public schools of the city or district where the minor resides."　.　.　. [Footnote by the Court.]

systems, including parochial systems, strongly suggests that a wide segment of informed opinion, legislative and otherwise, has found that those schools do an acceptable job of providing secular education to their students.[3] This judgment is further evidence that parochial schools are performing, in addition to their sectarian function, the task of secular education.

Against this background of judgment and experience, unchallenged in the meager record before us in this case, we cannot agree with appellants either that all teaching in a sectarian school is religious or that the processes of secular and religious training are so intertwined that secular textbooks furnished to students by the public are in fact instrumental in the teaching of religion. This case comes to us after summary judgment entered on the pleadings. Nothing in this record supports the proposition that all textbooks, whether they deal with mathematics, physics, foreign languages, history, or literature, are used by the parochial schools to teach religion. No evidence has been offered about particular schools, particular courses, particular teachers, or particular books. We are unable to hold, based solely on judicial notice, that this statute results in unconstitutional involvement of the State with religious instruction . . . .

Affirmed.*

Mr. Justice HARLAN, concurring.

Although I join the opinion and judgment of the Court, I wish to emphasize certain of the principles which I believe to be central to the determination of this case, and which I think are implicit in the Court's decision. . . . I would hold that where the contested governmental activity is calculated to achieve nonreligious purposes otherwise within the competence of the State, and where the activity does not involve the State "so significantly and directly in the realm of the sectarian as to give rise to . . . divisive influences and inhibitions of freedom" [Schempp], it is not forbidden by the religious clauses of the First Amendment.

In my opinion, § 701 of the Education Law of New York does not employ religion as its standard for action or inaction, and is not otherwise inconsistent with these principles.

Mr. Justice BLACK, dissenting. . . .

The Everson and McCollum cases plainly interpret the First and Fourteenth Amendments as protecting the taxpayers of a State from being compelled to pay taxes to their government to support the agencies of private religious organizations the taxpayers oppose. To authorize a State to tax its resi-

---

3. In 1965–1966 in New York State, over 900,000 students, or 22.2% of total state enrollment, attended nonpublic schools. The comparable statistic for the Nation was at least 10%. [Footnote by the Court.]

* Reliance on cases such as Allen did not save a Mississippi lending program to students in both public and private schools, where the State made no effort to exclude private schools with racially discriminatory policies.

Norwood v. Harrison, 413 U.S. 455 (1973) (see chap. 11, sec. 2). Chief Justice Burger stated that the "leeway for indirect aid to sectarian schools," though "narrow," was broader than the channel for permissible aid to racially discriminatory private schools. He noted that, "although the Constitution does not proscribe private bias, it places no value on discrimination as it does on the values inherent in the Free Exercise Clause."

dents for such church purposes is to put the State squarely in the religious activities of certain religious groups that happen to be strong enough politically to write their own religious preferences and prejudices into the laws. This links state and churches together in controlling the lives and destinies of our citizenship—a citizenship composed of people of myriad religious faiths, some of them bitterly hostile to and completely intolerant of the others. It was to escape laws precisely like this that a large part of the Nation's early immigrants fled to this country.   . . .

[Books in sectarian schools], although "secular," realistically will in some way inevitably tend to propagate the religious views of the favored sect. [I]t is not difficult to distinguish books, which are the heart of any school, from bus fares, which provide a convenient and helpful general public transportation service. With respect to the former, state financial support actively and directly assists the teaching and propagation of sectarian religious viewpoints in clear conflict with the First Amendment's establishment bar; with respect to the latter, the State merely provides a general and nondiscriminatory transportation service in no way related to substantive religious views and beliefs.

. . . It requires no prophet to foresee that on the argument used to support this law others could be upheld providing for state or federal government funds to buy property on which to erect religious school buildings or to erect the buildings themselves, to pay the salaries of the religious school teachers, and finally to have the sectarian religious groups cease to rely on voluntary contributions of members of their sects while waiting for the Government to pick up all the bills for the religious schools. . . . The First Amendment's prohibition against governmental establishment of religion was written on the assumption that state aid to religion and religious schools generates discord, disharmony, hatred, and strife among our people, and that any government that supplies such aids is to that extent a tyranny. . . .

Mr. Justice DOUGLAS, dissenting. . . .

The statute on its face empowers each parochial school to determine for itself which textbooks will be eligible for loans to its students. [The] initial and crucial selection is undoubtedly made by the parochial school's principal or its individual instructors, who are, in the case of Roman Catholic schools, normally priests or nuns.

The next step under the Act is an "individual request" for an eligible textbook, but the State Education Department has ruled that a pupil may make his request to the local public board of education through a "private school official." . . . The role of the local public school board is to decide whether to veto the selection made by the parochial school. This is done by determining first whether the text has been or should be "approved" for use in public schools and second whether the text is "secular," "non-religious," or "non-sectarian." The local boards apparently have broad discretion in exercising this veto power.

Thus the statutory system provides that the parochial school will ask for the books that it wants. Can there be the slightest doubt that the head of the parochial school will select the book or books that best promote its sectarian creed?

If the board of education supinely submits by approving and supplying the sectarian or sectarian-oriented textbooks, the struggle to keep church and state separate has been lost. If the board resists, then the battle line between church and state will have been drawn and the contest will be on to keep the school board independent or to put it under church domination and control.

Whatever may be said of Everson, there is nothing ideological about a bus. There is nothing ideological about a school lunch, or a public nurse, or a scholarship. . . . The textbook goes to the very heart of education in a parochial school. It is the chief, although not solitary, instrumentality for propagating a particular religious creed or faith. How can we possibly approve such state aid to a religion? . . . Even where the treatment given to a particular topic in a school textbook is not blatantly sectarian, it will necessarily have certain shadings that will lead a parochial school to prefer one text over another. . . .

Mr. Justice FORTAS, dissenting. . . .

This case is not within the principle of [Everson]. Apart from the differences between textbooks and bus rides, the present statute does not call for extending to children attending sectarian schools the same service or facility extended to children in public schools. This statute calls for furnishing special, separate, and particular books, specially, separately, and particularly chosen by religious sects or their representatives for use in their sectarian schools. . . .

THE BURGER COURT AND FINANCIAL AIDS

During the sixties, the mounting pressures for financial aid to parochial education led to the enactment of major federal and state programs. For example, congressional enactments [1] made parochial institutions eligible for federal financial aid, in the wake of extensive constitutional debates.[2] Would the varied programs pass muster under the establishment clause? The Court assured that it would play a significant role in delineating the constitutional limits when it recognized taxpayers' standing to challenge federal spending programs on establishment grounds in Flast v. Cohen, 392 U.S. 83 (1968) (chap. 15 below). And even without taxpayers' standing, access to the Court for some establishment clause attacks was possible, as Board of Education v. Allen illustrates. The Allen decision's application of

1. E. g., the Higher Education Facilities Act of 1963 (see the 1971 decision in Tilton v. Richardson, below) and the Elementary and Secondary Education Act of 1965.

2. See, e. g., the HEW Memorandum, The Impact of the First Amendment to the Constitution Upon Federal Aid to Education (1961), and the National Catholic Welfare Conference paper, The Constitutionality of the Inclusion of Church-Related Schools in Federal Aid to Education (1961), both reprinted in 50 Georgetown L.J. 349, 397 (1961). See also, e. g., Drinan, Federal Aid to Education (1962), and Religion, the Courts and Public Policy (1963); compare Freund, "Public Aid to Parochial Schools," 82 Harv.L.Rev. 1680 (1969), and Choper, "The Establishment Clause and Aid to Parochial Schools," 56 Calif.L.Rev. 260 (1968).

The HEW memorandum suggested as relevant criteria the closeness of the benefits to the "religious aspects" of the institution aided, the economic significance of the benefits, and "what alternative means are available to accomplish the legislative objectives without resulting in the religious benefits ordinarily proscribed."

the "purpose and primary effect" test of Schempp indicated some willingness to permit assistance to parochial education. But financial aid programs fared less well when challenges in profusion reached the Burger Court.

The Burger Court had its first opportunity to speak to the establishment issue in a case raising the problem of tax exemptions for church property; and in that Walz case, which follows, it added the strand of "entanglement" to the "purpose and effect" emphasis of Schempp.[3] These "purpose, effect, and entanglement" criteria proved fatal for most aid programs below the college level that reached the Burger Court in subsequent years, as the cases beginning with Lemon v. Kurtzman in 1971 illustrate. Are the modern criteria persuasive in statement and application? Should the New York textbook program in Allen survive scrutiny under those modern criteria?[4] What, if any, avenues for aid to parochial education remain open under the modern cases? Would a school voucher program, for example, survive constitutional challenge?[5] Does the barrier to many financial aid programs under the establishment clause raise questions of impinging on the free exercise guarantee, in view of the modern cases considered in sec. 2 below?

PROPERTY TAX EXEMPTIONS, THE WALZ CASE, AND THE "ENTANGLEMENT" EMPHASIS

WALZ v. TAX COMMISSION, 397 U.S. 664 (1970), rejected, by an 8 to 1 vote, a challenge to New York's property tax exemption for property used solely for religious purposes. The exemption was granted pursuant to a state constitutional mandate barring taxes on "real or personal property used exclusively for religious, educational or charitable purposes." In reviewing the past decisions, Chief Justice Burger's majority opinion commented: "In attempting to articulate the scope of the two Religion Clauses, the Court's opinions reflect the limitations inherent in formulating general principles on a case-by-case basis. The considerable internal inconsistency in the opinions of the Court derives from what, in retrospect, may have been too sweeping utterances on aspects of these clauses that seemed clear in relation to the particular cases but have limited meaning as general principles. The Court has struggled to find a neutral course between the two Religion Clauses both of which are cast in absolute terms, and either of which, if expanded to a logical extreme, would tend to clash with the other. . . . The course of constitutional neutrality in this area cannot be an absolutely straight line; rigidity could well defeat the basic purpose of these provisions, which is to insure that no religion be sponsored or favored, none commanded, and none inhibited. The general principle deducible [from the decisions] is this: that we will not tolerate either governmentally established religion or governmental interference with religion. Short of those expressly proscribed governmental acts there is room for play in the joints productive of a benevolent

3. See Bittker, "Churches, Taxes and the Constitution," 78 Yale L.J. 1285 (1969).

4. Note the sharp divisions on the Court in responding to that question in Meek v. Pittinger, 421 U.S. —— (1975) (in the final note in sec. 1).

5. See Note, "Education Vouchers: The Fruit of the Lemon Tree," 24 Stan.L.Rev. 687 (1972). See also Giannella, "Lemon and Tilton: The Bitter and the Sweet of Church-State Entanglement," 1971 Sup.Ct.Rev. 147.

neutrality which will permit religious exercise to exist without sponsorship and without interference. . . . No perfect or absolute separation is really possible."

Turning to the property tax exemption, the Chief Justice noted that its purpose "is neither sponsorship nor hostility." Rather, the State "has granted exemption to all houses of religious worship within a broad class of property owned by nonprofit, quasi-public corporations." The limits of permissible state accommodation to religion "are by no means co-extensive with the non-interference mandated by the Free Exercise Clause." He emphasized: "We find it unnecessary to justify the tax exemption on the social welfare services or 'good works' that some churches perform for parishioners and others." He explained: "To give emphasis to so variable an aspect of the work of religious bodies would introduce an element of governmental evaluation and standards as to the worth of particular social welfare programs, thus producing a kind of continuing day-to-day relationship which the policy of neutrality seeks to minimize."

Finding a justifiable legislative purpose was not the end of the scrutiny, however: "We must also be sure that the end result—the effect—is not an excessive government entanglement with religion. The test is inescapably one of degree." But that "effect" requirement was satisfied here as well: "Granting tax exemption to churches necessarily operates to afford an indirect economic benefit and also gives rise to some, but yet a lesser, involvement than taxing them. In analyzing either alternative the questions are whether the involvement is excessive, and whether it is a continuing one calling for official and continuing surveillance leading to an impermissible degree of entanglement." [Note the reliance on this "entanglement" theme in the 1971 Financial Aid Cases, which follow.] Here, the entanglement was not excessive: "Separation in this context cannot mean absence of all contact." Moreover, there was a long, widespread tradition of tax exemptions: this was a "kind of benevolent neutrality toward churches and religious exercise generally."

Justice Brennan submitted a lengthy concurring opinion on the basis of his approach in Schempp and accordingly examined "the history, purpose, and operation" of church tax exemptions. He emphasized that the principal effect of exemptions is "to carry out secular purposes—the encouragement of public service activities and of a pluralistic society." There was another concurring opinion, by Justice Harlan. Justice Douglas' dissent concluded: "The present involvement of government in religion may seem de minimis. But it is, I fear, a long step down the Establishment path."

LEMON v. KURTZMAN

403 U.S. 602, 91 S.Ct. 2105, 29 L.Ed.2d 745 (1971).

Appeal from the United States District Court for the Eastern District of Pennsylvania.*

Mr. Chief Justice BURGER delivered the opinion of the Court.

These two appeals raise questions as to Pennsylvania and Rhode Island statutes providing state aid to church-related elementary and secondary schools. . . .

. . . The Rhode Island Salary Supplement Act [of 1969] rests on the legislative finding that the quality of education in nonpublic elementary schools has been jeopardized by the rapidly rising salaries [and] authorizes state officials to supplement the salaries of teachers of secular subjects in non-public elementary schools by paying directly to a teacher an amount not in excess of 15% of his current annual salary. As supplemented, however, a nonpublic school teacher's salary cannot exceed the maximum paid to teachers in the State's public schools, and the recipient [must] teach in a nonpublic school at which the average per-pupil expenditure on secular educa-tion is less than the average in the State's public schools during a specified period. Appellant state Commissioner of Education also requires eligible schools to submit financial data. If this information indicates a per-pupil ex-penditure in excess of the statutory limitation, the records of the school in question must be examined in order to assess how much of the expenditure is attributable to secular education and how much to religious activity.

The Act also requires that teachers eligible for salary supplements must teach only those subjects that are offered in the State's public schools. They must use "only teaching materials which are used in the public schools." Finally, any teacher applying for a salary supplement must first agree in writing "not to teach a course in religion for so long as or during such time as he or she receives any salary supplements" under the Act. [All of the teachers who have applied for supplements teach in Roman Catholic schools. The District Court held the Act unconstitutional.] We affirm.

. . . Pennsylvania has adopted a program which has some but not all of the features of the Rhode Island program. [Like the Rhode Island law, it was enacted in response to the financial crisis in the nonpub-lic schools.] The [1968] statute authorizes [the State] to "purchase" speci-fied "secular educational services" from nonpublic schools. Under the "con-tracts" authorized by the statute, the State directly reimburses nonpublic schools solely for their actual expenditures for teachers' salaries, textbooks, and instructional materials. A school seeking reimbursement must maintain pre-scribed accounting procedures that identify the "separate" cost of the "secular educational service." These accounts are subject to state audit. . . . There are several significant statutory restrictions on state aid. Reim-bursement is limited to courses "presented in the curricula of the public schools." It is further limited "solely" to courses in the following "secular"

* Together with Earley v. DiCenso and Robinson v. DiCenso, both on appeal from the United States District Court for the District of Rhode Island.

subjects: mathematics, modern foreign languages, physical science, and physical education. Textbooks and instructional materials included in the program must be approved by the state Superintendent of Public Instruction. Finally, the statute prohibits reimbursement for any course that contains "any subject matter expressing religious teaching, or the morals or forms of worship of any sect." More than 96% of [the pupils in schools receiving aid] attend church-related schools, and most of these schools are affiliated with the Roman Catholic church. The [District Court held] that the Act violated neither the Establishment nor the Free Exercise Clause, Chief Judge Hastie dissenting. We reverse.

.   .   .   Candor compels acknowledgement [that] we can only dimly perceive the lines of demarcation in this extraordinarily sensitive area of constitutional law.   .   .   .   Every analysis in this area must begin with consideration of the cumulative criteria developed by the Court over many years. Three such tests may be gleaned from our cases. First, the statute must have a secular legislative purpose; second, its principal or primary effect must be one that neither advances nor inhibits religion [Board of Education v. Allen]; finally, the statute must not foster "an excessive government entanglement with religion." [Walz].

Inquiry into the legislative purposes of the Pennsylvania and Rhode Island statutes affords no basis for a conclusion that the legislative intent was to advance religion.   .   .   .   [The two legislatures sought] to create statutory restrictions designed to guarantee the separation between secular and religious educational functions and to ensure that State financial aid supports only the former.   .   .   .   We need not decide whether these legislative precautions restrict the principal or primary effect of the programs to the point where they do not offend the Religion Clauses, for we conclude that the cumulative impact of the entire relationship arising under the statutes in each State involves excessive entanglement between government and religion.

[Walz] tended to confine rather than enlarge the area of permissible state involvement with religious institutions by calling for close scrutiny of the degree of entanglement involved in the relationship. [T]otal separation is not possible in an absolute sense.   .   .   .   Fire inspections, building and zoning regulations, and state requirements under compulsory school-attendance laws are examples of necessary and permissible contacts.   .   .   . Judicial caveats against entanglement must recognize that the line of separation, far from being a "wall," is a blurred, indistinct, and variable barrier depending on all the circumstances of a particular relationship.   .   .   .   In order to determine whether the government entanglement with religion is excessive, we must examine the character and purposes of the institutions that are benefited, the nature of the aid that the State provides, and the resulting relationship between the government and the religious authority.   .   .   . Here we find that both statutes foster an impermissible degree of entanglement.

.   .   .   The District Court made extensive findings on the grave potential for excessive entanglement that inheres in the religious character and purpose of the Roman Catholic elementary schools of Rhode Island. [It] concluded that the parochial schools constituted "an integral part of the

religious mission of the Catholic Church." [The] process of inculcating religious doctrine is, of course, enhanced by the impressionable age of the pupils, in primary schools particularly. In short, parochial schools involve substantial religious activity and purpose.

The substantial religious character of these church-related schools gives rise to entangling church-state relationships of the kind the Religion Clauses sought to avoid. . . . The dangers and corresponding entanglements are enhanced by the particular form of aid that the Rhode Island Act provides. Our decisions from Everson to Allen have permitted the States to provide church-related schools with secular, neutral, or nonideological services, facilities, or materials [—e. g., bus transportation, school lunches, public health services, and secular textbooks]. In Allen the Court refused to make assumptions, on a meager record, about the religious content of the textbooks. [We] cannot, however, refuse here to recognize that teachers have a substantially different ideological character than books. In terms of potential for involving some aspect of faith or morals in secular subjects, a textbook's content is ascertainable, but a teacher's handling of a subject is not. We cannot ignore the danger that a teacher under religious control and discipline poses to the separation of the religious from the purely secular aspects of pre-college education. The conflict of functions inheres in the situation. In our view the record shows these dangers are present to a substantial degree. [Several] teachers testified, however, that they did not inject religion into their secular classes. And the District Court found that religious values did not necessarily affect the content of the secular instruction. But [the record] suggests the potential if not actual hazards of this form of state aid. The teacher is employed by a religious organization, subject to the direction and discipline of religious authorities, and works in a system dedicated to rearing children in a particular faith. . . .

We need not and do not assume that teachers in parochial schools will be guilty of bad faith or any conscious design to evade the limitations imposed by the statute and the First Amendment. We simply recognize that a dedicated religious person, teaching in a school affiliated with his or her faith and operated to inculcate its tenets, will inevitably experience great difficulty in remaining religiously neutral. Doctrines and faith are not inculcated or advanced by neutrals. . . .

[The State has] carefully conditioned its aid with pervasive restrictions. . . . A comprehensive, discriminating, and continuing state surveillance will inevitably be required to ensure that these restrictions are obeyed and the First Amendment otherwise respected. Unlike a book, a teacher cannot be inspected once so as to determine the extent and intent of his or her personal beliefs and subjective acceptance of the limitations imposed by the First Amendment. These prophylactic contacts will involve excessive and enduring entanglement between state and church.

There is another area of entanglement in the Rhode Island program that gives concern. [The] state inspection [of school records] and evaluation of the religious content of a religious organization is fraught with the sort of entanglement that the Constitution forbids. It is a relationship pregnant with dangers of excessive government direction of church schools . . . ..

. . . The Pennsylvania statute [also] fosters this kind of relationship. [That law], moreover, has the further defect of providing state financial aid directly to the church-related school. This factor distinguishes both Everson and Allen . . .. The history of government grants of a continuing cash subsidy indicates that such programs have almost always been accompanied by varying measures of control and surveillance. The government cash grants before us now provide no basis for predicting that comprehensive measures of surveillance and controls will not follow. In particular the government's post-audit power to inspect and evaluate a church-related school's financial records and to determine which expenditures are religious and which are secular creates an intimate and continuing relationship between church and state.

A broader base of entanglement of yet a different character is presented by the divisive political potential of these state programs. In a community where such a large number of pupils are served by church-related schools, it can be assumed that state assistance will entail considerable political activity [by supporters and opponents]. Candidates will be forced to declare and voters to choose. It would be unrealistic to ignore the fact that many people confronted with issues of this kind will find their votes aligned with their faith.

Ordinarily political debate and division, however vigorous or even partisan, are normal and healthy manifestations of our democratic system of government, but political division along religious lines was one of the principal evils against which the First Amendment was intended to protect. [Freund, 82 Harv.L.Rev. 1680, 1692 (1969).] It conflicts with our whole history and tradition to permit questions of the Religion Clauses to assume such importance in our legislatures and in our elections that they could divert attention from the myriad issues and problems which confront every level of government. . . . Here [unlike Walz] we are confronted with successive and very likely permanent annual appropriations that benefit relatively few religious groups. Political fragmentation and divisiveness on religious lines are thus likely to be intensified [and] are aggravated in these two statutory programs by the need for continuing annual appropriations and the likelihood of larger and larger demands as costs and populations grow. . . .

In Walz it was argued that a tax exemption for places of religious worship would prove to be the first step in an inevitable progression leading to the establishment of state churches and state religion. [That] progression argument [is] more persuasive here. We have no long history of state aid to church-related educational institutions comparable to 200 years of tax exemption for churches. [M]odern governmental programs have self-perpetuating and self-expanding propensities. These internal pressures are only enhanced when the schemes involve institutions whose legitimate needs are growing and whose interests have substantial political support. Nor can we fail to see that in constitutional adjudication some steps, which when taken were thought to approach "the verge," have become the platform for yet further steps. . . . The dangers are increased by the difficulty of perceiving in advance exactly where the "verge" of the precipice lies. As well as constituting an independent evil against which

the Religion Clauses were intended to protect, involvement or entanglement between government and religion serves as a warning signal.

Finally, nothing we have said can be construed to disparage the role of church-related elementary and secondary schools in our national life. Their contribution has been and is enormous. Nor do we ignore their economic plight in a period of rising costs and expanding need. . . . The sole question is whether state aid to these schools can be squared with the dictates of the Religion Clauses. . . .

The judgment of the Rhode Island District Court in [DiCenso] is affirmed. The judgment of the Pennsylvania District Court in [Lemon] is reversed, and the case is remanded . . . . .*

Mr. Justice DOUGLAS, whom Mr. Justice BLACK joins, concurring. . . . The intrusion of government into religious schools through grants, supervision, or surveillance may result in [establishment] when what the State does enthrones a particular sect for overt or subtle propagation of its faith. Those activities of the State may also intrude on the Free Exercise Clause by depriving a teacher, under threats of reprisals, of the right to give sectarian construction or interpretation of, say, history and literature, or to use the teaching of such subjects to inculcate a religious creed or dogma.

If the government closed its eyes to the manner in which these grants are actually used it would be allowing public funds to promote sectarian education. If it did not close its eyes but undertook the surveillance needed, it would, I fear, intermeddle in parochial affairs in a way that would breed only rancor and dissension. . . . In my view the taxpayers' forced contribution to the parochial schools in the present cases violates the First Amendment.†

* On remand, the District Court enjoined further payments under the program held unconstitutional, but permitted Pennsylvania to reimburse schools for services performed prior to the decision in the principal case. The Supreme Court affirmed in a 5 to 3 decision. Lemon v. Kurtzman, 411 U.S. 192 (1973). Chief Justice Burger's opinion was joined only by Justices Blackmun, Powell and Rehnquist. Justice White concurred in the result. The Chief Justice concluded that "the proposed distribution of state funds to Pennsylvania's nonpublic schools will not substantially undermine the constitutional interests at stake in Lemon I." He noted that "this is not a case where it could be said that appellees acted in bad faith or that they relied on a plainly unlawful statute." Justice Douglas' dissent stated: "Retroactivity of the decision in Lemon I goes to the very core of the integrity of the judicial process."

† Note also the separate opinions of Justices Brennan and White after Tilton below, applicable to these cases as well.

Justice Marshall took no part in the decision of the Pennsylvania case. As to the Rhode Island case, he noted: "While intimating no view as to the continuing vitality of [Everson], he concurs in Mr. Justice Douglas' opinion." [Note the disposition, on the same day as these decisions, of appeals challenging a Minnesota statute authorizing use of public funds to transport children to sectarian schools. The Court dismissed the appeals "for want of a substantial federal question"; Justice Douglas and Marshall dissented. Americans United, Inc. v. Independent School Dist. and Stark v. Mattheis, 403 U.S. 945 (1971).]

TILTON v. RICHARDSON

403 U.S. 672, 91 S.Ct. 2091, 29 L.Ed.2d 790 (1971).

Appeal from the United States District Court for the District of Connecticut.

Mr. Chief Justice BURGER announced the judgment of the Court and an opinion in which Mr. Justice HARLAN, Mr. Justice STEWART and Mr. Justice BLACKMUN join.

This appeal presents important constitutional questions as to federal aid for church-related colleges and universities under Title I of the Higher Education Facilities Act of 1963, which provides construction grants for buildings and facilities used exclusively for secular educational purposes. . . .

The Act is administered by the United States Commissioner of Education. He advises colleges and universities applying for funds that under the Act no part of the project may be used for sectarian instruction, religious worship, or the programs of a divinity school. The Commissioner requires applicants to provide assurances that these restrictions will be respected. The United States retains a 20-year interest in any facility constructed with Title I funds. If, during this period, the recipient violates the statutory conditions, the United States is entitled to recover an amount equal to the proportion of its present value that the federal grant bore to the original cost of the facility. During the 20-year period, the statutory restrictions are enforced by the Office of Education primarily by way of on-site inspections. [The lower court sustained the constitutionality of the Act.]

The stated legislative purpose [to assist colleges "in their efforts to accommodate rapidly growing numbers of youths"] expresses a legitimate secular objective entirely appropriate for governmental action. [T]he Act is challenged on the ground that its primary effect is to aid the religious purposes of church-related colleges and universities. . . . The crucial question is not whether some benefit accrues to a religious institution as a consequence of the legislative program, but whether its principal or primary effect advances religion. . . .

The Act itself was carefully drafted to ensure that the federally subsidized facilities would be devoted to the secular and not the religious function of the recipient institutions. . . . These restrictions have been enforced in the Act's actual administration, and the record shows that some church-related institutions have been required to disgorge benefits for failure to obey them. [None] of the four church-related institutions in this case has violated the statutory restrictions. . . .

Appellants instead rely on the argument that government may not subsidize any activities of an institution of higher learning which in some of its programs teaches religious doctrines. This argument rests on [Everson]. [A]ppellants' position depends on the validity of the proposition that religion so permeates the secular education provided by church-related colleges and universities that their religious and secular educational functions are in fact inseparable. [The record] provides no basis for any such assumption here.

[T]he schools were characterized by an atmosphere of academic freedom rather than religious indoctrination. . . .

Rather than focus on the [four institutions] involved in this case, however, appellants seek to shift our attention to a "composite profile" that they have constructed of the "typical sectarian" institution of higher education. . . . Individual projects can be properly evaluated if and when challenges arise. [W]e cannot, however, strike down an Act of Congress on the basis of a hypothetical "profile."

Although we reject appellants' broad constitutional arguments we do perceive an aspect in which the statute's enforcement provisions are inadequate to ensure that the impact of the federal aid will not advance religion. . . . Limiting the prohibition for religious use of the structure to 20 years obviously opens the facility to use for any purpose at the end of that period. . . . If, at the end of 20 years the building is, for example, converted into a chapel or otherwise used to promote religious interests, the original federal grant will in part have the effect of advancing religion.

To this extent the Act therefore trespasses on the Religion Clauses. The restrictive obligations of a recipient institution cannot, compatibly with the Religion Clauses, expire while the building has substantial value. This circumstance does not require us to invalidate the entire Act, however. [T]here is no basis for assuming that the Act would have failed of passage without this provision; nor will its excision impair either the operation or administration of the Act in any significant respect.

We next turn to the question of whether excessive entanglements characterize the relationship between government and church under the Act. [Walz.] Here, [compared to Lemon and DiCenso], three factors substantially diminish the extent and the potential danger of the entanglement.

There are generally significant differences between the religious aspects of church-related institutions of higher learning and parochial elementary and secondary schools. . . . There is substance to the contention that college students are less impressionable and less susceptible to religious indoctrination. Common observation would seem to support that view, and Congress may well have entertained it. . . . Furthermore, by their very nature, college and postgraduate courses tend to limit the opportunities for sectarian influence by virtue of their own internal disciplines. Many church-related colleges are characterized by a high degree of academic freedom and seek to evoke free and critical responses from their students.

Since religious indoctrination is not a substantial purpose or activity of these church-related colleges and universities, there is less likelihood than in primary and secondary schools that religion will permeate the area of secular education. This reduces the risk that government aid will in fact serve to support religious activities. Correspondingly the necessity for intensive government surveillance is diminished and the resulting entanglements between government and religion lessened. Such inspection as may be necessary to ascertain that the facilities are devoted to secular education is minimal . . . . .

The entanglement between church and state is also lessened here [in contrast to Lemon] by the nonideological character of the aid which the

Government provides. [Here], the government provides facilities that are themselves religiously neutral. The risks of Government aid to religion and the corresponding need for surveillance are therefore reduced. Finally, government entanglements with religion are reduced by the circumstance that, unlike [the Pennsylvania program], the government aid here is a one-time, single-purpose construction grant. There are no continuing financial relationships or dependencies, no annual audits, and no government analysis of an institution's expenditures on secular as distinguished from religious activities. Inspection as to use is a minimal contact.

No one of these three factors standing alone is necessarily controlling; cumulatively all of them shape a narrow and limited relationship with government which involves fewer and less significant contacts than the two state schemes before us in Lemon and DiCenso. . . . We think that cumulatively these three factors also substantially lessen the potential for divisive religious fragmentation in the political arena. . . . The potential for divisiveness inherent in the essentially local problems of primary and secondary schools is significantly less with respect to a college or university whose student constituency is not local but diverse and widely dispersed.

. . . Appellants claim that the Free Exercise Clause is violated because they are compelled to pay taxes, the proceeds of which in part finance grants under the Act. Appellants, however, are unable to identify any coercion directed at the practice or exercise of their religious beliefs. Their share of the cost of the grants under the Act is not fundamentally distinguishable from the impact of the tax exemption sustained in Walz or the provision of textbooks upheld in Allen. . . .

Vacated and remanded.

Mr. Justice WHITE, concurring in part and dissenting in part, [in state and federal grants cases].

. . . . It is enough for me that the [public is] financing a separable secular function of overriding importance in order to sustain the legislation here challenged. That religion and private interests other than education may substantially benefit does not convert these laws into impermissible establishments of religion. It is unnecessary, therefore, to urge that the Free Exercise Clause of the First Amendment at least permits government in some respects to modify and mould its secular programs out of express concern for free exercise values. . . . The Establishment Clause, however, coexists in the First Amendment with the Free Exercise Clause and the latter is surely relevant in cases such as these. Where a state program seeks to ensure the proper education of its young, in private as well as public schools, free exercise considerations at least counsel against refusing support for students attending parochial schools simply because in that setting they are also being instructed in the tenets of the faith they are constitutionally free to practice.

I would sustain both the federal and the Rhode Island programs at issue in these cases . . . .[1] Although I would also reject the facial challenge

---

1. I accept the Court's invalidation of the provision in the federal legislation whereby the restriction on the use of buildings constructed with federal funds terminates after 20 years. [Footnote by Justice White.]

to the Pennsylvania statute, I concur in the judgment in [Lemon] for the reasons given below.

The Court strikes down the Rhode Island statute on its face.   .   .   . The difficulty with this is twofold. [In the first place, the Court] points to nothing in this record indicating that any participating teacher had inserted religion into his secular teaching or had had any difficulty in avoiding doing so.   .   .   .   Secondly, the Court accepts the model for the Catholic elementary and secondary schools that it rejected for the Catholic universities or colleges in the Tilton case.   .   .   .

The Court thus creates an insoluble paradox for the State and the parochial schools. The State cannot finance secular instruction if it permits religion to be taught in the same classroom; but if it exacts a promise that religion not be so taught—a promise the school and its teachers are quite willing and on this record able to give—and enforces it, it is then entangled in the "no entanglement" aspect of the Court's Establishment Clause jurisprudence.

Why the federal program in the Tilton case is not embroiled with the same difficulties is never adequately explained. Surely the notion that college students are more mature and resistant to indoctrination is a makeweight, for in Tilton there is careful note of the federal condition on funding and the enforcement mechanism available.   .   .   .

[The Court] makes much of the fact that under the federal scheme the grant to a religious institution is a one-time matter. But this argument is without real force. It is apparent that federal interest in any grant will be a continuing one since the conditions attached to the grant must be enforced. More important, the federal grant program is an ongoing one. The same grant will not be repeated, but new ones to the same or different schools will be made year after year. Thus the same potential for recurring political controversy accompanies the federal program.   .   .   .

In [Lemon] I agree, however, that the complaint should not have been dismissed for failure to state a cause of action. [O]ne of the legal theories stated in the complaint was that the Pennsylvania Act "finances and participates in the blending of sectarian and secular instruction." [I would] remand the case for trial, thereby holding the Pennsylvania legislation valid on its face but leaving open the question of its validity as applied   .   .   . ..

Mr. Justice DOUGLAS, with whom Mr. Justice BLACK and Mr. Justice MARSHALL concur, dissenting.   .   .   .

The public purpose in secular education is, to be sure, furthered by the [federal] program. Yet the sectarian purpose is aided by making the parochial school system viable. [I]t is hardly impressive that rather than giving a smaller amount of money annually over a large period of years, Congress instead gives a large amount all at once. The plurality's distinction is in effect that small violations of the First Amendment over a period of years are unconstitutional (see Lemon and DiCenso) while a huge violation occurring only once is de minimis. I cannot agree with such sophistry.
.   .   .

[S]urveillance creates an entanglement of government and religion which the First Amendment was designed to avoid.   .   .   .   The price of the subsidy under the Act is violation of the Free Exercise Clause. Could a course in the History of Methodism be taught in a federally financed build-

ing? Would a religiously slanted version of the Reformation or Quebec politics under Duplessis be permissible? How can the Government know what is taught in the federally financed building without a continuous auditing of classroom instruction? Yet both the Free Exercise Clause and academic freedom are violated when the Government agent must be present to determine whether the course content is satisfactory. . . .

Mr. Justice BRENNAN [in state and federal grants cases].

I agree that the judgments in [DiCenso] must be affirmed. In my view the judgment in [Lemon] must be reversed outright. I dissent in [Tilton]. In my view [the Federal Act] is unconstitutional insofar as it authorizes grants of federal tax monies to sectarian institutions, but is unconstitutional only to that extent. I therefore think that our remand of the case should be limited to the direction of a hearing to determine whether the four institutional appellees here are sectarian institutions. . . .

[F]or more than a century, the consensus, enforced by legislatures and courts with substantial consistency, has been that public subsidy of sectarian schools constitutes an impermissible involvement of secular with religious institutions. If this history is not itself compelling against the validity of the three subsidy statutes, [other] forms of governmental involvement that each of the three statutes requires tip the scales in my view against the validity of each of them. . . . The picture of state inspectors prowling the halls of parochial schools and auditing classroom instruction surely raises more than an imagined specter of governmental "secularization of a creed." The same dangers attend the federal subsidy even if less obviously. . . .

The common ingredient of the three prongs of [my test in Schempp] is whether the statutes involve government in the "essentially religious activities" of religious institutions. My analysis of the operation, purposes, and effects of these statutes leads me inescapably to the conclusion that they do impermissibly involve the States and the Federal Government with the "essentially religious activities" of sectarian educational institutions. [Moreover], I think each government uses "essentially religious means to serve governmental ends where secular means would suffice." . . .

. . . I emphasize that a sectarian university is the equivalent in the realm of higher education of the Catholic elementary schools in Rhode Island; it is an educational institution in which the propagation and advancement of a particular religion are a primary function of the institution. I do not believe that construction grants to such a sectarian institution are permissible. The reason is not that religion "permeates" the secular education that is provided. Rather, it is that the secular education is provided within the environment of religion; the institution is dedicated to two goals, secular education *and* religious instruction. When aid flows directly to the institution, both functions benefit. . . .

The plurality also argues that no impermissible entanglement exists [in Tilton]. I do not see any significant difference in the Federal Government telling the sectarian university not to teach any nonsecular subjects in a certain building, and Rhode Island telling the Catholic school teacher not to teach religion. The vice is the creation through subsidy of a relationship in which the government polices the teaching practices of a religious school or university. . . .

FINANCIAL AID TO EDUCATION SINCE LEMON AND TILTON

Introduction. Two years after Lemon and Tilton, the Court considered new varieties of state support for sectarian education. In the 1973 decisions (notes 1 and 2), all state efforts to aid parochial education below the college level fell afoul of the establishment clause; only a scheme for assistance to a college survived attack. Justice Powell wrote the majority opinions in most of the cases. He accepted the three-pronged test, "purpose, effect, and entanglement." All of the programs were found to have acceptable secular "purposes." And, in contrast to the 1971 cases, the Court had relatively little to say about "entanglement." It was the "effect" criterion that proved the fatal obstacle in most of the cases. Chief Justice Burger, who had written the 1971 majority opinions, now found himself in dissent in several of the cases, insisting that the majority was imposing excessive restrictions on state aid.*

Justice Powell's majority opinion in the major case purported to apply the "now well-defined three-part test." But does his application of that test, and particularly his emphasis on the forbidden "effects," suggest that "the ingenious plans for channeling state aid to sectarian schools" face greater obstacles than ever in the Court? What if any channels to aid parochial education remained available after the 1973 cases? Note also the 1975 decision (note 3 below) striking down additional varieties of school aids —but once again sustaining textbook loans to children. Is the sharply divided Court's line between the permissible and the impermissible a justifiable one? Is it likely to be a stable one?

1. *Committee for Public Educ. v. Nyquist.* The major 1973 case was COMMITTEE FOR PUBLIC EDUC. v. NYQUIST, 413 U.S. 756. That decision invalidated New York's three-part program for financial aid to nonpublic elementary and secondary education. The scheme included: (1) direct grants to nonpublic schools in low income areas for "maintenance and repair" of facilities; (2) tuition reimbursement grants for low income parents of children in nonpublic schools; and (3) income tax relief for middle income parents. The Court found flaws in all parts of this latest of "the ingenious plans for channeling state aid to sectarian schools that periodically reach" the Court. Part 1 failed by an 8 to 1 vote; the other parts were struck down by 6 to 3 margins. Justice White was the sole dissenter as to the "maintenance and repair" grants; Chief Justice Burger and Justice Rehnquist joined him in dissenting as to the tuition and tax provisions.

Justice Powell concentrated on that prong of "the now well-defined three-part test" that requires a law to "have a primary effect that neither advances nor inhibits religion" in order to "pass muster under the Establishment Clause." The "maintenance and repair" provision fell because its

---

* That is a characteristic sequence in establishment cases: repeatedly, the author of the majority opinion in one round of the battle dissents in the next round. In addition to Chief Justice Burger's move from majority to dissent between 1971 and 1973, note, e. g., Justice Black in Everson (1947 majority) and Zorach (1952 dissent), and Justice White in Allen (1968 majority) and Lemon (1971 dissent).

"effect, inevitably, is to subsidize and advance the religious mission of sectarian schools." "Virtually all" of the recipients of grants under that part of the program were Catholic schools. There were no restrictions that would keep the schools from spending the money to maintain facilities used for religious purposes; "nor do we think it possible within the context of these religion-oriented institutions to impose such restrictions." Cases like Everson and Allen were distinguishable: the channel for indirect aid "is a narrow one."

The tuition reimbursement program also failed the "effect" test. The Court rejected the argument that, under Everson and Allen, aid was permissible if it went directly to parents rather than the schools. Aid for such services as busing and police and fire protection, "provided in common to all citizens," was sufficiently separate from the religious function and was consistent with neutrality. Here, by contrast, "the effect of the aid is unmistakably to provide desired financial support for nonpublic, sectarian institutions." [1] Justice Powell was not persuaded by the fact that the money went to parents for reimbursement *after* they paid tuition, so that parents were not mere conduits for money going to the schools: the grants were nevertheless "an incentive to parents to send their children to sectarian schools." Nor could the tuition program be justified as an aid to the free exercise of religion. The state had argued that without such assistance, the right of the low income parents "to have their children educated in a religious environment 'is diminished or even denied.'" Justice Powell replied that the state could not enhance the opportunities of the poor to choose among types of education by a method "which can only be regarded as one 'advancing' religion." [2]

---

1. Justice Powell noted also that Allen and Everson were distinguishable because in those cases "the class of beneficiaries included *all* school children, those in public as well as those in private schools." Here, most of the nonpublic school children went to sectarian institutions. Justice Powell noted that "we need not decide whether the significantly religious character of the statute's beneficiaries might differentiate the present case from a case involving some form of public assistance (e. g., scholarships) made available generally without regard to the sectarian-nonsectarian, or public-nonpublic nature of the institution benefitted."
Justice Powell also disagreed with Chief Justice Burger's suggestion that tuition grants were analogous to programs benefitting "*all* school children" as in Allen and Everson because they provided comparable benefits to all parents of school children whether enrolled in public or nonpublic schools. He thought that "argument proves too much, for it would also provide a basis for approving through tuition grants the *complete subsidization* of all religious schools on the ground that such action is necessary if the State is fully to equalize the position of parents who elect such schools—a result wholly at variance with the Establishment Clause."

2. In a footnote, Justice Powell also rejected the argument that the Court must decide whether the "primary" effect of the tuition grant program was "to subsidize religion or to promote" legitimate secular objectives. He stated: "We do not think such metaphysical judgments are either possible or necessary. Our cases simply do not support the notion that a law found to have a 'primary' effect to promote some legitimate end under the State's police power is immune from further examination to ascertain whether it also has the direct and immediate effect of advancing religion." Sunday Closing Laws were upheld in McGowan, he insisted, only because they had only a "remote and incidental" effect advantageous to religious institutions.

Similarly, the tax benefit provision for middle income parents produced an unconstitutional effect. In form, the provision was a tax deduction, but the lower court thought it was "in effect a tax *credit*," because the deduction was not related to the amount actually spent for tuition and was designed to yield a predetermined amount of tax forgiveness. According to the Court, the constitutionality of this "hybrid benefit" did not turn on any label: in practical terms, there was little difference between the tuition reimbursement and the tax benefit.[3] The finding of impermissible "effects," then, was central to the invalidation of the New York scheme. But Justice Powell also commented briefly on the "entanglement" aspects. He observed that "assistance of the sort here involved carries grave potential for entanglement in the broader sense of continuing political strife over aid to religion." He noted the "long experience" that "aid programs of any kind tend to become entrenched, to escalate in cost, and to generate their own aggressive constituencies." The prospect of such "divisiveness" was at least a significant "warning signal."

Chief Justice Burger's dissent insisted that, under Everson and Allen, "government aid to individuals generally stands on an entirely different footing from direct aid to religious institutions." He argued that the Constitution permits "general welfare" programs "under which benefits are distributed to private individuals, even though many of those individuals may elect to use those benefits in ways that 'aid' religious instruction or worship." That "fundamental principle," he stated, "is premised more on experience and history than on logic." To be sure, the tuition and tax benefits here went only to parents of private school children, while in Everson and Allen they were available to parents of public school children as well: "But to regard that difference as constitutionally meaningful is to exalt form over substance. It is beyond dispute that the parents of public schoolchildren [receive] the 'benefit' of having their children educated totally at state expense; the statutes [at] issue here merely attempt to equalize that 'benefit.' [It] is no more than simple equity to grant partial relief to parents who support the public schools they do not use." Accordingly he could find no constitutional flaw in the tuition and tax portions of the New York scheme. And Justice Rehnquist reached the same result, arguing that the tax scheme was valid under Walz, since it, like Walz, "was simply abstention from taxation," and that the reimbursement plan, like the assistance in Everson and Allen, was "consistent with the principle of neutrality." Justice White, finally, would have upheld the entire New York program. He reminded the majority that the test it relied on was "one of 'primary' effect, not *any* effect," and argued that the Court had made "no attempt at that ultimate judgment" here.[4]

2. *The 1973 companion cases: Additional examples of invalid state assistance to schools and valid aid to colleges.* One of the companion cases, Sloan v. Lemon, 413 U.S. 825, was easily disposed of on the basis of Nyquist.

3. Justice Powell commented in a footnote: "Since the program here does not have the elements of a genuine tax deduction, such as for charitable contributions, we do not have before us, and do not decide, whether that form of tax benefit is constitutionally acceptable under the 'neutrality' test in Walz."

4. Recall Justice Powell's response to that claim, in footnote 2 above.

Sloan involved Pennsylvania's tuition reimbursement scheme enacted after the decision in Lemon v. Kurtzman. Justice Powell's majority opinion found "no constitutionally significant difference" between the Pennsylvania and New York programs. The third case, LEVITT v. COMMITTEE FOR PUBLIC EDUC., 413 U.S. 472, presented still another New York program—a plan under which the state reimbursed private schools for certain costs of testing and recordkeeping. Chief Justice Burger wrote the majority opinion holding that plan, like the "maintenance and repair" program in Nyquist, unconstitutional. He noted that "the aid that will be devoted to secular functions is not identifiable and separable from aid to sectarian activities." This case involved "state-supported activities of a substantially different character from bus rides or state-provided textbooks," he argued. For example, routine teacher-prepared tests are "an integral part of the teaching process," and there was "substantial risk" that these tests "will be drafted with an eye, unconsciously or otherwise, to inculcate students in the religious precepts of the sponsoring church." He rejected the State's claim that it should be permitted to pay for any activity "mandated" by state law. The constitutional "primary purpose or effect" inquiry "would be irreversibly frustrated if the Establishment Clause were read as permitting a State to pay for whatever it requires a private school to do." [5]

The final case, HUNT v. McNAIR, 413 U.S. 734 (1973), like Tilton v. Richardson, involved aid to higher education, and it survived scrutiny. This was an attack on the South Carolina Educational Facilities Act as applied to authorize a financing transaction for the benefit of the Baptist College at Charleston. The point of the scheme was to permit the College to make use of the State's ability to borrow money at low interest rates—an ability stemming from the income tax exemption of interest on state bonds. The Act had established an Authority to assist—through the issuance of revenue bonds —colleges in construction projects. The assistance could not be used for any sectarian facility. Under the proposal under review, the Authority would make the proceeds of the bonds available to the College; in return, the College would convey the project to the Authority, which would then lease the property back to the College. All expenses of the Authority are payable solely from the revenues of the project, with no state financing or pledge involved. After repayment in full of the bonds, the project would be reconveyed to the College.

Justice Powell's majority opinion applied the "purpose, effect, and entanglement" tests. As to effect, he noted that here, as in Tilton, it had not been shown that the College was "pervasively sectarian," and aid was not barred simply because "aid to one aspect of an institution frees it to spend its other resources on religious ends." Moreover, no state funds were involved here. The entanglement aspect of the test provided the major difficulty, since the Authority had a right to inspect the project to insure that it was not being used for religious purposes as well as the right, on the face of the agreement, to participate in management decisions. The inspection provision was found to be no more entangling than that in Tilton. The "sweeping" powers of the Authority regarding management presented a

5.　Justices Douglas, Brennan and Marshall concurred in the result; Justice White dissented.

"closer issue." But as Justice Powell's majority opinion read it, the Authority was not justified in acting unless the college defaulted, e. g., with respect to rental payments: "In that event, the Authority or trustee might either foreclose on the mortgage or take a hand in the setting of rules, charges, and fees. It may be argued that only the former would be consistent with the Establishment Clause, but we do not now have that situation before us." On the facts here, the scope of the assistance to the secular aspects of the college was "confine[d]", and the arrangements "did not foreshadow excessive entanglement." Justice Brennan, joined by Justices Douglas and Marshall, dissented, insisting that "this scheme involves the State in a degree of policing of the affairs of the College far exceeding that called for by the statutes struck down in Lemon I."

3. *Aid to schools in 1975: Valid textbook loans; impermissible "auxiliary services" and instructional materials.* A Pennsylvania program adopted in 1972, after the Lemon decision, came before the Court in MEEK v. PITTINGER, 421 U.S. ___ (1975)—and, in most respects, failed to survive scrutiny under the various strands of modern establishment clause doctrine. The Pennsylvania scheme had three components: (1) textbook loans to children in nonpublic elementary and secondary schools; (2) loans of "instructional materials and equipment" to nonpublic schools;[6] and (3) "auxiliary services" provided in nonpublic schools by public school personnel.[7] All but the textbook loan provision were found unconstitutional. The opinions disclosed a 3 to 3 to 3 division on the Court: Justices Brennan, Douglas, and Marshall would have invalidated all elements of the program; Chief Justice Burger and Justices Rehnquist and White would have sustained all elements; a middle group—Justices Stewart, Blackmun and Powell—proved decisive in supporting textbook loans but rejecting all other elements.[8]

In invalidating most parts of the program, the Court drew upon four criteria developed in modern cases: "secular legislative purpose"; "primary effect"; "excessive entanglement" in administration; and "divisive political potential." With respect to the invalid elements, Justice Stewart's opinion, joined by Justices Blackmun and Powell, had the support of a separate opinion by Justice Brennan, joined by Justices Douglas and Marshall, with the latter

6. The "instructional materials and equipment, useful to the education" of nonpublic school children, included, as to "materials," periodicals, photographs, maps, charts, sound recordings, and films; and, as to "instructional equipment," projection equipment, recording equipment, and laboratory equipment.

7. "Auxiliary services" included counseling, testing, and psychological services, speech and hearing therapy, teaching and related services for exceptional children, for remedial students, and for the educationally disadvantaged, "and such other secular, neutral, non-ideological services as are of benefit to nonpublic school children and are presently and hereafter provided for public school children." The

services were provided in the nonpublic schools by public employees.

8. The holding clarified conflicting signals left by two decisions in 1974. Compare the summary affirmance invalidating a New Jersey program in Public Funds for Public Schools v. Marburger, 417 U.S. 961 (1974) (affirming 358 F.Supp. 29), with Wheeler v. Barrera, 417 U.S. 402 (1974), where the majority failed to reach a First Amendment challenge to federal funding of special programs for educationally deprived children (under the Elementary and Secondary Education Act of 1965), but where some of the separate opinions perceived hints in majority dicta that some special programs might be permissible.

group placing special emphasis on the "political divisiveness" factor. On the "instructional material and equipment" loans to schools, Justice Stewart emphasized "the unconstitutional primary effect of advancing religion because of the predominantly religious character of the schools benefiting" from the program. He noted that more than 75% of Pennsylvania's nonpublic schools were "church-related or religiously affiliated." He recognized that some "secular and non-ideological services" could be provided for church-related schools—e. g., bus transportation, school lunches, and public health facilities. But those were "indirect and incidental benefits" to the schools, in contrast to the "massive," "direct and substantial" aid provided by Pennsylvania.

When Justice Stewart turned to the "auxiliary services" aspect of the program, he emphasized the "entanglement" and "divisiveness" themes rather than the "primary effect" strand of prior doctrine. He concluded that the lower court had erred "in relying entirely on the good faith and professionalism of the secular teachers and counselors functioning in church-related schools to insure that a strictly nonideological posture is maintained." He recalled the fear of entanglement through supervision reflected in the Rhode Island companion case to Lemon, above. Here, to be sure, the teachers were public employees; but they were serving in sectarian schools, and the "potential for impermissible fostering of religion under these circumstances, although somewhat reduced, is nonetheless present." Moreover, that part of the program, like those in Lemon and Nyquist, created "a serious potential for divisive conflict over the issue of aid to religion." Accordingly, that "potential for political entanglement, together with the administrative entanglement which would be necessary to insure that auxiliary services personnel remained strictly neutral and nonideological when functioning in church-related schools," barred the program.

But in sustaining the textbook loan element, Justice Stewart's opinion explored none of the doctrinal criteria. Instead, he relied simply on precedent: the Pennsylvania program, he found, was "constitutionally indistinguishable from the New York textbook loan program upheld in Board of Education v. Allen," above. On that part of the case, Justice Stewart's middle group lost the support of the Brennan-Douglas-Marshall group and was supported by the Rehnquist-White-Burger position. But both of the latter groups criticized the Stewart position on textbook loans as being inconsistent with his analysis of the other elements of the program. Justice Brennan charged Justice Stewart with ignoring the "political divisiveness factor" which should invalidate textbook loans. Moreover, he questioned whether Allen could withstand overruling in light of Lemon and Nyquist. And he did not think textbook loans were distinguishable from the other elements because the formal recipients were students rather than schools: he insisted that textbook loans, though "ostensibly to students," were loans "in fact to the schools." He argued as well that the administrative guidelines in Pennsylvania made it much clearer than in Allen that the state and the sectarian schools worked in close cooperation: "neither parents nor students have a say."

Justice Rehnquist, by contrast, thought the Stewart position wholly arbitrary in invalidating the other elements of the program after sustaining textbook loans. Moreover, he found "a significant sub silentio extension" of Lemon in the striking down of the "auxiliary services" element. He claimed

that the majority had ignored the record showing nonentanglement and insisted that the Court was unjustified in invalidating simply because of the "potential" of entanglement. He also objected to the "overtones" of the majority view invalidating most of the program: the Court, he claimed, had gone beyond "neutrality" and had thrown "its weight on the side of those who believed that our society as a whole should be a purely secular one." A separate opinion by Chief Justice Burger similarly objected to the majority's "crabbed attitude": he thought it penalized not only *institutions* with a religious affiliation" but also *children*—children who have the misfortune" to require remedial assistance.

SECTION 2.   THE "FREE EXERCISE" OF RELIGION

INTRODUCTION: THE "BELIEF–ACTION" DISTINCTION AND THE PROTECTION OF RELIGION–BASED CONDUCT

What is the freedom of religion protected by the free exercise clause? To what extent does "free exercise" afford protections beyond those assured by the First Amendment protections of freedom of expression considered in chaps. 12 and 13? To what extent must the delineation of any additional protections assured by the free exercise guarantee take account of the other religion clause of the First Amendment, lest the immunizing of religious belief and conduct run afoul of the safeguard against "establishment"?

In the Court's early efforts to articulate the contours of freedom of religion, there were repeated reliances on a distinction between "belief" and "action." [1] At first, as the introductory notes below illustrate, the Court suggested that "free exercise" extended only to belief, and did not reach conduct at all. More recently, the Court has increasingly come to acknowledge that conduct based on religious belief may sometimes claim exemption from general regulatory statutes because of the free exercise guarantee. That growing recognition in turn has brought inherent tensions between the free exercise and establishment clauses to the forefront. The principal cases below emphasize these recent confrontations with the problem of arguably exempt conduct: When *must* regulatory statutes exempt religion-based conduct? When *may* a legislature exempt such conduct without violating the establishment clause? As background to the consideration of those contemporary problems, these introductory materials note some of the major steps in the evolution of the Court's analysis of the free exercise clause.

1.   *Mormons and polygamy: The "belief only" view of the Reynolds case.* REYNOLDS v. UNITED STATES, 98 U.S. 145 (1878), affirmed a conviction of a Mormon resident of the Territory of Utah under a federal law making bigamy a crime in the territories. The defendant testified that Mormon doctrine did not merely permit polygamy, but required it "when circumstances would admit." The trial judge refused to instruct the jury to acquit if they found that the defendant had entered into a plural marriage in

---

1. Recall the efforts to analyze the free speech guarantee in terms of a "speech-conduct" distinction, in the preceding two chapters.

"conformity with what he believed at the time to be a religious duty." Chief Justice Waite's opinion affirming the conviction drew a sharp belief-conduct distinction and accordingly found no violation of the First Amendment. Like the more recent establishment cases (see Everson, sec. 1A), he drew on the writings of Jefferson: he noted, for example, that Jefferson's bill "for establishing religious freedom" had drawn "the true distinction between what properly belongs to the church and what to the State." The preamble to that bill had condemned the intrusion of civil authority "into the field of opinion," but had added "that it is time enough for the rightful purposes of civil government for its officers to interfere when principles break out into overt acts against peace and good order." Chief Justice Waite noted, too, that "there never has been a time in any State of the Union when polygamy has not been an offence against society, cognizable by the civil courts and punishable with more or less severity." In view of that traditional condemnation of polygamy, "it is impossible to believe that the constitutional guaranty of religious freedom was intended to prohibit legislation in respect to this most important feature of social life." Turning specifically to the First Amendment claim, he concluded that "those who make polygamy a part of their religion" were not "excepted from the operation of the statute." He explained:

"Laws are made for the government of actions, and while they cannot interfere with mere religious belief and opinions, they may with practices. Suppose one believed that human sacrifices were a necessary part of religious worship, would it be seriously contended that the civil government under which he lived could not interfere to prevent a sacrifice? Or if a wife religiously believed it was her duty to burn herself upon the funeral pyre of a dead husband, would it be beyond the power of the civil government to prevent her carrying her belief into practice? . . . Can a man excuse his practices [in violation of the bigamy law] because of his religious belief? To permit this would be to make the professed doctrines of religious belief superior to the law of the land, and in effect to permit every citizen to become a law unto himself. Government could exist only in name under such circumstances."

Under that view suggesting that only belief, not practice, is protected by the free exercise clause, does the clause assure any protection beyond that already afforded by the free speech guarantee? [2]

2. Note also a case decided a few years after Reynolds, Davis v. Beason, 133 U.S. 333 (1890). That was an unsuccessful challenge to an Idaho territorial law directed at Mormons and requiring voters to take an oath that they were not members of any organization which "teaches, advises, counsels or encourages" its members to commit the crime of bigamy. Davis, a Mormon, was convicted of taking a false oath. Justice Field's opinion affirming that conviction viewed the case as similar to Reynolds: "To extend exemption from punishment for [crimes such as bigamy] would be to shock the moral judgment of the community. To call their advocacy a tenet of religion is to offend the common sense of mankind. If they are crimes, then to teach, advise and counsel their practices to aid in their commission, and such teaching and counseling are themselves criminal and proper subjects of punishment, as aiding and abetting crime are in all other cases. [Crime] is not the less odious because sanctioned by what any particular sect may designate as religion." Would the conviction in Davis v. Beason be sustained under modern interpretations of the free speech guarantee—even the interpretations of those who draw a speech-conduct distinction? Recall chaps. 12 and 13 above.

2. *The belief-action distinction in the 20th century: The Cantwell case.* One of the most widely cited passages about the scope of freedom of religion appeared in Justice Roberts' opinion for the Court in CANTWELL v. CONNECTICUT, 310 U.S. 296 (1940) (one of the Jehovah's Witnesses proselytizing cases; other aspects of the case are considered in chap. 12, sec. 2A, above). Cantwell, like Reynolds, spoke of a belief-action distinction; but unlike Reynolds, there was no longer the implication that conduct resting on religious belief is wholly outside the scope of the First Amendment. Instead, there was the suggestion that, though conduct is subject to greater regulation than belief, conduct too may be protected under appropriate circumstances. It was left to later cases to elaborate on the appropriate standards of scrutiny.

Justice Roberts stated in Cantwell: "The constitutional inhibition of legislation on the subject of religion has a double aspect. On the one hand, it forestalls compulsion by law of the acceptance of any creed or the practice of any form of worship. [On] the other hand, it safeguards the free exercise of the chosen form of religion. Thus the Amendment embraces two concepts,—freedom to believe and freedom to act. The first is absolute but, in the nature of things, the second cannot be. Conduct remains subject to regulation for the protection of society. [Reynolds; Davis v. Beason.] The freedom to act must have appropriate definition to preserve the enforcement of that protection. In every case the power to regulate must be so exercised as not, in attaining a permissible end, unduly to infringe the protected freedom. No one would contest the proposition that a State may not, by statute, wholly deny the right to preach or to disseminate religious views. Plainly such a previous and absolute restraint would violate the terms of the guarantee. It is equally clear that a State may by general and non-discriminatory legislation regulate the times, the places, and the manner of soliciting upon its streets, and of holding meetings thereon; and may in other respects safeguard the peace, good order and comfort of the community, without unconstitutionally invading the liberties protected by the Fourteenth Amendment."

Was Justice Roberts' distinction a helpful one? In that aspect of the Cantwell case, the Court reversed the conviction for soliciting funds for a religious cause without a permit, where the licensing statute required the administrator to "determine whether such cause is a religious one or is a bona fide object of charity." The Court concluded: "[T]o condition the solicitation of aid for the perpetuation of religious views or systems upon a license, the grant of which rests in the exercise of a determination by state authority as to what is a religious cause, is to lay a forbidden burden upon the exercise of liberty protected by the Constitution." If "conduct" may be regulated in some circumstances, what are the appropriate judicial standards for delineating those circumstances? Note the Court's efforts, and the reliances on Cantwell, in the modern cases which follow these notes.

3. *The relation between the religion and speech guarantees: The Flag Salute Cases.* In the Flag Salute Cases, Jehovah's Witnesses attacked school regulations which required participation in public school exercises of saluting the flag. The challengers insisted that their participation in the salutes was "forbidden by command of Scripture." In the first case, MINERSVILLE SCHOOL DIST. v. GOBITIS, 310 U.S. 586 (1940), the Court sustained the

flag salute requirement; three years later, however, in WEST VIRGINIA STATE BOARD OF EDUCATION v. BARNETTE, 319 U.S. 624 (1943), the requirement was struck down. Both cases elicited extensive discussions of the Court's responsibilities in the protection of individual liberties. And of special interest here are the relative emphases on the religion and speech guarantees in the cases.

a. *Gobitis.* In the Gobitis case (decided two weeks after Cantwell), Justice Frankfurter's majority opinion found little constitutional protection for conduct allegedly compelled by religious belief. He stated: "The religious liberty which the Constitution protects has never excluded legislation of general scope not directed against doctrinal loyalties of particular sects. . . . Conscientious scruples have not, in the course of the long struggle for religious toleration, relieved the individual from obedience to a general law not aimed at the promotion or restriction of religious beliefs. The mere possession of religious convictions which contradict the relevant concerns of a political society does not relieve the citizen from the discharge of political responsibilities. [E. g., Reynolds; Davis v. Beason.] . . . Nor does the freedom of speech assured by Due Process move in a more absolute circle of immunity than that enjoyed by religious freedom. . . . It is not our province to choose among competing considerations in the subtle process of securing effective loyalty [while] respecting at the same time individual idio-syncrasies . . . . So to hold would in effect make us the school board for the country. . . . Except where the transgression [of] liberty is too plain for argument, personal freedom is best maintained—so long as the remedial channels of the democratic process remain open and unobstructed—when it is ingrained in a people's habits. [T]o the legislature no less than to courts is committed the guardianship of deeply-cherished liberties." Justice Stone dissented: "This seems to me no less than the surrender of the constitutional protection of the liberty of small minorities to the popular will." He insisted on "careful scrutiny" of efforts "to secure conformity of belief [by] a compulsory affirmation of the desired belief."

b. *Barnette.* Three years later, in Barnette, Justice Jackson's majority opinion overruled Gobitis. To Justice Jackson, the central issue was not freedom of religion but freedom of expression: it was not whether Jehovah's Witnesses could be subjected to the requirement, but whether any person could be compelled to salute the flag contrary to personal belief. He explained: "Nor does the issue as we see it turn on one's possession of particular religious views or the sincerity with which they are held. While religion supplies appellees' motive of enduring the discomforts of making the issue in this case, many citizens who do not share these religious views hold such a compulsory rite to infringe constitutional liberty of the individual. It is not necessary to inquire whether non-conformist beliefs will exempt from the duty to salute unless we first find power to make the salute a legal duty."

And there was no such power, as Justice Jackson emphasized in a widely-quoted passage about a core theme of the First Amendment (recall the introduction to chap. 12 above): "The very purpose of the Bill of Rights was to withdraw certain subjects from the vicissitudes of political controversy, to place them beyond the reach of majorities and officials and to establish them as legal principles to be applied by the courts. One's right to life,

liberty, and property, to free speech, a free press, freedom of worship and assembly, and other fundamental rights may not be submitted to vote, they depend on the outcome of no elections." Justice Jackson added: "Much of the vagueness of the due process clause disappears when the specific prohibitions of the First become its standard. [First Amendment rights] are susceptible of restriction only to prevent grave and immediate danger to interests which the State may lawfully protect. . . . Nor does our duty [to apply the Bill of Rights] depend upon our possession of marked competence in the field where the invasion of rights occurs. [W]e act in these matters not by authority of our competence but by force of our commissions. . . . If there is any fixed star in our constitutional constellation, it is that no official, high or petty, can prescribe what shall be orthodox in politics, nationalism, religion, or other matters of opinion or force citizens to confess by word or act their faith therein." [3]

Justice Frankfurter's dissent concluded: "Of course patriotism cannot be enforced by the flag salute. But neither can the liberal spirit be enforced by judicial invalidation of illiberal legislation. Our constant preoccupation with the constitutionality of legislation rather than with its wisdom tends to preoccupation of the American mind with a false value. The tendency of focusing attention on constitutionality is to make constitutionality synonymous with wisdom, to regard a law as all right if it is constitutional. Such an attitude is a great enemy of liberalism. Particularly in legislation affecting freedom of thought and freedom of speech much which should offend a free-spirited society is constitutional. Reliance for the most precious interests of civilization, therefore, must be found outside of their vindication in courts of law." [4]

Transitional note. Many of the opinions sampled in the foregoing notes are marked by hesitation and skepticism if not outright rejection of claims that religion-based conduct must be exempt from general regulatory laws. In the cases which follow, however—cases of the sixties and seventies—a wide agreement developed that the religious objector can sometimes claim exemption from regulations of conduct. Those cases focus on the most difficult problems of the modern dimensions of the free exercise guarantee: When is religion-based conduct constitutionally exempt from regulation? Must the conduct be *compelled* by doctrine? May the Court inquire into the content of religious doctrine to determine whether the objector's grounds are central to that religious doctrine? Do constitutionally compelled exemptions threaten establishment values? What burden of justification must

---

3. Justices Roberts and Reed announced their adherence to Gobitis. Justice Black, joined by Justice Douglas, submitted a "statement of reasons for our change of view" since Gobitis. Justice Murphy also concurred. Justice Frankfurter submitted a lengthy dissent noted in the text.

4. Justice Frankfurter began his dissent with the following comment: "One who belongs to the most vilified and persecuted minority in history is not likely to be insensible to the freedoms guaranteed by our Constitution.

Were my purely personal attitude relevant I should wholeheartedly associate myself with the general libertarian views in the Court's opinion, representing as they do the thought and action of a lifetime. But as judges we are neither Jew nor Gentile, neither Catholic nor agnostic. . . .
As a member of this Court I am not justified in writing my private notions of policy into the Constitution, no matter how deeply I may cherish them or how mischievous I may deem their disregard."

the state meet to warrant regulation of religion-based conduct? Are the strict scrutiny criteria of the free speech cases—the emphases on "compelling" state interests and on resort to least restrictive alternatives—appropriate in this area? Is a distinction between "direct" and "indirect" burdens useful? Are other analyses necessary to assure the proper accommodation between free exercise and establishment values? Even if an exemption is not constitutionally compelled, *may* the state exempt conduct based on religious belief without impinging upon the "neutrality" theme of the establishment cases?

BRAUNFELD v. BROWN

366 U.S. 599, 81 S.Ct. 1144, 6 L.Ed.2d 563 (1961).

Appeal from the District Court for the Eastern District of Pennsylvania.

Mr. Chief Justice WARREN announced the judgment of the Court and an opinion in which Mr. Justice BLACK, Mr. Justice CLARK, and Mr. Justice WHITTAKER concur.

This case concerns the constitutional validity of the application to appellants of the Pennsylvania criminal statute [of 1959] which proscribes the Sunday retail sale of certain enumerated commodities. [T]he only question for consideration is whether the statute interferes with the free exercise of appellants' religion.

Appellants are merchants in Philadelphia who engage in the retail sale of clothing and home furnishings within the proscription of the statute in issue. Each of the appellants is a member of the Orthodox Jewish faith, which requires the closing of their places of business and a total abstention from all manner of work from nightfall each Friday until nightfall each Saturday. [They allege] that appellants had previously kept their places of business open on Sunday; that each of appellants had done a substantial amount of business on Sunday, compensating somewhat for their closing on Saturday; that Sunday closing will result in impairing the ability of all appellants to earn a livelihood and will render appellant Braunfeld unable to continue in his business, thereby losing his capital investment. [The lower court dismissed the complaint.]

Appellants contend that the enforcement against them of the Pennsylvania statute will prohibit the free exercise of their religion because, due to the statute's compulsion to close on Sunday, appellants will suffer substantial economic loss, to the benefit of their non-Sabbatarian competitors, if appellants also continue their Sabbath observance by closing their businesses on Saturday; that this result will either compel appellants to give up their Sabbath observance, a basic tenet of the Orthodox Jewish faith, or will put appellants at a serious economic disadvantage if they continue to adhere to their Sabbath. Appellants also assert that the statute will operate so as to hinder the Orthodox Jewish faith in gaining new adherents. And the corollary to these arguments is that if the free exercise of appellants' religion is impeded, that religion is being subjected to discriminatory treatment . . . . .

Certain aspects of religious exercise cannot, in any way, be restricted or burdened by either federal or state legislation. Compulsion by law of the

acceptance of any creed or the practice of any form of worship is strictly forbidden. The freedom to hold religious beliefs and opinions is absolute. [Cantwell; Reynolds; Barnette.] But this is not the case at bar; the statute before us does not make criminal the holding of any religious belief or opinion, nor does it force anyone to embrace any religious belief or to say or believe anything in conflict with his religious tenets.

However, the freedom to act, even when the action is in accord with one's religious convictions, is not totally free from legislative restrictions. [Cantwell; Reynolds.] And, in Prince v. Massachusetts, 321 U.S. 158 [1944], this Court upheld a statute making it a crime for a girl under eighteen years of age to sell any newspapers, periodicals or merchandise in public places despite the fact that a child of the Jehovah's Witnesses faith believed that it was her religious *duty* to perform this work.

It is to be noted that, in [Reynolds and Prince], the religious practices themselves conflicted with the public interest. In such cases, to make accommodation between the religious action and an exercise of state authority is a particularly delicate task [because] resolution in favor of the State results in the choice to the individual of either abandoning his religious principle or facing criminal prosecution. But, again, this is not the case before us because the statute at bar does not make unlawful any religious practices of appellants; the Sunday law simply regulates a secular activity and, as applied to appellants, operates so as to make the practice of their religious beliefs more expensive. . . . Fully recognizing that the alternatives open to appellants and others similarly situated—retaining their present occupations and incurring economic disadvantage or engaging in some other commercial activity which does not call for either Saturday or Sunday labor—may well result in some financial sacrifice in order to observe their religious beliefs, still the option is wholly different than when the legislation attempts to make a religious practice itself unlawful. To strike down, without the most critical scrutiny, legislation which imposes only an indirect burden on the exercise of religion, i. e., legislation which does not make unlawful the religious practice itself, would radically restrict the operating latitude of the legislature. . . .

Needless to say, when entering the area of religious freedom, we must be fully cognizant of the particular protection that the Constitution has accorded it. Abhorrence of religious persecution and intolerance is a basic part of our heritage. But we are a cosmopolitan nation made up of people of almost every conceivable religious preference. [I]t cannot be expected, much less required, that legislators enact no law regulating conduct that may in some way result in an economic disadvantage to some religious sects and not to others because of the special practices of the various religions. . . .

Of course, to hold unassailable all legislation regulating conduct which imposes solely an indirect burden on the observance of religion would be a gross oversimplification. If the purpose or effect of a law is to impede the observance of one or all religions or is to discriminate invidiously between religions, that law is constitutionally invalid even though the burden may be characterized as being only indirect. But if the State regulates conduct by enacting a general law within its power, the purpose and effect of

which is to advance the State's secular goals, the statute is valid despite its
indirect burden on religious observance unless the State may accomplish its
purpose by means which do not impose such a burden. See [Cantwell].[1]

As we pointed out in [McGowan v. Maryland, sec. 1B], we cannot
find a State without power to provide a weekly respite from all labor and,
at the same time, to set one day of the week apart from the others as a day
of rest, repose, recreation and tranquillity. [And we] found there that a
State might well find that [alternative means suggested in McGowan] would
not accomplish bringing about a general day of rest. . . . However,
appellants advance yet another means at the State's disposal which they would
find unobjectionable. They contend that the State should cut an exception
from the Sunday labor proscription for those people who, because of religious conviction, observe a day of rest other than Sunday. . . ,

A number of States provide such an exemption, and this may well be
the wiser solution to the problem. But our concern is not with the wisdom
of legislation but with its constitutional limitation. Thus, reason and experience teach that to permit the exemption might well undermine the State's
goal of providing a day that, as best possible, eliminates the atmosphere of
commercial noise and activity. Although not dispositive of the issue, enforcement problems would be more difficult since there would be two or more
days to police rather than one and it would be more difficult to observe
whether violations were occurring.

Additional problems might also be presented by a regulation of this
sort. To allow only people who rest on a day other than Sunday to keep their
businesses open on that day might well provide these people with an economic
advantage over their competitors who must remain closed on that day . . . .
With this competitive advantage existing, there could well be the temptation
for some, in order to keep their businesses open on Sunday, to assert that they
have religious convictions which compel them to close their businesses on
what had formerly been their least profitable day. This might make necessary a state-conducted inquiry into the sincerity of the individual's religious
beliefs, a practice which a State might believe would itself run afoul of the
spirit of constitutionally protected religious guarantees. Finally, in order to
keep the disruption of the day at a minimum, exempted employers would
probably have to hire employees who themselves qualified for the exemption
because of their own religious beliefs, a practice which a State might feel to
be opposed to its general policy prohibiting religious discrimination in hiring.
For all of these reasons, we cannot say that the Pennsylvania statute before us
is invalid, either on its face or as applied.

. . . Mr. Justice FRANKFURTER and Mr. Justice HARLAN have
rejected appellant's claim under the Free Exercise Clause in a separate opinion.

Affirmed.

---

1. Thus in cases like Murdock v. Pennsylvania, 319 U.S. 105, and Follett v.
McCormick, 321 U.S. 573, this Court
struck down municipal ordinances
which, in application, required religious colporteurs to pay a license
tax as a condition to the pursuit of
their activities because the State's interest, the obtaining of revenue, could
be easily satisfied by imposing this
tax on nonreligious sources. [Foot-
note by the Court.]

Mr. Justice BRENNAN [dissenting].

[T]he issue in this case [is] whether a State may put an individual to a choice between his business and his religion. The Court today holds that it may. But I dissent, believing that such a law prohibits the free exercise of religion.

The first question to be resolved [is] the appropriate standard of constitutional adjudication in cases in which a statute is assertedly in conflict with the First Amendment. [See Barnette.] The Court in such cases is not confined to the narrow inquiry whether the challenged law is rationally related to some legitimate legislative end. Nor is the case decided by a finding that the State's interest is substantial and important, as well as rationally justifiable. . . . The honored place of religious freedom in our constitutional hierarchy [must] now be taken to be settled. Or at least so it appeared until today. For in this case the Court seems to say, without so much as a deferential nod towards that high place which we have accorded religious freedom in the past, that any substantial state interest will justify encroachments on religious practice, at least if those encroachments are cloaked in the guise of some nonreligious public purpose.

Admittedly, these laws do not compel overt affirmation of a repugnant belief, as in Barnette, nor do they prohibit outright any of appellants' religious practices, as [in Reynolds]. That is, the laws do not say that appellants must work on Saturday. But their effect is that appellants may not simultaneously practice their religion and their trade, without being hampered by a substantial competitive disadvantage. Their effect is that no one may at one and the same time be an Orthodox Jew and compete effectively with his Sunday-observing fellow tradesmen. This clog upon the exercise of religion, this state-imposed burden on Orthodox Judaism, has exactly the same economic effect as a tax levied upon the sale of religious literature. And yet, such a tax, when applied in the form of an excise or license fee, was held invalid in Follett v. Town of McCormick, supra. All this the Court, as I read its opinion, concedes.

What, then, is the compelling state interest which impels the Commonwealth of Pennsylvania to impede appellants' freedom of worship? What overbalancing need is so weighty in the constitutional scale that it justifies this substantial, though indirect, limitation of appellants' freedom? It is not the desire to stamp out a practice deeply abhorred by society, such as polygamy, as in [Reynolds]. Nor is it the State's traditional protection of children, as in [Prince v. Massachusetts]. It is not even the interest in seeing that everyone rests one day a week, for appellants' religion requires that they take such a rest. It is the mere convenience of having everyone rest on the same day. It is to defend this interest that the Court holds that a State need not follow the alternative route of granting an exemption for those who in good faith observe a day of rest other than Sunday.

It is true, I suppose, that the granting of such an exemption would make Sundays a little noisier, and the task of police and prosecutor a little more difficult. It is also true that a majority—21—of the 34 States which have general Sunday regulations have exemptions of this kind. We are not told that those States are significantly noisier, or that their police are significantly

more burdened, than Pennsylvania's. [The Court] conjures up several difficulties with such a system which seem to me more fanciful than real. . . .

In fine, the Court, in my view, has exalted administrative convenience to a constitutional level high enough to justify making one religion economically disadvantageous. . . .

I [would] remand for a trial of appellants' allegations . . . ..

Mr. Justice STEWART, dissenting.

I agree with substantially all that Mr. Justice Brennan has written. Pennsylvania has passed a law which compels an Orthodox Jew to choose between his religious faith and his economic survival. That is a cruel choice. It is a choice which I think no State can constitutionally demand. . . .

SHERBERT v. VERNER

374 U.S. 398, 83 S.Ct. 1790, 10 L.Ed.2d 965 (1963).

Appeal from the Supreme Court of South Carolina.

Mr. Justice BRENNAN delivered the opinion of the Court.

Appellant, a member of the Seventh-day Adventist Church, was discharged by her South Carolina employer because she would not work on Saturday, the Sabbath Day of her faith.[1] When she was unable to obtain other employment because from conscientious scruples she would not take Saturday work, she filed a claim [for] benefits under the South Carolina Unemployment Compensation Act. . . . The appellee Employment Security Commission [found] that appellant's restriction upon her availability for Saturday work barred her within the [statutory] provision disqualifying for benefits insured workers who fail, without good cause, to accept "suitable work when offered [by] the employment office or the employer." [The highest state court affirmed, holding "that appellant's ineligibility infringed no constitutional liberties." [2]]

[If] the decision [is to stand] it must be either because her disqualification as a beneficiary represents no infringement by the State of her consti-

---

1. Appellant became a member of the Seventh-day Adventist Church in 1957, at a time when her employer, a textile-mill operator, permitted her to work a five-day week. It was not until 1959 that the work week was changed to six days, including Saturday, for all three shifts in the employer's mill. No question has been raised in this case concerning the sincerity of appellant's religious beliefs. Nor is there any doubt that the prohibition against Saturday labor is a basic tenet of the Seventh-day Adventist creed, based upon that religion's interpretation of the Holy Bible. [Footnote by the Court.]

2. It has been suggested that appellant is not within the class entitled to benefits under the South Carolina statute because her unemployment did not result from discharge or layoff due to lack of work. It is true that unavailability for work for some personal reasons not having to do with matters of conscience or religion has been held to be a basis of disqualification for benefits. . . . But appellant claims that the Free Exercise Clause prevents the State from basing the denial of benefits upon the "personal reason" she gives for not working on Saturday. Where the consequence of disqualification so directly affects First Amendment rights, surely we should not conclude that every "personal reason" is a basis for disqualification in the absence of explicit language to that effect in the statute or decisions of the South Carolina Supreme Court. . . . [Footnote by the Court.]

tutional rights of free exercise; or because any incidental burden on the free exercise of appellant's religion may be justified by a "compelling state interest in the regulation of a subject within the State's constitutional power to regulate." NAACP v. Button [chap. 13, sec. 4].

We turn first to the question whether the disqualification for benefits imposes any burden on the free exercise of appellant's religion. We think it is clear that it does. In a sense the consequences of such a disqualification to religious principles and practices may be only an indirect result of welfare legislation within the State's general competence to enact; it is true that no criminal sanctions directly compel appellant to work a six-day week. But this is only the beginning, not the end, of our inquiry. For "[i]f the purpose or effect of a law is to impede the observance of one or all religions or is to discriminate invidiously between religions, that law is constitutionally invalid even though the burden may be characterized as being only indirect." [Braunfeld.] Here not only is it apparent that appellant's declared ineligibility for benefits derives solely from the practice of her religion, but the pressure upon her to forego that practice is unmistakable. The ruling forces her to choose between following the precepts of her religion and forfeiting benefits, on the one hand, and abandoning one of the precepts of her religion in order to accept work, on the other hand. Governmental imposition of such a choice puts the same kind of burden upon the free exercise of religion as would a fine imposed against appellant for her Saturday worship. . . .

Significantly South Carolina expressly saves the Sunday worshipper from having to make the kind of choice which we here hold infringes the Sabbatarian's religious liberty. When in times of "national emergency" the textile plants are authorized by the State Commissioner of Labor to operate on Sunday, "no employee shall be required to work on Sunday [who] is conscientiously opposed to Sunday work." [§ 64–4.] No question of the disqualification of a Sunday worshipper for benefits is likely to arise, since we cannot suppose that an employer will discharge him in violation of this statute. The unconstitutionality of the disqualification of the Sabbatarian is thus compounded by the religious discrimination which South Carolina's general statutory scheme necessarily effects.

We must next consider whether some compelling state interest [justifies] the substantial infringement of appellant's First Amendment right. It is basic that no showing merely of a rational relationship to some colorable state interest would suffice; in this highly sensitive constitutional area, "[o]nly the gravest abuses, endangering paramount interest, give occasion for permissible limitation," Thomas v. Collins, 323 U.S. 516, 530. No such abuse or danger has been advanced in the present case. The appellees suggest no more than a possibility that the filing of fraudulent claims by unscrupulous claimants feigning religious objections to Saturday work might not only dilute the unemployment compensation fund but also hinder the scheduling by employers of necessary Saturday work. [But] no such objection appears to have been made before the [state courts, and] there is no proof whatever to warrant such fears of malingering or deceit as those which the respondents now advance. Even if consideration of such evidence is not foreclosed by the prohibition against judicial inquiry into the truth or falsity of religious beliefs, United States v. Ballard [sec. 1B]—a question as to

which we intimate no view since it is not before us—it is highly doubtful whether such evidence would be sufficient to warrant a substantial infringement of religious liberties. For even if the possibility of spurious claims did threaten to dilute the fund and disrupt the scheduling of work, it would plainly be incumbent upon the appellees to demonstrate that no alternative forms of regulation would combat such abuses without infringing First Amendment rights.

In these respects, then, the state interest asserted in the present case is wholly dissimilar to the interests which were found to justify the less direct burden upon religious practices in [Braunfeld]. [That statute was] saved by a countervailing factor which finds no equivalent in the instant case —a strong state interest in providing one uniform day of rest for all workers. That secular objective could be achieved, the Court found, only by declaring Sunday to be that day of rest. [Here] no such justifications underlie the determination of the state court that appellant's religion makes her ineligible to receive benefits. . . .

In holding as we do, plainly we are not fostering the "establishment" of the Seventh-day Adventist religion in South Carolina, for the extension of unemployment benefits to Sabbatarians in common with Sunday worshippers reflects nothing more than the governmental obligation of neutrality in the face of religious differences, and does not represent that involvement of religious with secular institutions which it is the object of the Establishment Clause to forestall. . . . Nor do we, by our decision today, declare the existence of a constitutional right to unemployment benefits on the part of all persons whose religious convictions are the cause of their unemployment. This is not a case in which an employee's religious convictions serve to make him a nonproductive member of society. . . . Our holding today is only that South Carolina may not constitutionally apply the eligibility provisions so as to constrain a worker to abandon his religious convictions respecting the day of rest. . . .

[Reversed and remanded.]*

Mr. Justice STEWART, concurring in the result.

Although fully agreeing with the result which the Court reaches in this case, I cannot join the Court's opinion. This case presents a double-barreled dilemma, which in all candor I think the Court's opinion has not succeeded in papering over. The dilemma ought to be resolved. . . .

[After deploring the Court's "distressing insensitivity" in Braunfeld and its "not only insensitive, but positively wooden," interpretations of the establishment clause in other cases, Justice Stewart continued:] But [the] decisions are on the books. And the result is that there are many situations where legitimate claims under the Free Exercise Clause will run into head-on collision with the Court's insensitive and sterile construction of the Establishment Clause. The controversy now before us is clearly such a case.

. . . The Court says that South Carolina cannot under these circumstances declare her to be not "available for work" within the meaning of its statute because to do so would violate her constitutional right to the free exercise of her religion. Yet what this Court has said about the Estab-

* A concurring opinion by Justice Douglas is omitted.

lishment Clause must inevitably lead to a diametrically opposite result. If the appellant's refusal to work on Saturdays were based on indolence, or on a compulsive desire to watch the Saturday television programs, no one would say that South Carolina could not hold that she was not "available for work" within the meaning of its statute. That being so, the Establishment Clause as construed by this Court not only *permits* but affirmatively *requires* South Carolina equally to deny the appellant's claim for unemployment compensation when her refusal to work on Saturdays is based upon her religious creed.

To require South Carolina to so administer its laws as to pay public money to the appellant under the circumstances of this case is thus clearly to require the State to violate the Establishment Clause as construed by this Court. This poses no problem for me, because I think the Court's mechanistic concept of the Establishment Clause is historically unsound and constitutionally wrong. . . . And I think that the guarantee of religious liberty embodied in the Free Exercise Clause affirmatively requires government to create an atmosphere of hospitality and accommodation to individual belief or disbelief.

South Carolina would deny unemployment benefits to a mother unavailable for work on Saturdays because she was unable to get a babysitter. Thus, we do not have before us a situation where a State provides unemployment compensation generally, and singles out for disqualification only those persons who are unavailable for work on religious grounds. This is not, in short, a scheme which operates so as to discriminate against religion as such. But the Court nevertheless holds that the State must prefer a religious over a secular ground for being unavailable for work . . . .

Yet in cases decided under the Establishment Clause the Court has decreed otherwise. It has decreed that government must blind itself to the differing religious beliefs and traditions of the people. With all respect, I think it is the Court's duty to face up to the dilemma posed by the conflict between the [religion clauses] as interpreted by the Court. [S]o long as the resounding but fallacious fundamentalist rhetoric of some of our Establishment Clause opinions remains on our books, to be disregarded at will as in the present case, or to be undiscriminatingly invoked as in [Schempp], so long will the possibility of consistent and perceptive decision in this most difficult and delicate area of constitutional law be impeded and impaired. And so long, I fear, will the guarantee of true religious freedom in our pluralistic society be uncertain and insecure. . . .

My second difference with the Court's opinion is that I cannot agree that today's decision can stand consistently with [Braunfeld]. The Court says that there was a "less direct burden upon religious practices" in that case than in this. With all respect, I think the Court is mistaken simply as a matter of fact. The Braunfeld case involved a *criminal* statute [and, as Justice Brennan's dissent there pointed out, involved a drastic impact on the challenger's business]. The impact upon the appellant's religious freedom in the present case is considerably less onerous [than in Braunfeld]. Even upon the unlikely assumption that the appellant could not find suitable non-Saturday employment, the appellant at the worst would be denied a maximum of 22 weeks of compensation payments. I agree with the Court that the possibility of that denial is enough to infringe upon the appellant's constitutional right

to the free exercise of her religion. But it is clear to me that in order to reach this conclusion the Court must explicitly reject the reasoning of [Braunfeld]. I think the Braunfeld case was wrongly decided and should be overruled, and accordingly I concur in the result reached by the Court in the case before us.

Mr. Justice HARLAN, whom Mr. Justice WHITE joins, dissenting.

. . .

The [highest state court] consistently held that one is not "available for work" if his unemployment has resulted not from the inability of industry to provide a job rather from personal circumstances, no matter how compelling. . . . The fact that these personal considerations sprang from her religious convictions was wholly without relevance to the state court's application of the law. Thus in no proper sense can it be said that the State discriminated against the appellant on the basis of her religious beliefs or that she was denied benefits *because* she was a Seventh-day Adventist. She was denied benefits just as any other claimant would be denied benefits who was not "available for work" for personal reasons.[1]

With this background, this Court's decision comes into clearer focus. What the Court is holding is that if the State chooses to condition unemployment compensation on the applicant's availability for work, it is constitutionally compelled to *carve out an exception*—and to provide benefits—for those whose unavailability is due to their religious convictions.[2] Such a holding has particular significance in two respects.

First, despite the Court's protestations to the contrary, the decision necessarily overrules [Braunfeld]. Clearly, any differences between this case and Braunfeld cut against the present appellant.[3]

Second, the implications of the present decision are far more troublesome than its apparently narrow dimensions would indicate at first glance.

1. I am completely at a loss to understand note [2] of the Court's opinion. Certainly the Court is not basing today's decision on the unsupported supposition that *some* day, the South Carolina Supreme Court may conclude that there is *some* personal reason for unemployment that may not disqualify a claimant for relief. In any event, I submit it is perfectly clear that South Carolina would not compensate persons who became unemployed for *any* personal reason, as distinguished from layoffs or lack of work, since the State Supreme Court's decisions would make it plain that such persons would not be regarded as "available for work" within the manifest meaning of the eligibility requirements. . . . [Footnote by Justice Harlan.]

2. The Court does suggest, in a rather startling disclaimer, that its holding is limited in applicability to those whose religious convictions do not make them "nonproductive" members of society, noting that most of the Seventh-day Adventists in the Spartanburg area are employed. But surely this disclaimer cannot be taken seriously, for the Court cannot mean that the case would have come out differently if none of the Seventh-day Adventists in Spartanburg had been gainfully employed, or if the appellant's religion had prevented her from working on Tuesdays instead of Saturdays. Nor can the Court be suggesting that it will make a value judgment in each case as to whether a particular individual's religious convictions prevent him from being "productive." I can think of no more inappropriate function for this Court to perform. [Footnote by Justice Harlan.]

3. The Court's reliance on South Carolina Code § 64–4, to support its conclusion with respect to free exercise, is misplaced. Section 64–4, which is not a part of the Unemployment Compensation Law, is an extremely narrow provision that becomes operative only during periods of national emergency and thus has no bearing in the circumstances of the present case. . . . [Footnote by Justice Harlan.]

[The meaning of the holding is that the State] must *single out* for financial assistance those whose behavior is religiously motivated, even though it denies such assistance to others whose identical behavior (in this case, inability to work on Saturdays) is not religiously motivated.

It has been suggested that such singling out of religious conduct for special treatment may violate the constitutional limitations on state action. See Kurland, Of Church and State and The Supreme Court, 29 U.Chi.L.Rev. 1. My own view, however, is that at least under the circumstances of this case it would be a permissible accommodation of religion for the State, if it *chose* to do so, to create an exception to its eligibility requirements for persons like the appellant. The constitutional obligation of "neutrality," see [Schempp], is not so narrow a channel that the slightest deviation from an absolutely straight course leads to condemnation. There are too many instances in which no such course can be charted, too many areas in which the pervasive activities of the State justify some special provision for religion to prevent it from being submerged by an all-embracing secularism. . . . [But] I cannot subscribe to the conclusion that the State is constitutionally *compelled* to carve out an exception to its general rule of eligibility in the present case. Those situations in which the Constitution may require special treatment on account of religion are, in my view, few and far between, and this view is amply supported by the course of constitutional litigation in this area. Such compulsion in the present case is particularly inappropriate in light of the indirect, remote, and insubstantial effect of the decision below on the exercise of appellant's religion and in light of the direct financial assistance to religion that today's decision requires. . . . *

WISCONSIN v. YODER

406 U.S. 205, 92 S.Ct. 1526, 32 L.Ed.2d 15 (1972).

Certiorari to the Supreme Court of Wisconsin.

Mr. Chief Justice BURGER delivered the opinion of the Court.

[We granted certiorari] to review a decision of the Wisconsin Supreme Court holding that respondents' convictions of violating the State's compulsory school-attendance law were invalid under the Free Exercise Clause. [We affirm.]

Respondents Jonas Yoder and Wallace Miller are members of the Old Order Amish Religion, and respondent Adin Yutzy is a member of the Conservative Amish Mennonite Church. . . . Wisconsin's compulsory school attendance law required them to cause their children to attend public or private school until reaching age 16 but the respondents declined to send their children, ages 14 and 15, to public school after they completed the eighth

---

* Compare the affirmance, by an equally divided Court, in Dewey v. Reynolds Metals Co., 402 U.S. 689 (1971): In an action under Title VII of the 1964 Civil Rights Act, the Court of Appeals [429 F.2d 324 (6th Cir. 1970)] had held, inter alia, that the Act did not bar the employer from discharging an employee who, because of religious beliefs, refused to comply with a union contract provision requiring him to work or obtain a replacement to work on Sundays. The case is discussed in Edwards and Kaplan, "Religious Discrimination and the Role of Arbitration under Title VII," 69 Mich.L.Rev. 599 (1971).

grade. [Respondents were convicted under the compulsory attendance law and were fined $5 each.] Trial testimony showed that they believed that by sending their children to high school, they [would] endanger their own salvation and that of their children. The State stipulated that respondents' religious beliefs were sincere. . . .

Formal high school education beyond the eighth grade is contrary to Amish beliefs, not only because it places Amish children in an environment hostile to Amish beliefs with increasing emphasis on competition in class work and sports and with pressure to conform to the styles, manners, and ways of the peer group, but also because it takes them away from their community, physically and emotionally, during the crucial and formative adolescent period of life. During this period, the children must acquire Amish attitudes favoring manual work and self-reliance and the specific skills needed to perform the adult role of an Amish farmer or housewife. . . .

[An expert] testified that compulsory high school attendance could not only result in great psychological harm to Amish children, because of the conflicts it would produce, but would also, in his opinion, ultimately result in the destruction of the Old Order Amish church community as it exists in the United States today. The testimony of [another expert] also showed that the Amish succeed in preparing their high school age children to be productive members of the Amish community. [The] evidence also showed that the Amish have an excellent record as law-abiding and generally self-sufficient members of society. . . .

[A] State's interest in universal education, however highly we rank it, is not totally free from a balancing process when it impinges on fundamental rights and interests, such as those specifically protected by the Free Exercise Clause of the First Amendment, and the traditional interest of parents with respect to the religious upbringing of their children . . . . It follows that in order for Wisconsin to compel school attendance beyond the eighth grade against a claim that such attendance interferes with the practice of a legitimate religious belief, it must appear either that the State does not deny the free exercise of religious belief by its requirement, or that there is a state interest of sufficient magnitude to override the interest claiming protection under the Free Exercise Clause. [O]nly those interests of the highest order and those not otherwise served can overbalance legitimate claims to the free exercise of religion. . . .

. . . In evaluating [respondents'] claims we must be careful to determine whether the Amish religious faith and their mode of life are, as they claim, inseparable and interdependent. A way of life, however virtuous and admirable, may not be interposed as a barrier to reasonable state regulation of education if it is based on purely secular considerations; to have the protection of the Religion Clauses, the claims must be rooted in religious belief. Although a determination of what is a "religious" belief or practice entitled to constitutional protection may present a most delicate question, the very concept of ordered liberty precludes allowing every person to make his own standards on matters of conduct in which society as a whole has important interests. Thus, if the Amish asserted their claims because of their subjective evaluation and rejection of the contemporary secular values accepted by the majority, much as Thoreau rejected the social values of his time and isolated

himself at Walden Pond, their claim would not rest on a religious basis. Thoreau's choice was philosophical and personal rather than religious, and such belief does not rise to the demands of the Religion Clause.

Giving no weight to such secular considerations, however, we see that the record in this case abundantly supports the claim that the traditional way of life of the Amish is not merely a matter of personal preference, but one of deep religious conviction, shared by an organized group, and intimately related to daily living. That the Old Order Amish daily life and religious practice stem from their faith is shown by the fact that it is in response to their literal interpretation of the Biblical injunction from the Epistle of Paul to the Romans, "be not conformed to this world . . . ." This command is fundamental to the Amish faith. Moreover, for the Old Order Amish, religion is not simply a matter of theocratic belief. As the expert witnesses explained, the Old Order Amish religion pervades and determines virtually their entire way of life, regulating it with the detail of the Talmudic diet through the strictly enforced rules of the church community. . . .

The impact of the compulsory-attendance law on respondents' practice of the Amish religion is not only severe, but inescapable, for the Wisconsin law affirmatively compels them, under threat of criminal sanction, to perform acts undeniably at odds with fundamental tenets of their religious beliefs. See [Braunfeld]. Nor is the impact of the compulsory-attendance law confined to grave interference with important Amish religious tenets from a subjective point of view. It carries with it precisely the kind of objective danger to the free exercise of religion which the First Amendment was designed to prevent. [It raises] a very real threat of undermining the Amish community and religious practice as they exist today; they must either abandon belief and be assimilated into society at large, or be forced to migrate to some other and more tolerant region. [In sum], enforcement of the State's requirement of compulsory formal education after the eighth grade would gravely endanger if not destroy the free exercise of respondents' religious beliefs.

. . . [The State does not challenge] the claim that the Amish mode of life and education is inseparable from and a part of the basic tenets of their religion—indeed, as much a part of their religious belief and practices as baptism, the confessional, or a sabbath may be for others. The Court must not ignore the danger that an exception from a general obligation of citizenship on religious grounds may run afoul of the Establishment Clause, but that danger cannot be allowed to prevent any exception no matter how vital it may be to the protection of values promoted by the right of free exercise. . . .

The State advances two primary arguments in support of its system of compulsory education. It notes, as Thomas Jefferson pointed out early in our history, that some degree of education is necessary to prepare citizens to participate effectively and intelligently in our open political system if we are to preserve freedom and independence. Further, education prepares individuals to be self-reliant and self-sufficient participants in society. We accept these propositions.

However, the evidence adduced by the Amish in this case is persuasively to the effect that an additional one or two years of formal high school for

Amish children in place of their long-established program of informal vocational education would do little to serve those interests. . . . It is one thing to say that compulsory education for a year or two beyond the eighth grade may be necessary when its goal is the preparation of the child for life in modern society as the majority live, but it is quite another if the goal of education be viewed as the preparation of the child for life in the separated agrarian community that is the keystone of the Amish faith.

The State attacks respondents' position as one fostering "ignorance" from which the child must be protected by the State. [But] this record strongly shows that the Amish community has been a highly successful social unit within our society, even if apart from the conventional "mainstream." Its members are productive and very law-abiding members of society; they reject public welfare in any of its usual modern views. The Congress itself recognized their self-sufficiency by authorizing exemption of such groups as the Amish from the obligation to pay social security taxes.[1] A way of life that is odd or even erratic but interferes with no rights or interests of others is not to be condemned because it is different.

The State, however, supports its interest in providing an additional one or two years of compulsory high school education to Amish children because of the possibility that some such children will choose to leave the Amish community, and that if this occurs they will be ill-equipped for life. . . . However, on this record, that argument is highly speculative. . . .

Contrary to the suggestion [in Justice Douglas' dissent], our holding today in no degree depends on the assertion of the religious interest of the child as contrasted with that of the parents. It is the parents who are subject to prosecution here [and] it is their right of free exercise, not that of their children, that must determine Wisconsin's power to impose criminal penalties on the parent. The dissent argues that a child who expresses a desire to attend public high school in conflict with the wishes of his parents should not be prevented from doing so. There is no reason for the Court to consider that point since it is not an issue in the case. The children are not parties to this litigation. The State has at no point tried this case on the theory that respondents were preventing their children from attending school against their expressed desires, and indeed the record is to the contrary.[2] . . .

Our holding in no way determines the proper resolution of possible competing interests of parents, children, and the State in an appropriate state

1. 26 U.S.C. § 1402(h) authorizes the Secretary of Health, Education, and Welfare to exempt members of "a recognized religious sect" existing at all times since December 13, 1950, from the obligation to pay social security taxes if they are, by reason of the tenets of their sect, opposed to receipt of such benefits and agree to waive them, provided the Secretary finds that the sect makes reasonable provision for its dependent members. . . .

The record in this case establishes without contradiction that the Green County Amish had never been known to commit crimes, that none had been known to receive public assistance, and that none were unemployed. [Footnote by the Court.]

2. The only relevant testimony in the record is to the effect that the wishes of the one child who testified corresponded with those of her parents. Testimony of Frieda Yoder, Tr. 92–94, to the effect that her personal religious beliefs guided her decision to discontinue school attendance after the 8th grade. The other children were not called by either side. [Footnote by the Court.]

court proceeding in which the power of the State is asserted on the theory that Amish parents are preventing their minor children from attending high school despite their expressed desires to the contrary.   Recognition of the claim of the State in such a proceeding would, of course, call into question traditional concepts of parental control over the religious upbringing and education of their minor children recognized in this Court's past decisions.   It is clear that such an intrusion by a State into family decisions in the area of religious training would give rise to grave questions of religious freedom . . . .   On this record we neither reach nor decide those issues.[3]

      . . .   It cannot be over-emphasized that we are not dealing with a way of life and mode of education by a group claiming to have recently discovered some "progressive" or more enlightened process for rearing children for modern life.   [In light of the "convincing showing" by the Amish here,] one that probably few other religious groups or sects could make, and weighing the minimal difference between what the State would require and what the Amish already accept, it was incumbent on the State to show with more particularity how its admittedly strong interest in compulsory education would be adversely affected by granting an exemption to the Amish.   Sherbert v. Verner.   . . . [4]

      Affirmed.

      Mr. Justice POWELL and Mr. Justice REHNQUIST took no part in the consideration or decision of this case.

      Mr Justice STEWART, with whom Mr. Justice BRENNAN joins, concurring.

      . . .   This case in no way involves any questions regarding the right of the children of Amish parents to attend public high schools, or any other institutions of learning, if they wish to do so.   [T]his record simply does not present the interesting and important issue discussed in Part II of the dissenting opinion of Mr. Justice Douglas.   . . .

      Mr. Justice WHITE, with whom Mr. Justice BRENNAN and Mr. Justice STEWART, join, concurring.   . . .

3. What we have said should meet the suggestion that the decision of the Wisconsin Supreme Court recognizing an exemption for the Amish from the State's system of compulsory education constituted an impermissible establishment of religion. . . . Accommodating the religious beliefs of the Amish can hardly be characterized as sponsorship or active involvement. The purpose and effect of such an exemption are not to support, favor, advance, or assist the Amish, but to allow their centuries-old religious society, here long before the advent of any compulsory education, to survive free from the heavy impediment compliance with the Wisconsin compulsory-education law would impose. Such an accommodation "reflects nothing more than the governmental obligation of neutrality in the face of religious differences, and does not represent that involvement of religious with secular institutions which it is the object of the Establishment Clause to forestall." [Sherbert v. Verner.] [Footnote by the Court.]

4. Several States have now adopted plans to accommodate Amish religious beliefs through the establishment of an "Amish vocational school." These are not schools in the traditional sense of the word. . . . There is no basis to assume that Wisconsin will be unable to reach a satisfactory accommodation with the Amish in light of what we now hold, so as to serve its interests without impinging on respondents' protected free exercise of their religion. [Footnote by the Court.]

This would be a very different case for me if respondents' claim were that their religion forbade their children from attending any school at any time. . . .

Decision in cases such as this [will] inevitably involve the kind of close and perhaps repeated scrutiny of religious practices, as is exemplified in today's opinion, which the Court has heretofore been anxious to avoid. But such entanglement does not create a forbidden establishment of religion where it is essential to implement free exercise values threatened by an otherwise neutral program instituted to foster some permissible, nonreligious state objective. I join the Court because the sincerity of the Amish religious policy here is uncontested, because the potential adverse impact of the state requirement is great, and because the State's valid interest in education has already been largely satisfied by the eight years the children have already spent in school.

Mr. Justice DOUGLAS, dissenting in part. . . .

It is argued that the right of the Amish children to religious freedom is not presented by the facts of the case. [I]t is essential to reach the question to decide the case, not only because the question was squarely raised in the motion to dismiss, but also because no analysis of religious-liberty claims can take place in a vacuum. If the parents in this case are allowed a religious exemption, the inevitable effect is to impose the parents' notions of religious duty upon their children. Where the child is mature enough to express potentially conflicting desires, it would be an invasion of the child's rights to permit such an imposition without canvassing his views. [I]t is an imposition resulting from this very litigation. As the child has no other effective forum, it is in this litigation that his rights should be considered. And, if an Amish child desires to attend high school, and is mature enough to have that desire respected, the State may well be able to override the parents' religiously motivated objections.

[Crucial] are the views of the child whose parent is the subject of the suit. Frieda Yoder has in fact testified that her own religious views are opposed to high-school education. I therefore join the judgment of the Court as to respondent Jonas Yoder. But Frieda Yoder's views may not be those of Vernon Yutzy or Barbara Miller. I must dissent, therefore, as to respondents Adin Yutzy and Wallace Miller as their motion to dismiss also raised the question of their children's religious liberty.

This issue has never been squarely presented before today. Our opinions are full of talk about the power of the parents over the child's education. [See Pierce and Meyer, chap. 9.] Recent cases, however, have clearly held that the children themselves have constitutionally protectible interests. [E. g., Tinker, chap. 12.] While the parents, absent dissent, normally speak for the entire family, the education of the child is a matter on which the child will often have decided views. . . . It is the student's judgment, not his parents', that is essential if we are to give full meaning to what we have said about the Bill of Rights and of the right of students to be masters of their own destiny. [The child] should be given an opportunity to be heard before the State gives the exemption which we honor today. . . .

I think the emphasis of the Court on the "law and order" record of this Amish group of people is quite irrelevant. A religion is a religion irrespec-

tive of what the misdemeanor or felony records of its members might be. I am not at all sure how the Catholics, Episcopalians, the Baptists, Jehovah's Witnesses, the Unitarians, and my own Presbyterians would make out if subjected to such a test. It is, of course, true that if a group or society was organized to perpetuate crime and if that is its motive, we would have rather startling problems akin to those that were raised when some years back a particular sect was challenged here as operating on a fraudulent basis. [United States v. Ballard.] But no such factors are present here, and the Amish, whether with a high or low criminal record,[1] certainly qualify by all historic standards as a religion within the meaning of the First Amendment.

The Court rightly rejects the notion that actions, even though religiously grounded, are always outside the protection of the Free Exercise Clause [and in so ruling] departs from the teaching of [Reynolds v. United States]. . . . What we do today, at least in this respect, opens the way to give organized religion a broader base than it has ever enjoyed; and it even promises that in time Reynolds will be overruled.

In another way, however, the Court retreats when in reference to Henry Thoreau it says his "choice was philosophical and personal rather than religious, and such belief does not rise to the demands of the Religion Clause." That is contrary to what we held in [Seeger and Welsh, the conscientious objector cases below]. . . .

SOME PROBLEMS IN INTERPRETING THE FREE EXERCISE GUARANTEE

1. *The criteria of Braunfeld, Sherbert and Yoder.* Note that Justice Brennan, who dissented in Braunfeld, wrote for the majority in Sherbert. Are Braunfeld and Sherbert reconcilable? On the basis of the criteria in the prevailing opinions in the two cases? On the basis of other criteria? Are Braunfeld, Sherbert, and similar cases in this section usefully analyzed in terms of "direct" and "indirect" burdens? In terms of a "belief"-"action" distinction? Does Wisconsin v. Yoder clarify the uncertainties left by Braunfeld and Sherbert? Do these recent cases make it clear that religiously based conduct may sometimes claim constitutional exemption from regulatory statutes? Has balancing become the appropriate—inevitable?—analysis? Is it similar to the balancing in First Amendment cases: Must the state show a compelling justification? Must it demonstrate that it has resorted to the least restrictive alternative?

---

1. The observation of Justice Heffernan, dissenting below, that the principal opinion in his Court portrayed the Amish as leading a life of "idyllic agrarianism," is equally applicable to the majority opinion in this Court. So, too, is his observation that such a portrayal rests on a "mythological basis." Professor Hostetler [one of the expert witnesses relied on by the Court] has noted that, "Drinking is common in all large Amish settlements." Amish Society, 283. Moreover, "[i]t would appear that among the Amish the rate of suicide is just as high, if not higher, than for the nation." He also notes an unfortunate Amish "preoccupation with filthy stories," as well as significant "rowdyism and stress." These are not traits peculiar to the Amish, of course. The point is that the Amish are not people set apart and different. [Footnote by Justice Douglas.]

Do constitutionally mandated exemption cases such as Sherbert and Yoder support Justice Stewart's concern, in Sherbert, about a "double-barreled dilemma"? Has the Court adequately addressed the problem of impinging on establishment clause values by finding some religiously based conduct exempt? In Sherbert? In Yoder? How should the tension between the religion clauses be resolved? Do Sherbert and Yoder rule out Professor Kurland's "neutrality" solution (see the introduction to this section), barring any "classification in terms of religion either to confer a benefit or to impose a burden"? * If pure neutrality is inappropriate, is Justice Harlan's suggestion in Sherbert the preferable one—that government may, but need not, carve out an exception in the face of religious scruples? Or does even that variety of accommodation with (special treatment of?) religion run into the principles of the establishment clause cases? The Sherbert and Yoder results require even more "accommodation" than Justice Harlan supported. Do those results reinforce the view that the "wall of separation" metaphor of some of the establishment decisions is not to be taken literally?

2. *State regulation and religious scruples: Some other examples.* Re-examine, in light of the criteria stated and applied in the recent cases, the earlier examples of conflicts of free exercise claims with state regulatory power—e. g., Barnette (flag salute), Reynolds (polygamy), and Prince v. Massachusetts (child labor). Consider, too, other illustrations of claims to constitutional exemption from general statutes on the basis of religious scruples: e. g., In re Jenison, 375 U.S. 14 (1963) (remanding for reconsideration in light of Sherbert a conviction of a woman who had refused jury duty for religious reasons); Jacobson v. Massachusetts, 197 U.S. 11 (1905) (compulsory vaccination); Memorial Hospital v. Anderson, 42 N.J. 421, cert. den., 377 U.S. 958 (1964), and Application of Georgetown College, 331 F.2d 1000 (D.C.Cir.), cert. den., 377 U.S. 978 (1964) (compulsory blood transfusion); People v. Woody, 61 Cal.2d 716 (1964) (ban on the drug peyote unconstitutional as applied to use in bona fide religious practices by the Native American Church),† see Comment, 17 Stan.L.Rev. 494 (1965); and compare Lawson v. Commonwealth, 164 S.W.2d 972 (Ky.1942) (use of poisonous snakes in religious ceremonies).**

---

* Can the course of decisions be reconciled with a "neutrality" principle by viewing "religion" as broadly as the Court has viewed it in interpreting statutory references to religion in the conscientious objector exemption to the draft laws? See cases such as United States v. Seeger, below.

† Compare Kennedy v. Bureau of Narcotics, 459 F.2d 415 (9th Cir. 1972) (challenge by the "Church of the Awakening" to a regulation exempting from federal control the use of peyote "in bona fide religious ceremonies of the Native American Church").

** See generally Clark, "Guidelines for the Free Exercise Clause," 83 Harv. L.Rev. 327 (1969); Giannella, "Religious Liberty, Nonestablishment, and Doctrinal Development: Part I, The Religious Liberty Guarantee," 80 Harv.L.Rev. 1381 (1967); and Fernandez, "The Free Exercise of Religion," 36 So.Cal.L.Rev. 546 (1963).

MILITARY SERVICE, THE CONSCIENTIOUS OBJECTOR, AND RELIGION

1. *The background.* Selective service laws have typically exempted from military service conscientious objectors opposed to "war in any form" on "religious" grounds. The Court has traditionally assumed that the exemption is a matter of legislative grace, is not compelled by the free exercise clause, and does not violate the establishment clause. Do the modern interpretations of the religion clauses cast doubt on those assumptions? (Compare the recent cases in notes 4 and 5 below.) For the traditional view, see the sustaining of the World War I version of the conscientious objector exemption in the Selective Draft Law Cases, 245 U.S. 366 (1918), where the Court summarily rejected free exercise and establishment clause objections. See also Hamilton v. Regents, 293 U.S. 245 (1934), where a requirement that all male students take military science courses was sustained against a claim that it violated the religious beliefs of a conscientious objector.

2. *The scope of "religion" in the modern draft law: The Seeger case.* Sec. 6(j) of the Universal Military Training and Service Act of 1948 exempted from combatant military service those persons who were conscientiously opposed to participation in war in any form by reason of their "religious training and belief." The quoted phrase was defined as a "belief in a relation to a Supreme Being involving duties superior to those arising from any human relation, but [not including] essentially political, sociological, or philosophical views or a merely personal moral code." [1] The section was attacked under the establishment, free exercise, and due process clauses, on the grounds that it did not exempt nonreligious conscientious objectors and that it discriminated among different forms of religious expression.

In three cases decided as UNITED STATES v. SEEGER, 380 U.S. 163 (1965), the Court did not reach these constitutional claims; rather, Justice Clark's opinion interpreted Section 6(j) and its references to religion very broadly, so that all petitioners proved entitled to the exemption: "We have concluded that Congress, in using the expression 'Supreme Being' rather than the designation 'God,' was merely clarifying the meaning of religious training and belief so as to embrace all religions and to exclude essentially political, sociological, or philosophical views. We believe that under this construction, the test of belief 'in a relation to a Supreme Being' is whether a given belief that is sincere and meaningful occupies a place in the life of its possessor parallel to that filled by the orthodox belief in God of one who clearly qualifies for the exemption. Where such beliefs have parallel positions in the lives of their respective holders we cannot say that one is 'in a relation to a Supreme Being' and the other is not." [2]

1. A 1967 amendment deleted the statutory reference to a "belief in a relation to a Supreme Being."

2. In discussing the application of this standard, the Court emphasized "that in resolving these exemption problems one deals with the beliefs of different individuals who will articulate them in a multitude of ways. In such an intensely personal area, of course, the claim of the registrant that his belief is an essential part of a religious faith must be given great weight. . . . The validity of what he believes cannot be questioned. Some theologians, and indeed some examiners, might be tempted to question the

In a concurring opinion, Justice Douglas discussed "the idea of God" in Hinduism and Buddhism to illustrate the "fluidity and evanescent scope of the concept." He stated, moreover, that he "would have difficulties" if he "read the statute differently" from the Court: "For then those who embraced one religious faith rather than another would be subject to penalties; and that kind of discrimination, as we held in [Sherbert v. Verner] would violate the Free Exercise Clause [and] would also result in a denial of equal protection by preferring some religions over others."

3. *The scope of "religion" and the draft law: The Welsh case.* In WELSH v. UNITED STATES, 398 U.S. 333 (1970), the plurality opinion rested reversal of petitioner's conviction on a statutory interpretation of § 6 (j) which elaborated on Seeger. But in Welsh, several of the separate opinions reached constitutional issues.[3] Justice Black's plurality opinion found no adequate reason to distinguish Welsh's case from Seeger's. Welsh, to be sure, had struck the word "religious" on his application, but that did not bar the exemption: "[V]ery few registrants are fully aware of the broad scope of the word 'religious' as used in § 6(j)." Moreover, Welsh's claim was not barred by the exclusion in § 6(j) of those persons with "essentially political, sociological, or philosophical views or a merely personal moral code." That language, Justice Black concluded, should not be read "to exclude those who hold strong beliefs about our domestic and foreign affairs or even those whose conscientious objection to participation in all wars is founded to a substantial extent upon considerations of public policy. The two groups of registrants that obviously do fall within these exclusions from the exemption are those whose beliefs are not deeply held and those whose objection to war does not rest at all upon moral, ethical, or religious principle but instead rests solely upon considerations of policy, pragmatism, or expediency."

Justice Harlan's opinion concurring in the result took a very different route. He found that the Seeger interpretation of § 6(j), which he had joined, exceeded the limits of permissible statutory interpretation; thought that § 6(j) must be read as limited to "those opposed to war in general because of

existence of the registrant's 'Supreme Being' or the truth of his concepts. But these are inquiries foreclosed to Government. [United States v. Ballard, sec. 1B.] Local boards and courts in this sense are not free to reject beliefs because they consider them 'incomprehensible.' Their task is to decide whether the beliefs professed by a registrant are sincerely held and whether they are, in his own scheme of things, religious. But we hasten to emphasize that while the 'truth' of a belief is not open to question, there remains the significant question whether it is 'truly held.'" See Rabin, "When is a Religious Belief Religious . . .," 51 Corn.L.Q. 231 (1966), and White, "Processing Conscientious Objector Claims: A Constitutional Inquiry," 56 Calif.L.Rev. 652 (1968).

3. Justice Black wrote the plurality opinion, joined by Justices Douglas, Brennan and Marshall. Justice Harlan thought he had "made a mistake" in Seeger and adopted a narrower reading of the conscientious objector exemption; he nevertheless joined the judgment reversing the conviction because he found the narrowly construed statutory provision unconstitutional. Justice White, joined by Chief Justice Burger and Justice Stewart, dissented. He did not think that petitioner qualified for an exemption under the Seeger interpretation; and he, like Justice Harlan but unlike the plurality opinion, addressed himself to the constitutional issue. Justice Blackmun did not participate in the case.

theistic beliefs"; went on to hold that interpretation unconstitutional under the First Amendment; and concluded that the Court, rather than nullifying the exemption entirely, should extend its coverage to those like Welsh who had been unconstitutionally excluded from its coverage. On the constitutional issue, he stated that Congress "cannot draw the line between theistic or nontheistic religious beliefs on the one hand and secular beliefs on the other. Any such distinctions are not, in my view, compatible with the Establishment Clause."

Justice White's dissent concluded that, whether or not Seeger was an accurate reflection of legislative intent, "I cannot join today's construction of § 6(j) extending draft exemption to those who disclaim religious objections to war and whose views about war represent a purely personal code arising not from religious training and belief as the statute requires but from readings in philosophy, history, and sociology." And if the establishment clause issue were reached, he added, he would find the "religious training and belief" requirement constitutional. Such an exemption would not constitute establishment even if it were not required by the Free Exercise Clause: "It is very likely that § 6(j) is a recognition by Congress of free exercise values . . .. That judgment is entitled to respect." It was surely "necessary and proper" in enacting laws for the raising of armies, Justice White explained, "to take account of the First Amendment and to avoid possible violations of the Free Exercise Clause. If this was the course Congress took, then just as in [Katzenbach v. Morgan, chap. 11], where we accepted the judgment of Congress as to what legislation was appropriate to enforce the Equal Protection Clause of the Fourteenth Amendment, here we should respect congressional judgment accommodating the Free Exercise Clause and the power to raise armies. This involves no surrender of the Court's function as ultimate arbiter in disputes over interpretation of the Constitution. But it was enough in Katzenbach 'to perceive a basis upon which the Congress might resolve the conflict as it did,' and plainly in the case before us there is an arguable basis for § 6(j) in the Free Exercise Clause." [4]

4. *Selective conscientious objection: The Gillette case.* The 8 to 1 decision in GILLETTE v. UNITED STATES (decided together with Negre v. Larsen), 401 U.S. 437 (1971), held that the congressional refusal to exempt selective conscientious objectors from the draft was constitutional. The petitioners did not oppose all wars, but they objected to participation in the Vietnam conflict as an "unjust" war. Negre, for example, claimed that it was his duty as a faithful Catholic to discriminate between "just" and "unjust" wars, and to refuse participation in the latter. Justice Marshall's majority opinion rejected at the outset the argument that petitioners were entitled to statutory exemption under § 6(j) because they were "conscientiously opposed to participation in war in any form": "This language, on a straightforward reading, can bear but one meaning: that conscientious scruples relating to war and military service must amount to conscientious opposition to participating personally in any war and all war."

---

4. See generally Note, "The Conscientious Objector and the First Amendment: There But for the Grace of God," 34 U.Chi.L.Rev. 79 (1966), and Note, "Religious and Conscientious Objection," 21 Stan.L.Rev. 734 (1969).

Justice Marshall then turned to the constitutional challenge and found the exemption as so construed valid. He stated that, "despite free exercise overtones, the gist of the constitutional complaint is that § 6(j) impermissibly discriminates among types of religious belief and affiliation." The Court rejected that attack because it found "neutral, secular reasons to justify the line that Congress has drawn." The statute did not discriminate between religions on its face; but that, Justice Marshall conceded, did not end the matter, "for the Establishment Clause forbids subtle departures from neutrality, 'religious gerrymanders,' as well as obvious abuses. [Still] a claimant alleging 'gerrymander' must be able to show the absence of a neutral, secular basis for the lines government has drawn." And that showing had not been made here: "We conclude not only that the affirmative purposes underlying § 6(j) are neutral and secular, but also that valid neutral reasons exist for limiting the exemption to objectors to all war, and that the section therefore cannot be said to reflect a religious preference."

In examining the asserted justifications for the limitation on the exemption, the Court was most impressed by the Government's argument that "the interest in fairness would be jeopardized by expansion of § 6(j) to include conscientious objection to a particular war." He noted the risk "that granting the claim in theory would involve the real danger of erratic or even discriminatory decisionmaking in administrative practice," and added: "Ours is a Nation of enormous heterogeneity in respect of political views, moral codes, and religious persuasions. It does not bespeak an establishing of religion for Congress to forgo the enterprise of distinguishing those whose dissent has some conscientious basis from those who simply dissent. There is a danger that as between two would-be objectors, [that] objector would succeed who is more articulate, better educated, or better counseled. There is even a danger of unintended religious discrimination—a danger that a claim's chances of success would be greater the more familiar or salient the claim's connection with conventional religiosity could be made to appear." Justice Marshall also noted an argument that recognition of such claims would "open the doors to a general theory of selective disobedience to law" and jeopardize the binding quality of democratic decisions. Justice Marshall commented: "Should it be thought that those who go to war are chosen unfairly or capriciously, then a mood of bitterness and cynicism might corrode the spirit of public service and the values of willing performance of a citizen's duties that are the very heart of free government."

Justice Marshall recognized that the free exercise claim had "a reach of its own." He added, however: "Nonetheless, our analysis of § 6(j) for Establishment Clause purposes has revealed governmental interests of a kind and weight sufficient to justify under the Free Exercise Clause the impact of the conscription laws on those who object to particular wars." Even with neutral laws having secular aims, "the Free Exercise Clause may condemn certain applications clashing with imperatives of religion and conscience, when the burden on First Amendment values is not justifiable in terms of the Government's valid aims. [Sherbert v. Verner.] However, the impact of conscription on objectors to particular wars is far from unjustified. [The laws] are not designed to interfere with any religious ritual or practice, and do not work a penalty against any theological position. The incidental

burdens felt by persons in petitioners' position are strictly justified by substantial government interests that relate directly to the very impacts questioned. And more broadly, of course, there is the Government's interest in procuring the manpower necessary for military purposes." [5]

Justice Douglas' dissent emphasized the "implied First Amendment right" of "conscience": "It is true that the First Amendment speaks of the free exercise of religion, not of the free exercise of conscience or belief. Yet conscience and belief are the main ingredients of First Amendment rights." And, he added, "[t]he constitutional infirmity in the present Act seems obvious once 'conscience' is the guide." He continued: "The law as written is a species of those which show an invidious discrimination in favor of religious persons and against others with like scruples."

5. *Denying veterans' benefits to conscientious objectors: Johnson v. Robison.* JOHNSON v. ROBISON, 415 U.S. 361 (1974), was a constitutional attack on the statutory scheme which denies veterans' educational benefits to alternate service conscientious objectors while granting them to veterans of the armed forces. After disposing of an equal protection challenge (see chap. 10), Justice Brennan's majority opinion rejected the free exercise claim on the basis of an analysis closely tracking that in Gillette. The Court was once again divided 8 to 1. Justice Brennan noted that members of the disadvantaged class were not required "to make any choice comparable to that required of the petitioners in Gillette. The withholding of educational benefits involves only an incidental burden upon appellee's free exercise of religion—if, indeed, any burden exists at all." [6] He found that "the Government's substantial interest in raising and supporting armies, Art. I, § 8, is of 'a kind and weight' clearly sufficient to sustain the challenged legislation."

Justice Douglas was once again the sole dissenter. He insisted that the line of free exercise cases culminating in Sherbert v. Verner and Wisconsin v. Yoder was applicable and he insisted that government "may not place a penalty on anyone for asserting his religious scruples." He thought Gillette "irrelevant": the conscientious objector claim here was concededly valid; the classification was not neutral; and the burden on religious belief was not "incidental." He noted, moreover, that "the only governmental interest here is the financial one of [denying] educational benefits."

5. Justice Marshall added in a footnote: "We are not faced with the question whether the Free Exercise Clause itself would require exemption of any class other than objectors to particular wars. A free exercise claim on behalf of such objectors collides with the distinct governmental interests already discussed, and, at any rate, no other claim is presented. We note that the Court has previously suggested that relief for conscientious objectors is not mandated by the Constitution. See Hamilton v. Regents, 293 U.S. 245, 264 (1934)."

6. Justice Brennan suggested in a footnote that "Congress' decision to grant educational benefits to military servicemen might arguably be viewed as an attempt to equalize the burdens of military service and alternate civilian service, rather than an effort by Congress to place a relative burden upon a conscientious objector's free exercise of religion."

Chapter 15

PROPER CONDITIONS FOR CONSTITUTIONAL
ADJUDICATION:
INTERESTED PARTIES; CONCRETE CONTROVERSIES;
JUSTICIABLE ISSUES

AN INTRODUCTORY NOTE

This chapter returns to and elaborates themes introduced in chap. 1. That first chapter explored the legitimacy and framework of constitutional adjudication. This chapter examines some recurrent problems of the constitutional adjudication process. What are the appropriate circumstances for constitutional adjudication? When may courts decide constitutional issues? At whose behest? At what stages of a dispute? As to what issues? The foundations of judicial authority in chap. 1 are essential but not adequate ingredients for an understanding of the institutional context of constitutional litigation. The "jurisdictional" and "procedural" materials which follow provide some minimal amplifications. The purpose of this chapter goes beyond the sharpening of professional skills in advancing constitutional claims for judicial consideration. The concern here is with court as well as with lawyer. What are the institutional limitations on constitutional adjudication? What are the justifications for those limits?

Some of the materials in this chapter will seem technical and esoteric. Frequently, the contours of the rules are unclear, the justifications perplexing, the applications chaotic. Yet these problems are not mere technicalities; they go to the heart of the Supreme Court's place in the governmental structure. This chapter seeks to provide a minimum of "federal jurisdiction" material essential to an understanding of the role of the Court, which, after all, only acts as an organ of constitutional elaboration because it is a *court*, a judicial body deciding cases. Who may go to court? When—at what stage in the evolution of a dispute? As to what constitutional issues? This chapter, then, explores the who, when and what of constitutional adjudication.[1]

The limits on adjudication: Sources and policies. Two related problems surface repeatedly with respect to each of the limits on constitutional adjudication considered in this chapter. *First, where does the limitation come from?* To what extent does each derive from the Constitution, especially Art. III? To what extent does it derive from congressional action with respect to jurisdiction and remedies? To what extent is the source simply

---

1. For a useful recent commentary on the "who" and "when," see Monaghan, "Constitutional Adjudication: The Who and When," 82 Yale L.J. 1363 (1973) (hereinafter cited as Monaghan, "The Who and When"). The themes of this chapter are more fully explored in federal jurisdiction courses. See generally Bator, Mishkin, Shapiro and Wechsler, Hart and Wechsler's The Federal Courts and the Federal System (2d ed. 1973) (hereinafter cited as Hart and Wechsler, Federal Courts); Wright, Federal Courts (2d ed. 1970); and Currie, Federal Courts —Cases and Materials (2d ed. 1975).

the Court's own elaboration of rules and doctrines reflecting its view of the appropriate scope of judicial authority and the optimum conditions for its exercise? The cases abound with obscurities and inconsistencies regarding these questions. But an effort to make sense of them is worthwhile, if only because of the practical consequences. Thus, if a barrier to court access is derived from Art. III of the Constitution, Congress cannot readily remove it; but if a court's refusal to decide rests simply on a self-imposed limitation —a limitation resting on judicial discretion rather than on constitutional mandate—Congress can probably remove the limitation and compel adjudication.

Second, what are the policies that give rise to each of the limitations— and to what extent does each limitation truly serve to implement those policies? Consider especially the limits examined in the opening sections of this chapter, the limits going to the who and when of constitutional adjudication. The "who" question is especially raised by the cases on "standing": How much of a personal stake must an individual have in the outcome of a controversy in order to obtain a court ruling? (See sec. 2 below.) The "when" question is especially raised by the concept of "ripeness" (sec. 3 below): How far advanced must a dispute be, how fully developed must the issues be, to elicit a judicial resolution? To what extent do the answers to those questions turn on the Art. III limitation of the "judicial Power" to "Cases" and "Controversies"? To what extent are the limitations explainable by a desire to assure the best possible conditions for reasoned elaboration and thoughtful decision by courts—a desire "to assure that concrete adverseness which sharpens the presentation of issues upon which the court so largely depends for illumination of difficult questions," as the Court put it in Baker v. Carr, 369 U.S. 186 (1962) (sec. 5 below)? To what extent do the limitations reflect notions of judicial restraint and prudential judgments of institutional self-protection: notions of minimizing the occasions for and scope of judicial interventions; judgments designed to delay or avoid adjudications that are perceived as being unusually complex or controversial? To what extent do the limitations reflect efforts to ration limited judicial resources?[2] To what extent do the limitations reflect considerations of federalism: the interest in respecting state autonomy in its policymaking and judicial processes; the interest in avoiding federal-state friction? And to what extent do the various limitations flow from the justifications which make any judicial review legitimate?

The relevance of Marbury v. Madison. That last question invites reference back to Marbury v. Madison in chap. 1. In the materials in this chapter, the implications and ambiguities of the Marbury defense of constitutional adjudication play a central role. Recall the questions in chap. 1 about the nature of the judicial power John Marshall defended in that case. The major thrust of Marshall's reasoning was that the power of constitutional adjudication was an incident of the Court's obligation to decide the particular "case" before it. That emphasis gives rise to a "private rights" model of constitutional adjudication: it looks to the kinds of "cases" ordinarily handled by courts, and it suggests that the kind of individual interest neces-

2. See Scott, "Standing in the Supreme Court—A Functional Analysis," 86 Harv.L.Rev. 645 (1973).

sary to assure "standing" in a constitutional case is guided by the courts' ordinary rules as to private rights warranting judicial attention.

Yet there are some aspects of Marbury—including its emphasis on the importance of judicial enforcement of constitutional limitations—which suggest a "special function" model for constitutional adjudication. The Court's growing role over the years—and its own broader assertions (recall, e. g., Cooper v. Aaron in chap. 1)—lend added weight to that theme. That approach views the Court as having a special role in interpreting constitutional norms. If constitutional adjudication is seen as the Court's primary function, and safeguarding constitutional values its special task, it is possible to argue that the "personal interests" that are a prerequisite to eliciting court decisions in private litigation are excessively confining limits for constitutional adjudication. In short, a broad view of Marbury reinforces arguments that courts can decide constitutional questions in proceedings which do not conform to the model of traditional private litigation and at the instance of litigants who have no special, personal stake in the outcome.[3] That competition of views—between constitutional adjudication as an incidental byproduct and constitutional adjudication as a special function—may underlie a number of developments traced in the materials below. Consider, for example, to what extent that tension as to views of the Court's authority explains the shrinkage of "standing" barriers during the Warren years, as well as the shrinkage of the types of issues thought to be nonjusticiable "political questions."

Rules, discretion, and the merits. Most of the opinions below speak about a number of separate prerequisites to the exercise of the federal judicial function in constitutional cases: e. g., standing, ripeness, political questions. But are these separately stated elements truly separable ones? Does each have a distinguishable content of its own? Are they primarily principled requirements? Are they largely exercises of prudential judgment?[4]

Or are these superficially separate requirements not truly separable at all, but rather merely illustrations of a single underlying institutional policy— e. g., of avoidance of constitutional questions unless absolutely necessary? See especially secs. 1 and 4 below. Is any such general policy compelled by the Constitution? Is it a permissible position? A principled one? Or is it mainly a discretionary policy of institutional prudence, a policy of ad hoc judgments about the political propriety of judicial intervention—judgments resting, for example, on balancing the desirability of a decision against such institutional costs as hostile political reactions?

And are those limits on adjudication—whether separable or an interrelated whole, whether externally imposed or Court-made, whether principled

3. For a discussion of the "private rights" and "special function" models, see Monaghan, "The Who and When," 82 Yale L.J. 1363 (1973).

4. For disagreement on the question of whether these and related requirements must be as principled in their content as substantive constitutional doctrines themselves, or whether they are properly exercises of prudential judgment rather than delineations of principle, compare Bickel, The Least Dangerous Branch (1962), with Gunther, "The Subtle Vices of the 'Passive Virtues'—A Comment on Principle and Expediency in Judicial Review," 64 Colum.L.Rev. 1 (1964). That dispute is more fully developed below, especially in sec. 4.

or ad hoc—ultimately best understandable as disguised judgments on the merits?   To what extent are the concerns of this chapter really not institutional ones at all?   The cases claim to worry about what courts are good for, and when.   But are they, at least occasionally, really concerned with how valuable the substantive claim is, and to whom?   To what extent do (and to what degree should) decisions about the availability of a judicial forum turn on the merits of the constitutional claim?

Scope Note.   Before turning to the major limits on constitutional adjudication, this chapter briefly considers, in sec. 1, the best-established outer boundary of judicial authority: the ban against "advisory opinions."   That section also explores some related themes, including overarching policy arguments that seek to tie the advisory opinion ban to other limits on constitutional adjudication.   The remaining sections consider more specific ingredients of the limitations.   Sec. 2 focuses on the requisite litigant interest—the ingredients of "standing" to sue.   Sec. 3 turns to problems of ripeness.   Sec. 4 considers additional, Court-developed restraints: the claim that the Court has discretion to refuse adjudication of cases, even cases within its obligatory appeal jurisdiction;   and restraints in the interest of federalism, reflected in doctrines about federal court abstention and about noninterference with controversies in the state courts.[5]   Sec. 5, finally, turns to the most open-ended ingredients of the "political questions" doctrine.

SECTION 1.   SOME PERVASIVE THEMES: ADVISORY OPINIONS, ART. III BARRIERS, AND DISCRETION-ARY INSTITUTIONAL CONSIDERATIONS

1.   *Advisory opinions: The 1793 refusal.*   In 1793 President Washington sought the advice of the Justices of the Supreme Court on some perplexing legal questions then confronting him.   The Justices declined to help.   That refusal illustrates the most prominent, most continuously articulated boundary of justiciability: federal courts will not give "advisory opinions."   What justifies that limitation?   What are the objections to advisory opinions?   What distinguishes forbidden "advice" from permissible adjudication?

George Washington's request to the Justices was understandable.   He genuinely needed legal assistance in dealing with a major national concern, America's neutrality toward the on-going war between England and France.   Accordingly, on July 18, 1793, Secretary of State Thomas Jefferson, on behalf of the President, wrote to Chief Justice John Jay and the Associate Justices as follows:

"The war which has taken place among the powers of Europe produces frequent transactions within our ports and limits, on which questions arise of considerable difficulty, and of greater importance to the peace of the

5.   Recall also the federalistic limits on Supreme Court review reflected in the   "adequate state grounds" barrier, considered in chap. 1, sec. 4, above.

United States. These questions depend for their solution on the construction of our treaties, on the laws of nature and nations, and on the laws of the land, and are often presented under circumstances *which do not give a cognizance of them to the tribunals of the country.* Yet their decision is so little analogous to the ordinary functions of the executive, as to occasion much embarrassment and difficulty to them. The President therefore would be much relieved if he found himself free to refer questions of this description to the opinions of the judges of the Supreme Court of the United States, whose knowledge of the subject would secure us against errors dangerous to the peace of the United States, and their authority insure the respect of all parties. He has therefore asked the attendance of such of the judges as could be collected in time for the occasion, to know, in the first place, their opinion, whether the public may, with propriety, be availed of their *advice on these questions?* And if they may, to present, for their advice, the abstract questions which have already occurred, or may soon occur, from which they will themselves strike out such as any circumstances might, in their opinion, forbid them to pronounce on." [1]

A few weeks later, on August 8, 1793, the Justices replied to President Washington: "We have considered the previous question stated in a letter written by your direction to us by the Secretary of State on the 18th of last month, [regarding] the lines of separation drawn by the Constitution between the three departments of the government. These being in certain respects checks upon each other, and our being judges of a court in the last resort, are considerations which afford strong arguments against the propriety of our extrajudicially deciding the questions alluded to, especially as the power given by the Constitution to the President, of calling on the heads of departments for opinions, seems to have been *purposely* as well as expressly united to the *executive* departments.[2]

"We exceedingly regret every event that may cause embarrassment to your administration, but we derive consolation from the reflection that your judgment will discern what is right, and that your usual prudence, decision, and firmness will surmount every obstacle to the preservation of the rights, peace, and dignity of the United States."

1. The Jefferson letter, some of the questions accompanying it, and the Justices' response are printed in Hart and Wechsler, Federal Courts (2d ed. 1973), 64–66.

Illustrative of the questions submitted to the Justices are: "Do the treaties between the United States and France give to France or her citizens a *right*, when at war with a power with whom the United States are at peace, to fit out originally in and from the ports of the United States vessels armed for war, with or without commission?" "If they give such a *right*, does it extend to all manner of armed vessels, or to particular kinds only? If the latter, to what kinds does it extend?" and "May we, within our own ports, sell ships to both parties,

prepared merely for merchandise? May they be pierced for guns?"

2. See Art. II, § 2, of the Constitution, stating that the President "may require the Opinion, in writing, of the principal Officer in each of the executive Departments, upon any Subject relating to the Duties of their respective Offices." There has been an Attorney General since the organization of the Government. But in the early decades of national history, the Attorney General was in effect a part-time official, typically carrying on a substantial private practice at the same time. And the Attorney General typically had no legal assistants. The Department of Justice was not organized until 1870. See Cummings and McFarland, Federal Justice (1937).

Most of President Washington's questions seemed "legal"; the need for answers was real; nevertheless, Chief Justice John Jay and his brethren refused. They relied in large part on separation of powers principles. Ever since, it has been accepted that federal courts cannot give advisory opinions. The desirability of early, authoritative resolution of constitutional doubts is often evident. For example, before the Court-Packing crisis in 1937, President Roosevelt briefly considered a plan "for Congress to pass an act taking away from all lower courts the right to pass upon the constitutionality of statutes. This right would be given to the Supreme Court as a matter of original jurisdiction. The Court would be required to give advisory opinions. It would be expected to say in advance of the passing of a law whether it was unconstitutional." [3] Yet that plan was soon abandoned, partly because of its obvious unconstitutionality. (Note, however, that several state constitutions authorize state courts to issue advisory opinions at the request of the legislature or chief executive.) [4] What, then, are the reasons that make advisory opinions by federal courts impermissible?

2. *The arguments against advisory opinions.* a. *Constitutional text and Framers' intent.* Are advisory opinions clearly barred by the Art. III limitation of judicial power to "cases" and "controversies"? [5] Does a case inevitably require adverse parties, so that the Court may be informed by opposing arguments? Could "the difficulty of lack of adversary parties have been met [in 1793] if the Court gave notice to England and France to brief and argue the issues raised?" [6] Could the Justices in 1793 have found other ways to assure the presentation of all relevant facts in sufficiently concrete form? Note that the Court has held that uncontested naturalization proceedings are a case or controversy within judicial power—though the Court noted that the United States "is always a possible adverse party." Tutun v. United States, 270 U.S. 568 (1926).

3. See The Secret Diary of Harold L. Ickes—The First Thousand Days, 1933–1936 (1953), 529. Secretary of the Interior Ickes was describing a conversation with the President on January 29, 1936. The plan under discussion would also have authorized Congress to enact the law after considering the advisory opinion, "in which event it would be the law of the land, whatever the Supreme Court might say." Ickes notes: "I made the obvious remark that the Supreme Court would declare unconstitutional such an act as the President had in mind and he said that of course it would." The President's alleged strategy was to "then go to Congress and ask it to instruct him whether he was to follow the mandate of Congress or the mandate of the Court. If the Congress should declare that its own mandate was to be followed, the President would carry out the will of Congress [and] ignore the Court."

4. See generally Field, "The Advisory Opinion—An Analysis," 24 Ind.L.J. 203

(1949); Note, "Advisory Opinions on the Constitutionality of Statutes," 69 Harv.L.Rev. 1302 (1956); Note, "Judicial Determinations in Nonadversary Proceedings," 72 Harv.L.Rev. 723 (1959); and a classic article by Felix Frankfurter, "Advisory Opinion," in 1 Encyclopedia of the Social Sciences 475 (1930).

5. As the Court has several times explained, "the term 'controversies,' if distinguishable at all from 'cases,' is so in that it is less comprehensive than the latter, and includes only suits of a civil nature." See, e. g., Muskrat v. United States, 219 U.S. 346 (1911), which also states: "By cases and controversies are intended the claims of litigants brought before the courts for determination by such regular proceedings as are established by law or custom for the protection or enforcement of rights, or the prevention, redress, or punishment of wrongs."

6. Monaghan, "The Who and When," 82 Yale L.Rev. 1363, 1373 (1973).

Can more persuasive arguments against advisory opinions be derived from the Framers' intent? Recall the rejection of Madison's proposals that Justices sit on a Council of Revision, chap. 1 above. (Note the reference to that aspect of history in several of the opinions in this chapter, including Justice Powell's opinion in United States v. Richardson, sec. 2 below.) The proposed Council of Revision was rejected in part because of opposition to having Justices pass on "the policy of public measures." Does that provide compelling reason against advisory opinions on questions of "law"? Note, moreover, that a proposal to permit Congress or the President to obtain advisory opinions on "important questions of law" was before the Constitutional Convention and was not adopted.

b. *Separation of powers and judicial finality.* Note that the Justices in 1793 referred to their "being judges of a court in the last resort." The view that it was essential to judicial decisions that they be final rather than tentative, and not subject to revision by the executive and legislative branches, had been voiced by the Justices a year before President Washington's request. In Hayburn's Case, 2 Dall. 409 (1792), most of the Justices, sitting on circuit, had refused to certify eligible pension claimants to the Secretary of War because the statute authorizing such proceedings improperly assigned duties "not of a judicial nature" to the courts. Among the reasons given for the refusal to undertake the function assigned by statute to the judges was the fact that the judicial actions might be "revised and controuled by the legislature, and by an officer in the executive department. Such revision and controul we deemed radically inconsistent with the independence of that judicial power which is vested in the courts."

Note the modern reiteration of that principle in Chicago & Southern Airlines v. Waterman S. S. Corp., 333 U.S. 103 (1948), holding that courts could not pass on CAB awards of international air routes because such decisions were ultimately subject to modification by the President. The Court stated: "Judgments within the powers vested in courts by the Judiciary Article of the Constitution may not lawfully be revised, overturned or refused faith and credit by another Department of Government. To revise or review an administrative decision which has only the force of a recommendation to the President would be to render an advisory opinion in its most obnoxious form . . . .. This Court early and wisely determined that it would not give advisory opinions even when asked by the Chief Executive. It has been the firm and unvarying practice of Constitutional Courts to render no judgments not binding and conclusive on the parties and none that are subject to later review or alteration by administrative action." Are those arguments persuasive? Recall the decisions in chap. 2 through 14: Were all of those Court decisions immune from subsequent modification by the political branches?

c. *Institutional considerations.* Does the refusal to give advisory opinions ultimately rest on institutional considerations? Because courts are less competent to give advice than to decide cases? Because courts would be too busy if they gave advice? Because courts would be more vulnerable to political attacks if they gave advice?

To what extent does the avoidance of advisory opinions reflect a concern with assuring conditions that will maximize the prospects for informed and accurate decisionmaking by the courts? Do courts need a concrete

factual context to develop law with adequate focus and understanding? Do courts need adversary presentations to assure adequately reasoned development of law? To what extent do those needs vary with the substantive issues presented? Would advisory opinions encourage judicial pronouncements at abstract, general, unreal levels and discourage attention to factual contexts and problems of degree? Does the significance of that risk in turn depend on the Justices' views of substantive law? Recall, e. g., the debates between "absolutes" and "balancing" in First Amendment adjudication, chap. 12 above. Would lack of a concrete record and lack of adversary argument present as much difficulty for a Justice reading the First Amendment "literally" and absolutely than for a Justice viewing the scope of freedom of expression as dependent upon contexts, circumstances, and competing interests? (Note also the discussion of the Adler case, sec. 3 below.)

Note the reflection of these institutional concerns with assuring the best possible conditions for reasoned and accurate constitutional adjudication in a passage in Flast v. Cohen, 392 U.S. 83 (1968) (sec. 2 below): "[T]he implicit policies embodied in Article III, and not history alone, impose the rule against advisory opinions. [The rule] implements the separation of powers [and] also recognizes that such suits often 'are not pressed before the Court with that clear concreteness provided when a question emerges precisely framed and necessary for decision from a clash of adversary argument exploring every aspect of a multifaced situation embracing conflicting and demanding interests.' United States v. Fruehauf, 365 U.S. 146, 157 (1961). Consequently, the Article III prohibition against advisory opinions reflects the complementary constitutional considerations expressed by the justiciability doctrine: Federal judicial power is limited to those disputes which confine federal courts to a role consistent with a system of separated powers and which are traditionally thought to be capable of resolution through the judicial process."

Finally, is the ban on advisory opinions necessary to conserve the Court's strength and energies? Would advisory opinions thrust courts into conflicts too early and too often? Is the ban on advisory opinions desirable because of the "value of having courts function as organs of the sober second thought of the community appraising action already taken, rather than as advisers at the front line of governmental action at the state of initial decision"? Hart and Wechsler, "Federal Courts" (2d ed. 1973), 67.

These questions about the justifications that may underlie the advisory opinions ban are not raised because the barrier to advisory opinions—a barrier which has existed from the beginning—is now vulnerable or likely to disappear. Rather, the questions are raised because the policies served by the ban on advisory opinions resemble some of the grounds for the traditionally strong and still vital "standing" and "ripeness" limits on constitutional adjudication, considered in secs. 2 and 3. To a considerable degree, views as to the weight of these concerns will govern one's position as to the justifiability of barring access to courts through broadly read standing and ripeness limitations. In short, the varying doctrines about the "who" and "when" of constitutional adjudication are interrelated not only in some of their governing criteria but also in the institutional concerns underlying them. For example, courts' concerns about optimum conditions for doing their job well and about protecting themselves from political controversy

are pervasive ones; and to some degree, all of the strands of doctrine considered in the several sections of this chapter can be seen as manifestations of those concerns. (See also the Court's statement about some of those interrelationships in note 4 below.)

3. *Declaratory judgments.* Declaratory judgment actions are commonplace in modern litigation. Many of the constitutional decisions in the preceding chapters arose in the context of such actions. Yet half a century ago, development of the declaratory judgment device was inhibited by fears that it might run afoul of the advisory opinions ban. Declaratory judgments were not among the characteristic remedies of courts at the time Art. III was drafted, and definitions of an Art. III "case" relying on traditional common law practice might, it was feared, cause difficulty for the development of the new declaratory remedy. And those fears were for a time spurred by dicta in WILLING v. CHICAGO AUDITORIUM, 277 U.S. 274 (1928).

a. Willing was a suit in a lower federal court "in the nature of a bill to remove a cloud upon title." The Supreme Court held "that the proceeding does not present a case or controversy." Consider the facts: The Association held long-term leases on land and had constructed an auditorium. The building had become obsolete, and the Association desired to erect a new building. The lease did not explicitly authorize the Association to tear down the old building and erect a new one. There were some negotiations between the Association and Willing, one of the lessors. During "an informal, friendly, private conversation," Willing stated to an officer of the Association that he did not think the old building could be torn down without the consent of the lessors and the bondholders. The Association "never approached" most of the other lessors or the bondholders. A year after the talk with Willing, the Association brought this action against all the lessors and the trustee for the bondholders, to establish the right to tear down the old building.

Justice Brandeis' opinion for the Court stated that there was "neither hostile act nor a threat." Willing had merely expressed an informal, oral opinion. "What the plaintiff seeks is simply a declaratory judgment. To grant that relief is beyond the power of the federal judiciary." The proceeding "is not a case or controversy within the meaning of Article III of the Constitution. The fact that the plaintiff's desires are thwarted by its own doubts, or by the fears of others, does not confer a cause of action. No defendant has wronged the plaintiff or has threatened to do so."

Why was this not an Article III controversy? Because the plans of the parties had not sufficiently jelled? Because there were too many contingencies on both sides—uncertainty as to precisely what the plaintiff would do, uncertainty as to precisely what the defendants would do? Was this, in short, a case where the controversy lacked such concreteness, was so contingent, was so "unripe" as to lack the minimum ingredients of adverseness for an Art. III case? (Compare the "ripeness" cases in sec. 3 below: all of those may be viewable as being concrete enough to meet minimum Art. III requirements, with the decisions not to adjudicate resting on discretionary considerations governing federal court remedies rather than on constitutional compulsion.) Assuming the Willing dispute was not within

Art. III, was Justice Brandeis' language too broad? Recall that he said: "To grant that [declaratory judgment] relief is beyond the power conferred upon the federal judiciary." Was that statement itself something of an advisory opinion?

b. Those doubts about the permissibility of declaratory judgments soon evaporated, however. In NASHVILLE, C. & St. L. RY. v. WALLACE, 288 U.S. 249 (1933), the Court reviewed a state court declaratory judgment after asking for argument on the question "whether a case or controversy is presented in view of the nature of the proceedings in the state courts." The case involved a company threatened with an allegedly unconstitutional tax and seeking a declaratory judgment that the tax constituted an unconstitutional burden on interstate commerce. The Court emphasized that the controversy was clearly concrete enough to be adjudicable in a traditional injunction action. And it noted that the state courts authorized declaratory judgments only "when the complainant asserts rights which are challenged by the defendant, and presents for decision an actual controversy to which he is a party, capable of final adjudication by the judgment [to] be rendered." In those circumstances, Justice Stone's opinion found no Art. III barrier to adjudication. Satisfying Art. III required concern "not with form, but with substance." Since the controversy would have been justiciable in the form of an injunction proceeding, it was no "less so because through a modified procedure appellant has been permitted to present it in the state courts, without praying for an injunction."

Justice Stone explained: "[T]he Constitution does not require that the case or controversy should be presented by traditional forms of procedure, invoking only traditional remedies. [Art. III] defined and limited judicial power, not the particular method by which that power might be invoked. It did not crystallize into changeless form the procedure of 1789 as the only possible means for presenting a case or controversy otherwise cognizable by the federal courts. [C]hanges merely in the form or method of procedure by which federal rights are brought to final adjudication in the state courts are not enough to preclude [Supreme Court review], so long as the case retains the essentials of an adversary proceeding, involving a real, not hypothetical, controversy, which is finally determined by the judgment below."

c. The decision in the Nashville case paved the way for the enactment of the federal Declaratory Judgment Act of 1934. That law authorizes federal declaratory judgments "[i]n a case of actual controversy" within federal jurisdiction. The Supreme Court sustained the constitutionality of the Act in AETNA LIFE INS. CO. v. HAWORTH, 300 U.S. 227 (1937). Chief Justice Hughes' opinion there emphasized that the law was "procedural only." Relief can be granted only if there is a "case" in the Art. III sense; and even when there is a "case," there is discretion to withhold relief. (See the ripeness materials, sec. 3 below.) [7]

7. In emphasizing that declaratory judgments were available only "to determine controversies which are such in the constitutional sense," Chief Justice Hughes explained: "A 'controversy' in this sense must be one that is appropriate for judicial determination. A justiciable controversy is thus distinguished from a difference or dispute of a hypothetical or abstract char-

4. *The relation of the advisory opinions ban to other limitations on constitutional adjudication: Policies of judicial restraint.* [A majority opinion by Justice Rutledge in RESCUE ARMY v. MUNICIPAL COURT OF LOS ANGELES, 331 U.S. 549 (1947), articulated some of the policy relationships between the advisory opinion ban and various other limitations on access to courts for constitutional adjudication. He emphasized the overarching theme of "strict necessity": the Court will not adjudicate constitutional issues unless such decisions are unavoidable. Though the application of these policies of restraint and avoidance in the Rescue Army case is questionable (see sec. 4 below), Justice Rutledge's survey of purposes and policies is worth attention here.]

From Hayburn's Case, [this] Court has followed a policy of strict necessity in disposing of constitutional issues. The earliest exemplifications, too well known for repeating the history here, arose in the Court's refusal to render advisory opinions and in applications of the related jurisdictional policy drawn from the case and controversy limitation. U.S. Const., Art. III. The same policy has been reflected continuously not only in decisions but also in rules of court and in statutes made applicable to jurisdictional matters, including the necessity for reasonable clarity and definiteness, as well as for timeliness, in raising and presenting constitutional questions. Indeed perhaps the most effective implement for making the policy effective has been the certiorari jurisdiction conferred upon this Court by Congress. . . .

The policy, however, has not been limited to jurisdictional determinations. For, in addition, "the Court [has] developed, for its own governance in the cases confessedly within its jurisdiction, a series of rules under which it has avoided passing upon a large part of all the constitutional questions pressed upon it for decision." [8] Thus, as those rules were listed in support of the statement quoted, constitutional issues affecting legislation will not be determined in friendly, nonadversary proceedings; in advance of the necessity of deciding them; in broader terms than are required by the precise facts to which the ruling is to be applied; if the record presents some other ground upon which the case may be disposed of; at the instance of one who fails to show that he is injured by the statute's operation, or who has availed himself of its benefits; or if a construction of the statute is fairly possible by which the question may be avoided.

---

acter; from one that is academic or moot. The controversy must be definite and concrete, touching the legal relations of parties having adverse legal interests. It must be a real and substantial controversy admitting of specific relief through a decree of a conclusive character, as distinguished from an opinion advising what the law would be upon a hypothetical state of facts. Where there is such a concrete case admitting of an immediate and definitive determination of the legal rights of the parties in an adversary proceeding upon the facts alleged, the judicial function may be appropriately exercised although the adjudication of the rights of the litigants may not require the award of process or the payment of damages."

8. The quotation is from a famous concurring opinion by Justice Brandeis, joined by Justices Stone, Roberts and Cardozo, in Ashwander v. Tennessee Valley Authority, 297 U.S. 288, 346 (1936). For a further examination of the Brandeis rules in Ashwander—and for a criticism of the "neo-Brandeisian fallacy" of viewing those rules as legitimating discretionary dismissals of cases within the Court's obligatory appeal jurisdiction (a "fallacy" reflected in the disposition of the Rescue Army case itself)—see the materials on discretionary abstention in sec. 4A.

Some, if not indeed all, of these rules have found "most varied applications." And every application has been an instance of reluctance, indeed, of refusal, to undertake the most important and the most delicate of the Court's functions, notwithstanding conceded jurisdiction, until necessity compels it in the performance of constitutional duty.

Moreover the policy is neither merely procedural nor in its essence dependent for applicability upon the diversities of jurisdiction and procedure, whether of the state courts, the inferior federal courts, or this Court. Rather it is one of substance * grounded in considerations which transcend all such particular limitations. Like the case and controversy limitation itself and the policy against entertaining political questions, it is one of the rules basic to the federal system and this Court's appropriate place within that structure.

Indeed in origin and in practical effects, though not in technical function, it is a corollary offshoot of the case and controversy rule. And often the line between applying the policy or the rule is very thin.† They work, within their respective and technically distinct areas, to achieve the same practical purposes for the process of constitutional adjudication, and upon closely related considerations.

The policy's ultimate foundations, some if not all of which also sustain the jurisdictional limitation, lie in all that goes to make up the unique place and character, in our scheme, of judicial review of governmental action for constitutionality. They are found in the delicacy of that function, particularly in view of possible consequences for others stemming also from constitutional roots; the comparative finality of those consequences; the consideration due to the judgment of other repositories of constitutional power concerning the scope of their authority; the necessity, if government is to function constitutionally, for each to keep within its power, including the courts; the inherent limitations of the judicial process, arising especially from its largely negative character and limited resources of enforcement; withal in the paramount importance of constitutional adjudication in our system.

All these considerations and perhaps others, transcending specific procedures, have united to form and sustain the policy. Its execution has involved a continuous choice between the obvious advantages it produces for the functioning of government in all its coordinate parts and the very real disadvantages, for the assurance of rights, which deferring decision very often entails. On the other hand it is not altogether speculative that a contrary policy, of accelerated decision, might do equal or greater harm for the security of private rights, without attaining any of the benefits of tolerance and harmony for the functioning of the various authorities in our scheme. For premature and relatively abstract decision, which such a policy would be most

* "If there is one doctrine more deeply rooted than any other in the process of constitutional adjudication, it is that we ought not to pass on questions of constitutionality [unless] such adjudication is unavoidable." . . . "It is not the habit of the Court to decide questions of a constitutional nature unless absolutely necessary to a decision of the case." . . . [Footnote by Justice Rutledge.]

† Indeed more than once the policy has been applied in order to avoid the necessity of deciding the "case or controversy" jurisdictional question, when constitutional issues were at stake on the merits, e. g., recently in declaratory judgment proceedings. See . . . United Public Workers v. Mitchell, 330 U.S. 75 [sec. 3 below]. . . . [Footnote by Justice Rutledge.]

likely to promote, have their part too in rendering rights uncertain and insecure.

As with the case and controversy limitation, however, the choice has been made long since. Time and experience have given it sanction. They also have verified for both that the choice was wisely made. Any other indeed might have put an end to or seriously impaired the distinctively American institution of judicial review.** And on the whole, in spite of inevitable exceptions, the policy has worked not only for finding the appropriate place and function of the judicial institution in our governmental system, but also for the preservation of individual rights.[9]

SECTION 2. STANDING TO LITIGATE: THE REQUISITE PERSONAL INTEREST

Some introductory comments and questions. a. *The ingredients.* What is standing? How does it differ from ripeness (sec. 3) and other ingredients of justiciability considered in this chapter? Consider the suggestion that "clarity would be gained by viewing standing as involving problems of the nature and sufficiency of the litigant's concern with the subject matter of the litigation, as distinguished from problems of the justiciability—that is, the fitness for adjudication—of the legal questions which he tenders for decision. More precisely stated, the question of standing in this sense is the question whether the litigant has a sufficient personal interest in getting the relief he seeks, or is a sufficiently appropriate representative of other interested persons, to warrant giving him the relief, if he establishes the illegality alleged—and, by the same token, to warrant recognizing him as entitled to invoke the court's decision on the issue of illegality." [1]

What are the criteria for determining whether a litigant may obtain adjudication of the issue he seeks to raise? The major emphasis in this section is on the problem of plaintiffs' standing—the problem of access to court. In most cases, the question of the plaintiff's access presents no great dif-

---

** It is not without significance for the policy's validity that the periods when the power has been exercised most readily and broadly have been the ones in which this Court and the institution of judicial review have had their stormiest experiences. See, e. g., Brant, Storm Over the Constitution (1936). [Footnote by the Court.]

9. Justice Rutledge's overview is printed here because of the light it throws on some of the reasons prompting the doctrines considered in the opening sections of this chapter. Some of the avoidance techniques he cites warrant further examination as to their scope and legitimacy. That examination is postponed to later materials, especially in sec. 4 below, on discretionary abstention.

1. Hart and Wechsler, Federal Courts (2d ed. 1973), 156. Note also the statement in the 1969 ruling in Flast v. Cohen, below: "The fundamental aspect of standing is that it focuses on the party [and] not on the issues he wishes to have adjudicated. [The question] is whether the person whose standing is challenged is a proper party to request an adjudication of a particular issue and not whether the issue itself is justiciable."

ficulty: we do not doubt that a plaintiff claiming physical injury in a tort action or economic damage in a contracts action can readily get to court. But in constitutional litigation such traditional bases for access to court are often lacking. For example, what of the plaintiff who claims that a law regulating protest demonstrations "chills" his or her First Amendment rights? What of the taxpayer who claims an unconstitutional expenditure of public funds? What of the citizen who is outraged by public officials' conduct allegedly violating separation of powers principles? Can and should there be access to court for plaintiffs claiming speculative or attenuated injuries? Is any injury in fact sufficient? Is injury in fact necessary? Must the plaintiff show some special injury singling the litigant out from the mass of citizens generally? Or should "public actions" be permissible? [2]

b. *Who decides?* To what extent is standing an aspect of Art. III? To what extent is it a discretionary judgment regarding federal court remedies? To the extent the ingredients of standing are not compelled by Art. III, institutions other than the Supreme Court (e. g., Congress and the states) may claim a larger voice in shaping standing. The materials in this section reveal an increasing recognition of congressional authority to grant standing to plaintiffs to whom federal courts would not grant access in the absence of the congressionally created remedy. (See especially the notes on congressional control over standing, below.)

c. *How decided?* How does the Court determine whether a litigant has a sufficiently distinctive personal interest to warrant rendering the constitutional adjudication sought? As already noted under a above, that is the central question of this section. Is the existence of injury in fact enough? Or must there be an invasion of "legal rights"? What is a "legal" injury? Does standing depend in part on the nature of the substantive claim raised? Can the traditional requirement of a distinctive individualized injury be dispensed with so long as a person genuinely wishes to litigate a claim in a concrete factual setting—e. g., are "public actions" by "mere" citizens permissible? Consider the Court's own description of the purpose of standing rules in assuring the best conditions for informed

---

2. The central concerns of this section are these problems of plaintiffs' standing: the extent to which a plaintiff must show some traditional or special injury to achieve access to court. The rather different problem of defendants' standing is considered only briefly, near the end of this section. That problem is not one of *access* to court: the defendant has been brought into court by someone else—a private plaintiff or the government. Defendants' standing problems involve instead the question of what *issues* the defendant may raise. Is the defendant limited to issues that immediately affect him? Or, once he is in court, may he assert the rights of others who may be subject to the statute under which he is charged? Must he be in some special relationship to the nonlitigant third party whose rights he seeks to assert?

Aspects of that problem have occasionally surfaced earlier—recall, e. g., the consideration of the overbreadth doctrine in chap. 12 above. Some additional examples of defendants' standing problems are noted below.

Note, too, that this section emphasizes problems of plaintiffs' access to *federal* courts. State courts of course have considerable autonomy to delineate their own standing rules. Those rules bear on federal litigation when Supreme Court review is sought in the case of a plaintiff who has obtained an adjudication in the state courts by who might not have been able to claim direct access to a lower federal court. The bearing of state standing rules on Supreme Court review is considered briefly below.

adjudication: the "gist of the question of standing," the Court said in Baker v. Carr, 369 U.S. 186 (1962) (sec. 5 below), is whether the litigant alleges "such a personal stake in the outcome of the controversy as to assure that concrete adverseness which sharpens the presentation of issues upon which the court so largely depends for illumination of difficult constitutional questions." Is injury in fact truly necessary to "assure that concrete adverseness," to encourage the best possible "presentation of issues"? May not a concerned citizen's readiness to go to court provide adequate assurance of optimizing the conditions for informed adjudication? The "mere" citizen may not in fact present the arguments as well as possible. But is there truly greater assurance of optimum argument by insisting on a traditional "injured" plaintiff with a personalized injury—even though the "injury" may consist of no more than a small financial loss? Would opening of the doors to "citizens" or "private attorneys general" actions raise too many of the dangers of advisory opinions? To what extent should a decision on standing turn on the needs of the parties and the society at large, and to what extent on institutional values pertaining to the courts?

Questions such as those run through all of the materials which follow and are raised in especially sharp form by the taxpayers and citizens cases culminating in United States v. Richardson. In the Richardson case, the next principal case (and in Reservists Committee, a companion case), lower courts had read the Court's leniency in standing cases of the 1960's and early 1970's as authorizing the recognition of standing to taxpayers and citizens seeking to raise constitutional issues. Indeed, the District Court in the Reservists Committee case had stated: "In recent years the Supreme Court has greatly expanded the concept of standing and in this Circuit [the District of Columbia] the concept has now been almost completely abandoned." Yet the Supreme Court reversed and found standing requirements unsatisfied in each case. The Justice recognized that standing concepts had indeed been "greatly expanded" in recent years; but, as the 1974 decision in Richardson demonstrates, the majority of the Court is unwilling to abandon standing requirements entirely. In the absence of congressional action, the Court suggested, federal court doors will not be wide open to every plaintiff seeking to litigate a constitutional issue. What explains the modern trends? Do the opinions adequately clarify the rules? Do they adequately articulate the underlying policies?[3] Are the modern resolutions of standing controversies sound?

---

3. Note the comment in Brown, "Quis Custodiet Ipsos Custodes?—The School-Prayer Cases," 1963 Sup.Ct. Rev. 1: "The fact, if it is a fact, that standards for standing may not be absolute does not mean that they do not exist. One can make some judgments, if only by history and analogy, of the occasions on which, and the facility with which, judicial power should be brought into action. One will, of course, be influenced if not guided by the extent to which one thinks of judges as specially appointed (or anointed) wardens and nurturers of our higher values and principles."

FEDERAL TAXPAYERS AND CITIZENS ACTIONS

1. *The Frothingham case.* In FROTHINGHAM v. MELLON, 262 U.S. 447 (1923), Mrs. Frothingham brought suit as a federal taxpayer to enjoin the Secretary of the Treasury from making expenditures under the Maternity Act of 1921, which provided for conditional grants to state programs "to reduce maternal and infant mortality." She argued that the Act "is a usurpation of power not granted to Congress by the Constitution—an attempted exercise of the power of local self-government reserved to the States by the Tenth Amendment." (Recall chap. 4 above.) She alleged that spending under the Act would increase her tax liability and that she would thereby be deprived of property without due process of law. A unanimous Supreme Court held that the suit "must be disposed of for want of jurisdiction" because the plaintiff "has no such interest in the subject-matter, nor is any such injury inflicted or threatened, as will enable her to sue."

Was the Court's decision based on Art. III? Or did the Court rely on its authority to fashion federal equitable remedies? Did the grounds of the decision preclude Congress from granting federal taxpayers standing to sue? Subsequent opinions and commentary divided on the question of whether the Frothingham decision rested on constitutional barriers. Consider the Court's statements in Frothingham:

"The right of a taxpayer to enjoin the execution of a federal appropriation act, on the ground that it is invalid and will result in taxation for illegal purposes, has never been passed upon by this Court. [Bradfield v. Roberts, 175 U.S. 291,] came here from the Court of Appeals of the District of Columbia, and that court sustained the right of the plaintiff to sue by treating the case as one directed against the District of Columbia, and therefore subject to the rule frequently stated by this Court, that resident taxpayers may sue to enjoin an illegal use of the moneys of a municipal corporation. The interest of a taxpayer of a municipality in the application of its moneys is direct and immediate and the remedy by injunction to prevent their misuse is not inappropriate. It is upheld by a large number of state cases and is the rule of this Court. [Crampton v. Zabriskie, 101 U.S. 601.] . . . The reasons which support the extension of the equitable remedy to a single taxpayer in such cases are based upon the peculiar relation of the corporate taxpayer to the corporation, which is not without some resemblance to that subsisting between stockholder and private corporation. But the relation of a taxpayer of the United States to the Federal Goverment is very different. His interest in the moneys of the Treasury—partly realized from taxation and partly from other sources—is shared with millions of others; is comparatively minute and indeterminable; and the effect upon future taxation, of any payment out of the funds, so remote, fluctuating and uncertain, that no basis is afforded for an appeal to the preventive powers of a court of equity.

"The administration of any statute, likely to produce additional taxation to be imposed upon a vast number of taxpayers, the extent of whose several liability is indefinite and constantly changing, is essentially a matter of public and not of individual concern. If one taxpayer may champion and litigate

such a cause, then every other taxpayer may do the same, not only in respect of the statute here under review but also in respect of every other appropriation act and statute whose administration requires the outlay of public money, and whose validity may be questioned. The bare suggestion of such a result, with its attendant inconveniences, goes far to sustain the conclusion which we have reached, that a suit of this character cannot be maintained. . . .

"The functions of government under our system are apportioned. . . . The general rule is that neither department may invade the province of the other and neither may control, direct or restrain the action of the other. . . . We have no power per se to review and annul acts of Congress on the ground that they are unconstitutional. That question may be considered only when the justification for some direct injury suffered or threatened, presenting a justiciable issue, is made to rest upon such an act. Then the power exercised is that of ascertaining and declaring the law applicable to the controversy. It amounts to little more than the negative power to disregard an unconstitutional enactment, which otherwise would stand in the way of the enforcement of a legal right. The party who invokes the power must be able to show not only that the statute is invalid but that he has sustained or is immediately in danger of sustaining some direct injury as the result of its enforcement, and not merely that he suffers in some indefinite way in common with people generally. If a case for preventive relief be presented the court enjoins, in effect, not the execution of the statute, but the acts of the official, the statute notwithstanding. Here [the plaintiff has] no such case. Looking through forms of words to the substance of [the] complaint, it is merely that officials of the executive department of the government are executing and will execute an act of Congress asserted to be unconstitutional; and this we are asked to prevent. To do so would be not to decide a judicial controversy, but to assume a position of authority over the governmental acts of another and co-equal department, an authority which plainly we do not possess."[1]

2. *Flast v. Cohen.* In FLAST v. COHEN, 392 U.S. 83 (1968), federal taxpayers challenged aid to religious schools under the Elementary and Secondary Education Act of 1965. The lower court dismissed their complaint because of Frothingham's "impenetrable barrier" to taxpayers' actions. Chief Justice Warren's majority opinion reversed, concluding that "the Frothingham barrier should be lowered when a taxpayer attacks a federal stat-

---

1. In a case decided in the same opinion as Mrs. Frothingham's, the State of Massachusetts proved no more successful in eliciting a constitutional ruling on the Maternity Act. Massachusetts v. Mellon, 262 U.S. 447 (1923). The Court held that the State "presents no justiciable controversy either in its own behalf or as the representative of its citizens." The complaint of invasion of states' rights was "political and not judicial in character." Nor could the State sue as representative of its citizens: "But the citizens of Massachusetts are also citizens of the United States. It cannot be conceded that a State, as parens patriae,

may institute judicial proceedings to protect citizens of the United States from the operation of the statutes thereof." But a State was permitted to bring an original jurisdiction action as parens patriae in Georgia v. Pennsylvania R. Co., 324 U.S. 439 (1945), an antitrust laws attack on rates as discriminatory. For cases where state interests were found sufficient for standing to challenge the constitutionality of federal laws, recall Missouri v. Holland, 252 U.S. 416 (1920) (protection of migratory birds) (chap. 4), and South Carolina v. Katzenbach, 383 U.S. 301 (1966), (Voting Rights Act of 1965) (chap. 11).

ute on the ground that it violates the Establishment and Free Exercise Clauses of the First Amendment." (Recall chap. 14.) In reexamining the Frothingham limit on standing,[2] the Chief Justice stated:

"Embodied in the words 'cases' and 'controversies' are two complementary but somewhat different limitations. In part those words limit the business of federal courts to questions presented in an adversary context and in a form historically viewed as capable of resolution through the judicial process. And in part those words define the role assigned to the judiciary in a tripartite allocation of power to assure that the federal courts will not intrude into areas committed to the other branches of government. Justiciability is the term of art employed to give expression of this dual limitation placed upon federal courts by the case-and-controversy doctrine.

"[T]he Government's position is that the constitutional scheme of separation of powers, and the deference owed by the federal judiciary to the other. two branches of government within that scheme, presents an absolute bar to taxpayer suits challenging the validity of federal spending programs. . . . An analysis of the function served by standing limitations compels a rejection of the Government's position. . . .

"[W]hen standing is placed in issue in a case, the question is whether the person whose standing is challenged is a proper party to request an adjudication of a particular issue and not whether the issue itself is justiciable.

. . . When the emphasis in the standing problem is placed on whether the person invoking a federal court's jurisdiction is a proper party to maintain the action, the weakness of the Government's argument in this case becomes apparent. The question whether a particular person is a proper party to maintain the action does not, by its own force, raise separation of powers problems related to improper judicial interference in areas committed to other branches of the Federal Government. Such problems arise, if at all, only from the substantive issues the individual seeks to have adjudicated. Thus, in terms of Article III limitations on federal court jurisdiction, the question of standing is related only to whether the dispute sought to be adjudicated will be presented in an adversary context and in a form historically viewed as capable of judicial resolution. It is for that reason that the emphasis in standing problems is on whether the party invoking federal court jurisdiction 'has a personal stake in the outcome of the controversy,' and whether the dispute touches upon 'the legal relations of parties having adverse legal interests.' A taxpayer may or may not have the requisite personal stake in the outcome, depending upon the circumstances of the particular case. Therefore, we find no absolute bar in Article III to suits by federal taxpayers challenging allegedly unconstitutional federal taxing and spending programs. There remains, however, the problem of determining the circumstances under which a federal taxpayer will be deemed to have the personal stake and interest that impart the necessary concrete adverseness to

2. The Chief Justice noted that there had been "some confusion" as to "whether Frothingham establishes a constitutional bar to taxpayer suits or whether the Court was simply imposing a rule of self-restraint which was not constitutionally compelled." He commented that the Frothingham opinion "can be read to support either position," and that the "prevailing view of the commentators is that Frothingham announced only a nonconstitutional rule of self-restraint."

such litigation so that standing can be conferred on the taxpayer qua taxpayer consistent with the constitutional limitations of Article III."

In examining that last question, Chief Justice Warren substituted for the simple Frothingham inquiry about the taxpayer's direct financial stake a more complex one involving a preliminary look at the substantive issues "to determine whether there is a logical nexus between the status asserted and the claim sought to be adjudicated." He elaborated: "The nexus demanded of federal taxpayers has two aspects to it. First, the taxpayer must establish a logical link between that status and the type of legislative enactment attacked. Thus, a taxpayer will be a proper party to allege the unconstitutionality only of exercises of congressional power under the taxing and spending clause of Art. I, § 8, of the Constitution. It will not be sufficient to allege an incidental expenditure of tax funds in the administration of an essentially regulatory statute. . . . Secondly, the taxpayer must establish a nexus between that status and the precise nature of the constitutional infringement alleged. Under this requirement, the taxpayer must show that the challenged enactment exceeds specific constitutional limitations imposed upon the exercise of the congressional taxing and spending power and not simply that the enactment is generally beyond the powers delegated to Congress by Art. I, § 8. When both nexuses are established, the litigant will have shown a taxpayer's stake in the outcome of the controversy and will be a proper and appropriate party to invoke a federal court's jurisdiction."

Under that double nexus approach, the Flast and Frothingham situations were distinguishable. In Flast, the Establishment Clause claim rested on a provision of the First Amendment which "operates as a specific constitutional limitation upon the exercise by Congress of the taxing and spending power conferred by Art. I, § 8." The "quite different" allegations in Frothingham failed to satisfy the second nexus: Mrs. Frothingham had not claimed that the Maternity Act violated "a specific limitation" on the taxing and spending power; she had merely argued that Congress "had exceeded the general powers delegated to it by Art. I, § 8, and that Congress had thereby invaded the legislative province reserved to the States by the Tenth Amendment." To be sure, Mrs. Frothingham had relied on due process as well; but that clause "does not protect taxpayers against increases in tax liability."

Chief Justice Warren concluded: "[W]e hold that a taxpayer will have standing consistent with Article III to invoke federal judicial power when he alleges that congressional action under the taxing and spending clause is in derogation of those constitutional provisions which operate to restrict the exercise of the taxing and spending power. The taxpayer's allegation in such cases would be that his tax money is being extracted and spent in violation of specific constitutional protections against such abuses of legislative power. Such an injury is appropriate for judicial redress, and the taxpayer has established the necessary nexus between his status and the nature of the allegedly unconstitutional action to support his claim of standing to secure judicial review. Under such circumstances, we feel confident that the questions will be framed with the necessary specificity, that the issues will be contested with the necessary adverseness and that the litigation will be pursued with the necessary vigor to assure that the constitutional challenge will be made in a

form traditionally thought to be capable of judicial resolution. We lack that confidence in cases such as Frothingham where a taxpayer seeks to employ a federal court as a forum in which to air his generalized grievances about the conduct of government or the allocation of power in the Federal System."

Justice Douglas' concurrence stated: "While I have joined the opinion of the Court, I do not think that the test it lays down is a durable one for the reasons stated [in Justice Harlan's dissent]. I think, therefore, that it will suffer erosion and in time result in the demise of [Frothingham]. It would therefore be the part of wisdom, as I see the problem, to be rid of Frothingham here and now." He added that, unlike Justice Harlan, he would not "view with alarm" the elimination of all barriers to taxpayers. Frothingham "was in the heyday of substantive due process": a contrary result in Frothingham "might well have accentuated an ominous trend to judicial supremacy. But we no longer undertake to exercise that kind of power." He was convinced that taxpayers "can be vigilant private attorneys general. Their stake in the outcome of litigation may be de minimis by financial standards, yet very great when measured by a particular constitutional mandate." He concluded that he would not be "niggardly [in] giving private attorneys general standing to sue. I would certainly not wait for Congress to give its blessing to our deciding cases clearly within our Article III jurisdiction."

There were also separate concurrences by Justices Stewart and Fortas, emphasizing that the Flast decision was limited to taxpayers' challenges to spending in violation of the Establishment Clause. Justice Stewart noted that since that Clause "plainly prohibits taxing and spending in aid of religion, every taxpayer can claim a personal constitutional right not to be taxed for the support of a religious institution." Justice Harlan was the sole dissenter. His elaborate opinion—further considered in some of the opinions in Richardson, which follows—insisted that the majority's criteria were "not in any sense a measurement of any plaintiff's interest in the outcome of any suit. [T]he Court's standard for the determination of standing and its criteria for the satisfaction of that standard are entirely unrelated." Excluding expenditures "incidental" to an "essentially regulatory program" had nothing to do with a plaintiff's interest in the outcome of a suit. Similarly, the "intensity of a plaintiff's interest in a suit is not measured, even obliquely, by the fact that the constitutional provision under which he claims is, or is not, a 'specific limitation' upon Congress' spending powers." He also questioned the argument that the Establishment Clause was "in some uncertain fashion a more 'specific' limitation upon Congress' powers than are the various other constitutional commands."

The basic difficulty, as Justice Harlan saw it, was that the Court was trying to retain a theoretical "personal interest" requirement while in fact recognizing the rights of "private attorneys general" to sue. The interests and rights claimed by plaintiffs in cases such as Frothingham and Flast "are bereft of any personal or proprietary coloration. They are, as litigants, indistinguishable from any group selected at random from among the general population, taxpayers and nontaxpayers alike. These are and must be, to adopt

Professor Jaffe's useful phrase, 'public actions' brought to vindicate public rights." [3]

Justice Harlan noted, however, that "private attorneys general" bringing "public actions" were not barred by Art. III. He thought it "clear that non-Hohfeldian plaintiffs as such are not *constitutionally* excluded from the federal courts. The problem ultimately presented [is] therefore to determine in what circumstances, consonant with the character and proper functioning of the federal courts, such suits should be permitted." His proposed solution was that the Court should not on its own grant access to taxpayers bringing "public actions," and that the permissibility of such suits should be left to Congress. He explained: "It seems to me clear that public actions [may] involve important hazards for the continued effectiveness of the federal judiciary. Although I believe such actions to be within the jurisdiction conferred upon the federal courts by [Art. III], there surely can be little doubt that they strain the judicial function and press to the limit judicial authority." Federal judicial authority should be "employed prudently." The majority evidently was aware of the hazards, but its limitations were "wholly untenable." A better resolution of the problem was available, one "that entirely satisfies the demands of the principle of separation of powers." Congress had authority to permit plaintiffs lacking economic or other personal interests to bring public actions, and the Court should wait for Congress to act: "Any hazards to the proper allocation of authority among the three branches of the Government would be substantially diminished if public actions had been pertinently authorized by Congress and the President." (Note the echoes of Justice Harlan's position in Justice Powell's opinion in Richardson, below.)

UNITED STATES v. RICHARDSON
418 U.S. 166, 94 S.Ct. 2940, 41 L.Ed.2d 678 (1974).

Certiorari to the United States Court of Appeals for the Third Circuit.

Mr. Chief Justice BURGER delivered the opinion of the Court.

We granted certiorari in this case to determine whether the respondent has standing to bring an action as a federal taxpayer alleging that certain provisions concerning public reporting of expenditures under the Central Intelligence Agency Act of 1949 violate Art. I, § 9, cl. 7, of the Constitution which provides:

> "No Money shall be drawn from the Treasury, but in Consequence of Appropriations made by Law; and a regular Statement and Account of the Receipts and Expenditures of all public Money shall be published from time to time."

3. The reference was to Jaffe, Judicial Control of Administrative Action (1965). Justice Harlan also referred to such plaintiffs as "non-Hohfeldian" plaintiffs. That was another phrase of Professor Jaffe's, derived from Hohfeld, Fundamental Legal Conceptions (1923). As Justice Harlan explained in a footnote: "I have here employed the phrases 'Hohfeldian' and 'non-Hohfeldian' plaintiffs to mark the distinction between the personal and proprietary interests of the traditional plaintiff, and the representative and public interests of the plaintiff in a public action."

Respondent brought this suit in the United States District Court on a complaint in which he recites attempts to obtain from the Government information concerning detailed expenditures of the Central Intelligence Agency. . . . In essence, the respondent asked the federal court to declare unconstitutional that provision of the Central Intelligence Agency Act which permits the Agency to account for its expenditures "solely on the certificate of the Director." The only injury alleged by respondent was that he "cannot obtain a document that sets out the expenditures and receipts" of the CIA but on the contrary was "asked to accept a fraudulent document." The District Court granted a motion for dismissal on the ground respondent lacked standing under [Flast], and that the subject matter raised political questions not suited for judicial disposition.

The Court of Appeals sitting en banc, with three judges dissenting, reversed, holding that the respondent had standing to bring this action. The majority relied chiefly on [the "two-tier test" of Flast]. . . . We conclude that respondent lacks standing to maintain a suit for the relief sought and we reverse.

I. . . . Recently in Association of Data Processing Service Organizations, Inc. v. Camp [1970-below], the Court, while noting that "[g]eneralizations about standing to sue are largely worthless as such," emphasized that "[o]ne generalization is, however, necessary and that is that the question of standing in the federal courts is to be considered in the framework of Article III which restricts judicial power to 'cases' and 'controversies.' " Although the recent holding of the Court in [Flast] is a starting point in an examination of respondent's claim to prosecute this suit as a taxpayer, that case must be read with reference to its principal predecessor, [Frothingham]. . . . While the "impenetrable barrier to suits against Acts of Congress brought by individuals who can assert only the interest of federal taxpayers," had been slightly lowered [in Flast], the Court made clear it was reaffirming the principle of Frothingham precluding a taxpayer's use of "a federal court as a forum in which to air his generalized grievances." . . .

II. Although the Court made it very explicit in Flast that a "fundamental aspect of standing" is that it focuses primarily on the *party* seeking to get his complaint before the federal court rather than "on the issues he wishes to have adjudicated," it made equally clear that

> "in ruling on [taxpayer] standing, it is both appropriate and necessary to look to the substantive issues for another purpose, namely, to determine whether there is a logical nexus between the status asserted and the claim sought to be adjudicated."

We therefore turn to an examination of the issues sought to be raised by respondent's complaint to determine whether he is "a proper and appropriate party to invoke federal judicial power" with respect to those issues.

We need not and do not reach the merits of the constitutional attack on the statute;* our inquiry into the "substantive issues" is for the limited purpose indicated above. The mere recital of the respondent's claims and an examination of the statute under attack demonstrate how far he falls

---

* For a discussion of that issue, see Note, "The CIA's Secret Funding and the Constitution," 84 Yale L.J. 608 (1975).

short of the standing criteria of Flast and how neatly he falls within the Frothingham holding left undisturbed. Although the status he rests on is that he is a taxpayer, his challenge is not addressed to the taxing or spending power, but to the statutes regulating the CIA, specifically 50 U.S.C. § 403J(b). That section provides different accounting and reporting requirements and procedures for the CIA, as is also done with respect to other governmental agencies dealing in confidential areas.

Respondent makes no claim that appropriated funds are being spent in violation of a "specific constitutional limitation upon the [taxing and spending power]." Rather, he asks the courts to compel the Government to give him information on precisely how the CIA spends its funds. Thus there is no "logical nexus" between the asserted status of taxpayer and the claimed failure of the Congress to require the Executive to supply a more detailed report of the expenditures of that agency.

The question presented thus is simply and narrowly whether these claims meet the standards for taxpayer standing set forth in Flast; we hold they do not. Respondent is seeking "to employ a federal court as a forum in which to air his generalized grievances about the conduct of government." Both Frothingham and Flast reject that basis for standing.

III. The Court of Appeals held that the basis of taxpayer standing "need not always be the appropriation and the spending of [taxpayer's] money for an invalid purpose. The personal stake may come from an injury in fact even if it is not directly economic in nature." [1]

The respondent's claim is that without detailed information on CIA expenditures—and hence its activities—he cannot intelligently follow the actions of Congress or the Executive, nor can he properly fulfill his obligations as a member of the electorate in voting for candidates seeking national office.

This is surely the kind of a generalized grievance described in both Frothingham and Flast since the impact on him is plainly undifferentiated and "common to all members of the public." Ex parte Lévitt, 302 U.S. 633, 634 (1937); Laird v. Tatum, 408 U.S. 1, 13 (1972). While we can hardly dispute that this respondent has a genuine interest in the use of funds and that his interest may be prompted by his status as a taxpayer, he has not alleged that, as a taxpayer, he is in danger of suffering any particular concrete injury as a result of the operation of this statute. As the Court noted in Sierra Club v. Morton, 405 U.S. 727 (1972), "a mere 'interest in a problem,' no matter how longstanding the interest and no matter how qualified the organization is in evaluating the problem, is not sufficient by itself to render the organization 'adversely affected' or 'aggrieved' within the meaning of the APA."

Ex parte Lévitt, supra, is especially instructive. There Lévitt sought to challenge the validity of the commission of a Supreme Court Justice who had

---

1. The Court of Appeals thus appeared to rely on Association of Data Processing Service Organizations, Inc. v. Camp, 397 U.S. 150 (1970). Abstracting some general language of that opinion from the setting and controlling facts of that case, the Court of Appeals overlooked the crucial factor that standing in that case arose under a specific statute, Bank Service Corporation Act of 1962. . . . In short, Congress had provided competitor standing. . . . [Footnote by the Court. See the notes, below.]

been nominated and confirmed as such while he was a member of the Senate. Lévitt alleged that the appointee had voted for an increase in the emoluments provided by Congress for Justices of the Supreme Court during the term for which he was last elected to the United States Senate. The claim was that the appointment violated the explicit prohibition of Art: I, § 6, cl. 2, of the Constitution.[2] The Court disposed of Lévitt's claim, stating: "It is an established principle that to entitle a private individual to invoke the judicial power to determine the validity of executive or legislative action he must show that he *has sustained or is immediately in danger of sustaining a direct injury* as the result of that action and it is not sufficient that he has merely a general interest common to all members of the public." (Emphasis supplied.)

Of course, if Lévitt's allegations were true, they made out an arguable violation of an explicit prohibition of the Constitution. Yet even this was held insufficient to support standing because, whatever Lévitt's injury, it was one he shared with "all members of the public." Respondent here, like the petitioner in Lévitt, also fails to clear the threshold hurdle of [Baker v. Carr and Flast].[3]

It can be argued that if respondent is not permitted to litigate this issue, no one can do so. In a very real sense, the absence of any particular individual or class to litigate these claims gives support to the argument that the subject matter is committed to the surveillance of Congress, and ultimately to the political process. Any other conclusion would mean that the Founding Fathers intended to set up something in the nature of an Athenian democracy or a New England town meeting to oversee the conduct of the National Government by means of lawsuits in federal courts. The Constitution created a *representative* Government with the representatives directly responsible to their constituents at stated periods of two, four, and six years; that the Constitution does not afford a judicial remedy does not, of course, completely disable the citizen who is not satisfied with the "ground rules" established by the Congress for reporting expenditures of the Executive Branch. Lack of standing within the narrow confines of Art. III jurisdiction does not impair the right to assert his views in the political forum or at the polls. Slow, cumbersome, and unresponsive though the traditional electoral process may be thought at times, our system provides for changing members of the political branches when dissatisfied citizens convince a sufficient number of their fellow electors that elected representatives are delinquent in performing duties committed to them.

2. "No Senator or Representative shall, during the Time for which he was elected, be appointed to any civil Office under the Authority of the United States, which shall have been created, or the Emoluments whereof shall have been encreased during such time . . . ." [Footnote by the Court.]

3. Although we need not reach or decide precisely what is meant by "a regular Statement and Account," it is clear that Congress has plenary power to exact any reporting and accounting it considers appropriate in the public interest. It is therefore open to serious question whether the Framers of the Constitution ever imagined that general directives to the Congress or the Executive would be subject to enforcement by an individual citizen. . . . Independent of the statute here challenged by respondent, Congress could grant standing to taxpayers or citizens, or both, limited, of course, by the "cases" and "controversies" provisions of Art. III. . . . [Footnote by the Court.]

As our society has become more complex, our numbers more vast, our lives more varied, and our resources more strained, citizens increasingly request the intervention of the courts on a greater variety of issues than at any period of our national development. The acceptance of new categories of judicially cognizable injury has not eliminated the basic principle that to invoke judicial power the claimant must have a "personal stake in the outcome" [Baker v. Carr], or a "particular, concrete injury" [Sierra Club], or "a direct injury" [Lévitt], in short, something more than "generalized grievances" [Flast]. Respondent has failed to meet these fundamental tests . . ..

Reversed.

Mr. Justice POWELL, concurring.

I join the opinion of the Court because I am in accord with most of its analysis, particularly insofar as it relies on traditional barriers against federal taxpayer or citizen standing. And I agree that [Flast], which set the boundaries for the arguments of the parties before us, is the most directly relevant precedent and quite correctly absorbs a major portion of the Court's attention. I write solely to indicate that I would go further than the Court and would lay to rest the approach undertaken in Flast. I would not overrule Flast on its facts, because it is now settled that federal taxpayer standing exists in Establishment Clause cases. I would not, however, perpetuate the doctrinal confusion inherent in the Flast two-part "nexus" test. That test is not a reliable indicator of when a federal taxpayer has standing, and it has no sound relationship to the question whether such a plaintiff, with no other interest at stake, should be allowed to bring suit against one of the branches of the Federal Government. In my opinion, it should be abandoned.

I. My difficulties with Flast are several. The opinion purports to separate the question of standing from the merits, yet it abruptly returns to the substantive issues raised by a plaintiff for the purpose of determining "whether there is a logical nexus between the status asserted and the claim sought to be adjudicated." Similarly, the opinion distinguishes between constitutional and prudential limits on standing. I find it impossible, however, to determine whether the two-part "nexus" test created in Flast amounts to a constitutional or a prudential limitation, because it has no meaningful connection with the Court's statement of the bare-minimum constitutional requirements for standing.

Drawing upon [Baker v. Carr], the Court in Flast stated the " 'gist of the question of standing' " as "whether the party seeking relief has 'alleged such a personal stake in the outcome of the controversy as to assure that concrete adverseness which sharpens the presentation of issues upon which the court so largely depends for illumination of difficult constitutional questions.' " [T]his is now the controlling definition of the irreducible Art. III case-or-controversy requirements for standing.[1] But, as Mr. Justice Harlan pointed out in his dissent in Flast, it is impossible to see how an inquiry

1. See also, e. g., Barlow v. Collins, 397 U.S. 159, 170–171 (1970) (Brennan, J., dissenting); Scott, Standing in the Supreme Court—A Functional Analysis, 86 Harv.L.Rev. 645, 658 (1973). The test announced in Baker and reiterated in Flast reflects how far the Court has moved in recent years in relaxing standing restraints. . . . [Footnote by Justice Powell.]

about the existence of "concrete adverseness" is furthered by an application of the Flast test. . . .

In my opinion, Mr. Justice Harlan's critique of the Flast "nexus" test is unanswerable. As he pointed out, "the Court's standard for the determination of standing [i. e., sufficiently concrete adverseness] and its criteria for the satisfaction of that standard are entirely unrelated." . . .[2]

The ambiguities inherent in the Flast "nexus" limitations on federal taxpayer standing are illustrated by this case. There can be little doubt about respondent's fervor in pursuing his case. [T]he intensity of his interest appears to bear no relationship to the fact that, literally speaking, he is not challenging directly a congressional exercise of the taxing and spending power. On the other hand, if the involvement of the taxing and spending power has some relevance, it requires no great leap in reasoning to conclude that the Statement and Account Clause, Art. I, § 9, cl. 7, on which respondent relies, is inextricably linked to that power. And that clause might well be seen as a "specific" limitation on congressional spending. Indeed, it could be viewed as the most democratic of limitations. Thus, although the Court's application of Flast to the instant case is probably literally correct, adherence to the Flast test in this instance suggests, as does Flast itself, that the test is not a sound or logical limitation on standing.

The lack of real meaning and of principled content in the Flast "nexus" test renders it likely that it will in time collapse of its own weight, as Mr. Justice Douglas predicted in his concurring opinion in that case. This will present several options for the Court. It may either reaffirm pre-Flast prudential limitations on federal and citizen taxpayer standing; attempt new doctrinal departures in this area, as would Mr. Justice Stewart; or simply drop standing barriers altogether, as, judging by his concurring opinion in Flast and his dissenting opinion today, would Mr. Justice Douglas.[3] I believe the first option to be the appropriate course, for reasons which may be emphasized by noting the difficulties I see with the other two. And, while I do not disagree at this late date with the Baker v. Carr statement of the constitutional indicia of standing, I further believe that constitutional limitations are not the only pertinent considerations.

II. Mr. Justice Stewart, joined by Mr. Justice Marshall, would grant citizen or taxpayer standing under those clauses of the Constitution that impose on the Federal Government "an affirmative duty" to do something on

2. Mr. Justice Harlan's criticisms of the Court's analysis in Flast have been echoed by several commentators. E. g., Scott, supra, n. 1, at 660–662; Davis, Standing: Taxpayers and Others, 35 U.Chi.L.Rev. 601, 604–607 (1968). As Professor [Kenneth] Scott notes, the Flast "nexus" test "can be understood as an expedient by a court retreating from the absolute barrier of Frothingham, but not sure of how far to go and desirous of a formula that would enable it to make case by case determinations in the future. By any other standard, however, it is untenable." [Footnote by Justice Powell.]

3. [Justice Brennan's view], that federal taxpayers are able to meet the "injury-in-fact" test that he articulated in Barlow v. Collins, renders his position, for me at least, indistinguishable from that of Mr. Justice Douglas. Furthermore, I think that Mr. Justice Brennan has modified the standard he identified in Barlow by finding it satisfied in this case. It is a considerable step from the "distinctive and discriminating" economic injury alleged in Barlow, to the generalized interest of a taxpayer or citizen, as Mr. Justice Brennan appears to have acknowledged in his opinion in that case. [Footnote by Justice Powell.]

behalf of its citizens and taxpayers. Although he distinguishes between an affirmative constitutional duty and a "constitutional prohibition" for purposes of this case, it does not follow that Mr. Justice Stewart would deny federal taxpayer standing in all cases involving a constitutional prohibition, as his concurring opinion in Flast makes clear. Rather, he would find federal taxpayer standing, and perhaps citizen standing, in all cases based on constitutional clauses setting forth an affirmative duty and in unspecified cases where the constitutional clause at issue may be seen as a plain or explicit prohibition.

For purposes of determining whether a taxpayer or citizen has standing to challenge the actions of the Federal Government, I fail to perceive a meaningful distinction between constitutional clauses that set forth duties and those that set forth prohibitions. In either instance, the relevant inquiry is the same—may a plaintiff, relying on nothing other than citizen or taxpayer status, bring suit to adjudicate whether an entity of the Federal Government is carrying out its responsibilities in conformance with the requirements of the Constitution? A taxpayer's or citizen's interest in and willingness to pursue with vigor such a suit would not turn on whether the constitutional clause at issue imposed a duty on the Government to do something for him or prohibited the Government from doing something to him. Prohibitions and duties in this context are opposite sides of the same coin. Thus, I do not believe that the inquiry whether federal courts should entertain public actions is advanced by line drawing between affirmative duties and prohibitions.[4]

In short, in my opinion my Brother Stewart's view fails to provide a meaningful stopping point between an all-or-nothing position with regard to federal taxpayer or citizen standing. In this respect, it shares certain of the deficiencies of Flast. I suspect that this may also be true of any intermediate position in this area. Mr. Justice Douglas correctly discerns, I think, that the alternatives here as a matter of doctrine are essentially bipolar. His preference is clear: "I would be as liberal in allowing taxpayers standing to object to . . . violations of the First Amendment as

---

4. Such an approach might well lead to problems of classification that would divert attention from the fundamental question of whether public actions are an appropriate matter for the federal courts. And, if distinctions between constitutional prohibitions and duties are to make a difference, there are certain to be some incongruous rules as to when such a public action may be brought. This is apparent when one attempts to categorize the provisions of the Constitution primarily addressed at limiting the powers of the National Government—Art. I, § 9, and the Bill of Rights. All of the clauses of Art. I, § 9, except the seventh, which is at issue here, are stated as prohibitions. In fact the seventh clause is in part a prohibition against expenditures of public money in the absence of appropriations and in part an affirmative duty to publish periodically an account of such expenditures. The rationale for according special treatment solely to one-half of Art. I, § 9, cl. 7, and not to the other and not to the remaining clauses of Art. I. § 9, is not immediately apparent.

The same observation may be made of the Bill of Rights. The First Amendment through the Fifth, the Eighth, and possibly the Tenth are stated in terms of prohibitions. The Sixth Amendment and portions of the Seventh can be classified as duties. The Ninth defies classification. Rational rules for standing in public actions are, it seems to me, unlikely to emerge from an effort to make the format of a particular Amendment determinative. [Footnote by Justice Powell.]

I would in granting standing to people to complain of any invasion of their rights under the Fourth Amendment or the Fourteenth or under any other guarantee in the Constitution itself or in the Bill of Rights." [Flast.] My view is to the contrary.

III. Relaxation of standing requirements is directly related to the expansion of judicial power. It seems to me inescapable that allowing unrestricted taxpayer or citizen standing would significantly alter the allocation of power at the national level, with a shift away from a democratic form of government. I also believe that repeated and essentially head-on confrontations between the life-tenured branch and the representative branches of government will not, in the long run, be beneficial to either. The public confidence essential to the former and the vitality critical to the latter may well erode if we do not exercise self-restraint in the utilization of our power to negative the actions of the other branches. We should be ever mindful of the contradictions that would arise if a democracy were to permit general oversight of the elected branches of government by a nonrepresentative, and in large measure insulated, judicial branch. Moreover, the argument that the Court should allow unrestricted taxpayer or citizen standing underestimates the ability of the representative branches of the Federal Government to respond to the citizen pressure that has been responsible in large measure for the current drift toward expanded standing. Indeed, taxpayer or citizen advocacy, given its potentially broad base, is precisely the type of leverage that in a democracy ought to be employed against the branches that were intended to be responsive to public attitudes about the appropriate operation of government. . . .

Unrestrained standing in federal taxpayer or citizen suits would create a remarkably illogical system of judicial supervision of the coordinate branches of the Federal Government. Randolph's proposed Council of Revision, which was repeatedly rejected by the Framers, at least had the virtue of being systematic; every law passed by the legislature automatically would have been previewed by the Judiciary before the law could take effect. On the other hand, since the Judiciary cannot select the taxpayers or citizens who bring suit or the nature of the suits, the allowance of public actions would produce uneven and sporadic review, the quality of which would be influenced by the resources and skill of the particular plaintiff. And issues would be presented in abstract form . . . .[5]

The power recognized in Marbury v. Madison, is a potent one. Its prudent use seems to me incompatible with unlimited notions of taxpayer and citizen standing. Were we to utilize this power as indiscriminately as is now being urged, we may witness efforts by the representative branches drastically to curb its use. Due to what many have regarded as the unresponsiveness of the Federal Government to recognized needs or serious inequities in our society, recourse to the federal courts has attained an unprecedented popularity in recent decades. Those courts have often acted as a major instrument of social reform. But this has not always been the case,

5. Some Western European democracies have experimented with forms of constitutional judicial review in the abstract, see, e. g., M. Cappelletti, Judicial Review in the Contemporary World 71–72 (1971), but that has not been our experience, and I think for good reasons. [Footnote by Justice Powell.]

as experiences under the New Deal illustrate. The public reaction to the substantive due process holdings of the federal courts during that period requires no elaboration, and it is not unusual for history to repeat itself.

Quite apart from this possibility, we risk a progressive impairment of the effectiveness of the federal courts if their limited resources are diverted increasingly from their historic role to the resolution of public-interest suits brought by litigants who cannot distinguish themselves from all taxpayers or all citizens. The irreplaceable value of the power articulated by Chief Justice Marshall lies in the protection it has afforded the constitutional rights and liberties of individual citizens and minority groups against oppressive or discriminatory government action. It is this role, not some amorphous general supervision of the operations of government, that has maintained public esteem for the federal courts and has permitted the peaceful coexistence of the countermajoritarian implications of judicial review and the democratic principles upon which our Federal Government in the final analysis rests.

The considerations outlined above underlie, I believe, the traditional hostility of the Court to federal taxpayer or citizen standing where the plaintiff has nothing at stake other than his interest as a taxpayer or citizen. . . .

To be sure standing barriers have been substantially lowered in the last three decades. The Court has confirmed the power of Congress to open the federal courts to representatives of the public interest through specific statutory grants of standing. E. g., [FCC v. Sanders Bros. Radio Station, 309 U.S. 470 (1940); Scripps-Howard Radio, Inc. v. FCC, 316 U.S. 4 (1942).] Even in the absence of specific statutory grants of standing, economic interests that at one time would not have conferred standing have been re-examined and found sufficient. . . . Noneconomic interests have been recognized. E. g., Baker v. Carr; Sierra Club v. Morton. A stringently limited exception for federal taxpayer standing has been created. Flast v. Cohen, supra. The concept of particularized injury has been dramatically diluted. E. g., United States v. SCRAP [below].

The revolution in standing doctrine that has occurred, particularly in the 12 years since Baker v. Carr, has not meant, however, that standing barriers have disappeared altogether. . . . Indeed, despite the diminution of standing requirements in the last decade, the Court has not broken with the traditional requirement that, in the absence of a specific statutory grant of the right of review, a plaintiff must allege some particularized injury that sets him apart from the man on the street.

I recognize that the Court's allegiance to a requirement of particularized injury has on occasion required a reading of the concept that threatens to transform it beyond recognition. E. g., Baker v. Carr; Flast v. Cohen, supra.[6] But despite such occasional digressions, the requirement remains,

---

6. Baker v. Carr may have a special claim to sui generis status. It was perhaps a necessary response to the manifest distortion of democratic principles practiced by malapportioned legislatures and to abuses of the political system so pervasive as to undermine democratic processes. Flast v. Cohen may also have been a reaction to what appeared at the time as an immutable political logjam that included unsuccessful efforts to confer specific statutory grants of standing. [Footnote by Justice Powell.]

and I think it does so for the reasons outlined above. In recognition of those considerations, we should refuse to go the last mile towards abolition of standing requirements that is implicit in broadening the "precarious opening" for federal taxpayers created by Flast or in allowing a citizen *qua* citizen to invoke the power of the federal courts to negative unconstitutional acts of the Federal Government.

In sum, I believe we should limit the expansion of federal taxpayer and citizen standing in the absence of specific statutory authorization to an outer boundary drawn by the *results* in Flast and Baker v. Carr. I think we should face up to the fact that *all* such suits are an effort "to employ a federal court as a forum in which to air . . . generalized grievances about the conduct of government or the allocation of power in the Federal System." . . . The Court should explicitly reaffirm traditional prudential barriers against such public actions.[7] My reasons for this view are rooted in respect for democratic processes and in the conviction that "[t]he powers of the federal judiciary will be adequate for the great burdens placed upon them only if they are employed prudently, with recognition of the strengths as well as the hazards that go with our kind of representative government." [Flast v. Cohen] (Harlan, J., dissenting).

Mr. Justice Douglas, dissenting.

I would affirm the judgment of the Court of Appeals on the "standing" issue. . . . Whatever may be the merits of the underlying claim, it seems clear that the taxpayer in the present case is not making a generalized complaint about the operation of Government. He does not even challenge the constitutionality of the Central Intelligence Agency Act. He only wants to know the amount of tax money exacted from him that goes into CIA activities. Secrecy of the Government acquires new sanctity when his claim is denied. . . .

From the history of [Art. I, § 9, cl. 7] it is apparent that the Framers inserted it in the Constitution to give the public knowledge of the way public funds are expended. No one has a greater "personal stake" in policing this protective measure than a taxpayer. Indeed, if a taxpayer may not raise the question, who may do so? . . .

---

7. The doctrine of standing has always reflected prudential as well as constitutional limitations. Indeed, it might be said that the correct reading of the Flast nexus test is as a prudential limit, given the Baker v. Carr definition of the constitutional bare minima. The same is undoubtedly true of, for example, the second test created in Association of Data Processing Service Organizations, Inc. v. Camp, 397 U.S. 150, 153 (1970)—"whether the interest sought to be protected by the complainant is arguably within the zone of interests to be protected or regulated by the statute or constitutional guarantee in question." . . . Whatever may have been the Court's initial perception of the intent of the Framers [e. g., Frothingham], it is now settled that such rules of self-restraint are not required by Art. III but are "judicially created overlays that Congress may strip away. . ." G. Gunther & N. Dowling, Cases and Materials on Constitutional Law 106 (8th ed. 1970). But where Congress does so, my objections to public actions are ameliorated by the congressional mandate. Specific statutory grants of standing in such cases alleviate the conditions that make "judicial forbearance the part of wisdom." [Flast] (Harlan, J., dissenting). [Footnote by Justice Powell.]

Mr. Justice STEWART, with whom Mr. Justice MARSHALL joins, dissenting.

The Court's decisions in [Flast and Frothingham] throw very little light on the question at issue in this case. For, unlike the plaintiffs in those cases, Richardson did not bring this action asking a court to invalidate a federal statute on the ground that it was beyond the delegated power of Congress to enact or that it contravened some constitutional prohibition. Richardson's claim is of an entirely different order. It is that Art. I, § 9, cl. 7, of the Constitution, the Statement and Account Clause, gives him a right to receive, and imposes on the Government a corresponding affirmative duty to supply, a periodic report of the receipts and expenditures "of all public Money." In support of his standing to litigate this claim, he has asserted his status both as a taxpayer and as a citizen-voter. Whether the Statement and Account Clause imposes upon the Government an affirmative duty to supply the information requested and whether that duty runs to every taxpayer or citizen are questions that go to the substantive merits of this litigation. Those questions are not now before us, but I think that the Court is quite wrong in holding that the respondent was without standing to raise them in the trial court. . . .

When the duty relates to a very particularized and explicit performance by the asserted obligor, such as the payment of money or the rendition of specific items of information, there is no necessity to resort to any extended analysis, such as the Flast nexus tests, in order to find standing in the obligee. Under such circumstances, the duty itself, running as it does from the defendant to the plaintiff, provides fully adequate assurance that the plaintiff is not seeking to "employ a federal court as a forum in which to air his generalized grievances about the conduct of government or the allocation of power in the Federal System." [Flast.] If such a duty arose in the context of a contract between private parties, no one would suggest that the obligee should be barred from the courts. It seems to me that when the asserted duty is, as here, as particularized, palpable, and explicit as those which courts regularly recognize in private contexts, it should make no difference that the obligor is the government and the duty is embodied in our organic law. Certainly after United States v. SCRAP, 412 U.S. 669 (1973), it does not matter that those to whom the duty is owed may be many. "[S]tanding is not to be denied simply because many people suffer the same injury." Id. . . .

Mr. Justice BRENNAN, dissenting.[*]

The "standing" of a plaintiff to be heard on a claim of invasion of his alleged legally protected right is established, in my view, by his good-faith allegation that " 'the challenged action has caused him injury in fact.' " Barlow v. Collins, 397 U.S. 159, 167 (1970) [separate opinion of Justice Brennan]. . . . Richardson plainly alleged injury in fact. My Brother Stewart demonstrates this in his analysis of Richardson's claimed right to have the budget of the Central Intelligence Agency pub-

---

[*] Justice Brennan's dissent applied to this case as well as to the Reservists Committee case, below.

lished. . . . Moreover, his complaint, properly construed, alleged that the violations caused him injury not only in respect of his right as a citizen to know how Congress was spending the public fisc, but also in respect of his right as a voter to receive information to aid his decision how and for whom to vote. These claims may ultimately fail on the merits, but Richardson has "standing" to assert them.

Unlike my Brother Stewart, who distinguishes [Richardson and Reservists], I would find that [Flast] supports the conclusion that these allegations of injury in fact are sufficient to give respondents in both cases "standing." [After noting that Flast reiterated the Baker v. Carr statement that standing turns on a plaintiff's "personal stake in the outcome of the controversy," Justice Brennan continued:] The two-pronged test fashioned by Flast was not a qualification upon these general principles but was fashioned solely as a determinant of standing of plaintiffs alleging only injury as taxpayers who challenge alleged violations of the [religion clauses] of the First Amendment. The extension of that test to the very different challenges here only produces the confusion evidenced by the differing views of the Flast test expressed in the several opinions filed today in these cases. Outside its proper sphere, as my Brother Powell soundly observes, that test is not "a reliable indicator of when a federal taxpayer has standing." We avoid that confusion if, as I said in Barlow, supra, we recognize that "alleged injury in fact, reviewability, and the merits pose questions that are largely distinct from one another, each governed by its own considerations. To fail to isolate and treat each inquiry independently of the other two, so far as possible, is to risk obscuring what is at issue in a given case, and thus to risk uninformed, poorly reasoned decisions that may result in injustice. . . . The risk of ambiguity and injustice can be minimized by cleanly severing, so far as possible, the inquiries into reviewability and the merits from the determination of standing."

OTHER MODERN STANDING CASES

1. *The Reservists case.* A case decided on the same day as Richardson, SCHLESINGER v. RESERVISTS COMMITTEE TO STOP THE WAR, 418 U.S. 208 (1974), reemphasized the majority's determination to maintain standing as a significant barrier to access to federal courts, despite the erosion of that concept in recent years. (See the sampling of pre-1974 cases, below.) The plaintiffs in Reservists were an association of present and former members of the Reserves, joined by some of the members of the association. They challenged the Reserve membership of certain Members of Congress as being in violation of the Incompatibility Clause—the clause in Art. I, § 6, cl. 2, stating that "no Person holding any Office under the United States, shall be a Member of either House during his continuance in Office." They alleged injury because members of Congress belonging to the Reserves were "subject to the possibility of undue influence by the Executive Branch" and subject to "possible inconsistent obligations which might cause them to violate their duty faithfully to perform as Reservists or as Members of Con-

gress," thus depriving "plaintiffs and all other citizens and taxpayers of the United States of the faithful discharge by members of Congress who are members of the Reserves of their duties as members of Congress, to which all citizens and taxpayers are entitled."

Chief Justice Burger's majority opinion found that the plaintiffs lacked standing either as taxpayers or as citizens. The taxpayer claim was disposed of readily: the Chief Justice simply noted that the plaintiffs had failed to satisfy the first nexus text of Flast, since they "did not challenge an enactment under Art. I, § 8, but rather the action of the Executive Branch in permitting Members of Congress to maintain their Reserve status." As to citizens' standing, the Chief Justice explained at length why "generalized citizen interest" is not a sufficient basis for access to the federal courts. He concluded that the claimed constitutional violation "would adversely affect only the generalized interest of all citizens in constitutional governance, and that is an abstract injury." In elaborating that barrier, he explained: "Concrete injury, whether actual or threatened, is that indispensable element of a dispute which serves in part to cast it in a form traditionally capable of judicial resolution. It adds the essential dimension of specificity to the dispute. [This] personal stake is what the Court has consistently held enables a complainant authoritatively to present to a court a complete perspective upon the adverse consequences flowing from the specific set of facts undergirding his grievance. Such authoritative presentations are an integral part of the judicial process, for a court must rely on the parties' treatment of the facts and claims before it to develop its rules of law. Only concrete injury presents the factual context within which a court [is] capable of making decisions."

Moreover, the "concrete injury" requirement served the function of assuring that constitutional adjudication "does not take place unnecessarily." The Chief Justice added: "To permit a complainant who has no concrete injury to require a court to rule on important constitutional issues in the abstract would create the potential for abuse of the judicial process, distort the role of the Judiciary in its relationship to the Executive and the Legislature and open the Judiciary to an arguable charge of providing 'government by injunction.'" Cases such as SCRAP, below, did not go so far as to "allow a citizen to call on the courts to resolve abstract questions." Though citizens might allege "an arguable conflict with some limitation of the Constitution, it can be only a matter of speculation whether the claimed violation has caused concrete injury to the particular complainant."

The fact that there was genuine adverseness between the parties, assuring able arguments, was not enough to justify recognition of standing: "[Plaintiffs'] motivation has indeed brought them sharply into conflict with [defendants, but] motivation is not a substitute for the actual injury needed by the courts and adversaries to focus litigation efforts and judicial decision-making." He added: "The proposition that all constitutional provisions are enforceable by any citizen simply because citizens are the ultimate beneficiaries of those provisions has no boundaries." And the fact that no one might be able to sue if plaintiffs could not was not determinative: "Our system of government leaves many crucial decisions to the political processes."

Justice Stewart, who had dissented in Richardson, concurred here, since the plaintiffs "do not allege that the [defendants] have refused to perform

an affirmative duty imposed upon them by the Constitution." And Flast did not help, "since there is simply no challenge to an exercise of the taxing and spending power." Moreover, his opinion in SCRAP was distinguishable: "Standing is not today found wanting because an injury has been suffered by many, but rather because *none* [of the plaintiffs] has alleged the sort of direct, palpable injury required for standing under Art. III."

Justices Douglas, Brennan and Marshall dissented. Justice Marshall thought the citizen standing here rested on a sufficiently "specific interest" and not on one shared by "all members of the public": "Not all citizens desire to have the Congress take all steps necessary to terminate American involvement in Vietnam, and not all citizens who so desired sought to persuade members of Congress to that end." Justice Douglas, finally, thought that "the interest of citizens in guarantees written in the Constitution seems obvious." He added: "The 'personal stake' in the present case is keeping the Incompatability Clause an operative force in government by freeing the entanglement of the federal bureaucracy with the Legislative Branch."

2. *Noneconomic injuries and standing: The Sierra Club and SCRAP cases.* Another effort by the Court to assert standing barriers, in the years immediately preceding Richardson and Reservists, proved a relatively insignificant one. In SIERRA CLUB v. MORTON, 405 U.S. 727 (1972), the majority imposed a limited restraint on the growing tendency of some lower federal courts to recognize the standing of organizations with a special interest in such problems as environmental control and consumer protection. But a year later, the decision in UNITED STATES v. SCRAP, 412 U.S. 669 (1973), indicated that the Sierra Club barrier was a minor, temporary, easily avoidable one.

a. *Sierra Club.* The Sierra Club, describing itself as an organization with "a special interest in the conservation and sound maintenance of the national parks [and] forests," brought suit to block the proposed development of Mineral King Valley by Walt Disney Enterprises. Mineral King, in the Sierra Nevadas, is part of Sequoia National Forest. Sierra Club claimed that federal authorities had violated federal laws governing the preservation of national parks, forests and game refuges in approving the Disney plans to develop Mineral King as a recreational area. It relied on § 10 of the Administrative Procedure Act authorizing judicial review by a person "suffering legal wrong" or "adversely affected or aggrieved" by agency action. Justice Stewart's majority opinion found that the kind of injury alleged, though noneconomic, could amount to "injury in fact" cognizable under § 10, but nevertheless concluded that Sierra Club lacked standing because it had failed to allege an individualized injury to itself.

Justice Stewart recognized that modern Court decisions [1] had expanded the coverage of § 10 beyond the traditional "legal wrongs" to encompass a

---

1. The reference was to such modern "competitors' standing" cases as Association of Data Processing Service Organizations, Inc. v. Camp, 397 U.S. 150 (1970), and Barlow v. Collins, 397 U.S. 159 (1970). In Data Processing, Justice Douglas emphasized two ingredients of standing: (1) the Art. III requirement that the challenged action caused the plaintiff "injury in fact"; and (2) "whether the interest sought to be protected by the complainant is arguably within the zone of interests to be protected or regulated by the statute or constitutional guarantee in question." Justice Brennan's separate opinion insisted that only the first inquiry was relevant to standing. Re-

broad category of "injuries in fact." The recent cases involved "palpable economic injuries," but that was not essential: noneconomic injuries, too, were "injuries in fact," and Sierra Club accordingly met the § 10 requirements in that respect. "Aesthetic and environmental well-being, like economic well-being, are important ingredients of the quality of life in our society, and the fact that particular environmental interests are shared by the many rather than the few does not make them less deserving of legal protection through the judicial process." But Sierra Club fell short in another respect: The "injury in fact" test "requires more than an injury to a cognizable interest. It requires that the party seeking review be himself among the injured." The Sierra Club "failed to allege that it or its members would be affected in any of their activities or pastimes by the Disney development." [2]

The Court rejected the Club's argument that allegations of individualized injury were superfluous because this was a "public" action: the Club claimed standing as a "representative of the public" in view of its special expertise and concern. That argument, Justice Stewart insisted, reflected a "misunderstanding" of "public actions" cases. Decisions such as Scripps-Howard and Sanders [3] merely held that a litigant properly in court because of an individ-

quiring the second, "nonconstitutional step," he insisted, "comes very close to perpetuating the discredited requirement that conditioned standing on a showing by the plaintiff that the challenged governmental action invaded one of his legally protected interests." He emphasized: "When agency action is challenged, standing, reviewability, and the merits pose discrete, and often complicated, issues which can best be resolved by recognizing and treating them as such." In arguing against the relevance of the second inquiry to the issue of standing, he commented: "I had thought we discarded the notion of any additional requirement when we discussed standing solely in terms of its constitutional content in [Flast]." Flast, he insisted, established that standing existed when the plaintiff alleged "that the challenged action has caused him injury in fact, economic or otherwise." That was enough to show "personal stake" in the outcome.

Was that a persuasive reading of Flast? Note that Flast had a dual nexus requirement. Was the second nexus requirement in Flast like the second requirement in Data Processing? Compare also an earlier case rejecting competitors' standing, Tennessee Electric Power Co. v. Tennessee Valley Authority, 306 U.S. 118 (1939), where private power companies sought to stop competition by the TVA on the ground that establishment of the TVA violated federalism limits on Congress. Though the plaintiffs' actual injury from competition was

plain, they were found to lack standing—because theirs was not a "legal" injury, because there was no "legal right" to be free from lawful competition. The reference to "legal right" caused considerable confusion in the commentaries and was attacked as being question-begging. Such modern cases as Data Processing reject the "legal right" inquiry—yet, Justice Douglas' second criterion, as to "zone of interest to be protected," indicates that "injury in fact" is not sufficient for standing without more. Justice Brennan, as his opinions in Barlow and later cases indicate, insists "injury in fact"—broadly read—is sufficient by itself. The standing barrier involved in the TVA litigation—requiring more than injury in fact—was one Congress could modify, as cases of the 1940's soon made clear. See footnote 3 below.

2. In a footnote, the Court added: "Our decision does not, of course, bar the Sierra Club from seeking in the District Court to amend its complaint." A few weeks after the decision, the Sierra Club accordingly amended its complaint in the lower court, alleging that some of its members use the Mineral King area for recreational purposes and would be injured by the resort development.

3. The cases referred to—FCC v. Sanders Bros. Radio Station, 309 U.S. 470 (1940), and Scripps-Howard Radio, Inc. v. FCC, 316 U.S. 4 (1942)—were among a series in which the Court indicated that Congress could modify the stand-

ualized injury could then argue the public interest in support of his claim; "a mere 'interest in a problem' "—though a longstanding one, by a qualified organization—"is not sufficient by itself to render the organization" an "aggrieved" party within § 10. In justifying that limitation, Justice Stewart explained: "[I]f any group with a bona fide 'special interest' could initiate such litigation, it is difficult to perceive why any individual citizen with the same bona fide special interest would not also be entitled to do so."

Justices Douglas, Brennan and Blackmun dissented. Justice Blackmun asked: "Must our law be so rigid and our procedural concepts so inflexible that we render ourselves helpless when the existing methods and the traditional concepts do not quite fit and do not prove to be entirely adequate for new issues?" Justice Douglas urged a standing rule permitting environmental issues to be litigated "in the name of the inanimate object about to be despoiled, defaced, or invaded by roads and bulldozers and where injury is the subject of public outrage." And those who have an "intimate relation with the inanimate object about to be injured" should be recognized as "its legitimate spokesmen."

b. *SCRAP.* Justice Stewart once again wrote for the majority a year later, in SCRAP. This time, he found that the limitations of Sierra Club had been overcome and that the appellees had adequately alleged standing—even though, as he noted, the federal action of which they complained was not as "specific and geographically limited" as that challenged in the Sierra Club case, and even though the injury alleged here was "far less direct and perceptible" than in Sierra Club. SCRAP (Students Challenging Regulatory Agency Procedures—an unincorporated association formed by five law students), joined by several other environmental groups, had challenged the ICC's failure to suspend a temporary railroad surcharge on most freight rates. SCRAP alleged that its members "suffered economic, recreational and aesthetic harm directly as a result of the adverse environmental impact of the railroad freight structure." The "attenuated line of causation" regarding the alleged injury was stated by Justice Stewart as follows: "a general rate increase would allegedly cause increased use of nonrecyclable commodities as compared to recyclable goods, thus resulting in the need to use more natural resources to produce such goods, some of which resources might be taken from the Washington area, and resulting in more refuse that might be discarded in national parks in the Washington area." (SCRAP had alleged that each of its members "breathes the air" within the Washington area and "uses the forests,

ing barrier involved in the TVA litigation, footnote 1 above—the requirement that the plaintiff allege a "legal right" as well as injury in fact. In the Sanders case, the Court noted that Congress could "confer" standing on an economic competitor even though the law did not assure an FCC licensee freedom of competition. And in Scripps-Howard, the Court stated that the Federal Communications Act gave "these private litigants [standing] only as representatives of the public interest." Justice Douglas' dissent argued that, if Congress did not grant a substantive right to be free

from competition, "I fail to see how an appeal statute constitutionally could authorize a person who shows no case or controversy to call on the courts to review an order of the Commission." What Art. III difficulty troubled Justice Douglas? In light of his later opinions—e. g., in Flast—Justice Douglas has apparently overcome that concern.

The problems raised by cases such as these and those in footnote 1 typically involve review of agency action and are pursued more fully in administrative law courses.

rivers, streams, mountains, and other natural resources" in the Washington area.) That was a sufficient allegation of "specific injury" for the Court. The fact that the injury was potentially widespread was no obstacle: "To deny standing to persons who are in fact injured simply because many others are also injured, would mean that the most injurious and widespread Government actions could be questioned by nobody. We cannot accept that conclusion."

Justices Douglas, Brennan, Marshall and Blackmun joined the standing part of Justice Stewart's opinion. Indeed, three members of the majority thought Justice Stewart was requiring more than was necessary. Justice Blackmun, joined by Justice Brennan, said that he would not require "injury in fact" to the appellees: "Rather, I would require only that appellees, as responsible and sincere representatives of environmental interests, show that the environment would be injured in fact." In a separate opinion, Justice Douglas agreed with that position. Justice White, joined by Chief Justice Burger and Justice Rehnquist, dissented: "The allegations here do not satisfy the threshold requirement of injury in fact for constituting a justiciable case or controversy." He added: "To me, the alleged injuries are so remote, speculative, and insubstantial in fact that they fail to confer standing." [4]

THE INGREDIENTS OF STANDING AND CONGRESSIONAL POWER

Introduction. a. Consider, in light of the preceding cases: To what extent are these standing barriers compelled by Art. III? To what extent are they judicially created overlays that Congress may strip away? Are the barriers to plaintiffs' access announced in cases such as Richardson prudential ones created by the courts? Or are they mandated by the Constitution? Most of the preceding decisions involved situations where Congress had not specifically sought to grant standing to the plaintiff. Are the Court's criteria for governing access in that context coherent? Are they responsive to the policies that standing doctrines may promote? What are the decisive policies in the various cases? Are the Court's standards apt implementations of those policies?

b. Does "injury in fact" remain as a core constitutional ingredient of standing requirements? Or has the modern dilution of standing requirements made personal injury in fact no longer necessary as a constitutional requirement? Note that even cases such as Richardson continue to recognize Flast and SCRAP. Is it realistic and persuasive to speak of "personal" "injuries in fact" in those cases? Or are they more realistically viewed as recognitions of "public actions" by "non-Hohfeldian" plaintiffs, as Justice Harlan claimed in his dissent in Flast? Note that Justice Harlan found no constitutional barrier to public actions; his reluctance to grant standing stemmed explicitly from prudential considerations; he would have seen no constitutional difficulty if Congress had chosen to grant standing. Note also Justice Brennan's willingness to find "injury in fact" in a wide range of situations.

4. Recall that the decisions in the text and in the preceding footnotes were discussed in the several opinions in the Richardson case, above.

Is Justice Powell persuasive in Richardson in claiming that Justice Brennan's position is ultimately indistinguishable from Justice Douglas' endorsement of a broad range of citizens' actions?

c.   One of the criticisms repeatedly voiced by the Court in standing cases is the need to assure a sufficiently concrete record, and sufficient adverseness, to assure informed decision of constitutional issues.   Does emphasis on "injury in fact" and on similar criteria truly promote those optimum conditions for constitutional adjudication?   Are groups such as the Sierra Club less likely to assure adverseness and concreteness than an individual plaintiff residing in the Mineral King area?   Are standing rules the proper vehicles for assuring adequate concreteness?   Would those needs be better met by emphasizing rules as to ripeness (sec. 3 below) rather than standing?

d.   To what extent do modern standing barriers stem from Court concerns about excessive judicial involvement in governmental operations and about risks of confrontation with other branches?   To what extent, in short, do they reflect the fear of excessive engagement in substantive constitutional decisionmaking?   Is invocation of standing rules an appropriate and legitimate expression of those concerns?   Should those concerns be treated as "political questions" problems of justiciability, see sec. 5 below?   If the constitutional issues presented are not nonjusticiable political questions, is the Court obligated to decide them?   Or is its control over remedies sufficiently broad to justify barriers to access in the absence of a congressional grant of standing?   These questions, raised by the preceding cases, are briefly pursued in the notes which follow.

1.   *The Court's criteria.*   a.   Are the Court's criteria for standing coherent and workable?   Are they responsive to the interests they purport to serve?   The most frequently reiterated ingredient, as noted, is "injury in fact."   Why should not a concerned citizen's outrage at allegedly constitutional behavior qualify as sufficient injury?   Is it a less significant injury, in terms of the purposes the standing doctrines purport to serve, than the economic and noneconomic injuries the Court has recognized as adequate for standing? *

What added ingredients do the Court decisions disclose?   Are the Flast double-nexus criteria plausible ones in terms of standing policies?   Do they contribute to concreteness?   Is their central purpose simply to limit the Court's role in constitutional decisionmaking?   Note Professor Kenneth Scott's comment: "The court may in effect set [a] higher access threshold [when] the case presents troublesome questions about the suitability of the issues tendered for decision by the judiciary.   Or, putting it another way, concern over the decision role the court would have to assume may lead it to reject standing for a plaintiff whose injury and stake would, in a different context, pass muster."   Scott, "Standing in the Supreme Court—A Functional Analysis," 86 Harv.L.Rev. 645 (1973).   Is that a proper use of standing doctrines?   Do the cases that do not meet the Flast nexus requirement present problems of political question justiciability?   Were the issues in Rich-

---

* Note the comment that the "idle and whimsical plaintiff, a dilettante who litigates for a lark, is a specter which haunts the legal literature, not the courtroom."   Scott, "Standing in the Supreme Court—A Functional Analysis," 86 Harv.L.Rev. 645 (1973).

ardson and Reservists political questions (see sec. 5 below)? If so, why did not the Court say so, instead of emphasizing standing rules?

c.   Are additional Court requirements for standing suggested by the decision in LINDA R. S. v. RICHARD D., 410 U.S. 614 (1972)? In that case, the majority found lack of standing in a federal court action by the mother of an illegitimate child who sought to compel the local prosecutor to enforce against the alleged father a Texas criminal law that punished parents who refused to provide for their children's support. The state courts had construed that statute to apply only to the parents of legitimate children, and the plaintiff claimed that that construction violated the equal protection clause. Justice Marshall's majority opinion held that she lacked standing, stating that she "has failed to allege a sufficient nexus between her injury and the government action which she attacks to justify judicial intervention. To be sure, appellant no doubt suffered an injury stemming from the failure of her child's father to contribute support payments. But the bare existence of an abstract injury meets only the first half of the standing requirement. 'The party who invokes [judicial] power must be able to show   .   .   . that he has sustained or is immediately in danger of sustaining some *direct* injury *as the result of* [a statute's] enforcement.' Massachusetts v. Mellon. .   .   . Here, appellant has made no showing that her failure to secure support payments results from the nonenforcement [of the law] as to her child's father. [I]f appellant were granted the requested relief, it would result only in the jailing of the child's father. The prospect that prosecution will, at least in the future, result in payment of support can, at best, be termed only speculative. Certainly the 'direct' relationship between the alleged injury and the claim sought to be adjudicated, which previous decisions of this Court suggest is a prerequisite of standing, is absent [here]." [1]   (Was the standing problem in the Linda R. S. truly one of constitutional dimensions?)

2.   *Public actions.* Should the Court—or Congress—be more generous in recognizing "public actions" by "private attorneys general"? Or would such actions bring the Court too close to being the Council of Revision rejected at the Constitutional Convention? (Recall Justice Harlan's opinion in Flast and Justice Powell's in Richardson.) Would general access to courts by "private attorneys general" risk bringing to the courts too many cases involving abstractions and resting on inadequately developed records? Do not the ripeness rules, sec. 3 below, adequately safeguard against that risk? Has not the Court in fact recognized public actions in some circumstances? Recall Justice Harlan's description of the Flast claim.[2]

Note Professor Jaffe's conclusion in "Standing to Secure Judicial Review: Private Actions," 75 Harv.L.Rev. 255, 305 (1961). After noting

1. A dissent by Justice White, joined by Justice Douglas, found standing. Another dissent, by Justice Blackmun, joined by Justice Brennan, thought the standing issue "a difficult one with constitutional overtones" but found it unnecessary to reach it: he urged a remand to determine whether intervening developments had made the controversy no longer a "live, ongoing" one.

2. On the desirability of authorizing public actions, compare Bickel, "Foreword: The Passive Virtues," 75 Harv. L.Rev. 40 (1961), with Jaffe, "Standing to Secure Judicial Review: Public Actions," 74 Harv.L.Rev. 1265 (1961).

the "potential correspondence between the lack of a conventional plaintiff and the lack of maturity" (see the ripeness materials below), he adds: "I find it difficult to accept the conclusion [that] an issue in every other respect apt for judicial determination should be nonjusticiable because there is no possibility of a conventional plaintiff—an issue in short in which everyone has a legitimate interest but only as a citizen." Note also his suggestion in Jaffe, Judicial Control of Administrative Action (1965), that where "the moving party is a citizen, the suit may be most appropriate when he purports to assert interests which are peculiarly citizen concern. 'Citizen concern' might be conceived of in terms of demands for the enforcement (1) of norms generally accepted as appropriate for the proper day-by-day conduct of government, or (2) of norms basic to the political and social process and to the citizen's participation in it." He suggests that the plaintiff "must convince" a court "that the dereliction of law has a real public significance" and "involves a 'public right.' " Would that suggestion significantly limit the availability of public actions? Are the suggested groundrules justifiable and workable?

3. *Congress and standing rules.* In the competitors' standing cases noted earlier, congressional lowerings of standing barriers were all on behalf of plaintiffs who were injured in distinctive ways by the challenged governmental action. May Congress grant standing even where the plaintiff's grievance is indistinguishable from the public at large? May Congress authorize "any taxpayer" or "any citizen" to bring suit against allegedly unconstitutional governmental action? Or would that be tantamount to directing advisory opinions in violation of Art. III? Are there any substantial constitutional barriers to congressional expansion of plaintiffs' access to courts? Do the modern Court opinions imply any barriers? Once again, the question of whether "injury in fact" is an aspect of Art. III or a prudential rule becomes important. Compare, e. g., Chief Justice Warren's opinion in Flast with that of Justice Harlan; and Chief Justice Burger's opinion in Richardson with that of Justice Powell. Note also a comment in Justice Stewart's majority opinion in Sierra Club, above: "Congress may not confer jurisdiction on Art. III federal courts to render advisory opinions [or] to entertain 'friendly' suits [or] to resolve 'political questions' [because] suits of this character are inconsistent with the judicial function under Art. III. But where a dispute is otherwise justiciable, the question whether the litigant is a 'proper party to request an adjudication of a particular issue' is one within the power of Congress to determine."

Does such a congressional power rest on Congress' Art. III control over the law of remedies and the use of the federal courts? Or is it necessary to look to sources outside of Art. III to justify congressional lowerings of standing barriers? Note Justice White's concurrence, joined by Justices Blackmun and Powell, in Trafficante v. Metropolitan Life Ins. Co., 409 U.S. 205 (1972). In that case, the Court gave a "generous construction" to the standing requirements under the fair housing provisions of the Civil Rights Act of 1968. Justice Douglas' opinion found that Congress had intended to define standing "as broadly as is permitted by Article III" and noted: "The role of 'private attorneys general' is not uncommon in

modern legislative programs." Justice White's brief concurrence voiced a different approach to the standing issue. If there were no statute, he explained, "I would have great difficulty in concluding that petitioners' complaint in this case presented a case or controversy" under Art. III. But the statute overcame his Art. III concerns: with the Civil Rights Act "purporting to give all those who are authorized to complain to the agency the right also to sue in court, I would sustain the statute insofar as it extends standing to those in the position of the petitioners [here]." He added a significant citation: "Cf. Katzenbach v. Morgan; Oregon v. Mitchell." Is the controversial congressional power under the Katzenbach v. Morgan interpretation of § 5 of the 14th Amendment sufficient to overcome Art. III limitations? Recall the discussions of the Morgan problem in chap. 11, sec. 4, above. Rather than invoking Katzenbach v. Morgan, should the Trafficante issue more properly be viewed as one presenting no genuine Art. III difficulty?

ADDITIONAL PROBLEMS: STATE STANDING RULES AND SUPREME COURT REVIEW; DEFENDANTS' STANDING; MOOTNESS

1. *Standing to sue in state courts and Supreme Court review.* a. State courts are not merely authorized but compelled to adjudicate federal constitutional questions in appropriate cases. And states have considerable autonomy with respect to the operation of their judicial systems.[1] Ordinarily, then, questions of standing to sue in state courts are questions of state law; and state rules as to access to state courts may and frequently do differ from federal court standing rules. But what if Supreme Court review is sought in a case in which a plaintiff has gained access to state courts under more lenient standing rules than the federal ones? Do the federal standing rules considered in the preceding materials then govern? May or must the Supreme Court refuse review in such a case? Or is the Supreme Court bound to adjudicate such a case?

As noted in sec. 1, some states authorize their courts to issue advisory opinions. Presumably, the Supreme Court could not review such a case: it cannot exercise power beyond the limits of the Art. III case and controversy requirement. But consider a more common situation, presented in the Doremus case in 1952—a state court action by a state taxpayer challenging a state's funding program on Establishment Clause grounds, during the period before Flast v. Cohen, at a time when federal taxpayers lacked standing. During that period, the Supreme Court repeatedly decided the merits in municipal taxpayers' suits challenging local action without even discussing the standing issue. See, e. g., Everson v. Board of Education, 330 U.S. 1 (1947) (local taxpayer challenging spending of public funds for transportation of parochial school students) (chap. 14 above). But in DOREMUS v. BOARD OF EDUCATION, 342 U.S. 429 (1952), the Court dismissed an appeal from a state court decision which had rejected

---

1. Recall, in connection with this note, the materials in chap. 1, sec. 4, on adequate state grounds and Supreme Court review.

an attack by taxpayers on the validity of Bible reading in the public schools. Justice Jackson's majority opinion stated:

"We do not undertake to say that a state court may not render an opinion on a federal constitutional question even under such circumstances that it can be regarded only as advisory.   But, because our own jurisdiction is cast in terms of 'case or controversy,' we cannot accept as the basis for review, nor as the basis for conclusive disposition of an issue of federal law without review, any procedure which does not constitute such.   The taxpayer's action can meet this test, but only when it is a good-faith pocketbook action.   It is apparent that the grievance which it is sought to litigate here is not a direct dollars-and-cents injury but is a religious difference."

Justice Douglas, joined by Justices Reed and Burton, dissented: "If this were a suit to enjoin a federal law, it could not be maintained by reason of [the Frothingham case].   But New Jersey can fashion her own rules governing the institution of suits in her courts.   If she wants to give these taxpayers the status to sue, [I] see nothing in the Constitution to prevent it. And where the clash of interests is as real and as strong as it is here, it is odd indeed to hold there is no case or controversy within the meaning of Art. III, § 2 of the Constitution." [2]

Were the majority's Art. III doubts justified?   Was not Justice Douglas' response persuasive?   And if there was no Art. III barrier, was there any justification for the Court's dismissal of a case within its obligatory appeal jurisdiction?   Nevertheless, there have been frequent statements by Justices suggesting that state grants of standing may not be binding for review purposes, even where there is no statutory or constitutional barrier to Supreme Court review.   Note Justice Frankfurter's comment in Coleman v. Miller, 307 U.S. 433 (1939) (sec. 5 below): "[T]he creation of a vast domain of legal interests is in the keeping of the states, and from time to time state courts and legislators give legal protection to new individual interests.   Thus, while the ordinary taxpayer's suit is not recognized in the federal courts, it affords adequate standing for review of state decisions when so recognized by state courts.   .   .   .   But it by no means follows that a state court ruling on the adequacy of legal interest is binding here."   Why not, if Art. III and the jurisdictional statute are satisfied?   What if the state courts in Doremus had decided for the plaintiffs?   Would the Supreme Court have adhered to its position on standing?   Would it have entered orders dismissing the appeals—and left intact the state injunctions based on federal substantive law?

Should the question of standing to raise federal issues in state courts be considered one of federal law?   Note Professor Freund's comment on Doremus, in Supreme Court and Supreme Law (Cahn ed., 1954), 35: "I think it is a needed change to make standing to raise a federal constitutional question itself a federal question, so that it will be decided uniformly throughout the country.   I disagree with the Doremus case in so far as it

2. Recall that in 1963, the Court reached the substantive issue Doremus had sought to present and held that Bible reading in schools violated the Establishment Clause. See School District of Abington Township v. Schempp, 374 U.S. 203 (chap. 14 above), where the majority found standing because the challengers were "school children and their parents directly affected" by the practices.

lets the state judgment stand and merely declines to review it. It seems to me that the Court should have [vacated the state court decree] so that it would not be a precedent even in the state court." What, if any, constitutional justification is there for an approach such as that?

b.   Note the similar problems raised by TILESTON v. ULLMAN, 318 U.S. 44 (1943), an early unsuccessful effort to challenge the Connecticut ban on the use of contraceptives—a challenge that succeeded on the merits 22 years later, in Griswold v. Connecticut (chap. 9 above). Tileston was a declaratory judgment action by a doctor alleging that the statute would prevent his giving professional advice to three patients whose lives would be endangered by child-bearing. The state court reached the merits and held the law constitutional. The Supreme Court dismissed the appeal: "We are of the opinion that the proceedings in the state courts present no constitutional question which appellant has standing to assert. The sole constitutional attack upon the statutes under the Fourteenth Amendment is confined to their deprivation of life—obviously not appellant's but his patients'. [The] patients are not parties to this proceeding and there is no basis on which we can say that he has standing to secure an adjudication of his patients' constitutional right to life, which they do not assert in their own behalf. No question is raised in the record with respect to the deprivation of appellant's liberty or property." The Court concluded "that appellant has no standing to litigate the constitutional question which the record presents"; and the Court therefore found it "unnecessary to consider whether the record shows the existence of a genuine case or controversy."

If there was no Art. III difficulty, what justified the Supreme Court's dismissal? Is there any source of Court discretion to decline adjudication in a case in which the state court decided the merits?[3] If the question of standing "is the question whether the litigant has a sufficient personal interest in getting the relief he seeks, or is a sufficiently appropriate representative of other interested persons," and, if, "[s]o viewed, the question becomes inextricably bound up with the law of rights and remedies"[4] —in short, if the Tileston variety of standing question is "one of remedy"[5] —why should not the Supreme Court bow to the state court's recognition of the physician's representative or fiduciary capacity to raise the interests of his patients?

2.   *Asserting the rights of others and defendants' standing.* As Tileston illustrates, the Court has frequently stated as a general rule that "one may not claim standing [to] vindicate the constitutional rights of some third party." E. g., Barrows v. Jackson, 346 U.S. 249 (1953), below. But "the Court has created numerous exceptions which lack a coherent pattern and leave the significance of the rule in doubt."[6] Though the major focus of

3.   See also the materials on discretionary abstention from the exercise of jurisdiction, in sec. 4A below.

4.   Hart and Wechsler, Federal Courts (2d ed. 1973), 156.

5.   Hart and Wechsler, Federal Courts (1st ed. 1953), 174.

On the problem of standing to raise the rights of others, note also the additional materials in note 2 below.

6.   See Note, "Standing to Assert Constitutional Jus Tertii," 88 Harv.L.Rev. 423 (1974), a recent, thoughtful effort to provide greater coherence in this area. See also Sedler, "Standing to

this section is on the minimal ingredients necessary to afford plaintiffs' access to federal courts, a brief view of the jus tertii problem—standing to assert the rights of others—is warranted here. Though that problem may arise in the plaintiffs' access context, it more commonly involves the standing of defendants who of course are in court and do not present an access problem. The central question is what issues—other than those immediately affecting them—those defendants may raise.

In the Court's numerous confrontations with the issue, the Court has identified three factors as being important in justifying the wide-ranging exceptions to the general barrier against raising the rights of third parties: "the presence of some substantial relationship between the claimant, and the third parties"; the impossibility of the third party rightholders "asserting their own constitutional rights"; and "the risk that the rights of third parties will be diluted" unless the the party in court is allowed to assert their rights. Consider the role of those factors in the illustrative cases noted below. Consider as well the suggestion that the last of these factors should be the critical one—that emphasis on it would create more "coherent doctrine" out of the present "patchwork of exceptions." That suggestion advocates a "practice of permitting claimants to assert jus tertii when the injury of which they complain also deprives third parties of constitutional rights." [7] Consider, then, the following "exceptions" to the allegedly general barrier against asserting the rights of others.

a. In Pierce v. Society of Sisters, 268 U.S. 510 (1925) (chaps. 9 and 14 above), where a parochial school challenged the constitutionality of a statute requiring parents to send children to public schools, the plaintiff in a federal court action was permitted to assert the rights of the parents in defending its own property rights. And in NAACP v. Alabama 357 U.S. 449 (1958) (chap. 13, sec. 5, above), the NAACP—in resisting a state order to disclose its membership lists—was permitted to assert the rights of its members. The Court stated that the Association "argues more appropriately the rights of its members [and] its nexus with them is sufficient to permit that it act as their representative before this Court." Why could not Connecticut, in the Tileston case above, find that the doctor's "nexus" with his patients was "sufficient" to permit him to "act as their representative"? Was it because the doctor in Tileston lacked minimal standing requirements because he alleged no injury to himself at all, whereas in all of the other cases, the claimants were in court asserting some rights of their own, and the Court permitted them to assert rights of others as well?

Compare the case in which the issues sought to be raised in Tileston were ultimately decided on the merits, Griswold v. Connecticut, 381 U.S. 479 (1965) (chap. 9). The appellants in Griswold had given birth control information at a clinic and were convicted as accessories to the violation of the "use" ban. The majority opinion noted: "We think that appellants have standing to raise the constitutional rights of the married people with whom they had a professional relationship. Tileston v. Ullman is differ-

---

Assert Constitutional Jus Tertii in the Supreme Court," 71 Yale L.J. 599 (1962), and generally, Hart and Wechsler, Federal Courts (2d ed. 1973), chap. 2, sec. 5.

7. Note, 88 Harv.L.Rev. 423 (1974) (footnote 6 above). The quoted passages in this paragraph are from that Note.

ent, for there the plaintiff seeking to represent others asked for a declaratory judgment. In that situation we thought that the requirements of standing should be strict, lest the standards of 'case or controversy' in Article III of the Constitution become blurred. Here those doubts are removed by reason of a criminal conviction for serving married couples in violation of an aiding-and-abetting statute. Certainly the accessory should have standing to assert that the offense which he is charged with assisting is not, or cannot constitutionally be, a crime. This case is more akin to Truax v. Raich, 239 U.S. 33 (below); to Pierce v. Society of Sisters (above); and to Barrows v. Jackson, 346 U.S. 249 (below). The rights of husband and wife, pressed here, are likely to be diluted or adversely affected unless those rights are considered in a suit involving those who have this kind of confidential relation to them."[8]

b. Note similarly the exceptions to the usual rule that one must be a member of the class discriminated against in order to have standing to attack a statute as denying equal protection. Thus, Truax v. Raich, 239 U.S. 33 (1915), permitted an alien employee to enjoin the enforcement of a statute limiting the percentage of aliens on the employer's work force: the employee was permited to raise the rights of the employer. And in BARROWS v. JACKSON, 346 U.S. 249 (1953) (noted after Shelley v. Kraemer, chap. 11, sec. 2, above), a defendant in a state court damage suit for breach of a racially restrictive covenant was permitted to challenge the enforcement of the covenant although he was not a member of the class discriminated against.

---

8. Note also the standing barriers overcome in a subsequent challenge to contraception laws, Eisenstadt v. Baird, 405 U.S. 438 (1972) (chap. 10, sec. 6). Baird was convicted under an anti-distribution law on the ground that he was not an authorized distributor. There was no indication as to the marital status of the woman to whom Baird gave the contraceptives. It was argued that Baird lacked standing "to assert the rights of unmarried persons denied access to contraceptives because he was neither an authorized distributor [nor] a single person unable to obtain contraceptives." Clearly, Baird had minimal standing to be in court: he was a defendant in a criminal case. The question was the issues he could raise: could he attack the statute in its application to potential recipients? Justice Brennan rejected the argument that Baird lacked standing: "[O]ur self-imposed rule against the assertion of third-party rights must be relaxed in this case just as in [Griswold]." The state in Baird argued that "the absence of a professional or aiding-and-abetting relationship distinguishes this case from Griswold." Justice Brennan replied that those relationships were "not the only circumstances in which one person has been found to have standing to assert the rights of another. [Barrows]." He concluded: "[H]ere the relationship between Baird and those whose rights he seeks to assert is not simply that between a distributor and potential distributees, but that between an advocate of the right of persons to obtain contraceptives and those desirous of doing so. . . . In any event, more important than the nature of the relationship between the litigant and those whose rights he seeks to assert is the impact of the litigation on the third-party interests." Here, as in Griswold, enforcement of the law "will materially impair the ability of single persons to obtain contraceptives." Indeed, here the case for recognizing standing to raise other parties' interests was stronger than in Griswold "because unmarried persons denied access to contraceptives in Massachusetts, unlike the users of contraceptives in Connecticut, are not themselves subject to prosecution and, to that extent, are denied a forum in which to assert their own rights. [Cf. NAACP; Barrows.]" Accordingly, Baird, who "plainly has an adequate incentive to assert the rights of unmarried persons denied access to contraceptives, has standing to do so."

Justice Minton's majority opinion in Barrows v. Jackson suggested that the Article III requirements at the core of the law of standing were encased in discretionary, prudential considerations: "Ordinarily, one may not claim in this Court to vindicate the constitutional rights of some third party. . . . The requirement of standing is often used to describe the constitutional limitation on the jurisdiction of this Court to 'cases' and 'controversies.' Apart from the jurisdictional requirement, this Court has developed a complementary rule of self-restraint for its own governance (not always clearly distinguished from the constitutional limitation) which ordinarily precludes a person from challenging the constitutionality by invoking the rights of others. . . . There are still other cases in which the Court has held that even though a party will suffer a direct substantial injury from application of a statute, he cannot challenge its constitutionality unless he can show that he is within the class whose constitutional rights are allegedly infringed." That was "salutary" as a general rule, but in this case "it would be difficult if not impossible for the persons whose rights are asserted to present their grievance before any court." Under these "peculiar circumstances," accordingly, "we believe the reasons which underlie our rule denying standing to raise another's rights, which is only a rule of practice, are outweighed by the need to protect the fundamental rights which would be denied by permitting the damages actions to be maintained." [9]

c.   Compare the problems of defendants' standing and the severability of statutes illustrated by UNITED STATES v. RAINES, 362 U.S. 17 (1960), in which the trial court was reversed for invalidating a law on the basis of constitutional defects "in applications not before it." The United States had brought suit against certain voting registrars under the Civil Rights Act of 1957, which allowed the United States to act against "any person" depriving citizens of the right to vote on account of race or color. Although the complaint charged only official action, the District Court dismissed because the statute on its face applied to private action, supposedly beyond the constitutional scope of the 15th Amendment. (See chap. 11.) Justice Brennan's majority opinion reversed on the basis of the general rule that "one to whom application of a statute is constitutional will not be heard to attack the statute on the ground that impliedly it might be taken as applying to other persons or other situations in which its application might be unconstitutional."

In explaining the rationale for the general rule, Justice Brennan commented: "The delicate power of pronouncing an Act of Congress unconstitutional is not to be exercised with reference to hypothetical cases." If an application of doubtful constitutionality were in fact concretely presented, "a limiting construction could be given to the statute by the court responsible

---

9. Justice Minton added: "The relation between the coercion exerted on respondent [the white seller who had sold property to a Black buyer in violation of the covenant] and a possible pecuniary loss thereby is so close to the purpose of the restrictive covenant, to violate the constitutional rights of those discriminated against, that respondent is the only effective adversary of the unworthy covenant in its last stand." In Raines, below, Justice Brennan distinguished Barrows and NAACP v. Alabama as cases "where, as a result of the very litigation in question, the constitutional rights of one not a party would be impaired, and where he has no effective way to preserve them himself."

for its construction." Moreover, the rule "frees the Court not only from unnecessary pronouncement on constitutional issues, but also from premature interpretations of statutes in areas where their constitutional application might be cloudy."

Justice Brennan found none of the exceptions to the "general rule" applicable. Prominent among the "exceptions" noted by him were two instances of nonseverable statutes: "[W]hen a state statute comes conclusively pronounced by a state court as having an otherwise valid provision or application inextricably tied up with an invalid one"; and "that rarest of cases where this Court can justifiably think itself able confidently to discern that Congress would not have desired its legislation to stand at all unless it could validly stand in its every application."

d. Among the "exceptions" considered by Justice Brennan in Raines were those akin to the First Amendment "overbreadth" doctrine. He stated: "This Court has indicated that where the application of these rules would itself have an inhibitory effect on freedom of speech, they may not be applied." Note also a passage in Dombrowski v. Pfister, 380 U.S. 479 (1965) (sec. 4 below): "We have consistently allowed attacks on overly broad statutes with no requirement that the person making the attack demonstrate that his own conduct could not be regulated by a statute drawn with the requisite narrow specificity. [This exception to the usual standing rules exists because of the] 'danger of tolerating, in the area of First Amendment freedoms, the existence of a penal statute susceptible of sweeping and improper application.'" Note that in the overbreadth situation, the claimant permitted to raise the rights of third parties stands in no special relationship to those parties, unlike most of the cases noted earlier—e. g., the physician in Griswold raising the rights of his patients. As the First Amendment "exceptions" to the rule illustrate, problems of standing to raise the rights of third parties, even more so than plaintiffs' access problems, are often closely linked to judgments as to the merits and the underlying substantive constitutional rights involved. (Recall the fuller consideration of the "overbreadth" doctrine in chap. 12, sec. 2, above.)

3. *Mootness.* The mootness barrier to constitutional adjudication is related to the previously considered problems of standing and advisory opinions. The cases presenting mootness problems involve litigants who clearly had standing to sue at the outset of the litigation. The problems arise from events occurring after the lawsuit has gotten under way—changes in the facts or in the law—which allegedly deprive the litigant of the necessary stake in the outcome. The mootness doctrine requires that "an actual controversy must be extant at all stages of review, not merely at the time the complaint is filed." In recent years, the Court has repeatedly insisted that the mootness doctrine is an aspect of the Art. III case or controversy requirement. See, e. g., Liner v. Jafco, Inc., 375 U.S. 301 (1964).

Yet, despite the supposed constitutional basis of the doctrine, the modern Court has frequently relaxed the mootness barrier, has found a number of exceptions to it, and has, in many observers' views, applied them erratically. To what extent do the exceptions rest on principled grounds? To what extent are they ad hoc invocations of prudential judgments? Note the attempt to summarize "the different kinds of harm which may prevent a case

from being held moot: a continuing harm to the plaintiff; [1] the likelihood of future recurrence of past harm, either to the plaintiff personally or to the group he represents; and the probability that similar cases arising in the future will evade judicial review." [2]   To what extent does and should the mootness doctrine serve as a discretionary avoidance device? [3]

For modern examples of erratic relaxations of mootness barriers, contrast the abortion decision, ROE v. WADE, 410 U.S. 113 (1973) (chap. 9), with the preferential admission program decision, DeFUNIS v. ODEGAARD, 416 U.S. 312 (1974) (chap. 10, sec. 2).   In the abortion case, Miss Roe's suit, brought in 1970, was not decided by the Supreme Court until January, 1973.   She obviously was no longer pregnant by then, yet the Supreme Court refused to dismiss the case as moot.   Justice Blackmun explained: "[W]hen, as here, pregnancy is a significant fact in the litigation, the normal 266-day human gestation period is so short that the pregnancy will come to term before the usual appellate process is complete.   If that termination makes a case moot, pregnancy litigation seldom will survive much beyond the trial stage, and appellate review will be effectively denied.   Our laws should not be that rigid.   Pregnancy often comes more than once to the same woman, and in the general population, if man is to survive, it will always be with us.   Pregnancy provides a classic justification for a conclusion of nonmootness.   It truly could be 'capable of repetition, yet evading review.' " [4]

However, a narrowly divided Court found a mootness barrier in the DeFunis case.   DeFunis had challenged a law school minority admissions program as racially discriminatory, but had attended the school while the case was in the courts.   The majority's per curiam decision took note of "DeFunis' recent registration for the last quarter of his final law school

1. For a common example of "continuing harm to the plaintiff" as barring a finding of mootness, note the growing reluctance to find appeals moot even though a convicted defendant has completed serving his sentence. The Court has reviewed such cases in recent years by finding a broad variety of "collateral consequences" to the conviction. See, e. g., Sibron v. New York, 392 U.S. 40 (1968), and North Carolina v. Rice, 404 U.S. 244 (1971). The Court has relied on "collateral consequences" which involved such disabilities as barriers to voting and to holding public office. Should adverse psychological or economic consequences be sufficient to bar a finding of mootness in such cases?

2. Note, "The Mootness Doctrine in the Supreme Court," 88 Harv.L.Rev. 373, 378 (1974). That Note observes that an appropriate mootness inquiry "should proceed sequentially, beginning with the interests of the plaintiff personally and proceeding to broader group interests."

3. See the Note cited in the preceding footnote, commenting: "The Court may be tempted in borderline cases to opt for holding the case moot when the substantive issues are particularly troublesome and avoidance is therefore especially welcome. [Cf. Justice Brennan's dissent in the DeFunis case, noted in the text.] So broad a consideration of the merits seems to be unwarranted, because it could deprive jurisdictional decisions of any principled content, see Gunther, ["The Subtle Vices of the 'Passive Virtues'— A Comment on Principle and Expediency in Judicial Review," 64 Colum. L.Rev. 1 (1964).]."

4. The "capable of repetition, yet evading review" exception stems from Southern Pacific Terminal Co. v. ICC, 219 U.S. 498 (1911). But in Southern Pacific, it was the same plaintiff who might be harmed by future action of the defendant. As Roe illustrates, the rule "has come to have independent significance apart from the possible repetition of injury to the particular plaintiff." Note, 88 Harv.L.Rev. 373, 386 (1974).

year, and the Law School's assurance that his registration is fully effective."
DeFunis had not brought a class action and the Court did not find in his
case the "exceptional situation" of an issue "capable of repetition, yet
evading review": "If the admissions procedures of the Law School remain unchanged, there is no reason to suppose that a subsequent case attacking those procedures will not come with relative speed to this Court."
Justice Brennan, joined by Justices Douglas, White and Marshall, insisted
the case was not moot: "Any number of unexpected events—illness, economic necessity, even academic failure—might prevent his graduation at
the end of the term." (The majority dismissed this argument as resting on
"speculative contingencies.") Moreover, the dissenters thought the dismissal disserved the public interest, since the issues "must inevitably return
to the federal courts and ultimately again to this Court."

The majority in DeFunis emphasized that the case had not been brought
as a class action. How significant should that factor be? To be sure, mootness challenges have been rejected in a number of cases even though the
plaintiff's controversy was no longer live, because the litigant had sued on behalf of a class. See, e. g., Dunn v. Blumstein, 405 U.S. 330 (1972), and
Richardson v. Ramirez, 418 U.S. 24 (1974) (both in chap. 10, sec. 4, above).
Yet the Court has sometimes accepted jurisdiction even though the interest
of the plaintiff had expired and even though the suit had *not* been brought
as a class action. Are the results in DeFunis and such voting rights cases
as Ramirez nevertheless justifiable? Note the suggestion that in DeFunis,
"neither the issues of law nor the groups of interested persons were as well
defined as in Ramirez."[5] Apart from considering whether a decision on the
merits will "obviate the necessity for future repetitious litigation," should the
decision on mootness also turn on "whether the area of substantive law which
[the Court] is asked to examine is one in which the legislature or the executive
is currently [altering] its policy"? Should the Court be more ready to find
mootness in situations where an adjudication "might unnecessarily restrict
policymaking by the other branches"?[6]

Are the usual considerations arguing against advisory opinions relevant
to the typical mootness problem? Note that a potentially moot case will
usually have a concrete record. Does a decision in such a case nevertheless
risk excessive judicial intervention in constitutional disputes? Is the lawsuit
less likely to be marked by adversariness if the litigant will not be affected
by the outcome? Does the growing practice of group litigation help
to explain the erratic modern refusals to sustain mootness claims?[7]

5. Note, 88 Harv.L.Rev. 373, 394 (1974).

6. Note, 88 Harv.L.Rev. 373, 395 (1974).

7. See the comment in Note, 88 Harv.L.
Rev. 373, 396: "Recognition for jurisdictional purposes of harm to a group
when there is no litigant with a stake
in the outcome plainly represents a departure from traditional notions of a
'case or controversy.' The Court has
been willing to continue the exercise of
jurisdiction in such cases only when
there are important justifications for
refusing to find the case moot."

For an illustration of the rarely invoked
ban on collusive suits, see United
States v. Johnson, 319 U.S. 302 (1943),
dismissing an action testing rent control because the nominal plaintiff, a
tenant, had been procured by and at
the expense of the defendant landlord.

SECTION 3. RIPENESS, CONTINGENCIES, AND ANTICIPATORY RELIEF

———

Introduction. When is a dispute sufficiently real, well developed, specific to elicit adjudication? Concerns about concrete records and premature interventions have surfaced repeatedly in the preceding materials. Those concerns are central to the problem of "ripeness," the focus of this section. How ripe must a controversy be to present appropriate circumstances for the exercise of judicial power? At one extreme lies the much-reiterated premise that federal courts will not render "advisory opinions" on legal questions even though private citizens or public officials have intense curiosity about the answer. At the other end of the scale is the common situation of the defendant resisting enforcement of a criminal law against him: in that situation, typically, the relevant facts occurred in the past and are on the record; in that context, courts regularly adjudicate constitutional challenges. Most problems of ripeness arise from situations in between— between disputes not yet fully born or already dead and disputes as fully developed as they can be. How fully must a controversy have jelled to elicit a ruling? How eyeball-to-eyeball must the disputants' confrontation be? That problem arises most characteristically with requests for anticipatory relief—where a plaintiff, for example, is seeking a ruling on the legality of an action that he fears may be taken against him, rather than waiting to raise the issues as a defendant in an enforcement proceeding.

It is in these actions for anticipatory relief that the problems of contingencies and uncertainties as to the facts are most prominent. In actions for declaratory or injunctive relief, courts may be most reluctant to intervene and may be most anxious to have the most clearly defined record to assure informed and narrow adjudication. The relationship between the parties is typically still in flux and developing. And the contingencies may affect both sides of the lawsuit. The plaintiff may not yet be able to say specifically what action he expects to take. Similarly, it may not yet be possible to say what specific actions the defendant will take against the plaintiff. The record in such a case will typically consist in part of predictions about the probable conduct of both parties; the parties' behavior turns on contingencies and requires guesses about the future. And those uncertainties give rise to the ripeness problem.

As the preceding materials have already indicated, the Court frequently speaks of the need for a concrete controversy, for a sufficiently nonhypothetical, nonabstract, "ripe" dispute between truly "adverse" parties. What do those requirements mean? And what justifies the requirements? Are they all derived from the Art. III "case or controversy" requirement? Or are some of these limitations nonconstitutional in origin? Based on the federal courts' authority to help shape the law of remedies? Based on judicially developed policies responding to institutional self-defense perceptions—on prudential decisions to conserve the energies (and the political capital) of federal courts for a limited number of truly important constitutional causes? Consider these problems in light of the materials and additional questions raised in this section.

CONCRETENESS AND THE PLAINTIFF'S PLANNED CONDUCT: THE MITCHELL AND ADLER CASES

The Mitchell and Adler cases examined here both involved constitutional challenges to restrictions on the conduct of public employees. (Recall the substantive problems raised by such restrictions, considered in chap. 13 above.) In Mitchell, the Court found most claims nonjusticiable; in Adler, by contrast, the Court reached the merits. Mitchell and Adler afford an initial opportunity to explore the nature and ingredients of ripeness: To what extent is ripeness derived from Art. III? What factors go into the determination of ripeness?

1. *The Mitchell case.* UNITED PUBLIC WORKERS v. MITCHELL, 330 U.S. 75 (1947), was an attack on the political activities ban in the Hatch Act of 1940. Section 9(a) prohibits federal employees in the executive branch from taking "any active part in political management or in political campaigns." Several employees and their union brought suit to restrain the Civil Service Commission from enforcing § 9(a) against them, and for a declaratory judgment that the section is unconstitutional. The three-judge District Court dismissed the suit on the merits. The Supreme Court affirmed the judgment, but on other grounds as to most of the plaintiffs. Justice Reed's opinion for the Court contained the following passages:

"It is alleged that the individuals desire to engage in acts of political management and in political campaigns. Their purposes are as stated in the excerpt from the complaint set out in the margin.[1] . . . None of the appellants, except George P. Poole, has violated the provisions of the Hatch Act. They wish to act contrary to its provisions [and] desire a declaration of the legally permissible limits of regulation. Defendants moved to dismiss the complaint for lack of a justiciable case or controversy. . . .

". . . At the threshold of consideration, we are called upon to decide whether the complaint states a controversy cognizable in this Court. We defer consideration of the cause of action of Mr. Poole . . .. The other individual employees have elaborated the grounds of their objection in individual affidavits for use in the hearing on the summary judgment. We select as an example one that contains the essential averments of all the others and print below the portions with significance in this suit.[2] Noth-

---

1. ". . . [T]he individual plaintiffs desire to engage in the following acts: write for publication letters and articles in support of candidates for office; be connected editorially with publications which are identified with the legislative program of UFWA [former name of the present union appellant] and candidates who support it; solicit votes, aid in getting out voters, act as accredited checker, watcher, or challenger; transport voters to and from the polls without compensation therefor; participate in and help in organizing political parades; initiate petitions, and canvass for the signa-

tures of others on such petitions; serve as party ward committeeman or other party official; and perform any and all acts not prohibited by any provision of law other than [the Hatch Act]. . . ." [Footnote by the Court.]

2. ". . . I wish to engage in such activities on behalf of those candidates for public office who I believe will best serve the needs of this country and with the object of persuading others of the correctness of my judgments and of electing the candidates of my choice. This objective I wish to pur-

ing similar to the [third] paragraph of the printed affidavit is contained in the other affidavits. The assumed controversy between affiant and the Civil Service Commission as to affiant's right to act as watcher at the polls on November 2, 1943, had long been moot when this complaint was filed. We do not therefore treat this allegation separately. The affidavits, it will be noticed, follow the generality of purpose expressed by the complaint. . . . They declare a desire to act contrary to the rule against political activity but not that the rule has been violated. In this respect, we think they differ from the type of threat adjudicated in Railway Mail Association v. Corsi, 326 U.S. 88. In that case, the refusal to admit an applicant to membership in a labor union on account of race was involved. Admission had been refused. . . . The threats which menaced the affiants of these affidavits in the case now being considered are closer to a general threat by officials to enforce those laws which they are charged to administer, than they are to the direct threat of punishment against a named organization for a completed act that made the [Corsi] case justiciable.

"As is well known, the federal courts established pursuant to Article III of the Constitution do not render advisory opinions. For adjudication of constitutional issues, 'concrete legal issues, presented in actual cases, not abstractions,' are requisite. This is as true of declaratory judgments as any other field. These appellants seem clearly to seek advisory opinions upon broad claims of rights protected by the First, Fifth, Ninth and Tenth Amendments to the Constitution. As these appellants are classified employees, they have a right superior to the generality of citizens, [but] the facts of their personal interest in their civil rights, of the general threat of possible interference with those rights by the Civil Service Commission under its

sue by all proper means such as engaging in discussion, by speeches to conventions, rallies and other assemblages, by publicizing my views in letters and articles for publication in newspapers and other periodicals, by aiding in the campaign of candidates for political office by posting banners and posters in public places, by distributing leaflets, by 'ringing doorbells', by addressing campaign literature, and by doing any and all acts of like character reasonably designed to assist in the election of candidates I favor.

"I desire to engage in these activities freely, openly, and without concealment. However, I understand that the second sentence of Section 9(a) of the Hatch Act and the Rules of the C.S.C. provide that if I engage in this activity, the Civil Service Commission will order that I be dismissed from federal employment. Such deprivation of my job in the federal government would be a source of immediate and serious financial loss and other injury to me.

"At the last Congressional election I was very much interested in the outcome of the campaign and offered to help the party of my choice by being a watcher at the polls. I obtained a watcher's certificate but I was advised that there might be some question of my right to use the certificate and retain my federal employment. Therefore, on November 1, 1943, the day before election, I called the regional office of the Civil Service Commission in Philadelphia and spoke to a person who gave his name as . . . . Mr. . . . stated that if I used my watcher's certificate, the Civil Service Commission would see that I was dismissed from my job at the . . . for violation of the Hatch Act. I, therefore, did not use the certificate as I had intended.

"I believe that Congress may not constitutionally abridge my right to engage in the political activities mentioned above. However, unless the courts prevent the Civil Service Commission from enforcing this unconstitutional law, I will be unable freely to exercise my rights as a citizen. (Identifying words omitted.)" [Footnote by the Court.]

rules, if specified things are done by appellants, does not make a justiciable case or controversy. Appellants want to engage in 'political management and political campaigns,' to persuade others to follow appellants' views by discussion, speeches, articles and other acts reasonably designed to secure the selection of appellants' political choices. Such generality of objection is really an attack on the political expediency of the Hatch Act, not the presentation of legal issues. It is beyond the competence of courts to render such a decision. . . .

"The power of courts, and ultimately of this Court, to pass upon the constitutionality of acts of Congress arises only when the interests of litigants require the use of this judicial authority for their protection against actual interference. A hypothetical threat is not enough. We can only speculate as to the kinds of political activity the appellants desire to engage in or as to the contents of their proposed public statements or the circumstances of their publication. It would not accord with judicial responsibility to adjudge, in a matter involving constitutionality, between the freedom of the individual and the requirements of public order except when definite rights appear upon the one side and definite prejudicial interferences upon the other.

"The Constitution allots the nation's judicial power to the federal courts. Unless these courts respect the limits of that unique authority, they intrude upon powers vested in the legislative or executive branches. . . . Should the courts seek to expand their power so as to bring under their jurisdiction ill-defined controversies over constitutional issues, they would become the organ of political theories. Such abuse of judicial power would properly meet rebuke and restriction from other branches. . . . No threat of interference by the Commission with rights of these appellants appears beyond that implied by the existence of the law and the regulations. . . . These reasons lead us to conclude that the determination of the trial court, that the individual appellants, other than Poole, could maintain this action, was erroneous.

". . . The appellant Poole does present by the complaint and affidavit matters appropriate for judicial determination. The affidavits filed by appellees confirm that Poole has been charged by the Commission with political activity and a proposed order for his removal from his position adopted subject to his right under Commission procedure to reply to the charges and to present further evidence in refutation. We proceed to consider the controversy over constitutional power at issue between Poole and the Commission as defined by the charge and preliminary finding upon one side and the admissions of Poole's affidavit upon the other. Our determination is limited to those facts. This proceeding so limited meets the requirements of defined rights and a definite threat to interfere with a possessor of the menaced rights by a penalty for an act done in violation of the claimed restraint." [Poole's constitutional challenge was rejected on the merits.]

Justice Rutledge dissented as to Poole and stated that he did not pass "upon the constitutional questions presented by the other appellants for the reason that he feels the controversy as to them is not yet appropriate for the discretionary exercise of declaratory judgment jurisdiction." Justice

Frankfurter concurred in a separate opinion, and Justice Black dissented. Justice Douglas dissented in part. As to justiciability, he said:

"It is clear that the declaratory judgment procedure is available in the federal courts only in cases involving actual controversies and may not be used to obtain an advisory opinion in a controversy not yet arisen. The requirement of an 'actual controversy,' which is written into the statute [and] has its roots in the Constitution, [seems] to me to be fully met here. What these appellants propose to do is plain enough. If they do what they propose to do, it is clear that they will be discharged from their positions. . . . Their proposed conduct is sufficiently specific to show plainly that it will violate the Act. The policy of the Commission and the mandate of the Act leave no lingering doubt as to the consequences.

". . . [T]o require these employees first to suffer the hardship of a discharge is not only to make them incur a penalty; it makes inadequate, if not wholly illusory, any legal remedy which they may have. Men who must sacrifice their means of livelihood in order to test their rights to their jobs must either pursue prolonged and expensive litigation as unemployed persons or pull up their roots, change their life careers, and seek employment in other fields. . . . Declaratory relief is the singular remedy available here to preserve the *status quo* while the constitutional rights of these appellants to make these utterances and to engage in these activities are determined. The threat against them is real not fanciful, immediate not remote. The case is therefore an actual not a hypothetical one."

2. *The Adler case.* ADLER v. BOARD of EDUCATION, 342 U.S. 485 (1952), attacked New York's Feinberg Law of 1949, designed to eliminate "subversive persons from the public school system." The Act included provisions for the compilation of a list of subversive organizations by the school authorities; membership in any such organization constituted "prima facie evidence of disqualification" for any school position. The plaintiffs were taxpayers, parents of school children, and teachers. The appellate courts of the state rejected their constitutional challenges on the merits. On appeal, the Supreme Court affirmed, without discussing justiciability.

Justice Frankfurter's dissent, however, made it clear that the justiciability issue in Adler was a substantial one that called for discussion, especially in light of Mitchell. Justice Frankfurter argued that the case was not justiciable and that the Court should not decide the merits. With respect to the taxpayer and parent plaintiffs, he found lack of standing to sue. His discussion of the ripeness-Mitchell problem came in the course of his insistence that the teacher plaintiffs, too, had failed to present a claim that could be adjudicated at this time:

"The allegations in the present action fall short of those found insufficient in the Mitchell case. These teachers do not allege that they have engaged in proscribed conduct or that they have any intention to do so. They do not suggest that they have been, or are, deterred from supporting causes or from joining organizations for fear of the Feinberg Law's interdict, except to say generally that the system complained of will have this effect on teachers as a group. They do not assert that they are threatened with action under the law, or that steps are imminent whereby they would incur the hazard

of punishment for conduct innocent at the time, or under standards too vague to satisfy due process of law. They merely allege that the statutes and Rules permit such action against some teachers. Since we rightly refused in the Mitchell case to hear government employees whose conduct was much more intimately affected by the law there attacked than are the claims of plaintiffs here, this suit is wanting in the necessary basis for our review."

Earlier in his dissent, Justice Frankfurter had noted that the case "comes here on the bare bones of the Feinberg Law only partly given flesh by the Regents' Rules." He stated further: "We are asked to pass on a scheme to counteract what are currently called 'subversive' influences in the public school system of New York. The scheme [is] still an unfinished blueprint. We are asked to adjudicate claims against its constitutionality before the scheme has been put into operation, before the limits that it imposes upon free inquiry and association, the scope of scrutiny that it sanctions, and the procedural safeguards that will be found to be implied for its enforcement have been authoritatively defined. I think we should adhere to the teaching of this Court's history to avoid constitutional adjudications on merely abstract or speculative issues and to base them on the concreteness afforded by an actual, present, defined controversy, appropriate for judicial judgment, between adversaries immediately affected by it. In accordance with the settled limits upon our jurisdiction I would dismiss this appeal." [3]

3. *Some questions about Mitchell and Adler.* a. *The Art. III and the Supreme Court review dimensions: Basis for reconciliation?* Mitchell and Adler raise questions on two levels—one involving the Art. III contours themselves, the other pertaining to the additional problems of Supreme Court review of state adjudications. As to Art. III: Does every dispute found not "ripe" fall short of being an Art. III "case"? Or may some disputes be concrete enough to fall within Art. III yet not ripe enough to warrant grant of a discretionary federal remedy? As to Supreme Court review: If a state court adjudicates a dispute concrete enough to be an Art. III case, must not the Supreme Court decide the merits on appeal—even though federal declaratory or injunctive relief would have been denied on the basis of the discretionary, remedial aspect of the ripeness doctrine if that case had started in a federal District Court? Are Mitchell and Adler reconcilable?

There is good reason to criticize the majority's failure even to mention the justiciability issue in Adler. But the result—the decision to adjudicate—may have been justifiable: there were reasons to reach the merits in Adler that were lacking in Mitchell. To be sure, Mitchell and Adler do not seem reconcilable if only the Art. III and ripeness dimensions are considered: Mitchell seems hardly less ripe than Adler. But if the Supreme Court review dimension is also taken into account, Mitchell and Adler may be able to stand together: review of Adler may have been justified (despite the dismissal in Mitchell) because Adler, unlike Mitchell, originated in the state courts—and was not so unripe as to fall short of being an Article III case. If Mitchell is viewed as a discretionary denial of a federal declaratory judgments remedy, as Justice Rutledge's separate opinion suggested, can it be au-

---

3. Recall that a renewed constitutional attack on the Feinberg Law, 15 years after Adler, proved more successful. Keyishian v. Board of Regents, 385 U. S. 589 (1967) (chap. 13, sec. 5, above).

thority for dismissing a state court appeal such as Adler—even if the dispute in Adler was at least as unripe as that in Mitchell, as Justice Frankfurter claimed? In reviewing a state court decision falling within the obligatory appeal jurisdiction, must not the Supreme Court decide the merits unless Article III is not satisfied? Is it accurate to say that the Court has no discretion to abstain from decision in such a case—unlike the discretion it may exercise over a federal court remedy like that sought in Mitchell? [4]

b. *Minimal concreteness: Art. III requirement or federal remedial discretion?* To what extent is ripeness an aspect of the "case or controversy" requirement of Art. III? To what extent is it a question of the law of remedies? What difference does it make? May a dispute fall so far short of ripeness that it does not present a minimal Art. III "case"? Was that the flaw in Willing v. Chicago Auditorium Ass'n, 277 U.S. 274 (1928) (sec. 1 above)? Recall that Justice Brandeis noted the contingencies there in both the lessee's and lessor's plans, expressed fears about "advisory opinions" and commented: "The fact that plaintiff's desires are thwarted by its own doubts, or by the fears of others, does not confer a cause of action. No defendant has wronged the plaintiff or has threatened to do so." Was that a case of so many contingencies on both sides of the dispute that Art. III barred judicial resolution? By contrast, may a dispute be sufficiently concrete to meet the minimum requirements of Art. III but nevertheless be sufficiently contingent to warrant dismissal on ripeness grounds in the exercise of judicial discretion as to the federal declaratory judgments remedy? Was Mitchell such a case?

c. *The premature, the concrete, and the underlying substantive issue.* In Adler, the state court thought some questions sufficiently "ripe" for adjudication. Was there not adequate ripeness to satisfy Art. III policies at least as to some issues in Adler? Obviously, the teachers in Adler could not complain of specific actions taken against them—that challenge would indeed have been premature. But could they not properly argue that there could be *no* constitutional applications of the Feinberg Law? And if the state courts chose to decide that claim, was not the Supreme Court compelled to review? Does not the importance of concrete, fully developed facts turn to some extent on the background of substantive law and on the plaintiff's legal theory? All that the decision in Adler held was that the Feinberg Law was not in all possible situations unconstitutional, that it was constitutional in some conceivable applications. Litigants may be unwise to present so broad an issue to the courts; but if they are willing to do so, is there any justification for refusal to adjudicate? [5]

4. Is it accurate to say, in other words, that discretionary considerations appropriate in federal court litigation have no place in Supreme Court review of state cases within the appeal jurisdiction? Or does the law of remedies become "federalized" in all cases of Supreme Court review? Because of the overriding institutional need of the Supreme Court to avoid premature and excessive interventions, and interventions based on inadequately developed records? These problems recur in

other contexts in this chapter. Recall the comments on the Doremus case on state taxpayers' standing, sec. 2 above, and note the materials on discretionary abstention in exercising Supreme Court review jurisdiction, sec. 4 below.

5. Note also Times Film Corp. v. Chicago, 365 U.S. 43 (1961), an attack on a city censorship ordinance in which the challenger refused to submit a film to the censoring agency and sued to enjoin enforcement of the ordinance on

d. *The contingent and the concrete in Mitchell and Letter Carriers.*
Were the issues in Mitchell so abstract and premature as to bar all exercise
of Art. III power? Are the "unfit for adjudication" assertions of the
majority more persuasive if they are read as going not to Art. III power
but merely to the issue of discretionary exercise of declaratory judgment
authority? A generation after Mitchell, the Court reaffirmed the constitutionality of the Hatch Act without mentioning the issue of ripeness. U.S.
Civil Service Comm'n v. Letter Carriers, 413 U.S. 548 (1973) (chap. 12
above). Contrast the plaintiffs' factual allegations in the 1973 case with
those found wanting in Mitchell. In 1973, one plaintiff, for example,
simply alleged "that she desired to become a precinct Democratic Committee Woman"; another, that "he desired to, but did not, file as a candidate
for the office of Borough Councilman" ; another, that "he desired to run
as a Republican candidate" in a mayoral election and that he feared losing
his job if he ran. Were those allegations more concrete than those found
inadequate in Mitchell? Did the specificity of the allegations in the two
cases differ so greatly as to justify failure to discuss the justiciability issue
in the 1973 case? [6] Note that the attack in Letter Carriers rested largely on
overbreadth and vagueness grounds—arguments which had not yet become
a well-developed part of constitutional doctrine at the time of the Mitchell
case. Note, moreover, that the particular facts of the case generally play
a less significant role when overbreadth and vagueness attacks are made.
(Recall chap. 12 above.) Since the Court's primary concern in overbreadth
analysis is the risks of application of a statute to those not before the
Court—to persons other than the plaintiff—concreteness and ripeness concerns, like standing barriers, tend to be less important.

4. *Some further questions on ripeness: Hardship to the parties and
shape of the issues.* a. *Hardship to the parties.* In a number of cases
involving review of administrative regulations, the Court's determinations
of ripeness issues have explicitly turned on considerations of "hardship

the ground that *no* prior restraint
mechanism could be constitutional.
The Court rejected that claim, emphasizing that it was simply rejecting
the argument that the First Amendment "includes complete and absolute
freedom to exhibit, at least once, any
and every kind of motion picture."
(See chap. 13, sec. 3, above.)

For a Justice viewing *all* prior restraints
as unconstitutional (e. g., Justices
Black and Douglas, see chap. 13 above),
the Times Film issue was easy, and no
more concrete record was necessary.
For Justices finding "balancing" more
congenial than "absolutes," a fuller record—in obscenity cases, typically a
view of the film itself—was desirable.
But even "balancing" Justices should
be able to reject the "absolute" urged
by the claimant in Times Film. Does
Justice Frankfurter's lonely objection
to the justiciability of Adler mainly
reflect the fact that he, especially, was
inclined to "balance": that his pre-

ferred mode of constitutional adjudication turned heavily on the particular
circumstances of the case?

Professor Bickel argued that the sparse-
ness of the record in Times Film
should have induced the Court to refuse review of the case. Is that defensible, if the litigant wanted to take
the risk of submitting his broad contention—and *only* his broad contention
—to the Court? Compare Bickel, The
Least Dangerous Branch (1962), with
Gunther, "The Subtle Vices of the 'Passive Virtues' . . .," 64 Colum.L.Rev.
1 (1964).

6. Note Justice White's description of
the justiciability aspects of Mitchell, in
his majority opinion in the Letter Carriers case: "The Court [in Mitchell]
first determined that with respect to
all but one of the plaintiffs there was
no case or controversy present within
the meaning of Art. III."

to the parties" and "fitness of the issues." [7] Does "hardship to the parties" play a significant, if less articulated, role in the constitutional adjudication cases as well? May the hardship of delaying relief to the litigant be so minimal as to make preenforcement adjudication inappropriate? Were the parties so unaffected by delay in Mitchell or Adler as to make immediate adjudication constitutionally improper?

Compare the Court's dismissal of the claim of one set of litigants in the abortion case, Roe v. Wade, 410 U.S. 113 (1973) (chap. 9). Though the Court adjudicated the complaint of Jane Roe (despite mootness questions, as noted in sec. 2), it dismissed the complaint of John and Mary Doe, a married childless couple claiming that pregnancy would risk Mrs. Doe's health and that they wanted assurance that there could be an abortion if she became pregnant. Justice Blackmun's opinion commented that the Does claimed "as their asserted immediate and present injury, only an alleged 'detrimental effect upon [their] marital happiness' because they are forced to [make] 'the choice of refraining from normal sexual relations or of endangering Mary Doe's health through a possible pregnancy.' Their claim is that sometime in the future Mrs. Doe might become pregnant . . . and at that time in the future she might want an abortion." Justice Blackmun stated: "This very phrasing of the Does' position reveals its speculative character. Their alleged injury rests on possible future contraceptive failure, possible future pregnancy, possible future unpreparedness for parenthood, and possible future impairment of health. Any one or more of these several possibilities may not take place and all may not combine. In the Does' estimation, these possibilities might have some real or imagined impact upon their marital happiness. But we are not prepared to say that the bare allegation of so indirect an injury is sufficient to present an actual case or controversy." Since the Does did claim a present "impact upon their marital happiness," why was that impact not sufficient to warrant Court adjudication? Was the dismissal of the Does' suit based on discretionary considerations, partly influenced by the fact that Miss Roe's claim *was* being adjudicated? Or is it really tenable to suggest that the Does' concern was so speculative as to take the controversy outside of Art. III limits?

Generally, to what extent should "hardship to the parties" affect ripeness? If ripeness is less of a barrier when delay in adjudication constitutes a hardship to the plaintiff, what of hardship to the defendant (and to the public interest) from early adjudication? Should assessment of hardship vary with the nature of the legal claim? In the course of his dissent in the modern administrative review cases (footnote 7 above), Justice Fortas commented: "Where personal status or liberties are involved, the courts may well insist upon a considerable ease of challenging administrative orders." Should the First Amendment claim in Mitchell have lowered the ripeness barrier there? •

7. See, e. g., three companion cases in 1967, Abbott Laboratories v. Gardner, 387 U.S. 136; Toilet Goods Ass'n v. Gardner, 387 U.S. 158; Gardner v. Toilet Goods Ass'n, 387 U.S. 167.

The issues raised by judicial review of agency actions are more fully discussed in administrative law courses.

b. *Shape of the issues.* In applying the "fitness of the issue" criterion in the administrative review cases (footnote 7 above), the Justices asked whether factual enforcement experience was necessary to decide the legal question. Does that need for facts itself depend upon what legal question is asked? On how the judge views the substantive law? Some legal standards are less dependent on factual variations than others. And some judges are more inclined than others to formulate legal standards as questions of degree. Recall the comment on Justice Frankfurter's dissent in Adler, above.

Does the focus on the shape of the issues and on the hardship to the parties unduly deemphasize the Court's institutional values, especially in constitutional litigation? Should ripeness be primarily concerned with protecting the Court from premature opinions—opinions with some of the effects of advisory ones, in quality and in vulnerability? Or should assessment of the parties' (and society's) need for an adjudication be the major ingredient of the ripeness determination?

CONCRETENESS, CONTINGENCIES, AND THE DEFENDANT'S BEHAVIOR

Concern about adequate development of the dispute, about adequate concreteness, goes to both sides of a lawsuit. Not only must the plaintiff seeking anticipatory relief ordinarily spell out his proposed conduct in some detail, but he must also demonstrate that some harm will befall him if he goes through with his plans. Is it enough that there is a statute on the books which may subject the plaintiff to criminal prosecution?[1] Or must the plaintiff challenging a law show that a governmental official has in fact threatened to take action against the plaintiff if the proposed course of conduct is undertaken? Consider the criteria announced in the modern cases below in which the Court requires that the existence of a genuine controversy be shown and that concrete injury be threatened. Are the criteria justifiable? Workable? What policies are they designed to serve? How effectively do they serve those policies?

1. *O'Shea v. Littleton.* In O'SHEA v. LITTLETON, 414 U.S. 488 (1974), Justice White's majority opinion found a federal court class action complaint inadequate "to satisfy the threshold requirement imposed by

---

1. Recall the emphasis on the "chilling effect" of governmental action threatening First Amendment rights, in chaps. 12 and 13 above. Compare Laird v. Tatum, below. And note another aspect of the abortion litigation: In Doe v. Bolton, 410 U.S. 179 (1973) (chap. 9), the companion case to Roe v. Wade, the Georgia doctors' complaint was found sufficient when they alleged that the laws "chilled and deterred" them from practicing their profession, even though the record did not disclose "that any one of them has been prosecuted, or threatened with prosecution, for violation of [Georgia's] abortion statutes." The Court explained: "The physician is the one against whom these criminal statutes directly operate in the event he procures an abortion that does not meet the statutory exceptions and conditions." Accordingly, the challengers were found to "assert a sufficiently direct threat of personal detriment. They should not be required to await and undergo a criminal prosecution as the sole means of seeking relief." But why were they not required to await a specific official *threat* to prosecute? See the cases which follow.

Art. III of the Constitution." The complaint grew out of years-long racial tension in Cairo, Illinois. It charged that the original defendants—a magistrate and a judge—were engaged in a continuing pattern of discriminatory bond, sentencing, and jury fee practices in criminal cases. Justice White commented: "The nature of [plaintiffs'] activities is not described in detail and no specific threats are alleged to have been made against them. Accepting that they are deeply involved in a program to eliminate racial discrimination in Cairo and that tensions are high, we are nonetheless unable to conclude that the case or controversy requirement is satisfied by general assertions or inferences that in the course of their activities respondents will be prosecuted for violating valid criminal laws." He concluded that "the threat of injury from the alleged course of conduct they attack is simply too remote to satisfy the 'case or controversy' requirement." Justice Douglas' dissent, joined by Justices Brennan and Marshall, insisted that the complaint alleged "a more pervasive scheme for suppression of Blacks and their civil rights than I have ever seen. It may not survive a trial. But if this case does not present a 'case or controversy' involving the named plaintiffs, then that concept has been so watered down as to be no longer recognizable."

2. *Boyle v. Landry.* In one of the companion cases to Younger v. Harris (sec. 4 below), BOYLE v. LANDRY, 401 U.S. 77 (1971), Black residents of Chicago sued city officials to enjoin enforcement of a number of state statutes and city ordinances. They alleged that some of the plaintiffs had been arrested under some of the laws, and that the laws were being used to harass them and to deny them their First Amendment rights. The lower federal court rejected the challenges to most of the statutes, but invalidated one provision prohibiting the "intimidating" of a person by threatening to commit a criminal offense. Justice Black's opinion holding that that issue should not have been decided found it "obvious" that the allegations fell "far short of showing an irreparable injury" from threatened or actual prosecutions and stated: "Not a single one of the citizens who brought this action had ever been prosecuted, charged, or even arrested under the particular intimidation statute which the court below held unconstitutional. . . . In fact, the complaint contains no mention of any specific threat by any officer or official [to] arrest or prosecute any one or more of the plaintiffs under that statute. . . . Rather, it appears from the allegations that those who originally brought this suit made a search of state statutes and city ordinances with a view to picking out certain ones that they thought might possibly be used by the authorities as devices for bad-faith prosecutions against them."

3. *Poe v. Ullman.* POE v. ULLMAN, 367 U.S. 497 (1961) (noted further in sec. 4 below), was one of a series of efforts to obtain a Supreme Court adjudication on the constitutionality of Connecticut's ban on the use of contraceptives. Poe came some years after Tileston v. Ullman (sec. 2 above) failed, some years before Griswold v. Connecticut (chap. 9 above) succeeded. In the controversial decision refusing to adjudicate the issue in Poe v. Ullman, Justice Frankfurter wrote the plurality opinion dismissing an appeal in a suit brought by two married couples and a physician. The couples claimed that they had sought contraceptive advice from the physician, who had not given it for fear of prosecution. Justice Frankfurter's

opinion noted that the allegations did not "clearly" state that the prosecutor threatened to prosecute the challengers. Rather, they merely asserted "that, in the course of his public duty, he intends to prosecute any offenses against Connecticut law, and that he claims that use of and advice concerning contraceptives would constitute offenses." Justice Frankfurter commented: "The lack of immediacy of the threat described by these allegations might alone raise serious questions of non-justiciability. [United Public Workers v. Mitchell.] But even were we to read the allegations to convey a clear threat of imminent prosecutions, we are not bound to accept as true all that is alleged on the face of the complaint and admitted, technically, by demurrer . . . . Formal agreement between parties that collides with plausibility is too fragile a foundation for indulging in constitutional adjudication."

In examining "plausibility," the Court noted that the Connecticut law had been on the books since 1879, that there had been only one reported prosecution, and that this and other circumstances showed the "unreality of these lawsuits." Contraceptives were commonly sold in Connecticut. "The undeviating policy of nullification by Connecticut of its anti-contraceptive laws . . . bespeaks more than prosecutorial paralysis: '[T]raditional ways of carrying out state policy are often tougher and truer law than the dead words of the written text.'" Justice Frankfurter added: "If the prosecutor expressly agrees not to prosecute, a suit against him [is] not such an adversary case as will be reviewed here. [Eighty years of state practice] demonstrate a similar, albeit tacit agreement [here]. To find it necessary to pass on these statutes now, in order to protect appellants from the hazards of prosecution, would be to close our eyes to reality." Moreover, the "deterrent effect complained of was [not] grounded in a realistic fear of prosecution."

Justice Douglas' dissent commented: "No lawyer, I think, would advise his clients to rely on that 'tacit agreement.' . . . What are these people—doctor and patients—to do? Flout the law and go to prison? Violate the law surreptitiously and hope they will not get caught? . . . It is not the choice they need have under the regime of declaratory judgment and our constitutional system." And in a strong and long dissent, Justice Harlan commented that it was "pure conjecture, and indeed conjecture which to me seems contrary to realities, that an open violation of the statute by a doctor [would] not result in a substantial threat of prosecution." He added: "Despite the suggestion of a 'tougher and truer law' of immunity from criminal prosecution and despite speculation as to a 'tacit agreement' that this law will not be enforced, there is, of course, no suggestion of an estoppel against the State if it should attempt to prosecute appellants. . . . What is meant is simply that the appellants are more or less free to act without fear of prosecution because the prosecuting authorities of the State, in their discretion and at their whim, are, as a matter of prediction, unlikely to decide to prosecute." (See the additional comments on this dissent in sec. 4 below.)

4. *Laird v. Tatum.* The 5 to 4 decision in LAIRD v. TATUM, 408 U.S. 1 (1972), found nonjusticiable respondents' First Amendment attack on the army's surveillance of "lawful and peaceful civilian activities." Army Intelligence in the late 1960's had established a "data-gathering system"

about "public activities" with a potential for "civil disorder." The Court of Appeals had held that the action was justiciable, since respondents contended that "the *present existence of this system* of gathering and distributing information, allegedly far beyond the mission requirements of the Army, constitutes an impermissible burden" on persons such as respondents and "exercises a *present inhibiting effect*" on their First Amendment rights: "under justiciability standards it is the operation of the system itself which is the breach of the Army's duty" and the case was "therefore ripe for adjudication." The basic claimed evil was overbreadth and "there is no indication that a better opportunity will later arise to test the constitutionality of the Army's action."

Chief Justice Burger's majority opinion reversed, quoting the United Public Workers v. Mitchell statement of hostility to advisory opinions and stating that "allegations of a subjective 'chill' are not an adequate substitute for a claim of specific present objective harm or a threat of specific future harm." He recognized that governmental action could be attacked "even though it has only an indirect effect" on First Amendment rights, but he insisted that an immediate risk of "direct injury" had to be shown. Here, by contrast, the essential claim was one of disagreement with executive use of Army data gathering or a "perception of the system as inappropriate to the Army's role" or a belief "that it is inherently dangerous for the military to be concerned with activities in the civilian sector" or a fear resting on the "less generalized yet speculative apprehensiveness that the Army may at some future date misuse the information in some way that would cause direct harm to respondents." Those concerns did not amount to "specific present objective harm" or "threat of specific future harm." [2]

Justice Brennan, joined by Justices Stewart and Marshall, dissented on the basis of the Court of Appeals decision on justiciability. Another dissent, by Justice Douglas, joined by Justice Marshall, insisted that the "present controversy is not a remote, imaginary conflict": the surveillance was "massive"; the intelligence reports were "widely circulated"; undercover techniques were used; and the Army had "misused or abused its reporting functions." And the lack of standing claim was "too transparent for serious argument": "One need not wait to sue until he loses his job or until his reputation is defamed." [3]

2. Chief Justice Burger added in a footnote that the challengers had not only "left somewhat unclear the precise connection between the mere existence of the challenged system and their own alleged chill, but they have also cast considerable doubt on whether they themselves are in fact suffering from any such chill." Before the District Court, respondents' counsel "admitted that his clients were 'not people, obviously, who are cowed and chilled' "; instead, they claimed to "represent millions of Americans not nearly as forward [and] courageous." The Chief Justice commented: "Even assuming a justiciable controversy, if respondents themselves are not chilled, but seek only to represent those 'millions' whom they believe are so chilled, respondents clearly lack that 'personal stake in the outcome of the controversy' essential to standing."

3. Soon after the decision in this case, the respondents moved that Justice Rehnquist disqualify himself, largely because he had testified as a Justice Department official at the Senate Subcommittee Hearings on army surveillance. (A 4 to 4 division of the Court would have produced an affirmance rather than a reversal of the Court of Appeals.) In denying that motion, Justice Rehnquist filed a lengthy opinion concluding that "neither the oath, the disqualification statute, nor the practice of the former Justices of this

SECTION 4. DISCRETION TO DECLINE THE EXERCISE OF JURISDICTION

A. SUPREME COURT REVIEW: DISCRETION AND THE OBLIGATORY APPEAL JURISDICTION

Introduction. The Supreme Court's appeal jurisdiction, unlike its certiorari jurisdiction, purports to be obligatory rather than discretionary. (Recall chap. 1, sec. 4, above.) May the Supreme Court nevertheless refuse to review a state court decision for reasons other than those grounded in the requirements of Art. III or the jurisdictional statute? Do the nonconstitutional ingredients of such doctrines as ripeness and standing considered in the preceding sections apply to the Court's exercise of its appeal jurisdiction, even though Congress directed the Court to hear those cases? Those questions were posed by some of the earlier materials; [1] they are the central concerns of this section. Considerations such as adequate concreteness and ripeness play a legitimate role in the exercise of the certiorari jurisdiction. But do nonconstitutional ingredients of justiciability properly enter into the exercise of the appeal jurisdiction?

Consider, first, the contending positions summarized in the opening materials below. Are the statements by Chief Justice Marshall and by Justice Brandeis wholly inconsistent? Or can Marshall's emphasis on the duty to decide be reconciled with Brandeis' stress on avoidance of constitutional adjudication?

Then consider the samples of dismissals of appeals which follow. In cases such as Rescue Army, Naim v. Naim, and Poe v. Ullman, the Court declined to reach the merits in cases apparently within its obligatory review jurisdiction. Did the Court give adequate justification for not deciding those cases? Do the institutional reasons which underlie some of the doctrines considered in the preceding sections justify those avoidances of decision? Do the Court's concerns about excessive intervention and assured conditions for optimum decisionmaking legitimately carry over to the disposition of appeals? [2]

Court guarantee a litigant that each judge will start off from dead center in his willingness or ability to reconcile the opposing arguments of counsel with his understanding of the Constitution and the law." Laird v. Tatum, 409 U.S. 824 (1972).

1. Recall, e. g., the dismissal of the appeal of a state suit by a taxpayer in Doremus, sec. 2, and the discussion of the Adler case, sec. 3.

2. Note the concluding materials in chap. 1, considering recent proposals which would eliminate the appeal jurisdiction and route all cases sought to be reviewed in the Supreme Court through the certiorari channel. Would adoption of those proposals still all doubts raised by the practices considered in this sec. 4A?

MARSHALL AND BRANDEIS: CONFLICTING VIEWS?

Chief Justice Marshall in COHENS v. VIRGINIA, 6 Wheat. 264, 404 (1821): "It is most true that this Court will not take jurisdiction if it should not: but it is equally true, that it must take jurisdiction if it should. The judiciary cannot, as the legislature may, avoid a measure because it approaches the confines of the constitution. We cannot pass it by because it is doubtful. With whatever doubts, with whatever difficulties, a case may be attended, we must decide it, if it be brought before us. We have no more right to decline the exercise of jurisdiction which is given, than to usurp that which is not given. The one or the other would be treason to the constitution. Questions may occur which we would gladly avoid; but we cannot avoid them. All we can do is, to exercise our best judgment, and conscientiously to perform our duty."

Justice Brandeis in ASHWANDER v. TVA, 297 U.S. 288, 346–348 (1936) (concurring opinion): "The Court developed, for its own governance in the cases confessedly within its jurisdiction, a series of rules under which it has avoided passing upon a large part of all the constitutional questions pressed upon it for decision. They are:

"1. The Court will not pass upon the constitutionality of legislation in a friendly, non-adversary, proceeding, declining because to decide such questions 'is legitimate only in the last resort, and as a necessity in the determination of real, earnest and vital controversy between individuals. It never was the thought that, by means of a friendly suit, a party beaten in the legislature could transfer to the courts an inquiry as to the constitutionality of the legislative act.' . . .

"2. The Court will not 'anticipate a question of constitutional law in advance of the necessity of deciding it.' . . .

"3. The Court will not 'formulate a rule of constitutional law broader than is required by the precise facts to which it is to be applied.' . . .

"4. The Court will not pass upon a constitutional question although properly presented by the record, if there is also present some other ground upon which the case may be disposed of. This rule has found most varied application. Thus, if a case can be decided on either of two grounds, one involving a constitutional question, the other a question of statutory construction or general law, the Court will decide only the latter. . . .

"5. The Court will not pass upon the validity of a statute upon complaint of one who fails to show that he is injured by its operation. . . .

"6. The Court will not pass upon the constitutionality of a statute at the instance of one who has availed himself of its benefits. . . .

"7. 'When the validity of an act of the Congress is drawn in question, and even if a serious doubt of constitutionality is raised, it is a cardinal principle that this Court will first ascertain whether a construction of the statute is fairly possible by which the question may be avoided.' . . ."

ASHWANDER AND THE "NEO–BRANDEISIAN FALLACY"

Note the comments on the content and uses of the Ashwander rules in Gunther, "The Subtle Vices of the 'Passive Virtues'—A Comment on Principle and Expediency in Judicial Review," 64 Colum.L.Rev. 1 (1964): * "[J]urisdiction under our system is rooted in Article III and congressional enactments; it is not a domain solely within the Court's keeping." The view that the Court has a general discretion not to adjudicate "frequently professes to find support in the Brandeis opinion in the Ashwander case. Brandeis' statement regarding "cases confessedly within [the Court's] jurisdiction" is "sound and of principled content; it is not an assertion of a vague Court discretion to deny a decision on the merits in a case within the statutory and constitutional bounds of jurisdiction. The Brandeis rules are a far cry from the neo-Brandeisian fallacy that there is a general 'Power To Decline the Exercise of Jurisdiction Which Is Given,' that there is a general discretion not to adjudicate though statute, Constitution, and remedial law present a 'case' for decision and confer no discretion. [The 'Power to Decline' quotation is from Bickel, The Least Dangerous Branch (1962), 127.]

"Of course the Court often may and should avoid 'passing upon a large part of all of the constitutional questions pressed upon it for decision.' Four of the seven Brandeis rules involve well-known instances of such avoidance—avoidance only of some or all of the constitutional questions argued, *not* avoidance of all decision on the merits of the case. . . . The remaining rules given by Brandeis deal with situations in which there is no 'case' or 'controversy' in terms of the jurisdictional content of Article III—as with the 'non-adversary' proceeding of his first rule—or where there is a lack of what Bickel calls 'pure' standing in the constitutional sense, or where the state of the remedial law prevents a 'case' from arising. In these Brandeis categories, decision on the merits is precluded because the jurisdictional requirements of Article III are not met; in the earlier ones, the jurisdiction to decide the merits is in fact exercised and all that is avoided is decision on some or all of the constitutional issues presented.

"The only possible Brandeis contribution to the fallacy lies in his reference to all of the categories as 'cases confessedly within' the Court's jurisdiction. But that referred to the fact that all of the jurisdictional requirements added by the statute had been met; and adjudication on the merits did in fact result in all of his categories, except where a jurisdictional requirement originating in the Constitution had not been satisfied. There is a sad irony in the transformation of the Brandeis passage into a veritable *carte blanche* for Court discretion as to jurisdiction; and there is sad irony too in the invocation of Brandeis' principled concern with threshold questions by members and appraisers of the Court who would assert a virtually unlimited choice in deciding whether to decide. The neo-Brandeisian fallacy has fortunately not yet gained a firm, persistent foothold on the Court." †

---

* Reprinted with the permission of the publisher, © copyright 1964, The Directors of the Columbia Law Review Association, Inc.

† Note also the reference to the Ashwander rules in the majority opinion

in Flast v. Cohen, sec. 2 above. Chief Justice Warren pointed to them as illustrations of "not always clearly distinguished" strands of policy considerations and constitutional limitations. The Flast opinion elaborated: "Because the rules operate in 'cases con-

SOME EXAMPLES OF DISCRETIONARY DISMISSALS OF APPEALS—AND SOME QUESTIONS

Introduction. Consider the following examples of Supreme Court refusals to adjudicate the merits of cases apparently within the Court's obligatory appeal jurisdiction. Was there any principled justification for any of these dismissals? Sometimes the Court purports to rely in substantial part on Justice Brandeis' statement in Ashwander. Is that reliance justified? Sometimes the Court merely states that the case is dismissed "for want of a properly presented federal question" or "because of the inadequacy of the record." Yet there was apparently nothing "improper" about the presentation of the federal question in those cases in the sense of compliance with governing statutes and Supreme Court rules. That variety of noncompliance would presumably have resulted in a simple dismissal for want of jurisdiction. If the record is indeed unclear, the Court may remand to the state court for clarification; but is dismissal justified? "If the technical requirements have been met, and the validity of a state statute 'drawn' in question within the meaning of the jurisdictional provision, is it appropriate to dismiss an appeal because the questions have not been 'properly presented' in some other sense?" [1] What, if any, justification is there, then, for the Court's exercise of discretion in these cases?

1. *The Rescue Army case.* In RESCUE ARMY v. MUNICIPAL COURT OF LOS ANGELES, 331 U.S. 549 (1947), the appeal concededly presented "substantial questions concerning the constitutional validity of ordinances of the City of Los Angeles governing the solicitation of contributions for charity." Moreover, the case was clearly within the appeal jurisdiction. Yet the majority disposed of the case without reaching the merits: "While [we] are unable to conclude that there is no jurisdiction in this cause, nevertheless compelling reasons exist for not exercising it." After making that statement, the majority opinion of Justice Rutledge contained the long passage quoted in sec. 1 tracing the evolution and varied ingredients of the Court's "policy of strict necessity in disposing of constitutional issues." Can that "policy of strict necessity" legitimately override the congressional mandate in the appeal statute?

The Rescue Army litigation arose as follows: Murdock, an officer of the Rescue Army, had been twice convicted in a local court of violations of specified sections of Los Angeles ordinances governing charitable solicitations. Each conviction was reversed on evidentiary grounds. After the second reversal, Murdock and his organization filed an action in the highest state court seeking a writ of prohibition against further prosecution. The state Supreme Court denied the writ on the merits, in part relying on a parallel case, Gospel Army v. Los Angeles. In examining the Rescue Army appeal, the Supreme Court was troubled by the "interlacing relationships" between the various statutory provisions and the "difficult problems" as to the

---

fessedly within [the Court's] jurisdiction,' they find their source in policy, rather than purely constitutional, considerations. However, several of the cases cited by Mr. Justice Brandeis . . . articulated purely constitutional grounds for decision."

1. See Hart and Wechsler, Federal Courts (2d ed. 1973), 658; see generally id., 656–62, for a sampling of additional orders summarily dismissing appeals seemingly within the obligatory jurisdiction.

bearing of the state court's Gospel Army opinion on the Rescue Army litigation. Justice Rutledge, after the general passages quoted in sec. 1, stated:

"One aspect of the policy's application—[the "policy of strict necessity" and avoidance of constitutional adjudication]—has been by virtue of the presence of other grounds for decision. But when such alternatives are absent, as in this case, application must rest upon considerations relative to the manner in which the constitutional issue itself is shaped and presented.

"These cannot be reduced to any precise formula or complete catalogue. But in general, as we have said, they are of the same nature as those which make the case and controversy limitation applicable, differing only in degree. To the more usual considerations of timeliness and maturity, of concreteness, definiteness, certainty, and of adversity of interests affected, are to be added in cases coming from state courts involving state legislation those arising when questions of construction, essentially matters of state law, remain unresolved or highly ambiguous. They include, of course, questions of incorporation by reference and severability, such as this case involves. Necessarily whether decision of the constitutional issue will be made must depend upon the degree to which uncertainty exists in these respects. And this inevitably will vary with particular causes and their varying presentations. [F]or a variety of reasons the shape in which the underlying constitutional issues have reached this Court [in this case] presents, we think, insuperable obstacles to any exercise of jurisdiction to determine them.

"Those reasons comprise not only obstacles of prematurity and comparative abstractness arising from the nature of the proceeding in prohibition and the manner in which the parties have utilized it for presenting the constitutional questions. They also include related considerations growing out of uncertainties resulting from the volume of legislative provisions possibly involved, their intricate interlacing not only with each other on their face but also in the California Supreme Court's disposition of them, and especially from its treatment of this case by reference in considerable part to the Gospel Army case, difficulties all accentuated for us of course by the necessity for dismissal of that cause here. . . .

"We are not unmindful that our ruling will subject the petitioner Murdock to the burden of undergoing a third trial or that this burden is substantial. Were the uncertainties confronting us in relation to this Court's historic policy less in number, and resolving them not so far from our appropriate function in cases coming from state courts, the inconvenience of undergoing trial another time might justify exercising jurisdiction in this cause. But, consistently with the policy, jurisdiction here should be exerted only when the jurisdictional question presented by the proceeding in prohibition tenders the underlying constitutional issues in clean-cut and concrete form, unclouded by any serious problem of construction relating either to the terms of the questioned legislation or to its interpretation by the state courts. . . . Accordingly, the appeal is dismissed, without prejudice to the determination in the future of any issues arising under the Federal Constitution from further proceedings in the Municipal Court." [2]

2. Justice Murphy, joined by Justice Douglas, dissented, finding it "difficult [to] believe" that the California Supreme Court opinion was "so ambiguous that the precise constitutional issues in this case have become too

2. *Poe v. Ullman.* a. *The decision.* POE v. ULLMAN, 367 U.S. 497 (1961), was the decision already discussed in part in sec. 3 above: Justice Frankfurter's plurality opinion there dismissed an appeal from a state court decision upholding the Connecticut ban on use of contraceptives, emphasizing especially the considerations noted earlier as to the absence of any specific threat of enforcement and the long history of nonenforcement of the law. Justice Frankfurter's opinion also included more general comments, including reliance on the Brandeis opinion in Ashwander. He stated, for example:

"The restriction of our jurisdiction to cases and controversies within the meaning of Article III of the Constitution [is] not the sole limitation on the exercise of our appellate powers, especially in cases raising constitutional questions. The policy reflected in numerous cases and over a long period was thus summarized in the oft-quoted statement of Mr. Justice Brandeis: 'The Court [has] developed, for its own governance in the cases confessedly within its jurisdiction, a series of rules under which it has avoided passing upon a large part of all the constitutional questions pressed upon it for decision.' [Ashwander]. In part the rules summarized in the Ashwander opinion have derived from the historically defined, limited nature and function of courts and from the recognition that, within the framework of our adversary system, the adjudicatory process is most securely founded when it is exercised under the impact of a lively conflict between antagonistic demands, actively pressed, which make resolution of the controverted issue a practical necessity. . . . These considerations press with special urgency in cases challenging legislative action or state judicial action as repugnant to the Constitution. . . . The various doctrines of 'standing,' 'ripeness,' and 'mootness,' which this Court has evolved with particular, though not exclusive, reference to such cases are but several manifestations—each having its own 'varied application'—of the primary conception that federal judicial power is to be exercised to strike down legislation, whether state or federal, only at the instance of one who is himself immediately harmed, or immediately threatened with harm, by the challenged action. . . .

"Justiciability is of course not a legal concept with a fixed content or susceptible of scientific verification. Its utilization is the resultant of many subtle pressures, including the appropriateness of the issues for decision by this Court and the actual hardship to the litigants of denying them the relief sought. Both these factors justify withholding adjudication of the constitutional issue raised under the circumstances and in the manner in which they are now before the Court." [3]

Justice Harlan's extensive dissent commented that the fact "that justiciability is not precisely definable does not make it ineffable." He noted that

blurred for our powers of discernment."

For a reliance on Rescue Army to dismiss an appeal from a three-judge District Court, see Socialist Labor Party v. Gilligan, 406 U.S. 583 (1972).

3. Justice Brennan, whose vote was necessary to make a majority for the disposition in Poe v. Ullman, concurred in the result on the ground that the "true controversy in this case is over the opening of birth-control clinics on a large scale." He stated: "It will be time enough to decide the constitutional questions urged upon us when, if ever, that real controversy [between the state and the clinics] flares up again." Justices Black, Douglas, Harlan and Stewart submitted separate dissents.

Justice Frankfurter had referred to virtually every ingredient of justiciability and proceeded to eliminate most as "*not* involved in the present appeals." For example, the fact that the case was one seeking anticipatory relief clearly did not make the case premature. Nor was this a situation where lack of "ripeness" could be charged: "No clarifying or resolving contingency" as to the plaintiffs' proposed conduct existed; there were "no circumstances besides that of detection or prosecution to make remote the particular controversy." And the lack of an actual prosecution was "not *alone* sufficient to make the case too remote, not ideally enough 'ripe' for adjudication, at the prior stage of anticipatory relief." Moreover, there was no lack of adversariness, nor lack of standing. There was simply the past history of failure to enforce the law. And as to that, Justice Harlan stated—as noted earlier—that it was "pure conjecture, and indeed conjecture which to me seems contrary to realities, that an open violation of the statute by a doctor [would] not result in a substantial threat of prosecution." He concluded: "I fear that the Court has indulged in a bit of slight of hand to be rid of the case." He insisted that "there is no justification for failing to decide these married persons' appeals. . . . It seems to me to destroy the whole purpose of anticipatory relief to consider the prosecutor's discretion [as] in any way analogous to those other contingencies which make remote a controversy presenting constitutional claims." [4]

b. *The justification.* Poe v. Ullman, like Rescue Army, was a refusal to adjudicate a state court case apparently within the Court's obligatory appeal jurisdiction. Was the Poe dismissal any more justifiable? Note Gunther, "The Subtle Vices of the 'Passive Virtues'—A Comment on Principle and Expediency in Judicial Review," 64 Colum.L.Rev. 1, 18 (1964), commenting on Bickel, The Least Dangerous Branch (1962): "[Bickel states] that it was 'wise' and proper that the Court withheld decision [in Poe v. Ullman]. And nothing but a 'dictum in Cohens v. Virginia' stood in the way of the Court's refusal to adjudicate. Was that all that really stood in the way? John Marshall, in Cohens, uttered words which Bickel repeatedly undertakes to disparage, for they flatly contradict his notions of permissible Court abstention. 'We have no more right to decline the exercise of jurisdiction which is given,' Marshall said, 'than to usurp that which is not given.' But the only way in which this can be viewed as insignificant dictum is to argue that there are no adequate reference points for determination of the jurisdiction assigned to the Court. But there are: there is the Constitution; there is the statute. Under Bickel's analysis as well as the Court's, Poe v. Ullman was a 'case' within Article III; moreover, it was one of that small group of cases Congress has made it the Court's duty to decide." [5]

---

4. Justice Harlan proceeded to find the statute unconstitutional on the merits, as a violation of substantive due process. Extensive excerpts from that part of the opinion are printed above, together with his concurring opinion in Griswold v. Connecticut, chap. 9, sec. 3.

5. See also Note, "The Discretionary Power of the Supreme Court to Dismiss Appeals from State Courts," 63 Colum.L.Rev. 688 (1963), and Note,

"Threat of Enforcement—Prerequisite of a Justiciable Controversy," 62 Colum.L.Rev. 106 (1962).

Note also Mattiello v. Connecticut, 395 U.S. 209 (1969), applying the Rescue Army principle to dismiss an appeal of an appellant challenging a statute pursuant to which he had been placed in juvenile detention. Is that dismissal even more questionable than those in Poe and Rescue Army, which were efforts to obtain anticipatory re-

c. *The Epperson case.* Compare with Poe v. Ullman the majority's summary disposition of the justiciability issue in EPPERSON v. ARKANSAS, 393 U.S. 97 (1968), a state court declaratory and injunction action challenging the constitutionality of a 1928 law barring the teaching of evolution (the "monkey law" case noted in chap. 14 above). Before reaching the merits, Justice Fortas' majority opinion simply noted: "There is no record of any prosecutions in Arkansas under its statute. It is possible that the statute is presently more of a curiosity than a vital fact of life in [Arkansas, Mississippi, and Tennessee]. Nevertheless, the present case was brought, the appeal as of right is properly here, and it is our duty to decide the issues presented." Only Justice Black dissented on this point.

Note the comment on Epperson in Hart and Wechsler, Federal Courts (2d ed. 1973), 657: "Doesn't Epperson confirm what Justice Frankfurter's opinion [in Poe v. Ullman] clearly implies—that the Poe disposition was not compelled by the 'case or controversy' requirements of Article III? Isn't that also true of Rescue Army? What, then, justifies such refusals to adjudicate appeals?"

3. *The Naim case.* a. *The litigation.* Mrs. Ruby Elaine Naim sued Mr. Ham Say Naim for an annulment of their marriage "on the ground of their racial ineligibility to marry one another," in view of the Virginia miscegenation law. The parties left Virginia in 1952 to be married in North Carolina, concededly "for the purpose of evading the Virginia law which forbade their marriage." After the marriage, they "immediately returned to Norfolk, Virginia, where they lived together as husband and wife." The state trial court found the marriage void and granted the annulment. The Supreme Court of Appeals of Virginia affirmed. It considered the federal constitutional objections to the miscegenation law at length—and rejected them all. 197 Va. 80, 87 S.E.2d 749 (1955). The case was brought to the United States Supreme Court by appeal. The full opinion of that Court, NAIM v. NAIM, 350 U.S. 891 (1955), follows:

"Appeal from the Supreme Court of Appeals of Virginia. *Per Curiam:* The inadequacy of the record as to the relationship of the parties to the Commonwealth of Virginia at the time of the marriage in North Carolina and upon their return to Virginia, and the failure of the parties to bring here all questions relevant to the disposition of the case, prevents the constitutional issue of the validity of the Virginia statute on miscegenation tendered here being considered 'in clean-cut and concrete form, unclouded' by such problems. Rescue Army v. Municipal Court, 331 U.S. 549, 584. The judgment is vacated and the case remanded to the Supreme Court of Appeals in order that the case may be returned to the Circuit Court of the City of Portsmouth for action not inconsistent with this opinion."

On remand, the Supreme Court of Appeals of Virginia stated [197 Va. 734, 90 S.E.2d 849 (1956)]: "[T]he material facts were not [in] dispute.

lief? Mattiello is noted in Hart and Wechsler, Federal Courts (2d ed. 1973), 660, with the comment: "Is there any justification for the Supreme Court declining an appeal in its 'discretion' when the result is to permit a state to act against a person who is assert-ing a federal constitutional defense against that action? If there is in such cases 'justice at the discretion of the Court,' what then is the significance of the Act of Congress creating appeal jurisdiction?"

The record showed that the complainant in the suit, a white woman, was an actual bona fide resident of, and domiciled in, Virginia, and had been for more than a year next preceding the commencement of the suit; that the defendant was a Chinese and a non-resident of Virginia at the time of the institution of the suit; that they had gone to North Carolina to be married for the purpose of evading the Virginia law which forbade their marriage, were married in North Carolina and immediately returned to and lived in Virginia as husband and wife. . . .

"The record before the Circuit Court of the City of Portsmouth was adequate for a decision of the issues presented to it. The record before this court was adequate for deciding the issues on review. The decision of the Circuit Court adjudicated the issues presented to that court. The decision of this court adjudicated the issues presented to it. The decree of the trial court and the decree of this court affirming it have become final so far as these courts are concerned.

"We have no provision either under the rules of practice and procedure of this court or under the statute law of this Commonwealth by which this court may send the cause back to the Circuit Court with directions to re-open the cause so decided, gather additional evidence and render a new decision. . . . We therefore adhere to our decision of the cause and to the decree of this court which affirmed the final decree of the Circuit Court of the City of Portsmouth holding that the marriage of the parties to this cause was void."

The case was once again taken to the United States Supreme Court. That Court's per curiam opinion on the second appeal, 350 U.S. 985 (1956), follows in full:

"Appeal from the Supreme Court of Appeals of Virginia. The motion to recall the mandate and to set the case down for oral argument upon the merits, or, in the alternative, to recall and amend the mandate is denied. The decision of the Supreme Court of Appeals of Virginia of January 18, 1956, in response to our order of November 14, 1955, 350 U.S. 891, leaves the case devoid of a properly presented federal question."

b. *The justification.* Was there any justification for the Court's disposition of the Naim case? In law? In policy? Do you agree with the comment that the dismissal of the appeal rested "on procedural grounds [that] are wholly without basis in the law"? Wechsler, "Toward Neutral Principles of Constitutional Law," 73 Harv.L.Rev. 1, 34 (1959). Note also the Bickel-Gunther differences on this issue reflected in Gunther, "The Subtle Vices of the 'Passive Virtues'—A Comment on Principle and Expediency in Judicial Review," 64 Colum.L.Rev. 1, 11–12 (1964): "Bickel's [Bickel, The Least Dangerous Branch (1962)] cavalier amalgamation of certiorari and appeal is a vast if not mischievous overstatement, in fact and in law. [He states:] 'Thus a decision on the validity of anti-miscegenation statutes was avoided through the dismissal of an appeal, which is to be explained in terms of the discretionary considerations that go to determine the lack of ripeness.' . . . In an earlier chapter, Bickel praised that dismissal as an example of the operation of 'techniques that allow leeway to expediency without abandoning principle'; 'the Court found no insuperable difficulty,' he notes with admiration, 'in leaving open the question

of the constitutionality of anti-miscegenation statutes, though it would surely seem to be governed by the principle of the Segregation Cases' decided two years earlier.' I will withhold comment for the moment on Bickel's judgment that this achievement was possible without 'abandoning principle'; the immediate question is Bickel's reliance on this dismissal for descriptive and normative purposes in handling appeals generally.

"Where [is] the legal basis for the discretion Bickel would condone and indeed advocate in this and similar cases within the appeal jurisdiction? No doubt there were strong considerations of expediency against considering the constitutionality of anti-miscegenation statutes in 1956. But does not the appeal jurisdiction, too, have a 'content of its own'? The content of this 'passive virtue' device is of course more than minimal: it derives from congressional regulation of the Supreme Court's appellate jurisdiction. . . . The Court, to be sure, has sometimes honored the appeal statute in the breach: the miscegenation case is on the books, and there are a very few dismissals similarly indefensible in law. But these are still only aberrations, and surely more can be expected of Bickel than to exaggerate them to the level of the commonplace and to elevate them to the level of the desirable and the acceptable." [6]

Note also a comment in Hart and Wechsler, Federal Courts (2d ed. 1973), 661–62. After quoting another passage from the late Professor Bickel's The Least Dangerous Branch,[7] the authors ask: "Is it a justification for the Court's action that decision of the case at the time would not have been 'wise'? If that is sufficient reason, what content is left to the obligatory nature of appeal jurisdiction? Professor Bickel has argued that there is none, and that there is a general 'power to decline the exercise of jurisdiction which is given'—pointing to Naim v. Naim as an example in support. But doesn't this view wholly neglect the Court's obligation of fidelity to law? Can that be so easily set aside without great harm, internal as well as external, to a body whose entire power to command ultimately rests on that precept? If, indeed, the Court believed that under the conditions of the time it had to avoid deciding Naim v. Naim without regard to cost, and had to violate the law to do so, isn't it far better to accept that fact rather than seek to rationalize and thus generalize the breach? See Gunther, supra."

6. Eleven years after Naim, the Court reached the merits of an appeal challenging the Virginia miscegenation statute: Loving v. Virginia, 388 U.S. 1 (1971), involving criminal convictions of a white man and his Black wife who had returned to Virginia after marrying in the District of Columbia, held the laws unconstitutional. Recall chap. 10, sec. 2, above.

7. "Actually a judgment legitimating such [miscegenation] statutes would have been unthinkable, given the principle of the School Segregation Cases and of decisions made in their aftermath. But would it have been wise, at a time when the Court had just pronounced its new integration principle, when it was subject to scurrilous attack by men who predicted that integration of the schools would lead directly to 'mongrelization of the race' and that this was the result the Court had already willed, would it have been wise, just then, in the first case of its sort on an issue that the Negro community as a whole can hardly be said to be pressing hard at the moment, to declare that the states may not prohibit intermarriage?" Bickel, The Least Dangerous Branch (1962), 172.

INTERPRETING STATUTES TO AVOID CONSTITUTIONAL QUESTIONS

The policy and its risks. a. *The principle.* "[I]t is a cardinal principle that this Court will first ascertain whether a construction of the statute is fairly possible by which the [constitutional] question may be avoided." So ended the last of Justice Brandeis' seven rules in the Ashwander case, above; and that statement echoes a principle enunciated by the Court from the beginning. Indeed, Chief Justice Marshall, in the very case juxtaposed with the Brandeis rules at the beginning of this section, decided the merits on the basis of statutory interpretation: where such a basis is available, he said, "it will be unnecessary, and consequently improper, to pursue any inquiries, which would then be merely speculative, respecting the power of Congress in the case." Cohens v. Virginia, 6 Wheat. 264, 441 (1821).

b. *The risks.* The principle has obvious limitations, however. See Chief Justice Vinson's warning in Shapiro v. United States, 335 U.S. 1, 31 (1948): "The canon of avoidance of constitutional doubts must, like the 'plain meaning' rule [in the interpretation of statutes], give way where its application would produce a futile result, or an unreasonable result 'plainly at variance with the policy of the legislation as a whole'."

This avoidance technique risks not only indefensible statutory interpretation but also irresponsible constitutional adjudication. There may be temptation to strain for a meaning in the statute beyond that "fairly possible" in order to avoid constitutional interpretation. Yet constitutional interpretation may not be wholly avoided: tentative interpretations may be ventured in the very process of stating *what* constitutional issues are being avoided; there may be temptation to launch constitutional trial balloons and indulge in free floating constitutional dicta without the restraints of fashioning constitutional law dispositive of the case.

Is the "constitutional trial balloon" risk illustrated by the disposition in KENT v. DULLES, 357 U.S. 116 (1958)? Were its constitutional statements akin to an advisory opinion? Is advice acceptable in this context because it is only tentative, because it serves to make Congress sensitive to constitutional issues, yet leaves to Congress the opportunity to change the scope of the statute? Was the Court exercising a "remanding" function— sending the issue back to Congress "for a second reading" a statutory problem "the implications of which Congress failed to see"? See Bickel and Wellington, "Legislative Purpose and the Judicial Process . . .," 71 Harv.L.Rev. 1 (1957). Is the Court authorized to "remand" to Congress?

In the Kent case, the challenger had been denied a passport for failing to submit an affidavit as to whether he was or had ever been a Communist, as required by a State Department regulation. The Court's holding was simply that the applicable statutes did not "delegate to the [Secretary of State] the kind of authority exercised here." Justice Douglas' majority opinion insisted that "we do not reach the question of constitutionality"; yet he wrote several passages elaborating the constitutional "right to travel" underlying the statutory interpretation. Though no prior decision had squarely said so, the Court announced (and explained) that the "right to

travel is a part of the 'liberty' of which the citizen cannot be deprived without the due process of law of the Fifth Amendment." A few years later, the Court relied squarely on that "right" (announced in a purportedly nonconstitutional decision) in holding unconstitutional a passport restriction in Aptheker v. Secretary of State, 378 U.S. 500 (1964) (chap. 12 above).

B. RESTRAINING THE EXERCISE OF JURISDICTION IN THE INTEREST OF FEDERALISM:
DISTRICT COURT ABSTENTION; NONINTERFERENCE WITH STATE COURT PROCEEDINGS

DISTRICT COURT ABSTENTION

Introduction. The Supreme Court is not the only tribunal that occasionally declines to adjudicate even though jurisdiction is granted by the Constitution and the statutes. The federal district courts, too, have exercised a discretion to abstain—more frequently than the Supreme Court, and at the behest of the Supreme Court's wavering and often unclear evolution of abstention standards. When should federal courts abstain so that state courts may decide? Is district court abstention more justifiable than the Supreme Court's failures to exercise its obligatory jurisdiction?

The abstention doctrine is a response to the problems caused by the existence of two sets of courts, state and federal, with authority to adjudicate questions of state and federal law. Federal district court abstention has been especially important and controversial in suits challenging state action on federal grounds—suits made more readily possible by the nationalizing impacts of the post-Civil War Amendments, the enactment of civil rights laws (recall chap. 11), and the 1908 Supreme Court decision in Ex parte Young. Congress was asked to curtail the exercise of that jurisdiction, but the legislative restrictions imposed were of limited scope. Beginning in 1940, Court-developed doctrines have created significant additional restraints on the exercise of federal jurisdiction; and those doctrines have produced much confusion and delay. Though these problems are more fully considered in courses on federal jurisdiction, the following materials briefly trace the major developments.

In form, the judge-made abstention exception to the obligatory jurisdiction of the lower federal courts does not mean the total denial of jurisdiction. Rather, it purports simply to be "postponement of the exercise" rather than "abdication" of federal jurisdiction. Typically, the district court retains jurisdiction, so that the litigant may go to the state courts to obtain an answer to unclear questions of state law; theoretically, the federal issues may then be brought back to the federal court, after the state litigation is completed. But when the case involves both federal and state issues, it may prove preferable—or the state courts may urge—that both sets of issues be presented to the state system. A decision there is then ultimately reviewable in the Supreme Court; and access to the lower federal courts may be

effectively lost. Alternatively, if the issues are divided, the resulting litigation may be marked by unusual expense and delay.

Arc such reasons as avoiding federal-state conflicts and avoiding unnecessary decision of federal constitutional issues sufficiently compelling to justify the tortured course of decisions traced below? Are they in any event sufficient to justify judge-made restraints on the exercise of congressionally mandated jurisdiction? Does the proposed ALI codification provide a better response? Do the materials below provide adequate reasons for so complex a scheme? Do they provide rules of adequate clarity?

1. *Statutory restrictions and Ex parte Young.* EX PARTE YOUNG 209 U.S. 123 (1908), made possible the broad and frequently invoked application of federal jurisdiction to state official action. A federal district court had ordered Young, a state attorney general, to cease enforcing a law regulating railroad rates, on the ground that it violated the 14th Amendment. The Supreme Court held that the 11th Amendment assurance of state immunity from federal court suits did not bar the suit against the state official: "If the Act which the state Attorney General seeks to enforce be a violation of the Federal Constitution, the officer in proceeding under such enactment, comes into conflict with the superior authority of that Constitution, and he is in that case stripped of his official or representative character and is subjected in his person to the consequences of his individual conduct." [And two years later the Court found that such "individual conduct" not entitled to the 11th Amendment state immunity nevertheless constituted "state action" within the reach of the 14th Amendment's restraints. Home Tel. and Tel. Co. v. Los Angeles, 227 U.S. 278 (1913).]

The pleas that Congress close the doors opened by Ex parte Young met only limited success: in 1910, a statute was enacted requiring that there be three-judge federal courts in most cases challenging state action; the Johnson Act of 1934 prohibits most federal injunctions against state rate orders where "a plain, speedy and efficient remedy" in state courts is available; and a 1937 law similarly bars federal injunctions against state taxes. But Congress left many doors to the federal courts open. Thereafter, the Supreme Court undertook to close some of the doors Congress had not seen fit to shut. Why? How adequate were the justifications?

2. *The Pullman Case.* RAILROAD COMMISSION v. PULLMAN CO., 312 U.S. 496 (1941), launched the modern history of judicially-developed doctrines encouraging District Court abstention. There, a state agency's order was challenged as violating state law as well as the federal Constitution. Justice Frankfurter's opinion for a unanimous Court directed the District Court to "stay its hand": "to retain the bill pending a determination of proceedings, to be brought with reasonable promptness, in the state court." Adjudication of the unclear state law issue might make decision on the constitutional question unnecessary. A lower federal court's decision of the state issue "cannot escape being a forecast rather than a determination"; the "resources of equity are equal to an adjustment that will avoid the waste of a tentative decision as well as the friction of a premature constitutional adjudication." And this judge-made doctrine was found appropriate even though it went beyond the limitations Congress had seen fit to impose: "This use of equitable powers is a contribution of the

courts in furthering the harmonious relation between state and federal authority without the need of rigorous congressional restriction of those powers."

3. *The Alabama Public Service case.* Compare Justice Frankfurter's separate opinion a decade later, in ALABAMA PUBLIC SERVICE COMMISSION v. SOUTHERN RY., 341 U.S. 341 (1951). A railroad suit in a federal court challenged, under the Due Process Clause, a state order barring discontinuance of certain railroad passenger service. The Court found no unclear state statutory issue, as in Pullman, and no constitutional challenge to the state statute as such. Nor was federal action barred by the Johnson Act. Nevertheless, Chief Justice Vinson's majority opinion concluded that the federal court's jurisdiction "should not be exercised in this case as a matter of sound equitable discretion." He noted that "adequate state court review of an administrative order based upon predominantly local factors is available."

Justice Frankfurter's opinion concurring in the result, joined by Justice Jackson, protested that the Court's order directing the District Court to dismiss the suit rested on "a line of argument in plain disregard of congressional legislation." He argued that the Court had in effect amended the statutory federal question jurisdiction grant and it did not "change the significance of the Court's decision to coat it with the sugar of equity maxims." Was Justice Frankfurter's Pullman opinion, note 2, subject to the same criticism?

4. *The consequences of abstention—Confusion and delay.* Are the institutional values of abstention (such as avoidance of needless constitutional adjudication and of federal-state friction) worth the cost? Not only has there been uncertainty in determining when abstention is appropriate, but there has been confusion as well about what should happen when a federal court chooses to abstain: Is abstention merely a postponement of federal adjudication, or a total relinquishment? Should the court stay or dismiss? Should the entire case go to the state courts, or only a portion? Should state adjudication (with the availability of Supreme Court review) end the litigation, or may the litigant return to the federal District Court?

The Court has repeatedly insisted, as in Harrison v. NAACP, 360 U.S. 167 (1959), that abstention does not "involve the abdication of federal jurisdiction but only the postponement of its exercise." Yet the federal as well as the state issues are often presented to the state court after the federal trial court abstains, and the state court's decision is often reviewable in the Supreme Court. Thus the case may never return to the federal trial court. Indeed, the Court has occasionally insisted that the federal as well as the state issue must be submitted to the state court. See Government Employees v. Windsor, 353 U.S. 364 (1957). But see the "clarification" in England v. Louisiana Medical Examiners, 375 U.S. 411 (1964): "The [Windsor] case does not mean that a party must litigate his federal claims in the state courts, but only that he must inform those courts what his federal claims are, so that the state statute may be construed 'in light of' those claims." What if the state courts then proceed to adjudicate the federal claim they have been "informed" about?

5. *The ALI proposal.* The American Law Institute's proposals for revision of Title 28 of the United States Code include a new § 1371 designed to set forth all of the circumstances in which a three-judge district court

may abstain in favor of state adjudication.[1] The ALI comments concede that there is "no wholly satisfactory answer" in fashioning acceptable abstention doctrines: "To litigate these cases entirely through the federal courts strains state-federal relations, may make necessary the premature decision of federal constitutional questions, and requires the federal court to pass on questions of state law in circumstances under which an erroneous decision may seriously interfere with state substantive policies. To litigate such cases entirely through the state courts, with review in the United States Supreme Court, deprives plaintiff of federal fact-finding, and of federal protection during the pendency of the state action. To shuttle the cases back and forth from state to federal court, as present doctrines permit, 'operates to require piecemeal adjudication in many courts.' "

Nevertheless, the ALI sets forth groundrules with considerable clarity and detail. (And, if adopted by Congress, they would remove the question of legitimacy about the judge-made evolution of abstention doctrines as an overlay on the congressionally mandated jurisdiction.) The core ALI provision, § 1371(c) provides: "A district court may stay an action, otherwise properly commenced in or removed to a district court under this title, on the ground that the action presents issues of State law that ought to be determined in a State proceeding, if the court finds: (1) that the issues of State law cannot be satisfactorily determined in the light of the State authorities; and (2) that abstention from the exercise of federal jurisdiction is warranted either by the likelihood that the necessity for deciding a substantial question of federal constitutional law may thereby be avoided, or by a serious danger of embarrassing the effectuation of State policies by a decision of State law at variance with the view that may be ultimately taken by the State court, or by other circumstances of like character; and (3) that a plain, speedy, and efficient remedy may be had in the courts of such State; and (4) that the parties' claims of federal right, if any, including any issues of fact material thereto, can be adequately protected by review of the State court decision by the Supreme Court of the United States."

Other provisions of the ALI proposals worth special note are the following: § 1371(f) bars abstention beyond the circumstances set forth above; it prohibits additional "judge-made notions of abstention." Subsection (d) clarifies the consequences of abstention: abstention produces a stay, not a dismissal; but ordinarily litigation through the state court route (with the possibility of Supreme Court review) ends the case. And subsection (g) excepts certain actions from the abstention authorization: suits by the United States; and some civil rights actions—on the ground that "there is an especially strong national interest in a federal forum for such cases.[2] Note that the ALI decided against authorizing abstention "merely

---

1. See ALI, Study of the Division of Jurisdiction within State and Federal Courts (1969), 48–50 (text), 282–298 (commentary). Compare Friendly, Federal Jurisdiction (1973); Currie, "The Federal Courts and the American Law Institute," 36 U.Chi.L.Rev. 268 (1969).

2. The propriety of abstention in suits to protect civil rights has long pro-

voked controversy. The Court has rejected arguments that federal courts should *always* refuse to abstain in civil rights cases. See, e. g., Harrison v. NAACP, 360 U.S. 167 (1959). Compare the ALI proposal barring abstention in some but not all civil rights cases. But see the principles of the Younger v. Harris-line of cases in the next group of notes.

to avoid a federal constitutional question." The commentary explains: "The risk that the federal court will decide a constitutional question unnecessarily, because it has made an erroneous determination of some question of state law, does not seem sufficiently grave to justify imposing on litigants the delay and expense of abstention."

   f. *Abstention and the Burger Court: Some examples.* a. *The Constantineau case.* The Court divided over the propriety of abstention in WISCONSIN v. CONSTANTINEAU, 400 U.S. 433 (1971). Justice Douglas' majority opinion rejected the claim that a challenge to the Wisconsin "posting" law should have been presented first to the state courts.[3] He found no unresolved question of state law with respect to the thrust of the federal constitutional challenge, the absence of notice and hearing, and concluded: "Where there is no ambiguity in the state statute, the federal court should not abstain but proceed to decide the federal constitutional claim." Two dissents disagreed with this view—one by Chief Justice Burger, joined by Justice Blackmun, and another by Justice Black, also joined by Justice Blackmun. Though Chief Justice Burger conceded that there was "no absolute duty to abstain," he argued that "a three-judge district court would be well advised in cases such as this, involving no urgency or question of large import, to decline to act."

   b. *The Lake Carriers' case.* Some lower federal courts, purporting to draw on hints in early Burger Court decisions, sought to discourage resort to federal courts in challenging state legislation and tried to channel more litigation into the state courts. That tendency was curtailed by the Court's disposition of LAKE CARRIERS' ASS'N v. MacMULLAN, 406 U.S. 498 (1972). This was an attack by Great Lakes shipowners on a Michigan pollution control law apparently prohibiting the discharge of sewage and requiring the installation of on-board sewage storage devices. The District Court dismissed the suit, relying in part on abstention considerations. But Justice Brennan's majority opinion found that "abstention was not proper on the majority of grounds given by the District Court." For example, "the availability of declaratory relief in Michigan courts" was held to be "wholly beside the point," in view of the federal courts' obligation to give "due respect to a suitor's choice of a federal forum." The only justification for abstention found applicable by the Supreme Court was the possibility that the state courts might resolve "ambiguities in the Michigan law" in such a way as to "avoid or significantly modify the federal questions appellants raise." More generally, Justice Brennan reemphasized that abstention is appropriate "only in narrowly limited 'special circumstances' justifying 'the delay and expense to which application of the abstention doctrine inevitably gives rise.' " [4]

---

3. The "posting law" permitted various local officials or a man's wife to designate—and thereby forbid selling liquor to—any person who, because of "excessive drinking," exposed his family to want or was dangerous to the peace. There had been no construction of the statute by the state courts; the law did not provide a hearing on its face; and the challenger's name had been posted without a hearing.

The lower court refused to abstain and held the lack of notice unconstitutional on procedural due process grounds.

4. Compare Harris County Commissioners Court v. Moore, 420 U.S. —— (1975), an 8 to 1 decision ordering abstention because of uncertain questions of state law underlying the federal constitutional claims.

LIMITS ON FEDERAL JUDICIAL INTERVENTION IN STATE COURT PROCEEDINGS: THE BACKGROUND AND IMPACT OF YOUNGER v. HARRIS

Introduction. The abstention doctrines considered above limit the exercise of federal jurisdiction not only because of federalism concerns but also, and often predominantly, because of the federal judiciary's interest in avoiding unnecessary constitutional decisions. Another doctrine—one that has produced considerable controversy in recent years—rests more heavily on federalism concerns. In a variety of settings, the Court has enforced a policy of noninterference in state judicial proceedings. While abstention (at least in form) merely means *postponement* of the exercise of federal jurisdiction, the nonintervention doctrine is a total *barrier* to district court adjudication.

Like abstention, the nonintervention policy rests in part on statutory grounds but even more heavily on judge-made doctrines. Thus, a federal statute, 28 U.S.C. § 2283, bars federal court injunctions "to stay proceedings in a State court except as expressly authorized by Act of Congress, or where necessary in aid of its jurisdiction, or to protect or effectuate its judgments." But that law, after a period of uncertainty, was held inapplicable to federal actions under the federal civil rights laws, including the wide-ranging 42 U.S.C. § 1983. (Recall chap. 11, sec. 1, above.) Since the bulk of modern constitutional litigation rests on the civil rights jurisdictional provision, the anti-injunction statute is of little force with respect to most constitutional litigation: Mitchum v. Foster, 407 U.S. 225 (1972), held 42 U.S.C. § 1983 to be an "expressly authorized" exception to § 2283. Hence it is judicially developed nonintervention doctrine that provides the major barrier to access to federal courts by those challenging the enforcement of state legislation. In DOMBROWSKI v. PFISTER, 380 U.S. 479 (1965), the Court seemed to open the federal doors wide to a variety of civil liberties claims, and that decision was read very broadly by many lower courts. However, beginning with Younger v. Harris, 401 U.S. 37 (1971), the Court imposed significant restraints on the Dombrowski developments. The impact of these cases has been particularly great on First Amendment litigation and on the availability of overbreadth and vagueness attacks. (Recall chap. 12 above.) The review of Younger v. Harris and related developments below is designed to convey a sense of recent developments.

In Dombrowski, the challengers claimed that state criminal statutes were about to be invoked against them in bad faith, as well as that those statutes were "overly broad and vague regulations of expression." Justice Brennan's majority opinion, emphasizing the "chilling effect" of such laws, concluded that in such a case "abstention and the denial of injunctive relief may well result in the denial of any effective safeguards against the loss of protected freedoms of expression, and cannot be justified."

In the wake of Dombrowski, constitutional challenges to state criminal statutes in three-judge federal courts proliferated. The Younger v. Harris group of cases in 1971 curbed that trend. Dombrowski itself had sustained federal relief against *future* state prosecutions. In most of the 1971 cases, the lower courts had gone beyond Dombrowski to grant injunctive or

declaratory relief against state criminal prosecutions already under way. The Court's specific holdings in 1971 were addressed to the latter situation, found federal relief against *pending* state proceedings justified only in exceptional circumstances, and concluded that the lower court interventions challenged here had all been improper.

Justice Black's opinion in Younger v. Harris was, however, written very broadly and was read by many as having an importance going beyond the specific situations before the Court. There were passages that appeared significant not only in cases of federal relief against *pending* state prosecutions but also in Dombrowski-like suits to block *future* prosecutions. Other passages suggested changing attitudes regarding the receptiveness of federal courts to "on the face" overbreadth attacks on legislation—a technique of constitutional litigation that had gained considerable added impetus as a result of Dombrowski. (Though later overbreadth opinions have not curtailed that technique as much as some of the dicta in Younger v. Harris suggested, Younger v. Harris did prove to be the beginning of a trend of limiting the availability of that variety of attack. Recall the materials on the curtailment of overbreadth and the new emphasis on "substantial overbreadth" in chap. 12, sec. 2, above.)

1. *Younger v. Harris.* YOUNGER v. HARRIS, 401 U.S. 37 (1971), was a federal action originally brought by Harris to hold a California criminal syndicalism act unconstitutional on its face under the First Amendment.[1] Harris had been indicted under the act and sued to enjoin prosecution.[2] The District Court found the act unconstitutional and enjoined "further prosecution of the currently pending action" against Harris. The Supreme Court held that the trial court should not have exercised jurisdiction.[3]

Justice Black concluded that the lower court should not have adjudicated Harris' claim because of "the settled doctrines that have always con-

1. The act had been held constitutional in Whitney v. California, 274 U.S. 357 (1927); Whitney was overruled by Brandenburg v. Ohio, 395 U.S. 444 (1969). See chap. 12, sec. 1, above.

2. The federal District Court had permitted three others to intervene as plaintiffs in Harris' suit: two members of the Progressive Labor Party who claimed that the prosecution of Harris would inhibit them from peaceful advocacy of the Party's programs; and a college history instructor who claimed that Harris' prosecution made him uncertain "as to whether he could teach about the doctrines of Karl Marx or read from the Communist Manifesto as part of his classwork." Justice Black's plurality opinion summarily disposed of those three additional plaintiffs. They had no "acute, live controversy" with the state: "None has been indicted, arrested, or even threatened by the prosecutor"; there was no "genuine controversy" with respect to them "sufficient to bring the equitable jurisdiction of the federal courts into play." Only Harris, who was actually being prosecuted, was found to be a proper plaintiff in the case.

3. Justice Black wrote an opinion joined by Chief Justice Burger and Justices Harlan, Stewart and Blackmun. But Justice Stewart, joined by Justice Harlan, also filed a concurring opinion—and the narrowness of that concurring opinion suggested that some of the passages in Justice Black's "opinion of the Court" represented only a plurality view. Justice Brennan, joined by Justices White and Marshall, filed a separate opinion concurring only in the result. Justice Douglas was the only dissenter in the case.

The statute challenged by Harris was subsequently held unconstitutional by a state court. In re Harris, 97 Cal. Rptr. 844 (1971).

fined very narrowly the availability of injunctive relief against state criminal prosecutions"—doctrines that, contrary to the lower court's views, had not been upset by Dombrowski. Justice Black reviewed the Court's repeated insistence "that the normal thing to do when federal courts are asked to enjoin pending proceedings in state courts is not to issue such injunctions." He relied on Fenner v. Boykin, 271 U.S. 240 (1926), where the Court had made clear, in Justice Black's words "that such a suit, even with respect to state criminal proceedings not yet formally instituted, could be proper only under very special circumstances." The Fenner case had spoken of "extraordinary circumstances where the danger of irreparable loss is both great and immediate." Justice Black emphasized that, because of "the fundamental policy against federal interference," it was necessary to show more than "irreparable injury, the traditional prerequisite to obtaining an injunction": "even irreparable injury is insufficient unless it is 'both great and immediate.' " He explained: "Certain types of injury, in particular, the cost, anxiety, and inconvenience of having to defend against a single criminal prosecution, could not by themselves be considered 'irreparable' in the special legal sense of that term. Instead, the threat to the plaintiff's federally protected rights must be one that cannot be eliminated by his defense against a single criminal prosecution." Under that "settled doctrine," an injunction was improper here: Harris had an opportunity to raise his constitutional claims in the pending prosecution against him; there was "no suggestion that this single prosecution against Harris is brought in bad faith or is only one of a series of repeated prosecutions to which he will be subjected."

Justice Black explained the underlying reasons for the "long standing public policy against federal court interference with state court proceedings" as follows: "One is the basic doctrine of equity jurisprudence that courts of equity should not act, and particularly should not act to restrain a criminal prosecution, when the moving party has an adequate remedy at law and will not suffer irreparable injury if denied equitable relief. The doctrine may originally have grown out of circumstances peculiar to the English judicial system and not applicable in this country, but its fundamental purpose of restraining equity jurisdiction within narrow limits is equally important under our Constitution, in order to prevent erosion of the role of the jury and avoid a duplication of legal proceedings and legal sanctions where a single suit would be adequate to protect the rights asserted. This underlying reason for restraining courts of equity from interfering with criminal prosecutions is reinforced by an even more vital consideration, the notion of 'comity,' that is, a proper respect for state functions, a recognition of the fact that the entire country is made up of a Union of separate state governments, and a continuance of the belief that the National Government will fare best if the States and their institutions are left free to perform their separate functions in their separate ways. This, perhaps for lack of a better and clearer way to describe it, is referred to by many as 'Our Federalism.' [T]he concept does not mean blind deference to 'States' Rights' any more than it means centralization of control over every important issue in our National Government and its courts. The Framers rejected both these courses. What the concept does represent is a system in which there is sensitivity to the legitimate interests of both State and

National Governments, and in which the National Government, anxious though it may be to vindicate and protect federal rights and federal interests, always endeavors to do so in ways that will not unduly interfere with the legitimate activities of the States."

Justice Black then turned to the impact of Dombrowski on this settled doctrine—and, contrary to the District Court, found none. (Some of his comments on Dombrowski, especially his criticism of the overbreadth technique, have been quoted earlier, in chap. 12.) Justice Black stated: "The district court, however, thought that the Dombrowski decision substantially broadened the availability of injunctions against state criminal prosecutions and that under that decision the federal courts may give equitable relief, without regard to any showing of bad faith or harassment, whenever a state statute is found 'on its face' to be vague or overly broad, in violation of the First Amendment. We recognize that there are some statements in the Dombrowski opinion that would seem to support this argument. [But] such statements were unnecessary to the decision of that case, because the Court found that the plaintiffs had alleged a basis for equitable relief under the long-established standards. In addition, we do not regard the reasons adduced to support this position as sufficient to justify such a substantial departure from the established doctrines regarding the availability of injunctive relief. . . .

"[T]he existence of a 'chilling effect,' even in the area of First Amendment rights, has never been considered a sufficient basis, in and of itself, for prohibiting state action. [T]he chilling effect that admittedly can result from the very existence of certain laws on the statute books does not in itself justify prohibiting the State from carrying out the important and necessary task of enforcing these laws against socially harmful conduct that the State believes in good faith to be punishable under its laws and the Constitution.

"Beyond all this is another, more basic consideration. Procedures for testing the constitutionality of a statute 'on its face' in the manner apparently contemplated by Dombrowski, and for then enjoining all action to enforce the statute until the State can obtain court approval for a modified version, are fundamentally at odds with the function of the federal courts in our constitutional plan. The power and duty of the judiciary to declare laws unconstitutional is in the final analysis derived from its responsibility for resolving concrete disputes brought before the courts for decision. [Marbury v. Madison.] But this vital responsibility, broad as it is, does not amount to an unlimited power to survey the statute books and pass judgment on laws before the courts are called upon to enforce them. [T]he task of analyzing a proposed statute, pinpointing its deficiencies, and requiring correction of these deficiencies before the statute is put into effect, is rarely if ever an appropriate task for the judiciary. The combination of the relative remoteness of the controversy, the impact on the legislative process of the relief sought, and above all the speculative and amorphous nature of the required line-by-line analysis of detailed statutes, see, e. g., Boyle v. Landry [sec. 3 above], ordinarily results in a kind of case that is wholly unsatisfactory for deciding constitutional questions, whichever way they might be decided. In light of this fundamental conception of the Framers as to the proper place of the federal courts in the governmental processes of passing and enforcing laws, it can seldom be ap-

propriate for these courts to exercise any such power of prior approval or veto over the legislative process.

"For these reasons, fundamental not only to our federal system but also to the basic functions of the Judicial Branch of the National Government under our Constitution, we hold that the Dombrowski decision should not be regarded as having upset the settled doctrines that have always confined very narrowly the availability of injunctive relief against state criminal prosecutions. We do not think that opinion stands for the proposition that a federal court can properly enjoin enforcement of a statute solely on the basis of a showing that the statute 'on its face' abridges First Amendment rights. There may, of course, be extraordinary circumstances in which the necessary irreparable injury can be shown even in the absence of the usual prerequisites of bad faith and harassment.[4] For example, as long ago as [Watson v. Buck, 313 U.S. 599 (1942)], we indicated: 'It is of course conceivable that a statute might be flagrantly and patently violative of express constitutional prohibitions in every clause, sentence and paragraph, and in whatever manner and against whomever an effort might be made to apply it.' Other unusual situations calling for federal intervention might also arise, but there is no point in our attempting now to specify what they might be."

2. *Samuels v. Mackell.* The Court relied on a similar approach in disposing of most of the companion cases. One of them, SAMUELS v. MACKELL, 401 U.S. 66 (1971), provided Justice Black with the occasion to discuss an issue not reached in his Younger v. Harris opinion—the question of *declaratory* rather than injunctive relief against *pending* state prosecutions. The appellants had all been indicted under New York's criminal anarchy law. They sought injunctive or declaratory relief in the federal court. Justice Black's opinion concluded that "under ordinary circumstances the same considerations that require the withholding of injunctive relief will make declaratory relief equally inappropriate." He explained his view that "the propriety of declaratory and injunctive relief should be judged by essentially the same standards" as follows:

"In both situations deeply rooted and long-settled principles of equity have narrowly restricted the scope for federal intervention, and ordinarily a declaratory judgment will result in precisely the same interference with and disruption of state proceedings that the long-standing policy limiting injunctions was designed to avoid. This is true for at least two reasons. In the first place, the Declaratory Judgment Act provides that after a declaratory judgment is issued the district court may enforce it by granting '[f]urther necessary or proper relief,' 28 U.S.C. § 2202, and therefore a declaratory judgment issued while state proceedings are pending might serve as the basis for a subsequent injunction against those proceedings to 'protect or effectuate' the declaratory judgment, 28 U.S.C. § 2283, and thus result in a clearly improper interference with the state proceedings. Secondly, even if the declaratory judgment is not used as a basis for actually issuing an injunction, the declaratory relief alone has virtually the same practical impact as a formal injunction would. . . . We therefore hold that, in cases where the state criminal prosecution was begun prior to the federal suit, the same equitable principles

---

4. For an elaboration of the "extraordinary circumstances" exception to the Younger v. Harris barrier, see Kugler v. Helfant, 421 U.S. —— (1975).

relevant to the propriety of an injunction must be taken into consideration by federal district courts in determining whether to issue a declaratory judgment, and that where an injunction would be impermissible under these principles, declaratory relief should ordinarily be denied as well."†

In stating his holding, Justice Black specifically limited it to "cases where the state criminal prosecution was begun prior to the federal suit." In those cases, where an injunction would be impermissible, "declaratory relief should ordinarily be denied as well." But, as with passages in his Younger v. Harris opinion, some of the broad reasons offered in support of the conclusion carried suggestions of applicability to the case of federal relief against *future* prosecutions as well. Because of these implications, the narrowness of some of the separate opinions warrants special emphasis. Justice Stewart, joined by Justice Harlan, joined Justice Black's prevailing opinion with a narrow restatement of the holding, emphasizing that it was limited to *pending* criminal proceedings. And in still another case—Perez v. Ledesma—401 U.S. 82, 98 (1971)—Justice Brennan, joined by Justices White and Marshall, had occasion to discuss the appropriateness of declaratory relief against *future* prosecutions—an issue the majority did not reach—and in the course of that opinion differed sharply from Justice Black's view of a practical identity of injunctive and declaratory relief. (And on that issue, Justice Brennan's position was subsequently embraced by the majority. See the next note.)*

2. *Threatened rather than pending state prosecutions and declaratory relief: Steffel v. Thompson.* Younger v. Harris and Samuels v. Mackell were explicitly limited to interference in *pending* prosecutions, despite some of the overtones in Justice Black's opinion. And three years later, the Court made it clear that the principles would not extend to interference in *threatened* state prosecutions. In STEFFEL v. THOMPSON, 416 U.S. 452 (1974), Justice Brennan had the opportunity in a majority opinion to adopt for the Court the views he had expressed in his separate opinion in one of the companion cases to Younger, Perez v. Ledesma, 401 U.S. 82, 93 (1971).

---

† Note also the partial reliance on Younger v. Harris principles to bar adjudication of a civil rights complaint, in O'Shea v. Littleton, 414 U.S. 488 (1974) (noted above). However, the Court has rejected lower court efforts to draw on the Younger principles to justify greater federal court abstention. See Lake Carriers' Ass'n v. MacMullan, 406 U.S. 498 (1972) (noted above).

* Are the Younger and Samuels principles applicable to federal court intervention in pending state civil proceedings? In his concurrence in Younger, Justice Stewart noted that in the context of civil rather than criminal cases, "the balance might be struck differently." Compare a later comment by Justice White, joined by Chief Justice Burger and Justice Blackmun, dissenting in Lynch v. Household Finance Corp., 405 U.S. 538 (1972): "Of course, [the Younger v. Harris group of cases] involved fed-

eral injunctions against state criminal proceedings, but the relevant considerations, in my view, are equally applicable where state civil litigation is in progress." Compare Gibson v. Berryhill, 411 U.S. 564 (1973), and note also Justice White's dissent in Fuentes v. Shevin, 407 U.S. 67 (1972). For a partial resolution of the question, see Huffman v. Pursue, Ltd., 420 U.S. — (1975), holding the Younger v. Harris principles applicable to intervention in a state civil action. The civil action was one to close, on "public nuisance" grounds, a theater allegedly showing obscene films. The majority emphasized that this was not a civil case between private parties, but "a state proceeding which [is] more akin to a criminal prosecution than are most civil cases." The dissenters feared that the decision was "obviously only the first step toward extending to state *civil* proceedings generally" the Younger principles.

Petitioners in Steffel had stopped distributing antiwar leaflets at a shopping center because of threats of prosecution under a state criminal trespass law. They sued for declaratory relief that the law was unconstitutional. The lower court had concluded that the bad faith harassment prerequisite for federal relief against *pending* state prosecutions, established in Younger v. Harris and Samuels v. Mackell, should be carried over to actions for *declaratory* relief against *threatened* state prosecutions as well. Justice Brennan's opinion for a unanimous Court in Steffel rejected that view and concluded instead that declaratory relief against a threatened rather than pending state prosecution is permissible without a showing of bad faith harassment. The Court concluded that "federal declaratory relief is not precluded when no state prosecution is pending and a federal plaintiff demonstrates a genuine threat of enforcement of a disputed state criminal statute, whether an attack is made on the constitutionality of the statute on its face or as applied." A concurring notation by Justice Stewart, joined by Chief Justice Burger, admonished that cases "where such a 'genuine threat' can be demonstrated will, I think, be exceedingly rare."

Justice Brennan explained the majority's conclusion as follows: "When no state criminal proceeding is pending at the time the federal complaint is filed, federal intervention does not result in duplicative legal proceedings or disruption of the state criminal justice system; nor can federal intervention, in that circumstance, be interpreted as reflecting negatively upon the state court's ability to enforce constitutional principles. In addition, while a pending state prosecution provides the federal plaintiff with a concrete opportunity to vindicate his constitutional rights, a refusal on the part of the federal courts to intervene when no state proceeding is pending may place the hapless plaintiff between the Scylla of intentionally flouting state law and the Charybdis of forgoing what he believes to be constitutionally protected activity in order to avoid becoming enmeshed in a criminal proceeding." Accordingly, when "no state proceeding is pending and thus considerations of equity, comity, and federalism have little vitality, the propriety of granting federal declaratory relief may properly be considered independently of a request for injunctive relief."

In explaining why the Court had recognized "that *different considerations* enter into a federal court's decision as to declaratory relief, on the one hand, and injunctive relief, on the other," Justice Brennan stated: "First, as Congress recognized in 1934, a declaratory judgment will have a less intrusive effect on the administration of state criminal laws. As was observed in Perez v. Ledesma, 401 U.S., at 124–126 (separate opinion of Brennan, J.):

> 'Of course, a favorable declaratory judgment may nevertheless be valuable to the plaintiff though it cannot make even an unconstitutional statute disappear. A state statute may be declared unconstitutional *in toto*—that is, incapable of having constitutional applications; or it may be declared unconstitutionally vague or overbroad—that is, incapable of being constitutionally applied to the full extent of its purport. In either case, a federal declaration of unconstitutionality reflects the opinion of the federal court that the statute cannot be fully enforced. If a declaration of total unconstitutionality is affirmed by this Court, it follows that this Court stands ready to reverse any conviction under the

statute. If a declaration of partial unconstitutionality is affirmed by this Court, the implication is that this Court will overturn particular applications of the statute, but that if the statute is narrowly construed by the state courts it will not be incapable of constitutional applications. Accordingly, the declaration does not necessarily bar prosecutions under the statute, as a broad injunction would. Thus, where the highest court of a State has had an opportunity to give a statute regulating expression a narrowing or clarifying construction but has failed to do so, and later a federal court declares the statute unconstitutionally vague or overbroad, it may well be open to a state prosecutor, after the federal court decision, to bring a prosecution under the statute if he reasonably believes that the defendant's conduct is not constitutionally protected and that the state courts may give the statute a construction so as to yield a constitutionally valid conviction. . . .'

"Second, engrafting upon the Declaratory Judgment Act a requirement that all of the traditional equitable prerequisites to the issuance of an injunction be satisfied before the issuance of a declaratory judgment is considered would defy Congress' intent to make declaratory relief available in cases where an injunction would be inappropriate. . . . Thus, the Court of Appeals was in error when it ruled that a failure to demonstrate irreparable injury—a traditional prerequisite to injunctive relief, having no equivalent in the law of declaratory judgments—precluded the granting of declaratory relief.

"The only occasions where this Court has disregarded these 'different considerations' and found that a preclusion of injunctive relief inevitably led to a denial of declaratory relief have been cases in which principles of federalism militated altogether against federal intervention in a class of adjudications. In the instant case, principles of federalism not only do not preclude federal intervention, they compel it. Requiring the federal courts totally to step aside when no state criminal prosecution is pending against the federal plaintiff would turn federalism on its head."

SECTION 5. NONJUSTICIABLE "POLITICAL QUESTIONS," "JUDICIALLY DISCOVERABLE AND MANAGEABLE STANDARDS," AND REAPPORTIONMENT LITIGATION

Introduction. This section pursues the consideration of the "political questions" doctrine begun in the concluding portions of chap. 7 above. Those materials, especially note 2 beginning at p. 473, should be reexamined at this point. As noted there, the concept that some constitutional issues are nonjusticiable because they are "political" is well established. But what the ingredients of that concept are has produced considerable controversy. There are at least three strands to the "political question" doctrine. The first, most confined, most clearly legitimate one is the "constitutional commitment" strand. That variety of political question reflects separation of powers principles and rests on the position that the Constitution commits the

final determination of some constitutional questions to agencies other than courts. But the Court's political questions decisions cannot all be explained on that "constitutional commitment" ground. As noted in chap. 7: "Some decisions on political questions nonjusticiability emphasize the nature of the question and its aptness for judicial resolution in view of judicial competence: that strand of the political questions doctrine finds some issues nonjusticiable because they cannot be resolved by 'judicially manageable standards,' or on the basis of data available to the courts. Still another, even more open-ended strand of the doctrine, suggests that the political questions notion is essentially a problem of judicial discretion, of prudential judgments that some issues ought not to be decided by the courts because they are too controversial or could produce enforcement problems or other institutional difficulties."

The political questions materials in chap. 7 emphasized the first, most clearly "constitutional interpretation" strand of the doctrine. It dealt with the arguable commitment of some issues to other branches for final decision, in such contexts as the reviewability of convictions upon impeachment and the Powell v. McCormack case. This section focuses on the more amorphous, "judicially discoverable and manageable" strand of the doctrine. The third, broadly prudential, ingredient of political questions notions has already surfaced in chap. 7 and underlies some of the materials in this section as well. After sampling some varieties of political questions contentions, this section explores at greater length one area once thought to be nonjusticiable and "political" and now a fertile source of constitutional litigation: the area of legislative districting. Baker v. Carr, Reynolds v. Sims, and their progeny provide the best modern examples of an area in which the "judicially manageable standards" obstacle proved a formidable but not insuperable one.

In examining the materials which follow, recall again the Court's effort to summarize the ingredients of the political questions doctrine, in the brief passage from Baker v. Carr, 369 U.S. 186 (1962), quoted in chap. 7 above and worth reiterating here: "It is apparent that several formulations which vary slightly according to the settings in which the questions arise may describe a political question, although each has one or more elements which identify it as essentially a function of the separation of powers. Prominent on the surface of any case held to involve a political question is found a textually demonstrable constitutional commitment of the issue to a coordinate political department; or a lack of judicially discoverable and manageable standards for resolving it; or the impossibility of deciding without an initial policy determination of a kind clearly for nonjudicial discretion; or the impossibility of a court's undertaking independent resolution without expressing lack of the respect due coordinate branches of government; or an unusual need for unquestioning adherence to a political decision already made; or the potentiality of embarrassment from multifarious pronouncements by various departments on one question."

The "textually demonstrable constitutional commitment" branch of the doctrine has already been examined, in chap. 7. To what extent are the other ingredients also "essentially a function of the separation of powers"? The "judicially discoverable and manageable standards" facet is a major concern below. Does the final group of factors listed in Baker v. Carr comprise essentially prudential considerations? Do the concerns about "lack of

the respect due coordinate branches" and "embarrassment from multifarious pronouncements" retain vitality, in view of the Court's handling of such concerns in Powell v. McCormack and United States v. Nixon, in chap. 7? To the extent that those prudential considerations remain an articulated part of the doctrine, do they represent a broad reservoir of discretion not to adjudicate? Is that a justifiable discretion? Is it consistent with the view of the bases of the Court's authority at the time of Marbury v. Madison? Is it an outgrowth of the view that has gained considerable acceptance since Marbury v. Madison, that the Court has a "special function" in constitutional interpretation, and that that special function justifies broad discretion as to the occasion for the exercises of the Court's powers? Is that discretion legitimate? Recall the related questions raised in sec. 4A above.

"LACK OF JUDICIALLY DISCOVERABLE AND MANAGEABLE STANDARDS" AND PRUDENTIAL CONSIDERATIONS: SOME EXAMPLES

1. *Lack of decisional criteria and relevant data: The Coleman v. Miller formulation.* a. *Chief Justice Hughes' opinion.* Does the passage below illustrate the "lack of judicially discoverable and manageable standards" strand of the political questions doctrine? To what extent is that lack an independent, justifiable ground of nonjusticiability? The passage below is from Chief Justice Hughes' opinion in COLEMAN v. MILLER, 307 U.S. 433 (1939). Chief Justice Hughes sought to explain why courts could not decide whether the Child Labor Amendment, proposed by Congress in 1924, had lost its vitality through lapse of time and accordingly could not be ratified by a state legislature in 1937. The proposed Amendment was designed to overturn the Court invalidations of congressional efforts to prohibit child labor.[1] In the Coleman case, members of the Kansas legislature who had voted against ratification of the Amendment sued to enjoin state officials from certifying the legislature's 1937 ratification resolution. One of the grounds of their suit was that "by reason [of] the failure of ratification within a reasonable time the proposed amendment had lost its vitality." The Court affirmed the state court's denial of relief. In explaining why the "reasonable time" issue was not justiciable, Chief Justice Hughes stated:[2]

"Where are to be found the criteria for such a judicial determination? None are to be found in Constitution or statute. In their endeavor to answer this question petitioners' counsel have suggested that at least two years should be allowed; that six years would not seem to be unreasonably long; that seven years had been used by the Congress as a reasonable period; that one year, six months and thirteen days was the average time used in passing upon amendments which have been ratified since the first ten amendments; that

---

1. Recall Hammer v. Dagenhart, chap. 3 above, and the Child Labor Tax Case, chap. 4 above.

2. Chief Justice Hughes' opinion was joined by only two other members of the seven-man majority. Several of the other Justices who joined in the result emphasized the legislators' lack of standing and the argument that problems of the amendment process were examples of issues wholly committed by the Constitution for final decision to a coordinate political department—to Congress. (The latter argument reflects the strand of the political questions doctrine considered in chap. 7 above.)

three years, six months and twenty-five days has been the longest time used in ratifying. To this list of variables, counsel add that 'the nature and extent of publicity and the activity of the public and of the legislatures of the several States in relation to any particular proposal should be taken into consideration.' That statement is pertinent, but there are additional matters to be examined and weighed. When a proposed amendment springs from a conception of economic needs, it would be necessary, in determining whether a reasonable time had elapsed since its submission, to consider the economic conditions prevailing in the country, whether these had so far changed since the submission as to make the proposal no longer responsive to the conception which inspired it or whether conditions were such as to intensify the feeling of need and the appropriateness of the proposed remedial action. *In short, the question of a reasonable time in many cases would involve, as in this case it does involve, an appraisal of a great variety of relevant conditions, political, social and economic, which can hardly be said to be within the appropriate range of evidence receivable in a court of justice and as to which it would be an extravagant extension of judicial authority to assert judicial notice as the basis of deciding a controversy with respect to the validity of an amendment actually ratified.* On the other hand, these conditions are appropriate for the consideration of the political departments of the Government. The questions they involve are essentially political and not justiciable. They can be decided by the Congress with the full knowledge and appreciation ascribed to the national legislature of the political, social and economic conditions which have prevailed during the period since the submission of the amendment." (Emphasis added.) *

b. *The adequacy of the formulation.* Does Chief Justice Hughes' formulation provide persuasive reasons for a finding of nonjusticiability? What were the critical reasons? The need for "appraisal of a great variety of relevant conditions, political, social and economic," not "within the appropriate range of evidence receivable" in the courts? Recall the variety of data relied on by the Court in constitutional decisions in the preceding chapters under such clauses as due process and equal protection and the First Amendment. For example, did Brown v. Board of Education involve a narrower range of "relevant conditions"? Did the Dennis case (chap. 12) involve greater difficulties in gathering relevant data?

---

* Are the constitutional amendment provisions in Art. V "textually demonstrable commitments" to another branch? In the Coleman case, Chief Justice Hughes, before turning to the "reasonable time" issue, disposed of the question whether a state legislature could ratify an amendment after a previous rejection: "[This question] should be regarded as a political question pertaining to the political departments, with the ultimate authority in the Congress in the exercise of its control over the promulgation of the adoption of the amendment." Note also the dispute in the battle over ratification of the proposed 27th Amendment, the Equal Rights Amendment, as to the effectiveness of ratification by two state legislatures who subsequently sought to revoke their ratification. Note also the concurring opinion by Justice Black in Coleman, for four of the Justices, objecting that the Court had not made it clear enough that the Constitution "grants Congress exclusive power to control submission of constitutional amendments."

The Court has however passed on amendment process issues in some contexts. See, e. g., Leser v. Garnett, 258 U.S. 130 (1922), finding the 19th Amendment validly adopted despite alleged procedural irregularities in the legislatures of two states. Moreover, Dillon v. Gloss, 256 U.S. 368 (1921), sustained the power of Congress to fix a time limit on ratification.

Instead of the "range of evidence" concern, was the central difficulty in Coleman that of formulating manageable judicial standards—the concern expressed in Chief Justice Hughes' opening question: "Where are to be found the criteria for such a judicial determination?" Selecting a particular time period as the "reasonable time" is awkward for courts, to be sure. But would it have been improper for the Court to select a period such as seven years? (Many amendments submitted by Congress in recent years have carried such a seven year time limitation.) Was it more difficult to formulate a seven-year limit in Coleman than, e. g., to devise the "one person-one vote" rule in Reynolds v. Sims, below?[3]

Did Coleman v. Miller rest ultimately on broader, prudential considerations? Note the comment that the Court's invalidations of congressional efforts to curb child labor were "difficult enough to square [with] democratic principle" and that "it would seem to be quite a different matter" if the Court, by imposing restrictions on the amendment process, had barred use of the amendment route to overturn the Court decisions. Though there might be constitutional flaws in the process of adopting a particular amendment, "this seems to be one instance in which the Court cannot assume responsibility for saying 'what the law is' without, at the same time, undermining the legitimacy of its power to do so." Scharpf, "Judicial Review and the Political Question: A Functional Analysis," 75 Yale L.J. 517 (1966).[4]

c. *Complexity, justiciability, and the merits.* Does the mere complexity of the question justify finding it nonjusticiable? Is that what Chief Justice Hughes suggested by his reference to "a great variety of relevant conditions"? Were the questions in Coleman truly more complex than those in many of the cases considered in the preceding chapters? Or in Baker v. Carr and Reynolds v. Sims, below? To what extent does the concern over complexity more properly go to the merits rather than to the issue of justiciability? Compare Justice Frankfurter's exploration of multiple variables in Baker v. Carr—and Justice Harlan's dissent in Reynolds v. Sims—with the simple "one person-one vote" rule ultimately adopted by the majority in Reynolds v. Sims. Was the majority's view on the merits the critical ingredient that turned the reapportionment issue once considered nonjusticiable into one the Court did undertake to decide: in short, was ultimate agreement on the "one person-one vote" rule critical to the surmounting of the "lack of manageable criteria" hurdle? Once so simple a rule was found justifiable on the merits, the difficulty as to the manageability of judicial cri-

---

3. Recall also the series of cases involving the permissible length of durational residency requirements in voting legislation, beginning with Dunn v. Blumstein, 405 U.S. 330 (1972) (chap. 10, sec. 4A, above).

4. Note also Professor Scharpf's more general effort to formulate the ingredients of the political questions barrier: "[The Supreme Court may find a political question] when its access to relevant information is insufficient to assure the correct determination of particular issues, when the Court would have to question the position taken by the government in an international dispute, or when an independent determination by the Court would interfere with the specific responsibilities of another department for dealing with a wider context which itself would be beyond the Court's reach. But even though one or more of these factors may be present, the Court will not usually apply the doctrine to the constitutional guarantees of individual rights and to conflicts of competence among the departments of the federal government and between the federal government and the states."

teria disappeared, did it not? (As to whether that simple rule was in fact a constitutionally justifiable one, and whether it has in fact promoted the values it was designed to serve, consider the contending positions in the reapportionment cases below.)

Even if the simple "one person-one vote" rule is unjustifiable, and even if the Justices who saw reapportionment issues as more complex were correct, was a finding of nonjusticiability defensible? Compare Justice Frankfurter's view in Baker v. Carr with that of Justice Harlan: What justification was there for finding Baker nonjusticiable, rather than holding on the merits that the challenged action was not unconstitutional?

2. *Lack of standards and criteria: Foreign affairs.* Some, but not all, questions in the foreign affairs area are nonjusticiable. Consider the Court's effort at summary in the passage below, from Justice Brennan's majority opinion in Baker v. Carr. What explains the nonjusticiability of some foreign relations issues? To what extent are they issues which are constitutionally "committed to another branch" for final decision? To what extent do the nonjusticiability rulings rest on prudential judgments? To what extent do they involve difficulties of access to relevant data or of lack of manageable criteria?[5] Justice Brennan stated in Baker v. Carr, 369 U.S. 186 (1962):

"There are sweeping statements to the effect that all questions touching on foreign relations are political questions. Not only does resolution of such issues frequently turn on standards that defy judicial application, or involve the exercise of a discretion demonstrably committed to the executive or legislature; but many such questions uniquely demand single-voiced statement of the Government's views. Yet it is error to suppose that every case or controversy which touches foreign relations lies beyond judicial cognizance. Our cases in this field seem invariably to show a discriminating analysis of the particular question posed, in terms of the history of its management by the political branches, of its susceptibility to judicial handling in the light of its nature and posture in the specific case, and of the possible consequences of judicial action. For example, though a court will not ordinarily inquire whether a treaty has been terminated, [if] there has been no conclusive 'governmental action' then a court can construe a treaty and may find it provides the answer."

3. *Prudential considerations.* a. *The Vietnam controversy.* Recall Professor Bickel's contention, noted in chap. 7, sec. 2, above, that the political questions doctrine does not involve "constitutional interpretation," insisting: "There is something different about it, in kind, not in degree, from the general 'interpretive process'; something greatly more flexible, something of prudence, not construction and principle."[6] To what extent

5. Recall the passage quoted in United States v. Nixon (chap. 7), in the discussion of judicial deference to executive decisions in the military and foreign affairs area: "The President, both as Commander-in-Chief and as the Nation's organ for foreign affairs, has available intelligence services whose reports are not and ought not to be published to the world. It would be intolerable that courts, without the relevant information, should review and perhaps nullify actions of the Executive taken on information properly held secret. Nor can courts sit *in camera* in order to be taken into executive confidences." Chicago and Southern Airlines v. Waterman Steamship Corp., 333 U.S. 103 (1948).

6. Note also Professor Bickel's comment, in The Least Dangerous Branch (1962),

do the materials considered in this section ultimately rest on prudential considerations? Were those considerations determinative, for example, in the Court's repeated refusals to consider the constitutionality of American military involvement in Indochina?

Recall the examples cited in chap. 7 above, especially Justice Stewart's dissent from the denial of certiorari in Mora v. McNamara, 389 U.S. 934 (1967), stating: "These are large and deeply troubling questions. Whether the Court would ultimately reach them depends, of course, upon the resolution of serious preliminary issues of justiciability." What issues of justiciability did those cases involve? Commitment of the issues to other branches? Judicial difficulties in formulating manageable criteria or getting access to relevant data? Or simply prudential avoidance? As noted in chap. 7, some lower courts did reach some of the issues presented in the challenges.

b. *Political party conventions.* Were prudential considerations predominant in the Court's refusal to intervene in a party convention dispute in O'Brien v. Brown, 409 U.S. 1 (1972)? That litigation reached the Court three days before the Democratic National Convention of 1972. The Convention's Credentials Committee had recommended seating groups of California and Illinois delegates. The excluded delegations challenged the Committee's actions in the federal courts. The California claimants, pledged to Senator McGovern, attacked a winner-take-all primary election scheme. The excluded Illinois delegation, led by Mayor Daley, had been excluded because it was not adequately representative, and the Illinois plaintiffs claimed, inter alia, that the Credentials Committee had established minority quotas in violation of equal protection. The District Court dismissed the actions as nonjusticiable, but the Court of Appeals reached the merits, holding for the California claimants and against those from Illinois. The Supreme Court's 6 to 3 per curiam ruling stayed the Court of Appeals decision: "In light of the availability of the convention as a forum to review the recommendations of the Credentials Committee, in which process the complaining parties might obtain the relief they have sought from the federal courts, the lack of precedent to support the extraordinary relief granted by the Court of Appeals, and the large public interest in allowing the political processes to function free from judicial supervision, we conclude the judgment of the Court of Appeals must be stayed." In the course of its brief opinion, the majority cited Luther v. Borden (below) and stated: "No case is cited to us in which any federal court has undertaken to interject itself into the deliberative processes of a national political convention." Justices Douglas, White, and Marshall dissented. Justice Marshall's dissent, joined by Justice Douglas, insisted that any claim of "poli-

that the political questions doctrine rests on "the Court's sense of lack of capacity, compounded in unequal parts of (a) the strangeness of the issue and its intractability to principled resolution; (b) the sheer momentousness of it, which tends to unbalance judicial judgment; (c) the anxiety, not so much that the judicial judgment will be ignored, as that perhaps it should be but will not be; (d) finally, [the] inner vulnerability, the self-doubt of an institution which is electorally irresponsible and has no earth to draw strength from." Did the Vietnam war and the party convention dispute, below, present such "momentous" issues? More momentous than the reapportionment dispute, below, and the school segregation dispute, chap. 10? Was Luther v. Borden, below, a case that fits Bickel's description? Do the criteria he lists justify Court refusals to adjudicate?

tical questions" nonjusticiability was misconceived since that doctrine dealt with the "very different problem" of avoiding conflict with the coordinate branches of government.[7]

4. *The Guarantee Clause.* a. The Court has consistently asserted—and reiterated in Baker v. Carr, below—that the opening provision of Art. IV, § 4, is nonjusticiable. That provision states: "The United States shall guarantee to every State in this Union a Republican Form of Government . . . ." Note, e. g., PACIFIC STATES TEL. & TEL. CO. v. OREGON, 223 U.S. 118 (1912), refusing to adjudicate a claim that a law enacted via Oregon's initiative and referendum procedure violated the Guarantee Clause. The Court's opinion emphasized "the inconceivable expansion of the judicial power and the ruinous destruction of legislative authority in matters purely political which would necessarily be occasioned by giving sanction to the doctrine which underlies and would be necessarily involved in sustaining the propositions contended for." Chief Justice White stated that adjudication of such an issue would mean examination of contentions "as to the illegal existence of a State"; and "if such contention be thought well founded to disregard the existence in fact of the State, of its recognition by all of the departments of the Federal Government, and practically award a decree absolving it from all obligation to contribute to the support of or obey the laws of such established state government." Courts would have to build new state governments on "the ruins of the previously established" ones, and would have to "control the legislative department of the Government of the United States in the recognition of such new government and the admission of representatives therefrom."

Would justiciability of the Guarantee Clause inevitably involve such cataclysmic consequences? Is this an example of "too momentous" an issue for the courts? The majority in Baker v. Carr, below, explained the decision on the ground that the clause "is not a repository of judicially manageable standards." Was Baker v. Carr nevertheless really "a Guarantee Clause claim masquerading under a different label," as Justice Frankfurter's dissent argued? Should the Clause be found justiciable, at least in some contexts? See Bonfield, "Baker v. Carr: New Light on the Constitutional Guarantee of Republican Government," 50 Calif.L.Rev. 245 (1962): "The clause is neither textually committed to the exclusive enforcement of another department, nor bare of judicially discoverable or manageable standards." [8]

b. The best known Guarantee Clause case is LUTHER v. BORDEN, 7 How. 1 (1849). In summarizing political questions decisions in Baker

---

7. Three days later, the Democratic National Convention reached results identical to those of the Court of Appeals: it seated the California McGovern slate but refused to seat the Illinois Daley delegation.

Cf. Cousins v. Wigoda, 419 U.S. 477 (1975), holding that a state court could not interfere with the selection of delegates to a national party convention. The Court stated that a national party and its supporters "enjoy a constitu-

tionally protected right of political association" and that a state's interest in the integrity of its electoral process is not a "compelling" justification for interference in the selection of delegates.

8. See also Bonfield, "The Guarantee Clause of Article IV, Section 4: A Study in Constitutional Desuetude," 46 Minn.L.Rev. 513 (1962).

v. Carr, below, Justice Brennan described the case as follows: "Luther v. Borden, though in form simply an action for damages for trespass was, as Daniel Webster said in opening the argument for the defense, 'an unusual case.' The defendants, admitting an otherwise tortious breaking and entering, sought to justify their action on the ground that they were agents of the established lawful government of Rhode Island, which State was then under martial law to defend itself from active insurrection; that the plaintiff was engaged in that insurrection; and that they entered under orders to arrest the plaintiff. The case arose 'out of the unfortunate political differences which agitated the people of Rhode Island in 1841 and 1842,' 7 How., at 34, and which had resulted in a situation wherein two groups laid competing claims to recognition as the lawful government. The plaintiff's right to recover depended on which of the two groups was entitled to such recognition; but the lower court's refusal to receive evidence or hear argument on that issue, its charge to the jury that the earlier established or 'charter' government was lawful, and the verdict for the defendants, were affirmed upon appeal to this Court.   .   .   .

"Clearly, several factors were thought by the Court in Luther to make the question there 'political': the commitment to the other branches of the decision as to which is the lawful state government; the unambiguous action by the President, in recognizing the charter government as the lawful authority; the need for finality in the executive's decision; and the lack of criteria by which a court could determine which form of government was republican."

But Chief Justice Taney's opinion in Luther v. Borden also expressed concerns similar to those of Chief Justice White in the Pacific Tel. & Tel. Co. case, above. He stated that if the Court were to enter the controversy and decide "that the charter government had no legal existence during the period of time above mentioned,—if it had been annulled by the adoption of the opposing government,—then the laws passed by the legislature during that time were nullities; its taxes wrongfully collected; its salaries and compensation to its officers illegally paid; its public account improperly settled; and the [judgments] of its courts in civil and criminal cases null and void, and the officers who carried their decisions into operation answerable as trespassers, if not in some cases as criminals." Does Justice Brennan's summary of the case adequately reflect that "momentousness" concern? Would that concern be present in every case in which a Guarantee Clause claim might be raised? [9]

9. For the political background of Luther v. Borden, see generally Gettleman, The Dorr Rebellion (1973); Wiecek, The Guarantee Clause of the U. S. Constitution (1972); Conron, "Law, Politics, and Chief Justice Taney: A Reconsideration of the Luther v. Borden Decision," 11 Am.J.Leg.Hist. 377 (1967); and Schuchman, "The Political Background of the Political Question Doctrine: The Judges and the Dorr War," 16 Am.J.Leg.Hist. 111 (1972). See also the comment that "the Court's political motivations in the case contradicted the very princi-

ple that it was enunciating," and noting "the paradox that in this classic statement of grounds for judicial restraint, Taney's refusal to accept jurisdiction was accompanied by an extended discussion of the substantive issues in the case." Fehrenbacher, "Book Review," 42 U.Chi.L.Rev. 216 (1974).

Note also a footnote in Justice Douglas' separate opinion in Baker v. Carr, below, insisting: "The statements in [Luther v. Borden] that this guaranty is enforceable only by Congress or the Chief Executive is not maintain-

LEGISLATIVE REAPPORTIONMENT: THE FORMULATION AND ELABORATION OF JUDICIALLY MANAGEABLE STANDARDS

Introduction. Before 1962, legislative districting controversies were thought to be nonjusticiable. But in that year, in Baker v. Carr, the divided Court rejected the claim that equal protection challenges to legislative apportionments were nonjusticiable. In that case, the Court expressed confidence that judicially manageable standards could be formulated. The formulation of standards began two years later, with the "one person-one vote" decision in Reynolds v. Sims. Since then, the Court has had frequent occasion to elaborate and administer the equal protection approach of Reynolds v. Sims.

In examining the predecessors and progeny of Reynolds v. Sims, consider the implications for the "judicially discoverable and manageable standards" strand of the political questions doctrine. Did the judgment in Baker v. Carr that manageable standards could be fashioned imply a preliminary judgment on the merits? Did it take the simple-sounding Reynolds v. Sims "one person-one vote" principle to lay to rest the doubts about the manageability of reapportionment standards? Are Reynolds v. Sims and its progeny adequately responsive to the values as to representation which the Court has found in the equal protection clause? What are those values?

The situation before Baker v. Carr. The pre-Baker v. Carr attitude as to the justiciability of districting disputes is reflected in Justice Frankfurter's opinion in COLEGROVE v. GREEN, 328 U.S. 549 (1946). In Colegrove, the majority refused to reach the merits of a federal court challenge to the congressional districting scheme in Illinois. Only seven Justices participated in the decisions. The challengers contended that the Illinois law prescribing congressional districts was unconstitutional because the districts were not approximately equal in population. Justice Frankfurter announced the judgment of the Court affirming the dismissal of the complaint, but his opinion was joined only by Justices Reed and Burton. He stated: "We are of opinion that the petitioners ask of this Court what is beyond its competence to grant. This is one of those demands on judicial power which cannot be met by verbal fencing about 'jurisdiction.' [E]ffective working of our government revealed this issue to be of a peculiarly political nature and therefore not meet for judicial determination. [T]his controversy concerns matters that bring courts into immediate and active relations with party contests. From the determination of such issues this Court has traditionally remained aloof. It is hostile to a democratic system to involve the judiciary in the politics of the

able. [T]he abdication of all judicial functions respecting voting rights, however justified by the peculiarities of the charter form of government in Rhode Island at the time of Dorr's Rebellion, states no general principle. It indeed is contrary [to] the modern decisions of the Court that give the full panoply of judicial protection to voting rights. [Recall chap. 10, sec. 4A.] . . . Moreover, the Court's refusal to examine the legality of the regime of martial law which had been laid upon Rhode Island is indefensible." Note also Justice Douglas' comment in another footnote in Baker v. Carr: "The category of the 'political' question is, in my view, narrower than the decided cases indicate."

people. [D]ue regard for the Constitution as a viable system precludes judicial correction. Authority for dealing with such problems resides elsewhere. [Art. I, § 4.] The short of it is that the Constitution has conferred upon Congress exclusive authority to secure fair representation by the States in the popular House and left to that House determination whether States have fulfilled their responsibilities. ". . . Courts ought not to enter this political thicket." The deciding vote was cast by Justice Rutledge, who concurred in the result. He thought the issue was justiciable, but concluded that the complaint should be dismissed for want of equity: "I think the case is of so delicate a character [that] the jurisdiction should be exercised only in the most compelling circumstances. . . . The right here is not absolute. And the cure sought may be worse than the disease. I think, therefore, the case is one in which the Court may properly, and should, decline to exercise its jurisdiction." Justice Black, joined by Justices Douglas and Murphy, dissented, insisting that "the complaint presented a justiciable case and controversy." [1]

BAKER v. CARR

369 U.S. 186, 82 S.Ct. 691, 7 L.Ed.2d 663 (1962).

Appeal from the District Court for the Middle District of Tennessee.

Mr. Justice BRENNAN delivered the opinion of the Court.

This civil action was brought under 42 U.S.C. §§ 1983 and 1988 to redress the alleged deprivation of federal constitutional rights. The complaint, alleging that by means of a 1901 statute of Tennessee apportioning the members of the General Assembly among the State's 95 counties, "these plaintiffs and others similarly situated, are denied the equal protection of the laws accorded them by the Fourteenth Amendment to the Constitution of the United States by virtue of the debasement of their votes," was dismissed by a three-judge court [which] held that it lacked jurisdiction of the subject matter and also that no claim was stated upon which relief could be granted. . . . We hold that the dismissal was error, and remand the cause to the District Court for [further proceedings] consistent with this opinion. . . .

. . . . Tennessee's standard for allocating legislative representation among her counties is the total number of qualified voters resident in the respective counties, subject only to minor qualifications. . . . In 1901 the General Assembly . . . passed the Apportionment Act here in controversy. In the more than 60 years since that action, all proposals in both Houses of the General Assembly for reapportionment have failed to pass.

---

1. See also South v. Peters, 339 U.S. 276 (1950), challenging Georgia's county unit system in state elections. The Supreme Court affirmed the lower court's dismissal of the suit: "Federal courts consistently refuse to exercise their equity powers in cases posing political issues arising from a state's geographical distribution of electoral strength among its political subdivisions." (The county unit system was held unconstitutional after Reynolds v. Sims, in Gray v. Sanders, 372 U.S. 368 (1963).)

Compare Gomillion v. Lightfoot, 364 U.S. 339 (1960) (chap. 10, sec. 2A, above), where Justice Frankfurter wrote for the Court in holding a redrawing of the city boundaries of Tuskegee, Alabama, unconstitutional as a device to disenfranchise Blacks, in violation of the 15th Amendment.

Between 1901 and 1961, Tennessee has experienced substantial growth and redistribution of her population. . . . It is primarily the continued application of the 1901 Apportionment Act to this shifted and enlarged voting population which gives rise to the present controversy. [The complaint alleges] that "because of the population changes since 1900, and the failure of the Legislature to reapportion itself since 1901," the 1901 statute became "unconstitutional and obsolete." Appellants also argue that, because of the composition of the legislature effected by the 1901 Apportionment Act, redress in the form of a state constitutional amendment to change the entire mechanism for reapportioning, or any other change short of that, is difficult or impossible. [Appellants] seek a declaration that the 1901 statute is unconstitutional and an injunction restraining the appellees from acting to conduct any further elections under it. . . .

. . . [W]e hold today only (a) that the court possessed jurisdiction of the subject matter; (b) that a justiciable cause of action is stated upon which appellants would be entitled to appropriate relief; and (c) because appellees raise the issue before this Court, that the appellants have standing to challenge the Tennessee apportionment statutes. Beyond noting that we have no cause at this stage to doubt the District Court will be able to fashion relief if violations of constitutional rights are found, it is improper now to consider what remedy would be most appropriate if appellants prevail at the trial . . .

In holding that the subject matter of this suit was not justiciable, the District Court relied on Colegrove v. Green [in the note preceding this case] and subsequent per curiam cases. [The District Court read those cases] as compelling the conclusion that since the appellants sought to have a legislative apportionment held unconstitutional, their suit presented a "political question" and was therefore nonjusticiable. We hold that this challenge to an apportionment presents no nonjusticiable "political question." . . .

Of course the mere fact that the suit seeks protection of a political right does not mean it presents a political question. Such an objection "is little more than a play upon words." Rather, it is argued that apportionment cases, whatever the actual wording of the complaint, can involve no federal constitutional right except one resting on the guaranty of a republican form of government [Art. IV, § 4], and that complaints based on that clause have been held to present political questions which are nonjusticiable.

We hold that the claim pleaded here neither rests upon nor implicates the Guaranty Clause and that its justiciability is therefore not foreclosed by our decisions of cases involving that clause. . . . To show why we reject the argument based on the Guaranty Clause we must examine the authorities under it. But because there appears to be some uncertainty as to why those cases did present political questions, and specifically as to whether this apportionment case is like those cases, we deem it necessary first to consider the contours of the "political question" doctrine. . . . [Our] review reveals that in the Guaranty Clause cases and in the other "political question" cases, it is the relationship between the judiciary and the coordinate branches of the Federal Government, and not the federal judiciary's relationship to the States, which gives rise to the "political question." . . .

It is apparent that several formulations which vary slightly according to the settings in which the questions arise may describe a political question, although each has one or more elements which identifies it as essentially a function of the separation of powers. Prominent on the surface of any case held to involve a political question is found a textually demonstrable constitutional commitment of the issue to a coordinate political department; or a lack of judicially discoverable and manageable standards for resolving it; or the impossibility of deciding without an initial policy determination of a kind clearly for nonjudicial discretion; or the impossibility of a court's undertaking independent resolution without expressing lack of the respect due coordinate branches of government; or an unusual need for unquestioning adherence to a political decision already made; or the potentiality of embarrassment from multifarious pronouncements by various departments on one question.

Unless one of these formulations is inextricable from the case at bar, there should be no dismissal for nonjusticiability on the ground of a political question's presence. . . . But it is argued that this case shares the characteristics of [cases] concerning the Constitution's guaranty, in Art. IV, § 4, of a republican form of government. A conclusion as to whether the case at bar does present a political question cannot be confidently reached until we have considered those cases with special care. We shall discover that Guaranty Clause claims involve those elements which define a "political question," and for that reason and no other, they are nonjusticiable. In particular, we shall discover that the nonjusticiability of such claims has nothing to do with their touching upon matters of state governmental organization. . . .

[T]he only significance that [Luther v. Borden, above] could have for our immediate purposes is in its holding that the Guaranty Clause is not a repository of judicially manageable standards which a court could utilize independently in order to identify a State's lawful government. The Court has since refused tō resort to the Guaranty Clause—which alone had been invoked for the purpose—as the source of a constitutional standard for invalidating state action. See, [e. g.], Pacific States Tel. Co. v. Oregon, 223 U.S. 118 (claim that initiative and referendum negated republican government held nonjusticiable); . . . Ohio ex rel. Bryant v. Akron Metropolitan Park District, 281 U.S. 74 (claim that rule requiring invalidation of statute by all but one justice of state court negated republican government held nonjusticiable); Highland Farms Dairy v. Agnew, 300 U.S. 608 (claim that delegation to agency of power to control milk prices violated republican government, rejected). . . .

We come, finally to the ultimate inquiry whether our precedents as to what constitutes a nonjusticiable "political question" bring the case before us under the umbrella of that doctrine. A natural beginning is to note whether any of the common characteristics which we have been able to identify and label descriptively are present. We find none: The question here is the consistency of state action with the Federal Constitution. We have no question decided, or to be decided, by a political branch of government coequal with this Court. Nor do we risk embarrassment of our government abroad, or grave disturbance at home if we take issue with Tennessee as to the constitutionality of her action here challenged. Nor need the appellants,

in order to succeed in this action, ask the Court to enter upon policy determinations for which judicially manageable standards are lacking. Judicial standards under the Equal Protection Clause are well developed and familiar, and it has been open to courts since the enactment of the Fourteenth Amendment to determine, if on the particular facts they must, that a discrimination reflects *no* policy, but simply arbitrary and capricious action.

This case does, in one sense, involve the allocation of political power within a State, and the appellants might conceivably have added a claim under the Guaranty Clause. Of course, as we have seen, any reliance on that clause would be futile. But because any reliance on the Guaranty Clause could not have succeeded it does not follow that appellants may not be heard on the equal protection claim which in fact they tender. . . .

We conclude then that the nonjusticiability of claims resting on the Guaranty Clause which arises from their embodiment of questions that were thought "political," can have no bearing upon the justiciability of the equal protection claim presented in this case. Finally, we emphasize that it is the involvement in Guaranty Clause claims of the elements thought to define "political questions," and no other feature, which could render them nonjusticiable. . . .

We conclude that the complaint's allegations of a denial of equal protection present a justiciable constitutional cause of action upon which appellants are entitled to a trial and a decision. The right asserted is within the reach of judicial protection under the Fourteenth Amendment. . . .

Reversed and remanded.*

Mr. Justice CLARK, concurring. . . .

. . . Try as one may, Tennessee's apportionment just cannot be made to fit the pattern cut by its Constitution. . . . An examination of Table I accompanying this opinion [omitted here] conclusively reveals that the apportionment picture in Tennessee is a topsy-turvical of gigantic proportions. This is not to say that some of the disparity cannot be explained, but when the entire Table is examined—comparing the voting strength of counties of like population as well as contrasting that of the smaller with the larger counties—it leaves but one conclusion, namely that Tennessee's apportionment is a crazy quilt without rational basis. . . .

Although I find the Tennessee apportionment statute offends the Equal Protection Clause, I would not consider intervention by this Court into so delicate a field if there were any other relief available to the people of Tennessee. But the majority of the people of Tennessee have no "practical opportunities for exerting their political weight at the polls" to correct the existing "invidious discrimination." Tennessee has no initiative and referendum. I have searched diligently for other "practical opportunities" present under the law. I find none other than through the federal courts. [T]he legislative policy has riveted the present seats in the Assembly to their respective constituencies, and by the votes of their incumbents a reapportionment of any kind is prevented. [We must] conclude that the people of Tennessee are stymied and without judicial intervention will be

---

* A concurring opinion by Justice Douglas is omitted. Justice Whittaker did not participate in the decision of the case.

saddled with the present discrimination in the affairs of their state government.   .   .   .

Mr. Justice STEWART, concurring.   .   .   .

Contrary to the suggestion of my brother Harlan, the Court does not say or imply that "state legislatures must be so structured as to reflect with approximate equality the voice of every voter."   .   .   .   The Court does not say or imply that there is anything in the Federal Constitution "to prevent a State, acting not irrationally, from choosing any electoral legislative structure it thinks best suited to the interests, temper, and customs of its people."   .   .   .   And contrary to the suggestion of my brother Douglas, the Court most assuredly does not decide the question, "may a State weight the vote of one county or one district more heavily than it weights the vote in another?"   .   .   .

[T]he Court today decides only: (1) that the District Court possessed jurisdiction of the subject matter;   (2) that the complaint presents a justiciable controversy;   (3) that the appellants have standing.   My brother Clark has made a convincing prima facie showing that Tennessee's system of apportionment is in fact utterly arbitrary—without any possible justification in rationality.   My brother Harlan has, with imagination and ingenuity, hypothesized possibly rational bases for Tennessee's system.   But the merits of this case are not before us now.   .   .   .

Mr. Justice FRANKFURTER, whom Mr. Justice HARLAN joins, dissenting.   .   .   .

A hypothetical claim resting on abstract assumptions is now for the first time made the basis for affording illusory relief for a particular evil even though it foreshadows deeper and more pervasive difficulties in consequence.   The claim is hypothetical and the assumptions are abstract because the Court does not vouchsafe the lower courts—state and federal—guidelines for formulating specific, definite, wholly unprecedented remedies for the inevitable litigations that today's umbrageous disposition is bound to stimulate in connection with politically motivated reapportionments in so many States.   In such a setting, to promulgate jurisdiction in the abstract is meaningless.   It is as devoid of reality as "a brooding omnipresence in the sky" for it conveys no intimation what relief, if any, a District Court is capable of affording that would not invite legislatures to play ducks and drakes with the judiciary.   For this Court to direct the District Court to enforce a claim to which the Court has over the years consistently found itself required to deny legal enforcement and at the same time to find it necessary to withhold any guidance to the lower court how to enforce this turnabout, new legal claim, manifests an odd—indeed an esoteric—conception of judicial propriety.   .   .   .   Even assuming the indispensable intellectual disinterestedness on the part of judges in such matters, they do not have accepted legal standards or criteria or even reliable analogies to draw upon for making judicial judgments.   .   .   .

Recent legislation, creating a district appropriately described as "an atrocity of ingenuity," is not unique.   Considering the gross inequality among legislative electoral units within almost every State, the Court naturally shrinks from asserting that in districting at least substantial equality

is a constitutional requirement enforceable by courts. Room continues to be allowed for weighting. This of course implies that geography, economics, urban-rural conflict, and all the other non-legal factors which have throughout our history entered into political districting are to some extent not to be ruled out in the undefined vista now opened up by review in the federal courts of state reapportionments. To some extent—aye, there's the rub. In effect, today's decision empowers the courts of the country to devise what should constitute the proper composition of the legislatures of the fifty States. . . .

. . . [T]here is not under our Constitution a judicial remedy for every political mischief, for every undesirable exercise of legislative power. The Framers carefully and with deliberate forethought refused so to enthrone the judiciary. In this situation, as in others of like nature, appeal for relief does not belong here. Appeal must be to an informed, civically militant electorate. . . .

The [Colegrove v. Green] doctrine, in the form in which repeated decisions have settled it, was not an innovation. It represents long judicial thought and experience. From its earliest opinions this Court has consistently recognized a class of controversies which do not lend themselves to judicial standards and judicial remedies. To classify the various instances as "political questions" is rather a form of stating this conclusion than revealing of analysis. Some of the cases so labelled have no relevance here. But from others emerge unifying considerations that are compelling. . . .

The influence of these converging considerations—the caution not to undertake decision where standards meet for judicial judgment are lacking, the reluctance to interfere with matters of state government in the absence of an unquestionable and effectively enforceable mandate, the unwillingness to make courts arbiters of the broad issues of political organization historically committed to other institutions and for whose adjustment the judicial process is ill-adapted—has been decisive of the settled line of cases, reaching back more than a century, which holds that Art. IV, § 4, of the Constitution, guaranteeing to the States "a Republican Form of Government," is not enforceable through the courts. . . .

The present case involves all of the elements that have made the Guarantee Clause cases non-justiciable. It is, in effect, a Guarantee Clause claim masquerading under a different label. But it cannot make the case more fit for judicial action that appellants invoke the Fourteenth Amendment rather than Art. IV, § 4, where, in fact, the gist of their complaint is the same— unless it can be found that the Fourteenth Amendment speaks with greater particularity to their situation. . . . Art. IV, § 4, is not committed by express constitutional terms to Congress. It is the nature of the controversies arising under it, nothing else, which has made it judicially unenforceable. . . .

What, then, is this question of legislative apportionment? Appellants invoke the right to vote and to have their votes counted. But they are permitted to vote and their votes are counted. They go to the polls, they cast their ballots, they send their representatives to the state councils. Their complaint is simply that the representatives are not sufficiently numerous or powerful—in short, that Tennessee has adopted a basis of representation

with which they are dissatisfied. Talk of "debasement" or "dilution" is circular talk. One cannot speak of "debasement" or "dilution" of the value of a vote until there is first defined a standard of reference as to what a vote should be worth. What is actually asked of the Court in this case is to choose among competing bases of representation—ultimately, really, among competing theories of political philosophy—in order to establish an appropriate frame of government for the State of Tennessee and thereby for all the States of the Union.   .   .   .

The notion that representation proportioned to the geographic spread of population is so universally accepted as a necessary element of equality between man and man that it must be taken to be the standard of a political equality preserved by the Fourteenth Amendment—that it is, in appellants' words, "the basic principle of representative government"—is, to put it bluntly, not true. However desirable and however desired by some among the great political thinkers and framers of our government, it has never been generally practiced, today or in the past.   .   .   .   Unless judges, the judges of this Court, are to make their private views of political wisdom the measure of the Constitution—views which in all honesty cannot but give the appearance, if not reflect the reality, of involvement with the business of partisan politics so inescapably a part of apportionment controversies—the Fourteenth Amendment, "itself a historical product,"   .   .   . provides no guide for judicial oversight of the representation problem. .   .   .

.   .   .   Apportionment, by its character, is a subject of extraordinary complexity, involving—even after the fundamental theoretical issues concerning what is to be represented in a representative legislature have been fought out or compromised—considerations of geography, demography, electoral convenience, economic and social cohesions or divergencies among particular local groups, communications, the practical effects of political institutions like the lobby and the city machine, ancient traditions and ties of settled usage, respect for proven incumbents of long experience and senior status, mathematical mechanics, censuses compiling relevant data, and a host of others.   .   .   .   The practical significance of apportionment is that the next election results may differ because of it. Apportionment battles are overwhelmingly party or intra-party contests. It will add a virulent source of friction and tension in federal state relations to embroil the federal judiciary in them.   .   .   .

Dissenting opinion of Mr. Justice HARLAN, whom Mr. Justice FRANKFURTER joins.   .   .   .

Once one cuts through the thicket of discussion devoted to "jurisdiction," "standing," "justiciability," and "political question," there emerges a straight-forward issue which, in my view, is determinative of this case. Does the complaint disclose a violation of a federal constitutional right   .   .   .?
The majority opinion does not actually discuss this basic question, but, as one concurring Justice observes, seems to decide it "sub silentio." However, in my opinion, appellants' allegations, accepting all of them as true, do not, parsed down or as a whole, show an infringement by Tennessee of any rights assured by the Fourteenth Amendment. Accordingly, I believe the complaint should have been dismissed for "failure to state a claim upon

which relief can be granted." Fed.Rules Civ.Proc., Rule 12(b)(6). . . .
Until it is first decided [whether] what Tennessee has done or failed to do
in this instance runs afoul of any [constitutional] limitation, we need not
reach the issues of "justiciability" or "political question" . . . .

The suggestion of my Brother Frankfurter that courts lack standards
by which to decide such cases as this, is relevant not only to the question of "justiciability," but also, and perhaps more fundamentally, to the
determination whether any cognizable constitutional claim has been asserted
in this case. Courts are unable to decide when it is that an apportionment
originally valid becomes void because the factors entering into such a
decision are basically matters appropriate only for legislative judgment. And
so long as there exists a possible rational legislative policy for retaining an
existing apportionment, such a legislative decision cannot be said to breach
the bulwark against arbitrariness and caprice that the Fourteenth Amendment
affords. . . .

. . . Those observers of the Court who see it primarily as the last
refuge for the correction of all inequality or injustice, no matter what its
nature or source, will no doubt applaud this decision and its break with the
past. Those who consider that continuing national respect for the Court's
authority depends in large measure upon its wise exercise of self-restraint
and discipline in constitutional adjudication, will view the decision with deep
concern.*

---

* For a sampling of the extensive commentary on Baker v. Carr, see Neal,
"Baker v. Carr: Politics in Search
of Law," 1962 Sup.Ct.Rev. 252;
McCloskey, "Foreword: The Reapportionment Case," 76 Harv.L.Rev.
54 (1962); Emerson, "Malapportionment and Judicial Power," 72 Yale
L.J. 64 (1962); and McKay, "Political Thickets and Crazy Quilts:
Reapportionment and Equal Protection," 61 Mich.L.Rev. 645 (1963).

Between Baker and Carr in 1962, and
Reynolds v. Sims in 1964, the Court
decided two important cases discussed
in the majority opinion in Reynolds
v. Sims, which follows. Gray v.
Sanders, 372 U.S. 368 (1963), struck
down Georgia's county unit system in
primary elections of state-wide officers. The Court purported not to
reach most of the questions left open
by Baker v. Carr. The majority insisted that this was "only a voting
case" and emphasized that the case
had nothing to do "with the composition of the state or federal legislature." Note also Justice Stewart's
concurrence in Gray v. Sanders: "We
do not deal here with 'the basic
groundrules implementing Baker v.
Carr.' . . . Within a given constituency, there can be room for but
a single constitutional rule—one voter,
one vote." Compare the use made of
Gray v. Sanders in Reynolds v. Sims.

In the second major case, Wesberry v.
Sanders, 376 U.S. 1 (1964), the
Court held—without reaching the 14th
Amendment claims—"that, construed
in its historical context, the command
of Art. I, § 2, that Representatives
be chosen 'by the People of the several States' means that as nearly as
practicable one man's vote in a congressional election is to be worth as
much as another's." The Court accordingly struck down Georgia's congressional districting statute. Note the
use made of this decision in Reynolds
v. Sims. (On the Court's use—or misuse—of historical materials in Wesberry, see, e. g., Kelly, "Clio and the
Court: An Illicit Love Affair," 1965
Sup.Ct.Rev. 119, 134.)

REYNOLDS v. SIMS

377 U.S. 533, 84 S.Ct. 1362, 12 L.Ed.2d 506 (1964).

Appeal from the District Court for the Middle District of Alabama.

[Within a year of Baker v. Carr, suits challenging state legislative apportionment schemes were instituted in over 30 states. The major decision answering some of the questions left open by Baker v. Carr came two years after, in Reynolds v. Sims. That case was a challenge to the malapportionment of the Alabama legislature. The challengers claimed discrimination against voters in counties whose populations had grown proportionately far more than others since the 1900 census. The complainants in Reynolds noted that the existing districting scheme was based on the 1900 census, even though the state constitution required legislative representation based on population and decennial reapportionment. A three-judge district court held that the old apportionment as well as two new ones devised by the legislature violated the equal protection guarantee. The lower court ordered temporary reapportionment for the 1962 election by combining features of the two plans newly devised by the legislature. Both sides in the lawsuit appealed.]

Mr. Chief Justice WARREN delivered the opinion of the Court.
. . .

II. Undeniably the Constitution of the United States protects the right of all qualified citizens to vote, in state as well as in federal elections. A consistent line of decisions by this Court in cases involving attempts to deny or restrict the right of suffrage has made this indelibly clear. [See, and compare, chap. 10, sec. 4A, above.] . . . The right to vote freely for the candidate of one's choice is of the essence of a democratic society and any restrictions on that right strike at the heart of representative government. And the right of suffrage can be denied by a debasement or dilution of the weight of a citizen's vote just as effectively as by wholly prohibiting the free exercise of the franchise. . . .

[Gray v. Sanders and Wesberry v. Sanders—both noted above—] are of course not dispositive of or directly controlling on our decision in these cases involving state legislative apportionment controversies. Admittedly, those decisions, in which we held that, in state wide and in congressional elections, one person's vote must be counted equally with those of all other voters in a State, were based on different constitutional considerations and were addressed to rather distinct problems. But neither are they wholly inapposite. Gray, though not determinative here since involving the weighting of votes in statewide elections, established the basic principle of equality among voters within a State, and held that voters cannot be classified, constitutionally, on the basis of where they live, at least with respect to voting in statewide elections. And our decision in Wesberry was of course grounded on that language of the Constitution which prescribes that members of the Federal House of Representatives are to be chosen "by the People," while attacks on state legislative apportionment schemes [are] principally based on [equal protection]. Nevertheless, Wesberry clearly established that the fundamental principle of representa-

tive government in this country is one of equal representation for equal numbers of people, without regard to race, sex, economic status, or place of residence within a State. Our problem, then, is to ascertain, in the instant cases, whether there are any constitutionally cognizable principles which would justify departures from the basic standard of equality among voters in the apportionment of seats in state legislatures. . . .

III. A predominant consideration in determining whether a State's legislative apportionment scheme constitutes an invidious discrimination violative of rights asserted under the Equal Protection Clause is that the rights allegedly impaired are individual and personal in nature. [T]he judicial focus must be concentrated upon ascertaining whether there has been any discrimination against certain of the State's citizens which constitutes an impermissible impairment of their constitutonally protected right to vote. Like Skinner v. Oklahoma, 316 U.S. 535 [chap. 10], such a case "touches a sensitive and important area of human rights," and "involves one of the basic civil rights of man," presenting questions of alleged "invidious discriminations . . . against groups or types of individuals in violation of the constitutional guaranty of just and equal laws." Undoubtedly, the right of suffrage is a fundamental matter in a free and democratic society. Especially since the right to exercise the franchise in a free and unimpaired manner is preservative of other basic civil and political rights, any alleged infringement of the right of citizens to vote must be carefully and meticulously scrutinized. . . .

Legislators represent people, not trees or acres. Legislators are elected by voters, not farms or cities or economic interests. As long as ours is a representative form of government, [the] right to elect legislators in a free and unimpaired fashion is a bedrock of our political system. It could hardly be gainsaid that a constitutional claim had been asserted by an allegation that certain otherwise qualified voters had been entirely prohibited from voting for members of their state legislature. And, if a State should provide that the votes of citizens in one part of the State should be given two times, or five times, or 10 times the weight of votes of citizens in another part of the State, it could hardly be contended that the right to vote of those residing in the disfavored areas had not been effectively diluted. . . . Of course, the effect of state legislative districting schemes which give the same number of representatives to unequal numbers of constituents is identical. . . . Weighting the votes of citizens differently, by any method or means, merely because of where they happen to reside, hardly seems justifiable. . . .

State legislatures are, historically, the fountainhead of representative government in this country. . . . Full and effective participation by all citizens in state government requires [that] each citizen have an equally effective voice in the election of members of his state legislature. Modern and viable state government needs, and the Constitution demands, no less.

Logically, in a society ostensibly grounded on representative government, it would seem reasonable that a majority of the people of a State could elect a majority of that State's legislators. To conclude differently, and to sanction minority control of state legislative bodies, would appear to deny majority

rights in a way that far surpasses any possible denial of minority rights that might otherwise be thought to result. . . . And the concept of equal protection has been traditionally viewed as requiring the uniform treatment of persons standing in the same relation to the governmental action questioned or challenged. With respect to the allocation of legislative representation, all voters, as citizens of a State, stand in the same relation regardless of where they live. Any suggested criteria for the differentiation of citizens are insufficient to justify any discrimination, as to the weight of their votes, unless relevant to the permissible purposes of legislative apportionment. Since the achieving of fair and effective representation for all citizens is concededly the basic aim of legislative apportionment, we conclude that the Equal Protection Clause guarantees the opportunity for equal participation by all voters in the election of state legislators. Diluting the weight of votes because of place of residence impairs basic constitutional rights under the Fourteenth Amendment just as much as invidious discriminations based upon factors such as race [or] economic status [cf. chap. 10]. Our constitutional system amply provides for the protection of minorities by means other than giving them majority control of state legislatures. And the democratic ideals of equality and majority rule, which have served this Nation so well in the past, are hardly of any less significance for the present and the future.

We are told that the matter of apportioning representation in a state legislature is a complex and many-faceted one. We are advised that States can rationally consider factors other than population in apportioning legislative representation. We are admonished not to restrict the power of the States to impose differing views as to political philosophy on their citizens. We are cautioned about the dangers of entering into political thickets and mathematical quagmires. Our answer is this: a denial of constitutionally protected rights demands judicial protection; our oath and our office require no less of us. . . . To the extent that a citizen's right to vote is debased, he is that much less a citizen. The fact that an individual lives here or there is not a legitimate reason for overweighting or diluting the efficacy of his vote. [T]he weight of a citizen's vote cannot be made to depend on where he lives. Population is, of necessity, the starting point for consideration and the controlling criterion for judgment in legislative apportionment controversies. A citizen, a qualified voter, is no more nor no less so because he lives in the city or on the farm. This is the clear and strong command of our Constitution's Equal Protection Clause. This is an essential part of the concept of a government of laws and not men. This is at the heart of Lincoln's vision of "government of the people, by the people, [and] for the people." The Equal Protection Clause demands no less than substantially equal state legislative representation for all citizens, of all places as well as of all races.

IV. We hold that, as a basic constitutional standard, the Equal Protection Clause requires that the seats in both houses of a bicameral state legislature must be apportioned on a population basis. Simply stated, an individual's right to vote for state legislators is unconstitutionally impaired when its weight is in a substantial fashion diluted when compared with votes of citizens living in other parts of the State. . . .

V. . . . Much has been written since our decision in Baker v. Carr about the applicability of the so-called federal analogy to state legis-

lative apportionment arrangements. . . . We agree with the District Court, and find the federal analogy inapposite and irrelevant to state legislative districting schemes. Attempted reliance on the federal analogy appears often to be little more than an after-the-fact rationalization offered in defense of maladjusted state apportionment arrangements. . . .

The system of representation in the two Houses of the Federal Congress is one ingrained in our Constitution, as part of the law of the land. It is one conceived out of compromise and concession indispensable to the establishment of our federal republic. Arising from unique historical circumstances, it is based on the consideration that in establishing our type of federalism a group of formerly independent States bound themselves together under one national government. . . . Political subdivisions of States —counties, cities, or whatever—never were and never have been considered as sovereign entities. Rather, they have been traditionally regarded as subordinate governmental instrumentalities created by the State. . . .

. . . The right of a citizen to equal representation and to have his vote weighted equally with those of all other citizens in the election of members of one house of a bicameral state legislature would amount to little if States could effectively submerge the equal-population principle in the apportionment of seats in the other house. . . . Deadlock between the two bodies might result in compromise and concession on some issues. But in all too many cases the more probable result would be frustration of the majority will through minority veto in the house not apportioned on a population basis. . . .

We do not believe that the concept of bicameralism is rendered anachronistic and meaningless when the predominant basis of representation in the two state legislative bodies is required to be the same—population. A prime reason for bicameralism, modernly considered, is to insure mature and deliberate consideration of, and to prevent precipitate action on, proposed legislative measures. Simply because the controlling criterion for apportioning representation is required to be the same in both houses does not mean that there will be no differences in the composition and complexion of the two bodies. . . .

VI. By holding that as a federal constitutional requisite both houses of a state legislature must be apportioned on a population basis, we mean that the Equal Protection Clause requires that a State make an honest and good faith effort to construct districts, in both houses of its legislature, as nearly of equal population as is practicable. We realize that it is a practical impossibility to arrange legislative districts so that each one has an identical number of residents, or citizens, or voters. Mathematical exactness or precision is hardly a workable constitutional requirement.

. . . So long as the divergences from a strict population standard are based on legitimate considerations incident to the effectuation of a rational state policy, some deviations from the equal-population principle are constitutionally permissible with respect to the apportionment of seats in either or both of the two houses of a bicameral state legislature. But neither history alone, nor economic or other sorts of group interests, are permissible factors in attempting to justify disparities from population-based representation. Citizens, not history or economic interests, cast votes. Considerations of area

alone provide an insufficient justification for deviations from the equal-population principle. Again, people, not land or trees or pastures, vote. Modern developments and improvements in transportation and communications make rather hollow, in the mid-1960's, most claims that deviations from population-based representation can validly be based solely on geographical considerations. Arguments for allowing such deviations in order to insure effective representation for sparsely settled areas and to prevent legislative districts from becoming so large that the availability of access of citizens to their representatives is impaired are today, for the most part, unconvincing.

A consideration that appears to be of more substance in justifying some deviations from population-based representation in state legislatures is that of insuring some voice to political subdivisions, as political subdivisions. . . . In many States much of the legislature's activity involves the enactment of so-called local legislation, directed only to the concerns of particular political subdivisions. And a State may legitimately desire to construct districts along political subdivision lines to deter the possibilities of gerrymandering. . . . But if, even as a result of a clearly rational state policy of according some legislative representation to political subdivisions, population is submerged as the controlling consideration, [the] right of all of the State's citizens to cast an effective and adequately weighted vote would be unconstitutionally impaired. . . .

[Affirmed and remanded.]

[In five companion cases to Reynolds v. Sims, the Court relied on its principles to invalidate apportionment schemes in Colorado, New York, Maryland, Virginia, and Delaware.* The Colorado case, LUCAS v. FORTY-FOURTH GENERAL ASSEMBLY, 377 U.S. 713, warrants special mention, because the defenders of the districting there argued that it should be sustained because it had been approved by the voters of the state. The Colorado scheme—relying on the federal analogy in apportioning only one of the two houses on the basis of population—had been approved in 1962 by a statewide referendum. Moreover, the voters had rejected a plan to apportion both houses on the basis of population. Chief Justice Warren's opinion concluded that that background did not justify deviation from the Reynolds v. Sims requirement. He stated:

["[T]his case differs from the others decided this date in that the initiative device provides a practicable political remedy to obtain relief against alleged legislative malapportionment in Colorado. . . . [W]e find no significance in the fact that a nonjudicial, political remedy may be available for the effectuation of asserted rights to equal representation in a state legislature. Courts sit to adjudicate controversies involving alleged denials of constitutional rights. . . . An individual's constitutionally protected right to cast an equally weighted vote cannot be denied even by a vote of a majority of a State's electorate, if the apportionment scheme adopted by the voters fails to measure up to the requirements of the Equal Protection Clause. Manifestly, the fact that an apportionment

---

* The Colorado case was Lucas v. Forty-Fourth General Assembly, 377 U.S. 713; the New York case was WMCA, Inc. v. Lomenzo, 377 U.S. 633. The others: Maryland Committee for Fair Representation v. Tawes, 377 U.S. 656; Davis v. Mann, 377 U.S. 678 (Virginia); and Roman v. Sincock, 377 U.S. 695 (Delaware).

plan is adopted in a popular referendum is insufficient to sustain its constitutionality or to induce a court of equity to refuse to act. . . . A citizen's constitutional rights can hardly be infringed simply because a majority of the people choose that it be. We hold that the fact that a challenged legislative apportionment plan was approved by the electorate is without federal constitutional significance, if the scheme adopted fails to satisfy the basic requirements of the Equal Protection Clause, as delineated in our opinion in Reynolds v. Sims."]

Mr. Justice HARLAN, dissenting [in all six cases]. . . .

The Court's constitutional discussion [is] remarkable [for] its failure to address itself at all to the Fourteenth Amendment as a whole or to the legislative history of the Amendment pertinent to the matter at hand. Stripped of aphorisms, the Court's argument boils down to the assertion that petitioners' right to vote has been invidiously "debased" or "diluted" by systems of apportionment which entitle them to vote for fewer legislators than other voters, an assertion which is tied to the Equal Protection Clause only by the constitutionally frail tautology that "equal" means "equal." . . .

The history of the adoption of the Fourteenth Amendment provides conclusive evidence that neither those who proposed nor those who ratified the Amendment believed that the Equal Protection Clause limited the power of the States to apportion their legislatures as they saw fit. Moreover, the history demonstrates that the intention to leave this power undisturbed was deliberate and was widely believed to be essential to the adoption of the Amendment. [An extensive review of the history is omitted.] . . .

Although [the Court] provides only generalities in elaboration of its main thesis, its opinion nevertheless fully demonstrates how far removed these problems are from fields of judicial competence. Recognizing that "indiscriminate districting" is an invitation to "partisan gerrymandering," [the] Court nevertheless excludes virtually every basis for the formation of electoral districts other than "indiscriminate districting." In one or another of today's opinions, the Court declares it unconstitutional for a State to give effective consideration to any of the following in establishing legislative districts:

    (1) history;
    (2) "economic or other sorts of group interests";
    (3) area;
    (4) geographical considerations;
    (5) a desire "to insure effective representation for sparsely settled areas";
    (6) "availability of access of citizens to their representatives";
    (7) theories of bicameralism (except those approved by the Court);
    (8) occupation;
    (9) "an attempt to balance urban and rural power";
    (10) the preference of a majority of voters in the State.

So far as presently appears, the *only* factor which a State may consider, apart from numbers, is political subdivisions. But even "a clearly rational state policy" recognizing this factor is unconstitutional if "population is submerged as the controlling consideration . . .."

I know of no principle of logic or practical or theoretical politics, still less any constitutional principle, which establishes all or any of these exclusions. . . . So far as the Court says anything at all on this score, it says only that "legislators represent people, not trees or acres" . . . .. All this may be conceded. But it is surely equally obvious, and, in the context of elections, more meaningful to note that people are not ciphers and that legislators can represent their electors only by speaking for their interests —economic, social, political—many of which do reflect the place where the electors live. The Court does not establish, or indeed even attempt to make a case for the proposition that conflicting interests within a State can only be adjusted by disregarding them when voters are grouped for purposes of representation. . . .*

Mr. Justice STEWART, whom Mr. Justice CLARK joins, dissenting [in the Colorado and New York cases].† . . .

I. What the Court has done is to convert a particular political philosophy into a constitutional rule, binding upon each of the 50 States, . . . without regard and without respect for the many individualized and differentiated characteristics of each State, characteristics stemming from each State's distinct history, distinct geography, distinct distribution of population, and distinct political heritage. My own understanding of the various theories of representative government is that no one theory has ever commanded unanimous assent among political scientists, historians, or others who have considered the problem. But even if it were thought that the rule announced today by the Court is, as a matter of political theory, the most desirable general rule which can be devised, [I] could not join in the fabrication of a constitutional mandate which imports and forever freezes one theory of political thought into our Constitution, and forever denies to every State any opportunity for enlightened and progressive innovation in the design of its democratic institutions, so as to accommodate within a system of representative government the interests and aspirations of diverse groups of people, without subjecting any group or class to absolute domination by a geographically concentrated or highly organized majority.

Representative government is a process of accommodating group interests through democratic institutional arrangements. Its function is to channel the numerous opinions, interests, and abilities of the people of a State into the making of the State's public policy. Appropriate legislative apportionment, therefore, should ideally be designed to insure effective representation in the State's legislature, in cooperation with other organs for political power, of the various groups and interests making up the electorate. In practice, of course, this ideal is approximated in the particular apportion-

* Justice Clark concurred in the results in all of the cases except those from Colorado and New York. In his concurrence in Reynolds v. Sims, he argued that the majority had gone "much beyond the necessities of this case in laying down a new 'equal population' principle," suggesting: "It seems to me that all that the Court need say in this case is that each plan considered by the trial court is 'a crazy quilt,' clearly revealing invidious discrimination in each house of the Legislature."

† Justice Stewart concurred in the results in the Alabama, Delaware, and Virginia cases, finding those apportionment schemes "completely lacking in rationality." In addition to the dissent printed here, he also submitted a brief dissent in the Maryland case.

ment system of any State by a realistic accommodation of the diverse and often conflicting political forces operating within the State. . . .

[L]egislators do not represent faceless numbers. They represent people, or, more accurately, a majority of the voters in their districts—people with identifiable needs and interests which require legislative representation, and which can often be related to the geographical areas in which these people live. The very fact of geographic districting, the constitutional validity of which the Court does not question, carries with it an acceptance of the idea of legislative representation of regional needs and interests. Yet if geographical residence is irrelevant, as the Court suggests, and the goal is solely that of equally "weighted" votes, I do not understand why the Court's constitutional rule does not require the abolition of districts and the holding of all elections at large.[1]

The fact is, of course, that population factors must often to some degree be subordinated in devising a legislative apportionment plan which is to achieve the important goal of ensuring a fair, effective, and balanced representation of the regional, social, and economic interests within a State. And the further fact is that throughout our history the apportionments of State Legislatures have reflected the strongly felt American tradition that the public interest is composed of many diverse interests, and that in the long run it can better be expressed by a medley of component voices than by the majority's monolithic command. What constitutes a rational plan reasonably designed to achieve this objective will vary from State to State, since each State is unique, in terms of topography, geography, demography, history, heterogeneity and concentration of population, variety of social and economic interests, and in the operation and interrelation of its political institutions. But so long as a State's apportionment plan reasonably achieves, in the light of the State's own characteristics, effective and balanced representation of all substantial interests, without sacrificing the principle of effective majority rule, that plan cannot be considered irrational.

II. This brings me to what I consider to be the proper constitutional standards to be applied in these cases. . . . I think that the Equal Protection Clause demands but two basic attributes of any plan of state legislative apportionment. First, it demands that, in the light of the State's own characteristics and needs, the plan must be a rational one. Secondly, it demands that the plan must be such as not to permit the systematic frustration of the will of a majority of the electorate of the State. I think it is apparent that any plan of legislative apportionment which could be shown

1. Even with legislative districts of exactly equal voter population, 26% of the electorate (a bare majority of the voters in a bare majority of the districts) can, as a matter of the kind of theoretical mathematics embraced by the Court, elect a majority of the legislature under our simple majority electoral system. Thus, the Court's constitutional rule permits minority rule. Students of the mechanics of voting systems tell us that if all that matters is that votes count equally, the best vote-counting electoral system is proportional representation in statewide elections. . . . It is just because electoral systems are intended to serve functions other than satisfying mathematical theories, however, that the system of proportional representation has not been widely adopted. . . . [Footnote by Justice Stewart.]

to reflect no policy, but simply arbitrary and capricious action or inaction, and that any plan which could be shown systematically to prevent ultimate effective majority rule, would be invalid under accepted Equal Protection Clause standards. But, beyond this, I think there is nothing in the Federal Constitution to prevent a State from choosing any electoral legislative structure it thinks best suited to the interests, temper, and customs of its people. In the light of these standards, I turn to the Colorado and New York plans of legislative apportionment.

III. COLORADO. The Colorado plan creates a General Assembly composed of a Senate of 39 members and a House of 65 members. The State is divided into 65 equal population representative districts, with one representative to be elected from each district, and 39 senatorial districts, 14 of which include more than one county. In the Colorado House, the majority unquestionably rules supreme, with the population factor untempered by other considerations. In the Senate rural minorities do not have effective control, and therefore do not have even a veto power over the will of the urban majorities. It is true that, as a matter of theoretical arithmetic, a minority of 36% of the voters could elect a majority of the Senate, but this percentage has no real meaning in terms of the legislative process.[2] Under the Colorado plan, no possible combination of Colorado senators from rural districts, even assuming arguendo that they would vote as a bloc, could control the Senate. To arrive at the 36% figure, one must include with the rural districts a substantial number of urban districts, districts with substantially dissimilar interests. There is absolutely no reason to assume that this theoretical majority would ever vote together on any issue so as to thwart the wishes of the majority of the voters of Colorado. Indeed, when we eschew the world of numbers, and look to the real world of effective representation, the simple fact of the matter is that Colorado's three metropolitan areas, Denver, Pueblo, and Colorado Springs, elect a majority of the Senate. . . .

It is clear from the record that if per capita representation were the rule in both houses of the Colorado Legislature, counties having small populations would have to be merged with larger counties having totally dissimilar interests. Their representatives would not only be unfamiliar with the problems of the smaller county, but the interests of the smaller counties might well be totally submerged by the interests of the larger counties with which they are joined. Since representatives representing conflicting interests might well pay greater attention to the views of the majority, the minority interest could be denied any effective representation at all. Its votes would not be merely "diluted," an injury which the Court considers of constitutional dimensions, but rendered totally nugatory. . . .

2. The theoretical figure is arrived at by placing the legislative districts for each house in rank order of population, and by counting down the smallest population end of the list a sufficient distance to accumulate the minimum population which could elect a majority of the house in question. It is a meaningless abstraction as applied to a multimembered body because the factors of political party alignment and interest representation make such theoretical bloc voting a practical impossibility. For example, 31,000,000 people in the 26 least populous States representing only 17% of United States population have 52% of the Senators in the United States Senate. But no one contends that this bloc controls the Senate's legislative process. [Footnote by Justice Stewart.]

The present apportionment, adopted overwhelmingly by the people in a 1962 popular referendum as a state constitutional amendment, is entirely rational, and the amendment by its terms provides for keeping the apportionment current. Thus the majority has consciously chosen to protect the minority's interests, and under the liberal initiative provisions of the Colorado Constitution, it retains the power to reverse its decision to do so. Therefore, there can be no question of frustration of the basic principle of majority rule.

IV. NEW YORK. . . . Legislative apportionment in New York [is] not a crazy quilt; it is rational, it is applied systematically, and it is kept reasonably current. The formula reflects a policy which accords major emphasis to population, some emphasis to region and community, and a reasonable limitation upon massive overcentralization of power. In order to effectuate this policy, the apportionment formula provides that each county shall have at least one representative in the Assembly, that the smaller counties shall have somewhat greater representation in the legislature than representation based solely on numbers would accord, and that some limits be placed on the representation of the largest counties in order to prevent one megalopolis from completely dominating the legislature. . . .

A policy guaranteeing minimum representation to each county is certainly rational, particularly in a State like New York. It prevents less densely populated counties from being merged into multicounty districts where they would receive no effective representation at all. Further, it may be only by individual county representation that the needs and interests of all the areas of the State can be brought to the attention of the legislative body. The rationality of individual county representation becomes particularly apparent in States where legislative action applicable only to one or more particular counties is the permissible tradition. . . .

In addition to ensuring minimum representation to each county, the New York apportionment formula, by allocating somewhat greater representation to the smaller counties while placing limitations on the representation of the largest counties, is clearly designed to protect against overcentralization of power. To understand fully the practical importance of this consideration in New York, one must look to its unique characteristics. New York is one of the few States in which the central cities can elect a majority of representatives to the legislature. As the District Court found, the 10 most populous counties in the State control both houses of the legislature under the existing apportionment system. Each of these counties is heavily urban; each is in a metropolitan area. . . . Obviously, [the] existing system of apportionment clearly guarantees effective majority representation and control in the State Legislature.

But this is not the whole story. New York City, with its seven million people and a budget larger than that of the State, has, by virtue of its concentration of population, homogeneity of interest, and political cohesiveness, acquired an institutional power and political influence of its own hardly measurable simply by counting the number of its representatives in the legislature. . . . Surely it is not irrational for the State of New York to be justifiably concerned about balancing such a concentration of political power, and certainly there is nothing in our Federal Constitution

which prevents a State from reasonably translating such a concern into its apportionment formula. . . .

V.   In the allocation of representation in their State Legislatures, Colorado and New York have adopted completely rational plans which reflect an informed response to their particularized characteristics and needs. The plans are quite different, just as Colorado and New York are quite different.   But each State, while clearly ensuring that in its legislative councils the will of the majority of the electorate shall rule, has sought to provide that no identifiable minority shall be completely silenced or engulfed. [I] believe that what each State has achieved fully comports with the letter and the spirit of our constitutional traditions.*

THE PROGENY OF REYNOLDS v. SIMS: SOME ELABORATIONS OF THE "ONE PERSON–ONE VOTE" THEME

Introduction.   Did Reynolds v. Sims provide a "judicially manageable standard"?   Was that standard a justifiable inference from the equal protection clause?   Is individual voter equality sufficiently promoted by insisting on legislative districts of equal population?   Is Justice Stewart persuasive in arguing that proportional representation would more fully promote that principle?   Does the Reynolds v. Sims principle assure adequate political equality, given the other variables in districting schemes such as organized political parties and interest groups?   Do the "distorting" effects of party cohesion on the equality principle justify or require the Court to limit gerrymandering?   (See note 3 below.)[1]   Would Justice Stewart's emphasis on searching for "systematic frustration of the majority" be a preferable, more realistic focus for judicial inquiry?   Would Justice Stewart's standard be a "judicially manageable" one?   Do the emphases on voter equality and majority rule make supermajority requirements impermissible?   (See note 5 below.)   Do the Reynolds v. Sims principles permit excluding some voters from special purpose elections—e. g., by im-

---

* In the wake of Reynolds v. Sims, an intense but ultimately unsuccessful drive was launched to overturn it by constitutional amendment (and to delay its implementation by congressional statute—recall chap. 1 above).   The most widely supported proposal would have permitted one house of a state legislature to be apportioned on a basis other than population, if a majority of the state's voters approved the plan.   (Recall Lucas, the Colorado apportionment case, above.)   A widely publicized plan was to promote such a proposal through the alternative "Convention" method of initiating constitutional amendments.   That campaign reached its high water mark in the late 1960's, when over thirty states were reported to have approved "Applications" to Congress for a call of a constitutional convention.   See Bonfield, "The Dirksen Amendment and the Article V Convention Process," 66 Mich.L.Rev. 949 (1968).

1. Note the comment in Neal, "Baker v. Carr: Politics in Search of Law," 1962 Sup.Ct.Rev. 252: After questioning the utility of the equal voting requirement in assuring adequacy of representation, he notes that "the principle of apportionment-by-population may be of only marginal significance unless all other factors in the equation can be made to remain constant. An asserted constitutional principle that may not be much more useful than one half of a pair of pliers ought to be viewed with some skepticism." Chief Justice Warren thought Reynolds v. Sims the most important decision of his tenure.   How significant has its impact been, in view of the Court's implementations—and the Court's limits—noted below?   For skeptical views about the contribution of Reynolds v. Sims, note not only the early comment by Neal, above, but also the later assessment in Bickel, The Supreme Court and the Idea of Progress (1970).

posing property requirements or by weighing votes according to property holdings? Consider these questions in examining some of the problems of elaborating and implementing Reynolds v. Sims summarized in the following group of notes.[2]

1. *Application of Reynolds v. Sims to local government.* AVERY v. MIDLAND COUNTY, 390 U.S. 474 (1968), was the first decision to apply the equal districting requirement to a unit of local government. The case involved a Texas county Commissioner's Court—an agency with "general governmental powers." The county had been divided into four districts for purposes of representation on the Commissioner's Court. The city of Midland located in the county constituted one district, with over 67,-000 people; the rural area was divided into three districts, with less than 1,000 people each. Justice White's majority opinion rejected the argument that the Commissioner's Court was an administrative rather than a legislative body and concluded "that the Constitution permits no substantial variation from equal population in drawing districts for units of local government having general governmental powers over the entire geographic area served by the body." Whether state power was exercised through the legislature or through local elected officials, the equal protection clause required assurance "that those qualified to vote have the right to an equally effective voice in the election process."[3] Justices Harlan, Fortas and Stewart submitted separate dissents.

A divided Court extended the principles of Avery to a case involving the election of trustees of a junior college district in HADLEY v. JUNIOR COLLEGE DISTRICT, 397 U.S. 50 (1970). The junior college district comprised eight local school districts, and the Court found it impermissible to give a district with more than half of the junior college district population the right to elect only half of the trustees. The majority stated the "general rule" as follows: "[W]henever a state or local government decides to select persons by popular election to perform governmental functions, [equal protection] requires that each qualified voter must be given an equal opportunity to participate in that election, and when members of an elected body are chosen from separate districts, each district must be established on a basis which will insure, as far as is practicable, that equal numbers of voters can vote for proportionally equal numbers of officials. It is of course possible that there might be some case in which a State elects certain functionaries whose duties are so far removed from normal governmental activities and so disproportionately affect different groups that a popular election in compliance with [Reynolds v. Sims] might not be required."[4]

---

2. For additional evaluations of Reynolds v. Sims and its progeny, see generally McKay, "Reapportionment: Success Story of the Warren Court," 67 Mich.L.Rev. 223 (1968); Dixon, Democratic Representation: Reapportionment in Law and Politics (1968); Reapportionment in the 1970's (Polsby ed. 1971).

3. Justice White left open the possibility that deviations from equal population districting might be permissible for special purpose units of government. And he insisted that the Court would be sensitive to "the greatly varying problems" of local government, pointing to earlier decisions in Sailors v. Board of Education, 387 U.S. 105 (1967) ("administrative" school board), and Dusch v. Davis, 387 U.S. 112 (1967).

4. See generally, "Symposium: One Man-One Vote and Local Government," 36 Geo.Wash.L.Rev. 689 (1968).

2. *Mathematical inequalities: Permissible deviations from "one person-one vote."* In the years since Reynolds v. Sims and Wesberry v. Sanders, the Court has adhered rigidly to the maximum possible mathematical equality in districting for congressional elections. But the Court has gradually permitted somewhat greater deviations from equality in state districting, over the dissents of some Justices claiming that the Reynolds v. Sims principles were being undercut.

a. *Congressional districting.* KIRKPATRICK v. PREISLER, 394 U.S. 526 (1969), drew from the congressional districting principles of Wesberry v. Sanders the requirement "that as nearly as is practicable, one man's vote in a congressional election is to be worth as much as another's." Kirkpatrick rejected a Missouri plan which varied from the "absolute population equality" ideal within a range of 2.8% below and 3.1% above. Justice Brennan's majority opinion insisted that variations from absolute equality could not be justified on de minimis grounds, nor by a desire to avoid fragmenting political subdivisions or even to deter political gerrymandering. Instead, states were required to "make a good-faith effort to achieve precise mathematical equality." [5]

In 1973, WHITE v. WEISER, 412 U.S. 783, adhered to the precise equality approach for congressional districting, even while the Court drifted away from that strictness in a group of state legislative reapportionment cases noted below. The majority insisted that even "small" population variances were impermissible in congressional districting. In a concurring opinion, Justice Powell, joined by Chief Justice Burger and Justice Rehnquist, argued that the state redistricting cases, below, "strengthen the case against attempting to hold any reapportionment scheme—state or congressional—to slide-rule precision." But since Kirkpatrick was "virtually indistinguishable," he agreed to follow it "unless and until the Court decides to reconsider that decision."

b. *State districting.* After rejecting a state's redistricting plan involving substantial variations from population equality in Swann v. Adams, 385 U.S. 440 (1967), the Court in the 1970's began to manifest considerable tolerance toward smaller deviations from the equality ideal. In ABATE v. MUNDT, 403 U.S. 182 (1971), the Court found justification for an 11.9% total deviation from population equality in the apportionment of a county legislature—a larger deviation than those found impermissible in a few earlier cases. Justice Marshall's majority opinion insisted that deviations "must be justified by legitimate state considerations," but found adequate justifications here—including the fact that the local body reflected a "long history of, and perceived need for, close cooperation between the county and its constituent towns." Justice Brennan, joined by Justice Douglas, thought the majority had permitted a dilution of Reynolds v. Sims standards.

Even greater tolerance was manifested in a leading modern case, a case involving a state legislature—MAHAN v. HOWELL, 410 U.S. 315 (1973). That decision made it clear that the new majority was more receptive to claimed justifications for deviations from equality. And other decisions,

5. See also the companion case, Wells v. Rockefeller, 394 U.S. 542 (1969), another decision by a divided Court rejecting a New York congressional redistricting plan.

soon after, indicated that the Court would not even demand justification for "minor" (apparently, up to 10%) deviations. Mahan approved a redistricting of the lower house of the Virginia legislature with a maximum variance of 16.4% from population equality. Justice Rehnquist's majority opinion stated that "more flexibility was constitutionally permissible with respect to state legislative reapportionment than in congressional redistricting," because of the interest in "the normal functioning of state and local governments." Here, the deviations from the equality ideal were justified by "the State's policy of maintaining the integrity of political subdivision lines." But even rational state justifications, he insisted, could not "be permitted to emasculate the goal of substantial equality." The deviation in Virginia "may well approach tolerable limits," but "we do not believe it exceeds them."

Justice Brennan's dissent, joined by Justices Douglas and Marshall, thought the state plan demonstrated "a systematic pattern of substantial deviation from the constitutional ideal." And he objected to the notion of "different constitutional *standards*" as to state and congressional districting. A state might have a broader range of interests to submit as justifications for deviations, but the state burden of proof or the applicable standard should not be any lighter.

The loosening of Court reins on state reapportionment plans became even more manifest a few months later, in two decisions which not only reaffirmed the Mahan v. Howell receptiveness to a broader range of state justifications, but also found a new category of "minor" deviations in population equality requiring no justifications at all. The cases focused on reapportionment of the houses of the Connecticut and Texas legislatures. In the Connecticut case, GAFFNEY v. CUMMINGS, 412 U.S. 735 (1973), there was a maximum variation among districts of about 8% and an average deviation of about 2% from the ideal. In the Texas case, WHITE v. REGESTER, 412 U.S. 755 (1973), there was a maximum deviation of 9.9% and an average deviation of less than 2%. Justice White's majority opinion found these to be "relatively minor" population deviations, insufficient to meet the "threshold requirement of proving a prima facie case of invidious discrimination" and accordingly requiring no justifications from the States. He distinguished these cases from the "enormous," unjustifiable variations struck down in the "early cases beginning with Reynolds v. Sims" and from cases such as Mahan v. Howell, involving deviations "sufficiently large to require justification" but nonetheless justifiable. "It is now time to recognize," he added, "that minor deviations from mathematical equality among state legislative districts are insufficient to make out a prima facie case [so] as to require justification by the State." Attainment of the "worthy goal" of Reynolds v. Sims "does not in any commonsense way depend upon eliminating the insignificant population variation" here. He added: "That the Court was not deterred by the hazards of the political thicket when it undertook to adjudicate the reapportionment cases does not mean that it should become bogged down in a vast, intractable apportionment slough, particularly when there is little, if anything, to be accomplished by doing so." When "only minor population variations" are proved, judicial involvement "should never begin."

Justice Brennan, joined by Justices Douglas and Marshall, dissented. He commented that "one can reasonably surmise," in view of the fact that justification had been required for the 11.9% deviation in Abate v. Mundt in 1971, above, "that a line has been drawn at 10%—deviations in excess of that amount are apparently acceptable only on a showing of justification by the State; deviations less than that amount require no justification whatsoever." He insisted that the plans now sustained involved "substantial inequalities" and thought that the majority approach "effects a substantial and very unfortunate retreat from the principles established in our earlier cases."

3. *The unwillingness to scrutinize gerrymanders.* The challengers in the Connecticut case above, GAFFNEY v. CUMMINGS, 412 U.S. 735 (1973) raised a claim going beyond that of population equality: they argued "that even if acceptable population-wise, the [plan] was invidiously discriminatory because a 'political fairness principle' was followed." The plan was admittedly drawn to create districting "that would achieve a rough approximation of the statewide political strengths of the Democratic and Republican Parties," and the challengers characterized the plan "as nothing less than a gigantic political gerrymander, invidiously discriminatory under the Fourteenth Amendment."

In the course of rejecting that claim, Justice White's majority opinion chilled most hopes that gerrymanders might be subjected to careful judicial scrutiny. He conceded that a plan could be constitutionally vulnerable despite substantial population equality, as in the multi-member district discrimination considered in the next note. But gerrymandering as such is apparently not a source of such vulnerability: Justice White reminded in a footnote that "compactness or attractiveness have never been held to constitute an independent federal constitutional requirement of state legislative districts." And the "political fairness" principle was permissible: "Politics and political considerations are inseparable from districting and apportionment. . . . It is not only obvious, but absolutely unavoidable, that the location and shape of districts may well determine the political complexion of the area. District lines are rarely neutral phenomena. They can well determine what district will be predominantly Democratic or predominantly Republican, or make a close race likely. . . . The reality is that districting inevitably has and is intended to have substantial political consequences. It may be suggested that those who redistrict and reapportion should work with census, not political, data, and achieve population equality without regard for political impact. But this politically mindless approach may produce, whether intended or not, the most grossly gerrymandered results, and, in any event, it is most unlikely that the political impact of such a plan would remain undiscovered by the time it was proposed or adopted, in which event the results would be both known and, if not changed, intended."

Justice White added: "It is much more plausible to assume that those who redistrict and reapportion work with both political and census data. Within the limits of the population equality standards of the Equal Protection Clause, they seek, through compromise or otherwise, to achieve the political or other ends of the State, its constituents, and its office-holders. What

is done in so arranging for elections, or to achieve political ends or allocate political power, is not wholly exempt from judicial scrutiny under the 14th Amendment. [F]or example, multimember districts may be vulnerable, if racial or political groups have been fenced out of the political process and their voting strength invidiously minimized. [See the next note.] Beyond this, we have not ventured far or attempted the impossible task of extirpating politics from what are the essentially political processes of the sovereign States. Even more plainly, judicial interest should be at its lowest ebb when a State purports fairly to allocate political power to the parties in accordance with their voting strength. [N]either we nor the district courts have a constitutional warrant to invalidate a state plan, otherwise within tolerable population limits, because it undertakes, not to minimize or eliminate the political strength of any group or party, but to recognize it and, through districting, provide a rough sort of proportional representation in the legislative halls of the State." [6]

4. *Multimember districts and racial minorities.* In one of the early post-Reynolds v. Sims cases, Burns v. Richardson, 384 U.S. 73 (1966), the Court held that multimember rather than single-member districts were permissible, absent a showing that they were "designed to or would operate to minimize or cancel out the voting strength of racial or political elements of the voting population." See also Fortson v. Dorsey, 379 U.S. 433 (1965). In the 1970's, the Court began to undertake the difficult task of scrutinizing the impact of multimember districting schemes. WHITCOMB v. CHAVIS, 403 U.S. 124 (1971), rejected a claim that a multimember district underrepresented minorities, but articulated standards that laid the groundwork for future challenges. Those guidelines bore fruit in 1973: in WHITE v. REGESTER, 412 U.S. 755 (1973), the Court for the first time sustained such a claim.

a. *Whitcomb v. Chavis.* This was a two-pronged attack on the Indiana districting system constituting Marion County, which includes Indianapolis, a multimember district for electing state senators and representatives. Indiana has a house of representatives of 100 members and a senate of 50 members. Several districts in each house are multimember districts—i. e., "districts which are represented by two or more legislators elected at large by the voters of the district." Under the challenged scheme, the Marion County multimember district elected 8 senators and 15 members of the house.

The Court described appellees' "two quite distinct challenges" as follows: "The first charge is that any multi-member district bestows on its voters several unconstitutional advantages over voters in single-member districts or smaller multi-member districts. The other allegation is that the Marion County district, on the record of this case, illegally minimizes and cancels out the voting power of a cognizable racial minority in Marion County." The District Court upheld the second claim and found the first "sufficient-

---

6. Does this refusal to scrutinize political gerrymandering minimize the impact of Reynolds v. Sims in achieving the ideal of political equality? Recall the skeptical comments above, especially at footnote 1.

On the Court's assumption that racial factors in gerrymandering may be unconstitutional—though difficult to prove—see Wright v. Rockefeller, 376 U.S. 52 (1964).

ly persuasive to be a substantial factor in prescribing uniform, single-member districts as the basic scheme of the court's own plan." The Supreme Court disagreed, in an opinion by Justice White, joined by Chief Justice Burger and Justices Black, Blackmun and, in substantial part, Stewart. The basis for the rejection of the first claim was essentially that it rested on mere theory and was not supported by "real-life" evidence.

Justice White next turned to the second prong of the attack, the one that had explicitly prevailed in the trial court. That court had emphasized discrimination against voters *within* the Marion County district, rather than those outside. As summarized by Justice White, the trial court "identified an area of the city as a ghetto, found it predominantly inhabited by poor Negroes with distinctive substantive-law interests and thought this group unconstitutionally underrepresented because the proportion of legislators with residences in the ghetto elected from 1960 to 1968 was less than the ghetto's proportion of the population, less than the proportion of legislators elected from [a less populous district], and less than the ghetto would likely have elected had the county consisted of single-member districts."

Justice White found "major deficiencies in this approach." The challengers had relied on the statements in earlier cases, reiterated by the Court here, that multimember districts were subject to challenge where the circumstances of a particular case may "operate to minimize or cancel out the voting strength of racial or political elements of the voting population." But, Justice White reminded, "we have insisted that the challenger carry the burden of proving that multi-member districts unconstitutionally operate to dilute or cancel the voting strength of racial or political elements." The Court had "not yet" sustained such an attack, and it did not sustain one here: "We have discovered [nothing] indicating that poor Negroes were not allowed to register or vote, to choose the political party they desired to support, to participate in its affairs or to be equally represented on those occasions when legislative candidates were chosen."

Justice White also noted a more general objection to the trial court's approach. Though it was invoked here to protect one racial group, it was an approach "not easily contained": "It is expressive of the more general proposition that any group of distinctive interests must be represented in legislative halls if it is numerous enough to command at least one seat and represents a majority living in an area sufficiently compact to constitute a single-member district." That approach would make it difficult to reject claims of other political or interest groups who are regularly submerged in a one-sided multimember district vote: "There are also union oriented workers, the university community, religious or ethnic groups occupying identifiable areas of our heterogeneous cities and urban areas."

Justice Douglas, joined by Justices Brennan and Marshall, dissented, insisting that the District Court had "done an outstanding job." The central question, as he saw it, was "whether a gerrymander can be 'constitutionally impermissible.' The question of the gerrymander is the other half of [Reynolds v. Sims]. Fair representation of voters in a legislative assembly— one man, one vote—would seem to require (1) substantial equality of population within each district and (2) the avoidance of district lines that weigh the power of one race more heavily than another." Racial motivation did

not have to be shown: "[T]he test for multi-member districts is whether there are invidious effects." Justice Douglas rejected the argument that "if we prevent racial gerrymandering today, we must prevent gerrymandering of any special interest group tomorrow, whether it be social, economic, or ideological." The Constitution "has a special thrust" with respect to racial discrimination in voting.

b. *White v. Regester.* Three years later, in White v. Regester, 412 U.S. 755 (1973), the Court found the difficult requirements of Whitcomb v. Chavis satisfied and for the first time sustained an attack on the use of multimember districts. The Court sustained findings that the Texas redistricting scheme had established two multimember districts which unconstitutionally tended "to cancel out or minimize the voting strength of racial groups." (The lower court had found that the Bexar County district discriminated against Mexican-Americans, and the Dallas district, against Blacks.)

5. *Supermajorities.* West Virginia requires that political subdivisions may not incur bonded indebtedness or exceed constitutional tax rates without the approval of 60% of the voters in a referendum election. A county school bond proposal received only slightly more than 50% of the vote and was accordingly defeated. The highest state court found that the 60% requirement violated equal protection because "the votes of those who favored the issuance of the bonds had a proportionately smaller impact on the outcome of the election than the votes of those who opposed issuance of the bonds." The Supreme Court reversed. GORDON v. LANCE, 403 U.S. 1 (1971).

Chief Justice Burger called the state court's reliance on Gray v. Sanders, the Georgia county unit plan case above, and Cipriano v. City of Houma (chap. 10, sec. 4A, above) "misplaced." He explained: "The defect this Court found in those cases lay in the denial or dilution of voting power because of group characteristics—geographic location and property ownership—that bore no valid relation to the interest of those groups in the subject matter of the election; moreover, the dilution or denial was imposed irrespective of how members of those groups actually voted." More generally, his majority opinion stated:

"Certainly any departure from strict majority rule gives disproportionate power to the minority. But there is nothing in the language of the Constitution, our history or our cases that requires that a majority always prevail on every issue. . . . The Federal Constitution itself provides that a simple majority vote is insufficient on some issues . . . .. The constitutions of many States prohibit or severely limit the power of the legislature to levy new taxes or to create or increase bonded indebtedness, thereby insulating entire areas from majority control. . . . We conclude that so long as such provisions do not discriminate against or authorize discrimination against any identifiable class they do not violate the Equal Protection Clause." In a footnote, he added: "We intimate no view on the constitutionality of a provision requiring unanimity or giving a veto power to a very small group. Nor do we decide whether a State may, consistent with the Constitution, require extraordinary majorities for the election of public officers."

Can this holding be reconciled with Reynolds v. Sims and its emphasis on political equality? Were not the apportionment plans invalidated in Reynolds v. Sims attempts to protect minorities? Why were those attempts invalid, while the West Virginia supermajority requirement was valid? Is there adequate explanation in Chief Justice Burger's comment in Gordon v. Lance that, "[u]nlike the restrictions in our previous cases, the West Virginia Constitution singles out no 'discrete and insular minority' for special treatment. The three-fifths requirement applies equally to all bond issues for any purpose, whether for schools, sewers, or highways"?

*

APPENDIX

TABLE OF JUSTICES †

Two sets of dates are given for each Justice, indicating his entire life as well as his years on the Supreme Court; but only the term of office is indicated for a President. Those Presidents who made no appointments to the Supreme Court are not included in the table. They are Presidents William H. Harrison (Mar.–Apr. 1841), Zachary Taylor (1849–50), and Andrew Johnson (1865–1869).

The symbol * and the figure (1) designate the Chief Justices. The other figures trace lines of succession in filling vacancies among the Associate Justices. For example, by following the figure (2) it can be seen that Justice Rutledge was succeeded by Justice Thomas Johnson, he by Justice Paterson, he in turn by Justice Livingston, etc.

Appointed by President Washington, Federalist from Virginia (1789–1797)

* (1) Jay, John (1745–1829). Fed. from N.Y. (1789–1795). Resigned.

(2) Rutledge, John (1739–1800). Fed. from S.C. (1789–1791). Resigned without ever sitting.

(3) Cushing, William (1732–1810). Fed. from Mass. (1789–1810). Died.

(4) Wilson, James (1724–1798). Fed. from Pa. (1789–1798). Died.

(5) Blair, John (1732–1800). Fed. from Va. (1789–1796). Resigned.

(6) Iredell, James (1750–1799). Fed. from N.C. (1790–1799). Died.

(2) Johnson, Thomas (1732–1819). Fed. from Md. (1791–1793). Resigned.

(2) Paterson, William (1745–1806). Fed. from N.J. (1793–1806). Died.

* (1) Rutledge, John (1739–1800). Fed. from S.C. (1795). [Unconfirmed recess appointment.]

(5) Chase, Samuel (1741–1811). Fed. from Md. (1796–1811). Died.

---

† This table was originally prepared by Professor Margaret Spahr, Hunter College of the City University of New York. [For recent biographical sketches of each of the Justices, see the four-volume collection, The Justices of the United States Supreme Court 1789–1969: Their Lives and Major Opinions (Friedman and Israel, eds., 1969).]

*(1) Ellsworth, Oliver (1745–1807). Fed. from Conn. (1796–1800). Resigned.

*Appointed by President John Adams, Federalist from Massachusetts
(1797–1801)*

(4) Washington, Bushrod (1762–1829). Fed. from Pa. and Va. (1798–1829). Died.

(6) Moore, Alfred (1755–1810). Fed. from N.C. (1799–1804). Resigned.

*(1) Marshall, John (1755–1835). Fed. from Va. (1801–1835). Died.

*Appointed by President Jefferson, Republican from Virginia
(1801–1809)*

(6) Johnson, William (1771–1834). Rep. from S.C. (1804–1834). Died.

(2) Livingston, [Henry] Brockholst (1757–1823). Rep. from N.Y. (1806–1823). Died.

(7) Todd, Thomas (1765–1826). Rep. from Ky. (1807–1826). Died.

*Appointed by President Madison, Republican from Virginia
(1809–1817)*

(5) Duvall, Gabriel (1752–1844). Rep. from Md. (1811–1835). Resigned.

(3) Story, Joseph (1779–1845). Rep. from Mass. (1811–1845). Died.

*Appointed by President Monroe, Republican from Virginia
(1817–1825)*

(2) Thompson, Smith (1768–1843). Rep. from N.Y. (1823–1843). Died.

*Appointed by President John Quincy Adams, Republican from Massachusetts
(1825–1829)*

(7) Trimble, Robert (1777–1828). Rep. from Ky. (1826–1828). Died.

*Appointed by President Jackson, Democrat from Tennessee
(1829–1837)*

(7) McLean, John (1785–1861). Dem. (later Rep.) from Ohio (1829–1861). Died.

(4) Baldwin, Henry (1780–1844). Dem. from Pa. (1830–1844). Died.

(6) Wayne, James M. (1790–1867). Dem. from Ga. (1835–1867). Died.

*(1) Taney, Roger B. (1777–1864). Dem. from Md. (1836–1864). Died.

(5) Barbour, Philip P. (1783–1841). Dem. from Va. (1836–1841). Died.

Appointed by President Van Buren, Democrat from New York
(1837–1841)

(8) Catron, John (1778–1865). Dem. from Tenn. (1837–1865). Died.

(9) McKinley, John (1780–1852). Dem. from Ky. (1837–1852). Died.

(5) Daniel, Peter V. (1784–1860). Dem. from Va. (1841–1860). Died.

Appointed by President Tyler, Whig from Virginia
(1841–1845)

(2) Nelson, Samuel (1792–1873). Dem. from N.Y. (1845–1872). Resigned.

Appointed by President Polk, Democrat from Tennessee
(1845–1849)

(3) Woodbury, Levi (1789–1851). Dem. from N.H. (1845–1851). Died.

(4) Grier, Robert C. (1794–1870). Dem. from Pa. (1846–1870). Resigned.

Appointed by President Fillmore, Whig from New York
(1850–1853)

(3) Curtis, Benjamin R. (1809–1874). Whig from Mass. (1851–1857). Resigned.

Appointed by President Pierce, Democrat from New Hampshire
(1853–1857)

(9) Campbell, John A. (1811–1889). Dem. from Ala. (1853–1861). Resigned.

Appointed by President Buchanan, Democrat from Pennsylvania
(1857–1861)

(3) Clifford, Nathan (1803–1881). Dem. from Me. (1858–1881). Died.

Appointed by President Lincoln, Republican from Illinois
(1861–1865)

(7) Swayne, Noah H. (1804–1884). Rep. from Ohio (1862–1881). Resigned.

(5) Miller, Samuel F. (1816–1890). Rep. from Iowa (1862–1890). Died.

(9) Davis, David (1815–1886). Rep. (later Dem.) from Ill. (1862–1877). Resigned.

[3]

(10) Field, Stephen J. (1816–1899). Dem. from Cal. (1863–1897). Resigned.

*(1) Chase, Salmon P. (1808–1873). Rep. from Ohio (1864–1873). Died.

Appointed by President Grant, Republican from Illinois
(1869–1877)

(4) Strong, William (1808–1895). Rep. from Pa. (1870–1880). Resigned.

(6) Bradley, Joseph P. (1803–1892). Rep. from N.J. (1870–1892). Died.

(2) Hunt, Ward (1810–1886). Rep. from N.Y. (1872–1882). Resigned.

*(1) Waite, Morrison (1816–1888). Rep. from Ohio (1874–1888). Died.

Appointed by President Hayes, Republican from Ohio
(1877–1881)

(9) Harlan, John Marshall (1833–1911). Rep. from Ky. (1877–1911). Died.

(4) Woods, William B. (1824–1887). Rep. from Ga. (1880–1887). Died.

Appointed by President Garfield, Republican from Ohio
(Mar.–Sept. 1881)

(7) Matthews, Stanley (1824–1889). Rep. from Ohio (1881–1889). Died.

Appointed by President Arthur, Republican from New York
(1881–1885)

(3) Gray, Horace (1828–1902). Rep. from Mass. (1881–1902). Died.

(2) Blatchford, Samuel (1820–1893). Rep. from N.Y. (1882–1893.) Died.

Appointed by President Cleveland, Democrat from New York
(1885–1889)

(4) Lamar, Lucius Q. C. (1825–1893). Dem. from Miss. (1888–1893). Died.

*(1) Fuller, Melville W. (1833–1910). Dem. from Ill. (1888–1910). Died.

Appointed by President Harrison, Republican from Indiana
(1889–1893)

(7) Brewer, David J. (1837–1910). Rep. from Kansas (1889–1910). Died.

(5) Brown, Henry B. (1836–1913). Rep. from Mich. (1890–1906). Resigned.

(6) Shiras, George (1832–1924). Rep. from Pa. (1892–1903). Resigned.

(4) Jackson, Howell E. (1832–1895). Dem. from Tenn. (1893–1895). Died.

Appointed by President Cleveland, Democrat from New York (1893–1897)

(2) White, Edward D. (1845–1921). Dem. from La. (1894–1910). Promoted to chief justiceship.

(4) Peckham, Rufus W. (1838–1909). Dem. from N.Y. (1895–1909). Died.

Appointed by President McKinley, Republican from Ohio (1897–1901)

(10) or (8)
McKenna, Joseph (1843–1926). Rep. from Cal. (1898–1925). Resigned.

Appointed by President Theodore Roosevelt, Republican from New York (1901–1909)

(3) Holmes, Oliver Wendell (1841–1935). Rep. from Mass. (1902–1932). Resigned.

(6) Day, William R. (1849–1923). Rep. from Ohio (1903–1922). Resigned.

(5) Moody, William H. (1853–1917). Rep. from Mass. (1906–1910). Resigned.

Appointed by President Taft, Republican from Ohio (1909–1913)

(4) Lurton, Horace H. (1844–1914). Dem. from Tenn. (1909–1914). Died.

(7) Hughes, Charles E. (1862–1948). Rep. from N.Y. (1910–1916). Resigned.

*(1) White, Edward D. (1845–1921). Promoted from associate justiceship. (1910–1921). Died.

(2) Van Devanter, Willis (1859–1941). Rep. from Wyo. (1910–1937). Retired.

(5) Lamar, Joseph R. (1857–1916). Dem. from Ga. (1910–1916). Died.

(9) Pitney, Mahlon (1858–1924). Rep. from N.J. (1912–1922). Retired.

Appointed by President Wilson, Democrat from New Jersey (1913–1921)

(4) McReynolds, James C. (1862–1946). Dem. from Tenn. (1914–1941). Retired.

(5) Brandeis, Louis D. (1856–1941). Dem. from Mass. (1916–1939). Retired.

(7) Clarke, John H. (1857–1945). Dem. from Ohio (1916–1922). Resigned.

Appointed by President Harding, Republican from Ohio
(1921–1923)

*(1) Taft, William H. (1857–1930). Rep. from Conn. (1921–1930). Resigned.

(7) Sutherland, George (1862–1942). Rep. from Utah (1922–1938). Retired.

(6) Butler, Pierce (1866–1939). Dem. from Minn. (1922–1939). Died.

(9) Sanford, Edward T. (1865–1930). Rep. from Tenn. (1923–1930). Died.

Appointed by President Coolidge, Republican from Massachusetts
(1923–1929)

(8) Stone, Harlan F. (1872–1946). Rep. from N.Y. (1925–1941). Promoted to chief justiceship.

Appointed by President Hoover, Republican from California
(1929–1933)

*(1) Hughes, Charles E. (1862–1948). Rep. from N.Y. (1930–1941). Retired.

(9) Roberts, Owen J. (1875–1955). Rep. from Pa. (1930–1945). Resigned.

(3) Cardozo, Benjamin N. (1870–1938). Dem. from N.Y. (1932–1938). Died.

Appointed by President Franklin D. Roosevelt, Democrat from New York
(1933–1945)

(2) Black, Hugo, L. (1886–1971). Dem. from Ala. (1937–1971). Retired.

(7) Reed, Stanley F. (1884–——). Dem. from Ky. (1938–1957). Retired.

(3) Frankfurter, Felix (1882–1965). Ind. from Mass. (1939–1962). Retired.

(5) Douglas, William O. (1898–——). Dem. from Conn. and Wash. (1939–——).

(6) Murphy, Frank (1893–1949). Dem. from Mich. (1940–1949). Died.

(4) Byrnes, James F. (1879–1972). Dem. from S.C. (1941–1942). Resigned.

(1) Stone, Harlan F. (1872–1946). Promoted from associate justiceship (1941–1946). Died.

(8) Jackson, Robert H. (1892–1954). Dem. from N.Y. (1941–1954). Died.

(4) Rutledge, Wiley B. (1894–1949). Dem. from Ia. (1943–1949). Died.

Appointed by President Truman, Democrat from Missouri
(1945–1953)

(9) Burton, Harold H. (1888–1964). Rep. from Ohio (1945–1958). Retired.

*(1) Vinson, Fred M. (1890–1953). Dem. from Kentucky (1946–1953). Died.

(6) Clark, Tom C. (1899–——). Dem. from Texas (1949–1967). Retired.

(4) Minton, Sherman (1890–1965). Dem. from Indiana (1949–1956). Retired.

Appointed by President Eisenhower, Republican from New York
(1953–1961)

*(1) Warren, Earl (1891–1974). Rep. from Cal. (1953–1969). Retired.

(8) Harlan, John Marshall (1899–1971). Rep. from New York (1955–1971). Retired.

(4) Brennan, William J., Jr., (1906–——). Dem. from New Jersey (1956–——).

(7) Whittaker, Charles E. (1901–1973). Rep. from Missouri (1957–1962). Retired.

(9) Stewart, Potter (1915–——). Rep. from Ohio (1958–——).

Appointed by President Kennedy, Democrat from Massachusetts
(1961–1963)

(7) White, Byron R. (1917–——). Dem. from Colorado (1962–——).

(3) Goldberg, Arthur J. (1908–——). Dem. from Illinois (1962–1965). Resigned.

Appointed by President Lyndon B. Johnson, Democrat from Texas
(1963–1969)

(3) Fortas, Abe (1910–——). Dem. from Tenn. (1965–1969). Resigned.

(6) Marshall, Thurgood (1908–——). Dem. from N.Y. (1967–——).

Appointed by President Nixon, Republican from California
(1969–1974)

*(1) Burger, Warren E. (1907–——). Rep. from Va. and Minn. (1969–——).

(3) Blackmun, Harry A. (1908–——). Rep. from Minn. (1970–
——).

(2) Powell, Lewis F., Jr., (1907–——). Dem. from Va. (1972–
——).

(8) Rehnquist, William H. (1924–——). Rep. from Ariz. (1972–
——).

INDEX

[9]

END OF VOLUME